Oxford Dictionary of National Biography

Volume 29

Oxford Dictionary of National Biography

IN ASSOCIATION WITH

The British Academy

From the earliest times to the year 2000

Edited by
H. C. G. Matthew
and
Brian Harrison

Volume 29
Hutchins–Jennens

OXFORD
UNIVERSITY PRESS

OXFORD

UNIVERSITY PRESS

Great Clarendon Street, Oxford OX2 6DP

Oxford University Press is a department of the University of Oxford.
It furthers the University's objective of excellence in research, scholarship,
and education by publishing worldwide in

Oxford New York

Auckland Bangkok Buenos Aires Cape Town
Chennai Dar es Salaam Delhi Hong Kong Istanbul Karachi
Kolkata Kuala Lumpur Madrid Melbourne Mexico City Mumbai Nairobi
São Paulo Shanghai Taipei Tokyo Toronto

Oxford is a registered trade mark of Oxford University Press
in the UK and in certain other countries

Published in the United States
by Oxford University Press Inc., New York

British Library Cataloguing in Publication Data
Data available

Library of Congress Cataloging in Publication Data
Data available: for details see volume 1, p. iv

ISBN 0-19-861379-2 (this volume)
ISBN 0-19-861411-X (set of sixty volumes)

Text captured by Alliance Phototypesetters, Pondicherry
Illustrations reproduced and archived by
Alliance Graphics Ltd, UK
Typeset in OUP Swift by Interactive Sciences Limited, Gloucester
Printed in Great Britain on acid-free paper by
Butler and Tanner Ltd,
Frome, Somerset

LIST OF ABBREVIATIONS

1 General abbreviations

AB	bachelor of arts	BCnL	bachelor of canon law
ABC	Australian Broadcasting Corporation	BCom	bachelor of commerce
ABC TV	ABC Television	BD	bachelor of divinity
act.	active	BEd	bachelor of education
A$	Australian dollar	BEng	bachelor of engineering
AD	*anno domini*	bk *pl.* bks	book(s)
AFC	Air Force Cross	BL	bachelor of law / letters / literature
AIDS	acquired immune deficiency syndrome	BLitt	bachelor of letters
AK	Alaska	BM	bachelor of medicine
AL	Alabama	BMus	bachelor of music
A level	advanced level [examination]	BP	before present
ALS	associate of the Linnean Society	BP	British Petroleum
AM	master of arts	Bros.	Brothers
AMICE	associate member of the Institution of Civil Engineers	BS	(1) bachelor of science; (2) bachelor of surgery; (3) British standard
ANZAC	Australian and New Zealand Army Corps	BSc	bachelor of science
appx *pl.* appxs	appendix(es)	BSc (Econ.)	bachelor of science (economics)
AR	Arkansas	BSc (Eng.)	bachelor of science (engineering)
ARA	associate of the Royal Academy	bt	baronet
ARCA	associate of the Royal College of Art	BTh	bachelor of theology
ARCM	associate of the Royal College of Music	*bur.*	buried
ARCO	associate of the Royal College of Organists	C.	command [identifier for published parliamentary papers]
ARIBA	associate of the Royal Institute of British Architects	*c.*	*circa*
ARP	air-raid precautions	c.	*capitulum pl. capitula*: chapter(s)
ARRC	associate of the Royal Red Cross	CA	California
ARSA	associate of the Royal Scottish Academy	Cantab.	Cantabrigiensis
art.	article / item	cap.	*capitulum pl. capitula*: chapter(s)
ASC	Army Service Corps	CB	companion of the Bath
Asch	Austrian Schilling	CBE	commander of the Order of the British Empire
ASDIC	Antisubmarine Detection Investigation Committee	CBS	Columbia Broadcasting System
ATS	Auxiliary Territorial Service	cc	cubic centimetres
ATV	Associated Television	C$	Canadian dollar
Aug	August	CD	compact disc
AZ	Arizona	Cd	command [identifier for published parliamentary papers]
b.	born	CE	Common (*or* Christian) Era
BA	bachelor of arts	cent.	century
BA (Admin.)	bachelor of arts (administration)	cf.	compare
BAFTA	British Academy of Film and Television Arts	CH	Companion of Honour
BAO	bachelor of arts in obstetrics	chap.	chapter
bap.	baptized	ChB	bachelor of surgery
BBC	British Broadcasting Corporation / Company	CI	Imperial Order of the Crown of India
BC	before Christ	CIA	Central Intelligence Agency
BCE	before the common (*or* Christian) era	CID	Criminal Investigation Department
BCE	bachelor of civil engineering	CIE	companion of the Order of the Indian Empire
BCG	bacillus of Calmette and Guérin [inoculation against tuberculosis]	Cie	Compagnie
		CLit	companion of literature
BCh	bachelor of surgery	CM	master of surgery
BChir	bachelor of surgery	cm	centimetre(s)
BCL	bachelor of civil law		

Cmd	command [identifier for published parliamentary papers]
CMG	companion of the Order of St Michael and St George
Cmnd	command [identifier for published parliamentary papers]
CO	Colorado
Co.	company
co.	county
col. *pl.* cols.	column(s)
Corp.	corporation
CSE	certificate of secondary education
CSI	companion of the Order of the Star of India
CT	Connecticut
CVO	commander of the Royal Victorian Order
cwt	hundredweight
$	(American) dollar
d.	(1) penny (pence); (2) died
DBE	dame commander of the Order of the British Empire
DCH	diploma in child health
DCh	doctor of surgery
DCL	doctor of civil law
DCnL	doctor of canon law
DCVO	dame commander of the Royal Victorian Order
DD	doctor of divinity
DE	Delaware
Dec	December
dem.	demolished
DEng	doctor of engineering
des.	destroyed
DFC	Distinguished Flying Cross
DipEd	diploma in education
DipPsych	diploma in psychiatry
diss.	dissertation
DL	deputy lieutenant
DLitt	doctor of letters
DLittCelt	doctor of Celtic letters
DM	(1) Deutschmark; (2) doctor of medicine; (3) doctor of musical arts
DMus	doctor of music
DNA	dioxyribonucleic acid
doc.	document
DOL	doctor of oriental learning
DPH	diploma in public health
DPhil	doctor of philosophy
DPM	diploma in psychological medicine
DSC	Distinguished Service Cross
DSc	doctor of science
DSc (Econ.)	doctor of science (economics)
DSc (Eng.)	doctor of science (engineering)
DSM	Distinguished Service Medal
DSO	companion of the Distinguished Service Order
DSocSc	doctor of social science
DTech	doctor of technology
DTh	doctor of theology
DTM	diploma in tropical medicine
DTMH	diploma in tropical medicine and hygiene
DU	doctor of the university
DUniv	doctor of the university
dwt	pennyweight
EC	European Community
ed. *pl.* eds.	edited / edited by / editor(s)
Edin.	Edinburgh
edn	edition
EEC	European Economic Community
EFTA	European Free Trade Association
EICS	East India Company Service
EMI	Electrical and Musical Industries (Ltd)
Eng.	English
enl.	enlarged
ENSA	Entertainments National Service Association
ep. *pl.* epp.	*epistola(e)*
ESP	extra-sensory perception
esp.	especially
esq.	esquire
est.	estimate / estimated
EU	European Union
ex	sold by (*lit.* out of)
excl.	excludes / excluding
exh.	exhibited
exh. cat.	exhibition catalogue
f. *pl.* ff.	following [pages]
FA	Football Association
FACP	fellow of the American College of Physicians
facs.	facsimile
FANY	First Aid Nursing Yeomanry
FBA	fellow of the British Academy
FBI	Federation of British Industries
FCS	fellow of the Chemical Society
Feb	February
FEng	fellow of the Fellowship of Engineering
FFCM	fellow of the Faculty of Community Medicine
FGS	fellow of the Geological Society
fig.	figure
FIMechE	fellow of the Institution of Mechanical Engineers
FL	Florida
fl.	*floruit*
FLS	fellow of the Linnean Society
FM	frequency modulation
fol. *pl.* fols.	folio(s)
Fr	French francs
Fr.	French
FRAeS	fellow of the Royal Aeronautical Society
FRAI	fellow of the Royal Anthropological Institute
FRAM	fellow of the Royal Academy of Music
FRAS	(1) fellow of the Royal Asiatic Society; (2) fellow of the Royal Astronomical Society
FRCM	fellow of the Royal College of Music
FRCO	fellow of the Royal College of Organists
FRCOG	fellow of the Royal College of Obstetricians and Gynaecologists
FRCP(C)	fellow of the Royal College of Physicians of Canada
FRCP (Edin.)	fellow of the Royal College of Physicians of Edinburgh
FRCP (Lond.)	fellow of the Royal College of Physicians of London
FRCPath	fellow of the Royal College of Pathologists
FRCPsych	fellow of the Royal College of Psychiatrists
FRCS	fellow of the Royal College of Surgeons
FRGS	fellow of the Royal Geographical Society
FRIBA	fellow of the Royal Institute of British Architects
FRICS	fellow of the Royal Institute of Chartered Surveyors
FRS	fellow of the Royal Society
FRSA	fellow of the Royal Society of Arts

FRSCM	fellow of the Royal School of Church Music	ISO	companion of the Imperial Service Order
FRSE	fellow of the Royal Society of Edinburgh	It.	Italian
FRSL	fellow of the Royal Society of Literature	ITA	Independent Television Authority
FSA	fellow of the Society of Antiquaries	ITV	Independent Television
ft	foot *pl.* feet	Jan	January
FTCL	fellow of Trinity College of Music, London	JP	justice of the peace
ft-lb per min.	foot-pounds per minute [unit of horsepower]	jun.	junior
FZS	fellow of the Zoological Society	KB	knight of the Order of the Bath
GA	Georgia	KBE	knight commander of the Order of the British Empire
GBE	knight or dame grand cross of the Order of the British Empire	KC	king's counsel
GCB	knight grand cross of the Order of the Bath	kcal	kilocalorie
GCE	general certificate of education	KCB	knight commander of the Order of the Bath
GCH	knight grand cross of the Royal Guelphic Order	KCH	knight commander of the Royal Guelphic Order
GCHQ	government communications headquarters	KCIE	knight commander of the Order of the Indian Empire
GCIE	knight grand commander of the Order of the Indian Empire	KCMG	knight commander of the Order of St Michael and St George
GCMG	knight or dame grand cross of the Order of St Michael and St George	KCSI	knight commander of the Order of the Star of India
GCSE	general certificate of secondary education	KCVO	knight commander of the Royal Victorian Order
GCSI	knight grand commander of the Order of the Star of India	keV	kilo-electron-volt
GCStJ	bailiff or dame grand cross of the order of St John of Jerusalem	KG	knight of the Order of the Garter
		KGB	[Soviet committee of state security]
GCVO	knight or dame grand cross of the Royal Victorian Order	KH	knight of the Royal Guelphic Order
		KLM	Koninklijke Luchtvaart Maatschappij (Royal Dutch Air Lines)
GEC	General Electric Company	km	kilometre(s)
Ger.	German	KP	knight of the Order of St Patrick
GI	government (*or* general) issue	KS	Kansas
GMT	Greenwich mean time	KT	knight of the Order of the Thistle
GP	general practitioner	kt	knight
GPU	[Soviet special police unit]	KY	Kentucky
GSO	general staff officer	£	pound(s) sterling
Heb.	Hebrew	£E	Egyptian pound
HEICS	Honourable East India Company Service	L	lira *pl.* lire
HI	Hawaii	l. *pl.* ll.	line(s)
HIV	human immunodeficiency virus	LA	Lousiana
HK$	Hong Kong dollar	LAA	light anti-aircraft
HM	his / her majesty('s)	LAH	licentiate of the Apothecaries' Hall, Dublin
HMAS	his / her majesty's Australian ship	Lat.	Latin
HMNZS	his / her majesty's New Zealand ship	lb	pound(s), unit of weight
HMS	his / her majesty's ship	LDS	licence in dental surgery
HMSO	His / Her Majesty's Stationery Office	*lit.*	literally
HMV	His Master's Voice	LittB	bachelor of letters
Hon.	Honourable	LittD	doctor of letters
hp	horsepower	LKQCPI	licentiate of the King and Queen's College of Physicians, Ireland
hr	hour(s)	LLA	lady literate in arts
HRH	his / her royal highness	LLB	bachelor of laws
HTV	Harlech Television	LLD	doctor of laws
IA	Iowa	LLM	master of laws
ibid.	*ibidem*: in the same place	LM	licentiate in midwifery
ICI	Imperial Chemical Industries (Ltd)	LP	long-playing record
ID	Idaho	LRAM	licentiate of the Royal Academy of Music
IL	Illinois	LRCP	licentiate of the Royal College of Physicians
illus.	illustration	LRCPS (Glasgow)	licentiate of the Royal College of Physicians and Surgeons of Glasgow
illustr.	illustrated	LRCS	licentiate of the Royal College of Surgeons
IN	Indiana	LSA	licentiate of the Society of Apothecaries
in.	inch(es)	LSD	lysergic acid diethylamide
Inc.	Incorporated	LVO	lieutenant of the Royal Victorian Order
incl.	includes / including	M. *pl.* MM.	Monsieur *pl.* Messieurs
IOU	I owe you	m	metre(s)
IQ	intelligence quotient		
Ir£	Irish pound		
IRA	Irish Republican Army		

m. *pl.* mm.	membrane(s)
MA	(1) Massachusetts; (2) master of arts
MAI	master of engineering
MB	bachelor of medicine
MBA	master of business administration
MBE	member of the Order of the British Empire
MC	Military Cross
MCC	Marylebone Cricket Club
MCh	master of surgery
MChir	master of surgery
MCom	master of commerce
MD	(1) doctor of medicine; (2) Maryland
MDMA	methylenedioxymethamphetamine
ME	Maine
MEd	master of education
MEng	master of engineering
MEP	member of the European parliament
MG	Morris Garages
MGM	Metro-Goldwyn-Mayer
Mgr	Monsignor
MI	(1) Michigan; (2) military intelligence
MI1c	[secret intelligence department]
MI5	[military intelligence department]
MI6	[secret intelligence department]
MI9	[secret escape service]
MICE	member of the Institution of Civil Engineers
MIEE	member of the Institution of Electrical Engineers
min.	minute(s)
Mk	mark
ML	(1) licentiate of medicine; (2) master of laws
MLitt	master of letters
Mlle	Mademoiselle
mm	millimetre(s)
Mme	Madame
MN	Minnesota
MO	Missouri
MOH	medical officer of health
MP	member of parliament
m.p.h.	miles per hour
MPhil	master of philosophy
MRCP	member of the Royal College of Physicians
MRCS	member of the Royal College of Surgeons
MRCVS	member of the Royal College of Veterinary Surgeons
MRIA	member of the Royal Irish Academy
MS	(1) master of science; (2) Mississippi
MS *pl.* MSS	manuscript(s)
MSc	master of science
MSc (Econ.)	master of science (economics)
MT	Montana
MusB	bachelor of music
MusBac	bachelor of music
MusD	doctor of music
MV	motor vessel
MVO	member of the Royal Victorian Order
n. *pl.* nn.	note(s)
NAAFI	Navy, Army, and Air Force Institutes
NASA	National Aeronautics and Space Administration
NATO	North Atlantic Treaty Organization
NBC	National Broadcasting Corporation
NC	North Carolina
NCO	non-commissioned officer
ND	North Dakota
n.d.	no date
NE	Nebraska
nem. con.	*nemine contradicente*: unanimously
new ser.	new series
NH	New Hampshire
NHS	National Health Service
NJ	New Jersey
NKVD	[Soviet people's commissariat for internal affairs]
NM	New Mexico
nm	nanometre(s)
no. *pl.* nos.	number(s)
Nov	November
n.p.	no place [of publication]
NS	new style
NV	Nevada
NY	New York
NZBS	New Zealand Broadcasting Service
OBE	officer of the Order of the British Empire
obit.	obituary
Oct	October
OCTU	officer cadets training unit
OECD	Organization for Economic Co-operation and Development
OEEC	Organization for European Economic Co-operation
OFM	order of Friars Minor [Franciscans]
OFMCap	Ordine Frati Minori Cappucini: member of the Capuchin order
OH	Ohio
OK	Oklahoma
O level	ordinary level [examination]
OM	Order of Merit
OP	order of Preachers [Dominicans]
op. *pl.* opp.	opus *pl.* opera
OPEC	Organization of Petroleum Exporting Countries
OR	Oregon
orig.	original
OS	old style
OSB	Order of St Benedict
OTC	Officers' Training Corps
OWS	Old Watercolour Society
Oxon.	Oxoniensis
p. *pl.* pp.	page(s)
PA	Pennsylvania
p.a.	per annum
para.	paragraph
PAYE	pay as you earn
pbk *pl.* pbks	paperback(s)
per.	[during the] period
PhD	doctor of philosophy
pl.	(1) plate(s); (2) plural
priv. coll.	private collection
pt *pl.* pts	part(s)
pubd	published
PVC	polyvinyl chloride
q. *pl.* qq.	(1) question(s); (2) quire(s)
QC	queen's counsel
R	rand
R.	Rex / Regina
r	recto
r.	reigned / ruled
RA	Royal Academy / Royal Academician

RAC	Royal Automobile Club
RAF	Royal Air Force
RAFVR	Royal Air Force Volunteer Reserve
RAM	[member of the] Royal Academy of Music
RAMC	Royal Army Medical Corps
RCA	Royal College of Art
RCNC	Royal Corps of Naval Constructors
RCOG	Royal College of Obstetricians and Gynaecologists
RDI	royal designer for industry
RE	Royal Engineers
repr. *pl.* reprs.	reprint(s) / reprinted
repro.	reproduced
rev.	revised / revised by / reviser / revision
Revd	Reverend
RHA	Royal Hibernian Academy
RI	(1) Rhode Island; (2) Royal Institute of Painters in Water-Colours
RIBA	Royal Institute of British Architects
RIN	Royal Indian Navy
RM	Reichsmark
RMS	Royal Mail steamer
RN	Royal Navy
RNA	ribonucleic acid
RNAS	Royal Naval Air Service
RNR	Royal Naval Reserve
RNVR	Royal Naval Volunteer Reserve
RO	Record Office
r.p.m.	revolutions per minute
RRS	royal research ship
Rs	rupees
RSA	(1) Royal Scottish Academician; (2) Royal Society of Arts
RSPCA	Royal Society for the Prevention of Cruelty to Animals
Rt Hon.	Right Honourable
Rt Revd	Right Reverend
RUC	Royal Ulster Constabulary
Russ.	Russian
RWS	Royal Watercolour Society
S4C	Sianel Pedwar Cymru
s.	shilling(s)
s.a.	*sub anno*: under the year
SABC	South African Broadcasting Corporation
SAS	Special Air Service
SC	South Carolina
ScD	doctor of science
S$	Singapore dollar
SD	South Dakota
sec.	second(s)
sel.	selected
sen.	senior
Sept	September
ser.	series
SHAPE	supreme headquarters allied powers, Europe
SIDRO	Société Internationale d'Énergie Hydro-Électrique
sig. *pl.* sigs.	signature(s)
sing.	singular
SIS	Secret Intelligence Service
SJ	Society of Jesus
Skr	Swedish krona
Span.	Spanish
SPCK	Society for Promoting Christian Knowledge
SS	(1) Santissimi; (2) Schutzstaffel; (3) steam ship
STB	bachelor of theology
STD	doctor of theology
STM	master of theology
STP	doctor of theology
supp.	supposedly
suppl. *pl.* suppls.	supplement(s)
s.v.	*sub verbo* / *sub voce*: under the word / heading
SY	steam yacht
TA	Territorial Army
TASS	[Soviet news agency]
TB	tuberculosis (*lit.* tubercle bacillus)
TD	(1) *teachtaí dála* (member of the Dáil); (2) territorial decoration
TN	Tennessee
TNT	trinitrotoluene
trans.	translated / translated by / translation / translator
TT	tourist trophy
TUC	Trades Union Congress
TX	Texas
U-boat	*Unterseeboot*: submarine
Ufa	Universum-Film AG
UMIST	University of Manchester Institute of Science and Technology
UN	United Nations
UNESCO	United Nations Educational, Scientific, and Cultural Organization
UNICEF	United Nations International Children's Emergency Fund
unpubd	unpublished
USS	United States ship
UT	Utah
v	verso
v.	versus
VA	Virginia
VAD	Voluntary Aid Detachment
VC	Victoria Cross
VE-day	victory in Europe day
Ven.	Venerable
VJ-day	victory over Japan day
vol. *pl.* vols.	volume(s)
VT	Vermont
WA	Washington [state]
WAAC	Women's Auxiliary Army Corps
WAAF	Women's Auxiliary Air Force
WEA	Workers' Educational Association
WHO	World Health Organization
WI	Wisconsin
WRAF	Women's Royal Air Force
WRNS	Women's Royal Naval Service
WV	West Virginia
WVS	Women's Voluntary Service
WY	Wyoming
¥	yen
YMCA	Young Men's Christian Association
YWCA	Young Women's Christian Association

2 *Institution abbreviations*

All Souls Oxf.	All Souls College, Oxford
AM Oxf.	Ashmolean Museum, Oxford
Balliol Oxf.	Balliol College, Oxford
BBC WAC	BBC Written Archives Centre, Reading
Beds. & Luton ARS	Bedfordshire and Luton Archives and Record Service, Bedford
Berks. RO	Berkshire Record Office, Reading
BFI	British Film Institute, London
BFI NFTVA	British Film Institute, London, National Film and Television Archive
BGS	British Geological Survey, Keyworth, Nottingham
Birm. CA	Birmingham Central Library, Birmingham City Archives
Birm. CL	Birmingham Central Library
BL	British Library, London
BL NSA	British Library, London, National Sound Archive
BL OIOC	British Library, London, Oriental and India Office Collections
BLPES	London School of Economics and Political Science, British Library of Political and Economic Science
BM	British Museum, London
Bodl. Oxf.	Bodleian Library, Oxford
Bodl. RH	Bodleian Library of Commonwealth and African Studies at Rhodes House, Oxford
Borth. Inst.	Borthwick Institute of Historical Research, University of York
Boston PL	Boston Public Library, Massachusetts
Bristol RO	Bristol Record Office
Bucks. RLSS	Buckinghamshire Records and Local Studies Service, Aylesbury
CAC Cam.	Churchill College, Cambridge, Churchill Archives Centre
Cambs. AS	Cambridgeshire Archive Service
CCC Cam.	Corpus Christi College, Cambridge
CCC Oxf.	Corpus Christi College, Oxford
Ches. & Chester ALSS	Cheshire and Chester Archives and Local Studies Service
Christ Church Oxf.	Christ Church, Oxford
Christies	Christies, London
City Westm. AC	City of Westminster Archives Centre, London
CKS	Centre for Kentish Studies, Maidstone
CLRO	Corporation of London Records Office
Coll. Arms	College of Arms, London
Col. U.	Columbia University, New York
Cornwall RO	Cornwall Record Office, Truro
Courtauld Inst.	Courtauld Institute of Art, London
CUL	Cambridge University Library
Cumbria AS	Cumbria Archive Service
Derbys. RO	Derbyshire Record Office, Matlock
Devon RO	Devon Record Office, Exeter
Dorset RO	Dorset Record Office, Dorchester
Duke U.	Duke University, Durham, North Carolina
Duke U., Perkins L.	Duke University, Durham, North Carolina, William R. Perkins Library
Durham Cath. CL	Durham Cathedral, chapter library
Durham RO	Durham Record Office
DWL	Dr Williams's Library, London
Essex RO	Essex Record Office
E. Sussex RO	East Sussex Record Office, Lewes
Eton	Eton College, Berkshire
FM Cam.	Fitzwilliam Museum, Cambridge
Folger	Folger Shakespeare Library, Washington, DC
Garr. Club	Garrick Club, London
Girton Cam.	Girton College, Cambridge
GL	Guildhall Library, London
Glos. RO	Gloucestershire Record Office, Gloucester
Gon. & Caius Cam.	Gonville and Caius College, Cambridge
Gov. Art Coll.	Government Art Collection
GS Lond.	Geological Society of London
Hants. RO	Hampshire Record Office, Winchester
Harris Man. Oxf.	Harris Manchester College, Oxford
Harvard TC	Harvard Theatre Collection, Harvard University, Cambridge, Massachusetts, Nathan Marsh Pusey Library
Harvard U.	Harvard University, Cambridge, Massachusetts
Harvard U., Houghton L.	Harvard University, Cambridge, Massachusetts, Houghton Library
Herefs. RO	Herefordshire Record Office, Hereford
Herts. ALS	Hertfordshire Archives and Local Studies, Hertford
Hist. Soc. Penn.	Historical Society of Pennsylvania, Philadelphia
HLRO	House of Lords Record Office, London
Hult. Arch.	Hulton Archive, London and New York
Hunt. L.	Huntington Library, San Marino, California
ICL	Imperial College, London
Inst. CE	Institution of Civil Engineers, London
Inst. EE	Institution of Electrical Engineers, London
IWM	Imperial War Museum, London
IWM FVA	Imperial War Museum, London, Film and Video Archive
IWM SA	Imperial War Museum, London, Sound Archive
JRL	John Rylands University Library of Manchester
King's AC Cam.	King's College Archives Centre, Cambridge
King's Cam.	King's College, Cambridge
King's Lond.	King's College, London
King's Lond., Liddell Hart C.	King's College, London, Liddell Hart Centre for Military Archives
Lancs. RO	Lancashire Record Office, Preston
L. Cong.	Library of Congress, Washington, DC
Leics. RO	Leicestershire, Leicester, and Rutland Record Office, Leicester
Lincs. Arch.	Lincolnshire Archives, Lincoln
Linn. Soc.	Linnean Society of London
LMA	London Metropolitan Archives
LPL	Lambeth Palace, London
Lpool RO	Liverpool Record Office and Local Studies Service
LUL	London University Library
Magd. Cam.	Magdalene College, Cambridge
Magd. Oxf.	Magdalen College, Oxford
Man. City Gall.	Manchester City Galleries
Man. CL	Manchester Central Library
Mass. Hist. Soc.	Massachusetts Historical Society, Boston
Merton Oxf.	Merton College, Oxford
MHS Oxf.	Museum of the History of Science, Oxford
Mitchell L., Glas.	Mitchell Library, Glasgow
Mitchell L., NSW	State Library of New South Wales, Sydney, Mitchell Library
Morgan L.	Pierpont Morgan Library, New York
NA Canada	National Archives of Canada, Ottawa
NA Ire.	National Archives of Ireland, Dublin
NAM	National Army Museum, London
NA Scot.	National Archives of Scotland, Edinburgh
News Int. RO	News International Record Office, London
NG Ire.	National Gallery of Ireland, Dublin

NG Scot.	National Gallery of Scotland, Edinburgh
NHM	Natural History Museum, London
NL Aus.	National Library of Australia, Canberra
NL Ire.	National Library of Ireland, Dublin
NL NZ	National Library of New Zealand, Wellington
NL NZ, Turnbull L.	National Library of New Zealand, Wellington, Alexander Turnbull Library
NL Scot.	National Library of Scotland, Edinburgh
NL Wales	National Library of Wales, Aberystwyth
NMG Wales	National Museum and Gallery of Wales, Cardiff
NMM	National Maritime Museum, London
Norfolk RO	Norfolk Record Office, Norwich
Northants. RO	Northamptonshire Record Office, Northampton
Northumbd RO	Northumberland Record Office
Notts. Arch.	Nottinghamshire Archives, Nottingham
NPG	National Portrait Gallery, London
NRA	National Archives, London, Historical Manuscripts Commission, National Register of Archives
Nuffield Oxf.	Nuffield College, Oxford
N. Yorks. CRO	North Yorkshire County Record Office, Northallerton
NYPL	New York Public Library
Oxf. UA	Oxford University Archives
Oxf. U. Mus. NH	Oxford University Museum of Natural History
Oxon. RO	Oxfordshire Record Office, Oxford
Pembroke Cam.	Pembroke College, Cambridge
PRO	National Archives, London, Public Record Office
PRO NIre.	Public Record Office for Northern Ireland, Belfast
Pusey Oxf.	Pusey House, Oxford
RA	Royal Academy of Arts, London
Ransom HRC	Harry Ransom Humanities Research Center, University of Texas, Austin
RAS	Royal Astronomical Society, London
RBG Kew	Royal Botanic Gardens, Kew, London
RCP Lond.	Royal College of Physicians of London
RCS Eng.	Royal College of Surgeons of England, London
RGS	Royal Geographical Society, London
RIBA	Royal Institute of British Architects, London
RIBA BAL	Royal Institute of British Architects, London, British Architectural Library
Royal Arch.	Royal Archives, Windsor Castle, Berkshire [by gracious permission of her majesty the queen]
Royal Irish Acad.	Royal Irish Academy, Dublin
Royal Scot. Acad.	Royal Scottish Academy, Edinburgh
RS	Royal Society, London
RSA	Royal Society of Arts, London
RS Friends, Lond.	Religious Society of Friends, London
St Ant. Oxf.	St Antony's College, Oxford
St John Cam.	St John's College, Cambridge
S. Antiquaries, Lond.	Society of Antiquaries of London
Sci. Mus.	Science Museum, London
Scot. NPG	Scottish National Portrait Gallery, Edinburgh
Scott Polar RI	University of Cambridge, Scott Polar Research Institute
Sheff. Arch.	Sheffield Archives
Shrops. RRC	Shropshire Records and Research Centre, Shrewsbury
SOAS	School of Oriental and African Studies, London
Som. ARS	Somerset Archive and Record Service, Taunton
Staffs. RO	Staffordshire Record Office, Stafford
Suffolk RO	Suffolk Record Office
Surrey HC	Surrey History Centre, Woking
TCD	Trinity College, Dublin
Trinity Cam.	Trinity College, Cambridge
U. Aberdeen	University of Aberdeen
U. Birm.	University of Birmingham
U. Birm. L.	University of Birmingham Library
U. Cal.	University of California
U. Cam.	University of Cambridge
UCL	University College, London
U. Durham	University of Durham
U. Durham L.	University of Durham Library
U. Edin.	University of Edinburgh
U. Edin., New Coll.	University of Edinburgh, New College
U. Edin., New Coll. L.	University of Edinburgh, New College Library
U. Edin. L.	University of Edinburgh Library
U. Glas.	University of Glasgow
U. Glas. L.	University of Glasgow Library
U. Hull	University of Hull
U. Hull, Brynmor Jones L.	University of Hull, Brynmor Jones Library
U. Leeds	University of Leeds
U. Leeds, Brotherton L.	University of Leeds, Brotherton Library
U. Lond.	University of London
U. Lpool	University of Liverpool
U. Lpool L.	University of Liverpool Library
U. Mich.	University of Michigan, Ann Arbor
U. Mich., Clements L.	University of Michigan, Ann Arbor, William L. Clements Library
U. Newcastle	University of Newcastle upon Tyne
U. Newcastle, Robinson L.	University of Newcastle upon Tyne, Robinson Library
U. Nott.	University of Nottingham
U. Nott. L.	University of Nottingham Library
U. Oxf.	University of Oxford
U. Reading	University of Reading
U. Reading L.	University of Reading Library
U. St Andr.	University of St Andrews
U. St Andr. L.	University of St Andrews Library
U. Southampton	University of Southampton
U. Southampton L.	University of Southampton Library
U. Sussex	University of Sussex, Brighton
U. Texas	University of Texas, Austin
U. Wales	University of Wales
U. Warwick Mod. RC	University of Warwick, Coventry, Modern Records Centre
V&A	Victoria and Albert Museum, London
V&A NAL	Victoria and Albert Museum, London, National Art Library
Warks. CRO	Warwickshire County Record Office, Warwick
Wellcome L.	Wellcome Library for the History and Understanding of Medicine, London
Westm. DA	Westminster Diocesan Archives, London
Wilts. & Swindon RO	Wiltshire and Swindon Record Office, Trowbridge
Worcs. RO	Worcestershire Record Office, Worcester
W. Sussex RO	West Sussex Record Office, Chichester
W. Yorks. AS	West Yorkshire Archive Service
Yale U.	Yale University, New Haven, Connecticut
Yale U., Beinecke L.	Yale University, New Haven, Connecticut, Beinecke Rare Book and Manuscript Library
Yale U. CBA	Yale University, New Haven, Connecticut, Yale Center for British Art

3 Bibliographic abbreviations

Adams, *Drama* W. D. Adams, *A dictionary of the drama*, 1: *A–G* (1904); 2: *H–Z* (1956) [vol. 2 microfilm only]

AFM J O'Donovan, ed. and trans., *Annala rioghachta Eireann / Annals of the kingdom of Ireland by the four masters*, 7 vols. (1848–51); 2nd edn (1856); 3rd edn (1990)

Allibone, *Dict.* S. A. Allibone, *A critical dictionary of English literature and British and American authors*, 3 vols. (1859–71); suppl. by J. F. Kirk, 2 vols. (1891)

ANB J. A. Garraty and M. C. Carnes, eds., *American national biography*, 24 vols. (1999)

Anderson, *Scot. nat.* W. Anderson, *The Scottish nation, or, The surnames, families, literature, honours, and biographical history of the people of Scotland*, 3 vols. (1859–63)

Ann. mon. H. R. Luard, ed., *Annales monastici*, 5 vols., Rolls Series, 36 (1864–9)

Ann. Ulster S. Mac Airt and G. Mac Niocaill, eds., *Annals of Ulster (to AD 1131)* (1983)

APC *Acts of the privy council of England*, new ser., 46 vols. (1890–1964)

APS *The acts of the parliaments of Scotland*, 12 vols. in 13 (1814–75)

Arber, *Regs. Stationers* F. Arber, ed., *A transcript of the registers of the Company of Stationers of London, 1554–1640 AD*, 5 vols. (1875–94)

ArchR *Architectural Review*

ASC D. Whitelock, D. C. Douglas, and S. I. Tucker, ed. and trans., *The Anglo-Saxon Chronicle: a revised translation* (1961)

AS chart. P. H. Sawyer, *Anglo-Saxon charters: an annotated list and bibliography*, Royal Historical Society Guides and Handbooks (1968)

AusDB D. Pike and others, eds., *Australian dictionary of biography*, 16 vols. (1966–2002)

Baker, *Serjeants* J. H. Baker, *The order of serjeants at law*, SeldS, suppl. ser., 5 (1984)

Bale, *Cat.* J. Bale, *Scriptorum illustrium Maioris Brytannie, quam nunc Angliam et Scotiam vocant: catalogus*, 2 vols. in 1 (Basel, 1557–9); facs. edn (1971)

Bale, *Index* J. Bale, *Index Britanniae scriptorum*, ed. R. L. Poole and M. Bateson (1902); facs. edn (1990)

BBCS *Bulletin of the Board of Celtic Studies*

BDMBR J. O. Baylen and N. J. Gossman, eds., *Biographical dictionary of modern British radicals*, 3 vols. in 4 (1979–88)

Bede, *Hist. eccl.* *Bede's Ecclesiastical history of the English people*, ed. and trans. B. Colgrave and R. A. B. Mynors, OMT (1969); repr. (1991)

Bénézit, *Dict.* E. Bénézit, *Dictionnaire critique et documentaire des peintres, sculpteurs, dessinateurs et graveurs*, 3 vols. (Paris, 1911–23); new edn, 8 vols. (1948–66), repr. (1966); 3rd edn, rev. and enl., 10 vols. (1976); 4th edn, 14 vols. (1999)

BIHR *Bulletin of the Institute of Historical Research*

Birch, *Seals* W. de Birch, *Catalogue of seals in the department of manuscripts in the British Museum*, 6 vols. (1887–1900)

Bishop Burnet's History *Bishop Burnet's History of his own time*, ed. M. J. Routh, 2nd edn, 6 vols. (1833)

Blackwood *Blackwood's [Edinburgh] Magazine*, 328 vols. (1817–1980)

Blain, Clements & Grundy, *Feminist comp.* V. Blain, P. Clements, and I. Grundy, eds., *The feminist companion to literature in English* (1990)

BL cat. *The British Library general catalogue of printed books* [in 360 vols. with suppls., also CD-ROM and online]

BMJ *British Medical Journal*

Boase & Courtney, *Bibl. Corn.* G. C. Boase and W. P. Courtney, *Bibliotheca Cornubiensis: a catalogue of the writings … of Cornishmen*, 3 vols. (1874–82)

Boase, *Mod. Eng. biog.* F. Boase, *Modern English biography: containing many thousand concise memoirs of persons who have died since the year 1850*, 6 vols. (privately printed, Truro, 1892–1921); repr. (1965)

Boswell, *Life* *Boswell's Life of Johnson: together with Journal of a tour to the Hebrides and Johnson's Diary of a journey into north Wales*, ed. G. B. Hill, enl. edn, rev. L. F. Powell, 6 vols. (1934–50); 2nd edn (1964); repr. (1971)

Brown & Stratton, *Brit. mus.* J. D. Brown and S. S. Stratton, *British musical biography* (1897)

Bryan, *Painters* M. Bryan, *A biographical and critical dictionary of painters and engravers*, 2 vols. (1816); new edn, ed. G. Stanley (1849); new edn, ed. R. E. Graves and W. Armstrong, 2 vols. (1886–9); [4th edn], ed. G. C. Williamson, 5 vols. (1903–5) [various reprs.]

Burke, *Gen. GB* J. Burke, *A genealogical and heraldic history of the commoners of Great Britain and Ireland*, 4 vols. (1833–8); new edn as *A genealogical and heraldic dictionary of the landed gentry of Great Britain and Ireland*, 3 vols. [1843–9] [many later edns]

Burke, *Gen. Ire.* J. B. Burke, *A genealogical and heraldic history of the landed gentry of Ireland* (1899); 2nd edn (1904); 3rd edn (1912); 4th edn (1958); 5th edn as *Burke's Irish family records* (1976)

Burke, *Peerage* J. Burke, *A general [later edns A genealogical] and heraldic dictionary of the peerage and baronetage of the United Kingdom* [later edns *the British empire*] (1829–)

Burney, *Hist. mus.* C. Burney, *A general history of music, from the earliest ages to the present period*, 4 vols. (1776–89)

Burtchaell & Sadleir, *Alum. Dubl.* G. D. Burtchaell and T. U. Sadleir, *Alumni Dublinenses: a register of the students, graduates, and provosts of Trinity College* (1924); [2nd edn], with suppl., in 2 pts (1935)

Calamy rev. A. G. Matthews, *Calamy revised* (1934); repr. (1988)

CCI *Calendar of confirmations and inventories granted and given up in the several commissariots of Scotland* (1876–)

CCIR *Calendar of the close rolls preserved in the Public Record Office*, 47 vols. (1892–1963)

CDS J. Bain, ed., *Calendar of documents relating to Scotland*, 4 vols., PRO (1881–8); suppl. vol. 5, ed. G. G. Simpson and J. D. Galbraith [1986]

CEPR letters W. H. Bliss, C. Johnson, and J. Twemlow, eds., *Calendar of entries in the papal registers relating to Great Britain and Ireland: papal letters* (1893–)

CGPLA *Calendars of the grants of probate and letters of administration* [in 4 ser.: *England & Wales, Northern Ireland, Ireland,* and *Éire*]

Chambers, *Scots.* R. Chambers, ed., *A biographical dictionary of eminent Scotsmen*, 4 vols. (1832–5)

Chancery records chancery records pubd by the PRO

Chancery records (RC) chancery records pubd by the Record Commissions

CIPM   *Calendar of inquisitions post mortem*, [20 vols.], PRO (1904–); also *Henry VII*, 3 vols. (1898–1955)

Clarendon, *Hist. rebellion*   E. Hyde, earl of Clarendon, *The history of the rebellion and civil wars in England*, 6 vols. (1888); repr. (1958) and (1992)

Cobbett, *Parl. hist.*   W. Cobbett and J. Wright, eds., *Cobbett's Parliamentary history of England*, 36 vols. (1806–1820)

Colvin, *Archs.*   H. Colvin, *A biographical dictionary of British architects, 1600–1840*, 3rd edn (1995)

Cooper, *Ath. Cantab.*   C. H. Cooper and T. Cooper, *Athenae Cantabrigienses*, 3 vols. (1858–1913); repr. (1967)

CPR   *Calendar of the patent rolls preserved in the Public Record Office* (1891–)

Crockford   *Crockford's Clerical Directory*

CS   Camden Society

CSP   *Calendar of state papers* [in 11 ser.: *domestic, Scotland, Scottish series, Ireland, colonial, Commonwealth, foreign, Spain* [at Simancas], *Rome, Milan,* and *Venice*]

CYS   Canterbury and York Society

DAB   *Dictionary of American biography*, 21 vols. (1928–36), repr. in 11 vols. (1964); 10 suppls. (1944–96)

DBB   D. J. Jeremy, ed., *Dictionary of business biography*, 5 vols. (1984–6)

DCB   G. W. Brown and others, *Dictionary of Canadian biography*, [14 vols.] (1966–)

Debrett's Peerage   *Debrett's Peerage* (1803–) [sometimes *Debrett's Illustrated peerage*]

Desmond, *Botanists*   R. Desmond, *Dictionary of British and Irish botanists and horticulturists* (1977); rev. edn (1994)

Dir. Brit. archs.   A. Felstead, J. Franklin, and L. Pinfield, eds., *Directory of British architects, 1834–1900* (1993); 2nd edn, ed. A. Brodie and others, 2 vols. (2001)

DLB   J. M. Bellamy and J. Saville, eds., *Dictionary of labour biography*, [10 vols.] (1972–)

DLitB   Dictionary of Literary Biography

DNB   *Dictionary of national biography*, 63 vols. (1885–1900), suppl., 3 vols. (1901); repr. in 22 vols. (1908–9); 10 further suppls. (1912–96); *Missing persons* (1993)

DNZB   W. H. Oliver and C. Orange, eds., *The dictionary of New Zealand biography*, 5 vols. (1990–2000)

DSAB   W. J. de Kock and others, eds., *Dictionary of South African biography*, 5 vols. (1968–87)

DSB   C. C. Gillispie and F. L. Holmes, eds., *Dictionary of scientific biography*, 16 vols. (1970–80); repr. in 8 vols. (1981); 2 vol. suppl. (1990)

DSBB   A. Slaven and S. Checkland, eds., *Dictionary of Scottish business biography, 1860–1960*, 2 vols. (1986–90)

DSCHT   N. M. de S. Cameron and others, eds., *Dictionary of Scottish church history and theology* (1993)

Dugdale, *Monasticon*   W. Dugdale, *Monasticon Anglicanum*, 3 vols. (1655–72); 2nd edn, 3 vols. (1661–82); new edn, ed. J. Caley, J. Ellis, and B. Bandinel, 6 vols. in 8 pts (1817–30); repr. (1846) and (1970)

DWB   J. E. Lloyd and others, eds., *Dictionary of Welsh biography down to 1940* (1959) [Eng. trans. of *Y bywgraffiadur Cymreig hyd 1940*, 2nd edn (1954)]

EdinR   *Edinburgh Review, or, Critical Journal*

EETS   Early English Text Society

Emden, *Cam.*   A. B. Emden, *A biographical register of the University of Cambridge to 1500* (1963)

Emden, *Oxf.*   A. B. Emden, *A biographical register of the University of Oxford to AD 1500*, 3 vols. (1957–9); also *A biographical register of the University of Oxford, AD 1501 to 1540* (1974)

EngHR   *English Historical Review*

Engraved *Brit. ports.*   F. M. O'Donoghue and H. M. Hake, *Catalogue of engraved British portraits preserved in the department of prints and drawings in the British Museum*, 6 vols. (1908–25)

ER   The English Reports, 178 vols. (1900–32)

ESTC   *English short title catalogue, 1475–1800* [CD-ROM and online]

Evelyn, *Diary*   *The diary of John Evelyn*, ed. E. S. De Beer, 6 vols. (1955); repr. (2000)

Farington, *Diary*   *The diary of Joseph Farington*, ed. K. Garlick and others, 17 vols. (1978–98)

Fasti Angl. (Hardy)   J. Le Neve, *Fasti ecclesiae Anglicanae*, ed. T. D. Hardy, 3 vols. (1854)

Fasti Angl., 1066–1300   [J. Le Neve], *Fasti ecclesiae Anglicanae, 1066–1300*, ed. D. E. Greenway and J. S. Barrow, [8 vols.] (1968–)

Fasti Angl., 1300–1541   [J. Le Neve], *Fasti ecclesiae Anglicanae, 1300–1541*, 12 vols. (1962–7)

Fasti Angl., 1541–1857   [J. Le Neve], *Fasti ecclesiae Anglicanae, 1541–1857*, ed. J. M. Horn, D. M. Smith, and D. S. Bailey, [9 vols.] (1969–)

Fasti Scot.   H. Scott, *Fasti ecclesiae Scoticanae*, 3 vols. in 6 (1871); new edn, [11 vols.] (1915–)

FO List   *Foreign Office List*

Fortescue, *Brit. army*   J. W. Fortescue, *A history of the British army*, 13 vols. (1899–1930)

Foss, *Judges*   E. Foss, *The judges of England*, 9 vols. (1848–64); repr. (1966)

Foster, *Alum. Oxon.*   J. Foster, ed., *Alumni Oxonienses: the members of the University of Oxford, 1715–1886*, 4 vols. (1887–8); later edn (1891); also *Alumni Oxonienses … 1500–1714*, 4 vols. (1891–2); 8 vol. repr. (1968) and (2000)

Fuller, *Worthies*   T. Fuller, *The history of the worthies of England*, 4 pts (1662); new edn, 2 vols., ed. J. Nichols (1811); new edn, 3 vols., ed. P. A. Nuttall (1840); repr. (1965)

GEC, *Baronetage*   G. E. Cokayne, *Complete baronetage*, 6 vols. (1900–09); repr. (1983) [microprint]

GEC, *Peerage*   G. E. C. [G. E. Cokayne], *The complete peerage of England, Scotland, Ireland, Great Britain, and the United Kingdom*, 8 vols. (1887–98); new edn, ed. V. Gibbs and others, 14 vols. in 15 (1910–98); microprint repr. (1982) and (1987)

Genest, *Eng. stage*   J. Genest, *Some account of the English stage from the Restoration in 1660 to 1830*, 10 vols. (1832); repr. [New York, 1965]

Gillow, *Lit. biog. hist.*   J. Gillow, *A literary and biographical history or bibliographical dictionary of the English Catholics, from the breach with Rome, in 1534, to the present time*, 5 vols. [1885–1902]; repr. (1961); repr. with preface by C. Gillow (1999)

Gir. Camb. opera   *Giraldi Cambrensis opera*, ed. J. S. Brewer, J. F. Dimock, and G. F. Warner, 8 vols., Rolls Series, 21 (1861–91)

GJ   *Geographical Journal*

Gladstone, *Diaries*	*The Gladstone diaries: with cabinet minutes and prime-ministerial correspondence*, ed. M. R. D. Foot and H. C. G. Matthew, 14 vols. (1968–94)
GM	*Gentleman's Magazine*
Graves, *Artists*	A. Graves, ed., *A dictionary of artists who have exhibited works in the principal London exhibitions of oil paintings from 1760 to 1880* (1884); new edn (1895); 3rd edn (1901); facs. edn (1969); repr. [1970], (1973), and (1984)
Graves, *Brit. Inst.*	A. Graves, *The British Institution, 1806–1867: a complete dictionary of contributors and their work from the foundation of the institution* (1875); facs. edn (1908); repr. (1969)
Graves, *RA exhibitors*	A. Graves, *The Royal Academy of Arts: a complete dictionary of contributors and their work from its foundation in 1769 to 1904*, 8 vols. (1905–6); repr. in 4 vols. (1970) and (1972)
Graves, *Soc. Artists*	A. Graves, *The Society of Artists of Great Britain, 1760–1791, the Free Society of Artists, 1761–1783: a complete dictionary* (1907); facs. edn (1969)
Greaves & Zaller, *BDBR*	R. L. Greaves and R. Zaller, eds., *Biographical dictionary of British radicals in the seventeenth century*, 3 vols. (1982–4)
Grove, *Dict. mus.*	G. Grove, ed., *A dictionary of music and musicians*, 5 vols. (1878–90); 2nd edn, ed. J. A. Fuller Maitland (1904–10); 3rd edn, ed. H. C. Colles (1927); 4th edn with suppl. (1940); 5th edn, ed. E. Blom, 9 vols. (1954); suppl. (1961) [see also *New Grove*]
Hall, *Dramatic ports.*	L. A. Hall, *Catalogue of dramatic portraits in the theatre collection of the Harvard College library*, 4 vols. (1930–34)
Hansard	*Hansard's parliamentary debates*, ser. 1–5 (1803–)
Highfill, Burnim & Langhans, *BDA*	P. H. Highfill, K. A. Burnim, and E. A. Langhans, *A biographical dictionary of actors, actresses, musicians, dancers, managers, and other stage personnel in London, 1660–1800*, 16 vols. (1973–93)
Hist. U. Oxf.	T. H. Aston, ed., *The history of the University of Oxford*, 8 vols. (1984–2000) [1: *The early Oxford schools*, ed. J. I. Catto (1984); 2: *Late medieval Oxford*, ed. J. I. Catto and R. Evans (1992); 3: *The collegiate university*, ed. J. McConica (1986); 4: *Seventeenth-century Oxford*, ed. N. Tyacke (1997); 5: *The eighteenth century*, ed. L. S. Sutherland and L. G. Mitchell (1986); 6–7: *Nineteenth-century Oxford*, ed. M. G. Brock and M. C. Curthoys (1997–2000); 8: *The twentieth century*, ed. B. Harrison (2000)]
HJ	*Historical Journal*
HMC	Historical Manuscripts Commission
Holdsworth, *Eng. law*	W. S. Holdsworth, *A history of English law*, ed. A. L. Goodhart and H. L. Hanbury, 17 vols. (1903–72)
HoP, *Commons*	*The history of parliament: the House of Commons* [1386–1421, ed. J. S. Roskell, L. Clark, and C. Rawcliffe, 4 vols. (1992); 1509–1558, ed. S. T. Bindoff, 3 vols. (1982); 1558–1603, ed. P. W. Hasler, 3 vols. (1981); 1660–1690, ed. B. D. Henning, 3 vols. (1983); 1690–1715, ed. D. W. Hayton, E. Cruickshanks, and S. Handley, 5 vols. (2002); 1715–1754, ed. R. Sedgwick, 2 vols. (1970); 1754–1790, ed. L. Namier and J. Brooke, 3 vols. (1964), repr. (1985); 1790–1820, ed. R. G. Thorne, 5 vols. (1986); in draft (used with permission): 1422–1504, 1604–1629, 1640–1660, and 1820–1832]
IGI	*International Genealogical Index*, Church of Jesus Christ of the Latterday Saints
ILN	*Illustrated London News*
IMC	Irish Manuscripts Commission
Irving, *Scots.*	J. Irving, ed., *The book of Scotsmen eminent for achievements in arms and arts, church and state, law, legislation and literature, commerce, science, travel and philanthropy* (1881)
JCS	*Journal of the Chemical Society*
JHC	*Journals of the House of Commons*
JHL	*Journals of the House of Lords*
John of Worcester, *Chron.*	*The chronicle of John of Worcester*, ed. R. R. Darlington and P. McGurk, trans. J. Bray and P. McGurk, 3 vols., OMT (1995–) [vol. 1 forthcoming]
Keeler, *Long Parliament*	M. F. Keeler, *The Long Parliament, 1640–1641: a biographical study of its members* (1954)
Kelly, *Handbk*	*The upper ten thousand: an alphabetical list of all members of noble families*, 3 vols. (1875–7); continued as *Kelly's handbook of the upper ten thousand for 1878* [1879], 2 vols. (1878–9); continued as *Kelly's handbook to the titled, landed and official classes*, 94 vols. (1880–1973)
LondG	*London Gazette*
LP Henry VIII	J. S. Brewer, J. Gairdner, and R. H. Brodie, eds., *Letters and papers, foreign and domestic, of the reign of Henry VIII*, 23 vols. in 38 (1862–1932); repr. (1965)
Mallalieu, *Watercolour artists*	H. L. Mallalieu, *The dictionary of British watercolour artists up to 1820*, 3 vols. (1976–90); vol. 1, 2nd edn (1986)
Memoirs FRS	*Biographical Memoirs of Fellows of the Royal Society*
MGH	Monumenta Germaniae Historica
MT	*Musical Times*
Munk, *Roll*	W. Munk, *The roll of the Royal College of Physicians of London*, 2 vols. (1861); 2nd edn, 3 vols. (1878)
N&Q	*Notes and Queries*
New Grove	S. Sadie, ed., *The new Grove dictionary of music and musicians*, 20 vols. (1980); 2nd edn, 29 vols. (2001) [also online edn; see also Grove, *Dict. mus.*]
Nichols, *Illustrations*	J. Nichols and J. B. Nichols, *Illustrations of the literary history of the eighteenth century*, 8 vols. (1817–58)
Nichols, *Lit. anecdotes*	J. Nichols, *Literary anecdotes of the eighteenth century*, 9 vols. (1812–16); facs. edn (1966)
Obits. FRS	*Obituary Notices of Fellows of the Royal Society*
O'Byrne, *Naval biog. dict.*	W. R. O'Byrne, *A naval biographical dictionary* (1849); repr. (1990); [2nd edn], 2 vols. (1861)
OHS	Oxford Historical Society
Old Westminsters	*The record of Old Westminsters*, 1–2, ed. G. F. R. Barker and A. H. Stenning (1928); suppl. 1, ed. J. B. Whitmore and G. R. Y. Radcliffe [1938]; 3, ed. J. B. Whitmore, G. R. Y. Radcliffe, and D. C. Simpson (1963); suppl. 2, ed. F. E. Pagan (1978); 4, ed. F. E. Pagan and H. E. Pagan (1992)
OMT	Oxford Medieval Texts
Ordericus Vitalis, *Eccl. hist.*	*The ecclesiastical history of Orderic Vitalis*, ed. and trans. M. Chibnall, 6 vols., OMT (1969–80); repr. (1990)
Paris, *Chron.*	*Matthaei Parisiensis, monachi sancti Albani, chronica majora*, ed. H. R. Luard, Rolls Series, 7 vols. (1872–83)
Parl. papers	*Parliamentary papers* (1801–)
PBA	*Proceedings of the British Academy*

Pepys, *Diary* — *The diary of Samuel Pepys*, ed. R. Latham and W. Matthews, 11 vols. (1970–83); repr. (1995) and (2000)

Pevsner — N. Pevsner and others, Buildings of England series

PICE — *Proceedings of the Institution of Civil Engineers*

Pipe rolls — *The great roll of the pipe for . . .*, PRSoc. (1884–)

PRO — Public Record Office

PRS — *Proceedings of the Royal Society of London*

PRSoc. — Pipe Roll Society

PTRS — *Philosophical Transactions of the Royal Society*

QR — *Quarterly Review*

RC — Record Commissions

Redgrave, *Artists* — S. Redgrave, *A dictionary of artists of the English school* (1874); rev. edn (1878); repr. (1970)

Reg. Oxf. — C. W. Boase and A. Clark, eds., *Register of the University of Oxford*, 5 vols., OHS, 1, 10–12, 14 (1885–9)

Reg. PCS — J. H. Burton and others, eds., *The register of the privy council of Scotland*, 1st ser., 14 vols. (1877–98); 2nd ser., 8 vols. (1899–1908); 3rd ser., [16 vols.] (1908–70)

Reg. RAN — H. W. C. Davis and others, eds., *Regesta regum Anglo-Normannorum, 1066–1154*, 4 vols. (1913–69)

RIBA Journal — *Journal of the Royal Institute of British Architects* [later *RIBA Journal*]

RotP — J. Strachey, ed., *Rotuli parliamentorum ut et petitiones, et placita in parliamento*, 6 vols. (1767–77)

RotS — D. Macpherson, J. Caley, and W. Illingworth, eds., *Rotuli Scotiae in Turri Londinensi et in domo capitulari Westmonasteriensi asservati*, 2 vols., RC, 14 (1814–19)

RS — Record(s) Society

Rymer, *Foedera* — T. Rymer and R. Sanderson, eds., *Foedera, conventiones, literae et cuiuscunque generis acta publica inter reges Angliae et alios quosvis imperatores, reges, pontifices, principes, vel communitates*, 20 vols. (1704–35); 2nd edn, 20 vols. (1726–35); 3rd edn, 10 vols. (1739–45); facs. edn (1967); new edn, ed. A. Clarke, J. Caley, and F. Holbrooke, 4 vols., RC, 50 (1816–30)

Sainty, *Judges* — J. Sainty, ed., *The judges of England, 1272–1990*, SeldS, suppl. ser., 10 (1993)

Sainty, *King's counsel* — J. Sainty, ed., *A list of English law officers and king's counsel*, SeldS, suppl. ser., 7 (1987)

SCH — Studies in Church History

Scots peerage — J. B. Paul, ed. *The Scots peerage, founded on Wood's edition of Sir Robert Douglas's Peerage of Scotland, containing an historical and genealogical account of the nobility of that kingdom*, 9 vols. (1904–14)

SeldS — Selden Society

SHR — *Scottish Historical Review*

State trials — T. B. Howell and T. J. Howell, eds., *Cobbett's Complete collection of state trials*, 34 vols. (1809–28)

STC, 1475–1640 — A. W. Pollard, G. R. Redgrave, and others, eds., *A short-title catalogue of . . . English books . . . 1475–1640* (1926); 2nd edn, ed. W. A. Jackson, F. S. Ferguson, and K. F. Pantzer, 3 vols. (1976–91) [see also Wing, *STC*]

STS — Scottish Text Society

SurtS — Surtees Society

Symeon of Durham, *Opera* — *Symeonis monachi opera omnia*, ed. T. Arnold, 2 vols., Rolls Series, 75 (1882–5); repr. (1965)

Tanner, *Bibl. Brit.-Hib.* — T. Tanner, *Bibliotheca Britannico-Hibernica*, ed. D. Wilkins (1748); repr. (1963)

Thieme & Becker, *Allgemeines Lexikon* — U. Thieme, F. Becker, and H. Vollmer, eds., *Allgemeines Lexikon der bildenden Künstler von der Antike bis zur Gegenwart*, 37 vols. (Leipzig, 1907–50); repr. (1961–5), (1983), and (1992)

Thurloe, *State papers* — *A collection of the state papers of John Thurloe*, ed. T. Birch, 7 vols. (1742)

TLS — *Times Literary Supplement*

Tout, *Admin. hist.* — T. F. Tout, *Chapters in the administrative history of mediaeval England: the wardrobe, the chamber, and the small seals*, 6 vols. (1920–33); repr. (1967)

TRHS — *Transactions of the Royal Historical Society*

VCH — H. A. Doubleday and others, eds., *The Victoria history of the counties of England*, [88 vols.] (1900–)

Venn, *Alum. Cant.* — J. Venn and J. A. Venn, *Alumni Cantabrigienses: a biographical list of all known students, graduates, and holders of office at the University of Cambridge, from the earliest times to 1900*, 10 vols. (1922–54); repr. in 2 vols. (1974–8)

Vertue, *Note books* — [G. Vertue], *Note books*, ed. K. Esdaile, earl of Ilchester, and H. M. Hake, 6 vols., Walpole Society, 18, 20, 22, 24, 26, 30 (1930–55)

VF — *Vanity Fair*

Walford, *County families* — E. Walford, *The county families of the United Kingdom, or, Royal manual of the titled and untitled aristocracy of Great Britain and Ireland* (1860)

Walker rev. — A. G. Matthews, *Walker revised: being a revision of John Walker's Sufferings of the clergy during the grand rebellion, 1642–60* (1948); repr. (1988)

Walpole, *Corr.* — *The Yale edition of Horace Walpole's correspondence*, ed. W. S. Lewis, 48 vols. (1937–83)

Ward, *Men of the reign* — T. H. Ward, ed., *Men of the reign: a biographical dictionary of eminent persons of British and colonial birth who have died during the reign of Queen Victoria* (1885); repr. (Graz, 1968)

Waterhouse, *18c painters* — E. Waterhouse, *The dictionary of 18th century painters in oils and crayons* (1981); repr. as *British 18th century painters in oils and crayons* (1991), vol. 2 of *Dictionary of British art*

Watt, *Bibl. Brit.* — R. Watt, *Bibliotheca Britannica, or, A general index to British and foreign literature*, 4 vols. (1824) [many reprs.]

Wellesley index — W. E. Houghton, ed., *The Wellesley index to Victorian periodicals, 1824–1900*, 5 vols. (1966–89); new edn (1999) [CD-ROM]

Wing, *STC* — D. Wing, ed., *Short-title catalogue of . . . English books . . . 1641–1700*, 3 vols. (1945–51); 2nd edn (1972–88); rev. and enl. edn, ed. J. J. Morrison, C. W. Nelson, and M. Seccombe, 4 vols. (1994–8) [see also *STC, 1475–1640*]

Wisden — *John Wisden's Cricketer's Almanack*

Wood, *Ath. Oxon.* — A. Wood, *Athenae Oxonienses . . . to which are added the Fasti*, 2 vols. (1691–2); 2nd edn (1721); new edn, 4 vols., ed. P. Bliss (1813–20); repr. (1967) and (1969)

Wood, *Vic. painters* — C. Wood, *Dictionary of Victorian painters* (1971); 2nd edn (1978); 3rd edn as *Victorian painters*, 2 vols. (1995), vol. 4 of *Dictionary of British art*

WW — *Who's who* (1849–)

WWBMP — M. Stenton and S. Lees, eds., *Who's who of British members of parliament*, 4 vols. (1976–81)

WWW — *Who was who* (1929–)

Hutchins, Edward (1557/8–1629), Church of England clergyman, was born of poor parents; according to Wood he was a native of Denbighshire. In 1576 he matriculated at Brasenose College, Oxford, aged eighteen, and graduated BA on 6 February 1578, proceeding MA on 8 July 1581. Earlier that year, on 4 February, he had been elected a perpetual fellow of the college, and in 1589 he became first bursar and then vice-principal. He may in the meantime have been active in Cheshire, on the evidence of two sermons which were published after being preached at Chester in the autumn of 1586. One of them, delivered on 8 October, was dedicated to Thomas Egerton, the attorney-general, and exhorted the assize judges to deal severely with 'stubborn and perverting papists'. On 9 November 1590, however, Hutchins was removed from his Brasenose fellowship in consequence of his having married. Nevertheless he supplicated for the degree of BTh on 21 November following.

Hutchins acquired two Wiltshire livings, Brinkworth and Nettleton, both near Salisbury, and on 28 December 1589 he was instituted to the prebend of Chisenbury and Chute in Salisbury Cathedral. In 1581 he had published a collection of prayers and meditations entitled *Davids Sling Against Great Goliah*, several times reprinted. In addition to his sermons preached at Chester, and one preached at Oxford, again before Egerton, in 1590, he also published a theological treatise entitled *Sampsons Jawbone Against the Spiritual Philistine* (1601). Hutchins seems to have spent the rest of his life in Wiltshire. In his will, drawn up on 8 February 1623, he directed that he be buried in Nettleton parish church. Apart from small bequests to the poor of Nettleton and Brinkworth, and to the fabric of Salisbury Cathedral, Hutchins's legacies, which totalled just over £100, were left entirely to his own family, to his five sons and four daughters, and in some cases to their children. His executor and residuary legatee was his wife, Jane (maiden name unknown). Hutchins did not die until early in 1629, a successor to his prebend being appointed on 30 March.   STEPHEN WRIGHT

Sources [C. B. Heberden], ed., *Brasenose College register, 1509–1909*, 2 vols., OHS, 55 (1909) · T. Phillipps, *Institutiones clericorum in comitatu Wiltoniae* (1825) · *Fasti Angl., 1541–1857*, [Salisbury], 34 · E. Hutchins, *A sermon preached in Westchester, 8 Oct, 1586* (1586) · Wood, *Ath. Oxon.*, new edn, 2.452–3 · B. Williams, ed., *The subscription books of bishops Townson and Davenant, 1620–40*, Wilts RS, 32 (1977) · PRO, PROB 11/156, sig. 64
Wealth at death over £100—plus unknown fixed and moveable property: PRO, PROB 11/156, sig. 64

Hutchins, Elizabeth Leigh (1858–1935), social investigator and socialist, was born on 20 April 1858 at 25 Hanover Square, London, the daughter of Frederick Leigh Hutchins, a solicitor, and his wife, Emily Every. Little is known about her early years. Privately educated, she later attended King's College for Women in London and in 1896 became a student at the new London School of Economics, where she was taught by Beatrice Webb.

Remaining in London, she joined the Women's Industrial Council in 1899, became a member of its executive committee by 1904, and served as the editor of its journal, the *Women's Industrial News*. She was a member of the Fabian Society, serving on its executive committee between 1907 and 1912, and a founder member of the Fabian Women's Group in 1908.

A prolific researcher, investigator, and author, Hutchins published at least twenty works between 1901 and 1917. Her meticulously researched works contain a wealth of statistics and information on the conditions of women's work, their wages, and the history of labour laws affecting them. Her book *A History of Factory Legislation* (1903), co-written with Amy Harrison, provided detailed information about the development of factory regulations from their inception until 1901 and covered the campaigns for shorter hours, the extension of legislation to workshops, the creation of measures to safeguard the health and safety of workers, and special regulations for women. Hutchins viewed protective labour legislation as progressive reforms that reflected the state's responsibilities towards its female workers. This perspective led her to criticize middle-class 'women's rights' groups, as she called them, whose individualism led them to argue that protection violated women's freedom in the workplace. As a result she participated in the contemporary debate among women's organizations about the effects of protection on women workers. In his preface to this work, Sidney Webb praised it for being the first systematic treatment of the subject. By the time of Hutchins's death it was considered the standard work on factory legislation, and it has been routinely cited by historians ever since.

Many of Hutchins's other publications dealt with the contemporary issues of women's home work and sweated labour. She contributed an article about a sweated industries exhibition held in Berlin in 1905 to the handbook for the Sweated Industries Exhibition held in London in 1906, an event intended to bring sweated labour to public and governmental attention. Her Fabian tract, *Home Work and Sweating: the Causes and the Remedies*, appeared in 1907. She also contributed to the Women's Industrial Council's investigation of home work, *Home Industries of Women in London* (1908), the sections that examined legislative initiatives regarding home work in Australia, New Zealand, and Germany. She supported the creation of minimum wage legislation for sweated trades.

In 1907 and 1908 Hutchins delivered a series of lectures on women's work and public health. When the Women's Industrial Council offered a course at King's College entitled 'The relation of the state to women's work', in 1907 Hutchins lectured on the history of legislation affecting women in trade and industry. In the following year she presented four lectures at the London School of Economics on the nineteenth-century public health movement. The latter lectures were published in 1909 as *The Public Health Agitation, 1833–1848*.

During the pre-war years Hutchins was part of a wide network of social reformers actively working to improve the conditions of women's work. Her activities and writings brought her into contact with the Webbs, Margaret and Ramsay MacDonald, Clementina Black of the Women's Industrial Council, J. J. Mallon of the Anti-

Sweating League, and Mary MacArthur of the Women's Trade Union League.

Hutchins's career as a social investigator and writer ended with *Women in Industry after the War* (1917). Thereafter she turned her attention and support towards the League of Nations, on whose committee she served. Formerly of Holland Park, London, Hutchins died at her home, 6 Granville Court, Granville Road, Eastbourne, on 17 October 1935. She had previously established a scholarship at the London School of Economics and provided for its permanent maintenance.

Hutchins's obituary in *The Times* characterized her as an accomplished woman with a wide circle of friends. She was a talented linguist and musician who enjoyed concerts, plays, and country walks. Friends and relatives described Bessie, as she liked to be called, as a woman who lived an unselfish life of private and civic service. Hutchins epitomizes the highly educated 'new woman' of the period who did not marry, but rather directed and devoted her immense energies and talents to a cause: the cause of working women. CAROLYN MALONE

Sources *The Times* (26 Oct 1935) · *The Times* (14 Dec 1935) · O. Banks, *The biographical dictionary of British feminists*, 2 (1990) · *The Labour who's who* (1927) · E. Mappin, *Helping women at work: the Women's Industrial Council, 1889–1914* (1985) · P. Pugh, *Educate, agitate, organize: 100 years of Fabian socialism* (1984) · b. cert. · d. cert. · *CGPLA Eng. & Wales* (1935)
Wealth at death £30,379 7s. 7d.: resworn probate, *CGPLA Eng. & Wales* (1935)

Hutchins, Ellen (1785–1815), botanist, was born on 17 March 1785 at Ballylickey House, Bantry Bay, co. Cork, Ireland, the second youngest child of two surviving daughters and four surviving sons of the twenty-one children of Thomas Hutchins (1735–1787) JP, and Elinor (d. 1814), only child and heir of Arthur Hutchins of Thomastown and Cregane Castle, Limerick. While completing her education in Dublin she began to suffer from poor health and a family friend, Dr Whitley Stokes, took her into his care for treatment. While recovering, she developed an interest in botany, having browsed in Stokes's library and met the botanist James Townsend Mackay. Stokes encouraged her pursuit as providing both outdoor exercise and indoor occupation. On returning home to Ballylickey, Hutchins became a keen collector of algae, mosses, liverworts, and lichens, as well as establishing her own garden.

By 1806 Hutchins's skills had become so acute that she was regularly sending specimens of algae to Mackay, who forwarded rare discoveries to Dawson Turner of Yarmouth, then working on seaweeds, and Lewis Weston Dillwyn of Swansea, who studied freshwater algae. While respecting Hutchins's stipulation that her name should not appear in print Mackay did reveal her role as collector to Turner. This opened her lifelong correspondence with the latter, who guided Hutchins through classificatory systems of cryptogamic plants and overcame her isolation by sending not only books but also named specimens to act as stepping stones towards increasing her knowledge. Hutchins's exquisitely preserved specimens, beautiful botanical drawings, and capacity to find plants deeply impressed Turner.

Although Hutchins never published she was persuaded to allow her name to appear when her discoveries were described in the later volumes of the *English Botany* (1790–1814) of James Sowerby and James Edward Smith as well as in Dillwyn's *British confervae* (1802–9) and Turner's *Fuci* (4 vols., 1808–19), which also included seven of her drawings. In 1809 Dillwyn and Joseph Woods visited Ballylickey, finding Hutchins 'a very sensible, pleasing, square made & tolerably good looking woman' whom both considered 'almost the best Botanist, either Male or Female that we ever met with' (Dillwyn to Dawson Turner, 22 July 1809, TCC).

Hutchins's reputation among men of science appears formidable and even threatening. James Edward Smith claimed that she could find almost anything and William Jackson Hooker, overwhelmed by her contributions to his monograph on liverworts, *British Jungermanniae* (1816), told Turner in December 1811 that 'Miss Hutchins' discoveries alone will form an Appendix as large as the work itself' (RBG Kew, Hooker MS 1, fols. 134–6). A year later he confided to Robert Brown that 'Miss Hutchins is a *mine*, but I never intend to bore her lest she should be too prolific' (BL, Add. MSS 32439, fols. 370–71). None the less, Hooker opened his monograph with *Jungermannia hutchinsiae*, a new species found by Hutchins, and acknowledged her discovery of Bantry Bay habitats for almost half the species he described. Brown also honoured Hutchins by naming a genus of alpine plants *Hutchinsia* in 1812.

Hutchins's last years were disrupted by illness and family troubles. Her brother Thomas was paralysed and required much attention. From 1810 she also nursed her elderly mother, with whom she moved to Bandon, 30 miles from Bantry Bay, in the summer of 1813, after her eldest brother Emanuel took possession of Ballylickey House and drove them out. In Bandon, Hutchins became desperately ill and barely able to care for her mother, who died in March 1814.

By May that year Hutchins was back in Bantry Bay living at Ardnagashel, the estate belonging to another brother, Arthur. Although mercury treatment for a liver complaint had reduced her to a 'mere skeleton', her cousin Thomas Taylor reported in a letter to Dawson Turner of 26 October 1814 that her physician believed she would recover (corresp., Trinity College Cambridge). Taylor, however, thought this unlikely given her proximity to her eldest brother. Hutchins attributed her mental and physical suffering to family disputes and increasingly relied on Turner's epistolary friendship as a source of pleasure in her unhappy life. Her illness worsened and she died on 9 February 1815, shortly before her thirtieth birthday. She was buried in Bantry churchyard.

Hutchins bequeathed her herbarium to Turner but its shipment was delayed when, following her death, fighting broke out between two of her brothers, one of whom attempted to seize Ballylickey House with forty armed men. Eventually Turner received Hutchins's specimens and drawings and ensured their continued use by botanists. Although they never met, Turner expressed deep and abiding sorrow at Hutchins's death in the concluding volume of his *Fuci* (4, 1819, 152). Bringing together their shared love of botany and poetry, he lamented her loss and praised her qualities by quoting from James Hurdis's 1794 poem, 'Tears of Affection; a Poem Occasioned by the Death of a Sister Tenderly Beloved'. ANNE SECORD

Sources D. Turner, letters to E. Hutchins, Royal Collection · E. Hutchins, letters to Dawson Turner, Trinity Cam. · Burke, *Gen. Ire.* (1958) · H. W. Lett, 'Census report on the mosses of Ireland', *Proceedings of the Royal Irish Academy*, 32B (1913–16), 65–166, esp. 70–71 · memoir of Ellen Hutchins, Representative Church Body Library, Dublin, MS 47 · W. H. Pearson, 'Ellen Hutchins—a biographical sketch', *The Bryologist*, 21 (1918), 78–80 · M. C. Knowles, 'The lichens of Ireland', *Proceedings of the Royal Irish Academy*, 38B (1928–9), 179–434, esp. 182 · J. Bevan, 'Miss Ellen Hutchins (1785–1815) and the garden at Ardnagashel, Bantry, county Cork', *Moorea*, 3 (1984), 1–10 · G. J. Lyne, 'Lewis Dillwyn's visit to Waterford, Cork and Tipperary in 1809', *Journal of the Cork Historical and Archaeological Society*, 2nd ser., 91 (1986), 85–104 · G. J. Lyne and M. E. Mitchell, 'A scientific tour through Munster: the travels of Joseph Woods, architect and botanist, in 1809', *North Munster Antiquarian Journal*, 27 (1985), 15–61, esp. 27 · *Irish women artists: from the eighteenth century to the present day* (1987) [exhibition catalogue, NG Ire., the Douglas Hyde Gallery, TCD, and the Hugh Lane Municipal Gallery of Modern Art, Dublin, July–Aug 1987] · D. Turner, *Fuci, or, Colored figures*, 4 vols. (1808–19) · W. J. Hooker, *British Jungermanniae: being a history and description, with colored figures, of each species of the genus, and microscopical analyses of the parts* (1816) · H. C. G. Chesney, 'The young lady of the lichens', *Stars, shells, and bluebells: women scientists and pioneers*, ed. [M. Mulvihill and P. Deevy] (Dublin, 1997), 28–39 · *Early observations on the flora of south-west Ireland: selected letters of Ellen Hutchins and Dawson Turner, 1807–1814*, ed. M. E. Mitchell (1999)
Archives NHM, herbarium · priv. coll., family MSS · RBG Kew · RBG Kew, botanical drawings · Sheffield City Museum, botanical drawings | Trinity Cam., corresp. with Dawson Turner

Hutchins, Sir George (*bap.* 1640, *d.* 1705), lawyer and politician, was baptized on 16 August 1640, at Georgeham, Devon, the only son and heir of Edmund Hutchins of Georgeham, parish clerk of Barnstaple, and Elizabeth Perriman. His father's lowly origins were once the butt of the wit of Edmund Hickeringill in a chancery case in 1700 when he referred to their being something akin to each other—not by consanguinity, but by affinity, for he was a clerk and Hutchins's father was a parish clerk. Hutchins entered Gray's Inn on 19 May 1666, and was called as early as 3 August 1667, as the privilege of the reader, William Lehunt. He was given chambers there on 28 November 1684. He was made a serjeant-at-law in April 1686, his patrons being the earl of Nottingham and Heneage Finch, both leading tories. He was probably the Mr Hutchins appointed as solicitor to the customs in 1687, but he seems to have transferred his allegiance to the Williamite regime with little difficulty. He was the first king's serjeant of the reign, appointed on 2 May 1689, and was knighted on 31 October 1689. He was returned to the House of Commons for Barnstaple in the election of 1690, and on 14 May he was named as a commissioner of the great seal. He made at least five recorded speeches in the Commons during this parliament. When Sir John Somers became lord keeper in March 1693 Hutchins returned to private practice. His initial attempt to claim his former position as king's serjeant was rebuffed by the judges, but on 6 May the king reappointed him to that rank. Hutchins was not returned to the Commons at the 1695 election.

Hutchins buried his first wife (whose identity is unknown) on 26 July 1695, in a 'very magnificent' (Kerr and Duncan, 208) funeral in Hatton Garden. In October 1697 he married his two daughters to Richard Minshall of the Temple and Peere Williams of Gray's Inn, both lawyers, each with a reputed portion of £20,000. On 27 December 1697 he married as his second wife, Sarah (1667–1700), daughter of Sir William Leman, second baronet, of Northaw, Hertfordshire. She died in August 1700 shortly after the birth of twins.

Hutchins's patent as king's serjeant was revoked on 23 June 1702, shortly after the accession of Queen Anne. However, by this date his health seems to have been poor. Hutchins was resident at Northaw when he died on 6 July 1705, a codicil to his will in April 1698 referring to the purchase of property there. His body was then taken to London for burial on 12 July at St Andrew's, Holborn. He was succeeded by his son, Leman Hutchins. STUART HANDLEY

Sources HoP, *Commons, 1690–1715* [draft] · Sainty, *King's counsel*, 23, 34 · Baker, *Serjeants*, 449, 520 · R. Clutterbuck, ed., *The history and antiquities of the county of Hertford*, 2 (1821), 413–15 · N. Luttrell, *A brief historical relation of state affairs from September 1678 to April 1714*, 4 (1857), 289, 651; 5 (1857), 341, 570 · *The parliamentary diary of Narcissus Luttrell, 1691–1693*, ed. H. Horwitz (1972), 46, 117, 148, 415, 469 · *The Portledge papers: being extracts from the letters of Richard Lapthorne … to Richard Coffin*, ed. R. J. Kerr and I. C. Duncan (1928), 208 · will, PRO, PROB 11/481, sig. 243 · J. Foster, *The register of admissions to Gray's Inn, 1521–1889, together with the register of marriages in Gray's Inn chapel, 1695–1754* (privately printed, London, 1889), 300 · R. J. Fletcher, ed., *The pension book of Gray's Inn*, 1 (1901), 80 · *The Genealogist*, new ser., 31 (1914–15), 233 · Foss, *Judges*, 7.320–21 · IGI · DNB

Hutchins, Henry [*known as* Harry Hutchens] (1857–1939), athlete, was born on 27 November 1857 at Ellisfield, near Basingstoke, Hampshire, the son of Charles Hutchins, a farm labourer, and his wife, Ann Myrtle. Known as Harry Hutchens, he competed mostly in handicaps at the main centres for professional meetings, Sheffield and Edinburgh. He was a 'marked man' from the time he won a Sheffield handicap in 1878, but running off scratch he won there in 1879, 1882, and 1891. Handicapped severely, he never won the 120 yards at the new year gala meeting at Powderhall, Edinburgh, regarded as the blue riband event for professionals. Indeed, Hutchins's reputation was to some extent based on what people thought he could have achieved if he had run flat out more often than he did, for he sometimes found it more profitable to lose races he might well have won.

In Australia in 1886 Hutchins beat the expatriate Irishman Tom Malone in a three-race series, then lost twice to Charles Samuels, an Aborigine. He beat Samuels so decisively in a third race, however, it seemed likely, as was claimed, that he deliberately lost the first two. On 13 September 1887 he was involved in a fiasco that virtually ended the claim of professional races to be genuinely competitive. At Lillie Bridge Stadium, London, he was due to meet Harry Gent of Stockton over 120 yards. With several thousand spectators present, the race was cancelled at the last moment because their backers could not agree which runner should lose the race. The crowd rioted and burnt down the grandstand.

Hutchins's fame, however, spanned several generations, and people who had not seen him run repeated the cliché of those who had: that he was the finest sprinter who ever lived. Three examples of performances when he was apparently moving at top speed show that he was very fast by any standard: 131 yards (120 metres) in 12.4 seconds, and 50 yards in 4.5. He always used a standing start, and was still competing and starting off scratch in his late thirties. At Paisley, a month before his thirty-seventh birthday, he was timed at 11.8 seconds for 120 yards and 21.8 for 220. Hutchins, described as a 'professional athlete (retired)', died at 134 Brookdale Road, Catford, London, on 2 January 1939, fifty-five years to the day after he had covered 300 yards in 30 seconds on a cold winter's day in Edinburgh, a performance that still impresses historians of athletics. He was survived by a daughter, Hilda.

WILFRED MORGAN

Sources D. A. Jamieson, *Powderhall and pedestrianism* (1943) · P. Lovesey, 'Flash Harry (Harry Hutchens)', *Athletics Weekly* (25 Dec 1982), 44–7, 52 · G. Nicholson, *The professionals* (1964) · R. E. Walker, *Sprinting* (1922) · P. Lovesey, *The official centenary history of the Amateur Athletics Association* (1979) · A. Newton, *Races and training* (1949) · b. cert. · d. cert.
Likenesses Gale & Polden Ltd, photograph · photograph (in old age), repro. in Newton, *Races and training*

Hutchins, John (1698–1773), county historian, was born on 21 September 1698 at Bradford Peverell, Dorset, the son of Richard Hutchins (1667–1734), Church of England clergyman, and his wife, Anne (d. 1707). He came from a well-established Dorset clerical family. His grandfather John Hutchins had been vicar of Sydling St Nicholas from 1665 until his death in 1701, and his father was curate of Bradford Peverell and from 1693 was also rector of All Saints', Dorchester. His mother died on 9 April 1707, when he was only eight years old, and Hutchins reveals nothing about her. A note in the second and third editions of his *History of Dorset* following the description of her memorial in Bradford Peverell church states that 'She was related to Mr Seward, a Portugal merchant, on St Mary Hill, London' (Hutchins, 2.536).

Hutchins's early education was under William Thornton, rector of West Stafford, Dorset, and master of Dorchester grammar school. In his *History of Dorset* Hutchins paid tribute to Thornton, describing him as 'a person of great worth, piety and virtue' and as 'a sincere friend, and even a father to the author of this work' (Hutchins, 2.517). Thornton had been educated at Hart Hall, Oxford, and Hutchins matriculated there on 30 May 1718, but in April 1719 he transferred to Balliol College, and graduated BA on 18 January 1722. He was ordained deacon in February 1722 and priest in December 1723, then returned to Dorset, where he was to spend the rest of his career. In

John Hutchins (1698–1773), by J. Collimore, pubd 1813 (after Charles Bestland)

1730 he received the degree of MA from Magdalene College, Cambridge, presumably because he had not kept sufficient residence to satisfy the requirement at Oxford.

In 1723 Hutchins became curate and assistant schoolmaster to George Marsh, vicar of Milton Abbas and master of the grammar school there. At Milton Abbas he became known to the wealthy landowner Jacob Bancks, who presented him to the rectory of Swyre in 1729 and to the rectory of Melcombe Horsey in 1733. Hutchins vacated Melcombe Horsey when he was instituted to the rectory of Holy Trinity with St Martin's and St Mary's, Wareham, on 8 March 1744. Thereafter he continued to hold Swyre and Wareham until his death. On 21 December 1733 he married Anne (1709–1796), daughter of Thomas Stephens, rector of Pimperne, Dorset. They had only one child, Anne Martha (d. 1797).

Hutchins was a conscientious clergyman, but his reserved and studious manner did not appeal to all his parishioners. In a *Memoir* written soon after Hutchins's death his friend George Bingham, rector of Pimperne, described him as 'a sound Divine rather than … an eminent preacher' and increasing deafness meant that 'his elocution was scarce improved by age' (Hutchins, 1.xix–xxiii). In 1761 the vestry of Wareham complained to the bishop that they could not hear when he read the service nor when he preached. At Wareham, Hutchins was also involved in difficulties with the numerous nonconformists and in political controversies in the borough. Further problems were caused by a curate who was eventually confined in a lunatic asylum. On Sunday 25 July 1762 the town of Wareham was devastated by fire, and the rectory house was badly damaged and his library destroyed. Hutchins was away at the time, and his notes, together with the partly completed manuscript of his *History* were only saved through the remarkable exertions of his wife. The episode is commemorated on the title-page of the *History* by the quotation 'Reliquiae Troia ex ardente receptae'.

It was while he was at Milton Abbas and at the instigation of his patron, Jacob Bancks, that Hutchins began the research on Dorset history which was to occupy the rest of his life. In 1736 the antiquary Browne Willis, who was a native of Dorset, persuaded him to undertake a complete history of the county. Three years later he circulated a list of six queries together with a general appeal for information; this had been drawn up and printed by Willis. The work proceeded slowly, hampered by parochial duties, illness, and the expense of visiting libraries and record repositories. By 1750 it was already reported that progress was almost at a standstill. In 1761 a subscription was raised by the local gentry enabling Hutchins to pursue his research in Salisbury, London, and Oxford. He was assisted in the collection of material by various local antiquaries and corresponded with other historians, including William Stukeley, William Borlase, Charles Goodwyn, Richard Gough, and Charles Lyttleton. In his last years his research was much hindered by ill health. In the summer of 1771 he suffered a stroke and, although he continued to work on the *History*, he never fully recovered and died at Wareham on 21 June 1773. He was buried in the church of St Mary, Wareham.

Hutchins's *History* was still uncompleted at his death but, owing to the efforts of Gough and William Cuming, a family friend and Dorchester physician, it was finally published in 1774 in two folio volumes entitled *The History and Antiquities of the County of Dorset*. The editors were able to remit £170 from the proceeds for the support of his widow and his daughter, who was a ward of both Gough and Cuming. On 3 June 1776 Anne Martha Hutchins married John Bellasis (*d.* 1808), then in the service of the East India Company and afterwards major-general and commander of the forces at Bombay. Anne Hutchins died on 2 May 1796, aged eighty-seven, and a year later Anne Martha Bellasis died in Bombay on 14 May 1797.

The wealth of information contained in the first edition of Hutchins's *History*, including detailed pedigrees of gentry families, histories of estates, religious houses, parish churches, towns, and villages, together with the numerous illustrations and extracts from documentary sources, ensured that the book was well received, and a second edition was soon planned. This was again edited by Gough and Cuming. It was produced in four volumes, with additional material and many more illustrations. The expenses were met by Hutchins's son-in-law, John Bellasis. The first volume of the second edition was issued in 1796, and the second volume in 1803, but on 8 February 1808 a fire at the printing house of John Nichols destroyed all the unsold copies and all copies of the third volume except for one which remained in Gough's possession. Gough died in 1809, and the third and fourth volumes

were finally published by J. B. Nichols in 1813 and 1815 respectively. A third edition was edited by W. Shipp and J. W. Hodson and was published in four volumes, dated 1861, 1863, 1868, and 1870. This edition was reprinted in 1973 with a new introduction by Robert Douch.

The third edition is the fullest and most reliable, containing many additions on the antiquities, archaeology, and social and economic history of the county. It also includes numerous new illustrations, plans, references, and extracts from documentary sources, reflecting the growing interest in these aspects of local history. Hutchins's *History of Dorset* became and has remained an indispensable reference book and the essential starting point for any historical study of Dorset.   J. H. BETTEY

Sources G. Bingham, 'Biographical anecdotes of the Reverend John Hutchins', *Bibliotheca topographica Britannica*, 34 (1785) · J. Hutchins, *The history and antiquities of the county of Dorset*, 3rd edn, ed. W. Shipp and J. W. Hodson, 2–3 (1863–8) · R. Douch, 'John Hutchins', *English county historians*, ed. J. Simmons (1978), 112–58 · parish register, Sydling St Nicholas, 1665–1764, Dorset RO, PE/SSN/RE 1/2 [note on genealogy of Hutchins family inside front cover] · brief notes on Hutchins family, Dorset RO, D/RGB/LL 595 · complaint of Wareham vestry concerning Hutchins, Dorset RO, PE/WA/CW 6 · *IGI*

Archives Bodl. Oxf., Dorset antiquarian collections and corresp. | BL, letters to Charles Lyttleton, Stowe MSS 753–754 · Bodl. Oxf., corresp. with William Stukeley, MS Eng. misc. c. 321, fols. 23–7 · Bodl. Oxf., letters to Browne Willis, MS Willis 43, fols. 224–91; 60, fol. 122; 83, fol. 111 · Dorset RO, letters to Sir Peter Thompson

Likenesses J. Collimore, engraving (after C. Bestland), BM, NPG; repro. in G. Bingham, *Biographical anecdotes of the Reverend John Hutchins*, 2nd edn (1813) [see illus.]

Hutchinson [*née* Marbury], **Anne** (*bap.* 1591, *d.* 1643), dissident prophet in America, was baptized on 20 July 1591 at Alford, Lincolnshire, the eldest child of the Revd Francis Marbury (*c.*1556–1611) and his wife, Bridget Dryden, both from gentry families. While her father was a militant presbyterian who none the less eventually conformed, Anne herself combined an intimate acquaintance with scripture with a thoroughly non-deferential attitude to ecclesiological structures and representatives. On 9 August 1612 she married William Hutchinson (*bap.* 1586, *d.* 1642), an Alford merchant; they had fourteen children, of whom Faith (1617–1652) married the merchant and army officer Thomas Savage.

Of the little that is known of Anne's life in England two points are salient to her later public role. She found assurance of her salvation not through her holiness, or sanctification, as most puritan ministers advocated, but through a charismatic experience of scripture texts. This technique was grounded in the teaching of two ministers she admired, the prominent preacher John Cotton, and her brother-in-law John Wheelwright, but it could easily be interpreted by unsympathetic ministers as verging on the heresies of familism and antinomianism. She also used scripture texts as the basis for temporal prophecies. Once, while seeking divine insight into the state of the Church of England, she received verses that revealed to her the nature of Christ's union with the souls of the elect and enabled her to evaluate the doctrinal soundness of ministers. Wheelwright and Cotton were the only ministers she knew of whom she regarded as completely sound.

Influenced by the example of Cotton, and of her brother-in-law and her eldest son, both called Edward Hutchinson [see below], in emigrating to Massachusetts, and in possession of what she felt was divine encouragement, Anne Hutchinson and her immediate family followed them, arriving in mid-September 1634. Anne joined the Boston church on 2 November 1634, after satisfying some of their concerns about her doctrinal soundness and her lack of respect for ministers whose doctrine she did not agree with. The Hutchinsons quickly became important members of the Boston community. While her husband, William, served as a deputy to the general court, town selectman, and deacon of the church, Anne herself was valued in part for her help at childbirth and in part because of her ability to lead people to what her ministers regarded as genuine conversions.

When Henry Vane arrived and joined the Boston church in November 1635 he was greatly taken with Anne's spiritual abilities. Elected governor in May 1636 he encouraged her to set up well-attended conventicles in which she expounded and developed her own theology, a more extreme variant of Cotton's. A millennial enthusiasm spread in the Boston church. John Winthrop, a hostile witness perhaps engaging in rhetorical excess, claimed that some persons in the colony considered Anne to be a divinely appointed prophet for the conversion of the Jews and that more persons visited her than any minister for spiritual counselling. When theological rifts between Boston and the other churches escalated into a dispute known to historians as the antinomian controversy, Anne was pitted with Cotton, the most prominent minister in Massachusetts, John Wheelwright, who had arrived in May 1636, and their supporters and admirers against most of the ministers and magistrates in the colony.

The dispute seriously weakened Massachusetts, already suspect among English puritans for its radical ecclesiology and under the threat of having its charter revoked by Charles I's government, and in 1637 its ministerial and magisterial élite pulled the Boston church back into line. While Cotton finally threw in his lot with his fellow ministers, the most vocal dissidents, including Wheelwright and Anne Hutchinson, were tried for sedition. At her civil trial in November 1637 Anne warned her judges that she had a divine message that they and the colony would be destroyed if they punished her. The court compared her to the Anabaptists of Munster and decided that her revelations were at the root of the colony's disturbances. Sentenced to be banished she was meanwhile placed under house arrest through the winter. During that time she expressed theological opinions more radical than most of her supporters suspected and, as a result, in March 1638 she was tried for heresy by the Boston church. She recanted, but the church judged that she had lied about how radical her views had become, and excommunicated her.

After her banishment in 1638 Anne and her family helped set up Aquidneck colony in an area that later became part of Rhode Island. They were riven by political and religious disputes. In 1642, as Massachusetts made moves to annex the colony and her husband died, Anne, fearing for her safety, moved to what is now Westchester County, New York, territory then claimed by the Dutch. Tensions between the Dutch and the local Indians were high, and the latter warned her not to settle among them, but she had a scriptural revelation that God would protect her. She and fifteen members of her family died in an Indian attack in August or September 1643.

Anne's eldest son, **Edward Hutchinson** (1613–1675), arrived in Boston in 1633 with his uncle Edward Hutchinson, with whom he is frequently confused. Hutchinson was admitted to the Boston church on 10 August 1634 and was made a freeman a month later on 3 September. He went to Rhode Island along with his mother when she was banished in 1638, but he returned to Boston within a few years. From 1658 to 1675 he was periodically a deputy to the general court and opposed the persecution of Quakers and Baptists. A militia captain, in July 1675, after the outbreak of King Philip's War, he went to negotiate with the Nipmuck Indians at Brookfield and was killed by them.

MICHAEL P. WINSHIP

Sources J. L. Chester, 'The Hutchinson family of England and New England, and its connection with the Marburys and Drydens', *New England Historical and Genealogical Register*, 20 (1866), 355–67 · *The journal of John Winthrop, 1630–1649*, ed. R. S. Dunn, J. Savage, and L. Yeandle (1996) · D. D. Hall, ed., *The antinomian controversy, 1636–1638: a documentary history*, 2nd edn (Durham, NC, 1990) · F. Johnson, *The wonder working providence of Sion's saviour in New England*, ed. J. F. Jameson (1910), 124–36, 186–7 · N. B. Shurtleff, ed., *Records of the governor and company of the Massachusetts Bay in New England*, 5 vols. in 6 (1853–4), vol. 1, pp. 207, 212, 225–6, 368–9; vol. 3, p. 27; vol. 4/1, pp. 320, 369; vol. 4/2, pp. 449, 485, 507, 551, 561 · E. Battis, *Saints and sectaries: Anne Hutchinson and the antinomian controversy in the Massachusetts Bay colony* (1962) · R. C. Dudding, *History of the parish and manors of Alford* (1930), 147–52 · T. Hutchinson, 'Hutchinson in America', BL, Egerton MS 2664, 13 · S. Gorton, *Simplicity's defence against seven-headed policy*, ed. W. R. Staples (1835), 270 · R. D. Pierce, ed., *The records of the First Church in Boston, 1630–1868*, 3 vols. (1961), 19 · 'Memoir of Governor Hutchinson', *New England Historical and Genealogical Register*, 1 (1847), 299–300 · J. R. Bartlett, ed., *Records of the colony of Rhode Island and Providence plantations, in New England*, 10 vols. (1856–65), vol. 1, pp. 52, 55–6, 111 · F. L. Gay, 'Rev. Francis Marbury', *Proceedings of the Massachusetts Historical Society*, 48 (1914–15), 280–81 · *DNB* · M. P. Winship, '"The most glorious church in the world": the unity of the godly in Boston, Massachusetts, in the 1630s', *Journal of British Studies*, 39 (2000), 71–98

Hutchinson, Arthur (1866–1937), mineralogist, was born in London on 6 July 1866, the only child of George Hutchinson, of Woodside, Westmorland, silk merchant, of London, and his wife, Deborah Richardson, of Culgaith, Cumberland. He was educated at Clifton College, Bristol, and in 1884 went with a scholarship to Christ's College, Cambridge, where he was awarded first classes in both parts of the natural sciences tripos (1886 and 1888). After a year's research work in chemistry with Matthew Moncrieff Pattison Muir he went to the University of Würzburg in Germany where he studied under Emil Fischer and W. K. Röntgen and obtained the degree of PhD. In 1891 he was appointed a demonstrator in the chemical laboratory at

Gonville and Caius College, Cambridge, and in 1892 was elected into a fellowship at Pembroke College and appointed college lecturer in natural science.

Hutchinson's work as a mineralogist began in 1895 when he was appointed demonstrator in mineralogy in the University of Cambridge. In this capacity he conducted, almost unaided, for twenty-eight years the whole of the course in mineralogy for the first part of the natural sciences tripos. He was appointed university lecturer in crystallography in 1923 and finally in 1926 he succeeded William James Lewis as professor of mineralogy. He devoted himself to the development of his department, encouraging research in X-ray crystallography and preparing for the organization of the two new departments, of mineralogy and petrology and of crystallography, which were established on his retirement from the professorship in 1931.

Hutchinson's first notable contribution to mineralogical research was the discovery of a new mineral, stokesite, in 1899. In the same year he began work on the diathermancy and optical characters of stibnite, showing that the mineral, ordinarily supposed to be opaque, transmitted light of long wavelength, and he successfully measured its refractive indices, and proved its orthorhombic symmetry. He devised an inverted form of goniometer for the determination of the crystallographic and optical characters of small crystals, and a protractor for the construction of stereographic and gnomonic projections, adapting this in 1925 to the interpretation of Laue X-ray photographs of crystals. Several charts, for the graphical solution of crystallographic problems, for the correction of specific gravity determinations, and for the solution of some formulae in crystal optics, were published between 1915 and 1925. From 1904 to 1912 he wrote the section on mineralogical chemistry in the annual reports of the Chemical Society.

In 1901 Hutchinson married Evaline Demezy, second daughter of Alexander Shipley, of Datchet, Buckinghamshire, and sister of Sir Arthur Everett Shipley. They had two sons and a daughter; the elder son became professor of zoology in Yale University. Hutchinson was a governor of Gresham's School, Holt, for twenty-two years, and of St Bees School, Cumberland, and was an active member of the council of Clifton College. He was elected FRS in 1922 and an honorary fellow of Christ's College in 1935, and was appointed OBE for his research work on gas masks during the First World War. In addition to his mineralogical work he was assistant tutor of Pembroke College from 1901 to 1926, and was elected master of the college in 1928, a post from which he retired only five months before his death, at home at 62 Grange Road, Cambridge, on 12 December 1937. He was survived by his wife.

W. C. Smith, rev.

Sources W. C. Smith, *Obits. FRS*, 2 (1936–8), 483–91 · *The Times* (13 Dec 1937) · personal knowledge (1949) · CGPLA Eng. & Wales (1938) **Likenesses** W. Stoneman, photograph, 1926, NPG · W. Rothenstein, oils, Pembroke Cam. · photograph, repro. in *Obits. FRS* **Wealth at death** £21,436 11s. 1d.: resworn probate, CGPLA Eng. & Wales (1938)

Hutchinson, Benjamin (*bap.* 1733, *d.* 1804), Church of England clergyman and antiquary, was baptized on 29 August 1733 in St Nicholas's Church, Durham, the son of John and Ann Hutchinson. His mother may have been Ann, *née* Sowerby (*b.* 1697?), the widow of Thomas Brass. The Hutchinsons of co. Durham were numerous, and included the antiquary William Hutchinson (1732–1814) and several mayors of Durham, but Benjamin's immediate family were probably tradespeople of no special note. Modest origins may explain why his education, of which nothing is known, did not include either Oxford or Cambridge, in spite of which he was ordained to the priesthood, and why his earliest publication, *An Humble Address to the Clergy of England* (1764), was concerned with the financial precariousness of the clergy and especially that of their widows and children. Nevertheless, he successfully climbed the ladder of ecclesiastical preferment: his principal livings were the vicarage of Kimbolton (1761–88) and the rectory of Holywell-cum-Needingworth (1788–1804), both Huntingdonshire churches in the gift of the duke of Manchester, whose seat was at Kimbolton Castle, but his income was supplemented from 1773 by the prebend of Welton Painshall in Lincoln Cathedral and from 1788 by the rectory of Rushden, Northamptonshire. Huntingdonshire thus became his adopted county, a connection he cemented by marriage on 26 November 1761 to Jane Peet (1737–1820x24), daughter of William Peet (*d.* 1740) of Wornditch.

Hutchinson's literary skill is apparent from two poems, 'Kimbolton Park' and 'Marriage: an Ode', both published in 1765, the first obviously in honour of his patron. Doubtless, too, the appearance in print of his sermon preached on a public fast day in 1778 which questioned recourse to arms against fellow citizens in America was due to Manchester, who was a relentless critic of Lord North's policy there. About this time he turned increasingly to matters antiquarian and scientific, compiling climatic records at Kimbolton, from which he published a paper in 1782, and contributing meteorological notes to the *Philosophical Transactions of the Royal Society* in 1789–90. Cambridge, where one of his sons, Benjamin, entered Sidney Sussex College in 1793, and the Royal Society of London provided sources of scholarly contact; at each he could meet or correspond with the eminent, such as Emanuel da Costa, the fossilist, and Thomas Martyn, botanist and professor at Cambridge. In 1795 he was elected FRS.

It was a short step to natural history and local archaeology. According to Martyn, who inherited, albeit briefly, Hutchinson's manuscripts, Hutchinson visited every Huntingdonshire parish, the purpose of which was announced in 1794 as the publication of *The Natural History and Antiquities of Huntingdonshire*. The production of folio county histories was at its height, but the particular stimulus was surely William Hutchinson's *History of County Durham* (1785–94), to which Benjamin was a subscriber. A bundle of correspondence, a mere fragment compared to the '20 small memorandum books' last recorded when sold in 1888, is all that certainly survives of the Huntingdonshire history, but these are enough to reveal its author's scientific inclination. The Durham precedent of giving local population statistics, for example, was evidently to be extended by giving mortality rates and making observations on longevity, mineral waters, and such like. Much material was contributed by others, a neighbouring clergyman, Charles Favell of Brington, being especially keen, while the Cambridge botanist Richard Relhan had particular reason to regret the book's non-appearance as he had submitted details of 800 plants but failed to keep a copy. Antiquities too are well represented among the letters, which have the appearance of reports of archaeological finds from clerical colleagues in response to a systematic enquiry.

Sadly, mental illness interrupted Hutchinson's work and controversially it was necessary for a curate to take over his religious duties. Hutchinson died on 23 March 1804 in the rectory, Holywell, and was buried in Holywell church on 28 March 1804. The *Cambridge Chronicle* mourned the loss to the literary world 'of such a virtuoso' as the *Natural History* was said to be on the eve of publication. The family, comprising his widow, two sons and three daughters, is described by more than one source as virtually destitute and indeed, for some years after, Jane Hutchinson and the unmarried daughters received benefactions from the Huntingdonshire Clergy Charity.

P. C. SAUNDERS

Sources C. P. Lewis, 'Huntingdonshire', *English county histories: a guide*, ed. C. R. J. Currie and C. P. Lewis (1994), 196–207 · *VCH Huntingdonshire*, 1.xv–xvi, 38 · letters to B. Hutchinson, 1785–98, Wilts. & Swindon RO, Stourhead Archive, 383/921 · parish records, Kimbolton, Cambs. AS, Huntingdon, Acc. 2774 · parish records, Holywell-cum-Needingworth, Cambs. AS, Huntingdon, Acc. 2280 · T. Martyn, letter to D. Lysons, 1824, BL, Add. MS 9458, fols. 134–5 · F. Knight, ed., *Letters to William Frend from the Reynolds family of Little Paxton and John Hammond of Fenstanton, 1793–1814* (1974) · G. C. Gorham, *History of Eynesbury and St. Neots*, 2 vols. and supplement (1820–24) · annual reports, Huntingdonshire Clergy Charity, Cambs. AS, Huntingdon, Acc. 4197 · *Cambridge Chronicle and Journal* (31 March 1804) · Venn, *Alum. Cant.* · H. I. Longden, *Northamptonshire and Rutland clergy from 1500*, ed. P. I. King and others, 16 vols. in 6, Northamptonshire RS (1938–52) · IGI
Archives BL, letters to E. M. da Costa, Add. MS 28538, fols. 258–9
Wealth at death family described as 'distressed' in 1802 during subject's madness, and 1822 as 'left in a manner destitute'; but son groom of wardrobe of George III and reasonably beneficed; three of five daughters married well

Hutchinson, Beryl Butterworth (1892–1981), volunteer ambulance driver and member of the FANY, was born on 22 August 1892 at Tenter House, Spotland, near Rochdale, Lancashire, the only child of Robert Arthur Lord Hutchinson (1860–1925), woollen manufacturer, and his wife, Florence Mark (1866–1945). She grew up in Lancashire and learned to drive at the age of twelve. At the outbreak of the First World War she joined the First Aid Nursing Yeomanry (FANY) corps, an all-women voluntary organization. Founded in 1907 as a mounted ambulance unit the FANY soon mastered mechanized transport and was the first women's organization to go to France, on 27 October 1914. FANYs drove ambulances and ran hospitals and casualty clearing stations for the British, Belgian, and French armies all along the western front.

Beryl Hutchinson, known as Hutch, arrived in Boulogne on 1 January 1915, having brought with her a mobile kitchen that she had purchased herself, 'the price of my being allowed to go to France. In appearance it was like a hen-house mounted on a Ford chassis' (Hutchinson). On 24 May 1915, while attached to a joint British–Belgian mounted artillery unit, she was involved in one of the first gas attacks, near Ypres:

> A procession of British came staggering up the lane … they had the silliest bits of chewed cotton wool fastened to their faces … We remembered we had 'Mr Southall's conveniences for ladies' … also at that time one used Rimmel's toilet vinegar for cleansing one's face, etc. We cut the pads in half, poured the vinegar on and … lashed it to the men's faces. It got them along the road to the dressing station. We often wondered if the medics there recognised our 'first aid equipment!' (ibid.)

Hutchinson was second in command of the joint FANY-VAD St Omer convoy. On the night of 18 May 1918, during the German spring offensive, under heavy bombardment, the women successfully evacuated the wounded, and Beryl Hutchinson was responsible for keeping the engines of the ambulances running. She was not one of the many decorated on that occasion—'There was no glamour in starting up engines but the girls said I should have been awarded a "mangle handle rampant"' (ibid.)—but she was appointed MBE in 1919 for her war service.

After her return from France and the death of her father Beryl Hutchinson lived with her mother in the New Forest, where they bred horses, and later moved to London. She maintained her membership of the FANY and at the outbreak of the Second World War she was appointed company commander, 8th (London) motor transport company, and then motor transport instructor in the newly created ATS. After the war she lived in Kenya for four years but the dominant interest of her later life was palmistry. In 1945, with Noel Jaquin, she co-founded the Society for Study of Physiological Patterns, of which she was made life president in 1971. She did research into the signs of Parkinson's disease in a person's palm and kept a library of palm prints sent to her from all over the world. In 1953 she published *A Handbook on Hands*, which was followed by *Your Life in your Hands* in 1967. She was a post-war pioneer in the field of radionics, the practice of hands-on healing. Beryl Hutchinson died at Vicarage Gate Nursing Home, Kensington, on 6 November 1981.

LYNETTE BEARDWOOD

Sources Beryl Hutchinson, reminiscences, Duke of York's HQ, Mercury House, London, FANY archives · I. Ward Hutchinson, *FANY Invicta* (1955) · H. Popham, *FANY, the story of the Women's Transport Service* (1982) · *CGPLA Eng. & Wales* (1982) · *Daily Telegraph* (26 May 1971) · *Sunday Telegraph* (24 Oct 1976) · b. cert. · d. cert.
Archives U. Leeds, Liddell Collection | SOUND IWM · U. Leeds, Liddell Collection
Likenesses photographs, 1918, Women's Transport Service, Duke of York's HQ, Mercury House, London, FANY archives
Wealth at death under £25,000: probate, 6 May 1982, *CGPLA Eng. & Wales*

Hutchinson, Christopher [Kit] **Hely-** (1767–1826), soldier and politician, the fifth son of John Hely-*Hutchinson

(1724–1794), politician and provost of Trinity College, Dublin, and Christiana Nikson (*bap.* 1732, *d.* 1788) of Munny, co. Wicklow, was born in Ireland on 5 April 1767. John Hely-*Hutchinson, second earl of Donoughmore (1757–1832), and Richard Hely-*Hutchinson (1756–1825) were his elder brothers. Educated at Trinity College, Dublin (1784), and at Lincoln's Inn (1791), he was called to the Irish bar in 1792. The study and practice of law was little to his taste, but his father's influence soon secured him a respectable position, which the more easily reconciled him to his profession. In 1795 he succeeded his father by purchasing the representation of the borough of Taghmon, co. Wexford. He entered parliament during the viceroyalty of Earl Fitzwilliam (1794–5), and was an ardent supporter of his administration. Accordingly, he was strongly opposed to the government of his successor Lord Camden (1795–8), and resigned his seat in disgust in 1796. On the outbreak of the rebellion of 1798 he enlisted as a volunteer under his brother John, for whom he had a profound admiration, and was actively engaged at Ballinamuck, co. Longford, where he was instrumental in capturing the French generals Lafontaine and Sarrazin, and was commended by Lord Cornwallis for his bravery.

Hely-Hutchinson was strongly opposed to the union, and at a meeting of the bar proposed to resist it with the sword. After the passing of the measure, he quitted Ireland and, having developed a taste for military life, he took part as aide-de-camp of his brother in the expedition against The Helder, and was wounded in the battle of Alkmar. In January 1801 he was raised to the rank of lieutenant-colonel, and accompanied his brother John as a volunteer in the expedition to Egypt under Sir Ralph Abercromby. On the elevation of his brother to the peerage as Lord Hutchinson, in June 1802 he took his seat for the city of Cork, which he continued to represent, except from 1812 to 1818, when he was displaced by Colonel Longfield, until his death in 1826. He congratulated the government on the suppression of Emmet's rebellion, but pressed for an inquiry into the causes of Irish distress, declaring that he saw more supineness and negligence respecting Irish affairs than he had ever witnessed respecting the smallest English interest. In 1805 he voted for the Irish Habeas Corpus Suspension Bill, 'but was of opinion that the union would be of little benefit if it was not followed up with other marks of attention to Ireland than continued suspensions of the Habeas Corpus Act'. He was a strenuous advocate of the war, and made an offer, which was, however, declined, to raise a regiment at his own expense. In 1806 he accompanied Lord Hutchinson on a diplomatic mission to St Petersburg and Berlin. In 1807 he took part in the Polish campaign, fighting in the Russian ranks. He was wounded in the battle of Eylau, and was also present in the mêlée at Friedland. After the peace of Tilsit he visited Moscow, and on his return to Britain at the beginning of 1809 he vehemently opposed the ministry for their mismanagement of the war, and particularly for the convention of Cintra, which he declared had mortified the troops and disgusted the nation. In 1810 he was highly critical of the Scheldt expedition.

As he had opposed the union when it was first mooted, so Hely-Hutchinson regarded the refusal to fulfil the conditions of the bargain, in particular Catholic emancipation, as the chief cause of Irish disturbances. Against Lord Castlereagh he was particularly indignant, and on more than one occasion was reprimanded in the Commons by the speaker for the violence of his language. In 1812 he moved the repeal of the union describing it as 'degrading and abominable' (HoP, *Commons*). He voted in favour of Sir Francis Burdett's plan of parliamentary reform, and one of the last speeches he made was directed against emigration to Canada as a panacea for Irish distress.

Unlike the rest of his family, who were notorious placehunters, Kit Hely-Hutchinson was determinedly independent and he proved a thorn in the side of successive governments. There was delight in government circles when he was defeated for Cork in 1812, and proportionate gloom when he was returned in 1818. However, his increasingly violent language caused him to be viewed as an eccentric or crank, and this ensured that the family did not suffer any loss of office for his wayward views. He was in fact beyond control, as his brother John, to whom he was closest, ruefully admitted:

> Kit and I live upon the best terms possible. I have but one reason for so doing: I do not endeavour to control him in any one thing, either public or private. All my friends here are perfectly aware that I have no influence over him. (PRO NIre., Donoughmore papers, T.3459/D/42/15)

After the conclusion of the war with France, Hely-Hutchinson was accustomed during the recesses of parliament to visit Paris with his family; but becoming objectionable to the French government, owing to his intimacy with the liberal chiefs and his opposition to the legitimist intervention in Spain, he was compelled to withdraw from France. Constantly short of money, his family had to supply his property qualification for parliament and to fund his election campaigns. His elder brother John also supported his second marriage, to his (Kit's) mistress of the previous eighteen years. His first wife, whom he had married on 24 December 1792, was Anne Wensley, the daughter of Sir James Bond, MP for Naas, co. Kildare; she died on 30 March 1796, having had a son, John. His second marriage took place on 1 October 1818, to Anne, the widow of John Brydges Woodcock, daughter of the Hon. Maurice Crosbie, dean of Limerick, and sister of William, fourth Lord Branden. They had two sons and two daughters. Hely-Hutchinson died after a lingering illness at his residence, Ben Lomond House, Downshire Hill Road, Hampstead, on 26 August 1826.

ROBERT DUNLOP, *rev.* THOMAS BARTLETT

Sources HoP, *Commons, 1790–1820*, vol. 4 · Burke, *Peerage* · *GM*, 1st ser., 96/2 (1826), 370–71 · PRO NIre., Donoughmore papers, T.3459/D/42/15
Archives TCD | PRO NIre., Donoughmore papers
Likenesses C. Turner, mezzotint, pubd 1813 (after J. Corbett), BM

Hutchinson, Edward (1613–1675). *See under* Hutchinson, Anne (*bap.* 1591, *d.* 1643).

Hutchinson, Francis (1660–1739), bishop of Down and Connor, second son of Edward Hitchinson (*bap.* 1625), was born on 2 January 1660 at Carsington, Derbyshire, according to the parish register, in which the family name is invariably spelt Hitchinson. His mother was Mary Tallents, sister of Francis Tallents (1619–1708), the ejected minister. He matriculated as a pensioner on 4 July 1678 at St Catharine's College, Cambridge, and graduated BA (1680) and MA (1684). Francis Tallents directed his historical studies, and employed him about 1680 in taking the manuscript of his *View of Universal History* to Benjamin Stillingfleet, William Beveridge, and Richard Kidder for their corrections before it was printed.

Hutchinson's first preferment was the vicarage of Hoxne, Suffolk. Before 1692 he became perpetual curate of St James's, Bury St Edmunds, Suffolk. On 3 July 1698 he commenced DD at Cambridge. His residence in Suffolk turned his attention to the earlier proceedings against witches in that county and resulted in his treatise on the history of witchcraft (1718), with many particulars collected by personal inquiry from survivors. Although the work was prepared more than a decade earlier, Hutchinson delayed publication out of deference to the anxieties of Archbishop Tenison. The treatise applied a consciously rational approach to the phenomenon and deprecated how witchcraft prosecutions divided and unsettled communities. At the same time, Hutchinson was obliged to concede the existence of both good and evil spirits in the world, so weakening his arguments against the existence of witches. Nevertheless, this contribution, together with his sermons in support of the Hanoverians, aligned him clearly with the whig and latitudinarian groups in the church, and assisted his advancement.

Hutchinson married Anne (*d.* 1758/9) on 15 April 1707 at Bury St Edmunds. In 1720 he was appointed bishop of Down and Connor, and was consecrated on 22 January 1721. Having taken up residence at Lisburn in co. Antrim he quickly threw himself into the business of the diocese. Notable was his interest in the problems of Irish-speakers, specifically on Rathlin Island, suspected as a haven of Jacobites. For their benefit he had printed a bilingual catechism and primer, with the Irish rendered phonetically in a roman script. Rathlin itself was made a separate parish and a church was built there. In 1722 he issued the church catechism in Irish in the same font. He continued to explore the culture and history of his adopted country, making contact with scholars such as Cornelius Nary and Anthony Raymond, and in 1734 published his elaborate and learned *Defence of the Antient Historians*. Inspired by the belief that God-given natural resources lay unregarded and unused, he advocated more exact surveys in order to facilitate material improvements. He published pamphlets on the need for a national bank in Ireland, bog reclamation, improved navigation on the River Bann, better exploitation of the fisheries, and how to reduce poverty and unemployment. None of this was original, but Hutchinson was in the vanguard of a public-spirited band of projecting and pamphleteering landowners. His readiness to

share his ideas in print was mocked by some contemporaries. He attended closely to his responsibilities in the diocese and House of Lords. In 1729 he established himself on a newly purchased estate at Portglenone in co. Antrim, for which he paid £8200. Here he lived in some style, true to his conviction that social and economic hierarchies were needed. His private chapel at Portglenone, completed in 1739, subsequently became the parish church in 1840. Hostile to the material and ethical impact of Catholicism, he nevertheless lived on good terms with local Catholics. Similarly, Presbyterians in the neighbourhood respected his industry and piety.

Hutchinson died on 23 June 1739 at Portglenone, and was buried in the chapel there on 25 June. His widow survived him by nineteen years. Of their two children, their son, Thomas, had died before Hutchinson's death, and their daughter, Frances, married first John Hamilton (*d.* 1729), dean of Dromore; second, in 1732, Colonel O'Hara (*d.* 1745) of Crebilly, co. Antrim; and third, in 1748, John Ryder (1697?–1775), afterwards archbishop of Tuam. It was to her eldest son, the Revd Hutchinson Hamilton (*d.* 1778), that Hutchinson left the bulk of his estate. His library was sold at auction in Dublin on 26 April 1756: an annotated copy of the catalogue is in the library of Queen's University, Belfast.

TOBY BARNARD

Sources F. Hutchinson, notebooks and account books, PRO NIre., D/o 1/22/1–2 · Hutchinson's notebook, Dean and Chapter of Down MSS · computation of Hutchinson's estate at Portglenone, NL Ire., PC 223 · T. C. Barnard, 'Protestants and the Irish language, c.1675–1725', *Journal of Ecclesiastical History*, 44 (1993), 243–72 · W. G. Wheeler, 'Bishop Francis Hutchinson: his Irish publications and his library', *An uncommon bookman*, ed. J. Gray and W. McCann (1996) · N. J. A. Williams, 'Thomas Wilson, Francis Hutchinson agus litriúna Gaelige', *Eighteenth-Century Ireland*, 1 (1986) · Venn, *Alum. Cant.* · I. Bostridge, *Witchcraft and its transformations, c.1650–c.1750* (1997) · IGI · DNB · H. Cotton, *Fasti ecclesiae Hibernicae*, 6 vols. (1845–78)

Archives Down Cathedral, notebook · PRO NIre., notebooks and account books

Hutchinson, Francis Ernest (1871–1947), literary scholar and Church of England clergyman, was born at Forton, near Gosport, Hampshire, on 17 September 1871. He was the third son of the vicar, the Revd Charles Pierrepont Hutchinson (1831/2–1898), who was descended from the father of the regicide John Hutchinson, and his wife, Louisa, daughter of the Revd Alleyne Higgs Barker, vicar of Rickmansworth, Hertfordshire. Hutchinson was educated at Lancing College and at Trinity College, Oxford, where he read modern history, graduating with a second-class degree in 1894. He was ordained deacon in 1896 and priest in 1897.

After some years as a schoolmaster at Radley College (1895–1900) and Cooper's Hill College (1900–03), Hutchinson was appointed chaplain of King's College, Cambridge, in 1904. In the same year he married Julia Margaret Crawford, daughter of Colonel G. A. Crawford; they remained in Cambridge until 1912, when Hutchinson became vicar of Leyland, Lancashire. He spent eight years in this industrial parish, working hard for the cause of adult education in the Workers' Educational Association, before returning

Francis Ernest Hutchinson (1871–1947), by Walter Stoneman, 1945

to Oxford as secretary to the university's delegacy for extramural studies, a post which he held with great success from 1920 to 1934. In 1934 Hutchinson accepted a canonry of Worcester, thus severing for a time his association with Oxford, to which he had become bound more closely by his appointment in 1928 to be chaplain, and, in March 1934 to be a fellow, of All Souls. In 1943 he resigned his canonry and returned to Oxford, where he devoted himself to literary work, maintaining none the less his old associations, notably with Lady Margaret Hall (he was a member of its council for more than twenty-three years) and All Souls, where he again enjoyed and enriched the society of the common room as a quondam fellow. He was awarded a DLitt by Oxford in 1942 and elected FBA in 1944.

Hutchinson was an Anglican of the old school, who felt an affinity with the Caroline divines he studied and became an authority on Caroline poetry. He was a modest, careful, sensitive scholar in that field, as is evident in his contributions to the Cambridge *Bibliography of English Literature* and *History of English Literature*, his edition of the works of George Herbert (1941), and his life of Henry Vaughan (1947). He published also *Christian Freedom* (1920, the Hulsean lectures of 1918–19) and *Milton and the English Mind* (1946), and at his death was at work on a life of John Donne. A brief study of *Cranmer and the English Reformation* (1951) and an account of *Medieval Glass at All Souls College* (1949) based by Hutchinson on the notes of G. McN. Rushforth, were published posthumously.

Hutchinson died suddenly at his home, 3 Church Walk, Oxford, of heart failure, on 21 December 1947, and was survived by his wife, a son, and a daughter. His funeral was held at All Souls College, Oxford, on 24 December 1947.

JOHN SPARROW, *rev.* NILANJANA BANERJI

Sources *The Times* (23 Dec 1947) · *The Times* (30 Dec 1947) · Venn, *Alum. Cant.* · *CGPLA Eng. & Wales* (1948) · private information (1959) · personal knowledge (1959)
Archives Bodl. Oxf. | BL, corresp. with Albert Mansbridge, Add. MSS 65257 A–B · Bodl. Oxf., papers relating to poems of Henry Vaughan · King's Cam., letters to Oscar Browning
Likenesses W. Stoneman, photograph, 1945, NPG [*see illus.*]
Wealth at death £13,741 18s. 1d.: probate, 31 March 1948, *CGPLA Eng. & Wales*

Hutchinson, Horatio Gordon [Horace] (1859–1932), golfer and writer, was born in London on 16 May 1859, the third son of General William Nelson Hutchinson (1803–1895), of the Grenadier Guards, the author of standard works on brigade drill and dog breaking, and his wife, Mary, daughter of John *Russell, headmaster of Charterhouse. In 1864 his father went to live near Northam in Devon, the same year that the Royal North Devon Golf Club was founded, and here Hutchinson learned golf as a boy. He went to school first at Charterhouse, which he left owing to ill health, and later at the United Services College, Westward Ho!. In 1878 he went up to Corpus Christi College, Oxford, and captained the university that year in the university golf match, the first to be held; this was a role he repeated in 1879, 1880, and 1882 (there was no match in 1881). Generally known as Horace, he was a keen sportsman: in 1881 he won the university cue and played for Oxford in the doubles match at billiards. He was also a competent oarsman and cricketer and enjoyed shooting and angling. Graduating BA with third-class honours in *literae humaniores* (1881), he entered the Inner Temple with a view to reading for the bar, but his health, always frail, temporarily broke down. Later, in 1890, he had thoughts of being a sculptor and worked for some time in G. F. Watts's studio, but this project was likewise abandoned; he then embraced no regular profession but took gradually to authorship. He married in 1893 Dorothy Margaret, youngest daughter of Major Frederick Barclay Chapman, of the 14th hussars.

In 1886 Hutchinson wrote a small book, *Hints on the Game of Golf*, which coincided with the great increase in the popularity of the game in England, and had considerable success. In 1890 he edited and wrote a large part of the volume on golf in the Badminton Library series, and from that time he became a prolific writer on golf both in books and newspapers, as well as on shooting, fishing, and natural history. When *Country Life* was founded in 1897, he wrote regularly for it on all these subjects and edited several volumes in the Country Life Library. He wrote several not unsuccessful novels, among them *Peter Steele, the Cricketer* (1895), and *'Bert Edward, the Golf Caddie* (1903), in which the hero rises from a poor Scottish background to win the Open at Sandwich. However, he was essentially an essayist rather than a novelist.

Horatio Gordon [Horace] **Hutchinson** (1859–1932), by Elliott & Fry, pubd 1904

When in 1886 the amateur golf championship was formally instituted Hutchinson beat Henry Lamb in the final. This was the year that two of the forty-four entrants were disqualified because they had acted as caddies and were thus deemed professionals. In 1887 Hutchinson won against John Ball at Hoylake but resigned from the organizing committee in protest at the barring of Douglas Rolland for having once won a small money prize against a professional. He also championed the activities of the club professionals, whom he saw as 'nature's gentlemen who never step out of their position, and yet never fail to make us feel that by right of courtesy they are equals with the best'. Hutchinson played for England against Scotland in the first international match in 1902 and in each subsequent year until 1907, except 1905, when he was ill. In 1908 he was the first Englishman to be elected captain of the Royal and Ancient Golf Club of St Andrews. As a golfer, Hutchinson was for a long time one of the leading amateur players in the country, with a dashing and characteristic style in which 'the wrists are shaken about in the most warlike fashion'. His career would have been even more successful but for intermittent ill health. During the last eighteen years of his life he was incapacitated by

grave illness. He left his home at Forest Row in Sussex and moved to 29 Lennox Gardens, Chelsea, London, where he committed suicide on 27 July 1932. He was survived by his wife. BERNARD DARWIN, rev. WRAY VAMPLEW

Sources J. Lowerson, *Sport and the English middle classes, 1870–1914*, new edn (1995) · P. N. Lewis, *The dawn of professional golf* (1995) · J. L. Low, *Concerning golf* (1903) · *The Times* (29 July 1932) · T. Barrett, *The Daily Telegraph golf chronicle* (1994) · *DNB* · d. cert.
Likenesses Elliott & Fry, photograph, pubd 1904, NPG [*see illus.*] · O. Birley, oils, 1909, Royal and Ancient Golf Club, St Andrews · Spy [L. Ward], caricature, chromolithograph, NPG; repro. in *VF* (19 July 1890) · Walery, photograph, NPG · photographs, repro. in Lewis, *Dawn of professional golf* · photographs, repro. in Barrett, *Daily Telegraph golf chronicle*
Wealth at death £26,337 2s. 6d.: probate, 30 Aug 1932, CGPLA Eng. & Wales

Hutchinson, John (*bap.* 1615, *d.* 1664), parliamentarian army officer and regicide, was baptized on 18 September 1615 at St Mary's, Nottingham, the son of Sir Thomas Hutchinson (1589–1643) of Owthorpe, Nottinghamshire, and Margaret, daughter of Sir John Byron. Educated at free schools in Nottingham and Lincoln and at Peterhouse, Cambridge, where he graduated in 1634, he was admitted to Lincoln's Inn in May 1636 but found the study of law uncongenial. On 3 July 1638 he married Lucy Apsley (1620–1681) [*see* Hutchinson, Lucy], daughter of Sir Allen *Apsley, lieutenant of the Tower of London. Hutchinson negotiated for the purchase of a Star Chamber office but the deal was incomplete when the court was abolished. In March 1642, on Henry Ireton's recommendation, he was appointed to the Nottinghamshire commission of the peace but refused to act, though he joined the shire's gentry who at the end of the month presented a petition to Charles at York. He was among those in Nottingham who prevented Viscount Newark seizing for the king the gunpowder of the Nottinghamshire militia, but Mrs Hutchinson's claim that her husband led the opposition is not substantiated in other contemporary accounts. Though he believed 'the defence of the just English liberties' to be 'so clear a ground for the war' (Hutchinson, 1.137), it was royalist attempts to take control of the county which led him in the last months of 1642 to accept a commission in the Nottinghamshire parliamentarian forces and to join in the defence of Nottingham.

On 29 July 1643 Hutchinson was appointed governor of Nottingham Castle by Sir John Meldrum and the local parliamentarian committees. An inadequate number of troops to defend an unfortified town led him to take the town's ordnance into the castle while his arrest of townsmen who protested began the often fractious relations with the civic leaders. At first he retained the support of the county committee for at its request parliament appointed, and Lord Fairfax confirmed, him as governor of the castle and town, but did not define his authority. Disputes, however, arose between Hutchinson and the committee about its command over local forces and culminated in the refusal of the Nottinghamshire troops to obey the orders of parliament and the governor to fight in Wales. A joint request was duly made to the committee of both kingdoms to define their respective powers, Hutchinson travelling to London for the hearing in September 1644. The accusation that he was preparing to betray the town infuriated the colonel, who had rejected and reported a previous royalist approach. The report of 11 November 1644 from the committee of both kingdoms recommended restricting his independent military action but did not give the Nottinghamshire committee the authority it sought. It was overtaken by a petition from the common council of Nottingham, which criticized the governor and supported the demands of the committee. In the event royalist attacks on the town ended the proceedings in London for on 22 April 1645 Hutchinson was ordered to return. Again he led a successful defence but his bitterness at his accusers remained as they and their supporters were appointed by parliament to local committees. When he was elected a burgess of Nottingham in November 1645 his services received some recognition, but the sympathy of the colonel and his wife to religious separatists and their rejection of infant baptism continued their disputes with the town's Presbyterians.

Elected an MP for Nottinghamshire, formerly represented by his father, on 16 March 1646, Hutchinson took little part in the proceedings of the Commons. The Commons' acceptance of the limited concessions offered by the king in the treaty of Newport led him to join the unsuccessful attempts of opponents to record their dissent on 4 December 1648. Though he 'infinitely disliked' Pride's purge of the Commons, he remained in the house and was appointed to the court to try the king. It was a service he 'durst not refuse … holding himself obliged by the covenant of God and the public trust of his country'. Edmund Ludlow remembered him as having exceeded most of the members of the court in his zeal to execute Charles; according to Mrs Hutchinson it was only after a long and serious debate and prayer that her husband signed the death warrant [see also Regicides]. In subsequent months Hutchinson had few doubts about the legitimacy of these proceedings. In June 1650 he was a teller for an unsuccessful motion, which would have obliged all who rejoined the house after 11 January 1650 to accept that parliament had the authority to establish the court. He was a member, though only a moderately active participant, in the work of the council of state from its inception in February 1649 to 10 February 1651. In the spring of 1651 he returned to Nottinghamshire, where he acted as a justice of the peace, but he refused office during Oliver Cromwell's protectorate. This hostility explains Major-General Whalley's opposition to Hutchinson's nomination by 'the honest part' (Thurloe, State papers, 4.299) of the county to represent Nottinghamshire in the 1656 parliament. Hutchinson was persuaded to serve as sheriff by Richard Cromwell and it was not until 20 June 1659, when he was released from this duty, that he could attend the restored Rump Parliament. An active member in July and August, on 30 September he was fined for absence. Lambert's expulsion of the Rump Parliament in October 1659 led Hutchinson with other supporters of the Commonwealth to prepare for armed action, which the recall of parliament prevented. Holding moral and practical objections to the imposition of an oath abjuring the Stuarts he was a teller against this motion and gave his support to George Monck and Anthony Ashley Cooper because he believed at this time they favoured the Commonwealth. He later claimed to have proposed that Monck be given sole command of the army. He attended conferences called by Monck between sitting members, those excluded after 1648, whose readmission he supported, and the representatives of the officers. His persuasion of Monck to countermand an order to allow troops to take reprisals in Nottingham contributed to his election for the town in the 1660 Convention Parliament.

On 12 May 1660, during a Commons debate about the king's trial, Hutchinson offered himself as a sacrifice for the public peace and settlement. Mrs Hutchinson claimed that to prevent such an action she disobeyed her husband and wrote a letter in his name to the speaker. Hutchinson's explanation to the house that 'if he had erred' it came from 'the inexperience of his age and the defect of his judgment and not the malice of his heart' was now described as an insufficient 'expression of that deep and sorrowful sense which so heavily presses my soul'. It was claimed that for more than seven years he had attempted to redeem his crime, as was demonstrated by his hostility to Cromwell and his actions in the last session of the Rump Parliament. On 9 June the Commons voted that Hutchinson should be discharged from the house and be incapable of holding public office, but he was allowed to retain his liberty and estates. It was, as his wife admitted, 'providential' that the vote was taken before a detailed investigation of the king's trial. The vote of the House of Lords that signatories of the king's death warrant were to be excepted from the Bill of Indemnity led Hutchinson again to stress his repentance and present a certificate signed by royalists and Cooper. They testified, in a number of 'good natured fictions' that he had expressed support for the return of the king, and supported the interpretation of his conduct presented to the Commons. The Lords accepted the pleas and on 23 June 1660 struck his name from the record of those present at the king's trial. However, he faced financial ruin when a bill promoted by Lord Lexington to recover from him £2690 granted by parliament from money lent to the king at Newark was passed in the Lords. The bill failed in the Commons, as did a second attempt in the Cavalier Parliament. As he saw others punished, Hutchinson 'suffered with them in his mind' and believed he was 'kept for some eminent service or suffering in this cause' (Hutchinson, 2.262–4). When in October 1663 information from the Yorkshire rebels implicated him in their plot he was arrested by the Nottinghamshire militia. Though searches failed to discover the arms he was alleged to have collected, he was kept a close prisoner and taken to London. The imprisonment was the 'happiest release in the world to him' and though the allegations remained unproven, he was incarcerated in Sandown Castle in Kent where he died on 11 September 1664. He was buried at Owthorpe.

Hutchinson's most important contribution to parliament's cause was to lead the successful defence of Nottingham. He believed he was called by God to this service and he remained resolute in the face of danger and the unwarranted accusations of his opponents there. Lucy Hutchinson's *Memoirs of the Life of Colonel Hutchinson* often gives an undue prominence to her husband's activities, but as one of the great English biographies her portrait of Hutchinson will endure. P. R. SEDDON

Sources L. Hutchinson, *Memoirs of the life of Colonel Hutchinson*, ed. J. Hutchinson, new edn, ed. C. H. Firth, 2 vols. (1885) · L. Hutchinson, *Memoirs of the life of Colonel Hutchinson*, ed. J. Sutherland (1973) · BL, Add. MS 25901 · *JHC*, 2–8 (1640–67) · *JHL*, 11 (1660–66) · P. R. Seddon, 'Colonel Hutchinson and the disputes between Nottinghamshire parliamentarians, 1643–45', *Transactions of the Thoroton Society*, 98 (1994) · Notts. Arch., MSS C. A. 3419, 3420 · Notts. Arch., MS DDP 37/3 · *CSP dom.*, 1641–64 · *The memoirs of Edmund Ludlow*, ed. C. H. Firth, 2 vols. (1894) · Thurloe, *State papers*, vol. 4 · *The diurnal of Thomas Rugge, 1659–1661*, ed. W. L. Sachse, CS, 3rd ser., 91 (1961) · R. Scrope and T. Monkhouse, eds., *State papers collected by Edward, earl of Clarendon*, 3 vols. (1767–86), vol. 3 · M. A. E. Green, ed., *Calendar of the proceedings of the committee for advance of money, 1642–1656*, 3 vols., PRO (1888) · *To the king's most excellent majesty: a petition presented … by the inhabitants of the county of Nottingham* (1642) [Thomason tract 669.f.6(6)] · Keeler, *Long Parliament* · G. W. Marshall, ed., *The visitations of the county of Nottingham in the years 1569 and 1614*, Harleian Society, 4 (1871) · parish register, Nottingham, St Mary's, 18 Sept 1615 [baptism] · W. P. Baildon, ed., *The records of the Honorable Society of Lincoln's Inn: admissions*, 1 (1896), 230
Archives BL, 'The notebook', Add. MS 25901 · Castle Museum, Nottingham, 'Memoirs' · U. Nott. L., letters, NeD3759/19
Likenesses I. Neagle, line engraving, pubd 1806 (after R. Walker), BM, NPG · R. Walker, oils, priv. coll. · engraving, Castle Museum and Art Gallery, Nottingham; repro. in Hutchinson, *Memoirs*

Hutchinson, John (1674–1737), naturalist and theologian, was born at Spennithorne, near Middleham, Yorkshire. His father, also John Hutchinson, was of yeoman status and possessed an estate worth £40 per annum. At first he wanted his son to qualify as an estate steward, and sent him to school at Spennithorne. Before long, however, a gentleman who came to lodge with Hutchinson's father offered to educate young John himself. Hutchinson later recalled that he had learnt mathematics and history from this gentleman and 'as much as he could see there was use for either upon the earth, or in the heaven, without poisoning him with any false notions fathered upon the Mathematics' (Spearman, ii). In 1693 Hutchinson duly became steward to Mr Bathurst of Skutterskelf, Yorkshire, moving shortly afterwards to the service of the earl of Scarbrough. A vacancy having occurred on the staff of the duke of Somerset, Hutchinson soon entered that nobleman's service, worked hard to restore the fortunes of his estates, and rose quickly to become his chief steward. His work for the duke of Somerset took him to London about 1700, where he satisfactorily managed a law suit between his master and Lord Wharton.

This move marked a turning point in Hutchinson's career, since in London he made the acquaintance of Dr John Woodward, who acted as physician to his patron. Woodward apparently cured Hutchinson of the effects of lead poisoning, contracted through work in the mines. Hutchinson soon fell under the spell of Woodward's natural philosophical ideas and offered to assist his friend in the search for minerals and fossils that would prove his theories about the history of the earth and the effects of the biblical flood. From 1702 until 1706 Hutchinson travelled on business through much of England and Wales, reporting to Woodward on the nature of the countryside and its inhabitants and regularly sending boxes of specimens to him. In 1706 his travels took him in particular to Wales, the west country, and Cornwall, and led to the compilation of his own *Observations Made by J. H. Mostly in the Year 1706*, which was published shortly afterwards and included annotations by Woodward. However, Woodward became gradually more and more dissatisfied with Hutchinson's work, above all with his failure to classify the materials that he collected. At the same time, Hutchinson began to be suspicious that Woodward was plagiarizing his findings and that the great work on which he claimed to be engaged was nothing more than a fraud. One day, when Woodward was distracted, Hutchinson managed to sneak a look through his papers and 'found that the Doctor was playing fast and loose with him' (Spearman, iv). Woodward, for his part, felt that Hutchinson had 'shaken off the Miner, & started up at once into a Philosopher; … soaring at Things he could not reach, & neglecting Those in his Power' (BL, Add. MS 5860, fol. 156r). Hutchinson later attempted to reclaim the specimens that he had provided for Woodward, but desisted on his adversary's death, when his collections were bequeathed to the University of Cambridge.

From about 1712, therefore, Hutchinson set out for himself as a natural philosopher and sought to make sense on his own of the observations and experiments that he had made in the previous decade. He initially intended to leave the service of the duke of Somerset, but was persuaded instead to become the duke's riding purveyor at a salary of £200 and with lodgings in the mews at Somerset House. The duke's support for Hutchinson's work later extended to granting him the presentation to the living of Sutton in Sussex, where Hutchinson eventually installed one of his most committed supporters, Julius Bate. One of the first among Hutchinson's independent ventures as a natural philosopher concerned his claim to have invented a timepiece with an improved movement. He sought an act of parliament to protect his property in this discovery, which he claimed would help to solve the longitude problem. He was opposed successfully by the London clockmakers, who argued that Hutchinson's modifications did not constitute a new invention. Thereafter, and with the duke of Somerset's support, Hutchinson's work adopted a more theoretical slant.

Hutchinson's natural philosophical writings were deliberately polemical in nature. They took as their principal target the publications of Isaac Newton and drew heavily for their scientific content on Woodward's unpublished work on the nature of spirit. Hutchinson perceived early on the connection between Newton's ideas and the antitrinitarian writings of Samuel Clarke, and denied wholeheartedly both the philosophy and the theology that underpinned these works. He rejected the idea of a vacuum and the concepts of attraction and of gravity, as they appeared in the writings of both Newton and Woodward, because they seemed to him to endow matter with activity and to imply that God might himself be material. Instead, Hutchinson argued that knowledge derived from the senses could not reach to the microscopic level at which God acted to create and govern the world. Revelation was the only sure key to these processes. Moreover, human understanding of revelation, which was provided by the Bible and in particular by those passages of the Hebrew text of the Old Testament that dealt with God's creative power, had been corrupted.

Like Woodward, Hutchinson rejected contemporary arguments that Hebrew religious practices and knowledge of nature had been derived from the wisdom of the Egyptians. However, he also went further than his former mentor, in jettisoning contemporary ideas of the way in which one should read and understand Hebrew. He argued that later generations of Jewish writers and other commentators had corrupted the pristine Hebrew tongue, especially through the introduction of written vowel points. For Hutchinson, the unpointed text of the Old Testament could be read and vocalized in order to bring out the essential affinities between words that shared a similar spiritual meaning. Thus Hutchinson was able to argue that the text of Genesis concealed an account of creation in which God separated out gross from subtle matter, and subsequently endowed this subtle matter or spirit with motion, incubating the earth and shaping the heavens. He suggested that this subtle matter could also take on the form of fire, light, or air, circulating backwards and forwards from the sun. The circulatory motion of these fluid elements explained both the movements of the heavens and the operation of other systems in which heat generated circulation, such as the human body. Hutchinson's new physics was encapsulated in his system for reading Hebrew, in which, for example, a single word might imply both the idea of making something heavy, or gravitation, caused by light, and the divine glory represented by the light emanating from Christ. Hutchinson also claimed that his system made apparent the role of the Christian Trinity in creation and throughout the Old Testament, and undermined the arguments of contemporary Arian and Socinian writers, including the leading Newtonian authors.

The first publication to embody Hutchinson's ideas was *Moses's principia*, part one of which appeared in 1724. A stream of other works by Hutchinson came out over the next thirteen years, including the second part of *Moses's principia* in 1727, and Hutchinson built up a wide following in England and Scotland, particularly at Oxford and at Edinburgh. Although many of his admirers shared high-church sympathies, Hutchinson's writings were also popular with those who were persuaded by John Wesley's views on electricity and other philosophical matters. The editors of the twelve volumes of Hutchinson's *Works* (1748–9), Robert Spearman and Julius Bate, quoted their author as saying that he had '*learnt his Hebrew under-ground*'

(Spearman and Bate, vii). Readers of Hutchinson's impenetrable English prose might well have shared the sensation of tunnelling ever deeper into obscurity. The creation of a system of Hutchinsonianism thus owed much to the writings of his followers, notably Bate, Alexander Catcott, Benjamin Holloway, George Horne, and William Jones of Nayland.

It had been Hutchinson's practice during his writing career to retire to the country in the months of June and July each year. In 1737 he remained in London during the summer, preparing the second part of the *Data of Christianity*, part one of which had been published in 1736. Neglecting to take exercise for a time, Hutchinson was injured by the unfamiliar movements of his horse when riding in Hyde Park. He died in London sixteen days afterwards on 28 August 1737. He left several books in manuscript, which were subsequently published by Spearman and Bate as part of his *Works*.   SCOTT MANDELBROTE

Sources R. Spearman, *A supplement to the works of J. Hutchinson … To this work is prefixed, Mr. Hutchinson's life* (1765) · R. Spearman and J. Bate, Preface, in J. Hutchinson, *The philosophical and theological works of J. H.*, ed. R. Spearman and J. Bate, 12 vols. (1748–9), 1 · BL, Add. MS 5860, fols. 154v–156r · Bodl. Oxf., MS Gough Wales 8 · *The clockmakers reasons against Mr Hutchinson's pretended invention* [n.d.] · J. C. English, 'John Hutchinson's critique of Newtonian heterodoxy', *Church History*, 68 (1999), 581–97 · G. N. Cantor, 'Revelation and the cyclical cosmos of John Hutchinson', *Images of the earth*, ed. L. Jordanova and R. Porter (1995), 17–35 · C. B. Wilde, 'Hutchinsonianism, natural philosophy and religious controversy in eighteenth-century Britain', *History of Science*, 18 (1980), 1–24 · J. M. Levine, *Dr Woodward's shield: history, science, and satire in Augustan England* (1977) · D. S. Katz, 'The Hutchinsonians and Hebraic fundamentalism in eighteenth-century England', *Sceptics, millenarians and Jews*, ed. D. S. Katz and J. I. Israel (1990), 237–55 · A. Thackray, *Atoms and powers* (1970) · A. J. Kuhn, 'Glory or gravity: Hutchinson vs. Newton', *Journal of the History of Ideas*, 22 (1961), 303–22
Archives Bodl. Oxf., MS Gough Wales 8 · Bristol Central Library, MS B 2 6063

Hutchinson, John (1884–1972), botanist and writer, was born at Blindburn Cottage, Wark-on-Tyne, Northumberland, on 7 April 1884, the second in the family of four sons and three daughters of Michael Hutchinson, head gardener at nearby Blindburn Hall, and his wife, Annie Willey. On leaving the village school in 1900 Hutchinson first worked under his father as a garden boy and a year later, to gain further experience, he moved to Callerton Hall, near Ponteland, and then to Axwell Park, Blaydon-on-Tyne, where he attended evening classes in botany at Rutherford College. Later, he attended evening classes at Chelsea and Regent Street polytechnics in London. His abilities as an artist had been noted and encouraged in childhood and he continued to practise drawing and watercolour painting.

In April 1904 Hutchinson moved to the Royal Botanic Gardens, Kew, and worked in the arboretum as a gardener. His abilities caught the attention of his superiors and, after about a year, he was offered a post in the herbarium as a preparer. Between 1907 and 1916 he was appointed assistant, first for India and then Africa. In 1910 he married

Lilian Florence, daughter of James Firman Cook, decorator, of Richmond, Surrey. They had two sons and three daughters. In 1917 Hutchinson joined the permanent staff taking charge of the African section, a responsibility he retained until, in 1936, he became keeper of the museums at Kew, a post he held until he retired in April 1948. However, he continued to work daily in the herbarium up to and including the Saturday on which he died.

Work on the African flora dominated Hutchinson's earlier years and his first major contributions were to the *Flora of Tropical Africa* (1912, 1915) and the *Flora Capensis* (1915). In 1923 he began work on a *Flora of West Tropical Africa* which, with the assistance of J. M. Dalziel, he completed in 1937. This flora set a new pattern of conciseness for such works. Hutchinson contributed greatly to knowledge of the horticulturally important genus *Rhododendron*, on which he wrote large parts of several major works. The Royal Horticultural Society in 1945 awarded him their Victoria medal of honour. The work for which Hutchinson is most noted is on the classification of flowering plants. Although that set out in his *Families of Flowering Plants* (2 vols., 1926 and 1934) has not been generally followed, this work, together with his *Evolution and Phylogeny of Flowering Plants* (1969)—each fully illustrated by his own line drawings—provided a powerful stimulus to others, while his keys and descriptions have been widely used.

In 1949 Hutchinson began a major revision of all genera and families of flowering plants. The first volume of *The Genera of Flowering Plants* was published in 1964, the second three years later, and at the time of his death he was working hard on the third (of a projected seven volumes). Hutchinson's record of publications is incomplete, however, without mention of his popular books. In 1945 Penguin published his *Common Wild Flowers* which sold 250,000 copies in the first year. This was followed by *More Common Wild Flowers* (1948) and *Uncommon Wild Flowers* (1950) which, together, were revised and expanded into the two-volume *British Wild Flowers* (1955), in all of which the text was complemented by his own illustrations. With Ronald Melville he also wrote *The Story of Plants and their Uses to Man* (1948).

Hutchinson travelled widely, collecting plants and making observations. His journeys in southern Africa in particular are noteworthy, especially that in 1930, accompanied by his friend General J. C. Smuts, to Lake Tanganyika, experiences described in his book, *A Botanist in Southern Africa* (1946). In 1934 the University of St Andrews conferred on Hutchinson an honorary LLD. The Linnean Society, of which he had become a fellow in 1918, presented him with their Darwin–Wallace centenary medal in 1958 and their highest award, the Linnean gold medal, in 1965. In 1947 he was elected FRS and in 1972 appointed OBE. He was very proud of his humble origins and wrote an unpublished autobiography, *From Potting Shed to FRS*, a copy of which is deposited in the library at Kew. He died at his home, 12 Kenmore Close, Kent Road, Kew, on 2 September 1972; his wife died a week later. His remains were cremated at Mortlake.   P. S. GREEN, *rev.*

Sources J. P. M. Brown, 'Dr. John Hutchinson, 1884–1972', *Kew Bulletin*, 29 (1974), 1–14 · C. E. Hubbard, *Memoirs FRS*, 21 (1975), 345–65 · personal knowledge (1986) · private information (1986)
Archives RBG Kew, corresp. and papers
Likenesses portrait, repro. in Hubbard, *Memoirs FRS*
Wealth at death £10,393: probate, 12 Oct 1972, *CGPLA Eng. & Wales*

Hutchinson, John Hely- (1724–1794), politician, was born John Hely, the son of Francis Hely of Gortroe, co. Cork, and his wife, Prudence, daughter of Matthias Earbery. He was educated at Trinity College, Dublin, whence he graduated in 1744. In 1748 he was called to the Irish bar. On 8 June 1751 he married Christiana (*bap.* 1732, *d.* 1788), eldest daughter of Abraham Nikson and Mary Hodson, and the grandniece and heir of Richard Hutchinson; Hely adopted the additional surname Hutchinson when his wife inherited the Knocklofty estate in co. Tipperary in 1759. It was an expensive marriage, as along with the 3000 acre estate his wife brought £11,000 of her great-uncle's debt, which he agreed to pay off. They had six sons and four daughters.

In 1759 Hely-Hutchinson entered the Irish parliament as MP for Lanesborough; after the dissolution on the death of George II he disposed of this seat, and from 1760 to 1790 sat as MP for the city of Cork. He immediately became a leading spokesman for the independent patriot interest. According to the duke of Bedford, the lord lieutenant (1757–61), Hely-Hutchinson was, 'in order to satisfy his ambition, and promote himself, stirring up all kinds of contention in this unsettled time' (BL, Add. MS 32899, fol. 365). During the parliamentary session beginning in October 1759 he was responsible for proposing a number of motions in the Commons relating to Ireland's constitutional grievances. However, it is clear that Bedford's judgement was sound as his successor Lord Halifax was able to procure Hely-Hutchinson's services by appointing him as prime serjeant in December 1761. Hely-Hutchinson acted as chief government spokesman in the Commons, and though he temporarily fell out of favour during Lord Northumberland's viceroyalty (1763–5), he quickly resumed his leading role, and was sworn of the Irish privy council in 1764.

Hely-Hutchinson was expected to play a prominent part in Lord Townshend's lord lieutenancy (1767–72), for Townshend regarded him as 'by far the most powerful man in parliament' (McDowell, 223). But he was alienated from government by his failure to secure either the office of lord chancellor or provision for his two sons, and by the British ministry's determination to push through the controversial augmentation scheme. Hely-Hutchinson, however, was not necessarily averse to the strengthening of the Dublin Castle government planned by Townshend and the British ministry. He argued that 'there never was a time when the mild executive government of this country required firmness and system more than [at] present' (*Beaufort MSS*, 264). But to his mind this should not include the dismissal of unreliable office-holders. On returning to government Hely-Hutchinson was instrumental in devising the alternative augmentation scheme that was carried

John Hely-Hutchinson (1724–1794), by Sir Joshua Reynolds, 1788

on 21 November 1768. His rather mercurial support for government was generously rewarded. He accepted the sinecure place of alnager, a reversionary grant of the principal secretaryship of state, to which he succeeded in 1777, and a commission of major in a cavalry regiment, which he later sold for £3000. Henry Flood was indignant at his betrayal of the patriot cause, and in the anti-Townshend satire *Baratariana* he declared that Hely-Hutchinson, under the alias of Sergeant Rufinus, had received more for ruining one kingdom than Admiral Hawke had received for saving three.

Hely-Hutchinson was willing to take a leading role in the Commons under the new viceroy, Lord Harcourt, though the prime serjeant was advised that 'while your capacity is admitted by everybody, the exorbitance of your demands is arraigned on all hands' (*Beaufort MSS*, 270). In 1774 Harcourt appointed Hely-Hutchinson as provost of Trinity College, Dublin, in spite of the fact that he was academically unqualified, and that the post usually went to one of the senior fellows. Harcourt was warned that:

> the most imprudent thing administration could do would be to place him there, for then he would have three places under, but independent of, government. Consequently, he would relapse into patriotism, make a borough of the university and return his sons for it and he would halloo the college boys as he did the liberty boys in Bedford's ad[ministratio]n against government or individuals whenever he pleased.   (PRO NIre., D572/4/26)

Hely-Hutchinson's rapacious reputation certainly made him a surprising choice as provost. The chief secretary Sir John Blaquiere wryly commented that 'the church meek and humble as we know it were alarmed for the morals as

well as the piety of the rising generation' (*Beaufort MSS*, 281).

The *Freeman's Journal*, a patriot newspaper, published a number of letters mocking this appointment. A compilation was eventually published under the title *Pranceriana*, a reference to Hely-Hutchinson's attempt to establish a dancing and fencing school in the college in imitation of the University of Oxford. Dr Patrick Duigenan, a senior college fellow and follower of Philip Tisdal, the attorney-general, was author of many of the *Pranceriana* letters. He also published a book entitled *Lachrymae academicae*, which attacked the conduct of the provost since his appointment. Hely-Hutchinson sued for libel, but the judge dismissed the case, announcing that he 'left the school to its own correctors' (Johnston, 158). Hely-Hutchinson's appointment as provost further embittered his relationship with Tisdal, who was MP for Dublin University and the provost's chief rival in the Commons. Although Tisdal planned legal and perhaps even physical retribution after being driven out of his parliamentary seat by Hely-Hutchinson's son Richard in 1776, his death the following year meant that these threats came to nothing. Richard Hely-Hutchinson was unseated on an election petition. A similar charge was made against the provost on the election to parliament in 1790 of another of his sons, Francis. However, when the case was heard before a Commons select committee, Hely-Hutchinson was acquitted by a majority of one.

Hely-Hutchinson's appointment as provost—as many government supporters predicted—did not guarantee his loyalty, and in October 1775 he refused to support a motion condemning the rebellious American colonists. He also opposed a troop transfer scheme in December. In part Hely-Hutchinson was repositioning himself to take advantage of the resurgence of patriotism in the Commons. However, he still came close to losing his Cork seat in the 1776 general election. Throughout the period in which he represented Cork he was careful to take account of the views of the merchant community. When an embargo on the export of Irish goods became an incendiary issue in Cork, Hely-Hutchinson's support for government became increasingly unreliable. During Lord Buckinghamshire's administration he moved into opposition, and made clear his support for the free trade movement. He wrote a memorandum to the viceroy on the subject of Ireland's commercial distress and the possible means of alleviation, which was eventually published as *The Commercial Restraints of Ireland* in 1779. Even when a version of free trade was conceded in December of that year, Hely-Hutchinson was dissatisfied and clearly wished for a more generous settlement. In the spring of 1780 he attempted to move retaliatory measures against English goods.

Yet by August Hely-Hutchinson had returned once again to government, and was willing to support its version of the mutiny bill. He was a staunch Castle supporter during the Carlisle viceroyalty (1780–82) and took the lead in opposing Henry Flood's challenge to Poynings' law in December 1781. In response to Henry Grattan's address declaring the independency of Ireland in February 1782, Hely-Hutchinson put forward the case for allowing the Declaratory Act to go unchallenged, though in private he saw no real reason for retaining it. The duke of Portland, appointed as viceroy by the Rockingham ministry, initiated a cull of the Castle party, but Hely-Hutchinson retained his influence and at the opening of the session relayed Portland's address to the Commons. During this administration he was broadly in favour of Irish legislative independence. He was equally supportive of Catholic relief, probably because it coincided with his electoral interests in Cork City.

Hely-Hutchinson was out of favour during the viceroyalty of the earl of Northington, appointed by the Fox–North coalition. Charles James Fox was particularly critical of Hely-Hutchinson's love of jobbing. Fox viewed Ireland's demands for parliamentary independence in the light of such placehunting:

> Ireland appears to me now to be like one of her most eminent jobbers, who, after having obtained the Prime Serjeancy, the Secretaryship of State, and twenty other great places, insisted upon the Lord Lieutenant's adding a major's half-pay to the rest of his emoluments.   (*Memorials and Correspondence*, 2.170)

Despite the opposition of his constituents, who censured him for his conduct, Hely-Hutchinson supported William Pitt's commercial propositions of 1785. He did have some reservations, but defended his actions in *A Letter from the Secretary of State to the Mayor of Cork*. Hely-Hutchinson's views were also influential during the negotiations over Ireland's adoption of the British Navigation Act of 1786. He initially described the measure as an attempt to 'bind Ireland by an absolute coercive law' (Kelly, *Prelude*, 226). On 15 January 1787 he was sworn of the British privy council. During the regency crisis, however, he supported the opposition, though following George III's recovery his inconstancy was pardoned by the viceroy. In the early 1790s he gave his support to the revived parliamentary reform movement. In 1790 he was elected for the borough of Taghmon, co. Wexford, which he continued to represent until his death.

Hely-Hutchinson, very much a self-made man, was a gifted politician. Noted for his sarcastic wit, he was as accomplished at oratory as he was at intrigue, and his practical abilities made him invaluable to government. He made many useful contacts throughout his career, including Primate Stone, William Gerard Hamilton, Edmund Sexton Pery, and Edmund Burke, but his ambition often stood in the way of close friendships. In the Irish Commons he had enemies on both sides of the house, and was widely viewed as an unprincipled placehunter, prepared to back whichever side would offer the greatest reward. Lord North claimed that if he were offered the country of Great Britain as his estate he would still ask for the Isle of Man as his potato garden. Hely-Hutchinson clearly misused his influence over the two parliamentary seats representing Trinity College, Dublin, and attempted to turn the university into a close borough.

Yet he was also a very efficient provost and was responsible for establishing the college's modern languages professorships, and the better organization of the medical school. He was determined to extend the curriculum, so that graduates would leave Trinity as accomplished gentlemen as well as scholars. To this end he promoted composition in Latin and English, and the establishment of junior common rooms and a riding house. He also improved the economic standing of the college, by raising the rents, having the college estates surveyed, and securing generous building grants from parliament. He was an admirer of drama, and in March 1794 he was made a fellow of the Royal Society. He was also involved in prison reform and was responsible for introducing a measure abolishing the payment of gaol fees by prisoners who were acquitted.

In 1783 Hely-Hutchinson accepted a peerage for his wife, who became Baroness Donoughmore in her own right. He died on 4 September 1794 at Buxton, Derbyshire, while visiting the spa for health reasons. His eldest son, Richard Hely-*Hutchinson, succeeded his mother in 1788 as second Baron Donoughmore, was created an earl in 1801, and was in turn succeeded by his brother John Hely-*Hutchinson. Two other sons, Francis and Christopher Hely-*Hutchinson, sat as MPs for Dublin University and for the city of Cork respectively.

MARTYN J. POWELL

Sources DNB · M. J. Powell, 'An early imperial problem: Britain and Ireland, 1750–1783', PhD diss., U. Wales, 1997 · A. P. W. Malcomson, *John Foster: the politics of the Anglo-Irish ascendancy* (1978) · R. B. McDowell, *Ireland in the age of imperialism and revolution, 1760–1801* (1979) · E. M. Johnston, *Ireland in the eighteenth century* (1974) · J. Kelly, *Prelude to Union: Anglo-Irish politics in the 1780s* (1992) · Newcastle papers, BL, Add. MS 32899 · PRO NIre., Macartney MSS, D 572 · *Memorials and correspondence of Charles James Fox*, ed. J. Russell, 4 vols. (1853–7), vol. 2 · E. Magennis, *The Irish political system, 1740–1765* (2000) · GEC, *Peerage* · J. Kelly, *Henry Flood: patriots and politicians in eighteenth-century Ireland* (1998) · *The manuscripts of the duke of Beaufort … the earl of Donoughmore*, HMC, 27 (1891)

Archives Bodl. Oxf., vols. 1–2 (of 7) of typescript copy of his 'Essay towards a history of Trinity College to 1730' · TCD, corresp. and papers | BL, corresp. with first earl of Liverpool, Add. MSS 38208, 38210, 38221, 38306–38309, 38375 · NL Ire., letters to Charles O'Hara · NL Ire., letters to Thomas Orde · PRO NIre., letters to George Macartney · Sheff. Arch., corresp. with Edmund Burke

Likenesses J. Watson, mezzotint, pubd 1778 (after J. Reynolds), BM · J. Reynolds, oils, 1788, NG Ire. [*see illus.*] · J. Peacock, oils, *c*.1815 (after J. Reynolds), TCD · F. Wheatley, group portrait, oils (*The Irish House of Commons, 1780*), Leeds City Art Gallery

Hutchinson, John Hely-, second earl of Donoughmore (1757–1832), army officer and politician, was born on 15 May 1757, the second son of John Hely-*Hutchinson, formerly Hely (1724–1794), and his wife, Christiana (*bap.* 1732, *d.* 1788), the daughter of Abraham Nikson of Munny, co. Wicklow. His elder brother was Richard Hely-*Hutchinson, first Viscount Donoughmore and first earl of Donoughmore in the Irish peerage, and first Viscount Hutchinson in the peerage of the United Kingdom (1756–1825), who died unmarried. John Hely-Hutchinson was educated at Eton College (1767–73) and Magdalen College, Oxford (1773). He entered the army in May 1774 as cornet, and was promoted lieutenant in 1775, captain in 1776, major in 1781, and lieutenant-colonel in 1783.

The family interest had a crucial role in his career. Hely-Hutchinson became a politician due to the wealth and prominence acquired by his father through the latter's legal practice and his marriage to the heiress of the Hutchinson property at Knocklofty, near Clonmel, co. Tipperary: in 1774 he was provost of Trinity College, Dublin, and in October 1783 his wife was created Baroness Donoughmore in the Irish peerage. He was instrumental in having his son returned to the Irish parliament for Lanesborough (1776–83) and later for Cork City (1790–1800), which, he hoped, would become the family's political flagship. As MP, Hely-Hutchinson pursued a line broadly similar to that of his father, supporting the Catholic petition in February 1792, acceding to the enfranchisement of forty-shilling Catholic freeholders in 1793, though preferring a higher valuation, and eventually supporting the Union on the grounds that it would extirpate intolerance and lead to Catholic relief. He sat briefly for Cork City after the Union, but resigned on 16 December 1801.

After eleven years on half pay, during which he travelled on the continent and studied at the Strasbourg military academy, in 1792 Hely-Hutchinson visited the French revolutionary armies. He went to the allied armies under the duke of Brunswick, and in 1793 he became a volunteer in the duke of York's army before Valenciennes and served for some time as an extra aide-de-camp to Sir Ralph Abercromby. In 1794 he was appointed colonel of the 94th (raised by his elder brother Richard), which he commanded until it was drafted. Following his promotion to major-general (3 May 1796) he was appointed to the Irish staff. In August 1798, in the Irish uprising, he commanded at Castlebar when 1000 French under General Joseph Humbert landed in Killala Bay. Hely-Hutchinson had 1500 men, mostly English and Scottish fencibles and Irish militia. On 30 August, when the French veterans attacked, most of Hely-Hutchinson's inexperienced troops fled—an action nicknamed the Castlebar races. Hely-Hutchinson offered to resign but retracted when Cornwallis, the viceroy and commander-in-chief, seemed to approve his conduct. Privately, however, Cornwallis spoke of him 'as a sensible man, but no general' (*Correspondence of … Cornwallis*, 3.360).

Hely-Hutchinson served in the ill-fated attack on the Batavian Republic (August–October 1799) and was wounded in the thigh in October. In 1801 he commanded the first division of Abercromby's army, which landed in Egypt on 10 March. The French were defeated at the battle of Alexandria, Abercromby was killed, and Hely-Hutchinson succeeded him by seniority. In May he was made a KB. Henry Addington's new government and the commander-in-chief, the duke of York, favoured his retaining command until General Fox's arrival, but in the British camp near Alexandria senior officers apparently tried to deprive him of the command—which seems to have been foiled by General Sir John Moore's refusal to support it. The reasons for Hely-Hutchinson's unpopularity are obscure but may have been an unkempt appearance and unattractive personality. Accounts differ, however, with one author describing him as gentlemanlike, with agreeable manners.

Hely-Hutchinson successfully blockaded Menou's army in Alexandria, forced the French in Cairo to surrender, and then besieged Alexandria until the French there surrendered on 2 September 1801. Late in October he returned to England, and in December 1801 he was created Baron Hutchinson of Alexandria and of Knocklofty, co. Tipperary, with a pension of £2000 a year. He also received the new Turkish order of the Crescent in brilliants (March 1802).

On the renewal of the war in May 1803 Hely-Hutchinson held the rank of major-general in the southern district (Kent and Surrey) until promoted lieutenant-general in September 1803. He served as colonel of various regiments (the 74th highlanders in 1803, the 57th foot in 1805, and, to his great pleasure, the 18th Royal Irish foot in 1811) and was three times considered as commander-in-chief in Ireland (in 1804, in 1806, and at the prince regent's request in 1812). In April 1806 he became governor of Stirling Castle. In 1811 he made known his opposition to corporal punishment in the army, and in 1813 he was promoted general. He became GCB on 2 January 1815.

From about 1803 Hely-Hutchinson was a well-known confidant of the prince of Wales, to whom he became 'entirely & irrevocably attach'd' (*Correspondence of George, Prince of Wales*, 4.454), and he was 'a great feature' (ibid.) at Brighton Pavilion. This relationship was politically significant. In 1803, on Fox's advice, he was one of three men consulted by the prince on the possibility of establishing a new system of government in Ireland, including Catholic relief; and in spring 1804, when the king's illness raised the possibility of a regency, he was sent to Pitt to underline the prince's 'political importance'. Pitt rejected him.

Following the French victories over the Prussians, Lord Grenville's new whig government sent Hely-Hutchinson on a special mission to the Prussian military headquarters in October 1806 as part of a diplomatic initiative designed to prevent a Franco-Prussian settlement. He was instructed to negotiate a subsidy treaty for the immediate assistance of the army and to report on its condition. Hely-Hutchinson was chosen principally for his military knowledge but also because of his friendship with the prince, who had become concerned about the future of Hanover as a result of the representations of the Hanoverian envoy in London. In private, however, Hely-Hutchinson cared little for Hanover; had no time for his immediate master, Lord Morpeth, the envoy to Prussia, whom he called 'a wretched thing'; and, in view of Napoleon's military dominance, regarded the enterprise as 'a wild goose chase' (John Hely-Hutchinson to Francis Hely-Hutchinson, 31 Oct 1806, Donoughmore papers). He had his first meeting with the Prussian commander-in-chief on 23 December and, despite his own misgivings, signed a treaty on 28 January 1807 by which Britain would again subsidize Prussia and would sacrifice captured French colonies for a general peace settlement. In parliament Grenville congratulated Hely-Hutchinson on the treaty. Howick, the foreign secretary, noted to his satisfaction that his special envoy had not been lured into anything other than a single very modest subsidy. Following the Grenville government's resignation, Hely-Hutchinson remained at his post with the support of the king, the prince of Wales, and the duke of York until the new administration appointed a permanent minister.

Hely-Hutchinson travelled to Memel in April 1807 for discussions with Frederick William III of Prussia and Tsar Alexander I and was instrumental in summoning British ships off Danzig to relieve the Prussian garrison. In June he reported from Memel about the meeting between Napoleon, Frederick William, and Alexander which led to the peace of Tilsit (July 1807). He went to St Petersburg in July and had discussions with the tsar, and he was still there late in August when news arrived of the pre-emptive attack by the British on Copenhagen to prevent the French gaining the Danish fleet—an event which helped turn Russia against Britain. In November, Hely-Hutchinson returned to Britain. In February 1808 Canning claimed in defence of the attack at Copenhagen that one of Hely-Hutchinson's dispatches indicated Russia had already turned against Britain before the attack took place. Hely-Hutchinson denied this, arguing that Copenhagen had been both decisive and disastrous.

Thereafter Hely-Hutchinson faded from active politics. His relationship with the prince fluctuated, but in 1820 the new king sent him as his envoy to Queen Caroline. He met her at St Omer on 4 June, but she refused to listen to his offer and went to England.

Hely-Hutchinson spent the remainder of his life mostly in Ireland, disillusioned and discontented. He succeeded his brother as second earl of Donoughmore and second Viscount Hutchinson on 25 August 1825. Although his requirements were modest, he inherited money problems, largely because of his brother's commitments and his Cork City electoral interest. He became convinced that British rule in Ireland was doomed, that most Irish protestants were Orangemen, and that Catholic emancipation was essential to any medium-term stability. He supported the 1829 Relief Bill and, although alarmed by the extent of the reform bills, stated that he preferred the whigs to the tories, who would only provoke revolution, the end result of which would be despotism. He died, unmarried, at Knocklofty, co. Tipperary, on 29 June 1832, when the barony of Hutchinson became extinct. The pension attached to it, and a pension of £900, for an abolished sinecure in the Irish custom house, also ceased. He was succeeded as earl and viscount by his nephew John Hely-Hutchinson (1787–1851).   P. J. JUPP

Sources *Public characters of 1801–1802* (1802) · *DNB* · GEC, *Peerage* · *Correspondence of Charles, first Marquis Cornwallis*, ed. C. Ross, 3 vols. (1859) · *Memoirs and correspondence of Viscount Castlereagh, second marquess of Londonderry*, ed. C. Vane, marquess of Londonderry, 12 vols. (1848–53) · H. Bunbury, *Narrative of some passages in the great war with France, from 1799–1810* (1854) · *The manuscripts of J. B. Fortescue*, 10 vols., HMC, 30 (1892–1927), vols. 4, 7–10 · *GM*, 1st ser., 102/2 (1832), 265–6 · *Report on the manuscripts of Earl Bathurst, preserved at Cirencester Park*, HMC, 76 (1923) · *The correspondence of Edmund Burke*, 7, ed. P. J. Marshall and J. A. Woods (1968) · *The later correspondence of George III*, ed. A. Aspinall, 5 vols. (1962–70) · *The correspondence of George, prince of Wales, 1770–1812*, ed. A. Aspinall, 8 vols. (1963–71) · *The letters of King George IV, 1812–1830*, ed. A. Aspinall, 3 vols. (1938) · P. Mackesy, *British victory in Egypt, 1801* (1995) · *The diary and correspondence of Charles Abbot, Lord Colchester*, ed. Charles, Lord Colchester, 3 vols. (1861) · *The Farington diary*, ed. J. Greig, 8 vols. (1922–8) · T. Pakenham, *The year of liberty: the history of the great Irish rebellion of 1798* (1969) · *The Creevey papers*, ed. H. Maxwell, 3rd edn (1905); rev. edn, ed. J. Gore (1963) · *Lord Granville Leveson Gower: private correspondence, 1781–1821*, ed. Castalia, Countess Granville [C. R. Leveson-Gower], 2nd edn, 2 vols. (1916) · H. R. V. Fox, third Lord Holland, *Further memoirs of the whig party, 1807–1821*, ed. Lord Stavordale (1905) · K. Bourne and W. B. Taylor, eds., *The Horner papers* (1994) · S. Romilly, *Memoirs of the life of Sir Samuel Romilly*, 3 vols. (1840) · TCD, Donoughmore papers

Archives TCD, corresp. and papers | BL, corresp. with Sir James Willoughby Gordon, Add. MS 49496 · BL, letters to Sir Robert Wilson, Add. MSS 30125–30126 · Bodl. Oxf., corresp. with Bruce family · NA Scot., letters to Sir Alexander Hope · NA Scot., corresp. with lords Melville · NL Ire., letters to Dennis Scully · priv. coll., corresp. with Maurice FitzGerald · PRO, FO papers, Prussia and Russia · PRO NIre., corresp. with Lord Anglesey · U. Durham, corresp. with second Earl Grey

Likenesses Goss, mezzotint, pubd 1802, BM · T. Phillips, oils, c.1809, Royal Collection · J. Heath, stipple (after Knight), BM, NPG; repro. in J. Barrington, *Historic memoirs of Ireland*, new edn, 2 vols. (1835) · H. Mackenzie, stipple (after T. Phillips), BM, NPG; repro. in *Contemporary portraits* (1809) · W. Nicholls, stipple, BM, NPG; repro. in *Military panorama* (1814)

Hutchinson, John Hely-, third earl of Donoughmore (1787–1851), army officer, eldest son of Francis Hely-Hutchinson (1759–1827), who was the third son of John Hely-*Hutchinson (1724–1794), and his wife, Frances Wilhelmina, daughter of Henry Nixon of Belmont, co. Wexford, was born at Wexford. He entered the army in September 1807, and served with the 1st foot guards in the Peninsula. He was promoted captain on 9 November 1812, and fought at Waterloo. On the allied occupation of Paris he was on the staff there, and became known for his role in the escape of General Lavalette, formerly Napoleon's postmaster-general and under sentence of death. Together with Lieutenant Bruce of his own regiment and Sir Robert Wilson, he was put on trial for his life in Paris. Public sympathy was on the side of the accused, and the judge leniently sentenced them to three months' imprisonment and the expenses of the trial.

After release Hely-Hutchinson returned to England and in 1816 was deprived of his commission, but was soon restored to his regiment. He was whig MP for co. Tipperary in 1826–30 and 1831–2; he became a Conservative about 1839. In 1832 he succeeded his uncle, John Hely-*Hutchinson (1757–1832), as third earl of Donoughmore; in 1834 he was made KP and in 1842 was appointed one of the commissioners of charitable donations and bequests in Ireland. He married on 15 June 1821 the Hon. Margaret Gardiner (1796–1825), seventh daughter of Luke, first Viscount Mountjoy; they had one son, Richard John, who succeeded his father, and a daughter, Margaret, who died young. He was married for a second time on 5 September 1827, his wife being Barbara (d. 11 Dec 1856), second daughter of Lieutenant-Colonel William

Reynell of Castle Reynell, co. Westmeath; they had one son and three daughters. Hely-Hutchinson died at his residence at Palmerston House, near Dublin, on 14 September 1851. A memorial tablet was erected by his widow in Chapelizod church, co. Dublin.

ROBERT DUNLOP, rev. JAMES FALKNER

Sources *Army List* · Burke, *Peerage* · F. W. Hamilton, *The origin and history of the first or grenadier guards*, 3 vols. (1874) · *Colburn's United Service Magazine*, 2 (1849) · Comte de Lavalette, *Memoires et souvenirs* (1831) · GEC, *Peerage* · *GM*, 2nd ser., 36 (1851)
Archives TCD, corresp. and papers
Likenesses print, c.1815, BM

Hutchinson, Sir Jonathan (1828–1913), surgeon, was born at The Quay, Selby, Yorkshire, on 23 July 1828, the second son of Jonathan Hutchinson (1797–1872), a middleman in the flax trade, and his wife, Elizabeth Massey (1803–1867). He belonged to a group of distinguished medical contemporaries of Quaker origin, which included Thomas Hodgkin, T. B. Peacock, Lord Lister, Wilson Fox, and D. H. Tuke. His ancestors had farmed for generations the same small estate near Boston in Lincolnshire, and among them were some of the early followers of George Fox. He was brought up as a strict Quaker, but by middle life he had freed himself from the outward forms of Quakerism, though its serious influence upon him was obvious throughout his life. A scientific training, the close study of nature, and the influence of Darwin left him at last far from orthodox, but—to quote the words which he directed to be engraved upon his tombstone—'a man of hope and forward-looking mind'.

After being apprenticed to Dr Caleb Williams of York in 1845, he spent four years at the small York school of medicine (1846–50), where he came under the influence of Thomas Laycock. He completed his training by attending lectures at St Bartholomew's Hospital, London. At first disliking the thought of private practice, he began his life in London by writing for medical journals, coaching, and making the elaborate clinical records for which he afterwards became famous. On 31 July 1856 he married Jane Pynsent West (1835–1887), and about this time began private practice at 14 Finsbury Square. As his family grew— he and his wife had ten children—Hutchinson became more involved in private practice, but he always considered himself primarily a clinical investigator and medical teacher. He held minor hospital appointments until in 1859 he obtained a post as assistant surgeon at the London Hospital. Here, as well as at the Metropolitan Free Hospital and the special hospitals on the surgical staff of which he served (the Royal London Ophthalmic Hospital, the Blackfriars Hospital for Skin Diseases, and the Royal Lock Hospital), the greater part of his life's work was carried out. In 1862 he obtained the fellowship of the Royal College of Surgeons, and in that year he was appointed lecturer on surgery at the London Hospital; in 1863, when he became full surgeon, he took on the additional subject of medical ophthalmology. In 1874, by now well-renowned, he moved to more fashionable quarters, 15 Cavendish Square, next door to his famous medical colleague Sir Andrew Clark. He left the active staff of the London Hospital in 1883 with the title of emeritus professor of surgery, and the Hutchinson triennial prize essay was then instituted to commemorate his services. He served on the council of the Royal College of Surgeons from 1879 to 1895 and was president in 1889. He was Hunterian professor from 1879 to 1883 and in 1891 delivered the Hunterian oration. In 1882 he was elected a fellow of the Royal Society. Hutchinson was also president in turn of most of the London medical societies, and he received many honours both in Britain and from overseas. He served on the royal commissions on smallpox and fever cases in London hospitals (1881) and on vaccination (1890–96), and was knighted in 1908.

Hutchinson was a specialist of great repute in at least three subjects: he was a leading authority on ophthalmology, dermatology, to some extent on neurology, and above all on syphilis; so that he was described as the greatest general practitioner in Europe and 'a specialist in all medicine'. He was extraordinarily diligent, a laborious and accurate observer, and an inveterate note-taker. His vast collection of pathological drawings was probably unequalled. He had a retentive memory, a logical mind, a love of discussion, and an enthusiasm for diffusing knowledge. His teaching was made impressive by ingenious arguments, apt illustrations, vivid metaphors, and quaint expressions, and was driven home by the simplicity and solemnity with which it was delivered. He thus naturally attracted a large following of students, young and old, and his clinic at the London Hospital was filled with patients referred to him with unusual diseases.

Among other outcomes of Hutchinson's labours were the publication of his *Illustrations of Clinical Surgery* (2 vols., folio, 1878–84), *A Smaller Atlas of Illustrations of Clinical Surgery* (1895), and a series entitled *Archives of Surgery* (1889–1900), a periodical edited by himself to which he was the sole contributor. He was a strong advocate of the value of museums and his medical collection of specimens and drawings was first housed at 1 Park Crescent, London, and was moved in 1889 to the 'polyclinic', a pioneering postgraduate medical college in Chenies Street near University College Hospital in which Sir William Broadbent and Fletcher Little were also greatly interested. Here courses of lectures and demonstrations were given by Hutchinson and others, and free consultations were held in public for impecunious patients. The polyclinic was the first systematic establishment in Britain for the purpose of encouraging postgraduate training by doctors.

Hutchinson spent some time early in his career as a medical journalist, and he spent eighteen months editing the *British Medical Journal* during a break in Ernest Hart's long reign there. He wrote easily and published on many medical as well as cultural topics. His work on syphilis was of lasting value and included the first description of the three common manifestations of congenital syphilis seen in infants born to infected parents. These are still known as Hutchinson's triad. Hutchinson also described for the first time several rare skin diseases as well as the more common chronic disease called sarcoidosis. Although widely recognized as one of the most astute dermatologists in Europe, his impact was mitigated by the fact that he paid little attention to previous classifications of skin diseases.

Hutchinson was always concerned with the hereditary aspects of disease, a legacy of Laycock's teaching and of Darwin's influence on him. As he became doubtful of personal immortality he became more convinced that real immortality was achieved through one's offspring and through working for social melioration. He served for more than half a century as the secretary and moving spirit of the New Sydenham Society, the Victorian publishing enterprise which sponsored translations of major European medical works as well as the republication of classic works from English-language sources.

Hutchinson had many interests outside his profession. He was an omnivorous reader, and by inheritance and inclination a country man. In his early days in Surrey he had a small house at Reigate, and when he became prosperous he bought a property at Haslemere to which he added from time to time until it reached 300 acres. Over this he would walk with his gun, and part of it he farmed. Here, with such companions as Hughlings Jackson, he studied natural history and geology with the same energy which he devoted to surgery and medicine in London. He also established in Haslemere in 1891 at his own expense an educational museum of specimens scientifically arranged for methodical instruction and study; this, he hoped, would be a model for similar museums elsewhere. Here and at a hall near his own house he gave Saturday and Sunday lectures and demonstrations to his neighbours and guests, on scientific, literary, and religious subjects. He gave a museum arranged on the same lines to his native town, Selby.

Hutchinson's fame does not rest on his achievements in general surgery. He can hardly be placed among the pioneers; and he was too early in the field to become identified with the advances in pathology and bacteriology which laid the foundations and raised the structure of modern surgery. He has been described as an indifferent though a successful operator. His special gift was that of observation, and the accumulation and collation of clinical facts. It was impossible to doubt their accuracy, but his deductions from them were not always equally convincing. Thus, having come to the conclusion as early as 1855 that the chief cause of leprosy was the eating of decomposed fish, he did not change his opinion even after the discovery of Hansen's bacillus. He held that leprosy was only slightly contagious, and strongly condemned segregation. To corroborate his theory he journeyed to Norway in 1869, South Africa in 1901, and India and Ceylon as late as 1903. His book *Leprosy and Fish-Eating* (1906) was meant for a wider reading public, but his views did not meet with wide acceptance, though he upheld them stoutly to the last. Although the theory became something of an obsession with him in his later life, it is unfortunate that he is remembered historically for this, to the exclusion of so much else.

Hutchinson died at his home, The Library, Inval, in Haslemere, on 23 June 1913, and was buried in Haslemere churchyard, beside his wife.

R. J. GODLEE, *rev.* W. F. BYNUM

Sources H. Hutchinson, *Jonathan Hutchinson, life and letters* (1946) • A. E. Wales, 'Sir Jonathan Hutchinson', *British Journal of Venereal Diseases*, 39 (1963), 67–86 • J. T. Crissey and L. C. Parish, *The dermatology and syphilology of the nineteenth century* (1981) • *BMJ* (28 June 1913), 1398–1401 • *The Lancet* (28 June 1913), 1833–5 • G. G. Meynell, *The two Sydenham societies* (1985) • private information (1927) • personal knowledge (1927) • *CGPLA Eng. & Wales* (1913)
Archives RCP Lond., corresp. and papers
Likenesses H. J. Brooks, group portrait, oils (*Council of the Royal College of Surgeons of England of 1844–85*), RCS Eng. • Spy [L. Ward], caricature, chromolithograph, NPG; repro. in *VF* (27 Sept 1890) • portraits, repro. in Hutchinson, *Jonathan Hutchinson* • portraits, repro. in *BMJ* • portraits, repro. in *The Lancet*
Wealth at death £92,269 18s. 6d.: probate, 20 Aug 1913, *CGPLA Eng. & Wales*

Hutchinson, Sir Joseph Burtt (1902–1988), geneticist and agriculturist, was born on 21 March 1902 in Burton Latimer, Northamptonshire, the eldest of the three sons (there were no daughters) of Edmund Hutchinson, who farmed at Cransley Grange, near Kettering, and his wife, Lydia Mary Davy, both of whom were Quakers. Jack, as he was known within the family, was encouraged to participate in the activities of the farm, learning skills which served him well in later years. He was educated at Ackworth School in Yorkshire and then at Bootham School in York, where he showed an aptitude for science, winning an exhibition to St John's College, Cambridge. Although keen to farm, he was encouraged by his uncle, Joseph Burtt Davy, a distinguished African plant taxonomist, to read botany. After gaining second-class honours in part one (1922) and part two (1923) of the natural sciences tripos, he went to study at the Imperial College of Tropical Agriculture in Trinidad.

From his earliest years Hutchinson brought together the charity and discipline of his Quaker upbringing, a common-sense approach learned through practical farming, and his excellence in science. His direct and attentive gaze and upright bearing, his capacity to listen, speak clearly and with authority, and to blend the thoughts of those around him with his own radical and incisive thinking, were treasured by those he knew and with whom he worked. From 1924, in Trinidad, he worked on the breeding of cotton, using the new genetical science. He was assigned research on the African and Asian species. Seizing a chance to work in India in 1933, he went as geneticist and botanist to the Institute of Plant Industry at Indore, where he found the prevailing Indian Civil Service attitude to research utilitarian and myopically short-term. Here he excelled by harnessing the power of numerous young Indian scientists, whom he trained to work on the biodiversity of native cottons. He became a legend in India and left behind him an embryonic programme for improved crop breeding. He returned to Trinidad in 1937 to head the Empire Cotton Growing Corporation's cotton genetics programme. He was appointed CMG in 1944 before becoming chief geneticist at the corporation's station near Khartoum, Sudan (1944–9).

Apart from his major taxonomic work on cotton, for which he became a fellow of the Royal Society in 1951, Hutchinson's principal plant-breeding achievement was in developing cotton varieties resistant to disease, the descendants of which formed the principal cottons grown in sub-Saharan Africa in the late twentieth century. He became director of the Empire Cotton Growing Corporation's Namulonge research station in Uganda in 1949. It was in Uganda that he ensured a continuing and high profile for agricultural research in English-speaking Africa, never losing sight of the needs of the African smallholder. In Uganda, a country which depended on cotton and coffee, Hutchinson played a major role in developing agricultural education at school, technical, and university levels. He chaired the Makerere College council (1953–7) in the last days of a relatively enlightened protectorate government. Knighted in 1956 for his services in east Africa, he 'retired' in 1957 when offered the Drapers' chair of agriculture at Cambridge and a fellowship at St John's College.

Hutchinson's years at Cambridge were celebrated by the wide vision of his undergraduate teaching and writing, but they were uneasy ones, for in 1969 the school of agriculture was eventually forced to close, under government pressure, despite the reinvigoration which he latterly brought to it. He was a figure of national standing in British agriculture and, with his global view, he continually challenged the conventional wisdoms of his times. He was particularly proud of his governing-body associations with the John Innes and Plant Breeding institutes and the Norfolk agricultural station. He was president of the British Association in 1965–6, received the Royal Society gold medal in 1967, and was awarded an ScD from Cambridge (1948) and the honorary degree of DSc from the universities of Nottingham (1966) and East Anglia (1972). Among his books were *The Evolution of Gossypium* (1947) and *Application of Genetics to Cotton Improvement* (1959).

Hutchinson was a humble man who consistently and unobtrusively adhered to the precepts of the Society of Friends. He was chairman of the board of governors of a local Friends' school, a preacher in Cambridge churches and college chapels, and 'a weighty Friend' in his own Quaker meeting. He was an immensely positive person with a deep faith in the essential goodness of human beings. In 1930 he had married Martha Leonora (Lena) Johnson (d. 1988); she was the daughter of George Frederick Johnson, who trained as an engineer and worked in his own brass and ironmongery business in Malton, Yorkshire. The couple had a son and a daughter. Their marriage was a lifelong partnership marked by a real devotion; in their home simplicity and *gravitas* were combined with quiet humour and occasional frivolity. Joseph Burtt Hutchinson died on 16 January 1988 at his home, Huntingfield, Huntingdon Road, Girton, near Cambridge; he was cremated and his ashes were interred at St Andrew's Church, Girton.   STEPHEN P. TOMKINS, *rev.*

Sources M. H. Arnold, *Memoirs FRS*, 37 (1991), 278–97 · personal knowledge (1996) · *CGPLA Eng. & Wales* (1988) · D. W. Altman, P. A. Fryxell, and R. D. Harvey, 'Sydney Cross Harland and Joseph B. Hutchinson', *Huntia*, 9/1 (1993), 31–49
Archives John Innes Centre, Norwich, papers · RS · St John Cam. | John Innes Centre, Norwich, corresp. with G. D. H. Bell and Ralph Riley | SOUND priv. coll., archive tapes
Likenesses photographs, priv. coll.
Wealth at death £325,734: probate, 19 Feb 1988, *CGPLA Eng. & Wales*

Hutchinson, Leslie Arthur Julien [*performing name* Hutch] (**1900–1969**), cabaret entertainer, was born on 7 March 1900 on the Caribbean island of Grenada, the son of George Hutchinson and Marianne Simm Turnbull; he was of mixed African, Caribbean, Indian, Scottish, and French ancestry. His father, a local businessman (a hatter and dry-goods merchant), played the organ in church, and Leslie operated the handpump for him. By the age of twelve Leslie had shown talent for playing the piano. After leaving school he joined the civil service, but at the age of sixteen Hutch, as he became known, left Grenada for New York. He later recalled that he arrived:

> with a few dollars and a lot of ambition. I became an elevator boy [but] in the Winter of 1917 I was without a job and absolutely broke. So I offered my services as a pianist at private parties. And that's how it all started.   (Breese and Palmer)

After turning professional he was so alarmed by the Ku Klux Klan during an engagement in Palm Beach that he decided to leave America for good. In Paris, where he went to study the classical piano, Hutch played in Joselli's bar, where he was adopted by the rich and famous, and met Cole Porter, the songwriter who was to become his friend and musical *alter ego*. Hutch became the best-known interpreter of Cole Porter's songs, and there was even a joke that said Hutch knew the lyrics before Porter had written them.

In 1927 Hutch was invited by Britain's top theatrical impresario, C. B. Cochran, to appear at the London Pavilion in the revue *One Dam Thing After Another*, with music and lyrics by Richard Rodgers and Lorenz Hart. Hutch accompanied the star of the show, Jessie Matthews, in its big hit—'My heart stood still'. During the next three years he appeared in three more West End revues for Cochran: Noël Coward's *This Year of Grace*, Cole Porter's *Wake Up and Dream*, and *Cochran's 1930 Revue*. Hutch's trademark was a white handkerchief which he used to mop his brow. As a singing pianist cabaret entertainer, he was befriended and lionized by the pre-war rich and famous. Charlotte Breese described the legend—and some of the tensions in Hutch's life—in *Salutations*, a BBC Radio 2 tribute broadcast on 11 September 1993:

> Hutch was a remarkably elegant man. Outwardly he conformed entirely and he became part of the set that were his clients. He was certainly invited to their houses at weekends although of course it would have been different at official functions in London where he was still expected to enter by the tradesmen's entrance. For a man with as much pride as Hutch it must have been extraordinarily humiliating. He was a walking threat in a kind of way because he was so good-looking.   (*Salutations*)

Leslie Arthur Julien Hutchinson [Hutch] (1900–1969), by Paul Tanqueray

In London, Hutch performed in society nightclubs such as the Café de Paris, Café Anglais, and Quaglino's. He was equally loved by the ordinary public, and became a top-of-the-bill attraction in music-halls all over the country. In 1930 he made his film début with a guest appearance in the musical *Big Business* (1930). Hutch enlivened several other British films of the 1930s and 1940s with his guest appearances, as well as a number of Pathetone Weekly and New Sound Pictorial films. With regular radio broadcasts and many recordings his popularity grew throughout the 1930s, and during the war years he gave many concerts for the armed forces. In 1942 he reappeared in a West End revue after an absence of more than a decade. This was *Happidrome*, and in 1943 he was featured in the screen version of *Seventy Years of Song*, a variety spectacular staged at the Royal Albert Hall by Cochran for the Toc H war relief fund.

After the Second World War Hutch's sophisticated style of performing, so popular with the pre-war smart set, was no longer in fashion, and his health was deteriorating. Though he continued performing (he returned to, and remained at, Quaglino's in 1954) he only occasionally recaptured the level of popularity he had enjoyed in pre-war Britain. In 1953 he was Roy Plomley's guest on the popular BBC radio programme *Desert Island Discs*, and in 1964 he realized his ambition to play an acting role when he appeared as a jazz musician in a British television drama called *A Really Good Jazz Piano*. His wife Ella Byrd (1894/5–1958), whom he married in New York and with whom he had at least one daughter, died in Hampstead in 1958. Hutch himself died on 18 August 1969 in New End

Hospital, Hampstead. His *Times* obituarist noted his 'fanatical' devotion to the game of cricket, and deemed him 'the ideal artist for the relaxed hour after dinner' (*The Times*).

STEPHEN BOURNE

Sources C. Breese and H. Palmer, *Hutch sings Cole Porter, Noel Coward and others* (1994) [disc notes; Happy Days, UK, B00001CE9] · S. Bourne, *Black in the British frame: black people in British film and television, 1896–1996* (1996) · *The Times* (19 Aug 1969) · d. cert. [Ella Byrd Hutchinson] · *Salutations*, BBC Radio 2, 11 Sept 1993 [Ladbroke Radio production for the BBC, produced J. Hiley] · C. Breese, *Hutch* (1999)
Archives FILM BFI NFTVA, performance footage | SOUND BL NSA, documentary recording · BL NSA, oral history interview · BL NSA, performance recordings
Likenesses P. Tanqueray, photograph, priv. coll. [*see illus.*]
Wealth at death £3128: administration, 25 Nov 1969, *CGPLA Eng. & Wales*

Hutchinson, Leslie George [*known as* Leslie Jiver Hutchinson] (**1906–1959**), trumpeter and bandleader, was born on 18 March 1906 at Hope Road, Cross Roads, St Andrew parish, Jamaica, the only son and the younger child of John Hutchinson, a soldier and farmer, and Nora French or Ffrench, a washerwoman. Both parents were Jamaican. As a boy he joined the band of the West India regiment, where he learned to play the trumpet, and he travelled with the band to Toronto in 1922 for the Canadian National Exhibition and to London in 1924 for the British Empire Exhibition held at Wembley. On his return to Jamaica he played with several dance bands, including that of the alto saxophonist Bertie King.

Hutchinson returned to London in 1936 to work with the nightclub band led by the Trinidadian drummer Happy Blake. In the same year, as featured singer and trumpeter, he joined the Emperors of Jazz, the all-black band formed by the trumpeter Leslie Thompson and conducted by the dancer Ken 'Snake Hips' Johnson. After this re-formed under Johnson's leadership, he had an intermittent relationship with Johnson, leaving him to play in nightclubs with other black leaders, including the Yorkshire-born double bass player Jack Davies. He worked in the co-operative band of drummer Al Craig and dancer Lewis Hardcastle and was trumpet soloist with the Nigerian pianist Fela Sowande at the Florida Club in Mayfair, where he accompanied the American singer Adelaide Hall. He was also seen on screen, leading Sowande's band in the film *Traitor Spy* (1939). On 26 April 1939 he married Phyllis Adela Swaby (1917–1969), a Jamaican beautician who had travelled to London to join him and whom he had known since she was a schoolgirl. They had three children, Pamela Elaine (*b.* 1939; the singer known as Elaine Delmar), Ivor Kenrick (1943–2000), and Maria Angela Lesley (*b.* 1953).

Hutchinson had returned to Johnson by the time his West Indian Dance Orchestra opened at the Café de Paris in 1939, and was on stage there when a bomb fell on the nightclub on 8 March 1941, killing Johnson. Hutchinson was unhurt and, with the ranks of musicians depleted by war service, was rapidly in demand for his professional services. Regimental discipline and the musical grounding he had received in the military band stood him in good embarked on a similarly gruelling series of one-night stands throughout Britain. He worked in Belgium and Switzerland before being forced to disband. Geraldo remained his greatest champion, holding his first trumpet chair open and enabling Hutchinson to come back on the payroll whenever his own ventures failed. He became an indispensable part of the organization, restricted mainly to playing in the trumpet section and featured infrequently as a jazz soloist, but, like other improvising musicians who earned a living with similar dance bands, he found opportunities for self-expression as a frequent and enthusiastic jam-session participant.

In 1949 Hutchinson re-formed his own band, employing some of the young musicians who had recently arrived from the Caribbean alongside his contemporaries. They travelled to Sweden and Czechoslovakia, Hutchinson subsequently dividing his time between his own projects and Geraldo's band. He still hoped to keep a well-organized black band in the public eye, but the musical and economic climate had changed, and this was now an expensive and complicated proposition. Furthermore, as the new Caribbean arrivals found better paid work in nightclubs, he was no longer able to retain an all-black personnel. In 1952 he worked alongside the American pianist Mary Lou Williams. As all-black variety shows were revived, he went on tour with several such productions and formed a new group, the Ebony Knights. He was music director in 1958 for a London production of Langston Hughes's play *Simply Heavenly*, then, with his daughter Elaine Delmar as band singer, he returned to the touring life. He was driving the band bus between engagements when, on 22 November 1959, he hit a telegraph pole at Weeting, near Brandon, Suffolk. He died two hours later at the West Suffolk General Hospital, Bury St Edmunds, of the injuries he received, and was buried at St Pancras Roman Catholic cemetery, East Finchley. He was survived by his wife, Phyllis, and their three children.

Hutchinson was a pioneering figure who worked hard to bring black British and Caribbean musical achievement to public attention. If he was never able to match the success enjoyed by Ken 'Snake Hips' Johnson, it was not through want of instrumental ability or lack of trying. A solidly built man with a ready smile and easy-going nature, he was much loved in the music business, where he was regarded as a gentleman whose personal integrity and trusting nature sometimes stood in the way of his progress.   VAL WILMER

Sources J. Chilton, *Who's who of British jazz* (1997) · L. Thompson and J. P. Green, *Leslie Thompson: an autobiography* (1985), 89, 90, 93, 98 · 'Hutchinson no more "Jiver"', *Melody Maker* (24 Jan 1948), 5 · M. Burman, *Melody Maker* (28 Nov 1959), 4 · K. Graham, 'Tribute to Leslie "Jiver" Hutchinson', *Melody Maker* (5 Dec 1959) · personal knowledge (2004) · private information (2004) · b. cert. · m. cert. · d. cert.

Likenesses photographs, 1922–4, repro. in Thompson and Green, *Leslie Thompson* · photograph, *c*.1940, priv. coll. [*see illus.*] · A. Bender, photograph, 1944, priv. coll. · photographs, priv. coll.

Leslie George Hutchinson (1906–1959), by unknown photographer, *c*.1940

stead, and he earned a solid reputation in London for his reading ability, instrumental competence, and reliability. After playing with Bert Ambrose and the clarinettist Sid Phillips, he began a long association with the popular orchestra leader Geraldo (Gerald Bright). With this band he broadcast frequently and made numerous recordings, and also travelled to Egypt and the Middle East to play for British troops.

In 1944 Hutchinson united several former members of Johnson's orchestra to form his own All-Star Coloured Band. Like his erstwhile colleague Carl Barriteau, who had embarked on a venture of his own, Hutchinson's ambition was to emulate the success of Ken Johnson. Unlike Barriteau, however, he wanted to fulfil this with another all-black band. In doing so, he was forced to change his professional name. Confusion with the pianist and popular entertainer Leslie Hutchinson (Hutch) led him to adopt 'Jiver' as a stage name, although it was an appellation he never liked, as he considered it belittled his musicianship and was racially stereotyping. The full form Leslie 'Jiver' Hutchinson was used for professional purposes at his insistence, but he was always known as Leslie or Les by his intimates. In 1948 he announced that he was dropping the name, although it appeared to have crept back five years later.

At the end of the Second World War, Hutchinson's band spent three months entertaining the forces in India, then

Hutchinson [*née* Apsley], **Lucy** (1620–1681), poet and biographer, was born, according to her own account, on 29 January 1620 in the Tower of London, the second of the ten children of Sir Allen *Apsley (1566/7–1630), lieutenant of the Tower, and his third wife, Lucy (c.1589–1659), daughter of Sir John St John of Lydiard Tregoze, Wiltshire, and his wife, Lucy Hungerford.

Education and marriage Her father was no scholar—after a period of service he had worked as a military victualler, with a long stint in Ireland—but he encouraged her in an education unusual for a girl of the period, ensuring that she was particularly well versed in Latin. Her mother was a strong influence: a youthful stay on Jersey had instilled in her a love of the 'Geneva discipline' (*Memoirs*, 1973, 284), and her Puritan sympathies emerged in her support for lectureships and in her encouraging her daughter to memorize sermons from an early age. Despite an intellectual precocity that came to alarm her mother as inappropriate for a girl, Lucy Apsley also loved tales of amatory intrigues and poems, and at an early age began to compose songs herself.

Lucy Apsley's father's last years were clouded by financial difficulties and on his death in 1630 her mother was left with a large family and large debts. Her second marriage, to Sir Leventhorpe Francke of Hatfield Broad Oak, Essex, seems to have been unhappy, leading to an early separation. Lawsuits of the 1630s show glimpses of the young Lucy Apsley being shuttled between different, and frequently discordant, branches of the family. The pressure was strong for her to make a dynastically advantageous marriage, and this seems to have led to tensions between mother and daughter. Pages apparently dealing with an unsuitable early passion were torn from the manuscript of her autobiography, which is now largely lost. According to her account in the *Memoirs*, the pressures of resistance to a series of arranged matches were causing her acute distress when she encountered her future husband, John *Hutchinson (*bap.* 1615, *d.* 1664) of Owthorpe in Nottinghamshire. He had been lodging at Richmond with the musician Charles Coleman, with whom Lucy Apsley's sister Barbara also studied. A much cited, and unusually lyrical, passage in the *Memoirs* tells of the courtship from his point of view, thus enabling her to draw attention to the role of her poetic and scholarly gifts in kindling his love: this was a marriage that would respect her aspirations as a writer. He was considered a suitable match, belonging to a moderately prosperous gentry family, and the couple were married at St Andrew's Church, Holborn, on 3 July 1638.

Mother and translator of Lucretius The north of England, Lucy Hutchinson later recalled, had 'a formidable name among the London ladies' (*Memoirs*, 1973, 34), and her husband allowed her time to wean herself away from her friends, renting a house a little out of town at Monken Hadley, Middlesex. While she brought up her first, twin, children, who were born in September 1639, John Hutchinson engaged in theological studies that intensified his Calvinism. His wife persuaded him to take an opportunity of staying in the south by seeking a vacancy in the Star Chamber, but before the negotiations were completed

that court had been abolished. Viewing this as providential the couple travelled to take possession of the Owthorpe estate in October 1641, soon after the birth of their third son, John. After a period of hesitation John Hutchinson enlisted in the parliamentary army and in 1643 was appointed governor of Nottingham and of Nottingham Castle. Lucy Hutchinson compiled a manuscript account of her husband's services for parliament which seems to have been designed to vindicate him in his quarrels with the civic leaders and other rivals (BL, Add. MSS 25901, 39779, 46172N).

Once peace had returned it took the Hutchinsons some time to bring the Owthorpe estate back to good order, and it was probably during the 1650s that Lucy Hutchinson began her first major literary project, a translation of Lucretius's *De rerum natura*. She later self-deprecatingly presented it as an accompaniment to her needlework, but it was a difficult and ambitious undertaking. Representing Lucretius's Latin in not many more lines of English, the translation belonged to a mode of very close verbal rendition that was becoming outmoded by freer approaches, but this discipline contributed to the characteristic force and economy of her later writings, and the translation displayed considerable philological judgement and was attentive to the poetic effects of the original. Another work plausibly ascribed to Hutchinson from this period is a line by line refutation of Edmund Waller's *A Panegyrick of my Lord Protector* (BL, Add. MS 17018), a vigorously republican assault not just on Cromwell but on the compliance of poets with his rule.

At the Restoration, John Hutchinson's life was endangered as a signatory of Charles I's death warrant. According to Lucy Hutchinson's own account, which may have been designed to clear his name, she tricked him into recanting his republicanism by a forged letter (*Memoirs*, 1973, 229–30); certainly her St John and Apsley connections were powerfully deployed on his behalf. There followed a renewed period of peace, and the couple's last child was born, but in 1663 Lucy Hutchinson's world collapsed with her husband's arrest for alleged involvement in an armed rising. She again played an active role in fighting for his interests, writing, and on one occasion threatening to print, letters on his behalf.

Widow and memorialist Like her mother before her Lucy Hutchinson was left by her husband's death in captivity to deal with a dynastic as well as a personal crisis. The memorial inscription she prepared for John Hutchinson recorded four sons, the twins Thomas and Edward, Lucius, and John (the second of that name, the first having died in 1647), and four daughters, Barbara, Lucy, Margaret, and Adeliza, the last of whom was already dead by 1664. Thomas, the eldest son, married Jane Radcliffe in the early 1660s but his wife died in childbirth soon afterwards. He was soon effectively disinherited. To help with her husband's debts Lucy Hutchinson sold off his estates first at Lowesby in Leicestershire, where local tradition claims she composed the *Memoirs*, and then at Owthorpe, which was sold in 1672 to her husband's half-brother, Charles Hutchinson. She seems to have continued to live at

Owthorpe. Thomas allegedly later tried to challenge the validity of this sale, and Charles Hutchinson claimed that mother and son were intriguing to reclaim the property, though it is difficult to disentangle the actuality from the legal fictions of chancery suits. Surviving correspondence from 1674–5 presents a bleak picture of family worries, with one son mortally ill and great difficulties in financing her youngest children's education and finding them employment. Another son, John, married a Miss Morgan, with whom he had two children, both of whom emigrated. Her daughter Barbara married Andrew Orgil, a London merchant who later emigrated to Jamaica, on 19 August 1668 at St Clement Danes, Strand, at the age of twenty-three. Some time after the marriage Lucy Hutchinson complained to her that 'outward ill successes have much weakened my authority, and made it of no force with all persons' (*Principles*, 1). Barbara Orgil's daughters were recorded in their old age as living 'in the utmost distress & want' (BL, Add. MS 22221, fol. 488*r*).

Despite all these practical difficulties, after her husband's death Lucy Hutchinson entered a remarkable new phase of literary productivity. Her first project was to clear his name, a task the more urgent because she thought that her own actions had served to tarnish it: royalists and republicans alike viewed him as a traitor. She celebrated him in a work which she entitled austerely 'The life of John Hutchinson of Owthorpe in the county of Nottinghamshire'—*Memoirs* was a later editor's addition. For the central portions she drew heavily on her earlier wartime narrative, though she cut down on some detail and added the character sketches that give the work so much of its vituperative vividness. For the wider narrative she drew heavily on Thomas May's history, but she gave it a distinctive cast by incorporating a Harringtonian sociological analysis of the origins of the war, as well as intensifying the apocalyptic rhetoric. Woven into this narrative of the providential clash of absolutes is a more personal story in which the author's presence, though unobtrusive, is frequently felt, especially towards the end. Though far from the simple truth-telling she claimed, the work has been found of continuing value by local historians, for whom indeed it often remains the only source. Hutchinson seems to have been stimulated by the process of composition to follow it with an autobiography of her own. Though the date of this work is uncertain, the reference to 'my house at Owthorpe' would seem to place it after the completion of the *Memoirs* (by 1671) and before she sold the estate.

Later writings Underlying Lucy Hutchinson's later writings was an intensified religious dedication. She had long shown an independent cast of mind: during the 1640s she had taken the lead in questioning the validity of infant baptism and after her husband's death she pursued a spiritual journey of her own. Statements of her belief composed in 1667 and 1668 reveal her engaging intensely but critically with Calvin, affirming double predestination but rejecting any single church as the source of truth: while she opposed state intervention in religious practice, her name does not appear in the records of any particular

denomination. The same notebook indicates that in 1673 she attended the sermons of the congregationalist divine John Owen. The link here may have been her neighbour Sir John Hartopp, one of the purchasers of Lowesby, who took notes on Owen's sermons in the same year. Owen regularly preached at Hartopp's London home, Fleetwood House, which had become a refuge for former supporters of the puritan revolution. As Latin tutor for her son Lucius she chose Robert Ferguson, an associate of Owen who later became involved in the Rye House Plot against Charles II. A manuscript now lost contained a translation of part of a Latin treatise by Owen, *Theologoumena pantodoupa*, a rearguard action against the natural theology that was becoming more and more popular at the Restoration. As a former republican who had held equally firmly to Calvinist doctrine, Owen offered for Hutchinson a continuity with the previous age. It was apparently fear of backsliding in Calvinist belief that led her to compose a lengthy treatise warning her daughter Barbara against joining a sect and posthumously published as *On the Principles of the Christian Religion* (1817).

If heresy moved Lucy Hutchinson to write, atheism troubled her still more. In the new political order atheism was becoming fashionable among courtiers, notably the earl of Rochester, son of her cousin Anne Wilmot, who had intervened for her husband in 1660. Her own early translation of Lucretius was now returning to haunt her. Learning that an unauthorized manuscript was in circulation, she had a new copy made and presented to her friend Arthur Annesley, earl of Anglesey, with a dedication denouncing modern atheists as even worse than the deluded pagan poet (BL, Add. MS 17018; *Translation of Lucretius*, 23–7).

In 1679 there appeared anonymously a biblical poem entitled *Order and disorder, or, The world made and undone, being meditations upon the creation and fall, as it is recorded in the beginning of Genesis*. The preface, like the Lucretius dedication, expresses the author's concern at the renewed circulation of an early pagan poem; its wording is often virtually identical to the dedication, and many affinities with Hutchinson's writings confirm that the poem is hers. The poem was ascribed by Anthony Wood to her brother, Sir Allen Apsley, but he had been a committed royalist and was now a servant of the duke of York, a world remote from this poem's millennial radicalism. The printed version has only five cantos, down to the story of Adam and Eve; one manuscript, formerly in the possession of the countess of Rochester (Beinecke Rare Book and Manuscript Library, Yale University Library, Osborn collection, fb100), carries the narrative down to Jacob and Laban. It is hard to determine the poem's date, but it coheres with the project of all her later writing and thought. She was determined to use all her powers to hold the fort against the atheism and scepticism that in her view were undermining political as well as moral virtue, but she retained her early humanist belief in the importance of language and poetry. In composing a biblical epic she could redeem her muse, making the Lucretius translation not just a dangerous lapse but a preparation for further, godly epic verse.

The publication of *Order and disorder* suggests that at the time of her death Hutchinson still had energy and ambition as a writer. It also indicates that poetry continued to be a prime love: she had mourned her husband in verse, in some impassioned elegies, and her theological manuscript and the lost autobiographical manuscript also contained verse (Nottinghamshire Archives, DD/HU2, HU3). She died at Owthorpe in October 1681; she was buried there in the tomb she had prepared for her husband, but was given no memorial herself.

Assessment Lucy Hutchinson prided herself on remaining unchanged in her principles in a backsliding world, but her own life and writings reveal intense contradictions. In a society where female authorship was still widely frowned on, she herself insisted on women's intellectual inferiority; yet she was ready to have herself painted by Robert Walker proudly holding in her lap a laurel wreath, emblem of her literary aspirations. There is a strong vein of social criticism in her later writings, and she supported a Harringtonian agrarian law to limit landed wealth, but she could write of base-born adversaries with patrician hauteur. Intensely suspicious of the abuse of the imagination in pagan idolatry, she none the less devoted great care to entering the imaginative life of a pagan. Her anguish at her susceptibility to intellectual error is counterbalanced by an unflagging Calvinist conviction of ultimate rectitude. In dealing with the large masses she deemed ungodly her pen is unfailingly censorious, yet she can show warmth and tenderness in describing her inner circle, and in compassionate and wondering descriptions of the natural world.

Many of Hutchinson's papers passed like the Owthorpe estate to a different branch of the family, for whom her uncompromising defence of the regicide would have been an embarrassment. Though it is likely that Hutchinson hoped the *Memoirs* would ultimately reach an audience beyond her family, the work remained in manuscript (Nottinghamshire Archives, DD/HU4) and it was not until 1806 that a later Julius Hutchinson brought the *Memoirs* and the autobiography into print. The book became an immediate success, quickly passing into a cheaper edition and being regularly reprinted thereafter, and her strongly moralistic account of the civil war helped to mould both professional historiography and popular opinion. Mrs Hutchinson regularly figured in Victorian books about notable women, though the emphasis was almost always on her devotion to her husband rather than her own role in narrating his life. Though post-Victorian writers have often been less sympathetic to her puritan bias, the *Memoirs* has remained an important source for historians, while literary scholarship has directed attention to her lifelong commitment to poetry. DAVID NORBROOK

Sources L. Hutchinson, *Memoirs of the life of Colonel Hutchinson*, ed. J. Sutherland (1973) • L. Hutchinson, *Memoirs of the life of Colonel Hutchinson*, ed. J. Hutchinson, new edn, ed. C. H. Firth (1906) • commonplace book, Notts. Arch., DD/HU1 • elegies, Notts. Arch., DD/HU2 • religious notebook, Notts. Arch., DD/HU3 • memoirs, Notts. Arch., DD/HU4 • legal papers, Notts. Arch., M 691–693, M 701–713 • BL, Add. MSS 17018, fols. 213–17 (reply to Waller); 19333 (Lucretius translation); 25901; 39779; 46172N (memoirs drafts); 60671, fol. 248r; 63788B, fol. 143r (letters) • 'Order and disorder', Yale U., Beinecke L., Osborn collection, fb100 • *Lucy Hutchinson's translation of Lucretius, De rerum natura*, ed. H. de Quehen (1996) • L. Hutchinson, *On the principles of the Christian religion addressed to her daughter* (1817) • PRO, C5/56/126, C5/496/2, C5/503/56, C5/582/7, letter F, C24/604, C24/624/136, SP 29/361/18 • A. B[athurst], *History of the Apsley and Bathurst families* (1903) • J. G. Taylor, *Our Lady of Batersey* (1925) • J. T. Wharton, 'Monumental inscriptions', *Friends of Lydiard Tregoz*, 5 (1972), 63–79 • K. Narveson, 'The sources for Lucy Hutchinson's On theology', *N&Q*, 234 (1989), 40–41 • J. T. Godfrey, *Notes on the parish registers of St Mary's, Nottingham, 1566 to 1812* (1901) • J. Ainsworth and others, eds., *Index to administrations in the prerogative court of Canterbury*, 2, ed. C. H. Ridge, Index Library, British RS, 74–5 (1952) • bishops' transcripts, Owthorpe parish register, Southwell Minster

Archives BL, letters, Add. MSS 60671, fol. 248r; 63788B, fol. 143r • BL, memoirs of her husband and a fragment of a notebook, Add. MSS 25901, 39779, 46172N • BL, reply to Waller, Add. MS 17018, fols. 213–217 • Northants. RO, treatise addressed to daughter, Fitzwilliam Misc. vol. 793 • Notts. Arch., commonplace book, DD/HU1 • Notts. Arch., elegies, DD/HU2 • Notts. Arch., religious notebook, DD/HU3 • Notts. Arch., memoirs, DD/HU4 • Notts. Arch., legal papers, M 691–725 | PRO, sales of Lowesby and Owthorpe, C5/56/126, C5/496/2, C5/503/56, C5/582/7 • PRO, letter F, C24/604 • PRO, depositions, 1635, 1637, C24/624/136 • Yale U., Osborn collection, 'Order and disorder', fb100

Likenesses Freeman, line engraving (with child; after R. Walker), BM, NPG; repro. in Hutchinson, *Memoirs* (1973), facing p. 67 • R. Walker, oils, priv. coll. • engraving (after R. Walker), repro. in Hutchinson, *Memoirs* (1906), facing p. 1 • engraving (imaginary portrait), repro. in E. Starling, *Noble deeds of women* (1859), facing p. 108 • engraving (imaginary portrait), repro. in Mrs N. Crosland, *Memorable women: the story of their lives* (1864)

Hutchinson, Ralph (1552?–1606), biblical scholar and college head, was born in London and educated at Merchant Taylors' School. Concerned that his father, John Hutchinson, was 'greatly charged with a great nombre of children', Joan White (in her capacity as the widow of the founder, Sir Thomas White) nominated Ralph in 1568 to a scholarship at St John's College, Oxford, and he was finally admitted two years later on 26 June 1570 (Stevenson and Salter, 164). In 1578 Hutchinson graduated MA and in 1579 he was elected to the rhetoric readership, which he resigned in 1581 when he became medical fellow—presumably to the relief of those among his colleagues who had attempted to deprive him of the rhetoric readership in 1580 on grounds of his neglect of duties. By December 1583 he was vice-president, but he then resigned his fellowship from Lady day 1586, probably in order to marry Mary, daughter of Katherine Willis (from her first marriage). In June 1590 he was elected president, by which time he had taken holy orders. He became vicar of Charlbury, Oxfordshire, in 1593, the advowson of which he ultimately bequeathed to St John's in perpetuity. He was also vicar of Cropthorne, Worcestershire. He became BTh on 6 November 1596, DTh in 1602, and in 1604 he was appointed one of the translators of the Authorized Version of the Bible, to work at Westminster with six others from the Greek version of the epistles. Hutchinson died on 16 January 1606 in Oxford, proud that his college had been 'much blessed and increased during the tyme of [his] governement there', and he was survived by nine children (PRO, PROB 11/108). As requested in his will, he was buried in the college chapel, where his widow (and executor) placed a stone effigy in remembrance of his life and achievements.   ALEXANDRA SHEPARD

Sources W. H. Stevenson and H. E. Salter, *The early history of St John's College, Oxford*, OHS, new ser., 1 (1939) · W. C. Costin, *The history of St John's College, Oxford, 1598–1860*, OHS, new ser., 12 (1958) · A. W. Pollard, ed., *Records of the English Bible: the documents relating to the translation and publication of the Bible in English, 1525–1611* (1911) · C. J. Robinson, ed., *A register of the scholars admitted into Merchant Taylors' School, from AD 1562 to 1874*, 2 (1883) · F. W. M. Draper, *Four centuries of Merchant Taylors' School, 1561–1961* (1962) · C. M. Clode, ed., *Memorials of the Guild of Merchant Taylors of the fraternity of St John the Baptist* (1875) · PRO, PROB 11/108 · PRO, PROB 11/109
Archives St John's College, Oxford, college muniments lii
Likenesses effigy, 1606, St John's College, Oxford

Hutchinson, Ray Coryton (1907–1975), novelist, was born on 23 January 1907 at Doucina, Dollis Park, Church End, Finchley, London, the son of Harry Hutchinson (1866–1946) of Watford in Hertfordshire, a chief clerk in the insurance business, and his second wife, Lucy Mabel Coryton (1871–1936), the daughter of an army officer, of an Irish-Cornish family which had produced a steady line of clergymen and army officers. Hutchinson's half-brother Sheldon (1902–1962), was an Anglican clergyman, and his sister Madge (1909–1990) was in the Probation Service and latterly a probation inspector and tutor at the Home Office. Hutchinson was educated at Monkton Combe School in Somerset. A diary he kept at school relates his constant homesickness, and how he hated rugger and loathed the food. While there he wrote a 20,000-word novel called 'The Hand of the Purple Idol' (unpublished). He then proceeded to Oriel College, Oxford, to read for a degree in philosophy, politics, and economics. He rowed for his college (thereby gaining the friendship of A. J. P. Taylor), and he also joined the cavalry section of the Officers' Training Corps, and the university air squadron.

While at Oxford Hutchinson became attracted to a fellow undergraduate, Margaret Owen (1906–1992), daughter of Captain Owen Jones, a merchant navy officer. Hutchinson pursued her anonymously, leaving notes and small presents in her bicycle basket. It was not until some time after she identified him that she came to reciprocate his feelings, and they eventually married, on 2 April 1929. It was a very happy union, and produced two sons and two daughters. Meanwhile, having graduated a year ahead of Margaret with a third-class degree in 1927, Hutchinson moved to Norwich, where he worked as an assistant manager in the advertising department of Colman's Mustard. In the evenings he wrote short stories, some of which, including his first 'Every Twenty Years', were published in the *English Review*. He started very boldly by retelling the gospel story, with Christ as a motor mechanic in 'Strainland' at an unspecified time in the distant future. As *Thou hast a Devil* it was published in 1930 under the name R. C. Hutchinson. *The Answering Glory* (1932) tells of how an aged missionary forced to leave Africa, is replaced by a distinctly non-pious sixth-form hockey captain. Although all his work is informed by his Christian faith, he moved away from overt Christian themes and started

using contemporary European history as the main setting of novels such as *The Unforgotten Prisoner*, which was an instant best-seller when it appeared in 1933.

One Light Burning (1935), about an explorer in Siberia, was so successful that his wife encouraged Hutchinson to leave Colman's and devote his energy to writing. They moved to Birdlip in Gloucestershire; *Shining Scabbard* appeared the following year. *Testament* (1938), which won the Sunday Times gold medal for fiction, is a brilliant and monumental account of the Bolshevik Revolution. A spin-off from this was *Last Train South*, Hutchinson's only staged play; it was produced by Basil Dean and J. B. Priestley at the St Martin's Theatre, London, with Flora Robson in the leading role, but August 1938 was not a propitious time for such a venture and the play was not a commercial success. By the end of that year the family had moved to Crondall in Hampshire, where Hutchinson was a churchwarden. They lived here until 1955, after which, their children grown up, the couple moved nearer London, to Dysart, Bletchingley in Surrey, where Hutchinson lived for the rest of his life.

When the Second World War broke out Hutchinson enlisted, and he served as an army officer throughout, first with the 8th battalion of the East Kent regiment. His writing had to take second place, but *The Fire and the Wood* appeared in 1940; it was a powerful tale of a German doctor and his tuberculous patient suffering under the Nazi regime. *Interim* appeared five years later, having been written in difficult conditions amid air raids and the vagaries of army life. In 1943 he was transferred to the Staff College at Camberley, and he was later posted to the Home Guard directorate at the War Office. In 1944 he wrote the speech delivered by George VI at the standing-down of the Home Guard. After that he went to Baghdad to write the official history of the Persian and Iraq command, eventually published anonymously as *Paiforce* (HMSO, 1948). A few astute journalists recognized it as Hutchinson's work. He was discharged in October 1945 and attended a few sessions of the Nuremberg war crimes trial.

Elephant and Castle, a story of an unlikely marriage between a socially aspirant woman and a working-class man, appeared in 1949, to be followed in 1952 by one of the most powerful of Hutchinson's works, *Recollection of a Journey*, which related the deportation of Poles to Siberia in ghastly conditions. Later works were *The Stepmother* (1955), a domestic tale, and in contrast *March the Ninth* (1957), a gripping story of post-war vengeance in Yugoslavia. This was his last best-seller; in the 1960s sales of his books tailed off and he never quite regained his earlier popularity. *Image of my Father* followed in 1961. *A Child Possessed* (1964), a beautifully told tale of the love of a Marseilles lorry driver for his retarded daughter, won the W. H. Smith & Son literary award in 1966. *Johanna at Daybreak* (1969) is told through the eyes of a German female psychotic, while *Origins of Cathleen* (1971), the last novel published in Hutchinson's lifetime, was his only comic novel. As Mervyn Horder has outlined, Hutchinson's novels, which have a distinctive style, usually incorporate characteristics such as inappropriate infatuations, hazardous journeys, and 'an individual's single-minded pursuit of an all-but-unobtainable object' (Horder). Hutchinson also had the extraordinary ability to describe places he had never visited. He was particularly fond of outlandish epithets, the provision of 'dummy' prefaces crediting the events of a novel to plausible but non-existent sources, and violent switches in scene from chapter to chapter.

Some people found Hutchinson shy. He certainly avoided literary parties and London social life, but he was a warm, witty, and kindly host. He was a handsome man, of slightly less than average height. Mervyn Horder described him as:

> markedly dolichocephalic [with] grey-white hair swept back from a furrowed brow, sunken grey eyes, a husky voice, and a general expression of slight puzzlement which broke quickly either way into a smile or frown as he took in what you were saying, to which he paid the compliment of always listening as if nothing else mattered.

Hutchinson was struggling to complete a novel (subsequently published under the title *Rising*) when he died of a heart attack on 3 July 1975 at his home in Bletchingley. He was buried at St Katherine's Church in Merstham, which he regularly attended. *Rising* was short-listed for the Booker prize in 1976. This last book returns in some ways to the theme of his first novel: it tells of a healer in a South American village in 1903 who has come back to life after being tortured to death, and who has the power to transform the wicked hero.

In 1979 Rupert Hart-Davis edited *Two Men of Letters*, a selection by Margaret Hutchinson of a sequence of witty, compassionate, and lively letters between her husband and the poet Martyn Skinner from 1957 to 1974. *The Quixotes*, a collection of Hutchinson's short stories, was edited in 1984 by Robert Green, who also produced in the following year a useful reference work, *R. C. Hutchinson: the Man and his Books*. The foreword to this book includes Rupert Hart-Davis's tribute: 'Genius is impossible to define, and the word has become tarnished by exposure, but I believe R. C. Hutchinson had it'.

STEPHEN GREEN

Sources WWW · *The Times* (5 July 1975) · R. Green, *R. C. Hutchinson: the man and his books* (1985) · D. Severn, *Remembering R. C. Hutchinson, the author* (2000) · M. Horder, 'One light burning: the world of R. C. Hutchinson', *London Magazine, a Monthly Review of Literature*, new ser., 17/6 (1977), 65–72 · private information (2004) · b. cert. · m. cert. · d. cert.
Archives Ransom HRC, letters and papers | Bodl. Oxf., corresp. with Martyn Skinner · JRL, letters to Richard Church
Likenesses R. C. Hutchinson, self-portrait, drawing, repro. in R. Hutchinson, *A child possessed* (1964)
Wealth at death £11,181: probate, 30 Sept 1975, *CGPLA Eng. & Wales*

Hutchinson, Richard (*b.* 1597, *d.* in or before **1670**), colonist in America and naval administrator, was born in Alford, Lincolnshire, on 3 January 1597, the fourth child and fourth son in the family of six sons and two daughters (one of whom died young) of Edward Hutchinson, a merchant, and his wife, Susannah. Little is known of his early life. In 1621 he married Mary Hiley. They had six surviving sons and four daughters. His descendants included the earls of Donoughmore; the colonial governor and historian of Massachusetts, Thomas Hutchinson, was a collateral descendant. The commercially successful Hutchinson family emigrated to Massachusetts in 1633 and 1634. The Hutchinsons were involved in the great antinomian religious conformity controversy by which the infant colony was riven in 1636–8, Richard's sister-in-law being the religious leader Anne *Hutchinson and his brother-in-law her closest ally, the Revd John *Wheelwright. Richard had become a freeman—that is, a full church member—in 1634 but, along with others considered theologically unsound, was ordered to be disarmed in 1637, and with the rest of his family moved to the more tolerant atmosphere of Providence in 1638. He seems to have returned briefly to Massachusetts, perhaps in connection with his property there, but was back in England by 1643, in the service of the younger Sir Henry Vane, who as governor of the Massachusetts Bay colony at a precociously early age had been something of a fellow-traveller with the alleged heretics.

Hutchinson's first official work was under the navy and customs committee of the Long Parliament; by 1645 he was acting as Vane's deputy in the very important post of navy treasurer. In view of Vane's other commitments, Hutchinson must have had practical charge of parliamentarian naval finance, although it would seem that he was only paid a salary out of the treasurer's profits. Then in 1650 Vane was voted out of the position and Hutchinson succeeded him, holding it from the beginning of 1651 until the Restoration. With the outbreak of the First Anglo-Dutch War (1652–4), the treasurership became much more lucrative, its holder being remunerated partly on a poundage basis related to naval expenditure. Hutchinson was also active in the Ironmongers' Company of London, of which he had purchased the freedom. His earlier association with Vane (who had tried to resist being replaced by his own deputy) did not prevent Hutchinson from remaining in office under the Cromwellian protectorate. Though inevitably losing office in 1660, he cleared his accounts successfully, and years later Samuel Pepys believed that the finances of the navy had never been better handled than while he was treasurer. Hutchinson seems to have resumed his part in a family transatlantic trading network; although according to tradition his losses in the great fire of London exceeded £60,000, he seems to have died a wealthy man about 1670.

Confusingly, it was another Richard Hutchinson, of the City and later of Stepney, who was co-treasurer for sick and wounded soldiers, widows, and orphans from 1643 to 1660 and a judge for imprisoned debtors in 1653–4, and who served as co-paymaster of the navy under the treasurers in 1668–71, appearing in the latter part of Pepys's diary. The will of the former naval treasurer, the subject of this entry, was proved in April 1670, and the co-paymaster was still serving the following year and being called to account after that.

G. E. AYLMER, *rev.*

Sources G. E. Aylmer, *The state's servants: the civil service of the English republic, 1649–1660* (1973) • Pepys, *Diary* • V. A. Rowe, *Sir Henry Vane the younger: a study in political and administrative history* (1970) • B. Bailyn, *The New England merchants in the seventeenth century* (1955) • declared accounts, navy, PRO, E 351 • PRO, PROB/11/PCC, 47 Penn, 129 North, 174 Pett
Wealth at death substantial

Hutchinson, Richard Hely-, first earl of Donoughmore (1756–1825), politician, was born on 29 January 1756, the eldest of the six sons and three daughters of John Hely-*Hutchinson (1724–1794), politician, of Palmerstown, co. Dublin, and Knocklofty, co. Tipperary, and his wife, Christiana (*bap.* 1732, *d.* 1788), the daughter of Abraham Nickson of Munny, co. Wicklow, and the grandniece of Richard Hutchinson of Knocklofty. At the age of eight he was appointed lord treasurer in the Irish exchequer. Educated at Eton College from 1767, he entered Lincoln's Inn in 1770, matriculated from Magdalen College, Oxford, in 1772, and proceeded to Trinity College, Dublin, where his father was provost; he graduated BA (1775) and MA (1780). Hely-Hutchinson was called to the Irish bar in 1777, having the year before been appointed commissioner of stamps and imprest and elected to parliament for the university seat. His election annulled, he sat for Sligo borough from 1778 to 1783, when he became LLB and LLD, and switched constituency to Taghmon. From 1785 he was a revenue commissioner. Some of his parliamentary speeches were studiedly competent, notably on parliamentary reform and the prosecution of the sheriff of Dublin (29 November 1783 and 24 February 1785). He seems to have wintered in Naples in December 1787: his health was seldom robust.

On his mother's death, on 24 June 1788, Hely-Hutchinson succeeded to her barony of Donoughmore, created in 1783, and on 5 February 1789 he took his seat in the Lords, where he increasingly voiced criticisms of Irish ruling circles. He was grand master of the Irish freemasons from 1789 to 1813. In 1792, having ten years earlier supported his father's championship of Catholic enfranchisement, he mustered delegates for the Catholic convention in Dublin. In 1793 he exchanged his revenue commissionership for one of excise, to which the former was added in 1799, and which he held until 1806; he was chief commissioner from 1801. Donoughmore raised the 112th foot in 1794, serving as lieutenant-colonel under his brother John, and became a governor of Tipperary; he was promoted major-general in 1805 and lieutenant-general in 1812. He was sworn of the Irish privy council on 26 October 1796, and on 20 November 1797 he was created Viscount Donoughmore; he took his seat in the Irish Lords on 23 February 1798. His support for the Anglo-Irish union obtained him the earldom of Donoughmore on 31 December 1800. Hoping that the Union would facilitate Catholic relief, he became an Irish representative peer at Westminster in 1801, though Lord Cornwallis restrained him from raising Catholic aspirations then. He was therefore reluctant to attend.

When his political friends the 'talents' came to power in 1806, Donoughmore gave up his commissionerships to be joint postmaster-general in Ireland. He was sworn of the British privy council on 7 May 1806, joined the Board of Trade on 23 May, and became fellow of the Society of Antiquaries a month later. He resigned office with the ministry in April 1807. From 1810 he was a leading advocate of Catholic relief in the Lords, and each year until 1821, apart from 1818 and 1820, presented petitions from the Irish Catholics, despite the sporadic distrust between him and the Irish Catholic board. He was a cogent critic of coercive legislation for Ireland, and in 1819 for Britain—especially from 1814, when his debating range embraced the post-war plight of the downtrodden nations of Europe.

In 1820 Donoughmore sided vociferously with George IV on Queen Caroline's trial, and was rewarded with a British peerage, as Viscount Hutchinson, at the coronation on 14 July 1821. In 1822 he reluctantly conceded support for the Irish Insurrection Bill. His brother John's association with George IV had drawn him into court circles, although, consorting with Lord Lansdowne, he still professed opposition to the ministry. He was promoted general just before his death. His last political act, a vote on the Catholic question in the Lords on 17 May 1825, when he was already ill, showed him to be true to Catholic claims. Following his death, on 22 August 1825 at his home at 4 Bulstrode Street, Manchester Square, Marylebone, Middlesex, the Catholic Association hailed him as their hereditary patron. Since he was unmarried, his brother John succeeded to the earldom.   ROLAND THORNE

Sources *GM*, 1st ser., 95/2 (1825), 371 • *DNB* • J. Porter, P. Byrne, and W. Porter, eds., *The parliamentary register, or, History of the proceedings and debates of the House of Commons of Ireland, 1781–1797*, 17 vols. (1784–1801), vols. 2, 4 • B. C. MacDermot, ed., *The Catholic question in Ireland and England, 1798–1822: the papers of Denys Scully* (1988) • *The correspondence of Daniel O'Connell*, ed. M. O'Connell (1972–80), vols. 1–3 • *The manuscripts of J. B. Fortescue*, 10 vols., HMC, 30 (1892–1927), vol. 1, pp. 420, 441; vol. 8, pp. 70, 74–5, 104, 110, 116, 120, 122, 125; vol. 10, pp. 144, 151, 225, 233, 240, 244, 299, 341, 394 • *Hansard 1* (1805–20), vols. 16–41 • *Hansard 2* (1820–23), vols. 1–8; (1825), vol. 12 • *The manuscripts of the duke of Beaufort … the earl of Donoughmore*, HMC, 27 (1891) • *Diary and correspondence of Lord Colchester*, ed. C. Abbot, 3 vols. (1865), 2.377, 469, 593; 3.370, 385 • *The Creevey papers*, ed. H. Meakwell, 2 vols. (1904), 1.48, 138, 317, 326; 2.178, 234, 236 • H. R. V. Fox, third Lord Holland, *Further memoirs of the whig party, 1807–1821*, ed. Lord Stavordale (1905), 124–5, 286, 293 • *Memoirs and correspondence of Viscount Castlereagh, second marquess of Londonderry*, ed. C. Vane, marquess of Londonderry, 12 vols. (1848–53), vol. 2, 240; vol. 3, 483; vol. 4, 21 • *The later correspondence of George III*, ed. A. Aspinall, 5 vols. (1962–70), vol. 3, p. 2315; vol. 4, p. 2699 • *The correspondence of Edmund Burke*, ed. T. W. Copeland and others, 10 vols. (1958–78), vol. 4, p. 435; vol. 5, p. 289; vol. 10, p. 21 • *The letters of King George IV, 1812–1830*, ed. A. Aspinall, 2 (1938), 881, 884 • *The correspondence of George, prince of Wales, 1770–1812*, ed. A. Aspinall, 6: 1806–1809 (1969), 2375
Archives Royal Arch. • TCD, corresp. and papers | BL, Add. MS 758, fol. 138 • BL, Peel MSS • BL, letters to Lord Grenville, Add. MS 58963 • BL, corresp. with Lord Hardwicke, Add. MSS 35688, 35731, 35734–35738, 35740, 35748, 35754, 35759–35761, 35764 • Royal Library, Windsor • U. Durham L., letters to second Earl Grey
Likenesses W. Leney, stipple, pubd 1797, BM, NPG • G. Hayter, group portrait, oils, 1820 (*The trial of Queen Caroline, 1820*), NPG • H. Brocaw, stipple (after B. Stoker), NPG • J. Reynolds, oils
Wealth at death under £2000 • cash bequests of £1429 18s. 6d.: will, PRO, PROB 12/230

Hutchinson, Richard Walter John Hely-, sixth earl of Donoughmore (1875–1948), politician, was born at 18 Charles Street, Berkeley Square, London, on 2 March 1875, the eldest child and only son in the five children of John Luke George Hely-Hutchinson, fifth earl of Donoughmore (1848–1900), and his wife, Frances Isabella (d. 1924), daughter of General William Frazer Stephens of the East India Company's service. Until he succeeded to the earldom in 1900 upon the death of his father, he bore the courtesy title of Viscount Suirdale. He was educated at Eton College (1889–93) and at New College, Oxford, where he obtained a second class in modern history in 1897 and was elected an honorary fellow in 1931. From 1898 to 1900 he was private secretary to Sir Henry Blake, governor of Hong Kong. On 21 December 1901 he married Elena Maria (d. 1944), second daughter of Michael Paul Grace, of New York, a founder of the ship-owning firm W. R. Grace & Co.

As a Conservative peer Donoughmore was appointed to the position of under-secretary of state for war in 1903 and held this position until the fall of the Balfour government at the end of 1905. After this time Donoughmore became a leading member of the opposition peers' committee—known as the 'Apaches'—formed by Lord Onslow to co-ordinate efforts in the upper house 'to embarrass the Liberals and fight off threats to landowners' (Adonis, 68). Onslow was until 1910 lord chairman of committees, the holder of which post was said by *The Times* to exercise 'more than any other Member of the House, the control of its everyday business' (Adonis, 87). It was with Onslow's support that Donoughmore was selected in 1911 to succeed him.

Yet the most noteworthy and dramatic events of Donoughmore's public life perhaps related to his position as an Irish peer, at a time of exceptional turmoil. A prominent freemason, he became in 1913 the grand master of the grand lodge of Ireland. In 1916 he was required to lead the defence of the freemason order against charges of 'bigotry and sectarianism', made during the parliamentary debate on the Irish Police Bill, which sought to introduce an order preventing members of the police forces in Ireland from belonging to the order. In the same year he was caught up in the events of the Easter rising while travelling through Dublin and was slightly wounded by a bullet.

Donoughmore was among the southern unionists who refused to acknowledge that home rule was a widespread popular demand in Ireland, claiming that the nationalist movement was representative only of the Roman Catholic hierarchy and financed by Irish migrants to the United States. Donoughmore declared in 1910 that the home rule movement was becoming 'less and less Irish and more and more American' (Buckland, 10).

After the Irish settlement in 1921 Donoughmore became a member of the southern Ireland senate, which was seen by Unionists as central to their protection against 'hasty legislative proposals at the expense of the 350,000 loyalists who will be practically unrepresented' in the new lower house (Buckland, 266). He was heavily involved in the political negotiations in 1922 over the establishment

of further 'minority safeguards' under the new arrangements. But when in November that year the Irish peers as a group agreed not to attempt to extend the powers of the Free State senate in the debates over the new constitution bill, Donoughmore and others refused to sit in this body, condemning it as 'a puppet assembly' (Buckland, 295). In 1931 he was forced by ill health to resign from his positions and committee work, having earlier chaired inquiries into the constitution of Ceylon (1927–8) and ministerial powers (1929). He suffered badly in later life from the effects of arthritis.

In 1916 Donoughmore was appointed KP and was sworn of the privy council in 1918. He was also chairman of the National Radium Commission. He died on 19 October 1948 at his home at Knocklofty, Clonmel, co. Tipperary, shortly after being involved in a serious motor accident, and was buried on 22 October.   MARC BRODIE

Sources *The Times* (21 Oct 1948) · P. Buckland, *Irish unionism*, 1: *The Anglo-Irish and the new Ireland* (1972) · A. Adonis, *Making aristocracy work: the peerage and the political system in Britain, 1884–1914* (1993) · Burke, *Peerage* · *The Eton register*, 6 (privately printed, Eton, 1910) · GEC, *Peerage* · *CGPLA Eng. & Wales* (1949)

Archives TCD, corresp. and papers | CUL, corresp. with Lord Hardinge · PRO, corresp. with Lord Midleton, 30/67 · Rhodes University, Grahamstown, South Africa, Cory Library for Historical Research, letter to Sir John Sprigg

Likenesses A. J. Munnings, oils, 1921, Jockey Club, Newmarket · L. Palmer, oils, 1922 (after unknown portrait), Jockey Club, Newmarket · J. Lavery, oils, 1923, Royal Scot. Acad. · W. Stoneman, photographs, 1931, NPG · Spy [L. Ward], lithograph caricature, NPG; repro. in *VF* (9 Feb 1905)

Wealth at death £164,274 14s. 4d. save and except settled land: probate, 23 Feb 1949, *CGPLA Eng. & Wales* · £17,400 limited to settled land: further grant, 1 July 1949, *CGPLA Eng. & Wales*

Hutchinson, Roger (d. 1555), religious writer, has been variously described as coming from the north of England and from Hertfordshire. His father's name was William. Roger Hutchinson was educated at St John's College, Cambridge, where he graduated in 1541, was elected a fellow in 1543, and commenced MA in 1544. He became a senior fellow on 28 March 1547. In May that year Thomas Dobbe, one of his junior colleagues, was expelled for challenging the rule of clerical celibacy and wanting to marry. Since Hutchinson himself eventually married and became a noted evangelical, it may seem surprising that according to John Foxe he was one of Dobbe's three accusers, along with the master, John Taylor, who was also an evangelical. Probably Hutchinson and Taylor felt that Dobbe was endangering their common cause by the assertive, even provocative, way in which he advanced his opinions. In October 1547 Hutchinson and Thomas Lever took part in a disputation in St John's in which they argued against the mass, and Hutchinson subsequently became closely linked to an evangelical group centred upon Archbishop Thomas Cranmer and Nicholas Ridley, successively bishop of Rochester and London.

In 1550 Hutchinson was made a fellow of Eton College, and in the same year was one of the theologians who disputed with Joan Bocher, alias Joan of Kent, in the hope of persuading her to renounce her heretical views on the human and divine natures of Christ. Joan was burnt on 2

May, and less than two months later Hutchinson published *The Image of God, or, Laie Mans Booke*, dedicated to Cranmer, which gave particular attention to her Christological opinions. Two years later Hutchinson was again a spokesman for the new ecclesiastical establishment. The delay in the appearance of a revised Book of Common Prayer was causing concern in advanced protestant circles, and in April 1552 he found it necessary to preach at Eton in defence of the 1549 prayer book's retention of the traditional practice whereby communicants received the consecrated bread in their mouths rather than in their hands, as the more radical evangelicals demanded and as the revised prayer book eventually provided. His sermons were published in 1560 as *A Faithful Declaration of Christes Holy Supper*.

Following Mary's accession Hutchinson remained in England, where he was deprived of his Eton fellowship because he had married. He died in 1555, between drawing up his will on 23 May and its being proved on 15 June (PRO, PROB 11/195, fol. 201r–v). He bequeathed his soul simply 'into thandes of Almightie God thoroughe the merits of Jesus Christ'. He made bequests of £20 to his son Thomas, and of £10 apiece to his daughters Anne and Elizabeth. His cousin William Box was to have 'my Xeniphons works in greek in smale volumes', everything else, including 'my lease of Seynt Ellyns and my advowson of Rickmansworthe', was to go to his wife, Agnes, who was also his executor. Hutchinson's reputation was that of a learned and acute divine, hot-tempered, and passionate about the furtherance of the Reformation in England. His writings, which also include two sermons on oppression, affliction, and patience, were published by the Parker Society in 1842.   JOHN F. JACKSON

Sources DNB · Cooper, *Ath. Cantab.*, 1.126, 546 · *The works of Roger Hutchinson*, ed. J. Bruce, Parker Society, 4 (1842) · will, PRO, PROB 11/195, fol. 201r–v · D. MacCulloch, *Thomas Cranmer: a life* (1996) · *The acts and monuments of John Foxe*, ed. S. R. Cattley, 8 vols. (1837–41), vols. 5, 7

Wealth at death £40 cash bequests: will, PRO, PROB 11/195, fol. 201r–v

Hutchinson, Thomas (*bap.* 1698, *d.* 1769), classical scholar, the son of Peter Hutchinson of Cornforth, in the parish of Bishops Middleham, co. Durham, was baptized there on 17 May 1698. He matriculated at Lincoln College, Oxford, on 28 March 1715, and graduated BA in 1718, MA in 1721, BD (from Hart Hall) in 1733, and DD in 1738. In 1731 he was appointed rector of Lyndon, Rutland, having acquired some reputation as a scholar with the publication of an edition of Xenophon's *Cyropaedia* (1727). This was followed by his edited volume of Xenophon's *Anabasis* (1735); both books passed through numerous editions in the eighteenth century. Hutchinson was also the author of *The Usual Interpretation of Daimones and Daimonia* (1738), an essay on demoniacal possession and several published sermons including a survey of the use of ceremonial law (1740).

In 1748 Thomas Herring, archbishop of Canterbury, presented him to the vicarage of Horsham, Sussex; he held also the rectory of Cocking in the same county, and a prebendal stall in Chichester Cathedral. He died at Horsham, and was buried there on 7 February 1769.

    C. J. ROBINSON, *rev.* PHILIP CARTER

Sources Foster, *Alum. Oxon.* · Nichols, *Lit. anecdotes*, 8.467

Hutchinson, Thomas (1711–1780), colonial politician and historian, was born in Boston, Massachusetts, on 9 September 1711, the son of Colonel Thomas Hutchinson (1674–1739), a wealthy merchant, and his wife, Sarah, *née* Foster (*b.* 1686, *d.* after 1739). Raised in a mansion filled with works of art on historical themes, he displayed a studious bent from his early years, and from 1723 attended Harvard College, from which he graduated in 1727 aged sixteen. In 1734 he married Margaret (Peggy) Sanford (1716–1754); they had twelve children, of whom only three sons and two daughters survived to adulthood.

In May 1737 Hutchinson, already a successful merchant, secured election to the Massachusetts assembly. He headed a revived pro-government faction that competed on at least equal terms with the anti-prerogative group dominated by the caucus, an anti-prerogative political machine, until the 1760s. Hutchinson became speaker of the house in 1746, a post he held until 1748. On 17 November 1747 he mediated between Governor William Shirley and a crowd angered that the British fleet in Boston harbour had impressed perhaps as many as 300 men to fill the places of sailors who had deserted with local connivance. Hutchinson stood up for the rights of colonial sailors throughout his lifetime.

Hutchinson's proposal in 1748 to place the Massachusetts currency on a sound footing severely divided the province. A general court worn out by five weeks of debate voted forty to thirty-seven to approve his proposal to use the £183,649 (Massachusetts) received as reimbursement for its war expenses to retire its inflated paper money. His Boston constituents responded by giving him only 200 of 700 votes in the next election. His mansion burned down, as did the old state house, under mysterious circumstances. Some bystanders cried out 'let it burn!' as the fire companies arrived. Nevertheless, Hutchinson's plan gave Massachusetts the only stable, specie-backed currency in British North America.

Having been elected to the council in 1749, Hutchinson joined with Benjamin Franklin in co-authoring the unsuccessful Albany plan of union in 1754. Representatives of various colonies had hoped to establish an American parliament to tax the colonies in the impending war with France, but neither the colonial legislatures nor the British parliament would accept this infringement on their autonomy. Hutchinson became lieutenant-governor in 1758, and even his adversaries respected his dedication and competence in public affairs.

Troubles that never left Hutchinson began when in 1760 the new governor, Francis Bernard, chose him as chief justice of the superior court. Hutchinson did not want the post, and accepted it only after Bernard assured him that under no circumstances would it go to the elder James Otis, who claimed that the previous two governors had promised him the job. However, the Otises concocted the story that Hutchinson, who with members of his family held numerous high offices, had sought the post as a step in his scheme to establish an aristocracy that would trample on American liberty.

One of the reasons Bernard selected Hutchinson played into the Otises' hands. The governor sought the court's approval of the writs of assistance being used by newly appointed customs officers Charles Paxton and Thomas Lechmere. They were seeking out illegal cargoes with vigour, and claimed the right of British officials to do so by a general writ authorizing them to search anywhere. Hutchinson sidestepped the argument of James Otis jun. that such writs violated the rights of Britons, postponed the case until he could discover how the customs service operated in Britain, and then ruled that Massachusetts should follow suit. Ironically, Lord Camden, chief justice of England's court of common pleas, later ruled against Hutchinson on the ground that parliament had never approved such writs for the colonies.

Hutchinson's behaviour as the colonies were threatened with the Stamp Act in 1764 convinced many that the Otises were right. Hutchinson persuaded the Massachusetts legislature to oppose the proposed law as a matter of favour rather than of right, a moderate stand that fell far short of the protests of other colonial legislatures. He correctly believed telling parliament it had no right to tax the colonies would prove futile, but his own petition was ignored as well. Hutchinson's opponents spread the idea that he had dreamed up the Stamp Act himself. Ironically, Hutchinson had expressed his opposition to the Stamp Act as eloquently as anyone based on right as well as expediency, but only in private letters to Britain; Isaac Barré, the colonies' friend in parliament, appears to have cribbed liberally from Hutchinson in his denunciation of the act.

Hutchinson's unwillingness to state his true opinions publicly came back to haunt him on 26 August 1765. Twelve days after the Boston mob had forced his brother-in-law Andrew Oliver to resign as the colony's stamp master, the crowd called on Hutchinson's elegant North End mansion and demanded that he deny responsibility for the Stamp Act. Refusing to do so, he insisted on remaining in the house as violence loomed; his life was probably saved by his daughter Peggy, who refused to leave unless he did. The mob then totally destroyed the house, stealing £900 in cash, drinking up his liquor, and trampling on his manuscripts (which were rescued). The following day, wearing borrowed clothes rather than his judicial robes, Hutchinson appeared in the superior court and swore that he had nothing to do with initiating or supporting the Stamp Act.

Despite his belief that British incursions on colonial liberties played into the hands of his adversaries, Hutchinson always tried to stand on the side of what he regarded as law. Thus during the Stamp Act crisis he refused to convene the superior court because it could not proceed legally without the stamps the Bostonians had prevented from landing. On the other hand, in 1768, after British troops had been sent to Boston, he refused to employ them to silence crowds or their leaders on the legal ground that he could only do so with the concurrence of the provincial council or a local magistrate.

Hutchinson became acting governor when Sir Francis Bernard sailed for England on 1 August 1769, and in 1771 received the actual position. In the interim he prevented the event known as the Boston Massacre of 5 March 1770 from escalating. He plunged into the crowd that had provoked six British soldiers to fire upon it, escorted the six to gaol, and removed the rest of the forces from town. He then delayed the trial until defence attorneys John Adams and Josiah Quincy could develop a case based on self-defence and a sympathetic jury could be chosen.

Paradoxically, the Hutchinson who reduced tension after the 'massacre' revived it between 1770 and 1773 when the British government was doing little or nothing to provoke the colonies. He entered into a dispute with the assembly on the nature of royal authority and colonial rights, and on 6 January 1773 penned a phrase that returned to haunt him: 'no line can be drawn between the supreme authority of Parliament and the total independence of the colonies' (A. Bradford, *Speeches of the Governors of Massachusetts*, 1818, 339–40). Hutchinson's detractors twisted these words to mean that parliament was absolutely sovereign, whereas he was merely reasserting the traditional, flexible relationship where authority was pragmatically divided without a precise line.

Because of the presence of British warships in Boston harbour, Hutchinson, alone of the royal governors, thought that he could enforce the act of parliament that required East India Company tea to be sold in the colonies. The tea had been consigned to his sons, who, like their father, owned East India Company stock and did much business with the company. The result was the Boston Tea Party of 16 December 1773, when the tea from three ships was emptied into the harbour by anti-government protesters. The event provoked parliament to issue the Coercive Acts (known in the colonies as 'Intolerable'), which closed Boston harbour, forbade town meetings except those to choose local officers, and replaced the elected council of Massachusetts with an appointed one.

Although Hutchinson had lamented the lack of law and order in Boston and attributed it to the town meeting and lack of support from the council, he abhorred institutional change that would only inflame the opposition and prevent the provincial élite from asserting its authority. (He preferred punishment of resistance leaders.) Hutchinson asked leave to resign his post and arrived in England on 29 June 1774 to lobby against these acts. He also correctly considered his usefulness finished when his letters to the ministry, provided by Benjamin Franklin, were published by his enemies. Here again, Hutchinson's words were wrenched out of context to demonize him: his statement that there needed to be 'an abridgment of what are called British liberties' (to Thomas Whately, 20 Jan 1769 Massachusetts Commonwealth Archives, 26.339) referred to the exaggerated claims of the patriots, not real liberty as he understood it.

Hutchinson was treated cordially in Britain, met George III, and received a doctorate of laws from Oxford, ironically on 4 July 1776. However, his efforts to reconcile the two parties came to naught. Like other loyalists Hutchinson found himself increasingly marginalized, and he longed to return home and escape the arrogant British ruling class. He died suddenly in London on 3 June 1780, and was buried in Croydon. He divided his estate among his surviving three children, who lived comfortably on government pensions. His Massachusetts properties were seized by the state by an act of 1779: his beloved cottage in Milton, purchased by his arch-enemies James and Mercy Otis Warren, survived until 1946.

Hutchinson was a notable historian and political thinker as well as a political figure. His three-volume *History of the Colony and Province of Massachusetts Bay* (published in 1760, 1768, and posthumously in 1828) has been praised for over two hundred years, even by historians who condemn his deeds. Hutchinson's main point was that British authority and colonial liberty had co-existed traditionally in a healthy tension that could only be preserved if neither side insisted on absolute sovereignty. Although Hutchinson's conservatism was as profound and deep as Edmund Burke's, his thought has been overlooked both because the loyalists lost and because his style, while precise and elegant, lacked flair.

Modern historians have argued over whether Hutchinson was a dedicated idealist (Shipton, Freiberg, Pencak), failed pragmatist (Bailyn), or corrupt, self-serving, hypocrite (Hoerder, Brown). But all agree that some interpretation of his complicated writings, policies, and personality is essential to understanding the outbreak of the American War of Independence.   WILLIAM PENCAK

Sources DNB • B. Bailyn, *The ordeal of Thomas Hutchinson* (1974) • M. Freiberg, *Prelude to purgatory: Thomas Hutchinson in Massachusetts politics, 1760–1770* (1990) • W. Pencak, *America's Burke: the mind of Thomas Hutchinson* (1982) • C. K. Shipton, 'Hutchinson, Thomas', *Sibley's Harvard graduates: biographical sketches of those who attended Harvard College*, 8 (1951), 149–217 • R. E. Brown, *Middle-class democracy and the revolution in Massachusetts, 1691–1780* (1955) • D. Hoerder, *Crowd action in revolutionary Massachusetts, 1765–1780* (1977) • R. M. Calhoon, 'Hutchinson, Thomas', *ANB* • Massachusetts Commonwealth Archives Division, Boston, vols. 25–7
Archives BL, corresp. and papers, Egerton MSS 2659–2666 • Devon RO, letters and diary • Massachusetts Commonwealth Archives Division, Boston, corresp. • NYPL, Humanities and Social Sciences Library, corresp. and papers • U. Mich., Clements L., letters and copies of letters relating to American rebellion | BL, letters to Lord Hardwicke, Add. MS 35427 • NA Canada, corresp. with Lord Dartmouth • U. Mich., Clements L., corresp. with Thomas Gage
Likenesses E. Truman, oils, 1741, Mass. Hist. Soc.

Hutchinson, (Christian) Victor Noel Hope Hely- (1901–1947),

composer and music administrator, was born on 26 December 1901 at Newlands House, Newlands, Cape Town, Cape Colony, the youngest son of Sir Walter Francis Hely-Hutchinson (1849–1913), son of the earl of Donoughmore and last governor of Cape Colony, and his wife, May Justice (1861–1938).

As an infant Hely-Hutchinson grew up in Kent, where his talent for music was recognized by Charles Hoby, director of music of the Royal Marines at Chatham. After he returned to South Africa in 1907 his training was undertaken by Barrow Dowling, organist of Cape Town Cathedral. Shortly after his father's retirement to England, he was taken to the Royal College of Music on 25 January 1910 to see Sir Hubert Parry, who recommended study with a former pupil, Donald Tovey. (In October 1918 he would be pallbearer at Parry's funeral at St Paul's Cathedral.) In order to be near Tovey, he was educated at Heatherdown preparatory school, Ascot, and he won a scholarship to Eton College in 1914. Having studied harmony and counterpoint with some thoroughness under Tovey, he took extra-mural composition lessons in the later war years from Sir Charles Stanford, who had moved to Windsor to escape the bombing of London, and later from Gustav Holst; he also studied conducting with Adrian Boult.

In 1919 Hely-Hutchinson won the Lewis Nettleship memorial scholarship to Balliol College, Oxford, though his time at the university (September 1920 to December 1921) was curtailed by the offer of a lecturing post at the South African College of Music (later part of the University of Cape Town) from its director, W. H. Bell. In South Africa he married on 22 June 1925 Marjorie Anna Hugo (1900–1988), a capable violinist and a silver medal winner at the Royal Academy of Music in 1919. They had two sons, John and Christopher. Hely-Hutchinson's work as a lecturer was supplemented by broadcasting on *Children's Hour* for the South African Broadcasting Corporation (where he was known as 'Uncle Porps'), experience which served him well when he returned to England in 1926 as a musical assistant for the BBC at Savoy Hill.

Hely-Hutchinson's work at the BBC involved not only programme planning but also conducting, arranging, accompanying (he was an able pianist), and appearances on *Children's Hour* as 'Uncle Bunny'. In 1933 he moved to Birmingham as the BBC's midland regional director of music and founded the BBC Midland Orchestra. A year later, in succession to Granville Bantock, he was appointed professor of music at Birmingham University, a post he held until 1944. In Birmingham, Hely-Hutchinson was active as the president of the Brass Bands Association and conducted the city orchestra. During the Second World War he enrolled as an ARP warden and joined the university cadet force, and in order to raise money for the city orchestra he gave a series of recitals of all Beethoven's piano sonatas; he subsequently repeated this at Oxford in aid of a memorial to Tovey. In 1944 he returned to London as the BBC's director of music, succeeding Arthur Bliss. During the severe winter at the beginning of 1947 he developed influenza, and he died of acute meningitis on 11 March at 26 Queen's Grove, St John's Wood, London; he was cremated at Golders Green crematorium. He was only forty-five. Months before, he had been involved in controversy when he oversaw the termination of Constant Lambert's connection with the Promenade Concerts and the appointment of Malcolm Sargent as chief conductor.

Though his professional creative life was relatively

short, Hely-Hutchinson was highly productive. He composed a wide range of incidental music for films and plays; the latter included productions of C. K. Munro's *The Rumour*, Laurence Housman's *The House Fairy*, and Walter de la Mare's *Yes, and Back Again* (all 1930). Like Armstrong Gibbs and Herbert Howells, he evinced a penchant for the poetry of de la Mare, which is reflected in his many songs, but his most enduring settings are those of Edward Lear's nonsense rhymes (1927), 'Old Mother Hubbard' (1929), an amusing Handelian parody, and *Ruthless Rhymes*, to words by Harry Graham (1945–6). His chamber works include a piano quintet, a string quartet, and a viola sonata, none of which was published. The more impressive *Variations, Intermezzo, Scherzo and Finale*, dedicated to W. H. Bell, was published by the Carnegie Trust and first performed at a Promenade Concert in 1927. Described by the composer as a set of symphonic variations, the work exhibits a fresh, vibrant technique and a polished, colourful orchestral palette. An affinity for classical structures was foreshadowed in the *Three Fugal Fancies* for strings (1925) and echoed with greater aplomb in *The Young Idea* for piano and orchestra (1928), though it was in the popular *Carol Symphony* (1927), a suite of movements based on popular Christmas carols, that his lighter style achieved a particular eloquence alongside passages of greater warmth and even pathos. Some of his film music was later reworked into a symphony for small orchestra. Undergoing revision at the time of his death, this was heard during the 1947 season of promenade concerts. JEREMY DIBBLE

Sources J. Hely-Hutchinson, *Victor Hely-Hutchinson 1901–47: a many-sided composer* [forthcoming] · P. Scowcroft, *British light music composers* (1997) · D. Brook, *Composer gallery* (1946), 74–7 · *MT*, 88 (1947), 142 · M. Grierson, *Donald Francis Tovey* (1952) · d. cert. · *CGPLA Eng. & Wales* (1947) · private information (2004) [family]
Archives BBC WAC, corresp. · South African Broadcasting Association, Johannesburg, corresp. | TCD, corresp. with T. Bodkin
Wealth at death £8678 15s. 9d.: probate, 19 Sept 1947, *CGPLA Eng. & Wales*

Hutchinson, William (1715–1801), mariner and writer on seamanship, presumed to be a native of Newcastle upon Tyne, was at a very early age employed on colliers, as cook, cabin-boy, and beer-drawer for the men. He gradually worked his way through all the most active employments as a seaman.

Hutchinson referred to his various experiences in his later book on seamanship, beginning with his time as a 'forecastle man' on board an East Indiaman in 1738–9, and making the voyage to China; he was also mate of 'a bomb's tender in Hyères Bay' with the Royal Navy about 1743. His later experiences included a time cruising in the Mediterranean, prying on French shipping in the employ of Fortunatus *Wright, merchant and privateer, and Hutchinson was himself in command of a privateer in 1747.

In 1750 Hutchinson commanded the *Lowestoft*, an old twenty-gun frigate sold out of the navy and bought by Wright, and in her traded to the West Indies and the Mediterranean. At some unspecified date his ship was wrecked, Hutchinson and his men escaping in a boat. They were

without food, and cast lots to determine which one should die for the others. The lot fell on Hutchinson, but at the last moment he was saved by a vessel coming in sight. To the end of his life he kept the anniversary as a day of 'strict devotion'. In 1759 he was appointed a dock master at Liverpool, afterwards also water bailiff and harbour master, posts he held for more than twenty years, part of the time in conjunction with a younger Fortunatus Wright, a kinsman of his old companion.

In 1763 Hutchinson set up the first parabolic reflectors on the Bidston light. These were made up from sheets of tin soldered together and lined with pieces of mirror-glass; he afterwards had larger reflectors made, up to 12 feet in diameter, plastered inside to a smooth bowl and similarly lined with glass. These reflectors were so successful that Hutchinson was asked to procure examples for the Dublin harbour authorities' lighthouses.

Prompted by a friend, the astronomer James Ferguson, Hutchinson began in 1764 to observe the times and heights of tides flowing at the old dock gates in Liverpool, and fixed a tide-pole in the bed of the river itself, to gauge the lowest point of the ebb. On plotting the readings he found that they formed a parabolic curve, and he attributed the difference between his observed measurements and the predictions given by tide-clocks to lunar effects which had not previously been properly considered. Hutchinson's data was incorporated in *Holden's Tide Tables*, published in 1773. His record of tides, barometer, weather, and winds, 1768–93, was presented to Liverpool Public Library. In 1777 he published a *Treatise on Practical Seamanship*, which dealt also with the proper form and dimensions of merchant ships. This contained autobiographical material, and it ran through several enlarged editions.

Hutchinson was one of the founder members of the Liverpool pilot committee, founded in 1766. In 1779 he and some companions set out on horseback to find a refuge for the pilot boats, riding across Anglesey where they paused to view the great Parys copper mine; they identified a cove, which they named Pilot's Bay, where the boats might safely shelter to await incoming shipping. He also subscribed 100 guineas to the Liverpool Marine Society, established in 1789 to care for needy mariners and their families. He died, unmarried, on 11 February 1801 in Liverpool, and was buried in the churchyard of St Thomas's, Liverpool. J. K. LAUGHTON, *rev.* ANITA MCCONNELL

Sources J. S. Rees, *History of the Liverpool pilotage service* (1984) · D. B. Hague and R. Christie, *Lighthouses, their architecture, history and archaeology* (1975), 164 · R. Brooke, *Liverpool as it was during the last quarter of the eighteenth century* (1853), 101–2, 393 · W. Hutchinson, *A treatise on practical seamanship* (1777) · J. K. Laughton, *Studies in naval history: biographies* (1887) · will
Archives Lpool RO, tide journals · RS, tide journals
Wealth at death effects and administration to sister

Hutchinson, William (1732–1814), topographer, was born in Durham on 31 December 1732, the eldest son of William Hutchinson (1705–1777), attorney of Durham, and Hannah Doubleday of Butterby by Durham. He was probably educated at Durham School and, having served his articles as a solicitor, on 30 September 1756 he married Elizabeth

William Hutchinson (1732–1814), by Joseph Collyer the younger, pubd 1814 (after J. Hay) [right, with his friend George Allan]

Marshall (d. 1814) of Stockton, co. Durham. By 1760 he had set up practice at Barnard Castle, co. Durham. He was also clerk to the lord lieutenancy of Durham. His leisure, which was abundant, as he ruefully admitted, was devoted to literary and antiquarian pursuits.

Before 1771 Hutchinson had become friendly with George Allan of Blackwell Grange near Darlington, a wealthy solicitor who was a compulsive transcriber of legal and other manuscripts, which he hoped would form the basis for a history of co. Durham. In 1772 Hutchinson published his first literary work, *The Hermitage: a British Story*, which was followed by other tales and plays. He then published *An Excursion to the Lakes in Westmorland and Cumberland, August 1773* (1774) and *A View of Northumberland, with an Excursion to the Abbey of Mailross in Scotland* (2 vols., 1776–8). In 1778 he came to an amicable agreement with the antiquary and travel writer Thomas Pennant not to compete with each other in publishing tours of the northern counties. The appearance of Hutchinson's *Excursions*, meanwhile, may have decided Allan to turn over to Hutchinson the material for a history of Durham, which Allan advertised from his private press in June 1781. Subscribers were solicited and the work was to be published in two demi-quarto volumes by Solomon Hodgson, printer, proprietor, and editor of the *Newcastle Chronicle*.

The first volume of *The History and Antiquities of the County Palatine of Durham*, devoted to an account of the see and bishops of Durham, appeared in 1786, and the second, which continued with the bishops and cathedral, hardly touched the rest of the county, which was left to a third volume, undesired by the publisher. The matter was tried at the Newcastle assizes of 1793 and eventually was referred to the arbitration of Mr Jonathan Raine of Lincoln's Inn. Subscribers were invited to choose between acceptance of the original continuation or an enhanced

third volume 'richly embellished with plates' that would require a modest additional payment. This was printed by F. Jollie in Carlisle and published in 1794. The same year, Hutchinson published *The History of the County of Cumberland, and Some Places Adjacent* in two volumes. Having overestimated the market for the Durham volume, he disposed of 400 copies for a trifling sum to the publisher John Nichols, 200 of which were converted into waste paper and most of the remainder consumed by fire in February 1808. Another edition, however, was issued posthumously in Durham in 1823 in three quarto volumes; this was revised from the author's corrected copy and contained additional pedigrees issued in a separate part. An octavo edition of the Durham history, published in 1823, is regarded as pirated.

Hutchinson was an ardent freemason; he was master of his local lodge and wrote a spirited defence of the craft, *The Spirit of Masonry* (1775), which ran to several editions, the last being published in 1843. He was elected FSA on 15 February 1781. He died at The Grove, Barnard Castle, on 7 April 1814, having survived his wife by only five days, and was buried in St Mary's churchyard, Barnard Castle. They left three daughters, known to their friends as Faith, Hope, and Charity, and to their detractors as Plague, Pestilence, and Famine. Their surviving son, Robert Marshall Hutchinson, followed his father in the law and died in 1821.　　　C. M. FRASER

Sources J. C. Hodgson, 'William Hutchinson', *Archaeologia Aeliana*, 3rd ser., 13 (1916), 166–83 · *Weekly Chronicle* [Newcastle] (31 July 1880), 3 · Nichols, *Illustrations*, 1.421–58 · *GM*, 1st ser., 84/1 (1814), 515–16 · *DNB* · *IGI* · Bodl. Oxf., MS Gen. Top. u1, fol. 311
Archives U. Durham L., accounts and literary MSS
Likenesses J. Collyer the younger, line engraving (after J. Hay), BM, NPG; repro. in Nichols, *Lit. anecdotes*, 8 (1814), frontispiece [see illus.] · R. Scott, engraving, repro. in W. Hutchinson, *The spirit of masonry* (1802)

Hutchison, Sir (William) Kenneth (1903–1989), gas industrialist, was born on 30 October 1903 at Dooria, Assam, India, the third of the five children of William Hutchison (1855–1932), a tea planter, and his wife, Barbara, née McCormack (1880–1906). On the death of their mother the children were brought up by an aunt near Dumfries; they later moved to Edinburgh. Hutchison was educated at Edinburgh Academy, won a scholarship to Corpus Christi College, Oxford, and graduated with first-class honours in chemistry. At the instigation of Harold Hartley, a director of the Gas Light and Coke Company, Hutchison joined the company as a research chemist in 1926, and for the next fifteen years helped to bring more scientific method to the empirical traditions of gas engineering. In 1939 he married Dorothea Marion Eva Bluett (c.1905–1987x9); they had one daughter.

During the war Hutchison was given an opportunity to escape from the laboratory. He was attached to the Air Ministry, where within a couple of years he had become director of hydrogen production for barrage balloons; then, in 1944, he was appointed director responsible for the supply of all compressed gases, especially oxygen, for the British and American air forces. Apart from gaining invaluable direct management experience and learning the ways of Whitehall, he came to meet many senior figures in the gas industry. On his return to Gas Light and Coke he was appointed controller of by-products (coke, tar), and in 1947 became a director of the company. On nationalization in 1949 he was appointed first chairman of the South Eastern Gas Board.

Hutchison recognized that the gas industry had little control over its raw material costs and could be held to ransom as long as coal was its predominant feedstock. He placed great emphasis on developing new processes to use whatever oil feedstocks were available cheaply and in quantity. As an extension of this policy, he was closely involved in developing new technology for importing liquified natural gas by sea from Algeria. Even before 1964 when the gas tankers entered service, another possibility had been opened up by the discovery of natural gas in the Netherlands. In 1960 Hutchison was appointed deputy chairman of the Gas Council, which co-ordinated the activities of the twelve area gas boards. He foresaw the prospects of huge reserves of natural gas in the British sector of the North Sea, and fought to ensure that the gas industry would participate in the risks of exploration and production (and incidentally gain inside knowledge of the economics of the business) rather than remain a passive customer of the oil industry.

Making cheaper gas affordable was not enough if customers were abandoning gas for electricity or oil. Hutchison was the driving force behind national publicity campaigns, notably for 'high-speed gas', to persuade customers to buy gas fires and gas central heating. Such strategies, together with improved appliances and the likelihood of markedly cheaper gas, transformed the prospects of the industry. Sales of gas had been falling steadily since the war but they began to expand in 1961; and when Hutchison retired in 1966 they were increasing at 10 per cent a year. Supplies of North Sea gas had not yet started to flow, but Hutchison had already foreseen the way the market might expand and how the industry could accommodate this, both organizationally and technically.

Hutchison's move from scientist to entrepreneurial general manager came when he had turned forty. Despite this late start, more than any other single person he was the driving force behind the technical, commercial, and organizational changes which transformed the gas industry in the mid-twentieth century. From the fragmented, coal-dependent concerns which had survived from the nineteenth century, gas became a taut, centralized, organized industry, able to deal on equal terms with international oil companies. Lacking statutory powers, Hutchison had the strength of character to impart direction to the activities of the twelve semi-autonomous gas boards; and at the same time Sir Henry Jones, the chairman of the Gas Council, liaised with government and the civil service.

Hutchison was made a CBE in 1954 and knighted in 1962. He was president of the Institution of Gas Engineers (1955–6) and the Institution of Chemical Engineers (1959–

61). In 1966 he was elected a fellow of the Royal Society. Generally taciturn and proud of being a scientist, he found it easier to make friends with lovers of literature. He was a keen golfer and sailor until late in life, and a first-class chef. He died a widower on 28 November 1989, from heart disease, at his home, 2 Arlington Road, St Margaret's, Twickenham.   FRANCIS GOODALL

Sources K. Hutchison, *High speed gas: an autobiography* (1987) · T. I. Williams, *A history of the British gas industry* (1981) · S. Everard, *The history of the Gas Light and Coke Company, 1812–1949* (1949) · *The Times* (5 Dec 1989)
Archives CAC Cam., corresp. and papers
Likenesses portrait, British Gas
Wealth at death £171,098: probate, 19 April 1990, *CGPLA Eng. & Wales*

Hutchison, Patrick (1740/41–1802), minister of the Relief church and author, was born the son of a farmer in Dunblane parish, Perthshire. He was educated at the Divinity Hall of the General Associate or Anti-Burgher Synod, where he received his MA in 1764. He left the Anti-Burghers for the Relief church soon thereafter and served as assistant to James Baine in the South College Church of Edinburgh. On 19 November 1774 he was called to the Relief congregation at St Ninians in Stirling, and on 22 May 1783 he was translated to the church at Canal Street in Paisley, Renfrewshire, where he spent the remainder of his career.

The Anti-Burghers were noted for their strict adherence to Scotland's covenanting traditions, and when Hutchison left that communion for the Relief he entered a church noted for its far more liberal and tolerant theology and ecclesiology. At the time of its publication in 1779 his *Compendious View of the Religious System, Maintained by the Synod of Relief* was the most extensive articulation of the principles of the Relief church to appear in print. It described the evangelical theology to which the group subscribed, as well as their differences with the Presbyterian establishment and Scotland's other denominations of seceders. The occasion for the *Compendious View* was a 1778 pamphlet by James Ramsay, Anti-Burgher minister in Glasgow, entitled *The Relief Scheme Considered*, which accused that persuasion of following an 'unscriptural plan of church communion' by accepting all who wanted to come without demanding their renunciation of every alleged error of the established church. Hutchison's reply criticized the Anti-Burghers for their intolerance and for their narrowness in accepting only those who adhered to the most conservative understanding of Presbyterian traditions dating back to the covenanters. Shortly thereafter Hutchison and the Relief came under attack from Ramsay again, as well as from the other branch of the original secession, the Burgher synod, provoking in turn several additional replies from Hutchison.

In addition to his controversial writings Hutchison published *A Dissertation on the Nature and Genius of the Kingdom of Christ* (1779) and *Three Discourses on the Divine and Mediatorial Character of Jesus Christ* (1788). His *Sermons on Various and Important Subjects*, which he was preparing for publication at the time of his death aged sixty-one in Paisley on 10

January 1802, appeared posthumously in the same year. He left a wife and children, although their names are not known. Although his fame has generally been limited to those with a particular interest in the histories of the seceders and the Relief church, Hutchison was a pivotal figure in the broadening of Presbyterian dissent in Scotland, away from its early eighteenth-century roots among those who insisted that communicants remain faithful to every detail of Presbyterian orthodoxy and Scotland's covenanting traditions, and towards a more enlightened, tolerant, and evangelical faith.   NED C. LANDSMAN

Sources G. Struthers, *The history of the rise, progress, and principles of the Relief church* (1843) · R. Small, *History of the congregations of the United Presbyterian church from 1733 to 1900*, 2 vols. (1904) · W. Mackelvie, *Annals and statistics of the United Presbyterian church*, ed. W. Blair and D. Young (1873) · N. R. Needham, 'Hutchison, Patrick', *DSCHT* · G. Struthers, *The history of the rise of the Relief church* (1848) · P. Hutchison, *Sermons on various and important subjects* (1802)

Hutchison, Sir Robert, first baronet (1871–1960), physician and paediatrician, was born at his family home of Carlowrie House, Kirkliston, Linlithgowshire, on 28 October 1871, the youngest of seven children and fourth son in the family. His father, Robert Hutchison (1834–1894), was a partner in the family wine business in Leith but in later life played the part of a minor country gentleman with a keen interest in forestry, on which he was an acknowledged expert and the author of a number of papers. His mother was Mary Jemima (d. 1912), daughter of the Revd Adam Duncan Tait, minister of Kirkliston. His eldest brother, Sir Thomas Hutchison, first baronet (1866–1925), of Hardiston, was lord provost of Edinburgh in 1921–3.

Although Hutchison's parents were well off, his early life was not pampered. He was educated at the collegiate school and at the University of Edinburgh, where he took his basic medical degrees with the highest honours in 1893. Of his subsequent resident hospital appointments the most significant was at the Sick Children's Hospital in Edinburgh. After this he paid visits to Strasbourg and Paris, and was appointed to a junior post in the department of chemical pathology in Edinburgh. He obtained his MD in 1896 and in the same year moved to London to become junior resident at the Hospital for Sick Children, Great Ormond Street. A post in the department of physiology at the London Hospital medical school was followed in 1900 by appointment to the visiting staff of Great Ormond Street Hospital and assistant physician to the London Hospital, where he looked after both adults and children. He was elected FRCP in 1903. In 1905 he married a medical practitioner, Laetitia Nora (d. 1964), eldest daughter of the Very Revd William Moore-Ede, dean of Worcester in 1908–34. They had five children, of whom one died at birth and a son died from an infection sustained during his anatomical studies as a medical student at Oxford. Two sons and one daughter survived.

Hutchison early showed a talent for teaching and for writing textbooks. His *Clinical Methods* (1897, with H. Rainy) was long a standard work, and in 1900 he published his famous *Food and the Principles of Dietetics*. His chief paediatric publication was *Lectures on Diseases of Children* (1904).

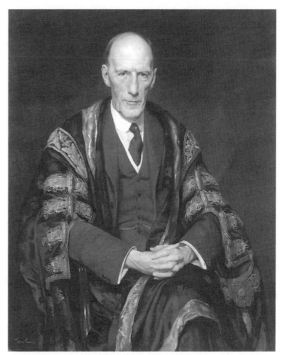

Sir Robert Hutchison, first baronet (1871–1960), by Sir James Gunn, 1938

The 1951 issue of the *Archives of Disease in Childhood*, which marked his eightieth birthday, listed 276 publications and lectures on paediatric subjects. He developed a busy consultant practice in London and received many distinctions, including honorary degrees from Edinburgh, Oxford, Birmingham, and Melbourne. He was president of the Royal Society of Medicine (1934–5) and of the Royal College of Physicians (1938–41) and Harveian orator in 1931.

Hutchison's tall, slim figure, his Scottish accent, and his scathing tongue, all created a distinctive personality. His academic and scientific eminence inspired admiration, and his advice was sound, kindly, and helpful. He gave up his hospital appointments in 1934 and was created a baronet in 1939. After retirement to Thurle Grange, Streatley, Berkshire, in 1940, he held court for his previous pupils and successors, who readily acknowledged his influence. As a doting grandfather he belied much of what his sharp attitude to parents and children had suggested in earlier days. The eldest son, Peter (b. 1907), succeeded his father when he died at Thurle Grange on 12 February 1960.

ALAN MONCRIEFF, *rev.* ELIZABETH BAIGENT

Sources *The Times* (13 Feb 1960) · *BMJ* (20 Feb 1960) · *The Lancet* (20 Feb 1960) · A. Moncrieff, 'Sir Robert Hutchison, bart, 1871–1960', *Journal of Pediatrics*, 58 (1961), 137–9 · private information (1971) · personal knowledge (1971) · *WWW* · Burke, *Peerage* · *CGPLA Eng. & Wales* (1960)
Likenesses J. Gunn, oils, 1938, RCP Lond. [*see illus.*]
Wealth at death £33,512 18s. 6d.: probate, 9 May 1960, *CGPLA Eng. & Wales*

Hutchison, Sidney Charles (1912–2000), art administrator and art historian, was born on 26 March 1912 at 14

Swinton Street, St Pancras, London, the only child of Henry Hutchison, carpenter, and his wife, Augusta Rose, *née* Timmons, who died three weeks after his birth. His paternal grandmother and his paternal grandfather, a piano maker, brought him up with the assistance of five aunts. At an early age Hutchison discovered a love of music, practising on the household piano before joining the choir of St Paul's, Camden Square. Soon he began to play the organ, a lifelong passion, and from 1933 to 1937 he was senior organist at St Matthew's, Westminster. He left Holloway grammar school (to which he had won a scholarship) in 1929 and began work as a junior clerk in the Royal Academy of Arts; he always maintained that initially he believed that the job was to be at the Royal Academy of Music. His arrival coincided with a grand cycle of international exhibitions staged at the Royal Academy in the 1930s. Landmarks in this series included 'Italian Art, 1200–1900' (1930), 'Persian Art' (1931), 'French Art, 1200–1900' (1932), and 'Chinese Art' (1935). As his involvement with exhibition planning increased he developed the record-keeping skills that were to underpin the academy's subsequent loan exhibition programme. Hutchison married Nancy Arnold (1911/12–1985), daughter of Alfred Brindley, electrical engineer, at Christ Church, Southgate, on 24 July 1937; they had no children. That same year he began to study art history at London University.

Hutchison volunteered for the Royal Navy at the outbreak of the Second World War. He was eventually called up in 1941, commissioned in March 1942, and appointed to the aircraft-carrier HMS *Furious*, serving on her until the war's conclusion. He reached the rank of lieutenant commander. The *Furious* travelled extensively, assisting in D-day operations and support of Maltese convoys. His service culminated in leading one of the earliest detachments to enter Hong Kong.

On demobilization Hutchison returned to work at the Royal Academy while completing his diploma in art history. In 1949 he was appointed librarian to the academy, and in 1955 he was in addition created secretary of loan exhibitions in recognition of his continued responsibilities. A sustained proximity to the academy's workings combined with a broad knowledge of art history made him indispensable to the institution. He was lecturer at the extra-mural department of London University from 1957 to 1968 and wrote articles for the *Walpole Society Journal*, *Apollo*, the *Encyclopaedia Britannica*, and others on aspects of the academy's history. This research resulted in the publication of *The Homes of the Royal Academy* (1956) and, in the bicentenary year of 1968, *The History of the Royal Academy, 1768–1968*, a revised edition being published in 1986. The latter work remains the pre-eminent institutional history of the academy. He also contributed a number of articles to the *Dictionary of National Biography*.

In 1968 Hutchison succeeded Humphrey Brooke as secretary to the academy, a post he held until his retirement in 1982. He ably served two presidents, Sir Thomas Monnington and Sir Hugh Casson. Notable exhibitions of the period carrying his mark were 'Turner' (1974), 'Pompeii'

(1977), and the 'Great Japan' exhibition of 1981 to 1982. As secretary he oversaw a tumultuous period of the academy's history as it struggled to remain both independent and financially viable. Ground-breaking approaches were developed in the areas of corporate sponsorship and fundraising. In 1977 he helped launch an organization of subscription supporters of the Royal Academy, the first national institution to devise such a scheme.

By his own admission Hutchison was a short man of portly appearance but he displayed erudition, not least in his role of after-dinner speaker. A courteous manner was combined with great resolve, valuable assets in the strong currents of the international art world. On retiring after fifty-two years of service he did not relinquish all academy duties and was active as honorary archivist (1982–2000) and antiquary (1992–2000). In addition he remained secretary to the E. A. Abbey memorial fund for mural painting (1960–87), the E. A. Abbey scholarships fund (1965–92), and the E. Vincent-Harris fund for mural decoration (1972–87). He was awarded the LVO (1977) and CVO (1987). He died on 21 April 2000 at Chase Farm Hospital, Enfield.

MARK POMEROY

Sources audio interview, 1996, RA · S. C. Hutchison, *The history of the Royal Academy, 1768–1986*, 2nd edn (1986) · *The Times* (9 May 2000) · *The Independent* (11 May 2000) · *The Guardian* (13 May 2000) · *WWW* · personal knowledge (2004) · private information (2004) · b. cert. · m. cert. · d. cert.
Archives RA, archives
Likenesses photograph, 1969, repro. in *The Times* · L. H. Rosoman, acrylic, 1979–84, NPG · R. Matthews, photograph, repro. in *The Independent*

Hutchison, Sir William Oliphant (1889–1970), landscape and portrait painter, was born at Kirkcaldy on 2 July 1889, the fifth child in the family of four sons and two daughters of Henry William Hutchison of Kinloch, a Kirkcaldy businessman, and his wife, Sarah Hannah Key. He was educated at Kirkcaldy high school, Cargilfield School, Edinburgh, and later at Rugby School. As a boy he showed considerable promise as an artist and wished to become a painter but his family were set on him entering business. In 1911 he spent a period in Paris, primarily to perfect his French but he also took this opportunity to study at the Atelier Delacluse. It was during this year that he struck up a lifelong friendship with another Scottish artist, James H. Gunn. After his return from Paris he dutifully entered the timber business but after a short time he rebelled and obtained his father's permission to enter the Edinburgh College of Art. He used to say that his father agreed to this because he had had a picture accepted by the Royal Scottish Academy. This was a portrait of his younger sister Nancy, exhibited in 1911.

It was while he was studying in Edinburgh that Hutchison came under the influence of the watercolourist E. A. Walton, an influence evident in much of his early work, especially his landscapes. He became very friendly with Walton and his family and eventually, in 1918, married Margery (d. 1977), the Waltons' youngest daughter. The marriage was a particularly happy one. They had two sons,

Sir William Oliphant Hutchison (1889–1970), by Sir James Gunn, exh. RA 1952

Henry Peter (*b.* 1919) and Robert Edward (*b.* 1922), and one daughter (*b.* 1935).

Hutchison served in the Royal Garrison Artillery during the war of 1914–18, in Malta and in France, where he was severely wounded. Shortly after his demobilization, late in 1918, he and his wife took a studio flat in York Place in Edinburgh. They remained there only until 1921, when they moved to London. At first they lived at Mulberry Walk in Chelsea but two years later moved to Ladbroke Road, Holland Park, and became near neighbours of James F. Pryde, another Scottish artist who had long been settled in London. Hutchison practised as a portrait painter and had some measure of success. He exhibited regularly at the Royal Academy. He joined the Savage Club and had a wide circle of friends, mainly connected with the arts. In particular, he became a close friend of James Pryde.

In 1929 Hutchison bought an old vicarage in Suffolk near Wickham Market and he spent his time either in London or Suffolk. In 1932 he was persuaded to apply for the post of director of the Glasgow School of Art, was successful in the competition, and took up his post in the following year. He remained director until 1943, when he retired to devote more time to painting. Although he had had no teaching experience, he made an excellent director. He painted very much in the academic tradition but was always ready to help and encourage students and young artists who aspired to the avant-garde. Sir Basil Spence, who for a time served on Hutchison's staff, said of him:

> his liberal understanding and enthusiasm for everything young brought the activities of the school into close harmony with the building itself [designed by Charles Rennie Mackintosh, a close friend of Hutchison]. It was during Bill Hutchison's term that many distinguished artists

were produced as confidence was high and enthusiasm was a characteristic of those years. (letter to *The Times*, 14 Feb 1970)

After he relinquished the directorship in Glasgow, Hutchison moved to Edinburgh and took the upper part of a house in Eglinton Crescent in the west end of the city. He converted the principal floor into a handsome studio and elegant living-room. He again devoted his energies to portrait painting and became deeply involved in the affairs of the Royal Scottish Academy, of which he had been elected an associate in 1937 and a full academician in 1943. He served on the council of the academy and in 1950 succeeded Sir Frank Mears as president, a post he held until 1959. He was knighted in 1953. Shortly after he relinquished the presidency he returned to London, where he had maintained a studio at Cheniston Gardens Studios in Kensington since shortly after the Second World War. He held an exhibition in London in 1964. He continued to be very active as a portrait painter and from 1965 served as president of the Royal Society of Portrait Painters, of which he was elected a member in 1948.

Hutchison is best-known for his portraiture but throughout his career he painted landscapes of great charm and sensitivity. He painted many distinguished people, including the queen, Prince Philip, and the queen mother. His full-length portrait of the queen in Thistle robes, painted for the Edinburgh Merchant Company in 1956, is probably one of his finest works. Among his other portraits can be mentioned Ramsay MacDonald (House of Commons), Dorothy L. Sayers (National Portrait Gallery, London), Sir James Gunn (his diploma picture in the Royal Scottish Academy, which is perhaps his finest male portrait), and Sir Sydney A. Smith, for which he received a gold medal in the Paris Salon of 1961.

Hutchison was a retiring and modest man but he had a good speaking voice and was in demand as a public speaker. He was also a great raconteur and his reminiscences of his early days in London were a never-failing source of pleasure and amusement to his family and friends. In appearance he was a tall, fair, distinguished-looking man with strong features, his face scarred by a war wound.

Hutchison continued working right up until his death at home at 30 Oakwood Court, Kensington, London, on 5 February 1970. He died very suddenly while writing a letter to *The Times*, leaving two uncompleted commissions in his studio. Kirkcaldy Art Gallery has a group of paintings, both portraits and landscapes, given by the artist: these include a portrait of the artist's mother, which he himself considered to be one of his most successful works.

R. E. HUTCHISON, *rev.*

Sources NL Scot., Hutchison MS · *The Scotsman* (10 Feb 1970) · *Glasgow Herald* (10 Feb 1970) · *The Times* (9 Feb 1970) · *The Times* (12 Feb 1970) · *The Times* (14 Feb 1970) · *Annual Report of the Council of the Royal Scottish Academy of Painting, Sculpture, and Architecture*, 143 (1970), 9–10 · private information (1981) · personal knowledge (1981) · *CGPLA Eng. & Wales* (1970) · CCI (1970)
Archives NL Scot., corresp. and papers

Huth, Alfred Henry (1850–1910), book collector, was born in London on 14 January 1850, the second son of Henry *Huth (1815–1878), book collector, and his wife, Augusta Louisa Sophia, née Westenholz. When almost twelve, he was taken from a private school at Carshalton in Surrey to travel with his elder brother in the Middle East in the company of the historian Henry Thomas Buckle. They set off on 20 October 1861, landed at Alexandria, and by 22 December 1861 had reached Aswan. They returned to Cairo and in March 1862 set out for Palestine. Somewhere along the road Buckle fell ill, probably with typhoid; he died at Damascus on 22 May 1862. The brothers returned to England and in August 1864 Alfred was sent to Rugby School, which he left at the end of 1866. After a brief enrolment at London University in 1867, he was sent to the University of Berlin (1867–8). In January 1872 he married his first cousin Octavia, youngest daughter of Charles Frederick Huth.

Alfred Huth was a rich man, with no personal involvement in the banking firm founded by his grandfather, Frederick *Huth, although at one time he was a director of the Alliance Assurance Company. He was able to devote his life to study, and from 1878 to the cultivation of his father's valuable library. In 1875 he published *The Marriage of Near Kin Considered with Respect to the Laws of Nations*, an anthropological and historical work which shows wide reading. A second revised edition was published by Longmans in 1887. The subject of consanguinity and close breeding interested him (his marriage with his cousin was childless) and he wrote on the subject in the field of botany also. In 1880 he published a lively two-volume life of his old mentor Buckle, a work which had two American editions in the same year, and was translated into German (1881). He also published a pamphlet, *On the Employment of Women* (1882), and, in 1889, a verse translation of part 1 of Goethe's *Faust*, the latter couched in language which is partly Jacobean and partly modern. In 1894 he published a novel, *A True Relation of the Travels and Serious Adventures of Matthew Dudgeon*, adopting a typography and design intended to give the book a somewhat early appearance.

Huth became the first treasurer of the Bibliographical Society at its foundation in 1892, and was active in the affairs of the society for some years, becoming president in 1903. Elected to the Roxburghe Club in 1883, he was treasurer from 1892 to 1903 and vice-president from 1903 until his death. In 1888 he presented to the club an edition of *The Miroure of Mans Saluacionne*, a fifteenth-century English translation of the *Speculum humanae salvationis*. He

himself transcribed the manuscript and edited the volume. His work on his own collections resulted in the publication in 1910 of *A Catalogue of the Woodcuts and Engravings in the Huth Library*.

Huth, like his father, allowed access to his library and was an active lender to exhibitions: he loaned nearly forty bindings to the 1891 Burlington Fine Arts Club exhibition of bookbindings and a number of manuscripts to their exhibition of manuscripts in 1908.

For a large part of his life Huth lived in London at Bolney House in Ennismore Gardens (his brother Edward lived at Bolney in Sussex). Later he bought a house at Fosbury in Wiltshire. He died suddenly on 14 October 1910 at Fullerton Wherwell, Hampshire, while out shooting with a neighbour, and was buried at Fosbury.

At his death Huth left in personalty well over £200,000, and in his will (dated January 1903) he made it clear that should his heirs decide after his death to sell the library, the trustees of the British Museum should have the right to select fifty volumes. He stipulated that the books be marked Huth Bequest, and that a catalogue of them be published. A handsome illustrated catalogue was published in 1912. It contains descriptions of the manuscripts and printed books; the last item is the collection of over seventy ballads bound in one volume.

The sale of the Huth library took place at Sotheby, Wilkinson, and Hodge, between 1911 and 1920 and totalled 8357 lots spread over nine sections. The first section covered the letters A and B and the Shakespeare collection. Before the sale took place, the entire Shakespeare collection was sold to Alexander Cochrane for £40,000 and presented to the Elizabethan Club at Yale University. The first part (without Shakespeare) fetched over £50,000, and by the time the sales had been concluded, over £350,000 had been raised. Many items found their way into institutional libraries, particularly in the USA, with the British Museum also buying heavily. Other items were snapped up by private collectors and still turn up from time to time in the salerooms. The sale catalogue itself was modelled on the printed catalogue of 1880 and gave a substantial amount of bibliographical information.

P. R. QUARRIE

Sources DNB · *The Times* (18 Oct 1910) · *The Times* (19 Oct 1910) · *The Times* (21 Oct 1910) · *The Times* (19 Dec 1910) · *The Times* (24 Dec 1910) · A. W. Pollard and others, *Catalogue of the fifty manuscripts and printed books bequeathed to the British Museum by Alfred H. Huth* (1912) · *Catalogue of the famous library of printed books, illuminated manuscripts, autograph letters, and engravings, collected by Henry Huth and since maintained and augmented by his son Alfred H. Huth*, 9 vols. (1911–20) [sale catalogues, Sotheby, Wilkinson, and Hodge] · [F. Temple], ed., *Rugby School register from 1675 to 1867 inclusive* (1867) · CGPLA Eng. & Wales (1910)
Archives BL, Add. MSS 38114–38126
Likenesses Maull & Co., photograph, repro. in Pollard and others, *Catalogue*
Wealth at death £252,409 3s. 4d.: probate, 21 Dec 1910, CGPLA Eng. & Wales

Huth, (John) Frederick Andrew [formerly (Johann) Friedrich Andreas] (1777–1864), merchant and merchant banker, was born at Stade, Hanover, on 29 October 1777, the second son of Johann Friedrich Huth (*d.* 1801), a soldier of the Scharnhorst regiment, and his wife, Marie Amelia (*d.* 1812), daughter of Johann Thee, farmer. The family settled in 1781 at nearby Harsefeld, where Johann Huth worked as a tailor and where Friedrich attended local schools.

In 1791 Huth was apprenticed to the Spanish merchants at Hamburg, Brentano Urbieta & Co., led by Juan Antonio Urbieta, and twice weekly he attended the Handelsakademie to receive a formal education in commerce. Urbieta promoted him to a senior clerkship and in 1796 took him on his annual linen-buying tour of Silesia. A year later, when a change in Spanish law enabled foreign protestants both to live and to work in Spain, Urbieta dispatched Huth to his Corunna house which was managed by his brother, Cypriano. Germany's trade with Spain was then expanding rapidly, while liberalization of Spain's trade with South America presented further opportunities. From 1799 to 1803 Huth, acting as Urbieta's supercargo, made two voyages to the west coast of South America, taking out German manufactures and bringing back hides from Buenos Aires. On his return he was appointed chief clerk in Corunna.

Notwithstanding his strong commitment to the Lutheran church, in January 1805 Huth married, at Corunna, Manuela Felipa Mayfren (1785–1856), a Catholic and an orphan believed to be the daughter of a senior member of the king of Spain's court; the duke of Veragua was then her guardian. Between 1805 and 1821 they had five sons and six daughters.

Following his marriage Huth set up in business on his own account but this was short-lived. In 1809 the invasion of Spain by France and the subsequent attack on Corunna forced the Huths' evacuation to London; apparently they took with them, for safe keeping, jewels and money belonging to the recently deposed king of Spain. In London, Huth established himself as a commission merchant, initially working with a capital of £700 and doing business with Spain, in particular supplying the British army there. His business prospered and in 1815 he took into partnership a Bremen merchant, John Frederick Gruning, formerly of De Jaslet & Co. As Frederick Huth & Co., they moved to South Place, off Finsbury Square. Later on Huth was to move his family home to Clapton, on the outskirts of London, and then, in the late 1830s, to the fashionable residential district of Upper Harley Street in London's West End. As confirmation of the family's long-term commitment to Britain, in 1815 Huth's wife and children gave up Roman Catholicism and joined the Church of England; in 1819 the family also became naturalized British citizens by act of parliament.

By 1832 Huths' capital was £32,000, of which £22,000 was owned by Huth. In the mid-1820s the business was described as being much connected with Spain and Norway, whence arrived consignments of wool and timber respectively. 'Colonial produce' was also exported occasionally to the continent; an important link existed in South America with a Lima house; and coffee cargoes were handled for a firm at San Domingo. 'There is no doubt but that their means are most ample for anything they may undertake', concluded Barings in the 1820s; 'Mr Huth is a most prudent & circumspect man and highly thought of' (Baring archives, HC 16.1). Huths' South American business was becoming a noted specialization, following the establishment of sister houses at Lima and Valparaiso in the 1820s.

Huth's prestige was considerably enhanced in 1829 when the Spanish queen, Maria Christina, later queen regent, appointed him her financial adviser and banker in London; by 1836 Huth had invested £300,000 of her assets in British government securities. Also in these years, Huths became financial agents for the Spanish government, charged in particular with making diplomatic payments around the world. Huth's personal reward came in 1834 with his appointment as knight of the order of Charles III; in 1852 he was advanced to commander *de número extraordinario*.

In 1833 Huth took into partnership his clerk and future son-in-law, Daniel Meinertzhagen, originally of Bremen. This served to reinforce the German character of the firm, but it also marked Huths' commencement of new areas of business and in a new part of the world. The company was now emerging as a major accepting house concerned with financing international trade and as a house which marketed securities. An important focus of this new business was North America, and in 1839, to facilitate north Atlantic merchanting and trade finance, especially in cotton, a Liverpool house was opened. By the end of 1839 Huths' American business accounted for £430,000 out of a total balance of £1.2 million.

Huths became a 'major conduit' (M. Wilkins, *The History of Foreign Investment in the United States*, 1989, 56) for the passage of American securities to Europe, for the most part placing them with rich private investors in Spain and Germany. But it steered clear of public issues; no public prospectus carried its name. Its American business was damaged by the financial crisis of 1841, which resulted in a lock-up of funds, but elsewhere headway continued to be made. By the late 1840s capital had grown to over £300,000 and Huths were now one of London's leading houses, ranking immediately below such companies as Barings and Rothschilds.

In 1850 Huth retired from day-to-day management, leaving the business in the hands of Meinertzhagen, who was assisted by Huth's first, third, and fifth sons, Charles Frederick, Henry *Huth, and Louis. Huth's reputation was then second to none. Notwithstanding his small, slight stature, he had great presence; an obituary states that he had been known as 'Napoleon of the City'.

Huth maintained links with his native Germany. At least two of his sons, Fernando and Henry, worked in Hamburg when young. In retirement he himself returned regularly to the country, and at Harsefeld in the 1840s he paid for the establishment of a library and a continuation school for able children; in 1855 he created a fund to support the village's poor; and in the late-1850s he funded the reconstruction of the local church.

Frederick Huth died at his residence at 33 Upper Harley

Street, London, on 14 January 1864, and was buried in the family mausoleum he had had constructed in 1837 at Kensal Green cemetery. His firm remained one of the City's most prestigious houses, but after Meinertzhagen's death in 1869 it went into relative decline; it was eventually wound up in 1936, when led by Huth's great-grandsons.   CHARLES JONES

Sources A. J. Murray, *Home from the hill: a biography of Frederick Huth, 'Napoleon of the City'* (1970) · J. Mayo, *British merchants and Chilean development, 1851–1886* (1987) · J. R. Freedman, 'A London merchant in the Anglo-American trade, 1835–1850', PhD diss., U. Lond., 1968 · S. D. Chapman, *The rise of merchant banking* (1984) · G. Meinertzhagen, *A Bremen family* (1912) · d. cert.
Archives Duke U., Perkins L., business corresp. · GL, MSS 10700–10706, 22305, 25049 · UCL, letter-books, corresp., ledger books, and account books | Baring Brothers, Baring Brothers records
Likenesses Berthon, double portrait (with Manuela Huth), probably Vancouver; copy, Tunbridge Wells, 1970 · portrait, probably Ratshaus, Harsefeld, Germany
Wealth at death under £500,000: probate, 26 Feb 1864, *CGPLA Eng. & Wales*

Huth, Henry (1815–1878), book collector, was the third son of (John) Frederick Andrew *Huth (1777–1864), a German banker who in 1809 settled in London from Corunna, Spain, and his wife, Manuela Felipa Mayfren (1785–1856), daughter of Barbara Kastner and ward of the duke of Veragua. Henry's brothers included Charles Frederick Huth, merchant banker and art collector. In 1819 the family was naturalized. The Huth firm became, after the Rothschilds, the biggest in London, and at his death Frederick Huth (as Henry's father was known) left a large fortune.

Originally intended by his father for the Indian Civil Service, Henry Huth was educated at a school at Leith Hill in Surrey run by a Mr Rusden, where among other things he studied oriental languages and developed a strong interest in chemistry, which his father encouraged. In 1833 he left to join the family firm. After spending three years in Germany, first at Hamburg for commercial reasons and then at Magdeburg to perfect his German, he went in 1839 to the USA and Mexico, and returned to England in 1843. In 1844 he married Augusta Louisa Sophia Westenholz, third daughter of Friedrich Westenholz of Waldenstein Castle, Austria. They had three daughters and three sons, one of whom, Alfred Henry *Huth also became a noted bibliophile. He first settled in Hamburg but returned to London in 1849 and rejoined his father's firm.

Huth's interest in old books went back to his school-days, and he was said to have been fired with enthusiasm by seeing 'a curious old book' in Baldock's Holborn bookshop. In Mexico in 1840 he acquired a number of rare Spanish books and a Chinese Bible from a man who stopped him in the street, but it was in the later 1840s that he began collecting in London with his brother Louis (d. 1905) from whom he bought a copy of the 1512 Burgos edition of the *Cronica del Cid*. Louis later became a well-known collector of oriental porcelain. In 1852 Huth met the bookseller Joseph Lilly, who exercised a good deal of influence on his purchases over the years and was generally his agent, but Huth bought throughout the trade and made it his practice on his way from the City to his home at 30

Princes Gate, London to stop at a number of leading booksellers. Books of American interest he acquired from Henry Stevens of Vermont. Several of his grandest purchases were through Bernard Quaritch, including, in 1874, a copy of the 42-line Bible of Johann Gutenberg (Mainz, c.1455) which had been bought at the sale of the Perkins library from Hanworth Park in 1873. From Quaritch also, and from the same sale, he obtained the magnificent 1462 Fust and Schoeffer Bible on vellum.

Huth bought extensively at the important sales of the period—Utterson, Hawtrey, Perkins, Tite—and especially at the sale of George Daniel's library in 1864, and the sales from 1867 to 1872 of the library of Thomas Corser. His celebrated collection of Elizabethan ballads came from the Daniel sale; they had been acquired some forty or so years earlier by the Suffolk antiquary William Stevenson Fitch, who had bought a parcel of 'old songs' from a countryman in the market. Daniel had disposed of some, which ended up in the Christie–Miller library at Britwell Court, but the rest were bound up.

Huth owned twelve books printed by Caxton, mostly bought in the 1860s from Lilly, and much early English literature, including many unique or very rare items. He did not, unlike the collectors of an earlier generation for whom first editions of the classics of Greece and Rome were of paramount importance, strive to collect wonderful copies from the presses of Aldus, Estienne, and so on. But splendid books in German, French, Italian, and Spanish, many of them illustrated, he did collect. Of the fifty books chosen for the British Museum Library after the death of his son Alfred, most are vernacular, and most are in English. Some, like the Longus of 1598, were and remained unique. The influence of William Carew Hazlitt in the creation and documentation of the Huth library was strong, and certainly it was the Huth collection on which Hazlitt drew largely for his own works. Huth was very liberal in allowing scholars and others access to his collection.

In 1863 Huth became a member of the Philobiblon Society, and in 1866 of the Roxburghe Club, being elected together with Henry Bradshaw. In 1867 he had printed for the Philobiblon Society *Ancient Ballads and Broadsides Published in England in the Sixteenth Century*. In 1870 he published *Inedited Poetical Miscellanies 1584–1700 Selected Chiefly from Mss. in Private Hands*; in 1874 *Prefaces Dedications Epistles Selected from Early English Books*; and in 1875 *Fugitive Tracts Written in Verse* (two series, 1493–1600 and 1600–1700). All were edited by Hazlitt and had prefaces by Huth. They were privately printed in fifty copies only by C. Whittingham at the Chiswick Press. In the late 1860s Huth conceived the idea of a catalogue of his collection, a work he began himself, but which from 1871 was worked on by Hazlitt and F. S. Ellis, though Huth himself read the proofs. The work lasted some years, eliciting adverse remarks from Huth about its cost, and he did not live to see its completion in five volumes in 1880. Huth was found dead on 11 December 1878, having had a stroke on the stairs of his house at 30 Princes Gate, and fallen backwards, fracturing his skull. His wife and family were away for the weekend and he was believed to have died the previous day. His son Alfred took over the care of the collection, which was finally sold by Sotheby, Wilkinson and Hodge between 1911 and 1920, raising over £350,000. Before the sale the British Museum was allowed to select fifty volumes. Of the remaining books many found their way into the British Museum's library and other institutional libraries, especially in the United States. Although not a very sociable man, Huth was said to be a charming talker. He was a generous benefactor of charitable causes and for many years he was treasurer and president of the Royal Hospital for Incurables.   P. R. QUARRIE

Sources W. C. Hazlitt, *Four generations of a literary family*, 2 (1897), 267–84 · A. H. Huth, 'Mr Henry Huth, 1815–1878', *Contributions towards a dictionary of English book-collectors*, ed. B. Quaritch, 2 (1892), 1–8 · S. Parks, *The Elizabethan Club of Yale University and its library* (1986) · H. Huth, W. C. Hazlitt, and F. S. Ellis, *The Huth library: a catalogue of the printed books, manuscripts, autograph letters, and engravings, collected by Henry Huth*, 5 vols. (1880) · *N&Q*, 5th ser., 10 (1878), 505 · *DNB*

Archives BL, letters to W. C. Hazlitt, Add. MSS 38899–38902 · U. Edin. L., corresp. with James Halliwell-Phillipps

Likenesses Aldis, medallion engraving, repro. in A. B. Grosart, *Prospectus of the Huth Library* (privately printed, London, [1881]) · Lenthall, photograph · T. D. Scott, pencil drawing (after photograph by Lenthall) · C. W. Sherborn, etching, NPG · etching (after photograph by Lenthall), repro. in Huth, Hazlitt, and Ellis, *The Huth library*

Wealth at death under £300,000: probate, 23 Jan 1879, *CGPLA Eng. & Wales*

Huthwaite, Sir Edward (bap. 1793, d. 1873), army officer, was baptized at the parish church of St Peter, Nottingham, on 24 June 1793, the son of William Huthwaite, a draper and sometime mayor of Nottingham, and his wife, Lucy.

Huthwaite was nominated for a cadetship by Edward Parry, a director of the East India Company. He entered the Royal Military Academy, Woolwich, on 19 August 1807, joined the East India Company as a cadet in 1809, and was appointed second-lieutenant in the Bengal artillery on 13 November 1810. His first recorded military employment was recruiting for *golundauze* (Indian foot-artillerymen) at Chittagong in 1812. He served as a lieutenant-fireworker in the campaigns in Nepal in 1815–16, was present at the capture of various forts in Oudh in 1817, and fought in the Third Anglo-Maratha War of 1817–18. He was promoted lieutenant on 25 September 1817.

When the Burmese invaded Cachar, which was under British protection, in January 1824, Huthwaite was sent there with a contingent of *golundauze*. Brigadier Innes, in his report on the engagement at Tachyon, on 8 July 1824, expressed himself much indebted to Huthwaite. The latter, having contracted fever in Burma, went afterwards on sick leave to Singapore and China. He was made brevet captain on 12 November 1825, and commanded a foot-battery at the siege and capture of Bharatpur in 1825–6. He was promoted substantive captain on 30 August 1826.

From November 1836 to January 1837, and again from October 1837 to January 1839, Huthwaite commanded the Marwar artillery division. He was promoted major on 20 January 1842, posted to the 2nd brigade horse artillery on 15 March 1842, and placed in command of two troops of his brigade at Ludhiana. He then commanded the artillery of the Marwar field force from 30 December 1842 until 1844. The India Office inspector commended him for his 'zeal, ability, and firmness', and he was promoted lieutenant-colonel on 3 July 1845. During the First Anglo-Sikh War, of 1845–6, he commanded the 3rd brigade Bengal horse artillery, and was present at the battles of Ferozeshahr and Sobraon. He was made CB for his services on 3 April 1846. During the Second Anglo-Sikh War, of 1848–9, he was brigadier of the foot-artillery with Lord Gough, and was present at the two passages of the Chenab, and the battles of Chilianwala and Gujrat. He then commanded the artillery of the force under General Sir W. R. Gilbert, which crossed the Jhelum, received the surrender of the Sikh army, and pursued their Afghan allies to the entrance of the Khyber Pass.

Huthwaite was promoted brevet colonel and colonel-commandant on 23 January 1854, colonel on 20 June 1854, major-general on 14 March 1857, and lieutenant-general on 6 March 1868. He was made a KCB on 2 June 1869. After his retirement he remained in India, and died at his residence, Sherwood, Naini Tal, North-Western Provinces, on 5 April 1873.   H. M. CHICHESTER, rev. ALEX MAY

Sources *Indian Army List* · E. Buckle and J. W. Kaye, *Memoirs of the services of the Bengal artillery* (1852) · V. C. P. Hodson, *List of officers of the Bengal army, 1758–1834*, 4 vols. (1927–47) · G. Bruce, *The Burma Wars, 1824–1886* (1973) · H. C. B. Cook, *The Sikh wars: the British army in the Punjab, 1845–1849* (1975) · R. G. Burton, *The First and Second Sikh wars* (1911)

Hutt, (George) Allen (1901–1973), journalist and political activist, was born at 57 Harvist Road, Willesden, London, on 20 September 1901, the son of Edwin George Wellington Hutt, a commercial clerk and later general manager in the paper industry, and his wife, Marion de Witt, a headmistress. He was educated at Kilburn grammar school and at Downing College, Cambridge, where he gained a first in the history tripos in 1923.

By this time Hutt was a committed Marxist. In its latter stages he was 'vehemently' opposed to the First World War, and at Cambridge he was active in the university socialist society, eventually becoming the national secretary of the communist-dominated University Socialist Federation. Briefly, in 1920–21, he was a member of the Independent Labour Party, but it was his adhesion to the Communist Party in 1922 that set the course for the rest of his political life.

Equally fateful in professional terms was Hutt's recruitment to the *Daily Herald*, then a congenial home for communists, in 1923. Through a paternal lineage of master printers, Hutt took pride in a family involvement in the publishing industry dating from the seventeenth century. Combining political commitment with exacting professional standards, he was a priceless asset to a left-wing press disproportionately endowed with only the first of these. In addition to the *Herald*, he worked on or for the communist *Workers' Weekly*; the Soviet news agency TASS; Palme Dutt's *Labour Monthly*, which he briefly claimed to edit 'in fact if not in name'; and *Trade Union Unity*, a short-lived venture of TUC 'lefts' like A. A. Purcell for which Hutt functioned as a self-designated 'factotum' (Hutt to Karl August, 29 Dec 1925, Hutt papers, People's History Museum, Manchester). These trade union contacts were reflected in his first book *Communism and Coal* (1928), a collaboration with Arthur Horner, and a voluminous correspondence with the Fife miners' leader David Proudfoot.

After a spell at the International Lenin School and two years as chief sub-editor at the newly launched *Daily Worker* (1930–32), Hutt produced a series of books on British working-class politics, most of them developing historical narratives which seemingly culminated inexorably in the current policy of the Communist Party. Perhaps the best of them, however, was *The Condition of the Working Class in Britain* (1933), an early example of the decade's committed documentary style, revealing a flair for the investigative side of journalism as well as its technical aspects.

Nevertheless, it was to the latter that Hutt owed a reputation extending well beyond the left. In 1936 he joined the co-operative-owned *Reynolds News* as chief assistant to the editor with a special brief for the paper's redesign. Six years later he rejoined the *Daily Worker*, then being relaunched after a temporary wartime ban. These were halcyon days for British communists, and much of their optimism for the post-war world was focused on the prospect of the 'new' *Daily Worker* that, from its own distinct perspective, would match the best that Fleet Street had to offer. Hutt as chief sub-editor made perhaps the outstanding contribution to such a goal, turning 'a squad of unqualified and in some cases poorly qualified people into journalists' (MacEwen, 109). Famously rude—the paper's editor, William Rust, likened him to 'a combination of a dragon and a porcupine'—he nevertheless earned the tremendous respect of both his colleagues and his profession. While the *Worker*'s circulation figures never matched expectations, and from the late 1940s declined steadily, the paper won prestigious awards for newspaper design, and Hutt himself gained the rare distinction of being named a royal designer for industry. His book *Newspaper Design* (1960), a summation of his technical experience, cemented the high professional regard in which he was held.

For a quarter of a century from 1946 Hutt also sat on the executive of the National Union of Journalists and edited its monthly paper *The Journalist*. Here too he achieved high honour when in 1967 he was made the union's president. If he had a great frustration, it was that on the *Daily Worker* the positions of editor and assistant editor were the preserve of leading communist functionaries, politically dependable but often unpractised in journalism. When these posts were filled in this fashion on Rust's untimely death in 1949, Hutt was driven by the 'most bitter disappointment and humiliation' to consider his resignation (draft statement, 14 Feb 1949, Hutt papers, People's History Museum, Manchester). Through finesse or party discipline he was persuaded to change his mind, and he remained with the paper until his retirement in 1966. That same year, to his fervent dismay and contempt, the paper changed its name to the *Morning Star*.

Both the issue and the reaction were typical. A disciplined communist not known to have had any major disagreements with the party line, Hutt was nevertheless fiercely independent on the matters which he knew best. He married three times, in each case to an active communist, and left children by both his first marriage, to Norma, and his second, to Sheena. He died of cancer at his home, 8 Regent's Park Terrace, Camden, London, on 10 August 1973; his third wife, Avis, a nurse, survived him.

KEVIN MORGAN

Sources W. Rust, *The story of the Daily Worker*, ed. A. Hutt (1949) • K. Morgan, 'The communist party and the *Daily Worker*, 1930–1956', *Opening the books: essays on the social and cultural history of British communism*, ed. G. Andrews, N. Fishman, and K. Morgan (1995), 142–59 • M. MacEwen, *The greening of a red* (1991) • *Militant miners: recollections of John McArthur, Buckhaven, and letters, 1924–26, of David Proudfoot, Methil, to G. Allen Hutt*, ed. I. MacDougall (1981) • b. cert. • d. cert.
Archives Kirkcaldy Central Library, papers • People's History Museum, Manchester, papers
Likenesses photograph, 1930?–1939, repro. in McDougall, ed., *Militant miners*
Wealth at death £14,652: probate, 30 Nov 1973, *CGPLA Eng. & Wales*

Hutt, Sir George (1809–1889). *See under* Hutt, Sir William (1801–1882).

Hutt, John (1746–1794), naval officer, uncle of Sir William Hutt, became lieutenant of the *Lively* on 10 April 1773, while serving in North America; later he moved to the *Hind* (7 January 1774) and *Scarborough* (20 April 1774). In 1780 he was serving in the West Indies in the brig *St Lucia*; in October he was moved to the *Sandwich* by Sir George Rodney, who, on 12 February 1781, promoted him to the command of the brig *Antigua* (14 guns).

On 28 May, during De Grasse's attempt to recapture the island of St Lucia, the *Antigua* was lying in Dauphin Creek; she was seized and burnt, Hutt and the ship's company being made prisoners. In November he was allowed to return to England on parole, and, being shortly afterwards exchanged, was tried for the loss of his ship, and acquitted. In July 1782 he was appointed to command the sloop *Trimmer* in the channel, and in the following year he was posted to the *Camilla* (20 guns), in which he went out to Jamaica. The *Camilla* returned to England in November 1787, and in July 1790 Hutt became captain of the frigate *Lizard*. In September he was sent to a position off Ferrol to gather intelligence of the Spanish force, and brought back the news that the Spanish fleet had retired to Cadiz.

In 1793 Hutt was appointed to the *Queen* (98 guns) as flag captain to Rear-Admiral Sir Alan Gardner, whom he had already known as commodore on the Jamaica station, and during that year he was involved in the unsuccessful attempt to retake Martinique. He was still in the *Queen*, in Howe's fleet, when, on 29 May 1794, in an engagement preliminary to the battle of 1 June, he lost a leg. No serious danger to his life was at first apprehended, but after the return of the fleet to Spithead his condition deteriorated and he died on 30 June 1794.

J. K. LAUGHTON, *rev.* RANDOLPH COCK

Sources PRO, commission and warrant books, ADM 6/20, 21 · W. L. Clowes, *The Royal Navy: a history from the earliest times to the present*, 7 vols. (1897–1903) · *GM*, 1st ser., 64 (1794), 674
Archives PRO, commission and warrant books, ADM 6/20, 21
Likenesses Bartolozzi, Landseer, Ryder & Stow, engraving, pubd 1803 (after R. Smirke *Naval victories, Commemoration of the victory of June 1ˢᵗ 1794*), BM, NPG · J. Bacon jun., medallion on monument, 1804, Westminster Abbey

Hutt, Sir William (1801–1882), politician, third son of Richard Hutt, of Appley Towers, Ryde, Isle of Wight, was born at 2 Chester Place, in the parish of St Mary, Lambeth, on 6 October 1801, and was privately baptized in February 1802. He was educated at private schools at Ryde and Camberwell, matriculated from St Mary Hall, Oxford, on 15 February 1820, where he remained until August 1820, and then studied with a private tutor at Hatfield, Essex, until he entered at Trinity College, Cambridge. He graduated BA in 1827, and MA in 1831. A Cambridge friend, Lord Arran, introduced him to Mary (*d.* 1860), daughter of J. Milner, of Staindrop, Durham, and widow of the tenth earl of Strathmore, whom he married on 16 March 1831. She was an heiress, and in her lifetime Hutt resided at Streatlam Castle, Durham, and at Gibside, also in Durham.

Hutt was MP for Hull from 13 December 1832 to 23 June 1841, and for Gateshead from 29 June 1841 to 26 January 1874. He supported free trade, took an active part in colonial and commercial questions, was a commissioner for the foundation of South Australia, and received the thanks of the London shipowners for his exertions in the extinction of the Stade and Sound dues. As a member of the New Zealand Company, he was instrumental in annexing New Zealand to Great Britain. He was made paymaster-general and vice-president of the Board of Trade, and was sworn of the privy council on 22 February 1860. In 1865 he successfully negotiated at Vienna a treaty of commerce with Austria, and on 1 March 1865 was appointed a member of the mixed commission to examine the Austrian tariff. He was made KCB on 27 November 1865.

Hutt's first wife, Lady Strathmore, died on 5 May 1860, leaving him collieries which produced about £18,000 a year. He married as his second wife, on 15 June 1861, Fanny Anna Jane (*d.* 1886), daughter of the Hon. Sir Francis Stanhope, and widow of Colonel James Hughes. He had no recorded children by either marriage. He died at Appley Towers, Ryde, on 24 November 1882, leaving his landed property to his brother, **Sir George Hutt** (1809–1889), army officer, who served with credit through the Sind and Afghan campaigns of 1839–44; for the performance of his battery at Meanee he was made a CB. He commanded the artillery in the Anglo-Persian War of 1856–7, and rendered valuable aid to Sir Bartle Frere in Sind during the mutiny. When he retired in 1858 the government of Bombay thanked him for his services. In 1865 he became registrar

and secretary to the commissioners of Chelsea Hospital, and held that appointment until 1886, in which year he was made KCB. He married, in 1862, Adela, daughter of General Sir John Scott KCB, with whom he left a family. He died at Appley Towers, Ryde, on 27 September 1889.

G. C. BOASE, *rev.* H. C. G. MATTHEW

Sources *Morning Post* (27 Nov 1882), 4 · Boase, *Mod. Eng. biog.* · *Broad Arrow* (2 Nov 1889) · W. P. Morrell, *British colonial policy in the age of Peel and Russell* (1930) · private information (1891)
Archives Tyne and Wear Archives Service, Newcastle upon Tyne, travel journals in Europe, incl. details of diplomatic mission to Vienna, album of autograph letters and cuttings book | BL, corresp. with W. E. Gladstone, Add. MSS 44367–44783 · BL, letters to Sir A. H. Layard, Add. MSS 39000, 39113–39117 · Lambton estate office, Lambton Park, Chester-le-Street, co. Durham, letters to earl of Durham · PRO, corresp. with Lord John Russell, PRO 30/22
Likenesses J. Livesay, etching, BM
Wealth at death £70,317 14s. 3d.: resworn probate, Nov 1884, *CGPLA Eng. & Wales* (1883) · £8263 12s. 8d.—George Hutt: resworn probate, July 1892, *CGPLA Eng. & Wales* (1890)

Hutten, Leonard (1556/7–1632), Church of England clergyman and antiquary, of unknown origins, was educated on the foundation at Westminster School in London and in 1574 was selected one of its three scholars sent triennially to Christ Church, Oxford, where he remained for the rest of his life. He became a student—that is, a fellow—in 1575, graduated BA on 12 November 1578, proceeded MA on 3 January 1582, commenced BD on 27 April 1591, and was admitted DD on 14 April 1600. He took holy orders, and held the rectories of Long Preston, Yorkshire (1587–8); Rampisham, Dorset (1595–1601); Floore, Northamptonshire (1601 until his death); and Weedon Beck, Northamptonshire (1602–4). He was made canon of the seventh prebend in Christ Church Cathedral, Oxford, in 1599, and later became subdean, and he was collated to the prebend of Reculversland in St Paul's, London, on 1 October 1609.

Hutten was a prominent figure in early seventeenth-century church and university life. He officiated at the opening of the Bodleian Library in 1602. A copy of his sermon for the queen's accession day in the same year is preserved in the Bodleian (MS Rawlinson C.79, fol. 140). A pro-vice-chancellor in 1603, he was then and later involved in theological disputes within the university. In 1604 he was appointed by King James to be one of the translators of the Bible, one of the group working on the gospels, Acts, and Apocalypse. His first published work appeared the following year, entitled *An Answere to a Certaine Treatise of the Crosse in Baptisme*. A response to William Bradshaw's work attacking ceremonies, it was dedicated to Archbishop Bancroft. In 1606 Hutten contributed to the collection of verses by ninety-eight Oxford dons, 'Charites Oxonienses, sive, Laetitia musarum' (BL, Royal MS 12 A LXIV), commemorating the visit of Christian IV of Denmark. Two books he gave to the library of Christ Church in 1582 are still there.

Hutten left two antiquarian works in manuscript. A copy of his 'Historia fundationum ecclesiae Christi Oxon', now lost, was seen by Anthony Wood in the hands of Dr John Fell. The original of Hutten's other work, his

'Antiquities of Oxford', is also now lost, but the text survives in print, published by Thomas Hearne, as part of his 1720 edition of the Textus Roffensis, and by Charles Plummer in his *Elizabethan Oxford*, of 1887. Wood disliked this 'Discourse', claiming it was a mere copy of Brian Twyne's work, yet Twyne's influence is readily acknowledged throughout. The text is of value in conveying a colourful sense of the streetscapes of Elizabethan Oxford, interspersed with a number of historical anecdotes. Wood was 'informed by one who knew this Dr. Hutten well, that he was author of a tragic comedy', the 'Bellum grammaticale' performed for the queen in 1592, but dismissed this claim on the grounds that the play had been published as early as 1574. Nevertheless it has not been attributed to another author, and it is conceivable that Hutten could have written at least part of it.

Hutten married Anne Hampden about 1600, and they had a daughter, Alice (1602–1628), who married Richard Corbet, then dean of Christ Church and later bishop of Oxford. Hutten died, presumably in Oxford, on 17 May 1632, aged seventy-five, and was buried in the north transept of Christ Church Cathedral, where a brass inscription in Latin records that he 'gave back to God a soul learned, straightforward, godly'. His widow was still alive in 1635, when she was involved in litigation in her capacity of executor of her son-in-law Bishop Corbet.

PETER SHERLOCK

Sources Wood, *Ath. Oxon.*, new edn, 2.532–4 · C. Plummer, ed., *Elizabethan Oxford: reprints of rare tracts*, OHS, 8 (1887) · Wood, *Ath. Oxon.: Fasti* (1815) · J. Arthur, *A guide to the memorial brasses, Christ Church Oxford* [n.d.] · C. M. Dent, *Protestant reformers in Elizabethan Oxford* (1983) · Foster, *Alum. Oxon.* · Bodl. Oxf., MS Tanner 135 · *Hist. U. Oxf. 3: Colleg. univ.*, 506–7 · *DNB*
Archives BL, 'Charites Oxonienses, sive, Laetitia musarum', Royal MS 12 A LXIV | Bodl. Oxf., MS Rawlinson C.79, fol. 140

Hüttner, Johann Christian (1766–1847), translator, was born at Guben in Lusatia, Germany. He studied philology at Leipzig University and was awarded his doctorate on the basis of his work *De mythis Platonis*, which was published in Leipzig in 1788. He travelled to England in 1791 as tutor to George Thomas Staunton, son of Sir George Leonard Staunton. He accompanied father and son on Lord Macartney's diplomatic mission to China in 1793–4, and was occasionally employed to write diplomatic documents in Latin. He sent accounts of his experiences to friends in Germany, who had promised not to publish them. A copy of them was, however, sold to a Leipzig bookseller, and his friends in Germany then decided to bring out an authentic text, which was published in Berlin in 1797, under the title of *Nachricht von der brittischen Gesandtschaftsreise durch China und einen Theil der Tartarei*. The work, which pre-empted Staunton's official account of the mission, excited considerable attention. Two French translations of it were published in 1799 and 1804.

In 1807 Hüttner was appointed as a translator to the Foreign Office, a position he held for forty years. In 1808 he translated from Spanish into German Don Pedro Cevallos's appeal to the nations of Europe against Napoleon's invasion of Spain, which was believed to have had a powerful effect in raising sympathy in Germany for the Spanish cause.

Hüttner maintained close contacts with Germany, and was a correspondent on England and a travel writer for a number of German newspapers and periodicals, and for a long period acted as literary agent to the grand duke of Saxe-Weimar.

Hüttner was twice married, but had no children. He was hit by a cab in Fludyer Street, Westminster, and died two weeks later on 24 May 1847. He was buried at Kensal Green cemetery in London beside his second wife on 29 May 1847.   FRANCIS WATT, *rev.* JANETTE RYAN

Sources *GM*, 2nd ser., 28 (1847) · F. Ratzel, 'Hüttner, Joh. Christ', *Allgemeine deutsche Biographie*, ed. R. von Liliencron, 13 (Leipzig, 1881), 480

Hutton, Alfred (1839–1910), swordsman, born at Beverley, Yorkshire, on 10 March 1839, was eleventh and youngest child and seventh son of Henry William Hutton (1787–1848) of Walker Gate, Beverley, captain in the 4th (Royal Irish) dragoon guards (retired 1811). His mother was Marianne (*b.* before 1795, *d.* 1879), only child of John Fleming of Beverley. A brother, Edward Thomas, was the father of Lieutenant-general Sir Edward Hutton KCMG (1848–1923). Educated at Blackheath, Alfred matriculated at University College, Oxford, on 25 November 1857, but left without graduating to join the 79th (Cameron) Highlanders (31 May 1859). At the age of twelve he had taken his first fencing lessons at the school in St James's Street from Henry Angelo the younger (*d.* 1852), his father having been a pupil of Henry Angelo the elder. On arrival at the depot of his regiment at Perth he soon proved himself an expert fencer. Upon joining the headquarters of his regiment in India, at the request of his commanding officer, Colonel Hodgson, he organized in the regiment the Cameron Fencing Club, for which he prepared his first book, *Swordsmanship* (1862). In 1864 he exchanged into the 7th hussars, and in 1866 into the 1st (King's) dragoon guards, and he popularized fencing in both regiments. He was gazetted captain on 30 September 1868, and retired from the service in 1873.

Invalided home in 1865, Hutton had become the pupil and friend of McTurk, Angelo's successor at the school of arms in St James's Street. On leaving the army he devoted himself to the practice of modern fencing with foil, sabre, and bayonet, but chiefly to the study and revival of older systems and schools. His chief work, published in 1889, was devoted to the sabre—*Cold Steel* (a title sometimes transferred by his friends from the book to the writer). Hutton successfully advocated the use by cavalry of a straight pointed sword for thrusting rather than an edged sword for cutting. In 1890 he published *Fixed Bayonets*, in which he insisted that a competently wielded bayonet should beat a good swordsman, but his views of bayonet fighting were regarded in the army as too theoretical for modern practical instruction. He retorted by deploring

Alfred Hutton (1839–1910), by John Ernest Breun, pubd 1889
[*Cold Steel*]

military reliance on Italian theories of swordsmanship to the exclusion of effective French practice.

Under Hutton's instruction the school of arms of the London rifle brigade reached a high level of all-round swordsmanship. For its benefit *The Swordsman* was written in 1891 (enlarged edn, 1898). In 1892 he published *Old Sword Play*, a summary history of fencing as practised in the fifteenth, sixteenth, and seventeenth centuries. In 1894 he was elected FSA, and an honorary member of the Cercle d'Escrime de Bruxelles, on whose invitation he took the chief part with several English pupils in a historical display, 'L'escrime à travers les âges', held at the opera house on 22 May.

From 1895 until his death Hutton was first president of the Amateur Fencing Association, originally the fencing branch of the Amateur Gymnastic Association, the earliest attempt at organizing British fencing. He promoted the beginning of national championships for men from 1898 and for women from 1907. When English fencers first participated in the international cup (at Paris in 1903), he was on the jury. In 1909 he became fencing delegate to the British Olympic Council.

Hutton was one of the founders in 1874 of the Central London Throat and Ear Hospital, and for thirty years he was its first chairman. Of tall and picturesque figure, handsome face, and chivalrous bearing, traits suggestive

to friends of Don Quixote, he was wholehearted in his devotion to the science of arms, which he did much to rescue from neglect. He died unmarried at his chambers in 76 Jermyn Street, London, on 18 December 1910, and was buried in Astbury churchyard, near Congleton, Cheshire, three days later. A memorial tablet was unveiled at Astbury church by Lieutenant-general Sir Edward Hutton on 8 October 1911. Hutton bequeathed his fine collection of fencing and duelling literature, with some admirable specimens of oriental sword-cutlery, to the Victoria and Albert Museum. The Captain Alfred Hutton memorial shield was instituted for the amateur foil championship; a challenge cup was also instituted for ladies' foil, but was melted down in the Second World War. The historian of the Amateur Fencing Association concluded, 'The revival of interest in, and the development of, fencing in Great Britain during the first decade of this century were undoubtedly due chiefly to his enthusiasm and untiring work' (de Beaumont, 37).

A. F. SIEVEKING, *rev.* JULIAN LOCK

Sources *The Times* (19 Dec 1910) · C. L. L. A. de Beaumont, *Modern British fencing: a history of the Amateur Fencing Association of Great Britain* (1950) · A. W. Hutton, *Some account of the family of Hutton of Gate Burton, Lincolnshire* (privately printed, Devizes, 1898) · A. Hutton, *Cold steel* (1889) · private information (1912) · CGPLA Eng. & Wales (1911)
Likenesses J. E. Breun, photogravure, repro. in Hutton, *Cold steel*, frontispiece [*see illus.*] · Jest, chromolithograph caricature, NPG; repro. in *VF* (13 Aug 1903) · W. H. Robinson, portrait, repro. in *The Field* (25 June 1910) · relief portrait (on memorial shield), Amateur Fencing Association
Wealth at death £15,586 8s. 10d.: resworn probate, 25 Jan 1911, CGPLA Eng. & Wales

Hutton, Catherine (1756–1846), novelist and letter-writer, was born on 11 February 1756, probably in Birmingham, the only surviving daughter of William *Hutton (1723–1815), a Birmingham-based bookseller and topographer, and his wife, Sarah Cock (1731–1796). The family was a close and affectionate one, and, although she was tempted to marry, filial devotion prevented Catherine Hutton from ever leaving home. She nursed her mother through five years of illness before her death, and continued to care for her father in his old age. He repaid her with admiring sympathy: in his autobiographical *Life*, he praised both her character—she was 'incapable of an ill-natured speech'—and her abilities—'whatever lies within the bounds of female reach she ventures to undertake, and whatever she undertakes succeeds' (Jewitt, 45).

From the ages of seven to fourteen Catherine Hutton attended an undistinguished day school in Birmingham; subsequently, she hoped to attend a boarding-school in Worcester, but was prevented by her father, and continued her own education at home. In Birmingham, she was in the midst of a stimulating scientific, intellectual, and religious community: her father, the author of a history of Birmingham, promoted the development of education and science in the city and, as a Unitarian, moved in progressive dissenting circles. Catherine herself joined Joseph Priestley's congregation in the 1780s, and became a friend of the radical novelist Robert Bage. The confidence

Catherine Hutton (1756–1846), by William Read, pubd 1824

of both Catherine Hutton and her contemporaries was, however, severely dented by the 1791 Birmingham Church and King riots: rioters attacked both William Hutton's town house and business, and his country house on the outskirts of Birmingham at Bennett's Hill, Washwood Heath.

From an early age, Catherine Hutton was a keen letter-writer. The Coltman family of Leicester and Mrs Andre of Enfield, Middlesex, were lifelong correspondents. She also wrote to her cousin the mathematician Charles Hutton (1737–1823), Sarah Harriet Burney (Fanny Burney's half-sister), the radical author Sir Richard Phillips, Eliza Cook, and, latterly, Edward Bulwer Lytton, and Charles Dickens. Her letters are full of anecdotes and shrewd observations on her acquaintance and are seasoned with a self-deprecating wit, their direct address and dry cheerfulness recalling the epistolary style of Jane Austen. Hutton delighted in Austen's novels, and believed that 'her character is either something like mine, or what I would wish mine to be' (Reminiscences, 183).

In 1778 Catherine Hutton visited London (the first of twenty-six visits) and became a keen tourist, travelling throughout England and Wales in the course of her life. Although she described herself as 'a worshipper of mountains' (Reminiscences, 118), her reflections were not limited to romantic commonplaces. She commented on the condition of inns and boarding-houses and the eccentricities of her fellow guests, and she visited industrial towns, factories, and (in 1801) a slave ship in Liverpool. Her observations were characteristically frank. She described

Aberystwyth, which she visited in 1787, as 'a poor, petty place', uninfluenced by having received two proposals of marriage during her stay (ibid., 52). The spa town of Malvern, which she first visited in 1802, was more to her taste; she revisited it annually for the next thirty-two years.

In 1813 Catherine Hutton published The Miser Married: a Novel, which she dedicated to her father. An epistolary novel, it related the tale of the second marriage of debt-ridden and deceitful widow, Lady Montgomery, to the miserly Mr Winterdale. Her characterization was lively; she created fine cameos including Mrs Thacker, the vulgar parvenu wife of the local clergyman, and her nephew, the chatty and shallow Mr Sharp. She made attempts to imitate the orthography, as well as the style, of the lower-class characters. The extensive space given to descriptions of a tour of mid-Wales and to literary criticism of novels, including Bage's Hermsprong, foreshadowed features of her other novels. The Monthly Review of November 1813 praised the novel as 'a promising first attempt' (p. 326).

Hutton's next novel, The Welsh Mountaineer (1817), portrayed the country-bred maiden abroad in fashionable London, where her innocence highlights the corrupt superficiality of society life. The minimal plot often flags, burdened with lengthy descriptions of visits to the midlands and Scarborough. Oakwood Hall (1819), the last of Hutton's novels to be published but the first to be written, also contains much travel writing, although the concentration of the majority of the narration in the hands of Miss Oakwood, a shrewd middle-aged spinster, gives the novel a piquant unity absent from The Welsh Mountaineer. Although her novels are the most significant of her publications, Hutton published other works, including an edition of her father's autobiography (1815) and The Tour of Africa (1819–21), a selection from the writings of travellers in the dark continent, and left in manuscript a history of the queens of England. She also wrote about sixty pieces for periodicals. In 1827, she remarked wryly that writing for La Belle Assemblée 'does not require exertion, and … keeps me from stagnating' (Beale, 179).

In an account of her occupations written in July 1844, Catherine Hutton described some of the other activities which absorbed her: needlework, including 'patchwork beyond all calculation' (GM, 476); pastry and confectionery; collecting prints of costumes in 8 large volumes; and collecting more than 2000 autographs. By 1843 Catherine Hutton was losing her sight; she died on 13 March 1846 at Bennett's Hill, and was buried in a vault under Ward End church. Bridget Hill rightly concludes that her life 'illustrates the particular problems of the educated, intelligent, single daughter of the middle class' in late eighteenth- and early nineteenth-century Britain (Hill, 47).   ROSEMARY MITCHELL

Sources Reminiscences of a gentlewoman of the last century: letters of Catherine Hutton, ed. C. H. Beale (1891) • C. H. Beale, ed., Catherine Hutton and her friends (1895) • B. Hill, 'Catherine Hutton (1756–1846): a forgotten letter-writer', Women's Writing, 1/1 (1994), 35–50 • 'Miss Hutton', GM, 2nd ser., 25 (1846), 436–7 • 'A female collector', GM, 2nd ser., 25 (1846), 476–7 • The life of William Hutton, ed. L. Jewitt (1872) • 'The miser married', Monthly Review, new ser., 72 (1813),

326 · *Monthly Review*, new ser., 90 (1819), 214 · Blain, Clements & Grundy, *Feminist comp.*
Archives Birm. CA, corresp., literary MSS, and papers · U. Birm. L., diary and papers · Wellcome L., MSS collection | Birm. CA, letters and papers · CUL, collected papers of eighteenth- and early nineteenth-century booksellers · Herts. ALS, letters to Lord Lytton · Leics. RO, letters to Mrs Coltman and to Miss Ann Coltman · NL Wales, letters to her brother, Thomas Hutton
Likenesses lithograph, *c.*1799, repro. in Beale, ed., *Reminiscences*, frontispiece · T. Woolnoth, stipple, pubd in or before 1825 (after T. Wageman), NPG · lithograph, *c.*1826, repro. in Beale, ed., *Reminiscences*, facing p. 192 · J. W. Cook, stipple (aged forty-three), BM, NPG · J. W. Cook, stipple (aged eighty-three), BM, NPG · W. Read, stipple, BM, NPG; repro. in *La Belle Assemblée* (1824) [*see illus.*]

Charles Hutton (1737–1823), by Andrew Morton, 1823

Hutton, Charles (1737–1823), mathematician, was born in Newcastle upon Tyne on 14 August 1737, the youngest son of Henry Hutton, an overseer in a local colliery, who died in June 1742; Hutton's mother, Eleanor, married again the same year; her second husband was Francis Fraim (or Frame), who also worked in a colliery, as pit overman. When he was seven Hutton dislocated his right elbow in a street fight; he could not recover the full use of his right arm so was considered unfit for hard labour and, while his brothers were sent to the mine, Hutton went to school. His first teacher was an old Scottish woman who taught in Percy Street, where the Huttons lived. His next teacher was one Mr Robson, who kept a school at Benwell. When the family moved to High Heaton, Hutton went to a school run by Ivison, an Anglican clergyman, in Jesmond, then a village near Newcastle. After a short period in which he worked as a coal cutter in a pit at Long Benton, he was able, about 1756, to take the place of Ivison, who had obtained a curacy at Whitburn. Hutton's income was now higher than the wage that he could earn as a handicapped miner—coal cutters were paid on the basis of the amount of coal they could work and wage notes for September 1755 and March 1756 prove that Hutton was the least productive of the workforce. Notwithstanding his youth, Hutton's tenure at the school in Jesmond was a success, and he had to move the school to Stott's (or Stote's) Hall, a mansion where he could accommodate the increasing number of pupils. In the meantime he attended evening classes in mathematics in a school in Newcastle run by a Mr James. During his residence in Jesmond, Hutton became a follower of the Methodists; he wrote sermons and even preached, but was soon, however, to distance himself from the church.

In 1760 James left, and Hutton moved his school from Jesmond to Newcastle. On 14 April 1760 the opening of Hutton's 'writing and mathematical school' was announced. Hutton established himself as one of the most successful mathematics teachers of the region. His syllabus was orientated towards applied mathematics—bookkeeping, navigation, surveying, dialling, and so on. Pupils at the local grammar school were sent to his mathematical lessons, and among his students was Robert Shafto of Benwell Hall, who made available to Hutton his rich mathematical library. In 1766 Hutton began a course intended for mathematics schoolmasters, to be attended during the

Christmas holidays. This course was probably based on *The Schoolmaster's Guide* (1764), Hutton's first publication. His next work, *Treatise on Mensuration*, was published by subscription (more than 1000 subscribers) in numbers, the last appearing in 1770. Hutton's early works were engraved by Ralph Beilby, whose assistant, Thomas Bewick, who was to become one of the great masters of woodcuts, contributed to the *Treatise*. In 1770 Hutton was asked by the mayor and corporation of Newcastle to prepare a survey of the town. The destruction on 11 November 1771 of several bridges across the Tyne, caused by a flood about 9 feet higher than the usual spring tides, motivated him to study bridge building: in 1772 he published *The Principles of Bridges*.

In 1773 the chair of mathematics at the Royal Military Academy became vacant on the retirement of John Lodge Cowley, and a public examination was held for the election of the new professor: Hutton was appointed on 24 May 1773. His researches centred on the convergence of series, experiments in ballistics, the building of bridges, and measurement of the density of the earth. His elaborate calculations of the mean density of the earth, based on Maskelyne's observations on the deviation of the plumb line close to Mount Schiehallion, Perthshire, were praised by Pierre-Simon Laplace. In 1778, for his papers on the relationships between the 'force' of gunpowder and the velocity of projectiles, he was awarded the Copley medal of the Royal Society, of which he had been elected fellow in 1774.

In 1779 the University of Edinburgh awarded Hutton the degree of doctor of laws, and in the same year he became foreign secretary of the Royal Society. It is not surprising that his publishing career and his teaching at Woolwich did not allow him much time for these additional duties. In 1783, when the council decided that the foreign secretary should reside in London, he was compelled to resign. In fact, his expulsion was engineered by Joseph Banks, president of the Royal Society. A group of Hutton's supporters tried unsuccessfully, in February 1784, to reinstate him as foreign secretary, and then tried to support his candidacy as secretary. When this second attempt failed, Hutton, among other 'mathematicians', resigned from the society. It is a reasonable view that the controversy between Hutton and Banks reflects two different views on the role of mathematicians in the Royal Society, and that this opposition was also determined by the lower social status of the mathematical practitioners in comparison with other members.

From 1771 to 1775 Hutton published in numbers, bound in 1775 in five volumes, an annotated edition of the literary and mathematical parts of the *Ladies' Diary* from the first issue in 1704 to the 1773 issue, and he was the editor of this famous periodical from 1773-4 to 1818. In 1781 and 1785 he published volumes of mathematical tables. In addition, he wrote *A Mathematical and Philosophical Dictionary* (1795-6) and a two-volume *Course of Mathematics* (1798-1801). The *Course* was published in various editions in a period of fifty years: it was even translated into Arabic. The dictionary reveals a deep and extensive knowledge of British and continental works and is still used by historians as a valuable source. The British reader was provided with bibliographical and biographical information on continental mathematicians such as D'Alembert, Euler, and Lagrange. The entries on engineering are particularly valuable, while mechanics, optics, and astronomy are less complete, especially from the point of view of mathematical treatment. Hutton referred very often to Euler with great esteem; the article 'Euler' is very detailed and appreciative. He did not hide his admiration for analytical methods and his belief, at odds with most of his countryfellows, that geometrical constraints are extraneous to research. However, the dictionary did not include technical details of the foreign works. It is revealing that the brief entries for 'differential' and 'integral' referred to 'fluxions' and 'fluents'. The explanation for this last entry went as far as the integration of rational functions, but almost nothing was said about differential equations. In the dictionary the 'new analysis' of the continentals was advocated, but Hutton was unable to convey a detailed idea of it. The second edition contains among its additions a ten-page presentation, written by 'a friend', of Edward Waring's mathematical achievements. From 1803 to 1809 Hutton, together with the physician Richard Pearson and the naturalist George Shaw, worked to the preparation of the abridgement of the *Philosophical Transactions* from 1665 to

1800, in eighteen volumes: from this work he obtained at least £6000.

Hutton's publications guaranteed him a good income and in 1786 he moved into the building business. He built several houses for letting on Shooter's Hill, the hill south of the Thames overlooking Woolwich. He also manufactured bricks and tiles. When the academy was moved from the riverside to the hilltop, the decision was taken to buy Hutton's houses; these were then sold by Hutton to the crown and subsequently converted into official residences for artillery field officers and professors of the academy.

Hutton married first in 1760, 'a hasty and unhappy marriage'. He married again and his second wife died in 1817. From these marriages he had two daughters and at least one son, George Henry Hutton [*see below*]. His second daughter married Henry Vignoles, captain of the 43rd regiment, and, with her husband, died of yellow fever in June 1794 at Guadeloupe, where they were prisoners of war. In July 1807, Hutton, suffering from pulmonary disorders, resigned his professorship and the Board of Ordnance assigned him a pension of £500 per year. He moved to Bedford Row, London, where he died of a severe cold on 27 January 1823. He was buried at St Luke's, Charlton, on 4 February, perhaps alongside his wife, as a Margaret Hutton was buried there on 27 March 1817; his grandson, Charles Henry Hutton, was buried there on 16 February 1815.

Hutton patronized the study of mathematics in several ways: he was influential in the choice of Captain William Mudge as suitable for conducting the trigonometrical survey of England and Wales; he supported the appointment of Francis Bonnycastle, Peter Barlow, Lewis Evans, and Olynthus Gregory at the Royal Military Academy at Woolwich, and the appointment of Edward Riddle at the Trinity House School in Newcastle and at the Naval Hospital in Greenwich; he encouraged and assisted Margaret Bryan in the publication of her *Compendious System of Astronomy* (1797) of which he was one of the subscribers; he financed several institutions in his native Newcastle and subscribed £5 per year to public lectures in the Literary and Philosophical Society of Newcastle; and he supported the Royal Jubilee School and the Protestant Schoolmasters' Association.

Hutton belonged to a group of mathematicians, interested in applied mathematics and open to innovations from the continent, active in the military schools of Woolwich and Sandhurst at the end of the eighteenth and the first decades of the nineteenth century, who prepared the ground for the reformation of British mathematics during the first half of the nineteenth century.

George Henry Hutton (*d.* 1827), only surviving son of Charles Hutton, was appointed second lieutenant in the Royal Artillery in 1777. His early service was in the West Indies where, in action against the French forces who were occupying Guadeloupe, he discovered imprisoned the infant son and nursemaid of his sister and her husband. Hutton was able to free the two and send them back to England. In a later action, a musket ball caused the loss of his right eye, and he was held prisoner of war for about a year, until his exchange in 1796.

Hutton was twice married; his first wife died at Canterbury in 1802 leaving a son, Charles, who died while he was a cadet at the Royal Military Academy. Hutton then married a Miss Barlow of Bath, about 1807, by which time he had been promoted to major, then to lieutenant-colonel, and appointed to command the artillery in Ireland, rising in 1811 to major-general and in 1821 to lieutenant-general. Their only son Henry (1809–1863) graduated BA and MA at Wadham College, Oxford, and was rector of St Paul, Covent Garden, until his death.

George Hutton cultivated a passion for architecture and antiquarian pursuits and was elected fellow of the Society of Antiquaries. He was often resident at Aberdeen, and amassed a sizeable collection of documents and drawings of Scottish ecclesiastical antiquities. He founded bursaries and a prize at the University of Aberdeen, which in 1816 conferred the degree of LLD on him. He died at his residence, Moate, co. Westmeath, Ireland, on 28 June 1827.   NICCOLÒ GUICCIARDINI

Sources G. Howson, *A history of mathematics education in England* (1982), 59–74 • D. P. Miller, 'The revival of the physical sciences in Britain, 1815–1840', *Osiris*, 2nd ser., 2 (1986), 107–34 • O. Gregory, 'Brief memoir of the life and writings of Charles Hutton', *Imperial Magazine*, 5 (1823), 201–27 • J. Bruce, *A memoir of Charles Hutton* (1823) • R. Welford, *Men of mark 'twixt Tyne and Tweed*, 3 vols. (1895) • *Public characters*, 10 vols. (1799–1809), vol. 2. pp. 107–30 • C. Knight, ed., *The English cyclopaedia: biography*, 3 (1856) • W. Johnson, 'Charles Hutton, 1737–1823: the prototypical Woolwich professor of mathematics', *Journal of Mechanical Working Technology*, 18 (1989), 195–230 • J. L. Heilbron, 'A mathematicians' mutiny, with morals', *World changes, Thomas Kuhn and the nature of science*, ed. P. Horwich (1993), 81–129 • I. Grattan-Guinness, 'French calcul and English fluxions around 1800: some comparisons and contrasts', *Jahrbuch Überblicke Mathematik* (1986), 167–78 • *GM*, 1st ser., 97/2 (1827), 561–2 [George Henry Hutton]

Archives Yale U., Farmington, Lewis Walpole Library, catalogue of mathematical library

Likenesses B. Wyon, bronze medal, 1821, NPG; repro. in *Imperial Magazine*, 5 (1823), 201 • S. Gahagan, marble bust, 1822, Literary and Philosophical Society, Newcastle upon Tyne • A. Morton, portrait, 1823, Literary and Philosophical Society, Newcastle upon Tyne [*see illus.*] • stipple, pubd 1823 (after medal by B. Wyon), BM • J. Thomson, stipple (after S. Gahagan), BM, NPG; repro. in *European Magazine* (1823) • C. Turner, print (after H. Ashby), BM, NPG; repro. in C. Hutton, *Tracts on mathematical and philosophical subjects* (1812) • portraits, Newcastle City Library

Hutton, Christopher William Clayton (1893–1965), intelligence officer and inventor, was born at 102 Willow Road, Birmingham, on 16 November 1893, the son of Christopher Hutton, brass manufacturer, and his wife, Edith Eliza, *née* Clayton. He had a sister. His uncle and godfather William Clayton ran a large timber business on the outskirts of Birmingham at Saltley, where he worked on leaving school. Aged nineteen he bet Houdini the escaper £100 that the latter could not get out of a box built by one of his uncle's workmen; Houdini bribed the workman and won the bet.

Hutton had a variegated First World War. An early attempt to enter the Royal Flying Corps and learn to fly failed. On Boxing day 1914 he was commissioned into the South Lancashire regiment, but stayed with its 8th battalion for only a few months before transferring into the Northumberland Fusiliers, where he served with the 25th battalion (2nd Tyneside Irish) for most of 1915 before transferring again, into the Yorkshire regiment. By March 1916 he was a captain in its 13th battalion and three months later became adjutant of its 15th (reserve) battalion. Almost at once, he was yet again posted, this time to be captain and adjutant of the 10th battalion of the training reserve, which had over a hundred battalions. He remained in the *Army List* at this rank until the end of the war; but he did manage, still as a captain, to talk his way into the Royal Air Force on its formation in April 1918. After two months' administration he passed pilot training, and served briefly at Salonika. He was demobilized in January 1919.

Between the wars Hutton held a variety of jobs, none of them for long, save that he was a reporter for some years on the *Daily Chronicle*. He tried living in Berlin; he tried film; he tried advertising; nothing seemed to last. Nevertheless, early in the war against Hitler he found his niche, thanks to the accident that someone remembered the Houdini affair. After a brief interview he was appointed to help Norman Crockatt set up a new semi-secret service, MI9, whose tasks included training fighting men in how to evade capture or escape if they found themselves in enemy-held territory. Hutton (known to his colleagues as Clutty) was to provide them with any devices they might need. He was recommissioned in May 1940, this time as a captain on the general list of the army; was promoted major in 1943; and was then allowed to retire into plain clothes, which suited his work better.

Hutton quickly saw the need for maps, and secured their printing on silk—which does not rustle—so that they could be hidden in uniforms. He devised and secured miniature compasses, hidden in buttons, studs, tobacco pipes, pen tops, and so on; over two and a quarter million of these were issued. He worked out a plastic box full of food and devices, including a rubber water-bottle, water purifying tablets, and benzedrine tablets to provide extra energy. He thought up a pack of playing cards, which when dropped into water revealed a fifty-two-part detailed map, for example of the frontier between Switzerland and Germany. Code messages exchanged by post with prisoner-of-war camps enabled him to warn prisoners how to secure the goods he sent them. Parcels he supervised also included blankets which, when soaked, were marked out for conversion into civilian overcoats: a useful escaper's device in winter.

By 1941 no aircrew left Britain for an operational flight over Europe, and no commando went on a raid, without having at least an escape box with him. Similar facilities were provided for the United States air forces. Hutton managed to get all this done in the teeth of every sort of shortage of materials, and of much bureaucratic obstruction. He was often in hot water with police and with supply authorities of various kinds, but was unreservedly backed by Crockatt. A cartoon sketch of MI9 staff, *c*.1941, showed Hutton with sparse straight hair, a clean-shaven oval face, and RAF wings.

After the war, short as always of money, Hutton wrote a book about his wartime experiences to match all the stories about escapes he had seen in the newspapers. To his surprise he encountered difficulties with the security authorities, always nervous about revelations by former members of secret or semi-secret services. After eight years' official obstruction, *Official Secret* eventually came out in 1960, and went into paperback two years later. By that time he had retired to Ashburton, on the eastern side of Dartmoor; he died at the Royal Devon and Exeter Hospital, Exeter, of a brain haemorrhage, on 3 September 1965. He was buried in Devon.   M. R. D. FOOT

Sources C. Hutton, *Official secret* (1960) · M. R. D. Foot and J. M. Langley, *MI9* (1980) · D. M. Green, *From Colditz in code* (1971) · *Army List* (1914–19) · *Army List* (1940–44) · *Daily Telegraph* (7 Sept 1965) · permanent display of escape devices, RAF Museum, Hendon · private information (2004) [J. M. Langley *et al.*] · b. cert. · d. cert.
Archives PRO, WO 208 · Royal Air Force Museum, Hendon, permanent display of escape devices
Likenesses group portrait, caricature, *c.*1941 (with staff of MI9), priv. coll.
Wealth at death £2021: probate, 1965, *CGPLA Eng. & Wales*

Hutton, Sir Edward Thomas Henry (1848–1923), army officer and military reformer, was born on 6 December 1848 at Torquay, Devon, the only son of Edward Thomas Hutton (d. 1849), a banker, and his wife, Jacintha Charlotte, the daughter of the Revd J. P. Eyre. He was educated at Eton College from 1864 and in 1867 he joined the 60th rifles. From 1879 to 1885 he was on active duty in Africa and took part in the Anglo-Zulu War (1879), the First South African War (1880–81), the occupation of Egypt (1882), and the Nile expedition (1884–5). He was impressed by the Boers' use of mounted infantry, and later became the leading authority on this form of cavalry in the British army. Following reports he sent to the War Office, he was given responsibility for raising and training mounted infantry at Aldershot (1888–92), where he worked out the strategical and tactical principles for this new mobile force.

On 1 June 1889 Hutton married, at St Paul's, Knightsbridge, Eleanor Mary, the daughter of the Revd Lord Charles Paulet and the niece of Field Marshal Lord William Paulet. Three years later he was promoted colonel and made aide-de-camp to Queen Victoria.

At the height of his career Curly Hutton commanded the military forces of New South Wales (1893–6), Canada (1898–9), and Australia (1902–4), all of which were composed primarily of militia. Associated with the Wolseley ring, he was committed to modernizing and reforming the army, and under his energetic leadership in all these appointments a systematic organization was adopted, discipline was improved, and education and training were encouraged. With the support of the War Office and the Colonial Office, he also sought to instil an imperial spirit in the troops and to persuade the Australians and Canadians to see the defence of the empire as the joint responsibility of the mother country and those he called 'Our Comrades in Greater Britain' (*Evening News*, 28 Nov 1896).

At the same time Hutton's sense of mission and impatience with colonial politicians caused much friction. Shortly after arriving in Sydney he criticized the government of Sir George Dibbs for reducing defence expenditure and made speeches looking forward to the day when the colonial forces would be fighting with imperial forces. This brought a rebuke from the New South Wales premier, who declared that the commandant had 'come here with a lot of strong Imperial opinions, and he has to learn that things in the colony have to be done in a far different style' (Mordike, 35). In Canada he encountered even greater opposition, which after he tried to manoeuvre the Ottawa government into offering a contingent for the Second South African War, forced his resignation in 1899.

In the following year Hutton was appointed KCMG, and the War Office promoted him to the substantive rank of major-general and sent him to South Africa, where he commanded with much success a brigade of mounted infantry that included Canadians, Australians, and New Zealanders. The experience confirmed his view that these troops were particularly suited for such a military role, and that the empire should be able to draw on the dominions' resources for the common defence. He hoped that the co-operation exhibited in the Second South African War would 'go far towards bringing forward that consolidation of the Empire … which in some crisis not far distant perhaps will prove the salvation of the mother country and her children' (Hutton to Eleanor Hutton, 7 April 1900, NL Aust. 1215).

In January 1902 Hutton arrived in Australia to take command of the federation's military forces. He welded the six colonial organizations into one national body, which initially comprised almost 30,000 men—1730 permanent and 28,000 militia. Though the colonial secretary, Joseph Chamberlain, had told him that he was the servant of the Australian government, the British authorities expected him to use his position to advance the imperial cause. Thus in his minute of April 1902 setting out the basis for a defence scheme he argued that the federal army should be divided into two parts, a garrison force to protect ports and fixed defences and a mobile field force which could be sent wherever Australian interests might be threatened. Aware of the dominion's sensibilities, Hutton had moved with a certain cunning to compass his ends. He wrote to the Colonial Office, 'I have been careful to leave the deductions to be drawn as to what is really comprised under this head "Australian interests"; the keynote is a "Co-operative System of Defence"' (Meaney, 60–61). In the event, however, Hutton failed in his object. The Defence Act of 1904 refused to allow the government to compel any military forces to serve outside Australian territory. Though insensitive in his ambition, Hutton was nevertheless dedicated to his profession.

In 1907 Hutton was made lieutenant-general, and five years later he was appointed KCB. With the onset of the First World War he was brought out of retirement and given charge of the 21st division of the Third Army, but in April 1915, as a result of an illness brought on by a hunting accident, was compelled to surrender his command. He died at his home, Fox Hills, Chertsey, Surrey, on 4 August 1923 and was buried on 9 August according to Anglican rites at Lyne village, near Chertsey. He was survived by his wife. There were no children of the marriage.

NEVILLE MEANEY

Sources N. Meaney, *The search for security in the Pacific* (1976) • J. Mordike, *An army for a nation: a history of Australian military developments, 1880–1914* (1992) • R. Preston, *Canada and 'imperial defense': a study of the origins of the British Commonwealth's defense organization, 1867–1919* (1967) • *The Times* (6 Aug 1923) • *The Times* (10 Aug 1923) • E. Hutton, *The defence and defensive power of Australia* (1902) • W. Perry, 'Military reforms in the colony of New South Wales, 1893–96: the work of the commandant, Major-General E. T. H. Hutton', 1996, Mitchell L., NSW, MLMSS 6114 • W. S. Hamer, *The British army: civil–military relations, 1885–1905* (1970) • A. J. Hill, 'Hutton, Sir Edward Thomas Henry', *AusDB*, vol. 9 • BL, Hutton MSS, Add. MSS 50078–50114

Archives BL, official, military, and personal corresp. and papers, Add. MSS 50078–50114 • NL Aus., corresp. and press cuttings | Mitchell L., NSW, Parkes MSS • NA Canada, corresp. with Sir George Parkin • NL Aus., letters to second Baron Tennyson • NL Scot., letters to fourth earl of Minto

Likenesses Freeman & Co. Ltd, photograph, 1895, Mitchell L., NSW • T. Roberts, oils, 1896, Victoria Barracks, Sydney • T. Roberts, oils, 1912, Royal Military College, Duntroon, Australia

Wealth at death £6926 19s. 3d.: probate, 29 Sept 1923, *CGPLA Eng. & Wales*

Hutton, Frederick Wollaston (1836–1905), geologist and zoologist, was born on 16 November 1836 at Gate Burton, Lincolnshire, the second son of the Revd Henry Frederick Hutton and his wife, Louisa, daughter of the Revd Henry John Wollaston of Scotter, Lincolnshire. He was educated at the Revd L. Fletcher's Grammar School in Southwell, Nottinghamshire, and at the Royal Navy Academy, Gosport. In 1851 he failed to secure a place in the navy because he was over the stipulated age of fourteen, and instead joined the India mercantile marine. In 1854 he enrolled at King's College, London, but the following year he joined the Royal Welch Fusiliers, serving in the Crimea, India during the mutiny, Malta, England, and Ireland. During a period at Sandhurst in 1860–61 he studied geology and worked with the geological survey in southern England. On 4 February 1863 he married Annie Gouger (1844/5–1916), sixth daughter of Dr William Montgomerie, former superintendent surgeon of the Bengal medical service of the East India Company, and his wife, Elizabeth Graham.

Hutton retired from the army in November 1865 with the rank of captain, a title he retained for the rest of his life, and early in 1866 emigrated to New Zealand, arriving at Auckland in June that year. Unable to obtain permanent employment in geology in Auckland, he engaged in sheep farming and flax milling but with little financial success. In 1871 Hutton did obtain a scientific position, as assistant geologist in the New Zealand geological survey, and he moved to Wellington. His three years or so in Wellington were the most active and productive of his career.

In October 1873 Hutton took up the position of provincial geologist of Otago and at the same time was appointed curator of the provincial museum and lecturer in geology at the university. On 15 February 1877 he was appointed professor of natural science but three years later he

made his final move—to Christchurch—which proved to his liking. He worked there for the remaining twenty-five years of his life, as professor of biology until 1892 and then as curator of the museum until his death in 1905.

Hutton was distinguished in both geology and zoology and it was as a systematist that he made his main contribution, publishing manuals on a large number of animal groups. As a field geologist he was less competent than his contemporaries, Julius von Haast (1822–1887) and James Hector (1834–1907), but he was their superior in the laboratory and lecture hall. He can rightly be called the father of New Zealand zoology and in the geology laboratory he was the pioneer in petrology and palaeontology. Hutton was however, more than a systematist; again in contrast to both Haast and Hector, he was both scientist and philosopher. In the last fifteen years of his life he was the leader of scientific thought in New Zealand and gave much consideration to the fundamental questions of natural science. He had a lifelong interest in evolution. Indeed, his first paper was 'Some remarks on Mr. Darwin's Theory', published in *The Geologist* in 1861. It showed such an understanding of both the virtues and limitations of the theory that it drew an appreciative letter from Darwin.

Although Hutton's military background made him stiff and formal towards his classes, he was a successful teacher. His lectures were clear and he had the ability of imparting his own enthusiasm to his students. His contribution to New Zealand scientific literature comprised over 600 varied books, papers, catalogues, addresses, and newspaper articles. However, his writings were often controversial and many were merely destructive criticism of other opinions. Throughout his forty years in the country Hutton was active in the New Zealand Institute, its premier scientific body. Uniquely he successively held office in branches of the institute in all four of the main cities. A long-time critic of Hector's management of the institute, Hutton was one of the architects of its reconstruction in 1903 and he became its first elected president. His service to it is commemorated in the Hutton memorial medal and the Hutton research grants. Hutton was elected FGS in 1860, corresponding member of the Zoological Society of London in 1872, and FRS in 1892. In 1904 he was made a life member of the Australasian Association for the Advancement of Science.

Hutton was of medium build, with good bearing, and has been described as gentle, courteous, and amiable, yet he did not always have a smooth relationship with his associates. In 1905 he and his wife returned to England for the first time, but he died during the return journey, on 27 October 1905, and was buried at sea off Cape Town. His wife continued to live in Christchurch until her death on 30 June 1916, aged seventy-one. She was survived by their three sons and three daughters.

ALAN MASON

Sources E. W. Dawson, 'F. W. Hutton, 1836–1905, pioneer New Zealand naturalist', *Occasional Papers of the Hutton Foundation New Zealand*, 5 (1994) [contains bibliography] • S. H. Jenkinson, *New Zealanders and science* (1940), 60–69 • P. Burton, *The New Zealand geological survey, 1865–1965* (1965), 19–20, 32, 35 • H. F. von Haast, *The life and times of Sir Julius von Haast* (1948), 665–73 • C. A. Fleming, *Science,* *settlers, and scholars* (1987), 131–2 • A. Wall, *Long and happy: an autobiography* (1965), 91 • G. M. Thomson, 'Biographical notices II—Frederick Wollaston Hutton', *New Zealand Journal of Science*, 2 (1885), 301–6 • C. Chilton, *PRS*, 79B (1907), xli–xliv • J. D. Campbell, 'F. W. Hutton in Otago', *Geological Society of New Zealand Historical Studies Group Newsletter*, 9 (1994), 15–19 • D. R. Oldroyd, 'Geology in New Zealand prior to 1900', MSc diss., U. Lond., 1967, 11–12, 163–73, 271–4, 277–8

Archives Canterbury Museum, Christchurch, New Zealand | National Museum of New Zealand, Wellington, Colonial Museum • NL NZ, Turnbull L. • University of Otago, Dunedin, Hocken Library, Hector MSS

Likenesses W. A. Sutton, portrait (after R. Wallwork), Royal Society of New Zealand Science House, Wellington • R. Wallwork, portrait, University of Canterbury, New Zealand, zoology department • photograph, National Museum of New Zealand, Wellington • photograph, NL NZ, Turnbull L. • photograph, Auckland Museum, Finn scrapbook

Hutton, George Clark (1825–1908), Free Church of Scotland minister, born at Perth on 16 May 1825, was the eldest of twelve children, of whom only three outlived childhood. His father, George Hutton, a teacher and a strong Secessionist, taught at a private school in Perth, took an active interest in deaf mute people, and invented a sign language; another of his children, James Scott *Hutton, became principal of the Deaf and Dumb Institution, Halifax, Nova Scotia. George's mother, Ann Scott, came of a Cromarty family. Hutton, who received his early education from his father, was for a time a teacher, and at the age of fifteen had sole charge of a school near Perth. In October 1843 he entered Edinburgh University, where he won prizes for Latin and Greek, the gold medal for moral philosophy under John Wilson (Christopher North), and three prizes for rhetoric, one for a poem, 'Wallace in the Tower', which his professor, W. E. Aytoun, caused to be printed.

Hutton entered the Divinity Hall of the United Secession church, Edinburgh, in July 1846, was licensed to preach by the presbytery of Edinburgh on 5 January 1851, and on 9 September of the same year was ordained and inducted as minister of Canal Street United Presbyterian Church, Paisley. There he remained for the rest of his life, celebrating his ministerial jubilee on 21 October 1901. He married, on 16 May 1853, Margaret Hill; they had five children and she died in 1893.

Hutton was an able evangelical preacher and a capable exponent of traditional theology, but he was mainly known throughout his life as an obsessive anti-establishmentarian. In 1858 he joined the Society for the Liberation of Religion from State Patronage and Control, and from 1868 until death was a member of its executive. He was the chief spokesman of a branch of the society formed in Scotland in 1871, and in 1886 helped to form the disestablishment council for Scotland. From 1872 to 1890 he was the convener of a disestablishment committee of the synod of the United Presbyterian church, which encouraged his increasingly strident views. He spoke in support of disestablishment in tours through Scotland, and urged his views not merely in pamphlets, and in the press but also privately to Gladstone. On his representations the Teinds (Scotland) Bill in 1880 was dropped by the government. In 1883 Hutton was mainly responsible for drafting an abortive bill for the disestablishment and disendowment of the Church of Scotland, which John Dick Peddie, MP for Kilmarnock burghs, introduced into the House of Commons. To Hutton's pertinacity may be partly attributed Gladstone's support of a motion for Scottish disestablishment in the House of Commons in 1890. When in January 1893 Gladstone's government announced a measure to prevent the creation of vested interests in the established churches of Wales and Scotland, Hutton wrote urging the substitution of a final measure for the suspensory bill. On 25 August Gladstone gave a somewhat evasive reply to a deputation from the disestablishment council, who pressed the government to accept Sir Charles Cameron's Scottish disestablishment bill. With Gladstone's resignation in March 1894 legislative action was arrested. Gladstone's cautious attitude to the Scottish disestablishment question disappointed Hutton, but friendly relations continued between them, and in May 1895 he was invited to Hawarden, and was cordially received.

Hutton also promoted temperance and educational legislation. In regard to education, he held strongly that a state system must be entirely secular. He strenuously opposed the provision in the Education Bill of 1872 for the continuance of 'use and wont' in regard to religious teaching. In 1873 he was elected a member of Paisley school board; he lost his seat in 1876, but served again from 1879 to 1882.

Hutton exerted a dominant influence on the affairs of the United Presbyterian church in the years preceding its union in 1900 with the Free Church. He represented his church at the pan-Presbyterian council at Philadelphia in 1880 and at Toronto in 1892. In 1884 he was moderator of synod, in 1890 he became convener of the synod's business committee, and in 1892 principal of the theological hall of his church, succeeding Dr John Cairns. He gave only qualified supporter to first negotiations for the amalgamation of the Free and United Presbyterian churches (1863–1873), and when the negotiations were resumed in 1896 and were brought to a successful issue in 1900, he did not favour an early union. Union seemed to him to endanger the cause of disestablishment, but he finally accepted the assurance that in the united church there would be no attempt to limit the expression of his 'voluntary' opinions. Once the union was accomplished he became one of its most enthusiastic champions and was co-principal with G. C. Monteath Douglas of the United Free Church college, Glasgow, until 1902. In 1906 he was elected moderator of the general assembly of the United Free Church in succession to Robert Rainy. True to the last to his 'voluntary' principles, he unflinchingly opposed the movement for a reunion of the established and United Free churches, and his final words in the general assembly of his church, on 27 May 1908, resisted a proposal of conference on the subject from the established church. He died two days later, on 29 May 1908, in his hotel at Edinburgh, and was buried in Woodside cemetery, Paisley.

Hutton was a born controversialist—trenchant, argumentative, and sometimes obsessive—with an intense belief in the spiritual mission of the church and the need of freeing it of civil ties. His opinions made him unpopular with a large and influential section of his countrymen. In his later years there was little enthusiasm for his cause, even in his own church, where attendance markedly declined. He failed to show the Liberal leadership that the Scots as a nation wanted disestablishment.

W. F. GRAY, rev. H. C. G. MATTHEW

Sources A. Oliver, *Life of G. C. Hutton* (1910) · P. C. Simpson, *The life of Principal Rainy*, 2 vols. (1909) · A. L. Drummond and J. Bulloch, *The church in late Victorian Scotland* (1978) · Gladstone, *Diaries*
Archives BL, letters to W. E. Gladstone, Add. MSS 44444–44526, *passim*
Likenesses G. Reid, oils, 1901, United Free Church assembly hall, Edinburgh
Wealth at death £3920 11s.: confirmation, 30 July 1908, CCI

Hutton, George Henry (d. 1827). *See under* Hutton, Charles (1737–1823).

Hutton, Henry (d. 1671), satirist, can almost certainly be identified as the Henry Hutton born at Durham, fifth son of Edward Hutton BCL, bailiff to the bishop of Durham, and his wife, Anne, daughter of Francis Lascelles of Allesthorpe in Yorkshire. His father had matriculated at Cambridge as a sizar in 1573; in 1613 Henry Hutton also went to Cambridge, matriculating from St John's College as a pensioner at Easter 1613. According to Anthony Wood (Wood, *Ath. Oxon.*, 2.277), the poet at some point studied at Oxford, but 'minding more the smooth parts of poetry and romance than logic, departed, as it seems, without a degree'; no archival trace remains to confirm Wood's story. On 1 November 1616 Henry Hutton was admitted to study at Gray's Inn, with which there were strong family connections. In 1619 he published *Follie's Anatomie, or, Satyres and Satyricall Epigrams* and in the same year he took his BA at Cambridge. There then follows a period in which nothing can be said about his movements.

On 4 August 1635 Hutton was appointed as curate of Witton Gilbert, outside Durham. In 1638–9, he executed the will of his brother Ralphe Hutton; in 1641 he and his churchwardens signed the parliamentary protestation; and he remained in office at Witton Gilbert until his death in 1671. He was buried on 24 April 1671 at Witton Gilbert. About his widow, Margery (d. 1674), and their four sons and three daughters, very little is known.

Follie's Anatomie, Hutton's one known publication, falls into three main sections, divided up by dedicatory poems which include one from a 'kinsman', R. H., and one to Sir Timothy Hutton of Marske, Yorkshire, son of the archbishop of York. The author is identified at the end as 'Henry Hutton, Dunelmensis'. The first part is a series of pen portraits of satirical types; the second, a collection of sixty short satirical epigrams; the third, 'Ixion's Wheel', a strange comic epyllion in pentameters rhyming ABABCC which tells the story of Ixion's crime and punishment. Hutton's work is interesting for its ear for legal terms and slang and its intense topicality of reference; the satires show this off rather better than the stilted satirical epigrams.

One H. Hutton prefixed commendatory verses to the 1647 edition of Thomas Fuller's *The Historie of the Holy Warre* (sig. A5v), and has been identified as the satirist, but this seems unlikely. MATTHEW STEGGLE

Sources *Follie's anatomie, or, Satyres and satyricall epigrams by Henry Hutton*, ed. E. F. Rimbault (1842) · H. M. Wood, ed., *Durham protestations*, SurtS, 135 (1922), 3 · [H. M. Wood], ed., *Wills and inventories from the registry at Durham*, 4, SurtS, 142 (1929), 280–81 · Wood, *Ath. Oxon.*, new edn, 2.277 · Venn, *Alum. Cant.*, 1/2.442 · J. Foster, *The register of admissions to Gray's Inn, 1521–1889, together with the register of marriages in Gray's Inn chapel, 1695–1754* (privately printed, London, 1889), 142

Hutton, Isabel Galloway Emslie [*née* Isabel Galloway Emslie], **Lady Hutton** (1887–1960), physician specializing in mental disorders and social worker, was born in Edinburgh, the eldest daughter of James Emslie, advocate and deputy keeper of the privy seal of Scotland. She was educated at Edinburgh Ladies' College and Edinburgh University, training in the women's medical school with hospital years at Edinburgh Royal Infirmary. She graduated in medicine in 1910 and gained her MD in 1912 with a thesis on the Wasserman reaction to the test for syphilis in the blood and cerebro-spinal fluid of the insane. The thesis, undertaken during her first appointment as pathologist at the Stirling District Asylum at Larbert, was concerned with the condition known as general paralysis of the insane, and marked the first step in Emslie's growing interest in the study and treatment of mental and nervous disorders. Still in Edinburgh she then moved to the Royal Sick Children's Hospital before becoming the first woman to be appointed physician in charge of the women's side of the Royal Mental Hospital, Morningside.

In August 1915 Emslie joined the Scottish Women's Hospitals Organisation, a voluntary body whose services were welcomed by the French, Russian, and Serbian governments. She was posted first to France, and then with the Armée d'Orient to Salonika. She commanded the unit which accompanied the Serbian army in its victorious advance in 1918, caring for the soldiers and their prisoners, as well as the local population as they succumbed to various epidemics. She herself undertook the necessary surgical procedures. When the Serbian hospital closed Emslie took over Lady Muriel Paget's mission, which was serving in the Crimea on the Russian side. One of the last to leave the field, she brought a number of orphaned children to Constantinople and played a significant role in organizing relief for the Russian refugees. Her account of these years, *With a Woman's Unit in Serbia, Salonika and Sebastopol* (1928), was praised in *The Times* (23 November 1928, 11c) for its shrewd comments on political and economic aspects of the region and for its lively descriptions of Serbian and Russian customs.

In Constantinople, Emslie had met Major Thomas Hutton, eldest son of W. H. Hutton of Clevedon; Hutton had been commissioned into the Royal Artillery in 1909. On return to Edinburgh in 1920 she was reinstated in her former post, but resigned at her marriage in 1921 to Hutton, then on a posting at the Staff College, Camberley. There were no children of the marriage. Thereafter she adopted the name of Emslie Hutton, and on moving to London obtained a temporary research post at the Maudsley Hospital, which resulted in a joint paper with Sir Frederick Mott as well as honorary consultancies at the Maudsley and at the West End Hospital for Nervous Diseases (then at the British Hospital for Nervous and Mental Diseases). She drew on this experience to publish *Mental Disorders in Modern Life* (1940). The intervening summer of 1925 was spent in Albania on an anti-malarial mission sent by Elizabeth, countess of Carnarvon.

Although her own qualifications and determination carried Emslie Hutton onward and upward throughout her career, she was sensitive to the penalties which most of her female colleagues paid on marriage. In 1928 she wrote a long and passionate letter to *The Times* (26 March 1928, 12c), regretting the universal dismissal of medically qualified women as soon as they married, and the way in which women were ignored as candidates for honorary positions. Women were not barred in many foreign countries, and to ignore them was a dreadful waste of trained and eager women.

Emslie Hutton's affection for sick children led her to take responsibility for the Ellen Terry Home for blind and mentally handicapped children at Reigate; and finding nothing written on the care of such children she wrote a treatise which, however, was not published. She gave up this responsibility in 1938 when Hutton was posted to India, following him to make their home in Quetta. Her offers of medical help were initially rejected, and she turned to charity work, broadcasting, and translating secret dispatches for the external affairs department. Eventually she accepted the post of director of the Indian Red Cross welfare service. Hutton was in command in Burma at the time of the Japanese invasion in 1941; he returned to India and retired from the army in 1944, when the order of KCIE was conferred on him in June. He held a civilian post until he and his wife returned to England in 1946. Lady Hutton was appointed CBE in 1948.

Now senior consultant psychiatrist at the British Hospital, Emslie Hutton served one year beyond the normal age for retirement, and was thereafter consultant emeritus. She was elected fellow of the Royal School of Medicine and was a member of the Royal Medico-Physical Association; she was awarded the French Croix de Guerre, and decorated by Serbia and Russia. She enjoyed the cultural life of London, being a member of the Mercury Theatre ballet club and a lover of art and theatre. She wrote books on married life seen from the woman's viewpoint, then a somewhat delicate subject, and contributed to medical journals, and latterly wrote an autobiography, *Memories of a Doctor in War and Peace* (1960). She died on 11 January 1960 at her home, 5 Spanish Place, St Marylebone, London. Queen Marie of Yugoslavia, and representatives of other nations and groups to which she had devoted so much of her energy were represented at her funeral, held in London on 15 January at St Columba's Church of Scotland, Pont Street.

ANITA McCONNELL

Sources I. Hutton, *Memories of a doctor in war and peace* (1960) · *The Times* (12 Jan 1960) · *The Times* (15 Jan 1960), 14c · *BMJ* (30 Jan 1960), 353–4 · *The Lancet* (23 Jan 1960), 231–2 · *The Times* (20 Jan 1981), 16f–h · *WWW* · d. cert. · *CGPLA Eng. & Wales* (1960)

Wealth at death £35,226 12s. 4d.: probate, 12 April 1960, *CGPLA Eng. & Wales*

Hutton, James (1715–1795), Moravian minister and bookseller, was born on 3 September 1715 in College Street, Westminster, the son of John Hutton (*bap.* 1676, *d.* 1750), a nonjuring clergyman who took in Westminster School boarders, and his wife, Elizabeth, *née* Ayscough (*d.* 1752). Educated at Westminster School and apprenticed to the bookseller William Innys in 1731, he opened a bookshop at the Bible and Sun in Little Wild Street, London, in 1736.

In 1735 Hutton met the Wesleys, was 'awakened' by them, and, unable (as an apprentice) to accompany them to Georgia, saw them off at Gravesend. He read the journal which John Wesley sent him to the Methodist religious societies, collected money for the poor, and founded a new society, which in 1737 was swollen in numbers by George Whitefield's preaching. It was in Hutton's bookshop home that on 1 May 1738 Peter Böhler established a Moravian-style band, Hutton being one of nine founder members. This quickly grew into the Fetter Lane Society, which became the headquarters of the English evangelical revival, with Hutton its pivotal figure. From April to October 1739 Hutton visited the Moravians in Marienborn and Herrnhut, Germany. He married the Swiss Moravian Louise Brandt (1709–1778) in Marienborn on 3 July 1740—an arranged marriage which proved very happy, although their five children died in infancy. That month the Wesleys withdrew from the society, Hutton having failed before leaving London to restrain their opponents from making inflammatory statements. In March 1741 Whitefield, too, broke with Hutton, his London publisher, for refusing to publish two pamphlets by Whitefield with which he disagreed.

In August 1741 Hutton was elected first president of the Fetter Lane Society, now controlled by Moravians, but owing to business commitments served as one of two stewards. When the London Moravian congregation was established in October 1742 the Huttons were appointed its wardens. Recognition as joint Moravian leader in England in July 1743 did not last, but Hutton was frequently the only Englishman in the provincial conference. Until 1749, when he was ordained deacon on 19 September, he remained a bookseller, based from 1745 in Fetter Lane, and published the Moravians' English publications. He visited the continent for synods and conferences, and differed from Zinzendorf, the Moravian leader, in advocating public dissent from the Church of England (to which he was hostile by 1743) and Moravian sponsorship of evangelistic preaching. Abroad from 1747 to 1749, the Huttons made an extended visit to Switzerland.

James Hutton (1715–1795), by John Raphael Smith, pubd 1786 (after Richard Cosway)

Hutton's parental home in College Street, Westminster, was Zinzendorf's headquarters from 1751 until 1753, when his household, which included the Huttons, moved to Lindsey House, Chelsea. In May 1752 Hutton was appointed secretary of the Unity (Moravian church). He responded to anti-Moravian tracts with advertisements (1754–5) and *An Essay towards Giving some Just Ideas of the Personal Character of Count Zinzendorff* (1755), and edited Zinzendorf's two-volume *Exposition* (1755). When Zinzendorf left England in March 1755 the Huttons accompanied him to Herrnhut.

In September 1756 the Huttons returned to Switzerland to consolidate Moravian work in the French-speaking area and strengthen relations with French protestantism. As an educated bookseller, Hutton mixed easily with people of all classes and made influential friends. Although now deaf, he led worship in Basel. As in England a decade earlier, Hutton questioned the Moravians' 'too great fear of proselytizing' (Reichel, 108). After Zinzendorf's death in 1760 the church's directory sought an even lower profile, but in 1763 Hutton, who was already disaffected, became involved in Genevan politics. He was recalled and sent to England to sort out various financial affairs.

Back in Lindsey House, the Huttons' relations with the German provincial leaders were cool and, forbidden to be active in English Moravian life, they felt obliged to avoid contact with English members. Hutton was distressed by the leadership's apparent lack of confidence, further evidenced by a request to convey Lindsey House and estates in North Carolina, which he owned on the church's behalf, to German Moravians. Relations improved after

Benjamin La Trobe became provincial leader in 1768, however, and in the 1770s Hutton occasionally conducted worship—especially children's services—in Fetter Lane. He attended the 1764 and 1769 general synods, and was acting provincial leader during that of 1775.

In 1765–6 Hutton revived the Society for the Furtherance of the Gospel, of which he had been a founder member in 1741, and was chairman when he died. His *Letter to a Friend* (1769) described its history and work supporting Moravian missions. Hutton's contacts and friendships with influential people (some dating from schooldays) benefited his church, and he played a key part in negotiations which in 1769 secured a grant of land for a mission in Labrador.

From 1773 Hutton became friends with Charles and Fanny Burney, and between 1775 and 1780 was a royal favourite, frequently visiting the king and queen. With the king's permission, in January 1778 he visited his old friend Benjamin Franklin in France to request terms for peace with the American colonies. Gregarious, affectionate, principled, and eccentric, Hutton, with his old wig and shabby clothes, was by now a well-known character. Hannah More mentions 'Hutton the Moravian' among the aristocrats, diplomats, and celebrities she encountered at a party in 1778 (*Early Diary*, 1.305). In 1784 Hutton was painted, with his ear-trumpet, by Richard Cosway—an excellent likeness.

From about 1775 the Huttons lived in Queen's Row, Pimlico; after Louise's death on 10 November 1778 the philosopher John Andrew de Luc was Hutton's companion there. Ever generous, Hutton gave to the needy instead of buying new clothes. Through charitable activity he met two sisters, Misses Biscoe and Shelley, who by November 1791 had taken him into their home, Oxted Cottage, near Godstone, Surrey. There he died on 3 May 1795. He was buried in the Moravian burial-ground in Chelsea on 11 May.   C. J. PODMORE

Sources D. Benham, *Memoirs of James Hutton* (1856) · C. J. Podmore, *The Moravian church in England, 1728–1760* (1998) · H. Reichel, 'Die Anfänge der Brüdergemeine in der Schweiz mit besonderer Berücksichtigung der Sozietät in Basel', *Unitas Fratrum*, 29/30 (1991), 9–127 · *GM*, 1st ser., 65 (1795), 552–3 · *The early diary of Frances Burney, 1768–1778*, ed. A. R. Ellis, rev. edn, 1 (1907) · *The early journals and letters of Fanny Burney*, ed. L. E. Troide, 2: 1774–1777 (1990) · *The letters of Dr Charles Burney*, ed. A. Ribeiro, 1 (1991) · *The correspondence of King George the Third from 1760 to December 1783*, ed. J. Fortescue, 3 (1928); repr. (1967) · *Diary and letters of Madame D'Arblay*, ed. [C. Barrett], new edn, 5 (1854) · *The last journals of Horace Walpole*, ed. Dr Doran, rev. A. F. Steuart, 2 (1910) · D. F. McKenzie, ed., *Stationers' Company apprentices*, [3]: 1701–1800 (1978) · *Old Westminsters*, vol. 1 · R. Green, *The works of John and Charles Wesley: a bibliography*, 2nd edn (1906) · *DNB* · *IGI* · JRL, Eng. MS 1069

Archives Moravian Church House, London, corresp. · NL Wales, letters | JRL, letters to Miss Cooper · Unitätsarchiv, Herrnhut, Germany

Likenesses J. V. Haidt?, oils, 1740–1749?, Unitätsarchiv, Herrnhut, Germany; repro. in Reichel, 'Anfänge der Brudergemeine' · R. Cosway, oils, 1784, probably Moravian Church House, London · J. R. Smith, mezzotint, pubd 1786 (after R. Cosway), BM, NPG [*see illus.*] · W. Dickes, engraving (after R. Cosway), repro. in Benham, *Memoirs of James Hutton* · J. R. Smith, mezzotint, copy, Unitätsarchiv, Herrnhut, Germany

Wealth at death seemingly income from houses in Westminster for lifetime: will in Benham, *Memoirs of James Hutton*, 550–53

Hutton, James (1726–1797), geologist, was born in Edinburgh on 3 June 1726, the younger son of William Hutton (*d.* 1729), a prosperous merchant, and Sarah (*b.* 1698), daughter of John Balfour of Braidwood, Edinburghshire, merchant, and his wife, Elizabeth. Hutton's life spanned the greatest years of the Scottish Enlightenment and, of its number, only Joseph Black made a greater contribution to science. The principal source of information about his life is the masterly biography by Professor John Playfair published in *Transactions of the Royal Society of Edinburgh* in 1805; little of his correspondence and none of his papers—barring one manuscript—survives. His father and elder brother died when he was very young, so Hutton grew up with his mother and sisters.

Education and early researches Hutton was sent to the Royal High School and then, in 1740, to Edinburgh University where he studied the humanities and developed a taste for chemistry. Originally destined for a career in law, his apprenticeship to a writer to the signet was swiftly curtailed as he was often found entertaining his fellow apprentices with chemical experiments. In 1744 he returned to the university as a medical student, moving to Paris to continue his studies in late 1747, a move which may have been connected with the birth of a natural son (who was also known as James Hutton) at about this time. During nearly two years in Paris he studied anatomy and chemistry, probably attending the lectures of G. F. Rouelle. He finally graduated MD in Leiden in 1749 with a thesis entitled *De sanguine et circulatione microcosmi*. However, Hutton never practised medicine. Back in Edinburgh he and John Davie set up a plant to manufacture sal-ammoniac (ammonium chloride) by a process they had discovered some years before, using the soot from Edinburgh's chimneys as the raw material. The business, managed by Davie, flourished until the early nineteenth century and, together with Hutton's inherited wealth, made him rich.

In 1752, in an abrupt change of direction, Hutton decided to farm and, with Norfolk as his base, spent two years studying new agricultural methods. After a tour through Picardy and the Low Countries in 1754, he settled at Slighhouses, a farm belonging to his family, which lay in the fertile Tweed valley near Duns, Berwickshire. His few surviving letters from this period suggest Hutton was restless and unhappy at first, but he remained there for about thirteen years, bringing the land into good order, testing different crops and fertilizers, studying plant growth and diseases, and keeping meteorological records. He also introduced the Norfolk two-horse plough into the Borders and this proved his most lasting innovation. He failed to complete 'Elements of agriculture', a lengthy manuscript dealing with economics as well as plant and animal husbandry, which he was revising during his final illness and which still remains unpublished. Since 'the husbandman maintains the nation in all its ease, its affluence and its splendour' (NL Scot., Hutton, 'Agriculture',

James Hutton (1726–1797), by Sir Henry Raeburn

681). Hutton believed governments should actively support agriculture.

Middle years in Edinburgh In or before 1767 Hutton returned to Edinburgh. He bought a share in the Company of the Proprietors of the Forth and Clyde Navigation and spent seven years on the committee of management for this huge project, helping surveyors decide the route and finding suitable supplies of building stone for its thirty-nine locks. In 1777 he published *Considerations on the Nature, Quality and Distinctions of Coal and Culm*, a pamphlet urging the government to lift the tax on culm carried by sea, which was almost certainly written with traffic on the canal in mind. The tax was subsequently lifted, the pamphlet—according to Playfair—having contributed significantly to its repeal.

Of Hutton's circle of friends the closest were Joseph Black, Adam Smith (who appointed Hutton and Black as his literary executors), George Clerk Maxwell (later Sir George Clerk of Penicuik), his brother John Clerk of Eldin, and James Watt. Hutton spent more time with Black than anyone else, often in scientific pursuits. Playfair, who probably first met Hutton in the 1770s, gave a vivid description of him. In figure he was slender, vigorous, and plainly dressed; in manner, impetuous and candid, careless of convention, and notable for his 'powerful and imperious' (Playfair, 96) desire for knowledge, which encompassed mechanical contrivances, exploration—he advised Joseph Banks how to make a geological survey of unknown terrain when he was planning to go on Cook's second voyage—and social philosophy as well as the sciences. For relaxation in his later years he used 'regularly to unbend himself with a few friends' (ibid., 98) at the Oyster Club, an informal group he formed with Black and

Smith where they got together with savants, manufacturers, and entrepreneurs. He never married but enjoyed the company of intelligent women. This somewhat ascetic image is fleshed out by Hutton's few remaining letters which show he relished bawdy jokes and though, in Playfair's words, 'he ate sparingly, and drank no wine' (ibid., 93) he was certainly not averse to hard liquor.

In the early 1770s Hutton moved to 3 St Johns Hill, a house (now demolished) which he had built overlooking the Salisbury Crags and where he lived with his sisters until the end of his life. He had established a reputation as a geologist and mineralogist but although he gave several papers to the Edinburgh Philosophical Society he published nothing except the pamphlet on culm until after the foundation of the Royal Society of Edinburgh in 1783. Thereafter he became one of its most active members, reading papers on chemistry, meteorology, natural history, geology, and the origin of speech and writing; six of these were published in the society's *Transactions*, the others were incorporated in his books. Much noticed at the time, and opposed by Jean André de Luc, was his *Theory of Rain* (1788), in which he proposed that the solubility of water vapour must increase with temperature at an accelerating, rather than a constant, rate, since precipitation occurs when masses of air at different temperatures and humidities collide. However, it was a paper given in the spring of 1785, 'Theory of the earth, or, An investigation of the laws observable in the composition, dissolution, and restoration of land upon the globe', which was to bring him lasting fame. An abstract was printed the same year; the full text, perhaps elaborated, appeared in the first volume of the society's *Transactions* in 1788. Hutton's final geological statement, *Theory of the Earth with Proofs and Illustrations*, preserved much of the 1788 text but added new evidence. The first two volumes appeared in 1795. The third volume may never have been completed; the manuscript of chapters four to nine found its way, long after Hutton's death, to the Geological Society of London and was eventually published in 1899.

Geological researches According to Playfair, Hutton's interest in geology had developed in the 1750s in parallel with his interest in agriculture. During the next three decades he made extensive journeys through much of England and Wales and most regions of Scotland except the northwest and the Hebrides. Only the journeys he made in the 1780s are well documented and some historians of science have branded him as a theorist, unaware that his theories were preceded by thirty years of investigation at home and effort in the field. Indeed, long hours in the saddle led him to write, on an arduous journey through north Wales in 1774, 'Lord pity the arse that's clagged to a head that will hunt stones' (Hutton to George Clerk Maxwell, August 1774, NA Scot., GD 18/5937/2). On his excursions he invariably collected many specimens and in his writings he laid great weight on the evidence they provided.

At the outset of his geological researches Hutton observed, as others had done before him, that the majority of rocks on the surface of the earth are formed from the debris of former rocks and that the earth's surface is gradually being destroyed by erosion. However, he was the first to perceive the connection between these phenomena, arguing that the sediments produced by erosion must be consolidated on the seabed and then uplifted to form land—'a new and sublime conclusion' (Playfair, 56). He believed that heat was the agent of consolidation and uplift and that it also generated, in the interior of the earth, hot fluids from which all crystalline rocks originated. Hutton went further still, claiming that erosion, uplift, and igneous activity were continuous processes which had always, and would always, operate in the same way and thus that the surface of the earth was continually being recycled, leaving no evidence of how many times this had happened in the past or would happen in the future. In his most famous dictum: 'we find no vestige of a beginning—no prospect of an end' (Hutton, 'Theory of the earth', 304).

At the time of his 1785 paper Hutton was still uncertain whether granite, like trap or whinstone, was igneous. In summer 1785 he made the first of three famous excursions to prove this point. In the bed of the River Tilt, in Perthshire, he found the junction between the granite of the Cairngorms and the 'marble' (schists and limestones) of the mountains to the south. Here branching veins of granite penetrated deep into the marble, which could have happened only if the granite were younger than the marble and had been fluid. Hutton's companion, John Clerk of Eldin, made several drawings, so accurate that more than 200 years later it is possible to identify the exact site. Excursions to examine the granite of southwest Scotland and Arran followed in 1786 and 1787.

Hutton summarized his findings on granite in a paper published in 1794 and wrote a full account of his excursions for volume three of the *Theory of the Earth*. When it was published in 1899 the geological community had long lost sight of Clerk's drawings, which were not identified and published until 1978. Their detail, admirable even by modern standards, confirms Hutton's mastery in the field and suggests that Clerk, too, was a skilful observer.

During the visit to Arran, Hutton noticed strata of two different sedimentary rocks lying at an angle to each other (a conformation later called an unconformity). In 1788 he found another example of the same phenomenon in the banks of the River Jed, in this case horizontal strata of sandstone resting on vertical strata of 'schistus' (shales and mudstones). Subsequently, accompanied by Playfair and Sir James Hall, he found a magnificent exposure of the sandstone and schistus on the east coast at Siccar Point. He realized that there was only one way their configuration could be explained: the schistus had been laid down horizontally on the ocean floor, then elevated, folded, and the tops of its folds eroded, subsequently sinking back into the ocean where it formed the base on which the sand was later deposited and consolidated. Such a sequence of events could only have taken place over an immense period of time. Hutton advanced this explanation with such eloquence that it made an indelible impression on his companions whose minds 'seemed to grow giddy looking so far into the abyss of time' (Playfair, 73).

Later years In the autumn of 1791 Hutton fell dangerously ill with what Black described as 'a suppression of urine' (Joseph Black to James Watt, 1 Dec 1791, Birmingham City Archives, JWP: 4/44/30), probably caused by kidney stones. To save his life Black and a colleague operated on his bladder, after which he made a slow recovery. Thereafter he set about publishing a lifetime's work on a wide range of subjects. *Dissertations on Different Subjects in Natural Philosophy* (1792) contains his published papers on meteorology; a defence of phlogiston based on debates at the Royal Society of Edinburgh with Sir James Hall (who was one of Lavoisier's first British converts); and an exposition of his theory of matter, which he held to be composed of particles with no magnitude—a hypothesis which resembles that of R. G. Boscovich but was probably arrived at independently. In *A Dissertation upon the Philosophy of Light, Heat, and Fire* (1794) he discussed the connection between these phenomena—a connection he had striven to understand all his adult life—and concluded that heat and fire were 'different modifications of solar matter, alike destitute of inertness and of gravity' (Playfair, 81) lying dormant in matter. The same year he published a long, uneven, work in three volumes, *An Investigation of the Principles of Knowledge and the Progress of Reason, from Sense to Science and Philosophy*. Having stated that the true merit of scientific investigation lies in providing the facts on which to base a sound guide to conduct and belief, he constructed a complete metaphysical system partly derived from Locke, Berkeley, and Hume. Causation is a major topic but he also dealt with time, space, religion, morality, politics, and education. He referred, in passing, to the disadvantageous position of women, whom society considered 'only fitted for domestic service, and for the idle entertainment of the little tyrant, in the thoughtless moments in his life' (*An Investigation of the Principles of Knowledge*, 3.588), and argued that their education was necessary 'for the perfection of the state' (ibid., 1.xiii).

Hutton's illness recurred in 1794, after which he was never again able to leave the house. His last years were spent in considerable pain which he endured with 'a wonderful degree of Courage and good spirits' (Joseph Black to James Watt, 29 Sept 1795, Birmingham City Archives, JWP: 4/44/21). He died on 26 March 1797 at his home, 3 St John's Hill, and was buried in Greyfriars kirkyard, Edinburgh, where, on the 150th anniversary of his death, a memorial tablet was placed above his unmarked grave. He left no will and his considerable property passed to his only surviving sister, Isabella. Subsequently she distributed it between young cousins on the Balfour side of the family and Hutton's seven impoverished grandchildren, whose father had made only a meagre living as a clerk in the London post office.

Influence Hutton's theory of the earth was studied on the continent and in America but had few supporters at first except for Black, Playfair, and Hall; it was fifty years before his theory was universally accepted in all its essentials.

Though he was certainly a theist, claiming time and again that a beneficent deity had designed all the operations of the earth for the ultimate benefit of man, his theories offended many Christians by implicitly rejecting the biblical account of the creation and Bishop Ussher's chronology for the age of the earth. Some natural philosophers, following the ideas of Robert Hooke, Thomas Burnet, and de Luc, opposed his contention that the surface of the earth is slowly recycled by the same natural processes which operate at present (a view later called 'uniformitarianism'); instead they maintained that sudden catastrophes had given the earth's surface a permanent form. Even more fiercely contested were Hutton's ideas about the heat of the earth and the igneous nature of crystalline rocks. Some of these objections focused on limestone and fossils, which Hutton held are not decomposed by the heat of the earth because of the high pressures in the crust. Although he and Black demonstrated this point in a small way using a Papin's digester, he concluded that attempts to replicate the heat and pressure in the earth were futile. It was not until after his death that his suppositions, both about limestone and the igneous origin of crystalline rocks, were verified experimentally by Hall whose work did much to rebut the criticisms of the Wernerians led by Robert Jameson, professor of natural philosophy at Edinburgh. Hutton's other powerful advocate, John Playfair, recast his prolix arguments into a more lucid form (*Illustrations of the Huttonian Theory*, 1802) and it was often through this book rather than Hutton's own work that his ideas were taken up by the next generation of geologists, most notably Charles Lyell. From the mid-nineteenth century onwards they became received wisdom to such an extent that Hutton's name was sometimes forgotten.

JEAN JONES

Sources J. Playfair, 'Biographical account of the late James Hutton, FRS Edinburgh', *Transactions of the Royal Society of Edinburgh*, 5/3 (1805), 39–99 · G. Y. Craig, ed., *James Hutton's theory of the earth: the lost drawings* (1978) · D. R. Dean, *James Hutton and the history of geology* (1992) · J. Hutton, 'Theory of the earth, or, An investigation of the laws observable in the composition, dissolution, and restoration of land upon the globe', *Transactions of the Royal Society of Edinburgh*, 1/2 (1788), 209–304 · J. Hutton, 'Elements of agriculture', 1797, NL Scot., MSS 23165–23166 [2 vols., unfinished MS] · *Partners in science: letters of James Watt and Joseph Black*, ed. E. Robinson and D. McKie (1970) · J. Hutton, two letters to George Clerk Maxwell, July 1774, NA Scot., GD18/5937/1 · J. Hutton, *Dissertations on different subjects in natural philosophy* (1792) · J. Hutton, *A dissertation upon the philosophy of light, heat, and fire* (1794) · J. Jones, 'James Hutton and the Forth and Clyde Canal', *Annals of Science*, 39 (1982), 255–63 · J. Jones, 'James Hutton: exploration and oceanography', *Annals of Science*, 40 (1983), 81–94 · J. Jones, 'The geological collection of James Hutton', *Annals of Science*, 41 (1984), 223–44 · J. Jones, 'James Hutton's agricultural research and his life as a farmer', *Annals of Science*, 42 (1985), 573–601 · J. Jones, H. S. Torrens, and E. Robinson, 'The correspondence between James Hutton and James Watt', *Annals of Science*, 51 (1994), 637–53; 52 (1995), 357–82

Archives FM Cam., papers · GS Lond., 'Theory of the earth', chaps. 4–9 · NL Scot., elements of agriculture | Birm. CA, letters to James Watt · BL, corresp. with John Strange, Eng. MS 2001, fol. 27 · FM Cam., letters to James Lind and Joseph Banks · NA Scot., letters to John Bell · NA Scot., letters to George Clerk Maxwell

Likenesses J. Kay, caricature, etching, 1787, BM; repro. in J. Kay, *A series of original portraits and caricature etchings*, 2 vols. (1837) · J. Kay, caricature, etching, 1787 (with Joseph Black), BM, NPG; repro. in J. Kay, *A series of original portraits and caricature etchings*, 2 vols. (1837) · J. Tassie, ceramic medallion, 1792, Scot. NPG · J. Tassie, wax model, 1792 (for ceramic medallion), Royal College of Physicians of Edinburgh · J. Kay, caricature, etching, BM, NPG · P. Park, bust, Geological Museum, London · H. Raeburn, oils, Scot. NPG [*see illus.*] · wash drawing, Scot. NPG

Hutton, James Scott (1833–1891), teacher of deaf people and author, was born on 10 May 1833 in Perth, Scotland, son of George Hutton (1801–1870) and Ann Scott (*b.* 1803/4), both natives of Perthshire. Raised on Melville Street, Perth, in a strongly Secessionist family, James Scott Hutton was one of twelve children, of whom only three survived past childhood, including his eldest brother, George Clark *Hutton (1825–1908), a leading Free Church divine. In devoting his life to the 'children of silence' (*Eleventh Annual Report of the Institution for the Deaf and Dumb at Halifax, Nova Scotia*, 1869, 12) Hutton was led by the example of his father, a schoolmaster, who tutored deaf students in Perth for nearly forty years. As a self-taught specialist in deaf education and ardent Secessionist, George Hutton moulded his son's vigorous intellect as well as his earnest Christian principles.

In 1847 Hutton moved to Edinburgh, where he was engaged for seven years as an apprentice teacher at Henderson Row's Edinburgh Royal Institution for the Education of Deaf and Dumb Children. He remained at the school for another three years as an assistant teacher while pursuing his studies in arts at the University of Edinburgh during 1855 and 1856. In April 1857 Hutton accepted the position of principal at the Institution for the Deaf and Dumb in Halifax, Nova Scotia. Despite the hindrances of inadequate funding, textbooks, and apparatus, the school was transformed by Hutton's dedicated service. Within a year it had twenty-seven students and was quickly gaining respectability.

During his term as principal Hutton shared the heavy burden of responsibilities with his wife, Mary (*b.* 1836/7), daughter of William Burton, a merchant, and his wife, Margaret, *née* Sinclair. They married in Edinburgh on 21 August 1860, and worked together with Hutton's father, who was a full-time volunteer at the school for ten years. Hutton routinely lobbied for legislative grants and toured the Atlantic provinces lecturing and holding public meetings to awaken public interest in the residential school. His overriding objective was to secure permanent state support for deaf education. In April 1884 this goal was realized in Nova Scotia; it was due in no small part to Hutton's persistence.

Hutton's professional and personal life was virtually coterminous with the Halifax school; he remained principal for almost thirty years. Despite a demanding schedule of commitments as an administrator, teacher, fund-raiser, and writer, he also addressed the needs of deaf persons outside the school. By 1875 he had established a Sunday morning service and Bible classes for adult deaf people in Halifax. There was one brief interruption in Hutton's long career in Canada: in 1878 he moved to Belfast, where he served as vice-principal at the Ulster Institution for the Deaf and Dumb and the Blind. For four years he assumed 'sole charge' of the school's educational programme, and initiated several 'fresh developments', most notably lip-reading and articulation (McClelland, 124).

As an acknowledged expert in deaf education, Hutton added liberally to the literature of his profession. He authored several textbooks, including *The Deaf-Mute's Question Book* (1867) and *Language Lessons for the Deaf and Dumb* (1878). He was an active contributor to the *American Annals of the Deaf and Dumb*, and an energetic participant at international meetings such as the Convention of American Instructors of the Deaf and Dumb, the Conference of Superintendents and Principals of Institutions for Deaf Mutes, and the Conference of Head Masters of Institutions for the Education of the Deaf & Dumb. In 1888 Hutton was vice-president of the so-called Gallaudet Conference held in Jackson, Mississippi. These public forums enabled him to further several personal crusades, especially the professional, educational, and social elevation of teachers of deaf people. He also strove to secure recognition of his father's inventive lexicon of pictured signs called mimography (*Thirteenth Annual Report of the Institution for the Deaf and Dumb at Halifax, Nova Scotia*, 1871, 10).

As a principal Hutton was a cautious but informed innovator. Although he started experimenting with articulation in 1852, he was a self-proclaimed manualist in the early part of his career. He stressed the acquisition of written language and regarded audible speech and lip-reading as 'impossible attainments' for the 'great majority' of deaf persons (Hutton, 'Deaf mute instruction', 75). His curriculum highlighted the 'natural language' of deaf people, reviled by many experts as arbitrary and imperfect signs, as well as writing and the single-and two-handed manual alphabets as the chief instruments of communication. He also had little sympathy for traditional grammatical instruction and favoured a more holistic and practical system based on the principles of 'living realism', which enabled students to learn in whole sentences and to connect words with the 'familiar realities' of their daily experiences (Hutton, 'The teaching of language', 93–4). He described his approach as a mixture of 'action-writing', 'picture-teaching', and 'story-telling' (ibid., 98–102).

By the 1880s Hutton's position had undergone modification. As the polarities between the manualists and oralists sharpened, Hutton eschewed the zealotry of these camps and conceded the merits of both techniques. He advocated the 'Combined Method' of manual spelling in conjunction with articulation and lip-reading, and refused to endorse the pure oralism of the Milan Convention and its proscription of signing, the suppression of which he likened to stifling 'the very life of the soul' (Hutton, 'Deaf mute instruction', 76). The annual reports for the Halifax school indicate that Hutton closely monitored international trends and debates, especially programme content in other deaf schools. By the 1880s this institution featured penmanship, the manual alphabet, composition, geography, history, lip-reading, articulation, drawing, clay modelling, calisthenics, and occupational training. In line with Hutton's own evangelical presbyterian beliefs, this regimen was heavily infused with religion and morality.

At a time when deaf education was overshadowed by the near deification of Alexander Graham Bell for his work in this area, Hutton toiled quietly and unostentatiously. Although he did not seek celebrity, his work did not go unrecognized. In 1869 he received an honorary master's degree from the National Deaf-Mute College (now Gallaudet University) in Washington. His death at the Halifax school on 25 February 1891 was widely mourned as the loss of a beloved teacher, 'noble benefactor', and one of the profession's 'brightest ornaments' (Fearon, 313). LAURIE C. C. STANLEY-BLACKWELL

Sources *Morning Herald* [Halifax, Nova Scotia] (26 Feb 1891) · *Morning Herald* [Halifax, Nova Scotia] (28 Feb 1891) · bap. reg. Scot. · m. cert. · m. cert. [G. Hutton] · *Annual Report of the Institution for the Deaf and Dumb at Halifax, Nova Scotia* (1857–92) · Public Archives of Nova Scotia, Halifax, School for the Deaf (Halifax, Nova Scotia), boxes 1990-205/001–1990-205/003 · J. Fearon, *Quarterly Review of Deaf-Mute Education* (1888–91), 307–13 · J. S. Hutton, 'Posthumous papers of the late George Hutton', *American Annals of the Deaf and Dumb*, 19 (Oct 1874), 205–16 · J. Guildford, 'Hutton, James Scott', *DCB*, vol. 12 · J. S. Hutton, 'Deaf mute instruction in the British maritime provinces', *American Annals of the Deaf and Dumb*, 14 (April 1869), 65–82 · 'Death of James Scott Hutton', *Presbyterian Witness and Evangelical Advocate* (28 Feb 1891) · J. S. Hutton, 'The teaching of language', *Proceedings of the (Gallaudet) Sixth National Conference of Superintendents and Principals of Institutions for Deaf Mutes* (1888), 90–104 · C. F. Carbin, *Deaf heritage in Canada*, ed. D. L. Smith (1996), 117–19 · J. G. McClelland, 'The development of educational facilities for handicapped children in Ireland, with particular reference to the deaf in Ulster', MA diss., Queen's University of Belfast, 1965 · *Annual report of the Ulster Society for Promoting the Education of the Deaf and Dumb and the Blind* (1879–83) · *Report of the Edinburgh Institution for the Education of the Deaf and Dumb* [Edinburgh] (1847–57) · A. Oliver, *Life of George Clark Hutton* (1910), 1–6 · register of births and baptisms, High Street Middle Church, Perth, 26 May 1833 · minute books of directors, 1854–68, 1869–90, Edinburgh Royal Institution for the Education of Deaf and Dumb Children, NL Scot., dep. 263.113–263.114 · minute book of Deaf and Dumb Institution, 1846–54, Donaldson's College, Edinburgh, Edinburgh Royal Institution for the Education of Deaf and Dumb Children archives

Archives Alexander Graham Bell Association for the Deaf, Washington, DC | Donaldson's College, Edinburgh, minute books · Gallaudet University, Washington, Edward M. Gallaudet MSS, box 7, folder 2 · NL Scot., minute books, dep. 263.113–263.114 · Public Archives of Nova Scotia, Halifax, boxes 1990-205/001–1990-205/003

Likenesses W. Notman, photograph, c.1888, Alexander Graham Bell Association for the Deaf, Washington, Volta Bureau Library

Wealth at death left estate to wife: Halifax County will book, vol. 10, p. 575, mfno. 19361, Public Archives of Nova Scotia, Halifax

Hutton, John (d. 1712), physician, a native of Caerlaverock, Dumfriesshire, Scotland, began life as a herd-boy to the Episcopalian minister of that parish. Through his master's kindness he received a good education, and became a physician, graduating MD at Padua. Hutton chanced to be at hand when Mary Stuart, princess of Orange, met with a fall from her horse in the Netherlands. He gained the regard of Prince William, helped to run William's intelligence service, and accompanied William as physician-general to the army that invaded England in 1688. On ascending the English throne William appointed Hutton his first physician and acting physician-general to all the forces. During the preparations for the Irish campaign in the spring of 1690 Hutton took on the responsibilities of inspecting the military hospitals, inquiring into the qualifications of everyone employed as army physician, surgeon, or apothecary, overseeing the care of the sick and wounded, and guaranteeing the provision of the necessary medicines, nursing, and attendance. Bishop Burnet wrote of 'Dr Hutton … who took care to be always near' the king during his campaigns: he was certainly with him at the battle of the Boyne and at the siege of Limerick. In 1691 he earned the new title of physician-general to the armies and land forces. At some time before 1702 Hutton also became head of the commission for sick and wounded soldiers, and physician-general to the hospitals.

Hutton was admitted a fellow of the Royal College of Physicians on 30 September 1690, when he presented the college with a sum of money, and intimated that he hoped to be able to repeat his generosity. On 9 November 1695 he was incorporated MD at Oxford, and was elected FRS on 30 November 1697. Queen Anne continued him as first physician. Hutton provided liberally for his poor relatives. At his own expense he built in 1708 a manse for the minister at Caerlaverock, bequeathed to the parish £1000 sterling for pious and educational purposes, and also gave all his books to the ministers of the presbytery of Dumfries 'to be carefully kept in that town'. In 1710 Hutton was elected MP for the Dumfries burghs, and sat until his death in 1712, when he was apparently buried in the chapel of Somerset House, London. In his will, dated 13 August 1712 and 2 September 1712, and proved on the following 4 December, he describes himself as living in the parish of St Clement, Westminster.

GORDON GOODWIN, rev. HAROLD J. COOK

Sources annals, RCP Lond. · 'Appointment by William and Mary of Dr John Hutton as physician-general of the army, 1691', GL, MS 10, 494 · *CSP dom.*, 1689–91 · W. A. Shaw, ed., *Calendar of treasury books*, 9–17, PRO (1931–47) · *Bishop Burnet's History of his own time*, ed. G. Burnet and T. Burnet, 2 vols. (1724–34) · Munk, *Roll* · Foster, *Alum. Oxon.* · A. Peterkin and W. Johnston, *Commissioned officers in the medical services of the British army, 1660–1960*, 1 (1968) · J. Carswell, *The descent on England: a study of the English revolution of 1688 and its European background* (1969) · H. J. Cook, 'Practical medicine and the British armed forces after the "Glorious Revolution"', *Medical History*, 34 (1990), 1–26

Hutton, John (1739–1806), writer on topography and etymology, was born in Westmorland. The identity of his parents is unknown; Venn states that he was a brother of William *Hutton (1737–1811), but his will shows the two to have been cousins. John Hutton was educated at Sedburgh School and matriculated from St John's College, Cambridge, in 1759. He was made a scholar in 1762, graduated BA in 1763 as third wrangler, and was ordained deacon in June 1763 and priest in September 1763. In that year he became curate of Croydon with Clapton, Cambridgeshire, and in 1764 was presented by his family to the vicarage of Burton in Kendal, Westmorland. In 1765 he became fellow and tutor of his college and in 1766 he proceeded MA. In

1774 he proceeded BD and in 1789 he was chosen moderator and senior taxor at Cambridge. On 7 November 1781 he married Agnes Miles of Ambleside and they had an only daughter, Agnes, who married Captain Johnson of Mains Hall, Hereford. Hutton was treasurer and secretary to the Humane Society in the archdeaconry of Richmond, Yorkshire.

Hutton made a summer tour of the karst (carboniferous limestone) areas around Malham Tarn, publishing his account as *A tour to the caves in the environs of Ingleborough and Settle in the West-Riding of Yorkshire with some philosophical conjectures on the Deluge, remarks on the origin of fountains … and observations on the ascent and descent of vapours* (1781). Though his descriptions of the towns and villages he visits are unremarkable, Hutton makes a point of visiting relatively inaccessible peaks and, particularly, of entering many caves and potholes. His is the first detailed account of the caves, though he was by no means the first to visit them; he notes with sorrow, for example, the destruction wrought by previous visitors who have taken away stalactites and stalagmites as trophies. He follows many conventions of eighteenth-century travel accounts; when he makes his first entrance into a 'gloomy cavern', for example, his imagination is so excited by the experience that several passages of Ovid and Virgil apparently spring instantly into his mind.

By far the most interesting part of Hutton's book is the philosophical conjectures at the end. Evidently well read in the geological debates of the day, he observes the geomorphology, drainage, and geology of the area with care and interprets his observations in the light of current theories. He comes, however, to very largely erroneous conclusions, mostly because of his attempts to reconcile explanations with biblical accounts and because of his persistent reliance on the operation of processes not observable at the time. He suggests, for example, that limestone pavements were formed as the rock, originally a slurry, was dried by the sun's warmth, shrank, and cracked. He specifically rules out solution by rainwater, now known to cause such pavements. Similarly he finds explanation of dry valleys in the Deluge, when large volumes of water moulded the earth's surface, and he accounts for uplift by postulating an increase in the speed of rotation of the earth about its axis. His excursions into etymology are similarly hindered by his classical education: in footnotes he traces Celtic and Germanic words back to Phoenician and Greek roots respectively. His appended glossary of dialect words in use in the areas he visited is interesting, if unsystematic, and he offers no explanation for them. The glossary was reprinted by the English Dialect Society in 1873. Still of considerable local interest as the first detailed description of the caves, Hutton's *Tour* was reprinted in Wakefield in 1970.

Hutton left a manuscript, 'A treatise on the etymology of words in the English language derived from that of the Greek'. His will shows that he owned extensive property in the north of the country and he left legacies to a large circle of kin. He died in August 1806; his wife survived him.   ELIZABETH BAIGENT

Sources Venn, *Alum. Cant.* · *GM*, 1st ser., 76 (1806), 875 · *N&Q*, 9 (1854), 144 · *N&Q*, 10 (1854), 19 · will, PRO, PROB 11/1453, fols. 65v–68v · D. C. Mellor, foreword, in G. Hutton, *A tour to the caves* (1970), v
Archives Cumbria AS, Kendal, corresp. and papers · NL Wales, papers · Yale U., Beinecke L., letters
Wealth at death see will, PRO, PROB 11/1453, fols. 65v–68v

Hutton, John Henry (1885–1968), anthropologist, was born on 27 June 1885 at West Heslerton, Malton, Yorkshire, the son of Joseph Henry Hutton, a Church of England clergyman, and his wife, Clarissa Marshall, *née* Barwick. He was educated at Chigwell School and at Worcester College, Oxford, where he took a third in modern history in 1907. He became a member of the Indian Civil Service in 1909 and spent most of his administrative career in Assam, on the border between India and Burma, particularly in the Naga hills. From 1917 to 1919 he was political officer with responsibility for the Kuki operations. He became increasingly interested in the culture and society of the peoples with whom he worked, and with the encouragement of Henry Balfour, the curator of the Pitt Rivers Museum, who visited him in the Naga hills, decided to document their lives in various ways. From 1920 onwards he wrote many articles about the Nagas, and in 1921 published two seminal monographs, *The Angami Nagas* and *The Sema Nagas*. On 6 March 1920 he married a widow, Stella Eleanora (*d*. 1944), daughter of the Revd Rhys Bishop. They had two sons and a daughter.

Hutton's most important administrative work came when he was appointed census commissioner for the census of India in 1929, a position he held until 1933. The first and third parts of the first volume of the census report bear the clear imprint of Hutton; he played a vital role in collating and organizing the mammoth undertaking. He applied the knowledge he had gained in this work in the writing of his most frequently cited book, *Caste in India* (1946; 4th edn, 1963), which anticipated many subsequent developments in the field, for example concerning the diversity of caste groups and their hierarchical ordering. He also played an important part in the discussions which determined the treatment of the tribal populations of India in the legislation concerning scheduled castes and scheduled tribes and their rights during the fifteen years before independence.

In 1936 Hutton resigned from the Indian Civil Service, and took up the prestigious William Wyse chair of social anthropology in Cambridge, becoming the second holder of the post and successor to another Naga expert, T. C. Hodson. He was elected a fellow of St Catharine's College at that time, and an honorary fellow in 1951. In the department of anthropology he built up connections with students being trained for the colonial civil service and encouraged, among other things, the teaching of material culture. His distinction as an anthropologist was recognized by the award of the degree of DSc by Oxford University, and his presidency of the Royal Anthropological Institute (1944–5). He had won the Rivers memorial medal of the institute in 1929. He gave the Frazer memorial lecture in 1938, and in 1932 won the silver medal of the Royal Society of Arts. His first wife died in 1944, and on 7 December 1945 Hutton married Maureen Margaret O'Reilly (b. 1901/2), an assistant museum curator. He retired from his professorship in 1950, and died on 23 May 1968 at his home, 4 Rectory Lane, New Radnor, in Radnorshire, the county of which he had been high sheriff in 1943.

It is clear from a number of sources that Hutton became very involved with the lives, diverse histories, and cultures of the various tribal groups who lived in the eastern Himalayas. He became interested in their connections with other megalithic cultures in south-east Asia and Oceania, and wrote important articles on the possible links between them. He provided important clues to the function of head-hunting in the area. He worked closely with, and guided, his younger colleague John Philip Mills, and inspired the next generation of experts in the area, particularly Christoph von Fürer-Haimendorf. The monographs of these three writers covered most of the major Naga tribes, the Angami, Sema, Lhota, Ao, Rengma, and Konyak. Hutton's ethnography and deep knowledge of the people he wrote about evidently set a very high standard. As well as these extensive writings, Hutton, Mills, and Haimendorf set out to collect objects, from the everyday to the ornate. Most of Hutton's extensive collections are in the Pitt Rivers Museum at Oxford, where many of his photographs and some rare wax cylinder recordings which he made are also to be found. Combined with the detailed reports of his tours and other administrative papers in the Oriental and India Office collections at the British Library, his work helped to make the Nagas one of the best documented tribal groups in the world. This is particularly important since he was working just at the point when an ancient and forest-dwelling population, enormously rich in its material culture and varied in every way, was being incorporated into the British empire.

ALAN MACFARLANE

Sources *The Times* (30 May 1968) · *WWW* · b. cert. · m. certs. [Stella Eleanora, *née* Bishop; Maureen Margaret O'Reilly] · d. cert. · Kelly, *Handbk* (1947) · BL OIOC, Hutton MSS · CUL, Hutton MSS · J. D. Saul, review, *Man*, new ser., 4 (1969), 677
Archives BL OIOC, papers [copies] · U. Cam., Centre of South Asian Studies, papers · U. Cam., Museum of Archaeology and Anthropology, corresp. and papers · U. Oxf., Pitt Rivers Museum, artifacts, collection | FILM BFI NFTVA, current affairs footage
Wealth at death £16,612: probate, 12 Sept 1968, CGPLA Eng. & Wales

Hutton, Kurt [*formerly* Kurt Heinrich Hübschmann] (1893–1960), photojournalist, was born in Strasbourg, Alsace (then Germany), on 11 August 1893, the son of J. Heinrich Hübschmann (d. c.1908), an authority on the Armenian language and professor of comparative philology at Strasbourg University, and his wife, Anna Meyer (d. c.1933), a dressmaker and distant relative of Aby S. Warburg of the international banking family. Anna Hübschmann was Jewish but her son did not realize this until years later, when the Nazis stamped his passport with a 'J'. Indeed, his schooling was at the Protestant *Gymnasium* in Strasbourg (1902–11); he went on to study in Heidelberg, probably at the university there. In 1911 he attended Queen's College,

Oxford, for one or perhaps two years but did not graduate: he wrote in 1947 of 'half hearted studies of law interrupted by the War' (Hutton, introduction). He also spoke of a failed career in law and banking, perhaps in connection with his mother's relations.

During the First World War Hübschmann was a cavalry officer, and was awarded the Iron Cross, second class, for carrying dispatches. Early in 1918 he contracted tuberculosis and was invalided out of the army, and spent the next two years in a sanatorium at St Moritz in Switzerland. As a boy he had used a quarter-plate camera; while in the sanatorium he experimented with a stereo-camera. He had been a keen tennis and hockey player and at St Moritz began to ski. His skiing companions included Margareta Malvina Rosena Anna Ratchitzky (1899–1962), a dressmaker, and her friend's sister, Frau Gertrude Englehardt; Margareta (known as Gretl) became his wife about 1921, and Gertrude later became his business partner in a photographic studio.

About 1921 Hübschmann had started his own portrait studio but, within two years, he realized that it was beyond his business ability. Accordingly, he went to work in a large fashionable studio while studying, it is said, with the well-known photographer Germaine Krull. By 1926 he and Gertrude Englehardt had founded the Atelier Englehardt und Hübschmann in the Berlin suburb of Dahlem; from this period only family portraits have survived. Hübschmann became dissatisfied with the big studio camera for formal portraiture and began experimenting with the new revolutionary miniature cameras, the Leica and the Contax.

Success still eluded Hübschmann until Simon Gutmann, the legendary head of the Dephot agency, persuaded him to do a photo-story on a children's festival in nearby Zehlendorf: the photographs were published in the popular weekly *Die Woche* in 1929. Hübschmann became a successful photojournalist working not only for Dephot but for other agencies such as Weltrundschau and Mauritius. His stories appeared in many German magazines including the *Münchner Illustrierte Presse*, run by the brilliant Stefan Lorant.

When the Nazis came to power Hübschmann, with his family, and Lorant left Germany in 1933 for England. In 1934 Lorant founded the British *Weekly Illustrated*, and he employed Hübschmann, thus guaranteeing him regular work. (Lorant left the *Weekly Illustrated* soon after it was launched and Tom Hopkinson became editor.) At least eighty of Hübschmann's photo-stories for the publication have been identified between 1934 and 1938.

Edward Hulton founded the *Picture Post* in October 1938 with Lorant as editor and Hopkinson as his assistant; Hübschmann became one of its regular freelance photographers. In June 1940 he was interned as a German alien in the Isle of Man, but when released in June 1941 he continued working for *Picture Post*, now as a staff photographer. His son Peter became a captain in the army recce corps and changed his name to Hutten in the belief that this was the spelling of the name of the famous cricketer. Kurt, though always called Hubsch by his friends, used the same name but spelt it correctly as 'Hutton'; however, when he officially changed it in 1947 it was to his son's spelling of 'Hutten' (though he never used that spelling professionally). Hutton photographed for *Picture Post* until 1951, when following a heart attack he and Gretl moved from their rented house at 81 Brooklands Rise in Hampstead Garden Suburb, Middlesex, to Aldeburgh in Suffolk.

Hutton still did occasional stories for *Picture Post* with his son's friend Ronald Blythe, later famous as the author of *Akenfield* (1969). He continued to photograph the early Aldeburgh festivals, which he had covered since 1947, for his own enjoyment; Benjamin Britten admired his photography, finding that his unobtrusive presence and almost silent Leica never disrupted rehearsals. These swansong photographs, now in the Britten–Pears Library, are in constant demand worldwide for music programmes and magazines; his *Picture Post* photographs are in the Hulton-Getty Library, while much of his earlier work for the *Weekly Illustrated* is held by Popperfoto. Ironically, after failing as a studio portrait photographer in Berlin, his informal British portraits are among his best-known today, some of which are in the collection of the National Portrait Gallery, London.

Hutton died on 14 March 1960 at his home, 36 Crag Path, Aldeburgh, and was buried in Aldeburgh parish churchyard. Gretl Hutton died of cancer in 1962. Their son Peter emigrated with his family to Australia; some of his father's photographs were still in his possession in the 1990s.   COLIN OSMAN

Sources K. Hutton, *Speaking likeness* (1947) · *The Times* (20 March 1961) · *Creative Camera Year Book* (1975) · private information (2004) · taped interviews, U. Wales, Cardiff, Tom Hopkinson Centre for Media Research, Tom Hopkinson archive · Hutton MSS, priv. coll. · CGPLA Eng. & Wales (1960) · tombstone, Aldeburgh parish churchyard, Aldeburgh, Suffolk
Archives priv. coll. | Hult. Arch., *Picture Post* collection · NPG, *Weekly Illustrated* negatives · Popperfoto, Nottingham, *Weekly Illustrated* negatives | SOUND U. of Wales, Cardiff, Tom Hopkinson archive, interviews with sources
Likenesses photographs, 1948–53, Hult. Arch. · K. Hutton, photograph, priv. coll.
Wealth at death £1989 14s. 6d.: probate, 22 April 1960, CGPLA Eng. & Wales

Hutton, Sir Leonard (1916–1990), cricketer, was born on 23 June 1916 at 5 Fulneck, near Pudsey, Leeds, the youngest of the six children of Henry Hutton (1876–1947), builder and foreman joiner, and his wife, Lily Swithenbank (1875–1952). Moravians, the earliest protestant sect in Europe, had come to Fulneck in 1732 and within a generation Benjamin Hutton, a tailor from Scotland, had been the first of his family to settle there. Moravian traditions of discipline, hard work, self-sufficiency, and craftsmanship would be the lodestars of Leonard Hutton's life and professional career. He was brought up in one of the community terraced houses 'in a home which was strict but caring' (Howat, 3) and attended the chapel, but there were not the financial resources to send him to Fulneck School, despite the emphasis it gave to cricket. Instead, he went to Littlemoor council school in Pudsey, practising on the concrete playground or at the Pudsey St Lawrence club, where his

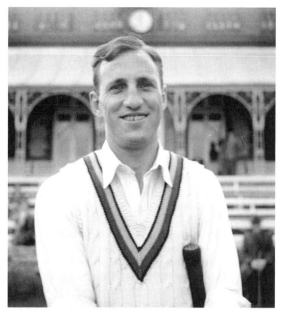

Sir Leonard Hutton (1916–1990), by unknown photographer, 1947

three elder brothers all played in Yorkshire league cricket.

Yorkshire batsman At thirteen Hutton made his début for the club's first eleven and in 1930, on the recommendation of his near neighbour Herbert Sutcliffe, he reported to the Yorkshire indoor shed at Headingley, where he was coached by George Hirst. In the same year he watched Donald Bradman make his 334 in a test match, a record in Anglo-Australian tests which Hutton himself would eclipse eight years later. That autumn the fourteen-year-old began a year at Pudsey grammar school, where he studied technical drawing and quantitative work before joining the building firm of Joseph Verity. He would remain with them in the winters until 1939 and retain a practical interest in woodwork all his life.

In the season of 1933 Hutton opened the batting both for Pudsey St Lawrence and Yorkshire second eleven (where he averaged 69.90), the prelude to his first eleven début in 1934 against Cambridge University. He was still six weeks off his eighteenth birthday and the youngest player to have appeared for Yorkshire. In anxious pursuit of his first run, a throw from Jack Davies dismissed him for 0. But against Worcestershire he became the youngest Yorkshire centurion when he made 196. Neville Cardus wrote that he was mature at an age when other brilliant beginners were merely showing promise. But the young man, whom the press were idolizing, remained 'the most retiring and unconceited personality that anyone could meet' (Howat, 20).

In playing for Yorkshire, Hutton had joined the strongest county side of the inter-war years, to whom winning the championship was almost a prescriptive right. Their tight ranks only welcomed a newcomer once he had proved his worth. From men such as Maurice Leyland,

Hedley Verity, and Bill Bowes he learned the folklore of the Yorkshire cricket tradition. Sutcliffe remained his strongest advocate, and declared in print, in 1935, that at fourteen he had been good enough to play for most county sides. Hutton (and others) found the eulogy embarrassing: the more so, as the seasons of 1935 and 1936 were not without their pitfalls. He averaged under 30 in both and—never the most robust of men—had to be rested through physical strain. The press were beginning to criticize his reluctance to display the strokes at his command. Yorkshire, however, kept faith and he became, in July 1936, their youngest capped player in the twentieth century.

Record innings Hutton's test début, against New Zealand at Lord's in 1937, was as inglorious as his first-class one three years earlier. He was dismissed for 0 and 1, but redeemed himself with a century at Old Trafford a month later. Then, in August 1938, after two months' absence through injury, came his innings of 364 against the Australians at the Oval in the fifth test. In beating Bradman's record to make what remains the highest individual score in Anglo-Australian tests, Hutton fulfilled all the attributes of skill, concentration, and endurance so often credited to him. If the press were lost for words, they hid the fact successfully enough in column upon column of reporting. Not since the abdication crisis two years earlier had the thoughts of millions throughout the British empire been so centred on one person. Even the American magazine *Time* reported on his innings. Hutton, ever after, would be conscious of his obligations to those, especially the young, who came to watch him. He would play better innings in the years to come (six, at least) but '364' remained for the rest of his life as much a millstone as a milestone.

While not fulfilling the highest expectations in South Africa (1938–9), Hutton averaged 96.00 against the West Indies in 1939. The Second World War broke out twelve days after he had made 165 not out at the Oval in the third test. Pelham Warner summed him up at the time as possessing 'every stroke conceivable' (Howat, 50). The first wartime *Wisden* called him 'one of the world's greatest batsmen' (*Wisden*, 1940, 513).

On 16 September 1939 Hutton married in Wykeham parish church Dorothy Mary (*b.* 1916), daughter of George Dennis, foreman joiner on Lord Downe's estate at Wykeham, Yorkshire. He had known her since 1935. The happiness of that marriage proved central to an understanding of his later success. She was as vital to her husband in his cricket career as in his later business one. Over the years they successfully faced the twin hazards of fame and separation. Of their two games-playing sons, Richard (*b.* 1942) would play for Cambridge University, Yorkshire, and England.

Hutton's war service, as a sergeant in the Army Physical Training Corps, ended in 1941. He fell in a gymnasium while on a commando course. The resultant fracture of his left arm put his cricket future in doubt. There followed operations and graftings and he would eventually resume his cricket career with an arm 2 inches shorter and a need to adjust his batting technique. He was able, in 1943, to

captain Pudsey St Lawrence (not without some differences of opinion with club officialdom) and in 1944 he played in two matches at Lord's—for the Rest, and then for England, both against Australia. He was 'the real Hutton of brilliant and elegant stroke-play' (*The Times*, 29 May 1944). In 1945, when the war in Europe was over, he played in the victory internationals against Australia, although Pudsey, who paid him £100 a season, resented his absences for these national occasions and had released him most reluctantly.

In the immediate post-war era Hutton was the mainstay of England's batting against dominating Australians, challenging South Africans, and burgeoning West Indians. A cameo of 37 in the second test at Sydney during England's 1946–7 tour of Australia evoked the Yorkshire journalist J. M. Kilburn to flights of fancy: 'Hutton scattered light, loveliness and brave beauty and took cricket to the pinnacles of artistry' (*Yorkshire Evening Post*, 19 Dec 1946). His 158 in the second test at Johannesburg in 1948–9 helped England to a record first-wicket partnership of 359 while his double century (in which he carried his bat) against the West Indies at the Oval in 1950 was a masterly display on a difficult wicket. He had also been flown out to the West Indies in February 1948 to strengthen a struggling MCC side and, in the five matches which remained of the tour, achieved an average of 64.22.

Captain of England In 1952 Hutton became England's first professional captain in the twentieth century, an invitation more widely welcomed than he allowed himself to realize. India were defeated 3–0 and the captain topped the batting averages. Meanwhile, he had never ignored his obligations to Yorkshire, whose senior professional he became soon after the war, though he was never made their captain. The county gave him a benefit match in 1950, which realized £9713, tax free. It was by far the highest ever received by a Yorkshire player. Hutton, who was an assiduous follower of the stock market, did not get the capital sum back, invested on his behalf by the county (as was the custom), until 1972. Cricket did not make even the top players of his generation rich and he would always assess his own financial worth. 'How much will we make?' he had asked when *Cricket is my Life* was published in 1949. For Yorkshire he continued to make runs as consistently as he did for England.

In coronation year (1953) Hutton brought the mythical Ashes back to England after nineteen years in Australian custody, the outcome decided by England's victory at the Oval in August 1953, in which he scored 82 in the first innings. Again he topped the averages. He took MCC to the West Indies in 1953–4 at a time when the movement for national independence in the Caribbean was gaining strength. *The Times* called the tour 'the second most controversial in cricket history' (Howat, 141) and the demands upon Hutton's captaincy were compounded by umpiring disputes and crowd riots. Yet again he led from the front with a test average of 96.71 and a double century in the final test, which ensured that England drew the series. Despite his unfitness during the Pakistani visit to England in 1954, he made himself available for the forthcoming tour of Australia. Both he and his rival for the captaincy, David Sheppard—both men of strong moral fibre—conducted themselves with dignity during the summer. Hutton was eventually appointed and, though less successful as a batsman, he retained the Ashes. On his return from Australia he was elected to membership of the Marylebone Cricket Club, the first serving professional to be so honoured. But, stricken with lumbago, he relinquished the England captaincy in May 1955. If his had been a pragmatic appointment three years earlier, pragmatism had triumphed and the plaudits were generous. His diplomacy off the field, when abroad, could not be faulted. On the field undue caution and slow over rates had been the negative aspects of his leadership. But he had been quietly effective rather than demonstrative and displayed a tenacity of will which embodied total dedication. Only Peter May, in the long banner roll of England captains, would match his achievements as leader and performer.

Knighthood and retirement In June 1955 Hutton made 194 for Yorkshire against Nottinghamshire in his 129th and last century in first-class cricket, but in the following January he retired on medical advice. With a few more appearances his career record would be 40,140 runs (55.51), nearly three-quarters of which had been made for Yorkshire. In seventy-nine test matches he scored 6971 runs (56.67), with nineteen centuries. Harry Altham, in a broadcast, declared that a great chapter in the history of cricket had ended. But for Sir Leonard Hutton—knighted in June 1956—another one had to open. At first, work as a broadcaster and journalist came his way. Both the London *Evening News* and *The Observer* employed him for many years but the significant change was an invitation to join the firm of J. H. Fenner, power transmission engineers. He would work for them longer than he had played first-class cricket. At first his role was to talk cricket to the firm's associates. The fitting of Fenner mechanical products to a new MGB model gave cars 'as smooth a performance as a Hutton innings'. However laboured the analogy or the pun, his name would be linked and his presence required. But events took an unexpected turn as Hutton, who became a director in 1973, found himself selling the products of his firm even in non-cricketing countries, where his name was of no consequence.

The Hutton family had taken the decision in 1961 to leave Pudsey and settle in London. Living in Kingston upon Thames came to suit both his role in business and his work as a journalist. He served briefly (1975–7) as an England selector but felt he could not spare the time from his work for Fenner. He published three books, of which *Fifty Years in Cricket* (1984) was the most illuminating. John Arlott called it a model cricket autobiography. Hutton identified with Surrey in his later years, especially with the 'Save the Oval' campaign, but he also accepted an invitation in January 1990 to become president of Yorkshire at a time of some 'political' unrest in the club.

Achievement and fulfilment were all-in-all to Hutton, and always those stern puritan voices from his upbringing were calling him to succeed. His cricket was never meant to be a joyride, yet he was not a joyless man without

humour. His own brand was never far away and might be seen in the twinkle in his blue eyes, a warm smile, in his delphic utterances and enigmatic remarks. Humour lurked in the wings but he was aware that he was expected to be centre-stage and he took the trouble to talk to people and to remember them.

Hutton died in Kingston Hospital, Surrey, on 6 September 1990, five days after watching a Natwest final at Lord's. His wife survived him. His funeral took place on 13 September at St Peter's, Kingston, and he was cremated at Putney Vale crematorium. There was a memorial service in York Minster, at which the bishop of Liverpool, his former colleague David Sheppard, gave the address.

GERALD M. D. HOWAT

Sources G. Howat, *Len Hutton*, rev. edn (1990) · L. Hutton, *Fifty years in cricket* (1984) · L. Hutton, *Just my story* (1956) · D. Trelford, *Len Hutton remembered* (1992) · *Wisden* (1938) · *Wisden* (1950) · *Wisden* (1956) · *Wisden* (1991) · *The Times* (7 Sept 1990) · *Daily Telegraph* (7 Sept 1990) · A. A. Thomson, *Hutton and Washbrook* (1963) · L. Kitchin, *Len Hutton* (1953)
Archives Headingley, Yorkshire cricket club committee | priv. coll., Lady Hutton's scrapbooks | FILM BFI NFTVA, 'The greatest', 6 May 1996 · BFI NFTVA, advertising film footage · BFI NFTVA, sports footage · priv. coll. | SOUND BBC WAC
Likenesses photograph, 1938, Central Press · photographs, 1938–56, Hult. Arch. · photograph, 1947, Empics Sports Photo Agency, Nottingham [*see illus.*] · H. Carr, oils, 1951, MCC, Lord's, London; [on loan] · D. Glass, photograph, 1952 · P. Mennim, acrylic, repro. in *The Observer* (16 Aug 1992), 34
Wealth at death £385,465: probate, 29 Oct 1990, *CGPLA Eng. & Wales*

Hutton, Luke (*d.* 1598), highwayman and writer, is of uncertain origins. Sir John Harington states that he was the younger son of Matthew *Hutton (1529?–1606), archbishop of York, an opinion also adopted by Cooper. However, according to Thomas Fuller, whose account is accepted by Ralph Thoresby and William Hutchinson, Luke was the son of Robert Hutton, prebendary of Durham, and his wife, Grace (*née* Pilkington), making him the nephew of Archbishop Hutton. He matriculated as a sizar of Trinity College, Cambridge, in October 1582, but left without a degree. Described as 'so valiant that he feared not men nor laws' (Harington, 192), Hutton took to a life of crime, specializing in highway robbery. In 1598 he robbed nineteen men in Yorkshire on St Luke's day, 18 October (also Hutton's birthday). After a long hue and cry, he was arrested and committed to Newgate in London. He was subsequently transferred to York, where he was tried and hanged the same year.

Hutton is the author of *Luke Hutton's Repentance*, a lost poem dedicated to Henry, earl of Huntingdon, and entered in the Stationers' register on 3 November 1595; and of *The Black Dogge of Newgate* (*c*.1596). This was reprinted as *The Discovery of a London Monster* in 1638. The preface of *The Black Dogge* reveals that the *Repentance* had been printed, although no copy now remains; the manuscript of the 'Repentance', also now lost, once belonged to the antiquarian Ralph Thoresby. *The Black Dogge of Newgate* is dedicated to Chief Justice Sir John Popham, possibly in gratitude for Popham's successful intercession on Hutton's behalf when he was convicted on a capital charge in

1595. The text, which comprises a ballad about the author's experience in Newgate and a prose dialogue between the author and 'Zawney', an inmate of Newgate, subverts the coney-catching genre. Instead of titillating the reader with a glimpse into the criminal underworld, this is an impassioned document, protesting at prison conditions and the brutality and corruption of prison officials. The 'criminals' here are not those imprisoned in Newgate, but their warders and the so-called instruments of justice. A lost 'comodye' in two parts called *The Black Dog of Newgate* and written by Hathway, Wentworth, Smith, John Day, and one 'other poet' was produced by the Earl of Worcester's Company in 1602 and 1603. No record of the play is known to exist, so any connection with Hutton's text is unascertainable.

Soon after Hutton's execution a broadside ballad was published, dubiously ascribed to Hutton and entitled 'Luke Huttons Lamentation which he Wrote the Day before his Death'. Set to the tune of 'Wandering and Wavering', the ballad narrates how Hutton, despite his lineage 'of good degree', was led astray by 'many a graceless mate'. By the age of twenty he was a fully-fledged criminal, accompanied by twelve henchmen, whom he irreverently dubbed his 'twelve apostles'.

CATHY SHRANK

Sources L. Hutton, *The black dogge of Newgate* (c.1596) · [L. Hutton?], *Luke Huttons lamentation* (1598) · A. V. Judges, *The Elizabethan underworld* (1930) · Cooper, *Ath. Cantab.*, vol. 2 · *The correspondence of Dr Matthew Hutton, archbishop of York*, ed. [J. Raine], SurtS, 17 (1843) · T. Fuller, *The church history of Britain*, ed. J. S. Brewer, new edn, 6 vols. (1845), vol. 5 · J. Harington, *A briefe view of the state of the Church of England* (1653) · W. Hutchinson, *The history and antiquities of the county palatine of Durham*, 1 (1785) · R. Thoresby, *Vicaria Leodiensis, or, The history of the church of Leedes in Yorkshire* (1724) · L. Hutton, *The discovery of a London monster* (1638) · *Henslowe's diary*, ed. R. A. Foakes and R. T. Rickert (1961) · W. W. Rouse Ball and J. A. Venn, eds., *Admissions to Trinity College, Cambridge*, 2 (1913) · *Musaeum Thoresbyanum, a catalogue of the collection of Ralph Thoresby* [1764]

Hutton, Matthew (1529?–1606), archbishop of York, was the son of Matthew Hutton of Priest Hutton in the parish of Warton, Lancashire. He went to Cambridge at the very end of the reign of Henry VIII, matriculating from Trinity College in 1546. He graduated BA early in 1552 and proceeded MA in 1555, when he was also elected a fellow of Trinity.

Early career Hutton delayed entering the church until 1560. That year he received a prebend in Ely Cathedral and the next year he became Lady Margaret professor of divinity and chaplain to Edmund Grindal, bishop of London, whom he succeeded in 1562 as master of Pembroke. In the same year he proceeded BD and exchanged the Lady Margaret chair for the regius professorship of divinity, gaining a particular reputation as a patristic scholar. It was probably in Cambridge that he amassed a considerable library of the early fathers in addition to the works of Bucer, Calvin, Marlot, and Musculus, which he mentioned in his will. Also in 1562 he was presented by Grindal to a prebend in St Paul's Cathedral and he acquired the Huntingdonshire rectory of Abbots Ripton (which he resigned in 1565); in 1563 he obtained the rectory of Boxworth,

Matthew Hutton (1529?–1606), by unknown artist, in or before 1606

Cambridgeshire. By 1564 Hutton had resigned his fellowship: that year he married Katherine Fulnetby, niece of Thomas Goodrich, the late bishop of Ely and lord chancellor, but she died soon afterwards, without children. In August 1564 Hutton, as regius professor, presided over the formal disputation during the queen's visit to Cambridge, and the next year he preached at court at the invitation of Archbishop Matthew Parker. In 1565 the earl of Leicester procured him a prebend in Westminster Abbey. In November that year, as the vestiarian controversy unfolded, Hutton, with John Whitgift (then Lady Margaret professor), and three other heads of houses, wrote to the chancellor, Sir William Cecil, begging him to moderate the imposition of conformity within the university. In 1567 Hutton married Beatrix (d. 1582), daughter of Sir Thomas Fincham of the Isle of Ely.

Dean of York The preferment for which Hutton seemed destined came the same year when the queen appointed him to the deanery of York. Although he relinquished the mastership of Pembroke and the regius chair, his prebends in Ely and Westminster, and the rectory of Boxworth, he held the deanery in conjunction with a prebend in Southwell, the rectory of West Leake, Nottinghamshire, and the rectory of Settrington, Yorkshire. This combination of livings produced an annual income of over £440 in 1575.

Hutton immediately made his presence felt in York, persuading the mayor and corporation in spring 1568 to discontinue the performance of the medieval creed play, which he considered contained much contrary to scriptural truth. An assiduous member of both the chapter and the ecclesiastical commission he worked tirelessly for the advancement of protestantism. On the death of Thomas Young in June 1568 Hutton urged upon Cecil the necessity of choosing a learned, discreet, and courageous man as the new archbishop of York before recommending his own patron Grindal for the post, but it was only after the rebellion of the earls had revealed the extent of conservatism in the north that the queen sanctioned the translation of the bishop of London to York in April 1570.

Decades after the event Elizabeth Russell, Lady Russell, reminded her nephew Sir Robert Cecil that some forward protestants had hoped that Hutton would then replace Grindal at London. Archbishop Parker, however, while granting him to be 'an honest, quiet and learned man … thought him not meet for that place' (Strype, *Parker*, 2.6). Still relatively young in 1570 Hutton could afford to wait, and working with Archbishop Grindal and later also the godly Henry Hastings, third earl of Huntingdon (from October 1572 president of the council in the north), he lent his aid with renewed vigour to the building of a protestant commonwealth in the north of England.

To win over waverers and further the protestant cause Huntingdon arranged for a general communion to be held in York Minster on 23 September 1576. The sermon Hutton delivered on this occasion was the only one of his works to be published in his lifetime; it appeared as *A Sermon Preached at Yorke* (1579). Taking as his text 'Consider and inquire of the old ways, which is good and walk therein', he cited the fathers as evidence that it was not the church of Rome but the newly restored Church of England which possessed 'the old, ancient, catholic and apostolic religion'.

Clashes with Archbishop Sandys Grindal's removal to Canterbury in 1576 brought an abrupt end to this period of active co-operation between the most senior representatives of church and state in the north. Fiercely loyal to Grindal during his public confrontation with the queen later in the year over the necessity for frequent preaching, Hutton and Huntingdon held that the new archbishop of York, Edwin Sandys, through his exaggerated reports of the extent of puritanism in the northern province, was at least partly responsible for the primate's continued sequestration. For his part, Sandys resented the friendship between the dean and the lord president. These tensions came to a head on Sandys's visitation of Durham in October 1578. When the archbishop tried to deprive the dean, William Whittingham, for his failure to obtain ordination within the Church of England, Hutton declared in open court 'that the orders at Geneva are more agreeing with the Word of God than popish orders'. Goaded yet further by Sandys he went on to claim a better title than the archbishop himself, 'for I was made a minister by the order of the queen's majesty and laws now established, and your grace a priest after the order of popery' (Borth. Inst., BP C and P XIX).

The subsequent formal apology extracted from Hutton did little to heal the breach. When in 1585 Sandys on his own initiative attempted to impose a total ban on usury in York, the dean again showed no hesitation over correcting him in public, asserting on the authority of Calvin, Bullinger, Beza, Bucer, and others that the word of God allowed many practices forbidden by the law of Moses. The archbishop turned to the privy council for redress, but this time, since the 1571 statute permitted some taking of interest, he had to admit defeat.

The enmity between the two clerics seems effectively to have barred Hutton from further promotion for over a decade. During his disgrace Grindal had hoped that his protégé might have been given the bishopric of Carlisle in 1577. Sandys, desperate to rid himself of his troublesome dean, had wanted him dispatched outside the province to Coventry and Lichfield, but Hutton had prevented this manoeuvre. Then, on the death of Sandys in 1588, his fortune changed and at the age of about sixty he finally attained a bishopric. Five years earlier Hutton, a widower since May 1582, had married, on 20 November 1583, Frances, widow of Martin Bowes, son of the London alderman Sir Martin Bowes.

Bishop of Durham While not Burghley's first choice for Durham in 1589, Hutton subsequently attributed his advancement to the chief minister's patronage and indeed the two men had much in common in their churchmanship. With other senior clergy, in 1573 Hutton had deplored the emergence of presbyterianism with its threat to remove the monarch's authority in ecclesiastical matters, despoil the church of its patrimony, and bring in an equality of ministers. Just after his nomination to Durham he once again aired his opinions on matters of church and state over a private dinner in London with Sir Francis Walsingham and Burghley. A convinced supporter of the royal supremacy he held that it was the duty of 'godly princes to advance true religion, put down idolatry and punish idolaters and to deal with matters and persons ecclesiastical'. To counter presbyterian claims he now cautiously affirmed apostolic sanction for episcopacy, maintaining that Titus and Timothy had exercised an office distinct from that 'of them who had only authority to preach and minister the sacraments, but not to appoint priests and censure offenders' (Strype, *Whitgift*, 3.224–8).

As bishop of Durham, Hutton inherited many secular responsibilities alongside his ecclesiastical duties, working harmoniously with the dean, Tobie Matthew, despite the fact that the latter had been a rival contender for the see. Although unswerving in his hostility to Catholicism, Hutton believed that papists should be won over to protestantism only by persuasion, not compulsion. Having procured her conversion, he sued repeatedly on behalf of Lady Margaret Neville, one of the daughters of the late earl of Westmorland, who had been condemned to death for sheltering a seminary priest, eventually obtaining for her both a pardon and a pension.

After about five years at Bishop Auckland, in January 1595 Hutton was offered the archbishopric of York, this time the uncontested candidate following the death of John Piers. As dean of York he had refused a request from

Archbishop Parker for a prebend for the son of civil lawyer John Hammond, prevented the confirmation of leases to members of Sandys's family, and rallied the chapter to resist the claims of Dr Gibson, dispensed by the queen to enjoy the revenues of residentiary canon though non-resident. It was, therefore, entirely predictable that Hutton should have withstood Sir Robert Cecil's attempt to extract a grant of Marton Priory for his brother-in-law, George Brooke, as the price of his elevation to York. 'I never hurt any ecclesiastical living in my life', he informed Cecil, 'and I am loth to begin now when one of my feet is almost in the grave' (*Salisbury MSS*, 5.95). Under pressure from his father and Lady Russell, Cecil made a strategic retreat.

Archbishop of York Within months of his return to York, Hutton became immersed in theological controversy in Cambridge, where to the consternation of the senior members a young Frenchman, Peter Baro, had been questioning the doctrine of predestination in his public lectures. The heads of houses then appealed to the archbishop of Canterbury and at this juncture Whitgift turned to Hutton for support. He responded by writing a short Latin treatise on predestination, and the three-way collaboration of Whitgift, Hutton, and the Cambridge heads eventually resulted in the production of the impeccably Calvinist Lambeth articles. Disconcerted by the court's hostile reaction to this declaration of faith Whitgift failed to see Hutton's tract through the press as he had hoped, but it appeared posthumously in a composite volume published in the Netherlands in 1613.

Hutton had been back in York for less than a year when the earl of Huntingdon died unexpectedly in December 1595. Lamenting 'that her Majesty hath lost so precious a jewel, the gospel so true a professor, and this country so worthy a governor' he immediately impressed upon Burghley the need to replace him with a nobleman of a similar calibre, only to find that the government required him to execute the office himself for much of the rest of the decade (BL, Lansdowne MS 79, no. 47).

Always ready to spring to the defence of the protestant cause, as he aged Hutton became even more willing to take on a prophetic role. Sir John Harington recalled one celebrated occasion which took place apparently early in 1596. Summoned to preach at court before Elizabeth and the lords spiritual and temporal, Hutton chose for his text 'The kingdoms of the earth are mine'. After a short summary of English history, and obligatory eulogy upon the blessings of the present reign, he urged upon his auditory the necessity of establishing the succession, without any circumlocution naming the king of Scots. The queen reacted with a 'sharp message' which left the archbishop scarcely knowing whether 'he were a prisoner or a free man' (Harington, 186–91).

This rebuff notwithstanding, Hutton still continued as the acting president of the council in the north, devoting the greater part of his time to overseeing the execution of justice, securing the defence of the region, and raising troops and horse for Ireland. In 1597 he and the council reported at length to Burghley and Sir Robert Cecil on a contested county election. Later in the year he had to accept custody of Scottish hostages sent into England to secure peace on the borders. In the late summer of 1599 the queen at last granted him his discharge.

Reluctantly involved in the factional struggle between the earl of Essex and Sir Robert Cecil, Hutton persisted in seeing the earl almost until the end as the great protector of the protestant cause. He sent an edifying message to Essex during his imprisonment after his precipitate return from Ireland in autumn 1599, and the following year, only days before the earl's removal from the privy council, confided to Whitgift his hope that the queen might yet be reconciled 'to that noble gentleman now abiding the frowns of fortune' (*Correspondence*, 153–5). After Essex's rebellion and execution in February 1601, in a letter to Cecil the archbishop felt constrained to clear himself of ever having been involved in any treasonable dealings with the earl of Leicester's political heir.

Given his tense relationship with Cecil, from the first Hutton seems to have been ill at ease with his elder brother, Thomas Cecil, second Lord Burghley, the new president of the council in the north. Even before Burghley reached York, Whitgift had warned Hutton of rumours circulating at court concerning the latter's responsibility for the increase of Catholicism in the region. On his arrival Burghley pointedly introduced a scheme forcing recusant prisoners to attend a course of protestant sermons, though their unruly behaviour brought the experiment to a speedy end. In 1602 Hutton became entangled in a precedence dispute with Burghley, again considering it necessary to assure Cecil that he did not doubt that the friendship between himself and his brother would soon be restored.

There seems to have been some substance in the privy council's concern that Hutton, when acting president of the council in the north, had not given sufficient attention to the threat from Catholicism. In contrast to his time as dean, as archbishop he rarely appeared in the high commission, delegating most of the routine business of prosecuting recusants to his clerical subordinates. His commitment to evangelical protestantism, on the other hand, never slackened: in 1597, for example, Whitgift admonished his fellow archbishop for referring to Christ's tide rather than Christmas in official letters. Two thirds of the young men ordained by Hutton during his ten years as archbishop were graduates or had at least studied for a time at a university. He took great pride in the rising educational standards of the clergy generally over the course of the reign, and when fighting an attempt to dissolve the collegiate church of Southwell in 1602, boasted that the English church then possessed 'the greatest number of learned men … that ever was' (*Salisbury MSS*, 12.7).

On the accession of James I, brought up in Scotland under a different protestant church order, the very future of the Church of England seemed open to doubt, and the bishops immediately rallied to its defence. Dispensed on account of his age and infirmity from attending the first parliament of the reign, in autumn 1603 Hutton submitted to Whitgift his opinion on propositions likely to be discussed at the forthcoming Hampton Court conference, reiterating his belief that an episcopal form of church government best suited an aristocratic state, and that bishops derived their authority from the apostles themselves. The following spring Tobie Matthew wrote to reassure him that James intended to preserve the church unscathed. The same report brought news of the death of Whitgift, mourned by Hutton as 'an ancient, constant and dear friend' (Strype, *Whitgift*, 408–9).

Very conscious now of being one of the last survivors of those evangelical protestants entrusted half a century earlier with reforming the English church, Hutton in his final months became increasingly troubled by the court's readiness to regard popery and puritanism as equivalent threats to the state, and in December 1604 singlehandedly set about trying to reverse government policy. Writing to Cecil (now Viscount Cranbourne) what was in effect an open letter, he deplored the 'fantastical zeal' of the puritans, but went on to emphasize that 'though they differ in ceremonies and accidents, yet they agree with us in substance of religion' adding that 'all, or the most of them, love his majesty and the present state; and I hope will yield to conformity'. On the other hand, 'the papists are opposite, and contrary in very many substantial points of religion, and cannot but wish the pope's authority and popish religion to be established'. It was, he assured Cranbourne, 'high time to look to them'. He then characteristically added an appeal that the king might restrain his passion for hunting 'both that poor men's corn may be less spoiled, and other his majesty's subjects more spared' (Borth. Inst., Abp 3A).

Neither James nor Cranbourne took kindly to this censure, but despite a stinging rebuke Hutton still succeeded in thwarting the campaign by the new archbishop of Canterbury, Richard Bancroft, for the strict enforcement of protestant conformity in the north. In reply to a government circular he asserted that there were very few puritans in his province and that it would be necessary to take proceedings against only the most wilful and obstinate, and he in fact deprived only four.

Hutton's petition for non-separating puritans proved to be his swan song. He made his will on 20 November 1605, conducted his last ordination ceremony nine days later, and died at Bishopthorpe on 16 January 1606, leaving a widow and a considerable estate; he was buried at York Minster. He had secured the future of his six surviving children, all from his second marriage, long before his death. In 1592 he had settled £1900 upon his eldest son, Timothy, on his marriage to the daughter of Sir George Bowes of Streatlam. Both Timothy Hutton of Marske and his younger brother, Thomas Hutton of Nether Poppleton, married to a daughter of his father's chancellor, Sir John Bennet, established county families in Yorkshire. Hutton also obtained appropriate matches for his daughters: the eldest married George Slater, rector of Bainton;

Elizabeth married Richard Remington, archdeacon of Cleveland; Thomasine married Sir William Gee, secretary to the council in the north; and Anne married John Calverley, gentleman.

In his lifetime Hutton had founded at Warton a grammar school and almshouse with an annual rent charge of £24. In his will he bestowed an annuity of £100 upon his wife to augment her jointure. He intended the manor of Darton and property in Pontefract to pass to his son Thomas after his stepmother's death, and then apart from donations to the poor he reserved most of the remainder of his bequests for his grandchildren. His heirs erected a monument to his memory in the south choir aisle of York Minster.   CLAIRE CROSS

Sources chancery will, 20 Nov 1605; high commission act books, 1568–1603, Borth. Inst., BP C and P XIX; Abp. 3A; HC AB 4–13 · dean and chapter act book, 1567–89, York Minster Archives, H 4 · York City Archives, housebook 1565–72, fol. 106; housebook 1572–4, fol. 27 · BL, Lansdowne MS 79, no. 47 · *The correspondence of Dr Matthew Hutton, archbishop of York*, ed. [J. Raine], SurtS, 17 (1843) · *Calendar of the manuscripts of the most hon. the marquis of Salisbury*, 24 vols., HMC, 9 (1883–1976), vol. 2, p. 60; vol. 4, p. 557; vols. 5–13, 16–17 · J. Harington, *A briefe view of the state of the Church of England* (1653), 186–91 · J. Strype, *The life and acts of Matthew Parker*, new edn, 3 vols. (1821), vol. 2, p. 6; vol. 3, pp. 125–6, 392–402, 408–9 · J. Strype, *The life and acts of Archbishop Whitgift* (1821), vol. 3, pp. 224–8, 420–21 · J. Strype, *Annals of the Reformation and establishment of religion … during Queen Elizabeth's happy reign*, new edn, 4 (1824), 545–9 · C. Cross, ed., 'The third earl of Huntingdon's death-bed', *Northern History*, 21 (1985), 100–01 · C. Cross, ed., *York clergy ordinations, 1561–1642*, Borthwick List and Index, 24 (2000), 81–9 · D. M. Meads, ed., *The diary of Lady Margaret Hoby* (1930), 73 · P. Lake, 'Matthew Hutton: a puritan bishop?', *History*, 64 (1979), 182–204 · P. Lake, *Moderate puritans and the Elizabethan church* (1982) · B. Usher, *Lord Burghley and episcopacy* [forthcoming] · I. P. Ellis, 'The archbishop and the usurers', *Journal of Ecclesiastical History*, 21 (1970), 33–42 · P. Collinson, *Archbishop Grindal, 1519–1583: the struggle for a reformed church* (1979) · R. Marchant, *The puritans and the church courts in the diocese of York, 1560–1642* (1960) · J. C. H. Aveling, *Catholic recusancy in the city of York, 1558–1791*, Catholic RS, monograph ser., 2 (1970), 50, 65 · R. R. Reid, *The king's council in the north* (1921) · Venn, *Alum. Cant.* · J. T. Cliffe, *The Yorkshire gentry from the Reformation to the civil war* (1969), 372–3 · A. C. Ducarel, 'Memoirs of the Hutton family', in *The correspondence of Dr Matthew Hutton, archbishop of York*, ed. [J. Raine], SurtS, 17 (1843), 1–49
Archives Hatfield House, Hertfordshire, letters · N. Yorks. CRO, letters
Likenesses portrait, in or before 1606; Sothebys, 19 Feb 1969, lot 168 [*see illus.*] · F. Perry, etching, *c.*1760 (after oil painting), BM, NPG · tomb effigy, York Minster; repro. in G. E. Aylmer and R. Cant, eds., *A history of York Minster* (1977), facing p. 137 · two portraits, Bishopthorpe Palace, York; repro. in J. Ingamells, *A catalogue of portraits at Bishopthorpe Palace* (1972), pls. 2 A and B
Wealth at death substantial: *Correspondence*, ed. [Raine], xxii–xxiii; Cliffe, *Yorkshire gentry*

Hutton, Matthew (1638/9–1711), antiquary, was born in Nether Poppleton, Yorkshire, the third son of Richard Hutton (1613–1648) and his wife, Dorothy (*d.* 1687), daughter of Ferdinando, Baron Fairfax of Cameron, Scotland. He was the great-grandson of Matthew Hutton, archbishop of York. Hutton was educated at Brasenose College, Oxford, where he was elected a fellow, graduating MA in 1661 and BD in 1669. While at Oxford he became a friend of

Anthony Wood, who described him as an excellent violist. He also developed an interest in antiquities, as evidenced by Wood's reference to a joint visit they paid to local churches and other archaeological sites and to his surviving church notes for Oxfordshire (Bodl. Oxf., Rawlinson B 397). In March 1677 he became rector of Aynho, Northamptonshire, and in 1689 he secured a second benefice at Croughton, Northamptonshire. In the following year he obtained his doctorate. At this comparatively late stage in his life he married Elizabeth (1663–1723), the daughter of Sir Roger Burgoyne of Sutton, Bedfordshire, and his second wife, Anne, granddaughter of Sir Thomas Hutton of Poppleton. Their two sons survived him.

Hutton was well known for his volumes of extracts from monastic registers and public records and for his heraldic collections. He also made collections of epitaphs. He corresponded widely and was generous in allowing other antiquaries access to his collections. In 1703 he was chosen along with John Anstis and Humphrey Wanley to prepare a report on the Cotton Library for its newly appointed trustees. According to Thomas Hearne, Francis Atterbury 'had most of the materials for writing his book about *Convocations* of Dr. Hutton' (*Remarks*, 1.283), while Atterbury's opponent White Kennett in turn provided Hutton with material useful for continuing Godwin's *Catalogue of Bishops*. In 1706 it was contended that he would willingly undertake such a continuation, if he 'were but encouraged with a dignity in the church' (ibid., 1.285–6), and his collections certainly contained material appropriate for the task. The lack of preferment may well be the excuse of a natural collector with little inclination for synthesis justifying himself to his contemporaries. Equally, Hutton's need to provide for his sons, the elder of whom was shortly to go to Oxford, may have led him to consider composition as a means of securing a larger income. Whatever the truth, no evidence of composition remains among his papers.

Although *Three Letters Concerning the Present State of Italy* (1687) has been attributed to Hutton, the grounds for this attribution are flimsy and it seems certain that Hearne was correct in stating that he never published anything. Nevertheless, the value of his collections was widely recognized and it was hoped that he would leave them to the public library in Oxford. When he died at Aynho on 29 June 1711, aged seventy-two, their fate was unsettled and they are not mentioned in his will. The collection of about forty volumes of extracts and indexes was subsequently purchased by the earl of Oxford for £150 and is now in the British Library. Hutton was buried at Aynho on 30 June 1711.

JAN BROADWAY

Sources *Remarks and collections of Thomas Hearne*, ed. C. E. Doble and others, 11 vols., OHS, 2, 7, 13, 34, 42–3, 48, 50, 65, 67, 72 (1885–1921), vol 1, pp. 71, 283–6; vol. 3, pp. 182, 280 · *The correspondence of Dr Matthew Hutton, archbishop of York*, ed. [J. Raine], SurtS, 17 (1843) · Foster, *Alum. Oxon., 1500–1714* [Mathew Hutton] · Wood, *Ath. Oxon.*, new edn, 1.xxxiv–xxxv, lxi · will, PRO, PROB 11/525, sig. 30 · C. Cooper and T. Cooper, 'Three letters concerning the present state of Italy', *N&Q*, 3rd ser., 4 (1863), 164

Archives BL, Harley MSS 6950–6985, 7519–7521, 1232, 5329, 5348 · Bodl. Oxf., letters and copies of MSS · York Minster, Antiquities of Yorkshire | CUL, letters, mostly to John Strype
Wealth at death lands in Mowthorp, Yorkshire, and £200 to son, Roger; lands in Poppleton, Yorkshire, and £200 to son, Thomas

Hutton, Matthew (1693–1758), archbishop of Canterbury, was born on 3 January 1693 at Kirby Hill, near Richmond in Yorkshire, the second son of John Hutton and his wife, Sarah, and a lineal descendant of Matthew Hutton, archbishop of York from 1596 to 1606. He attended the school at Kirby Hill but moved, with his headmaster, Mr Loyd, to the free school in Ripon. In June 1710 he entered Jesus College, Cambridge, as an exact contemporary of Thomas Herring, whom he succeeded in all three of his episcopal offices. Having graduated in 1713 he moved to Christ's College, of which he was a fellow from 1717 to 1727. In March 1732 Hutton married Mary, daughter of Henry Lutman of Petworth, and they had two daughters, Dorothy and Mary.

In 1736, already a royal chaplain and, from 1728, a DD, Hutton accompanied George II on a visit to Hanover and, as chaplain to the duke of Somerset, received preferment as rector of Trowbridge and also of Spofforth in Yorkshire. Elected to a canonry of Windsor he exchanged this, in 1739, for a prebend at Westminster; he had acquired a prebend at York from Archbishop Lancelot Blackburne in 1734. When Herring moved from Bangor to York in 1743, Hutton succeeded him as bishop of Bangor, and subsequently, when Herring was translated to Canterbury (1747), Hutton became archbishop of York. He followed Herring a third time, in 1757, when he himself became archbishop of Canterbury. However, he died the following year, never having occupied the house at Lambeth, there having been a dispute with Herring's executors over dilapidations. He occupied instead a house in Duke Street, Westminster. Hutton died on 18 March 1758, following a bowel rupture, and was buried on 19 March in Lambeth parish church.

Some of Hutton's sermons were published. They embodied plain, practical teaching, free from doctrinal nuances and reflecting the latitudinarian outlook of their author. The patronage of George II was a potent influence on Hutton's career and the friendship of the duke of Newcastle made Hutton's tenure of the northern and southern primacies more agreeable than had been the case with Herring. Hutton's demeanour was aristocratic; he was reputed never to have let himself down below the dignity of an archbishop. Apart from the patronage of George II his advancement was chiefly due to the favour of the duke of Somerset, chancellor of Cambridge University. He was said to be over-fond of money but said also to be of a cheerful and amiable disposition. A. C. Ducarel, in a memoir published in 1834, offered a glowing estimate of Hutton. However, his tenure of high office was unmemorable and, although personally agreeable, he was an undistinguished primate.

ROBERT T. HOLTBY

Sources Venn, *Alum. Cant.* · York registers and act books, Borth. Inst. · M. Bateson, 'Clerical preferment under the duke of Newcastle', *EngHR*, 7 (1892), 685–96 · N. Sykes, *Church and state in England* *in the XVIII century* (1934) • E. Hailstone, *Portrait of Yorkshire worthies*, 2 vols. (1869) • A. C. Ducarel, 'Memoirs of the Hutton family', in *The correspondence of Dr Matthew Hutton, archbishop of York*, ed. [J. Raine], SurtS, 17 (1843), 1–49

Archives BM, MSS • Borth. Inst., corresp. and papers • Leeds Central Library, MSS • LPL, papers relating to York • York Minster, chapter acts | BL, corresp. with duke of Newcastle etc., Add. MSS 32700–32878, *passim*

Likenesses T. Hudson, oils, *c*.1754, LPL • J. Faber junior, mezzotint (after T. Hudson), BM, NPG • B. Wilson?, portrait • oils (after T. Hudson, 1749), Bishopthorpe Palace, York

Hutton, Sir Richard (*bap.* 1561, *d.* 1639), judge, was a younger (second or third) son of Anthony Hutton (*d.* 1590), of Hutton Hall, Penrith, and his wife, Elizabeth (or Eleanor) Musgrave, formerly of Hayton Castle, Cumberland, and was baptized on 2 May 1561 at St Andrew's Church, Penrith. Richard possibly attended Penrith grammar school, where his father served as governor, before proceeding to Jesus College, Cambridge. There (according to Thomas Fuller) he originally studied for the church, but was persuaded to try the common law, entering Gray's Inn in June 1580 from its satellite Staple Inn. Called to the bar in 1586, five years later Hutton married Agnes Briggs (*d. c.*1648), who came from Westmorland, may have been a lawyer's daughter, eventually bore her husband nine children, and still outlived him. By 1592 Hutton had moved across the Pennines to the West Riding of Yorkshire, where he became escheator of the county and acquired the substantial manor of Goldsborough. While continuing to buy land in Cumberland, Westmorland, and Yorkshire, Hutton also accumulated honours and offices, as member of the council of the north (1599), serjeant-at-law (1603), receiver-general and chancellor of the bishopric of Durham (1608–9), and recorder of York, Doncaster, and Ripon (1608–10).

Hutton's remarkably swift rise to professional eminence was plainly assisted by some powerful clients and friends, including George Clifford, third earl of Cumberland, and Matthew Hutton, archbishop of York. His inclusion as the only northerner in the 1603 call of serjeants appears to have been something of an afterthought, possibly secured by Clifford. But whereas most of those called gained judgeships over the next decade, Hutton was to wait until 1617 for his next major promotion, as puisne justice of common pleas. This delay is partly explained by Hutton's relative youth and junior standing when he first became serjeant, and perhaps also by his lack of effective patrons after the deaths of both Cumberland and Archbishop Hutton early in James I's reign. Further, it may be that unfavourable notice was taken of his leading role as counsel for the defence in two major early Jacobean trials, *R.* v. *Bate* (1606) and *Calvin's Case* (1606–7), as well as his arguments on behalf of Serjeant John Hele (1604) and against the broad jurisdictional claims made by the council of Wales and the marches (*c.*1608). The predominantly regional orientation of Hutton's career, coupled with his lack of experience as a member of parliament and apparent low profile among the serjeants practising in Westminster Hall, may also have told against him. Finally,

Sir Richard Hutton (*bap.* 1561, *d.* 1639), by unknown artist, 1618

there could have been doubts about his religious sympathies, the lingering aftermath of two intercepted letters allegedly written by Hutton in the early 1580s, which then caused him to be labelled a papist, although these documents hardly provide conclusive evidence of popish leanings, and there is ample subsequent proof of his zealous protestantism.

Given his strong regional identification, it is appropriate that Hutton first learned of his impending judgeship (possibly secured by the newly appointed lord keeper, his Gray's Inn colleague Francis Bacon) during James I's visit to York in 1617. As recorder he naturally played a leading role in this important municipal event, and was knighted by the king after a convivial mayoral banquet in the Guildhall. Summoned next day into the royal presence and told he was to become a judge, Hutton claims that he asked to be spared. According to his account, the king replied that he had been spared too long, and 'he would hold a good opinion of me as an honest man' (*Diary*, 18). This passage comes from the extensive manuscript journal which Hutton started in 1614 and kept up until a few weeks before his death. Although overwhelmingly a record of public and professional events, rather than an inward-looking autobiographical memoir, it provides a unique participant-observer account of contemporary legal and political events, institutions, and personalities. Hutton's diary, as it has come to be known, bears strong similarities in form and language to his law reports, covering cases on which he sat as justice of common pleas, which survive both in manuscript copies and as printed texts published posthumously in 1656 and 1682.

After his promotion to the bench, as indeed before it, Hutton's name rarely occurs except in more or less official contexts and sources, with the partial exception of a run of correspondence with his Yorkshire neighbour Sir Thomas Wentworth, whose sister had married the judge's eldest son. Lack of estate or family papers precludes detailed reconstruction of his domestic and professional lives, although these must have been full and busy ones. Frequently commissioned by the privy council to advise, arbitrate, and report, Hutton also served regularly as an assize judge on the western and midland circuits. He attended most parliaments of the 1620s as one of the legal assistants to the House of Lords, and presided over the court of common pleas for twelve months from December 1625, during the vacancy which followed the death of Chief Justice Hobart. Hutton was thus at the forefront of the judges' persistent refusal to lend their collective endorsement to the forced loan raised by the crown in 1626, and experienced the king's angry reaction at first hand. He again found himself in direct confrontation with his royal master following the stormy finale to the second parliamentary session of 1628–9, when all the judges were summoned individually before the king in an effort to obtain their sanction for a Star Chamber prosecution of the imprisoned MPs, which Hutton and a majority of his colleagues refused.

In 1635 Hutton refused to join the other eleven common-law judges in endorsing the legality of extending ship money writs from maritime counties to the country as a whole. Although eventually subscribing under great pressure to the unanimous judicial opinion of 1637 in favour of ship money, when the case of *R. v. Hampden* came to trial in November of that year he gave the crown's case short shrift. Hutton's judgment, issued six months later, declared that such a charge might not be imposed by the king alone, without parliamentary assent, unless in times of actual invasion and war. Widely circulated, and applauded, this decision undoubtedly helped stiffen resistance to the collection of ship money. It also impelled a Laudian clergyman to accuse Hutton publicly in Westminster Hall of high treason, a charge which led to the Revd Thomas Harrison's prosecution by the crown, and a civil verdict of £10,000 damages for Hutton from a sympathetic jury.

Having long complained of 'infirmities, companions of age, especially the sciatica' (*Diary*, xxiin.), Hutton died at Serjeants' Inn, Chancery Lane, on 26 February 1639 following a brief illness. He was buried next day at St Dunstan-in-the-West, Fleet Street, 'without funeral sermon, save what his own virtues preached to posterity' (Fuller, 1.344). While clearly possessing strong religious convictions and deep piety, Hutton seems to have steered a middle way through the sectarian divisions of his time; in 1635 he presented both a communion table and a pulpit to Serjeant's Inn, and although his will commences with an orthodox protestant statement of faith, it only implicitly asserts a

personal assurance of election. In temporal matters Hutton was equally judicious, a political realist who could keep his own counsel as well as a deeply conservative legal traditionalist firmly conscious of his duty to God, the Commonwealth, and the common law. So while his ship money judgment won popular acclaim, and a posthumous eulogy depicted him as a 'grave Patriot', Charles I himself echoed his father in terming Hutton 'the honest judge' (*Diary*, xiii, xxxv). WILFRID PREST

Sources *The diary of Sir Richard Hutton, 1614–1639*, ed. W. R. Prest, SeldS, suppl. ser., 9 (1991) · Baker, *Serjeants* · W. R. Prest, *The rise of the barristers: a social history of the English bar, 1590–1640*, 2nd edn (1991) · Fuller, *Worthies* (1840), 1.344 · C. E. Whiting, 'The Huttons of Hooton Pagnell', *Transactions of the Hunter Archaeological Society*, 6 (1944–50), 26
Archives BL, mid-seventeenth-century collections of law cases collected by Hutton, Hargrave MS 46 · CUL, journals, Add. MSS 6862–6863 · Gloucester Cathedral library, law report
Likenesses oils, 1618, Gray's Inn Hall, London [*see illus.*] · portrait, *c.*1620, priv. coll.; ex Christies, 1985 · W. Hollar, etching, BM
Wealth at death manors, tithes, rectories, mills, and lands in Westmorland, Cumberland, Lancashire, and Yorkshire: PRO, C 142/586/108 · substantial: *Diary*, ed. Prest, 136–41; Prest, *Rise*, 371

Hutton, Richard Holt (1826–1897), journalist and theologian, was born at Leeds on 2 June 1826. He was the son of Joseph Hutton (1790–1860), a Unitarian minister, first at Mill Hall Chapel, Leeds, and later (from 1835) at Carter Lane, London, and his wife, Susannah Grindal, eldest daughter of John Holt of Nottingham. His grandfather Joseph Hutton (1765–1856), also a Unitarian minister, preached at the Eustace Street congregation, Dublin, where he was said to have 'wept easily in the pulpit' (Woodfield, 2). In 1831–2 his assistant was James Martineau, who would become Richard's first mentor and a powerful influence on his intellectual development. Hutton seemed destined to follow the profession of his grandfather and father. After attending University College School, he achieved signal distinction for his studies in philosophy and mathematics at University College, London (1841–5), and continued his studies at the University of Bonn (1845–6, where Theodor Mommsen, the distinguished German historian of the Roman empire and Switzerland, was his tutor) and the University of Heidelberg (1846–7). But his preparation for a Unitarian ministry at Manchester New College (1847–8)—where James Martineau, John James Tayler, and F. W. Newman were teaching—led, according to Gaylord C. LeRoy, to an invitation to take a pulpit, one which Hutton gave up almost as soon as he accepted it (LeRoy, 811). This account is disputed by other authorities.

In 1850 Hutton assumed the duties of vice-principal and chaplain of University Hall, Gordon Square, London, which had been founded in 1848 to accommodate liberal dissenting students, almost all of whom were Unitarians. He assisted Arthur Hugh Clough, the principal, and then succeeded him, serving in that position until the end of 1853.

In 1851 Hutton married Anne Roscoe, the sister of William Caldwell Roscoe, his colleague and close friend, on whom Hutton would later write a moving memoir. Illness

Richard Holt Hutton (1826–1897), by Frederick Hollyer

interrupted his administrative duties, and his convalescence in the West Indies (to which his doctor had ordered him) was brutally delayed by a yellow fever outbreak in Barbados. He and Anne both fell ill; she died in 1852. In 1858 Hutton married for the second time; his bride was Eliza Roscoe, a first cousin of his first wife, and the daughter of Robert Roscoe. The ceremony was in accordance with the rites of the established church. There were no children of either marriage.

Within a decade Hutton's faith, and that of his brother, Joseph Henry, was seriously shaken by the teachings of F. D. Maurice, professor of English literature and modern history at King's College, London, and his doubts about the divinity of Jesus permanently undermined his interest in joining any ministry. Though he held the professorship of mathematics at Bedford College, London (1856–7), an academic career, like the life of an Anglican clergyman, proved unsatisfactory to him over the long haul. For the major part of his life he was an editor and a journalist, turning out thoughtful, substantial essays that attracted a growing audience of serious readers, among them Gladstone, who regarded him as the finest critic of the century. (Years later, Maurice claimed that Hutton's talents were better used as an editor than as a Unitarian minister or as an Anglican clergyman.) Essays clearly identified as Hutton's number 3600, and a strong case can be made for an equal number of unsigned efforts. The more important of his twelve books (all his collections are representative of

major interests, but none is a complete gathering) are *Essays Theological and Literary* (1871), *Essays in Literary Criticism* (1876), *Essays on some of the Modern Guides of English Thought in Matters of Faith* (1887), *Criticisms on Contemporary Thought and Thinkers* (1894), and *Religious and Scientific Thought* (posthumously published in 1899).

Most of Hutton's essays can be read at a single sitting. (The life of Sir Walter Scott that he contributed to John Morley's English Men of Letters series, and his life of Cardinal Newman, printed in the English Leaders of Religion series, edited by H. C. Beeching, are unusually long.) He found ready outlets for his theological and literary concerns in several periodicals. He held a joint editorship at the Unitarian *Inquirer* (1853–5), during which time the paper generated much controversy by its liberal views and lost circulation as a consequence. He also contributed articles regularly to, and served as main editor of, the *Prospective Review* (1850–55). Writing primarily on literary matters, he worked with Walter Bagehot, his co-editor, at the *National Review* (1855–62); the journal folded in 1864. His literary essays and political leaders, written for *The Economist* (1857–62), the quarterly *North British Review*, and the weekly *Saturday Review*, also helped to establish his national reputation, and led to his becoming the proprietor and joint editor of the weekly *Spectator* (1861–97). He employed the young H. H. Asquith, who wrote leaders when Hutton was on holiday. Hutton's hostility to Irish home rule ended the connection. Approximately half of all Hutton's articles were written for the *Spectator*, and, during his first few years as a co-editor with Meredith Townsend (who covered politics), Hutton's revulsion against slavery and consequent support of the Northern cause during the American Civil War stirred up harsh criticism, and led to the cancellation of several subscriptions. He attacked materialism wherever he saw it in the writings of such public figures as Darwin, Spencer, Huxley, Mill, and Tyndall. Among his other interests were the Metaphysical Society (of which he was an original member) and anti-vivisection (in 1875 he served on a royal commission dealing with this subject, and helped to draft the act of parliament that limited experiments with live animals).

Hutton wrote in a letter (1865) that Martineau had shown him 'that the old Unitarianism was as weak as it was unsuccessful', and that 'the Incarnation could be held on a Protestant basis' (Woodfield, 49). The significance of these changes in Hutton's religious views can hardly be overemphasized. But perhaps even more important than the influence of Martineau was the friendship of Hutton and Walter Bagehot (1826–1877). It began at University College, when Hutton was sixteen, and lasted more than a half-century. An anecdote recounted by Hutton tells of the two young men wandering 'up and down Regent Street for something like two hours in the vain attempt to find Oxford Street', while arguing whether the so-called logical principle of identity (A is A) should be considered 'a law of thought' or only 'a postulate of language' (*The Works of Walter Bagehot*, ed. F. Morgan, 1, 1889, xxvii–xxviii). The two men tied for classical honours at graduation, and Hutton often recorded his admiration of, and respect for, Bagehot's rhetorical and intellectual gifts. Many of Bagehot's most famous epigrams were first recorded in the memoir that Hutton contributed to the first of his three collections of Bagehot's writings: *Bagehot's Literary Studies* (1879), *Economic Studies* (1880), and *Biographical Studies* (1881). Hutton, having little sympathy for the grey world of economic 'science', had little to say about Bagehot's interest in the subject. But he spoke with glowing enthusiasm about the sharpness of Bagehot's wit, the vividness of his imagination, the emphasis upon character in both his literary and political writings, the lucidity of his style, and (more than once) the strenuousness of his effort to translate into practical, personal terms the teachings of Darwin.

In addition to Martineau and Bagehot, the significant influences on Hutton's intellectual development included his brother-in-law William Caldwell Roscoe, Coleridge, Arthur Hugh Clough (who, Hutton believed, was also the primary intellectual influence on Bagehot), Frederick William Robertson, Frederick Denison Maurice, William George Ward, Dean Richard Church, and Canon Henry Parry Liddon. But Hutton's most significant influences derived from his reading. The authors he admired, whom he judged by aesthetic as well as moral standards, ranged widely. He had little to say about continental literature, and American authors, with the notable exceptions of Nathaniel Hawthorne and James Russell Lowell, were not treated in depth. He was fascinated by Newman (thirty-six articles in addition to the book) and Arnold (more than fifty essays and reviews), while his deep interest in the contemporary novel as a literary genre led to the writing of some 1500 reviews, some of them extended discussions of fairly minor fictions.

Entering the Church of England in 1862 was, as might be expected, a reasoned choice, and Hutton was to become a high-churchman for most of his remaining life. (He would also find the Roman Catholic church attractive, though the evidence for a possible conversion is not convincing.) The eulogy he wrote for Arthur Penrhyn Stanley approved, somewhat unexpectedly, the dean of Westminster's 'picturesque sensibility' (*Criticisms on Contemporary Thought and Thinkers: Selected from 'The Spectator'*, 1894, 130)—Hutton was quoting Disraeli—and, equally important in Hutton's view, the liberal theologian's avoidance of religious symbols.

Hutton placed great emphasis upon words as indices of power. He argued that such a term as realism, characterizing works of fiction, ought to be redefined as an analogue of phrases used in the defining of religious beliefs. This personalized employment of literary terms may have proved helpful to Hutton in describing a religious text (for example, Newman's *Oxford Sermons*) as well as a poem or novel, but it ran the risk of censure from both literary critics and theologians. Many of Hutton's religious speculations did not attract converts as much as they appealed to already formed opinions. The failure of his non-literary

writings to hold their audience after the turn of the century derived from a widespread sentiment (held by even Hutton's admirers) that the theological and social issues of greatest concern to him had either been solved, however unsatisfactorily, or had become anachronisms.

Nevertheless, Hutton's view of secular literature as an opportunity for Christian believers to reconsider and improve the quality of their faith was one that he held to consistently over his long life, and a strong case may be made for the unitary wholeness of his essays, however diverse their subject matter. In 'The poetry of the Old Testament', an essay that resembles, in its core conviction, hundreds of Hutton's analyses of both religious and literary texts, he characteristically rejects 'the absurd doctrine of absolute verbal dictation, by the Divine Spirit, through the mechanical instrumentality of certain chosen men, which obviously degrades them from poets into amanuenses at once' (*Essays Theological and Literary*, 2.254). While respecting the Hebrew poet's intense interest in the spiritual element of man, he compares and contrasts narrative moments with similar scenes in Greek and Scandinavian literature. He does not restrict himself to a consideration of the truth of the insights contained in the drama of Job, but delights in the story as a '*conscious* effort of imagination', as 'the only important book in the Old Testament which is not closely interwoven with the real history and life of the nation' (ibid., 2.288).

After injury in a carriage accident in 1888, Eliza Hutton sank into a deep depression and barely spoke to her husband right up until her death on 9 February 1897. Asquith commented: 'His devotion to his poor mad wife makes an almost unique story' (Matthew, 149). Within half a year of her death Hutton fell into a coma that lasted several weeks, and died at his home at Crossdeep Lodge, Twickenham, Middlesex, on 9 September 1897. He was buried in the Twickenham parish cemetery.   HAROLD OREL

Sources M. Woodfield, *R. H. Hutton: critic and theologian* (1986) · *DNB* · R. H. Hutton, 'Memoir', in *Poems and essays by the late William Caldwell Roscoe*, 1 (1860), ix–cvii · R. H. Hutton, 'Memoir', *Fortnightly Review*, 28 (1877), 453–84 [of Walter Bagehot] · J. Hogben, *Richard Holt Hutton of 'The Spectator': a monograph*, 2nd edn (1900) · A. J. Church, 'Richard Holt Hutton', *Memories of men and books* (1908), 202–20 · W. Ward, 'Three notable editors: Delane, Hutton, Knowles', *Ten personal studies* (1908), 48–77 · H. Orel, 'Richard Holt Hutton', *Victorian literary critics* (1984), 58–89 · G. C. LeRoy, 'Richard Holt Hutton', *Publications of the Modern Language Association of America*, 56 (1941), 809–40 · D. Young, *F. D. Maurice and Unitarianism* (1992) · W. B. Thomas, *The story of The Spectator, 1828–1928* (1928) · R. A. Colby, 'How it strikes a contemporary: *The Spectator* as critic', *Nineteenth-Century Fiction*, 11 (1956), 182–206 · P. J. Creevy, 'Richard Holt Hutton on Matthew Arnold', *Victorian Poetry*, 16 (1978), 134–46 · R. H. Tener, 'The writings of Richard Holt Hutton: a check-list of identifications', *Victorian Periodicals Newsletter*, 5/3 (1972), 1–179 · R. H. Tener, 'R. H. Hutton: some attributions', *Victorian Periodicals Newsletter*, 6/2 (1973), 14–65 · H. C. G. Matthew, 'H. H. Asquith's political journalism', *BIHR*, 49 (1976), 146–51 · *IGI* · d. cert.

Archives Hunt. L., letters | BL, corresp. with W. E. Gladstone, Add. MS 44215 · BL, corresp. with Macmillans, Add. MS 55040 · DWL, letters to Henry Allon · JRL, letters to E. A. Freeman · New York Historical Society, letters to Richard Grant White · U. St Andr. L., corresp. with Wilfrid Ward · University of Sheffield, letters to Maria Theresa Mundella

Wealth at death £39,939 0s. 2d.: probate, 8 Nov 1897, *CGPLA Eng. & Wales*

Hutton [Hutten], **Robert** (*d.* 1568/1574), Church of England clergyman, is first recorded in 1548, when, under the name Robert Hutten, he published *The summe of divinitie drawen out of the holy scripture, very necessarie for curates and yong studentes in divinitie, and also meete for al Christian men and women whatsoever age they be of. Drawn out of Latin into English*. This was a translation of the *Margarita theologica* of the Lutheran theologian Johann Spangenberg. The original was published in London in 1566, probably because Hutton's translation had proved popular. Copies survive from editions dated 1560, 1561, and 1567.

In the original preface to the reader William Turner, then fellow of Pembroke College, Cambridge, described Hutton as 'my scholar sometime, and servant' (*The summe of divinitie*, sig. A2r), but nothing else is known of his origins or his university career. A man of these names was ordained deacon at York on 2 July 1553. No evidence survives to support the claim that the writer went abroad during Mary's reign. If not, he was perhaps the 'chambre keper' to Sir Thomas Benger who, along with his master, was committed to the Fleet by the privy council on 28 April 1557.

Insoluble problems of identity obscure the writer's career thereafter. Two clerics of these names were active in London diocese at the beginning of Elizabeth I's reign, one subscribing the oath of supremacy in autumn 1559 as curate of St Swithin 'at London Stone for the time' (LPL, 'Carte antique et miscellanee', fol. 2r). It was doubtless this man who was collated on 9 April 1560 to the rectory of Wickham Bishops, Essex, by Edmund Grindal, bishop of London, and at some time after May 1561 instituted to the neighbouring, impoverished rectory of Little Braxted. Robert Hutton 'clerk' was cited before the Essex quarter sessions in 1563 along with Margaret Hutton, spinster, and Richard Hutton, yeoman, all of 'Witham' (that is, Wickham Bishops). The sequel is unknown but the indictment suggests that Hutton sprang from a local family who had abetted him in the forcible distraint of tithes. He was buried at St Mary-le-Bow, London, on 5 September 1568 as 'parson in Essex'.

Thus he can be safely identified with the Robert Hutton who on 13 May 1568 was granted letters patent for the vicarage of Catterick, Yorkshire, since on 8 September of that same year Grindal mentioned to Sir William Cecil that Catterick was now void by 'Mr Hutton's' death.

Another Robert Hutton was ordained deacon and priest by Grindal on 29 September and 21 December 1561. It was probably this man who, being 'now minister of the parish church', was on 24 March 1567 granted the whole benefice, with the tithes, of St Mary Colechurch, a perpetual curacy in the gift of the Mercers' Company (Mercers' Company archives, acts of court, fol. 103v). As 'minister of St Mary Colchers' he made a hasty and undated will leaving

everything to his wife, Judith, who was granted probate by the London consistory court on 8 December 1574.

George Hennessy, in his *Novum repertorium* (1898), misdated the probate record to 1514, in the process providing an entirely fictitious reference to the earliest surviving diocesan will register.   BRETT USHER

Sources Venn, *Alum. Cant.*, 1/2.443 · state papers, Elizabeth I, PRO, SP12/47/62 · W. H. Frere, *The Marian reaction in its relation to the English clergy: a study of the episcopal registers* (1896), 218 · C. H. Garrett, *The Marian exiles: a study in the origins of Elizabethan puritanism* (1938) · Wood, *Ath. Oxon.*, new edn, 1.364 · 'Carte antique et miscellanee', LPL, XIII/57, fol. 2r · GL, MS 9537/2 fol. 61v · Cooper, *Ath. Cantab.*, 1.261–2 · Essex RO, QS/R/10/17 · GL, MS 9535/1, fols. 103v, 105v · acts of court, 1560–95, Mercers' Hall, London · London diocesan records, GL, MS 9531/13, fols. 149, 151 · will, 1574, LMA, DL/C/419/9, no. 14 · CPR, 1566–9, no. 1880 · G. Hennessy, *Novum repertorium ecclesiasticum parochiale Londinense, or, London diocesan clergy succession from the earliest time to the year 1898* (1898)
Wealth at death see will, 1574, LMA, DL/C/419/9, no. 14

Hutton, Robert Howard (1840–1887), bone-setter, was born at Soulby, Westmorland, on 26 July 1840, one of the seven children of Robert Hutton and his wife, Mary. He was a member of a family of farmers who for upwards of two hundred years had lived in the north of England, where they had been bone-setters for the benefit of their neighbours. Robert's uncle, Richard Hutton, was the first of the family to make bone-setting a profession. He set up in practice in London at Wyndham Place, Crawford Street, and died at Gilling Lodge, Watford, on 6 January 1871, aged seventy.

The younger Hutton was from 1863 to 1869 at Milnthorpe in Westmorland, where he farmed, and as a sideline set bones. About 1869 he went to London, and for some time lived with his uncle Richard. He then set up for himself, first at 74 Gloucester Place, Portman Square, and afterwards at 36 Queen Anne Street, Cavendish Square. He soon obtained a name and a position. Hutton owed his reputation to his mechanical tact and acute observation of the symptoms of dislocations. His general method of procedure was to poultice and oil the limb for a week, and then by a sudden twist or wrench set the bone to rights; in fact this treatment often effected an immediate cure. Hutton's extensive practice brought him a large fortune, but his tastes were expensive. He was devoted to all field sports, and was well-known as a huntsman at Melton Mowbray. He was kind to animals, and often set their broken limbs. In 1875 Miss Constance Innes Leslie, daughter of Charles Leslie, was thrown from her horse and broke her arm. After many months, having, as she believed, a permanently stiff arm, she went to Hutton, who restored it to its use. They were married on 26 July 1876 and had one child, Gladys.

On 16 July 1887, a servant at his address in Queen Anne Street, gave Hutton some laudanum instead of a black draught (a purgative containing liquorice extract). He died soon afterwards at University College Hospital. A verdict of death by misadventure was returned at the inquest. Hutton's career as a bone-setter shows the success which could be achieved by the unqualified medical practitioner.   G. C. BOASE, *rev.* MICHAEL BEVAN

Sources J. M. Jackson, *Bonesetter's mystery* (1882) · 'The rationale of bone-setting', *St Bartholomew's Hospital Reports*, 14 (1878), 339–46 · 'Clinical Society of London', *The Lancet* (17 April 1880), 606–8 · W. P. Hood, *On bonesetting* (1871) · S. Smiles, *George Moore, merchant and philanthropist*, 2nd edn (1878), 320–21 · 'Bone-setters', *Chambers's Journal* (9 Nov 1878), 711–13 · 'The bone-setter's mystery', *Chambers's Journal* (22 Feb 1879), 113–15 · 'Hutton the bone-setter: an explanation', *Chambers's Journal* (26 April 1879), 272 · *The Times* (18 July 1887), 7 · *The Times* (19 July 1887), 11 · *DNB* · *IGI*
Wealth at death made 'a large fortune' but had 'expensive tastes': *DNB*

Hutton, Sibilla (*d.* 1808), milliner and shopkeeper, was the daughter of the Revd William Hutton, minister of the Secession church at Dalkeith, Edinburghshire, and Sibilla Tunnock, daughter of William Tunnock, an Edinburgh brewer; they married on 7 November 1742. Sibilla was well known as a milliner in Edinburgh in the second half of the eighteenth century. Her portrait, with brief biographical notes, appears twice in *Original Portraits* by John Kay, the Edinburgh caricaturist, once in conversation with a Mr Johnston: 'two of the stoutest shopkeepers in Edinburgh'. At one point she had her shop in the Royal Exchange Buildings (founded 1754), which housed several shops, a coffee house, and other facilities. By 1786, according to the records of the inhabited house tax, she was living in Advocates' Close. She advertised her business in the Edinburgh newspapers, informing the public about special sales of goods with bargains to be had 'for ready money only'; goods were priced 'to prevent words and spending of time' (*Edinburgh Evening Courant*, June–July 1783). Such advertisements show that women shopped in person and did not only commission from home even though Edinburgh shops were very small for most of the century. Like other women shopkeepers Sibilla went to London to buy goods, her advertisements showing that she brought back the latest in fashionable millinery. She went to court in person in order to sue clients for non-payment of bills. Her sister Nellie (Mrs Kidd) was also a milliner, who in the 1780s was found at the 'Haberdashery and Millinery Warehouse, Princes Street', and in 1785 was living in Bridge Street, where she also offered 'to board young ladies, besides carrying on her other business' (ibid., December 1785).

Sibilla Hutton appears to have had an eye to the advantages of the civic improvements in Edinburgh in the latter part of the century, and in 1781 decided to improve her shop by creating a bow window. This desire, however, landed her in a lawsuit when she went ahead with the alterations without permission from the dean of guild, who was responsible for building control. She was ordered to replace the stairs she had had removed or pay a fine of £100. She went to London in 1790, presumably to find more scope for her ambitions for she opened a shop there, which was later taken over by her sister; no further information about it has come to light. She eventually returned to Edinburgh, where she died, unmarried, in 1808.   ELIZABETH C. SANDERSON

Sources J. Kay, *A series of original portraits and caricature etchings … with biographical sketches and illustrative anecdotes*, ed. [H. Paton and others], 2 vols. in 4 (1837–8) · Edinburgh dean of guild book, 1772–82, Edinburgh City Archives · *Edinburgh Evening Courant* (June–July 1783) · *Edinburgh Evening Courant* (Dec 1785) · Edinburgh inhabited house tax schedules, NA Scot., E 326 · *Scots Magazine and Edinburgh Literary Miscellany*, 70 (1808), 239 · H. Paton, ed., *The register of marriages for the parish of Edinburgh, 1701–1750*, Scottish RS, old ser., 35 (1908)
Likenesses two caricatures, *c.*1786, repro. in Kay, *Series of original portraits*

Hutton, Thomas (1565/6–1639), Church of England clergyman and religious controversialist, was born in London, perhaps the son of William Hutton who was baptized in St Margaret's, Westminster, on 1 June 1566. His father, being a merchant tailor, sent him to the Merchant Taylors' School in 1573. He continued on a foundation scholarship, equivalent to a fellowship, at St John's College, Oxford, being admitted in 1583, matriculating on 2 July 1585, aged nineteen, graduating BA in 1587, and proceeding MA in 1591 and BD in 1597. From 1596, probably at the request of the corporation, he lived in Coventry and preached the Wednesday sermon. The mayor and aldermen certified the college in 1603 that 'he might with the good liking, desire and love of the inhabitants have continued still if he had been so minded, and that he has most lovingly, honestly, and godly behaved himself' (Stevenson and Salter, 363).

In December 1604 Hutton became rector of Huxham, Devon, and quickly became involved in public disputations with clergy not prepared to subscribe to the Lambeth articles of that year, and in preaching sermons in Exeter Cathedral, defending the prayer book. He took an agnostic viewpoint on who was elect, and was prepared to justify practices such as the threefold ministry from the fathers. He accepted God's calling of the unlearned but godly to ministry, the pastoral value of homily reading by such, and in many cases defended prayer book practices as valid even if not explicitly the same as New Testament ones. This work led to publication in *An Answer to Several Reasons for Refusall to Subscribe to the Book of Common Prayer* (1605), and *The Second and Last Part of Reasons for Refusall … with an Answere to Bothe* (1606), the latter expressing in the dedication his gratitude to Archbishop Bancroft and the king for their favour 'in the prime of his studies'. The printed controversy with an anonymous opponent, probably Samuel Hieron, one of the organizers in the west country of the millenary petition for further reformation, continued until 1608.

This zeal probably led to Hutton's presentation by the king to the vicarage of St Kew, Cornwall, in January 1607, and by John Sprott for the king to the rectory of North Lew, Devon, in July of that year. He resigned his fellowship of St John's in September 1607, probably about the time of his marriage to Dorothy, about whom no details are known. They had five known sons, of whom the eldest, William, was born in October 1608 and one died in infancy, and four known daughters.

Hutton was collated to a prebend in Exeter Cathedral in 1616, though not installed until 1618, and may have held one until his death. He continued as a preacher to the end of his life, and was described on his memorial as second to none in the work of the gospel, quick to attack as a theologian, and diligent in reading the liturgy. His love of learning, in theology and the four foreign languages he knew, was undiminished in old age. His library was valued at £200 in his inventory. He died at St Kew vicarage in December 1639, and was buried in the church there on 27 December. He had prospered, leaving movables valued at £1661 6s. 8d. including a striking clock: his largest legacies were £20 to his wife, Dorothy, and all his land to his son William, by that time rector of North Lew.

ELIZABETH ALLEN

Sources W. H. Stevenson and H. E. Salter, *The early history of St John's College, Oxford*, OHS, new ser., 1 (1939), 363 · Wood, *Ath. Oxon.*, 1st edn, 1.532–3 · *Fasti Angl.* (Hardy), 1.422–4 · Boase & Courtney, *Bibl. Corn.*, 1.261 · O. Murray, collection of will abstracts, Devon RO, 8/36 · Devon RO, Chanter 21 MFC4/7/14, Huxham, Dec 1604; St Kew, Jan 1607; North Lew, July 1607 · parish register, St Kew, Cornwall, Cornwall RO [marriage, Oct. 1608; baptism, burial (Hutton's children)] · C. J. Robinson, ed., *A register of the scholars admitted into Merchant Taylors' School, from AD 1562 to 1874*, 1 (1882), 21 · Foster, *Alum. Oxon.* · parish register, St Margaret's, Westminster, City Westm. AC, 1 June 1566 [baptism] · K. Fincham, *Prelate as pastor: the episcopate of James I* (1990), 215
Wealth at death £1661 6s. 8d. moveables; also land: will and inventory, Devon RO, Oswin Murray collection, 8/36

Hutton, William (1723–1815), historian, was born on 30 September 1723 at Full Street, Derby, the fourth or fifth of the nine children of William Hutton (1691–1758), woolcomber, and the first of his three wives, Anne (1691/2–1733), daughter of Matthew Ward of Mountsorrel, Leicestershire. The elder William Hutton was, according to his son, well informed, a man of good judgement, and 'by far the best speaker I ever heard in low life and nearly the best in any life' who 'read, and taught his children to read, religious books', denounced intemperance, but was given to drink (*Life*, 20). His business failed about 1725 and he became a journeyman.

The younger William Hutton 'owed much to Nature, and nothing to Education' (*GM*, 277). He has been called the English Benjamin Franklin, a comparison that is far-fetched. After attending school in Derby between the ages of five and seven, he served a seven-year apprenticeship in the Derby silk mill, followed by a second apprenticeship to his father's brother George Hutton, a stocking-maker in Nottingham. Having completed that apprenticeship in 1744, he remained with his uncle, on whose death in 1746 he reluctantly continued to work as a journeyman stocking-maker in Nottingham. While his rudimentary schooling had, by his own account, turned him away from learning, his father's encouragement of reading, informal teaching by a former schoolmistress who went to live with the Huttons in Derby in 1736, and the influence of his sister Catherine, five years older than him, helped to develop his mind. Catherine, with whom he lived from 1746 to 1750, had spent seven years in the service of two dissenting ministers, was widely read, dominating, resourceful, and a rigid Calvinist. To a large extent, however, Hutton was self-educated. At the age of seventy-five he characterized the predominant activity of his life from twenty-nine

William Hutton (1723–1815), by James Basire, pubd 1804

to fifty-six as reading; thereafter it was 'writing history'. He had no Latin, his prose occasionally revealed a lack of grammatical training, and his spelling was sometimes wayward.

In 1746 Hutton bought three unbound volumes of the *Gentleman's Magazine* which he fastened together in a rough way, and began to teach himself bookbinding on books bought cheaply, seeing bookbinding as an alternative occupation to stocking-making. The binding materials and tools available locally were inadequate, and in 1749, to acquire better, he borrowed 3 guineas from his sister and walked to London and back, covering the 129 miles each way in three days and spending 10s. 8d. on board and lodging. He resolved to set up as a bookseller, bookbinder, and stationer in Birmingham, which had impressed him with the beauty of its buildings and the vivacity of its people in 1741, when he had briefly run away from his apprenticeship with his uncle. As a preliminary step he took a shop in the market place in Southwell, where there was no other bookseller, and every Saturday walked the 14 miles from Nottingham and back, carrying up to 30 lb.

A year after his visit to London, in May 1750, Hutton settled in Birmingham, at 6 Bull Street. The best part of his stock was the 'refuse' of the library of the Presbyterian minister Ambrose Rudsdell (1707–1750), for whom his sister had worked, which he bought at a very low price on an undated promissory note. He soon prospered, saving £20 in his first year, moving into a better shop in the High Street, and opening Birmingham's first circulating library in 1751. By 1755 he was sufficiently confident to get married. His wife was Sarah Cock (1731–1796), the niece and housekeeper of his next-door neighbour in the High

Street, and daughter of John Cock of Ashton upon Trent, Derbyshire. They married on 23 June 1755 and in his writings Hutton frequently expressed his extreme happiness with his wife. They had a daughter, Catherine *Hutton (1756–1846), a novelist and historical writer, a son, Thomas Hutton (1757–1845), a collector of books and prints who died childless, and two other sons who died in infancy.

In 1756 Hutton set up a paper warehouse in the High Street, the first in Birmingham, which was profitable enough to encourage him to build a paper mill on Handsworth Heath in 1759. The mill was not a commercial success, and he abandoned it in 1762. In 1766 he began to speculate in land, an activity which he continued with success into old age, and in 1769 he bought half an acre at Bennett's Hill, Saltley, 4 miles north-east of the centre of Birmingham, where he built himself a country house. He enjoyed many recreations, which included music, boating, fishing, fives, excursions around Birmingham, and visits to the races at Nottingham. He entered public life in 1768 by becoming an overseer of the poor, and later a commissioner under the Birmingham Improvement Act of 1769 and in the Birmingham court of requests (for settling small debts), of which he became president. He afterwards recalled how on his arrival in the town in 1750 he had had trouble with the overseers because he lacked a settlement certificate, and how he had led opposition to the improvement act because it proposed the demolition of property which he owned in New Street.

When living with his sister in Nottingham in 1747, Hutton had begun writing verse. In 1752 he resumed versifying, and some of his poems were published in local magazines. In or shortly before 1775 he started to collect material for the history of Birmingham but then briefly abandoned the project. He may have been stimulated to begin it by the discovery of medieval remains below a house in the High Street which he bought in 1772 and rebuilt in 1775; alternatively, his taking on the supervision of the rebuilding may have induced him to reduce his other activities. His energy, however, was such that he 'bud forth in history at fifty-six' (*History of Birmingham*, 53). Written in 1780 and published in 1782 (though bearing the date 1781), *An History of Birmingham* was his first book and the most successful, the most enduring, and, as later enlarged, the most substantial. 'This was afterwards considered the best book I ever wrote. I considered it in a much less favourable light' (*Life*, 196). One object in publishing it was to glorify the town and, for all its digressions and the sometimes ponderous humour of the author's asides, it presents a spirited portrait of a great commercial and industrial town in the most vigorous phase of its growth. William Withering, friend of Joseph Priestley, declared it the best topographical history he had ever seen. A second edition was published in 1783 and three further editions appeared within forty years, besides two reissues and five abridged versions.

Having embarked on authorship with diffidence, Hutton found both the activity and the reputation enjoyable.

His wife's ill health provided a reason for annual excursions to places some way from Birmingham, beginning with Buxton in 1785. In the ten years from 1781 he wrote and published accounts of a journey to London, courts of requests, the battle of Bosworth, juries and hundred courts, and the history of Derby, and in the first decade of the nineteenth century he published works on Hadrian's Wall, north Wales, Scarborough, and a trip to Coatham, in each instance drawing on his own experience or on his holiday excursions. He was proud of his election in 1782 as a fellow of the Society of Antiquaries of Scotland, 'for a fool and an antiquary is a contradiction' (*History of Birmingham*, 274). His topographical writing was always clear, and aimed to emulate not so much Dugdale's *Antiquities of Warwickshire* (his debt to which he acknowledged) as Pilkington's *Present State of Derbyshire*: 'to read Dugdale is drudgery, but to peruse Pilkington a delight. One conveys intelligence without pleasure; the other conveys both' (*History of Derby*, 1791, 34).

Well known as a dissenter and as one of the group of radical thinkers of which Joseph Priestley was the most prominent member, Hutton suffered severely in the rioting which followed a dinner held in Birmingham on 14 July 1791 to celebrate the second anniversary of the storming of the Bastille, even though he had taken no part in the political and religious disputes of the time and had declined an invitation to attend the dinner. In Priestley's opinion his attitude to religion was too latitudinarian, and he professed himself 'a firm friend to our present establishment, notwithstanding her blemishes' (*Life*, 224). Nevertheless, the mob attacked Hutton's house in High Street on 15 July. He offered to buy them off, and they dragged him to the Fountain tavern, where he was presented with a bill for 329 gallons of ale. Even so, his house and furniture were destroyed that evening, and the next day his house at Bennett's Hill was burnt. He estimated his losses at £8243, not counting the loss of business resulting from the destruction of his stock in trade; more than two years later he received £5391 in compensation. Hutton wrote that the riots 'totally destroyed that peace of mind which can never return, nearly overwhelmed me and my family, and not only deprived us of every means of restoring the health of the best of women, but shortened her life' (ibid., 210). No fewer than seventeen of Hutton's friends, all but one of them churchmen, offered him their houses after the riots.

Among the things destroyed in the riots were Hutton's juvenile verses, written forty years earlier and, after writing down what he could remember of them, he began again to compose verses and published two volumes of poems in 1793. He published no historical writing between 1791 and 1802, and seems to have turned inward on himself. He relinquished active control of the paper merchant's business to his son, Thomas, on the latter's marriage in 1793. An injury to his leg in that year restricted his pedestrian habits. Sarah died in January 1796. Later that year Hutton began a curious compilation, 'Memorandums from memory, all trifles and of ancient date' (Birmingham City Archives, MS 467141), in which he recorded for each day of the calendar an incident remembered as occurring on that date, choosing, when two or more incidents were remembered for the same day, the more remote and insignificant; about a year later only nine days were left with no recorded incident.

In 1796 Hutton and his daughter, Catherine, resumed their annual excursions, and in 1801, shortly before his seventy-eighth birthday, they set out from Bennett's Hill for Penrith, she riding behind a servant on a coach horse while he walked, 'the mode of travelling which of all others' he preferred (*Life*, 279), agreeing to meet at certain inns for refreshment and rest. At Penrith, Catherine turned west to visit the lakes and Hutton continued to Carlisle to walk the length of Hadrian's Wall and back, examining the Roman remains, before walking back to Birmingham. In intensely hot weather he walked 601 miles in thirty-five days. His gait, described by Catherine, looked like a saunter but was a steady 2½ miles an hour. He was nearly 5 feet 6 inches tall, of stocky build, and inclined to corpulence, with a large head and a youthful look: at ninety-two his face was scarcely wrinkled.

The tour not only provided Hutton with material for his book *The History of the Roman Wall* (1802), but it also confirmed him in the character of a geriatric wonder. His interest in healthy longevity, noticeable in his *History of Birmingham* and increasingly so in later editions, is marked in his memoirs. In 1811, when 'sensible of decay', he claimed that at the age of eighty-two he had considered himself a young man and could without fatigue walk 40 miles a day (*Life*, 308). At eighty-eight he walked 12 miles with ease, and in 1812, in his ninetieth year, he walked from Bennett's Hill into Birmingham for the last time. He died at Bennett's Hill on 20 September 1815, apparently of pneumonia, although his apothecary diagnosed total wearing out of the structure, without disease. He was buried in Aston parish churchyard on 26 September. He had been living comfortably in his country house and a few years earlier had invested substantially in landed property, but he left no will, and his son said that his personal property did not amount to £20.　　　　C. R. ELRINGTON

Sources *The life of William Hutton*, ed. L. Jewitt (1872) · *The life of William Hutton* (1816); repr. (1998) · W. Hutton, *An history of Birmingham*, 2nd edn (1783) · C. R. Elrington, 'Introduction', in W. Hutton, *An history of Birmingham*, new edn (1976) · W. Hutton, 'Memorandums From Memory', Birm. CA, MS 467141 · *DNB* · *GM*, 1st ser., 85/2 (1815), 277–8 · C. Hartley, *British genius exemplified in the lives of men who … have raised themselves to … distinction* (1820) · administration papers for William Hutton, 1815, Lichfield RO · *VCH Warwickshire*, vol. 7 · R. Bage, letters to William Hutton, *c*.1778–*c*.1801, Birm. CA, MS 486802 · W. Hutton, notebooks, *c*.1798–*c*.1814, Birm. CA, MS 390702 · *IGI* · parish register (burial), 26/9/1815, Aston, Warwickshire

Archives Birm. CA, account book, corresp., family and personal MSS · Derby Local Studies Library, corresp.

Likenesses J. Basire, line engraving, pubd 1804, BM, NPG [*see illus.*] · line engraving, pubd 1804 (after J. Basire), NPG · P. Hollins, marble bust on monument, 1851, St Margaret's Church, Ward End, Birmingham · J. Basire, engraving (aged eighty), repro. in W. Hutton, *An history of Birmingham*, new edn (1976) · T. Ransom, engraving (aged eighty-one), repro. in C. Hutton, *Life of William Hutton*, 2nd edn (1817) · F. Wentworth, engraving, repro. in R. K. Dent, *Old and new Birmingham* (1880), 167 · engraving, repro. in Jewitt, ed., *Life of William Hutton* · photograph (after oils), Birmingham City Archives · portrait; formerly in the Public Library, Birmingham; disappeared long before 1872 · portrait; formerly in the Union Street Library, Birmingham; untraced

Wealth at death under £20—personal property: administration, Lichfield RO, probate records

Hutton, William (1737–1811), antiquary and Church of England clergyman, was born on 29 January 1737 at Beetham, Westmorland, the son of George Hutton (*d.* 1736) of Overthwaite in the parish of Beetham, and his wife, Eleanor (*d.* 1758), daughter of William Tennant of York and Bedale. William attended Sedbergh School about 1750 and was at Trinity College, Cambridge, in 1759. In 1760 he became curate and in September 1762 rector of the family living of Beetham, where he remained for the rest of his life. On 10 June 1765 he married Mary (1738/9–1768), daughter of John Hutton, of the same parish. Following Mary's death aged twenty-nine on 5 July 1768, Hutton remarried, on 23 April 1771. His second wife was Lucy (1744/5–1788), the third daughter of Rigby Molyneux, MP for Preston, with whom he had two sons.

Hutton is remembered for his curious tract in imitation of the local Westmorland dialect: *A bran new wark, by William de Worfat [Overthwaite], containing a true calendar of his thoughts concerning a good nebberhood*, of which fifty copies were printed in Kendal in 1785. Another version of the study was issued with slight variations, and was reprinted as *Specimens of English Dialect* by the English Dialect Society in 1879; its editor, Walter Skeat, spoke of the work as evidence of a man of 'kindly feeling and excellent sense' (Skeat, 180). While rector, Hutton also kept a large folio book, the 'Repository', in the vestry of Beetham church, in which he entered a record of parish affairs. This review was carefully preserved and continued by his successors before its publication as *The Beetham Repository, 1770* by the Cumberland and Westmorland Antiquarian and Archaeological Society in 1906. Hutton died in August 1811 and was survived by one son, William (will, PRO, PROB 11/1525, fol. 353*r*).　　　　GORDON GOODWIN, rev. PHILIP CARTER

Sources J. Ormandy Crosse, 'Sketch of the life of the Revd William Hutton, 1737–1811', *The Beetham repository, 1770*, ed. J. Ford (1906) · Burke, *Gen. GB* (1886), 1.962 · *GM*, 1st ser., 81/2 (1811), 291 · *IGI* · J. Nicolson and R. Burn, *The history and antiquities of the counties of Westmorland and Cumberland*, 1 (1777), 219 · will, PRO, PROB 11/1525, fol. 353*r* · W. de Worfat [W. Hutton], *A bran new wark*, ed. W. Skeat (1785); repr. in *Specimens of English dialects* (1879)

Hutton, William (1797–1860), geologist and palaeontologist, was born on 26 July 1797 in Sunderland, second of the four children of Michael Hutton (1763–1840), a grocer in Sunderland, and his wife, Jane Coxon, of Laverick Hall, Boldon, co. Durham. The family originated from Stainton in Yorkshire. He had little formal education and probably attended Gowan Lock's School in Sunderland. By 1827 he is recorded as living in Newcastle upon Tyne, where he was employed as an agent of the Norwich Union Insurance Company. He joined the Newcastle upon Tyne Literary and Philosophical Society in 1818 and the Society of Antiquaries of Newcastle upon Tyne in 1825. By this date he had become an honorary curator of the George Allan

Museum, purchased by the Literary and Philosophical Society in 1822, and was developing his own collection of minerals and fossil plants.

In 1828 he was made a fellow of the Geological Society of London. He became a founder member, co-secretary, and one of the honorary curators of mineralogy and geology of the Natural History Society of Northumberland, Durham and Newcastle upon Tyne which was founded in 1829. From 1830 until 1835 he was also co-secretary of the Newcastle Literary, Scientific and Mechanical Institution and from 1835 a vice-president.

Hutton's major academic work, *The Fossil Flora*, was published between 1831 and 1837 and co-authored by John Lindley (1799–1865). This was one of the first significant published works dealing with fossil plants. His other major contribution was his work on the nature of coal, published in 1833. His efforts were recognized in 1837 when Sternberg named a fossil plant *Huttonia* after him and in 1840 when he was made a fellow of the Royal Society. By 1845 Hutton had taken on the post of treasurer of the Natural History Society and the extra work may have contributed to the breakdown in his health which occurred in 1846. He left Newcastle for the Mediterranean and settled in Malta. He had returned to Newcastle by 1851 and by 1853 had moved to Tynemouth. Soon afterwards he moved to West Hartlepool where he became involved with the local Literary and Mechanics Institution, playing a leading role in the move to establish a museum in the Athenaeum. He died a bachelor at 53 Scarborough Street, West Hartlepool on 20 November 1860 and was buried in West Hartlepool cemetery three days later.

ANDREW NEWMAN

Sources A. Newman and J. Chatt-Ramsey, *A catalogue of the specimens figured in 'The fossil flora' by John Lindley (1799–1865) and William Hutton (1797–1860) … including a biography of William Hutton* (1988) • T. R. Goddard, *History of the Natural History Society of Northumberland, Durham and Newcastle upon Tyne, 1829–1929* [1929] • R. M. Richardson, 'The Hutton family (Papermakers)', *Antiquities of Sunderland*, 9 (1908), 169–79 • *Stockton and Hartlepool Mercury and Middlesbrough News* (24 Nov 1860) • parish register (baptism), co. Durham, Bishopwearmouth, St Michael, Sunderland Library Archives, 15 June 1799 • *South Durham Herald* (28 June 1879)
Archives GS Lond., papers • U. Newcastle, Hancock Museum, natural history of Northumbria | GS Lond., letters to Sir R. I. Murchison • NHM, corresp. with John Lindley • NL Scot., corresp. with George Combe • U. Newcastle, Robinson L., letters to Sir Walter Trevelyan
Likenesses Carrick, watercolour, repro. in Goddard, *History of the Natural History Society*; formerly in possession of North of England Institute of Mining Engineers, now lost

Hutton, William Holden (1860–1930), dean of Winchester and historian, was born at Gate Burton, Lincolnshire, on 24 May 1860, the younger son of the Revd George Hutton, rector of Gate Burton, and his wife, Caroline, daughter of Robert Holden, of Nuttall Temple, Nottinghamshire. His mother was sister to Sophia Holden, wife of the Hon. and Revd Alfred Curzon, grandfather of George Nathaniel *Curzon, first Marquess Curzon of Kedleston (1859–1925), who was a lifelong friend. Hutton, who was of

delicate health, attended a preparatory school at Bengeo, Hertfordshire, but received no further school education. He matriculated from Magdalen College, Oxford, in 1879. One of the original members of the Stubbs Society (a history society for undergraduates), he won the Stanhope prize in 1881 for an essay on political disturbances in the German Reformation and gained an expected first class in modern history in December 1882. In 1884 he became fellow of St John's College, Oxford, holding his fellowship until 1923. He was ordained deacon in 1885 and priest in 1886. From 1913 until 1920 he was reader in Indian history, having visited India with Curzon. Hutton's rooms in St John's and even more so his house in Burford became something of a centre for his mostly rather conservatively minded group of friends. Hutton's residence in Burford led to *By Thames and Cotswold* (1903) and *Burford Papers* (1905), and to various magazine articles.

Hutton was proctor in 1891–2, examiner in modern history 1892–5 and 1908–10, and select preacher from 1898 to 1900. He wrote a history of St John's College (2 vols., 1891–8) and biographies of Wellesley (1893), Thomas More (1895), and Laud (1895). He produced *Philip Augustus* in the Foreign Statesmen series, 1896, a monograph *Hampton Court* (1897), *Constantinople* (1900), *A Short History of the Church in Great Britain* (1900), *The English Church from the Accession of Charles I to the Death of Anne, 1625–1714* (vol. 6 of W. R. W. Stephens and W. Hunt, *The History of the English Church*, 1903), and *The Church and the Barbarians* (1906). In addition he wrote many articles and reviews for learned periodicals. These were works 'of moderate dimensions', as his close friend Charles Oman recorded (*DNB*).

In 1909, when James Bellamy resigned the presidency of St John's, some in the university expected Hutton would be his successor. However, a younger group in St John's, anxious to set that college on an academic footing commensurate with its wealth and reforming in its politics, favoured a change of tone, for Hutton was a crusty conservative, and he was not elected (though neither was Sidney Ball, the reformers' candidate). He resigned as modern history tutor in the same year. Two years later (1911) he was appointed archdeacon of Northampton, where he became well known for his sermons (he had already been a successful Bampton lecturer at Oxford in 1903, the lectures being published as *Lives of the English Saints*, 1903). In 1919 he was appointed dean of Winchester.

In 1928 Hutton began to be troubled by rheumatic and nervous complaints, which sapped his energy and vitality; after a long illness he died, unmarried, while undergoing treatment at Freiburg im Breisgau, Germany, on 24 October 1930.

H. C. G. MATTHEW

Sources *WWW* • *DNB* • M. Brock and M. C. Curthoys, *Victorian Oxford*, 2 (1999)
Archives Bodl. Oxf., papers relating to work as archdeacon, incl. notes on Northamptonshire churches • Pusey Oxf., corresp. • St John's College, Oxford, commonplace book and corresp. | BL, corresp. with Macmillans, Add. MS 55079 • LPL, letters to *Church Quarterly Review*
Wealth at death £23,778 7s. 11d.: probate, 23 Dec 1930, *CGPLA Eng. & Wales*

Huxham, John (*c*.1692–1768), physician, was born at Harberton, Devon, the son of a butcher. Orphaned early, he had as a guardian Thomas Edgerley, a nonconformist minister, who placed him at the school of Isaac Gilling, a Presbyterian minister in Newton Abbot. Later Edgerley sent him to the dissenting academy at Exeter. On 7 May 1715 Huxham entered as a student under Boerhaave at Leiden, but he was unable to stay the requisite three years and graduated MD at Rheims in 1717. He took a house at Totnes, Devon, but soon moved to Plymouth.

The dissenters generally consulted Huxham, but his practice did not grow as fast as he wished. Consequently, Huxham may have resorted to charlatanry in an attempt to gain attention for his work: allegedly, he would arrange to be conspicuously called from a conventicle to attend fictitious patients and would ride out of town on bogus visits. He afterwards conformed to the established church. According to the customs of the time, he walked with a gold-headed cane and was followed by a footman bearing his gloves; he usually wore a scarlet coat. A contemporary noted that, having married money, 'he began to look bigger, and to effect much more gravity than usual. And here was the beginning of that stiff and affected behaviour for which he hath been so very remarkable' (Schupbach, 416).

Huxham filled up his spare hours with study. He read Hippocrates in the original, and made observations in meteorology as well as in physic. He wrote a paper in the *Philosophical Transactions of the Royal Society* in 1723, and in 1739 he published *Observationes de aere et morbis epidemicis* in two volumes. In this work meteorological records, made at Plymouth between 1728 and 1737, were collated on a monthly basis with the diseases observed there.

Huxham was elected FRS on 5 April 1739, and received the Copley medal in 1755 for his observations on antimony, which were published first in *Philosophical Transactions*, and then as a separate book in 1756. Also in 1755 the College of Physicians of Edinburgh elected him a fellow. His most important work was *An Essay on Fevers and their Various Kinds* (1750). The book is written in a lucid style and begins with a historical introduction in praise of Hippocrates, Celsus, and Aretaeus; it goes on to describe the course and treatment of simple fevers, intermittent fevers, nervous fevers, smallpox, pleurisy, inflammation of the lungs, and bronchitis (then designated 'peripneumonia notha'). Huxham was a follower of Thomas Sydenham. He derived most of his information from his own observations, but also drew upon original observations found in the works of ancients or of moderns. He approved Hippocrates' dictum that whoever knows the nature of the disease knows the method of cure, but he was at the same time careful in his use of drugs and other treatments. The compound tincture of cinchona bark in the *British Pharmacopoeia*, which also contains bitter orange peel, serpentary root, saffron, and cochineal mixed in spirit, was devised by him, and was for some time called 'Huxham's tincture'.

Huxham's book gave him a wide reputation, and his practice grew large. A Leipzig professor asked in 1764,

John Huxham (*c*.1692–1768), by Thomas Rennell

'Who has as much as hailed our art from the threshold, who has yet never heard the great name of Huxham?' (Schupbach, 416). The physician to the trading station at Lisbon declared that the queen of Portugal, whom he cured of a fever, owed her life to Huxham's treatise. The queen ordered it to be translated into Portuguese, and sent a finely bound copy to the author. On 30 September 1747 Huxham wrote from Plymouth to the *General Evening Post* on the occasion of the return, after a voyage of only thirteen weeks, of Admiral Martin's fleet, with 1200 men suffering from scurvy; Huxham recommended vegetable food as a preventive, and urged a fuller supply of it to the navy. These remarks, with additions, were reprinted as a book, *De scurbuto*, at Venice in 1766.

In 1752 Huxham published a short book, *De morbo colico damnoniensi*. He had observed that the colic was commonest when the fresh cider came in, but he did not discover that it had any relation to the lead dissolved in the cider. In 1757 he published a dissertation *On the Malignant, Ulcerous Sore-Throat*, which contains an excellent account of what later became known as diphtheria, and he was the first to observe the palsy of the soft palate, which was common in the disease, though he failed to distinguish diphtheria from scarlatina anginosa.

Huxham married Ellen Corham (*d*. 1742); after her death he married Elizabeth Harris (*d*. before 1768). He died at Plymouth on 11 August 1768, and was buried in the north aisle of St Andrew's Church, Plymouth. He left two daughters and one son, John Corham Huxham, who graduated at Exeter College, Oxford, became FRS, and edited several of his father's works. A complete edition of Huxham's work was published in Latin at Leipzig in 1764; a new edition appeared in 1773, and a revised edition was printed at Leipzig in 1829.   NORMAN MOORE, *rev.* RICHARD HANKINS

Sources W. Schupbach, 'The fame and notoriety of Dr John Huxham', *Medical History*, 25 (1981), 415–21 · R. M. S. McConaghey, 'John Huxham', *Medical History*, 13 (1969), 280–87 · W. Munk, 'Biographica medica Devoniensis', *Western Antiquary*, 6 (1887), 258–62

Likenesses E. Fisher, mezzotint (after T. Rennell), Wellcome L. · J. Jenkins, stipple (after T. Rennell), NPG, Wellcome L. · T. Rennell, oils, RS [*see illus.*]

Huxley, Aldous Leonard (1894–1963), writer, was born at Laleham, a house near Godalming, Surrey, on 26 July 1894, the third son of Leonard *Huxley (1860–1933), an assistant master at Charterhouse School and subsequently editor of the *Cornhill Magazine*, and his first wife, Julia Frances *Huxley (*née* Arnold) (1862–1908) [*see under* Huxley, Leonard], an educator and daughter of the literary scholar Thomas *Arnold (1823–1900), granddaughter of Dr Thomas *Arnold (1795–1842) of Rugby School, and niece of Matthew *Arnold (1822–1888). As a grandson of T. H. *Huxley (1825–1895) and great-grandson of Dr Arnold, Aldous Huxley inherited a passionate interest in science, education, and human psychology. Mrs Humphry Ward [*see* Ward, Mary Augusta], the novelist, was his aunt; Julian *Huxley (1887–1975) his eldest brother.

Education and early career Huxley attended Prior's Field in Surrey, a school founded by his mother on a progressive-education model. He continued at Hillside, a preparatory school adjacent to Charterhouse, where his father taught. The four children (Julian, Trevenen, Aldous, and Margaret) grew up in the shadow of Thomas Henry Huxley, 'children from whom nothing but the best would be tolerated' (Clark, 130). Huxley's arrival at Eton College in autumn 1908 coincided with the first of the great traumatic experiences which marked his life and work: the unexpected death of his mother, Julia. The pale, blue-eyed boy with the oversized head had been very close to her; his devastation was complete, 'as if a great explosion had taken place in the family', according to Juliette Huxley (Julian's wife): 'it was to Aldous the irreparable loss, a betrayal of his faith in life' (Hunt. L., Huxley, 1985). Then in 1911 Huxley was struck down by a staphylococcic infection in the eye (keratitis punctata) untreated over term-break at Eton. It left him purblind for eighteen months. A central theme in Huxley's writing flowed from this disaster: sight and insight, light and shadow, transcendent vision and human opacity. At home Huxley taught himself to read Braille, to touch-type, and to play the piano. His eyesight improved to one-quarter of normal vision in one eye (he spent half a century experimenting with alternative therapies and surgery). With tutoring, he won a scholarship to Balliol College, Oxford, to read English language and literature. By dilating his eyes with drops and using a large magnifying glass, Huxley was able to read sufficiently to win a first and the Stanhope prize in 1916.

Huxley later noted that his adolescent near-blindness precluded his chosen career: 'I had of course before I went blind intended to become a doctor but I couldn't go on

Aldous Leonard Huxley (1894–1963), by Man Ray, 1934

with that kind of scientific career because I couldn't use a microscope' (University of California, Los Angeles, Huxley, 1957). A few weeks after the outbreak of the First World War his older brother Trev, having failed to win a place in the civil service list, succumbed to a cyclical depression and committed suicide. In a letter Huxley reflected that it was the highest and best in his brother which caused his downfall: 'his ideals were too much for him' (*Letters*, 68). These tragedies left Huxley detached from the world; in time detachment turned to cynicism: few of his characters shared his brother's idealism.

Huxley's Oxford career was characterized by intellectual jousting and the discovery of the French symbolist poets, particularly Mallarmé. Rake-thin and 6 feet 4½ inches tall, Huxley became a university character. His steps had the tentativeness of the ill-sighted. According to the fashionable journalist Beverley Nichols, 'Quantities of Aldous Huxley reclined on my sofa, spreading over the cushions, and stretching long tentacles to the floor' (Nichols, 136). Despite this imposing physical presence, Huxley exuded a quiet charm. He had an unforgettably mellifluous voice, and exhibited a formidable mental archive. Bertrand Russell—an occasional fellow guest with Huxley at Garsington Manor, home to Lady Ottoline Morrell—said he could tell which volume of the *Encyclopaedia Britannica* the student Huxley was reading by the prominence of subjects with that letter in their conversation. At Garsington, Huxley consorted with the Sitwells, Lytton Strachey, Maynard Keynes, and others in the Bloomsbury circle. In his writings—he started writing poetry but also short stories at Oxford—and often in person, Huxley managed controversy without belligerence.

He had an unending, gentle curiosity which endeared him to most.

After Oxford, Huxley moved briefly to London for a secretaryship at the Air Board, then taught at Repton School and at Eton, where among his students were Harold Acton and Eric Blair (George Orwell). By twenty-six Huxley's poetry had matured into four volumes: *The Burning Wheel* (1916), *Jonah* (1917), *The Defeat of Youth* (1918), and *Leda* (1920), arguably his most powerful poetic statement. Virginia Woolf praised the 'high technical skill and great sensibility' of his writing, while Proust placed him in the first rank of young British authors. But Huxley's need to finance a family drove him to work as a literary journalist for John Middleton Murry at *The Athenaeum*. On 10 July 1919 in Bellem, Belgium, he married Maria Nys (*d*. 1955), a Belgian refugee who had lived at Garsington. They had one son, Matthew, born in April 1920. They set up in a small flat in Hampstead, London, as Huxley moved on to the *Westminster Gazette* and *Vogue*; New York's *Century* magazine published his short story 'The Tillotson Banquet'. Huxley was proud of living by his pen.

Early fiction Huxley's first extended fiction—a novella, 'The Farcical History of Richard Greenow' (in *Limbo*, 1920)—echoes his years of pacifism and a brief stint as a Fabian at Oxford. It was his first novel, *Crome Yellow* (1921), based on goings-on at Garsington, which brought instant fame. This novel is the first of three 'house party' society novels, followed by *Antic Hay* (1923) and *Those Barren Leaves* (1925), which satirized social behaviour in post-war Britain using friends and family as fodder for incisive characterizations. The Morrells were particularly offended by their thinly disguised portraits in *Crome Yellow*; these led to a rift between Lady Ottoline and Huxley lasting for many years. Of *Crome Yellow*, F. Scott Fitzgerald wrote that 'this is the highest point so far attained by Anglo-Saxon sophistication'; Huxley was 'the wittiest man now writing in English' (Watt, 73). The comic lightness of the novels was undermined by much wider social concerns. In *Crome Yellow*, Mr Scogan imagines the creation of 'an impersonal generation': 'in vast state incubators rows upon rows of gravid bottles will supply the world with the population it requires' (p. 28), a theme developed in *Brave New World* (1932). Moreover, a dark thread runs through Huxley's musings on corruption in the smart set; his characters are torn between pleasures of the flesh and an austere dedication to the spirit, and Huxley was willing to expose human frailty, to illuminate hypocrisy. We have in us a higher essence, Huxley suggested, but it is understood by apes. The early novels were interspersed with brilliant collections of short stories, including *Mortal Coils* (1922), *Little Mexican* (1924), and *Two or Three Graces* (1926). In *Point Counter Point* (1928) Huxley turned his friendship with D. H. Lawrence into an international best-seller, and in *Proper Studies* (1929) he abandoned social satire and took a more didactic direction. In these years Huxley found his three-a-year contract with his publisher Chatto and Windus (usually a volume of essays, short stories, and a novel) daunting.

Huxley moved in a world of wit and erudition, 'yet wore his learning lightly, with an off-hand, man-of-the world air which was disarming' (Brooke, 6). Gertrude Stein considered him part of the 'lost generation', a group made cynical and numb by human suffering in the First World War. Yet Huxley's own life in the mid-1920s was harmonious and satisfying. A round-the-world tour in 1925 brought him before readers in Bombay, Kyoto, and Los Angeles. With his royalties he purchased small villas in southern France (first in Bandol, then in Sanary) and a Bugatti convertible for Maria, specially stretched to accommodate his huge height. The Huxleys summered in Italy, at Forte dei Marmi, and in France. The period 1921 to 1933 was the most productive and perhaps the happiest of his life.

As the 1930s opened, the Huxleys lived outside Paris in Suresnes, visiting London for the production of his plays, such as *The World of Light* (1931). Huxley published an enormous number of articles for the Hearst newspaper group and elsewhere, only recently collected (Sexton, Bradshaw). Key themes of the later, socially conscious Huxley, such as population control and the psychological roots of fascism, appear in these essays, and in publications such as *Nash's Pall Mall Magazine*, *Time and Tide*, and *The Star*. He also worked on *Now More than Ever* (1931), a play based on the notorious Swedish financier Ivar Kreuger, which was his most explicit attack on the evils of free-market capitalism. In summer 1932 Huxley published *Brave New World*, which enhanced his fortunes and reputation as the best-known British novelist between the wars. It was an international best-seller, particularly in paperback editions in the 1950s, and was translated into twenty-eight languages. The novel, the first about human cloning, is a dystopia set five centuries in the future, when overpopulation has led to biogenetic engineering. Through computerized genetic selection, social engineers create a population happy with its lot. All the earth's children are born in hatcheries, and Soma, a get-happy pill, irons out most problems. Huxley wrote to George Orwell suggesting that *Nineteen Eighty Four*'s vision of governmental autocracy was less likely than *Brave New World*'s society amusing itself to death: owing to infant conditioning and drugs 'an all-powerful executive of political bosses and their army of managers control a population of slaves who do not have to be coerced because they love their servitude' (*Letters*, 604). In a new foreword written in 1946 Huxley had second thoughts. His original vision denied the possibility of social sanity, which in 1946 he considered the book's 'most serious defect'. He went on to catalogue the possibility of sanity, 'the conscious and intelligent pursuit of man's Final End' (*Brave New World*, iii), and 'unitive' spiritual knowledge in his commentaries in the anthology *The Perennial Philosophy* (1946).

In winter 1934 Huxley returned to England from France and took a seven-year lease on a flat in the Albany, Piccadilly, London, where he worked on *Eyeless in Gaza* (1936). This novel catapults the reader and its hero, Anthony Beavis, across time periods, a structure Huxley found both troubling and challenging. Like the chorus in Greek drama, the effect of this time-shifting is fatalistic and oddly moving. The book's message, 'I know what I ought to do, and I do what I oughtn't', is articulated repeatedly. This was Huxley's most autobiographical fiction; upon publication, friends and family were again furious at their characterizations.

Crisis and emigration Toward the end of 1934 Huxley suffered a severe writer's block. He had hoped that London would inspire him, but its grey, sooty skies dimmed his vision. Maria Huxley wrote to friends of insomnia and 'gloom, irritation, lack of work' (*Letters*, 392). A niece recalls him as 'stooped, intense, sort of tortured' (private information). After fifteen years as England's cynic, Huxley had exhausted his stock-in-trade. Physically and spiritually he sank to his nadir; bright, fishy eyes peered out from black-rimmed bottle-glass lenses, his face lined with worry. Pressures from his multi-book contract mounted. According to Sybille Bedford, the Huxleys' house guest at Sanary and the Albany, and later Huxley's biographer, *Brave New World* had become a burden to live up to.

Huxley's depression yielded to various therapies, including F. M. Alexander's spine-straightening exercises. He also underwent a near-religious conversion to pacifism, a cause sweeping America in the early 1930s and England with the 'Oxford oath' against participation in armies. 'The thing finally resolves itself into a religious problem', he wrote to a friend (*Letters*, 398). Pacifism (and his new friend Gerald Heard) inspired him to give public lectures, which initially terrified him. Publication of *Eyeless in Gaza* (1936) did little to improve Huxley's situation. His hankering after physical and spiritual re-education, and through these transcendence, was not well received by colleagues. C. Day Lewis called him 'the prophet of disgust', while Stephen Spender was unconvinced: 'we had to wait for Aldous Huxley to propose that prayers are an exercise for the soul, like an elastic exerciser or a dose of Eno's fruitsalts' (Spender, 'Open letter to Aldous Huxley', *Left Review*, June 1936). Fellow pacifists, by July 1936 abandoning the creed in defence of Republican Spain, attacked the novel as muddled thinking.

Finally in spring 1937 the Huxleys (with Gerald Heard and his friend Christopher Wood) sailed for New York and began a five-week car journey across the United States, summering in San Cristobal, New Mexico, where Aldous Huxley finished a volume of metaphysics and pacifism, *Ends and Means* (1937). Promised sales of his books to Hollywood studios—a promise never fulfilled—he continued west to Los Angeles and planned a speaking tour on pacifism around the country with Heard. At the end of this tour in January 1938 the Huxleys returned to California, attracted by its isolationism, its interest in Hinduism and Buddhism, and its clear, bright air which aided Huxley's vision. Huxley, who had been an atheist in his youth, and who in his early fiction had derided Catholicism, protestantism, and Indian religions, became a Hindu Vedantist (with Buddhist leanings), along with Heard and Christopher Isherwood, whom he met in California. Huxley had been interested in religious mysticism from the mid-1930s but this interest was strengthened by his move to California and a study of the Veda. His most extensive writings on

this are found obscurely in essays in *Vedanta for the Western World*, a magazine co-edited by Isherwood (1945), and in an introduction to Isherwood's translation (with Swami Prabhavananda) of the *Bhagavad Gita* in 1944 (published in 1954).

Screenwriting in Hollywood Though hoped-for sales to Hollywood film studios did not materialize, screenwriting jobs came through the assistance of Anita Loos. The Huxleys were soon enmeshed in Hollywood's new immigrant community, which included Bertolt Brecht, Thomas and Heinrich Mann, and George Cukor. Huxley's films were on topics of great personal interest: *Madame Curie*, a bio-pic drafted in 1938 (and later rewritten by F. Scott Fitzgerald); *Pride and Prejudice* also for Metro-Goldwyn-Mayer, (1940) and *Jane Eyre* (1943), whose screenplay Huxley wrote with the director Robert Stevenson and John Houseman. But Huxley found himself tethered to writers' buildings and awaiting contract renewals. Disaffected by his meetings with studio executives, he wrote to his brother Julian that they 'have the characteristics of the minds of chimpanzees, agitated and infinitely distractible' (*Letters*, 439). Huxley, who worked as an active screenwriter for five years, was also derisive of Hollywood film, considering it a soporific, a bone to the poor, the powerless, and the plain who 'are themselves and not somebody else': 'hence those Don Juans, those melting beauties, those innocent young kittens, those beautifully brutal boys, those luscious adventuresses. Hence Hollywood' (*The Olive Tree*, 1936, 38–40).

In the early 1940s the Huxleys settled into Santa Monica canyon, where many European expatriates lived, including Isherwood. The Huxleys were delighted by the oddities of California, such as what Maria called 'its fancy un-dress costume'. The tide of screenwriters from abroad (H. G. Wells, P. G. Wodehouse, and Anthony Powell, among others) washed up in the banquet hall at W. R. Hearst's San Simeon castle, the backdrop for Huxley's *After Many a Summer* (1939; published in the United States as *After Many a Summer Dies the Swan*). Here Huxley satirized a classic American tycoon, while insisting that the quest for immortality by physical means is as pointless as the quest for fulfilment by possessions. Huxley's first full-length biography, *Grey Eminence* (1940), was a study of Père Joseph, Cardinal Richelieu's aide. This neglected work shows a cinematization of Huxley's prose and some parallels with his own search for transcendence, as Père Joseph opens himself 'to its purifying transforming radiance' (p. 12). In 1942 Huxley used savings from his screenwriting work to buy a cottage in Llano del Rio in the Mojave desert. He wrote for the screen until America's involvement in the Second World War, at which point the pacifist Huxley could not find (and was not asked to write) patriotic, win-the-war films.

Later years In the midst of petrol and tyre rationing Huxley, in isolation, produced three extraordinary volumes as he approached his fiftieth birthday. *The Art of Seeing* (1942) is an autobiographical study of the physical rehabilitation methods of D. W. E. Bates, which greatly improved his vision. Huxley had practised the Bates method of visual re-education avidly throughout the war years and after, with regular tutorials. In January 1940 he wrote to Julian of a breakthrough: 'Yesterday for the first time [since childhood] I succeeded, for short stretches, in getting a single fixed image from both eyes together' (*Letters*, 450). But opinions in his circle of friends differed as to the effectiveness of this treatment. In *The Art of Seeing*, however, Huxley suggests that there is a parallel in the way physical discipline could perfect vision while spiritual discipline could perfect insight. Meanwhile *The Perennial Philosophy* (1946) was an effort to find common ground among the world's religions in mysticism, and *Time Must Have a Stop* (1945), Huxley's response to a world at war, took his concerns with spiritual discipline into fiction.

The post-war years alternately haunted Huxley with visions of devastated cities and populations and hope that humanity might triumph over its increasingly potent weaponry. In *Science, Liberty, and Peace* (1946) and *Ape and Essence* (1949) he offered twin visions, light and dark, of humanity's future. The former is a hopeful appeal to scientists to consider humane values in research. *Ape and Essence*, Huxley's second novel of science fiction, is a darkly comic satire, in the form of a screenplay, of life in a post-apocalyptic Los Angeles. His play *The Gioconda Smile* (1948) was adapted for the screen as *A Woman's Vengeance*, but except for fanciful projects such as Walt Disney's *Alice in Wonderland* and an adaptation of Cervantes for the cartoon character Mr Magoo, his film-writing career was firmly at an end. He was satirized as the ineffectual scriptwriter Boxley in F. Scott Fitzgerald's *The Last Tycoon* (1941).

In June 1948 the Huxleys left America for Europe for the first time since 1937. In England they found a warmer reception than earlier headlines in the press, such as 'Gone with the wind up', might have suggested. Many critics dismissed Huxley's writings in America, considering him *Barmy in Wonderland*, as P. G. Wodehouse entitled one of his Hollywood novels. In a symposium organized by the *London Magazine* in 1955, of the work he had published while living in America only *After Many a Summer* was discussed, and that was roundly attacked. Huxley the Vedantist, the pacifist, the experimenter in education, health, and psychoactive phenomena, was disregarded. The Huxleys returned to the United States in autumn 1950. In the following spring Huxley had a recurrence of iritis following a bout of influenza, which may have shaped perhaps the darkest of his writings, *The Devils of Loudun* (1952), a historical recreation of a story of demonically possessed French nuns and exorcists. The depression which accompanied his physical illness only increased alongside Maria Huxley's half-acknowledged cancer. Searching in May 1953 for personal balance, and for new ways of seeing, Huxley took a tablet of mescaline, the laboratory-synthesized derivative of the peyote cactus used for centuries by native Americans, which produced effects similar to those of LSD. Humphrey Osmond MD guided him through an odyssey which culminated in Huxley briefly retrieving the stereoscopic vision which had eluded him since his teenage years. Huxley had sought clear sight

through pills, operations, visual retraining, and spiritual disciplines; it eluded him. Under the influence of mescaline he 'saw as painters see', as he wrote in an autobiographical account, *The Doors of Perception* (1953). A similar theme—the universality of transcendence—appears in *Heaven and Hell* (1956), while the quest for physical sight and vision (which characterized his American period), recurs in *Themes and Variations* (1950), in *Tomorrow and Tomorrow and Tomorrow* (1956), and *Brave New World Revisited* (1958), as well as in major essays in American publications such as *Esquire*, in which he had a monthly column from July 1955 to April 1957, and *World Review*, in which he published the two-part essay 'The double crisis'.

Just over a year after Maria Huxley's death on 12 February 1955, Huxley married Laura Archera, an Italian violinist, writer, and psychotherapist, on 19 March 1956. They moved into the Hollywood hills. Huxley had begun his last novel, *Island* (1962), an earnest, overlong story of an American cynic plane-wrecked on an island, and his recovery through participating in the island society's unorthodox health and educational practices.

In his last half-dozen years, Aldous Huxley—who twenty-five years before could barely be persuaded to speak in public—earned his living principally as a lecturer, including at the University of California, Berkeley, Massachusetts Institute of Technology, Menninger Clinic in Topeka, Kansas. In 1960 a dentist in Kansas removed a pre-cancerous lesion incompletely, failing to stop what developed into cancer of the tongue. By 1962 this had metastasized throughout his body. Huxley refused surgery for the cancer because it would have impaired his speech. His declining health only increased the fervour with which he finished *Island*—'this is what *Brave New World* should have been, and wasn't', his son Matthew said (private information)—although Huxley found a utopia far more difficult to write than a dystopia. His valedictory sense was hastened in May 1961 by a fire which destroyed his home in the Hollywood hills along with his manuscripts. Huxley was stoically detached about this. His stepdaughter Ellen Hovde described his final mood: 'He is one of the few people who got more open and available as he grew older. I think by the time he died, he was very young' (Hunt. L., Hovde, 1986). News of his death at his home, 6233 Mulholland Highway, Los Angeles, on 22 November 1963 was lost in coverage of John F. Kennedy's assassination. Huxley was cremated in Los Angeles on 23 November 1963, and in 1971 his ashes were returned to England and interred on 27 October in his parents' grave at Compton cemetery, Surrey.

Subsequent reputation During his lifetime Aldous Huxley had two distinct audiences: first, a largely European and British one, for his potent satires of his social milieu; second, the audience created by the didactic writings of the 1950s, particularly *The Doors of Perception*, which, with *Island*, heralded the youth culture of the 1960s. For the second audience, Huxley's appeal was social and philosophical, rather than literary. Later this audience gave way to a third, that was interested in his social prophecy, distanced from the bitter response to his experiments with psyche-delics, which in England was extreme. 'The Witch Doctor of California produces another prescription for his suffer-ing tribe', wrote Alistair Sutherland in typical response (*Twentieth Century*, May 1954). As late as 1989 the *Oxford Companion to English Literature* disregarded the work of his American years.

The Aldous Huxley Centenary Symposium in 1994 in Münster, Germany, and the International Aldous Huxley Society which emerged from that gathering, reflect a con-tinuing and widespread interest in Huxley, with two or three volumes of criticism appearing each year. Recent Huxley scholarship has made available new, and more complete, texts of his writing and has diminished the gap between appreciation of his early English (and European) years and his last quarter-century in the United States. *Brave New World* has returned to popular culture as the first novel about human cloning. Public radio in the United States and the BBC produced features and documentaries on him in the 1990s. Today Huxley is an icon of the avant-garde, a development which began with his friend Stra-vinsky composing the *Variations* for orchestra, subtitled 'In Memory of Aldous Huxley' in 1963–4 (also known as the 'Huxley Variations'). In 1968 Huxley appeared on the cover of the Beatles' *Sergeant Pepper's Lonely Hearts Club Band*: 'we came up with a list of our heroes', remembered Paul McCartney; 'it was about time we let out the fact that we liked Aldous Huxley' (Associated Press, 1 June 1987). This second audience bought sixteen printings of *Island* and twenty-three of *The Doors of Perception*. Huxley's name has been memorialized in the name of a street in Los Angeles, and his life-size image commercialized in an advertisement for Bass ale in 1999. In forthcoming dec-ades Huxley may be read not primarily as a novelist but as a metaphysical savant open to the psychological dimen-sions of healing and the psychic capacities of human intelligence.   DAVID KING DUNAWAY

Sources E. Bass, *Aldous Huxley: annotated bibliography* (1981) • S. Bedford, *Aldous Huxley: a biography*, 2 vols. (1973–4) • J. Brooke, *Aldous Huxley* (1954) • R. Clark, *The Huxleys* (1968) • D. Dunaway, *Hux-ley in Hollywood* (1989) • *Letters of Aldous Huxley*, ed. G. Smith (1969) • J. Meckier, ed., *Critical essays on Aldous Huxley* (1996) • D. Watt, *Aldous Huxley: the critical heritage* (1975) • Hunt. L., Aldous Huxley oral his-tory collection • U. Cal., Los Angeles, Aldous Huxley collection • J. Baxter, *Hollywood exiles* (1976) • D. Bradshaw, ed., *The hidden Huxley* (1994) • D. Dunaway, *Aldous Huxley recollected* (1999) • P. Firchow, *Aldous Huxley: satirist and novelist* (1972) • J. Huxley, *Aldous Huxley, 1894–1963* (1965) • L. Huxley, *This timeless moment* (1968) • J. Huxley, ed., *Aldous Huxley: a memorial volume* (1963) • J. Sexton, ed., *Aldous Huxley's Hearst essays* (1994) • J. Meckier, *Aldous Huxley: satire and structure* (1969) • B. Nichols, *Are they the same at home?* (1927) • private information (2004) • A. Huxley, foreword, *Brave new world* (1946)
Archives Princeton University, New Jersey, letters • Stanford University, California, corresp. and literary papers | BL, letters to S. S. Koteliansky, Add. MS 48975 • BL, letters to Sydney and Violet Schiff, Add. MS 52918 • Bodl. Oxf., corresp. with Sibyl Colefax • King's AC Cam., letters to W. G. H. Sprott • King's Lond., Liddell Hart C., corresp. with B. H. Liddell Hart • LPL, letters to H. R. L. Sheppard • U. Aberdeen, letters (with others) to J. B. Chapman • U. Reading L., letters to H. E. Herlitschka • Wellcome L., corresp. in Eugenic Society papers

Likenesses W. Rothenstein, chalk drawing, 1922, Man. City Gall. • E. Kapp, drawing, 1924, Barber Institute of Fine Arts, Bir-mingham • J. Collier, portrait, 1926, priv. coll. • A. Wolmark, ink and wash drawing, 1928, NPG • A. Wolmark, ink drawing, 1928, AM Oxf. • J. Davidson, terracotta head, 1930, Smithsonian Institution, Washington, DC, National Portrait Gallery • P. Hamann, bronze cast of mask, 1930, NPG • D. Wilding, photograph, 1930–39, NPG • D. Low, caricatures, four pencil sketches, 1933, NPG • M. Ray, bromide print, 1934, NPG [*see illus.*] • G. Schrieber, pencil drawing, 1937, U. Texas • D. Low, double portrait, pencil, chalk and ink draw-ing, 1938 (with H. R. L. Sheppard), Tate collection • W. Suschitzky, two photographs, 1958, NPG • M. Petrie, bronze cast of head, *c.*1960, NPG • D. Bachardy, sketches, 1960–69, priv. coll. • F. Topol-ski, oils, 1961, U. Texas • C. Beaton, photograph, NPG • H. Coster, photographs, NPG • W. Rothenstein, drawing, repro. in *Twenty-four portraits*, 2nd ser. (1923) • W. Suschitzky, double portrait, photo-graph (with Julian Huxley), NPG • photographs, Hult. Arch.
Wealth at death £14,186—in England: administration with will (limited), 27 Aug 1964, *CGPLA Eng. & Wales*

Huxley [*née* Grant], **Elspeth Josceline** (1907–1997), author and journalist, was born Elspeth Josceline Grant in Sussex Square, Bayswater, London, on 23 July 1907, the only child of Major Josceline Charles Henry (Jos) Grant (1873–1947), soldier and farmer, and his wife, the Hon. Eleanor Lilian (Nellie) Grosvenor (1885–1977), daughter of Richard de Aquila Grosvenor, first Baron Stalbridge, brother of the first duke of Westminster, and his second wife, Eleanor Francis Beatrice Hamilton. In 1912 her parents decided to invest their small capital in growing coffee in the newly opened British East Africa Protectorate, later renamed Kenya, and the next year she joined them on Kitimuru Farm, near Chania Bridge (later Thika), 30 miles from Nairobi. Though for her parents there was much hard labour, Huxley thoroughly enjoyed the life, with her mother taking charge of her schooling. But in 1914 their life was disrupted by the First World War. Her father returned to Britain to rejoin the 3rd Royal Scots, with whom he had fought in the Second South African War, and his wife and daughter followed him to England in 1915. Huxley was sent to boarding-school at Aldeburgh, Suffolk, which she hated. When her parents returned to Kenya at the end of the war, she managed to follow them by getting herself expelled, and her unconventional edu-cation was continued at home. The coffee farm proved so unprofitable that it had to be sold, and in 1923 the Grants made a new start on a farm called Gikammeh, near Njoro in the Rift valley. Huxley's mother experimented with many crops, while her father, a gentle, humorous, but impractical Scottish highlander, spent much of his time promoting a variety of unsuccessful schemes. For a year Huxley attended the government European school in Nairobi, and in 1925 she was accepted to study for a dip-loma in agriculture at Reading University, followed by a year at Cornell University in the United States. Her mother's hope that she would take over the farm never materialized, but they remained very close; their corres-pondence was regular, and in 1980 Huxley published *Nellie: Letters from Africa*, a selection of her mother's letters with an editorial memoir and insertions providing infor-mation on family events. She was very like her mother,

Elspeth Josceline Huxley (1907–1997), by Granville Davies, 1982

not only in physical characteristics—a square figure with dark hair cut short—but more importantly in her energy, optimism, enthusiasm for new enterprises, dry sense of humour, and fluent and entertaining writing style. The family were all agnostics, and she had little to do with organized religion.

Huxley did not live in Africa again, although she made frequent visits and travelled widely on the continent throughout her life. In 1929 she became a press officer with the newly created but short-lived Empire Marketing Board, and there she met Gervas Huxley (1894–1971), cousin of the biologist Sir Julian Huxley and of the novelist Aldous Huxley. They married on 31 December 1931. Huxley turned to writing to earn money; as a teenager she had been polo correspondent of the *East African Standard*. When her husband was appointed in 1933 to establish the Ceylon Tea Propaganda Board (later the International Tea Market Expansion Board), a task which involved worldwide travelling, she accompanied him when possible. However, she went first to Kenya, to undertake a commission to write the life of Hugh Cholmondeley, third baron Delamere, the pioneer farmer who had become leader of the European settlers. The title of the two-volume work, *White Man's Country: Lord Delamere and the Making of Kenya* (1935), came from Delamere's insistence that Europeans could live permanently in this equatorial highland region.

The work became the standard history of European settlement in Kenya, but having described the settlers' views, Huxley was eager to learn more of the African reaction to the invasion. She and her mother spent some weeks in a Kikuyu reserve, and she also attended a course in anthropology at the London School of Economics. The result was the novel *Red Strangers* (1937), describing the cataclysmic changes to the life of a fictional Kikuyu family. During the long sea voyages she undertook with her husband she also wrote detective novels: three were published between 1937 and 1940. Of her later novels *The Walled City* (1949) was the best known.

In 1938 the Huxleys bought a farm in Wiltshire (Woodfolds, at Oaksey, near Malmesbury), and while Elspeth worked during the Second World War at the BBC, in the war propaganda department, and as a liaison officer with the Colonial Office, they escaped there as often as possible. Their only child, Charles, was born in February 1944. Oaksey remained Huxley's home for the rest of her life, where, between overseas travels, London visits for official duties and broadcasts, and writing, she dealt with the problems of cows, pigs, and chickens. Early in 1971 they sold the farm and moved a short distance to a cottage named Green End, where Gervas died later that year.

After the publication of *White Man's Country*, Huxley was regarded as the spokeswoman in England of the settlers of Kenya, a position further confirmed by *Race and Politics in Kenya* (1944), a debate with Margery Perham, in which Huxley argued for a constitution giving more power, especially over matters concerning Africans, to the settlers, who were familiar with the conditions of the country, and Perham argued for the retention of power by the Colonial Office. Yet their long-term aims for Kenya were very similar, for Huxley believed in the education and eventual full participation in government of Africans. At the end of the war she was invited to east Africa to spend three months investigating the provision of reading matter for Africans, and in 1946 she produced a report which led to the establishment of the East Africa Literature Bureau. She was never politically active, but supported attempts to develop multiracial parties, and made contact with African leaders. Conservative settlers regarded her as dangerously radical, while to the British left she was an old-fashioned colonialist.

Huxley kept up a continuous output of articles on Africa, farming, and related subjects in the journal *Time and Tide* between the years 1944 and 1958, as well as in *The Times*, the *Sunday Times*, the *Telegraph*, and the *New York Times*. She gave talks on the BBC, and from 1950 to 1961 was one of the panel for the radio discussions *The Critics*. From 1952 to 1959 she was a member of the BBC's General Advisory Council. In 1959–60 she travelled in central Africa as an independent member of the Monckton commission to advise on the future of the region. But her major subject continued to be Kenya. She was commissioned to write a history of the Kenya Farmers' Association: *No Easy Way* (1958). Then she recalled her early memories of the country, and the stories she had been told of it, and remodelled the account into the semi-fictional *The Flame Trees of Thika*

(1959) and its sequel, *The Mottled Lizard* (1962). These became her best-loved books, reinforced by the television adaptation of *The Flame Trees* in 1981. Two other books described travels through east Africa, *The Sorcerer's Apprentice* (1948) and *Forks and Hope* (1964). She continued to collect and edit accounts of the early days: *Out in the Midday Sun: my Kenya* (1985) contained tales of the pioneer European settlers. Her work for Africa was recognized with her appointment as CBE in 1962.

As African colonies attained independence, and controversies over their future died down in Britain, Huxley developed her other interests. She was always concerned with farming in Britain, and this led to an involvement in all environmental issues. Her book *Brave New Victuals* (1965) was a study of the potential for harm in the developing techniques of food production. She also turned to writing biographies of those characters who fascinated her: David Livingstone, Florence Nightingale, and Scott of the Antarctic. Admiring the work of the explorer's son, her last book was *Peter Scott: Painter and Naturalist* (1993). She continued to be much involved in the life of her village and district. She was a justice of the peace from 1947 to 1977; and of her recreations as listed in *Who's Who*, 'resting' would seem an aim rarely achieved, but 'gossip' indicated her enjoyment of the company of family and friends. She died in a nursing home in Tetbury, Gloucestershire, on 10 January 1997. She was survived by her son.

MARY BULL

Sources *The Times* (13 Jan 1997) · *The Independent* (13 Jan 1997) · *Daily Telegraph* (13 Jan 1997) · Bodl. RH, Huxley MSS · E. Huxley, *Nellie: letters from Africa* (1980) · E. Huxley, *The flame trees of Thika* (1959) · E. Huxley, *The mottled lizard* (1962) · G. Huxley, *Both hands: an autobiography* (1970) · R. Cross and M. Perkin, *Elspeth Huxley: a bibliography* (1996) · WWW
Archives Bodl. RH, corresp., diaries, and literary papers, part I (1966), MS Afr. s. 782 · Bodl. RH, family corresp. and papers, part II (1993), MS Afr. s. 2154 | Bodl. RH, letters relating to Kenya · Bodl. RH, corresp. with Margery Perham and related papers · Bodl. RH, letters to C. W. G. Walker · CUL, corresp. and papers relating to biography of Sir Peter Markham Scott · U. Reading, Chatto and Windus archive |FILM BFI NFTVA, documentary footage |SOUND BBC WAC · BL NSA, oral history interview · BL NSA, performance recordings
Likenesses G. Davies, photograph, 1982, NPG [*see illus.*] · photograph, repro. in *The Times* · photograph, repro. in *The Independent* · photograph, repro. in *Daily Telegraph*
Wealth at death £670,948: probate, 24 Sept 1997, *CGPLA Eng. & Wales*

Huxley, Julia Frances (1862–1908). *See under* Huxley, Leonard (1860–1933).

Huxley, Sir Julian Sorell (1887–1975), zoologist and philosopher, was born on 22 June 1887 at 61 Russell Square, Bloomsbury, London, the eldest of three sons and a daughter of Leonard *Huxley (1860–1933) and his first wife, Julia Frances Arnold (1862–1908). Leonard Huxley was at this time a schoolmaster at Charterhouse but later became known for his writing and as editor of the *Cornhill Magazine*. Huxley's mother, likewise a schoolteacher, was a granddaughter of Thomas Arnold of Rugby; his middle name derived from her maternal grandfather, William Sorell (1733–1848), lieutenant-governor of Van Diemen's

Sir Julian Sorell Huxley (1887–1975), by Howard Coster, 1939

Land. The second son, Trevenen Huxley (1889–1914), committed suicide; the novelist Aldous Leonard *Huxley (1894–1963) was the youngest son.

Academic career Julian Huxley followed the traditional path for a member of the intellectual aristocracy—Eton College and Balliol College, Oxford. By 1909 he had collected two poetry prizes, one at Eton, the other at Oxford, the Shakespeare and biology prizes at Eton, the Naples biological scholarship, and a first-class honours degree in natural science (zoology). After a year spent at the Naples Zoological Station he returned to Oxford, where Balliol College appointed him lecturer and the university made him demonstrator at the department of zoology and comparative anatomy. Seeking promotion he left Oxford in 1913 for Texas to take up an assistant professorship and charge of the new department of biology at Rice University in Houston. There he persuaded H. J. Muller, the redoubtable young fruit-fly geneticist and subsequent Nobel laureate, to join him. But by 1916 Huxley had become homesick for England and concerned to join in the war effort. He returned and joined the Army Service Corps intelligence unit. While on leave he met his future bride, (Marie) Juliette (b. 1896/7), daughter of Alphonse Baillot, a solicitor of Neuchâtel, Switzerland. When the war ended Huxley returned to England and in 1919 was appointed a fellow of New College, Oxford, and made senior demonstrator in zoology. His marriage to Juliette on 29 March 1919 at St Martin-in-the-Fields, London, brought them two sons, Anthony Julian Huxley (1920–

1992), who became an anthropologist, and Francis Huxley (*b.* 1923), who became a botanist.

Six years later Huxley moved to the chair of zoology at King's College, London. H. G. Wells, who had made over £60,000 on his very popular *The Outline of History*, had persuaded Huxley to join him and his son, G. P. Wells, in writing a similar work on biology for the intelligent reader, entitled *The Science of Life*. Each could hope to receive about £10,000 for the effort. Under persistent prodding and demands for rapid progress from Wells—Huxley had promised 1000 words per day—he gave up his chair in 1927 to concentrate on the book. The resulting work was a great success and established Huxley as a master of scientific exposition.

Popular science Now Huxley had to live by his pen, by lecturing and his radio talks—the most famous being with Professor C. E. M. (Cyril) Joad and Commander Archibald Bruce Campbell in the BBC's very popular programme *The Brains Trust*, which continued throughout the Second World War. He also enjoyed some seven years of salaried employment starting in 1935 when the Zoological Society appointed him its secretary. Here his flair as a popularizer and science educator found full scope for action. But friction developed between the headstrong Huxley and the more conservative fellows and council of the society. When he outstayed his leave in America in the winter of 1941–2 he returned to a hostile council, and soon his resignation was requested. In 1945 the British government appointed him secretary-general of the UNESCO preparatory commission. With the establishment of the commission a year later he became its first director-general. Although the statutory term of appointment was six years Huxley was only appointed for two, a reduction sought, apparently, by the American delegation. When his term ended he was sixty-one. This proved to be his last salaried position but by no means the end of his work as a scholar and writer. Nor did he withdraw from the world of biology, for he helped to found the Ecological Society, the Society for the Study of Animal Behaviour, and the Society for the Study of Evolution.

As befitted his lineage Huxley was a man of great intelligence. He was also driven by a passion to experience life to the full, and to spread the gospel of evolutionary humanism. Whether it was saving wild places, religion without revelation, or the population problem, he threw himself into each topic, published what he believed, and aided organizations that supported his views or helped to found one where none existed. As his wife, Juliette, has explained: 'There were, in fact, so many Julians within the tall carelessly dressed wanderer bent on his various ploys, escaping from one activity by diving into yet another'. 'So many fingers in so many pies', she once said to him. 'What a pity you haven't got a few more fingers!' In truth there was no single niche for this 'Globe-trotter of Science', this whirlwind spirit, whose restlessness was driven by a 'deep compulsion' to experience and triumph in fresh encounters.

Huxley was a naturalist, experimentalist, and theoretician. He was at home in the field and in the biological laboratory, but not the physiological laboratory. Edmund Selous's observations of courtship in birds inspired him as much as did the experimental embryology (or *Entwicklungsmechanik* as the German embryologists christened it) practised at the zoological station in Naples and across the Atlantic at the marine biology station in Woods Hole. Despite his atheism Huxley could appreciate Teilhard de Chardin's vision of evolution, and like his grandfather T. H. Huxley he believed progress could be described in biological terms. Julian Huxley, however, held that a system of ethics could be constructed on the basis of man's knowledge of biology. He belonged to a generation of British intellectuals among whom was a number of stimulating, industrious, and influential biologists, several of them very successful in communicating biology to a wide audience, who had political commitments, who took eugenics seriously, and who wanted humanity to take control of evolution.

Huxley's greatest strength was surely his pen, and the notice given by the national press in 1920 to his work on that strange amphibian, the axolotl, was the stimulus that launched him on a new part-time career, that of popular scientific writing. The experience of working with H. G. Wells on *The Science of Life* between 1926 and 1931 must surely have developed his skill in this role. Book 4, entitled 'The essence of the controversies about evolution', offers perhaps the clearest, most readable, succinct, and informative popular account of the subject ever penned. It was here that he first expounded his own version of what later developed into the evolutionary synthesis. In 1936 he outlined the same subject to the British Association for the Advancement of Science. To his surprise, many biologists urged him to expand the address. The result was his famous *Evolution: the Modern Synthesis*, a work that won considerable acclaim.

Early researches When Huxley was a student experimental embryology was considered the way of the future for biology. In the mysterious unfolding of the organism lay the keys to understanding how like begets like. Although one key had been provided by Mendelian genetics, rediscovered in 1900, that theory did not explain how the several parts of the organism differentiate, some forming the head, others the tail, and so on, yet all parts are furnished with identical genetic material. Other factors were therefore invoked to achieve a causal account of the successive stages through which the embryo passes in development. Rejecting the claim of the recapitulationists that these stages represent a rapid journey through the evolutionary history of the species, Huxley, like his Oxford mentor, J. W. Jenkinson, used experimental manipulation of the embryo in his search for mechanistic alternatives. These studies led to his co-authorship with Gavin De Beer of their important book *Elements of Experimental Embryology* (1934), in which a prominent role is awarded to what they call biological or morphogenetic fields. Within such a field, the authors explain, there is a gradient, either of a metabolic kind or of the concentration of a specific chemical substance, established by external agencies. Thus the distribution of yolk granules in the egg—many at the bottom, few at the top—determines the polarity of head and tail. The point of entry of the sperm determines the symmetry of left and right sides of the embryo, and indirectly the dorsal–ventral polarity. As for the ultimate fates of individual cells, these are termed 'presumptive' but not irrevocably fixed until an internal factor, known as the organizer—presumed to produce a specific chemical substance—causes them to lose their plasticity. This book publicized the work of numerous zoologists, principal among them Charles Manning Child on gradients, Hans Spemann on the organizer, and Otto Mangold on the plasticity of tissues.

The experimental work for which Huxley is best-known concerns his study of relative growth, or allometry, and his attempt to relate Mendelian genetics and development through the concept of rate genes. Both subjects concerned relative rates. In allometry one measures the rates of increase of two characteristics of an organism over time and compares them, for instance the body weight and claw weight of fiddler crabs. These studies led him to establish the allometric formula representing the straight line yielded from the plot of the logarithm of the two values. The resulting book, *Problems of Relative Growth* (1932), was a landmark in the subject. In it he drew attention to the systematic and evolutionary importance of allometry.

The study Huxley conducted with E. B. Ford and E. W. Sexton on rate genes concerned the differing rates in the formation, and hence depth of colour, of the eyes of the freshwater shrimp (*Gammarus chevreuxi*). By breeding experiments they showed the Mendelian nature of the genetic determination of these rates in different strains. Had Huxley made his intended move to the United States of America following his visit in 1932, he would have pursued this work. He saw it as bringing together Mendelian genetics and the study of development, a rapprochement sorely needed.

Evolution Huxley's major text on this theme, *Evolution: the Modern Synthesis* (1942), was an expansion of his 1936 British Association address 'Natural selection and evolutionary progress'. The title of the book linked the author's name with the term 'synthesis', and thus with this important phase in the development of evolutionary biology, for it was in the thirties that the new knowledge of the genetics of populations and of mutation were being brought into productive union with the doctrine of natural selection. Huxley began with a sketch of the changing fortunes of Darwinian evolution. He pointed to the weakness in the theory as presented by Darwin, singling out Darwin's mistaken views on heredity and variation. So clamorous had Darwin's critics become, wrote Huxley, that one could speak of the 'Eclipse' or 'Death' of Darwinism, a reaction that, he claimed, set in during the 1890s. However, in the two decades following the First World War, he

said, Darwinism was reborn as the fruit of a process of synthesis that he described in the following words:

> Biology in the last twenty years after the period in which new disciplines were taken up in turn and worked out in comparative isolation has become a more unified science. It has embarked upon a period of synthesis, until today it no longer presents the spectacle of a number of semi-independent and largely contradictory sub-sciences but is coming to rival the unity of older sciences like physics, in which advance in any one branch leads almost at once to advance in all other fields, and theory and experiment march hand-in-hand. (J. S. Huxley, *Evolution*, 72)

The text is packed with information, and although Huxley had trained and carried out research as a zoologist, the work is noteworthy for the breadth of treatment and balance between the plant and animal kingdoms. Attending to plants as well as animals was just one example of the way in which his eclectic approach allowed him to adopt an open position on the significance of different sources of variation and the extent of gradualist evolution and by implication the extent of the creative action of natural selection.

Progress Progress, claimed Huxley, can be defined in terms of 'control over the environment, and independence of it'. These properties, he added, 'consist in size and power, mechanical and chemical efficiency, increased capacity for self-regulation and a more stable internal environment, and more efficient avenues of knowledge and of methods for dealing with knowledge'. Huxley claimed that the natural selection of the modern synthesis could account for adaptation and for long-range trends of specialization; therefore, it could account for evolutionary progress too. Evolution he pictured as a 'series of blind alleys'. All, save that of man, have 'terminated blindly'. Man's future is therefore of central importance to the future of life as a whole. For Huxley, man was the 'organ' of evolutionary progress. In this 'cosmic office' it was man's role to realize the highest possible spiritual experience. Man needs, Huxley claimed, a Columbus to explore the geography of the mind so that he can be taught techniques 'of achieving spiritual experience (after all, one can acquire the technique of dancing or tennis, so why not of mystical ecstasy of spiritual peace?)'. Huxley admitted that other authorities regarded the idea of progress as a myth, but he professed that the scientific doctrine of progress will in due time replace all other myths of human destiny, becoming the major external support for human ethics.

Religions Huxley treated as 'social organs whose function it is to adjust man to his destiny', and he classified as religious any system or teaching that concerned man's destiny. The evolutionary concept of progress was thus religious, but in contrast to old religions that helped man maintain his morale in the face of the unknown, religions today must 'utilize all available knowledge in giving guidance and encouragement for the continuing adventure of human development'. In 1931 Huxley described the role of religious mysticism as submerging the ego in a greater being. Whereas earlier religions identified such a being with a god, the evolutionary 'religion' of humanism identified it with the human species. Despite the struggle of the First World War, Huxley glimpsed the progress of coalescence of minds into super-minds taking place. At the end of his vista of progress he pictured man 'consciously controlling his own destinies and the destinies of all life upon this planet'. These views he expressed some sixteen years before he first met Pierre Teilhard de Chardin and found common ground with this mystic Catholic.

Historians tend to view the Russian-born American zoologist Theodor Dobzhansky as a more significant figure internationally than Huxley in the establishment of the neo-Darwinian synthesis, but in Britain, Huxley was one of the major contributors. In his activities for the biological community, especially conservation, he was possibly the most important figure.

Among his many awards Huxley received the Kalinga prize for the popularization of science (1953), the Lasker award for his contributions to planned parenthood (1959), the Darwin medal of the Royal Society for his contributions to the theory of evolution (1956), and a gold medal from the International Union for the Conservation of Nature and the World Wildlife Fund for his research relating to conservation (1970). He had been elected to the Royal Society in 1938, and was knighted in 1958. In 1966 he began to write his autobiography. The second volume of this two-volume work, *Memories*, appeared in 1973, the year he suffered a stroke. He died at his home, 31 Pond Street, Hampstead, on 14 February 1975; following cremation his ashes were buried at Compton Chapel, Puttenham, Surrey. A memorial meeting was held at St John's, Smith Square, London, on 18 April, and another at UNESCO headquarters in Paris on 5 May. His wife survived him. ROBERT OLBY

Sources C. Waters and A. J. Van Helden, eds., *Julian Huxley: biologist and statesman of science* (1992) · J. R. Durant, 'Julian Huxley and the development of evolutionary studies', *Evolutionary studies: a centenary celebration of the life of Julian Huxley* [London 1987], ed. M. Keynes and G. A. Harrison (1989) · A. Huxley, 'The Galton lecture for 1987: Julian Huxley—a family view', *Evolutionary studies: a centenary celebration of the life of Julian Huxley* [London 1987], ed. M. Keynes and G. A. Harrison (1989) · J. R. Baker, *Memoirs FRS*, 22 (1976), 207–38; repr. in *Julian Huxley: scientist and world citizen 1887–1975* (1978) [incl. bibliography compiled by J. P. Green, pp. 53–184] · J. Huxley, *Leaves of the tulip tree* (1986) · M. Ridley, 'Embryology and classical zoology in Great Britain', *A history of embryology: the eighth symposium of the British Society for Developmental Biology*, ed. T. H. Horder, J. A. Witkowski, and C. C. Wylie (1985), 35–67 · J. Huxley, *Memories*, 2 vols. (1970–73) · R. C. Clark, *The Huxleys* (1968) · J. S. Huxley and G. D. De Beer, *Elements of experimental embryology* (1934) · H. G. Wells, J. S. Huxley, and G. P. Wells, *The science of life: a summary of contemporary knowledge about life and its possibilities*, 3 vols. (1934–7) · J. S. Huxley, *Evolution: the modern synthesis*, 1st edn (1942); 2nd edn (1963); 3rd edn (1974) · S. J. Gould, 'The hardening of the modern synthesis', *Dimensions of Darwinism: themes and countertheories in twentieth-century evolutionary theory*, ed. M. Grene (1983), 71–93 · J. P. Green, *Krise und Hoffnung der Evolutionshumanismus Julian Huxleys* (1981) · b. cert. · m. cert. · d. cert.

Archives Pusey Oxf., family papers · Rice University, Houston, Texas, Woodson Research Center, corresp. and papers · U. Oxf., department of zoology, corresp. and papers relating to fiddler crabs · U. Oxf., Edward Grey Institute of Field Ornithology, ornithological diaries and papers | American Philosophical Society, Philadelphia, letters to H. T. Clarke · BL, corresp. with Marie Stopes, Add. MS 58473 · BLPES, corresp. with Lord Beveridge · BLPES, letters to E. K. Collard · Bodl. Oxf., corresp. with C. D. Darlington · Bodl. Oxf., corresp. with Sir Alister Hardy · Bodl. Oxf., corresp. with Gilbert Murray · Bodl. Oxf., corresp. relating to Society for Protection of Science and Learning · Bodl. RH, corresp. with Arthur Creech Jones · Bodl. RH, corresp. with E. B. Worthington · CUL, corresp. with Meyer Fortes · CUL, corresp. with Joseph Needham · CUL, corresp. with Sir Peter Markham Scott · ICL, corresp. with J. W. Munro · JRL, letters to *Manchester Guardian* · King's Lond., Liddell Hart C., corresp. with Sir B. H. Liddell Hart · McMaster University, Hamilton, Ontario, corresp. with Bertrand Russell · NA Scot., corresp. with Lord Lothian · NHM, corresp. with W. R. Dawson · Nuffield Oxf., corresp. with Lord Cherwell · Society for Psychical Research, London, corresp. with Sir Oliver Lodge · Tate collection, corresp. with Lord Clark · U. Glas., corresp. with E. Hindle · U. Lond., Institute of Education, corresp. with World Education Fellowship · U. Sussex, letters to J. G. Crowther · University of East Anglia Library, corresp. with J. C. Pritchard · Wellcome L., corresp. with Eugenics Society · Wolfson College, Oxford, corresp. with H. B. O. Kettlewell

Likenesses H. Coster, photograph, 1939, NPG [*see illus.*] · D. Low, caricature, pencil, 1945, U. Hull · W. Stoneman, photograph, 1956, NPG · W. Suschitzky, double portrait, photograph, 1958 (with Aldous Huxley), NPG · R. Shephard, chalk drawing, 1960, NPG · W. Suschitzky, photographs, 1961, NPG · M. Gerson, photograph, 1965, NPG · G. Argent, photograph, 1968, NPG · C. Beaton, photograph, 1970, NPG · H. Coster, photographs, NPG · E. Kapp, drawing, Barber Institute of Fine Arts, Birmingham

Wealth at death £23,741: probate, 12 June 1975, *CGPLA Eng. & Wales*

Huxley, Leonard (1860–1933), biographer and writer, was born in London on 11 December 1860, the second, but elder surviving, son of the scientist Thomas Henry *Huxley (1825–1895) and his wife, Henrietta Ann, daughter of Henry Heathorn, of Bathurst, New South Wales, Australia. He was educated at University College School, London, at St Andrews University, and at Balliol College, Oxford, of which he was an exhibitioner and where he obtained a first class in classical moderations (1881) and in *literae humaniores* (1883).

In 1884 Huxley became an assistant master at Charterhouse School, Godalming, Surrey, until in 1901 he joined the publishing firm of Smith, Elder & Co., becoming the close friend and literary adviser of Reginald John Smith and his assistant in the editorship of the *Cornhill Magazine*. After the death of Smith in 1916 and the amalgamation of his firm the following year with John Murray's, Huxley willingly relocated to Albemarle Street, London, and there continued his role of valued friend and adviser. He became sole editor of the *Cornhill*, a position which gave him full scope for his almost paternal encouragement of honest literary effort.

On 16 April 1885 Huxley married Julia Frances Arnold [*see below*]. They had a daughter, Margaret, and three sons, the second of whom, Trevenen, committed suicide in 1914 after being treated for depression. Their other two sons were Sir Julian *Huxley (1887–1975), scientist and director-general of UNESCO, and Aldous *Huxley (1894–1963), novelist. On 23 February 1912, after the death of his first wife from cancer, Huxley married Rosalind, third daughter of

Leonard Huxley (1860–1933), by Elliott & Fry

William Wallace Bruce; they had two sons. Huxley was also the brother-in-law and good friend of John *Collier, the well-known portrait painter.

Huxley's generous nature, combined with his veneration for the memory of his father and his enjoyment of the successes of his sons, saved him from any sense of being overshadowed. Nevertheless, it was a great pleasure to him when in 1919 his old university of St Andrews conferred upon him the honorary degree of LLD in recognition of his own literary achievements. He wrote an outstanding biography of his father, *The Life and Letters of Thomas Henry Huxley* (2 vols., 1900; 2nd edn, 3 vols., 1903), and also *The Life and Letters of Sir Joseph Dalton Hooker* (2 vols., 1918). His volume of poems, *Anniversaries* (1920), showed some talent, and, among other works, he skilfully edited *Jane Welsh Carlyle: Letters to her Family, 1839–1863* (1924) and *Elizabeth Barrett Browning: Letters to her Sister, 1846–1859* (1929), and wrote an account of the publishing firm where he had worked, *The House of Smith Elder* (privately printed, 1923). He always maintained his inherited interest in biology and was an enthusiast for music and the delights of open-air life. Leonard Huxley died at his home, 16 Bracknell Gardens, Hampstead, London, on 3 May 1933. His remains were interred on 6 May at Compton, Surrey. He was survived by his second wife.

Leonard Huxley's first wife, **Julia Frances Huxley** [*née* Arnold] (1862–1908), schoolmistress, was the eighth of the nine children of Thomas *Arnold (1823–1900), literary scholar, and his wife, Julia Sorell (1826–1888). Her grandfather was Thomas *Arnold (1795–1842), headmaster of Rugby School, and her sister was Mary Augusta *Ward (1851–1920), the novelist known as Mrs Humphry Ward. As children, she and her two young sisters, Lucy Arnold (1858–1894) and Ethel *Arnold (1864/5–1930), caught the eye of Charles Dodgson (Lewis Carroll) in Oxford and became among his favourite photographic models; he also invented a word game, 'doublets', in their honour. Born relatively late into a liberal-minded family with an educational bent, Julia was able to reap the benefits of more advanced thinking on education for women than had been the lot of her sister Mary. She attended Oxford High School for Girls and went on to Oxford University, first as a home student (on a Clothworkers' scholarship) and finally earning a first-class degree in English literature from Somerville College in 1882.

In her youth Julia was described as 'a tall raven-haired girl with a face which managed to be thin without being angular' (Sutherland, 166). She had a marvellous sense of humour and, like most of the women in the Arnold family, a great deal of resourcefulness and ambition to supplement her intelligence. On 16 April 1885 she married Leonard Huxley [*see above*] and they went to Godalming, Surrey, where he had taken up a teaching post at Charterhouse School the year before. Their house was named Laleham in tribute to Thomas Arnold of Rugby. Unlike her sister Mary, Julia supported the women's rights movement, including the suffragettes. She combined her own marriage and motherhood of four children with a teaching career, founding an experimental girls' school near Godalming, Prior's Field School, in January 1902. It was a great success, having fifty pupils within two years and eventually expanding to a student body of two hundred. Julia acted as its headmistress until her death, maintaining that it was 'what I've always wanted to do' (Sutherland, 167).

Julia Huxley, like her mother before her, contracted cancer, and, after a protracted struggle with the disease, which included newly instituted 'X-ray treatments', died at Prior's Field on 29 November 1908; her husband survived her.

JOHN MURRAY, *rev.* M. CLARE LOUGHLIN-CHOW

Sources *The Times* (4 May 1933) · C. E. L. [C. E. Lawrence], *Cornhill Magazine*, [3rd] ser., 74 (1933), 641–8 · [V. Stephen], review of *Letters of a betrothed*, *TLS* (31 May 1907), 170 · [O. J. R. Howarth], review of *Scott's last expedition*, *TLS* (6 Nov 1913), 501 · [H. H. Turner], 'The Victorian botanist', *TLS* (18 July 1918), 334 · [D. L. Murray], 'Mrs Carlyle's letters', *TLS* (8 May 1924), 283 [review] · *TLS* (7 Nov 1929), 893 [review] · personal knowledge (1949) · J. Sutherland, *Mrs Humphry Ward: eminent Victorian, pre-eminent Edwardian* (1990) [J. F. Huxley] · V. M. Brittain, *The women at Oxford: a fragment of history* (1960) [Julia Frances Huxley] · *CGPLA Eng. & Wales* (1933) · m. certs. · d. cert. [Julia Frances Huxley]

Archives BL, corresp. with Macmillans, Add. MS 55211 · U. Leeds, Brotherton L., letters to Edward Clodd

Likenesses J. Collier, portrait (as older man), priv. coll. · M. Collier and J. Collier, portrait (as young man), priv. coll. · Elliott & Fry, photograph, NPG [*see illus.*]

Wealth at death £14,863 17s. 8d.: probate, 24 June 1933, *CGPLA Eng. & Wales* • £27,477 19s. 8d.—Julia Frances Huxley: probate, 9 March 1909, *CGPLA Eng. & Wales*

Huxley, Sir Leonard George Holden (1902–1988), physicist, was born on 29 May 1902 at 14 Beauval Road, Dulwich, London, the son of George Hambrough (or Hamborough) Huxley (1868–1944), schoolmaster, and his wife, Lilian Sarah Smith. He was descended from an uncle of the Victorian scientist T. H. Huxley, and was a third cousin once removed of Aldous and Julian Huxley. His family moved to Australia when he was three years old, and he entered the Hutchins School in Hobart, Tasmania, in 1915. In 1920 he won a science and general scholarship to the University of Tasmania. As an undergraduate he gained distinction in the sciences, particularly in physics and mathematics. He was awarded the Philip Fysh prize for physics and was elected a Rhodes scholar for 1923. He entered New College, Oxford, in 1923 reading physics in the honours school of natural sciences.

Huxley's anxiety to do research before the expiry of his Rhodes scholarship led him to take his BA degree in two years. He gained second-class honours and began research in the electrical laboratory, Oxford, under J. S. Townsend. The award of the J. T. Bowden scholarship by New College enabled him to continue his research in Oxford after the expiry of the Rhodes scholarship and in 1928 he was awarded a DPhil for his thesis, 'Corona discharge in helium and neon'. He was appointed a lecturer, demonstrator, and tutor in the electrical laboratory in 1926 where he remained until 1929, taking his MA in that year. He married, on 5 October 1929, Ella Mary Child (1904/5–1981), daughter of Frederick George Copeland, a clergyman. They had one son and one daughter.

From 1929 to 1931 Huxley was on the staff of the Australian Radio Research Board. Before sailing for Australia he worked for some months with the British Radio Research Board at Datchet. In Australia he collaborated with the department of electrical engineering in Sydney University on the development of a cathode ray tube direction finder, and carried out investigations on atmospherics at the Commonwealth Solar Observatory, Mount Stromlo, Canberra.

Huxley's sojourn in Australia was brief and in October 1931 he was appointed lecturer in physics in the University College, Nottingham. His teaching duties took him to University College, Leicester, for one morning each week and in July 1932 he made a successful application for the Frederick W. Bennett lectureship in physics in that college. In Leicester he continued his researches on collision of electrons with gas molecules and in the related problems of the conduction of electricity in gases. At that stage he became interested in the propagation of electromagnetic radiation and this proved of great value when he was released for wartime duties in 1940.

The Air Ministry radar establishment, originally at Bawdsey Manor in Suffolk, had been evacuated to Dundee on the outbreak of war and to Dorset in the spring of 1940, where it remained until 1942, at first on a cliff site at Worth Matravers and at Swanage. It was at this stage with the name in transition to Telecommunications Research Establishment (TRE) that Huxley joined as a scientific officer. Many radar devices, already in operational use by the Royal Air Force, had evolved from TRE and it was clear that it was of little use devising complex equipment unless RAF personnel were taught how it worked and how to use it. That problem was handed to Huxley and led to the genesis of the TRE radar school. In the beginning Huxley was the sole lecturer, but his efforts were so greatly valued by the RAF that the school soon grew in strength.

After the move of TRE to Great Malvern in May 1942 the development of the vital new radar systems working in the centimetre waveband—such as the blind bombing aid known as H_2S and the anti-submarine radar—increased the importance of the radar school, and under Huxley's guidance many thousands of civilians and service personnel had passed through the school by the end of the war.

Huxley conversed and lectured in a quiet and undemonstrative voice but with such authority that he soon attracted high-ranking RAF officers anxious to understand the basis of the new radar systems under their command. In paying tribute to the TRE school after the war A. P. Rowe, the chief superintendent, recalled that the air officer commanding, RAF Training Command, had remarked that even if the rest of TRE did not exist, the teaching school would be well worth visiting.

Huxley had been appointed principal scientific officer and after the end of the war he wrote an important book, *Wave Guides* (1947), based on the lectures he had given in the TRE school. Much of the material in this book related to technical developments in the microwave region, which until then had been available only in secret documents. Huxley had been given leave of absence from University College, Leicester, which had been placed on the list to receive exchequer grants in 1946. He did not apply for the newly established chair of physics but moved to the University of Birmingham as reader in electromagnetism in the department of electrical engineering. His stay there was brief and in 1949 he was elected to the Elder chair of physics in the University of Adelaide.

Huxley soon became an important figure in Australian education and research. He continued as the Elder professor of physics until 1960 when he was appointed vice-chancellor of the Australian National University, Canberra. As the secretary of the physical science committee of the Australian Academy he became deeply involved with the British proposal to build a large optical telescope, as a joint project, in Australia. He was a member of the Australian large telescope committee which had discussions with the British delegation in 1964 and remained one of the principal Australian advisers in the complex negotiations that ultimately led to the joint decision of the British and Australian governments in 1967 to proceed with the construction of the Anglo-Australian 150 inch telescope at Siding Spring in New South Wales, for many years an outstanding instrument for astronomical research.

Huxley remained vice-chancellor of the Australian National University until December 1967. During this period he served on many educational and scientific committees. He was created KBE (1964) and was awarded the honorary degree of DSc by Tasmania in 1962 and by the Australian National University in 1980.

In his youth Huxley was a prominent athlete. He was captain of athletics at the Hutchins School and during his years in Oxford he was awarded the New College colours for athletics. He died during a visit to London on 4 September 1988 in the Royal Free Hospital, Camden.

BERNARD LOVELL

Sources L. G. H. Huxley file, University of Leicester Archives · private information (2004) · *WW* · B. Lovell, 'Sir Leonard Huxley', *The Guardian* (9 Sept 1988) · A. P. Rowe, *One story of radar* (1948) · b. cert. · m. cert. · d. cert.

Huxley, Margaret Rachel (1854–1940), nurse and promoter of nurses' training, was born on 21 December 1854 at Thornton Heath, Croydon, Surrey, the daughter of William Thomas Huxley, clerk at the Brighton railway, and his wife, Esther Hopkins. Margaret was a niece of Thomas Henry Huxley (1825–1895). At an early age she was influenced by the work of Florence Nightingale, and, in spite of strenuous opposition from her family, she decided to take up nursing. Miss Huxley began her training in 1880 at St Bartholomew's Hospital, London, shortly before Ethel Manson, the future Mrs Bedford Fenwick, was appointed matron of the hospital. Miss Manson was passionate about the development of nursing as a profession for women and Miss Huxley was influenced by her ideas. The two young women became friends, and for the rest of their lives they worked to promote the professional development of nurses and nursing.

On completing her two years' training Miss Huxley was appointed matron of the National Eye and Ear Infirmary in Dublin. Her talents were soon recognized and within a year she was invited to take up the position of matron of Sir Patrick Dun's Hospital, a small general hospital serving a working-class area of Dublin. As matron and lady superintendent with responsibility for training the nurses, she was able to introduce a 'modern' training scheme with lectures and a final examination. The standard of nursing improved so much that Miss Huxley proposed the establishment of a central school that would extend the benefits of theoretical instruction to nurses in the many small hospitals in Dublin. The Dublin Metropolitan Technical School for Nurses opened in 1894, with the support of the medical establishment, and it operated successfully for over sixty years.

Miss Huxley retired from Sir Patrick Dun's Hospital in 1902 but continued to be involved in nursing work through her private nursing home Elpis, in Lower Mount Street, Dublin. This nursing home, which opened in 1890, was the first of its kind in Ireland, providing private patients drawn from Dublin's middle-class protestant community with medical and surgical nursing care. The nursing staff were trained at Sir Patrick Dun's and the reputation of the nursing home brought credit to the hospital. Miss Huxley was honoured by the hospital when she was appointed the first woman governor in 1912.

After her retirement Miss Huxley became more

Margaret Rachel Huxley (1854–1940), by unknown photographer

involved in the professional side of nursing. Through her London contacts she was a founder member of the British Nurses' Association (later the Royal British Nurses' Association) in 1887, of the Matrons' Council in 1894, and of the International Council of Nurses (ICN) in 1899. In Ireland she was the prime mover behind the founding of the Irish Matrons' Association in 1903 and the Irish Nurses' Association (INA) in 1904. The priority of all these organizations was to achieve state registration for nurses. As vice-president of the National Council of Nurses of Great Britain and Ireland (NCN) she attended the international conferences of the ICN over many years, meeting the leading personalities in the nursing field. In 1913, during her term as president of the INA, she hosted the annual conference of the NCN, bringing a professional nurses' conference to Dublin for the first time.

Throughout the long campaign for state registration Miss Huxley represented Irish nurses at a national level, giving evidence to the House of Commons select committee on registration for nurses in 1904, as the representative of the INA on the central committee for the state registration of nurses, and as vice-president of the Society for the State Registration of Trained Nurses in 1914. By the time the British government passed the Nurses' Registration Acts in 1919, introducing state registration in England and Wales, Scotland, and Ireland, Ireland was seeking independence and Irish nurses were forming their own organizations. Miss Huxley was not sympathetic to Irish nationalism, believing more in the international aims of professional nurses. Although she was a member of the first General Nursing Council for Ireland, from 1920 to 1923, and also acted as an examiner for the council for several years, her role as a leader of Irish nurses was over.

Miss Huxley took a special interest in public health and the housing of the poor, a subject with which she was familiar through her work at Sir Patrick Dun's. She devoted time and money to improving housing conditions in Dublin, advocating that better living conditions would improve the hygiene and health of the poor. She set up the Huxley Trust Fund, through which well-planned cottages were built in the Coombe area of the city. During the First World War she worked on behalf of the Red Cross Society and as the matron of Dublin University Voluntary Aid Detachment Hospital. After the war she served for many years on the committee of the Nation's Tribute to Nurses, a fund to assist nurses whose health had been broken by war service. She played an active role in the politics of her profession until she was over eighty years old. She died at Elpis on 10 January 1940 after a short illness. Her funeral was held on 13 January at the Unitarian church, Dublin, and she was buried in the city's Mount Jerome cemetery. She was unmarried.

Miss Huxley was a woman of simple tastes who preferred deeds to words. When she retired as matron from Sir Patrick Dun's Hospital she inaugurated the Margaret Huxley memorial medal for the best nurse in training. She disliked publicity and honours and refused to accept the Royal Red Cross for her work during the First World War, though she accepted honorary membership of the Finnish Nurses' Association in 1925 and an honorary MA degree from Dublin University in 1928.

SUSAN McGANN

Sources records, Sir Patrick Dun's Hospital, board of governors, minutes, 1877–1909, Royal College of Physicians of Ireland, Dublin, ref. 1/6–9 · annual reports, 1883–99, Royal College of Physicians of Ireland, Dublin · Dublin Metropolitan Technical School for Nurses, minute book, 1893–1952, Royal College of Surgeons of Ireland, Dublin, Faculty of Nursing · Irish Matrons' Association, minute book, 1910–38, Royal College of Surgeons of Ireland, Dublin, Faculty of Nursing · General Nursing Council for Ireland, minutes, 1920–43, An Bord Altranais, Dublin · Rules Committee, minutes, 1925–46, An Bord Altranais, Dublin · *Irish Times* (11 Jan 1940) · *British Journal of Nursing* (Feb 1940), 27–8 · *Nursing Times* (27 Jan 1940), 102 · 'Select committee on the registration of nurses', *Parl. papers* (1904), 6.701, no. 281; (1905) · *Nursing Record and Hospital World* (1894–June 1902) · *British Journal of Nursing* (July 1902–1940) · S. McGann, 'Margaret Huxley: pioneer of scientific nursing in England', *The battle of the nurses: a study of eight women who influenced the development of professional nursing, 1880–1930* (1992), 130–159 · b. cert.
Archives Royal College of Physicians of Ireland, Dublin, records of Sir Patrick Dun's Hospital · Royal College of Surgeons of Ireland, Dublin, Faculty of Nursing, Dublin Metropolitan Technical School for Nurses, minute book
Likenesses portrait, repro. in *British Journal of Nursing* (Sept 1925), 204 · portrait, repro. in *British Journal of Nursing* (April 1928), 89 · two photographs, Royal College of Nursing, Edinburgh, archives [*see illus.*]
Wealth at death £2834 2s. 4d.: probate, 9 July 1940, *CGPLA Éire*

Huxley, Thomas Henry (1825–1895), biologist and science educationist, was born on 4 May 1825 in Ealing, the youngest of the six surviving children of George Huxley (1780–1853) and Rachel Withers (1785–1852); an elder sister and younger brother died in infancy. His mother was born in London's East End, but was of Devon descent. She was a high Anglican, and it was she who bequeathed Huxley's black eyes and lightning intellect. His grandfather, also Thomas Huxley, had owned an inn and farm in Coventry

Thomas Henry Huxley (1825–1895), by John Collier, 1883

but had died in debt, and by 1825 Huxley's father had been a mathematics teacher for eighteen years at the Ealing School run by Dr George Nicholas.

Student years, 1833–1846 The Ealing School was Anglican and evangelical, and in decline. It was here that Huxley had his only formal schooling—two years (1833–5) which he detested. The school's standards had collapsed and his sole memory was of fighting a bully, William Poideoin (who was transported to Australia, where Huxley met him again in April 1848), but even so his life was to be marked by the institution's evangelicalism. By 1835 the school's forty remaining pupils supplied insufficient fees, and in that year George Huxley took his family to Coventry, where, however, a job in the savings bank proved equally unsuccessful. Huxley, grown tall with raven hair, spent his early teens (1835–41) in the ribbon-weaving city, where a feeling of neglect turned him into 'one of the most secretive thin-skinned mortals in the world' (Huxley to H. Heathorn, 23 Nov 1848, Imperial College, Huxley MSS). He escaped into the world of science, reading James Hutton's *Theory of the Earth* at the age of twelve and later conducting galvanic experiments. He also now began to question his parents' Anglicanism. From Thomas Carlyle's books he learned that religion was distinct from theology, and he immersed himself in German Romanticism. He mixed with ribbon masters, dissenters who were then ousting the Anglican gentry from the town halls. These marginal men, with their cause-and-effect philosophy, encouraged him to question the duality of soul and matter (and sources of knowledge about them), and to challenge the state's right to force dissenters to pay church rates. One such dissenter, George May, introduced Huxley to the Unitarian Thomas Southwood Smith's *Illustrations of the Divine Government*, with its deterministic science and reforming imperative. Huxley responded to the prevailing sectarian bitterness by jotting in his 'Thoughts & doings' notebook 'It is not error but sectarian error—nay & even sectarian truth w^h. causes the unhappiness of mankind' (Imperial College, Huxley MS 3.123, fol. 10).

Huxley's sisters, Ellen and Eliza, both married medical men in 1839, by which time Huxley himself was apprenticed to Ellen's husband, John Charles Cooke, a hard-drinking practitioner who was editing the materialist John Elliotson's lectures for publication. However, the trauma of seeing a cadaver at this impressionable age resulted in a strange lethargy in Huxley, the sort that would subsequently dog his life. In 1841 Cooke transferred him to the mesmerist Thomas Chandler, whose dockside Rotherhithe practice exposed Huxley to London's garret-paupers during the economic depression. Late in 1841 he moved in with Eliza and her husband, John Salt, in Euston Place. Cooke was teaching forensic medicine at nearby Sydenham College: this was a private anatomy school on Grafton Street, whose teachers included Marshall Hall (then berating the Anglican exclusivity of the College of Physicians). Courses at the college were cheap and Huxley enrolled in October 1841; he described himself at this time as having the lowlife looks typical of those of the students of this cut-rate medical community—'a very pale, thin, lanky, ugly body' was capped 'with dreadfully long hair … and a generally neglected style of attire' (Huxley to H. Heathorn, 27 March 1850?, Imperial College, Huxley MSS). Besides anatomy and surgery he studied botany under Richard Hoblyn, and walked twice weekly to Chelsea to hear John Lindley at the Physic Garden. He took Hoblyn's class prize and a second-place silver medal at the Society of Apothecaries' competition in August 1842. Bathed in this radical dissenting milieu, Huxley accepted morality as a cultural product and Sir William Hamilton's logic that reason could not reveal God behind the veil of phenomena. Nevertheless, he still accepted God's existence.

As sons of a distressed professional, Huxley and his brother James gained free scholarships to the new Charing Cross Hospital in October 1842. There George Fownes (Justus von Liebig's protégé) had Huxley experimenting with the new organic chemistry, breaking down proteins to understand muscle activity. However, it was Thomas Wharton Jones's physiology lectures and comparative anatomy studies that most inspired Huxley. Huxley's intellect was 'acute & quick [rather] than grasping or deep' (Huxley to H. Heathorn, 8 Feb 1848, Imperial College, Huxley MSS), but physiology and chemistry met his need for exactitude and he gained medals in both subjects in 1843. Jones's fascination with 'electrophysiology'—he envisioned muscles as tightening electromagnets—helps to explain Huxley's growing love of the 'mechanical engineering of living machines' (*Collected Essays*, 1.7), but

he rejected Fownes's and Jones's divine-design explanations of body architecture and wrote Jacob Henle's epigraph on his notebook: 'To explain a Physiological fact means in a word to deduce its necessity from the physical and chemical laws of Nature' (Imperial College, Huxley MS 3.124, fol. 1).

Huxley's early skill in microscopy showed in his discovery of a new membrane—a single layer of cells next to the human hair follicle. Jones called it 'Huxley's layer', and he helped Huxley publish 'On a hitherto undescribed structure in the human hair sheath' in the *London Medical Gazette* in 1845. In the same year Huxley passed part one of London University's bachelor of medicine exam, winning William Sharpey's gold medal for anatomy and physiology, but, his scholarship having expired, he was forced to forgo part two (he never did get a degree). He was too young to obtain a practitioner's licence from the Royal College of Surgeons and his disintegrating family threw him onto his own resources. Also in 1845 his three brothers all married (although one, William, so antagonized the others that they cut him dead for life) and a scandal, the details of which remain unknown, forced his brother-in-law John Salt to flee the country. He went first to Antwerp (where Huxley secretly took Eliza to join him) and then, under the name Scott, to Tennessee. The following year, on 13 March, Huxley joined the navy in order to be able to repay debts owed to Cooke and his eldest brother, George.

The *Rattlesnake* voyage, 1846–1850 At Haslar naval hospital in Gosport, Sir John Richardson (1787–1865) placed Huxley in the museum, from where he was recruited by Captain Owen Stanley, who wanted a scientific assistant surgeon for his *Rattlesnake* expedition. Stanley's brief was to 'sweep' the Great Barrier Reef's 'inner passage' to make it safe for the new screw steamers out of Sydney, and to survey southern New Guinea. The obsolete 'donkey' frigate was well refitted by Stanley, with a large chart room where Huxley could lash his microscope. Despite hardships—he slept in an alcove off the gun-room and supervised twenty-two midshipmen—he would be able to study and dissect around the globe while earning 7s. 6d. a day. Before setting sail Huxley was introduced to Edward Forbes, who, at the British Association for the Advancement of Science meeting at Southampton, initiated him into tow-netting and dredging techniques.

The *Rattlesnake* left England on 11 December 1846, with Huxley resolved to specialize in the perishable pelagic jellyfish and sea nettles. On leaving Madeira, where he climbed the Curral Mountain (starting his obsession with mountain scenery), he dissected Diphydae (siphonophores), ascidians, and the arrow worm *Sagitta*. The Portuguese man-of-war *Physalia* and tiny *Velella* became his daily study while *en route* for Rio de Janeiro and Cape Town. Whether *Physalia* was an individual organism or a complex colony was a contemporary problem—Huxley's first paper, on *Physalia* (Imperial College, Huxley MS 34.1), made it a single individual composed of 'organs'. This, like the other papers, was posted by Stanley to his father, the bishop of Norwich and figurehead president of the

Linnean Society—an act of *noblesse oblige* that galled the independent Huxley, who already equated scientific rank with ability rather than status.

At the Cape, Huxley began a monograph on the mollusc archetype and the variations shown in the structure of the 'foot', but as the ship reached Mauritius he suffered the first of the depressions that bedevilled his trip, brought on by his hatred of service life and exacerbated as the voyage progressed by his religious dislocation and despair of making his scientific mark. At Hobart in June 1847 he was taking strength from his research on the tiny *Diphyes*, and three months in Sydney saw him finishing a paper on the unity of organization of the Diphydae and Phosphoridae, which would group the siphonophores around a structural archetype. He wrote to Forbes that he was removing the hydras, sea anemones, sea nettles, and jellyfish from Cuvier's rag-bag, the Radiata, and combining them in a new class, the Nematophora (Rudolph Leuckart simultaneously coined the word Coelenterata). He tried out his ideas at the colony's scientific salons, including Philip Parker King's, and in 1848 that of William Sharp Macleay, whose quinarianism would influence the romantic Huxley's search for nature's pattern.

In July 1847, shortly after arriving in Sydney, Huxley met Henrietta (Nettie) Anne Heathorn (1825–1914), a brewer's daughter born in the West Indies and currently keeping house for her brother-in-law William Fanning. Impulsive as ever, Huxley became engaged to her on their sixth meeting. Although his mother had hoped that the tropics would distance him from the 'Scoffer and the Unbeliever' (R. Huxley to T. H. Huxley, 26 Oct 1847, Imperial College, Huxley MSS), his religious doubts continued to grow. After church on Sunday 10 October 1847, the eve of the *Rattlesnake*'s departure for the Barrier Reef, his talk evidently distressed Nettie, and his subsequent explanatory letter to her gives the first details of his scepticism: he was already mooting the moral responsibility of weighing evidence, and of not accepting orthodox dogmas for their social value—an honest doubt which he clearly distinguished from the atheism of the demagogues (Huxley to H. Heathorn, 16 Oct 1847, Imperial College, Huxley MSS).

The first survey of the Barrier Reef's inner passage (October 1847 – January 1848) reached Cape Upstart. It introduced Huxley to Aboriginal life, and he rode inland towards the Darling downs with a squatter guide. In February 1848 he visited Melbourne and Tasmania, where homesickness was alleviated by his working on another paper, 'On the anatomy and the affinities of the medusae'. Here he made the existence of two 'foundation membranes' (to be called endoderm and ectoderm by George Allman in 1853) the defining characteristic of the Nematophora, proving from the growth stages that the organs of siphonophores and medusae were homologous. He casually suggested that these membranes were related to one another in the same way that the two cell layers were related in the early vertebrate embryo. Another zigzag up the inner passage (April 1848 – January 1849) took place as a thirteen-man team under Edmund Kennedy trekked overland from Rockingham Bay. Huxley had been invited by Kennedy to join them but was not permitted to—fortunately, as it turned out, for all but three died. However, the broiling heat of the Coral Sea still caused a mental collapse of sorts in Huxley as he buried himself in Dante's *Inferno*. From Cape York the *Rattlesnake* sailed to Port Essington's crumbling settlement, where Huxley pondered the fate of a shipwrecked missionary, 'a soldier of his church' (*T. H. Huxley's Diary*, 151), as he put it, already honing his military metaphor.

Huxley continued his scientific studies. He investigated larval comb jellies, sea urchins, and sea butterflies before the ennui returned as the *Rattlesnake* sailed for New Guinea (May 1849 – January 1850). A visit to the Louisiade archipelago, off eastern New Guinea, provided the opportunity to sketch Papuans, although Stanley, his mind by then beginning to fail, never allowed the crew to step onto the New Guinea mainland itself. At Cape York a shipwrecked Scottish woman, who had lived with the Aborigines for five years, gave Huxley his first insights into tribal beliefs. Although no collector, Huxley was a brilliant anatomist. Studying the Coral Sea ascidians, he noted that the larval *Appendicularia* had tail muscles like a tadpole's (Imperial College, Huxley MS 34.168). He elucidated the life cycle of salps, which comprise a chained, sexually reproducing form and a solitary asexual form, and he considered the latter not individuals, but 'zoöids', budded reproductive organs.

Stanley had a seizure on the return voyage to Sydney, and on 13 March 1850 another fit left him dying in Huxley's arms. The final survey was cancelled and the *Rattlesnake* sailed for home on 2 May 1850. Huxley was still £100 in debt: Cooke's teaching had failed and George Huxley had lost his fortune in the crash of 1847, so Huxley and Nettie (who remained in Australia) resolved not to marry until he could pay his own way. The homeward journey took in the Bay of Islands (New Zealand), where Huxley trekked to the Waimate mission, while the seas approaching a bitter Cape Horn provided him with the phosphorescent *Pyrosoma* to complete his work on the ascidians. Sailing via the Falklands and Azores, the *Rattlesnake* reached England on 23 October 1850.

Establishing himself in London, 1850–1854 The returned Huxley was lionized for his researches and London's scientific élite, including Sir Charles Lyell, Sir Roderick Murchison, and Richard Owen, backed Huxley's claim for Treasury funding for a book on oceanic hydrozoa. With typical gall Huxley applied to the sea lords for a year's leave on half pay to write it up, which he obtained after Owen's intercession. He was posted to the commodore's ship *Fisguard* at Greenwich on paid leave. In London he joined others from the anatomy theatres and dissenting outskirts, including Edwin Lankester and George Busk, whose sharp-witted wife, Ellen, became Huxley's sounding board on free thought. In 1851 the Royal Society, looking increasingly to scientific commitment over social distinction, elected him a fellow for his *Rattlesnake* memoirs. He was the youngest of the candidates in that year, but even so was only just pipped for the royal medal, worth 50 guineas (he took it in 1852). Having debated the value of an unpractical science with his businessman brother George, Huxley saw the medal as a vindication, which was reinforced with his election to the Royal Society council in 1853. However, he could not obtain a chair, nor a Treasury grant, despite the support of George Airy, president of the British Association for the Advancement of Science, at Ipswich in 1851, where Huxley had gone to talk on the ascidian archetype (the subject of two papers in 1851). Three futile years (1851–4) spent job-hunting led to fits of despair and self-doubt, even as the struggle fostered Huxley's adversarial attitude and led him to sharpen his critique of the state for failing to support science or reward talent.

Huxley's bullishness made a protagonist of Owen. Huxley loathed Owen's hauteur and his 'divine archetype' at the service of cloth and gown. Their belligerence was symptomatic of the widening social divide in an industrializing culture. An older historiography marked Owen as the 'aggressor' (*Life and Letters*, 1.97–8), but the bitterness partly reflected Huxley's inability to get a job, and dislike of Owen's deference to the landed élite: indeed in a confrontation on 14 March 1852 Huxley accused Owen of being too 'conservative' in science (Huxley to H. Heathorn, 15 March 1852, Imperial College, Huxley MSS). At the Royal Institution on 30 April 1852, in his first public lecture (on animal individuality), Huxley introduced his ascidian and siphonophore zoöids and contradicted Owen's explanation of alternation of generations. Then, in 1853, Huxley insisted that the 'archetypal' mollusc was an abstraction with no real Platonic existence. He blended it with Macleay's circles, visualizing a central archetype from which all the mollusc types stood equidistantly. From this it followed that there was no progression from one type to another, which meshed with Lyell's non-progressionist palaeontology, so influential to Huxley. These were to be his pre-Darwinian themes. He proved as iconoclastic in his classification: he related worms, rotifers, and starfish in a new (and unsuccessful) group, the Annuloida.

During this period Herbert Spencer introduced Huxley to the freethinkers of the *Westminster Review* at John Chapman's soirées. Marian Evans (George Eliot) saw Huxley 'becoming celebrated in London', with a penchant for '*paradox* and *antagonism*' that seemed the price for his 'brilliant talents' (*George Eliot Letters*, 8.89–90). Chapman asked Huxley to review the *Narrative of the Voyage of H.M.S. Rattlesnake* by the ship's naturalist, John MacGillivray (Huxley, a gifted artist, had drawn the book's illustrations), then gave him his own scientific column (1854–7). To make money Huxley also translated part of Karl Ernst von Baer's monograph on foetal specialization, wrote reviews, including one of the new cell theory, and even tried reportage on Sultan Schamyl's resistance to the Cossacks in the Caucasus (Huxley made the ascetic Schamyl's hostility to Russian Orthodoxy a metaphor for his own scientific 'war' to purify theology). The *Westminster* column mingled rationalist sense with outright provocation: he denied

that fossil life showed an increasing specialization, and also denied a Christian biology that made man the end point—to Huxley mankind was an 'aberrant modification' (*Westminster Review*, 62, 1854, 247). But he none the less castigated positivism and the evolutionary *Vestiges of the Natural History of Creation* (1844) by Robert Chambers. He was learning to polish his prose, and anticipations of some later essays appeared here. The columns also reveal his influences: for instance, Robert Latham's racial geography, first reviewed in the *Westminster*, re-emerged in Huxley's 1890 paper on the origin of the Aryans west of the Urals.

Teaching and marriage, 1854–1860 Huxley was struck off the list of naval surgeons for refusing to join the training ship *Illustrious* at Portsmouth in 1854. He instead took over Edward Forbes's lectureships in natural history and palaeontology at the School of Mines in Jermyn Street in July 1854. He trained science teachers at the Department of Science and Art and, with courses at the London Institution and the post of naturalist to the Geological Survey (whose duties included a coast survey), he was banking on £700 per annum by late 1854. Although in a utilitarian institution turning out industrialists and teachers, he emphasized the moral benefits of science. In 'The educational value of the natural history sciences' (1854), delivered at St Martin's Hall, Huxley the scientific Calvinist saw zoology as pointing up the universality of pain in nature (and teaching humankind courage). After an eight-year engagement Nettie arrived in London in May 1855; she and Huxley were married at All Saints' Church, Finchley Road, on 21 July. Their Tenby honeymoon doubled as the coastal survey, with Huxley dredging or dissecting goose barnacles for ovaria (Charles Darwin had misidentified these in a work which Huxley had recently reviewed; Huxley now detected them in the organism's stalk). After their return to London the couple lived at 14 Waverley Place, St John's Wood, where Nettie became an unsung helpmate, translating German and drawing diagrams to accompany her husband's lectures. Huxley confirmed his meteoric rise by taking the Fullerian professorship of physiology at the Royal Institution (1855–8). In 1855 he also started his winter evening lectures to the working classes, and for two decades he was effectively to pull them behind his *arriviste* scientific professionals and divert them from the socialist track.

Darwin and Huxley diverged on key points: the romantic Huxley saw nature as a 'poem', not a Benthamite cost-benefit mechanism, and his anti-progressionism and archetypal geometry of nature worried Darwin. The latter, shortly to write the *Origin of Species*, quizzed Huxley at Downe on 26 April 1856. Darwin apparently did not tip his hand on natural selection, but nevertheless Huxley's attitude changed. His secular needs were well served by opposing supernaturalism and in class he questioned the evidence for creative acts 'independent of the whole vast chain of causes and events in the universe' ('Lectures', *Medical Times and Gazette*, 12, 1856, 482). Those who did not accept a naturalistic development he labelled 'creationists' and his caricature of the first elephants flashing together from atoms was incorporated by Darwin in the *Origin of Species*. Huxley's dissenting strategy against the church had been distilled into an evolution versus creation slogan. The professional, vying for educational and moral territory with the church, canvassed artisan support by portraying a low-caste dissenting image of science, where the book of nature was open to all rather than the prerogative of a priesthood. The demise of 'Parsondom', he said, would usher in a 'new Reformation' (Huxley to F. Dyster, 30 Jan 1859, Imperial College, Huxley MSS) as his marginal men of science assumed positions of cultural leadership.

In the summer of 1856 Huxley climbed in the Alps with John Tyndall: here faithless Victorians could worship nature's indomitable force, and Huxley would frequently revisit Switzerland. In the following year the wire squadron, then attempting to lay a transatlantic cable, dredged sea-bed mud containing shells of the planktonic foraminiferan *Globigerina*, which had Huxley speculating that these were the source of the world's chalk rocks (this was the gist of his lecture 'On a piece of chalk' in 1868—a talk that, like many of Huxley's best, was an odyssey into an exotic past).

By January 1859 Huxley was telling his workers that animals and humans '*must* have proceeded from one another in the way of progressive modification' ('Science and religion', *The Builder*, 15 Jan 1859, 35–6). Darwin would avoid human ancestry in the *Origin of Species*, but Huxley made it the ideological crux. Thus he challenged Owen's new subclass Archencephala for humankind (erected in 1857 and based on the cerebral hemispheres dividing into a unique third lobe, with a 'hippocampus minor' projecting into its lateral ventricle). In his 1858 Royal Institution course Huxley first made his claim 'that there is very little greater interval *as animals* between the *Gorilla* & the *Man* than exists between the *Gorilla* & the *Cynocephalus* [baboon]' (Imperial College, Huxley MS 36.97). Thus Huxley's and Owen's sciences became fundamentally antagonistic: Huxley's Croonian lecture to the Royal Society in 1858 demolished Owen's older romantic idea of the vertebral skull and ridiculed his Platonic idealism.

The links with the Darwins tightened: of the Huxleys' first four children—Noel (1856–1860), Jessie Oriana (1858–1926), Marian (1859–1887), and Leonard (1860–1933)—Jessie and Leonard *Huxley were the godchildren of Emma and Charles Darwin respectively. In turn Darwin needed the support of this charismatic professionalizer: Huxley was the teacher of the teachers, the examiner at the War Office and London University, with growing Whitehall contacts (in 1858 he was inspecting catches for the fisheries commission). He was also agitating (successfully) for a London University science faculty and the introduction of the BSc degree, and starting a column in the *Saturday Review*.

Meanwhile Huxley's fossil studies forced the redating of the 'Devonian' Elgin sandstones. The socketed teeth of the Elgin reptile *Stagonolepis*, supplied by the Revd George Gordon, were like those of Mesozoic crocodiles, and *Hyperodapedon gordoni* (as Huxley named it) was so similar to a Triassic rynchosaur that these deposits were accepted as Triassic, even by Lyell, who abandoned his non-progressionist views. However, Huxley, discussing 'persistent types' (unchanging fossil lineages) in 1859, only partly shifted to a progressionist palaeontology: he restricted all evolutionary development to pre-Silurian times and saw no new animal types evolve thereafter. As secretary at the Geological Society from 1858 he studied the fish *Pteraspis*, monographed the Devonian lobe-fin fishes—Crossopterygians he called them—and by 1865 had added eleven new genera of labyrinthodont amphibians to the three previously known. As the society's secretary he stood in to deliver the anniversary address in 1862, talking again on persistent types and delivering a critique of contemporary views on the contemporaneity of scattered geological deposits.

Publicizing evolution, 1859–1870 Huxley's *Rattlesnake* monograph, *Oceanic Hydrozoa*, was published by the Ray Society in late 1859, only to be eclipsed by Darwin's *Origin of Species*. Huxley wrote supportive reviews of the *Origin* in *The Times*, *Macmillan's Magazine*, and *Westminster Review* (he was now a shareholder in the Westminster Review Company) but downplayed Darwin's utilitarian natural selection and thought that the analogy with artificial selection would remain incomplete until Darwin's fancy runts and tumbler pigeons refused to breed, or produced sterile hybrids. Moreover, he explained the lack of transitional forms between the classes of animals by mooting an inherent power of variation which produced saltations (abrupt evolutionary changes). However, he shared Darwin's overwhelming faith in evolutionary naturalism and Huxley praised the *Origin*—that 'Whitworth gun in the armoury of liberalism' (*Collected Essays*, 2.23)—for extending 'the domination of Science'. In an age of patriotic volunteers (he was one himself), Huxley tied liberalism, industry, and Darwinism to national salvation. With his passion for Tennyson, he exhorted audiences to cherish this sort of science or 'see the glory of England vanishing like Arthur in the mist' (Imperial College, Huxley MS 41.56).

At the Oxford meeting of the British Association for the Advancement of Science in 1860 Owen's reassertion of humanity's unique hippocampus minor brought Huxley to his feet. So began a rancorous public dispute, ostensibly over an anatomical fact, but actually about the social and moral implications of evolution. It was at this meeting that Bishop Samuel Wilberforce turned to Huxley and apparently enquired jokingly whether the apes were on his grandfather's or grandmother's side (his exact words are unclear, but he might have been exploiting contemporary sensibilities about chaste maidens). To this purple-vested jest Huxley, a puritan who saw virtue as the true nobility, replied that he would 'rather have a miserable ape for a grandfather' than a man 'possessed of great means of influence & yet who employs … that influence for the mere purpose of introducing ridicule into a grave scientific discussion' (Huxley to Dyster, 9 Sept 1860, Imperial College, Huxley MSS). Huxley repeated his words to his liberal Anglican friend Frederick Dyster to correct press reports that had him saying 'I would rather be an ape than a bishop'. (At a personal level this clash did not prevent Huxley, as a vice-president of the Zoological Society, from collaborating with Bishop Wilberforce in 1861 behind the scenes at the society.)

There was a political dimension to this repartee: the vice-chancellor Francis Jeune's liberal clergy entertained Huxley to dinner on two nights of the meeting. They disliked Wilberforce's castigation of a new multi-authored book of biblical criticism, *Essays and Reviews*, and Jeune thought the bishop 'got no more than he deserved' (G. Rolleston to Huxley, n.d., Imperial College, Huxley MS 25.150). This fits with other evidence of Darwinian and liberal Anglican sympathies. Captain Stanley's brother, the Revd Arthur Stanley, alerted Huxley to his own anonymous defence of *Essays* and was in turn put up for the Royal Society's Philosophical Club. Bishop John William Colenso attended Huxley's lectures and was introduced by him at the Athenaeum. Huxley backed the Anglicans William Henry Flower and George Rolleston for chairs at the College of Surgeons and Oxford, and was supported in turn on ape anatomy and evolution. The alliance was mirrored inside the home, and not only by the Anglican Nettie: her reforming vicar, Llewelyn Davies, was at ease with evolution and comfortable in the Huxley house.

Indeed, it was the Christian socialist Charles Kingsley who reanimated Huxley after the death of his son Noel from scarlet fever in 1860. In May 1861 the Huxleys moved to a larger house in Abbey Place to break the morbid associations. A grieving Huxley finished his landmark 'On the zoological relations of man with the lower animals', which ran in the opening number of his new Darwinian house-organ, the *Natural History Review*, on 1 January 1861. The paper was a vote-catching masterpiece which insisted that a 'pithecoid pedigree' did not lower the 'princely dignity of perfect manhood, which is an order of nobility, not inherited, but to be won by each of us, so far as he consciously seeks good and avoids evil' (*Scientific Memoirs*, 2.472). None the less, as a human evolutionist, Huxley knew that his morality was always suspect and as late as 1886, in 'Science and morals', he had to rebut W. S. Lilly's charge that scepticism led to debauchery; even so Bishop A. C. Tait's wife was surprised to hear that he was a devoted husband. In 1861 Huxley lectured on human ancestry to London's workers, whose gutter presses had long advocated such notions, and in 1862 at the Edinburgh Philosophical Institution. Reports of his talks on the *Origin* in 1862 were published by Robert Hardwicke in weekly parts and bound as *On our Knowledge of the Causes of the Phenomena of Organic Nature*.

The continuing contretemps with Owen over ape brains in *The Athenaeum* in 1861–3 gave the Victorian crisis of faith its anatomical edge. Huxley developed new techniques for comparing skulls in his study of the recently unearthed Neanderthal man to show that its supposed ape-like features were superficial. His Royal Institution lecture 'On the fossil remains of man' in 1862 was considered shocking, as was his seminal *Evidence as to Man's Place in Nature* (1863): written to be accessible, this was ignored by the highbrows and abominated by the religious press, but acquired a cachet among the middle-class public no less than among *National Reformer* secularists and Russian and German socialists.

With the American Civil War raging Huxley's group took over the abolitionist Ethnological Society, where John Lubbock and Huxley, as the next two presidents, turned it against the ultra-racist Anthropological Society. To his plural livings Huxley added the Hunterian professorship at the Royal College of Surgeons (1862–9). Here he refuted the anthropologicals' linking of black anatomy with slavery and he supported the Union in the American Civil War, even though his brother-in-law John Scott was a Confederate army surgeon. His course was published as *Lectures on the Elements of Comparative Anatomy* (1864) and accompanied by an *Atlas of Comparative Osteology* (1864), illustrated by Benjamin Waterhouse Hawkins.

Co-opted onto the royal commission on fisheries in 1862, Huxley made continual trips to Scotland to examine catching methods. His was becoming a whistle-stop life: his diary shows that he travelled some 4000 miles by train in 1862. The family called him 'the lodger', so rarely was he at home. The debts, however, persisted, and when his brother George died of tuberculosis in 1863 Huxley had to sell his own royal medal to settle the estate. He took over as family banker: he financed his sister Ellen and acted *in loco parentis* to his broken-down brother James's children, Katie and Jim. Jim was put through the School of Mines, while Katie, like Ellen's daughter Alice, was sent at Huxley's expense to Nettie's old school in Germany. Huxley was crushed under an inverted financial pyramid. His own family had increased with the birth of Rachel (1862–1934), Nettie (1863–1940), Henry (1865–1946), and Ethel Gladys (1866–1941), making a total of seven surviving children.

In 1864 Huxley, with Spencer, Busk, Lubbock, Tyndall, Hooker, Thomas Archer Hirst, William Spottiswoode, and Edward Frankland, formed the informal X-club. All bar Lubbock had begun as establishment outsiders, and they were men of a mind on *Essays and Reviews*, who showed their appreciation of Darwin by helping him to gain the Royal Society's Copley medal. Huxley became a director of Thomas Hughes's revamped *Reader* in 1864, but his editorial on 31 December 1864 so damned Benjamin Disraeli's 'electioneering' buffoonery in posing the question at Oxford 'Is man an ape or an angel?', and so incensed his Anglican allies by predicting that science would achieve 'uncontrolled domination over the whole realm of the intellect' ('Science and "Church policy"', *The Reader*, 4, 1864, 821), that the ailing paper was sold in 1865. Nevertheless, *The Reader* provided a test run, and a similar team was responsible for founding *Nature* in 1869.

Huxley soon added a third gown by gaining (for the second time) the Fullerian chair at the Royal Institution

(1866–9), where he lectured on ethnology. With his authority undermined by the racists (who actually considered the races separate species), he moved to amalgamate the Ethnological and Anthropological societies. He compromised by treating the races as persistent modifications, and at the Ethnological he restricted women to special events, in line with the all-male Anthropological Society. Negotiations stalled when in 1866 he joined J. S. Mill's Jamaica committee to prosecute Governor Edward John Eyre for hanging an assembly member after the rebellion, but the merger into the Anthropological Institute succeeded in 1871 and the ultra-racists were purged. In 1870–71 Huxley carried out a photographic collation of the empire's far-flung peoples, using a network of colonial correspondents.

Defending a male meritocracy Huxley considered the learned societies forums for adepts, but he wanted daughters educated at school alongside sons to order to qualify them to join the men. Despite society's evangelical hardening against the aspirations of black people and of women, he defended the free operation of the 'laws of social gravitation', while proclaiming in 'Emancipation—black and white' (1865) that educated women and black people would still be held to their stations by a discriminatory biology. The 'dispassionate' professional was appealing to all sides as nature's power-broker. That the strategy was successful was shown by the women crowding to see him. His launch of the 'Sunday evenings for the people' lectures in 1866 resulted in 2000 being unable to get in to hear him declare blind faith 'the one unpardonable sin' (*Collected Essays*, 1.40). When the Royal Institution announced Huxley's talk on the fossil pedigree of the horse, Tyndall was 'torn to pieces by women in search of tickets' (J. Tyndall to Huxley, 6 April 1870, Imperial College, Huxley MSS).

The campaign to get science into schools expanded as Huxley joined the Harrow School master the Revd Frederick William Farrar in 1866 to modernize the classics-dominated public schools. The influx of teachers (particularly after the 1870 Education Act) required the writing of science textbooks, which Huxley himself began to fulfil with his *Lessons in Elementary Physiology* (1866). He developed a child's course based on a rounded 'earth knowledge', which he launched at the London Institution in 1869 and published as *Physiography* (1877). The number of students sitting the Department of Science and Art's countrywide classes increased fourfold in 1867–72, and the physical geography courses set by Huxley had the largest attendance. To Macmillan's ninepenny science primer series Huxley contributed the *Introductory Science Primer* (1880), which sold 19,000 copies within weeks.

Huxley's next evolutionary phase began in 1867. He had been classifying birds on the basis of their palate bones at the Zoological Society, but after studying Ernst Haeckel's morphological approach to constructing 'phylogenies' (Haeckel's neologism) Huxley began drawing 'trees' of living gallinaceous birds. His work also showed an increasing biogeographic awareness: it was Huxley at this time

who coined the term 'Wallace's line' to divide the Australian and Asian faunal zones. However, his most spectacular pedigree was a dinosaur ancestry for birds. Since 1864 he had been uniting the birds and reptiles in a new morphological province, the Sauropsida, and in Oxford University Museum on 24 October 1867 he noticed a dinosaur ilium that was avian-like. Reconstructing the British Museum's *Iguanodon* as a biped gave it 'a considerable touch of a bird about the pelvis & legs!' (Huxley to J. Phillips, 31 Dec 1867, Oxford University Museum, 29) and in 1868 Huxley talked at the Royal Institution on the ratites (ostrich group) as the descendants of *Compsognathus*-like dinosaurs.

In 1868, after examining some samples of deep-sea mud, Huxley believed he had discovered a protoplasmic 'jelly', which he named *Bathybius haeckelii*. However, he later had to recant his *Blunderibus*, as he called it in a letter to N. Lockyer dated 13 August 1875 (Imperial College, Huxley MSS), when HMS *Challenger*'s naturalists discovered that it was a precipitate in the preserving alcohol. Nevertheless, Huxley's popularization of protoplasm in 'On the physical basis of life' sent the *Fortnightly Review* into a record seven editions in 1869.

The agnostic In 'The physical basis' Huxley justified the materialist investigation of life, while insisting—as he had since at least 1857 (Imperial College, Huxley MS 38.53)—that materialism as a philosophy of ultimate existence was no more legitimate than spiritualism. On this basis he coined a new label for himself in 1869—'agnostic'. Agnosticism was founded on his 1840s sympathy with a dissenting secularist bulwark against Anglican privilege, bounded by his belief that morality rested in judging evidence, and was justified by Hamilton's logic. He shifted the emphasis from the grounds of existence to the ground rules, the study of nature's laws, effectively putting his professionals in the priest's seat. In the 1860s he had echoed Herbert Spencer's talk of the 'unknowable' beyond the senses, but soon ditched that as another fetish. He was considered a positivist by default, but he loathed their empty ritualism; and *The Spectator*'s calling him an atheist in 1866 showed that he needed a new badge to sanction his scientific method of 'consecrated doubt'. So, at the first meeting of the Metaphysical Society on 21 April 1869, denying the certain 'gnosis' that was claimed by Christians, he called himself an agnostic. It suggested a professional detachment and went with his claim to the Young Men's Christian Association that the sciences are 'neither Christian, nor Unchristian, but are Extra-christian'; they are 'unsectarian' (*Collected Essays*, 1.195). With his hatred of sectarianism, he was positioning his experts on neutral ground.

In 1868 F. D. Maurice's Christian socialists appointed Huxley principal of a new south London working men's college on the Blackfriars Road, a post he held until 1880. There he used his chess analogy for the world, calling the rules of the game the laws of nature. It was an analogy tailored to the local factory hands: a personification of Darwin's all-powerful natural selection which rewards or exterminates. To learn the 'rules' the workers had to attend science's altar. Not surprisingly, R. H. Hutton dubbed him Pope Huxley in 1870.

Huxley's professionals were by now pushing a causal, deterministic science onto the cultural agenda, and his first collection of essays, *Lay Sermons* (1870), capped the move. At the Metaphysical Society, Huxley used the philosopher David Hume's arguments against his rivals' faith in the miraculous. Furthermore, on 11 January 1876, he responded to the Roman Catholic theologian William George Ward's challenge to deal with a specific miracle by dissecting the testimony supporting Christ's alleged resurrection. It was the society's most notorious paper, and such a 'deadly routing of the most sacred article in theology' (J. Morley to Huxley, 9 Jan 1876, Imperial College, Huxley MSS) that even John Morley declined to publish it in the *Fortnightly*.

Huxley gained a reputation as Darwin's 'bulldog': when a Worthing solicitor, Anthony Rich, offered to leave Darwin his fortune, it was Huxley who vetted the man (and as a consequence was himself bequeathed Rich's house in 1891). Put up in opposition to Darwin for the Académie Française in 1877, Huxley stepped aside (he was never subsequently elected). In 1869 he countered Sir William Thomson's claim that an earth apparently only 100 million years old militated against Darwin's chancy natural selection having had time to operate.

For a decade Darwinism (a word coined by Huxley) covered all manner of beliefs in nature's development. As the word evolution took over in the 1870s and Huxley ostracized the providentialists, his label, agnosticism, would legitimate only a naturalistic evolution. One casualty was his own former pupil, the liberal Catholic St George Mivart. In 'Mr. Darwin's critics' (1871), Huxley bypassed the biological arguments in Mivart's *Genesis of Species* to show that scholastic theologians had never (despite Mivart's assertion) anticipated evolution. Huxley's words now carried added weight, by dint of his position in several of science's learned societies. He was president of the Geological (1869–71) and Ethnological (1868–71) societies, and biological secretary of the Royal Society (1872–81). In addition, despite the politicking—as the outgoing president, Sir Stafford Northcote, tried to engineer the succession of another grandee—Huxley was elected president of the British Association for the Advancement of Science at the Liverpool meeting in 1870.

Laboratory teaching at South Kensington, 1871–1878 The marriage of dissenting industry and Darwinian academia was consummated when the Huxleys began staying with the manufacturers Sir Joseph Whitworth and Sir William Armstrong. They echoed Huxley's call—repeated as he sat on the duke of Devonshire's royal commission on scientific instruction (1870–75)—for more science teachers to meet Germany's industrial threat. For Huxley 'truth' did not come from recycling Greek texts at Oxford or Cambridge; it had to be ascertained experimentally. The laboratory, he said in *Hume* (1878), was 'the fore-court of the temple of philosophy' (*Essays*, 6.61). But while 'research' was to be his professionals' path to power, his Jermyn Street school, ironically, lacked a biological laboratory.

The Devonshire commission recommended the amalgamation of the Jermyn Street Royal School of Mines and the Royal College of Chemistry, and their relocation to the new Science Schools building in South Kensington. Here Huxley's 60 foot laboratory would be a symbol of the industrial age, to contrast with Owen's Romanesque Natural History Museum over the road. In 1871 the Royal Engineers were still on site—the visible military underbelly of Henry Cole's Department of Science and Art—and their presence augmented the martial image of Huxley's science. So the General, as the students nicknamed Huxley, taught his 1871 summer course in South Kensington Museum. Huxley, having argued that daughters should be educated, took women schoolteachers as students at South Kensington; indeed, the solitary schoolmistress among thirty-eight men took that first term's prize, which helped to destroy Huxley's own image of a discriminatory biology holding women down. By 1874 a woman demonstrator had joined a brilliant team comprising Michael Foster, E. Ray Lankester, William Rutherford, and William Kitchen Parker.

This yearly summer course, transmitted via the teachers to the new schools, became the foundation of the modern discipline of biology. Huxley simplified conventional comparative anatomy by concentrating on a dozen 'types' of plants and animals, which were studied in a 'philosophical' way, from simple to complex. Later he cut the number of types and reversed the order, publishing the result in his and Henry Newell Martin's *A Course of Practical Instruction in Elementary Biology* (1875).

Although the training was regimented, Huxley's mellifluous voice augmented a beguiling style as he hung his arm over a gorilla's skeleton as he talked. (He was the pupils' favourite countrywide, and was elected by the students at Aberdeen University as lord rector in 1872, in which post, held for two years, he attempted to obtain bursaries for Scottish dissenters and to introduce modern languages.) His descriptive morphology kept him firmly in the nineteenth-century mainstream and, despite his popular talks on evolution, he kept his 'types' discrete for the masters, believing that introducing evolution into class would 'throw Biology into confusion' (*Manual of the Anatomy of Invertebrated Animals*, 1877, 4). Religious controversy too was kept out of class, which explains why the Catholic Mivart and Methodist literalist Parker could put their sons under him (in 1874 the nineteen-year-old Jeffrey Parker was already marking papers for Huxley).

Huxley defended responsible laboratory vivisection (under anaesthetic) as a member of the royal commission on vivisection (1875–6), against Francis Power Cobbe's alliance, which questioned the new researchers' accountability. Another issue of great interest during the 1870s was the origin of the vertebrates. Huxley supported and reinforced a relationship between the primitive lancelet *Amphioxus*, a fish-like sand burrower without heart, eyes, brain, or distinct head, and the agnathans (jawless fishes). And, given his observations aboard HMS *Rattlesnake* on the tadpole-like tail musculature of the larval ascidian *Appendicularia*, he now readily accepted Alexander

Kovalevskii's proposed larval ascidian ancestry for vertebrates. Huxley thus endorsed a route for vertebrate origins, via ascidians and *Amphioxus*, that quickly took its place in the textbooks. Ernst Haeckel and E. Ray Lankester also revived Huxley's suggestion (made in his *Rattlesnake* paper on the jellyfish or Medusae in 1849) that the coelenterate's ectoderm and endoderm layers were homologous to the germinal layers of the vertebrate embryo—which itself showed how simple invertebrates could be related structurally to vertebrates. By 1875 Huxley, relaxing his emphasis on persistent types, showed that Mesozoic crocodiles had evolved by developing a secondary palate. He connected his Crossopterygian fish with labyrinthodont amphibians, and in 1876 studied the newly discovered Queensland lungfish *Ceratodus*, noting its amphibian-like skull bones and 'autostylic' jaw suspension.

Scientific naturalism was founded on the uniformity of nature, and Huxley broached another axiom with his lectures on mind as an epiphenomenon (1871–4). He was never an extreme determinist, but by 1874 he was hardening as he discussed reflex arcs (familiar since his Sydenham College days) and Descartes's brutes as self-adjusting machines, while his British Association for the Advancement of Science talk at the Belfast meeting, 'On the hypothesis that animals are automata' (1874), was the closest he would come to rejecting 'free will'.

In 1874 Sophia Jex-Blake appealed to him when Edinburgh University withdrew the women students' teacher. While Huxley supported the professorate (he was to join them, standing in for Wyville Thomson as Edinburgh's professor of natural history in summer 1875 and 1876), he sat on a co-ordinating committee to establish Jex-Blake's own London School of Medicine for Women in 1874.

Even as Huxley's reputation grew, his financial position remained precarious—a situation which contributed to his taking on more and more. Despite his prodigious capacity for work, he had badly overloaded himself by 1871. In that year he had travelled to Manchester as a governor (1870–75) of Owens College, and to Birmingham, where he had given his Chamberlainite 'Duties of the state' address as president of the Birmingham and Midland Institute (it attacked Spencer's anti-state-interventionism and was subsequently published as 'Administrative nihilism'). He also presided over two societies, delivered seven courses, sat on the Devonshire commission and the royal commission on contagious diseases (1870–71), and was acting as governor of the International School (from 1865), president of his working men's college, and chairman of the Metaphysical Society (1871–2). The final straw was his election to the London school board (1870–72); his education committee published its blueprint for London's schooling in 1871.

Huxley broke down in December 1871 and was ordered to go away by his doctors, Andrew Clark and Bence Jones. Since he was studying the moth *Ephestia* which infested the naval stores at Gibraltar, he took a cruise (January–April 1872) via Gibraltar and Tangier to Egypt. In Cairo he painted mosques, investigated the Mokattam hills, and was escorted round the pyramids and museum by Sir William Gregory; he then sailed up the Nile to Aswan in a *dahabieh* with Frederick Ouvry. He returned little better.

In 1871–2 the architect James Knowles oversaw the conversion of a cottage at 4 Marlborough Place, St John's Wood, into a substantial house for the Huxleys but the £4000 costs kept them in debt and Nettie could rarely afford to accompany Huxley to British Association meetings. The worry increased in 1873 when a neighbour sued him over a well which allegedly made the neighbour's basement damp. Huxley won but was unable to extract costs. He tried to recoup by writing on Charles Wyville Thomson's voyage aboard HMS *Challenger* and issuing a new set of essays, *Critiques and Addresses* (1873), but his depression shook Fanny Hooker, Emma Darwin, and Mary Lyell (the women were the family's traditional philanthropists); they prevailed on the X-clubbers and their industrial allies to collect £2100 in April 1873 to send Huxley on holiday to the Auvergne, where he recovered his health.

Senior statesman of science, 1876–1885 Huxley, at the forefront of the transatlantic science movement, was on the committee of E. L. Youmans's International Science Series (to which he contributed *The Crayfish* in 1880), but only an unexpected £1000 bequest from the Quaker manufacturer Thomas Thomasson in March 1876 enabled the Huxleys to visit America (July–September 1876). At Yale, Othniel C. Marsh showed Huxley his Cretaceous bird *Hesperornis* and fossil horses from Nebraska. (The ascent of horses from Eocene ancestors finally forced Huxley to accept a Tertiary time-scale for human evolution.) He visited Alexander Agassiz at Harvard, stayed with John Fiske, and attended the American Association for the Advancement of Science meeting at Buffalo. The couple spent four days with Huxley's sister Eliza in Nashville, where he delivered a 'Sermon in Stone' (on evolution) at the Masonic Hall. He inaugurated a guest lecture series at Johns Hopkins University, then visited Washington, DC, Philadelphia, and the Centennial Exposition before finishing in New York with three days of lectures at Chickering Hall. These talks extolled Huxley's dinosaur ancestry of birds, and proclaimed Marsh's horses the 'demonstrative evidence of evolution', although the headlines of 'Huxley Eikonoklastes' were for his parody of Milton's days of creation. The lectures appeared as *American Addresses* in 1877. Huxley was first called a 'scientist' during this trip, although it was never a word he used.

Huxley's achievements were recognized in honorary doctorates from Edinburgh (1866), Dublin (1878), and Cambridge (1879), and the Swedish order of the North Star (1873). He accepted a seat on the royal commission to inquire into the universities of Scotland (1876–8), where he fought for the admission of women, and the presidency of the Quekett Microscopical Club (1878–9), but it was joining the Eton College governing board (1879–88) (a Royal Society representative was required under the Public Schools Act to help modernize the school) that established his respectability. Even more did the Huxleys now fear a scandal breaking around his sister Ellen, who was drinking heavily and running up debts using his name.

Huxley's Whitehall influence paid off with his appointment as inspector of fisheries (1881–5) at £700 per annum. Although he discovered the fungal cause of the contemporary salmon disease, his time was taken up by disputatious fisherfolk. Simultaneously he sat on the royal commission on the Medical Acts (1881–2) to systematize Britain's licensing bodies. Bureaucracy interfered with research, and Huxley's eclecticism did not help (he veered into Greek studies in 1879 to discover why Aristotle saw only three chambers in the human heart): as a result his 1877 monograph on the cephalopod *Spirula* remained unfinished. However, his *Manual of the Anatomy of Invertebrated Animals* finally appeared in 1877, twenty years after it was commissioned, as did *Physiography*, which—by starting with local parish terrain and familiar causes and moving outwards to the universe and big results—established the pattern for post-Darwinian geography.

Huxley was now calling for vocational training in 'technical education' (1877) and advised the City livery companies on their plan for a central institution for technical education—the City and Guilds Institute, opened in 1884. He wanted not an apprentice-shop but a red-brick teaching institution under professional control. Stressing the moral discipline to be gained from pure science—to make it rival the classics—he was partly responsible for the theoretical bent of technical education. He was made a freeman of the City of London in 1883, and in 1887 supported a City, rather than South Kensington, site for an imperial institute to celebrate the jubilee, industry, and empire.

From the later 1870s Huxley accompanied his notes with tentative evolutionary trees. In 1879 he depicted two vertebrate trunks, one (the Monocondylia) passing from the amphibians via reptiles to birds (his Sauropsida), while the Dicondylia connected the amphibians via some unknown group to the mammals. He lumped Owen's fossil mammal-like reptiles with the Sauropsida, and only in 1882 did he begin to query this, as Edward Drinker Cope postulated a pelycosaur ancestry for mammals (Imperial College, Huxley MS 2.75, fol. 10). These trees were private heuristic devices, rarely surfacing in his finished monographs. In his 1878 Davis lectures at the Zoological Society he used gill development to classify the crayfishes and to construct a logical tree of the extant forms. *The Crayfish* (1880) portrayed crayfish evolution from a diffusionist, geographical perspective, in line with his 'physiographic' approach. With evolution becoming more acceptable, Huxley justified the principle of teaching it in schools in his introduction to the English translation of Haeckel's *Freedom in Science and Teaching* (1878). Huxley's 'Coming of age of the *Origin of Species*' (1880) itself suggested Darwinian maturity. It celebrated with a propagandist revision of history, which repositioned the catastrophist extremists at centre stage in 1859 to highlight the *Origin*'s coup, and in so doing encouraged the trend to deprecate the 'pre-Darwinians'. At the same time he made science's 'retrospective prophecies' appear magical, as he equated the palaeontologist, able to predict the existence of five-toed Eocene horses before a fossil had been found, with the Babylonian Zadig of Voltaire's legend.

In 1878 Huxley's daughter Jessie married the architect Fred Waller; Marian married the artist John Collier in 1879, and Rachel the civil engineer Alfred Eckersley in 1884. The Huxleys' regular Sunday 'tall teas' saw the gathering of the liberal intelligentsia, including Spencer, Tyndall, Matthew Arnold, Leslie Stephen, Henry James, and Benjamin Jowett (who would steer Huxley's son Leonard to Balliol College, Oxford). Robert Browning and the artist Briton Riviere were Nettie's favourites (the Huxleys put all of their daughters through the Slade School of Fine Art at University College). Huxley held his own in a world of humanities. Indeed, in his address 'Science and culture', given at the opening of Josiah Mason's science college in Birmingham in 1880 (reprinted in *Science and Culture*, 1881), he made the point that the study of modern literature, combined with a knowledge of science (and its anti-authoritarian spirit), was a better tool than classical literature to evaluate life—a point increasingly debated by Matthew Arnold. The politics of professionalization and classical reaction of 'young Oxford' only widened the cultural split, which was equally evident inside Huxley's house as Leonard married Arnold's niece Julia in 1885 and became a classics master at Charterhouse.

Nevertheless, Huxley had growing influence at both Oxford and Cambridge. He examined candidates for science fellowships (advising the Revd George Bradley at Oxford and designing practical exams for Trinity College, Cambridge). On Bradley's departure for Westminster Abbey, Huxley was offered the mastership of University College, Oxford, in 1881, and it was Huxley's intimacy with Bradley and Farrer that clinched the X-club's effort to have the agnostic Darwin interred in the abbey in 1882. Again he was offered the Linacre chair of anatomy after Rolleston died in 1881, but that year Huxley's Science Schools was renamed the Normal School of Science (Huxley's idea, after the French *École normale*) and he was appointed professor of biology and dean of the school. Alexander Agassiz at Harvard cavalierly offered 'say $10,000 a year for the benefit of your presence' (A. Agassiz to Huxley, 8 Nov 1882, Imperial College, Huxley MSS), guessing that Huxley would refuse.

Huxley the agnostic had made his evolutionary world-view seem non-partisan. His patriotism was being noted: his briefing of the Eton volunteer corps on Nile geology in 1883 followed General Garnet Wolseley's victory over the Egyptian nationalists. His acceptance of family values showed when he refused to press for George Eliot's burial in Westminster Abbey in 1880 because of her cohabitation with G. H. Lewes. He was tying agnosticism to middle-class mores, which made it acceptable to the establishment. How much so became apparent in 1883, on Chief Justice J. D. Coleridge's ruling in the trial of G. W. Foote for his blasphemous cartoons in *The Freethinker*. Coleridge ruled that Christianity was no longer the law of the land, and that it was the manner rather than substance which constituted a blasphemous libel. Huxley's reverent tone was acceptable, while a coarse working-class atheism was outlawed.

Huxley became president of the Royal Society (1883–5), where he unsuccessfully attempted to abolish the society's fees to help the poorer fellows. He recommended Flower as director of the Natural History Museum on Owen's retirement and, being in charge of the Darwin Fund, arranged for Joseph Edgar Boehm's statue of Darwin to be manoeuvred into the museum too. Huxley contributed a chapter to R. S. Owen's *The Life of Richard Owen* (1894), but forty years had done nothing to increase his estimate of Owen's idealistic science.

Huxley became a senator at London University (1883–95), and in 1892–5 was active in the Association for Promoting a Teaching University in London. He was president of the Marine Biological Association (1884–90)—where he supported Lankester's effort to build a marine station at Plymouth—and sat on the royal commission on trawl, net, and beam trawl fishing (1884)—his tenth and final commission.

Work was Huxley's escape during the years 1882–7, a period of personal tragedy. His highly strung daughter Marian, an acclaimed artist, had been his gifted heir (her painting *The Sins of the Father* was hung at the Royal Academy) but she collapsed in 1882. Marian's husband, John Collier, was himself painting his famous portrait of Huxley in 1883, and when in 1884 Marian's hysteria worsened, it triggered Huxley's own breakdown. He spent from October 1884 to the following April travelling through Italy. Coca extract eased him through his last South Kensington lectures in spring and summer 1885, which is when, as an adoring student, H. G. Wells first encountered him.

Theological and political controversy in retirement, 1885–1895
As he turned sixty Huxley voluntarily retired from the presidency of the Royal Society, preferring, as he put it, to 'step down from the chair [rather] than dribble out of it' (*Life and Letters*, 2.106). He also retired from the inspectorship of fisheries and the Normal School (he remained honorary dean). Oxford conferred on him an honorary doctorate of civil laws, while Gladstone awarded a £1200 per annum pension for the man who had made science education central to an imperial nation. (The incoming tory government added a £300 civil-list pension.)

Gladstone promptly sparked a controversy by claiming in a review that the Genesis days of the creation accorded with modern palaeontology—to which Huxley responded that the Jurassic *Archaeopteryx* (fowl) appeared after the 'creeping' things. Not only were the professionals loath to let a statesman speak for science, but Huxley abhorred Gladstone's home rule policy and was encouraged by Tyndall to expose him for political reasons. Huxley refused to vote Liberal in the 1886 election for the first time and thereafter supported Chamberlain's Liberal Unionists.

In 'The evolution of theology' (1886) Huxley applied the higher criticism to the books of Judges and Samuel to elucidate the emergence of a single God, Jehovah, from earlier polytheistic ancestor-worshipping beliefs. He extended the naturalistic critique in an unfinished book,

'The natural history of Christianity', to show how theology had appropriated society's ethical code. His essays were polished and pointed: 'On the reception of the *Origin of Species*' in Francis Darwin's *Life and Letters of Charles Darwin* (1887) began the mythologizing of the 1860 encounter with Wilberforce, while three in the *Nineteenth Century* dissected the older vision of the duke of Argyll (George Douglas Campbell) of natural law as a divine edict.

Huxley extended the Darwinian–dissenting competitive ethos into the social-industrial realm in his campaigns for technical education by depicting foreign competition as industrial warfare, with starvation the price of defeat. But while his 'Progress of science, 1837–1887' in the jubilee volume, *The Reign of Queen Victoria* (1887), offered technological salvation, the poor had begun to look to direct action. On 'black Monday', 8 February 1886, the mob rampaging through the West End evidently overran Huxley's bus, and it was about this time that his opposition to the socialist revival stiffened.

Beatrice Webb thought that the 'old lion' was himself showing a 'strain of madness' (*Diary*, 202–3) as he worried about Marian, who died in Paris on 20 November 1887, from pneumonia, on her way to Jean-Martin Charcot's hospital. Huxley buried his grief in work. In an apocalyptic early draft of 'The struggle for existence in human society' he indicted an amoral nature driven by 'battle murder & sudden death' (Imperial College, Huxley MS 42.61). He saw Malthusian over-population force a ceaseless struggle which undercut all co-operative panaceas. Where once Huxley had anthropomorphized natural selection as a 'calm angel', in an 'Apologetic irenicon' (*Fortnightly Review*, 52, 1892, 569), he now swore to the 'primacy of Satan in this world'. Politics and personal tragedy had fully Darwinianized him. Humanity was 'doomed forever to be at war' (Imperial College, Huxley MS 42.67). In part this war was an industrial one, and for that reason he supported Manchester's efforts to raise rates to provide money for scientific and technological retraining.

Huxley's warning of failure in the industrial struggle, mated to Lankester's emphasis on degeneration, was to be recast by H. G. Wells in *The Time Machine* (1895). But Huxley's cynicism caused scathing reviews, none more enduring than Peter Kropotkin's rebuttal 'Mutual aid among animals' (1890) in the *Nineteenth Century*.

As Huxley's views were changing, so was his domestic life. The last children were leaving—in 1889 he took Ethel to Norway to marry John Collier, Marian's widower (it remained illegal in England as Chamberlain failed to carry a deceased wife's sister bill), and Nettie married the mining engineer Harold Roller in 1889. Harry, before settling into medical practice, was taken by his father to Madeira in 1890, forty-four years after the *Rattlesnake* surgeon's last visit. Prone to heart trouble and pleurisy, Huxley escaped London's smog by moving to Eastbourne in 1890, where Fred Waller designed a house, Hodeslea (the archaic form of Huxley's name). Since a Swiss trip in 1886 alpine gentians had been Huxley's interest and at Hodeslea the garden was his passion.

Huxley's exegesis of agnosticism in three articles (1889–

90) was less a discussion of his naturalism than an undermining of the miraculous props of a rival Anglican authority. He made a test case of the Gadarene swine, which spawned more controversy with Gladstone in 1890–91. He published prolifically on theology and politics, with seven articles in the *Nineteenth Century* alone in 1890. Nettie begged him to give up controversy, but in 1891 he turned the biblical plagiarism of Babylonian flood stories into more ideological weapons. He characterized Christ as an orthodox Jewish teacher and thus another 'infidel' in post-Pauline Christian eyes (as Huxley was accused of being by Henry Wace). The puritan was as happy running his pike through Canon Henry Liddon for his attack on the progressive *Lux mundi*, with its allegorical explanation of biblical miracles, as he was demolishing *Lux mundi* itself (Imperial College, Huxley MS 46.125). He republished these polemics in *Essays upon some Controverted Questions* (1892), adding a prologue which continued to replace Christianity's 'Supernature' with the new 'scientific Naturalism'.

Days after the publication of *Controverted Questions* Lord Salisbury's government offered Huxley a privy councillorship. (The office of crown adviser was, Donnelly assured Salisbury, one that Huxley could accept, despite his hatred of honours.) It was awarded by the queen on 25 August 1892. The anomaly of tory dissolution honours going to Huxley is explained by the increasingly anti-socialist function of his science, not that his belittling of Gladstone went unheeded by Conservatives pledged to the union. He received the Royal Society's Copley medal in 1888 and Darwin medal in 1894, and the Linnean medal of the Linnean Society in 1890.

Huxley, with his state-spending solutions to education and science, clashed with Spencer the *laissez-faire* extremist in *The Times* (1889–90), leaving the old friends estranged. He then turned on Henry George's socialist belief in human equality: the first article in the *Nineteenth Century* Knowles titled 'On the natural inequality of men' (1890) to influence working-class readers. Huxley himself planned to republish the pieces in a book, 'Letters to working men', which never appeared but showed his intent on using a Malthusian biology to police the crowds. The term 'social Darwinism' would be deployed shortly after 1890, and Huxley's stress on over-population, struggle, and inequality served to emphasize its anti-socialist roots.

It was the mix of rival deliverance and 'socialist' regimentation that Huxley disliked about the Salvation Army. Asked by a philanthropist to vet the scheme proposed in William Booth's *In Darkest England and the Way Out*, Huxley penned a series of letters to *The Times* on this standing army's threat, and republished them as a shilling pamphlet, *Social Diseases and Worse Remedies* (1891).

The more family tragedy and socialist equality forced Huxley to emphasize nature's struggle, the more he had to detach human ethics. The young romantic had given nature a moral spine; now the sexagenarian drove a wedge between Darwin's 'war' as the natural state and the civilized curbing of these 'anti-social' instincts. Deafness had stopped his public speaking after Marian's death, but

he broke his silence with the Romanes lecture (the second in the series) 'Evolution and ethics' at Oxford in 1893. He staked his liberal ethics midway between the Spencerian and socialist extremes—insisting on Darwinism in nature, but disdaining a *laissez-faire* foundation for a naturalistic ethics. Social progress entailed selecting, not the 'fittest', but 'ethically the best' (*Collected Essays*, 9.81–3). Huxley left a conundrum for the twentieth century: care and altruism had evolved as part of nature, yet they were antagonistic to Darwinism.

A heroic mythology shrouded Huxley himself at the end of his life. He made a guest appearance at the British Association for the Advancement of Science at Oxford in 1894, where, after Lord Salisbury's address, waves of applause saw him to his feet to bear the standard one last time. His preface on evolution to mark the twenty-fifth anniversary of *Nature* was covertly aimed at Salisbury for his Oxford caveats about natural selection. Huxley was rebutting Salisbury's nephew Arthur Balfour's *Foundations of Belief* (1895)—with its attempt to discredit 'naturalism'—when his final illness struck. To the end agnosticism was the old puritan's shield in a hostile world. Influenza in early March 1895 led to bronchitis. Severely weakened, he suffered a heart attack, and died on the afternoon of 29 June 1895 at his home in Eastbourne. He was buried on 4 July, by his own wish alongside his son Noel in St Marylebone cemetery, East Finchley.

Changing historiographical interpretations Huxley published over 400 essays, papers, letters, reviews, and books. Many of his papers on invertebrate anatomy and vertebrate palaeontology were amassed by Foster and Lankester into five volumes as *The Scientific Memoirs of Thomas Henry Huxley* (1898–1903) and Huxley had himself republished his best articles in nine volumes of *Collected Essays* (1893–4)—a tenth was in preparation but never appeared. For the fast wit, famous irony, suave hectoring, and commonsense cleverness in these essays, Huxley was declared 'perhaps the greatest virtuoso of plain English who has ever lived' (Fawcett, 208). With their reinterpretation of duty, belief, and morality in a secularizing, industrializing culture, they provide a partisan insight into the Victorian move to a naturalistic world-view.

Huxley's historiographic fortunes in the twentieth century fall into roughly three phases. The first was set by Leonard Huxley's hagiographic *Life and Letters of Thomas Henry Huxley* (1900). By judiciously extracting letters, Leonard Huxley highlighted Huxley's fast and often funny vernacular, but the *Life* started the trend for interpreting Huxley's 'struggle' against benighted aggressors and religious obscurantism. Biographers saw their duty in backing biologists in their continuing debate with creationists and deploying Huxley as a rationalist hero. Nevertheless, Cyril Bibby's informed *T. H. Huxley: Scientist, Humanist and Educator* (1959) considerably widened Huxley studies, and this phase ended when historians of science became professionalized in the 1960s. The church-turned-Darwin historian James R. Moore, working in an anti-Vietnam War climate, 'demilitarized' Huxley historiography in his *Post-Darwinian Controversies* (1979). At the same time Frank

Turner (in papers subsequently collected in *Contesting Cultural Authority*, 1993) began to reassess the 'war' with theology as a professional territorial dispute, while James G. Paradis in *T. H. Huxley: Man's Place in Nature* (1978) relocated the scientist into the literary culture of his day. The third phase began in the 1980s with the contextualizing of science history. Social historians now seek to assess the dissenting and industrializing forces which sustained Huxley and conditioned his naturalistic thought, and to understand the way his resulting agnostic ideology functioned to help his marginal professionals—the 'scientists'—usurp Anglican prestige.   ADRIAN DESMOND

Sources ICL, Huxley MSS · A. Desmond, *Huxley*, 2 vols. (1994–7) · *The T. H. Huxley family correspondence*, ed. A. Darwin and A. Desmond, 4 vols. [forthcoming] · L. Huxley, *Life and letters of Thomas Henry Huxley*, 2 vols. (1900) · C. Bibby, *T. H. Huxley: scientist, humanist and educator* (1959) · J. G. Paradis, *T. H. Huxley: man's place in nature* (1978) · M. Di Gregorio, *T. H. Huxley's place in natural science* (1984) · T. H. Huxley, *Collected essays*, 9 vols. (1893–4) · *The scientific memoirs of Thomas Henry Huxley*, ed. M. Foster and E. R. Lankester, 5 vols. (1898–1903) · A. Desmond, *Archetypes and ancestors: palaeontology in Victorian London, 1850–1875* (1982) · A. Barr, ed., *Thomas Henry Huxley's place in science and letters: centenary essays* (1997) · J. V. Jensen, *Thomas Henry Huxley: communicating for science* (1991) · *T. H. Huxley's Diary of the voyage of H. M. S. Rattlesnake*, ed. J. Huxley (1935) · D. A. Roos, 'Neglected bibliographical aspects of the works of Thomas Henry Huxley', *Journal of the Society of the Bibliography of Natural History*, 8 (1976–8), 401–20 · M. S. Helfand, 'T. H. Huxley's *Evolution and ethics*', *Victorian Studies*, 20 (1976–7), 159–77 · J. G. Paradis and G. C. Williams, eds., *Evolution and ethics* (1989) · W. P. Randel, 'Huxley in America', *Proceedings of the American Philosophical Society*, 114 (1970), 73–99 · M. Bartholomew, 'Huxley's defence of Darwin', *Annals of Science*, 32 (1975), 525–35 · J. R. Moore, *The post-Darwinian controversies* (1979) · F. M. Turner, 'The Victorian conflict between science and religion: a professional dimension', *Isis*, 69 (1978), 356–76 · S. Gilley and A. Loades, 'Thomas Henry Huxley: the war between science and religion', *Journal of Religion*, 61 (1981), 285–308 · E. Richards, 'Huxley and woman's place in science', *History, humanity and evolution*, ed. J. R. Moore (1989), 253–84 · S. Forgan and G. Gooday, 'Constructing South Kensington: the buildings and politics of T. H. Huxley's working environments', *British Journal for the History of Science*, 29 (1996), 435–68 · R. Barton, 'Evolution: the Whitworth gun in Huxley's war for the liberation of science from theology', *The wider domain of evolutionary thought*, ed. D. Oldroyd and I. Langham (1983), 261–86 · P. White, *Thomas Huxley: making the 'man of science'* (2003) · 'Professor Huxley's homes', *ILN* (6 July 1895) · R. M. MacLeod, *Public science and public policy in Victorian England* (1996) · B. Lightman, *The origins of agnosticism: Victorian unbelief and the limits of knowledge* (1987) · D. W. Dockrill, 'T. H. Huxley and the meaning of "agnosticism"', *Theology*, 74 (1971), 461–77 · D. R. Stoddart, '"That Victorian science": Huxley's *Physiography* and its impact on geography', *Transactions of the Institute of British Geographers*, 66 (1975), 17–40 · J. R. Moore, 'Deconstructing Darwinism', *Journal of the History of Biology*, 24 (1991), 353–408 · M. Collie, *Huxley at work: with the scientific correspondence of T. H. Huxley and the Rev. Dr George Gordon of Birnie, near Elgin* (1991) · R. Barton, 'Scientific opposition to technical education', *Scientific and technical education in early industrial Britain*, ed. M. D. Stephens and G. W. Roderick (1981), 13–27 · St G. Mivart, 'Some reminiscences of Thomas Henry Huxley', *Nineteenth Century*, 42 (1897), 985–98 · *The correspondence of Charles Darwin*, ed. F. Burkhardt and S. Smith, 1–10 (1985–97) · *The George Eliot letters*, ed. G. S. Haight, 9 vols. (1954–78) · *The diary of Beatrice Webb*, ed. N. MacKenzie and J. MacKenzie, 4 vols. (1982–5), vol. 1 · J. W. Fawcett, 'Thomas Henry Huxley', *Unity*, 95 (1925), 207–10 · *BMJ* (6 July 1895), 30–32 · *The Times* (5 July 1895) · S. L. Lyons, *Thomas Henry Huxley: the evolution of a scientist* (1999)

Archives Hunt. L., letters · ICL, corresp., diaries, notebooks, and papers · NHM, manuscripts, sketches of flowers, insects, and birds · NL Wales, lecture notes · U. Oxf., department of zoology, lecture notes · Wellcome L., lecture notes | American Philosophical Society, Philadelphia, letters to Sir Henry Cole · American Philosophical Society, Philadelphia, letters to Sir Charles Lyell · BGS, letters to Trenham Reeks · BL, corresp. with Macmillans, Add. MS 55210 · Co-operative Union, Holyoake House, Manchester, letters to George Holyoake · CUL, corresp. with Charles Darwin; corresp. with Sir George Stokes · Elgin Museum, letters to George Gordon · ICL, letters to Lord Playfair · LUL, corresp. with Herbert Spencer · NHM, corresp. and papers relating to Huxley Memorial Committee · NHM, letters to Andrew Murray [copies] · RCP Lond., letters to Sir Michael Foster · Royal Institution of Great Britain, London, letters to Sir John Tyndall · U. Edin. L., letters to Sir Archibald Geikie · University of Exeter Library, letters to Sir Norman Lockyer · Wellcome L., letters to J. T. Knowles

Likenesses Walker & Cockerell, photogravure, 1857 (after Maull & Polyblank), NPG · plaster busts, 1866? (after J. Forsyth), U. Cam., department of zoology · T. B. Wirgman, pencil drawing, 1882, NPG · J. Collier, oils, 1883, NPG [*see illus.*] · J. Collier, oils, 1891; on loan to RS · R. Lehmann, drawing, 1892, BM · Ape [C. Pellegrini], caricature chromolithograph, NPG; repro. in *VF* (28 Jan 1871) · A. Bassano, cabinet photograph, NPG · J. Collier, oils, 1883, other versions, ICL, RCS Eng. · M. Collier, pencil drawings, NPG · W. & D. Downey, woodburytype, NPG; repro. in W. Downey and D. Downey, *The cabinet portrait gallery*, 1 (1890) · E. Edwards, photograph, NPG; repro. in L. Reeve, ed., *Portraits of men of eminence*, 1 (1863) · Elliott & Fry, cabinet photograph, NPG · E. O. Ford, plaster bust, NPG · A. Legros, oils, V&A · Lock & Whitfield, woodburytype, NPG; repro. in T. Cooper, *Men of mark: a gallery of contemporary portraits* (1880) · Walker & Boutall, photogravure (after daguerreotype, 1846), NPG · cartes-de-visite, NPG · chalk drawing, U. Cam., department of earth sciences · medallion on frieze, School of Science and Art, Strand

Wealth at death £9290 10s. 9d.: probate, 27 July 1895, *CGPLA Eng. & Wales*

Huxtable, Anthony (1808–1883), agriculturist and Church of England clergyman, was born on 30 November 1808 in Williton, Somerset, the eldest of the three sons of Anthony Huxtable, a Bristol surgeon. He was educated at Trinity College, Cambridge, where he obtained his BA in 1833. He was ordained deacon in 1833 and after being made priest in 1834 became vicar of Sutton Waldron, north-east Dorset, a small parish and one of the most backward agriculturally in that county. He was an energetic builder and engineer, and made use of innovative designs and newly available materials, such as indiarubber. He demolished the existing Saxon church and erected St Bartholomew's (1847), which was noted for the interior decorations by Owen Jones. A tractarian, whose work for the Society for the Propagation of the Gospel attracted national attention, he became archdeacon of Dorset in 1862 but resigned, through ill health, nine months later.

Aided by the wealth of his first wife, Maria Langstone (d. 1874), whom he married in 1840, and by the patronage of the first Viscount Portman, a prominent member of the Royal Agricultural Society, Huxtable rented two farms in the parish to pursue experimental scientific farming with the object of relieving the misery of farmer and labourer alike in the face of the impending repeal of the corn laws. In 1845 he published in volume six of the *Journal of the*

Royal Agricultural Society of England the results of a successful experiment in cultivating swedes to determine what would happen when the essential constituents of a plant were supplied to 'barren' land. This attracted national attention, causing Huxtable to be appointed to the chemical committee of the society, of which he was a member until 1867. His farming methods were unique in that all stock were housed and fed in sheds; there were no fences or trees. Employing a steam-engine, liquid animal and artificial manures were pumped through ceramic pipelines to delivery points in the fields and, in collaboration with the sanitation pioneer Edwin Chadwick, Huxtable also carried out experiments to test the possibilities of disposing of urban sewage by pumping it on to farm land. In 1845 Huxtable passed liquid farm manure through a bed of Dorset loam, the emerging liquid being clear and free of any offensive smell. This made a fundamental contribution to knowledge of the phenomenon of absorption and led to changes in the composition of artificial manures. It also inspired the Revd Henry Moule of Dorchester to design his patent earth closet, which enjoyed great commercial success.

Huxtable was an effective propagandist, by the spoken or written word, for his innovative ideas for recycling waste materials and conserving resources; his principal publication, *The 'Present Prices'* (1850), went through seven editions. Although his farms attracted many distinguished visitors, including Sir Robert Peel, he attracted great controversy, both for his support of the Dorset farm labourers and for his novel practices. This probably exacerbated his tendency to long periods of nervous exhaustion, which caused his absence from his parish while he recovered.

Huxtable's second marriage, in 1875, was to a Yorkshire widow, Susannah Maria Gott, who outlived him. There were no children of either marriage. He died at St Leonards, Sussex, on 12 December 1883 and was buried in Sutton Waldron.   EDWARD R. WARD, *rev.*

Sources E. R. Ward, 'Archdeacon Anthony Huxtable, 1808–1883, radical parson, scientist, and scientific farmer', *Proceedings of the Dorset Natural History and Archaeological Society*, 101 (1979), 7–25 · *The Times* (15 Dec 1883), 7b · *Dorset County Chronicle* (27 Dec 1883) · *Western Gazette* (28 Dec 1883)

Likenesses photograph, repro. in Ward, 'Archdeacon Anthony Huxtable'

Wealth at death £88,714 14s. 1d.: probate, 5 Feb 1884, *CGPLA Eng. & Wales*

Huxtable, William John Fairchild (1912–1990), Congregational minister and college head, was born on 25 July 1912 at Ladysmith Villa, Plumpton Green, near Lewes, Sussex, where his father, Percy John Fairchild Huxtable (1883–1922), lately of West Moors Congregational Church, Devon, was minister. His mother, Florence Watts (1885–1968), who had been apprenticed in the bakery and confectionery trade, married Percy in the Baptist church, Barnstaple, in March 1911. Following a pastorate at Blenheim Road Mission, Crouch End (1913–19), and service with the YMCA (1919–21), the family moved to Leghorn, Italy, where Percy had taken a post with the British and

Foreign Sailors' Society, and where, within two months of arriving, he died on 13 July. His widow, with John and his sister Kathleen, returned to Devon and associated themselves with the Congregational church in Barnstaple, whose minister, George Herbert King Chick (1892–1973), greatly influenced the young Huxtable.

A pupil at Barnstaple grammar school until 1930, from there John went to Western College, Bristol, under the distinguished scholar Robert Sleightholme Franks, where he graduated BA (Bristol) in English and philosophy, and then began his theological studies. The latter were completed during two years at Mansfield College, Oxford (1935–7), where his teachers included Nathaniel Micklem, H. Wheeler Robinson, T. W. Manson, and A. M. Hunter. Deeply appreciative of the catholic roots of the faith, and valuing Congregationalism's reformed heritage, he joined the Church Order Group, whose leaders included Micklem, John Whale, and Bernard, Lord Manning.

On 2 September 1937 Huxtable was ordained at Newton Abbot Congregational Church, Micklem delivering the charge to the minister, and Chick that to the church. Here he met Joan Lorimer Snow (*b.* 1912), whom he married on 6 September 1939. They had a son, Peter, and two daughters, Janet and Felicity. With the approach of war Huxtable came to review the pacifism which had led to his becoming a member of the Peace Pledge Union, and found that 'With much hesitation I had become and remain a very reluctant non-pacifist' (Huxtable, 23).

In September 1942 Huxtable was inducted to the pastorate at Palmers Green, London, a large suburban church which gave him many families to care for, a pulpit of some significance, and opportunities to serve the denomination, but fewer civic duties than he had enjoyed in Barnstaple. In 1948 he was a delegate to the first assembly of the World Council of Churches, and from 1948 to 1974 he served on the translation committee of the *New English Bible*.

After twelve happy years at Palmers Green, Huxtable was called to the principalship of New College, London, in succession to Sydney Cave (1883–1953). Here Congregational ministers were trained within the orbit of London University, and here Huxtable's colleagues included the church historian Geoffrey F. Nuttall, whom he had known at Mansfield College, but not intimately. The two came to have a high regard for one another, notwithstanding their differing emphases on matters historical, liturgical, and ecumenical.

Under the leadership of Howard Stanley, its general secretary, the Congregational Union of England and Wales (CUEW) inaugurated ten commissions to review the denomination's life and witness. Huxtable chaired that on the nature of the church—a 'hot potato', given the reluctance of some to conceive of a denomination as a churchly body, and the fears of some conservative evangelicals that the authority of scripture was in danger of being compromised. In the midst of these excitements Huxtable chaired the CUEW (1962–3). In 1964 he left New College to follow Stanley as general secretary of the CUEW, and two years later he became the first minister-secretary of the newly covenanted Congregational church in England and Wales. Meanwhile his ecumenical activities had been increasing. He was a vice-president of the British Council of Churches, and served the International Congregational Council and, after that body's union in 1970 with the World Presbyterian Alliance, the World Alliance of Reformed Churches. He also served on the central committee of the World Council of Churches, and was intimately involved in conversations between the Congregationalists and the Presbyterian Church of England. The last bore fruit in the union in 1972 of the latter church with the majority of English and English-speaking Welsh Congregationalists to form the United Reformed church, of whose general assembly Huxtable became the first moderator. With his Presbyterian opposite number, Arthur MacArthur, he became joint secretary of the new church. In the same year he became the first free church minister to be honoured by the then archbishop of Canterbury (A. M. Ramsay) with the Lambeth DD, a similar honour being bestowed a few months later by Aberdeen University. He was moderator of the Free Church Federal Council in 1976–7.

Meanwhile in 1974 Huxtable had become the executive officer of the Churches' Unity Commission. He worked tirelessly for a cause dear to his heart, and convened the first meeting of the Churches' Council for Covenanting, which met on 24 November 1978. He then retired to Devon, fearful that the covenanting scheme would founder, as it did.

Huxtable was a faithful minister, a gifted expository preacher, a lover of liturgical decency and order, and a trusted ecumenist. His publications reflect these interests. Thus his first book, *The Ministry* (1943), which he later regarded as his 'young man's book', was nevertheless a manifesto expressive of convictions concerning the ministry of Word, sacrament, and pastoral care in the context of the gathered church which remained with him throughout his life; and these were reinforced by his study of John Owen, whose *The True Nature of a Gospel Church* (1689) he abridged and edited (1949). He shared with John Marsh, E. R. Micklem, and J. M. Todd in the preparation of *A Book of Public Worship* (1949), a reformed yet catholic volume in which the relation of Word with sacrament was clearly displayed; and his published sets of broadcast talks testify to his ability to communicate with a wide audience. In 1962, expressing his indebtedness to P. T. Forsyth and John Oman (though perhaps borrowing his title from the evangelist Billy Graham's constantly reiterated phrase), he published *The Bible Says*. He here adjusted himself to traditional Roman Catholic and protestant attitudes to the Bible, and, over against fundamentalism and the views of J. I. Packer, he presented his view of the authority of scripture and the place of the Bible in the worship and life of the church. There followed *The Preacher's Integrity* (1966) and two books of ecumenical interest: *Christian Unity, some of the Issues* (1966) and *A New Hope for Christian Unity* (1977). In the wake of the failure of the ten propositions for covenanting—itself a successor to the failed Anglican–Methodist unity proposals—Huxtable came to

the rueful conclusion that because of its (then) attitude towards the ordination of women and its sectarianism concerning non-episcopal ordinations the Church of England was destined to be 'the bridge Church over which no traffic ever flows' (Huxtable, 71). Huxtable died on 16 November 1990 at Torbay Hospital, Torquay, and was cremated on 23 November at Torquay. ALAN P. F. SELL

Sources *CGPLA Eng. & Wales* (1991) · b. cert. · m. cert. · d. cert. · d. cert. [P. J. F. Huxtable] · d. cert. [F. Huxtable] · J. Huxtable, *As it seemed to me* (1990) · *WW* · *Yearbook* [United Reformed church in the UK] (1991–2), 229 · A. MacArthur, 'The end of an epoch? John Huxtable (1912–1990), ecumenist', *Reformed Quarterly*, 3/2 (1992), 1–5 · private information (2004) · J. Huxtable and A. Snow, *Our fathers that begat us: the story of the protestant dissenters of Newton Abbot, 1662–1984* (privately printed, 1984)
Archives DWL, notes, papers, and sermons
Likenesses photograph, repro. in *Daily Telegraph* · portrait, repro. in *The Congregational Year Book* (1962), frontispiece
Wealth at death under £115,000: probate, 8 Feb 1991, *CGPLA Eng. & Wales*

Huysmans [Huysman], **Jacob** [Jaques] (*c.*1630–1696), portrait painter, was probably born in Antwerp. George Vertue and Horace Walpole claimed that he was a pupil of Gilles Backereel, but their accounts cannot be substantiated. He may be identified with the Jaques Huysman listed in the registers of the Academy of St Luke in Antwerp as an apprentice in the workshop of Frans Wouters in 1649–50.

Huysmans emigrated to England from Flanders shortly before the Restoration of 1660, and quickly became one of the leading portrait painters at Charles II's court. On 26 August 1664 Pepys made the first of three visits to the painter's studio in Westminster, noting that 'some pictures at one Hiseman's, a picture-drawer … which is said to exceed Lilly; and endeed there is … as good pictures I think as I ever saw' (Pepys, 5.254). The diarist saw there some of the artist's most important works: a full-length portrait of Queen Catherine of Braganza as a shepherdess (*c.*1664; Royal Collection), another of the queen as St Catherine of Alexandria (*c.*1664; versions at Gorhambury, Hertfordshire, and Drumlanrig, Dumfriesshire), as well as several portraits of the queen's maids of honour, among which Pepys singled out that of Frances Teresa Stuart, later duchess of Richmond, 'in a buff doublet like a soldier' (Pepys, 5.254) (*c.*1664; Royal Collection).

The number and quality of Huysmans's portraits of the Roman Catholic Queen Catherine suggest that he worked as her principal portrait painter, and apparently he called 'himself her Majesty's Painter' (Vertue, *Note books*, 2.124). It is generally thought that he was suited—perhaps even chosen—for this role because of his own (presumed) Roman Catholicism. Certainly all his paintings demonstrate an affinity for the traditions of the baroque style practised by continental painters working for the Roman Catholic church and the predominantly Roman Catholic courts of Europe. One of his few known remaining subject pictures, *Cupid* (*c.*1659; Kingston Lacy, Dorset), directly reflects the images of martyrs and saints by Guido Reni and the early seventeenth-century Bolognese school of painters.

Similarly, Huysmans's portraits generally adhere to the continental fashions of portraiture and show his female sitters most often in disguise, either as saints and shepherdesses or in elaborate costumes—possibly worn by the sitters in court masques or other theatrical events (such as *Portrait of a Lady, as Diana?*, *c.*1674, Tate collection). Unlike the more simplified and generalized treatment of such subjects by his rival Sir Peter Lely, Huysmans's most elaborate compositions of the 1670s and 1680s, such as the monumental group portrait *Four Children of John Coke of Melbourne* (1680; Melbourne Hall, Derbyshire), feature the sitters in fantastical guises—allegorical or mythological—posed self-consciously in floral Arcadian settings populated by lambs and dogs with putti flying overhead. Such ornate compositions have led his work to be labelled idiosyncratic, even vulgar, and modern scholars, despite recognizing his talent, have characterized his work as an 'absurd climax of the Van Dyck pattern' (Baker, 1.212) or 'devoid of taste, crowded with accessories, and painted in cold, liverish colour' (Whinney and Millar, 182). His unique approach to colour was best described as a 'broken ... treatment, from which an impressionistic, shot quality results' (Baker, 1.212) and is recognizable by a preponderance of reddish lights in the flesh tones, highly keyed colours in the fabrics, and an overall 'opaquely shiny' and 'smooth' surface (ibid., 2.214).

In addition to the many elaborate allegorical portraits for which Huysmans is best-known, he painted a number of well-executed but conventionally treated portraits of Restoration statesmen, such as *John Maitland, 1st Duke of Lauderdale* (*c.*1665–*c.*1670; National Portrait Gallery, London), and a few more restrained portrait heads, foremost among these that of Izaak Walton (*c.*1675; National Portrait Gallery, London). Although he was based in London from his arrival until his death, the artist seems to have spent some time in Chichester after the great fire of London in 1666, possibly because his status as a foreigner—and in particular his religious affiliation—may have caused him to fear for his security in the city, then full of anti-Catholic fervour. He continued, however, to enjoy court patronage throughout his career, and in 1683 he was paid £230 to paint the cupola and high altar for the Queen's Chapel in St James's Palace. Christopher Wren described the altarpiece as 'painfully don and like an able Artist' (Colvin, 5.251), but Vertue hailed it as the 'most Famous Piece of his Performance' (Vertue, *Note books*, 2.124). Huysmans died in 1696 in London, possibly in Jermyn Street, and was buried in St James's, Piccadilly, London. JULIA MARCIARI ALEXANDER

Sources C. H. C. Baker, 'Jacob Huysmans', *Lely and the Stuart portrait painters: a study of English portraiture before and after van Dyck*, 2 (1912), 209–19 · Pepys, *Diary*, 5.254, 276, n. 30; 6.113 · Vertue, *Note books*, 1.25, 69, 83, 116; 2.30, 67, 124; 4.3, 35, 63, 91, 102, 119 · H. M. Colvin and others, eds., *The history of the king's works*, 5 (1976), 251 · P. Rombouts and T. Van Lerius, *De liggeren en andere historische archieven der Antwerpsche Sint Lucasgilde*, 2 (The Hague, 1876); repr. (Amsterdam, 1961), 208–9 · O. Millar, 'Huysmans [Houseman], Jacob', *The dictionary of art*, ed. J. Turner (1996) · 'Huysmans, Jacob', Thieme & Becker, *Allgemeines Lexikon*, 18.204 · Bénézit, *Dict.*, 3rd edn · H. Walpole, 'James Huysman', in H. Walpole, *Anecdotes of painting in England: with some account of the principal artists*, ed. R. N. Wornum, new edn, 3 vols. (1849); repr. (1876); repr. in 4 vols. (New York, 1969), vol. 2, pp. 121–3 · M. Whinney and O. Millar, *English art, 1625–1714* (1957), 169, 182, 186, 300 · E. Waterhouse, *Painting in Britain, 1530–1790*, 4th edn (1978); repr. (1994), 104–6 · A. Laing, 'Sir Peter Lely and Sir Ralph Bankes', *Art and patronage in the Caroline courts: essays in honour of Sir Oliver Millar*, ed. D. Howarth (1993), 107–31, 121–5 · DNB

Archives GL, 'Booke of orders' and constitutions of the painter-stainers guild, ii, fol. 71

Huyssing, Hans. See Hysing, Hans (1678–1752/3).

Huysum, Jacobus van (1687×9–1740), flower painter, was born at Amsterdam. He was one of four sons, all painters, of the painter Justus van Huysum the elder (1659–1716), the other three being Justus van Huysum (1685–1707), Michiel van Huysum (1704–1760), and Jan van Huysum (1682–1749), the celebrated flower painter. Van Huysum came to England in 1721, in which year he was living in the house of a patron, Mr Lockyear, of the South Sea House, London. He drew many of the plates in J. Martyn's *Historia plantarum rariorum* (1728–37) and in the Society of Gardeners' *Catalogus plantarum* (1730). Subsequently he was patronized by Sir Robert Walpole, in whose house at Chelsea he lived; there he was employed to paint flower pieces and copies from the old masters in Walpole's collection, including paintings by Caravaggio and Claude, for the decoration of Walpole's great house, Houghton Hall, in Norfolk. The 1736 catalogue of Walpole's collection records that all the pictures hung over the doors and the chimneys in the attic storey of Houghton were by 'a brother of van Huysum' (MS, PML 7586, Pierpont Morgan Library, New York). However, because of his drunk and disorderly habits Walpole dismissed him after two years. He subsequently died in obscurity in London in 1740.

Although van Huysum did sometimes copy his brother Jan's paintings he did not necessarily seek to emulate his style, and in his most famous work, the series of flower pieces representing the twelve months of the year (priv. coll.), the flowers are rendered in a more naturalistic manner than those in the work of his brother. Examples of his drawings are in the British Museum, the Royal Society of Arts, and the Natural History Museum, London.

SARAH HERRING

Sources P. Mitchell, *European flower painters* (1973), 141–2 · I. Haberland, 'Huysum, van', *The dictionary of art*, ed. J. Turner (1996) · Thieme & Becker, *Allgemeines Lexikon* · M. H. Grant, *The twelve months of flowers: Jacobus van Huysum* (1950) · Vertue, *Note books*, 1.26, 80, and n.; 5.121 · H. Walpole, *Anecdotes of painting in England: with some account of the principal artists*, ed. J. Dallaway, [rev. and enl. edn], 4 (1827), 46–7 · Bryan, *Painters* (1903–5), 3.91–2 · P. Taylor, *Dutch flower painting, 1600–1750* (1996), 86 [exhibition catalogue, Dulwich Picture Gallery, London, 3 July – 29 Sept 1996] · J. B. Descamps, *La vie des peintres flamands, allemands et hollandois*, 4 (Paris, 1763), 231–2 · A. Bredius, ed., *Künstler-Inventare*, 8 vols. (The Hague, 1915–22), vol. 4, pp. 1186, 1189, 1199 · J. van Gool, *Die nieuwe schouburg der Nederlantsche kunstschilders en schilderessen*, 2 (The Hague, 1751), 30–31 · Desmond, *Botanists*, rev. edn

Likenesses J. van Huysum, self-portrait, oils, *c.*1739, AM Oxf.

Hwicce, kings of the (*act. c.*670–*c.*780), ruled over a people in the west midlands, in what is now Gloucestershire, Worcestershire, and part of Warwickshire. The kingdom of the Hwicce, assessed at 7000 hides in the short seventh- or eighth-century text known as the Tribal Hidage, emerges in the late seventh century, already under Mercian overlordship, and was completely absorbed into Mercia in the eighth. It was probably coterminous with the early medieval diocese of Worcester, which reached as far south as Bath; the first extant charter issued by a king of the Hwicce (Osric, with the Mercian king's consent) is the foundation charter for Bath monastery, on the West Saxon border, in 675 (*AS chart.*, S 51). While Osric is styled *rex*, Ealdred, a century later, is described in a charter of Offa as 'my underking [*subregulus*], that is to say ealdorman [*dux*] of his own people the Hwicce' (S 113), and his brother Uhtred is described as 'holding a certain degree of rule over his own people the Hwicce' (S 57).

The origin of the Hwiccian dynasty is obscure; the connection with the Northumbrian royal family asserted in twelfth-century sources, and in the *Dictionary of National Biography*, is implausible. Attempts to draw up a family tree for the kings of the Hwicce (as by W. G. Searle and H. P. R. Finberg) rely on guesswork and forged charters, but the recurrence of certain name elements and the uniform alliteration of their names make it certain that the kings listed below were all somehow related. The first known members of the dynasty, the brothers Eanfrith and Eanhere, are mentioned by Bede in his account of Wilfrid's conversion of Sussex in 680 or 681; Bede says that the South Saxon queen Eaba was the daughter of **Eanfrith** (*fl. c.*670), brother of **Eanhere** (*fl. c.*670), who were Christians along with their people, the Hwicce (Bede, *Hist. eccl.*, 4.13). This implies that Eanhere had been king, and perhaps that Eanfrith had ruled jointly with him. Bede also refers to King **Osric** (*fl.* 674–679), apparently as patron of Bishop *Oftfor; charters imply that he ruled at least from 674 to 679, and associate him and his brother Oswald with the foundation of Gloucester and Pershore monasteries respectively. Oswald may be the father of an **Æthelmund** (*d.* before 746), son of Oswald, whom Æthelbald of Mercia (*d.* 757) slew, afterwards making reparation to Gloucester monastery (in 746: *AS chart.*, S 1679). Gloucester tradition says that the first abbess Cyneburh was Osric's sister. The third, Eafe, was conceivably the same woman as the Eaba mentioned above. Osric was evidently succeeded as king of the Hwicce by **Oshere** (*fl. c.*680–*c.*693), the alleged founder of the see of Worcester in 679, whose charters begin in 680 and reach into the 690s. He is possibly the Oshere whose death is lamented by his sister *Ecgburh in a letter which St Boniface received *c.*717; she is conceivably the abbess called Eadburh in Gloucester sources, the successor of Cyneburh and widow of Wulfhere, king of Mercia (*d.* 675).

By 709 Oshere's four sons, Æthelheard, Æthelweard, Æthelberht, and **Æthelric** (*fl. c.*693–736), were attesting charters without him. The last of these is best evidenced in charters; these extend from the 690s to 736, when he is styled *subregulus* of the Mercian king Æthelbald (*AS chart.*, S 89). He may be associated with the church at Wootton Wawen, Warwickshire. It is not known whether he succeeded Oshere directly; or whether one or more of his three brothers reigned first. Another member of the family who witnesses Æthelbald's charters was Osred, but he may not have ruled. There is in fact a gap in the record of Hwiccian *reguli* between Æthelric and the appearance together, in charters of 757 and 759, of three brothers, **Eanberht** (*fl.* 757–759), **Uhtred** (*fl.* 757–777), and **Ealdred** (*fl.* 757–777), each styled *regulus*. This is the first unequivocal evidence of joint rule among the Hwicce. Uhtred and Ealdred were active at least until 777. A relative of theirs was Æthelburh, the abbess of Fladbury, Withington, and Twyning in the 770s; she was the daughter of the thegn Ælfred, and was no doubt related to Oshere's son Æthelheard, who had also been associated with Fladbury. No member of the dynasty is known to have ruled after the 770s; Æthelmund, ealdorman of the Hwicce (*d.* 802), may be unrelated. His wife Ceolburh may have been the abbess of Berkeley who died in 807, and his son Æthelric refers to an extensive inheritance in the kingdom of the Hwicce in the will that he made in 804. Æthelric's wish to be buried at Deerhurst may indicate a break with the traditions of the Hwiccian kings, for Osric is said to have been buried at Gloucester, and the bodies of the ancestors of the brothers Eanberht, Uhtred, and Ealdred were said to lie in the church of St Peter at Worcester. There is a post-medieval effigy of Osric in Gloucester Cathedral.

PATRICK SIMS-WILLIAMS

Sources P. Sims-Williams, *Religion and literature in western England, 600–800* (1990) · P. Sims-Williams, *Britain and early Christian Europe: studies in early medieval history and culture* (1995) · W. G. Searle, *Anglo-Saxon bishops, kings, and nobles* (1899) · H. P. R. Finberg, *The early charters of the west midlands*, 2nd edn (1972) · *AS chart.*, S 51–63, 64, 70, 74–5, 79, 89, 94, 1252, 1679 · Canon Bazeley and M. L. Bazeley, 'Effigies in Gloucester Cathedral', *Transactions of the Gloucestershire and Bristol Archaeological Society*, 27 (1904), 304, 306
Likenesses effigy?, repro. in Bazeley and Bazeley, 'Effigies in Gloucester Cathedral'

Hyatt, John (1767–1826), Independent minister, was born at Sherborne on 21 January 1767, the son of a publican. He was educated at a day school, and at fourteen was apprenticed to a cabinet-maker, on whose death Hyatt carried on the business. Young, successful, and worldly, his first real contact with Christian society came through Elizabeth Westcombe (*d.* 1834). She was the niece of a deceased dissenting minister, and it was her example, as well as her uncle's library, which secured Hyatt's conversion. They married in 1787.

Hyatt was a tireless defender of Calvinist theology against Arminianism, despite a close friendship with one of Wesley's preachers. In 1794 he began to conduct services, acting in the local area as a lay preacher. In 1798 he gave up his business and moved with his family to Mere, Wiltshire, where he was eventually ordained a minister. The need to provide adequately for his growing family led him to leave Mere for Zion Chapel in Frome, Somerset, in 1800, where his reputation as a preacher was established. Shortly afterwards he was invited to become minister of the London Tabernacle, which, along with its sister church, Tottenham Court Chapel, he served until the end of his life. In 1811 he published *Sermons on Select Subjects*.

Hyatt died in London on 30 January 1826 and was buried

in Bunhill Fields. He was survived by his wife and only son, Charles, who edited another volume of his sermons (1828) and *Sketches of Fifty Sermons of the Late J[ohn] H[yatt]* (1827).

W. A. J. ARCHBOLD, rev. L. E. LAUER

Sources *New Baptist Magazine*, 2 (1826), 113 · *Sermons on various subjects by the late John Hyatt: to which is prefixed, a memoir of the author, by the Revd John Morrison*, ed. C. Hyatt, 2nd edn (1828) · J. A. Jones, ed., *Bunhill memorials* (1849), 94–100 · A. W. Light, *Bunhill Fields: written in honour and to the memory of the many saints of God whose bodies rest in this old London cemetery*, 1 (1913), 176–8
Archives E. Sussex RO, sermons
Likenesses engraving, pubd 1804, Regent's Park College, Oxford · Freeman, stipple, pubd 1819 (after painting), NPG · R. Woodman, engraving, repro. in C. Hyatt, ed., *Sermons on various subjects*

Hyde, Alexander (1596×8–1667), bishop of Salisbury, was born in the parish of St Mary, Salisbury, Wiltshire, the fourth son of Sir Laurence Hyde (*c*.1562–1642), barrister, and his wife, Barbara Castilian (1574–1641); Robert *Hyde (1595/6–1665) and Edward *Hyde (1607–1659) were his brothers. He appears under the year 1610, aged twelve, in the register of Winchester College. From here he was appointed a scholar of New College, Oxford; he matriculated on 17 November 1615, when he was said to be aged eighteen, and was admitted to a fellowship in the same year. On 24 April 1623 he graduated BCL and he was awarded his doctorate on 4 July 1632. In 1634, on the presentation of the earl of Pembroke, he was instituted to two Wiltshire rectories, Little Langford and Wyly, both on the death of John Lee. He was collated on 19 May 1637 to the office of subdean of Salisbury, vacant through the death of Giles Thornborough, and in early 1639 to the prebend of Grantham Australis in the diocese of Salisbury, with its attached vicarage in Lincolnshire. His installation there took place either on 5 January 1639 or by Archbishop Laud on 4 March. Probably about this time Hyde married Mary, daughter of Robert *Townson (*bap.* 1576, *d.* 1621), former bishop of Salisbury, and niece of John Davenant, current bishop of Salisbury; of their children the eldest known, Laurence, was baptized at Salisbury in 1641 but died at an early age as did a daughter, Mary. When their father's will was drawn up only Robert, Barbara, Ann, Elizabeth, and Margaret, who had married Henry Parker, had survived.

Hyde, together with his brother Robert, then MP for Salisbury, supported the royalists during the civil war. On 1 December 1645 Hyde was charged with taking the oath of association and of corresponding with the royalist party. On 14 May 1646 the county committee ordered each of his Wiltshire rectories to be let at £100. On 5 June 1647 a James Harris was authorized to rent the house of the subdean from the government in order to provide accommodation for Hyde's wife. It seems also that the prebendal vicarage of South Grantham had been sequestered by the Lincolnshire county committee, and on 15 July 1647 the committee for sequestrations granted Mary Hyde the fifth of the value of each. From these arrangements it seems that Hyde went abroad for a time, and indeed in February 1647 he was reported to be staying in Rouen. From 1649 to

1654, however, he was resident in Salisbury, baptizing a son and three daughters there in that period.

In 1658 John Thurloe was informed that Hyde had been privy to the conspiracy of John Hewitt: Hyde's first cousin Edward Hyde, the future earl of Clarendon, had written to him with a request 'to furnish them with some money to buy arms, which he refuseth to do, alledging, that the business is so laid, that they will quickly be provided of arms' (Thurloe, *State papers*, 1.712). But, as his will reveals, Hyde did advance £400 to Charles Stuart. It seems safe to assume that it was through Edward Hyde's influence that on 9 July 1660 his cousin received the crown's nomination as dean of Winchester in the place of John Young, his installation following on 8 August. Hyde also returned to the diocese of Salisbury, becoming canon residentiary (South Grantham) and was admitted to residence at the cathedral on 15 September 1660. Having been granted the royal assent on 21 December 1665 Hyde was consecrated bishop of Salisbury in the chapel of New College, Oxford, on 31 December. Hyde became a very wealthy man with extensive property, chiefly in Wiltshire, and was able to bequeath in land and money £1000 to each of his unmarried daughters. He continued in the see until his death on 22 August 1667. Hyde was buried near the south transept in Salisbury Cathedral, and an inscribed black marble stone was set there to mark his grave.

STEPHEN WRIGHT

Sources *Walker rev.* · Wood, *Ath. Oxon.*, new edn · T. F. Kirby, *Winchester scholars: a list of the wardens, fellows, and scholars of … Winchester College* (1888) · Thurloe, *State papers* · *Fasti Angl., 1541–1857*, [Salisbury] · *Fasti Angl., 1541–1857*, [Canterbury] · *Calendar of the Clarendon state papers preserved in the Bodleian Library*, ed. O. Ogle and others, 5 vols. (1869–1970) · R. C. Hoare, *The history of modern Wiltshire*, 6 vols. (1822–44) · R. Rawlinson, *The history and antiquities of the cathedral church of Salisbury, and the abbey church of Bath* (1723)

Hyde, Anne. *See* Anne, duchess of York (1637–1671).

Hyde, David de la (*fl.* 1549–1561), scholar and recusant, is of unknown parentage. Anthony Wood believed him to be of Irish birth. Sir Walter and his son Sir James de la Hyde of Moyclare, King's county, were proscribed for supporting the rebellion of Thomas Fitzgerald, tenth earl of Kildare, in 1535. David de la Hyde appears to have had some Irish connections, and his association with King's county is at least likely. He certainly sought refuge in Ireland in times of difficulty and was esteemed there.

Hyde was admitted a probationer fellow of Merton College, Oxford, in June 1549 and was confirmed as a fellow there in July 1550. He proceeded to his MA in 1553 and in 1556 was allowed to study canon and civil law, subjects which in Merton required special licence. His supplication for a degree was later refused, perhaps on political grounds. That course of studies suggests that he was thinking in the 1550s of an administrative career in the church or state, but in the meantime he had conscientiously discharged his duties in college, serving as a bursar in 1555–7 and 1559, as dean and a keeper of the Rede chest in 1557–8, as a prelector, and as garden-master in 1558–9. He accompanied the warden on at least one visitation of the college estates, in the winter of 1556–7. He was renowned as an orator and disputant in the schools, and Wood preserved the text of an address by Hyde, 'De ligno et foeno', delivered in praise of Jasper Heywood when Heywood was *rex fabarum* (king of the beans), the traditional lord of Christmas misrule in Merton.

Heywood resigned his fellowship in 1558 and migrated to the Jesuits in Rome by way of All Souls College. Hyde was formally expelled from Merton in December 1560, with two other fellows, for refusing to take the oath of supremacy. He then went to Ireland, which suggests that he had some confidence in kinship or patronage there, but he returned to England in 1561, when he was noted as a recusant to be watched closely and forbidden to come within 20 miles of either Oxford or Cambridge. He seems then to have spent some further time in Ireland and may later have moved to the continent. In Ireland Hyde had a reputation for learning which extended to a mastery of Latin, Greek, and mathematics, and was credited with many books by Richard Stanyhurst in the description of Ireland which he appended to Holinshed's *Chronicles* (1578). Stanyhurst, who entered the Catholic church in the 1580s, graduated in Oxford after Hyde had left Merton, and probably met him in Ireland. Wood says that Hyde's books were printed abroad, but that seems to have been by way of explaining that he had not been able to find them. If they were published in Hyde's own name they appear all to have perished.

Hyde's reputation owes most to Wood, though Stanyhurst is the more explicit witness to his scholarship. Wood approved of Hyde as a collegial man, distinguished in the schools yet readily willing to take office in Merton, and perhaps even as a recusant, although Wood's own sympathies were staunchly Anglican. Wood was a traditionalist, and lingered over reminiscences of the communal life in hall. Hyde's energies and wit had been directed to traditional ends, not least at twelfth night, and they earned him particular notice from Wood.   G. H. MARTIN

Sources DNB · Wood, *Ath. Oxon.*, new edn · J. M. Fletcher, ed., *Registrum annalium collegii Mertonensis, 1521–1567*, OHS, new ser., 23 (1974) · R. Stanyhurst, 'Description of Ireland', in R. Holinshed, *Chronicles* (1578)

Hyde, Douglas (1860–1949), writer and president of Éire (Ireland), was born near Castlerea, co. Roscommon, on 17 January 1860, the third son and fourth child of the Revd Arthur Hyde (*c*.1820–1905), rector of Kilnactranny, co. Sligo, and his wife, Elizabeth (1834–1886), daughter of the Ven. John Orson Oldfield, archdeacon of Elphin. The Hyde family, originally from Berkshire, had been granted land in Cork by Queen Elizabeth, and a junior branch had produced a long line of Church of Ireland clergymen. In 1867 Hyde's father became rector of Tibohine, co. Roscommon, and the family, related by marriage to the French family, moved to nearby Frenchpark. Here he began to learn Irish from native speakers, devising his own phonetic spelling to record words and phrases and starting to transcribe the poems and stories he heard from country people. His first encounter with the written language and with Irish grammar was in an old Church of Ireland catechism found in

Douglas Hyde (1860–1949), by John Butler Yeats, 1906

his father's rectory. Apart from a brief, unsuccessful interval at a school in Kingstown (now Dunlaoghaire) in 1873, he was informally educated at home by his father, a classicist and eccentric polymath, developing a particular interest in languages and trying his hand at verse and prose in Irish.

Hyde's father's intention was that he should become a Church of Ireland clergyman like so many of his family, and he entered Trinity College, Dublin, in 1880, though he still lived mainly at home until 1882. In 1881 he won the Bedell scholarship, intended to encourage Church of Ireland preaching in Irish; he later graduated in modern literature (1884, with gold medal) and divinity (testimonium, 1885). Other medals and prizes followed. He had already decided against entering the church, and turned instead to the law, graduating LLB in 1887 and LLD in 1888. But he did not pursue a legal career either, having already begun to establish himself as a writer and literary scholar. In 1890–91 he was interim professor of modern languages at the University of New Brunswick. On his return he applied unsuccessfully for professorships in Belfast and Dublin and settled in Frenchpark, co. Roscommon, from 1892. He married Lucy Cometina Kurtz (*d*. 1939) on 10 October 1893, and they had two daughters: Nuala, who died of tuberculosis in 1916, and Una.

Hyde's failure to obtain academic posts stems probably from conservative dismay at his growing prominence as a campaigner for the revival of Irish as a spoken language. In 1880 he had joined the Gaelic Union, a militant offshoot of the rather staid and scholarly Society for the Preservation of the Irish Language, and he began to publish poems in Irish under the pseudonym An Craoibhín Aoibhinn ('The Pleasant Little Branch'). In his own name he contributed to the *Dublin University Review* essays entitled 'The unpublished songs of Ireland' (August 1885) and 'A plea for the Irish language' (August 1886). Associated with the new Young Ireland societies established in the 1880s, he contributed, with W. B. Yeats and Katharine Tynan among others, to *Poems and Ballads of Young Ireland*, published in 1888, forty years after the Young Ireland rebellion, with a dedication to the veteran Fenian journalist John O'Leary, though Hyde personally found O'Leary tiresome and autocratic. In 1889 he published *Leabhar sgeulaigheachta* ('Book of story-telling'), a collection of folk tales gleaned from Irish speakers in the west, and this was followed in 1890 by *Beside the Fire*, containing rhymes, riddles, and stories, again collected from Irish speakers, prefaced by a long critical discussion of previous attempts to gather Irish folklore. These books, the first of Georges Dottin's French translations of some of his collected stories (1892–3), and learned papers such as 'Oscar au fléau, légende ossianique' in the *Revue Celtique* for 1892, established Hyde's international credentials as a folklorist and scholar of Irish.

The year 1892 also saw the founding of the National Literary Society in Dublin, of which Hyde was elected president. Chairing the meetings proved difficult as he had to try to mediate between the sharply conflicting views of W. B. Yeats and the aged Young Irelander Charles Gavan Duffy. On 25 November he delivered a stirring and influential presidential lecture, 'On the necessity for de-Anglicising the Irish people', insisting on a contradiction between the assertive political nationalism of the day and Ireland's servile willingness to operate culturally through the forms and language of the alien English. Yeats welcomed it but worried that Hyde's purist rhetoric dismissed the possibility of a credibly Irish literature in English to which Yeats himself was firmly committed.

Hyde's lecture helped to focus the patriotic enthusiasm which led in 1893 to the founding of the Gaelic League, devoted to language revival with local meetings to promote Irish music, dancing, and the recitation of poetry and stories. Once again Hyde was elected president. Under his vociferous and energetic leadership, despite constant tensions and disputes among members, the league grew steadily, with more than forty branches by 1897. In 1899 it brought about the Palles commission on intermediate education, which considered the teaching of Irish. The prominent Trinity classicist J. P. Mahaffy and the professor of Sanskrit and comparative philology Robert Atkinson, whose only interest in Irish was historical and philological, disparaged Irish literature and folklore and recommended that Irish should not be taught in schools. Hyde's indignant letter of protest to the *Daily Express* contributed to the vigorous ensuing controversy, and his own evidence to the commission and his reply to Atkinson were published as Gaelic League pamphlets in 1901. His American lecture tour (1905–6) raised substantial funds for the league, which could claim some 550 branches in

different parts of the country by 1908. But by 1915 his cautious policy of steering clear of divisive separatist politics had proved unsustainable, and he resigned as president.

Despite all the demands of the league Hyde had continued to collect and translate oral material. *The Love Songs of Connacht* appeared in book form in 1893, eventually followed by *The Religious Songs of Connacht* (2 vols., 1905–6). The best Irish scholar among the leading activists of the Gaelic revival, Hyde was a gifted and imaginative translator in prose and verse, pioneering a form of Irish English which was sensitive to the syntax and idiom of Irish, though his much anthologized verse translations sometimes diverged considerably from the sense of the original. His most important scholarly work in these crowded years was his comprehensive, epoch-making study *A Literary History of Ireland* (1899), from which all writing in English was deliberately and provocatively excluded. He edited the first volume of the Irish Texts Society's series of editions with English translations in 1899, subsequently contributing two further volumes. He also wrote short plays in Irish, beginning in 1901 with *Casadh an tsúgain* ('The twisting of the rope'), the first play in Irish to be performed on the professional stage, though this aspect of his work was best-known through the English translations subsequently provided by Lady Gregory.

Appointed to the royal commission on university education in 1906, Hyde campaigned successfully for Irish as a compulsory matriculation subject for the new national university. In 1908 he was appointed first professor of modern Irish at University College, Dublin, a post he held until his retirement in 1932. He continued to publish widely for both scholarly and popular audiences, now taking a more modest part in public life as a co-opted Free State senator (February–September 1925) and as chairman of the Irish Folklore Institute (1930–34).

In 1938, under the new constitution of the previous year, Hyde was unexpectedly elected first president of Ireland as a non-partisan compromise candidate. Despite a stroke in 1940 which confined him to a wheelchair, he continued to attend to official business, working closely with the Taoiseach Eamon de Valera during the war years when Ireland preserved her status as a neutral country. He completed his term of office in 1945 and, after being bedridden in his last years, died at his home, Little Ratra, Phoenix Park, Dublin, on 12 July 1949. He was accorded a state funeral, with a Church of Ireland service held in St Patrick's Cathedral while the now overwhelmingly Catholic establishment of the new nation waited outside. Then he was taken across Ireland by motorcade to be buried in Frenchpark churchyard, co. Roscommon, on 14 July.

Sometimes accused of equivocation, Hyde was both a passionate partisan and a peacemaker with the same genial manner for everyone, equally at ease with poachers and professors. During his long life he was overtaken as a cultural activist by a more extremist and more political younger generation, and overtaken in technical scholarship by the rigorous new professionalism associated with the Dublin Institute of Advanced Studies (founded 1940), but his reputation as scholar, writer, and cultural patriot has grown since his death. His exclusivist 'Irish Ireland' approach to Irish culture has not worn well in more pluralist times, but he has come to be generally recognized as an important pioneer and cultural enabler, described by the writer James Stephens as 'the fairy godmother of the new Ireland'. New editions of his plays, translations, and essays have continued to be published, and there are biographies and other modern studies in both Irish and English. NORMAN VANCE

Sources J. E. Dunleavy and C. W. Dunleavy, *Douglas Hyde: a maker of modern Ireland* (1991) · DNB · *The collected letters of W. B. Yeats*, 1, ed. J. Kelly and E. Domville (1986) · R. Welch, ed., *The Oxford companion to Irish literature* (1996) · [J. H. Todd], ed., *A catalogue of graduates who have proceeded to degrees in the University of Dublin, from the earliest recorded commencements to … December 16, 1868* (1869) · *A catalogue of graduates who have proceeded to degrees in the University of Dublin … from the year 1868 to … 1895* (1896) · www.pgil-eirdata.org/html [Princess Grace Irish Library, Monaco], 17 Sept 2001 · CGPLA Éire (1949)

Archives National University of Ireland, Galway, papers · NL Ire., corresp. and papers · NYPL, corresp. · TCD · University College, Dublin, Irish folklore department | NL Ire., letters to William Bulfin · NL Ire., letters to Alice Stopford Green · NL Ire., letters to Maurice Moore · NL Wales, letters to John Glyn Davies · NL Wales, corresp. with E. T. John · priv. coll., letters to Edith Œnone Somerville · University College, Dublin, Irish folklore department · University College, Dublin, letters to D. J. O'Donoghue | FILM BFI NFTVA, 'Eire installs president', British Paramount News, 30 June 1938 · BFI NFTVA, news footage | SOUND Southern Illinois University, Eoin O'Mahony collection, interview

Likenesses J. B. Yeats, pencil drawing, 1895, NG Ire. · J. B. Yeats, oils, 1906, NG Ire. [*see illus.*] · T. Spicer-Simson, plasticine medallion, 1922, NG Ire.; bronze cast, NG Ire. · W. Conor, oils, *c.*1937–1945, University College, Dublin · S. O'Sullivan, oils, *c.*1938, NG Ire. · H. A. Kernoff, pencil on card, 1939, NG Ire. · S. O'Sullivan, oils, 1944, TCD · G. de Gennaro, pastel drawing, President's Lodge, Dublin · S. Murphy, bust, President's Lodge, Dublin · S. O'Sullivan, drawing, repro. in *Irish Press* (1938) [Christmas] · S. O'Sullivan, drawing, NG Ire. · S. Purser, oils, NG Ire. · L. Whelan, oils, President's Lodge, Dublin · J. B. Yeats, oils, Hugh Lane Municipal Gallery of Modern Art, Dublin

Wealth at death £27,874: probate, 5 Dec 1949, CGPLA Éire

Hyde, Edward (1607–1659), Church of England clergyman, was baptized on 10 May 1607, the fifth of the eleven sons of Sir Laurence Hyde (*c.*1562–1642), lawyer of Salisbury, and his wife, Barbara Castilian (1574–1641) of Benham Valence, Berkshire; Alexander *Hyde (1596x8–1667) and Robert *Hyde (1595/6–1665) were his elder brothers. He was educated at Westminster School and elected to Trinity College, Cambridge, in 1625, where he graduated BA in 1630, became a fellow in 1632, proceeded MA in 1633, became a tutor in 1636, and proceeded BD in 1640. In 1643 he was created DD of Oxford (16 January), married Anne, probably daughter of Stephen Hurst of Cowsfield, Whiteparish, Wiltshire, and was made rector of Brightwell, Berkshire.

After the county committee sequestered his living in 1647 Hyde quarrelled bitterly with his puritan successor, John Ley. Ley stated that he had permitted Hyde and his family to remain in the rectory until 1 April 1650 while making arrangements to move. However, he objected to the order that he pay a fifth of its income to Hyde because Hyde had ample personal means. Nor, Ley said in *An Acquittance or Discharge from Dr. E. H.* (1654), would Hyde 'abate any whit of his rigid misconceits, and disaffection to the present Government' (Ley, *Acquittance*, 17). In a later pamphlet Ley claimed that Hyde had attempted to undermine his ministry at Brightwell by describing the Westminster assembly directory as sacrilegious, and he said he had frequently heard Hyde proclaim himself 'a Seraphical zealot for the Service-book'. Hyde rejected only the word 'seraphical' in that description and insisted that it was indeed sacrilegious 'to rob God of his worship' (Ley, *Debate*, 1–3).

Hyde took his family to Oxford, and (perhaps as late as January 1657) he preached frequently at Holywell, where 'all the loyal party of that city flocked to hear his doctrine' (Wood, *Ath. Oxon.*, 3.643). After the Restoration his contemporary at Westminster and Trinity, Robert Boreman, published, as *Allegiance and Conscience not Fled out of England* (1662), sermons that Hyde had preached at the time of Charles I's trial that explained his appeal for that audience. Hyde had proclaimed that the 'King of Kings' had given to earthly kings their 'Allegiance and Supremacy'. Therefore only 'the Calendar of Antichrist' would celebrate those who murdered their kings as 'S. Faux, S. Garnet … our homebred traitors' (*Allegiance*, 1, 33–4). Like his late diocesan John Davenant, to whose books and person he was devoted, Hyde held to a Calvinist soteriology. He was not, as has been asserted, the Edward Hide junior who published *A Wonder and yet No Wonder: a Great Red Dragon in Heaven* (1651) and *The Mystery of Christ in Us* (1651)—both of a millenarian cast such as he abominated—but, beginning with *A Christian Legacy* (1657), which addressed the subject of death, he published three works in Oxford. In *A Christian Vindication of Truth* (1659), he attacked as superstitious such Roman Catholic practices as prayer to saints and image worship while also swiping at the 'irreligion … in Faction, which hath no Liturgie' (p. 292). By 'Faction', he meant all opponents of the Church of England's ceremonies. In *Christ and his Church* (1658), he called the directory 'the Anti-prayer Book' (p. 627) and considered it a subtle plot to destroy all set forms of prayer and bring in 'a full Dictatorship in Religion' (p. 634) controlled by the factious ministers. Such men, with their extemporary prayers, were 'guilty of worse Idolatry then many of the Heathen' because they forced their congregations to 'resign up their souls in a blind obedience' to their notions of worship (p. 291).

On 16 August 1659 Hyde died at Salisbury (where he had moved about two years previously), too soon to enjoy the deanery of Windsor that the influence of his eponymous cousin, Charles II's lord chancellor, had obtained for him in 1658. According to one of Clarendon's correspondents Hyde had 'strained a vein in his breast with too much preaching at Carfax Church or elsewhere' (Clarendon, *Hist. rebellion*, 4.414), although other sources speak of his suffering from the stone. As requested in his will, he was buried in the south aisle of Salisbury Cathedral, near his parents and siblings. He left £10 to be spent on the cathedral fabric and made numerous bequests to fellow dispossessed clerics. He bequeathed Melchett Park, probably the property that, according to Ley's assertion in 1652, brought Hyde £80 per annum (Ley, *Acquittance*, 16). Consistent to the end with his polemical message, in his will he described his wife as 'well grounded and settled in the true Catholicke Religion of the Church of England and not inclined either to superstition or faction'. Appropriately, his final and posthumous publication was issued as *The true Catholicks tenure, or, A good Christians certainty which he ought to have of his religion* (1662).   J. SEARS MCGEE

Sources Wood, *Ath. Oxon.*, new edn, vols. 3–4 • D. Lloyd, *Memoires of the lives … of those … personages that suffered … for the protestant religion* (1668) • Venn, *Alum. Cant.*, 1/1–4 • *Old Westminsters*, vol. 1 • *Walker rev.* • J. Welch, *The list of the queen's scholars of St Peter's College, Westminster*, ed. [C. B. Phillimore], new edn (1852) • Foster, *Alum. Oxon.* • J. Ley, *An acquittance or discharge from Dr. E. H.* (1654) • J. Ley, *A debate concerning the English liturgy* (1656) • E. Hyde, *Allegiance and conscience not fled out of England* (1662) • *Calendar of the Clarendon state papers preserved in the Bodleian Library*, 4: *1657–1660*, ed. F. J. Routledge (1932) • *VCH Wiltshire* • will, PRO, PROB 11/298, fols. 337r–339r

Hyde, Edward, first earl of Clarendon (1609–1674), politician and historian, was born on 18 February 1609 at Dinton, Wiltshire, and baptized there on 22 February, the sixth of the nine children of Henry Hyde (*c.*1563–1634), gentleman, and his wife, Mary (*bap.* 1578, *d.* 1661), daughter of Edward Langford of Trowbridge. The Hyde family in Wiltshire owed its rise into the higher ranks of the gentry through the exercise of the law, and Hyde's father and two of his uncles attended the Middle Temple. The uncles went on to become prominent practitioners but Henry Hyde abandoned the law on his marriage to a local heiress and retired to the country, living a life marked, according to his son, by quiet piety, wide reading, and good, though temperate, fellowship.

Legal career, marriage, and intellectual circles Edward, Henry's third but second surviving son, was originally intended for a clerical career. A place was sought for him at his father's college, Magdalen, Oxford, and probably through the influence of his uncles the king's recommendation was obtained for a demyship there; the fellowship successfully ignored it, leaving him to find a place at the socially less desirable Magdalen Hall, where he matriculated in 1623. The early death of his elder brother caused the abandonment of the plan to go into the church. Edward completed his Oxford degree, and in Michaelmas term 1626 he embarked on a legal training at the Middle Temple, although a serious illness late in the year delayed its beginning in earnest. Not that he was as yet deeply committed to it: his memoir confesses to an interest in soldiery generated by the preparations in 1627 for the expedition to the Île de Ré, as well as an exposure to 'signal debauchery'. His continuance at the law may have owed much to the encouragement of his younger uncle, Sir Nicholas Hyde, lord chief justice of king's bench. A second illness—smallpox—struck Edward in July 1628; on his recovery he seems to have become more set on his legal career. He made the acquaintance of John Selden, the most significant legal mind of the day, and of Selden's intellectual heir, John Vaughan, and spent much time

Edward Hyde, first earl of Clarendon (1609–1674), after Adriaen Hanneman, *c.*1648–55

with other pious and studious Middle Templars—Bulstrode Whitelocke, Geoffrey Palmer, and Harbottle Grimston. Yet even though, as the lord chief justice told his father in November 1629, he 'studieth hard and is very orderly and frugal' (G. Davies, 'The date of Clarendon's first marriage', *EngHR*, 32, 1917, 407), preparation for legal practice still occupied only a part of Hyde's mind. His interests in 'polite learning and history', particularly Roman history (*Life*, 1.8–9), helped him to become involved in the circles of London intellectuals more or less closely attached to the inns of court, especially those around Ben Jonson.

The death of Hyde's principal patron, the lord chief justice, in August 1631 left him with considerably reduced prospects of a successful legal practice. But he found a replacement for his uncle's influence in his marriage, on 4 February 1632, to Anne (*d.* 1632), daughter of Sir George Ayliffe of Grittenham, Wiltshire. The marriage was one of strong mutual affection, although the bride's mother, Anna, was a child of John St John, of Lydiard Tregoze in the same county, and brought Hyde a train of connections not only with Wiltshire gentry, but also with the Villiers family: another of the St John daughters had married Sir Edward Villiers, the half-brother of the duke of Buckingham. Hyde appears to have celebrated the connection with his essay countering an argument of Sir Henry Wotton about the similar trajectories of the careers of the earls of Essex and Buckingham, a piece which brought him to the favourable notice of the king. The association was more immediately valuable in providing a group of wealthy and prominent potential clients. All this was jeopardized by Anne's death in July. Hyde's grief—as with subsequent bereavements—was profound: an intention to go abroad 'to enjoy his own melancholy' was only prevented by what appears to have been his father's opposition (*Life*, 1.12). His relationship with the St John and Villiers families survived, though, and assisted him to make some impact at court through managing the Villiers interest in 1633 in the delicate matter of the affair of the daughter of Sir Edward Villiers, Eleanor, with Henry Jermyn, the queen's secretary. The affair:

> accidentally introduced him into another way of conversation than he had formerly been accustomed to, and which in truth by the acquaintance, by the friends and enemies he then made, had an influence upon the whole course of his life afterwards.   (*Life*, 1.13)

Jermyn himself was probably the enemy he meant.

Hyde was called to the bar on 22 November 1633. Already relatively well known in court circles as well as in legal ones, he was selected along with Bulstrode Whitelocke to represent the Middle Temple on a committee established by the inns of court to prepare a masque in response to the assault on court culture made by William Prynne in his *Histrio-Mastix*. The *Triumph of Peace* was performed on 3 February 1634. Bringing together Hyde's literary, legal, and court concerns, his involvement attracted valuable attention. Whitelocke reported the great condescension shown him and Hyde by the lord chamberlain, the earl of Pembroke, and both men were among those who attended the king and queen concerning the performance. Hyde, oddly, failed to mention it in his own *Life*, perhaps because it seemed to contradict his account of the increasingly serious tenor of his activity after 1630.

By the time he had become utter-barrister Hyde had probably known Lucius Cary, Viscount Falkland, for about three years. Their friendship, commemorated famously by Hyde in the *History* and in the *Life*, is likely to have arisen in the circle of Ben Jonson. It may have begun about 1630, after Cary's retirement to the estate of his maternal grandfather at Great Tew. The open personality and intellectual sophistication of Cary (who became Viscount Falkland on the death of his father in 1633) profoundly affected Hyde, as they did others; but Falkland's practice of keeping open house for a combination of London intellectuals and Oxford divines made for an extraordinarily stimulating atmosphere which suited Hyde enormously—'one continued *convivium philosophicum*, or *convivium theologicum*, enlivened and refreshed with all the facetiousness of wit, and good humour, and pleasantness of discourse' (*Life*, 1.39). Among the regulars, apart from Hyde himself, were William Chillingworth, John Hales, Gilbert Sheldon, and George Morley; although there were also many visitors who were more concerned with secular and polite learning, the presence of these divines and Falkland's own interests ensured that the *convivium* concerned itself more with the relationship between the Roman and protestant churches than with anything else. Spurred by Falkland's reading in Plato, it also became much engaged with the place of authority and reason in religion. The atmosphere was pietistic but rationalist, and strongly influenced by the Roman, stoical moralism of Jonson. Richard Hooker, too, was a powerful influence on those who frequented Falkland's house, and especially on Hyde, who folded Hooker's defence of religious ceremony and the foundation of the church in human law into his own thought.

Hyde's second marriage, on 10 July 1634, was to Frances (*d*. 1667), daughter of Sir Thomas Aylesbury, the master of the mint and a master of requests. It may have been—like his first—an astute professional move, yet it seems, also like his first, to have been founded on genuine affection. Children were born in 1637, 1638, and 1640. The death of Hyde's father in Salisbury in September 1634 marked out the year as a clear break with the past. Hyde 'grew every day more intent on business and more engaged in practice, so that he could not assign so much time as he had used to do to his beloved conversation' (*Life*, 1.56). What little evidence of his practice that there is suggests one typically dependent on fees from friends and relatives—St Johns and Mompessons—but Hyde made much of the advantages that came his way: after a meeting with Archbishop Laud in 1635 or 1636 concerning a petition he had drawn up for clients, Laud 'desired his service in many occasions, and particularly in the raising monies for the building of St Paul's Church' (ibid., 1.25). Hyde's association with Laud flourished, and he became close enough to the archbishop to attempt to mediate in his long-standing disputes with the earls of Hertford and Essex.

The Short and Long parliaments Although involved with the court and government ministers in the late 1630s, Hyde claimed to have kept his distance, and 'as he had those many friends in court, so he was not less acceptable to many great persons in the country, who least regarded the court, and were least esteemed by it' (*Life*, 1.57). In his *History* he recalled a period of unusual prosperity and peace: 'this kingdom, and all his majesty's dominions, … enjoyed the greatest calm and the fullest measure of felicity that any people in any age for so long time together have been blessed with' (Clarendon, *Hist. rebellion*, 1.93). Hyde may have supported Laud's political or religious projects in the late 1630s, although certainly by the late 1640s he had recognized their political inexpediency. What did trouble him in the late years of the personal rule was what he saw as attempts by the government to abuse the law for political purposes, and the connivance of the judges at the abuse. For him, as for many other common lawyers, the judicial decision (especially that of Lord Finch) in the ship-money case was of particularly worrying significance. Ship money was tolerable when demanded as a response to an emergency; but when claimed as a prerogative right of the crown, and when it was:

> by sworn judges of the law adjudged so, upon such grounds and reasons as every stander-by was able to swear was not law … and by a logic that left no man any thing which he might call his own   (ibid., 1.87)

it became in effect the abnegation of law. For Hyde the ship-money judgment and its aftermath demonstrated the centrality of law and the certainty of legal rules and process to the achievement of political stability, an insight which would be fundamental to his approach not just to the crisis of 1640–42 but throughout his career.

Looking back on it from the other side of the civil war, Hyde regarded the Short Parliament of April–May 1640 as a tragically wasted opportunity for undoing the damage caused by the policies of the end of the personal rule. He owed his election at Wootton Bassett in Wiltshire to the St John family. Appointments to committees suggest his associations with prominent critics of the regime such as Robert Holborne and Oliver St John (John Hampden's counsel in the ship-money case), Sir Walter Earle, and John Pym, and Hyde made something of a speciality out of cataloguing the abuses of the prerogative courts: his first speech, condemning proceedings in the earl marshal's court, was widely reported. Hyde's co-operation with the government's critics, though, was tempered by a commitment to the search for an accommodation with the court. He visited Laud in the hope of preventing a dissolution; and he distanced himself from the beginnings of the parliamentary assault on the Laudian regime in the church, defending Laudian altar policy at a conference with the Lords at the end of April. In the long debate on supply on 2–4 May Hyde supported the government's offer to abandon ship money in exchange for twelve subsidies. In hindsight, he saw the dissolution which followed its failure as having been part of the scheme designed by Pym and others: St John, he wrote, had assured him that 'all was well: and that it must be worse before it could be better; and that this Parliament would never have done what was necessary to be done' (Clarendon, *Hist. rebellion*, 1.183).

At the summons of the second parliament of 1640 Hyde found a seat at Saltash in Cornwall. His failure to be elected in Wiltshire may indicate the truth of his claim that some efforts were made to prevent or overturn his election because he was regarded 'as a man they knew well to have great affection for the archbishop, and of unalterable devotion to the government of the Church' (*Life*, 1.70). Once securely there, however, he was wooed by the principal opponents of the regime, and continued his attacks on the prerogative courts and the judiciary. He chaired committees on the earl marshal's and the two regional courts; and—with Falkland and Sir John Colepeper, as well as with his Middle Temple associates Palmer and Whitelocke—he took a leading role in the inquisition of the judges and their judgments in the ship-money case. Yet Hyde's collaboration with the parliamentary leadership was strained by the attempt by the Scots and their city allies to push forward the abolition of episcopacy. In a debate on 10 March 1641 Hyde opposed a demand for the removal of the right of the bishops to sit and vote in the House of Lords—something which, he said, was 'changing the whole frame and constitution of the kingdom, and of the Parliament itself'—only to be taken aback by the willingness of Falkland and Colepeper to accept it in the hope that it would satisfy anti-episcopal sentiment (Clarendon, *Hist. rebellion*, 1.311). Despite his worries about the aims of the parliamentary leadership, his failure—along with Falkland, Colepeper, and Palmer—to oppose

the impeachment or the attainder of the earl of Strafford testifies to a still lively impression of the excess of power, injustice, and oppression of government in the 1630s.

The Lords' rejection of the bill for exclusion of the bishops and the introduction in May of the root and branch bill for the abolition of episcopacy raised the political stakes. Hyde, chairman of the committee of the whole house considering the bill, delayed progress on it well into the summer while he worked elsewhere to hasten the disbandment of the Scottish and English armies. The acts which received royal assent shortly before the king left for Scotland in August included reforms of royal prerogative jurisdiction which Hyde regarded as a sufficient, perhaps even over-generous, response by the king to the abuses of the 1630s. By about the summer of 1641 he, Falkland, and Colepeper had become the nucleus of a group working informally to secure a full settlement of the political crisis. During the autumn their energies and those of what the diarist Simonds D'Ewes now referred to as the 'episcopal party' (*Journal*, ed. Coates, 150) were channelled into resisting increasingly strident demands for religious and political reform. In November, Hyde's demand to enter a protestation in the journal against the grand remonstrance, seconded by Palmer, helped to provoke serious disorder in the house which came close to violence.

In an attempt to build on moderate conservative support the king appointed Colepeper and Falkland as respectively chancellor of the exchequer and secretary of state on 1 January 1642; Hyde refused the post of solicitor-general on the grounds that it would cause unnecessary offence to the current incumbent, St John, but he agreed to continue to co-operate with Colepeper and Falkland in the Commons, and to allow his draft of a pamphlet against the remonstrance to be adopted—as *His Majestie's Declaration, to All His Loving Subjects*—as an official response to it. The *Declaration*'s themes—a powerful commitment to the Church of England tempered by an offer not to enforce ceremony where it involved matters indifferent, and an insistence on the king's determination to stand by the law—established themselves as the constant themes of Hyde's, and much other royalist, polemic.

Three days after the new appointments Charles disastrously attempted to arrest Pym, Hampden, Holles, Strode, Mandeville, and Hesilrige in the House of Commons—an action which Hyde attributed, in part at least, to one of his friends and allies among the defenders of episcopacy, Lord Digby. Hyde, Colepeper, and Falkland were caught 'between grief and anger that the violent party had by these late unskilful actions of the Court gotten great advantage and recovered new spirits' (Clarendon, *Hist. rebellion*, 1.487). The three may have offered to resign, but warily accepting the king's renewed assurances that he would make no step in parliament without their advice, they agreed to continue to co-ordinate the government's activities in the house. But the court had largely lost any prospect of influencing proceedings in the Commons, and at the beginning of February, under the pressure of popular disturbances in London, serious opposition to parliamentary control of the militia collapsed in the Lords. The king made a string of concessions including giving his assent to the bill for the exclusion of the bishops from the Lords. Its acceptance split the triumvirate. Colepeper, and possibly Falkland, advised it. For Hyde, it destroyed any confidence that the king would resist unacceptable compromise. Many, he wrote:

> never after retained any confidence that he would deny what was importunately asked; and so, either absolutely withdrew themselves from those consultations, thereby avoiding the envy and the danger of opposing them, or quietly suffered themselves to be carried by the stream, and consent to any thing that was boldly and lustily attempted.   (ibid., 568)

Even so Hyde believed that the king accepted it only in order to secure the queen's safe passage to France. Having seen her off at Dover on 23 February and, with some assistance from Hyde himself, secured custody of his eldest son, the king planned to leave London. In a series of interviews with the king over the weekend of 25–27 February Hyde agreed to remain at Westminster, and to take on the draftsmanship of statements of royal policy. The first of a long series of royal declarations drafted by Hyde was issued by the king from Huntingdon on 15 March, as a response to the militia ordinance. It, and its successors, rehearsed the themes of the earlier declaration: the king's determination to adhere to the law, and parliament's failure to do the same.

Hyde's position in London was risky, particularly after the king's failure to gain admission to Hull; he was widely suspected of having a role in the composition of royal propaganda. He remained long enough to participate in the rapid exchange of votes and declarations following the events before Hull, and to assist in the delicate task of ensuring the removal of the lord keeper, Lord Littleton, with the great seal, to the king. He probably left very soon after the agreement by both houses in their declaration of 19 May. On his way to York to join the king he composed answers to it, and to a further declaration of 26 May.

The two answers were possibly Hyde's most sustained and most accomplished pieces of polemic. In them he developed his analysis of the arbitrary nature of parliamentary rule much further than before, underlining the threat it posed to the security of property. 'If the major part of both Houses declare that the law is, That the younger brother shall inherit, what is become of all the families and estates in the kingdom?' (Clarendon, *Hist. rebellion*, 2.145). The parliamentary leadership was a:

> faction of malignant, schismatical, and ambitious persons; whose design was, and always had been, to alter the whole frame of government, both of Church and State, and to subject both King and people to their own lawless, arbitrary power and government.   (ibid., 2.149)

In a particularly influential passage Hyde summed up in seven points what he claimed were the parliamentary doctrines, among them, '*That no precedents can be limits to bound their proceedings. So they may do what they please*'; and that 'they may depose his majesty when they will, and are not to be blamed for so doing' (ibid., 2.163–4). As a result he found himself on the parliamentary blacklist as one of the 'authors of a civil war' (ibid., 2.240). Hyde's own view of royalist strategy was that the king should take no further aggressive steps which would—like the attempted arrest of the five members—only help to draw the uneasy coalition of different interests at Westminster closer together. He, though, was still marginal to royal counsels, and was not the only publicist used by the king, for an answer to parliament's nineteen propositions was drafted not by him, but by his associates Falkland and Colepeper. Its acceptance that the king was one of the three estates not only ousted the bishops from their status as an indispensable part of the constitution—on which Hyde and they had previously differed—but also reduced the king from a position of lofty superiority to that of a participant in a political struggle.

Hyde arrived in York about 4 or 5 June 1642. Unlike Colepeper and Falkland he was not a councillor, and was not involved in the official decision-making machinery of the court. But the king valued his advice, and employed him in several projects aimed at attracting support. By now his views were hardening. He reported it as the 'general, received doctrine' at court in July and August that parliament would not take the argument so far as fighting; but that even if it did, the first of the parties which made preparations for civil war would find its support ebbing away. Hyde indicated some impatience with this view and the idea 'that the softest and gentlest remedies might be most wholesomely applied to these rough and violent diseases' (Clarendon, *Hist. rebellion*, 2.250, 288).

The civil war Hyde went with the king to Nottingham, where he witnessed the 'melancholic' scene of the raising of the standard, and accompanied him as he trawled through Derbyshire, Staffordshire, and Shropshire looking for troops. He was present at Edgehill, though not as a combatant—he was given the role of looking after the two princes. In Oxford during the autumn and winter Hyde was effectively acting as under-secretary of state to Falkland.

In late February 1643 the king knighted Hyde and appointed him to the privy council; shortly afterwards he was made chancellor of the exchequer. The preferment was a token of the king's appreciation of Hyde's ability and constitutional views (he had recently told the queen that he would appoint him to the secretaryship 'for the truth is I can trust nobody else'; *DNB*); but it was probably also connected to the contacts between the parliamentary peace party and Oxford in February. Despite his belief in the autumn of the need for firm action, once war had been joined Hyde became closely associated with a political, rather than military, solution, but his approach to achieving it was not to offer compromises on central prerogatives or the church, but to chip away at parliament's support. When commissioners from London (including Bulstrode Whitelocke) arrived in Oxford at the end of March, Hyde and Falkland were closely involved in the negotiations for a ceasefire, but his main purpose seems to have been to detach individual moderates from the parliamentary party. By the middle of April the treaty negotiations had been abandoned, with Hyde blaming the unwillingness of parliament to provide a realistic basis for discussions. His own side's real interest in negotiations was in fact strictly limited, and the influence of the privy council on royalist policy small: the 'soldiers did all they could to lessen the reverence that was due to them, thinking themselves the best judges of all counsels and designs, because they were for the most part to execute them' (Clarendon, *Hist. rebellion*, 2.537). The king may have appreciated Hyde's opposition to the concession of prerogative powers, but he was less enthusiastic about his commitment to a peaceful conclusion of the war; Hyde interpreted his decision to remove command of the army from the marquess of Hertford and give it to Prince Maurice as an indication that he believed 'that he should sooner reduce his people by the power of his army than by the persuasions of his Council, and that the roughness of the one's nature might prevail more than the lenity and condescension of the other' (ibid., 3.128).

The death of Falkland—'the joy and comfort of his life'—at the battle of Newbury on 20 September 1643 left Hyde as grief-stricken as he had been at the loss of his first wife. The secretaryship was filled by Lord Digby but if anything Falkland's death increased Hyde's involvement in royal policy-making. He was now one of a junto—the effective part of the council—including the duke of Richmond, Lord Cottington, Digby and the other secretary, Sir Edward Nicholas, and Sir John Colepeper, 'where all matters were to be consulted before they should be brought to the council-board' (*Life*, 1.177).

Yet the court's failure to provide Bedford and Holland, the defectors from the parliamentary cause in August, with a more enthusiastic welcome showed how little support there was in the royalist camp for Hyde's strategy of reuniting the moderate parliamentary élite. His proposal for a gathering at Oxford of those who had seceded from the parliament in London was partly designed to efface the impression that further migrations would be coldly received, as well as to demonstrate that those who remained at Westminster were merely 'a handful of desperate persons, who, by the help of the tumults raised in the city of London, had driven away the major part of the Parliament' (Clarendon, *Hist. rebellion*, 259–60). What Hyde described (probably with some exaggeration) as almost 300 members of the Commons and more than sixty peers met at Oxford between January and April 1644 and October 1644 and March 1645. Hyde and Colepeper acted as parliamentary managers. Hyde was, though, unwilling to claim for it the title of parliament and provide a propaganda coup for Westminster, and the king was unhappy with the pressure to negotiate which it created: beyond unsuccessful approaches to the earl of Essex and some political cover for raising money, the assembly made little impact.

Nevertheless, Hyde regarded other strategies—such as Prince Rupert's determination to tackle the combined parliamentarian and Scottish army outside York, or Lord Wilmot's informal approaches to Essex in 1644, offering concessions—as endangering the success of his own attempts to split the parliamentary coalition. During the autumn of 1644 the revival of the old tensions in the parliamentary alliance—between the Scots and the English and presbyterians and sectaries—enabled Hyde to try again to exploit them. In late November parliament sent commissioners with new propositions for peace, and negotiations began at Uxbridge at the end of January 1645. The king's commissioners included Hertford, Richmond, Southampton, Colepeper, Geoffrey Palmer, and Hyde, who seems to have acted as their secretary as well as taking an active part in the proceedings. He was convinced that many of the parliamentary commissioners—who again included Whitelocke—were so keen on a peace that they would have been prepared to settle on 'much honester conditions then they durst own', and he was, for a time, almost willing to go along with a temporary transfer of the militia to commissioners (Clarendon, *Hist. rebellion*, 3.497). But Hyde changed his mind, and there had been in any case little willingness on either side to accept a real compromise, at least on this central issue. In its absence Hyde's main efforts were directed towards exposing disagreements between the Scots and parliamentary commissioners over forms of presbytery. By the second half of February the failure of the treaty was obvious, and both sides parted on the 23rd, exhausted:

> they who had been most inured to business had not in their lives ever undergone so great fatigue for twenty days together as at that treaty; the commissioners seldom parting during that whole time till one or two of the clock in the morning, and they being obliged to sit up long after who were to prepare such papers as were directed for the next day, and to write letters to Oxford.   (ibid., 3.501)

The failure of the Uxbridge treaty further reduced the influence in royal counsels of the advocates of negotiation. The king had already decided to move his elder son, Prince Charles, away from Oxford to the greater safety of the west. In the previous year the king had appointed a council for the prince which included some of those who had been involved in the negotiations—Richmond, Southampton, Colepeper, and Hyde. Now he commanded it to accompany the prince. Richmond and Southampton refused, insisting on remaining with the king. Hyde was deeply reluctant to be removed from court, but complied. On 4 March 1645 he left Oxford with Colepeper and the rest of the prince's entourage. Shortly afterwards the king dismissed the Oxford parliament.

What followed was one of the unhappiest periods of Hyde's career—made worse by the onset of the gout which intermittently cursed him for the rest of his life. The prince's role in the west had been determined only vaguely; the council lacked influence; and the lines of command in the royalist forces in the west were already confused. The fifteen-year-old prince was not close to any of the members of the council. When they arrived in Somerset the council attempted to bring some co-ordination to the activities of generals Lord Goring and Sir Richard Grenville. They succeeded mainly in upsetting both: Hyde's lawyerly attitudes and confidence in his own views came to be especially resented by Goring and Grenville and the rest of the soldiery. After the king's defeat at Naseby on 14 June 1645 the western campaign became in any case merely a holding operation, as Fairfax advanced into Somerset and Devon. At the beginning of July the king commanded that the prince should go to France as soon as his position became dangerous. Hyde went into Cornwall to make contingency plans for a crossing, whenever it should be required; but the council in general, and Hyde in particular, were deeply opposed to the idea of a move into France—into the hands of the Catholic queen and a government which Hyde viewed with intense suspicion—and wrote to the king querying his instructions. After the fall of Bristol on 11 September the question became more urgent still. The council risked outright disobedience in arguing that the prince's going abroad would be 'an argument against his Majesty's sincere intentions'. Instead, they proposed either Jersey or the Scillies—still within the king's dominions.

At the beginning of 1646 the royalist defence in the west fell apart and the council fixed on an escape to the Scillies, arriving on 4 March; but it became clear that the islands were untenable against a determined attack. A parliamentarian fleet appeared before them on 12 April, and taking advantage of its dispersal in a storm the council moved a few days later to Jersey. Jersey was relatively secure, and it seemed possible to remain there for some time, but the queen now insisted that the prince come to France. The question of where to go became linked to wider discussions about royalist strategy and to an offer of mediation by, perhaps even alliance with, France. In June a large delegation, including Colepeper, Digby, Wilmot, and Jermyn, arrived in Jersey and thrashed out the issue in a heated series of meetings from 20 to 22 June. The decision to leave Jersey and go to Paris was taken by the prince himself. Of his council only Colepeper agreed to accompany him, and with the prince's embarkation on 25 June most of the remaining members of the council dispersed, leaving only lords Capel and Hopton and Hyde himself in Jersey. Hyde came to regard the division between those who went and those who remained as marking an almost permanent estrangement between royalist factions.

Jersey and the *History of the Rebellion* Hyde stayed in Jersey for almost two years. Much of it he spent reading and writing. He had begun a *History of the Rebellion* in the Scillies, and by the middle of June he had reached the end of what is now book 3; but after the move to Jersey and the departure of the prince he broke off to compose instead a lengthy vindication of the activities of the prince's council in the west over the previous fifteen months. He returned quite quickly to the *History*, however; by the beginning of October he was up to the arrival of the king in York in March 1642, the present book 5. Writing for three hours a day, he was estimating by November 1646 that the full work 'would exceed what Daniell hath written of twelve kings; to what a Book of Martyrs will the whole volume swell' (*Clarendon State Papers*, 1.341–2). As he began to deal with the war itself, though, the rate of production fell: he needed information from others, which was not always forthcoming, or not as quick to come as

required. By November 1647 he was finding the attempt to extract information from others increasingly frustrating: 'I often wish I had never begun, having found less assistance for it than I thought I should have done, as if all men had a desire the ill should be remembered, and the good forgotten' (Firth, 46).

Hyde nursed considerable literary ambitions for his *History* and in correspondence with friends discussed what models—both Roman and more recent—it might follow. Read now, with parts of his later autobiography spliced into it as they were in 1671–2, it is a much less formal and much more revealing record than it originally was. Though he disclaimed publication in print for the *History*, it was intended to be a very public statement of Hyde's own political beliefs and of the essentials of royalism which might at least circulate privately—'to inform myself and some others what we are to do, as well as to comfort us in what we have done' (Clarendon, *Hist. rebellion*, 1.3). The accounts of misgovernment in the 1630s and of the debates in the Long Parliament and the inclusion of the royalist declarations of 1642 make at least the first few books of the *History* into an argument for and vindication of the carefully balanced form of royalism set out in the declarations. Monarchical rule had to be firmly founded in law; concessions to parliamentary pressure might upset the fine balance of a constitution which had already been damaged by the government's failure to recognize the importance of those legal foundations in the past. The existing church government had to be defended as part of that constitution and legal foundation. Hyde intended to make a long digression, as book 5, on the theory and practice of the constitution, covering:

> the just regal power of the King of England, and of his negative voice, of the militia, and of the great seal by the laws of England, of the original, at least of the antiquity and constitution of parliaments, of their jurisdiction and privileges, of the power of the House of Peers by the law, and of the natural limits and extent of the Commons.
> (Firth, 39)

But the little treatise on constitutional law never emerged, perhaps because of the unavailability of the sources he needed.

Hyde had removed himself from royalist counsels but he remained closely in touch with sympathetic figures in what passed for the royal court—Sir Edward Nicholas, Lord Digby, and Sir John Berkeley among others—and to these friends provided a commentary on aspects of royalist policy and events in England. He continued to argue against an alliance with France; he objected to the view that the king should negotiate on the basis of the Scots' Newcastle propositions; and he harangued friends to persuade them against taking the covenant and compounding. The experience of defeat may have made him engage more deeply than he had since Great Tew in the 1630s with ecclesiastical issues. He wrote against sacrilege, concerned both by the possibility that the king might accept damaging concessions on the church and by parliament's first radical move against the church (the ordinance of

October 1646 appropriating church lands), and he was disgusted by the attitude of the continental reformed churches to the difficulties of the Church of England.

Despite this, Hyde's period in Jersey was one of almost blissful distance from the struggles and frustrations of the previous few years. He 'enjoyed … the greatest tranquillity of mind imaginable' (*Life*, 1.205); he moved into Castle Elizabeth, and had painted over his door a line from Ovid, 'Bene vixit, qui bene latuit' ('He has lived well, who has led a quiet life'). Yet he doubted that he could stay for ever; the departure of Capel, then Hopton by early March, deprived him of company; and even in January he was feeling that his stay might be self-indulgent. He doubted whether he would be happily received back as a royal counsellor, especially by the queen. But as the unity of parliament disintegrated in 1647, the possibility opened up of encouraging and exploiting divisions inside the enemy camp. Although Hyde was extremely concerned by the king's negotiations with the Scots, and believed that he had conceded too much in the treaty and engagement that followed, he nevertheless returned to polemic in January 1648 to gnaw at the worries of moderates in England about the vote of no addresses. His short attack on parliament's account of the failure of negotiations with the king, *An Answer to a Pamphlet, Entitled a Declaration of the Commons of England*, was circulating in London in May; a lengthier version, *A Full Answer to an Infamous and Traiterous Pamphlet*, was published in July.

The Hague and the embassy to Madrid, 1648–1651 The crisis initiated by the vote of no addresses, and the preparations for a royalist rising and a Scottish invasion of England in the summer, finally brought Hyde back into royal counsels. At the beginning of June 1648, a command was sent from Paris to a number of councillors to gather at Paris: Hyde dropped the *History of the Rebellion* and scrambled to comply, but it was more than two months after he left Jersey on 26 June before he could catch up with the court. He found Nicholas, Lord Cottington, and the earl of Bristol at Rouen, where they discovered that Prince Charles had left the queen at St Germain to rendezvous with the mutinied parliamentarian fleet. With Cottington he chased the prince as far as Dunkirk only to find him gone; he took another ship at Dunkirk but it was captured, and they were robbed, by pirates. Not until 17 September did they finally find Charles at The Hague.

By then the rebellions in England had clearly failed, and information was reaching the Netherlands of the disastrous defeat of the Scots, just as the earl of Lauderdale arrived to attempt to persuade Charles to come to Scotland. Hyde's distaste for court politics, learned at Oxford, was quickly reawakened. The court, in his sketch of it, was riven by recriminations for the collapse of the counter-revolution: Colepeper and Robert Long, the prince's secretary, were blamed for the ill-starred Scottish alliance. Hyde lent his weight to those opposing the alliance, making as his first contribution to a council meeting for over two years a typically offensive and punctilious demand for Lauderdale to withdraw as they discussed the terms he offered. It soon became apparent that the Scots were now

in no position to offer an alliance anyway. But the opening of new negotiations between the king and parliamentary commissioners at the Isle of Wight in September meant that the possibility of unwelcome concessions both on the church and the constitution continued to exist. Hyde was deeply opposed to the proposals discussed at the treaty of Newport and to the king's offer to suspend episcopacy for three years and to confer military power on parliament for twenty; but he recognized the enormous pressure on both the king and the parliamentary moderates to secure an agreement, and copied into the *History* the apology for the terms which the king sent to The Hague: 'Censure us not for having parted with so much of our own right; the price is great, but the commodity was security to us, peace to our people' (Clarendon, *Hist. rebellion*, 4.454). The council at The Hague could only look on at the negotiations, and then, with increasing horror, at the army's coup on 1–6 December, the trial of the king, and his execution on 30 January 1649.

However great the international revulsion at the killing of Charles I, his eighteen-year-old successor found it extraordinarily difficult to translate this into support for his cause. The best hopes for royalist recovery remained either for the marquess of Ormond to defeat parliament in Ireland, or for an alliance with the kirk party in Scotland (which, although it had been opposed to the 1648 invasion, had now proclaimed Charles II, and sent him messages of support). Hyde was keen to undermine any undertaking with the kirk party—the scheme backed by the queen and Colepeper—as much as he could. And although his attempts to forge a coalition between its enemies, Montrose and the engagers of 1648, were doomed to failure, Montrose's presence at The Hague when commissioners arrived from the kirk party to consider the basis of co-operation with the king severely reduced the (already small) likelihood of its happening. Hyde also opposed concessions designed to attract domestic presbyterian support: he resisted the prince of Orange's suggestion that the continental protestant churches be included in any proposed synod to consider the religious question. By the end of May hopes of an alliance with the Scots were abandoned. On 29 May it was resolved that the king should sail to Ireland to join Ormond. Hyde did not go with him. Instead he allowed himself to be persuaded by Lord Cottington to accompany him on a mission to Spain, to raise support for the cause there. Hyde's dislike of the court had a great deal to do with his decision to leave: he:

> did believe that he should in some degree improve his understanding, and very much refresh his spirits, … by his absence from being continually conversant with those wants which could never be severed from that court, and that company which would always be corrupted by those wants. (Clarendon, *Hist. rebellion*, 5.37)

Hyde and Cottington left The Hague at the very beginning of June 1649, going via Antwerp (where Hyde saw his wife and children for the first time since leaving Oxford), Brussels, Paris, and St Germain. An interview with the queen at St Germain helped to dampen the queen's hostility, and it may have been as a result of this meeting that Hyde drafted a memorandum on royalist strategy. It considered the likelihood of an alliance with either of the English republic's principal internal enemies—the presbyterians or the Levellers. It suggested a line to take with either group, accepting their lack of involvement in the king's death, and rejecting the idea of reconquest with foreign assistance. He insisted that there should be no acceptance of the solemn league and covenant and no agreement to change the law except in a full and free parliament, and that church government should be debated in a parliament to be called by the king's writ. The key was for the king to be resolute on these conditions: 'if they shall once believe him fixed and resolved upon his owne grounds (which can only restore him and preserve him being restored) they will entirely cast themselves at his Majesty's feet and be of his parties' (Warner, 1.147).

By the time Hyde and Cottington arrived at St Germain the Irish expedition had been abandoned because of the success of the Commonwealth's armies against Ormond. The plans for the Spanish embassy held, however, and they left on 29 September for Bordeaux. Passing through the battle lines of the Fronde, they finally arrived in Madrid on 26 November. Hyde was much struck with Spain, noting the cruelty of the bullfights and the modesty of the women, but the prospects of securing any more than moral support from Philip IV were negligible. With the parlous state of Spanish royal finances, the king's promise to obtain Catholic help may have been the most he could do.

Hyde was isolated from affairs elsewhere, and was seriously under-employed. He knew little about the beleaguered state of Ormond in Ireland, or the decision of an expanded council in January 1650 to reopen discussions with the Scots. When he found out, in the middle of March, he was appalled, and he was even more concerned when the king actually went to Scotland, although the king's possession of a kingdom and an army enhanced the prestige of his own embassy. Hyde's and Cottington's situation was complicated, though, by the murder in Madrid of the republic's agent, Anthony Ascham, by a group of royalist thugs in June; after the defeat of the king and the Scots at Dunbar in September they were given broad hints that they should go. By the beginning of December the advice had become explicit. Cottington decided to remain, privately, in Spain; Hyde left in March 1651, uncertain of his ultimate destination.

Paris, 1651–1654 Hyde's return journey through France was plagued with gout and sickness. With privileges granted by the king of Spain he was allowed to settle in Antwerp, with the character of ambassador. Permitted his own chapel, he became the resort of the English community in the town. How he financed himself and his family—and the acquisition of a growing library—is not at all clear, but he discussed and continued vigorously to resist a return to England in exchange for composition. It is possible that he (like a number of other royalists) wavered in that resistance in the nervous weeks between the king's

defeat at Worcester and the confirmation in late October of his survival and escape. When Charles at last reached Paris he summoned Hyde to join him. Having left his wife and children at Breda in the hands of the princess of Orange, Hyde travelled painfully back to Paris, arriving by 30 December. He found himself one of the most senior political figures there, the only member, so he noted, of the king's original privy council in Paris. As a long discussion with the king shortly after his arrival indicated, he was one of the few whom the king was now prepared to trust. Another was Ormond, who had been forced to abandon Ireland, and with whom Hyde now formed a close political alliance and personal friendship. There could be little unity in royal policy-making, however, while the court remained in Paris. The queen was determined to be involved in decisions—often through Hyde's old adversary, Jermyn. An added complication was the duke of York's determination to assert his independence of his brother and the council. A skeleton council was formed with Hyde, Ormond, Jermyn, and Lord Wilmot, the king's companion during the escape from Worcester. Others slowly drifted back or were added, including Lord Digby in March 1652.

The reconstituted court spent more of its energy on power struggles than on efforts to regain the throne. God's intention, Hyde commented in some distraction, must be:

> either to make us worthy of that destruction He hath assigned us, or, if He intends to preserve us, that we may have no pretence to virtue of our own that might bear a part in our recovery, but that we may owe all intirely to the miracle of His mercy.   (*Clarendon State Papers*, 2.218)

Sir Robert Long, the new secretary of state, appears to have fallen foul of the queen, and was turned out of the court early in 1652 after a lengthy investigation of allegations of treason made against him, in which Hyde—perhaps seeking to retain the queen's favour—was heavily involved. Hyde was left again performing the role of secretary. His long-standing friendship with Sir John Berkeley, the duke of York's old governor, was wrecked over a combination of political and personal disagreements. He fell out with other long-standing councillors as well, including Sir Edward Herbert, the attorney-general. Part of the court's trouble stemmed from the lack of money and of any obvious strategy for political recovery. The queen's pension from France was its only reasonably reliable source of income; a few months after his return from England, the king managed to obtain his own separate grant, although its payment was no more than sporadic because of the instability of the French government. Hyde's insistence that the king refuse to satisfy demands for provisional grants of office or land in England in lieu of more valuable reimbursement for their services made him increasingly unpopular among the king's servants.

While many schemes existed for risings in England, Scotland, and Ireland, few of them appeared to have much chance of success. A project for royalist resistance in Scotland under the command of John Middleton and the earl of Glencairn was developed slowly in 1652–3, and the court conducted long-drawn-out negotiations with the duke of Lorraine in the hope of persuading him to finance and fit out an expedition to Ireland. Hyde, though, doubted the value of armed intervention. He and Ormond, he wrote, believed:

> that the King had nothing at this time to do but to be quiet, and that all his activity was to consist in carefully avoiding to do any thing that might do him hurt, and to expect some blessed conjuncture from the unity of Christian princes, or some such revolution of affairs in England by their own discontents and divisions amongst themselves, as might make it seasonable for his majesty again to shew himself. (Clarendon, *Hist. rebellion*, 5.240)

It was in effect an extension of the strategy which Hyde had favoured during the war years, and it was far from simple to follow. Hyde's attempts to avoid actions which he thought would harm the prospects of a Restoration required him to upset a good many other parties. He objected to the proposal for the king's participation in the services of the French protestant church at Charenton (intended to attract presbyterian support). It would be taken, he argued, to mean either that the king had abandoned hope of the revival of the Church of England, or else that he thought that the differences between it and the French church were indifferent—something which would threaten the status of the bishops in the English church. Likewise, Hyde opposed steps to the marriage of either the duke of York or the king himself: he and Ormond 'besought him to set his heart entirely on the recovery of England, and to indulge to nothing that might reasonably obstruct that, either by making him less intent upon it, or by creating new difficulties in the pursuing it' (ibid., 5.250).

Attempts to create a united front against the republic among Christian princes found little success. When a breach in relations between the republic and the Dutch appeared likely in the summer of 1652, Hyde devoted considerable time and effort to discussions with Boreel, the Orangist Dutch ambassador in Paris, about how to turn the likely war to the advantage of the Orange faction in the Netherlands and the royalists in England. By late August royalist hopes were growing of creating a grand coalition of continental powers against England, drawing in the French, the Swedes, and the Danes. But the Dutch responded with extreme caution to offers of a royalist naval squadron or even royalist privateering, and by the end of the year, when France sent an ambassador to England, the court recognized that the coalition scheme was unlikely ever to become a reality. France's courting of the republic made the search for alternative support imperative: the republic was bound to demand the expulsion of the king as a price of an alliance. Wilmot, now earl of Rochester, left in December to attend the imperial diet at Ratisbon in the hope of obtaining financial backing, and an embassy was prepared to go to Rome in March 1653—but Hyde had little more expectation of the latter than that it should encourage Irish support, and the idea was dropped (according to Hyde, because of difficulties with the queen over the choice of ambassadors).

The promotion of domestic dissent within England proved still more difficult to achieve, even after the dismissal of the Rump Parliament by Cromwell in April 1653. Setting up a network of those prepared to accept instructions from Paris was regarded as the best means of co-ordination and preventing poorly prepared and amateurish swipes at the regime. Early in 1654 the most promising attempt to do so—the Sealed Knot—was handled by Hyde and Ormond. But it was severely affected by a disorganized plot to assassinate Cromwell in June, and all royalist conspiracy was disturbed by the divisions within the court in Paris. Hyde wanted to discourage such efforts: he wrote of 'the vanity of imagining that any insurrection could give any trouble to so well formed and disciplined army, and the destruction that must attend such a rash and uncounsellable attempt' (Clarendon, *Hist. rebellion*, 5.347–8). The best that could be hoped for was to wait for either the death of Cromwell or a schism in the army to weaken its hold over England. The worst would be Cromwell's assumption of the title of king, and his more secure establishment in power.

Royalist options were narrowing sharply as negotiations continued between France and Cromwell during 1654, until the news which arrived in April of Rochester's success in obtaining promises of cash. Hyde began to talk, with much relief, of moving to Germany. By mid-1653 the strain of Paris politics had begun to tell on him: he was weary of trying to get the pleasure-loving king to concentrate on business, while resentment at his influence with the king, and his forthright views on the opinions or value of others, made him deeply loathed by a wide variety of enemies. Early in 1653 bands of Scots presbyterians and Catholics at court, apparently with the support of the queen, requested his removal; towards the middle of the year Jermyn and Sir Edward Herbert planned an attack on his influence by means of an attempt to restore Sir Robert Long to favour and his place as secretary. The king accepted the queen's request that Herbert be made lord keeper in April; by July Herbert and Jermyn were putting together a treason charge against Hyde. The charge backfired, ending in a full hearing in council and a vindication of Hyde by the king on 14 January 1654. Yet as long as he stayed in Paris, Hyde seems to have felt threatened, and the atmosphere remained poisonous.

From June 1654 a move to Germany had become possible, and essential, as the Anglo-French negotiations progressed. The queen remained in Paris along with a number of Hyde's more bitter opponents, including Herbert, allowing a respite from the bitter conflicts of the past few years. Also remaining with her, however, was her youngest son, the fourteen-year-old duke of Gloucester, whom the king allowed to stay as a result of her pleading, despite a well-founded suspicion that she planned to have him received into the Roman church. On 10 July the royal household finally made its way out of Paris, thankful to be leaving but conscious that it was leaving for a far more uncertain future than ever before. Hyde wrote that 'the King is as low now as to human understanding he can be' (*Clarendon State Papers*, 2.381).

Germany, Flanders, and the Spanish alliance, 1654–1658 Hyde took the opportunity, as the court moved first to Aachen, to visit his family at Breda, but had rejoined it by the time it moved on to Cologne at the end of September. Despite difficulties about securing the money pledged at Ratisbon, residence at Cologne vastly improved the temper of king, court, and Hyde himself, with just enough diversions—such as the passage through the town of the abdicated Queen Kristina, who impressed Hyde enormously—to keep it amused without diverting it from what Hyde saw as the task in hand. Yet Paris could not be escaped. At the end of October the king heard at Cologne that as had been feared the queen had begun a campaign to make his young brother change his religion, packing off his tutor and sending the duke to stay with her confessor, the Abbé Montagu. Ormond efficiently sorted out the exceptionally delicate situation, but the incident considerably reduced the prospect of securing financial help from the pope, despite a promising approach via the duke of Newburg.

The court's main problem, however, was to keep some control over the varied schemes of royalist insurgency being hatched across the channel. Hyde's view—at least retrospectively—was that most of these were wildly impractical, but that to try to prevent them would be to kill off royalist conspiracy altogether. Worst of all was the mutual jealousy that existed among the various groups: 'everybody chose their own knot with whom they would converse, and would not communicate with anybody else' (Clarendon, *Hist. rebellion*, 5.368–9). From time to time Hyde did have some hopes of a reasonably successful rising, and the winter of 1654–5 was occupied with planning for one early in the new year. But with little understanding of the true disposition of forces in England the king could not co-ordinate or lead it, nor take decisions about whether or not it should go ahead. It was regularly postponed. At last, in February 1655, the king, accompanied by Ormond, left Cologne for the coast, and was followed a little later by Hyde. The rising in late March proved a messy failure: only in Wiltshire did it result in a significant public-order problem for the army, and even that was over by the 25th (NS). Hyde (whose return from Breda was delayed by illness) was widely blamed in royalist circles for the mess.

By the summer, however, hopes of external assistance rose as news arrived in August of Cromwell's aggression against Spanish colonies in the West Indies. When the Anglo-French treaty was signed at the beginning of November (NS), preparations were already being made for the renewal of hostilities between Spain and allied forces in Flanders. The king and Hyde fired off letters to the Spanish ministers in Madrid and Brussels offering co-operation. The Spanish were highly reluctant to commit themselves, but by February 1656 they had agreed to let the king, accompanied by Ormond, come to Flanders; Hyde, apparently at Spanish insistence, remained at Cologne. In April the king agreed with the Spanish ministers a treaty (ratified by Philip IV in June) promising a small amount of military and naval assistance in England if the royalists were able to seize a port for a landing, but,

more practically, allowing the king to reside in Flanders. The court began hasty preparations for a further move.

With the Spanish alliance, the royalists had for the first time what seemed to be a serious promise of military help, and something around which they could build a domestic insurgency. Over the next four years Hyde and his colleagues, with an increasing sense of frustration, worked hard to take advantage of it. Hyde, having gone to visit his pregnant wife at Breda, met the king at Antwerp by the middle of May 1656. Over the summer he shuttled between Brussels and Bruges to discuss with the Spanish ministers the terms of their co-operation and the payment of the subsidy; reopened contact with the conspirators of the Sealed Knot and other active royalists; began discussions with William Howard, a representative of the Levellers; and struggled with the huge logistical problems caused by the recruitment of a royalist army under Spanish pay. By October and November Hyde was buried under work, even though negotiations with the governor of Flanders, Don Juan of Austria, and the other ministers were increasingly handled by Lord Digby, now earl of Bristol, who was appointed secretary of state on the first day of 1657.

Despite Bristol's charm and ability to get on with Don Juan, the collaboration was doomed by the financial squeeze on the Spanish, and the inability of the royalists to make any practical commitments about securing a port. Planning for a rising in the winter of 1656–7 was abandoned by February, and postponed to the following year. Hyde's frustration and ill-temper at what he generally saw as the inefficiency and dishonesty of the Spanish were not improved by the difficulty of getting any activity going in England. From having lamented the keenness of royalists at home to engage in poorly planned attacks, he now regretted the apparent absence of any interest in rebellion at all; royalists:

> seem to have so little confidence in each other that they rarely confer together, or send advice, or declare what part they can take, but seem so heart-broken as only to wait for some extraordinary act of Providence; if the King were to land to-morrow in England with as good an army as can be hoped for, he would be overpowered as he was at Worcester while men sit still and wait for the effect of the first battle. (*Clarendon State Papers*, 3.359)

To add to his worries, the king's enjoyment of and involvement in the activities of the army both threatened his life and (to Hyde's eyes) rendered him unfit for anything else.

In the following winter Spanish interest in the invasion of England grew, at least to divert Cromwell from his participation in the attack on Flanders. Towards the end of 1657 there seemed a real prospect that they were finally prepared to commit themselves. In December Hyde declared that:

> the conjuncture seems as favourable as can be wished, nor can it ever be presumed that the King can be in a greater readiness than he is at present ... Every paper from England cries to haste away, matters cannot be better prepared. (Underdown, 216)

But when Ormond, at Spanish insistence, secretly visited England in February 1658 he recognized the inability of conspirators to support an invasion. The appearance of the English fleet in strength in the channel finally forced the plans—to Hyde's frustration—again to be put off to the next winter. A new gloom descended on the royal cause. The arrests of royalist conspirators which followed destroyed the remaining influence of the Sealed Knot. In an attempt to get a more positive commitment from Spain, the king considered going there himself. Hyde was in Breda in August 1658, probably hoping to draw the Dutch into an alliance against France and England. He was there still when news arrived in September of Cromwell's death.

The Restoration, 1658–1660 The quiet transfer of power to Cromwell's son Richard disappointed royalist hopes of Leveller risings or other disturbances; it also considerably reduced the briefly reawakened interest of the Spanish in their alliance with Charles. By November they were actively seeking to negotiate peace with England. But it did encourage the abandonment of the fruitless search for a strategy based solely on military success. Anticipating a new parliament, Hyde made strenuous efforts to encourage royalists and his contacts among the Levellers to seek election. It proved difficult to coax all the forces hostile to the protectorate into active co-operation in the parliament which opened on 27 January 1659, and by April much of Richard's new constitution had been accepted. Some ascribed the failure to block it to Hyde's reluctance to make sufficient approaches to presbyterians; after the confrontation between Richard and the army in April, more strenuous efforts were made to attract them. As a consequence, the debate about political and ecclesiastical concessions—largely dormant since 1651—was revived.

The scale of Hyde's efforts at intervention in English affairs grew rapidly as 1659 wore on. He used his Leveller contacts to exacerbate the divisions between the recalled Rump and the army and within the army, and sought with increasing difficulty to co-ordinate a range of conspiracies. New instruments—especially Lord Mordaunt—had been found to replace the discredited Knot, and by mid-May these were trying to put together plans for a royalist–presbyterian rising. In July they were judged to be well enough advanced for the king to make preparations to cross to England, while Hyde waited nervously in Brussels. In the event the rising was a dismal failure, with only the presbyterian Sir George Booth in Cheshire offering any significant resistance to the army. In its aftermath the king's hope of an alliance of the two crowns of France and Spain to help him to recover his own seemed more practical than to wait for another chance to capitalize on the insecurity of the army and the Rump. Hyde, who had previously been reluctant to see the king supported by an invasion, hoped that the declaration by the two crowns of their intention to help would encourage defections to his cause. Charles left to attend the negotiations between France and Spain, in company with the earl of Bristol.

While the king was *en route* for the Pyrenees news came of the army's dismissal of the Rump on the night of 13/14 October, which set off the final moves leading to the Restoration. Speculation mounted about the intentions of General George Monck, the commander of the army in Scotland, whose army was capable of challenging the forces under the control of the committee of safety in England, commanded by John Lambert. Hyde resisted any premature action, wanting nothing to prevent the likelihood of a conflict developing between Lambert and Monck. Depressed at news of the agreement between Monck's commissioners and Lambert on 12 November, Hyde was relieved when it was disowned by Monck himself on the 22nd. In December Monck moved slowly south, the army council collapsed in confusion, the Rump was restored, and Lambert's army disintegrated. Keenly watching developments, Hyde—always highly sceptical about Monck's intentions—grew concerned about the possibility that he might form a firm alliance with the Rump. His agents were encouraged to do their best to disrupt the relationship and to make approaches to prominent presbyterians such as Manchester, Fairfax, and Waller. But after Monck arrived in London in February 1660, the readmission of the secluded members and the decision of the Long Parliament to dissolve and to call new elections brought a Restoration within grasp for the first time.

In March and April Hyde once again exhorted all his contacts to obtain election to the new parliament. He was by now almost confident that, as he had hoped for many years, the logic of events should enable the king to return without concessions; but there were still dangers to be avoided. Keen not to jeopardize success at the elections, he tried to suppress the provocative activities of some royalist clergy. The presbyterians in the council of state identified Hyde as the principal obstacle to any negotiation, and tried, fruitlessly, to mobilize their allies at court to insist on his removal. Monck's views on the terms which the army would accept, crucial to the shape of the restored monarchy, remained frustratingly opaque. Not until 19 March did he give any indication of them: they alarmed Hyde further, particularly the request for a general liberty of conscience, which 'was a violation of all the laws in force, and could not be comprehended to consist with the peace of the kingdom' (Clarendon, *Hist. rebellion*, 6.197). But a confident expectation by late March that the elections would produce a well-disposed parliament confirmed a long-standing policy 'to make a general reference of all things which he could not reserve to himself to the wisdom of the Parliament, upon presumption that they would not exact from him more than he was willing to consent to' (*Clarendon State Papers*, 4.197). This was reflected in the declaration, drafted by Hyde, but amended at a meeting at Hyde's lodgings in Brussels by Nicholas, Ormond, and the king and published from Breda at the beginning of April.

Hyde had already made approaches to the states general concerning a move to the Netherlands; Monck's advice hastened it. Hyde, preparing letters for the king to send to the new House of Commons, the House of Lords, and the City of London, arrived at Breda on 5 April (os), the day after Charles. In the few weeks before the new parliament was due to sit his agents in London, especially Mordaunt and George Morley, were conducting intense discussions with the principal presbyterians to overcome any attempt to insist on conditions and to break what was widely rumoured to be an alternative negotiation, conducted from the queen's court, based on acceptance of some conditions. After parliament opened the royal court was still unsure what success the presbyterians were likely to have; a management committee full of Hyde's political allies—the earl of Southampton, Sir Orlando Bridgeman, Geoffrey Palmer, and others—ran the royalist interest. The failure of the presbyterians to hold back the train of events set the course for the Restoration. In response to the votes of both houses, the king moved to The Hague on 15 May (os) and welcomed a committee of both houses on the 16th. Hyde sailed for England with the king on 22 May.

The convention and the establishment of the Restoration monarchy Early in 1660 the king had been advised by a relatively tightly knit junto of four: apart from Hyde himself (who had been made lord chancellor in January 1658), they were Ormond, Colepeper, and Nicholas. The only one of these with whom Hyde's relationship was not uniformly good was Colepeper, who died very shortly after the Restoration. The influence of the queen mother and her associates was no longer significant, particularly following the alliance with Spain. The influence of Bristol, who had been so heavily involved in negotiations with the Spanish in 1657–9, had decayed rapidly after his entry into the Roman Catholic church towards the end of 1658—Hyde's disapproval of which had resulted in a breach of their old friendship—and he had been forced to give up the secretaryship. Others were brought into the inner circle after the Restoration. Monck's inclusion was unavoidable, but it was soon clear that he had little interest in exercising much influence over policy. The earl of Southampton, among the few remaining members of Charles I's and the prince of Wales's councils, was also brought in and became a powerful political ally of the chancellor. Some presbyterians were brought into government office, but generally in less significant or in subordinate places.

Hyde was left apparently in a dominant position: he was 'the highest in place and thought to be in trust, because he was most in private with the King, and managed most of the secret correspondence in England, and all despatches of importance had passed through his hands' (*Life*, 1.309). He claimed to want nothing more than to act as lord chancellor and recorded his indignant rejection of Ormond's suggestion that he resign the office and act more simply as principal counsellor to the king. He eventually shed his chairmanship of the Treasury commission established at the Restoration when Southampton was appointed lord treasurer in September, and not until September the following year did he cease to act as chancellor of the exchequer. But he found it impossible to extricate himself from the rest of his burden while the king looked on him as the most reliable of his advisers and himself shrank from hard work or difficult decisions. As a result Hyde continued to be occupied with a phenomenal amount of business, both domestic and foreign, and including much involvement in the affairs of Ireland and Scotland. The

exact extent of Hyde's responsibility for policy is difficult to pin down, for despite his strong views on political and constitutional affairs he insisted on procedural propriety and claimed to accept, and argue for, decisions with which he did not necessarily agree. Nevertheless, the government's strategy in the 1660s reflected Hyde's central concern to rebuild the monarchy by creating confidence in the government's respect for law and due process.

It was an obvious concern for a chancellor, and Gilbert Burnet noted how Hyde was regarded as a 'very good chancellor … very impartial in the administration of justice' (*Burnet's History*, 1.i.169). Hyde's encouragement of reforms of chancery procedure was designed with the same ends in mind. But it also ran through many other of the government's actions—in particular its efforts to prevent a bloody counter-revolution. The question of retribution was among the most dangerous issues to be addressed, and made more dangerous by the abandonment in the declaration of Breda of a long-established policy of excepting from a general pardon a few specific individuals, or else those who had been Charles I's judges—a policy which had been intended to make any blood-letting as relatively legal and certain a process as possible. Monck had insisted instead on the reference of the issue to parliament, expecting it to reduce the number of exceptions. Instead it converted it into an exercise in political trading, leading to lengthy and bitter debates in the convention. Hyde describes himself as playing a leading role in restricting the number excepted from the pardon in the Act of Indemnity: 'no man was more impatient to remove all causes which obstructed that work' (*Life*, 1.401). But in the process the king—and more particularly Hyde—were seen as failing to acknowledge the sacrifice and sufferings of their closest allies.

The perception that Hyde neglected the interests of royalists grew as the government grappled with the ecclesiastical settlement. Hyde aimed to re-establish an episcopal Church of England with a basic uniformity of practice. But presbyterianism had a powerful voice in the convention, and the government's—Hyde's—strategy appears to have been to avoid a final determination of ecclesiastical affairs until it was in a stronger position to influence it. Hyde and the king held lengthy discussions with senior presbyterians during June 1660 and the government reluctantly accepted a bill to confirm existing incumbents in their livings in September. Shortly before parliament rose for a late summer adjournment, they floated a scheme of slightly moderated episcopacy. In meetings based on the scheme at Hyde's London residence, Worcester House, on 22–25 October, presbyterians won some further concessions, especially concerning the roles of bishops and presbyters. The fact that Hyde left the conference early with the king, and the final agreement was drawn up by the earl of Anglesey and Lord Hollis—both presbyterian moderates—has sometimes been seen as an indication that Hyde opposed the concessions offered in the Worcester House declaration. Yet there is no evidence that he objected to the offers, nor that the episcopal clergy did; the declaration was cast as a temporary expedient until conditions were right for a more complete restoration of the pre-war church. Hyde was irritated by presbyterian attempts to convert it into a more permanent constitution for the church when parliament sat again during late November and early December, which were thwarted with some difficulty.

Hyde's handling of the ecclesiastical politics of the Restoration was complicated by two other issues of equal delicacy. One was the position within the religious settlement of Independents. During the conference Hyde had raised with the presbyterian leaders the question of whether Independents might be allowed to worship outside the formal structure of the church, a suggestion which they thought designed to open the subject of toleration for Roman Catholics. Hyde used their dismissive response to obtain Independent opposition to the attempt to make the Worcester House declaration permanent in November; but there was probably some truth in the idea that the king at least was considering a form of linkage with the position of Catholics. Some obscure approaches in the summer of 1660 suggest an opening of unofficial negotiations of which Hyde may not have been aware—although more formal discussions were conducted in the course of 1661 in which he certainly took part.

The other issue was more personal. Hyde's eldest child, his daughter *Anne, duchess of York (b. 1637), had been taken under the wing of the princess of Orange in 1655 as one of her maids of honour. Anne's affair with James, duke of York [see James II and VII (1633–1701)], probably began in the Netherlands in 1659. By the spring of 1660 the chancellor's daughter was pregnant; York sought the king's permission to marry her. When Hyde found out—Ormond and Southampton were asked by the king to tell him—his reaction was melodramatic, urging that his daughter be put on trial. Southampton said that he 'was mad, and had proposed such extravagant things, that he was no more to be consulted with' (Life, 1.327). Extravagant or not, Hyde recognized his vulnerability to a charge that he was deliberately insinuating himself into the royal family. The queen and the princess of Orange regarded the marriage with extreme distaste, and for several months tried to prevent it. Their pressure and some inept scandalmongering by members of his own household almost persuaded York to cast Anne adrift but the two were married in secret on 3 September 1660, and after a son was born to Anne on 22 October the opposition was slowly overcome. By 20 December York had publicly acknowledged Anne to be his wife; and on 18 February a special meeting of the privy council was summoned in order to affirm the genuineness of the marriage.

In some ways the marriage of his daughter greatly increased Hyde's significance and power within government, allying him closely to the king and the royal family. His election as chancellor of Oxford University on 27 October 1660 indicated the influence which he was now believed to wield. His new status was acknowledged when in November 1660 the king created him Baron Hyde of Hindon and in April 1661 further advanced him as Viscount Cornbury and to the earldom of Clarendon, adding

a gift of £20,000 to enable him to maintain the latter position. But the marriage also made his position more problematic. As he later professed to be acutely aware, it exposed him to considerable jealousy; it complicated his relationship with the king, allying him awkwardly with the reversionary interest; and it made it more difficult for him to cut himself off from court politics.

1661–1662: constitutional reconstruction and the regrouping of court faction Clarendon's growth in slightly uncertain political strength at the turn of the year was paralleled by the Church of England's return to a shaky monopoly of religious power. The convention was dissolved at the end of December 1660. Over the autumn and winter the reconstruction of the church hierarchy had placed it in a politically dominant position; the elections for a new parliament in March and April 1661 virtually destroyed presbyterianism as a political force, within parliament at least. The new, highly royalist parliament which opened on 8 May 1661 might have provided an opportunity for a constitutional counter-revolution. But some—York and Burnet especially—regarded the Restoration reaction as much weaker than it might have been, and believed that Clarendon, clearly implicated in placing limits on the prerogative in 1641–2, had held it back. Clarendon's rejection of the view that acts agreed to by the Lords and king under duress were *ipso facto* void meant that repeal would have to be sought through legislation; and it is likely to have been his views which principally determined the government's approach to the constitutional and legal settlement in the early sessions of the Cavalier Parliament. The exclusion of the bishops from parliament—which Clarendon believed had been the essential breach of constitutional fundamentals which had allowed parliament to assume power—was repealed in July 1661. The government eventually secured the repeal of the Triennial Act in 1664. But when it came to other acts passed in 1641 or 1642—the abolition of the prerogative courts, and various prerogative rights of taxation—it was much more circumspect. Clarendon had approved of the concessions in 1641, but had not ruled out the possibility of re-establishing the courts, and it is unclear whether it was his view of what was desirable, or of what was politically possible, which prevented it now. Burnet claimed that Clarendon had moderated attempts to provide the king with an adequate financial settlement; but there is no corroboration of the claim, and it seems inherently unlikely, unless he felt too heavy a demand was politically inexpedient.

Clarendon's approach to the religious settlement seemed just as equivocal. The temper of the new parliament permitted a full re-establishment of the Church of England, and at its opening Clarendon encouraged it. Yet, as before, he indicated a willingness to provide temporary relaxation of laws at least for presbyterians:

> if the good old known laws be for the present too heavy for their necks which have been so many years without any yoke at all, make a temporary provision of a lighter and easier yoke, till ... they recover strength enough to bear, and discretion enough to discern, the benefit and the ease of those laws they disliked. (Cobbett, *Parl. hist.*, 4.191)

Over the following fifteen months, though Clarendon welcomed the reaffirmation of legal uniformity, he became alarmed at parliament's failure to allow the temporary relaxation which he had proposed. His personal efforts to introduce concessions on ceremonial and on the covenant into the Act of Uniformity were unavailing, and the bill received royal assent at the end of May 1662. Even afterwards, Clarendon proposed an arrangement which might allow ministers effectively to keep their livings without complying fully with the Book of Common Prayer: at a privy council meeting on 28 August the opposition of the new bishop of London, his old friend Gilbert Sheldon, convinced the king to drop the idea.

Clarendon's support for moderation in the Act of Uniformity helped to lower his reputation among Anglican royalists, just when he was regarded as having lost the position of pre-eminence with the king that he had enjoyed in 1660 and early 1661. As ever, Clarendon's distaste for and inability to manage court politics was the source of many of his difficulties. The king's mistress, Barbara Palmer, now countess of Castlemaine, and the companion of his youth, the duke of Buckingham, were at the centre of the king's social circle, which viewed the chancellor as a pompous prig. Clarendon in return held Castlemaine in contempt and loathing—he could not be brought to write her name—and deeply deprecated the time the king spent with her. Buckingham, whose contacts with the Cromwells in the 1650s had compromised his claims to political office after the Restoration, he treated with more circumspection. The most immediate threat to Clarendon's position, though, came from the return of the earl of Bristol to active politics. Bristol sought to replace his lost secretaryship with a more informal influence, and planned to place at least one protégé, Sir Henry Bennet, in a position close to the king. In 1661 Bristol's advocacy of toleration for Catholics, his joining forces with the queen and seeking alliances with protestant dissenters to promote it, revived a combination of forces and issues against which Clarendon had struggled during the 1650s. Every contact between the two appeared to embitter a relationship which had once been very close.

Bristol's bid for influence gained plausibility from the divide which opened up between Clarendon and the king over Charles's marriage. Preoccupied with the domestic settlement, the government had given little attention to foreign affairs in the year of the Restoration, beyond closing the now virtually dormant war with Spain. Its main objective from a foreign alliance was to obtain financial support. Finding a bride for the king who brought with her a substantial dowry was one means of obtaining it, and the offer from Portugal in late summer 1660 of the infanta Catherine of Braganza with far-flung possessions and a very large sum of money was highly attractive. The Spanish mobilized their connections to oppose it: Bristol, on their behalf, offered instead one of the princesses of Parma, a Spanish client state. In choosing the Portuguese option, French support was decisive. The marriage was agreed in May 1661, although Catherine did not arrive until a year later.

The new queen's arrival seriously destabilized the court. The king insisted on continuing his affair with Castlemaine, and even demanded that she be made a lady of his wife's bedchamber. Catherine appealed to Clarendon, but Clarendon's intervention provoked Charles into what was probably his first serious row with his chancellor: 'you know how true a friend I have been to you', he wrote:

> if you desire to have the continuance of my friendship, meddle no more with this business ... whosoever I find to be my Lady Castlemaine's enemy in this matter, I do promise, upon my word, to be his enemy as long as I live. (Lister, 3.202–3)

The affair badly dented Clarendon's prestige and political influence. The departure of Ormond to take up residence in Ireland as lord lieutenant in July, shortly after the end of the 1661–2 session of parliament, removed a crucial ally. In October another, Sir Edward Nicholas, was eased out of the secretaryship and the job handed over to Bennet. By late 1662 the emergence of a coalition of forces against Clarendon, based around Bristol, the queen mother, and the court, looked set to produce a palace coup which would end his influence for good.

Clarendon was left more vulnerable still by the unpopularity of Dunkirk's sale to France, which he negotiated in the autumn of 1662. The sale was in part a product of the warmer relations with France which followed the death in March 1661 of Mazarin—always regarded by Clarendon with deep suspicion. In April Clarendon had asked, on a precautionary basis, for a loan of £50,000. Charles was eager to secure a closer alliance with Louis XIV, and to prevent a Franco–Dutch treaty; Clarendon was closely involved in the unsuccessful attempts to achieve either object. The Dunkirk project had not originated with Clarendon, nor had he been the sole adviser, but he became closely identified with it; although he described proudly in his memoir how he had indignantly turned down the offer of £10,000 from the French government, the abandonment of England's only possession in western Europe for less than £400,000 was widely attributed to his being bribed. It gave him an unenviable public reputation and made him an easy target for political attack. Bennet's active courting of members of the Cavalier Parliament late in 1662 may well have been connected to a scheme to seek his impeachment, and to offer an alternative political and religious programme in the following session.

The court crisis of 1663 In the end Clarendon survived because the attempt was premature, the king resisted having his hand forced, and Clarendon was recognized to represent some powerful political forces. The struggle during the parliamentary session of 1663 centred on Bristol's plans to offer an alternative religious policy. A declaration of indulgence, drafted by Bennet and issued on 26 December 1662, indicated the king's intention to seek a statutory power to dispense with the Act of Uniformity. Clarendon did not oppose it, as it appeared similar to the scheme he had advanced in the summer. But the declaration left unclear the exact nature of the dispensation that was being sought, and the bill drafted to give effect to it, shown to the chancellor in February 1663, horrified him. The power to dispense being sought was not specific, but wide and general; not temporary, as Clarendon had proposed in the previous August, but permanent. He saw it as a dangerous replacement of law by royal discretion—'ship money in religion, that nobody could know the end of, or where it would rest', and in the House of Lords he attacked the 'wildness and illimitedness' of the bill (*Life*, 2.98). Clarendon's feelings against it were far from unique, and the bill was opposed so vehemently in both houses that within a few weeks of the opening of the session it was dropped.

Clarendon's antipathy to the bill had brought him to a dangerously low point in the king's favour; his opponents began to marshal their strength in the Commons and at court and his dismissal was confidently expected from March onwards. Clarendon himself complained in April to Ormond that Bennet:

> hath credit enough to persuade the king that because I did not like what was done I have raised all the evil spirit that hath appeared upon and against it which, I think, you will absolve me from, for without doubt, I could as easily turn turk as act that part.   (Bodl. Oxf., Carte MS 47, fol. 45)

With the backing of the duke of York, however, and the evidence that Clarendon's views were shared by a large segment of Anglican royalist and presbyterian opinion, the king refused to remove the chancellor. Bristol's poorly prepared attempt to have Clarendon impeached for high treason by the Commons in July indicated that he saw that his chance to seize power was slipping through his fingers; he obtained the backing of very few, despite his efforts to attract not only those opposed to Clarendon's religious views, but also those Anglican royalists who believed that he had deliberately obstructed their own interests. Even his court allies, especially Bennet, found it expedient to drop him as quickly as possible.

The return to a relatively unified court was helped by renewed concern about radical subversion during the course of 1663, which encouraged the king to adopt a more consistently Anglican royalist religious policy—although there is little evidence that Clarendon personally promoted the anti-dissenting legislation of 1664 and 1665 to which his name later became attached (the Clarendon code). The presence of Bennet (created Baron Arlington in 1665), however, meant that policy-making was no longer dominated by Clarendon to anything like the same extent as in 1662 and before. A wary truce prevailed between the two. Clarendon was also highly sensitive to the growth in influence of Sir William Coventry, an able servant of the duke of York, who became a privy councillor in 1665; of Sir Charles Berkeley, from 1665 the earl of Falmouth, another servant of York's and increasingly an intimate of the king's; and of Lord Ashley, councillor of state under the protectorate, now chancellor of the exchequer and a threat to the position of Southampton, Clarendon's only powerful ally within the English council. In Scotland the earl of Middleton, the royalist conspirator of the 1650s and closely associated with Clarendon, had been replaced in 1663 as commissioner of the parliament; Lauderdale, his old engager adversary, took a dominant position in Scottish affairs, cutting out Clarendon almost completely.

How effective a member of the government Clarendon remained into the later 1660s is uncertain: his conservative instincts and insistence on constitutional propriety became irritating to those who—like Coventry—were keen to see a more effective and dynamic approach to the difficulties of the government, and his objections to projects such as the appropriation of taxation to the repayment of loans in 1665 could seem merely captious. There were signs, too, that his age and illnesses made him no longer capable of carrying his earlier workload. Pepys remarked on his 'sleeping and snoring the greater part' of one meeting in November 1666. Yet only six weeks before, Pepys had come home after a meeting about the affairs of Tangier to write in his diary 'I am mad in love with my Lord Chancellor, for he doth comprehend and speak as well, and with the greatest easiness and authority, that ever I saw man in my life' (Pepys, *Diary*, 7.377, 321).

It was perhaps an indication that Clarendon was no longer so central to government business that he began to build on a substantial scale. Hugh May rebuilt his house at Cornbury, his estate near Oxford, in the early 1660s, and in 1664 Clarendon commissioned Roger Pratt to build him a house in London. Clarendon House in Piccadilly was one of the first and best classical houses in London. Clarendon lavished on it much personal interest, paying particular attention to the library, and procuring a collection of portraits of 'most of our ancient and modern wits, poets, philosophers, famous and learned Englishmen' to decorate the house (Evelyn, *Diary*, 3.520). It proved, though, to be a serious mistake. The expense was a heavy burden, but more significant was its political cost: for many Londoners 'Dunkirk-House' (because it was believed to have been financed by Clarendon's proceeds from the sale) symbolized what was seen as the corruption and dynastic ambition of the chancellor. Corruption formed a large element of the charges against him in 1663 and 1667, and Clarendon had certainly gained from the bounty of the king and his officers and from new years' presents which 'I could not refuse without some affectation': beyond the gift of 1661, he had received several gifts of land and, like other prominent courtiers, had been provided with some profits out of the Irish land settlement. But he made much of his incorruptibility, and while he held a profitable office, there is no clear evidence of his benefiting improperly from it.

The Second Anglo-Dutch War and government collapse, 1664–1667 To one so exposed as Clarendon the political crisis engendered by the Second Anglo-Dutch War of 1664–7 was highly dangerous. Clarendon had little time for the Dutch, whose politics he opposed and whose treatment of the royalists during the interregnum he resented; but he viewed the prospect of war—engineered by courtiers, merchants, and individuals keen to emulate the success of the English republic in the 1650s—with extreme misgiving. Nevertheless, he helped to choreograph the vote by the Commons of an unprecedented grant of money to permit preparations in late 1664, if only in the hope that it would persuade the Dutch to negotiate more seriously; and, once war was joined in earnest, he was as involved as anyone in the domestic and financial aspects of the government's war effort.

By September 1666 the plague, the fire, and an agricultural depression had contributed to a growing reluctance to contribute any more money towards the war, a reluctance which was fed by claims of large-scale corruption and encouraged by the duke of Buckingham in a campaign to become a leading minister. A government desperate to finance the war became deeply divided about the extent to which concessions might be offered in order to secure supply. Clarendon vehemently opposed the Irish Cattle Bill, intended to ease the problems of farmers, in part because it was designed expressly to deny the king any prerogative right to suspend it or dispense with it, and also an attempt by the government's critics to establish a statutory commission to review government finance, although he seems to have initiated the compromise offer of a royal commission to achieve the same object. Clarendon's hostility to concessions may have contributed to moves which were widely interpreted as testing the ground for impeachment proceedings against him—a challenge to the Canary Company's patent, and an impeachment against Viscount Mordaunt, the governor of Windsor Castle, in December 1666 and January 1667. Despite Clarendon's opposition the government finally accepted defeat on the Irish Cattle Bill at a meeting in mid-January in order to unblock essential grants of money. Clarendon dissented from the decision, but it largely achieved its purpose and enabled the government to end the session on 8 February.

The money came too late to allow the fitting out of a major fleet, and the government was forced to pin its hopes on an early conclusion of the peace conference which began at Breda in mid-May. The attack by the Dutch on the almost undefended Medway on 10–13 June produced panic in London: 'they who remember that conjuncture', wrote Clarendon with evident feeling:

> and were then present in the galleries and privy lodgings at Whitehall, whither all the world flocked with equal liberty, can easily call to mind instances of such wild despair and even ridiculous apprehensions, that I am willing to forget, and would not that the least mention of them should remain. (*Life*, 2.418–19)

The political atmosphere, both in the country at large and in council, became extremely heated. The chancellor became the favourite object of public anger; at its height a gibbet was meaningfully set up outside his new house by a crowd of rioters. Desperate for money to mount a defence against further attack, the government considered recalling parliament; Clarendon advised against it, as it was unlikely to be of any practical value, and argued instead for a dissolution. In the meantime, before a new parliament could meet, he suggested a return to an old expedient—the forced loan, to be repaid later out of parliamentary subsidies.

Clarendon's advice was not taken, and parliament was summoned for 25 July. In the end it met only briefly before the news of the conclusion of the treaty of Breda allowed it to be dismissed, relieving the political crisis but adding significantly to parliament's sense of grievance. Clarendon was its most likely target: his suggestion of using prerogative powers to raise money had been widely reported, and (possibly because of a confusion with comments made by York) he was said to be in favour of rule by the military. The death of Southampton in late May had removed his one remaining significant ally from the heart of the government. When his wife died on 9 August 1667 Clarendon's strongly expressed grief seems to have fathered the suggestion that he should resign from his position. Clarendon refused, both because it would seriously reduce an income heavily charged with building debts, and because he had no wish to take responsibility for the débâcle of June. Over the following two weeks Clarendon's survival in government was the subject of intense discussion, York arguing with the king for his father-in-law's retention.

Clarendon's removal was only delayed. The king had certainly come to accept the view of Arlington and Coventry that parliament would be impossible to manage unless he had gone. But more significantly, his own relationship with the chancellor had deteriorated rapidly: stories circulating attributed the king's attitude both to his anger at a rumoured attempt by Clarendon to interfere with his choice of mistresses by arranging for Frances Stewart to be married to the duke of Richmond, and to a more generalized irritation with the extent to which Clarendon's exercise of the role of chief adviser compromised his own command of his government. In a long interview with the king Clarendon may only have compounded his offence by emphasizing the need to assert royal authority: he drew a parallel with the reign of Richard II, 'when they terrified the King with the power and the purposes of the Parliament, till they brought him to consent to that from which he could not redeem himself, and without which they could have done him no harm' (*Life*, 2.451). On 30 August 1667 the king sent the secretary of state, Sir William Morrice, to collect the seals.

Impeachment and exile, 1667–1674 Impeachment proceedings against Clarendon were widely expected when parliament sat again in October, but it was only the king's mounting hostility that made them serious. Clarendon prepared his defence against the coming storm with his old energy, and the continued loyalty of the duke of York to his father-in-law began to convert Clarendon's personal struggle into a more dangerous confrontation between the two royal brothers. When parliament met on 10 October the king made the dismissal of his chancellor his principal peace-offering, and privately pressed for an impeachment. The first accusations were presented in the Commons on 26 October. Clarendon's support there turned out to be far larger than anticipated, but on 11 November a set of charges, including one of high treason, was presented to the Lords. There the support of the duke of York and the bishops helped Clarendon to avoid committal to the Tower, and occasioned an escalation of the factional dispute and an enormous procedural row between the two houses. Various possibilities for overcoming the deadlock were suggested, including—ominously for Clarendon—the prorogation of parliament and the removal of the prosecution into the court of the lord steward.

Until this moment Clarendon had been confident that he could defend himself, but he recognized the difficulty of a trial before a picked jury. Having received two strong hints from the king to leave, on 30 November he accepted defeat and embarked for France, possibly hoping that compliance with the king's demand and a temporary exile might permit his later return. The news of his departure broke after the weekend, when his son Lord Cornbury [see Hyde, Henry, second earl of Clarendon] presented to the Lords Clarendon's lengthy and defiant petition, written in transit to France. In fact, Clarendon's departure was regarded in most quarters as damaging to his case, and in some as proving his guilt. Although a bill of attainder was avoided, by Christmas the king had given his assent to a bill banishing Clarendon for life unless he returned by the beginning of February 1668.

Initially treated with respect by the French government, Clarendon headed first for Rouen, an old haunt of English exiles during the civil war. Within a week or two, however, the attitude of the French changed and he was ordered to leave. Clarendon expressed an intention to return to England in obedience to the Act of Banishment, but the onset of gout made it impossible to do so immediately. By the time he had found his way to Calais it was too late to return under the act, and he was too ill. He was not well enough to travel again until March, by which time Louis XIV's relations with Charles II had cooled considerably, and he was willing to allow Clarendon to pass through France on his way to the papal enclave of Avignon. On the way, at Évreux, he was assaulted and badly beaten by a group of drunken English sailors who held him responsible for their arrears of pay. He did not arrive at Avignon until about the middle of June. In July he was allowed to move on to Montpellier, a popular resort with the English.

At Montpellier, Clarendon settled into a routine of writing, reading, and meditation, which recalled his time in Jersey in the 1640s. Very soon after his arrival he wrote a detailed refutation of the impeachment charges; almost at the same time, he had begun to write an account of his own life. The latter became a franker version of the *History*—a less accurate one, for Clarendon had brought little, if any, documentary material with him; but as it did not have to act as an official defence of the conduct of Charles I, it emphasized even more than the *History* had done the mistakes in royalist policy and anatomized with some relish the character failings of many of the principal actors, particularly those—Bristol and Berkeley—who had become his enemies. The *Life* was completed in August 1670, at least as far as the Restoration. Clarendon had returned in December 1668 to the devotional writing that

he had begun in Jersey: his drafts for 'Contemplations and reflections upon the Psalms of David' were sent to him by mistake instead of other papers he had requested, and he completed that work by February 1671. He also had time to complete a sustained critique of Hobbes's *Leviathan* in which he set out his objections to 'conclusions, which overthrow or undermine all those principles of government, which have preserved the peace of this kingdom through so many ages, even from the time of its first institution' (E. Hyde, earl of Clarendon, *A Brief View and Survey of the Dangerous and Pernicious Errors to Church and State, in Mr. Hobbes's Book Entitled Leviathan*, 1676, 6).

Despite the contentment that his retirement at Montpellier brought him, Clarendon still cherished hopes of returning home. In the spring of 1671 he secured permission from Louis XIV to move further north, closer to England. He settled at Moulins in the heart of France, where in June he was able to meet his second son, Laurence *Hyde, first earl of Rochester. Laurence brought with him some of his father's papers, including, probably, the original drafts of the *History*. Clarendon set to work to merge it with the *Life* he had just completed—plus some additions—to create a full account of events from the accession of Charles I to the Restoration; after he had finished the task in early 1672 he continued the *Life* up to the present. In 1674 he turned to writing against Rome, perhaps especially because of the distressing news that his daughter, the duchess of York, had been converted. His response to the Catholic Hugh Cressy's attack on Stillingfleet's description of the Roman Catholic church as fanatical was published anonymously in England in November that year. He then wrote, remarkably, a long history of the growth of papal temporal power, which he had finished by February 1674. A visit of his elder son, Henry, Viscount Cornbury, possibly in 1673 or very early in 1674, and permission to move further north still, to Rouen, in the summer of 1674 may have suggested that the hostility of the king was beginning to fade. Clarendon began to believe that a return from exile could be imminent. But at Rouen in December he suffered a stroke; he died there on 9 December.

Royalism and conservatism Clarendon's body was returned to London and was buried privately in Westminster Abbey on 4 January 1675. A year later his *Brief View and Survey* of Hobbes's *Leviathan* was published at Oxford—a sign, perhaps, of the revival of Anglican royalist fortunes from the mid-1670s. The remainder of Clarendon's manuscripts remained unpublished for more than twenty-five years, although his sons allowed certain politically sympathetic individuals—among them Archbishop Sancroft—to see them. The first volume of the *History of the Rebellion*, the text put together in 1671–2 out of the *History* and the *Life*, was not published until 1702, after the accession to the throne of Clarendon's granddaughter, Anne. Laurence Hyde, earl of Rochester, contributed a carefully nuanced defence of his father to the first volume; by the time the second and third volumes were published in 1704, Rochester's dismissal from government made him give a more partisan, tory edge to their dedications to the queen.

Some whigs rose to the tory agenda revealed in the dedications. One in particular—John Oldmixon—sustained for more than twenty years his attack on the *History*'s veracity, with repeated claims that the text had been tampered with by a knot of high tories at Christ Church, Oxford. The identification of Clarendon with his tory defenders encouraged whigs for the remainder of the century to regard him as a sower of discord, rather than a promoter of unity, a view which the publication in 1759 of the *Life* did nothing to dispel. A more common reaction to the *History*, though, was to see in its moderate version of the royalist cause a sort of tory precursor to the 1688–9 revolution settlement. But to the more progressive nineteenth-century interpreters of the history of the constitution—Macaulay, or Gardiner—such praise appeared seriously misconceived. Clarendon's resistance to the development of parliamentary government was the work of a Canute who had no grasp of the processes of historical change. Brian Wormald's subtle analysis of 1951 did something to refurbish the moderate tory view. He emphasized the efforts Clarendon had made in the 1640s to achieve a political settlement: his role had been that of a 'bridge builder' between king and parliament, although his attitude towards concessions had hardened after the king's defeat. Nor had he been a prominent defender of the church until after a similar point.

Clarendon had undoubtedly recognized in 1640–41 the threat that existed to the liberty and property of the subject and contributed to efforts to redress it. Even in 1647, writing his will, he proudly claimed to have always 'endeavoured to observe the bounds between the King's power and the subject's right' (*Clarendon State Papers*, 1.370–71). Those bounds were set by law, the proper observation and administration of which was—as the history of the ship-money case amply demonstrated—fundamental to the achievement of political stability: 'all governments subsist and are established by firmness and constancy, by every man's knowing what is his right to enjoy, and what is his duty to do' (Clarendon, *Brief View … Leviathan*, 1676, 124). The effect, though, of so insistent a stress on the constitution as an intricate balance of law and prerogative was to make constitutional growth and development exceptionally difficult. Temporary relaxation of laws might be permitted if absolutely necessary, but anything more than that had the potential to upset the entire structure, and there is no evidence that Clarendon favoured anything but small and temporary concessions to parliamentary opposition throughout the period from 1640 to 1667. His main purpose in encouraging negotiations throughout the 1640s was not to try to forge a compromise settlement, but to open up divisions inside parliament and to encourage the defections of the more moderate parliamentarians—an activity which could be seen as attempting to reunite a broken political élite.

For Clarendon the church formed a part of that constitution, and to his commitment to episcopacy and a uniformity of religious practice Anglicanism owed something of its survival and post-war reconstruction. Yet to his clerical allies Clarendon's commitment was less than total, as from time to time he seemed to be regrettably willing to subordinate ecclesiastical aims to political objectives and to offer presbyterians some concessions in liturgy and ceremonial. Great Tew had drawn with it an association with a rationalist approach to religion and a recognition of the indifference of much religious practice which seemed to go with a tolerant view of the ecclesiastical polity, and though he was sympathetic to a Laudian approach to liturgy and ceremonial there is no evidence that Clarendon regarded their imposition as especially important. But as with his attitudes in constitutional law, Clarendon saw a fundamental stability in the ecclesiastical laws as essential to their survival, and his acceptance of compromise was limited to temporary relaxations which might encourage eventual compliance and outward uniformity.

Clarendon liked to assume that, with time, circumstances could be altered to fit the law and the constitution, rather than the other way round. It was perhaps as unrealistic a view as his whig critics claimed, and Clarendon compounded it as he mourned, but did not accept, the passing of a unitary, pre-war political and social world:

> the nation was corrupted from that integrity, good nature and generosity, that had been peculiar to it, and for which it had been signal and celebrated throughout the world; in the room whereof the vilest craft and dissembling had succeeded. (*Life*, 1.307)

But if it is unsustainable to argue, as Wormald contended, that it was 'Hyde's conception of the constitution rather than that of anybody else which did come to be permanently adopted after the Revolution of 1688' (Wormald, 152–3), Clarendon's development of a secular royalist ideology, which depended little on the divine right of kings and set them firmly within a framework of law, did provide a key to the way in which royal power could ultimately be reconciled with parliamentary control—albeit within a constitution which Clarendon himself would no longer regard as monarchical.

That legacy was ultimately more important than Clarendon's political achievement. For although his confidence in his own prescriptions for a royalist strategy and his capacity for hard work which made him dominate royalist counsels in the 1650s and early 1660s were among the factors which helped the royalist cause to survive throughout the interregnum, that lawyerly confidence went with a prickliness and a lack of political art which were almost legendary. The earl of Norwich—a political ally in the 1650s—complained that his 'overvallewing himselfe and undervallewing others, together with his grasping at too much, hath and will, if it be still permitted, bring irrecoverable inconveniences, if not ruin, to affaires' (Warner, 2.279). Clarendon wrote proudly of the occasion on which Queen Henrietta Maria said that he was 'so far from making promises, or giving fair words, and flattering her, that she did verily believe that "if he thought her a whore he would tell her of it"' (*Life*, 1.225); but such forthrightness was a liability in court politics, a sphere which Clarendon could never master and which played a large part in his undoing.

But still more than for his political role or his intellectual legacy, Clarendon remained in the mind because of his literary achievement—the fashioning of the most sophisticated and finely balanced history yet written in English (or written for a long time afterwards)—and for an unmistakable rhetorical voice. Clarendon's writings—and his own life—were steeped in the literary stoicism of the early seventeenth century; but in the *History* he created a distinctive work of art based on a highly wrought style, a forensic dissection of character and issue, and a sense of the depth of individuals' moral responsibility for their actions: a description of:

> the pride of this man, and the popularity of that; the levity of one, and the morosity of another; the excess of the court in the greatest want, and the parsimony and retention of the country in the greatest plenty; the spirit of craft and subtlety in some, and the rude and unpolished integrity of others, too much despising craft or art; like so many atoms contributing jointly to this mass of confusion now before us.
>
> (Clarendon, *Hist. rebellion*, 1.4)

PAUL SEAWARD

Sources *The life of Edward, earl of Clarendon … written by himself*, 2 vols. (1857) · Clarendon, *Hist. rebellion* · T. H. Lister, *The life and administration of Edward earl of Clarendon, with original correspondence and authentic papers never before published*, 3 vols. (1837–8) · R. Ollard, *Clarendon and his friends* (1987) · *Calendar of the Clarendon state papers preserved in the Bodleian Library*, ed. O. Ogle and others, 5 vols. (1869–1970) · B. Wormald, *Clarendon: politics, history and religion* (1951) · G. Roebuck, *Clarendon and cultural continuity* (1981) [bibliography] · J. C. Hayward, 'The mores of Great Tew', PhD diss., U. Cam., 1982 · C. H. Firth, 'Clarendon's *History of the rebellion*', *EngHR*, 19 (1904), 26–54, 245–62, 464–83 · M. Dzelzainis, '"Undoubted realities": Clarendon on sacrilege', *HJ*, 33 (1990), 515–40 · M. Brownley, *Clarendon and the rhetoric of historical form* (1985) · H. R. Trevor-Roper, *Edward Hyde earl of Clarendon* (1975) · *Burnet's History of my own time*, ed. O. Airy, new edn, 2 vols. (1897–1900) · *The Nicholas papers*, ed. G. F. Warner, 4 vols., CS, new ser., 40, 50, 57, 3rd ser., 31 (1886–1920) · *The diary of Bulstrode Whitelocke, 1605–1675*, ed. R. Spalding, British Academy, Records of Social and Economic History, new ser., 13 (1990) · J. A. R. Marriott, *The life and times of Lucius Cary, Viscount Falkland* (1907) · C. Russell, *The fall of the British monarchies, 1637–1642* (1991) · D. L. Smith, *Constitutional royalism and the search for settlement* (1994) · D. Underdown, *Royalist conspiracy in England, 1649–1660* (1960) · R. Hutton, *The Restoration: a political and religious history of England and Wales, 1658–1667* (1985) · P. Seaward, *The Cavalier Parliament and the reconstruction of the old regime* (1989) · C. Roberts, 'The impeachment of the earl of Clarendon', *Cambridge Historical Journal*, 13 (1957), 1–18 · Evelyn, *Diary* · Pepys, *Diary* · *The journal of Sir Symonds D'Ewes: from the beginning of the Long Parliament to the opening of the trial of the earl of Strafford*, ed. W. Notestein (1923) · *The journal of Sir Symonds D'Ewes: from the first recess of the Long Parliament to the withdrawal of King Charles from London* / edited by Willson Havelock Coates, ed. W. H. Coates (1942) · R. Gibson, *Catalogue of portraits in the collection of the earl of Clarendon* [1977] · GEC, *Peerage* · G. D. Squibb, ed., *Wiltshire visitation pedigrees, 1623*, Harleian Society, 105–6 (1954) · *DNB* · Wood, *Ath. Oxon.*, new edn, vol. 3 · *Hist. U. Oxf.* 4: *17th-cent. Oxf.* · C. H. Hopwood, ed., *A calendar of the Middle Temple records* (1903) · BL, Althorp MSS · P. Beal and others, *Index of English literary manuscripts*, ed. P. J. Croft and others, [4 vols. in 11 pts] (1980–), vol. 2 · Bodl. Oxf., Clarendon MSS

Archives BL, corresp. and papers, Add. MSS 10614, 14269, 32093–32094, 33233, 34727 · BL, MS 'A short view of the state of Ireland 1640 to the present time', Egerton MS 1625 · Bodl. Oxf., corresp.

and papers · CUL, copies of 'View of the state of Ireland' · Longleat House, Wiltshire, family corresp. and related material · NRA, corresp. and literary papers | BL, papers relating to impeachment, Harley MSS · Bodl. Oxf., corresp. with Sir Henry Coventry and Lord Holles · Bodl. Oxf., letters to Gilbert Sheldon · Herts. ALS, corresp. with Sir H. Grimstone · Leics. RO, corresp. with earl of Winchelsea · St John Cam., corresp. with John Barwick · Valence House Museum, Dagenham, letters to Sir R. Fanshawe

Likenesses oils, *c.*1648–1655 (after A. Hanneman), Clarendon collection [*see illus.*] · P. Lely, oils, *c.*1660–1665, Bodl. Oxf. · T. Simon, silver medal, 1662, NPG · D. Loggan, line engraving, 1666, BM, NPG · R. Dunkarton, mezzotint, pubd 1812 (after D. Loggan), NPG · M. Burghers, line engraving (after P. Lely), BM, NPG · T. Johnson, mezzotint (after G. Soest), BM, NPG · R. White, line engraving (after P. Lely), BM · oils (after P. Lely, *c.*1660–1665), Clarendon collection; on loan to Palace of Westminster, London; copy, Middle Temple, London · oils (after A. Hanneman), second version, NPG

Wealth at death two houses in London, land in Wiltshire, Leicestershire, Oxfordshire, and Rutland, plus money and other gifts totalling £15,600, and a legacy of £200 a year: will, 1666, Bodl. Oxf., Clarendon MS 83, fols. 35–42

Hyde, Edward, third earl of Clarendon (1661–1723), army officer and colonial governor, was born on 28 November 1661, the only child of Henry *Hyde, second earl of Clarendon (1638–1709), and his first wife, Theodosia (*bap.* 1640, *d.* 1662), daughter of Arthur, first Baron Capel. He was named after his grandfather Edward *Hyde (1609–1674), lord high chancellor of England under Charles II, and took the title Viscount Cornbury in 1674. He was first cousin of Mary II and Queen Anne owing to the marriage of his aunt, Anne Hyde (1637–1671), in 1660 to the duke of York, later James II.

Although he was enrolled at Christ Church, Oxford, at the age of thirteen, Cornbury's formal education took place primarily at the Académie de Calvin in Geneva from 1680 to 1682. He was appointed lieutenant-colonel of the Royal regiment of dragoons in 1683, and his valiant service at the battle of Sedgemoor during Monmouth's rebellion (1685) earned him a full colonelcy and command of the dragoons at the age of twenty-three. On 10 July 1688 he married Katherine O'Brien, Baroness Clifton of Leighton Bromswold (1673–1706) on her mother's death in 1702, a descendant of the Irish earls of Thomond and the duke of Richmond and Lennox, yet with only distant financial prospects. The marriage produced two daughters and a son, who predeceased their father.

The revolution of 1688 broke Cornbury's allegiance to James II, as he was the first English officer to defect to the invading Prince William of Orange. His sturdy devotion to the Church of England was a leading motive, as was his connection to the protestant court of Princess Anne, where in 1685 he had been appointed master of the horse to Prince George. William of Orange vowed in 1688 never to forget the 'seasonable service' of Cornbury's timely defection (*Correspondence*, 2.213–15). Yet, when in 1689 Clarendon and his son urged Anne's right of succession above William's, both William and Mary turned against them. As a nonjuror Clarendon received no offices, and Cornbury's regiment was taken from him. The family now confronted a time of financial distress from which it never fully recovered. Cornbury's sole office after 1690 was as MP for Wiltshire (1685–7, 1690–95) and for Christchurch (1695–1701), where his fundamental loyalty to the crown soon became apparent.

In 1702 William appointed Cornbury governor-general of the royal colony of New York; later that year Queen Anne added the governorship of the newly royal colony of New Jersey. Well qualified for these posts by military experience and imperial allegiance, Cornbury strengthened the defences and political stability of New York. Fractious New Jersey, often beset by land disputes, was less easily tamed. An opposition party, led by gentleman landowner Lewis Morris, employed slander and Grub Street satire—newly emergent in colonial politics—to assail the governor's reputation for financial and moral integrity. Accused of venality, bigotry, and transvestism, Cornbury was replaced as governor in December 1708. After successfully defending his administration and reputation in England and succeeding to the title third earl of Clarendon (1709), he was sworn of the privy council, took a leading role in the House of Lords from 1710 to 1723, and in 1714 served as Queen Anne's envoy-extraordinary to the court at Hanover. He died on 31 March 1723 at Chelsea, Middlesex, and was interred in the family vault at Westminster Abbey on 5 April.　　PATRICIA U. BONOMI

Sources The correspondence of Henry Hyde, earl of Clarendon, and of his brother Laurence Hyde, earl of Rochester, ed. S. W. Singer, 2 vols. (1828) · N. Luttrell, A brief historical relation of state affairs from September 1678 to April 1714, 6 vols. (1857) · P. U. Bonomi, The Lord Cornbury scandal: the politics of reputation in British America (1998) · GEC, Peerage, new edn · M. Rubincam, 'The formative years of Lord Cornbury, the first royal governor of New York and New Jersey', New York Genealogical and Biographical Record, 71 (1940), 106–16

Archives Bodl. Oxf., MSS · New York Historical Society, MSS · Society for the Propagation of the Gospel in Foreign Parts, letterbooks | BL, letters to earl of Strafford, Add. MS 22211 · John Carter Brown Library, Providence, Rhode Island, letters · LPL, corresp. with Society for the Propagation of the Gospel · New York State Library, Albany, New York, Colonial MSS · PRO, Colonial Office MSS, class 5

Wealth at death inconsiderable: will, PRO, PROB 11/592

Hyde, Harford Montgomery [H. Montgomery Hyde] (1907–1989), politician and historian, was born on 14 August 1907 at Ranelagh, Malone Road, Belfast, the son of James Johnstone Hyde JP, linen merchant, and his wife, Isobel Greenfield, née Montgomery. He was later very proud of the part played by his family in developing the Ulster linen industry. His great-grandfather, he told the House of Commons, had in the 1840s spent several years in the USA in 'a not unsuccessful endeavour to stimulate the export of Irish linen', and Hyde himself during the First World War spent part of the school holidays in helping to pull flax. From Sedbergh School (1921–5) he went to Queen's University, Belfast, where he graduated in 1928 with a first-class degree in history. Encouraged by J. E. Todd, the professor of history, who 'lectured in the grand manner', he proceeded to Oxford, entering Magdalen College as an exhibitioner, and in 1930 obtained a second-class degree in jurisprudence. A member of the Middle Temple, he was called to the bar in 1934 and practised for a short time on the north-east circuit. He also travelled widely, visiting, among other countries, the Soviet Union. In 1933 he published his first book, The Early Life of Castlereagh, swiftly followed by The Russian Journals of Martha and Catherine Wilmot (1934) and More Letters from Martha Wilmot (1935), both with the marchioness of Londonderry. In 1935 he became librarian and then private secretary to Charles Stewart Henry Vane-Tempest-Stewart, seventh marquess of Londonderry, Conservative politician. Hyde became very attached to the Londonderry family and was the author of several further books on the family and their possessions. On 15 April 1939 he married Dorothy Mabel Brayshaw Crofts (b. 1903/4), daughter of James Murray Crofts, secretary to the joint matriculation board of the northern universities.

After the outbreak of the Second World War Hyde worked as a censor in Gibraltar. In 1940 he was commissioned in the intelligence corps and after serving in Bermuda was engaged in counter-espionage work in the United States under Sir William Stephenson, 'the quiet Canadian', whose life he published in 1962. He also described his own war experiences in his lively Secret Intelligence Agent (1982). In 1944 he was attached to Supreme Headquarters Allied Expeditionary Force, and in 1944–5 he worked for the Allied Control Commission for Austria, retiring with the rank of lieutenant-colonel.

After short stints as an adviser to Alexander Korda's film company and as an assistant editor of the Law Reports Hyde was in 1950 elected as Ulster Unionist MP for East Belfast. For ten years he was an energetic backbencher, concerned especially with the economic development of Northern Ireland. He sat on standing committees dealing with copyright and the Public Record Office and was a member of the United Kingdom delegation to the Council of Europe consultative assembly. On two issues, which cut across party lines, he intervened vigorously: in 1956 he seconded a measure for the abolition of capital punishment, and in 1957 he strongly supported the recommendations of the Wolfenden committee, 'a humanitarian document'. Hyde's attitude on these highly controversial issues, together with the feeling that he was not seen often enough in his constituency, contributed to his losing his seat in 1959. The constituency selection committee by a small majority readopted him but the association rejected him at a meeting from which Hyde was absent, being in the West Indies on parliamentary business. After leaving parliament he held, from 1959 to 1961, an academic post as professor of history and political science in the University of the Punjab, Lahore. He and his first wife, Dorothy, were divorced in 1952, and in 1955 he married Mary Eleanor, daughter of Colonel L. G. Fischer, of the Indian Medical Service. This marriage also ended in divorce, in 1966, and on 28 October in the same year he married Rosalind (Rose) Roberts (b. 1908/9), daughter of Commander James Francis William Dimond, naval officer.

Though Hyde practised many avocations, all of which provided him with experience and expertise, he was essentially a man of letters, with a prolific and varied output. His *British Air Policy between the Wars* (1976) was a balanced and lucid survey of a complex subject. He produced numerous biographies, his subjects ranging from the Emperor Maximilian of Mexico to Mrs Beeton, and including several eminent lawyers. From his undergraduate days, when he occupied Oscar Wilde's rooms in Magdalen, he was interested in Wilde and built up a valuable collection of Wildeana. He published a life of Wilde (1975), an edition of his trials (1948), a detailed account of his imprisonment and last years (1963), an edition of his plays (1988), and a life of Lord Alfred Douglas (1984). He had an intense, dispassionate interest in the homosexual world. His *The Other Love* (1970) was a history of homosexuality in England from the sixteenth century which fused legal knowledge with illustrative anecdotage; and *The Cleveland Street Scandal* (1976) was a full and enthralling account of a Victorian *cause célèbre*, involving all levels of society. He also published several works dealing with another secretive world, that of espionage.

Versatility, it is sometimes suggested, implies superficiality. This was certainly not so as regards Hyde. He was diligent, widely and thoroughly read, and assiduous in tracking down manuscript material: when the PRO released files on a subject in which he was interested he was first in the queue. His books were carefully crafted and very readable. Though chained to his desk for long stretches he enjoyed congenial company, conversation, and his clubs. A hospitable host, he encouraged and helped other writers, and was a splendid raconteur and a good listener (two roles which do not always go together). For many years he lived in Rye, where he wrote *Henry James at Home* (1969), but in his closing years he lived at Westwell House, Tenterden, Kent. He died at the William Harvey Hospital, Ashford, Kent, of acute pulmonary oedema and ischaemic heart disease on 10 August 1989. He was survived by his third wife, Rosalind, who bequeathed £10,000 to Queen's University, Belfast, to provide an annual Dr Harford Montgomery Hyde award for the top history graduate.

R. B. MCDOWELL

Sources WWW, *1981–90* · *The Times* (12 Aug 1989) · personal knowledge (2004) · private information (2004) · b. cert. · m. cert. [Dorothy Mabel Brayshaw Crofts] · m. cert. [Rosalind Roberts] · d. cert. **Archives** CAC Cam., papers · PRO NIre., corresp., news cuttings, and papers | HLRO, corresp. with Lord Beaverbrook **Likenesses** photograph, repro. in *The Times* **Wealth at death** £28,387: probate, 30 Oct 1989, *CGPLA Eng. & Wales*

Hyde, Henry, second earl of Clarendon (1638–1709), politician, was the eldest son of Edward *Hyde, first earl of Clarendon (1609–1674), and his second wife, Frances (1617–1667), daughter of Sir Thomas *Aylesbury. He was born in England on 2 June 1638, and baptized at St Margaret's, Westminster, nine days later, but went into continental exile with his parents following the royalist defeat in the civil war. When he was about seventeen his father began to use him as an amanuensis 'so that he was generally half the day writing in cipher or deciphering, and was

so discreet as well as faithful that nothing was ever discovered by him' (*Bishop Burnet's History*, 1.473). He continued to be employed in this capacity after the Restoration.

Early political career Hyde was returned as member for the borough of Lyme Regis in the Convention Parliament, and became a commissioner of trade in November 1660, a post he held until 1668. During that time he is also recorded, in 1661, as attending the Middle Temple. At the elections for the Cavalier Parliament he became a knight of the shire for the county of Wiltshire, holding the seat until the death of his father in 1674, when he succeeded him as second earl of Clarendon. Before that he was known by the courtesy title of Viscount Cornbury. In January 1661 he married Theodosia (*bap.* 1640), the daughter of Arthur *Capel, first Baron Capel; she died in March 1662. Their only child, Edward *Hyde, was born in 1661. In 1662, being 'much in the queen's favour' (*Bishop Burnet's History*, 1.473), he became the queen's private secretary, and was made her lord chamberlain in 1665. As an MP he was regarded as a court supporter, and was satirized by Andrew Marvell as 'leading the peers' sons to reinforce the court party in the house astride a hobby horse', perhaps an allusion to his activities in the Oxfordshire militia (*HoP, Commons, 1660–90*, 2.627). Cornbury inadvertently fell foul of the king about the time of his father's disgrace, when Charles discovered that a woman he was minded to make his mistress had clandestinely married the duke of Richmond, and wrongly suspected Cornbury of being involved in the intrigue. Cornbury defended his father at the time of his impeachment, and went into opposition when Clarendon went into exile. When he got the chance in 1674 to round on those he held responsible for the coup he attacked them with vigour. Thus he denounced the duke of Buckingham for murdering the earl of Shrewsbury and living with his widow, and castigated the earl of Arlington's religious indifference. He continued to oppose the ministry of the earl of Danby, whom he also considered to be one of his father's chief opponents. This led to the loss of his post under the queen in 1675.

In 1677, however, his brother Laurence *Hyde went on an embassy to the Dutch Republic, and Clarendon became a court supporter. Laurence wrote to him from The Hague in January 1678 to obtain his support for a treaty he had negotiated 'by the influence you have over a great many of the House of Commons' (Singer, 1.4). This was the beginning of a political partnership between the two brothers which was to last until the revolution. In 1680 Laurence entered the ministry and Henry was sworn of the privy council, and was restored to the queen's favour, becoming her treasurer and receiver-general of her revenues. By then he was himself in serious financial difficulties, despite his second marriage, on 19 October 1670 to Flower (1641–1700), daughter of Sir John Backhouse and widow of Sir William Backhouse (her second husband), having brought him the estate of Swallowfield in Berkshire. When he succeeded as earl of Clarendon he owed scriveners £19,860. In 1678 he sold land in an attempt to reduce his debt, and lived at Swallowfield rather than at the Hyde family seat at Cornbury, which he could not afford to maintain. Instead he stripped it of its assets and later sold it to his brother, though the sale was kept secret to avoid embarrassment. Clarendon's support of the court in the exclusion crisis led to his being named in the Commons in January 1681, along with Laurence and three other peers, as men inclined to popery who should therefore be removed from the king's service. The Hydes, who were both staunch Anglicans, particularly resented the accusation of Catholicism. Henry's attachment to the Church of England led him to write 'Some account of the tombs and monuments in the cathedral church of Winchester' which he 'finished this 17th day of February 1683 [1684]' (*The history and antiquities of the cathedral church of Winchester … begun by the Right Honourable Henry late earl of Clarendon and continued to this time by Samuel Gale*, 1715, preface). When James II came to the throne he indicated his public commitment to maintain the established church by employing the Hydes, the brothers of his first wife, as ministers. Laurence, by now earl of Rochester, became lord treasurer while Henry was made lord privy seal. After the defeat of his rebellion the duke of Monmouth appealed to them to intercede with the king for his life, but in vain.

Lord lieutenant of Ireland In September 1685 Clarendon was appointed lord lieutenant of Ireland. He had long shown an interest in Irish affairs, having headed a Commons committee on the state of Ireland in 1673. His brother as lord treasurer had a particular interest in Irish revenues, and Clarendon undertook to follow his advice about improving them. Thus after becoming lord lieutenant he continued investigations into their administration which his brother had already initiated. These retrospective inquiries antagonized some of those investigated, such as Sir William Talbot, so that as Clarendon was informed 'the height of their impudence is such that they spare not your Lordship' (Bodl. Oxf., Clarendon state papers, 88.200). Reform of the revenue administration also brought about the first overt criticism from Richard Talbot, Lord Tyrconnell, not because he objected to it, but because he thought he could make a better job of it. Tyrconnell became Clarendon's arch-rival in Ireland, heading the interests which James wished to foster against those of the Anglican ascendancy. While this involved replacing protestants with Catholics in the corporations, the commissions of the peace, and the army, as Clarendon observed 'the great contention here was more between English and Irish than between Catholic and Protestant' (Singer, 1.296). He wished, if Catholics were to be appointed to Irish offices, they would be sent over from England and not recruited in Ireland. When Tyrconnell returned from a visit to England in the summer of 1686 he had a commission giving him charge of military matters in Ireland; Clarendon, upon hearing of this, was reluctant to believe it, thinking it was 'more for the King's disservice to have it thought he has one here whom he will not trust, than it will be to my disrepute' (ibid., 1.288). He later confided to Rochester:

> It is a new method of doing business that all that the King thinks fit to have done should be performed by those in subordinate authority, and he, who is vested in all the power the King can give him, must sit like an ass and know nothing. (ibid., 2.10)

Tyrconnell proceeded to replace 'English' soldiers with 'Irish natives', many of whom spoke only Irish, while Clarendon was instructed to alter the judiciary in favour of

Henry Hyde, second earl of Clarendon (1638–1709), by Sir Peter Lely, 1661 [with his first wife, Theodosia Capel]

Catholics 'of old Irish race'. As he ruefully expressed it in a letter to Rochester: 'I believe it was never yet known, that the sword and the administration of justice were put into the hands of a conquered people' (ibid., 1.357). 'It is not so much the King's employing Roman Catholics in the army which disquiets men', he observed to the earl of Sunderland, 'as that there are such from whom, by their own words and actions, they fear to be oppressed instead of being protected' (ibid., 1.486). Such fears led to an exodus of many of the 'English' back to England, disrupting the trade of Ireland which Clarendon was concerned to promote. His concern about Irish commerce perhaps accounts for his choosing to accompany him to Dublin as secretary Sir Paul Rycaut, who had been employed by the Levant Company. At all events he had tried to persuade William Blathwayt, the secretary to the committee for plantations, that the navigation laws should be relaxed in order to permit American produce, such as tobacco, to clear customs in Ireland rather than exclusively in England.

Clarendon also did his best to allay people's fears of the consequences of James II's policies in Ireland. Thus he issued a proclamation granting indemnity for any words spoken against James before he became king. He also urged James to assure his subjects in Ireland that there would be no undoing of the Act of Settlement, which had resolved conflicting property claims at the Restoration. Consequently, when Tyrconnell went to England in August 1686 with a view to persuading James to revise the settlement, the reassurances Clarendon had given the 'English' that their property was secure were contradicted. He was convinced that Tyrconnell, in collusion with the earl of Sunderland, was undermining his position in England, with the queen as well as with the king, and that his tenure of the lord lieutenancy would soon be terminated. His hunch was correct. In October he received a list of five 'heads sent by His Majesty's command to the Lord Lieutenant of Ireland' (Bodl. Oxf., Clarendon state papers, 88.296). These were complaints about Clarendon's behaviour laid before the king by Tyrconnell. The first was that he had confirmed appointments to corporations despite Tyrconnell's objections to them, while the fifth complained that he had not acted on the king's directions to put Catholics on the corporation of Dublin. The second was that he had allowed disbanded soldiers to keep their arms when 'to leave men that must be displeased for being disbanded with arms in their hands' was 'against all prudence and reason' (Singer, 2.17). The third was that he had recalled an officer from raising men for a regiment of guards, thus countermanding Tyrconnell's orders. The fourth claimed that, though Clarendon had consented to the changes in favour of Catholics, he showed that he did not approve of them. As Clarendon riposted 'what account can a man give of his looks?' (ibid., 2.19). Though he defended himself against all the charges, and wrote a grovelling letter to the king, he knew that his days as lord lieutenant were numbered. This became clearer when he received a letter from Rochester conveying 'the terrible news of the king's displeasure', who thought his reply

unconvincing (ibid., 2.39). The decline in Rochester's influence with the king was rapidly diminishing the credit of the Hyde brothers at court. Clarendon, though the elder, was very much the junior partner, as he readily acknowledged, and he accepted that his tenure of office could not long outlast that of Rochester. On 8 January 1687 he learned that his brother had resigned, that he himself had been recalled to England, and that Tyrconnell was to be appointed lord deputy for the government of Ireland.

Counter-revolutionary James II did not wish to disgrace Clarendon. Thus Clarendon continued to be nominally lord lieutenant, with Tyrconnell technically his deputy, though in practice viceroy of Ireland. The king sought to sweeten the pill by granting Clarendon a pension of £2000 per annum. There was even a rumour that he would be restored to the privy seal, which had been kept in commission since his appointment to the lord lieutenancy, though James scotched this in March by giving it to the Catholic Lord Arundel of Wardour. Clarendon then had little option but to withdraw into private life, retiring to Swallowfield, where John Evelyn visited him in August 1687. Yet he felt sufficiently confident of the king's favour to attend his levee on new year's day 1688, and again on 12 and 28 January, when he intended to speak with James but could not get an opportunity. At the next levee, however, he did get the chance to talk to the king in private about a dispute that had arisen between himself and Catherine, the queen dowager. She claimed that Clarendon owed her money from the time when he had been in her service, and was suing him for its repayment. Clarendon, who desperately needed all the cash he could keep after losing his Irish post, maintained that others in her employ had been allowed to enjoy the payments the queen now demanded from him. James was naturally reluctant to get involved, but thought she would be advised not to take Clarendon to court. Nevertheless she did take proceedings against him in the court of exchequer. The case went on for months, adding significantly to Clarendon's debts.

Although Clarendon continued to attend the king's levee, he became involved in the resistance to James's order to read the second declaration of indulgence from all Anglican pulpits. On 12 May, a week after it was ordered, he dined at Lambeth Palace with the archbishop of Canterbury and five bishops. When the bishops of Chester and St David's, who disapproved of disobeying the royal command, left, the rest determined to summon more bishops to town to reinforce their resolution not to consent. The bishop of St Asaph, William Lloyd, one of those who answered the summons, stayed at Clarendon's house and kept him informed of their petition to the king. On 23 May Clarendon was apprised by Lord Chancellor Jeffreys that the king knew he had been involved in the consultation of the bishops. If this was a warning it did not prevent him from continuing to be involved, advising them about how best to defend themselves against the charges laid against them. Nor did it stop him going to congratulate James on the birth of his son, before going to the Tower to visit the seven bishops. After they were declared not guilty he was approached by the lord chancellor to act as a go-between with Archbishop Sancroft. This was the first hint of a rapprochement between the king and the Anglican tories. It was not followed up in earnest until 22 September, the day after James learned that William of Orange had launched an expedition to England. Then Clarendon went to the king's levee and afterwards to the lord chancellor's, where he was informed by Jeffreys that 'the King intended to send for my Lord of Canterbury, my brother, myself and some other of his old friends to discourse with us upon the whole state of his affairs' (Singer, 2.188).

When the king summoned such peers as were in town to a council meeting on 22 October, to deny the accusation that the birth of his son was supposititious, Clarendon at first hesitated to attend, not wishing to sit with Father Petre. Upon James assuring him that the Jesuit would not be there he still insisted on sitting as a peer rather than as a councillor. Nevertheless he accepted the king's denial, and remonstrated with Princess Anne when she appeared to lend credence to rumours about the circumstances of the prince's birth. He was actively involved in attempts to get the peers spiritual and temporal to address the king on the occasion of the invasion of William of Orange. When he learned on 15 November that his own son, Lord Cornbury, had gone over to William, he was mortified. Cornbury had given him enough trouble that summer by clandestinely marrying the under-age Katherine O'Brien, but that was nothing in comparison to the shame he felt as a parent now. 'O God, that my son should be a rebel!' he wrote in his diary (Singer, 2.204). The very next day he waited on the king, who 'said he pitied me with all his heart, and that he would be still kind to my family' (ibid., 2.205). Between then and 1 December events conspired to make Clarendon join Cornbury at the prince of Orange's camp. Princess Anne's flight to Nottingham perhaps relaxed his resolve to stay loyal to James, as he admired her decision, and wished he had had a share in her plan. When James returned from Salisbury and called a meeting of peers, Clarendon by his own admission spoke very indiscreetly, making assertions about the infiltration of the army with Catholics until the king felt obliged to interrupt him to deny them. It seems that this apparently heated exchange determined Clarendon to desert to William, using as an excuse the issuing of writs for a new parliament, which conveniently required him to journey to Salisbury for the elections. Curiously when Clarendon got down to Wiltshire he found that the prince was staying in Berwick, 2 miles from Hindon, with the widow of his own cousin, and that his son Cornbury was there too. The prince welcomed him.

Although he signed the association, Clarendon clearly felt that it was still possible for a parliament to meet and for the kingdom to be settled along the lines of the prince of Orange's declaration, without any change of monarch. Burnet, who could not even see how any parliament could possibly meet in the circumstances, was exasperated at his attitude, recording that 'he suggested so many peevish and peculiar things when he came that some suspected all

this was but collusion, and that he was sent to raise a faction among those that were about the prince' (*Bishop Burnet's History*, 4.340). The arrival of lords Halifax, Godolphin, and Nottingham as commissioners from the king to treat with William led the prince to appoint three of his own, including Clarendon, to parley with them. Clarendon was dismayed when a majority of William's supporters demanded that the writs for a new parliament should be superseded, calling off the elections. To his relief William refused to go along with their demands. Then to his great chagrin James played into their hands by fleeing from Whitehall down the Thames, throwing the great seal into the river as he fled, effectively cancelling the polls. Unfortunately the king was captured by fishermen, from whom he had to be rescued and escorted back to London. Clarendon joined the peers who had met at Windsor on 17 December to advise William what to do in this unexpected, and unwelcome, development. When he learned that they had advised sending the king to Ham House he dissented. What his own advice was is now hard to determine, since there is a conflict of evidence. According to some accounts he recommended that James be confined in the Tower. On the other hand, Burnet claimed that William himself told him that Clarendon vehemently proposed sending James to Breda 'on account of the Irish protestants' (*Bishop Burnet's History*, 4.355). This was in the context of the effect of the crisis on Ireland, where Tyrconnell was suspected of consolidating the Catholic position so that James could find a secure base there. Certainly Clarendon was concerned about the situation in Ireland, and might have approved of getting the king as far away from that kingdom as possible, but he himself recorded that he favoured allowing James to go to one of his own houses, such as Hampton Court or Windsor. The apparent inconsistencies can be resolved if it is supposed that, in the discussions of how to solve the problems posed by the king's return, several possibilities were scouted, and that he went along with different suggestions as they were raised. The one he did not support, that James be sent to Ham, was the one accepted by William. On his return to London from Windsor, Clarendon observed that 'I thought it the most melancholy day I had ever seen in my whole life' (Singer, 2.230). In the event the king's request to be allowed to go to Rochester was honoured. Clarendon sensed that this was a convenient device to enable him to escape again, and when James Graham, privy purse to James, visited him he urged him 'to beseech the King not to go from Rochester'. He was convinced even at this late stage that there were enough loyalists to address James to return, and 'that nothing could be so destructive to him and the public as his going out of the kingdom' (ibid., 2.232). On 23 December Clarendon was admitted to an audience in William's bedchamber, and was giving him the advice that his declaration should be the basis of their proceeding, when the prince cut him short and told him that James had fled. 'I was struck to the heart', Clarendon recorded, 'and, without saying one word, I made my leg, and went home as fast as I could' (ibid., 2.234).

James's departure from his kingdom was a shattering blow to those who wished him to remain their king. As Clarendon put it, 'it is like an earthquake' (Singer, 2.234). Events now outran all efforts of loyalists such as himself to control them. He was prepared to advise William on Irish affairs, but when the convention met in January 1689 he made a last-ditch effort to avoid replacing James with the prince. Along with his brother, Lord Rochester, and the earl of Nottingham he led those peers who proposed that there should be a regency 'under the style of King James II; which after a long debate was carried in the negative by two votes' (ibid., 2.256). He then opposed the motion that the throne was vacant, but found himself in a minority of forty-seven to sixty-two. His opposition to filling it by making William and Mary king and queen was so vehement that, according to John Evelyn, it 'putt him by all preferments, which must doubtlesse (have) been as greate as could have ben given him' (Evelyn, 4.626). Burnet attributed Clarendon's advocacy of James to his disappointment at not getting from William a promise of the lord lieutenancy of Ireland. However, though he had displayed apparently inconsistent behaviour since the invasion of the prince of Orange, thwarted ambition does not seem to have motivated it. On the contrary, like many who became nonjurors, whose loyalties were divided between church and crown, his conscience was severely tested in these months. If it had been less scrupulous, like Rochester's, he could have accommodated himself to the new regime.

Nonjuror In the spring of 1689 Clarendon contemplated going overseas to avoid arrest, and applied to Lord Nottingham, the secretary of state, for a pass. Nottingham 'wondered how I should enter into the Association at Salisbury and now refuse to take the oaths' (Singer, 2.268). His own answer to the secretary's question he gave to Bishop Lloyd of St Asaph:

> I told him I could not take them; thinking myself bound by the oaths of allegiance and supremacy which I had already taken. He told me those oaths did no longer oblige me, than the King, to whom I took them, could protect me; and that these new oaths were no more than to live quietly under King William; and he would fain have persuaded me to take them. But I answered, that I was fully satisfied that I could not be absolved from the oaths I had taken; to which these new ones were contradictory; that, having already taken the former oaths, my allegiance was due to King James, and not in my power to dispose of. (ibid., 2.266)

Instead of going abroad Clarendon stayed away from Whitehall, spending much of his time at his country houses. He came out of internal exile early in 1690 to take part in the parliamentary elections, using his influence in Hampshire and Wiltshire to back tory candidates, and appearing at the election of knights of the shire for Berkshire. That spring he had several meetings with 'friends', including James Graham and his brother Lord Preston, at Somerset House, home of the dowager Queen Catherine. These were almost certainly Jacobite cabals. William III warned him at the end of May that he suspected these meetings were held to plot against the regime, and that he had even thought of omitting Clarendon from an act of

grace, but had been dissuaded by the queen. On 24 June he was arrested on a charge of treason and confined to the Tower until 15 August, when he was released on bail. Two days later he went to Somerset House to see his friends. He became embroiled in another Jacobite intrigue which came to light in December when Lord Preston was arrested on board a ship carrying incriminating letters to James II in France, including one from Clarendon. He was again arrested and imprisoned in the Tower from 6 January 1691 to 3 July, when he was released on bail of £20,000. Towards this sum he found £10,000 himself, Rochester lent him £5000, and Lord Lovelace supplied the remaining £5000. Another condition was that he resided under the surveillance of a warder at Cornbury.

Clarendon spent the rest of William's reign in seclusion. Upon the accession of Queen Anne there were rumours that he would at last take the oaths, but he remained a nonjuror, and was therefore not permitted into her presence at court, although she did grant him a pension of £1500 a year. The publication of his father's *History of the Rebellion* in three volumes between 1702 and 1704 was largely his brother's work, but Clarendon took pride in it and presented a copy of the third volume to Evelyn on 9 December 1704. He died in London of asthma on 31 October 1709, and was buried four days later in Westminster Abbey, the charge of his burial being paid by the queen.

W. A. SPECK

Sources *The correspondence of Henry Hyde, earl of Clarendon, and of his brother Laurence Hyde, earl of Rochester*, ed. S. W. Singer, 2 vols. (1828) · Clarendon state papers, Bodl. Oxf., MSS Clarendon 87–90 · *Bishop Burnet's History* · Evelyn, *Diary* · HoP, *Commons, 1660–90* (1980) · S. Gale, *The history and antiquities of the cathedral church of Winchester … begun by the right honourable Henry late earl of Clarendon, and continued to this time by Samuel Gale* (1715) · R. Beddard, ed., *A kingdom without a king: the journal of the provisional government in the revolution of 1688* (1988) · 'Notes of a noble lord', *A parliamentary history of the Glorious Revolution*, ed. D. L. Jones (1988) · GEC, *Peerage*

Archives BL, corresp. and papers, Add. MSS 10613–10614, 15892–15898, 21485, 22551, 22558, 22578, 28190, 28792 · BL, diary, Stowe MS 770 · Bodl. Oxf., Clarendon state papers · U. Glas. L., corresp. | BL, letters to Sir J. Nicholas, Egerton MSS 2537–2540 · BL, letters to Sir William Trumbull · Bodl. Oxf., letters to Lord Abingdon, Clarendon MS 128

Likenesses P. Lely, oils, 1661, Badminton House, Gloucestershire [*see illus.*] · W. Wissing, portrait, priv. coll.

Hyde, Henry, **Viscount Cornbury and fifth Baron Hyde of Hindon** (1710–1753), politician, was born on 28 November 1710 at The Cockpit, Whitehall, the third but eldest surviving son of Henry Hyde, fourth earl of Clarendon and second earl of Rochester (1672–1753), politician, and his wife, Jane (1670–1725), the daughter of Sir William Leveson-Gower, fourth baronet, of Sittenham, Yorkshire. Styled Viscount Cornbury, he was educated at Christ Church, Oxford, whence he matriculated on 21 May 1725 and was created DCL on 6 December 1728. He was a friend and admirer of Viscount Bolingbroke, and his political allegiances were to the tory party and the Jacobite cause. In 1731 he met the Pretender (James Stuart) in Rome and offered his support for a Stuart restoration. On his return to England he declined a pension of £400 per annum from the crown and became MP for the University of Oxford, a seat which he retained until his elevation to the Lords in 1751. He then joined the parliamentary opposition to Sir Robert Walpole and became involved in Jacobite negotiations with the French government for a possible Stuart restoration. By the end of the decade, however, Cornbury's Jacobite sympathies were fading and he began distancing himself from the opposition, even to the extent of opposing the attempt to remove Walpole from office in 1741. From 1742 to 1745 he voted mostly with the ministry, though doubts about his loyalty to the Hanoverians persisted. These seemed justified during the rising of 1745, when he voted against the government's proposals to recall troops from Flanders and to send Hessian troops to Scotland. Increasingly disillusioned with politics, he requested permission from George II in 1748 to leave the country to restore his health.

Cornbury spent most of the next three years in France and returned to England in December 1750, having sold his Oxfordshire estate of Cornbury in an attempt to restore his finances. He successfully petitioned the king to succeed to his father's barony, and in January 1751 he took his seat in the Lords as Baron Hyde of Hindon, though he continued to be known by his courtesy title of Viscount Cornbury. He continued to eschew party politics and spent most of his remaining years in France.

Cornbury never married, though he may have been engaged in 1737 to Lady Frances (d. 1761), the daughter of his Oxfordshire neighbour George Henry Lee, second earl of Lichfield, and his wife, Frances Hales; she subsequently entered the convent of the blue nuns in Paris, of which she became abbess in 1757. Through his close connection with Bolingbroke, Cornbury enjoyed the friendship of Alexander Pope, Jonathan Swift, and Sir Charles Hanbury Williams. Bolingbroke was clearly the most formative intellectual as well as political influence on his life; the latter's *A Letter on the Spirit of Patriotism* (1736) and *Letters on the Study and Use of History* (1752) were both addressed to Cornbury. Cornbury's own writings were modest: in addition to various political pamphlets, he wrote a comedy, *The Mistakes, or, The Happy Resentment*, which was published posthumously in 1758.

Cornbury died in Paris on 26 April 1753, after a fall from his horse, and was buried in Westminster Abbey on 12 June. The barony reverted to his father, who died six months later, and most of his property was inherited by his niece, Lady Charlotte Capel, who took the name Villiers.   A. W. WARD, rev. M. J. MERCER

Sources E. Cruickshanks, 'Hyde, Henry, Viscount Cornbury', HoP, *Commons, 1690–1715* [draft] · GEC, *Peerage* · T. Lewis, *Lives of the friends and contemporaries of Lord Chancellor Clarendon*, 3 vols. (1852), 3.422–3 · Foster, *Alum. Oxon.* · A. Chalmers, ed., *The general biographical dictionary*, new edn, 32 vols. (1812–17) · J. Ingamells, ed., *A dictionary of British and Irish travellers in Italy, 1701–1800* (1997), 242
Archives BL, corresp. with the first Lord Hardwicke · BL, corresp. with the duke of Newcastle · BL, notes to Mrs Herbert and Lady Suffolk · U. Nott. L., corresp. with Henry Pelham
Likenesses G. Knapton, oils, 1741, Brooks's Club, London, Society of Dilettanti

Hyde [*née* Leveson-Gower], **Jane**, **countess of Clarendon and Rochester** (*c*.1672–1725), courtier, was the second

Jane Hyde, countess of Clarendon and Rochester (*c*.1672–1725), by Michael Dahl, *c*.1691

daughter of Sir William Leveson-Gower, fourth baronet (1647–1691), and his wife, Lady Jane Granville or Grenville (*c*.1653–1697), daughter of John *Grenville, first earl of Bath. Her father had been a firm whig and sympathizer of James Scott, duke of Monmouth, although he seems to have played no part in the rising of 1685. However, he angered William III by his attack on George Savile, first marquess of Halifax, which led to the king's denying him a peerage. Leveson-Gower then became a moderate tory and a supporter of Princess Anne. Before his death in 1691 he arranged Jane's marriage to Anne's first cousin Henry, Lord Hyde (1672–1753), son of Laurence *Hyde, first earl of Rochester. They married on 2 March 1692 and had three sons and five daughters. Portraits of Jane, a beauty at her marriage, by Michael Dahl and Godfrey Kneller, inspired at least one commemorative poem.

In contrast to the Leveson-Gowers' influence in Staffordshire, the Hydes' main estate of Wootton Bassett in Wiltshire did not support a secure political base; the borough was usually controlled by the St John family, and Jane's cousin George Granville, Baron Lansdowne, provided Lord Hyde with his Commons seat at Launceston, held from 1692 to 1711. Jane's politics were tory like those of her brother John Leveson-*Gower, first Baron Gower, but both were alarmed when in 1703–4 their nephew Sir William Wyndham, supported by Jane's uncle John, Baron Granville of Potheridge, Lady Henrietta's stepfather, proposed that he marry Lady Henrietta Somerset. Although this would have seemed a sensible alliance among tory families, Jane and her brother objected on the grounds of madness in Lady Henrietta's mother's family, the Childs, and her poor health. To their relief Sir William changed his mind and married Lady Catherine Seymour, daughter of Charles, sixth duke of Somerset. On her brother's death in 1709 Jane assumed the political stewardship of the Leveson-Gower interest and used it to ensure that a loyal friend of the family, William Burslem, became MP for Newcastle under Lyme in 1710.

During the formation of the Harley ministry in 1710, Queen Anne summoned her uncle Rochester to become lord president of the council in a bid to ensure the ministry's tory character. Jane and her husband followed in his wake, Hyde becoming joint vice-treasurer and paymaster of Ireland and a privy councillor, and Jane becoming lady of the bedchamber to the queen. Jane became countess of Rochester when her husband succeeded to the title in 1711. At court, Jane was a witness of the last days of Queen Anne. She wrote to her sister-in-law Katherine, Lady Gower, on 7 August 1714 that 'the death of this poor Queen puts everybody into a new world and tell the King comes, nobody knows who they depend on or what they depend upon' (Leveson and Leveson-Gower correspondence, 6.23a). She remained the object of admiration from poets, all of them tories in politics: Matthew Prior praised her as Myra in his *Judgement of Venus*; Jonathan Swift wrote about her to John Gay; and in 1716 Alexander Pope visited her in her house at Petersham Lodge, Richmond, where he admired the gardens ascending the hill in an artful confused manner. Her prominence in literary circles may have aroused the unfriendly interest of Lady Mary Wortley Montagu, who was at pains to stress that, of her eight children, Catherine (Kitty) [*see* Douglas, Catherine, duchess of Queensberry and Dover] was in fact the child of Henry *Boyle, Baron Carleton (1669–1725). He certainly left Catherine a life interest in part of his estates and £5000, while her mother was bequeathed all his diamond and ruby rings. The story was probably confirmed when Jane's only surviving son, Henry *Hyde, Viscount Cornbury (1710–1753), left all his estates to the daughter of his sister Jane, countess of Essex (*d.* 1726), completely ignoring his only living sister Catherine.

In the reign of George I, Jane continued to take a keen interest in her Leveson-Gower nephews and in the families of her married daughters, Jane and Catherine. She, with all the family, survived the catastrophic destruction of Petersham Lodge by fire on 1 October 1721, when between £40,000 and £50,000 worth of damage was done, including the loss of the important library of Lord Chancellor Clarendon. Jane died on 24 May 1725, not long after Lord Carleton, and was buried in Westminster Abbey on 1 June. Her husband, who succeeded to the earldom of Clarendon in 1724 on his cousin's death, died many years later on 10 December 1753, a few months after Lord Cornbury. His titles became extinct, with the estates descending to his Essex granddaughter Lady Charlotte Villiers (*née* Capel) under the terms of Lord Cornbury's will.

RICHARD WISKER

Sources Leveson and Leveson-Gower corresp., Staffs. RO, Sutherland-Leveson-Gower family papers, D 868, vol. 2, letters at beginning *THOS. TATE*; vol. 6, 18a–29b, 34c–37; vol. 7, 25b, 29b, 35a · Staffs. RO, Sutherland papers, D 593, C18, C/19/2, P/12/7, R/1/5/2, R/1/61, R/7/24 · T. Lewis, *Lives of friends and contemporaries of Lord Chancellor Clarendon* (1852), vol. 3, pp. 410–15 · *The complete letters of Lady Mary Wortley Montagu*, ed. R. Halsband, 3 vols. (1965–7), vol. 2, 48; vol. 3, 48 · A. M. Mimardiere, 'Leveson-Gower, Sir William', HoP, *Commons, 1660–90* · *VCH Wiltshire*, 9.188, 198–9 · *VCH Surrey*, 3.529 · *The correspondence of Alexander Pope*, ed. G. Sherburn, 1 (1956), 431; 3 (1956), 97, 148 · M. R. Brounell, *Alexander Pope and the arts of Georgian Britain* (1978), 154 · J. C. Wedgwood, 'Staffordshire parliamentary history [2/1]', Collections for a history of Staffordshire, William Salt Archaeological Society, 3rd ser. (1920), 207 · J. D. Stewart, *Sir Godfrey Kneller and the English baroque portrait* (1983), 50–51, pl. 41D · V. Biddulph, *Kitty, duchess of Queensberry* (1935), 8–11, 15, 29 · H. Walpole, *Anecdotes of painting in England*, ed. R. Wornum, new edn, 3 vols. (1849); repr. (1876), vol. 2, pp. 212–13 · R. Gibson, *Catalogue of portraits in the collection of the earl of Clarendon* [1977] · O. Manning and W. Bray, *The history and antiquities of the county of Surrey*, 2 (1809), 439 · GEC, *Baronetage*, 1.147 · GEC, *Peerage*, new edn, 2.21; 3.26–7, 268

Archives Staffs. RO, letter-books, D 868 | Staffs. RO, Sutherland MSS, D 593

Likenesses M. Dahl, oils, *c*.1691, priv. coll. [*see illus.*] · G. Kneller, oils, *c*.1692; Christies, 27 May 1960 · J. Faber junior, mezzotint (after G. Kneller), BM, NPG

Wealth at death £16,000 portion for younger children; plus £3513 from mother's estate: Staffs. RO, Sutherland MSS, D 593, C/18, C/19/2

Hyde, Laurence, first earl of Rochester (*bap.* 1642, *d.* 1711), politician, was the second son of Edward *Hyde, first earl of Clarendon (1609–1674), and Frances, *née* Aylesbury (1617–1667), his second wife. He was born in England and baptized at St Margaret's, Westminster, on 15 March 1642, but spent much of the interregnum in exile with his family on the continent. When they returned at the Restoration Laurence, though he was only eighteen, became a member of the Convention at a by-election held in August 1660 for the borough of Newport in Cornwall. In April 1661, still under age, he was elected for the University of Oxford, from which he had received an MA the preceding February, and of which his father was chancellor 'and then in the heighth of his power' (*An Essay*, 4). In October 1661 he went with William Crofts and Sir Charles Berkeley to France to congratulate Louis XIV on the birth of the dauphin. The following May 'by the interest of his father [he] was made Master of the Robes to his Majesty, in whose Favour he daily improved' (ibid., 4). He held the office until 1678, when he sold it to Sidney Godolphin. While he held it 'he was thought the smoothest man in the court' (*Bishop Burnet's History*, 1.474). Hyde married in 1665, before 14 June, Lady Henrietta Boyle (1645/6–1687), a younger daughter of Richard *Boyle, first earl of Burlington and second earl of Cork, and his wife, Elizabeth Clifford, Baroness Clifford. Their only son, Henry, was to succeed both his father as earl of Rochester and his uncle Henry *Hyde as earl of Clarendon. Of their four daughters Anne was the first wife of James Butler, second duke of Ormond; Henrietta married James Scott, earl of Dalkeith; Mary became the first wife of Francis Seymour, first Lord Conway; and Catherine never married.

When parliament met in Oxford in October 1665 because of the plague in London, Hyde was appointed with three other members to give the thanks of the House

Laurence Hyde, first earl of Rochester (*bap.* 1642, *d.* 1711), by Sir Godfrey Kneller, 1685

of Commons to the university for its loyalty during the civil wars. Along with his brother Henry Hyde he defended their father when he was impeached in 1667, making a speech in the Commons which impressed another member with 'its greatness and worthiness' enough to compare Hyde with Brutus. In it he assured the house 'that if he shall be found guilty no man shall appear more against him than I; if not, I hope everyone will be for him as much as I' (HoP, *Commons, 1660–90*, 2.629). Reflecting on the episode later, in some 'Meditations' composed on 9 December 1675, the first anniversary of Clarendon's death, he confessed that he was 'too earnest and overweening in my own thoughts, in persuading him to provide for the security of his person, by going out of England' and thought himself 'in the wrong for advising his going away' (Singer, 1.645–50). In Hyde's view it would have been better if Clarendon had stayed and faced his accusers, for then his innocence of their charges would have been proved. He noted that he had only seen his father twice between his exile and his death. The second of these visits was apparently to Moulins in June 1672 when he helped Clarendon with his critique of Hobbes's *Leviathan*.

Diplomat Hyde was chosen by Charles II to go as his ambassador-extraordinary to the king of Poland, John Sobieski, in June 1676. His credentials were to compliment the king on his accession and to take presents to his daughter Teresa, to whom Charles had stood as godfather

by proxy. Hyde arrived on 11 August in Danzig, where he was received by the queen and presented the princess with her gifts. He then went from Danzig to Leopol in Russia where John Sobieski was based, fighting the Turks. Unfortunately when he got there the king had left the town for the camp some distance away. Hyde kept a diary of his embassy, which records his growing impatience at not being able to gain access to the king. At one stage he was so frustrated that he sent a Scot with a trumpeter to the king's camp. Much to Hyde's distress the party was set upon by Tartars, and the Scottish messenger was killed. Hyde passed the time visiting churches of various denominations, and a synagogue. He also discussed the merits of protestantism and Catholicism with Polish ministers. When one claimed to have been converted from protestantism to Catholicism because protestants were divided on the topics of predestination and the eucharist, Hyde:

> told him I wished he could understand English, that I might give him a book (I meant Chillingworth) where he would see a man of our Church, of great learning and piety, of no interest nor passion, to have changed three times, and giving the reasons every time for so doing. (Singer, 1.597)

His acquaintance with such disputes was to stand him in good stead when James II tried to convert him to Catholicism. His ecumenical activities during his embassy included interceding with John Sobieski, on Charles's instructions, on behalf of Polish protestants (when he finally reached the Polish king in October). Subsequently a peace was negotiated between Poland and the Turks in which, according to Robert South, who accompanied Hyde as his chaplain, he 'had no small share of the management' (South, 23).

Eventually, in November, Hyde left on the second stage of his mission, which was 'to condole with the Emperor upon the late Empress's death … but upon his coming from thence to Vienna found the Emperor married and so passed privately home and arrived at Nimeguen' (Temple, 241). He then proceeded to Rotterdam where he found a commission from England appointing him as one of the mediators at the peace conference being held in Nijmegen. Not knowing whether to continue his journey home or to stay in the Netherlands, at The Hague he consulted Sir William Temple, who saw that the commission was intended:

> to introduce him into those kinds of characters and employments; and so advised him to go back to Nijmegen, which he did, and made a part of the Ambassy during a short stay there, but excused himself from entering into the management of any conferences or dispatches. (ibid., 242)

Hyde stayed at the conference for two or three weeks and then went to England.

In July 1677 Temple was recalled to London by the king who briefed him on an approach to William of Orange to accept terms of peace. Temple was reluctant to take on the commission, having failed previously to persuade the prince, and, when Charles insisted that he knew nobody who could undertake the task, recommended Hyde. The latter had clearly impressed Temple with his ability on his brief visit earlier in the year, after which they became friends as well as colleagues. Significantly the duke of

York was the first to respond positively to Temple's suggestion. Hyde, whose sister Anne was James's first wife, was already firmly in the duke's camp, and was to remain his stalwart supporter until the duke tested his loyalty to the limit. Since Temple remained in England until July 1678, Hyde was effectively the English ambassador to the Dutch republic from the summer of 1677 to that of 1678. His initial attempt to persuade William to accept the proposed peace terms was abortive, for instead of accepting them the prince went himself to England to marry James's daughter Mary. As a result of his visit Charles agreed to ally with the Dutch to put pressure on France to make peace. A treaty was sent over to Hyde on 23 December with instructions to urge William to accept it before parliament met on 15 January, so that the king could announce to the houses that 'according to their desires he has entered into an alliance with the States for the preservation of Flanders' (Bodl. Oxf., MS Firth b. 1, p. 13). Hyde thus found himself as an agent of Charles II's tortuous foreign policy at this juncture. The king sought the agreement of his allies and of the Commons for an effort to force Louis XIV to accept his terms for peace, backed up by the threat that, should the French king refuse, England would declare war on France. The Anglo-Dutch treaty required the United Provinces to pressurize their Spanish allies to accept the proposed terms, while England put similar pressure on the French. Hyde, who admitted that he was a novice in these negotiations, allowed William to alter the terms of the treaty so as to relax the intensity of the Dutch pressure on Spain. It even appears that his grasp of Latin, in which language the treaty was drafted, was inadequate for the occasion (certainly when Hyde had been obliged to address John Sobieski in that language his chaplain, South, had translated a speech for him from English into Latin). At all events, when Charles received the draft thus altered in this respect, he expressed his displeasure that Hyde had exceeded his instructions, and returned the treaty for the original terms to be restored. Hyde was mortified, and tried to get the prince to make the required changes. Although the Dutch demurred treating an ally as harshly as the enemy, amendments were made which, while they did not fully restore the original clauses, were acceptable to the king and the committee of the privy council on foreign affairs. Indeed, Sir Joseph Williamson wrote on 22 January 1678 to congratulate Hyde 'with all my heart your happy winding up so important and so difficult a work' (ibid., 107).

In addition to this treaty, Hyde was sent the draft of a defensive alliance between England and the Dutch republic which he was urged to persuade the prince and Pensionary Fagel to accept. This ran into the quagmires of the anarchic constitution of the United Provinces and of Dutch politics. The states of Holland considered it and then referred it to the towns. The fact was that Amsterdam was suspicious of Orangist intentions, especially after the marriage of William and Mary, and sought to make peace with France on much easier terms than those proposed by England. The treaty was thereby delayed until towards the end of February, when the whole diplomatic and military situation was drastically altered in favour of the French by their taking Ghent. All Hyde's diplomacy was thwarted by this development. Although he tried to keep William and Fagel interested in an Anglo-Dutch treaty against France, the anti-Orangist party in the republic proved too strong to resist its demands for peace. While Hyde continued to send letters to Williamson to inform the king and the committee on foreign affairs that a treaty with the Dutch could still be ratified, he also bypassed the privy council by writing to the earl of Danby on 26 February, informing him that the demands for peace were 'a torrent too great to be opposed' (Bodl. Oxf., MS Clarendon 87, fol. 275). Louis XIV encouraged these demands by offering terms in mid-April which had to be accepted by 10 May. The proposals were clearly designed to appeal to the peace party in the United Provinces. Hyde was convinced they would accept. As a critic observed 'he was so ingenuous as to acquaint the Court that Holland absolutely desired the Peace, even upon the terms proposed by France' (An Essay, 7). When the deadline came the French demanded a response. The states general of the United Provinces accepted the proposals as far as they related to the Dutch republic, but requested an extension of the time so that the allies could consider them. The French refused, upon which the Dutch agreed to sign a separate peace. Charles, furious with the delays, called off the proposed treaty with the Dutch, prorogued parliament until October, and recalled Hyde to England, where he arrived in the middle of June. He was back in the Netherlands before the end of August. According to Temple, who had returned as ambassador to the Dutch republic, 'Mr Hyde arrived at the Hague from England without the least intimation given me of his journey or his errand' (Temple, 362–3); its purpose was in fact to try to get the Dutch to repudiate the peace treaty they had signed with France, and to join England in a declaration of war. Temple took Hyde to William immediately to break the news to him, but the prince took it very coldly. When Hyde went out to visit Princess Mary, William vented his exasperation on the English court for blowing so hot and cold. A joint declaration of war with France would have been of great moment before the Dutch made peace. 'As it comes now it will have no effect at all', he told Temple, 'tho I would not say so to Mr Hyde' (ibid., 365). Consequently 'Mr Hyde had the mortification to return to England with the entire disappointment of the design upon which he came' (ibid., 373).

Court politician What little time Hyde could devote to parliamentary affairs in the late 1670s led to his being identified as a courtier. One opposition libel claimed he had received £20,000 in perquisites, while the first earl of Shaftesbury marked him down as 'thrice vile' in his list of MPs, the worst degree of servility to the court in that compilation. Hyde showed that he was loyal to the court when he defended the duke of York against moves to exclude him from the House of Lords. At the general election held in the spring of 1679 he was returned for the borough of Wootton Bassett, the manor of which he had purchased in

1676, allegedly for £36,000. On the fall of Danby the Treasury was put into commission, and Hyde became a commissioner. As a lord of the Treasury, and later lord treasurer, he came to be identified with reforms which have earned for him the reputation of putting the royal finances on a more professional basis. Of his work on the commission, of which he became first lord in November 1679, it was noted that he was 'always early plodding at the scrutiny of accounts and estimates before the other lords came' (HoP, *Commons, 1660–90*, 2.629). With Sidney Godolphin and Robert Spencer, earl of Sunderland, Hyde led the ministry which succeeded the collapse of Temple's privy council scheme in 1680. The three were immortalized as the 'Chits' from a doggerel verse which claimed that, because of their inexperience:

Sunderland, Godolphin, Lory [Hyde's nickname]
will appear such Chits in story,
'Twill turn all Politics to jests.
(J. P. Kenyon, *Robert Spencer, Earl of Sunderland*, 1958, 35n.)

In the previous parliament Hyde had not spoken on the Exclusion Bill, though he had voted against it, but in 1680 he emerged as one of the leading court speakers, contributing no fewer than fourteen speeches to the debates on exclusion. Thus on 21 October he came out in favour of 'such limitations as may secure the Protestant religion', and on 11 November urged that exclusion could not be made binding, for there was 'a loyal party which will never obey, but will think themselves bound by their oaths of allegiance and duty, to pay obedience to the Duke, if ever he should come to be King, which must occasion civil war' (*An Essay*, 10, 13). On 7 January 1681 the opposition passed a resolution for his removal from the king's service along with four peers, including his brother Henry, the earl of Clarendon. This incident deeply affected him, reducing him to tears. It apparently led him to resolve to lower his profile, for he did not stand for election to the third Exclusion Parliament, and apparently advised its early dissolution. By then he was in a position to assure Charles II that he could manage without parliamentary supply. Although the royal finances were taking a turn for the better largely because of a growth in overseas trade, which boosted the customs, they were also benefiting from Hyde's measures at the Treasury. Severe pruning of expenses had cut expenditure, while efforts to increase revenue, such as abandoning tax farming, were showing dividends. Every little helped, including the subsidy from Louis XIV which was seen by earlier historians as 'the worst act of his political life' (*DNB*). Hyde's prudent management of the king's finances presumably account for his being raised to the peerage as Viscount Hyde of Kenilworth in April 1681, and earl of Rochester in November 1682. His favour with Charles led Dryden to praise him in *Absalom and Achitophel* as Hushai, 'the friend of David in distress', whose 'frugal care supply'd the wanting throne' (part 1, lines 888–97).

Rochester was even more in the favour of the duke of York, who became a leading force in the government upon his return from Scotland in spring 1682. Together they supervised church appointments through a commission for ecclesiastical promotions, and encouraged the suppression of protestant dissent. Consequently when Charles began to cool towards his brother in the summer of 1684, Rochester's interest at court also went cold. Before that James had been able to protect him from adversaries, who were numerous, for Rochester notoriously made enemies. As the earl of Dartmouth recalled:

> I never knew a man that was so soon put into a passion, that was so long before he could bring himself out of it, in which he would say things that were never forgot by any body but himself; therefore he had always more enemies than he thought he had; though he had as many professedly so, as any man of his time. (*Bishop Burnet's History*, 1.474)

At this time they included the marquess of Halifax, who charged Rochester with peculation in the hearth tax to the tune of £40,000, even accusing him of tearing pages out of the accounts to cover his tracks. In August Rochester was removed from the Treasury commission and 'kicked upstairs' to the post of lord president. Shortly afterwards the duke managed to obtain for him the lord lieutenancy of Ireland but Rochester never went to Dublin and early in 1685 the charges of peculation were being pressed so hard that there were rumours he would be sent to the Tower. Rochester himself meditated on the vanity of human wishes in a memoir written on the anniversary of his daughter's death in January 1686. He recorded how he had then contemplated retirement from public life because of his private affliction, not mentioning the accusations he was then facing. In the midst of his distress came the sudden and unexpected news that Charles II had died. By the favour of the duke of York, now James II, Rochester was:

> immediately snatched out of these peaceable and quiet intentions and contemplations, to attend him and his service in the entering on the throne, and quickly after was translated in my own person into a more eminent and splendid station in the world than I had seen before. (Singer, 1.174)

On the accession of James, Rochester became lord treasurer and in June 1685 was made a knight of the Garter. This was the high point of his career. The defeat of the duke of Monmouth's rebellion that summer, however, marked a change in the king's attitude towards the Anglican church, of which Rochester emerged as one of the chief defenders. Rochester dated the withdrawal of the king's favour from the day of Monmouth's execution in July. Convinced that providence was on his side James demanded concessions from Anglicans to his fellow Catholics. Thus he requested parliament's approval of the continuation of commissions he had given to Catholics in the army raised to suppress the rebels. When parliament refused he prorogued it in November. Rochester's reaction to these developments can only be surmised. He was probably not in favour of the commissions to Catholics, since the earl of Sunderland chose this moment to begin his intrigue at court to undermine him. Thereafter Rochester was involved in a rearguard action to forestall his own fall from the king's grace. He apparently cultivated Catharine Sedley, the king's mistress, who was so much in the ascendant early in 1686 that James had her made countess of Dorchester. This did little to endear Rochester to the queen, who was Sunderland's main ally at court. Something of the strain Rochester was undergoing might be detected behind his extraordinary display of public drunkenness in the company of Lord Chancellor Jeffreys in February 1686, when 'they stripped into their shirts, and had not an accident prevented had gott upon a sign-post to drinke the King's health' (*The Memoirs of Sir John Reresby*, ed. A. Browning, 2nd edn, ed. M. Geiter and W. A. Speck, 1991, 411). Although Jeffreys was a notorious drunkard, Rochester, albeit a heavy drinker, was not. In the summer of 1686 he joined the commission for ecclesiastical causes, an action later laid against him by his opponents; even his brother Clarendon criticized his membership, and hoped he would not use it to harm the church. His supporters excused it on the grounds that he sought to use his membership to protect the church from greater damage. James then sought to convert Rochester to Catholicism, for which purpose a disputation was held in December between Anglican divines chosen by Rochester and Catholic priests selected by the king. Rochester professed to have been unconvinced by the arguments of the priests. James had tested his loyalty to the limit, and on 4 January 1687 he was dismissed from the treasurership. The king sweetened the pill with a pension of £4000 a year out of the Post Office and grants of land valued at £20,000. Three months later, Rochester lost his wife: Countess Henrietta died on 12 April and was buried four days later in Westminster Abbey.

Although no longer at the centre of public affairs Rochester remained a court politician. Thus that summer he went over to the Netherlands 'to take care of the king's interests there, and to do him all the service he could that was consistent with his honour and the Protestant Cause' (*An Essay*, 18). On his return he was made lord lieutenant of Hertfordshire, and in November and December put to the local gentry the three questions drawn up by James to test the attitude of his subjects to his attempt to obtain a parliament willing to repeal the Test Act and penal laws. Indeed he allegedly put them with some acerbity, which they resented, but if this was the case their resentment does not seem to have been remembered against him after the revolution of 1688: his role in the turbulent events of 1688–9 was still that of a firm supporter of James II. When James learned of the imminence of a Dutch invasion he hastily abandoned his pro-Catholic and dissenter policies and turned to his former allies the Anglican tories, prominent among whom was Rochester. On his return from Salisbury in November James summoned a meeting of peers to advise him. Among them Rochester took a leading part in advocating the summoning of parliament. James initially took this advice, but then abandoned it in favour of flight to France on 11 December. That very day Rochester, with the bishop of Ely, summoned a meeting of peers to the Guildhall to fill the vacuum left by the king's departure. They hoped to use the provisional government to rally the loyalists behind an attempt to reconcile James and William, but were outmanoeuvred by the prince's

supporters, who had no desire for a reconciliation. One sign of this was that Rochester had to yield the chair of their meetings to the marquess of Halifax. Another was the cold reception he received from William when his brother Clarendon took him down to Windsor to meet the prince on 16 December. James's return to London following his apprehension by fishermen in Kent temporarily raised the spirits of the loyalists and dampened those of the Williamites, but the king's second and successful attempt to reach France ended all Rochester's hopes of an accommodation between him and William. Nevertheless Rochester was still prepared to fight a rearguard action, and in the Convention was one of the chief advocates of a regency, which many suspected to be a stalking horse for the return of James.

High-church tory Rochester is often labelled a high-church tory before the revolution, but his political attitude under Charles II and James II was much more that of a court politician. Tories criticized him for his membership of the commission for ecclesiastical causes, while his browbeating of the Hertfordshire gentry to support repeal of the Test Act was scarcely a distinguishing mark of toryism. After the revolution, however, he threw in his lot with the tory party. Unlike his brother he took the oaths to the new regime and worked his way back into the favour of the new monarchs, and especially of Mary, whom he came to advise on church matters. In 1692 he was admitted to the privy council. Burnet, who claimed the credit for reconciling Rochester with the queen, asserted that he 'went into an interest very different from what I believed he would have pursued' when he joined with the high-church tories to attack the Williamite bishops (*Bishop Burnet's History*, 4.211). After Mary's death he found himself in opposition to the whig government but, again unlike Clarendon, never flirted with Jacobitism. On the contrary, Rochester suggested a form of words which allowed tories to join the associations in support of William at the time of the assassination plot. He also supported the high-church campaign for the recall of convocation in the later 1690s, insisting upon its being elected along with parliament as a condition for taking office as lord lieutenant of Ireland in December 1700. His leading role in the tory ministry which William constructed at that time was seen by one MP as making 'Lord Rochester now prime minister of state' (*Diary of Sir Richard Cocks*, 61, 72). His prominence in the ministry made him the target of a hostile pamphlet, *The True Patriot Vindicated* (1701). The title was inspired by the dedication to Rochester of sermons by his chaplain, Charles Hickman, which fulsomely praised his devotion to the Church of England, concluding that he had 'given the world so glorious an example, both of a *Patriot* and a *Confessor* such as I am sure this Age cannot equal' (Hickman, 'epistle dedicatory'). *The True Patriot* was a vicious satire, raking up all the charges it could against Rochester going back to Charles II's reign. When it was reprinted after his death in 1711 it prompted a riposte, *An Essay towards the Life of Laurence, Earl of Rochester*. The author of this claimed that:

in the latter part of King William's reign he had also the chief direction of Scotch affairs. That Prince had a wonderful esteem for his Lordship, and even courted his friendship, giving him frequent visits at his charming seat in Petersham. (*An Essay*, 24)

There is no strictly contemporary evidence to support these claims. On the contrary, Rochester advocated foreign policies diametrically opposed to those of the king, which did not endear him to William. Thus he recommended the acceptance of Carlos II's will, which would have given the whole of the Spanish empire to the Bourbon claimant. Such appeasement of Louis XIV led to Rochester's dismissal from the lord lieutenancy on 25 January 1702. When William died and Anne succeeded on 8 March, however, Rochester retained the post since 'his commission was never superseded' (bishop of Clogher to Bishop King, 12 March 1702, TCD, Lyons collection, 888). By then war had broken out, so that advocacy of appeasement was no longer feasible. Rochester did, however, on one of his rare attendances at the cabinet, promote a tory 'blue water' policy against Marlborough's insistence on continental strategy. He had consistently advocated such a policy since 1692, and enshrined it in the preface to the first volume of his father's *History of the Rebellion* which he saw through the press in 1702: 'this Kingdom cannot be useful to the common cause in any other way so much as at sea' (p. ix). Rochester developed this argument about strategy to point a finger at Marlborough:

> The perpetual jealousy that, some time or other, endeavours may be used by the increase of land forces, to advance another greatness, and another interest, will fix the genius of the nation still to depend on its greatness and its security by sea.   (p. x)

He even used his influence with tories in the Commons to oppose a grant to Marlborough of £5000 from the Post Office. Rochester was perhaps relying on his relationship with Queen Anne to influence her counsels, but even though he was the queen's uncle, if there is any truth in Lady Marlborough's story that he had taken the side of his other niece, Mary, against Anne a decade earlier—and Sarah's tales lost nothing in the telling—then her decision to stick by the Marlboroughs had been effectively taken then too. At all events Anne took their side on this occasion, and in February 1703 ordered Rochester to go to Ireland. He preferred to resign the lieutenancy rather than obey.

In opposition Rochester championed high-church causes such as the occasional conformity bills. When the second and third volumes of Clarendon's *History of the Rebellion* appeared in 1703 and 1704 he again used the prefaces to develop tory arguments. Thus in the second he posed the rhetorical question 'what can be the meaning of the several seminaries and as it were universities, set up in various parts of the kingdom … where the youth is bred up in principles directly contrary to monarchical and episcopal government?' (pp. v–vi). Again, in the third, he warned that 'there may want the concurrence of a parliament to prevent the return of the same mischievous practices, and to restrain the madness of men of the same

principles in this Age, as destroyed the last' (p. x). Rochester was singled out in a celebrated pamphlet, *The Memorial of the Church of England* (1705), as one of the leading tories whose departures from the ministry had brought the church into danger. Although Anne in her speech from the throne at the opening of parliament in October denounced those who supported its arguments, Rochester defied her by asserting in the Lords, when she was present, that he thought the church was in danger. After a heated debate the upper house passed a resolution that those who held such views were enemies to the queen, the church, and the kingdom. It was because he feared they threatened the church that Rochester opposed both the Regency Bill and the union with Scotland. In the first parliament of Great Britain following the union Rochester joined in the attacks on the conduct of the Admiralty under Prince George which, though justified, did much to offend the queen. Although there were rumours that he was included in Robert Harley's schemes to replace the whig ministers with tories, this was categorically denied and seems intrinsically unlikely. He did not feature in Harley's original plans which underlay the ministerial revolution of 1710, and to some extent these were blown off course by Rochester's appointment to the lord presidency of the council, since it was a bigger concession to the tories than Harley desired. How he obtained the post remains mysterious, though it does appear to have been Anne's own decision, for in mid-July she 'sent for' him to go to court (Bromley to Grahme, 16 July 1710, Kendal RO, Levens MSS). Quite how he had come back into her favour is unknown. There was no love lost between him and Harley, and it was not until 21 September that he was appointed. In office, however, he displayed responsible statesmanship. Consequently when he died unexpectedly, in London on 2 May 1711, he was sorely missed by the queen and the prime minister. He was buried in Westminster Abbey eight days later.   W. A. SPECK

Sources *The correspondence of Henry Hyde, earl of Clarendon, and of his brother Laurence Hyde, earl of Rochester*, ed. S. W. Singer, 2 vols. (1828) • Bodl. Oxf., MSS Firth b. 1, b. 2 • Bodl. Oxf., Clarendon MSS • E. Hyde, earl of Clarendon, *The history of the rebellion and civil wars in England*, 3 vols. (1702–4) • *The true patriot vindicated* (1701) • *An essay towards the life of, Laurence, earl of Rochester* (1711) • C. Hickman, *Fourteen sermons preach'd at St James' Church in Westminster* (1700) • R. South, *Posthumous works* (1717) • W. Temple, *Memoirs of what passed in Christendom from the war begun in 1672 to the peace concluded in 1679* (1692) • *Bishop Burnet's History* • HoP, *Commons, 1660–90* • *The parliamentary diary of Sir Richard Cocks, 1698–1702*, ed. D. W. Hayton (1996) • GEC, *Peerage*

Archives BL, corresp. and papers, Add. MSS 8103–8124, 15892–15898, 17016–17019 • Bodl. Oxf., letters, Don MS c 68 | BL, corresp. with Henry Coventry, Add. MSS 25119, 25125 • BL, letters to Henry Sydney, Add. MSS 32680–32681, *passim* • BL, corresp. with James Vernon, Add. MS 40775 • BL, letter-book of corresp. with Sir Joseph Williamson, Ref: 69 • Bodl. Oxf., Clarendon state papers • Bodl. Oxf., corresp. with Sir Joseph Williamson, MSS Firth b. 1, b. 2 • CAC Cam., corresp. with Thomas Erle • PRO NIre., letters to Lord Coningsby • TCD, Lyons MSS

Likenesses G. Kneller, oils, 1675–1700, Ranger's House, London • G. Kneller, oils, 1685, NPG [*see illus.*] • J. Houbraken, line engraving, pubd 1741 (after G. Kneller, 1685), NG Ire. • G. Kneller, portrait, Devonshire Arms, Bolton Bridge, North Yorkshire • oils (after W. Wissing, *c*.1685–1687), NPG • oils (after W. Wissing), Audley End House,

Essex • portrait (after W. Wissing), Bodl. Oxf., NPG; version, Hardwick Hall, Derbyshire

Hyde, Sir Nicholas (*c*.1572–1631), barrister and politician, was born at Wardour Castle, Wiltshire, the fourth and youngest son of Laurence Hyde (*d*. 1590) of Gussage St Michael, Dorset, and West Hatch, Tisbury, Wiltshire, and his second wife, Anne, *née* Sibell (*d*. 1606), widow of Matthew Colthurst of Claverton, Somerset, but originally of Kent. Supposedly bequeathed £30 a year at his father's death, he probably received additional support from his widowed mother, 'who was left very rich' (*Life of … Clarendon*, 1.3). After entering Exeter College, Oxford, in May 1590, Nicholas joined his two older brothers Laurence and Henry in membership of the Middle Temple on 14 July following, although he was not formally admitted to a chamber there for another three years. In 1597 he gained a parliamentary seat for the pocket borough of Old Sarum, and the next year was called to the bar.

Hyde's first professional preferment was to a workaday clerkship of assize on the Norfolk circuit, which he held between 1600 and 1604. In 1601 he married Mary, the daughter of Arthur Swayne, of Sarson, Amport, Hampshire; their first son, Nicholas, was baptized in July 1603 at Dinton, Wiltshire. Now a veteran MP, having sat for Andover in the 1601 parliament, Hyde was again returned to James I's first parliament (1604–10), this time for Christchurch, Hampshire. A letter of recommendation from John Foyle, the previous member, described Hyde as 'a very sufficient gent. He is Clarke of Assize in my lord chief Justices Circuite, he dwelleth in Wiltshire where he payeth subsidie and is every way a fytt man' (History of Parliament Trust, photocopy from Christchurch borough muniments). While the continued presence of his still more experienced MP and barrister brother Laurence makes it difficult to distinguish Nicholas's own interventions, he was noted in 1610 as resisting the great contract 'upon theise conditions proposed', and also argued against the legality of impositions (Gardiner, 120, 130). In the 1614 parliament (where he sat for Bath as the borough's recorder) his involvement in preparations for a proposed conference with the Lords on impositions was attested by his lower house colleague Edwin Sandys, who characterized Hyde as 'a zealous member' (Jansson, 226). After the dissolution Hyde and other dissident MPs were summoned before the privy council and forced to watch the burning of their notes, presumably in order to prevent subsequent publication. Hyde was also temporarily removed from the Wiltshire commission of the peace.

Such public retribution may well have facilitated Hyde's succession to his brother as recorder of Bristol in 1615, drawing attention to his commitment to economic and political attitudes which Laurence had espoused since the 1590s. Besides a small annual fee, the recordership offered various opportunities for associated legal work. This appointment also strengthened his involvement with the Atlantic maritime trades, an association he shared with other Middle Templars; already a director of the Virginia Company, he later became a founding member of the Somers Island Company.

Hyde was raised to the bench of the Middle Temple in 1617; extensive notes of his Lent reading on the Henrician statutes of wills (32 Hen. VIII c. 1 and 34 & 35 Hen. VIII c. 5) survive in manuscript. According to Simonds D'Ewes, his father's witticism that now 'the Middle Temple bench was Hide-bound' incurred Nicholas's lasting enmity (*Autobiography*, 2.48). Reciprocal ill feeling colours D'Ewes's claim that before his promotion to the judiciary in 1627, 'this man was … but plain Mr Nicolas Hyde, and of mean esteem, having a small estate and practising chiefly in his chamber' (ibid.). On the eve of his call to the Middle Temple bench, Hyde does not indeed appear among the first rank of barristers pleading before the superior courts of Westminster Hall. Yet his practice seems to have been widely distributed across a number of jurisdictions, both common law and equity. He also held substantial urban office (by 1619 he had added the recordership of Bath to that of Bristol), while possessing numerous mercantile connections and investments, including a founding share in the New River enterprise supplying London with fresh water. Such commercial links may well have contributed to Hyde's next major professional achievement, when he was chosen in 1624 as one of two legal advisers allowed by the House of Lords to Lionel Cranfield, the impeached lord treasurer, himself a former merchant.

Returned to the first parliament of the new reign in 1625 by both Bath and Bristol, Hyde chose to represent the latter; although named to a number of committees he played little other part in the business of the Commons. Next year the duke of Buckingham, possibly impressed by the quality of advice Cranfield had received, retained Hyde to help draft responses to his articles of impeachment. This commission led directly to Hyde's knighting and appointment as chief justice of king's bench on 5 February 1627, filling a vacancy left by Randolph Crew's dismissal. There seems no reason to doubt Hyde's avowal that against Buckingham's insistence he himself sought only a serjeant's place (*Diary of Sir Richard Hutton*, 87). Nevertheless, his meteoric rise inevitably attracted adverse comment, including the following verse supposedly repeated at Bury St Edmunds during the new chief justice's first assize circuit in Lent 1627:

Learned Coke, Court Montague
The aged Lea, and honest Crew
Two preferred, two set aside
And then starts up Sir Nicholas Hyde!
(*Autobiography*, 2.49)

Despite the circumstances of his appointment, Hyde's performance as chief justice displayed some independence. Although in *Darnell's case* (1627) he and his colleagues refused to bail the five imprisoned loan resisters, they seem to have been moved by the crown's arguments rather than coerced at a pre-trial interview with the king, Buckingham, and other councillors. They also effectively resisted Attorney-General Heath's attempt to have their interim rule entered as a final judgment. These proceedings inevitably became a major issue in the subsequent parliament, where the judges' explanation of their actions broadly escaped censure. Despite considerable pressure, they then refused to provide the king with the undertaking he sought as to future judicial interpretations of the petition of right. However, in the aftermath of the dissolution of 1629, Hyde did prove more amenable to executive coercion than his colleague Chief Baron Walter. Although the full extent of his tractability is difficult to determine, a progressive pliancy is discernible during the complex manoeuvres which concluded in February 1630 with the conviction of the dissident MPs imprisoned nearly a year before.

By his will made in May 1630 Hyde bequeathed manors in Hampshire, Wiltshire, and Devon, East India stock, and London waterworks shares to his wife, daughter, and three surviving sons. His death at home at Hinton Daubney, Catherington, Hampshire, on 25 August 1631 was attributed by D'Ewes to a fever caught following a 50 mile ride on a hot day, undertaken 'out of his penurious and base disposition to save charges', although others thought it resulted from an impostume, a surfeit, or some gaol infection. While overdrawn, D'Ewes's further claim that (besides having 'a yellowish complexion like tallow, and … a mean aspect') Hyde's 'poverty made him very worldly-minded and griping' (*Autobiography*, 50) gains some credence from the latter's retention of his recordership at Bristol after becoming chief justice, until a direct conflict of interest forced his resignation in January 1631. Judicial colleagues, nevertheless, eulogized Hyde's 'good, fair and aimiable demeanour in his place' (*Diary of Sir Richard Hutton*, 87), besides his 'Integrity and prudence in those difficult times' (Whitelocke, 16). Hyde was buried at Catherington.   WILFRID PREST

Sources R. C. Gabriel, 'Hyde, Nicholas', HoP, *Commons, 1558–1603*, 2.364 [and draft biography] · W. R. Prest, *The rise of the barristers: a social history of the English bar, 1590–1640*, 2nd edn (1991) · L. J. Reeve, *Charles I and the road to personal rule* (1989) · *The autobiography and correspondence of Sir Simonds D'Ewes*, ed. J. O. Halliwell, 2 (1845) · *The life of Edward, earl of Clarendon … written by himself*, new edn, 3 vols. (1827), vol. 1 · *The diary of Sir Richard Hutton, 1614–1639*, ed. W. R. Prest, SeldS, suppl. ser., 9 (1991) · *The parliamentary diary of Robert Bowyer, 1606–1607*, ed. D. H. Willson (1931) · M. Jansson, ed., *Proceedings in parliament, 1614 (House of Commons)* (1988) · D. H. Sacks, *The widening gate: Bristol and the Atlantic economy, 1450–1700* (1991) · S. R. Gardiner, ed., *Parliamentary debates in 1610*, CS, 81 (1862) · *DNB* · [B. Whitelocke], *Memorials of the English affairs* (1682) · C. T. Martin, ed., *Minutes of parliament of the Middle Temple*, 4 vols. (1904–5), vol. 1 · Baker, *Serjeants* · J. J. Hammond, 'Notes on the Hydes of Wilts. and Cheshire', *Wiltshire Notes and Queries*, 6 (1908–10) · C. H. Hopwood, ed., *Middle Temple records*, 1–2 (1904) · will, PRO, PROB 11/160, fols. 394v–395v

Archives BL, law reports, Hargrave MSS 27, 132 | CUL, cases from Hyde's reading, MS Ee.6.3, fols. 122–52

Wealth at death substantial; significant lands, equities, plate: will, PRO, PROB 11/160, fols. 394v–395v; PRO, C 142/720/9, cited Baker, *Serjeants*

Hyde, Pearl Marguerite (1904–1963), leader of women's voluntary work and politician, was born in north London, the only girl among five children of Harman Bigby and his wife, Ellen Amelia, *née* Abbey. Her mother died when she was four and her father was killed in a car accident five years later, in 1913. At the time of his death he was licensee of The Vine inn in Waltham Cross, Hertfordshire; Pearl subsequently lived with a married elder brother in a Birmingham hotel run by her uncle. In 1920 she moved to Coventry to live at the White Lion public house in Smithfield Street, where the licensee, a former friend of her father, taught her the family trade. In 1923 she married Walter Eric Hyde, with whom she lived at 40 Westwood Road, Coventry, until 1939 and with whom she had one son, Eric.

Pearl Hyde, whose interest in politics was awakened by unemployment in the 1920s, joined the Labour Party in 1931, having gained her political education by sitting night after night in the public gallery of the council chamber. After fighting three unsuccessful elections in the Westwood ward, where with other members of the Women's Co-operative Guild she started a maternity and child welfare clinic staffed by volunteers, she was finally elected to the council for the Walsgrave ward in 1937.

What made Pearl Hyde's name was the Coventry blitz. Shortly before the war, overcoming pacifist reservations, she had accepted appointment as leader of the local Women's Voluntary Service (WVS), to the chagrin of local social leaders who had expected a woman of more established social status to be given this post. The energy, courage, and leadership that she displayed in the chaos following the November 1940 air raid on Coventry earned her an MBE. Something of her presence survives in *Heart of Britain*, a documentary film made by Humphrey Jennings in 1941 in which she features briefly. While the camera lingers on a shot of WVS women getting tea from an urn Jennings's voice-over intones: 'Here, in Coventry, those everyday tasks of the women came right through the fire and became heroic'. Speaking to camera Hyde explains: 'You know you feel such fools standing there in a crater with a mug of tea … until a man says "it washed the blood and dust from my mouth" and you know you really have done something useful'.

'Our Pearl', as the chief constable called her, was a large woman 'with heart and sympathy to match her generous proportions' (G. Hodgkinson, quoted in *Coventry Evening Telegraph*, 15 April 1963). On duty in the blitz she wore the chief constable's trousers, not only literally but also on occasions metaphorically, leaving her superiors in the WVS to appease those on whose authority she had trespassed in her practical determination to get things done. She was, according to her mentor, the Coventry Labour politician George Hodgkinson, 'the leading lady, the queen bee, dicing with death and embarrassing the Regional Commissioner [Lord Dudley] by kissing him in public' (Hodgkinson, 150). Cinema audiences cheered her in neutral New York, and a model was set up on Broadway of the 'devil's kitchen', from which, in the cellars of Coventry police station, the WVS produced tea and sandwiches for civil defence workers. Even when not kissing aristocrats she had an ebullient sense of fun. An unpublished memoir written by her WVS second in command has Pearl conniving at the procurement of alcohol for the residents of an old people's home and, to the disgust of the matron, entertaining them with a rendition of 'Knees up Mother Brown'.

After the war Pearl Hyde was active in local Labour politics, becoming an alderman in 1952 and serving as Coventry's first woman lord mayor in 1957, a post in which she arranged to be supported by a lady mayoress, her daughter-in-law, Elizabeth Hyde. Pursuing with enthusiasm Coventry's international links, she once again impressed the citizens of New York, where 'her magnificent presence in her robes of office literally stopped the traffic', while in Czechoslovakia peasants mistook 'her regal figure driving past in an open car' for the queen of England (*The Times*, 8 May 1963). She carried out her political work in an undoctrinaire and unpartisan spirit, and was active in a wide range of charitable activities in the city. She remained leader of the local WVS until 1958. During her mayoral year, with characteristic flourish she established a trust to finance a narrow boat, named the *Pearl Hyde*, to take parties of elderly people for day trips on local canals. Her public interests included the presidency of the Business and Professional Women's Club (which she had founded in 1942), chairmanship of Coventry's annual music festival, and a leading role in the campaign to establish the city aerodrome. Between 1943 and 1959 she earned her living as a welfare officer at Lea Francis Cars, and subsequently as a public relations executive, briefly with Massey-Fergusons and, from 1960, with Associated Television (ATV).

Pearl Hyde, like her father, died in a road accident. On 15 April 1963 the car that she was driving while on holiday in Scotland collided with a lorry on the Glasgow–Carlisle road in Crawford, killing both herself and her friend Mrs Phyliss Thrift, co-founder of the Business and Professional Women's Club and a well-known Coventry spiritualist and faith healer. The guest list at her funeral in Coventry Cathedral reads like a roll call of Coventry's great and good, whose tributes bore witness to the breadth of her engagement in the public life of her adoptive city. Her employer, ATV, presented the council with a short film of her life but no copies appear to have survived.

JAMES HINTON

Sources *Coventry Evening Telegraph* (15 April 1963) · *Coventry Evening Telegraph* (19 April 1963) · *Coventry Evening Telegraph* (23 April 1963) · *Coventry Standard* (19 April 1963) · *Coventry Standard* (26 April 1963) · M. Edelman, *The Times* (8 May 1963) · 'She will be city's first woman lord mayor', *Coventry Evening Telegraph* (22 May 1957) · G. Hodgkinson, *Sent to Coventry* (1970) · M. Thacker to 'Dear Minnie', 2 Jan 1968, Coventry RO, PA 705 · W. Baruch to M. Thacker, 8 April 1941, Coventry RO, PA 1753/1 · Pam Keyner, 'Pearl Hyde', Coventry RO, PA 1753/1 · S. Fletcher Moulton to Lady Reading, 7 Dec 1940; to P. Hyde, 21 May 1941; to Patterson, 21 May 1941, Women's Royal Voluntary Service, archive, WVS, files on West Midlands Regional Office · L. K. Huxley to Miss Nanson, 16 June 1941, Women's Royal Voluntary Service, archive, WVS, files on West Midlands Regional Office · H. Jennings, *Heart of Britain*, Crown Film Unit (1941) · M. Lodge, 'Women and welfare: an account of the development of infant welfare schemes in Coventry, 1900–1940 with special reference to the work of the Coventry Women's Co-operative Guild', *Life and labour in a twentieth century city: the experience of Coventry*, ed. B. Lancaster and T. Mason (1986), 81–97 · K. Richardson, *Twentieth-century Coventry* (1972) · *Coventry Directory* (1926–7) · *Coventry Directory* (1939) · P. Hyde, 'Women's voluntary service', *The city we loved* (1941?) · d. cert.

Archives Coventry RO, Women's Volunteer Service, PA 1753/1 · Women's Royal Voluntary Service, archive, WVS, Coventry narrative reports · Women's Royal Voluntary Service, archive, WVS, files on West Midlands Regional Office

Likenesses photograph, 1957–8, Coventry RO, CCA/TC/2/9/39 · photographs, Coventry RO

Wealth at death £3234 17s. 0d.: administration, 4 June 1963, *CGPLA Eng. & Wales*

Hyde, Sir Robert (1595/6–1665), barrister and politician, was the second son of the barrister Sir Laurence Hyde (*c*.1562–1642), of Salisbury and Woodford, Wiltshire, and his wife, Barbara Castilian (1574–1641), and was baptized in Salisbury Cathedral on 24 February 1596. Only twelve years old when he was specially admitted to the Middle Temple during his father's reading in 1608, Robert enrolled as a student at Magdalen Hall, Oxford, on 9 March 1610. Admission to his father's Middle Temple chamber in November of that year may have marked the beginning of Hyde's legal studies, which were supported by an initial allowance of £50 per annum. After his call to the bar in 1617, his younger associates included Bulstrode Whitelocke and his cousin Edward Hyde, the future earl of Clarendon. He married on 17 August 1631 Mary Baber (*d*. 1668). By 1639, when Hyde delivered his reading on the statute 43 Eliz. I c. 4 (charitable uses), he had a respectable practice in Westminster Hall and on the western assize circuit. Besides holding a reversion to the position of common pleader in the City of London, and minor local office for the duchy of Lancaster, he was justice of the peace for Wiltshire, and since 1635 had served as Salisbury's recorder.

In the spring of 1640 a campaign against Hyde's election as MP for Salisbury accused him of furthering the cathedral's interference in town affairs and excessive zeal in collecting ship money, although a few years before he and his father had been charged with negligence in that service. Following the Short Parliament, where Hyde kept a low profile, he was joined to the general call of serjeants held in June 1640, naming Pembroke and Hertford, the two leading Wiltshire magnates, as his patrons. In October the Salisbury corporation again returned Hyde, but he was rejected in a second return also sent to Westminster, purportedly from the citizenry at large. The corporation's return and thus Hyde's election was eventually ratified in March 1641, just before he joined the minority voting against Strafford's attainder. No more is heard of him until July 1642, when he was brought to London on charges of promoting the royalist cause in Salisbury. Disabled from membership of the house and imprisoned in the Tower from 4 to 18 August, Hyde subsequently joined the king at Oxford. Yet despite 'having for a long tyme absented himself from this Cittie' (*Various Collections*, 4.240) and being sequestered in September 1645, he was not dismissed from his recordership until May 1646, and in December of that year was permitted to compound on the Oxford articles.

Little is known of Hyde's activities over the next thirteen years. He was not present after the battle of Worcester when the fugitive Charles II stayed in his house outside Salisbury. He evidently resumed practice in London, serving as treasurer of Serjeant's Inn, Chancery Lane, from 1653 to 1655. At the Restoration he was knighted, restored to his recordership, and made a justice of common pleas on 31 May 1660. In this capacity his expertise as criminal lawyer, apparent in a surviving analytical digest of his compilation, was brought to bear against the regicides. His cousin Clarendon secured his elevation as chief justice of common pleas on 19 October 1663. While Samuel Pepys was amused by Hyde's unfamiliarity with nautical terminology when he presided over a maritime case at the Guildhall that December, Henry Townshend carefully transcribed his admonition that legal questions arising at quarter session should be determined by legally qualified JPs, not 'put to the vote of many ignorant justices' (Horle, 31). Despite his prominent role in judicial proceedings against nonconformists, at Yarmouth in April 1664 Hyde possibly attempted to protect Quakers against their local persecutors (ibid., 259, 274n.). Hyde died in London of an apoplectic fit on 1 May 1665, and was buried about the 11th in Salisbury Cathedral, where there is a memorial bust. As his marriage was childless, he left most of his Wiltshire estates and his London house to his nephews. His argument in the case of *Manby* v. *Scott* (1663), on married women's contractual capacity, was separately published in 1732.

WILFRID PREST

Sources W. R. Prest, *The rise of the barristers: a social history of the English bar, 1590–1640*, 2nd edn (1991) · Keeler, *Long Parliament* · J. J. Hammond, 'Notes on the Hydes of Wilts. and Cheshire', *Wiltshire Notes and Queries*, 6 (1908–10) · C. T. Martin, ed., *Minutes of parliament of the Middle Temple*, 4 vols. (1904–5), vol. 2 · Baker, *Serjeants* · P. Slack, 'An election to the Short Parliament', *BIHR*, 46 (1973), 108–14 · D. Hirst, *The representative of the people?* (1975) · Pepys, *Diary*, vols. 4, 6 · C. W. Horle, *The Quakers and the English legal system, 1660–1688* (1988) · *The diary of Bulstrode Whitelocke, 1605–1675*, ed. R. Spalding, British Academy, Records of Social and Economic History, new ser., 13 (1990) · J. S. Cockburn, ed., *Western circuit assize orders, 1629–1648* (1976) · *Report on manuscripts in various collections*, 8 vols., HMC, 55 (1901–14), vol. 4 · *Report on the manuscripts of the late Reginald Rawdon Hastings*, 4 vols., HMC, 78 (1928–47), vol. 2, p. 158 · *DNB*

Archives L. Cong., analytical index of criminal law and matters relating to JPs, Law MS 53

Likenesses portrait, 1672 (posthumous); in Salisbury council chamber in 1910 · P. Besnier, marble bust in medallion, Salisbury Cathedral · T. Flatman, miniature, V&A · C. Gardiner, oils, Salisbury Corporation, Wiltshire

Wealth at death significant; five Wiltshire manors; numerous messuages, lands, etc.; also newly built house in Chancery Lane: will, PRO, PROB 11/316, fols. 362–363A

Hyde, Sir Robert Robertson (1878–1967), industrial welfare promoter, was born on 7 September 1878 in London, the second son among the five children of Robert Mettam Hyde, of Paisley, and his wife, Marjorie Stoddart Robertson, of Inveraray. His father was a constructional civil engineer who had been responsible for laying the first submarine cables in South America, but he fell upon hard times; he died in 1888. Hyde grew up in circumstances of considerable poverty: his formal education ended at Westbourne Park School in 1893 when he went on to work in commerce. In 1901 he was able with the help of friends to enter the theological faculty of King's College, London. He was ordained deacon in 1903 and priest in 1904, and began his ministry in the East End as curate at St Saviour's, Hoxton.

From the beginning Hyde was concerned with boys' clubs, and in 1907 he became warden of the hostel settlement in Hoxton founded in memory of F. D. Maurice. There he came into contact with many movements, interests, and people normally beyond parish bounds. From 1912 to 1916 he combined his work at the Maurice Hostel with the living of the parish church of St Mary. In 1917 Hyde married Eileen Ruth (*d.* 1970), second daughter of Dr George Parker, of Cuckfield. They had one daughter and a son, who was reported missing in Italy in 1943.

In 1916 there came a dramatic change in Hyde's career when he was asked by Seebohm Rowntree, who was helping Lloyd George, to take charge of the boys' welfare department in the Ministry of Munitions. Hyde knew the essential nature of boys and how well they could respond if given the opportunity to develop. He was a born leader, whose humanity, kindliness, and humour shone out of him, and he soon had a band of friends and admirers, among them the reputedly cold industrialists and employers with whom he came in contact. These men rallied round him when in 1918, irked by the constrictions of civil service procedures, he broke away from the munitions ministry and set up an organization of his own: the Boys' Welfare Association. Sir William Beardmore (later Lord Invernairn) was his first chairman and, with a characteristic flash of imagination and audacity, Hyde obtained the consent of George V to his son's, Prince Albert's, becoming the first president.

Entirely self-financing, supported by industry itself, and dedicated to the advancement of humanitarianism in industry, the association was soon firmly established as a repository of valuable and practical knowledge which prompted and led the way to new legislation, and as a reliable instrument for the selection and training of welfare practitioners. This was due largely to Hyde's practical idealism, enormous energy, and powers of persuasion. On royal suggestion the name was changed in 1919 to that of the Industrial Welfare Society (IWS) to conform with the wider responsibilities it had been urged to undertake; and it was with the IWS, as it became familiarly known, that Hyde's name was principally associated.

Hyde made a considerable impact on British industry and commerce in the provision of basic welfare such as lavatories, canteens, changing rooms, and other amenities. He campaigned for pension funds for workers, for apprentice schemes for young people, for the introduction of medical officers in factories, for recreational facilities where the community did not provide them, for works magazines, and for suggestion schemes. His whole method of working was by widespread visiting, walking factory floors, talking to all and sundry, and by providing the very practical expertise necessary to introduce these schemes. He had the ability of not boring people or putting over his ideas in highfalutin terms. He argued that it was just common sense to treat human beings decently if you wanted them to work and co-operate decently.

Between the duke of York, as Prince Albert had now

become, and Hyde a genuine friendship developed, to their mutual benefit. Hyde was able to give the duke an intimate understanding of the industrial and commercial life of Britain such as no previous member of the royal family had possessed. Together they conceived and carried through the venture known as the Duke of York's camps, where boys from industry and the public schools met and mixed, to their great mutual benefit, at summer camps in an unselfconsciously egalitarian atmosphere. The last of these camps was held at Balmoral in 1939 by invitation of the duke, by then George VI.

In 1932 George V conferred the MVO upon Hyde in personal recognition of his services to his son who in 1949 himself bestowed a KBE upon his old friend. To Hyde's deep sorrow, his acceptance of the knighthood led to his being required by the Church of England, as was customary, to relinquish holy orders.

In 1950 Hyde retired as director of the IWS and was given the official title of founder. The society, subsequently renamed the Industrial Society, became the largest joint management–union body specializing in man management, industrial relations, communication, and the development of young people.

Hyde was an unpretentious and lovable man of medium stature and buoyant step. He loved people, and his impelling charm and sincerity when talking to anyone made that person feel that no one mattered more. He published a comprehensive book, *The Boy in Industry and Leisure*, in 1921, and an autobiography appeared in 1968. Hyde died at his home, Glevering, Beech Road, Haslemere, Surrey, on 31 August 1967.   JOHN GARNETT, rev.

Sources R. R. Hyde, *Industry was my parish* (1968) • personal knowledge (1981) • private information (1981) • *WWW* • *The Times* (1 Sept 1967) • *CGPLA Eng. & Wales* (1968)

Likenesses J. Gunn, oils, c.1952, Industrial Society, London

Wealth at death £32,503: probate, 16 Jan 1968, *CGPLA Eng. & Wales*

Hyde, Thomas. *See* Hide, Thomas (1524–1597).

Hyde, Thomas (1636–1703), oriental scholar, was born on 29 June 1636 at Billingsley in Shropshire, the son of Ralph Hyde, rector of the parish, and of his wife, Anne Jennings of Barrowden, Rutland. He was educated at Eton College for some four years before being admitted to King's College, Cambridge, in 1652. There his aptitude for oriental languages, apparently nurtured by his father, quickly caught the attention of Abraham Wheelocke, the professor of Arabic, who recommended him to Brian Walton, the editor of the polyglot Bible. Hyde worked on correcting proofs in Syriac and Arabic and on transcribing a Persian version of the Pentateuch from Hebrew characters back into Persian ones and then in making a Latin translation of it.

In 1654 Hyde moved from Cambridge to Queen's College, Oxford, from where he proceeded MA in 1659. That year he was appointed sub-librarian of the Bodleian Library, becoming its librarian in 1665, a post which he held until he resigned in 1701, being weary of 'the toil and drudgery of daily attendance in all times and weathers' (Macray, 170). In 1674 a new catalogue of the library was

published under his name, although it was believed that he had done little of the actual work involved. He was appointed a canon of Salisbury, rector of a parish in Gloucestershire, and archdeacon of Gloucester. Having proceeded DD in 1682, he became Laudian professor of Arabic at Oxford in 1691 and acquired the regius professorship of Hebrew together with a canonry at Christ Church in 1697. He served the government for many years as translator of diplomatic correspondence with the Ottoman empire or the states of north Africa.

Hyde was described as a 'corpulent man', often rapt in thought and disregarding all around him, 'wonderfull slow of speech, and his delivery so very low that 'twas impossible to hear what he said'. On one occasion he preached inaudibly for an hour-and-a-half until he had emptied the cathedral and the vice-chancellor 'sent to him to come down'. Yet 'he would be merry and facetious in discourse' (*Remarks*, 11.368–9). His first wife, Anne, whom he married about 1670, was the widow of John Hill, cook at Queen's. She was maliciously called 'an old whore … who hath domineered over the old fool so imperiously' and was said once, on suspicion that he had been 'too familiar with her mayd', to have beaten him so severely that he was confined to his rooms for two months (*Letters of Humphrey Prideaux*, 46–7). She died in 1687, deemed 'a mad woman' (*Life and Times of Anthony Wood*, 3.213). The following year he married Elizabeth, *née* Oram, who was evidently a talented singer; Hyde later thought it inappropriate for her, as a 'Divine's wife', to take part in a competition 'in a Play-House' (letter to T. Bowrey, 29 Jan 1701, BL OIOC, MS Eur. E 192, no. 11). There appear to have been no children by either marriage.

Hyde has been assessed as 'a mediocre orientalist' (Feingold, 495–6) and his tenure of the chairs in Arabic and Hebrew was not notably distinguished. His linguistic abilities above all in Persian and also in Arabic were remarkable, but he did little teaching. He proposed or started many projects which he never finished, so that his published work was mostly confined to essays (with many others left unpublished at his death), apart from his *magnum opus*, the *Historia religionis veterum Persarum*, published towards the end of his life in 1700. The *Historia* was an attempt to present for the first time in Europe the beliefs of the ancient Zoroastrians of Persia through material acquired by Hyde from Parsis in western India by the good offices of men in the East India Company's service. Financially the book was a disaster. Hyde was 'left in the lurch' by promised subscribers, so that 'a great part of the charge fell upon myself' (letter to H. Sloane, 24 Jan 1701, BL, Sloane MS 4038, fol. 292), and he was warned that his book was not to the taste of 'the men of phantasy and the young fry of wits and poets' (Hyde, 2.492–3). The book gained in reputation after Hyde's death, however, to the point that a second edition was successfully issued in 1760. By the end of the eighteenth century the *Historia* had been displaced by the first deciphering of the Avestan texts which Hyde, who had relied on Persian, could not read.

The lethargic manner in which Hyde seems to have discharged his official duties at Oxford gives a misleading impression of a man whose correspondence reveals an intense intellectual curiosity about all things Asian, a curiosity which went far beyond the usual biblically inspired concerns of a seventeenth-century orientalist for the ancient languages of the Near East. He assiduously collected books and manuscripts, seeking them not only in Europe but in Asia, and he bombarded men who had travelled in Asia with requests for books and curiosities. Asian people who turned up in England were for him the most authentic source of knowledge. 'I, for my own benefit and pleasure, do catch at all opportunities of discoursing with the natives of those countries in their own languages', he wrote (*Works of … Boyle*, 6.563). He spoke Turkish to a couple captured by the Austrians, but was forced to use Latin in communicating with a 'very knowing and excellent' young Chinese who visited Oxford (ibid., 6.574).

Hyde was an avid collector of languages. The deciphering of ancient Persian was his prime concern, but he sought out grammars or vocabularies of other languages, ancient or modern. He asked his friends in India to get him 'the alphabets and languages of all the sorts of Tartars who trade there', including 'the Mogul Tartars about Samarcand and Ouzbek' (letter to Bowrey, 13 April 1701, BL OIOC, MS Eur. E 192, no. 15). He spent a great deal of time and money personally cutting plates of characters for printing in Asian languages, including the 'old Persian' for the *Historia* and Chinese, and supervised the printing of a published version of the gospels in Malay at Oxford that appeared in 1677.

Hyde collected religions as well as languages and was broadly tolerant in his attitude to non-Christian beliefs. He asked that the Parsis be assured that he was 'a great lover of their religion' (letter to Bowrey, 13 April 1701, BL OIOC, MS Eur. E 192, no. 15). Tolerance did not, however, imply that Hyde was in any sense a freethinker. He assured Robert Boyle that he primarily studied 'eastern authors' in order to help in 'the explication of the Scriptures' and 'for the edification of others in the truth and right understanding of His word' (*Works of … Boyle*, 6.559). He was enthusiastic about the prospect of Christian missions in Asia, for which the gospels in Malay were intended to be a contribution.

Hyde died at Christ Church on 18 February 1703, survived by his wife, and was buried two days later at Hanborough in Oxfordshire. By then his reputation may have been somewhat equivocal in his own university, but a Dutch scholar commented on the news of his death: 'Decessit Hydius stupor mundi' ('Hyde, the wonder of the world, has died'; *Remarks*, 1.295).   P. J. MARSHALL

Sources P. J. Marshall, *Thomas Hyde: stupor mundi*, Hakluyt Society [1983] · M. Feingold, 'Oriental studies', *Hist. U. Oxf. 4: 17th-cent. Oxf.*, 449–503 · T. Hyde, *Syntagma dissertationum … Thomas Hyde*, ed. G. Sharpe, vol. 2 (1767) · W. D. Macray, *Annals of the Bodleian Library, Oxford*, 2nd edn (1890) · *Remarks and collections of Thomas Hearne*, ed. C. E. Doble and others, 1, OHS, 2 (1885) · *Remarks and collections of Thomas Hearne*, ed. C. E. Doble and others, 11, OHS, 72 (1921) · *The life and times of Anthony Wood*, ed. A. Clark, 3, OHS, 26 (1894) · *Letters of Humphrey Prideaux … to John Ellis*, ed. E. M. Thompson, CS, new ser., 15 (1875) · BL OIOC, MS Eur. E 192 [Bowrey letters] · BL, Sloane MSS 4037–4038 [Sloane letters] · *The works of the Honourable Robert Boyle*, ed. T. Birch, new edn, 6 (1772) · BL, Harley MS 3779 [Wanley letters] · W. Sterry, ed., *The Eton College register, 1441–1698* (1943) · Wood, *Ath. Oxon.*, new edn, 4.522 · Venn, *Alum. Cant.*
Archives BL, catalogue of books and papers, Sloane MSS 3323, 4062 · Bodl. Oxf., catalogue of the Selden MSS | BL, letters to Sir Hans Sloane, Sloane MSS 4037–4038 · BL, letters to Humfrey Wanley, Harley MS 3779 · BL OIOC, letters to Thomas Bowrey, MS Eur. E 192 · Bodl. Oxf., corresp. with Thomas Smith
Likenesses F. Perry, line engraving, bust, repro. in Sharpe, ed., *Syntagma* · portrait, Bodl. Oxf.
Wealth at death no debts: will, Oxf. UA, chancellor's court wills, Hyde

Hyde [*formerly* Bayaert], **William** (1597–1651), Roman Catholic priest, was born on 27 March 1597 in the parish of St Mary-at-Hill, London, the son of William Bayaert or Bayarde (*d.* 1622), a merchant and native of Ypres, and his wife, Anne. Following three years of classical studies at Leiden University he entered Christ Church, Oxford, where the authorities allowed him to include a term's study of logic at Leiden towards his BA, awarded in December 1614. He proceeded MA on 15 May 1617. Converted to Roman Catholicism as a result of reading books of Catholic theology during his time at Oxford, Bayaert, henceforth known as Hyde, entered the English College at Douai on 6 January 1623 to train for the priesthood. Ordained at Cambrai on 24 September 1625, he taught philosophy at Douai until his return to England on 3 June 1631. There he spent a year as chaplain to John Preston at Furness Abbey, Lancashire, and a similar length of time at what we may presume to have been the Essex home of Henry Parker, Baron Morley and Monteagle. In 1633 he was recalled to Douai to teach theology, but because of an outbreak of plague there in 1636 he resumed his pastoral ministry in England, serving as chaplain to the Blount family of Soddington in Worcestershire for three years, holding also the honorary office of archdeacon of Worcester and Shropshire. He then moved to Humphrey Weld's house at Arnolds, Southgate, Edmonton, Middlesex.

In January 1641 George Muscott (*vere* Fisher), 'the flower of the English clergy' (Burton and Williams, 2.484), though still a prisoner in the Clink in London, was appointed president of Douai College following the death of Matthew Kellison. As Muscott was not immediately available Hyde agreed in September to become his vice-president and arrived at the college on 12 October to begin his duties as acting president and professor of theology. In the event, through the intervention of the queen, Muscott was unexpectedly released from prison within the month and immediately travelled to Douai, where he arrived on 14 November. Thereafter, as vice-president Hyde aided Muscott in a most successful presidency.

Muscott died in December 1645 and Hyde was appointed by Rome as his successor seven months later, on 21 July 1646. In February 1647 he sought permission from the cardinal protector of the college to seek the degree of DD from the University of Douai, and this was conferred on him after the necessary disputations in the October of that year. With Hyde the irksome system of Rome's licensing of students to proceed to academic degrees came to an end, largely, it must be said, by default. Since the days of Robert Persons it had been a grievance of the English missioners that the system used *de facto* prevented many of them acquiring academic standing in the eyes of their English contemporaries. Two years after obtaining his DD Hyde was appointed regius professor of history in the university and during 1650 he gave a course of public lectures on the works of Baronius. It is said that he was also professor of eloquence and / or public orator in the university, which may explain why he was designated to welcome Charles II to the abbey of Anchin on 20 March 1650 as he passed through Flanders from France. In turn the king chose him to offer his thanks to the university. Hyde died at the English College at the age of fifty-four on 22 December 1651 after an illness lasting three months, thus cutting short a promising career. He was buried on Christmas eve in the lady chapel of the church of St Jacques close by the college. Half of the fifth Douai diary is concerned with Hyde's presidency. He showed himself a good administrator, bringing a welcome period of peace and stability to the college, lessening by 40,000 florins the substantial debt with which it had been saddled for many years. He was an able teacher of not only history but theology. According to Dodd he had a fine reputation as a moralist, leaving a manuscript concerning the resolution of certain cases. He built up a collection of books for the use of future presidents, to which three medieval manuscripts in the municipal library at Douai seem to have belonged. In death he proved to be a generous benefactor to the college, leaving it most of his wealth. Evidence of his good standing in the local church as well as in the seminary and university is provided by his appointment as *censor librorum* for the diocese of Arras in 1648 and installation as a canon of St Amatus. D. MILBURN

Sources E. H. Burton and T. L. Williams, eds., *The Douay College diaries, third, fourth and fifth, 1598–1654*, 2, Catholic RS, 11 (1911), 484–514, 541–4 · G. Anstruther, *The seminary priests*, 2 (1975), 19–20 · Gillow, *Lit. biog. hist.*, 3.527–30
Archives Sacra Congregazione di Propaganda Fide, Rome, report on the state of the college in 1651, Collegia, 365, fol. 64
Wealth at death 9842 florins and 18 stivers to Douai College: Burton and Williams, eds., *The fifth Douay College diary* (1911), vol. 2, p. 543

Hygbald (d. 802/3), bishop of Lindisfarne, took over the duties of the aged Cynewulf, his predecessor as bishop of Lindisfarne, at Cynewulf's retirement in 780. He was consecrated later (in 780 or 781), after Cynewulf's death. Nothing is known of Hygbald's background, but it may be assumed from his name that he was English. It is possible that he had been educated in the religious community at Lindisfarne; certainly he was known to its members, since he was chosen by unanimous consent. No writings by him survive. Lindisfarne had long been regarded as one of the holiest sites in Britain, but the constitution of the community of which Hygbald took charge is unclear. From Alcuin's letters it seems that Bishop Hygbald was the head of a single monastic *familia*, and no other abbot or prior is attested during his term of office.

In the 780s Hygbald was present at at least one Northumbrian episcopal consecration and at the Legatine Council of 786, the acts of which he subscribed. In the 790s he continued to attend episcopal consecrations. Meanwhile, the serious disturbances in Northumbria of those years affected Hygbald directly. Lindisfarne was sacked by the vikings in 793. Although no demonstrably contemporary account gives precise information about the extent of the material damage, Alcuin's writings occasioned by the event show that it was intellectually and spiritually devastating, comparable in some respects to the sack of Rome. Yet Alcuin did assume that the community's regular life could continue (and indeed it was not until the following century that the monks had to leave their exposed location). As a result of the attack, Hygbald may have been burdened with the worry that the sinfulness of the community had occasioned divine vengeance. Alcuin consoled him with letters and his third-longest poem, but also admonished and exhorted him and the community to a better life.

The final decade of the eighth century was a time of violent contests for the Northumbrian throne, two of which impinged on Hygbald. In 796, after a reign of twenty-seven days, one former king, Osbald, took refuge on Lindisfarne and then fled from there by boat. Hygbald's possible role in that episode is unknown, but not long afterwards he attended the consecration and enthronement of Osbald's successor, King Eardwulf, in York Minster. Hygbald died on either 25 May 802 or 24 June 803.

Almost nothing is known of the condition of learning or monastic discipline on Lindisfarne in Hygbald's time; a century earlier, its scriptorium had been notable. Alcuin's letters to the community indicate that standards were at least adequate and that its reputation as a holy place was outstanding. The Carolingian scholar Candidus, known for his contributions to logic and speculative thought, began his education with Hygbald at Lindisfarne. Hygbald subsequently dispatched Candidus to the continent for further instruction from Alcuin.

It has been conjectured that Hygbald is identifiable with the Wigbald who was the chief scribe of the Barberini gospels (Vatican City, Biblioteca Apostolica Vaticana, MS Barb. lat. 570) and whose signature may be seen on folio 153 of that manuscript. The suggestion must be rejected because the scribal signature there reads 'Uuigbald', an entirely different and not uncommon name, frequently recorded (with the spelling Uigbald) in the Durham *Liber vitae*. The ninth-century portion of that work includes the name Hygbald, but the absence of the bishop-section in the manuscript makes it impossible to determine which of the attestations might refer to the bishop of Lindisfarne. From the nineteenth century Hygbald was equated with Alcuin's correspondent Speratus, but that identification has now been disproven. MARY GARRISON

Sources W. A. Searle, *Anglo-Saxon bishops, kings and nobles: the succession of the bishops and the pedigrees of the kings and nobles* (1899) · E. Dümmler, ed., *Epistolae Karolini aevi*, MGH Epistolae [quarto], 4 (Berlin, 1895) · E. Dümmler, ed., *Poetae Latini aevi Carolini*, MGH Poetae Latini Medii Aevi, 1 (Berlin, 1881) · Symeon of Durham,

Opera • D. A. Bullough, 'What had Ingeld to do with Lindisfarne?', *Anglo-Saxon England*, 22 (1993), 93–125 • *ASC*, s.a. 780, 785, 793, 795, 803 [text D] • [A. H. Thompson], ed., *Liber vitae ecclesiae Dunelmensis*, SurtS, 136 (1923) • John of Worcester, *Chron.* • Henry, archdeacon of Huntingdon, *Historia Anglorum*, ed. D. E. Greenway, OMT (1996) • J. Gerchow, *Die Gedenküberlieferung der Angelsachsen: mit einem Katalog der libri vitae und Necrologien* (Berlin, 1988) • R. Müller, 'Untersuchungen über die Namen des northumbrischen *Liber vitae*', *Palaestra*, 9 (1901) • C. Cubitt, *Anglo-Saxon church councils, c.650–c.850* (1995) • Barberini gospels, Biblioteca Apostolica Vaticana, Vatican City, MS Barb. lat. 570, fol. 153 • M. Brown, 'The Lindisfarne scriptorium from the late seventh to the early ninth century', *St Cuthbert, his cult and community to AD 1200*, ed. G. Bonner, D. Rollason, and C. Stancliffe (1989), 151–63, 161, and pl. 7

Hygdon, Brian (*d.* 1539), dean of York, is of unknown origins. John *Hygdon was his brother. He studied at Oxford, proceeding BCL in 1499 and DCL in 1506. A proctor in the chancellor's court in 1504, on 9 September 1505 he was appointed principal of Broadgates Hall. Earlier that year he was ordained deacon, but he is not recorded as becoming a priest. Nevertheless he began to accumulate benefices, in an ecclesiastical career that owed much to the support of Thomas Wolsey and Richard Fox (the latter had earlier employed him as an envoy to Rome). In 1505 he became rector of Bucknell, Oxfordshire, while in 1508 he was collated to the prebend of Welton Ryval in Lincoln Cathedral, subsequently exchanging it for Clifton (1513) and then Aylesbury (1523). He was also subdean of Lincoln from 1511 to 1523. A licensed pluralist from 1511, he received the living of Kirkby Underwood, Lincolnshire, in that year and Nettleton in the same county in 1513. On 15 May 1515 he was collated to the archdeaconry of the West Riding in the diocese of York, but resigned it the following year, when on 14 June he was elected dean of York. On the same day he was collated to the prebend of Ulleskelf (where Leland reports that he built a house) in York Minster.

Hygdon owed his deanery to his services to Wolsey. The latter had been translated from Lincoln to York on 15 September 1514, and on 13 November following he made Hygdon his vicar-general. Recorded as involved in proceedings against heretics in 1528, and as supervising the elections of a number of Yorkshire abbots, Hygdon was also active in secular government, and showed himself a good servant of the crown. From 1525 he was chancellor of the duke of Richmond's council, and he was regularly appointed to commissions of the peace. On 15 January 1526, with the earl of Westmorland and Thomas Magnus, he concluded a peace treaty with Scotland. He was also a conscientious dean, unusual both in being resident and in the frequency with which he attended chapter meetings. He was clearly a visible presence in York, processing to the minster every Christmas with a retinue of fifty liveried gentlemen and thirty yeomen. Letters to Wolsey of 20 May 1527, reporting complaints that ecclesiastical causes were being transferred from York to London, and of 26 January 1528, begging the cardinal 'to remember the great decay and poverty of York' (*LP Henry VIII*, vol. 4/2, no. 3843), suggests that Hygdon was mindful of the city's well-being.

After Wolsey's fall Hygdon seems to have maintained good relations with Thomas Cromwell, and from 1530 he served on the king's council in the north parts which succeeded the duke of Richmond's council as the principal agency of royal government in Yorkshire. But his health began to fail, and on 12 January 1536 the treasurer of York reported to Cromwell that 'The dean of York is so ill that I think he cannot recover' and described him as 'a crasytt [decrepit]' (*LP Henry VIII*, vol. 10, no. 84). Plans for allowing the dean to retire with a pension came to nothing, and he remained in office until his death. His sickness presumably explains his failure to resist, or even to flee from, the Pilgrimage of Grace in 1536. Still able to write to Cromwell on business on 2 March 1539, Hygdon died on 5 June following and was buried in the minster. He is probably commemorated by a monument on the outer wall of the north choir aisle, though the loss of its original brass precludes certainty. In his will, drawn up on 3 June 1539 and approved by him next day, Hygdon bequeathed £13 6s. 8d. to works on the minster, to which he had earlier given a fine cope. There were also bequests to the clergy attending his funeral, to his servants, to his relations, and to the poor, and in some cases the churches, of his various livings. He also remembered Broadgates Hall in Oxford, where he had given £110 to found a fellowship at Brasenose College.

W. A. J. ARCHBOLD, *rev.* ANDREW A. CHIBI

Sources Emden, *Oxf.*, 2.930–31 • *LP Henry VIII*, vols. 1–14 • P. Gwyn, *The king's cardinal: the rise and fall of Thomas Wolsey* (1990) • A. A. Chibi, *Henry VIII's conservative scholar: Bishop John Stokesley and the divorce, royal supremacy and doctrinal reform* (1997) • will, PRO, PROB 11/26, fol. 144r–v • R. R. Reid, *The king's council in the north* (1921); facs. edn (1975) • A. G. Dickens, *Lollards and protestants in the diocese of York, 1509–1558* (1982) • *John Leland's itinerary: travels in Tudor England*, ed. J. Chandler (1993) • *Fasti Angl., 1300–1541*, [Lincoln; St Paul's, London; York] • D. M. Palliser, *Tudor York* (1979) • G. E. Aylmer and R. Cant, eds., *A history of York Minster* (1977) • Wood, *Ath. Oxon.*, new edn

Hygdon, John (*d.* 1532), college head, was the brother of Brian *Hygdon. After attending Westminster School, he was elected a fellow of Magdalen College, Oxford, about 1495, and by 1498 he had proceeded MA. He was subsequently lecturer in sophistry, senior dean of arts, and second bursar. His own and John Stokesley's conduct as bursars prompted a chancery action by the president and scholars in 1502–3, but Hygdon was nevertheless vice-president of the college in 1504–5. Shortly afterwards, however, he vacated his fellowship. He had been ordained subdeacon, deacon, and priest in 1500. Magdalen presented him to the vicarage of Beeding, Sussex, in 1502, and then to the Nottinghamshire rectory of East Bridgford in 1504; he held the latter living for the rest of his life. He also became vicar of Sutterton, Lincolnshire, in 1510. Presumably his benefices financed his continuing studies—he was licensed for DTh on 29 January 1514.

On 17 December 1516 Hygdon was elected president of Magdalen. His relations with the fellows were not always easy, and in 1520 some of them presented a number of complaints against him to the college visitor, notably that he was negligent in financial matters, had erected unnecessary buildings at the college's expense, and was an overstrict disciplinarian. Hygdon emerged unscathed, and on 26 December 1521 was admitted to the prebend of Milton Manor in Lincoln Cathedral. On 2 December 1524 he also became prebendary of Weighton in York Minster, exchanging this for Wetwang in 1529. On good terms with Wolsey—in this it doubtless helped that his brother Brian was the cardinal's vicar-general for the diocese of York—he was present when St Frideswide's Priory, Oxford, was dissolved in April 1524, and when the priory site became the basis for Wolsey's Cardinal College in the following year, Hygdon was appointed its dean. He resigned as president of Magdalen and went to live in what had been the house of the prior of St Frideswide's. His 'daybook' survives, recording the expenditure of £1276 on building in the first year of the new college's short life. He was also active both in countering heresy among his students and in supervising the college estates. On 3 July 1528 Wolsey appointed him to head a commission 'to reform and amend the statutes of his colleges at Ipswich and Oxford' (*LP Henry VIII*, vol. 4/2, no. 4460).

On Wolsey's fall Hygdon exerted himself to save the college from sharing the cardinal's fate. In 1530 he and one of the canons petitioned the king at Windsor, and had a reassuring reply: 'Surely we purpose to have an honorable college there, but not so great and of such magnificence as my lord Cardinal intended to have … yet we will have a college honorably to maintain the service of God and literature' (*LP Henry VIII*, vol. 4/3, no. 6579). Hygdon remained in Oxford during 1531, and when the college was refounded as King Henry VIII College, on 18 July 1532, he was appointed its dean. On 30 September he gave £180 to found exhibitions for four probationary fellows and four demies at Magdalen. The end of his life was sudden. On 15 December following the subdean of his college informed Cromwell that:

> There is no way but one with Mr Dean, for he has lain speechless this 20 hours … His goods are all conveyed to Magdalene, Corpus, and New College, on which he has bestowed large sums, but nothing to this college, where he had his promotion. (*LP Henry VIII*, vol. 5, no. 1632)

Hygdon died about the 20th, and was buried in the choir of Magdalen College chapel, under a stone with an engraved brass, now lost. The same fate has befallen a stained-glass window which he presented to Balliol College chapel in 1530. W. A. J. ARCHBOLD, *rev.* ANDREW A. CHIBI

Sources Emden, *Oxf.*, 2.931–2 · *LP Henry VIII*, vols. 1–5 · J. E. Oxley, *The reformation in Essex to the death of Mary* (1965) · P. Gwyn, *The king's cardinal: the rise and fall of Thomas Wolsey* (1990) · A. A. Chibi, *Henry VIII's conservative scholar: Bishop John Stokesley and the divorce, royal supremacy and doctrinal reform* (1997) · J. G. Milne and J. H. Harvey, 'The building of Cardinal College, Oxford', *Oxoniensia*, 8–9 (1943–4), 137–53 · W. D. Macray, *A register of the members of St Mary Magdalen College, Oxford*, 1 (1894) · *Hist. U. Oxf. 3: Colleg. univ.* · J. R. Bloxam, *A register of the presidents, fellows … of Saint Mary Magdalen College*, 8 vols. (1853–85) · *The acts and monuments of John Foxe*, ed. J. Pratt, [new edn], 8 vols. in 16 (1853–70) · *Fasti Angl., 1541–1857*, [York; Lincoln] · H. A. Wilson, *Magdalen College* (1899); repr. (1998) · Wood, *Ath. Oxon.*, new edn

Archives Magd. Oxf., bursars' indentures 189/1–2

Hygeberht [Higbert] (*d.* in or after 803), archbishop of Lichfield, received his see in 779 (*AS chart.*, S 114). His origins are unknown, though he was presumably a Mercian. Lichfield was the chief see of Mercia, close to the royal residence at Tamworth. It was made an archbishopric at the 'contentious' Synod of Chelsea in 787. The dominance in southern England of Offa, king of the Mercians, had been threatened by the resurgence of Kent under Ecgberht II (*fl.* 765–779), of whom Jænberht, archbishop of Canterbury, had been an adherent. When Offa re-established control of Kent after Ecgberht's death, he persuaded Pope Hadrian I to divide the province of Canterbury, and the Mercian and East Anglian sees became the new province of Lichfield. Jænberht retained control of the West Saxon, South Saxon, and Kentish bishoprics, and as the senior archbishop took precedence over Hygeberht in attesting charters. After Jænberht's death in 792, Hygeberht took precedence over his successor, the Mercian Archbishop Æthelheard.

Soon after his elevation at the Synod of Chelsea, Hygeberht consecrated Offa's son Ecgfrith as king of the Mercians. The dependence of Lichfield's enhanced status on Offa's line becomes evident after the deaths of Offa, on 29 July 796, and of Ecgfrith, on 16 December in the same year. In 797 Æthelheard was driven from his see in a Kentish rising, and by 798 the new king of the Mercians, Cenwulf, was negotiating with Pope Leo III for the restoration of an undivided southern province. Objections had always been to the advancement of Lichfield, not to Hygeberht personally, and in 797 Alcuin wrote to Æthelheard advising that 'the pious father' Hygeberht should not be deprived of his pallium, but that ordination of bishops should revert to Canterbury, which is what seems to have transpired. Hygeberht retained his archiepiscopal title until at least 799, but at the Synod of Chelsea in 801 he attests, albeit in first place, only as bishop. Cenwulf's attempt to transfer the archbishopric from Canterbury to London (then a Mercian city) failed, and in 803 a council at 'Clofesho' demoted Lichfield and restored the rights of Canterbury. Hygeberht attested the proceedings as abbot, but the location of his monastery and the date of his death are unknown. ANN WILLIAMS

Sources N. Brooks, *The early history of the church of Canterbury: Christ Church from 597 to 1066* (1984) · *English historical documents*, 1, ed. D. Whitelock (1955) · A. W. Haddan and W. Stubbs, eds., *Councils and ecclesiastical documents relating to Great Britain and Ireland*, 3 (1871) · S. Keynes, *The councils of Clofesho* (1994) · *ASC*, s.a. 785

Hylton. For this title name *see* Jolliffe, William George Hylton, first Baron Hylton (1800–1876).

Hylton, Jack (1892–1965), band leader and impresario, was born in Bolton, Lancashire, on 2 July 1892, the son of George Hilton, a Bolton millhand, and his wife, Mary Greenhalgh. He was educated at the higher grade school in Bolton. He learned to play the piano as a child, becoming an accompanist at the age of ten. He later changed the spelling of his name to Hylton. His first professional engagement was at Rhyl, in the summer of 1905, as assistant pianist and singer with a pierrot troupe. Afterwards he conducted for touring revues, musical comedies, pantomimes, and ballet.

Hylton went to London in 1913 and worked in a music publisher's office. He made his London début in October 1913 when he was engaged as cinema organist at the Alexandra, Stoke Newington. In 1920 he worked as a double act with Tommy Handley at Bedford music hall. He was assistant pianist in cabaret at Queen's Hall roof, joined the resident band, and became its leader. On 28 May 1921 he made his first records with the Queen's Dance Orchestra for His Master's Voice and, as Jack Hylton's Jazz Band, for Zonophone. When he heard the first American records by Paul Whiteman's Orchestra, he set out to emulate the style of orchestration. In this he was very successful. He left Queen's Hall roof briefly in 1922, but returned to install a new band, and ensured that his name appeared on the labels of all his subsequent records.

It was then that Hylton opened a London office, employing many first-class dance-band musicians and placing bands in the Piccadilly Hotel and the Kit-Cat Club (1925), while at the same time touring with his principal band, which was generally recognized as the finest showband in the British Isles. On 4 September 1927 he took his band in an Imperial Airways biplane from Croydon to Blackpool, circling the tower and playing a new song ('Me and Jane in a 'Plane') so that holiday-makers could hear it. He appeared with his band in *Shake your Feet* (London Hippodrome, 20 July 1927); *Life Begins at Oxford Circus* (Palladium, March 1935); *Swing is in the Air* (Palladium, 29 March 1937); and *The Band Wagon* (Prince's, 26 December 1938).

Hylton toured Europe many times, with great success, particularly in Germany (1928, 1928–30, 1931, 1932), France (1928–31), and Italy (1931). However, he was unable to take his band to the USA owing to restrictions imposed by the American Federation of Musicians. He went there alone in December 1935 and appeared conducting a specially formed American band for six months.

Through his agency he was responsible for bringing a large number of American jazz musicians to Britain, most notably tenor saxophonist Coleman Hawkins, who appeared with Hylton's orchestra (and that of his wife Ennes Parkes) in 1934–5 and again in 1939. He brought the Duke Ellington Orchestra to England in 1933.

Hylton created a sensation in the popular-music world in October 1931 by signing a contract with the fairly recently formed Decca Record Company after ten years with His Master's Voice. However, he returned to the latter early in 1935 and remained with this label until war conditions prompted him to disband in April 1940.

In 1935 Hylton had appeared in the film *She Shall have Music* and the theatre also made a strong appeal to him. He began a new career as a theatrical impresario immediately after disbanding, touring with the London Philharmonic Orchestra. He became associated with the Daniel Mayer Company and revived *Peter Pan* (1940), continuing the annual presentation of this popular show until December 1948. He entered the West End field of theatre

management by presenting *Lady Behave* (His Majesty's, 24 July 1941), following the success of this with such outstanding productions (mostly musical) as *Jack and Jill* (Palace, 26 December 1941); *The Merry Widow* (revived, His Majesty's, 4 March 1943); *Hi-de-hi* (Palace, 3 June 1943); *The Love Racket* (Victoria Palace, 26 October 1943); *Duet for Two Hands* (Lyric, 27 June 1945); *For Crying out Loud* (Stoll, 6 August 1945); *Follow the Girls* (His Majesty's, 25 October 1945); and *No Room at the Inn* (Winter Garden, 3 May 1946). One of his longest-running productions was *Salad Days*, which he took over three weeks into its run in 1954, finally closing in 1960.

Hylton composed many popular songs, especially at the outset of his career as a bandleader—'Mooning' (1921); 'Singing' (1922); 'Little Miss Springtime' (1922); and 'Joyce' (1923) among them. He featured as a vocalist on a number of early recordings, with label-credit, which was very unusual at that time.

Hylton provided opportunities and encouragement to others. Over the years he featured many prominent musicians and popular vocalists, such as Sam Browne, Dolly Elsie (his own sister), Arthur Askey, Stanley Holloway, George Formby jun., Tommy Handley, and Leslie Sarony. He also launched the bandleading careers of several famous personalities by giving them employment, including the trumpeter Jack Jackson, the trombonist Ted Heath, the saxophonists Noel Chappie d'Amato and Billy Ternent, and the violinist Hugo Rignold. He often employed European musicians, such as the trumpeter Philippe Brun, the trombonist and arranger Leo Vauchant, and the saxophonist André Ekyan. In 1921–2 one of his colleagues at the Queen's Hall roof was the black American clarinettist Ed (Edmund Thornton) Jenkins, thus affording one of the earliest examples of a mixed-race dance or jazz band in England.

Hylton was thrice married: first, in 1922, to Florence Parkinson (Ennis Parkes), the revue artist, bandleader, and composer, who died in 1957. This marriage was dissolved, as was Hylton's second marriage, to Friederike Kogler (*d.* 1973). He married, third, in 1963, Beverley Prowse, who in 1973 married Sir Alex McKay. There were two daughters of the second marriage. Hylton also had a son.

Hylton made musical history on 10 February 1927 by taking down the music of 'Shepherd of the Hills', which was dictated to him over the newly opened transatlantic cable by the British composer Horatio Nicholls, who was then in New York. While motoring to Hayes, Middlesex, to record the new song the following morning Hylton was involved in a near fatal car accident in fog. He survived, and died nearly four decades later on 29 January 1965 at 20 Devonshire Place, London.

For most of the two decades of his bandleading Hylton set the standard for most of the others to follow, offering a variety act in the band itself, playing not only dance music, for which it is said Sir Edward Elgar and William Walton wrote some arrangements, but modern concert music, 'hot' jazz, comedy routines, and even ballet music. He appeared in six royal command variety performances, received the decoration of the Légion d'honneur, and was made officier de l'instruction publique by the French government. BRIAN RUST, rev.

Sources *The Times* (30 Jan 1965) · private information (1990) · P. Oliver, ed., *Black music in Britain: essays on the Afro-Asian contribution to popular music* (1990) · J. Godbolt, *A history of jazz in Britain, 1919–1950* (1984) · P. W. Logan, *Jack Hylton presents* (1995) · CGPLA Eng. & Wales (1965)

Likenesses D. Low, pencil sketches, NPG · photographs, Hult. Arch.

Wealth at death £242,228: probate, 19 May 1965, CGPLA Eng. & Wales

Hyman, Joe [*formerly* Joseph] (1921–1999), businessman, was born on 14 October 1921 at 4 Heaton Terrace, Broughton, Salford, Manchester, the youngest son of Solomon Hyman (1885–1961), textile merchant, and his wife, Hannah, *née* Goodman. He was named Joseph, but at a later date changed his first name to Joe by deed poll. His great-grandparents had been textile merchants in Russia, and his father specialized in buying up and reselling clearance lines from the Bradford Dyers' Association. Born into the Jewish community of north Manchester, Hyman was educated at the North Manchester grammar school, which he left at sixteen in order to join his father's business. Within a few years it was clear that he had unusual abilities as a trader, and was earning between £2000 and £3000 a year. With his father's blessing, he looked for an opportunity to establish his own business. In 1939 he went into textile converting, organizing the finishing and distribution of cloth. By the end of the war, when he was twenty-three, he had overdraft facilities for £10,000 with Martin's Bank.

Gainsborough Fabrics In 1945 Hyman judged the time right to set up on his own. He registered the business name of Gainsborough Fabrics, after his favourite painter, and launched into buying and selling cloth (chiefly linings for ladies' garments) on his own account from a small office in Manchester. His income grew to between £25,000 and £30,000 a year. With assets of £130,000, he moved in 1950 to London to be nearer his customers, the multiple stores, and the clothing trade. Meanwhile, on 3 March 1948 he married Corinne Abrahams, teacher of elocution, and daughter of Maurice David Abrahams, company director. They had a son, Howard Jonathan, and a daughter, Penelope Ann.

Hyman realized that to make significant progress he must move into manufacturing. His first attempt, the purchase of two weaving firms, brought losses of £40,000. He got rid of them and turned his attention to knitting. In 1957 he paid £187,000 for Melso Fabrics, a small knitting firm at Cornard in Suffolk, coincidentally the birthplace of Thomas Gainsborough. Renaming the firm Gainsborough Cornard Ltd in 1958, Hyman constructed an integrated warp knitting, dyeing, and finishing business, switching from rayon to nylon. One of the small textile firms he acquired was Cooper Bros. (Nottingham), who made clothing for Marks and Spencer. Marks and Spencer became his principal customer. By June 1960 he headed five subsidiaries and was waiting to move his head office from Regent Street to Hanover Square, London, where his salesmen could meet overseas customers. His business now extended across the gamut of producing and marketing synthetics, such as acrylic for ladies' wear. Between 1957 and 1960 the Gainsborough Cornard group's turnover rose from £200,000 to £2 million. With great prescience the *Financial World* on 28 November 1959 commented, 'With an established position in the UK in the field of circular knitted rayon fabrics, the group has been preparing for what looks like the beginning of a "textile revolution" and intends to be in the vanguard'. Less than fifteen months later Hyman made the move which catapulted him into the circle of big players in the UK's textile industry.

Viyella International Hyman's success with warp knitting and synthetics was noted by the old-established firm of William Hollins Ltd of Nottingham, most famous for their Viyella brand, garments made of speciality mixture yarns of wool and cotton prized in the children's nursery and the old people's home alike. Chaired by Sir Edward Herbert, an ageing and ailing lawyer, and employing 4500 people, the Hollins board were looking for an entry into man-made fibres. In 1961 they bought Gainsborough Cornard for £1.35 million, including £423,000 of Hollins shares. A new Hollins board chaired by Sir Nutcombe Hume, a financier and merchant banker, with Hyman as deputy chairman and managing director, was appointed. It did not take Hyman long to discover a lack of dynamic leadership. One employee told him 'it was like working for a scaled-down nationalised industry … no one minded what you did so long as it was not too noticeable' (*Drapery and Fashion Weekly*, 28 Sept 1961). By the end of the year Hyman was both chairman and chief executive, and was shaking up the company. The firm was renamed Viyella International. The old plant was closed and new equipment was concentrated at Pleasley, near Nottingham (spinning), and at Boden Street, Glasgow (weaving). A multi-divisional structure was established. Most devastating to the old guard, the 700-strong company headquarters in Nottingham, Viyella House, was closed and relocated in London. The Viyella image was revamped with advertising featuring, as Hyman put it later, 'Colour, sex, romance, fast cars, and all that sort of thing. I got Viyella worn by the jet set' (*Financial Times*, 11 Dec 1969). Meanwhile, his first marriage having ended in divorce, on 3 February 1963 he married Simone Duke, daughter of Isaac Duke, knitwear manufacturer. They had a son, Spencer, and a daughter, Daphne.

By the time Hyman was appointed chairman and chief executive of Viyella, the UK textile industry was in chronic decline. At mid-century its capacity was half the size it had been at its height in 1921. Between 1950 and 1961 the output of the UK cotton industry slumped from 2207 million yards per annum to 1315 million yards. Including synthetics, the picture was slightly less dismal, the output of synthetic fabrics falling from 666 million yards per annum in 1951 to 528 million yards in 1961. Nevertheless employment in the industry was also collapsing, from 382,000 (cotton spinning and man-made fibre production) in 1950 to 185,000 in 1961. Faced with this situation, Hyman concurred with other commentators, and examples he had encountered on many visits to the USA, in arguing that the horizontal, atomized structure of the industry needed to be swept aside and replaced with large, internationally competitive businesses which were vertically integrated. Hollins had just such a potential. With this vision, Hyman began developing the means to attain it. He assembled a small core of able executives, several picked from the firms he was taking over. One of them offered the complementarities Hyman urgently needed. This was David Brunnschweiler, whom he recruited in 1960, before the Hollins coup. While Hyman was essentially emotional and intuitive, Brunnschweiler was cool, rational, and dispassionate. Equally importantly, while Hyman's strengths lay in strategy formation, selling, and marketing, Brunnschweiler, the son of a Manchester textile family and a university textile technology lecturer, had the technical skills necessary to translate Hyman's grand visions into practice. Sound estimates of strategic choices were supplied by John A. Blackburn, an economist who joined the Viyella board in 1966, and his small team of business analysts.

Alliance with Imperial Chemical Industries Viyella was the vehicle for Hyman's ambitions. However, he lacked a commensurate injection of large-scale finance. Surprisingly, this came from Imperial Chemical Industries (ICI), which was looking for long-term customers in its struggle against Courtaulds to capture market share on the synthetics side of the UK textile industry. ICI's strategy became clear in the summer of 1963 when it backed the take-over by English Sewing Cotton (ESC) of Tootal Broadhurst Lee Company. In addition ICI publicly announced that its willingness to promote the reorganization of the UK textile industry was not confined to the ESC–Tootal merger. But Hyman looked an upstart compared to Sir Cyril Harrison, the highly experienced, innovative, and entrepreneurial ESC chairman, and Viyella was less than a quarter the size of ESC. However, Hyman had unshakeable confidence in his vision of a 'multi-fibre, multi-process' (a term he coined) organization, one which included spinning, weaving, warp knitting, weft knitting, carpets, dyeing, printing and finishing, synthetic yarn texturizing, garments, and utilizing all fibres, natural and synthetic. His considerable powers of persuasion convinced the ICI chairman, Sir Paul Chambers. On 4 November 1963 it was announced that the boards of ICI and Viyella had entered an agreement to promote a more efficient and compact structure in the UK textile industry. To this end ICI lent £10 million to Viyella and purchased £3 million of Viyella shares (£2 million ordinary, £1 million preference). At the same time ICI declared that it had no intention of wishing to control textile companies, only to make them more efficient and progressive. This surprising move allowed Hyman to cut large swathes through the UK's jungle of textile firms.

Just before the ICI cash injection, Viyella International bought up two textile companies, R. H. and S. Rogers, the men's shirt group, and John Binns & Sons, synthetic fibre weavers and bulk yarn producers. With ICI capital Hyman went on a renewed take-over spree. Within ten days of the ICI agreement he spent most of his new capital on his biggest acquisition, British Van Heusen, a major vertical group, costing £11.343 million (£9.955 million in cash). Two other take-overs were notable. Combined English Mills, one of the largest cotton spinners in the UK, was a venture into the risky end of the cotton industry, spinning. Bradford Dyers' Association, a very large dyer and finisher (which cost £9.186 million, £8.1 million of it paid in shares), was positioned as a finisher of Viyella products. In all, nineteen acquisitions (including Binns) between October 1963 and January 1965 cost Viyella £33.309 million, £19.246 million paid in cash, the rest in Viyella shares.

From his acquisitions Hyman built his multi-fibre, multi-process organization. In 1965, when most of the additions were incorporated into Viyella, the group comprised sixty-one firms grouped in ten divisions, with 25,320 employees. By 1969 the group (now seventy-six firms) was slimmed to seven divisions and 23,532 employees. Using these resources, Hyman achieved remarkable growth rates. While the UK's output of man-made fibres slightly more than doubled between 1961 and 1969, Viyella turnover between 1963 and 1969 rose twelvefold (from £7.9 million to £94 million) and profits rose sevenfold (from £0.8 million to £5.9 million). The acquisitions of 1963–4 brought the fastest expansion in both turnover and profits. By 1965 Viyella International was the largest weaver in the industry and the second largest spinner. It ranked second in warp knitting and had between 30 and 40 per cent of synthetic spinning, weaving, dyeing, and finishing. It also had 80 per cent of the UK's shirt finishing capacity.

Parting of the ways Meanwhile, ICI in its tussle with Courtaulds widened its policy of spotting and backing likely winners. Stakes of about 20 per cent were taken in a number of Viyella's rivals. Hyman was no longer ICI's favourite. At first he carried on regardless, adding to his group firms like Mekay, Gaunson, Hadfield, and Sixsons. At the end of 1967, however, there was an acrimonious parting of the ways with ICI. The situation had changed since 1963 for differing reasons. First, Courtaulds, ICI's rival, changed its technological strategy. Under Sir Frank Kearton in the 1960s Courtaulds aggressively followed a strategy of acquisition and diversification which added polyesters (nylon variants) to the viscose and acetate fibres (cellulose) production they had dominated for fifty years. In addition Courtaulds were building a vertically integrated organization with large-scale plants. ICI watched these developments with growing concern. So did Hyman. Courtaulds were undercutting Gainsborough Cornard's nylon fabric prices by supplying their warp knitting company (Furzebrook) with Celon (their nylon fibres) at below market prices. Yet ICI would make no parallel concessions to Viyella. Hyman initially wanted ICI to retaliate against Courtaulds by becoming more financially involved in Viyella. He considered ICI's strategy of backing a string of companies against Courtaulds a mistake. Scale and scope were the business principles that he believed were the only way to counter Courtaulds and re-establish the UK in international markets. He became more and more frustrated with ICI and threatened to build his own polyester and nylon plants. Eventually in October 1967 he severed his financial ties with ICI. Viyella repaid the ICI loan and ICI sold its Viyella shares. Viyella's financial gearing rose steeply.

Yet Hyman still held to his vision of building up a multi-fibre, multi-process giant, focused on cotton-polyester production. In autumn 1968, for example, he purchased the tufted carpet business of Cyril Lord Ltd, whose founder had recently retired. In February 1968 he suggested the creation of a new holding company to acquire both Viyella International and ESC, Viyella holding 60 per cent and ESC 40 per cent, with projected sales of £150 million. ESC rejected it out of hand, revealing they had been in talks with the Calico Printers' Association (CPA) for some time. A few weeks later ESC and CPA merged to form English Calico. ICI and Courtaulds each took a 12.5 per cent share in the new company. In January 1969 Courtaulds announced a £105 million bid for English Calico. ICI objected and in June the Labour government's secretary of state for trade, Edmund Dell, imposed a freeze on mergers, domestic or foreign, involving the top five textile firms.

On 10 December 1969 Hyman was deposed from his £30,000 a year post as chairman of Viyella International by his fellow directors, though he remained a director and a large shareholder. Exactly why he was removed was much debated. It was rumoured that he intended merging with an American multinational, such as Burlington Industries, a scheme choked by the government's freeze. Thereafter he could not deliver any practical scheme to support his strategic vision. Another view was that he stepped down so that his personal prejudices would not hinder a merger of interests between Viyella and a fibre producer (ICI or Courtaulds). Another was that the take-over of the Cyril Lord business had provoked an internal crisis on the Viyella board. Possibly linked to this, Hyman had fallen out bitterly with fellow board members because he had demoted David Brunnschweiler from executive responsibility. Certainly the exit of Hyman allowed ICI to step in. With government permission they were allowed to buy 35 per cent of Viyella with the intention of merging it with Carrington and Dewhurst. This was done in September 1970 when Carrington Viyella was created.

Character and assessment On two matters all commentators were agreed: the volatile and controversial nature of Hyman's personality and the huge impact he made on the UK textile industry. Sheila Black characterized his personality thus:

> The best word is his own, 'passionate', for he does nothing without doing it passionately. His love of art and music; his grand designs for an international company; his obsession with finding young men to train whether they had experience or not—Hyman would hire them on hunch; his almost fanatic paternalism and his insistence on spending time with his sons. (*Financial Times*, 11 Dec 1969)

In fact, he assessed potential trainees by shrewd personal

scrutiny and, before being ousted, was planning a Viyella management training college. These interests, and his readiness to publish his views on the political economy of British industry, earned him the nickname 'the Professor'. As for his impact, he was the catalyst for a long overdue reorganization and modernization of the UK textile industry. At the height of his success he had flats in London, Manchester, and New York, as well as an estate at Ewhurst, Surrey.

Sixteen months after leaving Viyella, Hyman became chairman of John Crowther & Co., a Huddersfield woollen business. He never recovered his old dynamism and retired in 1981. He later emerged as Tiny Rowland's nominee to become chairman of House of Fraser, had Rowland won control of that group. Between 1967 and 1970 he had made serious, but over-ambitious and eventually futile, attempts to enter national politics, but appeared not to harbour such ambitions thereafter. He was a trustee of the Pestalozzi Children's Village, a governor of the London School of Economics, and president of the Textile Benevolent Fund. He died of heart failure at the Chelsea and Westminster Hospital, Chelsea, London, on 6 July 1999. He was survived by his wife, Simone, their two children, and the two children of his first marriage.

DAVID J. JEREMY

Sources J. Hyman, collection of press cuttings, 3 vols., priv. coll. · *Annual Report*, Viyella International Ltd (1961–9) · F. A. Wells, *Hollins and Viyella* (1968) · J. A. Blackburn, 'The British cotton textile industry since World War II: the search for a strategy', *Textile History*, 24 (1993), 235–58 · G. Turner, *The north country* (1967) · C. H. King, *The Cecil King diary, 1965–1970* (1972) · *The Times* (8 July 1999) · *Daily Telegraph* (9 July 1999) · *The Guardian* (12 July 1999) · *The Independent* (12 July 1999) · *Financial Times* (11 Dec 1969) · *Sunday Times* (14 Dec 1969) · *The Observer* (14 Dec 1969) · WWW · personal knowledge (2004) · private information (2004) [Simone Hyman] · b. cert. · m. certs. · d. cert.

Archives priv. coll., newspaper clippings | FILM D. Frost, *The Frost programme*, interview with Joe Hyman (17 Nov 1967) · M. Goldring, *In the public eye*, interview with Joe Hyman (7 March 1968) | SOUND W. Harms, *Meet the British*, interview with Joe Hyman, by BBC Overseas Services, for broadcasting in Australia, n.d.

Likenesses photograph, 1968, repro. in *The Times* · photograph, 1970, repro. in *Daily Telegraph* · T. McGrath, photograph, repro. in *The Guardian* · photograph, repro. in *The Independent* · photograph, repro. in *Financial Times*

Hymers, John (1803–1887), mathematician, was born on 20 July 1803 at Ormesby, near Middlesbrough, Yorkshire, the son of Thomas Hymers, a tenant farmer under Sir James Pennymon, and his wife, the daughter of John Parrington, rector of Skelton in Cleveland. After attending schools at Witton-le-Wear and Sedbergh, Hymers gained a sizarship at St John's College, Cambridge, in 1822. He graduated as second wrangler in 1826, and was elected fellow of St John's College in 1827. For some years Hymers was a successful tutor of private pupils, and then became assistant tutor of his college in 1829 and tutor in 1832, and was moderator in the mathematical tripos in 1833–4.

Hymers was esteemed a conscientious tutor, but his most important influence was exerted through his mathematical textbooks. His *Treatise on the Analytical Geometry of Three Dimensions* (1830) was followed by his *Treatise on Conic*

Sections (1837), which became the standard textbook on analytic geometry at Cambridge. Most of his books reveal a vast acquaintance with the development of mathematics on the continent. For instance, in the second edition of his *Integral Calculus* (1835) he introduced English students to the topic of 'elliptic functions', then newly discovered by C. G. J. Jacobi (1804–1851) working in Königsberg. Hymers was quick to appreciate any new mathematical technique; the most outstanding example concerns his use of differential operator methods for the solution of differential equations. In particular, his *Differential Equations and the Calculus of Finite Differences* (1839) incorporated the new solution of the Laplacian equation for the figure of the earth as given by Thomas Gaskin in symbolic form; it was the elaboration of this original solution by R. L. Ellis in 1841 which led largely to George Boole's masterpiece 'On a general method in analysis' in 1844 (*PRS*, 5, 1843–50). Boole's novel comprehensive method, which applied now to a wide class of differential equations important in physics, was, in its turn, presented by Hymers in the revised edition of his *Differential Equations* (1858) in an unusually clear manner.

Hymers became a deacon in 1833 and was ordained priest in the following year. He received the BD in 1836 and was elected senior fellow of his college and fellow of the Royal Society in 1838. In 1841 he was Lady Margaret preacher, and received the DD; he was made president of his college in 1848. In 1852 he was presented by his college to the rectory of Brandesburton in Holderness, in the East Riding of Yorkshire, where he spent the last thirty-five years of his life. Appointed JP for the East Riding in 1857, his decisions as a magistrate were noted for their precision.

As a textbook writer, Hymers marked an era in the history of St John's College at Cambridge; he was also a good classical scholar. He numbered among his pupils J. W. Colenso and William Cavendish (1808–1891). He presented to the college library some manuscripts of Wordsworth, with whom he was distantly connected, and a portrait of Wordsworth was painted under his care for the college. An active traveller, Hymers enjoyed good health all his life. He died at Brandesburton on 7 April 1887. He was unmarried. By his will of 24 August 1885, he bequeathed some of his property to the mayor and corporation of Hull, to provide for the foundation of a grammar school, 'for the training of intelligence in whatever social rank of life it may be found among the vast and varied population of the Town' (will). An obscurity in the wording of the will rendered the bequest invalid, but his heir, his brother Robert Hymers, voluntarily granted the sum of £50,000 for the establishment of Hymers College, Hull.

R. E. ANDERSON, *rev.* MARIA PANTEKI

Sources R. F. S., *The Eagle*, 14 (1887), 398–402 · J. B. Mullinger, *St John's College* (1901), 278–81 · M. Panteki, 'Relationships between algebra, logic and differential equations in England, 1800–1860', PhD diss., Middlesex University, 1992, chap. 4 · Boase, *Mod. Eng. biog.* · Venn, *Alum. Cant.* · *DNB* · will, proved 9 May 1887, York · d. cert.

Archives U. Hull, Brynmor Jones L., papers
Wealth at death £167,997 18s. 9d.: probate, 9 May 1887, *CGPLA Eng. & Wales*

Hynd, John (*fl. c.*1592–1606), writer of romances, was probably the grandson of the judge Sir John *Hynde, according to a family tree in the British Library (Add. MS 14049, fol. 49). About 1592 he entered Trinity College, Cambridge, from which he graduated BA in 1595–6 and MA in 1599. His major work was *Eliosto libidinoso, described in two bookes, wherein their imminent dangers are declared, who guiding the course of their life by the compasse of affection, either dash their ship against most dangerous shelves, or else attaine the haven with extreame prejudice* (1606). The title is largely borrowed from the subsidiary title of Robert Greene's *Gwydonius: the Card of Fancie* (1584). Such borrowing is a feature of Hynd's literary output. Of the poems in the romance, one, 'Eliostoes Roundelay', is taken from Greene's *Never Too Late* (1590), where it is called 'Francescoes Roundelay', and another, 'Among the Groves', is from Nicholas Breton's romance, *The Historie of the Life and Fortune of Don Frederigo di Terra Nuova* (1590). The four poems by Hynd himself are signed 'Dinohin'. The dedicatee is Philip Herbert, earl of Montgomery, and there is a prefatory poem signed Alexander Burlacy.

Hynd also wrote another romance, called *The most excellent historie of Lysimachus and Varrona, daughter to Syllanus, duke of Hypata in Thessalia* (1604). The title-page bears the initials 'I. H. R.' but the dedication, which is addressed to Henry Wriothesley, earl of Southampton, is signed 'I. H.'. *Lysimachus and Varrona* borrows directly from John Dickenson's *Arisbas* (1594), as does *Eliosto libidinoso*. Other authors plagiarized by Hynd in these romances are Robert Greene, George Pettie, Thomas Lodge, William Braunche, Robert Smythe, and Henry Roberts. John Weld thus describes Hynd's creative technique as 'literary masonry' (Weld, 173). It is likely that Hynd's involvement with Greene's works continued after the latter's death. In 1617 another edition of *Greenes Groatsworth of Wit* (originally published in 1592) was published, proclaiming itself 'newly corrected'. It also included a new preface addressed 'to wittie Poets' and the concluding 'Greenes Epitaph'; these additions are signed 'I. H.', who is tentatively identified as Hynd in the *Short-Title Catalogue*. Another text, *Work for Chimny-Sweepers, or, A Warning for Tabacconists* (1602), also carries an introductory verse signed 'I. H.'; according to Atkins, 'I. H.' may be the author of the whole pamphlet. In both cases an alternative author has been advanced (Jasper Heywood for the additions to *Greenes Groatsworth* and Joseph Hall for *Work for Chimny-Sweepers*) but Hynd's is the most likely identification.

Hynd also wrote a moral tract called *The Mirrour of Worldly Fame* (1603), which is dedicated to his uncle William Hynd and which has been reprinted in the *Harleian Miscellany* (vol. 8, p. 33). The *Dictionary of National Biography*, following Thomas Corser's *Collectanea Anglo-poetica* (pt 8, 1878, 294–8), confused this John Hynd with John Hind, steward to Anne, Lady Twysden, *c.*1620–1651, who was the author of two letters now in the British Library (Harley MS 376, art. 51; Add. MS 34173, fol. 20). The confusion perhaps arose from the Latin poem signed 'Johannes Hind' which precedes *Eliosto libidinoso*.   HELEN MOORE

Sources Cooper, *Ath. Cantab.*, 2.446 · Venn, *Alum. Cant.* · *STC, 1475–1640* · W. R. Davis, 'The plagiarisms of John Hynd', *N&Q*, 214 (1969), 90–92 · J. S. Weld, 'Notes on the novels of John Hind', *Philological Quarterly*, 21 (1942), 171–8 · S. Halkett and J. Laing, *A dictionary of anonymous and pseudonymous publications in the English language*, ed. J. Horden, 3rd edn, 1 (1980), 88, 219 · BL, Add. MS 14049, fol. 49 · A. B. Grosart, ed., *The life and complete works in prose and verse of Robert Greene*, 8 (1881), 92–3 · *Poems (not hitherto reprinted) by Nicholas Breton*, ed. J. Robertson (1952), l–li · S. H. Atkins, 'Joseph Hall', *TLS* (3 April 1937), 256

Hynde, Sir John (*c.*1480–1550), judge, was probably of a London family, though he was the first to achieve prominence and established the family seat at Madingley near Cambridge. He is probably the John Hynde who was an undergraduate at King's College, Cambridge, in the early 1490s. At any rate, he became a member of Gray's Inn about 1500 and was autumn reader there in 1518. Some cases from this first reading, concerning uses and wills, are in the Harvard law school (MS 125, nos. 169–71). He gave a second reading in 1527 and a third, as serjeant-elect, in 1531. Cases from the third reading also survive (BL, Hargrave MS 253, fol. 19). By the time of his first readership he was settled in Cambridgeshire, probably at Girton, serving as a justice of the peace for the county from 1512 and as counsel to the borough of Cambridge by 1515; in 1520 he became recorder of Cambridge, holding the office until he became a judge; and by 1526 he was the bishop of Ely's steward of the Isle of Ely. In 1529 he represented Hindon, Wiltshire in parliament and about that time he was regarded as one of the best counsel of his day.

Hynde was twice married. His first wife, Elizabeth (*d. c.*1530), was the daughter of Sir John Heydon of Baconsthorpe, Norfolk, and his second wife, Ursula (*d.* 1555), the daughter of John Curson of Belaugh, Norfolk. Towards the end of his life Hynde built the mansion house at Madingley, where a figure carved on the bay window is said to represent him. Hynde took the coif in 1531 and four years later was appointed one of the king's serjeants, obtaining the further office of surveyor of the liveries in 1537. As a justice of assize Hynde took the home circuit until 1538, and then the northern. On 24 November 1545 he was appointed a puisne justice of the common pleas and he received a knighthood the following year. He was ousted from the surveyorship of the liveries in 1546, to make way for Robert Keilwey, not because he was a judge but on the grounds that the office had ceased to exist when the court of wards was established; after a suit in council in 1550 Keilwey was obliged to pay him £50 a year as compensation. Edward VI reappointed Hynde as a judge in 1547, and he died in office on 17 October 1550. He was buried in St Dunstan-in-the-West, Fleet Street, on the following day, the judges and serjeants coming in procession 'two and two together, and the clarkes syngyng' (*Diary of Henry Machyn*, 2). Dame Ursula provided a great dole of money, meat and drink, and gowns for the poor, in Cambridgeshire, 'for ther was myche a doo ther for hym' (ibid., 4). He left two sons and four daughters.   J. H. BAKER

Sources HoP, *Commons, 1509–58*, 2.432–4 · Sainty, *King's counsel*, 14 · Sainty, *Judges*, 72 · Baker, *Serjeants*, 168, 520 · Harvard U., law school, MS 125 · BL, Hargrave MS 253, fol. 19 · PRO, CP 40/1050, m. 629 · PRO, CP 40/1131/21, m. ld · BL, Lansdowne MS 874, fol. 94*v* · *The diary of Henry Machyn, citizen and merchant-taylor of London, from AD 1550 to AD 1563*, ed. J. G. Nichols, CS, 42 (1848), 2, 4 · PRO, PROB 11/37, fols. 261*v*–262 [widow's will] · APC, 1547–50, 386 · J. W. Clay, ed., *The visitation of Cambridge … 1575 … 1619*, Harleian Society, 41 (1897), 113 · inquisition post mortem, PRO, C/142/90/22
Likenesses carving on bay window, Madingley Hall, Cambridge-shire

Hyndford. For this title name *see* Carmichael, John, first earl of Hyndford (1638–1710); Carmichael, John, third earl of Hyndford (1701–1767).

Hyndley. For this title name *see* Hindley, John Scott, Viscount Hyndley (1883–1963).

Hyndman, Henry Mayers (1842–1921), socialist leader, was born on 7 March 1842 at 7 Hyde Park Square, London, the eldest son of John Beckles Hyndman (1812–1874), a West India merchant and benefactor of east London churches, and his wife, Caroline, daughter of Henry Adams Mayers of Barbados. He had two brothers and two sisters. The Hyndmans originally came from the north country and settled in Ulster. Robert Augustus Hyndman, his grandfather, made a fortune by land speculation in Demerara, and developed West Indian connections through trade, marriages, and local politics. After his mother's death in 1848, Henry was placed under the care of private tutors, latterly at Oxburgh, Norfolk, before matriculating at Trinity College, Cambridge, in 1861. He attended lectures on political economy by Henry Fawcett and read Auguste Comte and John Stuart Mill, and he graduated BA in 1865. A good cricketer, he played for the Sussex County eleven between 1863 and 1868.

After graduation Hyndman read for the bar, but found the law uncongenial. His visit to Italy in 1866 coincided with the Italian war for Venice; he became a war correspondent of the *Pall Mall Gazette* and followed the Garibaldian forces heading for the Tyrol. On his return he made a study of European nationalism, and visited the exiled Mazzini. In 1869 he embarked on a journey to the Antipodes, where he was convinced that 'little Englanders' were wrong in refusing responsibilities in the south seas, and returned to London by way of America early in 1871. He contributed extensively to review literature and from 1871 to 1880 he was on the staff of the *Pall Mall Gazette*, where he took a special interest in Indian questions, later reflected in his *The Awakening of Asia* (1918). In his study of the Indian famine of 1876–8 he was helped by his friend Dadabhai Naoroji, and criticized the 'drain' of Indian wealth represented by a vast trade gap.

On 14 February 1876 Hyndman married Matilda Ware, the daughter of William Ware of Newick, Sussex, a yeoman farmer. Hyndman had a round face, wore a flowing beard, and was of medium height and sturdy build, with a fair complexion and blue eyes. From his parents he had

Henry Mayers Hyndman (1842–1921), by George Charles Beresford, 1919

inherited a substantial legacy amounting to £21,000, part of which he invested in the mining industry of the American West. Financial security also allowed him to stand for Marylebone as an independent at the general election of 1880: in his election manifesto he described the 'free-governed colonies' as 'the special heritage of our working classes' (Lee and Archbold, 275), but his 'reform' proposals were modest. The rebuff he received from the workers of the Marylebone Radical Association was decisive, and he withdrew from the contest. Early in 1881 he had an interview on social questions with Benjamin Disraeli, who suggested that tory democracy had become untenable.

Hyndman had already visited Karl Marx at Hampstead early in 1880, and read the French translation of *Das Kapital* during his last business trip to America. On his return he expounded to his new mentor the idea of reviving the Chartist movement and took advantage of an agitation among the radical workers in London against coercion in Ireland to launch a 'New Party', the object of which was 'the direct representation of labour' (Tsuzuki, 38). On 8 June 1881 the inaugural conference of the Democratic Federation was held at the Memorial Hall, Farringdon Street, presided over by Hyndman, who distributed copies of his booklet entitled *The Text-Book of Democracy: England for All*. It contained a summary of *Kapital* but suppressed the name of its author. This annoyed Marx and led to a rupture between the two.

The Democratic Federation soon outgrew radicalism,

and in 1883 adopted its first socialist manifesto, *Socialism Made Plain*, which embodied a nationalization programme as well as reformist measures including an eight-hour day. Hyndman at this time published *The Historical Basis of Socialism in England* (1883). In January 1884 the first number of *Justice*, the 'Organ of Social Democracy', came out; Hyndman edited the paper for some years. At the annual conference in August 1884 the federation changed its name to the Social Democratic Federation (SDF), but differences of opinion over socialist tactics, foreign policy, and international co-operation were accentuated. William Morris and his allies on the executive council seceded in December, complaining of Hyndman's 'absolutism, jingoism and political opportunism' (*Justice*, 31 Jan 1885): they formed the Socialist League. Hyndman, in spite of the provocative frockcoat and top hat in which attire he invariably appeared before working-class audiences, was defended by their representatives on the council for his 'sincerity for socialist principles as he advocate[ed] them at street corners on sixty-six consecutive Sundays' (ibid.). On 8 February 1886 a meeting of the unemployed in Trafalgar Square degenerated into a riot in the West End, for which Hyndman together with three other SDF orators—John Burns, H. H. Champion, and Jack Williams—were indicted for sedition, but they were all acquitted. He was found among the socialist speakers who spoke from an orange-box at the dock gate early in the morning for weeks before the London dock strike in the summer of 1889. Socialists had made contact with the masses: while the Independent Labour Party was formed at Bradford in 1893, the SDF had established its largest branch at Burnley, where Hyndman fought his first parliamentary contest at the general election of 1895, though without success (he polled 1498 votes against 5454 for the Gladstonian Liberal).

It was in defence of the principle of national autonomy and a variety of tactics in the socialist movement that Hyndman sided with the French possibilists against the German Marxists. From the two rival socialist congresses held simultaneously in Paris in July 1889 emerged the second international, but Hyndman continued to criticize the German leadership. He joined the pro-Boer agitation in the Second South African War, but later opted for a British victory as a lesser evil, for he believed that the future of South Africa should belong to the indigenous Africans.

Hyndman did not stand for parliament at the general election of 1900. After a period of money-making through company promotions, he started a campaign against Joseph Chamberlain's tariff reform movement and contested the Burnley seat again; he was narrowly defeated at the general election of 1906, polling 4932 votes against 5288 for the successful Labour candidate, Fred Maddison. He was also unsuccessful in contests for the seat at the two general elections in 1910. Against the background of labour unrest, Hyndman's party merged with other dissident groups to form the British Socialist Party in 1911. Hyndman continued to attack the German party for its 'impotence and timidity' (Tsuzuki, 201) in spite of its numbers, and declared that naval superiority was 'to Great Britain a necessity: to Germany a luxury' (p. 209).

Matilda Hyndman died on 27 June 1913 after a long illness, and on 14 May 1914 Hyndman married Rosalind Caroline Travers (1874–1923), a poet and the only daughter of Major John Amory Travers of Tortington House, Arundel, Sussex, and chairman of the North Borneo Trading Company. Hyndman served on the War Emergency Workers' National Committee and also on a food consumers' council to protect workers' interests in wartime. In 1916 he and his followers left the anti-war British Socialist Party and formed a National Socialist Party (NSP). His vituperations against the Bolsheviks were due to his belief that Russia, being economically backward, was not ready for socialism. The NSP resumed its old name, the SDF, in 1920. It had been affiliated with the Labour Party since 1918, and Hyndman's socialist legacy went into that party. He died of pneumonia at his home, 13 Well Walk, Hampstead, London, on 22 November 1921. He had no children. The funeral, agnostic and socialist in character, took place at Golders Green crematorium. Rosalind Travers Hyndman, having published her memoirs of Hyndman, took an overdose of sleeping tablets and died on 7 April 1923. By her will all her possessions were to go to such causes as would keep alive the memory of her husband.

CHUSHICHI TSUZUKI

Sources *Justice* (19 Jan 1884–22 Jan 1925) · H. M. Hyndman, *The record of an adventurous life* (1911) · H. M. Hyndman, *Further reminiscences* (1912) · R. T. Hyndman, *The last years of H. M. Hyndman* (1923) · C. Tsuzuki, *H. M. Hyndman and British socialism* (1961) · F. J. Gould, *Hyndman: prophet of socialism* (1928) · H. W. Lee and E. Archbold, *Social-democracy in Britain: fifty years of the socialist movement*, ed. H. Tracey (1935) · H. Pelling, *The origins of the labour party, 1880–1900* (1954) · E. P. Thompson, *William Morris: romantic to revolutionary* (1955) · E. Hobsbawm, *Labouring men: studies in the history of labour* (1964) · A. Briggs, 'H. M. Hyndman', *People for the people*, ed. D. Rubinstein (1969), 113–21 · *Wellesley index* · b. cert.

Archives BLPES, corresp.; letters relating to Social Democratic Federation [microfilm] · JRL, Labour History Archive and Study Centre, corresp. and papers | BL, letters to Sir Charles Dilke, Add. MSS 43915–43916, 43920–43921, *passim* · BL, corresp. with Macmillans, Add. MS 55242 · BL, William Morris MSS · BL, corresp. with George Bernard Shaw, Add. MS 50538 · Internationaal Instituut voor Sociale Geschiedenis, Amsterdam, corresp. with Karl Marx and Friedrich Engels · L. Cong., letters to C. E. Russell · McGill University, Montreal, McLennan Library, letters to Mrs Cobden-Sanderson · U. Edin. L., corresp. with Charles Sarolea

Likenesses Barratt's Photo Press Ltd, photograph, 1906, repro. in Tsuzuki, *H. M. Hyndman*, frontispiece · E. Kapp, drawing, 1914, Barber Institute of Fine Arts, Birmingham · G. C. Beresford, photographs, 1919, NPG [*see illus.*] · photograph, 1919, Hult. Arch.; repro. in Gould, *Hyndman*, frontispiece · M. Beerbohm, caricature drawing, 1920, AM Oxf. · E. H. Lacey, bronze bust, 1922, NPG

Wealth at death £237 10s. 0d.: probate, 7 July 1922, CGPLA Eng. & Wales

Hyne, Charles John Cutcliffe Wright

Hyne, Charles John Cutcliffe Wright [*known as* C. J. Cutcliffe-Hyne; *pseud.* Weatherby Chesney] (1865–1944), novelist, was born at Arlington, Bibury, Gloucestershire, on 11 May 1865, the elder son (he had one sister) of the Revd Charles Wright Noble Hyne (1830–1912), then curate of Bibury and from 1868 vicar of Bierley, Yorkshire, and

his wife, Frances (1840–1923), only child of Robert Wootton of Bedford. He was educated at Bradford grammar school, which he called 'a beastly place' (Cutcliffe-Hyne, 136), and at Clare College, Cambridge, where he read natural science, and was president of the college Alpine Club, in which capacity he distinguished himself by jumping 'across the canyon which then divided the chapel from Trinity Hall, leaving there a marmalade pot which long remained as a token of his achievement' (Venn, *Alum. Cant.*, 3.511).

After graduating in 1887 Hyne moved to London and became a hack writer for four years, of which period he says in his entertaining autobiography, 'I wrote potboilers for the baser press, and the more evil of the publishers' (Cutcliffe-Hyne, 260). He also wrote a column of advice to the lovelorn in a women's magazine under the name Aunt Ermyntrude. He then started to travel widely and adventurously: there was a period as winch-man and barber on a North Sea whaler, and another as a doctor on a tramp steamer sailing across the Atlantic from New Orleans. He also travelled up the Congo River. In 1895 he contributed a story called 'The Great Sea Swindle' to the Harmsworth magazine *Answers*, which was to be the turning point in his career. (It was later published in one volume as *Honour of Thieves*, 1895, and again in 1902 under the title *The Little Red Captain*.) Alfred Harmsworth (1865–1922), later first Viscount Northcliffe, told Hyne to take a minor character, Captain Kettle, and turn him into a serial character like Sherlock Holmes. While engaged on a particularly hazardous walk across Finland and Sweden, chronicled in *Through Arctic Lapland* (1898), Hyne received the staggering offer from *Pearson's Magazine* of 50 guineas apiece for six Kettle stories, which were successfully serialized during 1897, eventually came out as *The Adventures of Captain Kettle* (1898), and were followed by nine other Kettle books of which the last was *Ivory Valley: an Adventure of Captain Kettle* (1938). In the course of a second series of Kettle stories, which appeared in *Pearson's* during 1898, the hero becomes a riverboat pilot in the Congo. It has been argued that these episodes anticipated and influenced the plot and characterization of Joseph Conrad's *Heart of Darkness* (first published in *Blackwood's Magazine* in 1899). Another story by Hyne, 'The Transfer', first published in the *Pall Mall Magazine* (December 1897) and collected in a volume called *The Derelict* (1901), is also claimed as an influence on Conrad's tale.

On his return from the north Hyne became engaged to Mary Elizabeth Haggas (1868/9–1938), known as Elsie, daughter of John Haggas, manufacturer, of Keighley, whom he married at St John's, Ingrow, Yorkshire, on 24 February 1897. They had a son, who died in 1916 of wounds received in the battle of the Somme, and a daughter. His marriage does not seem to have put an end to Hyne's adventures, because he writes of a period as a mine owner in Mexico, which was ended by the fall of Porfirio Díaz, which took place in 1910. The admiration he expresses in his autobiography for Díaz, as an effective administrator, like his unwillingness to deplore all aspects of King Leopold's government of the Congo, is characteristic of his world-view. His books are written in a bracing tone, with frequent expressions of contempt for weaklings and whiners, and of belief in hard work and the salutary effect of the school of hard knocks.

As well as the Kettle books, Hyne's fiction under his own name includes *Kate Meredith, Financier* (1907), a rather racist romance set in west Africa; *McTodd* (1903); Kiplingesque stories about a disreputable engineer; historical fiction; and boys' books. He also wrote thirteen novels between 1898 and 1908 under the name Weatherby Chesney. Hyne died of a cerebral embolism at his home, Darnside, Kettlewell in Craven, near Skipton, Yorkshire, on 10 March 1944.   CHARLOTTE MITCHELL

Sources Venn, *Alum. Cant.* · C. J. Cutcliffe-Hyne, *My joyful life* (1935) · Burke, *Gen. GB* (1937) · G. P. Winnington, 'Conrad and Cutcliffe Hyne: a new source for *Heart of darkness*', *Conradiana*, 16 (1984), 163–82 · R. Ruppel, '*Heart of darkness* and the popular exotic stories of the 1890s', *Conradiana*, 21 (1989), 3–14 · b. cert. · m. cert. · d. cert.

Archives probably priv. coll., inscribed photographs

Wealth at death £17,356 6s. 10d.: probate, 25 Oct 1944, *CGPLA Eng. & Wales*

Hysing [Hyssing, Huysing, Huyssing], **Hans** (1678–1752/3), portrait painter, was born in Stockholm, the son of Diedrich Hysing (*fl.* 1676–1707), a goldsmith. After a three-year apprenticeship as a goldsmith with V. E. Schröder, he turned to painting in 1694, studying under the Swedish painter David von Krafft. In 1700 he went to London, where his compatriot Michael Dahl maintained a good portrait practice. Hysing became his pupil and 'lived with him for many years' (Vertue, *Note books*, 3.11). On 7 October 1721 'Hans Hysing of St Ann, Westminster' married Frances Breton of the same parish at St Benet Paul's Wharf (Harleian Society, publications, register section, 39, 1910, 228), and by 1733 he was living in Leicester Fields.

In 1711 Hysing had subscribed to Kneller's academy in Queen Street and in 1720 to the St Martin's Lane Academy. By this time he had achieved a certain reputation. In 1714 the third earl of Bristol commissioned a portrait of the musician William Babel and in the following year one of his second wife, Elizabeth Felton. During the next decade Hysing received increasingly distinguished sitters: in 1721 the first earl of Ducie (ex Christies, 17 June 1949); in 1726 the thirteen-year-old earl of Danby, later fourth duke of Leeds (formerly Hornby Castle, Lancashire, and once wrongly identified as the Young Pretender); and the first Earl Cadogan (Goodwood House, Sussex). In 1728 he painted the speaker of the House of Commons, Arthur Onslow (Wadham College, Oxford; National Portrait Gallery, London), and his most eminent commissions came in 1730: the eldest daughters of George II, the princesses Anne, Amelia, and Caroline (each engraved by John Faber the younger), and Sir Robert Walpole (King's College, Cambridge). He had meanwhile painted several of London's cosmopolitan colony of artists, including Nicolas Dorigny in 1722; Christian Zincke, Jacques Parmentier, and Pieter Tillemans, all in 1723; James Gibbs by 1726; John Faber in 1729; and George Vertue in 1733.

In 1732–3 the young Allan Ramsay went to London from Edinburgh to be the pupil of this 'very ingenious painter' whose professional behaviour was 'a Vertuous & valuable example of the present age' (Vertue, *Note books*, 3.44). The first earl of Egmont sat to him in 1733–4 (ex Christies, 12 December 1930, lot 101, as Kneller; engraved) and was still expressing his admiration for Hysing's beautiful hands and draperies in 1743 (*Egmont Diary*, 3.275). There is an elegant half-length of Peter Halkett, dated 1735 (Scottish National Portrait Gallery, Edinburgh), and an untraced three-quarter-length of the Hon. John Spencer of 1739. Hysing's last known dated work is of 1741 (an unidentified lady; ex Sothebys, 23 March 1977). On 24 November 1752 he witnessed the will of Dorothy Dahl, Michael Dahl's daughter, and on 6 February 1753 his widow, Frances, was granted the administration of the estates of 'Hans Hysing late of the parish of St James, Westminster' (Hultmark, 105). He was buried in St James's, Piccadilly, London. Hysing appears as a tall, imposing figure in Gawen Hamilton's group of the virtuosi 'that usually meet at the Kings Armes, New Bond Street', painted in 1735 (National Portrait Gallery, London).   JOHN INGAMELLS

Sources W. Nisser, *Michael Dahl and the contemporary Swedish school of painting in England* (1927), 131–4, 178 [catalogue, 97–105] · Vertue, *Note books*, 3.11, 12, 38, 44, 69, 71; 4.169–70 · E. Hultmark, 'An interesting portrait by the Swedish painter Hans Hysing', *The Connoisseur*, 35 (1913), 103–5 · W. A. Littledale, ed., *The registers of St Bene't and St Peter, Paul's Wharf, London*, 2, Harleian Society, register section, 39 (1910), 228 · C. H. C. Baker, *Lely and the Stuart portrait painters: a study of English portraiture before and after van Dyck*, 2 (1912), 185 · *Manuscripts of the earl of Egmont: diary of Viscount Percival, afterwards first earl of Egmont*, 3 vols., HMC, 63 (1920–23), vol. 1, pp. 329, 385; vol. 2, p. 154; vol. 3, pp. 275, 336 · J. Kerslake, *National Portrait Gallery: early Georgian portraits*, 2 vols. (1977), 74

Likenesses G. Hamilton, group portrait, oils, 1735 (*A conversationn of virtuosi … at the Kinges Armes*), NPG

Hyslop, James (1798–1827), poet, was born on 23 July 1798 at Damhead, in the parish of Kirkconnel, Dumfriesshire. From a young age he worked as a cowherd at Dalblair, then, after a year's schooling, as a shepherd at Bughead in Ayrshire. From 1812 to 1816 he worked on Nether Wellwood Farm, in the parish of Muirkirk, and his contributions to the *Greenock Advertiser* and other newspapers were frequently signed the Muirkirk Shepherd. Between 1816 and 1818 Hyslop worked at Corsebank, then moved to Carcoe, where he studied languages and mathematics for a time before opening an evening school. He then went to Greenock, opened a day school, and wrote for the *Edinburgh Magazine*. After some success he lost money through acting as security for a friend, and returned to Carcoe. During this time he studied European literature and published a number of poems in the *Edinburgh Magazine*, including his best-known piece, 'The Cameronian dream'. The persecution of the covenanters was a favourite subject in both his verse and his prose.

Hyslop opened a school in Edinburgh next, but left about 1821 to work as a tutor on board HMS *Doris*, during a three-year voyage to South America. After its completion he returned to Carcoe, and contributed the series 'Letters from South America' to the *Edinburgh Magazine*, which was reprinted in volume form in 1825. In the following year he went to London and worked briefly as a reporter on *The Times*, meeting Allan Cunningham and Edward Irving, among others, before returning to teaching, first as headmaster of a charity school, and in 1827 as tutor on board HMS *Tweed*, bound for the Mediterranean. The vessel sailed for the Cape of Good Hope in October 1827, and on 4 November of that year Hyslop died of fever off the Cape Verde Islands, in the Atlantic. He was buried at sea with military honours.   SARAH COUPER

Sources C. Rogers, *The modern Scottish minstrel, or, The songs of Scotland of the past half-century*, 3 (1856), 254–6 · Anderson, *Scot. nat.* · J. G. Wilson, ed., *The poets and poetry of Scotland*, 2 (New York, 1876), 181–2 · J. McDiarmid, *Sketches from nature* (1830), 337–48 · Irving, *Scots. · Poems, by J. H., with a sketch of his life*, ed. P. Mearns (1887) · *Scottish Presbyterian Magazine* (1840) · *Scottish Presbyterian Magazine* (1853) · R. Simpson, *Traditions of the covenanters* (1867), 93–100

Hyslop [*née* Reid], **Janet Kerr** [Jenny] (1898–1989), community activist, was born on 13 July 1898 at 90 Westmoreland Street, Gorbals, Glasgow, the only daughter and youngest of three children of Thomas Reid (*d.* 1914), dairyman, and his wife, Mary Kerr Hyslop. Her father owned two shops on the south side of Glasgow in the Pollokshaws area, and Jenny delivered milk for him in the mornings and evenings. She attended Strathbungo School in Craigie Street, Glasgow, but after her father's death had to help her mother in the shop and so could not go on to secondary school. She managed to learn Esperanto, however, and secured a job with the Esperanto Society as a secretary in 1917. She subsequently taught the language in Abbotsford Street School and Whitehill School, Glasgow.

On 9 March 1921 at Pollokshields register office Jenny Kerr married a cousin, George Hyslop, a shipyard worker from Glasgow; they had a son and two daughters. The couple settled in Clydebank, where a rent strike was then under way, in opposition to the Rent and Mortgages Interest (Restrictions) Act which had nullified the 1915 Rent Restrictions Act. Approached by neighbours they were asked to pay only the standard rent and to ignore paying any increase. Jenny Hyslop became actively involved in fighting the rent increases and was herself taken to court for non-payment of extra rent. By ringing a large bell through the streets to warn people of the arrival of officials representing the landlords, and by devising schemes to mislead and divert the officers from evicting the intended families, she helped frustrate the process of eviction and prevent families from ending up out on the street. In the course of organizing female opposition Jenny Hyslop often found herself negotiating through letter boxes with the sheriff's officers sent to evict people. The strikers were initially successful in getting the 'notice of increase' invalidated in certain cases. However, the landlords eventually gained a legal ruling in their favour, and by 1928 the rent strike had collapsed.

During these struggles of the early 1920s Jenny Hyslop became an active member of the Communist Party on Clydebank. The party managed to elect a number of candidates on to the district council there, and Jenny Hyslop herself represented Clydebank fifth ward from 1938 to

1946. Although she retained a keen interest in the party (and was a supporter of the later rent strike campaigns of 1958 and 1972–3), Jenny Hyslop became occupied with community projects rather than direct political action. A member of the Kinning Park co-operative society in Glasgow before her marriage, in 1926 Jenny Hyslop helped run the Clydebank co-operative society, and was also an active member of the local branch of the Women's Co-operative Guild and chaired the Kilbowie and Whitecrook branch.

During the Second World War Jenny Hyslop was a senior officer in the air raid protection service and the first female sectional head for the ARP in the west of Scotland. She was in charge of a post in Clydebank and mounted rescue operations during the Clydebank blitz on the nights of 13–14 March 1941 when the town was continuously bombed and suffered fatalities totalling 534. In the worst of circumstances Jenny Hyslop had to make decisions as to who should have immediate medical treatment and who would have to wait until reinforcements arrived. She also had to try to identify bodies. She organized hot meals for the rescuers digging for survivors and arranged for families to be evacuated to other towns in the west of Scotland. Like many others she lost her house during the two-day blitz.

In the years after the Second World War Jenny Hyslop became deeply involved in the campaign to provide better services for disabled children. She was herself the mother of a child with a major disability and was the first secretary of the Voluntary Association for Handicapped Persons formed in Clydebank in 1955. She later worked with the Disablement Advisory Committee, and attacked the tendency to hide disabled children away instead of involving and employing them in the community, and was critical of government centres for concentrating on 'teachable' handicapped persons. In October 1971 she started to raise funds for a handicapped home with the 170 members of the association and in 1978 she performed the opening ceremony for a hostel for the handicapped in Drumry Road, Clydebank. On 2 June 1978 she was voted Glasgow *Evening Times* 'Scotswoman of the year' for her devoted work for disabled children in Clydebank. She remained secretary of the association until 1981.

In appearance Jenny Hyslop was well built, approximately 5 feet 5 inches tall, with short black hair. She died on 13 September 1989 at Canniesburn Hospital, Bearsden, Glasgow, at the age of ninety-one. A funeral service was held on 16 September at Clydebank crematorium.

NEIL RAFEEK

Sources Janet Hyslop, tape recording, 9 March 1983, Clydebank Public Library, 0060-2 · *Co-operative News* (14 June 1978), 1 · brochure, Clyde Regional Centre (1 Dec 1978) · S. Damer, *Rent strike: the Clydebank rent struggles of the 1920s* (1982), 3, 4, 9, 12 · I. M. M. Macphail, *The Clydebank blitz* (1974), 29, 55–6 · 'The Bankie Street fighter', *Glasgow Herald* (16 Feb 1984) · *Evening Times* [Glasgow] (19 May 1978), 8–9 · *Evening Times* [Glasgow] (2 June 1978) · *Clydebank Post* (21 Sept 1989), 1 · *Evening Times* [Glasgow] (13 March 1981) · d. cert.

Archives Clydebank Central Library, photographic album | SOUND Clydebank Public Library, Reference Room, Tape 0060-2

Likenesses two photographs, 1945? (with civil defence wardens) · photograph, 1983? (aged mid-eighties) · photograph, priv. coll.

Hythe [Hethe], **Hamo** (*b. c.*1270, *d.* in or after **1357**), bishop of Rochester, was born in the parish of St Leonard, Hythe, about 1270. Professed as a Benedictine monk, in 1307 he became chaplain to Bishop Thomas Wouldham of Rochester. On the resignation of John Greenstreet in May 1314 he became prior of Rochester, and although rivals procured a visitation from the archbishop of Canterbury to the chapter, they failed to overturn his appointment.

Following Wouldham's death the monks of Rochester elected Hythe as bishop on 18 March 1317. On 19 March, however, Pope John XXII (*r.* 1316–34) reserved the see for Giovanni di Puzzuoli, chaplain of Edward II's queen, Isabella. The contest between the two candidates was first fought out before cardinals Gaucelin and Luca (Fieschi) in England, but in 1318 the case was revoked to the papal curia at Avignon, where Hythe was himself constrained to go in early 1319. His biographer, as represented by the *Historia Roffensis*, attributes the protracted proceedings there to Hythe's unwillingness to bribe the cardinals (although it is clear that he retained at least Cardinal Guillaume Testa at the curia), as well as to the proliferation of other candidates with royal support. His election was confirmed on 21 July 1319, and he was consecrated at Avignon on 26 August. By the end of the year he had obtained livery of his spiritualities and temporalities, receiving the latter from Archbishop Walter Reynolds on 2 December and from the king on 5 December. He was enthroned on 13 January 1320. However he was engaged in a protracted and bitter dispute for over a year with Archbishop Reynolds over the sums Hythe claimed as due to him from the period during which the see of Rochester had been in the archbishop's hands. During this time Hythe was desperately pressed with debts and with the payment of his common service of 1450 florins to the curia, which he effected by February 1321.

Nothing in Hythe's episcopate matches the activity surrounding his election. His natural caution kept him on the political sidelines, although he was well placed to know what was going on at the highest level, as the *Historia Roffensis*, written by a clerk in his entourage, demonstrates. He excused himself from diplomatic assignments on the grounds of (often genuine) ill health and the poverty of his bishopric, and spent much time improving episcopal residences, especially at Halling and Trottiscliffe (both in north Kent). He appears as sympathetic to the regime of Edward II's last years and clearly distrusted the baronial opposition in 1321. In 1326 he advised the king against an attempt to divorce his wife, and was especially commended by Edward to Hugh Despenser the younger (*d.* 1326). Caught in London during the revolution of that year, he refused to join either John Stratford, bishop of Winchester (*d.* 1348), or the archbishop of Canterbury in embassies to Queen Isabella, and fled to Rochester. He was one of four prelates who refused to do fealty to Edward III in January 1327, although he took part in the new king's

coronation in February. He is said to have affirmed his support for the new fourth clause of the coronation oath, under which the king swore to observe such laws and customs as should be approved by the community of the realm, at this time.

Hythe soon made his peace with the new regime, meeting the queen and the young king when they went on pilgrimage to Canterbury in Lent 1327. He refused to join Archbishop Simon Mepham (*d.* 1333) in his precipitate support for the opposition to the Mortimer regime. But when in June 1329 he was urged by Roger Mortimer, first earl of March (*d.* 1330), to serve on the council, he declined. In Lent 1330 he opposed a grant of clerical taxation to the regime of Mortimer and Isabella. His biographer comments that Hythe might have become treasurer in 1332 but for his reluctance to buy the office. In 1333 he rallied the men of the Cinque Ports to defend the country during Edward III's absence in Scotland, and throughout the early stages of the Hundred Years' War was inevitably involved in the organization of coastal defence. But he firmly eschewed political involvement and devoted his time to his diocese and to building. The new bell-tower at Rochester Cathedral was raised under his auspices. He clashed with the monks of Rochester on several occasions, and in Mepham's visitation of 1329 was accused of not preaching and of being impatient and irascible. But he supported Mepham in 1332 when the other prelates appealed to the curia. In 1333 he made a rare journey abroad to deliver the pallium to the new archbishop of Canterbury, John Stratford, at Rue in Ponthieu. From 1331 to 1336 he was engaged in a bitter dispute with Bishop William Airmyn of Norwich (*d.* 1336).

Illness prompted Hythe's resignation of the bishopric no later than 1352. He was succeeded by John Sheppey (*d.* 1360), whom he had himself chosen as prior in 1333. In June 1353, at Sheppey's request, Hythe was granted a papal pension of £40. The grant specifies that he was more than eighty years old. He was still living in May 1357.

M. C. BUCK

Sources BL, Cotton MS Faustina B.5 · C. Johnson, ed., *The register of Hamo de Hethe, bishop of Rochester, 1319–52*, 2 vols. (1948) · R. M. Haines, 'The episcopate of a Benedictine monk: Hamo de Hethe, bishop of Rochester', *Revue Bénédictine*, 102 (1992), 192–207 · [H. Wharton], ed., *Anglia sacra*, 1 (1691), 356–77 · *CEPR letters*, 2.1305–42 · BL, Arundel MS 68, fol. 26*v*
Archives CKS, register

Hywel [*called* Hywel Fychan] (*d.* **825**), king of Gwynedd, ruled the kingdom of Gwynedd in north Wales perhaps from as early as 798 but most certainly from 816 until his death in 825. He was one of two protagonists in a struggle for the kingship of Gwynedd witnessed in the chronicles between the years 813 and 816. Whereas his rival, Cynan, has been identified as Cynan Dindaethwy of the main ruling line of Gwynedd whose father, Rhodri Molwynog ab Idwal, had died in 754, Hywel's genealogical affiliations and political origins are more enigmatic. Two chronicles represent Hywel as a brother of Cynan and their rivalry would thus be seen as a fraternal struggle for their father's kingdom. This was the view taken by early modern antiquaries and inspired Hywel's cognomen Bychan (lenited Fychan), meaning 'little' and thus 'junior'. Alternatively Hywel has been regarded as Hywel Farf-fehinog of the related dynasty of Rhos. This Hywel's father, Caradog ap Meirion, had ruled Gwynedd in the second half of the eighth century, possibly succeeding Rhodri Molwynog in 754, and had died in 798. Hywel Farf-fehinog would thus have sought to retain his father's hold of the kingship in the face of the traditional dynasty represented by Cynan. A third possibility is that Hywel was the mysterious Hywel ap Cadwal mentioned in the prophetic poem *Cyfoesi Myrddin a Gwenddydd* which lists the 'Kings of the Britons', mostly those of Gwynedd.

The first recorded encounter between Hywel and Cynan Dindaethwy occurred in 813, when Hywel was victor (though one account has Cynan). In the following year they fought on Anglesey, where again Hywel was victorious, expelling Cynan from that island. As Anglesey was the traditional base of Cynan's dynasty as kings of Gwynedd, this was no doubt an important victory for Hywel. He possibly maintained himself for a further two years until 816, when Cynan in turn is said to have expelled him from Anglesey. Cynan was recognized as king at this point (the Irish chronicles call him 'rex Brittonum'—'king of the Welsh'—the traditional title of the kings of Gwynedd) but he was unable to capitalize on this success for he died in the same year. That Hywel was now unchallenged king of Gwynedd is probable, though the battle at Llan-faes (perhaps that on Anglesey) fought in 817 may have been an attempt by Cynan's kinsmen to unseat him. If so, they failed for Hywel survived for a further nine years. However, records of his death in 825 do not credit him with a title, except one case as 'king of Manaw' (that is Man), no doubt an error for Môn, or Anglesey. On his death the kingship passed to Merfyn Frych, the maternal grandson of Hywel's erstwhile rival Cynan Dindaethwy.

DAVID E. THORNTON

Sources J. Williams ab Ithel, ed., *Annales Cambriae*, Rolls Series, 20 (1860) · T. Jones, ed. and trans., *Brenhinedd y Saesson, or, The kings of the Saxons* (1971) [another version of *Brut y tywysogyon*] · T. Jones, ed. and trans., *Brut y tywysogyon, or, The chronicle of the princes: Peniarth MS 20* (1952) · T. Jones, ed. and trans., *Brut y tywysogyon, or, The chronicle of the princes: Red Book of Hergest* (1955) · P. C. Bartrum, ed., *Early Welsh genealogical tracts* (1966) · *Four ancient books of Wales containing the Cymric poems attributed to the bards of the sixth century*, ed. and trans. W. F. Skene, 2 vols. (1868) · P. C. Bartrum, 'Disgyniad pendefigaeth Cymru (Descent of the sovereignty of Wales)', *National Library of Wales Journal*, 16 (1969–70), 253–63 · *Ann. Ulster* · J. E. Lloyd, *A history of Wales from the earliest times to the Edwardian conquest*, 3rd edn, 2 vols. (1939); repr. (1988) · D. E. Thornton, *Kings, chronologies and genealogies: studies in the political history of early medieval Ireland and Wales* [forthcoming]

Hywel ab Edwin (*d.* 1044), king of Deheubarth, was the son of Edwin ab Einion ab Owain ap Hywel Dda. In 1033, after the death of Rhydderch ab Iestyn, ruler of Deheubarth since 1023, Hywel and his brother Maredudd succeeded to the kingdom. The sons of Rhydderch seem to have contested Hywel's and his brother's claim, and the next year a battle was fought at Irathwy between the rival houses, but

it is not known which was victorious. In 1035 Maredudd was slain by the sons of one Cynan, possibly Cynan ap Seisyll (*d.* 1027), but before the year was out the death of Caradog ap Rhydderch equalized the position of the combatants. After a few years of comparative peace Hywel's son Meurig was captured by the vikings in 1039. In the same year Gruffudd ap Llywelyn became king of north Wales, and after devastating Llanbadarn, drove Hywel out of his territory. In 1041 Hywel made an effort to win back his dominions, but was defeated by Gruffudd at Pencader. Hywel's wife became Gruffudd's captive, and subsequently his concubine.

In 1042 Hywel fought a battle at Pwlldyfach, where he defeated some vikings who had been raiding Dyfed. In the same year (though not necessarily in a connected event), Gruffudd was taken prisoner by the vikings of Dublin, but he soon escaped and reoccupied Hywel's territory. In 1044 Hywel collected a great fleet of his viking allies, and entered the mouth of the Tywi in another effort to win back his own. The final battle was fought at the mouth of the river. Gruffudd won a complete victory, and Hywel was slain.   T. F. TOUT, *rev.* DAVID E. THORNTON

Sources J. Williams ab Ithel, ed., *Annales Cambriae*, Rolls Series, 20 (1860) · T. Jones, ed. and trans., *Brenhinedd y Saesson, or, The kings of the Saxons* (1971) [another version of *Brut y tywysogyon*] · T. Jones, ed. and trans., *Brut y tywysogyon, or, The chronicle of the princes: Peniarth MS 20* (1952); 2nd edn (1973) · K. L. Maund, *Ireland, Wales, and England in the eleventh century* (1991) · J. E. Lloyd, *A history of Wales from the earliest times to the Edwardian conquest*, 3rd edn, 2 vols. (1939)

Hywel ab Ieuaf (*d.* 985), king of Gwynedd, was the son of Ieuaf ab Idwal Foel of Gwynedd. He was a contender for the kingship of Gwynedd and other parts of north Wales perhaps from *c.*969, and certainly held that kingship from 979 or 980 until his death in 985. His father, Ieuaf, seems to have shared the kingship of north Wales with his brother *Iago from the death of Hywel Dda in 949 or 950.

The first notice of Hywel may date to 955: a later tradition claims that he was summoned from Maen Gwynedd (possibly in Powys) to Ceredigion to aid his father and uncle Iago in an encounter, which may refer to the raid on Ceredigion by the sons of *Idwal Foel in 955. When, in 969, Iago imprisoned and (according to one chronicle) hanged his brother Idwal, it seems likely that Hywel became the senior representative of his branch of the dynasty. Like his father he seems to have shared power in some way with Iago, though in the light of the events of 969 this can hardly have been an amicable arrangement. Both men, however, were among the Welsh kings said to have submitted to Edgar soon after his 'coronation' at Bath in 973 and to have rowed the English king up and down the River Dee. In the following year Hywel exacted revenge upon his fratricidal uncle who, it is said, was expelled from his kingdom (it is not specified by whom) and replaced by Hywel. However, this new state of affairs in Gwynedd was not permanent and Iago managed to re-establish himself at least by the end of the decade. Thus, in 978, Hywel (with English support) raided the church at Clynnog Fawr and the Llŷn peninsula: this would seem to be a surprising act for a north Welsh ruler unless these areas were under the rule of a rival, in this case probably Iago. In the following year Iago is said to have been captured by Hywel (or in some versions, by vikings) and once again Hywel ruled in his stead. It is possible that Iago died (perhaps slain by Hywel) at this time, for he is not mentioned in the sources subsequently. Thus, it was Iago's son Custennin Ddu who, with Godred Haraldsson (Gofraid mac Arailt), king of Man, ravaged Llŷn and Anglesey in 980: this was no doubt directed against Hywel, for Custennin was slain in the same year by Hywel, possibly at Hiraddug (in modern Clwyd).

These events appear to have put an end to the dynastic rivalry characteristic of Hywel's reign until this point, and he subsequently turned his attention southwards against the north Welsh kings' traditional enemies in Deheubarth. In alliance with Ealdorman Ælfhere of Mercia he raided Brycheiniog and all the territories of Einion, son of Owain ap Hywel Dda, king of Deheubarth. This raid proved not to be a great success, for many of Hywel's forces are said to have been destroyed by those of Einion. Hywel's alliance with Ælfhere does not seem to have been long-lived, because two years later, in 985, Hywel was himself slain by the English, though which English is not known. On Hywel's death the kingship of Gwynedd was contended by a number of rival kinsmen, until it appears to have been annexed by Maredudd, another son of Owain of Deheubarth. Hywel's son Cynan reclaimed the kingship on Maredudd's death in 999.

David E. Thornton

Sources J. Williams ab Ithel, ed., *Annales Cambriae*, Rolls Series, 20 (1860) · T. Jones, ed. and trans., *Brenhinedd y Saesson, or, The kings of the Saxons* (1971) [another version of *Brut y tywysogyon*] · T. Jones, ed. and trans., *Brut y tywysogyon, or, The chronicle of the princes: Peniarth MS 20* (1952) · T. Jones, ed. and trans., *Brut y tywysogyon, or, The chronicle of the princes: Red Book of Hergest* (1955) · P. C. Bartrum, ed., *Early Welsh genealogical tracts* (1966) · R. Bromwich, ed. and trans., *Trioedd ynys Prydein: the Welsh triads*, 2nd edn (1978) · *Florentii Wigorniensis monachi chronicon ex chronicis*, ed. B. Thorpe, 1, EHS, 10 (1848), 142–3 · *Willelmi Malmesbiriensis monachi de gestis regum Anglorum*, ed. W. Stubbs, 2 vols., Rolls Series (1887–9), vol. 1, p. 165 · J. E. Lloyd, *A history of Wales from the earliest times to the Edwardian conquest*, 3rd edn, 2 vols. (1939); repr. (1988) · D. E. Thornton, 'Edgar and the eight kings, AD 973: textus et dramatis personae', *Early Medieval Europe*, 10/1 (2001), 49–79

Hywel ab Iorwerth (*d*. in or before **1216**). *See under* Iorwerth ab Owain (*d*. 1175x84).

Hywel ab Owain Gwynedd (*d*. **1170**), prince of Gwynedd and poet, was the eldest son of *Owain Gwynedd (*d*. 1170), king of north Wales; his mother, Pyfog (or Ffynod), was Irish. After the reconquest of Ceredigion in 1136 by Owain and his brother Cadwaladr, Hywel held lands there and in 1143, following the murder of his cousin Anarawd ap Gruffudd ap Rhys of Deheubarth by Cadwaladr's men, he drove Cadwaladr out of northern Ceredigion. Two years later he and his brother Cynan raided Cardigan and in 1146, with Anarawd's brother Cadell, he captured Carmarthen. Hywel joined Cadell, his brothers Maredudd and Rhys, and William fitz Gerald in 1147 in a successful attack on the castle of Wiston and later the same year Hywel and

Cynan combined in an attack on Cadwaladr in Meirionnydd and took his castle of Cynfal near Tywyn. In 1150 Hywel captured and imprisoned Cadwaladr's son Cadfan and seized his lands. By 1153 he had been expelled from Ceredigion by Cadell, Maredudd, and Rhys. In 1159 he and Cynan took part in an inconclusive campaign led by the earl of Cornwall, against Rhys ap Gruffudd, which ended in a truce.

Hywel was probably Owain Gwynedd's designated heir. Owain died in October 1170, but Hywel's succession was challenged by his two youngest half-brothers, Dafydd [*see below*] and Rhodri [*see below*], the sons of Owain's second wife, Cristin. He was defeated and killed by them near Pentraeth in Anglesey in 1170. Five of his six foster brothers, the sons of Cydifor Wyddel (the Irishman) were killed with him, and their elegy and that of Hywel were sung by the only survivor, Peryf ap Cydifor. He was buried at Bangor. The name of his wife is unknown but he had at least one son, Gruffudd.

The poet Cynddelw praised him as a soldier, as did Llywarch ap Llywelyn (Prydydd y Moch) in a poem to Dafydd. Hywel himself was also a distinguished poet and eight of his poems survive. As a member of a royal house he was not constrained by the conventions of court poetry and he composed some of the earliest surviving Welsh love and nature poems.

Dafydd ab Owain Gwynedd (*d*. 1203), king of Gwynedd, was Hywel's half-brother and the elder of the two sons of Owain Gwynedd and his cousin Cristin. In 1157 Dafydd and his brother Cynan ambushed Henry II in the forest near Hawarden during the king's invasion of north Wales; by 1165 he appears to have been holding Dyffryn Clwyd when he raided and plundered the adjacent cantref of Tegeingl. In 1170 he seized power in Gwynedd after killing Hywel at Pentraeth.

The next few years saw him consolidating his power. Although he had the kingship, the territory had been divided between the surviving brothers but he gradually brought all Gwynedd under his rule. When Henry II's sons went to war against him in 1173–4 Dafydd gave Henry his unswerving support and it may have been this loyalty that led to his marriage to the king's illegitimate half-sister Emma of Anjou in 1174. This was a significant dynastic alliance; it was the first time that a member of a Welsh ruling house had married outside Wales.

Dafydd had imprisoned his brother Rhodri, who had sought a share of the inheritance, but towards the end of 1175 Rhodri escaped and drove Dafydd out of Gwynedd west of the Conwy. After this a certain equilibrium seems to have been achieved; Dafydd held Gwynedd east of the Conwy, Rhodri the west, and Gruffudd and Maredudd, the two sons of Cynan, who had died in 1174, Meirionnydd and Llŷn and the lands in between. Dafydd, however, retained the kingship; in a grant of the tithes of Nefyn in Llŷn to Haughmond Abbey some time between 1177 and 1190 he is described as 'Rex Norwallie' ('king of north Wales') and in other grants he used the titles 'David Rex filius Owini' ('David the King, son of Owain') and 'Princeps Norwallie' ('prince of north Wales').

In May 1177 most of the Welsh rulers attended the Council of Oxford, but only Dafydd and Rhys ap Gruffudd of Deheubarth did homage to Henry II. This may suggest a polarization of native political authority in Wales with Dafydd and Rhys being recognized as the dominant rulers in the north and south. Henry granted him and Emma the lordship of Ellesmere in Shropshire and the manor of Hales in Worcestershire. In June 1177, according to the Chester annalist, Dafydd aided the earl of Chester in his occupation of Bromfield or Maelor, part of northern Powys.

During their journey through Wales in 1188 Gerald of Wales and Archbishop Baldwin of Canterbury were entertained by Dafydd at his castle at Rhuddlan, and Gerald commented on the way in which his host succeeded in maintaining a neutral position between the Welsh and the English. He also stated that at the time of the visit Dafydd's nephew, the young Llywelyn ab Iorwerth, had already begun to challenge his uncles.

According to *Brut y tywysogyon* Llywelyn, Rhodri, and the sons of Cynan allied against Dafydd in 1194, defeated him near Aberconwy, and ejected him from north Wales, leaving him only three castles. He was imprisoned by Llywelyn in 1197 and in 1203 he was driven out of Gwynedd and retired to his lands in England where he died in the same year. He had one son, **Owain** (d. 1212), from whom the manor of Hales came to be called Halesowen. He appears to have been a competent ruler and a good soldier, but the circumstances of his accession to power probably meant that his position could never be unchallenged and he was eventually overthrown by one of the greatest of all Welsh rulers, Llywelyn ab Iorwerth.

Rhodri ab Owain Gwynedd (d. 1195), prince, was the younger son of Owain and Cristin. In 1175 he was imprisoned by Dafydd but escaped and expelled his brother from Gwynedd west of the Conwy; he was ruling there in 1188 when he met the archbishop of Canterbury and his party in Anglesey, but, according to Gerald, none of his *teulu* or retinue was willing to take the cross. He appears to have been ejected from Anglesey, possibly by the sons of Cynan ab Owain Gwynedd, about 1190; in 1193 he returned with Manx aid in a campaign described as *haf y Gwyddyl* ('the summer of the Gaels'), but before the end of the year he was again driven out. *Brut y tywysogyon* states that he took part in the campaign of Llywelyn ab Iorwerth and the sons of Cynan against Dafydd in 1194 but this is not certain; in the same year Llywelyn won victories at Porthaethwy and Coedana in Anglesey, presumably over him. He died in 1195 and was buried at Holyhead. His wife was a daughter of Rhys ap Gruffudd of Deheubarth; he was subsequently betrothed to a daughter of the Manx king Ragnvald I but the marriage does not seem to have taken place and Llywelyn ab Iorwerth was later to seek a papal dispensation to marry her. He had three sons; some of his descendants were in the service of the thirteenth-century princes of Gwynedd and his great-granddaughter Senena was the mother of Llywelyn ap Gruffudd.

There is a substantial body of poetry addressed to Dafydd and Rhodri. Prydydd y Moch addressed three poems to the former and four to the latter, Gwalchmai one to each of them, and Gwilym Rhyfel two to Dafydd; Elidir Sais sang Rhodri's elegy. A. D. CARR

Sources T. Jones, ed. and trans., *Brut y tywysogyon, or, The chronicle of the princes: Peniarth MS 20* (1952) · J. Williams ab Ithel, ed., *Annales Cambriae*, Rolls Series, 20 (1860) · J. E. Lloyd, *A history of Wales from the earliest times to the Edwardian conquest*, 3rd edn, 2 vols. (1939); repr. (1988) · J. B. Smith, 'Owain Gwynedd', *Transactions of the Caernarvonshire Historical Society*, 32 (1971), 8–17 · Gerald of Wales, *The journey through Wales' and 'The description of Wales'*, trans. L. Thorpe (1978) · *Gwaith Llywarch ap Llywelyn*, 'Prydydd y Moch', ed. E. M. Jones and N. A. Jones (1991), 39–75 · J. Morris-Jones and T. H. Parry-Williams, eds., *Llawysgrif Hendregadredd* (1933), 28–33, 98–107, 182–5, 315–21 · A. D. Carr, 'Prydydd y Moch': ymateb hanesydd', *Transactions of the Honourable Society of Cymmrodorion* (1989), 161–80 · M. Richter, 'The political and institutional background to national consciousness in medieval Wales', *Nationality and the pursuit of national independence*, ed. T. W. Moody (1978), 37–55 · U. Rees, ed., *The cartulary of Haughmond Abbey* (1985) · D. M. Lloyd, 'The poets of the princes', *A guide to Welsh literature*, ed. A. O. H. Jarman and G. R. Hughes, 1: *Late sixth century to c.1300* (1976), 157–88 · D. Walker, *Medieval Wales* (1990) · E. Anwyl, ed., *The poetry of the Gogynfeirdd from the Myfyrian Archaiology of Wales* (1909), 168, 227
Wealth at death presumably wealthy

Hywel ap Goronwy (d. 1366?). *See under* Tudor family, forebears of (*per.* c.1215–1404).

Hywel, Sir, ap Gruffudd [called Syr Hywel y Fwyall] (d. 1381?), soldier, was a son of Gruffudd ap Hywel ap Maredudd of Bron-y-foel near Cricieth. There is no evidence of his early military career, though he may have fought at Crécy in 1346, but he had been knighted by 25 June 1355 when the chamberlain of north Wales was ordered to pay him half of the yearly fee due to him while in the Black Prince's service for the forthcoming campaign in France. He fought at Poitiers in 1356 and was popularly believed in Wales to have captured King John II of France. He is said to have performed such feats with his battleaxe that the prince ordered a ration of food to be served before it daily, the food being then distributed to the poor; according to Sir John Wynn of Gwydir this ritual continued until the beginning of the reign of Elizabeth I. In 1359 Hywel was leading troops from north Wales to Sandwich for service in France. Although he is said to have been granted the rents of the Dee mills at Chester, there is no reference to such a grant in the Chester recognizance rolls. He was, however, about 1359, appointed constable of Cricieth Castle, being probably the first Welshman to be appointed to such an office in the principality of north Wales. He was still there in 1378, when he was being paid an annual fee of 10 marks as well as an annuity of £20; he had ceased to hold office by 10 September 1380, when another constable was appointed, and he probably died not long afterwards.

The poet Iolo Goch composed a poem in his praise in which he referred to his exploits at Poitiers and to the open house he kept at Cricieth. Some pedigrees call his wife Tangwystl and others Lleucu; they had two sons and two daughters. His elegy was sung by Rhisierdyn and by Gruffudd ap Maredudd ap Dafydd, both of whom refer to his burial at Clynnog Fawr. A. D. CARR

Sources J. Wynn, *The history of the Gwydir family and memoirs*, ed. J. G. Jones (1990) · A. D. Carr, 'Welshmen and the Hundred Years

War', *Welsh History Review / Cylchgrawn Hanes Cymru*, 4 (1968–9), 21–46 • D. L. Evans, 'Some notes on the history of the principality of Wales in the time of the Black Prince (1343–1376)', *Transactions of the Honourable Society of Cymmrodorion* (1925–6), 25–110 • D. R. Johnston, ed., *Gwaith Iolo Goch* (1988), 6–12, 185–91 • J. G. Evans, ed., *The poetry in the Red Book of Hergest* (1911) • H. Lewis, 'Gruffwdd ap Maredudd ap Dafydd a Rhisierdyn', *BBCS*, 1 (1921–3), 123–33

Wealth at death probably wealthy on the proceeds of campaigns and offices

Hywel ap Gruffudd ab Ednyfed (d. 1282). *See under* Tudor family, forebears of (*per. c.*1215–1404).

Hywel Dda [Hywel Dda ap Cadell] (d. **949/50**), king in Wales, was son of *Cadell ap Rhodri Mawr (*d.* 910). He ruled the kingdom of Deheubarth in south-west Wales from 903 or 904 and, in addition, Gwynedd and other parts of north Wales from 942 or 943 until his death in 949 or 950. The gradual extension of his power over most of Wales, with the exception of the kingdoms of the south-east, was achieved through a combination of marriage alliance, fortuitous deaths of rivals, and, no doubt, a certain amount of violence. He is most famous as the king who supposedly first codified and promulgated Welsh customary law. It was perhaps because of this attribute, rather than due to any notably moral personal conduct, that he came to be known as Da, lenited as Dda (the Good).

Hywel's father, Cadell, may have ruled the kingdom of Ceredigion from 878 until 910. Hywel was himself married to Elen (d. 929), the daughter of Llywarch ap Hyfaidd, king of Dyfed from 892 or 893 until his death in 903. Hywel may have inherited Llywarch's kingdom in 903 on account of his marriage to Elen. However, the fact that one Rhodri (less correctly Rhydderch), brother of Llywarch, is said to have been decapitated in the region of Arwystli in the following year may indicate that Hywel also used more violent means to achieve this end. That he also succeeded his father to Ceredigion is by no means certain: the list of Welsh kings who submitted to Edward the Elder at Tamworth in 918 mentions Hywel but also includes his brother Clydog. The location of Clydog's kingdom is not known, but if it was Ceredigion he lost it in 920 when he was slain by a third brother, Meurig. This was not the end of Hywel's dynastic rivals: Clydog's son Hyfaidd (not called king) and a Meurig (possibly Hywel's brother) both lived until 938, and a Gwriad (whose genealogical affiliations are unknown) witnessed Anglo-Saxon charters in 928 and 932. It is therefore possible that Hywel's power in south-west and west Wales was not free from threat until the late 930s. Finally, in 942 on the death of Idwal Foel, king of Gwynedd and the dependent parts of north Wales, Hywel seems to have annexed these areas to his rule, expelling Idwal's sons Iago and Ieuaf. That this point marked a significant upturn in his fortunes is possibly implied in the English charters witnessed by him, which from now on distinguish Hywel from his fellow Welsh royal witnesses as *rex* or *regulus* rather than mere *subregulus*.

Hywel's relations with contemporary English kings have been a point of some controversy. Mention has already been made of his submission, along with Clydog

and Idwal Foel, to Edward the Elder at Tamworth in 918. However, it is with Edward's son and heir Æthelstan that Hywel is most frequently linked. In 926, when Æthelstan annexed Northumbria, he is said to have received the submission of all the kings in the island of Britain. Hywel and the other Welsh rulers possibly made their submissions, not at Eamont Bridge, but at Hereford, where Æthelstan is said to have exacted an annual tribute from them. For the remainder of his reign Hywel regularly attended this English king and later his brother Eadred: at Exeter in 928, Worthy (in modern Hampshire) and Luton in 931, 'Middleton' in 932, Winchester and Nottingham in 934, and Dorchester twice in 935. The 'Topsham charter' of 937 may be spurious, though there is no reason to suppose Hywel took part in the anti-English coalition at 'Brunanburh' in that year. There is then a gap (perhaps reflecting the decline in English fortunes after Æthelstan's death rather than a deterioration in Anglo-Welsh relations) until 946 when Hywel witnessed Eadred's charter at Kingston, and again at 'Chetwode' and Bourton three years later, not long before his death. The later tradition that one *Lolinus*, or *Loelinus*, king of Dyfed (possibly the name Llywelyn, but probably an error for Hoel or Hywel), accompanied King Edmund on a raid into Cumbria in 946 is of uncertain reliability. Hywel's frequent visits to England, combined with other factors such as the naming of one son Edwin, led to the view that Hywel was, in the words of the historian J. E. Lloyd, 'a warm admirer' of things English; more recently this alleged Anglophilia has been questioned, some historians suggesting rather that Hywel and his fellow Welsh rulers were sufficiently astute politicians to recognize the greater authority of the English kings such as Æthelstan, and visited England more out of political expediency than out of enthusiasm for that more powerful neighbour.

One of Hywel's supposed pro-English acts was the introduction of elements of English law into those of Wales. This was not impossible, since according to the prologues to the Welsh law books of the thirteenth and later centuries, he was responsible for the first codification and promulgation of Welsh law, known consequently as *cyfraith Hywel* ('the law of Hywel'). He is said to have convened an assembly of ecclesiastics from throughout Wales at Whitland (in Dyfed) and after forty days and nights of deliberation the laws were amended and redacted. In some accounts Hywel journeyed to Rome with three bishops to obtain papal approval for these laws. The authenticity of the prologues has come under increasing scholarly criticism and the whole account may owe more to the extent of Hywel's power over much of Wales than to historical fact. He did indeed travel to Rome, probably on pilgrimage, in 929 (thus thirteen years before he would have been in a position to impose any legal reforms upon the north Welsh), and it may be significant that his wife, Elen, died in the same year.

Hywel Dda is also notable as possibly the only early medieval Welsh ruler to have issued coinage. However, the single example, bearing the legend 'Howæl Rex', may have had more a ceremonial than a monetary function, and was a product of the English mint at Chester. Hywel's

Welsh 'empire' was short-lived, and on his death in 949 or 950 his southern territories were ruled by his sons, while those in the north were contended for successfully by the sons of Idwal Foel. Hywel's sons were called Edwin (Gwyn), *Owain, Rhain (Rhun), and Rhodri; and late sources add Hywel Fychan and Einion, both probably dubious.   DAVID E. THORNTON

Sources J. Williams ab Ithel, ed., *Annales Cambriae*, Rolls Series, 20 (1860) · T. Jones, ed. and trans., *Brenhinedd y Saesson, or, The kings of the Saxons* (1971) [another version of *Brut y tywysogyon*] · T. Jones, ed. and trans., *Brut y tywysogyon, or, The chronicle of the princes: Peniarth MS 20* (1952) · T. Jones, ed. and trans., *Brut y tywysogyon, or, The chronicle of the princes: Red Book of Hergest* (1955) · P. C. Bartrum, ed., *Early Welsh genealogical tracts* (1966) · *ASC*, s.a. 921, 926 [texts A, D] · *AS chart.*, S 400, 407, 413, 416, 417, 425, 433, 434, 435, 520, 544, 550, 1497 · Paris, *Chron.*, 1.455 · H. R. Luard, ed., *Flores historiarum*, 3 vols., Rolls Series, 95 (1890) · D. P. Kirby, 'Hywel Dda: Anglophil?', *Welsh History Review / Cylchgrawn Hanes Cymru*, 8 (1976–7), 1–13 · H. R. Loyn, 'Wales and England in the tenth century: the context of the Athelstan charters', *Welsh History Review / Cylchgrawn Hanes Cymru*, 10 (1980–81), 283–301 · J. E. Lloyd, *A history of Wales from the earliest times to the Edwardian conquest*, 3rd edn, 2 vols. (1939); repr. (1988) · H. Pryce, 'The prologues to the Welsh lawbooks', *BBCS*, 33 (1986), 151–87 · A. D. Carr and D. Jenkins, *A look at Hywel's law* (1985)

Hywel Fychan. *See* Hywel (*d.* 825).

Hywel of Caerleon. *See* Hywel ab Iorwerth (*d.* in or before 1216) *under* Iorwerth ab Owain (*d.* 1175x84).

Hywel, Syr, y Fwyall. *See* Hywel, Sir, ap Gruffudd (*d.* 1381?).

I. A. *See* Andrewes, John (*b.* 1582/3).

Iaco ab Dewi [James Davies] (1647/8–1722), copyist and translator, was born in Llandysul, Cardiganshire. There is no record of his birth or baptism and nothing is known of his family antecedents, but he appears to have lived to early adulthood in Carmarthenshire. Under the influence of Stephen Hughes he joined the Presbyterian (Independent) church at Pencader (founded by Hughes in 1672) and was a member of that church 'for many years', according to the Pant-teg church book. He was living in the area in 1684, and perhaps in 1686. He lost many of his belongings in a fire at his home, either in south Wales or following his move to Penllyn, around Bala, Merioneth. Some time before 1710, perhaps even by 1696, Iaco returned to Carmarthenshire and spent the rest of his life at Blaengwili, Llanllawddog.

Although Iaco ab Dewi was highly respected as an antiquary and as a knowledgeable collector and transcriber of manuscripts—'a very considerable man, a man of very few words, but of very extensive knowledge', claimed Christmas Samuel in the Pant-teg church book—and though he was well known as a literary figure, he led a solitary life, dogged by ill health and poverty. South Cardiganshire and the Teifi valley, where Iaco spent his early years, were in the second half of the seventeenth century and the first part of the eighteenth an area remarkable for the vitality of its literary and religious culture. Religious zeal and care for the Welsh literary tradition merged in the work of many local antiquaries, clerics, and their gentry patrons and there is no doubt that Iaco was influenced in his work both by the local scholarly tradition and by the

importance which was attached to popular devotional literature. A dissenter of conviction, he was associated with Stephen Hughes, whose mission was to ensure the publication and distribution of Welsh religious literature to ordinary folk, and he assisted Hughes in collecting the poems of Rees Prichard, the Old Vicar, which were published by Hughes in parts between 1659 and 1670.

More importantly, Iaco was a significant figure in the literary antiquarian movement of the seventeenth century which revived interest in the Welsh literary tradition and which safeguarded, often through scribal activity and energetic manuscript collecting, much of the work of the *Cywyddwyr of the preceding centuries. Iaco's earliest extant manuscript (Cardiff Central Library MS 2.623, Havod 13) is dated *c.*1690, and he had a part in transcribing some twenty-five other manuscripts (listed and discussed by G. H. Hughes in *Iaco ab Dewi*). He copied some texts, both prose and poetry, more than once, and his fine clear hand suggests that he was a professional copyist. He may have acted in this capacity for Edward Lhuyd. He co-operated with Samuel Williams, vicar of Llandyfrïog, in compiling the important collection of poetry in Aberystwyth, Llanstephan 133 (1712), a manuscript as remarkable for the number of unique copies of poems which it contains as for its beautifully executed hands.

But Iaco was not simply an assiduous copyist: he was, rather, an intelligent and critical scribe able to compare different copies of the same text to create an improved or more comprehensive version, and knowledgeable enough in the native literary tradition to be able to comment on the sources and attributions of what he transcribed. Moses Williams in his *Repertorium poeticum* (NL Wales, Llanstephan MS 57) remarked upon Iaco's 'fine taste in his Native Language both in Prose and Verse'. Though not named in the pamphlet, Iaco was probably responsible for the 1710 edition of *Flores poetarum Britannicorum*. In addition to the poetry of the *cywyddwyr* Iaco also collected popular verses from both manuscript and oral sources but his primary loyalty was to the classical tradition of Welsh poetry. He composed a few poems in popular carol metres but more in the strict metres—occasional *englynion*, many referring to his personal circumstances, and a *cywydd* in praise of Christ. His poetry is not, however, inspiring, and it is significant that Iaco showed little interest in the bardic *eisteddfodau* of the day.

Iaco's other important role was as a translator, between 1714 and 1730, of eight devotional and instructional religious books. These works and others of a similar nature were commissioned by gentry and by dissenters in south Cardiganshire and elsewhere, and represent a continuation of the ideals of the Welsh Trust in the 1680s. Iaco was sympathetic to these aims but was glad to accept the commissions as a means of eking out his livelihood. His translations are careful and literal, sometimes too close to the original to avoid complexity of style, and he does not reveal the literary flair and confidence of other more successful translations made in the same period. His most important or popular translations are *Cyfeillach beunyddiol a Duw* (1714: *Daily Conversations with God, Exemplify'd in the*

Holy Life of Armelle Nicolas), *Meddylieu neillduol ar grefydd* (1717: William Beveridge, *Private Thoughts upon Religion*), *Catechism o'r scrythur* (1717: Matthew Henry, *A Scripture-Catechism*), *Tyred a groesaw at Iesu Grist* (1719: John Bunyan, *Come, and Welcome to Jesus Christ*), and *Yr ymarfer o lonyddwch* (1730: George Webb, *The Practice of Quietness*). A Welsh translation of Bunyan's *The Pilgrim's Progress, Taith neu siwrnai y pererin*, appeared in 1688, attributed in the preface to four unnamed translators, including 'a man from Pencadair'. It has been assumed that this is Iaco ab Dewi but the attribution is not certain. Iaco died aged seventy-four at Llanllawddog on 24 September 1722 and was buried there three days later.   BRYNLEY F. ROBERTS

Sources G. H. Hughes, *Iaco ab Dewi, 1648–1722* (1953) · Pant-teg church book, NL Wales, MS 12362D · J. Davies, *Bywyd a gwaith Moses Williams* (1937) · G. H. Jenkins, *Literature, religion and society in Wales, 1660–1730* (1978) · G. H. Jenkins, 'Bywiogrwydd Crefyddol a Llenyddol Dyffryn Teifi, 1689–1740', *Cadw tŷ mewn cwmwl tystion: ysgrifau hanesyddol ar grefydd a diwylliant* (1990) · G. H. Hughes, 'Iaco ab Dewi: rhai ystyriaethau', *National Library of Wales Journal*, 3 (1943–4), 51–5

Iago ab Idwal ap Meurig (*d.* 1039). *See under* Gruffudd ap Cynan (1054/5–1137).

Iago ab Idwal Foel (*d. c.*979), king of Gwynedd, was the son of *Idwal Foel ab Anarawd, king of Gwynedd, who died in 942. Iago jointly ruled Gwynedd and dependent regions in north Wales from 950 until 979, when he was possibly slain. On Idwal's death the kingdom had come under the rule of the famous Hywel Dda ap Cadell, king of Deheubarth in south Wales, who expelled Iago and his brother Ieuaf. When Hywel Dda himself died in 949 or 950 these sons of Idwal Foel sought to reassert their claim to their father's northern kingdom, and the early 950s were characterized by a series of encounters between them and the sons of Hywel who ruled the southern kingdom. In 950 they fought at Nant Carno, in Arwystli, and according to some accounts the sons of Idwal were the victors, thus securing their hereditary position in the north. Two years later they were sufficiently strong to take the fight into Dyfed twice, and in 952 or 953 they (or according to some accounts, vikings) slew one Dyfnwal (or Dyfnwallon), a possible son of Hywel Dda. In 954 or 955 Owain ap Hywel and his brothers retaliated and the two groups met at Llanrwst (in the Conwy valley, Gwynedd). Iago and Ieuaf were probably the victors, slaying Edwin ap Hywel Dda and subsequently raiding Ceredigion.

For most of these early actions Iago and Ieuaf are simply referred to jointly as the 'sons of Idwal' and it seems that they shared political power in north Wales. Of the two there are hints that Iago was the senior or more powerful brother: thus, it was he who witnessed a charter of the English king Eadred in 955. Relations between the brothers were by no means always harmonious. In 969 Iago imprisoned Ieuaf and, according to one chronicle, had him hanged, though it is also possible that Ieuaf survived until 988. Iago may have thereby established his dominance in Gwynedd, but it appears that *Hywel ab Ieuaf then sought to assume his father's position. Thus Iago and his nephew Hywel were among the Welsh rulers

who submitted to Edgar at Chester soon after his 'coronation' at Bath in 973 and rowed the English king up and down the Dee. The dynastic rivalry continued apace. A year later, in 974, Hywel exacted revenge upon his fratricidal uncle when Iago was expelled from his kingdom (it is not specified by whom) and Hywel ruled in his place. Iago seems to have succeeded in re-establishing himself at least by the end of the decade. In 978 Hywel (with English support) raided the church at Clynnog Fawr and the Llŷn peninsula: this would seem to be a surprising act for a north Welsh ruler unless these areas were under the rule of a rival, in this case probably Iago. In 979 Iago was taken captive by Hywel (or by vikings) and again Hywel ruled in his stead. This is the last record of Iago and he may well have died soon afterwards, perhaps at Hywel's instigation. This inference is supported by the fact that in the following year it was his son Custennin Ddu who, with the help of Godred Haraldsson (Gofraid mac Arailt), king of Man, raided the Llŷn peninsula and Anglesey, no doubt against his rival Hywel.   DAVID E. THORNTON

Sources J. Williams ab Ithel, ed., *Annales Cambriae*, Rolls Series, 20 (1860) · T. Jones, ed. and trans., *Brenhinedd y Saesson, or, The kings of the Saxons* (1971) [another version of *Brut y tywysogyon*] · T. Jones, ed. and trans., *Brut y tywysogyon, or, The chronicle of the princes: Peniarth MS 20* (1952) · T. Jones, ed. and trans., *Brut y tywysogyon, or, The chronicle of the princes: Red Book of Hergest* (1955) · *AS chart.*, S 566 · P. C. Bartrum, ed., *Early Welsh genealogical tracts* (1966) · *Florentii Wigorniensis monachi chronicon ex chronicis*, ed. B. Thorpe, 1, EHS, 10 (1848), 142–3 · *Willelmi Malmesbiriensis monachi de gestis regum Anglorum*, ed. W. Stubbs, 2 vols., Rolls Series (1887–9), vol. 1, p. 165 · J. E. Lloyd, *A history of Wales from the earliest times to the Edwardian conquest*, 3rd edn, 2 vols. (1939); repr. (1988) · H. R. Loyn, 'Wales and England in the tenth century: the context of the Athelstan charters', *Welsh History Review / Cylchgrawn Hanes Cymru*, 10 (1980–81), 283–301 · D. E. Thornton, 'Edgar and the eight kings, AD 973: textus et dramatis personae', *Early Medieval Europe*, 10/1 (2001), 49–79

Iago ap Ieuan. *See* James, James (1832–1902).

Iago Trichrug. *See* Hughes, James (1779–1844).

Iain Glas. *See* Campbell, John, first earl of Breadalbane and Holland (1634–1717).

Iain Lom. *See* MacDonald, John (*c.*1624–*c.*1710).

Ian, Leslie Charles Bowyer Charteris [*formerly* Leslie Charles Bowyer Yin; *pseud.* Leslie Charteris] (1907–1993), writer, was born Leslie Charles Bowyer Yin in Singapore on 12 May 1907, the son of Dr Suat Chuan Yin (1876–1958), a wealthy Chinese surgeon who claimed descent from the Shang emperors, and Lydia Florence, *née* Bowyer (1876–1953).

Yin's part-Chinese origins, which were clear from his good-looking features, grated with him and he reinvented himself as often as his famous fictional character Simon Templar, 'the Saint'. He was brought up speaking Chinese and Malay as well as English. At ten he produced a four-page magazine, with his own illustrations of matchstick men—the prototype for the Saint's distinctive haloed logo.

After the breakup of his parents' marriage in 1919, Yin

and his mother went to England, where he attended Rossall School in Fleetwood, Lancashire, from 1920 to 1924 and King's College, Cambridge, which he left in 1926 after a year because, to his father's dismay, he wanted to write thrillers like Edgar Wallace and Sapper.

To support himself initially, Yin worked in a goldmine in Malaya and as a bartender, professional bridge player, and temporary policeman in Britain. He published his first stories as Leslie C. Bowyer. On 16 October 1926 he changed his name by deed poll to Leslie Charles Bowyer Charteris Ian; he adopted 'Charteris' after Colonel Francis Charteris, the eighteenth-century rake who was a founder member of the Hellfire Club. From then on he was known as Leslie Charteris.

Charteris's first book, *X Esquire*, published in 1927, told of a plot to destroy Britain with poisoned cigarettes. He experimented with a couple of heroes—a Bulldog Drummond lookalike, Terry Mannering, and the cavalier Ramon Francisco de Castila y Esproneda Manrique—before settling on the debonair Templar, who first appeared in *Meet the Tiger* in 1928. The character also appeared in stories for the magazine *The Thriller* and found popularity with *Enter the Saint* in 1930.

On 24 June 1931 Charteris married Pauline Schishkin (d. 1975), daughter of a Russian former tsarist diplomat. Unlikely to grow rich on *The Thriller*'s rate of 2 guineas per 1000 words, Charteris began visiting the United States in 1932 and wrote Hollywood film scripts, starting with *Midnight Club*, adapted from an E. Phillips Oppenheim novel.

Charteris continued his increasingly successful Saint books—the mix of light humour, sophisticated settings, and story-line emphasizing the role of a crusader tackling the forces of evil having special appeal in the depression. He enjoyed the quasi-mythical element evident in his hero's *nom de guerre*, derived from the initials of Simon Templar—itself a nod to the legend of the knights templar.

During the 1930s the Saint, who had many similarities with his author, went through a process of Americanization, apparent in the harder-edged *The Saint in New York* (1935). In 1938 the first Saint film was produced in Hollywood, starring the South African Louis Hayward. George Sanders later took up the role in 1939 in *The Saint Strikes Back*. By then Charteris was effectively living in North America, where his divorce from his first wife in 1937 was followed by marriage to Barbara Meyer (d. 1950) on 15 May 1939. His second marriage ended in divorce in 1943.

The Saint in Miami (1941) was an anti-Nazi thriller designed to encourage the United States to enter the Second World War. After Pearl Harbor, the Saint was transformed into a sober patriotic hero who worked alongside FBI chief Edgar Hoover's G-men.

On 7 October 1943 Charteris married his third wife, Elizabeth Bryant Borst (b. 1909), and in 1946 he became a naturalized American. He was divorced again in 1951, but the following year he married British actress Audrey Long. From 1953 his stories appeared in his own *Saint Magazine*, as well as in ongoing novels, films, radio features, and cartoon strips.

The Saint metamorphosed again into a mere private detective, operating in colourful locations, but after more than a quarter of a century Charteris was tiring of his creation. In 1962 he sold the rights to make twenty-six television episodes of *The Saint* for £500,000. The series starring Roger Moore gave Simon Templar a new lease of life, though, in reality, the Saint had been superseded in the public imagination by Ian Fleming's James Bond, a figure whom Charteris found vulgar and violent.

Having returned to Europe, Charteris became increasingly right-wing politically, backing Enoch Powell and capital punishment. Wealthier than ever, he devoted his time to pleasures such as eating, drinking, and racing. (He was a columnist for *Gourmet Magazine* and ran his own racehorses.) He maintained his intellectual interests, becoming a fellow of the Royal Society of Antiquaries and inventing a pictorial language called Paleneo. He also founded the Saint Club which raised money for east London charities. In the early 1970s he was resident in Dublin for tax purposes, though his main house was a large bungalow in Surrey and he also kept a hotel apartment in the south of France.

Further television adaptations of *The Saint* followed in the 1970s (featuring Ian Ogilvy) and 1980s (with Simon Dutton) and Charteris was happy for 'novelizations' by others to appear under his name. He spent his final years in Britain as something of a recluse. He and his reputation were cared for by his fourth wife. In 1992 he won the Crime Writers' Association's diamond dagger award for lifetime achievement. In all he wrote fifty books, which were translated into twenty-one languages. Though his later novels were formulaic, his early work had a mischievous *jeu d'esprit* and understated sophistication not unlike that depicted by Roger Moore in his cinema James Bond—significantly after he had played the Saint on television. Leslie Charteris died at the Princess Margaret Hospital, Windsor, on 15 April 1993 and his remains were cremated at Woking on 20 April.   ANDREW LYCETT

Sources *The Times* (17 April 1993) · *The Independent* (20 April 1993) · private information (2004) [the Saint Club] · deed poll, 1926 · d. cert. · *WW*
Archives Boston University, Massachusetts, corresp. and papers | GL, corresp. with Hodder and Stoughton
Likenesses J. Bratby, portrait, c.1980, priv. coll.

I'Anson, Edward (1811–1888), architect, was born on 25 July 1811, at 18 Laurence Pountney Lane, City of London, the eldest son of Edward I'Anson (1775–1853), surveyor and architect, and his wife, Lavinia Ann Woolloton (d. 1825). He was educated at Merchant Taylors' School, London, and at the Collège Henri IV, Paris. He was articled to his father, but also trained with John Wallen, then the principal London quantity surveyor, and in 1832 enrolled in the Royal Academy Schools. In 1835–6 he travelled on the continent, to Italy, Athens, and Constantinople. In 1842 he married Catherine Blakeway (1821–1866); they had six children. They lived in Clapham, London, where I'Anson was district surveyor. She died in 1866, and in July 1876 he married Caroline Susannah de Champs (b. 1833).

I'Anson joined his father in practice, and in 1844–5 he

Edward I'Anson (1811–1888), by unknown photographer

built Royal Exchange Buildings for Magdalen College, Oxford, and Sir Francis Graham Moon. The first successful office block in the City of London, it established his reputation and brought him a leading practice as an architect of city offices. Those in the Italianate style, such as the buildings of the British and Foreign Bible Society (1866), in Queen Victoria Street, London, were the most successful.

I'Anson was surveyor to several corporate bodies with London estates: for the Merchant Taylors' Company he designed new school buildings in the Gothic style, on its move to the Charterhouse, London (1873); for St Bartholomew's Hospital he designed the library and museum (1878–9): Ecclesiastical work included the restoration of St Mary Abchurch, London, and he also designed schools and almshouses, mainly in south London. As a surveyor, he had a large practice as a referee, arbitrator, and expert witness. In his later work he was assisted by his eldest son, Edward Blakeway I'Anson (1843–1912).

I'Anson was elected a fellow of the Royal Institute of British Architects in 1840, and was president from 1886 to 1888. He contributed papers to the *Transactions* of the institute; many were based on his frequent travels on the continent. His paper 'Office buildings in the City of London' (*Transactions of the Royal Institute of British Architects*, 15, 1864,

25–31) is a leading source for its subject. He was a founder member of the Surveyors' Institution and president in 1885–6, and was also a fellow of the Geological Society.

I'Anson died at home at 28 Clanricarde Gardens, Kensington, on 30 January 1888, from the effects of an operation for cancer. He was buried on 4 February at Headley, Hampshire, near his country home at Grayshott. I'Anson was noted by his contemporaries for combining the artistic side of his profession with his surveyor's skills. He combined great industry with a genial and unostentatious manner. His place in architectural history rests on his leading role in the development of city offices.

L. H. CUST, rev. PETER JEFFERSON SMITH

Sources *The Builder*, 54 (1888), 77–8, 99–100 · *Building News*, 54 (1888), 177–8 · B. I'Anson, *The history of the I'Anson family* (c.1915), 43–4 · parish records, London, St Laurence Pountney · registers, RA, Royal Academy Schools · registers of Merchant Taylors' School, Merchant Taylors' Company archives, London · Magd. Oxf. · *CGPLA Eng. & Wales* (1888) · d. cert.
Archives RIBA, topographical and measured drawings of continental subjects | RIBA, Royal Institute of British Architects nomination papers · RIBA, biography file · RIBA, photographic collection
Likenesses photograph, c.1865, priv. coll. · oils, c.1888, RIBA; repro. in *Architects' and Builders' Journal* (30 Dec 1913) · engraving (after photograph?, c.1865), repro. in *The Builder*, 29 (1871), 1006 · photograph, RIBA [*see illus.*]
Wealth at death £5520 11s. 1d.: probate, 12 April 1888, *CGPLA Eng. & Wales*

Iarlaithe [St Iarlaithe, Jarlath] (*supp. d.* 481), supposed bishop of Armagh, is attested in the Irish annals, in the early twelfth-century list of the heirs of Patrick, and in the saints' genealogies. In the earliest of the Irish martyrologies, the martyrology of Tallaght, there is one Iarlaithe at 11 February, who is given neither patronymic nor title; another, at 25 December, is entitled bishop. By the late seventh-century work of Muirchú and Tírechán, a fifth-century history of Ireland had been constructed on two premises (both probably false): Palladius, known from the chronicle of Prosper to have come as first bishop in 431, was replaced in 432 by Patrick; Patrick himself was the contemporary of Lóegaire, a son of Niall Noígíallach (Niall of the Nine Hostages), ancestor of the Uí Néill. By the final date of the original chronicle of Ireland, 911, this chronology had been largely adopted by the annalist. A further representative of this same conception was the early section of the list of heirs of Patrick. For Armagh, the essential message was that Patrick was its first bishop (later, archbishop); that he was succeeded by Benignus (or Benén; *d.* 467); and that Benignus was succeeded by Iarlaithe, son of Trian.

Even in the exiguous evidence for Iarlaithe, however, there remained inconsistent elements. In the genealogies of the saints, his father, Trian, is reckoned to be a descendant of Fiatach Find and thus a member of the ruling group (*gens*) of Ulster, Dál Fiatach. Their principal kingdom lay in what is now south-east co. Down, around Downpatrick. This is consistent with the claim that Patrick was buried at Saul, a few miles to the east of Downpatrick, or at Downpatrick itself. More particularly, Iarlaithe was said to be paternal first cousin to Díchu, who first welcomed Patrick to Ulster and whose descendants had a claim to the church of Saul. A later saint, Findbarr of Movilla (d. 579), was likewise attached, probably falsely, to the lineage of Díchu. While Benignus was already claimed in the late seventh century to have come from Brega, then the most powerful kingdom of the Uí Néill and the scene of Patrick's legendary struggle with Lóegaire, Iarlaithe was associated by the genealogists with Patrick's final resting-place. On the other hand, in the list of the heirs of Patrick, Iarlaithe is said to have come from Cluain Fiacla, which is plausibly identified with Clonfeacle, 5 miles to the north-west of Armagh, just into Tyrone (the site is marked by an early cross). This location for Iarlaithe is thus entirely inconsistent with his genealogy (itself indicated by the patronymic given him in the annals). Who or what Iarlaithe was in reality cannot be known; but he undoubtedly became an important figure in the bold attempt made by the clergy of Armagh to reconstruct the earliest history of Irish Christianity as a history of their church.

T. M. CHARLES-EDWARDS

Sources P. Ó Riain, ed., *Corpus genealogiarum sanctorum Hiberniae* (Dublin, 1985), p. 26, no. 150 · *Ann. Ulster*, s.a. 481 · H. J. Lawlor and R. I. Best, 'The ancient list of the coarbs of Patrick', *Proceedings of the Royal Irish Academy*, 35C (1918–20), 316–62 · R. I. Best and H. J. Lawlor, eds., *The martyrology of Tallaght*, HBS, 68 (1931), 11 Feb, 25 Dec · L. Bieler, ed. and trans., *The Patrician texts in the Book of Armagh*, Scriptores Latini Hiberniae, 10 (1979) · D. N. Dumville, 'The Armagh list of "Coarbs of St Patrick"', *Saint Patrick, AD 493–1993*, ed. D. N. Dumville and others (1993), 273–8 · Lord Killanin and M. V. Duignan, *The Shell guide to Ireland*, 2nd edn (1967), 120

Iarlaithe mac Loga (*fl.* 6th cent.). *See under* Connacht, saints of (act. *c.*400–*c.*800).

Ibach, Josias (*fl.* 1679–1696), brass founder, is thought to be the son of Constantin Ibach, the organist at St Pankratius at Stade, on the River Elbe. (Stade was then the capital of the Swedish duchy of Bremen and Verden.) Constantin Ibach had married there in 1640; his family came from Meissen and were organ builders, which is probably how Josias—named after his grandfather—learned brass founding and pipe making. The young Josias Ibach emigrated to London, obviously attracted by work opportunities after the great fire in 1666; he was subsequently naturalized in 1694. Christ Church, Newgate Street, records the burials of two members of an 'Ibeck' family, Hester on 2 January 1677 and John on 4 November 1679, who may well be related to him.

In 1679 Ibach cast the bronze statue of Charles II on horseback that Tobias Rustat commissioned from Grinling Gibbons to stand in the courtyard of Windsor Castle. Christopher Wren noted that 'the horse at Windsor was first cut in wood by a German and then cast by one Ibeck a founder in London' (Bolton and Hendry, 22, letter no. 7, 9 Sept 1682). Clearly at that time he still regarded himself as a citizen of Stade, since on one of the horse's hoofs he inscribed 'Josias Ibach Stada Bramensis 1679 Fundit'. In 1689 Ibach recast and repaired the original brass shells on the fountain in the privy garden at Hampton Court, for which he was paid £121. At Chatsworth

House he assisted Jean Tijou and was paid £17 for seventeen 'brass vauses gilt' in 1692 with another £60 the following year in part payment for an 'artificial tree of brass for a fountain' (Thompson, 36, 124)—which was a copper willow tree designed to surprise visitors with a sudden shower—together with further payments for minor repairs in 1696. His place and date of death are not known.

PHILIP LEWIN

Sources A. T. Bolton and H. D. Hendry, *Wren Society*, 5: *Designs of Sir Christopher Wren for Oxford, Cambridge, London, etc.* (1928) · G. Beer, *Orgelbau Ibach, Barmen, 1794–1904* (1975) · F. Thompson, *History of Chatsworth* (1949) · H. M. Colvin and others, eds., *The history of the king's works*, 6 vols. (1963–82) · list of denizations, 22 June 1694, PRO · P. Lewin and J. Renfrew, 'Tobias Rustat: best of royal servants', 1999, Jesus College, Cambridge · K. Gibson, '"Best belov'd of kings": the iconography of King Charles II', PhD diss., Courtauld Inst., 1997

Ibar mac Lugna (d. 500/01). *See under* Munster, saints of (act. *c.*450–*c.*700).

Ibbetson [*née* Thomson], **Agnes** (1757–1823), botanist, was born in London, the daughter of Andrew Thomson, merchant. She attended a finishing school, and her early life was said to have been 'devoted to gaiety, frivolity, and dissipation' (Webb, 54). She married James Ibbetson (1755–1790), barrister, who died at Bushey, Hertfordshire, after a long illness. From the late 1790s she lived on a comfortable annuity in Bellevue, at Cowley Bridge, near Exeter, and pursued scientific interests in plant chemistry, galvanic electricity, and microscopy. By her own testimony, she devoted 'thirteen out of twenty-four hours' to botany for many years (Nicholson, 28, 1811, 256). Manuscript folio volumes on grasses contain drawings, botanical descriptions, and reports on observations and dissections.

When in her fifties Agnes Ibbetson began reporting to scientific journals on her research work in plant physiology, illustrated by her own drawings. She published thirty-three essays in Nicholson's *Journal of Natural Philosophy, Chemistry, and the Arts* (1809–13) and twenty-two papers in the *Philosophical Magazine* (1814–22). Her first two letters to Nicholson's *Journal* were signed 'A. Ibbetson'. She did not correct their attribution to 'A. Ibbetson, Esq.' until her third letter, and thereafter was identified as 'Mrs Ibbetson'. She also published essays about soil and applied botanical knowledge in *Letters and Papers of the Bath and West of England Society* (1816) and *Annals of Philosophy* (1818–19). Her botany was observational and experimental. She used microscopes extensively, and invented her own tools to be able to 'cut vegetables' more precisely. She dismissed ideas about plant sensitivity and volition, and argued for mechanical explanations of plant functions. She stepped into contemporary discussions about 'perspiration' in plants and about the 'circulation' of sap, and put forward the theory that seeds, pollen, and flower buds all are formed in the root of a plant.

Ibbetson sought recognition from contemporary scientists for her theories about plant physiology. In 1810 Dr Sims named the genus *Ibbetsonia* (now *Cyclopia genistoides*) for her as 'the author of several very ingenious and instructive papers on vegetable physiology' (*Curtis's Botanical Magazine*). However, Ibbetson worked in relative isolation from the scientific community, and had a sense of grievance about the reception of her ideas. She sent material to Sir James Edward Smith of the Linnean Society in 1814, but he was not interested in promoting her work. In 'A new view of vegetable life' (*Philosophical Magazine*, 1816) she acknowledged that her views about plant physiology would 'appear bold language, especially in a woman'. Throughout her later years Ibbetson compiled her findings in an unpublished 'Botanical treatise', written in the form of letters. A prefatory 'Address to the public', probably written at the end of her life, opens with these words:

> Aweful as it is, as it must be to a woman to present to the Public a work of science: The reflection that it is the result of near 16 years hard study can alone give me courage to offer it.

Ibbetson died at Exmouth in February 1823 and was buried on 17 February at Littleham, Devon.

ANN B. SHTEIR

Sources A. B. Shteir, *Cultivating women, cultivating science: Flora's daughters and botany in England, 1760–1860* (1996), 120–35 · W. Webb, *Memorials of Exmouth* (1872), 53–4 · Linn. Soc., MSS 120a, 120b, 490 · NHM, Agnes Ibbetson MSS, MS IBB [5 vols.] · *Journal of Natural Philosophy, Chemistry, and the Arts*, 23–36 (1809–13) [various articles] · *Curtis's Botanical Magazine*, 31 (1810), pl. 1259
Archives Linn. Soc., 'Phytology' and letters, MSS 120a, 120b, 490 · NHM, corresp. and notebooks

Ibbetson, Sir Denzil Charles Jelf (1847–1908), administrator in India and author, was born on 30 August 1847 at Gainsborough in Lincolnshire. He was the elder son of Denzil John Holt Ibbetson, civil engineer and clergyman, and his wife, Clarissa Elizabeth, daughter of the Revd Lansdowne Guilding. His grandfather was commissary general at St Helena during Napoleon's captivity, which he recorded in a series of humorous caricatures. At the time of his son's birth, Ibbetson senior was a civil engineer employed in the construction of the Manchester, Sheffield, and Lincolnshire Railway. He was subsequently ordained in the Church of England and became vicar of St John's in Adelaide, South Australia. Denzil Ibbetson was educated first at St Peter's College, Adelaide, and then at St John's College, Cambridge. In 1868 he passed third in the open competition for the Indian Civil Service, and the following year graduated BA at Cambridge as a senior optime in the mathematical tripos. On 2 August 1870 he married Louisa Clarissa, daughter of Samuel Coulden of the College of Arms; they had two daughters.

The Punjab Ibbetson proceeded to India and joined the Punjab commission at the end of 1870. He formed part of a new élite of 'competition-wallahs' which intellectually outshone the earlier generation of Punjabi military political officials and well-connected alumni of Haileybury College. In December 1871 he was appointed assistant settlement officer for the south-eastern Karnal district of the Punjab. Four years later he assumed sole responsibility for the settlement operations. Settlement officers assessed the value of agricultural output so that revenue

demands could be fixed, and defined rights in land. These tasks provided officials with a unique opportunity to get to know Indian rural society. During an eight-year period of constant cold-weather tours, Ibbetson personally inspected thousands of holdings in an 892 square mile portion of land between the Jumna on the east and the high-lying lands of Jind on the west. He questioned large numbers of the Jat peasant proprietors who dominated the area's agrarian structure. Ibbetson established his reputation when he submitted the assessment reports (1877–8) and settlement report (published 1883) on his handiwork. His work was admired for its scholarly investigation of 'tribal' organization, and of the social life of the villagers and their systems of agriculture. He received the thanks of government for the 'ability, patience and skill' with which he had discharged his duty. Ibbetson's *Karnal Settlement Report* marked him out as the leading practitioner of the historicist anthropology inspired by Sir Henry Maine which was to dominate the Punjab's settlement literature of the 1870s and 1880s. Indeed, Ibbetson advocated the inclusion of Maine's book *Early History of Institutions* as a set text for the Indian Civil Service examination.

Publications in India Ibbetson's three-volume *Census of the Punjab, 1881* was the most impressive product of the historicist methodological revolution, the result of his work as superintendent of the census operations. Parts of his intellectual *tour de force* were reprinted as *Outlines of Punjab Ethnography* (1883), *The Religion of the Punjab* (1883), and *Punjab Castes* (1916). His treatment of the Punjab census remains a classic text for the study of the caste system. Ibbetson embarked on a fresh task when he edited the 1883–4 *Karnal District Gazetteer*. He had by now established a reputation among his colleagues for brilliance backed up by thoroughness and efficiency. In the words of one of his associates, 'any subject which he dealt with was explained to its beginnings, brought up to date and despatched of for years to come' (Maconochie, 91).

In a move away from revenue work and agrarian questions, Ibbetson was appointed director of publication instruction in 1884. During the next twenty months he introduced a number of reforms in the administration of the Punjab's education which made good the defects pointed out by Lord Ripon's commission. At the end of this period, in 1887, he went on furlough to England, having completed sixteen strenuous years of service. When he returned to India at the end of the following year he was given responsibility in the political field for the first time, being entrusted with the conduct of British relations with the princely state of Kapurthala. Other special duties falling to him were conferences on census operations and gaol administration in 1890, followed by an inquiry regarding cantonment administration. The next year he represented the Punjab on a commission which was established to investigate the working of the Deccan Agriculturalists' Relief Act of 1879. The inquiry resulted in an amendment which more efficiently prevented the transfer of agriculturalists' holdings to the trading and moneylending classes.

Land reform By the late 1880s a growing number of Punjabi officials were concerned about the problem of indebtedness and the threat posed to the stability of the 'sword arm' of India by the moneylenders' expropriation of the 'yeoman class'. Ibbetson believed that rural indebtedness was a result of peasant extravagance and suggested protecting the peasant from the 'wiles' of the moneylender by removing the cultivators' right to alienate land. His colleagues Charles Rivaz and Septimus Smet Thorburn shared these views, which were eventually implemented, although the lieutenant-governor, Dennis Fitzpatrick, was uneasy about government intervention in hitherto sacrosanct property rights.

Ibbetson's laborious investigations for the Deccan Agriculturalists' Relief Act commission earned him appointment in 1896 as secretary of the revenue and agricultural department of the government of India. His remit was to consider more widely the issue of indebtedness and the measures which might be taken to ameliorate the lot of the peasant. Ibbetson, in a note to the viceroy, Lord Elgin, elaborated the justification for a possible restriction on the transfer of land. He emphasized that the first 'duty' of the government of India was to secure the 'loyalty and contentment of our sturdy yeomanry from whose ranks we draw our native soldiers'. These arguments prepared the ground for the Punjab Alienation of Land Act. That measure was piloted through the legislative council in 1900 by Charles Rivaz, the new revenue secretary, against the wishes of the lieutenant-governor of the Punjab, Mackworth Young. It alleviated the problem of land transfers to the commercial castes by barring sales of agricultural holdings to individuals who were not members of 'agricultural tribes' gazetted by name in each district. The act also had the effect of privileging the 'tribe' as opposed to religion in the construction of rural identities. It thus paved the way for the domination of Punjabi politics by the cross-communal Unionist Party during the closing period of British rule. Ibbetson's significant role in shaping government thinking on this issue of indebtedness was his greatest practical achievement and legacy. In 1896, in reward for his services, he was made CSI.

Chief commissioner for Central Provinces Ibbetson was sent in 1898 to the Central Provinces, where he became chief commissioner. He could not have taken up this position at a more difficult time. The province—at that period 87,000 square miles in extent—was still suffering from the effects of the 1897 famine when, in October 1899, another failure of the monsoon coincided with the ravages of epidemics of fatal diseases. By July 1900 relief was required for two and a quarter million of the famished population. The pressures of work took an inevitable toll on Ibbetson's health and he was compelled to seek rest on furlough.

In 1902, after his return from England, Ibbetson joined Lord Curzon's executive council. He was immediately put to work with a vengeance. One task involved collating the reports of the famine commissioners of 1898 and 1901, translating their recommendations into rules and regulations for the conduct of future relief strategies. He also took responsibility for schemes of reform relating to the police and to irrigation. In addition to these duties he also played a leading part in legislative business. He was responsible for a number of significant measures, including the Co-operative Credit Act of 1904, a Poison Act, the transfer of property amendment, and the Punjab Village Sanitation and the Central Provinces Municipal Acts. In 1903 he was promoted KCSI.

Lieutenant-governor of the Punjab Ibbetson was appointed temporary lieutenant-governor of the Punjab in 1905 and was confirmed in the office when Sir Charles Rivaz retired on 6 March 1907. Unfortunately, rather than proving to be the crowning achievement of his career, Ibbetson's period as lieutenant-governor was dogged by mounting controversy and by his own ill health. Rural disturbances in the province in 1907 were rooted in the resentment which had been generated the preceding year by the Punjab Colonization of Land Bill and by the drastic increase in the charge on canal water on the Bari Doab Canal. The cultivators in the irrigated areas had already been hard hit by disease in their cotton crop and were increasingly bitter about the irregular supply of water and the bribery and corruption of petty officials. The Colonization Bill was thus ill-timed. In a spirit of benevolent despotism, it legalized the system of fines for the cultivators' transgression of sanitary rules and the prohibition on tree felling. It also enforced strict primogeniture. Rivaz was determined to rush through the legislation before his retirement in March, despite evidence of growing rural disquiet.

Ibbetson had been absent from the Punjab for the best part of fifteen years. He was thus out of touch with its political and social developments. He clung to the view that intervention in the canal colonies was for the good of the people and was as necessary as the earlier Alienation of Land Act. While he was acting governor he had in fact defended the proposals which forbade transfer of property by will. In a serious political misjudgement, he refused to accept that the rural protests could be based on genuine grievances. Instead they were blamed on the activities of 'outside agitators'. He thus embarked on a policy of repression which made scapegoats of the urban politicians Lajpat Rai and Ajit Singh, who had taken up the cultivators' cause. His action was further encouraged by the exaggerated reports by the local criminal investigation department of Russian assistance in a plot to subvert the Indian army. Lajpat Rai and Ajit Singh were deported without trial, meetings were banned in five districts of the Punjab, and anyone planning or attending illegal meetings was subject to six months' imprisonment.

In June, while Ibbetson was receiving medical treatment in London for a persistent lip ulcer which he had discovered was malignant, there was intense debate in the government of India over the Colonization Bill. The viceroy, Lord Minto, despite his personal respect for Ibbetson, decided that the veto of a 'poor piece of legislation' outweighed the need to back up the 'man on the spot'. The Punjabi agriculturalists ironically attributed the subsequent veto to Ibbetson's change of mind and he received a hero's welcome on his return to the province in August

1907. His final months in office were marked by a reversal of policy regarding the increases in canal water rates, following the appointment of a small committee to investigate this problem, and by attempts to limit the damage to the Punjab's reputation in the eyes of the viceroy and the executive council.

Resignation and death On 21 January 1908 Ibbetson resigned from office because of ill health, and immediately left India for the final time. He died at his home, 60 Montague Mansions, York Street, London, on 21 February, survived by his wife, and his body was cremated at Golders Green. When the news of his death reached the Punjab, a public subscription was launched, part of which paid for a portrait executed by H. Oliver which was hung in the Lawrence Hall at Lahore. Lord Curzon personally gave a memorial tablet which was erected in Christ Church, Simla.   IAN TALBOT

Sources N. G. Barrier, *The Punjab Alienation of Land Bill of 1900* (1966) · N. G. Barrier, 'The Punjab disturbances of 1907: the response of the British government in India to agrarian unrest', *Modern Asian Studies*, 1 (1967), 353–83 · N. G. Barrier, ed., *The census in British India* (1981) · I. Ali, *The Punjab under imperialism, 1885–1947* (1988) · C. Dewey, *The settlement literature of the Greater Punjab: a handbook* (1991) · D. Gilmartin, *Empire and Islam: Punjab and the making of Pakistan* (1988) · I. Talbot, *Punjab and the raj, 1849–1947* (1988) · C. E. Buckland, *Dictionary of Indian biography* (1906) · P. H. M. van den Dungen, *The Punjab tradition: influence and authority in nineteenth-century India* (1972) · E. Maconochie, *Life in the Indian civil service* (1926) · Burke, *Peerage* (1902) · *The Times* (22 Feb 1908) · *CGPLA Eng. & Wales* (1908) · *Debrett's Peerage*
Archives BL OIOC, Elgin MSS · BL OIOC, Ilbert MSS · BL OIOC, letters to Sir Henry Richards, MSS Eur F 122 · BL OIOC, corresp. with J. R. Dunlop Smith, MSS Eur D 573 · Trinity Cam., letters to Sir Henry Babington Smith
Likenesses H. Oliver, oils, 1908, Lawrence Hall, Lahore
Wealth at death £9167 4s. 3d.: probate, 2 May 1908, *CGPLA Eng. & Wales*

Ibbetson, Sir Henry, first baronet (1708–1761), cloth merchant, was born in Leeds, the third surviving son of James Ibbetson (1674–1739) and his wife, Elizabeth, the coheir of Dr John Nicholson, York's premier medical practitioner in the late seventeenth century. Ibbetson was a fourth-generation cloth merchant and a member of one of the town's leading merchant dynasties. His father had made a large fortune in exporting West Riding cloth; he was also a considerable buyer of land in the county, and in 1717 purchased the 2000 acre Denton Hall estate, near Ilkley, from the Fairfax family. Nothing is known of either Henry's education or his training; in both cases it was likely to have been expensive. On 23 December 1736 he married Catherine (1717–1740), the fourth daughter of Francis Foljambe of Aldwarke, a prominent Yorkshire landowner. She died childless within four years of the marriage, and on 6 October 1741 he married Isabella (d. 1757), the elder daughter of Ralph Carr of Cocken Hall, co. Durham. They quickly produced a family of ten children, four sons and six daughters, of whom three failed to survive infancy.

James Ibbetson was a ruthlessly successful man, and when he died in 1739 he passed on to his favourite and, by then, younger son, a great deal of scattered property in Leeds and the West Riding, which produced more than £1000 per annum, as well as one of the leading merchant houses in Leeds. Henry lacked his father's cutting edge, and his career developed in a variety of not entirely reconcilable directions. Clearly, extending the family fortunes to support and launch a large family with landowning connections and pretensions was uppermost in his mind. The export house in Leeds was continued until his death in 1761, for the last thirteen years of its existence with the aid of an active German partner, John Koster. A letter-book survives for the 1750s showing the firm to be one of high repute and tradition, dealing with importers in Germany, Flanders, and the western Mediterranean. By this stage it was probably past its zenith, for Ibbetson became increasingly involved in coalmining ventures and, after 1758, with a fellow merchant, Peter Birt, in farming the extremely lucrative Aire and Calder navigation tolls. He had long been handling the remittances of the East and West Riding land tax receivers, an activity which meshed well with his merchanting activities.

Although Ibbetson never lived at Denton, it became clear that it would pass to him, or his eldest son, since his elder brother, a barrister, produced no male heir. Certainly by the 1750s he was buying further land at Denton from the proceeds of property sales in Leeds and elsewhere. His ambition to launch his eldest son as a major West Riding landowner was fuelled by a baronetcy bestowed on him in 1748 as a reward for zealously raising a hundred men at his own expense in the Jacobite rising of 1745 and serving as high sheriff of Yorkshire two years later. But Ibbetson appears never to have lived elsewhere than in Leeds, either in villas on its edge or in the family's town house in Kirkgate, which John Carr (it was one of his earliest commissions) extended in 1752. He was mayor of Leeds in 1753—a record promotion, since he had served only three months on the corporation—and he also acted as a justice of the peace and deputy lieutenant for the West Riding of Yorkshire. He died on 22 June 1761 in York (while consulting a doctor there) after a protracted illness, and was buried in Leeds parish church. The firm's letter-book records his earlier visits to Bath and London in search of a medical cure. His wife had predeceased him four years earlier. Ibbetson's ambitions were realized within a decade of his death when his son James (1746–1795), the second baronet, inherited Denton (where Carr built the Ibbetsons a splendid new house in the 1770s) in 1768, the same year in which he married Jenny Caygill, the heir of a Halifax merchant with an estate in Essex.

R. G. WILSON

Sources R. G. Wilson, 'Merchants and land: the Ibbetsons of Leeds and Denton, 1650–1850', *Northern History*, 24 (1988), 75–100 · R. G. Wilson, *Gentlemen merchants: the merchant community in Leeds, 1700–1830* (1971) · R. Thoresby, *Ducatus Leodiensis, or, The topography of … Leedes*, ed. T. D. Whitaker, 2nd edn (1816), 146 · R. V. Taylor, ed., *The biographia Leodiensis, or, Biographical sketches of the worthies of Leeds* (1865), 168–9 · J. Hunter, *Familiae minorum gentium*, ed. J. W. Clay, 4 vols., Harleian Society, 37–40 (1894–6) · will, PRO, PROB 11/874, sig. 113
Archives priv. coll. | N. Yorks. CRO, Wyvill MSS
Likenesses P. Mercier, portrait, 1740, Constable Burton Hall, North Yorkshire

Wealth at death see will, Borth. Inst.

Ibbetson, Henry John Selwin-, Baron Rookwood (1826–1902), politician, born in London on 26 September 1826, was only son of Sir John Thomas Ibbetson-Selwin, sixth baronet (d. 1869), and his wife, Elizabeth, daughter of General John Leveson-Gower of Bill Hill, Berkshire. His father had assumed the surname of Selwin on inheriting in 1825 the Selwin estates at Harlow, Essex. After education at home Henry was admitted a fellow-commoner at St John's College, Cambridge, on 2 July 1845. He graduated BA in 1849, and proceeded MA in 1852. In 1850 he married Sarah Elizabeth (1821–1865), daughter of John Singleton *Copley, first Baron Lyndhurst, and his wife, Sarah; they had no children. In the early 1850s Selwin travelled widely, and was present in the Crimea at the declaration of peace in 1856. In the same year he embarked, as a Conservative, upon his political career. After twice suffering defeat at Ipswich, in March 1857 and in April 1859, he headed the poll for South Essex in July 1865. When the Essex constituencies were redistributed, he was returned unopposed for the western division in 1868, again in 1874, and by a large majority in 1880. Subsequently (after the redistribution in 1885) he sat for the Epping division until his elevation to the peerage in 1892.

Selwin took from the first a useful part in parliamentary discussion, cautiously supporting moderate reforms. In 1867 he married his second wife, Eden, née Thackrah (d. 1899), widow of his cousin Sir Charles Henry Ibbetson, fifth baronet; they had no children. On their marriage he resumed the old family name of Ibbetson in addition to that of Selwin, and in 1869 he succeeded his father in the baronetcy. In the same year, while in opposition, he carried a bill which aimed at diminishing the number of beerhouses by placing all drink-shops under the same licensing authority and by leaving none under the control of the excise. He encouraged the Liberals to take up the licensing question. In 1870 he supported the Liberals' Elementary Education Bill, and in 1873 he backed Plimsoll's Merchant Shipping Bill.

In 1874 the Conservatives were returned to power, and Selwin-Ibbetson became under-secretary to the Home Office after declining the chairmanship of ways and means. He proved a laborious and efficient administrator, but was perhaps too prone to deal with details which might have been left to subordinates. During his tenure of office, acts were passed for the improvement of working-class housing in 1875, for the amendment of the labour laws so as to relax the stringency of the law of conspiracy, and for the provision of agricultural holdings, a measure which was largely based on information he had himself collected. He was unsuccessful in persuading his colleagues to introduce further licensing law reforms. Selwin-Ibbetson was at this time frequently ill, but would not resign. He became something of an embarrassment to the government. In 1878 he became parliamentary secretary to the Treasury, and piloted through the house the bill which made Epping Forest a public recreation ground, as well as the Cattle Diseases Bill. As early as 1871 he had championed in the house public rights in Epping Forest.

In 1879 Selwin-Ibbetson declined the governorship of New South Wales. In October, while in Ireland with the chancellor of the exchequer, Sir Stafford Northcote, he sanctioned a scheme for improving the navigation of the Shannon, and planned a reconstruction of the Irish board of works which never became law but led to changes in the personnel of the board. In 1880 Selwin-Ibbetson retired from office with the Conservative government. He acted as second church estates commissioner from 7 July 1885 to 2 March 1886, and again from 8 September 1886 to 20 June 1892. At the general election of 1892 he was raised to the peerage by Lord Salisbury as Baron Rookwood, the title being taken from an old mansion in Yorkshire long in the possession of the Ibbetson family. On 5 September 1900, aged seventy-three, he was married for the third time; his new wife was Sophia Harriet (d. 1932), first daughter of Digby Lawrell of Jersey.

Through his life Rookwood devoted himself to county business, frequently presiding at quarter sessions with efficiency and impartiality. He also did much work for hospitals and charities, especially in the Essex area, where his seat, Down Hall, was situated. A keen sportsman, he was master of the Essex hounds from 1879 to 1886. In March 1893 Essex men of all parties presented him with his portrait by W. Q. Orchardson, which was installed at Down Hall, Harlow. Rookwood died childless at 51 Welbeck Street, London on 15 January 1902, following an operation, and was buried on 21 January at Hatfield Broadoak, Essex, his titles becoming extinct.

W. B. DUFFIELD, rev. H. C. G. MATTHEW

Sources The Times (16 Jan 1902) · Essex County Chronicle (17 Jan 1902) · GEC, Peerage · P. Smith, Disraelian Conservatism and social reform (1967) · Venn, Alum. Cant. · R. Shannon, The age of Disraeli, 1868–1881: the rise of tory democracy (1992) · R. F. Ball and T. Gilbey, The Essex foxhounds (1896) · H. B. Yerburgh, Leaves from a hunting diary in Essex, 2 vols. (1900) · Irish Times (13 Oct 1879) · CGPLA Eng. & Wales (1902)
Archives Bodl. Oxf., Disraeli MSS · UCL, corresp. with E. Chadwick
Likenesses W. Q. Orchardson, oils, 1893; formerly at Down Hall, Essex, 1912 · J. Brown, stipple (after photograph by J. Mayall), NPG; repro. in Baily's Magazine (1882) · R. T. & Co., wood-engraving (after photograph by G. Jerrard), NPG; repro. in ILN (4 June 1892) · engraving (after W. Q. Orchardson) · photograph, NPG
Wealth at death £106,265 8s. 1d.: probate, 13 May 1902, CGPLA Eng. & Wales

Ibbetson, Julius Caesar (1759–1817), landscape and watercolour painter, was born on 29 December 1759 at Farnley Moor, Leeds, the second child of Richard Ibbetson (d. 1791), a clothier of Yorkshire descent. According to the 'Memoir', Ibbetson's nineteen-year-old mother went into premature labour as a result of a fall on ice and died, with her son being delivered by caesarean section, hence the unusual middle name which he strove to suppress throughout his life. The details of Ibbetson's earliest education are unknown, but it is probable that he was supervised first by a local Moravian community (with whom his father had been connected before marriage), and then by Quakers in Leeds. Its unusual thoroughness is reflected in the fluent prose, both of his published painting manuals and of his regular, often entertaining, and rewarding correspondence with patrons. Between 1772 and 1777 he was apprenticed to John Fletcher, a ship painter in Hull, where he also enjoyed some success as a theatrical scene painter. This contract ended with his abrupt move to London, where his only regular employment over the next decade was as a picture restorer, principally for one Clarke of Leicester Fields. About 1780 he married Elizabeth (d. 1794), and two years later sent an account of his early life to Benjamin West (seen and transcribed by Joseph Farington in 1805).

Ibbetson's thirty years as an exhibitor of landscapes and genre scenes at the Royal Academy began in 1785 with *View of North Fleet*. *George Biggin* of 1783 (Yale U. CBA) is one of Ibbetson's earliest known works and, as an accomplished full-length portrait in the Gainsborough tradition, should be considered as a milestone in the development of an artist who was entirely self-taught. Through the connoisseur Captain William Baillie, Ibbetson was appointed draughtsman to Colonel Charles Cathcart on the first British embassy to Peking (Beijing) in 1787, and he made numerous watercolour drawings of the fauna and the scenery *en route*, for example *False Bay, Cape of Good Hope* (V&A). His *Landing of the Remains of the Hon. Col. Cathcart for Interment … in Java* (priv. coll.), worked up from a detailed sketch made on the spot (V&A) and shown at the Royal Academy in 1789, alludes to the expedition's abortive end after only six months, and 'the wreck of cherished dreams' (Clay, 24) for Ibbetson. During his absence in 1788, *The Ascent of George Biggin, esq. from St. George's Fields, June 29th 1785 ('Lunardi's Balloon')* (Neue Pinakothek, Munich) was an acclaimed exhibit at the Royal Academy and remains his best-known painting.

In 1789 Ibbetson was the guest of Viscount Mountstuart (later first marquess of Bute) at Cardiff Castle, the beginning of a decade-long association with Wales. His detailed watercolours of iron furnaces, coal staithes, and copper mines foreshadow the work of Joseph Wright of Derby and J. M. W. Turner and constitute an important record of the early industrial developments in that region, but are less well known than his more numerous scenes of folk life and picturesque scenery. From an extensive tour of Wales in 1792 with a patron, Colonel Greville, and the watercolour painter John 'Warwick' Smith arose his only major foray into the sublime: *Aberglaslyn: the Flash of Lightning* (Temple Newsam House, Leeds). A visit to the Isle of Wight in 1790 opened another rich seam of subjects, including shipwrecks and smugglers. His wife's death in 1794 and sole responsibility for three small children provoked a minor nervous breakdown, exacerbated by near destitution and relieved only by employment on a decorative scheme at Kenwood. Ibbetson was commissioned by David Murray, second earl of Mansfield, and his wife to decorate the music room with large painted borders, terracotta red in colour, with clustered musical instruments and painted ovals representing various pastoral scenes and views in north Wales. The scheme was unfinished, but the oil sketches remain at Kenwood, although

not *in situ*. In 1798 Ibbetson moved to Liverpool to begin working for the dealer Thomas Vernon and from there made his first visit to the Lake District. The 'Memoir' records that he 'fixed his residence in that paradise of painters and poets' (Ibbetson, *Accidence*, x) in 1799 but it was not until 1801, with his marriage to a local weaver's daughter, Bella Thompson (c.1780–1835), that he settled at Ambleside. Meanwhile through Sir George Beaumont, the Liverpool patron William Roscoe, and a stay in Edinburgh in 1800, Ibbetson acquired a number of other important patrons, including Sir Henry Nelthorpe (for whom George Stubbs had worked) and the countess of Balcarres, the latter encouraging him to produce his instruction manual *An Accidence, or Gamut, of Painting in Oil*, published in 1803. In that year Ibbetson met the Yorkshire landowner and philanthropist William Danby, and by 1805 had moved to Masham as his protégé. Here, surrounded by his young family and a welcoming community, he spent the only settled period of his life and 'Years glided by away in comfort, though not in affluence' (ibid., xi). Ibbetson died on 13 October 1817 and was buried in the churchyard of St Mary's, Masham. A good likeness of him was taken in 1807 by John Raphael Smith (pastels, Temple Newsam, Leeds) and shows him to have been a large, portly man. Benjamin West accurately dubbed him the 'Berchem of England' in acknowledgement of his debt to the Dutch seventeenth-century landscape painters. His watercolours are prized for their delicacy and sureness of line; many were engraved for such diverse projects as John Church's publication *A Cabinet of Quadrupeds*, and John Boydell's *Shakspeare Gallery*. His son from his first marriage, Julius Caesar Ibbetson the younger (1783–1825), was a drawing master and innkeeper at Richmond, North Riding of Yorkshire.

JAMES MITCHELL

Sources J. C. Ibbetson, *An accidence, or gamut, of painting in oil and water colour*, 2nd edn (1828) [incl. anonymous 'Memoir of the author'] • R. M. Clay, *Julius Caesar Ibbetson* (1948) • J. F. Mitchell, *Julius Caesar Ibbetson, 1759–1817* (1999) • M. H. Grant, *A chronological history of the old English landscape painters*, 3 vols. (1926–47) • J. C. Ibbetson, *A process of tinted drawing* (1795) • private information (2004) • Farington, *Diary* [23–4 Jan 1805]

Archives priv. coll., letters

Likenesses G. Cuitt, oils, c.1777, Temple Newsam, Leeds • J. C. Ibbetson, self-portrait, oils, 1804, NPG • J. R. Smith, pastel drawing, 1807, Temple Newsam, Leeds • R. Cooper, crayon, line and stipple print (after J. R. Smith), BM, NPG; repro. in Ibbetson, *Accidence*

Ibbot, Benjamin (1680–1725), Church of England clergyman, was born at Beachamwell, Norfolk, the son of Thomas Ibbot (d. 1720?), vicar of Swaffham and rector of Beachamwell. Admitted as a sizar at Clare College, Cambridge, on 25 July 1695, he graduated BA in 1699; his tutors included Richard Laughton, follower of John Locke and Isaac Newton, who may have first brought him into contact with Samuel Clarke. He was made scholar of Corpus Christi College in 1700 and graduated MA in 1703. His territorial nexus gained him a Norfolk fellowship there in 1706 but he resigned it the next year on being appointed librarian, and subsequently Cambridge chaplain, to Thomas Tenison, the whiggish latitudinarian archbishop of Canterbury. This position opened up to Ibbot a network of connections through the church, as Tenison preferred to conduct formal church business through his chaplains, a consequence of his old age and political differences with other senior churchmen. Since Oxford parochial clergymen applying to become pluralists (a procedure disapproved of by Tenison) were examined by the Oxford chaplain, and Cambridge applicants by the Cambridge chaplain, the position was potentially one of great influence. Ibbot was installed as treasurer of Wells Cathedral on 13 November 1707 by Tenison's choice; Tenison also presented him to his peculiar in London, the rectory of the united parishes of St Vedast-alias-Foster and St Michael-le-Querne.

Ibbot joined the preachers and writers defending Christianity against deism, which upheld the existence of God by reason rather than by revealed religion—and, it now seemed, would engulf English society. During 1714 and 1715 Tenison, as sole survivor of the original trustees, appointed Ibbot to preach the sixteen Robert Boyle lectures at Oxford, established for the defence of Christianity against unbelievers by employing contemporary advances in natural philosophy. He declared 'wherein the true notion of the exercise of Private Judgment, or Freethinking, in matters of Religion is stated' (B. Ibbot, *A Defence of Natural and Revealed Religion*, 2, 1739). This replied to the *Discourse of Free-Thinking in Matters of Religion* published in 1713 by the deist Anthony Collins, which had argued that freedom of thought was sufficient for the discovery of truth, while doubting biblical evidence.

On 28 July 1714 Ibbot married Susanne Powell at the church of St Martin Outwich in Threadneedle Street, London. He was a zealous supporter of the Hanoverian succession, and George I appointed him a chaplain-in-ordinary in 1716; when the king visited Cambridge on 6 October 1717 Ibbot was by royal mandate made a DD.

Ibbot became involved in the Bangorian controversy as a defender of Benjamin Hoadly's position. In 1719 he brought out a translation of Samuel Pufendorf's *De habitu religionis Christianae ad vitam civilem*, which distinguished between the Christian and the civil life. This was followed in 1720 by the publication of six occasional sermons, including 'The nature and extent of the office of the civil magistrate, considered in a sermon preached ... Sept. 29 ... being the election day of a lord mayor for the year ensuing', on Acts 18: 14–15. In this sermon Ibbot upheld the judgement of Gallio, a Roman proconsul, who, when the Jews at Corinth accused St Paul of persuading 'men to worship God according to the (Mosaic) law', indicated that he 'cared for none of these things' because the empire should abstain from religious matters. From this Ibbot argued that it was not religion's role in society to ordain the civil government, nor was it the role of the civil power to interfere in an individual's spiritual affairs beyond allowing members of society to worship God in the way they chose, provided that this did not lead them to commit injustices against their neighbour. The sermon aroused much hostile criticism and was answered by Silas Drayton in a pamphlet entitled *Gallio Reproved* (1721), by Joseph Slade in *Gallionism Truly Stated* (1721), and by another writer under the pseudonym Philoclesius.

Ibbot was appointed preacher-assistant in 1718 to his friend and fellow opponent of deism Samuel Clarke at St James's, Piccadilly, and rector of St Paul's, Shadwell. He was presented by George I to a prebend of Westminster Abbey on 19 November 1724 and installed on 26 November. He died at Camberwell, Surrey, on 5 April 1725 and was buried in Westminster Abbey. *Thirty Discourses on Practical Subjects* was selected from his manuscripts by Clarke and published in 1726 to benefit his widow. It was republished in 1776, with an introduction by Roger Flexman.

LEONARD W. COWIE

Sources R. Masters, *The history of the College of Corpus Christi and the B. Virgin Mary ... in the University of Cambridge* (1753) [incl. appx of lives of members (1755)] · R. Flexman, preface, in B. Ibbot, *Thirty discourses on practical subjects*, ed. S. Clarke, 2nd edn, 2 vols. (1776) · J. Le Neve, *Fasti ecclesiae anglicanae* (1716) · W. T. Lowndes, *The bibliographer's manual of English literature*, 4 vols. (1834) · N. Sykes, *Church and state in England in the XVIII century* (1934) · C. J. Abbey and J. H. Overton, *The English church in the eighteenth century*, new edn (1896) · E. Carpenter, *Thomas Tenison, archbishop of Canterbury* (1948) · Venn, *Alum. Cant.*, 1/2

Archives BL, Add. MS 3873, fol. 43

Likenesses mezzotint (after unknown artist), BM, NPG

Wealth at death all worldly goods left to wife: will, PRO, PROB 11/603, sig. 113

Ibbotson, Henry (*bap.* 1814, *d.* 1886), botanist, was born at Ganthorpe, near Castle Howard, Yorkshire, and baptized at nearby Terrington on 7 May 1814, the son of a gardener, John Ibbotson, and his wife, Elizabeth. Richard Spruce (1817–1893) grew up with him in Ganthorpe and as youths the two together investigated the flora of the local dales and woods. Unlike Spruce, who became a plant collector overseas, Ibbotson settled for the humdrum life of schoolmaster of a local village, Mowthorpe. However, finding that occupation ultimately uncongenial he opted instead to wander the British Isles in search of plants. He was an active contributor to Henry Baines's *Flora of Yorkshire* (1840), to its supplement (1854), and to J. G. Baker's *North Yorkshire* (1863). He also published two local plant lists in *The Phytologist* in 1844 and a pamphlet on the ferns of Yorkshire in 1884. His chief production, a laborious compilation of all the synonyms of British flowering plants known to him, entitled *A Catalogue of the Phænogamous Plants of Great Britain*, came out in parts, from 1846 to 1849, and is said to have received a wide circulation. He also sold sets of dried and named specimens of the rarer plants of the northern counties. That Ibbotson had unrestricted access to the grounds of Castle Howard (where his father was probably employed) is revealed by his publications, especially a detailed *Visitors Guide* to Castle Howard (1851). A follow-up volume on the history and topography of forty of its surrounding villages, which he planned, was never completed.

By the 1850s, however, Ibbotson had turned to drink and effectively become a vagrant, sinking into an often penniless state and scraping a scanty livelihood by using his botanical expertise to collect herbs from the countryside and sell them to druggists. He died in York on 12 February 1886, intestate.   D. E. ALLEN

Sources H. J. Wilkinson, 'Historical account of the herbarium of the Yorkshire Philosophical Society', *Annual Report* [Yorkshire Philosophical Society] (1907), 67–8 · R. L. Gulliver, 'Henry Ibbotson, 1814–1886', *York History*, 5 (1979), 269–70 · *Journal of Botany*, 4 (1845), 496–7 · *Natural History Journal and School Reporter* (15 March 1886), 42
Archives South London Botanical Institute, herbarium, F. Townsend, plants

Ibrahim, Sir Kashim (1910–1990), politician and governor of Northern Nigeria, was born on 10 January 1910 in Gargar ward, Yerwa, in the Borno province of Nigeria, youngest son of Mallam Ibrahim Lakanmi (*b. c.*1840), a Kanuri aristocrat, and of a Badawi mother, Falmatta Bosumami (*b. c.*1875). Kashim Ibrahim became not only the first indigenous governor of Northern Nigeria (1962–6) but was also the last: following the 1966 coup, the military dissolved the northern region.

Brought up in a strict Muslim household, Kashim Ibrahim received a thorough Koranic education before entering the Borno provincial school in 1922. When only fifteen he was admitted to the premier Katsina College, where he graduated as a teacher in 1929. During his early years at the Borno middle school, he wrote a teacher's guide to mathematics and a Kanuri reader. He was advanced to the native administration's education inspectorate in 1933, and in recognition of his work in education the shehu (emir) of Borno conferred on him the traditional scholarly title of Shettima in 1935. At the end of the war Shettima Kashim, as he was now known, played an important part in the strategy for resettling former servicemen.

In 1947 Shettima Kashim was promoted to the government senior service as a provincial education assistant, and two years later became one of the first northern education officers. His horizons now broadened beyond Borno. He accompanied the shehu to the opening of the University College Ibadan in 1948, visited Britain, and in 1950 found himself a member of the government's study mission to the teacher training centre at Bakht-el-Ruda in the Sudan. An obvious choice for nomination to the new northern house of assembly in 1946, he was made special member for education, and in 1952, as a founding Borno member of the Northern People's Congress (NPC), he was elected MP. By now a national figure, Shettima Kashim was among the four northerners nominated to ministerial office in Lagos, taking the portfolio of welfare and social services. A year later he became Nigeria's minister of education. Unwilling to remain in Lagos, he did not contest the 1954 federal election; instead he returned to the north and in 1955 was made minister of development and surveys in Kaduna.

In 1956 a crisis erupted in Borno, where the corruption of the waziri (the title of the native administration's chief executive) and the inability of the ageing shehu to take corrective action led to the colonial government's intervention and the removal of the waziri. This was the second major purge of Borno native administration in three years. In helping to resolve both crises Shettima Kashim took a positive lead, yet ensuring his 'loyalty to the Shehu was unimpaired' (Sharwood-Smith, 250). He was now invited to return to Maiduguri, where the shehu turbanned him waziri of Borno. In this key position he implemented a much-needed improvement in the probity and modernization of the administration's bureaucracy. Still a pillar of the NPC, both he and the ruling party were humiliated when in 1956 he lost the regional election to a local lorry driver.

Nationally, too, Kashim Ibrahim's administrative talents and educational experience were in continual demand. He was a member of the governing councils of University College Ibadan and of the Nigerian College of Arts, Science, and Technology at Zaria, and chairman of the council of the new Ahmadu Bello University, whose library was named after him. Later he was successively chancellor of the universities of Ibadan (1967) and Lagos (1977). A notable appointment was his membership of the Ashby commission, set up in 1959 to consider the future of higher education in Nigeria. Kashim Ibrahim was also a key member of the international panel of jurists, which in 1958 reviewed the north's legal system. He was appointed a senator in 1959.

During the final months of the governorship of Sir Gawain Westray Bell (1909–1995), the last expatriate governor of Northern Nigeria, the emir of Kano had stood in for him while he was on leave. But relations between the premier, Sir Ahmadu Bello, and the emir deteriorated, and when Bell retired in 1962 the queen, on the recommendation of the premier, appointed Kashim Ibrahim as the northern governor. He was made CBE in 1960 and KCMG in 1962.

Kashim Ibrahim's governorship was brief. When the military overthrew the Nigerian government in January 1966, he was detained. On his release he was appointed civilian adviser to the military governor, Hassan Katsina. His cool head and seasoned experience proved invaluable during the disturbances of 1965 and 1966 and the subsequent civil war, and he played a significant role in the successive conferences on Nigeria's constitutional future.

As part of the creation of states in 1967, the town of Bauchi was named capital of the new North-East State. However, Kashim Ibrahim's vigorous advocacy of Maiduguri's prior claim won the day. Yet the division of the region into states meant the end of his post as adviser to the military governor. He retired to Maiduguri in 1968, spending time on his farm and leaving only now and then to attend to his chancellorial duties. If he had withdrawn from public politics, he remained an influence in Borno's king-making. One event gave him particular pleasure. This was the extension of the railway line to Maiduguri, a project he had long supported.

Ibrahim Kashim's recreations included riding and polo. Among his awards were the Nigerian honour of grand commander of the Niger and honorary doctorates from three Nigerian universities. He died on 25 July 1990, survived by three wives and fourteen children.

Like so many of the founding generation of NPC ministers, Kashim Ibrahim was a graduate of Katsina College (the north's Eton) who acquired his administrative skills in native administration service and was recognized by promotion to a traditional titled office. 'A patrician of correct etiquette' (Osuntokun, 142), his philosophy embraced both conservatism and change. Emanating a palpable sense of wisdom and discipline, his natural dignity and innate courtesy once encountered could never be forgotten.   A. H. M. KIRK-GREENE

Sources A. Osuntokun, *Power broker* (1987) · C. S. Whitaker, *The politics of tradition* (1970) · B. Sharwood-Smith, *But always as friends* (1969) · G. W. Bell, *An imperial twilight* (1989) · A. Bello, *My life* (1962) · B. J. Dudley, *Parties and politics in Northern Nigeria* (1968) · R. L. Sklar, *Nigerian political parties* (1963) · N. C. McClintock, *Kingdoms in the sand and sun* (1992) · *West Africa* (3–9 Sept 1990), 2399 · *Legacy of leadership: lives and times of some of Nigeria's great leaders*, Federal Ministry of Information, Lagos (1995) · Burke, *Peerage* · *WW* (1988) · personal knowledge (2004)

Likenesses photograph, repro. in *West Africa*, 2399 · portraits, repro. in Osuntokun, *Power broker*, cover

Ickham, Peter of (*d.* 1295), chronicler and Benedictine monk, doubtless took his name from the village of Ickham near Canterbury; he was a monk of Christ Church Cathedral priory, Canterbury, almost certainly by 1264, and remained there until his death on 4 May 1295. It is highly likely that he had a legal training, for seven of the ten books that passed from him to the cathedral's library were of law: three civil-law texts and four canon-law texts and commentaries. He acted in a judicial capacity for the cathedral priory in 1271 during an archiepiscopal vacancy. The library at Dover Priory in the early fifteenth century contained a canon-law compilation ascribed to him, the gift of a former Christ Church monk, Walter Causton.

The sixteenth-century historian John Bale states that Ickham spent some time at the University of Paris and that he was a friend of its chancellor, Philippe. Paris was not a centre for civil-law studies, but it is certainly possible that Ickham studied canon law there. That he was one of the seven monks appointed to act as compromissors in the archiepiscopal election of 1270 further suggests that when he joined the cathedral community he was a mature man, perhaps even middle-aged.

Ickham is generally regarded, apparently on the authority of Archbishop Matthew Parker (in his edition of Dr John Caius's *De antiquitate Cantabrigiensis academiae*, 1574), as having composed a Latin chronicle of the kings of England from Brutus to Edward I. Over a dozen manuscripts survive of this summary compilation, which is avowedly compiled from such writers as Bede, Geoffrey of Monmouth, William of Malmesbury, and Pierre de Poitiers; it terminates at dates that in different manuscripts vary from 1272 to 1483. It has no distinctive focus on Canterbury, however, and it is unclear what prompted Parker to make the ascription. Moreover, in BL, Cotton MS Domitian A.iii, fol. 38*v*, the chronicler refers to himself as having been present in the Franciscan church, Worcester, at the burial of William Beauchamp, earl of Warwick, in 1298; this postdates Ickham's life. The ascription of the chronicle's authorship to Ickham must therefore be regarded as doubtful, even if the later part of Domitian A.iii is to be regarded as the work of a continuator. The chronicle has not been printed.

Bale records that, while still in France, Ickham wrote a French genealogy of the kings of England and Britain, down to 1274; Bale states that the historian John Leland himself owned a copy of this, but unfortunately neither provides further details of it. It is perhaps to be identified as the two separate works (in what would now be called Anglo-Norman), *Le livere de reis de Brittanie* and *Le livere de reis de Engleterre*, which were edited by John Glover for the Rolls Series in 1865. These provide no clear indication of their authorship, but the latter work does come down to 1274. Their historical value is rather limited, since they are largely derived from well-known Latin chronicles.
                                                     NIGEL RAMSAY

Sources T. D. Hardy, *Descriptive catalogue of materials relating to the history of Great Britain and Ireland*, 3, Rolls Series, 26 (1871), no. 454, pp. 251–2; no. 488, pp. 271–3 · Bale, *Cat.*, 1.327–8 · Bale, *Index*, 323 · J. Glover, ed., *Le livere de reis de Brittanie e le livere de reis de Engleterre*, Rolls Series, 42 (1865) · M. R. James, *The ancient libraries of Canterbury and Dover* (1903), pp. 128–9, nos. 1538–42; p. 425, no. 263 · J. C. Russell, 'Dictionary of writers of thirteenth century England', *BIHR*, special suppl., 3 (1936) [whole issue], esp. 99–100 · N. Adams and C. Donahue, eds., *Select cases from the ecclesiastical courts of the province of Canterbury, c. 1200–1301*, SeldS, 95 (1981), 19 · J. Greatrex, *Biographical register of the English cathedral priories of the province of Canterbury* (1997), 207 · R. Sharpe, *A handlist of the Latin writers of Great Britain and Ireland before 1540* (1997), 427 · J. Caius, *De antiquitate Cantabrigiensis academiae* (1574), 61

Ida (*d.* 559/60), king of Bernicia, from whom the Northumbrian royal family traced their origin, began his reign in 547 and ruled for twelve years. This statement, which appears in similar form in Bede's chronological summary at the end of the *Historia ecclesiastica gentis Anglorum* and in the earliest Northumbrian regnal list, known as the Moore memoranda, is the principal evidence from English sources for the establishment of the Anglian kingdom of Bernicia, the northern, and later dominant, part of Northumbria. Bede does not mention Ida in the main part of the *Historia ecclesiastica*, possibly because Ida was irrelevant to Bede's Christian theme.

This statement and the date 547 are clearly a later construction, since the kingdom of Northumbria did not come into being until the mid-seventh century. But because the ruling family of Bernicia eventually also established control over the southern Northumbrian kingdom of Deira, Ida became the dynastic ancestor of the rulers of Northumbria, and all later claimants to the throne traced their ancestry back to him, even when the main line of succession broke down at the beginning of the eighth century. The date 547 was probably calculated by adding together the reign lengths in a king-list like the Moore memoranda. The accuracy of this form of dating depends on the assumption that all the kings in the list reigned successively. However, it has been argued that a number of the early Bernician kings may have been rivals, in which case this form of dating breaks down, and Ida's reign may have begun later in the sixth century.

The eighth- or ninth-century Bern chronicle fragment

which is based on Bede's summary provides the additional information that Ida's grandfather Oesa (Oessa, Eosa) was the first of his line to come to Britain. It also names his father Eoppa (Eobba). Both these names appear in one of the Bernician genealogies where Ida's ancestry is traced back to Woden, but Oesa was eclipsed as the traditional founder of the dynasty, possibly because Ida was the first of the family to rule. The source of the later claim in two twelfth-century documents, the life of St Oswald and *De primo Saxonum adventu*, that Ida came with his father Eoppa and forty or sixty ships and first landed at Flamborough Head, in what is now Yorkshire, is unknown.

Mirroring the information in Bede and the Moore memoranda, the 'common stock' of the Anglo-Saxon Chronicle, compiled in the late ninth century, gives the accession of Ida in 547. The northern recension (represented by text E), probably compiled in the tenth century, adds a statement to the effect that he built Bamburgh. The date of 560 (or 559 in text F) for Ida's death is unlikely to be any more than a mechanical calculation on the part of a chronicle compiler who already knew, from Bede, that Ida reigned for twelve years.

Ida is also linked with Bamburgh in the ninth-century *Historia Brittonum*, where he is said to have joined Din Guayrdi to Bernicia. In a later passage, Din Guaroy (generally accepted as the same name) is said to have been given by Ida's grandson *Æthelfrith to his wife Bebba, from whom it derived its Anglian name Bamburgh. The statement that he joined Din Guayrdi to Bernicia is amplified in subsequent editions of the *Historia Brittonum* by a passage which states that these two countries, namely Deira and Bernicia, became one. This appears, however, to be a gloss conceived in the light of later political geography, after Northumbria had become one kingdom.

Sir Frank Stenton and Peter Hunter Blair saw the initial Anglian settlement of Bernicia as confined to a pirate stronghold on Bamburgh Rock. This picturesque image appeared to be supported by references in the *Historia Brittonum* to Ida's sons and successors still fighting the British in this coastal zone, and also by the lack of distinctive Anglo-Saxon burials in Bernicia, but it has been challenged by the results of the excavations at the royal site of Yeavering, and by further analysis of the cemetery material at Norton and elsewhere, which suggests that the Anglians penetrated the region from the south along Dere Street. It is therefore possible that the passage claiming that Ida joined Din Guayrdi to Bernicia implies that Bamburgh was one of the last British forts to fall into Anglian hands.

From the king-lists and genealogies mentioned above, it can be deduced that three of the later rulers of Bernicia, **Adda** (*d.* 565?), Æthelric, and Theodric, were sons of Ida. But because these kings did not rule successively, it is probable that the other three early Bernician kings, Glappa, Frithuwald, and Hussa, were rivals who failed to establish their own dynasties. Two more sons, Ocga and Eadric, are named as ancestors of later Northumbrian kings. In other sources Ida is said to have had twelve sons.

Only seven of these are named in the *Historia Brittonum*, together with a queen, Bearnoch. In post-conquest writings of minimal value all twelve sons are named, and it is said that six were born of his queen and six from concubines. The names include the three kings, Adda, Æthelric, and Theodric (though in John of Worcester's chronicle the order is changed), but the other three kings of Bernicia are not mentioned.   D. J. CRAIG

Sources Bede, *Hist. eccl.*, 5.24 • *ASC*, s.a. 547, 560; s.a. 559 [text F] • E. Faral, ed., 'Historia Brittonum', *La légende Arthurienne, études et documents: les plus anciens textes*, 3: *Documents* (1929), 1–62 [Harleian recension] • P. H. Blair, 'The *Moore* memoranda on Northumbrian history', *The early cultures of north-west Europe: H. M. Chadwick memorial studies*, ed. C. Fox and B. Dickins (1950), 245–57 • D. N. Dumville, 'The Anglian collection of royal genealogies and regnal lists', *Anglo-Saxon England*, 5 (1976), 23–50 • D. N. Dumville, ed., 'A new chronicle-fragment of early British history', *EngHR*, 88 (1973), 312–14 • P. H. Blair, 'The Bernicians and their northern frontier', in H. M. Chadwick and others, *Studies in early British history* (1954); [new edn] (1959), 137–72 • K. H. Jackson, 'On the northern British section in Nennius', *Celt and Saxon: studies in the early British border*, ed. N. K. Chadwick (1963), 20–62 • B. Hope-Taylor, 'The historical significance of Yeavering', *Yeavering: an Anglo-British centre of early Northumbria* (1977), 276–324 • D. P. Kirby, 'Bede and Northumbrian chronology', *EngHR*, 78 (1963), 514–27 • M. Miller, 'The dates of Deira', *Anglo-Saxon England*, 8 (1979), 35–61 • Symeon of Durham, *Opera* • F. M. Stenton, *Anglo-Saxon England*, 3rd edn (1971)

Iddesleigh. For this title name *see* Northcote, Stafford Henry, first earl of Iddesleigh (1818–1887).

Iddison, Roger (1834–1890), cricketer, was born at Bedale, in the North Riding of Yorkshire, on 15 September 1834, the eldest of the four children of Roger Iddison (*b.* 1809) and his wife, Jane, *née* Jefferson; his father was a ropemaker. Having begun life as a butcher Iddison played cricket for Bedale as early as 1849. He made his first professional appearance for The 14 of Yorkshire against the United All England eleven in 1853. Iddison was an all-rounder; he fielded at point and was originally regarded as a round-arm fast bowler, but later changed his technique to deliver 'insidious' lobs. As a batsman he favoured the off drive, and in both 1867 and 1869 he was third in the national batting averages. At the Oval in 1870 he won a silver cup given by a Yorkshire gentleman for the best all-round performance by one of the Yorkshire eleven.

From 1853 until 1876 Iddison played for Yorkshire in seventy-four matches and, from 1863 to 1872, was the county's first captain. Throughout the 1860s he was among the leading batsmen in England and in October 1861, one of only two northerners, he joined the first team to tour Australia, led by H. H. Stephenson. The All England eleven sailed on the *SS Great Britain* and won six out of their twelve matches, in all of which Iddison played. He took the most wickets in Australia, had the fourth highest batting average, and made twenty-seven catches; in Melbourne he was presented with two commemorative bats. By 1864 he had moved to Manchester, where with his younger brother, William Holdsworth Iddison (1840–1898), a professional cricketer for Lancashire, he set up a sports equipment business in Corporation Street. In the years 1865–70 Roger Iddison also played for Lancashire, in sixteen matches; against Surrey at the Oval in 1866 he became the first batsman to score a century for the county. He featured in the north versus south division in cricket and, with four others of the Yorkshire team, refused to play against Surrey in 1865.

In 1869 Iddison moved to York, where he worked as a commission agent and cattle auctioneer and set up a sports goods shop at 20 Blake Street. In the same year he founded the United North of England eleven and was its first secretary; he was also joint secretary of the short-lived Yorkshire United eleven, founded in 1874 under the patronage of Lord Londesborough, president of the MCC in 1876. In 1872, when the MCC played Yorkshire, Iddison took the wicket of W. G. Grace. Iddison was given a benefit match (29–31 July 1872) at Bramall Lane, Sheffield, against Gloucestershire; this was the first time that Grace played at Sheffield, and he scored 150 not out. The legendary bowler George Freeman came out of retirement for the match, which was watched by some 17,000 spectators, who saw Iddison caught and bowled by Grace for 4 runs. Iddison was cricket coach at various public schools, including Uppingham (1866–72). He made his last professional appearance in 1876, for Yorkshire against Middlesex, but continued to play in local games, such as that at Malton in 1885.

Relatively under-appreciated as a cricketer, Iddison clearly had organizational qualities and was known to be 'effusive in his vernacular' style of speech on the field (West, 44). Like Grace, Iddison had become increasingly portly by the end of his cricket career, allegedly weighing some 17 stone. He died at his family home, 8 Portland Street, York, on 19 March 1890 and was buried three days later in the city cemetery, where his grave still can be found. Large crowds attended his funeral, to which the city butchers sent 'a handsome wreath … in a glass case' (*Evening Press*, 21 March 1890). He was survived by his wife, Elizabeth Webster (*b.* 1834) of Halifax, whom he had married on 19 January 1857, and by their only child, Elizabeth Jane (1858–1938); his widow later married again.

JOAN LANE

Sources R. S. Holmes, *The history of Yorkshire county cricket* (1904) • P. Thomas, *Yorkshire cricketers, 1839–1939* (1973) • G. D. West, *Twelve days of Grace* (1989) • *Seventy-one not out: reminiscences of William Caffyn* (1899) • S. Rae, *W. G. Grace: a life* (1998) • P. Bailey, P. Thorn, and P. Wynne-Thomas, *Who's who of cricketers*, rev. edn (1993) • *Wisden* (1872–3) • *James Lillywhite's cricketers' annual* (1891) • A. Haygarth, *Arthur Haygarth's cricket scores and biographies*, 5 (1875), 5. 273 • *MCC scores and biographies from 1855 to 1875*, 7 (1877) • D. Frith, *The trailblazers* (1999) • W. F. Paterson, *Sixty years of Uppingham cricket* (1909) • *Evening Press* [Yorkshire] (20–22 March 1890) • parish register, Bedale, 10 Feb 1835, N. Yorks. CRO [baptism] • D. Hodgson, *The official history of Yorkshire county cricket club* (1989) • m. cert., Halifax register office • *CGPLA Eng. & Wales* (1890)
Archives priv. coll., family MSS
Likenesses photograph, 1861 • photograph, *c.*1865, repro. in Holmes, *History of Yorkshire county cricket*, facing p. 44 • photograph, *c.*1870, Castle Museum, York • double portrait, photograph (with George Anderson), repro. in West, *Twelve days*, 38 • wood-engraving, lithograph, repro. in *The Cricketer* (Nov 1986), 64
Wealth at death £535: probate, 22 April 1890, *CGPLA Eng. & Wales*

Idrisyn. *See* Jones, John (1804–1887).

Idwal ap Meurig (*d.* 996/7), dynast, was son of Meurig ab Idwal Foel. He was an aspiring (and possibly actual) king of Gwynedd and dependent regions of north Wales in the early 990s. On the death of Hywel ab Ieuaf, king of Gwynedd, in 985, the kingdom had been contended by a number of rival kinsmen until in 986 Maredudd ab Owain, of the ruling line of Deheubarth in south Wales, possibly slew Meurig ab Idwal Foel and then Cadwallon ab Ieuaf, and took the kingdom for himself. He continued to rule north Wales as well as Deheubarth (after 988) until his death in 999. However, Idwal and the other sons of Meurig ab Idwal challenged Maredudd's position in the north during the early 990s. In 993 they launched an attack on Gwynedd, presumably directed against Maredudd's authority in that kingdom (or, by a different account, because their hostages 'were in Gwynedd'). In 994 they inflicted a heavy defeat upon Maredudd near Llangwm (in Dinmael, north Wales), where his nephew Tewdwr ab Einion was slain. It has been suggested that Idwal had established himself in north Wales before this battle and that it represented an attempt by Maredudd to oust him thence; alternatively, it may have been a further attempt by Idwal and his brothers to regain their rightful kingdom. As it transpired, Idwal ap Meurig died in 996 or 997 (slain by Swein Forkbeard in some accounts), thus predeceasing Maredudd by three years. Whether he ever held actual political power or not, Idwal is notable as ancestor of the famous Gruffudd ap Cynan, and thereby the later rulers of Gwynedd through his son Iago.

DAVID E. THORNTON

Sources J. Williams ab Ithel, ed., *Annales Cambriae*, Rolls Series, 20 (1860) • T. Jones, ed. and trans., *Brenhinedd y Saesson, or, The kings of the Saxons* (1971) [another version of *Brut y tywysogyon*] • T. Jones, ed. and trans., *Brut y tywysogyon, or, The chronicle of the princes: Peniarth MS 20* (1952) • T. Jones, ed. and trans., *Brut y tywysogyon, or, The chronicle of the princes: Red Book of Hergest* (1955) • P. C. Bartrum, ed., *Early Welsh genealogical tracts* (1966) • *The historie of Cambria, now called Wales*, ed. D. Powell, trans. H. Lhoyd [H. Llwyd] (1584); repr. (1811) [repr. (1811)] • O. Jones, E. Williams, and W. O. Pughe, eds., *The Myvyrian archaiology of Wales, collected out of ancient manuscripts*, new edn (1870) • J. E. Lloyd, *A history of Wales from the earliest times to the Edwardian conquest*, 3rd edn, 2 vols. (1939); repr. (1988) • D. E. Thornton, 'Maredudd ab Owain (d.999): the most famous king of the Welsh', *Welsh History Review / Cylchgrawn Hanes Cymru*, 18 (1996–7), 567–91

Idwal Foel [Idwal Foel ab Anarawd] (*d.* 942), king of Gwynedd, was the son of *Anarawd ap Rhodri Mawr (*d.* 916) of Gwynedd. Idwal ruled the kingdom of Gwynedd in north Wales from the death of his father in 916 until his own demise in 942. Knowledge of his reign is limited almost entirely to his relations with contemporary English rulers. It should not be assumed that Idwal was significantly less powerful than his more famous kinsman Hywel Dda ap Cadell, who ruled Deheubarth in south Wales during the same period and annexed Gwynedd on Idwal's death.

In 918 Idwal Foel (the epithet means 'the Bald'), along with Hywel and Hywel's brother Clydog, submitted to Edward the Elder at Tamworth, probably late in the summer of that year. Edward reinforced his position in north

Wales in 921 with the building of a fortification at the mouth of the River Clwyd, probably the *burh* ('fortified settlement') at Rhuddlan. While this was perhaps primarily a defence against vikings active in the Irish Sea, it no doubt restricted Idwal's actions considerably. However, according to William of Malmesbury, Idwal may not have been totally submissive in his dealings with the English: Malmesbury puts Edward at Chester in 924, a few days before his death at Farndon-on-Dee, in order to put down a rebellion by the men of that city in alliance with the Welsh. Idwal would seem the most likely Welsh ruler to have been implicated in this rebellion, if it did take place.

Relations with Edward's son and successor, Æthelstan, were more peaceful, though this is perhaps on account of the extent of his power rather than any pro-English policy on the part of Idwal and the other Welsh kings. Thus in 926, when Æthelstan annexed Northumbria, he is said to have received the submission of all the kings in the island of Britain. The Welsh kings, no doubt including Idwal, possibly made their submissions not at Eamont Bridge, but at Hereford, where Æthelstan is said to have exacted an annual tribute from them. Again William of Malmesbury states that Æthelstan deprived Idwal 'king of all the Welsh' and Constantine, king of Scots, of their thrones at this time, but subsequently re-established them ('Idwal' here may of course be an error for Hywel). Æthelstan's dominant position in relations with Idwal Foel and the other Welsh kings is also reflected in their frequent visits to England where they witnessed royal charters. Idwal did so at Exeter in 928, at Worthy, Hampshire, and Luton in 931, 'Middleton' in 932, Winchester and Nottingham in 934, and finally Dorchester twice in 935. His relations with Æthelstan probably continued in a similar vein for the remaining four years of the English king's life, and there is no reason to assume Idwal took part in the anti-English coalition at 'Brunanburh' in 937. The decline in English fortunes after Æthelstan's death in 939 may have encouraged Idwal to withhold submission to his brother and successor, Edmund, or even to take more offensive action against this English king. Either way, Idwal and his brother Elise are said to have met their deaths at English hands in 942. That Edmund reconquered Mercia in this year is perhaps not coincidental. On Idwal's death, his kingdom did not pass directly to his sons *Iago and Ieuaf but was annexed by Hywel Dda. Idwal's other sons included Meurig, Cynan, and Idwal Fychan; a less reliable source would add Anarawd, probably an error for his father.   DAVID E. THORNTON

Sources J. Williams ab Ithel, ed., *Annales Cambriae*, Rolls Series, 20 (1860) · T. Jones, ed. and trans., *Brenhinedd y Saesson, or, The kings of the Saxons* (1971) [another version of *Brut y tywysogyon*] · T. Jones, ed. and trans., *Brut y tywysogyon, or, The chronicle of the princes: Peniarth MS 20* (1952) · T. Jones, ed. and trans., *Brut y tywysogyon, or, The chronicle of the princes: Red Book of Hergest* (1955) · P. C. Bartrum, ed., *Early Welsh genealogical tracts* (1966) · *ASC*, s.a. 921, 926 [texts A, D] · William of Malmesbury, *Gesta regum Anglorum / The history of the English kings*, ed. and trans. R. A. B. Mynors, R. M. Thomson, and M. Winterbottom, 2 vols., OMT (1998–9) · *AS chart.*, S 400, 407, 413, 416, 417, 425, 434, 435 · J. E. Lloyd, *A history of Wales from the earliest times to the Edwardian conquest*, 3rd edn, 2 vols. (1939); repr. (1988) · H. R. Loyn, 'Wales and England in the tenth century: the context of the Athelstan charters', *Welsh History Review / Cylchgrawn Hanes Cymru*, 10 (1980–81), 283–301 · D. N. Dumville, 'Brittany and "Armes Prydein Vawr"', *Études Celtiques*, 20 (1983), 145–59

Iestyn ap Gwrgant (*fl. c.*1081–*c.*1120), nobleman, was an important Welsh magnate, of whom little is known outside two references to him in the Book of Llandaff, datable to the time of Bishop Herwald (1059–1104). In one, he made reparations to the episcopal community at Llandaff for the rape of a woman under the bishop's protection, which had been carried out by a member of his household and by his nephew Einion. In another, dating to before 1081, he appears as a member of the entourage of Caradog ap Gruffudd, dominant king of Glamorgan. That he was a man of great influence in eastern Glamorgan and southern Brycheiniog can be deduced from the wide spread of the lands of his sons in the 1120s and 1130s. The annals of Margam note three of them—Gruffudd, Caradog [*see below*], and Goronwy—engaged in warfare with Anglo-Norman colonists around Kenfig in 1127. Gerald of Wales also alludes to the 'sons of Iestyn' as being engaged in warfare to the north, in the lordship of Brycheiniog, in the 1130s. Iestyn ap Gwrgant was probably (if sources were available to detail it) a key figure in relations between native Welsh and incoming Anglo-Norman settlers in Glamorgan in the reigns of William Rufus and Henry I. But Iestyn's later historical importance chiefly derives from the place he acquired in the legendary history of the Winning of Glamorgan, written over four hundred years after his death. This fictionalized history of the Norman conquest of Glamorgan by Robert fitz Haimon and his twelve knights (the supposed forebears of the great gentry families of later Glamorgan) was probably created by fifteenth-century itinerant bards, and a version of it copied into the (now lost) register of Neath Abbey. The register's Tudor owner, Sir Edward Stradling, used this earlier material as the basis for his popular account of the Winning, written between 1561 and 1566, and published by Humphrey Llwyd in 1584. In this account Iestyn plays a role not dissimilar to that of Vortigern in medieval legends of the Saxon conquest of Britain. He is made to invite Robert fitz Haimon and his knights into Glamorgan to help him fight off his rival Rhys ap Tewdwr; but when Iestyn reneged on the contract, Robert took Glamorgan for himself. The Winning is responsible for giving Iestyn his posthumous and unmerited status of lord of all Glamorgan, whereas in fact his dynasty had a rather more limited importance.

Caradog ab Iestyn (d. before 1175) appears to have held the primacy among his brothers, and the extent of his territories is indicated by the fact that the lords of Afan, Glynrhondda, and Meisgyn (between the Neath and the Taff valleys) were descended from him. The greatness of this Caradog in his lands is indicated by his marriage to Gwladus, sister of the Lord Rhys ap Gruffudd of Deheubarth. There were however other sons of Iestyn politically active in the 1130s, whose existence shows that Iestyn's lands had extended further westwards and southwards than those which Caradog held. Neath Abbey sources record a Rhys ab Iestyn (ap Gwrgant) who ruled over upland Gower between the Neath and the Tawe rivers, and who also possessed a detached estate around Llanilid (perhaps the predecessor of the later lordship of Ruthin), further east in lowland Glamorgan. A Rhiwallon ab Iestyn is also noted as ruling lands between the rivers Clydach and Leiros in the 1130s. Little is known of the later history of the dynasties founded by Caradog's siblings, although Rhys ab Iestyn's sons were still in control of Llanilid at the end of the twelfth century.

Caradog's estates were divided at his death, before 1175. Gerald of Wales mentions four sons: Morgan, Maredudd, Cadwallon, and Owain. The principal fragment of his upland lordship went to **Morgan ap Caradog** (d. c.1208), who controlled what became the lordship of Afan, between the Neath and Rhondda valleys, and including the coastal district around Baglan, where Morgan appears to have constructed (or taken over) a substantial castle with a square, stone keep. Morgan's style of lordship seems therefore to have followed the Anglicizing precedent of Morgan ab Owain in Gwent, and this was to be consummated under his grandsons, Lleision and Morgan (III), who integrated into the Glamorgan gentry. Another substantial fragment went to his brother Maredudd, who exercised lordship over Meisgyn, the area roughly between the Taff and the Ely valleys, extending south as far as the demesne lordship of Cardiff. He was succeeded in it by his son Hywel ap Maredudd. A further lordship (Glynrhondda) was created in the Rhondda valleys for Cadwallon ap Caradog, who was succeeded in the thirteenth century by his son, Morgan. Although politically fragmented after Caradog's death, there is some evidence in the Margam charters that Morgan ap Caradog of Afan was able to continue to exert an overlordship in the uplands of Glamorgan until the end of the twelfth century, extending the life of the political entity created by Iestyn ap Gwrgant into the third generation. In 1175 it was Morgan alone of the brothers who attended the Council of Gloucester with Henry II. In 1183–4 it was Morgan who, after the death of Earl William of Gloucester, directed the native Welsh campaign against the keepers of the lordship of Glamorgan, involving the areas of Neath and Kenfig, which had been lost by Caradog ab Iestyn to the Normans. Morgan's limited success is known from the cession to him of the castle and lordship of Newcastle, opposite Bridgend.

After Morgan ap Caradog's death the various dynasties deriving from Iestyn went their own way. The principal line continued in his son **Morgan ap Morgan** [called Morgan Gam] (d. 1241), nobleman, who became lord of Afan. Morgan appears to have had to contend with his brothers for overall control of Afan, and during his first years as lord he lost his father's acquisition of Newcastle. His tenure of the lordship was marked by continued fighting with the earls of Gloucester, with (it appears) the overall

aim of re-establishing his father's control of the lowland area west of the Ogwr River. The abbey of Margam also apparently found itself challenged to acknowledge his advocacy, rather than the earl's. His ambitions led Morgan to ally with Prince Llywelyn ab Iorwerth of Gwynedd, with whom in 1231 he assaulted and destroyed Neath Castle, and in 1232 attacked the castle of Kenfig. The next year Morgan was among those Welsh lords who assisted Earl Richard Marshal in his war against the king in the southern march. The ultimate defeat of the Marshals seems to have cancelled any territorial gains they may have promised him in Glamorgan. After Morgan's death in February 1241 his lands were inherited successively by his sons Lleision ap Morgan and Morgan ap Morgan (Morgan Fychan). Lleision's policy of complete Anglicization is evident from the late 1240s, when he appears as a member of the county court of Glamorgan. He assumed a toponymic name, de Avene, derived from Afan, and under him and his brother, Morgan, the family assumed the guise and lifestyle of the surrounding Anglo-Welsh gentry.   DAVID CROUCH

Sources J. G. Evans and J. Rhys, eds., *The text of the Book of Llan Dâv reproduced from the Gwysaney manuscript* (1893) · *Gir. Camb. opera*, vol.6 · *Ann. mon.*, vol. 1 · B. Ll. James, ed., *Morganiae Archaiographia*, *South Wales and Monmouth RS* (1983) · D. Crouch, 'The slow death of kingship in Glamorgan, 1067–1158', *Morgannwg*, 29 (1985), 20–41 · G. Williams, ed., *Glamorgan county history*, 3: *The middle ages*, ed. T. B. Pugh (1971), chaps. 1–2 · *The historie of Cambria, now called Wales*, ed. D. Powell, trans. H. Lhoyd [H. Llwyd] (1584) [incl. 'Winning of Glamorgan']

Ieuan ap Hywel Swrdwal (d. c.1470). *See under* Swrdwal, Hywel (*fl.* c.1450).

Ieuan ap Rhydderch ab Ieuan Llwyd (*fl.* 1430–1470). *See under* Rhydderch ab Ieuan Llwyd (c.1325–1392x8).

Ieuan Ddu. *See* Thomas, John (1795–1871).

Ieuan Ddu ap Dafydd ab Owain (*fl.* c.1400x50), Welsh poet, was associated with the Dyffryn family of Aberdâr in Glamorgan by the unreliable Edward Williams (Iolo Morganwg), who in the years on either side of 1800 was often intent on inflating Glamorgan's literary tradition. On this basis Ieuan was described in nineteenth-century Welsh biographical dictionaries as a gentleman of estate and a patron of poets. It may, however, be significant that some poetry manuscripts associate the poet with Brycheiniog (Brecknockshire) rather than Glamorgan. Of the half dozen poems attributed to Ieuan in manuscript, only one can safely be regarded as his work, a poem addressed to the Glamorgan poet Ieuan Gethin ab Ieuan ap Lleision responding to a lost satirical poem. Ieuan Ddu alludes to the poetic contention between Dafydd ap Gwilym and Gruffudd Gryg, so the poem may be part of a similar exchange.

GRUFFYDD ALED WILLIAMS

Sources G. J. Williams, *Traddodiad llenyddol Morgannwg* (1948) · MALDWYN, NL Wales [computerized database of Welsh strict-metre poetry in manuscript] · NL Wales, MS 970E · W. O. Pughe, ed., *The Cambrian biography: or, historical notices of celebrated men*

among the ancient Britons (1803) • R. Williams, *Enwogion Cymru: a biographical dictionary of eminent Welshmen* (1852)
Archives NL Wales, MS 970E

Ieuan Ebblig. *See* Griffiths, Evan (1795–1873).

Ieuan Fardd. *See* Evans, Evan (1731–1788).

Ieuan Glan Alarch. *See* Mills, John (1812–1873).

Ieuan Lleyn. *See* Pritchard, Evan (1769–1832).

Ifor ap Llywelyn [*called* Ifor Hael] (*fl. c.*1320–1380), landowner and patron of poetry, owned Gwernyclepa in the parish of Basaleg, lordship of Newport. His father was Llywelyn ab Ifor of St Clears and Gwynfe in Carmarthenshire, who married (as the first of her three husbands) Angharad the daughter of Morgan ap Maredudd, son of the dispossessed lord of Edeligion, Llebenydd, and Machen in Gwent; Morgan led the uprising of 1294 in Glamorgan but remained loyal during Llywelyn Bren's insurrection in 1316. Llywelyn and Angharad had three sons, of whom Ifor was the second, and a daughter; the eldest son Morgan founded the important family of Morgan of Tredegyr. Ifor married Nest, daughter of Rhun of the commote of Cibwr in Glamorgan, and at least two sons and a daughter were born to them. He may have married again after Nest's death.

It is thought that Llywelyn's connections with Carmarthenshire (and perhaps Angharad's second marriage, to Dafydd ap Llywelyn of Rhydodyn in the same county) may have contributed to Dafydd ap Gwilym's coming to Gwernyclepa. He was made welcome by Ifor and Nest and he repaid them with seven remarkable poems: an *awdl*, a series of *englynion*, four *cywyddau* in praise of Ifor, and a mock elegy in *awdl* metres for both of them. The *cywyddau* were probably the first ever composed in praise of anyone, and they incorporate nature and love motifs from Dafydd's love poetry, which set them apart from all later examples of the genre [*see* Cywyddwyr (*act. c.*1330–*c.*1650)]. In one of them Dafydd calls Ifor 'hael' ('generous'), thus equating him with the three exemplars of generosity in sixth-century north Britain, 'Tri hael ynys Prydain', praised in the early medieval triads.

R. GERAINT GRUFFYDD

Sources P. C. Bartrum, ed., *Welsh genealogies, AD 300–1400*, 8 vols. (1974), vol. 1 • T. Parry, ed., *Gwaith Dafydd ap Gwilym* (1952) • C. W. Lewis, 'The literary tradition of Morgannwg down to the middle of the sixteenth century', *Glamorgan county history*, ed. G. Williams, 3: *The middle ages*, ed. T. B. Pugh (1971), 449–554, esp. 490–93 • E. Rolant, 'Ifor Hael', *Y Traethodydd*, 136 (1981), 115–35 • D. J. Bowen, 'Dafydd ap Gwilym ac Ifor Hael', *Y Traethodydd*, 137 (1982), 29–30 • R. Bromwich, ed. and trans., *Trioedd ynys Prydein: the Welsh triads*, 2nd edn (1978) • E. R. Ll. Davies and E. Edwards, 'Teulu Ifor Hael a'r traddodiad nawdd', *Ysgrifau Beirniadol*, 12 (1982), 143–56
Wealth at death presumed wealthy

Ifor ap Meurig [*called* Ifor Bach] (*fl.* 1158), nobleman, is of obscure origins. Little is known of the antecedents of Ifor's dynasty: even the unreliable royal genealogies have nothing to say of his forebears. The likelihood is that Ifor and his father, Meurig, emerged into notice out of the lesser nobility of Glamorgan during the reign of Henry I of England, while greater families fell victim to the Anglo-Norman conquerors. Ifor, known as 'the Little' (*bach*, *parvus*), was certainly an important lord of upland Glamorgan in the reign of Stephen, and based his power in the lordship of Senghennydd, between the sons of Iestyn ap Gwrgant to the east, and the great power and prestige of King Morgan ab Owain ap Caradog to the west. Early in the reign of Henry II, Ifor fell foul of both King Morgan and his Norman ally, Earl William of Gloucester. Ifor's later fame derived from his coup of defeating both greater rulers in the same year, 1158. Attacked by both, he first killed King Morgan somewhere in the uplands. As Gerald of Wales tells the story, Ifor then penetrated the region of Cardiff, and led a daring raid on the castle where the earl and his wife were in residence, protected by a strong garrison of mercenary troops. He and his men climbed the walls by night and abducted Earl William and Countess Hawise, holding them hostage in the hills until the assault on Senghennydd was abandoned. It is some measure of Ifor's political success that he was courted by the Lord *Rhys of Deheubarth, and had a marriage arranged between him and Rhys's sister, Nest ferch Gruffudd ap Rhys.

Ifor's son and heir, **Gruffudd ab Ifor** (*d.* 1210), had succeeded his father by 1175, when, as Gruffudd ab Ifor ap Meurig of Senghennydd, he accompanied his uncle, the Lord Rhys, to Henry II's court at Gloucester. Gruffudd's relationship with Earl William seems to have been less antagonistic than his father's. The earl confirmed Gruffudd's grants in the upper reaches of the Taff Vale around Bargoed and Capel Gwladus to Margam Abbey. Gruffudd also made grants in the vicinity of Leckwith, on the hills west of Cardiff, to the same abbey. It has been suggested that the lands his family held near Cardiff were part of an inducement offered to his father by Earl Robert, William's father, for Ifor's adherence in Stephen's reign (parallel to those in Wentloog offered by the earl to Ifor's neighbour, Morgan ab Owain). Gruffudd's brothers Cadwallon and Meriadoc are recorded in 1188 as leading a party of some 300 Welsh foot and mounted sergeants from Glamorgan to London for service in Henry II's campaigns against Philip Augustus. Gruffudd himself served in King John's armies in Normandy. His death in 1210, and his burial at the Cistercian abbey of Llantarnam, are recorded by the *Cronica de Wallia*.

Gruffudd was succeeded by his son **Rhys ap Gruffudd** (*d.* 1256). There seems to have been a division of lands. Rhys ap Gruffudd ruled over Senghennydd, and his younger brother, Gruffudd Bychan ap Gruffudd, succeeded (under his brother's overlordship) to the detached lands in the hills west of Cardiff, living at Beganston (a toponym derived from his surname), near Leckwith. Gruffudd Bychan married a daughter of Roger Sturmi, receiving a marriage portion in Stormy Down, near Kenfig, and was integrated into lowland society. He had died by 1234, leaving eight sons, who acknowledged Rhys, their uncle, as lord. Rhys supported Earl Richard Marshal in his confrontation with Henry III in 1233–4, during the minority of Earl Richard de Clare. In 1242 Rhys was involved in fighting with Gilbert de Turberville, lord of

Coety, but their dispute was settled later in the county court of Cardiff. He died in 1256. His successor, **Gruffudd ap Rhys** (*fl.* 1256–1267), became unwisely involved with the ambitions of Prince Llywelyn ap Gruffudd in south Wales, and as a consequence was seized in January 1267 by Earl Gilbert de Clare, who imprisoned him first in Cardiff and later in his Irish castle of Kilkenny. Senghennydd remained in contention between the earl and Prince Llywelyn ap Gruffudd of Gwynedd, who supported the claims of Maredudd ap Rhys (presumably Gruffudd ap Rhys's brother) until 1272. Senghennydd was thereafter incorporated in the demesne of the lord of Cardiff, but descendants of Ifor ap Meurig remained important tenants, while *Llywelyn Bren, who rebelled against English lordship in 1316, was the son of Gruffudd ap Rhys.

DAVID CROUCH

Sources T. Jones, ed. and trans., *Brut y tywysogyon, or, The chronicle of the princes: Red Book of Hergest* (1955) · *Gir. Camb. opera*, vol. 6 · R. B. Patterson, ed., *Earldom of Gloucester charters* (1973) · T. Jones, ed., 'Cronica de Wallia and other documents from Exeter Cathedral Library, MS 3514', *BBCS*, 12 (1946–8), 27–44 · *Ann. mon.*, vol. 1 · G. Williams, ed., *Glamorgan county history*, 3: *The middle ages*, ed. T. B. Pugh (1971), chaps. 1–2 · G. T. Clark, ed., *Cartae et alia munimenta quae ad dominium de Glamorgancia pertinent*, ed. G. L. Clark, 6 vols. (1910) · BL, Harley Charters 75 B6; 75 B7 · D. Crouch, 'The slow death of kingship in Glamorgan, 1067–1158', *Morgannwg*, 29 (1985), 20–41

Ifor Bach. *See* Ifor ap Meurig (*fl.* 1158).

Ilbert, Sir **Courtenay Peregrine** (1841–1924), parliamentary draftsman, administrator in India, and legal writer, was born at Kingsbridge, Devon, on 12 June 1841, the eldest of six sons of the Revd Peregrine Arthur Ilbert, rector of Thurlestone, Devon, and his wife, Rose Anne, daughter of George Welsh Owen, of Lowman Green, Tiverton, Devon.

Ilbert went to Marlborough School (1852–60) and then Balliol College, Oxford, where he obtained first classes in classical moderations (1862) and in *literae humaniores* (1864). President of the Oxford Union in 1865, he won, successively, the Hertford, Ireland, Craven, and Eldon scholarships (1861–7). Elected a fellow of Balliol in 1864 he was bursar of the college (1871–4) and became a friend of Benjamin Jowett, master of Balliol, for whom he was to act as literary executor. In 1874 he married Jessie (*d.* 1923/4), daughter of the Revd Charles Bradley and niece of George Granville Bradley, formerly headmaster of Marlborough; they were to have five daughters, the eldest of whom, Lettice *Fisher, was first chair of the National Council for the Unmarried Mother and her Child.

Ilbert was called to the bar at Lincoln's Inn in 1869, and he began to establish a practice in property law with an emphasis on drafting trusts and other instruments. Ilbert's ability as a draftsman soon attracted the attention of Sir Henry Thring, who had become parliamentary counsel to the Treasury and was reforming both the style of legislation and the administrative arrangements for the drafting of bills. At Thring's invitation Ilbert played a significant role in the preparation of bills which became the Statute Law Revision Act of 1881 and the Civil Procedure Act of 1883.

G. F. Robinson, first marquess of Ripon, was a reforming viceroy of India in 1880–84, and he requested Hartington, the secretary of state for India, to send him an able and imaginative constitutional lawyer who should also be a sound Liberal. Such a person would become the law member of the viceroy's council; predecessors in this office, or its equivalent, had included Lord Macaulay, Sir Henry Maine, and Sir James Fitzjames Stephen. Ilbert was offered the position and was soon in India working on major bills. He drafted a code of laws for Burma (then under the control of the viceroy) in 1885, and provided clauses for the Bengal Tenancy Act which assisted tenants and caused concern to white 'planters' in the interior. These proposals were soon eclipsed in the public mind by a measure in 1883 which became known as the Ilbert Bill. The measure was designed to remove judicial disqualifications based on race, and its practical effect was that it would become possible for Indian judges to sit in judgment on Europeans in certain circumstances where this had not previously been possible. The extent of Ilbert's personal commitment to the measure is unclear. It is likely that he gave the principle in the bill unequivocal support but that he had doubts as to the political expediency of pursuing the matter at that time. In the event the reaction of some white people in India was very hostile, and their protests against the proposal were supported by influential men in London such as Sir Fitzjames Stephen. The dispute rapidly gave rise to an international debate about imperial purposes and values. Reformers argued that the empire should be used as an instrument to advance the interests and dignity of all who came within its boundaries: this was an opportunity for mutual progress and forms of partnership between races. Their opponents stated that the empire had been won by force and would only be kept by force—there could be no question of subjecting white people to the judgment of local people of a different race. The Ilbert Bill was very heavily modified in response to the opposition, but the early draft came to have symbolic force in political debates; the existence of the draft was a reminder that statute law could be used in attempts to secure equality between races within the empire.

In 1886 Ilbert returned to England and was appointed assistant parliamentary counsel to the Treasury. He retained his interest in laws elsewhere and a paper he gave at the Imperial Institute in 1894 resulted in the creation of the Society for Comparative Legislation. He published *The Government of India* in 1898, which he had begun working on as early as 1873. In substance, it was a study of Indian legislation and a proposal for a code, which became the basis for the consolidation introduced in 1915. As a draftsman during these years he achieved a high reputation and became a parliamentary counsel in 1899. In 1902 he was appointed clerk of the House of Commons and, between then and 1921, he gave advice on procedural issues arising out of bills, such as the Parliament Act of 1911, which were often the subject of strong political controversy. He was respected, as he had been throughout his life, for his independence, approachability, courtesy, and knowledge.

While he was working at the House of Commons, Ilbert began to reflect on the nature of statute law and the way it was created. He wrote *Legislative Methods and Forms* (1901), a brief study of *Parliament, its History, Constitution, and Practice* (1911), and *The Mechanics of Law-Making* (1914). The book on parliament was popular for many years and was moderate and general in tone; it avoided the committed approach of his contemporary, A. V. Dicey, and did not attempt the erudition of other authorities writing at this time, such as Anson. Ilbert's other books explored the detailed problems associated with the preparation and debating of bills. They revealed how the governments and parliaments of those years attempted to turn political initiatives into legal form. In later years jurists such as Sir Carleton Kemp Allen praised Ilbert's knowledge of parliamentary procedures but criticized him for failing to see what was happening to twentieth-century laws. In particular it was thought that Ilbert had too much faith in the power of public opinion to exert its influence and correct legislative abuses. Also it was claimed that he had not recognized the increasing importance of delegated legislation.

Contemporaries saw how strange it was that a man who had always tried to avoid public contention had come to have his name linked to an intense dispute about imperial values and race. Ilbert consistently sought high legal standards in the framing of bills rather than personal participation in political arguments. His public role was that of a lawyer with scholarly inclinations who was interested in reflecting on the legal instruments of political change rather than on the substance of reforms. He had considerable influence on the production and style of modern legislation, but very little impact on its content.

Ilbert was created KCSI in 1895, KCB in 1908, and GCB in 1911. He was made one of the original fellows of the British Academy (1903). He died a few months after his wife at his country home, Troutwells, Penn, Buckinghamshire, on 14 May 1924.   R. C. J. COCKS

Sources *Law Times* (24 May 1924), 435–6 · F. Pollock, 'Sir Courtenay Peregrine Ilbert, GCB, 1841–1924', *PBA*, 11 (1924–5), 441–5 · *Men and women of the time* (1899) · A. Seal, *The emergence of Indian nationalism: competition and collaboration in the later nineteenth century* (1968) · C. K. Allen, *Law and orders* (1965) · S. Gopal, *The viceroyalty of Lord Ripon, 1880–1884* (1953) · M. Bennett, *The Ilberts in India, 1882–1886* (1995) · *CGPLA Eng. & Wales* (1924) · *DNB*
Archives BL OIOC, corresp. and papers · HLRO, diaries · priv. coll. | BL OIOC, letters to Arthur Godley, Eur MS F 102 · Bodl. Oxf., letters to Herbert Asquith · Bodl. Oxf., letters to Lord Bryce · Bodl. Oxf., letters to H. A. L. Fisher · Bodl. Oxf., corresp. with Lord Kimberley
Likenesses S. P. Hall, pencil drawing, 1888–9, NPG · O. Rejlander, carte-de-visite, NPG · photograph, repro. in *The Times* (15 May 1924) · portrait, repro. in *ILN*, 120 (1902), 234
Wealth at death £11,356 11s. 1d.: probate, 28 July 1924, *CGPLA Eng. & Wales*

Ilchester. For this title name *see* Strangways, Giles Stephen Holland Fox-, sixth earl of Ilchester (1874–1959).

Ilchester, Richard of (*d.* 1188), administrator and bishop of Winchester, was born in the diocese of Bath, quite possibly at Sock Dennis, Somerset, close to Ilchester, where he later held a hide of land by grant of Robert de Beauchamp. His family name is variously reported. The annals of Tewkesbury call him Richard Hokelin, a law case of 1224 Richard Tokeliv, his tomb Ricardi Toclyve, the *Life of St Nectan* Richard Tokelin. For other names—Le Poer, Poore, or More—there is only later evidence. His family background, too, is uncertain, although Gilbert Foliot records that they were kinsmen. In the lawsuit of 1224 John le Deneys, a young knight, claimed a hide in Sock Dennis, tracing his claim back to 'his kinsman, Richard, once bishop of Winchester, whose heir he was' (*Curia Regis Rolls*, 11, no. 2539). John's father had made a grant to the church for the soul of Richard of Ilchester, and it sounds as if Richard may have been a fairly close relative of John's, either through the Deneys or the Clevedon family. In either case his background would be of knightly Somerset families, with kinship or tenurial connections to the bishopric of Bath, and perhaps involvement in royal administration. Richard of Ilchester had at least two sons, and it is conceivable, although far from certain, that he was married before he took such clerical orders as would render the sons illegitimate.

Relations with Henry II and Thomas Becket The *Life of St Nectan* tells that Richard of Ilchester advanced as a notary through the household of the earls of Gloucester during Stephen's reign. Indeed this may well have ensured that he met the future Henry II before the latter became king. Quite logically, therefore, he moved into the administration of Henry II. A grant to Athelney Abbey by Robert de Beauchamp, probably of the 1150s, was witnessed by Richard of Sock, the king's scribe. Also Henry II's earliest pipe roll records that the king had granted Richard his scribe the mill at Ilchester worth 40s. p.a. From 1162/3 pipe rolls with increasing frequency record his accounts for expenditure in royal service. Throughout the reign he was prominent in the lists of those who witnessed the king's charters, often as the first or second witness. In England there are concentrations of his witnessing at Westminster, Winchester, and Woodstock, but he was also a frequent witness on the continent. His scribal work brought him into early contact with the chancellor, Thomas Becket, and in 1159 the two joined in witnessing a royal confirmation at Rouen. It may have been partly through Thomas's influence that in 1162 or 1163 Ilchester became archdeacon of Poitiers, later being appointed treasurer of the same church, posts that he held until his promotion to the bishopric of Winchester in 1173. The early 1160s also saw him gaining increasing influence in judicial matters. In 1163–4 the abbot of St Albans was seeking to persuade the king that the church of Luton belonged to the abbey rather than to the royal demesne. Henry temporarily restored the church and promised to consider the matter:

> hence the aforesaid abbot, having been put at ease, secretly went to see [Richard], who had the king's ear, to obtain that he would persuade the king effectively to grant the said church to St Albans. To this Richard agreed on condition that

the two parts of the church which the clerics Baldric and Adam had held should be granted to him (van Caenegem, no. 405)

Such efforts to accumulate churches seem characteristic of Ilchester, although during the vacancy of 1171–5, the prior and convent of Battle refused to grant him the parish church he was seeking. Nevertheless he succeeded in becoming a noted pluralist, holding, for example, a prebend of Lincoln Cathedral.

Despite his earlier contacts with Becket, Ilchester was prominent as a royal supporter in Henry's dispute with the archbishop. Such indeed would be the expected stance of a well-rewarded royal servant and a kinsman of Gilbert Foliot. In late 1163 Henry sent Richard with Arnulf of Lisieux to Pope Alexander III (r. 1159–81) in France to beg for confirmation of royal customs, but with no success. Also in 1163–4 he may have brought to the diocese of Poitiers 'the unheard of harshness of new mandates', limiting the activities of church courts (Robertson and Sheppard, 5.38–9). Likewise, *Thómas saga* states that he was one of those entrusted with publicizing the constitutions of Clarendon, an activity for which he may have had particular responsibility in the diocese of Poitiers. In 1164, too, he reputedly instructed Henry's mother, the Empress Matilda, in criticism of the clergy. With other distinguished figures, Ilchester was sent by Henry to the French king Louis VII in order to turn him against Thomas Becket, and then on with a further mission to the pope. His diplomatic activity took him to Germany in May 1165, when at a meeting at Würzburg on Whitsunday he and John of Oxford, in Henry's name, promised adherence to the antipope Pascal III. It seems only to have been the intervention of John of Salisbury, mindful of their earlier friendship, that delayed Ilchester's excommunication until 1166. Then Henry sent Ilchester and others to explain his absence at Vézelay, but on 12 June Becket excommunicated him, notably because of his contact with the schismatic archbishop of Cologne, Rainald von Dassel. The impact of the excommunication on his relations with the king was ambiguous. Henry prevented some templars from embracing Ilchester because he was an excommunicate, but Ilchester's royal service continued and he may have been sent on a mission to Rome. Spiritually Ilchester may have been more worried, and he received a letter of advice from his friend Ralph Diceto telling him to accept the sentence with due humility. Again, perhaps because of the former friendship of Becket supporters such as John of Salisbury, Ilchester was absolved from his excommunication before or during January 1168.

A royal administrator and justice At this very time Richard of Ilchester was extremely prominent in royal administration, notably of justice; according to one account, 'by the king's order he exercised the greatest power throughout England' (van Caenegem, no. 446). A case of Michaelmas 1165 records him sitting as a royal justice at the exchequer, while in 1168–9 he served as an itinerant justice in several shires in the south, the west, and the midlands. His prestige also ensured that he was used as a conduit for claims in disputes not directly involving him. Furthermore he undertook a wide range of non-judicial duties. He was 'keeper' of the vacant bishopric of Lincoln from Christmas 1166 to 1173, during which time an annual payment of £10 was made to Herbert of Ilchester, presumably Richard's son. Between April 1167 and 1178/9 Ilchester also had control of the honour of Montagu, following the death of Richard Montagu, and was custodian of the see of Winchester and abbey of Glastonbury after the death of Henry de Blois in the summer of 1171. In 1168–9, he was one of the justices responsible for collection of an aid for the marriage of Matilda, Henry II's daughter. His prominence in financial matters is clear from the statement in the *Dialogus de Scaccario* that Ilchester 'is a great man and should not be busied except in important affairs'. Interestingly, one of Ilchester's tasks was to prevent the treasurer from falling asleep. He was also very concerned with record keeping, and pipe rolls of the mid-1160s mention rolls of the archdeacon (of Poitiers) or of the archdeacon and the justiciars; these do not survive, but may have been records of amercements. The *Dialogus* also describes Ilchester's introduction of a scheme whereby a copy was kept of every summons sent to a sheriff concerning his debts:

so when the sheriff was sitting at his account and the chancellor's clerk was reading the summons, the archdeacon's clerk, with his eye on the copy, watched him to see that he made no mistake. But as time went on, and the number of debtors enormously increased so that a whole skin of parchment was scarcely enough for a single summons, the number of names and the labour involved became over-powering, and the barons were satisfied, as of old, with the original summons. (*Dialogus*, 74–5)

The degree of Ilchester's loyalty to the king and his regime in both judicial matters and ecclesiastical is illustrated by a letter of Gilbert Foliot from c.1168–9. Foliot, a staunch opponent of Becket but not an enemy to the liberties of the church, wrote to Ilchester and other justices asking that two clerks whom they had arrested be handed over to the church courts. It would appear that for Ilchester, though not for Foliot, service to the king was more important than protection of ecclesiastical rights. On 15 May 1169 Ilchester attended a meeting organized by Gilbert Foliot and aimed at producing an appeal against Becket. On Ascension day, 29 May, Becket again excommunicated Ilchester, who was none the less one of those to whom Henry directed a new set of constitutions against Becket and his supporters in late September 1169. In June 1170 Ilchester was with the king's son Henry, escorting him from Caen to the coast with the aim of hastening his voyage to England for his coronation, and thereafter he shuttled between England and the continent, being with the young Henry at Westminster in early October and early December 1170, and with Henry II in Normandy in mid-October. In December he returned to Normandy to inform the king of Becket's dispute with the bishops who had participated in the Young King's coronation.

Bishop of Winchester Despite his prominence among Henry's supporters, Richard of Ilchester seems to have avoided a lasting ill repute with churchmen. It is uncertain when his excommunication was lifted, but Gerald of

Wales tells a story of his regret that he had misjudged the archbishop, and of the miracles that had influenced him, and it is also known that after 1173 Ilchester gave assent and permission for the construction of a chapel at Portsea in honour of St Thomas. At the beginning of March 1173 Ilchester helped in an attempt to end a conflict over who was to announce the election of a new archbishop of Canterbury, and himself recited the choice of Roger, abbot of Bec, who, however, refused the see. During 1173 Henry filled various bishoprics with men who had been loyal to him during the Becket dispute, and Ilchester received Winchester. Famously, according to his oldest son, Henry sent a writ before the election to the monks of the church of Winchester: 'I order you to hold a free election, but nevertheless forbid you to elect anyone but Richard, my clerk, archdeacon of Poitiers' (Duggan, 'Richard of Ilchester', 14). However, he also enjoyed the support of, among others, John of Salisbury and Gilbert Foliot, and the latter wrote on behalf of Richard his kinsman to Cardinal Guglielmo di Pavia. He seems initially to have been enthroned before consecration on Ascension day (17 May) 1174, then consecrated at Canterbury on 5 or 6 October, and finally enthroned again on 13 October. Although in his first seven years as bishop he was absent from his see for at least a third of the time, this need not mean that he was neglecting wider ecclesiastical affairs, notably the reconciliation of king and church that followed the compromise of Avranches of 1172. Although there is no sign that he had any academic legal training, Ilchester acted on occasion as a papal judge-delegate, and some of the papal instructions he received were incorporated in canonical collections. He also took care to provide suitable administrators to compensate for his absence, and according to Peter of Blois was the person responsible for the introduction of the position of bishop's 'official' into England.

Richard of Ilchester remained prominent among the king's counsellors. The close-knit character of the central group of Henry's servants is illustrated by a charter of c.1181 witnessed by Richard, Ranulf de Glanville, Richard fitz Nigel, and, making his first known appearance, Hubert Walter. In the early stages of the revolt of 1173–4 Henry II concentrated his attentions on his continental lands, but in mid-1174 the justiciars were desperate for his personal help in overcoming the rebellion in England. They unanimously agreed to use Ilchester as their messenger, 'knowing that he would speak to the king much more familiarly, warmly and urgently than anyone else', and he duly found the king at Bonneville on 24 June (Diceto … opera historica, 1.381). After the civil war he was present at an ecclesiastical council at Westminster on 18 May 1175, where he sat at the archbishop of Canterbury's left hand 'because he was most eminent in the office of cantor' (Works of Gervase of Canterbury, 1.251). On 1 July he was at a council at Woodstock, where the election of a new bishop of Norwich and various abbots was discussed, and then on 6 October he was the first in the list of witnesses to an agreement between Henry II and the king of Connacht. In late July 1176 Cardinal Vivian, a papal legate, landed in England without royal permission and Ilchester was sent to make him swear that he would do nothing to prejudice the king or kingdom. Then in August he arranged for an escort and other necessities for Henry's daughter Joanna during her journey to Sicily, whose king she was to marry. At Michaelmas, Ilchester went as justiciar to Normandy, where he probably took a leading role in the restoration or reform of the Norman exchequer, and in June 1177 he was sent on a peace embassy to France. He was present at court at Verneuil in September, and witnessed the treaty of Ivry in September 1177. After a year and a half in Normandy he returned to England on 21 March 1178.

Further royal service and death Richard of Ilchester was specially favoured in being excused attendance at the Third Lateran Council, his absence perhaps being necessitated by recent judicial reforms. Ralph Diceto named him as one of three bishops among the five justices Henry appointed in 1179, although the pipe rolls of the following years do not actually reveal his participation in the consequent eyre. On 5 March 1180 he was sent on a mission to the king of France, and he was present at the renewal of the treaty of Ivry on 28 June 1180. By Michaelmas he had returned to England, and on 23 October he was sitting as a baron of the exchequer. On 21 February 1182 Ilchester entertained the king at his manor house at Bishops Waltham, Hampshire, and there Henry made his will, in which Ilchester appeared as a witness and as a trustee of certain bequests. On 28 February he blessed Samson, the new abbot of St Edmunds, at Marwell, on the Isle of Wight. In 1182 and 1183 he is recorded as sitting as a baron of the exchequer and as a justice in final concords. Ilchester was present at the council at Westminster that elected Baldwin of Forde as archbishop of Canterbury on 2 December 1184, but in the following years there are signs of decreasing activity. He was with the king at Dover on 10 April 1185. A cirograph, preserving Ilchester's autograph signature and a fine impression of his seal, was issued there, recording that the bishop had taken back from the hospitallers the custody and administration of the hospital of St Cross, outside the walls of Winchester, and raised the number of poor entertained there from 113 to 213. At the end of April 1186 Henry visited him at Marwell. Richard of Ilchester died on 21 or 22 December 1188 and was buried at Winchester on the north side of the presbytery. After his death he was praised for his alms and his buildings, while Gerald of Wales described him as a man of 'common sense rather than learning, more astute in worldly deeds than in the liberal arts' (Ann. mon., 2.245–6; Gir. Camb. opera, 7.70). He probably left two sons. Herbert *Poor had a successful royal administrative and ecclesiastical career, probably working at the exchequer under Henry II and as a royal justice under Richard I; he was a canon of Lincoln in 1167–8, archdeacon of Canterbury in 1175, and bishop of Salisbury in 1194. Richard *Poor was successively bishop of Chichester (1215–17), Salisbury (1217–28), and Durham (1228–37).   JOHN HUDSON

Sources V. D. Oggins and R. S. Oggins, 'Richard of Ilchester's inheritance', Medieval Prosopography, 12 (1991), 57–122 • Curia regis rolls preserved in the Public Record Office (1922–) • Pipe rolls • C. Duggan, 'Richard of Ilchester, royal servant and bishop', TRHS, 5th ser., 16

(1966), 1–21 • C. Duggan, 'Bishop John and Archdeacon Richard of Poitiers: their roles in the Becket dispute', *Thomas Becket* [Sédières 1973], ed. R. Foreville (1975), 72–83 • J. C. Robertson and J. B. Sheppard, eds., *Materials for the history of Thomas Becket, archbishop of Canterbury*, 7 vols., Rolls Series, 67 (1875–85) • R. C. van Caenegem, ed., *English lawsuits from William I to Richard I*, 2 vols., SeldS, 106–7 (1990–91) • *Letters and charters of Gilbert Foliot*, ed. A. Morey and others (1967) • *Radulfi de Diceto … opera historica*, ed. W. Stubbs, 2 vols., Rolls Series, 68 (1876) • W. Stubbs, ed., *Gesta regis Henrici secundi Benedicti abbatis: the chronicle of the reigns of Henry II and Richard I, AD 1169–1192*, 2 vols., Rolls Series, 49 (1867) • *The historical works of Gervase of Canterbury*, ed. W. Stubbs, 2 vols., Rolls Series, 73 (1879–80) • R. Fitz Nigel [R. Fitzneale], *Dialogus de scaccario / The course of the exchequer*, ed. and trans. C. Johnson, rev. edn, rev. F. E. L. Carter and D. E. Greenaway, OMT (1983) • *Gir. Camb. opera* • *Ann. mon.* • E. Searle, ed., *The chronicle of Battle Abbey*, OMT (1980) • *Chronica magistri Rogeri de Hovedene*, ed. W. Stubbs, 4 vols., Rolls Series, 51 (1868–71) • R. W. Eyton, *Court, household, and itinerary of King Henry II* (1878) • *The letters of John of Salisbury*, ed. and trans. H. E. Butler and W. J. Millor, rev. C. N. L. Brooke, 2 vols., OMT (1979–86) [Lat. orig. with parallel Eng. text] • C. R. Cheney, *Hubert Walter* (1967) • C. R. Cheney, *From Becket to Langton: English church government, 1170–1213* (1956) • G. H. Doble, trans., *Life of St Nectan*, Cornish Saints, 45 (1941) • G. F. Warner and H. J. Ellis, eds., *Facsimiles of royal and other charters in the British Museum* (1903)

Iles, (John) Henry (1871–1951), brass-band promoter and entertainment entrepreneur, was born at 8 Clarence Road, Bristol, on 17 September 1871, the son of John Thomas Iles and his wife, Mary Ann Butler. After leaving Ashville College, Harrogate, he entered his father's timber business. At the same time he built on his strong interest in music to develop a business career of his own. A keen church organist, choirmaster, and singer, he began by buying the journal *Organist and Choirmaster* before turning his interest to the brass-band movement. He appears first to have encountered brass bands when attending a contest while on a business trip to Belle Vue, Manchester, in 1898. Almost immediately after this he purchased the band music publishing house, Richard Smith & Co., turning its journal, the *British Bandsman* (founded 1887), into the movement's only weekly paper in March 1902. With its combination of regional news and gossip, technical hints, and extensive advertising columns, it rapidly became the most important element of the band press.

In January 1900 Iles, a highly effective publicist for the band movement, persuaded Sir Arthur Sullivan to conduct massed bands in a rendition of the composer's setting of Kipling's 'The Absent-Minded Beggar' during a concert at the Royal Albert Hall in London in aid of Second South African War charities. Building on the enthusiasm that this engendered and using Sullivan's influence as a director of the Crystal Palace, he established the National Brass Band Championship, which was held at the palace from 1900 until it was destroyed by fire in 1936. Until the early twentieth century, brass-band contest music typically comprised operatic selections and Iles was instrumental in the decision to encourage composers to produce complete pieces specifically designed for the brass band's distinctive configuration. In 1913 *Labour and Love*, an unsolicited work by the light orchestral and theatre music composer, Percy Fletcher, was selected as the championship test piece with this consideration in mind. Gustav

Holst (1928), Sir Edward Elgar (1930), John Ireland (1932), and Arthur Bliss (1936) were among the many composers commissioned to produce test pieces in the next decades: Iles was especially proud of his achievement in securing a work from Elgar. The best of these pieces did much to increase the level of technical ability within bands.

These commissions, the positive publicity that Iles consistently brought to a movement prone to suffer from an inferiority complex, and, not least, his personal popularity, made 'John Henry' an immensely respected figure within the band movement. On his death, a number of obituaries termed him 'our chief' and many commentators clearly saw him essentially as a philanthropist and not a businessman. At a memorial service, the composer Eric Ball claimed that for Iles, the band movement was 'a crusade, an ideal; material gain from it did not worry him'. Certainly, by the inter-war period, Iles seemed to see his band work as more hobby and social obligation than money-making venture, but this had not been the case at the outset, when philanthropy and profit fused in fruitful combination.

Iles's band work also led him indirectly into the business ventures which were to be the eventual basis of the considerable wealth which he enjoyed at one stage. In 1906 he managed a 'world tour' undertaken by the Besses o' th' Barn Band, during which he was much inspired by the amusement parks of North America. He returned with the British rights to the switchback ride and with plans for the 'scenic railway', a feature which he soon introduced at Blackpool and the White City in London. Eventually Iles was to enjoy major interests in amusement parks in Barcelona, Berlin, Brussels, Cairo, Copenhagen, Paris, and Pittsburgh. In terms of the English outdoor entertainment industry, he was most closely associated with Margate, where he developed the Dreamland Amusement Park and the Cliftonville Lido on a seafront site purchased in 1919. He also had interests in greyhound racing, introducing the sport into Kent in the late 1920s, at which time he also became a director of Belle Vue, Manchester. Unsuccessful investment in the British film industry in the later 1930s effectively destroyed Iles's business empire, a loss of some £250,000 resulting in his bankruptcy in July 1938. He resigned from all his directorships, though he maintained control of the brass-band National Championship until 1945, when he finally relinquished it to the *Daily Herald*.

Iles served as master of the Worshipful Company of Musicians in 1933. He was appointed OBE for his services to the band movement in 1944 and was also made an officer of the Académie Française. A keen sportsman, he was an occasional member of the Gloucestershire county cricket side in 1890–91 (he was proud once to have bowled W. G. Grace in a net practice), enjoyed a lifelong enthusiasm for golf, and wrote a cyclist's guide to Bristol and its environs in 1898. In 1893 Iles married Eleanor Marion (b. 1869/70), daughter of Frederick Bird, a merchant of Midsomer Norton; they had a daughter and three sons, the eldest of whom, H. F. B. Eric Iles, took over a number of his father's directorships after 1938. The family made their home at Birchington in Kent from the 1920s, Iles serving as a Margate JP from 1935 to 1938.

Iles died at his home, 'Aurora', Cliff Road, Birchington, on 29 May 1951 and was buried in Birchington on 7 June. He was survived by his wife. A well-attended memorial service, held at St Sepulchre's, Holborn, saw a number of leading figures in the band world pay verbal and musical tributes to a man whose respect for bandsmen's skills and commitment led him, directly and indirectly, into fertile business operations and the band movement into a level of public exposure beyond anything it had previously received.   DAVE RUSSELL

Sources *British Bandsman* (9 June 1951) · *Isle of Thanet Gazette* (1 June 1951) · *WWW* · T. Herbert, ed., *Bands: the brass band movement in the 19th and 20th centuries* (1991) · A. R. Taylor, *Brass bands* (1979) · *CGPLA Eng. & Wales* (1951) · b. cert. · m. cert. · d. cert.
Likenesses photograph, repro. in *British Bandsman* (2 June 1951)
Wealth at death £10,318 10s. 7d.: probate, 30 Oct 1951, *CGPLA Eng. & Wales*

Iliffe, Edward Mauger, first Baron Iliffe (1877–1960), newspaper and periodical proprietor, was born on 17 May 1877 in Coventry, the second son of William Isaac Iliffe (1843–1917), printer and stationer, and his wife, Annette, daughter of James Coker, of Guernsey. His grandfather had founded the family stationery, wallpaper, and printing business. This venture's early success ensured that the Iliffes soon became pillars of the local community, not least in their enthusiasm for civic politics and evangelism. Iliffe's father appreciated that late Victorian Coventry was at the heart of a revolution in engineering, and thus the ideal place from which to pioneer specialist transport magazines intended for a mass market. *The Cyclist* (1878) was so successful that it absorbed two rivals and moved to London as *Bicycling News*. *Autocar* followed in 1895 and *Flight* in 1909. By this time Iliffe & Sons had diversified beyond printing and periodicals, having relaunched a moribund weekly, the *Coventry Times*, in 1879 and more significantly having secured control in 1891 of the *Midland Daily Telegraph*.

After schooling in Coventry, Iliffe joined the family firm at seventeen and served his proprietorial apprenticeship on the new *Coventry Evening Telegraph*. Managerial responsibility grew throughout the Edwardian period, and there was a smooth transition when he succeeded his late father in 1917. Iliffe Press was jointly owned with his elder brother, W. Coker Iliffe, and wartime confidence in the company is confirmed by Iliffe's willingness to be seconded to the Ministry of Munitions, where he spent the final two years of the First World War as controller of the machine tool department. Although with the end of the war Iliffe looked to advancement via national rather than local politics, his newspapers faithfully backed Coventry's 'shopocracy' of retailers, professionals, and businessmen in control of the city council. In the late 1920s he fostered links between the Liberal–Conservative 'coalition' and Coventry's major engineering employers. Iliffe himself won Tamworth for the Conservatives in 1923 and held the seat until 1929. His war efforts had earned him a CBE in 1918, and a knighthood followed in 1922. In 1933 he

was made a peer. The family home was Yattendon, a large estate in the Berkshire countryside acquired in 1926. Iliffe had married Charlotte, daughter of Henry Gilding JP, of Gateacre, Liverpool, as early as 1902. They had a daughter and two sons.

Life as a tory back-bencher scarcely distracted Iliffe from his business ventures, which by now were based in London. In 1924 he formed Allied Newspapers Ltd, in partnership with William and Gomer Berry, the future lords Camrose and Kemsley. The Berry brothers were from south Wales, with a similar background in magazine publishing. With Iliffe they raised sufficient capital to buy from Lord Rothermere a clutch of provincial and metropolitan papers the latter had purchased from the first Sir Edward Hulton only a year earlier. When these titles were later auctioned off they made Allied Newspapers Ltd a profit of £2.4 million, by which time the company had acquired the *Sunday Times* and the *Daily Telegraph*. Secured from Lord Burnham in 1928, the latter became a mass-circulation daily, not through changing either its format or its hard-tory politics but via successful marketing and a halving of the 2*d*. price in December 1930.

In January 1937 falling sales and cash flow problems led to the breakup of Allied Newspapers, with Iliffe absorbing an assortment of titles into the family business. More crucially, as part of the deal he acquired the well-established and highly lucrative Kelly's directories. Iliffe's last major acquisition was the holding company for the *Birmingham Post* and the *Birmingham Mail*, and in 1943 he became chairman, thereby consolidating his west midlands power base. During the Second World War, Iliffe chaired the duke of Gloucester's Red Cross and St John Fund. His spectacularly successful fund-raising efforts were rewarded by appointment as GBE in 1946.

Iliffe chose to be a major regional newspaper proprietor rather than a minor player in Fleet Street. But like his father and grandfather he was always ready to diversify, enjoying a parallel career in insurance. A name at Lloyd's, between the wars Iliffe not only sat on the board of the London Assurance, but was chairman of the Guildhall Insurance Company. At the heart of the City establishment, he was the master of three livery companies, and presided over the Association of British Chambers of Commerce in 1932–3, and the Periodical Proprietors' Association from 1935 to 1938. He enjoyed a lengthy presidency of the International Lawn Tennis Club of Great Britain, from 1945 to 1959, and presided over the Shakespeare Memorial Theatre's trust fund from 1933 to 1958. Iliffe always retained a keen interest in midlands affairs, not least the rebuilding of Coventry after 1945: as early as 1938 the *Coventry Evening Telegraph* was promoting planning schemes and exhibitions. Iliffe gave £35,000 towards the new Coventry Cathedral, as well as funding local school initiatives. Apart from his newspapers Iliffe's most visible legacy is Allesley Hall, on the western edge of Coventry: 47 acres of land were given to the city council in the late 1930s for recreational use. When Iliffe died in the Middlesex Hospital, London, at the age of eighty-three on 25 July

1960 his eldest son—Edward Langton Iliffe (b. 1908)—succeeded to the title and the chairmanship of Coventry Newspapers Ltd. He also inherited his father's reputation as a major public benefactor, handing over a further 51 acres of parkland to the Allesley Hall estate.

ADRIAN SMITH

Sources *The Times* (26 July 1960) · K. Richardson, *Twentieth-century Coventry* (1972) · S. E. Koss, *The rise and fall of the political press in Britain*, 2 (1984) · E. B. Newbold, *Portrait of Coventry* (1982) · B. Lancaster and T. Mason, eds., *Life and labour in a twentieth century city: the experience of Coventry* [n.d., c.1987] · *CGPLA Eng. & Wales* (1961)

Archives NRA priv. coll., family papers | Coventry Newspapers Ltd, Coventry, *Coventry Evening Telegraph*, MSS · U. Birm., corresp. with Lord Avon | FILM BFI NFTVA, news footage · IWM FVA, actuality footage · IWM FVA, news footage

Likenesses W. Stoneman, photograph, 1937, NPG · W. Stoneman, photograph, 1945, NPG · F. O. Salisbury, oils, priv. coll.

Wealth at death £510,367 11s.: probate, 30 Jan 1961, *CGPLA Eng. & Wales*

Ilive, Jacob (*bap.* **1705**, *d.* **1763**), printer and religious polemicist, baptized at St Botolph, Aldersgate, London, on 6 July 1705, was the son of Thomas Ilive (*d.* 1724), a printer of Aldersgate Street, one of those 'said to be highflyers' (Nichols, *Lit. anecdotes*, 1.309). His mother, Jane (1669–1733), daughter of Thomas James, printer, and his two brothers, Abraham (*bap.* 1706, *d.* 1777) and Isaac (*bap.* 1704), were also printers and members of the Stationers' Company. Jacob was apprenticed to his father on 6 July 1719, was freed by his mother on 2 August 1726, and was called to the livery on 7 August 1733. His mother's will made the family business go to Jacob, even though he was not the eldest son. About 1730:

> he applied himself to letter-cutting, and carried on a foundry and a printing-house together. In 1734 he lived at Aldersgate … afterwards he removed to London House, the habitation of the late Dr. Rawlinson, on the opposite side of the way … in 1746, but his foundry had been purchased 3 July 1740 by Mr. John James. (Mores, 64)

Ilive abandoned typefounding, but maintained the printing office to the end of his life.

Ilive was among the most persistent and original of England's mid-eighteenth-century religious radicals, lecturing frequently in London's guildhalls between 1730 and 1750 regarding the exotic religious ideas he had derived from gnosticism. In 1730 Ilive printed his chief religious work, *The Layman's Vindication of the Christian Religion, in 2 Parts*. This work sets out his views on creation, human nature, and the destiny of the human race. Ilive questioned the historical reliability of the Pentateuch and cited ancient authors condemning the Hebrews. At Brewers' Hall, on 10 September 1733 and at Joyners' Hall, on 24 September, Ilive delivered an oration on the plurality of worlds which he had written in 1729. The work was made public in 1733 (2nd edn, 1736), 'pursuant to the will' of his mother, who shared and may have been a source of his religious views. In these orations Ilive argues that life exists on many planets and that a human being is 'an apostate Angel and a Body'. *A dialogue between a doctor of the Church of England and Mr. Jacob Ilive upon the subject of the oration spoke at Joyners' Hall* followed in the same year, in support of the oration. At Carpenters' Hall, London Wall, Ilive

lectured on natural religion. In 1738 he brought out another oration, this one 'spoke at Trinity Hall, in Aldersgate Street', on 9 January of the same year, and directed against Henry Felton's discourses on personal identity in the resurrection. In these lectures Ilive denied the resurrection of the body, affirmed the pre-existence of the soul, maintained that earth is hell and that human beings are embodied pre-existent spirit beings whose destiny is to inhabit and rule other planets. Some of Ilive's theological ideas were derived from William Derham's *Astro-Theology* (1715). Ilive, like other deists, argued that Christianity was a corruption of early, primitive, rational religious beliefs.

In 1751 Ilive printed anonymously a forgery purporting to be a translation of the lost biblical book of Jasher, issued 'with Testimonies and Notes explanatory of the Text, to which is prefixed various Readings translated into English from the Hebrew by Alcuin of Britain, who went a Pilgrimage into the Holy Land'. This work retold crucial stories from the Pentateuch, and portrayed Adam as practising a pure religion of reason. In 1829 Jasher was revised and reissued by the Revd C. R. Bond at Bristol.

Bishop Thomas Sherlock sought to prevent Ilive's publishing works by other deists. On 20 June 1756 Ilive was sentenced to three years' imprisonment with hard labour in the house of correction at Clerkenwell for writing, printing, and publishing *Some remarks on the excellent discourses lately published by a very worthy prelate* [Thomas Sherlock] *by a searcher after religious truth* (1754). Rewritten and enlarged as the anonymous *Remarks on the Two Volumes of Excellent Discourses Lately Published by the Bishop of London* (1755), it was declared to be 'a most blasphemous book … denying in a ludicrous manner the divinity of Jesus Christ's well as all revealed religion'. Ilive remained in gaol until 10 June 1758, engaged 'continually in writing'. Surviving prison, he continued writing and lecturing. As part of his effort to bring about prison reforms, Ilive published *Reasons Offered for the Reformation of the House of Correction … with a Plan of the Prison* (1757), and a *Scheme* (1759) for the employment of persons sent there as disorderly. The two pamphlets contain a detailed account of a prisoner's daily life. 'Ilive was somewhat disordered in his mind,' says Nichols (Nichols, *Lit. anecdotes*, 1.309), an opinion apparently based upon the printer's unorthodoxy.

Other works by Ilive include a rival to Cave's *Gentleman's Magazine* published between 1736 and 1738. Written in response to a dispute within the Stationers' Company, Ilive also published a *Speech to his brethren the master printers on the great utility of the art of printing at a general meeting 18th July 1750*. In 1762 Ilive became involved in a dispute with the Stationers' Company, as a result of its decision to exclude journeymen from the livery. Ilive called a general meeting of the yeomanry (compositors, pressmen, and journeymen bookbinders) and proposed that they should 'rescue their liberties' (Blagden, 232) by electing their own master, wardens, and committee. 'At their next meeting they bound apprentices, admitted men to their freedoms and called freemen to the Livery' (ibid., 233). In the following year Ilive encouraged members of the yeomanry to refuse to pay quarterage. As a result the company sued the defaulters in the court of requests, where Ilive acted as defence counsel. The company won the case and 'from this date the Yeomanry, as one of the "estates" of the Company, is heard of no more' (ibid.). Ilive died in 1763.

JAMES A. HERRICK

Sources J. A. Herrick, 'The religious rhetoric of Jacob Ilive', *The radical rhetoric of the English deists* (1997), 181–204 · Nichols, *Lit. anecdotes* · T. B. Reed, *Old English letter foundries* (1887), 346–9 · C. Blagden, *The Stationers' Company: a history, 1403–1959* (1960) · private information (2004) [M. Treadwell] · D. F. McKenzie, ed., *Stationers' Company apprentices*, [3]: *1701–1800* (1978) · E. R. Mores, *A dissertation upon English typographical founders* (1778) · T. H. Horne, *Introduction to the critical study and knowledge of the holy scriptures* (1856), 4.741–6
Archives BL

Ilkeston. For this title name *see* Foster, Balthazar Walter, first Baron Ilkeston (1840–1913).

Illiam Dhône. *See* Christian, William (1608–1663).

Illidge, Thomas Henry (1799–1851), portrait painter, was born on 26 September 1799 at Birmingham, and was that day baptized at Bond Street Baptist Church, Birmingham, the son of John Illidge and his wife, Mary. His family were resident near Nantwich in Cheshire. His father moved to Manchester when Illidge was a child, and dying young left his family with scant means of support. Illidge was educated at Manchester grammar school, and was taught drawing. Afterwards he became the pupil successively of Mather Brown and William Bradley. He tried landscape painting, but married early, and with a young family to support resorted to portrait painting as a more profitable option. He succeeded as a portraitist in the large manufacturing towns of Lancashire, painting many of the local civic and financial celebrities. He exhibited at the Manchester Royal Institution between 1827 and 1837; from 1827 to 1850 he also frequently exhibited works at the Liverpool Academy. His portrait of Benjamin Robert Haydon (NPG), was reproduced in the *Illustrated London News* following Haydon's death in 1846. His portrait of Colonel Clayton hangs in the court house at Preston; his portraits of Sir Joshua Walmesley (1794–1871), mayor of Liverpool 1839–1840 (exh. Liverpool Academy, 1840), and the Revd William Shepherd LLD (1768–1847), eminent Unitarian minister in Liverpool and political and educational reformist (exh. Liverpool Academy, 1843), hang in the Walker Art Gallery, Liverpool. He was commissioned to paint portraits for the town hall, Birkenhead, and the Royal Free Hospital, London. In 1842 he moved to London, and from that time exhibited fourteen works at the Royal Academy. He also exhibited five works at the British Institution and thirteen works, including the portrait *James Montgomery, Author of 'The World before the Flood'*, at the Society of British Artists, Suffolk Street, between 1843 and 1851. His portrait of the fashionable miniature painter Sir William Charles Ross was reproduced in the *Art Journal* in 1849. In 1844, on the death of H. P. Briggs RA, he purchased the lease of his house at 33 Bruton Street, Berkeley Square, where he continued to practise as a popular and fashionable portrait painter. He died there unexpectedly of fever after a short illness on 13 May 1851, leaving a widow, Ellen.

L. H. CUST, *rev.* RUTH STEWART

Sources Redgrave, *Artists* · *Merseyside painters, people and places: catalogue of oil paintings*, Walker Art Gallery, Liverpool, ed. M. Bennett (1978) · R. Ormond, *Early Victorian portraits*, 2 (1973) · E. Morris and E. Roberts, *The Liverpool Academy and other exhibitions of contemporary art in Liverpool, 1774–1867* (1998) · Wood, *Vic. painters*, 3rd edn, vol. 1 · IGI · will, LMA, DL/C/421 · B. Stewart and M. Cutten, *The dictionary of portrait painters in Britain up to 1920* (1997) · T. Fawcett, *The rise of English provincial art: artist, patron and institution outside London, 1800–1830* (1974)
Archives Walker Art Gallery, Liverpool, archive

Illing, Vincent Charles (1890–1969), petroleum geologist, was born on 24 September 1890 at Jullundur, Punjab, the younger son of Thomas Illing (1863–1934), a non-commissioned officer in the 3rd rifle brigade of the Indian army, and his wife, Annie *née* Payton (1857?–1954). His early education came from army and other schools in India and Malta. He was thirteen when his father retired to Hartshill, near Nuneaton, Warwickshire. His mother, who came from a family long established in that area, was ambitious on his behalf and sent him to King Edward VI Grammar School, Nuneaton. From there in 1909 he won an open scholarship to Sidney Sussex College, Cambridge.

At Cambridge, Illing became interested in geology—largely through the influence of W. G. Fearnsides (then a young university demonstrator in petrology). As a result, Illing abandoned his early ambition to join the Indian Civil Service. He was a keen athlete and soccer player, though an ankle injury ruled him out of university selection. Illing graduated with first-class honours in part one (1911) and part two (1912) of the natural sciences tripos, at the same time winning the Harkness scholarship. The award financed his research on trilobite fossils in the Cambrian rocks at Hartshill, begun as an undergraduate. The result of this work, a paper on the Paradoxidian fauna of the Stockingford Shales, was published in 1915 in the *Quarterly Journal of the Geological Society*.

In 1914 Illing was appointed demonstrator in petroleum at Imperial College, London, and was requested to develop a course in petroleum technology. This decision by the college seems to have been prompted by growing interest in the use of petroleum fuels in warfare. Starting almost from scratch, Illing saw clearly that geology was an integral part both of exploration for petroleum and of its production. He was appointed lecturer in 1915, assistant professor of petroleum in 1921, assistant professor of oil technology in 1923, and full professor of oil technology in 1937. An inspiring lecturer and geology teacher, he seemed to have almost inexhaustible energy in the field.

After contributing a short note on British oil-shale prospectivity to *Nature* in 1917, Illing's first significant publication on exploration for oil was a somewhat pessimistic assessment of the potential for oil occurrence in Britain. This work was a lucid scientific review of the search then current for subterranean 'oil-pools' in the British landscape, and was his considered reaction to exaggerated ideas held by politicians of the day. It was published in 1919 in the *Geological Magazine*.

On 20 December 1919, Illing married Frances Jean Leslie, eldest daughter of Hugh Leslie, a headmaster of Perth

Academy. They had one son and four daughters. In the following year, with a two-year leave of absence, he set out with his wife on a return visit to Trinidad, where he had begun work on oil production some five years previously; this time he went to map the Naparima region for a local oil company. Fieldwork was very arduous: he examined more than 9000 pits and 100 trenches using particular occurrences of 'heavy mineral' sand grains to distinguish and identify various sandstone bodies, a technique probably first used by him in 1916.

After returning to Imperial College, Illing carried out geological studies on Polish and Romanian oilfields, and the Pechelbronn oil-mine in France. That work engendered curiosity of what the maximum possible amount of oil recoverable from a reservoir might be, which in turn led to practical experiments on the movement of oil and gas in porous media. Later assessments deem this to have been his chief laboratory-research contribution to petroleum geology. The principal results appeared in 1933 in the *Journal of the Institute of Petroleum Technology*, under the title 'The migration of oil and gas'. In this article Illing introduced the concept of primary and secondary migration, primary migration being a movement of hydrocarbons from source-rock to reservoir, and secondary migration further movements and hydrocarbon concentration within the reservoir. Other papers followed, notably seven articles in 1938 for the encyclopaedic *Science of Petroleum*, and in 1945 a review of the role of stratigraphy in oil discovery for the *Bulletin* of the American Association of Petroleum Geologists.

In 1942 Illing made what was later seen to be a significant address to the Geologists' Association, entitling it 'Geology applied to petroleum'. It was a synopsis and statement of his philosophy of geological education—the equal value of academic and practical studies. He had himself decided early in his career to combine academic and consulting work to ensure that his teaching had the authority of practical experience. He held a lifelong conviction that acquiring scientific knowledge should not be an exclusive aim, and he commented disparagingly on the use of divisive terms such as 'pure' and 'applied' in geological science, asserting that geology is one, and that its purity depends on its truth not on its application.

In the early 1920s Illing began to consult on behalf of the Cowdray Group, and thereafter he practised widely in the role of petroleum consultant. He travelled much. For part of every summer from 1928 to the beginning of the Second World War he carried out geological surveys in Venezuela, leading to a long association with the Ultramar Company and the discovery in 1948 of the Mercedes oilfields in Guarico State. In 1946, Illing formed Petroleum Scientific Services Ltd as a vehicle for his advisory work on behalf of companies in the Caribbean. In 1950, as work expanded, its name was changed to V. C. Illing & Partners. He also helped to form Seismograph Services Ltd in the days of inhibiting currency-exchange controls. In 1947, at the request of the British government, he successfully arbitrated with the government of Mexico on compensation due to the Mexican Eagle Oil Company for their

nationalized properties. He also assisted the government of Nigeria on the development of its oil resources.

In 1958 Illing was appointed adviser to the Gas Council on natural-gas exploration of inland Britain. Discovery of a large gasfield at Groningen in the Netherlands had rekindled interest in the British oil and gas potential, especially in the North Sea basin, because American industry was developing offshore marine equipment in the Gulf of Mexico that could be used in the North Sea. Illing advised the Gas Council to leave exploration to the industry, but to purchase any gas that was found. His last assignment was a search for suitable reservoirs underground for storage of town-gas against peaks of demand. This called for many shallow borings, which incidentally revealed much new information on Cotswold geology.

Illing joined the Geological Society in 1913. He was awarded its Lyell fund in 1918 and its Murchison medal in 1944. He served on its council from 1927 to 1928, and on the council of the Institute of Petroleum from 1930 to 1941 and 1947 to 1948. He was a vice-president of the institute from 1942 to 1945 and again in 1948. He was the first English geologist to be elected to honorary membership of the American Association of Petroleum Geologists (1961). He was elected FRS in 1945, honorary associate of the Royal School of Mines in 1951, and fellow of Imperial College in 1958. On his retirement in 1955 he was honoured also with the title of professor emeritus of geology (oil technology) in the University of London.

Though he might be said to have been short in build and of a quiet disposition, Illing was a man of great presence and determination. He had physical and mental energy in abundance. Spiritually he was religious, as also had been his mother. He was upright in business and his scrupulous honesty won the confidence of all with whom he worked and advised. His career was characterized by enduring personal relationships; he inspired his students, and took care to follow their subsequent careers. He lived unostentatiously, always mindful of the needs of others, and was immersed in the work he loved until his final days. He died of cancer on 16 May 1969 at his home, 24 The Avenue, Cheam, Surrey, and his body was cremated six days later at Leatherhead.   J. G. C. M. FULLER

Sources G. D. Hobson, 'The history of the oil technology course and its offshoots', *Seventy-five years of progress in oil field science and technology* (1990), 9–17 · N. L. Falcon, *Memoirs FRS*, 16 (1970), 365–84 · *DNB* · b. cert. · private information (2004)

Archives BGS, trilobite faunas

Likenesses portrait, c.1950, ICL, department of geology · E. Blacker, oils, 1969, priv. coll.

Wealth at death £108,075: probate, 17 Sept 1969, *CGPLA Eng. & Wales*

Illingworth, Alfred (1827–1907), worsted spinner and politician, was born on 25 September 1827 at Kent Street, Bradford, Yorkshire, the elder son of Daniel Illingworth (1792–1854), worsted spinner, and his wife, Elizabeth, daughter of Michael Hill of Bradford. He was educated at a private academy in Little Horton, Bradford, run by a Moravian, Joseph Hinchcliffe, who contributed to the education of a number of Bradford's leading industrialists from middle-class dissenting families. Its curriculum appears to have paid attention to the needs of business, by providing modern and commercial subjects, alongside the traditional syllabus of the day. In 1839 Alfred transferred to the newly opened Huddersfield College, which directed its teaching to those sons of nonconformist businessmen in the West Riding of Yorkshire, intending to pursue a business career. Although from a nonconformist background, and brought up in the Baptist faith, in adult life he was never a full member of any church.

Alfred Illingworth joined the family textile business in 1843 at the time when the Bradford worsted trade was about to expand rapidly, through the use of cotton warps in its cloth, and its discovery of a satisfactory means of dyeing cloths containing both wool and cotton fibres. His grandfather Phineas Illingworth had the first, unsuccessful, steam-powered factory in Bradford. His uncle, Phineas's eldest son, and his father, Daniel, set up a new textile business in Bradford in 1820, bringing in a partner, William Murgatroyd, who provided the business with capital. In 1837 Daniel decided to start his own business at Providence Mill, Thornton Road, Bradford. There is no detailed record of the activities of the firm in its early years. However, on Daniel's death in 1854, Alfred and his younger brother Henry (1829–1895) took over the firm as joint partners. They built a new factory, Whetley Mills, nearby. Opened in 1865, it was one of the largest in Bradford, with almost 1000 workers by 1873. It specialized in combing and spinning. Machine combing had been perfected through the 1850s and 1860s, and provided the worsted industry with a means to experiment in providing the growing international markets for worsted cloth. Samuel Cunliffe Lister's patent rights were running out in the mid-1860s and Daniel Illingworth & Sons was free to use the new combing machinery without the previous legal constraints. Within the firm, Alfred was responsible for wool buying and marketing. Henry looked after internal management. The brothers appear to have been very capable, and may have suffered less than many of their competitors from the trading problems of the 1870s and 1880s. They had a workforce of 1000 in 1893.

On 8 August 1866 Alfred married Margaret (d. 1919), daughter of Sir Isaac *Holden, one of the pioneers of wool-combing machinery, and established a home at Daisy Bank, in Allerton, next door to his brother who, six years earlier, had married Margaret's sister, Mary. Angus Holden, the girls' brother, married Margaret Illingworth, the eldest sister of the Illingworths. Thus a close connection between two major Bradford industrial families was established. It is possible that the Illingworth firm benefited from the technical expertise for which the Holdens were renowned. The families lived in close proximity to one another, and Isaac Holden's new Bradford mill, Alston works, was about 1 mile from Whetley Mills.

In 1865 Isaac Holden was invited to stand as a Liberal candidate for Knaresborough in the West Riding of Yorkshire. He held the seat until 1868, when he gave it up to Alfred, who then embarked on a significant political career, leaving the management of the firm mainly to Henry.

Alfred Illingworth represented Knaresborough until 1874, and Bradford from 1880 to 1895. He was highly influential in the Liberal–radical interest, wielding great power in Bradford politics and pursuing a wide range of local and national political causes with vigour. The disestablishment of the Anglican church was a matter of great importance to him and he was a very active member of the Liberation Society. He fought for freedom of individual action in many areas of social, economic, and political affairs. He was opposed to the campaign of W. E. Forster, the other Bradford MP, for education reform. He took issue with the 1870 Elementary Education Act, but recognized the need for improvements in the availability of technical education. Government intervention in economic affairs was a matter of continual anathema for him; he was very much a member of the Manchester Liberal free-trade school. He was a member of the Peace Society, opposing many of Britain's military campaigns and supporting freedom for Ireland. He believed in the rights of workers, including the secret ballot and the working-class vote, and helped to organize the Bradford Working Men's Reform Committee, which campaigned for the extension of the franchise. But with his strong belief in individual freedom he opposed anything that interfered with the rights of the individual. Thus he saw the relationships between employer and employee as private matters, not to be constrained by government or trade unions. He fought wages and hours legislation and many proposals for social reform. His views found less and less sympathy in the changing social context of the late nineteenth century and moved out of line with developing Liberal policy. The rise of the Independent Labour Party in Bradford, it has been argued, owed a great deal to the intransigence of Illingworth and his associates. He withdrew from politics in 1900, disillusioned by the Liberal Party and frustrated by the success of the Labour Party. But he continued to fight particular issues which injured his personal convictions. He opposed the Balfour Education Act of 1902, which he felt gave too much power to the Anglican church in education. He was made a freeman of the city of Bradford in 1902.

Illingworth was described as a rather humourless man, with unswervingly strong emotional, passionate, and bitter convictions for his causes. He was tall, spare, alert, ruddy-bearded, and hawk-visaged. He doggedly supported what he saw as the interests of the Bradford trade, and failed to recognize the need to change with the changing times. Sir Henry Campbell-Bannerman described him as a 'sound, staunch, fearless politician' (*Bradford Daily Telegraph*). His leisure interests were few. At his country house at Stanbury near Haworth, West Riding of Yorkshire, at which he spent most of his time after 1900, he occasionally entertained, played billiards, and engaged in leisurely shooting. Alfred Illingworth died of heart failure on 2 January 1907 at home at Daisy Bank; his funeral took place on 5 January. His wife died in 1919. Two of his six surviving sons, Hampden Holden Illingworth and Eustace Holden Illingworth, entered the family firm along with two of Henry Illingworth's sons.   D. T. Jenkins

Sources *Bradford Daily Telegraph* (2 Jan 1907) · A. Illingworth, *Fifty years of politics: Mr Alfred Illingworth's retrospect* (1905) · J. Reynolds, 'Illingworth, Alfred', *DBB* · *Bradford Daily Argus* (3 Jan 1907) · *Yorkshire Post* (3 Jan 1907) · K. Honeyman and J. Goodman, *Technology and enterprise: Isaac Holden and the mechanisation of woolcombing in France, 1848–1914* (1986) · *Industries of Yorkshire* (1888) · m. cert. · d. cert.
Archives BL, corresp. with W. E. Gladstone, Add. MSS 44492–44789, *passim* · U. Leeds, Brotherton L., letters to Isaac Holden and corresp. as president of the Northern Counties Education League · University of Bradford Library, J. B. Priestley Library, letters to Isaac Holden
Likenesses photograph, repro. in *Bradford Daily Telegraph*
Wealth at death £172,470: Reynolds, 'Illingworth, Alfred'

Illingworth, Cayley (*c.*1758–1823). *See under* Illingworth, William (*bap.* 1764, *d.* 1845).

Illingworth, Sir Charles Frederick William (1899–1991), surgeon, was born on 8 May 1899 at 33 West View, Halifax, Yorkshire, the only child of John Illingworth, an iron and steel merchant, and his wife, Edith, *née* Boys. He attended the Heath grammar school, Halifax, until 1915, when he joined the Sea Scouts, taking part in coastguard duties on the Yorkshire coast. Subsequent work in a munitions factory and then as a farm labourer provided more rigorous training and experience, and promoted his physical fitness. In 1916 he began medical studies at the University of Edinburgh. Although completion of his first year entitled him to exemption from military service, he chose to enlist in the Officers' Training Corps and volunteered for the Royal Flying Corps: after training at Farnborough and Oxford, he was based near Amiens, flying Sopwith Camels on sorties over the battle lines. In August 1918 he made a forced landing over enemy lines and was imprisoned in Bavaria, until the imminent end of the war was intimated by a letter from his father, reporting the homecoming of his (non-existent) brother. Illingworth made his way home, arriving on Christmas day. The spirited determination with which he met the challenges of these early experiences was maintained throughout his subsequent career, in which his outstanding achievements were particularly remarkable for a man of small stature and outwardly retiring disposition. However, his devotion to high standards in all his activities, and his insistence on the same qualities in the work of his associates, constituted an inspiring (albeit daunting) example to students and professional colleagues alike.

Illingworth began his delayed medical studies at Edinburgh University, graduating MB ChB in 1922. He gained valuable experience during six months' work at the Royal Infirmary as house surgeon to Sir Edward Stiles, who was famed for his surgical skill.

Following his term as a house physician, at Derbyshire Royal Infirmary, Illingworth returned to Edinburgh, becoming clinical tutor to Sir David Wilkie, a specialist in abdominal surgery. In this post he acquired experience in gastroenterology, a subject in which he retained a practical interest throughout his career. On 12 April 1928 he married Eleanor Mary Bennett (1901/2–1971); they had four sons.

Illingworth's pre-eminence in the practice and teaching of surgery was based on strict adherence to certain principles of technique, which demanded scrupulous attention to economy of manipulation. Accordingly, the conduct of his own surgical operations was deft, rapid, and decisive. His success and reputation were further enhanced by the warm sympathy that he showed in the care of his patients. A model of punctiliousness, he would not tolerate any slackness among his staff.

In 1939 Illingworth was appointed to the regius chair of surgery in Glasgow. Strongly encouraged by the principal, Sir Hector Hetherington, he embarked on major initiatives, in staff appointments and in the establishment of collaborative work, both within the medical school and in association with other departments. These developments were especially admirable in view of the dispersed nature of the various sections of the medical school. Under Illingworth's leadership, the Glasgow school achieved worldwide renown for excellence in the practice and teaching of medicine and surgery, and also in research (which Illingworth did not pursue personally but strongly encouraged). The work of the school entailed substantial collaboration with other departments. Illingworth recognized that such working relationships were to become essential adjuncts to medicine and surgery.

The end of the war made possible major rebuilding, allowing the establishment of a modern surgical research unit, contiguous with the wards, and having first-class facilities. These improvements, together with Illingworth's personal distinction, attracted numerous visiting specialists, including many from the USA. Glasgow also provided professors of surgery for numerous universities in the UK and overseas.

Illingworth was a prolific author. Among his most important and best-selling works were *A Textbook of Surgical Pathology* (twelve editions, 1932–79) and the *Short Textbook of Surgery* (nine editions, 1938–72). His monograph, *The Story of William Hunter* (1967), celebrated the eighteenth-century surgeon noted for his great benefactions to Glasgow University.

Notwithstanding his eminence and high honours, including CBE (1946), knighthood (1961), and appointment as honorary surgeon to the queen (1961–5), Sir Charles retained a characteristic modesty and an inveterate dislike of pretentiousness. As a patient himself, undergoing open-heart surgery at the age of eighty-two, he elected for a bed in a general ward. Dismissive of convalescence, he quickly resumed his leisure pursuit of hill-walking.

Retirement in 1964 gave Sir Charles the opportunity for further enterprises. He appreciated the need to provide for new techniques which were essential for modern medical practice and cognate research. Accordingly, in order to secure additional resources for funding work in the relevant disciplines, Sir Charles persuaded a group of ten distinguished associates and patrons to establish, in 1967, a foundation for the support of research in Scotland in medical and related fields. The name, Tenovus-Scotland, was derived from the similarly sponsored, but more specialized, Tenovus Institute for Cancer Research in Cardiff.

Sir Charles's committee ensured that Tenovus-Scotland would be sufficiently endowed to continue its independent support of an increasing variety of projects. Sadly, the founder did not survive long enough to participate in the dinner celebrating the thirtieth anniversary of Tenovus-Scotland.

With indefatigable determination and industry, when approaching ninety, Sir Charles resumed authorship, publishing *There is a History in All Men's Lives* (1988), an informal autobiographical memoir, in which his own matchless achievements are given scant attention. He assigned the profits from its sale to Tenovus-Scotland. Charles Illingworth died at 234 Crow Road, Glasgow, on 23 February 1991.   C. J. W. BROOKS

Sources C. Illingworth, *There is a history in all men's lives* (1988) · *The Times* (26 Feb 1991) · A. P. Forrest, *The Independent* (30 March 1991) · *Glasgow Herald* (26 Feb 1991) · *Daily Telegraph* (28 Feb 1991) · A. W. Kay and others, 'Appreciations by colleagues', *Tenovus-Scotland Newsletter*, no. 36 (June 1991) · L. McQueen and A. B. Kerr, *The Western Infirmary* (1974) · U. Glas., Archives and Business Records Centre · b. cert. · m. cert. · d. cert.

Wealth at death £190,286.75: confirmation, 9 May 1991, NA Scot., SC/CO 554/298

Illingworth, Leslie Gilbert (1902–1979), cartoonist and illustrator, was born at 8 or 9 Harbour Road, Barry, Glamorgan, on 2 September 1902, the youngest son of Richard Frederick (Dick) Illingworth (1866–1956), who later became chief clerk in the engineers department of the Barry Railway and Docks Company, and Helen MacGregor (1874–1952), a teacher. His uncle Frank William Illingworth (1888–1972) drew the famous *Punch* First World War cartoon *Do I know if the Rooshuns has really come through England?* (23 September 1914). Illingworth began drawing at the age of four and was educated at Palmerston Road infants' school, Cadoxton, where he won a scholarship to Barry county (grammar) school (fellow pupils included Ronald Niebour—who later became NEB, pocket cartoonist of the *Daily Mail*). At the age of fifteen he won a scholarship to study art under Wilson Jagger at the City of Cardiff Technical School (later known as Cardiff Art School), where he won a gold medal for drawing. He studied in the mornings, and in the afternoons worked in the lithographic department of the *Western Mail* in Cardiff. His first paid humorous drawing was a design for a railway timetable cover and he later drew police court drawings for the paper and a regular weekly rugby football cartoon ('Dai Pepper') for its sister publication the *Football Express*.

In 1920 Illingworth won a scholarship to study under Sir William Rothenstein at the Royal College of Art, London. Meanwhile he continued to work for the *Western Mail* and his first political cartoon appeared in the paper on 11 October 1921. When the *Mail*'s political cartoonist, J. M. Staniforth, died on 17 December 1921, he took over his job (aged nineteen) at the salary of £6 a week but continued to study and live in London. By the time he was twenty he was earning the then high sum of £1000 p.a. and so decided to give up his studies and return home.

In November 1923 Owen Aves—art editor of the humorous weekly *Passing Show*—invited him to submit work and

when Aves left and became an agent in June 1924 he took on Illingworth. He subsequently worked for *London Opinion*, *The Humorist*, *Pearson's*, *Strand*, *Nash's*, *Good Housekeeping*, *London Life*, *Red Magazine*, *Wills' Magazine*, *Answers*, *Tit-Bits*, and others. Later the same year he returned briefly to London to study part-time at the Slade School of Fine Art under Henry Tonks while still freelancing and working for the *Western Mail*. During the general strike of 1926 he continued to work for the paper, producing his own plates when the print department refused to make them, but resigned later that year. He then moved to Paris (with his mother) to study at the Académie Julian, supporting himself with freelance illustrations, cartoons, and advertising work dispatched to London by air.

In 1927 Illingworth went to the USA with his sister Phyllis; he worked for three months as a political cartoonist for Hearst newspapers in New York and also drew for *Life Magazine*. He returned to London to study briefly again under Tonks at the Slade (1928–9) and then in 1929 went back to Wales and took up freelancing once more, producing advertisements for the Beer is Best campaign and for such clients as Winsor and Newton, Grey's cigarettes, Symingtons soups, Eiffel Tower lemonade, and Wolsey underwear. About this time he also began to work for *Punch*, his first drawing (an illustration for someone else's joke) being published on 27 May 1931 and his first 'big cut' or whole-page political cartoon appearing on 21 April 1937.

When Poy (Percy Fearon; 1874–1949) retired as the *Daily Mail*'s political cartoonist in 1938, Illingworth applied for the job using the name MacGregor (his mother's maiden name) in the belief that his humorous work for *Punch* and other magazines would count against him. His ruse was detected but he got the job, his first drawing, *Feeding Time*, appearing on 30 October 1939. He remained as political cartoonist through eight editors until 1969 when he retired. He drew four cartoons a week for the paper (alternating after 1957 with Emmwood) and also contributed occasional journalism, illustrating his own international travel pieces. He also later worked briefly as political cartoonist on the weekly *Sunday Dispatch* (part of the same group), until it closed in 1961.

During the Second World War Illingworth served in the Home Guard and was later (1942–4) on night duty as an anti-aircraft gunner in Hyde Park. In the daytime he continued to work for the *Daily Mail*, *Punch*, and others and drew aerial leaflets and produced propaganda drawings for the Ministry of Information, Ministry of Labour, and Ministry of Defence. He also made a film (with NEB) called *The Birth of a Notion* (1945). (After the war *Daily Mail* cartoons by Illingworth and NEB were found in Hitler's bunker in Berlin.)

On the death of *Punch*'s principal cartoonist, Sir Bernard Partridge, in 1945 Illingworth became second cartoonist under E. H. Shepard. He was elected to the *Punch* Table in 1948, and in 1949 succeeded Shepard as principal cartoonist. Some of his best work for *Punch* was under the editorship of Malcolm Muggeridge (1953–7). After Muggeridge left, Illingworth did little work for the magazine but returned from 1962 until 1968, alternating as cartoonist with Norman Mansbridge.

Illingworth travelled widely, especially in the USA, where he met Lyndon B. Johnson and Richard Nixon, and contributed to *Washington Daily News*, *Life*, *Time* (including a cover in 1963), and others. After leaving *Punch* he retired to his home in Sussex but continued to travel, visiting the USA again in 1968 and, as president of the British Cartoonists' Association, was involved in its major cartoon exhibition 'Drawn and quartered', opened by Princess Margaret at the National Portrait Gallery, London, in 1970. In December 1973 he returned to Fleet Street briefly as a guest cartoonist on the *Sun* during Rigby's absence. This led to a commission from the *News of the World* to draw a weekly leader-page cartoon from 10 February 1974 until he finally retired from newspaper cartooning on 6 June 1976.

Perhaps Illingworth's most memorable cartoons were those drawn during the war, especially *The Bus* (*Daily Mail*, 7 May 1940) attacking Chamberlain, and the powerful symbolic colour drawing *The Combat* (*Punch*, 6 Nov 1939). His post-war work included a controversial attack on the ageing prime minister, Winston Churchill (*Punch*, 3 Feb 1954). Though he produced many magazine and advertising drawings, both in colour and black and white, his book illustrations were few. Unlike Low, Vicky, Strube, and others he did not produce collections of his cartoons, but seventy-one of his *Daily Mail* drawings were published in *400 Famous Cartoons from the Daily Mail, Evening News, Sunday Dispatch* (1944). He had few solo exhibitions of his drawings, the most notable being at: Lewis's Stores, Glasgow (1943); Wiggin Gallery, Boston Public Library, Massachusetts (1970), including a catalogue *Illingworth on Target* by Draper Hill; and the Arts Club, Dover Street, London (1971), organized by Dr Frank Hoar (the cartoonist Acanthus).

Illingworth always wanted to be a cartoonist and early influences included the magazine illustrator Frank Craig (whose paintings hung in County Hall, Cardiff) and the artists of *Punch*. As well as drawing in pen, brush and ink, and watercolour, he used crayon and was a pioneer in the use of scraperboard in cartoons. Though a political cartoonist and broadly in sympathy with the Conservative Party line of the *Daily Mail*, he was not politically committed and mistrusted zealots of any kind. None the less he wrote a course on political cartoons for Percy Bradshaw's Press Art School and influenced other political cartoonists such as Trog (Wally Fawkes)—who depicted him as the Welsh farmer character Organ Morgan in the satirical strip 'Flook' in the 1970s. Praised by Sir Alfred Munnings, Illingworth held that in art 'You should represent the absolute truth even if you distort it' (*The Observer*, 23 Aug 1970) and said his cartoons gave people 'symbols to think with' (*Queen*, 12 June 1962). He rarely used models and disliked drawing caricatures of women. Illingworth was described by William Hewison (*Punch*'s art editor, 1960–84) as having a 'faultless pen-and-ink technique, a technique which is essentially naturalistic yet masterly in its variety of textures, arrangement of tones, and subtle

atmospheric perspective' (Hewison, 68–9) and in his *Guardian* obituary Malcolm Muggeridge believed that Illingworth's cartoons would last longer than Low's: 'Illingworth's go deeper, becoming, at their best, satire in the grand style rather than mischievous quips; strategic rather than practical' (*The Guardian*, 22 Dec 1979).

Voted political and social cartoonist of the year by the Cartoonists' Club of Great Britain in 1962 and given a special award for distinguished services to cartooning in 1965, Illingworth was the first president of the British Cartoonists' Association when it was founded in 1966. In addition he was made an honorary DLitt by the University of Kent (1975). He was a member of the Toby Club, Chelsea Arts Club, and the Royal Automobile Club.

Illingworth never married, calling himself 'an optimistic bachelor', but lived for many years with his long-term companion Enid Ratcliff, whom he met in 1936 when she had leased him a flat in Bayswater (she later worked for the art agency Clement Danes). In appearance he had bright red hair in his youth and very large bushy eyebrows overhanging blue eyes. He wore glasses when drawing and spoke softly with a strong Welsh accent. Illingworth had an operation for gallstones in 1979 and later suffered from a stroke. He died in Hastings Hospital on 20 December 1979. His funeral was held at Salehurst church, Sussex, on 31 December 1979 and he was cremated in Hastings. A memorial service was later held in St Bride's, Fleet Street, on 26 February 1980. Illingworth's drawings are much sought after by cartoonists and cartoon historians. Examples of his drawings are in the Swann Collection, New York; the British Museum and the Victoria and Albert Museum, London; the Royal Collection, and several private collections in England and America.

MARK BRYANT

Sources R. Illingworth, 'Lived beloved and died lamented', typescript, priv. coll. [Illingworth family history] · taped interviews with Illingworth made by Francis Wilford-Smith (Smilby) and Keith Mackenzie · private information (2004) [Wally Fawkes, Nicholas Garland, Bill Hewison] · D. Hill, *Illingworth on target* (1970) [exhibition catalogue, Boston Public Library, MA] · M. Bryant, *Dictionary of twentieth-century British cartoonists and caricaturists* (2000) · M. Bryant and S. Heneage, eds., *Dictionary of British cartoonists and caricaturists, 1730–1980* (1994) · M. Horn, ed., *The world encyclopedia of cartoons* (1980) · A. Horne, *The dictionary of 20th century British book illustrators* (1994) · P. V. Bradshaw, *They make us smile* (1942) · W. Hewison, *The cartoon connection* (1977) · M. Bateman, *Funny way to earn a living: a book of cartoons and cartoonists* (1966) · W. Feaver, *Masters of caricature: from Hogarth and Gillray to Scarfe and Levine*, ed. A. Green (1981) · R. G. G. Price, *A history of Punch* (1957) · WWW

Archives NL Wales, *Daily Mail* cartoons, and letters · University of Kent, Canterbury, cartoons, letters, photographs, tape recordings | Daily Mail Archive, London, press cuttings · Punch Library, London, letters | FILM 'Here & now', interview, Rediffusion TV, 17 Aug 1962 · *The birth of a notion*, film (with Neb [Ronald Niebour]), 1945 | SOUND 'Two of a kind', Illingworth and Vicky, BBC Radio Home Service, 6 March 1962 · Desert island discs, BBC Radio, March 1963

Likenesses G. E. Le Pelley, photograph, 1964, repro. in Hill, *Illingworth on target*, frontispiece · K. Jonzen, bronze head, RA · Joss, caricatures · Trog, caricatures · photographs, University of Kent · photographs, Daily Mail Archive, London

Illingworth, Ronald Stanley (1909–1990), expert in child health, was born on 7 October 1909 in Harrogate, Yorkshire, the younger son and youngest of the three children of Herbert Edward Illingworth, architect, and his wife, Ellen Brayshaw. He was educated at Clifton House School in Harrogate and at Bradford grammar school, and went with a West Riding scholarship in classics to read medicine at Leeds University. He graduated MB, ChB in 1934. In the following five years he held various posts and obtained the MD and MRCP in 1937, and the DPH with distinction and DCH in 1938. He worked at the Hospital for Sick Children in Great Ormond Street, London, before taking up a Nuffield research studentship at Oxford in 1939. He joined the Royal Army Medical Corps in 1941 and by the end of the Second World War was a lieutenant-colonel and in charge of a medical division in the Middle East.

After the war Illingworth worked at the Hammersmith and Great Ormond Street hospitals in 1946, before going to the USA on a postponed Rockefeller research fellowship. In 1947 he married Cynthia, a paediatrician, daughter of Arthur Blenkinsop Redhead, engineer. They had one son and two daughters, and all the family were fellows or members of the Royal College of Physicians.

Also in 1947, the year he became an FRCP, he was appointed to the foundation chair of child health at the University of Sheffield. Over the next twenty-eight years he made the Sheffield Children's Hospital and his department of child health a port of call for aspirant academics and future consultants. When he arrived at Sheffield the department was in a near derelict house, and from there he led a team of clinical academics, which at any one time was composed of a stimulating mixture of doctors from home and abroad. Illingworth possessed a fine instinct for picking future leaders in paediatrics and child health. In the post-war years he was one of the medical magnets which drew bright young men from all over the empire and Commonwealth to the Sheffield Children's Hospital. When he retired in 1975 no fewer than fifteen of his former staff had become full professors and two had become ministers of health in their own countries.

Illingworth was an astute clinician and meticulous clinical researcher. By the time the endemic diseases of rheumatic fever, tuberculosis, and rickets had disappeared, he had become the foremost clinical expert on developmental paediatrics. It was in this area of clinical practice that he left his greatest legacy, through his prodigious output of papers and books. He had more than 650 publications, including forty-six translations of new editions of his books. He was undoubtedly the most widely read paediatrician of his time. His best-known books are *The Normal Child* (first published 1953; ten editions in all), *The Development of the Infant and Young Child* (1960, nine editions), and *Common Symptoms of Disease in Children* (1967, nine editions), all three of which were translated into many languages. He had an eminently readable style of writing, being economical with words and precise in their use. His writings were a model of clarity and very popular with students and postgraduate scholars.

Illingworth's hobby of photography, for which he received over seventy awards, was practised to a high professional standard. He was awarded the fellowship of the Royal Photographic Society in 1936, having exhibited at its annual international exhibition while still a medical student. His superb use of illustrated material, combined with his effortless and lucid style of delivery, made him a much sought-after lecturer. He gave more than 500 invited lectures, including more than 180 abroad in places as far apart as the USSR and South Africa. On his eightieth birthday in 1989 he gave masterly lectures on medical education and walking in the Alps, without recourse to notes and, as always, illuminated by admirable photographic material.

Illingworth served on major committees of the Medical Research Council and Department of Health, and was the paediatric adviser to the parliamentary commissioner (ombudsman). For twenty-six years he was a member of the council of the Medical Defence Union. He was uncompromisingly honest in his expression of opinion whether in court, committee, or personal discussion. Illingworth was not a 'clubbable' person, for he was very modest and avoided self-publicity. He was elected an honorary fellow of five foreign academies of paediatrics and received the Aldrich award and medal of the American Academy of Pediatrics (1978). He also received the Spence medal of the British Paediatric Association (1979) and the Dawson Williams prize of the British Medical Association (1981). He was awarded the freedom of the city of Sheffield and honorary doctorates from Baghdad (1975), Sheffield (1976), and Leeds (1982). He was never awarded any civil honour, though he had fought long and hard to develop and protect hospital services for children. He may well have antagonized those in authority who were determined to see an end to children's hospitals in the 1950s and 1960s. After he retired in 1975 he started anew as a clinical medical officer, running a well baby clinic in Derbyshire, and he published a further seventy worthwhile papers and new revised editions of his books.

Illingworth was of medium height and relatively slender build, and could be of forbidding mien. With the exception of his taste in ties, his style of dress was subdued. He died in Bergen, Norway, on 4 June 1990 while on holiday, among the mountains and lakes where he had been so fond of walking and taking photographs.

FRANK HARRIS, *rev.*

Sources *BMJ* (23 June 1990), 1644 · *The Lancet* (21 July 1990) · personal knowledge (1996) · *CGPLA Eng. & Wales* (1990)
Wealth at death £532,004: probate, 10 Sept 1990, *CGPLA Eng. & Wales*

Illingworth, William (*bap.* 1764, *d.* 1845), archivist, baptized at St Mary's, Nottingham, on 3 January 1764, was the third son of William Illingworth (*d.* 1782), tradesman, of Nottingham, and his wife, Elizabeth. After attending Nottingham and (from 1779) Manchester grammar schools, William was articled to a Nottingham attorney named Story. By 1788 he had established himself in practice in London as an attorney of the king's bench. In 1800 he published a learned *Inquiry into the Laws, Antient and Modern, Respecting Forestalling, Regrating, and Ingrossing*. His skill in deciphering manuscripts led to his being appointed in the same year a subcommissioner on public records. He transcribed and collated the *Statutes of the Realm* from Magna Carta to nearly the end of the reign of Henry VIII; transcribed and printed the *Quo warranto Pleadings* (1818) and the *Hundred Rolls* (1812–18), and wrote the preface and compiled in Latin the index rerum to the *Abbreviatio placitorum* (1811). With John Caley he edited the *Testa de Nevill* (1807), and assisted in the preparation of the first volume of the *Rotuli Scotiae* (1814). He sorted and arranged the records in the chapter house at Westminster, and in 1808 drew up a press catalogue of their contents. His *Index cartarum de Scotia* in the chapter house was privately printed in folio by Sir Thomas Phillipps at Middle Hill about 1840. With T. E. Tomlins he visited all the English and Irish cathedrals to search for original statutes. In Ireland he also examined the condition of public records.

About 1805 Illingworth was chosen deputy keeper of the records in the Tower of London, under Samuel Lysons. His notoriously bad temper subsequently hindered his advancement, but his unrivalled knowledge with old law and records was several times exhibited during court cases: in the case of *Roe v. Brenton*, he produced from the lord treasurer's remembrancer's office an important extent of the assessionable manors of the duchy of Cornwall in the reign of Edward II, and in the case of the *Mayor and corporation of Bristol* v. *Bush* he presented rolls of the reign of Henry VI, which established the rights of the corporation of Bristol to all the tolls upon shipping coming in and out of the port. Illingworth became a fellow of the Society of Antiquaries of London in 1805.

When Henry Petrie succeeded Lysons as keeper in August 1819, he refused to retain Illingworth as deputy keeper, although he offered to allow him to remain as his 'clerk'. Illingworth objected to this title and resigned. He then established himself as a record agent and translator. On 25 June 1825 he entered himself at Gray's Inn, but was not called to the bar. In expectation of becoming a subcommissioner under the new record commission at Christmas 1832, he drew up for the private use of the commissioners, in May 1831, *Observations on the public records of the four courts at Westminster, and on the measures recommended by the committee of the House of Commons in 1800 for rendering them more accessible to the public*, of which fifty copies were printed by the board. He advised the secretary, Charles Purton Cooper, on numerous issues, but never received the appointment, and alleged that Cooper made extensive use of his notes and suggestions without acknowledgement. Illingworth was examined by the second committee of the House of Commons respecting the record commissioners on 2 March 1836. In his later years Illingworth became blind and fell into poverty; a subscription was made for him at the Incorporated Law Society in Chancery Lane. He died at 13 Brooksby Street, south Islington, on 21 February 1845.

William's elder brother **Cayley Illingworth** (*c*.1758–1823) was educated at Pembroke College, Oxford, and graduated BA in 1781, proceeding MA in 1787, and DD in 1811. In 1783 he was presented to the rectory of Scampton

in Lincolnshire, of which parish he wrote a topographical history, published in 1808. He subsequently held other livings in the county, and was a prebendary of Lincoln Cathedral from 1802 to 1808, when he became archdeacon of nearby Stow. On 8 May 1783 he married Sophia Harvey, with whom he had two sons and four daughters. He was elected FSA in 1809, and died at Scampton on 28 August 1823, his wife surviving him.

GORDON GOODWIN, rev. BERNARD NURSE

Sources J. F. Smith, ed., *The admission register of the Manchester School, with some notes of the more distinguished scholars*, 2, Chetham Society, 73 (1868) · 'Select committee on … the record commission: minutes of evidence and appendix', *Parl. papers* (1836), 16.1–937, no. 565 · C. P. Cooper, *Papers and documents relating to the evidence of certain witnesses* (1837) · J. Foster, *The register of admissions to Gray's Inn, 1521–1889, together with the register of marriages in Gray's Inn chapel, 1695–1754* (privately printed, London, 1889) · Browne's *General Law List* (1788) · Foster, *Alum. Oxon.* · *GM*, 1st ser., 53 (1783), 451 [marriage of Cayley Illingworth and Sophia Harvey] · *GM*, 1st ser., 93/2 (1823), 279

Archives BL, translation of Domesday of Ipswich, Add. MS 25341 · NL Scot., calendar of records in Westminster Chapter House

Illtud [St Illtud, Illtyd] (*fl.* **5th–6th cent.**), abbot of Llantwit Major, the monastery in the south of Glamorgan of which he was also patron, was famous during the middle ages (and perhaps in his own lifetime) for his erudition and wisdom. His school at Llantwit is said to have attracted to him such renowned disciples as saints David, Gildas, Samson of Dol, Paul (Paulus Aurelianus), and Leonorius of St Lunaire. Analysis of ecclesiastical dedications to Illtud shows that, next to St Cadog, he was the most important saint whose cult was based in south-east Wales. Information relating to his life comes almost entirely from later hagiographical sources and is therefore of dubious historical reliability. His own extant Latin life, probably composed at Llantwit no earlier than *c*.1140 and preserved in BL, Cotton MS Vespasian A.xiv, is extremely derivative; and the earlier traditions recorded in two Breton saints' lives—that of St Samson (now thought to have been composed *c*.750), chapters 7–12, and that of St Paul of St Pol-de-Léon (written by Wrmonoc in 884), chapters 2–5—are perhaps more useful up to a point.

The account of Illtud's miraculous encounter with a floating altar given among the *Mirabilia* appended to the *Historia Brittonum*, compiled *c*.830, is the earliest surviving notice from Wales of the saint. The *Vita sancti Samsonis* describes how at the age of five Samson was brought to the master Eltut, 'the most learned of all the Britons', and was ordained deacon by him, and adds that Illtud had himself been a disciple of St Germanus of Auxerre, by whom he had been ordained. This synchronism would suggest that Illtud was a youth in either 429 or *c*.445 (the dates of Germanus's two visits to Britain), in which case he must have been of advanced years when Samson (who is known to have attended the Synod of Paris in 561 or 562) entered Llantwit. This chronology, though stretched, is not wholly impossible, but equally it may encourage suspicion regarding Illtud's connection to Germanus. The account of how two of Illtud's nephews resident at Llantwit conspired unsuccessfully against Samson, since one of them, as a presbyter, might be 'deprived of his hereditary right in the monastery' by Samson, possibly demonstrates something of the internal organization of Illtud's church. Samson's life also contains a detailed description of Illtud's death at Llantwit. The early chapters of Wrmonoc's *Vita sancti Pauli* similarly describe the education of its subject at Llantwit but imply that Paul was first brought to Illtud on Caldy Island: this has been taken to show that Illtud's first hermitage was on the island, but it may rather have arisen from a textual error. A completely separate tradition about Illtud is preserved in the twelfth-century life of St Cadog by Lifris of Llancarfan, which recounts that he had been a veteran warrior who was ordained through the influence of Cadog and thus became his disciple. This tradition probably underlies Illtud's later epithet Marchog ('horseman', 'knight') but probably reveals more about the rivalry between the houses of Llantwit and Llancarfan in the twelfth century than it does about Illtud's origins.

The extant *Vita sancti Illtuti* seems to be a mixture of local Llantwit traditions, such as the date of his death as 6 November, with material extracted, often very clumsily, from earlier saints' lives. For example, the claims that Illtud was son of a Breton warrior Bicanus and of Rhieinwylydd, daughter of Anflawdd 'King of the Britons', and thus a cousin of King Arthur, are no doubt wholly fictional. Indeed, the detailed episodes of the life are of interest from a hagiographical rather than historical perspective. Archaeology offers little extra help in this regard. There are no surviving traces of Illtud's original monastic site at Llantwit Major and, while the later insertion of Christian burials at the nearby Roman villa (abandoned *c*.350) have been connected by some scholars with the saint or his community, there is no direct evidence to support this view. The handful of inscribed memorial stones housed in the present church are of a later date, possibly eighth century, although one contains the name form Iltuti. The cult of Illtud in Wales, like that of Cadog, is focused on the south-east and, in addition to some dedications near Llantwit itself (including Llantrithyd and Llanhari), follows the coastal routes into Wales (on the Gower peninsula and the opposite Carmarthenshire coast) and the inland routes (through north Glamorgan and Brecon). Otherwise, there is one outlying dedication to him at Llanelltyd, near Dolgellau in Merioneth. Illtud has no known dedications in Cornwall, but has seven or eight in Brittany, in the dioceses of Léon, Tréguier, and Vannes, which appear to parallel those of St Tudwal.

DAVID E. THORNTON

Sources A. W. Wade-Evans, ed. and trans., *Vitae sanctorum Britanniae et genealogiae* (1944) [incl. twelfth-century life of Illtud] · *La vie ancienne de Saint Samson de Dol* ('Vita Sancti Samsonis episcopi Dolensis'), ed. and trans. P. Flobert (1997) · *Gildae de excidio Britanniae / Gildas' the ruin of Britain*, ed. H. Williams (1899) · G. H. Doble, *The saints of Cornwall*, pt 1 (1960) · G. H. Doble, *Lives of the Welsh saints*, ed. D. S. Evans (1971) · E. G. Bowen, *The settlements of the Celtic saints in Wales*, 2nd edn (1956) · V. E. Nash-Williams, *The early Christian monuments of Wales* (1950) · A. H. A. Hogg, 'The Llantwit Major villa: a reconsideration of the evidence', *Britannia*, 5 (1974), 225–50

Image, Selwyn (1849–1930), designer, was born at Bodiam, Sussex, on 17 February 1849, the second son of the Revd John Image, vicar of Bodiam, and his wife, Mary Hinds. The family had emigrated from France on the revocation of the edict of Nantes in 1685. Image was educated at Marlborough College, Wiltshire, where his artistic nature was first evident, and proceeded to New College, Oxford, as an exhibitioner in 1868, graduating BA in 1872, and MA in 1875. For the rest of his life he worked in London. At Oxford, Image studied drawing under John Ruskin, who was appointed the first Slade professor of fine art in 1870. He later stated that, 'Whatever small power of design I possess, I date the dawn of it from that lesson' (Jervis, 246).

In 1872 Image was ordained deacon, and priest in the following year. He was successively curate of All Hallows, Tottenham (1872–7), and of St Anne's, Soho (1877–80). He continued to design and exhibited his designs for stained glass at the Paris Exhibition of 1878. In 1881 he shared a studio with Ruskin's assistant, Arthur Burgess, and resigned from holy orders the following year.

Image was interested in design of all sorts, but he became best-known for his designs for stained glass, remarkable for their austere dignity and a rare feeling for the capacities and limitations of the medium. The west window of St Luke's, Camberwell, four archangels in a window of Mortehoe church, Devon (for which he later designed a mosaic), two windows in Marlborough College chapel, and one in memory of Bishop Lancelot Andrewes in Gray's Inn chapel, are his most important works of this kind. He also designed decorative panels for the Century Guild, founded by his friend A. H. Mackmurdo in 1883, which undertook the designing of houses and furniture, and published a magazine, the *Century Guild Hobby-Horse* (continued as the *Hobby Horse*), for which Image designed the cover (1886) and to which he contributed tail-pieces as well as poems and essays. During the 1890s he designed a number of decorative title-pages, covers, and bindings for books. In 1892–3 he designed a fine Greek type for the publishers Macmillan. He also designed embroideries for the Royal School of Needlework. Image married in 1901 Janet McHale, youngest daughter of Thomas Hanwell, of London; they had no children.

In later life Image devoted much time to lecturing on art, to landscape drawing and to watercolour painting. He found his favourite motifs in Epping Forest, which he also frequented on moth-hunting expeditions, for he was an ardent entomologist and made a collection of British butterflies, exquisitely arranged and labelled, now in the Hope entomological collections at the University of Oxford Museum of Natural History. In 1894 he published *Poems and Carols*, and he continued writing occasional poems until his death. In 1896 he assisted with the decoration of the first harpsichord made by Arnold Dolmetsch. In 1900 Image was elected master of the Art Workers' Guild, and in 1910 Slade professor of fine art at Oxford, holding the latter post until 1916. He was a member of the

Design and Industries Association. He was happiest in lecturing on English artists, such as Thomas Bewick and Thomas Rowlandson, for whom he had special admiration. Lawrence Binyon wrote of him:

> Image would have produced more original work had he not always been at the service of his friends and ready to undertake labours of love. A selection of his *Poems* and a selection of his *Letters* were published in 1932, after his death, both edited by A. H. Mackmurdo, and both containing a photographic portrait. His beautiful penmanship added to the charm of his letters. In conversation the wisdom and sweetness of his nature, his zest in life, and the fervour of his convictions, were even more intimately revealed. There was choiceness and a sense of beauty in all he wrote, said, and produced. (*DNB*)

He died at his home at 78 Parkhurst Road, Holloway, London, on 21 August 1930; he was survived by his wife. Drawings by him are in the British Museum and the Victoria and Albert Museum, London, and the Ashmolean Museum, Oxford; his cartoons for stained glass are in public collections at Birmingham, Glasgow, Newcastle, Nottingham, Bristol, Dublin, and Melbourne.

HELEN CAROLINE JONES

Sources *DNB* · A. H. Mackmurdo, ed., *Century Guild Hobbyhorse* (1884) [engravings incl. pls. and title-page designed by S. Image] · A. H. Mackmurdo, ed., *Selwyn Image letters* (1932) · S. Image, *The art of dancing: on a question of dress* (1891) · S. Image, 'Colour in relation to internal decoration', *National Association for the Advancement of Art Transactions* (1890), 68–77 · S. Image, 'Of designing for the art of embroidery', in *Arts and Crafts essays*, Arts and Crafts Exhibition Society (1893), 414–20 · S. Image, 'Cartoons for stained glass', *Practical designing*, ed. J. White (1893), 161 · J. Mawer, 'Image, Selwyn', *The dictionary of art*, ed. J. Turner (1996) · S. Image, 'Architecture in paintings (with discussion)', *Architectural Association Journal*, 26 (1911), 112 · S. Image, introduction, in H. L. de Boisbaudran, *The training of the memory in art and the education of the artist* (1911) · *The poems of Selwyn Image* (1932) · S. Image, 'Cosmopolitan art, a friendly dispute between Mr Selwyn Image and Mr Lewis F. Day', *Art Journal*, new ser., 22 (1902), 374–5 · *CGPLA Eng. & Wales* (1930) · S. Jervis, *The Penguin dictionary of design and designers* (1984) · L. F. Day, 'How to make the most of a museum', *Journal of the Royal Society of Arts*, 56 (1907–8), 146–55
Archives Bodl. Oxf., corresp., poems, and MSS · Oxf. U. Mus. NH, notebooks · Royal Entomological Society of London, entomological notebook · William Morris Gallery, London, papers | LUL, letters and poems to T. S. Moore · V&A NAL, poems and letters to C. W. Whall
Likenesses W. S. Frith, bust, Art Workers' Guild, London
Wealth at death £185 18s. 3d.: probate, 21 Nov 1930, *CGPLA Eng. & Wales*

Image, Thomas (*bap.* 1772, *d.* 1856), geologist, baptized on 7 August 1772 at Peterborough, was the son of the Revd John Image (1747–1786), vicar of St John the Baptist, Peterborough, and rector of Etton, Cambridgeshire, and his wife, Mary Cox. Image was educated at Corpus Christi College, Cambridge, and graduated BA 1795 and MA 1798. Following his ordination as a priest in 1797, he became curate of Etton, then rector of Whepstead (1798), and of Stanningfield (1809), both in Suffolk. On 15 January 1799 Image married Frances, daughter of the Revd John Freeman, rector of Lyndon, Rutland. The couple had at least one son, John (1820–1878), who in turn was father of the artist Selwyn Image (1849–1930).

From an early age, Image devoted his leisure to the study of geology. He spent more than fifty years diligently collecting minerals and fossils. His specimens in the museum at Whepstead fully illustrated the geology of the eastern counties of England. In 1843 he was elected FGS. In 1856 his collection of fossils was bought by the University of Cambridge (owing to the efforts of the geologist Adam Sedgwick), and is now housed in the Sedgwick Museum. Image died at Whepstead rectory on 8 April 1856 and was buried at Whepstead on 14 April. Following his death, his collection of minerals was sold by auction.

W. A. J. ARCHBOLD, *rev.* YOLANDA FOOTE

Sources *GM*, 3rd ser., 1 (1856), 534, 554 · *Cambridge Chronicle* (23 Feb 1856) · Venn, *Alum. Cant.* · *GM*, 1st ser., 69 (1799) · *GM*, 1st ser., 56 (1786) · *Clergy List* (1850) · Ward, *Men of the reign* · *IGI* · parish register (burial), Whepstead, Suffolk, Suffolk RO, Bury St Edmunds · private information (2004) [W. Bradford]

Imhoff, von. For this title name *see* Hastings, Marian [Marian von Imhoff, Baroness von Imhoff] (1747–1837).

Imison, John (*d.* 1788), clockmaker and printer, was in business at Manchester in 1781–5 as a clock and watch maker, optician, and printer. His parentage is unknown, but it is known that he and his wife, Mary, had at least one child, a daughter, Zillah (*bap.* 1781). A report is given by Loomes of an 'arched brass-dial long-case clock … in carved case signed "Imison-Mossley"', while a London watch hallmarked 1786 is recorded by Baillie (Loomes, 110, 192). Lemoine states that 'the ingenious Imisson … among other pursuits made some progress in the art of letter-founding, and actually printed several small popular novels at Manchester, with woodcuts cut by himself'. *The History of the Lives, Acts, and Martyrdoms of those Blessed Christians* was printed by Imison at Black Swan Yard, Smithy Door, Manchester, in 1785. Other imprints include *Drill Husbandry Perfected* by the Revd James Cooke (*c.*1783), Richard Falconer's *Voyages* (1785), and *The Politick Squire's Garland*, an undated chapbook. Imison was also an author. His main work was *The School of Arts, or, An Introduction to Useful Knowledge* (1785). This ran to four editions, and was later issued as *Elements of Science and Art*. A portion of the work was separately issued too, as *A Treatise on the Mechanical Powers* (1787). Imison also wrote *A Compendium of Arithmetic* (1787) and a pamphlet on *The Construction and Use of the Barometer or Weather Glass*, which he printed himself. By 1786 Imison had moved to London, where he died on 16 August 1788. Lemoine records his death incorrectly as occurring in 1791.

C. W. SUTTON, *rev.* JULIE RAMWELL

Sources H. Lemoine, *Typographical antiquities* (1797), 81 · *GM*, 1st ser., 58 (1788) · *Manchester Mercury* (26 Aug 1788) · J. P. Earwaker, ed., *Local gleanings relating to Lancashire and Cheshire reprinted from the Manchester Courier*, rev. edn, 2 (Jan 1877–Dec 1878), 6,17,292, 298 · G. R. Axon, 'Ingenious Imisson', *Manchester City News* (9 March 1929) · B. Loomes, *Lancashire clocks and clockmakers* (1975) · G. H. Baillie, *Watchmakers and clockmakers of the world* (1929) · G. R. Axon, *The Manchester press before 1801: a list of books. pamphlets and broadsides printed in Manchester in the 18th century* (1931) · *IGI*

Imlah, John (1799–1846), poet and songwriter, was born on 15 November 1799, in Aberdeen, the son of Peter Imlah, a stabler, and his wife, Elizabeth. On completing his education at Aberdeen grammar school, he was apprenticed to a local music-seller as a piano-tuner, and ultimately gained an appointment with the London firm of Broadwood.

Imlah composed verse from boyhood, and published the collections *May Flowers* (1827) and *Poems and Songs* (1841). Several of his songs became popular, notably 'Oh gin I were where Gadie rins' and 'There lives a young lassie far down yon lang glen'. While visiting a brother in Jamaica, Imlah contracted yellow fever, and died in St James's, Jamaica, on 9 January 1846.

J. C. HADDEN, *rev.* DOUGLAS BROWN

Sources Irving, *Scots.* · C. Rogers, *The modern Scottish minstrel, or, The songs of Scotland of the past half-century*, 6 vols. (1855–7) · W. Walker, *The bards of Bon-Accord, 1375–1860* (1887) · bap. reg. Scot.

Imlay, Gilbert (1754–1828), land speculator and author, was born on 9 February 1754 in Monmouth county, New Jersey, the son of Peter Imlay, landowner. His upbringing remains obscure but it is known that he served as a paymaster and lieutenant in the American revolutionary army in the American War of Independence between 1777 and 1778 before being wounded in action. Following his military service Imlay moved to Kentucky and by 1783 he had acquired an interest in vast tracts of land in the area. Between 1784 and 1786 he became a deputy county surveyor and a renowned land speculator in Kentucky, through which dealings he acquired a close association with the likes of Daniel Boone and James Wilkinson. Imlay, however, was soon confronted with financial problems that required him to liquidate his holdings in 1786, after which he left Kentucky without trace. While his whereabouts for the next six years remains unknown it is most likely that he immediately left America bound for Europe. In the early months of 1792 he was probably in London where his first book, *A Topographical Description of the Western Territory of North America* (1792), was published. Styling himself on the book's title page as 'Commissioner for laying out lands in the Back Settlements', Imlay presents a series of letters designed to promote settlement in America. The book was well reviewed in the *British Critic* and *Monthly Review* of July 1792, and two further editions were printed in London in 1793 and 1797—the latter with substantial additions from John Filson, Thomas Hutchins, and others—as well as editions printed in Dublin and New York, and a German translation appearing in 1793. A similar textual format, encompassing a series of letters, was adopted in Imlay's novel *The Emigrant* (1793), published in London in three volumes. Capturing the lives of an emigrant English family in the Ohio valley and their relatives and friends in England, *The Emigrant* also criticized the discrimination against women in English law and the custom of marriage; this makes the contribution or at least the influence of Mary *Wollstonecraft (1759–1797), with whom Imlay was intimately connected by 1793, a distinct possibility. For Imlay, influenced by patriotic feeling and the utopian ideas of some of his radical associates in London, the purpose of *The Emigrant* was the portrayal of America as the ideal destination for an emigrant and

to place a mirror to their [the English] view, that they may behold the decay of those features which were once so lovely. And that they may take into consideration the establishing, by a more enlightened policy, laws that will in future prevent the sacrilege which the present practice of matrimonial engagements necessarily produces. (Emerson, 425)

The novel, however, never achieved any real literary prominence and for the most part it remains of interest to scholars more for the speculative involvement of Wollstonecraft than for its contribution to literature.

By the early months of 1793 Imlay was in Paris and through a letter of introduction from Thomas Cooper of Manchester he became acquainted with Brissot de Warville and the Girondist group. He presented to the French government two proposals to seize Spanish Louisiana and Brissot came to praise Imlay as someone 'very proper to give information on the manner of executing the plan' (Emerson, 418). His proposals, both dated 1792, outlined the strategic importance of Louisiana and her West Indian possessions to France, estimated the expense of carrying out the plot, and suggested that Americans were in need of rescuing from Spanish tyranny and should be encouraged to support France in any cause against despotism. Imlay's motives in the scheme are unclear, but he probably hoped to promote both his own and his country's well-being through it.

In France, Imlay was well connected through an established association with St Jean de Crèvecœur and an affiliation with a circle of radical Britons then residing in Paris which included Thomas Paine, Helen Maria Williams, and Thomas Christie. Through these mutual friends Imlay and Wollstonecraft struck an almost immediate union. She regarded their relationship in the same manner as a true marriage but apparently did not pursue a matrimonial tie with Imlay: knowing that he had no property she did not want to place an extra financial burden on him. Imlay appears to have had no intention of marrying Wollstonecraft though he allowed her to use his surname and declared her to be his spouse in order to afford her some protection as an American citizen in revolutionary France. At much the same time that France declared British subjects should be imprisoned, in August 1793, Wollstonecraft fell pregnant to Imlay. In the following month Imlay moved to Le Havre on business, and it was not until February 1794 that Wollstonecraft was able to join him. Their daughter, Fanny Imlay, was born in May 1794 but despite discussions about moving to the United States with Wollstonecraft and the baby, like the characters in *The Emigrant*, Imlay proved to be a less than attentive father and partner. In March and August 1794 he left Wollstonecraft to travel on business before moving to London in September. He was reunited with Wollstonecraft in April 1795, but his European business dealings were in disarray by this time and Wollstonecraft volunteered to settle matters in Sweden and Norway on his behalf. On her return to London in late 1795 she discovered that Imlay was with another woman of unknown identity, but believed by some to be an actress. Imlay's relationship with Wollstonecraft thereafter was distant and discordant and it is upon her accounts of their separation that his unflattering reputation has been based, Imlay having left no comparable personal papers.

Imlay travelled to Paris for three months in 1796 with his new partner, before returning to London where he had several passing meetings with Wollstonecraft. The remainder of Imlay's life remains shrouded in mystery, but some time after 1801 he apparently moved to the Isle of Jersey, where he died on 20 November 1828.

MICHAEL T. DAVIS

Sources O. F. Emerson, 'Notes on Gilbert Imlay, early American writer', *Publications of the Modern Language Association of America*, 39 (1924), 406–39 • J. P. McClure, 'Imlay, Gilbert', *ANB* • R. L. Rusk, 'The adventures of Gilbert Imlay', *Indiana University Studies*, 10, Study 57 (1923) • J. L. Fant, 'A study of Gilbert Imlay (1754–1828): his life and works', PhD diss., University of Pennsylvania, 1984 • *DNB*

Imms, Augustus Daniel (1880–1949), entomologist, was born on 24 August 1880 at Moseley, Worcestershire, the only son and elder child of Walter Imms, a member of the staff of Lloyds Bank. His mother, Mary Jane Daniel, was born in the United States, of British parents who returned to England a few years later. He was educated at St Edmund's College, Birmingham, but his schooldays, and indeed his whole working life, were constantly interrupted by attacks of asthma. Debarred from strenuous physical activity, he became interested in collecting insects and when, on leaving school, he joined the science classes at Mason College, Birmingham, the attraction of biology was such that he abandoned his father's intention that he should become an industrial chemist, and in 1903 graduated with second-class honours in zoology in the University of London.

After spending two years at Birmingham in research on the anatomy of fishes, Imms was awarded an 1851 Exhibition science scholarship and in 1905 entered Christ's College, Cambridge. From that time onwards Imms devoted himself entirely to entomology. After carrying out a fine piece of work on the anatomy of the larva of the *Anopheles* mosquito, for which he was awarded the Darwin prize of Christ's College (1907), and having obtained his BA, Cambridge, and DSc, Birmingham, in the same year, he accepted the newly established professorship of biology at the University of Allahabad. Here he had to build up his new department from the foundations. In 1911, when appointed forest entomologist to the government of India, with headquarters at Dehra Dun, he again had to design new laboratories.

In 1913 Imms left India for reasons of health and was appointed reader in agricultural entomology at the Victoria University, Manchester. The same year he married Georgiana Mary, daughter of T. W. French, resident magistrate of co. Tyrone, and first cousin of Sir John French. There were two daughters of the marriage. During the First World War he acted as crop-pest inspector and reporter for the Board of Agriculture and Fisheries.

In 1918 an entomological department was founded at Rothamsted Experimental Station in Harpenden, Hertfordshire, and Imms was appointed chief entomologist at the experimental station. Once more he had to plan and equip extensive laboratories, occupying the whole upper floor of the new Institute of Plant Pathology. During his time at Rothamsted, Imms's efforts were largely put into the writing of his famous textbook of entomology. In 1931 Imms was appointed to a newly established readership in entomology at Cambridge. He retired in 1945, becoming an honorary fellow of Downing College, of which he had been elected a fellow in 1940.

Imms's published researches, primarily on insect morphology, are limited in number. His main contribution to entomology was his books. The most important of these was his *General Textbook of Entomology*, first published in 1925, which passed through seven editions in his lifetime. This became at once the standard treatise in the English language, and introduced a more scientific outlook on the subject. Other books, including *Recent Advances in Entomology* (1931), *Outlines of Entomology* (1942), and *Insect Natural History*, added to the New Naturalist series in 1947, all helped to spread Imms's influence among a wide circle of entomologists.

Imms was a reserved man, and few people knew him intimately. But he was an excellent judge of promise in young research workers and the real investigator could count on him for unswerving support. He was elected FRS in 1929, was president of the Royal Entomological Society of London (1936–8), and (1930–31) of the Association of Economic (later Applied) Biologists, of which he was also a co-founder. He was an honorary member of the entomological societies of the Netherlands, Finland, and India, and in 1947 he was elected a foreign member of the American Academy of Arts and Sciences. He died at his home, Faldonside, Tipton St John, Sidmouth, on 3 April 1949, survived by his wife and daughters.

V. B. WIGGLESWORTH, rev. V. M. QUIRKE

Sources V. B. Wigglesworth, *Obits. FRS*, 6 (1948–9), 463–70 • W. H. Thorpe, 'Dr A. D. Imms', *Nature*, 163 (1949), 712–13 • personal knowledge (1959)
Archives ICL, corresp. with J. W. Munro • Royal Entomological Society of London, letters to C. J. Wainwright
Likenesses P. Drury, pencil drawing, 1945, U. Cam., department of zoology • black and white photograph, repro. in Wigglesworth, *Obits. FRS*, 463
Wealth at death £25,782 16s. 10d.: probate, 12 Sept 1949, *CGPLA Eng. & Wales*

Immyns, John (d. 1764), founder of the Madrigal Society, became a lawyer in his youth, but, reduced to poverty by dissolute living, he became clerk to a city attorney. He was an amanuensis of the composer and professor of music John Christopher Pepusch, and was copyist to the Academy of Ancient Music, of which he was an active member. At the age of forty he taught himself to play the lute using Thomas Mace's *Musick's Monument* (1676); he became sufficiently skilled to be appointed lutenist to the Chapel Royal in 1752, in succession to John Shore.

Immyns had a 'cracked counter-tenor voice' (Hawkins), and he was devoted to performing madrigals. In 1741 he founded the Madrigal Society, which has been in continuous existence ever since, the oldest musical association in the country. Its fourteen original members were mostly tradesmen and craftsmen, including some Spitalfields weavers. They met at the Twelve Bells alehouse in Bride Lane, Fleet Street, and sang the works of early composers such as Ruffo, Lassus, and Gesualdo, and the English madrigalists. By the nineteenth century, membership of the society had moved away from the labouring classes toward the aristocracy. Immyns was an enthusiastic collector of the musical manuscripts of the early composers, but had no taste for the music of his own time. He died of asthma in Coldbath Fields, London, on 15 April 1764. His son John was for some time organist of Surrey Chapel.

R. F. SHARP, *rev.* K. D. REYNOLDS

Sources N. Temperley, 'Immyns, John', *New Grove* · J. Hawkins, *A general history of the science and practice of music*, 5 vols. (1776)

Impey, Catherine (1847–1923), political activist and temperance reformer, was born at Street in Somerset on 13 August 1847. Her parents were Robert Impey (1820–1886), originally a tanner, who grew seeds, became an innovative farmer, and sold agricultural equipment, and his wife, Mary Hannah Clothier (1823–1895), whose father was a tanner. Catherine, their second daughter, attended a school for girls at Weston-super-Mare. The Impey family belonged to the Religious Society of Friends.

Catherine Impey (known as Katie) was active in the temperance movement with a special commitment to work on behalf of children. She served for over forty years as the treasurer of the village mission and Band of Hope in Street. She was also a vice-president of the Western Temperance League, an office-holder in the Independent Order of Good Templars (a fraternal temperance society), and a member of the Street Teetotal Society, the Somerset Band of Hope Union, and the British Women's Temperance Association. She travelled to North America several times for meetings of the Good Templars and of the Woman's Christian Temperance Union.

During the Good Templar schism of 1876–87 Impey served as honorary secretary of a British mission committee which attempted to organize black people on a nonracial basis in the former slave states, an enterprise financed almost entirely by Quakers. Initiated by Good Templars in England and Scotland opposed to racism, the schism combined conflicts over human rights and Good Templar constitutional procedures with a struggle for power within the order. During this period many prominent Good Templars visited her home. The celebrated black writer William Wells Brown was her guest at Street, and she stayed at his home while visiting Massachusetts. Impey was outraged when in 1886 Joseph Malins (1844–1926), the head of the Grand Lodge of England, negotiated an end to the schism on a basis of racial segregation, a compromise which she deplored as unchristian and contrary to Good Templar principles of brotherhood and sisterhood. Three years later she withdrew from the Good Templar order.

Devoting much of the rest of her life to the fight for racial equality, Impey had already started a monthly newssheet called *Anti-Caste* in 1888. It campaigned against the racial bigotry suffered by non-white peoples throughout the world, particularly in the British empire and the United States. Impey also belonged to the anti-slavery committee of the mid-Somerset monthly meeting of the Society of Friends and the British and Foreign Anti-Slavery Society.

In the early 1890s Impey acquired an ally, Isabelle Fyvie Mayo (1843–1914), a Scottish novelist. The two women invited Impey's friend Ida B. Wells, a former slave, to speak in Britain against the lynching of black Americans accused of such crimes as sexual offences against white women. Impey and Mayo organized the Society for the Recognition of the Universal Brotherhood of Man. Its organ, variously called *Fraternity* and the *Bond of Brotherhood*, first appeared simultaneously with *Anti-Caste* and then replaced it.

Impey fell in love with Mayo's Ceylonese protégé, a dentist named George Ferdinands, and in 1893 she wrote to him proposing marriage. She believed that racial difference made him hesitant to declare his own love. Ferdinands, who had no interest in marrying Impey, showed the letter to Mayo. Infuriated at Impey's initiative, Mayo severed her relations with Impey and tried unsuccessfully to make Wells do the same. Mayo wrote to Frederick Douglass and other prominent African-Americans in a vain attempt to turn them against their old friend. The breakup of the alliance between Impey and Mayo explains Impey's brief revival of *Anti-Caste* in 1894; it ceased publication in 1895.

In addition to her work for temperance and against racism Catherine Impey was active in local government. Serving on the Street urban district committee, the Wells poor-law board of guardians, and the Long Sutton school committee, she advocated women's suffrage in parliamentary elections.

Impey's family supported her throughout all her public and private controversies. Although at one time engaged to T. Beavan Clark, whose family operated a shoe factory at Street, Impey never married, and resided all her life at her family home. From 1879 she was a vegetarian; so apparently was the rest of the household, but meat was served to non-vegetarian guests. Long before their father's death in 1886, Impey's elder sister Ellen (or Nellie) took charge of the family seed business despite her poor health. The Impeys also attempted jam making but with little success.

Impey combined militancy with affability, near austerity with generosity. Outspoken and uncompromising, she had a gift for friendship and served local needs as well as worldwide humanitarian causes. By living simply, she found the income to maintain a furnished house for retired teachers and missionaries on furlough. A devout member of the Society of Friends, she wrote frequently for the monthly magazine of Street's Quaker community. Impey died at her home, 3 Wraxhill Road, Middle Leigh, Street, on 14 December 1923 after a short illness; she was buried in Street on 18 December.

DAVID M. FAHEY

Sources 'Dictionary of Quaker biography', RS Friends, Lond. [card index] · R. L. I. [R. L. Impey], 'Catherine Impey', *The Friend*, new ser., 64 (1924), 19 · V. Ware, *Beyond the pale: white women, racism and history* (1992) · D. M. Fahey, *Temperance and racism: John Bull,*

Johnny Reb, and the Good Templars (1996) · *Crusader for justice: the auto-biography of Ida B. Wells*, ed. A. M. Duster (1970) · E. A. Impey, *About the Impeys* (1963) · S. C. Morland, 'Catherine Impey and Ida B. Wells', 1987, priv. coll. · E. H. Cherrington and others, eds., *Standard encyclopedia of the alcohol problem*, 6 vols. (1924–30) · *The collected writings of Jessie Forsyth, 1847–1937*, ed. D. M. Fahey (1988) · *Clarks of Street, 1825–1950*, C. & J. Clark Ltd. (1950?) · private information (2004) · d. cert. · b. cert. · S. Stanley Holton, 'Segregation, racism and white women reformers: a transnational perspective, 1840–1930', 1999 [unpublished paper]

Archives Bodl. RH, anti-slavery MSS

Likenesses drawing, repro. in Fahey, *Temperance and racism* · photograph (with sister, Nellie), priv. coll.; repro. in Ware, *Beyond the pale*

Wealth at death £2660 13s. 6d.: probate, 14 Feb 1924, *CGPLA Eng. & Wales*

Impey, Sir Elijah (1732–1809), judge in India, was born on 13 June 1732 at Butterwick House, Hammersmith, the third and youngest son of Elijah Impey (1683–1756), merchant, and his second wife, Martha (1692–1776), daughter of James Fraser, secretary and registrar of the Royal Hospital, Chelsea, and his wife. Impey went to Westminster School in 1740, where he was a contemporary of Warren Hastings. In 1751 he was admitted to Lincoln's Inn and next year entered Trinity College, Cambridge, becoming a fellow in 1757. Impey was called to the bar in 1756 and practised for seventeen years on the western circuit. He was appointed recorder of Basingstoke in 1766. Impey married, on 18 January 1768, Mary, the daughter of Sir John Reade, bt, of Shipton Court, Oxfordshire [see Impey, Mary, Lady Impey (1749–1818)]. They had five sons and two daughters. Impey also had two illegitimate children with Elizabeth Curbyshire, including a son born in 1766. Mary joined her husband in Calcutta in 1777, where she became one of the earliest British patrons of Indian artists.

In 1773 the East India Regulating Act established the Bengal supreme council and a supreme court. Hastings was appointed governor-general and Impey chief justice. Impey was knighted on 30 March 1774, immediately before he and the three nominated puisne judges embarked for Calcutta, where they arrived in October. Structural and operational defects in both the court and the council soon became apparent: first, the court's jurisdiction and the council's powers were inadequately defined; second, consequent upon this, friction developed between the two bodies; third, the council, consisting of the governor-general and four councillors, was irreconcilably split into pro- and anti-Hastings factions, Philip Francis being particularly influential in the latter.

In March 1775 Impey and his colleagues became immersed in the litigation centred on Nandakumar, a Brahman who had charged Hastings with corruption. The outcome of the Nandakumar affair led the historian Lord Macaulay, reviewing a biography of Hastings in the *Edinburgh Review*, to repeat contemporary allegations that Hastings and Impey had conspired to perpetrate judicial murder in sanctioning Nandakumar's execution for forgery on 5 August 1775. The charges and counter-charges preceding Nandakumar's committal, the febrile political climate in which the trial took place, and the uncertainties surrounding the supreme court's jurisdiction ensured

Sir Elijah Impey (1732–1809), by Johan Zoffany, *c.*1771–2

that the two questions of motive and morality in his prosecution and sentence would long be debated, but Macaulay's widely disseminated rhetoric heightened a popular impression of Impey's partiality and subservience to Hastings.

Latterly the conspiracy theory has been largely discounted by historians and, in the context of an application of English law in unusual and unfamiliar circumstances, Impey's conduct of the trial has been adjudged fair and impartial. However, his refusal to allow a reprieve or a stay of execution when ample grounds existed is much more questionable. If, as has been argued, he wanted to assert the supremacy and independence of the court against a hostile executive council, his selfish want of compassion was matched, each for their own reasons, by the acquiescence of the other judges and the councillors.

In 1776 Impey, in collaboration with Hastings, drew up a plan to improve the system of justice in Bengal, and to reduce the growing discord between the supreme court and the supreme council, which he believed arose out of the absence of any constitution defining the limits of the organs of government. The plan was sent home but not acted upon by Lord North's government. Meanwhile, Impey sought a place on council, ostensibly to enable him to act as a bridge between court and council although he privately conceded that he needed to bolster his personal income.

Civil cases, especially revenue cases, were the main cause of dispute between the supreme court and the Bengal supreme council, and two cases in the years 1778 to 1780 precipitated a crisis. Impey wanted to extend the supreme court's jurisdiction into the provinces, and to try defendants who were neither inhabitants of Calcutta nor British subjects. This, he claimed, was necessary to protect Indians from the oppressions of East India Company officials and company courts, as in the Patna case (1778). Impey believed that the supreme court should determine who was and who was not amenable to its jurisdiction, while the supreme council claimed that its decision on this point was final and authentic. An impasse between court and council was reached during the Kasijora case (1779–80), but a temporary truce between Hastings and Francis in council signalled a reverse for Impey. The supreme court's jurisdiction was restricted to Calcutta and Impey's amity with Hastings was momentarily shaken. However, in the latter part of 1780 Hastings was again able to assume firm control of the council. In October, in a modification of the plans of 1776, he obtained council's agreement to offer Impey the superintendency of the *sadr diwani adalat*, or central civil court, which was serviced by councillors assisted by Indian officials. Hastings saw this as a means of alleviating differences between the supreme court and the supreme council, and a contribution to the co-ordination of the machinery of justice. Impey accepted Hastings's offer. To Macaulay it was a bribe to head off any further attempts at aggrandizement by the supreme court which made Impey 'rich, quiet and infamous' (Macaulay, 204). Although Impey took his salary, he set it aside while writing home to seek assurance that he had not acted improperly.

In his new role Impey, who was conversant with Persian and Hindustani, prepared a code of procedure for the *diwani adalats*, or district civil courts. In July 1781, partly for his health and partly to inspect the district *adalats*, he left Calcutta on a tour of Bengal and Bihar. Concurrently, Hastings left for Benares and Lucknow. At Hastings's request, Impey went to Benares, where he approved the former's punitive measures against Chet Singh, the raja of Benares, and took affidavits. He returned to Calcutta in December.

In May 1782, following consideration of the first report of the Commons select committee on the administration of justice in Bengal, the house resolved to recall Impey for having accepted the presidency of the *sadr diwani adalat*. His action was held to have infringed the provisions of the Regulating Act. He relinquished the appointment in November. Impey embarked for England on 3 December 1783, but did not resign the chief justiceship until 1787.

Impey made his London residence first in Grosvenor Street and then in Wimpole Street. He hoped to obtain a seat in parliament in order to strengthen his position against his adversaries, but did not succeed until 1790, when he was returned for New Romney, by which time the inquest into his conduct in India had been abandoned. This had been initiated on 12 December 1787 by Sir Gilbert Elliot, afterwards earl of Minto, who presented charges to the Commons which Impey repudiated in an address at the bar of the house on 4 February 1788. The first article of impeachment, which concerned the trial of Nandakumar,

was considered by a committee of the whole house on 7 and 9 May 1788. The motion was lost, and after a discussion on the Patna case on 27 May the impeachment was dropped.

Impey did not lack skill in the law but, as is intimated in the full and fleshy face represented in his portraits, he was complacent and unimaginative. In retirement he ultimately settled at Newick Park, Uckfield, Sussex. His financial position was only moderately good and in December 1801 he went to France to try to recover funds lost during the revolution. The resumption of war prevented his return until July 1804. He died at Newick Park on 1 October 1809 and was buried in St Paul's Chapel, Hammersmith.

T. H. BOWYER

Sources B. N. Pandey, *The introduction of English law into India: the career of Sir Elijah Impey in Bengal, 1774–1783* (1967) · original correspondence of Sir Elijah Impey, 1774–83, BL, Add. MSS 16259–16264 · E. B. Impey, *Memoirs of Sir Elijah Impey, knt* (1846) · [Lord Macaulay], *EdinR*, 74 (1841–2), 160–255 · T. Faulkner, *An historical and topographical account of Fulham* (1813) · *The parish of Hammersmith*, Survey of London, 6 (1915), 1–32 · L. S. Sutherland, 'New evidence on the Nandakuma trial', *EngHR*, 72 (1957), 438–65 · HoP, *Commons, 1790–1820* · *Old Westminsters*, 1.501 · W. P. Baildon, ed., *The records of the Honorable Society of Lincoln's Inn: admissions*, 1 (1896) · W. P. Baildon, ed., *The records of the Honorable Society of Lincoln's Inn: the black books*, 3 (1899) · Venn, *Alum. Cant.* · J. P. Losty, *Calcutta: city of palaces* (1990) · W. A. Shaw, *The knights of England*, 2 (1906)
Archives BL, corresp. and papers, Add. MSS 16259–16271 · BL OIOC, corresp. relating to India | BL, Hastings correspondence, Add. MSS 63090, 63104 · RA, corresp. with Ozias Humphry
Likenesses J. Zoffany, oils, *c*.1771–1772, NPG [*see illus.*] · T. Kettle, oils, 1775, High Court, Calcutta · J. Zoffany, oils, 1783, High Court, Calcutta · J. Zoffany, group portrait, *c*.1783–1784, Thyssen-Bornemisza Museum, Madrid; *see illus. in* Impey, Mary, Lady Impey (1749–1818) · T. Lawrence, pastel drawing, 1786, NPG · P. Roun junior, monument, 1809, St Paul's Church (formerly Chapel), Hammersmith, London
Wealth at death very modest; earned little by Indian service: Impey, *Memoirs of Sir Elijah Impey* · amassed immense wealth in India: GM, 79/2 (1809), 988

Impey, John (*d.* 1829), legal writer, was the only son of Robert Impey of Bedford. Admitted to the Middle Temple on 4 November 1771, he remained a member for nearly sixty years and practised as an attorney at 3 Inner Temple Lane. He was for many years, until 1813, one of the attorneys of the sheriff's court of London and Middlesex. John Thelwall, the lecturer, spent three and a half years of his unsettled youth in Impey's office, and acknowledged that Impey's 'only fault was swearing'. Impey and his wife, Susanna, had several children, one of whom, Walter John Impey, also became a legal writer. During the last three years of his life Impey lived in retirement at Hammersmith, where he died on 14 May 1829.

Impey's books contain the first systematic account of the practice of the two great common law courts, and in 1797 he related in a letter that he stood high as an authority on this subject even with the bench (BL, Add. MS 21507, fol. 311). He wrote *The new instructor clericalis, stating the authority, jurisdiction, and practice of the court of king's bench* (1782), which reached a tenth edition in 1823, and *The new instructor clericalis*, stating the authority, jurisdiction, and practice of the court of common pleas (1784), which reached a seventh edition in 1826. He also produced works on the offices of sheriff (1786) and coroner (1800; 5th edn, 1822), and on the role of the pleader (1794).

JAMES TAIT, rev. JONATHAN HARRIS

Sources letter of Impey, 7 Nov 1797, BL, Add. MS 21507, fol. 311 · H. A. C. Sturgess, ed., *Register of admissions to the Honourable Society of the Middle Temple, from the fifteenth century to the year 1944*, 1 (1949), 373 · *GM*, 1st ser., 99/2 (1829), 282 · *Clarke's New Law List* (1803–28) · PRO, PROB 11/1757/361 (will) · Mrs Thelwall, *The life of John Thelwall* (1837) · T. Lee, *A dictionary of the practice in civil actions, in the courts of King's bench and common pleas*, 2nd edn, 1 (1825), v · J. Thelwall, *Poems written chiefly in retirement*, 2nd edn (1801), xv–xviii

Impey [*née* Reade], **Mary**, **Lady Impey** (1749–1818), natural historian and patron of the arts, was born on 2 March 1749, the daughter of Sir John Reade (1721–1773) of Shipton Court, Oxfordshire, and his wife, Harriet, *née* Barker (*d.* 1811). She was the eldest of three children—the others, John and Thomas, being twins born in 1762. Of her early life nothing is known. On 18 January 1768 she married the rising barrister Elijah *Impey (1732–1809) at Hammersmith parish church (the parish church of the Impey family). Her husband, a bachelor of thirty-six, now brought to an end his long-standing relationship with another woman, Elizabeth Curbyshire, with whom he had two children, and he provided her with an annuity for life. Impey fully acknowledged his illegitimate children, but the effect of their existence on his young bride is not known. The newly married pair lived first in a retiring manner in a house in Essex Street off the Strand, while he pursued his career as a barrister. This was the happiest time of their life according to her son's recollection of his mother (E. B. Impey, 12). While her husband practised at the bar, and on the western circuit, Mary stayed at home

with their four children born before 1773, when Impey was made chief justice of Fort William in Bengal.

Leaving the infant children under the care of his brother Michael at Hammersmith, the newly knighted Sir Elijah and Lady Impey sailed with the other members of the new supreme court on the *Anson* from Portsmouth in April 1774, landing at Calcutta on 19 October. The Impeys took a large house south-east of Fort William, in a virtual rural location, off the road then known as Burying Ground Road (subsequently Park Street), surrounded by a deer park, formerly the garden (or country) house of Henry Vansittart, governor of Bengal from 1760 to 1764. According to H. E. A. Cotton, 'Time was when it was customary for wayfarers to form into large parties before braving the terrors of Burying Ground Road; and a guard of sepoys paraded nightly to scare away the dacoits and protect my Lord Chief Justice's person and property' (Cotton, 286).

The Impeys joined in Calcutta a society where the educated had unrivalled opportunities for new cultural and scientific pursuits. Sir Elijah had studied Persian with a munshi on the voyage out, and now began to collect Persian and Indian manuscripts and paintings, many from the nearest court studio at Murshidabad, the capital of Mughal Bengal. On all his collections is impressed his Persian seal, which he had had made in 1775. Lady Impey channelled her own investigative spirit, perhaps newly discovered through enforced leisure, into natural history, and kept birds and wild animals in the gardens of their mansion. Between 1777 and 1782 she commissioned a series (nearly 200 in all) of large drawings (mostly double folios) of her natural history collection from three Indian artists, Sheikh Zain al-Din (responsible for more than half the drawings), Bhavani Das, and Ram Das. The drawings are meticulously numbered and inscribed by clerks with

Mary Impey, Lady Impey (1749–1818), by Johan Zoffany, *c.*1783–4 [with her husband, Sir Elijah Impey, and their three children]

the names of the subjects in Persian, sometimes with an English equivalent if known, and described as being 'in the collection of Lady Impey' with the name of the artist (in Persian) and the date. Of the over 120 drawings whose whereabouts are now known, more than 100 are of birds.

The work commissioned by Lady Impey is important for two reasons. The bird drawings sometimes include the earliest depictions of Indian species, and were used by subsequent ornithologists to identify new species or new habitats for existing ones. John Latham (in the supplement of 1787 to his *General Synopsis of Birds*) often refers to the drawings, and cites Lady Impey's authority for information on both habitat and Indian name. Aesthetically also they are among the most beautiful bird drawings ever attempted, in which each bird is depicted from the life, perched not on the dead stump of European convention, but on a branch of the living tree which it frequented. They are painted life size where possible (with measurements where this would have been impractical). The three artists are described on the drawings as natives of Patna, whither the Murshidabad School had been transported with Nawab Kasim Ali in 1763. They used the Mughal technique of building up the bird's body feather by feather, creating passages of iridescent brilliance, but also suggesting the volume of the bird's body beneath. This unusual combination of scientific accuracy with Mughal technical expertise suggests that Lady Impey did much herself to create the style of the drawings. The careers of the artists are unrecorded before 1777 or after 1782, although the style they inaugurated continued in Calcutta under other patrons such as lords Wellesley and Valentia. On a more mundane level, Lady Impey's ornithological interest popularized for the table the Himalayan pheasant which is named after her.

Sir Elijah Impey was recalled in 1783. A further four children had been born to the couple in India, of whom the eldest died in infancy. Before their departure on 3 December of that year, the Impey family was painted on the terrace of their mansion by Zoffany (newly arrived in Calcutta) in one of his grand conversation pieces in which young Marian (*b*. 1778) dances to the music of a group of Indian musicians, while parents, siblings, ayahs, and servants look on. Both Lady Impey and Sir Elijah appear to have been interested in Indian music, since one of their major Indian albums was a *Ragamala* or set of pictures illustrating thirty-six of the ragas of Indian music. Lady Impey also had herself and her children painted in their rooms by her Indian artists.

The family arrived back in England in June 1784. One more child was born after their return, in February 1785, while their eldest son was married soon afterwards. There were eventually to be some thirty grandchildren in all. The reunited family lived on their return in Grosvenor Street, and then Wimpole Street, London, before finally settling in the country at Newick Park, near Lewes, Sussex. Both Sir Elijah and Lady Impey were in Paris in 1801–3, when her husband described her as becoming 'the complete Frenchwoman, gay as a butterfly, busy as a bee' (E. B. Impey, 28). They had great difficulty in securing a passport

after war was redeclared, but managed to get out of France via the Low Countries to Hamburg on passports signed by Bonaparte himself. Sir Elijah died at Newick Park in 1809. Beside a life interest in his estate, he left his wife 100 books of her choice, all his jewels, paintings, Asiatic and European drawings, furniture, horses, carriages, wine, gold, and silver plate. She died on 20 February 1818, and was buried like her husband in the family vault at Hammersmith parish church.   J. P. LOSTY

Sources E. B. Impey, *Memoirs of Sir Elijah Impey* (1846) • E. A. Impey, *About the Impeys* (1963) • H. E. A. Cotton, *Calcutta old and new: a historical and descriptive handbook to the city* (1907) • T. Falk and G. Hayter, *Birds in an Indian garden* (1984) [exhibition catalogue, London, June 12 – July 14 1984]
Likenesses T. Gainsborough, portrait, before 1774 • attrib. Shaykh Zain al-Din, portrait, *c*.1780, priv. coll. • J. Zoffany, group portrait, *c*.1783–1784, Thyssen-Bornemisza Museum, Madrid [*see illus.*]

Imray, James (1803–1870), hydrographer and stationer, was born on 16 May 1803 in Spitalfields, London, the third child and eldest son of the six children of James Imray (1761/2–1830), a Scottish dyer, and his wife, Elizabeth Cooper (1779/80–1842). In 1818, shortly before his fifteenth birthday, Imray was apprenticed to William Lukyn, a stationer, of George Street, Mansion House. Six years later, on 16 May 1824, he married Elizabeth Cutbill (1805–1836), the daughter of another Spitalfields silk family, and when their first child, Elisabeth Ann, was baptized in 1825 James described himself as a bookseller. In 1827 and 1828 he was trading briefly on his own account as a bookbinder specializing in account books, first in Cheapside and then at 116 Minories, the premises of the chart publisher Robert Blachford. There is no further record of his trading until 1835 when he opened in Budge Row, just west of Cannon Street, again specializing in account books. In 1836 he was also trading as a dealer in marine stores in Patriot Row, Bethnal Green; that year, on 24 October, Elizabeth died of consumption leaving him with three young children, but before the year was out he had returned to the Minories to join Michael Blachford as a partner in the Blachford chart publishing business.

Blachford and Imray traded together for ten years and brought a new vitality to the business, which had been lagging sadly behind its rivals; they enlarged and updated the chart list, published new sailing directions, and opened a nautical academy. During these years Imray was still involved in stationery, with a share in the Budge Row account book business, having taken in a partner, William Fitch, and an interest in another unsuccessful stationery venture. In 1846 Imray sold out to Fitch and committed himself to a future in chart publishing, acquiring Michael Blachford's share of the chart business and becoming sole proprietor. A period of rapid growth followed and in 1850 he moved to larger premises at 102 Minories. Imray's own particular interest was in chart compilation and he expanded his list beyond home trade waters with new charts of American and eastern seas. The publication of sailing directions, the manufacture and sale of nautical instruments (with which the firm had widened its services to navigators), and the nautical academy all flourished. In 1854, when his elder son, James Frederick Imray (1829–1891), became a partner in the book and instrument sides of the business, the firm became James Imray & Son.

By the 1860s Imray had become the leading British commercial chart publisher and was operating from three premises: 89 Minories housed chart publication, 102 Minories chart and books sales and the nautical academy, and 1 Postern Row the instrument shop. The majority of the fast-growing British merchant fleet used his charts because, although accurate Admiralty charts were now available, merchant shipmasters still preferred the charts of commercial publishers, named 'blue backs' from their distinctive blue paper backing, and particularly James Imray's blue backs. They were popular because they retained the traditional format of a small-scale general chart with many large-scale insets of harbours. They were designed to answer the needs of a particular voyage conveniently and used modern survey material, now available from Admiralty and foreign government charts. They were more expensive than Admiralty charts, but fewer of them were needed because for some voyages they provided all that was required on a single chart; they were also accompanied by complementary sailing directions.

As official surveys of Australia, New Zealand, the northwest coast of America, and the coast of Chile became available, Imray used them to compile charts designed for wool clippers, gold rush ships, and copper and nitrate clippers. As the influence of the East India Company waned and eastern seas opened to all British ships he published new charts of the Indian and Pacific oceans, followed by popular series of larger scale charts for the intricate passages through the eastern archipelago and on to China. Charts for particular trades were promoted with labels such as 'Rice ports of India' and 'Cotton ports of Georgia'. Before he died his catalogue listed over 150 charts. He also led the defence of the private publishers against increasing Admiralty competition and in 1865 acquired the *Mercantile Marine Magazine*, the mouthpiece of the private publishers, edited by his navigation teacher W. H. Rosser.

Imray's success was founded on shrewd business skills and an appreciation of his customers' needs. Although he expanded the firm's other activities his heart was in chart publishing and he always kept personal control of this. He was the leading private chart publisher of the day, standing head and shoulders above his competitors. His name was virtually synonymous with the term 'blue back': Thomas Gray, of the marine department of the Board of Trade, wrote in 1875 that 'I only know of Imray's charts (i.e. the blue backs) as running the Admiralty charts close' (*Memorandum relating to the Supply and Correction of Charts*, Board of Trade departmental paper, no. 79, 1882).

In his later years Imray and his second wife, Ann Hilton (1809–1892), whom he married on 4 January 1838, lived in Manor Park, Streatham, where his granddaughter remembered him in old age as a red-haired, very stockily built, florid faced man who was fond of children. He died there on 15 November 1870 at the age of sixty-seven after a long illness; the cause of death was given as cardiac dropsy.

James Frederick Imray inherited the business on his father's death. Although he also drew charts, his principal contribution was authorship of many of the firm's sailing directions. His *North Pacific Pilot, Part I* (1870) was considered the best available and supplied by the Admiralty for use in warships. However, James Frederick lived the comfortable life of a second generation proprietor and lacked his father's business acumen. In the face of increasing Admiralty competition, the firm began to decline slowly and after his death his inexperienced young sons had to agree to amalgamation with their competitors Norie and Wilson in 1899. Five years later they were joined by the only other surviving private chart publisher, R. H. Laurie.

The amalgamated firm, Imray, Laurie, Norie and Wilson Ltd, under the leadership of the Wilson family, carried the tradition of British private chart publishing on through the twentieth century. They survived the near monopoly of government charting, finding a role in meeting the needs of specialist users such as fishermen and yachtsmen. They are still publishing charts today.

SUSANNA FISHER

Sources S. Fisher, *The makers of the blueback charts: a history of Imray, Laurie, Norie and Wilson Ltd.* (2001) · catalogues, charts and sailing directions published by Blachford and Imray, James Imray, and James Imray and Son (1836–70), *passim* · parish registers, London, Spitalfields, Christ Church · private information (2004) · trade directories, London · land tax assessments · census returns
Archives BL, charts · NMM, charts
Wealth at death under £35,000: probate, 20 Jan 1871, *CGPLA Eng. & Wales*

Ince, Edward Lindsay (1891–1941), mathematician, was born on 30 November 1891 in King William Street, Amblecote, Staffordshire, the only son of Edward Ince, an Inland Revenue officer, and his wife, Caroline Clara Cutler. He attended Cricieth School and the county school at Portmadoc, and, after his family moved to Scotland, completed his secondary education at the Perth Academy. In 1909 he went to Edinburgh University to read mathematics, and graduated in 1913 with first-class honours. He played a prominent part in the communal life of the university as senior president of the students' representative council and convener of the international academic committee. A scholarship awarded to him on graduation enabled him to remain in Edinburgh for research. After being rejected for war service on medical grounds, he entered Trinity College, Cambridge, in 1915 as research student, and was a Smith's prizeman in 1917, but after four terms left for a national service appointment.

In 1924 Ince married Phyllis Fry, with whom he had two daughters. After the war he held lectureships, first at Leeds and then in 1920–26 in Liverpool. In 1926 he was elected to the chair in pure mathematics at the newly founded Egyptian University, Cairo. Building up a new department was congenial to him and he proved a most successful teacher and organizer, but in 1931 he decided to return to Britain because of lack of facilities for educating his children and the effect of the climate on his health. After spending the session 1931–2 as lecturer in Edinburgh, and 1932–5 at Imperial College, London, he returned to Edinburgh as head of the department for technical mathematics, where he remained until his death.

Ince's main work was in the theory of differential equations. E. L. Mathieu in 1868 had, in the study of vibrations of an elliptic membrane, introduced and solved the differential equation now bearing his name, but a thorough study, using modern function-theoretic methods, was only beginning when Ince graduated; he was to make important contributions to the theory of Mathieu equations, proving the uniqueness of periodic solutions, now called Mathieu functions, and extending this work to Hill's equation. He found that the equation admits a solution of period π or 2π for certain values of a parameter, the 'eigenvalues'. A knowledge of these eigenvalues is prerequisite for numerical computations with Mathieu functions; Ince felt that providing tables of these values for physicists and astronomers was essential, though he realized that a practicable method of construction depended on progress in theoretical analysis. By the use of convergent infinite determinants and continued fractions, with asymptotic formulae for large values, he succeeded in making computations practicable and after eight years' devotion to this task he published in 1932 tables of eigenvalues for Mathieu's equation, and zeros of Mathieu functions. These tables were useful not only in the problems originally envisaged but also in more recent investigations such as quantum-mechanical problems leading to Mathieu's equation.

Ince's interests extended over a large part of analysis, and he put this to good use in his book *Ordinary Differential Equations*, which gave a modern presentation of the theory, using methods from algebra as well as analysis. Published in 1927, it immediately became a classic and remained in print for many years. In two papers published in the last year of his life he made important contributions to the theory of Lamé's equation; in particular he introduced orthogonal functions for their expansions, thus simplifying and extending results of previous authors.

In 1923 Ince was elected fellow of the Royal Society of Edinburgh; he was awarded its Makdougall Brisbane prize but did not live to receive the award. He was also a member of the London Mathematical Society and of the Royal Astronomical Society. He died of leukaemia at St Raphael's Home, Blackford Avenue, Edinburgh, on 16 March 1941. He was survived by his wife.   P. M. COHN

Sources WWW · E. T. Whittaker, *Journal of the London Mathematical Society*, 16 (1941), 139–44 · A. W. Y. [A. W. Young], *Year Book of the Royal Society of Edinburgh* (1940–41), 18 · b. cert. · d. cert.
Wealth at death £4023 2s. 4d.: confirmation, 11 June 1941, CCI

Ince, Sir Godfrey Herbert (1891–1960), civil servant, the eldest son of George Alfred Reynolds Ince, solicitor's clerk, and his wife, Emma Budgen, was born at Redhill, Surrey, on 25 September 1891. From Reigate grammar school he went with a county major scholarship to University College, London, where he graduated BSc in 1913 with first-class honours in mathematics. He was a keen games player and excelled at football. He organized and captained the first University of London team and, as he never tired of recalling in his later life, took it to Moscow, returning triumphant.

In the First World War Ince held commissioned rank in the East Lancashire brigade of the Royal Field Artillery, and was wounded in action while attached to the Royal Engineers. In 1918 he married Ethel Dorris, daughter of Charles Maude, of Northallerton, Yorkshire, with whom he had three daughters. The following year he entered the Ministry of Labour, where he was to remain for his whole career. His early years were concentrated on industrial relations, and he acted as secretary to a number of courts of inquiry including, ironically, that on dock labour (1920) where Ernest Bevin made his reputation as the 'Dockers' KC'. In 1928 Ince was transferred to the employment and insurance department where his phenomenal memory and mathematical brain enabled him to become quickly an expert on unemployment insurance. Two years later he was appointed principal private secretary to the minister, Margaret Bondfield, and acted in a similar capacity to her immediate successors. In 1933 he was appointed chief insurance officer with the rank of assistant secretary and in that capacity was loaned in 1936–7 to the commonwealth government of Australia to advise on national unemployment insurance. For his comprehensive report, which fully reflected his delight in analytical tables, he was rewarded with an honorarium of £400 by the Australian government.

In 1939 Ince was put in charge of the military recruitment department where, under the Military Training Act and then the National Service (Armed Forces) Act, he was heavily involved in the call-up. The success with which he handled this exacting task was recognized by Ernest Bevin, who became minister of labour in May 1940. Ince was first given the delicate task of integrating the old factory department of the Home Office into the ministry, and was then appointed director-general of manpower in June 1941. This new post was designed to bring under a single control the national service, military recruiting, and labour supply departments with their related problems. Under the permanent secretary the director was made immediately responsible to the minister for all matters affecting the call-up to the forces and the supply of civilian labour. This was work for which, as a strong-willed man of action who was imperturbable and indefatigable in times of crisis, he was admirably suited. Crucially, he and Bevin were also able to enjoy an exceptional mutual trust. Ince was in close sympathy with the aims and ideas of his minister, but he was not afraid to criticize his schemes when necessary. Bevin on his side valued Ince's judgement, and found it easy to work with a man whose advice was plain and direct and not hedged about with debating subtleties.

In the following three years of constant strain and ever-expanding responsibilities Ince's gifts found their greatest fulfilment. However, H. M. D. Parker was correct to write in the *Dictionary of National Biography* that:

> with an innate streak of vanity and personal ambition he enjoyed the power which fell into his own hands and the wide appreciation of his achievements. Convinced of the soundness of his own judgements he was not always an easy person with whom to negotiate. He was at times unwilling, or perhaps unable, to admit the honesty of opinions running counter to his own, and the strident tones in which he tried to dominate a conference tended to exacerbate, when a little persuasiveness might well have reconciled, his opponents.

It was because of these defects that many of his colleagues doubted whether, beyond a mastery of manpower policy, he had much to contribute to the wider responsibilities of the ministry.

In November 1944 Ince was nevertheless chosen to succeed Sir Thomas Phillips as permanent secretary of the ministry, and this post he held until his retirement on 1 February 1956. The plan for demobilization owed much of its success to his insistence upon a procedure which would be simple, equitable, and intelligible. He was also personally much involved in plans for the resettlement of service personnel in civilian life and, in particular, for the provision of careers advice and vocational training for the young. He chaired a committee of educationists and industrialists to inquire into the working of the Juvenile Employment Service and its report in 1946 helped to lay the foundations of the Youth Employment Service.

As wartime controls were gradually relaxed or removed, there were calls for reductions in the ministry's large staff. To its ultimate detriment, Ince did not take kindly to these suggestions. He had built up a departmental empire and he was loath to accept any diminution of its powers. There was another and more commendable reason for his intransigence. He was always deeply interested in the welfare of his staff, and encouraged social gatherings and athletic contests in which he liked to take part. He was therefore anxious to ensure that as far as possible they should continue in post until reaching the normal age of retirement. This concern for his staff, however, met with little apparent response. His fairly frequent visits to local offices, for example, tended to frighten rather than stimulate. This was because, apart from his work and sport, Ince had few if any outside interests, and he had no small talk. He was shy and taciturn, he neither drank nor smoked, and he was a little intimidating to a stranger or a junior. This was particularly true if they were women, with whom he was not above abusing his position of authority.

On his retirement, until his death at the Nelson Hospital, Merton, Surrey, on 20 December 1960, Ince was chairman of Cable and Wireless and its associated overseas telecommunication companies. He enjoyed the travelling which his duties made possible, especially on one occasion when his arrival in Australia coincided with the opening of the Olympic games. This insatiable appetite for watching sport—he was a familiar figure at White Hart Lane and the Oval—made him in 1957 an obvious choice for membership of the Wolfenden committee on sport.

Ince was appointed CB (1941), KBE (1943), KCB (1946), and GCB (1951). His old college elected him to a fellowship in 1946, and in 1951 he received an honorary LLD from the University of London.   RODNEY LOWE

Sources DNB · *The Times* (21 Dec 1960) · H. M. D. Parker, *Manpower: a study of wartime policy and administration* (1957) · *The Observer* (19 Nov 1944) · A. Bullock, *The life and times of Ernest Bevin*, 2 (1967) · E. Wigham, *Strikes and the government, 1893–1974* (1976) · CGPLA Eng. & Wales (1961)
Archives JRL, Manchester Guardian archive, letters to the *Manchester Guardian* · PRO, Ministry of Labour papers, LAB 79
Likenesses W. Stoneman, photograph, 1943, NPG · W. Stoneman, photograph, 1954, NPG · H. Knight, portrait, priv. coll. · double portrait, photograph (with Ernest Bevin), repro. in Bullock, *Life and times*, 210
Wealth at death £14,612 8s. 7d.: probate, 9 Aug 1961, CGPLA Eng. & Wales

Ince, Joseph Murray (1806–1859), painter, was born at Presteigne, Radnorshire, Wales. In 1823 he became a pupil of David Cox the elder in Hereford, and remained working under him until early 1826, when he went to London. He exhibited in that year for the first time at the Royal Academy, and was also an occasional exhibitor at the British Institution, the Society of Artists, where he exhibited up to 1858, and other galleries. In 1832 he was residing at Cambridge, where he made many architectural drawings. About 1835 he returned to Presteigne, where he spent much of the rest of his life, inheriting some property on the death of his parents, and making a good income out of his profession. He died at his London home, 9 George Street, Portman Square, on 24 September 1859, and was buried in Kensal Green cemetery, London. A monument was erected to his memory at Presteigne. Ince was a good painter of landscape in watercolours. There are examples of his drawings at the Victoria and Albert Museum, such as *Coasting Vessels, with Harbour*, 1836, and in the print room at the British Museum.

L. H. CUST, rev. PATRICIA MORALES

Sources private information (1891) · Redgrave, *Artists* · M. Hardie, *Water-colour painting in Britain*, ed. D. Snelgrove, J. Mayne, and B. Taylor, 2nd edn, 3: *The Victorian period* [1968] · J. Turner, ed., *The dictionary of art*, 34 vols. (1996) · CGPLA Eng. & Wales (1859)
Wealth at death under £10,000: probate, 11 Nov 1859, CGPLA Eng. & Wales

Ince, Peter (1614/15–1683), clergyman and ejected minister, was the son of Peter Ince of Chester. He was admitted as a plebeian to Brasenose College, Oxford, on 3 December 1630, aged fifteen, matriculating on 9 December 1631. He graduated BA in 1634 and MA in 1637. He was chaplain to the parliamentarian garrison at Weymouth between 1644 and 1646, publishing in 1644 *A brief relation of the surprise of the forts of Weymouth, the siege of Melcombe, the recovery of the forts and raising of the siege*. Indeed, the parishioners of Melcombe Regis wished to keep him as their minister because, they claimed, the inspiration he had given the troops had been instrumental in preserving the place. Instead he became rector of Donhead St Mary, Wiltshire, where he was admitted on 1 March 1647, and where he stayed until his ejection in the summer of 1660. He was one of the Wednesday lecturers at Shaftesbury in 1647. He was nominated to the Warminster classis for the Wiltshire province and was one of the signatories of *An Apology for the Ministers of Wiltshire* (1654). For part of the time between 1660 and his death (probably in Ferne) in the first half of 1683 Ince lived with the patron of his living, his great friend Thomas Grove, at Donhead St Andrew. Calamy mentions a wife in relating an incident in 1664 or 1665. She was a member of the Thornhill family and Ince left property to his niece by marriage, Margaret Thornhill, in his will. His wife predeceased him. In 1669 he was reported at the houses of Grove and his son. Ince was licensed as a presbyterian to preach at his own house at Thornhill (Stalbridge parish, Dorset) in May 1672. Calamy recalled him as 'An excellent Practical Preacher, he had an admirable Gift in Prayer … call'd by the Name of Praying Ince' (*Calamy rev.*, 288).

Ince is best known through his correspondence with Richard Baxter, of whom he was an admirer, but not an uncritical one. Like many who wrote to Baxter he had reservations about Baxter's first work, *Aphorismes of Justification* (1649), and none about his second, *The Saints Everlasting Rest* (1650). In the first of many letters to Baxter he struck a familiar note among Baxter's correspondents: Baxter was so good with his practical divinity; why did he lose himself in controversies? (16 Nov 1652, DWL, Baxter correspondence, 4, fol. 181). Baxter would have concurred with the sentiment, but somehow there was a slip between precept and practice. On 7 May 1653 (ibid., 6, fol. 111) Ince would rejoice that rumours of Baxter's death had been exaggerated. Perhaps Baxter had a responsibility for that story having credence. He had called his 1649 work his 'dying thoughts' but lived on to 1691. Ince was in at the start of the Wiltshire Association of Ministers, modelled on Baxter's Worcestershire Association. He confided to Baxter, on 25 October 1653, his hope that 'the foundation of some good amongst us had been laid' (ibid., 1, fol. 10). Thereafter he would keep Baxter informed of parallel developments in other counties: the ecumenical basis for the national 'Holy Commonwealth' in 1659 which Baxter advocated under Richard Cromwell's protectorate. Was Baxter too soft on Arminianism, too inclined to listen to Moïse Amyraut, John Cameron, John Davenant, and their 'third way' between Calvinism and Arminianism? Ince called their views those of 'the proud and profane'. Baxter retorted, on 21 November 1653, that he was no 'Arminian', because it was incompatible with praying to God. However, unlike antinomianism, Arminianism was only contingently, not causally, related to impiety (ibid., 1, fol. 11). A fellow puritan minister, Henry Bartlett, put the question to Baxter on 6 November 1654: 'how I and my Brother Ince put you on Controversy, while in the Generall we take you off, I do not conceive' (ibid., 5, fol. 107). It was practical help again which Ince required from Baxter on 1 March 1655. It was all very well for Baxter in Kidderminster effecting a revolution there by catechizing: he had superior material to work on. Ince blamed his predecessor, George Pope, for the shambles which he had inherited in Donhead St Mary. Therefore he could not accept Baxter's bland reassurance that 'there would not be many

found notoriously ungodly amongst our people' (ibid., 4, fol. 245). But Ince identified the Penruddock rebels with those who were 'notoriously opposite to godlinesse' (13 April 1655, ibid., 3, fol. 168). He wondered, on 21 April 1655, why Baxter allowed himself to get so steamed up about the Quakers, who were in any case 'incapable (as far I understand them) of a rationall confrontation' (ibid., 3, fol. 179). Yet only a few months on Ince is himself asking Baxter: 'I pray you let me know what your neighbour quakers doe' (3 Dec 1655, ibid., 5, fol. 172). He continued to ask Baxter for guidance on catechizing on 7 January 1656, because no central lead was being provided by London (ibid., 5, fol. 177).

At the Restoration Ince would twice fall foul of the authorities. With his fellow prisoner John Sacheverell he was imprisoned for eighteen months at Dorchester upon their refusal to be bound to their good behaviour after they had been convicted of illegal preaching at Shaftesbury. Eventually, 'the Persuasion of Friends, and the Tears of a Wife, prevail'd with Mr. Ince to yield, and he did so, with Mr. Sacheverel' (*Calamy rev.*, 288). Their companion in the cells, Francis Bampfield, remained defiant from 1663 until the declaration of indulgence freed him in 1672. Ince was presented again at quarter sessions on 18 June 1676 for preaching at a conventicle at the home of Thomas Grove. Baxter's influence on both men is reflected in their words before 1660 and in their deeds afterwards.

WILLIAM LAMONT

Sources *Calendar of the correspondence of Richard Baxter*, ed. N. H. Keeble and G. F. Nuttall, 2 vols. (1991) • W. M. Lamont, *Richard Baxter and the millennium: protestant imperialism and the English revolution* (1979) • P. Ince and others, *An apology for the ministers of Wiltshire* (1654) • *The county of Wilts divided into four classes* (c.1650) • *Calamy rev.*, 288–9 • P. Ince, *A brief relation of the surprise of the forts of Weymouth, the siege of Melcombe, the recovery of the forts and raising of the siege* (1644) • D. Underdown, *Fire from heaven: the life of an English town in the seventeenth century* (1992) • will, PRO, PROB 11/373, sig. 71 • DWL, Baxter correspondence • E. Calamy, ed., *An abridgement of Mr. Baxter's history of his life and times, with an account of the ministers, &c., who were ejected after the Restauration of King Charles II*, 2nd edn, 2 vols. (1713) • [C. B. Heberden], ed., *Brasenose College register, 1509–1909*, 2 vols., OHS, 55 (1909)

Archives DWL, Baxter corresp.

Wealth at death modest sums divided between nephews, nieces, and wife's relatives: will, 1683, PRO, PROB 11/373, sig. 71

Ince, William (1825–1910), university professor, born in St James's parish, Clerkenwell, London, on 7 June 1825, was the son of William Ince, sometime president of the Pharmaceutical Society of London, and his wife, Hannah Goodwin Dakin. He was educated at King's College School, London (being made an honorary fellow of King's College in 1861); there he began a lifelong friendship with William Henry Smith, who became leader of the House of Commons. He was elected to a Hutchins' scholarship at Lincoln College, Oxford, on 10 December 1842. He graduated BA with first-class honours in classics in Michaelmas term 1846, proceeding MA on 26 April 1849 and DD on 7 May 1878. He was ordained deacon in 1850 and priest in 1852.

Early in 1847 Ince was elected to a Petrean fellowship in Exeter College; he became tutor of the college in 1850 and sub-rector in 1857, holding all three posts until 1878. He was elected an honorary fellow in 1882. He was at once recognized as 'one of the ablest and most popular tutors of his day' (W. K. Stride, *Exeter College*, 1900, 181), his lectures on Aristotle's *Ethics* and on logic being especially helpful. As sub-rector he earned the reputation of a tactful but firm disciplinarian. He was a constant preacher in the college chapel.

Ince served the university offices of junior proctor in 1856–7, of select preacher before the university in 1859, 1870, and 1875, of Oxford preacher at the Chapel Royal, Whitehall, in 1860–62, and of classical examiner in 1866–8. From 1871 until 1889 he was examining chaplain to J. F. Mackarness, bishop of Oxford, who was fellow of Exeter (1844–6).

On 6 April 1878 Ince was appointed regius professor of divinity at Oxford and canon of Christ Church. Keenly alive to the intellectual side of his official duties, he read widely and gave his pupils the benefit of his studies. His duties included that of presenting candidates for honorary degrees in divinity, and his happily expressed and enunciated Latin speeches on such occasions recalled the days when Latin was still a spoken language. He took an active share in the administration of Christ Church, both as a cathedral body and as a college, and showed a well-informed and even-minded judgement in such university offices as curator of the Bodleian Library, chair of the board of theological studies, and member of the hebdomadal council. Ince's theological position was that of an old-fashioned high-churchman, but inclining, especially in his later days, to evangelical interpretations, and rejecting ritualism alike in form and doctrine. Ince published many occasional sermons and other pieces, including *The Education of the Clergy at the Universities* (1882), but nothing of real substance. His two inaugural lectures given in 1878 were published as *The Past History and Present Duties of the Faculty of Theology in Oxford*, and led to a published correspondence with H. R. Bramley (1879).

Ince married at Alvechurch, Worcestershire, on 11 September 1879, Mary Anne, younger daughter of John Rusher Eaton of Lambeth. He died, after some years of failing health, in his official house at Christ Church on 13 November 1910, in his eighty-sixth year, and was buried on 16 November in the cemetery at the east end of Christ Church Cathedral. His wife died at Fairford, Gloucestershire, on 21 March 1911, and was buried next to her husband. ANDREW CLARK, rev. H. C. G. MATTHEW

Sources *The Times* (14 Nov 1910) · *Oxford Times* (19 Nov 1910) · 'Memoir by W. Walrond Jackson', *Stapledon Magazine*, 3, 6 · C. W. Boase, ed., *Registrum Collegii Exoniensis*, new edn, OHS, 27 (1894) · J. S. Reynolds, *Canon Christopher of St Aldate's, Oxford* (1967)

Likenesses oils, Christ Church Oxf.

Wealth at death £44,693 12s. 1d.: resworn probate, 11 Jan 1911, *CGPLA Eng. & Wales*

Inchbald [*née* Simpson], **Elizabeth** (1753–1821), writer and actress, was born on 15 October 1753 in Standingfield, near Bury St Edmunds, Suffolk, the youngest child but one in the large family of John Simpson (*d.* 1761), farmer, and

Elizabeth Inchbald (1753–1821), by Sir Thomas Lawrence, *c*.1796

his wife, Mary (*d.* 1783), daughter of William Rushbrook of Flimpton.

Early life, marriage, and first acting roles Elizabeth Simpson's family was Roman Catholic and had many friends in local Catholic circles. Her biographer calls her father's living a 'moderate farm', but does not indicate how well the family fared after his death. Educated with her sisters at home while her brother went to school, Elizabeth later remarked that the girls, but not their brother, learned to spell: this showed, she thought, that girls were more 'inclined to literature' (Boaden, *Inchbald*, 1.6). Her own literary interests were sharpened by her speech difficulties. Ambitious from an early age to become an actress, she worked hard to overcome her stammer, and in early 1770 attempted to get an engagement at the Norwich Theatre. Her family visited theatres and had acquaintances among actors, and there were dramatic readings at home; but Elizabeth's acting ambitions were discouraged. Her brother George became an actor in 1770. In April 1772 Elizabeth set off without permission for London, leaving her mother a defensive note: '[I] cannot *prove* my affection;—yet time may' (ibid., 1.18). She took lodgings and tried to get stage engagements, but soon decided to stay with her sister for protection. She encountered harassment, including sexual advances from the theatre manager Dodd, which she is said to have answered with a faceful of hot water; and within a couple of months she agreed to marry the actor Joseph Inchbald (1735–1779), who had been courting her since the previous year. Boaden remarks that he was not 'the object of her romantic love' (ibid., 1.96), and it is likely that she decided upon marriage as a way of gaining a protected entrance into her chosen profession. They were married in a Catholic ceremony on 9 June 1772 and by protestant rites the following day. Immediately afterwards they went to Bristol, where her husband had acting engagements, and where she made her début as Cordelia to his Lear on 4 September.

From 1772 to 1776 the Inchbalds toured Scotland with West Digges's theatre company, acting in Glasgow, Edinburgh, and Aberdeen. Despite her determined practising, walking the hills and shores with her husband listening to her recitals, Inchbald was never a very good actress, but she continued to perform a variety of roles and to supplement her wages by 'walking on' in the pantomime. The touring life was a hard one: travelling, they were caught in storms and had to walk long distances in the rain, and her health was undermined by the consequent attacks of ague and fever. Her marriage was difficult, too. She did not enjoy her role as stepmother to her husband's illegitimate son Robert, whose mother is not known. Robert was in the same company playing children's roles, and Elizabeth insisted on his lodging separately from the couple in Edinburgh. Her husband also had another, older son, George, whose mother may or may not have been the same as Robert's. Elizabeth and her husband quarrelled over money and her independence: he objected to her receiving her own salary separately from his, and to her friendships with other men, and she objected to his drinking sessions with friends.

In 1776 the Inchbalds left Digges's company after an incident in which Joseph had antagonized the audience. They now had to find alternative ways of earning a living. Joseph decided to study painting in France, while Elizabeth, who had already been studying the language, resolved to continue her French studies and to try and write for the stage. After their brief stay in France, abandoned because of their shortage of money, they were for a while destitute in Brighton, where they 'once went into the fields to eat turnips instead of dining' (Boaden, *Inchbald*, 1.68). At this point Elizabeth was still on bad terms with her mother, and the latter had refused to help the couple with money. Later Elizabeth seems to have been reconciled with her mother, visiting her in Standingfield several times before Mary Simpson's death in 1783. Her family connections were important to her, and she sent money to members of her family whenever she could, from her acting wages and later from the profits of her writing. Perhaps she hoped in this way to make up for running away to the stage and marrying Inchbald.

Later in 1776 the Inchbalds managed to get another theatrical engagement, with Younger in Liverpool. Here Elizabeth met the actress Sarah Siddons, who became a lifelong friend, and her brother, the actor John Philip Kemble. Her friendship with Kemble was intense, and sometimes quarrelsome; the relationship between the coquettish, passionate Miss Milner and her stern guardian in *A Simple Story* may be based in part on it. Like her other friendships it aroused her husband's jealousy. Siddons and Kemble seem to have been an intellectual stimulus to the incipient writer, who was educating herself during this period by reading in English, and in Latin literature in translation. She began writing a novel (possibly, but not certainly, an early version of *A Simple Story*), and corresponded with Kemble about it. She tried unsuccessfully to get this novel published in 1779.

The Inchbalds continued to change company, moving to Dimond's company in Canterbury, where Elizabeth acted with Thomas Holcroft, and then to the Yorkshire company led by Tate Wilkinson, who remembered her as 'my well-beloved, my beautiful Mrs. Inchbald' (Wilkinson, 1.277). Joseph Inchbald died suddenly in 1779. His widow carried on acting for Wilkinson for a while, and then spent the next few years acting in London and Dublin. With the freedom of widowhood came, once again, the pitfalls of being a young single woman on the stage in a society that judged women by increasingly stringent criteria of delicate behaviour. She enjoyed a lively social life, risking censorious comment on the one hand, and unwanted sexual attention on the other. Boaden recounts a number of flirtations enjoyed and proposals refused in these years.

Writing for the stage Inchbald acted for seventeen years, taking a great number of different roles in Shakespearian drama, seventeenth-century comedies and tragedies, and more recent plays. Her leading roles in tragedies included the heroine of *Jane Shore*, Calista in *The Fair Penitent*, Monimia in *The Orphan*, and Desdemona in *Othello*. In comedies her roles included Violante in *The Wonder*, Angelica in *The Constant Couple*, and Indiana in *The Constant Lover*. She also played the cross-dressing heroine Bellario in *Philaster*. She acted in new plays of the 1780s, including Hannah Cowley's *The Belle's Stratagem*. She was painted as Lady Jane Grey and as the Lady Abbess in *The Comedy of Errors*; but apart from this she never seems to have become well known for any particular role, and her acting was never critically acclaimed. From at least the mid-1770s, she was considering writing as a possible alternative to this only moderately successful stage career. Her acting experience gave her a knowledge of stage techniques, and familiarized her with a wide range of stage plots and character types that she drew on for her own plays. Her stage experience was also put to use in her fiction, with its tight, dramatic dialogues and its use of themes from earlier dramatists. Her Shakespearian roles included Hermione in *The Winter's Tale* and Perdita in an adaptation from the same play, *Florizel and Perdita*; and in *A Simple Story* she used several motifs from this play including the tyrannical husband and father, the mother–daughter pair of heroines, and the jump in time.

Inchbald's first farces were submitted to the theatre managers Harris and Colman in 1781, but were refused. Eventually her farce *The Mogul Tale*, submitted to Colman under an assumed name, was accepted. Three English characters fly to the Orient in a balloon; the topical interest of balloon ascents helped make the play popular, and it had a good run at the Little Theatre in the Haymarket in July and August 1784. Inchbald acted in it herself—stammering with nerves on the first night—and, once its success was assured, declared her authorship and took applause for it from the stage. Colman paid her 100 guineas for the farce, and agreed to accept a comedy she had sent him previously, which he altered and put on at the Haymarket as *I'll Tell You What* in 1785. This five-act comedy of contemporary life was also a success, and as well as bringing her £300 for three benefit nights, it gave her a fame which increased her value, and her wages, as an actress.

From this time on Inchbald became a prolific and highly popular dramatist, whose most successful productions brought high financial rewards. She estimated her proceeds from *Such Things Are* (1787) as £900. She used her earnings to buy annuities, and by 1789, with an investment income of £58 a year, she was able to give up her acting engagement at Covent Garden and rely on her writing. Altogether nineteen of her comedies, sentimental dramas, and farces were performed at the London theatres between 1784 and 1805. Some were original plots; others were translations or adaptations from French plays, which she read in the original, and German ones, which she had to approach through English translations. Her work ranged from broad farce such as *Appearance is Against them* (1785), which was criticized for indecent expressions, to serious sentiment, as in *Such Things Are*, which has topical interest in its fanciful portrait of the prison reformer Howard as Haswell, a benevolent Englishman visiting Sumatra, freeing prisoners—one of them the beloved wife of the very sultan who incarcerated her by mistake—and generally sorting life out for the English expatriates. Like other dramatists of the time, Inchbald wrote comedy about marriage and its problems, and parent–child relations. *To Marry, or not to Marry* (1805) is a typically light-hearted exploration of its theme, ending by answering the question it poses with a clear, sentimental affirmative. She was interested in challenges to social convention: she included divorced couples in some plays, and a favourite character type is the witty, irreverent young lady, a role in which her friend the actress Elizabeth Farren specialized. One of her plays, *Lover's Vows* (1798) from August Kotzebue's *Child of Love*, gave sympathetic treatment to a 'fallen woman' and her illegitimate son, and has since become famous as the dangerous drama performed in Austen's *Mansfield Park*. However, there were strict limits to how far unconventionality could be explored in popular comedy at this date: *All on a Summer's Day* (1787) was hissed by the audience and criticized in the reviews for portraying a flirtatious, imprudent wife with sympathy. In general Inchbald managed to please her audience by combining relatively liberal social views with the maintenance of social order, often through the actions of a benevolent male authority figure. In *Everyone has his Fault* (1792), for example, Mr Harmony manages to reconcile Sir Robert Ramble to the virtuous former wife he had failed to appreciate, and Lord Norland to the daughter he had disowned on her marriage to a poor man; to induce Mr Placid to take a firmer line with his domineering wife, and to marry the old bachelor Solus to Miss Spinster. A strong theme throughout this play is the critique of aristocratic extravagance and the championship

of poverty-stricken middle-class virtue, also found in *Next Door Neighbours* (1791), one of her French adaptations. *Wives as they Were and Maids as they Are* (1797) takes a sharp look at modern life, touching on the current questioning of female subordination; but though there is a memorably disturbing moment when a mistreated wife confirms that she fears her husband and refuses to say she loves him, the comedy concludes in a conservative way, with wifely submission praised and the witty, independent-minded Miss Dorrillon learning that she cannot manage without fatherly guidance.

Social and political opinions and other writing Inchbald's social and political views were radical. Her close friends included Thomas Holcroft, who was tried in the treason trials of 1794, and William Godwin, until she broke with him over his marriage to Mary Wollstonecraft. In her plays she generally avoided any strong expression of her political sympathies, which would have endangered her popular success. When she did use drama to explore current controversy, the theatre managers refused to stage it. *The Massacre*, a historical play about the St Bartholomew's day massacre which made clear the parallels between this subject and events during the French Revolution, was never performed, and in 1792 she withdrew it from publication on the advice of Holcroft and Godwin. Although its main thrust is to expose the horror of the civil unrest that leads to the murder of Madame Tricastin and her children, the play is not anti-revolutionary: its portrait of Glandeve, the 'sworn friend to Liberty' (Boaden, *Inchbald*, 1.375) and tribunal president who rebukes the bloodthirsty Dugas, indicates support for a moderate, Girondist stance, and would have marked Inchbald as a revolutionary writer to a 1790s audience.

Once she was established as a playwright, Inchbald also returned to writing fiction, this time with much greater success, and her first novel, *A Simple Story*, was highly praised on its appearance in 1791. The £200 she got for it, though good pay for a novel at this time, compared badly with the proceeds from dramatic hits, such as the £700 she made from *Every One has his Fault* (1793). However, if novels were less lucrative than drama, they opened up new artistic opportunities, leaving her freer to develop her challenging views both on family and sexual relations and on class relations and political order. *A Simple Story* explores in much greater psychological depth issues and behavioural patterns that also preoccupied her in her plays: paternal authority as exercised by a stern father who rejects his dependants, and the challenge to that authority represented by a passionate and wilful young woman. Miss Milner's desire for a man who is a priest and her guardian makes her a disruptive heroine, and though the novel concludes on a conventional note, its overall effect is to disturb eighteenth-century complacency about the benevolence of paternal power in a way Inchbald's drama did not. Her second and final novel, *Nature and Art* (1796), was openly critical of English social institutions and class structures. Through the story of two brothers and their children, one selfish father–son pair, both of whom rise in a corrupt world, and one unselfish pair, condemned to poverty, Inchbald attacks the system of patronage, the administration of justice, and the cruelties and hypocrisies of sexual morality.

After her last comedy, *To Marry or not to Marry*, was performed at Covent Garden in 1805, Inchbald turned to critical and editorial work, producing *The British Theatre*, a twenty-five-volume collection of plays with critical introductions, in 1806–9; a seven-volume *Collection of Farces and Afterpieces* in 1809; and ten volumes of *The Modern Theatre* in 1811. She wrote an article about the novel for the periodical *The Artist* in 1807, but declined invitations to write for the *Quarterly Review* and to edit *La Belle Assemblée*.

For many years Inchbald was a well-known figure in London society, with a wide circle of friends and a lively social life. Her fair, freckled, sandy-haired, slender beauty was greatly admired and often painted. Her independent attitude, and her ability to nudge the limits of acceptable feminine behaviour without ever laying herself open to scandal, struck her contemporaries as remarkable. George Hardinge commented: 'She lives alone—her character has no *tache* upon it—and Mrs Siddons said she was as cold as ice: but I cannot believe it' (Nichols, *Illustrations*, 3.38). She kept meticulous records of her considerable earnings and shrewd investments; but despite her growing wealth she always lived very frugally, scrubbing her own floor and carrying her own coals. She kept in touch with members of her family, all of them in much poorer circumstances than she was, and helped them with money. For some time she was estranged from her sister Debby, who seems to have entered prostitution; and though they were reconciled before Debby's death in 1794, Inchbald felt guilty about her earlier attitude. The sympathetic portrait of Hannah Primrose in *Nature and Art* may owe something to her feelings about her sister. Another social outcast for sexual reasons, the actress Mary (Becky) Wells, found Inchbald a constant friend and source of financial support.

Final years Inchbald's life was marked by tensions between, on the one hand, political radicalism, a passionate nature evidently attracted to a number of her admirers, and a love of independence, and on the other hand, a desire for social respectability and a strong sense of the emotional attraction of authority figures. If her own analysis of it contained anything like the psychological skill of her novels, it would have been a marvellous insight into the making of a woman writer in the eighteenth century. Unfortunately, the four-volume autobiography, which she began in 1795 and for which at one stage she was offered £1000, was destroyed on the advice of her confessor. She did leave extensive diaries, used by her biographer, which give a detailed account of her reading, writing, earnings, investments, moods, migraines, dizzy spells, flirtations, proposals, and friendships over fifty years. Some of these volumes still survive.

Inchbald's last years were spent in retirement and increasing seclusion. After what she called her years of no religious existence, from the late 1770s until 1810, she renewed her faith. She corresponded with and met Maria Edgeworth and Germaine de Staël, but on the whole she avoided socializing, spending her time instead in religious observances and studies. She died at Kensington House, Kensington, on Wednesday 1 August 1821, of 'an inflammation of the intestines' (Boaden, *Inchbald*, 2.278) and was buried on 4 August in Kensington churchyard.

Inchbald had great popular success and some critical praise for her witty comedies, several of which remained available to the nineteenth-century public in her own edited collection of English plays, *The British Theatre*. *A Simple Story* soon became her greatest claim to fame. It was frequently reprinted in the nineteenth century, and its appeal in an age of realist writing is indicated by Maria Edgeworth's praise:

> I never read any novel that affected me so strongly, or that so completely possessed me with the belief in the real existence of all the people it represents ... I believed all to be real, and was affected as I should be by the real scenes as if they had passed before my eyes.   (Littlewood, 123)

In the twentieth century, too, Inchbald was mainly remembered as a novelist, and is now receiving increasing critical attention, especially from those interested in women's literary history and in the revolutionary novels of the 1790s.　　　　　　　　　　　JANE SPENCER

Sources *Memoirs of Mrs Inchbald*, ed. J. Boaden, 2 vols. (1833) · T. Wilkinson, *The wandering patentee, or, A history of the Yorkshire theatres from 1770 to the present time*, 4 vols. (1795) · S. R. Littlewood, *Elizabeth Inchbald and her circle* (1921) · R. Manvell, *Elizabeth Inchbald: England's principal woman dramatist and independent woman of letters in 18th century London* (1987) · P. Sigl, 'The Elizabeth Inchbald papers', *N&Q*, 227 (1982) · P. Sigl, 'The literary achievement of Elizabeth Inchbald', PhD diss., U. Wales, 1980 · Highfill, Burnim & Langhans, *BDA* · Nichols, *Illustrations* · G. L. Joughin, *An Inchbald bibliography* (1934) · J. Boaden, *Memoirs of the life of John Philip Kemble*, 2 vols. (1825) · C. Kegan Paul, *William Godwin: his friends and contemporaries*, 2 vols. (1876) · D. C. Sutton, *Location register of English literary MSS and letters*, 1 (1995)

Archives BL, diaries, RP2266, 4730 [copies] · Folger, diary · V&A NAL, corresp. | Bodl. Oxf., letters to William Godwin; letters to John Taylor [copies]

Likenesses J. Russell, oils, *c*.1788, priv. coll. · G. Dance, pencil drawing, 1794, NPG · T. Lawrence, oils, *c*.1796, priv. coll. [see illus.] · G. Romney, oils, 1904, Tennant collection; repro. in R. S. Gower, *George Romney* (1904) · W. Daniels, engraving (after G. Dance) · S. De Wilde, oils (as Lady Jane Grey), Garr. Club · S. De Wilde, watercolour drawing, Garr. Club · S. Freeman, stipple (after T. Lawrence, 1796), BM; repro. in *Monthly Mirror* (1807), pl. · G. H. Harlow, pencil and sanguine drawing, Garr. Club · Heath, engraving (after portrait by G. Romney, 1904) · J. Opie, oils, priv. coll. · J. Opie, oils, Petworth House, Sussex · W. Ridley, engraving (after S. Drummond), repro. in *Monthly Mirror* (1797), pl. · Woodring, engraving (after J. Russell), repro. in *European Magazine* (1788), pl. · miniature (after J. T. Barber-Beaumont), Garr. Club · prints, BM · silhouette, Garr. Club

Wealth at death £5000–£6000: Boaden, *Memoirs*; *DNB*

Inchbold, John William (1830–1888), landscape painter, was born on 29 April 1830 in Leeds, one of at least two sons of Thomas Inchbold (*c*.1785–1832), one-time proprietor and editor of the *Leeds Intelligencer*, and his wife, Rachel, whose maiden name was probably Mawson. His father died when he was still a child, and from this time forward the family depended on a stationery and printing firm run by his mother. While still only fifteen or sixteen years old he moved to London to be apprenticed to the lithographic printers Day and Haghe. Soon after, he took up painting under the instruction of Louis Haghe, a Flemish-born artist who was a watercolourist as well as a lithographer; he may also have been enrolled in the Royal Academy Schools.

Inchbold's career as a professional artist began in 1849 when he exhibited sketches of Yorkshire coastal subjects at the Society of British Artists. Various of his early works are lost, but one surviving painting, *The Chapel, Bolton* (Northampton Museums and Art Gallery), shown at the Royal Academy in 1853, demonstrates Pre-Raphaelite principles of observation in its meticulous representation of vegetation and architecture and intense colour. By about 1854 he seems to have made contact with the Pre-Raphaelite circle of painters, being asked to join a sketching club then under discussion, and eliciting the support of John Everett Millais when his painting *Anstey's Cove* (Fitzwilliam Museum, Cambridge) was rejected by the selection committee of the Royal Academy. John Ruskin believed that Inchbold was among the most promising of the younger generation of landscape painters, and in *Academy Notes*—his annual commentary on the exhibitions, published for the first time in 1855—he seized with enthusiasm on various of his works. 'The Moorland': (*Dewar-Stone, Dartmoor*) (Tate collection), which appeared at the 1855 Royal Academy show, was, for example, 'the only thoroughly good landscape in the rooms of the Academy … more exquisite in its finish of lichenous rock painting than any work I have ever seen' (E. T. Cook and A. Wedderburn, *The Works of Ruskin*, 39 vols., 1903–12, 14.21–2). Other paintings by Inchbold of the mid-1850s offer minutely detailed inspections of the forms of nature and at close range. For example, *Mid-Spring* (exh. RA, 1856; priv. coll.), ostensibly an illustration to Tennyson's poem 'The Two Paths', shows a woodland floor with the dense textures of flowers and foliage spread upwards over the entire picture space.

Inchbold was one of a number of younger British landscape painters to be inspired to turn to mountain subjects by volume four of Ruskin's *Modern Painters*, which bore the subtitle 'Of mountain beauty' and which was published in the spring of 1856. In June of the same year Inchbold stayed with Ruskin at Lauterbrunnen in Switzerland. The resulting painting, *Jungfrau, from the Wengern Alps*, was shown at the Royal Academy in 1857 and later in the same year as part of a private exhibition in Leeds. It was praised by the *Leeds Mercury* as bearing 'the minutest examination, and yet its high finish does not interfere with the general effect' (21 Feb 1857). Inchbold returned to the Alps in the autumn of 1857 to carry out a commission to make watercolour drawings of Swiss vernacular architecture for Ruskin. On this occasion he stayed for a while at Sallanches, France, where he painted *A By-Path to Chamouni*. His oil painting *The Lake of Lucerne* (Victoria and Albert Museum, London), executed in the late summer of 1857, represents the fulfilment of his Pre-Raphaelite landscape style. In 1858 Ruskin and Inchbold were again in the Alps together,

at Fluelen on Lake Lucerne, and later at Bellinzona in Ticino, but clearly their ideas about landscape painting were diverging: as the former looked increasingly for subjects which would edify and uplift their audience, the latter moved away from strict observation towards a style of landscape painting which was both more indulgent and more technically experimental. In consequence Ruskin turned to John Brett (whose adoption of a Pre-Raphaelite landscape style owed much to the influence of Inchbold) as an acolyte and tester of his own artistic theories.

In 1860 Inchbold stayed at Cornwood and then at Tintagel in Cornwall. Thomas Woolner, Francis Palgrave, and Alfred Tennyson encountered him there while they were on a walking tour, as described by Palgrave: 'At a turn in the rocks [we met] that ever graceful, ill-appreciated landscapist Inchbold: whose cry of delighted wonder at sight of Tennyson still sounds in the sole survivor's ear' (H. Tennyson, *Alfred Lord Tennyson—a Memoir by his Son*, 1897, 1.461–2). Inchbold's *King Arthur's Island, Tintagel, Cornwall* (priv. coll.) was inspired by this visit. In 1864 he returned to Cornwall, lodging at the schoolhouse in Boscastle and having as his guest Algernon Charles Swinburne who was then working on the poem 'Atalanta in Calydon'.

In the period between his two stays in Cornwall, Inchbold lived in Venice, remaining there for about two years from the spring or summer of 1862. His Venetian subjects represent an original and challenging departure in the context of British landscape painting. Almost always avoiding familiar landmarks and yet remaining painstakingly accurate wherever a known topography occurred, works such as *From Saint Helena, Venice* (1863–4; priv. coll.) treat the more obscure parts of the city or outlying islands of the Venetian lagoon in terms of abstract pattern and texture. He was particularly attracted to effects of atmosphere and half-light, and he was one of the first among his generation to explore the possibilities of city views at dusk in works such as *Venice from the Public Gardens* (c.1862–1864; priv. coll.), which conjures the sights and sensations of the city and lagoon by evocative means rather than documentary ones.

Inchbold gained very little public recognition as an artist. His works were repeatedly rejected by the Royal Academy selection committees, and he depended for his livelihood on a small circle of patrons and friends, notably George Rae of Liverpool and James Leathart of Gateshead; even with these two sympathetic men relations were difficult. In 1863 Inchbold had participated in an exhibition of paintings refused by the Royal Academy which was held at the Cosmopolitan Club in Charles Street, and in 1868 his friend and patron Dr John Russell Reynolds set up a display of his paintings in his house in Grosvenor Street. On two occasions, in 1885 and 1887, works by Inchbold were shown at the Grosvenor Gallery. He also wrote poems, often on landscape themes, a collection of which appeared under the title *Annus amoris* in 1876.

Periodic financial crises were the cause of concern among Inchbold's circle of friends, and in 1868 he was forced to give up the studio in Lincoln's Inn Fields which he had occupied since 1857. D. G. Rossetti's unkind limerick

> There is a mad artist named Inchbold
> With whom you must be at a pinch bold:
> Or else you may score
> The brass plate on your door
> With the name of J. W. Inchbold
> (D. G. Rossetti, *Rossetti Papers*, ed. W. M. Rossetti, 1903, 495)

presumably dates from this period of near indigence. From 1869 onward Inchbold stayed at the Charing Cross Hotel in London but spent long periods on the Isle of Wight and elsewhere, finding country lodgings cheaper than accommodation in London. He also continued to travel abroad, reaching north Africa in 1876 and then in 1879 moving semi-permanently to Switzerland; here he was once again inspired to paint mountains and lakes, and with a new ethereal and serene quality. In 1886–7 he made his last long painting tour, exploring the Mediterranean coast from the south of France to Naples. He died, unmarried, on 23 January 1888 while staying at his sister's house, 13 Ebberstone Terrace, Headingley, Leeds. He was buried on 25 January in Woodhouse cemetery, Leeds. A. C. Swinburne's poem 'In Memory of John William Inchbold' (first published in an issue of *The Athenaeum* in December 1888) paid tribute to the artist, Swinburne recalling the stay in Cornwall the two had made together in 1864.

CHRISTOPHER NEWALL

Sources [F. G. Stephens], *The Athenaeum* (4 Feb 1888), 154 · *DNB* · *Loan exhibition of works by G. J. Pinwell, Sam Bough [and] J. W. Inchbold* [exhibition catalogue, Royal Water-Colour Society Art Club] · C. Newall, *John William Inchbold—Pre-Raphaelite landscape artist* (1993) [exhibition catalogue, Leeds City Art Gallery] · A. Staley, *The Pre-Raphaelite landscape* (1973) · d. cert.
Archives U. Leeds | Bodl. Oxf., letters to F. G. Stephens · University of British Columbia, Imogen Dennis collection · University of British Columbia, Leathart MSS
Likenesses wood-engraving, NPG; repro. in *ILN* (11 Feb 1888), 142
Wealth at death £981 2s. 2d.: resworn administration with will, Sept 1889, *CGPLA Eng. & Wales*

Inchcape. For this title name *see* Mackay, James Lyle, first earl of Inchcape (1852–1932); Mackay, Kenneth James William, third earl of Inchcape (1917–1994).

Inchiquin. For this title name *see* O'Brien, Murrough, first earl of Inchiquin (c.1614–1674); O'Brien, William, second earl of Inchiquin (c.1640–1692).

Inchyra. For this title name *see* Millar, Frederick Robert Hoyer, first Baron Inchyra (1900–1989).

Incledon, Benjamin (*bap.* 1730, *d.* 1796), antiquary and genealogist, baptized on 6 June 1730 at Pilton, near Barnstaple, was the second son of Robert Incledon of Pilton House, Barnstaple, and his second wife, Penelope, daughter of John Sanford of Nynehead, Somerset. He was educated at Blundell's School in Tiverton. Following the death of his father in 1758, he inherited his estate, his elder brother James having died in 1741. In 1757 he married Margaret (*d.* 1803), second daughter and coheir of John Newton of Tiverton; they had two sons and a daughter.

Incledon was elected recorder of the borough of Barnstaple in 1758, a position he held until his death. He carried out much research into Barnstaple's municipal history and produced a list of the town's mayors dating from 1303, and its parliamentary representatives from 1295. His researches into other aspects of Devon's history included papers on monumental inscriptions from Devon churches; inscriptions from churches and churchyards containing Devon family names; and pedigrees of Devon families. One such was the *Stemmata Fortescuana*, used by Lord Clermont in his *History of the Family of Fortescue*. Incledon's unexplained failure to reply to Richard Polwhele, who had written to him seeking genealogical material for his forthcoming *History of Devonshire*, resulted in an angry letter from Polwhele which was published in both the *Gentleman's Magazine* (1791, 308) and Polwhele's *Traditions and Recollections* (1826).

Incledon was elected a feoffee of Blundell's School in 1765; he was also a trustee of Comyn's or Chilcott's free English school at Tiverton. In 1792 he printed, at his own expense, *Donations of Peter Blundell and other Benefactors to the Free Grammar School at Tiverton*. His account of the leper hospital of St Margaret at Pilton was published in *Archaeologia*, volume 12.

Incledon died at Barnstaple on 7 August 1796 and was buried in Pilton church. His widow died at Castle House, Barnstaple, on 8 September 1803. His collection of papers remained with the family until 1830, when his son Robert sold them for £100 to Strong, an Exeter bookseller. They were subsequently bought by Thomas Thorpe and in 1834 they were sold to Sir Thomas Phillips. Most of these were subsequently deposited in the North Devon Athenaeum, Barnstaple.

W. P. COURTNEY, *rev.* J. A. MARCHAND

Sources J. L. Vivian, ed., *The visitations of the county of Devon, comprising the herald's visitations of 1531, 1564, and 1620* (privately printed, Exeter, [1895]), 498–9 · J. R. Chanter, *Sketches of the literary history of Barnstaple* [1866], 66 · R. Dymond, 'The customs of the manors of Braunton', *Report and Transactions of the Devonshire Association*, 20 (1888), 254–303, esp. 298 [biographical notice] · 'Seventh report of the committee in Devonshire records', *Report and Transactions of the Devonshire Association*, 28 (1896), 110–73, esp. 112–13 · B. W. Oliver, 'The long bridge of Barnstaple, pt 2', *Report and Transactions of the Devonshire Association*, 78 (1946), 177–91, esp. 180 · will, PRO, PROB 11/1290, sig. 336
Archives North Devon Athenaeum, Barnstaple, Devon · North Devon RO, Barnstaple, papers | priv. coll., Fortescue MSS
Wealth at death see will, PRO, PROB 11/1290, sig. 336

Incledon, Charles (*bap.* 1763, *d.* 1826), singer, was baptized Benjamin—a name he later forsook for Charles—at St Keverne, Cornwall, on 5 February 1763, the son of Bartholomew Incledon, a surgeon, and his wife, Loveday. At the age of eight he entered the Exeter Cathedral choir, where he studied under William Jackson. In circumstances still unclear he joined the navy as a seaman and served in the latter stages of the War of American Independence; his officers are said to have encouraged his singing. In 1784 he was paid off and made his first stage appearance at Southampton with Collins's company, as Alphonso in Arnold's *The Castle of Andalusia*; he later said that he knew what it was to be a strolling player earning half a guinea a week. In 1785 he reached Bath, where he appeared as Belville in Shield's *Rosina*; he was taught, and presented in concerts at Bath and Bristol, by the retired castrato Venanzio Rauzzini. He continued to appear at Bath through the late 1780s, and also sang each summer from 1786 at Vauxhall, performing mainly patriotic songs.

Incledon made his London stage début at Covent Garden on 17 September 1790, as Dermot in Shield's *The Poor Soldier*. Until 1815 he appeared there each season, apart from a few weeks in 1797–8 after a tiff over a part he thought unworthy, and a year's break in 1811–12 caused by a dispute over pay; he joined seven other actors, among them Joseph George Holman, in 1801 in their 'statement of differences' with the proprietors, but remained in the company. He also sang in oratorio, including the first London performance of Haydn's *Creation* (28 March 1800). His initial salary of £6 a week rose gradually to £20 and then fell back in 1812–15 to £17, but his annual benefit almost doubled the total sum. In the summers he appeared in Dublin (in 1803 he and his second wife were nearly drowned in the wreck of their ship on the harbour bar) or made extensive concert tours to Liverpool, Manchester, York, Edinburgh, and other British towns. He was quickly recognized as the finest English tenor of his day, who could hold his own with ease opposite Mrs Billington in Arne's virtuoso opera *Artaxerxes*. The taste of the time, however, required him to sing in ballad operas such as Bates's *The Woodman* and (as Macheath) *The Beggar's Opera*, besides many farces. In concert his repertory included sailor songs and patriotic pieces, but he was most famous for the songs 'Black-ey'd Susan' and his standby 'The Storm', a dramatic work, said to have astonished the great French tragedian Talma.

Incledon was none the less generally thought a poor actor. He stood out for his 'full and open' voice, which 'seemed to flow as from a copious spring' (Robson, 216–17), his high, brilliant falsetto, quite unlike his chest voice but just as strong, and his skill in ornamentation, particularly his shake; Haydn noted in 1791 'a good voice and quite a good style, but he uses the falsetto to excess. He sang a trill on high C and ran up to G' (quoted in Robbins Landon). Complaints of his lack of musical education and contradictory accounts of his character (vanity and plainspokenness, frugality and extravagance) seem due in part to his vulgarity: he never lost his west-country accent— (Byron liked to mimic his 'Thaut's impossible!'; *Letters and Journals*, 5.182, 8.97)—his clumsy manner, or his liking for low, mainly theatrical, company.

Of Incledon's three wives, the first two were from Bath: on 17 August 1787 he married Jane Lowther (1768/9–1800), mother of at least six of his eight children, and, on 8 February 1801, Mary Ann Howell (*d.* 1811). In 1813 he married a widow, Martha Hart, who survived him. After 1815 his voice was worn and he needed money; he now sang in minor London theatres or on tour, travelling in 1817–18 to New York (where he had a mixed reception) and other

North American cities. After two London farewell concerts in 1817 and 1822 he retired to Brighton. He made a last farewell appearance at Southampton in 1824. He died on 11 February 1826 of a stroke while on a visit to Worcester Glee Club, and was buried on the 20th in Hampstead churchyard, together with his first wife and five of their children who had died in infancy. His eldest son, **Charles Venanzio Incledon** (1788–1865), made a reluctant and unsuccessful début at Drury Lane (as Meadows in *Love in a Village*, 3 October 1829) and spent the latter part of his life teaching English in Vienna; he died at Bad Tüffer, Austria. JOHN ROSSELLI

Sources Highfill, Burnim & Langhans, *BDA* · [Clarke], *The Georgian era: memoirs of the most eminent persons*, 4 (1834), 289 · Boase & Courtney, *Bibl. Corn.*, 3.1241, suppl., 263 · G. C. Boase, *Collectanea Cornubiensia: a collection of biographical and topographical notes relating to the county of Cornwall* (1890), 405 · W. Robson, *The old play-goer* (1846), 216–17 · *GM*, 1st ser., 70 (1800), 93 · *GM*, 1st ser., 81/1 (1811), 597 · C. Mathews (elder), *Memoirs*, ed. Mrs Mathews (1838–9), 1.152, 154 · T. J. Walsh, *Opera in Dublin, 1705–1797: the social scene* (1973) · G. C. D. Odell, *Annals of the New York stage*, 15 vols. (1927–49), vol. 2, pp. 495–9, 502, 510–15 · *Diary, reminiscences, and correspondence of Henry Crabb Robinson*, ed. T. Sadler, 1 (1869), 343; 2 (1869), 418 · *Byron's letters and journals*, ed. L. A. Marchand, 5 (1976), 182; 8 (1978), 97 · H. C. Robbins Landon, *Haydn in England: 1791–1795* (1976), vol. 3 of *Haydn: chronicle and works*

Likenesses G. Dance, pencil drawing, 1798, NPG · attrib. M. A. Shee, portrait, oils, *c.*1815, Royal College of Music, London · Alais, engraving (after Forster), Harvard TC · S. De Wilde, two oil paintings, Garr. Club · S. De Wilde, watercolour (as Captain Macheath in *The beggar's opera*), Garr. Club · Thomson, engraving (after Singleton; singing 'The storm', in *Ella Rosenberg*), Harvard TC · Woolnoth, engraving (after Wageman), Harvard TC · mezzotint (after J. T. Barber-Beaumont; singing 'The storm', in *Ella Rosenberg*), Garr. Club · prints, BM

Wealth at death financial difficulty in last few years; £50 annuity to wife: will, Highfill, Burnim & Langhans, *BDA*

Incledon, Charles Venanzio (1788–1865). *See under* Incledon, Charles (*bap.* 1763, *d.* 1826).

Inderwick, Frederick Andrew (1836–1904), lawyer, the fourth son of Andrew Inderwick, Royal Navy officer, and his wife, Jane, daughter of J. Hudson, was born in London on 23 April 1836. He was educated privately at Brighton, and then at Trinity College, Cambridge, where he matriculated in Michaelmas term 1853, but did not graduate. He was admitted a student of the Inner Temple on 16 April 1855, and was called to the bar on 26 January 1858. On 4 August 1857 he married Frances Maria, the daughter of John Wilkinson of the Exchequer and Audit Department.

In 1857 the jurisdiction of Doctors' Commons over matrimonial and testamentary causes was abolished, and the courts of probate and divorce were created. Inderwick attached himself to this branch of the profession which speedily developed a special bar of its own. He had learned during his pupillage the working of the old 'Commons' practice and he soon made his reputation as a very capable and effective advocate. He took silk on 19 March 1874, and was made a bencher of his inn on 5 June 1877. He rapidly obtained a complete lead in what became from 1876 the Probate, Divorce, and Admiralty Division of the High

Court of Justice, while still occasionally accepting briefs on the south-eastern circuit, which he had joined immediately after his call. His elevation to the bench was confidently predicted; but promotion never came, and in August 1903, in the full enjoyment of a highly lucrative practice, he accepted the post of commissioner in lunacy.

After two unsuccessful attempts to enter parliament as a Liberal—for Cirencester in 1868 and Dover in 1874—Inderwick was returned for Rye in April 1880, but was defeated at the general election in December 1885, when he stood for the Rye division of the county of Sussex.

Inderwick's interests were closely bound up with the Cinque Ports, and he twice (1892–3) served as mayor of Winchelsea, near which he had a residence. Inderwick was a prolific writer on historical and antiquarian subjects, including the English civil war, and his work on the records of the Inner Temple was well regarded. He was elected FSA in 1894. He died at 10 Rothesay Place, Edinburgh, on 16 August 1904, and was buried at Winchelsea.

J. B. ATLAY, rev. ERIC METCALFE

Sources WWBMP · WWW · J. Foster, Men-at-the-bar: a biographical hand-list of the members of the various inns of court, 2nd edn (1885) · The Times (19 Aug 1904) · Venn, Alum. Cant. · private information (1912)
Likenesses Spy [L. Ward], caricature chromolithograph, 1896, NPG; repro. in VF (30 July 1896) · G. Frampton, marble bust, 1906, Gov. Art Coll.
Wealth at death £34,252 9s. 2d.: resworn probate, 30 Aug 1904, CGPLA Eng. & Wales

Indian visitors (act. c.1720–c.1810) came from many social classes and backgrounds. They rose in number from a few in the seventeenth century to over a thousand annually by the first decade of the nineteenth century. Indian seamen and male and female servants proved most numerous among them. Indian businessmen, diplomats, and travellers often appeared more individually prominent in British society. In addition, the Indian wives, mistresses, and children of Europeans occasionally visited Britain. Further, some Indians, for example Sake Deen *Mahomed (1759–1851), remained in Britain as immigrants.

Some élite Indian visitors wrote books describing their explorations in Britain for the edification of Indian readers, thus shaping Indian perceptions of Britain; others wrote for British audiences, thus influencing how Britons viewed Asia and Asians. Male élite Indian visitors repeatedly commented about their relatively free social intercourse with British women of their own social class, a level of association convention in India would not have permitted between their own womenfolk and European male visitors. They also uniformly remarked on how parochial the British public proved to be, as illustrated by the large number of mystified but well-disposed Britons who gathered round them whenever they appeared in public wearing their Indian clothing. During the eighteenth century none of these Indian accounts mentions any racial hostility against them, rather only the celebrity status they enjoyed. The far more numerous lower-class Indian visitors rarely described their own experiences. Nevertheless, British judicial documents, newspaper reports, and manuscripts and books record their presence. Many occasionally encountered less hospitable and more prejudicial attitudes from Britons than did élite Indian visitors.

Over the eighteenth century growing seaborne trade between India and Europe created demand for Indian sailors. Ships leaving India faced shortages of European seamen due to European wars, high levels of shipboard deaths from disease or injury, and desertions by Europeans on arrival in India. In their places Indian sailors (lascars) consequently shipped in growing numbers for Britain, especially London, despite the Navigation Acts and other parliamentary legislation seeking to minimize or prohibit their employment on British ships. These Indian sailors were often recruited by Indian labour contractors (ghat sarangs) and commanded by Indian petty officers (sarangs and tindals). In Britain the East India Company and British government attempted to isolate these Indian sailors and return them quickly to India. Nevertheless, countless Indian sailors, including Emin Joseph *Emin (1726–1809), evaded these attempts and remained as visitors in Britain for considerable periods. Many such Indian visitors found temporary work in England, especially as dock workers, chimney sweeps, crossing sweepers, street entertainers, and itinerant vendors. Some ran lodging houses for other Indian visitors. Marriage between male Indian visitors and British women of their class appears to have been fairly common, with their children staying on even when their fathers returned to India.

Higher-class Europeans and Indians travelling from India to Britain often brought Indian servants with them. Some of these servants appear in British paintings and, dressed in 'oriental' livery, added exotic dignity to élite British households. Numerous Indian servants advertised in British newspapers for employment. Most eventually left Britain, often working for Britons on the voyage to India. Included among Indian servants were domestic slaves, such as **Nabob** (fl. 1780), imported in 1780 by the lawyer William Hickey (1749–1830). Some Asian slaves, like Nabob, converted to Christianity, which granted them manumission according to popular belief (although not yet British law); Nabob did not remain free after his return to India.

Middle-class Indians also visited England. **Munshi Isma'il** (fl. 1771–1773) came as Indian secretary and Persian language teacher to an East India Company official, Claud Russell (b. 1732). Although employed by Russell, Isma'il brought along two Indian servants of his own. Isma'il later wrote Tarikh-i jadid ('New history') in Persian. He was particularly impressed with the hot springs of Bath and with Britain's extensive newspaper industry and numerous coffee houses.

Many Indian businessmen believed that direct personal appeals to the East India Company's court of directors or the British government could override adverse actions or policies by company officials in India. **Naorozji Rastamji** (fl. 1724–1725), son of a Parsi broker to the company, ventured to London in April 1724, pursuing his family's commercial dispute with the company's Bombay government.

During his year-long stay in England he won in arbitration, receiving over £50,000 in compensation and a dress of honour from the company's directors. Similarly, **Gregore Cojamaul** (*fl.* 1768–1770) and **Johanes Padre Rafael** (*fl.* 1768–1770), Armenian Christians long domiciled in India, arrived in London in 1769 with a petition for the company's directors against its officials in India. When this petition failed, they turned to the House of Commons, testifying before its select committee on Indian affairs about abuses by company officials against Indians.

Several Indian diplomatic missions visited England. **Mirza I'tizam al-Din** (*fl.* 1765–1785) left India in January 1766 as part of a diplomatic mission from the Mughal emperor Shah Alam, seeking British government support against the company. Robert Clive, however, blocked the emperor's letter and £10,000 gift for King George III, frustrating I'tizam al-Din, who returned to India late in 1768. In 1785 I'tizam al-Din completed a Persian-language account of his visit to France, England, and Scotland: *Shigurf-nama-i Vilayat* ('Wonder book of Europe'). While he appreciated the cordial reception he received from the British, he noted their inability to read cultured literature in Persian or to appreciate the advantages of Islam over Christianity. **Hanumant Rao** (*fl.* 1781–1782), a Brahman, and his assistant **Maniar** (*fl.* 1781–1782), a Parsi, visited England in 1781–2 as emissaries to the English court, representing the Maratha peshwa Raghunath Rao (*d.* 1783). Edmund Burke arranged for this Brahman diplomat to live for a time in his greenhouse at Beaconsfield; living in a separate building, he could prepare his food and dine in isolation without being polluted by Europeans.

Among Indian travellers **Mirza Abu Talib Khan Isfahani** (1752–1806) visited Ireland in 1799, England in 1800–3, and the continent. British high society received him under his self-styled title 'the Persian prince'. He later wrote in Persian both a prose account of his travels (and critical opinions of British society), *Masir-i Talibi fi bilad-i Afranji* ('Talib's travels in the lands of the Europeans', completed by 1805), and also a *mathnavi* (poem in rhyming couplets) of 1000 verses about his visit. He particularly noted the loose habits of European women, compared to élite Muslim Indians. To prove his point he wrote an essay, 'Vindication of the liberties of the Asiatic women', which demonstrated how the cold climate, monogamy, provincialism, and commercial activities of England forced Englishwomen into close quarters with their husbands and also into the degrading public sphere of business. In contrast, Abu Talib asserted that, owing to the more cosmopolitan and diverse society of India, Muslim women there enjoyed life in a separate, autonomous, luxurious, and congenial women's sphere, protected by purdah.

Additionally, many Indian wives or mistresses of European men of various classes, from private soldiers to aristocrats, visited Britain, some remaining as immigrants. For example **Halime Banu** [*known as* Nur Begam] (1770–1853), mistress or wife (by Islamic rite) of Benoît de Boigne (1751–1830), visited England in 1797 with him and their two children, Ali Bakhsh (otherwise Charles Alexander (1792–1853)) and Banu, or Anna (1789–1804).

A significant proportion of these visiting sailors, servants, wives, mistresses, and children were born in India of European, especially Portuguese, ancestry or were of mixed Indian and European descent. The East India Company classed such people as 'natives of India', although it officially distinguished those of them having patrilineal European ancestry as legally distinct from 'non-European natives of India'. MICHAEL H. FISHER

Sources 'Papers relating to the care of Lascars', East India Company, Marine Department, 1793–1818, BL OIOC, L/MAR/C/902, vols. 1–2 · E. J. Emin, *Life and adventures of Emin Joseph Emin*, ed. A. Apcar, rev. 2nd edn (1918) · A. T. Khan, *Travels of Mirza Abu Taleb Khan in Asia, Africa, and Europe during the years 1799, 1800, 1801, 1802 and 1803; written by himself in the Persian language*, trans. C. Stewart, 3 vols. (1814) · M. Itesa Mudeen, *Shigurf Namah-i Velaet or excellent intelligence concerning Europe; being the travels of Mirza Itesa Modeed in Great Britain and France translated from the original Persian manuscript into Hindoostanee, with an English version and notes*, trans. J. E. Alexander (1827) · S. Digby, 'An eighteenth century narrative of a journey from Bengal to England: Munshi Isma'il's "New History"', *Urdu and Muslim South Asia: studies in honour of Ralph Russell*, ed. C. Shackle (1989) · *The correspondence of Edmund Burke*, ed. T. W. Copeland and others, 10 vols. (1958–78) · W. Hickey, *Memoirs of William Hickey*, ed. A. Spencer, 3rd edn (1919–25), vol. 2 · H. Das, 'The early Indian visitors to England', *Calcutta Review*, 3rd ser., 13 (1924), 83–114 · R. Visram, *Ayahs, lascars and princes: Indians in Britain, 1700–1947* (1986) · G. Khan, *Indian Muslim perceptions of the West during the eighteenth century* (1998) · D. F. Karaka, *History of the Parsis* (1884) · J. J. Hecht, *Continental and colonial servants in eighteenth century England*, Smith College Studies in History, 40 (1954) · P. Fryer, *Staying power: the history of Black people in Britain* (1984) · R. B. Saksena, *European and Indo-European poets of Urdu and Persian* (1941) · D. Young, *Fountain of the elephants* (1959)

Archives BL OIOC

Likenesses portrait (Mirza I'tizam al-Din), repro. in Itesa Mudeen, *Shigurf Namah-i Velaet or excellent intelligence concerning Europe*, trans. Alexander, frontispiece

Indulf [Illulb mac Causantín] (*bap.* **927**?, *d.* **962**), king in Scotland, was the son of *Constantine II (*d.* 952). He had at least one (probably older) brother, who was killed at the battle of 'Brunanburh' in 937, and a sister who married Olaf Guthfrithson, king of Dublin (*d.* 941). It is indicative of the extent of Scandinavian influence upon Scotland at this time that his own name, and the names of two of his sons, should have been Norse in origin. He became king on the death of *Malcolm I in 954. During his reign Edinburgh was taken from the earl of Northumbria, to be held by the Scots thereafter. Indulf is said (in a late and debatable source) to have expelled Bishop Fothad (*d.* 963) from St Andrews. His kingship witnessed renewed Scandinavian pressure in the east of Scotland. A viking fleet was destroyed in Buchan, but he was killed in 962 by a Norse host at 'Invercullen', probably either Cowie (near Stonehaven, which was important strategically) or Cullen (Banffshire). He is said to have been buried on Iona. He was succeeded by *Dubh, son of Malcolm I. He had three sons, *Culen (*d.* 971), who became king, Eochaid (*d.* 971), and Olaf (*d.* 977). DAUVIT BROUN

Sources A. O. Anderson, ed. and trans., *Early sources of Scottish history, AD 500 to 1286*, 1 (1922), 409 n. 3, 468–70 · M. O. Anderson, *Kings and kingship in early Scotland*, rev. edn (1980), 249–53, 265–89

Industrial spies (*act. c.*1700–*c.*1800) were among numerous Europeans with an interest in technology who visited Britain during the seventeenth and eighteenth centuries, knowing that the country was ahead of the rest of Europe in its manufacturing techniques and organization.

Industrial grand tourists Depending on the particular field, an 'industrial grand tour' could include much of Great Britain and Ireland. Not all these men were entirely innocent visitors. Some were industrial spies, sent by their governments or acting on behalf of their own or family businesses, and knowing that they were not welcome at every door, while some of them concocted elaborate deceptions to cover their real purpose. The focus of interest changed over time, from the early Scandinavian concern with the iron and brass industries, through the Russian and French interest in shipbuilding and gun founding, to the later study of steam engines, textiles, pottery, and glass, but most took the opportunity to view whatever was available to them. Some already spoke good English, others took steps to learn. They also needed to recognize the important elements of what they were seeing, and to record these as notes and/or technical drawings. Many of these documents, having been submitted to authority on return and preserved in official archives, are now being studied and, in a few cases, published for the benefit of scholars.

As British technology improved on that of its neighbours, steps were taken to prevent the recruitment of skilled men and the transfer overseas of information and actual machines. In 1696 an act was passed to ban export of machinery: it was aimed primarily at the export of knitting frames. Other legislation followed, to prohibit the export of various types of machines and tools and prevent skilled men from leaving the country, with France seen as the principal attraction. The act of 1774 applied to 'any machine, tool, press, paper, utensil or implement whatsoever', and the 1785 Tools Act prohibited all exportation of tools, with an emphasis on manufacturing machines and engines of all sorts. Despite these restrictions, many skilled machine makers and operatives were tempted to emigrate, and, by more or less devious methods, various foreigners managed to take down descriptions and drawings of machinery and processes for replication in their own countries. British manufacturers were often in a difficult situation; while they sought to keep certain processes secret, they were at the same time eager to show off their manufacturing facilities and their products, with a view to selling overseas. A number of young men went to London as apprentices or journeymen with the leading scientific instrument makers. While expected to learn, some undoubtedly contravened the law by taking home drawings, models, and even machinery.

The reverse process also operated, albeit on a smaller scale, since Britain was a leader in so many fields. In the seventeenth century the art of making crystal glass was jealously guarded in Venice, and was furtively investigated by English merchants and travellers. They found, as was often the case, that written descriptions were unsatisfactory, for only experienced workmen could make the apparatus and carry out the operations necessary for many of these technical processes. Despite strict laws prohibiting their movement, many Venetian glassworkers were enticed to various parts of western Europe, including London. In the eighteenth century similar attempts were made to bring from France the manufacture of large crystal plates for mirrors, leading by the 1770s to their production at St Helens in Lancashire. The most successful British spying mission seems to have been that of John *Lombe [*see under* Lombe, Thomas], who in 1716 went to Leghorn and managed to see and draw the machinery for twisting silk thread. Small quantities of this thread had hitherto been illicitly imported into Britain, but with the arrival of immigrant Huguenot silk weavers far more was needed. John's brother Thomas secured a patent and the necessary capital and erected a vast silk throwing mill, powered by the River Derwent, near Derby.

Scandinavians By the end of the seventeenth century Britain still imported the bulk of her needs of bar iron and copper from Sweden, but copper refining was already under way around Bristol, an area of mercantile importance close to ample supplies of fuel and water. Other products of the Bristol area included iron, brass, pottery, glass, and gunpowder. The Swedish mining industry therefore had cause for concern lest the advancement of refining processes in Britain diminish the need for Swedish goods. As early as 1696 the Bergskollegium ('College of Mines') sent a mining expert, Thomas Cletcher, to inspect the copper works of Elton and Wayne at Bristol. In 1710 Göran Wallerius, a metallurgist, visited Redbrook copper works near Bristol, but he was taken for a spy and told to leave.

A more professional approach was that of **Jonas Alströmer** (1685–1761), who arrived in Britain in 1707, settled down as a successful businessman, took British nationality, and became Swedish consul in London. In 1714–15 and in 1719–20 he made extensive tours, paying much attention to industries in the Bristol region but also looking at textile manufacture. On his return to Sweden in 1724 he introduced new breeds of sheep and set up a manufactory for woollen goods.

Alströmer introduced **Henrik Kalmeter** (1693–1750), mining engineer, who had been sent abroad by the Bergskollegium. He arrived in Britain in 1719 and went to stay with his uncle, a music teacher, in Edinburgh. He toured the mining region of Leadhills, examining the process of extracting the lead, which was mainly sent to Holland for use in lead glaze, and also its by-product, silver. He visited several great houses on the way to St Andrews, noting forestry and plantings. At Leith he visited salt works, sugar boilers, and soap manufactories. He took in a coalmine near Kinghorn, and at Dryden saw working one of the earliest Newcomen engines to reach Scotland. Kalmeter also toured England; in Bristol he called on Nehemiah *Champion (1649–1722) [*see under* Champion family (*per. c.*1670–1794)], who allowed him to look over his brass-foundry. Kalmeter wrote two important works on the iron industry, parts of which were incorporated with Emanuel Swedenborg's *Opera philosophica and mineralia* (1734). Swedenborg (1688–1722) was better known as a philosopher, but he travelled in England in 1710–12 before being appointed to the Bergskollegium in 1716.

A known spy was **Reinhold Rütker Angerstein** (1718–1760), ironmaster, a member of Jernkontoret, the Swedish ironmasters' association, founded in 1747. Its purpose was to find a solution to the difficulties then besetting the Swedish iron industry, principally poor demand and low prices. As chemical and technical learning advanced, the Swedes realized that they should concentrate on high quality. When English ironmasters discovered how to use coal in the manufacture of wrought iron the Swedes were eager to inspect the process. Between 1753 and 1755 Angerstein was welcomed by Champion in Bristol; he also looked at the manufacture of steel, tinplate, and glass, and the process of desilvering lead. He traversed England and left voluminous notes on prices, wages, and conditions of commerce and industry, with comments on London's Swedish colony.

John Ludwig Robsahm (*fl.* 1760–1761) extended spying techniques because he was eager to obtain all sorts of secret information. He arrived in 1760 and stayed for a year. He was in Bristol in 1761 and visited Champion's works after dark, although Champion was one of the few industrialists to keep relatively open house for foreign visitors. Robsahm managed to see Benjamin *Huntsman's famous steel casting works, but did not fully comprehend the secret process; he also investigated a zinc works near Bristol. Huntsman's secret was finally uncovered by Benkt Qvist Andersson, a mining engineer who was in England in 1766–7. He set up near Stockholm the first cast-steel works outside England.

The astronomer **Bengt Ferrner** (1724–1802) came to England as tutor to a young nobleman. After having left his pupil at Bath he went to Bristol, where he took elaborate steps to avoid detection. He tried to make contacts with workmen in order to learn covertly about Champion's works, and visited a tinplate mill and lead and calamine mines. He also tried to entice skilled men to emigrate to Sweden, a practice which became increasingly common. In 1754–6 the Norwegian **Morton Waern** (*fl.* 1754–1756) was in England to learn about crown glass manufacture, the first project proposed by the Konglige Allernaadigst Octrojerade Norske Compagnie, set up to exploit Norway's natural resources. He travelled to Newcastle upon Tyne, then the centre of the industry, and also to Leith, Hull, Bristol, Liverpool, and Yarmouth, obtaining drawings of furnaces and information on the composition of the glass and sending home reports and samples of raw materials. All his correspondence went through intermediaries so as to prevent detection. His most important task was to persuade skilled men to move to Norway, and he tried to recruit a team consisting of master, gatherer, blower, and finisher from the same glasshouse, so that they could work well together. But suspicion was aroused when he tried to suborn workmen; he was arrested and imprisoned in Newgate. Granted bail, he fled the country, taking his notes and papers with him. He had earlier succeeded in recruiting men in Newcastle and Liverpool, and

they set up the first crown glass factory at Hurdal, 80 kilometres north of Christiania.

Equally covert in his approach was **Jøns Mathias Ljungberg** (1748–1812), a Swede by birth who became professor of mathematics and astronomy at Kiel and a Danish civil servant. He asked for six months' leave to travel abroad in order to study mathematics and astronomy and to purchase instruments. His first visit to Britain in 1777 was uneventful, but when he made another request in 1778 he was seen as the ideal person to bring back a spinning-machine and associated equipment. He failed to acquire the machine, but brought sufficient information to allow one to be constructed in Copenhagen. In 1780 he severed his association with Kiel and moved to Kommercekollegiet. In 1787 Ljungberg was arrested in London just as he was loading three years' harvest of technical espionage onto a ship bound for Denmark. The customs inspectors uncovered patented machinery, scientific instruments, models, drawings, and notebooks. The haul included items from the Wedgwood potteries at Etruria and also containers of cobalt, lead, and manganese ores. His notes indicated visits to Staffordshire, Cornwall, Birmingham, Coalbrookdale, Derby, Manchester, Leeds, Matlock, and Nottingham. Ljungberg had earlier been caught bribing workmen to bring him measurements of kilns and other equipment. Before the government could arrange for his notes to be translated and encourage manufacturers to bring charges, the Danish legation put up the £300 bail set, and he was freed and fled; furthermore, the legation bought his confiscated goods at auction, and eventually most of his plunder was returned to him. He went back to Kommercekollegiet, and the fruits of this expedition gradually appeared in the pottery and porcelain manufactories of Denmark. In 1793 he was back in England, this time studying the canal system.

The Dane **Jesper Bidstrup** (1763–1802) was sent by his government to acquire skills and knowledge in scientific instrument making; he arrived in London in 1787 and spent the next ten years in improving his skills, making wooden models, and acquiring the machinery, including tube drawing and glass cutting machines and a dividing engine, to establish himself back in Copenhagen. By 1797 everything was ready, including the first coal-fuelled cupola furnace to reach Scandinavia. The machines were dismantled and hidden among other goods on separate ships destined for Cuxhaven and Copenhagen. Bidstrup did not live long enough to enjoy the fruits of his labours. He fell ill on his return and died in 1802, leaving the most splendid workshop and machinery, which was taken as state property and handed over to other instrument makers in Copenhagen.

Russians **Nikolay Ivanovich Korsakov** (1749–1788) was sent by the Petersburg Engineering Corps to study canal building. He arrived in London in April 1775, studied in Oxford for a year, and set out the following May for Scotland, bearing letters of introduction to John *Smeaton, who recommended that he look first at the Forth and Clyde Canal. Throughout his tour Korsakov took copious detailed notes of canals, mills, foundries, manufactories, and machines, concerning not just their construction, but also their adoption and development, not omitting the patent system. He managed to get into a number of otherwise closed places by providing himself with letters of introduction, and thus at Newcastle saw a machine for gun boring. At the Carron ironworks he was not permitted to see the gun boring machinery and could make only general sketches. He spent three months in Glasgow, was made a freeman of the city, and visited Glasgow and Edinburgh universities. On his way south he spent time on the Leeds and Liverpool Canal, and on the Bridgewater, the latter with its aqueduct over the River Irwell being a famous sight. He called on Josiah *Wedgwood, then hurried on to the Soho works of Matthew *Boulton and John Fothergill. While these two men were eager to publicize their products with a view to entering the Russian market, there was always a reluctance to admit foreigners freely to the works. Fothergill went to Russia in 1776; James *Watt, who had been invited to settle there in 1771, was hoping to sell engines to Russia, but Korsakov, while admiring Watt, did not realize the full potential of Watt engines and advised his masters to keep to Newcomen engines if Watt's charges seemed high.

Korsakov was also invited to John *Wilkinson's foundries at Bilston and Broseley, where he saw a blowing machine for coke smelting of iron ore and lesser machines. He next visited Southampton and Portsmouth before returning to Leeds, where at last he was able to meet Smeaton in person. His last six months were spent in Oxford drawing up his canal plans. Korsakov was impressed by what he saw, noting it with an observant and critical eye and appreciating both craft skills and the university education which he sampled. He spent two years in France and Italy before returning to Russia. He was not employed on canals but went to the newly annexed Crimea, where he built the city that became Sevastopol. He died in an accident during the Turkish War in 1788.

In 1719 **Andrey Konstantinovich Narkov** (1680?–1756), an outstanding machine tool engineer, went to London with orders to seek information on the newly invented improved methods of steaming and bending the oak used in shipbuilding. He failed in this task, but was able to see a screw cutting lathe for the Royal Mint, a lead drawing machine for the Admiralty, dies for coining, gear cutting machinery, a boring machine, and a silver and gold sheet rolling mill. He also discovered the secret of steel smelting, which made possible the casting of hollow steel cylinders for lathe chucks.

Nikolay Galaktionovich Chizhov (1731–1767) was a trained instrument maker who went to London in 1760 to improve his skills under George *Adams the elder [see under Adams family (per. 1734–1817)]. He bought as many instruments as possible and carefully examined larger ones, such as James *Short's new 12 foot telescope at Greenwich. Another Russian, Vorobyov, worked in 1781 under Kenneth McCulloch, compass maker. Osip Ivanovich Shishorin worked for five years with John Stancliffe; Vasily Konstantinovich Sveshnikov was five years with Simon Spicer. When writing home for money, they

explained that they had to bribe knowledgeable workmen in order to acquire information that their masters would not disclose to foreigners.

Frenchmen and Belgians Charles Albert (b. 1767, d. in or after 1834), originally from Strasbourg, had previously spent a year in Manchester when in 1790 he was approached by two acquaintances who intended to set up a cotton mill in Toulouse. They asked him to go to England to examine textile machinery and recruit workmen for the Toulouse mill. Albert settled again in Manchester and found an accomplice, with whose help he set about his tasks. He was in London in November 1791 to meet the two men he had recruited, but one failed to appear and Albert heard that the man planned to denounce him. Albert sent his recruit to France with the notes and drawings and returned to Manchester, where he was arrested in December. Offered his freedom in exchange for helping to extradite the man who was in France, Albert refused for the patriotic reason that France needed skilled men.

Albert was sent to Lancaster Castle to await trial; meanwhile the French envoy and the acquaintances who had sent him to England pledged support and raised £500 for his bail. However, at Newgate three charges were laid against him with bail set at £500 on each, and as this sum was not forthcoming Albert was returned to Lancaster. In August 1792 he was found guilty, sentenced to a year in prison, and fined £500. When his term expired no money was produced, and he spent another four years in prison as a debtor. Meanwhile the Toulouse mill prospered, especially as the French Revolution had increased the need for military uniforms.

Eventually John Higgin, the prison governor, petitioned for Albert's release. Albert was befriended by the Johnson family of Bolton-le-Sands, and on his release in December 1796 he married their daughter Elizabeth (d. 1834) and left England with instructions not to return unless the fine was paid. He sought to recover the promised money from his acquaintances, but they had no time for him; at length he took them to court, won his case, and later still was reimbursed for his pains. He settled in Strasbourg as an engineer and inventor. His years in England were not wasted; in the Paris Exhibition of 1806 he won a gold medal and 6000 francs for his invention of spinning and weaving machinery and a small steam engine. After his wife's death in 1834 Albert sent to her family medals commemorating her birth, marriage, and death and a précis of his story.

Gabriel Jars (1732–1769) was the son of an owner of copper mines in the Lyonnais, where he was trained before coming to the attention of Trudaine, minister of commerce, under whose patronage he visited mines in central Europe. His brief was to learn about minerals, metallurgy, and dyestuffs derived from minerals. In July 1764 he was sent to Britain, ostensibly on a scientific and educational tour but in fact with detailed instructions to discover many aspects of industry and manufacture. Jars went first to Newcastle where he learned English. He then examined coalmines in that district and in lowland Scotland, looking at the regulations, the prices, and the uses of the various types of coal, including that for coke, a substance not known in France. He then looked at the lead–silver mines and their management and the Cornish tin mines with their stannary laws, calling in on any copper mines which happened to lie on his route. He was also commanded to investigate the iron smelting practices, steel making, and the source of iron ore for cementation, and he was to obtain drawings of the machinery for imparting a high polish to steel and copper artefacts. He was to discover how English files were cut and tempered to make them harder than those manufactured in Germany. Besides this exhaustive set of demands, Jars was to look at sulphuric acid production and the manufacture of earthenware, pottery, and paper, and to investigate the breeding of English sheep and to enquire whether it was possible to obtain any of these animals.

Before he left France, Jars asked the expatriate Englishman John Holker to recommend a trustworthy agent, and on arrival he contacted the marquis de Blosset, intelligence adviser at the French embassy. On his northern tour he was able to compile detailed reports on the Newcastle mines, coke works in Cumberland, the use of coal in glasshouses, and the various practices of forging and casting. He visited the famous Carron ironworks in southern Scotland where 800 workers were employed mining coal and iron ore, making coke, smelting, and casting. He also visited the alum mines of Whitby and the salt mines in Northwich.

On the manufacturing side, Jars reported on earthenware manufacture in the north-east, in Staffordshire and at Liverpool, and also on porcelain and the invention of printing on pottery. He examined the process of file manufacture at Newcastle and at Sheffield. He visited the briefly important copper mines in Yorkshire and Staffordshire, and smelting works near Derby, Bristol, and Hayle in Cornwall, although at Derby and at the brass making works at Cheadle he was prevented from seeing as much as he wished. He was able to see over the lead mines and to compare the technology with that in Europe. On his way back to London he visited a sulphuric works in Wandsworth, but could only glance round the laboratory, which the owner had staffed with Welsh women whose limited English prevented them from disclosing the secrets of manufacture. On his return, Jars was rewarded with government and academic favours, and he was later sent on further strenuous tours within Europe. He died from sunstroke in the Auvergne in August 1769.

Le Camus de Limare (b. 1736), a Louviers industrialist, went to England in 1781 at the height of the war against France (part of the American War of Independence) to examine the production of copper sheathing for warships and to recruit workmen for its manufacture. As a good English speaker, he was able to travel in England. His route is not known, but may have taken in Thomas *Williams's works at Holywell in Flintshire and on the Thames at Marlow and Wraysbury. He managed to find workmen to operate a plant which he set up at Romilly, using water power and emulating the English manufacture of regularly rolled copper plates and nails of a better shape than those previously used in French vessels.

The problem with sheathing was that catalytic corrosion took place in sea water when copper sheets were fastened by iron nails, and this could leave the hull literally leaking like a sieve. The solution was first found in Britain with the manufacture of hardened copper bolts. French scientists were eager to learn about this, and when the war ended a party consisting of one of the de Wendel family of ironmakers and other French officers called on several iron and copper masters, including Wilkinson's Ravenhead smelter. While their visits were open, care was taken to prevent the party from seeing more than they already knew, except at Ravenhead, since the Parys mine which supplied it was already negotiating for contracts with the French navy.

Bartélemy Faujas de St-Fond (1741–1819), author of *A Journey through England and Scotland to the Hebrides* (trans. A. Geikie, 2 vols., 1907), visited Britain in the guise of a mineralogist with an interest in allied technical matters. He was attached to the French inspectorate concerned with converting French industries to coal fuel, and this naturally led him to visit Wedgwood's potteries and the Newcastle glassworks, both of which were coal-fuelled and in some respects superior to similar establishments in France which were wood-fuelled. As a foreigner he was presumably suspect, for at Prestonpans, seeking to visit a sulphuric acid works, he could do no more than describe the walls surrounding the plant, so high that not even the tall chimneys were visible, while other walls surrounded the port so that the ships delivering sulphur and taking the acid away could not be seen. At the Carron ironworks he was told that although he would be taken round, there were several processes he would not see. In his supposed role as an innocent visitor he felt unable to take notes and thus had to memorize everything until he could write his reports at night.

Pierre Alexandre Forfait (1752–1807) and **Daniel Lescallier**, Baron Lescallier in the French nobility (*fl.* 1789–1790), were sent to England in 1789–90 to get the latest information on naval technology. Forfait was an experienced naval architect who rose to be in charge of administration at Le Havre. Lescallier had spent five years in England as a young man and was a fluent English speaker. He had travelled in Russia and Sweden on naval business and had held various colonial administrative posts. Their visit was not entirely successful. They arrived in the short days of early winter, the daylight hours were further reduced by bad weather, and Forfait was ill for much of the time. They found the navy yards closed to them, but this was not a handicap as they were freely admitted to the yards building vessels for the Greenland and East India trades. The men in these yards, which also built for the navy in times of war, had technical knowledge and skills equal to those in the royal dockyards. The Frenchmen also found easy access to navy and contractors' gun parks. They paid considerable attention to the process of coppering and took back samples of the new cast-iron pulleys running on copper bearings. Forfait's report remained in manuscript; plans for a possibly more secret and important mission were abandoned when Forfait was appointed to the legislative assembly.

Lieven Bauwens (1769–1822), of a noble Belgian family who engaged in industry and commerce, was sent to England at the age of seventeen to spend three years at the tannery of Underhall and Fox. Three years later he built a large tannery in Ghent, and, after the annexation of Belgium by France, another in Paris. Bauwens had relations in England and also in Hamburg, where his brother had a banking house. He was therefore able to mask his espionage behind genuine mercantile activities, and before he was twenty-nine he had made over thirty journeys to England. In 1797 he and François de Pauw, who was a relation and business associate, went to London and there recruited Saul Harding, whom they sent to Manchester to buy textile machines. Bauwens also bought machines and a small Boulton and Watt steam engine, and recruited a machine maker, a turner, and a factory manager. The first consignment consisted of machines which had been dismantled and concealed in bales of colonial goods and put on a Danish ship, but they were noticed by customs officials, who impounded the ship and cargo and fined the master. Bauwens hastily left the country, but returned when a second shipment was successfully effected. He recruited more workmen, took delivery of more machines, and with de Pauw and Harding prepared to sail from Gravesend in November 1798. They were exposed, however, when Harding's wife noisily objected to being left behind with her children, magistrates were alerted, and cover stories had to be concocted. Some of the men were taken to Yarmouth and reached Hamburg. Others deserted and informed. Harding and his men were seized and were each sentenced to a fine of £500 and a year in prison. Besides the considerable loss from the seizure of his goods, a deposit of 250,000 francs lodged with an agent was also stolen. Bauwens was condemned by Lord Erskine in the House of Lords for his transfers of knowledge first of tanning and later of the cotton machinery—he had smuggled out large mules and ancillary textile equipment, calico printing machinery, and fly-shuttle looms—and for the suborning of workmen. He subsequently built large steam-powered textile works at Passy in 1798 and at Ghent in 1799, eventually employing some three thousand people. His high-quality products earned him major prizes at the French industrial exhibitions at the turn of the century, and some of his British workmen also earned prizes for their skills. He married Mary Kenyon, daughter of the head of the Manchester workshop which had sold him the first mules. Two sons were established as industrialists in Paris and London. The Frenchman François Antoine Jecker spent some time in the workshop of Jesse *Ramsden (1735–1800), the noted scientific instrument maker, before returning to his father's instrument workshop in Paris and there building a replica of Ramsden's straight-line dividing engine.

Spaniards A young Spanish naval officer, **Jorge Juan y Santacilla** (1713–1773), was sent in 1748 with two colleagues on a secret mission to London with wide-ranging instructions to examine every aspect of shipbuilding and outfitting, to send home plans of each type of ship, and to note any new techniques and apparatus likely to be of value to the Spanish navy, and to acquire new books and scientific instruments relating to navigation. They were also to seek to persuade some of the master shipbuilders, skilled riggers, and sailmakers to emigrate to Spain.

The ostensible purpose of the visit was to contact members of the Royal Society (Juan was elected a fellow of the Royal Society in November 1749) with a view to improving their mathematics, and they were to enter the dockyards in the guise of simple sightseers. Juan was given a cipher for communicating with Richard Wall, the Spanish minister in London. Juan had no difficulty in purchasing scientific and medical instruments. As well as on aspects of naval science, he reported on printing and other techniques. An Irishman, Patrick Lahey, explained that Irish sailcloth was judged the best, and he agreed to go to Spain with his wife, some workmen, and a loom on which this superior cloth was produced. Juan managed to send in addition three shipbuilders and a rigging master, with their workmen and families, to Spain. He too, however, was betrayed by the wife of a shipbuilder; word passed to the man's employer and to the duke of Bedford, and Juan was obliged to flee in disguise on a Spanish ship. Despite being stopped and searched several times while going downriver, they were not arrested and reached France safely, where Juan bought some more books before returning to Cadiz. Under the auspices of the Sociedade Real Maritima, Gaspar José Marquez and João Maria Pedroso were apprenticed to the scientific instrument maker Jesse Ramsden for a considerably larger fee than was usual.

Conclusion It is likely that other nationals, including diplomats and chaplains, were able to take home industrial and technical information of a secret nature. The Swiss for example had an interest in textiles, and the cook at the Austrian embassy was apparently a conduit for recruiting workmen to that country. The extent and value of such activities remains undiscovered, though current research on industrial espionage is bringing home its extent, the ingenuity of the individuals concerned, and the amount of official involvement in the practice.

ANITA MCCONNELL

Sources J. R. Harris, *Industrial espionage and technology transfer* (1998) · M. W. Flinn, 'The travel diaries of Swedish engineers of the 18th century as sources of technological history', *Transactions* [Newcomen Society], 31 (1957–9), 95–110 · A. G. Cross, *'By the banks of the Thames': Russians in eighteenth-century Britain* (1980), 175–85 · T. C. Smout, 'Journal of Henry Kalmeter's travels in Scotland', *Scottish industrial history: a miscellany*, 4th ser., 14 (1978) · A. P. Woolrich, *Mechanical arts and merchandise: industrial espionage and travellers' accounts as a source for technology historians* (1986) · A. Birch, 'Foreign observers of the British iron industry during the eighteenth century', *Journal of Economic History*, 15 (1955), 23–33 · A. G. Cross, 'A Russian engineer in eighteenth century Britain: the journal of N. I. Korsakov, 1776–77', *Slavonic and East European Review*, 55 (1977), 1–

20 • A. Deprechins, *Liewen Bauwens et sa famille* (1954) • M. W. Flinn, *Svedenstierna's tour in Great Britain, 1802–3* (1973) • G. B. Gregg, ed. and trans., *The précis historique of Charles Albert: a story of industrial espionage in the 18th century* [1977] • G. McKay, 'Lichtenberg's friend: the progress of genius in the latter half of the eighteenth century', *Lychnos* (1979–80), 207–30 • J. L. Morales, 'Jorge Juan en Londres', *Revista General de Marina*, 184 (1973), 643–70 • B. F. de St-Fond, *A journey through England and Scotland to the Hebrides in 1784*, trans. A. Geikie, 2 vols. (1907) • D. C. Christensen, 'Technology transfer or cultural exchange', *Polhem*, 11 (1993), 301–32 • P. Leulliot, 'La "Biographie industrielle" de F. C. L. Albert (1764–1831)', *Annales Historiques de la Révolution Française* (1952) • S. G. Londberg, 'Bengt Ferrner', *Svenskt biografiskt lexikon*, ed. B. Hildebrand, 15 (1956), 635–43 • G. Arpi, 'The Swedish ironmasters' association', *Scandinavian Economic History Review*, 8 (1960), 77–90 • E. Naumann, 'Reinhold Rüdker Angerstein', *Svenskt biografiskt lexikon*, ed. B. Boëthius, 1 (1918), 792–3 • R. Vallerö, 'Henrik Kalmeter', *Svenskt biografiskt lexikon*, ed. E. Grill, 20 (1973–5), 574–6

Ine [Ini] (*d*. in or after 726), king of the West Saxons, was the son of Coenred, also West Saxon king (*c*.670–*c*.694), and brother of *Cuthburh and Cwenburh, supposed founders of Wimborne (and the former the widow of the Northumbrian king *Aldfrith). Ini may be a hypocoristic form of a dithematic name beginning Ing- or In-: he had a brother called Ingeld.

Background and succession to the West Saxon kingship By *c*.1175 a series of more or less absurd legends about Ine's origins were current, in evident connection with efforts to backdate the history of the see of Wells, and perhaps with the emergent saga of Glastonbury's origins. A more plausible reconstruction of his background must reckon with the complexities of the early West Saxon power structure. Coenred, who is called Ine's father in West Saxon genealogies (which are not demonstrably earlier than *c*.780) and also in the prologue to his laws, was not in the main (again later) West Saxon king-list. But he is found granting Dorset land in the earliest West Saxon charter (dated to between 669 and 676), and a Sussex charter of, perhaps, 692 lists him as 'king of the West Saxons' ahead of Ine, who has no title at all. Further, early records from Abingdon and probably relating to a minster at Bradfield, in what is now Berkshire, have both him and his son as donors. Bede says that, after the death of Cenwalh in 672, *subreguli* divided the kingdom between them for 'about ten years', until removed by Cædwalla in 685 or 686. The Anglo-Saxon Chronicle, however, reports the successive rule of Queen Seaxburh, Æscwine, and Centwine, while the genealogies which precede John of Worcester's chronicle cite the *Dicta regis Ælfredi* for a two-year reign by Æscwine's father between those of Seaxburh and Æscwine himself. It is likely that later sources were trying to give the impression that all of Wessex was governed consecutively rather than partitioned. Yet the Anglo-Saxon Chronicle readily reveals that no king between Cenwalh and Æthelwulf (*r*. 839–58) succeeded his father on the throne. One possible resolution of these contradictions is that Bede was basically right. The West Saxons' kingdom dissolved in the 670s into the constituents from which it was formed. Then, after Cædwalla (or conceivably Centwine) re-established mastery of the whole, it became the norm for kingship over Wessex to be held in turn by the leading families of its various segments, in the name of a putative common descent from the kingdom's founder, Cerdic; comparable arrangements are attested from early Christian Ireland, whose genealogical records, unlike the English, are rich enough to document it in detail. Coenred would then be a provincial *subregulus* whose son attained overall supremacy in his own lifetime; and Ine would himself be the *de facto* founder of the political order that prevailed in Wessex for the next century. He certainly anticipated most of his successors throughout this period in being challenged by rivals, one of whom is called by one text of the Anglo-Saxon Chronicle an *ætheling* ('prince of the blood').

Internal and external politics The recorded challenges to Ine come late in his reign (721, 722–5). The Irish analogy shows that a succession circulating between the segments of a notional common dynasty was far from proof against attempts to speed up the cycle by violence; and Ine's prolonged rule may have occasioned restlessness among those (as it were) awaiting their turn. The Anglo-Saxon Chronicle and later sources record few other events in the reign, and Bede seems to have known much less about it than about Cædwalla's. In 694 Ine is said to have extracted a royal wergeld of 30,000 pence from the men of Kent for burning Mul, brother of Cædwalla; in 710 he campaigned against the British king Geraint of Dumnonia in alliance with King Nothhelm (Nunna) of the South Saxons, called by one text of the chronicle his kinsman, and grantor of the afore-mentioned charter of perhaps 692; in 716 he fought the Mercian king with no recorded result.

The mysterious reference to the demolition of Taunton, which Ine had earlier built, by his queen, Æthelburh, in 722 may, as guessed in the twelfth century, be connected with the challenge of the atheling Ealdberht. That crisis certainly prompted his 722 or 725 attack on the South Saxons, as Ealdberht was said to have fled 'into Surrey and Sussex' (*ASC*, s.a. 722). The clear implication is that Ine had by then lost the power in the south-east which he inherited from Cædwalla, and which he had exercised when Nothhelm issued his charter, and when Earconwald, bishop of London and abbot of Chertsey, counselled him on his law-code. An important letter of 704 or 705 shows that by then London was beyond his control, though still subject to his threats. It would be hard to conclude from this evidence that he played any signal role in English expansion south-westwards; Welsh annals report a Cornish victory in 722. The great period of territorial gains seems to have ended by the 680s (as in Northumbria and perhaps Mercia). The era of expansion was that of what historians once called the 'heroic age': meaning that, by a process epitomized in heroic poetry, power blocks could be formed (or dissolved) in a very short time through the capacity of successful war leaders to offer the rewards of conquest to heavily armed warrior specialists. Ine's reign can be seen as a time when the process slowed down, prompting warriors to trade their services between rivals for the same throne; hence the rising internal instability.

Ecclesiastical patronage Ine can also, however, be seen as one of the kings who sought to balance the recession in the profits of war by developing alternative resources. One was the church. The Alfredian Anglo-Saxon Chronicle sought to bring out his link with the founders of the royal minster at Wimborne. He had an obscure and perhaps ambiguous role in the early history of Bradfield. Glastonbury thought him its founder at the time of later-tenth-century insertions in the West Saxon genealogy and a chronicle manuscript; but William of Malmesbury's researches persuaded him that Ine merely built a new church to stand beside a much older structure. William was faced with a more than usually outrageous forgery making this and other claims, but it is upheld by three generally acceptable grants as if to an ongoing foundation. Respectable texts also attest Ine's endowment of Muchelney, Malmesbury, and perhaps Sherborne, which was converted to a bishopric in 705 (at much the same time as South Saxon Selsey; and, judging by the 704 or 705 letter, only after prolonged resistance to Canterbury's orders, presumably by Hædde, bishop of Winchester, who died then). But Ine's major contribution to the church was a privilege now known to be substantially genuine and dated to 704: it frees churches 'from the obstacle of secular affairs and … tribute of fiscal business, that they might serve God with freed minds … and … offer prayers for the condition and prosperity of our reign' (*AS chart.*, S 245). It was the classic seventh- or eighth-century bargain of church and king, already established in Frankish and also Kentish kingdoms; and it is extended in Ine's case by the tribute *to* the church made compulsory by his laws. Besides the expected supernatural benefits, it is now clear that in early Christian England, as in Ireland, minsters functioned as prototowns, focuses of settlement and economic activity sufficient to sustain increasingly permanent market sites. As so often in the early medieval West, investment in heavenly futures paid earthly dividends.

The West Saxon economy Whether Ine also promoted his kingdom's economic development more directly is not yet clear. It was apparently in his time that Hamwih, equivalent to modern Southampton, was becoming one of the largest and most densely—if not necessarily continuously—occupied sites in pre-viking England. An early series of *sceatta* coins was perhaps minted here; yet this is not known to have been under his control and so a source of royal revenue. His laws, like those of Alfred (certainly an urban organizer), give instructions for reputable countryside trading, and offer royal protection to kinless foreigners. But unlike a Kentish code of the time, they do not refer to a king's 'market-reeve' or to a royal hall in this context. An economy could hardly fail to gain from good order, nor the king to profit as a result; but there need as yet have been no more direct connection.

Ine's law code It is above all Ine's law-code (of between 688 and 694) that underpins his fame. It survives only as an appendix to Alfred's, in nearly all manuscripts of the latter. This need not mean that Alfred made any great changes in its terms. Since several of his own laws differ from Ine's, it seems inconceivable that he would have left the discrepancies in Ine's code intact, had he tampered with it in any way. It may still be too much to hope that the code is as Ine left it. The Burgundian and (in some manuscripts) Salic laws include later decrees in continuously numbered sequence after the original codes. Careful analysis of Ine's code reveals a level of repetition, of reversion to topics already covered, and of variation in legislative style, unmatched by any other 'Germanic' legislation except Alfred's, which is modelled upon it. It is reasonable to deduce that the code actually comprises a series of enactments, starting with the one introduced by Ine's prologue, and going on to others issued later; to judge from the Frankish analogy, these may not even be in their original order. A serious implication is that some of Ine's code may in fact be laws of his successors; but it can be said that contents and vocabulary are in general archaic enough to make it unlikely that much is significantly later than 725. A more positive deduction is that Ine and his heirs were not so much issuing codified statements of custom as responding in writing to problems as they arose. Their most insistent concern was theft, especially the propensity to avenge thieves legitimately slain *in flagrante* (one of these laws is borrowed by Wihtred's Kentish code of 695). There are also striking measures on compulsory baptism, on Sunday observance (again close to Wihtred's), and on agricultural practices; there is an account of the food render to be expected from every 10 hides; and (as in Salic law) the arrangements for the wergeld and compurgation of non-English subjects are such as to give them a powerful incentive to adopt English identity. Ine's prologue already spoke, as the earlier Kentish codes had not, 'about the salvation of our souls and the security of our kingdom' (*English Historical Documents*, 1.364); and it demanded the obedience of his officials as well as subjects. Penalties and fines payable to authority are a great deal more prominent than in Kentish laws. This is already interventionist (and of course profitable) law making as it was understood by the Romans and their clerical avatars.

Death and assessment Like Cædwalla and several other early Christian English kings, if to rather less sensational effect, Ine demitted office in 726 and died as a pilgrim in Rome at an unknown date. He was later said to have founded the Schola Saxonum near St Peter's, and even to have inaugurated the payment of Peter's Pence. If not the most spectacular of Cerdic's line, it is easy to see why he loomed so large for King Alfred's family. Not only could he be delineated as their most nearly related royal predecessor; as a successful player by the rules of West Saxon politics, as a patron of the church and devoted son of Rome, and as a vigorous promoter of wealth and good order in the era of the maturity of St Boniface, he set the style of West Saxon kingship before the days of its greatness. He was a model of post-'heroic' rule because he was more than a warrior.   PATRICK WORMALD

Sources Bede, *Hist. eccl.*, 4.12, 15; 5.7 · ASC, s.a. 672–726 · William of Malmesbury, *Gesta regum Anglorum / The history of the English kings*, ed. and trans. R. A. B. Mynors, R. M. Thomson, and M. Winterbottom, 2 vols., OMT (1998–9) · *English historical documents*, 1, ed.

D. Whitelock (1955), no. 32 • F. Liebermann, ed., *Die Gesetze der Angelsachsen*, 3 vols. in 4 (Halle, 1898–1916) • *AS chart.*, S 238–52, 45, 1170, 1176, 1179, 1670–73 • H. Edwards, *The charters of the early West Saxon kingdom* (1988) • M. A. O'Donovan, ed., *Charters of Sherborne*, Anglo-Saxon Charters, 3 (1988) • S. E. Kelly, ed., *Charters of Shaftesbury Abbey*, Anglo-Saxon Charters, 5 (1996) • S. E. Kelly, ed., *Charters of Selsey*, Anglo-Saxon Charters, 6 (1998) • F. M. Stenton, *Anglo-Saxon England*, 3rd edn (1971) • D. N. Dumville, 'The West Saxon genealogical regnal list and the chronology of early Wessex', *Peritia*, 4 (1985), 21–66, esp. 55–65 • W. G. Hoskins, *The westward expansion of Wessex* (1970) • H. P. R. Finberg, *Lucerna* (1964) • D. P. Kirby, *The earliest English kings* (1991) • B. Yorke, *Wessex in the early middle ages* (1995) • P. Grierson and M. Blackburn, *Medieval European coinage: with a catalogue of the coins in the Fitzwilliam Museum, Cambridge*, 1: *The early middle ages* (5th–10th centuries) (1986) • P. Wormald, 'Inter cetera bona ... genti suae': law-making and peace-keeping in the earliest English kingdoms', *Settimane di studio del centro italiano di studi sull'alto medioevo*, 42 (1995), 963–96; repr. in P. Wormald, *Legal culture in the early medieval West: law as text, image and experience* (1999), 179–99 **Likenesses** miniature, 1321, BL, Cotton MS, Claudius D II, fol. 25

Inett, John (1646/7–1718), Church of England clergyman and ecclesiastical historian, was the younger son of Richard Inett of Bewdley, Worcestershire, who was of Huguenot extraction, and his wife, a member of the Hungerford family of Down Ampney, Gloucestershire. Educated at Bewdley grammar school, on 2 August 1661 John was awarded an earl of Leicester exhibition at University College, Oxford. He matriculated on 17 July 1663, aged sixteen, graduated BA in 1666, and proceeded MA in 1669. According to White Kennett, he was 'much favoured and encouraged' (Griffiths, 5) by John Fell, then dean of Christ Church. He was ordained deacon by William Nicholson, bishop of Gloucester, on 22 September 1667 and priest by Walter Blandford, bishop of Oxford, three years later. Some time after this he began to act as minister at St Ebbe's, Oxford: his name appears as such in the register in September 1672 and at Easter 1675.

Perhaps through Fell, who kept in close touch with his former student Sir Richard Newdigate (1644–1710), Inett was brought to the latter's attention. In December 1678 he was presented by the crown to the vicarage of Nuneaton, Warwickshire, and after his institution in February 1679 he acted as chaplain to Newdigate at his nearby seat of Arbury Hall; a shared religious and political perspective grounded on vigorous protestantism and militant anti-popery evidently made for a close bond between the two. In an assize sermon at Warwick on 1 August 1681, delivered as the tory reaction to exclusion began to gather pace, Inett made a strong appeal to 'the duties our religion and our country challenge from every true Englishman and every orthodox Protestant' (Griffiths, ix). On 27 February 1682 the similarly minded Thomas Barlow, bishop of Lincoln, appointed Inett precentor at Lincoln Cathedral. Meanwhile, probably in 1680, Inett had married Mary (*d.* 1727), daughter of Richard Harrison (*d.* 1676), late chancellor of Lichfield; their eldest child, Mary, was baptized at Nuneaton on 14 September 1681.

On the presentation of the dean and chapter of Lincoln, Inett was instituted on 20 November 1685 to the rectory of Tansor, Northamptonshire. Three years later he published

A Guide to the Devout Christian, dedicated to Mary, Lady Newdigate, and containing daily prayers, prayers for special occasions, and meditations on holy communion. In *A Guide to Repentance* (1692), dedicated to Sir Richard Newdigate, Inett commended the practice of 'private fasts' as part of the 'primitive discipline' of the church, later corrupted by Rome. Both works proved very popular over the succeeding century.

Following the death of Samuel Fuller in March 1700, Inett took his place as chaplain to William III, and he retained this role into the next reign. In 1701 his MA was incorporated at Cambridge and he proceeded DD from St John's College there; his second son, John (*bap.* 1684), was admitted to the college on 27 September the same year. By this time, encouraged by White Kennett, then dean of Peterborough, Inett was probably already working on his *Origines Anglicanae*, the first volume of which was published in 1704. Dedicated to the queen, it aimed to complement, through its study of Christianity in England from the conversion of the Saxons to the Norman conquest, John Stillingfleet's *Origines Britannicae* and Gilbert Burnet's *History of the Reformation*. Inett's theme was the corruption of the doctrine and discipline of the primitive church in England, and through it the subversion of state, by the invasive 'Steps and Arts' (p. ix) of the bishops of Rome; his immediate target was the writings of the Catholic historians Serenus Cressy and Matthew Alford, who had promoted papal claims. Although not in the same league as that of Burnet and Stillingfleet, being recognized as generally derivative and prone to errors, Inett's work was clearly organized and accessibly written, and received a moderately favourable response at the time. A second volume, taking the story from 1066 to the death of King John, appeared in 1710; time, old age, expense, and the difficulty of access to manuscripts had evidently pre-empted a third volume, intended to reach the sixteenth century, but Inett none the less ended with an affirmation of the Reformation, which had 'restor'd rights of the Church and the Monarchy and resettl'd the liberties of the English nation' (J. Inett, *Origines Anglicanae*, 1710, 2.502).

In the meantime, further preferment led Inett to leave Tansor in the hands of his eldest son, Richard (*bap.* 1683, *d.* 1745), first as curate, then from 24 March 1707 as rector. Three weeks later, on 14 April, Inett was instituted to the rectory of Clayworth, Nottinghamshire, where he also installed his sons as curates. Generous to all his family members, in 1708 he helped William Gardiner, husband of his elder daughter Mary, to the living of Hambleton, Rutland, and in 1715 he relinquished Clayworth to Samuel Hurst, who had married his younger daughter, Elizabeth (*bap.* 1690). That year he was presented by the crown to the more valuable vicarage of Wirksworth, Derbyshire. Inett died in Lincoln on 3 March 1718 and was buried in Bishop Flemming's chapel. His widow, who died on 26 November 1727, was buried next to him. Both volumes of *Origines Anglicanae* were edited and republished in 1855.

VIVIENNE LARMINIE

Sources J. Griffiths, preface, in J. Inett, *Origines Anglicanae, or, A history of the English church from the conversion of the English Saxons till the*

death of King John, ed. J. Griffiths, 2 vols. in 3 (1855) • Foster, *Alum. Oxon.* • Venn, *Alum. Cant.* • H. I. Longden, *Northamptonshire and Rutland clergy from 1500*, ed. P. I. King and others, 16 vols. in 6, Northamptonshire RS (1938–52), 7.197–9 • Wood, *Ath. Oxon.: Fasti* (1820), 308 • *Remarks and collections of Thomas Hearne*, ed. C. E. Doble and others, 2, OHS, 7 (1886), 269, 337, 341 • E. Gooder, *The squire of Arbury: Sir Richard Newdigate, second baronet, 1644–1710, and his family* (1990), 26, 28–9 • J. A. I. Champion, *The pillars of priestcraft shaken: the Church of England and its enemies, 1660–1730* (1992) • *DNB*
Archives Warks. CRO, letters to R. Newdigate, CR136, B227
Likenesses Kneller?, portrait, Lincoln Cathedral Library

Ing, (Harry) Raymond (1899–1974), chemical pharmacologist, was born at Alford, Lincolnshire, on 31 July 1899, one of the three sons of Arthur Frank William Ing, a solicitor's clerk originally from Herefordshire, and his wife, Anne Garrard. At the age of twelve he won a scholarship to Oxford high school. In 1917 he entered New College, Oxford, with an exhibition. After serving in the postal censorship department during the First World War he resumed his studies and attained first-class honours in chemistry in 1921; he went on to study for a DPhil under the younger W. H. Perkin while also teaching chemistry at Wadham College.

Although Ing enjoyed this combination of research and instruction no college fellowship was available on completion of his DPhil, so, in 1926, he moved to Manchester University. There he worked with Robert Robinson as a Ramsay memorial fellow and subsequently as a chemist with the Manchester committee on cancer. He became dissatisfied with this work and moved to University College, London, as a lecturer in 1929. In 1937 he was appointed reader in pharmacological chemistry, the first chemist ever to hold such an appointment in a British pharmacology department.

At London, Ing was content and he considered his time in the college as 'a flowering period, full of intellectual excitement and warm friendships'. These friendships included not only fellow scientists, but also, due to his interest in the arts, many members of that faculty.

In 1938 Ing's professor, J. H. Gaddum, obtained for him a fellowship at the Rockefeller Institute in New York to work with the organic chemist Max Bergmann. On Ing's return to England in 1939 the Second World War had begun, and he moved to Oxford to join a chemical research group. He was later asked to join Professor J. H. Burn at the department of pharmacology, giving the first lectures in chemical pharmacology in 1945. Oxford suited Ing; it was in many ways his spiritual home, and he stayed there for the rest of his life. In 1941 he married Catherine Mills Francis (*d.* 1983), daughter of Bertie Mills, professional musician, and Sarah Francis. She taught English literature at Lady Margaret Hall and St Hilda's College, Oxford. They had no children.

Ing's Manchester postgraduate essays in organic chemistry dealt with the determination of the molecular structure of substances from natural sources, which was then still in its earliest days. Without the aid of modern spectrometry these structural elucidations required considerable ingenuity and experimental skill, using a combination of degradative and synthetic methods including substitution into aromatic molecules. Ing began work on aromatic substitution with Robinson, who had recently developed a concept in which the position of entry of new substituents into benzene derivatives, for example, was governed by the particular distribution of the electronic charges in the conjugated ring system. Ing also helped to break new ground during his time in Manchester, working with a medical collaborator on mule-spinners' cancer. Together, they were able to show which fractions of the petroleum oils used in the cotton industry were the more carcinogenic (in mice) and to relate this for the first time to the degree of unsaturation or aromaticity in the hydrocarbon chains.

The years at Oxford saw Ing applying these early ideas to more general concepts of biological activity, helping to establish the pharmacologist as a distinct scientist, rather than a 'physiologist in disguise'. Most of his experimental work and theoretical writing was devoted to the elaboration and rationalization of structure–action relationships, particularly in terms of physical and chemical properties. His work laid the foundation of many of the principles that are practised in modern drug discovery. He retired from his university post in 1966, but continued to live in Oxford.

The importance of Ing's work was recognized in 1951 by his election to the Royal Society, but throughout his life he remained a modest and lovable person. His main dislike was abuse of the English language, something he shared with his wife. He was living at 6 Linton Road, Oxford, at the time of his death on 23 September 1974.

FRANK L. ROSE, *rev.*

Sources H. O. Schild and F. L. Rose, *Memoirs FRS*, 22 (1976), 239–55 • personal knowledge (1976)
Archives Wellcome L., corresp. with Sir Ernst Chain
Likenesses Ramsey & Muspratt, photograph, repro. in Schild and Rose, *Memoirs FRS*
Wealth at death £1092: probate, 10 April 1975, *CGPLA Eng. & Wales*

Ingalton [Ingleton], **William** (*bap.* 1794, *d.* 1866), painter and builder, was the son of William Ingleton, a shoemaker, and Sarah, and was born at Worplesdon, Surrey, and baptized on 9 June 1794 at Eton, Buckinghamshire. He lived for most of his life at Eton and he painted domestic and rustic scenes. From 1816 to 1826 he exhibited at the Royal Academy (nine pictures), the British Institution (nineteen pictures), and the Society of British Artists (five pictures). His exhibited works include *The Wedding Ring*, *Skittle Players*, and *The Battle Interrupted*. In 1821 he published lithographed views of Eton. about 1826, owing to ill health, he gave up painting and became an architect and builder at Windsor. He lived at Clewer, Berkshire, and later moved to the Isle of Wight. He died, apparently unmarried, at Clewer on 6 August 1866.

L. H. CUST, *rev.* CHLOE JOHNSON

Sources Redgrave, *Artists* • Graves, *Artists* • Bryan, *Painters* • *The exhibition of the Royal Academy* (1816–26) [exhibition catalogues] • private information (1891) [R. I. Drake] • *CGPLA Eng. & Wales* (1866) • *IGI*
Wealth at death under £8000: probate, 25 Oct 1866, *CGPLA Eng. & Wales*

Inge, Hugh (*d.* 1528), archbishop of Dublin and lord chancellor of Ireland, was a native of Somerset, recorded successively at Wells and Shepton Mallet. Admitted a scholar at Winchester College in 1480, two years later he went to New College, Oxford, again as a scholar, and he became a fellow there in 1484. He graduated in 1488 and later proceeded MA. Between 28 May and 17 December 1491 he was ordained subdeacon, deacon, and priest, and soon began to accumulate benefices, being admitted rector of Stonar, Kent, on 14 January 1492. Most of his livings were in Somerset and Gloucestershire, and three came to him at the presentment of Richard Bere, abbot of Glastonbury. In 1501 he was admitted prebendary of Cudworth in Wells Cathedral, exchanging this for Eastharptree in 1503, when he was also made succentor of the cathedral.

By 1504 Inge was in Rome. This may have been associated with a resumption of his studies which by 1508 had led to an unidentified foreign university's bestowing on him the degree of DTh, incorporated at Oxford in 1511. But it is also possible that he went to Italy with his benefactor Richard Bere, who headed a diplomatic mission to the curia in 1503. Once in Rome, Inge became a papal penitentiary, and in 1504 helped administer the oaths of allegiance to Silvestro Gigli and Adriano Castellesi as bishops of Worcester and of Bath and Wells respectively. On 4 November 1504 he also became warden of the English Hospice in Rome, having been nominated by Henry VII. In 1508 he returned to England, carrying with him candles blessed by Julius II for presentation to the king, Henry's mother and son, and the court. He himself benefited from a papal dispensation granted on 7 February enabling him to hold multiple benefices. He was admitted vicar of Doulting, Somerset, on 19 November 1509.

Inge seems to have linked his fortunes to those of Thomas Wolsey, and it was to the latter that he owed his elevation to the Irish see of Meath; he was provided on 28 January 1512. Unlike many English clerics advanced to important positions in Ireland, Inge was conscientious and active. He had transcripts made of all his see's ancient rolls of proxies and synodals, and acted as vicar-general to John Kite, archbishop of Armagh. On 27 February 1523 he was translated to the archbishopric of Dublin, after delays caused by wranglings over the consistorial taxes payable to the curia. Because of Irish raids he was able to secure a reduction from 1600 ducats to 1000. He also became closely involved in the secular government of Ireland, being made lord chancellor on 7 March 1522. He gained the reputation of a just and honest man, committed to establishing 'the administration in such good order as the mischief of the wild Irish would allow' (*Anglica historia*, 309). He showed himself deeply concerned to prevent disorder and to maintain the security of the English pale.

Inge became a close friend of the ninth earl of Kildare, to the extent of clouding his relationship with Wolsey, who by 1524 was blaming the ineffectiveness of his Irish policy on the archbishop's unwillingness to co-operate. On 23 February 1528 Inge urged Wolsey to give greater support to the king's vice-deputy, Sir Thomas Fitzgerald, whom he felt did not have the wherewithal to resist incursions from outside the pale, and also to allow Kildare, who had been detained at the English court since the end of 1526, to return to Ireland. Inge died in Dublin of sweating sickness on 3 August 1528 and was buried in St Patrick's Cathedral there. He is said to have restored his archiepiscopal palace of St Sepulchre. D. G. NEWCOMBE

Sources Emden, *Oxf.*, 2.1000–01 · T. W. Moody and others, eds., *A new history of Ireland*, 2: *Medieval Ireland, 1169–1534* (1987); repr. with corrections (1993) · H. Cotton, *Fasti ecclesiae Hibernicae*, 3 (1849) · S. G. Ellis, *Ireland in the age of the Tudors* (1998) · S. G. Ellis, 'Tudor policy and the Kildare ascendancy in the lordship of Ireland, 1496–1534', *Irish Historical Studies*, 20 (1976–7), 235–71 · A. Gwyn, *The medieval province of Armagh, 1470–1545* (1946) · P. Gwyn, *The king's cardinal* (1990) · T. F. Kirby, *Winchester scholars: a list of the wardens, fellows, and scholars of … Winchester College* (1888) · *LP Henry VIII*, vols. 1–4 · *Fasti Angl., 1300–1541*, [Bath and Wells] · *The Anglica historia of Polydore Vergil, AD 1485–1537*, ed. and trans. D. Hay, CS, 3rd ser., 74 (1950) · W. E. Wilkie, *The cardinal protector of England* (1974)

Inge, Sir William (*c.*1260–1322), lawyer and justice, was probably born in or before 1260 at or near Dunstable, Bedfordshire, the son of Thomas Inge of Dunstable, a minor local landowner active in local administration. Between 1281 and 1285 he acted as the attorney of a number of different litigants in the common bench and the exchequer, perhaps while studying law as an apprentice of the king's court. He was retained by the king as one of his serjeants between 1287 and 1293, and is to be found acting for him on the Gloucestershire eyre of 1287 and on the northern circuit eyres of 1292–3, as well as in the common bench and in the exchequer. Surviving reports show that he also acted for other litigants during the same period, both in the common bench and on eyres. In 1293 he became a regular assize justice but continued to act for private clients in the common bench until the court moved to York in 1298. By 5 April 1300 he had been knighted.

In 1303 Inge accompanied Edward I to Scotland, and in 1305, and again in 1307, was appointed a justice of one of the trailbaston circuits. By 1303 he had also entered the service of the future Edward II, and become one of his closest and most trusted advisers. In 1305 it was only Edward's intervention that prevented him being appointed a justice in Scotland. Inge remained close to Edward II after his accession, being retained as part of the king's household, and in 1310–11 he was sent to Gascony as one of the English commissioners at the Process of Périgueux, which was intended to resolve Anglo-French differences. In Hilary term 1313 he was appointed a justice of the common bench and served in that capacity for just over three years.

When Roger Brabazon (*d.* 1317) retired from the chief justiceship of king's bench, Inge replaced him (at Easter term 1316). But serious allegations had already been made against him by this date. It was claimed that he had purchased the Surrey manor of Woodmansterne from its tenant while litigation about the manor was pending in the common bench before him and his colleagues. This allegation seems never to have been proved, but, in connected proceedings brought against the sheriff of Surrey, a jury found that Inge had borrowed the plaintiff's original writ from the sheriff and tampered with it. Inge was not himself a party to the latter proceedings, and the verdict came only after his dismissal from the chief justiceship (in June 1317), but it seems probable that the dismissal was connected with these charges. Inge took no further part in public life.

Inge's first wife, Margery (1277–1310/11) (whom he married between 1298 and 1300), was one of four daughters and coheirs of Henry Grapinel, a landowner in Essex and Sussex. His second wife, Isolda (whom he married between November 1311 and March 1312), was the widow of Urian de Sancto Petro. His only surviving child at the time of his death was Joan, the daughter of his first marriage, who had married Eon la Zouche. He died shortly before 10 May 1322.   PAUL BRAND, *rev.*

Sources court of common pleas, plea rolls, PRO, CP 40 · P. A. Brand, ed., *The earliest English law reports*, 2, SeldS, 112 (1996) · *Chancery records* · *Law reports* · unpublished law reports · W. C. Bolland, ed., *Year books of Edward II*, 17: *8 Edward II*, SeldS, 41 (1925) · G. J. Turner and W. C. Bolland, eds., *Year books of Edward II*, 19: *9 Edward II*, SeldS, 45 (1929) · *CIPM*, 6, no. 328

Inge, William Ralph (1860–1954), dean of St Paul's and writer, was born at Crayke, in the North Riding of Yorkshire, on 6 June 1860, the eldest son of William Inge (1829–1903), curate of Crayke, and his wife, Susanna Mary Churton (*d.* 1917). His father was subsequently provost of Worcester College, Oxford; his mother was the daughter of Edward Churton, archdeacon of Cleveland, who had been a prominent associate of the Tractarians in the 1830s. Inge's staunchly high-church upbringing had two important bearings on his later career. On the one hand it left him with an aversion to the 'fierce bigotry' of the Oxford Movement. The family home was one in which 'the slightest concession to liberalism in theology was denounced with unqualified indignation', and Inge's mother never forgave him when, as a young man, he rejected Tractarianism and embraced modernism (Inge, *Vale*, 10). On the other hand Inge, who was educated by his parents until he was thirteen, retained a fierce pride in the family's accomplishments. His fascination with his family's position in the Victorian intellectual aristocracy led him to an interest in the inheritance of intelligence, and hence to a strong belief in eugenics.

Ralph Inge won a scholarship to Eton College in 1874. Here he met A. C. Benson, who became a lifelong friend, and with whom he was caned for making an indoor bonfire out of blotting paper. Inge went to King's College, Cambridge, as a scholar in 1879, and was garlanded with prizes. He won the Craven, Bell, and Porson scholarships, took a first in both parts of the classical tripos (1882–3), and was senior-chancellor's medallist. But Inge and Benson (who had followed him to King's) were both susceptible to bouts of acute depression, which Inge later attributed to overwork.

After graduation Inge spent four years teaching at Eton, but concluded that he was not especially suited to schoolmastering. He was more settled as a fellow of Hertford College, Oxford, from 1888, where he taught classics, and developed an interest in philosophy. Inge was ordained

William Ralph Inge (1860–1954), by Philip A. de Laszlo, 1934

deacon in 1888, but religious doubts meant that he did not proceed to the priesthood for four years. It was through his friendship with another Hertford tutor, Hastings Rashdall, that Inge was able to work out the religious ideas which he retained for the rest of his life. He came to believe that a church which rested its claims on miracle would be exposed to scientific and biblical criticism. Instead, he argued, Christianity must concentrate upon personal experience of God and upon mysticism. By mysticism he did not mean the miraculous, but the union with God which could be attained through prayer and contemplation. While at Hertford, Inge began his studies of the Christian mystical tradition, delivering the Bampton lectures of 1899, *Christian Mysticism*. His work reawakened English interest in mysticism and inspired other scholars such as Evelyn Underhill.

In 1905 Inge was appointed vicar of All Saints', Ennismore Gardens, in central London. The same year he married Mary Catharine (Kitty) Spooner (1880–1949). Like him, she came from a notable clerical dynasty. Her father was archdeacon of Canterbury, her uncle, William Spooner—of 'spoonerism' fame—was warden of New College, and her grandfather was Bishop Harvey Goodwin of Carlisle. This marriage was immensely successful, and Kitty succeeded in alleviating Inge's depression and in helping him to overcome his shyness.

Inge's experience of parish life was brief, because in 1907 he became Lady Margaret professor of divinity at Cambridge. Here he developed his study of mysticism by beginning his study of the fourth-century pagan Neoplatonist, Plotinus, which eventually appeared as the Gifford lectures, *The Philosophy of Plotinus* (two volumes, 1918). Inge argued that Plotinus's ideas, through their reception by Augustine, had played an important part in Christian tradition. Inge examined the influence of Platonism on the Church of England in his book *The Platonic Tradition in English Religious Thought* (1926), which argued that Platonism had been as important as the protestant and Catholic traditions, and which highlighted the work of seventeenth-century Cambridge Platonists such as Benjamin Whichcote.

In 1911 the prime minister, Asquith, made Inge dean of St Paul's. In many ways he was an inauspicious choice. He hated choral music, which was central to the cathedral's traditions, asking 'are we quite sure that the deity enjoys being serenaded?' He found the daily services 'dreary and interminable', and was often seen reading a book in his stall. As a modernist he was often at odds with his Anglo-Catholic canons, over whom he had little power, likening the dean to 'a mouse watched by four cats' (Inge, *Diary*, 9, 11). But Asquith had appointed Inge in order to revive the literary eminence which St Paul's had enjoyed under predecessors such as John Colet, John Donne, and R. W. Church, and in this respect Inge was a great success. His writings attained their widest readership through his weekly columns in the *Evening Standard*, which ran, with some interruptions, from 1921 to 1946. These articles—on literary and political, as well as religious, themes—were reprinted in collections such as his two volumes *Outspoken Essays* (1919–22) and *Lay Thoughts of a Dean* (1926). His 1911 lectures 'The church and the age' led the *Daily Mail* to dub him 'the Gloomy Dean', a nickname which stuck, though his newspaper columns were in fact often light, witty pieces. A contemporary joke had it that he was 'a pillar of the Church of England and two columns of the *Evening Standard*'.

Inge, who was fond of money, was lavishly rewarded for his literary efforts. He calculated that his writing earned him £4000 in 1927 alone. He used his columns to expound his political ideas, which combined the individualism of Herbert Spencer with the authoritarianism of Plato's *Republic*. He disliked democracy, which he believed would inevitably lead to class conflict and mob rule, and preferred government by an educated élite of Platonic guardians. He opposed state welfare provision on the grounds that it penalized the successful while subsidizing the weak and feckless, and thus encouraged the breeding of a new class of slum dwelling 'sub-men'. Such intemperate views were expressed at length in Inge's study of national character, *England* (1926), which drew heavily on the American philosopher George Santayana. Inge wrote this book at the time of the general strike, when he believed the nation was on the brink of civil war. His comments about the unemployed caused an outcry, and he was forced to retract them in a later edition.

Between the wars Inge was one of the most vociferous defenders of the rights of the middle classes. One of his most pressing social concerns was the shortage of domestic servants, which he called 'a matter of national importance'. 'Nobody can deny that the plight of ladies who have

to run a house is becoming desperate,' he wrote in *Our Present Discontents* (1938, 224–5). In 1921 Archbishop Davidson upbraided him for writing an article in the *Evening Standard* in which he complained that by providing university bursaries for working-class children the state was 'taking the bread out of our children's mouths' (*Evening Standard*, 9 Feb 1921). Inge was also concerned that the working classes were breeding too fast and that unless measures were taken to stop them they would overwhelm the middle classes. His interest in eugenic theory had deepened through his friendship with Sir Francis Galton, and he served on the council of the Eugenics Society. In books such as *Christian Ethics and Moral Problems* (1930) Inge promoted the use of birth control in marriage, but elsewhere he went much further, suggesting that the state could control which couples were allowed to procreate. Such an authoritarian eugenics policy sat uneasily with his individualism.

Inge was a romantic and iconoclastic Conservative who deplored economic competition and frequently invoked John Ruskin. Like his contemporary Stanley Baldwin he lamented the despoliation of the countryside wrought by the industrial revolution, and was much given to extolling the English landscape. His anti-industrialism was part of a wider aversion to what he termed 'the superstition of progress', which he denounced in his Romanes lecture of 1920, 'The idea of progress'. As his Rede lecture of 1922, 'The Victorian age' showed, Inge always longed to return England to the culture and values of the nineteenth-century country parsonages of his youth.

Inge's iconoclastic side was most clearly seen in his attitude to the prevailing currents of opinion in the Church of England. He denounced Christian socialist clergy as the 'court-chaplains of King Mob' (Inge, *More Lay Thoughts*, 38), and was critical of their attempts at intervening in the coal dispute in 1926. However, as part owner of a Staffordshire colliery he had something of a personal interest. Inge strongly held that the gospels offered precepts only for personal, and not for social, action, and that all attempts to extrapolate social ethics from them were erroneous. The only way forward for the church, he argued, was to emphasize the spiritual: social Christianity was a blind alley. This extreme stance led to public disagreement with his old friend Hastings Rashdall (with whom he had briefly joined the moderate socialist Christian Social Union as a young man), though the two men remained friends.

By the 1920s Inge had become a leading spokesman for the modernist wing of the Church of England, and he succeeded Rashdall as president of the Modern Churchmen's Union (1924–34). He was at pains to distance his own brand of modernism from that of Roman Catholics like A. F. Loisy and George Tyrell, whom he accused of overemphasizing the institutional church. Like many other modernists Inge was an Erastian who believed in parliamentary control of the church, and so he defended parliament's right to throw out the revised prayer book in 1927–8, clashing with his closest friend, Hensley Henson, bishop of Durham. The two men had hitherto been leading champions of modernism and of the national church. But Henson's conversion to disestablishment after the prayer book crisis and his decision to distance himself from the Modern Churchmen's Union led Inge to regard him as a turncoat.

Although a scholar of mysticism, Inge was no ascetic. Indeed, he had a penchant for worldly trappings. He was made CVO in 1918 and KCVO in 1930. He received a BD and DD from Cambridge in 1909, was an honorary fellow of several Oxford and Cambridge colleges, and was elected FBA in 1921. As his *Diary of a Dean* (1949) showed, Inge was something of a snob. He maintained close friendships with Lord Beaverbrook and R. B. Haldane, and with George Bernard Shaw. Another friend was H. H. Asquith, who astutely described Inge in his memoirs as 'a strange isolated figure, with all the culture in the world, and a curiously developed gift of expression, but with kinks and twists both intellectual and temperamental' (Asquith, 2.232).

The isolation detected by Asquith was certainly mitigated by Inge's very happy domestic life, and by his three sons and two daughters. But he suffered two family tragedies. In 1923 his eleven-year-old daughter, Paula, died of diabetes. Inge was devastated, and published a tribute to her in his book *Personal Religion and the Life of Devotion* (1924), which sold 50,000 copies. In 1941 his youngest son, Richard, who had followed him into the ministry, was killed in an RAF training flight.

In 1934 Inge retired to Brightwell Manor near Wallingford. He continued to publish collections of essays with elegiac titles such as *A Rustic Moralist* (1937) and *The End of an Age* (1949). Though not a pacifist in the strict sense, he opposed Britain's entry into the Second World War on the grounds that she had no quarrel with Germany. After the outbreak of war he continued to call for a negotiated peace. Towards Nazism he was ambivalent, admiring its strong government while condemning it as a tyranny. He was interested in Nazi race theory, but concluded that it was pseudo-scientific and based on poor eugenics. Inge's thoughts on the war were expressed in *A Pacifist in Trouble* (1939), *Talks in a Free Country* (1942), and *The Fall of the Idols* (1940).

Inge's later years were marred by increasing deafness, and by the double blow of his son's death, and that of his wife in 1949. He died at Brightwell Manor on 26 February 1954 and on 2 March was buried in the village churchyard beside his wife and son.   MATTHEW GRIMLEY

Sources A. Fox, *Dean Inge* (1960) · W. R. Inge, *Diary of a dean, St Paul's, 1911–34* (1949) · W. R. Inge, *Vale* (1934) · W. R. Inge, *Our present discontents* (1938) · *The Times* (27 Feb 1954) · *DNB* · H. H. Asquith, *Memories and reflections, 1852–1927*, ed. A. Mackintosh, 2 vols. (1928), vol. 2 · J. Garnett, 'Hastings Rashdall and the renewal of Christian social ethics, c.1890–1920', *Revival and religion since 1700: essays for John Walsh*, ed. J. Garnett and C. Matthew (1993), 279–316 · W. R. Inge, *More lay thoughts of a dean* (1931) · A. N. Wilson, 'The Gloomy Dean', *Penfriends from Porlock* (1988) · Inge diaries, Magd. Cam. · *WWW* · *CGPLA Eng. & Wales* (1954)

Archives GL, St Paul's Cathedral archives, sermons · Magd. Cam., diaries and papers | BL, letters to E. H. Blakeney, Add. MS 63089 · BL, corresp. with George Bernard Shaw, Add. MS 50538 · BLPES, letters to Violet Markham · Bodl. Oxf., letters to Sir James Marchant · HLRO, corresp. with Lord Beaverbrook · King's AC Cam., letters to Oscar Browning · King's Lond., Liddell Hart C., corresp. with Sir B. H. Liddell Hart · NL Scot., corresp. with Lord Haldane

Likenesses J. Russell & Sons, photograph, c.1915, NPG · W. Rothenstein, chalk drawing, 1920, King's Cam. · C. Dodgson, drawing, 1923, King's Cam. · W. Stoneman, photograph, 1925, NPG · D. Low, caricature, pencil drawing, c.1927, NPG · E. Kapp, drawing, 1930, U. Birm. · M. Coster, photographs, 1930–39, NPG · C. Dodgson, chalk drawing, 1934, King's Cam. · P. A. de Laszlo, oils, 1934, NPG [*see illus.*] · A. Norris, oils, c.1934, NPG · B. Partridge, pen and ink, and watercolour caricature, NPG; repro. in *Punch* (21 May 1928) · R. S. Sherriffs, ink and charcoal? caricature, NPG · W. H. [W. Hester], mechanically reproduced caricature, NPG; repro. in *VF* (31 Jan 1912) · print on cigarette card, NPG

Wealth at death £98,198 4s. 9d.: probate, 1 April 1954, *CGPLA Eng. & Wales*

Ingelend, Thomas (*fl.* 1550–1560), playwright, is identified solely from the appearance of his name on the title-page of *A Pretie and Mery New Enterlude, called 'The Disobedient Child'*, printed in London, without date, by Thomas Colwell. This play, a free adaptation of a continental play based on the prodigal son story, has been conjecturally identified with 'an enterlude for boyes to handle and to passe tyme at christmas', entered against Colwell's name in the Stationers' register in 1569. An epilogue (evidently added later) indicates a performance in the presence of Queen Elizabeth, but allusion earlier in the text to a reigning king suggests that it may have been composed during the reign of Edward VI. The title-page refers to Ingelend as 'late student in Cambridge', and tradition has associated him with Christ's College, but there is no record of his having taken a degree.   RICHARD BEADLE

Sources J. Peile, *Biographical register of Christ's College, 1505–1905, and of the earlier foundation, God's House, 1448–1505*, ed. [J. A. Venn], 1 (1910), 14

Ingelo, Nathaniel (1620/21–1683), author, was born at Bristol. His parentage is as yet unknown. In 1641 'Nathanaell Ingeley, *Anglus*' graduated MA at Edinburgh University. Ingelo's decision to study at Edinburgh, at the height of the struggles around the covenant, would seem to indicate strong presbyterian convictions, but, at some point in the early or mid-1640s he changed his position dramatically and became an Independent. In 1644 he was incorporated at Cambridge on his Edinburgh degree, and Anthony Wood asserts that he was temporarily a fellow of Emmanuel College. On 11 June of that year he was appointed a fellow of Queens' College, Cambridge, by the parliamentary visitors. He was appointed Greek lecturer on 24 June 1644, junior bursar on 31 January 1645, and dean in 1645, but in December 1645 he was granted a year's leave, and he had ceased to be a fellow by 6 October 1647. By the end of 1646 Ingelo had been appointed minister of All Saints', Bristol, where he was invited by a small Independent congregation to be its pastor. He served this congregation and administered communion to its members; alongside their Sunday and Thursday afternoon meetings they generally also attended his Sunday morning services in the parish church. After a few years, pastor and congregation fell out over his elegant dress and his love of music. The later chronicler of the congregation (which was to evolve into the Broadmead Baptist Church) records how many members began to be offended with Ingelo's:

> Flaunting apparell, for he, being a Thin, spare, slender person, did goe very neate in a costly trimm, and in some time began to Exceed in some garments not becoming to the gospell, much lesse a Minister of Christ; which together with his being given so much to Musick, not only at his owne house, but at houses of entertainments out of Towne, sometimes with some of his Relations, and gentry of the Citty of his acquaintance, he would be at his Musick.
> (Hayden, 102)

Remonstrated with 'to leave his Musick, nor his soe frequent nor publique use thereof', Ingelo memorably retorted, 'take away his Musick, take away his life' (ibid.). The summer of 1649 saw one example of such 'publique use' when he put on a musical entertainment at Bristol for his friend John Worthington, the vice-chancellor of Cambridge University. On 18 March 1650 Ingelo was appointed to a fellowship at Eton College, again probably through the intercession of the parliamentary visitors. It was during his years as a minister in Bristol that he would have courted and probably married his wife, Mary (their first known child was born at Bristol in 1651).

Ingelo accompanied Bulstrode Whitelocke on the Swedish embassy (1653–4) as one of his chaplains and as *rector chori*. Ingelo and Whitelocke had probably become acquainted while the latter was recorder of Bristol, but Ingelo had formerly agreed to join the Swedish embassy under the leadership of Lord Lisle, the original choice as ambassador. Whitelocke described Ingelo as 'a Person of admirable Abilities in the Work of the Ministery and … a well Studied Scholar, perfect in the Latin tongue, Conversant in the Greek and Hebrew and could speak good Italian, he was much delighted in Musick … and carried persons and instruments with him for that Recreation' (BL, Add. MS 4995, appx 5, fol. 11). He presented some compositions of Benjamin Rogers to Queen Kristina, and they were performed by her Italian musicians 'to her great content' (*Poems and Letters of Andrew Marvell*, 1.318). Andrew Marvell addressed a Latin poem to Ingelo in Sweden. He enquires after his friend's health in the cold Swedish climate, but most of the lines are written in praise of Kristina, for whom the poem was really meant. Ingelo and Marvell had probably met after the latter's move to Eton in June 1653. The embassy sailed in November, so their acquaintance must have been short. Whitelocke's embassy was back in London early in July 1654.

Ingelo received the degree of doctor of divinity at Cambridge in 1658. In the same year he arranged for the degree of bachelor of music to be conferred on Benjamin Rogers at Cambridge. Two years later he composed a Latin hymn, which was set to music by Rogers in four parts and performed at the Guildhall on 5 July 1660, the occasion being the entertainment of the royal family and the parliament by the corporation of London. Ingelo was readmitted to his Eton fellowship on 12 July 1660. According to Anthony Wood, Joseph Glanvill involved Ingelo in a plot to discredit Robert Crosse, a polemicist against the Royal Society. Ingelo was rector of Piddlehinton, Dorset (1671–7).

Ingelo died at Eton in August, September, or October 1683, aged sixty-two, and was buried in Eton College chapel. His wife, Mary, outlived him: he made her an executor of his will and among the personal effects he bequeathed her was 'the golden Medall of the Queene of Sweden wch she gave to mee' (PRO, PROB 11/374/114, fol. 105r). Four of their sons attended Eton: Nathaniel (*b*. 1651), Richard (born at Eton in 1655), Robert (*b*. 1663), and Samuel (*b*. 1666). Ingelo's will also reveals the existence of a daughter, Elizabeth. His will points to strong kin connections with the Vickris family, leading godly members of Bristol's mercantile élite. The trustees of his estate were Richard and Robert Vickris, very probably the puritan mayor of Bristol in 1646 and his son, and among Ingelo's personal effects was 'the Picture of my brother and sister Vickris which I gave to my cousin Richard Vickris' (ibid.). The relationship appears to be through marriage, but whether through his mother, wife, or sister can only be speculated.

Ingelo's major literary project was *Bentivolio and Urania*, published in two instalments (1660, 1664), a best-selling work of religious and moral instruction in the form of a fictional narrative. The work is dedicated to William Brereton, the eldest son of the civil war general. *Bentivolio and Urania* was conceived in terms of the Platonic doctrine of the heterogeneity of the soul set out in Henry More's long poem *Psychozoia* (1641). Rochester mocked the platitudes of Ingelo's satire, which urges a return to the traditional humanist marriage of learning and piety, but this is an indication of its popularity. There were four editions between 1660 and 1682. Alexander Brome commends the work in 'On Dr. [Ingelo] his divine romant' (Brome, 141–2) and Worthington called it 'that excellent scheme of divine morality' (*Diary and Correspondence*, 1.244–5). Samuel Hartlib used his friendship with Worthington to procure a complimentary copy of *Bentivolio and Urania* from the author.   IAN WILLIAM MᶜLELLAN

Sources R. Spalding, *Contemporaries of Bulstrode Whitelocke, 1605–1675*, British Academy, Records of Social and Economic History, new ser., 14 (1990) · *The diary and correspondence of Dr John Worthington*, ed. J. Crossley, 1, Chetham Society, 13 (1847) · *The diary of Bulstrode Whitelocke, 1605–1675*, ed. R. Spalding, British Academy, Records of Social and Economic History, new ser., 13 (1990) · Wood, *Ath. Oxon.*, new edn · *The poems and letters of Andrew Marvell*, ed. H. M. Margoliouth, rev. P. Legouis, 3rd edn, 1 (1971), 104–7, 318 · J. Evans, *A chronological outline of the history of Bristol* (1824) · BL, Add. MS 4995, appx 5, fol. 11 · epitaph of Nathaniel Ingelo, BL, Cole MS 5831, fol. 55 · D. Laing, ed., *A catalogue of the graduates … of the University of Edinburgh*, Bannatyne Club, 106 (1858), 59 · W. Sterry, ed., *The Eton College register, 1441–1698* (1943) · R. Hayden, ed., *The records of a church in Christ in Bristol, 1640–1687*, Bristol RS, 27 (1974) · PRO, PROB 11/374/114, fols. 104r–105v · *The complete works: John Wilmot, earl of Rochester*, ed. F. H. Ellis (1994) · A. Brome, *Songs and other poems* (1661) · N. Ingelo, *The perfection, authority, and credibility of the holy scriptures* (1659) · N. Ingelo, *A discourse concerning repentance* (1677) · N. Ingelo, *Hymnus eucharisticus* (1660)

Ingelow, Jean [*pseud.* Orris] (**1820–1897**), poet and writer, was born on 17 March 1820 in South Place, Boston, Lincolnshire, the first of ten children of William Ingelow (1794/5–1855), a Boston banker and shipping merchant, and his

Jean Ingelow (1820–1897), by Maull & Polyblank

Youth Magazine (which she edited for one year). These were republished in *Tales of Orris* (1860), illustrated by Ingelow's Kensington neighbour John Everett Millais.

Poems by Jean Ingelow (1863) brought the first public recognition of Ingelow's merit as a poet; this volume went through thirty editions in Ingelow's lifetime. It opens with 'Divided', a wistful lyric about lovers walking along opposite banks of a stream that eventually divides them forever. *Poems* also includes her popular ballad 'The High Tide on the Coast of Lincolnshire, 1571', an understated and affecting poem about loss of life in a sixteenth-century flood, and 'Songs of Seven', a meditation on the seven stages of woman's life, published separately in 1881 in a lavish illustrated edition. Ingelow's friend Charlotte Barnard (Claribel) set several pieces to music, notably the elegy 'When sparrows build' from 'Supper at the Mill'.

The long title poem of *A Story of Doom, and other Poems* (1867) recounts Noah's flood; this volume also contains many sea songs, inspirational verses, and nature lyrics. The gentle adventure narrative 'Gladys and her Island' has recently been revived for its schoolteacher heroine and its reflections upon artistic temperament in women. Subsequent collections of poetry proved very successful in England and abroad. By 1901 200,000 copies of Ingelow's works had been sold in the USA.

The nostalgic tone, simple style, and natural and domestic scenes of Ingelow's poetry connect it with Wordsworth's. Her lyrics also resonate with those of her Lincolnshire countryman Alfred Tennyson, who reportedly proclaimed to Ingelow on one occasion, 'Miss Ingelow, I do declare you do the trick better than I do' (Peters, 61). Ingelow's work compares favourably, too, with that of Christina Rossetti, who in 1863 wrote to her publisher, 'Miss Ingelow … would be a formidable rival to most men, and to any woman' (Peters, 62). When Tennyson died in 1892, a group of Americans sent Queen Victoria an unsuccessful petition supporting the appointment of Jean Ingelow as the first woman poet laureate of England.

Besides Tennyson and Christina Rossetti, Ingelow was acquainted with many other poets, painters, and writers, including John Ruskin, J. A. Froude, Robert Browning, Jane and Ann Taylor, Anna Sewell, and Henry Wadsworth Longfellow. She belonged to the Portfolio Society begun in the 1850s by Barbara Bodichon and Bessie Rayner, where Christina Rossetti, Adelaide Procter, Dora Greenwell, and other women shared their artwork and poetry. Ingelow's political and religious views were conservative, but she was very concerned about the poor and routinely expended profits from her writing serving 'copyright dinners' in Holland Street, Kensington, to convalescent poor people identified by local clergy.

Although poetry was Ingelow's chief gift, she also published adult novels and children's stories. *Off the Skelligs* (1872) and its sequel *Fated to be Free* (1875) are tales of romance and adventure set in the islands off the Irish coast; *Off the Skelligs*, autobiographical in part, remains quite readable. The plot of *Sarah de Berenger* (1879) resembles sensational women's novels of the 1860s such as *East Lynne* and *Lady Audley's Secret*. *Don John* (1881) contrasts

Scottish wife, Jean (1798/9–1876), daughter of George Kilgour and his wife, Jean Thornborough of Aberdeenshire. The Lincolnshire fen country and the Boston waterfront figure prominently in Ingelow's poetry.

After William Ingelow's bank failed, the family lived for a time in Ipswich, and then moved to London in 1850. Ingelow lived in Kensington, London, from 1855 until her death. Ingelow was educated at home by her mother and spinster aunt Rebecca. She never married. The prominent theme in her work of a lover or husband lost at sea provoked speculation from her biographer Maureen Peters, but aside from one paragraph in the anonymous *Recollections of Jean Ingelow* (1901), no contemporary reference to marriage prospects for Ingelow exists. Apparently she lived contentedly, taking an active interest in her nieces and nephews.

In 1850 Ingelow published an anonymous volume of poems, *A Rhyming Chronicle of Incidents and Feelings*, edited by a family friend, the Revd Edward Harston of St Stephen's Church in Ipswich. In the following year her anonymous novel *Allerton and Dreux*, exploring tensions between evangelicals and traditional Anglicans in the Church of England, appeared. (Like her mother, Ingelow had evangelical leanings.) Also during this decade, Ingelow published a series of fanciful didactic children's stories under the pseudonym Orris in the evangelical monthly upper- and lower-class family life in a melodrama about children switched in infancy. *John Jerome* (1886), probably Ingelow's least successful book, is an eccentric narration by a comical young man-about-town.

Besides *Tales of Orris*, Ingelow's best children's books include *Studies for Stories* (1864), also illustrated by Millais, and a striking prose fantasy *Mopsa the Fairy* (1869), reissued in 1972 and 1992. This tale, written in a graceful Pre-Raphaelite style reminiscent of George MacDonald or William Morris, and in a fantasy mode comparable to Lewis Carroll's *Alice in Wonderland* or Christina Rossetti's *Speaking Likenesses*, led one critic in 1972 to call Jean Ingelow 'a lost Pre-Raphaelite' (Lewis, 1487). Jean Ingelow died at her home, 6 Holland Villas Road, Kensington, London, on 20 July 1897, and was buried in Brompton cemetery.

KATHLEEN HICKOK

Sources M. Peters, *Jean Ingelow: Victorian poetess* (1972) · *The Times* (21 July 1897) · *The Athenaeum* (24 July 1897), 129 · *DNB* · N. Lewis, 'A lost Pre-Raphaelite', *TLS* (8 Dec 1972), 1487 · N. Auerbach and U. C. Knoepflmacher, eds., *Forbidden journeys: fairy tales and fantasies by Victorian women writers* (1992) · A. Leighton, *Victorian women poets: writing against the heart* (1992) · J. Wagner, 'In her "proper place": Ingelow's fable of the female poet and her community in *Gladys and her island*', *Victorian Poetry*, 31 (1993), 227–39 · K. Hickok, *Representations of women: nineteenth-century British women's poetry* (1984) · R. L. Green, *Tellers of tales: British authors of children's books from 1800 to 1964*, rev. edn (1965) · H. C. Black, *Notable women authors of the day* (1893) · M. Bell, 'Jean Ingelow', *The poets and poetry of the century*, ed. A. H. Miles, 7 (1892) · d. cert.

Archives Harvard U., Houghton L., MSS | Hunt. L., letters and literary MSS · University of Lancaster, Ruskin Library, letters to Miss Fall

Likenesses C. Barraud, photograph, 1891, repro. in J. Ingelow, *Jean Ingelow's poems* (Boston, 1896), frontispiece · Elliott & Fry, two cartes-de-visite, NPG · Maull & Polyblank, photograph, NPG [*see illus.*] · H. W. Smith, engraving, repro. in J. Ingelow, *A story of doom and other poems* (1867), frontispiece · portrait, repro. in J. Ingelow, *Poems*, new edn (1913) · stained-glass window, St Botolph's parish church, Boston, Lincolnshire

Wealth at death £6018 5s. 6d.: probate, 20 Aug 1897, *CGPLA Eng. & Wales*

Ingelram. *See* Ingram (d. 1174).

Ingen-Housz [Ingenhousz], **Jan** (1730–1799), physician and natural philosopher, was born on 8 December 1730 at Breda, the Netherlands, the second son of Arnoldus Ingen-Housz, an affluent leather merchant, and his wife, Maria Beckers. After qualifying as a physician at the University of Louvain in 1753, he continued his studies at Leiden, Paris, and Edinburgh. In 1765 he left his successful Breda medical practice and went to London, where his colleagues included Benjamin Franklin, who became a lifelong friend. An early proponent of the controversial new practice of smallpox inoculation, he worked with William Watson at the Foundling Hospital, and was selected by Sir John Pringle in 1768 to inoculate several members of the imperial family in Vienna. In 1769 the Archduchess Maria Theresa rewarded him with a life pension as court physician. Although Ingen-Housz disliked court life, this financial independence enabled him to travel throughout Europe, promoting inoculation and experimenting in natural philosophy. He became a fellow of the Royal Society in

Jan Ingen-Housz (1730–1799), by William? Tassie

1771, and delivered the Bakerian lecture in 1778. In 1775 he married Agatha Maria Jacquin; they had no children. Between 1773 and 1782 he contributed nine papers to the *Philosophical Transactions of the Royal Society*, five on electricity and magnetism, and four on atmospheric gases. He settled permanently in England after the French Revolution, often staying with the marquess of Lansdowne at Bowood House, near Calne, Wiltshire. Ingen-Housz produced important research on inoculation, electricity, and plant respiration; but he avoided public controversy, so the importance of some of his contributions was not fully recognized. Besides his papers sent to the Royal Society, his chief book was *Experiments upon Vegetables* (1779), in which he established that the green parts of plants 'restore' the air when illuminated by sunlight, and that it is the sun's visible light rather than its heat which is effective. He also found that all parts of plants respire continuously day and night. A skilled experimenter, he subsequently extended his studies of plant respiration, and investigated and wrote about soil renovation, the chemistry of gases, and algae. He designed devices to relieve respiratory ailments, and an electrically ignited lighter. Ingen-Housz died at Bowood House, Wiltshire, on 7 September 1799.

CHARLES CREIGHTON, *rev.* PATRICIA FARA

Sources P. Smit, 'Jan Ingen-Housz, 1730–99: some new evidence about his life and work', *Janus*, 67 (1980), 125–39 · P. W. van der Pas, 'Ingen-Housz, Jan', *DSB*

Archives U. Glas. L., corresp. with William Hunter · University of Utrecht, Biohistorical Institute, corresp. with Jacob van Breda

Likenesses D. Cunego, engraving, 1769, Wellcome L. • W. (?) Tassie, medallion, Wedgwood Museum, Barlaston, Staffordshire [see illus.] • engraving, repro. in J. Ingen-Housz, *Experiments upon vegetables* (1779), frontispiece

Wealth at death probably quite wealthy; generous life pension; moved in élite circles

Ingham, Albert Edward (1900–1967), mathematician, was born at Northampton on 3 April 1900, the son of Albert Edward Ingham (1875–1954) and his wife, Annie Gertrude Whitworth (1875–1923). He had an elder brother and three younger sisters. His father was a craftsman employed by a firm of boot and shoe manufacturers and was awarded a modest honorarium for the original idea of making shoes waterproof—the 'veldtschoen'. Ingham was educated in Northampton and at King Edward VI's Grammar School, Stafford, where he won the available prizes for academic achievement. In December 1917 he gained an entrance scholarship at Trinity College, Cambridge, going into residence in January 1919 after a few months in the army. In part two of the mathematical tripos (1921) he was a wrangler with distinction and in 1923 won a Smith's prize and an 1851 senior exhibition.

In 1922, his first year of candidature, Ingham was elected a prize fellow of Trinity, Cambridge. The electors saw in his dissertation a depth and maturity already marking him out as a leading scholar of his generation. He enjoyed four years of research (1922–6) without commitments to teach, spending some months in Göttingen. In 1926 he was appointed reader in the University of Leeds. In 1930, on the sudden and untimely death of F. P. Ramsey, he returned to Cambridge as fellow and director of studies at King's College, with a university lectureship. Ingham was an outstanding member of the G. H. Hardy and J. E. Littlewood school of mathematical analysis, which from its beginnings in the first decade of the twentieth century attained worldwide fame in the third. He was elected a fellow of the Royal Society in 1945. In 1953 (after two years as Cayley lecturer) he was appointed reader in mathematical analysis. He retired from regular college teaching in 1957.

Ingham was meticulously accurate; nothing slipshod came from his hand, his tongue, or his pen. A successful lecturer and tutor, he encouraged his pupils to aim for perfection. By nature shy, modest, and reserved, he was friendly and hospitable, kind to anyone lonely or troubled, and quick to win the affection of children. He had no car, radio, or television set. He was an expert photographer, and enjoyed cricket as both spectator and player.

Ingham's thirty-two research papers, models of incisive reasoning, solved difficult problems and opened up avenues for other workers. Ingham's method and Ingham's theorem are quoted repeatedly in mathematical works. His one book, *The Distribution of Prime Numbers* (1932), is a classic and his perspicacious and meticulous editing of the papers in number-theory in volume two of G. H. Hardy's *Collected Papers* (1967) has proved most valuable.

From 1932 Ingham had the devoted support of his wife Rose Marie (Jane; 1897–1982), a botanist and daughter of

Albert Edward Ingham (1900–1967), by unknown photographer

Canon Albert Darell Tupper-Carey. They had two sons, Michael and Stephen. Michael, an astronomer, followed his father in 1961 as a fellow of King's; later he moved to the observatory at Oxford, and became a fellow of New College in 1968. Stephen graduated in mathematics at New College, Oxford, in 1959 and entered the oil industry.

Every summer Ingham and his wife walked among mountains, and it was on such a holiday that he died. On 6 September 1967, on a high path near Mont Buet in France, his heart failed; he lived for only a few hours before he died in a mountain shelter, the refuge de la Pierre à Berard, Vallorcine, Haute Savoie. His body was cremated in Geneva the same day, and his ashes were scattered in Hayley Wood, near Cambridge.

J. C. BURKILL, rev. P. M. COHN

Sources WW • J. C. Burkill, *Memoirs FRS*, 14 (1968), 271–86 • personal knowledge (1981) • private information (2004) • CGPLA Eng. & Wales (1967)

Archives Trinity Cam., corresp. | Trinity Cam., corresp. with Harold Davenport

Likenesses photograph, priv. coll. [see illus.] • photograph, repro. in Burkill, *Memoirs FRS*

Wealth at death £13,153: probate, 15 Dec 1967, CGPLA Eng. & Wales

Ingham, Alice [name in religion Mary Francis] (1830–1890), Roman Catholic nun, was born in Rochdale on 8 March 1830 and baptized a Catholic at St John Baptist, Rochdale. She was the third daughter of George Ingham (1806–1865), cotton carder, baker, then woollen and linen draper of 149 Yorkshire Street, and his second wife, Margaret (née

Astley; *d.* 1842). She had a sister, half-brother, and two brothers who survived childhood; three or four other siblings died. After her mother's death in 1842, her father married a childless widow, Elizabeth Cheetham, who owned a dressmaker's and milliner's shop in the same street. All the family except her father were Roman Catholics, and he converted to Catholicism in 1851.

Alice Ingham is said to have received four years' elementary education and went to Sunday school. Afterwards, she worked in a woollen mill, and then became apprenticed to the family trades. In 1855 she spent several months with the Sisters of the Cross and Passion, the Manchester-based working-class Catholic congregation of her former Sunday school teacher, Sister Mary Paul Taylor, but returned to the family business. By 1861 the two shops had been amalgamated as Ingham's Caps and Confectionery, and later she became its proprietor. Her extensive charitable giving earned her the nickname Threepenny Bit Lady.

At about the time of her father's death, Ingham sought spiritual guidance from a Belgian Franciscan, Father Gomair Peeters, at West Gorton friary, Manchester. Supported by Taylor and Peeters, she started a small community of women, which included her stepmother, in 1871. She became a member of the lay society the third order of St Francis in 1872 and made a vow of voluntary chastity in 1874, thus setting the pattern for her community. The process of becoming a formally recognized religious congregation, however, was neither rapid nor smooth. For six years they ran the shop in Yorkshire Street, living on the premises and using it as the base for their charitable work. As numbers grew, a second shop was taken in John Street. The shops, both a livelihood and a means of being part of the community, echoed the Rochdale co-operative tradition and gave them a unique religious approach. Although persevering, no progress on status was made until 1878, when Alice Ingham accepted a proposal from Herbert Vaughan, bishop of Salford and founder of the Mill Hill Missionaries, that her members undertake the domestic work at St Joseph's College, Mill Hill, London. Her acceptance came from a realistic assessment of the community's situation but caused it to split, as some members could not accept the move and the substitution of domestic service for direct welfare work. The Rochdale shops were closed and the community moved to Mill Hill.

In 1880 Alice Ingham received a habit and was accorded the title Mother Mary Francis, a first step towards formal ecclesiastical recognition of her congregation. The official date of foundation was 8 September 1883, when Ingham and eleven sisters professed temporary vows. Professing permanent vows in 1884, Alice Ingham became the congregation's first 'good mother' (superior general). She sustained their Franciscan spirituality with support from a friary in Stratford, east London, and ensured their future in welfare work by writing it into the constitutions. Houses were opened in Wiltshire and in London at Hampstead. From 1886 the sisters began a return to Lancashire, moving first to Ardwick Hall to run Bishop Vaughan's Children's Rescue and Protection Society, then, in 1888, to a house in Blackburn. This realization of the congregation's original vision proved vital to its growth. Alice Ingham's desire that the community should undertake missionary work was also realized in 1885 when sisters went to Borneo with the Mill Hill Fathers. By the last decades of the nineteenth century the congregation, which remained working-class in membership and leadership, had four main operations: domestic management for priests; missionary activity in Borneo; welfare work with children in Lancashire; and parish work. Alice Ingham died at the Blackburn convent, 111 Paradise Street, of heart disease, on 24 August 1890, and was buried at Mill Hill. In 1925 the congregation which she had founded became part of the first and second orders of Franciscans and in 1930 gained pontifical status. Houses were established in the Netherlands, Germany, Kenya, the United States, Peru, Chile, and Ecuador.   SUSAN O'BRIEN

Sources *Franciscan missionaries of St Joseph: a short history on the occasion of the centenary of the congregation, 1883–1983* [1983] • A Sister, *Light after darkness: Mother Mary Francis (Alice Ingham)* (1963) • L. Nemer, 'Anglican and Roman Catholic attitudes on missions', PhD diss., U. Cam., 1979 • d. cert.

Archives St Joseph's College, Mill Hill, London, archives of the Mill Hill missionaries • St Joseph's Convent, Worsley, Manchester, archives of the Franciscan missionaries of St Joseph

Likenesses photograph, repro. in *Franciscan missionaries of St Joseph*

Ingham, Benjamin (1712–1772), evangelist and preacher, was born on 11 June 1712, probably at 7–9 Town End, Ossett, Yorkshire, the third son of William Ingham, a farmer and hatter, and his wife, Susannah (*d.* 1755). Ingham was good-natured and is said to have been extremely good-looking—'too handsome for a man' (Seymour, 1.302). He was educated at Batley grammar school and at Queen's College, Oxford (1730–34). After meeting the Wesleys in 1733 he became an 'Oxford Methodist' and after graduating held religious meetings in his mother's home. Ordained deacon by Bishop Potter in June 1735 he sailed to Georgia that October (after a brief curacy in Matching, Essex) with the Wesleys, Charles Delamotte, and some Moravians, who so attracted him that in May 1736 he (unsuccessfully) requested reception into their church. He left Georgia in February 1737, visiting Moravians in Pennsylvania on his way home. He preached in churches around Ossett, and by April 1738 had societies in neighbouring villages. In June he crossed to the continent with John Wesley, visiting Moravian congregations in Marienborn (where he met Count Zinzendorf and was admitted to communion) and Herrnhut, and returning in October. His December visit to his schoolfriend Jacob Rogers kindled a revival in Bedford. In February 1739 Ingham began a remarkable evangelistic ministry in Yorkshire. Banned from the churches in June, he preached in houses, barns, yards, and fields, and soon led some forty societies. Having vainly attempted to reunite the Fetter Lane Society behind the Wesleys in 1740, in 1741 he sided with the Moravians, barring the Wesleyan John Nelson from preaching for him. On 12 November 1741 he married the earl of Huntingdon's sister Lady Margaret Hastings

(1700–1768). They resided at Aberford Hall, near Tadcaster, Yorkshire.

In July 1742 the Moravians told Ingham they would only work with his societies if he handed them over completely, which he did—without joining them. He attended their 1743 general synod in Germany, and in 1744 purchased and leased them the site for their Yorkshire settlement, Fulneck, but soon felt that he had been made to surrender his societies under duress. He complained about the Moravians' authoritarianism, abuse of the lot, debts, extravagance with wealthy supporters' money, and separation from the Church of England, also finding their developing spirituality difficult.

In the later 1740s Ingham gradually developed his own preaching circuit, concentrating on the Craven area of Yorkshire, Lancashire, and (from 1749) Westmorland, but also visiting Cheshire, Derbyshire, and even Lincolnshire. He first visited Craven in May 1742, at the invitation of the family of William Delamotte's Cambridge contemporary Lawrence Batty. Invited to Colne, Lancashire, in February 1743, he met William Grimshaw, the vicar of Haworth, on the way; they later often preached for and with each other. (Ingham also toured with George Whitefield in 1749, 1750, and 1756.) In July 1748 the vicar of Colne, George White, roused a mob to break up one of Ingham's meetings; the following week Ingham had a number of places registered under the Toleration Act, and settled his first society in Craven. His *Collection of Hymns* also appeared in 1748.

Ingham had attended the Moravians' 1747 general synod in Germany, and in 1748 placed his son Ignatius (1746–1815) in their boarding-school. Secretly received into Moravian membership in July 1749, in 1750–52 he occasionally led worship and preached at Fulneck. Tensions resurfaced in 1751, however. In April 1752 (having expended in total more than £2300 on Fulneck and borrowed £1000 more on the Moravians' behalf), Ingham expressed himself 'desirous to be at peace and to part in mutual love' (Unitätsarchiv, R13.A17.44: Ingham to Zinzendorf, 22 April 1752). In February 1753 he withdrew Ignatius from the school and publicly distanced himself from the Moravians. Ingham's friendly visits to Fulneck (which the Moravians eventually purchased) continued, however; in 1761 the Moravians noted that his preachers tried to prevent him from meeting them, because 'it takes him 14 days until he is himself again' (Clarke, 172).

From 1752 Ingham's circuit gradually became a connexion. The first chapel having been built in 1750, others followed in 1752, 1754 (three), and 1757 (two). Ingham sought union with the Wesleys, but in May 1753 their conference decided that it could only unite with him 'when he returns to the old Methodist doctrine' (Clarke, 117). John Wesley rejected a further approach in May 1755, allowing Ingham to attend the Leeds conference as an observer, but not his preachers. Meanwhile one of the societies had declared its separation from the Church of England. Ingham was forced to organize his connexion as a separate denomination. In June 1756 a preachers' conference chose him as general overseer, and William Batty and James Allen as his assistants; he ordained them in September. He made one final approach to the Wesleys; Charles was favourable, but John was not.

In 1759 Ingham read the writings of the Scottish congregationalist John Glas (1695–1773) and his son-in-law Robert Sandeman (1718–1771). In June 1761 Batty and Allen were commissioned to visit the Glasites in Scotland. 'That horrid blast from the North', as William Romaine described Glasite influence (Tyerman, 140), fragmented the connexion. Objecting to Ingham's authority, the use of the lot, and delays in introducing a fully Glasite church order, Allen seceded in November 1761. Some followed him, but many more joined other groups. Ingham gave the ten or eleven remaining societies a quasi-Glasite church order in 1762, and in 1763 defended Sandemanian teaching in *A Discourse of the Faith and Hope of the Gospel*. According to Seymour the disruption of Ingham's connexion affected his mental stability, leaving him 'liable to sudden transitions from the highest flow of spirits to the utmost depression' (Seymour, 1.301). Lady Margaret died on 30 April 1768 and Ingham on 2 December 1772 at Aberford Hall. He was buried at Ledsham parish church, Yorkshire, on 10 December.

C. J. PODMORE

Sources D. F. Clarke, 'Benjamin Ingham (1712–1772), with special reference to his relations with the churches (Anglican, Methodist, Moravian and Glassite) of his time', MPhil diss., U. Leeds, 1971 · H. M. Pickles, *Benjamin Ingham, preacher amongst the dales, forests and fells* (1995) · Unitätsarchiv, Herrnhut, Germany, Ingham letters, R13.A17.22–50 · Moravian Church House, London, AB88.A3.14.1–40 · Pilgrim House diary, Moravian Church House, London · Fulneck Congregation diary, Yorkshire · L. Tyerman, *The Oxford Methodists: memoirs of the Rev. Messrs Clayton, Ingham, Gambold, Hervey, and Broughton, with biographical notices of others* (1873) · [A. C. H. Seymour], *The life and times of Selina, countess of Huntingdon*, 2 vols. (1839) · 'Richard Viney's diary, 1744', ed. M. Riggall, *Proceedings of the Wesley Historical Society*, 13–15 (1922–6) · F. Baker, *William Grimshaw, 1708–1763* (1963) · W. Batty, 'An account of Benjamin Ingham and his work', JRL, Eng MS 1062 · T. Moore, 'The beginnings of the revival in Yorkshire', JRL, Eng MS 1076, no. 21 · *Diary of an Oxford Methodist: Benjamin Ingham, 1733–1734*, ed. R. P. Heitzenrater (1985) · R. W. Thompson, *Benjamin Ingham (the Yorkshire evangelist) and the Inghamites* (1958) · DNB

Archives JRL, Methodist Archives and Research Centre, diary in cipher; papers incl. Inghamite committee minute book 1755 | Fulneck Moravian Church, Yorkshire, corresp. · Moravian Church House, London, corresp. · Unitätsarchiv, Herrnhut, Germany, corresp.

Likenesses Freeman, stipple, BM · engraving, repro. in Pickles, *Benjamin Ingham*, frontispiece

Ingham, Charles Cromwell (1796–1863), portrait and miniature painter, was born in Dublin. Of his parents nothing is known. He entered the Dublin Society's drawing school in 1809, and was awarded prizes for drawing in 1810 and 1811. He also studied under the portrait painter William Cuming (1769–1852), to whom he was apprenticed.

Ingham began exhibiting his work at the Irish Society of Artists' annual exhibition in 1812. In 1815 his *Death of Cleopatra* was awarded a prize of £34 2s. 6d. by the Irish Institution and it was exhibited at the 'Artists of Ireland' exhibition that year. He exhibited work again in 1816, and then emigrated to the United States of America.

In New York Ingham quickly established himself as a

portrait painter. He was one of the first artists to exhibit at the American Academy of Fine Arts, founded in New York in 1816. He became a member of the New York Drawing Association. In 1826 Ingham was one of the founders of the National Academy of Design, later becoming its vice-president. In 1829 he was involved in the establishment of the Artists' Sketch Club and was its first president. He oversaw its reorganization into the Century Association, New York's most intellectual gentleman's club.

Ingham was a fashionable portrait painter, gaining prestigious commissions from affluent New York society. His work is highly finished, employing a miniature painting technique—well suited to conveying details of costume, jewellery, and hair. The smooth surface of his miniatures was achieved by applying minute stippled brushstrokes. His sitters were usually women, young girls, or children. He painted them in a sentimental vein, often with a distant look in their eyes, which gave the portraits a romantic quality. Although Ingham concentrated on portraiture in oils, and miniature painting in watercolour on ivory, he also painted subject pictures such as his *Warrior at the Last Judgement* (New-York Historical Society). Examples of his work are in the Metropolitan Museum of Art, New York (Manney collection), and in the collection of the New-York Historical Society. Ingham died in New York on 10 December 1863.   PAUL CAFFREY

Sources W. G. Strickland, *A dictionary of Irish artists*, 1 (1913), 541–2 · D. T. Johnson, ed., *American portrait miniatures in the Manney collection* (1990), 13–26, 139–41 · R. J. Koke and others, *American landscape and genre paintings in the New-York Historical Society: a catalog of the collection*, 2 (1982), 217–19 · R. J. Koke, ed., *Artists by themselves, artists' portraits* (1983), 64 [catalogue from the National Academy of Design] · A. T. E. Gardener, 'Ingham in Manhattan', *Metropolitan Museum Bulletin*, 10/9 (May 1952), 245–53 · W. Dunlap, *History of the rise and progress of the arts of design in the United States*, 2 (New York, 1834), 273 · A. Crookshank and the Knight of Glin [D. Fitzgerald], *The watercolours of Ireland: works on paper in pencil, pastel and paint, c.1600–1914* (1994), 237–8 · A. M. Stewart, ed., *Irish art loan exhibitions, 1765–1927*, 1 (1990), 355 · A. M. Stewart, ed., *Royal Hibernian Academy of Arts: index of exhibitors and their works, 1826–1979*, 2 (1986), 113 · B. S. Long, *British miniaturists* (1929), 235 · P. Caffrey, 'Irish portrait miniatures, c.1700–1830', PhD diss., Southampton Institute, 1995 · D. Foskett, *Miniatures: dictionary and guide* (1987), 574

Likenesses C. C. Ingham, self-portrait, oils, c.1840–1850, National Academy of Design, New York

Ingham, Sir James Taylor (1805–1890), police magistrate, was born on 17 January 1805 at Mirfield, Yorkshire, a younger son of Joshua Ingham of Blake Hall, Yorkshire, and his wife, Martha, daughter of James Taylor, of Halifax. He was educated at school in Richmond, Yorkshire, and at Trinity College, Cambridge, matriculating in 1823 and graduating BA in 1829 and MA in 1832. He was admitted to the Inner Temple in November 1828 and was called to the bar in 1832. On 4 August 1835 he married Gertrude, fifth daughter of James Penrose of Woodhill, co. Cork; they had several children.

Ingham joined the northern circuit and practised at the West Riding sessions. In 1849 he was appointed magistrate at Thames police court, and from there he was successively transferred to Hammersmith and to Wandsworth.

Sir James Taylor Ingham (1805–1890), by Sydney Prior Hall, pubd 1889

In July 1876 he was made chief magistrate of London, sitting at Bow Street. On 21 July 1876 he was knighted at Osborne. Ingham was a man of dignified appearance, and, having jurisdiction over a great many extradition cases, did much to settle the rules of procedure of that time. He died at his home, 40 Gloucester Square, Hyde Park, London, on 5 March 1890.

W. A. J. ARCHBOLD, *rev.* ERIC METCALFE

Sources Venn, *Alum. Cant.* · Boase, *Mod. Eng. biog.* · *The Times* (6 March 1890) · *Law Journal* (8 March 1890) · *ILN* (15 March 1890) · E. Lodge, *Peerage, baronetage, knightage and companionage of the British empire*, 81st edn, 3 vols. (1912) · *VF* (20 Feb 1886) · *The Graphic* (9 April 1881) · *CGPLA Eng. & Wales* (1890)

Likenesses S. P. Hall, pencil drawing, pubd 1889, NPG [*see illus.*] · Spy [L. Ward], caricature chromolithograph, NPG; repro. in *VF* · portrait, repro. in *The Graphic*, 341 · wood-engraving (after photograph by J. C. Smallcombe), NPG; repro. in *ILN* (5 Aug 1876)

Wealth at death £22,709 19s. 3d.: probate, 30 April 1890, *CGPLA Eng. & Wales*

Ingham, Oliver, Lord Ingham (c.1287–1344), soldier and seneschal of Aquitaine, was son and heir of Sir John Ingham (1260–1309), of Ingham, Norfolk, and his wife, Margery. His father served in Edward I's Scottish wars and he was himself summoned for military service in Scotland in 1310 and 1314. He received livery of his inheritance on 22 May 1310 and held lands in Norfolk, Suffolk, Wiltshire, and Hampshire. With his wife, Elizabeth, daughter of Lord Zouche, he had two sons, Oliver (d. 1326) and John (d. 1339), and two daughters, Elizabeth and Joan.

A household knight of Edward II, Ingham was the recipient of many royal grants, including the custody of the castle of Ellesmere, Shropshire, in June 1321. During the disturbances of the early 1320s, he served Edward II against the baronial rebels led by Thomas, earl of Lancaster (d. 1322), subsequently receiving grants of offices in Wiltshire and Shropshire and becoming keeper of Chester and Flint. As a knight-banneret, he served in Scotland with the king in August 1322. In 1324 he was appointed adviser to the king's half-brother Edmund, earl of Kent (d. 1330), who represented Edward as lieutenant in Aquitaine. Anglo-French tensions had led to the outbreak of war with France, and Ingham, dispatched to Aquitaine with a force of Spanish and other mercenary troops, conducted a successful campaign against the French in the Agenais.

As a trusted lieutenant of both the king and the Despensers, Ingham was appointed seneschal of Aquitaine on 7 October 1325, and in April 1326 extensive powers were granted him over the financial administration of the duchy. He appears to have gained the confidence of many members of the Gascon nobility, but the terms of an agreement made with the French in 1327 led to his temporary banishment from Aquitaine. Although he had been an associate of the Despensers, Ingham largely escaped the recriminations unleashed in England against the latter and their clients following the crises of 1326–7. Having become an adherent of Roger Mortimer, earl of March, he was summoned to parliament between June 1328 and September 1330, and was a partisan judge in the trial of the conspirators who attempted to overthrow Mortimer in February 1329. In October 1330, when Mortimer was toppled from power, Ingham was seized by the young Edward III at Nottingham and sent for trial to London. On 22 October his lands and goods were declared forfeit.

Nevertheless, Ingham was pardoned on 8 December 1330 because the young king acknowledged his loyal service to Edward II. His property was restored to him, with the important exception of grants from the crown. From this time onwards he was to serve the king in Aquitaine, and rarely returned to England until his death. On 29 June 1331 he was reappointed as seneschal in Aquitaine, an office he was to hold for twelve years—an unusually long tour of duty. Ingham was responsible for the peace, order, and defence of the duchy during a period of crisis in Anglo-French relations which led to the outbreak of the Hundred Years' War in 1337. By August 1336 the duchy was on a war footing and Ingham was ordered to forbid all Gascon men-at-arms to leave the land without licence, and to ensure that all major strongholds were properly garrisoned, equipped, and victualled.

Philippe VI of France confiscated Aquitaine on 24 May 1337. It fell to Ingham, as seneschal, to receive the French commissioners appointed to take possession of the duchy. He met them at Libourne, but refused to surrender his charge. Like their predecessors in 1294, the French envoys departed, proclaiming the duchy's confiscation. Ingham's services in Aquitaine were acknowledged on 15 July 1337, when his and his ancestors' debts were written off. Relieved of this burden, Ingham began military operations in Aquitaine, generally confined to the Agenais, but, despite the loss of Penne and Bourg, he successfully defended Bonnegarde, Montlaur, and other strongholds. He fought off a French attack on Bordeaux in 1339 and, financial stringency notwithstanding, retained substantial companies of Gascon nobles in his service.

In January 1342 Ingham was summoned to a council in England in order to report upon the state of affairs in Aquitaine, and on 6 April 1343 he was relieved of his post as seneschal. He died, probably at Ingham, on 29 January 1344. Both his sons had predeceased him, and his inheritance was divided between his granddaughter Mary, aged eight years, daughter of his elder daughter, Elizabeth, who had also predeceased him, and his younger daughter, Joan, aged twenty-four years. She had married Sir Roger Lestrange (d. 1349), lord of Knokyn, Shropshire. She married as her second husband Sir Miles Stapleton (d. 1364) of Bedale, and in June 1360 they founded a chantry at Ingham to commemorate the souls of, among others, Sir Oliver Ingham and his wife, Elizabeth.

The inquisition post mortem for Ingham recorded that he held the manor and advowson of the church at Ingham, and he was buried there, although as early as June 1317 he was licensed to alienate land in mortmain in order to rebuild a chantry chapel at East Codford, Wiltshire, in which masses were celebrated for Edward II, himself, and his ancestors. His widow, Elizabeth, died on 11 October 1350 and was buried beside him. His tomb survives, a masterly and unusual monument, in which Ingham lies upon a bed of stones, in a twisted posture, one hand grasping his sword as if to do battle with the Devil for possession of his soul. The significance of the bed of stones is unclear, but it may refer either to a cult of penitence or to Ingham's essentially martial qualities. A huge, publicly displayed, recumbent figure of a river-god on a bed of stones at Rome was popularly regarded as a statue of Mars during the middle ages, and the allusion to the god of war may have been reinforced by wall-paintings (now lost) above and behind Ingham's effigy which depicted hunting scenes and, perhaps, astrological references to the month of March (Mars). Whatever the case, Ingham's tomb is one of the finer examples of the monumental sculpture of the period. MALCOLM VALE

Sources PRO, Chancery, Gascon Rolls, C 61 · PRO, Exchequer, Queen's Remembrancer, accounts various, E 101 · PRO, Special collections, ancient petitions, SC 8 · PRO, Chancery, inquisition miscellaneous, C 145 · *DNB* · *Chancery records* · GEC, *Peerage* · F. Palgrave, ed., *The parliamentary writs and writs of military summons*, 2 (1830–34) · Rymer, *Foedera*, vol. 2 · *CEPR letters*, vol. 2 · *CIPM*, vol. 8 · W. Stubbs, ed., *Chronicles of the reigns of Edward I and Edward II*, 2 vols., Rolls Series, 76 (1882–3) · V. H. Galbraith, 'Extracts from the *Historia aurea* and a French "Brut" (1317–47)', *EngHR*, 43 (1928), 203–17 · G. P. Cuttino and T. W. Lyman, 'Where is Edward II?', *Speculum*, 53 (1978), 522–43 · M. Vale, *The Angevin legacy and the Hundred Years War, 1250–1340* (1990) · J. Weever, *Ancient funerall monuments* (1631) · C. A. Stothard, *The monumental effigies of Great Britain* (1817) · A. Martindale, 'The knights and the bed of stones: a learned confusion of the 14th century', *Journal of the British Archaeological Association*, 142 (1989), 66–74

Likenesses effigy on tomb, *c.*1344, parish church, Ingham, Norfolk

Ingleby. For this title name *see* Peake, Osbert, first Viscount Ingleby (1897–1966).

Ingleby, Sir Charles (*bap.* 1645, *d.* 1719), judge, was the third son of John Ingleby (*d.* 1648) of Lawkland, Yorkshire, and his second wife, Mary (*d.* 1667), daughter of Sir Thomas Lake of Cannons, Middlesex, and was baptized on 20 February 1645 at Clapham, Yorkshire. He was a descendant of Sir Thomas Ingleby, judge of the king's bench in the reign of Edward III. Ingleby was admitted to Brasenose College, Oxford, on 26 November 1662, and Gray's

Inn on 25 June 1663. He was called to the bar on 22 November 1671. As a Roman Catholic he suffered under what the earl of Clarendon called 'Oates's usurpation and imposition' (Keeton, 399), being charged by the informers Robert Bolron and Lawrence Mowbray in February 1680 with complicity in the plot of Sir Thomas Gascoigne, and was committed to the king's bench prison. He was one of 'several persons of quality' (*Memoirs of Sir John Reresby*, 197) acquitted in July 1680 at his trial in York. He married Alathea (*d*. 1715), daughter of Richard Eyston of Saxton, Yorkshire, five of his children being baptized at Clapham during the 1680s.

The reign of James II opened up avenues of promotion for Ingleby which had been closed hitherto. On 23 April 1686 he was appointed a baron of exchequer in Ireland, but he was reluctant to take up his post, and on 27 May Lord Chief Justice Jeffreys informed the lord lieutenant, the earl of Clarendon, that Ingleby had been excused. In April 1687 Ingleby was made a serjeant-at-law, his patrons being the earl of Thanet and Viscount Carrington, the latter peer being a Catholic. On 6 July 1688 he was appointed a baron of the exchequer, being knighted later in the month. Bramston at this point calls him 'always a papist' (*Autobiography*, 311). Ingleby's appointment was officially revoked on 3 November 1688, and he returned to private practice. In April 1693 he was fined 40s. at York assizes for refusing to take the oaths of allegiance to William and Mary. He headed the register of Roman Catholic landholders in the West Riding of Yorkshire in 1717, residing at Austwick Hall, midway between Clapham and Lawkland. Ingleby was buried at Clapham on 5, 6, or 9 August 1719. His son Thomas also became a barrister.

STUART HANDLEY

Sources *Dugdale's visitation of Yorkshire, with additions*, ed. J. W. Clay, 3 (1917), 3 · IGI · Sainty, *Judges*, 127 · Baker, *Serjeants*, 520 · Foster, *Alum. Oxon.* · J. Foster, *The register of admissions to Gray's Inn, 1521–1889, together with the register of marriages in Gray's Inn chapel, 1695–1754* (privately printed, London, 1889), 295 · R. J. Fletcher, ed., *The pension book of Gray's Inn*, 2 (1910), 19 · *The autobiography of Sir John Bramston*, ed. [Lord Braybrooke], CS, 32 (1845), 311 · *Memoirs of Sir John Reresby*, ed. A. Browning, 2nd edn, ed. M. K. Geiter and W. A. Speck (1991), 197 · G. W. Keeton, *Lord Chancellor Jeffreys and the Stuart cause* (1965), 398–401 · *Ninth report*, 1, HMC, 8 (1883), 327 · Foss, *Judges*, 7.246–7

Ingleby, Clement Mansfield (1823–1886), literary scholar, was born on 29 October 1823 at Edgbaston, Birmingham, the only son of Clement Ingleby (1786–1859), a solicitor of Birmingham, and his wife, Elizabeth (*d*. 1877), daughter of John Jukes of Birmingham. His grandfather was William Ingleby, a country gentleman of Cheadle, Staffordshire. Ingleby suffered from ill health for much of his life, and was educated privately before proceeding in 1843 to Trinity College, Cambridge, from where he graduated BA in 1847, later receiving the degrees of MA (1850) and LLD (1859). Ingleby returned to Birmingham and joined his father's law firm, becoming a partner in 1850. On 3 October of that same year he married Sarah Oakes (*d*. 1906), only daughter of Robert Oakes, a magistrate of Gravesend, Kent.

Ingleby's son later wrote that Ingleby found the legal

Clement Mansfield Ingleby (1823–1886), by unknown artist, pubd 1883

profession 'distasteful' (*DNB*), and although he remained with the family firm until 1859, he devoted much of his time to pursuing his interests in philosophy and literature. He gave classes in logic in the industrial department of the newly formed Birmingham and Midland Institute and published several textbooks on logic. He also published articles on Shakespearian topics in the local press and in *Notes and Queries* and gave a lecture entitled, 'On the neology of Shakespeare' at the institute in 1856. This was one of his earliest contributions to the controversy surrounding the 'Perkins folio' emendations which John Payne Collier claimed to have discovered. Ingleby was among the first to examine the 'Perkins folio' when it became available for inspection at the British Museum in 1859 and shortly afterwards he published *The Shakspeare Fabrications, or, The MS Notes of the Perkins Folio Shown to be of Recent Origin*. He followed this up at the end of 1860 with *A complete view of the Shakspere controversy, concerning the authenticity and genuineness of manuscript matter affecting the works and biography of Shakspere, published by Mr J. P. Collier as the fruits of his researches*, a very effective (though far from impartial) presentation, running to more than 300 pages, of the case against Collier, which concluded by charging him unequivocally with forgery. Collier did not reply, and for more than a century Ingleby's *Complete view* was regarded as the authoritative account of the affair (the controversy was reopened in 1982, however, by Dewey Ganzel's biography of Collier, which strongly challenged Ingleby's handling of the evidence). Ingleby returned to the attack on Collier (whom he had never met) in the pamphlet *Was Thomas Lodge an Actor?* (1868), and in later essays and letters to *The Times*. Ingleby's attacks were fierce, but were motivated in part by a more general concern to preserve Shakespeare's text from casual emendation or modernization, a process which he feared would lead to the deterioration of the English language itself. Ingleby set out his views on legitimate emendation in *The Still Lion: an Essay towards the Restoration of Shakespeare's Text*, first published in Germany in 1867, enlarged and presented to every member of the New Shakspere Society in 1874, and finally published under the title *Shakespeare Hermeneutics* (1875).

By this time, following his father's death in 1859, Ingleby had severed his connections with the law and moved to London, taking up residence eventually at Valentines, the seventeenth-century mansion and estate in Ilford owned by Sarah Ingleby's uncle Charles Thomas Holcombe, which passed to the Ingleby family after Holcombe's death in 1870. There Ingleby completed his *Introduction to Metaphysics*, published in two parts in 1864 and (after a period of ill health) 1869. Ingleby remained interested in philosophical issues, and in 1880, at the request of the Royal Society, he produced a short report, with C. H. Monro, on the papers in the society's possession relating to contact between Isaac Newton and Gottfried Wilhelm Leibnitz. He also wrote articles for the *British Controversialist* on Bacon, Coleridge, and De Quincey. His main interest was in Shakespeare, however, and in 1874 he published *Shakespeare's Century of Prayse*, a compilation of allusions to Shakespeare in literature from the period 1592–1692; this work was republished in several later editions, with additional material provided by Lucy Toulmin-Smith, F. J. Furnivall, and others, as *The Shakespeare Allusion Book*. In 1877 and 1881 Ingleby published two volumes of occasional essays under the title *Shakespeare: the Man and the Book*. In addition to textual criticism, his subjects included Shakespeare's birthday, the spelling of the playwright's surname, and the various portraits of Shakespeare. Interest in this last topic, together with a lifelong interest in phrenology, led to the controversial and somewhat eccentric essay, *Shakespeare's Bones* (1883), in which Ingleby argued, in support of an earlier American proposal, that Shakespeare's skull should be disinterred in order to verify his likeness. The proposal was attacked in the press and firmly rejected by Stratford upon Avon town council. One of Ingleby's last publications was *Shakespeare and the Enclosure of Common Fields at Welcombe*, reproducing a contemporary reference to Shakespeare in a manuscript found at Stratford.

Ingleby read a number of papers before the Royal Society of Literature, and was elected a vice-president of the society in 1876, having previously served as its foreign secretary. He was also a member of the first committee of the New Shakspere Society (though he was among those who later resigned), and edited one of the first series of its publications, the Shakspere-Allusion Books. He was also a trustee of the Shakespeare Birthplace Trust and an honorary member of the Weimar Shakespeare Society and of the Shakespeare Society of New York. He was admired by his contemporaries for his mastery of minute detail in textual and biographical matters, but he is now chiefly remembered for his part in the 'Perkins folio' controversy, and for his work as a compiler of allusions to Shakespeare, which provided a useful resource for later generations of scholars. Though much concerned with questions of editorial responsibility, he published only one edition himself, of Shakespeare's *Cymbeline*, in 1886.

Ingleby died at Valentines on 26 September 1886, and was survived by his wife and four children. A further collection of his essays, on Shakespearian and other topics, was published in 1888, edited by his second son, Holcombe Ingleby (later MP for King's Lynn and high sheriff of Norfolk).　　　　　　　　　　　RICHARD STORER

Sources C. M. Ingleby, *A complete view of the Shakspere controversy* (1861) · 'Edgbastonians, past and present, no. 22: Clement Mansfield Ingleby', *Edgbastonia*, 3 (1883), 64–8 · S. Timmins, 'In Memoriam: C. M. Ingleby 1823–1886', *Shakespeariana*, 3 (1886), 543–7 · Burke, *Gen. GB* (1886) · *DNB* · D. Ganzel, *Fortune and men's eyes: the career of John Payne Collier* (1982) · S. Schoenbaum, *Shakespeare's lives*, new edn (1991)

Archives Folger, letters · NL Scot., corresp. · NL Scot., Scottish journal | BL, letters to W. C. Hazlitt and others, Index of MSS V, 1985 · LMA, corresp. with C. J. Monro · Shakespeare Birthplace Trust RO, Stratford upon Avon, corresp. and papers relating to Thomas Greene's diary · TCD, corresp. with W. R. Hamilton · U. Edin. L., corresp. with James Halliwell-Phillipps

Likenesses drawing, repro. in 'Edgbastonians, past and present' [*see illus.*]

Wealth at death £40,343 15s. 1d.: probate, 1 Nov 1886, *CGPLA Eng. & Wales*

Ingleby, John (1434?–1499), bishop of Llandaff, came of the distinguished family of Ingleby of Yorkshire. He may have been the only son of Sir William Ingleby of Ripley and Joan, daughter of Sir Brian Stapleton of Carlton, in which case he was born on 7 July 1434, married Margery, daughter of Sir James Strangways of Harsley, and 'died' (when he became a monk) on 21 September 1457. He was ordained subdeacon and deacon as a monk of Mount Grace, Yorkshire, a Charterhouse with which his family was closely connected, in 1457. He was elected prior of Hinton, Somerset, in 1476–7, but the Carthusian general chapter of 1477 refused to confirm his election and appointed him rector only. After he was elected prior of Sheen in 1477, the general chapter confirmed him as prior between 1478 and 1496, appointed and confirmed him as first visitor of the English province between 1478 and 1496, and made him a diffinitor of the general chapter in 1487–8 and 1490–91. As prior of Sheen he was among the co-founders of the Guild of St Mary, Bagshot, in 1480.

Ingleby acquired the confidence of kings and queens who with increasing regularity attended services at Sheen throughout his time there. Edward IV's queen, Elizabeth, who gained permission from Pope Sixtus IV (r. 1471–84) to attend services at Sheen in 1479, made him the first of three executors in 1492. Henry VII asked him to deliver to Pope Innocent VIII (r. 1484–92) a letter dated 10 February 1490, in which he extolled the Carthusians above the Cistercians and referred to Ingleby as his 'captain and envoy'. Henry also appointed him to oversee the works, which, between 1495 and 1499, transformed the manor house of Sheen into the palace of Richmond. At Henry's request he was provided to the see of Llandaff by Pope Alexander VI

(r. 1492–1503) on 27 June 1496. He continued to be active in Carthusian affairs, however, visiting Sheen on 28 October 1496 when he probably presented to his successor, Ralph Tracy, a copy of Chrysostom's Homilies on St John. Such a visit, combined with his works at Richmond, make it likely that he was usually a non-resident bishop, but since his diocese does not appear to have suffered from his absences, it may be assumed that he took steps to ensure continuity of administration. Ingleby's episcopal register and seal have been lost, although his armorial bearings have survived as those of his family: sable, an estoile argent. According to the acts of the general chapter and a brass inscription from Sheen, he died on 7 September 1499.   W. N. M. BECKETT

Sources J. Foster, ed., *Pedigrees of the county families of Yorkshire*, 1 (1874) · J. Hogg and others, eds., *The chartae of the Carthusian general chapter*, Analecta Cartusiana, 100/1–24 (1982–94) · W. N. M. Beckett, 'Sheen Charterhouse from its foundation to its dissolution', DPhil diss., U. Oxf., 1992 · C. B. Rowntree, 'Studies in Carthusian history in later medieval England', DPhil diss., York University, 1981 · J. Hogg, 'The pre-Reformation priors of the *Provincia Angliae*', *Analecta Cartusiana*, new ser., 1 (1989), 25–59 · L. Le Vasseur, *Ephemerides ordinis cartusiensis*, 3 (1891) · J. Page-Phillips, *Palimpsests: the backs of monumental brasses*, 2 vols. (1980) · *Chancery records* · PRO, exchequer, accounts various, E101 · *CSP Venice, 1202–1509* · W. de Gray Birch, *Memorials of the see and cathedral of Llandaff* (1912) · D. H. Williams, 'A catalogue of Welsh ecclesiastical seals, as known down to AD 1600, part 1: episcopal seals', *Archaeologia Cambrensis*, 133 (1984), 100–35
Archives Gon. & Caius Cam., MS 732/771 · Jesus College, Cambridge, MS Q. A. 12 · PRO, E101

Inglefield, Sir Edward Augustus (1820–1894), naval officer and Arctic explorer, was born in Cheltenham on 27 March 1820. He was the eldest son of Rear-Admiral Samuel Hood Inglefield (1783–1848), who died when commander-in-chief in the East Indies and China, and his wife, Priscilla Margaret, eldest daughter of Vice-Admiral Albany Otway; and grandson of Captain John Nicholson *Inglefield. He entered the Royal Naval College, Portsmouth, in October 1832, and, passing out in October 1834, was appointed to the *Etna*, and then to the *Actaeon*, from which, early in 1835, he was moved to the *Dublin*, flagship of Sir Graham Eden Hamond, on the South American station. He continued on the same station, in the *Dublin* and afterwards in the *Imogene*, until 1839. Having passed his examination, Inglefield was appointed in March 1840 to the *Thunderer*, in which he took part in the operations on the coast of Syria, the storming of Sidon, and the capture of Acre. He was afterwards for a short time in the West Indies and in the royal yacht, from which he was promoted lieutenant on 21 September 1842. From November 1842 to 1845 he was in the *Samarang* with Sir Edward Belcher. In March 1845 he joined the *Eagle* as flag-lieutenant to his father, then commander-in-chief on the South American station, and was shortly afterwards appointed to command the *Comus* (16 guns), in which he took part in the operations in the River Parana and in forcing the passage at Obligado on 20 November 1845. In recognition of his services on this day, his acting commission as commander was confirmed to 18 November. In 1852 Inglefield commanded Lady Franklin's private steamer, *Isabella*, in a summer expedition to the

Arctic, and looked into Smith Sound for the first time since it had been named by William Baffin. On his return he published *A Summer Search for Sir John Franklin* (1853), was elected FRS (2 June 1853), was awarded the gold medal of the Royal Geographical Society, and the silver medal of the Paris Geographical Society, and was presented with a diamond snuff-box by Napoleon III. In 1853 he went again to the Arctic in the *Phoenix* with relief to Sir Edward Belcher, and in October brought home the news of the discovery of the north-west passage by Robert John Le Mesurier McClure, for which he was promoted captain on 7 October 1853. In 1854, still in the *Phoenix*, he went for the third time to the Arctic, and brought back the crews of the *Resolute* and *Investigator*.

In July 1855 Inglefield was appointed to the *Firebrand* in the Black Sea, where he took part in the capture of Kinburn. In the following March he was moved into the *Sidon*, which he brought home and paid off. In April 1857 he married Eliza Fanny (d. 1890), daughter of Edward Johnston of Allerton Hall, near Liverpool. They had several children. From 1861 to 1864 he commanded the *Majestic*, coastguard ship at Liverpool, and from 1866 to 1868 the ironclad *Prince Consort* in the channel and the Mediterranean. On 26 May 1869 he was promoted rear-admiral, and on 2 June he was nominated a CB. From August 1872 to December 1875 he was second in command in the Mediterranean and superintendent of Malta Dockyard, vacating the post on promotion to vice-admiral on 11 December. On 13 August 1877 he was knighted, and from April 1878 until his promotion to admiral, on 27 November 1879, he was commander-in-chief on the North American station.

On 27 March 1885 Inglefield was put on the retired list; but in 1891, on the occasion of the naval exhibition at Chelsea, he was chairman of the arts section, to the success of which he contributed substantially. On 21 June 1887 (the queen's jubilee) he was nominated a KCB. In 1893, he married Beatrice Marianne, daughter of Colonel Hodnett of the Dorsetshire regiment.

Inglefield was a man of cultivated taste and mechanical ingenuity. He collected old Venetian glass, and was an exceptional amateur painter; some of his pictures—including portraits of the queen and princess royal—were exhibited at the Royal Academy. He had a good workshop in his house, and was the inventor of the hydraulic steering gear, which was highly thought of in the navy until it was superseded by steam, and of the Inglefield anchor. He also wrote pamphlets on naval subjects. Inglefield died at his home, 99 Queen's Gate, South Kensington, London, on 5 September 1894, and was buried at Kensal Green cemetery, London.   J. K. LAUGHTON, rev. ANDREW LAMBERT

Sources A. D. Lambert, *The Crimean War: British grand strategy, 1853–56* (1990) · O'Byrne, *Naval biog. dict.* · *Navy List* · *The Times* (7 Sept 1894) · *The Times* (10 Sept 1894) · personal knowledge (1901) · Boase, *Mod. Eng. biog.* · Kelly, *Handbk* (1893) · Burke, *Peerage* (1889) · *CGPLA Eng. & Wales* (1895)
Archives Mariners' Museum, Newport News, Virginia, logbook of HMS *Agamemnon*, 1855; HMS *Firebrand*, 1855–6; and HMS *Sidon*, 1856
Likenesses S. Pearce, oils, c.1853, NPG; copy, NPG · J. Collier, oils, 1897, NPG · Fradelle & Young, cabinet photograph, NPG · cabinet

photograph, NPG · photograph, RGS · wood-engraving (after photograph by Claudet), NPG; repro. in *ILN* (15 Oct 1853)

Wealth at death £12,992 1s. 3d.: probate, 2 Jan 1895, *CGPLA Eng. & Wales*

Inglefield, John Nicholson (1748–1828), naval officer, details of whose parentage and upbringing are unknown, entered the navy in 1759. After passing his examination he was, in April 1766, rated able seaman on the *Launceston*, going to North America with the flag of Vice-Admiral Philip Durell. In May 1768 he was made lieutenant and moved into the *Romney*, bearing the broad pennant of Commodore Samuel Hood before returning to the *Launceston* in October. In the following July he returned to the *Romney*, and from that time his active career was very closely connected with that of Hood. With him Inglefield left the *Romney* in December 1770, served in the *Marlborough* and *Courageux*, and in 1778 in the *Robust*, with Hood's brother Alexander. In the *Robust* he was present in the action of Ushant on 27 July. About 1775 Inglefield had married a daughter of the shipbuilder, Sir Thomas *Slade, and they had children.

In June 1779 Inglefield was promoted to the command of the sloop *Lively*. On 11 October 1780 he was promoted captain and posted to the *Barfleur* (90 guns), in which his patron, Sir Samuel Hood, hoisted his flag, and sailed to the West Indies as second in command. He thus had an important share in the skirmish with the French fleet off Fort Royal, Martinique, on 29 April 1781. In the following August he was moved by Hood to the *Centaur* (74 guns), and commanded her in the action off the Chesapeake on 5 September, in the action with the comte de Grasse at St Kitts on 25 January 1782, in the skirmish on 9 April, and in the decisive action of 12 April 1782 at the Saints.

In August the *Centaur* sailed for England with the convoy, under the command of Rear-Admiral Thomas Graves, and after much bad weather was overtaken by a hurricane on 16 September. Many of the ships, apparently including the *Centaur*, lay-to on the wrong tack. In a violent shift of the wind she was dismasted, lost her rudder, and was thrown on her beam ends. The crew struggled to keep the ship afloat, but towards evening on the 23 September she foundered. The sea ran very high, but Inglefield, with the master, a midshipman, and nine seamen, got into the pinnace, and after sixteen days' wild navigation and fearful suffering reached Fayal in the Azores, one of the men dying a few hours before they sighted land. These eleven men were all that remained of the crew of almost 600 men.

On returning to England, Inglefield, with the other survivors, was subjected to the usual court martial and fully acquitted.

Inglefield was then appointed to the guardship *Scipio* in the Medway. In 1788–9 he commanded the *Adventure* (44 guns) on the west coast of Africa, and from 1790 to 1792 the *Medusa* (also 44 guns) on the same station. In 1793 he commanded the frigate *Aigle* (36 guns) in the Mediterranean, and in the following year succeeded Sir Hyde Parker as captain of the fleet. Towards the close of 1794 he returned

to England with Samuel (now Viscount) Hood. Thenceforth he was successively in Corsica, Malta, Gibraltar, and Halifax, Nova Scotia, as resident commissioner of the navy, effectively relinquishing claims to further active service. In 1799 he was placed on the list of retired captains, retaining his civil appointment until 1811. Inglefield's daughter married Sir Benjamin Hallowell *Carew. A son, Samuel Hood Inglefield, who was rear-admiral and commander-in-chief in China in 1848, was father of Admiral Sir Edward Augustus Inglefield (*d.* 1894). John Nicholson Inglefield died in 1828.

J. K. LAUGHTON, rev. P. L. C. WEBB

Sources J. Marshall, *Royal naval biography*, 3 (1831–2) · J. Ralfe, *The naval biography of Great Britain*, 4 vols. (1828) · [J. N. Inglefield], *Captain Inglefield's narrative concerning the loss of the 'Centaur'*, new edn (1783) · D. Syrett and R. L. DiNardo, *The commissioned sea officers of the Royal Navy, 1660–1815*, rev. edn, Occasional Publications of the Navy RS, 1 (1994)

Likenesses B. Smith, stipple, pubd 1815 (after G. Engleheart), BM

Inglethorp, Thomas. *See* Ingoldisthorpe, Thomas of (*d.* 1291).

Inglis, Brian St John (1916–1993), journalist, was born on 31 July 1916 at 89 Lower Baggot Street, Dublin, the only child of Sir Claude Cavendish Inglis (1883–1974), civil engineer to the Bombay government, and his wife, Vera Margaret St John Blood (*d.* 1972). He lived with his parents at Poona, India, from 1918 until 1921 but saw little of them thereafter; at the age of five he was sent to England to board at St Catharine's School, Bexhill-on-Sea, before passing to the Dragon School, Oxford (1925–9), which he liked far better than Shrewsbury School (1929–35). His holidays were spent with his grandmother Sophie Blood at Malahide, co. Dublin, in an old-fashioned Anglo-Irish milieu.

In 1935 Inglis went to Magdalen College, Oxford. He obtained a second-class degree in history in 1939, by which time he had imbibed vaguely left-wing ideas. Studying Irish history made him cease to think of the English as his fellow countrymen, but he would always be aware of conflicting loyalties arising from an Irish Protestant background. He left for Dublin when the war began and reported local news for the *Irish Times*.

From June 1940 to January 1946 Inglis served voluntarily in the Royal Air Force, piloting flying boats for Coastal Command in west Africa and reaching the rank of squadron leader. The *Irish Times* re-engaged him on his return to Dublin as Quidnunc of 'An Irishman's Diary'. Patrick Campbell, Conor Cruise O'Brien, and Erskine H. Childers were numbered among his friends. A supporter of the Irish Labour Party, Inglis went freelance for two years from 1948 while completing a doctoral thesis at Trinity College, Dublin, on the freedom of the press in Ireland (1784–1841). From 1951 to 1953 the *Irish Times* carried his parliamentary sketches of the Dáil.

Inglis moved to London in June 1953 to work for the tabloid *Daily Sketch*. Highly sociable, he appeared at home in Fleet Street bars and clubs. There was nothing loud or pushy about Brian; standing quietly at the side of parties, he let other people come to him for lively talk, which spiced scholarly syntax with swear words. He never had an Irish accent. After a year he gave up his job, intending to write a novel, but in September 1954 he was asked to be assistant editor of *The Spectator*, a prestigious weekly. This placed him third within its hierarchy, rising to second in 1956. The editor-in-chief was the proprietor, Ian Gilmour.

On 5 November 1956 Inglis appeared on television for the first time, as writer–presenter of Granada TV's press review *What the Papers Say*. He reappeared on 160 editions over the next twenty years. Inglis in 1958 married Ruth (Boo) Woodeson (*b.* 1928), otherwise Ruth Langdon, an American journalist with a daughter from a previous marriage. They had a son in 1962.

When Inglis thought about leaving *The Spectator* in 1959, Gilmour responded by making him editor. Its circulation rose from 39,000 to 48,000 during his term. The journal boasted 'star' columnists in Bernard Levin (politics), Alan Brien (theatre), and Cyril Ray (wine). Often satirical in tone, it refrained from endorsing the Conservatives in the general election of 1959 and aired support for easier divorce, tolerance of homosexuality, and ending the death penalty. Gilmour began to complain that the content was becoming too lightweight—which Inglis took to mean too liberal. When he heard that Gilmour aimed to be a Conservative MP he resigned as editor in February 1962, fearing that the political independence of *The Spectator* would be compromised. He remained on its board, however, until November 1963, when he severed all ties in protest at the appointment as editor of tory politician Iain Macleod.

To a wider public Brian Inglis became familiar as the presenter of *All Our Yesterdays* (1962–73), Granada TV's weekly look at the events of twenty-five years earlier as shown in Pathé newsreels. He enjoyed the social life of a television celebrity but liked even more the short hours and high income which enabled him to devote most of his time to writing books. The industrial revolution, the First Opium War, and Roger Casement were among his historical subjects. Having himself coined the term 'fringe medicine' in 1960, he now wrote extensively on homoeopathy, acupuncture, and the like. When he separated from his wife in 1972—they divorced in 1974—his home ceased to be a large house in Paddington and became a small basement flat, full of books, at 23 Lambolle Road, Belsize Park. He was a founder member of the British-Irish Association (1972), an educational charity intended to promote better relations.

Arthur Koestler encouraged Inglis to pursue research into supernatural and paranormal phenomena. His later books concern dreams, intuition, coincidence, trances, spontaneous combustion, dowsing, levitation, poltergeists, fire walking, and ghosts. He condemned scientists for overlooking these matters and privately regretted his own lack of psychic experience. He never forced his opinions on his friends, many of whom were young women. His reputation as a good-natured philanderer was deserved, but from 1984 he adored Margaret van Hattem (1948–1989), a Dutch-born Australian-educated journalist.

Brian Inglis died of ischaemic heart disease at the Royal Free Hospital, Camden, on 11 February 1993 after collapsing in the street. The body was cremated.

JASON TOMES

Sources B. Inglis, *Downstart* (1990) • *The Times* (13 Feb 1993) • *The Independent* (13 Feb 1993) • *The Observer* (14 Feb 1993) • *The Guardian* (13 Feb 1993) • *Daily Telegraph* (13 Feb 1993) • B. Inglis, *West Briton* (1962) • P. K. L., 'Brian Inglis: an appreciation', *Irish Times* (3 March 1993) • R. Inglis, 'Don't marry a television celebrity', *The Independent* (10 July 1994) • S. Lowry, 'Eulogy for a lost quartet of friends', *Daily Telegraph* (19 Nov 1993) • A. Berry, 'If St Joseph of Copertino could fly', *Sunday Telegraph* (7 Jan 1990) • T. Gray, 'An Irishman's diary', *Irish Times* (26 Feb 1993) • b. cert. • d. cert. • *CGPLA Eng. & Wales* (1993)
Archives JRL, letters to the *Manchester Guardian*
Likenesses photograph, repro. in *The Times* • photograph, repro. in *The Independent*
Wealth at death £194,229: probate, 19 April 1993, *CGPLA Eng. & Wales*

Inglis, Charles (1731?–1791), naval officer, was the fourth of five sons of Sir John Inglis of Cramond, second baronet (1683–1771), and Anne (*d.* 1772), daughter of Inglis's step-father, Adam Cockburn of Ormiston, and Susan, daughter of the fourth earl of Haddington. He entered the navy in 1745 on the *Ludlow Castle* (40 guns) with Captain George Brydges. He followed Brydges to the *Eagle* (60 guns), being present when Brydges took four valuable prizes in June 1747 from the French San Domingo convoy. He was present in the *Eagle* in Rear-Admiral Edward Hawke's action with L'Etenduère at the second battle of Cape Finisterre on 14 October 1747, when she was heavily engaged with the French *Neptune* (70 guns), suffering considerable damage. Peace the following year led to her decommissioning in August 1748 and Inglis was unemployed until 1750 when he was appointed to the *Tavistock* (50 guns), with Captain Francis Holburne, 'a capable and considerate officer' (Spinney, 41), a friend of Brydges and Hawke's flag captain in 1748, and like Inglis a lowland Scot. Inglis seems indeed to have been part of a network of lowland Scots naval officers. His early career was furthered by Holburne; perhaps too by Sir John Clerk of Penicuik, a family friend with considerable influence; and possibly by his mother's connection with John Cockburn of Ormiston, a member of the Board of Admiralty (1727–32 and 1742–44).

Inglis passed his examination on 6 February 1755 and was promoted lieutenant of the *Monarch* (74 guns, Captain Abraham North). In April 1756 he was appointed to the *Magnanime* (74 guns, Captain Wittewronge Taylor). Inglis was turned over with Taylor into the *Marlborough* (90 guns) and then into the *Royal William* (84 guns) on 3 June 1757; and on 17 June 1757 he was promoted to the command of the sloop *Escorte* (14 guns), a former French privateer taken in 1756, and attached to the Rochefort expedition in September 1757, under Sir Edward Hawke. In June 1759 he was appointed to the bomb-vessel *Carcass*, part of the force under Brydges which bombarded Le Havre and destroyed the intended invasion force of flat-bottomed boats there in July.

On 15 December 1761 he was posted to the *Newark* (80 guns), which, early in 1762, went to the Mediterranean

Charles Inglis (1731?–1791), by Sir Henry Raeburn, c.1783 [retouched c.1795]

bearing the broad pennant of Commodore Sir Peircy Brett, to strengthen Admiral Sir Charles Saunders's squadron, when war with Spain was deemed unavoidable. There was no fleet action but some valuable Spanish prizes were taken, the most famous being that of the *Hermione* by the *Active* and *Favourite* on 21 May 1762. At the peace in 1763 Inglis returned to England with Saunders and the bulk of the fleet. Further unemployment followed, but in September 1770, the Falkland crisis between Britain and Spain saw sixteen guardships and six frigates prepared. Inglis was appointed to command the frigate *Lizard* (28 guns), possibly through the patronage of Admiral Holburne, now a member of the Board of Admiralty. When the crisis had passed Inglis again became unemployed; he remained so until August 1778 when he commissioned the *Salisbury* (50 guns), going out to Jamaica; and on 12 December 1779 he captured the Spanish privateer *San Carlos* (50 guns), laden with military stores, in the Bay of Honduras. In the summer of 1780 he returned to England, and when the *Salisbury* was paid off, was appointed to the *St Albans* (64 guns), one of the fleet, under Vice-Admiral George Darby, which sailed to the relief of Gibraltar in April 1781. The *St Albans* was then sent to the West Indies to join Sir Samuel Hood at Barbados. Inglis had served with Hood in the *Ludlow Castle* and at the Le Havre bombardment. He was now part of Hood's attempt to relieve St Kitts (25 January to 14 February 1782). Two months later Inglis and the *St Albans* were part of Brydges' fleet at the battle of the Saints (12 April 1782); and in August Inglis took the ship to North America with Admiral Hugh Pigot, who had replaced Brydges (now Lord Rodney) in July. At the end of that year Pigot returned to the West Indies, and Inglis was given command of a small squadron of four ships cruising there. On 15 February 1783 they chased three French warships, the *St Albans* capturing the frigate *Concorde* (32 guns). Inglis returned to England in the summer of 1783. He saw no further service. He was a capable and competent officer without being inspired or presented with fortunate opportunities. He was promoted rear-admiral of the blue on 21 September 1790 and died on 10 October 1791.

There are no details of Inglis's having been married but he is known to have had at least one child, a son, Charles. Charles Inglis was first lieutenant of the *Penelope* in her engagement with the *Guillaume Tell*, was promoted post captain on 29 April 1802, and died in that rank on 27 February 1833.   P. K. CRIMMIN

Sources J. Charnock, ed., *Biographia navalis*, 6 (1798), 455 · W. L. Clowes, *The Royal Navy: a history from the earliest times to the present*, 7 vols. (1897–1903), vols. 3–4 · GEC, *Baronetage* · D. Syrett and R. L. DiNardo, *The commissioned sea officers of the Royal Navy, 1660–1815*, rev. edn, Occasional Publications of the Navy RS, 1 (1994) · D. Lyon, *The sailing navy list: all the ships of the Royal Navy, built, purchased and captured, 1688–1860* (1993) · D. Spinney, *Rodney* (1969) · R. F. Mackay, *Admiral Hawke* (1965) · *GM*, 1st ser., 61 (1791), 973
Likenesses H. Raeburn, oils, c.1783, Scot. NPG [see illus.]

Inglis, Charles (1734–1816), American loyalist and bishop of Nova Scotia, was born at Glencolumbkille, Donegal, the son of Archibald Inglis (d. 1745), a Church of Ireland clergyman descended from several generations of Anglican ministers. Inglis's hopes of an education at Trinity College, Dublin, were thwarted by his family's impoverishment following the death of his father. About 1754 he moved to Philadelphia, and between 1755 and 1758 taught at a free school in Lancaster, Pennsylvania. Here he was recommended to the Society for the Propagation of the Gospel in Foreign Parts (SPG) and experienced a period of profound religious self-scrutiny, which resulted in his ordination by Bishop Pearce of Rochester in Fulham Palace in 1758. Inglis returned to America, where he began work as an SPG missionary at Dover, Delaware. In 1764 he married Mary Vining, who later that year died in childbirth.

In the following year Inglis became assistant to Samuel Auchmuty at Trinity Church in New York city. Known for his powerful preaching style, in his first address Inglis declared himself a Methodist and sympathetic to the Calvinist teaching of George Whitefield. Later, however, Inglis called for the appointment of an American Anglican bishop, and published articles to this effect under the pseudonym Whip. While at Trinity Church he began a programme of self-education, which he combined with pedagogical work among the Mohawk Indians. He published a defence of infant baptism in this period and subsequently received the degrees of MA (6 April 1770) and DD (25 February 1777) from Oxford University. In 1773 Inglis married his second wife, Margaret (b. 1748/9), daughter of John Crooke of Ulster county, New York. The couple had two daughters and two sons, Charles (d. 1783) and John (d. 1850).

An ardent loyalist during the American War of Independence, Inglis published several pamphlets against the revolutionaries and continued to lead prayers for George III, despite threats to his safety. He became British army chaplain at New York and criticized what he considered to be George Washington's 'murder' of John André. After the death of Samuel Auchmuty in 1777 Inglis was appointed rector of Trinity Church. However, he was ejected in 1779, when the state of New York attainted him for treason and confiscated his property. Inglis remained as rector of Trinity Church until his resignation on 1 November 1783. He then returned to England, where he worked for John Moore, archbishop of Canterbury.

In August 1787 Inglis was appointed the first colonial bishop of Nova Scotia, and later became bishop over Quebec, New Brunswick, and Newfoundland. During his episcopate between 1787 and 1816 he supervised the establishment of forty-four Anglican churches, as well as the foundation of King's College at Windsor, Nova Scotia. In contrast to his earlier sympathy for Methodism, Bishop Inglis was a vigorous critic of religious enthusiasm. He died at his home, Clermont, near Aylesford in Nova Scotia, on 24 February 1816. His son, John, became the third bishop of Nova Scotia, in 1825, and was the father of the army officer Sir John Eardley Wilmot Inglis.

PHILIP CARTER

Sources D. E. Maas, 'Inglis, Charles', *ANB* · B. Cuthbertson, *The first bishop: a biography of Charles Inglis* (1987) · R. V. Harris, *Charles Inglis: missionary, loyalist, bishop, 1734–1816* (1937) · J. Wydekker, *The life and letters of Charles Inglis* (1936) · M. Dix, *A history of the parish of Trinity Church in the city of New York* (1898)
Archives Anglican Diocesan Archives, Halifax, Nova Scotia · Archives of Protestant Episcopal Church, Austin, Texas · Bodl. RH, archives of Society for the Propagation of the Gospel · NA Canada, corresp. and papers [microfilm] · Public Archives of Nova Scotia, Halifax
Likenesses R. Field, oils, 1810, NPG

Inglis, Sir Charles Edward (1875–1952), civil engineer, was born on 31 July 1875 at Worcester, the second surviving son of Alexander Monro Inglis MD of Auchindinny and Redhall and his first wife, Florence (*d.* 1875), the second daughter of John Frederick Feeney, proprietor of the *Birmingham Daily Post*. His father moved from Worcester to Cheltenham and from 1889 Inglis was educated at Cheltenham College, of which he became senior prefect; for more than twenty years before his death he was a member of the college's council. In 1894 he went up to Cambridge with a scholarship at King's College, and in 1897 he was classed as 22nd wrangler in the mathematical tripos; in the following year he gained first-class honours in the mechanical sciences tripos. He next became a pupil of Sir John Wolfe-Barry & Partners, consulting engineers.

After a few months in the drawing office Inglis was transferred to the staff of Alexander Gibb, Wolfe-Barry's resident engineer for the new extension to the Metropolitan Railway between Whitechapel and Bow. He was engaged in particular on the design and supervision of the nine bridges crossing the railway, an experience which was of great value to him later in life when he became particularly interested in the behaviour of bridges. At this

Sir Charles Edward Inglis (1875–1952), by D. Gordon Shields, 1926

time, however, he also began a study, which lasted throughout his life, on the subject of mechanical vibration, and when, in 1901, he was made a fellow of King's College, Cambridge, the subject of his thesis was 'The balancing of engines'. In this year he returned to Cambridge as assistant to the professor of engineering, James Alfred Ewing. Ewing was succeeded two years later by Bertram Hopkinson, who held the chair of mechanism and applied mechanics, as it was then called, until his death in 1918. Under Hopkinson, Inglis was appointed to a lectureship in engineering (1908) and continued his work on vibrations. His interests were, however, by no means confined to vibrations. In 1913 he published a paper on the stresses in a plate due to the presence of cracks and sharp corners. This may well be his most far-reaching contribution, since A. A. Griffith's classic explanation of the discrepancy between observed and calculated strengths of amorphous substances, such as glass and silica fibres, was based on it. In 1901 Inglis married Eleanor Mary, younger daughter of Lieutenant-Colonel Herbert Belasyse Moffat of the South Wales Borderers. In 1904 they built Balls Grove, Grantchester, Cambridgeshire, where they lived until 1925 and where their two daughters were born.

On the outbreak of war in 1914 Inglis was commissioned in the Royal Engineers. Earlier he had designed a light tubular bridge, readily transportable and easy to erect, which the War Office adopted. From 1916 to 1918 he was in charge of the department responsible for the design and supply of military bridges; for this work he was appointed OBE. His bridge came to the fore when the army was faced in 1917–18 with the tank bridging problem. His designs were superseded by the Bailey bridge in the Second World War.

In 1918 Inglis returned to Cambridge and became, in 1919, professor of mechanism and applied mechanics (called mechanical sciences after 1934) and head of the department of engineering in succession to Hopkinson, a post which he held until his retirement in 1943. Before the war the number of undergraduates reading engineering at Cambridge had risen to 250, taxing to their utmost the laboratories in Free School Lane. In 1919 Inglis was met by an overwhelming entry of 800 and it became essential to move the department from the cramped central area. The 4 acre Scroope House site in Trumpington Street was acquired, and there, between 1920 and 1923, the Inglis Building was erected. It was so well planned that it accommodated the main teaching laboratories of the department until the end of 1964.

Between the wars the department became the largest in the university and one of the most important engineering schools in the world. Having spent seventeen years as a lecturer, and worked with Ewing and Hopkinson as successive heads of department, it is not surprising that Inglis, on his return, made no striking innovations. He was strongly opposed to premature specialization and he thought it 'hardly an overstatement to say that the soul and spirit of education is that habit of mind which remains when a student has completely forgotten everything he has ever been taught' (Inglis). Later in life he advocated the study of aesthetics for engineers as much for its cultural value as for its direct influence on their designs. About the teaching of mathematics and the need for the subject to occupy a prominent position in any university engineering course he held strong views, but on the position that research should occupy in a university engineering department he did not seem so clear. He was critical of the Cambridge PhD course, since he felt that teamwork was an essential introduction for a beginner. Perhaps because of this he did not, unfortunately, found or lead a research team at Cambridge. However, his own research continued to be distinguished. He played a most prominent part in the work of the bridge stress committee, set up in 1923 to determine the behaviour of railway bridges under moving loads, providing all the mathematics and much of the impetus which kept the experimental work going. He contributed papers to the Institution of Civil Engineers describing this research and also published *A Mathematical Treatise on Vibrations in Railway Bridges* (1934).

Inglis served on the councils of the institutions of naval architects and of civil, of structural, and of water engineers. He was president of the Institution of Civil Engineers in 1941–2, received the Telford and Parsons medals, and was an honorary member of the Institution of Mechanical Engineers. He received an honorary LLD from Edinburgh (1929), was elected FRS (1930), and was knighted in 1945. From 1943 to 1946 he was vice-provost of King's College. Though he made no secret of his enjoyment of these honours, his overwhelming interest and pleasure was in research and above all in teaching. In the last year of his life he saw the publication of his book *Applied Mechanics for Engineers* (1951) and spent three months in South Africa as a visiting lecturer, where he continued to teach and inspire young engineers. Inglis died at Southwold on 19 April 1952, only eighteen days after his wife.

J. F. BAKER, rev. JACQUES HEYMAN

Sources J. F. Baker, *Obits. FRS*, 8 (1952–3), 445–57 · T. J. N. Hilken, *Engineering at Cambridge University, 1783–1965* (1967) · C. E. Inglis, Presidential address, November 1941, *Journal of the Institution of Civil Engineers*, 17 (1941–2), 1–18
Archives CUL, papers
Likenesses D. G. Shields, oils, 1926, U. Cam., department of engineering [see illus.] · H. Lamb, oils, 1942, Inst. CE · H. Lamb, oils, 1942, King's Cam. · photograph, repro. in Baker, *Obits. FRS*
Wealth at death £17,139 10s. 11d.: probate, 5 Dec 1952, CGPLA Eng. & Wales

Inglis, Sir Claude Cavendish (1883–1974), hydraulic engineer, was born in Dublin on 3 March 1883, the sixth son of seven children of Sir Malcolm John Inglis JP, deputy lieutenant of co. Dublin, and his wife, Caroline Johnston. He was educated at St Helen's School, Dublin (1892–6), at Shrewsbury School (1896–1900), and at Trinity College, Dublin, under Professor John Joly; he graduated BA and BAI (bachelor of engineering) in 1905. Inglis was appointed to the India service of engineers in 1906 and served first in Sind. In 1911 he was promoted to the Bombay Deccan as executive engineer, Godavari canals, to introduce there the northern Indian methods of irrigation. In 1912 he married Vera Margaret St John (d. 1972), daughter of John Redmond Blood JP of Malahide, co. Dublin, brewer, company director, and commissioner for Irish lights. She had a subtle sense of humour and at times exerted a modifying influence on her husband. They had one son, Brian St John Inglis, writer and broadcaster.

Inglis moved in 1913 to Poona irrigation district in charge of the Nira canals, where he carried out research into waterlogging at an experimental station at Baramati. His success in drainage later involved him in a survey of half a million acres in the Bombay Deccan to improve conditions. Against opposition from farmers, he persuaded the government to control the type of irrigated crops most suitable for the nature of the soils and also demonstrated the benefits of using sewage mixed with canal water. In 1928 Inglis advised on the large Sukkur barrage in Sind, and on five major points the design was changed on his recommendations.

Hydraulic research was then transferred to Khadakwasla, downstream of a dam near Poona, where clear water and climatic conditions enabled large models to be used in the open. This Poona station was probably the first to use mobile beds (artificial terrain to research forced flow and effects), and after much lobbying by Inglis, Bombay was selected in 1937 as the central station for the whole of India with Inglis as its first director. General studies were carried out in river meanders, scour, and sediment control as well as specific investigations on barrages, bank protection, river training, and canal intakes. Inglis was in charge for eight years, playing a major part in all the work of the station until his retirement in 1945. He was succeeded by K. K. Framji, and subsequently D. V. Joglekar, who had served with him for twenty-one years.

As an independent consulting engineer in England, Inglis continued to advise on river problems in India, Burma, and Iran. In 1947 he was back in harness as the first director of research for the United Kingdom Hydraulics Research Board formed by the government to solve the urgent problems of river training, harbours, and coastal erosion. Inglis had to fight hard for a site for hydraulic research near to London. By 1955, when the first stage of construction had been completed at Wallingford in Berkshire, British hydraulic engineers were able greatly to benefit from the results of the model work on many schemes at home and overseas.

In the words later of his successor as director, Fergus Allen, Inglis 'with a judicious blend of pugnacity and charm' (Thomas and Paton, 377) ensured that the establishment would be of sufficient size, sophistication, and international standing. He retired in March 1958, aged seventy-five, but continued, despite failing eyesight, to work as a consultant with a lively interest in new developments. He enjoyed music, playing the cello and piano, and was a keen golfer.

Inglis was appointed CIE in 1936, knighted in 1945, elected FRS in 1953, and awarded the James Alfred Ewing gold medal by the Institution of Civil Engineers in 1958. He became an honorary MAI (master of engineering) in 1952. His main contributions to engineering were in irrigation canals and river training. He recommended safeguarding the major railway lines to Assam and to Calcutta by training the Ganges and Rup Narayan rivers. He pioneered the use of large models with mobile sand beds, but his recommendations in river training depended more on his personal judgement than the model results. In the words of his great friend Gerald Lacey, 'We might almost say that he studied river psychology … He asked himself the question "What would I do if I were the river?" and almost invariably got the answer right' (Thomas and Paton, 384).

Inglis died, shortly after a second operation for cataract, on 29 August 1974 at 7 Holmgarth, Furners Mead, Henfield, Sussex. ANGUS PATON, rev. DAVID JENNAWAY

Sources A. R. Thomas and A. Paton, *Memoirs FRS*, 21 (1975), 367–88 • B. Inglis, *Downstart* (1990) • *The Times* (31 Aug 1974) • d. cert.
Archives PRO, corresp. and MSS related to irrigation research in India, AY10
Wealth at death £50,716: probate, 6 March 1975, *CGPLA Eng. & Wales*

Inglis, Elsie Maud (1864–1917), physician and surgeon, was born at Naini Tal, in the Himalayan foothills of India, on 16 August 1864. She was the second daughter of John Inglis (1820–1894), who was in the service of the East India Company, and his wife, Harriet Thompson (c.1828–1885). Both of Elsie's grandfathers had held important posts in

Elsie Maud Inglis (1864–1917), by unknown photographer, c.1914–17

the East India Company, but John Inglis was opposed to the imperialist policies prevalent in the 1870s, and, having been passed over for promotion because of his views, he retired. The family went first to Tasmania for two years before moving, in 1878, to Edinburgh where they took a large house, 10 Bruntsfield Place. Inglis passed most of her life in Edinburgh. From 1878 to 1882 she attended the Edinburgh Institution for the Education of Young Ladies at 23 Charlotte Square, and at eighteen she went to a finishing school in Paris for a year. Three years later, in 1885, when her mother died, she became her father's mainstay. By that time she was keen to become a doctor (still an unusual ambition for a young woman, but no longer impossible). She would not have wanted to leave her father at such a time, but fortunately in 1886 Sophia Jex-Blake opened the Edinburgh School of Medicine for Women, and Elsie began her medical training there, with John Inglis's full support. Following a student rebellion against the over-controlling Dr Jex-Blake, Inglis, with the assistance of her father and his influential friends, helped to found in 1889 a rival establishment, the Medical College for Women, where she continued her training. Subsequently she studied for eighteen months at the Glasgow Royal Infirmary. Inglis qualified as a licentiate of the Royal College of Physicians and Surgeons, Edinburgh, and a licentiate of the Faculty of Physicians and Surgeons, Glasgow, on 4 August 1892, when she was twenty-seven.

Inglis's first post was resident medical officer at Elizabeth Garrett Anderson's New Hospital for Women in London, followed by a short spell at the Rotunda, Dublin, one of the world's leading centres for obstetrics, before returning to Edinburgh in 1894 where she nursed her father through his final illness. She then started a new general practice in the city, in partnership with Jessie Macgregor, who had been a fellow student at the Jex-Blake school. In 1899 she graduated MB CM of Edinburgh and was appointed lecturer in gynaecology at the Medical College for Women. In 1894, while working as a partner with Jessie Macgregor, Inglis opened a small hospital for women and children in George Square.

During the 1890s the women's suffrage movement was gaining new adherents and a new momentum, and Inglis was caught up in the campaign, becoming honorary secretary of the Edinburgh National Society for Women's Suffrage. She felt no sympathy for the militant wing of the movement which burst on the scene in 1905, but the volume of publicity generated by the Pankhursts gave an enormous boost to the non-militant, or 'constitutional' wing of the movement, and Elsie addressed many public meetings. When a Scottish Federation of constitutionalist societies was formed in 1909 Inglis became honorary secretary of that as well.

By 1904 the small hospital for women and children had outgrown its original premises and moved to the High Street as The Hospice. In 1905 Inglis was appointed senior consultant at the Bruntsfield Hospital, founded by Sophia Jex-Blake. In October 1909 she resigned in protest against the hospital's handling of a lawsuit over alleged negligence by a nurse. However, she was persuaded to reconsider and withdraw her resignation, and in 1911 the Bruntsfield Hospital was enlarged and united with The Hospice.

When war was declared on 4 August 1914 Inglis was nearly fifty, but both her patriotism and her zeal to prove the capabilities of medical women outside the fields of gynaecology and paediatrics spurred her to offer her services to the War Office, only to be rebuffed with the words, 'My good lady, go home and sit still.' She then had the idea of forming independent hospital units staffed by women. This she put to the executive committee of the Scottish Federation of Women's Suffrage Societies, which acclaimed the idea and formed a hospitals committee. An appeal for funds began via *The Common Cause*, the journal of the National Union of Women's Suffrage Societies, but soon attracted support far beyond suffrage supporters. After Inglis's inspiring speech at the Kingsway Hall in October on 'What women can do to help the war' funds began to pour in for the new organization, the Scottish Women's Hospitals for Foreign Service (SWH). The War Office may have spurned the idea of all-women medical units, but other allies were desperate for help, and both the French and the Serbs accepted the offer. The first unit left for France in November 1914 and a second unit went to Serbia in January 1915. Inglis was torn between her desire to oversee the fund-raising and organizational side of the SWH and her desire to serve in the field, but in mid-April

the chief medical officer of the first Serbian unit fell ill, and Inglis went out to replace her. During the summer she set up two further hospital units.

In the autumn Serbia was invaded; Inglis, and some other members of her unit, chose to remain behind. Her hospital in Kragujevac was taken over by the Germans, but she was put in charge of the only prisoner-of-war hospital in the town. She was interned until February 1916 when she was sent home via Vienna and Zürich. Another SWH unit served the French expeditionary force in Salonica, while further SWH units, attached to the Serbs, ended up in Corsica and Macedonia. After her return to Britain Inglis continued to be an impassioned advocate for aid to Serbia, and on 3 April 1916 she became the first woman to be decorated with the order of the white eagle, the highest honour that country could bestow. Given a choice, she would still have sought to help her own countrymen, but attempts to raise a unit for Mesopotamia, where conditions were believed to be particularly dire, were sabotaged by the War Office.

Unbeknown to the hospitals committee in Edinburgh, Inglis had been harbouring a host of grievances, some trivial, but others major. She believed that her vision of the future of the organization differed fundamentally from that of the committee, and that no *modus vivendi* could be found, and therefore, in June 1916, she abruptly resigned from the SWH. However, she was persuaded that a complete severance would do untold harm to the organization and she agreed to take out a new unit—under the auspices of the London committee—to southern Russia, where the Serbs were being formed into two divisions of the Russian army. The unit arrived in Russia in September 1916 and went on to the front at Megidia, Romania, but soon afterwards had to join the Russian retreat when the Germans attacked in strength. In December Inglis agreed to put the unit under the control of the Russian Red Cross until the Serbs re-formed; soon afterwards the women joined a second retreat, and in January 1917 a third. Each time a new hospital was created, though the Russian Revolution in March 1917 created fresh difficulties. The unit remained in Reni, Romania, until September, when it rejoined the Serbian division in the village of Hadji Abdul, Bessarabia.

Inglis knew before she left Britain that she had cancer, but other unit members thought she was simply suffering from dysentery and similar illnesses which they were all afflicted with that summer. However, at the end of September she collapsed, and after that she was unable to work as a surgeon, though she continued to direct the unit. Even though the political situation was deteriorating rapidly and a withdrawal was advised, Inglis refused to leave until the Serbs were transferred out of Russia. When the unit finally left Inglis sent a telegram home: 'Everything satisfactory and all well except me', the first intimation of her illness. After they landed at Newcastle, Inglis (who had been unable to digest solid foods since leaving Hadji Abdul) insisted on getting dressed and, wearing all her decorations, stood for nearly twenty minutes while the entire Serbian staff said goodbye. The following day,

26 November 1917, in the presence of her sisters, she dictated final messages, and died that same night in the Station Hotel, Newcastle upon Tyne.

Before its interment in Dean cemetery, Edinburgh, on 29 November Elsie Inglis's body lay in state in the city's St Giles's Cathedral. The royalty of Britain and Serbia were represented at the funeral and at the memorial service at St Margaret's, Westminster, a few days later. The SWH continued its work during the duration of the war, sending out more units, and raising about half a million pounds for the work. Afterwards the remaining money was divided between several Scottish hospitals and one in Belgrade. A memorial fund was started to help build the Elsie Inglis Memorial Maternity Hospital, which replaced The Hospice in Edinburgh in July 1925. It closed in October 1992 after maternity services were reorganized, though the building itself was saved by a vigorous campaign and became the Elsie Inglis Nursing Home.

Elsie Inglis had a strong network of family and friends and was adored by her patients. She could be ruthless in pursuit of her goals, but never out of self-interest. She believed that women had the capacity to be men's equals in every way (barring only physical strength), and much of her life was dedicated to proving that this was so. Elsie Inglis's greatest gift was that of inspiring others. From the Medical College for Women to The Hospice to the Scottish Women's Hospitals, she made things happen, not only because she came up with such practical, concrete ideas, but because she believed in them so fully herself and was able to fire others with her own vision.

LEAH LENEMAN

Sources L. Leneman, *In the service of life: the story of Elsie Inglis and the Scottish Women's Hospitals* (1994) · M. Lawrence, *Shadow of swords: a biography of Elsie Inglis* (1971) · L. Leneman, *Elsie Inglis: founder of battlefront hospitals run entirely by women* (1998) · F. Balfour, *Dr Elsie Inglis* (1918) · E. S. McLaren, *Elsie Inglis: the woman with the torch* (1920) · E. S. McLaren, ed., *A history of the Scottish Women's Hospitals* (1919) · d. cert. · *CCI* (1918)
Archives Mitchell L., Glas., letters and reports · priv. coll., family MSS | Lothian Health Services Archive, Edinburgh, administrative records, Hospice/Bruntsfield Hospital · Women's Library, London, Scottish Women's Hospitals collection
Likenesses photograph, *c.*1914–1917, Elsie Inglis Nursing Home, Edinburgh [*see illus.*] · I. Mestrovic, bronze bust, 1918, Scot. NPG · I. Mestrovic, bronze bust, IWM · photograph, repro. in Leneman, *In the service of life* · photograph, repro. in Lawrence, *Shadow of swords* · photograph, repro. in Balfour, *Dr Elsie Inglis* · photograph, repro. in McLaren, *Elsie Inglis* · photograph, repro. in McLaren, ed., *History of the Scottish Women's Hospitals* · photographs, repro. in Leneman, *Elsie Inglis*
Wealth at death £957 17s. 2d.: confirmation, 30 May 1918, *CCI*

Inglis [*married name* Kello], **Esther** (1570/71–1624), calligrapher, was probably born in London. She is generally known as Inglis, the Scottish form of Langlois. Her parents, Nicolas Langlois and Marie Presot, moved to London from Dieppe in France as Huguenot refugees about 1569. By 1574 they were settled in Edinburgh, where, after initially receiving assistance for debt, Nicolas became master of the French school and died in 1611. Esther, the second of five children, was taught calligraphy by her mother, who was a skilled scribe. She married Bartholomew Kello (*d.*

1631) about 1596. John Kello, her husband's father, had become minister of Spott, Haddingtonshire, in 1567, and was hanged for the murder of his wife, Margaret Thomson, in 1570. Bartholomew Kello was a minor government official who occasionally went abroad in the royal service. He and his family appear to have moved to London by 1604 and from 1607 to 1614 they were in Essex, where Bartholomew was rector of Willingale Spain. They returned to Edinburgh in 1615, and Esther died at Leith on 30 August 1624. She was survived by her husband and four children.

Samuel Kello (*d.* 1680), Church of England clergyman, her only surviving son, was educated at Edinburgh University (MA 1618) and also studied at Christ Church, Oxford. From 1620 until his death in December 1680 he was rector of Spexhall, Suffolk, where his wife, Marie, is recorded in the parish register. His *Carmen gratulatorium ad … Jacobum … sextum* (1617) was addressed to the king on his visit to Edinburgh that year; another poem was published in *The Muses' Welcome* (1618). He also wrote a treatise, 'Balme for the wounded soul', dated 1628 (Trinity College, Dublin, MS 695). He was buried in the church at Spexhall, Suffolk, on 9 December 1680.

Fifty-nine manuscript books written by Esther Inglis and dating from 1586 to 1624 are known. Most of them carry dedications to royalty, members of the nobility, or people of rank and influence, and were evidently presented in hope of reward. Two early works, 'Discours de la foy' in verse, dated 1591 (Huntington Library, HM 26068) and the Psalms in French of 1599 (Christ Church, Oxford, MS 180), were made for Elizabeth I, and four for Henry, prince of Wales; another patron was the poet and courtier Sir David Murray of Gorthy, whom she addressed as 'mon treshonoré Mecoenas' (BL, Harleian MS 4324, fol. 2). But despite these wealthy patrons the family was not well off, and Esther was in debt at the time of her death. The manuscripts are written in a wide range of scripts, including the French secretary hand, chancery script, mirror writing, and the highly ornamental hands practised by contemporary writing-masters. Some of her most ornate books, executed between 1599 and 1602, contain over thirty different styles, but from 1608 she tended to use only roman and italic, often on a tiny scale. Several manuscripts written in 1615 measure about 45 x 70 mm and contain lines of text less than a millimetre in height. The decoration in her manuscripts changed too. The earlier works often have introductory pages, headpieces, and initials incorporating designs and elements copied from printed books. In contrast, her later manuscripts make use of colour but have far less decoration, and this often takes the form of flower paintings. Many of the manuscripts contain a self-portrait in pen and ink or in colour, sometimes accompanied by verses in her praise by the Presbyterian divines Andrew Melville and Robert Rollock.

Esther Inglis signed and dated most of her work. Among the undated manuscripts are two collections (NL Scot., MS 2197, and Edinburgh University Library, MS La.III.522) probably intended as specimen books and modelled on the published works of writing masters such as John de Beauchesne. She certainly knew Clément Perret's

Exercitatio alphabetica (1569), since she copied parts of its decoration in several manuscripts written between 1599 and 1601, notably in 'Le livre de l'Ecclésiaste' dedicated to the vicomtesse de Rohan (New York Public Library, Spencer Collection, French MS 8). But the most striking example of adaptation is a manuscript made for Prince Charles in 1624 (BL, Royal MS 17.D.XVI), a version of Georgette de Montenay's *Emblemes ou devises chrestiennes* (1619), in which Esther dedicated each emblem to a different English courtier. As with eleven other books made for royalty, it is in an embroidered binding which is probably also her own work. Another outstanding manuscript (privately owned) is 'A book of the armes of England' made for Henry, prince of Wales, in 1609. It contains paintings of the arms of the nobility and its velvet binding is embroidered with the prince's crest in pearls.

In contrast to her elaborate manuscripts, Esther Inglis wrote at least ten small books between 1614 and 1617 which are relatively plain and very similar in design. They contain little decoration, the script is a small roman hand, and the texts are either the 'Quatrains' of Guy du Faur, Sieur de Pybrac, or the 'Octonaires sur la vanité et inconstance du monde' of Antoine de la Roche Chandieu. Esther frequently copied these texts as well as drawing heavily on both French and English versions of the Genevan Bible. She also wrote out an English translation by her husband and incorporated verses by him in her work.

While other women calligraphers are known from this period, the quantity of work by Esther Inglis to survive is remarkable and her manuscripts have always been admired. Although her draughtsmanship was weak and she lacked originality, preferring to reproduce designs by others, the delicacy and precision of her calligraphy, particularly when working on a very small scale, was outstanding.   ELSPETH YEO

Sources A. H. Scott-Elliot and E. Yeo, 'Calligraphic manuscripts of Esther Inglis', *Papers of the Bibliographical Society of America*, 84 (1990), 11–86 · D. Laing, 'Notes relating to Mrs Esther (Langlois or) Inglis', *Proceedings of the Society of Antiquaries of Scotland*, 6 (1864–6), 284–309 · D. J. Jackson, *Esther Inglis, calligrapher* (1937) · R. Williams, 'A moon to their sun', *Fine Print*, 11/2 (1985), 88–98 · R. E. G. Kirk and E. F. Kirk, eds., *Returns of aliens dwelling in the city and suburbs of London, from the reign of Henry VIII to that of James I*, Huguenot Society of London, 10/2 (1902), 15 · Commissariot of Edinburgh, register of testaments, NA Scot., CC8/8/48 (23 July 1614), CC8/8/53 (11 March 1625), CC8/8/55 (3 August 1631) · parish register of Spexhall, 1620–80, Suffolk RO · *N&Q*, 3rd ser., 2 (1862), 97, 330–31 · C. T. McInnes, ed., *Accounts of the treasurer of Scotland*, 13 (1978), 255

Archives NL Scot., MSS; summary of St Matthew's gospel [illuminated MS]

Likenesses oil on panel, 1595, Scot. NPG; loaned from National Museums of Scotland · E. Inglis, self-portrait, pen and ink, 1599, BL, Add. MS 27927, fol. 2 · E. Inglis, self-portrait, oils, 1606, Harvard U., Houghton L., MS Typ. 212, fol. 9*v* · E. Inglis, self-portrait, oils, 1612, Kungliga Biblioteket, Stockholm, Cod. Holm. A. 781, fol. 6 · E. Inglis, self-portrait, pen and ink, 1624, BL, Royal MS 17.D.XVI, fol. 7

Wealth at death debts of £156: commissariot of Edinburgh, 11 March 1625, register of testaments, CC8/8/53

Inglis, Henry David (1795–1835), traveller and writer, the only son of a Scottish advocate, was born in Edinburgh. He was educated for commercial life, but, finding it uncongenial, turned to travel writing. As Derwent Conway, he published his first work, *Tales of the Ardennes*, in 1825. Its success encouraged him to write *Narrative of a Journey through Norway, Part of Sweden, and the Islands and States of Denmark* (1826), *Solitary Walks through many Lands* (1828), and *A Tour through Switzerland and the South of France and the Pyrenees* (1830 and 1831). While these volumes were being published he edited a local newspaper at Chesterfield, Derbyshire, but soon relinquished it for further foreign travel. His *Spain in 1830* (1831) and *The Tyrol, with a Glance at Bavaria* (1833) were followed by a novel, *The New Gil Blas, or, Pedro of Peñaflor* (1832), delineating social life in Spain. This he regarded as his best work but it was a commercial failure. In 1832 he went to the Channel Islands, edited a Jersey newspaper, *The British Critic*, for two years, and published in 1834 a description, in two volumes, of the islands. The same year he published, after an Irish tour, *Ireland in 1834*, which was quoted as an authority by speakers in parliament in 1835, and reached a fifth edition in 1838. Inglis died—according to contemporaries, from brain disease brought on by overwork—at his home in Bayham Terrace, Regent's Park, London, on 20 March 1835. In 1837 *Colburn's New Monthly Magazine* published his *Rambles in the Footsteps of Don Quixote*, with illustrations by George Cruikshank.

Inglis's travel books met with commercial and critical success, but also with condemnation. Richard Ford described him as one of the travel writers 'who note down, print, and publish tales of horror … got up for the occasion by people who are laughing at them up their sleeve' and said of Inglis's Spanish works 'the tricks played on poor Mr Inglis and his note-book were the laughter of the whole Peninsula'. His books have fallen into well-deserved obscurity.

W. C. SYDNEY, *rev.* ELIZABETH BAIGENT

Sources *GM*, 2nd ser., 4 (1835), 325 · Chambers, *Scots.* (1855) · private information (1994) · *The Athenaeum* (28 March 1835), 246

Inglis, James (d. 1531), courtier, first appears in 1510–11 at the court of James IV. Nothing is known of his parentage or early life, and the name is too common for confident identification of all possible references. He must, however, be distinguished from the James Inglis 'that singis in Cambuskyneth for the King and Queen that last decessit' (*Compota*, 1507–13, 443), whose masses for the souls of James III and his wife continued into the 1530s and 1540s. Inglis seems not to have been a graduate: he is consistently referred to as sir, not master. On the other hand he possessed books on alchemy, which he lent to the king in 1510. 'Clerk to the closet' in 1511, he had become 'chapellane to the Prince'—James IV's infant son and successor (*b.* 10 April 1512)—before the reign ended disastrously at Flodden in 1513. Inglis's favour at court continued in the new reign. He presumably owed his crown presentation as chancellor of the Chapel Royal at Stirling on 5 June 1515 to the widowed queen, Margaret Tudor, whose secretary he then was and for whom he was acting in England during that year.

Inglis, however, was to make his way in the royal household rather than in the public service of the crown. Like—and indeed doubtless with—Sir David Lindsay of the Mount (who entered royal service at much the same time as Inglis), he was involved in organizing court entertainment. The treasurer's accounts record payments to him for the purchase of stage costumes and the like: 'xii elne [ells] taffetis' in February 1512 (*Compota*, 1507–13, 321); 'play cottis agane yule [for Christmas]' on 19 December 1526 (*Compota*, 1515–31, 396). More notably still, Inglis himself wrote what Lindsay was to call 'ballattis, farses, and … plesand playis' (*Testament of the Papyngo*, 1530, l.42). Unhappily, no surviving writings can be safely credited to Inglis: some attributions—the suggestion, for instance, that he wrote *The Complaynt of Scotland* (1549)—must be decisively rejected. His talents in any case were not solely literary. Under the heading 'Reparatioune of the Kingis Palaces besyde Halyrudhouse and Falkland' he appears in the treasurer's accounts in 1527 as master of works. Building went on, especially at Holyrood, during as well as after James V's minority, and Inglis must have played some part in overseeing if not in planning this.

Matters changed somewhat during what proved to be the last few years of Inglis's life. His appointment to the abbacy of Culross about 1529 (*in commendam*: there would be no question of his becoming a Cistercian monk) seemed to Lindsay to foreclose Inglis's literary career: 'Culrose hes his pen maid impotent' (*Testament of the Papyngo*, 1530, l.43). That was written in 1530; and Inglis appears to have surrendered his chancellorship of the Chapel Royal to his successor by mid-December 1529. Whatever future prospects the new abbot had were to be violently cut short. On 1 March 1531, in circumstances that remain mysterious, he was murdered by John Blackader of Tulliallan and William Lothian, a priest; he was probably buried in Culross Abbey. Tulliallan lies not far from Culross and it may be that the murder was the result of a dispute between the monastery and a neighbouring landowner. Both culprits (Lothian having been publicly degraded from his priestly orders) were beheaded for 'the cruel Slaughter of James Inglis, Abbot of Culross' (Pitcairn, 1.151). J. H. BURNS

Sources J. B. Paul, ed., *Compota thesaurariorum regum Scotorum / Accounts of the lord high treasurer of Scotland*, 4–5 (1902–3) • *LP Henry VIII*, vols. 1–2 • *The works of Sir David Lindsay*, ed. D. Hamer, 1, STS, 3rd ser., 1 (1931); 3, STS, 3rd ser., 6 (1934) • R. Pitcairn, ed., *Ancient criminal trials in Scotland*, 1, Bannatyne Club, 42 (1833) • D. E. R. Watt, ed., *Fasti ecclesiae Scoticanae medii aevi ad annum 1638*, [2nd edn], Scottish RS, new ser., 1 (1969) • *The letters of James the fourth, 1505–13*, ed. R. K. Hannay and R. L. Mackie, Scottish History Society, 3rd ser., 45 (1953) • *The letters of James V*, ed. R. K. Hannay and D. Hay (1954) • J. Lesley, *De origine, moribus, et rebus gestis Scotorum* (1675)
Archives BL, Cotton MSS, letters

Inglis, John (1762–1834), Church of Scotland minister and exponent of foreign missions, was born on 21 September 1762 in Perthshire, probably at Forteviot, the youngest son of Harry Inglis (1724–1799), Church of Scotland minister, and his second wife, Mary Bryce (d. 1802). He was educated in divinity at the University of Edinburgh and graduated in 1783. After being licensed by the Church of Scotland

Presbytery of Perth in 1785, he was presented by George III to be minister of Tibbermore, Perthshire, and was ordained there on 20 July 1786. A talented ecclesiastical politician, he was active in the duties of presbyterial administration. On 16 October 1798 he married Maria Moxham Passmore (d. 1864); the couple had five children of whom the most significant was John *Inglis, Lord Glencorse (1810–1891), the lord justice general of Scotland.

On 3 July 1799 Inglis became minister of Old Greyfriars Church in Edinburgh. Although not a popular preacher, he was a prominent figure in church politics, and became one of the most effective leaders of the dominant moderate party in the Church of Scotland. Henry Cockburn commented that 'no strong adversary ever measured mind against him without feeling his force' (*Memorials … by Henry Cockburn*, 233), and almost fifty years after his death, George Smith observed that he was 'the one man of the Moderate Party in the Church worthy, as an ecclesiastic at least, to rank with his great evangelical contemporaries' (Smith, 37). His qualities were widely recognized: the University of Edinburgh made him a DD in March 1804, and he served as the moderator of the general assembly the same year. In 1810 he was appointed as one of the deans of the Chapel Royal by George III, and he was continued in that office by William IV.

Inglis's greatest significance, however, is that he was probably the single most important figure in the inception of an institutionalized foreign missionary effort by the Church of Scotland. In particular, his emphasis on education and religion working together was extremely influential in determining the shape of Scottish missionary work throughout the world, and especially in India. On Friday 5 June 1818, he preached the annual missionary sermon before the Scottish Society for the Propagation of Christian Knowledge, a sermon that has been called 'the first public proposal of a great programme of educational missionary work' (Paton, 47). Unlike many of his contemporaries in the church, his vision was not limited to his own country, and, inspired by what Smith called his 'triumphant faith in the ultimate universal prevalence of Christianity' (Smith, 38–9), Inglis campaigned over the next decade for a foreign missions effort from the church. Eventually he triumphed when in 1824 the general assembly agreed to appoint a committee for foreign missions with Inglis as its first convenor. It was widely recognized by contemporaries and later commentators that it was principally owing to his persistence, diplomacy, and energy that the plan for a mission in India was successfully carried out: the minute book of the foreign missions committee of the Church of Scotland states that 'he alone was the author of its India mission' (Paton, 47). It was also due to the influence of Inglis—particularly his letter 'to the People of Scotland' of April 1826—that Alexander Duff, perhaps Scotland's most famous nineteenth-century missionary, went to work in India. Inglis died on 2 January 1834. JAMES LACHLAN MACLEOD

Sources *Fasti Scot.* • *Memorials of his time, by Henry Cockburn* (1856), 232–5 • G. Smith, *The life of Alexander Duff*, 1 (1879), 36–43 • W. Paton,

Alexander Duff, pioneer of missionary education (1923), 46–9 · J. Macleod, *Scottish theology in relation to church history since the Reformation* (1943) · *Acts of the general assembly of the Church of Scotland, 1638–1842* (1843) · information from the office of the principal clerk of the Church of Scotland, 1998

Archives U. Edin., New Coll. L., letters to Thomas Chalmers, CHA4

Likenesses A. Edouart, silhouette, 1830, Scot. NPG · A. Edouart, silhouette, Scot. NPG · T. Hodgetts, mezzotint (after J. Syme), NPG · oils, Scot. NPG

Wealth at death £4469 3s. 3½d.: inventory, 1835, Scotland

Inglis, John, Lord Glencorse (1810–1891), judge, was born in Edinburgh on 21 August 1810, the youngest son of John *Inglis (1762–1834), minister of Old Greyfriars, Edinburgh, and Maria Moxham Passmore (d. 1864), daughter of Abraham Passmore of Rollefarm, Devonshire. He went to Edinburgh high school and then to the University of Glasgow. From there he proceeded in November 1828 to Balliol College, Oxford, as a Snell exhibitioner. He graduated BA in 1833 and MA in 1837, and was admitted a member of the Faculty of Advocates in July 1835. His English education meant that, owing to a lack of contacts, his initial progress at the bar was slow, but, helped by a courtly manner, a growing reputation as a clear and convincing pleader, and success in an important patent case involving hot-blast techniques in the iron industry in 1842, he at length made an impact. On 11 July 1842 Inglis married Isabella Mary Wood (1820–1855), daughter of Alexander Wood, later judge of the court of session. Before her death a little over a decade later, they had two sons who were to survive Inglis and one who died aged eighteen in 1861.

Although not an ardent politician Inglis was a Conservative by family tradition and by personal conviction. His party recognized his sympathies and abilities by making him an advocate-depute in 1844. Inglis was appointed solicitor-general for Scotland in February 1852 in Lord Derby's first administration. In May of the same year he was raised to be lord advocate, an office which necessitated trying to find a seat in the House of Commons. Inglis stood for Orkney and Shetland at the general election of 1852, but was defeated. He made a further attempt, also unsuccessful, at a rowdy election at Lisburn in December 1852. By the end of that year, however, he was out of office with the fall of the ministry, being succeeded by his Liberal contemporary James Moncreiff, said by some to be his main rival at the bar.

Up to this point Inglis's progress had been rapid, the government positions he had held enlarging his experience in the criminal courts. The profession recognized this by electing him dean of the Faculty of Advocates immediately after he left office. His public reputation was enhanced by his defence, at the celebrated trial in 1857, of Madeleine Smith, on a charge of poisoning an intimate acquaintance. Pitched against Moncreiff and the solicitor-general, E. F. Maitland, and supported by George Young (later lord advocate), Inglis closed his case with a long and impressive speech which succeeded in breaking through the web of circumstantial evidence woven by the prosecution. Smith was acquitted on a verdict of 'not proven'.

John Inglis, Lord Glencorse (1810–1891), by Sir George Reid, 1882

Inglis was described at this time as a lithe, graceful figure, 'whose spontaneous movements seem to sympathise with the current and the emphasis of his argument' (Smith, 285). It was said that his features expressed shrewdness, with a clear, piercing expression, and that there was an undefinable persuasiveness about his manner and delivery.

On the return of Lord Derby to power in 1858 Inglis again became lord advocate. This time he succeeded in finding a seat and was returned for Stamford on 3 March. Once again he held office for only a short time, but he was nevertheless responsible during that period for the passing of a major measure, which reformed the Scottish universities (see below). He also became involved in controversies in which he was called on to defend the role of the lord advocate: one concerned suggestions that an undersecretary for Scotland be appointed to relieve the lord advocate of political responsibilities, and the other related to disappointment that there had been no public prosecutions over the failure of the Western Bank in Glasgow in 1857. In July 1858 Inglis was appointed lord justice-clerk and president of the second division of the court of session, with the title Lord Glencorse, in succession to

John Hope. It was suggested that he gave up party politics with some relief.

As a judge Inglis was to enjoy a high reputation among contemporaries to the extent that from 1867, when he succeeded Duncan McNeill as lord president of the court of session and lord justice-general of Scotland (the latter title he preferred for its historical associations), he came to be regarded as one of the great holders of that office. This reputation was founded on his defence of the independence of Scottish jurisprudence, notably against its encroachment by the English court of chancery, and on his leading role in implementing the act of 1868 designed to speed up and simplify court of session procedure. His contemporary on the bench, John McLaren, described him as a philosophical jurist, with a strong grasp of legal principle and logical order, whose decisions made law and developed it for codification. Inglis also played a leading role in developing mercantile law, and his judgment in the case involving the liquidation of the City of Glasgow Bank after its failure in 1878 broke new ground in the Scottish courts. His weaknesses in McLaren's view lay in an unfashionable partiality for jury trials and in a reluctance to overrule poor precedents. Perhaps this latter tendency contributed to the view that he was better at implementing than at originating reforms.

Despite the brevity of his tenure as lord advocate, Inglis was responsible for the passing of a significant piece of legislation—the Universities of Scotland Act of 1858. Based on a draft measure drawn up by his predecessor Moncreiff, Inglis's bill addressed problems such as the nature of university management, and the need to raise academic standards and to encourage graduation. University courts and general councils, the latter a concession to the graduate movement, were instituted. Other issues, such as the antiquated forms of patronage and appointments to chairs in Scottish universities, were brought up on amendment. This matter in particular led to a conflict, unintended on Inglis's part, over the vested interests of the Edinburgh town council, previously the effective managers of the city's university.

To become operational the act provided for the setting up of a commission, and Inglis's role in piloting the measure through the House of Commons was acknowledged by his election to the chairmanship. Over a four-year period in this position and as chairman of the Edinburgh Association for the Better Endowment of the University, Inglis played a major role in putting Scottish higher education, especially in the arts and law, on a new footing. His interest in this area was a major feature of his life. He held the distinction of having defeated W. E. Gladstone in 1869 in an election by the general council of Edinburgh University to become chancellor, an office he regarded over the succeeding years as more than honorary. This followed periods as rector of King's College, Aberdeen, from 1857, and of Glasgow University from 1865. Inglis also presided over another universities' commission, set up in 1876. His services were recognized by the award of a number of honorary degrees, and he had received an LLD from Edinburgh in 1858 and a DCL from Oxford in 1859.

Apart from the law and his interest in higher education, Inglis was active in other areas after the close of his political career. He was a member of the board of trustees for manufacturers (which despite its name was by then responsible chiefly for promoting the arts) and of the Scottish Text Society. He was a keen golfer and was a captain of the Royal and Ancient Golf Club of St Andrews. His interest in education led him to become a member of the governing bodies of Fettes College and of Donaldson's Hospital.

In 1855 Inglis had acquired the estate of Glencorse, south of Edinburgh. He later added the adjoining property of Belwood and in 1883 inherited the family estate of Loganbank, also in Glencorse parish. As an important local proprietor he was active in conserving the identity of the parish. In 1877 he wrote a paper in protest against a proposal to change its name to Glencross. His interest in tree cultivation led him in the late 1870s and early 1880s into successful litigation, taken as far as an appeal in the Lords, against the Associated Ironmasters of Scotland, over the damage caused to trees in the neighbourhood by air pollution.

Inglis published little. An article entitled 'Montrose and the Covenanters of 1638' appeared in *Blackwood's Magazine* in 1887. Earlier, during the ecclesiastical conflicts which culminated in the Disruption, he had published 'On the present position of the Church of Scotland' in 1839 in the same journal. For this, written from the point of view of the moderate party in the Church of Scotland, he came under attack from the evangelicals, who broke away in 1843 to form the Free Church of Scotland.

Despite failing health Inglis continued in office until the end of his life. This was perhaps hastened by the shock of a violent assault by a reportedly deranged assailant, which took place in early 1891. He died at Loganbank on 20 August 1891 and was buried at a well-attended public funeral in the new Calton cemetery, Edinburgh, five days later.

As a judge, university reformer, and defender of the interests of his locality, Inglis certainly showed his conserving instincts but also a desire for careful reconstruction. His refusal of the offer of a position as a lord of appeal showed his commitment to the work he was engaged on in Scotland. In the context of university reform he had defended distinctive Scottish traditions as a foundation on which to build. His belief, however, in bringing ideas from English education to Scotland, as shown in his trusteeship of the Fettes Endowment, demonstrated that this was not a narrow-minded nationalism. A self-contained man, he apparently gained the attachment of contemporaries through 'luminousness of mind' and 'a humanity of intelligence' (*Scots Observer*), and perhaps by the very moderation he embodied.

GORDON F. MILLAR

Sources *The Scotsman* (21 Aug 1891) · *The Scotsman* (22 Aug 1891) · *The Scotsman* (26 Aug 1891) · *Blackwood*, 150 (1891), 592–600 · *Juridical Review*, 22 (1910–11), 196 · G. W. T. Omond, *The lord advocates of Scotland, second series, 1834–1880* (1914), 203–21 · *Journal of Jurisprudence*, 35 (1891), 145, 449, 464–5, 576–9 · *Scots Observer* (19 July 1890), 219–

20 · *National Observer* (29 Aug 1891), 371 · F. J. Grant, ed., *The Faculty of Advocates in Scotland, 1532–1943*, Scottish RS, 145 (1944), 109 · S. P. Walker, *The Faculty of Advocates, 1800–1986* (1987), 82 · Foster, *Alum. Oxon.* · W. I. Addison, *A roll of graduates of the University of Glasgow from 31st December 1727 to 31st December 1897* (1898), 285 · WWBMP · A. D. Smith, ed., *The trial of Madeleine Smith*, Notable Scottish Trials (1905), 285 · R. D. Anderson, *Education and opportunity in Victorian Scotland: schools and universities* (1983)

Archives NL Scot., legal notebooks | Lpool RO, letters to four-teenth earl of Derby

Likenesses J. Watson-Gordon, oils, 1854, U. Edin. · D. Macnee, oils, 1872, U. Edin., Fettes College · G. Reid, oils, 1882, Parliament Hall, Edinburgh [*see illus.*] · E. Ljungh, silhouette, 1888, Scot. NPG · W. Brodie, marble bust, Faculty of Advocates, Parliament Hall, Edinburgh · J. Faed, chalk drawing, Scot. NPG · W. Hole, etching, NPG; repro. in W. B. Hole, *Quasi cursores* (1884) · drawing (after oils by G. Reid), Scot. NPG

Wealth at death £62,215 6s. 3d.: confirmation, 6 Oct 1891, *CCI*

Inglis, John. *See* Clifford, (Sophia) Lucy Jane (1846–1929).

Inglis, Sir John Eardley Wilmot (1814–1862), army officer, was born in Nova Scotia on 15 November 1814, the son of the Rt Revd John Inglis, who died on 27 October 1850, aged seventy-two, third bishop of Nova Scotia, and his wife, the daughter of Thomas Cochrane, member of the council of Nova Scotia. Charles *Inglis, first bishop of Nova Scotia, was his grandfather.

On 2 August 1833 Inglis was appointed ensign by purchase in the 32nd (Cornwall) foot. He served with his regiment during the insurrection in Canada in 1837, and was present at the engagements at St Denis and St Eustache. He was promoted lieutenant on 19 January 1839, and became captain by purchase on 29 September 1843 and major by purchase on 25 February 1848. During the Second Anglo-Sikh War, of 1848–9, he took part in the first and second sieges of Multan and in the attack on the enemy's position on 12 September 1848, succeeding to the command of the right column of the attack on the death of Lieutenant-Colonel D. Pattoun. He commanded the 32nd at Suraj Kund, and was present at the storm and capture of Multan, the action at Chiniot, and the battle of Gujrat. He was awarded the brevet of lieutenant-colonel on 7 June 1849.

On 19 July 1851 Inglis married the Hon. Julia Selina Thesiger (*b.* 1 April 1833), daughter of the first Lord Chelmsford. They had three sons. On 20 February 1855 Inglis was promoted regimental lieutenant-colonel, and on 5 June the same year he was made brevet colonel. He was in command of the 32nd at Lucknow on the outbreak of the mutiny in 1857. He was second in command under Sir Henry Lawrence in the action at Chinhat on 30 June 1857, and afterwards in the residency at Lucknow, to which the garrison, numbering 927 European officers and soldiers and 765 loyal Indian soldiers, withdrew on 1 July. When Lawrence was mortally wounded on 2 July, Inglis succeeded to the command, at Lawrence's wish, and led the defence until the arrival of Sir Henry Havelock on 26 September 1857. He remained there until the arrival of Sir Colin Campbell on 18 November. Inglis then commanded a brigade under Campbell, and took part in the attack on Tantia Topi on 6 December 1857. His wife and children had

Sir John Eardley Wilmot Inglis (1814–1862), by Charles Holl (after John Jabez Edwin Mayall)

been with him throughout the siege of Lucknow. His dispatch narrating the events of the siege was published in 1896. He was promoted major-general on 26 September 1857, and made KCB 'for his enduring fortitude and persevering gallantry in the defence of the residency'. The legislature of his native colony presented him with a sword of honour, the blade formed of steel from Nova Scotian iron.

Inglis was appointed colonel of the 32nd on 5 May 1860, and soon after was sent to Corfu to take command of the troops in the Ionian Islands. He died, while on leave from Corfu, at Hamburg on 27 September 1862.

H. M. CHICHESTER, *rev.* ALEX MAY

Sources *Army List* · *Despatch of Brigadier Inglis narrating the events of the siege of Lucknow* (1896) · Lady Inglis [J. S. Inglis], *The siege of Lucknow: a diary* (1892) · M. Edwardes, *A season in hell: the defence of the Lucknow residency* (1973) · V. Stuart, *Battle for Lucknow* (1975) · C. Hibbert, *The great mutiny, India, 1857* (1978) · D. Featherstone, *Victorian colonial warfare: from the conquest of Sind to the Indian mutiny* (1992) · H. C. B. Cook, *The Sikh wars: the British army in the Punjab, 1845–1849* (1975) · *CGPLA Eng. & Wales* (1862)

Archives NAM, letter-book

Likenesses T. J. Baker, oils, 1859, NPG · W. Gush, oils, Nova Scotia Legislative Library, Province House, Halifax, Canada · G. Hayter, mezzotint (after J. E. Coombs), NPG · C. Holl, stipple (after photograph by J. J. E. Mayall), NPG [*see illus.*] · J. J. E. Mayall, stipple (after photograph by C. Holl), NPG · D. J. Pound, mixed engraving (after photograph by J. J. E. Mayall), BM, NPG; repro. in *Illustrated News of the World*, 2 (1858) · portrait, repro. in E. H. Nolan, *The Illustrated history of the British Empire in India* (1879), 755

Wealth at death under £12,000: resworn probate, March 1863, *CGPLA Eng. & Wales* (1862)

Inglis [*née* Murray; *other married name* Finlay], **Margaret Maxwell** (1774–1843), poet, was born on 27 October 1774 at Sanquhar, Dumfriesshire, the daughter of Dr Alexander Murray. Her early literary and musical gifts were developed by her education. When very young she married a Mr Finlay, who was in the navy, and who soon died in the West Indies. In 1803, after some years living with her relatives in Dumfries, she married John Inglis, son of the parish minister of Kirkmabreck in east Galloway, and an officer in the excise. On his death in 1826, she and their three children were dependent on a small annuity devolving from his office. Inglis then studied hard, and wrote much, publishing a *Miscellaneous Collection of Poems, Chiefly Scriptural Pieces* in 1838. One of the lyrics, 'Sweet bard of Ettrick's glen', is a memorial tribute to James Hogg, whose manner Inglis followed with considerable success. According to Rogers, Burns commended her for her exquisite rendering of his songs, especially 'Ca' the yowes to the knowes' (4.73). She died in Edinburgh on 21 December 1843. T. W. BAYNE, *rev.* SARAH COUPER

Sources C. Rogers, *The modern Scottish minstrel, or, The songs of Scotland of the past half-century*, 4 (1857) · J. G. Wilson, ed., *The poets and poetry of Scotland*, 2 vols. (1876–7) · Irving, *Scots.* · bap. reg. Scot.

Inglis, Sir Robert Harry, second baronet (1786–1855), politician, was born in London on 12 January 1786, the only son of Sir Hugh Inglis (1744–1820), created baronet in 1801, and his first wife, Catherine (*d.* 1792), daughter and coheir of Harry Johnson of Milton Bryan, Bedfordshire. He had two younger sisters. His father was a self-made man, director and three times chairman of the East India Company, and MP for Ashburton from 1802 to 1806. Robert was educated at Winchester College, and at Christ Church, Oxford, where he matriculated in 1803, took his BA in 1806, his MA in 1809, and his DCL in 1826. At Christ Church, Inglis established a lifelong friendship with Sir Thomas Dyke Acland, and like him became loosely associated with the Clapham Sect of reforming Anglican evangelicals around William Wilberforce. Inglis's religious convictions were to remain a foundational influence on him: his evangelicalism was sometimes obscured by his passionate commitment to the establishment and to church order, but he was never to lose his deep personal faith, and his zeal for the spread of the Christian gospel and for the defence of national morality. On 10 February 1807 he married Mary (1787–1872), eldest daughter of Joseph Seymour Biscoe of Pendhill Court, Bletchingley, Surrey. They had no children of their own, but in 1815 became guardians to the nine orphaned children of Henry *Thornton (1760–1815) and his wife, Marianne Sykes, and themselves moved into the Thornton home at Battersea Rise, Clapham. Inglis's eldest ward, Marianne Thornton, was to become the subject of a 'domestic biography' by her great-nephew the novelist E. M. Forster, in which Sir Robert's kindly but rather solemn manner is vividly depicted.

In early adult life Inglis appears to have been something of a dilettante. He was admitted a student of Lincoln's Inn in 1806, but was not called to the bar until 1818 and never

Sir Robert Harry Inglis, second baronet (1786–1855), by George Richmond, in or before 1837

practised. He travelled extensively, and cultivated literary, historical, and scientific interests, becoming a fellow of the Royal Society in 1813 and a fellow of the Society of Antiquaries in 1816. Meanwhile he became increasingly involved in public affairs. He was for a time a private secretary to Lord Sidmouth, and in 1812 was appointed one of the commissioners responsible for settling the troubled financial affairs of the Carnatic. Having succeeded his father as second baronet in 1820, Inglis was at the coronation of George IV in 1821, deputed by the government to perform the delicate task of meeting Queen Caroline at the door of Westminster Abbey to inform her that she was to be denied admission to the ceremony. According to Marianne Thornton, 'the mingled gentleness and firmness of his manner induced her to give up the contest' (Forster, 88).

Inglis was first returned to parliament in May 1824 at a by-election for Dundalk, a pocket borough controlled by his fellow evangelical, the third earl of Roden. He strongly identified himself with tory and Irish protestant interests, seeing himself as linked to the cause of the Church of Ireland particularly through his close friendship with John Jebb, bishop of Limerick. In May 1825 he spoke forcefully in the Commons against Francis Burdett's Catholic Relief Bill. The dissolution of 1826 left him temporarily out of parliament, but his appetite for political life was now considerable, and he was returned again at a by-election in

February 1828, this time sitting for Ripon. He spoke against the repeal of the Test and Corporation Acts, and in May 1828 made a lengthy speech reaffirming his opposition to Catholic emancipation. Following Daniel O'Connell's victory at the County Clare election in July 1828, Inglis urged the government, through Robert Peel, who had been his contemporary at Christ Church and was a perceived political ally, to make a prompt demonstration of strength and determination. In the event, after initial irresolution, the government in February 1829 announced its intention to move for Catholic emancipation. Peel resigned his seat for Oxford University, and then stood at the by-election. Inglis, who had for several years been seen as a potential candidate for the university, stood against him. After a bitterly fought contest, although seemingly without personal animosity between the candidates, Inglis, supported disproportionately by the clergy, defeated the home secretary by a margin of 755 to 609. Thereafter he was to sit continuously for the university for the next quarter of a century.

Naturally, Inglis subsequently strenuously opposed the Catholic Relief Bill, and its passing left him politically disorientated. For the rest of his career he avoided firm party commitments, his natural affinities with the tories weakened by continuing distrust. He denounced the Reform Bill and Wellington's attempt at a compromise solution in May 1832, and in 1833 protested against the Irish Church Temporalities Act. He was only slightly disappointed when Peel did not invite him to join his short-lived first ministry in 1834, consoling himself with the thought that either acceptance or refusal of such an offer would have placed him in a difficult position (Inglis to T. D. Acland, 16 April 1835, Acland MSS, Devon RO). When the recommendations of the ecclesiastical commission set up by Peel began from 1836 to be implemented by the Melbourne administration, Inglis was in the forefront of opposition, perceiving the reforms as despoiliation and Erastianism. On 30 June 1840 he counter-attacked with a motion for a parliamentary grant for building churches, which failed by only nineteen votes. After Peel's return to office in 1841, Inglis hoped that the new government would adopt his proposals, but he was to be disappointed. Indeed in 1845 he was again to find himself firmly at odds with Peel when he led the opposition in the Commons to the prime minister's proposals for the permanent state endowment of the Roman Catholic seminary at Maynooth. Also in 1845 it was Inglis who memorably tagged the government's plans for colleges in Ireland 'a gigantic scheme of Godless education' (*Hansard 3*, 80, 1845, 378). In the late 1840s he resisted further concession to Roman Catholics, and in 1851 supported Russell's Ecclesiastical Titles Assumption Bill, although he considered it a very inadequate measure. Inglis's political importance at this juncture was confirmed by an invitation from Stanley to join his cabinet during his unsuccessful attempt to form a government in February 1851, but Inglis himself later observed to Stanley that 'you would have found me, I fear, … a more impracticable colleague than you might have expected or could have borne' (Inglis to Stanley, 31 Aug

1852, fourteenth earl of Derby MSS, Lpool RO). On 9 May 1851 Inglis reasserted his independence and the primacy of his protestant loyalties by voting with the whig government against David Urquhart's motion of censure, in order to secure the passage of legislation against the Roman Catholic hierarchy.

While the defence of church and protestantism dominated Inglis's parliamentary life, he also carried an address against the foreign slave trade (May 1838), and in 1842 he sought to limit the extent of income tax. He took a strong interest in Indian affairs and supported Lord Ashley in his campaign for factory reform. His exacting moral standards were illustrated by his vigorous opposition to the Deceased Wife's Sister Bill of 1850. He was an industrious and influential back-bencher, although he was hampered by a poor speaking voice and clumsy delivery. His strong convictions merged at times into prejudice, but his rugged political independence and integrity were softened by great charm and courtesy of manners. He had a rosy, corpulent, beaming appearance, graced with splendid floral buttonholes, and was regarded with affection and respect on all sides of the house. He was sworn of the privy council in August 1854.

Inglis also maintained and developed his intellectual and cultural interests. In 1831 he was appointed a commissioner on the public records and carried out a detailed examination of depositories. He was a trustee of the British Museum from 1834, and was a cogent defender of the maintenance of a broadly based collection 'of everything interesting in literature, natural science and ancient art' (Inglis to Peel, 13 March 1846, Peel MSS, BL). He was president of the British Association in 1847–8, and in 1850 was elected professor of antiquity at the Royal Academy. He was involved with numerous other philanthropic, religious, and educational societies, and published many devotional works and parliamentary speeches. He was hospitable and sociable, and his dinner table was a lively meeting-place for people of very diverse opinions and backgrounds.

Through his mother Inglis inherited the estate at Milton Bryan. In Bedfordshire he was a conscientious landlord, and served as sheriff of the county and chairman of quarter sessions. Nevertheless he was in spirit far more a Londoner than a country gentleman, and after ill health had in 1854 forced his retirement from his beloved House of Commons, it was at his London home, 7 Bedford Square, that he died on 5 May 1855. He was buried in the family vault in Milton Bryan church. The baronetcy became extinct on his death and, on the death of his wife in 1872, Milton Bryan passed to Marianne Thornton.

JOHN WOLFFE

Sources E. M. Forster, *Marianne Thornton, 1797–1887: a domestic biography* (1956) · *GM*, 2nd ser., 44 (1855), 640–41 · *DNB* · J. Wolffe, *The protestant crusade in Great Britain, 1829–1860* (1991) · G. I. T. Machin, *The Catholic question in English politics, 1820 to 1830* (1964) · G. I. T. Machin, *Politics and the churches in Great Britain, 1832 to 1868* (1977) · B. Disraeli, 'Sir Robert Inglis', Bodl. Oxf., Dep. Hughenden 26/2, fols. 110–11 · J. C. Colquhoun, *Christian Observer* (1865), 521–7, 610–18; repr. in *William Wilberforce: his friends and his times* (1866), 337–66 · *Fraser's Magazine*, 34 (1846), 648–53 · *The Times* (7 May

1855) · diaries, Canterbury Cathedral Library · corresp. with Sir Robert Peel, BL, Add. MSS 40182–40603 · correspondence with T. D. Acland, Devon RO · letters to John Jebb, TCD

Archives Canterbury Cathedral, corresp., journals, and papers; journal of parliamentary activity and travels in Europe; further travel journals and notebooks; mainly political diaries · Holborn Library, Camden, London, Camden Local Studies and Archive Centre, letters | BL, corresp. with Lord Aberdeen, Add. MSS 43238–43244 · BL, letters to Philip Bliss, Add. MSS 34570–34582 · BL, letters to Stanley Lees Gifford, Add. MS 56368 · BL, corresp. with W. E. Gladstone, Add. MSS 44352–44378 · BL, corresp. with Sir Robert Peel, Add. MSS 40182–40603 · Bodl. Oxf., letters to Samuel Wilberforce · CUL, Thornton MSS · Devon RO, corresp. with Sir Thomas Dyke Acland · Lpool RO, letters to fourteenth earl of Derby · NL Scot., corresp. with J. R. Hope-Scott; corresp. with John Lee · RS, corresp. with Sir John Herschel · TCD, letters to John Jebb · U. Edin., New Coll. L., letters to Thomas Chalmers

Likenesses G. Hayter, oils, 1833–43, NPG · G. Richmond, watercolour drawing, 1836, AM Oxf. · G. Richmond, watercolour, in or before 1837, Castle Museum and Art Gallery, Nottingham [*see illus.*] · G. Richmond, chalk drawing, 1845, NPG · G. Richmond, oils, 1854, Oxford, Examination Schools · J. Doyle, caricatures, drawings, BM · G. Hayter, group portrait, oils (*The House of Commons, 1833*), NPG · F. Holl, stipple (after C. W. Cope), NPG · F. C. Lewis, stipple (after J. Slater), BM, NPG · J. Partridge, group portrait (*The Fine Arts Commissioners, 1846*), NPG · J. Slater?, watercolour and pencil, Killerton, Devon

Wealth at death £40,000: probate, 1855

Inglis, Sir William (1764–1835), army officer, was the third son of William Inglis MD, who was three times president of the College of Surgeons, Edinburgh, and was descended from the Inglis family of Manner and Mannerhead, Roxburghshire. Nothing is known of the younger William's mother or his school education. On 11 October 1779 he was appointed ensign in the 57th regiment, which he eventually joined at New York in 1781, sailing with it for Nova Scotia at the end of the American War of Independence. In Canada he advanced to lieutenant on 3 May 1782, was appointed captain-lieutenant and captain on 1 July 1785, and secured his own company in the regiment as a captain in 1788, landing in England again on 14 November 1791. During most of 1792 and 1793 the 57th was assisting the civil power to maintain order in the midlands. In September 1793 it briefly served in Flanders with the duke of York, sailed to Brittany with an aborted expedition to assist French royalists early the next year, and returned to Flanders in June 1794. Inglis was with it throughout this period, and at the subsequent siege of Nijmegen and withdrawal to Bremen in the winter of 1794–5. He became a brevet major on 6 May 1795, took part in another unsuccessful excursion to Brittany, and obtained his majority in the 57th on 1 September. Shortly afterwards he embarked with the regiment for the West Indies, in charge of three companies on the *Charon*, the only vessel to reach Barbados in February 1796 as the others had turned back in stormy weather. He commanded his small force at the siege and fall of Morne Fortuné on St Lucia, and the capture of the island later that year. Until the belated arrival of regimental headquarters, he acted as second-in-command to Brigadier-General Sir John Moore, who described him as 'a good steady officer' (Kingsford, 58). After helping to secure Grenada, the regiment sailed to

Trinidad, from where Inglis returned to England towards the end of 1802.

Inglis had become a brevet lieutenant-colonel on 1 January 1800 and spent most of 1803 raising a second battalion at Ashford, Kent, before rejoining the 1st battalion, 57th regiment, and sailing with it to the Channel Islands, where he assumed command as regimental lieutenant-colonel on 16 August 1804. Inglis dubbed his battalion, which garrisoned Gibraltar from 1805 to 1809, 'fighting villains' (Kingsford, 61) because of their unruly behaviour when off duty. Nevertheless, successive inspecting general officers praised Inglis's zeal in improving its discipline and military competence. In June 1809 the 57th left Gibraltar to join the army under Lieutenant-General Sir Arthur Wellesley (later duke of Wellington) in the Peninsula. The battalion was attached to the brigade of Major-General Richard Stewart, whose illness caused its command to devolve on Inglis (promoted colonel on 25 July 1810) immediately before and during the battle of Busaco on 27 September 1810, and in the subsequent retreat to the lines of Torres Vedras before Lisbon. During the pursuit of Marshal Masséna from Santarém in March 1811, Inglis again commanded the brigade and led it in the action at Pombal on the 11th. After subsequently taking part with the battalion at Campo Mayor, Los Santos, and the first siege of Badajoz, he commanded the 57th at the battle of Albuera on 16 May 1811, where he took over the 3rd brigade when its commander fell mortally wounded.

During the battle of Albuera, the 57th came under heavy attack, and Inglis ordered all ranks to 'die hard'; the regiment is still known as the Die-hards. Inglis himself, besides having a horse shot under him, received a 4 oz grapeshot in the neck which, after he had carried it about with him for two days, was extracted from behind his shoulder. 'It was observed', wrote Marshal William Carr Beresford, 'that our dead, particularly the 57th, were lying as they fought, in ranks, and every wound was in front.' 'Nothing', he added, 'could exceed the conduct and gallantry of Colonel Inglis at the head of his regiment.' In 1828, Inglis would conduct a heated correspondence with the marquess of Londonderry, whose history of the Peninsular War falsely claimed that the 57th had lost its colours at Albuera.

Such was the severity of Inglis's wound that he surrendered command of the 57th and briefly returned to England before acting as president of a general court martial at Lisbon during 1812. By May 1813 he had sufficiently recovered to take the field as brigadier-general in command of the 1st brigade, 7th division. The following month Inglis, who had been made a major-general on 4 June, advanced with his brigade from San Esteban, and on 8 July he reached the top of the range of mountains immediately above Maya, overlooking the flat country of France. On 25 July, however, the French succeeded in turning the British right, and he retired in the direction of Pamplona. During the battle of the Pyrenees near by on 30 July, Inglis was ordered to capture the crest of a mountain occupied by the enemy, overlooking the high road which passed between that position and the main French force. 'General Inglis,' Sir William Napier later wrote:

> one of those veterans who purchase every step of promotion with their blood, advancing on the left with only five hundred men of the seventh division, broke at one shock the two French regiments covering Chauzel's right, and drove down into the valley of Lanz.   (Napier)

Wellington, in his dispatch, gave the highest credit to the conduct and execution of the attack, during which Inglis could muster merely 445 men against over 2000, lost 145 of them, and had a horse shot under him.

On 31 August 1813 Inglis's brigade fought in support of the 9th Portuguese brigade at Vera, where it suffered heavy casualties and Inglis had another horse shot from under him. His divisional commander, Lieutenant-General the earl of Dalhousie, reported to Wellington: 'The 1st brigade had to sustain the attack of two divisions of the enemy on a strong and wooded hill; the loss there was unavoidable.' After carrying fortified high ground above the village of Suré, on 10 November Inglis received orders from Marshal Beresford to cross the River Nivelle by a wooden bridge and attack the heights above Echallar; Inglis suffered severe bruising of one of his feet by a musket-ball during the ensuing, successful struggle. On 23 February 1814 the brigade was again engaged with the enemy near the village of Airgavé, and four days later in the battle of Orthez, when Inglis's horse was wounded.

For his services in the Peninsula, Inglis received the thanks of both houses of parliament and was created a KCB in 1815. He also received a field officer's medal for Albuera, a general's medal for the Pyrenees and Nivelle, and a gold cross with three clasps for the Pyrenees, Nivelle, and Orthez. In 1822 he married Margaret Mary Anne, eldest daughter of Lieutenant-General William Raymond of The Lee, Essex; they had two sons, William Inglis (1823–1888) and Raymond Inglis (1826–1880), both commissioned in the army. Promoted lieutenant-general on 27 May 1825, Inglis was appointed lieutenant-governor of Kinsale, Ireland, on 8 March 1827, then subsequently, on 8 January 1829, governor of Cork with respective annual allowances of £239 9s. and £318 8s., retaining the latter post until his death. On 16 April 1830 he was appointed colonel of the 57th regiment. He died at Ramsgate, Kent, on 29 November 1835 and was buried in Canterbury Cathedral in December.

W. R. LLUELLYN, rev. JOHN SWEETMAN

Sources Army List · C. L. Kingsford, The story of the duke of Cambridge's Own, Middlesex regiment (1916) · H. H. Woollright, History of the fifty-seventh, west Middlesex regiment of foot, 1755–1881 (1893) · G. Blaxland, The Middlesex regiment (1977) · W. F. P. Napier, History of the war in the Peninsula and in the south of France, 6 vols. (1828–40) · The dispatches of … the duke of Wellington … from 1799 to 1818, ed. J. Gurwood, 13 vols. in 12 (1834–9) · United Service Journal, 1 (1836), 237–40 · J. Philippart, ed., The royal military calendar, 3 vols. (1815–16) **Archives** NAM, corresp., journals, and papers **Likenesses** portrait, repro. in Woollright, History of the fifty-seventh, facing p. 166

Inglott, William (1553/4–1621), organist and composer, born probably at Norwich, was the son of Edmund Inglott (d. 1583), master of the choristers at Norwich Cathedral.

After serving as a chorister under his father in 1567–8, he was paid in 1582 for teaching the choristers during his father's illness. On 8 May 1588 he was formally granted the post of organist (and master of the choristers), which he held until Michaelmas 1591, when he seems to have left Norwich. Although Inglott would later return to Norwich, his career in the intervening period is obscure. But he is probably identical with the man of the same name who was admitted organist of Hereford Cathedral on 1 October 1597 and remained there until 1610. He was back at Norwich by 1611, when he was granted a fresh patent—as organist only, not master of the choristers as well—on 1 June. His first recorded payment was twice his predecessor's salary and may reflect a substantial increase in responsibility or workload.

Inglott, whose extant compositions amount to just three pieces for virginal, was held in great esteem by his contemporaries. A memorial inscription recording his burial in Norwich Cathedral praises his skill as a composer and as a player of organ and virginal. The two sets of variations attributed to William Inglott in the Fitzwilliam virginal book are well crafted, richly polyphonic, and technically demanding, and would seem to support this view of him. He was buried on 31 December 1621, at the age of sixty-seven.

IAN PAYNE

Sources H. W. Shaw, The succession of organists of the Chapel Royal and the cathedrals of England and Wales from c.1538 (1991), 135–6, 198–201 · J. Caldwell, 'Inglott, William', New Grove, 230 · I. Payne, The provision and practice of sacred music at Cambridge colleges and selected cathedrals, c.1547–c.1646 (1993), 236, 260–63 · J. A. Maitland and W. B. Squire, The Fitzwilliam virginal book (1899); repr. (1963), vol. 2, pp. 375, 381

Ingmethorpe, Thomas (bap. 1564, d. 1638), schoolmaster, was born in Worcester; he was baptized at the church of St Helen there on 3 December 1564 and attended the King's School under Thomas Bradshaw. On 31 May 1581 he matriculated at Brasenose College, Oxford, where his old headmaster's son, also Thomas, was already in residence. Ingmethorpe graduated BA from St Mary Hall on 7 February 1584, but it was as a member of Brasenose that he proceeded MA on 8 July 1586. By the following year he was ordained, and had returned to Worcester as usher of the King's School. On 9 August 1587 he engaged to marry Elizabeth, the elder daughter of the lately deceased Thomas Bradshaw senior. Their first child, Alice, was born in October 1589; she or another died in 1594. Ingmethorpe vacated the ushership in 1589; in the year of his daughter's death (and possibly in consequence of that sadness) he left his native town for ever, moving to co. Durham as rector of Great Stainton.

In 1598 Ingmethorpe published a sermon on 1 John 2 and in 1609 another sermon on the same chapter. In 1610 he was appointed headmaster of Durham School but he gave offence to his employers, the dean and chapter, by speaking in a sermon with 'biting invective' against one of their number, Archdeacon Tunstall (VCH Durham, 1.379). Ingmethorpe was called before the chapter on 9 July 1612, and was imprisoned until 13 June 1613 when he made his submission to the charge. The following Christmas he resigned from his headmastership, and spent the rest of his life at his rectory of Great Stainton, where he ran a small private school. Wood alludes to his 'admirable methods in pedagogy' and to his distinction as a Hebrew scholar (Wood, *Ath. Oxon.*, 2.592). Ingmethorpe's last and most important work was a Hebrew translation of the catechism, published in 1633 as *A Short Catechisme, by Law Authorised in the Church of England*. He died in 1638 and was buried at Great Stainton church on 1 November. The Thomas Ingmethorpe who was a king's scholar at Durham School between 1612 and 1614 was doubtless the headmaster's son.   C. S. KNIGHTON

Sources M. Craze, *King's School, Worcester* (1972), 38, 46, 48 · T. H. Burbidge, ed., *Durham School register*, 3rd edn (1940), 3, 75 · *VCH Berkshire*, 1.379 · Wood, *Ath. Oxon.*, new edn, 2.592 · *Reg. Oxf.*, 2.97; 3.119 · *STC, 1475–1640*

Ingold, Sir Christopher Kelk (1893–1970), chemist, was born on 28 October 1893 at 142 Windsor Road, Forest Gate, Essex, the first of the two children of William Kelk Ingold (1861–1898), commercial traveller, and his wife, Harriet Walker (1865–1943), daughter of Christopher Newcomb and his wife, Emma. Ingold's father suffered from tuberculosis, and although the family moved to the Isle of Wight he died in Shanklin in 1898. Despite her husband's death, Ingold's mother chose to remain on the Isle of Wight to ensure that her two young children were raised in a healthy, outdoor environment. Thus, from an early age, Ingold developed a love of birdwatching that continued throughout his life.

Education In 1905 Ingold entered Sandown county secondary school as a scholarship-supported day pupil, where he benefited from a group of young, gifted, and dedicated teachers, and learned not only science, but music and sports as well. He particularly liked cricket, which he played for a number of years; he played his Bösendorfer grand piano all his life.

After completion of the intermediate BSc at school, Ingold moved on to Hartley College, Southampton, in 1911, where he studied chemistry under Professor David Boyd, graduating with an external BSc of the University of London in 1913. This gained him acceptance to work with Professor Jocelyn Thorpe at the Royal College of Science, London, where Ingold received both a Royal College scholarship and a University of London exhibition, giving him £100 for the year 1913–14.

Ingold obtained his associateship of the Royal College of Science with first-class honours in 1914, and started immediately on a research programme. However, this was interrupted by the First World War when, in 1915, Thorpe sent him to Glasgow to run an industrial plant to manufacture SK lachrymator (a mixture of ethyl iodoacetate and alcohol), the tear gas extensively used by the British in shells throughout the war. For this work he was subsequently awarded the British Empire Medal. At the end of the war, his employer, the Cassel Cyanide Company, was anxious to retain his services, but Ingold had already decided that he wanted to follow an academic career. He had continued to collaborate with Thorpe throughout his sojourn in Glasgow, and submitted a thesis based on part of this

Sir Christopher Kelk Ingold (1893–1970), by Elliott & Fry

work for the MSc degree of the University of London in 1919. (He had already received the diploma of membership of Imperial College for his postgraduate research.) Early in 1920 Ingold took a considerable cut in pay to accept an offer from Thorpe to return to Imperial College as a demonstrator in industrial organic chemistry.

Early research and marriage In the five years from 1920 to 1924 Ingold published fifty-two research papers, was co-author of a 500-page book with Thorpe, obtained the DSc degree from the University of London and, for two years running, won the Meldola medal for the most outstanding research during the year by a chemist under thirty years of age. He was also elected to the Royal Society (at the age of thirty), and was appointed to the chair of organic chemistry at Leeds University, taking up his post on 1 October 1924. During this same period Ingold found the time to woo a brilliant young postgraduate student at Imperial College, (Edith) Hilda Usherwood [(**Edith) Hilda Ingold** (1898–1988)]. They were married on 11 July 1923.

Hilda Ingold was born on 21 May 1898 in Catford, London, the first of three children of Thomas Scriven Usherwood, and his wife, Edith. As all four of Hilda's grandparents were headteachers of London schools, and her father taught engineering at Christ's Hospital school in Horsham, Sussex, Hilda grew up in a learned and literary environment. She won many prizes in school and a scholarship to the renowned North London Collegiate School for Girls, which caused her father to move the family home to Finchley, Middlesex, in 1912, so that Hilda would have easy access to her new school.

After an outstanding academic career at school, Hilda

won the largest scholarship available, £50 per year for three years, to study chemistry and botany at Royal Holloway College. There she continued to win awards, including the Gilchrist scholarship, the Neil Arnott scholarship, and the Driver prize and scholarship (twice). In her graduating year, 1920, she won the Martin Holloway prize for the 'best and most efficient student, having regard to academic and intellectual distinction'. She graduated with first-class honours in chemistry.

In January 1921 Hilda entered Imperial College and started chemical research under Dr Martha Whiteley towards the PhD degree. Exactly twenty-four months later she submitted her thesis, and she was awarded the degree the following month. She published a number of research papers as sole author and with Martha Whiteley, but she was collaborating with Ingold as early as 1921. They immediately established a rapport, and their chemical collaboration matured rapidly to a personal one. They were both rather shy, but she nevertheless had an engaging vivacity which, coupled with her intelligence, made her the ideal companion for the tall, handsome young lecturer. After their marriage, Hilda became essential to all areas of Ingold's life, and her grace, kindness, good humour, and stalwart common sense enriched the forty-seven years that they were to live and work together.

After their marriage in 1923 Hilda Ingold continued her independent research, obtaining her DSc degree in 1926. However, after the birth of their first daughter, Sylvia, in 1927, research became a less important part of her life. Two more children completed their family, a son, Keith (*b.* 1929), and a second daughter, Dilys (*b.* 1932). Although Hilda continued to publish until 1947, she gradually shifted her support of Ingold to the administrative side, and it was in this field that she excelled at University College, London, from about 1939 until her retirement in 1968. She died on 8 August 1988 at Chelmsford.

Structure and mechanisms in organic chemistry In the mid-1920s an extraordinary debate took place in the chemical literature concerning the arrangements of electrons in organic molecules, and how the electrons move between molecules as chemical reactions take place. Many people took part in the debate, but the principal protagonists were Robert Robinson (1886–1975) and Christopher Ingold. During this period, which overlapped Ingold's stay at Imperial College and his time at Leeds, he gradually clarified in his own mind the mechanisms of electron movement in molecules and finally synthesized his ideas into a systematic scheme for reaction mechanisms for the whole of organic chemistry. This scheme gave rise to a new way of thinking about organic reactions and of teaching organic chemistry, which has been in use ever since. While at Leeds, Ingold developed a large, active research group. He also began mountain climbing, which became a major recreational activity almost until the end of his life.

In 1930 the chair of organic chemistry became vacant at University College, London, and Ingold was chosen to fill it. Almost immediately, however, he suffered medical problems with his eyes that required a rest from intensive

reading and thus a break from his very heavy load. He took this rest in the form of a six-month leave in California, during which he wrote a review article ('Principles of an electronic theory in organic reactions', *Chemical Reviews*, 15, 1934, 225) summarizing his ideas. When this was published in the USA, it quickly became the seminal statement in the field of organic chemistry and led to the acceptance on both sides of the Atlantic of Ingold's interpretation of the theory of organic reactions.

At the same time that Ingold arrived at University College, Edward Hughes (1906–1963) joined his research group as a postdoctoral fellow, and the two men began a collaboration that ended only with Hughes's death. Together they developed the system of reaction mechanisms for nucleophilic substitution reactions and elimination reactions at saturated carbon (S_N1, S_N2, E1, and E2) and elucidated the mechanism by which the Walden inversion occurred.

In the early 1930s deuterium, the isotope of hydrogen with twice its normal mass, was first prepared in quantity. Ingold realized how this could solve the problem, first defined by Kekulé in 1865, of the structure of the benzene molecule, on which Ingold had been working since 1922. In 1933 Hughes and co-workers started to separate pure heavy water in quantity from ordinary water, and Ingold and co-workers synthesized fully deuterated and half-deuterated benzene, C_6D_6 and $C_6H_3D_3$. Measurement of the infra-red and Raman spectra of these molecules in 1935 allowed the proof to be made that the benzene molecule did indeed have a plane regular hexagonal structure. The complete analysis of the structure required the synthesis of benzene molecules containing one, two, four, and five atoms of deuterium per molecule. This difficult task was interrupted by the Second World War, during which the research laboratories of University College were evacuated to Aberystwyth. The final experiments were completed in the autumn of 1943 and the results published in 1945. By an analysis of the infra-red and Raman spectra of ordinary benzene, fully deuterated benzene, and five partially deuterated benzenes, twenty-nine of the thirty normal vibrations that occur in the molecule were identified with particular observed absorption bands. This allowed Ingold to calculate the complete internal force system of the benzene molecule.

This was probably the greatest scientific contribution of Ingold's many research efforts. It won him the Bakerian lecture award in 1938, the Davy medal of the Royal Society in 1946, and, in 1953, an honorary degree from the University of Bologna, an ancient seat of learning that had rarely given such an award to a foreigner; in this last honour Ingold trod in the footsteps of Copernicus and Erasmus.

Ingold followed this work with further groundbreaking studies on the excited state of benzene and on the excited state of acetylene, C_2H_2. The latter study demonstrated the first example of an excited state that was radically different in its geometry from the ground state. The excited state of acetylene was found to have a bent geometry, whereas the ground state is linear. In the field of reaction mechanisms, major advances were the identification of the nitronium ion, NO_2^+, as the active reagent in the nitric acid nitration reaction of aromatic molecules, and the general elucidation of the mechanisms of these reactions. In 1949 Ingold wrote twenty-two papers on this subject which were published in 1950 in the *Journal of the Chemical Society*, running consecutively and occupying 285 pages.

In 1950 Ingold spent four months at Cornell University during which time he wrote his *magnum opus*, *Structure and Mechanism in Organic Chemistry*, published in 1953. It immediately assumed the status of 'bible' of organic chemistry in the Western world and eventually in the communist world, where Ingold's ideas had long been resisted. Ingold was finally received in Moscow in 1959, the year after he received a knighthood, and his book sold out on the first day of its publication in the USSR.

Later research and retirement During the 1950s and 1960s Ingold worked, in conjunction with R. Cahn and V. Prelog, on the sequence rule for the specification of the positions of four different groups tetrahedrally bonded to a chiral carbon atom. Since the mid-1950s their CIP sequence rule has been used throughout the world to specify the R (*rectus*) or S (*sinister*) handedness of a chiral (optically active) molecule.

Ingold officially retired in 1961 but University College continued to appoint him annually as a special lecturer. He continued to lecture there and to accept invitations to speak around the world. He gave his last major talk in Venice in June 1970, and then commenced a gentle decline leading to his death at his home of forty years at 12 Handel Close, Edgware, on 8 December 1970. The cause of death was recorded as cerebrovascular degeneration and arteriosclerosis.

Ingold received a great many honours, awards, honorary degrees, and visiting lectureships during his lifetime. His contribution to chemistry was succinctly encapsulated in the citation for the royal medal awarded to him by the Royal Society in 1952: 'it would be fair to say that no man has contributed with such detailed exactness and with such breadth of theoretical vision to our knowledge of the mechanism of organic reactions as has Ingold.'

KENNETH T. LEFFEK

Sources K. T. Leffek, *Sir Christopher Ingold: a major prophet of organic chemistry* (1996) · C. W. Shoppee, *Memoirs FRS*, 18 (1972), 349–411 · b. cert. · ICL, archives · D. Ingold, *Miscellany*, 23 (1971–2) [journal of the Ealing Arts Club] · private information (2004) · d. cert. · m. cert. · d. cert. [Edith Hilda Ingold] · b. cert. [Harriet Walker Newcomb, mother] · d. cert. [Harriet Walker Ingold, mother] · d. cert. [William Kelk Ingold, father] · m. cert. [William Kelk Ingold, father] · Sandown School archives, Isle of Wight · Hartley College archives, Southampton, Hampshire · b. cert. [co-s 56153: E. H. Ingold]

Archives Bodl. Oxf., corresp. with C. A. Coulson · RS, corresp. with Sir Robert Robinson

Likenesses Elliott & Fry, photograph, NPG [*see illus.*] · photographs, priv. coll.

Wealth at death £31,163: probate, 30 April 1971, *CGPLA Eng. & Wales*

Ingold, (Edith) Hilda, Lady Ingold (1898–1988). *See under* Ingold, Sir Christopher Kelk (1893–1970).

Ingoldisthorpe, Thomas of (*d.* 1291), bishop of Rochester, was probably a native of Norfolk and a member of the family of this name which provided county sheriffs in the 1220s and 1230s. He is almost certainly the M. Thomas Ingaldthorp, clerk, professor of civil law, who was chaplain to Octavianus Ubaldini, cardinal-deacon of Santa Maria in via Lata, in April 1261; at this time he received a papal dispensation on account of illegitimacy, thus opening the way to promotion to higher office, for which his studies, probably undertaken during this period abroad, would also have prepared him. Five years later he was archdeacon of Sudbury, and by 17 April 1268 he had changed dioceses to become archdeacon of Middlesex. Continuing family interests and connections may be inferred from a charter granting land at Dersingham near Ingoldisthorpe to Binham Priory, in which his name appears next to a *dominus* John de Ingoldesthorp. He was keeper of the spiritualities of London diocese during the vacancy of that see in 1274 and was elected dean of St Paul's Cathedral three years later, when he was described as holding the prebend of Newington. His election as bishop of Rochester, in succession to John Bradfield, occurred shortly before 9 July 1283, as the consequence of Archbishop Pecham's refusal to accept the chapter's previous choice. He made his profession of obedience to Canterbury on 26 September and his consecration probably followed on the same day, or perhaps on 3 October.

Within a few months Ingoldisthorpe found himself at odds with his monastic cathedral chapter. The prior was made to resign because of illegitimacy, and the monks objected to the bishop's selection of secular officers for the priory, and to his disregard of some of their rights and privileges. Appeal to the archbishop by both parties resulted in a severe reprimand for Ingoldisthorpe, who submitted to the judgment against him, harboured no ill feeling, and gave heed to wiser counsel from then on. The other dispute recorded by the Rochester annalist was a conflict with the abbot of St Augustine's, Canterbury, and the king. Entering into controversy with the abbot over a royal levy imposed on temporalities that involved abbey possessions within Rochester diocese, Ingoldisthorpe proceeded to exercise his power of excommunication until Edward I himself intervened and denounced his action; without delay he acceded to the royal command.

In 1283–4 Ingoldisthorpe acted as the archbishop's commissary in reconciling two churches polluted by bloodshed, St Mary-le-Bow in London and Maidstone in Canterbury diocese. He seems to have gone abroad for the next two years, 1285–6, as he appointed attorneys for this period in his absence; his return by 1 June 1287 is indicated by his presence in Canterbury at the episcopal profession on this date. He died on 11 or 12 May 1291, and was interred on the 17th in an altar tomb with effigy on the south side of the high altar of his cathedral. The Rochester annalist warmly commends him as 'a praiseworthy, mild and friendly man, a reverencer of the Trinity, agreeable, cheerful, and bountiful at table' (*Flores historiarum*, 3.72–3).

JOAN GREATREX

Sources J. Thorpe, ed., *Registrum Roffense, or, A collection of antient records, charters and instruments … illustrating the ecclesiastical history and antiquities of the diocese and cathedral church of Rochester* (1769) · [J. de Westerham], *Custumale Roffense*, ed. J. Thorpe (1788) · H. R. Luard, ed., *Flores historiarum*, 3 vols., Rolls Series, 95 (1890) · F. N. Davis and D. L. Douie, eds., *The register of John Pecham*, 2 vols., CYS, 64–5 (1908–69) · *Fasti Angl., 1066–1300*, [Monastic cathedrals] · *Fasti Angl., 1066–1300*, [St Paul's, London] · *Chancery records* · *CEPR letters*, vol. 1 · M. Richter, ed., *Canterbury professions*, CYS, 67 (1973) · A. Hughes, *List of sheriffs for England and Wales: from the earliest times to AD 1831*, PRO (1898); repr. (New York, 1963) · Binham cartulary, BL, Cotton MS Claudius D.xiii. · *Ann. mon.* · *Les registres d'Alexandre IV*, ed. C. Bourel de la Roncière and others, 2 (Paris, 1917), vol. 3 · C. Eubel and others, eds., *Hierarchia Catholica medii et recentioris aevi*, 2nd edn, 1 (Münster, 1913)
Likenesses tomb effigy, Rochester Cathedral

Ingoldsby, Sir Henry, first baronet (*bap.* 1623, *d.* 1701). *See under* Ingoldsby, Sir Richard, appointed Lord Ingoldsby under the protectorate (*bap.* 1617, *d.* 1685).

Ingoldsby, Sir Richard, appointed Lord Ingoldsby under the protectorate (*bap.* 1617, *d.* 1685), army officer and regicide, was baptized on 10 August 1617, the second son of Sir Richard Ingoldsby (*d.* 1656) of Lenborough, Buckinghamshire, and Elizabeth (*d.* 1666), daughter of Sir Oliver Cromwell, the uncle of the future lord protector. The family had been settled there since the fifteenth century; Ingoldsby's extravagant elder brother Francis had to sell the manor to his steward in the 1670s. Ingoldsby entered Gray's Inn on 4 May 1639. He was 'early attached to Puritanism' (Noble, 2.224), and married Elizabeth Lee (*d.* 1675), widowed daughter of the judge Sir George Croke, who had opposed ship money. A parliamentarian captain under his cousin John Hampden in 1642, by 1644 he was colonel of the regiment, now serving in Essex's Cornish expedition. Commanding the regiment after its transfer to the New Model, he was dispatched to the relief of Taunton and was distinguished at the storming of Bridgwater and Bristol.

Stationed at Oxford, the former royalist capital, after its fall, Ingoldsby was with the army at Saffron Walden in May 1647, and parliament attempted to dissolve his regiment. While his soldiers acquired a name for radicalism, he secured election as 'recruiter' MP for Wendover on 4 October. He was chosen as a judge for Charles I's trial, but only turned up to sign the death warrant [*see also* Regicides]. He later claimed he had refused to sign but Cromwell seized his hand and traced out his signature; his handwriting does not support this. Mutinous soldiers took him by surprise in September 1649 at Oxford, but he was rescued by Captain Wagstaff and speedily regained control. The regiment was dispatched to Scotland in 1651 and provided drafts for service at sea in February 1652. He was entrusted with the Tower of London during that summer's parliamentary recess, and on 24 November was appointed to the council of state for the following year. On 20 April 1653 he warned Cromwell of the Rump Parliament's attempt to retain power, precipitating its dissolution.

Trusted implicitly by Cromwell and his sons but not on their councils of state, Ingoldsby was prominent on local committees in Buckinghamshire, where he resided from 1651, at Waldridge. He represented Buckinghamshire in parliament in 1654 and 1656. In 1655 he switched his foot regiment for one of horse, and in December 1657 he was called to the upper house as Richard, Lord Ingoldsby. But his political and religious attitudes put him at variance with the radicals, as did his humour. In June 1654 Cromwell allegedly reprimanded him following an incident in which a Baptist claimed that Ingoldsby's parliamentary election would harm the Baptists, whereupon Ingoldsby offered to provide a practical demonstration and proceeded to box his ears. In 1657 he was one of only two officer MPs to support Cromwell becoming king. He was not invited to an important army prayer meeting as Cromwell was dying, and his isolation became more pronounced under Richard Cromwell. In a personal challenge, radical officers inspired his subordinate Cornet Sumpter to make official representations against his new, ex-royalist major. Richard Cromwell personally backed Ingoldsby, and according to Ludlow put his hand on his shoulder saying, 'Here is Dick Ingoldsby who can neither pray nor preach, and yet I will trust him before ye all' (*Memoirs of Edmund Ludlow*, 2.63).

Deprived of his regiment on Richard's removal, Ingoldsby turned towards royalism and in July offered his services if Richard was made the king's commander-in-chief. Despite the hostility caused by his role in 1649, by December he was encouraging Whitelocke to hand the great seal to the king. According to Clarendon and the earl of Northampton, he recognized the possibility of Charles's triumph leading to his execution, but gambled on proving his repentance. He had his chance when Monck restored him to his regiment in February 1660, and on 18 April he was sent after the fugitive General John Lambert to halt the final military threat to Charles's return. He caught Lambert and captured him in a skirmish outside Daventry on 22 April, rejecting Lambert's offer to support Richard Cromwell. On 26 April the Convention, in which he represented Aylesbury with his stepson Thomas Lee, voted thanks for his 'late great and eminent services to this Nation' (*JHC*, 8.2). He was added to the Act of Indemnity on 7 December, retained his English and Irish estates despite royalist claims, and was even made a knight of the Bath at the king's coronation. In addition to this unique honour for a regicide he served as gentleman of the privy chamber; his shameless claim that Cromwell had forced him to sign the death warrant may have caused ridicule, but Charles II saw fit to accept it.

Retaining his seat at Aylesbury, as Lee's junior, in the Cavalier Parliament and the three Exclusion Parliaments, Ingoldsby became deputy lieutenant for Buckinghamshire, and in January 1667 his regiment was briefly re-formed at the height of the emergency of the Second Anglo-Dutch War. He drifted into opposition in the 1670s, losing his place as JP in 1670 for religious reasons and being dismissed as deputy lieutenant in 1680 for supporting Shaftesbury. The projected marital alliance of his daughter and Whitelocke's son in 1671 collapsed due to his and his wife's 'high terms'. James II reckoned him dangerous enough to be lodged in the Tower briefly during Monmouth's rebellion. He died on 9 September 1685 and was buried at Hartwell, Lee's estate, with his wife. He had maintained a private Independent chaplain for years, and two prominent Presbyterians were among his executors. His son Richard succeeded him at Waldridge and died in 1703. A career soldier, loyal Cromwellian, and political moderate, his lack of religious zeal and refusal to equivocate undermined his effectiveness in 1659. He was not devoid of principles, and his ingenuity in explaining away his actions in January 1649 is blatant but effective.

Sir Henry Ingoldsby, first baronet (*bap.* 1623, *d.* 1701), army officer, was baptized on 16 January 1623 at Buckingham church, the younger brother of Sir Richard. He was a parliamentarian colonel when he volunteered to lead a regiment to Ireland in May 1647. Serving under Cromwell at Drogheda and Ireton at Limerick, he inflicted a decisive defeat on Colonel Richard Grace in the west midlands in June 1652. He acquired an uncompromising reputation and was accused by Clarendon of barbarity. He used his governorship of Limerick to acquire large estates in Clare and co. Meath, successfully petitioning Cromwell for lands valued at £2544 9s. 2d.

MP for counties Clare, Limerick, and Kerry in 1654, 1656, and 1659, on Richard Cromwell's deposition Ingoldsby sped the news to Henry Cromwell and promised to resist the generals 'to the wearing out of his old shoes' (*CSP dom.*, 1659–60, 19). Deprived of his command, he slipped over to England in December 1659 and seized Windsor Castle with its arsenal for parliament at a crucial moment. Accordingly on 22 May 1660, the Convention recommended to Monck his restoration to Limerick, and in April 1661 the king permitted him and his brother Richard to retain Irish lands valued at £4500. Charles also confirmed his Cromwellian baronetcy. He joined the Irish privy council, and sat in parliament for County Clare in 1661–6 and 1695–9. He raised a regiment for William III in 1689–90, which served in Ireland under Schomberg. He died late in March 1701; his wife, Ann, daughter of Sir Hardress Waller, died in 1709 and the baronetcy expired with his son William in 1726.   TIMOTHY VENNING

Sources M. Noble, *Memoirs of the protectoral-house of Cromwell*, 2 vols. (1787) · *A second narrative of the late parliament* (1658) · *The memoirs of Edmund Ludlow*, ed. C. H. Firth, 2 vols. (1894) · C. H. Firth and G. Davies, *The regimental history of Cromwell's army*, 2 vols. (1940) · HoP, *Commons, 1660–90*, vols. 1–2 · *A collection of original letters and papers, concerning the affairs of England from the year 1641 to 1660. Found among the duke of Ormonde's papers*, ed. T. Carte, 2 vols. (1739) · *DNB* · CSP dom., 1641–85 · CSP Ire., 1647–70 · J. T. Gilbert, ed., *A contemporary history of affairs in Ireland from 1641 to 1652*, 3 vols. (1879–80) · Bodl. Oxf., MSS Rawl. A. 259, C. 179 · *The diary of Bulstrode Whitelocke, 1605–1675*, ed. R. Spalding, British Academy, Records of Social and Economic History, new ser., 13 (1990) · *The writings and speeches of Oliver Cromwell*, ed. W. C. Abbott and C. D. Crane, 4 vols. (1937–47) · Pepys, *Diary*, vol. 8 · JHC, 7–8 (1651–67) · GEC, *Baronetage* · GEC, *Peerage* · W. H. Rylands, ed., *The visitation of the county of Buckingham*</br>

made in 1634, Harleian Society, 58 (1909) · *VCH Buckinghamshire*, vol. 3 · C. Polizzotto, 'Ingoldsby, Sir Richard', Greaves & Zaller, *BDBR*, 2.128–9
Archives Bodl. Oxf., material on involvement with royalists 1659, Rawl. MSS A. 259, C.179
Wealth at death estate at Waldridge, Buckinghamshire; also lands in Ireland, including Limerick (house); Ballybeg/Beggstown, Meath; Clonderalaw and Cratloe, Clare; lands retained as of 1661 value £4500: CSP Ire., 1647–70; GEC, vol. 3

Ingoldsby, Richard (1664/5–1712), army officer, was the son of Major Sir George Ingoldsby (*b. c.*1624, *d.* in or after 1678) of Ballybricken, co. Limerick, and his wife, Mary, daughter of James Gould. Having entered Charles II's Irish army before June 1678, and still serving under James II in June 1686, Ingoldsby quit Ireland during the troubles of James's reign and joined his uncle Sir Henry *Ingoldsby (*bap.* 1623, *d.* 1701) [*see under* Ingoldsby, Sir Richard] in raising a regiment in Staffordshire. He participated in the initial stages of the duke of Schomberg's Irish campaign and saw action on 24 November 1689 at Newry. It was intended that Richard, commissioned as major on 8 March 1689, would succeed his uncle as colonel, and a colonel's commission for Richard Ingoldsby is dated 8 November 1689; but in January 1690 the depleted regiment of Sir Henry Ingoldsby was disbanded before any change in its command became apparent. Richard Ingoldsby claimed in a petition that he had served in Ireland as a volunteer, at his own charge, as major and then as colonel, but had never received any pay, and was out of pocket by £11,000. Schomberg, writing to the king on 9 January 1690, observed that Colonel Sir Henry Ingoldsby's nephew was fit for a regiment; but none being immediately available Ingoldsby returned to England, taking no further part in the Irish campaign, and occupying himself with a petition to the House of Lords concerning his Irish property. Military employment came to him again on 30 June 1692, when, on the nomination of Meinhard Schomberg, duke of Leinster, he was appointed adjutant-general of the expedition to the coast of France. On 28 February 1693 he was appointed colonel of the Royal Welch Fusiliers, and commanded that regiment under King William in Flanders, being present at the siege of Namur. On 1 June 1696 he became a brigadier-general.

On 28 December 1697 Ingoldsby conveyed a challenge from Lord Kerry to John Methuen, for which action—the recipient of the challenge being the Irish lord chancellor—he was briefly committed to the Tower. Having left once more for Ireland with his regiment in the following year he was made constable of Limerick Castle on 17 October 1700. On 5 January 1701 care of the army in Ireland was entrusted jointly to him and to Brigadier Tiffin. Ingoldsby was appointed one of the original trustees and overseers of barracks on 12 February 1701; sworn a privy councillor in Ireland; and elected for Limerick in the Irish parliament of 1703.

Ingoldsby had command of the troops sent from Ireland to the Netherlands in November 1701. In the following years he divided his time between Ireland and the continent, declining in 1702 an offer to become governor of

Jamaica. Marlborough, under whom he commanded a division from 1702 to 1706, called him an 'extraordinary good man', 'a very brave, and a very honest man' (Snyder, 1.101). At the battle of Blenheim, Ingoldsby was second in command of the first line under Charles Churchill. Created a major-general on 9 March 1702, he was advanced on 1 January 1704 to what proved to be his final rank of lieutenant-general, although in the last months of his life he was writing to Harley seeking to be made a full general. On 1 April 1705 he was transferred from the colonelcy of the Royal Welch Fusiliers to that of the 18th Royal Irish foot, and on 30 July became master-general of the ordnance in Ireland. In 1706, besides organizing reinforcements for Marlborough's army and the purchase of muskets in the Netherlands, he commanded the British troops at the siege of Ath.

In February 1707, shortly after the death in office of Lord Cutts, commander-in-chief in Ireland, Luttrell recorded that Ingoldsby was to be his successor. The appointment, which came on 21 October 1707, inspired a publication in verse. Capable and ambitious, Ingoldsby enjoyed the friendship, and could command the support, of Marlborough and Ormond. In the absence of successive lords lieutenant, he acted on five occasions as one of the lords justices of Ireland. On 17 October 1711 Ormond, in asking that Ingoldsby be given a viscountcy, observed that he was 'truly devoted to her Majesty's service' and had 'estates sufficient to support the honour' (*Portland MSS*, 5.102). Swift, who mocked Ingoldsby, had heard that he was 'to be made a lord' (Swift, 2.405), but the honour was frustrated by the death of its intended recipient. On 29 January 1712 Ingoldsby, aged forty-seven, succumbed at his home in Mary Street, Dublin, to 'a quinsey in his throat after five days' illness' (*Frankland-Russell-Astley MSS*, 203). He was accorded a state funeral and was buried in Christ Church, Dublin, on 9 February 1712. He was survived by his wife, Frances (*d*. 1718), daughter of James Nap(p)er of Loghcrew in co. Meath, and by a son, Henry (*d*. 1757), of Carrtown, co. Kildare, who married Catherine Phipps.

Ingoldsby had a contemporary namesake in the service, with whom he is apt to be confused. This was the Major Richard Ingoldsby who on 10 September 1690 was appointed 'captain of the foot company lately raised for service at New York' (Dalton, *English Army Lists*, 3.162), and who on 17 March 1691 wrested from Jacob Leisler the control of Fort James on Manhattan Island. This Ingoldsby, whose relationship to the lieutenant-general is unclear, was afterwards lieutenant-governor of the province of New York, and died a colonel in 1719.

Richard Ingoldsby (1690?–1759), army officer, was probably the son of Richard Ingoldsby (1654–1703) of Waldridge, Buckinghamshire, and his wife, Mary, daughter of William Colmore of Warwick. Sir Richard *Ingoldsby (bap. 1617, d. 1685) the regicide was his grandfather, and Lieutenant-General Richard Ingoldsby his father's cousin. He was appointed ensign in the latter's regiment, the 18th foot, on 29 March 1707, lieutenant on 28 August 1708, and captain on 24 May 1711.

On 11 June 1715, as 'Captain Ingoldsby of Stearne's Foot',

he was transferred to the Grenadier Guards (Dalton, *George the First's Army*, 1.187), of which regiment on 16 November 1739 he became '2nd major' with the rank of colonel. He served in Flanders, and on 25 February 1744 was appointed by the duke of Cumberland a brigadier of foot. At Fontenoy (11 May 1745) Ingoldsby was stationed on the right flank of the British front with orders to take the redoubt d'Eu. French light troops stationed nearby in the wood of Barré, less numerous than their fire suggested, caused Ingoldsby, who was wounded, to fall back and ask for artillery. The battle was lost. On 15 July 1745 Ingoldsby was found guilty before a court martial of not having obeyed the duke of Cumberland's orders, and was sentenced 'to be suspended from pay and duty during his highness's pleasure' (Maclachlan, 192). The duke gave Ingoldsby three months to dispose of his company and retire, which he did; but George II refused to allow him to dispose of the regimental majority. Ingoldsby appealed to the duke of Cumberland and his case was debated in print. 'By consent of all the British commanders it was Ingoldsby's misunderstanding of his orders and his failure to capture the Redoubt d'Eu that lost the battle' (Fortescue, *Brit. army*, 2.119–20). Standing under no imputation of cowardice, but burdened with the 'error in judgment' (ibid., 2.120) that had precipitated 'England's greatest defeat since Hastings' (Maclachlan, 100), the brigadier-general died at his home in Lower Grosvenor Street, London, on 8 December 1759 and was buried on 16 December at the family seat, Hartwell, Buckinghamshire. His widow, named in the burial register Catherine, died on 28 January 1789, and was buried in the same place.

H. M. CHICHESTER, *rev.* KENNETH FERGUSON

Sources W. Betham, 'Pedigree of the family of Ingoldsby', NL Ire., MS 7340 · C. Dalton, *Irish army lists, 1661–1685* (1907) · C. Dalton, ed., *English army lists and commission registers, 1661–1714*, 6 vols. (1892–1904) · *The Marlborough–Godolphin correspondence*, ed. H. L. Snyder, 3 vols. (1975), 7, 77–8, 95, 101, 417, 504, 536, 542, 602, 637, 690, 846, 874, 881,1344 · *The letters and dispatches of John Churchill, first duke of Marlborough, from 1702 to 1712*, ed. G. Murray, 5 vols. (1845), vol. 1, pp. 401, 407; vol. 2. p. 599; vol. 4, pp.179, 473, 638; vol. 5, pp.20, 42 · P. B. Eustace, ed., *Registry of deeds Dublin: abstracts of wills*, vol. 1: *1708–1745* (1956), 26, 260 · NL Ire., genealogical MS 141, fol. 218 · M. Noble, *Memoirs of the protectoral-house of Cromwell*, 2 vols. (1807), vol. 2, pp.181–91 · J. T. Gilbert, *A history of the city of Dublin*, 3 vols. (1861), vol. 1, pp.126–7 · *The manuscripts of the marquis of Ormonde*, [old ser.], 3 vols., HMC, 36 (1895–1909), vol. 1, pp. 406, 427, 444; vol. 2, pp. 217, 224, 353 · *CSP dom., 1678–1712* · N. Luttrell, *A brief historical relation of state affairs from September 1678 to April 1714*, 6 vols. (1857) · A. N. C. Maclachlan, *William Augustus, duke of Cumberland* (1876), 65, 100, 189–92 · C. Dalton, *George the First's army, 1714–1727*, 2 vols. (1910–12) · J. Swift, *Journal to Stella*, ed. H. Williams, 2 vols. (1958), vol. 1, pp.129–30, 254, 350; vol. 2, pp. 405, 476 · A. Croke, *The genealogical history of the Croke family originally named Le Blount*, 2 vols. (1823), vol. 2, pp. 616–27 · F. W. Hamilton, *The origin and history of the first or grenadier guards*, 2–3 (1874), vol. 2, pp.118–26; vol. 3, pp. 445, 503 · Fortescue, *Brit. army*, 2.112–20 · R. Lascelles, ed., *Liber munerum publicorum Hiberniae … or, The establishments of Ireland*, later edn, 2 vols. in 7 pts (1852), vol. 2, pp.10, 103, 113, 117 · *The manuscripts of his grace the duke of Portland*, 10 vols., HMC, 29 (1891–1931), vol. 5, pp. 74, 102; vol. 10, pp. 68, 72 · *GM*, 1st ser., 29 (1759), 606 · *Calendar of the manuscripts of the marquess of Ormonde*, new ser., 8 vols., HMC, 36 (1902–20), vol. 7, p. 353 · BL, Add. MS 34195, fol. 124 · *Thirteenth*

report, HMC (1892), 245 · *Report on the manuscripts of Mrs Frankland-Russell-Astley of Chequers Court, Bucks.*, HMC, 52 (1900), 203
Archives BL, corresp. with Ormond, 1710, Add. MS 35933, fols. 22, 23

Ingoldsby, Richard (1690?–1759). *See under* Ingoldsby, Richard (1664/5–1712).

Ingram [Ingelram] (d. 1174), bishop of Glasgow, is of unknown origins, but his own name and those of his brothers, Simon and William, suggest that they were immigrants to Scotland. He was first clerk and then chancellor to Earl Henry, King David's son, from about 1140 until the earl's death on 12 June 1152, after which he served Malcolm IV as clerk, sometimes misleadingly called chancellor, until formally appointed to the latter office in 1161–2. He had been given the archdeaconry of Glasgow, and when the archbishop of York tried to act as legate to Scotland in the summer of 1164 (the sees of St Andrews and Glasgow being vacant), Ingram led a delegation to Norham to reject his pretensions and appeal to Rome. After some weeks he was elected bishop of Glasgow, probably on 13 September 1164; he was ordained priest six days later and obtained consecration from Pope Alexander III at Sens on 28 October. By then he had given up the chancellorship.

Ingram's representations to the pope were remarkably successful, for York failed in its claims from 1164 until their formal rejection in 1176. Apart from obtaining three bulls confirming the possessions of the see, he left little trace in the records of Glasgow and is not known to have encouraged the development of its chapter. As diocesan he probably participated at the establishment of a Cluniac priory at Paisley about 1169, and he presided at the opening of the tomb of Waltheof, abbot of Melrose, in 1171. In 1173 he vainly opposed King William's alliance with the young King Henry and his war with Henry II, which earned him the description of 'best of the clergy' from the chronicler Jordan Fantosme. But 'best of the administrator–politicians' would be a better modern assessment of a cleric who came to high ecclesiastical office too late to discharge its duties with any enthusiasm. He died on 2 February 1174, at a place unknown, after which the king plundered the possessions of the see.

A. A. M. DUNCAN

Sources J. Dowden, *The bishops of Scotland … prior to the Reformation*, ed. J. M. Thomson (1912), 297–8 · O. Engels and others, eds., *Series episcoporum ecclesiae Catholicae occidentalis*, 6th ser., 1, ed. D. E. R. Watt (1991), 59–60 · N. F. Shead, 'Origins of the medieval diocese of Glasgow', *SHR*, 48 (1969), 220–25 · N. F. Shead, 'The administration of the diocese of Glasgow in the twelfth and thirteenth centuries', *SHR*, 55 (1976), 127–50 · G. W. S. Barrow, ed., *Regesta regum Scottorum*, 1 (1960), 17, 28–9, 79, 108

Ingram [née Howard; *other married name* Douglas], **Anne**, **Viscountess Irwin** [Irvine] (c.1696–1764), poet, was born probably in Naworth, the second daughter and third child of Charles *Howard, third earl of Carlisle (1669–1738), and his wife, Anne (1675–1752), daughter of Arthur Capel, first

Anne Ingram, Viscountess Irwin (c.1696–1764), by Jonathan Richardson the elder [with her husband, Rich, fifth Viscount Irwin]

earl of Essex, and Elizabeth Percy, daughter of Algernon Percy, tenth earl of Northumberland.

As her parents' separation by 1712 assumed permanence, Anne's sharing of her father's interests in politics, literature, and landscaping acquired a vigour that is evident in her letters to him (those less personal, more objective, printed in *Carlisle MSS*). In December 1717 she married Rich Ingram, fifth Viscount Irwin (Irvine; 1688–1721), an army officer commonly known as Lord Irwin. Their financial distress, worsened by the collapse of the South Sea venture, was promised relief through his appointment in 1720 as governor of Barbados. Yet before they could sail he died of smallpox on 10 April 1721, leaving Anne childless to settle with the creditors.

In 1730 a trip through the Low Countries and France further developed Irwin's independence. In 1732, back in England, she published the anonymous *Castle-Howard*, a poem in heroic couplets that honoured Carlisle's character, his retirement from court, and creative management of the architecture, landscaping, and staff of their family seat. She saluted what she considered his English sensitivity to natural energies in the landscape. Admiration for Pope's verse prompted her response to his *Epistle to a Lady: on the Characters of Women*; her 'Epistle to Mr Pope. By a Lady' presumably first appeared in the *Gentleman's Magazine* for December 1736. Certainly later (if not already) an acquaintance of Pope, she attempted to tease him away from notions of innate gender differences:

In *Education* all the *Diff'rence* lies:
… A *Female Mind* like a rude *Fallow* lies,

Thorns there—& Thistles—all spontaneous rise.
… Culture improves all Soils.
(BL, Add. MS 28101, fol. 100v; the manuscript version of the text differs importantly from the version printed in GM)

Where Pope had focused on feminine caprice a male perspective shifting between fawning and scorn, Irwin distinguished the genders mainly by differing styles of a drive to power.

When Queen Caroline in 1736 sent Irwin to fetch Augusta of Saxe-Gotha to marry her son Frederick, prince of Wales, Irwin wrote,

she desired me in the strongest terms to recommend to the Princess to avoid jealousy, and to be easy in regard to amours, which she said had been her conduct, and had consequently procured her the happy state she had enjoyed for so many years. (Carlisle MSS, 167)

Irwin continued to attend Princess Augusta as lady of the bedchamber through the 1750s. On 11 June 1737 Irwin married a member of the prince's household, Colonel William Douglas, briefly piquing her father and siblings. Together they weathered the royal family's intergenerational feuds. Douglas rose to brigadier-general, serving on the continent with the allied army from 1742 until his death from a fever in August 1747. Irwin had his body returned for burial on 25 January 1748 in the chapel near their home at Kew where she herself was buried after her own death on 2 December 1764.

Beyond her shorter verse, and letters like her own reliving narrow escapes from highwaymen or seeking her father's blessing on her second marriage, Lady Irwin's characteristic high spirits are chronicled in the correspondence of Carlisle's architect Sir John Vanbrugh, one of John Nichols's subjects, and Horace Walpole.

RICHARD QUAINTANCE

Sources The manuscripts of the earl of Carlisle, HMC, 42 (1897), 98 [Ingram's authorship of Castle-Howard is confirmed] · T. Park, 'Anne Howard, Viscountess Irwin', in A catalogue of the royal and noble authors of England, Scotland, and Ireland … by the late Horatio Walpole, ed. T. Park, 5 (1806), 155–7 · J. Duncombe, The feminiad: a poem (1754), ll. 175–86 · Lady Mary Wortley Montagu: essays and poems and 'Simplicity, a comedy', ed. R. Halsband and I. Grundy (1977), 257–8 · K. Downes, Sir John Vanbrugh: a biography (1987), 539–40 · Nichols, Illustrations, 5.22–3 · Walpole, Corr., 9.207 · J. Todd, ed., A dictionary of British and American women writers, 1660–1800 (1984) · C. Dalton, George the First's army, 1714–1727, 1 (1910), 156 (n. 1), 178–9, 269 [Lord Irwin and Colonel Douglas] · C. Saumarez Smith, The making of Castle Howard (1990) · T. Gent, Pater patriae: being, an elegiac dialogue [on the] death of … Charles Howard earl of Carlisle (1738) · C. N. Thomas, Alexander Pope and his eighteenth-century women readers (1994), 146–50

Archives Castle Howard, North Yorkshire, letters, J8/1 | BL, A[shley] Cowper, Add. MSS 28, 101, fols. 99v–101v · BL, Taylor papers, Add. MS 37684, fol. 4b

Likenesses engraving, pubd 1806 (after Phillips), repro. in Walpole, Catalogue of the royal and noble authors of England · J. Richardson the elder, portrait, Temple Newsam House, Leeds [see illus.]

Wealth at death generous legacies to own relatives and those of both husbands: will, PRO, PROB 11/904, sig. 470

Ingram, Archibald (c.1699–1770), tobacco merchant and civic leader, rose to prominence from obscure origins, possibly in Ayrshire. He started in business as a street vendor while a boy and then married an armourer's daughter, Janet Simpson (d. 1742), on 16 August 1727, becoming a Glasgow burgess through her right. When Janet died in February 1742, after giving birth to nine children, he made a very good second marriage on 24 April 1743 to Rebecca Glassford (d. 1774), sister of John Glassford of Dougalston, a leading Glasgow tobacco magnate. He was never a partner in Glassford's main concern, though they entered into partnerships in other ventures.

Ingram's primary business was the Pollokshaws Print-Field Co., the pioneer firm in what would become a major Glasgow industry. In 1743 he bought 30 acres of land in then rural Pollokshaws in conjunction with Glassford. The linen trade was booming, but only coarse semi-bleached webs were being marketed. Ingram new-turfed a bleachfield, diverted a burn to make reservoirs, and trained workmen to hand-spin and weave finer cloth, and to bleach and dye. He printed linen, and later cotton, first with wooden blocks, then with copper plates, and finally with copper cylinders. Although he initially lost money, his faith in the product was justified by eventual large profits through domestic and colonial sales. Ingram also had a major share in an inkle manufactory, making linen tapes of all strengths on machinery smuggled into Britain from Holland in 1741, as well as in a stocking manufactory, Graham Liddell & Co., and in tobacco concerns. In November 1750 he was a founding member of the Glasgow Arms Bank, established by a co-partnery of Glasgow merchants to provide a circulating medium and credit.

Ingram was civic-minded, serving as a bailie on the town council in 1753–4 and then as lord provost in 1762–3 and 1763–4. He was also a man of taste. He owned a large library, contributed to an assembly hall for dancing that was begun in 1757, and, with John Glassford, financed Robert and Andrew Foulis's scheme to establish their fine arts academy in Glasgow in 1753, nine years before the opening of the Royal Academy in London. During his term as provost, in April 1764, the town's first playhouse burnt down in a riot on its opening night, after it was denounced as a 'temple of Satan' by pious critics. Shortly afterwards a concert hall was successfully opened with the provost's blessing. Ingram promoted tree-planting and housing development around Glasgow Green. In 1764 he attempted to protect the water quality and flow of the Molendar Burn (and the River Clyde into which it flowed) by leading the town council to take action against Glasgow's only water-driven sawmill, though the council was eventually required to pay its owner substantial damages after the court of session ruled in his favour.

Ingram died on 23 July 1770 at Cloberhill, in the parish of East Kilpatrick, the estate he had purchased some years earlier. He left Pollokshaw Printworks and Inkleworks to his third surviving son, James. He also owned a town house in the Back Cow Loan, Glasgow: in 1781 the town council, in the course of making improvements, drove a straight road through the loan, and called it Ingram Street. In 1818 a fanciful marble bas-relief depicting Ingram crowned by the genius of Glasgow was presented to the Merchants' House by his grandson, Robert Ingram.

MONICA CLOUGH

Sources J. R. Anderson, ed., *The provosts of Glasgow from 1609 to 1832* (1942) · T. M. Devine, *The tobacco lords: a study of the tobacco merchants of Glasgow and their trading activities, c.1740–1790* (1975) · D. R. [D. Robertson], rev., *Glasgow, past and present: illustrated in dean of guild court reports and in the reminiscences and communications of Senex, Aliquis, J.B., &c*, 3 vols. (1884) · J. O. Mitchell, *Old Glasgow essays* (1905) · C. W. Munn, *The Scottish provincial banking companies* (1981) · J. Gibson, *The history of Glasgow* (1778)
Likenesses marble bas-relief, 1809 (posthumous), Glasgow Merchants' House

Ingram, Sir Arthur (*b.* before 1571, *d.* 1642), financier and politician, was probably born in Fenchurch Street, London, the son of Hugh Ingram, a tallow chandler, and his wife, Anne, the daughter of Richard Goldthorpe, a haberdasher of York. After beginning his career as a factor in Italy, he then took over his father's moneylending business, and became comptroller of the London custom house by 1603. He lent customs receipts to courtiers and used contacts thus made to purchase trade concessions and crown lands, which he sold on through his business partner, Lionel Cranfield. His services were also used by Robert Cecil, first earl of Salisbury, who possibly engineered his return to the Commons for Stafford in 1609.

In 1611 Ingram's rapidly expanding business was saved from bankruptcy by a testimonial 'subscribed by three or four principal councillors' (*Letters of John Chamberlain*, 1.319), one of whom, Henry Howard, earl of Northampton, secured him a parliamentary seat at New Romney in 1614. Ingram gave up his customs post in 1613, when he was knighted and made secretary of the council in the north at York (a post worth £700 a year). Thomas Howard, first earl of Suffolk, whose personal finances he handled for many years, supported his purchase of the office of cofferer of the king's household in 1615, but his subordinates refused to work with him, and he was removed within months.

After his rebuff at court, Ingram invested most of his fortune in land, often exploiting the financial weakness of vendors (including his third wife's father) to drive a hard bargain. He eventually assembled an estate worth £6000 a year, and built on a lavish scale, at York and Temple Newsam, near Leeds. He leased the Yorkshire alum business from the crown in 1615; the industry grew, but was not a commercial success, although Ingram's political contacts helped him to avoid the bankruptcy which overtook one of his partners. He served as sheriff of Yorkshire in 1619–20, and canvassed for Sir Thomas Wentworth at the general election of December 1620, when he was elected for Appleby at the behest of Wentworth's father-in-law. He was returned at Appleby and Old Sarum at the next election, in 1624, but his growing local influence enabled him to sit for York in that year and in 1625, 1626, and 1628–9.

Ingram did little to stop Cranfield's impeachment in 1624, although he later helped his former partner out of the financial difficulties this caused. The removal of Cranfield's patronage allowed Ingram's enemies to wrest the alum farm from his grasp. From 1629 he found another patron in Wentworth, whom he helped to obtain farms of the Irish customs, the alum industry, and northern recusancy fines, but the two men quarrelled over the details of the last farm, and Ingram resigned the York secretaryship in 1633.

Ingram later attached himself to one of Wentworth's court opponents, Henry Rich, first earl of Holland, who probably secured his return for Windsor and Callington in the Short and Long parliaments. He attacked the secular and religious policies of the 1630s, but the evidence he gave about the Irish customs farm at Wentworth's trial was designed mainly to exonerate his own conduct.

Ingram married, first, by 1599, Susan, the daughter of Richard Brown(e) of London; secondly, in September 1613, Alice (*d.* 1614), the daughter of William Ferrers, a mercer of London, and the widow of John Halliday (or Holliday), a merchant of Bromley, Middlesex; and thirdly, in 1615, Mary, the daughter of Sir Edward Greville of Milcote, Warwickshire. There were children from each of these marriages. The king, who established his court at Ingram's house at York in the summer of 1642, offered him a peerage, but he remained active in parliament until May 1642, when he returned to York. He died there, at his home in Minster precincts, on 24 August 1642, and was buried in York Minster on 26 August. SIMON HEALY

Sources A. F. Upton, *Sir Arthur Ingram, c.1565–1642: a study in the origins of an English landed family* (1961) · R. B. Turton, *The alum farm, together with a history of the origin, development and eventual decline of the alum trade in north-east Yorkshire* (1938) · M. Prestwich, *Cranfield: politics and profits under the early Stuarts* (1966) · HoP, *Commons* · J. T. Cliffe, *The Yorkshire gentry from the Reformation to the civil war* (1969) · R. R. Reid, *The king's council in the north* (1921); facs. edn (1975) · *The letters of John Chamberlain*, ed. N. E. McClure, 2 vols. (1939) · W. A. Shaw, *The knights of England*, 2 vols. (1906) · J. Foster, ed., *Pedigrees of the county families of Yorkshire*, 3 vols. (1874) · will, PRO, PROB 11/190, sig. 107
Archives W. Yorks. AS, Leeds, corresp. and papers | CKS, letters to, and accounts with, Lionel Cranfield · York City Archives, houses book 34
Likenesses G. Geldorp, oils, Leeds City Art Gallery, Temple Newsam House, Yorkshire
Wealth at death approx. £9000 p.a.: Cliffe, *Yorkshire gentry*

Ingram, Arthur Foley Winnington- (1858–1946), bishop of London, was born on 26 January 1858 at the rectory, Stanford-on-Teme, Worcestershire, the fourth of the ten children of the rector, the Revd Edward Winnington-Ingram, and his wife, Maria Louisa, daughter of Henry *Pepys, bishop of Worcester. His father was also lord of the manor of Ribbesford. Through both parents he possessed connections with leading county families.

Winnington-Ingram was educated at Marlborough College and at Keble College, Oxford, where he gained first-class honours in classical moderations in 1879 and a second class in *literae humaniores* in 1881. Though he was to adhere broadly to the Tractarian principles he imbibed at Keble, he disavowed party labels and even described himself as an evangelical 'at heart'. Unspecified doubts about the truth of Christian doctrines at school and university delayed his ordination for three years, while he worked as a travelling tutor on the continent. Ordained deacon and priest in 1884, he served his title as assistant curate at St Mary's, Shrewsbury. The faith he now professed changed,

Arthur Foley Winnington-Ingram (1858–1946), by Olive Edis, 1923

on his own admission, not at all during the course of his long ministry. In 1885 he was appointed as domestic chaplain to W. D. Maclagan, bishop of Lichfield, whom he served for three years.

In 1888 Winnington-Ingram was appointed head of the recently founded Oxford House in Bethnal Green. This was a fortunate appointment. His uncomplicated character and sense of humour at once made him popular with people of the East End, and he transformed the work of the house within a few years by his energy and adroit use of his personal charm and social connections. By 1892 he had rebuilt the house, increased the number of residents from three to thirty, and trebled its annual income. His regular visits to Oxford colleges encouraged a stream of undergraduates to take up work in the East End. In addition to leading the clubs and charitable activities the house supported, he devoted considerable time to Christian apologetics, speaking against the secularists at open-air meetings in Victoria Park. From 1895 to 1897 he held the position of head of the house jointly with the rectory of St Matthew's, Bethnal Green.

Winnington-Ingram's success in the East End made him the obvious choice when, in 1897, Mandell Creighton, bishop of London, sought a suffragan bishop of Stepney,

to be also a canon of St Paul's. He was consecrated on St Andrew's day, 30 November 1897. His chief work as bishop was to begin a fund-raising campaign for the East London Church Fund. But his responsibilities here were short-lived: Mandell Creighton's death in 1901 gave Lord Salisbury the chance to nominate Winnington-Ingram to the see of London, and he was enthroned in St Paul's Cathedral on 30 April 1901. He held the see for thirty-eight years. He approached diocesan responsibility with characteristic energy, resisting pressure for the division of the diocese. An exacting weekly routine helped him to master a substantial volume of business. When in residence in London he visited four parishes every week to preach and meet his parish clergy. During his tenure of the see nearly 100 new parishes were created and 94 churches built. He prided himself on having ordained some 2205 men to the ministry by the time he resigned. Despite his energy he was ill at ease with matters of ecclesiastical discipline, and faced particular difficulties over militant protestant hostility to ritualist clergy. His policy of tolerating most innovations in ritual, and yet prohibiting certain practices, failed to satisfy either extreme.

The range of Winnington-Ingram's public concern was considerable. In 1917 he led the National Mission of Repentance and Hope, touring every diocese to stir up renewed zeal for the war effort, and then in 1919 led a national campaign to re-establish the Church of England Temperance Society. In London he chaired the Public Morality Council, working closely with police to close down brothels, clean up public parks, and oppose 'offensive' plays and birth control propaganda; in this work there was a somewhat rigid adherence to the values of his late Victorian upbringing. In the House of Lords he took a particular interest in the housing of the poor and in unemployment; his natural conservatism did not prevent him from speaking out against what he perceived to be social injustices, as when he attacked slum conditions in Paddington in the mid-1930s.

By far the most controversial aspect of Winnington-Ingram's episcopate was his tireless (and never modified) public advocacy of Britain's cause during the First World War. He saw the war as a 'great crusade to defend the weak against the strong' (Winnington-Ingram, 111), and accepted uncritically stories of atrocities perpetrated by German troops. In 1915 he toured the western front, in 1916 the Grand Fleet at Rosyth and Scapa Flow, and in 1918 Salonica. His skill at public speaking made him a successful recruiter of volunteers early in the war, and he took great delight in his position as chaplain to the London rifle brigade; later in the war he encouraged his own younger clergy to enlist as combatants. He had an unquestioning trust in the civilizing mission of the British empire, and freely used language about the German people which verged on xenophobia. H. H. Asquith considered that he had preached 'jingoism of the shallowest kind' throughout the war (Wilkinson, 70).

Winnington-Ingram travelled widely during his episcopate, making five trips in all to Canada and two to America. Through various official duties he built up links between the Anglican church in these countries and the Church of England. He was president of the British Columbia Association for over thirty years; his strong advocacy of English-speaking settlements in Canada, in response to immigration there from eastern Europe, was tactless and unfortunate. He extended his second visit to America, in 1926, to a tour of the Far East and Australasia the following year.

Winnington-Ingram's public reputation stood at its highest before 1918. A handsome, charismatic man, he had an ebullient, open, and straightforward personality which helped to make him a persuasive speaker. His Marlborough nickname, Chuckles, clung to him as an undergraduate and was entirely appropriate. His simplicity and boundless optimism put him at his best in situations where he was called upon to act as advocate of a particular cause, but they were positive handicaps when it came to appreciating the complexities of political and religious affairs. His failure to understand the depth of divisions within his own diocese meant that he was unable to develop a concerted policy for managing it; the discipline of the diocese seemed ever more unstable as the years passed by. He was unable to understand the mood of pessimism and disillusionment which set in after the First World War, and this, along with his essentially Victorian moral character, made him seem increasingly an anachronism in the inter-war years.

Winnington-Ingram was an enthusiastic sportsman, priding himself on his prowess at tennis and hockey, which he played into his seventies, and golf, which he played to the end of his life. His personal life was marked by moderation and simplicity. He was a teetotaller. He did not marry, though he was briefly engaged while bishop of Stepney. He resigned his see in 1939 and retired to Bournemouth, though he spent six months of the year at The Boynes, Upton-on-Severn, where he died on 26 May 1946. A private funeral service at Upton church was followed by a public one on 7 June 1946 at St Paul's Cathedral, where his remains were interred.					JEREMY MORRIS

Sources A. F. Winnington-Ingram, *Fifty years' work in London, 1889–1939* (1940) · P. Colson, *Life of the bishop of London* (1935) · S. C. Carpenter, *Winnington-Ingram* (1949) · A. Wilkinson, *The Church of England and the First World War* (1978)

Archives LPL, corresp. and papers | Borth. Inst., corresp. with second Viscount Halifax · LPL, corresp. with Lady Richardson at Duntisbourne; letters to H. R. L. Sheppard · LPL, corresp. with Temple | FILM BFI NFTVA, performance footage | SOUND BL NSA, performance recording

Likenesses H. von Herkomer, oils, 1908, Fulham Palace, London; replica, Keble College, Oxford · G. H. Neale, c.1916, London Diocesan Office · W. Stoneman, photograph, 1917, NPG · O. Edis, photograph, 1923, NPG [*see illus.*] · O. Edis, autochrome photographs, NPG · O. Edis, photographs, NPG · S. P. Hall, group portrait, watercolour (*The bench of bishops, 1902*), NPG · B. Partridge, pen-and-ink cartoon, NPG; repro. in *Punch* (16 June 1909) · J. Russell & Sons, photograph, NPG · Spy [L. Ward], caricature, chromolithograph, NPG; repro. in *VF* (23 May 1901) · P. Tonqueray, photograph, NPG · W. H., caricature chromolithograph, NPG; repro. in *VF* (22 May 1912) · E. White, portrait, priv. coll. · group portrait, photograph (*Anglican bishops*), NPG

Wealth at death £34,448 0s. 5d.: probate, 11 Sept 1946, CGPLA Eng. & Wales

Ingram, Sir Bruce Stirling (1877–1963), journalist and newspaper editor, was born in London on 5 May 1877, the second of three sons of Sir William James Ingram, first baronet (1847–1924), managing director of the *Illustrated London News* and Liberal MP, and his wife, Mary Eliza Collingwood Stirling (d. 1925). He was grandson of Herbert *Ingram, who founded the *Illustrated London News*, the world's first illustrated weekly newspaper, in 1842. Bruce Ingram was educated at Winchester College and at Trinity College, Oxford, where he took a third-class honours degree in jurisprudence (1897). After leaving Oxford he was given some technical training with a lithographic printing firm but was soon serving his journalistic apprenticeship by editing, with the help of a secretary and an office boy, the *English Illustrated Magazine*, and by producing, for the *Illustrated London News*, a special supplement on the war in Transvaal. He clearly impressed the directors with his journalistic potential, for when the editorship of the paper became vacant in 1900 he was offered the post, at first on a probationary basis.

As grandson of the founder Ingram may have been fortunately placed to have won so distinguished a position at the age of twenty-two, but he was quick to justify the family's confidence and to demonstrate his remarkable ability to adapt an essentially Victorian publication to respond to the rapid and at times almost revolutionary changes of the twentieth century without sensationalism and without discarding its tradition and authority. He took over at a difficult time. There were strong competitors in the field, and the recent development of the photographic half-tone gave daily newspapers the opportunity of carrying regular up-to-date illustrations. For the first time the daily press could challenge the illustrated weeklies, and daily picture papers such as *The Graphic* and the *Daily Mail*, which had been launched in the last decade of the nineteenth century, became a real threat to their continued existence. Ingram responded to the challenge by concentrating on the quality of printing, reproduction, and paper, exposing the weaknesses of the high-speed newsprint processes which the dailies had to use. He adapted the slow and expensive Rembrandt intaglio for rapid printing and after much patient experiment was able to introduce the photogravure process. He had a fine chance of emphasizing his point about the value of quality on the death of Queen Victoria. The memorial issues produced to mark the end of the reign, and of an era, were strikingly successful, and afterwards became valuable collector's items. They also provided sufficient reassurance for the company that the young member of the family was capable of upholding the traditions of his grandfather. His appointment was confirmed, and within a few years he was also made editor of *The Sketch*.

When the First World War broke out Ingram was a lieutenant in the East Kent yeomanry. From 1916 until the end of the war he served in the Royal Garrison Artillery on the French front, being promoted to the rank of captain and awarded the Military Cross (1917), appointed an OBE (military, 1918), and three times mentioned in dispatches. He

Sir Bruce Stirling Ingram (1877–1963), by Walter Stoneman, 1950

was able throughout the war to keep in reasonably close contact with his office in London, and thus to supervise the paper's coverage of the war, which extended to an additional weekly supplement history of the war, published on Wednesdays, as well as the normal weekly edition, published on Fridays. Because of its fairness and the high quality of its coverage of these events the *Illustrated London News* was used by the government to help make known abroad the extent of Britain's, and the Commonwealth's, war effort. The same compliment was paid to the publication in the Second World War when Ingram, still its editor but now too old for active service, was more directly involved in the day-to-day production. During this war he never missed a day at the office, even at the height of the blitz (when a bomb destroyed most of the paper's archives).

Ingram was always an active editor, and those who worked with him recall that even in his eighties he would crawl around the floor of his editorial office laying out the photographs for each weekly issue. He was astute in his judgement of writers—he chose G. K. Chesterton in 1905 to write the weekly 'Notebook' feature, and on Chesterton's death in 1936 picked the young Arthur Bryant to succeed him. Inevitably some parts of the paper reflected some of his prejudices: he was suspicious of modern art, so Picasso was ignored; and he was tone-deaf, so music tended to be neglected. But such eccentricities did not tarnish his reputation as an editor, which rested securely on his achievements in communicating, over a

period of sixty-three years, the actuality and atmosphere of Britain, its character, temper, and achievements, in a style that was not equalled.

Two of Ingram's particular interests throughout his life were archaeology and the collecting of pictures. He had, as a youth, twice visited Egypt, and these tours stimulated a lifelong curiosity about archaeology that was reflected in the regular reports on the subject which have always been a feature of the *Illustrated London News*. When he was twenty Ingram began to collect illuminated manuscripts, but after selling his collection in 1936 he concentrated his attention on collecting paintings and drawings, particularly on marine subjects. He published, in 1936, *Three Sea Journals of Stuart Times*, based on a study of naval manuscripts and journals, and from this developed his main preoccupation as a collector. Pre-eminent among his large collection were the works of the Dutch marine artists Willem van de Velde the elder and the younger (he contributed a note on their drawings to the catalogue of an exhibition held in 1937), 700 of which were presented to the National Maritime Museum to mark his eightieth birthday; but if the Dutch and Flemish schools remained his favourites, Ingram also collected many representative works by artists less well known, and the largest part of the collection, which at one time consisted of more than 5000 works, was devoted to the English schools. Among other museums that benefited from his collection were the Fitzwilliam at Cambridge, the Birmingham Art Gallery, and the Royal Scottish Museum. During the war Ingram commissioned, and subsequently presented to the nation, the battle of Britain roll of honour in the Royal Air Force chapel in Westminster Abbey.

As a collector Ingram was exceptionally generous in his attitude to lending, and many tributes were paid both to his readiness to deprive himself of large parts of his collection so that others could see and enjoy them in public exhibitions, and to the hospitality he showed towards other collectors and students at his home in Great Pednor, Buckinghamshire. He was honorary keeper of drawings at the Fitzwilliam Museum, vice-president of the Society for Nautical Research, vice-president of the Navy Records Society, and honorary adviser on pictures and drawings to the National Maritime Museum.

As well as editor of the *Illustrated London News* from 1900 to 1963, and of the *Sketch* from 1905 to 1946, Ingram was chairman of the Illustrated London News and Sketch Ltd, director of Illustrated Sporting and Dramatic News Ltd, and president of Illustrated Newspapers Ltd. He was knighted in 1950, awarded the Légion d'honneur by the French government in the same year, and given the honorary degree of DLitt by Oxford University in 1960. He married, on 14 July 1904, Amy, daughter of John Foy; she died in 1947. On 12 November 1947 Ingram married Lily, daughter of Sydney Grundy, who died in 1962. There was one son, who died in childhood, and one daughter of the first marriage. Ingram died at his home, Great Pednor Manor, Buckinghamshire, on 8 January 1963.

JAMES BISHOP, *rev.*

Sources *The Times* (9 Jan 1963) · A. Bryant, *ILN* (2 Jan 1960) · L. Herrmann and M. Robinson, 'Sir Bruce Ingram as a collector of drawings', *Burlington Magazine* (May 1963) · private information (1981) · personal knowledge (1981) · Burke, *Peerage* (1959) · *CGPLA Eng. & Wales* (1963)
Archives NMM, naval collection
Likenesses W. Stoneman, photograph, 1950, NPG [*see illus.*]
Wealth at death £207,668 11s. 6d.: probate, 8 May 1963, *CGPLA Eng. & Wales*

Ingram, Dale (*bap.* 1710, *d.* 1793), surgeon and man-midwife, the son of William Ingram and his wife, Catherine, was baptized at Spalding, Lincolnshire on 10 September 1710. He was apprenticed and studied in the country before entering practice as a surgeon and man-midwife at Barnet, but was working at Reading, Berkshire, in 1733. On 10 October 1734 he married Ann Reynell at Christ Church Greyfriars, Newgate, London. In 1743 he published *An Essay on the Gout*. Later in that year Ingram emigrated to Barbados, where he practised until 1750, when he returned to England and set up as a surgeon and man-midwife at Tower Hill, London. In 1751 he published *Practical Cases and Observations in Surgery*, his most important work. It contains records of cases observed in England and the West Indies. He described one successful and one unsuccessful operation in cases of abdominal wounds penetrating the bowel. In the successful case he washed the intestine with hot claret, and then stitched the peritoneum to the edge of the wound and the abdominal wall.

In 1754 Ingram went to live in Fenchurch Street, London, where he lectured on anatomy. In 1755 he published *An Historical Account of the Several Plagues that have Appeared in the World since the Year 1346*. It is a mere compilation. On 24 January 1759 Ingram was elected from among five candidates to the office of surgeon to Christ's Hospital, and lived there from then on. He sometimes visited Epsom, and in 1767 published *An Enquiry as to the Origin of Magnesia Alba*, the principal saline ingredient of the Epsom springs. Following the controversy which had arisen as to the cause of death of a potman who had received a blow on the head in an election riot at Brentford in 1769, Ingram published a lengthy pamphlet entitled *The Blow, or, Inquiry into the Cause of Mr. Clarke's Death at Brentford*, which demonstrated that blood poisoning arising from an ill-dressed scalp wound was the true cause of death. His claims were rejected in *A Letter to Mr Dale Ingram. In which the Arguments he has Advanced … are Refuted* (1769). In 1777 he published *A Strict and Impartial Inquiry into the Cause of Death of the Late William Scawen*, an endeavour to prove that poison had not been administered. The following year he produced *The Art of Farriery both in Theory and Practice*. In 1790 it was stated that he was too old for his work at Christ's Hospital, and as he would not resign he was superseded in 1791. Ingram died at Epsom on 5 April 1793.

NORMAN MOORE, *rev.* MICHAEL BEVAN

Sources S. C. Lawrence, *Charitable knowledge: hospital pupils and practitioners in eighteenth-century London* (1996) · *GM*, 1st ser., 63 (1793), 380 · journals of court of governors of Christ's Hospital, GL · lists of surgeons, RCS Eng. · parish register of St Bartholomew the Less, London · parish register of St Sepulchre-extra-Newgate, London · parish register of Christ Church Greyfriars, Newgate Street, London · *IGI*

Ingram [*née* Shepheard, Gibson]**, Frances**, Viscountess Irwin (1734?–1807), landowner and political manager, may have been born on 8 August 1734, the illegitimate daughter and heir of the wealthy speculator Samuel *Shepheard (*c.*1676–1748) [*see under* Shepheard, Samuel (*c.*1648–1719)]. Her mother's name was probably Gibson, as Frances is referred to as 'Miss Frances Gibson, commonly called Shepheard' on her marriage licence (GEC, *Peerage*). Shepheard seems to have had no qualms about recognizing her as his daughter: her correspondence not only makes it clear that she received an excellent education, it also indicates that she was accepted in the best circles. Her friends included young women from the most respectable families of the political élite. Most importantly, she was worth approximately £60,000, and was good-looking, shapely, assured, and intelligent—all arguments which would have swept away lingering doubts caused by her parentage. She was painted twice by Joshua Reynolds before her marriage.

This combination of wealth and beauty made Frances one of the most sought-after young women of her day. For aristocrats with good names but empty pockets such as Charles Ingram (1727–1778), who later succeeded his uncle as ninth Viscount Irwin (more correctly Irvine), in 1763, fortune came before parentage. Her father's lawyers drove a hard bargain, though—he had left her his fortune on the conditions that she did not marry an Irishman, a Scot, a peer, or the son of a peer—and the negotiations prior to her marriage to Ingram on 28 June 1758 were both protracted and extensive. Once married and secure in her inheritance, the young couple divided their time between London and Irwin's estates, Hills, near Horsham, Sussex, and Temple Newsam, at Whitkirk, Yorkshire. At Temple Newsam, where £20,000 of her fortune was used to pay off an outstanding mortgage, Lady Irwin immediately began redecorating, rebuilding, and landscaping. While Lord Irwin was still alive, James Wyatt was hired to build a new staircase for the house and Lancelot 'Capability' Brown was employed to relandscape the park. The art collection was improved by the purchase of pieces by Titian, Rubens, and Claude, among others. It was only after Irwin died, on 19 June 1778, with no male heir (albeit five daughters) that Lady Irwin, who inherited a life interest in the estate, began rebuilding in earnest. By the time that she died, in 1807, she had torn down and rebuilt the entire south wing of Temple Newsam with architectural advice from Robert Adam and John Carr; the builder was William Johnson, of Leeds. Thomas Chippendale the younger was responsible for much of the furniture.

It was during her long widowhood that Lady Irwin truly came into her own as a political figure. As an important landholder in Yorkshire and Sussex, she took over the Irwin family interest and put the Irwin seats and influence at the service of the administration. When John Robinson made up his famous list of borough patrons before the 1784 election, he simply noted, 'Horsham is Lady Irwin's Borough' (*Parliamentary Papers*, 91). As a politically active aristocratic widow safeguarding a family interest she was not at all unusual; what was unusual was that she was preserving the interest for her eldest daughter, Isabella (1760–1834), who in 1776 had married Francis Seymour-*Conway, later second marquess of Hertford, and not for a son or grandson.

Lady Irwin's extended struggle to maintain control of the family burgage borough of Horsham proved her to be as capable a politician as any of her male counterparts. When Charles Howard, eleventh duke of Norfolk, decided to wrest the borough away from her in the lead up to the 1790 election, he acted on the advice of his new steward, Thomas Charles Medwin, an ambitious and devious young lawyer. Lady Irwin, however, was to prove a far more formidable opponent than either Medwin or Norfolk expected. By 1788 she had a lifetime's worth of political experience, and was easily a match for Norfolk. She did everything that was necessary to win votes: she gave treats and entertainments, made scores of faggot votes, outbid Norfolk for burgages at highly inflated prices (as early as 8 September 1788 the *Sussex Advertiser* remarked that the price of houses with votes in Horsham had risen 1000 per cent), and approached the independent burgesses for their support, both personally and in writing. By the time of the election her victory was guaranteed, as long as her voters could be entered on the burgage roll at a court baron. Norfolk, through Medwin, controlled both the court baron and court leet. Medwin conveniently 'fixed' the proceedings. He scheduled the court baron for 9 a.m. on the day of the election, 19 June 1790, and the election itself for 11 a.m., thus making it impossible for Lady Irwin's voters to be enrolled before the voting started. When Lady Irwin's candidates were narrowly defeated, she pursued the matter to parliament. There, Medwin's sharp dealings were quickly exposed; Norfolk's candidates were unseated and Lady Irwin's installed on 10 March 1792. The irregularities of the contest were such that it spawned nine separate actions at law, the last of which was not settled until 1802. Norfolk returned to contest the borough again in 1806. Once again, Lady Irwin's candidates lost at the poll, but this time they failed to be returned on petition, as Norfolk's allies were in power as part of the Grenville administration. Norfolk's candidates won at the 1807 general election, but Lady Irwin's nominees again petitioned and, with a Pittite-led ministry again in power, this time succeeded in taking over the seats. In the seventeen years from 1790, Norfolk had spent at least £70,000 on the borough and still did not control it. Lady Irwin had not only succeeded in preserving the family interest at Horsham for her daughter, but had also ensured that the latter would benefit financially from its sale: when Norfolk finally did purchase the borough outright from Lady Hertford, in 1810–11, he did so for the record sum of £91,475.

Lady Irwin frustrated Norfolk's best efforts because she had a better understanding of the workings of politics, locally and nationally. She had the rank, status, and finances needed to compete against him; she also had proven political loyalty and useful contacts among the followers of William Pitt the younger. Finally, as a politically active aristocratic widow she was a landowner and the recognized head of a territorial political family: the place she occupied in eighteenth-century electoral politics was both acknowledged and respected. She died at Temple Newsam on 20 November 1807, and was buried at Whitkirk. Her estates passed to her eldest daughter and her husband, who assumed the surname Ingram-Seymour-Conway. As they had no second son, Temple Newsam passed on Lady Hertford's death to Lady Irwin's second daughter, Frances, Lady William Gordon, and then in 1841 to Hugo Meynell, the son of Lady Irwin's third daughter, Elizabeth. The property was sold to the city of Leeds in 1922.

E. H. CHALUS

Sources IGI · GEC, *Peerage*, new edn, 7.71–5 · W. Albery, *A parliamentary history of the ancient borough of Horsham* (1927) · A. F. Hughes and J. Knight, *Hills: Horsham's lost stately home and garden* (1999) · www.leeds.gov.uk/templenewsam/, 4 Dec 2001 · *The letters of Bysshe and Timothy Shelley*, ed. S. B. Djabri and J. Knight (2000) · *Parliamentary papers of John Robinson, 1774–1784*, ed. W. T. Laprade, CS, 3rd ser., 33 (1922) · M. H. Port, 'Horsham', HoP, *Commons, 1790–1820*, 2.394–5

Archives Horsham Museum, Horsham, West Sussex, Hills MSS, corresp.; Medwin papers · W. Sussex RO, Du Cane papers, corresp. · W. Yorks. AS, Leeds, Temple Newsam Archives, corresp.

Likenesses J. Reynolds, oils, 1755–8 · J. Reynolds, oils, 1755–8, Muncaster Castle, Cumbria · B. Wilson, oils, *c*.1758, Temple Newsam, West Yorkshire

Wealth at death see will, PRO, PROB 11/1477, sig. 308

Ingram, Herbert (1811–1860), newspaper proprietor and politician, was the son of Herbert Ingram (*b.* 1776), butcher, and his wife, Jane, *née* Wedd (*bap.* 1787), and was born on 27 May 1811 at Paddock Grove, Boston, Lincolnshire. His father having died before Herbert was a year old, his mother was left to provide for him and his elder sister, Harriet, by her own industry, and he learned at first hand the deprivations suffered by the poor and disadvantaged. After attending Boston's charity school and the national school, he was apprenticed to the printer Joseph Clarke, Market Place, Boston. From 1832, having higher aims than to remain a provincial printer, he worked in London for two years as a journeyman, then about 1834 he set up in Nottingham as printer, newsagent, and bookseller in partnership with Nathaniel Cooke (1810–1879). Cooke married Ingram's sister, Harriet, on 31 December 1835.

Ambitious to make money fast, Ingram became an agent for aperient pills, which made good profits. By some mutually advantageous arrangement with Manchester druggist and businessman T. Roberts, he became the sole distributor of Parr's Life Pills, said to have been concocted by Shropshire man Thomas Parr (*d.* 1635, aged 152), who attributed his longevity to the regular taking of his pill. Ingram printed a fictitious 'history' of Old Parr, with accounts of supposed incidents in his life, and engaged the engraver Henry Richard Vizetelly (1820–1895) to concoct a portrait of Old Parr, which Ingram then fraudulently attributed to Rubens. Many thousands of the booklet were sold—and of the pills!

Increasing profits encouraged Ingram in his ambition to found a newspaper. Some of his customers were always eager for London news; he also noticed the interest aroused when he displayed sketches and caricatures in his shop window, and that a newspaper sold well when it contained a picture or reported a shocking crime. These observations led him to plan an illustrated paper devoted mainly to such subjects. Accordingly, the partners moved to London and rented premises in Crane Court, where the *Illustrated London News* was first printed. On the advice of some of his more experienced London friends, Ingram, reluctantly at first, agreed that the paper should be of a higher tone. Frederick William Naylor *Bayley (1808–1852), the paper's first editor, set this tone in his article on the front page of the first issue on 14 May 1842. The paper, wrote Bayley, would:

> associate its principle with a purity of tone that may secure and hold fast for our journal the fearless patronage of families; to seek in all things to uphold the cause of public morality, … and to withhold from society no point that its literature can furnish or its art adorn. (Bailey, 211)

Such principles immediately set it apart from all other journals: its impact was explosive and changed the character of printed news for all time. Huge profits accrued and Ingram enjoyed the wealth and influence for which he had always hoped. Soon, larger premises at 198 Strand were acquired.

Writers and artists of the highest order were engaged. Innovative devices were introduced, featuring special places and events: fold-outs, supplements, and commemorative numbers, for example. At the time of the Great Exhibition of 1851, with some issues printed in continental languages, weekly circulation topped 200,000 and copies reached all parts of the civilized world. The *Illustrated London News* organization also launched many other journals, and several series of high-class and educational books. Competitive papers soon appeared; some survived but the *Illustrated London News* remained supreme.

In 1846 Ingram regained Swineshead Abbey, Lincolnshire, a 'lost' early seat of the family, which it had been one of his youthful ambitions to win back. In 1848 he acquired his own paper mills near Rickmansworth. Generous with his wealth and time, he endowed a school and a church, and served as magistrate in Hertford. In 1859 he got Brunel's ship the *Great Eastern* completed and launched after insuperable difficulties had ruined its builders and the strain of which had led to the death of its designer.

Ingram also campaigned for, and put money into, Boston's waterworks (opened 1849) and railway schemes (1850–59), and became its Liberal MP in 1856, serving until his death. Had he lived, he would have supported, with his influence and money, plans for radical improvement of the port and sea channel.

In the 1850s Nathaniel Cooke and William Little became disillusioned with their roles within the business, and Cooke left about 1854—in Little's view 'degraded and ruined by Ingram'. William Little (1816–1884), who, as well as being a highly trained chemist, had considerable skills with machinery, was printer and publisher of the paper for its first fifteen years. He was able on occasion to modify the machines to increase their rates of production, and he had also at one time lent Ingram £10,000 (the repayment of which Ingram continually postponed). Little thus contributed considerably to the success of the paper. Strangely, however, his name has never been mentioned in any histories of the *Illustrated London News* beyond the fact that he printed and published it.

In 1857 Little became aware of Ingram's sexual harassment, on a number of occasions, of Emma Little (*née* Godson), the wife of Charles Henry Little, and thus his own—and Ingram's—sister-in-law. In order that the matter should not become public and bring ruin upon all, the Little family agreed that an apology from Ingram would be sufficient and the matter would be at an end. The apology was made, but Ingram, resentful of being considered blameworthy in the matter, made William Little's position in the organization more and more intolerable, to the extent of physically assaulting him in the office. Rather than risk their disagreements becoming public knowledge, Little ceased his connection with the paper in January 1858. Serious embarrassment was thus avoided, the details of the causes of their breakup coming to light only in the late 1990s. It is doubtful whether Little's loan to Ingram was ever repaid. In 1862 Little settled in Heckington, Lincolnshire, the birthplace of his wife, to follow his family's traditional occupation of farming, and he became world famous for his innovative sheep dip and other agricultural improvements.

In the 1850s John Sadleir, MP for Sligo, had used Ingram's name when setting up fraudulent companies. His perfidy discovered, Sadleir committed suicide on 16 February 1856, and documents were later found among his papers that enabled Vincent Scully, former MP for Sligo, to sue Ingram for recovery of some losses incurred by him owing to Sadleir's frauds. Though the verdict went against Ingram, both judge and jury agreed that Ingram's honour was unsullied.

These events so depressed Ingram that he decided to take a holiday, and on 8 August 1860 he and his eldest son (Herbert), aged fifteen, went to America. In Chicago he changed his original plan and took a passage on the steamer *Lady Elgin*. During a storm on Lake Michigan on the night of 8 September the vessel was sunk by a schooner. Of the 393 people on board only 98 were saved. Young Herbert's body was never found, but Ingram's was washed ashore and was brought back to England and buried on 5 October in the cemetery at Boston, where his wife and daughter, Harriet, also lie. Ingram left his entire property to his wife. A statue of Ingram was later erected in Boston's Market Place, and two lifeboats for the Lincolnshire coast were subscribed for in his memory, named after him, and presented by his wife.

On 4 July 1843 he had married William Little's sister, Ann Little (1812–1896) of Eye, Northamptonshire, and they had ten children, several being either born or baptized at Swineshead. After Ingram's death, his friend, railwayman and MP Sir Edward William *Watkin (1819–1901), gratuitously managed the business until Ingram's sons William and Charles were old enough to do so. William (1847–1924), who was created baronet in 1893, served as Liberal MP for Boston three times between 1874 and 1895. His son, Bruce (1877–1963), who was knighted in 1950, succeeded him in 1900 as proprietor of the *Illustrated London News* until his death. The last Ingram to run the paper was Hugh (1910–1994).

Herbert Ingram's youngest son, **Walter Ingram** (1855–1888), born on 21 November 1855, was a military man and was killed by an elephant while on a hunting expedition in Africa, on 6 April 1888—an accident supposedly foretold by an inscription found inside an Egyptian mummy when he unwound its wrappings. One of Ingram's daughters, Emmeline Paxton Ingram (1851–1937), married Watkin's nephew, Edgar Watkin (1860–1908); their only son was Edward Ingram *Watkin. Another dynastic tie was made in 1892 when Sir Edward William Watkin married Ann Ingram, his friend's widow, in spite of great opposition from their families. Ann Watkin died on 25 May 1896.

ISABEL BAILEY

Sources I. Bailey, *Herbert Ingram esq., M.P.: founder of 'The Illustrated London News'*, 1842 (1996) · private information (2004) · *DNB* · *ILN* (16 May 1942) · *ILN* (1992) · *ILN* (14 May 1842) · *ILN* (21 May 1853), 401 · *ILN* (25 July 1857), 94 · *ILN* (13 June 1857), 578–81 · *ILN* (20 June 1857), 603 · *ILN* (13 Aug 1859), 160 · *ILN* (17 Sept 1859), 280–81 · *ILN* (29 Sept 1860), 285 · *ILN* (11 Oct 1862), 382–3 · *Stamford Mercury* (10 Oct 1845) · *Stamford Mercury* (14 July 1849) · *White's 1856 Directory of Lincolnshire*, 291 · A. Cartwright and S. Walker, *Boston, a railway town* (1987) · *Mid-Victorian Sleaford, 1851–1871*, Lincolnshire History Series, no. 4 (1981) · *Boston poll book* (1859) · *BL cat.* · *The Times* (10 Feb 1856) · *The Times* (18 Feb 1856) · *The Times* (10 March 1856) · *The Times* (28 Dec 1883) · *The Times* (11 April 1888) · H. Herd, *The march of journalism* (1952), 154, 155, 158, 159, 164, 165, 208–13 · H. Vizetelly, *Glances back through seventy years: autobiographical and other reminiscences*, 1 (1893), 221–59, 423–7 · *The Globe* [Toronto] (12 Sept 1860) · Knight, Frank and Rutley (auctioneers), conditions of sale relating to Ingram properties in and around Boston, 1912 · *Sleaford News* (1889) · *Boston Guardian* (13 April 1859), 2 · C. Kingsley, *Alton Locke* (1890), 171–2 · *Nottingham Guardian* (21 May 1927) · C. J. Courtney Lewis, *The story of picture printing in England during the nineteenth century* [1928] · *Hansard 3* [reports of Ingram's speeches in the House of Commons] · *CGPLA Eng. & Wales* (1889)

Archives priv. coll., letters and notes

Likenesses Baxter, portrait, c.1841, priv. coll. · J. Hogg?, wood-engraving, 1841 (after daguerreotype), repro. in *ILN* (14 May 1949) · A. Munro, marble statue, 1862, Market Place, Boston, Lincolnshire · bust, c.1890, parish church, St Botolph's, Boston, Lincolnshire · portrait, 1900, repro. in *Boston Society* (1900), 11 · portrait, 1992 (after woodcut), repro. in Bailey, 'Herbert Ingram' · Smyth, wood-engraving (after photograph by J. Watkins), BM, NPG; repro. in *ILN* (6 Oct 1860) · R. Taylor and Co., wood-engraving, BM; repro. in *ILN* (14 May 1892) · J. Watkins?, portrait, repro. in *Nottingham Evening Post* (5 May 1992) · print, NPG; repro. in *Illustrated Family Paper* (27 June 1857)

Wealth at death under £90,000: probate, 15 March 1861, *CGPLA Eng. & Wales* · £1405 18s. 2d.—Walter Ingram: probate, 4 March 1889, *CGPLA Eng. & Wales*

Ingram, James (1774–1850), Old English scholar and university teacher, son of John Ingram (1713/14–1785) and Elizabeth (1734/5–1814), his wife, was born on 21 December 1774 at Codford St Mary, near Salisbury, where his family had owned property for several generations. He was sent to Warminster School in 1785, and entered as a commoner at Winchester College in 1790. On 1 February 1793 he was admitted a commoner at Trinity College, Oxford, and was elected scholar of the college on 16 June 1794. He graduated BA in 1796, MA in 1800, and BD in 1808; he was from 1799 to 1803 an assistant master at Winchester, became fellow of Trinity College on 6 June 1803, and acted as tutor there.

From 1803 to 1808 Ingram was Rawlinsonian professor of Anglo-Saxon, and in 1807 he published his inaugural lecture on the utility of Anglo-Saxon literature. When the examination for undergraduates called responsions was introduced in 1809, Ingram acted as one of the 'masters of the schools'. From 1815 to 1818 he was keeper of the archives, and from 1816 to 1824 was rector of Rotherfield Greys, a Trinity College living, near Henley-on-Thames. On 24 June 1824 he was elected president of his college, and proceeded DD on 10 July. Ingram was too deeply absorbed in antiquarian research to take much part in the management of the college or in the affairs of the university. James Pycroft amusingly recalls Ingram about 1830 as a member of the 'church militant', who had been a Cornish wrestler in his youth, and who did not hesitate to lay about errant undergraduates. He violently roused one who had fallen asleep in chapel, and scattered an elaborate breakfast which another was bringing into college (Pycroft, 1.51–8). Ingram was rector at Garsington, near Oxford, in virtue of his presidency: there he superintended and largely paid for the erection of a new school, of which he sent an account to the *Gentleman's Magazine* (2nd ser., 15, 1841).

Ingram was elected a fellow of the Society of Antiquaries in 1824, and was a notable archaeologist. As an Old English scholar he was perhaps the best of his Oxford generation, and the most distinguished of John Mitchell Kemble's predecessors. His edition of the *Saxon Chronicle* (1823) was a great advance on Gibson's 1692 edition, for Ingram had thoroughly explored the Cottonian manuscripts in the British Museum. He also published an edition of Quintilian (1809), but he became best known for his admirable *Memorials of Oxford*, with a hundred plates by Le Keux, which appeared in three volumes between 1832 and 1837 and was reissued in two volumes in 1847. His other publications included *The church in the middle centuries, an attempt to ascertain the age and writer of the celebrated 'Codex Boernerianus'* (1842), *Memorials of the Parish of Codford St Mary* (1844), and the descriptions of Oxford and Winchester cathedrals in Britton's *Beauties of England and Wales*.

Ingram died on 4 September 1850 at his Trinity College lodgings, and was buried at Garsington, where a brass plate was put up to his memory. He was married, but had no family and survived his wife. He left most of his books, drawings, and so on to Trinity College, some pictures to

James Ingram (1774–1850), by Thomas Clement Thompson, in or after 1863

the university galleries, and some coins to the Bodleian Library. Two portraits of him hung in the president's lodgings at Trinity.   W. A. GREENHILL, rev. JOHN D. HAIGH

Sources personal knowledge (1891) · private information (1891) [Professor Earle] · J. Pycroft, *Oxford memories, a retrospect*, 2 vols. (1886), 1.51–8 · Foster, *Alum. Oxon.* · *ILN* (14 Sept 1850), 222 · G. V. Cox, *Recollections of Oxford* (1868), 158 · *Oxford University Calendar* (1850) · *GM*, 2nd ser., 34 (1850), 553–5 · *GM*, 2nd ser., 15 (1841) **Archives** Bodl. Oxf., rough sketches and notes, incl. drawings of tiles and pottery found at Trinity College, Oxford · Trinity College, Oxford, corresp. **Likenesses** S. Hewson, oils, 1803, Trinity College, Oxford · T. C. Thompson, oils, in or after 1863, Trinity College, Oxford [*see illus.*] **Wealth at death** money to three nieces: *GM*, 2nd ser., 34 (1850), 553

Ingram, John (*b.* 1721, *d.* in or after 1767), printmaker, was born in London, where he trained as an engraver. He went to Paris in 1755, and remained there for the rest of his life. He both etched and engraved, and is known for a number of plates after François Boucher and C. N. Cochin, and a set of emblematical figures representing the sciences, produced collaboratively with Cochin and one member of the Tardieu family of engravers. According to Bénézit, he also produced, with Jean-Michel Liotard, a series of *Sujets de la vie champêtre*. He was mainly employed in engraving small plates for book illustration, most notably for the *Transactions* of the Académie des Sciences. Ingram was considered by his contemporaries to be an illustrator of some merit. He appears to have been still active in 1767.

L. H. CUST, rev. ANNE PUETZ

Sources Bénézit, *Dict.*, 3rd edn · J. Gould, *Biographical dictionary of painters, sculptors, engravers and architects*, new edn, 2 vols. (1839) · Thieme & Becker, *Allgemeines Lexikon* · Redgrave, *Artists* · G. K. Nagler, ed., *Neues allgemeines Künstler-Lexikon*, 22 vols. (Munich, 1835–52) · Bryan, *Painters* (1886–9) · R. Portalis and H. Béraldi, *Les graveurs du dix-huitième siècle*, 3 vols. (Paris, 1880–82)

Ingram, John Kells (1823–1907), scholar and economist, born at the rectory of Temple Carne, near Pettigo, Donegal, on 7 July 1823, was the eldest son of William Ingram (1771–1829), then curate of the parish, and his wife, Elizabeth Cooke. Thomas Dunbar *Ingram was his younger brother. The family was descended from Scottish Presbyterians who settled in co. Down in the seventeenth century. John Ingram, the paternal grandfather, was a prosperous linen-bleacher at Lisdrumhure (now Glenanne), co. Armagh, who conformed to the established Church of Ireland. Ingram's father, who was elected in 1790 a scholar of Trinity College, Dublin, died in 1829, and his five children were brought up by his widow, who survived until 1884. Mother and children moved to Newry, and John and his brothers were educated at Dr Lyons's school there. At the early age of fourteen John matriculated (on 13 October 1837) at Trinity College, Dublin, where he won a sizarship the following year, a scholarship in 1840, and a senior moderatorship in mathematics in 1842. He graduated BA early in 1843.

In his undergraduate days Ingram showed precocious promise both as a mathematician and as a classical scholar. In December 1842 he helped to found the Dublin Philosophical Society, acting as its first secretary and contributing eleven papers in geometry to its early *Transactions*. He always said that the highest intellectual delight that he experienced in life was in pure geometry, and his geometrical papers won the praise of his Trinity mathematics teacher James MacCullagh. But from youth upwards Ingram showed that intellectual versatility which made him perhaps the most widely educated man of his age. After contributing verse and prose in boyhood to Newry newspapers, he published two well-turned sonnets in the *Dublin University Magazine* for February 1840, and three years later sprang into unlooked-for fame as a popular poet. On a sudden impulse he composed one evening in Trinity in March 1843 the poem entitled 'The Memory of the Dead', beginning 'Who fears to speak of '98?' It was printed anonymously in *The Nation* newspaper on 1 April, but Ingram's responsibility was at once an open secret. Though his view of Irish politics quickly underwent modification, the verses became for much of the nineteenth century the anthem of Irish nationalism. They were reprinted in *The Spirit of the Nation* in 1843 (with music in 1845); and were translated into Latin alcaics by Professor R. Y. Tyrrell in *Kottabos* (1870), and thrice subsequently into Irish. Ingram did not publicly claim the authorship until 1900, when he reprinted the poem in his collected verse.

In 1845 Ingram failed in competition for a fellowship at Trinity College, but was consoled as *proxime accessit* with the Madden prize. He was elected a fellow a year later, having obtained a dispensation from the obligation of taking

John Kells Ingram (1823–1907), by Sarah Purser, 1890

holy orders. He had thought of the law as a profession, in case he failed to obtain the dispensation. At a later period, in 1852, he was admitted a student of the King's Inns, Dublin, and in 1854 of Lincoln's Inn. But after taking his fellowship he was actively associated with Trinity College in various capacities for fifty-three years.

After being elected a member of the Royal Irish Academy on 11 January 1847, Ingram gave further results of geometrical inquiry in papers that he read in April and May of that year on 'Curves and surfaces of the second degree'. At the same time he was extending his knowledge in many other directions, in classics, metaphysics, and economics. Although Carlyle met him as a young member of Trinity during his tour in Ireland in 1849, he only recognized him as author of the 'Repeal' song, and described him as a 'clever indignant kind of little fellow' who had become 'wholly English, that is to say, Irish rational in sentiment' (Carlyle, 52–3). In 1850 Ingram visited London for the first time, and also made a first tour up the Rhine to Switzerland. In London he then made the acquaintance of George Johnston Allman, who became a lifelong friend. Other continental tours followed later.

In 1852 Ingram received his first professorial appointment at Trinity, becoming Erasmus Smith professor of oratory. Three years later the duty of giving instruction in English literature was first attached to the chair. Thus Ingram was the first to give formal instruction in English literature in Dublin University, although no independent chair in that subject was instituted until 1867. A public lecture that he delivered in Dublin on Shakespeare in 1863

showed an original appreciation of the chronological study of the plays, and of the evidence of development in their versification; it was published in *The Afternoon Lectures on Literature and Art* (1863). A notable paper on the weak endings of Shakespeare, which, first read before a short-lived Dublin University Shakespeare Society, was revised for the New Shakspere Society's *Transactions* (1874, pt 2), defined his views of Shakespearian prosody.

In 1866 Ingram became regius professor of Greek at Dublin, a post he held for eleven years. Although he made no great contribution to classical literature, he proved his fine scholarship, both Greek and Latin, in contributions—chiefly on etymology—to *Hermathena*, a scholarly periodical which was started at Trinity College in 1874 under his editorship. A sound textual critic, he had little sympathy with the art of emendation. Gladstone summoned him in January 1873 to assist in preparing the ill-fated Irish Universities Bill of that year.

In 1879 Ingram became librarian of Trinity College, and displayed an alert interest in the books and especially in the manuscripts under his charge. He had already described to the Royal Irish Academy in 1858 a manuscript in the library of Roger Bacon's *Opus majus*, which supplied a seventh and hitherto overlooked part of the treatise (on moral philosophy). He also printed *Two Collections of Medieval Moralised Tales* (1882) from medieval Latin manuscripts in the diocesan library, Derry, as well as *The Earliest English Translations of the 'De imitatione Christi'* from a manuscript in Trinity College Library (1882) which he fully edited for the Early English Text Society in 1893. Ingram was also well versed in library management. Two years before becoming university librarian he had been elected a trustee of the National Library of Ireland; he was re-elected annually until his death, and played an active part in the organization and development of that institution. When the Library Association met in Dublin in 1884, he was chosen president, and delivered the opening address on the library of Trinity College.

In 1881, on the death of the provost, Humphrey Lloyd, Ingram narrowly missed succeeding him. He became senior fellow in 1884, and in 1887 he ceased to be librarian on his appointment to the office of senior lecturer. The degree of DLitt was conferred on him in 1891. In 1893 he received the honorary degree of LLD from Glasgow University. In 1898 he became vice-provost, and on resigning that position the following year he severed his long connection with Dublin University.

Throughout his academic career Ingram was also active outside the university. He always took a prominent part in the affairs of the Royal Irish Academy, and served as secretary of the council from 1860 to 1878. While a vice-president in 1886 he presided, owing to the absence through illness of the president (Sir Samuel Ferguson), at the celebration of the centenary of the academy. He was president from 1892 to 1896. In 1887 Ingram became an additional commissioner for the publication of the Brehon laws. In 1893 he was made a visitor of the Dublin Museum of Science and Art, and he aided in the foundation of Alexandra College for Women in 1866.

Meanwhile, economic science divided with religious speculation a large part of Ingram's intellectual energy. His early adoption of Auguste Comte's creed of positivism accounted for his interest in economic questions and the position that he took as to the method of studying them. His attention was first directed to Comte's views when he read the reference to them in John Stuart Mill's *Logic* soon after its publication in 1843. It was not until 1851 that he studied Comte's own exposition of his religion of humanity: Ingram thereupon became a devoted adherent. In September 1855 he visited Comte in Paris. Though Ingram never concealed his religious opinions, he did not consider himself at liberty publicly to avow and defend them, so long as he retained his position in Trinity College. In 1900, the year after his retirement, when he was already seventy-seven, he published his *Outlines of the History of Religion*, in which he declared his positivist beliefs. In the same year there appeared his collected verse, *Sonnets and other Poems*, which was largely inspired by Comte's principles, and several other positivist works followed. Between 1904 and 1906 Ingram contributed to the *Positivist Review*, and on its formation in 1903 he accepted a seat on the Comité Positiviste Occidental. He sided with Richard Congreve in the internal differences of 1879 as to organization within the positivist ranks.

After his retirement Ingram himself stated that he had made a deliberate decision to devote much of the time and energy which he might have given to other academic subjects to studying and promoting Comte's religion of humanity. Like Comte, Ingram saw economics as an integral part of sociology, but one which in its more practical aspects could contribute towards the welfare of humanity. Hence arose his interest in a field apparently remote from his other studies, but in which he gained a considerable reputation in the 1870s and 1880s.

Ingram's first contributions to economic studies were strictly practical. In 1847 he had helped to found the Dublin Statistical Society. This owed its origin in part to the concern of men such as Richard Whately and William Nielson Hancock with the economic and social problems of Ireland, which had then just culminated in the great famine. Sharing those concerns, Ingram became a member of the society's original council, on which he served for ten years, acting as secretary from 1855 until 1857, when he became a vice-president; he was president from 1878 to 1880. Not until 1864 did he present a paper to the society—'Considerations on the state of Ireland'. Less radical than many contributors to the debate on Ireland's economic condition at the time, Ingram took an optimistic view of the growing rate of emigration and advocated the continuance of large farms rather than encouragement of small-holdings or peasant proprietorship. In later papers on poor-law administration his humanitarian sympathies became more clearly evident and were perhaps at their strongest in his address to the Trades Union Congress at Dublin in 1880 on 'Work and the workman', in which he stressed the need of workers for increased material comfort and security as well as higher intellectual and moral attainments. However, it was Ingram's earlier address,

'The present position and prospects of political economy', given as president of the section of economic science and statistics when the British Association met in Dublin in 1878, which first brought his economic philosophy to the attention of a wider audience, and subsequently to an international one.

In 1877 Sir Francis Galton had sought to persuade the British Association to close down its economic science and statistics section on the ground that 'few of the subjects treated of [therein] fall within the meaning of the word scientific'. Ingram responded to this challenge on Comtist lines, holding that economic phenomena were capable of scientific treatment, but only as part of sociology, which 'presides, in fact, over the whole intellectual system'. Nevertheless, the methods which economists had used in studying their subject needed to be reformed; such studies 'ought to be systematically combined with that of other aspects of social existence' and 'the *a priori* deductive method ought to be changed for the historical'.

Through this address and his *History of Political Economy* (1888) Ingram secured a niche in the history of economic thought as one of the founders of a small 'English historical school'. In his own time the *History of Political Economy* reached a world audience, being translated into ten languages. The book, like his *History of Slavery and Serfdom* (1895), appeared originally as one of sixteen on economic topics which Ingram wrote for the ninth edition of the *Encyclopaedia Britannica*; he was also a contributor to Palgrave's *Dictionary of Political Economy* (1892–9). While his economic writings thus covered a wide range, his adherence to Comtean philosophy tended to limit his ideas. Hence, while not denying that theoretical analysis had a place in economic studies, he made no contribution to such analysis and failed to foresee its growing importance for those studies.

Despite his sympathy with the Celtic people of Ireland and their history, Ingram distrusted the Irish political leaders of his time. He attended the great Unionist demonstration at Dublin in November 1887. In theory he judged separation to be the real solution of the Irish problem, but deemed the country unripe for any heroic change. To all military aggression he was hostile. He strenuously opposed the Second South African War (1899–1902). One of his finest sonnets commemorated the death of Sir George Pomeroy Colley at the battle of Majuba Hill on 27 February 1881. It formed a reply (in *The Academy*, 2 April 1881) to an elegiac sonnet by Archbishop Trench in *Macmillan's Magazine* of the same month. Ingram, while honouring Colley's valour, denounced as 'foul oppression' the cause for which he fought.

Ingram married on 23 July 1862 Madeline, daughter of James Johnston Clarke, of Largantogher, Maghera, co. Londonderry. She died on 7 October 1889, leaving four sons and two daughters. Many of Ingram's published sonnets are addressed to his wife; one of them, entitled 'Winged Thoughts', commemorates the death in South Africa, in 1895, of their third son, Thomas Dunbar Ingram, two of whose own sonnets appear in Ingram's volume of poems. Ingram died at his residence, 38 Upper Mount Street, Dublin, on 1 May 1907, and was buried in Mount Jerome cemetery.   [ANON.], *rev.* R. D. COLLISON BLACK

Sources *Proceedings of the Royal Irish Academy*, 27C (1908–9), 1–8 · T. W. Lyster, 'Bibliography of the writings of John Kells Ingram', *An Leabharlann*, 3/1 (1909) · C. Litton Falkiner, 'A memoir of the late John Kells Ingram, LLD', *Journal of the Statistical and Social Inquiry Society of Ireland*, 12 (1908), 105–23 · R. D. C. Black, *The Statistical and Social Inquiry Society of Ireland centenary volume, 1847–1947* (1947) · G. M. Koot, *English historical economics, 1870–1926* (1987) · Burtchaell & Sadleir, *Alum. Dubl.*, 2nd edn · *The Times* (2 May 1907) · T. Carlyle, *Irish journey* (1882) · Gladstone, *Diaries* · G. K. Peatling, 'Who fears to speak of politics?: John Kells Ingram and hypothetical nationalism', *Irish Historical Studies*, 31 (1998–9), 202–21
Archives Maison d'Auguste Comte, Paris, letters · PRO NIre., corresp. and papers · TCD, notebooks | BL, corresp. with Richard Congreve, Add. MSS 45228–45233 · BL, corresp. with W. E. Gladstone, Add. MSS 44332–44438 · NL Scot., corresp. with Sir Patrick Geddes
Likenesses S. Purser, pastel drawing, 1890, Ulster Museum, Belfast [*see illus.*] · S. Purser, oils, 1897, Royal Irish Acad. · S. Purser, oils (after her pastel drawing), TCD
Wealth at death £1825 11s. 5d.: Irish probate sealed in London, 31 July 1907, *CGPLA Ire.* · £8761 15s. 9d.: probate, 20 June 1907, *CGPLA Ire.*

Ingram, Robert (1727–1804), Church of England clergyman, was born at Beverley, Yorkshire, on 9 March 1727. His father was a merchant; his mother was Theodosia, younger daughter of Joseph Gascoigne, sometime tax revenue collector at Minorca. Ingram was descended from the family of Henry Ingram, Viscount Irwine (1616–1666) in the Scottish peerage. Soon after his marriage his father retired from business in London, and settled at Beverley.

Ingram was educated at Beverley grammar school under John Clarke (1706–1761), and in 1745 was admitted to Corpus Christi College, Cambridge, where he graduated BA in 1749 and MA in 1753. He subsequently became a fellow there. Ordained priest on 2 June 1751, Ingram became perpetual curate of Bredhurst, Kent, in 1758, and in the following year Dr Green, bishop of Lincoln, the former master of his college, who greatly respected him, presented him to the small vicarage of Orston, Nottinghamshire. In 1760 he obtained the vicarage of Wormingford, Essex, where he resided until within a year of his death. He also became, through the influence of his wife's family with Dr Terrick, bishop of London, vicar of Boxted, Essex. He married in 1759 Catherine, eldest daughter of Richard Acklom of Weireton, Nottinghamshire, and they had two sons, Robert Acklom *Ingram BD and Rowland Ingram, who succeeded William Paley as headmaster of Giggleswick School.

Ingram wrote a number of works of biblical exegesis, all of which were concerned with the elucidation of New Testament prophecies. All of these texts were strongly anti-Catholic and decidedly millenarian. Three of them—*An Exposition of Isaiah's Vision, Chap. vi* (1784), *A view of the great events of the seventh plague, or period, when the mystery of God shall be finish'd* (1785), and *A complete and uniform explanation of the prophecy of the seven vials of wrath, or the seven last plagues, contained in the Revelations of St. John, chapters xv. xvi.* (1804)—were separately, approvingly, and lengthily

noticed in the *Gentleman's Magazine*. He also wrote another apocalyptic work redolent of the political concerns of the period in his *Accounts of the ten tribes of Israel, originally published by Manasseh ben Israel, with observations thereon* (1792). He was very much a 'church and king' conservative, as all his writings attest. Ingram died at his eldest son's house at Seagrave, near Loughborough, Leicestershire, on 3 August 1804, survived by his wife.

THOMPSON COOPER, *rev.* B. W. YOUNG

Sources *GM*, 1st ser., 74 (1804), 343–8, 882 · *GM*, 1st ser., 55 (1785), 732 · *GM*, 1st ser., 72 (1802), 580 · W. H. Oliver, *Prophets and millennialists: the uses of biblical prophecy in England from the 1790s to the 1840s* (1978) · *DNB* · Venn, *Alum. Cant.*

Ingram, Robert Acklom (1763–1809), Church of England clergyman and economist, eldest son of Robert *Ingram (1727–1804) and his wife, Catherine, daughter of Richard Acklom, was probably born in Wormingford or Boxted, Essex, and was educated at Dr Thomas Grimwood's school, Dedham, and Queens' College, Cambridge, where he graduated BA as senior wrangler in 1784. He became fellow and tutor of his college, commenced MA in 1787, was moderator in 1790, and proceeded BD in 1796. On taking orders in 1790 he was appointed curate of Boxted, and in 1802 he was presented by the master and fellows of Queens' College to the rectory of Seagrave, Leicestershire, where he died on 5 February 1809, survived by his wife, Catherine, and three children.

In moving from a college fellowship to serve as a cleric in rural parishes of the Church of England, Ingram followed a career path typical in his time, but he was not altogether typical of those who followed it. He sincerely sought to discharge his duties towards all his parishioners, rich and poor, but realized clearly that his university education had not prepared him suitably for such a task. In *The Necessity of Introducing Divinity into the Regular Course of Academical Studies Considered* (1792) he contended that 'public reform … must be commenced by increasing the influence of religion'; existing university courses trained students to reason, but not in a way which enabled them readily to convey the tenets of religion 'to the illiterate part of mankind'. While not an evangelical himself, Ingram recognized that such an approach made religion more accessible to the common people, and still listed the inappropriate university training of Anglican clergy among *The Causes of the Increase of Methodism and Dissension* in a sermon published in 1807.

Ingram was similarly concerned that 'those who are designed to occupy a seat in either house [of parliament] should be perfectly instructed in the principles of government and the political interests of a community'. Consequently he became one of the earliest supporters of the view 'that the study of political economy be encouraged in the Universities', prefixing a proposal 'that a course of public lectures be delivered on that subject' to *A Syllabus or Abstract of a System of Political Philosophy*, which he published in 1799.

Ingram's first significantly economic work, *An Inquiry into the Present Condition of the Lower Classes, and the Means of Improving it*, had appeared in 1797, at the time of Pitt's Poor

Law Bill. In it Ingram traced the causes of distress beyond the scarcity and high food prices of the years since 1794 to the decline of small farms and the increase of manufactures, which between them created a great increase in the numbers solely dependent on the wages of daily labour. He opposed regulation of wages according to food prices or the giving to the poor of public relief beyond bare subsistence levels, but advocated giving 'industrious labourers' better opportunities to save and acquire property. Recognizing the dangers of wealth being concentrated in the hands of the few, Ingram advocated taxes on property and luxuries rather than essential foodstuffs. Although he realized that population had increased, Ingram saw no danger in this, and after the appearance of Malthus's *Essay on Population* he steadily opposed its doctrines, developing his arguments most fully in his last work, *Disquisitions on Population* (1808). In this, showing little recognition of the significance of diminishing returns in agriculture, he continued to assume that the ideal society would be a rural one, with only domestic manufactures, where intensive cultivation would allow all classes to live in sober comfort without the need to postpone marriage yet without fear of over-population. His arguments found no favour with orthodox political economists and were demolished, possibly by Malthus's friend Francis Jeffrey, in an anonymous article in the *Edinburgh Review* (no. 32, 1810).

R. D. COLLISON BLACK

Sources Venn, *Alum. Cant.* · *GM*, 1st ser., 79 (1809), 189, 275–6 · Watt, *Bibl. Brit.*, 2.534 · J. Foster, ed., *Index ecclesiasticus, or, Alphabetical lists of all ecclesiastical dignitaries in England and Wales since the Reformation* (1890), 96 · [S. Smith], *EdinR*, 11 (1807–8), 341–62 · [F. Jeffrey], 'Disquisitions on population', *EdinR*, 16 (1810), 464–76 · J. R. Poynter, *Society and pauperism: English ideas on poor relief, 1795–1834* (1969) · P. James, *Population Malthus* (1979)

Ingram, Thomas Dunbar (1826–1901), historian and lawyer, born in Newry, co. Down, on 28 July 1826, was the second son of William Ingram and his wife, Elizabeth Cooke. John Kells *Ingram was his elder brother. After a preliminary education in Newry, he was sent to Queen's College, Belfast, where he matriculated in 1849 and graduated BA and LLB in 1853. In 1851 he had been admitted to the King's Inns, but in 1854 he entered London University, where he graduated LLB in 1857. He entered Lincoln's Inn as a student on 24 January 1854, obtained a law studentship in January 1855, and was called to the bar on 17 November 1856.

In 1866 Ingram obtained the post of professor of jurisprudence in Hindu and Muhammadan law at Presidency College, Calcutta; he filled the chair until 1877, and at the same time practised in the high court of judicature. He left India in 1877, and settled in Dublin, where he devoted himself to historical research, chiefly on Irish themes. Ingram was a convinced unionist, and is best-known for his book *A History of the Legislative Union of Great Britain and Ireland* (1887), which was written in order to correct the view of W. E. H. Lecky that the union was brought about by corrupt means. It was reviewed in the *Nineteenth Century* by Gladstone, who sharply censured Ingram's account as 'no

history at all'. Although Ingram's research was acknowledged to be painstaking, he was criticized for his dogmatic views and for the vehemence with which his conclusions were presented. He also wrote a textbook on the law on compensation, a commentary on proceedings in the Indian government, and a history of the relationship between the papacy and the church in England between 1066 and 1688. Ingram died unmarried at his home, 13 Wellington Street, Dublin on 30 December 1901, and was buried in Mount Jerome cemetery.

D. J. O'DONOGHUE, rev. MARIE-LOUISE LEGG

Sources G. P. Macdonell, 'A history of the legislative union of Great Britain and Ireland, by T. Dunbar Ingram', *The Academy* (2 July 1887), 2–3 · *The Times* (20 Dec 1901) · W. E. Gladstone, 'Ingram's History of the Irish union', *Nineteenth Century*, 22 (1887), 445–69 · E. Keane, P. Beryl Phair, and T. U. Sadleir, eds., *King's Inns admission papers, 1607–1867*, IMC (1982) · University of London, *The historical record (1836–1926)*, 2nd edn (1926) · Gladstone, *Diaries*
Wealth at death £7244 18s. 10d.: resworn probate, 18 Feb 1902, *CGPLA Ire.* · £323 8s. 10d.: Irish probate sealed in England, 15 May 1902, *CGPLA Eng. & Wales*

Ingram, Walter (1855–1888). *See under* Ingram, Herbert (1811–1860).

Ingrams [*née* Shortt], **Doreen Constance** (1906–1997), actress and traveller, was born on 24 January 1906 at 70 Onslow Gardens, Kensington, London, the youngest daughter of Edward *Shortt (1862–1935), a lawyer and politician, and his wife, Isabella Stewart, *née* Scott. She grew up in Kensington, attended Glendower School in London, and had a governess, but was largely self-educated; she was influenced towards egalitarianism by reading Tolstoy. At the age of eighteen, a slim blonde, she joined the company of the actor–manager Sir Johnston Forbes-Robertson and acted for six years, playing leading Shakespearian roles, understudying Edith Evans, and forming a lasting friendship with Peggy Ashcroft. They travelled around Britain and Ireland, staying sometimes in squalid digs and seeing slums very different from her own affluent home. Doreen imbibed the leftist and anti-imperial views then fashionable among the 'bright young things' and prided herself on her 'rather unconventional approach' (Ingrams, 3).

In 1930 Doreen met William Harold *Ingrams (1897–1973). They were married on 3 June that year and she returned with him to Mauritius, where he was then assistant colonial secretary. However, she disliked colonial life and started to learn Arabic. In 1934 she accompanied her husband to Aden (where she disapproved of the Anglo-Indian influence), then on his visit to the Hadhramaut, and was the first European woman to visit Seiyun and Tarim. She helped him with his research, visiting harems and investigating women's lives. While Ingrams was resident in the Hadhramaut she helped him with confidential office work, including coding and decoding. They wore pseudo-Arab dress, a debatable practice—criticized by the Dutch traveller Colonel van der Meulen, who visited them, as a 'masquerade' (van der Meulen, 240), false to oneself and one's origins—and about which she was later defensive in her memoirs. She travelled, by donkey and camel, sometimes in areas where no European woman had been seen, and in her contacts with Arab women urged them to influence their menfolk in favour of the truce negotiated by her husband (known as the Ingrams peace) among the warring tribes. Doreen founded the first Bedouin girls' school and a school for the blind. In the famine of 1943–4 she established and worked in a hospital at Mukalla and set up a children's village for orphans. She accompanied Ingrams on visits to the Yemen, Ethiopia, Java, and Malaya. The couple had one daughter (Leila), and in 1937 had adopted a malnourished Arab baby girl, Zahra, given by her mother.

Doreen Ingrams returned to England in 1944 and lectured on the Hadhramaut and Arab women for the Central Office of Information. Her *Survey of social and economic conditions in the Aden protectorate* was published in 1949. From 1956 to 1967 she worked for the BBC Arabic service, in charge of talks and magazine programmes. She revisited the Hadhramaut and other Arab countries, and favoured the Palestinians against the Zionists. She supported Nasser and opposed the Suez intervention. An opponent of apartheid, she wanted improved British–Arab relations. She was a founder of the Council for the Advancement of Arab–British Understanding and served on its executive committee, and was patron of the Friends of the Hadhramaut. Britain should have left south Arabia ten years earlier, she argued, though admitting 'we would have left chaotic conditions behind us' (Ingrams, 151). Her publications included her memoirs, *A Time in Arabia* (1970), and *Palestine Papers, 1917–1922: Seeds of Conflict* (1972), blaming the British. With her daughter, Leila, she edited the sixteen-volume *Records of Yemen, 1798–1960* (1993), a labour of love. For their pioneering work in south Arabia she and her husband were awarded the Lawrence of Arabia medal of the Royal Central Asian Society (1939) and the founder's medal of the Royal Geographical Society (1940); in 1993 she was awarded the Sir Richard Burton medal of the Royal Asiatic Society.

Doreen Ingrams was energetic, resourceful, adventurous, curious, capable, and charming. Her marriage was dissolved, and she died suddenly on 25 July 1997 at the William Harvey Hospital, Ashford, Kent. She was commemorated by the Doreen Ingrams memorial lecture of the Royal Asiatic Society. ROGER T. STEARN

Sources *The Independent* (31 July 1997) · *Daily Telegraph* (13 Aug 1997) · *The Times* (11 Aug 1997) · *The Guardian* (6 Aug 1997) · 'Doreen Ingrams (1906–1997)', www.al-bab.com/bys/obits/ingrams.htm · D. Ingrams, *A time in Arabia* (1970) · D. van der Meulen, *Aden to the Hadhramaut: a journey in south Arabia* (1947) · b. cert. · m. cert. · d. cert. · CGPLA Eng. & Wales (1997)

Wealth at death under £180,000: probate, 1997, *CGPLA Eng. & Wales*

Ingrams, (William) Harold (1897–1973), colonial official, was born on 3 February 1897, at The Schools, Kingsland, Shrewsbury, the son of the Revd William Smith Ingrams (*b.* 1853/4), an assistant master at Shrewsbury School (1883–1921), and his wife, Gertrude Mary Payne. Ingrams was educated at Shrewsbury School (1910–14) and in the First World War served as a subaltern in the King's Shropshire light infantry on the western front. In Belgium in 1916 he was wounded, and subsequently worked as a temporary civil servant at the Ministry of National Service. His wound left him permanently lame, though he made light of it and led an active life.

In 1919 Ingrams entered the colonial service and was appointed assistant district commissioner in Zanzibar: in 1925 he was promoted second assistant secretary. His varied tasks included organizing for the sultan a picnic for British naval officers and in 1924 accompanying the sultan to the British Empire Exhibition at Wembley. In 1927 he was awarded fourth class of the order of the Brilliant Star, Zanzibar. He enjoyed friendly relations with local Arabs and acquired a lasting interest in the Arab world.

From 1927 to 1933 Ingrams was assistant colonial secretary in Mauritius, where white ants ate his pictures, books, and furniture. His first marriage, to Phyllis Mulgrave, ended in divorce. On 3 June 1930 he married at the Savoy Chapel, London, Doreen Constance Shortt (1906–1997) [*see* Ingrams, Doreen Constance], an actress, the youngest daughter of Edward *Shortt (1862–1935), a lawyer and politician; they had one daughter and one adopted Arab daughter.

In 1934 Ingrams went to Aden as political officer. From 1934 he journeyed, partly by camel and donkey, in the Hadhramaut, the hinterland of Aden—then little known to Europeans, and backward with slavery, armed feuding, and stinking insanitary villages—and reported on conditions there. From 1937 to 1940 he was British resident adviser at Mukalla, capital of the Qa'iti sultanate, in the eastern Aden protectorate. Later described by James Lunt as 'a strong man, with a deep understanding of the Arab psychology' (Lunt, 103), he negotiated a truce, known as the Ingrams peace, by which the tribes agreed to end their internecine warfare. He became known as Al Muslahi, 'the settler [of disputes]', and numerous fathers offered him their daughters in marriage. He encouraged the sultan to modernize his state by road building among other measures, and the sultan bestowed on him the title Friend of Hadhramaut and made him a pasha. According to his wife, he had 'quite uncolonial ideas' (D. Ingrams, 69) on how the Hadhramaut should be developed, with minimal British personnel and intervention, and he wrote: 'It is an Arab country and Arab it must remain' (H. Ingrams, *Arabia and the Isles*, 354). In 1938 he visited Major Glubb's desert patrol of the Arab Legion in Transjordan, and modelled on it the Hadhrami Bedouin legion, with former Arab Legion NCOs and the red-and-white shamagh of the Arab Legion.

Ingrams wore quasi-Arab dress—which he claimed was more comfortable and practical and was considered a compliment by the local people—and insisted his British staff did likewise. This was a debatable practice, criticized by the Dutch traveller Colonel van der Meulen, who visited them, as 'disguised Englishmen … a masquerade' (van der Meulen, 239–40), false to oneself and one's origins. *The Times* later commented that 'nothing could in fact have been more English than the burly figure and the quizzical blue eyes under a shock of white hair' (12 Dec

1973, 19). Ingrams was awarded an OBE in 1933 and a CMG in 1939. In 1939 he made a tour of Malaya to study the adviser system, and visited Hadhrami immigrants there and in Java and Hyderabad. He was acting governor of Aden in 1940, and continued to serve in various senior posts in Aden and the protectorate until 1945. In 1939 he and his wife were jointly awarded the Lawrence memorial medal of the Royal Central Asian Society, and in 1940 the founder's medal of the Royal Geographical Society. In 1942 he published his account of his life in Zanzibar, Mauritius, and south Arabia, *Arabia and the Isles*.

From 1945 to 1947 Ingrams was seconded as assistant secretary to the Allied Control Commission for Germany (British element). It was not untypical of the Colonial Office for Ingrams, an Arab expert with minimal African experience, to be transferred in 1947 from Arabia to sub-Saharan Africa, as chief commissioner of the northern territories of the Gold Coast. He drove there with his family and others, across the Sahara, and described their journey in *Seven across the Sahara* (1949), an unexciting travelogue praising French colonial officials and calling for Anglo-French co-operation in Africa. He was not entirely happy in his new post, and he retired from the colonial service in 1948. However, he continued to work for the Colonial Office in various advisory roles, finally retiring in 1968. He was a prolific writer, and his publications included a history of Zanzibar, official reports, textbooks, and pamphlets; he also broadcast. His second marriage was dissolved, and he married Henrietta Kathleen Box, who survived him.

Charming, genial, humorous, and a slightly eccentric 'character', Ingrams lived latterly at Uphousden, near Ash next Sandwich, Canterbury, Kent, and died on 9 December 1973 at the South Western Hospital, Stockwell, Lambeth.   ROGER T. STEARN

Sources *The Times* (12 Dec 1973) · *WWW, 1971–80* · H. N. Dawson, *Shrewsbury School register*, 2 (1964) · H. Ingrams, *Arabia and the isles* (1942) · D. Ingrams, *A time in Arabia* (1970) · Foster, *Alum. Oxon.* · *The historical register of the University of Oxford ... to the end of Trinity term 1900* (1900) · D. van der Meulen, *Aden to the Hadhramaut: a journey in south Arabia* (1947) · H. Ingrams, *Seven across the Sahara: from Ash to Accra* (1949) · J. Lunt, *The barren rocks of Aden* (1966) · J. B. Oldham, *A history of Shrewsbury School, 1552–1952* (1952) · m. cert. · *CGPLA Eng. & Wales* (1974) · b. cert. · d. cert.
Archives Bodl. Oxf., corresp. and papers · CAC Cam., papers as assistant secretary of the Control Commission in Germany · Commonwealth Institute, London, corresp. and papers · St Ant. Oxf., Middle East Centre, papers
Likenesses two photographs, c.1935, RGS
Wealth at death £58,020: administration, 1974, *CGPLA Eng. & Wales*

Ings, James (*bap.* 1794, *d.* 1820). *See under* Cato Street conspirators (*act.* 1820).

Ingulf (*c.*1045–1109), abbot of Crowland, is best-known as the supposed author of the earliest history of the Benedictine house of Crowland, covering the period from its first foundation in the early eighth century to his own time. This work in its surviving form is a forgery of the mid-fifteenth century. It shows that the Anglo-Norman Abbot Ingulf was remembered in his own monastery for his part

in preserving its Anglo-Saxon past. Recent study of the Pseudo-Ingulf serves to confirm the reliability of this tradition.

Contemporary sources give the barest outline of Ingulf's career, but Orderic Vitalis breathes some life into the man. He was probably born about 1045, of English birth—his name is Anglo-Scandinavian—and well educated. He had served as a royal scribe, whether before or after the conquest is not clear. He had gone on pilgrimage to Jerusalem. He became a monk at St Wandrille, one of the great monasteries of Normandy, and later was appointed prior of that house. About the time of his appointment as an abbot in England, the St Wandrille property which gave it a London base, a manor in Wandsworth, was held by the monk Ingulf. The English estates of the Norman monasteries were later termed priorates, and so it is possible that Ingulf was not the conventual prior of St Wandrille but the monk–warden of the house's English property. At the Christmas council at Gloucester in 1085–6, at which Domesday Book was commissioned, the English-born abbots of the monasteries of Thorney and Crowland were deposed by Archbishop Lanfranc. William I, who knew his man, nominated Ingulf to succeed at Crowland.

Ingulf was an active abbot. Early in his prelacy, in 1091, the abbey suffered a serious fire, which damaged buildings and vestments, and destroyed much of the archive. The abbey's history needed to be rediscovered, and Ingulf 'may have begun the work of collecting and restoring materials for the history of Crowland after the fire' (Ordericus Vitalis, *Eccl. hist.*, 2.xxv). As a part of the reconstruction, in 1091–2, the body of Earl Waltheof, beheaded for treason in 1076, was moved from the chapter house to the abbey church. His body, according to the monks, was found to be incorrupt, the head now reattached to the trunk, with only the faintest trace of a red line to mark where the axe had fallen. Many miracles were worked at the new tomb. Abbot Ingulf was at the royal court at Gloucester at Christmas 1093, and was at the abbey of Thorney on 1 December 1098, when it translated its own relics into a new church. These mark the only public record of him, outside the memory of his own house, although a nephew Robert occurs in the entourage of his successor, Abbot Geoffrey, in 1116. In his later years Ingulf suffered badly from gout. He died after an abbacy of twenty-four years on 16 November 1109.

The chronicle that bears Ingulf's name is written in the first person, from oral and from written sources, in a lively style. Its author claims to have been born in London; to have known Queen Edith (wife of Edward the Confessor), who would meet him on his way back from school, question him on his homework, and give him little treats; to have attended the University of Oxford, where he mastered the works of Aristotle; and to have been the dominant figure in the Conqueror's private household, where he ruled matters according to his whim. All this is fiction, building upon a single line of Orderic a great edifice of fantasy.

The first half of the work takes the history of the monastery from its first foundation c.714 to its destruction by the

Danes in 870; and then from its refoundation c.966 up to the time of the Norman conquest. The key part of the archive for this period, supposedly destroyed in 1091, was charters. Pseudo-Ingulf claims that some duplicates had been kept, for the instruction of the young monks, and these he presented to the king and copied into his text. The pre-conquest section of the Pseudo-Ingulf is in essence a commentary on these charters. For the commentary he claims to rely on the memory of five old monks, whom he calls 'sempects', all of whom lived to be well over a hundred years old. The charters are without exception forgeries. Pseudo-Ingulf explains—the nearest he gets to an admission of forgery—that he had been advised by Archbishop Lanfranc that the monks needed to present better evidence than they had to hand. This was the stimulus to forgery: a facsimile of one of the charters that survived in the eighteenth century suggests that it was written in the twelfth century. The forgeries at Crowland, as at other houses, were to support claims to the abbey's existing properties and the historic rights attached to them, as the monks understood these.

The identification of the forgery in the late nineteenth century led initially to the Pseudo-Ingulf being totally discounted as a historical source. This was an overreaction. The Pseudo-Ingulf draws at times on reliable chroniclers, and may at other times reflect authentic traditions. The forged charters incorporate pre-conquest boundary clauses. There is important information embedded in the account given of the drainage of the fenland of southern Lincolnshire. The list given of the property of Crowland in 1086 shows that it was copied from a Domesday 'satellite' record that predated the exchequer text. Pseudo-Ingulf says that this was one of 'the rolls of Winchester' (rotuli Wintonienses), and unhappily ascribes it to King Alfred (r. 871–99). In these sections of the work he is looking to explain 'sources that were clearly ancient and authoritative, but largely undated and of uncertain provenance' (Roffe, 96). He sought to provide a context for all the records he cited, and embroidered that context with much circumstantial detail. The figures from the post-conquest period, Abbot Ingulf's lifetime, are brought vividly to life. Hereward the Wake is a legendary figure, certainly larger than life, while the anti-hero is played by the Domesday sheriff, Ivo Taillebois. At its worst the Pseudo-Ingulf is a well-researched historical novel. At its best 'it may yet be proved to be a significant source for the history of eleventh century England' (Roffe, 108).

EDMUND KING

Sources D. Roffe, 'The *Historia Croylandensis*: a plea for reassessment', *EngHR*, 110 (1995), 93–108 · Ordericus Vitalis, *Eccl. hist.*, 2 · A. Gransden, *Historical writing in England*, 2 (1982) · Ingulf, 'Historia Ingulphi', *Rerum Anglicarum scriptorum veterum*, ed. [W. Fulman], 1 (1684), 1–107 · *Ingulph's Chronicle of the abbey of Croyland*, ed. and trans. H. T. Riley (1854) · F. Liebermann, 'Ueber Ostenglische Geschichtsquellen des 12, 13, 14 Jahrhunderts, besonders den falschen Ingulf', *Neues Archiv der Gesellschaft für ältere deutsche Geschichtskunde*, 18 (1892), 249–67 · W. G. Searle, *Ingulf and the Historia Croylandensis: an investigation*, Cambridge Antiquarian RS, 27 (1894) · H. E. Hallam, *Settlement and society: a study of the early agrarian history of south Lincolnshire* (1965) · J. Morris, ed., *Domesday Book: a survey of the counties of England*, 38 vols. (1983–92), vol. 3 [Surrey] · D. Knowles, *The monastic order in England*, 2nd edn (1963)
Wealth at death Crowland Abbey valued at £52 in 1086: Knowles, *Monastic order*, 702 · value of abbey improved by 1104: Hallam, *Settlement*

Ingworth, Richard of (*fl.* 1224–1239), Franciscan friar, was, according to Thomas Eccleston, the first Franciscan Friar Minor to preach to the peoples north of the Alps. He was among the friars who came to England with Agnellus of Pisa in 1224, and was already a priest and advanced in years. With eight other friars he established the first house of Franciscans in London; he then proceeded to Oxford, hired a house in the parish of St Ebbe, and thus founded the original convent in the university town; he also founded the friary at Northampton. Afterwards he became custodian of Cambridge, which was specially noted for its poverty under his rule. In 1230, when Agnellus attended the general chapter at Assisi, Richard acted as vicar of the English province. Soon after this he was appointed provincial minister of Ireland by the minister-general, John Parenti. He was released from this office by Alberto da Pisa in 1239, and set out as a missionary to Syria, where he died.

Richard was clearly a notable figure among the early friars: second in command in the Franciscan mission to England; first in their mission to Ireland; in old age a missionary to the East. He was known and respected by successive ministers-general of the order. In the manuscripts of Eccleston his name is nearly always 'Ingewrth', 'Ingewrd', or 'Ingewurde', with 'Indewurde' in one text and 'Kingesthorp' in a fourteenth-century *marginale* in the Phillipps manuscript (Bodl. Oxf., MS Lat. misc. c.75). This manuscript had links with Northampton, and Kingsthorpe is in Northamptonshire. But it is much more likely that Richard came from the only known Ingworth, in Norfolk.

A. G. LITTLE, rev. ROSALIND B. BROOKE

Sources *Fratris Thomae vulgo dicti de Eccleston tractatus de adventu Fratrum Minorum in Angliam*, ed. A. G. Little (1951), 4, 6, 9–10, 34n., 35 · Emden, *Oxf.* · J. R. H. Moorman, *The Grey friars in Cambridge, 1225–1538*, The Birkbeck Lectures (1952), 186 · E. B. Fitzmaurice and A. G. Little, eds., *Materials for the history of the Franciscan province of Ireland, AD 1230–1450* (1920), xi, 1

Inlander, Heinz Kurt [Henry] (1925–1983), painter, was born on 14 January 1925 in Vienna, Austria, the son of Rudolf Inlander (*b.* 1893) and his wife, Elly. The family, who were Jewish, lived in Trieste from 1935 to 1938, when they moved to London.

Inlander's schooling took place in Vienna, Trieste, and London (1939–41). He became a British subject on 13 December 1947 when he was single and living with his parents at 33 Greencroft Gardens, London. He married twice, the second time to Antonia Josephine O'Brien (*d.* 1982), a painter. He had no children. He studied at Camberwell School of Arts and Crafts (1945–9) and the Slade School of Fine Art (1949–52). Here he won first prize in the summer competition with *The Expulsion from Eden* (*Paradise Lost Book XII*) (oil, 1951), the first of several prizes and awards. Most importantly, in 1952 he won the prix de

Rome, a scholarship to work at the British School in Rome, where he remained until 1956. He was appointed art adviser to the school in 1955–6 and again in 1971. Inlander spoke Italian and loved Italy sufficiently to buy a house in Anticoli Corrado, in the hills to the east of Rome, which he owned for thirty years and where he and his wife worked for several months every year. It is said that, because of his beard and, perhaps, his penchant for dressing up as a member of the Mafia, he was known locally as Il diabolo (private information).

Though the countryside around Anticoli Corrado became his preferred subject, Inlander worked and exhibited principally in London. Here he shared a studio complex in the 1960s with the sculptor Bryan Kneale and others 'in a rather decrepit workshop belonging to a builders merchant in the Fulham Road' (*Henry Inlander*, 1976). Between 1957 and 1979 he taught painting at Camberwell School of Arts and Crafts. Students respected Inlander for having moved beyond the tired neo-romanticism prevalent when he began to teach and found him a kindly tutor who helped them to find their own direction. He had many friends, and was admired as 'a passionate painter' of great integrity (private information). His temperament was volatile, shifting rapidly from gloom and self-doubt to high spirits, and he seems always to have questioned his own identity.

Ambitious and focused, Inlander exhibited with the London Group as a non-member between 1947 and 1953. His first solo exhibition was at the Galleria La Tartaruga, Rome, in 1954 and the second at London's Leicester Galleries a year later. Subsequently he showed regularly with Roland, Browse, and Delbanco and the New Art Centre in London and at the Peridot Gallery, New York (1961–3). His paintings were selected for exhibitions organized by the Tate Gallery, the Contemporary Arts Society, and the Arts Council and are in numerous private and public collections in Britain and abroad. In the mid-1970s he held two exhibitions in Vienna. He spent 1960–61 in the United States on a Harkness Commonwealth scholarship and was visiting artist at the University of Calgary in Canada in 1969, though he remained untouched by American abstract expressionism. While he was described by colleagues as a romantic artist, his work, rooted in post-impressionism, was modern but not avant-garde. As a result it has been neglected by critics and historians since his death. His approach is exemplified by *Moving Surface* (oil on canvas, 1961; Tate collection). He wrote that it represented 'the study of movement in water' where the forms were based on accumulated leaves and branches which constantly shifted in the slow-moving river (*Tate Gallery: Report*, 1962). Even when his work looked abstract, it was grounded in the visible world, though Inlander seldom painted direct from a subject, preferring to work from drawings and memory. Predominantly a landscape painter, he also painted interiors, portraits, many self-portraits, and a variety of animals, for which he evidently had great sympathy. Inlander died at King's College Hospital, London, on 15 December 1983, as the result of a heart attack suffered during a party at Camberwell School of Art, and was buried in a Jewish cemetery in north-west London. MARGARET GARLAKE

Sources D. Buckman, *Dictionary of artists in Britain since 1945* (1998) · G. Hassell, *Camberwell School of Arts and Crafts: its students and teachers, 1943–1960* (1995) · M. Chamot, D. Farr, and M. Butlin, *The modern British paintings, drawings, and sculpture*, 1 (1964) [catalogue, Tate Gallery, London] · *Tate Gallery: report of the trustees for the year 1 April 1956 to 31 March 1957* (1957) · *Tate Gallery: report of the trustees for the year 1 April 1961 to 31 March 1962* (1962) · Tate collection, London Group archive · Tate collection, Women's International Art Club archive · *Henry Inlander* (1976) [exhibition catalogue, Arts Centre, Folkestone] · *Henry Inlander* (1984) [exhibition catalogue, New Art Centre, London] · *Henry Inlander* (1981) [exhibition catalogue, Wraxall Gallery, London] · private information (2004) [Bryan Kneale; others] · certificate of naturalization, PRO, HO 334/197, AZ35997 · certificate of naturalization, PRO, HO 334/179, AZ26558 [Rudolf Inlander, father] · d. cert. · *The Times* (22 Dec 1983) · *CGPLA Eng. & Wales* (1985)
Archives Tate Collection, catalogues of exhibitions
Likenesses H. Inlander, self-portrait, repro. in *Henry Inlander* (1976) · photograph, repro. in *Henry Inlander* (1970) [exhibition catalogue, University of Calgary Gallery]
Wealth at death £2811: administration, 19 June 1985, *CGPLA Eng. & Wales*

Inman, George Ellis (1814–1840), songwriter, was well educated and was for some time clerk in the office of a firm of wine merchants in Crutched Friars, London. He obtained some reputation as a songwriter; two of his compositions, 'The days of yore' and 'St George's flag of England', gained prizes of 10 and 15 guineas respectively from the Melodists' Club in 1838 and 1840. Other songs of his were 'Sweet Mary mine', which enjoyed a concert season's popularity; 'My Native Hills', set to music by Sir Henry Bishop; and 'Wake, wake, my love', set to music by Raffaelle Angelo Wallis. He wrote the libretto for Wallis's opera *The Arcadians*. Inman also contributed to various magazines. The *Bentley Ballads*, edited by Dr Doran (new edn, 1861), included two of his poems.

Inman died tragically at the age of twenty-six. He had begun taking opium, and he committed suicide, shooting himself on 27 September 1840, in The Mall, St James's Park, London. The coroner judged him to have been 'in a state of temporary insanity'. *La Belle Assemblée* for September 1844 published a piece by him, 'Le premier grenadier des armées de la république'. It was described as 'not high-class poetry … [but] very powerful' (*N&Q*, 226). He is said to have published a small volume of poems, but this has not been traced. FRANCIS WATT, *rev.* MEGAN A. STEPHAN

Sources *GM*, 2nd ser., 14 (1840), 550 · *N&Q*, 4th ser., 5 (1870), 225–6 · d. cert.

Inman, James (1776–1859), mathematician and writer on navigation, was the younger son of Richard Inman of Garsdale Foot, Sedbergh, Yorkshire. He attended Sedbergh grammar school, and subsequently became a pupil of John Dawson. Although entered at St John's College, Cambridge, in 1794, he did not go into residence until 1796. He graduated BA in 1800 as senior wrangler and first Smith's prizeman, and was elected to a fellowship.

With no immediate intention of taking orders, Inman decided to pursue mission work in the East, and set out for

Syria. He was unable to proceed further than Malta, where he studied Arabic. On his return to England he was recommended to the board of longitude for the post of astronomer on board the discovery ship *Investigator*, and joined her on her return journey to Port Jackson (later Sydney, New South Wales) in June 1803 [*see* Flinders, Matthew]. When the *Investigator*'s officers and men were transferred to the *Porpoise*, Inman was left at Port Jackson in charge of the instruments; but after the wreck and the return of Flinders, Inman accompanied him in the *Rolla*, and assisted him in determining the position of the reef on which the *Porpoise* had struck. With most of the crew he then returned to England, in the East India Company's ship *Warley*, in which he was present in the engagement with Rear-Admiral Durand Linois off Pulo Aor, at the entrance to the Strait of Malacca, on 15 February 1804. He received his MA in 1805, and was ordained, though he does not appear to have held any cure. He became BD in 1815, and DD in 1820.

On the conversion of the Royal Naval Academy at Portsmouth, in 1808, into the Royal Naval College, Inman was appointed professor of mathematics. In 1810, at his suggestion, the Admiralty established a school of naval architecture and Inman was appointed principal. In this office he turned to good account the knowledge of navigation and naval gunnery which he had acquired at sea. To supply the want of a textbook, he published, in 1820, *A treatise on shipbuilding by Frederick Henry de Chapman … translated into English, with explanatory notes, and a few remarks on the construction of ships of war*. The translation, made from the French, provided an excellent textbook. In 1821 appeared his well-known book *Navigation and Nautical Astronomy for the Use of British Seamen*, with accompanying tables. In the third edition (1835) he introduced a new trigonometrical function, the half-versine, or haversine, the logarithms of which were added to the tables, and enormously simplified the practical solution of spherical triangles. For many years the recognized textbook in the navy, the *Navigation* was gradually superseded, but the tables, with some additions, remained in use. Inman published, in 1828, *An Introduction to Naval Gunnery*, designed strictly as an introduction to the course of scientific teaching. It was during this period also that he produced for the use of his classes two short treatises—*Arithmetic, Algebra, and Geometry* (1810) and *Plane and Spherical Trigonometry* (1826). His other works include *The Scriptural Doctrine of Divine Grace: a Sermon Preached before the University* (1820) and *Formulae and Rules for Making Calculations on Plans of Ships* (1849).

Inman also taught design, and his students, notably Isaac Watts and Thomas Lloyd, dominated the design process between 1840 and 1870. Inman's own designs were competent, but he was bitterly opposed by the surveyor Sir William Symonds.

Inman married Mary, daughter of Richard Williams, vicar of Oakham, Rutland, a direct descendant of the mother of Sir Isaac Newton and her second husband; they had several children. In 1839 the naval college was again reorganized, and Inman retired. For the next twenty years he continued to reside in the neighbourhood of Portsmouth, and he died at his home in Gloucester Place, Southsea, on 7 February 1859.

J. K. LAUGHTON, *rev.* ANDREW LAMBERT

Sources M. Lewis, *The navy in transition, 1814–1864: a social history* (1965) • A. D. Lambert, *The last sailing battlefleet: maintaining naval mastery, 1815–1850* (1991) • D. K. Brown, *Before the ironclad* (1990) • personal information (1891) • *CGPLA Eng. & Wales* (1859)
Wealth at death under £8000: probate, 14 April 1859, *CGPLA Eng. & Wales*

Inman, Thomas (1820–1876), physician, was born on 27 January 1820 in Rutland Street, Leicester, the second son of eight children of Charles Inman (1791–1858), and his wife, Jane, *née* Clay. Charles Inman had been apprenticed in Liverpool to his cousin, as a cotton broker; later, he became a partner in Pickford & Co., and moved to Leicester. Twenty years later he withdrew from Pickfords and returned to Liverpool as a director of the Bank of Liverpool. Thomas Inman's younger brother, William *Inman (1825–1881), founded the Inman Steamship Company Ltd, which ran from Liverpool to New York. In the 1830s the brothers rode their ponies to school in Leicester, where they left them in their father's stables at Pickfords; *en route* they imitated circus feats, standing in the saddle and throwing themselves off their galloping ponies. At fourteen Thomas was sent to school at Wakefield and boarded with a Mr Bennett, a surgeon. Scholastically he made great progress and was also an excellent chess player. Two years later, in 1836, he was apprenticed to his father's younger brother, Richard Inman MD, surgeon at Preston, Lancashire, and in 1838 he entered King's College, London, where he distinguished himself; he graduated MB in 1842, and MD in 1844 with an exhibition and gold medal in materia medica and therapeutics. He returned to Liverpool in 1844 as house surgeon to the infirmary, but caught typhus within a month of starting his internship. Aware that the infection was caused by a bacterium-like organism carried by lice, which thrived in areas of human squalor, Inman worked hard to improve conditions, instituting proper baths and keeping registers to ensure regular cleansing.

On 10 June 1844 Inman married Janet Leighton, daughter of Daniel Newman of Douglas, Isle of Man. They raised six sons and two daughters. Inman enjoyed family life and when his children were away he wrote to them about the garden and new stables, and the new steamship (*City of Dublin*) that he and his brother had bought, and enquired after their progress at school. Also in 1844 Inman became a member of the Literary and Philosophical Society of Liverpool, which had united with the Natural History Society. He was a frequent speaker at the society's meetings, a favourite topic being the fossil wood which he found on his excursions to the submerged submarine forests exposed at low tide along the banks of the rivers Mersey and Dee.

At the infirmary Inman was appointed physician and part-time lecturer at the medical school, where he covered medical jurisprudence, botany, materia medica, and medicine; he also served as secretary to the school from 1847 to 1855. His neatly written lectures on materia medica started with the design of the course, followed by the history of medicines and their past and present usage. A textbook, *Foundation for a New Theory and Practice of Medicine* (1860), was followed by two works on public hygiene, *On the Preservation of Health, or, Plain Directions how to Avoid the Doctor* (1868) and *On the restoration of health, being essays on the principles upon which the treatment of many diseases is to be conducted* (1870).

Known in other circles as a freethinker, Inman took an interest in the origins and histories of pre-Christian religions. A controversial work, *Ancient faiths and modern: a dissertation upon worships, legends and divinities in central and western Asia, Europe, and elsewhere, before the Christian era, showing their relations to religious customs as they now exist* (1876), was published in New York and Edinburgh. In 1871 Inman gave up practice and retired to Clifton, near Bristol, where he died at his home, 8 Vyvyan Terrace, on 3 May 1876. He was buried at Arnos Vale cemetery, Bristol, and was survived by his wife.

ALEXANDER GORDON, rev. ANITA MCCONNELL

Sources U. Lpool L., special collections and archives, Thomas Inman MSS, MSS D. 398 · H. A. Ormerod, *The early history of Liverpool Medical School from 1834 to 1877* (1953) · *Medical Directory* (1876) · Boase, *Mod. Eng. biog.* · J. M. Wheeler, *A biographical dictionary of freethinkers of all ages and nations* (1889) · private information (2004) [A. Allen; Z. Inman] · personal knowledge (2004) · parish register, Braddon, Isle of Man, 10 June 1844 [marriage]
Archives U. Lpool L., MS D. 398
Likenesses photographs, U. Lpool, special collections and archives, D. 398/1/7, /1/10, /1/11
Wealth at death under £16,000: administration, 6 June 1876, *CGPLA Eng. & Wales*

Inman, William (1825–1881), shipowner, born at Leicester on 6 April 1825, was the fourth son of Charles Inman (*d.* 1858), a partner in the firm of Pickford & Co., and Jane (*d.* 1865), daughter of Thomas Clay of Liverpool. Thomas *Inman, the mythologist, was his elder brother. Educated at Leicester grammar school, Liverpool Collegiate Institute, and Liverpool Royal Institution, he served successively as a clerk to Cairns & Co., Cater & Co., and Richardson Brothers, all Liverpool merchants.

From 1846 Inman managed the Richardson ships trading between Liverpool and Philadelphia. He gained an intimate knowledge of the transatlantic emigrant trade and in 1849 became a partner in the firm. On 20 December 1849, he married Anne Brewis (*d.* in or after 1881), daughter of William Stobart of Picktree, Durham. They had nine sons and three daughters.

In 1850 Inman followed with interest the voyages of the *City of Glasgow*, an iron screw steamship recently built at Glasgow by Tod and Macgregor. He persuaded his partners to buy the vessel and set up the Liverpool and Philadelphia Steam Ship Company. In December 1850 the ship sailed from Liverpool carrying 400 emigrants and took twenty-two days to reach Philadelphia. It was the first time that emigrants had been taken across the Atlantic by steamship. It had previously been supposed that transatlantic steamship services could only be run if subsidized by a government mail contract, while the emigrant trade was left to sailing ships. Inman believed he could run a transatlantic steamship line without government support by using the latest marine technology—the iron screw steamer—to reduce costs. The viability of the line was further promoted by his strategy of ensuring a large and constant flow of emigrant passengers by offering a faster passage and better accommodation than could be provided by sailing ships.

By 1854 Inman had three steamers, with two others under construction, but then two of his ships were lost and the future of the line seemed in doubt. He was saved by the Crimean War which offered lucrative employment for steamships as transports. He returned to the Atlantic trade in 1856 with four steamers. In the following year he shifted the American terminus for most of his sailings to New York and changed the name of his firm to the Liverpool, New York and Philadelphia Steam Ship Company, although it was always popularly known as the Inman Line.

By the 1860s Inman's success had attracted other steamship lines into the emigrant trade and competition was strong. Inman was now ready to take on mail contracts to reduce his costs, and by 1869 he and his principal rivals, the Cunard, National, and Guion lines, had established a shipping conference to control rates and limit competition. The Inman Line probably reached its peak in 1870 when its eighteen ships carried 44,000 passengers, mostly emigrants, to New York.

The 1870s brought further competition, especially from the White Star Line, and Inman was forced to spend large sums on new ships. His 5500 ton *City of Berlin* of 1875 was the largest merchant ship in the world after Brunel's *Great Eastern*, but cost £200,000 at a time when passenger traffic had slumped. In the hope of raising more capital, a new public company, the Inman Steamship Company, was set up in 1875, but conditions were still difficult at the time of Inman's death.

Inman was a member of the local marine board, of the Mersey Docks and Harbour Trust, and of the first Liverpool school board; he was a captain of the Cheshire rifle volunteers, a magistrate for Cheshire, and chairman of the Liverpool Steam Shipowners' Association. He died at his home, Upton Manor, Upton, near Birkenhead, on 3 July 1881, and was buried in Moreton parish church, Cheshire, on 6 July.

ALAN G. JAMIESON

Sources Lpool RO, Inman Steamship Co. Ltd papers · *The Inman Steamship Company Limited official guide* (1878) · N. R. P. Bonsor, *North Atlantic Seaway* (1955) · 'Papers relating to … steam communication between Great Britain and Ireland and North America', *Parl. papers* (1859), session 1, 17.169, no. 230 · 'Select committee on … merchant shipping', *Parl. papers* (1860), vol. 13, no. 530 · 'Letter from agent of Liverpool … on restoration of Galway subsidy', *Parl. papers* (1863), 30.657, no. 68 · *Parl. papers* (1867–8), 41.185, no. 42; 41.249, no. 42-I; 41.259, no. 42-II; 41.261, no. 42-III [papers and correspondence on North American mail contracts] · 'Select committee to inquire into contracts … for conveyance of mails', *Parl. papers* (1868–9), 6.265, no. 106; 6.481, no. 106-I · 'Select committee on merchant ships', *Parl. papers* (1874), vol. 10, no. 309 [measurement of tonnage] · C. W. Jones, *Pioneer shipowners*, 2 vols. [1935–8] ·

D. B. Tyler, *Steam conquers the Atlantic* (1939) • F. E. Hyde, *Cunard and the north Atlantic, 1840–1973: a history of shipping and financial management* (1975) • W. S. Lindsay, *History of merchant shipping and ancient commerce*, 4 vols. (1874–6), vol. 4 • d. cert. • CGPLA Eng. & Wales (1881) • DNB • *The Times* (26 Jan 1877)

Archives Lpool RO, Inman Steam Ship Co. Ltd MSS

Wealth at death £121,359 5s.: probate, 25 Aug 1881, CGPLA Eng. & Wales

Innerpeffer. For this title name *see* Fletcher, Sir Andrew, of Innerpeffer, Lord Innerpeffer (d. 1650).

Innes, Cosmo Nelson (1798–1874), antiquary, was born on 9 September 1798 at the old manor house of Durris on Deeside, the youngest child but one of sixteen children of John Innes and his wife, Euphemia (*née* Russell). John Innes, who belonged to the family of Innes of Innes, had sold his property in Moray to buy Durris. He resided at Durris for many years, but was afterwards ejected by a legal decision, a leading case in the Scottish law of entail. Cosmo Innes was sent to the high school, Edinburgh, under James Pillans, and studied at King's College, Aberdeen, and Glasgow University. He afterwards matriculated at Balliol College, Oxford, on 13 May 1817, graduating BA in 1820 (with a third class), and MA in 1824. In 1826 he married Isabella, daughter of Hugh Rose; they had nine children. Their eldest daughter, Katharine, herself an author, married John Hill *Burton, the historian. Innes and his family lived chiefly in or near Edinburgh, first at Ramsay Lodge, then at 6 Forres Street, later at Hawes, South Queensferry, and finally rather grandly at Inverleith House, Edinburgh.

In 1822 Innes became an advocate at the Scottish bar. His practice was never large, but he was soon employed in peerage and other cases demanding antiquarian and genealogical research. His first case of this kind was the Forbes peerage case, about 1830–32. In the Stirling case he was crown advocate. For several years, from about 1833, he was advocate-depute. In 1840 he was appointed sheriff of Moray, and while in office had to deal with the Moray protesters, who at the time of the Irish potato famine resisted the export of produce from their own district. In 1845 he was a member of the municipal corporation (Scotland) commission. In 1852 he resigned his sheriffdom, and succeeded his friend Thomas Thomson as principal clerk of session.

About 1830 Innes had assisted Thomson in arranging the ancient documents in the Register House (cf. Innes, *Memoir of T. Thomson*, 1854). He was afterwards officially engaged in editing and preparing for the press the *Rescinded Acts*, and in partly editing the folio edition of the *Acts of the Scots Parliament* (1124–1707), to the first volume of which (1844) he wrote an introduction. In July 1865 he began to compile with his assistants the *General Index* to the whole work. This was published in 1875 after his death. Innes was an acute and learned student of ancient Scottish records, and singularly skilful as a decipherer. He was an active member and editor of the Bannatyne, Spalding, and Maitland clubs. He edited the cartularies of numerous Scottish religious houses, as well as various academical and municipal works of importance. In his *Scotland in the Middle Ages* (1860) and *Sketches of Early Scotch History* (1861)—the latter selected from his introductions to the cartularies—he showed a sympathetic interest in the pre-Reformation period, and was accused of being a Roman Catholic, though he was a member of the Episcopal church. From 1846 until his death Innes held the post of professor of civil history (from 1862 simply 'history') at the University of Edinburgh. His lectures were attractive. He also gave valuable lectures on Scottish legal antiquities to members of the Juridical Society, some being published as *Lectures on Scotch Legal Antiquities* (1872). While on a highland tour he died suddenly at Killin on 31 July 1874. He was buried in Warriston cemetery, Edinburgh, on 5 August. In appearance Innes was tall and handsome. He suffered from shyness, which sometimes took the form of nervous volubility in conversation. He was a keen sportsman, and amused himself with gardening. He had a great contempt for the mere bookworm, and said that more was to be learnt outside books than in them. As an antiquary he had no rival in his own line. In politics he was a whig. He advocated the claims of women students of medicine to graduate at the University of Edinburgh.

Innes's voluminous antiquarian publications, mostly for the Spalding and Bannatyne clubs, will chiefly be found listed in David Stevenson, *Scottish Texts and Calendars* (1987). In addition to works mentioned above, Innes wrote memoirs of friends, including one of E. B. Ramsay published in Ramsay's *Reminiscences* (22nd edn, 1874), and articles for the *Quarterly Review* and *North British Review*.

W. W. WROTH, *rev.* H. C. G. MATTHEW

Sources K. Burton, *Memoir of Cosmo Innes* (1874) • J. A. H. Murray, *The Academy* (15 Aug 1874), 181

Archives Elgin Museum, Elgin, letters to George Gordon • NL Scot., letters to E. D. Dunbar • NRA, priv. coll., letters to Sir Charles Dalrymple Fergusson relating to axe heads and sword remains • U. Edin. L., special collections division, letters to David Laing

Likenesses A. Edouart, paper silhouette, Scot. NPG

Wealth at death £6992 17s. 2d.: confirmation, 13 Oct 1874, NA Scot., SC 70/1/170, 142

Innes, James Dickson (1887–1914), painter, was born on 27 February 1887 at Greenfield Villas, Murray Street, Llanelli, one of the three sons of John Innes and his wife, Alice Ann Mary, née Rees. Although, as Augustus John put it, he felt bound to Wales 'by every tie of sentiment and predilection' (Holroyd, 352), his father, an engineer (or possibly, as recorded on Innes's birth certificate, an accountant) at a local tin-plate works, was in fact Scottish, and his mother was of French extraction. Innes was educated at the local higher grade school before being sent to Christ College, Brecon (1894–1904). He then studied art at Carmarthen Art School (1904–5) and from there won a scholarship to the Slade School of Fine Art (1906–8), where he fell particularly under the influence of Philip Wilson Steer. His other formative influences were the works of John Cotman and Turner (he always carried with him a copy of Turner's *Liber Studiorum*). While still a student he began to exhibit at the

New English Art Club. He had rooms in Fitzroy Street, London, and briefly experimented with the subject matter and techniques then being espoused by his neighbours Walter Sickert and Frederick Spencer Gore.

In 1908 Innes travelled to France with John Fothergill. They visited Caulbec, Bazals, and then—'because it looked so good on the map' (Holroyd, 352)—the little town of Collioure on the Mediterranean coast near the Spanish border. The revelation of southern light and colour had a lasting effect on Innes and his art. The trip had to be curtailed, however, when Innes fell ill. He returned to England and was diagnosed as consumptive. His mother took him to St Ives to rest and recuperate. During his convalescence he painted a series of idealized landscapes. When he was well enough Innes returned to France, where he took a studio in Paris. Outside a Parisian café he met and fell in love with Euphemia Lamb, the wife of the artist Henry Lamb. With her he travelled south again to Collioure. A one-man exhibition of his watercolours—many of which were done on this trip—was mounted at the Chenil Gallery, London, in January 1911. The work showed increasing stylization of forms and flatter bolder colours derived, perhaps, from his study of Japanese prints.

Innes returned to London in the autumn of 1910 and began to see much of Augustus John (whom he had first met while at the Slade). Together the two painters began to explore and paint in north Wales. In the spring of 1911 Innes 'discovered' the mountain of Arenig, which was to become one of his sacred sites; under a cairn on the summit he buried a casket of Euphemia Lamb's letters. John and he rented a cottage nearby, at Nant-ddu. Following John's example, Innes began to make quick oil sketches, rather than watercolours. These small landscapes—done at great speed—he charged with the colour and intensity that he had first discovered in the south of France.

At the end of 1911, after a third excursion to Collioure, Innes returned to London and contributed to the second *Camden Town Group show. His bohemian existence, and his refusal to compromise in the face of his illness, were, however, taking a heavy toll on his health. He travelled to Spain with Lord Howard de Walden (a new patron) and to Ireland (at the invitation of Lady Gregory), but suffered a collapse at Galway races and had to be taken back to England by John. In search of health, he made another visit to the south of France, accompanied by the young Australian painter Derwent Lees. Although frequently depressed, he produced some his best work, transforming the landscape through his heightened sense of colour and form. It was a style that, although essentially post-impressionist, also owed something to the symbolist tradition in its emotional intensity.

On his return to London in the spring of 1913 Innes enjoyed a successful one-man exhibition at the Chenil Gallery. It was his swan song. The money he earned was spent on a series of medical retreats, in England and then abroad—in Morocco and on Tenerife in the Canary Islands. He did no more work but his health continued to decline. Brought back to England by his brother Jack, Innes was nursed by his mother at Brighton, and then moved to a nursing home at Swanley, Kent, where he died on 22 August 1914.

Innes was an arresting and 'artistic' figure, with his broad-brimmed Quaker hat, coloured silk scarf, long overcoat, and gold-topped ebony cane. John described him as having:

> features of a slightly cadaverous cast, with glittering black eyes, a wide sardonic mouth, a prominent nose and a large bony forehead, invaded by streaks of thin black hair … [He] spoke with a heavy English accent, which had been imposed on an agreeable Welsh substratum.   (John, 'Fragment of an autobiography', 255)

Yet besides this pose, and a certain appetite for dissipation, his most telling characteristic was a rare and unselfconscious, almost visionary, directness.

MATTHEW STURGIS

Sources R. Schwabe, 'Reminiscences of fellow students', *Burlington Magazine*, 82 (1943), 6–9 · J. Fothergill, introduction, *James Dickson Innes*, ed. L. Browse (1946) · A. John, 'Fragment of an autobiography', *Horizon*, 11 (1945), 242–61 · A. John, *Chiaroscuro* (1952) · J. Rothenstein, *Modern English painters*, 2 (1956) · C. Hampton, 'Some of the sources for the art of J. D. Innes', BA diss., U. Cam., 1970 · M. Holroyd, *Augustus John*, new edn (1996) · A. D. Fraser Jenkins, *J. D. Innes at the National Museum of Wales* (1975) · J. Hoole, *James Dickson Innes* (1978) · b. cert.

Likenesses A. Rutherston, pencil drawing, 1908, NPG · A. John, oils, *c.*1910–1912, NMG Wales · I. Strang, oils, 1913, NMG Wales · I. Strang, pencil drawing, 1913, NPG · J. D. Innes, self-portrait, oils, repro. in Hoole, *James Dickson Innes*

Innes, James John McLeod (1830–1907), army officer, was born at Bhagalpur, Bengal, on 5 February 1830, the only son of surgeon James Innes of the Bengal army, of the family of Innes of Thrumster in Caithness, and his wife, Jane Alicia, daughter of Lieutenant-General Duncan McLeod (1780–1856) and sister of Sir Donald Friell McLeod (1810–1872). He was educated at a private school and at Edinburgh University, where he won the mathematical medal for his year.

Innes entered Addiscombe College in February 1847. He passed out at the head of his term, was awarded the Pollock medal (presented to the most distinguished cadet of the outgoing term), and was commissioned second-lieutenant in the Bengal Engineers on 8 December 1848. After the usual Chatham course he arrived in India in November 1850. He was at first employed in the public works department on the construction of the Bari Doab Canal in the Punjab. On 1 August 1854 he was promoted lieutenant. On 30 October 1855, at Jullundur, he married Lucy Jane, youngest daughter of Professor Hugh Macpherson of King's College, Aberdeen; they had three sons and one daughter.

In 1857, shortly after the annexation of Oudh, Innes was transferred to that province as assistant to the chief engineer. When the mutiny began in May 1857 he was at Lucknow. He was given charge of the old fort, the Machhi Bhawan, with orders to strengthen it; but the disastrous action at Chinhat made it necessary to concentrate the whole of the garrison at the residency. Orders were therefore given for the evacuation of the Machhi Bhawan and Innes, in very difficult circumstances, succeeded in blowing it up. He again distinguished himself on 20 July when the rebels assembled in large masses and exploded a mine in the direction of the Redan battery, leaving an enormous crater. They advanced boldly to the assault, but Innes and others, under the command of Lieutenant Loughman, drove them back after four hours' fighting. During the siege Innes was especially employed in mining. On 21 August, after sixty-four hours' hard work and no sleep, he blew up Johannes's house, from which the rebel sharpshooters had fired with deadly effect. During the relief by Sir Henry Havelock he took part in all the sorties, and after the general had entered the city on 25 September he was placed in charge of the mining operations in the new position occupied by Havelock's force in the palaces on the bank of the Gumti River. The defence was then chiefly confined to mining and countermining until the final relief by Sir Colin Campbell on 22 November.

Following the evacuation of Lucknow, Innes was posted to Sir Thomas Franks's division, and during its march through Oudh he was present at the actions at Miranpur, Chanda, and Amirpur. He especially distinguished himself at the battle of Sultanpur on 23 February 1858 when, far in advance of the leading skirmishers, he single-handedly captured two enemy guns, one of which was about to pour shot on the advancing British column. On 4 March, the day on which Franks effected his junction with Sir Colin Campbell to besiege Lucknow, Innes was severely wounded during an attack on the fort at Dhaurahra, 8 miles from Lucknow. For his services in the mutiny Innes was promoted captain on 27 August 1858 and brevet major on 28 August 1858, and received a year's service for the defence of Lucknow. He was awarded the Victoria Cross (24 December 1858) for his conspicuous gallantry at Sultanpur.

After the mutiny Innes was appointed garrison engineer at Fort William, Calcutta; he then served in the public works department in the Central Provinces and in the Punjab until 1867. In the following year he was appointed a member of the commission to investigate the failure of the Bank of Bombay. In 1869 he started the upper section of the Indus Valley Railway, and in the following year he was appointed accountant-general of the public works department, holding that important post for seven years. He was promoted first-captain in his corps on 29 February 1864, brevet lieutenant-colonel on 14 June 1869, regimental major on 5 July 1872, regimental lieutenant-colonel on 1 April 1874, and brevet colonel on 1 October 1877.

In 1882 Innes was appointed inspector-general of military works at Simla and member of the Indian defence committee. Many new defences were carried out under his orders. He was promoted colonel on 26 May 1883 and major-general on 28 November 1885, and retired from the service with the honorary rank of lieutenant-general on 16 March 1886. On the jubilee celebration of the defence of the residency at Lucknow, in June 1907, he was created CB, military division. After his retirement he devoted himself to literary pursuits. His works included two histories, *Lucknow and Oude in the Mutiny* (1895) and *The Sepoy Revolt of 1857* (1897), and biographies of Sir Henry Lawrence (1898) and

Sir James Browne (1905). Innes died, after a long illness, at his home, 5 Pemberton Terrace, Cambridge, on 13 December 1907.   R. H. VETCH, *rev.* ALEX MAY

Sources *Indian Army List* · *Army List* · *The Times* (16 Dec 1907) · J. Innes, *Lucknow and Oude in the mutiny* (1895) · private information (1912) · P. A. Wilkins, *The history of the Victoria Cross* (1904) · O'M. Creagh and E. M. Humphris, *The V.C. and D.S.O.*, 1 [1920] · M. Edwardes, *A season in hell: the defence of the Lucknow residency* (1973) · C. Hibbert, *The great mutiny, India, 1857* (1978) · H. M. Vibart, *Addiscombe: its heroes and men of note* (1894) · *CGPLA Eng. & Wales* (1908)
Archives BL, memorandum relating to siege of Lucknow, Add. MS 42807 · Bodl. Oxf., account of siege of Lucknow · NAM
Likenesses photograph, repro. in Wilkins, *History of the Victoria Cross*, 153
Wealth at death £813 11*s.* 5*d.*: probate, 5 Feb 1908, *CGPLA Eng. & Wales*

Innes, Sir James Rose- (1855–1942), politician and judge in South Africa, was born in Uitenhage, Cape Colony, on 8 January 1855, the eldest of the nine children of James Rose-Innes (1824–1906), magistrate and under-secretary for native affairs, and his wife, Mary Ann, *née* Fleischer. He was educated at Uitenhage and Bedford government schools, then at Gill College, Somerset East (a Presbyterian foundation), and received the degrees of BA (1874) and LLB (1877) from the University of the Cape of Good Hope. He was admitted to the Cape Town bar in 1878, and in 1890 became a QC. His gift for badinage, his good looks and engaging personality, and his ability in argument won him a brilliant reputation. In 1881 he married Jessie Dods Pringle (*d.* 1943), daughter of a prominent 1820 British settler, William Dods Pringle. Their only child, Dorothy, married Count Helmuth von Moltke of Kreisau, Germany; her eldest son, Count Helmuth James von Moltke, was the leader of the Kreisau circle which conspired against Hitler; he was executed in January 1945.

Rose-Innes combined his active legal practice with a distinguished parliamentary career. In 1884, with the help of the African leader John Tengo Jabavu, he was elected to the house of assembly for the racially mixed constituency of Victoria West, winning the black vote because of his liberal views on the 'native question'. He changed in 1888 to the more convenient Cape seat, which he represented until he retired from politics in 1902. His chief concerns were his championship of the rights of the black population and his battle to secure 'local option' for the sale of liquor to Africans—the paternalist side of his liberalism. As a politician he was sometimes indecisive on central issues and shirked the responsibility of opposition leadership.

In 1890 Rose-Innes became attorney-general in the first, ill-assorted Rhodes cabinet. Its struggling liberal trio, Rose-Innes, J. X. Merriman, and J. W. Sauer, were at odds with their Afrikaner Bond colleagues, especially the astute, unscrupulous James Sivewright, and were dismayed at Rhodes's dependence on the subtle Afrikaner Bond leader, J. H. Hofmeyr. Moreover, Rose-Innes distrusted Rhodes, who was obsessed with developing the north by means of the chartered British South African Company, and who shocked Rose-Innes by his political

Sir James Rose-Innes (1855–1942), by Walter Stoneman, 1919

misuse of his wealth. Rose-Innes's first crisis of conscience was in 1892, over the Bond-inspired attempt to weaken the 'native' vote by steeply increasing the property qualification. Rhodes, however, agreed to a compromise, which Rose-Innes unhappily accepted. The next collision followed swiftly, when Rose-Innes discovered that Sivewright, without calling for tenders or consulting the cabinet, had granted his friend J. D. Logan the catering monopoly on all Cape railways for eighteen years. On Hofmeyr's advice the contract was cancelled. But the liberal trio insisted on either Sivewright's resignation or their own. Rhodes intrigued to undermine them and after a long delay, during which 'the three mutineers' were persuaded not to resign, Rhodes suddenly re-formed his cabinet, dropping all four ministers, and, to Rose-Innes's disgust, taking in the opposition leader, Sir Gordon Sprigg (who was, incidentally, Rose-Innes's uncle).

At the end of 1895 the fiasco of the Jameson raid against the Transvaal polarized political loyalties and cost Rhodes his premiership. In Johannesburg the Kruger government charged the Reform Committee with high treason, and the British government gave Rose-Innes a watching brief over the trial. He came away convinced that the Uitlanders' grievances were authentic, and would lead to war if not promptly redressed. However, Merriman's priority was the cancellation of Rhodes's charter, and both his motion and Rose-Innes's Uitlander amendment were defeated. Instead, a parliamentary committee of inquiry was appointed: the motion was moved by W. P. Schreiner,

who was Hofmeyr's choice as Bond parliamentary leader. Rose-Innes served on the committee and welcomed the report's definitive finding on Rhodes's guilt.

In 1897 Sir Alfred Milner became Cape governor and high commissioner, and in the fraught period that followed Rose-Innes's inherent pacifism was shaken by the threat of war. His friendship with Merriman and Sauer lapsed as they moved towards the Bond in their effort to avert war. Yet he sympathized with Schreiner's troubled 'Peace Ministry' (October 1898 to June 1900) and sorrowed when war broke out in October 1899. Towards Milner—whose militancy was the prime cause of the war—Rose-Innes was ambivalent. When the Schreiner ministry broke up after the British government refused amnesty for the rank-and-file of Cape rebels, Rose-Innes agreed with their limited disfranchisement, and took office as attorney-general in Sprigg's stopgap cabinet. Rose-Innes's persistent scruples about civil rights added to his distress about the war: his protests against martial law abuses, however, caused him endless trouble with the military authorities. (The surprise of his knighthood in 1901 was the only offsetting event.) But when martial law was extended to the ports Milner intervened to modify it, and he also relieved Rose-Innes's miseries by appointing him judge president—later chief justice—of the new Transvaal supreme court. In this role Rose-Innes's tact, lucidity, fairness, and respect for individual rights significantly influenced the return to the habits of peace. And in his personal life, his friendship with Merriman, whom he intensely admired, was restored in 1907.

In May 1910, after South African union, Rose-Innes was appointed a judge of appeal, but he was distressed that Merriman (the last Cape prime minister), who on merit and experience should have been first prime minister of the union, was passed over in favour of General Botha (the Transvaal prime minister). In 1914 Rose-Innes reached the peak of his career when he became chief justice of South Africa. In 1919 he was made a privy councillor, and in 1924 the University of Stellenbosch awarded him an honorary doctorate in law. His judicious blending of common law and Roman-Dutch law heightened his prestige. Though not all his judgments won future acceptance, many jurists still rate him as the greatest of South African judges. Memorable examples include, on agency and company law, *Robinson* v. *Randfontein Estate Gold Mining Co.* (1921), on property, *Macdonald, Ltd.* v. *Radin N. O.* (1915), and, in criminal law, *R.* v. *Holliday* (1924).

Rose-Innes retired in February 1927. He continued to play a moderating role in public life, and in 1929 helped to found the Non-Racial Franchise Association, which sought vainly to prevent the destruction in 1936 of the Cape 'native' franchise. He remained until the end a dedicated and eloquent exponent of liberalism and upholder of the Cape tradition. He died in Wynberg, Cape Province, on 16 January 1942, at the age of eighty-seven.

PHYLLIS LEWSEN

Sources *James Rose-Innes … an autobiography*, ed. B. A. Tindall (1949) · *Sir James Rose-Innes: selected correspondence, 1884–1902*, ed. H. M. Wright (1972) · P. Lewsen, *John X. Merriman: paradoxical South*

African statesman (1982) • E. A. Walker, *W. P. Schreiner: a South African* (1937) • *Selections from the correspondence of J. X. Merriman*, ed. P. Lewsen, 4 vols. (1960–69) • B. Williams, *Cecil Rhodes* (1921) • E. Kahn, *Contract and mercantile law through the cases* (1971) • *Cape house of assembly debates* (1884–1902) • law reports of the Transvaal court and the South African court of appeal • *S. A. Law Journal*, 19–66 (1905–49) • J. H. Hofmeyr and F. W. Reitz, *The life of Jan Hendrik Hofmeyr (Onze Jan)* (1913) • (Sir) James Rose-Innes, Van Riebeeck Society, 2nd ser. (1972)

Archives National Library of South Africa, Cape Town | National Library of South Africa, Cape Town, Bower MSS; Merriman MSS; Rhodes MSS; Schreiner MSS

Likenesses W. Stoneman, photograph, 1919, NPG [*see illus.*] • M. Kottler, bust, South African National Art Gallery • N. Lewis, oils, Appeal Court Building, Bloemfontein, South Africa • G. C. Robinson, oils, Houses of Parliament, Cape Town, South Africa • W. H. Schroder, portrait, repro. in *Excalibur* (1 April 1887), appx • bust, Court of Appeal, Bloemfontein, South Africa • portrait, repro. in *The Graphic* (7 Aug 1897) • portrait, repro. in *Personality* (17 Oct 1963) • portrait, repro. in Rose-Innes, *James Rose-Innes*

Innes, John (*c.*1370–1414), bishop of Moray, was probably related to the Moray family of Innes of that ilk. The chronology of his academic career may indicate that he was born about 1370. He studied in Paris for an unknown period in the 1380s or 1390s and had become bachelor of civil law by 1396 and of both laws by 1407. His studies were supported by a grant which Bishop Alexander Bur of Moray made from the judicial profits of his diocese in 1396. Although he was appointed archdeacon of Caithness in 1396 and then dean of Ross at a date between 1399 and 1404, much of Innes's ecclesiastical career was spent in Moray. He had acquired a canonry in that diocese by February 1390, the prebend of Duffus between 30 May 1395 and 1 August 1398, and additionally the vicariate of Duffus after 1397. Having enjoyed the patronage of successive Moray bishops and apparently with strong familial ties in the area, Innes was elected bishop after the death of William Spynie in 1406. He was consecrated by Benedict XIII, probably on 23 January 1407 at Marseilles. His career following his return to Scotland remains obscure.

Innes has traditionally been credited with supervising the rebuilding of Elgin Cathedral after its destruction by Alexander Stewart, earl of Buchan, in 1390 and with building work at the episcopal palace of Spynie, but he played little part in national politics. His local political associations, in so far as they are known, suggest a willingness to follow his ecclesiastical superiors. On 22 February 1390, as a protégé of Bur, he witnessed the bishop's accommodation with Thomas Dunbar, son of the earl of Moray, against Buchan. In 1404, however, as dean of Ross, he joined Bishop Alexander Waghorn in witnessing several charters of Isabella, countess of Mar, shortly after her marriage to Buchan's son, also Alexander. Waghorn was probably an ally of Alexander junior and, a little less certainly, of Alexander senior. If Innes too can be associated with this clique, then he may well have had the tacit support of the younger Stewart, the leading magnate of the region, for his episcopal election. Innes died at Elgin on 25 April 1414 and was buried in the cathedral.

DAVID DITCHBURN

Sources D. E. R. Watt, *A biographical dictionary of Scottish graduates to AD 1410* (1977), 278–9 • C. Innes, ed., *Registrum episcopatus Moraviensis*, Bannatyne Club, 58 (1837) • J. Robertson, ed., *Illustrations of the topography and antiquities of the shires of Aberdeen and Banff*, 3–4, Spalding Club, 29, 32 (1857–62) • D. Forbes, *Ane account of the familie of Innes*, ed. C. Innes, Spalding Club, 34 (1864) • W. R. Macdonald, 'Notes on the heraldry of Elgin and its neighbourhood', *Proceedings of the Society of Antiquaries of Scotland*, 34 (1899–1900), 344–429

Innes, John (1739–1777), anatomist, was born at Callart in the highlands of Scotland. He went to Edinburgh as a boy, and was employed by Alexander Monro secundus, then professor of anatomy in the university. Innes became a dexterous dissector, and when eighteen was made dissector to the anatomical theatre. It was his duty to dissect out the parts for each of the professor's lectures, and he thus acquired a minute knowledge of human anatomy. The students liked him, and with Monro's consent he gave evening demonstrations of anatomy, and became so famous for the clearness of his descriptions that his audience numbered nearly two hundred students. In 1776 he published at Edinburgh *A Short Description of the Human Muscles, Chiefly as they Appear on Dissection*, and this book, with some additions by Monro, continued to be used in the dissecting rooms at Edinburgh for fifty years after his death. The book's descriptions are generally terse and lucid, and copies of the book often bear evidence that it was placed, as intended by the author, upon the body which the student was dissecting. Later in the same year he published *Eight Anatomical Tables of the Human Body*. The plates represent the skeleton and muscles, and are copied from Albinus, with brief original descriptions of each plate. Both books were published in second editions by John Murray in London in 1778 and 1779 respectively. After a long illness Innes died of phthisis on 12 January 1777, in Edinburgh.

NORMAN MOORE, *rev.* MICHAEL BEVAN

Sources J. Innes, *A short description of the human muscles* (1778) [incl. memoir by A. Monro]

Innes, John (1829–1904), property developer, and philanthropist, was born on 20 January 1829 in Hampstead, Middlesex, and baptized on 23 February 1829 at All Souls, St Marylebone, the sixth of seven known children of John Innes (1786–1869), a West Indies merchant of Mincing Lane and Moorgate Street in the City of London, and his wife, Mary Reid (1792–1849). His father was the author of reports to the government on the West Indies and the abolition of slavery, and his mother was the daughter of Andrew Reid MP, of Lyonsdown, Barnet, Hertfordshire, the founder of Reid's Brewery. His paternal grandparents were from Huntly, Scotland. John Innes never married.

After living in family homes in Kensington Square and then in Porchester Terrace in the parish of Paddington, Innes attended boarding-school in Brighton until the age of sixteen. He and his elder brother James, a London merchant (later of Roffey Park, Sussex), became wine importers of Mincing Lane, in the City. In 1864 they founded the City of London Real Property Company in Mark Lane; it subsequently became a subsidiary of Land Securities plc. In 1903 John followed James as director and chairman after the latter's death.

John Innes (1829–1904), by H. C. Osterstock, 1934

From the mid-1860s the brothers acquired land in Merton and Morden, Surrey, including several farms. John Innes rebuilt the farmhouse of Manor Farm, Merton, as his home, Manor House. He visited his father and sister in Porchester Terrace frequently. While James Innes concentrated on the City company, John, in association with the architect H. G. Quartermain, was more concerned with developing what was to be Merton Park, an early garden suburb centred on the old village, around the church of St Mary the Virgin. Quartermain built houses there between the early 1870s and 1904 (these are described by B. Cherry and N. Pevsner in *The Buildings of England, London 2, South*). The estate did not extend as far as planned during Innes's lifetime, but he achieved his aim of wide avenues of trees and holly hedges, houses for City men, cottages for farm and estate workers, a boys' club, a men's club, and a masonic hall. Lower Merton railway station was renamed Merton Park.

About 1872 Innes became lord of the manor of Merton. He was a JP, a churchwarden, and an overseer and guardian. He represented Merton on Croydon rural district council, and he was a trustee of the Merton schools and a manager of Abbey Road School. He purchased Bay Tree, a house on Kingston Road, to establish a place of temperance, and he considered the welfare of his estate workers and their widows; he also provided land for allotments and accommodated sports and fêtes in his gardens. He farmed pigs, sheep, and a dairy herd, in Merton, Morden, and Hedgerley, Berkshire. As chairman of the trustees of the Rutlish Charity, to finance the apprenticeship of poor

children of Merton he was closely involved when Rutlish Science School opened in 1895 to the east of the railway; he became chairman of its management board. As Rutlish School it later came to include Innes's original grounds, incorporating the building that was once his house.

John Innes died suddenly on 8 August 1904 at his home, Manor House, Merton, after a brief illness of uncertain cause. He was buried at Merton Park, Surrey, on 12 August at St Mary's Church, where four Burne-Jones windows, made in stained glass at Morris & Co. of Merton Abbey, were erected in his memory. An obituary on 13 August 1904 in the *Wimbledon News* described him as 'somewhat stern in demeanour', but generous, 'his purse always open for the furtherance of any good object'; and 'an all-round patron of all the social work of the parish'.

In his will Innes bequeathed his house and 5 acres of land for the establishment of a 'school of horticulture' with workshops, tools, scientific apparatus, libraries, and lecture and exhibition halls. The remainder of his estate was intended for a public park; later the John Innes Park came into being. The John Innes Horticultural Institution was founded in Merton Park in 1910, and was the earliest research institute for plant breeding and genetics in the UK. It later moved to Bayfordbury, Hertfordshire, where, in 1960, it became the John Innes Institute. In 1967 it transferred to Colney, near Norwich. It is now part of the John Innes Centre which is of international repute. The famous 'John Innes' compost was named after him.

JENNY WEST

Sources *Wimbledon News* (13 Aug 1904) · *The Times* (11 Aug 1904) · *London: south*, Pevsner (1983) · G. H. Godwin, 'John Innes: an appreciation', in G. H. Godwin, *Wimbledon and Merton Annual* (1905), 109–23 · *Some memories of Merton*, Merton Historical Society (1983) · L. Green, 'John Innes, 1829–1904', in E. M. Jowett, *History of Merton and Morden* (1951), 122–8 · J. Goodman, '100 years ago in Merton Park', *John Innes Society Newsletter* (1988–94) · J. Wallace, *Dorset Hall* (1991), 17–24 · K. Denbigh, 'John Innes: a story with a sequel', *History and heroes of Old Merton* (1975), 126–37 · *The Post Office London directory* (1853–1900) · *Royal blue book* (1830–42) [annuals] · parish registers (birth), St Marylebone, All Souls, 20 Jan 1829

Archives John Innes Centre, Norwich, John Innes archives, corresp., diaries, notebooks, and business papers | Surrey HC, deeds · Merton Park, London, John Innes Society MSS

Likenesses photograph, 1903, Manor Club, Kingston Road, Merton Park, London · H. C. Osterstock, portrait, 1934, John Innes Centre, Norwich [*see illus.*] · group portrait, photograph, John Innes Centre, Norwich, John Innes Archives

Wealth at death £338,026 14*s*. 7*d*.: probate, 11 Aug 1905, *CGPLA Eng. & Wales* · £17,560 5*s*.: administration, 21 March 1905, *CGPLA Eng. & Wales*

Innes, Lewis (1651–1738), Roman Catholic priest and courtier, was born at Walkerdales in the Enzie of Banff, the eldest son of James Innes of Drumgask (*c*.1617–1686), a Catholic laird from Aberdeenshire, and his wife, Jane Robertson (*c*.1619–1704), daughter of an Aberdeen merchant. The Inneses were a remarkable recusant family who produced an impressive line of priests for the Scottish Catholic mission from the time of James II to the reign of Queen Victoria: Lewis and three of his brothers, including Thomas *Innes, were educated for the priesthood. Lewis studied at the Scots College, Paris, and was ordained priest there about 1676. In 1682 he became its principal on the death of Principal Barclay. Like his brother Thomas, Lewis had a keen interest in Scottish history and in the conservation of the college's immensely rich archives: in 1694 he organized a ceremony of authentication by a team of world renowned French experts of a famous charter held by the college, which established the legitimacy of King Robert III, much to the delight of the exiled James II and his entourage.

Had it not been for the revolution of 1688 Lewis Innes would have been one of James II's nominees to be the first Catholic bishop to be appointed in Scotland since the Reformation. When the revolution postponed the deliberations on a Scottish vicar apostolic and sent James into exile in France, Lewis Innes instead became a close adviser to the deposed monarch when he set up court at St Germain in 1690 following his defeat in Ireland. He was also appointed almoner to the queen consort, Maria d'Este, retaining the position in 1701 when she became queen mother on the death of James II. On 23 December 1713 he became almoner to her son, James Francis Edward Stuart, the chevalier de St George, James VIII and III, the Old Pretender. On 17 March 1714 he was made lord almoner. By this time Innes was effectively acting as the Pretender's political secretary, and was obliged to resign from the principalship of the college in order to devote himself full time to politics. Having reluctantly left Paris in 1713 to accompany his royal master to the new home of the court at Bar-le-Duc in Lorraine he was a central figure in the diplomatic manoeuvres which tried without success to obtain James's right to the succession after the death of Queen Anne.

In 1718 Innes temporarily fell from grace with the Pretender but within a few years he had returned to favour, advising him notably in the matter of appointments of Scottish vicars apostolic. Of staunchly Gallican views Innes held that any senior ecclesiastical appointment required the consent of the sovereign as well as of Rome. He was one of the chief architects of the policy which aimed at effecting a Catholic restoration in Great Britain and Ireland via a political revolution. However sincere in his beliefs he must shoulder much of the responsibility for a strategy which did more harm than good to the cause of the Catholic religion in his native Scotland. He remains, however, a key figure in the annals of Jacobitism and at Innes's death, on 11 February 1738, in Paris, where he was buried, the Pretender paid fulsome tribute to his services to the cause of the Stuarts, praising him in a letter to Thomas Innes as 'a most faithful servant, who joynd capacity and zeal in my service, which are not always found in the same person' (Stuart, 2.379). The original memoirs written by James II had been deposited in the Scots College under the special care of Lewis and in his letter of condolence to Thomas, the Pretender expressed his gratitude for the college's custody of these manuscripts and confirmed that he wished them to remain there in the care of Thomas Innes and his nephew George Innes, the new principal of the college.   JAMES F. McMILLAN

Sources L. Innes, letters, Scots College Archives, Edinburgh · *Calendar of the Stuart papers belonging to his majesty the king, preserved at Windsor Castle*, 7 vols., HMC, 56 (1902–23), esp. vol. 1 · B. M. Halloran, *The Scots College, Paris, 1603–1792* (1997) · J. Stuart, ed., *The miscellany of the Spalding Club*, 2, Spalding Club, 6 (1842) · [E. T. Corp and J. Sanson], eds., *La cour des Stuarts* (Paris, 1992) [exhibition catalogue, Musée des Antiquités Nationales de Saint-Germain-en-Laye, 13 Feb – 27 April 1992] · E. Grew and M. S. Grew, *The English court in exile* (1911)

Archives Royal Arch., corresp. and related material · Scottish Catholic Archives, Edinburgh, letters

Innes, Michael. *See* Stewart, John Innes Mackintosh (1906–1994).

Innes, Ralph Hammond [*pseuds.* Hammond Innes, Ralph Hammond] (1913–1998), writer, was born on 15 July 1913 at 68 Clarence Road, Horsham, Sussex, the only child of William Hammond Innes, a bank clerk, and his wife, Dora Beatrice Chisford. Ralph went to Cranbrook School, and by the age of thirteen he knew he wanted to be a writer.

Innes left Cranbrook at eighteen, and tried a number of jobs in the early 1930s including teaching and publishing before joining the staff of the *Financial News* in 1934 as a trainee industrial correspondent. He stayed at the paper for the next six years. Wanting to raise some money in order to get married, he sent off a manuscript of a supernatural thriller to an agent (*The Doppelganger*, published in 1937), and was soon committed to producing three more thrillers in two years for Herbert Jenkins, with lower than usual advances. He met these arduous terms, though he later disowned these works, describing them as 'ham-fisted'. He did, however, acknowledge that the experience had been valuable: 'writing those four books I more or less taught myself how to do it' (*The Independent*). Innes married the actress, and later author, Dorothy Mary Lang (*d.* 1989) in Jevington, Sussex, on 21 August 1937.

Once he had worked out this first contract, Innes switched publishers, moving to Collins. He continued to write at a furious pace, and produced three more thrillers in the next two years. The first of these, *Wreckers must Breathe* (1940)—a story of U-boats operating out of Cornwall—met with considerable success. The third book for Collins, *Attack Alarm* (1941), was written largely during night watches defending an aerodrome during the battle of Britain. The book was serialized in an American newspaper, and has been credited with improving the image of Britain at this delicate stage in the Second World War.

Innes had volunteered for the Royal Artillery in 1940, served with the Eighth Army in the Middle East and Italy, and then transferred to the British army newspapers. By the end of the war he was editing the Florence edition of the forces' paper, and covering the invasion of southern France. After the war he left journalism to become a full-time writer. From then on he published a novel roughly every two years. *The Lonely Skier* (1947), a novel inspired by a gruelling skiing course taken just before he left the army, brought him to some prominence, and it was his first to be made into a film: *Snowbound* (1948). However, it was with *The 'Mary Deare'* (1956) that Innes secured his long-held status as a best-selling author. A film of the book, starring Gary Cooper, Charlton Heston, and Michael Redgrave,

Ralph Hammond Innes (1913-1998), by Godfrey Argent, 1970

was made in 1959 and was a tremendous success. Several more films of Innes's books followed, including *Campbell's Kingdom* (1952) starring Dirk Bogarde. In his heyday, in the 1950s and 1960s, Innes was selling more than 2 million copies of each book.

Innes's books are set in far-flung locations: from the western isles to Antarctica, the Indian Ocean, and the Australian outback. Each book was carefully researched. He never wrote about a place without having been there, and he and Dorothy—both compulsive travellers, and with no children to tie them down—spent months sailing around the world on these research trips in their 42 foot yacht the *Mary Deare*. His books fall into a familiar pattern. They are fast-moving adventure stories—Innes himself rejected the term 'thriller'—with a first-person male narrator, and stories of high action, played out against the hostile elements. He saw himself as one of the 'last romantics' in the tradition of Rider Haggard, Robert Louis Stevenson, and Rudyard Kipling. He valued the wide expanse of their tales, which countered the provincialism, as he saw it, of England after the war. Critics have often found the novels' characterization wanting, and the dialogue rather flat. Praise for his work tended to be of the faint variety (the common fate of popular literature)—for his workmanlike and unpretentious style. He did, however, maintain his commercial popularity over the length of his career, and V. S. Pritchett thought his depiction of action in a class of its own. His adventures have been translated into over forty languages.

Innes once described the theme of his books as being 'man's everlasting struggle against the enormous stature of nature' (*The Guardian*), and this passion evolved into a strong ecological theme in his later works, from *Black Tide* (1982), about oil spillage, and *High Stand* (1985), his 'tree' novel. With the profits from his early successes Innes had bought a medieval timbered house: Ayres End, in Kersey, Suffolk, and with it 233 acres of derelict woodland. He restored this, and went on to buy and reforest land in Wales and Australia, planting, at his estimation, about one and a half million trees.

In addition to his adventure novels, Innes wrote children's books under the pseudonym Ralph Hammond, and a number of non-fiction works, including two books of travels and a history of the conquistadors. He was appointed CBE in 1978, and was a member of the Society of Authors, the Royal Yacht Squadron, and the Timber Growers' Association. He was a dapper man, described by one interviewer in 1996 as a model of old-world courtesy and correctness. Innes died of cancer at Ayres End on 10 June 1998. He had amassed a fortune of nearly £7 million from his books; he left £5.4 million to the Association of Sea Training Organizations. ELERI LARKUM

Sources b. cert. · m. cert. · d. cert. · *WW* (1998) · *Daily Telegraph* (3 Aug 1996) · *Daily Telegraph* (12 June 1998) · *Financial Times* (14 May 1988) · *The Guardian* (13 June 1998) · *The Times* (12 June 1998) · *The Independent* (13 June 1998)

Likenesses G. Argent, photograph, 1970, NPG [*see illus.*]

Wealth at death approx. £7,000,000

Innes, Robert Thorburn Ayton (1861–1933), astronomer, was born at 66 Great King Street, Edinburgh, on 10 November 1861, the eldest of the twelve children of John Innes, a life assurance inspector, and his wife, Elizabeth Ayton. He attended a school in Dublin until he was twelve, then was self-taught, being especially gifted in computation. He married Anne Elizabeth Fennell in 1884 and soon afterwards emigrated to Australia, where he became a successful wine merchant. In Sydney he began observing with a 6¾ inch refracting telescope lent by the astronomer W. F. Gale, and contributed to the *Journal of the British Astronomical Association* and to *Monthly Notices of the Royal Astronomical Society*. He had very acute vision and discovered several double stars, of which he compiled a first list in 1894; with a larger reflecting telescope he then made further discoveries and began to pursue astronomy as a career.

Innes wrote to David Gill at the Cape of Good Hope observatory offering his services, but the only post available then was a combination of secretary, librarian, and accountant, at a salary much lower than he earned in the wine trade. He nevertheless accepted, and arrived at the Cape in 1896. By 1898 he had, in his spare time, discovered a further 280 double stars, and the following year he published his first *Reference Catalogue of Southern Double Stars*, containing 2140 pairs. He also measured proper motions and revised the *Cape Photographic Durchmusterung*. In 1903, on Gill's recommendation, Innes was appointed director of the new observatory in Transvaal. It was primarily a meteorological station, but, with the help of Gill and Dr Theodore Reunart of Johannesburg, Innes obtained a 9 inch refractor and began observations of Jupiter's satellites from October 1907. In 1909 he persuaded the government to order a 26½ inch refractor from Howard Grubb of Dublin; however, this was not installed until 1925, so Innes had only two years' use of it. Meanwhile he received the gift of a 10 inch photographic refractor from the wealthy English amateur John Franklin-Adams, who, just before his death in 1912, also presented his twin astrographic telescope.

When the four states merged to form the Union of South Africa the Transvaal observatory was renamed the Union Observatory, and Innes was given the title of first union astronomer in April 1912. Before his retirement in 1927 his achievements were numerous. He championed the use of the blink microscope and, with its aid, after a systematic search, discovered in 1912 Proxima Centauri, the nearest star to the solar system; he suspected the unusual shape, later confirmed, of the asteroid Eros; he found a star, ZC Vh.243, with the largest then known proper motion; he confirmed photographically the irregular variability of the star and associated nebula R Coronae Australis; and he discovered 'Innes's star', of the lowest then known luminosity. He was one of the first to offer proof of the variability of the rotation of the earth and to discuss evidence, from proper motions, of the rotation of the stellar system. In addition he continued to work on planets, comets, occultations, asteroids, Jovian satellites, and stellar magnitudes. In 1926 his work led to the proposal of the use of the parameters in orbit computation known as the Thiele–Innes constants. He issued his second catalogue of double stars in 1927, having discovered a total of 1628.

Innes drew attention to the exceptional seeing conditions on the high veld and encouraged the establishment of foreign observatories there. He forged an important link with Leiden University, which awarded him an honorary DSc in 1923. He was active in the affairs of the Johannesburg Public Library, and was one of the founders of the South African Association for the Advancement of Science, of which he was president in 1915–16. He was awarded the South Africa medal in 1918. He became a fellow of the Royal Astronomical Society in 1879, at the age of only seventeen, and a fellow of the Royal Society of Edinburgh in 1904. After he retired he became interested in cinematography and formed a film projection company.

Innes was an expert chess and bridge player, a delightfully informal and entertaining man, who cared little about official attitudes. Although physically strong and always in robust health, he died suddenly of heart failure at 27 Uxbridge Road, Kingston upon Thames, Surrey, on 13 March 1933, leaving his widow and three sons. His burial at Kingston cemetery on 17 March was conducted by the astronomer Revd Dr Martin Davidson and attended by the new astronomer royal, Harold Spencer Jones, a colleague and friend when at the Cape.   DAVID GAVINE

Sources *Monthly Notices of the Royal Astronomical Society*, 94 (1933–4), 277–81 · B. Warner, 'Innes, Robert Thorburn Ayton', *DSAB* · W. S. Finsen, 'Innes, Robert Thorburn Ayton', *DSB* · *Journal of the British*

Astronomical Association, 43 (1932–3), 260–62 · *South African Journal of Science*, 30 (1933), 1 · P. Moore and P. Collins, *The astronomy of southern Africa* (1977), 92–102 · *The Times* (15 March 1933) · *The Times* (18 March 1933) · *WWW* · B. Warner, 'Astronomical archives in southern Africa', *Journal for the History of Astronomy*, 8 (1977), 217–22 · *Proceedings of the Royal Society of Edinburgh*, 53 (1932–3), 367 · census returns, 1861
Archives Council for Scientific and Industrial Research, Pretoria, archives · RAS, corresp.
Likenesses photograph, South African Library and Africana Museum, Johannesburg · photographs, repro. in Moore and Collins, *Astronomy of southern Africa* · two photographs, South African Library and Africana Museum, Johannesburg

Innes, Thomas (1662–1744), Roman Catholic priest and historian, was born at Drumgask in the parish of Aboyne, Aberdeenshire, the third of eight children (of whom five became priests) of James Innes (*c*.1617–1686), wad-setter, and his wife, Jane Robertson (*c*.1619–1704), daughter of a merchant in Aberdeen. In 1679 he went to Paris where he attended lectures at the Collège de Navarre, though probably from the outset he was resident in the Scots College, Paris, where his brother Lewis, later principal, was already a student. He received the tonsure on 26 May 1684 and was ordained priest on 10 March 1691. Like most other Scottish Catholic priests of the period, he was commonly designated by aliases, the two most common being Fleming and Melville.

After ordination, Innes had some months' pastoral training with the Oratorians at Notre Dames des Vertus. Having returned to the Scots College in 1692, he graduated MA at the University of Paris in 1694. Between 1695 and 1697 he worked as an assistant priest in the parish of Magnay in the diocese of Paris. This was to prepare him further for an apostolate in Scotland on which he was engaged from June 1698 until October 1701, where he laboured mostly in the mission of Inveraven. Thomas Hearne, the English antiquary, recorded in his diary an incident in this period when Innes managed to avoid arrest by escaping through a window, but historical papers that he had been preparing for ten years were seized and burnt. Soon after Easter 1700 he was chosen to accompany Bishop William Nicolson on a six-month visitation of the western highlands and islands.

In 1701 Innes was appointed agent for the Scottish mission on being sent back to the Scots College, Paris, where he served as prefect of studies (1704–12 and 1718–27). From June 1727 until May 1729 he was in Britain arranging for the publication of *A Critical Essay on the Ancient Inhabitants of the Northern Parts of Britain or Scotland*. In this work he used precise historical methods to refute the mythic history of Scottish kings. Yet Innes had his own agenda, to vindicate primogeniture in the interest of the Jacobite cause, and his substitution of the Pictish line of kings is exceedingly suspect. A second work, which may be considered a continuation of the *Critical Essay*, existed only in manuscript form until published by the Spalding Club in 1853 under the title *The Civil and Ecclesiastical History of Scotland*.

Having heard in Scotland that he was suspected of Jansenism, Innes, on his return to Paris, resigned from the

Sorbonne, lest his membership of the university from which the appeal against the papal bull *Unigenitus* had been made bring opprobrium on the Scottish mission. He was appointed vice-principal of the Scots College, but was increasingly assailed by accusations of Jansenism. It was true that he could not accept *Unigenitus*, but he never wrote or preached against it, and made great efforts to avoid public dissent. Although he was accused of being an appellant, these charges were strenuously denied and have never been substantiated. Nevertheless, his views became widely known, and a movement for his ejection from the college, stirred up by a highland priest Colin Campbell, pressurized Bishop James Gordon to write to Rome in 1733 asking for Innes's removal.

At this point Innes voluntarily left the college, a move that severely restricted his archival work. This had begun about 1692 when he had embarked on the task of arranging in order the documents in the Scots College, Paris, and of copying the bulls and charters from Glasgow that had been deposited by Archbishop James Beaton in the Carthusian priory of Paris. In 1694 he made the great discovery of a charter of Robert II which proved the legitimacy of the Stuart dynasty. Innes liberally assisted all who visited the Scots College archives or wrote for information. Among these were Étienne Baluze, librarian of the Colbertine Library, the antiquary William Hamilton of Wishaw, Henry Maule, titular earl of Panmure, the publishers Robert and Andrew Foulis, the historian Thomas Carte, and David Wilkins, who in the first volume of *Concilia Magnae Britanniae et Hiberniae* published Innes's 'Letter on the ancient manner of holding synods in Scotland'.

Innes's scholarly competence was recognized by many in his lifetime, including Francis Atterbury, Thomas Ruddiman, the Maurist scholar Thiery Ruinart, and the Scottish Episcopalian bishops Archibald Campbell and Robert Keith. He was made a burgess of the city of Glasgow, but, on the debit side, he was twice rebuked by Bishop Gordon for neglecting his students.

In addition to Innes's published works a considerable amount of manuscript material has survived, including five volumes of historical collections in Edinburgh University Library, and numerous letters and historical papers in Columba House, Edinburgh, which also possesses an eighteenth-century transcript of charters of the church of Glasgow which Innes corrected. Some of his papers were published in *Miscellany of the Spalding Club* (vol. 2, 1908) and a few letters in Harry Maule's *Registrum de Panmure* (1874).

In 1738, in a private capacity, Innes was received back into the Scots College, Paris, where he died on 28 January 1744. He was buried on 30 January, probably in the churchyard of St Étienne du Mont, Paris. He was among the first to adopt the strict historical disciplines of Jean Mabillon, and his extant transcriptions have preserved the text of charters and manuscripts that perished in the French Revolution. The *Innes Review* is named after him.

BRIAN M. HALLORAN

Sources DNB · *The miscellany of the New Spalding Club*, 1–2, New Spalding Club, 6, 34 (1890–1908) · G. Grub, in T. Innes, *The civil and ecclesiastical history of Scotland*, ed. G. Grub (1853) [preface] · O. Blundell, *A notable family of priests* (c.1909) · T. Innes, 'The Inneses of Balnacraig', *Deeside Field*, 5 (1931), 76–83 · W. Clapperton, 'Memoirs of Scotch missionary priests', Scottish Catholic Archives, Edinburgh, CC 1/11 · letters of Thomas Innes and others, Scottish Catholic Archives, Edinburgh · T. Innes, 'A memoriall of my travels in England', 1679, Scottish Catholic Archives, Edinburgh, SCA/PT1/4/1 · *Reliquiae Hearnianae: the remains of Thomas Hearne*, ed. P. Bliss, 2nd edn, 2 (1869) · R. Wodrow, *Analecta, or, Materials for a history of remarkable providences, mostly relating to Scotch ministers and Christians*, ed. [M. Leishman], 4 vols., Maitland Club, 60 (1842–3) · B. M. Halloran, *The Scots College, Paris, 1603–1792* (1997) · G. Innes, letter to Bishop Gordon, Scottish Catholic Archives, Edinburgh, SCA/BL3/82/3, 31 Jan 1744

Archives NL Scot., notes on civil and ecclesiastical history · Scottish Catholic Archives, Edinburgh, eighteenth-century transcript of charters of Glasgow, corrected by Innes, vol. 1, JB 1/7; papers and letter-books; compilations of Thomas Innes, PT1/1/1–4; historical papers, PT1/2/1–11; Innes's letters [transcripts], PT1/3/1–4; miscellaneous, PT1/4/1–3 · U. Edin. L., collections relating to *History of Scotland* | Scottish Catholic Archives, Edinburgh, Blairs letter collection, letters · U. Edin. L., Laing collection, letters, 346

Wealth at death no income after 1733; owned books and papers: 29 March 1744, Scottish Catholic Archives, Edinburgh, SCA/BL3/82/4

Innes, Sir Thomas, of Learney (1893–1971), herald, was born in Aberdeen on 26 August 1893, the only son and elder child of Lieutenant-Colonel Francis Newell Innes of Learney (1845–1907), Royal Horse Artillery, and his wife, Margaret Anne (d. 1923), daughter of Archer Irvine-Fortescue, laird of Kingcausie, Kincardineshire. His ancient family descended through the Innes baronets of Innermarkie from Berowald the Fleming, granted the barony of Innes in 1160. He himself held the old territorial baronies of Learney, Kinnairdy, and Yeochrie, was superior of the town of Torphins, and restored Kinnairdy Castle, home of his ancestors, the thanes of Aberchirder.

Educated at Edinburgh Academy and at Edinburgh University, in 1922 Innes of Learney 'passed advocate' to the Scottish bar, where he practised for many years. His main interests were heraldic, and in 1926 he became Carrick pursuivant, soon establishing himself as a leading heraldic and peerage counsel. His principal case was perhaps Maclean of Ardgour, where he acted successfully for the heir, who held the principal inheritance, against her cousin, the heir male. This stimulated his later preference for the descent of both name and arms to immediate heirs female rather than remoter heirs male, though some heraldists felt that constant female line changes of name when the male line still existed were not to be encouraged when no 'principal inheritance' except the arms was involved. On 27 December 1928 he married Lady Lucy Buchan (b. 1902), daughter of the eighteenth earl of Caithness; they had three sons and a daughter.

Learney's authoritative work *Scots Heraldry* (1934), with its later revised edition (1956), as also his books on clans and tartans, played an important part in the remarkable development of public interest in heraldry, genealogy, and clans that gathered momentum under his leadership. More new coats of arms were recorded in the Lyon register during his time than during the whole previous three centuries put together. He learned the practical administration of Lyon office and court as interim Lyon clerk in 1929 and again in 1939–40. Promoted Albany herald in 1935, ten years later he became lord Lyon king of arms, being appointed KCVO in 1946. He was also secretary to the Order of the Thistle from 1945 to 1969 and was FSA (Scotland).

As lord Lyon, he felt himself custodian of the spirit of Caledonia allegorically embodied in the sovereign. He stage-managed the renewal of historic Scottish pageantry under Elizabeth II, who paid more official visits to Scotland than any other sovereign since 1603. His most important tasks were the ceremonial for the St Giles service after the coronation, at which the honours of Scotland appeared for only the second time since the union; the state visits of the kings of Norway and Sweden (the first ever by foreign sovereigns); the opening of the general assembly twice by the queen in person (she was the first sovereign since James VI to do this); and the silver jubilee. In 1967 the queen recognized his wise guidance by promoting him GCVO, an honour not bestowed on other modern kings of arms.

Learney distinguished carefully between his office as lord Lyon, the judge, and his ministerial capacity as king of arms. He had a natural modesty and sought no reward beyond his meagre official salary. His erudition and panoptical view of Scottish genealogical history enabled him to lay down a body of heraldic law by a series of considered judgments, though he sometimes tended to carry law to a logical conclusion that startled narrower historical specialists and he occasionally misused Gaelic expressions. Lyon sought to unite in goodwill Scotsmen worldwide and above all to maintain the extended family or clan. The standing council of Scottish chiefs was founded at his suggestion; he controlled claimants to chiefship, whose only unimpeachable right at law is to the undifferenced arms of their name; and he encouraged clan societies since the clan spirit cuts across social barriers, removing snobbery from heraldry and allowing all to share the traditions of their name.

Perhaps the last laird to speak naturally in the aristocratic but homely Doric, Sir Tam combined common sense with humour, was completely without pretension, and utterly unselfconscious: in his bar days it is said he even appeared in wig and gown over tartan bicycling-breeches, and once secured the acquittal of an accused criminal by assuring the jury: 'My client must be innocent. He tells me so himself.' He was probably the greatest Lyon since the seventeenth century. He was also a member of, and held office in, many Scottish learned societies.

Learney retired in 1969, becoming Marchmont herald, and died at Edinburgh on 16 October 1971. A knight of St John of Jerusalem and archer of the queen's bodyguard for Scotland, he was honorary LLD of St Andrews (1956). In 1981 his youngest son, Malcolm Innes of Edingight, also became the lord Lyon.

Iain Moncreiffe of That Ilk, *rev.*

Sources personal knowledge (1986) · *The Times* (18 Oct 1971) · *WWW* · Burke, *Peerage* (1939)
Likenesses D. Pottinger, oils, 1949, Court of the Lord Lyon, Edinburgh

Innrechtach ua Finnachtai (*d.* 854). *See under* Iona, abbots of (*act.* 563–927).

Inskip, Robert Andrew [Robin], **second Viscount Caldecote** (1917–1999), engineer and industrialist, was born on 8 October 1917 at 10 Eaton Square, Belgravia, London, the only child of Thomas Walker Hobart *Inskip, first Viscount Caldecote (1876–1947), barrister and Conservative politician and lord chief justice from 1940 to 1946, and his wife, Lady Augusta Helen Elizabeth (1876–1967), widow of Charles Lindsay Orr Ewing MP and eldest daughter of David Boyle, seventh earl of Glasgow. He had two stepbrothers and one stepsister, the children of his mother's first marriage. He was educated at Eton College and King's College, Cambridge, where he was awarded a first in mechanical sciences in 1939. In the same year he was commissioned in the Royal Naval Volunteer Reserve, which he had joined in 1937, and served in destroyers in the Mediterranean and the Far East during the Second World War. For his part in the evacuation of the army from Greece and Crete in 1941 he was awarded a DSC, ending the war as a lieutenant-commander. On 22 July 1942 he married Jean Hamilla (*b.* 1918), only daughter of Rear-Admiral Hugh Dundas Hamilton, of Haddenham, Buckinghamshire: they had one son and two daughters.

After the war Inskip studied naval architecture at the Royal Naval College, Greenwich, and in 1947, the year he succeeded to the viscountcy, he took a job as an assistant manager at the Vickers Armstrong shipbuilding yard at Walker-on-Tyne. In 1948 he was elected a fellow of King's College, Cambridge, and appointed a lecturer in the university engineering department. Already a director of the English Electric Company since 1953 he left Cambridge in 1955 to take on responsibility for the English Electric aircraft division. English Electric was producing the famous Canberra jet bomber, and under Caldecote developed the supersonic Lightning fighter, which entered operational service in 1959.

In 1960 English Electric, Vickers Armstrong, and the Bristol Aeroplane Company combined as the British Aircraft Corporation (BAC) at the government's insistence primarily in order to develop the TSR2, the successor to the Canberra bomber, an aircraft originally designed by English Electric. Caldecote, managing director of the newly formed English Electric Aviation Company from 1960 to 1963, was appointed executive director of the guided weapons division and in 1961 was also made deputy managing director of BAC, a position he held until 1967. In the reorganization of BAC in 1963 Caldecote became managing director of guided weapons. He brought great enthusiasm to the job of running this division, and was very disappointed in August 1962 when despite all his efforts to save it the government cancelled the Blue Water missile, the main new project and one that had been making excellent progress. He felt that Lord Portal, chairman of BAC, who had been chief of air staff during the war, was interested only in aircraft, and had not done enough to defend guided weapons projects against cancellation, although Portal was also unable to save the TSR2, cancelled by the Labour government in 1965. At that time Caldecote warned the government of the need to support a long-term development programme in order to protect the British aviation industry from being overtaken by its American competitors. Cancellation of Blue Water led to the closure of the Luton factory, causing more than a thousand redundancies and an exodus of engineers to jobs in the United States. But despite this blow Caldecote developed other projects, continuing with work begun by English Electric on the Thunderbird guided missile, and the Bloodhound missile developed at Bristol, and working on the Swingfire anti-tank missile. In 1964 work began on what was later called the Rapier, which became the best low-level anti-aircraft system in the Western world, and the BAC guided weapons operation came to be regarded as the best in Europe.

After the English Electric Company merged with GEC in 1968 Caldecote, who had opposed the merger, resigned as a director of the company and left BAC. In 1972 he became chairman of the Delta Metal Company (later the Delta Group), the electrical engineering company, a position he held until 1982. He was chairman of the Legal and General Group from 1977 to 1980, and from 1980 to 1987 chairman of Finance for Industry (from 1983 Investors in Industry), which provided smaller businesses with venture capital. He also held many public appointments and was chairman of the Design Council from 1972 to 1980, and a member of the British Railways board from 1979 to 1985. As president of the Fellowship of Engineering (later the Royal Academy of Engineering) from 1981 to 1986 he worked hard to promote excellence in engineering in British industry, and he was pro-chancellor of Cranfield Institute of Technology from 1976 to 1984. Through these bodies, and in debates in the House of Lords, he emphasized the importance of engineering to the economy, and the need for higher status for engineers. Although he remained a member of the Conservative Party he was worried about the decline of British manufacturing industry and the lack of government investment, and in 1991 he chaired a House of Lords committee which reported on the damage done to Britain's industrial base by the economic policies of the 1980s and the need for a high level of foreign investment to ensure its survival.

A member of the evangelical wing of the Church of England, Caldecote was chairman in 1990 of the Crown Appointments Committee which recommended the appointment of Dr George Carey as the next archbishop of Canterbury. He was patron of the Spirit of '88 group, which showed its opposition to the ecumenical movement in the Church of England, and especially the move towards closer links with the Roman Catholic church, by celebrating the defeat of the Spanish Armada in 1588 and of James II in 1688.

Caldecote was appointed KBE in 1987. He died on 20 September 1999 at his home, Orchard Cottage, South Harting, Sussex, near Petersfield, Hampshire.

ANNE PIMLOTT BAKER

Sources C. Gardner, *British Aircraft Corporation: a history* (1981) · D. Richards, *Portal of Hungerford* (1977), 384–5 · *The Times* (22 Sept 1999) · *Daily Telegraph* (22 Sept 1999) · *The Guardian* (22 Sept 1999) · *The Independent* (29 Sept 1999) · Burke, *Peerage* · *WW* · b. cert. · m. cert.
Archives Inst. EE, papers | Institution of Mechanical Engineers, London, corresp. with Lord Hinton
Likenesses photograph, repro. in *Daily Telegraph* · photograph, repro. in *The Independent* · photograph, repro. in *The Guardian* · photograph, repro. in *The Times*

Inskip, Thomas Walker Hobart, first Viscount Caldecote (1876–1947), lawyer and politician, was born at Clifton Park House, Clifton, Bristol, on 5 March 1876, the second son of James Inskip (1839–1909), a leading local solicitor, and the first son of his second wife, Constance Sophia Louisa (d. 1914), daughter of John Hampden. His elder half-brother, James Theodore Inskip (1868–1949), became bishop-suffragan of Barking; his younger brother, Sir John Hampden Inskip (1879–1960), became a prominent solicitor. He was educated at Clifton College and at King's College, Cambridge. He obtained a third class in the first part of the classical tripos in 1897. He was called to the bar by the Inner Temple in 1899 and over the next decade developed a successful practice on the western circuit, taking silk in 1914. However, he early had in mind a political career and stood unsuccessfully against Sir Edward Grey, the foreign secretary, at Berwick-on-Tweed in 1906 and January 1910.

On 30 July 1914 Inskip married Lady Augusta Helen Elizabeth Orr Ewing, eldest daughter of David Boyle, seventh earl of Glasgow, and widow of Charles Orr Ewing, Unionist MP for Ayr Burghs. They had one son. During the First World War he served in naval intelligence in London, rising to become head of the naval law branch in 1918. He represented the Admiralty on the war crimes committee (1918–19). He successfully stood for his native city at the general election of 1918, being elected as a Conservative for Bristol Central.

It was as a law officer that Inskip's political career developed. He became solicitor-general in the Bonar Law government in 1922 and continued under Baldwin. In March 1928 he succeeded Sir Douglas Hogg as attorney-general when, as Lord Hailsham, the latter became lord chancellor. He lost his Bristol seat in the general election of 1929. He returned to the Commons in 1931 as member for Fareham and became solicitor-general in the National Government. This step backwards was to enable Sir William Jowitt, who had been elected as a Liberal in 1929 but had then joined the Labour Party, to continue in office as attorney-general—since Jowitt shifted again and became a supporter, though without a parliamentary seat, of the National Government. Jowitt resigned in 1932 and Inskip once again became attorney-general, remaining in that post until 1936.

Inskip served as a law officer for a total of fourteen

years. In this capacity he was neither flamboyant nor brilliant. He did not possess a great legal mind. However, in the cases in which he appeared for the crown, whether criminal or civil, he made his points soberly and sturdily, largely without rhetorical embellishment. Sobriety, it might be added, came easily to a man who was almost a teetotaller and certainly a non-smoker. The stature he gained in legal circles derived not only from his physical stature—he was 6 feet 4 inches tall—but also from the manifest sincerity of his convictions. He had been raised as an Anglican evangelical and remained actively in that tradition. He served as chancellor of the diocese of Truro from 1920 to 1922 and lent his name to various evangelical causes. It is not surprising that he emerged as a strong opponent in 1927 and 1928 of the attempt to introduce a new prayer book for use in the Church of England. Inskip regarded the revisions it contained as undermining the protestant character of the church as established at the Reformation. His speech in the House of Commons against its introduction was widely regarded as being very influential in defeating the measure. A legal officer does not normally have a strong political profile and it was only in relation to his role in this matter that Inskip could be said to have appealed to a wider, though sectional, constituency. In 1928 he declined the suggestion that he might put himself forward for the speakership of the Commons when that office became vacant. It might confidently have been assumed, therefore, that his role would remain in the specialist legal area where his advice and experience were increasingly valued, not least in respect of the most complex legislation of the period, the Government of India Act of 1935. In that same year he declined the mastership of the rolls.

In February 1936, however, Inskip was unexpectedly appointed by Baldwin to the new post of minister for the co-ordination of defence. His First World War naval experience apart, Inskip had not otherwise expressed any great interest in or possessed any great knowledge of defence issues. In one sense this was an advantage because a co-ordinating minister with previous ministerial experience in a service department could easily be accused of prejudice because of that experience. He did not have party enemies—to the extent that Lloyd George even surmised in July 1936 that more Conservative back-benchers wanted Inskip rather than Neville Chamberlain to succeed Baldwin. Even so, despite these assets of neutrality and acceptability, in a situation in which the three service departments remained intact, with their own continuing ministerial heads, Inskip had no powerful position from which to operate. Since he was definitely not minister of defence, a man with a single office and two secretaries could scarcely be said to have a powerful departmental tradition behind him. He could persuade and cajole but not command. Co-ordination of defence was an objective with which few could disagree, particularly in a deteriorating international situation, but the minister's powers were not well defined. It was believed that his essential task was to act as an effective and impartial chairman in inter-service discussions and, somewhat ambiguously, he

was the prime minister's deputy in these matters. There were others, however, who found his appointment very odd indeed. Churchill unoriginally described it as the worst since Caligula made his horse a consul.

Even so, Inskip played a significant role in resolving the dispute which had long festered between the Admiralty and the Air Ministry concerning the control of aircraft in naval operations. The outcome in July 1937 was that the Air Ministry was persuaded to give way and accept what became the Fleet Air Arm. Another area in which he was heavily involved was the question of supply: he initially opposed the creation of a separate ministry, and had to consider how far there should be 'interference' in the priority assigned to military and civil requirements. Inskip was also necessarily at the heart of the debates which then raged about Britain's strategic priorities and the calculation of risks. His memorandum to the cabinet on 22 December 1937 was very important. It reflected in large measure a Treasury belief that it was as important to maintain economic stability as to maintain the armed forces. It fell to Inskip to try to establish a system of rationing between the services and to keep expenditure within the limits decreed by the Treasury. He felt, nevertheless, that Britain could not make proper provision in peace for the defence of the British empire against three different powers in three different theatres of war. It was up to diplomacy to reduce the number of potential enemies. In 1938 he was able to intervene to increase expenditure for the air force over Treasury objections and to maintain defence production at capacity. In January 1939, however, Chamberlain required him to resign, and it seems highly likely that this was because by this juncture Inskip had come to the view that appeasement had failed and war was inevitable.

Inskip then moved between several posts in swift succession. He was transferred to the Dominions Office in January 1939. In September 1939, on the outbreak of war, he was appointed lord chancellor in place of Lord Maugham, and was raised to the peerage as Viscount Caldecote of Bristol. In May 1940 he returned to the Dominions Office and was leader of the House of Lords. In neither office was he a member of the war cabinet. In October 1940, however, his political career came to an end on his appointment as lord chief justice, the first former lord chancellor to be appointed to the office. He remained in this position through the war, though towards its end his health deteriorated and he resigned in January 1946. As lord chief justice he took a keen interest in promoting legal education and continued his charitable works, notably with the Discharged Prisoners' Aid Society. He died at his home, Greystones, Enton Green, near Godalming, Surrey, on 11 October 1947; his wife survived him. He was buried at Baldock, Hertfordshire, near the grave of his grandfather, and was succeeded as second viscount by his son, Robert Andrew Inskip (1917–1999).

Inskip's most important role was that which he occupied between 1936 and 1939 in the co-ordination of defence. The qualities he brought to it were those he displayed throughout his career: calm judgement and a steady capacity to weigh evidence and draw unemotional conclusions. In that position at that particular time his limitations were also evident. Yet, given the ill-defined character of his role, he made a greater contribution than might have been assumed from the nature of his previous experience. In his various legal capacities he again left his mark by his courtesy and patience in dealing with the matters before him on a day-to-day basis, even if there are few specific decisions which continue to be linked to his name. His Christian convictions were throughout his life reflected in his commitment to charitable bodies; there his financial contributions were generous. He loved to be out of doors—shooting or playing golf—particularly in Scotland, with which country he became associated through his marriage. KEITH ROBBINS

Sources R. F. V. Heuston, *Lives of the lord chancellors, 1885–1940* (1964) · B. Bond, *British military policy between the two world wars* (1980) · M. Howard, *The continental commitment* (1972) · R. P. Shay, *British rearmament in the thirties: politics and profits* (1977) · G. C. Peden, *British rearmament and the treasury, 1932–1939* (1979) · K. Hylson-Smith, *Evangelicals in the Church of England, 1734–1984* (1988) · A. Hastings, *A history of English Christianity, 1920–1985* (1986) · P. Catterall, 'The party and religion', *Conservative century: the conservative party since 1900*, ed. A. Seldon and S. Ball (1994) · *CGPLA Eng. & Wales* (1948) · Burke, *Peerage*
Archives CAC Cam., diary | BL, corresp. with Albert Mansbridge, Add. MS 65253 · CAC Cam., corresp. with Lord Weir
Likenesses A. John, oils, 1942, Inner Temple, London · F. Brill, portrait, priv. coll.
Wealth at death £17,908 11s. 11d.: probate, 24 March 1948, *CGPLA Eng. & Wales*

Inskipp, James (1790–1868), painter, of whose parents nothing is known, was originally employed in the commissariat service, but in 1820 retired with a pension and became a painter in oils and watercolours. He began with landscapes and moved on to small subject pictures, and with less success to portraits. From 1825 he was a frequent contributor to the British Institution, the Society of British Artists, and the Royal Academy. Titles of his paintings include *Boy with a Fruit* and *Market Girls*. From 1835 he exhibited exclusively at the Royal Academy, showing pictures like: *An Italian Vineyard* (1839), *A Hen Coop* (1840), and *Zingarella* (1841), which was his last exhibited work. Although Inskipp never became an academician his pictures were admired at the time, and some were engraved by H. Robinson and others. He drew a series of illustrations for Sir Harris Nicolas's edition of Izaak Walton's *Compleat Angler*, published in 1833–6, and in 1838 he published a series of engravings from his drawings, entitled 'Studies of Heads from Nature'. His picture of *A Girl Making Lace* is at Bowood, Wiltshire, and *A Venetian Woman* is at Deepdene, Surrey. *Return to Market* is in the Museum of Montreal, Canada. His work became more popular later in the century on account of his bold brushwork and lack of finish, as seen, for example, in *The Fisher Boy*, noted for its 'free and fluent brushwork' (*Connoisseur*).

Towards the end of his life Inskipp lived in Cattshall Lane, Godalming, Surrey, and it was there that he died on 15 March 1868, aged seventy-eight. He was buried in Godalming cemetery. L. H. CUST, *rev.* CHLOE JOHNSON

Sources Redgrave, *Artists* · Graves, *Artists*, 3rd edn · Wood, *Vic. painters*, 3rd edn · B. Stewart and M. Cutten, *The dictionary of portrait painters in Britain up to 1920* (1997) · *The exhibition of the Royal Academy* (1825–41) [exhibition catalogues] · *Catalogue of the works of British artists in the gallery of the British Institution* (1825–35) [exhibition catalogues, British Institution] · *CGPLA Eng. & Wales* (1868) · 'Notes: our plates', *The Connoisseur*, 39 (1914), facing 102, 117–18
Archives V&A NAL, corresp. relating to exhibition of his work
Likenesses photograph, carte-de-visite, NPG
Wealth at death under £3000: probate, 7 July 1868, *CGPLA Eng. & Wales*

Instone, Sir Samuel (1878–1937), shipping and aviation entrepreneur, was born at Gravesend on 16 August 1878, the son of Adolphe Instone, and the eldest of three brothers. He was educated at Tunbridge Wells and at Boulogne. At the age of fifteen he went to work in the port, and soon acquired a very considerable knowledge of shipping between the United Kingdom and the continent. He married in 1910 Alice Maud Lieberman; they had five daughters. At a time unknown before the First World War he set up S. Instone & Co. Ltd of Cardiff to trade between Cardiff and Antwerp, and London and Antwerp, with coal as the principal cargo. Looking ahead at how he might expand his business, he bought the Bow Creek site of the Thames iron works, where he established the Instone wharf to allow direct trans-shipment to the Great Eastern Railway, later the London and North Eastern Railway (LNER), so as to avoid the congested lines through London itself. He worked closely with his brothers Theodore and Alfred, the latter of whom described their work in *Early Birds* (1924). This book concentrated on the airline which the brothers founded in 1921 to speed their bills of lading from Cardiff and London to Antwerp and so avoid demurrage charges. The Instone Air Line, which ran from London to Paris from 1919, was a pioneering enterprise. It merged with Imperial Airways in 1924, with Samuel Instone remaining on the board until his death in 1937.

In 1921 S. Instone & Co. Ltd went public with a nominal capital of £500,000 (of which £300,000 was issued). Instone himself was chairman of the Askern Coal and Iron Company Ltd, and of the Bedwas Navigation Colliery Company (1921). The combination of his modern ideas, introduction of machinery, and other cost-saving ideas, and the militancy of the declining mining industry with its rival unions, the South Wales Miners' Federation (SWMF) and the South Wales Miners' Industrial Union, resulted in a conflict that lasted a decade. In the shrill rhetoric of those depression years from the failed general strike of 1926 to the gradual recovery and amalgamation of the mines in the late 1930s, Instone was a leader in the fight for modern management and cost controls. This led him into a number of fights, and to his being labelled one of the 'bloodsucking rich'. The result is that his reputation now depends upon whether the literature is from the miners' or the owners' side, though recent scholarship has taken a more balanced view.

The battle with the SWMF lasted until 1936, and ran that colliery into a £1 million debt, when a compromise left the Instones in charge in return for recognition of the SWMF. The adventure into Benzol (an industrial solvent derived from coal tar) ended in constant bickering over coal quality, and the plant's cleansing powers. In truth the venture was ill timed. At the Askern in Yorkshire he was known for the establishment of a model housing estate at Instoneville, and for his successful prosecution of an action for slander against Herbert Smith, then president of the Miners' Federation of Great Britain. A hard worker himself, he had much sympathy for the miners in spite of the demands of modernization. He and Theodore were strong characters, but respected each other's judgements, and worked with Alfred in complete harmony and respect, as *The Times* noted (11 Nov 1937). Knighted in 1921, Sir Samuel was much liked for his many human qualities. He was a member of the lieutenancy of the City of London, and a liveryman of the Loriners' Company. Very interested in congestion in the streets, he started one of the waterbus services on the Thames. He lived at 11 Hanover Terrace, London, and died in the London Clinic on 9 November 1937 after an operation from which it was expected he would recover.

Sir Samuel was buried on 10 November in the Jewish cemetery, Beaconsfield Road, Willesden, London, and the memorial service was held at the West London Synagogue, Upper Berkeley Street. His wife outlived him. At death he left £1034 gross, presumably having previously made farsighted legal arrangements.

ROBIN HIGHAM

Sources R. Higham, 'Instone, Sir Samuel', *DBB* · *The Times* (10–12 Nov 1937) · A. Instone, *Early birds: air transport memories, 1919–1924* (1938) · R. Higham, *Britain's imperial air routes, 1918 to 1939* (1960) · D. Smith, 'The struggle against company unionism in the south Wales coalfield, 1926–1939', *Welsh History Review / Cylchgrawn Hanes Cymru*, 6 (1972–3) · M. W. Kirby, *The British coalmining industry, 1870–1946*, 4 (1977) · B. Supple, *The political economy of decline: 1913–1946* (1987), vol. 4 of *The history of the British coal industry* (1984–93) · *WWW* · d. cert. · *CGPLA Eng. & Wales* (1938)
Likenesses portrait, repro. in Instone, *Early birds*
Wealth at death £1034 15s. 6d.: probate, 19 Jan 1938, *CGPLA Eng. & Wales*

Insula, Adeliza de (*fl.* 1114–*c*.1130). *See under* Dunstanville, de, family (*per. c*.1090–*c*.1292).

Insula, Peter (*d.* in or before **1311**), scholastic writer, was MA and fellow of Merton College, Oxford, from at least 1284 until 1307. He was the author of a set of disputed questions on Aristotle's *On Generation and Corruption*, which survives in a late thirteenth-century English manuscript (Cambridge, Gonville and Caius College, MS 512/543), which contains numerous disputed questions by various English masters of that period, many of whom were associated with Oxford (and in particular with Merton College), including William Dalling, Walter Burley, John Felmyngham, Peter Insula, and masters Lyde and Henneymore (Hennore). Disputed questions were a characteristic feature of the scholastic method, being intended both to provide a way of presenting and reconciling diverse opinions on topics of substantial import, and also to give the disputants the opportunity to demonstrate their mastery of Aristotelian dialectics. They could take the form of academic exercises, which might take

place at many points in the university curriculum, or they might be public disputations by masters in which the leading issues of the day were discussed.

The questions in Gonville and Caius MS 512/543 are probably records of this last kind of debate. They deal with topics raised by Aristotle's books on logic (*On Interpretation*, *Sophistical Refutations*, *Prior Analytics*, *Posterior Analytics*, and *Topics*) and his works on natural philosophy (*Physics*, *On the Soul*, *Meteorology*, *On Sense and Sensibilia*, *On Generation and Corruption*, and *Ethics*). The work includes six questions by Insula grouped under the title 'On generation and corruption'. They are theoretical in nature and draw primarily upon Aristotle's *Physics* and his *Posterior Analytics* for their sources. The first question concerns generation as a form of motion which can be analysed as a series of continuous, contiguous, or successive states of change. The next question discusses generation as a change in state of being involving three different processes: that which changes; that in which it changes; and that to which it changes. The third question deals with generation as a transition from one successive state to another. The next two questions investigate how the nature of change may be logically determined and whether the nature of a thing can be formally demonstrated. The last question discusses whether matter can be an abstract entity separate from any given substantial form.

A number of other questions in the work may also be by Insula. Among the questions on the *Prior Analytics* are a group of seven under the title 'The same proposition is both true and false'. The first is attributed in a marginal gloss to Lyde, while the second is assigned to Insula. This question investigates the senses in which the written proposition 'I write' can be both true and false. The remaining five questions are preceded by a marginal comment explaining that the glossator did not know whether these questions were by Lyde or by Insula.

Insula was dead by November 1311, by which time he had presented Merton College with eighteen silver dishes and eighteen silver salt cellars. He should not be confused with two contemporary namesakes, of whom one became archdeacon of Exeter and of Wells, and the other subdean of York.

CORNELIUS O'BOYLE

Sources G. C. Brodrick, *Memorials of Merton College*, OHS, 4 (1885) · Emden, *Oxf.* · Emden, *Cam.* · M. R. James, *A descriptive catalogue of the manuscripts in the library of Gonville and Caius College*, 2 vols. (1907–8) · P. de Insula [P. Insula], 'Exposito de generatione et corruptione', Gon. & Caius Cam., MS 512/543
Archives Gon. & Caius Cam., MS 512/543

Inverarity [*married name* Martyn], **Elizabeth** [Eliza] (**1813–1846**), singer and actress, was born in Edinburgh on 23 March 1813 daughter of James Inverarity, merchant, of Grayfield Square and Helen McLagan. She was first taught by a Mr Thorne, and afterwards by Alexander Murray of Edinburgh, at one of whose concerts she appeared as an amateur singer in 1829. She made her début at Covent Garden in *Cinderella* on 14 December 1830. In 1832 she sang in *Robert le diable* at the same theatre and appeared at the Philharmonic Society's concerts. In 1836 she married Charles

Thomas Martyn, a bass singer, and in 1839 they went with an operatic company to New York, where they both sang in *Fidelio* and other works. She died from tuberculosis at 42 Grey Street, Newcastle upon Tyne, on 27 December 1846. She excelled greatly neither as a singer nor as an actress. With her husband she wrote some ballads, but they are of no particular merit. J. C. HADDEN, *rev.* J. GILLILAND

Sources J. C. Dibdin, *The annals of the Edinburgh stage* (1888) · J. D. Brown, *Biographical dictionary of musicians: with a bibliography of English writings on music* (1886) · Brown & Stratton, *Brit. mus.* · A. E. Heath, *Book of beauty* (1840) · O. Ebel, *Women composers: a biographical handbook of woman's work in music*, 3rd edn (1913) · D. Baptie, ed., *Musical Scotland, past and present: being a dictionary of Scottish musicians from about 1400 till the present time* (1894) · D. Baptie, *A handbook of musical biography*, 2nd edn (1887) · *The Scotsman* (6 Jan 1847)
Likenesses W. Sharp, lithograph, pubd 1832 (after lithograph by W. Booth), NPG · H. Robinson, stipple (after A. E. Chalon), BM, NPG; repro. in Heath, *Book of beauty*, 135 · prints, Harvard TC, NPG · prints, BM

Inverchapel. For this title name *see* Kerr, Archibald John Kerr Clark, Baron Inverchapel (1882–1951).

Inverclyde. For this title name *see* Burns, John, first Baron Inverclyde (1829–1901).

Inverforth. For this title name *see* Weir, Andrew, first Baron Inverforth (1865–1955).

Inverkeithing, Richard of (*d.* 1272), bishop of Dunkeld, was of Scottish birth, though Inverkeithing may have been his benefice, not his family name. First found as master and royal chamberlain in 1249 (his university is unknown), he was promoted to the see of Dunkeld by the Durward government in 1250 and consecrated in 1251. Having been out of favour during the Comyn ascendancy of 1251–5, he was appointed to the council in September 1255 and succeeded Gamelin as chancellor. In 1257, however, the Comyns seized the king and also took the seal from the dean of Dunkeld, who was acting as vice-chancellor. But Richard served the king again in various capacities in the more sedate 1260s. Within his diocese he did much building at Inchcolm Abbey and he founded the first Carmelite friary in Scotland at Tullilum in 1261–2. He collected procurations for the legate Ottobuono, whose council he attended at London in 1268, and was active as a papal judge-delegate. A very conventional career cleric who was lucky in his promotion, he died on 16 April 1272; his body was buried at Dunkeld, his heart at Inchcolm. A. A. M. DUNCAN

Sources J. Dowden, *The bishops of Scotland … prior to the Reformation*, ed. J. M. Thomson (1912), 57–8 · D. E. R. Watt, *A biographical dictionary of Scottish graduates to AD 1410* (1977), 280–82 · D. E. Easson and A. Macdonald, eds., *Charters of the abbey of Inchcolm*, Scottish History Society, 3rd ser., 32 (1938), xxiii · A. Myln, *Vitae Dunkeldensis ecclesiae episcoporum*, ed. T. Thomson, Bannatyne Club, 1 (1823), 11
Likenesses seal, U. Durham L., dean and chapter of Durham archives, misc. ch. no. 807

Invernairn. For this title name *see* Beardmore, William, Baron Invernairn (1856–1936).

Inverness. For this title name *see* Hay, John, of Cromlix, Jacobite duke of Inverness (1691–1740).

Inwood, Charles Frederick (1798–1840). *See under* Inwood, William (1771/2–1843).

Inwood, Henry William (1794–1843), architect and archaeologist, was born on 22 May 1794, and baptized on 25 June 1794 at St Pancras Old Church, London, the eldest son of William *Inwood (1771/2–1843), surveyor and architect, and his wife, Mary Townsend. He worked in his father's office from an early age and submitted his first design (for a garden seat) to the Royal Academy in 1809, when only fifteen. One of his earliest commissions was the completion of the tower of East Grinstead church, Sussex, in 1811–13, of which he sent a design to the 1812 Royal Academy. Much of his early professional activity consisted of the same sort of surveyor's work as his father specialized in: this included the design of a number of warehouses in London. Meanwhile he continued to exhibit a number of ambitious designs, such as a *Design for a Grecian Cathedral* (1813) and a *National Mausoleum to Commemorate Naval and Military Heroes* (1815) that hinted at a rather grander vision of his professional future.

The Inwoods' chance came when, in June 1818, they won first prize in the competition to design a new church for the swollen parish of St Pancras. Francis Bedford was placed second, and Thomas Rickman third. Building on James Gibbs's templar church formula of St Martin-in-the-Fields, the Inwoods steeped their design in convincingly correct Greek detail, thereby producing a church of distinction that coincided perfectly with the desires of the churchwardens. In order to ensure that the details were accurate and to enable his son to drink deep at the Athenian source, Henry Inwood was dispatched by his father to Greece later in 1818; he returned via Rome in time for the start of work on the church in May 1819.

On his arrival at Athens, Henry Inwood began a detailed study of the Acropolis (including the taking of casts and the removal of decorative specimens) that was to culminate in his most important published work, *The Erechtheion at Athens: fragments of Athenian architecture and a few remains in Attica, Megara and Epirus* (1827). Its professed intention was 'to increase more or less the general store of architectural understanding' (Crook, 60), and, by supplementing the coverage provided in J. Stuart and N. Revett, *The Antiquities of Athens*, it became an influential volume, dealing with the principal public buildings of Athens, and being published at the height of the Greek revival.

Henry Inwood's detailed observations soon made themselves felt upon St Pancras Church, where the two vestries on each side of the east end were copied directly from the Erechtheion tribunes. The distinctive caryatids, modelled in terracotta by John Rossi RA and his son Henry, were utterly unprecedented in an ecclesiastical setting: holding inverted torches (an addition by Inwood) and standing in front of a sarcophagus, they served as sentinels over the entrance to the vaults below the church. The building costs under the contractor, Isaac Seabrook, rose remorselessly. The final figure reached a staggering £76,679 (including £4300 paid to the Rossis for terracotta work) by the time of its completion in 1822. Sir John Summerson regarded it as 'the queen of early 19th century churches' (Crook, 138), but some contemporary assessments were less warm. C. R. Cockerell, in a diary entry in July 1821, dismissed it as 'simple Greek—radiates bad taste thro' the whole' (Watkin, 67). He attacked their total reliance on precedent, and in May 1822 observed sourly that 'wherever their authorities have ceased they as usual have been grounded' (ibid.). William and Henry Inwood jointly exhibited six drawings altogether of the church at the Royal Academy in 1819 and 1821. It was the ecclesiastical culmination of the Greek revival, and in 1854 was memorably described by Wightwick in *Bentley's Miscellany* as 'the epilogue of the Greek Play' (Crook, 128).

A number of lesser commissions for other churches in the parish followed: the Camden chapel (now the Greek Orthodox church) in Pratt Street was built in 1822–4, and St Peter's Chapel, Regent Square, was built in 1822–5 (dem. 1967; designs for both churches exhibited at the 1823 Royal Academy). Thereafter, for reasons which remain unclear, Inwood's career flagged. The only other classical church to come from his pen was St James's, Holloway (1837–8), which he designed in partnership with his pupil E. N. Clifton (1817–1889). Save for an Ionic temple designed for the earl of Onslow's seat at Clandon Park, Surrey, in 1838 (and exhibited under William and Henry Inwood's name in the Royal Academy of that year, their last known collaboration), no more overtly classical buildings were designed by the architect.

Henry Inwood turned his attentions to the Gothic in the 1820s, but with decidedly less impressive results. His first effort in this idiom, St Mary's Chapel, Somers Town (again in St Pancras), was built in 1824–7. A thin brick edifice with a mean sham front, it attracted the scorn of A. W. N. Pugin, who held it up for ridicule in his *Contrasts, or, A parallel between the noble edifices of the fourteenth and fifteenth centuries and similar buildings of the present day, shewing the present decay of taste* (1836). Inwood's other Gothic London church was St Stephen's, Canonbury Road, Islington (1837–9), designed once more in partnership with Clifton. Other buildings known to have been designed by Henry Inwood (listed in an 1840 letter to John Place of Nottingham) include Woburn Lodge, Upper Woburn Place, Bloomsbury (1824), a hotel at Windsor (c.1840), and an unidentified church near Rochester as well as a number of schools and houses.

A fellow of the Society of Antiquaries, Inwood's other published work besides *The Erechtheion at Athens* was *The resources of design in the architecture of Greece, Egypt and other countries obtained by the studies of architects of those countries from nature*, the first (and only) part of which appeared in 1834. This advanced the thesis that classical architecture was derived entirely from natural forms, and in particular those of shells. In 1843 he sold his collection of forty-odd objects from the Acropolis to the British Museum for £40 and embarked for a voyage to Spain. He never arrived as the ship on which he was sailing sank in a storm on 20 March 1843; all aboard drowned. Inwood never married, and left no children.　　　ROGER BOWDLER

Sources Colvin, *Archs.* · *DNB* · J. Lever, ed., *Catalogue of the drawings collection of the Royal Institute of British Architects: G–K* (1973), 156–7 · J. M. Crook, *The Greek revival: neo-classical attitudes in British architecture, 1760–1870* (1972) · D. Watkin, *The life and work of C. R. Cockerell* (1974), 67 · J. Summerson, *Architecture in Britain, 1530–1830*, 8th edn (1991), 489 · *IGI* · Graves, *RA exhibitors*
Archives RIBA BAL

Inwood, William (1771/2–1843), architect and surveyor, was born at Caen Wood, Highgate, the son of Daniel Inwood, bailiff to Lord Mansfield. He was brought up as an architect and surveyor, and became steward to Lord Colchester and practised as a surveyor. On 8 July 1793 he married, at St Pancras Old Church, Mary Townsend. In 1811 he published *Tables for the purchasing of estates … and for the renewal of leases held under … corporate bodies*. This well-known work, which was founded on the tables of Francis Baily and John Smart, reached its twenty-first edition in 1880, and was generally known as the 'Inwood tables'. From 1813 Inwood for several years exhibited designs at the Royal Academy: he designed numerous mansions, villas, barracks, and warehouses. In 1821 he planned the new galleries for St John's Church, Westminster, and in 1832–3 designed, with the assistance of his second son, Charles Frederick Inwood [*see below*], the new Westminster Hospital.

Inwood's most important work is St Pancras New Church, London (1819–22). In this design he was assisted by his eldest son, Henry William *Inwood, who designed the Greek models, basing them on the Erechtheion temple on the Acropolis, which he studied during a visit to Greece in 1818–19. Its style was severely criticized by James Fergusson, who said that its erection 'contributed more than any other circumstances to hasten the reaction towards the Gothic style, which was then becoming fashionable' (*History of Architecture*, 1874, 4.334–5). More recently it was re-evaluated by Howard Colvin, who described the church as 'a landmark in the history of the Greek Revival' (Colvin, *Archs.*). The most expensive church of its day, it is a Grecian version of the type of steepled Anglican church established by James Gibbs at St Martin-in-the-Fields. Adapted from authentic Greek prototypes, the architectural features combine to produce 'a tour de force whose elegance compels admiration' (ibid., 527). Inwood also erected in London, with the assistance of his eldest son, Camden chapel (1822–4; dedicated to All Saints in 1920 and in 1948 leased to the Greek Orthodox church), St Peter's Chapel, Regent Square (1822–5; dem. 1967), and the Gothic St Mary's Chapel, Upper Seymour Street, Somers Town (1824–7).

Inwood had several pupils, including William Railton; William Butterfield was in his office for a short time. In his later years he received assistance from the Sir John Soane Fund for Distressed Architects. He died at his house in Upper Seymour Street, London, on 16 March 1843, and was buried in the family vault in St Pancras New Church.

His second son, **Charles Frederick Inwood** (1798–

1840), architect, entered the Royal Academy Schools in 1822. He assisted his father in some of his buildings, in particular the Westminster Hospital (1832–4; dem. 1951). He designed All Saints' Church, Great Marlow (opened 1835), and the St Pancras national schools, London. He died on 1 June 1840. 			W. W. WROTH, *rev.* KAYE BAGSHAW

Sources Colvin, *Archs.* · C. E. Lee, 'A family of architects: the Inwoods of St Pancras', *Camden History Review*, 4 (Oct 1976)

Ioan ab Hywel. *See* Howell, John (1774–1830).

Iolo Goch (*fl.* **1345–1397**), poet, was the son of Ithel Goch (their shared epithet means 'the Red'), and could trace his genealogy back to Hedd ab Alunog of Uwch Aled. One of his ancestors bore the title herald, which is interesting in view of the detailed knowledge of heraldry displayed in Iolo's work. Genealogical sources also give the name of Iolo's wife as Margaret, and note a daughter called Nest. The survey of the lordship of Denbigh made in 1334 states that the family's hereditary holding of land was in the township of Lleweni in the Vale of Clwyd. Five-sixths of the holding had escheated to the crown, and the remainder had been exchanged for land in the township of Llechryd on higher ground to the north-west of Denbigh in order to make room for English settlers. A description of a journey home in one of his later poems suggests that Iolo lived in Llechryd in the parish of Llanefydd all his life.

It seems that Iolo was educated as a chorister, probably at the nearby cathedral church of St Asaph, and he certainly received patronage from the churchmen of that diocese throughout his life. His earliest datable poem is addressed to Bishop Dafydd ap Bleddyn, who died in 1345, and his latest to Bishop Ieuan Trefor on the occasion of his journey to Scotland in 1397. One of Iolo's principal patrons was Ithel ap Robert, archdeacon 1375–82, who was also his third cousin. But he visited patrons in all parts of Wales, as was customary for professional poets of that period, travelling particularly to the north-west where he was welcomed by powerful noblemen such as Sir Hywel ap Gruffudd, constable of Cricieth Castle, and the Tudor family of Penmynydd.

Iolo was one of the first of the *Cywyddwyr, and he seems to have pioneered the development of the *cywydd* as a medium for traditional eulogy, following the lead set by the slightly older Dafydd ap Gwilym in the field of love poetry. Johnston's 1988 edition of his work contains only thirty-nine authentic poems (although many more are falsely attributed to him in the manuscripts). These are varied in subject matter, showing him to have been a man of profound religious conviction, devoted in particular to the cult of the Virgin Mary, a sophisticated love poet, a vituperative bardic satirist, and above all an informed commentator on current affairs in the tradition of the political praise poets of thirteenth-century Gwynedd, projecting the aspirations of the new landed gentry class. Notable examples of Iolo's political verse are the poems which he addressed to Edward III *c.*1350, probably in support of Sir Rhys ap Gruffudd's military recruitment in south Wales, and to Sir Roger Mortimer, probably on the occasion in 1394 when Roger took part in Richard II's Irish

campaign—a poem expounding to the full the Mortimer genealogical descent and the claims arising from it. These and other poems reflect the contemporary obsession with warfare, stridently advocating the use of military power to maintain rightful authority.

Iolo's most famous patron was Owain Glyn Dŵr, to whom he addressed three poems in the 1380s. The association with Glyn Dŵr is largely responsible for Iolo's reputation as an ardent nationalist, but in fact this is not borne out by the poems themselves. Two of them present a conformist image of Glyn Dŵr prospering under English rule and living peacefully at his court at Sycharth where Iolo was an honoured guest in his old age. The third expresses discontent at the loss of Glyn Dŵr's rightful inheritance, but characteristically this is seen as a failure of justice to be remedied by recourse to the law, rather than by rebellion. The desire to maintain the status quo also lies behind another apparently radical poem by Iolo, that in praise of the ploughman, which was probably composed in response to the peasants' revolt of 1381 in England, stressing the humility of the ideal labourer in the interest of the landowning class. It is unlikely that Iolo lived to see Glyn Dŵr's rebellion in 1400. He is said to have been buried at Llanefydd. 			DAFYDD JOHNSTON

Sources D. R. Johnston, ed., *Gwaith Iolo Goch* (1988)

Iolo Morganwg. *See* Williams, Edward (1747–1826).

Iona, abbots of (*act.* **563–927**), played a major role in the history of Ireland and Britain from the foundation of Iona by *Columba (Colum Cille) in 563 until the tenth century. The evidence is unusually good up to the mid-eighth century. The lost annals of Iona formed the basis to *c.*740 for the chronicle of Ireland; the latter is no longer extant in its original form, but in derived texts, and especially in the annals of Ulster, much of the annals of Iona is preserved. Annalistic evidence for the sequence of abbots can be tested against a list preserved in the confraternity book of Salzburg, consisting, with the addition of Patrick, Ciarán, and Columbanus, of the abbots of Iona to Sléibíne (*d.* 767, the fifteenth abbot). A collection of genealogies of those abbots who belonged to Cenél Conaill (Columba's kindred) originally also extended as far as Sléibíne. In addition, texts about Columba himself reveal much about attitudes both at and to Iona; two of them were composed by abbots. These texts extend from the *Amra Choluim Chille* ('The wonderful [praise] of Colum Cille'), a difficult poem very probably composed shortly after the saint's death in 597, via two other poems of the mid-seventh century, to a fragment of a life by Cumméne (*d.* 669) and a complete life by Adomnán (*d.* 704), the ninth abbot. A text no later than *c.*700 gives an account of Columba's companions in his pilgrimage to Britain in 563 and of some of his relations by marriage. Bede's *Historia ecclesiastica gentis Anglorum* is revealing about Iona's relations with the English and, to a lesser extent, the Picts; for example, Bede says that Iona, an island off the west coast of Mull, was given to Columba by a Pictish king rather than by the ruler of Dál Riata (an

Irish kingdom including the north-eastern part of modern co. Antrim and also what is now Argyll in Scotland).

The companions of Columba The first three abbots of Iona, Baíthéne, Laisrén, and Virgno [*see below*], were all monks during Columba's lifetime. Baíthéne, indeed, was not only, like Laisrén, a kinsman of Columba from the royal lineage of Cenél Conaill, but he had also been one of the twelve companions said to have accompanied the saint on his pilgrimage to Britain in 563. Baíthéne, Laisrén, and another close kinsman and original companion of Columba, his uncle Ernán, appear in Adomnán's life as an inner core of trusted lieutenants and advisers. Baíthéne was prior of the daughter monastery of Mag Lunge on Tiree, Ernán of another Hebridean daughter house on the unidentified island of 'Hinba', and Laisrén was prior of the monastery of Durrow in the midlands of Ireland, probably founded between 585 and Columba's death in 597. Virgno, on the other hand, was not a kinsman of Columba; indeed a Middle Irish note to the martyrology of Óengus calls him a Briton; this is confirmed by the life of Baíthéne, discussed below, and also supported by his absence from the eighth-century collection of genealogies of Uí Néill abbots of Iona (almost all from Cenél Conaill). Yet, he apparently had Irish connections: his sister's son, Commán, bore an Irish name.

Baíthéne mac Brénainn [*formerly* Conin] (*d.* 598) was designated as abbot by Columba, that is, by the founder and *patronus* of the community—a community known as the *familia* ('household') of Columba or of Iona. Baíthéne, originally named Conin, was the subject of a short life of uncertain date, but probably of the eighth century, in which he was remembered as the pre-eminent pupil of Columba, inferior in knowledge of the scriptures only to his teacher. Columba was perceived by Adomnán as Baíthéne's 'foster-father' as well as his kinsman (Adomnán, 1.2, 3.18). Indeed, the bond between Columba and Baíthéne was not represented so much as one of physical as of spiritual kinship, expressed in the language of secular fosterage. The nature of the bond is represented by the story Adomnán tells of the designation of Baíthéne as successor. Columba was copying a psalter and got as far as the verse of Psalm 33, where it is written, 'But they that seek the Lord shall not want for anything that is good.' At this point, which was also the end of a page, he laid down his pen and declared, 'Here, at the end of the page, I must stop. Let Baíthéne write what follows' (Adomnán, 3.23).

This story is, however, something of an exception to the way in which Adomnán normally presented Columba. If the texts about Columba are compared, in particular the *Amra Choluim Chille* of *c.*597 and Adomnán's life of about a hundred years later, there are two striking contrasts which must be important for the history of the community in the seventh century. In the *Amra* the principal characteristic of Columba is his outstanding reputation as an exegete; Adomnán does not, of course, deny Columba's learning, but it is subordinated to his role as a prophet, a miracle worker, and one who enjoyed the companionship of angels. In this emphasis on scriptural knowledge, the

Amra is supported by the mid-seventh-century poems. Secondly, the *Amra* presents Columba as the missionary of the Picts, and not so much the northern Picts as those around the Tay. Any notion that the Picts were not effectively converted by Columba and his immediate disciples is incompatible with the *Amra*, and indeed has required an implausibly late dating for the poem.

The inheritance bequeathed by Columba to his chosen successor was, therefore, a demanding one. In Ireland there were dependent houses, perhaps mainly in the north-west, where Cenél Conaill was the ruling kindred, but also in the midlands; this confederation of monasteries was closely linked with the power of the Uí Néill, of whom Cenél Conaill was a branch. In Pictland, a full-scale mission was under way. And, for Iona itself, a reputation for outstanding learning had been established. It is worth noting that Baíthéne's short life concentrates on learning and says nothing of Pictland or of Ireland beyond a story implying both a respect for holy men who had remained in their native land and also Baíthéne's fitness to be included among the holiest as well as the most learned of their number. This is not surprising, since Baíthéne appears to have lived for only one year after Columba's death; he was said to have died on the very same day as his foster father, so that their feasts were celebrated together on 9 June.

Laisrén mac Feradaig [Laisrán] (*d.* 605) was also abbot for a fairly short period. Adomnán's life places him at a greater distance from Columba than was Baíthéne. The only story involving Laisrén in a role of any consequence concerned the latter's period as superior of the community at Durrow. He is said by Adomnán to have overworked the monks when they were erecting a large building. Columba, seeing this in a vision, was greatly distressed until Laisrén ordered the monks to stop, have a meal, and rest while the bad weather lasted. Columba ceased to weep and in his joy blessed Laisrén as 'the consoler of the monks' (Adomnán, 1.29). Since Columba's blessings were usually modelled by Adomnán on Old Testament benedictions, the story is likely to have been intended to imply that Laisrén was destined by Columba to succeed him in the future; it presumably also implied that he was remembered on Iona as a kindly abbot. He is said to have died on 16 September.

Virgno [Fergna Brit] (*d.* 623) was the first abbot with the time to emerge out of Columba's shadow. He was also the first not to be of Cenél Conaill. To judge by what Irish law had to say at a later date about churches controlled by the kin of the *patronus* (often, but not always, the founder), Virgno should have been a man of considerable ability. That he was very probably a Briton, presumably from what is now southern Scotland, makes his succession all the more remarkable. Iona later had an English bishop, Coeddi (*d.* 712), but Virgno was the only non-Irish abbot. This is also what Iona remembered: he is described by Adomnán (writing of Columba's lifetime) as 'a young man of good ability, who later, by divine authority, was in charge of this church' (Adomnán, 3.19). Adomnán's story told of Virgno praying during the night and so becoming by accident the witness of a visitation of heavenly light upon Columba. Virgno is said to have told this story to his sister's son, a priest called Commán, after Columba's death, and Commán told it to Adomnán. Virgno's death was commemorated on 2 March.

The height of Iona's influence It was probably during Virgno's time that Oswald of Bernicia (d. 642) and his brothers established contacts with Iona. Oswald was exiled together with his brothers, sons of the former king, Æthelfrith, when the latter's rival, Eadwin of Deira, came to power in 616. Both Oswald and Oswiu (d. 670) are shown by Bede to have been able to speak Irish, whereas their elder brother, Eanfrith, appears to have had closer connections with the Picts. When, therefore, Oswald came to power in Northumbria in 634, he sent a message to Iona requesting that a bishop be sent to preach to his people. The annals of Ulster record the foundation of Lindisfarne, by the Monk Áedán, (d. 651), in the very same year as Oswiu's victory over the British king Cadwallon. Whether Lindisfarne was really founded so quickly is doubtful, but what is striking is that it is given its British name (Medgoit) in the Irish annals, which may suggest some continued British presence close to Lindisfarne or British aid for Áedán's mission.

The abbot at the time was **Ségéne mac Fiachna** (d. 652), a kinsman of Columba. He appears to have taken a direct interest in the Northumbrian mission. A story told by Adomnán reveals Columba's support for Oswald's victory over Cadwallon. It was said to have been told by Oswald to Ségéne in the presence of Faílbe, Adomnán's predecessor as abbot and his informant. This meeting between abbot and king very probably took place in Northumbria rather than in Dál Riata, since the annals show that abbots of Iona not infrequently visited churches subject to their authority. Ségéne was also responsible for sending Fínán to Northumbria after Áedán's death in 651, the year before his own death. Earlier, in 635, he had founded a monastery called 'Rechru', probably Lambay Island, but possibly Rathlin Island. By the time of his death on 12 August 652, however, political conditions in the midlands of Ireland were becoming less favourable to Iona. After the death of Domnall mac Áeda, Cenél Conaill king of Tara, in 642, supreme power among the Uí Néill was divided between Cenél Conaill and the rulers of Brega (roughly modern co. Meath and north co. Dublin). The latter were forming close ties with Armagh, probably as a counterweight to the alliance between Iona and Cenél Conaill. It may be for this reason that Durrow is not once mentioned by the annals in the seventh century.

Ségéne's successor, **Suibne moccu Urthrí** [Suibhne] (d. 657), was the second abbot of Iona not to be a kinsman of the founder. His name shows that he came of a minor group, Corcu Urthrí (Corco Fhirthri), attested in connection with the people known as the Luigni, both in northern Connacht and in Meath. It may be have been felt to be wise not to bind Iona too closely to Cenél Conaill, whose power, after the deaths of Cellach Cóel (654) and Cellach mac Máele Coba (658), continued to decline from the peak it had reached c.640. During Suibne's time, Fínán, bishop of

the Northumbrians, sent missionaries to the Middle Angles and then Mercia, and also to Essex. When Suibne died (probably on 11 January), therefore, the authority of Iona, direct and indirect, stretched in a great arc from Durrow in the very centre of Ireland, through northern Ireland, Scotland, Northumbria, Mercia, and as far as the Thames. If Suibne's successor (and brother of Ségéne, Suibne's predecessor) **Cumméne Albus** [Cumine Ailbhe] (d. 669) had visited the churches of the Ionan mission to the English, as he may well have done, he could have visited the Saxon shore fort at Ythancæstir (Bradwell-on-Sea in Essex), where Cedd (d. 664) built a church, or have looked out from Cedd's other recorded church at Tilbury, across the Thames estuary to Kent.

It was, however, in Cumméne's time that Iona suffered the greatest blow to its power, the Synod of Whitby (664). Since the death of Áedán in 651, the Roman position on the dating of Easter and the tonsure had been advanced in Northumbria, first by an Irishman, Rónán, and subsequently by Wilfrid. Wilfrid had serious political backing from Oswiu's son and sub-king Alchfrith. Probably under pressure from Alchfrith, Oswiu summoned a council, over which he himself presided, at Whitby. Colmán, then bishop of the Northumbrians, could not have made any serious concession without authority from Iona; he, like his predecessor Fínán, was an Iona appointee. He appears from both accounts of the synod to have based his case principally on the holiness of Columba.

The continued identification of Columba's monks with their *patronus*, as well as his reputation for scriptural scholarship, made it exceedingly difficult for his heirs to make any major change. Ségéne had refused to change in the early 630s when an Irish churchman, Cummian, sent him an elaborate letter justifying change to the paschal reckoning of Victorius of Aquitaine, and also in 640, when he and other northern Irish churchmen had received a letter from the pope-elect John urging them to accept the Alexandrian Easter. It is consistent with his conservative attitude on Easter that he was also notably active in collecting stories about Columba. Similarly, Cumméne, whose death occurred on 24 February 669, was responsible for the first known life of Columba, in which he emphasizes the fearsome consequences for Dál Riata which flowed from their king having broken one of Columba's commands.

Iona after Whitby The effect of the Synod of Whitby was to remove Northumbria and other English churches from any control by Iona. Colmán had to leave and he was succeeded by an Englishman trained in southern Ireland. True, Wilfrid was to meet with opposition from those Northumbrians whom his disciples called Quartodecimans (that is, heretics on Easter), but there is no evidence that anyone sought to re-establish the authority of Iona. On the contrary, the terms of Pope Vitalian's letter to Oswiu and the eagerness of Wilfrid to extend his 'kingdom of churches' northwards *pari passu* with Ecgfrith's military aggression threatened an English intervention unfavourable to the authority of Iona, whether among the Picts or even in Dál Riata. When Wilfrid was expelled from the bishopric of York and thus attended a synod held by Pope Agatho in Rome in 680, he 'confessed the true and catholic faith for all the northern part of Britain and Ireland, and for the islands' (*Life of Bishop Wilfrid by Eddius Stephanus*, chap. 53). The ambition betrayed by this claim might well have been alarming to one such island, Iona: Wilfrid was hoping to make York the successor to Iona, not just in Northumbria but among the Picts and even in northern Ireland. He could entertain such ambitions only because Iona remained faithful to the Celtic Easter and tonsure. In Ireland, too, the shockwaves from Whitby were being felt. The arrival of St Theodore as archbishop of Canterbury (669) brought to England a man who believed that the community of Iona was heretical, and who almost certainly enjoyed a direct papal commission as archbishop of Britain (rather than as metropolitan bishop of a province embracing only southern Britain, as in Gregory the Great's scheme). Very probably in response to this event, the church of Kildare in Leinster (orthodox on paschal matters), and subsequently Armagh, developed claims to an archbishopric of Ireland. In the third quarter of the seventh century, the Uí Néill of Brega were at the height of their power (which explains why Brega was attacked by the Northumbrians in 684). They were more favourable to Armagh than to Iona. The ten years of the abbacy of **Faílbe mac Pípáin** (*d.* 679), whose death was commemorated on 22 March, and the early years of his successor, Adomnán, were, therefore, particularly unfavourable to Iona. Faílbe's long visit to Ireland, stretching from 673 to 676, may have enabled him to shore up Iona's position. Both of the two references to Faílbe in Adomnán's life of Columba show him in close association with Ségéne and as a link in the chain by which stories about Columba came to Adomnán. He was, perhaps, not likely to make any change in Iona's position on the Easter question.

His successor, *Adomnán (*d.* 704), bequeathed a position to his successors that was much stronger in terms of the political environment, but weaker in so far as the community of Columba was now divided over the Easter question. The defeat and death of Ecgfrith of Northumbria at the battle of Nechtansmere, 685, to be succeeded by his half-brother Aldfrith, brought to the throne a personal friend of Adomnán. The death of Fínsnechtae Fledach, king of Tara, ten years later, in 695, ended for the time being the domination of the kingship of Tara by the southern Uí Néill; Cenél Conaill would be the most powerful branch for the next generation. In the course of two visits to Northumbria to negotiate the release of captives held since the 684 attack on Brega, Adomnán had been persuaded to change to the Roman Easter. Armagh had probably abandoned the Celtic Easter *c.*685 and Adomnán's conversion may have been due as much to changes in Ireland as to the learning and eloquence of his Northumbrian hosts. The effect of these changes was that the northern half of Ireland had probably entirely conformed to the Roman Easter before the end of the seventh century.

The community of Iona itself, however, remained unwilling to change. The result was a split within the *familia* of Columba which was to endure until Iona itself finally conformed in 716. The split was almost certainly the reason why in the early eighth century there were often two abbots of Iona. The 'Hibernian' abbot of Iona in succession to Adomnán appears to have been **Conamail mac Faílbi** (*d.* 710); his 'Roman' counterpart from 707 was **Dúnchad mac Cind Fháelad** (*d.* 717). Initially, therefore, one abbot seems to have succeeded Adomnán; but his unwillingness to change and the difficulties likely to have been experienced by a Hibernian abbot in coping with Columban churches in Ireland that were now Roman made it easier to have two abbots. Their backgrounds were significantly different. Conamail belonged to the Uí Moccu Uais, a client people in what is now co. Londonderry; Dúnchad, on the other hand, was not merely of Cenél Conaill but also of its ruling branch: his grandfather and two uncles had been kings of Tara. Admittedly by the time he became abbot the descendants of his grandfather, Máel Coba, had lost power to those of Máel Coba's brother, Domnall mac Áeda; but none the less Dúnchad's genealogical position within Cenél Conaill was the strongest of any abbot of Iona including Columba. Not only was Conamail mac Faílbi likely to have enjoyed less influence in Ireland, but so also was another apparently 'Hibernian' abbot, **Dorbéne mac Altaíni** (*d.* 713), of a less powerful branch of Cenél Conaill. The likelihood is, therefore, that Adomnán had secured the adhesion of Cenél Conaill to the Roman Easter, as Bede's story implies, and that the abbacy of Dúnchad flowed partly from their desire to see Iona itself conform. They may have been in a position to put particular pressure on Iona because of an ambiguity in the law concerning family monasteries—should, on the one hand, an outsider, such as Conamail mac Faílbi, resign as soon as a kinsman of the *patronus* appeared who was fit for the office, or should he continue to rule until he died?

The background to the final decision to conform, taken in 716, can be inferred from Bede and from the annals. Of the abbots thought to have been Hibernian in sympathy, Conamail had died in 710, probably on 11 September, and Dorbéne obtained the *kathedra* of Iona in the summer of 713 only to die five months later on 28 October. Dorbéne was the person who possessed the Schaffhausen manuscript of Adomnán's life of St Columba, where he might have read how, more than a century earlier, Columba had prophesied the conflict over Easter. Meanwhile Dúnchad remained abbot. An English bishop of Iona, Coeddi, died on 24 October 712; and he may have been replaced by Ecgberht (*d.* 729), who, according to Bede, came to Iona at about this time and was strongly Roman in his sympathies. The Northumbrians defeated the Picts near Stirling in 711; the letter of Ceolfrith, abbot of Wearmouth–Jarrow, to Nechtan, son of Derilei and king of the Picts, which must have been written between 705 and 716, is perhaps more plausibly dated a year or two after this battle rather than before. In that case, the arrival of Ecgberht on Iona is unlikely to have been later than the letter to Nechtan. The letter was designed to persuade the king to conform to the Roman Easter and tonsure; but it included, as one of its arguments, a passage on Adomnán's work in northern Ireland in favour of the Roman cause. In other words, since Ecgberht probably worked closely with Dúnchad, the Roman abbot of Iona, the letter of Ceolfrith to Nechtan can best be seen as encouragement to Nechtan to bring the Picts into alliance with Dúnchad and Ecgberht. Given the warm appreciation of Adomnán by Ceolfrith and Bede, and Bede's exceedingly favourable attitude to Ecgberht, it is unlikely that the letter was intended to break the connection between the Picts and Iona.

In spite of this array of persuasive forces, the change was not accomplished easily. On Iona, Easter itself was changed in 716. This seems to have been followed by the resignation of Dúnchad, who was to die on 25 May 717. His successor was **Fáelchú mac Dorbéni** (d. 724), who belonged to a remote collateral branch of Cenél Conaill. By this stage Northumbria was in confusion, with the killing of the king, Osred, son of Aldfrith, in 716, and the death of the next king, Coenred, son of Cuthwine, in 718. In 717, however, apparently after the death of Abbot Dúnchad, King Nechtan drove the community of Iona out of Pictland, westwards into Dál Riata; and in 718 the community of Iona received the Petrine tonsure.

Nechtan's expulsion of the community of Iona in 717 is not easy to explain. Assuming that Dúnchad had been abbot for the Romani, his sphere would have included the Picts under Nechtan, if they had changed to the Roman Easter before 716 in response to Ceolfrith's letter. Nechtan may not have accepted the terms of the settlement, perhaps because he was not consulted, and perhaps because the influence he had over a Roman abbot of Iona would inevitably be greater than it was over an abbot accepted by all. Alternatively, it may have been that Nechtan expelled those who were making difficulties about accepting the Roman tonsure. It would, in any case, be very unsafe to infer from the annals that the link between the Picts and Iona was permanently broken in 717. Further difficulties are suggested by an entry in the chronicle of Ireland for 722, 'Feidilmid assumed the *principatus* of Iona' (*Ann. Ulster*, s.a. 722). Feidilmid is not included in the Salzburg confraternity book, which agrees with the picture of the succession given by another entry in the chronicle of Ireland s.a. 724: 'Fáelchú son of Dorbéne, abbot of Iona, slept; Cilléne the Tall succeeded him in the *principatus* of Iona' (ibid., s.a. 724). Although Fáelchú was nearly eighty by 722, neither the phrasing of the entry for that year nor the one for 724 suggests that Fáelchú had resigned. There were serious internal struggles among the Picts which might have had an effect on Iona, but these seem to have become serious only in 724.

The alliance with Cland Cholmáin In 724 when **Cilléne Fota** (d. 726) became abbot, Cináed mac Írgalaig was king of Tara. Cináed came from the Uí Néill of Brega, but he was to be the last of that branch to gain the kingship of Tara for many generations. After his death, Flaithbertach mac Loingsig of Cenél Conaill was king of Tara until 734; he also was the last member of his branch of the Uí Néill to gain the kingship of Tara for centuries. These branches,

dominant since the sixth century, were ousted by other Uí Néill kindreds, Cland Cholmáin, rulers of Mide, and Cenél nEogain from the valley of the Foyle, now supreme among the southern and northern Uí Néill respectively.

In 726 Cilléne the Tall (who died on either 14 or 19 April) was succeeded by his namesake, **Cilléne Droichtech** (d. 752), whose name is literally 'little man of the church [and] bridge builder'. He belonged to the southern Uí Néill, but to a collateral branch identified neither with the rulers of Brega nor with those of Mide. In 727 the relics of Adomnán were taken to Ireland and *Cáin Adomnáin* ('the law of Adomnán') was renewed. The *cáin* (*lex* or *rechtge*) of this kind was an edict established by a combination of royal and ecclesiastical authority, usually under the patronage of a saint, whose relics might be brought on circuit. The validity of the *cáin* was normally temporary (perhaps seven years), and it might thus be renewed; while it was in force, it was secured by an elaborate structure of sureties and pledges, designed to ensure that all authority, whether of kindred, lord, king, or church, had both an obligation and an interest in upholding the law. In the eighth and early ninth centuries these *cánai* or *leges* were to be the most dramatic expression of ecclesiastical influence on Irish society. A subsidiary purpose of Cilléne's renewal of the law of Adomnán was, according to a late text, to establish peace between the two great branches of the northern Uí Néill, Cenél Conaill and Cenél nEogain. Even though the information is from a late source, it is plausible: Adomnán's foundation at Raphoe was associated with his law, and it lay in the small kingdom of Cenél nÉndai, situated between Cenél Conaill and Cenél nEogain. The peace may indeed have lasted long enough to help Flaithbertach mac Loingsig of Cenél Conaill to defeat and kill Cináed mac Írgalaig in 728 and to reign for a few years as king of Tara. The relics of Adomnán were, however, brought back from Ireland in 730, and in 732 fighting broke out again between Cenél Conaill and Cenél nEogain, leading in 734 to the abdication of Flaithbertach mac Loingsig and the succession of his enemy Áed Allán mac Fergaile.

In 737 Áed Allán showed his appreciation of the significance of the *cáin* and his refusal to continue the alliance with Iona hitherto characteristic of the northern Uí Néill. He first held a meeting, situated close to the frontier, with Cathal mac Finguine, king of Munster, whereupon, in the words of the annals, 'the Law of Patrick was in force throughout Ireland' (*Ann. Ulster*, s.a. 737). He had done precisely what Adomnán and his kinsman Loingsech mac Óenguso, king of Tara, had done in 697 when they established *Cáin Adomnáin* at a great assembly at Birr on the borders between Munster and the lands of the Uí Néill; but this time it was the power of Patrick and Armagh which was displayed, not that of Adomnán or Columba. It may well have been Cilléne Droichtech who brought about a realignment in Iona's alliances in order to meet the new situation. The traditional allies of Armagh were the Uí Néill of Brega; its new allies were Cenél nEogain; Cland Cholmáin of Mide, however, had no strong and exclusive alliance among the great churches. The ruler of Mide in the middle years of the eighth century was Domnall mac Murchada (*d.* 763), who may have been buried at Durrow. A number of things may have conspired to forge the alliance between Cland Cholmáin and Iona, which was to rescue her influence in Ireland from the threat posed by the decline of Cenél Conaill: Domnall's friendship with Durrow, Cilléne Droichtech's family connections in the midlands, and Domnall's policy of using the king of Cenél Conaill (weakened and therefore not a dangerous rival) as a deputy ruler in the north.

The full effects of this realignment were visible in the time of Cilléne Droichtech's successor, **Sléibíne mac Congaile** (*d.* 767). Cilléne seems to have resigned the abbacy before his death on 3 July 752, since his obit gives him the title 'anchorite of Iona' (*Ann. Ulster*, s.a. 752). Resignation followed by a period as anchorite was a well-attested practice, found, for example, in the case of Áed, bishop of Sleaty in Carlow, who died as an anchorite in 700. Sléibíne also seems to have resigned before his death, which occurred perhaps on 2 March, since his successor, **Suibne** [Suibhne] (*d.* 772), was abbot by 766.

In 753 the law of Columba was proclaimed by Domnall mac Murchada, and in 754 Sléibíne went to Ireland. He was presumably still there when, in 757, he also promulgated the law of Columba. However, when Domnall mac Murchada died in 763, his successor, Niall Frossach, was from Cenél nÉogain; he, following the pattern established by his brother, Áed Allán, promulgated the law of Patrick in 767. Before Niall's death in 778 he had lost the kingship of Tara to Domnall's son Donnchad (*d.* 797). He, together with Suibne's successor as abbot, **Bresal mac Ségéni** (*d.* 801), promulgated the law of Columba in 778. The continued spiritual reputation of Iona in his time is attested by the pilgrimage in 783 of Artgal, son of Cathal, king of Connachta, to Iona, where he died in 791.

Bresal's successor, **Connachtach** (*d.* 802), was abbot for only a year; he died on 10 May 802 and is described in an obit as an excellent scribe, namely, in the terminology of the Irish annals, a scriptural scholar. This suggests that Iona had not abandoned the traditions of scholarship characteristic of the seventh and early eighth centuries. His successor, **Cellach mac Congaile** (*d.* 815), was responsible for building the new monastery at Kells, beginning in 807. When he had completed the buildings in 814, he resigned the abbacy and died the next year.

Iona and the vikings The building of 'the new monastery of Columba' (*Ann. Ulster*, s.a. 807) at Kells was an expression of the alliance between Cland Cholmáin and Iona. It may also have been intended as a refuge from viking attacks for vulnerable and precious possessions, among them, perhaps, the Book of Kells. The vikings began their attacks in 794. They burnt Iona in 802 and killed sixty-eight of the community in 806; this particular attack may have been behind the building of Kells. In 825 **Blaímac mac Flainn** [Blathmac] (*d.* 825) was martyred on Iona by 'the heathens'; his death was commemorated in a poem by Walafrid Strabo, abbot of Reichenau (*d.* 849).

In the long term the growing power of the vikings in the Western Isles was to make the position of Iona extremely insecure. The monastery inevitably found it difficult to maintain its role as the principal ecclesiastical link between Britain and Ireland. It attempted to do so by the same practice of making prolonged tours that had long been used to buttress the bonds of the *familia* of Columba in Ireland. At some point in the eighth century, Columba's remains appear to have been elevated from their grave in the monastic cemetery and enshrined. In 818 **Diarmait alumnus Daigri** (*d.* in or after 831), who had been abbot since 814, made a visit to Britain with the shrine of Columba; just as, in 849, his successor, **Innrechtach ua Finnachtai** (*d.* 854), went with the relics of Columba to Ireland. Innrechtach was martyred by Englishmen on 12 March 854, while on pilgrimage to Rome. His successor, **Cellach mac Ailella** (*d.* 865), is described in his obit as abbot of Kildare and Iona and as dying in Pictland; this combination is perhaps explained by the links of Cináed mac Ailpín, king of Scotland, with Leinster. Nothing is known of the next two abbots, **Feradach mac Cormaic** (*d.* 880) and **Flann mac Maíle Dúin** (*d.* 891), apart from their names and obits. Flann, who died on 20 April, was, however, succeeded by **Máel Brigte mac Tornáin** (*d.* 927), whose feast day is 22 February and who contrived to be both abbot of Armagh and abbot of Iona. It is quite uncertain whether Máel Brigte spent any significant time on Iona. The headship of the community of Columba was now passing to Kells.   T. M. CHARLES-EDWARDS

Sources J. Colgan, *Acta sanctorum veteris et maioris Scotiae seu Hiberniae* (Louvain, 1645); facs. edn with introduction by B. Jennings, *The Acta sanctorum Hiberniae of John Colgan* (Dublin, 1948) · *Adomnán's Life of Columba*, ed. and trans. A. O. Anderson and M. O. Anderson, rev. edn, rev. M. O. Anderson, OMT (1991) · Adomnán of Iona, *Life of St Columba*, ed. R. Sharpe (1995) · *Amra Choluim Chille*, ed. W. Stokes, 'The Bodleian "Amra Choluimb Chille"', *Revue Celtique*, 20 (1899), 31–55, 132–83, 248–89, 400–37; *Revue Celtique*, 21 (1900), 133–6 [corrections and additions] · Bede, *Hist. eccl.* · P. Ó Riain, ed., *Corpus genealogiarum sanctorum Hiberniae* (Dublin, 1985) · *Félire Óengusso Céli Dé / The martyrology of Oengus the Culdee*, ed. and trans. W. Stokes, HBS, 29 (1905) · 'Liber confraternitatis sancti Petri Salisburgensis', *Dioecesis Salisburgensis*, ed. S. Herzberg-Frankel, MGH Necrologia Germaniae, 2 (Berlin, 1904), 27 · R. I. Best and H. J. Lawlor, eds., *The martyrology of Tallaght*, HBS, 68 (1931) · F. Kelly, ed., 'A poem in praise of Columb Cille', *Ériu*, 24 (1973), 1–34 · F. Kelly, ed., *Tiughraind Bhécáin*, *Ériu*, 26 (1975), 66–98 · W. W. Heist, ed., *Vita S. Baithini abbatis Hiensis*, *Vitae sanctorum Hiberniae ex codice Salmanticensi nunc Bruxellensi* (Brussels, 1965), 379–82 · J. Bannerman, 'Notes on the Scottish entries in the early Irish annals', *Studies in the history of Dalriada* (1974), 9–26 · M. Herbert, *Iona, Kells, and Derry: the history and hagiography of the monastic familia of Columba* (1988) · E. Stephanus, *The life of Bishop Wilfrid*, ed. and trans. B. Colgrave (1927) · *Ann. Ulster* · *AFM*

Ionawr, Dafydd. *See* Richards, David (1751–1827).

Ionescu, (George) Ghita (1913–1996), political scientist, was born on 8 March 1913 in Bucharest, Romania, son of Alexandru Ionescu, manager of the Athenée Palace Hotel, and his wife, Hélène Sipsom. After graduating in law from the University of Bucharest, he threw himself into liberal politics and journalism as a supporter of the anti-fascist

Nicolae Titulescu. After Titulescu's defeat in the 1937 elections, Ionescu joined the diplomatic service, serving in Bulgaria and Turkey. Following the Soviet takeover of Romania and the abdication of King Michael in 1947, he emigrated to the West.

Ionescu did not find it easy to establish himself. Until 1953 he was based in London, where he broadcast on the BBC's Romanian service and taught Romanian at the School of Slavonic Studies. On 23 December 1950 he married Valence Ramsey de Bois Maclaren (1915/16–1996), stating that he was already a widower. They were a devoted couple, radiating warmth and humanity. In 1953 he became secretary of the Romanian national committee in New York, and in 1958 moved to Munich, where he directed the Romanian service of Radio Free Europe. But the role of propagandist did not suit him, and in 1963 he took up a research fellowship at the London School of Economics. Only then, at the age of fifty, could he begin what was to be his life's work.

After five years at the London School of Economics, Ionescu moved to Manchester University as reader in the department of government. He was promoted to a professorship in 1970, and soon became a vigorous and entrepreneurial departmental chairman. He showed the same flair as editor of the quarterly journal *Government and Opposition*, which he and a diverse group of political scientists and historians—including Bernard Crick, Leonard Shapiro, and the American historian Richard Hofstadter—founded during his time at the London School of Economics. *G & O*, as it was known to its friends, specialized in comparative politics, but it was resolutely interdisciplinary (as well as international) in approach; Ionescu's regular 'Reading notes'—sometimes quirky, sometimes profound, and almost always thought-provoking—epitomized its cosmopolitanism and disdain for narrow specialisms.

All this, however, was incidental to Ionescu's most important achievements as a scholar and thinker. He was, above all, the prophet, analyst, and moralist of interdependence. Industrial societies, he believed, were necessarily interdependent, in a sense not true of previous societies; the more advanced their industrial structures, the more interdependent they were bound to be. Irrespective of political forms, they depended on co-operation—at least in some degree voluntary—between the economic actors and the technical experts who kept the industrial machine turning. Ionescu first applied this approach to the communist world. No one could have been more hostile to communism, but he was too scrupulous a scholar to share the then common view that it was an unchanging monolith. In two path-breaking studies—*Communism in Romania* (1965) and *The Politics of the East European Communist States* (1966)—he argued that the logic of interdependence was beginning to make itself felt east of the iron curtain as well as in the West; and that as a result the communist regimes of eastern Europe would gradually become less communist and more European. Events bore him out; but in the 1960s it was a brave prophecy to make.

In the 1970s Ionescu shifted his focus to western Europe. Two themes preoccupied him—the impact of transnational interdependence within the EC, and the implications of socio-economic interdependence for his adopted country of Great Britain. His approach to the first was the mirror image of his approach to eastern Europe. Not only was the logic of interdependence undermining the 'apparat state' of the East, it was also undermining the traditional categories of national sovereignty in the member states of the EC. In *Centripetal Politics*, published in the inflation-haunted year of 1975, he offered a more pessimistic, but essentially similar, interpretation of the repeated economic and industrial crises of 1970s Britain. These, Ionescu argued, sprang from a dangerous mismatch between the realities of an interdependent society and the structures of conventional politics. In an interdependent society, an increasing range of actors—cities, regions, industrial firms, trade unions, and technical experts—had the power to wreck the economy, and, ultimately, to tear the society apart in internecine strife. These centrifugal pressures had to be countervailed by a new centripetal politics, in which systems of inter-group bargaining and concertation—alien to the British tradition—would supplement the familiar institutions of the parliamentary state.

It remained to explore the moral and philosophical implications of interdependence. In 1984, four years after his retirement, Ionescu set out the results of his meditations on this theme in a brief but haunting study, *Politics and the Pursuit of Happiness*. Social and political reforms, he had now come to think, were not enough. It was necessary to abandon the destructive fallacy, first applied by the Jacobins during the French Revolution, that the task of politics is to create a happy world and to sweep away the human and institutional obstacles to it. That fallacy lay at the heart both of totalitarian communism and of the mechanistic utilitarianism of the democratic West. Despite the conflict between them, they both sprang from a hedonistic and life-diminishing, because death-denying, materialism. What was needed was a new, more frugal conception of the tasks and possibilities of politics, based on 'the tragic sense of life' (a phrase which Ionescu borrowed from the Spanish philosopher Unamuno) which alone could generate a 'true sentiment of fraternity'. Ionescu continued working and writing until his death at 25 Southwood Lawn Road, Highgate, London, on 28 June 1996—producing, among other things, a path-breaking study of the implications of global interdependence for political leadership. But the passionate humanism of *Politics and the Pursuit of Happiness* is his true testament.

DAVID MARQUAND

Sources *Daily Telegraph* (9 July 1996) · *The Independent* (6 July 1996) · *The Guardian* (5 July 1996) · m. cert. · d. cert. · naturalization cert. · *WWW* · personal knowledge (2004) · private information (2004) · *CGPLA Eng. & Wales* (1996)
Likenesses photograph, repro. in *The Independent* · photograph, repro. in *Daily Telegraph*
Wealth at death £139,194: probate, 27 Nov 1996, *CGPLA Eng. & Wales*

Ionides, Alexander Constantine (1810–1890), art collector and patron, was born on 1 September 1810 in Constantinople, the fourth of eleven children of Constantine Ipliktzis (1775–1852) and his wife, Mariora Sendoukaki (1784–1857). Constantine had established a branch of his trading firm in London about 1815 and Alexander came to England at the age of sixteen, in 1827, completing his education at Mr Hine's school, Brixton. In 1832 he married Euterpe, *née* Sgouta (1816–1892), in Constantinople and settled in Cheetham Hill, Manchester; the couple had three sons and two daughters. He founded the firm of Ionides & Co., trading in textiles and wheat with the Balkans and the Near East, changing his name to Ionides at about the same time. The family moved to London in 1834, living first at 9 Finsbury Circus, and from 1838 or 1839 at Tulse Hill. He was naturalized in 1837, was Greek consul-general in 1854–66, became a director of the Crystal Palace in 1855, and had several directorships in banks.

Ionides, who joined in several of his father's charitable endowments, including the university at Athens, began his patronage of artists about 1829–30 when he acquired a set of engravings by his friend Edward Calvert, and in 1837 he commissioned the young G. F. Watts to copy a portrait of his father. He remained a patron and personal friend of Watts. In 1860 he was introduced by his son Alexander (Aleco; 1840–1898) to several artists who had befriended him in Paris, including Whistler, Edward Poynter, Thomas Armstrong, and George Du Maurier. At this time his house in Tulse Hill was a regular meeting place for artists, musicians, and writers who took part in the family's musical and theatrical entertainments. Rossetti was introduced to the circle in 1862 and he, in turn, introduced Edward Burne-Jones.

Philip Webb remodelled the interior of 1 Holland Park, to which the Ionides family had moved in 1864, and in 1870 Thomas Jeckyll was commissioned to decorate several rooms, notably the billiard room which was in the Japanese style with inset Japanese paintings. After 1875 the refurbishment was continued by Aleco, who commissioned William Morris and Walter Crane to undertake extensive decoration, and by 1890 the house had become a showpiece of the aesthetic movement. With Aleco also, Ionides built up a collection of Greek vases and tanagra figures. Of his other children, Constantine Alexander *Ionides (1833–1900), Aglaia Coronio (1834–1906), confidante of Morris and friend of Rossetti, and Luke Ionides (1837–1924), a lifelong friend of Whistler, were also art patrons and collectors.

Ionides bought mainly from his artist friends. About 1870 he was asked by the dealer Murray Marks to help finance an agency to deal in works by Watts, Burne-Jones, Rossetti, and Whistler. The partnership came to nothing, but Ionides acquired sixteen plates of Whistler's *Thames* set, from which he had 100 sets printed. His will lists eighty-six paintings and drawings, several by the artists mentioned and also, among others, by Fantin-Latour and Albert Moore. He is immortalized in Du Maurier's *Trilby*, in which the character of Sir Lewis Cornelys is based on both

Alexander Ionides and Arthur Lewis. Ionides moved to Hastings in 1875, and died there at his home, Windycroft, on 10 November 1890.   C. M. KAUFFMANN

Sources A. C. Ionides, *Ion, a grandfather's tale* (privately printed, Dublin, 1927) · A. C. Ionides, *Ion, a grandfather's tale: notes and index* (privately printed, London, 1927) · A. Leoussi, *Circles of light: the making of the Ionides art collection in the Victoria and Albert Museum* (2001) · D. S. Macleod, *Art and the Victorian middle class: money and the making of cultural identity* (1996), 278, 433 · L. Ormond, *Du Maurier* (1969), 98–100, 106 · *The young George Du Maurier: a selection of his letters, 1860–67*, ed. D. Du Maurier (1951) · L. Ionides, *Memories* (1925); facs. edn (1996) · L. F. Day, 'A Kensington interior', *Art Journal*, new ser., 13 (1893), 139–44 · G. White, 'An epoch-making home', *The Studio*, 12 (1897–8), 102–12 · T. Armstrong, *A memoir*, ed. L. M. Lamont (1912), 195 · E. Robins Pennell and J. Pennell, *The life of James McNeill Whistler*, 2 vols. (1908), vol. 1, pp. 78f., 153f. · A. Watson, 'Constantine Ionides and his collection of 19th century French art', *Journal of the Scottish Society for Art History*, 3 (1998), 24–31 · W. Blunt, *England's Michelangelo: a biography of George Frederic Watts* (1975) · J. Atkins, 'The Ionides family', *Antique Collector*, 58 (1987), 86–93 · T. Catsiyannis, *Constantine Ionidis-Ipliktsis, 1775–1852, and the Ionidis family* (1988) · M. L. Evans, 'Blake, Calvert, and Palmer: the album of Alexander Constantine Ionides', *Burlington Magazine* [forthcoming] · C. Dakers, *The Holland Park circle: artists and Victorian society* (1999)

Archives priv. coll., archives

Likenesses G. F. Watts, group portrait, oils, 1846, V&A · W. C. Ross, miniature

Wealth at death £28,874 18s. 10d.: resworn probate, Oct 1891, *CGPLA Eng. & Wales* (1890)

Ionides, Constantine Alexander (1833–1900), art patron and collector, was born on 14 May 1833 in Smedley Lane, Cheetham Hill, Manchester, the eldest of the five children of Alexander Constantine *Ionides (1810–1890), formerly Alexander Constantine Ipliktzis, and his wife, Euterpe (1816–1892), daughter of Lucas Sgouta. The family moved to London in 1834, living from 1838 or 1839 at Tulse Hill, where Constantine Alexander went to Miss Cole's school; in the 1840s he was at boarding-school near Geneva. He joined his father's trading firm in 1850 and, some years later, left England to represent the firm in the wheat trade in the Balkans and Turkey, living principally at Brăila in Romania. In 1860 he married Agathonike (c.1844–1920), daughter of Constantine Fenerli, at Constantinople; they had three daughters and five sons. They settled in England in 1864, living for almost thirty years at 8 Holland Villas Road, Kensington. Entering a career on the stock exchange, he worked at first for Clapham Brothers, and then, in 1866, set up his own firm, Ionides and Barker, subsequently Ionides & Co.

His son relates that Ionides was an autocrat in the home, as well as an enthusiast with wide interests who worked at his lathe, studied the Bible, and, in retirement, took up astronomy. During the period from 1878 to 1884 he built up the bulk of his art collection, of which he left all the paintings, prints, and drawings to the South Kensington Museum. His bequest, consisting of a total of 1156 items, including about 90 paintings, 300 drawings and watercolours, and 750 prints, headed by 123 etchings by Rembrandt and 78 by Piranesi, was subject to the condition that it should be kept as a separate collection and not distributed over the museum. Both in forming the collection and in this public benefaction, Ionides was following family tradition. His grandfather Constantine Ipliktzis had endowed schools and hospitals in Athens, and both his father and his brothers, Alexander and Luke, were collectors and patrons of artists, including Whistler and Rossetti.

Ionides's collection impressed his contemporaries and subsequent generations by its wide variety of different schools, periods, and artists. Outstanding among the old masters are paintings by Nardo di Cione (c.1350–c.1360), Botticelli (c.1470), Tintoretto (self-portrait, 1548), Rembrandt (1640), and Louis le Nain (c.1640–c.1648). Under the influence of the painter Alfred Legros, a close friend with whom he travelled abroad, Ionides bought a wide selection of nineteenth-century French paintings, of which the best-known are Delacroix's sketch for the *Shipwreck of Don Juan* (1840), Millet's *Wood Sawyers* (c.1850), and Degas's *Ballet Scene from the Opera 'Robert le Diable'* (1876), bought from the dealer Durand-Ruel in 1881 and the first painting by that artist to enter an English museum. He was also a patron of English artists, particularly G. F. Watts, who painted five generations of the Ionides family, and Rossetti and Burne-Jones.

In 1882 Ionides retired from active business and nine years later moved to his house at 23 Second Avenue, Brighton, where he died on 29 June 1900. He was buried at Hove cemetery on 2 July.   C. M. KAUFFMANN

Sources A. C. Ionides, *Ion, a grandfather's tale* (privately printed, Dublin, 1927) · A. C. Ionides, *Ion, a grandfather's tale: notes and index* (privately printed, London, 1927) · B. S. Long, *Catalogue of the Constantine Alexander Ionides collection*, 1 (1925) · *List of the bequests and donations to the South Kensington Museum to 31 Dec. 1900* (1901) · A. Leoussi, *Circles of light: the making of the Ionides art collection in the Victoria and Albert Museum* (2001) · archives and registers, V&A, department of prints and drawings · L. Ionides, *Memories* (1925); facs. edn (1996) · D. S. Macleod, *Art and the Victorian middle class: money and the making of cultural identity* (1996) · C. M. Kauffmann, ed., *Catalogue of foreign paintings: Victoria and Albert Museum*, 2 vols. (1973) · *The catalogue of the Constantine Alexander Ionides collection*, V&A (1904) · *The Times* (23 July 1900) · C. Monkhouse, 'The Constantine Ionides collection', *Magazine of Art*, 7 (1883–4), 36–44, 120–27, 208–14 · *Greek Gazette* (April 1981), 12 · *DNB* · J. Boardman, *Engraved gems: the Ionides collection* (1968)

Archives V&A, collection · V&A, museum registry | V&A library, letters from D. G. Rossetti and Jules Dalou

Likenesses G. F. Watts, group portrait, oils, 1840, V&A · W. C. Ross, miniature, 1853 · A. Legros, bronze medal, 1882 · G. F. Watts, oils, V&A

Wealth at death £155,584 14s. 8d.: probate, 11 Aug 1900, CGPLA Eng. & Wales

Iorwerth ab Owain (*d.* 1175×84), prince in Wales, lord of Caerleon, succeeded the king, his elder brother Morgan ab Owain, on Morgan's violent death in 1158. There is no indication that Iorwerth ever used the royal style, derived from their grandfather, *Caradog ap Gruffudd (*d.* 1081), one-time dominant king of Gwlad Morgan and client of William I. Iorwerth's first appearance is in 1136 when Gerald of Wales names him as the man responsible for the killing of Richard de Clare of Ceredigion in the pass of Grwyne Fawr between Abergavenny and Talgarth. In the subsequent conquest of Upper Gwent and Llefennydd by Morgan ab Owain, Iorwerth was closely associated with

his brother. They issued joint charters in Stephen's reign, and even appear to have possessed a joint seal (although no impression of it survives). Although King Morgan left at least two sons, it was his brother who succeeded him in 1158. This was quite clearly because Iorwerth had occupied the position of heir designate (*edling*) during his brother's lifetime.

Iorwerth (styled on one occasion of 'Gwynllŵg') presided over the decline of his family's fortunes in Gwent in the 1160s and 1170s. Before 1169 the castle of Usk (taken by his brother c.1136–7) was taken back by Earl Richard de Clare (Strongbow), lord of Chepstow. Iorwerth's failure to come to terms with Rhys ap Gruffudd of Deheubarth added to his problems. In 1171, on his way into the west, Henry II was persuaded by Rhys to join with him to oust Iorwerth from his castle of Caerleon and drive him back to his stronghold of Machen in Gwynllŵg. Iorwerth, his sons, and Morgan ap Seisyll, his nephew, retaliated by devastating the region of Llefennydd. Warfare continued into 1172, when Iorwerth's elder son, Owain, was assassinated by the earl of Gloucester's soldiers during a temporary truce. On 21 July 1173 Iorwerth retook Caerleon after a three-day siege and by mid-August had subdued all of lower Gwent, except the castles. He and his son Hywel [*see below*] appear to have maintained themselves by force in the area until early 1175, when family unity collapsed after Hywel blinded and castrated Owain Pen-Carn, his uncle (his father's younger brother). Iorwerth's nephew, Morgan ap Morgan ab Owain, seems always to have supported the English rather than his uncle. Caerleon Castle was once more lost.

Late in June 1175 Iorwerth came to an agreement with the Lord Rhys, with whose support he regained Caerleon from King Henry. The recovery of Caerleon may also have had something to do with the sexual liaison between the king and Iorwerth's daughter, Nest *Bloet, with whom the king had an illegitimate son, Morgan (surnamed Bloet, from his being brought up in the family of Nest's husband, Ralph Bloet (*d.* 1199) of Silchester). The date of Iorwerth's death is unknown, but he had been succeeded by his son Hywel ab Iorwerth of Caerleon by 1184. In Stephen's reign, probably before 1148, Iorwerth married Angharad, daughter of Bishop *Uthred of Llandaff. With her he had several known sons, Owain (killed in 1172), Hywel, his heir, and a younger pair, Gruffudd and Cadwallon, who appear at the court of King John at St Briavels in 1207, and also perhaps another son, Morgan. Iorwerth probably founded Llantarnam Abbey in Gwent and may have been buried there.

Hywel ab Iorwerth [Hywel of Caerleon] (*d.* in or before 1216) continued to rule as lord of Caerleon until the reign of John. A number of charters, in which he is styled Hywel of Caerleon, attest to his authority in the lowland area of Llefennydd, his control over Caerleon and the forest of Gwynllŵg (that is, upland Gwynllŵg), and his advocacy of Goldcliff Priory. In 1184–5 he was allied with the king of England, leading a company in the defence of the lordship of Glamorgan, where he acted as castellan of Newcastle, near Bridgend.

By 1216 Hywel had been succeeded by his son, **Morgan ap Hywel** [Morgan of Caerleon] (d. 1248), who in that year was carrying out a damaging campaign in Gwent against William (I) Marshal, earl of Pembroke and Striguil. The Marshal's biography suggests that Morgan had attempted to reclaim his dynasty's lost lands, which would imply an assault on the lordship of Usk. Morgan seems to have seized the opportunity presented by the invasion of England by Louis of France to press his claims by violence. The coming of peace in September 1217 removed his chance, and Morgan's men were driven from Caerleon at the end of the year by a bloody assault on the castle by the military household of William (I) Marshal. The campaign against him continued, as Morgan moved the centre of his resistance to his castle of Machen in upland Gwynllŵg. A conference at Worcester on 11 March 1218 led to Morgan's loss of Caerleon to the Marshal and the rest of Morgan's career is a story of his dogged attempts to reclaim his family's position in lower Gwent.

Morgan's principal opponents were the successive Marshal earls of Pembroke, each formidable in personal wealth and power. His chances of success against the younger Earl William Marshal were slim, for the earl maintained a great position at court, and married the king's sister. Even so, Morgan managed to challenge Earl William (II)'s continued possession of Caerleon in the *curia regis* and the castle remained in royal hands between 1223 and 1226 pending a resolution of the case. Morgan's failure led to a formal quitclaim of his rights in Caerleon to Earl William in or soon after 1227. But Morgan's great opportunity came with the succession of Richard Marshal in 1231. Earl Richard rapidly fell foul of Henry III and a war erupted in the marches and the south-west in 1232. Morgan was retained in the royal household for the campaign, and did great damage to the Marshal lands in Gwent. In the summer of 1233 his suit against the Marshals for possession of Caerleon was once again in the *curia regis*. By September 1233 he had a royal decision in his favour, but since the new earl, Gilbert Marshal (who succeeded his brother in 1234), would not give up the castle, Morgan had a grant of two English manors until he could repossess it. Morgan reoccupied the castle of Caerleon and lordships of Edlogan and Llefennydd early in 1236 (the *Brut* noting that it was 'for fear of the Lord Llywelyn') and also had damages assessed against Earl Gilbert, which the earl paid (reluctantly) in September. It seems that Earl Gilbert took the reverse badly, as is demonstrated by a remarkable indenture of 1236 between him and a local knight, Sir William de St Maur, by which Sir William undertook to support by any legal means possible the earl's attempts to oust Morgan from the manor of Undy, in lower Gwent. None the less, Morgan remained in control of Caerleon and its associated lordships until his death in 1248, before 15 March. He was childless, and was succeeded by Maredudd ap Gruffudd, who in one source appears to have been the descendant of Iorwerth ab Owain through Gwerfyl, the daughter of his youngest son, Morgan, but who could also conceivably have been the son of Gruffudd ab Iorwerth ab Owain (and therefore Morgan ap Hywel's first cousin once removed). Maredudd acquired lands in Llefennydd and elsewhere, but Caerleon was denied him (presumably on the pretext of its being a life grant to Morgan in 1233, and not therefore heritable except at the king's will).

The career of Morgan ap Hywel is the logical culmination of earlier choices of his family, such as the judicious collaboration of Morgan ab Owain with marcher powers in the reigns of Stephen and Henry II, and the choices of his grandfather and father at key points to ally with the king against the dominant Welsh power of their day (whether Deheubarth or Gwynedd). Morgan ap Hywel was an open Anglicizer: he operated through attorneys in courts of English law; served (as had his father) with English armies; adopted a toponym; and broke with the traditional Welsh families who supported and were tied to his dynasty, as can be seen from his aggression against his own hereditary *distain* ('steward'), Iorwerth ab Adam, in the 1240s. He prefigures several other Anglicizing Welsh dynasties, notably those of Powys and Afan. It is perhaps ironic that the ab Adam family, with whom he fell out, followed the same path and ultimately became peers of the English parliament in the reign of Edward I.

DAVID CROUCH

Sources T. Jones, ed. and trans., *Brut y tywysogyon, or, The chronicle of the princes: Peniarth MS 20* (1952) · T. Jones, ed. and trans., *Brut y tywysogyon, or, The chronicle of the princes: Red Book of Hergest* (1955) · *Chancery records* (RC) · *CPR, 1216–25* · P. Meyer, ed., *L'histoire de Guillaume le Maréchal*, 3 vols. (Paris, 1891–1901) · Rymer, *Foedera*, vol. 1 · Archives Départementales de l'Eure, H9 · Badminton deeds, NL Wales [1989 deposit] · J. E. Lloyd, *A history of Wales from the earliest times to the Edwardian conquest*, 3rd edn, 2 vols. (1939); repr. (1988)

Iorwerth ap Bleddyn (d. 1111). *See under* Bleddyn ap Cynfyn (d. 1075).

Iorwerth ap Madog ap Rhawd (fl. 1240), jurist, of whom hardly anything is known, was a member of a family traditionally learned in the law (like similar families in other Celtic lands), which held land in the vill of Dinlle, southwest of Caernarfon. Welsh medieval law, as known in manuscripts of the thirteenth and later centuries, is the product of a long development, by jurists rather than legislators. Among those jurists were Iorwerth ap Madog and his older relatives, Morgenau and his son Cyfnerth, whom some texts call 'the best in their time for remembrance and laws'. Others named in the family pedigree are given the epithet 'ynad', implying learning in law, and perhaps judicial office. The family was closely connected with the princes of thirteenth-century Gwynedd: Iorwerth's brother Einion wrote verse in praise of Gruffudd, the luckless elder son of Llywelyn ab Iorwerth (Llywelyn 'the Great'); and Gruffudd ab yr Ynad Coch, who mourned so strikingly the death of Gruffudd's son, Llywelyn (the so-called 'last prince'), was probably a distant relative. Ystrwyth, brother of Iorwerth's grandfather Rhawd, served Llywelyn ab Iorwerth as an administrative officer, and was the ancestor of several lawyers, including Sir John Glynne (1603–1666), as well as of Catherine Glynne, wife of W. E. Gladstone.

Iorwerth himself does not appear in the pedigree, and

survey material names no one who can be traced to him. This may be an accident, but it may mean that Iorwerth was a celibate cleric, for although Welsh law excluded the clergy from judicial office, it is clear that some law manuscripts were written by clerics, and the scribes may not have been mere copyists. Iorwerth is cited as an authority on one or two points in the thirteenth-century law texts from Gwynedd, and is credited with the editing which gave the most sophisticated and best-organized version of Welsh medieval law its classical form.

To the Welsh, their indigenous law was *cyfraith Hywel* ('the law of Hywel'), and although it is not clear what connection there was between the law and King Hywel Dda, who died in 949 or 950, most of the surviving manuscripts seem to have a common core, part of which may go back to Hywel's time. Some forty manuscripts (five in Latin, the rest in Welsh) survive from the period between about 1250 and 1536, when English law wholly replaced Hywel's law in Wales, and three classes of law book have long been recognized as represented among the manuscripts. In two of these classes a clear distinction is drawn between two books, those of the law of the court and the law of the country. The distinctive feature of the third class is its third book, the justices' test book (*llyfr prawf ynaid*), which brings together the material taken from the law of the country that those learned in the law were traditionally required to know: the 'three columns of law' (the law of homicide, of theft, and of arson) and the 'value of wild and tame'. Some manuscripts attribute the test book to Iorwerth, but the book was perhaps compiled before his day. In all manuscripts, however, an addition to the test book is thus explained: 'Iorwerth ap Madog saw that it would be useful to write the value of houses and equipment, and about joint ploughing and corn damage, in association with the test book'; Iorwerth was thus the final editor, and his significance is reflected in the name the 'Iorwerth redaction' by which this class is usually known. According to its preface, the test book was derived from the books of three named jurists (of whom Cyfnerth ap Morgenau is one) and 'the best books found in Gwynedd and Powys and Deheubarth'; the later law books of Powys and Deheubarth would draw freely on the Iorwerth redaction, for to the jurists Wales was united in law as it never was politically.   DAFYDD JENKINS

Sources D. Jenkins, 'A family of medieval Welsh lawyers', *Celtic law papers*, ed. D. Jenkins (1973), 123–33 • D. Jenkins, 'Iorwerth ap Madog', *National Library of Wales Journal*, 8 (1953–4), 164–70 • D. Jenkins, 'Yr Ynad Coch', *BBCS*, 22 (1966–8), 345–6

Iqbal, Sir Muhammad (1877–1938), philosopher and poet, was born at Sialkot in the Punjab on 9 November 1877. He was the younger son of Sheikh Nuruddin Muhammad, whose forebears were Hindu converts to Islam originally from Kashmir, and Imam Bibi, a devout woman of working-class background. He was educated at the Scotch Mission College at Sialkot and Government College, Lahore, where his brilliance gained him a post as lecturer in philosophy, first at the Oriental College and later the Government College. During these years he came under the influence of T. W. Arnold, who introduced him to

Western philosophy and the principles of critical scholarship. When Arnold left Lahore in 1904 Iqbal decided to continue his studies in England and in 1905 was admitted to Trinity College, Cambridge, where he read philosophy and came under the influence of the neo-Hegelians James Ward and John McTaggart. At the same time he attended law lectures at Lincoln's Inn and was called to the bar in 1908. From Cambridge he went to Germany and obtained the degree of DPh from Munich University for a thesis published in 1908 under the title *The Development of Metaphysics in Persia*. In 1908 Iqbal returned to India, and for the rest of his life practised as a barrister, a profession which he valued for its independence. In 1923 he was knighted, and from 1926 to 1930 was a member of the Punjab legislative council. Through his poems he had already won an outstanding position in the Indian Muslim community. He served as president of the All-India Muslim League in 1930 (when he expounded the concept of two nations in India and outlined the possibility of establishing a Muslim political entity in the north-west of the subcontinent) and as a delegate to the second and third round-table conferences held in London in 1931–2 to frame a constitution for India. In his last years he suffered from liver disease and took little part in politics.

Iqbal married first, in 1892, Karim Bibi, daughter of Khan Bahadur Atta Muhammad Khan, who bore three sons, but lived apart from him after his return from Europe; he married second and fourth (in 1909 and 1913) Sardar Begum, who bore one son; and third (about 1909) Mukhtar Begum. There is disagreement over the nature of his first marriage to Sardar Begum, but it appears that it was neither consummated nor ended with a formal divorce. In Europe he formed a deep and lasting friendship with Miss Atiya Begum Faizee, the first cousin of Sir Akbar Hayderi. He died at Lahore on 21 April 1938, and was buried there in a mausoleum of marble and lapis lazuli to the left of the steps leading to the Badshahi mosque.

For the last twenty-five years of his life Iqbal stood in a class by himself as a Muslim philosopher and poet. Impressed by the vigour and vitality of Europe and of Western thought, he saw in the social apathy of Muslim pantheism the cause of Muslim decadence, and in reaction against its negations he was drawn towards the evolutionary philosophy of Bergson and Nietzsche. It became his fixed purpose to infuse into Indian Islam the same spirit of activism. His first major work, a Persian *masnavi* sequence entitled *Asrar-i Khudi* (1915; translated into English, with an introduction, by Dr Reynold Alleyne Nicholson as *The Secrets of the Self*, 1920), with its gospel of the creative ego striving to achieve freedom and the fuller development of personality, took the younger generation of Indian Muslims by storm. But together with this he insisted that the true development of personality could be achieved only by sinking the self in the service of a community inspired by common spiritual traditions and in the pursuit of its highest values. Such a society could not be found in the West because of the evils inherent in Western civilization and social order, in the materialism of Western thought, and the corrupting influences of nationalism and imperialism. In contrast to these he saw in Islam the pattern within which the social endeavour and spiritual life of the developing personality should be integrated. This was the theme of his second major poetic work, *Rumuz-i Bekhudi* ('The mysteries of selflessness') issued in 1918.

These two doctrines, the sustained struggle of the awakened ego to raise humanity to a higher stage of evolution, and the moral, spiritual, and intellectual values of an idealized Islamic community, were developed and diversified in Iqbal's later poems. These were composed sometimes, like the first two, in Persian for the sake of a wider Muslim circle: *Payam-i Mashriq* ('The message of the East'), in reply to Goethe's *West-östlicher Divan* (1923); *Pas chih bayad kard, ay aqram-i sharq* ('What should be done, o nations of the East', 1926); *Zabur-i Ajam* ('Persian psalms', 1927); *Javid-Namah* ('The book of eternity', 1932), modelled after Dante's *Divina commedia*, and *Armaghan-i Hijaz* ('A gift of the Hijaz', 1938). Sometimes they were composed in Urdu for his own Indian public: *Bang-i-dara* ('Voice of the caravan', 1924); *Bal-i-Jibril* ('Gabriel's Wing', 1935); and *Darb-i-Kalim* ('The rod of Moses', 1936). A more systematic account of his thought was put together by Iqbal in a course of lectures delivered at Madras in 1928–9 and published as *The Reconstruction of Religious Thought in Islam* (1930; second edn, with a supplementary chapter, 1934). Throwing aside the traditional transcendentalist dogmas of Islam, as the imposition of an alien Hellenistic philosophy, he set out to reinterpret the Koran in evolutionary and immanentist terms. As a thinker Iqbal combines contradictory trends which enable him to appeal to Muslim modernist, conservative, and 'fundamentalist' alike. He had great influence over Muslims of his time, among them Saiyid Abdul Ala Mawdudi, who was to shape Muslim 'fundamentalism', and Muhammad Ali Jinnah, who was to found Pakistan. Many translations of Iqbal's work into Islamic and European languages in the late twentieth century brought his thought to a widely appreciative audience. In Pakistan he came to be regarded as the 'spiritual father' of the nation.

H. A. R. GIBB, *rev.* FRANCIS ROBINSON

Sources M. Iqbal, *The reconstruction of religious thought in Islam* (1934) · 'The secrets of the self' (*Asrār-i khudī*): *a philosphical poem by Sheik Muhammed Iqbal of Lahore*, ed. and trans. R. A. Nicholson (1920) · M. Iqbal, *The mysteries of selflessness*, trans. A. J. Arberry (1953) [Persian orig., *Rumūz-i Bēkhudī* (1918)] · A. J. Arberry, *Javid-Nama* (1966) · H. Malik, ed., *Iqbal: poet-philosopher of Pakistan* (1971) · A. Schimmel, *Gabriel's wing: a study into the religious ideas of Sir Muhammad Iqbal* (1963) · S. A. Vahid, *Iqbal: his art and thought* (1959) · K. G. Saiyidain, *Iqbal's educational philosophy* (1938) · Q. M. Haq and M. I. Waley, *Allama Sir Muhammad: poet-philosopher of the East* (1977) · A. Ahmed, *Islamic modernism in India and Pakistan, 1857–1964* (1967) · A. Schimmel, 'Ikbāl', *The encyclopaedia of Islam*, ed. H. A. R. Gibb and others, new edn, [10 vols.] (1960–) · K. A. Waheed, *A bibliography of Iqbal* (1965)
Archives Iqbal Museum, Lahore
Likenesses A. Kamal, oils, Department of Archaeology and Museums, Pakistan

Irby, Charles Leonard (1789–1845), naval officer and traveller, born on 9 October 1789, was sixth son of Frederick

Irby, second Baron Boston (1749–1825), and his wife, Christiana (*d.* 9 May 1832), only daughter of Paul Methuen of Corsham House, Wiltshire; he was the brother of Rear-Admiral Frederick Paul *Irby. He entered the navy in May 1801, and after serving in the North Sea and Mediterranean, at the Cape of Good Hope, the capture of Montevideo, and in the Bay of Biscay, was promoted lieutenant on 13 October 1808. He afterwards served at the capture of Mauritius, and on the coast of North America. On 7 June 1814 he was promoted to the command of the *Thames* (32 guns), in which he took part in the unsuccessful expedition against New Orleans.

Ill health compelled Irby to resign his command in May 1815, and in summer 1816 he left England with his old friend Captain James Mangles, intending to tour the continent. The journey was extended far beyond their original plan. They visited Egypt, went up the Nile, and, with Giovanni Baptista Belzoni and Henry William Beechey, explored the temple at Abu Simbel; they went across the desert and along the coast, with a detour to Balbec and the Cedars, and reached Aleppo, where they met William John Bankes and Thomas Legh, who with themselves were the earliest of modern explorers of Syria. Thence they travelled to Palmyra, Damascus, down the Jordan valley, and so to Jerusalem. They afterwards passed round the Dead Sea, and through the Holy Land. At Acre they embarked in a Venetian brig for Constantinople; but being both dangerously ill with dysentery, they were landed at Cyprus. In the middle of December 1818 they shipped on a vessel for Marseilles, which they reached after a rough passage of seventy-six days. Their letters during their journey were afterwards privately printed in 1823 as *Travels in Egypt and Nubia, Syria, and Asia Minor, during the Years 1817–18*. The work was published in Murray's Colonial and Home Library in 1844. After his return Irby married, on 8 February 1825, Frances, daughter of John Mangles of Hurley, Berkshire, and sister of his friend Captain Mangles. They had a son and a daughter.

In August 1826 Irby was appointed to command the sloop *Pelican* (18 guns), and suppressed piracy in the Levant and on the coast of Greece. On 2 July 1827 he was posted to the *Ariadne* (26 guns), but was not relieved from the command of the *Pelican* until the end of September. After the battle of Navarino he was appointed by Sir Edward Codrington to bring home the *Genoa*, which he paid off at Plymouth in January 1828. He had no further service, and died at Torquay on 3 December 1845.

J. K. LAUGHTON, *rev.* ANDREW LAMBERT

Sources *Piracy in the Levant, 1827–8: selected from the papers of admiral Sir Edward Codrington*, ed. C. G. Pitcairn-Jones, Navy RS, 72 (1934) · S. Searight, *The British in the Middle East*, rev. edn (1979) · O'Byrne, *Naval biog. dict.* · C. L. Irby and J. Mangles, *Travels in Egypt and Nubia, Syria, and Asia Minor, during the years 1817–18* (privately printed, London, 1823) · *GM*, 2nd ser., 25 (1846), 536 · J. Marshall, *Royal naval biography*, 3/2 (1832) · Burke, *Peerage* (1959) · GEC, *Peerage*

Irby, Frederick Paul (1779–1844), naval officer, was born on 18 April 1779, the second son of Frederick, second Baron Boston (1749–1825), and his wife, Christiana (*d.* 9

May 1832), only daughter of Paul Methuen of Corsham House, Wiltshire; he was the brother of Captain Charles Leonard *Irby. He entered the navy in 1791, served on the home and North American stations, and, as midshipman of the *Montagu*, was present at the battle of 1 June 1794 in the north Atlantic. On 6 January 1797 he was promoted lieutenant of the frigate *Circe*, in which he was present at the battle of Camperdown. He was afterwards in the *Apollo*, which was wrecked near the Texel on 7 January 1799. On 22 April 1800 he was promoted to command the bomb-vessel *Volcano*; in the following year was moved into the *Jalouse*, was employed in the North Sea, and was advanced to post rank on 14 April 1802. In 1805 he commanded the sea fencibles in the Essex district, and towards the end of 1807 was appointed to the frigate *Amelia* (38 guns), on the home station, one of the squadron under Rear-Admiral Robert *Stopford, which, on 24 February 1809, drove ashore and destroyed three large frigates near Les Sables d'Olonne. Irby's gallantry and the good conduct of his men gained the special approval of the Admiralty.

For the next two years Irby continued actively employed on the coast of France, and on 24 March 1811 he assisted in driving on shore and destroying the French frigate *Amazone*. Still in the *Amelia*, he was afterwards sent as senior officer of the squadron on the west coast of Africa, suppressing the slave trade and supporting British settlements. At the end of January 1813, as he was about to leave Sierra Leone for England, two French 40-gun frigates *Aréthuse* and *Rubis*, arrived on the coast, each stronger than the *Amelia*. Irby engaged and disabled the *Aréthuse* and, the *Amelia* being almost equally damaged, withdrew from the area. The *Amelia* was paid off in May 1813, and Irby had no further service. He settled in Norfolk, at Boyland Hall, near Norwich. He was made a CB in 1831, and a rear-admiral in 1837. He married on 1 December 1803 Emily Ives (d. 7 Aug 1806), youngest daughter of William Drake of Amersham; they had a son. On 23 January 1816 Irby married Frances (d. 16 Jan 1852), second daughter of Ichabod Wright of Mapperley Hall, Nottinghamshire; they had three sons, including the ornithologist Leonard Howard Loyd *Irby, and three daughters, including Paulina *Irby. Frederick Irby died on 24 April 1844.

J. K. LAUGHTON, *rev.* ANDREW LAMBERT

Sources D. Syrett and R. L. DiNardo, *The commissioned sea officers of the Royal Navy, 1660–1815*, rev. edn, Occasional Publications of the Navy RS, 1 (1994) · J. Marshall, *Royal naval biography*, 2/1 (1824) · W. James, *The naval history of Great Britain, from the declaration of war by France in 1793, to the accession of George IV*, [5th edn], 6 vols. (1859–60), vol. 6 · Burke, *Peerage* (1959)

Irby, Leonard Howard Loyd (1836–1905), army officer and ornithologist, born at Boyland Hall, Morningthorpe, Norfolk, on 13 April 1836, was the son of Rear-Admiral the Hon. Frederick Paul *Irby (1779–1844) and his second wife, Frances (d. 1852), daughter of Ichabod Wright of Mapperley Hall, Nottinghamshire. Irby's father was the second son of Frederick Irby, second Baron Boston.

After education at Rugby School and the Royal Military College, Sandhurst, Irby was commissioned ensign in the 90th (Perthshire) light infantry on 5 May 1854, and was promoted lieutenant on 8 December 1854. He served with his regiment in the Crimea from 5 December 1854 to 20 March 1855, and was present at the siege of Sevastopol.

Irby was promoted to be captain on 24 February 1857. Soon afterwards he was wrecked in the ship *Transit* with Captain Garnet Wolseley and his regiment in the Strait of Bangka, on his way to China. The arrival of the news of the Indian mutiny caused the regiment to be sent to Calcutta.

Irby served in India from 12 August 1857 until the end of the rebellion. He was engaged in the defence of Brigadier-General Sir Henry Havelock's baggage at the Alambagh, advanced to the relief of Lucknow with Lord Clyde, and after the relief and withdrawal of the garrison of Lucknow remained with Sir James Outram to defend the Alambagh until the final advance of Lord Clyde to the siege and capture of Lucknow. Irby was awarded a year's extra service. On 3 June 1864 he was promoted major. In October of that year Irby exchanged into the 74th highlanders, and was with the regiment at Gibraltar until 1872. He retired as a lieutenant-colonel on 1 April 1874.

On 31 August 1864 Irby married his first wife, Geraldine Alicia Mary, daughter of J. B. Magenis, rector of Great Horkesley. They had two sons. His wife died in 1882. On 22 January 1884 Irby married as his second wife Mary, daughter of Colonel John Brandling of Low Gosforth, Northumberland, and they had a daughter.

While stationed at Gibraltar, Irby devoted himself to ornithological study, and with his friend Thomas Littleton Powys, fourth Lord Lilford, pioneered investigation into Spanish ornithology. He published his *Ornithology of the Straits of Gibraltar* in 1875, and continued his ornithological studies after his retirement. He prepared a *Key List of British Birds* (1888) and contributed several papers to The *Ibis*. He denounced both the wanton destruction of bird life and the needless multiplication of species by scientists. In his later years he took up lepidopterology, and with the help of his sons formed a collection of European butterflies and British moths. He was a member of the council of the Zoological Society from 1892 to 1900, and assisted in the formation of the life groups in the British Museum (Natural History), where some of the most remarkable cases of British birds bear his name. Irby died on 14 May 1905 at his home, 14 Cornwall Terrace, Regent's Park, and was buried at Kensal Green.

H. M. VIBART, *rev.* ALEX MAY

Sources Army List · Hart's Army List · The Times (16 May 1905) · Nature, 72 (1905), 62 · The Ibis, 8th ser., 5 (1905) · Burke, Peerage · private information (1912) · Viscount Wolseley [G. Wolseley], The story of a soldier's life, 2 vols. (1903) · A. M. Delavoye, Records of the 90th regiment, 1795–1880 (1880) · J. H. Lehmann, All Sir Garnet: a biography of Field-Marshal Lord Wolseley (1964)
Wealth at death £49,823 14s. 4d.: probate, 13 July 1905, CGPLA Eng. & Wales

Irby, Nichola (d. 1395). *See under* Women in trade and industry in York (*act. c.*1300–*c.*1500).

Irby, (Adeline) Paulina (1831–1911), traveller and Balkan sympathizer, was the youngest daughter of Rear-Admiral

(Adeline) Paulina Irby (1831–1911), by unknown photographer

the Hon. Frederick Paul *Irby (1779–1844) of Long Stratton, Norfolk, and his second wife, Frances Wright (d. 1852), daughter of Ichabod Wright of Mapperley Hall, Nottinghamshire; she was the granddaughter of the second Baron Boston. Her long life, as traveller, relief worker, educationist, and Serbian patriot, was shaped by two events, one personal—she was arrested as a spy in 1859—the other of public concern—the 'Bulgarian atrocities' of 1876. In the first incident, she and her companion, Georgina Muir Mackenzie, while travelling in the Austrian Carpathians, were accused of showing 'pan-Slavistic tendencies'. Neither understood the term, knowing little of the Slav nationalities in Europe. In the next four years they remedied that ignorance through extensive journeys across Turkey in Europe, examining the conditions of the south Slavs, talking to Turkish authorities, and discussing the position and education of Christian women and girls. The evidence they obtained convinced them of Turkish misrule and made them advocates of Serbia and the south Slavs. They reported on their travels in some articles and speeches, and finally in 1867 in *The Turks, the Greeks and the Slavons: Travels in the Slavonic Provinces of Turkey-in-Europe*, a substantial and authoritative publication.

In 1865 Paulina Irby and Georgina Muir Mackenzie established an association to promote education among the Slavonic Christians, appealing for funds to set up a training school for Bosnian girls. The school was opened in Sarajevo, and in 1871 Paulina Irby, with a new companion, Priscilla Johnston (the granddaughter of the first Sir Thomas Fowell Buxton, the anti-slavery leader, of Northrepps, Norfolk), took over its management. The pattern of her life, nine months in Sarajevo followed by a summer of recuperation and fund-raising in England, was broken in 1875 by the uprising of the Christian population. She closed the school and set up a relief fund for Bosnian refugees fleeing into Austrian Slavonia, undertaking food distribution and the establishment of schools for refugee

children. By June 1876 seven schools were operating, and 3000 women and children had been fed, clothed, and vaccinated. She was in England in July 1876 when the 'Bulgarian atrocities' agitation swept the country: Turkish misrule and the condition of its subject Christian nationalities became the focus of public debate and practical action. Her relief fund was one among many that benefited from the generosity of the British public; she was recognized as an expert on Turkish matters, and relatives and influential friends, including Florence Nightingale, became active on behalf of the fund. References were made to her in parliament, and W. E. Gladstone wrote the introduction to the second edition of *Travels* (published in 1877).

During 1877 and 1878 in Dalmatia and Slavonia, Paulina Irby continued to administer relief, establishing twenty-one schools for 2000 pupils and distributing food, clothes, and pickaxes (for road building). Vivid descriptions of her work, written by Arthur Evans, appeared in the *Manchester Guardian*. Under the Berlin Congress of June 1878 Austria was given the mandate of Bosnia and Herzegovina, but the Austrian authorities were reluctant, because of her Serbian sympathies, to grant permission for her return to Sarajevo. Finally, in June 1879, the school was reopened. After Priscilla Johnston returned to England in 1885, Paulina Irby continued to maintain the school, which remained small, for Orthodox Christian girls only, an increasing number of whom were Slav and Serbian. Edith Durham, visiting in 1906, believed the school was the centre of the pro-Serb party. On 15 September 1911 Paulina Irby died, and her death was an occasion for public mourning in Belgrade as well as Sarajevo. As she had requested, her letters and papers were destroyed, but her work for the south Slav people became a legend. On the occasion of the centenary of her birth (postponed to 1934) there were celebrations throughout Yugoslavia in her honour. For some years there was an annual commemoration at her gravestone in Sarajevo of the day in June 1914 when the shot was fired that started the First World War.

DOROTHY ANDERSON

Sources D. Anderson, *Miss Irby and her friends* (1966) · D. Anderson, *The Balkan volunteers* (1968) · [G. M. M. Mackenzie and A. P. Irby], *Across the Carpathians* (1862) · G. M. Mackenzie and A. P. Irby, *The Turks, the Greeks, and the Slavons: travels in the Slavonic provinces of Turkey-in-Europe* (1867); 2nd edn as *Travels in the Slavonic provinces of Turkey-in-Europe* (1877) · *The Times* (18 Sept 1911)
Archives BL, Nightingale MSS
Likenesses photograph, repro. in Anderson, *Miss Irby* [see illus.] · portrait, Old Orthodox Church Museum, Sarajevo
Wealth at death £4453 14s. 5d.: resworn probate, 20 June 1912, *CGPLA Eng. & Wales*

Iredell, Francis (d. 1739), minister of the Presbyterian General Synod of Ulster and author, was born in co. Antrim, Ireland, and educated at a philosophical and theological school run in Antrim by the Revd Thomas Gowan. He was licensed by the Antrim meeting on 4 March 1684 and ordained in Donegore on 19 June 1688. That he was held in high esteem by his colleagues is indicated by the fact that in 1689 he was appointed as one of two ministers to present the address of the northern Presbyterians to the duke of Schomberg when he came to Ireland with the army of King William. He was clerk of the General Synod of Ulster from 1692 to 1696. In 1696 he resisted the command of synod to become minister of Armagh, and was rebuked for so doing.

In 1699 the synod compelled Iredell to become minister of the Capel Street congregation in Dublin, and there he remained until his death in 1739. On 22 April 1701 he preached before the societies for the Reformation of Manners in Dublin, taking as his theme national righteousness. This sermon was the first of his works to be published. It was followed in 1705 by a funeral sermon for his talented young colleague the Revd John Milling. On 25 May 1716 he married Eleanor McCartney, daughter of Arthur McCartney of Dublin.

Iredell was appointed moderator of the Synod of Ulster in 1701. Throughout his time in Dublin he continued to represent the cause of Irish Presbyterians in high places. Thus in 1711 the synod entrusted him to lay before the English government its answer to charges against them by the Irish House of Lords. A copy of his private instructions has been preserved, outlining the people to be met, the discretionary powers with which he was entrusted, the arrangements for consultation with leading members of the Synod of Ulster, and instances and explanations that he might employ to advance his arguments or counter those of his opponents. In 1715 he and Colonel Clotworthy Upton met George I to convey the grievances of their colleagues, chiefly regarding the operation of the Test Act of 1704. Although sympathetically received, they failed to secure the promises of relief they sought, but they were successful in obtaining the prompt renewal of the *regium donum*. In 1728 the lords justices of Ireland were alarmed by the excessive emigration from Ulster and turned to Iredell and his colleague the Revd Robert Craghead (*d.* 1738) for advice about its cause.

Although fully involved with his Dublin colleagues, Iredell represented an essentially northern presence in a congregation that belonged to the Synod of Ulster. Like them he was orthodox in doctrine. In the subscription controversy of the 1720s, however, he differed from them in being a subscriber by conviction. In 1726 he published *Remarks upon some passages relating to the confession of faith in Rev Mr Samuel Haliday's letter to the Rev Mr Gilbert Kennedy*. This produced a printed reply from Haliday, and as a rejoinder Iredell published in 1727 *A letter to the Rev Mr. Samuel Haliday, wherein the remarks upon some passages in his letter to the Rev Mr Gilbert Kennedy are defended*. In his writings he argued cogently that the Westminster confession in its teaching regarding the person of Christ was at one with classical defences of orthodoxy. Against the charge of Haliday that the Westminster confession made a merely scholastic point the ground of ministerial communion, he argued that the confession faithfully expressed the teaching of the church in its historic creeds and councils that Christ possessed a divine nature from all eternity, but assumed a human nature, and that these two distinct natures were inseparably joined in one person, the word made flesh. Such statements were valuable and necessary

safeguards against doctrinal error, including most notably the Nestorian and Eutychean heresies. Iredell also contended that the imposition of subscription was a legitimate way for church courts to suppress error and preserve truth.

Iredell was a reluctant controversialist, and generous to his opponents. Yet he could not remain silent when he felt truth was at stake. Both in his preaching, which was simple and direct, and in his writing he gave ample evidence of clear thinking and careful scholarship. His increasing disenchantment with the northern non-subscribers and with those who sympathized with them in the south indicated his growing unease at the direction in which he perceived those opposed to subscription to be heading. He died in Dublin on 31 January 1739. He was survived by two sons, Francis, a merchant in Bristol, and Thomas, a barrister and president of the council of Jamaica, where he owned considerable estates. A. W. GODFREY BROWN

Sources T. Witherow, *Historical and literary memorials of presbyterianism in Ireland, 1623–1731* (1879) · J. McConnell and others, eds., *Fasti of the Irish Presbyterian church, 1613–1840*, rev. S. G. McConnell, 2 vols. in 12 pts (1935–51), pt 3 · A. W. G. Brown, 'Irish Presbyterian theology in the early eighteenth century', PhD diss., Queen's University, Belfast, 1977 · C. H. Irwin, *A history of presbyterianism in Dublin and the south and west of Ireland* (1890) · J. S. Reid and W. D. Killen, *History of the Presbyterian church in Ireland*, new edn, 3 vols. (1867) · J. S. Reid, *History of congregations of the Presbyterian church in Ireland*, ed. W. D. Killen (1886) · T. Steward, MS correspondence, University of Ulster, Coleraine · Presbyterian Historical Society of Ireland, Belfast, Tenison Groves MSS · J. Armstrong, 'An appendix, containing some account of the Presbyterian churches in Dublin', in J. Armstrong and others, *Ordination service … of the Rev. James Martineau* (1829)

Wealth at death details of Irish prerogative grant of administration and goods: 19 Sept 1739, Presbyterian Historical Society of Ireland, Belfast, Tenison Groves MSS

Iredell, James (1751–1799), lawyer and jurist in the United States of America, was born on 5 October 1751 at Lewes, Sussex, the eldest of five sons of Francis Iredell (*d.* 1772), a Bristol merchant, and Margaret, *née* McCulloh, who came from a prominent Anglo-Irish family with influential links to London officialdom. After Iredell's father suffered a severe stroke, James, then about fifteen, dropped out of school in Bristol to help support his family. In 1768, through his well-connected McCulloh relatives, he became comptroller of customs at Edenton, North Carolina. Henry Eustace McCulloh, the port collector, held the post as a sinecure, so that Iredell had the full responsibility for the customs office. Iredell succeeded McCulloh as collector in 1774 and continued in that position until June 1776, the eve of the American Declaration of Independence.

Since his customs responsibilities had not been arduous, and since he had been sending most of his income to his widowed mother, Iredell studied law in order to develop a second profession. He read legal treatises and observed courtroom activity under the tutelage of Samuel Johnston, Edenton's leading citizen and nephew of Gabriel Johnston, a former North Carolina governor. On 18 July 1773 Iredell married Johnston's sister Hannah (*c*.1747–1826), with whom he had three surviving children.

James Iredell (1751–1799), by Charles Balthazar Julien Févret de Saint-Mémin, 1798–9

Indeed, Iredell wrote to his relatives in England that his personal universe revolved round the Johnston family. Johnston himself was educated in Connecticut, perhaps at Yale College, and his several sisters were cultivated women, well read in contemporary British literature.

As a lawyer Iredell paid particular attention to the constitutional aspects of the arguments between Britain's North American colonies and the Westminster government. Although he was a great admirer of William Blackstone's *Commentaries on the Laws of England*, Iredell rejected the idea of an empire based on indivisible sovereignty. Thus to him the various attempts to tax the colonies, and the passage of the Coercive Acts of 1774, were against the British constitution. Iredell embraced the idea, unique for its time, that the relationship between the colonies and the metropolis was what would become known in the twentieth century as the commonwealth idea of empire. As Iredell phrased it, the individual colonies and the mother country were equal spokes in the wheel of empire. The only binding tie was through the crown. Although he tried to conceal his identity, it seems to have been well known that, though a British official, Iredell was writing political essays. All of those that were written before independence appear to have circulated in unpublished form, or else were printed in editions of North Carolina newspapers that no longer survive. They include 'To the inhabitants of Great Britain' (September 1774), 'Principles of an American whig' (1775–6?), and an untitled essay on the causes of the American War of Independence (June 1776).

Although Iredell supported independence in July 1776, the break was painful. Separated from his mother and brothers, he also was disinherited by a wealthy bachelor uncle in the West Indies. Actively backing the new North Carolina revolutionary government, he accepted a seat on the state superior court in 1777 and in 1779 became the state attorney-general. Even so, he criticized state leaders for North Carolina's failure to comply with all the terms of the treaty of peace ending the revolutionary war. He also advocated that all the states strengthen the authority of the continental congress under the articles of confederation, America's first constitution, adopted in 1781. Politically conservative, Iredell preferred leaders of training and talent from established families who came primarily from the coastal sections. He criticized backcountry political figures, whom he deemed upstarts and rabble-rousers.

Iredell's political outlook revealed a strong measure of intellectual consistency throughout his life. He criticized the North Carolina state legislature for arbitrary behaviour, just as before independence he had sought to find ways to keep the British parliament within its constitutional boundaries. An early proponent of judicial review, he helped convince the North Carolina superior court in the 1787 case of *Bayard* v. *Singleton* to void a law enacted by the state legislature. Just as he had advocated divisible sovereignty under the old British empire, he favoured a similar relationship between the American states and the weak American central government under the articles of confederation. Frustrated with efforts to strengthen congress under the confederation, he and his brother-in-law Governor Samuel Johnston led the fight to ratify the federal constitution of 1787 in North Carolina. In January 1788, under the pen-name Marcus, Iredell published his *Answers to Mr. Mason's Objections to the New Constitution*. He demonstrated, among other things, that the legitimate rights of the states would not be sacrificed to a firmer form of union.

In 1790 President Washington appointed Iredell an associate justice of the United States supreme court. Conscious of creating support throughout the new union, Washington had yet to select a North Carolinian for high office before Iredell, who also appealed because of his reputation as a jurist and legal scholar. Iredell spent nine years on the high court, a formative if unspectacular period in the history of that tribunal. Besides two annual terms of the supreme court, its members did circuit duty twice yearly in the lesser federal courts, arduous responsibilities since the circuits extended the length of the thirteen states. Iredell's opinions show him to have been a strong nationalist, at the same time aware that divisible sovereignty meant that the states were supreme in their own designated sphere. There is no doubt that Iredell saw judicial review as a legitimate function of the federal courts as well as of the state courts. Iredell was possessed of a tough and independent mind, and his judicial prose and power of analysis have drawn praise from the greatest members of the supreme court, from John Marshall to Felix Frankfurter.

A devoted family man, Iredell deplored his weeks and months away from his family as a lawyer and jurist. A slave owner who recognized the immorality of the peculiar institution, he freed several of his bondsmen and was a kindly master. A devout Episcopalian, Iredell was neither staid nor prudish, enjoying parties, dances, and an occasional earthy story. He died in Edenton on 20 October 1799, and was buried in the nearby Johnston family cemetery at the Hayes plantation. Given Iredell's relative youth (he was forty-eight) and his seniority on the supreme court, there is a strong likelihood that he would have been appointed its chief justice had he lived only another year or two. He left several unpublished legal treatises, which seem to be incomplete.   DON HIGGINBOTHAM

Sources The papers of James Iredell, ed. D. Higginbotham, 2 vols. (1976) · G. McRee, Life and correspondence of James Iredell, 2 vols. (1857–8) · M. Marcus, J. R. Perry, and others, eds., The documentary history of the supreme court of the United States, 1789–1800, [6 vols.] (1985–) · D. Higginbotham, 'James Iredell's efforts to preserve the first British empire', North Carolina Historical Review, 49 (1972), 127–45

Archives Duke U., papers · North Carolina Division of Archives and History, Raleigh, North Carolina, papers

Likenesses C. B. J. F. de Saint-Mémin, engraving, 1798–9, Corcoran Gallery of Art, Washington, DC [see illus.] · attrib. C. B. J. F. de Saint-Mémin, pencil and crayon drawing, repro. in Higginbotham, ed., Papers

Ireland. For this title name see Vere, Robert de, ninth earl of Oxford, marquess of Dublin, and duke of Ireland (1362–1392).

Ireland, Alexander (1810–1894), journalist, was born at Edinburgh on 9 May 1810, the son of Thomas Ireland, a merchant, and his wife, Mary, née Keddie. Ireland worked in his father's business, but his literary interests and studies introduced him to an intellectual circle, including William and Robert Chambers and Dr John Gairdner. In 1833 Ralph Waldo Emerson came to Edinburgh with a letter of introduction to Gairdner, but the doctor's extensive medical duties prevented him from acting as a guide to the city. Ireland was asked to take Emerson under his wing, and this was the foundation of a lasting friendship between the two men.

On 4 September 1839 Ireland married Eliza Mary, daughter of Frederick Blythe of Birmingham. She died in 1842, and in 1843 Ireland moved from Birmingham to Manchester as representative of a Huddersfield firm. In the same year Robert Chambers not only entrusted him with the secret of the authorship of The Vestiges of Creation, divulged to only three other persons, but employed him to avert suspicion while the book was going through the press. The sheets were sent by the London publisher, who was himself in complete ignorance, to Ireland at Manchester, and transmitted to Chambers. The secret was strictly kept until 1884, when, every other depository of it being dead, Ireland revealed it in a preface to the twelfth edition, thus dismissing a host of groundless conjectures.

In 1846 Ireland succeeded Edward Watkin as publisher and business manager of the Manchester Examiner, a paper founded the year before by Watkin, John Bright, and William McKerrow in opposition to the Guardian. The first editor was Thomas Ballantyne. Before long the Examiner absorbed the other local exponent of advanced radicalism, the Manchester Times, and as the Manchester Examiner and Times held the second place in the Manchester press for forty years.

From 1847 to 1848 Emerson visited England again, at the instigation of Ireland. All the arrangements for Emerson's lectures were made by him; in his guest's words Ireland 'approved himself the king of all friends and helpful agents; the most active, unweariable, imperturbable'.

In 1851 Ireland was a member of the committee that organized the Manchester Free Library, where many books from his own library afterwards came to be deposited. He became friends with Thomas Carlyle and Leigh Hunt, and prepared a most useful bibliography of Hunt's writings, united in the same volume with a similar list of William Hazlitt's, and printed in a limited impression in 1868. On 13 September 1865 Ireland had remarried. His second wife was Anne Elizabeth, the daughter of John Nicholson of Penrith, and she later became well known under her married name, Annie Ireland [see below], as a biographer. They had five children: Lucy (b. 1866/7), Alice (b. 1867/8), Edith (b. 1872/3), John Nicholson *Ireland (1879–1962), and (Walter) Alleyne Ireland (d. 1951).

In 1889 Ireland edited a selection from Hazlitt's works, prefaced by a memoir. On Emerson's death in 1882 he published a biography of him, incomplete, but of value because of his own recollections; it was enlarged and reissued within the year as Ralph Waldo Emerson: his Life, Genius, and Writings. In the same year Ireland published at Manchester Recollections of George Dawson and his Lectures in Manchester in 1846–7. His best-known publication, however, was The Book-Lover's Enchiridion (1882), a collection of passages in praise of books selected from a wide range of authors. It was published under the pseudonym of Philobiblos, and went through five editions.

Ireland himself possessed a fine library, rich in the works of early English authors. He especially admired Daniel and Burton, and possessed all the seventeenth-century editions of the latter's Anatomy of Melancholy. Unfortunately, this treasured collection had to be sold owing to the reverse of fortune which overtook him in his latter days. There was a general transfer of Liberal support from the Examiner to the Guardian on the latter journal's acceptance of Gladstone's home rule proposals in 1886, and the Examiner, now an unprofitable property, passed into other hands, and soon ceased publication. Ireland bore his misfortunes with great dignity and fortitude, and, although an octogenarian, remained active to the last as a writer in the press. He died on 7 December 1894 at 31 Mauldeth Road, Fallowfield, Manchester. A collection of Ireland's books was presented in 1895 to the Manchester Free Reference Library by Thomas Read Wilkinson, and a special catalogue was issued in 1898.

Anne Elizabeth [Annie] **Ireland** (1842–1893), writer and biographer, was born in Penrith, the daughter of John Nicholson, a distinguished biblical scholar, and his wife, Annie Elizabeth, née Waring. Her elder brother was Henry Alleyne *Nicholson (1844–1899), regius professor of natural history at Aberdeen. She became well known as the biographer of Jane Welsh Carlyle, published in 1891, and as the editor of her correspondence with Geraldine Jewsbury. Her recollections of J. A. Froude were also published posthumously in the Contemporary Review. She was a member of the Browning Society, and lectured on Browning and Jane Welsh Carlyle in Manchester and other large provincial towns. Annie Ireland died at 31 Mauldeth Road, Fallowfield, Manchester, on 4 October 1893.

The Irelands' sons went on to distinguished careers: John Ireland became a composer and a professor at the Royal College of Music in London, and Alleyne became an expert on comparative government, writing works including *Tropical Colonization* (1889), *The Province of Burma* (1907), *Democracy and the Human Equation* (1921), and *The New Korea* (1926).

RICHARD GARNETT, *rev.* M. CLARE LOUGHLIN-CHOW

Sources *Manchester Guardian* (8 Dec 1894) · I. Mills, *From tinder-box to the 'larger' light: threads from the life of John Mills: interwoven with some early century recollections by his wife* (1899) · bap. reg. Scot. · m. cert. [Eliza Mary Blythe] · m. cert. [Anne Elizabeth Nicholson] · census returns, 1881 · *IGI* · *CGPLA Eng. & Wales* (1893) · *CGPLA Eng. & Wales* (1895) · *Gallery of Celebrities*, new ser., 1/2 (1891)
Archives BL, letters to W. C. Hazlitt, Add. MSS 38899–38906 · Hunt. L., letters to James Thomas and Annie Fields · U. Mich., letters to Moncure Conway and Ellen Conway
Wealth at death £10,696 7s. 4d.: probate, 11 Jan 1895, *CGPLA Eng. & Wales* · £1070 0s. 7d.—Anne Elizabeth Ireland: probate, 1893

Ireland, Anne Elizabeth (1842–1893). *See under* Ireland, Alexander (1810–1894).

Ireland [Irland], **Bonaventure** (1551–1608?), jurist, was born in Poitiers, France, the son of Robert *Ireland (d. 1561) and Claire Aubert. His father, who was professor of law at Poitiers, died when he was ten, and his education thereafter was provided for by his mother's family. He studied philosophy in Paris, where one of his teachers, presumably in the mid-1560s, was Petrus Ramus. In law his teacher, or one of them, was Étienne Forcadel (*c*.1518–1578): this must have been in the late 1560s or early 1570s in Toulouse, where Forcadel spent all his teaching career. At all events Ireland had achieved by his early twenties sufficient erudition to impress the great scholar J. J. Scaliger, who addressed him in flattering terms in a letter of 1574. It seems to have been in 1575 that his uncle Bonaventure Aubert resigned in Ireland's favour his position as *conseiller au présidial* in Poitiers (one of the courts of first instance established in 1551). In that capacity, doubtless, Ireland drafted in December 1575 a *Remontrance au roi Henri III au nom du pays de Poitou*, protesting against new taxes. By 1579, if not earlier, he was also professor of law in Poitiers, one of a notable group of expatriate Scots or Franco-Scots, which also included Thomas Bicarton and Adam Blackwood. Blackwood and Ireland are celebrated in verses by Scévole de Sainte-Marthe (reproduced by Dempster in his *Historia ecclesiastica*) as 'rara lumina' aiding France amid the afflictions of civil war. At an unknown date, probably in the 1580s, Ireland married Marie de Sanzay; their descendants were important members of the Poitevin *noblesse de la robe* until the revolution.

Ireland's only substantial work, published at Poitiers in 1598, is *De emphasi et hypostasi ad recte judicandi rationem consideratio*. (This, like an unpublished life of his father, Ireland dedicated to Philippe Hurault de Cheverny, chancellor of France, who had been Robert Ireland's pupil.) By 'emphasis' and 'hypostasis' Ireland meant something like 'appearance' and 'reality', though it would be confusing to use that Bradleyan terminology in translating his title. His concern was to distinguish clearly between the substantive truth of things and the false appearances put upon them to seduce and mislead the imagination. 'Right judgement' is possible only if that distinction is carefully observed. Ireland applies this not only to his own field of law, but far more broadly. The authors he refers to reflect both his professional and his wider interests. Thus besides contemporary and medieval jurists (from Gratian to Bodin) there are references to Gerson and to Pico della Mirandola. Rabelais is mentioned in terms suggesting that Robert Ireland's appearance in *Pantagruel* had provoked filial resentment: 'Confugite ad Rabelasium!' Ireland exclaims impatiently and scornfully (Ireland, fol. 36r). The names of Erasmus, Luther, Calvin, and Hotman, again, show that much of the book (which runs to 176 pages) is devoted to the religious issues of its day. Defending the Catholic position, Ireland deplores the defection to Calvinism of his Parisian teacher Ramus, criticizing the doctrine of the latter's posthumous *De religione Christiana* (1576). Ireland was particularly concerned to defend transubstantiation and to vindicate the use of the term 'missa' ('mass') for the eucharist against the charge of linguistic 'barbarity'.

Hardly anything has been established of Ireland's life after 1598. His only other known work, a Latin oration addressed to Henri IV on the birth of the dauphin, is said to have been published at Poitiers in 1605—somewhat tardily, since that event took place in May 1601. The date of his death is also problematic. He is sometimes said to have died about 1612; but Thibaudeau in his *Histoire du Poitou* states that Ireland died in 1608 and was buried in the church of St Cybard in Poitiers.   J. H. BURNS

Sources E. G., 'Ireland (Bonaventure)', *Biographie universelle, ancienne et moderne*, ed. L. G. Michaud and E. E. Desplaces, new edn, 25 (Paris, 1858), 252 · J. F. Dreux du Radier, *Bibliothèque historique et critique du Poitou*, 2 vols. (1842–9), 2.145–51 · C. Babinet, 'Le présidial de Poitiers: son personnel de 1551 à 1790', *Mémoires de la Société des Antiquaires de l'Ouest*, 2nd ser., 25 (1902), 151–341 · B. Ireland, *De emphasi et hypostasi ad recte judicandi rationem consideratio* (Poitiers, 1598) · A. R. H. Thibaudeau, *Histoire du Poitou*, 3 vols. (1839–40) · *Thomae Dempsteri Historia ecclesiastica gentis Scotorum, sive, De scriptoribus Scotis*, ed. D. Irving, rev. edn, 2 vols., Bannatyne Club, 21 (1829)

Ireland, Francis. *See* Hutcheson, Francis (1721–1780).

Ireland [Irland], **John** (*c*.1440–1495), theologian, was perhaps born in St Andrews, possibly son of a John Ireland who held property in Market Street in the mid-fifteenth century. It was probably in St Andrews that Ireland—still, he says, 'a very young man' (Esposito, 71)—met Thomas Livingston, who had been the leading Scots participant in the Council of Basel. Ireland was a determinant in the arts faculty of the University of St Andrews in 1455–6 (suggesting his approximate date of birth), but did not proceed to the MA degree he should have taken in 1458–9. The reason for this was a dispute over placing in the list of candidates for the licence, in the course of which he and two other bachelors of arts were accused of having 'raised a clamour in the public street' (Dunlop, 127–8). They were denounced for 'contumacy' in November 1458 and in April 1459 barred from the faculty until they made due submission for their 'contempt'. Alone of the three Ireland refused to submit. He went from St Andrews to Paris, where he entered the university as a bachelor of arts in 1459 and graduated MA in 1460, and spent the following fifteen years teaching in arts and studying theology; as a student in the latter faculty he was admitted to the Collège de Navarre in 1466. At Paris, Ireland held the usual sequence of arts faculty offices and was rector of the university twice, in 1469 (when he also became a bachelor in theology) and in 1476. He received his licence in theology on 5 February 1476, incepting as master (second in a list of nineteen) on 27 June.

Ireland began his teaching career in theology at a controversial time in Parisian academic life. Two years previously a royal decree had banned the use of certain key texts in the nominalist or *via moderna* tradition which looked back especially to William Ockham (*d.* 1349). In the preceding debates on the issue Ireland had taken the nominalist side, and in his writings during his years as an arts teacher (treatises, now lost, on logic and on Aristotle's *Physics*) he had by his own account 'followed' Ockham and the Ockhamist school. Ireland (who seems to have been a fairly combative academic politician) had earlier crossed swords on another issue with a leading figure in the now victorious *via antiqua* camp, the Dutchman Jacobus Houck, prior of the Sorbonne in 1474–6. Some degree of unease in his professional situation may thus have helped to take Ireland's career in a different direction at this stage.

On two occasions during his years in Paris, Ireland had procured letters of recommendation to James III of Scotland. It was, however, the king of France who was responsible for initiating a career in public service which interrupted and eventually ended his strictly academic activity. Possibly in 1479, certainly in 1480, Louis XI sent Ireland to Scotland, charged with seeking a reconciliation between James III and his brother Alexander, duke of Albany, and with inducing the king of Scots to reverse the 'diplomatic revolution' which had latterly brought about an Anglo-Scottish rapprochement. The second at least of these goals was achieved, and at the same time Ireland evidently commended himself to James III, whom he was later to serve in various capacities during the last years of the reign. Already in July 1480, during his diplomatic mission, Ireland sat as one of the lords of council to hear civil causes; but by the following winter he was back in Paris and had resumed his academic work at a time when, after seven years, the royal ban on nominalist texts was about to be lifted.

The next three years or so seem to have been for Ireland a period of intense intellectual activity, probably yielding his two surviving Latin works and major items that are no longer extant. His *Tractatus de immaculata conceptione virginis Mariae* (TCD, MS 965) was dedicated to Louis XI, having been written (Ireland says) 'last winter, after I had completed an embassy on your behalf' (Esposito, 69). A copy

was also sent to James III. Ireland's most substantial work, a commentary on the four books of Peter Lombard's *Sentences*, seemingly dates from the early 1480s: only books 3 and 4 have survived (University of Aberdeen, MS 264). Of other lost works mentioned in Ireland's extant writings, the most important was the treatise *De speciali auxilio*, in five books, 'made' (Ireland says) 'at the request of James III' (University of Aberdeen, MS 264, fol. 64). He also wrote, probably during this same fertile period, Latin treatises on the eucharist and on the passion. In 1483, however, his career again turned—this time for good—to the field of public service.

In this connection the political situation in Scotland calls for consideration. James III had experienced a 'time of troubles' in 1482, at the height, or depth, of which several of his familiars were hanged at Lauder Bridge. At one brief but critical moment there had even been a move to depose the king and set up his brother Albany as Alexander IV. The crisis passed; but afterwards James was evidently anxious to strengthen his government by recruiting new advisers. This is the likely context for the fact that Ireland had, by the autumn of 1483, been persuaded to go back permanently to Scotland. His position was to be at court, not in the academic world he had known virtually since boyhood. He returned to the judicial bench on which he had sat briefly in 1480. He sat in parliament and was sent on further diplomatic missions. In short, he fulfilled the varied tasks falling under the heading of counsel, so central to the functioning of medieval kingship. In all this Ireland had to be funded by preferment in the church. The intricacies this involved cannot be explored here. It suffices to say that, though he was not to enjoy permanently the archdeaconry of St Andrews he had evidently been promised, he acquired, thanks to royal patronage, an adequate number of benefices, including the subchantory of Moray and later a canonry of Glasgow. His passage was not uniformly smooth: in particular he was evidently *persona non grata* with William Scheves, archbishop of St Andrews, who had been a senior contemporary of Ireland at the university there.

The courtier–cleric, however, was still a cleric. Both James III and his son James IV emphasized in their references to Ireland his services as preacher and confessor. (In the latter role he may have heard James III's last confession before his death at Sauchieburn in 1488.) And his work as a theologian was to bear, perhaps, its most important fruit in the vernacular works he wrote after his return to Scotland (including a Scots version, now lost, of his work on Christ's passion). The short treatise *Of Penance and Confession* (*The Asloan Manuscript*, ed. W. A. Craigie, 2 vols., STS, new ser., 14, 16, 1923–5, 1.1–80), written in Edinburgh Castle, probably in Lent 1484, is noteworthy for its author's approval, subject to the authority of the church, of having the Bible in the vernacular. Much more substantial—and indeed one of the major works in Middle Scots prose—is *The Meroure of Wyssdome*, written originally for James III and dedicated, on its completion in 1490, to James IV. This 'ABC of Christianity', in seven books, ends with a 'mirror of princes' which, though largely deriva- tive (drawing particularly on Jean Gerson, but also on Chaucer), is important for the history of Scottish political ideas. The bulk of the text, however, is a popularized com- pendium of scholastic theology, reflecting (like Ireland's *Sentences* commentary) its author's special interest in the problems of predestination, divine foreknowledge, and human free will. Ireland is firmly opposed to any kind of Pelagian or semi-Pelagian view of the role of human will and endeavour in the work of salvation, adopting a reso- lutely Augustinian position somewhat reminiscent of the fourteenth-century theologian Gregorio da Rimini. More generally, his theology has room both for the *via moderna* thinkers he calls 'the new doctors' and for 'the old doc- tors' whom he also respects—notably Duns Scotus (*d.* 1308), whom he cites more frequently than any other post- patristic author. In ecclesiology Ireland's position is one of moderate conciliarism, where papal prerogatives are rec- ognized, but the pope's authority is ultimately subordin- ate to that of a council representing the universal church. There is an absence of radicalism in this, matching in its way Ireland's attempt in his account of temporal govern- ment to combine the advantages of hereditary and elect- ive monarchy.

Despite the presentation of his *Meroure of Wyssdome* to the young James IV, Ireland seems to have been less prom- inent and perhaps less in favour in the new reign. There is at all events no evidence of his having been active at court during the last five years or so of his life. He died some time between April and August 1495. The preamble (all that survives) of his will is the last trace we have of 'John Ireland, servant of Christ Jesus' (Ireland, *Meroure of Wyssdome*, 1.xxxii).   J. H. BURNS

Sources J. H. Burns, 'John Ireland: theology and public affairs in the late fifteenth century', *Innes Review*, 41 (1990), 151–81 · J. de Irlandia [J. Ireland], *The meroure of wyssdome*, ed. C. Macpherson, F. Quinn, and C. Macdonald, 3 vols., STS, new ser., 19; 4th ser., 2, 19 (1926–90) · A. I. Dunlop, ed., *Acta facultatis artium universitatis Sanctiandree, 1413–1588*, 2 vols., Scottish History Society, 3rd ser., 54–5 (1964) · H. Denifle, A. Chatelain, and others, eds., *Auctarium chartularii universitatis Parisiensis*, 2–3 (Paris, 1897–1935); 6 (Paris, 1964) · H. Boece, *Scotorum historiae a prima gentis origine*, ed. G. Fer- rerio, 2nd edn (Paris, 1574), appx, fols. 391–4 · [T. Thomson], ed., *The acts of the lords of council in civil causes, 1478–1495*, 1, RC, 41 (1839) · *APS*, 1424–1567 · D. E. R. Watt, ed., *Fasti ecclesiae Scoticanae medii aevi ad annum 1638*, [2nd edn], Scottish RS, new ser., 1 (1969) · N. Mac- dougall, *James III: a political study* (1982), 194–6, 314–15 · M. Esposito, 'An unpublished work by John Ireland', *EngHR*, 34 (1919), 68–71 · U. Aberdeen, MS 264, fol. 64

Archives TCD, MS 965, press mark 1.5.21 · U. Aberdeen, MS 264

Ireland, John (*c.*1742–1808), biographer, was born near Wem, Shropshire, at the Trench Farm, the birthplace of dramatist William Wycherley. He was the son of Thomas Ireland, farmer, and his wife, Sarah, daughter of the Revd Thomas Holland and great-granddaughter of noncon- formist minister Philip Henry; his parents were married on 17 April 1742 at St Alkmund's Church, Shrewsbury, Shropshire. Intended for the ministry, John Ireland dis- played in his youth both a talent for mechanics and an interest in art and literature. Wycherley's widow, Mrs

Elizabeth Shrimpton, who had inherited the Trench Farm on Wycherley's death, took the young Ireland to London, intending to provide for him, but died intestate soon after. He was then apprenticed to the Shrewsbury watchmaker Isaac Wood, and by 1769 had set up as a watchmaker in Maiden Lane, Covent Garden, London. Later he 'subsisted by trafficking in pictures, prints, &c. for which he had a correct taste' (Chalmers, 19.241). By 1772 he had married a woman of similar temperament and interests.

The convivial Ireland frequented the Three Feathers cof- fee house and was a member of the Shandean Society, 'an evening society, consisting of about twelve or fourteen members', whose meetings united 'the festivity of Anac- reon, the humour of Prior, the harmony of Pope; and, above all, the sensibility and pleasantry of Sterne' (Ire- land, 26). Among his intimate friends were the artists Thomas Gainsborough and John Hamilton Mortimer and the actor John Henderson, to the last of whom Ireland offered much support during Henderson's early career. Ireland's 'thin, fasting, formal face' (ibid., 296) was painted by Mortimer.

While claiming that his life of Henderson (1786) was 'the first book I ever ventured before the awful tribunal of the public' (Ireland, xii), Ireland had published a poem 'The Emigrant' (1785). He also wrote for the newspapers, though his work brought him little monetary reward and 'chiefly consisted of anecdotes of the stage, of pictures and artists, with such other matters as he gleaned from an extensive range of acquaintance' (Beloe, 203). He wrote a life of his friend William Julius Mickle for Mickle's *Poems, and a Tragedy* (1794).

Ireland admitted

> a habit I have of preserving any thing, however trifling, which is the production of a friend. On my once shewing a number of little sketches by the late Mr. Mortimer, a gentleman asked me, if I had hoarded up the cuttings of his pencils. (Ireland, vii)

His tendency to collect and preserve led Ireland to publish the first scholarly studies of William Hogarth whom he had long admired. From Mrs Mary Lewis of Chelsea, executrix of Mrs Jane Hogarth's will, Ireland purchased prints, plates, and manuscripts of Hogarth, publishing *Hogarth Illustrated* (2 vols., 1791; 2nd edn, corrected, 1793; presentation copy with additional material in the Hun- tington Library) and, subsequently, a biography—the standard for many years—based on Hogarth's manu- scripts and autobiographical notes, entitled *A Supplement to Hogarth Illustrated* (1798; 2nd edn 1804). In his proposal for the supplement (dated 7 July 1796), Ireland made clear there was no connection between himself and Samuel Ire- land, author of *Graphic Illustrations of Hogarth*.

A tall, thin, kindly man, 'full of literary anecdote, which he liberally dispensed' (Chalmers, 19.242), Ireland had the misfortune to outlive his closest friends. The loss of Morti- mer left 'a chasm in one's life and happiness, which is very, very, rarely filled up' (Ireland, 55). In later life, 'afflicted with a complication of disorders, which had ren- dered society irksome to him' (Chalmers, 19.242), and with 'his sufferings ... aggravated by pecuniary difficulties' (Mogg, 160), Ireland moved to the vicinity of Birmingham, where he died in November 1808. His books, twelve original pictures by Hogarth, as well as other prints and drawings, were sold by auction by Messrs King and Lochee, Covent Garden, on 5 March 1810.   PAGE LIFE

Sources J. Ireland, *Letters and poems, by the late Mr John Henderson, with anecdotes of his life* (1786) · *Public characters*, 10 vols. (1799–1809) · A. Chalmers, ed., *The general biographical dictionary*, new edn, 32 vols. (1812–17) · J. B. Blakeway and W. G. D. Fletcher, 'History of Shrewsbury hundred or liberties [pt 3]', *Transactions of the Shropshire Archaeological and Natural History Society*, 2nd ser., 2 (1890), 319–58 · *GM*, 1st ser., 78 (1808), 1189 · G. H. F. Vane, ed., *Diocese of Lichfield: Wem registers*, 9, Shropshire Parish Registers (1908) · J. T. Smith, *A book for a rainy day, or, Recollections of the events of the years 1766–1833*, ed. W. Whitten (1905) · E. Mogg, *Paterson's roads*, 18th edn (1826) · W. T. Whitley, *Thomas Gainsborough* (1915) · W. Connely, *Brawny Wycherley* (1930) · A. Dobson, *William Hogarth* (1907) · A. H. Cash, *Laurence Sterne: the later years* (1986) · *DNB* · W. Beloe, *The sexagenarian, or, The recollections of a literary life*, ed. [T. Rennell], 2nd edn, 2 vols. (1818)

Archives BL, descriptions of Hogarth's prints, Add. MS 27994, fol. 25 | BL, Hogarth MSS formerly owned by Ireland, Egerton MSS 3011–3016 · BL, corresp. with Mary Lewis, Add. MS 27995, fols. 27–8

Likenesses J. H. Mortimer, group portrait, oils, *c.*1760–1770, Yale U. CBA, Paul Mellon collection; repro. in *John Hamilton Mortimer, ARA, 1740–1779* (1968) [exhibition catalogue, Tower Art Gallery, Eastbourne, 6 July–3 Sept 1968 and Iveagh Bequest, Kenwood, 10 Sept–8 Oct 1968] · J. H. Mortimer, oils, 1763?–1767, Yale U. CBA, Paul Mellon collection; repro. in *John Hamilton Mortimer, ARA, 1740–1779* (1968) [exhibition catalogue] · W. Skelton, line engraving, before 1779 (after J. H. Mortimer), BM, NPG; repro. in J. Ireland, *Hogarth illustrated*, 3 vols. (1791–8) · T. Tagg, line engraving, 1806? (after W. Skelton; after J. H. Mortimer), repro. in J. Ireland, *Hogarth illustrated*, 2nd edn, 3 vols. (1804–6), frontispiece · I. Mills, line engraving, pubd 1834 (after drawing by J. R. Smith), BM, NPG · R. Westall, watercolour over pencil drawing, BM · drawing, BM

Wealth at death see Mogg, *Paterson's roads*, 160

Ireland, John (1761–1842), dean of Westminster, was born at Ashburton, Devon, on 8 September 1761, the son of Thomas Ireland, a butcher of that town, and his wife, Elizabeth. He was educated first at the free grammar school of Ashburton, under the Revd Thomas Smerdon. He matriculated as Bible clerk from Oriel College, Oxford, on 8 December 1779 and graduated BA on 30 June 1783. He did not take his MA until June 1810 and proceeded to the degrees of BD and DD the following October.

After serving a curacy near Ashburton for a short time Ireland travelled on the continent as tutor to the son of Sir James Wright. From 15 July 1793 until 1816 he was vicar of Croydon in Surrey. Sermons preached during the early years of his ministry there were published as *Five Discourses ... for and against the Reception of Christianity by the Antient Jews and Greeks* (1796). While at Croydon he also acted as chaplain to the first earl of Liverpool, who procured his appointment to a prebendal stall at Westminster Abbey. He was installed on 14 August 1802 and his connection with the abbey lasted for life.

Ireland became subdean in 1806 and the theological lectureship established at Westminster by the statutes of Elizabeth I was revived for him at the same time. Between 1806 and 1808 he gave a series of lectures to the king's

John Ireland (1761–1842), by James Stow, pubd 1823 (after George Perfect Harding)

scholars of Westminster School, which were subsequently published as *Paganism and Christianity Compared* (1809; new edn 1825). He continued the lectures, now entitled 'The history and principles of revelation', until the summer of 1812 but never published them. In March 1813 he preached before the House of Commons at St Margaret's, Westminster, and in the same year he declined the offer of the regius professorship of divinity at Oxford.

On the death of William Vincent in December 1815 Ireland was promoted to the deanery of Westminster, where he was installed on 9 February the following year. He was also dean of the Order of the Bath and, from 1816 to 1835, rector of Islip in Oxfordshire (a Westminster living). Not long after his appointment as dean, Ireland was accused of malversation as a trustee of Archbishop Whitgift's hospital in Croydon. He staunchly refuted the allegation in *A Letter to Henry Brougham, Esq. MP* (1818).

As a result of his preferments Ireland acquired considerable wealth, which he used with great generosity. In 1825 he gave £4000 for the foundation at Oxford University of four scholarships 'for the promotion of classical learning and taste'. Mindful of the advantages that he had derived from his early education he spent £2000 in acquiring a house at Ashburton as a residence for the master of its grammar school, left an endowment for its repair, and drew up statutes for remodelling the school. For the support of six old persons of the town he settled a fund of £30 per annum. To Westminster School he gave £500 to establish prizes for poems in Latin hexameters.

As dean of Westminster, Ireland held the crown at the coronations of George IV and William IV; he was too infirm to attend the coronation of Queen Victoria and the subdean, Lord John Thynne, took his place. It has been said of Ireland that he was 'essentially an eighteenth-century clergyman who lived long enough to feel the winds of change blowing around him' (Carpenter, 214). His occupancy of the deanery was uneventful but coincided with a period when the fortunes of Westminster School were beginning to decline and when decisive action by the dean to increase the proportion of chapter revenues allocated to it would have done much to revive the school's fortunes. Ireland has been justly criticized for this negligence, although the task of persuading his capitular colleagues to accept the consequent reduction in their own incomes would doubtless have been a considerable one.

Ireland indeed had little appetite for reform, and a conservative spirit emerges from his writings on the political and religious issues of the day, the earliest of which, *Vindicae regiae, or, A Defence of the Kingly Office*, was published in 1797. In 1801 appeared *Letters of Fabius*, in which he set out his opposition to the proposed removal of the Test Act for Irish Roman Catholics, and in 1807 he published *The Claims of the Establishment*, a sermon in which he considered what degree of tolerance and civil rights was due to those who dissented from the established doctrines of the church. His most influential work, however, was *Nuptiae sacrae, or, An Enquiry into the Scriptural Doctrine of Marriage and Divorce* (1801), which appeared anonymously as a contribution to the debate on Lord Auckland's bill to prevent the intermarriage of the offending parties when a marriage was dissolved on grounds of adultery. In 1821 the pamphlet was plagiarized by a proctor in Doctors' Commons for an *Essay on the Scriptural Doctrine of Adultery and Divorce*. Ireland exposed the fraud in the *Quarterly Review* in 1823, and a new edition of the original pamphlet appeared under his own name in 1830. His last works were two lectures on the plagues of Athens and Marseilles, read to the Royal College of Physicians by Sir Henry Halford and published in 1832 and 1834 respectively.

Ireland enjoyed a close and lifelong friendship with William Gifford, first editor of the *Quarterly Review*, whom he had known since they were schoolboys together in Ashburton. He gave valuable assistance to Gifford in editing the works of Massinger, and Gifford cordially acknowledged his help in his translation of Juvenal, every part of which had been submitted for Ireland's inspection. In the 'Maeviad' (ll.303 ff.) are some touching allusions by Gifford to their long friendship, and among the odes is an 'Imitation of Horace' addressed to Ireland. At the close of the 'Memoir of Ben Jonson' (*Works of Ben Jonson*, 1.ccxlvii) Gifford describes his friend as 'my delight in youth, my pride and consolation in age', and in announcing to Canning his retirement from editing the *Quarterly Review* in September 1824 he mentions that Ireland had stood closely by him during the whole period of its existence and urges (in vain, as it transpired) that the dean be considered for promotion to the episcopate. Ireland is said to have contributed many articles to the early numbers of the review but none has been identified. He was executor

of Gifford's will and arranged for his burial in Westminster Abbey.

Ireland married Susannah (1754/5–1826), only daughter of John Short of Bickham, Devon. They had no children and Susannah died at Islip rectory on 9 November 1826, aged seventy-one.

For four years before his death Ireland was in feeble health but he lived to a great age and died at the deanery, Westminster, on 2 September 1842, in his eighty-first year. He was buried on 8 September by the side of Gifford, in the south transept of the abbey; a marble bust by John Ternouth was erected nearby. In accordance with Ireland's wishes his manuscripts were destroyed after his death.

In his will Ireland made provision for further charitable bequests from his substantial estate, notably £10,000 to the University of Oxford to establish the professorship of the exegesis of holy scripture that bears his name, £5000 for the erection of a new church in Westminster (a bequest subsequently invalidated under the Mortmain Acts), and £2000 to Oriel College for exhibitions.

TONY TROWLES

Sources E. Hawkins, *An inaugural lecture upon the foundation of Dean Ireland's professorship … with brief notices of the founder* (1848) · C. Worthy, *Ashburton and its neighbourhood* (1875) · J. L. Chester, ed., *The marriage, baptismal, and burial registers of the collegiate church or abbey of St Peter, Westminster*, Harleian Society, 10 (1876) · E. Carpenter, ed., *A house of kings: the history of Westminster Abbey*, rev. edn (1972) · J. Sargeaunt, *Annals of Westminster School* (1898) · *Some official correspondence of George Canning*, ed. E. J. Stapleton, 2 vols. (1887) · *GM*, 2nd ser., 18 (1842), 549–50 · Foster, *Alum. Oxon.* · *The plays of Philip Massinger*, ed. W. Gifford, 4 vols. (1805) · *Memoir of William Gifford written by himself* (1827) · *The works of Ben Jonson*, ed. W. Gifford, 9 vols. (1816) · *DNB* · will, PRO, PROB 11/1969/684
Archives BL, corresp. with earl of Liverpool, Add. MSS 35230–35311, 38424, 38473, *passim*
Likenesses W. Bond and S. Reynolds, engraving, hand-coloured copy, *c*.1821 (after E. Stephanoff), Westminster Abbey Library · F. Chantrey, bust, Bodl. Oxf. · F. Chantrey, pencil sketch, NPG; repro. in G. Nayler, *The coronation of George the Fourth* (1824) · S. Reynolds and W. Bond, mezzotint (after F. Stephanoff), BM · J. Stow, engraving (after drawing by G. P. Harding), NPG; repro. in E. W. Brayley, *History and antiquities of the abbey church of St Peter, Westminster*, 2 (1823) [*see illus.*] · J. Ternouth, bust, Westminster Abbey
Wealth at death over £20,000: will, PRO, PROB 11/1969/684

Ireland, John Nicholson (1879–1962), composer and organist, was born on 13 August 1879 at Inglewood, St Margaret's Road, Dunham Massey, in the sub-district of Altrincham, Cheshire, the youngest of five children of Alexander *Ireland (1810–1894), writer and publisher, and his second wife, Anne Elizabeth (Annie) *Ireland, *née* Nicholson (1842–1893) [*see under* Ireland, Alexander], author and critic. His father was of Scottish descent, his mother from Cumberland. Within the household there was a strong emphasis on literature, and John developed a love and understanding of poetry that remained with him for the rest of his life. His patchy and rather unhappy early schooling included periods at the local dame-school in Bowdon and at Dinglewood preparatory school, Colwyn Bay, and just two terms at Leeds grammar school in the first part of 1893. In September 1893, a week before his mother died, Ireland enrolled at the Royal College of Music. The death of his father the following year left him

John Nicholson Ireland (1879–1962), by Herbert Lambert, c.1920

in the charge of a guardian, and it was therefore the college that provided Ireland with an extended period of security. While there he studied the piano with Frederick Cliffe and the organ with Sir Walter Parratt. From these earliest years at the college, little survives save for a few short piano works. In 1897 Ireland produced two string quartets, and in the same year he became a pupil of Sir Charles Villiers Stanford, whose demanding, disciplined teaching methods and breadth of knowledge made a considerable impression.

Early career The two string quartets were followed in 1898 by a sextet for clarinet, horn, and string quartet and by a large-scale choral work, *Vexilla regis*, written during the period of Ireland's first important post as an organist, at Holy Trinity Church, Sloane Street, Chelsea. After leaving the Royal College of Music in 1901, Ireland experimented with a range of musical genres and media. In 1904 he took up a new appointment as organist and choir trainer at St Luke's, Sydney Street, Chelsea. This was a significant post, both professionally and personally. It occasioned the composition of the bulk of his music for the Anglican church which, while not extensive, includes a number of pieces for organ, services and canticle settings, hymn tunes, carols, and anthems.

In 1906 Ireland completed a lyrical and skilfully organized *Phantasie* for piano trio, which was followed in 1908–9 by his first violin sonata. In 1912 he wrote a 'meditation' for passiontide, 'Greater love hath no man', a blend of the

sweetly transcendent and affirmative melodic motifs that constitute his church music. By 1913 it was clear that an assured and individual voice was emerging, influenced in part by the semi-autobiographical writings of Arthur Machen. In this year there were works for voice and piano, among them the song cycle *Marigold* and 'Sea Fever'. There were also some piano pieces, notably *Decorations* and *Preludes*, and the first of his significant 'pagan' works, *The Forgotten Rite*, for orchestra. This piece is associated with historic place and ritual. Characteristically of his pagan works, it features a ternary structure carrying personal resonances. And what is evident from all the works of 1913 is Ireland's passion for French music.

In 1914 Ireland was exempted from military service, and he spent the war years living in London. In 1915 he purchased 14A Gunter Grove, a studio in Chelsea, which became his primary residence for the next few decades. In this year, soon after writing a short anthem intended for use by troops serving in the war and a rhapsody for piano, Ireland began work on his second violin sonata in A minor, which he completed in 1917. In many ways this sonata is a landmark in Ireland's composing career. The first performance was given by the violinist Albert Sammons and the pianist William Murdoch. The work was an immediate success with the general public, with the performance of Sammons and Murdoch contributing to the emotions evoked by the piece: both men were on leave from service with the Grenadier Guards, and played in khaki uniform. Each of the three movements is tightly constructed, and there are strong motivic links between them. It is also a powerful example of the images, ideas, symbols, and connections with which the composer's music is invested. The work that followed, the second piano trio (1917), is a good example of the emotional outpourings and prevalent use of march rhythms and 'military' motifs that colour the composer's 'war' music.

From this point on, the number of works carrying descriptive titles increased dramatically, and Ireland later stated that these titles 'give some idea of the emotions involved' (Schafer, 33) and that personal experiences often instigated a composition. In 1917 he produced the piano miniature 'Chelsea Reach', the first of a sequence of London-inspired works. Ireland's musical representations of London are imbued with history and tradition, but at the same time are always personal to him. His musical cityscape is either a progressively shifting panorama, effected through a succession of new sections of music, or a tiny character sketch, 'Ragamuffin' being an example.

1918 was a year of focus on the English countryside, and there are a number of pieces, such as the piano work *The Towing Path* and the song 'Earth's Call', that embody Ireland's pastoral response, their common theme a sense of time and action standing still in the landscape. During the next few years Ireland worked on a large-scale piano sonata which integrates autobiographical and compositional features of the years 1917–20.

The 1920s The 1920s have generally been perceived as the period of Ireland's most personal and intimate music.

This is because the composer's closest and most inspirational relationships took place during this decade. His music from the 1920s expresses a gamut of emotions associated with love, from ecstatic passion to a cramped, tortured angst. Like most of Ireland's works, the music about love is linked to specific people, places, and literature. In the first two months of 1920 Ireland wrote two songs, 'The Trellis' and 'My True Love Hath my Heart', which are positive musical declarations of love. Later in the same year he started work on his Housman song cycle, *The Land of Lost Content*, which he completed in 1921. In 1922 he wrote the piano solo *On a Birthday Morning*. This bore the dedication 'Pro amicitia' ('For friendship'), and was dated 22 February 1922. It was a present for a former St Luke's choirboy, Arthur George Miller (1905–1986), who was seventeen on that day. Between 1922 and 1929 Ireland dedicated a series of works to Miller, most of them intended as birthday gifts. Though the nature of their relationship remains elusive, this young man was a central figure in Ireland's life, provoking the composer's most intense music. He was a constant companion, accompanying Ireland on holidays. During the 1920s Ireland visited Dorset several times and wrote a number of pieces linked to the county, among them the orchestral *Mai-Dun*, intended as an overtly programmatic depiction of the Roman invasion of Maiden Castle, effected through a series of contrasting musical episodes. During this decade he also spent much time in Sussex and there too composed associated works, such as two florid nature tone poems for piano, *Amberley Wild Brooks* (1921) and *April* (1925). In the meantime he had been appointed professor of composition at the Royal College of Music in 1923 (where his pupils included E. J. Moeran, Alan Bush, Benjamin Britten, and Geoffrey Bush), and had also expanded his studio in Gunter Grove by buying the remainder of the property at no. 14.

In 1926 Ireland produced a piano sonatina and a cycle entitled *Three Songs*. This was a momentous year for him, and the start of a period of bleak despair, reflected in his music. In October he left St Luke's. On 17 December he married a seventeen-year-old pianist and student at the Royal Academy of Music, Dorothy Phillips (*b.* 1909), Arthur Miller acting as his witness. The work dedicated to Miller two months later, February 1927, was the tortured Housman cycle *We'll to the Woods no More*. Miller married in 1927, and on 19 September 1928 Ireland was divorced. In the meantime he had acquired another protégée, the beautiful young pianist Helen Perkin (1909–1996), for whom he wrote the piano concerto in E♭ in 1930. This piece marks the end of a phase of music of great intimacy and intensity, and displays Ireland's coherent, organic approach to structure, with the three movements all interrelated.

The 1930s and 1940s Between 1929 and 1931 Ireland wrote his *Songs Sacred and Profane*, which as a group of six songs embodies various aspects of his life and musical language. The songs span years of personal crisis, and Ireland's transference of infatuation from Arthur Miller to Helen Perkin. In 1932 he received an honorary doctorate from Durham University. By now he had become a regular worshipper at St Cuthbert's, Kensington, where the priest in charge was Kenneth Thompson. This was a meeting of minds, and Thompson became a close and lifelong friend of the composer. In 1933 Ireland was preoccupied with pagan legends and ceremonies, producing *Legend* (1933) for piano and orchestra, which has strong connections with Harrow Hill in the Sussex Downs, and *Month's Mind*, for piano.

In June 1934 Helen Perkin married an affluent architect, George Mountford Adie (1901–1989), with whom she went on to have three children. Ireland was deeply shocked by the marriage, as his friendship with Perkin had been a possessive one. For a short time the composer produced very little, but then in his orchestral piece *London Overture* of 1936 he created a musical composite of memories of Edwardian London and personal experiences of that year, most significantly the death of a close friend, Percy G. Bentham.

By now Ireland was beginning to speak more openly of what might be called an 'aesthetic' interest in young boys. In 1936 he moved to Deal, and while there he produced three major works, each of which had connections with the worsening situation in Europe: *These Things Shall Be* (1937), the third piano trio (1938), and the *Concertino Pastorale* (1939). In July 1939 Ireland decided to leave England for Guernsey, ostensibly to consider settling on the island, and in 1940 he became director of music at St Stephen's, St Peter Port. But as early as May 1940 Ireland was forced to leave Guernsey because of the imminent German invasion of the Channel Islands. On his return he completed a piano suite, *Sarnia*, which reverberates with associations with Guernsey. Thenceforth Ireland spent the war years relying on the hospitality of friends. He went first to Alan Bush's home in Radlett, and from there to Banbury and Essex.

During these years Ireland's fascination with youths found expression in his music, notably in the *Three Pastels* for piano of 1941. At the same time he wrote a number of war-commissioned works, including the patriotic *Epic March* (1942). But perhaps the most significant of the pieces of the 1940s is the fantasy-sonata for clarinet and piano, which stands within Ireland's output as a late flowering, drawing together the musical meanings and structural techniques from across his composing career. This was followed in 1944 by a potent little anthem for boys' voices, *Ex ore innocentium*. There were two major projects in 1944–6: the orchestral overture *Satyricon* and the film score for *The Overlanders*.

Final years After this point Ireland composed very little music, suffering from medical problems including arteriosclerosis and a deterioration in his eyesight. In 1947 Norah Kirby was appointed as his housekeeper, and in 1953 he left London to settle in a converted windmill: Rock Mill, Washington, Sussex. Two works of 1958 mark the end of his composing career. These are an unaccompanied setting of Psalm 23 and an organ piece, the *Meditation on John Keble's Rogationtide Hymn*, which quotes from earlier works. Ireland died at Rock Mill on 12 June 1962 at the age of eighty-two. He was buried in Sussex, in the church of St Mary the Virgin, Shipley, on 16 June.

Both as a person and as a composer, John Ireland has always been difficult to place. Though he led a life that was in many ways uneventful, his highly individual musical style discloses an expressive, often contradictory personality. He could be gloomy but also exuberant and witty, passionate yet taciturn. Ireland was a practising Anglican for most of his life, though as he grew older his faith was increasingly tinged with doubt, cynicism, and an attraction to paganism. He loved the English countryside, in both its most rosy and most rugged aspects, but also had a strong attachment to London, the city in which he lived for most of his life. His works are deeply personal, nearly always closely linked to a specific event or place or person in his life, and a complex system of personal musical symbols and images permeates his output. It is this personal approach that makes his music so special and causes it to speak with such an individual voice.

FIONA RICHARDS

Sources F. Richards, *The music of John Ireland* (2000) [incl. complete work list and bibliography] • S. Banfield, *Sensibility and English song* (1985) • J. Longmire, *John Ireland: portrait of a friend* (1969) • S. Craggs, *John Ireland: a catalogue, discography, and bibliography* (1993) • A. Rowlands, 'John Ireland: a significant composer?', *RCM Magazine* (summer 1992), 18; (spring 1993), 13–19 • E. Evans, 'John Ireland', *MT*, 60 (1919), 394–6, 457–62 • C. Scott-Sutherland, *John Ireland* (1980) • M. Searle, *John Ireland: the man and his music* (1979) • J. Brooke, 'The music of John Ireland: an appreciation', *MT*, 99 (1958), 600–02 • R. M. Schafer, *British composers in interview* (1963) • G. Bush, *Left, right and centre: reflections on composers and composing* (1983) • Grove, *Dict. mus.* (1954) • records of Leeds grammar school • m. cert. • archives of Royal College of Music, London
Archives BL, letters • CUL, music MSS, Add. MS 65528 • CUL, scores, Add. MS 52871–52901 • John Ireland Trust, London • Ransom HRC, letters • Royal College of Music, London | BL, letters to K. C. Thompson, Add. MSS 60535–60536 | SOUND BBC WAC • BL NSA
Likenesses H. Lambert, photograph, c.1920, NPG [see illus.] • H. Lambert, photogravure, c.1920, NPG • G. L. Roddon, oils, 1960, NPG
Wealth at death approx. £39,725 19s.: probate, 13 Sept 1962, *CGPLA Eng. & Wales*

Ireland, Maud (*fl.* 1380). *See under* Women traders and artisans in London (*act. c.*1200–*c.*1500).

Ireland [Irland], **Robert** (*d.* 1561), jurist, was the son of Alexander Ireland and Margaret Coutts of Auchtertool, Fife. His grandfather was laird of Burnbane, Perthshire (in the parish either of Little Dunkeld or of Caputh), and Robert seems to have been born there. In 1500 he matriculated at St Andrews as a member of the university nation of Angus (north of the River Tay), but plague forced him to leave for France. He studied the laws at Poitiers, and is claimed to have become doctor of laws by 1502. One of his students was François Rabelais, who describes him as 'decretalipotens' in his *Pantagruel*. He was much admired by the Poitiers jurist Eguinaire Baron, who dedicated his *Pandectarum juris civilis oeconomia* of 1535–6 to him. In his capacity of professor of the laws Ireland is said to have encountered the young Calvin, who held evangelical

salons in the city soon after his conversion to protestantism, and to have been so angry with the youth's unorthodoxy that he tossed his bonnet at the reformer's head. Ireland married twice: his first wife was Marie Sauvetau, with whom he had a son, Jean, and his second was Claire Aubert, who was the mother of Bonaventure *Ireland, later a well-known jurist in Poitiers, and of Louis, who became a member of the Académie Française. Robert Ireland became a naturalized Frenchman on 1 May 1521, and died on Christmas day 1561.

JOHN DURKAN

Sources R. K. Hannay, ed. and trans., *Rentale Dunkeldense*, Scottish History Society, 2nd ser., 10 (1915), 105, 327 • J. Durkan, 'Scottish reformers: the less than golden legend', *Innes Review*, 45 (1994), 1–28, esp. 18 • J. M. Anderson, ed., *Early records of the University of St Andrews*, Scottish History Society, 3rd ser., 8 (1926), 198 • A. H. Thibaudeau, *Histoire du Poitou* (1839–40), 3.419–21 • P. Boissonnade, *Historie de l'Université de Poitiers (1432–1932)* (1932) • G. Dez, *Histoire de Poitiers* (1969), 95 n. 182

Ireland, Samuel (*d.* 1800), printmaker and writer, originally traded as a silk weaver at 19 Prince's Street, Spitalfields, London, but by 1789 he was listed in trade directories as a 'merchant' at 3 Arundel Street, off the Strand. Here he lived with 'Mrs Freeman' (Anna Maria de Burgh Coppinger; *d.* 1802), ostensibly his housekeeper, but assumed by his contemporaries to be the mother of his son, William Henry *Ireland (1775–1835), and his two daughters. From about 1758, however, Ireland had pursued a parallel career as a draughtsman and engraver. He was awarded a medal by the Society of Arts in 1760 and exhibited a drawing at the society's exhibition in 1765. In 1768 he became an honorary member of the Royal Academy of Arts, and in 1784 he exhibited there a view of Oxford. During the 1780s he etched many plates after William Hogarth and others and produced a number of portraits and architectural views. He offered Horace Walpole the dedication of two prints, and visited Strawberry Hill with Paul Sandby to trace prints by Hogarth in 1786. The following year Walpole accused him, probably with some exaggeration, of bribing his engraver to supply a limited edition print for the purpose of counterfeiting it. In 1794 Ireland published *Graphic Illustrations of Hogarth* from prints and drawings in his own possession; the authenticity of some of these was disputed, but a second volume appeared in 1799, and the work remained in use at the end of the twentieth century.

In 1790 Ireland published *A Picturesque Tour through Holland, Brabant, and Part of France*, beginning a series of moderately successful travel books featuring his own illustrations. *Picturesque Views on the Upper, or Warwickshire Avon* (1795) was derived from a tour which had allowed him free imaginative rein in the obsessional domain of Shakespeare memorabilia. The *Confessions* (1805) of his son William Henry Ireland record Ireland's gullibility in accepting spurious Shakespearian legends and objects. In December 1794 the younger Ireland began to produce the so-called Shakespeare Papers, which his father accepted as genuine; in February 1795 Ireland placed these on display at his house at 8 Norfolk Street, Strand, where the family had moved about 1791. A volume of facsimiles, *Miscellaneous Papers and Legal Instruments under the Hand and Seal of William Shakespeare*, was published on Christmas eve 1795, with 122 subscribers at 4 guineas. Edmond Malone's caustic *Inquiry* into the forgery of the documents was published in March 1796, just before the disastrous opening (and closing) performance of the supposedly Shakespearian *Vortigern* (Drury Lane, 2 April 1796). Ireland published in November 1796 *Mr Ireland's Vindication of his Conduct*, and later attacked Malone in *An Investigation of Mr Malone's Claim to the Character of Scholar, or Critic* (1797). Many, however, believed him to be the chief perpetrator of the fraud, and he was caricatured on stage in Frederick Reynolds's *Fortune's Fool* (1796). Gillray's print of 1 December 1797, based on an earlier self-portrait by Ireland, bore the title *Notorious Characters, No. I*, and carried accusatory inscriptions by George Steevens and William Mason. Ireland planned to sue for libel, but his lawyers advised him that to do so would mean calling his unreliable son as a witness.

Ireland died at his home in Norfolk Street in July 1800 of diabetes, bequeathing his son his watch and £20 as a token of forgiveness. The obituary in the *Gentleman's Magazine* thought his 'complicity' in the fraud seemed 'obvious'; a defence of his character, probably by John Byng, was published in the same magazine some months later, in September 1800. According to his son, Ireland did on one occasion tear off a tellingly anachronistic date from a document, but his manifest disbelief in his son's authorship of the papers, and his surviving letters to the fictional 'gentleman' in whose possession they were supposedly discovered, support the deathbed declaration which he made to his doctor, John Latham: 'that he was totally ignorant of the deceit, and was equally a believer in the authenticity of the manuscripts as those which were even the most credulous' (Latham, 176). His guilt has, however, been reasserted by Jeffrey Kahan (*Reforging Shakespeare*).   PAUL BAINES

Sources S. Schoenbaum, *Shakespeare's lives*, new edn (1991) · B. Grebanier, *The great Shakespeare forgery* (1966) · J. Mair, *The fourth forger* (1938) · W.-H. Ireland, *The confessions of William-Henry Ireland* (1805) · J. Latham, *Facts and opinions concerning diabetes* (1811) · E. Malone, *An inquiry into the authenticity of certain miscellaneous papers* (1796) · *Mr Ireland's vindication of his conduct* (1796) · *GM*, 1st ser., 70 (1800), 901–2, 1258 · Walpole, *Corr.*, 12.226; 15.338; 33.575; 42.120 · BL, Add. MS 30348, fol. 35 · J. Kahan, *Reforging Shakespeare: the story of a theatrical scandal* (1998)
Archives BL, corresp. relating to Shakespeare forgeries, Add. MSS 30346–30350 · Bodl. Oxf., papers · Boston PL, corresp. · Hunt. L., journal of tours in England and France | Bodl. Oxf., letters to John Charles Brooke
Likenesses H. D. Hamilton, chalk drawing, 1776, NPG · J. Nixon, engraving, 1796, BM · engraving, 1796, repro. in Grebanier, *Great Shakespeare forgery*, facing p. 149 · J. Gillray, engraving, 1 Dec 1797, repro. in Mair, *Fourth forger*, facing p. 224 · S. Ireland, self-portrait, engraving (after H. D. Hamilton), NPG
Wealth at death some details of will, Grebanier, *Great Shakespeare forgery*, 284 · collections sold by Leigh, Sotheby & Son, 7–15 May 1801: annotated sale catalogues, BL and Folger

Ireland [*alias* Ironmonger], **William** (1636–1679), Jesuit, was born in Lincolnshire, the eldest of four children of

William Ireland (1636–1679), by Cornelis van Merlen

William Ireland of Crofton Hall in Yorkshire and Eleanor, daughter of Ralph Eure of Washingborough, Lincolnshire. The Irelands were a well-connected Catholic gentry family. As a boy William was sent to the English College at St Omer and was admitted to the Society of Jesus on 7 September 1655. He was trained, and then himself taught, at the English Jesuit establishments at Watten, Liège, and St Omer; in 1667 he was ordained priest, and in 1673 was professed of the four vows. He acted as confessor to the Poor Clares convent at Gravelines for a number of years.

In 1677 Ireland was sent on the English mission and became procurator of the province. In the middle of the night of 28 September 1678, having postponed a journey abroad owing to an illness, he was arrested in London and charged with other Catholics, on the accusations of Titus Oates, with plotting to kill Charles II. He was examined by the privy council and then imprisoned in Newgate, and denied the opportunity to prepare his defence properly. At his trial on 17 December, Ireland, assisted by his sister Anne, who made desperate efforts to save his life, put up a stout defence of his innocence. The case against Ireland was that he had plotted at the triennial meeting of Jesuits, which Oates claimed to have attended, on 24 April 1678, and then again in late August at a more informal meeting of Jesuits in London. Ireland's hurriedly prepared defence was that he had been out of London from 3 August until 14 September, and also that Oates's testimony was that of a man known already to be a perjurer. Ireland's mother and sister testified that he had not been with them in London in August, while Harrison, the coachman of Sir John Southcote, gave evidence that he had driven Ireland from St Albans to Staffordshire at that time. Charles Gifford or Giffard was also called to confirm that the Jesuit had stayed with him in Wolverhampton. Sir Denny Ashburnham, MP for Hastings, where Oates had been brought up, was persuaded to testify that Oates had been a liar as a youth. But against them were Oates, his associate Bedloe, and one Sarah Paine, a serving girl who was willing to say that she had seen Ireland in London.

The lord chief justice, Scroggs, however, directed the jury in the strongest possible terms to find Ireland guilty, and he was duly convicted. Ireland's final throw at the trial had been to stress the royalism of his family, mentioning in particular his relationship to the Giffard and Pendrell families who had saved Charles II's life when he had hidden in the famous oak tree after the battle of Worcester.

The execution of Ireland was stayed over Christmas 1678 owing to royal intervention. It was well known in Staffordshire that Ireland had been there during the summer in question, and the king came under pressure to reprieve him. He consulted bishops and judges, and heard more evidence, but the atmosphere in London was tense and the political situation difficult. The king's scruples did not last long, especially after the appearance of Stephen Dugdale, bailiff to Lord Aston, with whom Ireland had stayed during the summer; Dugdale alleged that Ireland had not been there as he had claimed, and, furthermore, that Ireland had been involved in a wider plot with local Catholics. As a result Ireland was executed at Tyburn on 24 January 1679.

The subject of Ireland's innocence continued to be controverted. At a further trial of alleged plotters in July 1679 Robert Jenison gave evidence denying Ireland's alibi, while others testified that Ireland had been in Staffordshire as he had claimed. When Oates himself was tried for perjury in 1685 it was details of Ireland's case which formed much of the case against him, and over forty witnesses were produced to corroborate Ireland's alibi.

THOMAS SECCOMBE, *rev.* PETER HOLMES

Sources Gillow, *Lit. biog. hist.*, 3.551–5 · C. Dodd [H. Tootell], *The church history of England, from the year 1500, to the year 1688*, 3 (1742), 315–16 · R. Challoner, *Memoirs of missionary priests*, ed. J. H. Pollen, rev. edn (1924), 510–25 · H. Foley, ed., *Records of the English province of the Society of Jesus*, 5 (1879), 7–146, 223–33, 432, 448, 1004–6 · G. Holt, *The English Jesuits, 1650–1829: a biographical dictionary*, Catholic RS, 70 (1984) · G. Holt, *St Omers and Bruges colleges, 1593–1773: a biographical dictionary*, Catholic RS, 69 (1979), 144–5 · J. Hunter, *South Yorkshire* (1831), vol. 2, p. 215 · T. E. Gibson, *Lydiate Hall and its associations* (1876), 33 · G. Oliver, *Collections towards illustrating the biographies of the Scotch, English and Irish members of the Society of Jesus*, 2nd edn (1845) · J. Warner, *The history of English persecution of Catholics and the presbyterian plot*, ed. T. A. Birrell, trans. J. Bligh, 2, Catholic RS, 48 (1953) · [J. Keynes and T. Stapleton], *Florus Anglo-Bavaricus* (Liège, 1685); facs. edn with new introduction by T. A. Birrell (1970), 140–50 · J. Kenyon, *The Popish Plot* (1972) · J. Morris, *The troubles of our Catholic forefathers* (1972), vol. 1, pp. 373–8 · A. M. C. Forster, 'A Durham family: Jenisons of Walworth', *Biographical Studies*, 3/1 (1955–6), 9–10 · *State trials* · *Burnet's History of my own time*, ed. O. Airy, new edn, 2 (1900), 188–90

Likenesses print, line, pubd 1805, BM, NPG · C. van Merlen, engraving, NPG [*see illus.*] · engraving, repro. in H. Foley, *Records of the English province of the Society of Jesus* (1879)

Ireland, William Henry (1775–1835), literary forger and writer, was born on 2 August 1775 in London, the only surviving son of Samuel *Ireland (d. 1800), engraver and author, and Anna Maria de Burgh Coppinger, otherwise Mrs Freeman (d. 1802), who passed as the father's housekeeper but was known to be his mistress and mother of his children. After failing at English schools William Ireland was educated in northern France for about three years. At the age of sixteen he was articled to a conveyancer, William Bingley of New Inn, London, which left him ample time to indulge in self-aggrandizing fantasies of a Gothic nature: he read widely in medieval romances and collected old books and pieces of armour. The Ireland family visited the theatre often and read Shakespeare aloud among themselves; Ireland was also influenced by the story of Thomas Chatterton as melodramatically recounted in Herbert Croft's *Love and Madness* (1780): 'I used to envy his fate, and desire nothing so ardently as the termination of my existence in a similar cause' (Ireland, *Confessions*, 11).

Ireland's father was an obsessive and credulous collector of Shakespeariana in an age when a biographical basis for the study of Shakespeare was becoming dominant. His desire to own a document in Shakespeare's hand became poignantly obvious to his son in the summer of 1793 when the two men travelled to Stratford upon Avon while gathering materials for Samuel Ireland's *Picturesque Views on the Upper, or Warwickshire Avon* (1795). Ireland needed to gain favour with a father who regarded him with little affection or esteem, and after preliminary experiments with 'Elizabethan' ink, he announced on 2 December 1794 that he had found a deed signed by Shakespeare among documents owned by a mysterious 'Mr. H.'. The deed was produced on 16 December and was at once accepted by Samuel. Using old materials gathered from bookshops and the conveyancer's office, Ireland rapidly produced a sequence of legal and personal documents from the same supposed source, designed to cast Shakespeare in the light of a punctual and efficient businessman and well-regarded man of the world: a letter to the earl of Southampton (with a reply), a confession of faith proving the bard to be a good protestant, theatrical contracts, a love letter and poem to 'Anna Hatherreweye' with a lock of hair (proving the poet to be an affectionate husband), and a remarkably friendly letter from Queen Elizabeth. Shakespeare's library, with marginalia, was discovered; an original manuscript of *King Lear* showed that all the bawdy talk had been interpolated by actors. In February 1795 Samuel Ireland opened his house in Arundel Street, London, to display the papers. James Boswell, Croft, and John Pinkerton expressed their veneration of these 'relics' of the most personally enigmatic of all poets, though Joseph Ritson saw at once that they were forgeries. A new play supposedly by Shakespeare, *Vortigern*, was discovered and accepted by Sheridan for production at Drury Lane. Ireland's most audacious idea was to produce a deed of gift which ceded to an Elizabethan 'William Henry Ireland' all property in Shakespeare's papers as a reward for saving the poet from drowning; this at once secured the somewhat shaky copyright in the documents and invented a noble genealogy for Ireland himself. A further deed of gift mentioned an illegitimate child of Shakespeare, which opened the possibility that Ireland was himself a blood relative of the poet.

After Samuel Ireland published facsimile texts of the documents in *Miscellaneous Papers and Legal Instruments under the Hand and Seal of William Shakespeare* on Christmas eve 1795, more sceptical voices were heard. Newspapers parodied the bizarre doubled consonants of Ireland's compositions, and on 11 January 1796 James Boaden published *A Letter to George Steevens, Esq.* attacking them. Francis Webb asserted the authenticity of the documents on the basis of their Shakespearian spirit, but increasingly the documents were denounced as forgeries. *Vortigern* was eventually produced, without Shakespeare's name, on 2 April. (Kemble had tried to schedule it for April fool's day.) The play seemed to have a chance of success, but a packed and volatile crowd eventually turned against it and it was howled down in the fifth act. The theatre took £555 6s. 6d., of which Samuel Ireland received just over £100. The play's failure was also in part due to Edmond Malone, whose edition of Shakespeare (1790) was one of the inspirations for the forgeries, and who had published his very damaging *An Inquiry into the Authenticity of Certain Miscellaneous Papers* on 31 March 1796. Malone denounced the orthography of the papers and showed with facsimiles that the signatures did not match known exemplars, and that the chronology was wildly inaccurate. Ireland publicly exonerated his father in *An Authentic Account of the Shaksperian Manuscripts*, but Samuel Ireland refused to accept that his son was capable of creating the archive. Ireland left home on 5 June 1796 and married Alice Crudge on 4 July at St James's, Clerkenwell, London. He engaged in increasingly acrimonious correspondence with his father, from whom he attempted in vain to extract the full story of his parentage.

In 1798 Ireland ran for a time a circulating library at 1 Princes Place, Kensington, London. In that year Silvester Harding engraved a portrait showing him in a pose of poetic melancholy, apparently not much abashed by the scandal. In 1804 Ireland, now a widower, married the widow of Captain Paget Bayly RN. They had two daughters, the elder named, after Mrs Freeman, Anna Maria de Burgh. Ireland subsisted partly by producing new examples of Shakespeare forgeries as curiosities and by extra-illustrating copies of the *Miscellaneous Papers* and other books. In 1805 he published *The Confessions of William-Henry Ireland*, a highly readable if not entirely reliable account of his early life, and the motives for the forgeries and the techniques involved, spiced with anecdotes about the visitors who had worshipped the papers in his father's house. He continued to refer to the forgeries, which had briefly established his literary genius as equal to that of Shakespeare, with more pride than sorrow, in much of his subsequent work; he reissued *Vortigern* in

1832 with a new account of his unfortunate life. Ireland produced some ninety literary works: dramas, Gothic and sentimental novels, imitation ballads, satirical and political poems, romances, topographic works, and Chattertonian fantasies. (His *Neglected Genius* of 1812 was mockingly reviewed by Byron.) He was imprisoned in York Castle for debt in 1811; he spent the years from 1814 to 1823 in France and wrote many works about French history and culture. A portrait (c.1825) by Samuel Drummond shows Ireland still in sombre attitude. He was, however, described as high-spirited and engaging by contemporaries, though he had 'something gleaming out of his eyes that in the height of his hilarity forbad you to trust him' (Schoenbaum, 167). Ireland died at Sussex Place, St George's-in-the-Fields, London, on 17 April 1835 and was buried on 24 April at St George the Martyr, Southwark, London. A fictional account of the forgeries is given in James Payn's *The Talk of the Town* (1885).   PAUL BAINES

Sources J. Kahan, *Reforging Shakespeare: the story of a theatrical scandal* (1998) · S. Schoenbaum, *Shakespeare's lives*, new edn (1991) · B. Grebanier, *The great Shakespeare forgery* (1966) · J. Mair, *The fourth forger* (1938) · 'Ireland, Samuel', *DNB* · W.-H. Ireland, *The confessions of William-Henry Ireland* (1805) · W. H. Ireland, *An authentic account of the Shaksperian manuscripts* (1796) · S. Ireland, ed., *Miscellaneous papers and legal instruments under the hand and seal of William Shakespeare* (1796, i.e. 1795) · E. Malone, *An inquiry into the authenticity of certain miscellaneous papers* (1796) · J. Bate, 'Faking it: Shakespeare and the 1790s', *Essays and studies 1993: literature and censorship*, ed. N. Smith (1993), 63–80 · J. Boaden, *A letter to George Steevens, esq.* (1796) · F. Webb, *Shakspeare's manuscripts, in the possession of Mr. Ireland, examined* (1796) · *DNB*

Archives BL, corresp. and papers relating to his forgeries, Add. MSS 30346–30350 · BL, forgeries, Add. MSS 12051–37831; Egerton MS 2623; Stowe MS 994; RP 2041, 3770 · BL, papers, Facs Suppl VII(k) MS · Bodl. Oxf., Ireland MSS · Bodl. Oxf., papers relating to his forgeries · Boston PL, letters and papers · Folger, forgeries · Hunt. L., corresp., forgeries, and literary MSS · Shakespeare Birthplace Trust RO, Stratford upon Avon, collections on the Ireland forgeries · U. Edin. L., corresp. and specimens of forgeries · UCL, forgeries and papers | BL, Samuel Ireland MSS · Bodl. Oxf., letters to Messrs Vernor and Hood

Likenesses J. Nixon, engraving, 1796, BM · portrait, 1796 (*The spirit of Shakespere appearing to his detractors*), BM · S. Harding, stipple, 1798, BM, NPG · Mackenzie, stipple, 1818, BM · S. Drummond, miniature on ivory, c.1825, Shakespeare Birthplace Trust RO, Stratford upon Avon

Ireland, William Wotherspoon (1832–1909), physician and writer, was born in Edinburgh on 27 October 1832, the son of Thomas Ireland, a publisher and a descendant of Mrs Welsh, daughter of John Knox, the reformer. His mother was Mary, daughter of William Wotherspoon, writer to the signet and first manager and secretary of the Scottish Widows' Life Assurance Society. Ireland was educated at Edinburgh high school and afterwards at Edinburgh University and in Paris, where he studied medicine, graduating MD from Edinburgh in 1855. He served briefly as resident surgeon at Dumfries Infirmary before becoming an assistant surgeon in the East India Company with the Bengal horse artillery in 1856. He was present at the siege of Delhi, where he treated the wounds of Lieutenant Roberts (afterwards Lord Roberts, commander-in-chief in India). After seven months' service Ireland was seriously wounded by a bullet which destroyed one of his eyes and passed round the base of his skull to the opposite ear. A second bullet wounded his shoulder and back. It was a year before he could rise from his bed. He spent three years convalescing in India and was retired from the service with honours and a pension.

The next ten years of Ireland's life were devoted to convalescence in Madeira and travels in Europe. In 1861 he married Margaret Paterson. They had a daughter and a son, Thomas Ireland, later of the west India medical service. During this time he began his literary career. He published an eyewitness account, *History of the Siege of Delhi* (1861), *Randolph Mephyl* (1863), a novel based on his experience of Anglo-Indian life, and *Studies of a Wandering Observer* (1867), an account of his travels in Europe. In 1869 he returned to Scotland and to medicine, becoming medical superintendent of the Scottish National Institution for Imbecile Children at Larbert, Stirlingshire, where he remained for ten years. Ireland had no prior experience in this field, and institutional management may have provided a welcome opportunity for a man who had been seriously wounded and who had been absent so long from medical practice. His own experience of head injury may also have attracted him to the study of the brain.

Ireland soon established himself as a leading authority on idiocy, publishing articles in the *Edinburgh Medical Journal* and the *Journal of Mental Science*, and contributing to Hack Tuke's *Dictionary of Psychological Medicine*. In 1877 he published *On Idiocy and Imbecility*, an impressive synthesis of existing literature on the subject, which became the standard text in English for the rest of the century. Much of the book was devoted to a system of classification based on pathology, and this was adopted in some of the early idiot institutions.

In 1879 Ireland retired from Larbert to open private homes for idiots, first at Stirling, and afterwards at Prestonpans, near Musselburgh, and Polton, near Edinburgh. Over the next decade he returned to his historical and literary interests, developing a new field in which psychology and the study of heredity were used to cast light on historical events. Ireland's studies of the insanity of power, hereditary neurosis, and the effect of delusions on, among others, Mohammed, Luther, Joan of Arc, Caligula, Ivan the Terrible, and Swedenborg, were published in medical journals and in his *Blot upon the Brain* (1885) and *Through the Ivory Gate* (1889). Ireland did not romanticize hallucinatory experience. However, he pointed out that it could be a source of influence and power, particularly when it corresponded to the delusions of the public (as had been the case in the Indian mutiny). Written in non-technical language, these psycho-historical case studies fascinated the general public, pushing both books into second editions. He followed this popular success with *Golden Bullets* (1891), a novel which drew on his Indian experience and historical interests, and *The Life of Henry Vane the Younger* (1905), a more orthodox historical study based on original seventeenth-century documents.

Ireland remained active within the medical profession. In 1898 he had revised *Idiocy and Imbecility* under the new title *The Mental Affections of Children*. He was sceptical about the mounting alarm over degeneration, suggesting that any apparent increase in idiocy was most likely an illusion produced by earlier under-recording. His own survey of Glasgow schools suggested that the problem was not as bad as many were claiming. He continued to contribute to medical journals, who welcomed his ability to review and translate publications in French, German, Italian, Spanish, Norwegian, and Hindustani. In 1905 fellow professionals paid tribute to Ireland on the fiftieth anniversary of his MD graduation. He was admired for his striking individuality and his encyclopaedic knowledge.

Ireland was a member of the Psychiatric Society of St Petersburg, the New York Medico-Legal Society, and the Società Freniatrica Italiana. He also took an interest in local politics, and was chairman of the Prestonpans branch of the Unionist Association for some years. After the death of his wife he retired to Musselburgh, Midlothian, where he died at his home, 1 Victoria Terrace, on 17 May 1909. MATHEW THOMSON

Sources *Journal of Mental Science*, 55 (1909), 582–4 · J. S. C., *Edinburgh Medical Journal*, 3rd ser., 2 (1909), 563–4 · *The Lancet* (5 June 1909), 1643–4 · *BMJ* (29 May 1909), 1334 · DNB · *The Times* (27 May 1909)

Wealth at death £3858 17s. 2d.: confirmation, 26 June 1909, CCI

Ireton, Henry (*bap.* 1611, *d.* 1651), parliamentarian army officer and regicide, was baptized on 3 November 1611 in the parish church of Attenborough, Nottinghamshire. His father, German Ireton (*d.* 1624), who had settled in Attenborough about 1605, was the younger brother of William Ireton of Little Ireton, Derbyshire; his mother's name was Jane. Henry was the eldest of five sons, but the custom of ultimogeniture or 'borough English' prevailed in Nottinghamshire in the seventeenth century: all of German Ireton's landed estate went to his youngest son, Thomas. Lacking an inherited income, Ireton entered Trinity College, Oxford, as a gentleman commoner and graduated BA in 1629. From there he went to the Middle Temple, and, while he was never called to the bar, there is evidence that he practised as a professional lawyer before 1642.

The first civil war When armed conflict broke out in 1642 Ireton had already been active organizing the root and branch petition in his native county, and raising a company to protect the magazine at Nottingham from the royalists. Parliament accordingly nominated him captain of the troop of horse to be raised by the town. He brought this troop to Edgehill and fought under the earl of Essex, but led it back at the end of the year to Nottinghamshire where he became major of Colonel Francis Thornhagh's regiment. In July 1643 the Nottinghamshire horse contributed to the parliamentarian victory at Gainsborough, where Ireton met, and began his lifelong association with, Oliver Cromwell. Shortly afterwards he left Thornhagh's regiment to become deputy governor of the Isle of Ely under Cromwell. There, in addition to fortifying the area against the king, he put into practice his advanced religious beliefs. He had been raised in a firmly puritan family, both his parents having run into trouble for refusing to

Henry Ireton (*bap.* 1611, *d.* 1651), attrib. Robert Walker, *c.*1650 (after Samuel Cooper and Sir Anthony Van Dyck)

follow the rules of the Church of England on the churching of women and kneeling at communion. He now tried to turn the Isle of Ely into a godly commonwealth, to the dismay of religious and social conservatives. According to one unfriendly observer, under Ireton the Isle had become

> a meere Amsterdam, for in the chefest churches on the Sabbath day the souldiers have gonn up into the pulpitts both in the forenoone and the afternoone and preached to the whole parish, and our ministers have satt in their seatt in the church and durst not attempt to preach, it being a common thinge to preach in private houses night and day, they having gott whole famalyes of Independents into that Ile from London and other places. (Bruce and Masson, 73–4)

Ireton was promoted quartermaster-general in the earl of Manchester's eastern association army in 1644, and he fought both at Marston Moor (2 July) and the second battle of Newbury (27 October). Despite the demoralization of the cavalry for lack of money he chafed against Manchester's unwillingness to take an aggressive stance against the enemy. After the fiasco of Donnington Castle, when the king returned to Newbury and drew off his artillery under the noses of the parliamentarian forces, Ireton joined Cromwell in trying to overthrow the timorous earl. His testimony against Manchester helped the campaign to purge the parliamentarian armies of their moderate, aristocratic leadership and replace them by the more militant men of the New Model Army.

Ireton's name was not on the initial list of New Model officers, perhaps because it was feared that the House of Lords would veto his nomination, as they attempted to do with many other names on Sir Thomas Fairfax's list. However, once the new fighting season had begun in the spring of 1645 he was made colonel of a horse regiment, displacing Sir Michael Livesey. On the eve of the battle of Naseby (14 June 1645) he surprised the royalists' quarters in the village, taking many prisoners and alarming their whole army. The king was forced to flee to Harborough, and as a consequence decided to engage the New Model the next day. At the same time Fairfax acceded to Cromwell's request that Ireton be appointed commissary-general of horse with command of the cavalry's left wing. On the day of battle Ireton tried to gain the upper hand against the royalist cavalry, advancing under Rupert, by charging down the hill to meet them. The charge was ragged, however, and Ireton allowed himself to become distracted by the distress of the New Model infantry on his right. Turning to lead a charge against the king's musketeers, he had his horse shot under him, and was run through the thigh with a pike and struck in the face with a halberd. He was taken prisoner, but regained his liberty when the tide turned against the royalists; he recovered well enough from his wounds to be present at the storming of Bristol in September. Fairfax summoned Rupert to surrender in a letter, which contained an outline of the theory of parliamentary monarchy, and which Ireton may have written.

We next hear of Ireton in March 1646, when he was the chief negotiator of the treaty at Truro under which the royalist army in the west under Ralph, Lord Hopton, was disbanded. He then rode with several regiments of horse to blockade Oxford. There he was approached by the king, who tried to open negotiations with him. Ireton rejected the king's overtures and wrote to Cromwell asking him to relay the king's message to parliament. From his seat in the House of Commons, Cromwell denounced Ireton for even communicating with the king, since soldiers were forbidden to deal with political matters.

Marriage and family Ireton's exchange with Cromwell did not, however, betoken any animus between the two men, for on 15 June 1646, shortly after he had negotiated the capitulation of Oxford, Ireton married Cromwell's daughter Bridget (*bap.* 1624, *d.* 1662) [*see* Fleetwood, Bridget]. The ceremony was performed by William Dell, one of the New Model Army's radical Independent chaplains. Henry and Bridget Ireton had one son and three daughters: Henry, who married Katherine, daughter of Henry Powle, speaker of the House of Commons in 1689, and became lieutenant-colonel of dragoons and gentleman of the horse to William III; Elizabeth (*b. c.*1647), who married in 1674 Thomas Polhill of Otford, Kent; Jane (*b. c.*1648), who married in 1688 Richard Lloyd of London; and Bridget [*see* Bendish, Bridget (1649/50–1726)], who married in 1689 Thomas Bendish.

The fruit of an existing friendship between Cromwell and Ireton, the marriage drew the bonds of intimacy between the two men even tighter, with important political consequences over the five remaining years of Ireton's life. Each man influenced the other. Ireton had a logical and theoretical mind, had studied politics, and could express himself cogently in writing. Cromwell had the strengths of Ireton's defects: a man of broad sympathies, he was flexible, pragmatic, and eloquent in speech. By his willingness to accept compromises he was often able to control and moderate Ireton's zeal. Yet the two men were at one in aspiring to establish a godly commonwealth in England.

Politics and the army Ireton entered the House of Commons as a recruiter MP for Appleby on 30 October 1645. We hear of no parliamentary activity by him until he spoke out in defence of the army's petition of 29 March 1647. This involved him in a quarrel with Denzel Holles, the leader of Essex's party, who had framed a declaration of dislike against the petition, threatening that those who promoted it would be proceeded against as enemies of the state. The quarrel degenerated into physical threats; the two left the house with the intention of fighting a duel, but returned without doing so, and were ordered by the house to drop the matter.

Thomas Sheppard of Ireton's regiment was one of the three troopers who presented the appeal of the soldiers to their generals, which Philip Skippon laid before the house on 30 April. The house responded by dispatching the military MPs—Skippon, Cromwell, Ireton, and Fleetwood—to army headquarters at Saffron Walden to quieten the army's distemper. Ireton and the other commissioners listened to each regiment's grievances and communicated them to parliament. Ireton despaired of parliament's ability to grant adequate concessions. While he had initially attempted to discourage the militancy of the rank-and-file, he threw in his lot with them after the Holles-led majority attempted to force immediate disbandment on 25 May.

On 2 June 1647 Cornet George Joyce led a party of 500 troopers to Holdenby where they seized the king and took him two days later to Newmarket, where the army was planning a rendezvous. Fairfax demanded to know by what authority Joyce had acted. In fact the cornet had met Cromwell in his garden in Drury Lane at the end of May and received Cromwell's approval of the seizure. Cromwell must have been in close touch with Ireton too, for the latter told Fairfax that he was the one who 'gave orders … for securing the king' (Maseres, 2.398). This act marked the beginning of Ireton's intense involvement in the military politics. All the major documents issuing from the army in the next two-and-a-half years can be traced to his hand. 'Colonel Ireton was chiefly employed or took upon him the business of the pen', Whitelocke tells us, 'and was therein encouraged and assisted by lieutenant-general Cromwell, his father-in-law, and by colonel Lambert' (Whitelocke, 2.162–3).

Since the early spring the rank and file had been operating democratically, through the election of agitators (or representatives) in each troop and company. The grandees, or higher officers, now decided to take over this democratic movement. Probably under Ireton's leadership they moved, at the army rendezvous near Newmarket on 4–5 June, for the creation of a general council of the army. This, it was decided, would consist of four representatives from each regiment—two officers and two soldiers—plus the fifteen or more officers of the general staff, and it was thus shrewdly prearranged that the officers should have a permanent majority over the rank and file. Ireton too is the most likely candidate for authorship of the solemn engagement, adopted collectively on 5 June. By its terms the army entered into a covenant not to disband until its grievances had been redressed, and to conduct its political affairs through the forum of the general council.

The general council did not begin to meet until 16 July 1647; meanwhile on 14 June Fairfax's council of war issued a *Declaration or Representation*, again almost certainly drafted by Ireton. The document unveiled a full-dress political programme, with the justification that

> we were not a meer mercenary army hired to serve any arbitrary power of a state, but called forth and conjured by the several declarations of parliament to the defence of our owne and the peoples just rights and liberties; and so we took up armes in judgement and conscience to those ends.
> (*Declaration of the Engagements*, 39)

In the name of the people they called for a purge of all delinquent and corrupt members of parliament, a fixed limit on the life of future parliaments, an end to the king's arbitrary power of dissolution, the right of petition, and a public accounting for the vast sums levied during the war.

The Heads of Proposals While he attempted to fend off agitator demands for an immediate march on London and purge of parliament, Ireton worked with Lambert on 'the foundation of a treaty, or rather a whole map of every particular to be treated upon' with the king (R. Bell, ed., *Memorials of the Civil War*, 2 vols., 1849, 2.368). As he sketched out his 'whole map' Ireton was in daily contact with Lord Wharton, one of the parliamentary commissioners residing at army headquarters. Another peer, Lord Saye and Sele, was also closely consulted. When he introduced his projected settlement to the council of the army on 17 July Ireton requested that it be scrutinized by a joint committee of officers and rank-and-file agitators.

The terms of *The Heads of Proposals*, as they were called, were at once the most generous and the most radical settlement offered to Charles during the civil war. Parliament was to control the armed forces, and nominations of chief officers of state and judges, for only ten years. Bishops would not be abolished, but merely lose their coercive power. Use of the Book of Common Prayer would be permitted. There would be a tolerant state church, unsupported by tithes. Parliaments would become biennial, with seats redistributed according to taxation. In his anxiety to win over the king Ireton modified the proposals in several important points, and thereby imperilled his support among the soldiers. Cromwell and Ireton advised Charles to ignore the revised Newcastle propositions sent to him by parliament, and instead put his trust in the army. According to Major Huntington, who was their emissary, Ireton added 'that they would purge, and purge, and never leave purging the Houses, till they had made them of such a temper as should do his Majesty's business'

(Maseres, 2.403–4). Charles, however, believed that he could advance his own interests more effectively by negotiating simultaneously with the army, parliament, and a faction among the Scots, and playing one off against the others. The negotiations therefore went nowhere, their only effect being to bring discredit upon Cromwell and Ireton in the army. Radicals vilified them for the supposed obsequiousness of their dealings with the king. Why do they 'kneele, and kisse, and fawne upon him?' Wildman indignantly inquired. Greater blame was attached to Ireton 'by whose cowardly or ambicious policy Cromwel is betrayed into these mischievous practices; and by whose craft the power of your Adjutators is brought to nothing' (J. Wildman, *A Cal to All the Souldiers of the Armie by the Free People of England*, 1647, 5, 6). Edward Sexby told them to their faces that 'your creditts and reputation hath bin much blasted' by their flirtation with the king (Firth, *Clarke Papers*, 1.225). Ireton passionately disavowed any wrongdoing, swearing that he had pursued talks with the king in the belief that he had the army's support for them, and that they were in the best interests of the kingdom.

The Levellers, the Putney debates, and the *Agreement of the People* Ireton's fixation on achieving a settlement with the king was broken first by the radical challenge from the army, and second by the king's flight from Hampton Court to the Isle of Wight. Chronic irregularity of pay, along with parliament's failure to attend to its other grievances, made the army fertile ground for the insemination of Leveller ideas. Constant exhortation by John Lilburne and others bore fruit in the election of new agitators in five regiments in September, and eventually in six more. Proclaiming that 'the great Mansion House of this Commonwealth … [is] on fire', Edward Sexby and others published *The Case of the Armie Truly Stated* in October (Wolfe, 220). Ostensibly a call for thoroughgoing social and political justice, based on the dissolution of the present parliament and votes for all 'freeborn' (ibid.) men, the tract was also an indictment of the army grandees for failing to promote the interests of the soldiers and rendering the army odious to the people. They were guilty of nothing less than breaking the sacred engagement of 5 June. The grandees reacted by inviting the new agitators and their civilian supporters to debate the *Case* before the general council of the army. At the council's meeting in Putney church on 28 October Sexby attacked Cromwell and Ireton for their servility towards king and parliament. For his part Ireton denied any desire to set up the king; but neither could he countenance the destruction of parliament. After this skirmish another agitator, Robert Everard, laid before the meeting the recently drafted *Agreement of the People*, which was now read out to the council for the first time. Starting from the premise that all power resides in the people, it postulated two novel concepts: a written constitution that would be brought into being through the signatures of all Englishmen, and a set of powers reserved to the people, and which no parliament could exercise. Ireton raised two objections: first that the agreement might conflict with the army's previous engagements to uphold king and parliament; second, that the call for electoral redistribution according to the number of inhabitants implied universal manhood suffrage. Ignoring the appeal of Thomas Rainborowe's ringing statement that 'the poorest hee that is in England hath a life to live as the greatest hee' (Firth, *Clarke Papers*, 1.301) Ireton warned that votes for the propertyless majority would inexorably lead to the abolition of property. Unmoved by the silent disagreement of almost all who sat in the room with him, he stuck doggedly to his position that only those with 'a permanent fixed interest in this kingedome' (ibid.) should be eligible to elect representatives. By his tenacity he wearied his audience, especially with his insistence on defending his negotiations with the king. Although he shared the common desire to limit the veto of the king and the House of Lords, he opposed the demand to deny them any share in legislation. It was thanks mainly to Ireton that the Levellers backpedalled from their initial call for universal manhood suffrage, and agreed to exclude servants and beggars from the franchise. Yet the victory was pyrrhic: he and Cromwell had essentially lost the struggle for support within the army's general council. Therefore, with Fairfax's consent, they cut off further debate and sent the agitators back to their regiments. Before it was adjourned, the general council nominated an eighteen-man committee, which included Ireton, to draft a remonstrance for the approval of the regiments at the forthcoming rendezvous of the army. This document, probably written by Ireton, dwelt chiefly on the army's material grievances, and was instrumental in defusing the mutiny at the Ware rendezvous.

As late as 5 November Ireton was still adamant in supporting continued negotiations with the king. But when Charles fled Hampton Court to the Isle of Wight, pleading conspiracies against his life, Ireton abruptly changed his attitude. He now perceived the impossibility of a treaty with Charles, and took the position that the army's engagements with the king were ended. When a little later John Berkeley arrived with the king's proposals for a personal treaty Ireton received him with coldness and disdain instead of his former cordiality, and in January urged parliament to settle the kingdom without the king. Yet he was still not prepared to abandon monarchy as such, and for a time supported a plan of deposing the king and putting the duke of York on the throne.

The second civil war and the remonstrance of the army In the second civil war Ireton served under Fairfax in the campaigns in Kent and Essex. After the victory at Maidstone he was sent to attack Canterbury, which capitulated at his approach (8 June 1648). He then rejoined Fairfax at the siege of Colchester, and was one of the commissioners who negotiated the terms of its surrender (27 August). Royalist writers blamed the execution of Sir Charles Lucas and Sir George Lisle on the diabolical influence of Ireton over the supposedly mild and compassionate Fairfax. But there is no need to accept this speculation. Throughout his career Fairfax never shrank from severity when he thought it was called for, and on this occasion he enjoyed the solid support of his council of war. Ireton shared in the decision to send the two royalist officers to their deaths, and defended its justice both in an argument with Lucas himself at the time and subsequently as a witness before the high court of justice. According to the code of war in that century, officers who continued to hold an untenable position, thereby causing unnecessary bloodshed, forfeited their claim to quarter. Lucas was doubly guilty because, having been taken prisoner at Marston Moor, he had broken his parole by again taking up arms against the enemy. Finally, Lucas himself had put captured soldiers to the sword in cold blood.

When, following the royalist collapse, parliament opted to renew negotiations with the twice-defeated king, powerful figures within the army were outraged. Colonel Ludlow tried to persuade Ireton that they should at once put a stop to the negotiations at Newport. But Ireton held back. Better, he told Ludlow, to wait and see what king and parliament agreed to before moving against them. Then, despairing at his failure to persuade Fairfax of the need for any political action, he drafted a long letter of resignation from the army. However, as the secretary at headquarters noted, his letter 'was not agreed unto' (Worcester College, Oxford, MS 114, Clarke papers, fol. 80). Ireton then turned his energies to changing Fairfax's mind. Whether he had a hand in generating the thirty army petitions that were laid at Fairfax's door over the next three months is hard to say, but much of their content is echoed in the draft remonstrance that he laid before the council of officers. Many officers besides Fairfax were uncertain about what to do next, and it required a monumental exertion on Ireton's part at the meeting of 15–16 November to persuade them of the necessity of moving against parliament. He had to deal also with the Levellers, who opposed any plan to purge or dissolve parliament and cut off the king's head before a new constitution was secured. He therefore met Lilburne at Windsor at the beginning of November. It was agreed that a committee of sixteen—comprising Levellers, army officers, London Independents, and the 'honest party' in parliament—should hammer out a new version of the *Agreement of the People*. Leveller influence also brought Ireton to alter his remonstrance to commend the Leveller large petition of 11 September and to embrace a new constitution based on *An Agreement of the People*. In the end all obstacles to agreement among the officers were removed by the king's rejection of their last overtures. Wrote Ireton to Colonel Hammond:

> It hath pleased God miraculously to dispose the hearts of your friends in the army, as one man (together with the concurrence of the godly from all parts), to interpose in this treaty, yet in such wise …, as, we believe, will not only refresh the bowels of the Saints, and all other faithful people of this kingdom; but be of satisfaction to every honest member of Parliament. (Birch, 87–8)

He implored Hammond, in the national interest, not to let the king escape, and laboured to convince him that he should obey the army rather than parliament.

A remonstrance of his excellency Thomas Lord Fairfax ... And of the generall councell of officers Ireton's intellectual masterpiece became the army's blueprint for its actions in the critical months of December and January 1648–9, as well

as furnishing the theoretical justification for the revolutionary *coup d'état*. It therefore merits close attention. Ireton first justifies the army's speaking out on political matters by an appeal to the principle of the public safety being the highest law (*salus populi suprema lex*). He then reminds parliament of its vote of no addresses of the previous January. He next argues that the judgement of heaven had been rendered against the royalists 'in defeating [them] with a small handful [Fairfax's army]' (*A Remonstrance*, 11). Instead of chasing the chimera of reconciliation with the king, parliament ought to be upholding the public interest by calling offenders to account, even if they had broken no existing law. Against fierce Leveller hostility to creating *ex post facto* offences, Ireton insists that there could be no shred of justification for a royal trial unless parliament, the supreme council of the kingdom, possesses the retroactive power to declare certain acts punishable. According to the *Remonstrance* the king's great crime consists in breaking his covenant to protect the people's rights and liberties. He has thereby absolved them from their obligation of obedience towards him. More pointedly, since the king has been defeated in his attempts to overthrow the public interest, but has resumed that struggle causing bloodshed and desolation, 'wee may justly say [he] is guilty of the highest treason against the highest law among men … and … guilty of all the innocent blood spilt thereby' (ibid., 23). The wrath of God could not be appeased unless judgment were executed against him. Trying to reunite king and parliament was like trying to join 'light with darknesse … good with evill' (ibid., 26).

There was an apparent obstacle to bringing the king to judgment: the solemn league and covenant under which the Scots had aided parliament in its war against Charles. It obligated its adherents to preserve the king's person and authority. Ireton's answer was that this obligation must yield to the higher duty to defend religion and the public interest. Besides, since the king was not a party to the covenant, he could not claim benefit from it.

The core demand of the *Remonstrance* is 'that that capitall and grand Author of our troubles, the person of the King … may be speedily brought to justice, for the treason, blood and mischiefe, he is therein guilty of' (*A Remonstrance*, 62). Rather than calling for the outright abolition of monarchy, however, it stipulates 'that no king be hereafter admitted, but upon the election of, and as upon trust from the People by … [the] Commons in Parliament' (ibid., 67). It ends with an endorsement of the Levellers' September petition, underlining the latter's call for parliament to dissolve itself, for equal distribution of seats according to population, and for annual or biennial elections. The franchise is to be denied for the time being to all who had opposed parliament. This whole programme is to be embodied in 'a generall contract or Agreement of the People', whose benefits will be denied to all who refused to subscribe to it (ibid., 67).

Pride's Purge and the regicide The reading of the *Remonstrance* to the House of Commons took four hours, but in the end they laid it aside. That action, and the decision to accept the king's answer to the Newport propositions as a basis for continued negotiation, sealed their doom. At Ireton's instigation the army invaded the capital and threw a guard around the houses of parliament. His first intention had been to force a straightforward dissolution of parliament. However, the radical MPs prevailed upon him to opt for the less tidy alternative of merely purging the Commons of the army's most notable enemies. A small committee of officers and MPs, of which Ireton was a member, drew up a list of eighty to ninety MPs to be arrested and excluded from the Commons. The purge, carried out on the morning of 6 December, left the army with a remnant of the Long Parliament moulded to its will. The Rump, as it would later be known, obeyed Ireton's exhortation to bring Charles to trial as the 'capitall and grand offender and author of our troubles' (*Heads of the Charge Against the King … by the Generall Councell of the Armie*, 24 Dec 1648, 5). It erected a revolutionary tribunal, the high court of justice, to which Ireton was named as one of the commissioners. During the climactic month of January 1649 he and a small knot of officers met day and night to thrash out the details of the trial and execution. He sat regularly in the high court of justice, and his signature is among the first on the warrant for the king's execution.

The officers' *Agreement of the People* While the drama of the scaffold was being played out Ireton was also busily involved in the scheme for the settlement of the kingdom which was presented to the Commons on 20 January 1649 as the *Agreement of the People*. In the committee of sixteen Lilburne and the other radicals had 'a long and tedious tug' with Ireton, who was 'very angry and lordly in his debates' on two questions: liberty of conscience and whether parliament had the right to punish where no law existed (Lilburne, 35). In the second week of December the committee's draft was submitted to the council of officers, who spent much of the next month debating and amending it. All the participants, among whom Ireton was pre-eminent, appeared to share the conviction that they were taking part in deliberations of the greatest political and historical importance. The agreement took for granted the abolition of monarchy and House of Lords. It provided for biennial parliaments, electoral redistribution according to population, and a male householder franchise. Central to it was the distinctive constitutional concept of powers reserved by the people to themselves. Most notably, parliament would be deprived of the power of compulsion in religion or for military service.

Ireton presented a trenchant argument against absolute religious liberty in the name of the magistrate's obligation to preserve peace and restrain sin. Animated by the vision of a godly commonwealth, he wanted nothing to do with the religious pluralism of the radicals. In the end he prevailed, and the revised version of the agreement specified that Christianity would be 'held forth and recommended as the publike profession in this nation', with a ministry supported out of the public treasury (Wolfe, 348). The reserve against conscription was also modified, conscription now being prohibited only for foreign service. Ireton also tried to delete the sixth reserve, which forbade punishment for any act not explicitly prohibited by law.

Worried that it might be used to block the trial of the king, he nevertheless lost out to the lower officers who insisted on its retention. Ireton and the other grandees were also overruled by the lower officers' insistence that the representative should have no power over moral questions. The revised version submitted to the House of Commons explicitly excluded 'things spirituall or evangelicall' from the representative's sovereign power (ibid., 347). This was a galling defeat for Ireton, but in spite of losing on two key points, he continued to support the agreement. He understood that only the agreement, which explicitly barred royalists and any others who opposed the new constitution, would be a sufficiently strong bulwark to prevent the return of monarchy.

A delegation of officers laid the agreement before the Commons on 20 January 1649. After listening to their presentation the Commons ordered the agreement to be printed, and promised to consider it as soon as 'the present weighty and urgent affairs will permit' (*JHC*, 6.122). They never did, and the officers never reminded them of their promise. According to Lilburne the whole debate in December and January was staged merely as a sop to the radicals; it was a tactic for distracting them 'like children with rattles' while the grandees got on with the more serious business of cutting off the king's head (Lilburne, 35). The officers' acquiescence in the spurning of the agreement may be explained in part by the general preoccupation with the king's trial. It is also true that no one was passionately attached to the agreement. The most insistent pressure for its adoption had come from the lower officers, but their telling victories over Ireton in the council of officers may have robbed him of his initial enthusiasm for it as the constitution for the new republic [see also Regicides].

The expedition to Ireland Although he was the chief theoretician of the revolutionary army, and the man closest to Cromwell, Ireton made many enemies, and was not a successful politician. With his lengthy speeches, heavy-handed rhetoric, and overbearing manner he wearied many. Lilburne grudgingly recognized him as 'the Stearman himself … the Armie's Alpha and Omega', but resented his authoritarianism—'an absolute King if not an Emperor, against whose will no man must dispute'—and denounced him as 'the cunningest of Machiavilians' (Lilburne, 31, 35). In parliament he was feared as being too radical and too powerful. While the MPs had recognized his importance by adding him to the chief executive body, the Derby House committee, on 6 January 1649, a month later they denied him a place on the new council of state.

Nevertheless, in the spring of 1649 Ireton was fully taken up with reorganizing the army and selecting units to go to Ireland. In June he was once more acknowledged as indispensable when appointed Cromwell's second-in-command for the expedition. Two days after Cromwell, on 15 August, he set sail from Milford Haven in command of about 4000 troops in 77 vessels. He disembarked at Dublin about the end of the month. After participating in the storming of Drogheda and Wexford he took the reins of leadership during Cromwell's illness in November. With

Michael Jones he jointly commanded an expedition that resulted in the capture of Inistioge and Carrick, and in February 1650 he took Ardfinnan Castle on the Suir. In March he helped to prepare the capture of Kilkenny. Parliament had already appointed him president of the province of Munster, and when Cromwell was recalled to England at the end of May he made Ireton his deputy. Parliament ratified the choice and appointed Ludlow and three other commissioners to assist Ireton in the conquest of Ireland. Ireton and his commissioners, all deeply committed puritans, must have been satisfied with their instructions, chief among which was 'the advancement of religion and propagacion of the gospel …, and … suppression of idolatry, popery, supersticion and prophanesse in that land' (BL, Egerton MS 1048, fol. 192). Ireton and the commissioners continued the policies of Cromwell and the Rump for the plantation of Ireland. To colonize the country with English settlers, both military and civilian, was viewed as the only way to extirpate Catholicism and eliminate the military threat to England. Accordingly Ireton ordered the inhabitants of Limerick and Waterford to leave those towns with their families and goods within three to six months, on the ground that their support of the 1641 rising, combined with their obstinate adherence to Roman Catholicism, made it impossible to trust them in places of such strategic importance. He forbade all officers and men under his command to marry Catholic Irishwomen unless they could satisfactorily establish the sincerity of their conversion to protestantism.

Ireton, who had bought no confiscated land in England, invested heavily in Ireland. Before his death he had accumulated 13,753 acres, almost all of it in co. Kilkenny, with the rest in co. Tipperary. No other regicide acquired as big a stake in Ireland.

Ireton was less implacably hostile to the Irish than Cromwell. For example, he promised to show favour to any who had abstained from the massacres of 1641, and to make special provision for the support of the helpless and aged. By 1651 he and the parliamentary commissioners wrote to the council of state proposing a less rigid approach to the Irish. Without some assurance for 'lives libertyes and estates', they argued, the soil would continue to be untilled, flocks untended, the war lengthened indefinitely, and the financial burden on England incalculable (Bodl. Oxf., MS Tanner 56, fol. 253). The council of state took no action on this statesmanlike proposal, so that Ireland descended deeper into the maelstrom of violence.

Limerick When in the spring of 1650 Ireton assumed the lord deputyship of Ireland, Connaught, much of Munster, and parts of Ulster were still untamed, and the bubonic plague raged throughout the country. He began by summoning Carlow on 2 July 1650, which surrendered on 24 July. Then, resolving to combat the pestilence with supernatural weapons, he proclaimed the first of eight fast days on 6 August. Waterford capitulated on that same day, and Duncannon on 17 August. In September he joined Sir Charles Coote at the siege of Athlone, but soon gave it up as a bad job, and rejoined Sir Hardress Waller at Limerick,

which was summoned on 6 October. Ten days later he concluded that it was too late in the year for a successful operation, and so withdrew to winter quarters. Yet a vigorous attack on Limerick would almost certainly have toppled it. Though a formidable stronghold, the garrison was almost out of ammunition, and was riven by bitter dissension.

The following spring Ireton took his army on a sweep through co. Clare, and won several victories against Clanricarde, which he attributed to his first having set aside a day to seek the Lord. He then turned his attention towards Limerick again. This time he was confident that his preparations would be effective. By the time he took up his position opposite the town there was already a flotilla of parliamentarian ships in the mouth of the Shannon. The ships blocked the estuary, kept the army supplied with provisions, and later brought up the heavy guns for siege operations.

On 14 June 1651 Ireton commenced several days of bombardment of the castle. He displayed his essential humanity and honour as a soldier by court martialling Colonel Robert Tuthill for putting men to the sword who had been promised quarter. On the third day of bombardment the defenders asked to treat, but the talks foundered on the issue of liberty to practise the Catholic religion. The siege dragged inconclusively on into the autumn. Parliament had sent Ireton an additional 9000 troops, but disease and cold wasted many of them. Had Cromwell been in charge of the siege it would have been over much sooner. He would have found a way to exploit the fact that two-thirds of the town wanted to sue for peace, that the defenders continued to be racked by plague, and that the people were starving. Ireton, however, lacked his father-in-law's military decisiveness. For almost four months he relied on starvation to win the victory for him. Not until 27 October did he succeed in identifying a sector of the town wall that lacked an earthen backing. Once he unleashed his battery against it, the masonry collapsed forthwith, and the defenders gave up. While the soldiers were allowed to march out of Limerick unarmed, Ireton and his council of war found themselves divided over the fate of the governor, Hugh Dubh O'Neill. Twice Ireton compelled the council to vote for O'Neill's death because he had deceived Cromwell at Clonmel. When Ludlow reminded him that the actions at Clonmel were not pertinent to the present question, Ireton's conscience bothered him and he referred the case once more, this time not obstructing his fellow officers when they pursued their inclination to save O'Neill's life. This episode points up Ireton's harshness and his loyalty to Cromwell, but also his ability to listen to his colleagues and his flexibility in changing his mind.

Death and funeral The siege of Limerick cost Ireton his life. At the beginning of November 1651 the weather had become inclement and he succumbed to a bad cold. Unwilling to relax his tempo of work, he rode through a storm to co. Clare. His cold turned to fever, but still he insisted on carrying on. His illness was probably not helped by the orthodox Galenic medical treatments he received—a series of purges and bloodlettings. He died outside Limerick on 26 November.

Parliament ordered a lavish funeral. Ireton's body was brought to Bristol and conveyed to London, where it lay in state at Somerset House until its interment on 6 February 1652 in Henry VII's chapel in Westminster Abbey. The funeral sermon, entitled 'The labouring saints dismission to rest', was delivered by John Owen, a leading Cromwellian chaplain. A magnificent monument bearing a fervid epitaph was also erected. Many puritans were offended by the pomp and extravagance of these ceremonies and memorials. Ireton's admirer Ludlow wrote:

> If he could have foreseen what was done by them [Ireton] would certainly have made it his desire that his body might have found a grave where his soul left it, so much did he despise those pompous and expensive vanities; having erected for himself a more glorious monument in the hearts of good men, by his affection to his country, his abilities of mind, his impartial justice, his diligence in the publick service, and his other vertues, which were a far greater honour to his memory, than a dormitory amongst the ashes of kings. (*Memoirs of Edmund Ludlow*, 1.295)

Although Ludlow was a biased observer he was right about Ireton's austerity and self-denial. Compared to other leading revolutionaries, he did not grow rich during the interregnum. His military pay came through on a fairly regular basis, but when the Rump Parliament voted him, on top of his £3 a day as major-general, land worth £2000 a year, he turned it down, saying

> they had many just debts, which he desired they would pay before they made any such presents; that he had no need of their land, and therefore would not have it; and that he should be more contented to see them doing the service of the nation, than so liberal in disposing of the publick treasure. (*Memoirs of Edmund Ludlow*, 1.286)

Coming from a man who had no inherited estate, this was impressive. After his death, however, parliament renewed the grant, this time for the benefit of his widow, Bridget, and their children. Bridget, who married General Charles Fleetwood in 1652, died in 1662.

Soon after the Restoration the extravagant memorials to Ireton were laid to dust. The Commons ordered his corpse—along with those of Cromwell, Bradshaw, and Pride—to be disinterred, drawn on a hurdle to Tyburn, hanged up in its coffin for several days, and then buried under the gallows. The sentence was carried out at the end of January 1661, and his monument was also demolished.

Character, religion, and achievement During his lifetime Ireton aroused strong feelings among all those with whom he had dealings. To the royalists he was an arch villain. The newswriter of the *Man in the Moon* described him as 'a tall black thief, with bushy curl'd hair, a meagre envious face, sunk hollow eyes, a complection between choler and melancholly, a four-square Machiavillian head; and a nose of the fifteens' (1–8 Aug 1649, 135). Clarendon called him a man

> of a melancholic, reserved, dark nature, who communicated his thoughts to very few, so that for the most part he resolved alone, but was never diverted from any resolution he had taken, and he was thought often by his obstinacy to prevail over Cromwell, and to extort his concurrence

contrary to his own inclinations. But that proceeded only from his dissembling less; for he was never reserved in the owning and communicating his worst and most barbarous purposes, which the other always concealed and disavowed. (Clarendon, *Hist. rebellion*, 5.264)

At the other end of the political spectrum the Levellers detested him more than anyone except Cromwell. Lilburne, Sexby, and Wildman condemned him for bargaining with the king in 1647, as well as for double-crossing them over the *Agreement of the People*. He earned the wrath of the Leveller authors of *The hunting of the foxes from New-Market and Triploe-Heaths to White Hall, by five small beagles (late of the armie)* (1649) because he had 'destroied the Engagement and broke the faith of the Army' (p. 5). Few of them noticed that he took no part in their suppression in the late winter and spring of 1649.

Among republicans and fellow officers, on the other hand, Ireton commanded enormous respect and affection. Lucy Hutchinson, whose husband, Colonel John Hutchinson, was Ireton's cousin, had acerbic things to say about most actors in her husband's life. But Ireton won her approval as one who had been educated 'in the strictest way of godliness', and was 'a very grave, serious, religious person'. Being 'a man of good learning, great understanding, and other abilities, he was the chief promoter of the parliament's interest in the county [of Nottinghamshire]' (Hutchinson, 53). At his death John Hewson eulogized his selflessness:

> Wee that knew him can and must say truly, wee know no man like minded; most seeking their own things, few so singly minde the things of Jesus Christ, of publique concernment, of the interest of the precious sons of Zion. (*Severall Proceedings in Parliament*, 4–11 Dec 1651, 1780)

John Cooke, the chief-justice of Munster, in his preface to his *Monarchy No Creature of God's Making* (1652) dwelt on his industry, self-denial, love of justice, godliness, and extraordinary learning. He worked indefatigably, 'seldome thinking it time to eat till he had done the worke of the day at nine or ten at night, and then will sit up as long as any man had busines with him'. Ludlow also commended his industry, his frugality with the state's resources, and his complete lack of vanity.

> ... [H]e was so diligent in the public service, and so careless of every thing that belonged to himself, that he never regarded what clothes or food he used, what hour he went to rest, or what horse he mounted. (*Memoirs of Edmund Ludlow*, 1.278–9)

Bulstrode Whitelocke, the eminent lawyer, praised Ireton as

> a person very active, industrious, and stiff in his ways and purposes; he was of good abilities for counsel as well as action; and made much use of his pen; and was very forward to reform the proceedings in law.

Whitelocke went on to write that no one had more influence over Cromwell, and that '[h]is death struck a great sadness into Cromwell; and indeed it was a great loss to him of so able and active, so faithful and so near a relation and officer under him' (Whitelocke, 3.371).

As many of his contemporaries recognized, religion was the mainspring of Ireton's thought and action. An austere puritan, he was confident of God's providential favour, both in the political arena and on the battlefield. Disdainful of 'the frivolous impertinencies of a souldiers honour'—the phrase he used with General Preston when he summoned him to surrender Galway on 7 November 1651 (*Mercurius Politicus*, 5–12 Feb 1652, 1401)—he enjoyed a hard-won reputation as the 'best prayer-maker and preacher in the army' (Wood, *Ath. Oxon.*, 3.299). His combination of humility and other-worldliness compelled the respect of those closest to him. In Ireland he resorted frequently to days of prayer and fasting to advance his military campaign. Success he interpreted as God's 'answer to the weak, worthless and (almost) faithless prayers of his poor servants' (Bodl. Oxf., MS Clarendon 42, fol. 208). On one of his rare days of public thanksgiving (13 June 1651) he stipulated that

> [w]e are to stir up one another and humbly seek to God that … we may … not be lifted up in any conceit of ourselves, above our enemies, … and [we are] in trembling and fear before him, to declare, abominate, and oppose those evil practices amongst us that are so unworthy of him.
> (ibid., fol. 210)

One of the evil practices that upset him was Colonel Tuthill's killing of soldiers who had surrendered on the promise of quarter. 'Most justly the Lord hath rebuked us' was his interpretation of their repeated failure to capture Limerick. Yet that experience 'hath had some effects of humbling, melting and teaching many hearts amongst us' (*Severall Proceedings*, 31 July – 7 Aug 1651, 1490). Ireton rarely gave vent to the triumphalism so frequently found in Cromwell's writings. He co-signed a letter to his father-in-law during the Scottish campaign pleading 'that our conversation may tell the world we are not of itt, but are strangers and pilgrims here' (J. Nickolls, ed., *Originall Letters and Papers of State*, 1743, 74). But this other-worldliness was accompanied by a very this-worldly interpretation of God's purposes for mankind. God was 'a righteous Judge, pleading the quarrell of the innocent, and a severe revenger of their blood against those that spill it' (*Mercurius Politicus*, 5–12 Feb 1652, 1401).

Ireton's religious faith gave him the iron will, determination, and selflessness that are the mark of the great revolutionary. A man of indifferent military talent, he was nevertheless courageous on the battlefield. His genius lay in his ability to articulate with his pen a coherent vision of godly republicanism. Through his voluminous writings and political realism in action he forged a unity of purpose in the New Model Army between 1647 and 1649. To Ireton as much as any individual belongs the credit for calling monarchy to account and erecting the English republic on its ruins.   IAN J. GENTLES

Sources *The Clarke papers*, ed. C. H. Firth, 1–2, CS, new ser., 49, 54 (1891–4) · *A declaration of the engagements, remonstrances, representations, proposals, desires, and resolutions from his excellency Sir Tho. Fairfax and the generall councel of the army* (1647) [also known as the *Army book of declarations*; Thomason tract E 409(25)] · R. Ramsey, *Henry Ireton* (1949) · I. Gentles, *The New Model Army in England, Ireland, and Scotland, 1645–1653* (1992) · *A remonstrance of his excellency Thomas Lord Fairfax, lord generall of the parliaments forces. And of the generall councell of officers* (1648) · *The memoirs of Edmund Ludlow*, ed. C. H. Firth, 2 vols. (1894) · L. Hutchinson, *Memoirs of the life of Colonel Hutchinson*, ed. J. Sutherland (1973) · B. Whitelocke, *Memorials of English affairs*, new edn, 4 vols. (1853) · D. M. Wolfe, ed., *Leveller manifestoes of the puritan revolution* (1944) · J. Rushworth, *Historical collections*, new edn, 6–7 (1721–2) · H. Cary, ed., *Memorials of the great civil war in England from 1646 to 1652*, 1 (1842) · C. Walker, *The compleat history of Independency* (1661) · D. Underdown, *Pride's Purge: politics in the puritan revolution* (1971) · [E. Borlase], *The history of the execrable Irish rebellion*, new edn (1743), appx, 32–46 [incl. letters between Ireton and James Preston] · *CSP dom.*, 1643–51 · JHC, 6 (1648–51), 122 · JHL, 7–9 (1644–9) · J. Bruce and D. Masson, eds., *The quarrel between the earl of Manchester and Oliver Cromwell*, CS, new ser., 12 (1875) · R. Huntington, ed., *Sundry reasons inducing Major Robert Huntingdon to lay down his commission* (1648); repr. F. Maseres, ed., *Select tracts relating to the civil wars in England*, 2 (1815) · T. Birch, *Letters between Col. Robert Hammond, governor of the Isle of Wight and the committee of Lords and Commons at Derby House, General Fairfax, Lieut. General Cromwell, Commissary General Ireton, &c.* (1764), 19, 79, 87, 95 · Wood, *Ath. Oxon.*, new edn · BL, Egerton MS 1048, fol. 192 · Bodl. Oxf., MS Tanner 56, fol. 253 · Bodl. Oxf., MS Clarendon 42, fols. 208, 210 · K. S. Bottigheimer, *English money and Irish land* (1971) · *The trials of Charles the First, and some of the regicides: with biographies of Bradshaw, Ireton, Harrison, and others* (1832) · G. Vertue, *Medals, coins, greatseals, impressions from the elaborate works of Thomas Simon* (1753) · Clarendon, *Hist. rebellion* · J. Lilburne, *The legall fundamentall liberties of the people of England* (1649) [Thomason tract E 560(14)]; 2nd edn (1649) [E 567(1)] · A. Fletcher, *The outbreak of the English civil war* (1981) · J. L. Dean, 'Henry Ireton, the Mosaic law, and morality in English civil politics from April 1646 to May 1649', MPhil diss., U. Cam., 1990 · parish register, Attenborough, 1560–1643, Notts. Arch.

Archives Bodl. Oxf., letters | Worcester College, Oxford, contributions to Reading, Whitehall, and Putney debates

Likenesses S. Cooper, miniature, watercolour, 1649, FM Cam. · attrib. R. Walker, oils, c.1650 (after S. Cooper and A. Van Dyck), NPG; version, Petworth House, Sussex [*see illus.*] · attrib. R. Walker, oils, second version (after S. Cooper and A. Van Dyck), Petworth House, Sussex · engraving, Hunt. L. · medal, repro. in E. Hawkins, *Medallic illustrations of the history of Great Britain and Ireland to the death of George II*, ed. A. W. Franks and H. A. Gruber, 2 vols. (1885), vol. 1, p. 387 · oils (after R. Walker), Audley End House, Essex

Wealth at death over £6000—manors of Minshall (Mynshall) and Minshall Vernon, Cheshire; also lands in Kilkenny and Tipperary, Ireland: C. W. Russell and J. P. Prendergast, eds., *The Carte manuscripts in the Bodleian Library, Oxford* (1871), 174–5

Ireton, John [created Sir John Ireton under the protectorate] (1615–1690), mercer and mayor of London, was born at Attenborough, Nottinghamshire, and baptized there on 17 October 1615, the son of German Ireton (d. 1624) and his wife, Jane. Recent arrivals from Derbyshire, Ireton's parents were among the lesser gentry of Nottinghamshire, and his father was the lay appropriator of the Attenborough rectory. The Iretons were puritans: in 1609 Jane Ireton was presented to the archdeacon's court for refusing to be churched after a pregnancy, and German Ireton was subsequently cited for his refusal to kneel at communion. John and his elder brother Henry *Ireton (bap. 1611, d. 1651), the Cromwellian general and regicide, were childhood acquaintances of their neighbour and kinsman, Colonel John Hutchinson. Like his brother, John probably received 'an education in the strictest way of godlinesse' but, unlike Henry, John was destined for trade (Hutchinson, 94). He was apprenticed in 1634 to John Trussell of London. In 1641, he became a freeman of the corporation of London and a member of the Clothworkers' Company.

The civil war and early interregnum were years of capital acquisition for Ireton, who began his career as a mercer. He lived on Paternoster Row, near St Paul's Cathedral, with his wife, a daughter of Thomas Squire of the parish of St Bartholomew-the-Less, from whom he received a significant legacy. By 1646 he was acting as a receiver for the compositions of royalist delinquents in Nottinghamshire, where he eventually acquired land of his own. He became involved with sequestrations in several counties, and his political enemies claimed that he made a fortune off mortgages he provided to compounding royalists. He gained possession of the sequestered Highgate house and lands of the duke of Lauderdale, for instance, and he also speculated in recusant properties. In time he became a governor and treasurer of the Highgate grammar school, and was also involved in converting a former episcopal property in London into a prison. In 1648 he was made a parliamentary commissioner for the collection of arrears in the monthly assessment for the ward of Castle Baynard.

Ireton was among the members of the church gathered by George Cokayn, London Independent, who also included such prominent men as Bulstrode Whitelocke and Alderman Robert Tichborne. His political rise was assisted by the marriage of his brother to Oliver Cromwell's daughter, but he was entirely overshadowed by Henry Ireton until the latter's untimely death in 1651. In that year John Ireton was elected alderman for Bread Street. He served as sheriff of London and Middlesex for 1651–2 and as the master of the Clothworkers' Company in 1652. In the city he favoured shifting more authority from the lord mayor and aldermen towards common council and the freemen and declined many of the customary financial perquisites of civic office himself.

After Cromwell's dissolution of the Rump Parliament Ireton headed a sympathetic city delegation which conferred with army officers in May 1653. He became an exceptionally active London member of the nominated assembly (Barebone's Parliament), serving on several important committees and frequently acting as a teller. He showed particular hostility to the court of chancery and to lay patronage in the church, and he demonstrated his grasp of financial matters.

Ireton's family ties to Cromwell kept him heavily involved in the affairs of the protectorate, but they separated him from aldermanic colleagues who preferred a return to conventional parliamentary government. As a leading civic supporter of the protectorial regime he served on the London commission of the peace and on the London militia commission. From 1656 he served on the committee for trade, on the excise commission, and on a commission to secure the lord protector against treasonable actions. He was also acting as a government financier by 1657, when he lent £2500 for payment of wages to the fleet and was appointed to the assessments commissions for London, Middlesex, and Suffolk. He was knighted by Cromwell in 1658.

Lord mayor of London from October 1658 to October 1659, Ireton was caught up in the tumultuous political events that followed the death of Cromwell. He was unhappy with the election of presbyterian city MPs to Richard Cromwell's parliament, but he remained loyal to the protectorate until the army replaced it with the restored Rump. He then became a principal civic spokesman for republicanism and for the sectarian associates of the army. He was, for instance, among the intended members of a republican constitutional committee proposed by the circle of Commonwealthsmen around James Harrington. The Rump appointed Ireton to its London militia commission, named him colonel of a regiment of horse raised by that body, and retained him on the excise commission. He also served as colonel for one regiment of the trained bands in 1658–9 and as vice-president of London's Honourable Artillery Company in 1658–60. During the royalist insurrection of August 1659 he acted to prevent a rumoured rising of the London apprentices. By refusing to summon common council at that time he also blocked the efforts of civic presbyterians to petition for a free parliament or for the return of the MPs secluded by the army in 1648.

Ireton was rewarded by the Rump with a resolution that he should continue as lord mayor for a second year, but this mandate was defied in common council, which vigorously defended the city's right to choose its own chief magistrate. As a civic reaction against the Rump began to gather momentum, he would be accused of attempting '*to break the City Charter*' (*Apology*, 7). Indeed, he was so closely identified with the Rump as to become 'universally detested' in London (*CSP Venice, 1659–61*, 71). When the army expelled the Rump in October 1659, he was named to the new governing committee of safety. As alderman, he was outspoken in rebuffing overtures to the city from George Monck, commander of the Commonwealth's forces in Scotland. He was pointedly excluded from a civic committee of safety created in December 1659 by London leaders who preferred a free parliament to the rule of the army.

The council of state that governed after the dissolution of the recalled Long Parliament sent Ireton to the Tower in April 1660, at the time of John Lambert's republican rising. Freed upon his promise 'to live peaceably under the present government', he retired to Mortlake, Surrey, where he had maintained another residence (*CSP dom., 1659–60*, 575). He was one of several persons incapacitated by the Convention Parliament from holding further office. He was again sent to the Tower in November 1661 on suspicion of plotting against the Restoration regime with James Harrington, John Wildman, Praisegod Barebone, and other Commonwealthsmen. When his health deteriorated, he and Wildman were transferred to Scilly.

Ireton was eventually released and joined a circle of nonconformists in East Sheen, Surrey, who were ministered to by Revd Thomas Brooks, the ejected Independent divine. In 1665 he was forced by a king's bench judgment to surrender jewels and plate that had once belonged to Charles I, and he was also returned briefly to the Tower on suspicion of 'dangerous and seditious' practices (*CSP dom.*,

1664–5, 508). In 1668 Bulstrode Whitelocke provided testimony for a suit that Ireton had before the court of chancery. In 1670, Ireton contributed £200 to a loan by London dissenters to Charles II that was intended to wean the king away from enforcement of the recently adopted Conventicle Act. By 1677 he had relocated to Finsbury, Middlesex, near the London parish of St Giles Cripplegate. His nephew Henry, the son of his brother, was involved in the petitioning of London whigs in 1680 and was also a whig conspirator in 1683–5.

After the death of his first wife Ireton married, in 1658, Elizabeth, widow of Edmund Sleigh, who had been his colleague on the court of aldermen. She died in 1686, leaving money to the Independent divine George Griffiths, of whose church she and Ireton may have become members. Ireton himself survived to see the revolution of 1688 before dying in London, intestate, in March 1690. He was buried on 16 March at St Bartholomew-the-Less near three of his children.   GARY S. DE KREY

Sources A. Woolrych, *Commonwealth to protectorate* (1982), 124–7, 169, 172, 176, 201, 217–18, 303, 307n. · 318, 363, 386, 420–21 · R. W. Ramsey, *Henry Ireton* (1949), 1, 4, 47, 159, 199, 206 · A. Woolrych, 'Ireton, John', Greaves & Zaller, *BDBR*, 2.134–5 · *CSP dom.*, 1652–3, 337; 1654, 209–10, 241, 263; 1655, 43; 1655–6, 100, 189, 238; 1656–7, 41–2, 58; 1658–9, 17; 1659–60, 10, 32, 90–91, 93, 290, 574–5; 1661–2, 266, 460; 1664–5, 144, 447, 508; 1665–6, 448; 1683–4, 335 · Bodl. Oxf., MSS Clarendon 60, fols. 74, 465, 564; 63, fol. 243; 64, fols. 91, 95, 101–2; 65, fols. 31, 51 · *CSP Venice*, 1659–61, 54, 57, 70–72, 74 · R. Hutton, *The Restoration: a political and religious history of England and Wales, 1658–1667* (1985), 47, 49, 58, 60, 78, 88, 133 · *The apology of Robert Tichborn and John Ireton* (1660) · J. R. Woodhead, *The rulers of London, 1660–1689* (1965), 96 · A. B. Beaven, ed., *The aldermen of the City of London, temp. Henry III–[1912]*, 1 (1908), 50, 277, 349; 2 (1913), lvi, 78, 81 · J. Farnell, 'The politics of the City of London, 1649–1657', PhD diss., University of Chicago, 1963, 159–60, 163, 167, 212–13, 217–18, 267, 306, 404, 408 · C. H. Firth and R. S. Rait, eds., *Acts and ordinances of the interregnum, 1642–1660*, 1 (1911), 1129; 2 (1911), 619, 1039, 1073, 1081, 1293, 1349 · M. A. E. Green, ed., *Calendar of the proceedings of the committee for compounding … 1643–1660*, 1, PRO (1889), 43, 795; 2 (1890), 1072, 1439, 1532; 4 (1892), 2810, 3151, 3158 · M. A. E. Green, ed., *Calendar of the proceedings of the committee for advance of money, 1642–1656*, 1, PRO (1888), 509; 2 (1888), 949–51, 1008; 3 (1888), 1440 · *The diurnal of Thomas Rugge, 1659–1661*, ed. W. L. Sachse, CS, 3rd ser., 91 (1961), 16, 17, 54–5, 76 · P. Norman, *Cromwell House, Highgate*, London Survey Committee Monographs, 12 (1926), 17–19, 25, 27 · will of Elizabeth Ireton, PRO, PROB 11/384, sig. 96 · CLRO, MS 40/30 · *The diary of Bulstrode Whitelocke, 1605–1675*, ed. R. Spalding, British Academy, Records of Social and Economic History, new ser., 13 (1990), 530, 537, 548, 605, 732–3, 750 · Tai Liu, *Puritan London: a study of religion and society in the City parishes* (1986), 49, 203, 226 · L. Hutchinson, *Memoirs of the life of Colonel Hutchinson*, ed. J. Sutherland (1973), 62, 94, 319 · *JHC*, 4 (1644–6), 635

Wealth at death see Woodhead, *The rulers of London*, 96; Ramsey, *Henry Ireton*, 206

Ireton, Ralph. *See* Irton, Ralph of (d. 1292).

Irland, John. *See* Ireland, John (c.1440–1495).

Irland, Robert. *See* Ireland, Robert (d. 1561).

Irons, Evelyn Graham (1900–2000), journalist, was born on 17 June 1900 at 136 Hyndland Road, Kelvinside, Glasgow, the daughter of Joseph Jones Irons, stockbroker, and his wife, Edith Mary Latta. Her middle-class family possibly had connections with the Grahams of Montrose, and

she was descended from Henry Bell, developer of steam navigation. She was educated at St Bride's School, Helensburgh, and at Somerville College, Oxford (1918–21), where she was awarded a second-class degree in English and was a skilled canoeist.

Evelyn Irons had an early ambition to be a writer and moved to London to work in a bookshop. In 1927 she became the *Daily Mail*'s fashion correspondent for the women's page despite her characteristic rejection of cosmetics. She was a handsome and well-dressed woman with an open face and swept-back short hair. She became editor of the feature page by 1931 and was living in Chelsea with Olive Rinder when she interviewed Radclyffe Hall for an article entitled 'How other women run their homes'. She and Olive became part of Hall's circle, Hall and her partner, Una Troubridge, admiring the 'marriage' between Evelyn and Olive. In 1931 Irons was made editor of the women's page, and in March of that year interviewed Victoria Mary (Vita) Sackville-*West (1892–1962). She fell 'desperately in love' with Vita, who returned her feelings. The love poems in her *Collected Poems* that Sackville-West wrote in 1931 are addressed to Evelyn Irons, to whom she dedicated the entire collection. Olive Rinder, who 'actively encouraged' (Glendinning, 240) Irons's relationship with Sackville-West, was herself in love with Vita. The three entered into an uneasy ménage that culminated in a disastrous holiday in Cornwall, after which Irons put an end to both relationships. Vita had been extravagant both emotionally and materially, and once gave Evelyn a suitcase full of men's pyjamas, but she could be possessive and jealous. Though Vita was stung by Evelyn's desertion and sent her a poem, 'Valediction', they remained in touch until Vita's death. Olive moved into a cottage near Sissinghurst. On 14 July 1931 Evelyn Irons met Joy McSweeney (d. 1978) at a party, and spent the rest of her life with her. Four years later she saved McSweeney from drowning, for which she received the rare distinction of the Stanhope gold medal from the Royal Humane Society.

In 1935 Irons joined the *Evening Standard*, where she edited the women's pages until the outbreak of the Second World War. She worked for the air raid patrol and the London fire service, and transferred herself to the news desk on the *Evening Standard*, announcing to the unsuspecting chief news editor that she was now working for him. She managed to secure herself an assignment with a division of the free French forces under General Jean de Lattre de Tassigny, with whom she formed a close professional relationship throughout the war. With the Première Armée Française, Irons entered Germany with Charles de Gaulle early in 1945 as the only accredited British correspondent. She was the first woman to be awarded the croix de guerre, for her part in the French seizure of a Bavarian village. As she recalled it, she 'somehow had got ahead of the advance, and four of us in a jeep came to this village and found no allied troops had arrived. So we took it ourselves' (interview, in Knightley, 346). She was also probably the first female correspondent to reach Eagle's Nest—Hitler's summer retreat at Berchtesgaden—in

1945; she reported triumphantly that she had sampled Hitler's 'excellent Rhine wine'. She also secured an interview with Rudolf Hess's wife, Ilse, in a French prison.

After the war Irons continued at the news desk. In 1952 Lord Beaverbrook sent her to the United States to report on Eisenhower's presidential campaign. Having known very little about the subject she became so attuned to American politics that she was asked to stay on. She based herself in New York, settling in Brewster, and reported on a number of significant events. In 1954 she discovered the whereabouts of Edward Montagu, Michael Pitt-Rivers, and the marquess of Milford Haven after they had fled from Britain following an infamous homosexual trial. She was holidaying in Hungary with Joy McSweeney in 1956 when the revolution began, and had to cut short a house party to attend the wedding of Marilyn Monroe and Arthur Miller. She was one of the few reporters to break the United States news embargo on the Guatemalan revolution of 1957. Leaving many of her male colleagues languishing in a bar in Tegucigalpa, Honduras, she used rudimentary Spanish to hire a donkey and a guide to transport her through guerrilla-occupied jungle to the Guatemalan border. Her only worry was what Beaverbrook would say when she claimed expenses for the donkey.

From 1959 Evelyn Irons worked for the London *Sunday Times*, and stayed with the paper until she retired. Having enjoyed tending the grounds of Sissinghurst with Vita Sackville-West, she was a keen gardener, cultivating English roses in her wild riverside home in Brewster. She also had a holiday home in Skiathos. After Joy McSweeney's death in 1978 she learned to drive. Having been in good health until her late nineties, she died in Brewster on 3 April 2000, two months before her 100th birthday.

CLARE L. TAYLOR

Sources V. Glendinning, *Vita: the life of Victoria Sackville-West* (1983) · www.sbu.ac.uk/-stafflaglevelyvnirons.html, June 2002 · *The Independent* (25 April 2000) · b. cert. · www.goodbyemag.com/maroo/irons.html, Aug 2001 · *Oxford University Calendar* (1923) · A. Sebba, *Battling for news: the rise of the woman reporter* (1994) · P. Knightley, *The first casualty: the war correspondent as hero and mythmaker from the Crimea to Kosovo* (2000)

Irons, Joseph (1785–1852). *See under* Irons, William Josiah (1812–1883).

Irons, William Josiah (1812–1883), Church of England clergyman and theological writer, born at Hoddesdon, Hertfordshire, on 12 September 1812, was the second son of the Revd **Joseph Irons** (1785–1852) and his first wife, Mary Ann, daughter of William Broderick; she died in 1828. Joseph Irons was a popular evangelical preacher, born at Ware, Hertfordshire, on 5 November 1785, who began preaching in March 1808 under the auspices of the London Itinerant Society, and was ordained an Independent minister on 21 May 1814. He was stationed at Hoddesdon from 1812 to 1815, and at Sawston, near Cambridge, from 1815 to 1818; he was minister of Grove Chapel, Camberwell, Surrey, from 1818 until his death at Camberwell on 3 April 1852.

William Josiah Irons, after being educated at home, matriculated from Queen's College, Oxford, on 12 May

1829, and graduated BA in 1833, MA in 1835, BD in 1842, and DD in 1854. He was curate of St Mary, Newington Butts, Surrey, from 1835 until 1837, when he was presented to the living of St Peter's, Walworth, co. Durham. He became vicar of Barkway in Hertfordshire in 1838, vicar of Brompton, Middlesex, on 17 September 1840, prebendary of St Paul's Cathedral in December 1860, rector of Wadingham, Lincolnshire, on 6 April 1870, and on 7 June 1872 rector of St Mary Woolnoth with St Mary Woolchurch in the City of London, on the presentation of W. E. Gladstone. In 1870 he was Bampton lecturer at Oxford, and his published lectures, *Christianity as Taught by St Paul*, reached a second edition in 1876. Irons married first, in 1839, Ann, eldest daughter of John Melhuish of Upper Tooting, who died on 14 July 1853; and second, on 28 December 1854, Sarah Albinia Louisa, youngest daughter of Sir Lancelot *Shadwell; she died on 15 December 1887.

Irons's chief work was the *Analysis of Human Responsibility* (1869), written at the request of the founders of the Victoria Institute. There Irons lectured on Darwin's *Origin of Species*, Tyndall's *Fragments of Science*, Mill's *Essay on Theism*, and the *Unseen Universe*. He was an advocate of free and compulsory education, and suggested complete reform of the poor law. He was one of the most effective critics of *Essays and Reviews* (1860), writing 'The idea of a national church' in *Replies to 'Essays and Reviews'* (1862) and organizing a large deputation and petition in 1864. He was a dogged establishmentarian, and zealously defended it in a series of works, of which the earliest was a pamphlet called *The Present Crisis*, published in 1850, and the last a series of letters entitled *The Charge of Erastianism*. In 1855 a pamphlet, signed A. E., questioned 'Is the vicar of Brompton [Irons] a Tractarian?' He was one of the editors of the *Literary Churchman*, and wrote its leading articles from May 1855 to December 1861. He translated the 'Dies irae' of Thomas de Celano in the well-known hymn, 'Day of wrath! O day of mourning!'

Irons published many other works of a high-church character, including *Notes of the Church* (1845; third edn, 1846), *The Theory of Development Examined* (1846), and *Fifty-Two Propositions: a Letter to the Rev. Dr Hampden* (1848). In later life he published several works on Jesus Christ, *Psalms and Hymns for the Church* (1875), and collections of sermons. He died at his home, 20 Gordon Square, London, on 18 June 1883. G. C. BOASE, rev. H. C. G. MATTHEW

Sources *The Times* (20 June 1883) · *The Times* (21 June 1883) · *Guide to the church congress* (1883) · Foster, *Alum. Oxon.* · G. Bayfield, *A memoir of the Rev. Joseph Irons* (1852) · I. Ellis, *Seven against Christ: a study of 'Essays and reviews'* (1980) · G. Faber, *Oxford apostles* (1933)
Archives BL, letters to W. E. Gladstone, Add. MSS 44387–44785, *passim* · BL, corresp. with J. E. Hodgkin and others relating to Simonides, Add. MS 42502A, *passim* · LPL, corresp. with A. C. Tait
Wealth at death £2402 7s. 6d.: probate, 17 July 1883, *CGPLA Eng. & Wales*

Ironside, (William) Edmund, first Baron Ironside (1880–1959), army officer and farmer, was born on 6 May 1880 at Joks Lodge House, South Leith, Edinburgh, the second child and only son of William Ironside (1835–1881) of Athling, surgeon-major in the Indian army, and his wife,

(William) Edmund Ironside, first Baron Ironside (1880–1959), by Walter Stoneman, 1920

Emma Maria (1844–1939), daughter of William H. Richards of Stapleton House, Martock, Somerset. Intensely proud of his name and ancestors, whom he traced to John Ironside (b. 1636) at Rothie in the parish of Fyvie, Aberdeenshire (and proud of being a man of Buchan), Ironside was raised, he said, in the hard, simple ideas of a Scot by his widowed mother, attributing everything to her strength and intelligence. He was encouraged to learn languages, and famously succeeded, being credited with a working knowledge of anything from a dozen to eighteen.

An indifferent student in the town of St Andrews (at St Leonard's Kindergarten, St Salvator's School, and St Andrew's School), and at Tonbridge School (he later regretted missing a Scots secondary education), Ironside left Tonbridge for a crammer in 1896, and in January 1898 entered the Royal Military Academy, Woolwich, where he worked hard, boxed, and captained the second rugby fifteen. Something of a bruiser, as he said, at 6 feet 4 inches and 240 pounds, he acquired the nickname 'Tiny', by which he was known to friends, comrades, eminent supporters, and others ever after.

Career, character, and characteristics Ironside's soldiering—a mix of imperial adventure, wartime field command, routine peacetime posting, and high command in war—took him from the Cape to the Arctic, from the Atlantic to the Indian Ocean, to Europe east and west, and Whitehall. Meteoric in the First World War and its immediate aftermath (he was appointed CMG in 1918, became a KCB in August 1919, and GCB in June 1938), his career

slowed between the wars before unexpectedly taking him to the position of chief of the Imperial General Staff (CIGS) (4 September 1939–27 May 1940), then commander-in-chief, home forces (27 May–20 July 1940) at the outset of the Second World War.

Healthy, solidly built, handsome into old age, keenly observant, and with something like a photographic memory, he was warm, sensitive, impetuous, mercurial, and blunt. He had virtually no appreciation of music or poetry, little of theatre, none of dance, but wrote easily, indefatigably, better than he believed. Photography, architecture, and practical handicrafts delighted him. No stranger to the vulgar racial, cultural, and gender prejudices of his class, nation, and time, he made harsh judgements even of friends and often shattering criticism of others—especially air marshals, time-serving soldiers, politicians, pacifist university dons, diplomats, shipboard companions, nearly all women in what he considered the male domain, and most foreigners. Certain of British superiority, he professed special dislike of the Irish, Jews, Latins, and 'lesser races', that is, most of mankind. Readily excepting individuals, he acknowledged his prejudices: the fate of European Jewry appalled him. A good mixer, without side, as he remarked of others, he saw himself with some reason (although judging his military record superior to that of any contemporary) as a simple and humble person.

Ironside was as happy working under his car with his servant Kosti, or in the fields with a hired man, as hunting tigers with the nawab of Bhopal, golfing, fishing, shooting, or riding to hounds. Without inheritance, harassed by accounts and overdrafts, and obsessively worried about providing for wife and children—he married Mariot Ysobel Cheyne (d. 1984) on 26 June 1915, and had a daughter (b. 1917) and a son (b. 1924)—he lived comfortably, even in so-called hand-to-mouth periods. Accustomed to establishing an immediate ascendancy by name, personality, and reputation, and capable of both severity and great kindness, he knew he was not easy to live with, but was perpetually surprised to discover some considered him difficult—that he had enemies. A brilliant, high-spirited companion and amusing raconteur, a public speaker of charm, force, and wit, he was compulsively introspective. For all his worldly experience he avowed a lack of intimates, a need for solitude, an inability to open his soul to anyone. The love and loyalty of his dogs he held sacred: the accidental death at Gibraltar of his bull-terrier, Caesar, caused him grief beyond anything felt from almost any other loss.

Young Ironside prided himself on being a swashbuckler, a trainer, and leader of men, an almost self-educated soldier, a thinker in an institution inclined to intellectual decay. Sure of his destiny, he interpreted fate's (or the War Office's) decrees as inscrutable opportunities. Although tempted to nudge destiny by appeal to the political great whom he knew (against an obdurate army council or a CIGS deemed hostile), he mostly let matters take their course. His patrons included Sir John Asser, Sir Henry Wilson, Lord Byng, Lord Haldane, Lord Rawlinson, Sir Lyndon

Bell, Lord Chetwode, Sir Cyril Deverell, and not least, Winston Churchill, whom he judged ruthless, prodigiously energetic, imaginative, meddlesome, and infuriating, the greatest man he had ever known.

The South African and First World wars Commissioned second lieutenant, Royal Horse and Royal Field Artillery, on 28 June 1899, Ironside first savoured the joy of commanding men, was three times lightly wounded, and met Churchill, in the Second South African War. Proficient in Cape Dutch, he afterwards undertook intelligence work in South-West Africa, a clandestine escapade that lent support to the view that he was the inspiration for John Buchan's character, Richard Hannay. A season in India (August–November 1906), and a return to South Africa (February 1908–December 1912) preceded his becoming an unruly student at the Staff College, Camberley (January 1913–3 August 1914)—an arid experience cut short by the outbreak of war, which he greeted joyfully, leaving at once for France.

Staff and command skills made Ironside's reputation; he was appointed DSO in 1915, and mentioned in dispatches six times. Promoted major following duty at the Boulogne and St Nazaire bases (4 August–25 October 1914), he served with 6th division (29 October 1914–2 March 1916). Accompanied on inspections of the front by his bulldog Gibby (whose collar bore the Mons star), he was appointed temporary colonel and general staff officer, grade 1 (GSO1) to the 4th Canadian division (3 March 1916–6 January 1918) which he trained and effectively commanded through the Vimy and Passchendaele battles. Following a brief period as commandant of a small arms school at Camiers (7 January–26 March 1918) and then as brigadier-general commanding 99th infantry brigade, 2nd division (27 March–19 September 1918), he was sent to Archangel to bolster the faltering allied expedition in north Russia. It was, he said, his chance of chances.

Archangel and Persia As CGS in Russia (20 September–16 November 1918), Ironside was to prepare a winter campaign against German forces and/or revolutionary units, and to train a local army to take over. He found a tower of Babel of squabbling Russian politicians, motley diplomats, disconsolate officers, and ragtag international units. Although initially a temporary major-general, he became general officer commanding (GOC), north Russia (17 November 1918–3 March 1919), then GOC-in-chief, Archangel (4 March 1919–11 November 1919). For a year he was a whirlwind of proconsular activity in a sub-Arctic *opera bouffe*. By aeroplane, ship, and sled he travelled to ginger up or restrain units along the River Dvina. In Archangel, where, he said, he lived like a king, Ironside maintained order, lectured, arbitrated international squabbles, suppressed mutinies, reluctantly signed death warrants, and was saved from assassination by his young servant Kosti (earlier, in France, a Canadian soldier had saved his life), recording it all in his diary. But he saw that the enterprise, animated by Churchill, and less military than political, was doomed: the Whites could not win; the 'Bolos' would overwhelm the Russian army he had cobbled together. General Rawlinson, sent to co-ordinate allied evacuation, assumed the moral burden of abandoning Russia and left Ironside master of the affair.

After such northern excitements Ironside dreaded inaction and half pay. An almost comedic cross-European diversion as chief of military mission to supervise evacuation of Romanian troops from Hungary (1 March–May 1920), and a brief posting to Izmit (4 July–August 1920) to ginger up Sir George Milne's Black Sea army in preparing what Ironside called a 'second scuttle' (abandoning the Greeks), prefaced his command of the north Persia force (23 August 1920–February 1921), prelude to still another withdrawal. Proconsul again in a futile imperial cause, and trying to bring order, security, and reform to what he considered a degenerate, invertebrate society, he informally selected Colonel Rezha Khan as the rising power behind the decayed Peacock throne.

Summoned to the marathon colonial conference in Cairo (February–April 1921), and after surviving a snowbound forced landing *en route*, Ironside sat for Eric Kennington, mordantly sizing up T. E. Lawrence (as a charlatan with a wonderful pen), Gertrude Bell, and other notables, before succumbing to Churchill's seductive promise that they would do great things together: Ironside was to run Iraq (in co-operation with the RAF). Flattered that his superiors should turn to him in such outlandish places but convinced that empire could be of no interest to ordinary people, he doubted Britain should or could (employing the RAF alone) remain in Iraq. It made no difference: flying back to Persia, his aeroplane crashed near Basrah (8 April); after months spent reading Clausewitz and other military writers, he was invalided home.

Years of frustration Rescued from half pay by his appointment as commandant of the Staff College (1 May 1922–30 April 1926), and believing he was training, as he said, the army's future brains, he gave the school a distinguished quadrennium. Furiously active, and employing half a dozen languages with his visitors, he administered, lectured, published articles and a significant book, *Tannenberg: the First Thirty Days in East Prussia* (1925), while intermittently rushing about Europe to attend manoeuvres. Influenced by his brilliant colleague J. F. C. Fuller (as he had been by C. E. Callwell), he advocated an élite mechanized army with close air support for use in global small wars, and a unified Ministry of Defence. An often indiscreet, mutually self-interested correspondence with Basil Liddell Hart (whom he alternately dubbed a genius and a charlatan) dates from that time. Endemic army council anti-intellectualism and War Office failure to modernize ahead of the still constrained German army depressed him. His special grief was the half pay system, the old men clogging the promotion list. His criticisms brought reprimand in a serious row with Sir G. F. Milne, then CIGS.

After two years with 2nd division (1 October 1926–November 1928)—which he characterized as a phantom command, training infantry without modern weapons—Ironside was posted to the Meerut district, India (21 November 1928–31 May 1931). The move rekindled former emotions: rage at this veritable museum of antiquated weaponry, at officers he judged dead from the neck up, and mindless social obligations; pleasure from visiting cultural sites and participation in princely big-game hunting. India's problem, he discerned, was less north-west frontier defence than looming dominion status and religious war. Restless, teeming with ideas about mechanized forces, and yearning for a man's job (such as reorganizing Chiang Kai-shek's army), he sat calculating his pension, and conjuring his chances of ever becoming CIGS before his powers waned.

Promoted lieutenant-general (1 March 1931), home on half pay marginally augmented by a sinecure as lieutenant of the Tower of London (1 June 1931–October 1933), and so disgusted he threatened to throw his uniform away, Ironside fretted about War Office torpor while Hitler seized power in Germany. Judging war at least ten years distant, he still opposed sending an army to France. When posted back to India as quartermaster-general (4 October 1933–February 1936), he made the best of it, working with the commander-in-chief, his friend Sir Philip Chetwode, Indianizing the regiments, gingering things up, delegating the routine. Promoted general (30 June 1935), he fought the boredom by riding, hunting, and motoring enthusiastically to inspect the Khyber and other outposts.

Eastern command and Gibraltar After travelling home through the Far East and Canada to take up eastern command (12 April 1936–November 1938), Ironside found Sir Cyril Deverell's War Office (and an honorary degree from the University of Aberdeen) more cheering, but concluded that his own ten-year estimate was off: he thought the fat was in the fire all round the world. Britain's decayed imperial and home defences shocked him. Claiming to understand the German mind (though unfamiliar with current military literature), he neither knew how fast the Wehrmacht was moving nor resolved his own contradictions. Opposed both to Anglo-French staff talks and to sending men to France, he nevertheless believed France could not be let go under. But how a British army should be transported there and supplied under air attack he could not think. The September 1937 German manoeuvres (during which he had a five-minute talk with Hitler) suggested to him that war would come in 1940 when Britain could not be ready.

Eastern command palled; he could affect little. Being aide-de-camp to the king (from 12 October 1937) was devoid of interest. He witnessed Deverell frustrated, angry, unable to get the Baldwin government to take things seriously, and predicted they would all be hanged if they did not get on with it. Like the government, Ironside seemed to turn away from Europe. Recommending an all-purpose field force for landing and small operations wherever needed, he naturally envisioned himself as commander. Checked by Deverell's criticism (drafted by Alan Brooke) of his handling of the mobile division at Bedford, in September 1937, he was shocked (despite not desiring the post) when Deverell was replaced by Viscount Gort, whose abilities he deemed inferior to Sir John Dill's or his own. Some had feared Ironside would turn the office

upside down; the minister, Leslie Hore-Belisha, told him he was too old. Friends counselled patience. Churchill, considering Ironside the army's finest military brain, branded Hore-Belisha's decision a disaster. Believing he had missed the bus, Ironside proposed appointment as inspector-general for higher training (hoping to become wartime commander-in-chief, home forces); he then accepted a traditional *voie de garage*, Gibraltar.

Saying he had had a pistol to his head, Ironside argued that there was anyway no army at home to train, no men, no *matériel*, no tanks. When visiting Belgium in May 1938 he concluded an *attaque brusquée* would, within hours, take German armour deep into the Low Countries. The subsequent dismemberment of Czechoslovakia at Munich he judged inevitable. At Gibraltar he could save money, possibly obtain a field marshal's baton, have time to think. As governor (5 November 1938–30 June 1939) he vigorously strengthened defences, dug deep shelters, reinforced the garrison, reassured the citizenry, studied Spanish, and learnt to sail. Now orientated to the Mediterranean and Middle East (expecting the Middle East command in war) and sceptical of Britain's continental commitment, he reckoned the guarantee to Poland empty. Conscription he welcomed, but not a field force for France. The pursuit (unsuccessful) of alliance with the Soviet Union disturbed him, though he came round to it.

Chief of the Imperial General Staff Brought home as inspector-general of overseas forces (1 July–3 September 1939) and shifting outlook in his disconcerting way, he reasonably believed himself to be commander-in-chief designate of the field force. But the War Office, annoyed by his importunings, press coverage, and supposed intrigues, told him nothing, let him mark time. His reported comments led Hore-Belisha to warn him in Neville Chamberlain's name not to talk too freely to Churchill. As the Danzig crisis boiled up, he was dispatched to Warsaw (17–19 July) where the Poles satisfied him they intended no provocation. Alerted for a mission to Moscow, he worried about his rusty Russian but was not sent. Though realizing the Gort–Hore-Belisha quarrel might well make him CIGS two years after being told he was too old, he was upset when this decision came in the evening of 3 September. War had been declared; he felt he had to accept. Unhappy about certain cabinet opposition to him as CIGS (4 September 1939–27 May 1940), he was devastated to lose command of the skeletal British expeditionary force (BEF) to Gort.

Ironside's situation seemed far from ideal. Britain was allied with a nation he had long considered decadent. The Chamberlain cabinet, with one or two exceptions, he judged unfit to run a war. A strong British army was years distant. With no War Office experience, he was further weakened by removal of key officers to France. Denied Fuller as deputy (because of the latter's pro-fascist, anti-war views), he kept Ronald Adam, he said, against Hore-Belisha's opposition. Placing the BEF under French command was what he had reiterated should never be repeated. But assured by the French commander-in-chief,

Maurice Gamelin, that Gort's tiny force would not be sacrificed in mad offensives, Ironside settled down to raising twenty divisions for France (ten by spring 1940), and twelve for the Middle East where, anticipating stalemate on the western front, he foresaw decisive action. Fifty-five divisions was the goal.

Ironside was no warlord: Chamberlain kept firm control; the naval and airforce chiefs of staff (of whom he took a dim view) were peers. Scarcely understanding who commanded the BEF—Gamelin or his deputy Alphonse Georges (who were locked in a damaging personal struggle)—and mistakenly thinking Gamelin completely frank (he was unaware that the French had not wanted him (Ironside) as commander-in-chief), Ironside was readily manipulated. The enormous imbalance between French and British land forces weighed on him, limited his options. When in November, Gamelin settled on the 'Dyle plan' to wheel his First Army (including the BEF) into Belgium if called 'in good time', Ironside acquiesced for political and military reasons, despite his and BEF reluctance to leave frontier defences. The subordination of British to French strategy he had so long condemned was again a fact.

Ironside was without illusion; he knew it would be for his second or third successor to bring in victory. The BEF's build-up, though steady, was slow; production of tanks lamentable. Economic blockade showed no obvious results. No possibility of decisive action was then evident. Clearly Gamelin, far from planning offensives, did not intend to attack the Siegfried line for years, if ever: his written plan for 1940 was vacuous. Earlier allied notions of knocking out Italy had vanished; Ironside himself was now wary of 'Easterners'. Surprised by German failure to bomb and gas London, his scepticism of strategic air offensives almost forgotten, he regretted the lost opportunity to bomb Germany in the autumn of 1939. Expecting assault in the west, but with little firm intelligence, he was prone to underestimate the enemy.

Relations with his minister grew difficult. Despite his own prejudice and Hore-Belisha's insensitive methods and infuriating manners, Ironside had often been deferential and approving of his reforms. Now he was sometimes barely civil; his diary entries grew incandescent. That autumn, though forewarned, Hore-Belisha clumsily fell foul of Gort over a dominion report that the BEF was insufficiently constructing frontier defences. A campaign orchestrated by Gort's staff, and supported by the king, compelled Chamberlain to sack him, on 6 January 1940. Criticized by all parties, Ironside welcomed this outcome but had no direct hand in it. Two days later, as it happened, he and Gort received the *grande croix* of the Légion d'honneur from the puzzled and worried French.

The Norway campaign Frustrated, changeable, talking too freely in society, lecturing an indecisive cabinet, demanding closer RAF co-operation, Ironside was accused in Whitehall of throwing his weight about. Scathing about what he saw as Chamberlain's dithering and 'peace party' defeatism, and chastising Paul Reynaud for criticizing Britain's war effort, he wondered whether the empire was a spent force. Only the Russo-Finnish War seemed to offer an opening. In his mercurial way, influenced by Churchill (whose judgement he had often doubted and whose desire to halt Swedish iron-ore shipments to Germany he had resisted), Ironside rallied in late December 1939 to the idea of seizing the Gällivare mines under cover of dispatching a small allied force sent through Narvik to bolster the Finns. He remained reserved about landing in the Russian Arctic, bombing Soviet oil fields, and other fantastic schemes. The gamble was that by occupying or destroying the mines, the allies would cripple German war industry, forcing Hitler to react in Scandinavia and abandon attack elsewhere. Almost deaf to War Office and BEF opposition, and dismissing Gamelin's reservations, Ironside warmed to a scheme driven by the iron-ore illusion, sympathy for Finland, French domestic political warfare, and his own hunch that the Germans could be made to disperse, knocked off-balance in a trans-Baltic operation. This potentially calamitous enterprise, however, was aborted by allied delays, Scandinavian opposition, and above all, by Finland's accepting terms on 12 March, rather than appealing for the help it knew would be too little, too late, and certain to worsen its plight.

Unfazed by public criticism for failing Finland, Ironside was loath to proceed with the Gällivare scheme alone and to bomb Baku, but agreed to try to halt ore shipments by mining Norwegian waters: should Germany react, allied forces would secure Narvik and other Norwegian ports. Like Gamelin and Chamberlain, he despised Reynaud's insistence on action, but Ironside, too, believed destruction of its oilfields could immobilize Russia and seriously impede Germany. Blowing hot and cold about Hitler's intentions, and underrating German capacity, he wrestled with the French refusal to mine the Saar and Moselle rivers (which delayed North Sea mining until 8 April) and constant attempts to hasten arrival of British forces in France.

The unexpected publication, four days before the Germans suddenly struck Norway, of a background interview Ironside was asked to give in order to influence US opinion, quickly proved embarrassing. Apparently daring the Germans to attack, Ironside had no intelligence of their imminent Norwegian coup. Thereafter, events overwhelmed all improvisations. Allied procedures broke down, the higher direction in Whitehall grew tumultuous. Ironside proved unsuited to wrangling with admirals, civilians, and Churchill—then rapidly becoming *de facto* minister of defence and reaching, as was said, for the crown. Two weeks of argument and reverses persuaded him that the small allied force put into central Norway must get out—one more withdrawal. Doubtless nothing could then have repulsed the Germans, but he believed Churchill's early interference with the force sent 'bitched' the Norwegian campaign. Confrontation between them and long-simmering criticisms of Ironside led to Dill's recall from France as vice-CIGS on 23 April. Though momentarily fancying himself a kind of super-CIGS, Ironside discerned the writing on the wall.

Ironside's Dunkirk Amid rumours of his future posting to India as commander-in-chief (he would insist on the rank of field marshal) Ironside's immediate concern was the potential threat to the United Kingdom. The German blow, however, fell, on 10 May, on the Low Countries and France. Expecting a Dutch collapse but hoping Gamelin, responding to Belgian appeals, would get his forces to the Dyle line, Ironside was puzzled by the unopposed allied advance and suspicious of the apparent enemy thrust. The subsequent dramatic German breakthrough and French paralysis stunned him. Supporting the dispatch of fighter aircraft to France, and fearing that most of the BEF would be lost, he had visions of Germany's total triumph after a fight to the death. On 19 May he hurried to Gort with a cabinet order to cut south-west through the German-held corridor in order to join the French armies on the Somme. But Gort believed the BEF's sole hope was to reach the channel. Failure of an unco-ordinated Franco-British attempt at breakthrough brought cabinet approval of retreat and evacuation. Dunkirk was Ironside's final experience of military withdrawal.

Shaken but staying with him, Churchill agreed he should be commander-in-chief, home forces (27 May–20 July 1940), and promoted field marshal at an appropriate moment. Handing over to Dill but scarcely registering what had befallen him, Ironside reckoned his prestige would galvanize island defence. He rightly expected the Germans first to finish with France and seek air superiority; he was far from defeatist. Scornful of week-ending officials, meddlesome politicians, and the faint-hearted, he sounded an exaggerated fifth-column alarm, scrounged tanks and armoured cars, inspected defences, and consulted the royal family about their possible evacuation. He hoped to retain command, with Churchill (as he had imagined years before) as civilian dictator. Pondering France's fate, he thought of Pitt and quoted Cromwell in a prospective exordium to the populace. But the vice-chiefs of staff and experienced BEF commanders were critical of his plans. Brooke (whose abilities he admired) persuaded Churchill of his own views and of the need for stronger mobile reserves. At 2.45 p.m. on 19 July, learning that Churchill had reluctantly decided against him, Ironside immediately resigned. If he knew of disagreeable rumours about him at that time, he was silent. He had been, he was to say, a bad chief of staff, but would have been a good commander-in-chief: that was his trade.

Retirement Ten months earlier, at their first war cabinet, Churchill had remarked to Ironside that they two alone were not responsible for the situation. Ironside had replied that, all the same, when the crisis came they would share the lamp posts with the others. Partly mistaken, he now knew his forty-one years of soldiering were over. Receiving his baton, on 28 August, he reflected that he had done his best, he could not undo what he had done. Virtually shunned by the War Office, and grieving that Britain was beleaguered by such armies as he and his friend Fuller had been unable to obtain, he resented identification with the old 'Chamberlain gang'. Raised to the peerage on 29 January 1941, he constantly hoped for some military or civil mission. But though he gave lectures at home and wrote Ministry of Information commentaries for the Americas, no firm offer came. Residing at Hingham, Norfolk, he found visiting London expensive, the House of Lords unrewarding or comic. Irreparably wounded by his swift fall, he was stung by the incivility of more fortunate generals. He did not attend the London victory parade.

Compulsively introspective but deeply attached to his family, Ironside remained engaged with his times, criticizing the war crimes trials, predicting Bolshevism's inevitable collapse, applauding American intervention in Korea, and regretting the loss of India and the Suez disaster. Year after year, he worked his fields and orchards (without financial success), laboured to restore Morley Old Hall, enthusiastically travelled the country to lead his South African or old contemptible warriors, hunted, attended school and military occasions, but largely avoided clubland. Personal disappointments and a serious motor accident left him indomitable. He published *Archangel, 1918–1919* (1953) and numerous articles, worked on the posthumous *High Road to Command: the Diaries of Major-General Sir Edmund Ironside, 1920–1922* (1972) and *The Ironside Diaries, 1937–1940* (1962). And year after year he continued the remarkable diary kept almost without a break since 1918, an astonishingly full and vivid record set down at top speed almost without syntactical error.

Ironside was a gifted child of the fleeting high imperial moment. His professional itinerary, launched at 'the Shop' in the Victorian apogee, followed, for all its precocity and singularity, the Georgian decline of empire. Late in his career, in a war he had hoped might be avoided, fate placed him in a post he had contradictorily eyed and known was not for him. A larger than life *fin de siècle* romantic, imaginatively conjuring the possibilities of arms in his time without the discipline to formulate a clear doctrine, he resented civilian ascendancy in industrialized warfare. War as he loved and idealized it had seemed to him something quite different—the most interesting of crafts: the handling and leading of men.

When death, whose visit he anticipated, suddenly came for him at Queen Alexandra Military Hospital, London, on 22 September 1959, following his spirited recovery there from a fall at home, he still could catch the long-ago jingle of the horse artillery harness; still dreamt of adventure in an almost vanished landscape, of visiting or revisiting North Cape, Yugoslavia, Transylvania, Madeira, China, or St Helena, as he said, even for a day or two; longed to return to Buchan, and to glimpse once more his old haunts lying along the Orange River as they had been in the happy time sixty years before. With full military honours and a nineteen-gun salute, he was borne on a gun-carriage of the king's troop, Royal Horse Artillery, from Millbank to Westminster Abbey, on 30 September. A private funeral service followed at Hingham, on 1 October, where he was buried.   JOHN C. CAIRNS

Sources DNB · W. E. Ironside, *Archangel, 1918–1919* (1953) · *High road to command: the diaries of Major-General Sir Edmund Ironside, 1920–1922*, ed. Lord Ironside (1972) · *The Ironside diaries, 1937–1940*, ed.

R. Macleod and D. Kelly (1962) • B. Bond, 'Ironside', *Churchill's generals*, ed. J. Keegan (1991), 17–33 • W. K. Wark, 'Sir Edmund Ironside: the fate of Churchill's first general, 1939–40', *Fallen stars: eleven studies of twentieth century military disasters*, ed. B. Bond (1991), 141–63 • G. Powell, 'John Buchan's Richard Hannay', *History Today*, 37/8 (1987), 32–9 • private information (2004), priv. coll. [R. Macleod, Lord and Lady Ironside] • *CGPLA Eng. & Wales* (1959)

Archives IWM, letters relating to his career since 1914 • NAM, Persian General Staff diary • NRA, priv. coll., corresp., diaries, and papers | King's Lond., Liddell Hart C., corresp. with Sir B. H. Liddell Hart • King's Lond., Liddell Hart C., Roderick Macleod papers relating to Ironside • NAM, letters to Roderick Macleod • Royal Artillery Institution, London, letters to Roderick Macleod relating to First World War and north Russia | FILM IWM FVA, actuality footage • IWM FVA, documentary footage • IWM FVA, news footage | SOUND IWM SA, oral history interview

Likenesses G. Adams, photograph, 1919, Hult. Arch. • W. Stoneman, photograph, 1920, NPG [*see illus.*] • H. F. Davis, photograph, 1939, Hult. Arch. • E. Kennington, pastel, 1940, IWM • group portrait, photograph, 1940, Hult. Arch. • photographs, 1940, Hult. Arch. • K. Hauff, oils, *c.*1941, Tonbridge School, Kent • C. Corfield, oils, Royal Artillery, Woolwich • E. Kennington, portrait, priv. coll.

Wealth at death £4577 13*s.* 1*d.*: administration with will, 31 Dec 1959, *CGPLA Eng. & Wales*

Ironside, Edward (*c.*1736–1803), topographer, was the eldest son of Edward Ironside FSA, banker, of Lombard Street, London, who died while lord mayor on 27 November 1753. Ironside was a supercargo in the East India Company's service. He married on 17 December 1758 Elizabeth Havercamp at St Edmund, King and Martyr, Lombard Street. They had two daughters, Frances and Anna, and for many years lived at Twickenham. Ironside wrote *The history and antiquities of Twickenham; being the first part of parochial collections for the county of Middlesex*, which was published in 1797 in Nichols's *Bibliotheca Topographica Britannica* (vol. 10, no. 6). It was to have been followed by a history of Isleworth, which he did not complete. He died at Twickenham on 20 June 1803, and was buried on 28 June.   GORDON GOODWIN, rev. J. A. MARCHAND

Sources Nichols, *Lit. anecdotes*, 9.194 • *GM*, 1st ser., 73 (1803), 603 • D. Lysons, *Supplement to the first edition of 'The environs of London'* (1811), 319, 322 • *IGI* • will, PRO, PROB 11/1397, sig. 709

Archives Bodl. Oxf., inscriptions taken from Twickenham churchyard and parish register

Wealth at death £1900 left to widow: will, PRO, PROB 11/1397, sig. 709

Ironside, Gilbert (1588–1671), bishop of Bristol, was born on 25 November 1588 at Hawkesbury, near Sodbury, Gloucestershire, the eldest son of Ralph Ironside (1550?–1629), rector of the Dorset parishes of Long Bredy and Winterbourne Abbas, and his wife, Jane, daughter of William Gilbert MA of Magdalen College, Oxford. He matriculated at Trinity College, Oxford, on 22 June 1604 and became a scholar there on 28 May 1605. He graduated BA on 2 June 1608, proceeded MA on 5 May 1612, and was elected to a fellowship of Trinity in 1613. He proceeded BD on 1 July 1619, and was incorporated at Cambridge University in 1620. In 1618 Ironside was presented by Sir Robert Miller to the rectory of Winterbourne Steepleton, Dorset. In 1629 he succeeded his father as rector of Winterbourne Abbas, which he held in plurality. Some sources state that Ironside also held the rectory of Yeovilton, Somerset, but he

does not appear in lists of incumbents in the county. It was possibly during the 1620s that Ironside married his first wife, Elizabeth, daughter of Edward Frenchman of East Compton, Dorset, with whom he had four sons, the third of whom was Gilbert *Ironside (1631/2–1701). At some later date he married as his second wife Alice, daughter of William Glisson of Marnhull, Dorset.

Ironside was, in at least one area, probably in most, an ardent supporter of the Laudian reforms of the Church of England. His *Seven Questions of the Sabbath* (1637) was a substantial book against sabbatarianism, dedicated to Laud, which claimed that the author had held these views long before Charles I's declaration, and denounced sabbatarian tenets as novelties designed to raise schism in the church. Yet Ironside seems to have continued to hold his livings undisturbed during the civil wars. He was still officiating at Winterbourne Steepleton in 1650, but in 1659 his son Gilbert was admitted there by the triers. Gilbert Ironside the younger was officiating at Winterbourne Abbas in 1650, but his father did not resign it until 1657, when a J. Stoodley was admitted in his place. By 1660 Ironside described himself as 'an old man much decayed in strength, Lungs, Parts, plundered of Abilities as well as Books, by the Discouragements and Distractions of our late Confusions' (Ironside, *Sermon Preached at Dorchester*, sigs. A3–A3v). A man of considerable wealth, possibly amassed through his marriages, he lost, according to one of John Walker's correspondents, not only valuable rectories but three Dorset estates worth about £500 a year during the interregnum.

However, at the Restoration, Ironside was reinstated in both the Winterbourne livings and was not noticeably impoverished. Anthony Wood suggested that it was Ironside's personal fortune which best qualified him for promotion to the notoriously poverty-stricken bishopric of Bristol, and White Kennett remarks that although Ironside had never held a dignity in the church, nor a chaplaincy to a noble or a prince, he was seen as 'the fittest Person to enter upon that mean Bishoprick' (Kennett, 295). Whatever the reason, Ironside was elected in December 1660, consecrated on 13 January 1661 at Henry VII's chapel, Westminster, and enthroned on 17 January. His decade as bishop was unremarkable. Circumstantial evidence seems to suggest that he did not harry nonconformists in his diocese. A long discussion on conformity and the use of the prayer book between Ironside and John Wesley (1635?–1678) of Whitchurch was reported by Edmund Calamy and Kennett as evidence of Ironside's forbearance and leniency towards scrupulous consciences. The records of local nonconformist congregations and Quaker meetings indeed imply that Ironside was no persecutor, especially in comparison with his successor, Bishop Carleton. On the other hand, a letter from Archbishop Sheldon to Ironside on 11 October 1666 seems to imply that the latter had made some complaint (or at least return) to the primate about conventicles and some request to stir up the justices, although Sheldon explained he could take little action because Ironside expressed himself only in generalities. In 1670, under pressure from Sheldon to ensure that the new Conventicle Act was obeyed, Ironside is reported to have hired informers to identify members of nonconformist meetings. Gilbert Ironside died in Bristol on 19 September 1671 and was buried without any memorial near the steps of the bishop's throne in Bristol Cathedral.

JOHN SPURR

Sources J. Hutchins, *The history and antiquities of the county of Dorset*, 3rd edn, ed. W. Shipp and J. W. Hodson, 1 (1861), xxv; 2 (1863), 198, 280, 282; facs. repr. (1973) · G. Ironside, *Seven questions of the sabbath briefly disputed, after the manner of the schools* (1637) · G. Ironside, *A sermon preached at Dorchester in the county of Dorcet, at the proclaiming of his sacred majesty Charles the II, May 15. 1660* (1660) · Wood, *Ath. Oxon.*, new edn, 3.940–41 · Foster, *Alum. Oxon.* · W. Kennett, *A register and chronicle ecclesiastical and civil* (1728) · *Fasti Angl.* (Hardy), 1.217–18; 3.218 · R. Hayden, ed., *The records of a church in Christ in Bristol, 1640–1687*, Bristol RS, 27 (1974), 64, 72, 128, 295–6 · Archbishop Sheldon, letter to Ironside, 11 Oct 1666, Bodl. Oxf., MS Add. C 308, fol. 73v · *Walker rev.*, 134 · I. M. Green, *The re-establishment of the Church of England, 1660–1663* (1978)

Likenesses oils, 1662, Trinity College, Oxford

Gilbert Ironside (1631/2–1701), by unknown artist, c.1690

Ironside, Gilbert (1631/2–1701), bishop of Hereford, was born at Winterbourne Abbas, Dorset, the third of the four sons of Gilbert *Ironside (1588–1671), later bishop of Bristol, and Elizabeth, his first wife, daughter of Edward Frenchman. His family represented something of a clerical dynasty, the younger Gilbert being the third generation of his family to be ordained, and sons following fathers in certain Dorset livings, and the younger Gilbert ultimately following his father, if briefly, in the see of Bristol.

The younger Ironside's later royalism seems to have been mainly latent at the time of the interregnum. He found no difficulty in matriculating, aged eighteen, at Wadham College, Oxford, under the Commonwealth on 14 November 1650, becoming a scholar in 1651, graduating BA on 4 February 1653, and MA on 22 June 1655. He went on to be elected fellow in 1656 and appointed public reader in grammar in 1659, the same year that he became bursar of Wadham. He was said to be a great admirer of John Wilkins, until 1659 the intruded warden of Wadham and later bishop of Chester.

Nevertheless, Ironside was a known royalist in Oxford for at least a while before the Stuart Restoration seemed inevitable. This comes to light through a story gleefully narrated by Anthony Wood, of a London merchant who came to The Mitre inn in Oxford on 16 September 1659, posing as an Orthodox patriarch. Ironside was one of the known royalists from Wadham, who were taken in and sought the man's blessing.

The Restoration, when it came, helped to advance the Ironside family, the elder Gilbert becoming bishop of Bristol in 1661. The younger Gilbert continued his academic career at Wadham, where he became sub-warden in 1660 and was again elected bursar in 1661, became librarian in 1662, and took the degree of BD in 1664. In addition, he acquired the Dorset living of Winterbourne Faringdon in 1663 and succeeded his father at Winterbourne Steepleton in 1666. But his most prized acquisition was undoubtedly the wardenship of Wadham, in which he succeeded Walter Blandford, who became bishop of Oxford in 1665. He proceeded DD in June 1666.

However, Ironside's career at Oxford was not as trouble-free as such a list of honours might suggest. According to Wood, he was no friend of Dr John Fell, the dean of Christ Church, considering his approach to university affairs 'somewhat arbitrary' (Wood, *Ath. Oxon.*, 4.898), and this apparently explains the delay in Ironside's rise to the vice-chancellorship. For his part, attempting to discipline a dissolute scholar (one Francis Pyle) in 1669, brought Ironside into a head-on confrontation with Bishop William Piers, the nonagenarian visitor of Wadham. There was even talk of Ironside's being replaced as warden, before intervention from Archbishop Sheldon managed to still the storm and it was accepted that Ironside and the governing body had acted within their rights.

But Fell and Piers were not the only figures associated with Oxford who took a negative view of Ironside. Wood was savage, endorsing Fell's view of him as a 'prating and proud coxcomb' and adding that he was '[f]orward, saucy, domineering, impudent [and] lascivious' (*Life and Times*, 3.224). Dr John Hough, with more reserve, simply wrote him off as the roughest man he ever knew.

Such qualities did not, however, necessarily work against one at the court of Charles II, and Ironside rose to become a chaplain-in-ordinary to the king. A sermon he preached before Charles at Whitehall on 23 November 1684 was published and has survived. Much of it consists of a violent attack on the idea of religious toleration. But the tune of the court was to change under Charles's successor, James II, and when Ironside finally obtained the vice-chancellorship of Oxford in 1687, the change of policy was beginning to accelerate. Ironside was very much caught in the middle in the growing confrontation over Catholic intrusions between the king and the tory-dominated university. In particular, at Magdalen College, the royal attempt to procure the appointment of a president sympathetic to his cause was to lead to the opposition and ejection of the fellowship, and (after the brief tenure of Samuel Parker, bishop of Oxford) to a Catholic president admitting co-religionists to the fellowship. Ironside was not neutral in his personal feelings, bravely putting the case of the king's Oxford-based opponents to James II in person in September 1687. But Ironside was compelled by virtue of his office to hear complaints against those who were obstructing the king's policy. And he was even-handed in the discipline he enforced. He made his personal sentiments clear when he could, refusing on at least one occasion in November 1687 to dine with Bishop Parker and the commissioners when they were taking action against Magdalen College, remarking somewhat provocatively that in contrast to Colonel Kirke (notorious for his brutality in the aftermath of the Monmouth rising), he did not like to dine under the gallows. He obstructed Roman Catholic encroachments where he could, refusing to matriculate intruded Catholic priests and scholars and denying them the right to wear gowns. In April 1688 he boycotted a St Mark's day sermon, which was normally preached at Magdalen, and instead appointed a protestant to preach before him at the university church, though he did not boycott the remodelled college altogether, visiting the Roman Catholic president there in July.

But Ironside showed his true colours once again in August 1688, when he wrote the preface to a new edition of a treatise on the eucharist by Bishop Nicholas Ridley, the Oxford martyr, along with an account of a disputation he was involved in at Oxford on 20 April 1554. He wanted to bring the teaching and example of 'our Blessed Martyrs' to bear on the current crisis for the Church of England, while still glorying in its dutiful attitude to secular rulers.

In the revolution of 1688 Ironside came out strongly in support of William and Mary and was hard on nonjurors in Oxford. He was duly rewarded with his father's old bishopric of Bristol, which he accepted on the understanding that he would receive a better one, when it became free. He was consecrated on 13 October 1689 and stayed in Bristol just long enough to acquire an attractive widow from there named Marie (née Robinson) as his wife. In July 1691 he succeeded Herbert Croft as bishop of Hereford, in which see he lived out his days until his death in London, aged sixty-nine, on 27 August 1701. The oil painting of Ironside belonging to Wadham College appears to have been executed at the time of his translation: it shows him in a dark periwig and somewhat fat in the face. Ironside was buried at St Mary Somerset, Thames Street, London.

Wood refers to four other published sermons by him, which appeared in 1690 and 1691, but these do not seem to have survived.   ANDREW M. COLEBY

Sources Wood, *Ath. Oxon.*, new edn, vol. 4 · *The life and times of Anthony Wood*, ed. A. Clark, 5 vols., OHS, 19, 21, 26, 30, 40 (1891–1900) · J. R. Bloxam, ed., *Magdalen College and James II, 1686–1688: a series of documents*, OHS, 6 (1886) · R. B. Gardiner, ed., *The registers of Wadham College, Oxford*, 1 (1889) · J. Hutchins, *The history and antiquities of the county of Dorset*, 3rd edn, ed. W. Shipp and J. W. Hodson, 4 vols. (1861–74) · G. Ironside, *An account of a disputation at Oxford, A.D.1554* (1688) · G. Ironside, *A sermon preached before the king at Whitehall, November 23 1684* (1685) · M. Burrows, ed., *Collectanea: second series*, OHS, 16 (1890) · *Remarks and collections of Thomas Hearne*, ed. C. E. Doble and others, 1, OHS, 2 (1885) · *Hist. U. Oxf. 4: 17th-cent. Oxf.* · Wadham College, Oxford, Wadham College Archives · administration, PRO, PROB 6/77, fol. 159^r · *DNB*

Archives Bodl. Oxf. · Wadham College, Oxford | Bodl. Oxf., Carte MSS

Likenesses oils, *c*.1690, Wadham College, Oxford [*see illus.*]

Wealth at death see administration, Sept 1701, PRO, PROB 6/77, fol. 159^r

Ironside, Isaac (1808–1870), Chartist, was born at Pool Green, Masborough, near Rotherham, on 17 September 1808, the son of Samuel Ironside, clerk at an ironworks and lay preacher at Queen Street Congregational Church. After the family moved to Sheffield in 1809, Ironside was educated at Queen Street Sunday school and the Gibraltar Street Lancasterian school. At the age of twelve he was apprenticed as a stove-grate fitter, then worked at Longden and Walker's Phoenix foundry. He continued his education at John Eadon's night school and the Sheffield Mechanics' and Apprentices' Library, and won a mathematics prize awarded by the *Edinburgh Review*. In 1833 Ironside joined the accountancy and estate business firm that his father had founded the previous year. From the 1840s he was in complete control of the business and by the end of his life he had become a wealthy and successful accountant and sharebroker, with offices at 40 Queen Street.

Ironside began a long career in Sheffield politics in 1830, when he moved an amendment at a whig political meeting demanding universal suffrage, the ballot, and annual parliaments. The following year he joined the Sheffield Political Union and became the unpaid campaign secretary for the local radical candidate T. A. Ward. Despite the drift of his politics, Ironside collaborated closely with middle-class Liberals in establishing the Sheffield Mechanics' Institute in 1832. However, by September 1838, when he appeared at a Chartist meeting in Paradise Square, Ironside was demanding the franchise as a prelude to the disestablishment of the church, repeal of the corn laws, nationalization of the banks, the establishment of agrarian colonies, and national education.

Increasingly immersed in Chartism and socialism, at a Chartist meeting in September 1838 Ironside proposed the erection of agrarian communities and, on 17 March 1839, joined Robert Owen in opening the Hall of Science, Buckingham Street. In 1840 Ironside published *Brindley and his Lying Braggadocio*, a bitter attack on the acerbic Christian controversialist John Brindley; his increasing scepticism of orthodox religion had already ensured his dismissal as honorary secretary of the mechanics' institute library the previous year. Although soon disillusioned with orthodox Owenism, Ironside retained his interest in the Hall of Science, and launched the Workers' Educational Institute there in 1847; he continued his passion for education by helping raise the new mechanics' institution on Surrey Street in 1848. That year he took his *Address to the French Provisional Government* (a fusion of Chartist and Owenite aspirations) to Paris and, returning bearded, vowed never to shave until social justice had been achieved in Britain.

Ironside was one of two Chartists elected to the town council in 1846 and remained a councillor until 1868, first sitting for Ecclesall ward and latterly for Nether Hallam. He built up an ultra-radical grouping, calling itself the central democratic party, which numbered twenty-two by November 1849 and which forced several debates on the Charter and national education. On the practical side, Ironside established a health committee and, in 1848, gained council backing for the erection of a model workhouse farm at Hollow Meadows, near Sheffield, which by 1854 had seen 22 acres of wasteland reclaimed and farmed.

Inspired by the works of Toulmin Smith, Ironside successfully started experiments in anarchist political education. Central to the scheme was the creation of 'wardmotes', local parliaments attended by interested citizens. It was through the wardmotes' approval that Ironside, as chair of Sheffield's highway board in 1852–4, caused the town's streets to be paved and the first deep sewers to be laid, signalling his continued Owenite belief in environmental influences on character formation.

Ironside helped found the *Sheffield Free Press* in 1851 and through its pages he led the support of the controversial Russophobe ex-diplomat David Urquhart. He also published a pamphlet entitled *The Question; is Mr Urquhart a Tory or a Radical?* (1856). This lost him much local popular support and prestige, as did the opposition to his unsuccessful attempt to get Toulmin Smith elected to parliament for Sheffield in 1852. He remained involved with the foreign affairs committee (established in 1855) until his death, pressing his Urquhartist agenda and publishing *The Part of France and Russia in the Surrender of the Right of Search* in 1866. His only other work, *Trades Unions: an Address*, a defence of union rights, appeared the following year.

Ironside died after a long illness on 20 August 1870 at his Sheffield home, Alma Grange, Carr Road, Walkley, and was buried in Sheffield general cemetery. With his wife, who died in 1867, Ironside had four daughters (including Una, who lived on at Carr Road). MATTHEW LEE

Sources J. Salt, 'Ironside, Isaac', *DLB*, vol. 2 · J. Salt, 'Isaac Ironside the Sheffield Owenite', *Co-operative Review*, 24 (1960), 218–19 · *Sheffield Daily Telegraph* (22 Aug 1870) · J. F. C. Harrison, *Robert Owen and the Owenites in Britain and America: the quest for the new moral world* (1969) · R. G. Garnett, *Cooperation and Owenite socialist communities in Britain, 1825–48* (1972) · J. Salt, 'Experiments in anarchism, 1850–1854', *Transactions of the Hunter Archaeological Society*, 10/1 (1971), 37–53 · J. Salt, 'Isaac Ironside, 1808–1870: the motivation of a radical educationalist', *British Journal of Educational Studies*, 19 (1971–2), 183–201 · J. Salt, 'Isaac Ironside and the Hollow Meadows farm experiment', *Yorkshire Bulletin of Economic and Social Research*, 12 (1960), 45–51 · W. H. G. Armytage and J. Salt, 'The Sheffield land colony', *Politics for the People*, 35 (1961), 202–6

Archives Co-operative Union, Holyoake House, Manchester | BL, Gladstone MSS · Co-operative Union, Holyoake House, Manchester, letters to G. J. Holyoake · Sheffield Central Library, Leader MSS

Wealth at death under £1500: probate, 30 Sept 1870, *CGPLA Eng. & Wales*

Ironside, Robert Cunliffe [Robin] (1912–1965), painter and writer, was born on 10 July 1912 in London, the elder son of Reginald William Ironside, physician, and his wife, Phyllis Laetitia, daughter of Sir (Robert) Ellis Cunliffe, solicitor to the Board of Trade; she later married A. R. Williamson, a stockbroker. Ironside was educated at Bradfield College and studied art history at the Courtauld Institute. In 1937 he was appointed assistant keeper at the Tate Gallery, a post that he held until 1946, when he resigned in order to devote himself to painting, writing about painters, and occasional stage design. While at the Tate he served as assistant secretary (1938–45) to the Contemporary Art Society. Of his introductions to books, *Wilson Steer* was published in 1943, while he was still at the Tate. Other works were written in his years of independence afterwards: *Pre-Raphaelite Painters*, *British Painting since 1939*, and *David Jones* all appeared in 1948. He translated from French a work of E. de Goncourt and J. de Goncourt, published as *French XVIII Century Painters* (1948). His last writings were *Andrea del Sarto* (1965) and 'Van Eyck' (both for the Old Master Drawings series). The latter was unfinished at the time of his death.

Ironside's contributions to *Horizon* in the 1940s included the articles 'Burne-Jones and Gustave Moreau' (June 1940), 'The art criticism of Ruskin' (July 1943), and 'Comments on an exhibition of English drawings'—a circulating exhibition (September 1944). As an art historian and critic he combined complete independence from accepted opinions with a rare suavity and precision of style. In particular he rejected the respect and admiration accorded to the New English Art Club, the focus of the most serious British painting; he disliked the infiltration of innovations from the impressionists and other major continental artists. He believed that what he termed the club's 'crude corporate vigour', combined with the scandal of the Oscar Wilde trials and the early death of Aubrey Beardsley, had killed the imaginative tradition which had derived from William Blake and Samuel Palmer, and had been carried on by D. G. Rossetti and Edward Burne-Jones. It was a tradition that had been 'kept flickering in England ever since the end of the eighteenth century, sometimes with a wild, always with an uneasy light, by a succession of gifted eccentrics' ('Comments on an exhibition of English drawings', *Horizon*, 1944, 203). Ironside, unable to type, wrote with a stylish hand: his writings were original, highly informed, and elegantly presented.

Ironside's paintings, whether in oils or gouache, are mainly of esoteric subjects—for example, *Rose being Offered in a Coniferous Wood*, and *Musical Performance by*

Patients in a Condition of Hypomania. They are highly complex in colour and composition, and are skilfully executed. Ironside's rejection of generally accepted attitudes extended far beyond those of the relatively traditional New English school. His convictions were the precise opposite of those held by most of his own and the immediately preceding generation. 'He belonged in spirit to France of the 1850s, to the world of Berlioz (whom he so strikingly resembled), Baudelaire and Grandeville' (*The Times*, 9 Nov 1965).

Ideas accepted almost without question by those who regarded themselves as representing what was most progressive were almost all disregarded by Ironside in his practice as a painter, were questioned searchingly in his writings, and were often ridiculed in his talk. He rejected, for instance, the belief that '"formal relationships", "pattern", "structure", etc., have any absolute value in a picture as though it had practical functions requiring firmness or commodity', or that colour was 'an abstract element to be praised or criticized for its own sake as one would the colour variations of a wallpaper or a carpet' (*Horizon*, 1940, 420). He branded as an imposture any view of the arts as appealing to faculties that could be isolated from the hopes and frustrations of living ('The art criticism of Ruskin', *Horizon*, 1943). Ironside took nothing for granted, and at an early age had evolved his highly personal style of painting and his attitude towards the arts.

Ironside's achievements as a painter are the more remarkable in view of his total lack of formal training. They are remarkable, too, for the conditions under which a number of his paintings were created. At the end of a long working day at the Tate he would dine out, conduct himself with a leisurely calm, and then sit down to paint (or write) as though midnight were the dawn of a working day, until his strength failed him. Moreover, his constitution was frail and he neglected his health.

Ironside first exhibited in 1944 at the Redfern Gallery, London, with his brother Christopher and others; later at the Hanover Gallery, at the Arthur Jeffries Gallery, London, and at Durlachers, New York. He is represented at the Tate Gallery, the Boston Museum, and the Leicester Art Gallery. In spite of his accomplishments as painter and writer he could not have maintained himself after leaving the Tate without working for the theatre. He made designs for *Der Rosenkavalier* (Covent Garden, 1948), *Silvia* (Covent Garden, 1952), *A Midsummer Night's Dream* (Edinburgh Festival, 1954), and *La sylphide* (Sadler's Wells, 1960). The last three were in collaboration with his brother Christopher, with whom he also designed medals and coins, and a huge royal coat of arms as a centrepiece of Whitehall's coronation decorations—a rococo explosion of gilded aluminium, which is preserved in Australia.

Ironside was unmarried. He died at the National Hospital, Queen Square, Holborn, London, on 2 November 1965, and a retrospective exhibition was held the following year at the New Art Centre.

JOHN ROTHENSTEIN, rev. MARK POTTLE

Sources J. Rothenstein, 'Robin Ironside', *London Magazine*, new ser., 6 (1966), 81–5 · personal knowledge (1981) · *The Times* (4 Nov

1965) · *The Times* (9 Nov 1965) · G. M. Waters, *Dictionary of British artists, working 1900–1950* (1975) · F. Spalding, *20th century painters and sculptors* (1990), vol. 6 of *Dictionary of British art* · *Horizon: a Review of Literature and Art*, 1/6 (June 1940) · *Horizon: a Review of Literature and Art*, 8/43 (July 1943) · *Horizon: a Review of Literature and Art*, 10/57 (Sept 1944) · *CGPLA Eng. & Wales* (1965) · d. cert.

Archives Tate collection, corresp. with Lord Clark

Wealth at death £3172: administration, 20 Dec 1965, *CGPLA Eng. & Wales*

Irton [Ireton], **Ralph of** (d. 1292), bishop of Carlisle, may have belonged to the Cumbrian family of Irton of Irton Hall, near Ravenglass, but is more likely to have belonged to a family named from Irton near Harrogate, in the North Riding of Yorkshire. Several members of the latter family were benefactors of the nearby Augustinian priory at Guisborough, where Ralph of Irton became a canon. Elected prior between 1257 and 1261, he proved an effective upholder of the interests of his house, in 1263 securing for it a royal grant of a warren, market, and fair. In 1274 he obtained a royal protection to go abroad, probably to attend the Council of Lyons.

When Bishop Robert Chauze of Carlisle died in the autumn of 1278, the canons of Carlisle chose the dean of York, William Rotherfield, to succeed him, but when Rotherfield declined, they elected Irton, without obtaining a second royal licence to proceed. The see of York was then vacant, and the chapter of York refused to confirm the election, whereupon the Carlisle chapter appealed to Rome. Irton himself went there, presumably to press his own cause. Nicholas III (1277–80) quashed the election on the grounds of informality, but then provided Irton to the vacant see, 'in consideration of the character and learning of the said Ralph' (*CEPR letters*, 1.461). He was consecrated bishop by the cardinal-bishop of Tusculum, on 25 March 1280. Perhaps in deference to the source of his episcopal authority, Irton's seal as bishop was subsequently engraved with the heads of saints Peter and Paul. Their presumption in electing Irton cost the canons of Carlisle 500 marks (200 were later pardoned), and Irton himself found it prudent to pay 400 marks for the king's goodwill, which seems to have been genuine, since as bishop he later received several gifts of venison from Inglewood Forest. The temporalities of the see were restored on 10 July 1280.

Irton may have been less highly regarded in his diocese, owing to the taxation he imposed to finance the completion of Carlisle Cathedral. At a convocation held on 24 October 1280 he obtained the grant of a tithe for two years from all the churches in his diocese, payable according to a true valuation and in the new money issued in the recoinage of 1279/80. Unbeneficed priests, too, were taxed. The Lanercost chronicle denounced the bishop as 'a brigand rather than a high priest [*praedo non praesul*]', and as 'a wicked extortioner' (*Lanercost Chronicle*, 88–9). But the chronicler could not deny Irton's administrative competence. He retained a lawyer at York to safeguard his interests there, and was himself active in the courts, above all in bringing to a favourable end a protracted lawsuit over the valuable manor of Dalston. He secured from Edward I the Northumberland church of Rothbury, worth £133 6s.

8*d*. p.a., lost to the crown by Bishop Chauze. He provided for the water supply to the mill of the episcopal manor of Rose, improved the bishop's fishery in the River Eden, and was the first bishop of Carlisle recorded as keeping a register (now lost). In November 1291, having in mind the impoverished condition of his office at his election, he made elaborate provision for his successors, leaving books and furnishings of his own for them, and giving precise instructions for the stocking of the episcopal manors. These arrangements remained in force for centuries. Nor was he concerned only with temporal goods, for in 1285 he divided the revenues of the church of Dalston in order to provide for the support of twelve poor scholars in the bishop's school at Carlisle. Unfortunately he failed to secure royal assent to his scheme, and the project was quashed after his death.

In the meantime the king made use of Irton's secular skills. In 1290 he was one of the English commissioners who negotiated the treaty of Birgham, arranging for the marriage of the future Edward II to Margaret, the Maid of Norway, the heir to the Scottish throne, and in the following year he was appointed to collect the crusading tenth levied upon Scotland by the pope. And it was after attending a parliament in London that he died of a burst vein, at his manor of Linstock, on 28 February 1292. Provident as ever, in 1290 he had founded a chantry, for himself and his successors, in the parish church of Torpenhow, and in the following year he obtained papal licence to dispose of his personal possessions 'in funeral expenses and remuneration of servants and kinsmen' (*CEPR letters*, 1.534–5). He was buried in Carlisle Cathedral, where his tomb was destroyed shortly afterwards by a fire which ravaged the city. The Lanercost chronicle thought that this was no more than he deserved.   HENRY SUMMERSON

Sources *Chancery records* · *CEPR letters*, vol. 1 · H. Maxwell, ed. and trans., *The chronicle of Lanercost, 1272–1346* (1913) · W. Brown, ed., *Cartularium prioratus de Gyseburne*, 1, SurtS, 86 (1889) · *The chronicle of Walter of Guisborough*, ed. H. Rothwell, CS, 3rd ser., 89 (1957) · J. Wilson, *Rose Castle* (1912) · C. M. L. Bouch, *Prelates and people of the lake counties: a history of the diocese of Carlisle, 1133–1933* (1948) · H. Summerson, *Medieval Carlisle: the city and the borders from the late eleventh to the mid-sixteenth century*, 1, Cumberland and Westmorland Antiquarian and Archaeological Society, extra ser., 25 (1993), 28 · T. Astle, S. Ayscough, and J. Caley, eds., *Taxatio ecclesiastica Angliae et Walliae auctoritate P. Nicholai IV*, RC (1802)

Wealth at death approx. £600—temporal and spiritual revenues (in theory): Astle, Ayscough, and Caley, eds., *Taxatio*

Irvine. For this title name *see* Ingram, Anne, Viscountess Irwin [Irvine] (*c*.1696–1764).

Irvine, Sir Alexander, of Drum (*d.* 1657), royalist landowner, was the eldest son of Alexander Irvine of Drum (*d.* 1630) and Lady Marion (Mariota), daughter of Robert Douglas, earl of Buchan. Irvine was a knight by 1618, and in 1620 he married Magdalene (Mary), the daughter of Sir John Scrimgeour of Dudope. Some time thereafter he converted to Roman Catholicism, evidently under the influence of his wife, for Father Christie, the Jesuit who instructed him, had also instructed her 'ab infantia' ('from infancy'; Hay, 220). However, his conversion remained secret, allowing Irvine to play a role in public life, and as one of the richest men in Aberdeenshire after his father's death in 1630. He served as sheriff from 1634 to 1644, and sat as a shire commissioner in parliament in 1633.

Irvine's public opposition to the covenanters' rebellion against Charles I began on 5 October 1638 when in Aberdeen he and the marquess of Huntly proclaimed the king's orders for the signing of the king's covenant. As civil war approached, Irvine and other royalists fled by sea to England, leaving Aberdeen on 28 March 1639, and soon after this covenanting troops occupied his lands. However, he soon decided to return. By 2 June he was with Lord Aboyne's ships off Aberdeen, and they landed and occupied the town on 6 June. Hostilities were soon ended by the treaty of Berwick, but early in 1640 Irvine was fortifying Drum Castle in anticipation of a new war. He was absent when the Earl Marischal and Major-General Robert Monro summoned the castle on 2 June, and his wife surrendered it two days later. As part of the agreement then made Irvine surrendered himself to Monro on 9 June, and they 'drank kyndlie and blythlie togidder' (Spalding, 1.283) before he was sent to Edinburgh, where he was imprisoned in the Tolbooth and fined 10,000 merks (about £550 sterling). He was released after signing a bond on 6 February 1641 undertaking that he would behave peaceably, under pain of a £40,000 Scots (about £3300 sterling) penalty.

Irvine seems to have resolved thereafter to try to co-operate with the covenanting regime, though his being named as a commissioner to arrest Roman Catholic priests in 1642 may have been an attempt to test doubts as to his religion. In 1643 he sat in the convention of estates summoned in defiance of King Charles, and on 26 August he was appointed a member of the Aberdeenshire committee of war. The following month he was involved in raising levies for a new army, but on 22 November his underlying scruples began to show. When the other members of a committee of covenanters meeting in Aberdeen accepted the new solemn league and covenant Irvine declined to sign in so public a way, saying it should be sufficient to sign in his own parish church, Drumoak. As the parish minister had been deposed by the covenanters and only restored to office through Irvine's influence, he presumably expected to find some flexibility there. In January 1644 as sheriff of Aberdeen he led unsuccessful attempts to arrest the royalist Sir John Gordon of Haddo, but he evidently made no effort to obey orders to arrest Huntly. He did not join Huntly's abortive rising in Mar, but his sons' royalist activities [*see* Irvine, Alexander, of Drum] led to it being assumed that he had, and on 16 February 1644 he was one of those denounced for 'oppen and avowed rebellion' (*Acts of the Parliaments of Scotland*, 6.1.55).

In April or early May the marquess of Argyll garrisoned Drum Castle, which was plundered by Argyll's 'Irish [Highland] rogues' (Spalding, 2.355), the plunder being estimated (doubtless with exaggeration) at over £20,000 Scots (about £1700 sterling). All this was done 'without any fault committit be the old laird' (ibid., 2.356). He continued to try to prove that he was no threat to the covenanters, though in his talks with them he found 'littill comfort' (ibid.). As late as 24 May he was still trying to ingratiate himself, even sitting on a covenanting committee in Aberdeen which took action against royalists and 'excommunicat papists' (ibid.). By November, on the covenanters' orders, he was living in Edinburgh, his submissiveness having brought him this mild alternative to imprisonment in spite of suspicions about his beliefs. On 31 May 1645 he was given permission to return home, and though there is no evidence that he thereafter supported the marquess of Montrose's royalist rising he none the less came to be regarded as a rebel. On 24 July 1646 he submitted on being given assurance by Major-General John Middleton that his life and fortune would be safe, and subsequently he agreed on the 'transportatioune southward' of himself and his wife, on pain of a £50,000 Scots penalty. In spite of Middleton's assurance, in February 1647 he was ordered to pay £40,000 Scots under his 1641 bond, as he had not behaved peaceably, and in February the £50,000 penalty was also imposed as he had not moved south. He appeared before parliament and argued that he was protected by the assurance, but without effect. Finally, he was ordered to contribute to the government a loan of 10,000 merks. The covenanters' desperation for money to pay their armies made this rich landowner, who was known at heart to be an enemy, an attractive target for extortion, though Irvine's appeals eventually brought some reduction in the huge sums demanded from him.

Church as well as state sought satisfaction, for Irvine had been excommunicated. On 19 May 1647 he appeared before the commission of the general assembly but was found to be 'not sensible of his accession to the rebellion' and was therefore referred to the presbytery of Aberdeen 'to bring him to some sense of his guiltynes' (Mitchell and Christie, 1.259–60). The presbytery's efforts were in vain, for on 23 April 1651 he again appeared before the commission, expressing guilt and desiring to be relaxed from excommunication. Again he was referred to the presbytery, which was given power to receive him back into the church on his appearing in sackcloth in the kirk of Aberdeen. In all these proceedings Irvine was fighting for time, spinning out proceedings, seeking to remain true to his Roman Catholic conscience as far as was possible while conceding enough to avoid intensifying persecution. This time he succeeded in getting the sentence of excommunication lifted, but he was soon in trouble again, being summoned before the presbytery on 30 December 1651 for cursing the covenants, saying that sectaries were to be less hated than presbyterians, and that if he himself was not already a papist he would soon become one. His wife and son James were also accused of popery. Irvine denied the charges, but it is likely that they were true, and that he now said openly what he had thought for years. He had realized that his moment had come. The presbyterian church which had been persecuting him was deeply divided and demoralized, and Scotland had been conquered by an English sectarian army determined to destroy the church's power. Irvine could play one species of protestant heretic off against another. When he appeared before the presbytery on 30 December he denounced its intolerable tyranny and claimed its actions were illegal. Instead of submitting, he summoned it, in 'a very inorderly way … being in a great rage and passion' to appear before the English military authorities, in the person of Colonel Robert Overton, who would give him the benefit of English liberty (Firth, 352–3). A brief paper warfare ensued between the presbytery and Irvine, the former threatening renewed excommunication, the latter wittily and ironically defending himself, asking to be spared the presbytery's 'rhapsodies of confused nonsense' (ibid., 353–4). He was fulsome in declarations of loyalty to the English Commonwealth, praising its support for liberty and indicating his support for independency, even establishing a minister of 'the independent and congregational course' in Drumoak parish (Stuart, 222–3). The presbytery soon drove out this interloper, but Irvine won his main point, for he was left free of religious persecution in his final years. He had successfully exploited protestant divisions in order to survive as a Roman Catholic, and must have hugely enjoyed the secret joke that his protestations of sectarian sympathies and denials of Catholicism had been drafted by a Catholic priest tucked away in Drum Castle. Irvine had sent his son James to the Scots College at Douai in 1647, and after he returned in 1650 a Jesuit from there, John Walker, had settled in the castle. It was Walker who provided the intellectual bite of Irvine's papers. The English news-sheets which hailed the incident as an example of how Scots were welcoming English liberty would have been less happy had they realized it was a Roman Catholic who was benefiting. Irvine died in February 1657, after a long career of balancing his inner beliefs against the demands of the society he lived in, often evasive, sometimes lying outright in the interests of what he regarded as a higher truth.   DAVID STEVENSON

Sources DNB · J. Spalding, *Memorialls of the trubles in Scotland and in England, AD 1624 – AD 1645*, ed. J. Stuart, 2 vols., Spalding Club, [21, 23] (1850–51) · J. F. Leslie, *The Irvines of Drum* (1909) · M. V. Hay, *The Blairs papers, 1603–1660* (1929) · C. H. Firth, ed., *Scotland and the Commonwealth: letters and papers relating to the military government of Scotland, from August 1651 to December 1653*, Scottish History Society, 18 (1895) · J. Gordon, *History of Scots affairs from 1637–1641*, ed. J. Robertson and G. Grub, 3 vols., Spalding Club, 1, 3, 5 (1841) · M. D. Young, ed., *The parliaments of Scotland: burgh and shire commissioners*, 2 vols. (1992–3) · J. Stuart, ed., *Selections from the records of the kirk session, presbytery, and synod of Aberdeen*, Spalding Club, 15 (1846) · A. F. Mitchell and J. Christie, eds., *The records of the commissions of the general assemblies of the Church of Scotland*, 3 vols., Scottish History Society, 11, 25, 58 (1892–1909) · 'Protestation of Sir Alexander Irvine of Drum against the presbytery of Aberdeen, 1652', *The miscellany of the Spalding Club*, ed. J. Stuart, 3, Spalding Club, 16 (1846)
Archives NRA Scotland, Survey 1500

Irvine, Alexander, of Drum (*d.* **1687**), royalist landowner, eldest son of Sir Alexander *Irvine of Drum (*d.* 1657) and Magdalene, daughter of Sir John Scrimgeour of Dudope, was probably born soon after his parents' marriage in 1620. After the second bishops' war of 1640 he sailed, along with other royalists from north-eastern Scotland, from Aberdeen on 19 October to join the king in England, in the hope of favour and protection, but returned disillusioned in February 1641, 'moir foollis nor [than] thay went out' (Spalding, 2.5). He was then imprisoned in Edinburgh Tolbooth, being released only after being fined and forced to swear the national covenant. In December 1643 he married Lady Mary Gordon, daughter of the George *Gordon, second marquess of Huntly (c.1590–1649), at Bog of Gight (Gordon Castle) 'with gryte solempnitie, and mirth and myrriness' (Spalding, 2.296).

Three months later Alexander and his brother **Robert Irvine** (d. 1645) were among those who seized several Aberdeen burgesses (19 March 1644) to try to force his father-in-law into leading a royalist uprising. They were active (against their father's will) in the abortive rising that followed, and Alexander, 'being a brawe and most courageous youth' (P. Gordon, 51), led a bold raid on Montrose on 24 April. Excommunicated and facing arrest, Alexander and Robert sailed from Fraserburgh to Caithness, but there they were arrested and sent to Edinburgh Tolbooth where, on 4 February 1645, Robert died. On a petition Alexander, who was seriously ill, was transferred to Edinburgh Castle for fourteen days. An order to the keeper of the Tolbooth on 20 March 1645 to keep him 'a closse prisoner' (NA Scot., PA11/4, fol. 18v) may either mark his belated return from the castle, or an increase in the severity of his confinement. After the marquess of Montrose's victory at Kilsyth on 15 August 1645 Irvine was released, and early in 1646 he is recorded ambushing an enemy convoy on Deeside. In July he made his peace with the covenanters, receiving an assurance from Major-General John Middleton as to the safety of his life and property.

Irvine seems to have lived peaceably after this, though maintaining his family's Roman Catholic faith. He sent his son to the Scots Jesuit college at Douai in 1656, and in 1660 was being threatened with excommunication. Nothing came of this, as the confusion following the restoration of monarchy undermined the Church of Scotland's authority. During the Restoration decades Irvine served in such local offices as justice of the peace and commissioner for supply without his religion being questioned, though the escapades of his openly Catholic brother Francis in 1669–70 drew attention to the fact that priests were finding refuge at Drum Castle. By the 1680s, as Catholic influence at court grew, his religion began to count in his favour. His kinsman the earl of Aberdeen, chancellor of Scotland, called him in 1683 'a most deserving gentilman' to whom James, duke of York, was inclined to do kindness (*Buccleuch MSS*, 2.24), and when the Test Act was imposed in 1685 James, now king, included Drum's name on a list of those whose oath was to be dispensed with.

Irvine's last years were complicated by family problems. His only son was assumed to be incapable of marrying and producing heirs owing to mental incapacity. It was perhaps partly this that led him to the elderly indiscretion of marrying in the early 1680s a girl aged about sixteen, Margaret Coutts, who was, moreover, a former servant of his first wife, and was referred to contemptuously by his relatives as 'the shepherds daughter' (*Reg. PCS*, 1690, 170, 172).

Relatives hoping to eventually inherit Drum were infuriated when his new wife bore him a son, and she claimed that just before his death, which took place on 18 September 1687, Irvine had assigned Drum Castle and its grounds to him. Irvine was buried at St Nicholas's parish church in Aberdeen.   DAVID STEVENSON

Sources DNB · J. Spalding, *Memorialls of the trubles in Scotland and in England, AD 1624 – AD 1645*, ed. J. Stuart, 2 vols., Spalding Club, [21, 23] (1850–51) · J. F. Leslie, *The Irvines of Drum* (1909) · M. V. Hay, *The Blairs papers, 1603–1660* (1929) · J. Stuart, ed., *Selections from the records of the kirk session, presbytery, and synod of Aberdeen*, Spalding Club, 15 (1846) · J. Gordon, *History of Scots affairs from 1637–1641*, ed. J. Robertson and G. Grub, 3 vols., Spalding Club, 1, 3, 5 (1841) · P. Gordon, *A short abridgement of Britane's distemper*, ed. J. Dunn, Spalding Club, 10 (1844) · APS, 1124–1707 · *Reg. PCS*, 1st ser. · *The manuscripts of his grace the duke of Buccleuch and Queensberry … preserved at Drumlanrig Castle*, 2 vols., HMC, 44 (1897–1903), vol. 2
Archives NRA Scotland, Survey no. 1500

Irvine, Alexander (*bap.* 1794, *d.* 1873), botanist and bookseller, was born at Daviot, Aberdeenshire, the son of James Irvine of Skellarts, a well-to-do farmer, and baptized there on 27 April 1794. He was educated at the grammar school at Daviot and at Marischal College, Aberdeen, which he left in 1819 to become a private tutor and then a schoolmaster. His teaching career took him to London in 1824 and, having been interested in botany from an early age, he began making collecting trips into the surrounding countryside, often in the company of the philosopher John Stuart Mill (1806–1873) and the botanical bookseller William Pamplin. By 1834 he had compiled a manuscript list of more than six hundred species found by him within a 2 mile radius of Hampstead Heath. In 1836, at one of the first meetings of the Botanical Society of London, he advocated a collaborative flora of the environs of London by the circulation of printed forms with space under each species for the entering of habitat and other data—forerunners of modern botanical record cards.

About 1837 Irvine moved to Albury, in Surrey, one of the centres of the 'Irvingite' (Catholic Apostolic) sect with which he became associated and in which, in his last years, he held a ministerial office. While there he published, in 1838, a so-called *London Flora*, the first part of which included plants from all the south-eastern counties and the second, examples from the whole of Britain. Plants were arranged by the natural system, at that time still novel. *London Flora* sold sufficiently well to justify a second edition in 1846. After a further move, to Guildford, where he served as honorary secretary of Surrey Natural History Society, he finally returned to London for good. There in 1851 he opened a school of his own in Chelsea, which in due course achieved a considerable reputation. He also set up a bookselling business in partnership with his brother James, who shared his interest in botany.

For some years Irvine was a contributor to *The Phytologist*, the leading outlet for British field botanists, and when that ceased after the death of its editor, George Luxford, he and his friend Pamplin almost immediately sought to fill the gap with a periodical bearing the same title but with a less formal style. To the editorship of this Irvine brought a wide knowledge of botany and botanical history, but his discursive style and fondness for bitter personal attacks, most notably on H. C. Watson, increasingly alienated many readers. After eight years, and persistent financial loss, the venture finally folded in July 1863 on Pamplin's retirement from business. Undaunted and ever the popularizer, Irvine lost little time in producing a successor, with his brother James as its co-proprietor. This was a penny monthly, the *Botanists' Chronicle*, with which he circulated a catalogue of second-hand books which he had for sale. It proved no more commercially successful, however, and foundered in 1865 after only seventeen issues.

In addition to his botanical interests Irvine made a close study of the scriptures and compiled unpublished collections of folklore and proverbs. He died on 13 May 1873 at his home, 28 Upper Manor Street, Chelsea, and was buried in Brompton cemetery. His wife, Elizabeth, about whom almost nothing is known, outlived him. His extensive herbarium was subsequently sold at auction and some years later donated by its purchaser to Manchester Museum.   D. E. ALLEN

Sources *Journal of Botany, British and Foreign*, 11 (1873), 222–3 · *Gardeners' Chronicle* (26 July 1873), 1017–18 · G. C. Druce, *Flora of Northamptonshire* (1930), cxv–cxvi · D. E. Allen, *The botanists: a history of the Botanical Society of the British Isles through a hundred and fifty years*, St Paul's Bibliographies (1986), 13 · D. H. Kent and D. E. Allen, *British and Irish herbaria*, 2nd edn (1984), 174 · parish register (baptisms), Daviot, Aberdeen, 27 April 1794 · wills index, Principal Registry of the Family Division, London
Archives Manchester Museum, botanical specimens
Wealth at death under £100: administration, 6 June 1873, *CGPLA Eng. & Wales*

Irvine, Andrew Comyn (1902–1924). *See under* Mallory, George Herbert Leigh (1886–1924).

Irvine, Christopher (*c.*1620–1693), physician, was the son of Christopher Irvine of Robgill Tower, Annandale, barrister and member of the Irvine family of Bonshaw, Dumfriesshire, and brother of Sir Gerard Irvine, bt, of Castle Irvine, co. Fermanagh, who died at Dundalk in 1689. Irvine gained an arts degree at Edinburgh in 1645, having been ejected from the college previously for refusing to sign the national covenant in 1638, and subsequently graduated MD from an unknown university abroad. Irvine later became involved in the troubles in Ireland, and was deprived of his estate for his pains. 'After my travels', he wrote, 'the cruel saints were pleased to mortify me for seventeen nights with bread and water in close prision' (Irvine, preface). Irvine was allowed to return to Scotland, but was reduced to teaching in schools at Leith and Preston.

An ardent royalist, Irvine attended Charles II's camp at Atholl in June 1651, but after the defeat at Worcester took a pragmatic line, gaining an appointment as surgeon to General Monck's army of occupation, a post he retained until the Restoration, after which he was surgeon to the Horse Guards. He lost this office in the early 1680s because of a 'cruel misrepresentation' (Irvine, preface). Irvine became a master of the Incorporation of Surgeons of

Edinburgh on 28 December 1658, the first doctor of medicine to do so. He did not hold office within the incorporation and appears not to have practised surgery regularly in Edinburgh, as in 1689 John Monro, head of the dynasty of anatomists, was bound apprentice to Irvine, but was allowed also to attend his former master 'in respect that the Doctor does not keep a public shop whereby the said John Monro may get insight and knowledge into the art of chirurgerie' (Royal College of Surgeons of Edinburgh, minute of 9 Jan 1689). Irvine did submit a written opinion on a proposed order of precedence, formalized by the incorporation in its act of ranking of 1667.

When the Royal College of Physicians of Edinburgh was established in 1681 Irvine, a practitioner with long experience and good social connections, feared interference by the college in his medical practice. He petitioned the privy council, claiming that his education, qualifications, and army service meant that he should not 'be stated under the partial humours or affronts of the new College composed of men altogether his juniors' (Craig, 137). The privy council found in his favour, its decision ratified by an act of the Scottish parliament in 1685. Irvine's social standing and royal contacts were useful, and the Incorporation of Surgeons exploited these in 1676 when an itinerant mountebank, John Baptista, applied to the Edinburgh town council for a licence to practise. The incorporation wrote to Irvine and to the duke of Lauderdale asking them to petition the king on its behalf in opposition to Baptista.

Irvine was something of a polymath. He acted as historiographer to Charles II and published works on a variety of subjects. His *Medicina magnetica, or, The Rare and Wonderful Art of Curing by Sympathy* (1656) was dedicated to General Monck, despite his royalist sentiments. In 1660 he was commissioned by Edinburgh town council to translate the Bohemian covenant from Latin into Scots, and his other works included a drama in Latin, *Bellum grammaticale* (1658), inscribed to Dr George Sibbald; a treatise on Scottish place names, *Locorum, nominum propriorum … quae in Latinis Scotorum historiis occurrunt explicatio vernacula* (1664–5); and *Historiae Scoticae nomenclatura* (1682), an expanded version of *Locorum nominum … explicatio*, the dedication being to James, duke of York. He also translated Blochwitz's *Anatomia Sambuci* (1655) into the vernacular. Although perhaps a lesser figure, Irvine was very much in the mould of Sir Robert Sibbald, his publications demonstrating a range of skills and interests.

Irvine married Margaret Wishart, daughter of a minor landowner, the laird of Potterow; they had two sons, Christopher, also a physician, and James. The precise date of Irvine's death is not known, but appears to have occurred between 9 May and 19 June 1693, as his last quarterly payment to the Incorporation of Surgeons is noted on the former date, while the incorporation minutes refer to him as 'umquhile [deceased] Dr Irvine' on the latter.

                     HELEN M. DINGWALL

Sources J. D. Comrie, *History of Scottish medicine*, 2nd edn, 2 vols. (1932) · W. S. Craig, *History of the Royal College of Physicians of Edinburgh* (1976) · minute book, Royal College of Surgeons of Edinburgh · C. H. Creswell, *The Royal College of Surgeons of Edinburgh*

(1926) • *APS*, 1685, 530–31 • C. Irvine, *Historiae Scoticae nomenclatura* (1682) • Burke, *Gen. GB* • Chambers, *Scots.*, rev. T. Thomson (1875) • *DNB*

Irvine, James (1822–1889)

Irvine, James (1822–1889), portrait painter, was born at Meadowburn, Menmuir, Forfarshire, in 1833. He was the eldest son of John Irvine, who was a wright. Irvine was educated at Menmuir parish school and then became a pupil of the artist Colvin Smith, at Brechin. He subsequently studied at the Edinburgh Academy and soon afterwards was commissioned by Mr Carnegy-Arbuthnott of Balnamoon to paint portraits of the old retainers on his Forfarshire estate. Irvine practised as a portrait painter for some years in Arbroath, and then in Montrose.

Initially Irvine's sitters came from the local area. They included G. B. Smith and Dr Calvert, rectors of Montrose Academy, and Mr Campbell, the second curator of Montrose Museum, whom he painted in 1874. This portrait remains at the museum, along with a self-portrait of the artist and other portraits by Irvine of various provosts and church ministers of the area. Irvine exhibited his work at the Royal Academy in 1882 and 1884 and frequently at the Royal Scottish Academy between 1849 and 1885. He also contributed work to the annual exhibitions of the Glasgow Institute. He was an intimate friend of George Paul Chalmers and that artist's influence can be detected in the appearance of dramatic lighting, dark backgrounds, low tones, and rough brushstrokes in Irvine's later work. Irvine painted a portrait of Chalmers's mother, which he exhibited at the Royal Glasgow Institute in 1880. Irvine also painted some landscapes in which the influence of Chalmers is clearly evident: one, entitled *On the Tarf, Forfarshire*, was exhibited at the Royal Scottish Academy in 1879 and another, *A Highland Stream*, was shown at the Glasgow Institute in 1881.

As his reputation in the Forfar area grew, Irvine gradually became recognized further afield and ultimately was considered to be one of the best portrait painters in Scotland. His clientele became more widespread and more illustrious. He painted the earl of Mar and Kellie in 1880, James Spence, surgeon in ordinary to the queen in Scotland and professor of surgery at Edinburgh University, George Harrison, lord provost of Edinburgh, and the Most Revd J. Strain, archbishop of St Andrews and Edinburgh. Among his best-known portraits was that of James Coull, a survivor of the sea fight between the *Shannon* and the *Chesapeake* which took place off Boston on 1 June 1813. (This work was painted for Mr Keith of Usan, and so popular was it that Irvine painted four replicas.) Irvine's portrait of the classical scholar William Veitch (1794–1885) is in the Scottish National Portrait Gallery. He had begun memorial portraits of the earl and countess of Dalhousie for the tenantry on the Panmure estate when, in his fifty-seventh year, he died of congestion of the lungs at his home, Brunswick Cottage, Hillside, Montrose, on 17 March 1889.   L. H. CUST, *rev.* JENNIFER MELVILLE

Sources P. J. M. McEwan, *Dictionary of Scottish art and architecture* (1994) • archives/catalogue, Montrose Museum • J. L. Caw, *Scottish painting past and present, 1620–1908* (1908) • W. D. McKay, *The Scottish school of painting* (1906) • C. B. de Laperriere, ed., *The Royal Scottish Academy exhibitors, 1826–1990*, 4 vols. (1991)

Likenesses J. Irvine, self-portrait, oils, Montrose Museum, Montrose

Wealth at death £1378 6s. 4d.: confirmation, 14 May 1889, *CCI*

Irvine, Sir James Colquhoun (1877–1952)

Irvine, Sir James Colquhoun (1877–1952), chemist and educationist, was born in Glasgow on 9 May 1877, the younger son of John Irvine, who came of yeoman farmer stock but was himself a manufacturer of light iron castings, and his wife, Mary Paton Colquhoun, of highland descent, whose forebears had followed the sea, a love of which Irvine inherited and transmitted to his son; from his father, a close friend of Henry Drummond, author of *Natural Law in the Spiritual World*, came his interest in science. He won an open scholarship tenable at Allan Glen's School, Glasgow, and at the age of sixteen entered the Royal Technical College (later Strathclyde University); he became a pupil of G. G. Henderson. In 1895 he went to the University of St Andrews as a lecture assistant to Thomas Purdie, became a matriculated student, and graduated BSc in 1898 with special distinction in chemistry and natural science. His career in research began even before his graduation; in 1899 he was awarded an 1851 Exhibition scholarship and went to the University of Leipzig to work with Wislicenus, studying also under Ostwald and attending lectures by Bechmann, Stobbe, and Pfeffer. In 1901 his thesis 'Ueber einige Derivate des Orthomethoxy Benzaldehydes' gained him the degree of PhD *summa cum laude*.

Irvine returned to St Andrews in 1901 as a junior lecturer and to work with Purdie on investigations of the carbohydrates, in which subject he made his major contributions to scientific discovery. He obtained his DSc degree in 1903. He married on 28 June 1905 Mabel Violet, daughter of John Williams of Dunmurry House, co. Antrim. They had met in Leipzig, where Mabel was studying the piano and violin at the conservatorium of music. She was a gifted musician and did much for music in the university. Their marriage, which was a never-failing source of happiness and inspiration, produced two daughters and a son. Irvine was appointed professor of chemistry at St Andrews in 1909 and dean of the faculty of science in 1912, posts which he held until he was appointed principal in 1921.

While working in Leipzig, Irvine had the idea of applying Purdie's alkylation technique of hydroxyl groups with silver oxide and alkyl iodide to structural work in all branches of sugar chemistry and thus to elucidate the structure of the monosaccharides and polysaccharides. In particular this indicated the manner of linking of monosaccharide units. His work with his colleagues at St Andrews included studies of the chemistry of inulin, of cellulose, and of starch. Significant landmarks were the optical resolution of lactic acid by the use of morpholine in 1906 and studies of the process of mutarotation in 1910. During the First World War academic research on the carbohydrates was interrupted, but the experience gained enabled the St Andrews laboratories to make a significant contribution to the war effort. This included the production of

Sir James Colquhoun Irvine (1877–1952), by Elliott & Fry, 1910s

bacteriological sugars and related substances for the army and navy medical services. Production of dulcitol, inulin, fructose, and mannitol was followed by the preparation of novocain and orthoform. In addition many research problems were undertaken at the request of the chemical warfare department and the department of propellant supplies, among them a search for large-scale methods of preparing mustard gas. Research into carbohydrate chemistry at St Andrews became internationally famous, and remained so after Irvine's death.

As a teacher Irvine was outstanding. His eloquent presentation of his subjects commanded the attention of all his students and inspired many to follow chemistry as a career in both the academic and industrial fields. His enthusiasm for chemistry left a strong impression on all who were in his department while he was professor. He was a fine experimentalist, laying considerable emphasis on the practical side of his subject, and he preserved to the end of his life his sureness and delicacy of technique. He worked long hours and expected the same of his staff and students. A strict disciplinarian, he was yet easy to approach and always encouraging and helpful if the case was good. Like Bishop James Kennedy, the founder of St Salvator's College, he 'believed in the master–disciple relationship as the most effective method of inculcating knowledge and of transmitting knowledge into wisdom'. He was noted for his eloquence as a student and became internationally famous for it as a principal.

The welfare of his students was Irvine's prime concern

and he succeeded in making St Andrews largely a residential university as it had been in the past. He revived old customs and traditions, improved many buildings, and found donors for a graduation hall and for the renovation of St Salvator's Chapel and the restoration of St Leonard's Chapel. He widened the field of recruitment of students and raised the numbers to an economic level. In Dundee the schools of medicine, engineering, and chemistry were expanded, and he devised methods of improving the college finances. The hostility which arose between the two parts of the university in St Andrews and Dundee, resulting in a royal commission (1951–2), was most unfortunate. Irvine held strong opinions and so on occasion inevitably had to face opposition and criticism. The word autocratic was applied to him; but his was always benevolent autocracy and even his greatest enemies could not deny his unsparing devotion to his university.

Irvine travelled extensively in the interests of education. He went to India as chairman of the viceroy's committee on the Indian Institute of Science in 1936, and to the West Indies as chairman of the committee on higher education in 1944 and in subsequent years as the prime mover in founding the University College of the West Indies. He was chairman of the Inter-University Council for Higher Education in the Colonies from its formation in 1946 until 1951. The Carnegie Trust, the Scottish Universities Entrance Board, and the prime minister's committee on the training of biologists (1933) were among the educational bodies on which he served. He was always warmly received in America, where he had many friends, among them Edward Harkness, who sought his advice on the formation of the Pilgrim Trust on which he served, as on the committee of the Commonwealth Fund. Irvine impressed such men by his penetrating judgement and clarity of expression; practical in outlook, in action he was level-headed.

Irvine had a short, slim, athletic figure with a tanned skin and dark, bright eyes. In youth he was a good athlete, a versatile runner (his speciality the 100 yards), and a strong swimmer. Until late in life he played a good game of golf and tennis and maintained an interest in athletics and sport, which was encouraging to the students. He was very fond of music. He was a most engaging companion, of catholic tastes, and with a wide range of experience, backed by an astonishing memory for people and incidents. To scholarship he added wit, to knowledge wisdom, to sympathy discernment. Dignified in bearing, he compelled attention. When he was installed as principal the university was small and its financial resources had dwindled. By his skill, enthusiasm, and tact Irvine found the generous donors required to carry out his schemes for the improvement and expansion of the university.

Many honours came to Irvine, who was elected FRS in 1918, knighted in 1925, appointed CBE in 1920, and promoted KBE in 1948. He received a number of medals from learned societies and honorary degrees from many universities, and his services to Polish and Norwegian forces in Scotland during the Second World War were recognized by decorations from their countries. His later years were clouded by the accidental drowning of his son in Ceylon in 1944, when serving as a lieutenant in the Royal Naval Volunteer Reserve. Irvine died in St Andrews on 12 June 1952. DAVID TRAILL, *rev.* ANTHONY R. BUTLER

Sources *Alumnus Chronicle* [U. St Andr.], 42 (Jan 1953) · J. Read, *Obits. FRS*, 8 (1952–3), 459–89 · private information (1971) · personal knowledge (1971) · M. V. Irvine, *The avenue of years: a memoir of Sir James Irvine, principal and vice-chancellor of the University of St Andrews, 1921–1952* (1970)
Archives PRO, corresp., BW 90 · U. Edin. L., diaries and papers | Bodl. Oxf., corresp. relating to Society for Protection of Science and Learning · U. St Andr. L., letters to Cedric Thorpe Davie
Likenesses photograph, 1900, repro. in Irvine, *Avenue of years*, facing p. 66 · Elliott & Fry, photograph, 1910–19, NPG [*see illus.*] · photograph, 1921, repro. in Irvine, *Avenue of years*, facing p. 67 · W. Stoneman, photograph, 1925, NPG · O. Birley, oils, *c.*1934, U. St Andr. · K. Henderson, oils, U. St Andr.
Wealth at death £2231 3*s.* 0*d.*: confirmation, 11 Aug 1952, *CCI* · £1386 0*s.* 9*d.*: additional estate, 29 Dec 1952, *CCI*

Irvine, Robert (*d.* 1645). *See under* Irvine, Alexander, of Drum (*d.* 1687).

Irvine, William (1741–1804), army officer and revolutionary politician in America, was born on 3 November 1741 near Enniskillen, co. Fermanagh; details of his parents, who originally came from Scotland, are unknown. He was educated at Enniskillen grammar school and may have studied medicine at Trinity College, Dublin, though his name does not appear in lists of university graduates. After a brief period in the army he served as a naval surgeon during the Seven Years' War. In 1763 he moved to America, and in the following year he settled and began to practise medicine in Carlisle, Pennsylvania. About 1764 he married Anne, daughter of Robert Callender of Carlisle; the couple had ten children, five sons and five daughters.

Irvine sided with the revolutionaries following the outbreak of the American War of Independence. He was a member of the provincial convention assembled at Philadelphia on 15 July 1774, which recommended the establishment of a general intercolonial congress. On 9 January 1776 he was commissioned as colonel of the 6th Pennsylvania infantry regiment and ordered to Canada. In June he was captured during a surprise raid on the British at Three Rivers, on the north bank of the St Lawrence River. Paroled on 3 August, he was finally exchanged on 6 May 1778, when he resumed his military service. He was a member of the court martial that tried and convicted General Charles Lee for his conduct at the battle of Monmouth (June 1778). He commanded the 2nd Pennsylvania infantry in 1778, and in the following year was made brigadier-general and given command of the 2nd Pennsylvania brigade, with which he was involved in Lord Stirling's failed attack at Staten Island (January 1779) and in General Anthony Wayne's unsuccessful attempt on Bull's Ferry, New Jersey, on 21–2 July 1780. He tried to raise a corps of Pennsylvanian cavalry, without success. In March 1782 he was sent to Fort Pitt, on Washington's recommendation, to command on the western frontier. His period of command included the massacre of innocent Moravian Indians at Gnaddenhutten on 8 March 1782. Correspondence between Irvine and his wife indicates that in private

he had little sympathy for the Indians' plight. He resigned from the army in October of the following year.

In March 1785 Irvine was appointed agent for Pennsylvania to examine and distribute the donation lands promised to the soldiers of the revolution. He suggested the purchase of the piece of land known as the Triangle to give Pennsylvania an outlet on Lake Erie. Between 1786 and 1788 he was a member of the confederation congress, and was one of the assessors for settling the accounts of the union with individual states. He served as a representative in the third congress from 2 December 1793 to 3 March 1795, and commanded the Pennsylvania state militia against the whisky insurgents in 1794. In 1800 he moved to Philadelphia, and in March 1801 was appointed superintendent of military stores by President Jefferson. Irvine was president of the state society of Cincinnati from 1801 until his death, from cholera morbus at Philadelphia on 29 July 1804. PHILIP CARTER

Sources H. M. Ward, 'Irvine, William', *ANB* · C. W. Heathcote, 'General William Irvine: a trusted Pennsylvania officer and friend of Washington', *Picket Post*, 67 (1960), 6–14 · E. G. Williams, *Fort Pitt and the revolution on the western frontier* (1978) · 'Letters of General Irvine to his family', *Historical Magazine*, 7 (1863), 81–3 · *DNB*
Archives Hist. Soc. Penn. | L. Cong., Washington MSS

Irvine, William (1743–1787), chemist, was born in Glasgow, the only son of Michael Irvine, a merchant in that city. In 1756 he entered the University of Glasgow, where he studied medicine and chemistry under Joseph Black (1728–1799) and assisted him in his first experiments on latent heats. After graduating MD in 1766 and visiting London and Paris for the purposes of professional improvement, he was appointed in the same year as lecturer in materia medica at the University of Glasgow. He held the post until his death, together with (from 1769) the lectureship in chemistry, in which he succeeded John Robison (1739–1805).

Irvine's lectures were noted for their erudition and sagacity. His experimental work ranged widely, embracing not only thermal phenomena but also investigations of the water of petrifying springs, the effect of light on the growth of vegetables, and the processes of a large glassmaking factory in which he was concerned when he succumbed to a fatal fever on 9 July 1787. During his final illness he received an invitation from the Spanish government to assume a leading role in a glassworks and saltworks in Spain. He and his wife, Grace Hamilton, whom he married on 5 August 1774, had one son, William *Irvine (1776–1811), who published some of his father's papers, with others of his own (mainly defending and elaborating his father's work), as *Essays, Chiefly on Chemical Subjects*, in 1805. Irvine's views on specific heat, latent heat, and the absolute zero of temperature were developed by his pupil Adair Crawford, John Dalton, and others. However, his central belief that the heat absorbed in liquefaction and vaporization was the consequence of a change in specific heat (interpreted as a capacity to contain heat) was steadily overshadowed by the rival view of Black and the developing doctrines of Lavoisier and the partisans of the new chemistry, according to which

changes of state were caused by a quasi-chemical combination of the fluid of heat with ordinary ponderable matter.
ROBERT FOX

Sources W. Irvine, *Essays, chiefly on chemical subjects* (1873) · A. Kent, ed., *An eighteenth century lectureship in chemistry: essays and bicentenary addresses relating to the chemistry department, 1747, of Glasgow University* (1950), 140–45 · A. Duncan, ed., *Medical commentaries*, 2 (1788), 455–61 · W. Irvine, *Letters on Sicily* (1813), preface · J. Black, *Lectures on the elements of chemistry, delivered at the University of Edinburgh*, 1 (1803), 504–8 · R. Fox, *The caloric theory of gases from Lavoisier to Regnault* (1971)
Archives McGill University, Montreal, Osler Library, lecture notes

Irvine, William (1776–1811), military physician, was born in Glasgow on 22 August 1776, the son of William *Irvine (1743–1787), professor of chemistry and materia medica at Glasgow, and his wife, Grace Hamilton. He studied medicine at the University of Edinburgh, where he graduated MD on 25 June 1798. His thesis, *De epispasticis*, was based upon an unpublished essay by his father on nervous diseases. In 1805 he published his father's work as *Essays, Chiefly on Chemical Subjects*. He became a licentiate of the Royal College of Physicians in London on 25 June 1806, and a fellow of the Royal Society of Edinburgh in the same year.

Irvine's professional life was spent in the medical service of the army. In August 1807 he was appointed physician to the forces, and in 1808 he was stationed in Sicily. In 1810 he published *Some Observations upon Diseases, Chiefly as they Occur in Sicily*. This book was based upon observations of malarial fever and dysentery made by Irvine in the general army hospital at Messina, and was described by its reviewer in the *Edinburgh Medical and Surgical Journal* as 'the work of a man of independent mind, who views disease with a clear and unwarped understanding' (*Edinburgh Medical and Surgical Journal*, 7, 1811, 333–46). Irvine had compared his own observations with those of George Cleghorn and of James Currie on similar fevers, and had studied the observations of Hippocrates on diseases of the Mediterranean region.

Irvine died of fever while stationed at Malta, on 23 May 1811, aged thirty-five. His *Letters on Sicily* were published posthumously in 1813.

NORMAN MOORE, rev. CLAIRE E. J. HERRICK

Sources Munk, *Roll* · A. Peterkin and W. Johnston, *Commissioned officers in the medical services of the British army, 1660–1960*, 1 (1968), 184 · review of W. Irvine's *Some observations upon diseases*, *Edinburgh Medical and Surgical Journal*, 7 (1811), 333–46 · F. Bennet and M. Melrose, *Index of fellows of the Royal Society of Edinburgh: elected November 1783 – July 1883*, ed. H. Frew, rev. edn (1984) · *IGI*

Irvine, William (1840–1911), historian, was born at Aberdeen on 5 July 1840, the only son of William Irvine, an Aberdeen advocate, and his wife, Margaret, *née* Garden. After the death of her husband, Margaret moved to London, where young William was enrolled at St Anne's School, Brixton (*c*.1854–1855). At the age of fifteen he entered his uncle's saddlery business in Piccadilly. He later secured a clerkship at the Admiralty but surrendered it to attend King's College, London (*c*.1861–1862), to qualify for the Indian Civil Service. He passed well and in 1864

travelled from Calcutta to become an assistant magistrate at Saharanpur.

Irvine had inherited something of his father's legal ability and in 1869, while still an assistant, he published *The Rent Digest*, a 500-page compendium of Bengal's extensive revenue laws. At Mirzapur on 24 February 1872 he married Teresa Anne (1844/5–1901), the youngest daughter of Major T. A. Evans; three weeks later the couple left India for Britain on two years' furlough. When he returned in March 1874, Irvine was posted to Farrukhabad as joint magistrate and while there published in 1879 a novel history of the local Bangash nawabs, based on original Persian court letters, in the *Journal of the Asiatic Society of Bengal*.

In 1880 Irvine was appointed magistrate of Ghazipur, where he was charged with overseeing a new revenue settlement of the district. Again, as in Farrukhabad, he dug deep into local history, reconstructing detailed genealogies of Ghazipur's prominent landholders, but although his report, published in 1886, was praised fulsomely by his superiors more tangible rewards were not forthcoming. Irvine had only just been promoted to the first-class magistracy of Saharanpur in July 1885—slow progress after twenty years of solid, commendable work. In 1888 he resigned the service. By then he had mastered Persian, Urdu, and Hindi and amassed a large collection of Persian manuscripts. Aged forty-eight, he settled his family into the London suburb of Barnes and prepared himself to write a history of the later Mughal empire.

Even in London, Irvine tenaciously sought out original material, a habit which impeded his rate of publication. Gifts from Indian friends augmented his manuscript collection and he retained a scribe in India, Abdul Aziz, to purchase or copy new discoveries. He also pursued every known source in Europe. In articles appearing chiefly in the *Journal of the Asiatic Society of Bengal* he published sections of his history for the years 1707 to 1721. He also drafted a narrative taking the story up to 1738; but he was to make little further progress. Spurred by German competition, Irvine for a time concentrated on *The Army of the Indian Moghuls* (1903), which in its exploration of Persian, Eastern Turkish, and Hindi military terms remains a valuable source. But it was his rediscovery, in Berlin and Venice in 1899, of the manuscripts of Niccolao Manucci's famous history of the Mughals which finally killed off his own researches. Manucci had lived in India from 1656 until 1717, but for 200 years his history had been known to the world only through a corrupt and incomplete French translation. For years Irvine laboured to render Manucci's various French, Portuguese, and Italian manuscripts into a single, four-volume work in English, *Storia do Mogor*, which was published by the Royal Asiatic Society in 1907–8 at the expense of the government of India. Critics praised it, one observing that in its meticulous annotation it appeared to be the work of many scholars. Indeed Irvine may not have worked alone. His wife had died in 1901 and in 1903 his own health began to fail; it is likely that his daughter Margaret, who in 1913 abridged the *Storia* for popular consumption, had a hand in it as well.

In 1908 the Asiatic Society of Bengal made Irvine an honorary member and he also became a vice-president of the Royal Asiatic Society of Great Britain and Ireland. University honours, however, eluded him. He himself viewed history as a craft rather than an art and had little time for theorizing, believing that above all it was the historian's duty to establish a factually impeccable narrative. Inevitably, however, his ideas permeated his work and his emphasis on the personalities of the later emperors (especially that of Aurangzeb) as an influential factor in the decline of the empire was to dominate Mughal scholarship for years.

Irvine had a dry sense of humour and an open, strong-featured face, heavily bearded. Jadunath Sarkar, one of modern India's first Mughal specialists, remembered him with affection, in particular for the assistance which he gave to young historians. Sarkar was very much an heir to Irvine's personality-based historiography and he was an appropriate editor to bring together Irvine's articles in the posthumous *Later Mughals* (2 vols., 1922). Irvine died on 3 November 1911 at his home, Holliscroft, 49 Castelnau, Barnes, Surrey, after a long illness; he was buried at Barnes cemetery on 8 November. He was survived by a son, Henry, who became an electrical engineer in the West Indies, and his daughter Margaret, who became Mrs Seymour.

KATHERINE PRIOR

Sources J. Sarkar, 'William Irvine: a biography', *The later Mughals*, ed. J. Sarkar, 2 vols. (1922), 1.xiii–xxix • *The Times* (7 Nov 1911), 13 • *The Times* (4 Nov 1911), 1 • J. Kennedy, 'William Irvine', *Journal of the Royal Asiatic Society of Great Britain and Ireland* (1912), 299–304 • ecclesiastical records, BL OIOC • *Official quarterly civil list for the North-Western Provinces and Oudh, ... corrected up to 1 October 1888* (1888)
Likenesses photograph, repro. in Sarkar, ed., *The later Mughals*, vol. 1
Wealth at death £3448 14s. 1d.: probate, 5 Dec 1911, *CGPLA Eng. & Wales*

Irving, Alexander (d. 1659), army officer in the Swedish service, was born at Tulloch in Scotland, the son of George Irving, laird of Tulloch, and his wife, Isabella Makison. In the Swedish peerage, which often lists Scottish gentry as nobility, his mother is noted as baroness of Meldrum, daughter of Bishop Alexander Makison and his wife, Christina Duncan, but no trace of this has been found in Scotland. Irving came to Sweden with his father in 1608 where the latter served as under-governor-general of Kalmar.

Alexander Irving soon enlisted in the Swedish army and the military archives list him as an ensign for the Närke-Värmlands regiment in 1616. He had been promoted lieutenant-captain for the Uppland regiment by 1624, though some sources say that he was still an ensign in the Närke-Värmlands regiment until 1627. This probably means that he was retained by his first regiment while serving in the second one. After becoming a lieutenant in the Uppland regiment Irving appears to have served as a captain in two other regiments from 1630, including that of Lord Donald Mackay. He was still a captain in 1632, in Duke Bernhard of Weimar's regiment. The following year he returned to the company of fellow Scots in the Green

brigade as a lieutenant-colonel. In 1634 Irving held a position as major of the city militia in Regensburg, which had been occupied by the Swedes since 1633. There is further conflicting evidence as to Irving's position in 1639, both the Norrland infantry regiment and the Västerbotten regiment listing him among their officers. This implies that Irving had returned to Sweden after service in Germany, unlike many other Scottish officers who returned to Scotland during the bishops' wars.

At some stage Irving married Agneta Patkull, chief lady in waiting to Queen Kristina the elder. They had two sons and two daughters, which would have made leaving Sweden difficult. In 1643 Irving sought admission for his children to the Swedish house of nobility, and attention was drawn to this in the meeting of the Riksråd (Swedish state council) of 19 October. He claimed to have proof of his noble origins from Aberdeen, and he returned with the document the next day. To his dismay the Riksråd resolved that only documents from state councils, parliaments, or the monarch of a given nation would be accepted in future. Irving was still considered a nobleman, particularly on the merit of his service to the Swedish crown, but his children could not be admitted to the ranks of the Swedish nobility. The following year the Riksråd decided that Irving would receive four farms.

Irving's military career was still progressing and by 1645 he had been promoted colonel of the Småland regiment. The next year he was colonel and chief of the Kalmar regiment. In 1647 Irving was ennobled in Sweden and introduced to the house of nobility. After this not much is known of him until 1654 when his military expertise led to his appointment as commandant at Stade, a Swedish fort in the former province of Bremen on the Swedish border with the Danish duchy of Holstein. Irving left the Swedish service in 1656 because of old age, and died in 1659.

A. N. L. GROSJEAN

Sources military muster rolls, Krigsarkivet, Stockholm, MR 1626/8, 1627/12, 1629/12, 15, 17, 1630/3, 37, 38, 1632/30, 1639/9, 19, 20, 1640/8, 15–20, 1641/3, 9, 17, 1642/8, 1643/10, 1644/11, 1645/12 • G. Elgenstierna, *Den introducerade svenska adelns ättartavlor med tillägg och rättelser*, 9 vols. (1925–36), vol. 4 • N. A. Kullberg, S. Bergh, and P. Sondén, eds., *Svenska riksrådets protokoll*, 18 vols. (Stockholm, 1878–1959), vol. 10 • J. Grant, *Memories and adventures of Sir John Hepburn* (1851) • O. Donner, *A brief sketch of the Scottish families in Finland and Sweden* (Helsingfors, 1884) • H. Marryat, *One year in Sweden: including a visit to the isle of Gotland*, 2 vols. (1862)
Archives Riksarkivet, Stockholm, Krigsarkivet, muster rolls
Wealth at death 'Irving Holm' estate in Sweden: Elgenstierna, *Svenska adelns ättartavlor*, vol. 4

Irving, David (1778–1860), literary scholar and librarian, was born on 5 December 1778 in Langholm, Dumfriesshire, the youngest son of Janetus Irving, a baker, and Helen, *née* Little, whose family farmed at Canonbie, outside Langholm. He was educated both at the grammar school and at a small private school at Langholm, where he was introduced to classical languages. He entered Edinburgh University in 1796 and proceeded MA in 1801. There he met Robert Anderson, a literary critic who introduced him to Edinburgh's intellectual society.

Irving's first work to be published was *The Life of Robert*

Fergusson (1799), followed by *Lives of Scottish Authors* (1800), and the most successful of his early works, *Elements of English Composition* (1801). This work helped to establish Irving as a serious scholar, but the work which was to make his name was his life of Buchanan, towards which he began to work in 1804, and which was published as *Memoirs of the Life and Writings of George Buchanan* (1807) receiving much critical acclaim. On 1 June 1810 he married Anne Margaret, *née* Anderson. She died shortly after giving birth to their son, Robert, in 1812.

On graduating from university Irving abandoned his original intention of entering the ministry, and enrolled for classes in civil law at Edinburgh, although he never proceeded beyond the first year, as he began to devote more time to his literary career. The law remained one of Irving's major interests throughout his life, however, and he was to return to the subject in 1815 when he published *Observations on the Study of Civil Law*. He also contributed several important articles on law to the seventh edition of the *Encyclopaedia Britannica*, consisting of the entries on jurisprudence, canon law, civil law, feudal law, and on the development of Roman law. He received honorary degrees in civil law from Aberdeen (1808), in recognition of his life of Buchanan, and Göttingen (1837). A substantial body of correspondence on legal matters, between Irving and M. Jourdan (*d.* 1826), a French doctor of laws, survives. His most lasting contribution to legal writing, however, was his *Introduction to the Study of the Civil Law* (1837), which summed up all his previous work on the subject.

While making progress in his literary career Irving still required a permanent position for his own financial security, and in this cause he elicited support from Dugald Stewart, for applications for the classical chair at the College of Belfast in 1808, and for the professorship of moral philosophy at St Andrews in 1815. In 1820, however, Irving was appointed librarian of the Advocates' Library in Edinburgh, ahead of a list of notable applicants; this was largely due to the support of Sir William Hamilton of Preston, at the time one of the curators. Irving, although inexperienced in library matters, received training from Professor Beneke in Göttingen during his first year in post. Despite this lack of experience he steered the library through an important period in its history, during which he oversaw the move of some of the collections to new accommodation, and reorganized the remainder. He succeeded in cataloguing a large backlog of printed books, established the first strongroom for manuscripts in 1823, and generally improved the organization of the manuscript collections, rebinding long-neglected materials. Irving showed considerable enthusiasm for his position, actively pursuing publishers to deposit copies in terms of the copyright legislation, and he embraced even the most menial tasks with vigour. The seriousness with which he undertook his duties was such that he even had his erstwhile champion Sir William Hamilton barred from borrowing books, as at that time he had over 1000 volumes from the collections in his possession and refused to return them. His energies were rewarded by a grateful faculty which enhanced the staffing of the library to support

his efforts. Irving's time at the library was interrupted by a prolonged dispute with the deputy librarian, Thorleifur Gudmundsson Repp, a talented Icelander recruited in 1826 specifically to work on the large collections of German and Scandinavian material recently acquired. By 1830 personality disputes between Irving and Repp had divided the other staff into opposing camps, and the pressure began to tell on Irving, who wrote to MacVey Napier describing his position in the library as 'intolerable' (BL, Add. MS 34614, fol. 484*r*), and his relations with the rest of the library staff as 'excessively unpleasant' (ibid., fol. 484*v*). The situation was resolved when Repp resigned in 1834, and with this pressure gone Irving felt disposed to remain in post until 1848.

Irving married again on 28 October 1820, shortly after taking up his post in the Advocates' Library; his second wife was Janet Laing from Canonbie, his second cousin, with whom he had a daughter, Janet. At the Disruption of the Church of Scotland in 1843 he joined the Free Church, and became an active member of the new community. His interest in scholarly and literary work did not become subsumed in his library duties, and from 1820 to 1840 Irving produced some of his best literary work, editing Thomas Dempster's *Historia ecclesiastica gentis Scotorum* (1828–9), *Philotus, a Comedy* (1835) and David Buchanan's *De scriptoribus Scotis libri duo* (1837) for the Bannatyne Club, as well as *Clariodolus, a Metrical Romance* (1830) and *The Moral Fables of Robert Henryson* (1832) for the Maitland Club, all of which became standard scholarly editions for over a century. This latter period also saw Irving engage in correspondence with figures such as Thomas Carlyle, David Laing, Charles Kirkpatrick Sharpe, and Patrick Fraser Tytler. Carlyle in particular features as an important figure in Irving's professional life; as early as 1820 Carlyle spoke favourably of Irving's appointment to the Advocates' Library, and Irving wasted no time in cementing a friendship, helping Carlyle to find books, and securing introductions for him with visiting scholars. Carlyle even attempted to secure an exchange of duplicates between the Advocates' Library and the Royal Library at Munich in 1828, but Irving was not convinced that the idea was workable. In 1833 Irving tried to persuade Carlyle to apply for the vacant chair of astronomy at Glasgow, a suggestion which was not acted upon. In 1840 Carlyle wrote of Irving that he was 'a man known in Literary Biography, Bibliography and the like' (Carlyle to William Dougal Christie, 28 April 1840, in *Collected Letters*, 12.123–6), although by 1843 Carlyle had altered his opinion of him, referring to Irving as 'the same old stiff pedantic man, only flabbier a little' (Carlyle to Jane Welsh Carlyle, 7 Sept 1843, ibid., 17.121). Irving's *History of Scottish Poetry* (1861) was seen through the press by John Aitken Carlyle, who, together with David Laing, made numerous corrections and additions to Irving's original manuscript. He also collected a sizeable library of printed books, which, when dispersed at auction in 1863, required 2765 lots to dispose of the collection. Irving died at his home, 6 Meadow Place, Edinburgh, on 10 May 1860, and was buried in the Grange cemetery, Edinburgh.   RICHARD OVENDEN

Sources D. Laing, 'Memoir of Dr. Irving', in D. Irving, *The history of Scottish poetry*, ed. J. A. Carlyle (1861), xi–xxiv • A. M. Kinghorn, 'Two Scots literary historians: David Irving and John Merry Ross', *Studies in Scottish Literature*, 26 (1991), 78–89 • letters to MacVey Napier, 1830, BL, Add. MS 34614, fols. 346, 484 • Mitchell L., Glas. • library records, NL Scot., Faculty of Advocates MS VII, esp. FR5 • P. Wellburn, 'The living library', *For the encouragement of learning: Scotland's national library, 1689–1989*, ed. P. Cadell and A. Matheson (1989), 186–214 • *The collected letters of Thomas and Jane Welsh Carlyle*, ed. C. R. Sanders, K. J. Fielding, and others, [30 vols.] (1970–), esp. vols. 12, 17 • PRO • register of deaths, Edinburgh

Archives Mitchell L., Glas., corresp. | NL Scot., faculty records • U. Edin. L., letters to David Laing • U. Edin. L., letters to Joseph Cooper Walker

Likenesses D. O. Hill and R. Adamson, salted paper print from calotype negative, c.1844, NL Scot. • D. O. Hill and R. Adamson, salted paper print from calotype negative, c.1844, NG Scot.

Wealth at death £1267 9s. 5d.: confirmation, 11 June 1860, NA Scot., SC 70/1/104/900–904

Irving, David Daniel [Dan] (1854–1924), socialist organizer and politician, was born in Birmingham on 31 October 1854, the son of Samuel Irving, a commercial traveller, and his wife, Susannah. He attended Dawson's national school, Birmingham, went to sea at the age of thirteen, and then in 1875 settled in Bristol. After a year as a warehouseman, he was employed by the Midland Railway, where he rose to the grade of foreman shunter. An accident cost him a leg, a down-grading of his employment, and a wage cut of 8s. a week. This trauma and the response of his employer perhaps affected his political and religious views which hitherto had been Liberal and Baptist. Eventually he joined the Bristol Socialist Society. His shift was contemporary with the growth of new unionism and Irving became Bristol secretary of a gasworkers' union (later incorporated into the National Union of General Labourers). He was also involved heavily in attempts to organize so-called unskilled and women workers.

Irving participated in the ethical mobilization sometimes characterized as the religion of socialism. He married Clara Brock, daughter of a Bristol house decorator, in 1879; they had two daughters. Late in 1891, the Irving house acquired a lodger, Katherine Conway, a Newnham-educated socialist. She characterized herself as Irving's 'spirit-wife'. Irving and another Bristol socialist, Enid Stacey, were nominated by Katherine Conway as members of a home colony to be developed at Starnthwaite in Westmorland by a Unitarian minister, the Revd Herbert V. Mills. This venture, part of a broader attempt to develop a rural alternative to industrial society, proved during the winter of 1892–3 to be a disaster. Eventually, Irving and Stacey led a revolt against Mills's appointment of a foreman without a democratic vote. The colonists were evicted. Lengthy legal arguments resulted in costs to all parties, a payment of £75 to Irving, and the end of any relationship with Conway, who had supported Mills.

After a period as a socialist lecturer, in 1894 Irving was appointed full-time secretary of the Burnley branch of the Social Democratic Federation (SDF). Lancashire was a relative stronghold of the federation and Burnley was especially notable as the location of a sizeable branch. In the year of Irving's appointment, it boasted 1000 members.

Thereafter the durability of the branch owed much to Irving's organizational skills. At the 1906 election, the SDF was 350 votes from victory. The candidate was the SDF leader, H. M. Hyndman, who contested Burnley on four occasions and was highly appreciative of Irving's organizational work.

The political significance of Irving's activities is contestable. It would be simplistic to present Irving as the organizer of a Marxist and politically distinctive SDF presence. The federation branch fulfilled much the same role as the Independent Labour Party (ILP) in other towns; it was not a sectarian anomaly. When the national SDF broke with the Labour Representation Committee (LRC) in 1901 on account of the latter's lack of socialist commitment, Burnley, under Irving's leadership, continued much as before. His strategy included working with local trade unions in a broad alliance.

Irving's attempt to expand socialist influence in one community can be seen as a variant on the theme of municipal socialism. He was a member of the school board from 1898 until its abolition in 1903; he spent two periods on the board of guardians. Most significantly he was elected to the town council in November 1902 and, with a one-year gap, worked assiduously in this forum until his defeat in 1922. Beyond his Burnley base, he was a significant figure in the SDF, sitting on its executive from 1897, propagandizing, and fighting elections. In the 1906 election he secured a creditable vote against the sitting Liberal at Accrington; in both 1910 campaigns he contested Rochdale, a town with some record of socialist strength. A more specially propagandist intervention came in the North West Manchester by-election of April 1908. All these candidacies were on a specifically Social Democrat platform independent of the LRC and its successor, the Labour Party. Irving's support from local trade unionists therefore varied, but in Lancashire where support for socialist unity was relatively strong there was often backing from ILP members.

Socialist impatience with the Labour Party produced the formation, in 1911, of the British Socialist Party (BSP) as a left alternative. Irving was a member of its executive. Early optimism proved unfounded and by 1914 the BSP was moving towards affiliation to the Labour Party. War divided the BSP. Irving was already an advocate of national defence and he quickly moved to endorse a pro-war position. The recriminations culminated at the BSP conference of April 1916, when the pro-war delegates, outvoted on a procedural issue, withdrew. Irving was a signatory to the consequential statement which identified the prospects for socialism with the defeat of Germany; he helped to form a new organization, the National Socialist Party (NSP), which later adopted the old title of SDF. Under NSP auspices Irving was adopted as Burnley's Labour candidate for the 1918 election. Local reputation and wartime patriotism combined to give him a narrow victory in a three-cornered fight, a victory that was repeated in the elections of 1922 and 1923. Irving in parliament seemed a venerable figure almost from another age. Despite the limitations of the Parliamentary Labour Party between 1918 and 1922 he never made much of a mark.

Irving died of a heart attack on 25 January 1924 at his London home, The Chase, Clapham Common; he was survived by his wife. His effects were valued at £471. Contemporary assessments of Irving varied. Some saw him as a dogmatic follower of H. M. Hyndman; in Burnley where he was given the freedom of the borough shortly before his death, he was clearly revered by many. The electoral slogan 'Dan's the Man' evoked familiarity; the thousands who paid their respects at his funeral showed the impact of a socialist on a community.   DAVID HOWELL

Sources C. Tsuzuki, *H. M. Hyndman and British socialism* (1961) · *DLB* · L. Thompson, *The enthusiasts: a biography of John and Katharine Bruce Glasier* (1971) · G. Trodd, 'Political change in the working class in Blackburn and Burnley, 1880–1914', PhD diss., University of Lancaster, 1978 · D. Morris, 'Labour or socialism: opposition and dissent within the I.L.P., 1906–14, with special reference to the Lancashire division', PhD diss., University of Manchester, 1982 · H. M. Hyndman, *Further reminiscences* (1912) · H. W. Lee and E. Archbold, *Social-democracy in Britain: fifty years of the socialist movement*, ed. H. Tracey (1935) · W. Kendall, *The revolutionary movement in Britain, 1900–21* (1969) · S. V. Bracher, *The Herald book of labour members* (1923) · S. Pierson, *British socialists: the journey from fantasy to politics* (1979) · M. Crick, *The history of the social-democratic federation* (1994) · *Burnley Express* (26 Jan 1924)

Wealth at death £471 0s. 1d.: probate, 7 May 1924, *CGPLA Eng. & Wales*

Irving, Sir Edmund George (1910–1990), hydrographer, was born on 5 April 1910 in Sandakan, British North Borneo, the elder child and only son of George Clerk Irving, resident magistrate, British North Borneo, and his wife, Ethel Mary Frances Poole, of Kimberley, South Africa. After arriving in England at the age of nine, Irving was sent to St Anthony's preparatory school, Eastbourne, before being accepted for the Royal Naval College, Dartmouth, in 1923. Because of his distinctly prominent nose he was known to his classmates as Beaky.

Irving went to sea as a cadet in HMS *Royal Oak* in 1927. After completing the sub-lieutenants' courses, in 1931 he joined the Royal Naval Surveying Service, in which he served for thirty-five years. On 14 March 1936 he married Margaret Scudamore (d. 1974), daughter of Richard Edwards, of Ipswich and Birmingham, with whom he had a son and a daughter.

In 1941 Irving was mentioned in dispatches for his skill as navigating officer in HMS *Scott* when she was employed laying moored marker beacons in the Denmark strait (between Iceland and Greenland) to guide a squadron of British minelayers. While on the staff of the commander-in-chief, Mediterranean, Irving was again mentioned in dispatches for putting in place on the western side of the Strait of Messina three pairs of searchlights which, when illuminated vertically on the night of 2–3 September 1943, formed three sets of transit marks to guide the British landing craft to their beaches in Reggio di Calabria.

In 1944, when in command of HMS *Franklin*, Irving resurveyed a number of heavily damaged ports and harbours in north-west Europe as they fell into allied hands. Finally, after his ship was berthed in Terneuzen, his surveys of the River Schelde enabled allied shipping to bring vital military supplies to Antwerp. For this he received not only appointment as OBE in 1944, but also the thanks of Field Marshal Montgomery, who visited the ship and, at Irving's suggestion, 'spliced the mainbrace' (ordering the issue of an extra tot of rum). This action ruffled the feathers of their lordships at the Admiralty who considered that, apart from the monarch, only naval commanders-in-chief and the sea lords could give this beneficent order.

In 1948 'Egg' Irving, as he was now widely called because of his initials, carried out in HMS *Sharpshooter* a number of sea trials of the newly developed two-range Decca system for fixing the position of surveying ships when they were out of sight of land. This electronic invention brought about a radical change in sea surveying. Irving, by then a rear-admiral, was in 1960 appointed hydrographer of the Royal Navy, a post he held with distinction. During this period he convinced the Admiralty that converted warships made poor surveying vessels, and that new survey ships, custom-built to meet an increased oceanographic role—and to merchant ship rather than naval specifications—would save money by reducing the manpower needed to operate them. In December 1964 Irving's wife launched *Hecla*, the first of four successful ocean-going survey ships. He was appointed CB in 1962 and KBE in 1966, the year of his retirement. Meanwhile, in September 1966, Irving and his staff went to Leningrad in the survey ship HMS *Vidal* to confer with Admiral Rassokho, the Soviet hydrographer. It was eleven years since any British naval ship had visited the Soviet Union but, having been warned in advance of the quantity of vodka they would be expected to imbibe in the name of friendship, the British visitors established cordial relations and charts were exchanged to mutual benefit.

Irving was a man of great energy and enthusiasm with a flair for remembering people's names. When he took command of a ship he very quickly got to know the names of all his men. He was associated with a great number of institutes and associations, always playing an active part and often chairing vital committees, so that his retirement years were full and busy. He continued for a number of years to work for the Decca company, promoting the use of their electronic surveying equipment worldwide. He served on the council of the Royal Geographical Society, chairing the expeditions committee from 1965 to 1975, and as the society's president (1969–71). In 1976 he was awarded the society's patron's medal for 'services to the advancement of hydrographic science and encouragement for exploration'. As a member of the committee of management of the Royal National Lifeboat Institution from 1960, he was chairman of the boat committee from 1969 to 1978, when the faster *Waveney* and *Arun* class lifeboats were being developed. He was a fellow of the Royal Institution of Navigation and its president from 1967 to 1969. He also served in the Natural Environment Research Council from 1967 to 1974, and was acting conservator of the River Mersey from 1975 to 1985. He was a trustee of the National Maritime Museum (1972–81) and an active member of the Society for Nautical Research.

Of middle height and fairly stout, Irving had a light complexion and sandy hair (although his beard was red when he grew it in wartime), with vivid blue eyes and bushy eyebrows. His first wife died in 1974 and in 1979 he married Esther Rebecca, daughter of Joseph Ellison, a company director. He died of a heart attack at his home, Camer Green, Meopham, Kent, on 1 October 1990.

G. S. RITCHIE, *rev.*

Sources *The Times* (5 Oct 1990) · G. S. Ritchie, transcript of address given at the thanksgiving service for the life of Rear-Admiral Sir Edmund Irving, 24 Feb 1991 · G. S. Ritchie, *No day too long: an hydrographer's tale* (1992) · personal knowledge (2004) · private information (2004)

Wealth at death £212,806: probate, 20 Dec 1990, *CGPLA Eng. & Wales*

Irving, Edward (1792–1834), preacher and theologian, was born on 4 August 1792 in a plain, two-storied house in Butts Street, Annan, Dumfriesshire, one of nine children of Gavin Irving (1758–1832), tanner, and his wife, Mary Lowther (1764–1840), daughter of a small landowner. His father was the proprietor of a tanning yard and served as a bailie and long-term member of the Annan town council. His mother was energetic, high-spirited, and unconventional, 'the ruling spirit of the house' (Oliphant, 1.10). Edward attended small private schools in Annan and then briefly the Annan Academy, which opened when he was about twelve. With a love for outdoor sports, he developed into a tall, powerfully built young man, known for his physical strength. In 1805, at the age of thirteen, he matriculated with his older brother at Edinburgh University, graduating AM in 1809.

Early career in Scotland Through the influence of Professor John Leslie, Irving was appointed to teach at a school in Haddington, outside Edinburgh, in 1810. While in Haddington he also began part-time study in divinity at Edinburgh University, enrolling as an 'irregular student', which allowed him to complete his training for the ministry by attending classes for a certain number of weeks annually for six years, instead of through regular attendance over a course of four years. In 1812, again on the recommendation of Professor Leslie, Irving became master of a newly established academy in Kirkcaldy. Licensed to preach by the Church of Scotland in 1815, he occasionally assisted the parish minister in Kirkcaldy, John Martin, and he became engaged to Martin's eldest daughter, Isabella. His sermons were not well received, being regarded as formal and pretentious, modelled too much upon the style of seventeenth-century divines. His teaching also was not a great success. He gained a reputation for being unduly severe in disciplining his pupils, and in 1816 a rival academy was founded in Kirkcaldy. The new master was Thomas Carlyle, three years younger than Irving and a native of Ecclefechan, near Irving's birthplace of Annan. With his typical generosity Irving warmly welcomed his new rival, insisting that 'two Annandale people must not be strangers in Fife', and won a lifelong friend (Carlyle, 185).

In 1818 Irving resigned his teaching post and moved to Edinburgh in order to concentrate on his preparations for

Edward Irving (1792–1834), by unknown artist, *c.*1823

the ministry. He learned French and Italian, attended lectures in chemistry and natural philosophy, and read widely in sixteenth- and seventeenth-century theology. He also became fascinated with the eighteen-year-old Jane Welsh, who had been one of his pupils in Haddington eight years before. She was now a cultivated and attractive young heiress and she encouraged his affections. Irving inquired into the possibility of breaking his engagement with Isabella Martin, but her father insisted that he honour his commitment. Frustrated in love and disappointed in his search for a church living, Irving contemplated venturing into the overseas mission field. Then, through the influence of Andrew Thomson, a popular evangelical preacher in Edinburgh, Irving was introduced to Thomas Chalmers, who was looking for an assistant for an experiment in urban ministry he was planning in Glasgow. In October 1819 Irving accepted the offer to become Chalmers's assistant in the newly formed St John's parish.

It was a curious partnership. Chalmers was Scotland's most celebrated preacher and social reformer, with great gifts of organization. The aim of his St John's experiment was to demonstrate how parish communities could be revived and the cost of poor relief diminished in the new urban environment. His experiment involved the subdivision of the crowded urban parish and the recruitment of lay church officers who were to visit the families regularly and encourage self-help through delayed marriage, hard work, and habits of thrift. Irving shared Chalmers's goal of reviving the national church, but never entered into the spirit of his social experiment. While ardent in pastoral visiting among the labouring poor, he refused to treat them as human material to be moulded through moral instruction. In visiting he adopted a priestly character, solemnly blessing each household before entering. He was never patronizing, and would speak with labouring people on spiritual matters in the language of a traditional communal culture. He convinced one embittered shoemaker to return to church by being able to converse with him about the processes of tanning leather, which he had learned at his father's workshop. While he found many friends in Glasgow, his preaching and clerical manner failed to gain much favour. Some complained about his long hair, swarthy complexion, and erect, powerful walk, which gave him the appearance of a cavalry officer or brigand chief, rather than a Presbyterian minister. Chalmers, however, defended him, observing on one occasion that 'whatever they say, they never think him like anything but a leader of men' (Drummond, 33).

London and the years of fame Feeling eclipsed by Chalmers and undervalued in Scotland, Irving accepted in 1822 the invitation to become minister of the small Caledonian Chapel in Hatton Garden, London, which was part of the London presbytery and in communion with the national Church of Scotland. It was an unpromising position. There were only about fifty members of the congregation and it was in financial difficulties. Yet he was anxious for a church of his own and excited by the prospect of a new life in the metropolis. He was ordained to the ministry of the Church of Scotland by the presbytery of Annan, and in July 1822 he began his pastorate in London, being formally 'introduced' to his congregation by Chalmers later that summer.

In his first months in London, Irving experienced a sensational rise to fame as a preacher. Reports began circulating through London society of a strange new minister from the north, with an imposing figure, black eyes, and long, raven hair, a former assistant of the great Chalmers, who preached fearlessly a stern and demanding religion. What Scottish congregations had dismissed as affected and over-grand language, London society embraced as a unique combination of profound scholarship and prophetic fury. In early 1823 the foreign secretary, George Canning, observed during a debate on church endowments in the House of Commons that the most eloquent sermon he had ever heard was preached by the unendowed minister of the Caledonian Chapel. The rich and the cultivated, cabinet ministers, and peers now flocked to Irving's services, and there was a great crush for seats each Sunday, with hundreds unable to gain admission. After years of being unappreciated in his native land, Irving found himself lionized by London society. He was invited into wealthy and cultured social circles, especially that of Mrs Basil Montagu, wife of a successful barrister, who presided over what Carlyle termed 'a most singular social and spiritual *ménagerie*' in Bedford Square (Carlyle, 248). He became a regular visitor to Samuel Taylor Coleridge's Highgate home, where he absorbed the transcendental thought of the lake poets and German Romanticism. In

June 1823 he published his first book, *The Oracles of God and the Judgement to Come*, a plea for a heart-felt religion that quickly went through three editions.

With Irving's immense popularity came plans to erect a National Scotch Church for him in London, and in July 1824 the foundation-stone was laid for a magnificent neo-Gothic building in Regent Square. On 13 October 1823 he married Isabella Martin. Their London home provided generous hospitality to a host of visitors, including many friendless Scots. Irving took a leading role in the religious controversies of the day, combining devout evangelicalism with a romantic conservative vision of church and state. He opposed the inclusion of the Apocrypha in bibles distributed by the British and Foreign Bible Society, championed the established churches, and opposed Catholic emancipation. He struggled to revive the influence and authority of national religion, as the means of restoring harmony among the conflicting social orders and a sense of national purpose.

But Irving's dazzling popularity could not be maintained. His uncompromising stands on religious issues began to arouse hostility—as, for example, when he preached the anniversary sermon before the London Missionary Society in 1824. In the sermon Irving contrasted the unpractical and zealous idealism of the apostolic missionaries with the pragmatism, 'expediency', and 'prudence' of contemporary missionaries and missionary societies. He published the sermon in 1825 under the title *For Missionaries after the Apostolic School*, devoting the profits to the widow of a missionary in the British colony of Demerara who had been sentenced to death after a slave uprising and died as a result of mistreatment in prison. Irving boldly declared him a Christian martyr, though he had been condemned under British colonial law. Irving's insistence on faith and martyrdom was a challenge to the missionary societies, with their striving after political influence and respectability, and it made him not a few enemies.

Irving's fame as a preacher, moreover, began to fade. His congregations remained large, but after 1825 the wealthiest and most fashionable of his hearers departed, along with the rows of coroneted carriages outside the church. When the large Regent Square church was opened in May 1827, there were concerns about renting enough seats to pay off the debt. In part, his declining influence among the London élite resulted from the demanding nature of his regular worship. He would preach for inordinate lengths of time, sometimes over three hours. When Chalmers agreed to preach at the opening of the Regent Square church in 1827, Irving insisted on reading from the Bible for over forty minutes before Chalmers could begin, exhausting the patience of preacher and congregation alike. At the height of his fame Irving had been fired by the belief that he was contributing to the revival of true Christianity among the governing classes of the empire—that, as his friend Carlyle observed, 'Christian Religion was to be a truth again, not a paltry form, and to rule the world' (Carlyle, 254). Now, as his fashionable hearers drifted away and missionary societies viewed him with distrust, those hopes cooled.

Prophecy and the millennium In the mid-1820s, as he grew despondent about the prospects for Christianity in Britain, Irving was increasingly drawn to prophecy. In 1825 he delivered a sermon before the Continental Society, which was expanded and published in 1826 as *Babylon and Infidelity Foredoomed by God*. Reviewing history in the light of symbolism drawn from the books of Daniel and Revelation, he concluded that the French Revolution marked one of the signs of the imminent end of the world and that Christ's return in glory would occur in 1868. In 1827 he developed this theme further when he translated and wrote a lengthy preliminary discourse to a work by a tortured Chilean Jesuit, Ben-Ezra Lacunza. Irving was drawn into the circle of Henry *Drummond, a wealthy banker, who between 1826 and 1830 hosted annual week-long conferences on prophecy at his estate of Albury Park, Surrey. By the later 1820s Irving had emerged as a leading voice of the premillennialist movement in British evangelicalism, proclaiming the doctrine that the world was sinking into a state of evil and confusion which would culminate in the destruction of the church, the restoration of the Jews to Palestine, the return of Christ in glory, and the establishment of the 1000 years of rule by the saints on earth—to be followed by the last judgment and the end of the world. It was a pessimistic vision, which saw no real hope for improvement in this world. His growing obsession with prophecy and the millennium was perhaps strengthened by personal suffering. His first two children died in 1825 and 1827, leaving him devastated with grief. In June 1828, while preaching at a church in Kirkcaldy during a visit to his wife's family, the gallery of the church collapsed and thirty-five people were killed. Greatly distraught, he visited every bereaved family, but some blamed him for the tragedy, even suggesting Satanic possession.

Irving's gloomy premillennialism captivated many who were anxious over the dramatic changes associated with the French and industrial revolutions. But he also aroused hostility, especially from moderate evangelicals working for social improvement. Chalmers, for example, failed to appreciate Irving's premillennialism, pronouncing a series of lectures which Irving presented on the apocalypse to large audiences in Edinburgh in May 1828 to be 'quite woeful' (Drummond, 115). Early in 1828 accusations of heresy were raised against Irving, not for his views on prophecy but rather for his teachings concerning the human nature of Christ. Irving taught that at the incarnation Christ had taken on a fully human nature, including the rebellious tendency to sin. Christ had thus shared human doubts, suffering, and temptation, although he was preserved against actual sin by the indwelling of the Holy Spirit. It was only by becoming fully human that Christ had been able to redeem and transform suffering humanity. To maintain that Christ did not take on sinful human nature, Irving believed, was to make the incarnation a form of play-acting. His opponents, however, asserted the orthodox belief that Christ's flesh was inherently sinless, untainted by original sin. The controversy was

waged in the press throughout 1828–9, and late in 1830 formal charges against Irving were brought before the presbytery of London. After a trial in which Irving defended his views with passionate eloquence, the presbytery found him guilty of heresy. But Irving then refused to acknowledge the authority of the London presbytery to depose him, insisting that the presbytery did not truly represent the will of the Church of Scotland. With the unanimous support of his kirk session, he separated his church from the London presbytery and continued his ministry.

The gifts of the Spirit While Irving was locked in controversy over the human nature of Christ, reports began reaching him from Scotland of strange manifestations in the west highland parish of Rhu. The minister of Rhu was Irving's friend John Macleod Campbell, who for several years had been preaching God's universal love for all humankind and proclaiming that assurance of salvation was essential to Christian faith. Such teaching contradicted the Calvinist doctrines of the Westminster confession, the subordinate standard of faith in the Church of Scotland, which taught that Christ had died only for the elect, those predestined for salvation from before all time. Macleod Campbell's unorthodox preaching had a liberating effect on his parishioners, and unleashed new religious forces. In March 1830 the neighbourhood of Rhu experienced an outbreak of prophesying, faith healing, and speaking in tongues (utterances purporting to be in unknown languages), as individuals exhibited what they claimed were the gifts of the Spirit. Irving was initially sceptical, but his assistant minister in London, A. J. Scott, convinced him that the gifts of the Spirit, given to the church at Pentecost, had never been taken from the church; rather, they had been allowed to lapse through human faithlessness. Their revival at Rhu, argued Scott, might well be a further sign that the second coming was imminent. Moved by arguments which touched the heart of his premillennialist theology, Irving urged his congregation at Regent Square to pray for the return of the gifts of the Spirit, while his church sent a deputation north to observe the phenomena at Rhu.

In Scotland, the forces of Calvinist orthodoxy in the national church moved quickly to suppress the movement associated with Rhu. At the general assembly of May 1831, Irving's friends Macleod Campbell and Hugh Baillie McLean were deposed from the ministry for heresy, while A. J. Scott was deposed as a probationer minister. As part of a general reaction against new teachings, the same assembly condemned Irving's views on the human nature of Christ and instructed the presbytery of Annan, which had ordained him, to initiate proceedings for his trial. In April 1831, meanwhile, the spiritual phenomena had reached Irving's London congregation, and members began speaking in tongues and 'interpreting' the utterances in English at house prayer-meetings. On 30 October 1831 there was an outburst of tongues in Irving's church during the regular service, which caused distress among many in the congregation. It was a time of acute social tension: there had been revolution in France in the summer of 1830, Britain was in the midst of the agitation surrounding the Parliamentary Reform Bill, while the first epidemic of cholera had reached London. Irving initially silenced the tongues in his services, but after some weeks of agonized reflection he became convinced that they were genuine expressions of the Holy Spirit which he must not quench in the Lord's house. Late in November he began allowing 'gifted' persons to speak in tongues and 'interpret' during regular services.

The result, in the opinion of some church members, was bedlam. As reports of the tongues spread, Irving's church attracted not only genuine seekers but also the curious and the seriously disturbed. The popular press mocked and condemned the phenomena, respectable members began leaving the congregation, and the trustees of the church, who had responsibility for paying off the heavy debt, grew alarmed. In April 1832 the trustees appealed to the presbytery of London, whose jurisdiction they and their minister had previously disowned, against Irving's charismatic innovations in worship. The presbytery decided in favour of the trustees, and Irving and his supporters, who included the large majority of the congregation, were legally expelled from the Regent Square church. They worshipped for a time in a room in Gray's Inn Road, which they shared with an Owenite socialist society, while Irving conducted open-air services around London. After a few months they moved into a spacious house in Newman Street. In March 1833 Irving returned to Scotland to face trial for heresy before the presbytery of Annan. There was no reason to submit himself to the trial—he was now practically separated from the Church of Scotland—but he insisted upon defending his views in the town of his birth before the presbytery that had ordained him. Late on 13 March 1833, after a dramatic day-long trial, Irving was formally deposed from the ministry of the Church of Scotland for his views on the human nature of Christ. In the darkened church, as the sentence was pronounced, one of the 'gifted' burst out in tongues, then commanded the presbytery to flee the church they had defiled. The meeting broke up in confusion. The following day Irving preached to large crowds in the open air.

The Catholic Apostolic church, death, and reputation On his return to London Irving was on 5 April 1833 consecrated to the office of angel, or chief pastor, of the Newman Street congregation, in what was emerging as the Catholic Apostolic church, commonly called the Irvingites. This new denomination, which had developed out of Henry Drummond's Albury conferences and Irving's teachings, embodied premillennialist teaching and belief in the gifts of the Spirit. Irving's ministry in the new church, however, was not a success. He never expressed the gifts of the Spirit himself, and had to defer to those who did—difficult for a man who had spent his life in the presbyterian system, with its traditional respect for the authority of an educated ministry. His health, moreover, was declining and he showed signs of consumption. Seeing him after a lapse of two years in the summer of 1834, his old friend Carlyle was shocked by his grey hair, hollow, lined face,

and slow, unsteady walk. Carlyle desperately urged a trip to a warm climate for rest. But in September 1834 Irving decided to return to Scotland, there to open a new Catholic Apostolic church in Glasgow. Although winter was approaching, he was convinced that a return to his native air would hasten recovery. Reaching Liverpool, however, he collapsed and sent for his wife. With her aid he completed his journey to Glasgow by packet steamer and there, amid the scenes and old acquaintances of his first ministry, he gradually sank. He died, probably of consumption, on 7 December 1834, at the age of forty-two, survived by his wife, their son, and two daughters. He was buried in the crypt of Glasgow Cathedral, in a grave donated by a stranger, with many of the city clergy in attendance. Theological differences were set aside in recognition that a great Scottish Christian had fallen. As the mourners departed there remained a number of young women dressed in white, confidently expecting him to rise again.

Irving was, and has remained, a controversial figure. A learned man, who mastered several languages and published fifteen books between 1823 and 1831, he was none the less prepared to defer to semi-literate and often disturbed individuals claiming Spirit gifts. He sacrificed a promising career and a prosperous church living for his charismatic beliefs. He could be morose and despondent. Yet at other times he exhibited a countryman's sense of fun, was generous and trusting—almost to a fault—with a childlike innocence and sense of wonder. 'I call him', reminisced Carlyle in old age, 'on the whole, the best man I have ever, after trial enough, found in this world' (Drummond, 277). Physically he was for most of his life a powerful, broad-shouldered man, 6 feet 4 inches in height, with a handsome face marred slightly by a squint in one eye. His marriage with Isabella Martin was a happy one, though he might have benefited from a partner more prepared to exercise a critical influence. That was certainly the belief of Irving's early love, the strong-willed Jane Welsh, who married Carlyle. 'There would have been no tongues, had Irving married me', she later remarked (ibid., 274). Although some, including his biographers Margaret Oliphant and A. L. Drummond, have suggested that Irving became deluded in his final years, more recent biographers, such as Gordon Strachan and Arnold Dallimore, have emphasized his serious contributions as a theologian and forerunner of the modern Pentecostal movement.

STEWART J. BROWN

Sources E. Irving, *The works of Edward Irving*, ed. G. Carlyle, 5 vols. (1865) • E. Irving, *The prophetical works of Edward Irving*, ed. G. Carlyle, 2 vols. (1867–70) • M. Oliphant, *The life of Edward Irving*, 2 vols. (1862) • A. L. Drummond, *Edward Irving and his circle* [1937] • T. Carlyle, *Reminiscences*, ed. C. E. Norton, 2 vols. (1887) • C. G. Strachan, *The Pentecostal theology of Edward Irving* (1973) • S. Gilley, 'Edward Irving: prophet of the millennium', *Revival and religion since 1700: essays for John Walsh*, ed. J. Garnett and C. Matthew (1993), 95–110 • H. C. Whitley, 'Edward Irving: an interpretation of his life and theological teaching', PhD diss., U. Edin., 1953 • R. A. Davenport, *Albury Apostles* (1970) • A. Dallimore, *Forerunner of the charismatic movement: the life of Edward Irving* (1983) • E. Miller, *The history and doctrines of Irvingism*, 2 vols. (1878) • F. Miller, 'Edward Irving and Annan', *Records of the Scottish Church History Society*, 4 (1930–32), 87–92

Archives Alnwick Castle, Alnwick, letters to Henry Drummond · NL Scot., letters to Thomas Carlyle · U. Edin., New Coll. L., letters to Thomas Chalmers

Likenesses A. Robertson, watercolour, 1823, V&A · watercolour, c.1823, NPG [see illus.] · J. Atkinson, pencil and ink drawing, 1825, Scot. NPG · H. W. MacCarthy, marble bust, 1867, Scot. NPG · J. W. Dods, statue, 1892, outside Annan Old Kirk · J. Allan, oils, Scot. NPG · J. Slater, pencil drawing, NPG · D. Wilkie, oils, City Art Gallery, Auckland, New Zealand · D. Wilkie, pen-and-ink drawing, BM · oils, Scot. NPG · prints, BM, NPG · wax relief, NPG

Irving, (Kelville) Ernest (1877–1953), musical director and composer, was born on 6 November 1877 in Pound Hill, Godalming, the eldest child of Ashley Alfred Irving (b. c.1844/5, d. in or before 1898), ironmonger, and his wife, Emma Fenner (b. c.1854/5). His boyhood was much influenced by his maternal grandmother, whose late husband had been organist of Godalming parish church. Ernest became a choirboy at the same church at the age of seven and was later educated at Charterhouse School. On leaving school he sought musical engagements, and in 1895, at the age of seventeen, he became musical director of a musical burlesque in Maidenhead. There followed a succession of similar engagements around the country. At Fylde register office on 11 May 1898, aged twenty but claiming to be twenty-four, he married Bertha Newall (b. 1871/2) of Blackpool, the daughter of John Newall, a contractor. The marriage produced two children but did not last.

Among other subsequent touring engagements, Irving was musical director of a company playing British musical shows at the Teatro Comedia in Madrid in 1907. Then in 1910 he was engaged for the touring companies of George Edwardes, and in 1918 he finally obtained an extended London engagement as musical director of the Charles Cuvillier operetta The Lilac Domino at the Empire. He conducted the opening attraction of the Palace (later the Mogador) in Paris, and through membership of the Savage Club he became closely associated with Norman O'Neill. He conducted many of O'Neill's incidental scores, and through him was appointed to the committees of both the Savage Club and the Royal Philharmonic Society. During the 1920s and 1930s he conducted at virtually all London theatres, notably as musical director of Lilac Time from 1922 to 1924. He was also engaged for The Land of Smiles at Drury Lane with Richard Tauber, The Dubarry at His Majesty's with Anny Ahlers, and Henry IV at His Majesty's with George Robey. On 19 December 1930, following divorce from his first wife, he married Muriel (1898–1983), daughter of George Walter Heath, a woollen goods manufacturer. His wife was a contralto who had won prizes at the Guildhall School of Music and who had appeared in Lilac Time. They had one daughter; but the marriage was soon overshadowed by financial problems and bankruptcy from which, to avoid publicity, Irving never sought discharge.

Irving composed or arranged incidental music for forty-four plays in all, including The Circle of Chalk (1931) and eight Shakespeare scores for the Alhambra in London, the Hippodrome in Manchester, the Malvern Festival, and the Memorial Theatre in Stratford upon Avon. He also composed the operettas The Two Bouquets (1936) and An Elephant in Arcady (1938). During the Second World War he was musical director for the Entertainments National Service Association and also for the International Ballet.

Irving's most notable achievement was almost certainly his work in film music. Shortly after the First World War he had conducted music to accompany trade shows of the Gaumont-British Film Producing Company at the Empire Theatre, and this gave him early experience of fitting music to action on film. It led to other engagements and in due course brought him to the attention of Basil Dean, co-founder of Associated Talking Pictures. Irving directed the music for Dean's film Escape in 1930, and in 1935 was appointed musical director of Ealing Studios, a post he held almost until his death. He directed the music for over 100 films, including those of Gracie Fields and George Formby as well as such classics as Pink String and Sealing Wax (1945). He also composed film music, most notably for Whisky Galore (1949), and he arranged Handel's music for The Great Mr Handel (1943). Irving sought to raise the standard of film music by engaging distinguished composers, including John Ireland for The Overlanders (1946), Alan Rawsthorne for The Captive Heart (1946), and Ralph Vaughan Williams for The Loves of Joanna Godden (1947) and Scott of the Antarctic (1949). When Vaughan Williams based his Sinfonia antartica on the music for the latter film he dedicated it to Irving, who was also dedicatee of string quartets by William Walton and Rawsthorne.

Irving was well known as a lecturer and a writer on film music and was a member of the British Film Academy. He was for many years a committee member of the Royal Philharmonic Society and in 1951 was awarded the distinction of honorary membership. He also held an honorary degree of the Royal Academy of Music. A keen rock walker in his younger days, he was always an outstanding chess player. As such he was correspondent of the Illustrated London News and was known to frighten impresarios by playing chess with members of his orchestras during theatre performances.

After ill health compelled him to retire from Ealing Studios at the end of April 1953, Irving remained confined to bed at his home at 4 The Lawn, Ealing Green, adjoining the studios, and wrote a witty autobiography, Cue for Music, which was published posthumously in 1959. He died at home on 24 October 1953, aged seventy-five. A man of wide learning, Irving could—in his own words—be disputatious and didactic at times; but he was much valued as 'a character'.   ANDREW LAMB

Sources E. Irving, Cue for music (1959) · private information (2004) [daughter] · J. Huntley, British film music (1947) · New Grove · J. Parker, ed., Who's who in the theatre, 11th edn (1952) · b. cert. · m. certs. · d. cert.

Likenesses photographs, repro. in Irving, Cue for music

Wealth at death £1912 4s. 3d.: administration, 28 Aug 1956, CGPLA Eng. & Wales

Irving, George Vere (1815–1869), lawyer and antiquary, was the only son of Alexander Irving (b. c.1760) of Newton, Lanarkshire, afterwards a Scottish judge with the title of

Lord Newton. In 1837 George Irving was called to the Scottish bar. He took a great interest in the volunteer movement, and became captain of the Carnwath troop. He died at 5 St Mark's Crescent, Regent's Park, London, on 29 October 1869, aged fifty-three, survived by his wife, Leah Louisa, formerly Isaacs, whom he had married on 22 May 1844.

Irving was a fellow of the Society of Antiquaries (Scotland) and a vice-president of the British Archaeological Association, which he had joined in 1852 and to whose journal he was a frequent contributor. He also contributed frequently to *Notes and Queries*. He published a volume on the law of assessed taxes in Scotland in 1841, and a digest on the Inhabited House Tax Act, in 1852. With Alexander Murray he wrote *The Upper Ward of Lanarkshire* (1864), contributing an account of the archaeology and history of the area. He became interested in ancient camps and earthworks, particularly in British and Romano-British sites in St Albans. At the time of his death he was preparing for publication a section of the British Museum's Lauderdale papers.   GORDON GOODWIN, *rev.* C. A. CREFFIELD

Sources *Journal of the British Archaeological Association*, 26 (1870) · *N&Q*, 4th ser., 4 (1869), 398 · Irving, *Scots.*
Archives NL Scot., historical transcripts and notes
Wealth at death £1092 6s. 4d.: inventory, 1870, Scotland · £1203 10s. 2d.: confirmation, 1870 · £232 14s.—estate in England: 1870, NA Scot., SC 36/48/64, 303–6

Irving, Sir Henry [*real name* John Henry Brodribb] (1838–1905), actor, took the name Irving for his appearance at a private theatre in 1856 and made it official when he assumed it by royal licence in 1889, by which time it was famous. He was born at Keinton Mandeville, Somerset, on Saturday 6 February 1838; the house is marked with a plaque which was unveiled by Sir John Martin-Harvey on 31 October 1925.

A Methodist background Irving's father, Samuel Brodribb, of yeoman stock, was unsuccessful in a number of occupations; his mother, Mary Behenna, was Cornish; he was their only child. When he was four years old his parents moved to London, and he was left with his aunt Sarah Penberthy, in the mining village of Halsetown near St Ives. It was here, under the affectionate care of his aunt and her powerful, mercurial husband, Isaac, who was 'captain' of four tin mines, that Irving grew until his eleventh year, schooled in the Methodist teetotal religion of his foster parents, but also deep in the romance of the harsh but beautiful Cornwall of the time, when it was still a remote part of Britain. Those who knew him best said that he never wholly shook off the rusticity of his childhood. Ellen *Terry was amazed and amused that when, as Lear (1892), he picked her up to carry her onstage in their final scene, he invariably spat on his hands.

In 1849 Irving joined his parents in London, living at 65 Old Broad Street. It was his father who first introduced the boy to popular entertainment when he took him to see Van Amburgh, the 'Brute Tamer of Pompeii'. In his Cornwall days Irving had a repertory of recitations, and declared to his playmates that his ambition was to be an actor, a thing unthinkable in his Methodist world. But in London

Sir Henry Irving (1838–1905), by Sir John Everett Millais, 1883

he was sent to the City Commercial School by happy chance, for Dr Pinches, the headmaster, insisted that all his pupils be instructed in elocution for public performance, and young Irving quickly became his star turn. Dr Pinches remained a friend as long as he lived, and was succeeded as a friend by his son Edward, who in time advised Irving about the education of his own sons.

Irving's schooling ended when he was thirteen. He became a clerk in the solicitors' office of Peterson and Longman, in Milk Street, Cheapside; though the work was not disagreeable it led nowhere and in 1851 an opening was found for him in the offices of Thacker, Spink, & Co., East India merchants, in Newgate Street. It was during this time that he first attended a theatre, seeing Samuel Phelps as Hamlet, at Sadler's Wells. His ambition was now absorbing and he joined elocution classes and made the acquaintance of private theatres, where an aspirant might act a leading or subordinate role in a play of his choosing, upon payment of a fee—Richard III at £2, Buckingham at 15s. Squalid as these places were (*vide* Dickens in *Sketches by Boz*) they were an opening, and it was at the Soho that Irving made his first appearance under that name as Romeo.

Irving's determination to be an actor was a cause of grief and apprehension to his Methodist mother, and created a breach between them that never healed; it was the earliest evidence of the iron will that governed him all his life. His father encouraged him as long as he lived, and kept detailed scrapbooks of his son's notices.

When he was sixteen Irving became acquainted with a member of Phelps's company, William Hoskins, who gave him some instruction in acting and introduced him to Phelps. Learning of Irving's burning ambition Phelps warned him against the stage as 'an ill-requited profession', but seeing that this was unavailing he offered him an engagement in his company. With a wisdom beyond his years, Irving determined to gain experience in the provinces before seeking employment in London, and in 1856 Hoskins introduced him to E. D. Davis, who hired him for his stock company at the Lyceum Theatre, Sunderland.

Theatrical apprenticeship Here Irving made his first professional appearance, on 18 September 1856; his role was that of Gaston, duke of Orleans, in Bulwer-Lytton's *Richelieu*, and his first line, opening the play, was 'Here's to our enterprise'.

Thus began Irving's fifteen years of apprenticeship to what was indeed an ill-requited profession. Success came slowly and the craft was long to learn. Between 1856 and 1871 he played 'as cast' in stock companies in Sunderland, Edinburgh, Glasgow, Manchester, Liverpool, Oxford, and the Isle of Man; he endured a disastrous three weeks in Dublin in 1860 where, as he was replacing a popular favourite who had been dismissed, he was hooted down at every performance until at last he overcame the audience's hostility. He toured with his lifelong friend John L. Toole, the most popular low comedian of his day. In 1867 he appeared briefly in London at the Queen's Theatre in *Catherine and Petruchio*, David Garrick's drastically cut version of *The Taming of the Shrew*, as Petruchio to the Catherine of Ellen Terry; neither at that time thought much of the other. A detailed list of his engagements and roles is to be found in appendix B of Laurence Irving's fine biography of his grandfather.

In all Irving played more than 700 parts during this time, learning them hastily from 'sides' provided by the theatre's copyist; these were half-sheets of paper on which the words of a role were written, with cues that might be not more than three words in length, making a full understanding of the play difficult. Theatres provided basic costumes; actors were expected to provide any additional finery themselves, and Irving spent from his meagre earnings for swords, jewellery, and hats, which called attention to him as an actor who dressed his roles carefully, when many of the profession were careless. But he enjoyed no rapid success, and local critics 'cut him up' badly or ignored him entirely.

Irving played roles described as 'utility' or 'walking gentleman' much of the time but he appeared in all the stock favourites of the day. He played in fourteen of Shakespeare's plays and in the repertory of what was called old comedy. He played in raw-head-and-bloody-bones melodrama, imbecile farce, patriotic drama, both military and naval; he played drag roles in pantomime as an Ugly Sister in *Cinderella*, as Venoma in *The Sleeping Beauty*; he also appeared as an Ogre in *Puss in Boots* and as Scruncher the Wolf in *Little Bo-Peep*. Let no one scorn this as training for later and more sophisticated villainy. It was

during this period of his career that he gained his mastery of make-up, using the technique of water-based colours applied with brushes which he never abandoned, even after the virtually universal acceptance of greasepaint in the fourth quarter of the century.

On one occasion he sang a principal role in *Rob Roy* as substitute for Sims Reeves, one of the finest tenors of the day (Irving could sing, but not in the Sims Reeves class). As time wore on he gained a reputation as a reliable 'heavy' and in this category ranged from Bill Sikes in *Oliver Twist* to the sophisticated gambler Dudley Smooth in Bulwer-Lytton's *Money*. It was a prolonged and gruelling training, during which he became accustomed to criticism of his manner of speaking, the grotesquerie of his gestures, and his very thin legs, which never ceased even after he achieved an unassailable position as the leader of the British theatre.

During this time Irving regularly sent a portion of his salary, which could drop to 25*s*. a week, to his parents; he continued an allowance to his father throughout the latter's life. He knew want and hunger, and a gift of a suit of warm underwear from a more fortunate friend, Joe Robins, was a great moment of Christmas 1862.

Success, marriage, and *The Bells* At last Irving's fortunes began to turn. He secured a number of London engagements, in which he was well received, and on 4 June 1870 he appeared in a new play, *Two Roses*, by James Albery, in which the role of the pretentious and false-hearted Digby Grant suited him admirably. The play ran for almost 300 nights and Irving's place as a leading London actor was secured.

In another respect his fortunes had taken a wry turn. For some years Irving had been in love with Nellie Moore, a young actress of promise, but a false friend had come between them, and Nellie Moore's sudden death in January 1869 was unaccountable except perhaps as the result of a botched abortion. Until his death, Irving carried a photograph of her in his pocket book. At this time he had become acquainted with Florence O'Callaghan, the daughter of an Irish surgeon-general in the Indian service, and thus considerably the social superior of even a successful actor. Florence was wilful, and determined to marry Irving; she did so on 15 July 1869 at the parish church of St Marylebone. From the beginning the marriage was stormy, for Florence could not forget the social gulf between them, and Irving's bohemian habits did not make him an easy husband. They had met at the house of Clement Scott, another suitor, who later became the most influential critic of his time; it may well have been that Mrs Irving's interest in the theatre was predominantly critical.

In another respect, however, fortune had begun to smile—though somewhat reservedly—on Irving, for he was engaged by an American impresario, Colonel Hezekiah Linthicum Bateman, as leading man at the Lyceum Theatre, which Bateman had taken with the purpose of presenting his daughters Kate, Isabel, and Virginia before the London public. The girls had been actresses since childhood, in the 'infant phenomenon' mode, and it was now time for them to seek London stardom. Irving greatly liked the Bateman family, who were troupers to the depths of their souls, and they adopted him almost as a son. It was in their household that he sought refuge when home affairs were stormy.

It was clear, however, that with Colonel Bateman his daughters came first, second, and all the time, and Irving found himself playing uncongenial and unsuitable roles, such as Landry Barbeau in *Fanchette*, a much-mauled stage adaptation of George Sand's *La petite fadette*, prepared by Mrs Bateman, with Isabel's part grossly padded. Isabel Bateman was seventeen and, although unquestionably beautiful, she lacked the energy and charm of a leading actress. It was to 'support' her for an indefinite period that Irving had committed himself.

Irving's burning ambition would not suffer it. He persuaded the reluctant Bateman to mount a play which he had long had under his eye, an adaptation of Erckmann-Chatrian's *Le juif polonais* called *The Bells*, adapted by Leopold Lewis. Cheaply mounted, but rigorously rehearsed by Irving, *The Bells* first appeared on the night of Saturday 25 November 1871 before a small audience. During the following week London critics united to declare that they had seen a great actor.

In more than one way it was a turning point. The marriage was not going well. One son, Henry Brodribb, had been born on 5 August 1870; Florence was pregnant with the second; Laurence Sidney would be born in December 1871. As they drove home in their brougham, after the triumphant first night of *The Bells*, Irving said to his wife, 'Well, my dear, we shall soon have our own carriage and pair.' Her response was, 'Are you going to go on making a fool of yourself like this all your life?' Irving called to the driver to stop. He got out of the carriage and never returned to his home or spoke to his wife again. He had broken with his mother because of her disapproval of his profession, and thus he broke with his wife because she scorned it.

That night Irving went to his friends the Batemans, and during the subsequent months of despair they stood by him with exemplary loyalty, and Mrs Bateman in particular restrained the heavy drinking in which he sought forgetfulness. This association was complicated by the fact that Isabel was deeply in love with Irving, making affairs at the Lyceum difficult to maintain on a strictly professional footing, for he was now the unquestioned great attraction of the theatre, and it was the Bateman girls who were 'support'. His performances as King Charles I, as Eugene Aram, as Richelieu, and on 31 October 1874 as Hamlet, in which role he established himself as the unrivalled great Hamlet of his period, marked him as the foremost actor of the time. Bateman had generously subjected his ambition for his daughters to the advancement of his friend. *Hamlet* ran for 200 nights, an unheard of success for a Shakespearian play; it was on the day after the hundredth performance that Bateman died of a heart attack.

The management was carried on by Mrs Bateman, and from September 1875 until July 1878 she presented seasons in which Irving was unsatisfactory in *Macbeth* and *Othello* but magnificent as Richard III and as Louis XI in a poor play (rescued by a great part) by Dion Boucicault. It was at this time that he appeared in the 'dual role' of the virtuous Leserques and the villainous Dubosc in Charles Reade's *The Lyons Mail*, and this became one of his melodramatic standbys.

Managing the Lyceum, from 1878 By 1878 it became clear to Mrs Bateman that she could no longer maintain the Lyceum with Irving simply as a salaried actor, and that her daughters were not fated to realize the ambition that had inspired her husband. She therefore disposed of the theatre and management to Irving on 31 August of that year, and his great reign of twenty-three years in the theatre which he made world famous began on 30 December with a revival and handsome new mounting of his *Hamlet*.

The story of how the Lyceum passed into his hands is complicated. The best evidence shows that it was achieved with goodwill on both sides and a realistic acceptance of affairs by Mrs Bateman. A contrary account, suggesting great bitterness, is to be found in volume 2 of Compton Mackenzie's autobiography, in which it is asserted that Irving broke Mrs Bateman's heart. As Compton Mackenzie was a nephew of Isabel and the son of Kate Bateman, his version must be noted, highly coloured though it may be.

Much has been written of Irving's management, some of it neglectful of contemporary theatre practice, and of an actor–manager's primary obligation to make enough money to keep his theatre open. If Irving leant heavily on melodrama (a word he himself detested, thinking of such a play as *The Bells* as a psychological study, which is the quality he gave it) it was because his public delighted in his explorations of villainy, duplicity, and the tortures of remorse. He presented twelve of the plays of Shakespeare, of which, in 1896 and 1901 respectively, *Cymbeline* and *Coriolanus* can never have been thought of as crowd-pleasers. He presented Shakespeare's text of *Richard III* to audiences which had for 196 years been accustomed to Colley Cibber's coarse recension, and he restored the fifth act of *The Merchant of Venice*, which had for long been omitted by actors who thought that the disappearance of Shylock meant the end of interest in the plot. He cut the texts, though not as savagely as many of his contemporaries, because the extended scene changes of the time did not allow uncut versions, nor did popular taste call for them. Most people, and many critics, knew Shakespeare only through what they heard from the stage.

To his Shakespearian productions, as indeed to all his Lyceum offerings, Irving brought carefully considered and artistically refined physical mountings, employing as designers the finest artists of the day (Lawrence Alma Tadema for *Henry VIII*, Edward Burne-Jones for *King Arthur*), respected musicians (Charles Villiers Stanford and Arthur Sullivan to compose incidental music for *Lear* and *Macbeth*, to name but two), and scenic artists of the highest accomplishment such as Hawes Craven and Joseph Harker to provide the huge backcloths and set pieces for the *mise en scène*. He was a master of lighting, and rejected the new electric light in favour of the old-fashioned gaslight, with which he achieved effects hitherto unknown by using coloured silk mediums in front of the flames—dangerous but magical in result. It was Irving who finally established the custom of darkening the auditorium in order to concentrate attention on the stage picture. His productions were praised for their beauty and imagination, and he never yielded to elaboration for its own sake.

To bring about these results he gathered around him a staff of unusually able and loyal lieutenants, the most important of whom were Abraham (Bram) *Stoker, his manager of business and 'front of house', and H. J. Loveday, who had begun as a musical conductor but who was a sensitive and utterly accurate stage-manager, and in effect, under Irving, the director of the Lyceum productions. These two were with him until his death.

Irving spent without stint on everything that was needed to make his presentations perfect. He was lavish in payment of his actors and theatre staff—not all of whom neglected the chance to line their pockets at the expense of 'the Gov'nor'. As soon as he could afford it he had a long list of pensioners—old friends down on their luck, old actors, families of actors who had died in poverty. A friend estimated this expenditure as not less than £50 a week; at the end of his life he said ruefully that he had lived keeping an army. His personal expenditures were modest, and his lodgings at 15A Grafton Street (now marked by a plaque) were not luxurious, except for his large library, every volume of which related in some way to his stage work. He tipped with the open hand of a man who had known real poverty, and laughed when Ellen Terry told him in desperation (using the most dreadful of Victorian accusations) that such tipping was 'common'. But the guineas flowed on, and when Irving died every cabman in London tied a crepe ribbon on his whip, a tribute which the Gov'nor would have valued highly.

Stoker, at Irving's behest, made the Lyceum on a first night more like a party of distinguished persons than a theatre audience. After first nights, and hundredth nights, Irving entertained great numbers of the audience on the stage, which had been rapidly transformed into a pavilion, where Gunters served unlimited lobster, chicken, and champagne. In its original room in the back parts of the theatre, he revived the old Beefsteak Club, and it was there that he entertained his friends, and acquaintances whom he wished to become friends. His style of life was princely, but the money was not spent directly on himself.

Irving and Terry Irving's associate for twenty-five years, after 1878, was Ellen Terry (1847–1928), unquestionably the most charming, if not always the most artistically effective, actress of her time. She was an admirable foil for the darkling, sardonic Irving. Her expansive personality and exquisite but not wincing femininity gave a dimension to his productions that would otherwise have been lacking, so pervasive and powerful was the atmosphere he created. He was indulgent toward her lapses of memory,

her incalculability, and sometimes her irresponsibility on stage.

Under Irving's management Terry played memorably in seven of Shakespeare's greatest women's roles, and heroines in melodrama, which did not always tax her quality as an actress. It was at the beginning of their work together, in his *Hamlet* production of 30 December 1878, that she is thought by some to have become his mistress; she felt she had failed as Ophelia, and his sympathetic reassurance initiated a long association. The exact character of their relationship cannot now be known. It was soon assumed in the theatrical world that Terry was Irving's mistress, but the public was not encouraged to be curious, and when the Lyceum company toured Irving and Terry stayed at separate hotels, a delicacy of conduct that was much commented on, especially in the USA. The personal association did not last as long as their professional association, for Irving was not predominantly a man of sexual appetite, and Terry needed a variety of men to satisfy her exuberant tastes.

Irving's wife was bitter about the liaison, and instructed her sons to refer to Ellen Terry as 'the wench' (they were never permitted to speak of their father other than as 'Irving'). But Florence Irving did nothing to endanger her substantial allowance, which she was told by Irving's lawyers would be terminated at the first sign of public resentment. She was given a box for every first night, and appeared, a picture of feminine affront, with her sons, whom she sometimes encouraged to turn their backs on the stage and play cards in full view of their father. It was not until after their entry at Marlborough College in 1882 that the slow improvement in Irving's relations with his sons began; the bitterness inculcated and fostered by their mother was not wholly dispelled until, after Harry had studied for the bar and Laurence for the diplomatic service, both chose a stage career.

Irving and George Bernard Shaw Fame did not make Irving's life easy. The usual jealousies asserted themselves, and there were whispers that he suborned critics by taking options on their unproduced plays. This he certainly did, but not as extensively as was rumoured, and the critics who lent themselves to this sort of quid pro quo would have been quick to revenge if he had snubbed them. Such venality was not all-pervasive. This situation must be understood in terms of the theatre of its time, and retrospective high-mindedness achieves nothing.

One quarrel with a critic has, however, gained rather more notoriety than the circumstances justify. From January 1895 until 1898 George Bernard *Shaw was theatre critic for the *Saturday Review*, and during that time he pursued an implacable course of harassment against Irving, ostensibly because he did nothing for contemporary playwrights and ignored the new direction which the theatre had taken from the example of Ibsen. It was not true that Irving made use of no contemporary writers; he sought a play from J. M. Barrie, without result; he produced the earliest work of A. W. Pinero. He urged Alfred Tennyson to write for the theatre, for which the poet had little taste or aptitude; *Becket* and *The Cup*, the two Tennyson plays that

Irving brought to the stage, both needed extensive tinkering before they assumed anything like dramatic form.

The *Saturday Review* had long been severe on Irving, and when Shaw wrote of *King Arthur* in January 1895 he had an easy mark, for the play, begun by W. G. Wills and completed by Comyns Carr, was a feeble piece of uninspired verse, beautiful but empty. Shaw's campaign was severe on *Madame Sans Gêne* by Sardou (for whose master craftsmanship allied to commonplace inspiration Shaw coined the term Sardoodledom), and he thought little of *Olivia* (a dramatization of *The Vicar of Wakefield*). But it was in his criticism of *Richard III* (December 1896) that he may be thought to have overreached himself, for in 2500 words he compares the play with Punch, teaches most of the leading actors how to play their roles, and hints pretty broadly that Irving was drunk on the first night. This was understandably resented deeply by the Lyceum phalanx, and against it may be balanced Kate Bateman's declaration that, though drink went quickly to Irving's legs, it never affected his tongue.

This might have been passed over as the rough-and-tumble of theatrical life, except for two things: Shaw had a play to sell (*The Man of Destiny*) which was aimed straight at the heads of Irving and Terry, with whom Shaw professed himself in a long and enchanting correspondence (but never in a personal confrontation) to be in love. He saw himself as the hero rescuing the lovely maiden from the castle of the evil enchanter. He wanted the lovely maiden for the 'new drama', in the creation of which he had not, at this time, made a strong mark. Shaw was not venal but he was what may at times be something worse: he was a man of principle, and in the assertion of his principle his criticism veered between what his biographer St John Ervine called 'the Dublin smartie' and a spirit which might be called malignant.

Compare what he has to say about Irving with the criticism of J. T. Grein (1862–1935), a dominant figure in the Independent Theatre Club and later in the Stage Society, where he pressed the claims of the New Drama as assiduously as Shaw. Grein declares the Lyceum to be 'the National Theatre of the English world' ruled with tact and taste by a theatre autocrat who was 'no overstrained and vainglorious mummer, striving to concentrate all the lights and effects upon himself, thrusting everybody else into the shade'. Yet he finds space to deplore Irving's 'greater love for defunct dramatists than for the living'. Grein was a critic of international experience, in the theatres not only of England but of Germany, France, and his native Holland.

What was Irving? Appearance and voice Irving was a man of powerful and distinguished imagination, so concentrated on his profession that he had little time or energy for anything else. He was not a man of education, but his insights into Shakespeare astonished and delighted scholars of the stature of Sir Edmund Chambers. In pursuit of material to create his stage pictures he acquired and used a library both extensive and rare. By imagination and unremitting hard work he transformed a Cornish youth of somewhat dull appearance into a figure of extraordinary

distinction whose face was often described as beautiful, but which could turn (as Dubosc in *The Lyons Mail*) to coarse brutality. His psychological acuity was uncommon for, as Shaw says, he could reveal, under a humorous impishness 'glimpses of a latent bestial dangerousness'. This was never more in evidence than in his performance as Mephistopheles in his highly successful *Faust* in 1885. He was compelling and electrifying on the stage; off it he was of elegant demeanour and personal distinction that attracted, awed, and delighted a huge public. It is of interest that when Shaw was asked in old age who had been the greatest actor of his time he replied without hesitation that it had been Irving, and set to work at once to give an imitation of the great man—an imitation which has been recorded on film and which, though extraordinary, lacks magic.

Nothing could have reconciled the difference between Shaw, to whom the text of a play was its most important element—theatre as an adjunct to literature—and Irving, to whom the sub-text, provided by himself, and to which the total production offered an objective correlative, was supreme. It was this imaginative element that created the atmosphere of phantasmagoria and dream grotto that was the mark of every Lyceum production, even when the author was Shakespeare.

In person Irving was a little over 6 feet tall, and a tailor's bill gives his measurements, at the age of sixty: 'chest 40 inches, waist 37 inches, sleeve 33 inches'. From youth he wore his hair longer than was the fashion, and in his years of success it was carefully arranged and scented with bay rum. He was very short-sighted and wore a pince-nez everywhere except on the stage; it was one of the duties of his devoted valet and dresser, Walter Collinson, to see that he did not go on the stage with it, and that he was able to replace it the moment he was in the wings. This myopia may have contributed to the hypnotic quality of his gaze. Virtually everything about him was a gift to caricaturists, but the totality was transfixing.

A chief focus of criticism was Irving's voice and his idiosyncratic pronunciation. The quality of his voice was not sonorous and in great rhetorical passages it sometimes failed him, but in the main it served him well. A gramophone recording of a few lines from *Richard III* exists but its quality is poor and it cannot be trusted as evidence. Of his pronunciation, however, there are several authoritative accounts, and his enemy Shaw praised the purity of his speech and especially the firmness of his vowels, which contemporary English speech turned to diphthongs. Gordon Craig writes that Irving's speech had a Chaucerian ring and was expressive rather than refined. Ellen Terry records that in poetic passages his speech achieved great beauty.

Knighthood, decline, and death The pinnacle of Irving's career may be set at 1895, when his long campaign to have the theatre recognized as an art on an equal footing with painting and music was crowned by his knighthood, the first actor thus honoured. W. E. Gladstone—frequently in the audience at the Lyceum—wished to offer Irving a knighthood in 1883, but was dissuaded on the grounds that Irving's liaison with Ellen Terry would lead to a row with the queen about the proposal. However, Lord Rosebery gained him the knighthood in the birthday honours announced on 25 May 1895 and he was knighted on 18 July. The honour was greeted as the recognition of the theatre for which he had hoped: acclaim in his own country and in America, triumph over his detractors, and vindication in the eyes of his wife and the memory of his mother. As she touched his shoulder with the sword the queen said, unwontedly, 'I am very, very pleased'. What more was there to achieve?

A turn in Irving's fortunes was not long in coming. His strong physique was beginning to yield to the strains of overwork. A fall and a badly strained knee in 1897; serious pneumonia and pleurisy in 1898; respiratory troubles which made necessary his removal in 1899 from the gloomy Grafton Street rooms to 17 Stratton Street; a growing susceptibility to chills. Emphysema was at last diagnosed, but before that Stoker records that Irving was spitting pus from a damaged lung to such a degree that he required 500 handkerchiefs a week. Astonishingly, he managed to conceal his illness when on the stage, playing with his accustomed vigour and psychological penetration, but in private life he was ill indeed, and was at times unable to take any nourishment but beef tea laced with brandy.

This was inner grief. External misfortune was not wanting. On the night of 18 February 1898 a fire in the scene storage in the railway arches in Bear Lane, Southwark, destroyed the settings for forty-four of the plays that sustained Irving's touring enterprises, leaving only *The Bells* and *The Merchant of Venice* intact; the property was underinsured and replacement was out of the question. The American tours, always artistic triumphs, were markedly less profitable than they had been because of rising expenses. Eight such tours between 1883 and 1903, and his tours in the British provinces, had been the mainstay of the extremely expensive London Lyceum. Irving's immediate debts were pressing and the sale of his valuable library, in February 1899, only partly met them. With relief he accepted a proposal to turn the Lyceum into a joint-stock company administered by a syndicate. This was the end of his reign as autocrat of the most famous theatre in the world. His will, after he had generated great wealth, was probated at £20,090.

Irving made a brave show at the end. *Robespierre* at the Lyceum in 1899 and *Dante*, also by Sardou, produced at Drury Lane in 1903, were grandiose but empty plays in which he repeated his legerdemain of making bricks with very little straw. He toured, and was everywhere affectionately acclaimed, but it was plain to Stoker and Loveday that the exertion of such parts as Mathias was killing him. He collapsed on 13 October 1905 in the lobby of the Midland Hotel, Bradford, after performing Tennyson's *Becket*, and died in the arms of his faithful dresser, Walter Collinson.

Irving's death was greeted with an extraordinary show of national mourning. After some demurral, he was buried in Westminster Abbey on 20 October, at the feet of the statue of Shakespeare and beside the grave of David Garrick. His coffin was covered with an immense pall of laurel leaves, the gift of his last female confidante, Mrs Eliza Aria.

What was Irving really like? Perhaps the best evocation of him as man and actor is Max Beerbohm's essay in the *Saturday Review* of 21 October 1905 in which he gives Irving the Pre-Raphaelite title 'the Knight from Nowhere'. Public figure, leader of his profession, transfixing actor of tragedy and melodrama, always at the depths lurked the old bohemian, who had, with infinite relish, transformed the Cornish Methodist lad into one of the icons of Britain at the proudest reach of her history.

ROBERTSON DAVIES

Sources L. Irving, *Henry Irving: the actor and his world* [1951] · A. Brereton, *The life of Henry Irving*, 2 vols. (1908) · B. Stoker, *Personal reminiscences of Henry Irving*, 2 vols. (1906) · W. Winter, *Shakespeare on the stage* (1911–16) · G. Craig, *Henry Irving* (1930) · W. Winter, *Vagrant memories* (1915) · C. W. Scott, *From 'The bells' to 'King Arthur': a critical record of the first-night productions at the Lyceum Theatre from 1871 to 1895* (1896) · D. Mayer, ed., *Henry Irving and 'The bells'* (1980) [memoir by Eric Jones-Evans] · H. A. Saintsbury and C. Palmer, eds., *We saw him act* (1939) [a symposium on the art of Sir Henry Irving] · M. Beerbohm, *Around theatres*, new edn (1953) · E. Terry, *The story of my life* (1908) · *Ellen Terry and Bernard Shaw: a correspondence*, ed. C. St John (1931) · G. B. Shaw, *Our theatre in the nineties*, 3 vols. (1931) · J. Martin-Harvey, *The autobiography of Sir John Martin-Harvey* (1933) · J. Agate, *Ego: the autobiography of James Agate*, 9 vols. (1935–48) · W. H. Pollock, *Impressions of Henry Irving* (1908) · G. Sampson, *Seven essays* (1947) · H. C. Newton, *Cues and curtain calls* (1927) · C. Mackenzie, *My life and times*, 10 vols. (1963–71) · Gladstone, *Diaries* · St J. G. Ervine, *Bernard Shaw* (1956)

Archives Garr. Club · Russell-Cotes Art Gallery and Museum, Bournemouth, papers · Theatre Museum, London, corresp., diaries, and papers; scrapbook relating to his early career | BL, letters to T. H. S. Escott, Add. MS 58782 · BL, Gladstone MSS · BL, letters to George Bernard Shaw, Add. MS 50538 · Bodl. Oxf., corresp. with Lord Kimberley; letters to Lewis family · Hove Central Library, Sussex, letters to Lady Wolseley · Hunt. L., letters mainly to Clement Scott · U. Durham L., letters to Frances Burnand | SOUND BL NSA, performance recordings · L. Cong., performance recording

Likenesses J. Archer, oils, 1871–2, Museum of London · J. Archer, oils, 1871–2, Russell-Cotes Art Gallery, Bournemouth · J. M. Whistler, oils, 1875, Metropolitan Museum, New York · photographs, 1876–99, NPG · J. Bastien-Lepage, oils, 1880, NPG · J. E. Millais, oils, 1883, Garr. Club [*see illus.*] · E. O. Ford, marble statue, 1883–5, Guildhall Art Gallery, London · W. H. Margetson, double portrait, oils, probably *c.*1885 (with George Alexander), V&A · oil sketch, 1887, Russell-Cotes Art Gallery, Bournemouth · J. Blackwell, bronze medallion, 1893, Russell-Cotes Art Gallery, Bournemouth · M. Beerbohm, caricatures, drawings, 1895–1905, Garr. Club · M. L. Menpes, pencil drawing, 1898, Athenaeum, London · P. May, pencil sketches, 1899, NPG · W. Nicholson, coloured woodcut, 1899, NPG · F. C. Gould, pen, ink, and watercolour sketch, 1900 (for a caricature), V&A; repro. in H. Begbie, *The Struwwel Peter alphabet* · F. Eugene, photograph, *c.*1903, National Museum of Photography, Film and Television, Bradford, Royal Photographic Society collection · B. Partridge, oils, *c.*1903, Museum of London · R. Eves, oils, 1905–10 (after photograph by W. Crooke?, 1904), Museum of London · T. Brock, bronze statue, 1910, NPG · Ape [C. Pellegrini], chromolithograph caricature (in *The bells*), NPG; repro. in *VF* (19 Dec 1874) · W. H. Bartlett, group portrait, oils (*Saturday night at the Savage Club*), Savage Club, London · H. H. Cameron, photograph (as Thomas à Beckett), U. Texas, Gernsheim collection · E. O. Ford, figure on memorial (as Tamburlaine), Dane John Gardens, Canterbury · E. O. Ford, plaster bust, Man. City Gall. · G. Frampton, death mask, Museum of London · H. Furniss, pen-and-ink sketches, Garr.

Club, NPG · E. H. Gordon-Craig, ink and watercolour drawing (in *The bells*), V&A · F. C. Gould, silhouette, NPG · A. Maclaren, drawing, Garr. Club · G. G. Manton, group portrait, watercolour drawing (*Conversazione at the Royal Academy, 1891*), NPG · J. E. Millais, oils (copy by H. Allen), NPG · F. D. Niblett, watercolour drawing (as Hamlet), Museum of London · P. O'Malley, double portrait, oils (with Edward VII), Vancouver Club, Canada · B. Partridge, pencil drawings, Garr. Club, V&A · C. Pollock, bronze bust, Russell-Cotes Art Gallery, Bournemouth · C. Pollock, bronze bust, Garr. Club · W. Rothenstein, lithographs, BM, Harvard TC, NPG, V&A · W. Seymour, wash drawing (as Macbeth), V&A · drawing (as Wolsey), Garr. Club · oils (as Robespierre), Russell-Cotes Art Gallery, Bournemouth · photographs and photogravures, Theatre Museum

Wealth at death £20,090 4s. 11d.: resworn probate, 2 June 1906, *CGPLA Eng. & Wales*

Irving, James (1759–1791), naval surgeon and slave trader, was born at Langholm, Dumfriesshire, on 15 December 1759, the third and only surviving child of John Irving (1731?–1807), blacksmith and innkeeper, and his wife, Isobel, *née* Little (1725?–1791). As a surgeon and captain in the Liverpool slave trade Irving participated in the transportation of approximately 3000 Africans to slavery in the Americas. In July 1783, aged twenty-three, he undertook his first slave-trading voyage out of Liverpool, Europe's leading slave-trading port. By January 1789 he had completed five voyages, two of which were on board the *Princess Royal*, a ship which could carry 800 slaves.

From May 1786 Irving wrote to his wife, Mary (*née* Tunstall), at 9 College Lane, Liverpool, describing himself as surgeon. Official reference to his status is available in the examinations book of the Company of Surgeons, though there is no evidence to indicate where he was trained. Irving was passed as a surgeon to African ships on 2 April 1789. In this role he was involved in the physical examination of the slaves gathered for sale on the west coast of Africa, to which he made little reference in his letters written in Africa and the West Indies. However, in December 1786 Irving describes how he and the crew of the *Jane* were awaiting the sale of their 'disagreeable cargo' at Barbados. Impatient with 'our black cattle' who are 'intolerably noisy', he commented, 'I am almost melted in the midst of five or six hundred of them' (Schwarz, 112–13). The letters reveal a family man of liberal education, able to reconcile his occupation with his Christian beliefs.

In May 1789, at the comparatively young age of twenty-nine, Irving was promoted to his first captaincy of the *Anna*, a 'fine new vessell' (Schwarz, 140), capable of carrying eighty slaves. On 27 May 1789, twenty-four days after sailing from Liverpool, the *Anna* was shipwrecked on the Atlantic coast of Morocco. Irving and his crew were captured the following day by 'Arabs and Moors' (ibid., 118–21) and sold into slavery. In captivity Irving established a correspondence with British consular officials at Mogador and Tangier. On 24 June 1789 he pleaded with vice-consul John Hutchinson to 'rescue us speedily from the most intollerable slavery' (ibid.); after lengthy negotiations the consular officials secured their release. On 9 August 1790 Irving informed his wife of 'the termination of my bondage, which I have weathered with ten thousand difficulties' (ibid., 141–2).

Irving's journal indicates that enslavement did not prompt any reflection on his occupation. Nor did he recognize any irony in his situation; on the contrary he recorded that 'I could have died rather than devote my life to be spent in so abject a state, bereft of all Christian society, a slave to a savage race who despised and hated me for my belief' (Schwarz, 94–5). Irving's journal and letters offer a rare insight into the mindset of a participant in the Atlantic slave trade as he is one of the few slave-ship captains for whom personal papers survive.

On his arrival in London in November 1790 Irving wrote of his eagerness to see his son, James, who had been born on 4 December 1789 and baptized fourteen days later in the congregation of protestant dissenters at Benns Garden Chapel, Liverpool. By 14 December 1790 he had agreed to command the *Ellen*, owned by John Dawson. Following the ship's arrival on the Gold Coast of Africa on 5 April 1791, Irving purchased 341 Africans, eighty-eight of whom were transferred to other ships. On 16 September 1791 the *Ellen*, with 253 slaves, sailed for Trinidad. Forty-six Africans died during this middle passage. Irving died on 24 December 1791, the sixth and final member of the crew of twenty-seven to perish. There is no evidence to indicate how he died.   SUZANNE SCHWARZ

Sources S. Schwarz, ed., *Slave captain: the career of James Irving in the Liverpool slave trade* (1995) · J. Irving, journal, 1789–90, Lancs. RO, DDX 1126/1 [copy] · correspondence relating to James Irving, 1789–1809, Lancs. RO, DDX 1126/2–45 · James M. Matra, correspondence, 1789–90, PRO, FO 52/8–9 · parish registers, Langholm, 1688–1854, Dumfries Archive Centre, MF 67 · Liverpool muster rolls, 1782–92, PRO, BT 98/42–52 · customs registers of shipping, Merseyside Maritime Museum Archive, C/CX/L/4, vols. 4–8 · log and journal of the *Ellen* of Liverpool, House of Lords Main Papers, 28 June 1799 [extracts] · parish register, congregation of protestant dissenters, Benns Garden Chapel, 1734–1832, Lpool RO, MF 1/32 [birth, baptism] · S. D. Behrendt, 'The captains in the British slave trade from 1785 to 1807', *Transactions of the Historic Society of Lancashire and Cheshire*, 140 (1990), 79–140 · W. Lempriere, *A tour from Gibraltar to Tangier, Sallee, Mogodore, Santa Cruz, Tarudant, and thence over Mount Atlas to Morocco*, 3rd edn (1804)

Archives Lancs. RO, corresp. and journal

Irving, Joseph (1830–1891), journalist and antiquary, born at Dumfries on 2 May 1830, was the son of Andrew Irving, joiner. After education at the parish school of Troqueer, Maxwelltown, he served an apprenticeship as a printer in the office of the *Dumfries Standard*; he was subsequently a compositor and journalist in Dumfries and Sunderland and was for a time on the staff of the *Morning Chronicle*. In 1854 he became editor of the *Dumbarton Herald*. About this time he married Jane Walker Bell (1830?–1869). They had four children. For some years after 1854 he was a bookseller in Dumbarton, published a history of the county, and started in 1867 the *Dumbarton Journal*, which failed. In 1860 he became a fellow of the Society of Antiquaries of Scotland, and in 1864 an honorary member of the Archaeological Society of Glasgow, to whose *Transactions* he contributed an important paper on the 'Origin and progress of burghs in Scotland'.

Irvine disposed of his Dumbarton business in 1869 on the death of his wife, who had helped him much in all his undertakings, and after living a few years in Renton, Dunbartonshire, settled in 1880 in Paisley. There he wrote for the *Glasgow Herald* and other journals, and did much solid literary work. He was an authority on Scottish history and an excellent reviewer. He wrote a number of books about the west of Scotland and its history, including memoirs of the Smollett and Dennistoun families. Several of his works have been of lasting value: his *History of Dumbartonshire* (1857) and *The Book of Dumbartonshire* (3 vols., 1879), which was revised by his son John (3 vols., 1917–24), are still standard; his *Book of Eminent Scotsmen* (1882) also remains of use. He also published *Annals of our Time* (1869, and various subsequent supplements). Irving died at his home, Hillhead House, Paisley, of heart disease on 2 September 1891.   T. W. BAYNE, *rev.* H. C. G. MATTHEW

Sources *Lennox Herald* (5 Sept 1891), 4 · *Glasgow Herald* (5 Sept 1891) · family tree, Dumbarton District Libraries, Dumbarton **Archives** BL, corresp. with Macmillans, Add. MS 55077 **Wealth at death** £171 19s. 9d.: inventory, 27 Oct 1891, *CCI*

Irving, Lydia (1797–1893), philanthropist, was born on 15 May 1797 in Wellbury, Yorkshire, the eldest daughter of Hannah and John Irving; her father was clerk to W. Fry & Co., Tea Dealers and Poultry, London. She was brought up by her grandparents, who were both strict Quakers, until their deaths, when she returned to her parents' home.

In July 1825 Lydia Irving joined the British Ladies Society for promoting the reformation of female prisoners, which had been founded in 1821 by Elizabeth Fry as an expansion of her Newgate committee. Lydia immediately began to visit White Cross Street prison. From January 1826 she helped audit the society's accounts and in December 1836 she became sub-treasurer of the society. In 1828 she was instrumental in gaining funding from the Navy Board to purchase the gifts given to each woman on board the transport ships, which prior to this had been funded entirely by the British Ladies. Subsequently, she became a member of the convict ship subcommittee, visiting most of the ships to distribute the gifts of useful articles—which included aprons, a knife and fork, and needlework implements and materials—before they sailed.

A Quaker herself, Lydia Irving was regarded by Elizabeth Fry as one of her closest friends and helpers. In 1838 Lydia accompanied Elizabeth and Joseph Fry to France with Josiah Forster and William Allen, in the service of the Friends, although she and Elizabeth Fry also visited women's prisons there. Irving was also an overseer at the Ratcliff and Barking monthly meetings of the Society of Friends and later at Devonshire House.

After the death of Elizabeth Fry in October 1845 the British Ladies Society carried on with its reform work. In her memory the Elizabeth Fry Refuge was founded, for penitent females of the servant classes. It was run by a subcommittee of the British Ladies Society which Lydia Irving joined on 1 April 1850; by 1852 she was the assistant secretary to the refuge. She resigned from the society in 1877, when the onset of blindness made prison visiting impossible. A member for more than fifty years, she was held in high esteem by other members, who relied on her administrative skills and long experience, and her retirement was marked by the presentation of a Bible. In 1881, by way of appreciation for all her hard work, the British Ladies presented Lydia with £40; a further £20 was promised annually.

Lydia Irving had lived at 9 Hardwich Place, Commercial Road, London, but towards the end of her life she resided with her niece, Louisa Dodshon, also a member of the British Ladies Society, at 11 Victoria Grove, Stoke Newington, London, maintaining her strict adherence to the principles and dress of the Society of Friends to the end. Two years before her death at Stoke Newington on 22 February 1893, the British Ladies Society amalgamated with the Elizabeth Fry Refuge.   AMANDA PHILLIPS

Sources 'Dictionary of Quaker biography', RS Friends, Lond. [card index] · British Ladies Society committee minutes, 1823–35, 1855–91, Rose Lipman Library, Hackney Archives Department · *Annual Monitor* (1894), 98 **Wealth at death** £463 16s. 0d.: probate, 28 March 1893, *CGPLA Eng. & Wales*

Irving, Sir Paulus Aemilius, first baronet (1751–1828), army officer, was born on 30 August 1751, the son of Lieutenant-Colonel Paulus Aemilius Irving (*d.* 1796), who was wounded at Quebec when serving in the 15th foot under General James Wolfe, and died lieutenant-governor of Upnor Castle, Kent. His mother was Judith, the daughter of Captain William Westfield of Dover. Irving was appointed lieutenant in the 47th foot in 1764, became captain in 1768, and was promoted major in 1775. He served at Lexington in April 1775 at the outbreak of the American War of Independence, at the battle of Bunker Hill that June, and in Boston during the blockade. Later he accompanied the regiment to Quebec, and was present in the affair at Trois Rivières and the various actions of Lieutenant-General John Burgoyne's army down to the surrender at Saratoga on 17 October 1777. He was afterwards detained as a prisoner of war in America for three years.

Irving returned home in 1781 and in 1783 became lieutenant-colonel of the 47th foot. In 1790 he took the regiment out to the Bahamas, where he served until 1795, becoming brevet colonel in 1791 and major-general in 1794. On the death of Sir John Vaughan (21 June 1795) he succeeded to the West India command, in which he was replaced by Major-General Leigh in September of the same year. Irving then assumed the command in St Vincent, and on 2 October 1795 took the enemy's position at La Vigie with heavy casualties. For this he received the thanks of George III, conveyed by the duke of York. Irving returned home in December 1795. He was appointed colonel of the 6th Royal Veteran battalion in 1802 and was afterwards transferred to the colonelcy of his old corps, the 47th (Lancashire) foot. He was created a baronet on 19 September 1809 and became a full general in 1812. On 4 February 1786 he had married Lady Elizabeth St Lawrence, the second daughter of Thomas St Lawrence, first earl of Howth; the couple had two sons and a daughter. Irving died at Carlisle on 31 January 1828, and the baronetcy became extinct on the death of his younger son, the third and last baronet.

H. M. CHICHESTER, *rev.* PHILIP CARTER

Sources *GM*, 1st ser., 98/2 (1828), 269–70 · J. G. Wilson and J. Fiske, eds., *Appleton's cyclopaedia of American biography*, rev. edn, 7 vols. (1894–1900) · J. Philippart, ed., *The royal military calendar*, 3 vols. (1815–16)
Archives NL Scot., accounts and letter-books

Irwin. For this title name *see* Ingram, Anne, Viscountess Irwin (*c.*1696–1764); Ingram, Frances, Viscountess Irwin (1734?–1807).

Irwin, Eyles (*bap.* 1751, *d.* 1817), East India Company servant and writer, was born in Calcutta, where he was baptized on 23 February 1751, the son of Captain James Irwin, of Roscommon, Ireland, and his wife, Sarah, *née* Beale, the widow of Henry Palmer. He was educated in England, under William Rose at Chiswick, Middlesex, and at 'a celebrated academy in London', and, like his father, joined the service of the East India Company, being appointed a writer in 1766. Having returned to India, Irwin took up his post at Fort St George, Madras, and progressed upwards in the company's administrative hierarchy, becoming a factor in 1774 and a junior merchant two years later. In September 1771 he was appointed to survey the Black Town and was made superintendent of the lands belonging to Madras. During these years he wrote two works of poetry: *Saint Thomas's Mount: a Poem, Written by a Gentleman in India* (1774) and *Bedukah, or the Self-Devoted, an Indian Pastoral* (1776). Both were published in London and were the first fruits of literary activity that was to produce over a dozen published works during the remainder of Irwin's life. In 1776 he became caught up in the political storm that overtook the governor of Madras, George Pigot, who was placed in confinement by members of his own council. Irwin supported Pigot, and in August he was suspended from the company's service. Early in 1777 he left India in order to seek redress in England.

Irwin later published an account of his journey home, which was entitled *A series of adventures in the course of a voyage up the Red Sea, on the coasts of Arabia and Egypt, and of a route through the desarts of Thebais, in the year 1777* (1780). In this he displayed his classical education and described his experiences and observations during the journey, which lasted eleven months. On reaching England, Irwin found that he had already been reinstated by the directors of the company. His experiences appear to have prompted him to criticize the company's policy from an Indian perspective. In the third of his *Eastern Eclogues*, 'Ramah, or, The Bramin' (1780), for example, Irwin described the suicide of a Brahman in the face of the tyranny of British rule, concluding with a prophecy on the company's eventual defeat by the Muslim community. In 1778 he married Honor, daughter of the Revd William Brooke of co. Longford, with whom he had three sons and two daughters.

Irwin returned to India in 1780 as a senior merchant and his route was again overland, but this time via Aleppo, Baghdad, and the Persian Gulf. He again published an account of his adventures which also produced *Occasional Epistles, Written During a Journey from London to Busrah* (1783). Following his arrival at Madras in June 1781 he was appointed by the governor, Lord Macartney, to the committee dealing with assigned revenue and in 1783 was made the superintendent of revenue in the Tinnevelly and Madura districts. Irwin was successful in his work, which was later rewarded by the directors of the company, but ill health forced his return to England in 1785. Following an assignment to China in 1792, he left the company's service for good in 1794.

Having stood unsuccessfully as a candidate for a directorship of the company in 1795, Irwin devoted his retirement to literary pursuits. His publications included *An Enquiry into the Feasibility of the Supposed Expedition of Buonaparte to the East* (1798), *The Bedouins, or Arabs of the Desert: a Comic Opera in Three Acts* (1802), which played in Dublin for three nights, and *An Essay on the Origin of the Game of Chess* (1820). He was a member of the Royal Irish Academy.

Irwin died on 12 August 1817 at Clifton, near Bristol, and was buried in the churchyard there.   D. L. PRIOR

Sources DNB · R. H. Phillimore, ed., *Historical records of the survey of India*, 1 (1945) · C. C. Prinsep, *Record of services of the Honourable East India Company's civil servants in the Madras presidency from 1741 to 1858* (1885) · East India Company records, Calcutta baptisms, BL OIOC · *Annual Biography and Obituary*, 2 (1818) · D. E. Baker, *Biographia dramatica, or, A companion to the playhouse*, rev. I. Reed, new edn, rev. S. Jones, 3 vols. in 4 (1812) · *Asiatic Journal* (1817) · K. Teltscher, *India inscribed: European and British writing in India, 1660–1800* (1995) · H. D. Love, *Vestiges of old Madras, 1640–1800*, 4 vols. (1913) · Nichols, *Illustrations*, 8.359–60
Archives Bodl. Oxf., corresp. with Lord Macartney, MSS Eng. hist. b. 242, c. 1123 · FM Cam., letters to William Hayley · PRO NIre., letters to Lord Macartney, D 572
Likenesses J. Walker, mezzotint, pubd 1780 (after G. Romney), BM

Irwin, Sir John (1727/8–1788), army officer, born in Dublin, was the eldest son of Lieutenant-General Alexander Irwin and his wife, Catherine. Alexander Irwin entered the army in 1689, and was colonel of the 5th foot from June 1737 until his death in 1752, holding important commands on the Irish establishment. When very young John attracted the notice of Lionel Sackville, first duke of Dorset, lord lieutenant of Ireland (1730–37), who appointed him page of honour about 1735 or 1736. This began his connection with the Sackville family, which continued the rest of his life. He subsequently became the closest friend and confidant of the duke's younger son, Lord George Sackville (who changed his surname to Germain in 1770), continuing close despite the latter's disgrace following the battle of Minden (1 August 1759). Irwin was educated in Ireland, and owing to his patron's interest and his father's rank in the army, he was given a company in his father's regiment (the 5th foot) while a schoolboy. His commission as ensign was dated 8 July 1736, and on 14 January 1737 he became a lieutenant; he was promoted captain in 1745 and major in 1751. At the close of 1748 his father granted him a year's furlough to travel on the continent. Philip Dormer Stanhope, fourth earl of Chesterfield, who, while lord lieutenant of Ireland in 1745–6, seems to have taken a fancy to him and regularly corresponded with him for the following twenty years, gave him a letter of introduction to Solomon Dayrolles at The Hague. Chesterfield described him as 'a good pretty young fellow; and, considering that he has never been yet out of his native country, much more *presentable* than one could expect' (*Letters*, ed. Dobré, 4.1273). From The Hague Irwin went to Paris. He returned to Dublin at the end of 1749. He married on 16 December 1749 Elizabeth, youngest daughter of Hugh Henry of Dublin and Straffan, Kildare. His wife died in April 1750, and he was still in Dublin in 1751. In 1752 he was gazetted lieutenant-colonel of the 5th foot, his father's old regiment, and in April 1753 he married Anne (*d.* 1767), daughter of Sir Edward *Barry (1696–1776). In 1755 he visited Chesterfield at Bath, and reportedly Irwin then suggested to Chesterfield his paper entitled 'Good-breeding' which appeared in *The World* (no. 148) of 30 October 1755. Irwin and his wife were often in London after 1757, when his regiment left Ireland for Chatham. In 1758 he served in an attack on the French coast. In 1760 he served with distinction in Germany through the campaign under Prince Ferdinand of Brunswick. He became a full colonel on 1 March 1761, and was appointed to command the 74th foot. His regiment was disbanded in 1762, and for three years he had no military employment. On 10 July 1762 he was promoted major-general, and on 30 November he entered the House of Commons, in accordance with a desire he had expressed to Chesterfield eight years earlier, as MP for East Grinstead, Sussex, a burgage borough controlled by the Sackville family, who owned the majority of the burgages. He followed Lord George Sackville's political line, voting with the opposition until 1774, then with the government. He almost never spoke. He was re-elected in 1768, 1774, and 1780, and retired in 1783, but his attendance in the house was always irregular. On becoming an MP he took a prominent place in London society, and resided at Queen Anne Street, Cavendish Square.

From 1765 to 1767 Irwin was governor of Gibraltar, where his second wife died in 1767. While abroad he was gazetted colonel of the 57th regiment of foot on the Irish establishment (17 November 1767). He was in Paris on 26 June 1768, when Madame du Deffand wrote to Horace Walpole of her favourable impression of him. Chesterfield introduced him at the same time to Madame de Monconseil, writing of him, 'pour un Anglais, il a des manières' (*Letters*, ed. Dobré, 6.2847). Chesterfield afterwards told him that he believed him to be the first English traveller who could bring testimonials from Paris of having kept good company there.

Promoted lieutenant-general in 1772, in May 1775 Irwin was appointed, probably through Lord George Germain's influence, commander-in-chief in Ireland and a privy councillor there. On 15 December 1775 he was appointed KB, but he was not installed for four years. He was active in repressing the activities of the Whiteboys, a southern Irish agrarian insurgent movement of labourers, cottiers, and small farmers against enclosures, tithes, and other grievances. He lived mostly in Dublin, where he maintained a lavish establishment and was reportedly popular with all classes. In 1779, with the Irish situation threatening, Lord North wanted him removed, and in June wrote to George III that Irwin, 'though well esteemed as a gentleman, is in no great estimation as a general' (Brooke, 668). George refused and Irwin coped. In December 1779 he was installed a knight of the Bath, and joined the other new knights in giving a ball at the opera house, Haymarket, to all the nobility and distinguished persons in London. In November 1780 he became colonel of the 3rd regiment of horse or Carabiniers in Ireland (afterwards the 6th dragoon guards). At a banquet he gave at Dublin to the lord lieutenant (Frederick Howard, fifth earl of Carlisle) in 1781 he reportedly spent nearly £1500 on a centrepiece for the dinner table, a barley sugar model of the siege of Gibraltar. He retired from the post of commander-in-chief in Ireland on the fall of North's administration in March 1782; resided in his house in Piccadilly, overlooking Green Park; resumed his place in parliament; and became full general on 19 February 1783.

Irwin delighted in the pleasures of society, and his charm made him a general favourite. Charles James Fox thought him a fop but 'good-humoured' (Brooke, 667), and Sir Nathaniel Wraxall wrote, 'It was impossible to possess finer manners, without any affectation, or more perfect good breeding' (ibid.). With George III he was on especially good terms. Wraxall wrote that the king once said to him: 'They tell me, Sir John, that you love a glass of wine', to which Irwin replied: 'Those, Sir, who have so reported of me to your Majesty have done me great injustice; they should have said a bottle' (*Memoirs of … Wraxall*, 3.93). Wraxall related that Irwin's tall, graceful figure, set off by all the ornaments of dress and by the insignia of the Bath, which he constantly wore, even in undress, made him conspicuous when he attended the House of Commons. But his reckless extravagance dissipated his resources. At Paris Madame du Deffand noted his 'folles dépenses'. The loss of his appointment in March 1782 ruined him financially. Owing to his pecuniary difficulties he went to live in France, and retired from parliament in April 1783. He rented a château in Normandy. Reportedly George III sent him £1000. He moved to Italy, and resided at Parma, where he enjoyed the friendship of Duke Ferdinand and his consort, the Archduchess Amelia, and kept open house for all English visitors with characteristic hospitality. He died at Parma towards the close of May 1788, aged sixty. The *Gentleman's Magazine* believed he died in Brussels, but this is erroneous. Wraxall relates that, despite the duke's intervention, his remains were denied by the priesthood the rites of Christian burial, and the funeral service was read by an English gentleman. Irwin was survived by his third wife, Caroline, who died on 27 August 1805; they had two children. Her maiden name and the date of the marriage are not known. After her husband's death George III sent her £500 to enable her and her children to return home.

A. I. DASENT, rev. ROGER T. STEARN

Sources J. Brooke, 'Irwin, John', HoP, *Commons, 1754–90* • *Morning Post* (20 June 1788) • *Morning Chronicle* (20 June 1788) • J. Campbell, *Memoirs of Sir James Campbell, of Arkinglass*, 2 vols. (1832) • *The letters of Philip Dormer Stanhope, fourth earl of Chesterfield*, ed. B. Dobrée, 6 vols.

(1932) • *The historical and the posthumous memoirs of Sir Nathaniel William Wraxall, 1772–1784*, ed. H. B. Wheatley, 5 vols. (1884) • *Correspondance de Madame du Deffand* (1865) • *The Grenville papers: being the correspondence of Richard Grenville ... and ... George Grenville*, ed. W. J. Smith, 1–2 (1852) • *GM*, 1st ser., 58 (1788), 562 • J. Black, *Britain as a military power, 1688–1815* (1999) • A. Valentine, *Lord George Germain* (1962) • T. W. Moody and others, eds., *A new history of Ireland*, 4: *Eighteenth-century Ireland, 1691–1800* (1986) • R. F. Foster, *Modern Ireland, 1600–1972* (1989) • T. Bartlett and K. Jeffery, *A military history of Ireland* (1996)

Archives NL Scot., legal corresp. and papers | Norfolk RO, corresp. with the earl of Buckinghamshire • U. Hull, letters to Sir Charles Hotham-Thompson • U. Mich., Clements L., corresp. with Lord George Sackville

Irwin, Margaret Hardinge (1858–1940), women's labour activist, was born at sea on 13 January 1858 on the barque *Lord Hardinge*, after which she was named. She was the only child of James Richie Irwin, master mariner, of 3 Pine Terrace, Broughty Ferry, Forfarshire, and Margaret Hunter Cappon.

Educated privately, Margaret Irwin moved to St Andrews where she attended classes at the university. She was awarded the lady literate in arts (LLA) there in 1880 after studying French, German, and English. The LLA was then the only degree equivalent available to women prior to their admission to full matriculation rights in Scottish universities, granted only after the 1889 Universities (Scotland) Act. Irwin later moved into lodgings in Glasgow and from 1887 to 1889 attended classes at Glasgow School of Art. In the 1888–9 session she also attended classes in political economy at Glasgow's Queen Margaret College. After her studies, Margaret Irwin pursued a career which involved her with a number of organizations representing and campaigning for women's rights and improved working conditions. As well as engaging in campaign work, she acquired Sholach Fruit Farm, at Blairgowrie in Perthshire, which she ran on model lines.

Margaret Irwin became officially involved in campaigning for women's working rights in the early 1890s. What motivated her is not clear but she was committed to the suffrage movement and much of her work aimed to promote equal rights for women workers. In 1891 she was appointed by the Scottish branch of the Women's Protective and Provident League as its full-time organizer and in the same year was one of four women assistant commissioners responsible for gathering and returning information about the conditions of working women on behalf of the royal commission on labour. The Women's Protective and Provident League had developed from the Women's Trade Council and in the Glasgow area was associated with the Glasgow Council for Women's Trades. These were in turn linked to the National Federal Council of Scotland for Women's Trades, which in 1895 claimed affiliation to sixteen trades councils and twenty-five unions with over 100,000 members in all.

Margaret Irwin continued as organizer of the league until 1895 when she became secretary of the Scottish Council for Women's Trades (SCWT). Although her appointment as organizer of the league had negative coverage in the *Women's Trades Union Review*, where it was thought that she had been placed by the less radical interest, Irwin worked continuously to help organize women into unions, while at the same time collecting evidence on working conditions to aid their cause. As secretary of the SCWT, Irwin was instrumental in the formation of a separate Scottish Trades Union Congress (STUC). She became secretary of the STUC committee, was elected as secretary of the congress in 1897, and was elected top of the poll for the parliamentary committee.

Margaret Irwin's role as secretary of the parliamentary committee was a key aspect of her work for the congress. It was evident by the early 1900s, however, that problems were emerging over the extent of middle-class involvement and support of labour organizations across Britain. One major issue was over the eight-hour day and Margaret Irwin was attacked by Robert Smillie for her part in not pressing the issue when writing the parliamentary committee report. Moves to oust her as secretary of the parliamentary committee failed in 1899 but she determined the matter herself in 1900 by refusing nomination. In 1901 she gave evidence to the select committee of the House of Lords on the early closing of shops and throughout the 1900s she acted as a delegate for the SCWT at the congress in 1904, 1909, and 1910. She was instrumental in bringing to the attention of the home secretary the need to recognize and meet with the STUC by showing that its opinions were not in line with those of the TUC. In 1900 when elected to the parliamentary committee she campaigned for improved working-class housing and the cause of seasonal workers. It was she who was responsible in 1910 for the resolution to call for a parliamentary inquiry into the housing conditions of potato gatherers, fish curers, and fruit pickers.

In the period down to the 1920s Margaret Irwin wrote numerous reports on various industries connected with women's trades such as laundry and sweated tailoring work. Several articles by her on these subjects were published in the *Glasgow Herald*. She became interested in other issues connected to public health and factory acts. It was in this period that she established model working and housing conditions at her fruit farm in Perthshire. Her interest in the working conditions of women led her into involvement with land settlement schemes both in Britain and abroad. Her work with unemployed girls included a scheme to find them domestic work. This led her to be criticized yet again for associating work provision with a charity basis. By 1912 the National Federation of Women Workers objected to the rights of the SCWT to send delegates to the STUC. Margaret Irwin and the SCWT ceased affiliation to the congress soon after but she remained secretary of the council. She continued her writing and was appointed CBE in 1927. The council was dissolved in 1939. She was a fellow of the Royal Society of Arts.

It has been said of Margaret Irwin that she never 'threw off the middle-class philanthropic attitude of the Women's Protective and Provident League and the SCWT' (Lewenhak, 111). While interested in women's work she was not in a trade union and her association with the Fabian Women's Council and the SCWT linked her to the

Liberal Party. In certain respects Irwin's outlook and commitment to the league were to see her left behind and ignored by the labour movement, which became increasingly associated with the Labour Party after the First World War.

Margaret Irwin principally resided at 61 Kersland Street, Hillhead, Glasgow. It was there that she died on 21 January 1940. The cause of her death was registered as senility and influenza which had lasted for fourteen days. Following the Scottish tradition her funeral was from her home at 61 Kersland Street on 23 January 1940, thereafter to Glasgow crematorium. She never married.

Recognized 'as an authority on women's work' (Lewenhak, 111), Irwin has only from the 1970s been reappraised for her important contribution to the improvement of women's working conditions and to their organization in unions. She is seen by some as part of the middle-class Liberal tradition of radical involvement in reform. Her commitment to equal pay, women's right to the suffrage, and equal and fair working conditions was latterly obscured by those who emphasized her role as part of an establishment hindering change through vacillation. Yet Irwin achieved a high level of respect for her work, her determination, and her commitment to women's issues which continued until her death.

ELEANOR GORDON and CAMPBELL F. LLOYD

Sources S. Lewenhak, *Women and trade unions* (1977) · *Scottish biographies* (1938) · *WWW*, 1929–40 · *Glasgow Herald* (22 Jan 1940) · *Glasgow Herald* (23 Jan 1940) · b. cert. · d. cert. · *Glasgow Herald* (9 July 1918) · *Glasgow Herald* (11 Oct 1920) · *Glasgow Herald* (14 Jan 1921) · *Glasgow Herald* (10 Nov 1921) · *Glasgow Herald* (16 Dec 1921) · *Glasgow Herald* (14 April 1924) · MSS, St Andrew's University, Special collections · U. Glas. · MSS, Glasgow School of Art, Special collections **Archives** *Glasgow Herald* offices, articles index · Mitchell L., Glas., Glasgow United Trades Council MSS · NL Scot., Scottish TUC MSS · NL Wales, corresp. with Thomas Jones · U. Glas. L., Stack collection, education A5 1879-T **Likenesses** photograph, repro. in *Glasgow Herald* (22 Jan 1940) **Wealth at death** £10,809 10s. 1d.: confirmation, 7 April 1940, CCI

Irwin, Muriel Stuart [*pseud.* Muriel Stuart] (**1885–1967**), poet, was born at Kelsodene, St Helens Road, Norbury, London, on 20 March 1885, the daughter of Thomas Lennox Irwin (1849–1917), barrister, and his wife, Elizabeth Brewer, *née* Freeman (1850–1941). Her father's ancestry was Scottish, from Banff and the borders; her mother was English, from Gloucestershire. She was educated privately before studying design at Croydon School of Art. After a short-lived first marriage, and during the First World War and the immediate post-war years, she worked for the London publishers Herbert Jenkins and Heinemann. She began writing professionally as Muriel Stuart. Her early poems appeared in the *English Review* and her first collection, *Christ at Carnival*, was published in 1916. In 1917 she joined the To-Morrow Club, formed by Mrs 'Sappho' Dawson Scott to encourage young writers. A second collection, *The Cockpit of Idols*, followed in 1918.

In 1921 Stuart was a founder member of PEN. In the early 1920s, after the death of her first husband, she married the publisher Arthur William Board (1876–1967), with whom she had a daughter and a son. She was pregnant during May 1923 and unable to attend the first International Congress dinner of the PEN Club and has therefore disappeared from the club records. She published three further collections of poetry: *Poems* (1922), *New Poems and Old* (published in America in 1926 by Valentine Mitchell with an introduction by Henry Savage), and *Selected Poems* (1927).

Despite the interest of their themes, Muriel Stuart's first two collections of poetry draw formally on nineteenth-century traditions and it is therefore in her poetry of the 1920s that her most significant contribution is to be found. These later poems explore relationships between men and women in dramatic narratives whose voices and imagery belong recognizably to the modern world. Although written primarily from a woman's perspective, they speak powerfully of the need for a more equal partnership between men and women if true fulfilment for both is to be achieved. Their scenarios suggest that more than the removal of social and economic inequalities is required; it is, rather, what the introduction to 'Andromeda Unfettered' calls 'the deep-rooted antagonism of spirit' (*Poems*, 57) which needs to be overcome. This insight is given powerful dramatic form in poems such as 'In the Orchard', 'Mrs Effingham's Swan Song' (a fine opposing perspective to T. S. Eliot's 'Portrait of a Lady'), and 'The Father', where it is the young man in a relationship whose world collapses when his partner taunts him with the words 'Your child?' (*Poems*, 56).

In the 1920s Stuart's poems were anthologized in Hugh MacDiarmid's *Northern Numbers* and in the *Scottish Chapbook*. MacDiarmid claimed her as a leading writer in the inter-war Scottish renaissance movement (presumably on the evidence of her father's ancestry and her chosen name Stuart). Her early poems were published to critical acclaim and Thomas Hardy wrote her a letter saying that some of them were 'superlatively good'. *Poems* attracted wide and positive coverage in the leading newspapers and periodicals of the day, as did the American *New Poems and Old*. She was clearly seen as a writer of achievement, even if often designated a 'woman poet' at a time when such a label was often used condescendingly.

Stuart, however, published no more poetry after 1927, although she was involved in various publishing enterprises with her husband. Her play *The Marriage Bond* was produced in the West End and made into a film at Ealing Studios by Maurice Elvey (*c*.1935), and she wrote an unpublished life of Keats and Fanny Brawne. Gardening became a passion in the 1930s. The books *Fool's Garden* and *Gardener's Nightcap* were published in 1936 and 1938 respectively and she wrote articles on gardening until shortly before her death.

Stuart, who had a striking appearance, and was said to look 'like a poet', lived all her life in the south of England, mostly in or near London, with the last twenty-five years spent in the Berkshire countryside. She died at Halstock, Clappentail Lane, Lyme Regis, her daughter's home, on 18 December 1967, and was buried on 22 December at Uplyme, near Lyme Regis.

Stuart's work has been kept in public view in Scottish

anthologies as a consequence of Hugh MacDiarmid's claim, but she was absent from contemporary English anthologies in the 1920s, which may partially explain what has been the surprising neglect of her work. In the late twentieth century 'The Seed Shop', her war poem 'Forgotten Dead, I Salute You', and 'In the Orchard' occasionally appeared in collections, but she deserves to be more fully represented in the history of early twentieth-century poetry.   MARGERY PALMER McCULLOCH

Sources private information (2004) [daughter] · *National union catalog, pre-1956 imprints*, Library of Congress · *Bibliography of English* (1922), (1927) · *TLS* (13 July 1922), 462 · *TLS* (3 Aug 1922), 504 · *Nation and the Athenaeum* (9 Sept 1922), 773 · *Saturday Review*, 134 (7 Oct 1922), 510 · *English Review* (July 1922), 98 · *The Bookman* (Dec 1921), 137–41 · *The Bookman* (Aug 1922), 211 · M. McCulloch, 'Muriel Stuart: a cuckoo in the nest of singing birds?', *Scottish Literary Journal*, 16/1 (1989), 51–8 · M. McCulloch, 'Forgotten founder: the poetry of Muriel Stuart', *Pen International*, 45/1 (1995), 29–32 · C. M. Grieve, 'Muriel Stuart', *Contemporary Scottish Studies* (1926), 164–8 · J. Hendry, 'Twentieth-century women's writing: the nest of singing birds', *The history of Scottish literature*, 4: *Twentieth century*, ed. C. Craig (1987), 291–307 · M. Watts, *Mrs Sappho: the life of C. A. Dawson Scott, mother of International PEN* (1987) · b. cert.
Archives priv. coll., letters, newspaper cuttings, and MSS of unpublished life of John Keats and Fanny Brawne
Likenesses E. O. Hoppé, photograph, repro. in *The Bookman* (June 1922), 114 · K. Murray, photograph, repro. in *The Bookman* (Dec 1921), 141 · photograph, priv. coll.

Isaac, Mr (*fl.* 1675–1717), dancing-master, is of unknown origins and nationality. He may have had some connection with the Paris dancers Isac or Isecq, or with the Isaack family of musicians in London and Dublin. His own surviving dances, however, are English in construction and style.

According to John Aubrey's *Brief Lives* Isaac was apprenticed to the dancing-master John Ogilby, who was twice appointed master of the revels in Dublin. In 1675 Isaac took part in Crowne's masque *Calisto* at Whitehall Palace; by the 1690s he had become a respected dancing-master and teacher of deportment, both at court (although he never achieved any salaried status) and throughout fashionable London. His early pupils included the princesses Mary and Anne, John Evelyn's daughter Mary, and Katherine Booth, who looked—in vain—to Mr Isaac to secure her a place at court as a maid of honour.

Though several of Isaac's dances were performed on stage after they had been presented at court there is no evidence that he himself ever performed in the commercial theatre. Subscription lists to Weaver's and Pemberton's dance publications make it clear that the theatrical dancer L'Sac was a different person and had moved to Chester by 1711. Isaac is remembered as the creator of complex and beautiful dances for presentation at court in collaboration with the French-born composer Jacques Paisible, who had also performed in *Calisto* and subsequently worked both for the court and at Drury Lane Theatre.

In 1706 Isaac commissioned John Weaver's *Orchesography*, a translation of Raoul-Auger Feuillet's treatise *Chorégraphie* (1700) on dance notation; to further encourage its use Isaac also had six of his own dances notated and published by Weaver (*A Collection of Ball-Dances Perform'd at Court*, 1706), followed in 1707 by another dance (*The Union*). After 1707 Isaac turned to other notators, including the theatrical dancer Charles Delagarde (who notated Isaac's four birthday dances for Queen Anne between 1708 and 1711 and also performed three of Isaac's dances on stage between 1708 and 1716) and the dancing-master Edmund Pemberton (who notated at least seven of Isaac's dances from 1711 onwards). Most of Isaac's work was reissued at various times by the music firm of John Walsh, who claimed that they were all 'new' birthday dances for Queen Anne and supported that contention by adding different designs of title-page to the existing plates. In fact not all the extant twenty-two dances were created for the queen's birthdays; several almost certainly antedate her coronation by several years, two were created for celebrations at the court of George I, and the publication of *Chaconne* in 1711 was as part of Pemberton's *Essay for the Further Improvement of Dancing*, to encourage the wider use of dance notation.

Isaac may have been the Mr Lowsack who resided on the west side of Dean Street in the parish of St Anne, Soho, from at least 1706 to 1720; his collaborator Paisible resided for a few years on the east side of the same street. The 1721 rate book notes Isaac as 'gon away'. Indeed Isaac may have lived in one of the older houses on the east side of Dean Street before 1706, for a Luke Sacks is so noted in the rate books from 1696 (City of Westminster Archives Centre). The last definite reference to Isaac as a dancing-master, however, is on 8 July 1717, when he was paid for three months' teaching in London of Grisell Baillie's daughter Rachel.

The dancing-master John Essex described Mr Isaac as 'the prime Master in England for forty years together … he was both generous and charitable to all: he was an agreeable Figure in his Person, and had a handsome Mein [*sic*] joined to an easy Address and graceful Deportment' (Essex, xi–xii). According to Charles Burney the violinist Matthew *Dubourg (1703–1767) was the 'natural son of the celebrated dancing-master Isaac' (*Diary and Letters*, 38 n. 1). Musgrave's *Obituary* dates Isaac's death to 1740, in which year was published a mezzotint of his portrait by Louis Goupy, engraved by G. White; however, John Essex described him as 'the late Mr Isaac' in 1728 (Essex, xi). Isaac may have died in 1720, for despite their long collaboration he was not mentioned in Paisible's will of January 1721, nor did his name appear in the subscribers' list to Weaver's *Anatomical Lectures* (1721); also he was no longer the dedicatee of Weaver's *Orchesography* when its second edition was published in 1722. No burial or probate records, however, have yet been found for him.

JENNIFER THORP

Sources J. Weaver, *Orchesography* (1706) · J. Weaver, *A collection of ball-dances perform'd at court … all compos'd by Mr Isaac* (1706) · [P. Rameau], *The dancing master*, trans. J. Essex (1728) · E. Pemberton, *An essay for the further improvement of dancing* (1711) · *Memoirs of Dr Charles Burney, 1726–1769*, ed. S. Klima, G. Bowers, and K. S. Grant (1988) · *Brief lives, chiefly of contemporaries, set down by John Aubrey, between the years 1669 and 1696*, ed. A. Clark, 2 (1898) · R. Ralph, *Life and works of John Weaver* (1985) · M. Arnold-Forster, *Basset Down*

(1950) • J. Thorp, 'John Walsh entrepreneur or poacher: the publication of dance notations, 1705–c.1730', *Handbook for studies in 18th-century English music*, ed. M. Burden, 7 (1996), 1–36 • A. Ashbee and D. Lasocki, eds., *A biographical dictionary of English court musicians, 1485–1714*, 2 vols. (1998) • E. Boswell, *The Restoration court stage (1660–1702): with a particular account of the production of 'Calisto'* (1932) • A. R. Walkling, 'Masque and politics at the Restoration court: John Crowne's *Calisto*', *Early Music*, 24 (1996), 27–62 • Highfill, Burnim & Langhans, *BDA* • H. Bromley, *A catalogue of engraved British portraits* (1793) • W. Musgrave, *Obituary prior to 1800*, ed. G. J. Armytage, 3, Harleian Society, 46 (1900), 302 • St Anne's, Soho, King's Square division, parish rate book, 1691–1721, City Westm. AC, ref. A253, 80–81, 1146–1150, 1729–1731, MF 23–26 • *The household book of Lady Grisell Baillie, 1692–1733*, ed. R. Scott-Moncrieff, Scottish History Society, new ser., 1 (1911), 53 • *IGI*

Archives BL, dance notations, Music Library h.993/1–19 • BL, dance notations, Music Library d.64.h • Dundee Central Library, dance notations, G.10.4404

Likenesses G. White, mezzotint (after L. Goupy, c.1710), BM, NPG; repro. in Ralph, *Life and works*

Isaac of Norwich. *See* Norwich, Isaac of (c.1170–1235/6).

Isaac, Samuel (1812–1886), merchant and projector of the Mersey Tunnel, son of Lewis Isaac (c.1788–1879), a furniture broker, of Poole, Dorset, and his wife, Catherine (c.1789–1863), daughter of N. Solomon of Margate, was born at Chatham. He went to London as a young man and established a large business as an army contractor in Jermyn Street, trading as Isaac, Campbell & Co. His brother, Saul Isaac (1823–1903), JP, afterwards MP for Nottingham (1874–80), was associated with him in partnership. Isaac was married twice. His first wife was Isabella Simons (c.1814–1846). On 21 June 1848 he married Emma Hart (1814–1898).

Isaac, Campbell & Co. was the largest European commercial concern supporting the Confederacy during the American civil war. Its ships, conveying military stores to the southern states and returning carrying cotton, were regarded as the most enterprising of the British blockade-runners between 1861 and 1865. Having raised a regiment of volunteers for the Confederate army from among the workmen of his own factory at Northampton, Isaac was rewarded by the Confederacy with the military rank of major. He and his firm were large holders of Confederate funds, and were consequently ruined on the conclusion of the American war in 1865.

By 1881, however, Isaac had rebuilt his fortune and he was invited by the Mersey Railway Company to assist in fund-raising to construct the Mersey Tunnel. Isaac, with no engineering experience, nevertheless undertook to complete all the works and to pay all legal, parliamentary, and other expenses, until such time as the Board of Trade should certificate the tunnel for use. Isaac let the construction works to Messrs Waddell, employing James Brunlees and Douglas Fox as engineers. H. C. Raikes became chairman, with E. P. Bouverie as vice-chairman, of the company formed to carry through the undertaking. Money was raised, and the boring was completed under Isaac's supervision on 17 January 1884. The tunnel was opened on 13 February 1885, the first passenger train ran through on 22 December, and it was formally opened by the prince of Wales on 20 January 1886. Queen Victoria accepted from

Isaac a jewelled representation of the tunnel, in which the speck of light at the end of the excavation was represented by a diamond.

Isaac formed a collection of paintings containing some of the best works of B. W. Leader. He died at his home, 29 Warrington Crescent, Maida Vale, London, on 22 November 1886 and was buried in the United Synagogue cemetery, Willesden.   G. C. Boase, *rev.* Ralph Harrington

Sources *The Times* (24 Nov 1886) • *Jewish Chronicle* (26 Nov 1886) • S. W. Parkin, *The Mersey Railway* (1966), 6–8 • M. Jolles, *Samuel Isaac, Saul Isaac, and Nathaniel Isaacs* (1998) • d. cert. [Lewis Isaac, father] • d. cert. [Catherine Isaac, mother] • Boase, *Mod. Eng. biog.* • P. H. Emden, *Jews of Britain: a series of biographies* (1944)

Wealth at death £203,084: probate, 7 Jan 1887, *CGPLA Eng. & Wales*

Isaacs, Alick (1921–1967), virologist, was born in Glasgow on 17 July 1921, the eldest in the family of three sons and one daughter of Louis Isaacs, shopkeeper, of Glasgow, and his wife, Rosine, daughter of Jacob Lion, leather merchant, of London. The surname Isaacs was bestowed on his grandfather, Barnet Galinsky, when he arrived in England in the 1880s, having emigrated from Lithuania. Alick's mother, who trained as a schoolteacher, came from a more substantial Jewish family which had produced two lord mayors of London. His childhood was a happy one; among his early hobbies were music and chess, which became lifelong interests. At Pollokshields secondary school, where he was a popular pupil, he studied physics and chemistry but not biology. In 1939 he entered the faculty of medicine at Glasgow University; he proved an outstanding student, winning a number of prizes and medals, and graduated MB ChB in 1944.

After a year of house appointments at Glasgow Western Infirmary, Isaacs decided not to pursue a career in clinical medicine. Instead he accepted a scholarship to study under Professor Carl Browning in the department of bacteriology at Glasgow, where he conducted research on streptococci. In 1947 he was awarded a Medical Research Council studentship to work under Professor C. H. Stuart-Harris in the University of Sheffield. It was here that Isaacs began his work on influenza, which was his main field for the rest of his professional life. In 1948 a Rockefeller travelling fellowship enabled him to work under F. Macfarlane Burnet in Melbourne, where he remained for two years. In 1949 he married Susanna Gordon, a paediatrician and child psychiatrist, daughter of Hubert James *Foss, pianist and composer. The couple had met and become engaged during Isaacs's time in Sheffield. They subsequently had twin sons and one daughter.

Isaacs's research in Melbourne focused on viral interference, a phenomenon whereby one virus, live or inactivated, possesses the ability to interfere with the growth in a cell of another virus, even if the two viruses are unrelated. Working with Margaret Edney, Isaacs produced a series of papers, published in the *Australian Journal of Experimental Biology and Medical Science* in 1950 and 1951, analysing the interference between active and inactive influenza viruses in the allantoic cavities of developing hens' eggs. Their research suggested that the interfering

Alick Isaacs (1921–1967), by Walter Bird

virus did not prevent the adsorption or uptake of virus by the host cell but that interference took place within the cell's interior.

In 1951 Isaacs returned to England to work at the National Institute for Medical Research at Mill Hill, where he continued his research on viral interference and was assisted by a number of visiting scholars. During the second half of 1956 he carried out a series of critical experiments into the mechanism of interference with one of these visiting researchers, Dr J. Lindenmann, from Zürich. In a series of *in vitro* experiments, the results of which were published in two seminal papers in the *Proceedings of the Royal Society of London* in 1957, Isaacs and Lindenmann demonstrated that viral interference was mediated by a substance produced by infected cells. They named the active agent 'interferon'.

Initially, many scientists remained sceptical about the role of interferon in viral interference. However, hopes that interferon might prove to be a potent anti-viral agent (akin to penicillin in bacterial infections) gradually attracted interest from the media, the public, scientists, and pharmaceutical companies. Unfortunately, these early hopes for interferon as a natural chemotherapeutic agent in viral diseases were soon dashed. The difficulties involved in producing sufficient quantities of pure interferon, the troublesome side effects, and the poor results from trials contributed to a decline in commercial interest during the 1960s.

In the late 1970s and early 1980s, commercial and scientific interest in Isaacs's work was revived by hopes that interferon could be effective in treating a variety of cancers. Once again, the results of trials were largely disappointing and, although there is some evidence that interferon may be of value in the treatment of multiple sclerosis, the clinical uses of interferon have remained limited. Nevertheless, Isaacs had considerable impact in the fields of virology and immunology. Studies of the structure and function of the different types of interferon that have now been identified, and of their mechanisms of action, have contributed significantly to our understanding of natural defence-mechanisms against viruses and of the regulation of the immune system. A number of international symposia and scientific works have been devoted to interferon.

Isaacs's scientific projects, communicated in well over one hundred journal articles, were not limited to interferon. During his time at Mill Hill he was also busy with the work of the World Influenza Centre under the World Health Organization. This work involved comparing influenza strains from all over the world and monitoring changes in the antigenic composition of the virus. In 1955 Isaacs's work on influenza gained him an MD with honours at Glasgow University. In 1961 he succeeded C. H. Andrewes as head of the virus division at Mill Hill. One year later he received an honorary MD from the Catholic University of Louvain in Belgium, and he was elected FRS in 1966.

Isaacs was not only an outstanding scientist; he also had a great capacity for friendship and was generally full of *joie de vivre.* Unfortunately, following a subarachnoid haemorrhage due to an inoperable haemangioma in 1964, he suffered a number of episodes of intense depression. He continued working until, after a recurrence of intracranial haemorrhage, he died in University College Hospital, London, on 26 January 1967. He was survived by his wife.

C. H. ANDREWES, *rev.* MARK JACKSON

Sources C. H. Andrewes, *Memoirs FRS,* 13 (1967), 205–21 · T. Pieters, 'Interferon and its first clinical trial: looking behind the scenes', *Medical History,* 37 (1993), 270–95 · *The Times* (28 Jan 1967) · *Nature* (11 Feb 1967) · *The Lancet* (4 Feb 1967) · *BMJ* (4 Feb 1967) · D. J. Bibel, 'Interferon: 1957, Alick Isaacs and Jean Lindenmann', *Milestones in immunology: a historical exploration* (1988), 208–12 · J. Lindenmann, 'From interference to interferon: a brief historical introduction', *PTRS,* 299B (1982), 3–6 · S. Yanchinski, 'What next for interferon?', *New Scientist* (25 Sept 1980), 917–21 · personal knowledge (1981) · private information (1981)

Archives National Library of Medicine, Bethesda, Maryland, laboratory notebooks | priv. coll., Jean Lindenmann MSS · Wellcome L., corresp. with Ernst Chain

Likenesses W. Bird, photograph, RS [*see illus.*] · photograph, repro. in *The Lancet* · photograph, repro. in *BMJ*

Wealth at death £10,767: administration with will, 25 April 1967, *CGPLA Eng. & Wales*

Isaacs, George Alfred (1883–1979), trade unionist and politician, was born on 28 May 1883 in Holborn, London, the eldest of the nine children of Alfred Isaacs, a printer, and Martha Cook. He was educated at the Wesleyan elementary school at Hoxton, London. His childhood in the slums of Finsbury was hard. The family's poverty meant that he often had to depend on soup kitchens for a midday meal and it forced him to leave school at the age of twelve to begin work, although he later continued his education by attending classes organized by the Workers' Educational Association. He followed three generations of his forebears into the printing trade. He became a reader's boy, later a machine room assistant, and his fascination with printing led him to publish *The Story of the Newspaper Printing Press* in 1931. On 27 March 1905 he married Flora Beasley (*b.* 1884/5). They had a daughter and also adopted a nephew whose parents had died.

By the age of nineteen Isaacs was already active in the National Society of Operative Printers' Assistants and in 1909 he became its general secretary. At the time of his appointment the union was nearly bankrupt as a result of financial irregularities, and his immediate task was to restore its position. He remained general secretary of the union (renamed in 1911 the National Society of Operative Printers and Assistants) until his appointment to the cabinet in 1945. He was involved in the formation of the London Labour Party in 1914 and was mayor of Southwark from 1919 to 1921. He unsuccessfully contested the North Southwark constituency for Labour in the general election of 1918 and Gravesend in 1922. He won the Gravesend seat in 1923, making his maiden speech, on 24 May 1924, in support of a bill on industrial councils. He was defeated at Gravesend in the general election of 1924. He then tried his luck in North Southwark, unsuccessfully contesting a by-election in 1927. He managed to win the seat in the general election of 1929, but lost it in 1931 and was again defeated in 1935. However, in 1939 the sitting Liberal MP died: Isaacs won the subsequent by-election in May 1939 and was MP for the constituency from 1939 to 1950. The Southwark constituency was reorganized in 1950 and he was its MP until 1959.

Isaacs's parliamentary career included periods as parliamentary private secretary to J. H. Thomas as secretary of state for the colonies (1924) and the dominions (1929–31); he was also parliamentary private secretary to the first lord of the Admiralty (1942–5). In 1945 Clement Attlee appointed him minister of labour and national service, hoping that his status in the TUC (he was a member of the general council from 1932 and its chairman in 1945, though he had to resign both positions on joining the cabinet) would help to cement relations between the government and the trade unions. It was a challenging post, not least because his predecessor, Ernest Bevin, cast a long shadow which Isaacs, a relatively lightweight politician with no previous ministerial experience, never really escaped. There have been accusations that Isaacs's appointment was arranged by Bevin to allow him to dominate industrial policy (Wigham, 99) and, while pressure of work meant that Bevin could not interfere on a daily basis, his stature in cabinet often caused Isaacs to defer to his judgement.

Isaacs's first challenge at the Ministry of Labour and National Service was demobilization. This had been planned under Bevin but Isaacs's task was complicated by contrary pressures. On the one hand the Board of Trade and other departments pressed him to release manpower more quickly in order to provide the workers to increase exports (to pay for food and raw materials from abroad) and speed reconstruction. Service personnel and their families were also keen that they should return home. On the other hand Isaacs was under pressure from Bevin at the Foreign Office and from the Ministry of Defence to slow down demobilization in order to meet Britain's defence commitments in Germany and elsewhere. In the event, Isaacs managed to demobilize large numbers in a very short time—over 4 million men and women were released from the armed forces between August 1945 and December 1946, and more than another million in the subsequent two years. The pattern of demobilization, however, left something to be desired. The Bevin plan was certainly fair, demobilization being decided according to a combination of age and service, but the opposition of both Bevin and Isaacs to manpower planning resulted in essential workers being kept in the services unnecessarily. This may have contributed to the crisis in coal production during the winter of 1946/7 (Morgan, 132–3, 331–2), although Shinwell, then minister of fuel, was careful not to blame Isaacs for this (Shinwell, 194–5).

More seriously, Isaacs's commitment to free collective bargaining meant that he failed to appreciate the important role that the Ministry of Labour could play in the post-war world. In 1946 he successfully repealed the 1927 Trades Disputes Act, arguing that 'the right to strike is as much our inalienable right as the right to breathe' (*Hansard 5C*, 12 Feb 1946). For this he was widely fêted in the party and applauded by the TUC. But simply to repeal the legislation rendered the definition of a legal strike unclear and left the government with no effective instrument of control over the rising number of unofficial strikes, the conditions of employment and national arbitration order of 1942 (which effectively banned strikes and imposed compulsory arbitration) being almost impossible to exercise in such cases. The consequence of Isaacs's strong adherence to free collective bargaining, and his inability to address the changed nature of industrial relations in conditions of post-war full employment, was that other ministers seized the initiative in industrial policy. Cripps did so in incomes policy as did Wilson in regional policy. As Isaacs's parliamentary secretary, Frederick Lee, later pointed out, this contributed to the growing irrelevance of the Ministry of Labour to the government's industrial strategy (*DNB*).

In truth, Isaacs lacked the intellectual capacity and force of character needed to lead and represent such an important department. He leant heavily on his officials, particularly Sir Godfrey Ince, and the ministry found him a sore disappointment after Bevin. One official privately complained that Isaacs was 'a completely non-effective non-person' and another remarked that, whereas under Bevin the ministry had usually won its battles, 'under Isaacs it usually lost them' (private correspondence). His inability adequately to represent the ministry in cabinet also cost him the respect of his fellow ministers. Cripps soon concluded that 'Isaacs should go' (Davis Smith, 2) and Dalton thought him ineffectual (*Political Diary*, 455). Bevin's support ensured that he stayed in post until January 1951. Then, tired and in poor health, he was moved by Attlee to the Ministry of Pensions and remained there until the government fell in October 1951. He continued to be a popular figure in the House of Commons until his retirement from public life in 1959.

Short, thickset, and bespectacled, Isaacs was a friendly and unassuming man with a shrewd sense of humour. He was a committed advocate of temperance and a health enthusiast who delighted press photographers by taking an outdoor bathe before breakfast, whatever the weather. At heart he was reserved and shy, a family man who made few close friends among his trade union and political colleagues. He drew his political faith from the early, radical roots of the labour movement and fought vigorously for the interests of the poor and disadvantaged (of whom there were many in his constituency), and for this he was widely respected by his constituents. Isaacs died in the cottage hospital, Cobham, Surrey, on 26 April 1979.

HUGH PEMBERTON

Sources G. G. Eastwood, *George Isaacs* (1952) · *DNB* · E. Wigham, *Strikes and the government, 1893–1974* (1976) · K. O. Morgan, *Labour in power, 1945–1951* (1984) · J. Davis Smith, *The Attlee and Churchill administrations and industrial unrest, 1945–55* (1990) · *The political diary of Hugh Dalton, 1918–1940, 1945–1960*, ed. B. Pimlott (1986) · E. Shinwell, *I've lived through it all* (1973) · K. Harris, *Attlee* (1982) · H. A. Clegg, A. Fox, and A. F. Thompson, *A history of British trade unions since 1889*, 3 vols. (1964–94), vols. 1, 3 · press cuttings, Southwark borough library · b. cert. · m. cert. · d. cert.

Archives BL, corresp. with Lord Northcliffe, Add. MS 62171

Likenesses photographs, repro. in Eastwood, *George Isaacs*

Wealth at death £670: probate, 16 Oct 1979, *CGPLA Eng. & Wales*

Isaacs, Godfrey Charles (1866–1925), industrialist, was born in 1866, the fourth son and seventh of nine children of Joseph Michael Isaacs (1832–1908), a London fruit and ship broker, and his wife, Sarah (1835–1922), daughter of Daniel Davis. Godfrey Isaacs was of a Jewish family which had overcome considerable prejudice to make its mark in public life. His uncle, Sir Henry Isaacs (1830–1909), was lord mayor of London in 1889–90; an elder brother was Rufus Daniel *Isaacs, first marquess of Reading (1860–1935). Educated in London, and at universities in Hanover and Brussels, Isaacs travelled extensively in Europe as a young man. He then left the family firm and went into business on his own account, being associated with various mining enterprises and four taxicab companies. He married Leah Felicitie, daughter of Dr Seta, on 27 December 1892, in Paris. They had two sons, Marcel Godfrey and Dennys Godfrey.

In 1909 Isaacs met Guglielmo Marconi, founder of Marconi's Wireless Telegraph Company Ltd. Marconi invited Isaacs to take charge of the company's business affairs; he was appointed joint managing director in January 1910, assuming sole responsibility in August of that year, with effective control over the subsidiaries and associated companies overseas. The company was securely established with a good reputation, but had paid no dividend since its formation in 1897. Isaacs sought to remedy the situation with assiduous publicity, especially after the

successful use of radio in the arrest of the murderer Harvey Hawley Crippen in 1910 and the rescue of survivors from the *Titanic* disaster in 1912. He also sued the United Wireless Company for patent infringement. This successful action bankrupted the American company, enabling Marconi's to acquire their assets. The US Marconi subsidiary thus became the largest radio company in the New World.

Between 1911 and 1912, the value of contracts in hand increased fourfold to over £1 million. Marconi shares rose from just over £2 in 1911 to a peak of £9 in April 1912. They had twice as many radio installations worldwide as Telefunken, their nearest rival. From this position of relative strength, Isaacs was able to negotiate agreements with the German company to end the patent litigation, which had been costly for both parties.

But commercial success was overshadowed by political scandal. In March 1912 the government agreed a contract with Marconi's for an 'imperial chain' of high-powered radio stations. The agreement was widely criticized, as Isaacs's brother Rufus was then attorney-general. A select committee of the House of Commons dismissed the suggestion that he had used his position to influence the government's decision. But its investigations revealed that Rufus Isaacs, David Lloyd George (chancellor of the exchequer), and the master of Elibank (Liberal chief whip) had all speculated in US Marconi stock—a firm not involved in the imperial chain contract, but sharing in the consequent Marconi boom. The select committee divided along party lines and the ministers' careers were saved. But the imperial chain order was cancelled.

This 'Marconi scandal' provoked antisemitic attacks on the Isaacs brothers from three well-known writers, Hilaire Belloc, G. K. Chesterton, and Cecil Chesterton. Godfrey Isaacs brought a successful action for criminal libel against Cecil Chesterton in 1913. But the racially inspired campaign continued, causing distress among Isaacs's family and possibly influencing his conversion to Roman Catholicism about 1913. Isaacs's career was punctuated by a series of legal actions. In 1917 he sued Sir Charles Hobhouse, a former postmaster-general, for libel. The jury found against Isaacs; he offered to resign from the Marconi board, but stayed on after a vote of confidence at the company's annual general meeting in 1918.

The armed services had used radio extensively during the First World War. Marconi's Wireless Telegraph Company supplied much of the equipment and was responsible for important technical developments. But the company's reputation suffered from the political and legal controversies of 1913–19. There were widespread fears of a Marconi monopoly. They were excluded from government discussions of a revived imperial chain scheme in 1921–4. The United States government in 1919 forced the transfer of Marconi's US stock to the Radio Corporation of America (RCA), controlled by American shareholders. An agreement in 1921 between RCA and Telefunken prevented further Marconi expansion in South America.

Isaacs was appointed a director of the newly formed British Broadcasting Company in 1923. But internal stresses within Marconi's itself made his position there as managing director very insecure. His status was further weakened by injudicious investment of the Marconi assets, causing, his enemies claimed, losses of £6 million. He resigned from the board in November 1924, and from the BBC board at the same time. His chief recreation in retirement was golf, but he had little time left to enjoy this pursuit. Isaacs died, after a short illness attributed in part to overwork, on 17 April 1925, at his home, Lyne Grove, Virginia Water, Surrey. He was survived by his wife.

ROWLAND F. POCOCK

Sources *The Times* (18 April 1925) · R. P. T. Davenport-Hines, 'Isaacs, Godfrey Charles', *DBB* · W. J. Baker, *A history of the Marconi Company* (1970) · G. L. Archer, *History of radio to 1926* (1938) · S. G. Sturmey, *The economic development of radio* (1958) · F. Donaldson, *The Marconi scandal* (1962)
Likenesses portraits, Marconi Archives
Wealth at death £195,490 12s. 1d.: probate, 18 June 1925, *CGPLA Eng. & Wales*

Isaacs, Sir Isaac Alfred (1855–1948), judge and politician, was born at Elizabeth Street, Melbourne, on 6 August 1855, the eldest of the three children of Alfred Isaacs (*d.* 1904), a Polish-born tailor, of Auburn, Victoria, and his wife, Rebecca (*d.* 1912), the daughter of Abraham Abrahams of London. He was educated at an elementary state school in Yackandandah, at Beechworth grammar school, and at the University of Melbourne, where he graduated in 1880 with first-class honours in law, placed first of his year.

Isaacs was called to the bar on 9 April 1880 and rapidly acquired a good practice, particularly before appellate courts. His work was distinguished by extremely careful preparation of his cases, and he enjoyed a reputation as a pertinacious advocate. He was appointed QC on 4 December 1899. On 18 July 1888 he married the eighteen-year-old Deborah ('Daisy') Jacobs (1870–1960), the daughter of Isaac Jacobs, a tobacco merchant, of Melbourne: they had two daughters.

In 1892 Isaacs was elected to the legislative assembly of Victoria and in 1893 joined the government as solicitor-general. He held office as attorney-general from 1894 to 1899 and again from 1900 to 1901.

In 1897 Isaacs was one of ten Victorians elected by popular vote to be members, with representatives from the other colonies, of the Australasian federal convention. To this body was entrusted the task of drafting the commonwealth constitution, which was subsequently enacted as a statute by the parliament at Westminster. Alfred Deakin, a prominent federalist, wrote of Isaacs at this time: 'his will was indomitable, his courage inexhaustible and his ambition immeasurable. But his egotism was too marked and his ambition too ruthless to render him popular' (Deakin). Isaacs was a man of short stature, brisk in manner and speech, and, although he inspired affection in some, he was not generally liked or entirely trusted at the bar, in politics, or, later, on the bench.

On federation in 1901, Isaacs resigned from the Victorian parliament and was elected to the first federal house of

Sir Isaac Alfred Isaacs (1855–1948), by Walter Stoneman, 1921

representatives. In 1905 he was appointed attorney-general of the commonwealth. Sir Robert Garran has recorded his 'extraordinary photographic memory' and 'amazing' capacity for work: 'by day he carried the biggest practice of the Victorian Bar; by night he did full justice to the duties of Attorney-General' (Garran). Isaacs remained in that office until his appointment to the high court of Australia on 12 October 1906. On 2 April 1930 he was appointed chief justice of that court.

During his long period of service as a judge Isaacs established a great and lasting reputation. The general appellate jurisdiction enjoyed by the court enabled him to leave his mark in many fields of law, but his judgments on Australian constitutional law are of particular importance. He laid great emphasis on what he regarded as the predominant place of the commonwealth (as opposed to the states) in the federal compact.

The majority in the court held that the constitution must be read subject to implied prohibitions which denied to commonwealth legislation a power to bind the states and their instrumentalities and vice versa. For many years Isaacs and Henry Bournes Higgins found themselves in lone and consistent dissent on points of great importance. In refusing to follow previous decisions of the majority, they were of course departing from judicial habit and rendering the law less certainly ascertainable for those seeking to arrange their affairs in accordance with it. But the high court has always regarded itself as free to overrule its prior decisions, though the judges have not always agreed as to when it is proper to do so.

However, Isaacs said, in the *Australian Agricultural Co. case* (1913): 'It is not, in my opinion, better that the Court should be persistently wrong than that it should be ultimately right.' That proposition assumes, perhaps falsely, that there is always a discoverable 'rightness': Isaacs was, to a fault, convinced of the rightness of his opinions.

After the retirement of Chief Justice Sir Samuel Walker Griffith in 1919, the view reiterated by Isaacs prevailed, and in the *Engineers' case* (1920) the majority in the court held commonwealth legislation effective to bind the states and their instrumentalities—a monumental victory for the position which Isaacs had so consistently maintained.

Isaacs's interpretations of the commonwealth power to legislate with respect to industrial disputes also promoted the extension of central authority. He opposed the limitation of commonwealth power to situations arising out of existing industrial disputes, and gave a broad interpretation to the notion of industrial matters. The result enabled the commonwealth to vest, in the industrial courts and tribunals which it established, a wide power of control over industrial conditions in Australia.

Isaacs's interpretation of the supremacy clause in the constitution, under which inconsistent state legislation gives way to commonwealth laws, characteristically favoured the commonwealth. Again, in *Farey v. Burvett* (1916), where the high court held that the commonwealth defence power authorized the regulation of the price of bread in wartime, Isaacs took the most extreme position in the court in support of commonwealth power. He was also called upon to interpret section 92 of the constitution, which provides that 'trade, commerce and intercourse among the States … shall be absolutely free'. Isaacs held that this provision invalidated all forms of state control over inter-state trade, but that it did not bind the commonwealth. On both points relating to section 92 Isaacs's view has been rejected in subsequent decisions.

Isaacs's career was crowned by his appointment, at the age of seventy-five, as the first Australian governor-general of the commonwealth of Australia. His nomination to that office, proposed by the commonwealth government in March 1930, met with some opposition, notably from George V. However, the Imperial Conference of 1930 resolved that, in making such appointments, the king should act on the advice of his ministers in the dominion concerned: the government insisted and the appointment was reluctantly made. It marked an important stage in the constitutional development of the dominions, and in the changing role of the governor-general, who no longer represented the British government but had come to exercise purely vice-regal or monarchical functions in accordance with the constitution. Isaacs assumed his high office on 22 January 1931 and discharged his duties in full accordance with its traditions until his successor assumed the post on 23 January 1936.

Isaacs was sworn of the privy council in 1921, and was appointed KCMG in 1928, promoted GCMG in 1932, and appointed GCB in 1937. He died at Marne Street, South Yarra, Melbourne, on 11 February 1948, survived by his wife and daughters, and was buried in the Melbourne general cemetery two days later.

ZELMAN COWEN, *rev.* PETER BALMFORD

Sources Z. Cowen, introduction, *Isaac Isaacs*, new edn (1993) · C. Cunneen, *Kings' men* (1983) · J. Barry, 'From Yackandandah to Yarralumla: the enigma of Isaac Isaacs', *Meanjin Quarterly*, 26 (1967), 443–51 · A. Deakin, *The federal story: the inner history of the federal cause*, ed. J. A. La Nauze, 2nd edn (1963) · R. R. Garran, *Prosper the commonwealth* (1958) · G. Sawer, *Australian federalism in the courts* (1967) · A. Dean, *A multitude of counsellors: a history of the bar of Victoria* (1968) · *Commonwealth Law Reports* · roll of barristers admitted to practise in Victoria, Prothonotary of the Supreme Court of Victoria · *Victoria Government Gazette* (22 Dec 1899) · *Commonwealth of Australia Gazette* (13 Oct 1906) · *Commonwealth of Australia Gazette* (10 April 1930) · *Commonwealth of Australia Gazette* (22 Jan 1931) · *Commonwealth of Australia Gazette* (29 Jan 1931) · *Commonwealth of Australia Gazette* (23 Jan 1936) · T. G. Watson, *The first fifty years of responsible government in Victoria* [1906] · M. Gordon, *Sir Isaac Isaacs: a life of service* (1963) · J. G. Latham, 'Sir Isaac Isaacs', *Australian Law Journal*, 22 (1948), 66–7 · Z. Cowen, *Sir Isaac Isaacs* (Melbourne, 1979) · J. Rickard, *H. B. Higgins: the rebel as judge* (1984) · L. F. Crisp, 'The appointment of Sir Isaac Isaacs as governor-general of Australia, 1930: J. H. Scullin's account of the Buckingham Palace interviews', *Historical Studies: Australia and New Zealand*, 11 (1963–5), 253–7 · J. Robertson, *J. H. Scullin: a political biography* (1974) · H. Nicolson, *King George V: his life and reign* (1952) · *AusDB* · J. M. Bennett, *Keystone of the federal arch: a historical memoir of the high court of Australia to 1980* (1980)

Archives NL Aus.

Likenesses W. Stoneman, photograph, 1921, NPG [*see illus.*] · J. Longstaff, portrait, *c.*1930, Parliament House, Canberra · P. White, portrait, 1930, High Court Building, Canberra · B. Westwood, portrait, *c.*1950, High Court Building, Canberra · D. Low, caricature, repro. in Rickard, *H. B. Higgins*, 267 · photograph, repro. in Bennett, *Keystone of the federal arch* · photograph, High Court Building, Canberra · photographs, repro. in Cowen, *Isaac Isaacs* (1993), frontispiece

Isaacs, Jacob (1896–1973), writer and university teacher, was born in London on 6 December 1896, the son of the Revd Moses David Isaacs and his wife, Jessie, daughter of the Revd Moses Bregman. Isaacs's parents were Orthodox Jews, and he was brought up in the largely Jewish East End of London and educated at the Grocers' Company's School, Hackney Downs. In 1912 Isaacs joined the civil service where he worked until 1916. From 1916 Isaacs was on active service in France as a lieutenant (Territorial Army) in the Royal Garrison Artillery. After the 1918 armistice he became area commandant and brigade education officer. Of this period of active service, 'G. H.', writing in *The Times* after Isaacs's death, recalled that his 'talk and clowning as a young officer on the Western front solaced many a suffering fellow intellectual' (17 May 1973, 21h).

On 29 April 1919 Isaacs matriculated as a commoner reading English at Exeter College, Oxford. As there were very few fellows at his college at the time, he was assigned an outside tutor, Herbert Francis Brett-Smith. He seems not to have participated in the sporting activities at Exeter College. In March 1921 Isaacs was proposed as a member of the college Essay Club (the subjects ranging from Sappho to Shakespeare), was elected, and attended the meeting of 18 May 1921. He received a first-class honours degree in English language and literature, and took his BA degree

Jacob Isaacs (1896–1973), by Elliott & Fry

on 3 November 1921. His examiners were Sir Walter Raleigh, Sir Arthur Quiller Couch, Professor R. W. Chambers, and the historian of the English language Professor H. C. Wyld. On 11 June 1927 Isaacs received his MA degree from Oxford University.

In 1921 Isaacs was appointed assistant lecturer in English at the University College of North Wales, Bangor, where he worked under Professor Herbert G. Wright. In 1924 Isaacs became assistant lecturer in English at King's College, University of London, and in 1928 he was promoted to lecturer. 'G. H.' recalled in *The Times* that 'Oxford and London in the twenties knew him as a redoubtable controversialist in almost all the arts' (17 May 1973, 21h). On 15 July 1933 he married the non-Jewish Enid Austin Dickie (b. 1905/6), librarian, daughter of George Austin Dickie, architect; they had two daughters. In his dedication to *An Assessment of Twentieth-Century Literature* (1951) Isaacs wrote that his wife 'comforted me with apples and stayed me with flagons'.

In 1938, at the invitation of the Sir Moses Montefiore Commemoration Committee, Isaacs gave a highly successful series of twelve public lectures at the Mount Scopus campus of the fledgeling Hebrew University of Jerusalem in Palestine. In 1942 Isaacs was appointed the first Montefiore professor of English in the university, and he set about organizing and heading the new English department. At the end of 1945 Isaacs, his wife, and his family returned to England. Seven years later he was appointed to the chair of English language and literature at Queen Mary College, University of London. He gave his inaugural lecture, 'The nature of literary history', on 20 May 1952. Following a series of depressions Isaacs retired from the chair and in 1964 was appointed professor emeritus.

Isaacs's productivity ranged from critical exegesis to the textual editing of plays. He was author or editor of more than thirty books and articles, his field of concentration ranging from Shakespeare and his contemporaries, with a particular focus on Elizabethan and Restoration theatrical history, to Sir George Etherege, Samuel Taylor Coleridge, and twentieth-century poetry. Isaacs's strength lay in the lengthy article rather than the full-length monograph. His *Coleridge's Critical Terminology*, published as an English Association pamphlet in 1936, revealed a fine understanding both of critical theory and of Coleridge's critical importance. Isaacs's knowledge of bibliography and theatrical history was exhibited in, for instance, his *Production and Stage-Management at the Blackfriars Theatre*, a Shakespeare Association pamphlet of 1935. Professor C. L. Wrenn, with whom Isaacs worked at King's College, described Isaacs in a June 1945 testimonial as 'brilliant', noting that this was a quality 'especially displayed in [his] lectures … In King's College students of all faculties used to crowd into Mr. Isaacs' lectures as the most stimulating to minds of every kind.' Some of this brilliance was revealed in Isaacs's pioneering six BBC Third Programme broadcast lectures in 1949, published under the title *The Background of Modern Poetry* in 1951 and appealing to a wide rather than to a university-restricted audience. The talks were marked by clarity and scholarship and interlaced with wit, humour, irony, and choice poetic citation. Isaacs clearly revealed his bias as 'a literary historian' with 'the historical point of view' (Isaacs, *Modern Poetry*, 92). Demonstrating the range of his vision and taste, he concluded with citations from the poetry of Wallace Stevens and the Anglo-Jewish poet Lazarus Aaronson, and from the criticism of his friend T. S. Eliot.

Six lectures broadcast on the BBC Third Programme in September and October 1950 formed the foundation for Isaacs's *An Assessment of Twentieth-Century Literature* (1951). Isaacs's subjects ranged from the first forty years of the twentieth century, to scrutiny of 'the puzzling decade of the "forties"' (Isaacs, *Twentieth-Century Literature*, 41). A whole talk is devoted to 'T. S. Eliot and poetic drama'. Isaacs's religious Jewish upbringing and knowledge were reflected in a series of 1966 BBC Third Programme radio talks on the influence of the Hebrew Bible on English literature, English translations of the Bible, the Jew in English literature, and the Jewish contribution to art. Isaacs's eclecticism is reflected in the range of his publications. For instance 1954 saw the publication or reprinting of his 'Sixteenth century Bible versions' and 'The Authorised Version and after' in *The Bible in its Ancient and English Versions*; 'Dramatic criticism', an article in the *Encyclopaedia Britannica*; radio broadcasts entitled 'Robert Frost at eighty', published in *The Listener*; and a broadcast entitled 'The art of Peter Paul Rubens' for *London Calling* of the BBC overseas service. Also in 1954 he gave the British Academy Shakespeare lecture, 'Shakespeare's earliest years in the theatre', and a lecture entitled 'The academy labyrinth', published in *Art News and Review* (1954), and introduced a broadcast discussion between Robert Frost and R. Cook on Thoreau's *Walden*, published in *The Listener*.

Among Isaacs's other myriad interests was film criticism: he was a member of the London-based Film Society 'for which throughout the 1930s he edited, and wrote the bulk of, the unsigned programme notes' (*The Times*, 25 May 1973, 20h). In a letter to Isaacs's widow on his death, R. P. Tong, the registrar and secretary of Queen Mary College, referred to Isaacs's 'wit and humour', and particularly remembered Isaacs for the 'common interest in wines' which they shared. A fuller flavour of Isaacs's personality was revealed in the memorial reminiscences in *The Times* of 'G. H.', who noted that Isaacs:

> was for ever compiling material for what must surely prove one of the biggest and best books never written on the history of taste. Devastating as a critic, hardly ever known (and even less frequently proved) to be wrong, he went to inordinate length to help genuine students … he gave always much more than he took.

He concluded, 'the jovial, genial giant with his quietly patient corrective voice, wrongly deemed supercilious by strangers, has gone from us, leaving us the poorer for his going' (*The Times*, 17 May 1973, 21h). Lord Bernstein and Ivor Montague, in a *Times* obituary notice, referred to Isaacs as among the 'jovial sardonics' (19 May 1973, 16h). During a lengthy period of confinement to his home, Little Court, Court Yard, Eltham, London, and bed, suffering from depression, Isaacs was looked after by his beloved wife. Isaacs died at Lewisham Hospital on 12 May 1973.

WILLIAM BAKER

Sources *WWW, 1971–80* · *The Times* (15 May 1973), 18h · G. H., *The Times* (17 May 1973), 21h · Lord Bernstein and I. Montague, *The Times* (19 May 1973), 16h · T. D., *The Times* (25 May 1973), 20h · J. Isaacs, *An assessment of twentieth-century literature* (1951) · J. Isaacs, *The background of modern poetry* (1951) · *Jewish Chronicle* (18 May 1973) · A. A. Mendilow, 'The department of English, 1936–1982', Hebrew University of Jerusalem, Dept of English, 1984? · m. cert. · d. cert.
Archives Exeter College, Oxford · Queen Mary College, London
Likenesses Elliott & Fry, photograph, NPG [*see illus.*]
Wealth at death £28,966: probate, 26 June 1973, *CGPLA Eng. & Wales*

Isaacs, Lady Joan Alice Violet Rufus. *See* Zuckerman, Joan Alice Violet Rufus (1918–2000), *under* Zuckerman, Solly, Baron Zuckerman (1904–1993).

Isaacs, Nathaniel (1808–1872), trader and author, was born in Canterbury. His father, a merchant and inhabitant of Chatham, was married to Lenie Solomon, one of the many children of Nathaniel Solomon of Margate and Phoebe Mitz, a Dutch Jew; Saul Solomon, the merchant king of St Helena, was his uncle. Isaacs's father died during his early childhood and in 1822 the boy was sent to join his uncle Saul Solomon at St Helena. In 1825 he sailed for the British Cape Colony in the vessel *Mary*, commanded by Lieutenant James King, who aimed to join Lieutenant F. G. Farewell at Port Natal in order to participate in the ivory trade from that region. In October 1825 the *Mary* was wrecked on the sand bar at Port Natal and the crew left stranded. Isaacs was in contact with other members of Farewell's trading party, including Henry Fynn, Henry Ogle, and Thomas Halstead. James King's apprentice Charles Rawden Maclean ('John Ross') was also known to Isaacs.

In the absence of reliable evidence it is difficult to establish an accurate historical context for the white traders at Port Natal during the 1820s. Isaacs's early biographers noted his 'pioneering' qualities and his presence as a white explorer in the Shakan Zulu state. However, more recent researchers have moved away from this kind of depiction and have noted various kinds of interaction between the trading group and indigenous communities, based on trade in ivory. The South African historian Julian Cobbing has suggested that the Europeans were involved in the east African coastal slave trade, though this is still a debatable topic. While Isaacs and King were rivals with Farewell and Fynn for control of ivory supplies, this group later changed and after the death of King in 1828 Isaacs became Fynn's trading partner. By 1830 these traders had set out a business prospectus for their future economic activities at Port Natal. Isaacs did not, however, remain in the region; he left Natal for the Cape in 1831 aboard the American brig the *St Michael*.

Although he returned to England in 1832, Isaacs continued to show an economic and political interest in Natal and he wrote to the Cape governor, Sir Lowry Cole, asking for a land grant at Port Natal. This request was turned down and Isaacs then turned his attention to the idea of persuading the British government to annex Natal formally. He wrote to Fynn, suggesting that the latter publish his writing in which he could stress the savage nature of the Zulu in order to secure formal British intervention in defence of the white traders at Port Natal. In 1834 Isaacs and other Cape traders composed a 'merchants' memorial' which was sent to Governor D'Urban and then to London. This petition, which requested British annexation, was rejected by the Colonial Office on the grounds of expense.

Having failed to achieve annexation through these methods, Isaacs published in 1836 the book for which he is best known, *Travels and Adventures in Eastern Africa*. Despite encouragement from Isaacs, Fynn's reminiscences were only printed in Bird's *Annals of Natal* in 1888 and the *Diary of Henry Francis Fynn* was not published until 1950. Isaacs's publication thus became the earliest European writing on Shaka and the Zulu in the Natal region. Dan Wylie has suggested that Isaacs's writing, like other narratives on Shaka, was more in the nature of a character assassination than an objective account. His negative depiction of Shaka was clearly motivated by his desire to secure Natal as a political and economic sphere of British imperial expansion.

After his return to England in 1832 Isaacs formed a partnership with C. G. Redman in London for the purposes of commerce in the Senegal coastal region, and in 1835 petitioned the British government against French competition in the area. He also maintained his interest in Natal, and wrote to Fynn in 1840 stating that he planned to leave west Africa and return to southern Africa to control his commercial interests in the Natal coastal region. However, following the official British annexation of Natal in 1843, Isaacs was again refused a land grant in the colony and from this date he seems to have abandoned any further attempts to establish himself in South Africa.

During the early 1840s Isaacs established his trading headquarters in Old Calabar and bought property in Freetown in Sierra Leone. In 1844 he sold his Freetown properties and bought the island of Matacong, north of the Melakori River, as a trading post. The island was within the jurisdiction of the colony but remained outside customs. Isaacs took advantage of this fact and set up depots to ship goods to the mainland. He also acted as consular agent for the French government. From the 1850s he moved away from the European settlement where he cultivated arrowroot for export to England. He was suspected of being involved in the slave trade and in 1854 Governor Kennedy of Sierra Leone tried to have him arrested but he escaped to England. The evidence against Isaacs was later lost at sea while Kennedy was *en route* for Australia. In 1856 the British authorities dropped the prosecution against Isaacs. Isaacs lived in London from 1854 to 1858 but left England again in 1860 when he visited Matacong. He was in Freetown in 1863. He retired to Liverpool in 1868, and in 1870 he moved to 8 Church Street, Egremont, Cheshire, where he died in a coma on 26 June 1872.

JULIE PRIDMORE

Sources J. Bird, ed., *The annals of Natal, 1495 to 1845*, 2 vols. (1888); repr. (1965) · J. Cobbing, 'The Mfecane as alibi: thoughts on Dithakong and Mbolompo', *Journal of African History*, 29 (1988), 487–519 · C. R. Maclean, *The Natal papers of 'John Ross'*, ed. S. Gray (1992) · L. Herrman, 'Isaacs, Nathaniel', *DSAB* · N. Isaacs, *Travels and adventures in eastern Africa*, ed. L. Herrman, 2 vols. (1936) · N. Isaacs, *Travels and adventures in eastern Africa*, ed. L. Herman [L. Herrman] and P. R. Kirby (1970) · B. J. T. Leverton, *Records of Natal* (1984–92) · J. Pridmore, 'The reception of H. Fynn, c.1824–1992', *Current Writing*, 6 (1994), 80–92 · *The diary of Henry Francis Fynn*, ed. J. Stuart and D. Malcolm (1950) · E. C. Tabler, ed., *Pioneers of Natal and southeastern Africa, 1552–1878* (1977) · D. Wylie, 'Autobiography as adventure: history and projection in Nathaniel Isaacs' *Travels and adventures in eastern Africa* (1836)', *Current Writing*, 3 (1991), 72–90 · D. Wylie, 'Textual incest: Nathaniel Isaacs and the development of the Shaka myth', *History in Africa*, 19 (1992), 410–26 · D. Wylie, 'Language and assassination: cultural negations in white writers' portrayal of Shaka and the Zulu', *The Mfecane aftermath: reconstructive debates in southern African history*, ed. C. Hamilton (1995), 71–106 · d. cert.
Archives Natal Archives, South Africa, Fynn MSS

Isaacs, Rufus Daniel, first marquess of Reading (1860–1935), politician and judge, was born on 10 October 1860 at 3 Bury Street, in the parish of St Mary Axe, London, the second son and fourth of the nine children of Joseph Michael Isaacs (1832–1908), fruit importer, and his wife, Sarah (1835–1922), daughter of Daniel Davis of London. Joseph and his brother Harry carried on the business in Spitalfields founded by their father, Michael Isaacs. Michael's grandfather, the first Isaacs to settle in England, was probably of Spanish Jewish origin. Michael himself married Sarah Mendoza, whose father, Aaron, came from Madrid. Aaron's younger brother, the celebrated prize-

Rufus Daniel Isaacs, first marquess of Reading (1860–1935), by Sir William Rothenstein, 1925

fighter Daniel Mendoza, was Rufus Isaacs's great-uncle. Rufus's uncle Harry (later Sir Henry) Isaacs became an alderman and (1889–90) lord mayor of London. Rufus's sister Esther married the playwright Alfred Sutro. High-spirited and rebellious as a child—'he was wild, he was idle, he was volatile' (Reading, 1.11)—Rufus was sent away to school from an early age: to a kindergarten at Gravesend; between the ages of five and seven to a school in Brussels to learn French; then for some years as a boarder at an Anglo-Jewish school in Regent's Park. At all these schools he was precociously bright and exceedingly disruptive. In 1873 he entered University College School in Gower Street, London, where the headmaster noted his promise; but his father, seeing no future for him in higher education, removed him after less than a year in order to prepare him for the family business. Rufus was thirteen years old.

After six months in Hanover learning German, Rufus duly entered M. Isaacs & Sons as an apprentice; but he found the life irksome and uncongenial. There is no truth in the story that he ran away to sea; his father, feeling that discipline was his greatest need, arranged for him to join the sailing ship *Blair Athole*. Rufus refused to sign up for the two years laid down in the deed of apprenticeship, but he agreed to complete a round voyage as ship's boy—in effect, a deckhand. He was just sixteen years old. Conditions on board were harsh and menial; he jumped ship at Rio de Janeiro, but was caught and after punishment rejoined the vessel for the voyage to Calcutta. Here, briefly, he landed in the country over which he was to rule as viceroy forty-four years later. On his return to London in September 1877, his father sent him to Magdeburg to extend his knowledge of the import business; but his sojourn ended after eight months when he emptied a tureen of soup over a fellow lodger with whom he had fallen out. In 1879 he finally abandoned the family business to become a jobber in the foreign market at the stock exchange. At first he prospered. He became something of a man about town, bought his own horse, and regularly attended music-halls and dances. His stock exchange career ended disastrously, however, after a slump in 1884: he was 'hammered', owing debts of £8000. His father now determined that Rufus should seek his fortune in Panama, but after Rufus had left for the station his mother threw a fit of hysterics; his brother Harry pursued him to Euston and hauled him out of the Liverpool train at the last minute. His father at last agreed to let him read for the bar, a suggestion originally made by his headmaster at University College School. He was twenty-four years of age.

The law Isaacs began by attending for six months in the office of Algernon Sydney, the family solicitor, by way of experiment. He took instantly to the law; and the gadabout and seeming ne'er-do-well at last put his wild youth behind him and applied himself soberly and single-mindedly to his studies. In January 1885 he was admitted as a student to the Middle Temple. He read for a year as a pupil in the chambers of John Lawson Walton, and was called to the bar on 17 November 1887. Three weeks later, on 8 December, at the West London Synagogue, he married Alice Edith (c.1866–1930), third daughter of Albert Cohen, a City merchant, and set up house at 10 Broadhurst Gardens, near Finchley Road Station. The Isaacses were 'a remarkably good-looking couple', wrote his first pupil barrister, who noted their '*joie de vivre* and their radiant devotion to each other' (Oppenheimer, 99). They had a son.

Isaacs took the bold and unconventional step of setting up in chambers of his own, at 1 Garden Court, Temple. His confidence was vindicated. Work came flooding in. He earned £519 in his first year alone. He was soon bringing in an annual income of £7000, then a very considerable sum; and he repaid, within five years and with interest, the £8000 debt to his creditors. His firsthand experience of the stock exchange and close familiarity from the import trade with every sort of commercial document he put to good use, especially in the commercial court, established in 1895. He also became expert in trade-union law from his long association with the leading case of *Allen* v. *Flood*, which he argued through every court including the House of Lords. After only ten and a half years as a junior, he took silk in 1898, at the age of thirty-seven, and the Isaacses moved to the West End. Within five years he doubled his income; five years later he was earning an annual income, colossal for the time, of £30,000.

As a leader, Isaacs vied with such giants as Sir Edward Clarke and Sir Edward Carson. He practised chiefly in the commercial court or before special juries, occasionally in the divorce court or the Old Bailey. His triumphs included his defence of *The Star* newspaper in a libel action involving Joseph Chamberlain (1901), the Taff Vale litigation (1902), the prosecution of the fraudulent company promoter Whittaker Wright (1904), and the defence of Sir Edward Russell on a charge of criminal libel (1905) and of Robert Sievier on a blackmail charge (1908). Isaacs was exceedingly hard-working, and was blessed with an unusually robust constitution and, as he agreed, 'high animal spirits' (Jackson, 28). Able to do with little sleep, to take sleep when he chose, to ration his energy, and compartmentalize his mind, he invariably rose at 5 or 4 a.m. to prepare the day's work, arriving 'fresh and smiling' at the Temple (*The Times*, 31 Dec 1935). He made it a rule never to work after dinner, and though his wife's recurrent ill health often prevented her from accompanying him, she always encouraged him to seek an active social life and to enlarge his circle of acquaintances.

Isaacs was an engaging advocate: a slim, taut figure, with striking, chiselled features, and a melodious, beautifully modulated voice, delicate hands, firmly planted in the lapels of his coat, and an alert, compelling glance. His forensic strengths were his mastery of facts and figures, aided by a prodigiously retentive memory; great clarity of thought and expression; and total self-control. His opening speech in the Whittaker Wright case was considered 'an epic of lucidity and conciseness' (Muir, 35). His advocacy was the opposite of the rhetorical, browbeating technique then dominant. Always calm, always courteous, he never overstated his case, readily conceded his opponent's strong points, and knew how to put unpromising facts in the most favourable light. Never was he caught out or provoked into losing his temper. Beneath his impressive composure lay great tactical dexterity. He was among the first to put his client in the witness box under the Criminal Evidence Act 1898 to testify in his own defence. His mode of cross-examination—disarmingly quiet, polite, and equable—set a new and lasting standard. J. C. Davidson recalled:

> I was immensely struck by his capacity of exacting information without the giver of the information really realising it. He always asked questions with an anaesthetic in them, so that you really felt that if he was operating on you, you would never feel any pain. (*Memoirs of a Conservative*, 395)

His speeches in court—factual, couched in straightforward, almost conversational language—were singularly effective with both judge and jury. His acute judgement enabled him to seize the vital issue and press it home; to argue a point of law with ingenuity and persistence; and to sense the moment to compromise. His matter-of-fact, low-key approach also served him well in appeal cases. He handled the bench suavely, and he appeared frequently before the House of Lords. In the more measured assessment of his fellow lawyer and colleague John Simon, 'he was not a profound lawyer, but hard work and good sense made him the master of all the law that mattered for winning his case' (*DNB*).

Liberal MP and law officer In politics, Isaacs was a Liberal Imperialist, and his record of trade-union litigation stood him in good stead as a friend of the working man. After unsuccessfully contesting North Kensington in 1900, he was returned for Reading at a by-election in August 1904 and retained that seat, despite some close contests, until 1913.

In March 1910 Isaacs succeeded Sir Samuel Evans as solicitor-general and was knighted. In this capacity Sir Rufus Isaacs was immediately confronted by a painful dilemma in the case of George Archer-Shee, the naval cadet falsely accused of stealing a 5s. postal order and expelled from the Royal Naval College at Osborne. The case later became the subject of a well-known play by Terence Rattigan, *The Winslow Boy* (1946), and of two films (1948 and 1999). Perhaps over-cautious and relying too heavily on precedent and his predecessor's ruling, Isaacs declined to waive the Admiralty's crown privilege of immunity from suit. The Court of Appeal, however, decided that the facts should be heard; and after a full hearing Isaacs, on behalf of the Admiralty, acknowledged the boy's complete innocence.

In October 1910, after only six months as solicitor-general, Isaacs succeeded Sir William Robson as attorney-general. As such, in 1911 he secured the conviction for criminal libel of Edward Mylius, a republican agitator who circulated the falsehood that George V, when he married the future Queen Mary, was already married to another. The king wished to enter the witness box, but Isaacs advised that a reigning monarch cannot give evidence in his own courts. Shortly after, in June 1911, Isaacs was appointed KCVO. He prosecuted in the case of *R. v. Seddon* (1912), the only murder trial in which he took part—he did so reluctantly and only because the attorney-general customarily leads for the crown in poisoning cases. Seddon insisted on testifying in his own defence at the Old Bailey, where Isaacs's deceptive mildness of manner in cross-examination led Seddon fatally to expose his mercenary character to the jury and to entrap himself in the web of circumstantial evidence which Isaacs wove around him to prove that he had poisoned Eliza Barrow for her money. The same year, Isaacs prosecuted the militant suffragette Mrs Emmeline Pankhurst for conspiracy to commit injury and damage (though he personally favoured votes for women). In 1912 he represented the Board of Trade at the inquiry into the *Titanic* disaster.

Isaacs also helped pilot through the House of Commons the government's heavy and controversial legislative programme, including the Parliament Act, 1911; the Official Secrets Act, 1911, 'a very startling innovation', as he admitted (Hyde, 90); the National Insurance Act, 1911; the Trade Unions Act, 1913; and the Home Rule Act, 1914. He became the friend, perhaps the only close friend, of Lloyd George, and was much liked by the prime minister, Asquith. His 'outstanding quality was his tact' (Beaverbrook, 96) and a captivating charm which enabled him to win the confidence of men of very opposite characters and politics. His heavy legal practice took priority over attendance in the house, however: by the time he arrived in the evening, as he recalled, 'I was tired out' (Hyde, 61). His speeches there seldom caught the imagination, and he never became a 'House of Commons man'. He was appointed a privy councillor in the coronation honours of July 1911.

When, in June 1912, Lord Loreburn resigned from the woolsack, Isaacs, as attorney-general, expected to be appointed in his place. He was deeply affronted when Lord Haldane was appointed instead, deeming this a slur on his office and himself. At first he suspected that he was being passed over on grounds of religion. Asquith, however, had long since intended Haldane for the woolsack; but he assuaged Isaacs's pique by agreeing that the attorney-general should join the cabinet. This privilege, which Isaacs himself came to question, involved an inherent clash of interest with the functions of a law officer, and it was eventually discontinued.

The Marconi scandal Isaacs's career was interrupted and nearly terminated by what soon became known as the Marconi scandal. The Imperial Conference of 1911 having recommended the setting up of a chain of wireless stations across the empire, in March 1912 the Marconi Wireless Telegraph Company's tender was accepted by the postmaster-general, Herbert Samuel, subject to ratification by the House of Commons. The company's managing director was Rufus Isaacs's younger brother, Godfrey. Rufus Isaacs played no part in negotiating the contract, and apparently only learned of its existence from his brother a few days before it was concluded. Unsavoury rumours, however, began to circulate: first, that Godfrey Isaacs had secured the contract through the influence of his brother and Herbert Samuel; then that Rufus Isaacs and his friends—the chancellor of the exchequer, Lloyd George, and the government chief whip, Alec Murray, the master of Elibank—had made profitable speculations as a result of Isaacs's inside knowledge (the company shares having risen more than tenfold in value by April 1912). Neither allegation was true, as was later unanimously accepted by an all-party parliamentary select committee. What was true was that there was another company, the American Marconi Company, in which Godfrey Isaacs held a large block of shares, some of which he offered to Rufus and Harry. The American company had no interest, direct or indirect, in the profits of the English company; but while Harry purchased a large shareholding, Rufus wisely declined Godfrey's offer. In mid-April came the *Titanic* disaster, underlining the huge importance of wireless telegraphy. When Harry Isaacs then offered Rufus some of his American shares, this time Rufus accepted, and bought 10,000, though not at the jobbing price of 21s. which Harry offered, but at the market value of £2. The same day he transferred 1000 shares each to Lloyd George and Murray at the same price. Meanwhile the rumours concerning the English Marconi company abounded. The accusations were made openly in August in a highly offensive article by Cecil Chesterton (brother of G. K. Chesterton) in his journal *The Eye-Witness*. On Asquith's advice, Isaacs decided to do nothing rather than to stir up the controversy; but the effect of his inaction was precisely that.

When parliament reassembled in October 1912, Samuel moved for the appointment of a House of Commons select committee to investigate and report on the Marconi contract. Isaacs intervened in the ensuing debate. He denied having 'had one single transaction with the shares of that company', meaning the English Marconi company

(Reading, 1.246). He said nothing, however, about his shares in the American company, having satisfied himself before purchasing that while the English company might profit from the success of the American company, the reverse was not the case. His purchase and subsequent dealings were thus unexceptionable in themselves, and in fact the shares depreciated. His failure to mention them, however, was a cardinal and almost a fatal error of judgement, since it came close to disingenuousness and exposed his motives and actions to obvious misconstruction when the truth came out. The news broke in the course of an undefended libel action against the Paris newspaper *Le Matin* in March 1913, when Isaacs admitted that he, Lloyd George, and Murray had dealt in the American shares. Soon afterwards he appeared before the select committee. While even his political opponents on the committee were satisfied that the allegations of corruption were baseless, the question of 'grave impropriety' was raised in a minority report; but the final report, adopted by a majority of eight to six, accepted that Isaacs, Samuel, Lloyd George, and Murray had all acted in the belief that what they did was not in conflict with their public duty.

The press then discovered that when he joined the stock exchange at the age of nineteen, Isaacs had signed a false declaration that he was twenty-one. The fact admitted of an innocent explanation, but such revelations were extremely awkward at a time of acute political partisanship, when the Unionist opposition was out to embarrass the government and, in some quarters, to destroy both Isaacs and Lloyd George. In the Commons debate on the report on 18 June Isaacs admitted that, while at the time he believed there was nothing untoward in his American purchase, he had since concluded that 'it was a mistake to purchase those shares' (Reading, 1.271). The concession was belated and grudging. It was Asquith who, by treating the matter as a motion of censure on the government, throwing his personal authority behind his colleague, and vouching for his honesty, saved Isaacs's career. Isaacs, whose nature was essentially fastidious, suffered acutely during this long and painful controversy. 'As I walked across the lobbies or in the streets or to the courts', he said, 'I could feel the pointing of the finger as I passed' (Walker-Smith, 327). What was strange was that a man so sage in his counsel to others could himself have been so ill-advised.

Lord chief justice and ambassador In October 1913 the lord chief justice, Viscount Alverstone, resigned. As attorney-general Isaacs had a prescriptive right to the office; but the moment could hardly have been less propitious, and Asquith hesitated before offering him the post and Isaacs before accepting. To refuse would have been taken as an admission that he was not free from taint in the Marconi scandal, which in turn would have put in question his position as attorney-general. Other than quitting public life, therefore, 'he had very little option but to accept' (Judd, *Lord Reading*, 110). As it was, the appointment cut short his political career, which he was reluctant to abandon at the age of fifty-three, and revived hostile comment in sections

of the press. Rudyard Kipling joined the attack with 'Gehazi', a poem of stinging contumely. Isaacs was cheered by the abiding confidence which the bar showed in his integrity. In the new year's honours list of 1914, he was raised to the peerage as Baron Reading of Erleigh.

Reading had been in office barely half a year when, in August 1914, his help was urgently sought by Lloyd George to assist in coping with the unprecedented financial crisis brought on by the outbreak of war and in drafting the necessary emergency legislation. Almost daily after court Reading would repair to Whitehall, where an office was provided for him. His advice and his services were found to be indispensable: he himself considered this contribution the most gratifying of his career; and although he remained lord chief justice until 1921, his presence in court was to be intermittent. In *Porter v. Freudenburg* (1915) he ruled that an enemy alien, though he cannot sue, can be sued, and has the right to appear and defend himself. The most dramatic case over which he presided was the treason trial of Sir Roger Casement (1916). The main charge related to Casement's attempts while in Germany to recruit Irish prisoners of war to fight against England. Upholding the opinions of Coke, Hale, and Hawkins against the somewhat strained construction placed by the defence on the Statute of Treasons of 1351, Reading held that 'the offence, if proved in fact, has been committed in law' (Walker-Smith, 377).

As unofficial adviser at the highest level, Reading was entrusted by the government with a variety of wartime challenges at home and abroad. In June 1915 his services were rewarded with the GCB. In September, leaving Mr Justice Darling to deputize as lord chief justice, he headed an Anglo-French mission to the United States to seek American credits for urgently needed supplies. Despite much American neutralist and pro-German opposition, he secured from a consortium of American banks a loan of £100 million, though this was only half the amount hoped for and was restricted to purchases in the United States. During his six-week visit he made many influential contacts and left an excellent impression among his interlocutors, notably Colonel House, President Wilson's closest adviser. When House travelled to London early in 1916 to explore the possibilities of a compromise peace, Reading hosted his confidential meetings with the cabinet. The government continued to rely on his advice, and he was raised to a viscountcy in June 1916. In the political crisis of December 1916, he acted as intermediary between Lloyd George and Asquith in an attempt to keep both men in office; and after Lloyd George became prime minister, Reading tried to persuade Asquith to rejoin the cabinet as lord chancellor, while anticipating and indeed soliciting from Lloyd George further employment for himself.

Advancement was not long delayed. In September 1917 Reading returned to the United States with the special appointment of high commissioner (his mandate also extending to Canada). Although America was now an 'associated power', the war was going very badly for the allies. Reading's task—difficult, delicate, and calling for all his gifts—was to persuade the administration to integrate America's war effort more closely with that of the allies, to prioritize the deployment of military supplies and shipping, and to grant regular credits for the duration of the war. He persuaded William McAdoo, secretary to the treasury, to allow part of these credits to be spent on purchases in Canada. He helped to convince Wilson of the need for closer military co-ordination between America and the allies through a joint supreme war council at Versailles. In this, an observer commented, he 'achieved one of the biggest things of the war' (Hyde, 227). Reading himself was appointed to the supreme war council as financial adviser to the war cabinet. On his return to England in November, Lloyd George instigated his elevation to an earldom. Reading also helped to engineer the recall of the British ambassador, Sir Cecil Spring Rice, a jealous and unbalanced professional, who resented his success and obstructed his work.

In January 1918 Reading was appointed ambassador-extraordinary and high commissioner at Washington in place of Spring Rice. On his return to America in February, he engaged or re-engaged in many crucial and desperately urgent problems: the acceleration of food supplies to the allies, now within measurable distance of starvation; Britain's chronic and mounting overdraft with her American bankers; the fraught issue of allied intervention in Russia, and America's role therein; and the question of Irish home rule, always an irritant in Anglo-American relations (for the sake of which Reading urged Lloyd George to offer a generous settlement). Amid these daunting preoccupations, he continued to discharge, with unruffled aplomb, his public ambassadorial duties in the cause of Anglo-American co-operation. An observer recalls his diplomatic grace, as to the manner born, his 'sensitive hands toying with a chicken wing, sipping gingerly from a glass of good claret … elegant in evening dress' (Hyde, 218).

Reading's crucial mission proved successful. 'I do not know how we should get on without you', Lloyd George wrote feelingly (Hyde, 262). 'He can get more out of the Administration than anyone I can think of', Sir William Wiseman confirmed (Judd, *Lord Reading*, 165). Above all he faced and surmounted the dire problem of depleted allied military manpower following the collapse of Russia. Throughout the supreme crisis of the war in the spring and early summer of 1918 he instilled, at Lloyd George's behest, with infinite tact but infinite persistence, a greater sense of urgency in the president and the administration in transporting American troops to the western front in numbers and training sufficient to enable the hard-pressed forces of Britain and France to withstand the successive German onslaughts. Had he failed in this task, the war might have been lost. His absence in England, where he was recalled for consultation in August 1918, unforeseeably lasted for over six months in the second half of 1918, giving rise to complaints in Washington (where he returned to wind up his mission between February and May 1919). He regularly attended the war cabinet, and was Lloyd George's confidential emissary on high-level missions to France. He was present at cabinet discussion of the armistice, represented Great Britain in Paris on an inter-allied committee to discuss the revictualling of Europe, and perhaps aspired to a higher role at the Paris peace conference. If so, his hopes were not realized.

Viceroy of India Reading resumed with extreme reluctance his duties as lord chief justice. After the excitement of recent years—'the war, he would say, had spoilt him' (*The Times*, 31 Dec 1935)—he found the bench mundane and uninspiring, and the prospect of remaining there until retirement depressed him. Strolling in Paris with the new lord chancellor, the 46-year-old F. E. Smith, Lord Birkenhead, Reading, himself nearing sixty, exclaimed: 'Look here, F. E., you and I are both too young to be stuck for the rest of our lives as judges. Let's go back to the Bar!' (Reading, 2.149). In the case of *R. v. Beard* (1920), Reading held that drunkenness may reduce murder to manslaughter if it is sufficient to preclude the defendant from forming the necessary 'specific intent'. Birkenhead overruled Reading's judgment. A curious aspect of the case was that Reading, who also took part in the hearing of the appeal by the House of Lords, acquiesced without demur in the reversal of his own judgment. Perhaps he simply changed his mind, though his original ruling represents the law as it now stands. As lord chief justice 'he was a good judge' but 'not a great judge' (Walker-Smith, 389). The truth is that he was bored with the law, and hankered after the glamour of high politics and, noted the attorney-general, Hewart, 'the glitter of diplomacy' (Hyde, 313). He offered to return as ambassador to the United States, and continued through Lloyd George to have sight of the dispatches between London and Washington. He even angled for the British embassy at Paris.

Thanks to Lloyd George he soon secured another enviable position: in January 1921 he was appointed viceroy of India. After over thirty years in the law, he broke with his profession with unfeigned relief. 'I will never look at a law report again if I can help it!', he declared (Hyde, 327). The fresh challenge rejuvenated him: he showed himself 'marvellously bright and energetic' (Mersey, 314). The Government of India Act of 1919 envisaged increasing participation by Indians in the Indian Civil Service and army, and Reading was determined to implement it despite both die-hard tory hostility at home and widespread suspicion of British intentions among the Indians themselves. He took a principled stand against racial discrimination. 'I am convinced', he wrote to Edwin Montagu, the secretary of state for India, 'that we shall never persuade the Indian of the justice of our rule until we have overcome racial difficulties [i.e. discrimination]' (Hyde, 356). In charm and courtesy, Reading demonstrated his habitual qualities of political address. He believed in the reforms and in eventual Indian self-government, and he strove to show himself just, liberal, and sincere. He personally received both Gandhi and Jinnah. He made a point of visiting Amritsar as a gesture of reconciliation for the massacre of 1919. But he had to contend with Indian nationalism, now in the ascendant. Gandhi sought to rally Hindu and Muslim against the British on a common platform of non-co-operation. There was much unrest; and Reading showed patience and finesse in exploiting differences between the Hindu-dominated Congress Party and the Muslim League before marginalizing extremists on both sides. In 1921, however, he moved against two Muslim agitators, the Ali brothers; and in 1922, after long forbearance, he ordered Gandhi's arrest on a charge of sedition, for which the mahatma was sentenced to six years' imprisonment. Reading also cultivated the princely rulers, who governed a third of India; but again, his policy was even-handed, combining conciliation with firmness, as when, for cruelty to their subjects, he forced the abdication of two maharajas. In August 1921 he ordered the suppression of rebellion among the Moplahs, a fanatical Muslim sect in the Madras presidency, and in 1922 of Sikh unrest in the Punjab. Despite a volatile political situation, the prince of Wales's visit to India in November 1921, which took place largely at Reading's insistence, was a success.

In February 1922 Reading telegraphed a dispatch to Montagu in which he stressed the resentment among India's Muslims at Britain's post-war treatment of Turkey, and formally requested, in the name of the government of India, revision of the treaty of Sèvres. When at his request Montagu published this dispatch, but without seeking the consent of the prime minister or foreign secretary, Lloyd George forced Montagu to resign. Reading, as he informed Lloyd George, was 'very distressed by the resignation' (Hyde, 374). For a time he contemplated resigning himself, though he had not been at fault; and the treaty of Lausanne (1923) went far to relieve the Muslim anxieties which he had sought to allay.

Elder statesman On his return to England in April 1926, Reading was created a marquess, the first commoner to rise so high since the duke of Wellington. As before his Indian appointment, Reading 'faced a tremendous problem of readjustment' (Judd, *Lord Reading*, 232). In the first place, he had his income to consider. He had no pension, his investments had often failed, and he spent heavily. He was appointed to the boards of a number of companies (including the National Provincial Bank and the London and Lancashire Insurance Company, of which he became chairman). The most important of these remunerative posts was his directorship of Imperial Chemical Industries (ICI), the founder of which, Sir Alfred Mond, was the father of Reading's daughter-in-law. After Mond's death in 1930, Reading became president of ICI. He still yearned, however, for political office. He took part in efforts to heal the rifts in the Liberal Party which emerged after Asquith's retirement. As head of the Liberal Party delegation, he played a leading role in the three round-table conferences on the Indian constitution in 1930–32 and, during 1933–4, on the select committee appointed to draft the Government of India Act 1935.

On 30 January 1930, after forty-two years of marriage, Lady Reading died of cancer. She had encouraged Reading's ambitions throughout his career; a close observer even considered that 'she was the more gifted of the two' (Oppenheimer, 99). On 6 August 1931 Reading married Stella (1894–1971) [*see* Isaacs, Stella], third daughter of

Charles Charnaud, when he was nearly seventy-one and she was thirty-seven; she had served on his staff in India and thereafter as his private secretary. That same month, with the onset of the great depression, Ramsay MacDonald formed an all-party National Government and much to his delight appointed Reading, now Liberal leader in the House of Lords, as foreign secretary. The office, his son recorded, 'had always had a powerful attraction for him' (Judd, *Lord Reading*, 253) and he entered upon it with zest. It was a position which, but for the crisis, as he admitted, 'I could not have hoped to occupy' (ibid., 261). He also became leader of the House of Lords. In this capacity he was responsible for steering legislation through the upper house, notably on the suspension of the gold standard. He resigned the Foreign Office after the general election in October, though he negotiated to remain in government. However, he declined MacDonald's invitation to take office as lord privy seal in the second National Government.

Reading was appointed GCSI and GCIE in 1921 and GCVO in 1922. He received the freedom of Reading (1920) and of London (1926). He became a bencher of the Middle Temple in 1905 and served as treasurer in 1927. He received honorary degrees from the universities of Harvard, Yale, Princeton, Columbia, Toronto, and Calcutta, and from Cambridge and Oxford (1926). Having held the captaincy of Deal Castle since 1926, he was appointed lord warden of the Cinque Ports in 1934.

Retrospective survey Reading's career was a tale of dramatic success, the more remarkable in one whose schooling was patchy and ended before he was fourteen, who never, as he often regretted, attended university, whose early years were chequered, and whose soaring promise almost foundered in the Marconi scandal. To himself as to others, his life seemed a romantic adventure. 'Here I am,' he mused in 1918, 'ambassador, lord chief justice, peer, and I started from nothing' (Hyde, 284). As his son commented, visiting his parents in the viceregal lodge at Simla, they had come a long way since Broadhurst Gardens (Reading, 2.174). From his boyhood, Reading was bold and full of life, outgoing and ready to defy adversity. Aboard the *Blair Athole* he learned to use his fists (later, as an amateur boxer, he received a broken nose). These innate qualities of resilience and determination—to which he himself attributed his success—he applied assiduously in the furtherance of his career, while sublimating in that cause the too open pugnacity and recklessness which marred his early life. Both Margot Asquith and Frances Stevenson agreed that 'ambition was his ruling quality' (Stevenson, *Years that are Past*, 55); while the key to his continual advancement was his friendship with Asquith and Lloyd George. That he retained the favour of both without being harmed by the fall of either and tried, though unsuccessfully, to reconcile them was a mark of his suave and conciliatory character. The steely glint of Reading's ambition was screened by a velvet cover of ubiquitous amiability and genuine good nature. 'He did not challenge; he charmed' (Walker-Smith, 391); and his 'abundance of personal charm' (Beaverbrook, 96) won over colleagues and critics alike. His ambition, though constant and intense, was usually also tempered by prudence and reserve. According to Beaverbrook, he was 'so cautious that he never gave an opinion until he was forced to do so' (ibid.). J. M. Keynes noted this characteristic in 1918, when Reading hoped for a position of influence at the peace conference: he was 'terrified of identifying himself too decidedly with anything controversial' (Judd, *Lord Reading*, 145). Avoiding the rough and tumble of politics while forwarding his career from behind the scenes, he glided discreetly upwards from success to success, always with a modest smile and a friendly wave to those below him on the political escalator, though he had what Frances Stevenson called 'the "cafeteria" mind—self-service only' (Stevenson, *Years that are Past*, 55).

Reading's long and varied experience, dignity, and poise lent him in later years the authority of an elder statesman—'an affable Caesar' (Sitwell, 224)—and a reputation perhaps somewhat above his real merits, considerable though these were—and they included great industry and powers of concentration, as every stage of his career bears witness. Behind a certain elusive modesty he had not really much to say for himself. 'He owed much', Lord Birkenhead observed, 'to a very distinguished appearance' (Birkenhead, 106). In this sense the office of viceroy suited him admirably: a photograph of 1926 shows him acknowledging the obeisance of assembled Indian notables, politely doffing his sola topee. He was a diplomat and peacemaker—'this imperturbable negotiator' in the words of Colonel House (Hyde, 217), a conciliator rather than a leader of men. He attempted to mediate in the national strike of 1926. In politics he early became thought of as indispensable—'the inevitable Lord Reading', in C. P. Scott's somewhat peevish description (*Political Diaries*, 220)—and in his wartime mission to America, on which depended victory or defeat, he was undoubtedly the right man in the right place at the right time. While ambition drove him ever upward, the steady pursuit of advancement was for him perhaps an end in itself, the attainment of office more satisfying than the exercise. He had not, indeed, a commonplace mind, but perhaps a more bland, conventional, and even sentimental outlook than might have been expected. As a public speaker he was fluent but 'dignified and dull' (Beaverbrook, 96), saved from pomposity by a sense of humour. 'Few men indeed', Lord Birkenhead observed, 'have risen so high whose spoken words possessed so little literary distinction' (Birkenhead, 105–6).

Reading was no intellectual, though he enjoyed music and drama. He took up bridge, riding, shooting, tennis, and golf, at which last he was said to be a cheerful incompetent. Of a nature both tough and finely wrought, he shrank from crudity or emotional display, and as lord chief justice he was strangely embarrassed by cases of a sexual nature. His tastes were simple, though 'he thoroughly enjoyed the pomp and pageantry' (*The Times*, 31 Dec 1935), alternating formality with informality both as viceroy of India, where he introduced ballroom dancing to relieve the tedium of levees, and at Deal Castle and Walmer Castle, where he hosted festive family gatherings. In private he was good company, debonair, genial, and spontaneous. He would burst unexpectedly into music-hall songs or sea shanties. Motoring with Lloyd George in the south of France before the First World War, to his companion's astonishment he chanted in Hebrew the 'Song of Miriam', which he had learned at school. Kindly and generous—Marshall Hall and Asquith were among those to whom he proffered financial help in their time of need—he was 'a just and most likeable fellow' and 'a lovable man' (Beaverbrook, 96).

The first Jew to become lord chief justice or foreign secretary before Peter Taylor and Malcolm Rifkind in the late twentieth century, Reading was proud of his Jewish birth and he always spoke up for his co-religionists. But he had little feeling for religion as such: he seldom attended Jewish observances, his second wife was a gentile, and his grandson was baptized in the Anglican faith. Having scaled the heights and done service as an Englishman, he felt lukewarm towards Zionism, though he took pleasure in a visit to Palestine in 1931, and the advent of Hitler made him more sympathetic to the cause. Having helped to found the Anglo-German Association in 1929, he resigned as its president in 1933.

On holiday in Egypt in 1931, Reading nearly died of double pneumonia, though he made a quick recovery. In September 1935, while practising golf, he suffered a violent attack of cardiac asthma, and a further bout in December. He died at his home, 32 Curzon Street, London, on 30 December 1935, as he 'always said that he wished to die'—'in harness' (Mersey, 388). On 1 January 1936 his body was cremated and his ashes were interred near the remains of his first wife in the Golders Green Jewish cemetery. His estate was sworn for probate at £290,487 11s. 7d., a figure never exceeded hitherto by a practising member of the English bar. He was succeeded as second marquess of Reading by his only child, Gerald Rufus Isaacs (1889–1960).

A. LENTIN

Sources Marquess of Reading [G. R. Isaacs], *Rufus Isaacs, first marquess of Reading*, 2 vols. (1942–5) • H. M. Hyde, *Lord Reading: the life of Rufus Isaacs, first marquess of Reading* (1967) • D. Judd, *Lord Reading* (1982) • D. Walker-Smith, *Lord Reading and his cases* (1934) • *DNB* • M. A. Beaverbrook, *Men and power, 1917–1918* (1956) • Earl of Birkenhead, 'Lord Darling', *Contemporary personalities* [1924] • F. Donaldson, *The Marconi scandal* (1962) • *The Times* (31 Dec 1935) • *Memoirs of a Conservative: J. C. C. Davidson's memoirs and papers, 1910–37*, ed. R. R. James (1969) • F. L. Lloyd George, *The years that are past* (1967) • F. Oppenheimer, *Stranger within* (1960) • S. Jackson, *Rufus Isaacs: first marquess of Reading* (1936) • O. Sitwell, *Laughter in the next room* (1949) • *The political diaries of C. P. Scott, 1911–1928*, ed. T. Wilson (1970) • Viscount Mersey [C. C. Bigham], *A picture of life* (1941) • R. Muir, *A memoir of a public prosecutor* (1927) • W. B. Fowler, *British-American relations, 1917–1918: the role of Sir William Wiseman* (1969) • F. Stevenson, *Lloyd George: a diary*, ed. A. J. P. Taylor (1971) • *The Leo Amery diaries*, ed. J. Barnes and D. Nicholson, 1 (1980) • D. Judd, 'Reading, Lord', *The Blackwell dictionary of British political life in the twentieth century*, ed. K. Robbins (1990), 353–4

Archives BL OIOC, corresp. and papers; corresp. and papers relating to India, MSS Eur. E238, F118 • priv. coll., papers • PRO, corresp. and papers, FO800/222–6 • Royal Arch. | Balliol Oxf., letters to Sir Francis Oppenheimer • BL, corresp. with Arthur James Balfour, Add. MS 49741, *passim* • BL, corresp. with Lord Cecil, Add. MS

51082 · BL, corresp. with Lord Northcliffe, Add. MS 62156 · BL OIOC, letters to Lord Birkenhead, MS Eur. D703 · BL OIOC, letters to Sir Basil Blackett, MS Eur. E397 · BL OIOC, corresp. with Sir Harcourt Butler, MS Eur. F116 · BL OIOC, corresp. with Lord Goschen, MS Eur. D595 · BL OIOC, corresp. with second earl of Lytton, MS Eur. F160 · BL OIOC, corresp. with E. S. Montagu, MS Eur. D523 · Bodl. Oxf., corresp. with Herbert Asquith · Bodl. Oxf., H. A. L. Fisher papers · Bodl. Oxf., letters to the Lewis family · Bodl. Oxf., corresp. with Lord Sankey · Bodl. Oxf., corresp. with Lord Simon · Harvard U., Houghton L., Walter Hines Page papers · HLRO, corresp. with David Lloyd George · HLRO, corresp. with Herbert Samuel · NA Scot., corresp. with Lord Lothian · priv. coll., Birkenhead papers · priv. coll., Simon papers · PRO, Foreign Office papers · PRO, Grey papers · Yale U., Sterling Memorial Library, corresp. with Edward House · Yale U., Wiseman papers | FILM BFI NFTVA, documentary footage · BFI NFTVA, news footage

Likenesses G. C. Beresford, photographs, 1903, NPG · O. Birley, oils, c.1914, Reading Municipal Art Gallery · J. Russell & Sons, photograph, c.1915, NPG · W. Orpen, oils, 1919, NPG · W. Stoneman, photograph, 1919, NPG · G. F. Watt, oils, c.1920, Middle Temple, London; on loan to Palace of Westminster · K. Kennet, bronze bust, 1925, NPG · W. Rothenstein, chalk drawing, 1925, NPG [*see illus.*] · F. Bremner, photograph, c.1926, NPG · O. Birley, oils, 1928, Middle Temple, London · C. S. Jagger, statue, c.1928, New Delhi, India · E. Kapp, drawing, 1929, Barber Institute of Fine Arts, Birmingham · F. May, caricature, gouache, 1930–39, NPG · A. Lowental, bronze plaque, 1936, NPG · P. A. de Laszlo, portrait, viceroy's house, Delhi, India · Spy [L. Ward], caricature, lithograph, NPG; repro. in *VF* (14 Feb 1904) · Spy [L. Ward], mechanically reproduced caricature, NPG; repro. in *VF* (18 June 1913)

Wealth at death £290,487 11s. 7d.: probate, 28 Feb 1936, *CGPLA Eng. & Wales*

Isaacs [*née* Charnaud], **Stella, marchioness of Reading and Baroness Swanborough** (1894–1971), founder of the Women's Royal Voluntary Service, was born in Constantinople on 6 January 1894. Her father, Charles Charnaud, was of Huguenot descent, and was director of the tobacco monopoly of the Ottoman empire. In 1893 Charnaud married his second wife, Milbah Johnson, daughter of a Lincolnshire family, and Stella was their eldest child and Charnaud's third daughter. Because of a spinal ailment in her youth she never went to school but read and studied at the family home at Moda on the Asian side of the Bosphorus.

By 1914 Stella Charnaud, whose health was still regarded as delicate, was in London training as a secretary and it was in that capacity that she went to India in 1925 to assist Lady Reading, the wife of the viceroy, Rufus Daniel *Isaacs, earl (later marquess) of Reading (1860–1935). Later she worked as private secretary to the marquess of Reading, both at the headquarters of Imperial Chemical Industries, of which he was president, and at his London home in Curzon Street. In 1930 his wife died and the following year (6 August 1931) Reading married Stella Charnaud, on whom he had come increasingly to depend. They had no children.

For most young women the transition from private secretary to marchioness, wife of the foreign secretary (August–October 1931) and former viceroy, as well as marriage to a man nearly twice her age, would have been formidable. Yet Stella adapted quickly and easily, her natural dignity and authority, combined with her support of her

Stella Isaacs, marchioness of Reading and Baroness Swanborough (1894–1971), by Howard Coster, 1940

husband, earning her widespread acceptance in her new role.

During the remaining years of Reading's life Stella devoted herself almost exclusively to him, although in 1932 she became chair of the Personal Service League, a voluntary society concerned with the welfare of the needy. After a period of shock and disorientation following her husband's death in 1935 she stood out as a considerable figure in her own right: forceful, practical, and determined, finding various outlets for her abundant energy and idealism. In 1938 the dowager marchioness of Reading was sent for by the home secretary, Sir Samuel Hoare, and invited to form a service of women, to be attached to local authorities throughout the country and giving their services on a voluntary basis, in order to prepare for the dislocation that would inevitably be caused to the civil population if war was to come. The plan was farsighted, ambitious, and timely. The detailed structure was proposed by Lady Reading herself. Not for the first or the last time in her career, once her interest had been aroused and she had concluded there was a need, she lost no time in setting about finding ways of meeting it. Thus she was much more than simply the head of what was to become one of the largest and most remarkable of all voluntary organizations, mobilizing the resources of more than 1 million women by 1942, but was genuinely its founder and continuing inspiration.

Lady Reading served as the unchallenged leader of the Women's Voluntary Service for Civil Defence (WVS) throughout the Second World War and after. It became her life's work. From the start it was a service organized on original lines. Its founder had seen enough of well-intended charitable and philanthropic ventures to have developed a strong dislike of committees, bureaucracy, and fund-raising. The WVS had a minimum of committees, titles, and ranks, and efforts were made to enrol women from the widest possible social base. It was a uniformed service, directly funded by government and local authorities, and one that soon became established as a vital and highly valued part of the war effort. Conformity was never encouraged. Lady Reading retained absolute power and authority in her own hands, yet she was convinced that the strength of voluntary service lay in the character of each volunteer. She saw to it that individual initiative counted for more than regimentation, even in the matter of the strikingly different angles at which WVS hats were worn. Churchill was disapproving, but Lady Reading was unrepentant.

The wartime work of the WVS, particularly notable in the evacuation of many thousands of children from London and other cities, the caring for refugees and the victims of enemy bombing, and the provision of a wide variety of welfare services for the armed forces, as well as in a multitude of other useful ways, largely ended in 1945. By then the WVS was a national institution and Lady Reading met a heartening response when she called on her members to keep it in being. The needs of the British people in the immediate post-war era of shortages of food, fuel, and housing were different. But the opportunity the WVS afforded women to render practical service to the communities of which they were a part remained unchanged.

Although the WRVS (the accolade Royal was bestowed in 1966) was at the centre of her life, Lady Reading had many other interests. For more than thirty years, from 1936 to 1968, she was vice-chair of the Imperial Relations Trust and from 1946 to 1951 she served as a governor of the BBC and was its vice-chair from 1947 to 1951. Later she demonstrated once again her ability to keep up with the changing social problems of the day by seeking to improve the condition of Commonwealth immigrants to Britain and also of former prisoners. For the Home Office she chaired the Advisory Council on Commonwealth Immigration and a working party on the place of voluntary service in aftercare of prisoners. She was appointed DBE in 1941 and GBE in 1944. The universities of Reading (1947) and Leeds (1969) conferred honorary doctorates upon her, as did Yale (1958) and Smith College (1956) in the United States and Manitoba University in Canada (1960).

In character and appearance Lady Reading was a large woman with a deep voice and an evidently powerful personality. Although she never occupied herself with party politics she maintained an extensive network of political and official contacts which she used resolutely to achieve her objects. During the last decade of her life she epitomized the growing influence of non-party peers on the cross benches of the House of Lords. While she could be fierce and demanding at times, her charm and innate sense of modesty, as well as the laudable purposes of the causes which she championed, made her universally respected, and often loved. Throughout her long public career she was capable of acts of great personal kindness and consideration, while her qualities of leadership were underpinned by a consistent generosity of mind and sense of forward vision. She died, active to the last as chair of the WRVS, at her London home, 16 Lord North Street, on 22 May 1971. A service commemorating her life and work was held at Westminster Abbey.

Created Baroness Swanborough on 22 September 1958, she was the first woman life peer to take her seat in the House of Lords. Her coat of arms incorporated a WVS figure as one of the supporters, and in a letter to the membership she explained that in the upper part of the design were two bees, described as volant or flying, which naturally represented the industry of the WVS. The scroll on which the coat of arms rested bore the motto 'Not why we can't but how we can'. LORD WINDLESHAM

Sources *Stella Reading: some recollections by her friends* (1979) [privately printed] · *The Times* (24 May 1971) · *Women's Royal Voluntary Service, 1938–1998* (1998) [diamond anniversary brochure] · private information (2004) [College of Arms] · private information (1986)
Archives CUL, corresp. with Sir Samuel Hoare · Nuffield Oxf., corresp. with Lord Cherwell | FILM BFI NFTVA, documentary footage
Likenesses T. Gidal, photograph, 1939, Hult. Arch. · H. Coster, photograph, 1940, NPG [*see illus.*] · photograph, 1941, Hult. Arch. · J. Gunn, oils, Women's Royal Voluntary Service, Milton Hill, Oxfordshire
Wealth at death £74,370: probate, 12 Aug 1971, *CGPLA Eng. & Wales*

Isaacs [*née* Fairhurst], **Susan Sutherland** (1885–1948), educational psychologist and psychoanalyst, was born on 24 May 1885, at 32 Bradshaw Brow, Turton, Bolton, Lancashire, the seventh of eight children of William Fairhurst, journalist and Methodist lay preacher, and his wife, Miriam Sutherland. Fairhurst's personality was significantly influenced by crucial events in her early childhood: her sudden weaning from the breast when her infant brother caught pneumonia and the loss of her mother's devotion, regained only through the death of that brother when Susan was eight months old. Her mother died when Susan was six and her father soon married the nurse who had attended her mother during her fatal illness; this led to an unforgiving alienation from her father who died when Susan was twenty-four. Through her Kleinian analysis she later recognized guilt at the death that had secured her mother's attention and further guilt occasioned by her mother's death. She became further alienated from her father through conversion to atheistic socialism.

An intelligent, strong-minded child, eager to learn, frustrated at primary school, rebellious at Bolton secondary school, which she left after three years in 1900, Fairhurst resumed her education when she began training as an infant school teacher at Manchester University. Encouraged to enter graduate school she learned sufficient Greek and German in three months to meet the requirements. She obtained a first-class honours degree in philosophy under Professor S. Alexander followed by a year's scholarship to Newnham College, Cambridge (1910–11), which led

Susan Sutherland Isaacs (1885–1948), by Enoch Fairhurst, 1935

to her life's interest in psychology. She taught infant school teachers for one year at Darlington Training College (1913–14), then logic for one year at Manchester University (1914–15).

Fairhurst was a robust, rather short Lancashire girl of pale complexion, with a mass of fair hair and bright hazel eyes. She was challenging, tilting her head as she spoke, a little mischievous in her manner, but visibly friendly. She possessed a tautness of mind characterizing an able intellect which delighted in dialectic action. Trained in psychology, logic, philosophy, and psychoanalysis, her knowledge, which she used to the full, was tempered by humour.

On 11 July 1914 Fairhurst married botany lecturer William Broadhurst Brierley (b. 1888/9), son of Charles Henry Brierley, a brass moulder. Moving to London with her husband she became tutor to the Workers' Educational Association and from 1916 tutor in psychology to the University of London.

In 1922 the couple divorced and on 17 November that year she married Nathan Isaacs (b. 1894/5), the son of Isaac Isaacs, a retired general merchant. A manager of a metal merchant's, Nathan Isaacs became a brilliant collaborator in his wife's subsequent writings. Susan Isaacs's outstanding work on the intellectual and social development of young children was done at Malting House School, Cambridge, founded by Geoffrey Pyke, an eccentric genius who had made a fortune speculating on metal exchanges. He wanted to found a school as different as possible from Wellington, the public school where as a Jew he had suffered persecution and a rigid education. His ideal school

would enable children to encounter the ideas of discovery through play. Isaacs's association with the school lasted from 1924 to 1927, during which time thirty-one pupils with a mean IQ of 131 were closely studied for both their intellectual and their social development. The school collapsed as Pyke's grandiosity increasingly interfered with Isaacs's running of the school. (Subsequently Pyke lost his fortune, had a severe nervous breakdown, and committed suicide in 1948.) At Malting House School children were given great freedom for their intellectual and emotional development, supported by loving firmness rather than given punishment. The child was seen as a research worker; the teacher was an observer and provider of material and equipment required. Her work there had great influence on the education of children under seven in state schools, establishing play as central for the child's means of living and of understanding life.

Analysed by J. C. Flugel, Isaacs became an associate member of the newly formed British Psycho-Analytic Society in 1921, becoming a full member in 1923. Though already a full member of the society before her Malting House School days, she submitted herself to further analysis with Joan Riviere and to supervision to get personal experience and understanding of Melanie Klein's new ideas on infancy.

Susan Isaacs was an enthusiastic and early expositor of Jean Piaget's theories on the intellectual development of young children, though she combined her enthusiasm with criticism of his schemas for stages of cognitive development, which to her were over-schematic, not based on observation of the child in his natural environment, unlike her own, which came from the close observation of children at Malting House School. She published *The Intellectual Growth of Young Children* in 1930 and *The Social Development of Young Children* in 1933. In 1933 Susan Isaacs was appointed head of the newly formed department of child development of the University of London under Sir Percy Nunn. Despite under-funding she built a department of great influence in the teaching profession, overcoming the profession's reluctance to consider psychodynamic theory which she could bring together with developmental psychology.

Isaacs's influence as an educator extended widely. As Ursula Wise she answered parents' questions in the journals *The Nursery World* and *Home and School*. Her *Nursery Years* (1929) was a widely read and influential book in which understanding of the child's mind replaced punitive discipline. Isaacs developed cancer in 1935 and struggled with ill health for the next thirteen years, but nevertheless in 1937 she made an influential tour of Australia and New Zealand. Moving to Cambridge in 1939 she conducted the Cambridge Evacuation Survey on the effects of evacuation on children.

Isaacs was appointed CBE in 1948 for services to education; she had brought teaching and psychoanalysis into dialogue. Through her teaching she probably influenced the theory and practice of education in Britain more than any other person in the twentieth century. A pioneer, always a little ahead of her time, she introduced progressive educationist ideas to teachers and parents, wrote influential books on the intellectual and social development of young children, and responded generously to the needs of parents through journalism. A trained psychoanalyst, she supported and conceptualized the views of Melanie Klein on the fantasy life of children and introduced psychoanalytic ideas into general developmental psychology. Isaacs's great influence sprang from a combination of deep knowledge, sensitive observation and insight, robust common sense, and a sympathy which was extended not only to children but to those who care for them and bring them up. She died from cancer at her home, 30A Primrose Hill Road, London, on 12 October 1948. She was survived by her husband.

MALCOLM PINES

Sources D. E. M. Gardner, *Susan Isaacs* (1969) · *International Journal of Psycho-Analysis*, 29 (1950), 279–88 · L. A. H. Smith, *To understand and to help: the life and work of Susan Isaacs, 1885–1948* (1985) · A. Wooldridge, *Measuring the mind: education and psychology in England, c.1860–c.1990* (1994) · b. cert. · m. certs. · d. cert.
Archives U. Lond., Institute of Education, papers
Likenesses E. Fairhurst, photograph, 1935, NPG [*see illus.*]
Wealth at death £3398 3*s.* 1*d.*: probate, 4 Feb 1949, CGPLA Eng. & Wales

Isaacson, Henry (*bap.* 1581, *d.* 1654), chronologist and biographer, was baptized on 12 December 1581 at St Katharine Coleman, London, the eldest son of Richard Isaacson (*d.* 1620/21), painter–stainer, and his first wife, Susanna, daughter of Thomas Bryan of London. Of his early education nothing is known. He matriculated pensioner of Pembroke College, Cambridge, about 1599 and spent about two years there, but he left without taking a degree. However, during this period he formed a lasting association with Lancelot Andrewes, master of the college and royal chaplain, whom, on his own account, he attended at the courts of both Elizabeth and James I. When Andrewes became bishop first of Chichester (1605) and then Ely (1609), Isaacson remained in his household, being described variously as 'oeconomus' (treasurer) 'for many years' and 'amenuensis' (Pembroke College, Cambridge, Lib. MS II.77, fol. 27r; Isaacson, para. 5v). At Chichester he had overseen the receipt of episcopal revenues and on 22 June 1613 he was appointed principal registrar of the diocese of Ely. When his successor in this post, William Greene, was appointed in 1616, Isaacson was named as one of the deputies; on 17 October 1614 the two had been appointed joint constables of Wisbech Castle. It is unclear whether Isaacson followed Andrewes when the bishop was translated to Winchester in 1619.

By 1609 Isaacson had married Elizabeth, orphan daughter and sole heir of John Fan, leatherseller, of London, who had been his father's ward during her minority. Between 1609 and 1635 ten sons and nine daughters were born to the couple. In 1621 Isaacson inherited his father's properties in St Katharine Coleman and St Dionis Backchurch, London, as well as the manor of Hardings in Fyfield and Willingale Spain, Essex; the family divided their time between London and Fyfield. Like his father

and his uncle Paul Isaacson he took up the freedom of the Painter–Stainers' Company; he served as its upper warden in 1625, 1629, and 1630, and as its master in 1633, 1639, and 1640.

The influence of Andrewes can be discerned in Isaacson's churchmanship and civic service, the former marked by ceremonialist worship, and both by an emphasis on charity for the poor. While a churchwarden in 1620–21 he personally oversaw a complete refitting of the interior of St Katharine Coleman and, with his father and uncle, expanded parish poor relief. In November 1635 he was elected to the court of governors of Bridewell and Bethlem hospitals, and in March 1642 was elected its treasurer, a post he held until his death. In his will, drawn up in 1639, he left bequests to three Cambridge associates of Andrewes who had become zealous Laudians—Jerome Beale, Bishop Matthew Wren of Ely, and Samuel Collins, the last receiving 'the picture of Doctor Andrewes … in my studye at London' (will). Isaacson's son William, vicar of Swaffham Bulbeck, Cambridgeshire, was one of Wren's most extreme local supporters until deprived in 1643; his younger brother William, rector from 1619 of Woodford, Essex (where Isaacson was patron), and from 1629 of St Andrew by the Wardrobe, London, became a royal chaplain and was sequestered from the Essex living. As the presbyterian model was adopted in London, Isaacson himself was in 1646 elected an elder of St Katharine Coleman, but during the civil wars he administered relief to 'the kings souldiers' and to 'poor' (probably deprived) ministers (London, Guildhall, MS 1124/2). When in October 1651 he was elected by the mayor and aldermen of the city as the corporation's chamberlain, he declined to serve.

Andrewes also left a mark on most of Isaacson's published writings. In 1630 appeared *Institutiones piae*, attributed to 'H. I.' but in fact a rough compilation of extracts from Andrewes's devotional and catechetical writings, probably not assigned to their true author in deference to William Laud's exclusive copyright to Andrewes's works. When they were rightly attributed a year after Isaacson's death as *Holy Devotions … by L. Andrews*, the publisher described Isaacson as 'a kind foster-father' to them. From the late 1630s until his death several devotional and catechetical works appeared. All are marked by a churchmanship that can be described as Laudian, but that derives most directly from Andrewes. One of these, *Jacob's Ladder* (1638), is an unacknowledged translation of meditations by Cardinal Bellarmine. Much of these writings, especially the preface to *Jacob's Ladder*, and the whole of *Divine Contemplations* (1648), is so steeped in the language and style of Andrewes that here Isaacson was again probably 'foster-father' rather than original author.

Isaacson's most ambitious original work was the *Saturni ephemerides* (1633), 400 large-paper folio pages of chronological charts with a substantial index that summarized in parallel columns the major political, religious, and cultural events in Britain, Europe, and the biblical and Islamic East since the creation. In his preface Isaacson praised the superiority of chronology to narrative history for its greater 'delight, variety, and ease'. In addition to the dedication's reverent praise of Andrewes, other of the author's allegiances and enthusiasms appear in the work. Laudian connections are advertised in the choice of Richard Crashaw to write the poem glossing the engraved frontispiece by William Marshall, as well as in commendatory poems by Matthew Wren and Isaacson's brother William. Isaacson's ties to the Painter–Stainers' Company can be seen in the prominence given in the chronology to painters.

Isaacson has been most remembered for his *Exact Narration of the Life and Death of ... Lancelot Andrewes* (1651). It is written in the then traditional form of an 'exemplary life', which focuses more on the moral and intellectual virtues of its subject than biographical facts. Although uncompromisingly adulatory, the life does capture a genuine sense of Andrewes's piety and learning. However, this first biography of Andrewes, written partly as a reproach to the interregnum church and state, cast him in an oversimplified role as a high-church saint, a view that remained largely unquestioned until the twentieth century. Isaacson died on 7 December 1654 and was buried on 14 December at St Katharine Coleman. His widow died at Fyfield on 10 February 1674, survived by eight of their children. P. E. McCULLOUGH

Sources will, PRO, PROB 11/247 · will of Richard Isaacson, PRO, PROB 11/137 · benefactors' book, Pembroke Cam., Lib. MS II.77 · churchwardens' accounts, St Katharine Coleman, GL, MSS 1124/1–1124/2 · parish officers' book, St Katharine Coleman, GL, MS 1125/1 · parish register, St Katharine Coleman, GL, MS 17832, vol. 1 [baptism, burial] · court minute books, Painter–Stainers' Company, GL, MS 5667, vols. 1 and 2 · court minute books, Bridewell Royal Hospital, GL, MS 33011/9 · common hall book, CLRO, fol. 124 · common sergeant's book, CLRO, fol. 66 · *The visitation of London, anno Domini 1633, 1634, and 1635, made by Sir Henry St George*, 2, ed. J. J. Howard, Harleian Society, 17 (1883), 3–4 · Isaacson pedigree, Essex RO, MS T/G 18/1 · certificates of residence, king's remembrancer, E 115/222/135, 156, 129, 16, 37 · H. Isaacson, *Saturni ephemerides* (1633) · H. Isaacson, letter to Richard Juxon, W. Sussex RO, Ep. I/15/3/16, no. 35 · CUL, EDC 2/6/1, fols. 195–201 · *The obituary of Richard Smyth ... being a catalogue of all such persons as he knew in their life*, ed. H. Ellis, CS, 44 (1849), 39 · will of Elizabeth Isaacson, PRO, PROB 11/344
Archives GL, records of the royal hospitals of Bridewell and Bedlam · GL, records of the Painter–Stainers' Company · GL, records of the parish of St Katharine Coleman
Wealth at death £1000 in cash bequests; plus manorial lands in Fyfield, Essex; also messuages and tenements in two City parishes and Middlesex: will, PRO, PROB 11/247; PRO, PROB 11/344 [will of Elizabeth Isaacson]

Isaacson, Stephen (1798–1849), writer, was born on 17 February 1798, at The Oaks, Cowlinge, Suffolk, the son of Robert Isaacson (d. 1831), auctioneer, of Cowlinge, and afterwards of Moulton, Suffolk, and his second wife, Mary Anne, daughter of John Isaacson, rector of Lydgate and Little Bradley, Suffolk, and perpetual curate of Cowlinge. He was educated at a school in Norwich and, from 1816, at Christ's College, Cambridge, graduating BA in 1820. He was ordained as deacon in June 1824 and as priest in October of that year.

Both at school and at college Isaacson gained a reputation as a writer of humorous verse, and was even then a frequent contributor to the *Gentleman's Magazine* and

other periodicals. In 1822 he started the *Brighton Magazine*, which had a very brief existence. More successful was his translation of the sixteenth-century bishop John Jewel's *Apologia* (1825), with a life and a preliminary discourse on the doctrine and discipline of the Church of Rome in reply to some observations which the Roman Catholic historian Charles Butler had addressed to Robert Southey on his *Book of the Church* (1824). Butler answered Isaacson in a *Vindication of 'The Book of the Roman Catholic Church'* (1826).

Shortly afterwards Isaacson accepted the rectory of St Paul, in Demerara. In November 1826 he married Anna Maria Miller, youngest daughter of Bryan Bernard Killekelley of Barbados. In 1829 he edited his relative Henry Isaacson's *Life* of Bishop Andrewes, and prefixed a brief memoir of the author. By 1832 he had returned to England, and declared—from the results of his own experience—that the social and religious condition of West Indian slaves could not be bettered. On 8 August of that year he delivered a clever speech in vindication of the West Indian proprietors at Mansion House Chapel, Camberwell, which was afterwards published. For the next year or two he served as curate of St Margaret, Lothbury. In 1834 he was an unsuccessful candidate for the preachership of the Magdalen Hospital. He soon became curate of Dorking, Surrey, and remained there until February 1837. He again came forward as an anti-abolitionist in 1840, issuing part 1 of *An Address to the British Nation on the Present State and Prospects of the West India Colonies*, in which he argued in favour of an extensive system of immigration as the only means of extinguishing slavery and the slave trade.

From 1843 to 1847 Isaacson lived at Dymchurch, near Hythe, in Kent, taking duty as chaplain of the Elham union. During his residence there he became a member of the newly established British Archaeological Association, and contributed some papers on local antiquities to its journal. His quaint poem of the 'Barrow Digger' and other legends (printed in 1848) were suggested by the field operations of the association. He subsequently moved to Hoddesdon, Hertfordshire, but died on 7 April 1849 at 2 Tavistock Street, Bedford Square, London.

GORDON GOODWIN, rev. MARI G. ELLIS

Sources Venn, *Alum. Cant.* · *Clergy List* (1847) · *GM*, 2nd ser., 32 (1849), 101–2 · W. S. Robertson, 'Publications relating to Kentish archaeology', *Archaeologia Cantiana*, 15 (1883), 369, 372–3
Likenesses lithograph, 1852, NPG

Isabel of Lancaster (d. 1349), prioress of Amesbury, fourth daughter of *Henry, earl of Lancaster (d. 1345), second son of *Edmund, earl of Lancaster (Edmund Crouchback), and Maud, daughter and heir of Patrick of Chaworth, entered religious life at the Fontevrault priory of Amesbury where she was solemnly professed in 1327 and elected prioress in 1343.

The last direct connection between the Plantagenets and the order of Fontevrault, Isabel used her family connections to secure privileges for herself and the priory. She received a regular wine allowance from the king. Her brother, *Henry of Lancaster, then earl of Derby, obtained papal permission for the nuns to eat meat; at his petition the king confirmed the priory's possessions and he engineered the appropriation of the church at East Garston. In 1347, possibly as a reward for Isabel's having contributed some of the priory's wool clip towards the war effort, Amesbury was granted custody, for the duration of the war with France, of the alien priory of Ellingham in Hampshire.

Isabel's household accounts of 1333/4, while by no means illustrative of the lifestyle of all fourteenth-century religious women, portray nevertheless that of aristocratic women who joined religious life without cutting the ties of their previous existence. Isabel spent a large amount of her time outside the cloister, visiting family and friends and administering her personal property settled on her by her father. She gave and received expensive gifts, had expensive garments and furnishings, engaged in expensive leisure pursuits, and maintained her personal staff. She died at Amesbury Priory in 1349.

BERENICE M. KERR

Sources R. B. Pugh, ed., 'Fragment of an account of Isabel of Lancaster, nun of Amesbury, 1333–34', *Festschrift zur Feier des zweihundertjährigen Bestandes des Haus-, Hof-, und Staatsarchivs*, ed. L. Santifaller (1949), 487–98 • E. Hobhouse, ed., *Calendar of the register of John de Drokensford, Bishop of Bath and Wells*, Somerset RS, 1 (1887), 269 [see also J. Jackson, 'Consecration of nuns at Amesbury, AD 1327', *Wiltshire Natural History and Archaeological Magazine*, 18 (1879), 286–8, where names are listed] • *CClR, 1341–3*, 75; *1343–4*, 285; *1346–9*, 434; *1349–54*, 5 • *CPR, 1348–50*, 369 • *Calendar of the charter rolls*, 6 vols., PRO (1903–27), vol. 5, p. 20 • *CEPR letters*, 3.175 **Archives** Birm. CL, archives division, MS Hampton, 310v

Isabella, *suo jure* countess of Gloucester (*c.*1160–1217), first consort of King John, was the third and youngest daughter of *William, earl of Gloucester (*d.* 1183), and Hawisia (*d.* 1197), daughter of *Robert, earl of Leicester (*d.* 1168). Through her father she was first cousin once removed of Henry II. She emerged from obscurity in 1176, ten years after the death of her only brother, Robert, when King Henry and her father made her the centrepiece of a marriage agreement formalized on 28 September at Windsor. In his dynastic predicament Earl William betrothed Isabella to Henry's youngest son, *John, and declared John the heir to Gloucester. Should the pope prevent the marriage on the grounds of the couple's close affinity, the king pledged to arrange the best marriage possible for Isabella; and if a legitimate son of the earl were to survive him, that son would divide the earldom with John. Contrary to an earlier custom, whereby inheritances were divided equally among daughters, Isabella's two sisters, who were already married—Mabel to the future count of Évreux, and Amicia to Richard de Clare, earl of Hertford (*d.* 1217)—were excluded from the comital inheritance, explicitly in order to prevent its division, though they were to be provided with annuities of £100 each.

When Earl William died in 1183, still without a male heir, the king, instead of pressing for the marriage of Isabella and John, took Isabella into wardship as the unmarried heir of a tenant-in-chief, and enjoyed the income from her lordships and demesne estates. Only after Richard I's accession in 1189 was Isabella's wardship ended and

her marriage to John celebrated on 29 August at Marlborough. Archbishop Baldwin of Canterbury (*d.* 1190) reacted by summoning John before him to answer for his transgression against canonical prohibition of marriages within his degree of affinity to Isabella, and upon John's failure to appear, laid an interdict upon his lands. John appealed to an ecclesiastical council attended by the papal legate Giovanni di Anagni. Almost certainly out of deference to King Richard, the legate quashed the archbishop's penalty, and the pope never intervened. Some time between their marriage and 1199 Isabella and John visited Normandy, but by 1193 they seem to have become estranged. In that year, as part of his conspiracy with the French king, Philip Augustus, against his captive royal brother, John formally promised his continental overlord to marry the latter's half-sister Alice. John's implicit repudiation of Isabella probably resulted from their inability to have children, particularly a son.

After John became king upon Richard's death in 1199, he obtained an annulment of his marriage to Isabella on the grounds of consanguinity. Continental papal judges-delegate accomplished the desired divorce, whereupon the new king took his former wife, once again an unmarried heiress, into her second wardship along with most of her estates. John granted the comital title and a small fraction of the earldom's estates to Isabella's nephew, Amaury, count of Évreux, to compensate him for the loss of his county which John would surrender to Philip in the treaty of Le Goulet (22 May 1200). In 1213, perhaps in anticipation of her death, Isabella made a will disposing of her moveable goods. However, by the beginning of 1214 her wardship had ended and a new marital gambit begun. On 26 January John announced that he had sold the right to marry the countess of Gloucester to Geoffrey de Mandeville for 20,000 marks. Earl Amaury's death without issue (*c.*1213) had made Isabella once more heir of the earldom of Gloucester. Apart from being a possible source of financial gain for John, the marriage was more of a political tool to be exploited by the king in his baronial relations than a desirable asset for Mandeville, whose proffer may have been made unwillingly. Among other things the earldom's most valuable manor, Bristol, was specifically excluded from the new earl's grant. John also required Mandeville to liquidate his debt in four instalments during 1214, and when he failed to keep to the payment schedule, the king confiscated the earl's Gloucester estates. Although they were restored and John offered to negotiate Mandeville's debt, Isabella and her husband joined the baronial rebellion against John.

During the second phase of the barons' war with the king, on 23 February 1216, Mandeville died of wounds received in a tournament. For about a year Isabella, usually styling herself 'countess of Gloucester and Essex in my free widowhood' (Patterson, nos. 142–7) enjoyed possibly more personal freedom than at any other time during her adult life. But this situation ended some time in late 1217, possibly after 17 September, when Hubert de *Burgh, justiciar and one of the regents for Henry III, became Isabella's third husband. Hardly had this been accomplished than the countess of Gloucester died on 14 October, supposedly at her father's Augustinian foundation, Keynsham Abbey, near Bristol, and was buried at Christ Church, Canterbury. The Gloucester earldom then passed via Isabella's sister Amicia to the latter's son Gilbert (d. 1230), commencing the Clare tenure of the earldom which was to last until 1314.

ROBERT B. PATTERSON

Sources R. B. Patterson, ed., *Earldom of Gloucester charters* (1973), pp. 5–12, 15, 20–27, 29, 30; nos. 4, 8–9, 33, 57, 60, 62, 64, 76, 93, 114, 137, 139–50, 163n., 164, 234 · W. Stubbs, ed., *Gesta regis Henrici secundi Benedicti abbatis: the chronicle of the reigns of Henry II and Richard I, AD 1169–1192*, 2 vols., Rolls Series, 49 (1867), 1.124–5; 2.73, 78 · *Radulfi de Diceto … opera historica*, ed. W. Stubbs, 1: 1148–79 (1876), 385, 415; Rolls Series, 2 (1876), 72–3, 166–7 · *Ann. mon.*, 1.16, 56; 3, 45 · *Pipe rolls* · GEC, *Peerage*, new edn, vol. 5 · H. G. Richardson, 'The marriage and coronation of Isabella of Angoulême', *EngHR*, 61 (1946), 289–314 · F. A. Cazel and S. Painter, 'The marriage of Isabelle of Angoulême', *EngHR*, 63 (1948), 83–9 · H. G. Richardson, 'King John and Isabelle of Angoulême', *EngHR*, 65 (1950), 360–71 · F. A. Cazel and S. Painter, 'The marriage of Isabelle of Angoulême', *EngHR*, 67 (1952), 233–5 · N. Vincent, 'Isabella of Angoulême: John's Jezebel', *King John: new interpretations*, ed. S. D. Church (1999) · J. E. Sayers, *Papal judges delegate in the province of Canterbury, 1198–1254* (1971), 206–7 · R. V. Turner, *King John* (1994), 31, 42, 45, 104, 117, 186 · *The maire of Bristowe is kalendar, by Robert Ricart*, ed. L. Toulmin Smith, CS, new ser., 5 (1872), 20 · R. B. Patterson, *The scriptorium of Margam Abbey and the scribes of early Angevin Glamorgan* (2002), 27–8 and n.
Archives BL, Cotton MS Nero Evii · BL, Cotton MS Vespasian Exxiii · BL, Stowe MS 925 · NL Wales, Penrice and Margam charters and rolls
Likenesses seal, NL Wales, Penrice and Margam charters

Isabella [Isabella of Angoulême] (*c*.1188–1246), queen of England, second consort of King John, was the only child of Audemar, count of Angoulême (d. 1202), and his wife, Adalmues or Alice, widow of Guillaume, count of Jouy, and daughter of Pierre de Courtenay, a descendant of Louis VI of France. Isabella was about twelve years old at the time of her marriage to King *John, and so cannot have been born much before 1188. John had divorced his first wife, Isabella, countess of Gloucester, soon after his accession, and on 24 August 1200 he married Isabella of Angoulême. The chroniclers suggest that John had unexpectedly become besotted with the young girl, but in reality his decision reflects less romantic, political considerations. The counts of Angoulême controlled a wealthy and strategically significant province lying between the Plantagenet strongholds of Poitiers and Bordeaux. Earlier in 1200 Isabella had been betrothed to Hugues, count of Lusignan, who had recently been awarded the neighbouring lordship of La Marche by King John. The betrothal threatened to establish Hugues as lord of Lusignan, La Marche, and Angoulême, and hence as a dangerous rival to the Plantagenets. To counter this threat John stepped in to claim Isabella for himself. Following their marriage at Angoulême on 24 August Isabella accompanied John to Chinon and thence to England, where on 8 October 1200 she was crowned and anointed in Westminster Abbey.

John's actions caused uproar in France. Deprived of Isabella, his promised bride, and her inheritance, Hugues defected to the French king, Philip Augustus. In response

Isabella [of Angoulême] (*c*.1188–1246), tomb effigy

to his complaints Philip pronounced a sentence of forfeiture against John, which over the next three years was to serve as the pretext for a campaign of conquest in which the French drove John from Normandy and much of his continental inheritance. To this extent John's marriage with Isabella was directly responsible for his expulsion from the Plantagenet lands in France. In 1204, following the death of the king's mother, Eleanor of Aquitaine, Isabella was promised Eleanor's dower lands in England and Normandy, including the towns of Exeter, Wilton, Ilchester, and Malmesbury, the honour of Berkhamsted, the farm of Waltham in Essex, and the county of Rutland together with Rockingham. In addition, shortly after her marriage in 1200, she had been promised dower in Anjou and Poitou, consisting of the lordships of Niort, Saintes, and six other towns. During her husband's lifetime, however, she appears to have controlled no marriage portion of her own, her expenses being met by occasional payments from the king, and, perhaps, from the revenues of queen's gold, an additional levy charged upon fines with the crown.

In spite of stories of recrimination and infidelity retailed by some chroniclers, it is clear that, though Isabella was rarely in John's company after 1205, she continued to command his trust. She gave birth to five of John's legitimate children: the future king, *Henry III (1207–1272), *Richard (1209–1272), *Joan (1210–1238), *Isabella (1214–1241), and *Eleanor (1215?–1275). And in 1214 she crossed with her husband to Poitou, where John was able to establish control over her inheritance in Angoulême. During the ensuing civil war in England, she was kept in relative safety in the west country. The death of John and the accession of Henry III in October 1216 were followed by the release of Isabella's dower, from which, within the following six months, she made awards to the monks of Malmesbury and St Nicholas's, Exeter, in memory of her late husband. For the rest of her life she continued to use her title and her seal as queen of England. None the less, following John's death, she appears to have been excluded from the inner circle of the new royal council. Denied possession of the castles of Exeter and Rockingham, supposedly part of her dower, and refused payment of 3500 marks which she claimed to have been willed by John, in July 1217 she effectively abandoned her children in England in order to take up her family inheritance in France. Within the next three years she established her lordship over the city and county of Angoulême, despite resistance from the officials whom King John had appointed to administer the county in 1214, and in April or May 1220 she married for a second time.

Isabella's new husband, Hugues, count of La Marche, was the son of her former fiancé, repudiated in 1200 in order that she might marry King John. As a result, in 1220 the younger Hugues succeeded to precisely the combined lordship over Lusignan, La Marche, and Angoulême that John had been so anxious to disrupt twenty years before. In addition, via Isabella, he acquired a claim to Isabella's dower lands in England and the lordships of Saintes and Niort, assigned by John as part of her dower in France. The council of Henry III was in no position to resist the marriage, and Hugues was allowed possession of Isabella's English estates. However, disputes soon arose. The English estates of Isabella and Hugues were briefly seized in 1221, and confiscated for good after June 1224, when he joined in alliance with the French king, Louis VIII, effectively paving the way for a French invasion of Poitou. In 1226 a reconciliation was effected with the English court, and in 1230 Isabella met her son, Henry III, for the first time in more than a dozen years, during Henry's ineffective expedition to Brittany and Poitou.

However, Isabella and her husband continued to play a double game. In 1241 she is said to have persuaded Hugues to reopen negotiations with England, when French lordship in Poitou looked likely to become over-oppressive. At vast expense Henry III crossed to Poitou in 1242, but Hugues promptly abandoned him to rejoin Louis IX, and Henry's expedition collapsed in disarray. Isabella's marriage, too, proved unstable, shaken by Hugues's infidelities and by threats of divorce; Isabella and her second husband nevertheless had nine children (including Aymer de *Lusignan and William de *Valence) among whom the family estates were divided. She then retired to the great Plantagenet abbey of Fontevrault, where she died on 4 June 1246, having been veiled as a nun on her deathbed. Although her relations with Henry III had been badly soured by her desertion of him in 1217, and then by Hugues's treachery in 1242, her obsequies were celebrated in England, with royal gifts to the canons of Ivychurch in Wiltshire, the endowment of chantry chapels at Malmesbury and Westminster, and a feast for the poor scholars of Oxford and Cambridge. In 1254 Henry visited Fontevrault, and personally supervised the removal of his mother's body from its resting-place in the chapter house to a site within the abbey church, close to the tombs of his Plantagenet ancestors.

Isabella appears to have been a forceful character, capable of imposing her own rule in Angoulême after 1217, but apparently lacking in affection for the children she had had with John. Neither of her husbands was faithful to her, and this, combined with the fact that she was barely out of infancy when she married, may have contributed to the harshness of character attributed to her by some chroniclers.   NICHOLAS VINCENT

Sources Chancery records · Pipe rolls · Paris, *Chron.* · F. Michel, ed., *Histoire des ducs de Normandie et des rois d'Angleterre* (Paris, 1840) · M. Bouquet and others, eds., *Recueil des historiens des Gaules et de la France | Rerum Gallicarum et Francicarum scriptores*, 20–21 (Paris, 1850–55) [chronicles of William de Nangis and St Denis] · A. Teulet and others, eds., *Layettes du trésor des chartes*, 5 vols. (Paris, 1863–1909) · cartulary of St Nicholas Exeter, BL, Cotton MS Vitellius D.ix, fol. 65r–v · J. S. Brewer and C. T. Martin, eds., *Registrum Malmesburiense: the register of Malmesbury Abbey*, 2 vols., Rolls Series, 72 (1879–80) · Fontevrault obituary notices, Bibliothèque Nationale, Paris, MS latin 5480 pt 1, 1 · F. Marvaud, 'Isabelle d'Angoulême ou La Comtesse-Reine', *Bulletin de la Société Archéologique et Historique de la Charente*, 2nd ser., 1 (1856) · H. G. Richardson, 'The marriage and coronation of Isabella of Angoulême', *EngHR*, 61 (1946), 289–314 · F. A. Cazel and S. Painter, 'The marriage of Isabelle of Angoulême', *EngHR*, 63 (1948), 83–9 · H. G. Richardson, 'King John and Isabelle of Angoulême', *EngHR*, 65 (1950), 360–71 · F. A. Cazel and S. Painter, 'The marriage of Isabelle of Angoulême', *EngHR*, 67 (1952), 233–5 · P. Boissonnade, 'L'ascension, le déclin et la chute d'un grand état féodal du centre-ouest; les Taillefer et les Lusignans, comtes de la Marche et d'Angoulême', *Bulletins et Memoires de la Société Archéologique et Historique de la Charente*, 43 (1935) · H. S. Snellgrove, *The Lusignans in England, 1247–1258* (1950)

Likenesses seal · tomb effigy, Fontevrault, France [*see illus.*] · tomb effigy, replica, V&A

Isabella [Elizabeth, Isabella of England] (1214–1241), empress, consort of Frederick II, was the second daughter and fourth child of *John, king of England, and his queen, *Isabella of Angoulême. Her nurse, Margaret, who had an allowance of 1d. a day from the royal treasury in 1219, seems to have been the Margaret Biset who later accompanied Isabella to Germany. In the betrothal agreement of 1220 between Alexander II, king of Scots, and Isabella's sister *Joan (1210–1238) provision was made for Isabella to marry Alexander in her sister's stead if Joan could not return to England in good time, though in the event the marriage went ahead. *Henry III saw the diplomatic value of marriage alliances, and had plans to marry one of his sisters, probably Isabella, first to Heinrich VII, king of the Romans, the son of Frederick II whom Isabella eventually married, and later to Louis IX of France. Her sister *Eleanor (1215?–1275) married William (II) *Marshal, earl of Pembroke.

In November 1234 Frederick II, again a widower, was encouraged by an emollient Pope Gregory IX to take Isabella as his third wife, and a Sicilian embassy, headed by his close adviser, Piero della Vigna, came to England in February 1235. Within three days Henry III agreed to the proposal, ordering Isabella to be brought from the Tower of London to Westminster so that the ambassadors could interview her; they were eminently satisfied, and according to Roger of Wendover (followed by Matthew Paris) hailed her with the words 'Vivat imperatrix! Vivat!'. A marriage contract was signed on 22 February 1235. Henry gave his sister a dowry of 30,000 marks, to be paid in instalments over two years, half as much money again as had been paid when Henry II's daughter Joanna was sent to marry William II of Sicily in 1176; the English chroniclers were fascinated by the lavish gifts Henry bestowed upon her. She already possessed fine chapel silver of her own, as well as splendid robes described in the close rolls; but she was sent south with a magnificent trousseau and a service of gold and silver plate. Matthew Paris also records the irritation within England at the substantial marriage aid demanded of the king's subjects. Yet for Henry the German–Sicilian marriage offered both prestige and possible support against Louis IX of France. Her sister *Eleanor (1215?–1275) married William (II) *Marshal, earl of Pembroke.

In early May 1235 the archbishop of Cologne and the duke of Brabant arrived in London to accompany Isabella and the bishop of Exeter to Germany, where Frederick was then based. Her route took her via Canterbury to Sandwich, from where she sailed on 11 May; she arrived on 15 May at Antwerp. Some of the emperor's enemies were said to want to seize and carry her off, supposedly in league with Louis IX (an unlikely conspirator), but the guard provided by Frederick was strong enough to prevent any such attempt, and on Friday 24 May she arrived safely at Cologne. She is said to have endeared herself to the noble ladies of the city by throwing back her veil while riding in procession through the streets, to the acclaim of crowds of up to 10,000. She spent six weeks in the city, while Frederick was preoccupied with his war against his son Heinrich VII, before joining him at Worms, where Isabella married the emperor and was crowned empress by the archbishop of Mainz on Sunday 15 July. The wedding festivities lasted four days, and Matthew Paris says there were present four kings (it is hard to see which ones), eleven dukes, and thirty counts and marquesses, among others. On the advice of the court astrologers Frederick apparently refused to consummate the marriage until the second night.

Frederick was delighted with Isabella, who is described by Matthew Paris as beautiful and popular, but when the wedding guests had left Worms he sent away most of her English attendants except Margaret Biset and her maid Kathrein, a skilled practitioner of *opus anglicanum* (one or two other English women living later at Foggia may also have been in her service); she travelled with Frederick's Muslim slaves to his palace at Hagenau, where they spent the winter together. The emperor sent three leopards, the symbol of England, to Henry III as a mark of appreciation. There is doubt about the statement that Isabella's first child was a son named Jordan, born in Ravenna in 1236; Matthew Paris was clearly confused between a first child and her son Henry, born in Lombardy on 18 February 1238; probably the first child was in fact a daughter, Margaret, born in February 1237.

Isabella travelled extensively through Frederick's realms, living at Andria in Apulia until December 1238, when the archbishop of Palermo brought her back to Lombardy. Early in 1239 she resided at Noventa while her husband was at Padua; in February 1240 she was back in southern Italy, a little ahead of the emperor. Her travels suggest that he took pleasure in her company; he also expected her to live in some magnificence. On the other hand, Henry III was irritated that Isabella was only rarely

permitted to appear in public; Frederick had treated his second wife, Isabella-Yolanda of Jerusalem, similarly, and such practices gave rise to lurid tales of his sexual misdemeanours that are probably unfounded. In 1241, when her second brother, *Richard, first earl of Cornwall, went to visit Frederick, he saw Isabella, who was pregnant; a magnificent display was arranged at court, with jugglers and Muslim dancers who greatly delighted Richard and Isabella. Although Richard was not granted immediate access to her, this may reflect the protocol of the imperial–Sicilian court rather than Frederick's supposed practice of immuring his wives in a harem. Isabella died in childbirth at Foggia on 1 December 1241, while Frederick was in northern Italy besieging Faenza; her baby also died. Isabella's last words to her husband when they separated were to urge him to remain on good terms with Henry III, a source of concern since Henry was becoming increasingly compliant to the papacy. Isabella's marriage thus had genuine political uses, and she seems to have brought the emperor happiness, as well as some of the children Frederick craved. She was buried at Andria, beside Frederick's second wife, Isabella-Yolanda. Her son Henry, on whom Frederick had hoped to confer some of his minor crowns, appears to have died about 1254, and her daughter Margaret married the landgrave of Thuringia, thus becoming an ancestor of Prince Albert and Edward VII of England.   D. S. H. ABULAFIA

Sources Paris, *Chron.*, 3.319–27; 4.83, 147, 175 • *Rogeri de Wendover liber qui dicitur flores historiarum*, ed. H. G. Hewlett, 3 vols., Rolls Series, [84] (1886–9), 5.200 • J.-L.-A. Huillard-Bréholles, *Historia diplomatica Friderici secundi*, 4/2 (Paris, 1855), 728 • Riccardus de Sancto Germano [Richard of San Germano], *Chronica*, ed. C. A. Garufi, Rerum Italicarum Scriptores, new edn, 7/2 [1937] • G. Waitz, ed., *Chronica regia Coloniensis (Annales maximi Colonienses)*, MGH Scriptores Rerum Germanicarum, [18] (Hanover, 1880) • H. Bloch, ed., *Annales Marbacenses qui dicuntur*, MGH Scriptores Rerum Germanicarum, [9] (Hanover, 1979) • G. Masson, *Frederick II of Hohenstaufen* (1957) • D. Abulafia, *Frederick II* (1988)

Isabella [Isabella of France] (**1295–1358**), queen of England, consort of Edward II, was the only surviving daughter of Philippe IV of France (*r.* 1285–1314) and Jeanne de Champagne, queen of Navarre.

Early life and marriage Born late in 1295 Isabella was first proposed as a wife for *Edward I's eldest son in 1298, during negotiations for an Anglo-French truce in the duchy of Aquitaine. The renewal of the truce in 1299 led to Edward I's wedding to Philippe's sister Margaret, and again anticipated Isabella's marriage to the young Edward. Edward I may have been contemplating a Castilian bride for his son in April 1303, but a permanent Anglo-French peace the following month preceded Isabella's formal betrothal to Edward of Caernarfon [*see* Edward II] later that year. When Edward became king in 1307, at Philippe IV's behest he augmented Isabella's dower assignment before their wedding at Boulogne (25 January 1308), but Philippe refused to yield regarding Edward's rights in Aquitaine, and disputes continued.

Even before the couple reached England for their coronation on 25 February 1308, Edward had sent Philippe's wedding gifts to his favourite, Piers Gaveston (*d.* 1312). It was said that Edward visited Gaveston's bed more often than Isabella's; she complained to her father that Gaveston usurped her place and that her funds were inadequate. Her uncles Charles de Valois and Louis d'Évreux, who had accompanied her to England, left angered at her predicament. Isabella's dislike of Gaveston was well known and it was said that to eliminate him, she was in contact with her father, the pope and cardinals, and English earls. Wardrobe records refute Trokelowe's tale that in May 1312 Edward and Gaveston abandoned Isabella at Tynemouth to escape attack by Edward's cousin Thomas, earl of Lancaster (d. 1322); but already Lancaster (a half-brother of Isabella's mother) had promised her to expel Gaveston from England.

Relations with Edward II Gaveston's presence notwithstanding, Edward very regularly granted pardons and bestowed lands, money, or offices at his new wife's request. And, despite contemporary fears, Gaveston did not detain the king from his conjugal duties. Probably Edward at first avoided Isabella's bed because of her youth, and her first child, later *Edward III, born at Windsor Castle on 13 November 1312, was conceived well before Gaveston's death in July 1312. Children were born to Edward and Isabella regularly thereafter. In November 1313 the queen evidently lost a child, but bore a second son, *John, at Eltham on 15 July 1316; Eleanor (later countess of Gueldres) was born at Woodstock in July 1318, and *Joan (queen of Scots) at the Tower of London in June 1321. Edward in 1308 gave Isabella the county of Ponthieu to augment her revenue, and after Edward I's widow, Margaret, died in 1318, Isabella held the queen's usual dower lands. By 1311 she had induced Edward to favour her relatives, the Beaumonts. She was several times named custodian of the great seal, and was twice exposed to danger on Scottish campaigns with Edward: a plot in 1319 to abduct her was foiled by the capture of a Scottish scout, and when on 14 October 1322 the Scots routed and nearly seized Edward at Old Byland, Yorkshire, Isabella escaped with difficulty, enduring a perilous sea voyage during which two of her ladies perished.

Edward's consideration for his wife's dignity and revenues perhaps mollified her family, but their marriage was not without tension. He reputedly insisted he had married her unwillingly, and may have blamed her for continuing Anglo-French disputes over Aquitaine, which it had been hoped their marriage would end. His liking for rustic pastimes and low company sustained rumours in 1316–18 that he was not Edward I's son, humiliating Isabella who was aware of the mockery his behaviour elicited. During an episcopal election at Rochester in 1316 she independently sought papal approval for her confessor, Hamo Hythe, over Edward's favoured candidate, and also enlisted the help of the earl of Pembroke and the French king. In 1317 she induced Edward to support the election of her cousin, Louis de Beaumont (d. 1333), as bishop of Durham.

Involvement in politics Until the Despensers' rise, however, Isabella consistently took a supportive role in Edward's relations with his barons and the French crown. They were nobly received in Paris in May 1313, and took the cross there. (If, as has been suggested, it was Isabella who told Philippe IV of the adultery of his sons' wives, she must have detected it on that visit.) The queen and Gilbert de Clare, earl of Gloucester (d. 1314), mediated in October 1313 between king and barons in the wake of Gaveston's death; in August 1316 she and Humphrey (VII) de Bohun, earl of Hereford (d. 1322), mediated between Edward and Thomas of Lancaster, and she shared in negotiations for the treaty of Leake in 1318. She went with Edward in June 1320 to see her brother Philippe V (r. 1316–22) at Amiens, where Edward did homage for Ponthieu. Isabella and Aymer de Valence, earl of Pembroke (d. 1324), again procured peace between king and barons in August 1321, with the queen going down to Edward on her knees for the sake of the people; though by associating herself with those who sought the Despensers' exile, she incurred Edward's displeasure. Her efforts made her popular with the English, but her intercession alone could not have done as much to reconcile Edward with his opponents as has been supposed, and she had no lasting success as a mediator in either domestic or foreign affairs.

The well-known incident at Leeds Castle in Kent on 13 October 1321, when Isabella was refused entry by its custodian's wife and six of her men died in the resulting scuffle, was evidently set up by Edward to provoke a show of defiance, so that he could then use the insult to his wife as an excuse for attacking the barons. His siege of Leeds initiated the conflict that ended with Lancaster's execution after the battle at Boroughbridge (16 March) and Edward's triumph at the York parliament of May 1322. But Isabella now faced the Despensers' renewed dominance. The curtailment of her capacity for intercession with Edward after 1321 hints that her access to him was limited, either because he resented her actions in August 1321, or because the younger Hugh Despenser now controlled access to him. At the Despensers' urging Edward resumed her lands in September 1324, arguing the unwisdom of leaving them in her hands while Anglo-French relations worsened.

It is untrue that she was then allowed only 20s. daily for expenses; she had 8 marks daily, and £1000 yearly for her household, but she was left dependent on Edward for her funds, and many of her friends and French servants were thus dismissed. The younger Hugh Despenser's wife, Eleanor de Clare (Edward's niece), who had long served Isabella, now became Despenser's spy; the queen could allegedly no longer send letters without Eleanor's knowledge. When Despenser discovered Isabella in contact with his opponents, bishops Adam Orleton of Hereford (d. 1345) and Henry Burghersh of Lincoln (d. 1340), he reputedly sent Father Thomas Dunhead to ask the pope to divorce her from Edward. She was also suspected of intrigue with her relatives, especially Charles de Valois, who led the French army that again confiscated Aquitaine in 1324.

The deposition of Edward II Renewed conflict in Aquitaine gave Isabella the opportunity for reprisals. She induced

Edward to cease attacking the duchy and (perhaps at papal urging) to allow her to negotiate with her brother, Charles IV (r. 1322–8). Her household was restored before she departed for Paris in March 1325, but despite a staged reconciliation with the two Despensers as she left, it was already said she would never return while they were at Edward's side. The peace she arranged imposed heavy financial burdens on her husband. Charles agreed to accept her son's homage if the youth were made duke of Aquitaine and count of Ponthieu, as was suggested in January 1325 by Bishop John Stratford of Winchester (d. 1348) who, with other bishops, was perhaps already plotting with Isabella. Young Edward left England on 12 September with the king's brother Edmund, earl of Kent (d. 1330), but after he did homage he, his mother, and Kent stayed in Paris. Late in September Edward ordered Isabella to return home; she sent back many of her retinue but gave trivial excuses for not returning herself, and to Charles protested that the younger Despenser would kill her if she returned. English reports said that Despenser did indeed want her dead, that the earl of Richmond would kill her in France, or that Edward had sworn to crush her in his teeth if he had no weapon to kill her. Pretending Edward had expelled her from England, Charles supported Isabella in hopes of recovering Aquitaine. She now spent more time with Englishmen exiled as traitors than with the advisers Edward had given her. Among the exiles was the marcher lord Roger (V) *Mortimer, imprisoned in the Tower of London after Boroughbridge, who had escaped to Paris in 1323; by March 1326 it was known in England that he and Isabella were lovers.

So evident was Isabella's hostility to her husband's regime that by Christmas 1325 it was feared she would invade England. She left Paris early in 1326 for Ponthieu and then Hainault, where she betrothed her son to Count Guillaume (II)'s daughter Philippa, and used her dowry to hire mercenaries, who were commanded by Mortimer and the count's brother Jean. In March 1326 it was thought Isabella might yet return to England peacefully, and Pope John XXII (r. 1316–34) still hoped in May to reconcile the couple; but as his plan called for the Despensers' removal, the king refused, though he later swore to receive his wife and son honourably if they returned. On 23 September Isabella sailed from Dort with Kent, Jean d'Hainault, Mortimer, many English exiles, and perhaps 1000 men. She landed on 24 September near estates of the king's brother Thomas of Brotherton, earl of Norfolk (d. 1338), who (probably forewarned by Kent) joined her with Thomas of Lancaster's brother Henry (d. 1345). She met little resistance; Orleton, Burghersh, and Stratford hurried to her, and Archbishop Walter Reynolds (d. 1327) sent money. At Oxford Orleton preached that she sought to end misgovernment, and a proclamation she issued at Wallingford on 15 October violently denounced the Despensers. London rose to support her the same day, marking the collapse of Edward's authority.

Edward and the Despensers fled to Wales, and in pursuit of them Isabella was met at Gloucester by a force from the marches and a northern army under lords Wake (Kent's brother-in-law and Mortimer's cousin) and Percy, and her kinsman, Henry de Beaumont (d. 1340). Her military strength assured, she proclaimed her son guardian of the realm on 26 October. When Bristol submitted to her that day, the elder Despenser was captured and executed. Edward and the younger Hugh were taken, probably near Llantrisant in Glamorgan, on 16 November; Hugh Despenser the younger met his end at Hereford on 25 November. A parliament was summoned to London for 7 January 1327. Informed at Kenilworth of the assembly's decision he should no longer reign, Edward resigned the throne, and his son was crowned on 1 February. Orleton told the assembly Edward would kill Isabella if she rejoined him; an April council forbade her to do so, though she still sent him gifts. He was nearly rescued by a conspiracy in July 1327 led by Thomas Dunhead, and after another plot was exposed in September, the former king was killed in Berkeley Castle on 21 September, unquestionably at the new regime's tacit or express wishes.

The rule of Isabella and Mortimer Though neither figured on the young king's council, Isabella and Mortimer now governed. The pair seized all the Despensers' lands, and Isabella assigned herself so much of the royal demesne that only a third of its revenue remained to her son. In France she had secretly agreed to recognize Robert I as king of Scots and to abandon English claims to the overlordship of Scotland. A peace with France was concluded in September 1327, and after her son's failed Scottish campaign of 1327 the treaty of Edinburgh (17 March 1328)—perhaps only a sop to those who wished to continue the war—recognized Scottish independence and arranged the marriage of Isabella's daughter Joan to King Robert's son, *David. That Isabella kept much of the £20,000 paid by the Scots as reparations for devastations in northern England bore witness to the depletion of Edward II's vast cash reserves. Funds were needed to pay her mercenaries and to attract English loyalties, but for many the new regime's evident greed recalled the Despensers' avarice.

The treaty outraged many barons, including Henry de Beaumont and Henry, earl of Lancaster, who had been allowed to succeed to his brother's title and estates. Though a member of the council, Lancaster held no real power and his relations with the regime remained uncertain. He refused to attend a parliament at Salisbury in October 1328, and then tried to displace Mortimer's influence over the king. Isabella and Mortimer seized Lancaster's town of Leicester and ravaged his lands. Archbishop Mepham's mediation and defections among Lancaster's supporters staved off conflict; the earl submitted, while Beaumont fled abroad. But in March 1330 the queen and Mortimer procured the death of the more dynamic of the late king's brothers, Kent, by implicating him in a false plot to free the former king, who was rumoured to be still alive. Mortimer obtained his lands. This was a warning not to challenge the regime, but Isabella's greed and her lover's arrogance had alienated many. Evidence does not fully support the idea that the young king and Lancaster now connived to depose Isabella and Mortimer, but the latter pair were clearly apprehensive. At Nottingham for a parliament Isabella and Roger on 18 October 1330 examined Edward and several of his friends on their loyalty to the regime. Their evident intent to arrest her son's partisans set off a rapid chain of events that ended when Edward III and his friends arrested Isabella and Roger in her chambers in Nottingham Castle. Mortimer was soon executed as a traitor, but the only charge against him that named Isabella was that he had caused discord between her and the late king.

Retirement and death Isabella was briefly kept under guard, but later lived at Castle Rising in Norfolk and elsewhere, travelling freely and receiving all the deference due a queen dowager. She received her son regally on his many visits to her, and saw him on important occasions at Windsor and elsewhere; in her last months her daughter Joan came to live with her. Friends informed her on foreign affairs and she received notables, among them Jean II of France (r. 1350–64) (though a proposal in 1348 by Philippe VI (r. 1328–50) that Isabella should mediate between him and her son came to nothing). She gave up her illicit wealth, but was restored by 1337 to the lands and revenue she had enjoyed as consort; her son referred to her petitions touching her lands, and she vigorously sustained a lengthy dispute with the prior of Coventry over tenements and rights she claimed in that town. Her comfortable life is witnessed by gifts of wine and food from the corporation at Bishop's Lynn near Castle Rising, and by an inventory of her goods taken at her death. Isabella's varied library suggests a cultured woman, and the tomb of her son John of Eltham, which she probably commissioned, implies well-defined and cosmopolitan tastes. She owned religious books, furnished her chapel richly, gave alms, and made pilgrimages; but if she did take the habit of St Clare as reputed, it was on her deathbed.

Isabella's health had been poor for some time before she died at Hertford Castle on 23 August 1358, her end perhaps hastened by a purgative she insisted upon taking. Shrouded in the mantle worn at her wedding, she was buried with great pomp that November in the London Franciscan church in Newgate, of which she was a patron. Edward III richly endowed services for her soul. Her alabaster tomb, with Edward II's heart held in its effigy's breast and figures of the archangels at its corners, was lost when the priory was made a parish church about 1550. Contemporary manuscript illuminations and corbel heads represent Isabella, but there exist no authentic witnesses to the beauty so widely praised by her contemporaries.

Reputation A reasoned estimate of Isabella's career is impeded by the ambiguities of her reputation. Impressed by her high lineage, beauty, and tribulations, contemporaries regarded her as a lovely and tragic queen; the epithet 'She-Wolf of France', first used by Shakespeare for Margaret of Anjou, was applied to Isabella only in the eighteenth century. To represent Edward's liking for male favourites as marginalizing her during his reign, or emphasizing only her actions in 1325–30, obscures her important role between 1312 and 1325, which was clearly understood at

the time. It was above all in the queen's traditional role as intercessor that Isabella found a place at the centre of English politics, which she retained until the last years of Edward II's reign, when assaults on her dignity by her husband and the Despensers led her to the conclusion that her best hope of regaining wealth and influence lay in an alliance with those who could end the regime and crown her son. When the latter's homage as duke of Aquitaine proclaimed him of an age to take some part in state affairs, Edward II became redundant for Isabella's purposes. Her liaison with Mortimer perhaps renewed rumours about Edward's personal life, in the process further subverting his authority by exposing his failure to defend exclusive sexual rights to his wife's body.

The exact extent to which Mortimer really directed Isabella during the period 1326–30 will never be known, but their liaison inextricably linked her actions to his. It was inevitable that this should have been the case, when she attended public events like the marriage celebrations for Mortimer's daughters conducted at Hereford in the summer of 1328, while her closeness to Mortimer is vividly shown by her well-attested outcry at the moment of her lover's arrest in 1330, 'Good son, good son, have pity on gentle Mortimer' (*Chronicon Galfridi le Baker*, 46). Even if the spectacle of their relationship did not lead to her downfall as directly as was once thought, it is probably not surprising that Isabella was never able to attract to herself the lasting loyalty of those who had upheld her in 1326, loyalty rightly owed to the son in whom was legitimately vested the royal authority that his mother and Mortimer usurped. To determine Isabella's sense of responsibility or contrition for the events of 1326–30 is a virtual impossibility; but her burial with her wedding mantle and Edward's heart proves that these actions were on her mind to the end of her days.

JOHN CARMI PARSONS

Sources J. C. Davies, *The baronial opposition to Edward II* (1918) · T. F. Tout, *The place of the reign of Edward II in English history: based upon the Ford lectures delivered in the University of Oxford in 1913*, rev. H. Johnstone, 2nd edn (1936) · N. Fryde, *The tyranny and fall of Edward II, 1321–1326* (1979) · J. R. S. Phillips, *Aymer de Valence, earl of Pembroke, 1307–1324: baronial politics in the reign of Edward II* (1972) · J. R. Maddicott, *Thomas of Lancaster, 1307–1322: a study in the reign of Edward II* (1970) · E. A. R. Brown, 'The political repercussions of family ties in the early fourteenth century: the marriage of Edward II of England and Isabelle of France', *Speculum*, 63 (1988), 573–95 · S. Menache, 'Isabelle of France, queen of England—a reconsideration', *Journal of Medieval History*, 10 (1984), 107–24 · P. C. Doherty, 'Isabella, queen of England, 1296–1300', DPhil diss., U. Oxf., 1977 · H. Johnstone, 'Isabella, the she-wolf of France', *History*, new ser., 21 (1936–7), 208–18 · P. Chaplais, *Piers Gaveston: Edward II's adoptive brother* (1994) · F. D. Blackley and G. Hermansen, eds., *The household book of Queen Isabella of France for the fifth regnal year of Edward II* (1971) · F. D. Blackley, 'Isabella of France, queen of England, and the late medieval cult of the dead', *Canadian Journal of History*, 15 (1980), 23–47 · G. E. Trease, 'The spicers and apothecaries of the royal household in the reigns of Henry III, Edward I and Edward II', *Nottingham Medieval Studies*, 3 (1959), 19–52 · J. C. Parsons, 'The intercessionary patronage of queens Margaret and Isabella of France', *Thirteenth century England*, ed. M. Prestwich, R. H. Britnell, and R. Frame, 6: *Proceedings of the Durham conference, 1995* (1997), 145–56 · J. Vale, *Edward III and chivalry: chivalric society and its context, 1270–1350* (1982) · E. A. Bond, 'Notices of the last days of Isabella, queen of Edward the Second, drawn from an account of the expenses of her household', *Archaeologia*, 35 (1853), 453–69 · W. M. Ormrod, *The reign of Edward III* (1990) · S. L. Waugh, *England in the reign of Edward III* (1991) · H. G. Richardson and G. O. Sayles, eds., *Rotuli parliamentorum Anglie hactenus inediti, MCCLXXIX–MCCCLXXIII*, CS, 3rd ser., 51 (1935) · P. Binski, *Westminster Abbey and the Plantagenets: kingship and the representation of power, 1200–1400* (1995) · *Chronicon Galfridi le Baker de Swynebroke*, ed. E. M. Thompson (1889)

Archives Archives Nationales, Paris · BL · PRO · S. Antiquaries, Lond., expenses while in France, 1325, MS 543
Likenesses manuscript, *c.*1470–1480 (*Marriage of Edward II*), BL, Royal MS 15 E IV, fol. 295 · manuscript (*University of Oxford receiving queen at city gates*), Holkham Hall, Norfolk

Isabella, countess of Bedford (1332–1379), princess, was the eldest daughter and second surviving child of *Edward III and *Philippa of Hainault. Born at Woodstock on 16 June 1332, she shared a household, which was governed by William of St Omer and his wife, Elizabeth, with her brother *Edward the Black Prince (1330–1376) and her sister Joan (1333–1348). In June 1335 Edward III attempted to negotiate a marriage between Isabella and Pedro, later known as Pedro the Cruel (*d.* 1369), the eldest son of the king of Castile, but Joan was substituted. Meanwhile Isabella had by 1338 replaced Joan in marriage negotiations with the count of Flanders for a match with his heir Louis, later called de Male. The count's loyalty to the Valois, and English support of Jacob van Artevelde's revolt, stalled the talks. Edward III then began to seek the heir of the duke of Brabant for Isabella. Since the proposed groom was a descendant of Edward I, a papal dispensation was sought in 1344. During the delay the Flemish marriage was revived. The death of the count of Flanders at Crécy in 1346 made the new count, Louis de Male, even less willing, but he was placed under restraint by his subjects, who were eager for the English connection. Edward, Queen Philippa, and Isabella met with Louis de Male at Bergues near Dunkirk on 1 March 1347. Louis promised to marry Isabella, whose trousseau was in readiness, within a fortnight of Easter. The count, however, gave his subjects the slip while hawking, and soon married Marguerite de Brabant. In 1349 Isabella was offered to Charles IV of Bohemia (*d.* 1378), king of the Romans, but the offer was not pursued. When Isabella was nineteen, Edward in 1351 announced his consent to the marriage of 'our very dear eldest daughter whom we have loved with special affection' (Rymer, 5.702) to Bernard, heir of Bernard Ezi, sieur d'Albret, a loyal Gascon supporter. This was a useful but hardly spectacular match. It may have reflected Isabella's wishes. On 15 November five ships were ordered to take her to Gascony, but at the water's edge Isabella baulked, and the marriage was subsequently called off. She had managed to escape her role as a pawn in the marriage game.

Isabella was a favourite of her parents, with whom she spent more time than any of her siblings. She and *Edmund of Langley (1341–1402) were the only children to receive English lands in the period 1343–59. At Michaelmas 1358 Edward also gave her an annuity of 1000 marks, and in 1364 she received the valuable wardship of Edmund (III) Mortimer, earl of March and Ulster (1351–1381). Edward III had also lent his extravagant daughter 1000 marks in 1359 to redeem the jewels she had pawned. Some estimate of Isabella's resources can be found in a patent of 27 November 1377, issued when Richard II had to provide for his aunt after her husband's forfeiture of his English lands. Unfortunately it lists resources which were to be excluded from Isabella's revenues, rather than the extent of those revenues, and no inquisition post mortem survives to help to clarify the situation.

Although she was often at court, there is little trace that Isabella exerted any overt political influence. She had witnessed the naval engagement off Sluys in 1340; she was present during the siege of Calais of 1346–7. A frequent spectator at tournaments and participant in the hunt, Isabella was much involved with the martial and chivalrous pursuits that characterized the Edwardian court. She participated in the feasts of the Order of the Garter, and she remained a fixture at court even in the years of Alice Perrers's ascendancy.

On 27 July 1365 at Windsor, at the age of thirty-three, Isabella married Enguerrand (Ingram) (VII) de *Coucy (*c.*1340–1397), one of the hostages for the fulfilment of the treaty of Brétigny. Coucy had won Edward III's favour; he had been granted English lands claimed through his great-grandmother, a niece of John de Balliol. In consequence of the marriage Coucy was made a knight of the Garter, and was created earl of Bedford on 11 May 1366. In 1367 he received Soissons, surrendered to Edward by its count, another hostage, in return for his freedom. Once freed himself, he had taken Isabella to Coucy, where in April 1366 she gave birth to a daughter, Mary (Marie). A second daughter, Philippa, was born at Eltham in 1367. To escape his conflicting loyalties as England and France moved toward renewed war, Coucy went to fight in Italy in 1368, while Isabella stayed in England. The couple were briefly reunited in 1374 in France, but Isabella then returned to England, while her husband pursued his claims as a grandson of Leopold I, duke of Austria (*d.* 1326), to lands in Aargau and Alsace. They were again together in 1376, but Coucy was now firmly committed to his Valois lord, and on 26 August 1377 he courteously resigned all his English lands and honours in order to serve France. Isabella returned to her daughter Philippa in England; Mary remained in France with her father. Mary became heir to the French possessions and married Henri, son of Robert, duke of Bar. Philippa married Robert de Vere, earl of Oxford (*d.* 1392), the favourite of Richard II, who created great scandal in 1387 when he rejected her for a Bohemian woman.

Isabella, who was always a figure in her own right, received robes of the Order of the Garter in 1376, and did so again, after her husband's resignation, in 1379 under the style 'countess of Bedford'. She was joined in 1379 by Philippa. When Enguerrand de Coucy created the order of the Crown, it was an order that admitted women, a tribute—intended or not—to an independent wife.

Isabella was dead by 4 May 1379 and was buried in the Greyfriars Church in London. Her figure, along with those of her siblings, graced the tomb of Edward III in Westminster Abbey, but Isabella's image is not among those that survive. Enguerrand de Coucy erected her statue alongside his own in the Celestine church at Soissons, but this statue too is now lost.   JAMES L. GILLESPIE

Sources M. A. E. Green, *Lives of the princesses of England*, 3 (1851) • B. W. Tuchman, *A distant mirror* (1979) • W. M. Ormrod, 'Edward III and his family', *Journal of British Studies*, 26 (1987), 398–422 • Baron von Thurn und Zurlauben, 'Abrégé de la vie d' Enguerrand VII du nom, Sire de Couci', *Histoire de l'Academie royale des inscriptions et belles lettres*, 25 (1759) • *Chancery records* • J. L. Gillespie, 'Ladies of the fraternity of St George and of the Society of the Garter', *Albion*, 17 (1985), 259–78 • N. H. Nicolas, *History of the orders of knighthood of the British empire*, 2 (1842) • *Œuvres de Froissart: chroniques*, ed. K. de Lettenhove, 25 vols. (Brussels, 1867–77) • Rymer, *Foedera* • *CIPM*, 15, no. 176 • GEC, *Peerage*
Wealth at death see Green, *Lives*, appx

Isabella [Isabella of France] (1389–1409), queen of England, second consort of Richard II, was the daughter of Charles VI, king of France (*d.* 1422) (*r.* 1380–1422), and Isabella of Bavaria. She was born at the Louvre in Paris on 9 November 1389. *Richard II's first queen, Anne of Bohemia, died childless on 7 June 1394, and deeply though Richard mourned her, as a king he needed another wife and an heir. As early as the August after Anne's death, embassies were sent to the duke of Bavaria and the king of Scots, probably to make preliminary inquiries about marriage alliances, although their instructions, perhaps intentionally, were not very clear. But if these two embassies were not openly seeking a bride for Richard himself, another one which set out for Aragon in March 1395 certainly was. The possibility of an Anglo-Aragonese alliance alarmed Charles VI and the French court, who immediately began to suggest French princesses as brides for Richard. A secretary and a serjeant-at-arms of Charles VI were sent to London and proceeded to Ireland, where Richard was campaigning. Three French princesses were at first suggested, but none of them was a king's daughter, while Isabella, Richard's choice, was the daughter of the king of France, against whom the only objection that could be brought was her age, then only five years.

For Richard himself, anxious for peace with France, Isabella's extreme youth was evidently not unwelcome. It has been suggested that the impalement of his arms with those of Edward the Confessor on the Wilton diptych, probably painted in 1395 for Richard himself, was a sign that he was now 'wedded solely to the royal tradition of England' (Harvey, 6), a view supported by Barron, who argues that the extreme youth of his bride may have suited Richard: he had apparently committed himself to chastity in mourning for Anne, because he would have been unable under canon law to consummate the marriage for at least five years. But many of Richard's subjects, including his youngest uncle, the duke of Gloucester, were strongly opposed to peace with France and to the marriage, while historians from Adam Usk to T. F. Tout have emphasized less the youth of Isabella than the importance of the French alliance in strengthening Richard's position, and so preparing the way for his 'second tyranny'; Tout drew particular attention to the clause in Richard's instructions to his ambassadors asking the French to promise help against any of his own subjects.

For the French side Philippe de Mézières, who under the sobriquet of 'the Old Pilgrim' advocated peace with England in preparation for a joint crusade, wrote his *Letter to King Richard II* in the summer of 1395 recommending Isabella, and countered the argument that she was too young, by pointing out that it was easier to train elephants and camels when very young. A very young princess would be more easily educated by Richard to suit his wishes. The commissioning of this letter by Charles VI, the offer of the king's daughter, and the undertaking to pay a large dowry all show that the French were eager for peace. On 8 July 1395 the archbishop of Dublin, the earl marshal, and others were commissioned to go to Paris to treat for the marriage. According to Froissart the child princess said to the earl marshal, 'if it please God and my lord my father that I shall be queen of England, I shall be glad to, for I am told that I shall then be a great lady' (*Œuvres*, 15.186), and the commissioners were enthusiastic in praising her. Accordingly a treaty was sealed on 9 March 1396 and three days later the earl marshal, on a second mission to Paris, stood proxy for Richard at a betrothal in the Sainte-Chapelle. Meanwhile a separate truce for twenty-eight years was made between the two countries, a final peace proving impossible to achieve. The dowry agreed after some bargaining was 800,000 gold francs (300,000 to be paid on the wedding day and the remainder in annual instalments of 100,000), the whole being equal to about £130,000, or perhaps one year's receipts at the English exchequer.

Preparations were at once made for the young queen's journey to England. More than a hundred persons, including the dukes of Berri and Burgundy, lords, ladies, squires, serjeants, and servants, accompanied her to Calais at a cost of 100,000 francs. The two kings met near Calais in October, and on the 28th Isabella was handed over to Richard with elaborate ceremony. They were married by Archbishop Thomas Arundel in the church of St Nicholas at Calais. From there Isabella travelled to London and was crowned by the archbishop on 7 January 1397. Although he soon tired of the extravagance of her French ladies, headed by the Lady de Coucy, Richard treated Isabella well and she became devoted to him. Two years later in May 1399, after holding a tournament at Windsor in her honour, he set out on his second expedition to Ireland. When he was brought back to London as a prisoner Isabella was kept at Sonning in Berkshire, and not allowed to see him. Indeed, she never saw him again. In the autumn of 1399 Henry IV paid nearly £15,000 into the exchequer, the last instalment of her dowry to be received, thereby enabling his government to remain solvent at a very critical moment.

Isabella's presence as a virtual prisoner posed problems for the new king which his counsellors discussed at some length. Within weeks of his accession Henry IV sent an embassy to Paris to suggest a marriage alliance, possibly including that of Isabella with the prince of Wales, but, loyal to Richard, she would certainly have refused. The rebels of January 1400 found her at Sonning, and tore the Lancaster badges from her attendants, but their defeat left her in the king's custody. Following Richard's death, probably in February 1400, Charles VI demanded her return, with her dowry, jewels, and other property in accordance with the treaty of 1396, but the English exchequer had not the money to repay the dowry. Indeed, the English put in a counter-claim to money unpaid from the ransom of Jean II of France, captured at Poitiers in 1356. Negotiations continued, and a treaty was concluded at Leulighem in May 1401 by which Isabella was to be returned to France with her jewels and property. The dowry question was left open, and it was in fact never repaid. The earl of Worcester escorted her to Calais, where she was duly handed over to the count of St Pol on 31 July, and welcomed home. Five years later, on 29 June 1406, she was married to her cousin Charles, count of Angoulême, who was to become duke of Orléans on the assassination of his father, Louis, on 23 November 1407. Isabella died on 14 September 1409 in giving birth to her only daughter, Jeanne. She was buried at Blois in the chapel of the abbey of St Laumer, now the church of St Nicolas, and in 1624 her body was removed to the Orléans chapel in the church of the Celestines in Paris.

J. L. KIRBY

Sources A. de la Sante-Marie [P. de Guibours], *Histoire généalogique et chronologique de la maison royale de France*, ed. P. Ange and P. Simplicien, 3rd edn (Paris, 1726–33) · Rymer, *Foedera*, 1st edn, vol. 7 · Rymer, *Foedera*, 3rd edn, vol. 3 · *Choix de pièces inédites relatives au règne de Charles VI*, ed. L. Douet-d'Arcq, Société de l'histoire de France, 1 (1863) · J. J. N. Palmer, 'The background to Richard II's marriage to Isabel of France (1396)', *BIHR*, 44 (1971), 1–17 · J. J. N. Palmer, *England, France and Christendom, 1377–99* (1972) · P. de Mézières, *Letter to King Richard II*, ed. G. W. Coopland (1975) · J. Juvénal des Ursins, *Histoire de Charles VI, roy de France*, ed. J. F. Michaud and J. J. F. Poujoulat (Paris, 1850), ser. 1, vol. 2 of *Nouvelle collection des mémoires pour servir à l'histoire de France* · P. Chaplais, *English medieval diplomatic practice*, 1, PRO (1982), nos. 385–6 · *Œuvres de Froissart*, ed. K. de Lettenhove, 15 (Brussels, 1872) · *Œuvres de Froissart*, ed. K. de Lettenhove, 16 (Brussels, 1872) · A. B. Steel, *Richard II* (1941) · A. Steel, *The receipt of the exchequer, 1377–1485* (1954) · Tout, *Admin. hist.*, vol. 4 · J. H. Harvey, 'The Wilton diptych, a re-examination', *Archaeologia*, 98 (1961), 1–28 · D. Gordon and others, *Mastery and meaning: the Wilton diptych* (1993) [exhibition catalogue, National Gallery, London] · C. Given-Wilson, *The royal household and the king's affinity: service, politics and finance in England, 1360–1413* (1986) · L. Bellaguet, ed. and trans., *Chronique du religieux de Saint Denys*, 6 vols. (Paris, 1839–52), vol. 2 · N. H. Nicolas, ed., *Proceedings and ordinances of the privy council of England*, 7 vols., RC, 26 (1834–7), vol. 1 · *Thomae Walsingham, quondam monachi S. Albani, historia Anglicana*, ed. H. T. Riley, 2 vols., pt 1 of *Chronica monasterii S. Albani*, Rolls Series, 28 (1863–4), vol. 2 · *Chronicon Adae de Usk*, ed. and trans. E. M. Thompson, 2nd edn (1904) · B. Williams, ed., *Chronicque de la traison et mort de Richart Deux, roy Dengleterre*, EHS, 9 (1846)

Isabella of Castile, duchess of York (1355–1392). *See under* Edmund, first duke of York (1341–1402).

Isbister, Alexander Kennedy (1822–1883), headmaster and writer, was born on 18 April 1822 at Cumberland House, Fort Cumberland, on the Saskatchewan River, in Canada. He was the son of Thomas Isbister, an officer in the Hudson's Bay Company, and Mary, daughter of another Scot, Alexander Kennedy, and a Cree Indian, Aggathas. From the age of seven Isbister was educated at St Margaret's Hope School in the Orkneys, but subsequently attended the Anglican Red River Academy in Winnipeg. In 1838, two years after his father had been gored to death by a bull, Isbister entered the service of the Hudson's Bay Company, working first at Fort Simpson and subsequently at Fort McPherson. In 1841 he resigned from the company and, after a spell of teaching at his former Winnipeg school, in 1842 returned to Scotland, studying with distinction at the universities of Aberdeen and Edinburgh, from which he later graduated MA in 1858. His literary and educational talents found expression in contributions to the *Encyclopaedia Britannica*, and to Chambers's *Educational Course*. A barrister of the Middle Temple, he obtained an LLB degree from the University of London in 1866.

His obituaries (and the *Dictionary of National Biography* entry) state that Isbister was second master at the East Islington proprietary school from 1849, headmaster in 1850–55, headmaster of Jews' College, Finsbury Square, in 1855–8, and headmaster at the Stationers' Company's School in 1858–82. Hyamson's (1955) history of Jews' College, however, gives Dr Louis Lowe as headmaster in 1855–8, while Baynes's (1987) history of Stationers' states that Isbister was appointed on 5 February 1861 and retired in 1880. Isbister's evidence to the Taunton Commission, given in 1865, confirms that he was only in charge of the secular department at Jews' College. He was certainly the first headmaster of Stationers' which, although founded in 1858, did not admit boys until 1861, and he lived in the headmaster's house in Bolt Court, off Fleet Street, a residence whose previous inhabitants had included Dr Samuel Johnson. When Isbister retired, Stationers' had become an established middle-class school with a roll of some 200 pupils. He also became prominent in the work of the College of Preceptors. In 1861 when the *Educational Times* was adopted as the official journal of the college, Isbister became editor, and held the post until shortly before his death. In 1873 he was unanimously elected dean of the college, and during the rest of his life brought his naturally cautious and conservative approach to bear upon its proceedings.

Isbister was a prolific writer of textbooks on such subjects as arithmetic, geometry, English grammar, reading, elocution, bookkeeping, and accounts, and he produced popular editions of Xenophon's *Anabasis* and Caesar's *Commentaries*. His knowledge of Canada brought him into contact with geologists such as Sir Charles Lyell and Sir Roderick Murchison, and he was awarded the Albert medal of the Royal Geographical Society. He also acted as an adviser to Lady Franklin in her attempts to dispel the mystery which surrounded the fate of her husband and his companions in their search for the north-west passage. In a pamphlet of 1850 he recommended Canada as a suitable site for transportation. His criticisms of the Hudson's Bay Company ('the last stronghold of monopoly and barbarism in the British Empire') and his vigorous lobbying (which gained the support of Gladstone and the duke of Newcastle, and which secured the appointment of a parliamentary select committee in 1857) have been credited with influencing the eventual incorporation of the company's territories into the new dominion. Isbister never forgot his native land. As early as 1867 he endowed a fund for young scholars in the Red River area, to be distributed without considerations of sex or race. The bulk of his estate and his library were bequeathed to the University of Manitoba. Between 1894 and 1917 some $103,456 was distributed in Isbister scholarships. Isbister School, Winnipeg, which opened in 1899 was named in his honour, as was the Isbister Building at the University of Manitoba in 1961. Additionally, the copyright of all but one of his educational works was left to the College of Preceptors to establish a prize fund in connection with its examinations.

Isbister was a patient, determined, resourceful man, with a concern for detail. Although active in many causes, he was of a naturally retiring, even reclusive, disposition. In 1935 F. P. Knights, who had left Stationers' in 1879, remembered Isbister as:

> A great man, over six feet high, his gown, mortar board and person reeking with tobacco; his pipe had a hookah, and a large one at that, with ensuite tubing as large as could be seen outside illustrations from Arabian Nights Entertainments … a very likeable man and human.
> (Baynes, 19)

After his retirement from Stationers', Isbister, a bachelor, lived with his widowed mother, Mary, and unmarried sister, Eliza, at 20 Milner Square, Islington. He died there on 28 May 1883 of chronic Bright's disease and congestion of the lungs. RICHARD ALDRICH

Sources B. Cooper, *Alexander Kennedy Isbister: a respectable critic of the honourable company* (1988) · H. Knox, 'Alexander Kennedy Isbister', *Papers Read before the Historical and Scientific Society of Manitoba*, 3rd ser., 12 (1957), 17–28 · *Educational Times*, 36 (July 1883), 267 · *DCB*, vol. 11 · B. Cooper, 'Alexander Kennedy Isbister: a respectable Victorian', *Canadian Ethnic Studies*, 17 (1985), 44–63 · G. Bryce, 'In memoriam: late A. K. Isbister, MA, LL.B', *Manitoba Historical and Scientific Society*, 8 (1883–4), 1–4 · J. V. Chapman, *Professional roots: the College of Preceptors in British society* (1985) · *Isbister School, Winnipeg* (1984) · R. Baynes, *A history of the Stationers' Company's School, 1858–1983* (1987) · d. cert. · *CGPLA Eng. & Wales* (1883)
Archives RGS, notes relating to North America
Likenesses R. A. Ledward, bust, 1887, priv. coll.
Wealth at death £25,753 6s. 2d.: probate, 3 July 1883, *CGPLA Eng. & Wales*

Isham, Sir Charles Edmund, tenth baronet (1819–1903), rural improver and gardener, was born on 16 December 1819, the second son of Sir Justinian Isham, eighth baronet (1773–1845), and his wife, Mary Close (d. 1878). He was educated at Rugby School and at Brasenose College, Oxford, and succeeded to the baronetcy in 1846, following the unexpected death of his elder brother. The following year, on 26 October, he married Emily (d. 1898), daughter of Sir John *Vaughan, justice of the common pleas. His only experience of public office was as sheriff for Northamptonshire in 1851, which he did not enjoy. On the family estate of Lamport, Northamptonshire (held since 1560), Isham carried out a number of improvements; he rebuilt cottages in the village in a decorative style and concentrated much of his energy on the garden around the house.

In 1847 Isham embarked on his most ambitious project: the building of a large rockery alongside the house, which he maintained was inspired by the writings of the landscape gardener and horticulturalist John Claudius Loudon. Isham constructed with his own hands a high craggy wall of local ironstone, which looks from the lawns as though it might be a ruined remnant of a previous mansion—and indeed is often taken for that. Behind this wall, facing north, is the cascade of the rockery, falling into a deep dell. It was planted with a variety of alpines and miniature trees, many of some rarity, exciting considerable interest when it was described in the *Cottage Gardener* for September 1859. Several of these trees survive, now a little over-size, although the dell has now been largely filled in. Colour was not a major factor in the planting of the rockery, Isham preferring a green appearance throughout the year.

Among Isham's other interests were vegetarianism and spiritualism. The latter aroused a more than passing interest in fairies and gnomes, not least in the idea that mines were inhabited by races of tiny beings who by their lights and knockings led miners to the best seams of the various minerals to be found—ideas that he expressed in an article in *Medium and Daybreak* (1889). In an extraordinary way this interest manifested itself in the acquisition of hand-modelled tiny gnomes while on a visit to Nuremburg. He placed these little beings, wielding spades and pick-axes and pushing wheelbarrows, in the rockery, as though they were mining it, and for some he made banners protesting that they were 'On Strike'. Some of these figures he adorned with entertaining doggerel verses for occasions when the Ishams held fetes at Lamport for local orphanages. They seem to have been well established by the 1860s, and so may well be the first appearance of such figures as garden decoration. Photographs of Isham's work survive, and he himself produced small booklets printed on a spirit duplicator at Lamport, celebrating his passion. Various mottoes in plaster and stone that decorate the house at Lamport are further examples of his talent.

It was during Isham's tenure at Lamport that, in 1867, the hall became the scene of what has been described as the most important literary find of the nineteenth century. In a back lumber room a trunk was found that had not been opened for perhaps 200 years and that contained a small pile of books of great interest and value. A London bookseller offered Isham a paltry sum for these but he declined to sell. Some years later, when the library at Lamport was being catalogued, their identification caused a sensation, for among them were first-edition folios of Shakespeare and other treasures, which aroused the interests of experts at the British Museum and collectors elsewhere. Isham eventually made a deal, and today they are highly prized as part of the collection of the Huntington Library in California.

On the death of his wife in 1898 Isham made over Lamport to his cousin and abandoned his beloved garden, retiring to Horsham, Sussex, where he died at his home, The Bungalow, on 7 April 1903. His two surviving daughters disliked the gnome population, and the elder, Louisa, who had married Edward Corbett of Longnor, Staffordshire, ordered their removal. In the 1950s Sir Gyles Isham, twelfth baronet (1903–1976), set about restoring the hall and its garden. In excavating and recovering the structure of the rockery, in a crevice one tiny figure was found to have eluded Mrs Corbett's clearance. He now resides in the house, in the care of the Lamport Hall Preservation Trust, set up by Sir Gyles, and claims to be the earliest garden gnome in England.   BRUCE A. BAILEY

Sources private information (2004) [Sir Ian Isham, bt] · R. Fish, 'Lamport Hall', *Cottage Gardener*, 23 (1859–60), 84–6 · *Gardeners' Chronicle*, 3rd ser., 22 (1897), 209–10 · C. Isham, 'Visions of fairy blacksmiths at work', *Medium and Daybreak* (22 Nov 1889) · m. cert. · d. cert.
Wealth at death £11,179 8s. 8d.: probate, 8 June 1903, *CGPLA Eng. & Wales*

Isham, Elizabeth (*bap.* 1608, *d.* 1654), diarist, was baptized on 5 February 1608 at Lamport, Northamptonshire, the daughter of Sir John Isham (1582–1651) and Judith (*d.* 1625), daughter of William Lewyn of Otterden, Kent. She was educated at home, her curriculum consisting mainly of religious readings, needlework, some poetry reading, and some physical exercise. Her father and grandfather were learned men who collected a library that included many continental works as well as ones of natural science; her own reading, described in her diary, indirectly suggests that she had free access to this library. It is known that the children of her brother Justinian *Isham— including his daughters—were taught Latin and French and were also encouraged to keep diaries, so it is possible that he replicated his own father's educational practice. Lady Isham died when Elizabeth was seventeen, and from then on, as the eldest daughter, she took on the responsibilities of the domestic management of the house and estate.

Most existing knowledge of Elizabeth Isham's life comes from the short diary that she left, which has been preserved among the Isham papers at Northamptonshire Record Office. She never married, although serious negotiations were continued between her father and Sir Erasmus Driden on behalf of his grandson John Driden between April 1630 and May 1631. Agreement foundered because Sir John Isham felt that the amount that the Dridens were offering for her annual income was not sufficient in the light of her dowry, which was to have been £4000. There are extant letters from John Driden that suggest that the couple were eager to marry, although Elizabeth does not mention the courtship directly in her diary. She does, however, talk about her father's financial care of her and her sister in 1630, and comments: 'Now my father thought to marry me' (diary, fol. 2, entry 22). Her life was spent thereafter in helping with the responsibilities of the Lamport estate, including some charity visiting, helping with the accounts, a huge amount of intricate sewing for her family, and, after her brother's marriage, helping to educate his young daughters, who are mentioned with

great affection in the diary. She was responsible for the beehives on the estate, and records regular swarming and the volume of honey collected. During the years of the civil war she and her father were left at Lamport while Justinian was at Oxford with the king, and she educated and cared for his daughters. Her diary does record a few of the political events of these years. For example to her catalogue of the weather in 1642 she adds visitors, deaths, teaching her niece, sewing, and that the 'King fled to London' (ibid., fol. 4); in 1645 she notes simply 'Naseby field', although she later annotates 'God be praised at [his] scaping' (ibid.). It is known, from a letter of her brother's, that in 1644 parliamentary forces broke into the house, disturbing her and the children. She mentions this only obliquely: 'soldiers 3 or 4 days' (ibid.).

Elizabeth Isham's diary is composed in the manner and form conventional to the early seventeenth century, divided into small squares, each representing a year of her life. The first three squares—for the years between four and seven—are relatively empty. Subsequently each year from eight to forty is described, with later additions for some of the early and middle years, particularly as regards religious reading and spiritual feelings. It is unclear when exactly she began the diary but each basic annual entry is given retrospectively, perhaps at the end of the year, with some of the spiritual observations clearly made even later. Her key reading, which was increasingly religious as she aged, is noted each year, although she also records reading Sidney, Spenser, and Chaucer. The diary is a significant record of the domestic and interior life and responsibilities of the sister of a more famous brother. Isham died on 11 April 1654, after a short illness, and was buried at Lamport church.   KATE AUGHTERSON

Sources E. Isham, diary, Northants. RO, IL 3365 · *The correspondence of Bishop Brian Duppa and Sir Justinian Isham, 1650–1660*, ed. G. Isham, Northamptonshire RS, 17 (1951) · E. Isham, letters, Northants. RO, L.197; L.199–20 · M. E. Finch, *The wealth of five Northamptonshire families, 1540–1640*, Northamptonshire RS, 19 (1956) · parish register, Lamport, Northamptonshire, 5 Feb 1608 [baptism]
Archives Northants. RO, papers
Wealth at death £400 p.a.: Finch, *Wealth*; letters from or about Elizabeth Isham, Northants. RO

Isham [Isum], **John** (*c.*1680–1726), organist and composer, was born about 1680 and educated at Merton College, Oxford. He served as deputy organist of St Anne's, Westminster, under Dr William Croft, who resigned in his favour in 1711. Isham was admitted BMus at Oxford on 17 July 1713. Appointed organist of St Andrew's, Holborn, in April 1718, and of St Margaret's, Westminster, in 1719, he resigned from St Anne's in 1718 to take up the new appointments. He remained at St Andrew's and St Margaret's until his death in June 1726. He was buried in St Margaret's Church on 12 June 1726. Two of his anthems were included in Croft's *Divine Harmony* (1712), and with William Morley he published a collection of songs *c.*1710. One of these, a duet, 'Bury delights my roving eye', was reprinted by Sir John Hawkins in his *General History of the Science and Practice of Music* (1776).

THOMAS SECCOMBE, *rev.* K. D. REYNOLDS

Sources *New Grove* · Grove, *Dict. mus.* (1927) · J. Hawkins, *A general history of the science and practice of music*, 5 vols. (1776) · *N&Q*, 6th ser., 12 (1885), 288

Isham, Sir Justinian, second baronet (1611–1675), scholar and politician, was born on 20 January 1611 at Lamport Hall, Lamport, Northamptonshire, and was baptized at Lamport on 3 February. He was the third child and only son of Sir John Isham, first baronet (1582–1651), and his wife, Judith (1590–1625), youngest daughter of William Lewyn of Otteringden, Kent, a judge of the prerogative court of Canterbury. His mother's brother, Sir Justinian Lewyn, was his godfather and the source of his distinctive name which, due to the continued respect with which Justinian Isham was regarded, was to recur frequently in subsequent generations of Ishams. The family was established at Lamport in 1560 by John Isham, mercer and merchant adventurer of London, the great-grandfather of Justinian. He was initially taught at home by Mr Bunning, the curate of Lamport, and then studied with John Clerke at Uppingham School. From 18 April 1627 to Michaelmas 1628 he was a fellow-commoner at Christ's College, Cambridge, and on 11 October 1628 he was admitted to the Middle Temple. After travelling in the Netherlands in 1633–4, on 10 November 1634 he married Jane (1613/14–1639), eldest daughter of Sir John Garrard, baronet, of Lamer, Hertford. Over the next five years Jane gave birth to four daughters: Jane, twins Elizabeth and Judith, and Susan. She died on 3 March 1639 after giving birth to a premature son, John, who lived only thirteen days.

During the civil wars the Ishams supported the king. Justinian did not take up arms but for a time he was with the king at the royalist capital in Oxford. He succeeded to the baronetcy on his father's death in 1651. With other royalists he was imprisoned at St James's Palace in 1655, and again in 1658 at Northampton. During the fighting the family made loans to the king, and had been compelled to give financial support to the parliamentary forces. After the wars Sir Justinian was obliged to compound for his delinquency with a fine of £1100. In spite of these depredations he remained a wealthy man, and in the years following the wars he improved and extended Lamport Hall, purchased paintings (including an equestrian study of Charles I, still hanging there at the beginning of the twenty-first century) and added greatly to the library.

Apart from his commitment to the concerns of his family Isham's interests tended toward the scholarly. He was particularly attracted to mathematics, science, and the classics, and was one of the earliest fellows of the Royal Society. Sir Justinian had many friends and acquaintances who shared these learned pursuits: his old tutor at Cambridge, Joseph Mede, William Rawley (Bacon's chaplain and biographer), Charles Thynne, Sir Thomas Browne, Robert Boyle, Seth Ward, and Samuel Hartlib. He devoted himself to an extensive correspondence with these men. Isham was also a devout high-churchman, committed to the restoration of the Church of England, and he supported men such as his friend Brian Duppa, bishop of Salisbury, with whom he maintained a particularly warm and scholarly correspondence.

Sir Justinian Isham, second baronet (1611–1675), by Samuel Cooper, 1653

In 1653 Sir Justinian married his second wife, Vere (d. 1704), daughter of a fellow royalist, Thomas Leigh, Baron Leigh of Stoneleigh, and his wife, Mary, daughter and coheir of Sir Thomas Egerton. The daughters of his first marriage now lived primarily with Lady Denton, Sir Justinian's aunt, in Suffolk. Their relationship with their father was affectionate, but the six boys and two girls of his second marriage became the major focus of the remainder of Sir Justinian's life, and enabled him to combine his love of learning with devoted supervision of their education. Unusually for the time his daughters Mary and Vere were educated with their brothers. Mary was noted for her skill in Latin, and Vere was 'learned beyond her sex and years in mathematics and algebra' (*Correspondence of … Duppa and … Isham*, xliii). To Sir Justinian's great grief his daughter Vere died of smallpox at nineteen.

After the Restoration Isham was elected to the Cavalier Parliament for Northamptonshire in 1661. He was a largely inactive member and as a man of high moral principles disapproved of the dissolute court of Charles II. Away from Westminster he continued to devote himself to family concerns. While with his sons Thomas and Justinian at the house of a Mr Barret in St Mary's parish, Oxford he died 'of a sharp fit of the stone' (*Diary of Thomas Isham*, 36) on 2 March 1675. He was buried the next day at Lamport church, being survived by his wife, Vere; his daughters Elizabeth, Judith, and Susan from his first marriage; and his sons Sir Thomas [see below], Justinian, John, Ferdinando, and Henry, and his daughter Mary, from his second marriage. Several portraits of Sir Justinian survived into the twenty-first century at Lamport Hall (including one by Peter Lely and a miniature by Samuel Cooper). Each portrait shows a sober man of benevolent aspect, which would seem to be an appropriate representation of his character. His eldest son, **Sir Thomas Isham**, third baronet (1657–1681), diarist, was born at Lamport Hall on 15 March 1657 and baptized at Lamport on 20 March. Thomas is best-known for the diary he kept in Latin at his father's behest from 1671 to 1673. The diary gives a lively picture of the everyday country life of a boy of gentry class in his early teens—his studies, pleasures, and other interests. Thomas studied at home and then at Christ Church, Oxford, where his father had placed him just before his death, matriculating on 4 June 1675.

Sir Justinian had intended that his son travel in Europe, and Sir Thomas left England in October 1676 accompanied by his cousin and tutor, Zacheus Isham. After visiting France, Switzerland, and Italy they returned home in August 1679. Rome in particular fascinated Sir Thomas. His principal interest was in art and he acquired a significant collection of contemporary paintings, including several portraits of himself. In Italy he also purchased prints, books, and furniture. These acquisitions enhanced the Lamport estate, but at the time they added greatly to its financial burdens, and, together with the extravagance of Sir Thomas, made it necessary for him to contract a wealthy marriage. On the eve of his marriage to Mary, the daughter of Abram van den Bempde, a London merchant, this attractive, charming, but somewhat irresponsible young man died suddenly in London of smallpox on 27 July 1681. He was buried at Lamport on 9 August. His younger brother Justinian succeeded to the title upon his death. R. PRIESTLEY

Sources *The correspondence of Bishop Brian Duppa and Sir Justinian Isham, 1650–1660*, ed. G. Isham, Northamptonshire RS, 17 (1951) · *VCH Northamptonshire*, suppl. · *The diary of Thomas Isham of Lamport (1658–81)*, ed. G. Isham, trans. N. Marlow (1971) · R. Priestley, 'Marriage and family life in the seventeenth century: a study of gentry families in England', PhD diss., University of Sydney, 1988 · G. Isham, 'The historical and literary associations of Lamport', *Northamptonshire Past and Present*, 1/1 (1948–53), 17–28 · H. I. Longden, *The visitation of the county of Northampton in the year 1681*, Harleian Society, 87 (1935) · M. E. Finch, *The wealth of five Northamptonshire families, 1540–1640*, Northamptonshire RS, 19 (1956) · *The letters of Dorothy Osborne to William Temple*, ed. G. C. Moore Smith (1928) · G. Isham, 'Abram van den Bempde', *N&Q*, 202 (1957), 461–3 · E. R. Edwards, 'Isham, Sir Justinian', HoP, *Commons, 1660–90*, 2.638 · will, Northants. RO, IC 1404 [Sir Justinian Isham] · marriage indenture, 25 Aug 1653, Northants. RO, IC 468 [Sir Justinian Isham and Vere Leigh]
Archives Northants. RO, corresp. and papers
Likenesses S. Cooper, watercolour miniature, 1653, Lamport Hall, Northamptonshire [*see illus.*] · J. B. Gaspars, oils, *c.*1676, Lamport Hall, Northamptonshire · D. Loggan, line engraving, 1676 (Thomas Isham), BM, NPG · C. Maratti, oils, 1676 (Thomas Isham), Lamport Hall, Northamptonshire · attrib. G. Kneller?, oils, 1676–7 (Justinian Isham or Thomas Isham), Lamport Hall, Northamptonshire · P. Lely, oils, 1679–80 (Thomas Isham), Lamport Hall, Northamptonshire; copy by D. Loggan · D. Loggan, pencil drawing, 1681 (Thomas Isham), Lamport Hall, Northamptonshire · P. Lely, oils, Lamport Hall, Northamptonshire · oil miniature on copper, repro. in Marlow, trans., *Diary of Thomas Isham*
Wealth at death annual value of Lamport well in excess of £1000 (income from various sources at Lamport estimated by Mary Finch to be about £1000 in 1651, at the time of Sir John Isham's death; this income seems to have increased somewhat by 1675, when Sir Justinian died) and Shangton, an estate in Leicestershire, brought in at least £660 p.a.; made provision for payments to various children totalling £14,700, to be paid within a few years of death: Northants. RO, IC 468, indenture, 25 Aug 1653, marriage settlement of Sir Justinian Isham and Vere Leigh; will, Northants. RO, IC 1404 [Sir Justinian Isham], 20 Dec 1672; Finch, *Wealth*

Isham, Sir Thomas, third baronet (**1657–1681**). *See under* Isham, Sir Justinian, second baronet (1611–1675).

Isham, Zacheus (1651/2–1705), Church of England clergyman, was the son of Thomas Isham (1616/17–1676), rector of Barby, Northamptonshire, and his wife, Mary Isham (d. 1694). He matriculated from Christ Church, Oxford, aged fifteen, on 20 February 1667, graduating BA in 1671 and proceeding MA in 1674, BD in 1682, and DD in 1689. Between 1676 and 1678 he acted as tutor to his nineteen-year-old cousin Sir Thomas *Isham, third baronet [*see under* Isham, Sir Justinian], on his grand tour of Italy, and kept a record of their expenses and Sir Thomas's purchases. On his return he engaged in many of the usual activities of an Oxford don: acting as an interlocutor in the divinity school, giving set orations, attending university festivities, writing to and book hunting for a fellow scholar, Edmund Borlase, and following national politics closely.

About 1685 Isham was appointed chaplain to Henry Compton, bishop of London, and was collated successively to two prebends in St Paul's; in 1691 he was installed canon of the seventh prebend of Canterbury Cathedral. He held the rectory of Laindon in Essex from 1686 before being appointed rector of St Botolph without Bishopsgate, London, in 1688 in succession to Thomas *Pittis, whose daughter Elizabeth (d. 1703) he married. They may well have married after Isham acquired the living: of their four sons and four daughters the eldest was still just an infant when he was buried in St Botolph on 2 May 1692, while the others were all baptized within the parish between January 1693 and February 1701. Two more of their children died young. In 1700 Isham appeared first in a list of five conformist clergy who attested the accuracy of the ex-Quaker George Keith's use of quotations from Quaker works in *George Keith's Fourth Narrative of his Proceedings at Turners-Hall*. In 1701 he was appointed rector of Solihull, Warwickshire, then in the gift of the Archer family, though Thomas Hearne attributes the appointment to his cousin Sir Justinian Isham, fourth baronet. Zacheus Isham was a representative of the clergy of the diocese of Coventry and Lichfield in convocation, as before his move he had represented those of London diocese. In November 1695 Narcissus Luttrell reported that he had been chosen as a representative for the meeting of convocation (wrongly) expected to take place that winter.

Isham was a conscientious pastor who, like many others, made regular use of print. In 1694 he published anonymously *The Catechism of the Church with Proofs from the New Testament and some Additional Queries and Answers*, 'divided into XII sections for the use of a parish in London'. This was a medium sized supplement to the official church catechism for use in church and home on a three-monthly cycle. It cost 4d., and passed through more than a dozen editions between 1694 and 1735. Also in 1694 Isham published another work anonymously, *A Daily Office for the Sick Compil'd out of the Holy Scripture and the Liturgy of our Church*, with 'occasional prayers, meditations, and directions', again designed for use by his large London congregation. This work was republished in a revised and slightly enlarged edition in 1699 with a fine frontispiece by John Sturt.

Isham was also evidently in demand as a preacher on special occasions, and at least six of these sermons were published. In 1695 he delivered a sermon (reproduced more than once) at the funeral of a neighbouring London cleric, John Scott, author of the popular volumes entitled *The Christian Life* (1681–6). In 1697 Isham preached an anniversary sermon at the annual meeting of the Sons of the Clergy; in 1700 he gave a sermon before the mayor and aldermen and governors of the hospitals of London in Easter week; and in 1701 a fast sermon before the lower house of convocation. In 1704 he delivered a sermon at the consecration of a Welsh bishop at Lambeth Palace, and in 1705 preached a 'discourse of confirmation' at an episcopal visitation at Coleshill. Just before his death he was correcting the proofs of *Divine Philosophy* (1706)—the first part of a larger project designed to provide explanatory notes on different books in the Bible. In the Rawlinson collection in the Bodleian Library *Some passages in Dr Whitby's paraphrase ... contrary to scripture and the received doctrine of the Church of England* (1706) is also attributed to Isham.

Isham thus justified the memorial as 'Vir singulari eruditione et gravitate praeditus; in concionando celeberrime foecundus' ('a man of singular learning and endowed with authority; in public speaking most famously eloquent') that was placed in the chancel floor of Solihull church where he was buried. He died on 5 July 1705 'of an apoplexy' (Luttrell, 5.572).   IAN GREEN

Sources Wood, *Ath. Oxon.*, new edn, 4.654 · Foster, *Alum. Oxon.* · T. Isham, account book of grand tour, Northants. RO, Brooke MS B 74 · G. Burdon, 'Sir Thomas Isham: an English collector in Rome in 1677–8', *Italian Studies*, 15 (1960), 1–25 · letters to Edmund Borlase, 1679–81, BL, Sloane MS 1008 · W. Taswell, 'Autobiography and anecdotes', ed. G. P. Elliott, *Camden miscellany, II*, CS, 55 (1853), 28 · W. D. Macray, *Annals of the Bodleian Library, Oxford*, 2nd edn (1890), 151 · G. Hennessy, *Novum repertorium ecclesiasticum parochiale Londinense, or, London diocesan clergy succession from the earliest time to the year 1898* (1898), xxxiv, 112 · *Fasti Angl., 1541–1857*, [St Paul's, London], 36, 59 · *ESTC* · BL, Rawlinson MS J. 4°. 5, fol. 350 · R. Pemberton, *Solihull and its church* (1905), 27, 193 · *Remarks and collections of Thomas Hearne*, ed. C. E. Doble and others, 1, OHS, 2 (1885), 322–3 · *VCH Warwickshire*, 4.220, 228 · N. Luttrell, *A brief historical relation of state affairs from September 1678 to April 1714*, 6 vols. (1857), 3.552, 5.572 · *IGI* · W. Dugdale, *The antiquities of Warwickshire illustrated*, rev. W. Thomas, 2nd edn, 2 (1730), 944 · A. W. C. Hallen, ed., *The registers of St. Botolph, Bishopsgate, London*, 3 vols. (1889–95) · administration, PRO, PROB 6/81, fol. 185v [Zacheus Isham] · administration, PRO, PROB 6/97, fols. 31v, 33v [Justin Isham, son]
Archives BL, letters to E. Borlase, Sloane MS 1008

Isherwood, Annie Cecilia Ramsbottom [Cecile] (1862–1906), Anglican nun and educationist, was born on 14 November 1862 at Hillingdon Lodge, Uxbridge, the youngest of six children of Captain Richard Ramsbottom-Isherwood (*d.* 1874), an army officer, and his wife, Anna Clarendon Cox (*d.* 1870) of Fairfield, New South Wales. She was always known as Cecile. Her mother died when she was eight and her father was killed in an accident when she was thirteen. She attended a boarding-school at Brighton, after which she lived with the family of one of her father's fellow officers and continued her education in lectures and classes.

Entering by chance St Peter's Church, Eaton Square, in London, when she was sixteen, Cecile Isherwood heard a sermon by the vicar, G. H. Wilkinson (1833–1907), later primus of the Scottish Episcopal church, who was seeking missionaries. Deeply impressed by it, she was confirmed by him and devoted herself to social work in his parish. In 1883, on hearing the newly appointed bishop of Grahamstown, A. B. Webb (1839–1907), preach in the same church, she offered herself for service in his diocese, and was ordained deaconess.

Grahamstown, in the eastern Cape, had been bitterly divided by a quarrel between the previous bishop and the dean. Bishop Webb wished to recruit women who would be rooted in the diocese and help him in a mission of reconciliation. Ultimately he hoped to form a sisterhood which would extend mission and educational work to people of all races. On the voyage out in 1883, from among the dozen women whom he had recruited, he singled out Cecile Isherwood to be their leader, although she was only twenty-one years old. In 1884 the Community of the Resurrection of Our Lord was established in Grahamstown with Sister Cecile as the first novice. In 1887 she professed and became mother superior, with Bishop Webb as warden. The community rapidly expanded and opened schools in Grahamstown, for both paying and poor girls, and a boarding-house for children of itinerant railway workers. In Port Elizabeth nursing staff were provided for the hospital and a school was established for coloured children; a school and industrial centre was also set up for African girls. Having been an orphan herself, Mother Cecile was horrified by the practice by which orphans were lodged in prisons and she lobbied in the hall of the Cape legislature until funds were provided for an orphanage.

The most important work, however, was the establishment by the community of the Grahamstown Teaching College in 1894. Mother Cecile, unlike some of her more eager sisters, saw that it was even more important for the community to train teachers than to teach children themselves, and that this training in a local college, with a school attached, was likely to be much more effective than the preparation of girls as prospective teachers in Britain. Later she regarded the training of Dutch (Afrikaner) and British girls together as an important contribution to reconciliation after the Second South African War.

Dr Muir, the Cape superintendent-general of education, a Scottish Presbyterian, was not predisposed to favour denominational education. Mother Cecile, however, won his support and that of the Grahamstown community by the appointment, despite the misgivings of some Anglicans, of nonconformist governors and by the admission of nonconformist ministers to instruct their co-religionists. She believed strongly in co-operation with the state authorities, but this required that government standards must be maintained. Thus she had to spend much of her time raising money for the purpose, and visiting Britain to do so, particularly when—at Muir's request—the training was extended from the primary to the secondary level.

It was this unceasing effort, when her doctors had prescribed complete rest, which precipitated Mother Cecile's death at 14 Upper Hamilton Terrace, St John's Wood, London, after an operation for an internal growth, on 20 February 1906 at the age of forty-three. Her last message to her community, was 'Sparkle. … Don't let the fun go out of the place' (*Mother Cecile in South Africa*, 92). She died so young that the two men who had inspired her spiritual pilgrimage, bishops Wilkinson and Webb, were present at her funeral in the church where it had started. She was buried in Kensal Green cemetery on 24 February. She had been a remarkable institution builder, charming Joseph Chamberlain, the colonial secretary, and Dr L. S. Jameson, prime minister of the Cape, into financial support; but by her associates it was more for her spiritual leadership that she was remembered. She deliberately welcomed novices who would bring new kinds of gifts to the community, never trying to press them into a mould but allowing each personality to develop naturally. On the racial question she not only worked for reconciliation between British and Boers but also declared that the church could never do enough to make up for the great wrong which the white race had done to black people.

Mother Cecile was tall and slender with brown eyes which her contemporaries remembered as both magnetic and twinkling. Revd E. J. Bodington, who succeeded Bishop Webb as warden, described her as having 'The finished manners of a woman of the world with just a touch of the kindness of a saint' (*Mother Cecile in South Africa*, 143). She is commemorated in the calendar of the Anglican church in southern Africa.   RICHARD SYMONDS

Sources *Mother Cecile in South Africa, 1883–1906* (1930) · Sister Kate, *Mother Cecile* (1922) · [B. Imray], *Mother Cecile* (1960) · M. Roberts, *Mother Cecile of Grahamstown, South Africa* (1911) · K. S. Hunt, 'Isherwood, Annie Cecilia Ramsbottom', *DSAB* · M. Cropper, *Shining lights* (1963) · H. S. Holland, *A bundle of memories* (1915) · R. Symonds, *Far above rubies* (1993), chap. 8 · H. Davies, *Great Anglican Christians* (1957)
Archives Community of the Resurrection of Our Lord, Grahamstown, South Africa · Rhodes University, Grahamstown, South Africa, Cory Library for Historical Research
Likenesses photograph, repro. in *Mother Cecile in South Africa* · photograph, repro. in Sister Kate, *Mother Cecile* · photograph, repro. in Symonds, *Far above rubies* · stained-glass window, Liverpool Cathedral · stained-glass window, Cape Town Cathedral
Wealth at death £145 16s.: administration with will, 14 Nov 1906, *CGPLA Eng. & Wales*

Isherwood, Christopher William Bradshaw (1904–1986), writer, was born on 26 August 1904 at Wyberslegh Hall, High Lane, Cheshire, the elder son (there were no daughters) of Lieutenant-Colonel Francis Edward Bradshaw-Isherwood (1869–1915), professional soldier in the York and Lancaster regiment, of Marple, Cheshire, and his wife, Kathleen (1868–1960), the only child of Frederick Machell Smith, wine merchant, of Bury St Edmunds. His family followed the regiment to assorted garrison towns in England and Ireland, and this peripatetic childhood inaugurated a lifetime of travelling. Isherwood's sense of rootlessness was increased when his father was killed at the battle of Ypres in May 1915: his mother had no

Christopher William Bradshaw Isherwood (1904–1986), by Humphrey Spender, 1935

settled home until 1921, when she rented a house in Kensington, London.

Isherwood was educated at Repton School, where he met Edward Upward, who was to be a lifelong friend and, as he later put it, 'the judge before whom all my work must stand trial' (C. Isherwood, 'Introduction' to *All the Conspirators*, 1976, 9). He followed Upward to Corpus Christi College, Cambridge, ostensibly to read history. He spent most of his time, however, inventing a surrealist-Gothic world with Upward, which gradually crystallized around the imaginary village of Mortmere. The few surviving episodes of this constantly evolving saga were eventually published as *The Mortmere Stories* (1994).

The First World War, in which the certainties of the Edwardian world were destroyed, affected both Isherwood and his mother deeply, but in very different ways. Kathleen's romantic attachment to the past, a *paradis perdu* of ordered conservatism embodied by the Isherwood family seat, Marple Hall, increased in intensity. Isherwood reacted strongly against this, and much of his life may be seen as a search for some creed to replace the traditional, public-school, Christian values of his childhood. Determined to become a writer, he left university prematurely, having deliberately failed his tripos by submitting facetious answers to the examination questions. He began earning his living as secretary to the International String Quartet, and found the distinctly bohemian home of its leader, André Mangeot, far preferable to what he saw as the stultifyingly bourgeois ambience of his mother's residence.

In 1925 Isherwood was reintroduced to W. H. *Auden (1907–1973), whom he had known at preparatory school, and through him met Stephen Spender: the three men were to form a conspicuous literary, left-wing triumvirate of the 1930s. Auden sought Isherwood's approval for almost all his early work, and dedicated his first two volumes of poetry to him. The two men had a casual affair lasting over a decade, and Auden subsequently listed Isherwood among the 'great emotional milestones of his life' (E. Mendelson, *Later Auden*, 1999, 266). Auden's place in Isherwood's emotional life was less significant, but the two men remained close friends and occasional literary collaborators. Most of Isherwood's juvenilia reflected his obsession with public schools and the opportunities they provided for homosexual romance. His first published novel, *All the Conspirators* (1928), was an oblique story of family discord, influenced by the work of E. M. Forster and Virginia Woolf. The conflict between mother and son was to be as frequent a motif in his work as it was in his life, and resurfaced in *The Memorial* (1932), a remarkably acute and assured novel about the pre- and post-war generations, seen from both sides of the divide.

After a brief and unenthusiastic period studying medicine at King's College, London (October 1928–March 1929), Isherwood followed Auden to Berlin, partly in order to pursue a homosexual life in the unfettered atmosphere of the Weimar republic. He witnessed the rise of Nazism, and wrote two classic novels of the era, *Mr Norris Changes Trains* (1935) and *Goodbye to Berlin* (1939). Both were sardonic tragi-comedies, and the latter contains the famous sentence 'I am a camera with its shutter open, quite passive, recording not thinking', which (to Isherwood's increasing irritation) was often quoted as a summation of his fictional method. To this period also belonged the collaborations with Auden: three plays written for the experimental Group Theatre—*The Dog Beneath the Skin* (1935), *The Ascent of F6* (1936), and *On the Frontier* (1938)—and *Journey to a War* (1939), an account of their travels in China during the Sino-Japanese War. *Lions and Shadows* (1938), subtitled 'An Education in the Twenties', was a sly, self-deprecating, and very funny autobiography in which Isherwood reviewed his youth from the lofty eminence of thirty-four.

Isherwood spent much of the 1930s travelling in Europe with his young German lover, Heinz Neddermeyer, looking for somewhere they could settle without being harried by immigration officials and the German military authorities. The task of getting Neddermeyer a new passport was unwisely assigned to Gerald Hamilton, a colourful conman who had provided Isherwood with a model for the eponymous Mr Norris. Despite receiving large amounts of money, Hamilton failed to produce any papers and Neddermeyer was finally arrested in 1937. He was tried and imprisoned for draft evasion and sexual offences, after which Isherwood returned alone to London.

In January 1939 Isherwood and Auden emigrated to the United States of America, a controversial decision seen in some quarters as little short of 'desertion'. Uncertain of his future, Isherwood travelled to California to consult the exiled Irish mystic and pacifist Gerald Heard, who was to be one of several guru figures in his life. He settled in Los Angeles (he became an American citizen in 1946), but wracked by feelings of guilt, 'war-neurosis', and literary impotence, needed something to give order and a spiritual dimension to his life. He found this in Vedantism and became a disciple of Swami Prabhavananda, who had set up a temple in Hollywood. Through the Austrian director Berthold Viertel, with whom he had collaborated in England on the film *Little Friend* (1934), Isherwood found work as a screenwriter for MGM. His Hollywood career, though remunerative, was undistinguished, and included scripts for *The Great Sinner* (1949), loosely based on Dostoyevsky, and *Diane* (1956), a lavish and catastrophically miscast costume drama.

In 1941 Isherwood went to work in a Quaker-run hostel in Pennsylvania, where he helped refugees fleeing Europe acclimatize themselves to America and find work. When America entered the war, he registered as a conscientious objector and entered a Vedanta monastery, where he collaborated with Prabhavananda on a new translation of the *Bhagavad-gita* (1944), became co-editor of the movement's magazine, *Vedanta and the West*, and wrote *Prater Violet* (1945), a cinematic novella about his experiences with Viertel at Gaumont-British. Recognizing that he was unsuited to the monastic life (he found sexual abstinence particularly challenging), he left the monastery in 1945 and set up house with Bill Caskey, an ebullient, argumentative, and hard-drinking Irish-American. Their relationship was extremely volatile, which made it difficult for Isherwood to concentrate on his writing, but it resulted in *The Condor and the Cows* (1949), a book about their travels in South America, for which Caskey, a gifted photographer, provided the illustrations.

In April 1953 Isherwood met Don Jess Bachardy (b. 1934), a student almost thirty years his junior, who later became a renowned portraitist: they lived together until Isherwood's death. His attempt to write an 'American' novel, *The World in the Evening* (1954), took Isherwood a great deal of time and effort and pleased the author as little as it did the critics. *Down there on a Visit* (1962), which consisted of four lightly fictionalized interlinking episodes from Isherwood's past, was far more successful. Isherwood continued to work on film and television projects, sometimes in collaboration with Bachardy, but in 1960 also began teaching English literature at the University of California. An Isherwood-like professor was the protagonist of *A Single Man* (1964), a profound, witty, and touching book about being an outsider in American society. Its unapologetic, indeed combative, portrait of a homosexual man refusing the customary role of victim displeased many conservative critics, but the novel came to be widely regarded as

Isherwood's masterpiece. During the 1960s he wrote further books on Vedanta, including a biography of Ramakrishna (1965), and a novel on related themes, *A Meeting by the River* (1967), which he subsequently adapted for the stage.

In 1966 Isherwood published *Exhumations* (1966), a collection of stories, articles, and verses intended as 'fragments of an autobiography which tells itself indirectly, by means of exhibits' (prefatory note). Other fragments of autobiography included *Kathleen and Frank* (1971), a detailed portrait of his parents which he felt 'on closer examination' could be seen to be 'chiefly about' its author (*Kathleen and Frank*, 363), *Christopher and his Kind* (1976), which described his life—in particular his homosexual life—during the 1930s, and *My Guru and his Disciple* (1980), a somewhat proselytizing account of his relationship with Prabhavananda. He was an assiduous diarist, and although he destroyed or lost most of the journals covering his pre-war life, those he kept from 1939 onwards survive and run to over 1 million words. They were published posthumously in three volumes.

Isherwood's principal characteristic, both in his life and his work, was an apparent candour; he was also a professional charmer, and these two qualities offset his considerable vanity. He was of short stature, with a disproportionately large head, a prominent nose, and deep-set, penetrating eyes overhung by bristling eyebrows. Although he maintained a strikingly boyish appearance well into old age, he was a lifelong hypochondriac. He died of prostate cancer on 4 January 1986 at his home, 145 Adelaide Drive, Santa Monica, California. He had no funeral or grave and his body was left to science. He was survived by Don Bachardy.   PETER PARKER

Sources unpubd diaries and papers, Hunt. L., Isherwood papers · C. Isherwood, *Lions and shadows* (1938) · C. Isherwood, *The condor and the cows* (1949) · C. Isherwood, *Kathleen and Frank* (1971) · C. Isherwood, *Christopher and his kind* (1976) · C. Isherwood, *My guru and his disciple* (1980) · B. H. Finney, *Christopher Isherwood: a critical biography* (1979) · private information (2004) · Burke, *Gen. GB*

Archives Hunt. L., corresp. and papers · U. Texas, papers · Wichita State University, Kansas, transcripts of two interviews · Yale U., papers | King's AC Cam., letters to E. M. Forster · NYPL, literary papers · U. Durham L., archives and special collections, letters to William Plomer | FILM Hunt. L.

Likenesses H. Spender, photograph, 1935, NPG [*see illus.*] · H. Coster, photographs, c.1936, NPG · photograph, 1956, repro. in *Sunday Times* (11 July 1993) · D. Bachardy, portraits, c.1960–1980, priv. coll. · D. Hockney, lithograph, 1976, NPG · A. Springs, photograph, 1980, NPG · A. Springs, photograph, 1985, NPG · photograph, repro. in *The Times* (6 Jan 1986)

Wealth at death approx. $2,000,000: private information (2004)

Isherwood, Sir Joseph William, first baronet (1870–1937), naval architect, was born at Hartlepool, co. Durham, on 23 June 1870, the son of John Isherwood and his wife, Mary Ellen Dobinson, of Stockton-on-Tees; his parents were grocers. He was educated at Luggs School, Hartlepool.

When he was about fifteen years of age Isherwood entered the drawing office of Edward Withy & Co., shipbuilders, of Hartlepool, and, after serving in various other departments, in 1896 left that firm to become a ship surveyor for Lloyd's Register of Shipping. In 1892 he married Annie Mary, who survived him, daughter of Matthew Robson Fleetham. They had a son and a daughter.

At Lloyd's, Isherwood's duty was to classify the plans of ships, particularly cargo ships, and also examine the results of shipping accidents. Through this work he developed ideas for a new stronger, safer, and cheaper longitudinal girder form of ship construction to replace the traditional traverse construction method (of ribs placed at regular intervals along the keel). He patented what became widely acclaimed as the 'Isherwood system' of construction in 1906. He left Lloyd's in 1907 and the first ship constructed along the lines of his system was the *Paul Paix*, completed in August 1908, with others, in Britain and elsewhere, following soon after. He was briefly a director of the shipbuilding firm of R. Craggs & Sons of Middlesbrough, then began to practise as a naval architect in London, and made a number of other significant contributions to ship design. He developed an improved 'bracketless' system and in 1933 introduced a new design of hull form, namely, the 'arcform'. Several ships of this type were commissioned soon after.

By the time of Isherwood's death in 1937, 2500 ships, cargo vessels, and oil tankers incorporated one or more of his special designs and upwards of fifty 'Isherwood' ships were under construction in the shipyards in Britain and elsewhere representing the 'arcform' design and the 'combination' and 'bracketless' systems. Isherwood also introduced a new type of steel hatch cover.

Isherwood was created a baronet in 1921 in recognition of his contributions to the progress of naval architecture and his work for the government during the First World War. The *Shipbuilder and Marine Engine-Builder* on his death described 'the immense value of Sir Joseph's eminently practical inventions to shipbuilders and shipowners, and his name appears indelibly on naval architectural progress' (*Shipbuilder*, 576). He was a member of the Worshipful Company of Shipwrights, of the Institution of Naval Architects, of the North-East Coast Institution of Engineers and Shipbuilders, and of the Society of Naval Architects and Marine Engineers, New York. He was also a member for many years of the technical committee of Lloyd's Register of Shipping.

Isherwood died of pneumonia at his London home at 81 Grosvenor House, Park Lane, on 24 October 1937. He was succeeded as second baronet by his son, William (b. 1898).
                                        ARCHIBALD HURD, rev. MARC BRODIE

Sources D. J. Rowe, 'Isherwood, Sir Joseph William', *DBB* · *Shipbuilder and Marine Engine-Builder*, 44 (1937), 575–6 · Burke, *Peerage* · *The Times* (25 Oct 1937) · *The Times* (28 Oct 1937) · J. T. Sumida, *In defence of naval supremacy: finance, technology and British naval policy, 1889–1914* (1989) · CGPLA Eng. & Wales (1938)

Likenesses photograph, repro. in *Shipbuilder and Marine Engine-Builder*, 575

Wealth at death £176,638 19s. 1d.: administration, 1 Jan 1938, CGPLA Eng. & Wales

Islep [Islip], **Simon** (c.1300–1366), archbishop of Canterbury, came from Islip in Northamptonshire, being related

Simon Islep
(*c*.1300–1366), seal

to a family who had lordship of a manor there and lands elsewhere in the county. In 1322 his father was named as John Jossa; in 1348 both parents were identified, as John Islep and Margery, as were three brothers William, Thomas, and Richard. Two sisters are identified elsewhere as Isabella and Nichola. The William Islep who renounced the manor of Woodford, Northamptonshire, to endow Canterbury College, Oxford, was probably a nephew, as was William *Wittleseye (*d.* 1374), a successor as archbishop of Canterbury.

Early ecclesiastical career Simon Islep's early career is hidden. He first appears in November 1322, as the recipient of a papal expectative *in forma pauperum* (a promise of preferment for poor clergymen) drawn on the patronage of Peterborough Abbey. That suggests that he was then a student, and accordingly probably born about 1300. By 1331 he had risen to master, perhaps of Oxford (although the assertion that he was a fellow of Merton is unproven). From 1329 he appears as a collector of benefices, including prebends and archdeaconries at Lincoln, Canterbury, London, and Lichfield. During the 1330s his activities were apparently concentrated within the diocese of Lincoln. He appears as a greater residentiary of the cathedral from 1335 to 1340, and so must have spent more than two-thirds of the year there, in the process acquiring a good deal of experience in ecclesiastical administration. He was chancellor of the diocese in 1333, and its official from 10 April 1334 until at least 1339, also acting as vicar-general for Burghersh for periods of varied length from 1337 to 1340. An advocate of the court of arches in July 1331, by 1344 he was official of the court of Canterbury, a post he still held in 1346. He also sat at least once as a papal judge-delegate.

Islep secured the archbishopric of Canterbury by papal provision of 7 October 1349, after Thomas Bradwardine had fallen victim to the black death. The Canterbury monks had already elected him, on 20 September, but this was necessarily set aside. Temporalities were restored on 15 November, although he had already been granted the

custody during the vacancy. His consecration (by the bishops of London, Winchester, and St David's) occurred at St Paul's, London, on 20 December. He received the pallium in March 1350, until which point he styled himself only archbishop-elect.

That Islep secured the archbishopric without a previous episcopal post was extraordinary. He was, however, allegedly the candidate favoured by Archbishop John Stratford, whose death on 23 August 1348 had been followed by Bradwardine's election, and then in rapid succession by the provisions and deaths of John Offord and Bradwardine. The understanding he had gained of the church's bureaucratic and judicial apparatus doubtless also advanced his cause.

Secular employments Alongside his ecclesiastical administrative career Islep was active in the secular sphere. By 1337 at the latest he was a king's clerk (his acquisition of royal protection for a year in 1335 suggests earlier links with the crown), and owed his promotion to the archdeaconry of Canterbury in June 1343 to Edward III. It was presumably secular contacts that allowed him in October 1338 to gain the keepership of the English lands of Mortain Priory, confiscated as alien possessions during the French wars. In January 1342 he was appointed one of the envoys for peace negotiations with the French. In the following year he appears as a clerk of Edward, the Black Prince. The peak of his secular career came in 1346–9, with his appointment as keeper of the seal to Lionel of Antwerp, duke of Clarence, when the latter was guardian of England during Edward III's absence from 21 June 1346 to 27 September 1347; the following day he was appointed keeper of the privy seal, retaining that post until late in 1349—presumably until or just after his appointment as archbishop. During these years he also appears as a member of the royal council.

Islep's promotion to Canterbury did not end his involvement with the secular world, although he was not a prominent office-holder. In early 1353 he was again an envoy to discuss peace with the French, at Calais; and in 1355 was one of the guardians of the realm during Edward III's absence in France. Although there appears to be no formal identification as a member of the king's council, his continued involvement in state affairs suggests that he retained his place on that council at least during the early part of his pontificate. On 10 October 1361 he solemnized the marriage of the Black Prince to Joan of Kent, although reportedly under protest, because of objections to a spiritual relationship between the parties. As archbishop he also had local responsibilities in Kent, reflected in his appointment as overseer of the county's array in March 1360, against the threat of invasion.

The impact of the black death That Islep succeeded an archbishop who had died of plague set the tone for the immediate administrative demands of his archiepiscopate: to deal with the seismic impact of the black death on his diocese, and on the English church in general. His personal response to the threat of plague may be reflected in his concern for securing post-mortem commemoration. In

July 1348 he received a mortmain licence to establish a chantry in Lincoln Cathedral; further grants licensed the endowment of chantries at Thorney and Leicester abbeys, while in January 1362 he made provision for the celebration of an obit in Canterbury Cathedral.

Islep's most notable reaction as archbishop to the tensions generated within the church by outbreaks of plague was the attempt to regulate and place limits on stipends for the lower clergy, embodied in the decree *Effrenata*, issued on 28 May 1350. This was reinforced by a decree of 1351 requiring stipendiaries to take on cures of souls, and in 1353 by further action on clerical dress and salaries. A further epidemic of plague in 1361 produced more measures to control excessive clerical wage demands: a mandate of July 1362 and a reissue of *Effrenata* on 9 November 1362. Concern to maintain clerical standards appears in much of his legislation, and there are suggestions that he was something of a reformer. In order to increase lay awareness of the demands of the faith, he issued a manual of instruction for parish priests which may have paralleled the so-called *Lay Folks' Catechism* issued by his brother archbishop John Thoresby at York in 1357. Unfortunately, no copy of Islep's manual has been identified. In 1362 he also issued a decree reducing the number of feast days on which labour was prohibited.

Activities as primate Despite his concerns, Islep was not averse to exploiting his archiepiscopal status and powers to benefit his family. He certainly assisted the career of his nephew, William Wittleseye, and was active in promoting his kinsman Thomas Islep BCL. Others of the surname also gained promotion at his hands.

As archbishop, Islep was concerned to maintain his rights and status. He held metropolitan and diocesan visitations (the visitation of Chichester may not have been as perfunctory as is sometimes suggested), and generally maintained good oversight of his administration. His relations with his fellow bishops varied. On 20 April 1353 negotiations with the recently appointed Archbishop Thoresby of York produced a compromise on the longstanding dispute between the two archbishoprics over York's right to have a cross carried before him within the province of Canterbury, and on their precedence in seating. Canterbury's pre-eminence was clearly affirmed, and this time the settlement proved definitive. Similar determination to protect his archiepiscopal prerogatives appears in his prompt reaction when Bishop John Gynwell of Lincoln secured a papal bull of exemption from Canterbury's jurisdiction.

In 1350 Islep intervened in the quarrel between Bishop Gynwell and the University of Oxford, to confirm William Polmorva as the university's chancellor when Gynwell had refused to do so. However, the suggestion that he obstructed the promotion of the Black Prince's almoner and confessor Robert Stretton to Lichfield seems to be mistaken and unlikely. In 1363 he was appointed by the pope to try to resolve the dispute between Archbishop Thoresby and Bishop Thomas Hatfield of Durham, caused by the latter's acquisition of a bull of exemption. He also became embroiled in the defence of clerical rights and ecclesiastical jurisdiction which resulted from the indictment of Bishop Thomas Lisle of Ely on charges of homicide.

Islep was generally concerned with clerical rights. Under his auspices the statute *Pro clero* of 1352 among other things confirmed benefit of clergy for clerks convicted of felonies, and sought both to curtail regalian rights of ecclesiastical patronage and to limit interference with episcopal rights of patronage by lapse. In securing these concessions, Islep and the clergy had exploited royal financial need by delaying payment of a tax granted in 1351, until their grievances were addressed. In 1361 Islep again protested against secular judges' challenges to ecclesiastical liberties. In contrast, from the spring of 1362 he was involved in attempts to secure payment of a clerical subsidy of 100,000 florins to the papacy (in lieu of a threatened papal imposition of a biennial tenth), but was confronted by extensive opposition and inertia.

Islep's tenure of Canterbury involved him in the customary practical difficulties of the archbishopric, compounded by the economic impact of the black death. There was the perennial problem of maintaining the sea walls of the Romney Marshes, while in August 1359 he was pardoned for the escape of convicted clerks from his prison, a dereliction for which the usual penalty was a fine of £100 per escaper. There were also profits: in March 1358 he was licensed to export 200 quarters of wheat to Zeeland. Relations with the prior and convent of Canterbury were a major concern, but not always smooth. One monastic writer accused him of despoiling the endowments of his see for personal profit. Some of his correspondence with the priory, notably (and perhaps predictably) when dealing with visitation, suggests coolness in the relationship, and the monks' resentment of archiepiscopal interference. Islep was certainly concerned about the priory, and in 1356 complained of its failure to send monks to university. In 1361 he established Canterbury Hall in Oxford, initially as a mixed college of secular and monastic students under the supervision of his cathedral priory. The experiment was not a success, and under revised statutes of 1365 the college became wholly secular. Why Islep changed his mind is unknown, but perhaps this was linked to his general concern to raise the intellectual calibre of the secular clergy. His nominee as master was John Wyclif; but this is probably a comment on the scarcity of secular theologians rather than indicative of approval of Wyclif's ideas (which presumably were not seen as being particularly radical at this date).

Death and burial Islep was in poor health in his last years as archbishop, having suffered a stroke following a fall from his horse in January 1363. He died on 26 April 1366, probably at Lambeth, and was buried in Canterbury Cathedral. His tomb was among several destroyed in 1787. No will survives, although he did leave one, with Walter Dautre and Thomas Woltone being later identified as his executors. Some of his books are now in Merton College,

Oxford. The political tract *Speculum regis Edwardi* (known in an alternative version as *Epistola ad regem Edwardi III*), which was formerly attributed to him, is now ascribed to William Pagula. R. N. SWANSON

Sources Reg. Islip, LPL · *CPR* · Lincs. Arch., Ep. Reg. IV [Reg. Burghersh] · Lincs. Arch., Ep. Reg. IV [Reg. Bek] · B. H. Putnam, 'Maximum wage-laws for priests after the black death, 1348–1381', *American Historical Review*, 21 (1915–16), 12–32 · W. A. Pantin, *Canterbury College, Oxford*, 4, OHS, new ser., 30 (1985), 9–18 · [H. Wharton], ed., *Anglia sacra*, 2 vols. (1691) · J. B. Sheppard, ed., *Literae Cantuarienses: the letter books of the monastery of Christ Church, Canterbury*, 2, Rolls Series, 85 (1888) · *VCH Northamptonshire*, 3.216 · K. Edwards, *The English secular cathedrals in the middle ages: a constitutional study with special reference to the fourteenth century*, 2nd edn (1967), 339–40 · C. E. Woodruff, ed., *Sede vacante wills*, Kent Archaeological Society Records Branch, 3 (1914), 77–9 · L. E. Boyle, 'William of Pagula and the *Speculum regis Edwardi III*', *Mediaeval Studies*, 32 (1970), 329–36 · Emden, *Oxf.*, 2.1006–8

Archives LPL, register

Likenesses seal, BL; Birch, *Seals*, 1223 [*see illus.*]

Islington. For this title name *see* Poynder, John Poynder Dickson-, Baron Islington (1866–1936).

Islip, John (1464–1532), abbot of Westminster, was born on 10 June 1464, almost certainly at Islip, Oxfordshire, a manor belonging to Westminster Abbey. An isolated but trustworthy source implies that he took the name Patience on becoming a monk, but following an older convention he was normally known by his place of origin. He was probably related to Nicholas Barton, a yeoman who for many years leased the two watermills at Islip from the abbot and convent and whose executor he became. Islip also had a sister named Agnes, and from the fact that about 1490 he contributed to her expenses as a boarding pupil of a Mr Schybe it seems clear that she was considerably younger than he.

Islip was clothed as a Benedictine monk at Westminster on 21 March 1480. Although his abilities must soon have become apparent, it was perhaps equally clear that they fitted him better for an administrative career than for the university studies now undertaken by a small but growing number of monks of Westminster. In 1487, after seven years as a claustral monk, he became chaplain to Abbot Estney, and in 1492, after he had proved himself in that office and also as sub-almoner (a position carrying with it a measure of responsibility for the almonry school), his fellow monks elected him treasurer, monk–bailiff, warden of the abbey's appropriated churches, and warden of the royal manors. This combination of offices conferred on their holder control, under the abbot and prior, of the monastery's finances and estates. To these very large responsibilities were added in 1496 those of cellarer (the official who supplied bread and ale to the monastery and its dependants) and, for a short time, abbot's receiver. But he was by no means a desk-bound obedientiary, for he travelled to the manors to hold courts and transact other business. In 1493 he himself reckoned that he completed a circuit of some 250 miles in twenty-four days, including one devoted entirely to hunting. In the 1490s, however,

John Islip (1464–1532), by unknown artist [centre, top, with his monks (right) and a judge and ministers of the law (left)]

even more important matters were in hand at Westminster than the care of the manors. Early in 1498 Islip was engaged in the preparation of the abbey's claim to be the final burial place of Henry VI, and on 5 and 6 March he attended the hearings before the council at Greenwich at which a decision was given in favour of his house.

Islip's election to the offices he assumed in 1492, and especially those of treasurer and monk–bailiff, testify to the life of a Westminster obedientiary as a career open to talents, for at that time he was only twenty-first in order of seniority in a community numbering forty-two besides the abbot and prior. At the time of his own election as prior in July 1498 he had not yet presided at a meal in the refectory, a role always discharged by a monk of recognized seniority among those present and, in a period of much absenteeism, one that tended to be passed down the line. His election as abbot two years later, in succession to Abbot Fascet, was no doubt inevitable. Following the precedent of Fascet's own election in 1498, several secular observers were present at both the substantive discussion on 26 October 1500 and at the formal election next day. One of these, Edward Vaughan, presided on the second occasion, the prior (Islip himself) being for obvious reasons unable to do so. Islip was elected by the way of inspiration.

The new abbot did not put off the old obedientiary, although Islip now chose to hold different offices. In common with Estney and Fascet, his two immediate predecessors, he combined the offices of warden of the new work and sacrist with the abbacy. As warden he oversaw the new work in the nave, begun in the 1370s but long held up for lack of funds, to its completion in 1509; as sacrist he oversaw the integration of the new nave into the liturgical life of the monastery. His early years as abbot were dominated however by the taking down of the existing lady chapel of the abbey church, the building of the new lady chapel (envisaged as the shrine of a canonized Henry VI) at Henry VII's expense, and the acquisition, often in acrimonious circumstances, of manors and churches to the total value of approximately £800 per annum which were to support Henry's own anniversary and chantry. On 24 January 1503, with several others, and in the presence and name of the king, Islip laid the foundation-stone of the new chapel. As abbot he was *ex officio* warden of the new foundation. He left his personal mark in buildings erected during his abbacy in the form of his rebus, a visual pun on his name in the form of an eye next to the slip of a fig tree, from which a man falls. Perhaps Islip's sense of humour was not very sophisticated.

His diet book shows that from the beginning of his abbacy, like many of his predecessors, Islip was on friendly terms with some of the great men of the realm, in his case with Sir Reginald Bray, Bishop Richard Fox of Durham, and Archbishop William Warham. On 11 June 1501 he entertained Henry VII at Cheyneygates, and on 9 December following the king's mother, Lady Margaret Beaufort. But there is little in such relationships to suggest that in the years around 1500 Islip enjoyed much more than an *ex officio* eminence, arising from his abbatial position. Things had changed, however, by 1509, probably as a result of the competence with which Islip had handled the works at Westminster commissioned and funded by Henry VII. His circle of acquaintances now extended to include judges and administrators as well as bishops, on 23 August 1510 he baptized a child of the earl of Oxford, and he later lent money to the earl of Shrewsbury and duke of Buckingham. He also made regular visits to Greenwich and Lambeth, and at Christmas 1509 enjoyed the services of the king's minstrels and players, the master of the rolls's lord of misrule, and even the king's bear. He was a trier of petitions in the parliaments of 1510, 1512, and 1515, and a member of the king's council from no later than 1513 until his death. In 1519, for instance, he was a member of a committee of councillors appointed 'to hear the causes of poor men depending in the Sterred Chambre' (*LP Henry VIII*, 3/1, no. 571). He also attained national eminence in a more strictly monastic context, as a visitor (he was appointed in 1516 to visit three of the greatest Benedictine houses in southern and central England, at Gloucester, Worcester, and St Albans, as well as Colchester Abbey), and from no later than 1519 until 1527 was one of the presidents of the black monks in England.

Islip's advancement inevitably needed Wolsey's acquiescence. The abbot was present in 1515 when Wolsey received his cardinal's hat, and with Wolsey at other occasions both ceremonial and administrative, but there is no evidence for friendship, and when the cardinal decided in 1518 to conduct a legatine visitation, it was at Westminster that he chose to begin, with what Polydore Vergil describes as 'a drastic enquiry into the condition of the monks' (*Anglica historia*, 258–9). No more than any other head of an early sixteenth-century English monastery was Islip able to resist government pressure, but at least Wolsey seems to have valued his competence. The same can

doubtless be said of Henry VIII, who employed the abbot in his divorce proceedings in the late 1520s, and in 1531 referred to Islip as 'a good olde father' who could help settle the issue in England rather than in Rome (*State Papers, Henry VIII*, 7.312), but who also forced on him a distinctly detrimental exchange of property, whereby the abbey lost its valuable Westminster property of 'Petye Caleys' in what is now Hyde Park, in exchange for the possessions of the dissolved Berkshire monastery of Poughley. King Henry must also have appreciated Islip's standing as an upholder of theological orthodoxy, since he was employed in 1526 to examine Hanseatic merchants suspected of Lutheranism, and in 1529 in proceedings against John Tewkesbury (who later relapsed and was burnt).

Islip died at his manor house of La Neyte, a short distance from the abbey, between 4 and 5 p.m. on 12 May 1532. His funeral extended over two days, from the 16th to the 17th following. The body was carried into the abbey church in a huge procession, surrounded by his monks, the friars of Canterbury, and the priests and clerks of St Margaret's, Westminster. The Richmond and Lancaster heralds were present, as was a group of official mourners led by Lord Windsor, and twenty-four men carrying torches. In accordance with a long-standing arrangement between the two houses, the abbot of Bury St Edmunds conducted the requiem mass, and the vicar of Croydon preached when the corpse was finally interred in Islip's own chantry; proceedings concluded with 'a great Dole among the poor' (BL, Add. MS 5829, fol. 64*v*). The Islip roll has captured vividly for posterity this last display of the traditional magnificence of Westminster Abbey's monastic ceremonial. It was an appropriate setting for the exequies of the last abbot of Westminster to hold his office by the free choice of the community, and by any standards one of the most successful.

BARBARA F. HARVEY and HENRY SUMMERSON

Sources *Chancery records* · *LP Henry VIII*, vols. 1–5 · Westminster Abbey muniments 33320, 33324, 33290, 9462, and Register Book i · BL, Add. MS 5829, fols. 62*v*–64 · W. A. Pantin, ed., *Documents illustrating the activities of … the English black monks, 1215–1540*, 3 vols., CS, 3rd ser., 45, 47, 54 (1931–7), vol. 3 · *The Anglica historia of Polydore Vergil, AD 1485–1537*, ed. and trans. D. Hay, CS, 3rd ser., 74 (1950) · early chancery proceedings, PRO, C 1/371/30 · R. Widmore, *History of the church of St Peter, Westminster* (1751) · E. H. Pearce, *The monks of Westminster* (1916), 167–8 · T. H. Cocke, *900 years: the restoration of Westminster Abbey* (1995) · *State papers published under … Henry VIII*, 11 vols. (1830–52), vol. 7

Likenesses J. Basire, line engraving, BM, NPG; repro. in *Vetusta monumenta* (1808) · portrait, Westminster Abbey Muniment Room, The Islip Roll · portrait, BL, manuscript, 'A book of four indentures', Harley MS 1498, fol. 76 [*see illus.*] · stone head, Westminster Abbey Undercroft Museum

Islip, Simon. *See* Islep, Simon (*c*.1300–1366).

Ismail, Sir Mirza Mohammad (1883–1959), administrator and politician in India, was born in Bangalore on 23 October 1883, the son of Aga Jan, honorary aide-de-camp to the maharaja of Mysore. He was of Persian descent, his grandfather Ali Askar Shirazi having left Shiraz in 1824

and settled as an importer of horses in Bangalore. Mirza grew up with the young maharaja of Mysore, Krishnaraja Wodeyar, who was about the same age and who succeeded after the death of his father in 1894. Mirza was educated entirely in Bangalore, first at mission schools, then for five years under the tutorship of Sir Stuart Fraser, and finally at the Central College, graduating in 1905 at the Madras University. In 1906 he married Zeebenda Begum, daughter of Muhammad Mirza Shiraza, with whom he had one son and two daughters.

Mirza's first post was in the Mysore police but he was quickly transferred to the Mysore civil service. He soon joined the maharaja's own staff and eventually became *diwan* (principal administrator) in 1926. He remained in office until 1941, a year after the maharaja's death. He was an outstanding administrator and contributed to Mysore's reputation as one of the best-administered states in India. A born town planner, he made Mysore and Bangalore famous for their ordered beauty. He also created the celebrated gardens of Brindaban and Bangalore, which thousands still visit. But Mirza's ideal was to make Mysore not only beautiful, but also a 'truly Socialist State'. He started several state industries, in the face of considerable opposition from the government of India. He believed that in a backward country some state socialism was essential if industrialization was to make any substantial or rapid progress. By the middle of the twentieth century Mysore had a wide range of industries, some sponsored by the state, and others by the government of India or by private enterprise.

In all these activities Mirza was strongly supported by the maharaja, with whom he enjoyed an extremely close relationship. When the maharaja died in 1940 Mirza wrote to a friend that 'life without him can never be the same'. From 1942 to 1946 he was prime minister of Jaipur, where he tried to make his enlightened mark on the feudal administrative structure which he found. In 1946 he became president of the nizam of Hyderabad's executive council, but his tenure of office was a failure and he resigned after only ten months—a helpless witness to the final tragedy and end of that ancient dynasty. In 1950 he was appointed representative of the United Nations Technical Assistance Board for Indonesia, but he found the environment uncongenial and after nearly a year was glad to return to his beloved home in Mysore.

Mirza was always most carefully dressed and possessed an aloof dignity and bearing which compelled respect, if not affection. A devout and broad-minded Muslim, the *diwan* of a predominantly Hindu state and the servant and friend of an orthodox Hindu ruler, he was a living example of communal moderation and always believed in the essential unity of the Indian continent. He had little sympathy with the developments which led to the final creation of the two independent states of India and Pakistan. In 1930–32 he represented Mysore, and for part of the time the South Indian States, and Jodhpur and Jaipur, at the Round Table conferences in London, and he attended the meetings of the subsequent joint parliamentary select committee. In 1937 he led the Indian delegation to the conference of Far Eastern countries on hygiene in Indonesia. He was appointed OBE (1923) and CIE (1924), was knighted in 1930, and made KCIE in 1936. He died in Bangalore on 5 January 1959.

FREDERICK JAMES, *rev.* DAVID WASHBROOK

Sources M. Ismail, *My public life* (1954) · M. A. Sreenivasan, *Of the raj, maharajas and me* (1991) · *The Times* (6 Jan 1959) · *Times of India* (6 Jan 1959) · private information (1971) · personal knowledge (1971) **Archives** Bodl. Oxf., corresp. with Lord Monckton · Trinity Cam., papers of the joint select committee on constitutional reform | SOUND BL NSA, recorded talk
Likenesses portrait, repro. in Sreenivasan, *Of the raj*, pl. 7 · portrait, repro. in Ismail, *My public life*, frontispiece

Ismay, Hastings Lionel, Baron Ismay (1887–1965), army officer and public servant, was born at Naini Tal, India, on 21 June 1887, younger son of Sir Stanley Ismay, a member of the viceroy's legislative council and later chief judge of the Mysore court, and his wife, Beatrice Ellen, daughter of Colonel Hastings Read. He was educated at Charterhouse School and the Royal Military College, Sandhurst. Having entered the Indian army in 1905 he was posted in 1907 to the 21st Prince Albert Victor's Own cavalry, acquiring the frontier medal and clasp and becoming adjutant of his regiment. But he felt the need to gain wider military experience, and was thus by a quirk of fate forestalled from serving on any of the main fronts during the war of 1914–18, for he was seconded to the King's African rifles as captain, and landed at Berbera on 9 August 1914; in 1917–19 he was with the Somaliland Indian contingent, and with the newly formed camel corps in 1919–20. All efforts to return to his regiment failed, and he remained in Somaliland until 1920, distinguishing himself in operations against 'the mad Mullah'; he was appointed to the DSO and promoted major, having been temporary lieutenant-colonel in 1919.

Granted a year's leave on medical grounds, Ismay met and married in 1921 Laura Kathleen (*d.* 1978), only daughter of Henry Gordon Clegg, of Wormington Grange, Worcestershire; they had three daughters. His qualities, already recognized, then took him to the Staff College, Quetta, and they were confirmed in the passing-out report of his commandant, who declared: 'I consider this officer one of the two best, if not the best, of the students who have passed through my hands' (Wingate, 16–17). Thereafter Ismay was lost to regimental soldiering; in 1923 he spent a brief period on the staff at army headquarters, India, and in 1924 he was nominated to the vacancy reserved for an Indian army officer at the new RAF Staff College, Andover. At the end of 1925 he was appointed assistant secretary to the committee of imperial defence (CID) under Sir Maurice Hankey.

Five years at the CID, spent particularly in preparing the substratum of what became the war book, gave Ismay an exceptional insight into the ways of Whitehall. When his appointment ended in December 1930 his ability had already marked him as potential successor to Hankey, and the recognition of it in the new year honours list of 1931

Hastings Lionel Ismay, Baron Ismay (1887–1965), by Allan Gwynne-Jones, 1958

created a problem of protocol: by some failure of communications he was gazetted as both CB in the civil list and CIE in the India Office list: Ismay opted for the former.

The India Office wished to create a committee of imperial defence in Delhi, and Ismay was now pressed to accompany the new viceroy, Lord Willingdon, as military secretary with the organization of an Indian CID—a scheme which eventually proved abortive—among his duties. He was promoted colonel, and though he hoped for command of a cavalry regiment, in 1931 he obediently went east, where he enjoyed a privileged view of the raj in action. Nevertheless, those two years were a parenthesis and hardly equipped him for the responsibilities, which he took up on his return to the War Office in 1933, of GSO1, intelligence eastern Europe.

Shortly before he left India, Ismay's polo pony slipped while he was playing in the prince of Wales's tournament; the ensuring concussion left him deaf in the left ear, but he never allowed this disability to impede a long life of talk and conference. After his return to London there occurred a distressing sequence of deaths in his wife's family, which, however, brought her the inheritance of Wormington and substantial resources. Since Ismay was independent of mind, although a man of devoted loyalties, this independence of means merely increased his value as an objective adviser freed from the restrictions of an officer *de carrière*.

In 1936 Ismay moved into his predestined place as deputy secretary to Hankey at the committee of imperial defence. The succession was not inevitable, for the Treasury and the Foreign Office were eager to take over the Cabinet Office, and it was not without a struggle that the secretaryship of the CID (although not the rest of Hankey's empire) was handed over to Ismay after Hankey's retirement in 1938. Inadequacies of government policy made the months before and immediately after the outbreak of war in 1939 the most frustrating of his life. But in April 1940 Neville Chamberlain appointed Winston Churchill chairman of the ministerial co-ordinating committee, responsible for guiding and directing the chiefs of staff, assisted by 'a suitable central staff under a senior staff officer, who would be an additional member of the chiefs of staff committee' (Wingate, 43). The man he chose was Ismay, who had been promoted major-general in 1939.

Churchill planned to make a 'garden suburb' by assembling a central staff of his own henchmen. Ismay's first personal contribution to the war effort was to stonewall over this dubious proposal. In consequence when Churchill, on becoming prime minister and minister of defence in May 1940, retained Ismay as his chief staff officer, the military secretariat which Ismay evolved developed into a machine of unsurpassed quality because those whom he chose to man it—Leslie Hollis, Ian Jacob, and others who serviced the war administration—were apt for the task and not a prime minister's idiosyncratic miscellany. Moreover, drawn as they were from the staff of the CID or elsewhere in Whitehall, they provided continuity as well as competence.

For the remainder of the war Ismay's position was unique: none of the other belligerents, neither President Roosevelt's Harry Hopkins, nor Hitler's adjutants, provided an equivalent. Hundreds of Churchill's famous minutes and the replies to them were personally handled by Ismay, who commanded the prime minister's absolute trust. He was the essential link with the chiefs of staff, on whose committee he sat without executive powers of embarrassment. Difficult allies respected him as much as did difficult colleagues. On delicate missions abroad, amid growing responsibilities for the most secret matters, from 1940 to 1945 Ismay endured strains more continuous than any battle-commander, and sometimes equally intense. Not even Sir Alan Brooke was so exposed to the exigencies and exhaustion of intimate work with Churchill by day and by night. Shrewd, resilient, accessible, emollient in diplomacy but of an unbreachable integrity, Ismay created a role as entrepreneur which, in its range and value, surpassed that of his master Hankey in the previous war. As Ismay himself put it, 'I spent the whole war in the middle of the web'. He became lieutenant-general in 1942 and full general in 1944, and Churchill's 'resignation honours' gave his services the rather curious recognition of his appointment as CH. The next prime minister was not satisfied, and Clement Attlee's final victory list in June 1946 appointed Ismay GCB, and in the following new year honours he was created a baron.

Peace did not allow Ismay to 'put up his bright sword'. He retired from the army in December 1946, after largely reorganizing the defence system and setting up the Ministry of Defence. By the following spring he was back in India, as chief of the viceroy's staff and Lord Mountbatten's right-hand man in the days of the 'great divide'. He went there at his own suggestion, although he was anguished by the fear that the coming abandonment of India would be a betrayal of the guardianship to which he and his father had been dedicated, and as his country had also once seemed to be. He was by then a tired man, driven by a sense of duty; but again his performance as a catalyst, a tranquillizer, and a constructive negotiator was exemplary. Trusted by all parties, by his calmness and accumulated wisdom he balanced the mercurial energy of Mountbatten, who more than once dispatched him to London to conduct critical negotiations. Ismay took no pride in the clinical act of partition, although he accepted its draconian necessity, and he declined the grand cross in the Order of the Star of India, content merely with the order of release from what he described as the most distasteful assignment of his career.

In the event there was no release. He had been back in England for only a few weeks when—early in 1948—Attlee appointed him chairman of the council for the Festival of Britain—a job which, as Ismay himself said, called for strategic planning no less difficult than a military campaign. Shortly after its successful conclusion in September 1951 Churchill returned to power and, by a decision scarcely less idiosyncratic than his subsequent summons of Lord Alexander of Tunis to the Ministry of Defence, made Ismay secretary of state for Commonwealth relations. In practice the arrangement proved profitable, since Churchill drew heavily on Ismay's own experience of defence matters. It was a natural consequence when, only six months later, Ismay was chosen to be the first secretary-general of NATO and transferred to Paris.

Once more 'the man with the oil-can' went unwillingly; his achievement was brilliant and historic, for all his gifts—clarity of mind, winning charm, intellectual and social dexterity, combined with an unequalled *tact des choses possibles* and a keen appreciation of good press and public relations—were required and applied in the fusion of fourteen nations for a common, self-defensive end. When Ismay retired in April 1957, in his seventieth year, international acclaim recognized his unsparing efforts in providing NATO with an ordered structure and harmony of purpose which could hardly have been anticipated when he took office. He was immediately appointed KG. Other honours had already been bestowed: he was sworn of the privy council in 1951, and received honorary degrees from Queen's University, Belfast, Bristol, and Cambridge. He was chairman of the National Institute for the Blind in 1946–52, and president from 1952, as well as being director of various companies and schools, and a deputy lieutenant for Gloucestershire from 1950.

Ismay's retirement was marred by ill health, but in 1960 he was able to publish his self-effacing *Memoirs*. He had already assisted Churchill with *The Second World War* (1948–53). 'Pug' to all the world, he was the personification of honesty, loyalty, and human warmth, with an irresistible smile and that inner core of steel which made his presence at the heart of affairs so effective. An unashamed *bon viveur*, who also enjoyed racing and polo, tennis, and bridge, he nevertheless believed that the best thing in life is to seek to do the state some service. He died on 17 December 1965 at Wormington Grange, Broadway, Worcestershire. RONALD LEWIN, *rev.*

Sources R. Wingate, *Lord Ismay* (1970) · S. W. Roskill, *Hankey, man of secrets*, 3 vols. (1970–74) · W. S. Churchill, *The Second World War*, 6 vols. (Boston, MA, 1948–53) · *The memoirs of Lord Ismay* (1960) · *The Times* (20 Dec 1965) · private information (1981) · CGPLA Eng. & Wales (1966)
Archives King's Lond., Liddell Hart C., corresp. and MSS · PRO, corresp. and MSS, CAB 127/1–56 | BL, corresp. with Lord Keyes · Bodl. Oxf., corresp. with L. G. Curtis; corresp. with Lord Monckton · Bodl. RH, corresp. with C. Walker · Nuffield Oxf., corresp. with Lord Cherwell · U. Birm. L., corresp. with Lord Avon | FILM BFI NFTVA, news footage · IWM FVA, 'Inauguration of Lord Ismay as secretary-general of Nato', 1952, OTAN 4669 · IWM FVA, actuality footage · IWM FVA, news footage | SOUND BL NSA, 'Thinking soldier: Lord Ismay', P526RG1
Likenesses W. Stoneman, photograph, 1940, NPG · photographs, 1943–c.1952, Hult. Arch. · A. Gwynne-Jones, oils, 1958, NPG [see illus.] · A. Gwynne-Jones, portrait, 1959, priv. coll. · M. Birley, portrait, Cheltenham town hall · A. Devas, portrait, priv. coll. · A. John, drawing, priv. coll.
Wealth at death £49,612: probate, 24 Jan 1966, CGPLA Eng. & Wales

Ismay, Joseph Bruce (1862–1937), shipowner, was born at Enfield House, Great Crosby, near Liverpool, on 12 December 1862, the eldest son in a family of nine children of Thomas Henry *Ismay (1837–1899), shipowner and founder of the White Star Line, and his wife, Margaret, daughter of Luke Bruce. He was educated at Elstree School in Hertfordshire and at Harrow School, and on leaving the latter in 1878 went for a year to a tutor in Dinard, France.

On 30 September 1880 he began an apprenticeship of four years in his father's office and then sailed to Australia and New Zealand on the *Doric* to see how the new White Star service was working there. He was then sent to the White Star office in New York for a year, at the end of which time he was appointed agent for the White Star Line in New York. During this period he enjoyed a liberated lifestyle, which ended when he met a New York society belle, Julia Florence, daughter of George R. Schieffelin. They were married on 4 December 1888 and returned to England in 1891 so that Ismay could take up his partnership in the family firm. He and his wife had two sons and two daughters.

After his father's death in 1899, Ismay became head of the business. His management continued the tradition of commitment to quality, attention to detail, and firm grasp of commercial realities begun by his father. In 1901 he was approached by American interests towards forming an international shipping company, and after lengthy negotiations between him and J. P. Morgan (1837–1913), the International Mercantile Marine Company (IMM) was formed. C. A. Griscom, the ailing former chief of the American Steamship Line, became president. He was succeeded in 1904 by Ismay. During this period the White Star

Line reached its apogee in the building of the giant liners *Titanic*, *Olympic*, and *Britannic II*.

Ismay also held a number of appointments with other companies. He served as chairman of the Asiatic Steam Navigation Company, as well as being a director of Shaw, Savill, and Albion, and of several insurance companies. He was offered but declined the chairmanship of the London, Midland, and Scotland Railway (LMS). He was chairman of the Liverpool and London Steamship Owners' Protection Association and of the Liverpool and London War Risks Association.

Ismay was tall and handsome, with a somewhat contradictory personality. At times dogmatic, as in his decision to destroy many of the firm's archives after the *Titanic* disaster, he consulted in depth on big business decisions. He showed exceptional sympathy to the 'underdog', secretly helping all sorts of people, but he intensely disliked publicity. His reclusive characteristics no doubt sprang in part from being in his father's shadow, and were accentuated by the trauma of the *Titanic* sinking on 15 April 1912, which he survived. Though pilloried by the US press, he was cleared at the official inquiries. He reacted swiftly by ordering that there must be enough lifeboats for everyone on all his firm's vessels from that moment on. His resignation from the presidency of IMM and of White Star in 1913 was planned beforehand. He continued as an active director of many companies, and did not become a recluse. At the time of the White Star Line's near demise in 1934, he was considering a rescue operation, although in the end the company was saved by merging with Cunard.

Ismay inaugurated the cadet ship *Mersey* for training officers for the merchant navy. Following the *Titanic* disaster he gave £11,000 to found a fund to benefit widows of seamen who lost their lives afloat and in 1919 presented £25,000 to establish the National Mercantile Marine Fund in recognition of the role of merchant seamen in the First World War. A natural sportsman, he excelled at tennis and became a first-class shot. An expert fisherman, he owned a fishing lodge at Costelloe, co. Galway.

Ismay died of a stroke on 17 October 1937 at 15 Hill Street, Berkeley Square, London, where he had lived since 1920. He was survived by his wife. A memorial service was held in St Paul's, Knightsbridge, and he was buried in Putney Vale cemetery.   J. GORDON READ

Sources W. J. Oldham, *The Ismay line* (1961) · *The Times* (18 Oct 1937) · R. Anderson, *White Star* (1964) · J. G. Read, 'Ismay, Thomas Henry', *DBB* · W. H. Flayhart, *The American line* (New York, 2000) · *DNB* · *CGPLA Eng. & Wales* (1937)
Archives NMM | Northants. RO, Haselbech MSS · PRO, *Titanic* MSS
Likenesses photograph (aged thirteen), repro. in Oldham, *Ismay line* · photograph (aged nineteen), repro. in Oldham, *Ismay line* · photograph (shortly before maiden voyage of *Titanic*), repro. in Oldham, *Ismay line*
Wealth at death £693,305 17s. 6d.: probate, 25 Nov 1937, *CGPLA Eng. & Wales*

Ismay, Thomas Henry (1837–1899), shipowner, was born on 7 January 1837 at Maryport, Cumberland, the eldest son of Joseph Ismay, shipbuilder and shipbroker, and his wife,

Margaret, *née* Sealby. There was a long maritime tradition in the family. He was educated at Croft House School, Brampton, near Carlisle, from 1849 to 1853. This was an advanced school for its time, where Ismay learned science, including the elements of navigation, indulged his hobby of building ship models and developed the habit of chewing tobacco (hence his youthful nickname, 'Baccy').

At the age of sixteen Ismay was apprenticed to a firm of shipbrokers, Imrie, Tomlinson & Co., business acquaintances of his father, in Liverpool, and on the expiration of his time made a voyage to Chile as supercargo for a Maryport firm. On his return to Liverpool he started in business on his own account as a shipbroker, in partnership with a retired sea captain from Maryport, Philip Nelson, formally signing the articles on his twenty-first birthday. Ismay's advanced ideas proved incompatible with Nelson's conservatism and so Nelson retired and in 1862 Ismay moved into an office at 10 Water Street under the style of T. H. Ismay & Co. This was to be his head office until 1898.

The business mainly consisted of running sailing ships to Central and South America until 1867, then he entered the steam trade by becoming a director of the National Steam Navigation Company, a transatlantic line. In 1867, he took the step that made his name a household word by purchasing the flag, a white star on a red ground, along with the goodwill, of the bankrupt White Star Line of clippers to Australia, putting his own iron ships into this trade. In 1869 Ismay, in partnership with an old friend and fellow-apprentice, William Imrie, formed the Oceanic Steam Navigation Company. They were backed by Gustavus Schwabe, a Liverpool merchant, whose nephew, Gustav Wilhem Wolff (1834–1913), had recently joined with Edward James Harland (1831–1895) in a shipbuilding business in Belfast, on condition that all their ships would be ordered from Harland and Wolff. Its primary business was the north Atlantic passenger trade, and in 1871 they began running their steamers regularly between Liverpool and New York.

The White Star liners, which were highly innovative in design, earned a good reputation that rivalled that of Cunard for safety, comfort, and speed, despite the loss of the *Atlantic* in 1873 off the Nova Scotia coast. In 1878 Ismay placed his firm's steamers at the disposal of the Admiralty as transports or cruisers in the light of threats from the Russian fleet. This offer led to his proposal, in 1888, to build merchant vessels, with government subsidy, specifically for this purpose. This resulted in the building of two magnificent liners, one of which, the *Teutonic*, was sent to take part in the diamond jubilee naval review at Spithead. That year Ismay was offered a baronetcy, which he declined.

In 1892 Ismay retired from the firm of Ismay, Imrie & Co., but retained the chairmanship of the White Star Company, whose fleet then consisted of eighteen steamers, of an aggregate of 99,000 tons, which by 1899 was increased to 164,000. Ismay was also chairman of the Liverpool and London Steamship Protection Association, a director of the London and North Western Railway Company (LNWR), and of many other commercial enterprises. He was also a director of the British Workman Public House Company, founded to provide non-alcoholic refreshments for dockers and seamen. In 1884 he served on Lord Ravensworth's Admiralty committee on contract *versus* dockyard systems of building ships; in 1888 he served on the royal commission on army and navy administration; in 1891 on the royal commission on labour; and on several other important committees. He was chairman of the Board of Trade life saving appliances committee in 1889. He was a liberal supporter of the Liverpool Seamen's Orphan Institution. He was also chairman for over twenty-five years of the *Indefatigable* training ship for destitute boys, and in 1887 he contributed £20,000 towards a pension fund for worn-out Liverpool sailors. He was for some years a JP and deputy lieutenant of Cheshire, and high sheriff in 1892.

Ismay married, on 7 April 1859, Margaret, daughter of Luke Bruce, a local shipowner. The relationship was a supremely happy one. His first home was Enfield House, Great Crosby, 1859–65, then Beech Lawn, Waterloo; finally, in 1884, the magnificent mansion of Dawpool in Thurstaston, Wirral (demolished in 1926), designed by Norman Shaw, later architect of the White Star Line's grand new head office in Liverpool, opened in 1898 and still standing in the late twentieth century. He had nine children, of whom the eldest son, Joseph Bruce *Ismay (1862–1937), succeeded him as chairman of the line. He very much combined the virtues and the shortcomings of his era. Despite being something of a martinet in his family relationships, he clearly commanded immense affection and respect within and outside the family circle. Just as Dawpool was grand, but comfortless, so he was both compassionate, dutiful, and pious, yet aloof. His shipping line was the first to provide proper family accommodation for the third (steerage) class and his charitable largesse in both life and death was extensive, as was his magnanimity to business rivals in crisis. Ismay died at Dawpool, as a result of a liver abscess and heart attack combined, on 23 November 1899, and was buried four days later in the churchyard of Thurstaston, Cheshire, after a memorial service in St Nicholas's Church, Liverpool. He was survived by his wife.   J. GORDON READ

Sources W. J. Oldham, *The Ismay line* (1961) · R. Anderson, *White Star* (1964) · C. W. Jones, *Pioneer shipowners*, 2 vols. [1935–8] · J. G. Read, 'Ismay, Thomas Henry', *DBB* · *Journal of Commerce* (24 Nov 1899) · *Shipping Telegraph* (24 Nov 1899) · *Syren and Shipping* (29 Nov 1899) · *CGPLA Eng. & Wales* (1900)
Archives National Museums and Galleries on Merseyside, Liverpool · NMM, diaries, 1856 · priv. coll., Philip Nelson letter-books · priv. coll., G. H. Fletcher, diary extracts | NMM, diaries of Mrs T. H. Ismay
Likenesses T. Millais, oils, 1885, priv. coll. · H. von Herkomer, oils, priv. coll. · Lib [L. Prosperi], chromolithograph caricature, NPG; repro. in *VF* (15 Nov 1894) · photographs, repro. in *Teutonic*, presentation album, 1889 · photographs, Maritime Archive and Library
Wealth at death £1,297,881 14s. 1d.: probate, 9 March 1900, *CGPLA Eng. & Wales*

Issigonis, Sir Alexander Arnold Constantine (1906–1988), motor engineer and designer, was born on 18 November 1906 in Smyrna, Turkey, the only child of Constantine Issigonis (1872–1923), a marine engineer resident in Smyrna who was of Greek origin but had British citizenship, and his wife, Hulda Josephine Henriette Prokopp (1884–1972), whose family came from Bavaria and ran Smyrna's brewery. A comfortable childhood, during which Alec was taught by private tutors, was abruptly ended by the First World War, during which Greece and Turkey supported opposite sides and the Issigonis factory was confiscated. Following the war, the city came under Greek control until 1922, when Turkey invaded and the Issigonis family was evacuated along with other British citizens. Constantine Issigonis died in Malta in 1923, and his wife and son travelled to London alone. Hulda Issigonis wanted her son to continue his broken education, but despite suggestions that his drawing talent pointed to art school, Alec enrolled at Battersea Polytechnic as an engineering student in 1925.

Though he failed his final exams because of his weakness in mathematics and therefore obtained only a diploma rather than the honours degree he had hoped for, Issigonis was determined to pursue an engineering career and joined Edward Gillett in London in 1928, assisting in the design of a semi-automatic clutch. This earned him a job at Humber in Coventry in 1934, as a technical draughtsman, and he began experimental designs for independent front suspension, which he continued after joining Morris Motors in Oxford in 1936. During the Second World War Issigonis worked on various military projects, but simultaneously he began his first complete car design, which went into production in October 1948 as the Morris Minor. This small car was praised for its use of space, and its steering and road-holding capacities. It continued in production for twenty-four years, during which over 1.6 million were produced. Following this success, Issigonis was promoted to chief engineer in 1950. When Morris Motors merged with Austin Motors to form the British Motor Corporation (BMC) in 1952, he briefly moved to Alvis in Coventry, but in 1955 returned to BMC as deputy engineering co-ordinator, based in Birmingham.

Petrol rationing, arising out of the 1956 Suez crisis, prompted motor manufacturers to think about small, fuel-efficient cars, and Issigonis was asked to head a team to design such a car for BMC. Just two years later, in 1959, the Mini was launched and was quickly recognized to be a revolutionary vehicle. A transverse-mounted engine with front-wheel drive gave maximum space utilization, with room for four adults, while the strikingly functional bodyshell, shaped like a box, and only 10 feet long, resulted from Issigonis's insistence that a 'styled' car quickly dated. His instinct was vindicated by over three decades of continuous production, during which figures had reached 5 million by 1986. Though priced for the mass market, the Mini actually achieved its success as a 'cult' car, popular with the middle classes, particularly women, used by the rich and famous, and spectacularly successful

Sir Alexander Arnold Constantine Issigonis (1906–1988), by Snowdon, 1979

in motor sport. It was probably the last great product of one man's vision the car industry is likely to see.

Issigonis's career was at its high point. In 1961 he became technical director of BMC, in 1963 he was given a seat on the board, and in 1964 he became engineering director. He continued to design successful cars, including the 1100/1300 range, launched in 1962 and the best-selling car of its day; but when BMC became part of the car giant British Leyland in 1968 innovation was sacrificed for 'market research', something Issigonis abhorred. In 1971 he officially retired, and though he was retained by the company as consultant, continuing to produce original designs for a steam-engined car and a gearless Mini, neither of these was ever manufactured.

Issigonis never married, but was a man of great personal charm, occasionally irascible, who formed enduring friendships. Among his close friends were celebrities such as Lord Snowdon and Peter Ustinov. His working relationships seem to have been less relaxed, perhaps because of his need to be in complete control, his eye for detail, and his demanding work schedules. Colleagues were often irritated by his arrogant and impatient manner, but they also felt proud to be associated with one of his projects. His appearance was Mediterranean with his aquiline nose and large hands, yet his manner was very English and friends remembered his eloquent eyes and wry expression. He considered himself to be a creative artist rather than a number-cruncher, and his cars are very much the

creation of an individual with a strong personality, not pieces of styled metal constructed by a committee.

Issigonis's life was one of contrasts. His youth in Smyrna was relatively affluent but was followed by the privations caused by war. His middle years were spent in Oxford, where he built a career of personal achievement, while providing financial security for himself and his mother, who lived with him throughout her life. The years of his greatest success, which came when he was already over fifty, were spent in Birmingham, where he remained a man of simple tastes, which were reflected both in the practicality of his designs and the austerity which characterized his private life. His recreations were also modest, and included a model railway and love of Meccano sets.

His contribution to society brought him a number of distinctions. In 1964 he was elected a royal designer for industry and appointed CBE. In 1967 he became a fellow of the Royal Society. In 1969 he was knighted for 'services to automotive engineering'. In his later years Issigonis became increasingly reclusive because of the onset of Ménière's disease, a hearing impediment which affected his balance. His health deteriorated rapidly towards the end and the need to pay for constant nursing care forced him to sell the bungalow in Edgbaston, Birmingham, which he had shared with his mother until her death in 1972. He moved to a small flat in nearby Hindon Square where he died a few months later on 2 October 1988.

GILLIAN BARDSLEY, rev.

Sources A. Nahum, *Alec Issigonis* (1988) · L. Pomeroy, *The Mini story* (1964) · *The Times* (4 Oct 1988) · D. Downs, *Memoirs FRS*, 39 (1994), 199–212 · private information (1996) [family: Mrs M. Ransome] · R. Barker, 'Issigonis', *Car* (Dec 1988) · D. B. Tubbs, 'Parties to design', *The Motor* (28 Aug 1963)
Archives British Motor Industry Heritage Trust, Gaydon, Warwickshire, artefacts, photographs, and working and private papers
Likenesses Viner, photograph, 1965, Hult. Arch. · B. Griffin, photograph, 1978, NPG · Snowdon, photograph, 1979, NPG [see illus.]
Wealth at death £112,028: probate, 24 Nov 1988, *CGPLA Eng. & Wales*

Issouf Reis. *See* Ward, John (*c.*1553–1623?).

Íte ingen Chinn Fhalad (*d.* **570/577**). *See under* Munster, saints of (*act. c.*450–*c.*700).

Ívarr [Ívarr inn Beinlausi, Ingwaer, Imhar] (*d.* **873**), viking leader, is a figure the facts of whose life are difficult to disentangle from legendary accretions. In the saga tradition of the thirteenth century and later he was one of the many sons of Ragnarr Lodbrók (Ragnarr Hairy Breeches), a Danish king (or, alternatively, a Norwegian chieftain) whose historicity is very uncertain indeed.

Ívarr's earliest appearance in contemporary or near-contemporary sources comes in the Irish annals, which name an Ívarr (appearing there as Imhar) as the companion of Óláf the White. In 857 the two won a victory in Munster against a group of other Scandinavians and renegade Irish (*Ann. Ulster*, s.a. 856). The late medieval 'fragmentary annals' claim a victory for Ívarr over a similar force in the following year. By 859 Ívarr and Óláf had allied with Cerball mac Dúngaile (d. 888), king of Osraige, and together they attacked the lands in Meath of the high-king Máel Sechnaill mac Máele Ruanaid (d. 863). Cerball soon submitted to Máel Sechnaill, but it is likely that Ívarr and Óláf were the leaders of those 'foreigners' (that is, vikings) whom the annals record as the allies of the northern Uí Néill king Áed Findliath mac Néill (d. 879) in his campaigns in Meath in the following two years. The alliance did not last. In 863, in conjunction with Lorcán, king of Meath, and together with another viking leader named Auisl, Ívarr and Óláf plundered the territory of Áed's nephew Flann mac Conaing, including the spiritually significant Boyne tumuli of Knowth, Dowth, and Newgrange. The enmity with Áed thus created may account for Ívarr's absence from Irish sources, and from Ireland, for the next eight years.

Direct authority for the presence of an Ívarr among the leadership of the 'great heathen army' that arrived in England in the autumn of 865 is not contemporary, appearing first in the Latin version of the chronicle written by Æthelweard (d. 998?), where the name is given as Iguuar. The ninth-century Anglo-Saxon Chronicle, the most contemporary source, does not name him in its annals recording the army's progress, but indicates his status by naming him in connection with an event in which he took no part, the defeat of 'the brother of Ingwaer and Healfdene [Hálfdan]' in Devon in 878 (ASC, s.a. 878). Later sources tell of three brothers who were leaders of the army. As well as *Hálfdan, text F of the Anglo-Saxon Chronicle names Ubba along with Ívarr as heading the army in East Anglia, and the life of St Oswald by Byrhtferth (fl. c.986–c.1016) records that Oswald's grandfather had come to England from Scandinavia in the army led by Huba and Hinwaer. In addition, the life of St Edmund by Abbo of Fleury (d. 1004) makes Igwaer the conqueror of East Anglia. On the assumption that these sources are correct in identifying this Ívarr as a leader of the great army, his movements can be traced through the Anglo-Saxon Chronicle's record of the progress of the army through England. After wintering in East Anglia from autumn 865, the army moved to York, which it took on 1 November 866. A Northumbrian attempt to retake the city was repelled and the Northumbrian kings Osberht and Ælle killed on 21 March 867. The vikings established Ecgberht as their puppet king in the north before moving, in the autumn of 867, to Nottingham in Mercia. The army returned to York in 868, staying for a year before crossing Mercia to Thetford in East Anglia. At this point they engaged the East Angles, killing their king Edmund (d. 869).

According to Æthelweard, Ívarr died shortly afterwards. The failure of the main West Saxon source, the Anglo-Saxon Chronicle, to mention Ívarr in its record for the ensuing years, and his appearance in its annal for 878 only with the implication that he was no longer present, indicates that he did not participate in the army's campaign in Wessex, which began in the autumn or early winter of 870 with its move to Reading. Irish sources, however, suggest that Æthelweard's date for Ívarr's death is wrong. The annals of Ulster record a siege of 'Ail Cluaithe' by 'Amlaíb

and Ímar' in 870 (Ann. Ulster, s.a. 869; recte 870). It is hard to avoid the conclusion that these were the same Óláf and Ívarr who had been partners in Irish campaigns in the 850s and early 860s and that the chronological coincidence of the disappearance of the name Ívarr from the English scene with its reappearance in Ireland indicates the identity of the two. 'Ail Cluaithe' is a reference to Dumbarton, the chief fortress of the British kingdom of Strathclyde. Ívarr, it seems, having plundered Northumbria, Mercia, and East Anglia, had resuscitated his old alliance with Óláf, and the two are recorded as returning to Dublin from Scotland in the next year 'with two hundred ships, bringing away with them in captivity to Ireland a great prey of Angles and Britons and Picts' (ibid., s.a. 870; recte 871).

According to the annals of Ulster, Ívarr died in 873, 'king of the Norsemen of all Ireland and Britain' (Ann. Ulster, s.a. 872; recte 873). He is the only viking so described in a contemporary source. If the identity between the Irish and English Ívarrs is accepted, then the sheer range of his activities helps to justify this title. Later traditions suggest a high, perhaps unique, prominence among ninth-century viking leaders. Many of the generation that ruled the vikings at Dublin and York in the first half of the tenth century are named in Irish sources as 'the grandsons of Ívarr', including *Ragnall (d. 920/21) and *Sihtric Cáech (d. 927). One of his sons, Sigfrid, ruled in Dublin from c.881 until 888, when he was killed by his brother, probably named Sihtric (Sigtryggr in Norse), who was himself slain in 896. First named as the son of the more or less legendary Ragnarr Lodbrók by the eleventh-century writer Adam of Bremen, Ívarr was given a prominent place in the Icelandic saga tradition of the twelfth century and later, in which he acquired the obscure epithet inn Beinlausi (the Boneless), which may refer to a snake-like attribute, continuing an association in the saga literature in which Ragnarr died in a snake-pit and another son, Sigurd, bore the epithet Orm-í-Auga (Snake-in-the-Eye). English sources such as Abbo of Fleury's life of St Edmund and text F of the Anglo-Saxon Chronicle make Ívarr responsible for the martyrdom of the East Anglian king Edmund. Later Scandinavian sources claim that he disposed of both King Ælle of Northumbria and King Edmund by means of the bloodthirsty, and probably fictitious, 'blood-eagle' ritual, in which the victim's ribs were hacked from his spine and his lungs drawn out through his back.

MARIOS COSTAMBEYS

Sources ASC · Ann. Ulster · S. Keynes, 'The vikings in England', The Oxford illustrated history of the vikings, ed. P. H. Sawyer (1997), 48–82 · A. P. Smyth, Scandinavian kings in the British Isles, 850–880 (1977) · C. P. Wormald, 'Viking studies: whence and whither?', The vikings, ed. R. T. Farrell (1982), 128–56 · The chronicle of Æthelweard, ed. and trans. A. Campbell (1962) · Adam of Bremen, Magistri Adam Bremenensis gesta Hammaburgensis ecclesiae pontificum, ed. W. Trillmich and R. Buchner (1968) · Abbo of Fleury, Passio sancti Eadmundi, Three lives of English saints, ed. M. Winterbottom (1972), 67–87 · Fróði Ari þorgilsson, Íslendingabók / Landnámabók, ed. J. Benediktsson, 1 (Reykjavik, 1968) · J. N. Radner, ed., Fragmentary annals of Ireland (1978) · 'Ragnars saga loðbrókar ok sona hans', Fornaldarsögur Norðurlanda, ed. G. Jónsson and B. Vilhjálmsson, 1 (Reykjavik, 1943) · [Byrhtferth of Ramsey], 'Vita sancti Oswaldi auctore anonymo', *The historians of the church of York and its archbishops*, ed. J. Raine, 1, Rolls Series, 71 (1879), 399–475

Ive, Paul (*d.* 1604), military engineer, was English but of uncertain origin. He styled himself as 'gent.' and may have come from Stepney in Middlesex, to whose parish church he made a substantial but otherwise unexplained bequest for poor relief. Although he has been identified as the 'Ive' admitted to Corpus Christi College, Cambridge, in 1560 no further evidence has been found to support this claim.

One of the principal experts on fortification in the latter part of Elizabeth's reign, Ive was described by Sir Walter Ralegh in 1600 as having 'an excellent gift in these works, and that which is rarely joined to such knowledge, as much truth and honesty as any man can have' (*Salisbury MSS*, 10.352). Such praise was hard-earned: Ive travelled and consulted widely as a designer and overseer of construction. But he also served as a military intellectual, penning the first substantial discussion of fortification printed in English and making translations from the international literature of war. One of the most trusted of the Elizabethan state's small cadre of technicians, Ive was thus also an important figure in the introduction of continental military techniques to England.

Ive gained his early experience of fortification in the Low Countries, presumably fighting against the Spanish. He witnessed the construction of several forts from about 1567 onwards and by 1577 had become a military engineer rather than merely an observer. He is first securely recorded in England in 1584, newly arrived from Gravelines to work at Dover harbour and serving as an intermediary in securing the engineering skills of two 'strangers' from Dunkirk. He returned to the Low Countries at the end of 1585 with the earl of Leicester's expeditionary force, surveying forts at Ostend.

Ive refers to his experiences in the Netherlands in his *Practise of Fortification* of 1589, a succinct manual on the design and construction of Italian and Dutch style angle-bastioned fortifications. Dedicated to both Lord Cobham and Sir Francis Walsingham, the text exemplifies a pragmatic and non-doctrinaire approach doubtless attractive to his superiors, avoiding a rigid mathematicism and appealing to the experience and skills of both military men and masons. Likewise, though adept in the practical geometry of fortification design, Ive's surviving maps and plans are pictorial in style rather than severely mathematical. This textbook was issued along with Ive's translation of one of the most widely read of sixteenth-century military texts, Fourquevaux's *Instructions sur le faict de la guerre* (1548). Translated at the request of William Davison, and dedicated to him, the *Instructions for the Warres* was not, however, reissued when a new and expanded edition of *The Practise of Fortification*, dedicated to Elizabeth, appeared in 1597.

In 1593 Ive viewed proposed works at Rye and was also sent to the Channel Islands. Over the next two years he reported on and supervised improvements to existing castles on both Guernsey and Jersey, and also on Jersey was responsible for the new fort of Elizabeth Castle at St

Helier. In 1595 he was commissioned to implement plans at Portsmouth and was then sent by the privy council to consider the fortification of Milford Haven. From 1596 to 1599 he was charged with improving the defences of the Cinque Ports, particularly the strengthening of Dover and Queensborough castles.

Lord Cobham sent him to Ostend in October 1597 and a few months later he was at Falmouth advising on Pendennis Castle, whose new angle-bastioned trace was begun in February 1598. In 1600 he was again on military tour in the Low Countries, now with Henry Percy, ninth earl of Northumberland, to whom he dedicated a 1600 manuscript translation of Simon Stevin's Dutch treatise on fortification, *De sterctenbouwing*. This translation had at least some limited circulation because a second copy, for which Ive was evidently not responsible, survives in Trinity College, Cambridge.

Briefly back in Jersey in late 1600, Ive ended his career in Ireland. He arrived at the siege of Kinsale in late 1601, and he planned its new fort of Castle Park (James Castle). He was later responsible for Haulbowline Fort at Cork and surveys of Youghal and Kinsale harbours. Ive died in June 1604, survived by a daughter, Margaret. He was presumably predeceased by a wife and perhaps also by his son. From the provisions of his will it is likely that he was buried at Castle Park, Kinsale.   STEPHEN JOHNSTON

Sources H. M. Colvin and others, eds., *The history of the king's works*, 3–4 (1975–82) · *Calendar of the manuscripts of the most hon. the marquis of Salisbury*, 24 vols., HMC, 9 (1883–1976), vols. 4–7, 10–11, 17 · J. S. Brewer and W. Bullen, eds., *Calendar of the Carew manuscripts*, 4: *1601–1603*, PRO (1870) · *CSP Ire.*, *1601–3* · will, PRO, PROB 11/105, sig. 9 · R. A. Skelton and J. Summerson, *A description of maps and architectural drawings in the collection made by William Cecil, first Baron Burghley, now at Hatfield House*, Roxburghe Club (1971) · M. Biddle, 'Introduction', in P. Ive, *The practise of fortification* (1972) · G. R. Batho, 'The library of the Wizard Earl: Henry Percy, ninth earl of Northumberland (1564–1632)', *The Library*, 5th ser., 15 (1960), 246–61, esp. 249 · S. Stevin, *The art of war*, ed. W. H. Schukking (1964), 34–6 · S. Bendall, 'Enquire "when the same platte was made and by whome and to what intent": sixteenth-century maps of Romney Marsh', *Imago Mundi*, 47 (1995), 34–48, esp. 38 · *Masters' History of the college of Corpus Christi and the Blessed Virgin Mary in the University of Cambridge*, ed. J. Lamb (1831), 475 · J. Le Patourel, *The building of Castle Cornet, Guernsey* (1958) · R. Loeber, 'Biographical dictionary of engineers in Ireland, 1600–1730', *Irish Sword*, 13 (1977–9), 30–44, 106–22, 230–55, 283–314, esp. 240–41

Archives Hatfield House, Hertfordshire, Cecil papers and maps · LPL, Carew MSS

Wealth at death bequests totalling £660: will, PRO, PROB 11/105, sig. 9

Ive, Simon. *See* Ives, Simon (*bap.* 1600, *d.* 1662).

Ive [Ivy], William (*d.* 1486), theologian, is of unknown origins and parentage. He first came to prominence on his appointment as *magister informator* at Winchester College in 1444. The post was a relatively subordinate one and need not imply that Ive was already an experienced teacher, though it does suggest a reputation for learning in grammar. Ordained a priest in the following year, he remained at Winchester until 1453, receiving his first preferment, to the wardenship of Holy Trinity Chapel in St

Mary's Abbey, Winchester, in October 1450. On leaving Winchester he returned to Oxford to read for a higher degree; he was admitted as a bachelor of theology in 1456, and as a doctor of theology in 1460. While resident in the university he took a leading part in its government, acting as a proxy for William Waynflete, bishop of Winchester (d. 1486), in the endowment of Magdalen College, and as commissary to the chancellor, George Neville, bishop of Exeter (d. 1476), between 1461 and 1463. Such service and connections brought Ive rapid preferment: presented to the crown living of Tempsford, Bedfordshire, in December 1461, he was preferred by the university to the rectory of Appleby, Leicestershire, in the following year, and acquired the Salisbury prebend of Urchfont, Wiltshire, in 1463.

In July 1464 Ive secured the influential living of St Michael Paternoster Royal in London, which carried with it the mastership of Whittington College. Ive immediately took his place among a small group of London theologians, the holders of prosperous city livings, who acted as the arbiters and defenders of orthodoxy in the capital. He preached before Edward IV on several occasions, publicly protesting on one of them at the censorship of court sermons exercised by William Say, dean of the king's chapel, and also for several years 'kept the scolys at Poulys set up undyr the chapter house' (Gairdner, 203). It is possible that Ive was the author of the continuation of the London chronicle known as Gregory's chronicle, in which his own actions are prominently reported. He took a leading role in the controversy with the Carmelite friars that occupied the London secular clergy between 1464 and 1468. This centred on a revival of the doctrine of apostolic poverty by John Milverton (d. 1487), prior of the London Carmelite convent. The doctrine was disliked both by the London clergy, who suspected the friars of encouraging the laity to withhold their tithes, and by the city authorities, who feared an outbreak of public disorder. Ive refuted the Carmelite propositions in a series of public disputations, held both at St Paul's and in Oxford, between December 1464 and May 1465, and drew up an account of the incident that secured papal condemnation of Milverton's errors. His reward was preferment to the chancellorship of Salisbury in May 1470, still a position of considerable intellectual prestige, together with appointment to the mastership of De Vaux College, the small Salisbury house of studies situated just outside the cathedral close. He continued to hold both posts, together with the rectory of Odiham, Hampshire, a living annexed to the chancellorship, and the prebend of Brixworth, Northamptonshire, until his death in 1486, before 6 March. Ive was buried in Salisbury Cathedral, 'between the two piers on the south side, opposite the door called *speciosa*' (PRO, PROB 11/7, fol. 174).

A copy of Ive's *Lectiones de mendicitate Christi*, delivered during the Carmelite controversy, survives (Bodl. Oxf., MS Lat. theol. e.25, fols. 1–26), and several further sets of sermons and determinations are ascribed to him by Bale. He is also noted as supervising a translation of the New Testament into English for a devout laywoman (JRL, MS Eng.

77). Among the books he bequeathed in his will to Winchester, Magdalen, and New colleges were Peter Lombard's *Psalterium glossatum*, the epistles of Jerome, and works by Grosseteste, Neckam, and Wyclif. His career embodies the ideal of an active and spiritual churchmanship, combining learning with effective involvement in worldly affairs, which was displayed by many Wykehamist-trained clergy in this period.

Simon Walker

Sources Emden, *Oxf.*, 2.1008–9 · F. R. H. Du Boulay, 'The quarrel between the Carmelite friars and the secular clergy of London, 1464–1468', *Journal of Ecclesiastical History*, 6 (1955), 156–74 · Bodl. Oxf., MS Lat. theol. e.25, fols. 1–26 · PRO, PROB 11/7, fols. 173v–174 · J. Gairdner, ed., *The historical collections of a citizen of London in the fifteenth century*, CS, new ser., 17 (1876) · *VCH Wiltshire*, 3.369–85 · M. Deansley, *The Lollard Bible* (1920), 336 · J. A. F. Thomson, 'The continuation of *Gregory's Chronicle*—a possible author?', *British Museum Quarterly*, 36 (1971–2), 92–7
Archives Bodl. Oxf., MS Lat. theol. e.25

Iveagh. For this title name *see* Guinness, Edward Cecil, first earl of Iveagh (1847–1927); Guinness, Rupert Edward Cecil Lee, second earl of Iveagh (1874–1967); Guinness, Gwendolen Florence Mary, countess of Iveagh (1881–1966); Guinness, (Arthur Francis) Benjamin, third earl of Iveagh (1937–1992).

Ives, Edward (d. 1786), naval surgeon and traveller, is of obscure origins; of his early life little is known save that he had at least one sister, Gatty. He served in the navy as surgeon of the *Namur* in the Mediterranean from 1744 to 1746, and returned to England in the *Yarmouth*. He was afterwards for some time employed by the commissioners for sick and wounded. Ives married about 1751 Ann, daughter of Richard Roy of Titchfield; they had a daughter, Eliza, and three sons, the eldest of whom, Edward Otto, was in Bengal in 1786; the second, Robert Thomas, was appointed to a writership about the same year; the third, John Richard, was much the youngest.

From 1753 to 1757 Ives was surgeon of the *Kent*, bearing the flag of Vice-Admiral Charles Watson as commander-in-chief in the East Indies. The squadron sailed via the Cape of Good Hope and Madagascar to India, where they visited the chief English settlements and major cities, Ives attending the company hospitals and staff in each place. On the admiral's death in August 1757, his own health being somewhat impaired, he resigned his appointment, and travelled home overland from Basrah, through Baghdad, Mosul, and Aleppo, thence by Cyprus, to Leghorn and Venice, and so home through Germany and the Netherlands, arriving in England in March 1759.

Ives had no further service in the navy, but he continued on the half-pay list until 1777, when he was superannuated. In 1773 he published *A Voyage from England to India*, which described his journey to India, his experiences there, and his overland route home. Ives's presence at many of the events which he describes and his close relationship with Vice-Admiral Watson give his historical narrative an unusual importance, and his accounts of the manners and customs of the inhabitants, of the diseases and medical practices, of the natural history, and of the products of the countries he visited, some then little known to Europeans, are those of an acute and, for his time, relatively enlightened observer. During his later years Ives resided at Titchfield in Hampshire, dividing his time between literature and farming. He died at Bath on 25 September 1786.

J. K. LAUGHTON, rev. ELIZABETH BAIGENT

Sources *GM*, 1st ser., 56 (1786), 908 · will, proved, London, 1787, Principal Registry of the Family Division, London · *Navy List* · D. V. S. Reddy, 'Medical observations of Dr Edward Ives, a naval surgeon (1754–1757)', *Indian Journal of the History of Medicine*, 13/2 (1968), 31–44
Wealth at death see will, Principal Registry of the Family Division, London

Ives, Jeremiah (*fl.* 1646–1674), Leveller, was a cheesemonger by trade who spent most of his adult life in London. Of his birth and early years nothing is known, but in 1672 he recalled a thirty-year association with the Baptists, and this may suggest his conversion took place about the start of the civil war. Probably in 1646 Ives toured mid-Wales with Hugh Evans, the Radnor Baptist lay preacher. He may already have joined the parliamentarian army. It was reported that on 6 September 1646 Jeremiah Ives, together with Captain Henry Pretty and the Baptist evangelist Thomas Lambe, interrupted a church service at Devizes, 'armed in a most irreverent manner, to the abominable disturbance of the whole congregation' (Edwards, 3.30–31). On 3 January 1647 a trooper Ives preached at Buckingham, arousing violent opposition from local cavaliers and opponents of lay preaching; soldiers of Colonel Herbert's regiment came to his aid, and blood was shed.

Ives was a radical in politics as well as in religion. On 6 July 1647, as the 'agitator' of Hardress Waller's regiment, he co-signed a letter of protest at the presbyterian purge of the London militia. On 23 November that year he was one of five leading radicals imprisoned by order of the House of Commons, and spent time in Newgate prison. Ives and his collaborators were officially charged with sedition in canvassing in the army the Levellers' *Agreement of the People*; a hostile pamphleteer also accused them of planning to kill Charles I. By May 1648 Ives was a trooper in Whalley's horse regiment; about a year later he received a commission as its chaplain, and served the regiment in this capacity during its Scottish service, from May to October 1650.

In November 1653 Ives was reported to be preaching in Littlebury, Essex, but may not have stayed there long. In 1655, from his house in Red Crosse Street, Jeremiah Ives, cheesemonger, published an account of a public dispute, the first of many contests against Quakers and clergymen. In these, the conventions of formal debate were rarely honoured. Ives complained that the minister Thomas Willes had traduced him as a Jesuit, and that his own voice had been drowned by 'a tumultuous auditory: some pulling and hauling me; others threatening to throw me over the gallery' (Ives, *Confidence Questioned*, 'To the reader'). Ives was involved in continuing resistance to government attempts to restrict religious toleration: he was among those who campaigned on behalf of the imprisoned John Biddle, perhaps partly because Biddle's Socinianism was attracting support among General Baptists, but it is clear that political principles were also involved. When, in 1659, the re-restoration of the Rump Parliament was being canvassed, Ives opposed it. He recalled the names of those leading Levellers who had once been 'accounted the greatest asserters of their country's liberties, when they refused to comply with the votes of the then free and uninterrupted Parliament' (Ives, *Eighteen Questions*, 3).

Ives had been commissioned in July 1659 as a lieutenant of the London militia in the service of the Rump, but his preference in November was for the establishment of something along the lines of the Barebone's Parliament of 1653. Ives had helped build the radical General Baptist lay tradition of the 1640s, alongside men such as Samuel Oates and Thomas Lambe. In the next decade these veterans found themselves at odds with many of the newer generation of General Baptist leaders, who warned against political agitation and sought to introduce the ceremony of the laying-on of hands by ministers upon newly rebaptized members. Ives and his co-thinkers opposed these efforts; they did not attend, and refused the discipline of, the 'general assemblies' which sought to build a national denomination around such principles. Seventh day (Saturday) sabbath observance was also winning support among Baptists and in 1659, at the Stone Chapel near St Paul's, Ives debated with some of its leading adherents, including Peter Chamberlen.

In April 1660, following Lambert's escape from the Tower, a warrant was issued for the arrest of 'Hieronomo Ives', and it is also likely that he was in prison in the wake of the Venner revolt in January 1661. At first Ives refused the oath of allegiance, but later changed his mind, and (it was said) was freed as a result. *The Great Case of Conscience Opened*, of February 1661, rehearsed the traditional argument that oaths were permissible both as necessary devices of the common law and as civil duties, but also omitted the traditional view that they could be resisted as instruments of oppression. Quakers, and many General Baptists, remained in prison because of their refusal of all oaths on principle, and Ives was sharply criticized. He seems to have stayed in London, moving at some point before early 1672 to Walbrook, but he seems not to have abandoned entirely the itinerant ways of his youth. That year he was licensed to preach in Reading, where he had a correspondent, Daniel Roberts, and a contemporary complained in 1674 of his preaching in the market place at Croydon.

It was also reported that Charles II arranged a dispute at court between Ives, who was persuaded to dress as an Anglican clergyman, and a Roman Catholic priest. The king, it is clear, also expected that his champion would defend Baptist positions, and Ives did not disappoint. As the argument unfolded, the priest grew increasingly baffled by the wild unorthodoxy of the 'minister'; when the truth at last emerged, he broke off the discussion and departed in high dudgeon. 'This behaviour of the priest afforded his majesty and all present not a little diversion' (Crosby, 4.247–8). The story may be apocryphal, but Ives did win fame as a controversialist, especially against Quakers. In 1655–6 he took part in several ill-tempered public contests with James Nayler. Other opponents included James Parnell, and, in 1669, William Penn. In 1674 Ives also became involved in the case of one Thomas Hick, a Particular Baptist who, the Quakers claimed, had crudely misrepresented their views. It is interesting that Ives felt impelled to defend him, and persisted in debating with Quakers angry about the issue long after Hick's own co-thinkers, Kiffin and others, abandoned the fray.

For twenty years Ives was a favourite butt of Quaker criticism. This partly reflects the sheer persistence of his efforts against them, but it may also testify to his effectiveness, acquired through long experience as a popular speaker. It was charged that many 'discreet and sober' Baptists were themselves uneasy at Ives's theatrical technique: 'people say, it smells of ranter or atheism' (Rudyard, 23–4). His printed works were certainly sharp and popular in tone, unencumbered with the heavy machinery of syllogism and proof text; the writer's taste for poking fun at his opponents may well indicate his oratorical style. The Quaker Thomas Ellwood conceded that Ives knew both logic and scripture, but charged that he was too fond of his drink and that 'his chief Art lay in tickling the humours of rude, unlearned and injudicious hearers; thereby insinuating himself into their good opinion' (Ellwood, 313). Ellwood also reports that Ives died soon after the Hick controversy. So it may be: nothing further is known of the life, or death, of Jeremiah Ives.

STEPHEN WRIGHT

Sources J. Ives, *Confidence encountered* (1658) · J. Ives, *Confidence questioned* (1658) · J. Ives, *A contention for truth* (1672) · J. Ives, *The corrector corrected* (1672) · J. Ives, *Eighteen questions propounded* (1659) · J. Ives, *The great case of conscience opened* (1661) · J. Ives, *Infants baptism disproved* (1655) · J. Ives, *Innocency above impudency* (1656) · J. Ives, *The Quakers quaking* (1656) · J. Ives, *Saturday no sabbath* (1659) · J. Ives, *A sober request to the Quakers* (1674) · J. Ives, *A stop to a lying pamphlet ... Kellie* (1656) · J. Ives, *Vindiciae veritatis, or, An impartial account* (1672) · *A bloody independent plot discovered* (1647) · *A bloody plot discovered against the Independents* (1647) · *CSP dom.*, 1659–60, 547 · T. Crosby, *The history of the English Baptists, from the Reformation to the beginning of the reign of King George I*, 4 vols. (1738–40) · T. Edwards, *Gangraena, or, A catalogue and discovery of many of the errours, heresies, blasphemies and pernicious practices of the sectaries of this time*, 3 vols. in 1 (1646) · T. Ellwood, *The history of the life of Thomas Ellwood*, ed. S. Graveson (1906), 312–17 · I. Gentles, *The New Model Army in England, Ireland, and Scotland, 1645–1653* (1992) · R. L. Greaves, *Deliver us from evil: the radical underground in Britain, 1660–1663* (1986), 59 · S. Hodgkin, *A caution to the sons of Sion* (1661) · *JHC*, 5 (1646–8), 368 · *Kingdomes Weekly Intelligencer* (1647), 394–5 · A. Laurence, *Parliamentary army chaplains, 1642–1651*, Royal Historical Society Studies in History, 59 (1990), 138 · H. J. McLachlan, *Socinianism in seventeenth-century England* (1951) · T. Plant, *A contest for Christianity* (1674) · J. Price, *The sun outshining the moon* (1658), 10 · T. Rudyard, *The Anabaptists printed proposals* (1674) · W. Shewen, *The universality of the light which shines* (1674) · A. Taylor, *The history of the English General Baptists*, 2 vols. (1818), 253–9 · 'White, B. R.', Greaves & Zaller, *BDBR* · E. B. Underhill, ed., *Records of the Churches of Christ, gathered at Fenstanton, Warboys, and Hexham, 1644–1720*, Hanserd Knollys Society (1854) · G. Whitehead, *A serious search* (1674) · C. Whiting, *Studies in English puritanism* (1931), 165–9 · D. M. Wolfe, ed., *Leveller manifestoes of the puritan revolution* (1944), 237–41

Ives, John (1751–1776), antiquary and herald, was born at 65 Middlegate Street, Great Yarmouth, on 14 July 1751, son of John Ives (1719–1793), a rich merchant with several houses there and a country residence at Belton in Suffolk, and Mary Hannott (1718–1790), daughter of James Hannott, also a Yarmouth merchant, and granddaughter of a Congregationalist minister of the same name. He was baptized at the Congregationalist Old Meeting in Middlegate Street, and it was from a Congregationalist minister in the town that Ives received his earliest instruction before being sent, briefly, to Norwich grammar school in 1762. A further phase of private education was intended to be followed by residence at Gonville and Caius College, Cambridge, but this did not take place and in 1767 Ives went to work in his father's counting-house.

Employment was neither necessary nor convenient, however, for Ives had already developed a passionate and acquisitive interest in British antiquities which his father's affluence allowed him to indulge freely. In June 1770 he visited the Norfolk antiquary 'Honest Tom' Martin at his house in Palgrave, and a brief but advantageous friendship resulted. When Martin died the following March, Ives assisted his widow in the administration of the estate, buying large numbers of the deceased's important manuscripts in the process. Many of these had come to Martin from the antiquaries Peter Le Neve and Francis Blomefield and were of great value for the local history of East Anglia. When Martin's *History of Thetford* came out in 1771, Ives—who was elected FSA on 13 June 1771—paid for it to be prefaced with an engraving of the author. Largely working from the manuscripts he had acquired from Martin, Ives now began to assemble material for a history of Lothingland, the north-easternmost part of Suffolk where the family home of Belton was. His original contribution to the project, which was announced by prospectus in 1771, followed the traditional twin approach of church notes and a questionnaire circulated among the local clergy. No publication resulted, though a manuscript version was seen by D. E. Davy in 1831: his copy of it, entitled 'Collectanea Lothinglandia, or, The history and antiquities of the hundred of Lothingland', survives among his papers in the British Library. In part, Ives's energies were doubtless taken up by editing and seeing through the press the *History and Antiquities of Great Yarmouth* by Henry Swinden, another former habitué of Palgrave, who died just as printing of his work ended in 1772.

Backed by his father's money, Ives was also fully occupied both as a collector, retaining others to search for and acquire manuscripts, seals, and other artefacts on his behalf, and as a liberal patron and benefactor, paying for the engraving of portraits, which he distributed to interested parties, and facsimile seal impressions: his *Sigilla antiqua Norfolcensia*, nine woodcuts of medieval seals with commentary by himself, came out in 1772. Paternal munificence was presumably also responsible for Ives's acquisition of a private press at about this time, one early production of which was a rather leaden-footed 'pastoral

John Ives (1751–1776), by Peter Spendelowe Lamborn, pubd 1822 (after J. S.)

elegy' in memory of Thomas Martin. More useful was a printed copy, dated 5 September 1772, of the baptismal and burial registers of Great Yarmouth for the preceding nine years. Ives did not, however, print at his own press the three parts of his *Select Papers Chiefly Relating to English Antiquities* (1773, 1774, and 1775). Based upon the *Miscellaneous Antiquities* of Horace Walpole, to whom the first issue was dedicated, these three slim volumes contained editions of various documents in Ives's possession, including 'Remarks upon our English coins' by Archbishop Sharp of York, Dugdale's 'Directions for the search of records', Blomefield's 'Annals of Gonvile and Caius', and accounts of the coronations of Henry VII and Elizabeth.

Ives was elected FRS on 25 March 1773, and that summer eloped with a long-standing sweetheart, Sarah Kett (1750–1826), daughter of Wade Kett of Lopham in Norfolk, marrying her by special licence at Lambeth on 16 July 1773. Parental disapproval of this alliance soon abated, and his father gave the couple one of his houses in Great Yarmouth to live in on their return.

In 1774 Ives brought out his *Remarks upon the Garianonum of the Romans*, an essay on Burgh Castle near Belton. Following Camden, he identified this Roman camp (used as a castle in Norman times) with the site referred to as Garianonum by the fourth-century *Notitia dignitatum*: though the name is now usually rendered Gariannum this identification is now generally accepted. Despite misinterpreting the Norman motte as the praetorium of the Roman camp and engaging in certain speculations, now disproved, about the building techniques used, the work is of value for giving a detailed account of the contemporary state of the monument and a résumé of the site finds,

culled both from Blomefield's notes and from information deriving from Ives's own great-grandfather (to whom the site had belonged). Illustrations of the motte (levelled in 1837) and the Anglo-Saxon pottery found near by have also proved valuable. In October 1774 Ives was appointed Suffolk herald-extraordinary at the College of Arms: this did not necessarily give him access to the college records, but correspondence from late 1775 between him and J. C. Brooke, then Rouge Croix pursuivant, indicates that he was on friendly terms with the officers-in-ordinary. The same letters refer to the decline in his health, which was due to consumption: he died at Great Yarmouth on 9 January 1776. He was buried with his family in Belton church and commemorated by a Latin inscription there. In accordance with his will his collections were auctioned in the spring of 1777 in London, the proceeds going to Sarah, his widow. She married in 1796 the Revd David Davis, and later resided with him at Clifton in Bristol. Ives's boyish looks are preserved in several engravings, and companion miniatures of Ives (in herald's tabard) and his wife, belonging to a relative of her second husband, are held on loan at the College of Arms: they are thought to be by George Roth the younger.   C. E. A. CHEESMAN

Sources N. Scarfe, 'John Ives, FRS and FSA, Suffolk herald extraordinary, 1751–1776', *Proceedings of the Suffolk Institute of Archaeology*, 33 (1973–5), 299–309 • [D. Turner], 'Preface by the editor', in J. Ives, *Garianonum of the Romans*, 2nd edn (1803), iii–xx • D. Turner, *Sepulchral reminiscences of a market town* (1848), 47, 127–9 • *Letters between Rev. James Granger … and many of the most eminent literary men of his time*, ed. J. P. Malcom (1805), 99–101, 296–9, 299–300 • J. Fenn, 'Memoirs of the life of Thomas Martin, Gent.', *Norfolk Archaeology*, 15 (1903–4), 233–66 • C. J. Palmer, *The perlustration of Great Yarmouth*, 2 (1874), 42, 44–5, 71–2, 102, 119, 379–80, 401–8 • C. J. Palmer, *The perlustration of Great Yarmouth*, 3 (1875), 396–7 • J. Ives, 'Collectanea Lothinglandia, or, The history and antiquities of the hundred of Lothingland in the county of Suffolk', BL, Add. MS 19098 [D. E. Davy's Suffolk Collections, vol. 22], fols. 8r–10v, 376r–425r • J. Ives, 'Suffolk church notes', BL, Add. MS 19199 • J. Ives, notes and papers, Bodl. Oxf., MS Eng. misc. c. 136 • J. Ives, letters to J. C. Brooke, Bodl. Oxf., MS Eng. misc. c. 221, fols. 27, 32, 35 • D. Bonhote, letters to J. Ives, Ipswich Museum, Steward MSS • will, Norfolk, 1776 • Nichols, *Lit. anecdotes*, 3.197–200; 9.428–9, 610–11 • Nichols, *Illustrations*, 3.608–9 • M. Noble, *A history of the College of Arms* (1804), 445–7 • T. W. King, pedigree of Ives family, 1851, Coll. Arms, Collectanea Jernemuensia, vol. 34, pp. 10–11 • Congregationalist Old Meeting registers, PRO

Archives Bodl. Oxf., notes and papers • Coll. Arms, Suffolk collections • Yale U., Farmington, Lewis Walpole Library, journal, notes, and memoirs | Suffolk RO, Ipswich, Iveagh MSS

Likenesses attrib. G. Roth junior, miniature, oils, 1774–5, priv. coll.; on loan to Coll. Arms • P. S. Lamborn, etching, pubd 1822 (after J. S.), BM, NPG [*see illus.*] • P. Audinet, line engraving (after F. Perry), BM, NPG; repro. in Nichols, *Lit. anecdotes* • J. Basire, engraving (after drawing by E. Miles), repro. in J. Ives, *Remarks upon the Garianonum of the Romans*, 2nd edn (1803) • engraving, Ipswich Museum, album of Suffolk prints and drawings

Wealth at death books and MSS sold for £525 9s. 3d.: BL copy of sale catalogue, 824.b.17.3, with MS additions

Ives [Ive], **Simon** (*bap.* 1600, *d.* 1662), musician, was born at Ware in Hertfordshire and baptized on 20 July 1600. Nothing is known of his education or upbringing, but about 1626 he was living at Earl's Colne in Essex. Someone of that name was made groom of the chamber extraordinary at court on 27 April 1630, and about the same time he may have become organist of Christ Church, Newgate. Together with William Lawes, and at the invitation of Bulstrode Whitelocke (whom he assisted in composing 'Whitelocke's coranto'), he provided music for James Shirley's inns of court masque *The Triumph of Peace*, put on in honour of the king and queen at Whitehall on 3 February 1634, and ten days later at the Merchant Taylors' hall. He also sang countertenor and played the theorbo in the masque, receiving £100 for his part in the proceedings. The following year he became one of the London waits and may have remained teaching in London after the outbreak of the civil war. He is mentioned as one of Susanna Perwich's music masters in John Batchiler's *The Virgin's Pattern* (1661). At the Restoration he is listed as eighth minor canon of St Paul's, but he died at his house in Newgate Street, in the parish of Christ Church, on 1 July 1662, leaving his music and a chest of viols 'wherein are three tenors, one base, and two trebles; also another base' to his fellow petty canons. He bequeathed property to his daughter Mary Body, and other legacies to his son Andrew (including £100) and relatives in Hertfordshire and Essex. Another son, also Simon (*b*. 1626) and a minor composer, was already dead; he had graduated from Cambridge in 1648.

Whitelocke described Ives as 'an honest and able musitian, of excellent skill in his art' (Whitelocke); Wood noted that 'he was excellent at the lyra-viol, and improved it by excellent inventions' (Bodl. Oxf., MS Wood D19 [4]). A considerable amount of lyra-viol music by him, both solo and ensemble pieces, survives in manuscript. Some was published in collections such as John Playford's *Musick's Recreation on the Lyra-Viol* (1652). Also in manuscript are numerous ayres, pavans, and fantasias (including an In nomine) for viol consort, while several songs came out in Playford's *Select Musical Ayres and Dialogues* series (1652–9). Many catches by him were also printed in Playford's *Catch that Catch Can* (1652–85). On a more serious level he contributed an elegy on the death of William Lawes to Henry Lawes's *Choice Psalmes* (1648), but the music for his anthem 'Almighty and everlasting God' (feast of the purification) has not survived. Clearly he was a versatile composer, and, so far as his music has been studied, it seems to demonstrate a capable contrapuntal technique (in the fantasias, for example) as well as a pronounced melodic gift in his lighter music. IAN SPINK

Sources Highfill, Burnim & Langhans, *BDA*, 8.106–7 · N. Josephs, 'Ives, Simon (i)', *New Grove* · [B. Whitelocke], *Memorials of the English affairs* (1682) · A. Ashbee, ed., *Records of English court music*, 3 (1988), 51 · *IGI*

Ivie, Edward (1677/8–1745), Latin poet, was the son of Hugh Ivie, rector of Foscott, Somerset; where Edward was probably born. He was admitted to Westminster School in 1692, matriculated at Christ Church, Oxford, on 6 November 1696, aged eighteen, and graduated BA in 1700, and MA on 11 March 1703. He was given the honour of composing an extended hexameter poem, 'Articuli pacis', for recitation by three gentleman-commoners of the college at the *comitia* of 2 December 1697. This was sufficiently successful to be printed in *Examen poeticum duplex* (1698, 149–57).

The three speakers, Academicus, Mercator, and Colonus, engage in an entertaining discussion of the implications of peace, revealing their different preoccupations and prejudices. The farmer is suspicious of French wine, of Versailles (that affront to lovers of liberty), and of lasting friendship with the traditional enemy (about as likely, the scholar agrees, as lasting peace between the farmer and his wife); one must beware the venereal 'morbus gallicus' (at home, as well as abroad); there is praise of Ormond, and a dig at the Cambridge classicist Richard Bentley. Ivie contributed forty-three hexameters to the Oxford *Exequiae* for the duke of Gloucester (1700, sig. X1r–v), with some effective use of Virgilian allusion: 'tu Gulielmus eris', like the tragic Marcellus of *Aeneid*, vi.883. Another substantial hexameter poem appeared in *Pietas universitatis Oxoniensis in obitum augustissimi regis Gulielmi III* (1702).

After taking orders Ivie preached regularly in Oxford; Thomas Hearne notes several prominent sermons of 1716 and 1717. He was unable in 1713–14, despite the queen's warrant in his favour, to claim the post of schoolmaster at Ewelme—and despite fears in some quarters that under the rival candidate 'the place instead of a school will be a bawdy-house' (*Portland MSS*, 7.181–2). Ivie was appointed chaplain to George Smalridge, bishop of Bristol, formerly dean of Christ Church, and himself a distinguished Latin poet, who encouraged Ivie to complete his major publication, a Latin-verse paraphrase of Epictetus' *Enchiridion* (1715; reprinted 1723, 1804). Ivie thanks Richard Mostyn for additional patronage, and Dr Richard Frewin for ensuring that his health sufficed for the task. The Greek of each chapter is followed by loosely Horatian Latin hexameters, with many rhetorical additions and poetic expansions (so Socrates becomes 'inclytus ille senex patriis damnatus Athenis', 'that famous old man condemned by his native Athens'; ch. 10). Ivie's work reflects wide interest in Epictetus in the period, and a number of other editions in various languages appeared (notably Ellis Walker's English version of 1692, which was reprinted throughout the eighteenth century). Hearne welcomed the second edition of 1723:

> a very excellent Translation … Mr Ivy was several Years about this Translation, and it expresses the Sense of the Original better than any other Translation whatsoever, as, I remember, it was well observ'd by many good Judges soon after the first Edition came out. (*Remarks*, 8.75, 15 May 1723)

Ivie was instituted on 27 March 1717 to the vicarage of Floore, Northamptonshire, where he died on 11 June 1745, aged sixty-seven. D. K. MONEY

Sources Foster, *Alum. Oxon.* · *Remarks and collections of Thomas Hearne*, ed. C. E. Doble and others, 11 vols., OHS, 2, 7, 13, 34, 42–3, 48, 50, 65, 67, 72 (1885–1921), vols. 5–8 · *The manuscripts of his grace the duke of Portland*, 10 vols., HMC, 29 (1891–1931), vol. 7 · E. Ivie, *Epicteti Enchiridion*, 2nd edn (1723) · D. K. Money, *The English Horace: Anthony Alsop and the tradition of British Latin verse* (1998) · University of Oxford, *comitia* programme (1697) · *GM*, 1st ser., 15 (1745), 332

Ivie, John (*c*.1580–1665), magistrate and goldsmith, was born in Wincanton, Somerset, one of at least four sons of Hugh Ivie. He moved to Salisbury before 1600, perhaps as apprentice to his goldsmith uncle, Robert Tyte, and by 1612, when he married Jane Puxton (*d.* 1650), he was already embarked on a career in business and civic politics which, though locally circumscribed, was to last for half a century. Success in trade (silver spoons with his mark survive from the 1620s) accompanied a rapid rise up the civic ladder. He was elected common councillor of Salisbury in 1616, chamberlain in 1620, and alderman in 1623, and he served as mayor in 1626–7 and 1647–8. By the 1640s he was one of the richest men in town, and in 1652, two years after his first wife died, he married Jane Harwood, a widow already related by marriage to other Salisbury goldsmiths. She died in 1657.

Ivie's political associations were as close and effective as his business connections. His power base lay in St Edmund's parish (he was churchwarden during 1618–19), and rested on a formidable alliance with Henry Sherfield and Peter Thatcher, the godly minister they brought in as rector and preacher in 1623. When Sherfield became recorder of Salisbury, also in 1623, their party took control of the municipality and held it for a decade, undertaking a programme of civic reformation of a distinctively puritan kind. 'God's time is come', Sherfield told Ivie when inviting him to become justice of the peace in 1628 (Slack, *Poverty*, 124).

The centrepiece of the godly party's programme was a remodelling of poor relief through new institutions. In 1623 they set up a workhouse supported by a scheme for outdoor employment, and a municipal brewery, like that begun by John White in Dorchester in the previous year, intended to finance the whole effort. A third innovation, Ivie's own invention, was a storehouse, founded in 1627, where the poor obtained food and drink in exchange for tokens which they were given in lieu of the usual cash doles. The aim was to achieve a more perfect reformation of popular manners by adding deliberate control of a large sector of the local economy to the customary punishment of drunkenness and sexual misdemeanours in quarter sessions. The programme failed, partly because of opposition from vested interests, notably local brewers, and partly because the overheads of the new institutions were too great. The storehouse was closed down in 1640 and the brewhouse in 1646. In 1658 a younger generation of Salisbury puritans asked Ivie, now in his seventies, to revive the storehouse, but he failed to get it off the ground in the face of legal challenges from parish overseers. It was no longer, he noted, 'God's time to do any good in this city' (Slack, *Poverty*, 117).

Ivie described the history of the reformation programme in *A Declaration*, published in London in 1661. In breathless and scarcely punctuated prose (suggesting only rudimentary formal education), he defended its ambition and justified its purposes. He also gave a vivid account of the problems of civic government, especially during a plague epidemic in 1627, when, as mayor and the only magistrate still resident in town, he faced popular disorder and the task of relieving the sick and burying the dead. That was the kind of urban crisis which helped to stimulate quests for reformation in other early Stuart towns, like White's Dorchester and the Exeter of Ignatius Jourdain. Written in disillusioned old age, Ivie's *Declaration* is a unique firsthand account of the godly civic activism which motivated such men, and of the local contentions which it provoked between the 1620s and the 1650s.

Ivie was buried on 22 September 1665 in St Edmund's churchyard. He appears to have had no children of his own. After various cash bequests to the poor and to his surviving brothers, nephews, and nieces, he left the residue of his estate to a cousin, also John Ivie, merchant of Salisbury. It included six houses and gardens left in trust for 'six honest godly poor couples' of the town, 'worn out with age and labour' (PROB 11/322, fol. 340*r*).

PAUL SLACK

Sources P. Slack, *Poverty in early-Stuart Salisbury*, Wilts RS, 31 (1975) [incl. Ivie's *A declaration* (1661)] · P. Slack, 'Poverty and politics in Salisbury, 1597–1666', *Crisis and order in English towns, 1500–1700*, ed. P. Clark and P. Slack (1972), 164–203 · T. A. Kent, 'John Ivie, goldsmith', *Hatcher Review*, 3/23 (1987), 130–37 · will, PRO, PROB 11/322, sig. 180 · parish register, St Edmund's, Salisbury, Wiltshire, 1612 [marriage] · parish register, St Edmund's, Salisbury, Wiltshire, 22 Sept 1665 [burial]
Archives Hants. RO, J. L. Jervoise, Herriard collection, Sherfield corresp.
Wealth at death bequests to the poor and to surviving brothers, nephews, and nieces; residue of estate to a cousin, incl. six houses and gardens left in trust for 'six honest godly poor couples' of the town: will, PRO, PROB 11/322, sig. 180

Ivimey, Joseph (1773–1834), Particular Baptist minister and historian, was born on 22 May 1773 at Ringwood, the eldest of the eight children of Charles Ivimey (*d.* 1820), a tailor, and his wife, Sarah Tilly (*d.* 1830). His father's improvidence dictated that Joseph was to have only an elementary education before learning his father's trade. Owing to domestic difficulties, the young Ivimey went to live with a maternal uncle; it was in this household that he started to shed the Arian beliefs of his childhood. He began attending the Baptist church at Wimborne, where he formally espoused Calvinist principles by undergoing baptism on 16 September 1790. He journeyed to London in 1793, hoping for an improvement in his trade, but returned to Ringwood after four months. He left again in 1794 for Portsea, Hampshire, where he became an itinerant preacher, visiting in this capacity many towns in the district. On 7 July 1795 he married Sarah Bramble (*d.* 1807), with whom he had two sons and four daughters; only one son and one daughter were to survive him.

Early in 1803 Ivimey was recognized as a minister, and settled as an assistant at Wallingford. He was chosen minister of the Particular Baptist Church, Eagle Street, Holborn, in October 1804, and was ordained on 16 January 1805. His wife having died the previous year, on 7 January 1808 he married Anne Price (*née* Spence), a widow with three children of her own: she died 2 January 1820.

An advocate of foreign missions, Ivimey served from 1812 on the committee of the Baptist Missionary Society.

When that society declined to add Ireland to its sphere of operation, several London ministers formed the Baptist Society for Promoting the Gospel in Ireland. Ivimey served as (unpaid) secretary from the society's formation in 1814 until 1833. In 1817, and again in 1819, he made missionary journeys to the Channel Islands. Ivimey was the chief proposer of a national body to link the Baptist churches, and acted as one of the first co-secretaries of the Baptist Union from its formation in 1812. From 1821 to 1832 he was the union's sole secretary, maintaining its rather shadowy existence by his perseverance, and was still in office at his death. Ivimey was a conscientious minister and a tireless advocate of closed communion (reserving the sacrament for baptized church members only); in 1827 his strictness caused a secession of some fifty or sixty members of his church. A staunch anti-papist, he feared giving Roman Catholics any share in political power; on this ground he opposed the repeal of the Test and Corporation Acts, and in 1829 broke with the General Body of Protestant Dissenting Ministers of the Three Denominations once it became apparent that they were determined to agitate against all civil disabilities rooted in religious prejudice. On 21 September 1830 he married for a third time, taking as his wife the widowed Elizabeth Gratwick. Ivimey suffered from asthma in later life, and died on 8 February 1834; he was buried at Bunhill Fields, London, on 15 February.

Ivimey was a rapid writer and, from 1808 when he began to publish, a very prolific one. As Iota he contributed to the *Baptist Magazine* from 1809, but he is best known for his *History of the English Baptists*, started in 1809. The *History* swelled to four volumes (1811–30) and contains a great deal of information which should, however, be used only with caution. Most of his other works comprise memorial sermons and tracts and contain a strong anti-Roman Catholic element. He produced a life of Bunyan (1825); his *Pilgrims of the Nineteenth Century* (1827), an effort to continue Bunyan's *Pilgrim's Progress*, also served as a platform from which Ivimey advocated a resolute protestantism.

ALEXANDER GORDON, *rev.* L. E. LAUER

Sources E. C. Starr, ed., *A Baptist bibliography*, 11 (1966), 226–233 · *Baptist Magazine*, 26 (1834), 122–24 · *Baptist Magazine*, 28 (1836), 565–74 · G. Pritchard, *Memoir of the life and writings of the Rev. Joseph Ivimey* (1835) · A. W. Light, *Bunhill Fields: written in honour and to the memory of the many saints of God whose bodies rest in this old London cemetery*, 1 (1913) · 'The body', *Monthly Repository*, new ser., 3 (1829), 426–34 [review] · G. Gould, *Open communion and the Baptists of Norwich* (1860) · E. A. Payne, *The Baptist Union: a short history* (1959)

Likenesses Penny, mezzotint, pubd 1820 (after J. Linnell), NPG

Ivory, Sir James (1765–1842), mathematician and mill manager, born in Dundee, on 17 February 1765, was the eldest son of James Ivory, watchmaker. At the age of fourteen he matriculated at St Andrews University, and after six years' study with a view to becoming a minister of the Scottish church, he went to Edinburgh to complete his theological course. He was accompanied by John Leslie (1766–1832), a fellow student at Aberdeen, who like himself had already evinced a strong mathematical bias.

Ivory returned to Dundee in 1786, and for three years taught in the principal school, introducing the study of algebra and raising the standard of general instruction. He was afterwards one of the founders of a flax-spinning mill at Douglastown, on the Carbet, near Forfar, and acted as managing partner. Henry Peter Brougham (1778–1868), later first Baron Brougham, lord chancellor, but at the time a young advocate, cultivated his acquaintance and visited him at Brigton, near the factory.

Ivory devoted all his leisure to mathematical work, especially to mathematical analysis as it was then practised on the continent. His first papers, read to the Royal Society of Edinburgh in the mid-1790s, included rectifying the ellipse, approximating to the root of an equation, and Kepler's problem.

The flax-spinning partnership was dissolved in 1804 and soon afterwards Ivory was appointed professor of mathematics in the Royal Military College, then at Marlow, Buckinghamshire, and from 1812 at Sandhurst. His work at the college was thorough and successful, though the advanced parts of the science absorbed much of his attention; he also prepared an edition of Euclid's *Elements* for military students. In 1809 he published the paper for which he is best remembered: it contained a theorem relating in effect the components of the attractions at any surface point to those at a particular point in its interior (or alternatively to surface attractions on two confocal ellipsoids). Although it only unified two results due to the French mathematician P. S. Laplace, it was valuable (in generality, for example), and was praised even in Paris. In 1814 he produced a study of the orbits of comets which won the Copley medal of the Royal Society; the next year he was elected fellow.

On resigning his professorship in 1819 Ivory was allowed the full retiring pension, although his period of office was shorter than the rule required. He was then in his mid-fifties and retirement allowed him time for remarkable productivity; he published nearly eighty papers between 1821 and 1842, mostly in the *Philosophical Magazine*, but a dozen with the Royal Society. Several concerned attractions, including the properties of equipotential surfaces (where he was the loser in a dispute of 1827 with Laplace's disciple S. D. Poisson) and the conditions for the equilibrium of bodies (including the surprising cases of rotating fluid ellipsoids with three unequal axes, which had been discovered by C. Jacobi and J. Liouville). In celestial mechanics he examined the effects of perturbation upon the orbits of planets. For planetary mechanics he focused on the shape of the earth and its determination by use of pendula, and on methods of surveying. In planetary physics he examined capillarity and the use of hygrometers, and the 'graduation of heat' and especially the refraction of light in the atmosphere. For the latter two papers he was awarded royal medals of the Royal Society in 1826 and 1839 respectively.

In 1831, on the recommendation of Lord Brougham, then lord chancellor, Ivory received a knighthood, in company with Herschel and Brewster. While not in their rank as a researcher, his work was well acknowledged, not only at the Royal Society but also abroad, where he was elected a member of the Royal Academy of Sciences of France, the

Royal Academy of Berlin, and the Royal Society of Göttingen.

Ivory seems to have suffered from mental illness, maybe paranoia, in later life, thereby spoiling some of his personal relationships. He died, unmarried, at Hampstead, Middlesex, on 21 September 1842. In 1829 he had made an offer of his scientific library to the corporation of Dundee, his native town, and as there was then no public building suitable for the purpose, James *Ivory (Lord Ivory), his nephew and heir, kept the books in his own collection until his death in 1866, when they became part of the Dundee Public Library in the Albert Institute.

R. E. ANDERSON, rev. I. GRATTAN-GUINNESS

Sources *Abstracts of the Papers Printed in the Philosophical Transactions of the Royal Society of London*, 4 (1837–43), 406–13 • N. Guicciardini, *The development of Newtonian calculus in Britain, 1700–1800* (1989) • I. Grattan-Guinness, *Convolutions in French mathematics*, 2 (1990) • I. Todhunter, *A history of the mathematical theories of attraction and the figure of the earth*, 2 vols. (1873), vol. 2 • A. D. D. Craik, 'James Ivory, FRS, mathematician', *Notes and Records of the Royal Society*, 54 (2000), 223–47 • IGI
Archives NA Scot., papers | BL, letters to C. Babbage, Add. MSS 37182, 37185–37186, 37188, 37200 • BL, letters to Macvey Napier, Add. MSS 34611–34612 • RS, letters to J. W. Lubbock

Ivory, James, Lord Ivory (1792–1866), judge, son of Thomas Ivory, watchmaker and engraver, was born in Dundee on 29 February 1792. Sir James Ivory, mathematician, was his uncle. After attending Dundee Academy he studied for the legal profession at Edinburgh University, and was called to the Scottish bar on 9 July 1816. In that year he was enrolled as a burgess of his native town. When, in 1819, the select committee of the House of Commons was making inquiries into the state of the Scottish burghs, Ivory was examined with reference to the municipal condition of Dundee; he strongly advocated the abolition of self-election, which was then prevalent in the town councils of Scotland. Ivory married on 21 October 1817 Ann, second daughter of William Lawrie, deputy gazette writer for Scotland. Two of their sons followed their father to the Scottish bar.

Ivory acquired a considerable practice and he was chosen advocate-depute by Francis Jeffrey, lord advocate, in 1830; on 26 June 1833 he was appointed sheriff of Caithness, and on 1 July 1834 he was transferred to a similar office in Buteshire. He was solicitor-general of Scotland under Lord Melbourne's ministry in 1839, but he only held the post for just over a year. On 23 May 1840 he was raised to the bench of the court of session, on the retirement of Lord Glenlee. He took the courtesy title of Lord Ivory. In 1849 he transferred to the inner house of the court of session, and for several years before his retirement he was the court's senior judge. On 4 October 1862 he resigned all judicial duties, rather to avoid the onset of ill health than through any actual illness. He died at his residence in Edinburgh on 17 October 1866.

Although Ivory acquired an eminent position at the bar it was through his written rather than his oral pleadings that he made his name. While his arguments were thoroughly researched, highly detailed, and comprehensive, Ivory was no orator. His career is best summarized by a contemporary, John Clerk, who called him the worst speaker and the best writer he had known at the bar. As a judge of first instance he was wont to procrastinate upon matters of fact, to such an extent as 'materially to impair his usefulness while sitting alone in the Outer House' (*Journal of Jurisprudence*, vol. 10). This trait waned on his appointment to the inner house, as he now had to keep pace with his brother judges and was thus forced to reach decisions upon factual matters with greater speed and certainty. In the inner house, however, a new vice was discernible: in the perpetual legal struggle between substance and form, Ivory was very much on the side of the latter, and would often allow legal technicalities to triumph over the merits of the case. This was perhaps a natural progression from his days at the bar, where his arguments were often academic to the point of abstraction. None the less Ivory's was considered to have been an impressive legal career, both at the bar and the bench. He was a sound lawyer, and an honourable, upright judge. Politically Ivory was a lifelong Liberal, while in private life he was said to be unaffected, genial, and warm-hearted.

A. H. MILLAR, rev. NATHAN WELLS

Sources W. Norrie, *Dundee celebrities of the nineteenth century* (1873) • *Journal of Jurisprudence*, 10 (1866) • F. J. Grant, ed., *The Faculty of Advocates in Scotland, 1532–1943*, Scottish RS, 145 (1944) • Irving, *Scots.* • CCI (1867)
Archives NA Scot., letters to second Baron Panmure • NL Scot., letters to Andrew Rutherfurd
Wealth at death £21,536 4s. 5½d.—in UK: confirmation, 14 Jan 1867, NA Scot., SC 70/1/133/98–111 • £7527 18s.—debts due abroad: further action, NA Scot., SC 70/1/133/98–111

Ivory, Thomas (1709–1779), architect, purchased the freedom of the city of Norwich as a carpenter on 21 September 1745. His family background and details of his early life are unknown. A memoir of 1782 by his son William called him

> a publick spirited Man, with great activity of Mind and resolution, and a great knowledge in his business as a Master builder … being considerably employed in the profession of a Merchant in Exporting the Norwich Manufactory … into the Northern Countries and importing from thence large Quantities of Deals, Timber, Iron &c. (Wearing, 28)

In 1751 he was appointed carpenter to the Great Hospital in Norwich and built a house there, into which he moved with his family, from the parish of St Martin-at-Oak, in 1756. His timber yard was near by in Bishopsgate Street, where, in 1752–3, he built the Methodist meeting-house. The interior of the Octagon Chapel in Colegate of 1754–6 (a commission which he won against rival designs) is an attractive paraphrase of James Gibbs's first scheme for St Martin-in-the-Fields, published in 1721. The Norwich assembly house, which he began in 1754, has interiors designed by Sir James Burrough. In the construction of the adjoining theatre in 1758 Ivory combined the roles of architect, builder, and proprietor, before selling on the lease ten years later. In 1764 Ivory built another theatre in Colchester and in the following year began a series of extensive alterations at Blickling Hall for John, second earl of Buckinghamshire. Ivory's designs were usually dependent on what he could absorb from the publications of metropolitan architects. But at Blickling, with the guidance of an antiquarian-minded patron, he produced some of the most convincing neo-Jacobean architecture of the eighteenth century, including a great hall which reused and extended the original Jacobean stairs.

Ivory died on 28 August 1779, three months after an accident in which his leg had been crushed by a heavy piece of timber. He was buried in Norwich Cathedral, where in 1767–8 he had remodelled the choir furnishings in the Gothic style; he is commemorated there by a mural monument carved by his nephew the mason John Ivory, and a ledger slab. His wife, Hannah, *née* Lacey, whom he had married on 22 December 1735, died in 1787 aged eighty. They had two sons—William, who assisted his father as an architect, and Thomas, who settled in India and was excluded from the will—as well as a daughter, Sarah.

JOHN MADDISON

Sources W. Ivory, letters to John, second earl of Buckingham, Norfolk RO, 22702 Z 64, NRS 19180 • S. J. Wearing, *Georgian Norwich: its builders* (1926) • J. Maddison, 'Architectural drawings at Blickling Hall', *Architectural History*, 34 (1991), 75–135 • M. Carey Evans, 'The descendants of Thomas Ivory', *Norfolk Archaeology*, 39 (1984–7), 206–14 • Colvin, *Archs*.

Ivory, Thomas (1731/2–1786), architect, is of unknown parentage, and there is no evidence to suggest a connection with the Norwich architect of the same name. Information about his early life relies on an article in *Anthologia Hibernica* of May 1793, which states that he was born in Cork and became the pupil of a carpenter there before completing his apprenticeship in Dublin. After working for some time with the gunsmith Thomas Truelock, he decided to become an architect and took drawing lessons from a 'Mr Bell Myers', probably the surveyor and topographical draughtsman Jonas Blaymire. Ivory 'soon eclipsed his master, so as to be considered by far the best draughtsman in architecture at that time in Dublin' (*Anthologia Hibernica*, 335).

On 1 January 1764 Ivory married Elinor Lyons at St Werburgh's Church, Dublin. In the same year the Dublin Society opened a school to teach architectural draughtsmanship to boys from modest backgrounds. Ivory was appointed the first master of the school and, as the society acknowledged, took 'extraordinary Trouble' in instructing his pupils (Dublin Society minutes, 21 May 1772). In the early 1780s his health deteriorated, and his teaching duties were taken over increasingly by his apprentice Henry Aaron Baker. One of his pupils at this time recalled him as 'a gentle urbane character … in a delicate state of health' (Herbert, 57).

In 1773 Ivory won the competition for designing the Blue Coat School in Dublin. The realization of his scheme was curtailed through lack of funds, and he resigned from the commission in 1780 before the building was finished in its present reduced form. His other executed works in Dublin are 89 and 90 Harcourt Street, built in 1776 and 1780 respectively, and Newcomen's Bank, built c.1781. Elsewhere in Ireland he designed Kilcarty, co. Meath, in the 1770s for Dr George Cleghorn, professor of anatomy at Trinity College, and the bridge at Lismore, co. Waterford

(1773–9) for the fifth duke of Devonshire. In 1775 he succeeded John Smyth as architect to the revenue commissioners and in this capacity he designed the Custom House at Coleraine, co. Londonderry (1783).

Ivory died, aged fifty-four, on 27 December 1786 at his house at Mount Pleasant, Ranelagh, in the southern suburbs of Dublin. He was survived by his wife and two unmarried daughters, his twelve-year-old son having died two weeks before him. His buildings directly reflect the preference for a refined neo-Palladian manner which was common in the last third of the eighteenth century. Although highly esteemed as a draughtsman, he exhibited relatively little, and few of his architectural designs have been traced, apart from the magnificent set for the Blue Coat School now in the British Library. He is said to figure in a conversation piece by John Trotter, now in the King's Hospital, Palmerston, Dublin, which is believed to represent a meeting about the planning of the Blue Coat School.

A. M. ROWAN

Sources 'Mr. Thomas Ivory', *Anthologia Hibernica* (May 1793), 334–5 • E. McParland, 'Thomas Ivory', *Quarterly Bulletin of the Irish Georgian Society*, 17 (1974), 15–18 • D. O'Connor, 'Thomas Ivory', *RIAI Yearbook*, 1992, 68–73 • J. Turpin, *A school of art in Dublin since the eighteenth century: a history of the National College of Art and Design* (1995), 49–52 • *Faulkner's Dublin Journal* (7–11 Feb 1764) • *Faulkner's Dublin Journal* (23–5 Aug 1768) • *Faulkner's Dublin Journal* (17–20 Jan 1775) • *Faulkner's Dublin Journal* (22–5 April 1775) • *Faulkner's Dublin Journal* (26–8 Dec 1786) • J. D. Herbert, *Irish varieties for the last fifty years* (1836) • Dublin Society minutes, archive of the Royal Dublin Society, Dublin Archives BL, MSS, 7 Tab 16 • Chatsworth House, Derbyshire, archives, MSS, MSL/5 | Irish Architectural Archive, Guinness collection, acc. 96/98 Wealth at death not well off; widow had to sell interest in all his property to pay his debts: O'Connor, 'Thomas Ivory'

Iwan-Müller, Ernest Bruce. *See* Müller, Ernest Bruce John Iwan- (1853–1910).

Izacke, Richard (*bap.* 1624, *d.* 1698), antiquary, was baptized on 8 February 1624 at Ottery St Mary, Devon, the eldest son of Samuel Izacke of Exeter. On 20 April 1641 he was admitted a commoner of Exeter College, Oxford, but left the university at the end of the following year on account of the civil war. He had in the meantime, in November 1641, entered the Inner Temple, and he was called to the bar in 1650.

Izacke was elected chamberlain of Exeter on 25 October 1653 and town clerk on 15 December 1681. As chamberlain he had full access to Exeter's extensive archives and completed a manuscript history of the city, which he dedicated to the corporation in 1665. It was published as *Antiquities of the City of Exeter* in 1677 and reissued in 1681. It has been much criticized for his unacknowledged and inaccurate borrowings from the works of his predecessor in office, John Hooker, and for his own errors.

At an unknown date Izacke married Katherine, but appears to have displeased his father by 'his disobedience in his marriage' (Brushfield, 451). Nevertheless on his father's death in 1681 or 1682, he inherited a house in Holy Trinity parish, Exeter, and leasehold property in Tipton, Ottery St Mary, on condition of his future good conduct towards his stepmother, brothers, and sisters. Izacke himself was buried in the church of Ottery St Mary on 18 March 1698.

Izacke's son Samuel (*b.* 1663), who became chamberlain of Exeter in 1693, revised and continued his father's work to 1722, producing a second edition with the title *Remarkable Antiquities of the City of Exeter* (1723). Despite its inadequacies the work seems to have been adopted as an official history of the city, as reissues dated 1724, 1731, 1734, 1741, and 1757 are often to be found in standard red leather gilt bindings, probably intended for presentation. Izacke's grandson Samuel published another compilation from his manuscript in 1736 relating to legacies left to the city. Before the work of the charity commissioners this was considered to be a useful work as it reappeared in a variety of versions in 1751, 1757, 1785, and 1820.

IAN MAXTED

Sources T. N. Brushfield, 'Richard Izacke, and his *Antiquities of Exeter*', *Report and Transactions of the Devonshire Association*, 25 (1893), 449–71 · W. H. Cooke, ed., *Students admitted to the Inner Temple, 1547–1660* [1878], 218, 310 · Wood, *Ath. Oxon.*, new edn, 4.489 · R. G. [R. Gough], *British topography*, [new edn], 1 (1780), 305 · J. Davidson, *Bibliotheca Devoniensis* (1852) · parish register (baptism), 8 Feb 1624, Ottery St Mary · *DNB*
Archives Devon RO, Exeter City Archives, MS 'Memorials of the city of Exeter', book 53

Jabavu, John Tengo (1859–1921), journalist and politician in South Africa, was born on 11 January 1859 at Tyatyora village, near Healdtown in the eastern Cape, the youngest child of humble parents, Ntwanambi Jabavu and his wife, Mary, *née* Mpinda. Jabavu's family belonged to the Mfengu, who had fled from Natal during Shaka's wars (1818–28) and settled among the Xhosa of the eastern Cape. Strongly influenced by missionary teaching, the Mfengu had adopted Christian ideals, and were inclined towards European models of education and peasant agriculture. Jabavu was very much a product of this tradition. In 1875 he graduated from the Methodist institution at Healdtown and took up a teaching position at Somerset East in the eastern Cape.

While teaching at Somerset East, Jabavu became the local correspondent for some of South Africa's leading newspapers as well as apprenticing himself to a printer. He attracted the attention of Dr James Stewart of the Lovedale Mission School, who was looking for someone to edit the institution's Xhosa-language journal, *Isigidimi sama-Xosa* ('The Xhosa messenger'). As editor, Jabavu took a keen interest in Cape politics and during the Cape elections of 1883 he canvassed actively for one of the candidates. His partisan and controversial attitudes did not find favour with the missionary hierarchy and his editorial contract was not renewed.

But Jabavu had become convinced of the existence of a literate readership sufficient to support a Xhosa-language newspaper untrammelled by missionary inhibitions and willing to articulate their views and their opinions. In 1884 he launched his own newspaper, *Imvo Zabantsundu* ('Black opinion'), with financial backing from two white businessmen with political interests. The franchise of Cape Colony, though qualified, was at that time colour-blind and African voters held the balance of power in at least five eastern Cape constituencies. Jabavu's opinions thus carried considerable political weight, and he used his influence to fight various pieces of legislation which were designed to disarm and disenfranchise Cape Africans, to seize their lands, and to restrict their freedom of movement.

Jabavu was recognized for nearly fifteen years as the leading spokesman for African interests throughout southern Africa. He lost his pre-eminence, however, as the result of a split which occurred in Cape politics after Cecil Rhodes was deposed as premier of the Cape in 1896. Rhodes formed the Progressive Party, which was closely identified with the British imperial interests, whereas his opponents gravitated to the Afrikaner Bond. Several of Jabavu's white political allies tended towards the Bond, and Jabavu himself was impressed with the liberal racial attitude of its leader, Jan Hofmeyr. During the Cape elections of 1898, Jabavu backed the Bond candidates. Rhodes retaliated by sponsoring a rival newspaper with the assistance of Jabavu's long-term political adversary W. B. Rubusana. Because Jabavu was a Mfengu and Rubusana was a Xhosa, this rivalry acquired a nasty ethnic tinge.

Jabavu's association with the Afrikaner Bond led to the closure of *Imvo* by martial law during the Second South African War of 1899–1902. He became increasingly dependent on his white associates and this dependence, together with his jealousy of Rubusana, caused him to take idiosyncratic stands which lost him the confidence of many of his supporters. Jabavu refused, for example, to attend the inaugural meeting in 1912 of the South African Native National Congress (subsequently the African National Congress), and insisted on setting up his own organization instead. He later supported the notorious 1913 Native Land Act, which was introduced by his ally J. W. Sauer. In 1914 he challenged Rubusana, the sitting member, for the only African-held seat in the Cape provincial legislature. This split the African vote and threw the seat to the white candidate.

Jabavu married twice: in 1885 to Elda Sakuba, with whom he had four sons, and in 1901 to Gertrude Joninga, with whom he had three daughters. He died quite suddenly on 10 September 1921 while attending a meeting at the University College of Fort Hare. Though his historical reputation has been soured by the obstinacy and jealousy of his later years, his place in the pantheon of black journalism and African nationalism remains secure.

J. B. PEIRES

Sources L. D. Ngcongco, 'John Tengo Jabavu, 1859–1921', *Black leaders in southern African history*, ed. C. Saunders (1979) · D. D. T. Jabavu, *The life of John Tengo Jabavu* (1922) · A. Odendaal, *Uukani Bantu! the beginnings of black protest politics in South Africa to 1912* (1984) · S. Trapido, 'The friends of the natives: merchants, peasants and the political and ideological structure of liberalism at the Cape, 1854–1910', *Economy and Society in pre-industrial South Africa*, ed. S. Marks and A. Atmore (1980)
Likenesses photograph, repro. in Saunders, ed., *Black leaders*, 143 · photograph, repro. in Odendaal, *Uukani Bantu!*, xvi

Jac Glan y Gors. *See* Jones, John (1766–1821).

Jack of Newbury. *See* Winchcombe, John (*d.* 1520).

Jack the Ripper (*fl.* **1888**), serial killer, was known as 'the Whitechapel murderer' or 'Leather Apron' until on 27 September 1888 the Central News Agency received a red-inked, defiant, semi-literate letter signed Jack the Ripper. This letter was probably a hoax concocted by news agency staff. It is suitable that he is known by a name devised in a journalistic stunt, for he was the first criminal to become a figure of international mythology through the medium of global communications. The indivisibility of his crimes from reportage of them is shown in a few words of a cabinet minister, Lord Cranbrook, who on 2 October noted: 'More murders at Whitechapel, strange and horrible. The newspapers reek with blood' (Johnson, 716).

The Ripper was almost certainly male, probably right-handed, unmarried, and in work, and possessed either some anatomical training or sufficient education to study surgical textbooks; he was perhaps a foreigner. Although all his victims (possibly barring one) were destitute and drunken prostitutes, he did not rape or penetrate them; nevertheless, there was a sexual element to his homicidal excitement. He was daring, energetic, hate-ridden, cruel, and perhaps obsessed with wombs. Evidence as to his age and appearance from those who claimed to have seen him is inconclusive and contradictory. Nothing is certain of his life except for a few violent hours during the summer and autumn of 1888.

The first killings There was much routine violence against women in Whitechapel. Early on the morning of Tuesday 3 April 1888, following Easter bank holiday Monday, Emma Elizabeth Smith, aged forty-five, was attacked in Osborn Street. A blunt instrument, possibly a stick, was thrust into her. She died in the London Hospital next day. Her death is sometimes reckoned as the first in the series of crimes perpetrated by the Whitechapel murderer, but was probably an unrelated street robbery and rape by several ruffians.

Between 1.50 and 3.30 a.m. on Tuesday 7 August 1888 (after a Monday bank holiday) Martha Tabram (*b.* 1849), alias Turner, who was also known as Emma, was stabbed thirty-nine times on the first-floor landing of the communal stairs of George Yard Buildings, a block of model dwellings off Whitechapel High Street. Her clothes were disarrayed and her lower body exposed. Police investigations focused on an unidentified private in a guards regiment with whom Tabram had reportedly gone to George Yard shortly before midnight on 6 August. Some criminologists insist that Tabram's killer was an unidentified soldier; others identify this crime as the first of the series attributed to Jack the Ripper.

There is no controversy that at about 3 a.m. on Friday 31 August 1888 the Whitechapel murderer killed Mary Ann (Polly) Nichols (*b.* 1845) in the entrance to a stable yard in a narrow cobbled alley called Buck's Row, off Whitechapel Road. Like Tabram her skirts were raised almost to her stomach. Her abdomen was savagely ripped open and her throat cut; her private parts were twice stabbed. She had, however, probably been throttled before the stabbing and

mutilation. After her murder, suspicions focused on Jack Pizer (*c.*1850–1897), a Jewish slipper maker who for some time had been bullying prostitutes and was known as Leather Apron; he was eventually detained and eliminated from the enquiry.

The next victim was Annie Chapman, alias Annie Siffey (*b.* 1841). She was murdered (probably at 5.30 a.m.) on Saturday 8 September 1888 in the backyard of 29 Hanbury Street, Spitalfields. This was the only one of the serial killings committed in daylight. An eyewitness who saw the killer picking up his victim described him vaguely as shabby-genteel, foreign-looking, and aged about forty; a neighbour apparently heard him stifling her cries and throttling her to insensibility if not death. Chapman's throat was severed and her body mutilated. Some of her organs were removed from the scene, and her rings were wrenched off. The perpetrator seemingly had some knowledge of anatomical or pathological examinations; a small amputating knife or thin, sharpened slaughterman's knife was probably used.

The police response Police street patrols of Whitechapel and Spitalfields were increased after the Tabram murder and were soon intensified until the district was almost saturated with police at night-time. After Nichols's murder, when journalists raised the spectre of a homicidal lunatic stalking his victims through Whitechapel, Inspector Frederick Abberline of Scotland Yard, who had an extensive knowledge of the area, was sent there to co-ordinate the divisional detectives investigating the prostitute murders. Generally the police were reasonably efficient, if bewildered. The press sensation following Chapman's murder, however, raised bitter recriminations against the Metropolitan Police. Some of these attacks were intended to injure politically the home secretary, Henry Matthews, or to retaliate against stern police treatment of Irish nationalists, socialists, and the East End unemployed. The situation was exacerbated by Sir Howard Vincent's guidelines for the Criminal Investigation Department requiring secretiveness on the part of police officials in unsolved cases. Journalistic resentment of this policy led them to various ploys and dodges which impeded police investigations. There was a popular outcry for a large government reward to be offered for information on the killer, but the Home Office was set against this practice, which it knew could draw false information or induce the framing of innocent parties. The police nevertheless were showered with information from the public about lunatics, misfits, and unpopular neighbours. Chapman's death raised suspicions of Jewish ritual murder, and crowds assembled in the Whitechapel streets threatening Jews. This resulted in Samuel Montagu, MP for Whitechapel, offering a reward of £100 for the murderer's capture, and in the formation (largely by Jewish tradesmen) of the Mile End Vigilance Committee. Larger rewards were later offered.

The later murders Probably between 12.40 and 1 a.m. on Sunday 30 September, in Dutfield's Yard, flanking the socialist (and mainly Jewish) International Working Men's

Educational Club, at 40 Berner Street, Elizabeth Stride (*b.* 1843), a Swede, prone to drink but not a habitual prostitute, was murdered. A meeting of 100 members had only recently closed in the club, where members who had not dispersed were singing. Stride's throat had been cut, but her clothing was undisturbed. Her expression was peaceful and she still clutched in her left hand a packet of aromatic breath sweeteners wrapped in tissue paper. Some Ripperologists discount Stride as one of the serial killings because the corpse was not extensively slashed or mutilated, but it is more likely that the killer was disturbed before completing his work. A passer-by gave evidence suggesting that there were two men involved in this killing. Another witness, who saw a member of the socialist club leaving the yard carrying a small black bag, started the legend of Jack the Ripper carrying a doctor's bag.

After murdering Stride the killer went three-quarters of a mile eastward (12 minutes' walk) to Mitre Square, off Aldgate, within the eastern boundary of the City of London. In the south-east corner of this square, near a warehouse yard and some derelict or empty houses (the darkest corner of the square, favoured by prostitutes and their clients), between 1.30 and 1.44 a.m. on that same morning, he murdered Catherine Eddowes (*b.* 1842), alias Kate Conway or Kelly. She had been discharged from Bishopsgate Street police station (where she was held for drunkenness) only forty-five minutes before her corpse was discovered. She was found lying on her back with her clothes disarranged. Her throat was cut and her stomach opened. Further terrible mutilations were made, and again the murderer took organs away. He showed ruthless efficiency on this occasion, for he had only a quarter of an hour between two police patrols to inveigle his victim into the square, kill and mutilate her, and escape. The police reacted swiftly to the discovery in Mitre Square, but the killer fled eastwards, apparently stopping to leave a piece of Eddowes's bloody and faecal-stained apron at a stairwell entry at 108–19 Wentworth Model Dwellings, Goulston Street, where he chalked a message:

> The Juwes are
> The men That
> Will not
> be Blamed
> for nothing.

The chairman of Mile End Vigilance Committee received a parcel (16 October) putatively containing a portion of Eddowes's kidney together with an unsigned letter headed 'From Hell', purportedly from the murderer.

From the night of the double murder the police investigation became even more conditioned by public unrest and reactive to the press. The police were demoralized by false leads and failure. Relations became strained between Matthews and the commissioner of Metropolitan Police, Sir Charles Warren, who reported to the Home Office on 17 October, 'I look upon this series of murders as unique in the history of our country' (Evans and Gainey, 112); Warren resigned a few weeks later. The press agitation reached its shrillest pitch during October 1888, when

there were no Whitechapel prostitute murders: the pseudonym Jack the Ripper of the probably inauthentic letter publicized by the Central News Agency achieved worldwide notoriety in the early days of that month. This name represented a state of mind rather than an individual: that mentality being a paroxysm of horror, fear, and fascinated disgust.

In the aftermath of the Chapman murder a German hairdresser named Charles Ludwig was apprehended (18 September), and the evidence against him seemed powerful until the double murder was committed while Ludwig was in police custody. Other suspects at this time included Jacob Isenschmid, an insane Swiss pork butcher; Oswald Puckridge (1838–1900), a trained apothecary who had recently been released from Hoxton House Lunatic Asylum and had threatened to rip people up with a long knife; and three medical students, including John Sanders (1862–1901), who had attended London Hospital but had become insane. It was speculated whether the killer was a member of a barbaric sect, a mad freemason, a black magician, a dipsomaniac, a notoriety craver, a jewel thief, a midwife or abortionist, an individual or individuals intent on inciting antisemitism (many details of the Stride–Eddowes murders can be construed as intended to incriminate Jews), or (according to the mountebank Forbes Winslow) a religious monomaniac. Sir George Savage (who suspected '*post-mortem* room and anatomy room porters') hypothesized that 'imitative action may have come into play', and that the murders were maniacal acts of emulation by more than one killer, including someone bent on 'world regeneration' (Savage, 463). A looser speculation is that the killer was a social reformer such as Thomas Barnardo (who met Stride on 26 September) hoping to shock the national conscience about slum conditions. Certainly Whitechapel became the cynosure of 1888. Typically, Lord Sydney Godolphin Osborne characterized its inhabitants as living in 'godless brutality, a species of human sewage, the very drainage of the vilest productions of human vice' and called for a concentrated philanthropic effort (*The Times*, 18 Sept 1888, 11f.).

On Friday 9 November 1888 (perhaps between 1 and 4 a.m.) the Whitechapel murderer killed Mary Jane Kelly (*b.* 1862) in her room at a common lodging house, Miller's Court, off Dorset Street, Spitalfields. Her body was found almost naked on her bed with its throat cut. As her murderer was secure in her room, without fear of interruption, he had time to cut her to pieces in the light from her fireplace. The mutilations were horrific, apparently undertaken in an atrocious frenzy.

Kelly is usually treated as the last victim of the Whitechapel murderer. His death, incarceration in an asylum, or emigration may have terminated these crimes. (The deaths of Alice McKenzie, whose throat was cut between 12.25 and 12.50 a.m. in Castle Alley, off Whitechapel High Street, on 16 July 1889, and of Frances Cole, whose throat was cut under a railway arch in Swallow Gardens at 2.15 a.m. on 13 February 1891, have been tentatively attributed to the Whitechapel murderer.)

The Ripper as a continuing public phenomenon Over 130 suspects are listed in *The Jack the Ripper A to Z* (1991). Sir Melville Macnaghten of the Criminal Investigation Department believed in the guilt of Montague Druitt (1857–1888), a barrister and schoolmaster who drowned himself in the Thames after the Kelly killing. Another police official, Sir Robert Anderson, suspected Aaron Kosminski (*c.*1864–1919), a Polish Jew working in Whitechapel as a hairdresser, who was confined in Colney Hatch Asylum in 1891. Inspector Frederick Abberline of Scotland Yard, who was the most impressive detective involved in the investigation, suspected Severin Klosowski (1865–1903), a Pole who had studied surgery and emigrated to England in 1887. Klosowski (originally working as a hairdresser in Whitechapel) was a Roman Catholic who masqueraded as a Jew; under the name of George Chapman he was executed for poisoning his three common-law wives between 1897 and 1902. Chief Inspector John Littlechild specified an unbalanced woman-hating American quack, Francis Tumblety (*c.*1833–1903), who absconded abroad while on police bail after Kelly's death. Tumblety and perhaps Klosowski are the most plausible suspects. The guilt of an unidentified Jewish ritual slaughterman is also tenable. Sillier accusations include the eldest son of the prince of Wales, Albert Victor, duke of Clarence and Avondale; his tutor, James Kenneth Stephen (1859–1892); Sir William Gull; Walter Sickert; and Dr Thomas Neill Cream (1850–1892), an abortionist hanged for poisoning Lambeth prostitutes. Several Ripperologists accuse a fish porter called Joseph Barnett (1860–1927), who was in love with Kelly and was supposedly trying to frighten her off the streets.

The Ripper was the first sexual serial killer commanding international notoriety: he inaugurated the modern consciousness of such crimes. Since 1888 the phenomenon has proliferated: in England the atrocities of an unidentified serial killer of prostitutes in Notting Hill and Shepherd's Bush (1964–5), and of Peter Sutcliffe, the Yorkshire Ripper (1976–80), are comparable to the Whitechapel murders. Though the Victorian public had always revelled in the sanguinary details of murder, and popular journalism had always striven to shock, Jack's nightmarish mutilations were recognized in 1888 as new and strange. In an epoch when a glimpse of a woman's ankle could seem indecent, the violence of his mutilations was blasphemous. His attacks were reported in an explicit, pitiless detail that would be rendered impossible a generation later by voluntary journalistic self-censorship. The detectives' policy of not confiding their progress to journalists resulted in reporting that was often wild, irresponsible, and mendacious; accurate reports were contradicted with seeming authority by jealous or mischievous journalistic rivals. At their breakfast tables the British were confronted with the mechanisms of the vilest sexual homicide. After the Eddowes murder a 'sweet-natured and kindly-souled' middle-class girl who had been forbidden 'to read *Adam Bede*' was invited to east London, and asked enthusiastically, '"Shall we pass Mitre Court?"' (Barnett, 437). Knowledge of the crimes affected everyone, and there was no return to innocence.

Jack the Ripper is partly a literary phenomenon. There was already vigorous political and quasi-scientific debate among the intelligentsia in 1888 about the body, the city, and degeneration theory. The Whitechapel murders occurred two years after the publication of R. L. Stevenson's *The Strange Case of Dr Jekyll and Mr Hyde* and of Krafft-Ebing's *Psychopathia sexualis*, and two years before the publication of Oscar Wilde's *The Picture of Dorian Gray*. The graffiti clue left after the Eddowes murder seems adapted from an incident in Arthur Conan Doyle's 'A Study in Scarlet', published a few months earlier in *Beeton's Christmas Annual*. Much contemporary doggerel developed about the Ripper. Later, Leonard Matters's unreliable *The Mystery of Jack the Ripper* (1930) launched a massive literature of Ripperologists: some of it exploitative, asinine, or tawdry, but other books more fascinating. These crimes inspired one excellent novel, Marie Belloc Lowndes's *The Lodger* (1913), admired by Gertrude Stein and Ernest Hemingway, and first filmed by Alfred Hitchcock in 1926 (starring Ivor Novello), with four remakes to 1953. Phyllis Tate turned *The Lodger* into an opera (1960). A cognate novel is Colin Wilson's *Ritual in the Dark* (1960). By 1977 there were twenty films reflecting the Ripper story. The Ripper crimes influenced Wedekind's plays *Erdgeist* and *Die Büchse der Pandora* (and hence Berg's 1937 opera *Lulu*), as well as Brecht's *Dreigroschenoper*. RICHARD DAVENPORT-HINES

Sources P. Sugden, *The complete history of Jack the Ripper* (1995) · S. Evans and P. Gainey, *The lodger* (1995) · G. Savage, 'Homicidal mania', *Fortnightly Review*, 50 (1888), 448–63 · S. A. Barnett, 'East London and crime', *National Review*, 12 (1888–9), 433–43 · *The diary of Gathorne Hardy, later Lord Cranbrook, 1866–1892: political selections*, ed. N. E. Johnson (1981), 716, 718 · L. P. Curtis, *Jack the Ripper and the London press* (2002) · P. Begg, *Jack the Ripper* (1988) · D. Rumbelow, *The complete Jack the Ripper* (1975) · T. Cullen, *Autumn of Terror* (1965) · P. Begg, K. Skinner, and M. Fido, *The Jack the Ripper A to Z* (1991) · P. Harrison, *Jack the Ripper* (1991) · 'The Whitechapel mystery', *The Spectator* (15 Sept 1888), 1253–4 · 'The Whitechapel horrors', *The Spectator* (6 Oct 1888), 1352–3

Archives CLRO, Whitechapel murders files · PRO, HO 144/220/A49301 through to HO 144/221/A49301K · Scotland Yard archives, Abberline papers | FILM BFI NFTVA, 'Diary of Jack the Ripper', ITV, 20 Jan 1996

Likenesses engraving, Hult. Arch.; repro. in *Illustrated Police News* (1889) · portrait, repro. in *Illustrated Police News* (Aug–Nov 1888) · portrait, repro. in M. Harris, *The Ripper file* (1989)

Jack, Alexander (1805–1857), army officer in the East India Company, was born in Old Machar, Aberdeen, on 19 October 1805 into the family of four sons and two daughters of Revd William Jack (1815–1854), principal of University and King's College, Aberdeen, and Grace (1773–1850), daughter of Andrew Bolt of Lerwick, Shetland. Jack studied mathematics and philosophy at University and King's College, Aberdeen, in 1820–22, and obtained a Bengal cadetship in 1823. He was appointed ensign in the 30th Bengal native infantry on 23 May 1824, and arrived in India on 6 October. He was subsequently promoted lieutenant in the regiment on 28 September 1825, captain on 2 December 1838, and major on 19 January 1846.

During the First Anglo-Sikh War of 1845–6, Jack served with his battalion at the battle of Aliwal, and acted as brigadier of the force sent against the town of Kangra, when he received great credit for his extraordinary exertions in bringing up his 18-pounder guns. During the Second Anglo-Sikh War, of 1848–9, he commanded his battalion at the battles of Chilianwala and Gujrat. He was created CB on 9 June 1849, and promoted lieutenant-colonel in the 30th Bengal native infantry on 11 December 1851. He transferred to the 33rd native infantry in August 1852, to the 41st in December 1852, and to the 42nd in January 1853. He was made brevet colonel on 20 June 1854, took two years' furlough, and returned to join the 34th native infantry in May 1856.

On 9 August 1856 Jack was appointed brigadier at Cawnpore, the headquarters of Sir Hugh Wheeler's division of the Bengal army. On 7 June 1857 the mutiny broke out at Cawnpore. Wheeler maintained his position in an entrenched camp until the 27th, when an evacuation was made following an agreement with Nana Sahib. After the troops had embarked in boats for Allahabad, the mutineers treacherously shot down Wheeler, Jack, and all the British men except four. During the previous defence of the lines a brother, Andrew William Thomas Jack, who was on a visit from Australia, had his leg shattered and died during amputation.

H. M. CHICHESTER, rev. ALEX MAY

Sources Indian Army List · V. C. P. Hodson, List of officers of the Bengal army, 1758–1834, 4 vols. (1927–47) · G. O. Trevelyan, Cawnpore (1865) · C. Hibbert, The great mutiny, India, 1857 (1978) · J. W. Kaye, A history of the Sepoy War in India, 1857–1858, 9th edn, 2 (1880) · H. C. B. Cook, The Sikh wars: the British army in the Punjab, 1845–1849 (1975) · E. R. Crawford, 'The Sikh wars, 1845–9', Victorian military campaigns, ed. B. Bond (1967), 33–66

Jack, David Bone Nightingale (1898–1958), footballer, was born at 119 Chorley Old Road, Bolton, Lancashire, on 3 April 1898, the first son of Robert (Bob) Jack, a professional footballer from Alloa, Scotland, then playing for Bolton Wanderers, and his wife, Georgina Florence Nightingale. Educated largely at Leigh Road Presbyterian school, Southend, where the family had moved following his father's appointment as manager of Southend United in 1906, he eventually joined the navy as a writer, aged seventeen. Already showing great promise as a footballer, he attracted the attention of a number of major clubs, including Chelsea and Tottenham Hotspur. However, when football resumed its full programme in 1919 he chose to play under his father's managerial regime at Plymouth Argyle, before moving in December 1920 to Bolton Wanderers, where his brothers Rollo and Donald were to join him for a period in the 1920s. His place in football's record books was assured in 1923 when, after only two minutes, he scored the first goal in the first ever FA cup final to be played at Wembley stadium, the so-called 'white horse' final.

An intelligent observer of the game, Jack wrote an informative football column for *The Buff*, Bolton's Saturday football paper. Indeed, it was his awareness of the additional financial security that newspaper work could bring a player in the era of the maximum wage that eventually helped draw him away from Bolton in 1928. Rumours of his departure had been circulating for some time and when readers of the *Bolton Evening News* were informed on 12 October that Jack would not play the next day because 'he has developed a cold', they were quick to spot journalistic code for an impending transfer. A very healthy Jack was indeed *en route* for London to sign for Arsenal, whose manager, Herbert Chapman, had reputedly spent many hours skilfully dining and, more particularly, wining the Bolton directors, who were unwilling to lose their captain and leading player. Jack was initially uncertain about the move, but the offer of a weekly column with the London *Evening Standard* proved decisive. The transfer fee was variously reported to be £10,340, £10,670, and £10,890, but whatever the exact figure, he was the first player ever transferred for a five-figure fee and the consequent publicity saw his early appearances add 5000 to Arsenal's average home attendance. Arsenal were struggling at the bottom of the English first division when he arrived, but his purchase proved to be a crucial element in the building of a side that came to dominate English club football in the 1930s.

The elegant, long-striding Jack was undoubtedly one of the finest inside forwards of all time—he also played on the right wing and at centre forward while at Bolton—and, in fact, a number of informed commentators regarded him as the greatest player of his generation. The *Bolton Evening News* captured his strengths well: 'Players of his type are not made everyday, for he is remarkably clever with both feet and head, possessing an amazing swerve that has baffled many good defenders, passes superbly, and shoots goals from seemingly impossible positions' (*Bolton Evening News*, 15 Oct 1928). It was, above all, his ability to create opportunities for others as well as seizing his own scoring chances that made him such an admired player. Between 1920 and 1934 Jack played 555 games, scoring 291 goals, winning FA cup winners' medals with Bolton (1923, 1926) and Arsenal (1930), and league championship medals with Arsenal (1931, 1933, and 1934). A victim of the rather arbitrary selection policy that typified the period, he gained only nine English international caps spread between 1924 and 1932, although he captained the side in four of those games. All this was achieved despite his being a chain-smoker from an early age. In 1934 he wrote a coaching manual with the rather inelegant title *Soccer: experiences of the game with practical instruction on training and on play in each position*, which showed him to be a prescient observer of the emerging European game.

On his retirement in May 1934, Jack moved into management, first at Southend United, where he stayed until 1940, and then at Middlesbrough from 1944 to 1952, the gap between the two posts (caused by wartime disruption) being filled by spells in a London bank and as manager of a Sunderland greyhound stadium. Ill health, possibly relating to the stress of the game, forced his retirement in 1952, with one journalist remarking 'how time had left its mark on a once fine athlete' (*Bolton Evening News*, 10 Sept 1958). After a final brief spell managing the Irish club Shelbourne from 1953 to 1955, he finally left the game to work in the Air Ministry, leaving a managerial record generally unexceptional for one so knowledgeable and talented. Although a popular and affable individual—he was the pianist for club singsongs at Bolton—fellow player and journalist Charles Buchan's observation that 'a retiring, shy man off the field [he] had not the forthright personality to make a success of the manager's job' (*Charles Buchan's Football Monthly*, November 1958, 5) provides the most likely explanation for his underachievement in this area. Latterly resident in Streatham, he died of cancer at St Thomas's Hospital, London, on 10 September 1958 and was buried five days later in Streatham Park cemetery. His son David R. Jack was to be an influential Sunday football columnist and biographer in the 1950s and 1960s.

DAVE RUSSELL

Sources D. Hayes, *Bolton Wanderers: an A–Z* (1994) · C. Freddi, *The England football fact book* (1991) · E. Hapgood, *Football ambassador* (1945) · b. cert. · d. cert. · *Streatham News* (19 Sept 1958)
Archives FILM BFI NFTVA, news footage
Likenesses photographs, 1923–32, Hult. Arch.

Jack [Jacchaeus]**, Gilbert** (*bap.* **1577**, *d.* **1628**), philosopher and physician, baptized in Aberdeen on 23 May 1577, was the son of Isabel Cargill and Andrew Jack, a merchant who died when Gilbert was still young. His mother then entrusted his upbringing to Thomas Cargill. Jack attended the local grammar school and subsequently became a student of Marischal College, Aberdeen.

On the advice of Robert Howie, the principal, Jack continued his studies on the continent, first, from 1598, at the Lutheran University of Helmstadt and from 1601 at Herborn, where he was appointed professor *extraordinarius*. On 25 May 1603 he enrolled as student of theology at the University of Leiden. Jack wrote two theses that same year, one entitled 'Disputatio theologica de peccato', the other, 'Disputatio theologica de libero arbitrio'. In September 1603 he was given permission to teach the Isagoge by Porphyrius on Wednesdays and Saturdays, days on which no regular lectures were given at the university. As early as 1604 students defended their theses under his aegis, although his formal appointment as professor *extraordinarius* of rhetoric did not take place until August 1605. Two years later his duties were extended to include ethics. Despite his theological degree, the university senate strictly forbade Jack to touch on theological questions in his lectures.

In July 1606 Jack married a local woman, Marijtgen Wilemsd. Grossiers. The couple had at least nine children and lived for a time in a rented house at Rapenburg 18, a street for the wealthy where many university professors owned houses. In the meantime Jack also studied medicine and received his MD in 1611, with a dissertation on epilepsy, which was printed at Leiden the same year. In February 1612 his appointments in rhetoric and ethics were upgraded to that of a full professorship, but in 1617 he relinquished his philosophical work in order to become professor of physic. Jack, who used the name Jacchaeus in his professional life, was a strict follower of Aristotle's metaphysical ideas and wrote a number of textbooks, such as *Institutiones physicae* (1615), *Primae philosophiae sive institutionum metaphysicarum libri sex* (1616),

and *Institutiones medicae* (1624), all of which were reprinted more than once until well after his death.

Among Jack's friends were Arminians such as Caspar Barlaeus, Hugo Grotius, and G. J. Vossius and, although there is no direct evidence about Jack's religious affiliation, he was suspect enough to be suspended from his university posts in 1619 when many people lost their jobs in the aftermath of the Synod of Dort, when the conservative elements in the church won the day. However, in 1620 Jack was again permitted to lecture on physic for a period of three months, only being fully reinstated as professor in 1623. In 1621 he was offered the Whyte's professorship of moral philosophy at Oxford, but he declined.

Jack died in Leiden in April 1628 after an illness which had left him paralysed on one side and which, if his friend Barlaeus is to be believed, had also affected his mental capacities. He was buried in Leiden on the 18th of the same month. Nothing is known of Jack's wealth, but in the 1640s his widow let rooms to students from German and Swedish noble families.

MARJA SMOLENAARS

Sources P. C. Molhuysen and P. J. Blok, eds., *Nieuw Nederlandsch biografisch woordenboek*, 10 vols. (Leiden, 1911–37) · L. van Poelgeest, ed., *De Leidse hoogleraren en lectoren, 1575–1815*, part 4: *De wis—en natuurkundefaculteit* (Leiden, 1904) · T. Lunsingh Scheurleer and others, *Het Rapenburg, geschiedenis van een Leidse gracht*, part IVb (Leiden, 1989) · T. Lunsingh Scheurleer and others, eds., *Leiden university in the seventeenth century: an exchange of learning* (Leiden, 1975) · IGI
Likenesses J. Van de Velde, engraving, repro. in Meursius [J. van Meurs], *Athenae Batavae, sive, De urbe Leidensi* (Leiden, 1625) · line engraving, BM, NPG

Jack, Richard (*d.* **1759**), mathematician and military engineer, was born in Scotland, and was living at Broad Garth, Newcastle upon Tyne, in 1737 and in Edinburgh in 1739. In the *Caledonian Mercury* for 6 November 1739 and 26 September 1743 he advertised himself as giving a course on natural philosophy as well as a complete system of astronomy and geography, in which he would 'demonstrate both in Mathematics and Experiments'. During the Jacobite rising of 1745 Jack was engaged in protecting Edinburgh. In September 1746 he is known to have been in London, helping Henry Baker with astronomical work.

Jack gained a certain notoriety in 1746 as the only witness among forty persons who gave evidence against General Sir John Cope concerning his conduct and behaviour at the battle of Prestonpans during the Jacobite rising. Sir John's army was defeated after only a very short engagement against a gathering of poorly armed Scottish highlanders, and he had rapidly retired from the battlefield to Berwick Castle with a few hundred men. He was examined by a military court in 1746, the British public at large seeing him to have grossly mismanaged his command, if not reacted with cowardice. The court of inquiry found no one ready to give evidence against Sir John, save Richard Jack. He had been serving with the king's troop as a fortifications engineer and was able to give a clear account of the battle, the nature of which was quite contrary to that of Sir John and his witnesses. Benjamin Robins was put up to write a lengthy introduction to the report of the court members, though he was not named as its author. When the report was laid before the king it resulted in Sir John's being totally exonerated. The report, if not the whole court martial, seems to have been a whitewash.

Jack again advertised his lectures on natural and experimental philosophy in the *Daily Advertiser* in 1751 and 1754. He advertised his gunnery (with board and lodging) for young men, and on 1 December 1757 his teaching of fortification. He also announced courses in which he used a 'large model of a *regular* fortress' to 'discuss matters of outworks'. He served as an assistant engineer with the British expedition to Guadeloupe, which fell in May 1759, shortly before his death. Jack was noted for his co-operation with George Adams (1704–1773) in constructing a new type of refracting telescope. He was also mentioned in connection with the design of a sea quadrant made and sold by Adams: patent no. 656, 1750, was signed and sealed between them.

Jack published at least three books: the first was *The Elements of Conic Sections in Three Books* (1742). The subject of this work was frequently and profoundly addressed by the well-known contemporary Scot Robert Simson, and by Jack himself in a substantial article that appeared in the first edition of the *Encyclopaedia Britannica* (1771). Jack's book demonstrated the principal properties of the parabola, the ellipse, and the hyperbola. On this and his other title-pages he asserted himself to be a teacher of mathematics. His second book, entitled *The mathematical principles of the theory of the existence of God, geometrically demonstrated in three books* (1747), was dedicated to Hugh, third earl of Marchmont. In the course of the dedication Jack referred to his gaining the protection of the earl from his native countrymen, by whom he was driven out of Scotland after the rebellion. Jack's third work was *Euclid's Data Restored to their True and Genuine Order … Agreeable to Pappus Alexandrinus* (1756); it was dedicated to James Dawkins of Laverstoke in recognition of Dawkins's then widely acclaimed *Ruins of Palmyra and Balbec* (1753). In his advertisement in the *Caledonian Mercury* in 1743 Jack stated his intention to publish his *Elements of Arithmetic*, in which 'will be laid down the Doctrine of Proportion', adding 'This Scheme is quite new, having no Precedent that he knows of', but the book does not appear to have been published.

Jack died in Castle Street, Oxford Market, London, on 8 May 1759, leaving a widow, Elizabeth, and a son, also called Richard. A sale of his goods and books by auction took place in February the following year.

W. JOHNSON

Sources W. Johnson, 'Benjamin Robins's two essays: Sir John Cope's arraignment and Lord Anson's "A voyage around the world"', *International Journal of Impact Engineering*, 11 (1991), 121–34 · W. Johnson, 'Richard Jack, minor mid-18th century mathematician: writings and background', *International Journal of Impact Engineering*, 12 (1992), 123–40 · W. Johnson, 'Richard Jack and Henry Baker, FRS, in the late summer of 1746', *Notes and Records of the Royal Society*, 47 (1993), 225–31 · W. Johnson, 'Richard Jack, assistant engineer in the expedition to Guadeloupe, 1758/9: facts and hypotheses', *International Journal of Impact Engineering*, 15 (1994), 91–

6 · R. V. Wallis and P. J. Wallis, *Biobibliography of British mathematics and its applications: part II, 1701–1760* (1992)

Jack, Thomas (*d.* 1598), schoolmaster and Church of Scotland minister, served first as exhorter (or preacher) from 1563 to 1568 at Rutherglen and then as minister of that parish by 1569. A university graduate, probably of Glasgow, he also held office as master of Glasgow grammar school (he is perhaps to be identified with the pre-Reformation master of Cambuslang grammar school). In September 1570 he received a presentation from the crown to the vicarage of Eastwood, near Paisley, and by August 1574 he had resigned his mastership. He maintained close links with Glasgow University under Andrew Melville's reforming principalship, holding office as quaestor or bursar, and donating works of St Ambrose and St Gregory to the college library. On Melville's advice, in 1574 he consulted George Buchanan (then in Stirling Castle, acting as tutor to young James VI and busily at work preparing his history of Scotland) on a draft classical dictionary in verse, *Onomasticon poeticum, sive, Propriorum quibus in suis monumentis usi sunt veteres poetae, brevis descriptio poetica*, later printed in Edinburgh by Robert Waldegrave in 1592. He dedicated the work to James Hamilton (eldest son of Claud, commendator of Paisley Abbey) who had been educated in the grammar school under his supervision; a fellow pupil had been John Graham, later fourth earl of Montrose.

Jack's friendship with Melville and Buchanan probably also helped to shape his opposition to episcopal government of the church. As a minister from a neighbouring parish he sat as an elder on Glasgow general session, served as a commissioner to the general assembly, and in accord with the assembly's policy in 1582 opposed the appointment of Robert Montgomery, minister of Stirling, whom the crown had nominated to the archbishopric of Glasgow. Along with the university's principal, Thomas Smeton, Jack travelled to Edinburgh in May 1582 to inform the presbytery that Montgomery had contravened the general assembly's instructions and merited excommunication. His adherence to the presbyterian cause led to his imprisonment, along with Nicol Dalgleish, Patrick Melville, and other ministers, during the earl of Arran's anti-presbyterian administration of 1583–5. At the general assembly's request he was appointed by the privy council in 1590 as a commissioner for furthering the work of the reformed church in Renfrew and Lennox. Jack died in 1598, leaving a widow, Euphemia Wylie, who survived until about 1608, and a daughter, Elizabeth, who married Patrick Sharp, principal of Glasgow University and earlier Jack's successor as master of the grammar school.

RONALD BAYNE, *rev.* JAMES KIRK

Sources G. Donaldson, ed., *Accounts of the collectors of thirds of benefices, 1561–1572*, Scottish History Society, 3rd ser., 42 (1949) · M. Livingstone, D. Hay Fleming, and others, eds., *Registrum secreti sigilli regum Scotorum / The register of the privy seal of Scotland*, 5–8 (1957–82) · *Reg. PCS*, 1st ser., vols. 1–5 · T. Thomson, ed., *Acts and proceedings of the general assemblies of the Kirk of Scotland*, 3 pts, Bannatyne Club, 81 (1839–45) · D. Calderwood, *The history of the Kirk of Scotland*, ed. T. Thomson and D. Laing, 8 vols., Wodrow Society, 7 (1842–9) · C. Innes, ed., *Munimenta alme Universitatis Glasguensis / Records of* the University of Glasgow from its foundation till 1727, 4 vols., Maitland Club, 72 (1854) • R. Wodrow, *Collections upon the lives of the reformers*, ed. W. J. Duncan, 2 vols., Maitland Club, 32 (1832–48) • *Fasti Scot.*, new edn, 3.133, 486 • T. M'Crie, *The life of Andrew Melville*, new edn (1899) • J. Durkan and J. Kirk, *The University of Glasgow, 1451–1577* (1977) • J. Kirk, *The Second Book of Discipline* (1980) • C. H. Haws, *Scottish parish clergy at the Reformation, 1540–1574*, Scottish RS, new ser., 3 (1972)

Jack, William (1795–1822), botanist, was born on 29 January 1795 at University and King's College, Aberdeen, the eldest son in a family of at least three sons and two daughters of the Revd Dr William Jack (1768–1854), professor and principal of University and King's College, Aberdeen, and his wife, Grace, *née* Bolt (1773–1850). At just six years of age he entered the grammar school, Old Aberdeen, and in 1811 he graduated MA from University and King's College. An attack of scarlet fever prevented him from going to study medicine at Edinburgh but in October 1811 he went to London, where he qualified as a member of the Royal College of Surgeons in January 1812. Having been appointed by the East India Company to the Bengal medical service, he left for his post on his eighteenth birthday, travelling as surgeon's mate on the ship *Neptune*. He was appointed assistant surgeon on 12 August 1813.

Jack went through the Anglo-Nepal War in 1814–15, and after further service in other parts of India met Sir Stamford Raffles at Calcutta in 1818, whom he accompanied to Sumatra to investigate the island's natural history. After four years of research and collecting, particularly in botany, Jack's health had deteriorated. At Bencoolen Raffles was finally obliged to place him on the ship *Layton*, bound for the Cape of Good Hope, but Jack died on board of pulmonary tuberculosis complicated by malaria the next day (15 September 1822); he was buried at Bencoolen the following day.

Jack's major work 'Descriptions of Malayan plants' was published in the scarce *Malayan Miscellanies* (2 vols., 1820–22). Further plant descriptions appeared in the *Transactions of the Linnean Society* (1823). Jack's name is commemorated in the genus *Jackia*, Wallich (1824) among others. He was elected a fellow of the Geological Society of London in 1821, and one paper in his name appeared in its *Transactions* (1820). B. D. JACKSON, *rev.* ANDREW GROUT

Sources *Companion to the Botanical Magazine*, 1 (1835), 121–47 • [S. Raffles], *Letters of Sir Stamford Raffles to Nathaniel Wallich, 1819–1824*, ed. J. Bastin, Malaysian Branch of the Royal Asiatic Society, reprint, 8 (1981) • E. D. Merrill, 'William Jack's genera and species of Malaysian plants', *Journal of the Arnold Arboretum*, 33 (1952), 199–251 • M. J. van Steenis-Kruseman and C. G. G. J. van Steenis, eds., *Flora malesiana*, 1 (1950), 256–7 • M. J. van Steenis-Kruseman and C. G. G. J. van Steenis, eds., *Flora malesiana*, 8 (1978), 49 • F. A. Stafleu and R. S. Cowan, *Taxonomic literature: a selective guide*, 2nd edn, 2, Regnum Vegetabile, 98 (1979), 395–6 • D. Chatterjee, 'William Jack, the botanist (1795–1822)', *Journal of the Bombay Natural History Society*, 56 (1959), 449–56 • D. G. Crawford, ed., *Roll of the Indian Medical Service, 1615–1930* (1930)
Archives NA Scot., Hay MSS • RBG Kew, plants • Royal Botanic Garden, Edinburgh, plants

Jackman, Isaac (1752?–1831), journalist and playwright, was born in Dublin, the son of a clerk in the lord mayor's office. He practised as an attorney in Dublin before moving to England for a marriage which might restore his fortunes. His wife's annuity ended, however, when she died shortly after they married, and he ultimately moved to London and wrote for the stage. His comic opera, *Milesian*, met with an indifferent reception on its production at Drury Lane on 20 March 1777. It was published in 1777. *All the World's a Stage*, a farce by Jackman in two acts, was first performed at Drury Lane on 7 April 1777 and was revived frequently. It was printed in 1777, and reprinted in Bell's *British Theatre* and other collections. *The Divorce*, 'a moderate farce, well received', produced at Drury Lane on 10 November 1781, and afterwards twice revived, was printed in 1781. *Hero and Leander*, a burletta by Jackman (in two acts, prose and verse), was produced 'with the most distinguished applause', according to the printed copy, at the Royalty Theatre, Goodman's Fields, in 1787. Jackman prefixed a long dedication to Phillips Glover of Wispington, Lincolnshire, in the shape of a letter on *Royal and Royalty Theatres*, purporting to prove the illegality of the opposition of the existing theatres to one just opened by Palmer in Wellclose Square, Tower Hamlets. Jackman was one of two young Irishmen who edited the *Morning Post* for a few years between 1791 and 1795, and involved the printer and proprietor in several libel cases. Jackman died in 1831.

JAMES TAIT, *rev.* REBECCA MILLS

Sources A. J. Webb, *A compendium of Irish biography* (1878), 260 • [D. Rivers], *Literary memoirs of living authors of Great Britain*, 1 (1798), 305 • D. E. Baker, *Biographia dramatica, or, A companion to the playhouse*, rev. I. Reed, new edn, rev. S. Jones, 1 (1812), 393 • Genest, *Eng. stage*, 5.554 • *IGI* • R. Welch, ed., *The Oxford companion to Irish literature* (1996)

Jacks, Lawrence Pearsall (1860–1955), Unitarian minister, was born at Nottingham on 9 October 1860, the second son of Jabez Jacks, an ironmonger, and his wife, Anne Steere. His father died when he was thirteen, and at seventeen he left school to teach, unhappily, in several private schools, while working for an external London degree. Convalescing from an illness, he spent part of 1881 learning German at Göttingen.

Anglican by inheritance, Jacks was introduced to Unitarianism by Samuel Collinson, a cultivated stockbroker who lodged in the Jacks house. Attracted by Richard Acland Armstrong (1843–1905), Unitarian minister at Nottingham, and by Stopford Brooke (1832–1916), who had recently renounced Anglican orders for a non-denominational pulpit at Bedford Chapel, Bloomsbury, he himself decided to become a minister and, in 1882, entered Manchester New College, then situated in London with James Martineau (1805–1900) as principal, graduating BA (London) in 1883 and MA in 1886.

A Hibbert scholar at Harvard University in 1886, Jacks became assistant to Stopford Brooke, only to find that many in the fashionable congregation would walk out when they learned that the assistant was to preach. On 29 July 1889 he married Brooke's daughter, Olive Cecilia (1868/9–1948); they had five sons and a daughter. He also gave university extension lectures on political economy and came to know a brilliant group of Londoners, including Edward Burne-Jones, Oscar Wilde, G. B. Shaw, and the Webbs.

At last committed to Unitarianism, in 1888 Jacks was appointed to Renshaw Street Chapel, Liverpool, in daunting succession to the greatly admired Charles Beard (1827–1888), while Beard's venerated predecessor, John Hamilton Thom (1808–1894), still in attendance, sat in judgment: Jacks recalled Thom's rebuking him for the indignity of riding a bicycle. In 1894 he moved to the equally prestigious church of the Messiah in Birmingham, warning its leaders—it was Joseph Chamberlain's congregation—that he came to them a strong Gladstonian Liberal. In 1902 he was appointed first editor of the *Hibbert Journal*, devoted to free debate on a wide range of religious and kindred subjects. The competing demands of the editorship and a busy ministry led him in 1903 to a lectureship in philosophy at Manchester College, which had been in Oxford since 1889. In 1915 he became principal, succeeding J. Estlin Carpenter (1844–1927). Honorary degrees followed from Glasgow, McGill, Rochester, and Harvard universities.

Jacks's years at the college were increasingly frustrating. Disenchantment with institutional religion and a growing conviction that the future lay rather in a broad-based education (including physical education) gave some offence to both students and governing body. Loyal to the non-denominational myth he had inherited from Martineau, he kept the college from joining the general assembly of Unitarian and Free Christian Churches, a new central body established in 1928. In 1931 he retired from the principalship and formally withdrew from the roll of Unitarian ministers. Nevertheless, his acceptance of an invitation in 1934 to give three addresses at evening services in Liverpool Cathedral triggered a furious campaign led by Lord Hugh Cecil that forced the convocation of York, on a motion by Hensley Henson (1863–1947), bishop of Durham, to rebuke the cathedral authorities for offering the pulpit to a Unitarian.

Among his vast literary output—including many lectures given in Britain and America—were *The Alchemy of Thought* (1910); biographies of Stopford Brooke and Charles Hargrove (1840–1918), minister at Mill Hill Chapel, Leeds; the *Smokeover* series of allegorical stories; and translations of the New Testament writings of Alfred Loisy (1857–1940). He left a charming and candid autobiography, *The Confession of an Octogenarian* (1932).

In 1917 Jacks was president of the Society for Psychical Research, a subject in which he was keenly interested. As a disciple of Henri Bergson, he lacked sympathy for prevailing trends of academic philosophy in Britain. His chief memorial is the *Hibbert Journal*, which he conducted brilliantly until 1947. Jacks died after a coronary occlusion at his home, Far Outlook, Shotover Hill, near Oxford, on 17 February 1955. R. K. WEBB

Sources DNB · L. P. Jacks, *The confession of an octogenarian* [1942] · *The Inquirer* (2 June 1928) · *The Inquirer* (9 June 1928) · *The Inquirer* (16 June 1928) · *The Inquirer* (30 June 1928) · *The Inquirer* (7 July 1928) · *The Inquirer* (14 July 1928) · *The Inquirer* (21 July 1928) · m. cert. · d. cert. · CGPLA Eng. & Wales (1955)

Archives Harris Man. Oxf., corresp. and papers relating to the *Hibbert Journal* | BL, letters to Albert Mansbridge, Add. MSS 65257A, 65258 · Bodl. Oxf., letters to Francis Marvin · Bodl. Oxf., corresp. with Gilbert Murray · Incorporated Society for Psychical Research, London, corresp. with Sir Oliver Lodge · King's Lond., Liddell Hart C., corresp. with Sir B. H. Liddell Hart · NA Scot., corresp. with Lord Lothian · NL Aus., corresp. with Alfred Deakin · U. Edin. L., corresp. with Charles Sarolea

Likenesses G. Harcourt, oils, 1924, Harris Man. Oxf.

Wealth at death £41,241 9s. 6d.: probate, 14 March 1955, CGPLA Eng. & Wales

Jacks, William (1841–1907), ironmaster and author, was born on 18 March 1841 at Cornhill-on-Tweed, Coldstream, Northumberland, one of six children of Richard Jacks, a farmer and land steward, and his wife, Margaret Lamb. Educated at the village school of Swinton, Berwickshire, he left home at the age of fourteen to be apprenticed at a Hartlepool shipyard, where he quickly gained promotion. In the evenings he used his aptitude for the classics to learn modern European languages. He then worked for Seaham engine works in Sunderland, where he used his language skills to advantage in gaining business. On his own admission he made a fortune through his understanding of Italian, when he rescued a cargo of iron shipped to a fraudulent concern in that country. Jacks moved to Glasgow in 1869 to manage the firm of Robinows and Marjoribanks, iron and commission merchants, becoming a partner in 1875. He married in 1878 Matilda Ferguson, daughter of John Stiven, a Glasgow insurance agent. In December 1880 he set up his own firm of iron and steel merchants, William Jacks & Co. Five years later he took over the lucrative Scottish agency for the Blaenavon Iron and Steel Company and took Andrew Bonar Law (later the prime minister) into partnership. A London office was opened in 1886 and a Middlesbrough branch in 1892. Jacks played a prominent role in the British Iron Trade Association, serving as president in 1896 at a time when producers and agents were much concerned at the threat of foreign, particularly German, competition. He took the lead in trying to arrive at price agreements both nationally and locally through the Glasgow Iron Merchants Association, formed in 1899.

Jacks was well equipped to represent the concerns of the industry. A committed Liberal, he served briefly as MP for Leith burghs in 1885–6. He voted against Irish home rule in 1886 and at the following general election W. E. Gladstone was persuaded, just before the closing date, to oppose Jacks in Leith burghs. Jacks withdrew and Gladstone was returned unopposed, but sat instead for Midlothian. Jacks stood unsuccessfully as a Liberal Unionist at the consequent by-election in August 1886. He returned to the Liberal Party and was elected for Stirlingshire in 1892, narrowly losing the seat in 1895. In that parliament he served on the railway and canal rates committee. His wide knowledge of commercial questions led to his appointment as arbiter in the London chamber of commerce arbitration scheme.

Through the chamber of commerce Jacks became

involved in efforts to improve commercial education in Britain. When he failed to persuade the Glasgow chamber, of which he was chairman in 1904–5, to become involved in education and training, he encouraged the Glasgow Athenaeum to separate its commercial training and seek recognition from the Scottish education department. Jacks became the first chairman of the council of the new Commercial College with John Mann junior as his vice-chairman.

Outside his business and public life, Jacks maintained his interest in languages and scholarship, translating Lessing's *Nathan the Wise* in quiet moments in the House of Commons; it was published with an introduction by Dean F. W. Farrar in 1894. For the centenary of Robert Burns's death in 1896 he published *Robert Burns in other Tongues*, followed in 1899 by *The Life of Prince Bismark* and in 1901 by *The Life of James Watt*. Farrar suggested in an introduction that *Singles from Life's Gathering* (1902) was largely autobiographical. Jacks's last book was *The Life of His Majesty William II, German Emperor* (1904). It was for these academic pursuits that the University of Glasgow awarded him an honorary LLD in 1899. Jacks died on 9 August 1907 at his country house, The Gart, Callander, Perthshire. He had no children, but a large number of nieces and nephews. Among several educational endowments, he left £20,000 to the University of Glasgow to found the William Jacks chair in German language and literature. His wife survived him. Although the breadth of his interests was remarkable, Jacks was not unusual in late Victorian Glasgow. Many businessmen who came from relatively humble backgrounds encompassed very successful business careers with active public involvement and scholarly pursuits.

T. W. BAYNE, *rev.* MICHAEL S. MOSS

Sources Annual Report [Glasgow Athenaeum] (1904–7) · minutes of the University of Glasgow Court, 1907 · Glasgow Herald (10 Aug 1907) · M. D. Dykes, The Scottish iron merchant of one hundred years ago: Barclay and Matheson Ltd (1980) · J. R. Hume and M. S. Moss, A bed of nails: the history of P. MacCallum & Sons Ltd of Greenock, 1781–1981, a study in survival (1981) · WWBMP, 2.189 · Gladstone, Diaries · A. B. Cooke, 'Gladstone's election for the Leith district of burghs, July 1886', SHR, 49 (1970), 172–94 · DNB · CGPLA Eng. & Wales (1907)
Wealth at death £112,000 16s. 4d.: confirmation, 5 Dec 1907, CCI · £23,708 7s. 11d.: eik granted, 30 July 1908, CCI

Jackson. For this title name *see* individual entries under Jackson; *see also* Ward, Barbara Mary, Baroness Jackson of Lodsworth (1914–1981).

Jackson, Abraham (1588/9–1646?), Church of England clergyman, was born into a clerical family in Devon. He matriculated at Oxford from Exeter College in December 1607 and graduated in June 1611. By 1614, when he published *Sorrowes Lenitive: Written upon the Occasion of the Death of … John, Lord Harrington*, he had clearly for some time been chaplain to the Harington family of Exton; according to this work, dedicated to Harington's widow, Lady Anne, and his daughter, Lucy, countess of Bedford, and offering them spiritual consolation on their loss, he had previously written with their encouragement. After a period as chaplain of Christ Church, Oxford, during which he proceeded MA in June 1616, he became 'preacher

of God's Word' at Chelsea, from where he dedicated to Edward, Lord Russell, and the countess of Bedford his *God's Call for Man's Heart* (1618). Here he approaches with confidence 'your best friend, even your God', and, when discussing participation in the Lord's supper, commends the doctrine of 'the Church of Scotland' and dismisses the 'Papists'' belief in the 'Real Presence'.

Apparently Jackson was at some point in his career vicar of North Petherwin, Cornwall, but a continuing interest in London is suggested by his *The Pious Prentice*, published in 1640 and dedicated to all intending apprentices. In September of that year he was admitted prebendary of Peterborough; since there is no record of subsequent ejection it is assumed that he died shortly before 17 March 1646, the date when his successor there was admitted.

GORDON GOODWIN, *rev.* VIVIENNE LARMINIE

Sources Foster, Alum. Oxon. · Wood, Ath. Oxon., new edn, 2.267–8 · A. Jackson, Sorrowes lenitive: written upon the occasion of the death of John, Lord Harrington (1614) · Fasti Angl. (Hardy), 2.546

Jackson, Arnold Nugent Strode Strode- (1891–1972), athlete and army officer, was born on 5 April 1891 at The Hucket, Addlestone, Surrey, the son of Morton Strode Jackson (1848–1913), assistant secretary to the Inland Revenue, London, and his wife, (Edith Rosine) Diana Martin, a miniature portrait painter. He was educated at Malvern College and Brasenose College, Oxford (1910–14), where he took up running seriously on the advice of his uncle Clement Jackson, who was treasurer of the university athletics club. Even by the casual standards of the time, his training was less than arduous and consisted mainly of massage, golf, and walking. But with an abundance of natural talent he soon proved himself to be one of the world's finest middle-distance runners. He won the 1 mile against Cambridge in 1912 and on the strength of this performance alone he was selected to represent Great Britain in the 1912 Olympic games at Stockholm. Jackson was an absolute novice when he went to Stockholm to run in the 1500 metres. He had never before run on a 400 metres or 440 yards track or in an anti-clockwise direction (races at Oxford were run in a clockwise direction on a track of 3 laps to the mile). Thanks to some unselfish and unrehearsed pacemaking by Philip Baker (later Lord Noel-Baker), Jackson entered the home straight of the Olympic final in fourth place but his long, raking stride took him to the tape first in 3 min. 56.8 sec., a new Olympic and British record. Among those he beat were the American holders of the world record at 1500 metres and 1 mile. After again winning the 1 mile against Cambridge in 1913 and 1914 he anchored the winning Oxford 4x1 mile relay team at the 1914 Penn relays in Philadelphia before retiring after no more than half a dozen first-class races. He had never even entered for the Amateur Athletics Association championships.

In the First World War Jackson served on the western front with the King's Royal Rifle Corps and achieved distinctions which more than matched his sporting honours. He became the youngest brigadier-general in the British army, he was wounded three times, mentioned in dispatches six times, and was one of only seven officers to be

Arnold Nugent Strode Strode-Jackson (1891–1972), by Bassano, 1915

awarded a third bar to a DSO. After the war he was called to the bar at the Middle Temple. In 1920 he was appointed CBE for his work as a member of the British delegation at the Paris peace conference. He adopted Strode as an additional surname in 1919, and the change was registered at the College of Arms, but he still retained Strode as a forename and was henceforth known fully as Arnold Nugent Strode Strode-Jackson. In 1918 he married Dora Berryman, daughter of William Allen Mooney of Columbus, Indiana, and in 1921 he settled in the USA. He directed the first Kentucky derby festival in 1935, and was a colonel on the staff of the governor of Kentucky during the Second World War, serving in New York and Ottawa, where he was in charge of anti-sabotage precautions. In 1945 he became a naturalized US citizen but his final years were spent in Oxford, where he died at his home, Norham End, Norham Road, on 13 November 1972.   IAN BUCHANAN

Sources *The Times* (17 Nov 1972) · *Athletics Weekly* (25 Nov 1972) · WWW · b. cert.
Likenesses photograph, 1912, repro. in I. Buchanan, *British Olympians* (1991), 95 · Bassano, photograph, 1915, NPG [*see illus.*]
Wealth at death £17,827: administration, 29 Jan 1973, *CGPLA Eng. & Wales*

Jackson, Arthur (*c.*1593–1666), clergyman and ejected minister, was born at Little Waldingfield, Suffolk. His father, John Jackson, a Spanish merchant, died when he was young, and his mother afterwards married Sir Thomas Crooke and died in Ireland. Jackson's uncle and guardian, Joseph Jackson, sent him to Trinity College,

Cambridge, where he graduated BA in 1614 and proceeded MA in 1617 (incorporated at Oxford in the same year). He married in 1619 Mary, the eldest daughter of Thomas Bownest of Stonebury, Hertfordshire.

Ordained on 27 December 1620, Jackson was chosen not long after by the inhabitants of St Michael, Wood Street, London, first as lecturer and subsequently as pastor. He was also chosen by the Clothworkers' Company, of which both his father and his uncle had been members, as its minister, preaching on every quarter-day in the company's chapel, commonly known as Lamb's Chapel, where he sometimes used a 'turn-up table' (presumably a folding table) for the celebration of the communion. Laud apparently remonstrated with him, saying, rather revealingly, that 'I know not what you young Divines think, but for my part I know no other place of residence that God hath on earth, but the High Altar' (Jackson). True to his puritan belief in the sanctification of the Lord's day, he also refused to read the Book of Sports, which permitted parishioners to engage in lawful recreations and sports after attending Sunday church services. However, as Jackson was a quiet and peaceable man, Laud took no action against him.

In 1640, when the new ecclesiastical canons were issued, Jackson was opposed to the 'et cetera' oath which was suspected by the puritans as a mask for future innovations such as recognition of the pope and which, he wrote on 10 July, 'if God be with me, I hope I shall never take' (Birch, 2.286–7). On 6 August he and a group of London puritan clergymen met at Nag's Head tavern about a petition against it. In 1644 Jackson was appointed a commissioner for the ordination of ministers, and in the following two years he took part in the London ministers' campaign for a strong presbyterian church government, and was one of the leading signatories in their petitions both to the houses of parliament and to the common council of the City. He was also chosen president of Sion College, London, in 1646. He was an active participant in the London Provincial Assembly after its formation in 1647, and twice served as its moderator. In 1648 and 1649 Jackson was one of the signatories of three London ministers' declarations against toleration, the army, and the army's plan to put the king on trial—*A Testimony* (1648), *A Serious and Faithful Representation* (1649), and *A Vindication* (1649). Implicated in what was known as Love's plot in 1651, he was imprisoned with others for seventeen weeks in the Tower.

Jackson was a studious scholar and conscientious minister. The maintenance at St Michael, Wood Street, was small, and he was heard to say that he spent £2000 out of his own estate during the years of his ministry there. Having moved in late 1649 to the parish of St Faith's under St Paul's, he continued his pastoral work there until 1662. His publications consist of four volumes of 'annotations' on the Old Testament from the book of Genesis to the book of Isaiah. He took pride in pointing out that when he 'first undertook this work' there had not been 'any piece of this kind extant in English, saving only the Geneva marginall Notes' (*Annotations upon the Five Books*, 1658, preface). In early 1660 Jackson was again appointed a commissioner for the approbation of ministers. When in May Charles II entered the City, he waited at the head of the London clergy in St Paul's Churchyard to present a Bible to the king. In 1661 he was one of the commissioners on the presbyterian side in the Savoy conference, but does not appear to have taken an active part in it. Ejected in 1662 from St Faith's under St Paul's, he retired first to Hadley, Middlesex, and afterwards to Edmonton. It was reported, however, that he was living at Whitefriars and preaching at conventicles between 1663 and 1665.

Jackson died at Edmonton on 5 August 1666 and was buried on 7 August at St Michael, Wood Street. He was survived by his wife, two sons (Joseph and John), and two daughters (Elizabeth Hoare and Martha Jackson).

His son **John Jackson** (c.1621–1693), ejected minister, was also educated at Cambridge University, matriculating in 1638 at St Catharine's College, graduating BA in 1643 and proceeding MA in 1646 from Queens' College; he was made a fellow of Queens' in 1644. Ejected from Cambridge in 1650 for his refusal to take the engagement, he went to London where in 1653 he married Anne, daughter of Lawrence Brinley, a London merchant and lay presbyterian. In 1654, presented by the protector, he became rector of St Benet Paul's Wharf. He was suspended in early 1662 for refusing reading the Book of Common Prayer, and was kept out of the parish church by force. He was also ejected from Moulsey, Surrey, but after the ejection seems to have continued living at Moulsey, where he completed his *Index Biblicus* in 1668. Afterwards he preached at Brentford, Middlesex, in 1672 and 1689. He published a memoir of his father in the 1682 edition of Arthur Jackson's *Annotations upon the Whole Book of Isaiah*. He died in 1693, either at Edmonton or at Tottenham Cross.   TAI LIU

Sources J. Jackson, 'To the Christian reader (a memoir of Arthur Jackson)', in A. Jackson, *Annotations upon the whole book of Isaiah* (1682) · E. Calamy, ed., *An abridgement of Mr. Baxter's history of his life and times, with an account of the ministers, &c., who were ejected after the Restauration of King Charles II*, 2nd edn, 2 vols. (1713) · *Calamy rev.* · *Reliquiae Baxterianae, or, Mr Richard Baxter's narrative of the most memorable passages of his life and times*, ed. M. Sylvester, 1 vol. in 3 pts (1696) · journals, CLRO, court of common council, vol. 40, letterbooks QQ · St Michael, Wood Street, churchwardens' accounts, GL, MS 521/1 · St Benet Paul's Wharf, vestry book, GL, MS 877/1 · St Benet Paul's Wharf, churchwardens' accounts, GL, MS 878/1 · JHL, 7 (1644–5) · *CSP dom.*, 1640; 1651 · Venn, *Alum. Cant.* · [T. Birch and R. F. Williams], eds., *The court and times of Charles the First*, 2 vols. (1848) · C. E. Surman, ed., 'The records of the provincial assembly of London, 1647–1660', DWL [2 vols.] · A. Gordon, ed., *Freedom after ejection: a review (1690–1692) of presbyterian and congregational nonconformity in England and Wales* (1917) · P. S. Seaver, *The puritan lectureships: the politics of religious dissent, 1560–1662* (1970) · Tai Liu, *Puritan London: a study of religion and society in the City parishes* (1986)
Likenesses D. Loggan, line engraving (after Bownest), BM, NPG · portrait, repro. in A. Jackson, *Annotations upon the five books immediately following the historicall part of the Old Testament* (1658)
Wealth at death leasehold in London; interest in lands in Ireland: *Calamy rev.*

Jackson, Arthur Herbert (1851–1881), composer, was born on 29 October 1851 at 19 Poultry Street, London, the son of a piano tuner, Isaac Jackson, and his wife, Jane, *née* Dubbin. He was a student at the Royal Academy of Music from 1872, and was taught composition by Sir William Sterndale Bennett and Arthur Sullivan. He won, among other honours, the Lucas medal for composition, and was elected in 1878 a professor of harmony and composition.

Jackson was a prolific composer during his short life. His overture to the *Bride of Abydos* had its first performance at a Promenade Concert at Covent Garden. *Intermezzo* for orchestra was played at Alexandra Palace, and his concerto for piano and orchestra was performed by Agnes Zimmermann at a concert of the Philharmonic Society on 30 June 1880. His violin concerto in E was played by Prosper Sainton at Cowen's orchestral concert on 4 December 1880. He wrote many piano pieces, including *Andante con variazione* for four hands (1880). Among his vocal works were a cantata, *Jason and the Golden Fleece*, and a chorus, *Lord Ullin's Daughter* (1879).

Jackson died on 27 September 1881 at his home, 4 Oxford and Cambridge Mansions, Marylebone Road, London, from 'tubercular meningitis'. He left a widow, Kate, and some £44.

L. M. MIDDLETON, rev. ANNE PIMLOTT BAKER

Sources *MT*, 22 (1881), 581 · Boase, *Mod. Eng. biog.* · Brown & Stratton, *Brit. mus.* · *The Athenaeum* (3 July 1880), 27 · b. cert. · d. cert. · *CGPLA Eng. & Wales* (1881)
Wealth at death £43 19s. 8d.: administration, 4 Nov 1881, *CGPLA Eng. & Wales*

Jackson, Arthur Mason Tippetts (1866–1909). *See under* Jackson, Mason (1819–1903).

Jackson, Sir Barry Vincent (1879–1961), theatre director, was born at Northfield, a Birmingham suburb then in the county of Worcestershire, on 6 September 1879, the second son and the youngest child by ten years of George Jackson, provision merchant, and his wife, Jane Spreadborough. His father, founder of the Maypole Diaries, was a wealthy man who loved the arts; he named his younger boy after the actor Barry Sullivan. Unusually for that time, Barry Jackson was encouraged to go to the play; he never forgot his earliest experiences in Birmingham, particularly Shakespeare by the company of Frank Benson and by such artists as Wilson Barrett, Ada Rehan, and Hermann Vezin. Even before going to a preparatory school, he was taken abroad; later, except for eighteen months in Geneva, studying French and the theatre when he was sixteen, he was educated entirely by a tutor. In adolescence he began to paint; but his father wished him to be an architect. For five years he worked in a Birmingham office until he decided at twenty-three that this was not his vocation.

Thenceforward Jackson's life was in the theatre. In 1907 he and several of his friends, notably two young insurance officials, H. S. Milligan and a tall, black-haired youth, John Drinkwater, then beginning to write poetry, founded the Pilgrim Players. From the work of this amateur company which within five years presented twenty-eight plays of literary and aesthetic worth, there rose in February 1913 the Birmingham Repertory Theatre, later among the most honoured institutions of its kind in Britain; one intended, in Jackson's words, 'to serve an art instead of making that art serve a commercial purpose'.

After more than three years in planning, the Repertory took only four months to build. Once the site behind New Street Station had been secured in June 1912 and the plans had been completed that October, Jackson's life and the story of his theatre would be inextricably linked. In February 1913 the Repertory Company opened, with *Twelfth Night*, in the house—holding 464 people and called in a Drinkwater poem 'the captive image of a dream'—that would be used for over fifty years; a building ahead of its time, its auditorium descending to the stage in sharply raked steps. The money was Jackson's; he sent off the première by reading, 'rather bashfully', the rhymed iambics of Drinkwater's prologue and its often-quoted phrase:

We have the challenge of the mighty line;
God grant us grace to give the countersign.

A grey-eyed, urbane man, 6 feet tall and a conspicuous figure at any gathering, Jackson seemed, outwardly, to change little during his life. Although only a moderate actor (and he gave this up after the first Repertory years), he was always naturally authoritative. In those early days he would sometimes direct the play or design the sets. The programme he chose had an uncommon range; he saw his theatre not as a West End annexe but as 'a revolving mirror of the stage'. Birmingham, where some people spoke slightly of 'a rich man's toy', responded sluggishly. Jackson, to begin with, was uncompromising; although it was the period of the theatre theatrical, he had no orchestra at the Repertory and even banned curtain calls. Slowly the theatre did collect a following; when, midway through the war, Jackson was commissioned in the navy, Drinkwater carried on the work, and his own *Abraham Lincoln* (Birmingham, 1918) was the first of many Repertory plays to reach London (1919). On Jackson's return his life again became inseparable from the changes and chances in Station Street. He saw such a triumph as the opera *The Immortal Hour* (1921) by Rutland Boughton, which he presented later in London (1922); and in 1923 there arrived the famous production of the pentateuch *Back to Methuselah* by G. B. Shaw, directed by H. K. Ayliff, which established a lasting friendship between dramatist and manager. Jackson also experimented with the then radical idea of Shakespeare in modern dress by presenting *Cymbeline* (1923).

Birmingham remained oddly aloof. At length, among startled protests, Jackson—who for all his urbanity could be resolute—closed the theatre until an audience was guaranteed. Meanwhile he devoted himself to London and to the presentation of *The Farmer's Wife* (1924), the Dartmoor comedy by Eden Phillpotts, done long before in Birmingham and now a steady success at the Royal Court. The Repertory was reprieved; but Jackson continued a London career which was progressively complex. In 1925 he leased the Kingsway as well as the Royal Court; during that year, when he was knighted for services to the stage, he put on the modern-dress *Hamlet*, known popularly as '*Hamlet* in plus-fours', and in the next year *The Marvellous*

History of Saint Bernard, his own version of a French mystery play by Henri Ghéon.

The period from the mid-1920s to the early 1930s was Jackson's most strenuous time. At Birmingham his theatre prospered artistically. He believed in the inspiration of youth; no friend of the star system, he yet made his own stars. The Repertory had produced such players as Gwen Ffrangcon-Davies, Cedric Hardwicke, Ralph Richardson, and Laurence Olivier; people were speaking of it as the university of the English stage. In 1929, besides his active London management, Jackson increased his responsibilities by planning the Malvern summer festival with the lessee of the local theatre. Living now on the Malvern Hills, he thought the town would be unexampled for a festival, which he dedicated at first to Shaw. When Jackson left the London stage in 1935 he had still two or three Malvern seasons before he concentrated on Station Street. Birmingham had another scare; in the spring of 1934, after spending not less than £100,000 on the Repertory within twenty-one years, Jackson insisted that the city must finally prove itself. After a year he was able in 1935 to transfer his interest to a local trust, giving the theatre, in effect, to the city, although he remained its governing director. In 1938, tired of apathy among the townsfolk of Malvern, he withdrew from the festival after nine years of ardent and costly toil.

Generous and sensitive, Barry Jackson could not forgive ingratitude; several times he was sharply hurt. The last occasion came in 1948 when, after he had restored the fortunes of the Shakespeare Memorial Theatre at Stratford upon Avon during three celebrated post-war seasons of reorganization (which also established Paul Scofield as an actor and Peter Brook as a director), his contract was not renewed. Thereafter he gave himself entirely to the Birmingham Repertory, putting on, among other successes, the three parts of the rarely staged *Henry VI* (1953) and in 1956 a *Caesar and Cleopatra* which went to Paris. He relied more and more on a trusted staff. After severe illness he was in his theatre for the last time during the first two acts of *Antony and Cleopatra* at a matinée on 15 March 1961; on Easter Monday, 3 April, he died in the Queen Elizabeth Hospital, Birmingham. He was unmarried.

Barry Jackson, practical visionary, connoisseur, and philanthropist, asked, above all, for style and for living speech. He wrote, translated, or adapted, several plays himself, among them *The Christmas Party* for children (1914), *The Marvellous History of Saint Bernard* (1925), and *Doctor's Delight* (from Molière, 1945). He was an honorary freeman of Birmingham (1953); he held the honorary degrees of MA and DLitt from the University of Birmingham, the LLD from St Andrews, and DLitt from Manchester. A lover of opera, from 1949 to 1955 he was a director of the Royal Opera House, Covent Garden.   J. C. TREWIN, *rev.*

Sources J. Drinkwater, *Discovery: being the second book of an autobiography, 1897–1913* (1932) · G. W. Bishop, *Barry Jackson and the London theatre* (1933) · J. C. Trewin, *The Birmingham Repertory Theatre, 1913–1963* (1963) · personal knowledge (1981) · private information (1981) · *CGPLA Eng. & Wales* (1961)
Archives Birm. CL, corresp. with George Bernard Shaw · U. Birm. L., special collections department, letters, mainly to Edith Barling;

letters to John Ramsay Allardyce Nicoll and Josephine Nicoll |FILM BFI NFTVA, documentary footage |SOUND BL NSA, documentary recordings

Likenesses P. Evans, pen-and-ink drawing, before 1925, NPG · H. Coster, photographs, c.1930–1939, NPG · W. Stoneman, photograph, 1940, NPG · W. Stoneman, photograph, 1948, NPG · W. Bloye, bronze sculpture, c.1958, Birmingham Repertory Theatre · H. Knight, portrait; at Actors' Benevolent Fund Offices, London, in 1981 · H. Knight, portrait; at Birmingham Repertory Theatre in 1981 · A. Munnings, portrait, Birmingham Repertory Theatre

Wealth at death £231,131 15s.: probate, 12 May 1961, CGPLA Eng. & Wales

Jackson, Basil (1795–1889), military surveyor, born at Glasgow on 27 June 1795, was the son of Major Basil Jackson (1757–1849) of the royal wagon train. He entered the Royal Military College, Sandhurst, in 1808, obtained a commission in the Royal Staff Corps on 11 July 1811, and was promoted lieutenant on 6 May 1813. He was employed in the Netherlands in 1814–15, was at Waterloo as deputy assistant quartermaster-general, and was afterwards sent to St Helena, where he remained until 1819. He served in Canada and was employed in the construction of the Rideau Canal. He was promoted captain on 17 September 1825, and was given a half-pay majority on 7 February 1834. He married, on 28 March 1828, the daughter of Colonel George Muttlebury, CB; and they had at least one son and one daughter.

In February 1835 Jackson became assistant professor of fortification at the East India Company's college at Addiscombe. In December 1836 he became assistant professor of military surveying, a post he held until 30 December 1857, when he retired on a pension. His *Course of Military Surveying* (1838) was the textbook at Addiscombe, but as he did not vary his teaching over more than twenty years he came to find it wearisome and it was judged fortunate for the college when he retired. He had become lieutenant-colonel on 9 November 1846, and had sold out in 1847. He afterwards lived at Glewston Court, near Ross-on-Wye, Herefordshire, until September 1874, and later at Hillsborough, Ross-on-Wye, where he died on 22 October 1889; his will was proved at nearly £30,000. With Captain C. Rochford Scott he published *The Military Life of the Duke of Wellington* (2 vols., 1840), and other works on surveying and warfare. He was described by Vibart, historian of Addiscombe, as kindly and easygoing.

E. M. LLOYD, rev. ELIZABETH BAIGENT

Sources *The Times* (24 Oct 1889) · H. M. Vibart, *Addiscombe: its heroes and men of note* (1894) · C. Dalton, *The Waterloo roll call* (1890) · CGPLA Eng. & Wales (1889)

Wealth at death £29,787 18s. 2d.: probate, 18 Nov 1889, CGPLA Eng. & Wales

Jackson, Brian Anthony (1932–1983), educational reformer, was born on 28 December 1932 in Huddersfield, the son of (John) Henry Jackson, labourer at ICI, and his wife, Ellen O'Brien. Although he never wrote an autobiography he gave many glimpses of himself as a child in his writing, particularly in his first and most influential book, *Education and the Working Class* (1962), written jointly with Dennis Marsden, a fellow pupil at Huddersfield College.

The book is a brilliant study of the effect of grammar-school education on working-class children and their families in which the authors transform their old school into Marburton College. Jackson was a scholarship boy who went on to win an open exhibition to St Catharine's College, Cambridge, where he managed to hold on to working-class values without decrying the middle-class values which so often supersede them.

Some of the scholarship boys and girls became conformists, but not Jackson. He showed his independent spirit by the way he gained admission to university. Travelling by train to Cambridge, bearing the all-important headmaster's letter of reference, he wondered whether he might be the messenger for his own death sentence. He opened the letter and, finding his fears to be justified, threw it out of the window. When asked at the interview where the letter was, he said he had read it, decided it would do him no good, and destroyed it. To the credit of the college he was accepted, and in 1955 he gained a first-class honours degree in English.

Orthodox careers for Jackson might have been in Labour politics or in teaching. Instead, after four years in which he combined teaching in a primary school and supervising undergraduates in a Cambridge college, he took the path of research and reform which dominated his life. After writing *Education and the Working Class*, for which he conducted research while on the staff of the Institute of Community Studies in Bethnal Green, he was from 1962 to 1965 a visiting fellow at the department of applied economics at Cambridge. His next book again showed his empathy with children. *Streaming: an Education System in Miniature* (1964) was an attack on the manner in which children were winnowed, divided, and enjoined to become what their teachers expected them to become. Later the problems of culture and class were still under his microscope in *Working Class Community* (1968).

As a reformer Jackson achieved results not by haranguing his audiences (though he was a persuasive writer and speaker) so much as by running organizations where actions spoke louder even than his words. With his ever buoyant energy, his flair, and his talent for enthusing people to work hard for little money, he managed to be simultaneously director of the Advisory Centre for Education (ACE, 1962–74) and of the National Extension College (NEC). The ACE was an information co-operative for parents and teachers alike, and it played a part in every educational reform of the period. The NEC was expressly designed by Jackson and Lord Young of Dartington as a distance teaching initiative which would be a pilot for the idea of an open university. Until then correspondence education had been held in almost as low repute as television teaching. The NEC helped to raise the standard and standing of both by teaching home students effectively and making a convincing case for the Open University. Jackson managed to build up both the ACE and the NEC without substantial funding and with no money from the state. The NEC continued as a pre-university college for many thousands of students.

Jackson was a tireless advocate for a minister for children at cabinet level. The education shop which he set up in the Co-op shop in Ipswich has been copied many times. He also set up nursery groups in the camps in Britain which were created for the Ugandan Asians expelled by Idi Amin.

In 1976 Jackson started the National Research and Development Trust, from which sprang the National Children's Centre and Childminding Research Unit. For the first time he brought into focus the work of the small armies of women who looked after other people's children before they went to school; the results of his research were published in *Childminder* (1979), which he wrote jointly with Sonia Jackson. While chairman of the trust he became a research fellow at the department of child health at Bristol University, where he opened up yet another new subject in *Fatherhood* (1984). This book portrayed the 'invisible man', or rather the shadowy man feeling his way towards a new role in which releasing the full force of fatherhood would mean breaking the masculine taboo on tenderness.

In 1956 Jackson married Sheila Mannion, a childhood friend from Huddersfield and the daughter of John Henry Mannion, an employee of the gas board; they had a son and a daughter. They were divorced in 1977, and in 1978 Jackson married Sonia Abrams, who already had a son and a daughter; together they had another son and daughter. Sonia, who was the daughter of (Israel) Maurice *Edelman MP and formerly the wife of Philip Abrams, sociologist, became a lecturer at Bristol University, and their house in Bristol was the centre of an abundant life with the six children and numerous friends. Intellectual and family life were infused with the same zest and energy and hatred of humbug. Jackson died suddenly on 3 July 1983 in Huddersfield after taking part in a charity run there.

MICHAEL YOUNG, rev.

Sources *The Times* (5 July 1983) · *The Times* (13 July 1983) · S. Jackson, 'Preface', in B. A. Jackson, *Fatherhood* (1984) · H. Rée, foreword, in B. A. Jackson and D. Marsden, *Education and the working class* (1986) · personal knowledge (1990) · private information (1990) · *CGPLA Eng. & Wales* (1983)
Wealth at death under £40,000: administration, 6 Dec 1983, *CGPLA Eng. & Wales*

Jackson [*née* Elliott], **Catherine Hannah Charlotte**, **Lady Jackson** (1813/14–1891), historian, was the daughter of Thomas Elliott of Wakefield. In 1856, at St Helena, she became the second wife of the elderly diplomat Sir George *Jackson (1785–1861). After her husband's death, she edited his diaries and letters from 1801 to 1809, publishing them in two volumes in 1872. In the following year, *The Bath Archives* (2 vols.) appeared, a further instalment of her husband's papers, covering the period 1809 to 1816. On 19 June 1874 she was granted a pension of £100 from the civil list, in recognition of her husband's services.

After a tour of Portugal, which she boldly undertook without a companion, Lady Jackson published *Fair Lusitania* (1874), a lively and readable record of her travels. It was favourably noticed by the critic of the *Saturday Review*, who described it as 'light and pleasant reading' (6 Feb 1875,

195). Lady Jackson's subsequent works met with a less cordial reception. Her next work, *Old Paris, its Courts and Literary Salons* (2 vols., 1878), was the first of a series of lightweight publications dealing with French court and high society circles from the sixteenth century to the nineteenth. Reviews were uniformly condemnatory: *Old Paris* was described as a superficial and inaccurate work, consisting of 'seven hundred pages of downright gossip' (*Saturday Review*, 25 Jan 1879, 116), while *The Court of the Tuileries* (2 vols., 1883) was held up as an example of 'bookmaking to which it would not be easy to find up any inferior' (*The Athenaeum*, 305). Critics recognized, however, that Lady Jackson was widely read in standard authorities (and even unpublished papers), and admitted that her narrative style—bumptious and with 'a great deal of go' (*Saturday Review*, 25 Jan 1879, 117)—made her histories readable works of light literature.

Lady Jackson's last publication was *The First of the Bourbons* (2 vols., 1890). She died of bronchitis, aged seventy-seven, at her home, 13 Belvedere, Bath, on 9 December 1891.

ROSEMARY MITCHELL

Sources Boase, *Mod. Eng. biog.* · Allibone, *Dict.* · *DNB* · *The Times* (11 Dec 1891) · *Saturday Review*, 39 (1875), 193–5 · *Saturday Review*, 47 (1879), 116–17 · *The Athenaeum* (8 March 1884), 305–6 · d. cert.
Archives BL, corresp. with R. Bentley & Son, Add. MSS 46564–46661
Wealth at death £59 3s. 6d.: administration, 11 Jan 1892, *CGPLA Eng. & Wales*

Jackson, Charles (1809–1882), antiquary, was born on 25 July 1809 at Doncaster, where both his grandfather and his father served as mayor. He was the third son of the large family of James Jackson, a banker, and Henrietta Priscilla, the second daughter of Freeman Bower of Bawtry. In 1829 he was admitted of Lincoln's Inn, and was called to the bar there in 1834, but settled as a banker at Doncaster. He was treasurer of the borough from 1838, and trustee of numerous institutions, and he played a leading role in establishing the Doncaster Free Library.

Jackson edited a number of seventeenth- and eighteenth-century Yorkshire diaries for the Surtees Society and, at the time of his death, was engaged in editing a memoir of the Priestley family, of which Joseph Priestley (1733–1804) had been a member. He also contributed several papers to the *Yorkshire Archaeological Journal* and compiled *Doncaster Charities, Past and Present*, a comprehensive account published in 1881.

Jackson died at Balby, where he lived, near Doncaster, on 1 December 1882. From his marriage with a daughter of Hugh Parker of Woodthorpe, Yorkshire, he left four sons and four daughters.

JAMES TAIT, rev. WILLIAM JOSEPH SHEILS

Sources *The Times* (15 Dec 1882) · *Doncaster Chronicle* (8 Dec 1882) · *The Athenaeum* (16 Dec 1882), 815 · *N&Q*, 6th ser., 6 (1882), 500 · *CGPLA Eng. & Wales* (1883)
Likenesses photograph, repro. in C. Jackson, *Doncaster charities, past and present* (1881)
Wealth at death £5954: resworn probate, Dec 1883, *CGPLA Eng. & Wales*

Jackson, Clement Nugent (1846–1924), sports administrator, was born in Simla, India, on 2 April 1846, the second son of Lieutenant-General George Jackson (1812–1889), of the Bengal staff corps. Educated at Somerset College, Bath, in 1864 he was awarded a scholarship to Magdalen Hall, Oxford, where he graduated BA in 1869 and proceeded MA in 1871, having taken third-class honours in classics. He remained in Oxford as a private tutor, and also held a tutorship at Magdalen Hall, which he retained when the hall was transformed into Hertford College in 1874. He was a university proctor in 1881 and held a fellowship of Hertford from 1881 until 1886, when he relinquished it on his marriage to Ada Louise Martin on 15 July. He continued to teach for Hertford, was re-elected to a fellowship in 1897, and was college bursar from 1887 until 1914. Jackson played a large part in the successful establishment of the new college; during its early days he was 'the man whom everyone knew, consulted and respected' (*Hertford College Magazine*, 9, 1914, 46).

As an undergraduate, Jackson was an outstanding athlete and cricketer. In 1865 he set a world record of 16 seconds for the 120 yards hurdles on the 'unsuitable' Marston track, and in 1867 he won the high hurdles for Oxford against Cambridge in the first match of the series to be held in London. His athletic career was ended by an accident sustained while racing W. G. Grace over hurdles: 'I spiked a hidden oyster shell when going full bat in a hurdle handicap after the seven-leagued legs of W. G. Grace', recalled Jackson (Lovesey, 29), and 'from that day onward I never ran, never tasted an oyster, and never spoke to W. G. the Great' (quoted in P. Matthews, ed., *The Guinness Book of Track and Field Facts and Feats*, 1982, 149).

While his own participation in sport was limited to annual fishing trips to Norway, and to coaching the Hertford eight from a bicycle on the river bank, Jackson became an energetic sports administrator both inside and outside Oxford. He became the senior treasurer of the university athletic club in 1869, and it soon became a rule 'that any bankrupt club went to Jacky, and in a year or two it was showing a healthy balance' (*Hertford College Magazine*, 9, 1914, 47). He became senior treasurer of the rugby and association football clubs (1886), and later of lawn tennis (1900) and lacrosse (1903). The acquisition of the Iffley Road running ground in 1876 and of the football ground in 1899 were described as his two greatest triumphs, both 'practically unaided efforts, for … he never liked divided control' (ibid.). Jackson was an early supporter of the idea of amalgamated college clubs, and was treasurer of Hertford's clubs from 1883 to 1913.

Jackson was well known for his guidance of individual athletes at Oxford, and his nephew A. N. S. Strode-Jackson won the 1912 Olympic 1500-metre title as an Oxford undergraduate. One of the athletes he encouraged was Montague Shearman, who organized a conference in Oxford in 1880 to discuss the future of amateur athletics. Jackson, as 'guide, philosopher and friend of the OUAC' (*Hertford College Magazine*, 9, 1914, 46) gave his powerful support to this meeting, and to the Amateur Athletic Association (AAA) which was formed from it, and of which Jackson was treasurer until 1910. It was his intervention at the meeting which ensured that the definition of an amateur which the new association adopted did not exclude 'mechanics, artisans or labourers' from competition, unlike the definition supported by the metropolitan Amateur Athletic Club. Had the more exclusive definition of an amateur been adopted, a split in amateur athletics would have been likely; instead the new AAA was quickly accepted as the national governing body for the sport.

Jackson died on 28 October 1924 at his home, 12 Norham Road, Oxford, after a long period of ill health and seven years of paralysis caused by a stroke. His widow, the author of *Gordon League Ballads for Working Men and Women* (1897), survived him. A subscription provided two C. N. Jackson memorial cups, one competed for at the Oxford and Cambridge sports, and the other at the AAA championships. An undergraduate of the 1870s wrote in his memory, 'If a man is to be measured by his influence on other men Jackson must be accounted a great man' (*Hertford College Magazine*, 14, 1925, 7).   M. A. BRYANT

Sources 'C. N. Jackson', *Hertford College Magazine*, 14 (April 1925), 6–7, 20 · *Hertford College Magazine*, 8 (Dec 1913), 21 · 'Mr C. N. Jackson', *Hertford College Magazine*, 9 (May 1914), 46–7 · H. F. Pash, ed., *Fifty years of progress, 1880–1930: the jubilee souvenir of the Amateur Athletic Association* [1930] · P. Lovesey, *The official centenary history of the Amateur Athletics Association* (1979) · *The Times* (29 Oct 1929) · *Oxford Magazine* (6 Nov 1924)

Likenesses photograph, repro. in Lovesey, *Official centenary history* · photograph, repro. in Pash, ed., *Fifty years of progress* · portrait, repro. in *Hertford College Magazine*

Wealth at death £9087 15s.: probate, 10 Dec 1924, CGPLA Eng. & Wales

Jackson, Cyril (1746–1819), dean of Christ Church, Oxford, was born in Yorkshire, the elder son of Cyril Jackson (1717–1797), physician, and his wife, Judith Rawson, *née* Prescot (d. 1785), widow of William Rawson, through whom the manor of Shipley came into the family. Having been briefly educated at Halifax and at Manchester grammar school (1755), he migrated to Westminster School and became a king's scholar there in 1760. In 1764 he was elected a scholar of Trinity College, Cambridge, but with the prospect of a studentship at Christ Church he matriculated there as a commoner on 26 June 1764, and was appointed student the following Christmas. He graduated BA (1768), MA (1771), BD (1777), and DD (1781).

Jackson owed the flying start to his career to the favour of William Markham, the headmaster of Westminster, himself a social climber. When Markham became preceptor to the two eldest sons of George III he carried Jackson with him as sub-preceptor (12 April 1771). From this position Jackson (along with the whole entourage) was dismissed in 1776, but he had already established a claim on the favour of the prince of Wales, and a series of preferments followed: the preachership of Lincoln's Inn (1779–83), the rectorship of Kirkby in Cleveland (1781), and a prebendal stall at Southwell (1786). It was, however, in Christ Church that Jackson made his career and fame: he became a canon there in 1779 and succeeded Markham as dean in 1783 during the brief Indian summer of whig influence.

Jackson was in one sense fortunate in the moment of his

Cyril Jackson (1746–1819), by William Owen, 1810

promotion. The incubus which Christ Church had long borne in Oxford of being a great resource of crown patronage in a university of intense independent sentiments had been reduced as Oxford gradually came back to court in the reign of George III. Matriculations were already increasing. Access to political influence enabled Jackson both to build up the standing of the house among the political classes and to govern it effectively. The cancellarial election of 1792 in Oxford enabled Jackson to oblige both the duke of Portland (who became chancellor) and William Pitt, who was seeking to reinforce his government by the Portland whigs at the same time; these political connections were reinforced as men of his own generation at Christ Church (such as Lord Auckland and Charles Abbot) and others whom he launched into the world as dean (such as George Canning and Robert Peel) became prominent.

Jackson, moreover, sought to supplement backstairs information by backstairs influence. He was alarmed by the collapse of Pitt's ministry in 1801, and, strenuous protestant constitutionalist as he was, did not want to see Pitt forcing his way back to office at the head of the Grenvilles, Canning, and the whigs on a platform of Catholic emancipation. It was not Jackson's way to make a public demonstration—'my general idea in all such cases is, that the university shd. make itself felt before it makes itself heard' (Ward, 10)—and in May 1803 he brought the two sides together, in the dukes of York and Portland, with a view to bringing in Pitt at the head of a new ministry and 'placing Mr Addington upon a bed of roses' (*Diary and Correspondence*, 1.423).

Christ Church freemasonry was not strong enough to settle the destinies of state, and for the next few years Jackson confined himself to collecting political gossip and strengthening the king's protestant resolution through the duke of York. One of his fondest political ambitions was to secure the succession to Sir William Dolben, the senior MP for the university, for Charles Abbot, the speaker, and one of his own fervent admirers. To this end he secured a letter of resignation from Dolben in the summer of 1806 to produce at the most convenient time. It soon transpired that Abbot would neither interrupt parliamentary business nor take the political risks of fighting a by-election. In 1806, however, Grenville unexpectedly called a general election, and, after many alarms, Jackson steered his candidate home in second place, his majority over Richard Heber, the third candidate for the two-seat constituency, being less than the Christ Church poll.

At Christmas 1808 Jackson pulled the political wires for the last time, attempting to persuade Portland, a sick man at the head of a sick ministry, 'to resign, that he might even then render the King the service of superintending the formation of a new government' (*Diary and Correspondence*, 2.214). Thomas Grenville believed that it was the dean who finally persuaded Portland to resign a few days before his death in October 1809, but Jackson insisted that Portland refused to discuss the matter again as he was under the king's command to hold on. Portland's death led instantly to Jackson's resignation of his deanery, for it opened the way to an acrimonious conflict between Grenville and Liverpool for the Oxford chancellorship, a conflict in which Jackson knew that not even he could maintain the cohesion of his house, and which permanently crippled the authority of his successor, Charles Henry Hall. Jackson was still prepared to give moral advice to old pupils (such as the prince regent), but now assumed the character of one withdrawn, the hermit and philosopher of Felpham, Sussex.

Success by the backstairs guaranteed Jackson not merely the loyalty of the dons and politicians admitted to his circle, but the obloquy of those who were not. Holland described him as 'a worshipper of rank' (Holland, 323). He encouraged absurd exclusiveness at the house; indeed the mark of his success was that he attracted three-quarters of all the Oxford peers and sons of peers. J. W. Ward, later earl of Dudley, found him 'something of a mountebank' (*Letters of … Dudley*, 192), a character not unjustified by the literary opinions which he enforced after dinner. To Samuel Parr he was yet worse: he 'said, "Stung and tortured as he is with literary vanity, he shrinks with timidity from the eye of criticism" &c. meaning that Jackson had never presented himself to the public through the medium of the press' (Beste, 215–16). The immediate target of this barb was an edition of Herodotus which Jackson was preparing but which he withdrew from the Clarendon Press before it was ready.

Again to a man with Jackson's connections no ecclesiastical preferment was closed, and he is said to have refused various bishoprics and the primacy of Ireland. His preference for his deanery, and what Reginald Heber described as 'an absolute monarchy of the most ultra-oriental character' (Heber, 1.449), to a fully public station perhaps owed as much to weakness as to affection for the house. Yet Jackson was not just an early eighteenth-century head of house manipulating his society politically: he restrained the riotous propensities of the Westminsters and inculcated a strenuous ethic of work. His counsel to Peel was to 'work very hard, & unremittingly—work … like a Tigur, or like a Dragon, if Dragons work more & harder than Tygurs' (BL, Add. MS 40605, fol. 16). Moreover Christ Church filled its 101 places for students through the nomination of the dean (who had two choices) and the canons. The chapter clung tenaciously to this patronage, but exercised it judiciously enough to create a pool of prospective tutors who were able to reinforce the social pull of the college with an efficient education for those who wanted it, and to keep its reputation alive in the lax years which followed Jackson's retirement.

The same atmosphere of controversy surrounded both the methods and the objectives of Jackson's principal achievement in university politics, the examination statute of 1800, which he secured with the assistance of John Eveleigh, provost of Oriel, and John Parsons, master of Balliol, whose college ultimately made the greatest profit from the new system. On both fronts Jackson was relentlessly pursued by Edward Tatham, rector of Lincoln. The latter's accusation that Jackson attempted to avoid open debate in convocation by '*beckonings!* and *crossings!* and *whisperings!* and *consultations!*' and 'the tricks of a common borough' (E. Tatham, *A Letter to the Rev. the Dean of Christ Church*, 1807, 7) took the measure of his man, though it hardly allowed for the difficulty of securing new legislation from a university constitution designed to stop changes being made. At any rate Jackson and his allies played safe in terms of both academic and national politics, and though two sections of the statute were opposed by Edward Copleston of Oriel and 'Horse' Kett of Trinity as not going far enough, fifteen of the eighteen sections were accepted by convocation unanimously.

The new examinations were to be fully public, with 'as many members of the university as possible … present' and six candidates to be examined *viva voce* each day. The scope of the examination barely exceeded Oxford's ancient repertoire, namely grammar, rhetoric, logic, moral philosophy, and the elements of mathematics and physics. Additional subjects were to be offered in an examination for the master's degree which was dropped in 1807. The two great novelties were that 'at every examination, on every occasion, the Elements of Religion, and the Doctrinal Articles … must form a part' (Heywood, *Statutes*, 2.79), and that there was to be a supplementary examination for honours. The first of these provisions was Oxford's great pledge to the counter-revolutionary cause, a requirement which, so far as anyone knew, was not made by any other university for the first degree, an undertaking that, so far as it was in Oxford's power, the Church of England would never suffer by inadvertence the fate which had befallen the church of France. Candidates for the honours competition were to be examined by the whole board on a larger range of books, and the best twelve were to be listed in order of merit. As it was several years before twelve candidates presented themselves this provision was of no great importance.

The event showed that Jackson and his allies had gauged pretty accurately what could be got through convocation; this did not save them from the bitter complaints of Tatham that the new syllabus was narrow and obsolete: 'A violent affectation of Peripatetic learning has seized of late the fashionable college [Christ Church]' (E. Tatham, *A Letter to the Rev. the Dean of Christ Church*, 1807, 10), and all must follow suit. Tatham had for years raved against the reign of Aristotle in Oxford, and had rejoiced that under the unreformed system progressive colleges had been in no way inhibited by the official forms. This loss of liberty was the more galling because of the patronage questions which underlay it. The Greek chair had of late generally gone to the house, and the present incumbent, who had 'been completely dormant for more than twenty years' (E. Tatham, *A New Address to the Free and Independent Members of Convocation*, 1810, 17), was Jackson's younger brother, William *Jackson. On two fronts Tatham perceived disaster:

The old moral philosophy of Aristotle, Cicero, or Epictetus, however admirable in their days, is today not worth a louse … how much worse than absurd is it to send the youth of a Christian university in the nineteenth century, to learn their moral philosophy from Aristotle that uncircumcized and unbaptized Philistine of the Schools. (E. Tatham, *An Address to Members of Convocation*, 1807, 6)

Equally perilous were the prospects for science teaching, which had formed a modern offering in some colleges and in professorial classes. There seems no doubt that the new statute was instantly injurious in this field, and that the situation became worse in 1807 when 'the elements of mathematics and physics' (but not other sciences) attained the dignity of a separate school, and ceased to be obligatory subjects in the basic examination. On the other hand there is no doubt that the new system extracted more work from at least the conscientious undergraduates, that it encouraged the growth of a race of competitive tutors who thrived on the success of their pupils in the schools, and that the desire for competitive success in the long run weakened other Oxford rigidities. And in all this Jackson had benefited the university as a whole at the expense of the separate interest of his own society.

Jackson died at Felpham on 31 August 1819. His tombstone there was uncharacteristically modest, but his college had commissioned a portrait of him by Owen, and from this his pupils had a statue executed by Chantrey and placed in Christ Church Cathedral. W. R. WARD

Sources W. R. Ward, *Victorian Oxford* (1965) · *Hist. U. Oxf.* 5: *18th-cent. Oxf.* · E. Tatham, *Oxonia purgata* (1812) · *The diary and correspondence of Charles Abbot, Lord Colchester*, ed. Charles, Lord Colchester, 3 vols. (1861) · *Diaries and correspondence of James Harris, first earl of Malmesbury*, ed. third earl of Malmesbury [J. H. Harris], 4 vols. (1844) · H. R. V. Fox, third Lord Holland, *Further memoirs of the whig party, 1807–1821*, ed. Lord Stavordale (1905) · *The journal and correspondence of William, Lord Auckland*, ed. [G. Hogge], 4 vols. (1861–2) · *Letters of the earl of Dudley to the bishop of Llandaff* (1840) · H. D. Beste, *Personal and literary memorials* (1829) · A. Heber, *Life of Reginald Heber*

(1830) · J. Heywood, ed., *Oxford University statutes*, trans. G. R. M. Ward, 2 vols. (1845–51) · *DNB*

Archives W. Yorks. AS, Calderdale, family and estate papers | Balliol Oxf., Jenkyns MSS · BL, corresp. with Sir Robert Peel, Add. MSS 40226–40605, *passim* · BL, corresp. with earls of Liverpool, Add. MSS 38232, 38243, 38309–38310, 38423, 38471, *passim* · Flintshire RO, Hawarden, corresp. with Hugh Chambres Jones · LPL, letters to William Howley · Oxf. UA, MS hebdomadal register; MS minutes of hebdomadal meeting · PRO, Colchester diary and MSS, 30/9/33 · U. Nott. L., letters to third duke of Portland

Likenesses R. Dighton, double portrait, caricature, coloured etching, pubd 1807 (with James Webber), NPG · W. Owen, oils, 1810, Christ Church Oxf. [*see illus.*] · F. Chantrey, statue, exh. RA 1824, Christ Church Oxf.; repro. in *Hist. U. Oxf.* 6: *19th-cent. Oxf.*, pl. 2

Wealth at death considerable: *DNB*

Jackson, Sir Cyril (1863–1924), educationist, was born in London on 6 February 1863, the elder son of Laurence Morris Jackson (*d.* 1913) of South Park, Bodiam, Sussex, a member of the stock exchange, and his wife, Louisa Elizabeth Craven (*d.* 1915). He was educated at Charterhouse School and at New College, Oxford, where he obtained second classes in classical moderations (1883) and in *literae humaniores* (1885).

Inspired both by his family and by the Oxford movement for a university settlement to undertake social work among the poor in the East End of London, Jackson became a resident at Toynbee Hall in 1885, soon after its foundation, and remained there until 1895. He was called to the bar by the Inner Temple in 1893, but never practised as a lawyer. He possessed private financial means which enabled him to commit himself to educational work in the deprived industrial community of east London. He served as a member of the London school board (1891–6) and as secretary of the Children's Country Holiday Fund (1888–96). The boys' club which he ran at Northey Street School (later renamed the Cyril Jackson School) sought to mould Limehouse street boys into self-respecting citizens. His studies of Hebart, Pestalozzi, and Froebel drew him towards the ideas of the 'new education' movement, which rejected the rote-learning methods used in elementary schools.

In 1896 Jackson accepted an invitation to go to Western Australia as inspector-general of schools and permanent head of the education department. Between 1896 and 1903 he reorganized the system so completely that it was soon recognized throughout the commonwealth as equal to, if not the best, system in Australia. Although he was personally a devout Anglican, he welcomed the concession of the 'right of entry' to schools of all religious denominations. He returned to England in 1903 as chief inspector of elementary schools in the Board of Education, but resigned at the end of 1905 after a dispute with Robert Morant.

In July 1906 Jackson was appointed with John Christian Pringle of the Charity Organization Society one of two special investigators for the poor law commission, reporting on methods of relieving the unemployed outside the poor law. They concluded that these alternative forms of relief were completely ineffective. Jackson also wrote a report on boy labour for the commission, drawing on his concern that because of lack of training youths were drifting into unskilled, casual work. He was immersed in municipal work as elected member of the London county council, Limehouse division (1907–13), alderman (1913–16 and 1919), twice chairman of the education committee (1908–10 and 1922), leader of the Municipal Reform Party (formerly known as the moderates, and predominantly unionist in politics), and later chairman of the council (1915).

When war broke out Jackson took full charge of, and responsibility for, the council. A week later he was appointed chairman of the emergency committee. During 1916–17 he was vice-chairman, under the prince of Wales, of the national statutory committee on war pensions. He was created KBE in 1917. Among his other public offices, he served on the senate of London University (1908–21), on the Port of London Authority (1915–16 and 1919), on the royal commission on the superior civil services in India (1923), and as member of the memorial committee which presented to London the King Edward Park in Shadwell in 1922.

As a result of ceaseless work, regardless of his health, Jackson suffered breakdowns which, compounded by bouts of insomnia, sometimes made him a difficult person with whom to get on. He sought relief in sea voyages. His quick mind enabled him rapidly to puncture schemes or arguments which had major defects. In the municipal politics of London he was in advance of the bulk of his Conservative Party colleagues, whose feelings towards him were perhaps more admiring than affectionate. On the London county council he sought to curb unnecessary municipal expenditure, believed that voluntary organizations had an important part to play in providing welfare, and supported non-provided schools. More than anyone else he was responsible for co-operation between existing institutions in the medical treatment of school children, and for the creation of care committees of voluntary workers in London. While he was chairman of the education committee the London county council adopted a far-reaching scheme for reducing the size of elementary school classes, and established central schools. His report on boy labour, drawn up for a Board of Education committee in 1916, influenced the provisions in the 1918 Education Act for a school-leaving age of fourteen and part-time education thereafter. After the act was passed he gave enthusiastic support to the reorganization of evening education and to the compulsory day continuation system. His views on policy questions were set out in his books: *Unemployment and Trades Unions* (1910), *Outlines of Education in England* (1913), and *The Religious Question in Public Education* (1911, jointly with Michael Sadler and Athelstan Riley).

Jackson died unmarried at his beautiful home, Ballards Shaw, Limpsfield, Surrey, on 3 September 1924. He did not wear his heart on his sleeve: he never talked about the motive of his work, but those who knew him and had access to his papers concluded that Jackson, like many others of his generation, was driven by a profound belief in selfless public service.

R. BLAIR, *rev.* M. C. CURTHOYS

Sources personal knowledge (1937) · private information (1937) · Walford, *County families* (1919) · AusDB, vol. 9 · R. Aldrich and P. Gordon, *Dictionary of British educationists* (1989) · S. Maclure, *One hundred years of London education, 1870–1970* (1970) · R. J. W. Selleck, *The new education: the English background, 1870–1914* (1968) · A. Briggs and A. Macartney, *Toynbee Hall: the first hundred years* (1984) · J. Harris, *Unemployment and politics: a study in British social policy, 1886–1914* (1972) · A. M. McBriar, *An Edwardian mixed doubles, the Bosanquets versus the Webbs: a study in British social policy, 1890–1929* (1987) · CGPLA Eng. & Wales (1924)
Archives Bodl. Oxf., letters to Francis Marvin
Likenesses W. Stoneman, photograph, 1917, NPG · portrait, repro. in *Royal Academy Illustrated* (1917)
Wealth at death £38,885 12s.: probate, 17 Oct 1924, CGPLA Eng. & Wales

Jackson, Daphne Frances (1936–1991), physicist and champion of women in science and engineering, was born on 23 September 1936 at 34 Willesden Avenue, Peterborough, the only daughter and second child of Albert Henry Jackson (1893–1951), an engineering fitter and turner, and Frances Ethel, formerly Elliott (1897–1985), a dressmaker and designer until she married. She was educated at Peterborough county grammar school and Imperial College of Science and Technology; she graduated BSc (special physics) and became an associate of the Royal College of Science in 1958.

In 1958 Jackson was invited by L. R. B. Elton to join him as his first research student when he was appointed to the headship of the physics department at Battersea College of Advanced Technology. Two years later she was appointed to the academic staff as assistant lecturer (1960–62), earning her (University of London) PhD in 1962. She was appointed lecturer (1962–6) and with Elton helped to lay the foundations of an internationally respected group studying the theory of the structure of the atomic nucleus. Together they did important work on the theory of nuclear reactions and nuclear structure and Jackson soon began to publish individual contributions to the interpretation of nuclear reactions in which protons and other particles are knocked out of nuclei by a high-energy proton beam. Such studies yield important information about the constituents of nuclei. Her contributions were recognized by the award of a University of London DSc in 1970. In 1966 Battersea College was granted a royal charter and became the University of Surrey. Jackson was made reader in nuclear physics and leader of the nuclear physics group, which given this lead grew into the largest and most strongly supported such group in the UK, while the University of Surrey advanced into one of the UK's major research-led universities.

In 1971 Jackson was appointed professor and head of the physics department, the first woman to hold either post in the UK; she retained both until her death. It was a source of great frustration to her that she was the UK's only woman professor of physics for the first fifteen years of her appointment. Jackson proved a worthy successor to Elton. Her leadership qualities and wide perspective were recognized when the university appointed her dean, first of the faculty of mathematical and physical science during 1977–80, and thereafter of the faculty of science during 1984–8.

From about 1978 onwards Jackson's physics interests began to move away from fundamental questions and towards applications of nuclear physics, especially in medicine. She played an important role in strengthening these areas in physics at Surrey as well as serving on various relevant national committees. The department's two MSc courses in medical physics and in radiation and environmental protection, which came to prominence during her headship, soon attracted students from all over the world, providing an important source of trained personnel for hospital physics departments and industry, especially the nuclear industry.

The breadth of Jackson's interests is indicated by her publications—some eighty articles on nuclear physics (as well as four books and contributions to others), fifty-five articles on medical physics and its applications, and almost as many (forty-six) on issues of science and society. In 1965 she became the Institute of Physics's youngest fellow and later its vice-president. She was also fellow of the American Physical Society and the Institution of Electrical Engineers, a senior member of the Institution of Electrical Engineers (of which she was a member of council), and a liveryman of the Worshipful Company of Engineers. Various public bodies on which she served included the board of the Meteorological Office Agency, the Schools Examinations and Assessment Council, the Advisory Council on Research and Development for Fuel and Power for the Department of Energy, the BBC science consultative group, various boards of the Science and Engineering Research Council, the metrology and standards requirements board of the Department of Trade and Industry, the West Surrey and North East Hampshire District Health Authority, committees of several regional health authorities, the National Radiological Protection Board and the civil service commission final selection board. At various times she held visiting appointments in nuclear physics at the universities of Washington, Maryland, Louvain, and Lund, as well as at the Institute for Cancer Research of the Royal Marsden Hospital. She was also active in many roles within the Women's Engineering Society, most notably as its president.

In parallel with her interests in physics, Jackson found herself becoming increasingly active in 'encouraging women in science and engineering', which was listed as a recreation in her entry in *Who's Who* of 1991. This recreation had outstanding consequences, some with an importance equal to or exceeding that of her contributions to nuclear physics. Using her presidency of the Women's Engineering Society in 1983–5 as a springboard, she was instrumental in helping establish the national WISE (Women in Science and Engineering) initiative to attract schoolgirls into science and engineering. In the same period she conceived and launched the Women Returners' Fellowship scheme for women who had had to give up careers in science or engineering because of family commitments. These fellowships made it possible for such women to make an effective return to high-level technological or scientific careers, something many people had thought impossible. Her genius was to identify a genuine need in society, to plan an effective way of meeting this need, and to carry out that plan, raising the substantial funds needed and proving her many sceptics wrong in the process. Official recognition of these and related efforts came when she was appointed OBE in 1987. She was also awarded honorary degrees by the Open University and the universities of Exeter and Loughborough. Jackson's initiatives continued to flourish after her death, an effective testament to her vision and determination.

It was particularly poignant that, at a time when her professional interest was focused so much on the diagnosis and treatment of cancer using nuclear physics and other techniques, Daphne Jackson was herself diagnosed as having the disease. Throughout a long struggle with cancer she continued to work and make contributions both to science and society at university, national, and international levels. Her dedication to the Women Returners' scheme was particularly evident at this time. She died at her home in St Omer Road, Guildford, on 8 February 1991, having been involved only hours before in counselling one of her PhD students, and was cremated at Guildford six days later. Her memory has been perpetuated through her former research students, who hold positions as scientists all over the world, and through the Daphne Jackson Memorial Fellowships Trust which administers the Returners' Fellowship scheme she did so much to create.   R. C. JOHNSON and E A JOHNSON

Sources D. F. Jackson, curriculum vitae, Guildford, University of Surrey, 1990 · *The Guardian* (14 Feb 1991) · private information (2004) [R. H. Jackson, brother] · D. F. Jackson, 'President's inaugural message and introduction', *Woman Engineer*, 13/6 (1983), 1–2 · R. J. Huck, *Eighty years on—a brief history of the physics department of the University of Surrey, 1906–1986* · *WWW, 1991–5* · Daphne Jackson Memorial Fellowships Trust, University of Surrey · L. R. B. Elton, 'Daphne Jackson: the early years', *Register* (spring 1991) [University of Surrey Journal] · R. Douglas, *Surrey: the rise of a modern university* (1991) · b. cert. · d. cert.

Archives priv. coll. · University of Surrey, department of physics, Daphne Jackson Memorial Fellowships Trust

Likenesses J. Allison, oils, 2002, University of Surrey · photographs, University of Surrey

Wealth at death £266,032: probate, 5 April 1991, *CGPLA Eng. & Wales*

Jackson, Derek Ainslie

Jackson, Derek Ainslie (1906–1982), physicist, was born in Hampstead, London, on 23 June 1906, the younger of the twin sons of Sir Charles James Jackson (1849–1923), barrister and art historian, and his wife, Ada Elisabeth (d. 1924), daughter of Samuel Owen Williams. His elder identical twin, Charles Vivian, died in 1936, and his sister, Daphne (b. 1896), died during the First World War. Educated at Rugby School from 1920 to 1924, Jackson went to Cambridge in 1924 as a scholar at Trinity College. His parents having died, he was an affluent undergraduate but dependent for income until 1936 on a guardian who ran the family finances. He took a second-class degree in the

Derek Ainslie Jackson (1906–1982), by Bassano, 1935

natural sciences tripos in 1927, and was invited by Rutherford to undertake research on nuclear physics in the Cavendish Laboratory, but, stimulated by H. W. B. Skinner, his Cambridge tutor, and by a visit to the Berlin laboratory of H. Schüler, Jackson wished to work on the new topic of hyperfine structure of spectral lines. As a rich man Jackson could afford to defy Rutherford; he preferred to accept an offer from Lindemann, Dr Lee's professor of experimental philosophy at Oxford, to work in the Clarendon Laboratory, where he appeared in 1927 with all his spectroscopic apparatus bought by himself. Fearless, wild tempered, and wickedly amusing, he was the most prolific solo publisher in the Clarendon in the early 1930s. Neither his temperament nor his style of life permitted him to take on research students. He moved in artistic and literary circles, marrying Elizabeth Ann (Poppet; 1912–1997), daughter of Augustus Edwin *John, on 2 March 1931.

In 1933 Lindemann arranged for H. G. Kuhn, a refugee spectroscopist from Göttingen, to join Jackson in the Clarendon, where they worked fruitfully until 1939 on sharpening spectral lines, using sumptuous apparatus provided by Jackson. In 1934 Jackson became a stipendless lecturer in spectroscopy but spent much time at race meetings, fox hunts, and aristocratic dinner parties. In 1935 he rode for the first time in the Grand National, but fell. In the same year he was divorced, and on 29 December 1936 he married Pamela Freeman Mitford (b. 1907), second daughter of David Bertram Ogilvy Freeman Mitford, second Baron Redesdale, and thus became brother-in-law to the wife of Sir Oswald Mosley. Though no fascist Jackson was so fiercely independent that even in 1943 he gave accommodation in his spacious rural home, Rignell House, Oxfordshire, to the Mosleys on their release from internment.

When war broke out Jackson joined a small group of researchers working for the Admiralty in the Clarendon but in 1940, after Winston Churchill's intervention, Lindemann released him to join the Royal Air Force. Jackson flew as a navigator from spring 1941 until summer 1942 when, at Lindemann's instigation, he was made chief airborne radar officer of Fighter Command. He was involved in trials of 'window', metallic chaff thrown from aeroplanes to confuse enemy radar, and especially with ways of interfering with German night defences, either by jamming their transmissions or homing onto them. All told, Jackson flew 1100 hours as a navigator on active service and on dangerous trials. For his contribution to the air war he was awarded the DFC (1941), AFC (1944), was appointed OBE (1945) for valour, and was made an officer of the Legion of Merit (USA).

After the war Jackson found it difficult to resume academic life, even though in 1947 he was made stipendless professor of spectroscopy at Oxford and was elected FRS. Perhaps disappointed that no college made him a fellow, fiercely opposed to what he regarded as the socialism of Attlee's government, and wishing to avoid punitive taxation, Jackson moved in 1947 from Oxfordshire to Tullamaine Castle, Ireland. Keen to finish in the Grand National, he rode his own horse in 1947, when he fell, and 1948, and was lying second when his horse refused at the penultimate fence. In 1951 his second marriage was dissolved and he married Janetta, daughter of the Revd Geoffrey Harold Woolley (1892–1968), and former wife of Robert Kee. They had one daughter, Rose Janetta, but the marriage was dissolved in 1956. By this time, after much travelling in Europe and the USA, Jackson was working as a research professor in the spectroscopy laboratory at the Laboratoire Aimé Cotton, then at Bellevue, Paris, later transferred to Orsay, to which he had been invited by P. Jacquinot in 1952. Using his own equipment and photographic methods, and disdaining the photoelectric scanning techniques used by his French associates, Jackson continued to work on high resolution spectroscopy, mainly alone but occasionally with a few younger colleagues, almost until he died. For this research he was made a chevalier of the Légion d'honneur in 1966.

In his private life, however, Jackson was still unsettled. His fourth marriage in 1957 to Consuelo Regina Maria, daughter of the late William S. Eyre and widow of Prince Ernst Ratibor zu Hohenlohe Schillingsfürst, ended in 1959. That of 1966 to Barbara *Skelton (1916–1996), a writer, daughter of Eric George Skelton and former wife of Cyril Connolly and of A. G. (later Lord) Weidenfeld, lasted only a year. In 1968 he at last found happiness when he married Marie Christine, daughter of Baron Georges Reille and a young horse-loving widow with two daughters. They lived mainly in Lausanne where, after a major operation on a leg to cure poor circulation, Jackson died on 20 February 1982; he was buried in Lausanne on 25 February. He was survived by his sixth wife.

Jackson was a courageous and determined man whose independence, made manifest in five dissolved marriages, was reinforced by the sense of power that money gave him. As an affluent gentleman of science and the turf, he researched and rode hard. Intolerant of the second rate, he enjoyed part ownership of the *News of the World*, devastating repartee, and outrageous fantasy. Once he was fined £10 by the stewards for rough riding at an important race meeting. When he appeared before them he pulled out a £100 note and asked for the change. In 1954 Jackson went to Sweden to observe a total eclipse of the sun, which sadly was covered by clouds, and then proceeded to a big international conference where he solemnly told his colleagues that the silence of the eclipse had been shattered by gunshots: not daring to return home without results, astronomers from East Germany had committed suicide.   JACK MORRELL

Sources H. G. Kuhn and C. Hartley, *Memoirs FRS*, 29 (1983), 269–96 · private information (2004) · *The Times* (25 Feb 1982) · *The Times* (4 March 1982) · R. V. Jones, *Most secret war* (1978) · O. Mosley, *My life* (1968) · *WW* · *The Independent* (31 Oct 1997) · m. cert. [Poppet John] · m. cert. [Pamela Freeman Mitford]
Archives Nuffield Oxf., corresp. with Lord Cherwell
Likenesses Bassano, photograph, 1935, NPG [*see illus.*] · W. Stoneman, photograph, 1946, RS · photograph, 1953, repro. in Kuhn and Hartley, *Memoirs FRS*, facing p. 269 · photograph, repro. in Jones, *Most secret war*
Wealth at death reputed to be a millionaire

Jackson [*née* Hall], **Emily Emma Maude** (1845–1898), litigant for the rights of married women, was born on 10 February 1845 in Clitheroe, Lancashire, the daughter of Henry Hall, a solicitor. She was the youngest of a family of three sisters. Emily Hall was left a woman of independent means and lived, so far as can be gathered, an uneventful life until her marriage to (Edmund) Haughton Jackson (1840–1924), son of a captain in the Royal Navy and grandson of the lord chief justice of Jamaica. The marriage took place on 5 November 1887 in Blackburn, a date which may have hinted at the fireworks which were to follow. The bride was then aged forty-two, the bridegroom about forty-eight. When she was married she had, by her own account, an income of about £600 a year (E. Jackson, *Lancashire Evening Post*, 18 April 1891), a considerable sum at the time.

The marriage was doomed from the start. Haughton Jackson appears to have been a weak man who had made no success of any career before his marriage, though he claimed to have sufficient income to keep himself. Emily Jackson was heavily influenced by her sisters and brother-in-law, who knew nothing of her marriage until after it took place, when they immediately manifested their disapproval.

Haughton, who had previously been in government service in New Zealand, had arranged to go there again to try to establish himself in farming before Emily Hall finally accepted his repeated proposal of marriage. His intention of emigrating had been a barrier to the marriage, though in the end his friends thought that she was 'the stronger wooer of the two' (E. H. Jackson, 10). According to his account, he offered not to go to New Zealand until Emily could accompany him but, he complained, 'she virtually sent me abroad' (ibid., 44). After the wedding, the marriage unconsummated, he left for London and New Zealand, while Emily remained in Clitheroe in the care of her sisters and brother-in-law.

Soon after his departure for New Zealand Emily Jackson wrote to her husband saying that she did not want to leave England for a variety of reasons and asking him to return. He agreed to her request, but pointed out that he had insufficient funds to return and asked her to supply money for the passages of himself and his partner. Whether improperly influenced or not by her sisters and brother-in-law, she was shocked by this request; she had thought, she wrote, that he had taken capital to buy land which could be used for his return journey. 'I saw at once that things were wrong, and that I had been deceived … My eyes were opened. It was not for myself, as I had hoped and believed, that I had been loved and married' (E. Jackson, *Lancashire Evening Post*, 20 April 1891). Whoever was to blame, the marriage was now in danger, and attempts to repair it by correspondence and after Haughton's return to England in July 1888 only made matters worse.

Haughton Jackson felt himself to be a wronged man, having lost his opportunity to establish himself in New Zealand, having spent a good deal of money for nothing, and having been denied his wife's company by her unreasoning suspicions and the machinations of her family. He may have been a victim of a Victorian reluctance to explain his financial position to his wife before marriage, though her family seems to have had little doubt of his relative poverty.

Haughton obtained a decree for restitution of conjugal rights at the end of July 1889, but this was ignored by his wife, who continued to reside with her unmarried sister Esther at their parents' former home in Clitheroe. He remained at Blackburn, 11 miles away. On Sunday 8 March 1891, as Emily was leaving church in Clitheroe, she was seized by her husband and two accomplices and dragged backwards into a carriage. One of Haughton's accomplices told the Court of Appeal: 'No more force was used than was absolutely necessary' (*Times Law Reports*, 383), and Haughton himself wrote: 'we acted with the greatest forbearance possible under the circumstances' (E. H. Jackson, 29). The court was told, however, that Emily's arm was bruised in the struggle and she stated in her own account: 'From the rough handling I received in the struggle I felt sore all over my body for several days' (E. Jackson, *Lancashire Evening Post*, 22 April 1891). She was kept against her will at his house in Blackburn.

The Jackson (or, as it was sometimes called, the Clitheroe Abduction) case came at an appropriate time to clarify the legal rights of married women. The Matrimonial Causes Act of 1884 had specified that a decree for restitution of conjugal rights was to be enforced only by compensation by money or property, separation, or divorce, not by arrest and imprisonment of the offending spouse. Prior to 1891 the act had, however, not been tested before the courts.

Emily Jackson and her sisters were no less stubborn than Haughton and were unrestrained by financial considerations from taking legal action. The case went on 16 March to the Queen's Bench Division, where it became clear that male marital dominance still retained friends. One of the judges, Sir Lewis Cave, deplored the behaviour of Emily Jackson's sisters, both for systematically influencing Emily against her husband and for attempting to obtain her release by daily picketing of Haughton's house. His colleague Sir Francis Jeune agreed: 'where the relations are those between husband and wife, there may be a detention which is not illegal' (*Times Law Reports*, 680).

The Halls, however, were resolute, and the case was appealed. In the Court of Appeal on 19 March 1891 Lord Halsbury, the lord chancellor, and his two colleagues unanimously declared Emily Jackson wronged and freed her. Lord Halsbury was lord chancellor in the Unionist government of the day and was to be the champion of the House of Lords in the constitutional crisis of 1911. Even in 1891 he was thought of as an uncompromising legal conservative. In the Jackson case, however, he was a champion of Progressive views. He declared roundly: '[N]o English subject has a right to imprison, of his own motion, another English subject—whether his wife or anyone else—who is *sui juris*, and of age' (*Times Law Reports*, 683).

As in the Dreyfus case which soon followed in France, an important principle found an ambiguous champion. As in that case great public furore was aroused, though it did not have the same political repercussions. *The Times* recalled after Haughton's death: 'The events aroused extraordinary public interest, both husband and wife finding ardent and argumentative partisans' (16 June 1924). The decision in *R. v. Jackson* was hailed by feminists and their sympathizers as (in the words of the *Law Times*) 'the charter of the personal liberty of married women' (28 March 1891, 386), and the *Manchester Guardian* declared that the law had been brought in line with 'the modern conception of a just and decent relation between husband and wife' (20 March 1891).

Such sentiments were not universal. *The Times* (20 March 1891), without dissenting from the judgment, commented that it was a 'flagrant injustice' that Haughton Jackson was compelled to remain a married man; the Church of England paper *The Guardian* said (25 March 1891) that 'divorce by mutual consent', which it deplored, would be a logical next step, and *The Standard* wrote (13 April 1891) that:

> it will be an evil day for English society whenever the newly-married bride shall come to regard the companionship of her husband as a mere experiment, which she may abandon after a short trial without any excuse or any ceremony whatever.

'The modern conception' of marriage was not widely shared in Blackburn or Clitheroe, where there were riotous demonstrations outside Emily Jackson's sisters' homes and elsewhere. The *Blackburn Times* observed that '*everybody* in this district' put the blame on Emily Jackson and her supporters 'rather than on the husband' (4 April 1891), and the case gave an opportunity for sophisticated metropolitan opinion to dilate on the primitive sentiments and behaviour of the rough northerners.

After her vindication Emily Jackson continued to live with her sister in Clitheroe. There is no evidence that she was subsequently in the public eye after the press carried her detailed, serialized 'Vindication' (*Lancashire Evening Post*, 17–22 April 1891) or did anything further to support the emancipation of women. She died in Clitheroe aged fifty-three on 21 March 1898, after a cut in her foot developed into blood poisoning.

Emily Jackson left nothing to her husband in her will, and attempted to use it to revoke her marriage settlement. It seems that this may not have been successful: the *Clitheroe Times* noted (25 March 1898) that Haughton Jackson 'has been … very handsomely provided for'. This may have been the case, since the probate record showed that she left £7602 9s. 9d. He also succeeded his wife as patron of the living of Mitton church, near Clitheroe, where she was buried. A reconciliation of sorts may therefore have been reached, though the couple were not buried in the same grave.

Edmund Haughton Jackson died in his eighty-fifth year, on 11 June 1924. His occupation was described on his death certificate as 'of independent means'. His name and his wife's were not forgotten after a third of a century. The *Daily Mail* commented that his death 'reminds the public of the extraordinary revolution in the position of women which has been accomplished since that once-famous affair … If there are disabilities in marriage to-day they attach to the mere male' (*Clitheroe Advertiser and Times*, 20 June 1924).

Emily Jackson was important as a symbol, not as an active participant in feminist causes. However unlikely a heroine she might have been, it was she who established an important principle in English law: a wife was an independent human being, not a chattel. Married women's property, which within the previous twenty years had been the subject of important legal gains, henceforth included their own persons. DAVID RUBINSTEIN

Sources D. Rubinstein, *Before the suffragettes: women's emancipation in the 1890s* (1986), 54–8 · E. Reiss, *Rights and duties of Englishwomen: a study in law and public opinion* (1934), 45–9 · *Times Law Reports* (22 July 1891), 679–85 · *Queen's Bench Division*, 1G.B. (1891), 671–86 · *Times Law Reports*, 7 (25 March 1891), 382–8 · *Law Times* (25 July 1891) · 'The Clitheroe abduction case', *Englishwoman's Review*, 22 (1891), 107–13 · *The Times* (20 March 1891) · *The Times* (28 March 1891) · *The Times* (30 March 1891) · *Manchester Guardian* (20 March 1891) · *Manchester Guardian* (28 March 1891) · *Manchester Guardian* (30 March 1891) · *Clitheroe Times* (3 April 1891) · *Blackburn Times* (4 April 1891) · m. cert. · d. cert. · *CGPLA Eng. & Wales* (1898) · *CGPLA Eng. & Wales* (1925) [Edmund Haughton Jackson] · E. H. Jackson, *The true story of the Clitheroe abduction, or, Why I ran away with my wife*, ed. W. H. Burnett (1891) · E. Jackson, 'Vindication', *Lancashire Evening Post* (17–22 April 1891) · will

Wealth at death £7602 9s. 9d.: probate, 2 Dec 1898, *CGPLA Eng. & Wales*

Jackson, (John) Enderby (1827–1903), musician and impresario, was born in Mytongate, Kingston upon Hull, on 14 January 1827, the son of John Jackson who was a tallow chandler and soap-boiler, a trade which had been in the family for several generations. Enderby Jackson was a talented musician; he played several instruments and composed. But it was as an entrepreneur and impresario that he made his mark, inventing the brass band contest in its modern form.

Jackson's mother died when he was a child and his relationship with his father was not easy. He attended Hull grammar school, where he distinguished himself, but because music was not taught at the school, he took lessons privately with several teachers, becoming proficient on flute, French horn, piano, and in singing. He also took lessons in harmony and composition. He claimed to have been inspired to a career in music when, as a small boy enlisted to assist his father in the administration of footlight candles at the Theatre Royal, Hull, he heard Jullien's orchestra perform. He ignored the family business and became a professional musician playing in theatre and touring bands in northern towns. On 18 January 1860 Jackson married Eliza S. Smith (1837–1909) of Nettleham, Lincoln; they had four children.

Jackson's observation of the popularity of competitive agricultural events inspired the idea of brass band contests, which he organized under his 'National Musical Contests' enterprise. His first 'Open Contest' was held at the Belle Vue Gardens in Manchester in July 1856. Its success launched band contests as a feature of Victorian life, and many other provincial contests followed. Jackson negotiated tenaciously with railway companies to provide modestly priced transport for mass audiences travelling to his contests, with the result that the North Eastern Railway Company agreed to provide privileged prices for bands and their supporters. In 1859 the Crystal Palace Company engaged him to run a bell-ringing contest at Sydenham. The following year Jackson was similarly engaged to put on a band contest. This was spectacularly successful: 72 bands attended and they were listened to by an audience of over 22,000. Further contests were held at the Crystal Palace in the following two years.

Jackson was always ambitious to add an international dimension to the brass band contest, but though he visited many European countries to attend musical congresses and expositions, his vision of a 'Music Unity of Nations' was never entirely fulfilled. In September 1871 he left England for Australia and, more briefly, New Zealand and South Africa, with his London Star Company Comique. He returned to England in July 1873, and became the sole agent for many important foreign bands, including Lumbley's band from Copenhagen and Gilmore's from the USA. He was also agent for British and foreign instrument manufacturers.

Jackson died suddenly on 9 April 1903 of a brain haemorrhage, at his home, Sherwood House, 2 Sherwood Street, Scarborough, and was buried in Manor Road cemetery in the town. Although he was a man of eclectic talents, his surviving musical works show him to have been no more than a competent tunesmith. He dabbled in local politics and was a gifted painter and designer who, in 1891, put forward plans to join the two bays of Scarborough. Jackson's autobiographical writings reveal him as a man of considerable self-confidence and self-opinion, and he was one of the most effective impresarios of his time. His retrospective claim that his mission had been 'The Propagation of Music amongst the Working Classes' (Jackson) probably disguised more mundane, financial motives, but his impact on the musical life of ordinary Victorians cannot be denied.

TREVOR HERBERT

Sources U. Edin., Collection of Historic Musical Instruments, Arnold Myers collection · private information (2004) · *British Bandsman* (2 May 1903) · *Scarborough Gazette* (16 April 1903) · *CGPLA Eng. & Wales* (1903) · J. E. Jackson, manuscript autobiography, U. Edin., Collection of Historic Musical Instruments, Arnold Myers collection

Archives priv. coll.

Likenesses sketch, 1871, repro. in *British Bandsman* (24 Dec 1904), 917

Wealth at death £1759 8s. 1d.: probate, 7 May 1903, *CGPLA Eng. & Wales*

Jackson, Francis James (1770–1814), diplomatist, was born in December 1770, the eldest son of **Thomas Jackson** (1745–1797), Church of England clergyman. Thomas Jackson, a scholar of Westminster School, matriculated at Christ Church, Oxford, in 1763, and graduated BA in 1767, MA in 1770, and BD and DD in 1783. He was tutor to the marquess of Carmarthen, afterwards fifth duke of Leeds; minister of St Botolph, Aldersgate, London, until 1796; chaplain to the king, 1782; prebendary of Westminster Abbey, 1782–92; canon residentiary of St Paul's Cathedral, 1792; and rector of Yarlington, Somerset. He died at Tunbridge Wells on 1 December 1797.

Francis James entered the diplomatic service at the early age of sixteen, and was secretary of legation from 1789 to 1797, first at Berlin and afterwards at Madrid. He was appointed ambassador at Constantinople on 23 July 1796, and minister-plenipotentiary to France on 2 December 1801, after Cornwallis had returned from the peace congress at Amiens. In October 1802 Jackson was sent as minister-plenipotentiary to Berlin, where he married. Except for a brief period, when his younger brother George *Jackson was in temporary charge, Jackson stayed at Berlin until the breaking off of diplomatic relations following the occupation of Hanover in 1806. In 1807 he was sent on a special mission to Denmark before the bombardment of Copenhagen, which he witnessed. Afterwards, in 1809, he was sent as minister-plenipotentiary to Washington on the recall of David Montagu Erskine, second Lord Erskine, whose resolution of the difficulty arising out of the conflict between HMS *Leopard* and the US frigate *Chesapeake* in 1807 the British government refused to ratify. Jackson remained at Washington until the rupture between Great Britain and the United States in 1811, resulting in the Anglo-American War of 1812–14.

Jackson died at Brighton, after a lingering illness, on 5 August 1814.

H. M. CHICHESTER, rev. H. C. G. MATTHEW

Sources GM, 1st ser., 84/2 (1814), 198 · *The diaries and letters of Sir George Jackson*, ed. Lady Jackson, 2 vols. (1872) · Foreign Office registers, PRO

Archives PRO, corresp. and papers, FO 353 | BL, letters to Lord Auckland, Add. MSS 34430–34461, *passim* · BL, letters to Francis Drake, Add. MS 46833 · BL, letters to Lord Grenville, Add. MS 59016 · BL, letters to duke of Leeds, Add. MSS 28064–28067, *passim* · BL, corresp. with Sir Arthur Paget, Add. MS 48399 · Bodl. Oxf., corresp. with Sir James Bland Burges · NL Scot., corresp. with Robert Liston · NRA, priv. coll., corresp. with Joseph Ewart · PRO, letters to Lord Granville, PRO 30/29 · PRO, corresp. with Henry Manvers Pierrepont, FO/334 · Sandon Hall, Staffordshire, Harrowby Manuscript Trust, letters to Lord Harrowby · Som. ARS, letters to Francis Drake

Likenesses J. Sharples, pastel drawing, 1810, Bristol City Art Gallery

Jackson, Frederick George (1860–1938), explorer, was born at Alcester, Warwickshire, on 6 March 1860, the eldest son of George Frederick Jackson, landowner and farmer, and his wife, Mary Elizabeth, daughter of Frederick Alfred Crowe, rector of Alcester. Educated at Denstone College, he spent three years on a Queensland cattle station, and then for a brief period attended classes at Edinburgh University.

In 1887 Jackson sailed for a summer voyage in the Greenland Sea in the sealer and whaler *Eric*. Inspired by Fridtjof Nansen's projected voyage in the *Fram*, Jackson published in 1892 his plans for an attempt on the north pole, using Franz Josef Land, then supposed to extend far north, as a base. In order to test equipment and gain experience he explored Vaigach Island, in Arctic Russia, and made a sledge journey from Khabarova to Kirkenes in 1893–4. Having found a patron for his polar project in Alfred Harmsworth, he organized the Jackson–Harmsworth polar expedition which sailed in the *Windward* in 1894.

The expedition had its base at Cape Flora in Franz Josef Land for three years. Jackson and Albert Borlase Armitage explored British Channel and found to the north Queen Victoria Sea, which put an end to hopes of a poleward journey. Jackson wrote in his diary: 'Thus our explorations entirely upset existing maps, and our route towards the Pole as planned by land has been frustrated by the non-existence of it' (Jackson, *A Thousand Days in the Arctic*, 2.245). Jackson's travels revealed the main features of the western half of the group of islands. On 17 June 1896 he came across Nansen and Fredrik Hjalmar Johansen attempting a return from their northern record of latitude 86° 14′ N. They had wintered in the north of the group at Cape Norway, on an island subsequently named Jackson Island by Nansen, and were hoping to make their way to Spitsbergen. When Jackson met them they had hardly any food or ammunition left, and this chance encounter probably saved the lives of the two Norwegians. For his services Jackson was awarded in 1898 the Norwegian order of St Olav.

When in July 1897 the *Windward* arrived without the necessary supplies to continue the exploration, Jackson realized, with regret, that a decision had been taken in London to end the expedition; he had looked forward to its continuation into a fourth year. Back in London he found himself at the centre of 'a perfect maelstrom of jealousy mischief-making and intrigue' (Jackson, *The Lure of Unknown Lands*, 219). He became involved in a dispute with the Royal Geographical Society over arrangements for a lecture that he had promised to give, and over a peremptory demand for the three-years' subscription that he owed because of his time in the Arctic. He at once resigned from the society, and when his name was later put forward as the recipient of the society's gold medal for his work in Franz Josef Land, it was rejected. He was, however, awarded the gold medal of the Société Géographique de Paris (1899).

In 1898 Jackson married Mabel (d. 1918), the youngest daughter of Colonel Dalrymple Bruce. He was commissioned in the Manchester regiment and served with distinction with the mounted infantry in the Second South African War from 1899 to 1902. In the First World War he transferred to the East Surrey regiment and served on the western front where, in his own words, 'sniping snipers became a favourite sport with me' (Jackson, *The Lure of Unknown Lands*, 260). He was taken ill in November 1914 and after a period of convalescence in England was effectively invalided out of the war. He found employment as a recruiting service commander and after the armistice was in charge of Russian prisoners in Germany. In 1925, several years after the death of his first wife, he married Marguerite Emma Rosalie, elder daughter of Albert Hernu, of Boulogne, and widow of Henry James Wigan Fisher; there were no children from either this or Jackson's first marriage.

In 1925–6 Jackson made a long journey in search of sport by rail and boat and on foot through tropical Africa from Beira in Mozambique to Matadi in the Belgian Congo, via the Victoria Falls, Katanga district, the Lualaba River, lakes Tanganyika and Kivu, and the Congo River. Soon after his return to England he was appointed a member of the international commission of inquiry, set up by the League of Nations, into the existence of slavery and forced labour in the republic of Liberia. The report was published in 1930.

Jackson's travels were inspired chiefly by love of adventure and the opportunities of big-game hunting. He shared the imperial vision of Cecil Rhodes, after whom he named a fjord that was discovered during the Jackson–Harmsworth expedition, and throughout his polar travels he left union flags over cairns dotted on the landscape. His explorations were confined to his pioneer surveys in Franz Josef Land, where his scientific staff, including Albert Borlase Armitage, Reginald Koettlitz, and William Speirs Bruce were able to do much useful work.

Jackson was awarded the Royal Humane Society's medal (1885). He died in London at his home, sailing barge *Marguerite*, 162 Millbank, Westminster, on 13 March 1938 and was buried at Easthampstead church, near Bracknell, Berkshire, on 18 March; his second wife survived him. A memorial tablet was unveiled in St Paul's Cathedral in 1945. One of his colleagues remembered him as a man 'of great physical strength and endurance, modest and courageous, never failing to lead where danger threatened, and ever giving full credit to his companions' (A. B. Armitage, *The Times*, 16 March 1938).

R. N. RUDMOSE BROWN, *rev.* MARK POTTLE

Sources *The Times* (14 March 1938) · *The Times* (16 March 1938) · *The Times* (19 March 1938) · F. G. Jackson, *The great frozen land* (1895) · F. G. Jackson, *A thousand days in the Arctic*, 2 vols. (1899) · F. G. Jackson, *The lure of unknown lands: north pole and equator* (1935) · private information (1949) · *CGPLA Eng. & Wales* (1938)
Archives Scott Polar RI, journals and papers
Likenesses F. Stacpoole, oils, Scott Polar RI · oils; in possession of his widow, 1949
Wealth at death £260: probate, 27 May 1938, *CGPLA Eng. & Wales*

Jackson, Sir Frederick John (1860–1929), colonial governor and naturalist, was born on 17 February 1860 at Oran Hall, Catterick, Yorkshire, the only son of John Jackson of Oran and his wife, Jane Outhwaite. He was educated at Shrewsbury School (1874–8) and at Jesus College, Cambridge (1879–81), where he rowed in the college boat and was a university trialist, but did not take a degree. On 9 May 1904 he married Aline Louise Clifford Cooper (b. 1873/4), daughter of William Wallace Cooper, a barrister in Dublin. They had no children.

Jackson first visited east Africa in 1884 at the invitation of Rider Haggard's brother, who was vice-consul at Lamu. He spent two years exploring the region, and organized a hunting and collecting expedition to Kilimanjaro. Thus began his lifelong interest in the birds and natural history of Africa. The loss of his personal fortune obliged him, among other reasons, to take up a post with the British Imperial East Africa Company in 1888. The company, under the guidance of Sir William Mackinnon, was established to develop the region of east Africa which fell within the British sphere of influence. Early in 1889 Jackson was sent with Ernest Gedge, James Martin, and Dr Archibald Mackinnon (brother of Sir William), together with a force of 500 rifles, in command of an expedition to open up the region as far as Lake Victoria. He was to make treaties with African chiefs, buy ivory, and if possible make contact with Henry Morton Stanley, who was returning from his expedition to Lake Albert for the relief of Emin Pasha. It was later noted that Jackson crossed Kikuyu and Maasai country 'with not a single collision with the native tribes. The policy of conciliation, based upon justice in dealing and the formation of relations advantageous to the inhabitants, is thus proved to be not only possible in East Africa but eminently practicable' (*Morning Post*, 30 Nov 1889). However, Jackson also believed in forceful dealing with recalcitrant tribes such as the Nandi.

When Jackson reached Mumias he received letters from Mwanga, *kabaka* or king of Buganda, asking for his support in the civil war against his brother Kalema and the Muslim party. However, Jackson's instructions from the company were that he should not intervene in this troubled country. He offered help but only if concessions were made for the company and a treaty signed. He understood that help was no longer needed so he turned north to explore Mount Elgon and to seek Stanley and Emin Pasha. While he was away, Karl Peters, the German officer who had already laid claim to much of what was to become German East Africa, entered Jackson's camp and read his mail. On learning of Jackson's instructions not to enter Buganda, Peters seized the opportunity to do so, and persuaded Mwanga to sign a treaty. Jackson discovered

Sir Frederick John Jackson (1860–1929), by unknown photographer

this on his return to camp in March 1890 and speedily went to Buganda to reverse the setback for the company's interests. He obtained an agreement with Mwanga but not a treaty, and returned to the coast with two Ganda envoys to negotiate further. This imperial rivalry in the heart of Africa was in fact settled by diplomatic decisions in Europe in the Anglo-German treaty of 1890 which declared Uganda to be within the British sphere.

In 1894 the kingdom of Buganda was declared a British protectorate, and Jackson was appointed by the Foreign Office a first-class administrative assistant there. He became vice-consul in 1895, deputy commissioner in 1896, and on occasion acting commissioner. In 1897 the Sudanese troops who had been employed by the British in Uganda since 1892 began a serious mutiny. Jackson and Major J. R. L. Macdonald, with a force of Swahili and Ganda soldiers, managed to confine the mutineers in Luba's Fort, but they killed three British officers in the fort. Jackson was seriously wounded in the fighting which followed, and had to recuperate in England. He was afterwards successively employed in the East Africa Protectorate (later Kenya) as chief political officer (1900), deputy commissioner (1902–7), and lieutenant-governor (1907–11). During this period he was much involved with the wars against

Nandi resistance to colonial rule, and he believed firm action against them by punitive expeditions was necessary, but he clashed with Sir Charles Eliot, the commissioner, over the latter's harsh treatment of the Maasai and his strong encouragement of European settlers into the country, whom Jackson described as 'scalliwags'. However, as deputy commissioner, he assured Indians in 1902 that they were free to buy land, and later, as acting commissioner, he invited Indian agriculturalists to settle in the protectorate. Eliot did not confirm this policy.

Jackson was passed over for promotion in the East Africa Protectorate and instead was appointed governor of Uganda in 1911, staying until his retirement in 1917. As governor he was soon under pressure to develop the country for settler agriculture, a course recommended in 1911 by the Carter commission on land, but opposed by the director of agriculture and the provincial commissioner, eastern province. Jackson this time sided with the settler view, but in 1916 Bonar Law, the colonial secretary, decided in favour of the interests of peasant farmers instead, banning further grants of freehold land to non-Africans. Another issue was the problem of inefficient or corrupt chiefs, both local chiefs and Ganda agents as chiefs in other parts of the protectorate. Jackson's policy was to withdraw the latter whenever possible. During the First World War his main task was to keep up cotton production, which he placed under increasing government control, and in 1916 he issued a regulation that all Africans were required to grow at least a quarter of an acre of cotton.

Throughout his career Jackson devoted all his spare time to natural history, and became an authority on the habits of birds and their distribution in east Africa. He collected over 12,000 bird specimens, representing 774 species. From 1888 he wrote articles on birds for *The Ibis*, he contributed the east African chapters in Clive Phillips-Wolley's *Big Game Shooting* (1902), and he published *Notes on the Game Birds of Kenya and Uganda* (1926). His nearly completed book on the remaining birds was completed and edited by W. L. Sclater, and published as *The Birds of Kenya Colony and the Uganda Protectorate* (3 vols., 1938). Also published posthumously was his book of reminiscences about the earlier part of his service, *Early Days in East Africa* (1930). Lord Cranworth, in his foreword to *Early Days*, called Jackson 'the whitest gentleman who ever crossed the shores of Africa'. Jackson was very widely liked, and Charles Hobley, in his review of the book in the *Geographical Journal*, said that his sense of humour and fairness of mind were so apparent to Africans that his influence grew without any obvious effort on his part. A short, dark-haired man with a large moustache, he always wore a monocle, so that many said he was the model for Captain Good in Rider Haggard's *King Solomon's Mines*. Jackson died on 3 February 1929, aged sixty-eight, of heat exhaustion after bronchial pneumonia, at Victoria Lodge, Beaulieu-sur-Mer, France, where he was buried. He had been appointed CB in 1898, CMG in 1902, and KCMG in 1913, and made a grand officer of the order of Leopold of Belgium in 1917.   OLIVER FURLEY

Sources F. Jackson, *Early days in east Africa* (1930) · V. Harlow, E. M. Chilver, and A. Smith, eds., *History of East Africa*, 2 (1965) · K. Ingham, *The making of modern Uganda* (1958) · K. Ingham, *A history of East Africa*, new edn (1970) · G. H. Mungeam, *British rule in Kenya, 1895–1912: the establishment of administration in the East Africa Protectorate* (1966) · A. T. Matson, *Nandi resistance to British rule, 1890–1906* (1972) · DNB · WWW, 1929–40 · A. H. Kirk-Greene, *A biographical dictionary of the British colonial governor* (1980) · *The Times* (4 Feb 1929) · b. cert. · m. cert. · *CGPLA Eng. & Wales* (1930) · *Morning Post* (30 Nov 1889)

Archives CUL, Royal Commonwealth Society Library, papers · NHM, papers | Bodl. RH, corresp. with Ernest Gedge · Bodl. RH, corresp. with Lord Lugard

Likenesses H. Dixon, watercolour drawing, 1893, Scott Polar RI · Spy [L. Ward], caricature, watercolour drawing, NPG; repro. in *VF* · oils, Scott Polar RI · photograph, repro. in Jackson, *Early days in east Africa*, frontispiece [*see illus.*] · photographs, Scott Polar RI

Wealth at death £582 16s. 5d.: probate, 6 March 1930, *CGPLA Eng. & Wales*

Jackson, Frederick John Foakes (1855–1941), ecclesiastical historian, was born at Ipswich on 10 August 1855, the posthumous son of the Revd Stephen Jackson, proprietor of the *Ipswich Journal* and the fifth of his family to conduct the journal since 1739, and his wife, Catharine, daughter of Frederick Cobbold, of the 1st dragoon guards, a member of a distinguished Suffolk family. In 1858 his mother married Thomas Eyre Foakes, barrister, and when she sent her son to school at Brighton she entered him as Frederick John Jackson Foakes, by which name he was known later at Eton College. He subsequently changed it to Foakes Jackson, and when, many years later, he consulted an American lawyer about legalizing the name in that form he was told that 'he had already made it legal by making it famous'.

Foakes Jackson went up to Trinity College, Cambridge, and in 1879 was placed in the first class of the theological tripos. He won the Jeremie Septuagint and Scholefield prizes, the Crosse scholarship, and the Lightfoot scholarship. The last distinction indicated his predominating interest, which was in the field of ecclesiastical history. Ordained deacon in 1879 and priest in 1880, he served as curate at Ottershaw in Surrey, and at the churches of St Giles and St Botolph in Cambridge. In 1882 he was appointed chaplain and lecturer in divinity and Hebrew at Jesus College, Cambridge. Four years later he was elected to a fellowship, which he held for fifty-five years, and from 1895 to 1916 he was dean of the college. He proceeded BD in 1903 and DD in 1905.

Soon after Foakes Jackson settled in Cambridge his family became involved in a lawsuit, and only after some years of exacting work was he able to discharge the debt incurred. In spite of much teaching he early began to write, and in 1891 there appeared his often reprinted *History of the Christian Church*. The first edition dealt only with the period down to the death of Constantine, but the account was soon continued and brought down to the death of Pope Leo I (461). In 1921 Foakes Jackson followed this work with an *Introduction to Church History* (590–1314), which, though not always accurate, made livelier reading.

Foakes Jackson contributed to the second volume of the *Cambridge Medieval History* (1913), *Essays on some Theological Questions of the Day*, edited by H. B. Swete (1905), and volume 3 of the *Cambridge History of English Literature* (1909). In 1912 he edited *The Parting of the Roads*, a volume of essays on theological subjects by some of his former pupils. But his chief literary output belongs to his later years when, relieved of the burden of college teaching and removed from the allurement of Cambridge society, he published a number of books in rapid succession. His most considerable work was *The Beginnings of Christianity*, planned in co-operation with the more learned but less orthodox Kirsopp Lake. Five volumes on the Acts appeared between 1920 and 1933, but the partnership was not entirely successful (alienation resulted from Lake's divorce and remarriage) and Lake alone was responsible for editing the last two volumes. Foakes Jackson's last work, published in 1939, was entitled *A History of Church History*.

Foakes Jackson's range was wide, but he never specialized enough to win fame as an original scholar. He derived kudos from association with Lake, but his claim to distinction was as a teacher, and he was justly proud of the number of his pupils who rose to eminence as professors and bishops. He claimed that over a considerable period Jesus men won more first classes in the theological tripos than all the other candidates put together. He had a flair for penetrating a mass of detail to point out the essential facts, and he could make any subject interesting. This was mainly due to his remarkable personality. Never well off, he loved to be hospitable, and taught his students to appreciate good wine. He was described as the last eighteenth-century wit, and his conversation was characterized by shrewd humour; this, combined with his personal eccentricities and his unfailing kindness, made him immensely popular. The interest he took in the success of his pupils was rewarded by their unfailing devotion. Because he was loved, he escaped censure when he read his letters and the litany simultaneously.

In 1916 at the age of sixty-one Foakes Jackson crossed the Atlantic to deliver the Lowell lectures at Boston, and during his visit he was offered and accepted the Briggs graduate professorship of Christian institutions at the Union Theological Seminary, New York. In America he built up a reputation as teacher and talker (not as researcher, which disappointed some). Attempts to persuade him to retire failed: he stood firm on his contract, which finally expired in 1934, and outstayed his welcome in consequence.

In his younger days Foakes Jackson was a prominent oarsman and was for many years treasurer of the Cambridge University boat club. He was also fond of fishing and shooting. He held high office among the freemasons, being at one time grand chaplain of England. His scholarship brought him into touch with Jewish leaders: from 1924 to 1927 he held a lectureship at the Jewish Institute of Religion, New York, and in 1930 he published *Josephus and the Jews*. He received honorary degrees from the University of Strasbourg (DTh, 1933) and the University of the South, Sewanee, Tennessee (DLitt, 1935). He was an honorary canon of Peterborough (1901–26), a fellow of the Royal

Historical Society, honorary correspondent of the Institut Historique et Héraldique de France, and fellow of the American Academy of Arts and Sciences.

Foakes Jackson was twice married: first, in 1895, to Anna Maria (d. 1931), daughter of George Grimwade Everett of Hadleigh, Suffolk; and second, in 1932, to Clara Fawcett, widow of Arthur Jackson Tomlinson of New York. There were no children of either marriage. Foakes Jackson died at Englewood, New Jersey, on 1 December 1941.

P. GARDNER-SMITH, rev. HENRY CHADWICK

Sources personal knowledge (1959, 2004) · CGPLA Eng. & Wales (1942)
Archives BL, corresp. with Macmillans, Add. MS 55106 · LPL, letters to Church Quarterly Review · University of Toronto, letters to James Mavor
Likenesses F. Lutyens, oils, Jesus College, Cambridge
Wealth at death £4498 4s. 10d.: administration with will, 16 Sept 1942, CGPLA Eng. & Wales

Jackson, George. See Duckett, Sir George, first baronet (1725–1822).

Jackson, Sir George (1785–1861), diplomatist, born in October 1785, was the youngest son of Thomas *Jackson DD (1745–1797) [see under Jackson, Francis James (1770–1814)]. He was intended for the church but his father's death in December 1797 changed the plans of the family and in 1801 he joined the diplomatic mission to Paris under his brother Francis James *Jackson as an unpaid attaché. In October 1802 he accompanied his brother to Berlin and in 1805 he was presented at the Prussian court as chargé d'affaires and was sent on a special mission to Hesse-Cassel. In 1806 diplomatic relations with Prussia were broken off by Great Britain in consequence of the occupation of Hanover. But later in the year overtures were made by the Prussians for a renewal of friendly relations, and when Lord Morpeth went to conduct the negotiations in Berlin, Jackson, then a very young man, with pleasing manners and a good diplomatic training, was sent to north Germany to pick up what information he could. He returned home in February 1807, with a treaty signed in Memel by Lord Hutchinson, and was sent to Germany with the ratification of the treaty, and instructions to Hutchinson to reappoint him chargé d'affaires on leaving. Diplomatic relations were suspended after the treaty of Tilsit and Jackson returned home by way of Copenhagen, bringing with him the news of the seizure of the Danish fleet on 7 September 1807.

In 1808–9 Jackson was one of the secretaries of legation with the mission under John Hookham Frere to the Spanish junta. He was subsequently appointed in the same capacity to Washington, DC, where his brother Francis James was minister-plenipotentiary, but diplomatic relations with the United States were broken off before he could join. He afterwards did duty with the West Kent militia, in which he held a captain's commission from 2 July 1809 to 1812. In 1812 he married Cordelia, sister of Albany Smith, MP for Okehampton, Devonshire. She died in 1853.

In 1813 Jackson accompanied Sir Charles Stewart (afterwards third marquess of Londonderry) to Germany. He was present with the allied armies in Germany and France

during the campaigns of 1813–14 and entered Paris with them. On the return of the king of Prussia to Berlin, Jackson was appointed chargé d'affaires and minister at the Prussian court, and remained there until after the battle of Waterloo. In 1816 he was made secretary of embassy in St Petersburg. In 1822 he was sent by Canning on a secret and confidential mission to Madrid. The following year he was appointed commissioner in Washington, under article 1 of the treaty of Ghent, for the settlement of American claims. This post he filled until 1827.

Jackson's later services were in connection with the abolition of the slave trade. In 1828 he was appointed the first commissary judge of the mixed commission court in Sierra Leone. Afterwards he was chief commissioner under the convention for the abolition of the African slave trade in Rio de Janeiro from 1832 to 1841, in Surinam from 1841 to 1845, and in St Paul de Loando, in south-west Africa, from 1845 until his retirement on pension, after fifty-seven years' service, in 1859.

In 1856, in St Helena, Jackson married Catherine Hannah Charlotte (d. 1891), daughter of Thomas Elliot of Wakefield, Yorkshire [see Jackson, Catherine Hannah Charlotte, Lady Jackson]. She published selections from his Diaries and Letters (2 vols., 1872) and Bath Archives (2 vols., 1873). Jackson was knighted in 1832 and died in Boulogne on 2 May 1861. He was an effective workhorse, seen by his contemporaries as a model colleague.

H. M. CHICHESTER, rev. H. C. G. MATTHEW

Sources FO List (1861) · GM, 3rd ser., 10 (1861), 699 · The diaries and letters of Sir George Jackson, ed. Lady Jackson, 2 vols. (1872) · The Bath archives: a further selection from the diaries and letters of Sir George Jackson, ed. Lady Jackson, 2 vols. (1873)
Archives PRO, corresp. and papers, FO 353 | BL, corresp. with Lord Aberdeen, Add. MSS 43239–43244 · Chatsworth House, Derbyshire, letters from William Cavendish; letters from F. von Gentz
Wealth at death under £11,000: probate, 21 June 1861, CGPLA Eng. & Wales

Jackson, Georgina Frederica (1823/4–1895), writer on dialect, was born in Everton, Liverpool, daughter of William Jackson, a Liverpool wine merchant; her only other relative known by name was a married sister, mentioned in her will. Of Shropshire parentage, she lived in rural mid-Shropshire in childhood from the age of nine or ten. Evidently well educated, by 1871 she was running a school for young ladies at 13 White Friars, Chester, offering a 'sound English education' to boarders and day pupils. A photograph of her, probably taken in the 1870s, shows regular, strongly formed features, no less attractive for a slight severity of expression.

Casual reading in 1870 led Georgina Jackson to compile a list of Shropshire words remembered from childhood. Then a friend encouraged her to undertake a substantial work on the county dialect; the achievement for which she is remembered occupied a decade of her life, during which her vocation was teaching, literary work occupied her leisure hours, and holidays were devoted to dialecting tours. In three years she collected 3000 words, verifying them all herself. In 1873 she was advised by the philologist W. W. Skeat to record the locality from which each word came and to use the glossic symbols of A. J. Ellis (whom she also consulted). Applying their counsel thoroughly, she spent four years recasting her first three years' work.

In 1877 illness prevented Georgina Jackson's last planned tour, that of south-east Shropshire. She was awarded £100 from the Royal Literary Fund in 1878, and her *Shropshire Word-Book* was issued in three parts from 1879 to 1881. It included a grammar and was one of the very best of its kind, but by the time it was published its author was an invalid. Granted a civil-list pension of £40 about 1880, she gave up her school and moved to a smaller house nearby. She passed materials for her projected book on Shropshire folklore to her friend Charlotte Burne, who brought it out in 1883, duly acknowledging Georgina Jackson's work.

In later years, though confined to one room, often bedridden and in much pain, Georgina Jackson remained cheerful and courageous, living on very small means but keeping up her interest in dialect and etymology as correspondent and voluntary reader for the *English Dialect Dictionary*. She died aged seventy-one of chronic heart disease at her home, 11 Black Friars, Chester, on 16 October 1895. She was buried in Chester cemetery on 19 October; the dean and archdeacon of Chester officiated, both having been her parish priest. GEORGE C. BAUGH

Sources census returns for Everton, 1871, PRO, RG 10/3730, fol. 82v; 1871, RG 11/3558, fol. 88v; 1881, RG 12/2864, fol. 136 · d. cert. · *Bye-Gones Relating to Wales and the Border Counties*, 4 (1895–6), 209 · G. F. Jackson, preface, *Shropshire word-book, a glossary of archaic and provincial words … used in the county* (1879–81), ix–xiv · G. F. Jackson, 'Last words', *Shropshire word-book, a glossary of archaic and provincial words … used in the county* (1879–81), 521–3 · C. S. Burne, preface, *Shropshire folk-lore: a sheaf of gleanings from the collections of Georgina F. Jackson*, ed. C. S. Burne (1883) · Shrops. RRC, S. Morley Tonkin collection, 3217/57–83 · W. W. Skeat, *A student's pastime* (1896), lxviii–lxix · Ches. & Chester ALSS, DCE/1/5, no. 1656 · will, proved, Chester, 18 Nov 1895 · *Gore's Directory of Liverpool* (1825–32)

Archives Bodl. Oxf., papers and corresp. with Thomas Hallam relating to her work on Shropshire dialect · Shrops. RRC, S. Morley Tonkin collection, 3217/57–83

Likenesses photograph, *c.*1870–1879, Shrops. RRC

Wealth at death £111 4s. 5d.: probate, 18 Nov 1895, CGPLA Eng. & Wales

Jackson, Gilbert (*fl.* 1621–1643), portrait painter, was probably based in London but worked in different parts of the country painting the local gentry. His portrait of Edward Somerset, fourth earl of Worcester, signed 'Gilbertus Jackson' and dated 1621, is one of his earliest known works (Christies, 12 July 1996, lot 1) and was painted when the sitter was lord keeper of the privy seal. Another prominent sitter was Bishop (later Archbishop) John Williams (1625; St John's College, Cambridge).

Jackson appears to have been working in north Wales in the 1630s. He painted members of the Hickman family— Sir Willoughby, Bridget, Lady Hickman, and Master William—in 1634, and probably painted Lady Hickman's parents, Sir John and Lady Thornhaugh, in 1625 (priv. coll., Norfolk). He usually signed and dated his work, with his signature taking several forms: mostly Gil., Gl:, or G. Jack., Jac, or J., in various combinations.

One of Jackson's finest paintings is his portrait of John, Lord Bellasys (1636; NPG), in which he provides a rare example of a furnished English interior. His style is characterized by careful attention to detail on the clothing, especially lace, embroidery, buttons, and braiding, which contrasts with the two-dimensional, though often decorative, environments that his sitters inhabit. Although several works from Oxford colleges, including the portraits of Robert Burton (1635; Brasenose College) and Dr William Smyth (1635; Wadham College), are signed and dated according to R. Lane-Poole, their flat, archaic handling and lack of characterization are difficult to reconcile with his other signed and dated work of the same period.

Jackson was an independent picture-maker or one of the 'professors of that part of our art which they call to the Life' (MSS 5667/1, Guildhall Library, London), but he was made free of the Painter-Stainers' Company on 16 December 1640. That year the picture-makers approached the company with grievances about the increasing 'number of Strangers & others' (ibid.) contributing 'to the great impoverishing of the Society & the abuse of the subject in general' (ibid.). Because the painter-stainers shared these grievances, they agreed that the picture-makers who had served seven years but were not free of the company could take the oath of freemen and nominate six of their number as assistants to the company 'to confer, advise & be aiding to us' (ibid.) in redressing grievances and regulating those of their profession, and to attend the court when necessary. Jackson was sworn and admitted to the company as one of the six assistants.

Little else is known about Jackson's life. His *Lady of the Grenville Family and her Son* (1640) is in the Tate collection. His last-known signed and dated work is a head and shoulders portrait of Chief Justice Sir John Bankes (1643), at Kingston Lacy in Dorset, once the home of the Bankes family; a later three-quarter length copy is in the National Portrait Gallery, London. ARIANNE BURNETTE

Sources 'The booke of orders and constitutions to be made for the good gouerment of the Company of the Painters–Steyners', GL, MSS 5667/1 · O. Millar, 'Jackson, Gilbert', *The dictionary of art*, ed. J. Turner (1996) · Mrs R. Lane Poole, ed., *Catalogue of portraits in the possession of the university, colleges, city and county of Oxford*, 3 vols. (1912–25), vols. 2–3 · G. Jackson-Stops, ed., *The treasure houses of Britain: five hundred years of private patronage and art collecting* (1985) [exhibition catalogue, National Gallery of Art, Washington, DC, 3 Nov 1985 – 16 March 1986] · R. Poole, 'Gilbert Jackson, portrait-painter', *Burlington Magazine*, 20 (Oct 1911–March 1912), 38–43 · C. H. Collins Baker, 'More notes on Gilbert Jackson', *Burlington Magazine*, 21 (April–Sept 1912), 169–71 · J. Steegman, *A survey of portraits in Welsh houses*, 1: *Houses in north Wales* (1957) · A. Mitchell, *Kingston Lacy, Dorset* (1994) · O. Millar, *The age of Charles I: painting in England, 1620–1649* (1972) [exhibition catalogue, Tate Gallery, London, 15 Nov 1972 – 14 Jan 1973] · E. K. Waterhouse, *The dictionary of British 16th and 17th century painters* (1988) · E. Waterhouse, *Painting in Britain, 1530–1790*, 5th edn (1994) · M. Whinney and O. Millar, *English art, 1625–1714* (1957) · C. H. C. Baker, *Lely and the Stuart portrait painters: a study of English portraiture before and after van Dyck*, 2 vols. (1912) · D. Piper, *Catalogue of seventeenth-century portraits in the National Portrait Gallery, 1625–1714* (1963) · photographs, notes on collections, NPG, Heinz Archive and Library

Jackson, Gordon Cameron (1923–1990), actor, was born in Glasgow on 19 December 1923, the youngest of the five

Gordon Cameron Jackson (1923–1990), by Chris Capstick, 1978

children of Thomas Jackson, a foreman letterpress printer, and his wife, Margaret Fletcher. He left the city's Hillhead high school at the age of fifteen to pursue a career as an engineering draughtsman with Rolls Royce. However, like his contemporary Stanley Baxter, Jackson had been a child actor with the BBC in Scotland, and he was released by Rolls Royce during the war to play the first of over sixty film roles in the propagandist *The Foreman Went to France* (1941). It was not long before Jackson forsook industry for acting: he worked in repertory, initially at the semi-professional Rutherglen Repertory Theatre, and then at the fully professional Glasgow Citizens' Theatre, which was founded in 1943 by James Bridie. Further appearances followed in theatres in Scotland and England, and he made his London début in the long-running production of Hugh Hastings's farce *Seagulls over Sorrento* in 1951. In that year he married the actress Rona Anderson (*b.* 1928); they had played the romantic leads opposite each other in *Floodtide* (1949), one of the very few films about Scotland set on industrial Clydeside. They had two sons.

Gordon Jackson's career was steady, if not spectacular. His good looks, well modulated voice, and sensitivity to nuance of character ensured that he found work in a wide range of films including *Whisky Galore* (1948), *Tunes of Glory* (1960), *Mutiny on the Bounty* (1962), *The Ipcress File* (1965), *The Prime of Miss Jean Brodie* (1968), and *The Shooting Party* (1985).

He performed regularly on the stage, most notably as Ishmael in Orson Welles's London production of *Moby Dick* in 1955, as Banquo to Alec Guinness's Macbeth at the Royal Court in 1966, and Horatio to Nicol Williamson's Hamlet in Tony Richardson's 1969 production, which played on both sides of the Atlantic. For this last performance he gained the Clarence Derwent award for best supporting actor. Supporting actors are rarely as well known to the public as leading performers, yet the work they do can make or break productions. Jackson could be relied on to bring something distinctive to the roles he played, although until the end of his career he was apprehensive about every part he undertook, and had difficulty watching his own screen performances.

A much higher public profile than he had enjoyed thitherto came when, from 1970 until 1975, Jackson appeared in London Weekend Television's *Upstairs, Downstairs*, a series which explored the interaction of the parallel worlds of employers and servants in an Edwardian household. Jackson played the pivotal figure of the butler, Hudson, a dogged traditionalist who took his responsibilities very seriously indeed. For this portrayal he won the Royal Television Society's award for best actor in 1975, and an Emmy award in the United States in 1976. He followed Hudson by creating the much less attractive character of Cowley, the ruthless head of an anti-terrorist organization in *The Professionals* (1978–83); it ran for fifty-seven episodes but was unworthy of Jackson's talent.

Jackson was one of a number of Scottish actors—Andrew Cruickshank, Stanley Baxter, and Duncan Macrae were others—who sought in their careers to strike a difficult balance. On the one hand, there were available to them the ethnic parts at which they were effortlessly adept, but which could so easily lead to typecasting; on the other, there was a wider range of non-Scottish roles, which could extend them as performers and in the esteem of audiences. Jackson rose well to this challenge, and subsequently enjoyed a career which was rewarding both artistically and financially. He was appointed OBE in 1979. He died, from cancer, in the Cromwell Hospital, Kensington, London, on 14 January 1990.   DAVID HUTCHISON

Sources *The Times* (16 Jan 1990) · *Glasgow Herald* (16 Jan 1990) · *The Scotsman* (16 Jan 1990) · *WWW, 1981–90* · E. Katz, ed., *The Macmillan international film encyclopaedia*, 2nd edn (1994) · L. Halliwell and P. Purser, *Halliwell's television companion*, 3rd edn (1986) · H. Murdoch, *Travelling hopefully: the story of Molly Urquhart* (1981) · d. cert. · I. Herbert, ed., *Who's who in the theatre*, 16th edn (1977) · *CGPLA Eng. & Wales* (1990)

Archives FILM BFI NFTVA, *Invitation to remember*, LWT, 13 Aug 1989 · BFI NFTVA, documentary footage · BFI NFTVA, performance footage | SOUND BL NSA, oral history interviews · BL NSA, performance recordings

Likenesses photographs, 1947–81, Hult. Arch. · C. Capstick, photograph, 1978, Rex Features Ltd, London [*see illus.*] · photograph, Trinity College of Music, London, Jerwood Library of the Performing Arts, Mander and Mitchenson Theatre Collection · photograph, BFI

Wealth at death £742,068: probate, 28 March 1990, *CGPLA Eng. & Wales*

Jackson, Henry (1585/6–1662), Church of England clergyman and literary editor, was born in St Mary's parish,

Oxford, the son of Henry Jackson, mercer, and a kinsman of Anthony Wood. Jackson was admitted as scholar at Corpus Christi College, Oxford, on 1 December 1602, aged sixteen, graduated BA on 20 June 1605, proceeded MA on 18 March 1609, was elected a fellow in 1612, and proceeded BD on 18 June 1617.

John Spenser, shortly after his installation as president of Corpus Christi College in 1607, employed Jackson to prepare several of Richard Hooker's unpublished works for print. Between 1612 and 1614 Jackson saw through the press a number of Hooker's sermons as well as documents relevant to the controversy between Hooker and Walter Travers. Also by 1612 Jackson had organized and edited the fragments of the eighth book of Hooker's *Lawes of Ecclesiastical Politie*. It is widely (although not unanimously) believed that the manuscript of the eighth book at Trinity College, Dublin, 'is probably a copy of Jackson's manuscript' (Houk, 115). The Trinity manuscript is especially important because it is the primary source for modern editions of the eighth book.

Jackson was 'skillful and industrious' as an editor and translator (Keble, xxxi), but also of a 'somewhat jealous and cynical temperament' (Fowler, 173). Wood explains Jackson's lack of preferment beyond his rectorship by claiming that 'being a studious and cynical person he never expected or desired more' (Wood, *Ath. Oxon.*, 3.577). Further evidence of Jackson's cynicism comes from a letter written in 1612 in which he expressed concern that Spenser would try to publish Hooker's eighth book under his own name despite the fact that the text had been 'wholly restored to life' by Jackson ('a me plane vitae restitutum') (Hooker, 3.xviii–xix). In fact Spenser was not able to publish the eighth book at all before his death in 1614. Upon Spenser's death Hooker's papers passed into the custody of Bishop John King. There is speculation that, because of the considerable effort required to edit the remains of the eighth book, by 1614 Jackson had developed proprietary feelings toward the text. Accordingly it has been suggested that he handed over to King only the rough drafts of the eighth book that Spenser had entrusted to him, not the fair copy that he had constructed from them (Keble, li). Houk, however, argues that it is unlikely that Jackson withheld copies of the eighth book from Spenser and then King and thus that Jackson should 'be acquitted of suspicion of having unlawfully retained copies of the Eighth Book' (Houk, 130).

Regarding Jackson's ideology, Wood identifies him as a 'great admirer' of Sebastian Benefield (his former tutor) and also states that he 'was a great admirer of Richard Hooker and Joh. Rainolds [Reynolds]' (Wood, *Ath. Oxon.*, 2.489; 1.li). Keble offers the concurring opinion that Jackson was 'evidently of the Reynolds school in theology' (Keble, lvi). The testimony of Wood and Keble is supplemented by the fact that Jackson assisted the executors of Reynolds's will and also by Jackson's work as an editor. In addition to several pieces by Hooker, he translated and/or edited works by several more-or-less precisionist Reformed theologians within the Church of England including Reynolds, Benefield, and William Whitaker.

This evidence, in conjunction with recent arguments that Hooker himself was a proponent of Reformed theology, suggests that Jackson's theology was thoroughly Reformed, perhaps with tendencies toward puritanism, although Jackson, naturally, did not think of himself as a 'puritan'. In 1612 he wrote disparagingly of the 'Puritanos' who did not enthusiastically receive his edition of Hooker's sermon on justification (Hooker, 5.93). Jackson's work as an editor, translator, and writer also reflects an avid interest in humanist studies.

Only a few details of Jackson's later life are known. In 1622 he seems to have supervised a reprinting of Hooker's sermons and the first five books of the *Lawes* by William Stansby. In 1630 he became rector of Meysey Hampton, Gloucestershire. His library was plundered by parliamentarians in 1642, but he was not sequestered. In his later years he spent several days each summer in the company of Wood, sharing recollections from his days at Corpus Christi. He died, presumably at Meysey Hampton, on 4 June 1662 and was interred in the chancel of the church there the next day. DANIEL EPPLEY

Sources Wood, *Ath. Oxon.*, new edn · Foster, *Alum. Oxon.* · J. Keble, preface, in *The works of … Richard Hooker*, ed. J. Keble, 7th edn, 1, rev. R. W. Church and F. Paget (1888) · R. A. Houk, 'An introduction to the posthumous books of Richard Hooker's "Ecclesiastical polity"', *Hooker's 'Ecclesiastical polity': book VIII* (1931) · *The Folger Library edition of the works of Richard Hooker*, 1, 3, 5 (1977–90) · T. Fowler, *The history of Corpus Christi College*, OHS, 25 (1893) · *DNB* · Wood, *Ath. Oxon.: Fasti* (1815) · Cooper, *Ath. Cantab.*, vol. 2 · Walker rev., 175
Archives CCC Oxf., letters

Jackson, Henry (1831–1879), novelist, was born at Boston, Lincolnshire, on 15 April 1831, one of at least two sons of a brewer. After attending Sleaford and Boston grammar schools he was placed first in a bank and subsequently in his father's brewery. Severe illness left him an invalid for life at eighteen, and he devoted himself to literary work.

Jackson's earliest stories were published in *Chambers's Journal*, beginning with a brief tale called 'A Dead Man's Revenge'. His first novel, *A First Friendship*, was published in *Fraser's Magazine* while J. A. Froude was editor; it was reissued in one volume in 1863. His next novel, *Gilbert Rugge*, appeared in the same magazine and was published in three volumes in 1866. Both novels were reprinted in the United States, where they had a larger circulation than in England. In 1871 he published a volume of three stories, *Hearth Ghosts*. A novel in three volumes, *Argus Fairbairn* (1874), is his only piece of writing which appears under his own name. Jackson died at his home, Heathside Cottage, North End, Hampstead, London, on 24 May 1879 after a long illness.

GORDON GOODWIN, *rev.* MEGAN A. STEPHAN

Sources *CGPLA Eng. & Wales* (1879) · private information (1891) [F. Jackson] · d. cert.
Likenesses T. W. Huffam, mezzotint (after Herbert), BM
Wealth at death under £3000: probate, 25 June 1879, *CGPLA Eng. & Wales*

Jackson, Henry (1839–1921), classical scholar, was born at St James's Row, Sheffield, on 12 March 1839, the eldest son of Henry Jackson, an eminent surgeon there, and his wife, Frances, third daughter of James Swettenham, of Wood

End, near Winksworth. He was educated at the Sheffield collegiate school and Cheltenham College (1855–8), where he was taught by H. A. Holden; John Morley and F. W. H. Myers were among his fellow students. He went up to Trinity College, Cambridge, in 1858, taking his BA degree in 1862. His undergraduate contemporaries included R. C. Jebb, Henry Sidgwick, and G. O. Trevelyan. He became a fellow of Trinity in 1864, assistant tutor in 1866, praelector in ancient philosophy in 1875, and vice-master in 1914.

In his early years as a fellow, Jackson owed much to the friendship and support of W. H. Thompson, who became master in 1866. Thompson, who was instrumental in Jackson's appointment as a tutor, encouraged him, together with Jebb, Sidgwick, and W. E. Currey, in their scheme to provide individual teaching in composition and translation to all Trinity undergraduates studying classics. Such tuition had previously been provided—where it existed at all—by independent coaches in the town. This important reform soon spread to other subjects and other colleges, and was the basis of the system of supervisions which remains an invaluable characteristic of undergraduate teaching at Cambridge.

Thompson's recommendation of Jackson to the praelectorship in 1875 provided him with an opportunity to give lectures which were open to all members of the university. It also enabled him to marry without having to resign his fellowship, and in 1875, he married Margaret, daughter of the Revd Francis Vansittart Thornton, vicar of South-Hill with Callington, Cornwall. They had two sons and three daughters. Jackson's married life was clouded by the illness of his wife, for many years bedridden and unable to live at Cambridge.

In 1906 Jackson succeeded Sir R. C. Jebb as regius professor of Greek in the university, and in 1908 received, as crown of many other distinctions, the Order of Merit. As professor he continued to lecture on ancient philosophy, since no chair in the subject existed at the time. His lectures and articles proved highly influential on the later study of Greek philosophy at Cambridge. His principal contribution to learning was his doctrine of Plato's 'later theory of Ideas', published in a series of articles in the *Journal of Philology*, of which he was one of the editors from 1879 to his death. These articles were important not only in themselves but in giving an impulse to later speculation: he argued that Plato criticized and modified his own views, not remaining content with the crude form in which they were first put forth; he attempted to show that various statements of Aristotle's chimed in with what he found in Plato's later dialogues; and he held that the Ideas finally became 'natural kinds' like John Stuart Mill's. He also published an edition of Aristotle's *Ethics, Book v* (1879), translations, papers, articles in encyclopaedias dealing with ancient philosophy, and a book *About Edwin Drood* (1911).

Jackson's interest in school and college life was intense, and he took great pleasure at becoming a fellow of Winchester College. He took a leading part in college and university reform; his last appearance in public was when he was carried to the Senate House to vote for women's degrees. An ardent politician, he was a home-ruler before Gladstone. He was deeply interested in anthropology. In literature, after his beloved Greek philosophers, he was devoted to French and English fiction, Thackeray most of all; many years before his death he had read *Esmond* forty times. His rooms were crowded with all sorts of people, especially on Sunday evenings, and every distinguished visitor to Trinity would be taken under his wing. But he had some strong dislikes, hating all pretension and affectation. As vice-master he was a leader among those fellows who campaigned to deprive Bertrand Russell of his fellowship because of his pacifist views during the First World War.

Jackson's constitution was strong indeed. In teaching he never spared himself, and he was constantly occupied with college and university business during the day. He would often sit up late talking with a visitor until three or four o'clock, then work at a lecture, go to bed sometimes as late as six, and lecture at ten. And he took infinite pains over his work, taking great care over testimonials and letters of importance, and keeping up a large and delightful correspondence. Yet for many years all this had no visible effect upon him, and though he had to become more careful when about seventy, his health did not break down until just after he reached eighty. For two years he was a helpless invalid, yet even then was carried into the hall to lecture several days a week with indomitable spirit. He died at his home, Sunny Hill, St Stephen's Road, Bournemouth, on 25 September 1921.

J. A. PLATT, rev. RICHARD SMAIL

Sources R. St John Parry, *Henry Jackson, O. M.* (1926) · C. N. L. Brooke, *A history of the University of Cambridge*, 4: *1870–1990*, ed. C. N. L. Brooke and others (1993) · *CGPLA Eng. & Wales* (1921)
Archives CUL, corresp. and papers · Sheffield Central Library · Trinity Cam., corresp. | CUL, corresp. with Lord Morley · King's AC Cam., letters to O. Browning
Likenesses C. W. Furse, oils, 1889, Trinity Cam. · C. W. Furse, oils, 1889, NPG · W. Rothenstein, pastel drawing, 1904, Trinity Cam. · H. Lamb, chalk drawing, 1906, Athenaeum, London · W. Strang, chalk drawing, 1909, Royal Collection · V. H. Mottram, photograph, NPG · O. Rowland, oils, Trinity Cam. · D. Smith, photograph, NPG · portrait, repro. in St John Parry, *Henry Jackson*
Wealth at death £6,735 15s. 4d.: probate, 8 Dec 1921, *CGPLA Eng. & Wales*

Jackson, Sir Henry Bradwardine (1855–1929), naval officer and developer of wireless telegraphy, was born on 21 January 1855 at Barnsley, Yorkshire, the eldest son of Henry Jackson, a farmer in nearby Cudworth, and his wife, Jane, the daughter of Charles Tee of Barnsley.

Education and early naval service Jackson was educated at Chester and at Stubbington House, Fareham, entered the navy in December 1868, and was promoted sub-lieutenant in 1874 and lieutenant in 1877. He first specialized in navigation and served as junior lieutenant in the iron screw corvette *Active* on the Cape and west Africa station where he took part in the Anglo-Zulu War of 1879. He joined the *Vernon*, the torpedo school at Portsmouth, in September 1881 and qualified as a torpedo lieutenant. He served in the *Vernon* for three and a half years, part of the time in

Sir Henry Bradwardine Jackson (1855–1929), by Walter
Stoneman, 1918

command of the school's tender, the torpedo vessel *Vesuvius*. His interest in the scientific aspects of his profession were evident and in 1883 he was elected an associate of the Society of Telegraph Engineers, later the Institution of Electrical Engineers. He was promoted commander in January 1890 and that year married Alice Mary Florence, the eldest daughter of Samuel Hawksley *Burbury FRS, a barrister and mathematician; they had no children.

Telegraphy Jackson became interested in the work of Heinrich Hertz who had demonstrated the existence of electromagnetic waves. Jackson believed these 'Hertzian waves' might have a naval application, notably as a solution to the problem of identifying torpedo boats and distinguishing friend from foe, particularly at night. He made suggestions along these lines in 1891. In January 1895 he was appointed to command the *Defiance*, the hulk used as a torpedo school at Devonport. There in December he began the experiments that eventually led to the transmission and reception of wireless signals in Morse code in August 1896. The first transmission in the after cabin of the *Defiance* was apparently over only a few yards but the range was soon increased to 25 and then 50 yards. In late summer 1896 the War Office was interested in the wireless experiments and device offered by Guglielmo Marconi. Jackson, who had been promoted captain in June, served as the Admiralty's representative at a conference held at the War Office to discuss the subject and also attended the demonstrations of Marconi's device on Salisbury Plain in 1896 and 1897. Jackson and Marconi became friends

although they had developed rival systems and the friendship was complicated in the next few years by British official reluctance, eventually overcome, to pay Marconi an annual royalty of £100 for each of his devices installed in a warship. Jackson made no secret of his belief that Marconi's device was superior to his own but continued his experiments and in May 1897 in a demonstration before the commander-in-chief, Devonport, succeeded in transmitting a signal from the *Defiance's* tender *Scourge* to the *Defiance* at ranges of up to 2 miles. Within a few months he had reached ranges of 6000 yards and established a wireless link between the *Defiance* and Admiralty House at Plymouth.

Naval career from 1897 Jackson's work with wireless was interrupted when he was appointed naval attaché in Paris in November 1897. It was an interesting appointment for in 1898 France came close to war with Great Britain over Fashoda. He was particularly charged with reporting on French submarine construction. The Admiralty planned extensive experimentation with wireless at sea in the summer manoeuvres of 1899 and he was given command of the cruiser *Juno*, equipped with wireless, in order to report on the trials. The success of the latter led to Jackson's recommendation and the Admiralty's decision to provide warships with wireless sets. In October 1899 Jackson was appointed to the *Vernon* in order to give the officers of the *Vernon* the benefits of his experience with wireless, work out details for fitting wireless to ships, and establish a course to instruct operators. He emphasized the necessity of standardizing equipment to facilitate training of operators and minimize the number of spare parts to be provided. Jackson did not remain in the *Vernon* long, however, for in December 1899 he was appointed to command the torpedo boat carrier and depot ship *Vulcan* in the Mediterranean. The *Vulcan* received one of the first three sets introduced into the Mediterranean Fleet, then commanded by Admiral Sir John Fisher, for training. Fisher developed a high regard for Jackson, praising him in a private letter to the first lord in February 1902. In 1904 Fisher numbered Jackson among the 'seven brains', the select group (including Jellicoe and Bacon) that he intended to gather around him when he became first sea lord. Jackson's work also earned him recognition by scientists; in May 1901 he was elected fellow of the Royal Society and in 1902 published a paper in its *Proceedings*, 'On some phenomena affecting the transmission of electric waves over the surface of sea and earth'.

In February 1902 Jackson was appointed assistant director of torpedoes at the Admiralty and in February 1905 he became third sea lord and controller of the navy. He was chairman of the electrical committee on equipment of warships from 1902 to 1903. As one of Fisher's 'seven brains' he was a member of the committee on designs responsible for the introduction of the *Dreadnought* and the *Invincible*-class battle cruisers. He was also an aide-de-camp to Edward VII from September 1905 to October 1906 and was promoted rear-admiral in November 1906 and created KCVO. He left the Admiralty to command the 3rd (subsequently the 6th) cruiser squadron in the Mediterranean from October 1908 to October 1910 and was created a KCB in June 1910. He was also the Admiralty representative at the international conference on aerial navigation in Paris, October–December 1910. From February 1911 to February 1913 he commanded the Royal Naval College at Portsmouth; during this period he was promoted vice-admiral (March 1911) and temporarily commanded the old reserve ships in the seventh squadron during the naval manoeuvres of July 1912.

Onset of war This was his last sea-going command for in February 1913 he was appointed chief of the war staff. As chief of staff Jackson was critical of first lord Churchill's proposal in the event of war with Germany to revert to a more offensive strategy involving a close blockade of the German coast with the whole British flotilla fleet. Jackson argued that the British would be attacking the Germans in their home waters where they could easily concentrate while the British could employ only a limited number of large modern destroyers, which could stay out for only three days at a time. He was promoted admiral in February 1914 and in August was nominated commander-in-chief in the Mediterranean. However, when war broke out he was retained for special service at the Admiralty. He was president of the subcommittee of the committee of imperial defence dealing with overseas attack and largely concerned with planning attacks on the German colonies. In October 1914, after the first sea lord Prince Louis of Battenberg had been forced to resign following the agitation over his German birth, the king suggested Jackson as a possible replacement. Churchill did not accept; Jackson no doubt appeared too bland and mild. Churchill chose to recall Fisher.

The Dardanelles expedition At the beginning of 1915 Jackson was involved with planning for the Dardanelles expedition where he believed a methodical, although possibly protracted, naval bombardment would permit ships alone to force the straits. By mid-February he had revised his opinion and argued that ships alone would not suffice and a strong military force was necessary to assist in the operations. When the purely naval attack failed on 18 March he was one of those opposing a second naval attack without military support. The stalemate at the Dardanelles after the April landing and the clash between Churchill and Fisher over sending additional naval reinforcements to the Dardanelles led to Fisher's resignation and Churchill's dismissal. In May Balfour became the new first lord and Jackson first sea lord. Jackson appeared to be everyone's second choice and received the job only after Admiral A. K. Wilson declined. He was in some ways an odd selection for he had never commanded a fleet nor seen action at sea; and had been primarily involved in the scientific, technical, and administrative side of the navy. The Balfour–Jackson administration was in sharp contrast to the dynamic though volatile Churchill–Fisher combination. Jackson wrote to his predecessor Fisher, commenting that there was 'no senior officer who desired the appointment less than I' (Marder, *Fear God*, 3.253), and

acknowledging he had a very difficult job before him for which he was not fully qualified. On the other hand Jackson was generally acknowledged as highly intelligent, sound, and level-headed. Unfortunately he was also regarded as being in somewhat questionable health and had acquired a reputation for irritability. Barely a month after his appointment Jellicoe wrote to Beatty: 'I fear Jackson will only get irritated at all this bombardment of letters. I know him so well and told Balfour of this trait in his character' (Patterson, 1.170). Jackson complained that the mass of paperwork was 'overwhelming' and gave him no time for thought. To a certain extent he had himself to blame, for contemporaries alleged that he habitually concerned himself with trivial matters.

The Dardanelles expedition was a particularly pressing problem after Bulgaria entered the war and Serbia was overrun by an overwhelming German, Austrian, and Bulgarian force. An Anglo-French expedition to Salonika proved too little and too late. The loss of Serbia meant that direct rail communications between Germany and Constantinople would soon be supplying ammunition to the Turks. The allied expedition would also face the problem of supply of the army over open beaches at a time of winter gales. It became a problem of 'Get on or get out'. Jackson was at first inclined to favour another naval attempt and wrote to the naval commander, Admiral de Robeck, on 9 October 1915, '*Personally*, I say go for Constantinople tooth and nail, without further procrastination or delay' (Halpern, 5.476). But de Robeck was opposed and Jackson's doubts grew. Subsequently Jackson would consent to a renewed naval attack only if it was made in conjunction with an offensive by the army. This possibility was doomed when Kitchener returned from a tour of inspection at the Dardanelles and recommended evacuation.

Reputation for indecision Unfortunately Jackson appeared indecisive, particularly to those who favoured a renewed naval attack. Jackson, for his part, resented the naval commitments necessitated by the new Salonika expedition and found fault with his French and Italian allies in the Mediterranean. By 1916 the shortage of destroyers was evident; there were demands for them everywhere in the face of the submarine danger. Jackson, while admitting the shortage, claimed they were building all they could as rapidly as possible, and grew testy with Jellicoe when the latter complained of the Grand Fleet's shortages. The Balfour–Jackson administration in 1916 gave the impression of apathy and lassitude. It was a combination Admiral Bacon later termed 'the philosopher wedded to the scientist' (R. H. Bacon, *The Life of Lord Fisher of Kilverstone*, 1, 1929, xiii). The vigour associated with Churchill and Fisher was gone. There were no real disasters attributable to Jackson but the indecisive battle of Jutland meant the Admiralty could not bask in the glory of a great victory. There were more missed opportunities when the high sea fleet sortied on 19 August, and in the autumn the Admiralty had the appearance of failing to counter two raids by German destroyers into the channel. Critics of the Admiralty claimed that the Balfour–Jackson regime seemed more to be reacting to events and absorbing blows than initiating them. There was a widespread feeling that an offensive spirit was lacking at the Admiralty and some critics pointed out that the board in general lacked experience of command in battle. Jackson was vulnerable to these charges and despite his merits was not an inspiring wartime leader. The feeling of drift gave way to one of impending crisis as losses to submarines mounted and Jackson was openly pessimistic about defeating them. Asquith grew anxious to replace Jackson, although he was inclined to retain Balfour. By December 1916 Jackson himself was ready to go and indicated to Beatty that it was time a more energetic and experienced admiral replaced him as he had been away from the sea too long for someone who was responsible for naval operations. He was therefore ready to depart when Jellicoe replaced him as first sea lord on 4 December. A few days later the cabinet crisis resulted in a new coalition government with Lloyd George as prime minister, and on 11 December Sir Edward Carson replaced Balfour as first lord.

Later years and reputation A willing and obviously relieved Jackson left the Admiralty to become admiral-president of the Royal Naval College at Greenwich where he remained until July 1919. From April 1917 to July 1919 he was first and principal naval aide-de-camp to George V and in 1919 he was created a GCB. In July 1919 he was promoted admiral of the fleet and in 1920 appointed chairman of the Radio Research Board. Jackson retired from the navy in 1924 but remained active with scientific societies such as the Institution of Electrical Engineers. He was also a vice-president of the Institution of Naval Architects and vice-president of the Seamen's Hospital Society. He was awarded honorary degrees: DSCs from Oxford and Leeds and an LLD from Cambridge. He was also awarded Spanish, Russian, Japanese, and French decorations. Jackson died on 14 December 1929 at his home, Salterns, on Hayling Island, Hampshire, his wife surviving him. He was buried on 17 December in Hayling Island parish churchyard.

Jackson was not a great naval leader. In office between the Fisher and Jellicoe incumbencies, he appeared an interim figure who never aroused much enthusiasm. But that was only part of his career. His scientific and technical work was important, as contemporaries knew: his obituary in *The Times* carried the sub-heading, 'A pioneer of wireless'. Jackson was praised for this, not least because he refused to seek professional or financial profit from his experiments and readily acknowledged the superiority of Marconi's devices over his own. His priority was to ensure that the navy had the best equipment available. It is as a pioneer of the use of wireless at sea that he deserves to be remembered. PAUL G. HALPERN

Sources *The Times* (16 Dec 1929) • R. F. Pocock and G. R. M. Garratt, *The origins of maritime radio: the story of introduction of wireless telegraphy in the Royal Navy between 1896 and 1900* (1972) • A. J. Marder, *From the Dreadnought to Scapa Flow: the Royal Navy in the Fisher era, 1904–1919*, 5 vols. (1961–70) • M. H. Murfett, 'Admiral Sir Henry Bradwardine Jackson (1915–1916)', *The first sea lords: from Fisher to Mountbatten*, ed. M. H. Murfett (1995), 91–9 • M. Gilbert, *Winston S. Churchill*, 3: *1914–1916* (1971) • *The Jellicoe papers*, ed. A. T. Patterson, 2 vols., Navy RS, 108, 111 (1966–8) • P. G. Halpern, ed., 'De Robeck and the Dardanelles campaign', *The naval miscellany*, ed. N. A. M. Rodger, 5, Navy RS, 125 (1984) • *Fear God and dread nought: the correspondence of Admiral of the Fleet Lord Fisher of Kilverstone*, ed. A. J. Marder, 3 vols. (1952–9) • *The Keyes papers*, ed. P. G. Halpern, 1, Navy RS, 117 (1972) • S. W. Roskill, *Hankey, man of secrets*, 1 (1970) • A. J. Marder, *Portrait of an admiral: the life and papers of Sir Herbert Richmond* (1952) • B. Kent, *Signal! a history of signalling in the Royal Navy* (1993) • P. K. Kemp, ed., *The papers of Admiral Sir John Fisher*, 2 vols. (1960–64) • P. G. Halpern, *The naval war in the Mediterranean, 1914–1918* (1987) • R. F. MacKay, *Fisher of Kilverstone* (1973) • *Navy List* • *CGPLA Eng. & Wales* (1930) • *WWW*

Archives Naval Library, London • NMM, papers • Royal Naval Museum, Portsmouth, papers as first sea lord | BL, corresp. with Arthur James Balfour, Add. MS 49714, *passim* • BL, letters to Lord Jellicoe, Add. MS 49009 • CAC Cam., corresp. with Sir John de Robeck • NMM, corresp. with Sir Julian S. Corbett • NMM, Beatty MSS

Likenesses photograph, 1897, repro. in Pocock and Garratt, *Origins of maritime radio*, title-page • photograph, after 1914, IWM; repro. in Kent, *Signal!* • W. Stoneman, photograph, 1918, NPG [*see illus.*] • F. Dodd, charcoal and watercolour drawing, IWM

Wealth at death £10,924 18s. 11d.: probate, 3 March 1930, *CGPLA Eng. & Wales*

Jackson, Sir Herbert (1863–1936), chemist, was born in Whitechapel, London, on 17 March 1863, the only surviving son of Samuel Jackson and his wife, Clementina Rebecca Grant. He went to King's College School, and in 1879 entered King's College, London, where he worked for thirty-nine years, becoming successively demonstrator, lecturer, and professor of organic chemistry (1905), and Daniell professor of chemistry (1914). He was elected a fellow of the college in 1907, and became emeritus professor in 1918. In 1900 he married Amy, elder daughter of James Collister. They had no children.

Jackson covered an immense field in his investigations, but his publications give an entirely inadequate impression of the extent and importance of his work. About 1890, in the course of experiments on the excitation of phosphorescence by means of discharge tubes, he discovered that by using a concave cathode he could concentrate the phosphorescent response of material at the anti-cathode to a small area about the centre of curvature of the cathode. He also observed that phosphorescence was excited in screens held outside the tube, leading others to speculate on how near he had come to anticipating W. K. Röntgen's discovery of X-rays in 1895. With a discharge tube having a concave cathode and inclined anti-cathode, Jackson found that he was able in 1896 to reproduce all Röntgen's effects. This original Jackson 'focus-tube' became the prototype of later X-ray tubes.

Besides numerous investigations in pure chemistry, Jackson's enquiries extended to such subjects as the weathering of stone, and the action of soaps and solvents in laundry work; his advice on chemical matters was frequently sought by manufacturers. He was greatly interested in oriental ceramics, and his determinations of the colouring agents in glasses and glazes and reproduction of the effects gave much assistance to archaeologists and connoisseurs. He was an expert photographer, a skilled spectroscopist and user of optical instruments, and a master of microscope technique; his wide experience in the interpretation of microscopic observations was often the key to his success.

At the beginning of the First World War, British industry lacked the ability to produce glasses for special purposes, having previously imported supplies from Germany and France. Jackson headed an advisory committee appointed in October 1914 to define formulae for the scarcest types of laboratory, heat-resisting, and other glasses, including a full range of optical glasses. Formulae for the most crucial glasses were produced within six months, and published in *Nature* (1915). Working with his team at King's College and in his private laboratory, Jackson developed over seventy successful formulae. He also advised the glass manufacturers, and helped them to eliminate production problems. For these and other invaluable war services he was appointed KBE in 1917. In the same year he was elected a fellow of the Royal Society. In 1918 he resigned his professorship on being appointed the first director of research of the British Scientific Instrument Research Association, a post that he held successfully until his retirement in 1933. Through it, he became the friend and scientific adviser of the optical glass industry, which had been firmly established in Britain as a result of the war. He was president of the Röntgen Society (1901–03) and of the Institute of Chemistry (1918–21), a member of the senate of the University of London, and a governor of the Imperial College of Science; he gave valuable service on many government and scientific committees.

Jackson was a man of infinite resource, of very varied accomplishments, and great personal charm. As a young man he was a notable athlete. He was an entertaining talker, with a wealth of information on lesser known subjects. To those who worked with him, particularly younger colleagues, his help and encouragement were unfailing. He died, after a brief illness, at his home, 9 Parsifal Road, Hampstead, on 10 December 1936, survived by his wife. He was buried on 15 December at Hampstead parish church.   THOMAS MARTIN, rev. K. D. WATSON

Sources H. Moore, *Obits. FRS*, 2 (1936–8), 307–14 • *The Times* (12 Dec 1936), 6f • *The Times* (14 Dec 1936), 20a • *The Times* (16 Dec 1936), 17b • R. MacLeod and K. MacLeod, 'War and economic development: government and the optical industry in Britain, 1914–18', *War and economic development: essays in memory of David Joslin*, ed. J. M. Winter (1975), 165–203 • *Nature*, 139 (1937), 16–17 • *CGPLA Eng. & Wales* (1937)
Archives King's Lond., corresp. relating to King's College • RS | California Institute of Technology, Pasadena, Hale MSS • Nuffield Oxf., corresp. with Lord Cherwell • RBG Kew, Thiselton-Dyer MSS
Likenesses W. Stoneman, photograph, 1927, NPG • photograph, repro. in Moore, *Obits. FRS*
Wealth at death £29,464 0s. 6d.: probate, 24 Feb 1937, *CGPLA Eng. & Wales*

Jackson, Humphrey (*bap.* 1721, *d.* 1801), chemist and inventor, who was baptized at Hinderwell, Yorkshire, on 28 February 1721, was the son of Thomas Jackson, later of Stockton-on-Tees, co. Durham. He was apprenticed in 1735 to a Stockton apothecary and surgeon. He later moved to London, where he set up as a chemist in Upper East Smithfield during 1743. *Reflexions Concerning the Virtues of Tar Water* (1744), his first book, cogently argued the case for his product over the well-known medicine of George Berkeley, bishop of Cloyne. His chemical skill was further evidenced by experimental findings in 1751 in support of the famous fever powder patented by Dr Robert James and by his patent specification of 1753 (no. 680) for a very successful cordial bitter tincture. Jackson's next work, *An Essay on Bread* (1758), defended bakers and millers against allegations concerning adulteration of bread levelled by Peter Markham and Joseph Manning; it was the first reliable book on the chemical detection of food adulteration. In 1768 Jackson patented a method for hardening and preserving wood (no. 910), which was approved by the College of Physicians and effectively applied to several warships. It was publicized by an eight-page advertisement (1770) that described thirty-one items tested at his Great Tower Hill works, ranging from brewing implements, building components, and wooden pipes for London waterworks to twenty-five new standing gun carriages treated for the Tower of London garrison.

Jackson obtained another patent in 1760 (no. 749), following a journey to Russia, for manufacturing isinglass from British materials at his own factory, which employed fifteen workmen. His book, *An Essay on British Isinglass* (1765), graphically described his chemical method for producing isinglass from the air bladders of certain fishes. The Society of Arts, of which he became a member in 1760, serving on its chemistry and trade committees (1760–61), awarded him a premium in 1766 for importing American sturgeon and he informed Benjamin Franklin about a technique for making glue from this fish. Elected FRS on 19 November 1772, Jackson contributed a paper to the *Philosophical Transactions* for 1773, stressing that over forty tons of isinglass had been processed from fish in the Great Lakes which resembled those imported expensively from Russia. Captain James Cook, on completing his second global circumnavigation, highly praised Jackson's beer concentrate, which had been used for its antiscorbutic qualities. The *Resolution* and the *Discovery* also carried it on Cook's last voyage.

Jackson married three times; first, in 1743, to Elizabeth Savory (*d.* 1748). His second marriage, in 1763, was to Mary or Maria, daughter of Benjamin *Martin, public lecturer and instrument maker. She died at their home in Woolwich Common in 1784. His third marriage was to Jane (probably Chamberlain), a widow. Nothing is known of any children.

Jackson received an MD from Aberdeen University in 1761. A freemason, he wrote a Masonic ode and song, and was treasurer of the Soul Captain's Lodge near Hermitage Bridge, at London Docks, in the 1750s. He was a JP for the Tower of London Liberty (1772), Kent (1780), and Middlesex (1783), and wrote on 27 March 1791 to William Pitt, the prime minister, detailing improvements in the impress system. When he died in Tottenham on 29 June 1801, Jackson was the owner of property there and at Woolwich, Wapping, and Tower Street.   JOHN H. APPLEBY

Sources J. H. Appleby, 'Humphrey Jackson, FRS, 1717–1801: a pioneering chemist', *Notes and Records of the Royal Society*, 40 (1985–6), 147–68 • J. H. Appleby and J. R. Millburn, 'Henry or Humphrey?

The Jacksons, eighteenth-century chemists', *The Library*, 6th ser., 10 (1988), 30–43 • P. Mathias, *The brewing industry in England, 1700–1830* (1959), 206–7, 420–21 • F. A. Filby, *A history of food adulteration and analysis* (1934), 49–50, 65, 101–3 • J. C. Drummond and A. Wilbraham, *The Englishman's food: a history of five centuries of English diet*, rev. edn, rev. D. Hollingsworth (1958), 187–201 • *IGI* [baptism] • H. Jackson, 'Discovery of the manner of making isinglass in Russia', *The Philosophical Transactions of the Royal Society of London … abridged*, ed. C. Hutton, 13 (1809), 361–7, esp. 362 • Chancery files, Petty Bag Series, C 202/160/4

Likenesses portrait, priv. coll.

Wealth at death under £5000; excl. real estate in Tottenham, Wapping, Woolwich, and the Tower Hill areas of London: PRO, death duty registers, IR 26/52

Jackson, John (*c*.1621–1693). *See under* Jackson, Arthur (*c*.1593–1666).

Jackson, John (*d.* 1688), organist and composer, was successively master of the choristers at Ely Cathedral (1669) and Norwich Cathedral (1670), then organist and vicar-choral at Wells Cathedral from 1674, where, for a time, he was also master of the choristers. Music by him survives in manuscript from all three cathedrals.

So far as may be judged from mostly incomplete sources Jackson was a capable composer. At least two services are known (one in C major, the other in G minor), as well as twelve anthems, a burial service, and some chants. John Playford published his 'Let God arise' and 'Set up thyself, O God' in *Cantica sacra* (1674), and Thomas Tudway included 'Hallelujah, the Lord said unto my Lord' in his manuscript collection of church music (BL, Harleian MS 7338). Among other notable anthems are 'Many a time have they fought against me' ('Being a Thanksgiving Anthem for the 9th of September, 1683 [discovery of the Rye House plot]') and 'I said in the cutting off' ('An Anthem of Thanksgiving for Recovery for a Dangerous Sickness, Anno 1685'; Royal College of Music, London). Some catches, a single keyboard piece, and a suite of instrumental pieces are also attributed to him. Jackson died in 1688. His widow, Dorothea, was granted administration of his goods in December 1689.   IAN SPINK

Sources H. W. Shaw, *The succession of organists of the Chapel Royal and the cathedrals of England and Wales from c.1538* (1991), 287–8 • I. Spink, *Restoration cathedral music, 1660–1714* (1995), 357–60

Jackson, John (1686–1763), religious controversialist, was born at Sessay, near Thirsk, in the North Riding of Yorkshire, on 4 April 1686, the eldest son of John Jackson (*bap.* 1651, *d.* 1706), prebendary of Southwell and rector of Sessay, and his wife, Anne Revell, who came from a village near Chesterfield, Derbyshire. His grandfather John Jackson had been commissioned in the parliamentary army and subsequently served as vicar of Doncaster and rector of Rossington. Jackson was educated at Doncaster grammar school, and was entered at Jesus College, Cambridge, in 1702, going into residence in 1703. He studied Hebrew under Simon Ockley and graduated BA in 1707. He had overworked and was obliged to spend time with friends in the country, and so entered the household of Mr Simpson at Renishaw, in Derbyshire, where he acted as tutor for nine months in 1707. He took deacon's orders in 1708, and took up residence at Rossington, the living of which had been reserved for him by the corporation of Doncaster since his father's death; he became rector of Rossington in 1710, at the requisite age of twenty-four. On his marriage in 1712 to Elizabeth (*d.* 1760), daughter of John Cowley, collector of excise at Doncaster, he rebuilt the rectory at Rossington. They had twelve children. Through the recommendation of Samuel Clarke, master of Wigston's Hospital, Leicester, he was advanced to its confraternership in 1719 by Lord Lechmere, chancellor of the duchy of Lancaster. He moved to Leicester, which was better for his wife's health, and spent two to three months a year at Rossington, where he paid a curate a third of the living's value to work in the parish. In 1720 he became afternoon preacher at St Martin's, Leicester, for which he received a licence from Edmund Gibson, then bishop of Lincoln. In 1722 Sir John Fryer, an admirer of his writings, presented him to the prebend of Wherwell, in Hampshire. He inherited the mastership of Wigston's Hospital at the death of Samuel Clarke in May 1729, to which he was presented by John Manners, third duke of Rutland and chancellor of the duchy of Lancaster.

Jackson's long and prolific writing career began in 1714, when he anonymously went into print in defence of Samuel Clarke's *Scripture Doctrine of the Trinity*, the argument of which had persuaded him against belief in the orthodox doctrine of the Trinity. These three letters by 'A Clergyman of the Church of England' were to herald a career of constant opposition to 'orthodoxy' in favour of 'scriptural Christianity'. Jackson began to correspond with Clarke and subsequently met him at King's Lynn in 1714. He wrote against orthodox notions of the Trinity throughout the 1710s and 1720s, initially in three short tracts: *An examination of Mr. Nye's explication of the articles of the divine unity, the Trinity and incarnation* (1715), *A Collection of Queries* (1716), and *A Modest Plea for the Scriptural Notion of the Trinity* (1719). His attitude to his opponents was summed up in his criticism of Stephen Nye, whose detailed Socinian apologetic he misinterpreted as Sabellianism, when he declared that 'we live in an Age too knowing, to be impos'd on with old Sophistry instead of old Orthodoxy' (*An Examination of Mr. Nye's Explication*, 79). His exposition of such views prevented him from being able to take his MA at Cambridge in 1718. They were not well received by the high-church party in Leicester either, who prosecuted him for preaching heresy in 1721, and again in 1722; Jackson successfully defended himself against their accusations at the archdeacon's court in Leicester and at the chancellor's court in Lincoln. In the memoirs that he dictated to Dr Thomas Sutton of Leicester in 1762 he was keen to record that he had admitted people of many religious persuasions into Wigston's Hospital during his mastership, including some of his old high-church opponents. In 1716 he defended Hoadly's low-church principles in *The Grounds of Civil and Ecclesiastical Government Briefly Consider'd*, a second edition of which appeared in 1718. Something of the firmly whig tone of this work is apparent in a sermon that he preached to a company of dragoons camped near Leicester, which he published as *The Duty of Subjects towards their Governors* in 1723.

Jackson's chief high-church opponent was Daniel Waterland, to whom he had written in March 1718 in terms that would characterize their long exchange of sometimes vituperative pamphlets: 'But whether the *Orthodox* or *We* are more truly *Heretics*, the Arguments on both Sides from *Scripture* and *Reason* ought to determine, though I hope neither of us will be found so in God's Account at the *Great Day*' (Sutton, 7). Jackson was aided by Clarke in his encounters with Waterland, which amounted to four pamphlets published in the 1720s. The intricacies and insinuations of the debate were summarized in his *Memoirs of Waterland* (1731). Jackson had managed to become a figure of scandal to many in the church; all his preferments from 1719 onwards had been to posts that did not require him to subscribe to the Thirty-Nine Articles, in the authority of which he no longer believed. His refusal to subscribe cost him a prebend at Salisbury, which Hoadly had hoped to bestow on him in 1724. It was his trenchant sense of conviction that led to a significant contretemps at Bath in October 1735, when Dr Coney of St James's refused to give Jackson the sacrament on the grounds of his supposed non-belief in Christ's divinity. Jackson wrote an anonymous account of this event in 1736, denouncing Coney's '*Schismatical* Misbehaviour' and his 'Sacheverel Spirit' and portraying himself as a martyr in the 'Cause of true Religion' in 'a corrupt Age' (J. Jackson, *A Narrative of the Case of the Reverend Mr. Jackson being Refus'd the Sacrament of the Lord's Supper at Bath*, 1736, 13, 16, 21–2).

Jackson engaged in a debate with John Browne, a supporter of Edmund Gibson, bishop of London, which had been initiated by Jackson's *A Plea for Human Reason* (1730), a considered response to Gibson's attacks on freethinkers. Jackson had accused the bishop of slighting human reason; Browne turned on Jackson as 'an Obscure Writer', condemning his 'Pedantick Air' and 'assuming Style', and regretting his alleged confederation with infidels as a 'Dealer in *Demonstration*' (J. Browne, *A Defence of the Bishop of London's Second Pastoral Letter*, 1730, 3, 4, 59). Jackson considered Browne's response exceptionally insulting, and he replied in kind, describing Browne as 'a *Desperado* in Controversy' (J. Jackson, *Calumny No Conviction*, 1731, 71) before expanding his original argument in the *Second Part of the Plea for Human Reason* (1732). Jackson had in fact played his part in the Christian onslaught on the freethinkers. He had produced a considered response to the arguments of John Trenchard and Thomas Gordon in *A Defence of Human Liberty* (1725), which was followed by a repudiation of the arguments of Anthony Collins in *A Vindication of Human Liberty* (1730), and in a slim but effective tract against Matthew Tindal, *Remarks on a Book Intitled, Christianity as Old as the Creation* (1731). He continued the debate with freethinkers in *Christian Liberty Asserted* (1734) and attempted to deal with materialism in *A Dissertation on Matter and Spirit* (1734), a subject on which he further exchanged letters with William Dudgeon (whom he did not meet), which were published in 1737. He had continued to defend the natural theology of Samuel Clarke in *The Existence and Unity of God* (1734), which also acted as a

further critique of Waterland. In 1744 he produced *An Address to Deists*, a work that he had been desperate to reprint, which he felt had been made impossible through the indolence of his publisher, Knapton; he finally produced a second edition in 1762, admitting in a letter to Thomas Birch that it was better for 'the Instruction of Learned Believers' than it was for the reclamation of freethinkers (BL, Add. MS 4310, fols. 249–50). He also took on Conyers Middleton's critique of miracles in *Remarks on Dr. Middleton's Free Enquiry* (1749); his intervention in this debate won him the respect of some orthodox theologians and opened him up to criticism from Middleton's supporters. He had attacked Warburton's hypothesis that the ancient Jews had had no knowledge of a future life in *The Belief of a Future State Proved to be a Fundamental Article of the Religion of the Hebrews* (1745), an effective work which he defended in print in 1746 and 1747, and widened his argument to include ancient heathen philosophers in *A Critical Inquiry into the Opinions of the Ancient Philosophers Concerning the Soul* (1748). He denounced Warburton as a reader of texts, with some skill, in *A Treatise on the Improvements in the Art of Criticism Made by a Celebrated Hypercritick* (1748). His major work was his *Chronological Antiquities*, which appeared in three volumes in 1752, supported by a considerable list of subscribers, including many orthodox clergymen. The work was well received abroad, and a German translation appeared in the 1750s. In this work Jackson was concerned to further correct the chronology of classical and biblical history, a task that he had taken upon himself as a consciously Newtonian scholar in order to ensure the acceptance of a clear and proper periodization that would enable a scientific understanding of history to develop. His grounds for doing so were largely philosophical in character, and he was strongly criticized by a fellow clergyman, John Kennedy, who argued in *An Examination of the Reverend Mr. Jackson's Chronological Antiquities* (1753) that they ought, more properly, to have been astronomical in form.

Between 1742 and 1747 Jackson was master of Doncaster grammar school. He fell into a decline in the late 1750s, and he died at Leicester on 12 May 1763. He was buried at Rossington, survived by one of his sons, John, and three married daughters.

B. W. YOUNG

Sources T. Sutton, *Memoirs of the life and writings of John Jackson* (1764) · Nichols, *Lit. anecdotes* · J. Gascoigne, *Cambridge in the age of the Enlightenment* (1989) · B. W. Young, *Religion and Enlightenment in eighteenth-century England: theological debate from Locke to Burke* (1998) · Venn, *Alum. Cant.* · *DNB*

Likenesses J. Macardell, mezzotint, 1757 (after F. van der Mijn), BM, NPG

Jackson, John (1729/30–1806), actor and theatre manager, was born in 1729 or 1730, possibly in Keighley, Yorkshire, where his father, a Church of England clergyman, had his principal living. According to the autobiographical memoir he included in his *History of the Scottish Stage* (1793) Jackson was educated in Doncaster and Kirkby Lonsdale and was intended for the church. The intention was unfulfilled (because, the memoir hints, of straitened circumstances and lack of patronage). Instead he became an actor, making his début as Oroonoko on 9 January 1762 at the Canongate Hall in Edinburgh, and soon adding over a dozen leading roles to his repertory there. However, company tensions resulted in his quitting Edinburgh for London and joining Garrick's Drury Lane company, again first appearing as Oroonoko, on 7 October 1762. Garrick used him for only a few further roles that season. The *Theatrical Review* for 1763 was impressed by his figure and intelligence, but felt he lacked ease, strength of delivery, and refinement of pronunciation.

Jackson had two more seasons at Drury Lane, playing secondary but significant parts; but from the summer of 1765 (when he was a member of a company at Richmond in Surrey) to the winter of 1779–80 his career was largely that of a strolling player, outside London in the main. In the late 1760s he was acting again in Edinburgh, and was also at the Smock Alley Theatre in Dublin and in Cork and Belfast. In the summer of 1769 he married Hester (1751–1806), the daughter of the actor John Sowden. They had four children. Hester Sowden was a player herself, and the pair often acted together thereafter. In the early 1770s they appeared in Edinburgh, Dublin, York, and Liverpool, including performances in Jackson's own tragedy *Eldred, or, The British Freeholder* (given its première in 1774, published in 1782). In 1775 they were engaged for the summer season at the Haymarket in London, after which a London career took off for Hester Jackson but not for her husband. While she performed at Covent Garden, he was again in Edinburgh and Dublin and also in Bristol and Birmingham; he only returned to the capital to play in some of his wife's benefits, which included a performance of his second tragedy, *The British Heroine*, in 1778. (This had been first given in Dublin the previous year as *Gerilda, or, The Siege of Harlech*.)

A third play, *Sir William Wallace of Ellerslie, or, The Siege of Dumbarton Castle*, which received its première in Edinburgh in 1780, though less of a success even than the other two, indicated the focus of Jackson's activity from now on: Scotland and, more especially, the energetic management of its burgeoning theatre industry. He acquired managerial involvements in Dundee, Dumfries, and Aberdeen, but his main concern was Glasgow. He was planning as one of a triumvirate to take over the running of the Alston Street Theatre there, but was thwarted in May 1780 by arsonists, probably Church of Scotland anti-theatrical die-hards. He decided to build afresh on a more central site at Dunlop Street, near the Clyde. His clerical background was useful in helping to overcome the objections of the local burghers, and he was able to open his new playhouse in January 1782. Two months before that he had bought the patent of the Theatre Royal in Edinburgh from its first holder, David Ross; he refurbished Ross's Shakespeare Square house and reopened it on 1 December 1781. So by early 1782 he could run Edinburgh and Glasgow in tandem. His interests in other Scottish theatres involved them in the network too, giving him an unprecedented control over theatrical activity nationwide.

For eight years Jackson's managements prospered. If the theatres had very much a London-based repertory, this at least enabled Scots to see many of London's best performers on visits to Scotland under his aegis, notably (and sensationally) Sarah Siddons. However, by 1790 Jackson was finding himself financially overstretched. His Aberdeen interest had to be sold off; he withdrew from running the Edinburgh theatre, and in 1791 he was declared bankrupt. When the leases of the Edinburgh and Glasgow houses were auctioned the Edinburgh lease was acquired by Stephen Kemble, but under disputed conditions which led to much litigation (partly involving a third party, the actress and would-be lessee Harriet Esten). The matter was not finally resolved until 1794. In the interim Jackson had published his view of the case in *A Statement of Facts* (1792), which the following year he incorporated into his highly personal *A History of the Scottish Stage*. (Volumes 3 and 4 of Charles Lee Lewes's *Memoirs*, published in 1805, are largely an angry rebuttal of Jackson's 'facts'.)

Jackson was still acting in the late 1790s (in Dublin, Bury, Stockport, and Nottingham), but in 1800 he bought back the Edinburgh and Glasgow theatres and went into a management partnership with Francis Aickin. In 1805 they transferred their Glasgow operations from the Dunlop Street theatre to the new playhouse on Queen Street, but the partnership came to an end when Aickin sold his Edinburgh and Glasgow interests in 1806. Hester Jackson had died in January that year, and her husband followed, in Shakespeare Square, Edinburgh, on 4 December, when he succumbed to what the Calton burying-ground recorder's book called 'a Decline of Nature'. He was buried at Calton on 6 December. ROGER SAVAGE

Sources Highfill, Burnim & Langhans, *BDA* · J. Jackson, *The history of the Scottish stage* (1793) · J. C. Dibdin, *The annals of the Edinburgh stage* (1888) · G. W. Stone, ed., *The London stage, 1660–1800*, pt 4: 1747–1776 (1962) · C. L. Lewes, *Memoirs*, 4 vols. (1805) · Genest, *Eng. stage* · record book of Calton burying-ground, Edinburgh
Likenesses engraving (after unknown portrait), repro. in *Hibernian Magazine* (Feb 1777) · portrait (as Albertus in *Giralda*)

Jackson, John (d. 1794). *See under* Jackson, John (d. 1807).

Jackson, John (d. 1807), traveller, was freed by redemption in the Vintners' Company of London in January 1784, according to the 'Alphabet of City Freedoms' in the City Record Office, although he does not appear in any of the Vintners' Company's own records. It seems likely that in 1784 he had recently arrived in London (he is first recorded in land tax assessments for 31 Clement's Lane, City, in 1785) and perhaps came from another place which had its own Vintners' Company; this would explain his absence from London Vintners' Company records. Jackson was evidently a man of substance, since he held stock insured for £1000; the house at St Clement's Lane was separately insured for £300.

Jackson went to India on private business, visiting Ceylon and the Malabar coast while there. He travelled out by ship but took the overland route home. On 4 May 1797 he left Bombay by country ship for Basrah. He proceeded via the Euphrates and Tigris to Baghdad, and thence travelled through Kurdistan, Armorica, Anatolia, Bulgaria, Wallachia, and Transylvania, reaching Hamburg on 28 October of the same year. Under the title *Journey from India* towards England (1799) he published an account of his travels in which he showed that the use of the route he followed was practicable all the year round. Jackson's narrative of his journey is straightforward in style, with daily entries describing his party's progress, and observations on the people and places they encountered. Although he advocated greater use of the overland route, he conceded that it was only for the physically hardy, and his description made it clear that the route was potentially dangerous. He advised on how to seek help from the local people and how to travel inconspicuously. Jackson showed himself both curious and flexible in adopting local habits of dress, of wearing beard and moustache, and of eating, drinking, and smoking. The reviewer in the *Gentleman's Magazine* described the *Journey* warmly as 'a very useful and instructive guide' (1st ser., 70, 1800, 237–9).

Jackson did not return to his Clement's Lane address after his return to England. In 1803 he communicated to the Society of Antiquaries an account of some excavations made under his direction among the ruins of Carthage and at Udena, published in *Archaeologia* (vol. 15, 1806). He was elected fellow of the Society of Antiquaries on 2 February 1804. He also wrote *Reflections on the commerce of the Mediterranean, deduced from actual experience during a residence on both shores of the Mediterranean Sea, showing the advantages of increasing the number of British consuls, and of holding possession of Malta as nearly equal to our West Indian trade*. In August 1807 his death was reported to have taken place 'recently' (*GM*, 1st ser., 77, 1807, 795).

John Jackson the traveller has been confused with **John Jackson** (*d.* 1794) the antiquary. In 1786 the latter sent the topographer Richard Gough a description of Roman remains then lately discovered during some excavations in Lombard Street and Birchin Lane, which was printed, with plates, in vol. 8 of *Archaeologia*. He was elected a fellow of the Society of Antiquaries on 15 March 1787 and died in the first half of 1794. His effects were disposed of in two sales in 1794. ELIZABETH BAIGENT

Sources *GM*, 1st ser., 77 (1807), 795 · 'List of the fellows of the Society of Antiquaries of London, 1717–1796', S. Antiquaries, Lond. · *The London directory for the year 1789* (1789) · J. Jackson, *Journey from India towards England* (1799) · *GM*, 1st ser., 70 (1800), 237–9 · *Universal British directory, 1793–8* (1798) · land tax assessments and returns, Longbourne ward, 1782/3–1805/6, GL · Sun Fire insurance policy, GL, MS 11936/367, policy 501632 · private information (2004) [Adrian James, Society of Antiquaries] · F. Lught, *Repertoire des catalogues des ventes*, 1 (1938)

Jackson, John [*called* Gentleman Jackson] (1769–1845), pugilist, was the son of the builder who bridged the Fleet ditch. He was born in London on 28 September 1769, and appeared only three times in the prize-ring. His first public fight took place on 9 June 1788 at Smitham Bottom, near Croydon, when he defeated Fewterel of Birmingham in a contest lasting one hour and seven minutes, in the presence of the prince of Wales. He was defeated by George (Ingleston) the Brewer at Ingatestone, Essex, on 12 March 1789, owing to a heavy fall on the wet stage, which dislocated his ankle and broke the small bone of his leg. He offered to finish the battle tied to a chair, but this his

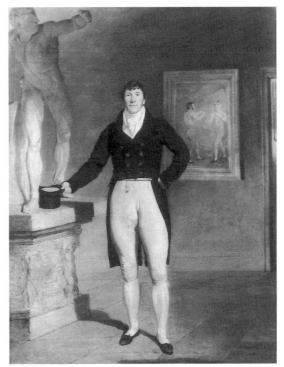

John Jackson [Gentleman Jackson] (1769–1845), by Benjamin Marshall, in or before 1810

opponent declined. His third and last fight was with Daniel Mendoza, whom he beat at Hornchurch, Essex, on 15 April 1795, in ten and a half minutes by seizing Mendoza's imprudently long hair and pounding him into submission. After some dispute, this was declared fair; Jackson therefore became champion of England. In 1803, still unchallenged, he retired and was succeeded by Jem Belcher.

After leaving the prize-ring, Jackson established a school at 13 Bond Street, jointly with the fencing school of Henry Angelo, where he gave instructions in the art of self-defence, and was largely patronized by the nobility of the day. He remained much in demand as a referee and master of ceremonies: according to Pierce Egan, he was 'the link that keeps the whole chain together' (Brailsford, 72). His school became headquarters of the Pugilistic Club, and he controlled the use of the fives court, Little St Martin's Street, for benefit exhibitions—a facility he denied to his old opponent Mendoza. He organized pugilistic demonstrations before visiting sovereigns in 1814; and at the coronation of George IV, Jackson was employed, with eighteen other prize-fighters dressed as pages—including Tom Cribb, Tom Oliver, and Thomas Winter—to guard the entrance to Westminster Abbey and Hall, especially against partisans of Caroline of Brunswick. He seems, according to the inscription on a mezzotint engraving by C. Turner, to have subsequently been landlord of the Sun and Punchbowl, Holborn, and of The Cock at Sutton. He died on 7 October 1845 at his home, 4 Lower Grosvenor Street West, London, in his seventy-seventh year, and was buried in Brompton cemetery, where a colossal monument to his memory was erected by subscription.

Jackson was a magnificently proportioned man. His height was 5 feet 11 inches and his weight 14 stone—3 stone heavier than Mendoza, whom he displaced. He was also a fine short-distance runner and jumper, and is said to have lifted, in the presence of Harvey Combe, 10¼ cwt, and to have written his own name with an 84 lb weight on his little finger (*GM*, 649). Egon kept a cast of his arm, while as early as 1790 Thomas Lawrence had chosen him as model for a muscular nude in the foreground of *Homer Reciting his Poems*. Jackson was said to make 'more than a thousand a year by teaching sparring' (Russell, 2.230). Lord Byron, who was one of his pupils, had a great liking for his company, despite criticism, and liked to refer to his training principles and exhortations against 'taking too much out of oneself' and 'putting it about' (*Byron's Letters and Journals*, 5.179, 162), even if he himself did not always observe these strictures. Byron depicted Jackson as Johnson in *Don Juan* (Canto V 10–11), and mentioned him in his *Hints from Horace*:

And men unpractised in exchanging knocks
Must go to Jackson ere they dare to box.
(*Complete Poetical Works*, 1.311)

Jackson's relative social acceptability was a by-product of the peak of Regency 'boximania'; it was also helpful that he established a formidable reputation with little actual fighting. By 1845 it was important to remember that 'Mr. Jackson is not to be confounded with the wretches who now disgrace society' in the prize-ring (*Annual Register*, 300). G. F. R. BARKER, *rev.* JULIAN LOCK

Sources *GM*, 2nd ser., 24 (1845), 649 · *Annual Register* (1845), 300 · *Bell's Life in London* (12 Oct 1845) · H. D. Miles, *Pugilistica: being one hundred and forty-four years of the history of British boxing*, 3 vols. (1880–81), vol. 1, pp. 89–102 · J. Ford, *Prizefighting: the age of Regency boximania* (1971) · J. C. Reid, *Bucks and bruisers: Pierce Egan and Regency England* (1971) · *Byron's letters and journals*, ed. L. A. Marchand, 12 vols. (1973–82) · D. Brailsford, *Bareknuckles: a social history of prize fighting* (1988) · *Lord Byron: the complete poetical works*, ed. J. J. McGann, 7 vols. (1980–93) · D. Johnson, *Bare fist fighters of the 18th and 19th century: 1704–1861* (1987) · *Memoirs, journal and correspondence of Thomas Moore*, ed. J. Russell, 8 vols. (1853–6) · N. S. Fleischer, *The heavyweight championship, 1719–1949* (1949)
Likenesses Gillray, portrait, 1788? (with Fewterel), BL · T. Lawrence, oils, 1790 (*Homer Reciting his Poems*), Tate collection · B. Marshall, oils, in or before 1810; Christies, 20 July 1951, lot 106 [*see illus.*] · C. Turner, mezzotint, pubd 1810 (after oils by B. Marshall), BM, NPG; repro. in Ford, *Prizefighting*, 49 · C. Turner, mezzotint, pubd 1821 (after his earlier work), BM, NPG · stipple, pubd 1823, NPG · T. Butler, medallion on monument, Brompton Cemetery, London · I. R. Cruikshank, aquatint and watercolour, V&A · W. Thomas, engraving (after painting), repro. in Miles, *Pugilistica*, vol. 1, facing p. 90 · group portrait, oils (with Mendoza in 1795), Garden and Country Park, Brodick Castle · oils, priv. coll.

Jackson, John (1778–1831), portrait painter and copyist, was born on 31 May 1778 at Lastingham in the North Riding of Yorkshire, the eldest son of John Jackson (1743–1822), tailor, and his wife, Ann Warrener (*d. c.*1837), who came from a Wesleyan missionary family. After a period at a private school at Nawton, some 15 miles away, Jackson worked in his father's tailoring business at Lastingham. In

John Jackson (1778–1831), self-portrait, *c.*1823

1797 he left home to make his way as a miniature painter on ivory based at York and Whitby. The miniatures were 'badly' done but he 'showed talent sketching likenesses on paper' (Farington, *Diary*, 8.299) and by January 1800 he had been introduced, probably through a dissenting clergyman (most likely Whitby's Presbyterian minister, Thomas Watson) to Lord Mulgrave at Mulgrave Castle. Executed with the local house-painter's colours, his copy of Sir Joshua Reynolds's portrait of the playwright George Colman (pencil version dated 13 January 1800; BM) showed promise and, encouraged by his friends, the collectors the earl of Carlisle and Sir George Beaumont, Mulgrave allowed Jackson to stay frequently for more copying, Lord Carlisle also inviting him to Castle Howard for several months.

Jackson often accompanied the Mulgrave family to their Harley Street house in London and he worked in Beaumont's Grosvenor Square painting room imbibing Reynolds's teaching from his eloquent host. In July 1802 he moved on to stay with Lord Mulgrave's nephew by marriage, Viscount Dillon, at Ditchley near Oxford but failed to please Beaumont in particular with a copy of a Van Dyck portrait. Previously, in January, Beaumont had written complaining that Jackson should 'abate his velocity & aim at correctness' and subsequent letters to Mulgrave advised stiff reprimands. A year later he feared 'a want of energy—of enthusiasm … the merest blockhead in the Academy can draw better than he can at present' and advised that withdrawal of support might activate him (Owen and Brown, x, 156). In fact Jackson did achieve admission to the Royal Academy Schools in March 1805 and Mulgrave paid for a London studio in the Haymarket from the previous year. Finished just in time, Lady Mulgrave's portrait with her sister-in-law hung in the 1806 exhibition: typically the carefree painter had been discovered playing battledore and shuttlecock with his patron's aide-de-camp instead of quickly dispatching it. In 1807 or 1808 Jackson married Maria Fletcher (c.1780–1817), with whom he had a daughter who was born on 9 July 1808.

Unselfishly Jackson introduced a fellow student, David Wilkie, to his patrons and Mulgrave followed Beaumont in immediately commissioning him. Benjamin Haydon also benefited. Haydon describes Jackson at this time as 'a good-natured looking man in black with his hair powdered whom I took as a clergyman' (Haydon, 19). Mulgrave was first lord of the Admiralty from 1807 to 1810 and the trio of painters dined at the Admiralty frequently in their patrons' company. For all his fine eye for colour Jackson, whose watercolour portraits improved, was too often diverted, enjoying the salerooms and lectures and sketching in the country—in 1810 he tried to attract John Constable to the New Forest—and he shared little of his friends' limelight.

In 1813 Jackson began his task of producing portraits of eminent Methodists for the *Wesleyan Methodist Magazine* while Cadell and Davies employed him for the *British Gallery of Contemporary Portraits*, likenesses being created by a synthesis of existing images. He also pleased the anatomist Sir Charles Bell with his copy, costing more than an original work by Sir Henry Raeburn, of Reynolds's *John Hunter*. James Northcote used the likeable younger painter as an occasional model and became the first of a series of academicians depicted and exhibited by Jackson prior to his election as an associate of the Royal Academy in 1815 and Royal Academician in 1818.

Jackson remained greatly attached to Yorkshire and to the Mulgrave family in particular. In 1816 he painted a group portrait of his patron (in 1812 created earl of Mulgrave and Viscount Normanby), his brothers General the Hon. Edmund and the Hon. Augustus Phipps with Sir George Beaumont (oil sketch; priv. coll.) that was engraved by William Ward (1820). He also made a five-week tour of the Low Countries with the general, visiting galleries in Antwerp and Brussels, where they were joined by the duchess of Richmond for an inspection of the Waterloo battleground. Only a few pencil sketches survive (V&A). Jackson exhibited two Yorkshire landscapes at the British Institution but was more successful with subject pictures and in 1827 with *A Negro's Head*, of which several versions survive (priv. coll.). The artist was delighted when the president of the institution, the marquess of Stafford, bought his *Little Moses* in 1815 for 50 guineas.

Jackson's wife, Maria, died on 4 March 1817 leaving two children, and on 11 August 1818 he married Matilda Louise (c.1796–1873), the daughter of James Ward RA, who also had a studio in Newman Street, Soho, where Jackson had moved in 1807. Farington wrote to Sir Thomas Lawrence that two days after marriage his wife was found to be mentally unbalanced; previously 'her singularity of manner' he had attributed to 'indifferent health and relaxed nerves' (MS letter, RA, LAW/2/249). Jackson's 'equanimity' enabled him to cope, and, although Matilda's expectations had been heightened by earlier admiration from Lord Chesterfield's nephew, she became inculcated with the Methodist faith and a devoted wife. The family settled happily in Hampstead then, in 1824, at 16 Grove End Road, St John's Wood, their youngest surviving child, Mulgrave Phipps, later aspiring to art criticism. Jackson retained his studio and owned a carriage, an indulgence he could barely afford while his charges for a half-length portrait remained about 50 guineas, giving him an income seldom reaching £1500 a year.

In December 1818 Jackson, long regarded as an amiable but silent member of the Beaumont circle, was invited to the baronet's Leicestershire seat, Coleorton Hall, to paint a portrait of its architect, George Dance RA (Leicester Art Gallery), and he also copied the Reynolds portraits of his hosts, one pair going to Constable. In the following year Jackson travelled with two Yorkshiremen—Francis Chantrey, the sculptor, and a Mr Read from Norton—through Paris and Geneva to Rome, where their president, Sir Thomas Lawrence, took his two new academicians in his carriage to see the sights. Chantrey was critical of Jackson's apathy and general indifference to art but the painter astounded observers with the speed and skill with which he worked copying Titian's *Sacred and Profane Love* in four days and on his outstanding portrait *Antonio Canova* (Yale U. CBA). Canova rewarded him by overseeing the Englishman's election to the Accademia di San Luca, Rome.

Jackson, like Northcote, was imbued with the Reynolds tradition and he showed little originality in composition. He was now at the height of his powers, and at the Royal Academy dinner in 1827 Lawrence described Jackson's portrait *John Flaxman, RA* as 'a grand achievement of the English School' (Redgrave, *Artists*, 245) and his *Lord Dover* was also approved by the critics. As George Agar Ellis, Dover played a leading political role in persuading the government to establish the National Gallery and he and Beaumont sometimes discussed the matter in Jackson's studio. Dover owned both portraits as well as a fine one of his wife by Jackson, who did not often succeed with portraits of women. Jackson was generally considered rarely to reach Lawrence's heights, although his portrayals were 'flesh and blood' according to Haydon, who cared less for the president's fine work.

In 1820 Mulgrave suffered a 'creeping palsy' that incapacitated him. Like Beaumont, who died in 1827, Jackson became gloomier over his last decade. In London he was often seen with Beaumont, Wilkie, and the Phipps brothers, while the general still welcomed him to Mulgrave Castle. But Jackson's religion was paramount. Constable suspected that he did many good works: equally at ease in church or chapel, he gave £50 in 1826 to improve the church at Lastingham and a smaller copy of Correggio's *Agony in the Garden* as an altarpiece. He was at Lastingham again in August 1830, having been in poor health, to see his mother, and he told Northcote he was ready for work again, 'now necessary for life' (RA, AND/40/

XXI). His final journey to Yorkshire to attend Mulgrave's funeral in 1831 proved too much for his weakened constitution and he died on 1 June at his home, 16 Grove End Road, St John's Wood, London.

Jackson's funeral and burial at Hinde Street Chapel, Marylebone, was attended mainly by Methodists. His family, left penniless, received £50 grants in 1831 and 1832 from the Royal Academy and his studio sale at Christies on 15 and 16 July 1831 yielded a disappointing £1032, although it included four works by Reynolds, his palette and Hogarth's; the former Jackson had used in youth and it was perhaps given him by Beaumont as a token of esteem. Fortunately he probably still owned his house and studio at his death; otherwise the Royal Academy would no doubt have continued its grants to his family, many of Jackson's friends being academicians who appreciated his virtues of kindness and generosity.   FELICITY OWEN

Sources H. Morgan, 'John Jackson', diss., U. Leeds, 1956 • Farington, *Diary* • B. Haydon, *Autobiography and memoirs*, ed. A. Penrose (1927) • A. Cunningham, *Lives of the most eminent British painters*, 3 (1880) • R. Redgrave and S. Redgrave, *A century of British painters*, new edn, ed. R. Todd (1947) • F. Owen and D. Brown, *Collector of genius* (1982) • W. Whitley, *Art in England*, 2 vols. (1973) • E. Lester, *A fine eye for colour* (privately printed, 2001) • *DNB* • Redgrave, *Artists*
Archives N. Yorks. CRO, letters mainly to his brother
Likenesses J. Jackson, self-portrait, 1808, Scarborough Art Gallery • J. Jackson, self-portrait, oils, c.1810–1812, V&A • J. Jackson, self-portrait, oils, c.1810–1812, Ferens Art Gallery, Hull • J. Jackson, self-portrait, c.1820–1825, Castle Howard, North Yorkshire • J. Jackson, self-portrait, oils, c.1823, NPG [*see illus.*] • M. Brewer, miniature, 1830, V&A • J. Jackson, self-portrait, watercolour drawing, Yale U. CBA
Wealth at death owned house and studio: Morgan, 'John Jackson'

Jackson, John (1801–1848), wood-engraver, was born at Ovingham, Northumberland, on 19 April 1801, the son of 'a poor cottager', John Jackson, and his wife, Mary Mason. Nothing else is known of his early circumstances except that his attempts at drawing were sufficiently promising to raise hopes that he could follow the career of Thomas Bewick, who had been born in the same parish. His parents were without the means to pay an apprentice's premium, but William Laws, steward of nearby Prudhoe Castle, had approached Bewick on his behalf in 1818 or 1819, and a letter from Bewick to Laws of 22 February 1819 reveals that Jackson had already spent some time on trial in the workshop, and that he was eager to learn, earnest in his ambition, and 'a clever boy and in every sense promising' [*see also* Bewick, Thomas, apprentices]. Bewick pointed out that, when no apprentice's fee was forthcoming, boys were kept by their parents or friends for the first three years, after which they received 5s. per week. If a fee of £60 were to be found, then the weekly rate would run from 5s. in the first year to 8s. in the seventh and final year. He emphasized that, as the parents were poor and that a subscription was to be raised, he would do everything possible to help. A few impressions from his work on wood were enclosed as an example of his promise.

The terms were refused by Jackson's sponsors, who by June of 1819 had sent a sample of Jackson's work on copper to Edward Walker of Newcastle upon Tyne, asking him to show it to likely employers who might visit his printing office. Bewick had been provoked by the sponsors' reaction and drafted a letter which, while not sent, declared that he blamed himself for letting the youth see 'for months past' everything of his trade that had taken him many years to perfect and more than he had ever seen when an apprentice himself. He continued by saying that he had been 'unsuspicious of any thing happening to prevent his becoming our Apprentice', and finished his note bitterly: 'having obtained all the information in the time he wished for—he leaves me in the Lurch' (letter, 15 April 1819).

Eventually Jackson was apprenticed to the Newcastle firm of Armstrong and Walker. (George Armstrong had himself been apprenticed to Bewick between 1802 and 1804.) The firm failed in 1823, and Jackson's sponsors were once more approaching Bewick to take him on for his final three and a half years. The 5s. a week first offered was considered insufficient, but a compromise was reached: Jackson was first on the workshop wages in the week ending 26 April 1823, and indentures were paid for on 19 June 1823. But by 12 June 1824 the work books record 'J. Jackson gone to London', and it was here that he finished his time, under William Harvey. No love was lost, and Bewick failed to notice Jackson in his *Memoir*. Jackson was eighteen when he began his time, four years later than was customary, and it is possible that his skills had developed more swiftly than usual, to the point where London could offer much more than the Newcastle trade. Despite having executed a few original drawings and watercolours, he was to become not a designer but an immensely successful reproductive engraver, working for the most part from the designs of others.

Jackson's London reputation was established on the extensive work he did for Charles Knight's *Penny Magazine* and its publisher, the Society for the Diffusion of Useful Knowledge. Here his hand appears workmanlike and vigorous but very mechanical, without much subtlety of tone, and suggesting the occasional use of the ruling machine. Among his other work for Knight, examples appear in the *Shakspeare*, *Pictorial Bible* and *Prayer-Book*. Two other notable contributions were made, after Harvey's designs, to Northcote's *Fables* of 1828 and 1833, and to Lane's *Arabian Nights* of 1840. The highly finished drawings on the wood were interpreted with extraordinary precision, in a manner very far from Bewick. W. J. Linton, while remarking on Jackson's want of artistry, admired the 'excellent cleanness' of his cutting (Linton, 192). Without his signature, which usually appears in minute capitals, it is difficult to attribute any idiosyncrasy of manner to his hand.

Jackson contributed articles to the *New Sporting Magazine* and to Hone's *Every-Day Book*, and he had an abiding interest in the history of wood-engraving. Provoked by the ignorance of the processes of engraving shown by earlier writers, he proposed, funded, and supplied engraved illustrations and much of the material for *A Treatise on Wood Engraving* (1839), which was put together and edited by his fellow Northumbrian W. A. Chatto. A valuable source of information on contemporary engravers and their technique, the work is generous in its praise of Bewick, and has often been referred to in relation to the discussion of the apprentice contributions to Bewick's major works. Chatto's preparatory notes for the book, now in the London Library, reveal that the source for this material was Edward Willis (apprenticed between 1798 and 1804) and his not altogether accurate recollection of events which had taken place thirty years earlier.

Jackson died in London of acute bronchitis on 27 March 1848, after several years of illness, and was buried in Highgate cemetery. He was the elder brother of Mason *Jackson (1819–1903), who also moved to London and was widely employed as a wood-engraver.   IAIN BAIN

Sources T. Bewick, *A memoir of Thomas Bewick written by himself*, ed. I. Bain (1975); rev. edn (1979) · MS corresp., priv. coll. · Beilby-Bewick workshop records, Tyne and Wear Archive Department, Newcastle upon Tyne, 1269 · R. Robinson, *Thomas Bewick: his life and times* (1887) · J. Boyd, *Bewick gleanings* (1886) · W. Chatto and J. Jackson, *A treatise on wood engraving* (1839) · W. J. Linton, *The masters of wood-engraving* (1889) · W. A. Chatto, MS notes for preparation of *Treatise*, 1839, London Library · A. Angus, *History of book trade in the north* (Nov 1993)

Archives Laing Art Gallery, Newcastle upon Tyne · Natural History Society of Northumbria, Newcastle upon Tyne · Tyne and Wear Archives Service, Newcastle upon Tyne | Central Library, Newcastle upon Tyne, Pease bequest · priv. coll., Thomas Bewick, family and business corresp. · UCL, letters to Society for the Diffusion of Useful Knowledge

Jackson, John (1811–1885), bishop of London, the only son of Henry Jackson, a merchant of Mansfield, Nottinghamshire, and afterwards of St Pancras, London, was born in London on 22 February 1811. He was educated at Reading School under the celebrated Richard Valpy, and on 10 June 1829 matriculated at Pembroke College, Oxford, where he was a scholar, taking first-class honours in *literae humaniores* and graduating BA in 1833, and proceeding MA three years later. He failed to obtain a fellowship at Oriel College, but in 1834 was awarded the Ellerton theological prize for an essay entitled 'The sanctifying influence of the Holy Ghost is indispensable to human salvation'.

Ordained deacon in 1835, Jackson was for a short time curate at Henley-on-Thames, Oxfordshire, but in the following year he was appointed headmaster of Islington proprietary school in London. He combined this post with the evening lectureship at Stoke Newington parish church and with the curacy and (from 1842) the incumbency of St James's, Muswell Hill, and soon gained a considerable reputation as a scholarly and cultured preacher with a grave and impressive delivery. It was at Stoke Newington that he delivered the sermons later issued as *The Sinfulness of Little Sins* (1849), his most successful and popular publication. He was a select preacher before the University of Oxford in 1845 and on several subsequent occasions. Jackson became rector of St James's, Piccadilly, in 1846, a chaplain to Queen Victoria in 1847, an honorary canon of Bristol Cathedral in 1852, and Boyle lecturer the following year. He had married in 1838 Mary Anne Frith, a daughter of Henry Browell of Kentish Town, London, with

John Jackson (1811–1885), by Walter William Ouless, exh. RA 1876

whom he had one son and ten daughters and who died on 6 January 1874.

In 1853 Jackson was consecrated as bishop of Lincoln, where he proved himself to be a good administrator and a diligent reformer, reviving the ruridecanal system, almost extinguishing non-residence, promoting the repair of dilapidated churches, and generally raising the spiritual tone of the clergy. He rarely spoke in the House of Lords, but was active in the convocation of Canterbury, where in 1864 he joined with A. C. Tait of London in opposing the condemnation of *Essays and Reviews* by the upper house of bishops.

When Tait was translated from London to Canterbury in 1868, Jackson was unexpectedly selected by Disraeli for the vacant see. However, he achieved much that was valuable through his painstaking, methodical ways. By the creation of the diocese of St Albans in 1877 and the consequent rearrangement of Rochester and Winchester, the diocese of London was made more workable, and two years later William Walsham How was appointed as suffragan bishop for east London. In 1873 Jackson reconstituted the Bishop of London's Fund, established a decade earlier by Tait, as a permanent institution to assist in the provision of additional personnel and buildings in the diocese. He encouraged and valued the contribution of the diocesan association of lay helpers, though he hesitated long before agreeing to the creation of a diocesan conference in 1882, believing that the see was too large for the laity to confer properly.

In London Jackson had to confront the growing problem of ritualism. He never had any sympathy for it and initially hoped that the Public Worship Regulation Act of 1874 would secure peace and conformity in the church.

However, faced with the intransigence of both the Church Association on the one side and the ritualistic clergy on the other he came to believe that the act led to lengthy litigation, unfair penalties, and public sympathy for the priests who were punished. By 1881, taking his lead from Tait, he had decided to use his powers of veto to stop prosecutions.

Though stern and reserved in manner, guarded and cautious in speech, and of a naturally conservative cast of mind, Jackson was widely respected as a conscientious and fair-minded church leader. Sometimes designated an evangelical, he was in fact a protestant low-churchman in the mould of A. C. Tait. He died suddenly of heart disease at Fulham Palace, London, on 6 January 1885, the eleventh anniversary of his wife's death, and was buried alongside her four days later in Fulham parish churchyard. His published works consist almost entirely of sermons and charges to his clergy. STEPHEN GREGORY

Sources Annual Register (1886), pt 2, pp. 135–6 · G. G. Perry and J. H. Overton, Biographical notices of the bishops of Lincoln: from Remigius to Wordsworth (1900) · Boase, Mod. Eng. biog., vol. 2 · Men of the time (1884) · Crockford (1885) · Foster, Alum. Oxon. · W. Benham and R. T. Davidson, Life of Archibald Campbell Tait, 2 vols. (1891) · O. Chadwick, The Victorian church, 2 (1970) · J. Bentley, Ritualism and politics in Victorian Britain (1978) · The Guardian (7 Jan 1885) · The Guardian (14 Jan 1885) · The Times (7 Jan 1885) · The Record (9 Jan 1885) · D. M. Lewis, ed., The Blackwell dictionary of evangelical biography, 1730–1860, 2 vols. (1995) · Clergy List (1842) · Clergy List (1846) · Clergy List (1847) · DNB
Archives BL, personal and family corresp., Add. MSS 63114–63115 · Lincs. Arch., letter-books · LPL, corresp. and papers | BL, letters to W. E. Gladstone, Add. MSS 44423–44489, passim · Durham Cath. CL, letters to J. B. Lightfoot · LPL, corresp. with E. W. Benson · LPL, letters to Archibald Tait · U. Nott. L., letters to J. E. Denison
Likenesses C. W. Sharpe, stipple, pubd 1854 (after G. Richmond), BM · W. W. Ouless, oils, exh. RA 1876, Fulham Palace, London [see illus.] · T. Woolner, sculpture, 1887, St Paul's Cathedral, London · Ape [C. Pellegrini], chromolithograph caricature, NPG; repro. in VF (12 Nov 1870) · H. Hering, carte-de-visite, NPG · Lock & Whitfield, woodburytype photograph, NPG; repro. in T. Cooper, Men of mark: a gallery of contemporary portraits (1876) · Maull & Polyblank, photograph, carte-de-visite, NPG · W. Walker, mezzotint (after W. Cooper), BM · photograph, carte-de-visite, NPG · portrait, repro. in Church Portrait Journal, 2 (1881), 89 · portrait, repro. in ILN, 54 (1869), 135, 137

Jackson, John (1833–1901), cricketer, was born at Bungay, Suffolk, on 21 May 1833. He was of illegitimate birth and was taken to Nottinghamshire in infancy. He was brought up at Wellow, near Newark, where in the hunting season he would run barefoot after the hounds. His first professional cricket engagement was at Southwell, and after others at Newark, Edinburgh, and Ipswich, he began a county career with Nottinghamshire (1855–66). For the North against the South at Lord's in 1857 he captured fifteen wickets for 91 runs and quickly became the most prominent bowler in England. In 1858, when helping Kent—as a 'given man' in two matches—against England, he took twenty-two wickets for 117 runs.

Jackson played in twelve matches (1859–64) for the Players against the Gentlemen, and in the match at Lord's in 1861 he and Edgar Willsher bowled unchanged through both innings of the Gentlemen. He was by far the most successful bowler in the annual matches between the All England eleven and United All England eleven, taking 107 wickets. In 1859 he went with the first England team to America with George Parr, meeting with great success against local teams. He was also a member of the team under Parr that visited Australia in 1863–4. In 1866 his career was cut short by an accident to his leg while playing for Nottinghamshire against Yorkshire.

Fully 6 feet in height, and weighing over 15 stone, 'Foghorn' Jackson was a round-arm bowler who combined variety and accuracy with tremendous pace, which gained for him the title of the Demon Bowler. He figured in many of the famous *Punch* cricket sketches by John Leech, where the village cricketer is seen bandaged after bruises inflicted by Jackson's lightning deliveries, but showing pride in his sufferings.

From 1870 until his death Jackson lived mainly at Liverpool, where he was professional (1870–72) at Princes Park, while also acting (1871) as caterer, groundsman, and bowler to the Liverpool club. He was the professional (1873–5) at Birkenhead grammar school. In 1875 he was employed in a Liverpool warehouse and was a first-class umpire (1884), but in later years he fell into poverty, depending on 5s. 6d. a week from the Cricketers' Fund Friendly Society. Jackson died, a pauper, in Liverpool workhouse infirmary on 4 November 1901, though the generosity of friends spared him a pauper's funeral. He provides one of the sadder examples of a nineteenth-century professional cricketer enjoying a brief spell of fame and later falling on hard times.

W. B. OWEN, rev. GERALD M. D. HOWAT

Sources A. Haygarth, Arthur Haygarth's cricket scores and biographies, 5 (1875) · Wisden (1902) · The Times (9 Nov 1901) · A. W. Pullin, Talks with old English cricketers (1900) · W. Caffyn, Seventy one not out (1899) · R. Daft, Cricket (29 June 1893) · F. S. Ashley-Cooper, Nottinghamshire cricket and cricketers (1923) · F. S. Ashley-Cooper, Cricket (28 Nov 1901) · P. Bailey, P. Thorn, and P. Wynne-Thomas, Who's who of cricketers (1984)
Likenesses Hennah, photograph, 1859, Trent Bridge, Nottingham, Nottinghamshire County Cricket Club · photograph, 1862, Trent Bridge, Nottingham, Nottinghamshire County Cricket Club · J. Leech, cartoon, 1863, repro. in Punch (29 Aug 1863) · photograph, c.1865, Lords, London, Marylebone Cricket Club Library
Wealth at death £15: administration, 23 Nov 1901, CGPLA Eng. & Wales

Jackson, Sir John (1851–1919), civil engineer and engineering contractor, was born on 4 February 1851 at 15 Coney Street, York, the youngest of the five children of Edward Jackson (1789–1859), goldsmith, and his wife, Elizabeth, daughter of David Ruddock of Horbury, Yorkshire. They were members of the Church of England. Jackson was educated at Holgate Seminary, near York, and in 1866 was apprenticed to William Boyd of Spring Gardens engineering works, Newcastle upon Tyne. In 1868 he proceeded to Edinburgh University, where he won prizes for engineering, surveying, and political economy. Later he was awarded an honorary LLD by the university and, in 1894, he was elected fellow of the Royal Society of Edinburgh. After leaving Edinburgh University he returned to Newcastle, where for a short time he worked for his brother, William Edwin Jackson, twenty-two years his senior and a well-established contractor, before establishing his own firm. On 31 May 1876 Jackson married Ellen Julia, the youngest child of George *Myers of Lambeth. They had nine children, three sons and six daughters; only five daughters survived.

Jackson was of average build with blue eyes and a small beard (which he claimed saved him many shaving hours in a year). He was bald from the age of nineteen, and as a consequence of this he gained his first contract. His was the most satisfactory tender for the Stobcross Docks contract no. 4 (Glasgow), but the dock owners, the Clyde Navigation Trustees, hesitated as Jackson was rumoured to be only twenty-five years old—which was true. A member of the committee pointed out that Jackson was quite bald and therefore the rumour should be discounted as absurd. In 1875 he founded his contracting business which was incorporated as Sir John Jackson Ltd in 1898. There were subsidiary companies in Bolivia, Canada, Chile, South Africa, and Turkey. He had his own shipping line, the Westminster Shipping Company Ltd, which transported his machinery and materials all over the world. In 1879 Jackson completed, in quicksands, the Stobcross Dock at Glasgow. His completion in 1894 of the Manchester Ship Canal in two-thirds of the contract time earned him a knighthood in 1895. At the same time he was laying the foundations of Tower Bridge, London.

Jackson's greatest work in Britain was the extension of the Admiralty works at Keyham, Devonport, in 1896–1907. This cost nearly £4 million and took ten years to complete. During this time Jackson and his family lived on the outskirts of Plymouth, while retaining a house in Holland Park, London. He later moved to 48 Belgrave Square, London, and leased a country house, Henley Park, Henley-on-Thames, Oxfordshire. He represented Devonport in parliament as a Unionist from 1910 to 1918, when he resigned.

Jackson undertook spectacular engineering works in many parts of the world. He constructed the naval harbour and graving dock at Simonstown in South Africa in 1910. For this he was made CVO by the duke of Connaught at the opening ceremony. He had expected to be given an earldom, but Asquith, the Liberal prime minister of the day, refused to countenance it as Jackson had made a derogatory remark about him in a speech a short time before. Jackson also carried out important harbour works at Singapore worth over £2 million, and constructed a breakwater at Victoria, British Columbia.

Foreign powers sought Jackson's services. He built the naval dock at Ferrol in Spain, for which he was awarded the grand cross of the order of merit of Spain. He advised the Austro-Hungarian government on the extension of the arsenal at Pola. In 1909 he built the railway from Arica in Chile to La Paz in Bolivia which crossed the Andes at a height of 14,500 ft. For this he was awarded the order of merit (first class) of Chile. For the Ottoman empire he carried out irrigation works in Lebanon and constructed a port at Salif on the Red Sea. Most impressive of all were the irrigation works in Mesopotamia which involved a barrage across the Euphrates at Hindiyyah. This work,

which entailed the temporary diversion of the course of the river, made possible once again the cultivation of the land said to have been the site of the Garden of Eden. 10,000 men were employed and the cost was £15 million.

Jackson was consulted by the French as to the feasibility of constructing a bridge across the channel between Calais and Dover. Negotiations with the Russians for a second trans-Siberian railway were broken off by the outbreak of war in 1914. His firm was appointed superintending engineers to the war department. Two years later it was suggested that he had used this position to obtain exorbitant commission on further government contracts. Jackson demanded an inquiry; a royal commission was appointed and he was exonerated.

Jackson had common sense, was a sound man of business, and inspired loyalty. He was interested in the welfare of his workmen, of whom he often had thousands in his employ. He had many friends, and was broad-minded and generous. Rowing, yachting, camping, and bicycling with his daughters (who very daringly wore bloomers), were his favourite pastimes. He was elected a member of the Royal Yacht Squadron in 1901.

From about 1910 Jackson had a mistress, a widow, Mrs Mabel Lydia Henderson of Hascombe Grange, Hambledon, Surrey. He appears to have visited her for the occasional weekend. Unfortunately, it was on one of these weekends that he died suddenly of heart failure in her house, on 14 December 1919. He left Mrs Henderson a large sum of money in his will, but an even greater sum to his widow. He was buried in Norwood cemetery in the family grave.

PATRICIA SPENCER-SILVER

Sources private information (2004) · *Proceedings of the Royal Society of Edinburgh*, 40 (1919–20), 182–4 · *The Times* (16 Dec 1919) · *Morning Post* (16 Dec 1919) · *Yorkshire Post* (16 Dec 1919) · *The Scotsman* (16 Dec 1919) · *Manchester Guardian* (16 Dec 1919) · *Daily Telegraph* (16 Dec 1919) · *News of the World* (21 Dec 1919) · 'Royal commission on Sir John Jackson, Limited', *Parl. papers* (1917–18), 15.189, Cd 8518 [Arthur M. Channell, report, 30 March 1917] · d. cert. · b. cert.
Archives CLRO · Inst. CE
Likenesses caricature, 1909; copy, priv. coll. · A. S. Cope, 1916, priv. coll. · R. J. Nathan, photograph, repro. in *Mayfair* (Sept 1919) · Spy [L. Ward], cartoon, repro. in *Vanity Fair Supplement* (1909)
Wealth at death £520,474 6s. 6d.: probate, 13 April 1920, CGPLA Eng. & Wales

Jackson, John (1881–1952), classical scholar, was born at Great Asby in Westmorland on 17 October 1881, the first son of Robert Jackson, farmer, and his wife, Elizabeth Austin. He was educated at Appleby grammar school and in 1899 matriculated as a Hastings exhibitioner at Queen's College, Oxford, where the tutors included Albert Curtis Clark and Thomas William Allen. A first class in classical honour moderations (1901) was followed by a third in Greats (1903), but he won the Ireland scholarship in 1901 and was elected Craven fellow in 1903. His lack of success in finals did not prevent him from being elected to a fellowship at Magdalen College in 1903; the competition was stiff, as the other candidates included Alexander Dunlop Lindsay. However, his career did not develop as expected, since he vacated his fellowship at the end of his probationary year. From the notebooks of the president, Herbert

Warren, it appears that Jackson's behaviour had caused unfavourable comment, leading to a complaint by the college staff to the president, who issued a warning to Jackson, evidently without achieving the desired effect.

Jackson's fellowship was not confirmed and he went to live on the family farm at Caldbeck in Cumberland, where he spent almost all the rest of his life. Although most of his energy was devoted to the farm, and he lacked access to a library, his publications were substantial. They included expert translations of Latin and Greek authors—the *Annals* of Tacitus in the Loeb Classical Library was particularly well received—and articles in the learned journals on the textual criticism of a wide range of Greek authors. His most important work is a posthumous publication which saw the light of day largely thanks to the efforts of Eduard Fraenkel, *Marginalia scaenica*, issued by the Oxford Press in 1955. It contains numerous discussions of difficult passages in Greek tragedy and Aristophanes, and proves that Jackson was a textual critic of the highest order, who would certainly have made an even greater name for himself had he been able to follow a more normal career. He died at the Royal Infirmary, Sheffield, of peritonitis on 20 November 1952, and his ashes were interred at Caldbeck.   N. G. WILSON

Sources E. Fraenkel, in J. Jackson, *Marginalia scaenica* (1955) [preface] · notebooks of President Warren of Magdalen College, Magd. Oxf., PR/2/15 · b. cert. · d. cert. · matriculation records, U. Oxf., archives · W. D. Macray, *A register of the members of St Mary Magdalen College, Oxford*, 8 vols. (1894–1915), vol. 7
Wealth at death £1429 19s. 3d.: administration, 11 March 1953, CGPLA Eng. & Wales

Jackson, John (1887–1958), astronomer, was born on 11 February 1887 at 9 Mossvale Street, Paisley, Renfrewshire, the fifth of the eight children of Matthew Jackson, a skilled mechanic, and his wife, Jeanie Millar. He attended Paisley grammar school and at the age of sixteen passed the entrance examination of the University of Glasgow. He graduated in 1907 and was awarded a Ewing fellowship for further study. During two years' graduate study he attended classes given by Professor Ludwig Becker and developed an interest in mathematical astronomy. To pursue a career, he entered Trinity College, Cambridge, in 1909 as an ordinary undergraduate; he graduated with distinction and received several awards, including the Tyson gold medal for astronomy. In 1913 Jackson was appointed a Mackinnon research student of the Royal Society and he determined the first reliable orbit for the faint eighth satellite of Jupiter, which had been discovered in 1908 and which had a highly disturbed retrograde orbit.

In 1914 Jackson was appointed as a chief assistant to the astronomer royal, Frank Dyson, at the Royal Observatory, Greenwich. (Harold Spencer Jones was then the other chief assistant.) As most of the junior members of staff had left for war service he undertook a large amount of observing, particularly on the Airy transit circle; it is said that he continued observing even when a bomb from a Zeppelin fell in the grounds of the observatory. In 1917 he

was given a commission in the Royal Engineers and served in France as a trigonometrical survey officer. He rejoined the observatory in February 1919.

At Greenwich Jackson carried out several special investigations in addition to supervising the regular work of observing and data reduction for the determination of star positions and of Greenwich Mean Time for national use. He collated and discussed the Greenwich observations on double stars made from 1893 to 1919; he derived orbits for some and estimated the distances of many of them. He also studied the performance of the new Shortt free-pendulum clock, which was installed as the standard observatory clock in 1925. He established that it was more regular than apparent sidereal time, which varies due to the nutation of the earth's axis of rotation; however, it was not yet accurate enough to detect any irregularities in the rate of rotation of the earth. He also collaborated with H. Knox-Shaw, the director of the Radcliffe Observatory, Oxford, in reducing the observations that had been made by Thomas Hornsby, the first Radcliffe observer, between 1774 and 1798. Other research concerned the rotation of Neptune, and Jackson reviewed the discoveries of Neptune and Pluto.

In 1933 Jackson succeeded Harold Spencer Jones as astronomer at the Royal Observatory at the Cape of Good Hope. There he continued successfully the astrometric programmes to improve the quality and coverage of the positions, proper motions, parallaxes, and magnitudes of the stars of the southern hemisphere. During the Second World War he once again carried out a large amount of observing himself, as many of the staff were absent on war service.

Jackson served as a member of the council of the Royal Astronomical Society for twelve years and was a secretary from 1924 to 1929. He was an active member of the International Astronomical Union; he was president of Commission 8 (meridian astronomy) for 1932–8 and of Commission 24 (stellar parallaxes) for 1938–52. He was elected a fellow of the Royal Society of South Africa in 1934, served on its council for many years and was president in 1949. He was elected FRS in 1938, and the honour of CBE was conferred on him in 1950. He was awarded the gold medal of the Royal Astronomical Society in 1952 and was president of that society in 1953–5. He was awarded the Gill medal of the Astronomical Society of South Africa in 1958.

Jackson was an unassuming and approachable man with a genial smile, and he retained his Scottish accent. He married Mary Beatrice Marshall in 1920; they had one son who died shortly after his birth. After retirement from the Cape the couple lived in Ewell, Surrey. Jackson died at Epsom District Hospital, Ewell, on 9 December 1958 after a cerebral thrombosis; his wife survived him.

GEORGE A. WILKINS

Sources H. Spencer Jones, *Memoirs FRS*, 5 (1959), 95–106 · H. Spencer Jones, *Monthly Notices of the Royal Astronomical Society*, 119 (1959), 345–8 · W. M. Witchell, *Journal of the British Astronomical Association*, 69 (1958–9), 178–9 · b. cert. · d. cert.

Jackson, John Baptist (b. c.1700, d. in or after 1773), woodcutter and designer of chintz and wallpaper, was the most remarkable English printmaker of his day, although he stands far apart from the mainstream. The main source of information on his life is an autobiography quoted in *An Enquiry into the Origin of Printing in Europe* (1752). This is the only such text known by any British printmaker before the nineteenth century.

Nothing is known of Jackson's birth or early training in England, and his only known early work is a cut in J. A. G. B. Tonson's 1717 edition of Dryden. In 1725, without any patronage, he moved to Paris where at first he cut small typographical ornaments for books, and became friends with the two leading woodcutters, Jean Michel Papillon and Vincent Le Sueur. Through the latter he met Comte Caylus who commissioned him to make some plates in woodcut after old master drawings for the collection of reproductions of outstanding paintings and drawings in France known as the *Cabinet Crozat*. According to Jackson's own account, this came to an end through the hostility of Crozat, and Caylus encouraged him to pursue his studies in Italy. So, after departing from Paris in April 1730, he made his way via Marseilles, Florence, and Bologna to Venice where he arrived in spring 1731.

The French had introduced Jackson to multiple-block woodblock printing in colours. This process had been much practised in the Renaissance, but was now obsolete and only of interest to a small group of connoisseurs and collectors. A leading figure among them was the Venetian Antonio Maria Zanetti, and Jackson first made in Venice two chiaroscuro woodcuts after drawings by Parmigianino for Zanetti. But the two men quickly quarrelled, apparently because Zanetti wished to take the credit for the blocks by signing them himself. Fortunately Jackson had recommendations to some of the major book publishers in Venice, and both the firms of Albrizzi and Pezzana commissioned him to make sets of small illustrations to the Bible. Meanwhile Jackson pursued the experiments he had already begun in Paris with printing in colours, building himself a cylinder press of a size to print large blocks, and strong enough to exert the necessary uniform pressure. The first result was a large print after Rubens's *Judgement of Solomon* in 1735 printed from four blocks.

At this point Jackson found himself undercut in the market for small book illustrations, and attempted instead to open a business in manufacturing coloured wallpaper for export to London (five sheets from this period survive in the British Museum). This failed, and in 1738 Joseph Smith, the British consul in Venice, came to his aid by lending him two paintings to turn into prints, and then enlisted the support of some nobles on the grand tour. With their help Jackson announced the publication by subscription of a series of plates after seventeen great paintings in Venice by Titian, Veronese, Tintoretto, and Bassano. Begun in 1739, distributed in parts, and completed in 1743, it was published in volume form by J. B. Pasquali two years later under the title *Opera selectiora*. This *tour de force* involved making twenty-four prints using ninety-six blocks (twenty-four of these are now in the museum at Bassano, in the archive of the Remondini firm which reprinted the blocks from 1784 onwards; five preparatory drawings are in the Victoria and Albert Museum, London). The paintings were reproduced in varying monochromatic tones, and, presumably through Smith's agency, sets were widely distributed and are in many collections today.

Jackson next, in 1744, produced his masterpiece, a set of six landscapes after gouaches by Marco Ricci dedicated to the earl of Holdernesse. These were in full colour, and as such unprecedented in western printmaking. They were however a commercial failure (they are now very rare) and Jackson tried to seek employment with Giambattista Remondini in Bassano to whom seven letters survive.

This came to nothing, and with his Italian wife, Lorenza, Jackson returned to England in 1745, and took up employment as a designer in a calico manufactory. In 1749 he took on an apprentice, giving an address at St Clement Danes, and soon after set up his own business in Battersea, returning to the wallpaper project that he had begun in Venice. In 1752 he launched a publicity campaign, of which his *Enquiry* was the beginning, and his better-known *Essay on the invention of engraving and printing in chiaroscuro … and the application of it to the making paper hangings of taste, duration and excellence* of 1754 the sequel. This includes some specimens of the paper (none survives otherwise), which confirm that the colours were printed in an oil-based ink in order that it should not fade. An advertisement for the paper published in the 1754 catalogue of the London print dealer Henry Overton is at pains to deny that the paper smelled badly, and this shows that the established wallpaper trade (which used stencils and water-based inks for colouring) was mounting a hostile counter-campaign. As a result Jackson's business collapsed. This was probably at the end of 1754, and no more is heard of him for a decade.

Jackson's later career was a sad decline, and he never again made any prints or designs of importance. Between 1765 and 1770 he provided patterns for textile manufacturers and taught apprentices at the Academy in Edinburgh established by the Scottish board of trustees for the improvement of fisheries and manufactures. He was still in Edinburgh in 1773 when he married Janet Wood, daughter of a farmer. He later met Thomas Bewick in Newcastle, who recorded that his last days were spent 'in an asylum … at some place on the border near the Teviot or on Tweedside' (T. Bewick, *Memoir*, ed. I. Bain, 1975, 194).

As a designer Jackson had real flair, and his surviving sheets of wallpaper in the British Museum, and the single furnishing chintz attributable to him in the Victoria and Albert Museum, are among the finest of their day. They are closely linked in their design to an album of his drawings in the Victoria and Albert Museum, which contains flower studies for floral chintzes made in 1740 and 1750–

54, as well as woodblock proofs and other designs, probably for wallpaper. *A Collection of Choice and Curious Flowers*, a set of six plates after Jackson's designs, engraved by J. S. Muller, was included in Robert Sayer's 1766 catalogue (a copy is in the Kunstbibliothek in Berlin).

Jackson's technical feats in woodcutting were extraordinary, and he created large monochrome and full-colour woodcuts of a type that had never been seen in European art. To do this he had to build a new press, devise new inks, and work out by eye colour separations and combinations by overprinting. But he was so far out on his own that he lost his market, and had no followers. His aesthetic values, which preferred a 'bold masterly way of drawing' to 'all the minute finishings done on copper' (Jackson, *Enquiry*, 22) were not those of his contemporaries, and his insistence on sticking to colour woodcut, while heroic in its single-mindedness, appears decidedly eccentric. The tone of his writings suggests that his obstinacy may have made him very difficult to deal with.   ANTONY GRIFFITHS

Sources J. B. Jackson, *An enquiry into the origin of printing in Europe: by a lover of art* (1752) · J. B. Jackson, *An essay on the invention of engraving and printing in chiaroscuro … and the application of it to the making paper hangings of taste, duration and elegance* (1754) · album, V&A, E.4486–4542–1920 · drawings for chiaroscuri, V&A, E.2504–2508–1938 · V&A, T.243–1979 [chintz] · J. Kainen, *John Baptist Jackson, eighteenth-century master of the color woodcut* (1962) · A. S. Cavallo, 'John Baptist Jackson in Scotland', *Art Bulletin*, 46 (1964), 233–7 · W. Hefford, *The Victoria & Albert Museum's textile collection: design for printed textiles in England from 1750 to 1850* (1992), 8–9; pls. 3–8 · G. Mastrapasqua, *John Baptist Jackson, chiaroscuri dalla collezione Remondini del Museo Biblioteca Archivio di Bassano del Grappa* (1996) · J. Ingamells, ed., *A dictionary of British and Irish travellers in Italy, 1701–1800* (1997) **Archives** V&A, album, E.4486 to 4542–1920 (pressmark 95 E2) · V&A, chintz, T.243–1979 **Wealth at death** indigent

Jackson, John Edward (1805–1891), antiquary, was born on 12 November 1805 in Doncaster, Yorkshire, the son of James Jackson, banker and sometime mayor of Doncaster, and his wife, Henrietta Priscilla, second daughter of Freeman Bower of Bawtry, near Doncaster. Charles *Jackson (1809–1882), also an antiquary, was a younger brother. John Jackson was educated at Charterhouse School (*c*.1818–*c*.1822) and matriculated at Oxford from Brasenose College on 9 April 1823. He graduated BA, with second-class classical honours in 1827, and proceeded MA in 1830. In 1834 he became curate at Farleigh Hungerford, Somerset, and in 1845 he was appointed rector of Leigh Delamere with Sevington, Wiltshire. In 1846 he became vicar of Norton Coleparle in the same county. He was also rural dean and honorary canon of Bristol (1855).

Jackson, who was elected FSA in 1857, was an advisory archivist to the marquess of Bath, and arranged and indexed the bulk of the manuscripts at Longleat. He was extremely hard-working and accurate, but inevitably his approach was that of an antiquary rather than a trained archivist. As a result, much of the routine estate material at Longleat was not listed at the time with the collection to which it belonged. His handwriting can be found on many documents besides those at Longleat, including parish records. His pioneering activities did much to ensure their preservation.

Jackson published several works on antiquarian topics, and was always ready to aid fellow students. Most of his works are histories of north Wiltshire parishes, but he also wrote the histories of two churches in Doncaster and a description of the Hungerford chapels in Salisbury Cathedral. He edited for the Wiltshire Archaeological and Natural History Society the *Wiltshire Topographical Collection* of John Aubrey (1862) and John Leland's *Journey through Wiltshire* (*c*.1875). For the Roxburghe Club he edited the *Glastonbury Inquisition of AD 1189, called 'Liber Henrici de Soliaco'* (1882). He was also an active contributor to the *Wiltshire Archaeological Magazine*. Articles by him included 'Charles, Lord Stourton, and the murder of the Hartgills, January 1557' and a study of the lost Wiltshire village of Rowley, alias Wittenham.

Jackson died unmarried at the rectory at Leigh Delamere, on 6 March 1891. He was buried in the churchyard there on 12 March.

GORDON GOODWIN, *rev.* PENELOPE RUNDLE

Sources J. Stratford, *Catalogue of the Jackson collection in Windsor Castle* (1981) · *The Athenaeum* (14 March 1891), 352 · Crockford (1890) · J. Foster, ed., *Pedigrees of the county families of Yorkshire*, 1 (1874) · Foster, *Alum. Oxon.* · *Wiltshire Archaeological and Natural History Magazine*, 25 (1891), 355–9 · parish register (burial), Leigh Delamere, 12 March 1891 **Archives** BGS, lecture notes · BL, collections, mainly relating to Wiltshire and the Hungerford family, Add. MS 34566 · Devizes Museum, Wiltshire, notes, papers, and collections; corresp. with John Britton · Longleat House, Warminster, Wiltshire · NRA, papers · S. Antiquaries, Lond., Wiltshire, collection **Likenesses** photograph, 1860–99, Library of Wiltshire Archaeological Society, Devizes, Wiltshire **Wealth at death** £34,505 9s. 2d.: probate, 14 July 1891, CGPLA Eng. & Wales

Jackson, John Hughlings (1835–1911), physician, born at Providence Green, Green Hammerton, Yorkshire, on 4 April 1835, was the youngest son in the family of four sons and one daughter of Samuel Jackson, a yeoman landowner and brewer, and Sarah, *née* Hughlings. His three brothers settled in New Zealand, where one, Major William Jackson, distinguished himself in the New Zealand wars, and was later accidentally drowned. From the village school of Green Hammerton Jackson moved on successively to schools at Tadcaster, Yorkshire, and at Nailsworth, Gloucestershire. Apprenticed later at York to William C. Anderson MRCS (father of Dr Tempest Anderson), he began his medical studies at the York Medical and Surgical School, continuing at St Bartholomew's Hospital, London, where James Paget was one of his teachers. After matriculating at London University and qualifying MRCS and LSA in 1856, he worked until 1859 as house surgeon to the York Dispensary, where he was closely associated with Thomas Laycock. Returning to London in 1859, he considered giving up medicine to study philosophy, but was dissuaded by Jonathan Hutchinson, and was, through Hutchinson's influence, appointed to the staff of the Metropolitan Free Hospital. In the same year he also became lecturer in pathology at the London Hospital,

John Hughlings Jackson (1835–1911), by Lance Calkin, c.1894

teaching histology and microscopy. In 1860 he graduated MD (St Andrews), and in 1863 became assistant physician to the London Hospital and lecturer in physiology: he was appointed physician in 1874, serving on the staff until 1894. He was also a clinical assistant at Moorfields Eye Hospital.

In May 1862 Jackson also became assistant physician to the National Hospital for the Paralysed and Epileptic in Queen Square, which had been established in 1859. When he joined the staff, Charles Edward Brown-Séquard, who was a physician there, persuaded him to concentrate on diseases of the nervous system. Jackson continued on the active staff of the hospital until 1906, then becoming consulting physician. He married his cousin, Elizabeth Dade Jackson (1836/7–1876), daughter of Thomas Jackson, farmer, in 1865; they had no children.

In 1868 Jackson, who had become MRCP (London) in 1860, was elected FRCP, and in 1869 delivered the Goulstonian lectures at the Royal College of Physicians—an honour conferred on the most distinguished newly elected fellow. His lectures were entitled 'Certain points in the study and classification of diseases of the nervous system'. He was also Croonian lecturer in 1884, discussing 'Evolution and dissolution of the nervous system', and Lumleian lecturer in 1890, when the title was 'Convulsive seizures'. Thus he had the unusual distinction of being chosen to deliver three courses of college lectures. He was a censor and member of council of the college in 1888 and 1889. He was elected FRS in 1878.

Though never an experimentalist, over a period of thirty years, Jackson 'out of a chaos of isolated and sometimes wild speculations and unrelated experiments,

organised and laid the foundations of modern neurology' (Munk, *Roll*, 162). Henry Head considered him to be the greatest scientific clinician of the nineteenth century. Jackson's investigations fell roughly into three groups. His earliest interest was in speech defect caused by brain disease, and by careful and detailed study of numerous cases he was able to associate such defects in most cases with disease in the left cerebral hemisphere. His papers on this topic were published chiefly in the *London Hospital Reports* in 1864. Two years previously Broca had associated loss of speech with disease of the posterior part of the third left frontal convolution. His work was unknown to Jackson at first, but on learning of it he generously acknowledged that his independent conclusions had on every point of importance been anticipated by Broca. The exceptions which Jackson noted were later explained in most instances by the observation that in left-handed persons the speech centre is usually situated in the right hemisphere.

The second series of Jackson's investigations dealt with the occurrence of localized (focal) epileptic discharges. Such focal epilepsy became known as Jacksonian epilepsy, although Jackson did not himself use that term. He always acknowledged Bravais's earlier recognition of this form of convulsion (1824), and the observation of 'epileptic hemiplegia'—temporary paralysis following such convulsions—by Robert Bentley Todd. But it was by observation of many such cases of convulsions starting locally, by careful identification of the subsequent paralysis or weakness, and by the correlation of these with the actual position of the causal brain lesion, that Jackson was able in 1870 to identify specific regions of the brain which controlled certain limb movements, while also confirming Broca's earlier work on the speech centre. Fritsch and Hitzig in Germany and Ferrier in England soon supplied experimental corroboration.

Jackson's third series of investigations related to the hierarchy of the nervous system, and although this seemed to some theoretical rather than practical, his hypotheses were regularly confirmed and illustrated by clinical observation and the study of disease. He concluded that the nervous system consists of three principal levels: a lower, a middle, and a higher. At the lowest level, movements are represented in their least complex form; such centres lie in the medulla and spinal cord. The middle level consists of the so-called motor area of the cortex, and the highest motor levels are found in the prefrontal area. Jackson did not attempt to apply this theory of levels to sensory structures. His view of the nervous system rendered intelligible the theory of nervous disease as a process of dissolution—a term borrowed from Herbert Spencer. The highest functions, most recently acquired in evolution, are those to go first as a result of disease. The removal of inhibition imposed by the highest centres results in the uncontrolled action of the lower. This was thought to explain such phenomena as post-hemiplegic spasticity. 'Negative' or destructive lesions, such as those causing paralysis, do not produce 'positive' symptoms;

the latter result from the action of normal structures acting without the control or restraint normally imposed by structures at a higher level. Another subject on which he worked was that form of epilepsy often called 'uncinate', because, as he first pointed out, its symptoms (hallucinations of smell or taste) are associated with a lesion in the uncinate gyrus of the temporal lobe.

Jackson's researches depended on meticulous clinical observation. Thousands of cases were carefully studied, and their symptoms and signs recorded in the greatest detail. As a teacher and writer, unlike W. R. Gowers, he lacked expositional gifts. He was famous, but never really popular; his modesty and love of truth led him to feel that a brilliant phrase might cloud the meaning he wished to convey. He had no hobbies and suffered from vertigo and migraine. It is said that once, approached by Henry Head who wished to discuss a new observation, Jackson said, 'Don't bother me now, Head, I'm making some observations on my own migraine'. He took little or no interest in public or administrative affairs, and while he received many academic honours, none were conferred upon him by the state. Nevertheless, he was and is revered as the 'father of English neurology'. He died of pneumonia at his home, 3 Manchester Square, London, on 7 October 1911, and was buried at Highgate cemetery.

Jackson wrote over 300 papers in various periodicals. The *London Hospital Reports*, 1864–1869, contain some of his earliest and most important work. He contributed many articles to *Brain*, the *West Riding Hospital Reports*, *The Lancet*, the *British Medical Journal*, and many other journals. A selection of his most important works, edited by James Taylor, was published in two volumes in 1958.

JAMES TAYLOR, *rev.* WALTON OF DETCHANT

Sources *The Times* (9 Oct 1911) · *BMJ* (14 Oct 1911), 950–54 · *The Lancet* (14 Oct 1911) · private information (1912) · Munk, *Roll* · W. Haymaker, ed., *The founders of neurology* (1953) · L. C. McHenry, ed., *Garrison's history of neurology* (1969) · M. Critchley and E. A. Critchley, *John Hughlings Jackson: father of English neurology* (1999) · m. cert. · personal knowledge (1912)

Likenesses L. Calkin, portrait, c.1894, RCP Lond. [*see illus.*] · portrait, repro. in Haymaker, ed., *Founders of neurology*

Wealth at death £23,220 12s. 5d.: resworn probate, 19 Oct 1911, CGPLA Eng. & Wales

Jackson, John Richardson (1819–1877), engraver, was born on 14 December 1819 at Portsea, Hampshire, the second son of Erasmus Jackson, a banker, and his wife, Barbara Helen. In 1836 he became pupil to Robert Graves ARA, from whom he learned the technique of line engraving. This he later abandoned for engraving in mezzotint. In 1847 he engraved *The Otter and Salmon*, after Sir Edwin Landseer, which was published by F. G. Moon; it was this work that brought him to public notice. On 28 September that year he married Eliza Jane, *née* Jackson, also of Portsea. Jackson obtained frequent employment as an engraver of portraits, and thereafter he devoted most of his time to such work, though he still produced some landscape and genre engravings. His engravings show careful drawing, and a great feeling for the colour in mezzotint. Between 1854 and 1876 he exhibited twenty-seven large portrait engravings at the Royal Academy,

including *Queen Victoria*, after William Fowler, *The Princess Royal and her Sisters*, after Franz Xavier Winterhalter, *William Howley, Archbishop of Canterbury*, after Margaret Carpenter, *Lady Gertrude Fitzpatrick*, after Sir Joshua Reynolds, and numerous portraits after George Richmond RA. These were published variously by Henry Graves, Paul Colnaghi, John Mitchell, Dixon and Ross, F. G. Moon, and Forres. He also engraved *St John the Baptist*, after the painting by Bartolomé Esteban Murillo in the National Gallery. Jackson died at Southsea of relapsing fever on 10 May 1877.

L. H. CUST, *rev.* ASIA HAUT

Sources R. K. Engen, *Dictionary of Victorian engravers, print publishers and their works* (1979) · A. Dyson, *Pictures to print: the nineteenth-century engraving trade* (1984) · Redgrave, *Artists* · J. Turner, ed., *The dictionary of art*, 34 vols. (1996) · Ward, *Men of the reign* · H. Guise, *Great Victorian engravings: a collector's guide* (1980) · *Printing Times* (15 June 1877) · IGI · CGPLA Eng. & Wales (1877)

Wealth at death under £1000: probate, 16 June 1877, CGPLA Eng. & Wales

Jackson, Joseph (1733–1792), typefounder, was born in Old Street, Shoreditch, London, on 4 September 1733, the son of James Jackson, feltmaker; he may have been the child baptized the following day at St Giles Cripplegate as the son of James and Alice Jackson. John Nichols, however, relates that Jackson was the first child to be baptized in St Luke's Church, which was completed in that year. He was educated at a school nearby, and in 1748 he was apprenticed to the typefoundry of William Caslon the elder, but according to Nichols he was frustrated in his wish to learn the cutting of punches, 'which in general is kept profoundly secret; his master and master's father locking themselves in whenever they were at that branch of the business'.

> This difficulty he surmounted by boring a hole through the wainscot, and observing them at different times, so as to form some idea of the mode in which the whole was performed; and applied himself at every opportunity to the finishing of a punch. When he had completed one to his own mind, he presented it to his master, expecting to be rewarded for his ingenuity: but the premium he received was a hard blow, with a threat that he should be sent to Bridewell if he again made a similar attempt. This circumstance being taken in dudgeon, his mother bought him what tools were necessary, and he improved himself at her house whenever he had an opportunity. He continued to work for his master, after he came out of his time, till a quarrel arose in the foundery about the price of work; and a memorial, which terminated in favour of the workmen, being sent to the elder Caslon (who was then in the commission of the peace, and had retired to Bethnal-green) young Jackson and a Mr. Cottrell (who had likewise been an apprentice) were discharged, as the supposed ringleaders. (Nichols, *Lit. anecdotes*, 2.359)

It is clear from the wording of this story that the 'master' who maltreated Jackson was William Caslon the younger.

Jackson went into a partnership with Thomas Cottrell, who set up a typefoundry in 1757, but left after his mother's death. During the war with France over colonial territories which had begun in 1756, he entered the frigate *Minerva* as a ship's armourer, transferring in May 1761 to the *Aurora*. At the peace of 1763 he received prize money of about £40. Having returned to London, he worked for a time again under Cottrell, then found two fellow workmen willing to supply capital to set up on his own and took a small house in Cock Lane. In 1762 he had married Elizabeth Tassell (*c*.1734–1783), a whinster (windster or winder of silk) in Spitalfields, whose 'care and industry' were a help to him when he first set up his business (Nichols, *GM*, 92). Within six months, encouraged by the younger William Bowyer, Jackson produced a first specimen of a single type. According to Nichols, the younger Caslon took this to his father 'with an air of contempt', but was advised 'to take it home, and preserve it; and whenever he went to cutting again, to look well at it' (ibid., 92). Jackson's business increased rapidly, and he moved to Dorset Street, Salisbury Square, Fleet Street. Edmund Mores, who describes Jackson as 'obliging and communicative', gives an account of his foundry that is apparently based on a specimen dated 1773, but which is not known to survive: it included Hebrew, Persian, and Bengali types (Mores, 83). Jackson cut and cast the type used in the reprint of the text of Domesday Book, printed by John Nichols in 1783. Its reception led to an invitation to cut type to reproduce the text prepared by Charles Woide and printed by Nichols in 1786 of the Greek New Testament contained in the Codex Alexandrinus, a fifth-century manuscript in the Royal Collection. He also made the type for the university press at Cambridge for the edition by Thomas Kipling of the Codex Bezae, a Greek biblical text of the fifth or sixth century that had been presented to the university by Theodore Beza in 1581. In 1790 his moulds and matrices were much damaged in a fire. He cut a two-line English type for Macklin's Bible, printed by Thomas Bensley in 1800, in seven folio volumes, and a double pica type for the same printer, which was used in Hume's *History of England* (1806).

No specimen of the roman and italic types issued by Jackson himself is known to survive, although the contents of a fragmentary small octavo specimen showing ornaments can be attributed to him, and there are two single-sheet specimens of the Devanagari type made about 1785 and intended for the Hindi grammar prepared by W. Kirkpatrick. He was among the most accomplished English punchcutters of the eighteenth century. His types are very well made, but being less innovative in design than those of some of his contemporaries they have attracted less attention. Notwithstanding his dismissal from the Caslon foundry, he not only had the respect of the elder Caslon but also the friendship of his grandson William Caslon (1754–1833), who bought the foundry after Jackson's death. Most of the roman and italic types and ornaments in the specimen books issued under Caslon's name from the Salisbury Square foundry in 1795, 1796, and 1798 can be attributed to Jackson himself.

Shortly after the death of his first wife in 1783 Jackson was married again, to Mary Pasham (1738/9–1791), said to be the widow of 'a printer' in Blackfriars, presumably Thomas Pasham; the ceremony took place in St Bride's, Fleet Street, on 5 July 1784 (Nichols, *GM*, 93). He died on 14 January 1792 and was buried beside his two wives in the burial-ground of Spa Fields Chapel, Clerkenwell. He was childless, and left most of his estate to his nephews and nieces. One of his executors was the printer John Nichols, who had used his types and was the author of the memoir from which most of the details of his life are derived. After Jackson's death his only apprentice, Vincent Figgins (1766–1844), set up a foundry of his own, which survived into the second half of the twentieth century.

JAMES MOSLEY

Sources [J. Nichols], *GM*, 1st ser., 62 (1792), 92–3 · Nichols, *Lit. anecdotes*, 2.358–61 · T. B. Reed, *A history of the old English letter foundries*, ed. A. F. Johnson (1952), 311–19 · E. R. Mores, *A dissertation upon English typographical founders and founderies*, ed. H. Carter and C. Ricks (1961); repr. with corrections (1963) · D. F. McKenzie, ed., *Stationers' Company apprentices*, [3]: *1701–1800* (1978) · J. Mosley, *British type specimens before 1831: a hand-list* (1984) · *IGI*
Likenesses engraving, repro. in Nichols, *Lit. anecdotes* · oils; formerly lent by William Blades to the Caxton Celebration exhibition in 1877

Jackson, Joseph Devonsher (1783–1857), judge and politician, was born in Cork on 23 June 1783, the eldest son of Strettel Jackson of Peterborough, Cork, a prosperous carrier, and his wife, Mary Cossens. His father was a descendant of an English family which had settled in Ireland in the early seventeenth century. Jackson's early education in Cork was at the hands of the Revd Mr Lee, an evangelical clergyman of the Church of Ireland. After matriculating at Trinity College, Dublin, in 1800, the protestant tradition of his boyhood was reinforced by his tutor Arthur H. Kenney, later rector of St Olave's, Southwark. He graduated BA with honours in 1806. In 1832 he proceeded AM and in 1835 became a Cambridge MA.

Jackson entered as a student of law in the King's Inns, Dublin, in 1803 and in the Middle Temple, London, the following year. In 1806 he was called to the Irish bar, and he took silk twenty years later. Initially attached to the Munster circuit, he was known as a zealous advocate and 'an amiable man, of courteous manners, and prepossessing appearance, with a fine forensic countenance' (Madden, 260). Although he lacked the wit, pathos, or imagination traditionally associated with distinguished advocates of the Irish bar, his scrupulous fair dealing and evangelical propensities led Hugh Percy, third duke of Northumberland, to appoint him chairman of the Londonderry quarter sessions in 1830. Service as a private in Westropp's grenadiers and membership of Hardinge's Orange lodge assured his acceptance by the Conservative establishment.

In 1811 Jackson married Sarah Lucinda (*d*. 1858), ninth daughter of Benjamin Clarke of Cullenswood, Dublin. In 1812 he was co-opted to the committee of the Kildare Place Society, established in 1811, where, as secretary, he strengthened the protestant influence. He gave detailed evidence in 1824–5 before the commissioners of the Irish education inquiry.

The borough of Bandon was reputed to have the most sectarian electorate in co. Cork, and in 1835 Jackson contested it as a Conservative, winning easily then and again in 1837. In 1841 he was returned unopposed for the borough, and a year later he became one of the members for

Dublin University. Success in politics led to professional advancement. In 1835 he was the third serjeant-at-law in Ireland and, shortly afterwards, second serjeant. In 1841 he was named solicitor-general and, on the death of John Leslie Foster in 1842, justice of the common pleas. He accepted the Chiltern Hundreds in September 1842.

Variously dubbed a 'biblical barrister' and a 'scriptural tory', Jackson's parliamentary interventions were largely confined to representing Irish loyalist interests. In 1837 he spoke for nearly four hours against the introduction of the Irish Corporation Reform Bill, which did not pass until 1840. Thoughtful and trenchant, his prolix arguments could often be tiresome, although Thomas Babington Macaulay thought his attack on the national board system, in the first debate on the issue when Sir Robert Peel came to power in 1841, led to 'the very best parliamentary set-to between the secretary and the solicitor-general for Ireland which has ever been witnessed'.

Jackson died at his home, Sutton House, Howth, co. Dublin, on 20 December 1857 and was interred there in St Fintan's cemetery.

V. A. McClelland, rev. Gerard McCoy

Sources F. E. Ball, *The judges in Ireland, 1221–1921*, 2 (1926) · *The Constitution or Cork Advertiser* (22 Dec 1857) · *Freeman's Journal* [Dublin] (24 Dec 1857) · D. O. Madden, *Ireland and its rulers since 1829*, 2 (1844) · I. d'Alton, *Protestant society and politics in Cork, 1812–1844* (1980) · R. B. McDowell, *Public opinion and government policy in Ireland, 1801–1846* (1952) · Kildare Place Society Records, I/MS 835
Archives BL, corresp. with Robert Peel, Add. MSS 40245–40575, *passim* · Church of Ireland College, Rathmines, Kildare Place Society records

Jackson, Julian (1790–1853), army officer in the Russian service and geographer, son of William Turner Jackson and his wife, Lucille, was born on 30 March 1790 and baptized at St Anne's, Westminster, on 24 May. He passed through the Royal Military Academy, Woolwich, was nominated to a Bengal cadetship by Sir Stephen Lushington in 1807, and was appointed second lieutenant in the Bengal artillery on 26 September 1808 and first lieutenant on 28 April 1809. He resigned his rank in India on 28 August 1813 to seek employment in Wellington's army in the Peninsula, but arrived too late. On 2 June 1815 Alexander of Russia appointed Julian 'Villiamovitch' Jackson to the quartermaster's staff of the imperial suite, with the rank of lieutenant. He did duty with the quartermaster-general's staff of the 12th Russian infantry division under Count Vorontsov, forming part of the allied army of occupation in France, until 6 November 1818, when he went to Russia with them in the rank of staff captain. On the augmentation of the Lithuanian army corps the following year Jackson was appointed to the quartermaster-general's staff and attached to the grenadier brigade. He remained with this part of the army during most of his service, becoming captain on 8 August 1821, and lieutenant-colonel on 29 March 1825. He was promoted colonel on the general staff of the army on 14 August 1829, and retired from the Russian service on 21 September 1830. On his retirement the imperial finance minister, comte de la Canerine, appointed him commissioner and correspondent in London for

the Russian department of manufactures attached to the Russian embassy.

While in Russia Jackson took a keen interest in physical geography, particularly in the freezing of water in the River Neva, on which he wrote useful memoirs in French and English. He was an enthusiastic supporter of the Royal Geographical Society from early on (though he was not a foundation fellow in 1830), and contributed several papers to its publications, all of which were in advance of their time for their scientific rigour; indeed, Hugh Mill, a meteorologist and long-time secretary of the society, sees in Jackson possibly the earliest British proponent of an independent science of geography (Mill, 148). In the *Journal of the Royal Geographical Society* for 1834, for example, he proposed a systematic terminology for river systems, some of which acquired currency. His *Guide du voyageur*, published in French in 1822 and in English in 1841 under the title *What to Observe, or, The Traveller's Remembrancer*, later became the core of the society's *Hints to Travellers*. Jackson was a member of the society's council from 1838, and throughout the late 1830s urged the society to remodel it so that fellows might participate in decision making; he also called for reform of exploration itself, which he believed not simply to be adventurous travel, but to have as its aim systematic scientific description. His advocacy of both systematic exploration and 'theoretical geography' or 'sedentary geography' based on library research brought him into conflict with those who wanted to keep the society the preserve of the amateur traveller. In 1841 he became the society's secretary at a salary of £300 a year. In this capacity he corresponded with senior officials in the home government and explorers throughout the world, encouraging the collection of geographical, economic, and political information regarding unmapped territories and areas in which British interests were in dispute, such as China, Oregon, and Afghanistan.

In 1844 Jackson took over the editorship of the society's *Journal*. He was an established contributor to the *Journal* on various subjects, mostly connected with physical geography, but failed to make his mark intellectually as editor. However, his index to the first ten volumes was a very valuable undertaking from which scholars still benefit. He continued to write, publishing *Minerals and their Uses* (1849), *On Military Geography* (1850), based on the French treatise by Antoine de La Vallée, and numerous other pamphlets, short works, and reviews.

While still editor of the *Journal* Jackson took over the librarianship of the society, at a salary of £52 a year. The 1840s were difficult years for the society, characterized by falling numbers of fellows and shortage of money, problems neither Jackson nor other well-intentioned officers managed effectively to remedy. Jackson's proposal to admit associates for a reduced fee was not accepted. Although the official society records are full of praise for his evident ability and energy, it is also clear that he was a difficult person to get on with. Jackson in particular and the society in general were attacked in the *Pictorial Times* of 12 September 1846, where Jackson's engrossment of offices and the society's general scientific torpor were criticized. The RGS council dismissed this report as trivial when Jackson brought it to their notice, but when a council member later questioned whether the secretary was worth his £300 a year Jackson resigned. The economizing society found another who filled the position on a reduced salary.

About the same time Jackson was suddenly superseded in his Russian post and emoluments, and was thus placed in very straitened circumstances. Through Sir Roderick Murchison, who also had strong Russian connections, he obtained a clerkship under the council of education, which he held until his death. Tsar Nicholas also gave him a small pension. Jackson was made a fellow of the Royal Society in 1845, and was a member or corresponding member of many learned societies. He was a knight of St Stanislaus of Poland. He died, after long suffering from hepatitis and chronic gastritis, at 32 Coleshill Street, London, on 16 March 1853. He had been married to Sarah Ogle, with whom he had several children.

ELIZABETH BAIGENT

Sources H. R. Mill, *The record of the Royal Geographical Society, 1830–1930* (1930) · *GM*, 2nd ser., 39 (1853), 562 · d. cert. · *DNB* · private information (2004) [R. Stafford] · RGS, Julian Jackson MSS · C. R. Markham, *The fifty years' work of the Royal Geographical Society* (1881) · F. Driver, *Geography militant: cultures of exploration and empire* (2001) **Archives** RGS, papers relating to travel | BL, Murchison MSS · GS Lond., Murchison MSS

Jackson, Julia Prinsep. *See* Stephen, Julia Prinsep (1846–1895).

Jackson, Kenneth Hurlstone (1909–1991), Celtic scholar, was born on 1 November 1909 at Melville, Lavender Vale, Beddington, Surrey, the younger child of Alan Stuart Jackson (1877–1964), stockbroker, and his wife, Lucy Jane, *née* Hurlstone (1879–1970). While his father's family included clerics and civil servants, his mother's contained several artists, notably Frederick Young Hurlstone (1800–1869). His sister Christine trained at the London College of Art. His early education, which was interrupted by ill health, was at Hillcrest School, Wallington (1916–19). He attended Whitgift Grammar School, Croydon, between 1920 and 1928. There his linguistic gifts blossomed, and he won an open scholarship to St John's College, Cambridge, in 1928.

Jackson did phenomenally well at Cambridge. After taking the classical tripos he transferred in 1931 to a new course on the cultures and literatures of north-west Europe, which was then being pioneered by Hector Munro Chadwick and Nora Kershaw Chadwick. Here, too, Jackson carried all before him. On being awarded a travelling studentship he opted to go to Ireland and Wales, to study with the most eminent Celtic scholars of the day—Osborn Bergin and Gerard Murphy in Dublin and Ifor Williams in Bangor—and to immerse himself in modern Irish and Welsh. It was through visiting the Blasket Islands that he met the great story-teller Peig Sayers, many of whose tales he published.

Jackson returned to Cambridge in 1934 as a lecturer in

Kenneth Hurlstone Jackson (1909–1991), by Walter Bird, 1959

Celtic. He built up the Celtic curriculum and established the parameters for his own scholarly career: a multi-disciplinary synthesis of philology, literary criticism, and history; a comparative approach, drawing in other traditions and languages; and recognition of the value of material collected in the field, such as place names, dialects, and folklore. In 1939 he moved to Harvard, where he soon became associate professor (1940). Harvard proved congenial, and it was there that he launched his most important scholarly work. Nevertheless, he missed the modern Celtic speakers, manuscript collections, and fellow Celticists of Britain and Ireland. He was considered for the chair of Celtic at Oxford in 1947 and, although promoted to a full professorship at Harvard in 1948, accepted the Edinburgh chair when it was offered to him in 1949.

While at Edinburgh (1950–79) Jackson emerged as the most respected of a brilliant generation of Celticists. He published on the ancient Celts, on the dark and middle ages, on all six modern Celtic languages, on folklore, place names, and dialects. Thus he spent much of his vacations during the 1950s recording Gaelic dialects for the Linguistic Survey of Scotland. Although he disliked academic politics he served his turn in other ways: in the university, as a fellow of the British Academy (elected 1957), and as a commissioner for the ancient and historical monuments of Scotland. When he retired he held honorary degrees from universities in England, Wales, Ireland, and Brittany. In 1985 his unique pre-eminence in Celtic studies was acknowledged with the honour of being made CBE.

On 12 August 1936 Jackson married Janet Dall Galloway

(*b.* 1909), whom he had met at Cambridge. She was a psychiatric social worker, and daughter of Alexander Galloway, farmer. Her family came from Kinross, and she combined a robustly practical outlook with a lifelong devotion to the arts, especially literature. Her support underpinned Jackson's productive but punishing work schedule throughout his life. Their children Alastar and Stephanie were born in the USA, but brought up and educated in Edinburgh.

To Jackson his most important work lay in the history of the Celtic languages, building on the achievements of the nineteenth-century philologists. His monumental *Language and History in Early Britain* (1953) traced the emergence of Welsh, Cornish, and Breton from the ancient British tongue. *A Historical Phonology of Breton* (1967) scrutinized Breton from the earliest British colonists to the modern Breton dialects. Jackson also planned a matching history of the Gaelic languages. His *Contributions to the Study of Manx Phonology* (1956) fed into this grand plan. Many of his shorter works were also philological; but they included in addition influential contributions in folklore (for example, *The International Popular Tale and Early Welsh Tradition*, 1961), literature (for example, *The Gododdin: the Oldest Scottish Poem*, 1969), and text edition (for example, *The Gaelic Notes in the Book of Deer*, 1972). His popular *Celtic Miscellany* (1951), containing translations from all the Celtic languages, showed high critical intelligence and the verbal sensitivity of a poet *manqué*.

As a scholar Jackson was outstandingly good at sorting complex things out. In all his best work he was comprehensive in grasp, penetrating in analysis, and lucid in exposition. Celtic studies needed all these qualities to counteract misunderstanding and ignorance—on Arthur or the Picts or 'Celtic twilight'. The degree of seriousness with which Celtic studies were treated by the time of his retirement owed much to the authority and force of Jackson's writing. Although subsequent research has altered scholarly understanding in many specialized areas, Jackson's works frequently contain the best statement of the case, and form the starting point for continuing scholarship. Few can claim such durability. His *Guardian* obituarist aptly placed him in an intermediate position between the nineteenth-century comparativists and the specialized scholars of today: they were the Gods, we are the mortals, and Jackson was a Hero.

Physically Jackson was slight but wiry; he coxed an eight while at St John's. He was an indefatigable walker, who harnessed his love of exercise and the countryside to his historical, archaeological, and place name interests. He enjoyed good food and wine in moderation, though in latter years moderation became extreme on account of persistent migraines. He had a keen eye for truth and beauty in art and literature. He drove others as hard as himself, but could see 'the other side', and even tell a story against himself, as when, in the early days of the Linguistic Survey, his attempts to interview Sutherland crofters on the sabbath met with a firm rebuff.

Jackson boasted that his job paid him to do what he enjoyed doing. Retirement consequently meant 'more of the same', and he had earmarked place names and Cornish studies as retirement projects. Since his big book on the Gaelic languages had eluded him, however, he decided to concentrate on that area. The result was his edition of *Aislinge Meic Con Glinne* (1990). Although he suffered a stroke in 1984, and could not work with the same intensity as before, this edition was sufficiently advanced for others to see it through the press. He died at the City Hospital, Edinburgh, on 20 February 1991 after a short illness. He was survived by his wife and two children. His funeral service, on 26 February, had been prescribed in all its details by himself. With typical modesty, he had instructed that a small chapel be booked, expecting that few would attend; in fact, the chapel was packed to overflowing. His remains were cremated at Mortonhall crematorium, Edinburgh, and his ashes were interred soon afterwards at the Surrey and Sussex crematorium, Worth, near Crawley, Sussex.
WILLIAM GILLIES

Sources J. E. Caerwyn Williams, 'Kenneth Hurlstone Jackson, 1909–1991', *PBA*, 80 (1993), 319–32 • J. E. Caerwyn Williams, 'Kenneth Hurlstone Jackson', *Studia Celtica*, 14–15 (1979–80), 1–4 • W. Gillies, 'The history of the survey', *Survey of the Gaelic dialects of Scotland*, ed. C. Ó Dochartaigh, 1 (1997), 25–47 • W. Gillies, 'Kenneth Hurlstone Jackson', *Edinburgh University Magazine* (summer 1991), 6 • *The Guardian* (23 Feb 1991) • *The Independent* (25 Feb 1991) • *The Scotsman* (23 Feb 1991) • *The Times* (8 March 1991) • *WWW*, 1991–5 • private information (2004) [family] • personal knowledge (2004) • m. cert. • d. cert.
Archives Bodl. Oxf., letters to O. G. S. Crawford • U. Edin., school of Scottish studies, linguistic survey of Scotland
Likenesses W. Bird, photograph, 1959, NPG [*see illus.*]
Wealth at death £332,305.40: confirmation, 14 May 1991, *CCI*

Jackson, Laurence (1691–1772), Church of England clergyman and religious writer, was born on 20 March 1691, the son of Laurence Jackson of London. He entered Merchant Taylors' School, London, on 12 March 1701 and in 1709 was admitted a pensioner of St John's College, Cambridge, where he graduated BA in 1712. He moved to Sidney Sussex College, where he was elected a fellow in 1715, and gained an MA in 1716 and BD in 1723. Ordained deacon at York in 1714 and priest at Ely in 1718 he was appointed vicar of Ardleigh, near Colchester, on 11 May 1723, rector of Great Wigborough, also in Essex, on 25 April 1730, and a prebendary of Lincoln Cathedral in 1747. He kept all these posts until his death.

In 1750 Jackson published two pieces in response to Conyers Middleton's debate with Thomas Sherlock, bishop of London. His other works include a response to Thomas Chubb (1739) and *A Letter to a Young Lady, Concerning the Principles and Conduct of the Christian Life* (1756), which was reprinted in 1758. Jackson, who was predeceased by his wife, died on 17 February 1772. His will shows that he possessed property in Somerset and almost £4000 in annuities by 1769. He left several small bequests to the SPCK and related charities.
THOMPSON COOPER, *rev.* EMMA MAJOR

Sources Venn, *Alum. Cant.* • will, PRO, PROB 11/977, fols. 310–11 • *ESTC* • *GM*, 1st ser., 42 (1772), 151 • *GM*, 1st ser., 48 (1778), 623 • Nichols, *Lit. anecdotes*, 1.418; 5.154 • *Fasti Angl.* (Hardy), 2.103 • P. Morant, *The history and antiquities of the county of Essex*, 1 (1768), 421,

435 • C. J. Robinson, ed., *A register of the scholars admitted into Merchant Taylors' School, from AD 1562 to 1874*, 2 (1883), 4 • Watt, *Bibl. Brit.* **Wealth at death** approx. £4000 in annuities; property in Somerset: will, PRO, PROB 11/977, fols. 310–11

Jackson [*née* Sanderson], **Margaret Anne** (1843–1906), mountaineer, was born on 27 September 1843, the daughter of George Samuel Sanderson, engineer of Birkenhead, and his wife, Jane. On 23 August 1865, at St John's Church, Birkenhead, she married Edward Patten Jackson (1842–1881), gentleman and colliery owner. He was the fourth son of Sir William Jackson, first baronet (1805–1876), an African merchant of Birkenhead and owner of a colliery in Chesterfield, who sat as a Liberal MP, and Elizabeth (d. 1875), daughter of Thomas Hughes of Liverpool. There were no children.

Margaret and Edward Jackson began climbing in the Alps in 1872, and he was elected to the Alpine Club in 1874. They both joined the Paris section of the Club Alpin Français in 1877; the British Alpine Club did not admit women until 1976. Together they climbed many peaks and passes around Chamonix, Zermatt, and Grindelwald, and her many first ascents by a woman included the Grand Dru and the Aiguille des Grandes Charmoz. Other mountaineers admired her penchant for making difficult first ascents by new routes, including on the east face of Weissmies, the western ridge and north-western face of the Dom, and the north-western ridge of the Täshhorn. After E. P. Jackson died on 17 January 1881 at Wynberg, Cape Colony, Margaret stopped climbing for two years. She attracted attention once again with a new route and first descent of the Dent Blanche by the western arête in 1884.

Margaret Jackson was best-known for a series of pioneering climbs in winter. In January 1888 she made first winter ascents of the Gross Lauteraarhorn, Pfaffenstöckli, the Gross Viescherhorn, and a traverse of the Jungfrau with Emil Boss. On the descent from the Jungfrau she and her guides spent the night in an ice cave on the Guggi glacier and suffered permanent injury from frostbite. As Mrs E. P. Jackson, she gave brief accounts of these climbs in 'A winter quartette' (*Alpine Journal*, 14, 1889, 200–10) and 'Winter mountaineering in 1888' (*Yorkshire Rambler's Club Journal*, 2, 1903, 97). By the time she gave up climbing in 1889, she had made over 140 grand ascents in the Alps.

Jackson died of acute pneumonia on 13 October 1906 at 14 Orsett Terrace, Paddington, London, the luxurious home where she had often hosted fashionable soirées for members of the Alpine Club. Contemporaries admired the manner in which she combined 'the elegance of fashionable society with the stoicism of the mountaineer' (*La Montagne*, 582), and recalled her as 'one of the foremost of lady mountaineers' (Mumm, 203). PETER H. HANSEN

Sources *La Montagne*, 2 (1906), 582 • *Rivista Mensile del Club Alpino Italiano*, 25 (1906), 486 • *Alpine Journal*, 10 (1881), 231 [obit. of Edward Patten Jackson] • Mrs E. P. Jackson, 'A winter quartette', *Alpine Journal*, 14 (1889), 200–10 • A. L. Mumm, *The Alpine Club register*, 2 (1925) • E. Lodge, *The peerage and baronetage of the British empire*, [new edn] (1877) [Sir William Jackson] • Burke, *Peerage* (1939) [Mather-Jackson] • m. cert. • d. cert.
Archives Ladies' Alpine Club, London, archives

Wealth at death £66,293 2s. 10d.: probate, 13 Nov 1906, *CGPLA Eng. & Wales*

Jackson, Mason (1819–1903), wood-engraver and journalist, was born at Ovington, Northumberland, the son of John Jackson, a husbandman, and the younger brother of the wood-engraver John *Jackson (1801–1848). The elder brother, having learned his craft with Thomas Bewick, went to London and was joined about 1830 by Mason, whom he then trained as a wood-engraver. By 1836 Mason Jackson was engraving after Richard Seymour for the green wrapper of Dickens's *Pickwick Papers* and for S. C. Hall's *Book of British Ballads* (1842). He married on 25 September 1849 Catherine Common of Gosforth, Northumberland; their daughter Catherine was born in 1851. From 1846 to 1863 Jackson was entered in directories as a wood-engraver, at 12 Cardington Street, off Hampstead Road, where after his wife's death he lived with his brother and his family. He married secondly Lucy Berriman Tippetts (b. 1838) on 16 July 1864, and thereafter worked from his home at 12 Pembroke Gardens, Kensington, where they brought up their three children, Arthur Mason Tippetts Jackson [*see below*], Herbert, and Lucy.

During the 1850s and 1860s Jackson produced engravings for numerous magazines and books, among them several series published by Charles Knight, the *Art Union of London* (1850–60), *Cassell's Illustrated Family Paper* (1857), and the *Illustrated London Almanack* (1850–51), signing 'M. JACKSON SC'. In 1850 he began engraving for the *Illustrated London News*, reproducing in full and double-page engravings the drawings and paintings of prominent contemporary artists. From 1860 to 1895 he was also the art editor of the *Illustrated London News*, and on retirement in 1896 he was briefly a director. His book *The Pictorial Press: its Origins and Progress* (1885) traced the rise of illustrated journalism from its hesitant beginnings to his own times. In addition, Jackson exhibited his landscape paintings from 1856 to 1879 at the Royal Academy and other London galleries. He died at his home, 79 Warwick Road, Brompton, on 29 December 1903 and was buried at Brompton cemetery. The *Times* obituarist commented, 'By his death journalism has lost one of its most respected veterans', and described him as 'a genial and upright man' (*The Times*, 2 Jan 1904, 4a).

Arthur Mason Tippetts Jackson (1866–1909) was born at the family home, 12 Pembroke Gardens, Kensington, on 30 December 1866. He was educated at Westminster School from 1880 to 1884, then went with a scholarship to Brasenose College, Oxford. A gifted oriental linguist, he gained the Boden prize for Sanskrit and graduated BA first class in 1888. He was called to the bar at Middle Temple in November of that year, by which time he had already secured the Indian Civil Service prize for Sanskrit, and was in India by December, where he rapidly increased his knowledge of vernacular languages.

Based in the Bombay presidency, Jackson held a number of legal and administrative posts, including that of private secretary to Lord Sandhurst, then governor of Bombay, from 1898 to 1900. He was also superintendent in charge of the revision of the *Imperial Gazetteer*. He was able to study in the library of the Royal Asiatic Society, was briefly its honorary secretary, and published in its journals. On the occasions when he was back in England, Jackson examined for Oxford University.

By December 1909 Jackson had risen to the rank of senior collector, stationed at Nasik, and was about to transfer to Bombay for a further promotion. On 22 December a farewell entertainment was being held in his honour at the theatre in Nasik; as Jackson and his wife entered, a young Hindu shot at him several times, and he died instantly. The assassination was undoubtedly political and part of a Brahman rebellion against the government; Jackson had earlier tried the killer's cousin for seditious conspiracy, and a higher court had sentenced him to transportation for life. But even in Nasik, a Brahmanical centre, Jackson's personal kindness had made him much loved, and he was admired and respected for his grasp of Indian languages. A large gathering accompanied his body to the local cemetery at Nasik for burial on 23 December.   ANITA MCCONNELL

Sources R. K. Engen, *Dictionary of Victorian wood engravers* (1985) · *The Times* (2 Jan 1904), 4a · *ILN* (2 Jan 1904) · *The Times* (23 Dec 1909), 3a, 9c · *Bombay Gazette* (23 Dec 1909), 4c–d · *Bombay Gazette* (25 Dec 1909), 7c · *Old Westminsters*, 1.506 · m. cert. · d. cert. · b. cert. [Arthur Mason Tippetts Jackson] · *CGPLA Eng. & Wales* (1910)

Wealth at death £770 11s. 1d.: probate, 25 Jan 1904, *CGPLA Eng. & Wales* · £16 11s. 5d.—Arthur Mason Tippetts Jackson: probate, 1910, *CGPLA Eng. & Wales*

Jackson, Nicholas Lane [*called* Pa Jackson] (1849–1937), sports administrator, was born on 1 November 1849 at 14 Southgate Road, De Beauvoir Town, Middlesex, the son of Nicholas Lane Jackson, a cheesemonger, and his wife, Mary Prior. His family had a long association with the west country. He grew up in London, and was interested in a wide range of sporting activities from an early age. Educated privately, he had intended to join the army, but a change in his family's financial circumstances led to his becoming a journalist instead. He married on 20 January 1869 Mary Ann, the daughter of Frank Williams, licensed victualler; by 1881 they had three sons and a daughter. At various times in the late 1860s and early 1870s he was a member of the London rifle brigade, played cricket for Devon, made a balloon ascent, fished, walked long distances, beagled, ran with the Thames hare and hounds and the London athletic club, and played association football for Upton Park. In addition, like many middle-class sportsmen of the period, he had a strong interest in amateur dramatics.

As well as competing, Jackson was involved in organizing and administering several different sports. In December 1866 he founded the Mutual Improvement Society in Edmonton, then a rapidly developing north London suburb. In the early 1870s, following his marriage, he lived in Finchley, where he founded an association football club, a cross-country running club, and a boxing club, and revived the local cricket club. In 1879 he was the organizer of the Finchley athletic sports. In the late 1860s and early 1870s, as he later recalled, Saturday afternoons off had yet to become customary—so permission was sought from the local vicar to play games on Sunday afternoons instead.

It was through his involvement with association football that Jackson became best known to the sporting public. In 1879 he was elected to the committee of the Football Association (FA), and he served as its assistant honorary secretary in 1881. He founded the London FA in 1882, became a member of the FA council in 1883, and in 1884 served on the FA subcommittee that recommended the removal of the bar on professionalism—a proposal adopted in 1885. In 1886 he was elected to the FA's international board, which gave him responsibility for the selection of international teams, a role he performed concurrently for the Lawn Tennis Association. He was a respected and influential writer on both sports.

In 1882, following a run of defeats for England in association football internationals against Scotland, Jackson founded the Corinthian Football Club, with the intention of providing an opportunity for leading amateurs to play together outside international matches. Membership was formally limited to the fifty leading amateurs of the day; but from the beginning the club was also socially exclusive, and members were invariably former public school or university players. After professionalism in the sport was legalized, the Corinthians quickly became the symbolic leaders of the amateur game, and their clashes with leading professional teams were eagerly anticipated by the sporting public. Jackson was the club's honorary secretary for seventeen years. As the Corinthian Casuals (following amalgamation with the Casuals in 1939) they remain, in the early twenty-first century, England's most famous amateur club.

In addition to the Corinthians, Jackson had long been associated with the organization of 'scratch' teams of amateur players, brought together for exhibition matches, often played against professional sides, with the gate money being given to good causes. Jackson helped to raise considerable sums for the Poplar Hospital, of which Rowland Hill, a rugby football administrator and writer, was also a patron. On one trip with a scratch team composed of Cambridge University players he was nicknamed Pa by the younger generation, and he was widely known as such thereafter. In 1894, by which time Jackson was a vice-president of the FA, the FA committee, in response to allegations of improper payments to amateurs, ruled that such scratch teams could not be formed without prior official permission. Jackson viewed this as unnecessarily restrictive, and resigned from the FA in protest; thereafter he gradually withdrew from involvement with the professional game.

Instead, Jackson directed his sporting enthusiasm elsewhere, and became involved with a variety of commercial sporting ventures. He had already founded the journals *Pastime* (in 1883) and the *Cricket Field* (1892), and in 1893 he became managing director of the Sports Club—a London club founded by a group of aristocratic sportsmen which included Sir John Astley. Jackson was regarded as a leading authority on many sports, and was visited by Baron Pierre de Coubertin when he visited Britain in 1894 as part of his campaign to revive the Olympic games. Jackson was involved with the design of several golf courses in Britain and France, including the development of Le Touquet as a leisure resort, a scheme which included among its financial supporters de Coubertin and Grand Duke Michael of Russia. Following the success of Le Touquet, Jackson attempted to introduce the concept of the country club to Britain, and chose a site at Stoke Poges, Buckinghamshire. Initially the project was successful; Edward VII visited in 1910, and by July 1914 the club had 900 full and 200 day members. But the war intervened, and Jackson's interests were diverted elsewhere: he became assistant director of the food production department. After 1918 the club was left in a precarious financial position, and Jackson eventually sold his interest in 1928.

Jackson continued his involvement with a variety of sports into his eighties: judging athletic competitions, serving on local and national golfing associations, driving motor cars, and playing golf. He continued to write books and articles until his death from pneumonia on 24 October 1937 at Avondale, Hermosa Road, Teignmouth, Devon. In his autobiography, *Sporting Days and Sporting Ways*, published five years earlier, he had written that he had enjoyed a 'longish life which thanks largely to sport has been a healthy one and a happy one'.   M. A. BRYANT

Sources N. L. Jackson, *Sporting days and sporting ways* (1932) · N. L. Jackson, *Association football* (1899) · 'Corinthian Casuals football club', www.corinthians.freeserve.co.uk, 23 Aug 2001 · E. Grayson, *Corinthian-Casuals and cricketers* (1983) · T. Mason, *Association football and English society, 1863–1915* (1980) · b. cert. · m. cert. · d. cert. · census returns, 1881 · WWW

Jackson, Sir Percy Richard (1869–1941), educational administrator, was born at Hebble Terrace, Huddersfield, Yorkshire, on 23 January 1869, the son of William Michael Jackson, tea merchant, and his wife, Anne Field. He attended Huddersfield collegiate school before entering business in the textile industry, where he became head of the firm of Field and Bottrill Ltd, plush manufacturers, of Skelmanthorpe, near Huddersfield. On 26 April 1893 he married Mary Elizabeth (1870/71–1938), daughter of Thomas Blacker, a contractor, at Skelmanthorpe Wesleyan Methodist Church, near Huddersfield. They had three sons, the eldest of whom was killed in the First World War, and four daughters.

As Jackson was an active member of the Methodist church and of the Liberal Party, his career in public affairs in the West Riding of Yorkshire strongly reflected local traditions of nonconformity and Liberalism. He was first elected to the West Riding county council in 1904 and remained a member until his retirement in 1937. He joined the education committee in 1905 and was chairman from 1918 until 1937; he was thus closely involved in the principal educational initiatives of one of the largest authorities in England. A man of abundant energy and a perceptive grasp of affairs, his special gift was an ability to reconcile sharply opposing interests without a sacrifice of principle—a gift that he had ample opportunity to exercise. Religious decisions over education were particularly contentious; so too were the problems thrown up by the

relationships between the county and the part III elementary education authorities (medium-sized boroughs and urban districts which gained the right to become local education authorities for specified purposes) and county boroughs which lay within the boundaries of the West Riding.

The strong local nonconformist tradition led to more difficulties in this authority than anywhere else in England after 1902, when the Education Act of that year required local education authorities to maintain church schools. The initial refusal of the activists among the Liberal members fully to accept their new legal responsibilities produced difficult relationships with both Roman Catholic and Anglican schools. While the position gradually settled down in the existing schools, attempts between the wars to reorganize schooling to give pupils aged over eleven separate senior or modern schools again excited traditional attitudes, for the churches certainly did not want to lose their older pupils to council senior schools. In the face of considerable opposition from some of his more entrenched councillors, Jackson managed in 1930, after an earlier, unsuccessful agreement in 1926, to secure a concordat on religious education with the Church of England diocesan authorities. This enabled some reorganization to go forward in the 1930s. The full significance of Jackson's achievement became clear when his compromise was used as an essential element in the national settlement in the Education Act of 1944.

After the First World War conflicts between counties and larger boroughs assumed sufficient importance for the government to appoint a royal commission in 1923. The West Riding, with nine county boroughs by this time, most of which seemed intent on enlarging their boundaries at the expense of the county, strongly defended its position in evidence. Yet in practice there was need for co-operation if the interests of the area as a whole were not to suffer, and this was particularly urgent in technical and further education. Jackson succeeded in bringing the main local authorities together in the Yorkshire council for further education in 1928. This became an effective organization for regional planning and co-operation in the 1930s. It served as the model in the wartime Board of Education for the planners of post-war technological education. The subsequent regional advisory councils set up from 1946 to cover the whole country followed its pattern. Jackson also managed to hold together the county councils of the three ridings in the Yorkshire council for agricultural education, although this broke up a few years after he ceased to be chairman.

Jackson, who was knighted in 1925, became a leading figure in education at national level. He was a member of the executive of the Association of Education Committees, of which he became president in 1924, and was chairman of the education committee of the County Councils Association. This dual responsibility gave him a position of considerable significance on the Burnham committee on teachers' salaries, of which he was deputy leader. He was a member of the consultative committee of the Board of Education from 1922 to 1938 when it produced the two major reports on schools of the inter-war years, the Hadow report, *The Education of the Adolescent* (1927), which recommended ending the all-age elementary school and separate provision for pupils over eleven, and the Spens report (1938) on secondary and technical education. He was a member of the royal commission on the civil service (1930–31).

In 1925 Jackson became a trustee of the United Kingdom Carnegie Trust, which supported many forms of social activity, and was appointed vice-chairman in 1934. He continued his work with the trust until his death. He gave up his membership of the county council in 1937 but remained a member of the executive of the Land Settlement Association, of which he had been a founder and the first chairman. Its purpose was to provide estates where unemployed men from depressed areas could learn how to run their own smallholdings. He took a particular personal interest in the work of the settlement at Carlton, Snaith, which was nearest to his home.

Following the death of his first wife in 1938 Jackson married Jessie Ewen Robertson (*b.* 1894/5), a schoolmistress, at Hove Presbyterian Church, Sussex, on 14 February 1939. He died of coronary thrombosis on 24 December 1941 at his home, Woodlands, Scissett, Skelmanthorpe, Yorkshire, and was buried on 28 December at Skelmanthorpe cemetery. He was survived by his second wife.

PETER GOSDEN

Sources P. H. J. H. Gosden and P. R. Sharp, *The development of an education service: the West Riding, 1889–1974* (1978) · *Yorkshire Post* (27 Dec 1941) · *Education* (1919–37) · *Yorkshire Post* (1918–39) · *Leeds Mercury* (1918–39) · *Huddersfield Daily Examiner* (1904–39) · b. cert. · m. certs. · d. cert.
Archives U. Leeds, Brotherton L., MSS of the Association of Education Committees
Likenesses photographs
Wealth at death £90,024 9s. 4d.: probate, 23 March 1942, CGPLA Eng. & Wales

Jackson, Ralph Ward (1806–1880), railway promoter and entrepreneur, was born on 7 June 1806 at Normanby Hall, near Middlesbrough, the third in the family of eight sons and one daughter of William Ward Jackson of Normanby Hall, and his wife, Susanna Louisa, daughter of E. Martin Atkins, esquire of Kingston Lisle, Berkshire. Educated at Rugby School, Jackson served articles at Preston, Lancashire. Living at Greatham Hall, Jackson practised as a solicitor in Stockton-on-Tees. Commercial speculation rather than the law fired his imagination. Exploitation of the Auckland coalfields entered a new era in 1825 with the Darlington–Stockton railway, soon extended closer to the sea at Middlesbrough, where a town arose with startling suddenness. The promoters, led by the Pease family (Edward Pease and his sons Henry and Joseph), saw Middlesbrough taking the lead over both Tyne and Wear. Their vision sparked rival ambitions in Jackson, subsequently dubbed 'a bottomless man' by Edward Pease (diary, 27 March 1857).

Jackson's counter-strategy emerged in the Stockton and Hartlepool Railway Company (1836) and Stockton and Durham County Bank (1838). The bank was merely a device to raise capital for railway and port construction and was transferred to the National Provincial after Jackson obtained parliamentary authority to build the West Hartlepool harbour and dock in 1844. Hartlepool then comprised 6000 people–no longer a simple fishing village since dock facilities had recently brought it into the coalexport and timber-import trades; but Jackson's sights were set on the adjacent hamlet of Stranton, with a population of 350. West Hartlepool grew there. Jackson liked to recall how he chased a rabbit as the first sod was cut to begin a dock (completed in 1847). Two more docks were added in 1852 and 1856. Jackson conceived that West Hartlepool would ultimately become the equivalent of the port of Liverpool on the east coast. He planned a trans-Pennine route to link the London and North Western Railway, and he promoted bills to eclipse the Pease interest in the north-east, where a struggle to control the movement of Cleveland ironstone intensified the original rivalry over coalfields.

Jackson's company became overextended financially, having invested in steamships and collieries as well as docks and railways. Malpractice and recklessness there were, but it would be wrong to ascribe Jackson's errors to fraudulent intent for personal profit. The agent of his downfall through protracted litigation, one Benjamin Coleman, was not motivated solely by shareholder's vigilance: he was embittered against Jackson's family and may even have been sponsored by rival railway interests, perhaps the North Eastern which subsequently absorbed Jackson's Hartlepool Company.

In 1861 the population of Stranton–West Hartlepool was 13,600. Separated for local government purposes, the Hartlepools were united as one parliamentary constituency in 1868. Jackson became the first MP by a majority of three votes. An election petition was initiated but withdrawn. His zeal for West Hartlepool had aroused antipathies, for he was apt to think that his personal preferences and the public good were synonymous. An unedifying dispute with the incumbent of Christ Church (a church built by his company) over control of local schools showed his uncompromising bent. Jackson's family tradition in politics was whig-Liberal; now he styled himself a Conservative opposed to all rash and hasty innovations. He voted against church disestablishment in Ireland, also against the secret ballot, though for temperance reform. In parliament Jackson's principal interest was not party politics, rather the promotion of West Hartlepool. He spoke rarely, his chief intervention being in the harbours of refuge debates, to solicit government money for docks improvements.

Jackson was not re-elected in 1874. His commercial reputation was now in shade, but Jackson was hatching speculative schemes to the last. He was never a utopian communitarian like Robert Owen. His founding of a town was the by-product of his business. Nevertheless, community building increasingly occupied his time and money, and his lasting reputation is that of an urban pioneer, the first and foremost West Hartlepool patriot.

In 1829 Jackson married Susanna (*d.* 1865), daughter of

Charles Swainson of Cooper Hill, Lancashire. They had one son. Jackson died on 6 August 1880 in London and was buried in Kensal Green cemetery.

PHILIP WALLER, rev.

Sources R. Martin, *Historical notes and personal recollections of West Hartlepool and its founder* (1924) · E. Waggott, *Jackson's town* (1980) · R. Wood, *West Hartlepool: the rise and development of a Victorian new town* (1969) · Boase, *Mod. Eng. biog.* · *The diaries of Edward Pease*, ed. A. E. Pease (1907)
Likenesses F. Grant, portrait, 1855 · statue, Christ Church, West Hartlepool

Jackson, Randle (1757–1837), lawyer, was the third son of Samuel Jackson of Paddington, Middlesex. He matriculated at Oxford on 17 July 1789, at the age of thirty-two. A member first of Magdalen Hall, afterwards of Exeter College, he was created MA on 2 May 1793. In the same year, on 9 February, he was called to the bar by the Middle Temple. He was also admitted *ad eundem* at the Inner Temple in 1805, became a bencher of the Middle Temple in 1828, and a reader in 1834.

Jackson won a considerable reputation at the bar, and acted as parliamentary counsel of the East India Company and of the corporation of London. He was said to have 'few rivals there in eloquence and legal knowledge' (*A New Biographical Dictionary*, 1825). Five or six of his speeches delivered before parliamentary committees or the proprietors of East India stock, on such issues as the grievances of clothworkers and the prolongation of the East India Company's charter, were printed. He also appeared before the Lords in privy council on behalf of those seeking a charter for a third London theatre. In addition to his speeches Jackson published a work, addressed to the magistracy, *On the Increase of Crime* (1828). In 1832 he wrote a pamphlet letter to Lord Henley, commenting on Henley's request for a vote for Middlesex, and with observations on his lordship's plan for reform of the church. Jackson died at Brixton, Surrey, on 14 March 1837.

JAMES TAIT, rev. ROBERT BROWN

Sources Foster, *Alum. Oxon.* · J. Hutchinson, ed., *A catalogue of notable Middle Templars: with brief biographical notices* (1902) · *GM*, 2nd ser., 7 (1837), 444 · [J. Watkins and F. Shoberl], *A biographical dictionary of the living authors of Great Britain and Ireland* (1816) · *A new biographical dictionary of 3000 cotemporary [sic] public characters, British and foreign, of all ranks and professions*, 2nd edn, 3 vols. in 6 pts (1825)
Archives BL, letters to Sir Arthur Wellesley, Add. MS 37278
Likenesses J. Thomson, stipple (after S. Drummond), BM, NPG; repro. in *European Magazine* (1820)

Jackson, Raymond Allen [*pseud.* Jak] (**1927–1997**), cartoonist and illustrator, was born in the Middlesex Hospital, London, on 11 March 1927, the only child of Maurice Jackson, formerly Jacobovitz (1894–1960), a journeyman tailor from Łódź, Poland, who had lived in France and then Brighton before moving to work in London's 'rag-trade' area around Great Titchfield Street. At first he changed his name to Jacob and then to Jackson and later set up his own ladies' tailoring shop in Kensington Mall, Notting Hill Gate. Raymond's mother was an Irishwoman, Marie (Polly) Murphy (*b.* 1904), who also worked in the clothing business. He was educated at Clipstone Road School, London, and Lyulph Stanley Central School, London. At fourteen he worked as a messenger boy in the Great Titchfield Street area before going to Willesden Technical College and School of Art (1941–4), where a fellow pupil was the illustrator Peter Jackson. There he spent two years in general education before studying art full-time for a further two years, training as a student teacher. On 3 April 1945 he enlisted for the Territorial Army and served at first as a driver in the Royal Army Ordnance Corps before joining its education division (1945–8). Teaching conscripts to paint, he was posted to Italy, Palestine (1945–7), and Egypt (he was an instructor at the Middle East Art College, 1947–8) and achieved the rank of sergeant. He then returned to Willesden Technical College (1948–50) to study commercial art, graduating with a national diploma in design.

In 1950 Jackson joined the Link House Publishing Group (1950–51) as a staff artist, retouching pubic hair on photos for *Health & Efficiency*, and drawing a series of cartoons about a character called Curly. He then moved to Keymers Advertising Agency as an artist (1951–2) while also contributing joke cartoons to *Punch*, *Lilliput*, and other publications. He joined the *Evening Standard* in 1952, first in the advertising department at 11 guineas a week, then as a freelance general illustrator for the paper before moving to the art department, producing drawings for the television and sports pages, illustrations for features (signing his drawings Ray Jackson), and occasional caricatures and pocket cartoons. In October 1954 he met his wife Claudie Grenier (*b.* 1936), a French au pair from Épernay, at the Linguists' Club in Kensington. They were married on 9 March 1957 and had three children: Dominique, Patrick, and Nathalie.

After the death of Vicky (Victor Weisz), Jak became the *Standard*'s political cartoonist (1966–97), while also drawing for its sister paper, the *Daily Express*, on Saturdays. When the *Evening Standard* was bought by Associated Newspapers in 1986, he stopped drawing for the *Express* and drew instead for the *Daily Mail* on Saturdays and the *Mail on Sunday*. Altogether he worked for the *Evening Standard* for forty-five years. In addition he contributed occasional journalism to the paper (especially travel articles with illustrations and photographs by himself in the 1960s), drew advertisements for Carling Black Label beer and others, illustrated several books including N. McWhirter and R. McWhirter, eds., *Guinness Book of Records* (1974) and *Russia Dies Laughing* (1982), and painted in watercolour. His own publications included thirty-one annuals of *Evening Standard* cartoons from *The Nutty World of JAK* (1966).

Jackson admired the work of Ronald Searle, Pat Oliphant, Ralph Steadman, and (the early) Carl Giles—whose detailed and realistic style influenced his own greatly. He roughed cartoons out in 2B pencil on A2 layout paper (usually six a day from which the editor chose one), and completed the drawing with a brush and mapping pen using Pelikan ink on board, tints being indicated with pale blue wash. Jak always drew hands with three fingers in the style of Disney animators and signed his name in capitals with 'blob' serifs. In his early drawings he often included a portrait of his wife (with a pony tail) and their boxer dog, Shamus. He was a technically proficient artist, good at backgrounds and architectural details, but (like Giles), 'excelled at drawing types: bumbling vicars and desiccated judges; crusty clubmen with quivering moustaches; bobbies and burglars and dimwitted bruisers; vast armour-plated matrons; long-legged lovelies, top-heavy on stiletto heels' (*The Times*). Though he supported no political party his cartoons were sometimes controversial. One drawing—'Homo-Electrical-sapiens Britannicus circa 1970' (9 December 1970)—which criticized a work-to-rule action by power-station workers, nearly resulted in the *Standard*'s closure as a result of sympathetic industrial action by print unions. Another ('The ultimate in psychopathic horror—THE IRISH', 29 October 1982), caused the Labour-controlled Greater London council to stop advertising in the *Evening Standard* as a protest.

Jak claimed to have been the first to break the (post-Victorian) unwritten prohibition on caricaturing the British royal family. The Labour prime minister Tony Blair called him 'one of the finest political cartoonists' and Lord Rothermere added that he was 'one of the all-time greats alongside Rowlandson, Gillray and Illingworth' (foreword to *Jak: his Life and Work*). He was voted political/social cartoonist of the year three times by the Cartoonists' Club of Great Britain (1964, 1965, 1985), British Press awards cartoonist of the year (1980), and Glen Grant sports cartoonist of the year (1981) and royal cartoonist of the year (1981). Jak was a founder member of the British Cartoonists' Association in 1966 and also belonged to the Chelsea Arts Club, the Saints' and Sinners' Club, and the Special Forces' Club. Examples of his work were included in the National Portrait Gallery exhibition 'Drawn and quartered: the world of the British newspaper cartoon' (1970) and can be found in such public collections as the Victoria and Albert Museum and the Centre for the Study of Cartoons and Caricature at the University of Kent at Canterbury.

'Small, wiry and as strong as an ox' (McKay and McGill, 5), Jak was 5 feet 8 inches tall, and was usually clean-shaven with prematurely thin dark brown (later grey) hair. He had brown eyes and wore thick spectacles from the age of two. At work he would always wear a butcher's apron. A judo blackbelt and a keen golfer, his motto was a variant of Disraeli's: 'Never explain; never complain'. Raymond Jackson died at his home, 21 Seymour Road, Wimbledon, London, on 27 July 1997 following a heart operation. He was cremated at Putney Vale crematorium, London, on 1 August 1997. **MARK BRYANT**

Sources private information (2004) [Claudie Grenier Jackson] · M. Bryant, *Dictionary of twentieth-century British cartoonists and caricaturists* (2000) · M. Bryant and S. Heneage, eds., *Dictionary of British cartoonists and caricaturists, 1730–1980* (1994) · M. Bryant, 'Jak', *World encyclopedia of the press*, ed. D. Griffiths [forthcoming] · P. McKay and A. McGill, *Jak: his life and work* (1997) · *Evening Standard* (29 July 1997) · *The Oldie* (Dec 1997) · M. Bateman, *Funny way to earn a living* (1966) · M. Horn, ed., *The world encyclopedia of cartoons* (1980) · *The Independent* (29 July 1997) · *Daily Mail* (29 July 1997) · *Daily Telegraph* (29 July 1997) · *The Times* (29 July 1997) · *The Guardian* (29 July 1997)

Archives priv. coll., photographs, letters, and drawings | FILM *Changing places*, BBC 1, 20 June 1989 (Jak and painter Michael Nokes) | SOUND 'The cartoonists', BBC Radio 4, 22 Dec 1988 · 'Jak', Derek Jameson programme, BBC Radio 2, interview by Nina Myskow, 20 June 1989

Likenesses R. A. Jackson, self-portrait, caricature, repro. in Bateman, *Funny way*, 33 · photograph, repro. in *Drawn and quartered: the world of the British newspaper cartoon* [exhibition catalogue, *Twentieth Century* magazine, 1970] · photograph, repro. in *Evening Standard* · photograph, repro. in *The Independent* · photograph, repro. in *Daily Mail*, 5, 45 · photograph, repro. in *Daily Telegraph*, 11, 21 · photograph, repro. in *The Times* · photograph, repro. in *The Guardian* · photographs, priv. coll. · photographs, repro. in McKay and McGill, *Jak*

Wealth at death £89,222: probate, 14 Oct 1997, *CGPLA Eng. & Wales*

Jackson, Richard (*fl.* 1567–1570), ballad writer, matriculated at Clare College, Cambridge, on 25 October 1567, graduated BA (1570), and was shortly afterwards appointed master of Ingleton School, in the West Riding of Yorkshire. The well-known ballad on the battle of Flodden Field, supposed to have been written about 1570, has been generally ascribed to him, either on the ground of vague tradition or from the fact that Ingleton borders on the Craven district, in the dialect of which the poem is written. The opening lines indicate that the author was no novice at ballad writing, while the partiality constantly shown for the house of Stanley and the Lancastrian forces seems to indicate some connection between the author and the Stanley family.

The earliest existing manuscript of the ballad is in the British Library (Harl. MS 3526), with a long title commencing 'Heare is the Famous Historie in Songe called Floodan Field'. It bears no date, but was probably written about 1636. The first printed edition was published under the title of *Floddan Field in nine fits, being an exact history of that famous memorable battle fought between the English and Scots on Floddan-Hill, in the time of Henry the Eight, anno 1513: worthy of the perusal of the English nobility* (1664). There were three more editions in the second half of the eighteenth century, and two critical editions in the nineteenth.

THOMAS SECCOMBE, *rev.* J. K. M^cGINLEY

Sources Cooper, *Ath. Cantab.*, 2.118 · T. D. Whitaker, *The history and antiquities of the deanery of Craven, in the county of York*, 3rd edn, ed. A. W. Morant (1878) · Watt, *Bibl. Brit.* · J. P. Collier, ed., *A bibliographical and critical account of the rarest books in the English language*, 2 vols. (1865)

Jackson, Richard (1623–1690x95), antiquary and physician, son of Gilbert Jackson (*d.* 1662) and his wife, Ann Leyland, was born at Cuerden, near Preston, Lancashire. Having been a pupil of Mr Sherburn at Leyland, Lancashire, he was admitted a commoner of St Mary Hall, Oxford, in 1638. On the outbreak of the civil war he moved to Emmanuel College, Cambridge, where he graduated BA in 1642.

In 1646 Jackson returned to Oxford, graduated MA on 22 March, and was elected vice-principal of St Mary Hall and tutor. He was a staunch royalist, and declined the office of proctor of the university rather than submit to the parliamentary government. He then began to study medicine, and in 1652 was appointed 'replicant to all inceptors of physic', an office which qualified him for the degree of MD. After paying the fees, however, he again declined to take the required oath, and it was not until some time after the Restoration, on 26 March 1663, that he was made MD.

At that time Jackson was already living in Preston and practising as a physician. He appears as a freeman of the borough on the guild merchant rolls of 1662 and 1682. According to Anthony Wood he neglected his practice, and devoted himself to the study of antiquities and genealogy. In conjunction with Christopher Townley of Carr Hall he contemplated the publication of a complete history of Lancashire, but the project was frustrated by Townley's death in 1674. Fourteen years later Jackson issued proposals for publishing his work under the title of 'Brigantia Lancastriensis restaurata, or, History of the honourable dukedom or county palatine of Lancaster, in 5 vols. in folio'. The work was not completed, but the collections for it remain in the College of Arms (abstract by John Palmer, 1842, in Bodl. Oxf., MS Eng. misc. e. 44), Chetham's Library, Manchester (MUN c. 1 6 1–3), the British Library (MS Harl. 7386), and the Lancashire Record Office (DDX 1348). A fragmentary itinerary of some parts of Lancashire by Jackson is given in J. P. Earwaker's *Local Gleanings* (1876).

Jackson was a friend of Sir William Dugdale, and acted as his deputy and marshal at a visitation held at Lancaster. He also associated with Catholic antiquaries, such as the former royalist officer William Blundell (1620–1698) of Little Crosby, whom he assisted in enquiries into Blundell's genealogy following Dugdale's heraldic visitation in 1664–5. He died between 1690 and 1695.

C. W. SUTTON, rev. D. R. WOOLF

Sources W. Blundell and others, 'The Great Hodge Podge', Lancs. RO, DDBI. Acc. 6121, fols. 76v–78r · Wood, *Ath. Oxon.*, new edn, 2.94, 275 · W. Dugdale, *The visitation of the county palatine of Lancaster, made in the year 1664–5*, ed. F. R. Raines, 3 vols., Chetham Society, 84–5, 88 (1872–3) · J. P. Earwaker, ed., *Local gleanings relating to Lancashire and Cheshire*, rev. edn, 1 (1876) · J. Whitaker, *The history of Manchester: in four years*, 2nd edn, 2 vols. (1773) · *The diary of Ralph Thoresby*, ed. J. Hunter, 2 vols. (1830) · E. Baines and W. R. Whatton, *The history of the county palatine and duchy of Lancaster*, new edn, ed. J. Croston and others, 5 vols. (1888–93)
Archives BL, Lancashire transcripts, 1688, Harley MS 7386 · Chetham's Library, Manchester, Lancashire notes and an index compiled in 1850, MUN c 1 6 1–3 · Coll. Arms, Kuerden MSS, Lancashire notes · Lancs. RO, historical notes on the townships of Leyland hundred, DDX 1348 | Bodl. Oxf., abstract of Kuerden's MSS at College of Arms by John Palmer, MS Eng. misc. e 44

Jackson, Richard (1704/5–1782), benefactor, was the son of Richard Jackson, a clerk, of Blurton, Staffordshire. He was educated at Mr Hargreaves's school at Trentham, Staffordshire, and at Trinity College, Cambridge, which he entered, aged eighteen, on 27 September 1723. He became a scholar in 1725, graduated BA in 1727, and was elected a fellow of the college in 1730; he proceeded MA in 1731 and was incorporated MA at Oxford in 1739. He married Katherine Willington (d. 1762), second daughter of Waldyve Willington of Hurley, Atherstone, Warwickshire; their marriage, the date of which is unknown, did not produce any children. By 1775 Jackson was living at Tarrington,

Herefordshire. He died on 24 September 1782 at Hurley Hall, Atherstone, Warwickshire, and was buried with his wife at Kingsbury in the same county. In his will Jackson bequeathed his library and an estate at Upper Longsdon, Staffordshire, to Trinity College for the founding of a professorship in experimental natural philosophy. The holder was to have a 'knowledge in natural Experimental Philosophy … and of Chymistry' but was permitted 'great latitude in the choice of the subjects of his lectures, provided they be of an experimental character' (Gascoigne, 277). The first Jacksonian professor was Isaac Milner, who between 1783 and 1792 followed the founder's request by giving, in alternate years, experiment-based lectures in chemistry and natural philosophy. Milner's successor, Francis Wollaston, continued this format until 1796, when he restricted himself to lectures on chemistry.

PHILIP CARTER

Sources Venn, *Alum. Cant.* · *GM*, 1st ser., 52 (1782), 503 · J. Gascoigne, *Cambridge in the age of the Enlightenment* (1989) · J. R. Tanner, ed., *Historical register of the University of Cambridge … to the year 1910* (1917) · H. M. Innes, ed., *Fellows of Trinity College, Cambridge* (1941)
Wealth at death estate at Upper Longsdon, Staffordshire, bequeathed to establish Jacksonian professorship at Cambridge, 1783: Venn, *Alum. Cant.*

Jackson, Richard (1721/2–1787), politician, was the only son of Richard Jackson (d. 1768) of Weasenham Hall, Norfolk, and his wife, Elizabeth, the daughter of Edmund Clarke. His father, who was from Dublin, was a merchant and a director of the South Sea Company. Although Jackson was brought up as a dissenter, he was educated at Queens' College, Cambridge, entered Lincoln's Inn as a student in 1739, and was called to the bar in 1744. On 22 November 1751 he was admitted *ad eundem* at the Inner Temple, where he became a bencher in 1770, reader in 1779, and treasurer in 1780. He was created standing counsel to the South Sea Company in 1764, was one of the counsel for Cambridge University, and held the post of law officer to the Board of Trade. He was elected FSA in 1781, and was a governor of the Society for the Propagation of the Gospel.

Jackson's main interest was American affairs. He was the agent for Connecticut (1760–70), Pennsylvania (1763–70), and Massachusetts (1765–70). In 1758 he wrote a controversial article on the *Constitution and Government of Pennsylvania*. It was published anonymously in 1759 as he did not want to alienate British public opinion, especially as he was keen to become an MP. On a chance vacancy he was returned to parliament on 1 December 1762 as member for the conjoint borough of Weymouth and Melcombe Regis, and from 1768 to 1784 he sat for the Cinque Port of New Romney. He was appointed secretary to the chancellor of the exchequer in the Grenville administration, but he was not, as Lord Edmund Fitzmaurice called him, 'the private secretary of George Grenville' in 1765, and there is no evidence of any correspondence between the two men.

Jackson's first and last speeches in the Commons concerned American issues. He had been a close friend of Benjamin Franklin since the early 1750s, and, not surprisingly, he warned the Commons against applying the

Stamp Act to the American colonies. The subsequent war severed his many connections and friendships in the colonies. In later years he was known as the intimate friend of Lord Shelburne. When Shelburne formed his ministry in July 1782, Jackson was made a lord of the Treasury, and he held that office until the following April. Jackson was admired by many of his contemporaries. Burke considered him 'a very sensible and informed man' (Burke, 2.329). From his extraordinary stores of knowledge he was known as Omniscient Jackson, but Johnson, in speaking of him, altered the adjective to 'all-knowing', on the ground that the former word was 'appropriated to the Supreme Being' (Boswell, 730). When Henry Thrale was considering a journey in Italy he was advised by Johnson to consult Jackson, who afterwards returned the compliment by remarking of the *Journey to the Western Islands* that 'there was more good sense upon trade in it than he should hear in the House of Commons in a year, except from Burke' (ibid., 826). He is introduced into 'The old benchers of the Inner Temple' in Lamb's *The Essays of Elia*.

Jackson died, unmarried, aged sixty-five, on 6 May 1787 at Southampton Buildings, Chancery Lane. His considerable fortune was divided between his two sisters.

W. P. COURTNEY, rev. J.-M. ALTER

Sources L. B. Namier, 'Jackson, Richard', HoP, *Commons* · *The papers of Benjamin Franklin*, 3–5, ed. L. W. Labaree and W. J. Bell (1961–2); 6, ed. L. W. Labaree and R. L. Ketcham (1963) · C. van Doren, *Benjamin Franklin* (1938) · [E. Burke], *The correspondence of Edmund Burke*, 2, ed. L. S. Sutherland (1960) · *Letters and papers of Benjamin Franklin and Richard Jackson, 1753–1785*, ed. C. van Doren (1947) · J. Boswell, *The life of Samuel Johnson*, 2 vols. (1791) · *Life of William, earl of Shelburne ... with extracts from his papers and correspondence*, ed. E. G. P. Fitzmaurice, 1 (1875), 321–2 · C. Lamb, *The essays of Elia*, [another edn], ed. A. Ainger (1883), 127 · *GM*, 1st ser., 34 (1764), 603 · *GM*, 1st ser., 57 (1787), 454 · Venn, *Alum. Cant.* · Nichols, *Lit. anecdotes*, 8.466

Wealth at death considerable fortune: DNB; GM, 57

Jackson, Robert (*bap.* 1750, *d.* 1827), military surgeon and medical writer, was born at Stonebyres, Lanarkshire, Scotland, and baptized on 15 July 1750 at Wandel, Lanarkshire, the son of Laurence Jackson, a small farmer. After an early schooling at Wandel and Crawford he was apprenticed for three years to a surgeon at Biggar. In 1768 he joined the medical classes at Edinburgh where he spent three winters. He left without a degree. In 1774 he sailed for Jamaica, where he acted as assistant to a doctor at Savanna-la-Mer from 1774 to 1778, and was called on to help the sick of the 60th regiment of foot. It is said he found slavery repugnant. He next made his way to New York, with the intention of fighting in the war against the American colonists. Instead he was given the duties of surgeon-mate in the 71st regiment in view of his medical background. His regiment travelled through the southern colonies of Georgia, the Carolinas, and Virginia, where he observed a high death rate due to fevers. He returned to Britain in the summer of 1782 before the end of the war and began two years of wandering through Europe. In 1784 he married his first wife, the daughter of Dr Stephenson of Edinburgh, and niece of Colonel Francis Shelley; they had four children. His second wife, whom he married much later, was the daughter of J. H. Tidy, the rector of Redmarshall. There are no known children from his second marriage. Marriage gave him financial security for the first time and he left Britain to pursue medical studies in Paris. From Paris he proceeded to Leiden, where he passed an examination for MD in 1785.

Jackson established a medical practice in Stockton-on-Tees, co. Durham, chosen for its association with Colonel Francis Shelley, his wife's uncle and a personal friend. While in Stockton he published in 1791 *A treatise on the fevers of Jamaica with observations on the intermittent fever of America; and an appendix containing some hints on the means of preserving the health of soldiers in hot climates* (German translation 1796). It marked the beginning of an extended medical preoccupation with fevers, particularly the yellow fever. With the outbreak of war with France in 1793, Jackson sought the post of physician to the army for service in the West Indies based on his previous experience. Not being connected with the College of Physicians of London he was ineligible for the office of army physician and accepted the post of surgeon to the 3rd regiment of foot, but he received the promotion in 1794, owing to the personal intervention of the duke of York, army commander in Europe, and Lieutenant-General Harcourt who recognized his abilities. They valued his experience of army diseases and held in low esteem those hospital physicians who had no experience of army diseases prior to appointment. Very shortly afterwards his rank was raised again to that of inspector of hospitals against the advice of the army medical board. His very rapid promotion quickly brought him into sustained conflict with medical chiefs in London. His next posting was with the British expeditionary force to Santo Domingo in 1796. He remained in Santo Domingo until 1798, when he returned to Stockton via the United States. In the same year he published *An outline of the history and cure of fever, epidemic and contagious; more especially of jails, ships, and hospital: the concentrated endemic, vulgarly the yellow fever of the West Indies* (German edition 1804). This was based on his observations of fever cases in Flanders, Holland, and Santo Domingo. Following the intervention of the duke of York he was promoted again in 1800 to the position of head of the army depot hospital at Chatham. While at Chatham he introduced changes to the diet of sick patients which led to controversy following an increase in deaths. An inquiry was instituted and although he was found blameless, he felt unable to serve under the officers who had instituted the inquiry. He retired from the army in 1802. Over the period 1802–8 he pursued private practice in Stockton and published works discussing principles for army discipline and for organizing medical departments. His book on army discipline, *A Systematic View of the Formation, Discipline and Economy of Armies* (1804), was the fruit of this period. It was the only work republished after his death. In 1808 he sought to return to army service, but this was blocked by the physician-general and surgeon-general, and in 1809 he assaulted Keate, the surgeon-general (by striking him across the shoulders with his gold-headed cane), for which he suffered six months' imprisonment. This did not end his career in the army. Jackson had many supporters, including Dr McGrigor, afterwards head of the army medical department. In 1811, his old enemies being out of the way, he was recalled from his retirement at Stockton to be medical director in the West Indies, a post he held until 1815. In 1817 he published a summation of his life work on fever: *A sketch of the history and cure of febrile diseases, more particularly as they appear in the West Indies among soldiers of the British army*. Although almost seventy, in 1819, when yellow fever was in Spain, he visited the Mediterranean. The results were published in 1821 as *Remarks on the epidemic yellow fever, which has appeared at intervals, on the south coast of Spain, since the year 1800*. Jackson died of paralysis at Thursby, near Carlisle, on 6 April 1827. He was survived by his second wife.

Jackson was of middle height, muscular, blue-eyed, and inclined to be florid. His army career was weakened, indeed damaged, by dramatic conflicts with more senior officers within the army medical department and his career may have suffered in the long run from excessive reliance on the duke of York for patronage. The medical subject of greatest interest to him was the study of fevers. He was able to study both the fevers that plagued British armies in Europe which he regarded as characteristically contagious, and the fevers that plagued British armies in the Caribbean which he regarded as characteristically non-contagious. At a symptomatic level he regarded these two categories of fever as not being easily distinguishable. He regarded yellow fever as the exemplary form fevers took in the Caribbean and North America (the 1793 Philadelphia epidemic, for example) and his views on it remained stable over time. In the debates over epidemic yellow fever he came down on the side of non-contagion and non-importation from a foreign source. Positively, he thought it characteristic of tropical climates, called forth by local conditions, and that it attacked newly arrived persons or strangers, particularly European strangers. When he observed yellow fever in Spain he emphasized significant differences between the Spanish and Caribbean forms of the disease, pointing out that in Spain it affected ordinary Spanish natives and not strangers, and arguing that the Caribbean form afflicted with more violence. In his views on non-contagion and non-importation from a foreign source he was firmly in line with much early nineteenth-century thinking about yellow fever.

NORRIS D. SAAKWA-MANTE

Sources R. Jackson, *A view of the formation, discipline and economy of armies*, 3rd edn (1845), xvii–cxx · T. Barnes, *Transactions of the Provincial Medical and Surgical Association*, 3 (1835), 405–31 · J. Borland, *Edinburgh Medical and Surgical Journal*, 29 (1828), 110–18 · *GM*, 1st ser., 97/1 (1827), 566 · *DNB*
Likenesses engraving, repro. in Jackson, *A view of the formation … of armies*

Jackson, Robert Edmund Scoresby- (*bap.* 1833, *d.* 1867), physician and geographer, was born Robert Edmund Jackson, probably at Whitby, Yorkshire, and was baptized there on 12 November 1833, the youngest of the eleven children born to Captain Thomas Jackson (1787–1873), merchant mariner and later shipowner of Whitby, and

Arabella (1792–1881), third and youngest daughter of William *Scoresby the elder (1760–1829), and sister of William *Scoresby the younger (1789–1857). Jackson trained for the medical profession at St George's Hospital, London, and afterwards at Paris and Edinburgh where he made a particular study of materia medica under Robert Christison. He became FRCS in 1859, FRSE in 1861, and FRCP in 1862. He lectured on materia medica and therapeutics in Surgeons' Hall, Edinburgh, and in 1865 was appointed physician to the Edinburgh Royal Infirmary; soon afterwards he became lecturer on clinical medicine. He published *Note-Book of Materia medica* (1866), and four revised editions of the work were issued after his death.

On the death of his uncle William Scoresby in 1857 Jackson assumed the additional name of Scoresby, and as Scoresby-Jackson on 14 September 1859 he married Elizabeth Whyte Johnston (*b.* 1830), only child of Sir William Johnston and his wife, Margaret Pearson, of Kirkhill House, Kirkhill, Edinburgh. They had two daughters, Margaret (*d.* 1939) and Arabella (*d.* 1927). Elizabeth's father was a well-known geographical publisher and the brother of Alexander Keith Johnston, the distinguished geographer. It was this geographical connection and his kinship with the Scoresby family which led Scoresby-Jackson to publish the works on which his reputation was made.

Scoresby-Jackson's interest in geography began with his MD thesis (1857) on climate, health, and disease. He went on to publish *Medical climatology: a topographical and meteorological description of localities resorted to in winter and summer by invalids* (1862); the work is based on his personal observations of European resorts between 1855 and 1861, though he also discusses the climates of places such as Australia, Canada, and the West Indies. Always tending to advise moderation, whether in bathing, exercise, or clothing, Scoresby-Jackson was assiduous in gathering climatic details which were sensibly interpreted: but he has little new to say and the work comes to life only when he quotes from *Physical Geography*, written by his wife's uncle, Keith Johnston. For some time Scoresby-Jackson was chairman of the medical department of the Scottish Meteorological Society and he published a paper on the influence of weather on disease and mortality in the *Transactions of the Royal Society of Edinburgh* in 1863. He remains best-known for his life of his uncle, William Scoresby, published in 1861. It is a sympathetic account of a man who captured the public imagination for his lonely scientific endeavours and selfless following of his Christian vocation.

Scoresby-Jackson died at 32 Queen Street, Edinburgh, on 1 February 1867, of typhus fever, in the presence of his father-in-law. An article by him on typhus fever had appeared in the *Edinburgh Medical Journal* just a month earlier. His medical and scientific writings, though not of the first order, together make a respectable body of work, particularly for one who died aged only thirty-three.

ELIZABETH BAIGENT

Sources m. cert. · *IGI* · *One hundred years of map making: the story of W. & A. K. Johnston* [1923] · C. Stamp, *The Scoresby family* (privately printed, Otley, 1989) · *DNB* · *The Scotsman* (2 Feb 1867) · *The Lancet* (9

Feb 1867) · *BMJ* (9 Feb 1867) · d. cert. · *The Athenaeum* (16 Feb 1867), 225–5

Likenesses photograph, repro. in Stamp, *The Scoresby family*, 14

Jackson, Sir **Robert Gillman Allen** (1911–1991), international administrator, was born on 8 November 1911 in Hawksburn, a suburb of Melbourne, Australia, the second son of Archibald Jackson (1858–1928), Scottish engineer and businessman, and his second wife, Kathleen Crooke (1872–1943), a nurse, daughter of Peter Williams, an Anglo-Irish farmer and vet, and his wife, Minnie Elizabeth, *née* Allen. He was given the names Wilbur Kenneth (after the doctor who delivered him) but changed them by deed poll in 1937 before he married. After attending Cheltenham state school from 1918 he went in 1922 to Mentone grammar school, which his father had helped to found. He excelled at work and games and became school captain. His father's death in 1928 deprived him of a university education, so he entered the Royal Australian Navy in 1929 as a paymaster-cadet, having won a cadetship, beating 180 candidates. Admiral Sir Wilbraham Ford, British commander of the Australian naval squadron, recognized his ability and in 1938 took him to Malta. British policy at that time was that Malta could not be defended. Paymaster-Lieutenant Jackson wrote a paper showing that it could, provided that the civilian population was protected and supplied with essentials, since its co-operation would be vital, particularly in maintaining the naval dockyard. Existing tunnels should be extended, and shelters, stores, and vital services put underground. Ford submitted Jackson's paper to the Admiralty; the arrival of their signal 'all proposals approved, proceed with all despatch' was one of the greatest moments of his life. But the RAF was not persuaded, and it was not until July 1939 that the British government accepted the navy's view and reversed its policy. Jackson spent the next two years organizing supplies and supervising the loading of convoys in England and Alexandria. Malta narrowly avoided starvation; its survival as an operational base played a crucial part in the allies' victory in north Africa. For his part, Jackson was appointed OBE in 1941.

In November 1941 the government posted Paymaster-Commander Jackson to Cairo—but as a civil servant. The Middle East Supply Centre (MESC) had been set up to develop local production of food and materials, so as to leave shipping space available for military supplies. MESC's operations extended over the Middle East and much of Africa. Jackson was appointed director in January 1942. He worked closely with the military authorities, introduced import licensing, and won the confidence of governments; given the variety of problems in the different territories this called for diplomacy and expertise. He inaugurated a long-term anti-locust campaign (for which he was appointed CMG in 1944). When the USA entered the war, he invited Americans to join the MESC team; this partnership flourished for two years. Jackson saw MESC as a model for future international co-operation, but as wartime pressures abated nations wanted independence. MESC was nevertheless the precursor of the regional economic commissions later set up by the United Nations.

In 1943 the United Nations Relief and Rehabilitation Administration (UNRRA) was created to bring relief and supplies to the peoples of nations devastated by war and to assist the millions of displaced persons. By the end of 1944 it was in difficulties, and in February 1945 the British government appointed Jackson senior deputy director-general—effectively chief executive (the director-general being the American Herbert Lehman). Jackson fired and hired on a large scale, recruiting generals as they were demobilized. After reorganizing the London office he was based in Washington, where he kept pressure on political leaders to provide financial support. UNRRA eventually sent relief to much of Europe and part of China. Some of these areas were under communist control and in 1946 the USA refused to provide further funds. Altogether UNRRA supplied $3 billion worth of food and equipment and dealt with 8.5 million displaced persons. It was the biggest UN relief operation ever mounted. When Jackson left UNRRA in August 1947 he had three major achievements to his credit. He was still only thirty-six, but after working non-stop for ten years was exhausted. His marriage to Una Margaret Dick (b. 1911), only daughter of Ronald Dick of Hobart, Australia, in 1937 had failed. He had fallen for Barbara Mary *Ward (1914–1981), the economist and leading Catholic, and had joined the Roman church.

In November 1947 Trygve Lie, secretary-general of the United Nations, offered Jackson a post as an additional assistant secretary-general for co-ordination. The British government agreed that he should go there provided the conditions were satisfactory. In the event they were not, but he took the job, maintaining that he was acting under orders. By mid-April 1948 he was in post; in mid-August he was fired. Lie had found him 'too strong'; some of the assistant secretaries-general also felt threatened. The post had, in Lie's view, proved unsatisfactory and was abolished. Jackson was shattered. He later claimed that the main reason for his dismissal was a disagreement with Lie concerning Israel. The British government then kept him occupied for two years; he spent the next two in Australia setting up a new ministry of national development, returning to England to marry Barbara Ward on 16 November 1950, having been granted a papal dispensation. During 1952 he advised the governments of India and Pakistan on their development plans.

In 1953 the British government appointed Jackson special commissioner in charge of the preparatory commission for the Volta River aluminium scheme in the Gold Coast. He reported in 1956 that the project—to build a dam, power station, aluminium smelter, and bauxite mine—was sound, provided that the aluminium companies could operate their smelter profitably; that would depend on the government's price for electricity. Nothing came of the project at that stage, partly because the Gold Coast was about to be granted independence as Ghana. Once again uncertain of his future, Jackson agreed to stay on as chairman of the Development Commission and adviser to President Nkrumah. In 1958 the American government became interested; the firm of Henry J. Kaiser then recommended major changes to the scheme (relocating the dam and using imported bauxite); in January 1962 the two governments and the World Bank agreed to provide the loans. The dam was inaugurated in 1966. Jackson was made KB in 1956 and KCVO in 1961 after organizing arrangements for the queen's visit to Ghana.

In 1962 Jackson returned to the UN as consultant to Paul Hoffman, then managing director of the special fund and later administrator of the United Nations Development Programme (UNDP). He advised on technical assistance and pre-investment aid to developing countries, inspecting projects in many parts of the world. Multi-purpose river projects (including the Mekong) were his particular interest. In 1968 Hoffman asked him to undertake a study of the capacity of the UN development system (then rapidly expanding), on the assumption that its funding would double in five years. He asked Margaret Joan Anstee (*b.* 1926), an experienced resident representative of UNDP, to be his chief assistant. This marked the start of a close and enduring personal and professional partnership. His marriage to Barbara Ward had failed; their son, aged twelve, was at school in England, under his father's caring eye. The 'Capacity study' was published in November 1969. One of its main conclusions was that many of UNDP's projects were not in the best interests of the nations they were intended to assist, being the result of selling pressure by the specialized agencies. It recommended that projects should be related to a country's own development plan. 'Country programming' required a new administrative structure: maximum devolution of responsibility to country level, where governments and 'resreps' could decide what should be provided by UNDP, combined with maximum central control of the agencies through UNDP's power of the purse as sole funding organization for technical assistance. The concept was simple but the study was exhaustive, covering all aspects of the system. Though welcomed by many, it was strongly opposed by the senior officials of UNDP and the agencies; its likening of the system to a dinosaur caused offence, particularly to Hoffman. Its recommendations were broadly accepted by the governing council, but somewhat watered down; the resulting 'consensus' was formally adopted in December 1970. In the event, over the next few years donor governments' support for UNDP declined sharply. Subsequent attempts to improve the system recognized that Jackson's analysis was right and was still relevant.

Hoffman dispensed with Jackson's services at the end of 1971; in March 1972 the new secretary-general, Kurt Waldheim, asked him to take charge of the UN relief operation in Bangladesh, then suffering from the aftermath of devastating floods and civil war. Millions of refugees were returning from India and there was a danger of widespread starvation. The main ports were blocked by sunken ships, the monsoon was approaching, and the UN relief operation had not been going well.

> At long last in Bangladesh we switched from quixotic amateurism to large-scale professionalism. Jackson's enormous experience was coupled with imagination, drive,

a world view, and a comprehensive approach which covered politics, finance, availability of supplies, shipping, transport and communications, the weather, crop prospects, grain futures, and the morale of all the people he was dealing with. (Urquhart, 231)

Not in good health, Jackson gave his all, saw what had to be done and what could wait, insisted that the UN system spoke with one voice, and briefed donor governments in his hard-hitting yet breezy style. He had a tiny office in New York and travelled frequently to Dacca. This was the most successful UN operation since UNRRA, handling $5 billion of aid, and a model of how these things could be done. Other appointments followed as co-ordinator of UN assistance, including that to Zambia, suffering as a result of UN sanctions against Rhodesia (1973–7), to Indo-China in the aftermath of the Vietnam War (1975–7), and finally to Kampuchea (1979–84). When Pol Pot was driven out by Vietnamese forces many thousands of Khmers (including Khmers Rouges) fled to the border with Thailand. Humanitarian aid was urgently needed within Kampuchea and on the border. The UN general assembly voted to give Kampuchea's seat to the Khmer Rouge, not to the new regime in Phnom Penh. In 1981 Western governments confined their support to the border relief operation, leaving Kampuchea dependent on the USSR and its allies. In this frustrating political minefield Jackson never put a foot wrong, with the result that hundreds of thousands of lives were saved within Kampuchea and on the border. In 1986 Jackson was made a companion of the Order of Australia. After suffering a severe stroke in New York in December 1987 he returned to England, where he died at his home, at Fairacres, Roehampton, Surrey, on 12 January 1991. He was cremated at Putney Vale on 21 January, and his ashes were taken to Australia for burial at Cheltenham, Victoria. He was survived by Dame Margaret Anstee and by the son of his second marriage.

Jacko (as he was nicknamed) was a world citizen, yet remained resolutely Australian with a sense of humour to match; he spoke no foreign languages, yet could communicate with ease. An imposing figure, with an air of authority, he was a natural leader who inspired the loyalty of his staff, of whom he expected much and to whom he was considerate and generous when they had personal problems. He did not suffer fools gladly, nor did he court popularity. He was held in great affection by many, yet remained a very private person. The 'Capacity study' was a landmark; nevertheless Jackson's greatest achievements were in actions not words, in Malta, UNRRA, and Bangladesh. As a relief operator and master of logistics he was unsurpassed.   JAMES GIBSON

Sources priv. coll. · private information (2004) · personal knowledge (2004) · *The Times* (17 Jan 1991) · *WWW* · British government's decision to defend Malta, July 1939, PRO, PRO/CAB2/9 · appointment to UN, Nov 1947–Jan 1948, PRO, PRO/FO371/72645 · B. Urquhart, *A life in peace and war* (1987)

Archives Bodl. Oxf., papers relating to service with UN, MSS Eng c 4676–4678, 4733 · priv. coll., MSS | Bodl. Oxf., transcripts of interviews with Richard Symonds on 4 April and 27 June 1990 for United Nations Career Records Project · Col. U., Herbert H. Lehman MSS, oral history memoir of Sir Robert G. A. Jackson concerning UNRRA with background information about Malta and MESC and personal reminiscences of Edith Lehman and Herbert Lehman • UN Archives Unit, New York, transcripts of oral history interviews carried out for the United Nations by William Powell between November 1985 and February 1986

Likenesses J. Erhardy, bronze bas-relief, 1993 (after photographs), Massachusetts Institute of Technology, Cambridge • J. Cassab, oils, 1996 (after photographs), Palais des Nations, Geneva • photograph, repro. in *The Times*

Wealth at death under £115,000—effects in England: probate, 18 Feb 1991, *CGPLA Eng. & Wales*

Jackson, Samuel (1786–1861). *See under* Jackson, Thomas (1783–1873).

Jackson, Samuel (1794–1869), watercolour painter, was born on 31 December 1794 in Wine Street, Bristol, the son of Samuel Jackson (*d. c.*1821), an accountant and later a partner in a firm of drysalters, and his wife, Margaret (*d. c.*1826). J. L. Roget in his *History of the 'Old Water-Colour' Society* called Jackson 'the father of the School' of Bristol artists (Roget, 2.87). However, Jackson, a kind-hearted, upright, and modest man would have justly rejected the title. He was the artist responsible for hanging the first Bristol artists' exhibition at the new Bristol Institution in 1824, the most important artist behind the first exhibition of the Bristol Society of Artists in 1832, and played a significant role in the early years of the Bristol Fine Arts Academy in the 1850s. He began his career in his father's office but Jackson, Schimmelpenning, and Tyndall ceased trading in 1821 and his earliest surviving watercolours date from the following year. These watercolours are strikingly accomplished and reflect the influence of Francis Danby, of whom one Bristol obituarist says Jackson was a pupil. However, early in 1823 both Jackson and James Johnson were collaborating on equal terms with Danby on a project for a folio of lithographs published later that year. In 1823 Jackson also first exhibited at the Society of Painters in Water Colours. One exhibit was titled *View of the Hotwells and Part of Clifton, Near Bristol* and is probably the large watercolour now in Bristol City Museum and Art Gallery. It shares Danby's fascination with evening sunlight and quiet, contemplative effects. It may also be the first of many occasions when Jackson took excellent advantage of W. H. Pyne's *Microcosm, or, A picturesque delineation of the arts, agriculture, manufactures, etc. … for the embellishment of landscape* (1806), integrating a group of figures borrowed from this book to apt effect. Jackson was elected an associate member of the Society of Painters in Water Colours in 1823, extraordinarily early, but he failed to progress to full membership and, despite exhibiting there regularly, if sparsely, he withdrew his support in 1848.

Jackson's exhibited works reflect his extensive travels. There were many views in Wales, which he certainly visited at least twice before his long walking tour with W. J. Müller and John Skinner Prout in 1833. He had earlier sketched at Lynmouth, Devon, in 1826 with another Bristol artist, E. V. Rippingille. In 1827 Jackson visited the West Indies, subsequently exhibiting views of Trinidad, St Vincent, and Tobago. Not until 1853 did he exhibit a Scottish scene, but Swiss views in both oil as well as watercolour,

resulting from visits in 1853 and 1858, dominated his late work. It is however for his Bristol watercolours that Jackson is now most highly regarded and particularly for those of the mid-1820s with their masterful control of even washes of strong, subtly balanced colours, rather than for the later and mellower works executed with increasingly complex techniques such as sponging and scratching out. Many of the earlier Bristol views were acquired by the Bristol antiquarian and collector G. W. Braikenridge, whose collection is now in the Bristol City Museum and Art Gallery. It provides crucial yardsticks against which to judge the inferior works of his many students, still too often attributed to him. Jackson was an industrious drawing master for over forty years and one obituary greatly lamented the time he had wasted 'teaching the unteachable of misses and masters in private academies' (*Western Daily Press*, 23 Dec 1869). Francis Danby drily observed that Jackson was 'a highly respected Drawing Master … able to screw his heart down for the getting of halfpence' (Danby to John Gibbons, 5 Dec 1835, Gibbons MSS). But Jackson, who is said to have been the best amateur pianist in Bristol, was also a most social artist and often attended the evening drawing parties of the 1820s and early 1830s. He produced many purely imaginary landscapes in monochrome wash as well as larger exhibition watercolours of purely fantastic scenes inspired by Danby's poetic landscape paintings. In 1828 Jackson married Jane Phillips, who was born in 1797 or 1798 at Wotton under Edge, Gloucestershire. They lived first at 2 Trelawney Place, Cotham, until 1831 and then until 1844 at 3 and subsequently 8 Freeland Place, Hotwells, overlooking the Avon. From 1845 the family lived at 1 Cambridge Place in Clifton. When Francis Danby visited his old friend there at Christmas 1860 he would also have met their son Samuel Phillips *Jackson, a successful painter of coastal scenes, and their three talented daughters, whom the census of 1861 described as a teacher of flower painting, a professor of music and singing, and a teacher of singing. Samuel Jackson died at his home on 8 December 1869 and was buried at Arnos Vale cemetery, Bristol. Examples of his work are in Bristol City Museum and Art Gallery; the British Museum and the Victoria and Albert Museum, London; the Yale Center for British Art, Paul Mellon collection; the National Library of Wales, Aberystwyth; Woodspring Museum, Weston-super-Mare; and the Somerset Archaeological and Natural History Society (Somerset County Council Library Service), Taunton. FRANCIS GREENACRE

Sources F. W. Greenacre and S. Stoddard, *The Bristol landscape: the watercolours of Samuel Jackson* (1988) [incl. bibliography] • *Western Daily Press* (23 Dec 1869) • *Daily Bristol Times and Mirror* (25 Dec 1869) • *Art Journal*, 32 (1870), 53 • H. S. Thompson, 'Samuel Jackson, artist, & his sketching club', *The Connoisseur*, 76 (1926), 163–9 • J. L. Roget, *A history of the 'Old Water-Colour' Society*, 2 vols. (1891) • N. N. Solly, *Memoir of the life of William James Müller* (1875) • H. S. Thompson, 'Bygone Bristol artists, 6', *Bristol Times and Mirror* (12 Dec 1925) • S. Stoddard, 'George Weare Braikenridge (1775–1856), a Bristol antiquarian and his collections', MLitt diss., University of Bristol, 1983 • Bristol RO, Gibbons MSS, 41197 • *Matthews' Bristol Directories*

Likenesses J. Fisher, watercolour, *c.*1840, Bristol City Museum and Art Gallery • S. P. Jackson, double portrait, photograph, *c.*1855 (with Francis Danby), Bristol City Museum and Art Gallery, Ada

Villiers album • E. F. West, photograph, c.1860, Bristol City Museum and Art Gallery

Jackson, Samuel Phillips (1830–1904), watercolour painter, was born in Bristol on 4 September 1830, the only son and the eldest of the four children of Samuel *Jackson (1794–1869), also a watercolour painter, and his wife, Jane Phillips (b. 1797/8). He had no formal training but would certainly have both watched and worked closely with his father, and he is known to have attended the life class of the Bristol Fine Arts Academy, of which he was elected a member in December 1850. His earlier works were mostly in oil.

Jackson first exhibited in London in 1851 at the British Institution, and in the following year exhibited at the Royal Academy for the first time. Then, in 1853, after showing six watercolours at the Old Watercolour Society, he became, at twenty-two, the youngest person ever elected a member of that society. Henceforth he worked almost exclusively in watercolour, exhibiting a total of 841 pictures at the society's exhibitions—perhaps more than any other artist; he was elected a full member in 1876. His subjects were mainly coastal scenes in Wales, Devon, and Cornwall. There were also views of the Thames, and he exhibited views of the Lake District in 1857 and 1858, and of the Yorkshire coast in 1863. Only a very small number of views in Switzerland resulted from his visit there in 1858 with his father.

From the early 1850s Jackson's watercolours show exceptional technical accomplishment, blending precise detail with considerable breadth of handling. J. L. Roget aptly observed that they are 'remarkable for clean handling and sober harmony of colour, in which the moist vapours of our west country are suggested by the use of well-concocted greys' (Roget, 2.380). Roget noted Jackson's friendship with the Bristol artist Charles Branwhite, whose use of opaque white may well have influenced him; Roget also mentions the landscape painter Francis Danby as a personal friend of Jackson's. Subsequent writers have assumed this to be a confusion with one of Danby's sons; however, Jackson based an early watercolour of 1852 on Danby's oil painting *An Enchanted Island* (1824) and it was certainly Jackson who photographed his father and Danby in the garden at Cambridge Place, Clifton, about 1855. There is a fine watercolour by Jackson of Danby's last home at Exmouth (1856; priv. coll.). His more ambitious exhibition watercolours—of sunsets, storms, and shipwrecks (which can be rather grandiose)—may well have been inspired by Danby's later oil paintings. His work continued to be based on fresh observation, however, becoming softer in colour, broader in handling, and less reliant on technical virtuosity.

From 1835 Jackson lived at 1 Cambridge Place (now 8 Canynge Square), Clifton, with his family. Only in 1870, the year following his father's death, did he move from the parental home to Rose Cottage, Streatley-on-Thames, near Reading. For the next two years he was seriously ill. In 1876 he moved to 1 River View Terrace, Henley-on-Thames; his elegant steam launch, *Ethel*, was a familiar sight on the river.

In 1888 Jackson returned to Clifton, where his three sisters lived. Isabella, now Mrs Wightwick, had been a teacher of flower painting. Jane was a pianist and a composer of piano music under the name Jules Sivrai; she had married the well-known composer J. L. Roeckel. The youngest sister, Mrs Ada Villiers, had been a teacher of singing and was herself well known locally as a vocalist. Jackson, who reputedly was a brilliant pianist, was also a skilled amateur mechanic and a successful photographer who exhibited widely and earned a prize from the Royal Photographic Society for the invention of an instantaneous shutter. His principal obituarist described him as punctilious, considerate, and generous.

Jackson, who never married, died at his home, 62 Clifton Park Road, Clifton, on 27 January 1904 and was buried at Arnos Vale cemetery. His closest companions had been his dogs, and he left bequests to two canine charities. Examples of his work are in the Bristol City Museum and Art Gallery, and in the Victoria and Albert Museum, London.   FRANCIS GREENACRE

Sources *Western Daily Press* (2 Feb 1904) • *Biographia. A record of public men: past and present—home and abroad*, vol. 1, pt 3 (Newhaven, Sussex, c.1895) • H. S. Thompson, 'Bygone Bristol artists', *Bristol Times and Mirror* (12 Dec 1925) • *DNB* • sale catalogue (1906), drawings and sketches [Alexander, Daniel & Co., Bristol, 28 June 1906] • J. L. Roget, *A history of the 'Old Water-Colour' Society*, 2 (1891), 379–81 • Graves, *RA exhibitors* • *The Royal Watercolour Society: the first fifty years, 1805–1855* (1992) • census returns, 1851

Likenesses J. Watkins, carte-de-visite, NPG • photographs, Bristol City Museum and Art Gallery; on loan

Wealth at death £2284: probate, 9 April 1904, *CGPLA Eng. & Wales*

Jackson, Sir (Francis) Stanley (1870–1947), cricketer and politician, was the second son and seventh child of William Lawies *Jackson, first Baron Allerton (1840–1917), and his wife, Grace, née Tempest (1845–1901). He was born on 21 November 1870 at Chapel Allerton, near Leeds. After schooling at Harrow, he graduated in 1893 from Trinity College, Cambridge. On 5 November 1902 he married Julia Henrietta (d. 1958), eldest daughter of Henry Broadley Harrison-Broadley, of Welton House, Brough, Yorkshire. They had a son, Henry. Stanley Jackson excelled at cricket from his childhood, first coming to prominence during the 1888 Eton–Harrow match, where he scored 80 and took eleven wickets for 68 runs. Awarded a blue by Cambridge, he captained his university's team in 1892 and 1893. In county cricket he represented Yorkshire and later became club president. He won a place in the English team for the 1893 series against Australia, and scored his maiden test century at the Oval. Under his captaincy England won the series against Australia in 1905. He retired from first-class cricket that year, having played twenty test matches and scoring 1412 runs with an average of 48 runs an innings. In 1921 he was elected the president of Marylebone Cricket Club (MCC). As chairman of a special committee appointed by the MCC in 1943, he also took an initiative in recommending important changes in the rules of the game.

Sir (Francis) Stanley Jackson (1870–1947), by Bassano, 1923

Jackson's cricketing career was cut short by his involvement in politics. He inherited an interest in politics from his father, who had represented Leeds in parliament and served as the chief secretary for Ireland in the closing days of Lord Salisbury's second administration. Jackson was first elected to the House of Commons in 1915 as a Conservative, for the Howdenshire division of Yorkshire, and he continued to represent that constituency until 1926. He had a brief stint in the War Office as its finance secretary in 1922–3. He had acquired considerable military experience, having been on the battle front during the Second South African War between 1900 and 1902, and commanded the 2nd / 7th West Yorkshire regiment in the First World War. He succeeded Lord Younger in 1923 as the chairman of the Conservative and Unionist Party and was a close confidant of the prime minister, Stanley Baldwin, a contemporary of his at Harrow. He became a privy councillor in 1926.

In 1927 Jackson was appointed GCIE and became the governor of Bengal presidency in British India, at a time when the province had become the nerve centre of Indian nationalist and protest politics. The outburst against the all-white Simon commission, which was appointed to review the workings of the 1919 constitutional arrangements in British India, Gandhi's civil disobedience movement, revolutionary terrorism, and the rising tempo of peasant and labour militancy combined to pose a threat to the stability of the raj. A committed conservative, Jackson proceeded to meet the crisis with strong-arm methods. He amended the Bengal criminal law and Bengal emergency powers ordinance and enacted the Indian Press Emergency Powers Act, thereby empowering the administration to take action against those suspected of sedition without furnishing prior evidence. Those believed to assist terrorism 'from background' were also brought within the ambit of these laws. The police budget was substantially enhanced. Special stringent regulations were imposed on districts like Chittagong, particularly vulnerable to terrorism. At risk of interfering with the principle of local self-government, Jackson disqualified from employment in the Calcutta corporation anyone with nationalist connections. The corporation was forbidden to sanction grants to institutions which in official eyes had 'politically dangerous' employees. Contemporary nationalist newspapers are replete with instances of police high-handedness against nationalists during Jackson's governorship, one of the worst examples of which was an unprovoked firing upon the detainees in the Hiji detention camp, which killed two and injured several. Mention may also be made of a police assault on an unarmed Congress Party procession on 26 January 1931 led by Subhas Chandra Bose, then mayor of Calcutta. But Jackson remained undeterred by nationalist condemnation for unleashing 'martial law in disguise' (Mitra, July–Dec 1932). Inaugurating the winter session of the Bengal legislative council on 1 February 1932, he remarked: 'I am not here to apologise for the Ordinances … forced upon the Government by those … [bringing] the administration to a standstill' (ibid., Jan–July 1932).

In its obituary The Times celebrated Jackson's contribution to the British administration in India, claiming he 'batted doggedly against bowling of all sorts—fair, unfair, and often malevolent' (The Times). He himself claimed to have kept 'the scales even' (DNB). But he failed to curb revolutionary terrorism in Bengal. Among the high-ranking British civilians who died at terrorist hands during his tenure as the governor of Bengal were R. R. Garlick, the district judge of Alipore; J. M. Peddie, the district magistrate of Midnapore; and C. G. B. Stevens, the district magistrate of Tippera. The Calcutta police commissioner Charles Tegart, the Dacca divisional commissioner A. Cassels, and the president of the Calcutta European Association E. Villers narrowly survived attempts on their lives. Three young Bengali revolutionaries even stormed into the administrative headquarters of Bengal, the Writers' Buildings, and went on a shooting rampage. Shortly before Jackson retired from office in March 1932 a daring attempt was made on his life by Bina Das, a woman graduate, while he was addressing the convocation of Calcutta University. Both he and his wife escaped unhurt, and the governor demonstrated extraordinary coolness by continuing with his speech, once the assailant was removed from the scene.

The Montagu–Chelmsford Act of 1919 had transferred administrative departments of lesser political importance, such as education, health, agriculture, and local administration, to ministers responsible to provincial legislatures. But Jackson considered the act too liberal for what he thought 'the politically discomforting climate' in

Bengal. He did not hesitate to dissolve the Bengal legislative council in April 1929, when he felt it 'showed a disposition to dispense with the assistance of Ministers' (*The Times*). He administered the transferred departments until the end of that year, when a ministry to his liking could be constituted. His governorship nevertheless witnessed the adoption of some developmental schemes. The Bengal (Rural) Primary Education Bill (1930) proposed to levy a cess for a gradual introduction of universal primary education in the countryside. The Bengal Opium Smoking Bill was enacted in 1931 to check use of the drug. To promote industrial growth, the state was authorized to invest in shares and debentures.

Jackson was honoured for his service to the empire. He was appointed GCSI on his retirement in 1932. He was also a knight of grace of the order of St John of Jerusalem. Calcutta and Dacca universities awarded him honorary DLitt degrees, while Sheffield University conferred upon him an honorary LLD. Despite his administrative and political preoccupations, he retained varied interests. For Harrow, his school, he had an abiding concern. He was a governor from 1923 to 1927, and again between 1939 and 1947, and in 1942 he was elected chairman of governors. He also served as a director of the Great Northern Railway, and of the *Yorkshire Post*. Upon his retirement from public life he spent much of his time at Lord's cricket ground, where his portrait by Gerald Reynell hung in the pavilion.

Sir Stanley Jackson met a tragic end. Having survived assassination attempts in India, he was knocked down by a taxi in London and never fully recovered from his injuries. He died on 9 March 1947 at the Hyde Park Hotel, Knightsbridge. SURANJAN DAS

Sources Venn, *Alum. Cant.*, 2/3 • N. N. Mirla, *Indian Annual Register* • *Report on the Administration of Bengal* (1927–32) • *WWW* • *The Times* (10 March 1947) • S. Sarkar, *Modern India* (1973) • *DNB* • B. Green, ed., *The Wisden book of obituaries* (1986) • Burke, *Peerage* (1939) • d. cert.
Archives BL OIOC, corresp. with Lord Birkenhead, Eur. MS D 703 • BL OIOC, corresp. with John Simon, Eur. MS F 77 | FILM BFI NFTVA, film footage
Likenesses Bassano, photograph, 1923, NPG [*see illus.*] • G. Reynell, oils, Lord's cricket ground, London • Spy [L. Ward], caricature, chromolithograph, NPG; repro. in *VF* (28 Aug 1902)
Wealth at death £85,620 1s. 1d.: probate, 15 May 1947, *CGPLA Eng. & Wales*

Jackson, Thomas (1570/71–1646), Church of England clergyman, was born in Lancashire and educated at Cambridge. A sizar of Emmanuel College in 1589, he graduated MA in 1600 and BD in 1608, and proceeded DD in 1615. At Emmanuel he learned a vigorous protestantism and became a diligent preacher.

Jackson served at Wye, Kent, from 1596 (and married about this time), and at Boughton Aluph from 1611 to 1614. On 30 March 1614 he was installed a prebendary in Canterbury Cathedral, holding with the prebend the east Kent livings of Great Chart, then Chilham and Milton by Canterbury, to which Ivychurch was added in 1629. At Canterbury Jackson took a great interest in the business side of the chapter's work, both domestic and external. With extreme application to detail he made himself an average income of £260 a year beyond the £40 of his prebend. His

account book includes lists of his many sermons; he lived in Canterbury but went out frequently to preach in his churches.

Jackson published eight volumes of sermons between 1603 and 1624, with the general theme of judgment upon a sinful nation and the safety of the elect. Anthony Wood says that he 'mostly seemed to be a true son of the church of England' (Wood, *Ath. Oxon.*, 2.669) and Archbishop Laud, considering him 'good and orthodox' gave him in 1636 the Canterbury hospitals of St John Northgate and St Nicholas Harbledon (*Works of … William Laud*, 4.298). However, Jackson testified against Laud at his trial in 1644 that he had in one of his statutes enjoined bowing towards the altar, earning the rejoinder from the archbishop that Jackson had often shifted his opinions in religion (ibid., 223).

Jackson evidently found favour with parliament, as he continued in office until his death in the precincts, Canterbury, in November 1646, but in a codicil to his will in 1644 he complained of a great loss of income 'in such troublesome times' (PRO, PROB 11/201, fols. 205–7). He was buried in Canterbury Cathedral on 13 November 1646. By the time his wife, Elizabeth, was buried there in March 1658, only four of their eleven children were living. One of his sons, also named Thomas, who was rector of St George's, Canterbury, had been among a number of local clergymen who in August 1636 were reported to Laud for tavern-haunting and drunkenness.

C. W. SUTTON, rev. MARGARET SPARKS

Sources Jackson's account book, Dean and Chapter archives, Canterbury, miscellaneous accounts 52 • Thomas Monins's account book, Dean and Chapter archives, Canterbury, Add. MS 50 • T. Jackson, *Davids pastorall poeme, or, A sheepheards song. Seven sermons on the 23. psalme* (1603) • T. Jackson, *Judah must into captivitie: six sermons* (1622) • *The works of the most reverend father in God, William Laud*, 4, ed. J. Bliss (1854), 223, 298 • Wood, *Ath. Oxon.*, new edn, 2.669 • will, Thos. Jackson, PRO, PROB 11/201, fols. 205–7 [Thomas Jackson] • will, Eliz. Jackson, PRO, PROB 11/275, fols. 342–4 [Elizabeth Jackson] • Venn, *Alum. Cant.* • *Fasti Angl.*, 1541–1857, [Canterbury] • *CSP dom.*, 1634–7 • Fourth report, HMC, 3 (1874), 125 • *Walker rev.*, 219 • Emmanuel College, Cambridge, records
Wealth at death owned at least four houses in Canterbury and land; expected annuities to be paid out of rents

Jackson, Thomas (*bap.* 1578, *d.* 1640), dean of Peterborough, was baptized at Witton-le-Wear, Durham, on 21 December 1578, one of six children and the second son of Henry Jackson of Smelthouse, a substantial yeoman farmer, and of his wife, Elizabeth. On his father's death, probably in late 1587 or shortly after, he inherited land in Ferrye on the Hill. The family intended him for commerce at Newcastle, where Jackson relations included merchants and civic dignitaries. At the urging of the local magnate, Lord Eure, however, he was sent to Queen's College, Oxford, where he matriculated on 25 June 1596; Richard Crakanthorpe was his tutor. Jackson obtained a scholarship at Corpus Christi College on 24 March 1597, and shortly afterwards a narrow escape from drowning convinced him he was reserved for some high purpose. Having graduated BA on 23 July 1599 and proceeded MA on 9 July 1603, he was ordained deacon and priest on 24 February and 22 September 1605 respectively, and was finally elected probationer fellow of the college on 10 May 1606. About 1609 he became tutor to two sons of Lord Spencer of Wormleighton, Edward and Richard. Afterwards he was 'ever in singular veneration with that whole Family, and their Alliances' (D. Lloyd, *Memoires*, 1668, 71). Jackson became BD on 25 June 1610 and received a university licence to preach on 11 June 1611. Meanwhile, he held offices in college and gave divinity lectures both there and at Pembroke. In 1616 he was granted the next vacancy of a college living at Trent, Somerset, which was so long in coming that he never took it up.

Jackson used his long wait for fellowship and preferment to become prodigiously, if idiosyncratically, learned. He immersed himself in Latin, Greek, Hebrew, oriental languages, and in many other studies. The college president, John Rainolds, for whose will Jackson was executor, may have inspired an interest in mathematical and occult sciences. According to his biographer, Vaughan, he was especially devoted to metaphysics as an introduction to theology; William Prynne thought he was 'transported beyond himself with Metaphysical contemplations to his own infamy' (W. Prynne, *Antiarminianism*, 1630, 270). Jackson had a predilection for natural theology and rational exposition of faith. His writings, and the books he is known to have possessed, moreover, show him to have been, for an Oxford man of his time, exceptionally steeped in Neoplatonism and unusually critical of Aristotle's indifference to matters divine; he had much in common with the Cambridge Platonists. Jackson became a friend of Joseph Mede, and knew the Little Gidding set and Nicholas Ferrar, for whose translation of a work by the Spaniard Juan de Valdés, posthumously published at Oxford in 1638, he was to provide a censure and possibly editorial help.

Jackson's independent mind led him, by his own account, to reject the Calvinist doctrine of absolute election or reprobation about 1605, and he was preaching against it privately in college by 1612. Prudently the theses for his DD on 27 June 1622 disputed anti-Catholic questions inoffensive to Calvinists, but from the mid-1620s, when the world was more receptive to Arminian ideas, he argued in print ever more daringly that Christ had died to save all, and that assertion of an absolute decree of reprobation drove men to hatred of God or to popery. He remained belligerently anti-Catholic, insisting that the pope was Antichrist and regarding infallibility and transubstantiation as major heresies upon which even apparently sound Catholic beliefs were falsely constructed. None the less, he allowed Rome to be in some sense a true church and was agnostic as to a pre-Reformation visible church.

In 1613 Jackson began publishing, in a volume dedicated to his patron, Lord Eure (*d.* 1617), the great series of commentaries on the apostles' creed in twelve books that is his major theological achievement. The first nine books and a portion of the twelfth were to be printed in his lifetime.

Preferment eventually came to Jackson, probably through the influence of Bishop Richard Neile of Durham, to whom he became chaplain [*see also* Durham House group]. He was instituted on 27 November 1623 to the important vicarage of St Nicholas, Newcastle, in the gift of Bishop Richard Milbourne of Carlisle, probably as a known anti-Calvinist with local connections, specifically to forestall a Cambridge-educated puritan and protégé of Seth Ward, Robert Jenison, who also had influential Newcastle relatives and desired the living. Jackson was allowed to remain in Oxford for most of 1624, and resigned his fellowship only in January 1625. In the latter year he was presented by Neile to the rectory of Winston, Durham, and dispensed to hold it with Newcastle. For six years he lived principally in the north. Finding Newcastle a place 'wherein Knox, Mackbray, and Udal had sown their tares' (T. Jackson, *Works*, 9, 1844, 550–51), he countered puritanism and assailed excessive reliance on predestination. He came into open doctrinal dispute with Jenison, who was assisted in upholding the synod of Dort by leading Calvinists such as Seth Ward, Thomas Gataker, and Bishop John Davenant. Jackson was ably assisted by his lecturer, and eventual successor at Newcastle, Yeldard Alvey. It was probably Neile who procured Jackson's nomination as a royal chaplain about this time.

In 1628 Jackson published the first part of his *Treatise of the Divine Essence and Attributes*, the sixth book of his commentaries, which openly argued against unconditional predestination and sided with Arminius on free will. Despite his eirenic suggestion that the approaches might be reconciled, he was censured the same year in the House of Commons, where his former pupil, Richard Spencer, was prominent in the minority of members who defended Arminians. From this time Jackson was publicly associated with Arminianism.

The *Treatise*, Jackson's most controversial publication, was dedicated to William, earl of Pembroke, chancellor of the university, which suggests a return to Oxford may have seemed imminent. Indeed, when Neile became bishop of Winchester and visitor of Corpus Christi College in 1628 he sought to replace the scandal-ridden president, Dr Thomas Anyan, with Jackson, who certainly visited Oxford around this time. Daniel Featley believed Neile's ulterior intention was to make Jackson regius professor of divinity to 'spaune yong Arminians' (MS Rawl. D.47, fol. 16r) as soon as the Calvinist John Prideaux could be removed by preferment. In the event Anyan was replaced in 1629 with John Holt and Prideaux remained, but after Holt's death the following year Jackson, recommended by Charles I, was elected president in January 1631. The college prospered in the nine years of his tenure, and a previously faction-ridden community lived peaceably. On election Jackson resigned his northern livings. On 18 July 1632 the king, during the vacancy at Winchester following Neile's elevation to York, presented Jackson to the vicarage of Witney, Oxfordshire.

Meanwhile, Jackson's *Treatise* was attacked in 1631 by William Twisse, the Aristotelian Calvinist rector of Newbury, in *A Discovery of D. Jackson's Vanity*, and he was among those targeted at Oxford in September 1632 in satirical verses entitled 'The academicall army of epidemicall Arminians'. None of this prevented further advancement. He was presented by the king on 16 March 1635 to a canonry of Winchester, obtaining royal dispensation for non-residence. Later, by Archbishop Laud's procurement, he received the deanery of Peterborough on 17 January 1639. He may have had scruples about pluralism, for he resigned his living at Witney in late 1637 and offered unsuccessfully to surrender his Winchester canonry. However, early in 1640 Laud intervened with the vice-chancellor to prevent Jackson publishing sermons which would have complemented collections printed previously in 1617, 1625, and 1637, but would have contravened the royal moratorium on controversial theology.

His biographer suggests that Jackson suffered much at this time from a presentiment of coming troubles and concern for his fellow north countrymen following invasion from Scotland. He died, unmarried, in college on 21 September 1640, and was buried by his request in the college chapel. By his will, dated 5 September, and proved on 2 October, he bequeathed a few books to his college and others to a servant. One-third of Jackson's residual estate went to a married niece. He left his manuscripts to the overseers of his will, his 'deare & loving Brother', Gilbert Sheldon, and his 'loving friend' (and successor) in college, Robert Newlin, 'to be perused & published as they thinke fitt'.

As urged by Archbishop Ussher of Armagh at the funeral, Newlin carefully preserved the papers, but it was Sheldon's advocacy and the editorial work of Barnabas Oley that brought most of Jackson's unpublished work, including the remaining books of commentaries on the creed, to print between 1653 and 1657, and a three-volume near complete edition of the works was published in 1672–3. Oley prefaced his 1653 re-edition of Jackson's first three books of commentaries with a biography by Edmund Vaughan, who had been at Corpus Christi College in the subject's presidency. A twelve-volume complete works appeared at Oxford in 1844. Jackson's works, despite a difficult style and some incoherence, were much esteemed by later generations of high-church and Anglo-Catholic theologians.   A. J. HEGARTY

Sources E. Vaughan, 'The life and death of the Reverend, learned and pious Dr. Jackson', in T. Jackson, *Works* (1844), 1.xxxix–lii · *Reg. Oxf.*, 1.36, 217; 2/2.214; 2/3.216 · Wood, *Ath. Oxon.*, new edn, 2.664–70 · T. Fowler, *The history of Corpus Christi College*, OHS, 25 (1893), 184–93 · R. Howell, *Newcastle upon Tyne and the puritan revolution: a study of the civil war in north England* (1967), 69–71, 84–7 · A. Milton, *Catholic and Reformed: the Roman and protestant churches in English protestant thought, 1600–1640* (1995) · S. Hutton, 'Thomas Jackson, Oxford Platonist, and William Twisse, Aristotelian', *Journal of the History of Ideas*, 39 (1978), 635–52 · N. Tyacke, *Anti-Calvinists: the rise of English Arminianism, c.1590–1640* (1987), 7, 64–7, 77–8, 83–4, 121, 143–4, 159–60 · CCC Oxf., MS 303, fols. 236r–v, 241r–v · CCC Oxf., MS 304, fols. 28r, 30r · M. H. Curtis, *Oxford and Cambridge in transition, 1558–1642* (1959), 209–10, 286–7 · PRO, SP 16/182/64; SP 16/308/98; SP 16/470/177 · J. Davies, *The Caroline captivity of the church: Charles I and the remoulding of Anglicanism, 1625–1641* (1992), 58, 113, 123 · parish register, Witton-le-Wear, SS Philip and John, 21 Dec 1578, Durham RO, EP/WW1 [baptism] · [W. Greenwell], ed., *Wills and inventories from the registry at Durham*, 2, SurtS, 38 (1860), 292–3 · Bodl. Oxf., MS Rawl. D. 47 · Oxf. UA, D-F hypo. 12, fol. 85r

Wealth at death £270 18s.—incl. £109 11s. books and £60 13s. 8d. cash: Oxf. UA inventories, D-F hypo. 12, fol. 85r, inventory of goods, 30/10/1640

Jackson, Thomas (*c*.1715–1781), organist and composer, is of obscure origin. Little is known of his early career, but in 1739 he was elected to the Royal Society of Musicians, and he had become a member of the king's band by 1767. In April 1768 he was appointed organist and master of the song school at Newark-on-Trent, Nottinghamshire, a sought-after post offering a salary of £36 a year, with a house in the churchyard of St Mary Magdalene. Newark was one of the few collegiate parish churches in England whose musical traditions survived after the Reformation, thanks to the munificent endowments provided by the diplomatist and churchman Thomas Magnus in the 1530s. Magnus stipulated that the song school master should select six boys 'apt and meet to learn to sing' and teach them 'their playn Song, pryk Song, descant and to play at the Organs' (*VCH Nottinghamshire*, 2.205). Jackson was married; his wife, Mary, was buried at St Mary Magdalene, Newark, on 18 April 1772.

As a composer Jackson was best known for his *Twelve Psalm Tunes and Eighteen Double and Single Chants*, published in London about 1780, which sold over 300 copies to about 130 subscribers. Many of these four-part pieces were included, invariably in association with different texts, in numerous similar collections up to 1820. His music for Psalm 47, often identified as 'Jackson's' or 'Byzantium', was reprinted no fewer than twenty-seven times and subsequently earned a place in *Hymns Ancient and Modern* (new edition, 1904). Jackson also published *A Favourite Lesson for the Harpsichord or Forte-Piano* (London, *c*.1778), but two songs attributed to him by E. B. Schnapper in *The British Union-Catalogue of Early Music* are actually by Joseph Jackson. In January 1780 he advertised a proposal to publish by subscription *Sixteen Marches, in Seven Real Parts*, but this project evidently never came to fruition. Jackson died in office at Newark, presumably at his house in St Mary Magdalene churchyard. He was buried in Newark, probably at St Mary Magdalene, on 11 November 1781.   IAN BARTLETT

Sources N. Temperley, *The music of the English parish church*, 1 (1979) · N. Temperley, *The hymn tune index*, 4 vols. (1998) · VCH Nottinghamshire, vol. 2 · E. B. Schnapper, ed., *The British union-catalogue of early music printed before the year 1801*, 1 (1957) · Brown & Stratton, *Brit. mus.* · N. G. Jackson, *Newark Magnus: the story of a gift* (1964) · B. Matthews, ed., *The Royal Society of Musicians of Great Britain: list of members, 1738–1984* (1985) · 'Jackson, Thomas', Grove, *Dict. mus.* (1954) · M. Frost, ed., *Historical companion to 'Hymns ancient and modern'* (1962) · *The Torrington diaries: containing the tours through England and Wales of the Hon. John Byng (later Viscount Torrington) between the years 1781 and 1794*, ed. C. B. Andrew, 4 (1938) · Notts. Arch., archives of St Mary Magdalene Church, Newark-on-Trent · account book, St Mary Magdalene Church, Newark-on-Trent, East Nottinghamshire Library, Newark-on-Trent, Nottinghamshire · parish register, Newark-on-Trent, St Mary Magdalene, 11 Nov 1781, Notts. Arch. [burial] · parish register, Newark-on-Trent, St Mary Magdalene, 18 April 1772, Notts. Arch. [burial of Mary, wife]

Archives Notts. Arch., archives of St Mary Magdalene Church, Newark-on-Trent

Jackson, Thomas (1745–1797). *See under* Jackson, Francis James (1770–1814).

Jackson, Thomas (1783–1873), Wesleyan Methodist minister and writer, born at Sancton, a village near Market Weighton, on 12 December 1783, was the second son of Thomas and Mary Jackson. His father was an agricultural labourer. His two brothers, Robert and Samuel, also became ministers in the Wesleyan Methodist Connexion. Thomas was mainly self-taught, being taken from school at twelve years of age to work on a farm. Three years later he was apprenticed to a carpenter at Shipton, a neighbouring village. At every available moment he read and studied, and in July 1801, converted through the preaching of Mary Taft, he joined the Methodist Society and threw his energies into biblical study and religious work. In September 1804 he was sent by the Wesleyan conference as an itinerant preacher to the Spilsby circuit in Lincolnshire and subsequently to Horncastle and Lincoln. In 1809 Jackson married Ann, daughter of Thomas Hollinshead of Horncastle. She died on 24 September 1854, aged sixty-nine. Their son Thomas *Jackson became a Methodist minister. For twenty years Jackson served some of the most important circuits, such as Preston, Wakefield, Manchester, Sheffield, Leeds, and London. His position and influence grew rapidly. From 1824 to 1842 he was editor of the connexional magazines, and, despite his lack of a liberal education in youth, he performed his duties with marked success. His own antiquarian researches did much to contribute to the success of the publications he edited. In 1842 he was appointed theological tutor at Richmond College, Surrey, where he remained until 1861.

In 1838–9 Jackson was for the first time chosen president of the Wesleyan conference. A hundred years had passed since the formation of the first Methodist Society by the Wesley brothers, and Jackson prepared a centenary volume describing the origin and growth of Methodism, and the benefits springing from it (1839). In the centennial celebration he played a leading part, and preached before the conference in Brunswick Chapel, Liverpool, the official sermon, which lasted for nearly three hours. The sermon was published, and had a very large circulation. Jackson's style as a preacher was simple and lucid. As a theologian he belonged to the school of Wesley and Fletcher of Madeley, defending the original principles of Methodism. Besides occasional sermons and pamphlets he wrote biographies of several notable Methodists and nonconformists. His works included a *Life of John Goodwin* (1822) and an edition of his *Exposition of Romans ix.* (1834), an edition of the works of John Wesley in fourteen volumes (1829–31), *Memoirs of the Life and Writings of the Rev. Richard Watson* (1834), and a *Life of the Rev. Charles Wesley* in two volumes (1841). He also edited the journal of the latter, with selections from his correspondence and poetry (1849). He wrote a *Life of the Rev. Robert Newton, D.D.* (1855), a portrait of a minister whom he saw as a role model for Methodism. In his later years he devoted much time to the *Lives of the Early Methodist Preachers*, first published in six volumes in 1865. This went into several editions and became the standard account of the history of the early years of Methodism, interest in which Jackson did so much to foster, as well as being a tool for evangelism.

Jackson was re-elected president of the conference in 1849, two years after his younger brother, **Samuel Jackson** (1786–1861), had occupied the president's chair. It was a time of great trial, as the Methodist community was agitated by the so-called reform movement and the expulsion of Everett, Dunn, and Griffiths. Jackson throughout the crisis showed great tact and dignity. He retired from Richmond College and from full-time work as a Wesleyan minister in 1861. At the same time his private library was bought by James Heald for £1000 and given to Richmond College. After leaving Richmond he resided with his daughter, Mrs Marzials, first in Bloomsbury, and afterwards at 29 St Stephen's Road, Shepherd's Bush, where he died on 10 March 1873.

W. B. LOWTHER, *rev.* TIM MACQUIBAN

Sources W. Hill, *An alphabetical arrangement of all the Wesleyan-Methodist ministers, missionaries, and preachers*, rev. J. P. Haswell, 9th edn (1862) · *Minutes of the Methodist conference* · R. E. Davies, A. R. George, and G. Rupp, eds., *A history of the Methodist church in Great Britain*, 1 (1965) · N. B. Harmon, ed., *The encyclopedia of world Methodism*, 2 vols. (1974) · T. Jackson, *Recollections of my own life and times*, ed. B. Frankland (1873) · private information (1891) · *CGPLA Eng. & Wales* (1873)
Archives JRL, Methodist Archives and Research Centre, corresp. and papers · Wesley's Chapel, London, letters and notes
Wealth at death under £200: probate, 2 April 1873, *CGPLA Eng. & Wales*

Jackson, Thomas (1812–1886), Church of England clergyman, was born in Preston, Lancashire, the son of Thomas *Jackson (1783–1873), Wesleyan minister, and his wife, Ann Hollinshead (*d.* 1854). He was educated at St Saviour's School, Southwark, and St Mary Hall, Oxford, where he matriculated in 1831 and graduated BA with third-class honours in classics in 1834, proceeding MA in 1837. While an undergraduate he compiled student manuals of examination questions on classical subjects and was employed in correcting Clarke's Homer for the university press. This inspired his *Uniomachia* (1833; 5th edn, 1875), compiled with John Sinclair, afterwards archdeacon of Middlesex, a comic poem in Homeric verse with a barbarous Latin translation and English couplets in the style of Alexander Pope, telling the story of the recent schism in the Oxford Union Society. Robert Scott, the lexicographer, supplied annotations. This humorous production removed much personal bitterness and restored good relations within the debating society.

Jackson was ordained in 1835, serving a curacy at Brompton before becoming in 1838 vicar of St Peter's, Stepney, a Brasenose College living. In 1844 he was appointed to succeed James Kay-Shuttleworth as principal of the teacher training college at Battersea run by the National Society for Promoting the Education of the Poor. For a while he was editor of the *English Journal of Education*, started in 1843. He became involved with the Canterbury Association, which aimed to establish a Church of England settlement on the South Island of New Zealand, and proved both a fervent platform speaker and a successful fund-raiser for the new colony. In 1850 he was appointed prebendary of Wedland in St Paul's Cathedral and in the same year was made bishop-designate of the projected see of Lyttelton, New Zealand. Following the first wave of 'Canterbury pilgrims' Jackson set out for New Zealand in the autumn of 1850 with his wife, Elizabeth Prudence, two sons, and several teachers from Battersea College, to make arrangements for churches and schools for the colony and to consult with Bishop Selwyn, primate of New Zealand, on the delicate question creating the new diocese. They arrived on 6 February 1851. The visit proved a fiasco and helped to undermine the original objects of the colony. The Jacksons shocked the settlement's co-founder, J. R. Godley, and mildly amused Bishop Selwyn by their social pretensions: Mrs Jackson disembarked in silks and ostrich feathers. When the lack of comforts became apparent, they set sail for England after only a month, the visit having cost the association some £3000. A disagreement with the association, which had become increasingly concerned about Jackson's casualness in financial matters, led to his resignation soon after his arrival in London.

Jackson enjoyed the support of Archbishop Sumner and of Blomfield, the bishop of London, who presented him in 1852 to the rectory of Stoke Newington. He rebuilt the parish church to the designs of Sir Gilbert Scott. A collection of his sermons was published (1859), and a number of more lightweight works, including *Curiosities of the Pulpit* (1868), a compilation of anecdotes about preachers, and *Our Dumb Companions* (2nd edn, 1864) and *Our Feathered Companions* (1870), both animal books for children. Jackson died at Stoke Newington rectory on 18 March 1886, survived by his wife. A mural monument to his memory was placed in Stoke Newington church.

M. C. CURTHOYS

Sources *The Times* (20 March 1886), 7 · *Men of the time* (1875) · Boase, *Mod. Eng. biog.* · Foster, *Alum. Oxon.* · S. Parr, *Canterbury pilgrimage: the first hundred years of the Church of England in Canterbury, New Zealand* (1951) · C. E. Carrington, *John Robert Godley of Canterbury* (1950) · H. A. Morrah, *The Oxford Union, 1823–1923* (1923)
Likenesses photograph, repro. in *The Church of England photographic portrait gallery* (1859), xiii
Wealth at death £503 17s. 7d.: probate, 8 June 1886, *CGPLA Eng. & Wales*

Jackson, Sir Thomas, first baronet (1841–1915), banker, was born on 4 June 1841 in Urker, Crossmaglen, co. Armagh, Ireland, the second son of the nine children of David Jackson (1814–1899), a schoolteacher, and his wife, Elizabeth, an educated woman of Huguenot descent, the daughter of Benjamin Oliver of Killinure, co. Armagh, and Elizabeth Bradford. In 1860, after attending Morgan's School, Castle Knock, Jackson joined the Bank of Ireland in Belfast, but, seeking advancement, contracted with Agra and Masterman's Bank for duty in the East. With the suspension of the Agra in 1866, Jackson, then in Hong Kong, joined the new Hongkong and Shanghai Banking Company. Within a year of his joining the bank he had been appointed 'accountant' in the important Shanghai office, and in 1868 he was sent into the interior of China to

Sir Thomas Jackson, first baronet (1841–1915), by London Stereoscopic Co., pubd 1907–9

open a branch in Hankow (Hankou), key to the finance of the tea trade. Within a year he was in Yokohama, Japan, as manager; then, while on his first leave, he served temporarily as manager of the London office. These early responsibilities reflected not only his ability but also the staff turnover on the China coast and the youth of the bank. In 1871, in Yokohama, he married Amelia Lydia (1848?–1944), the daughter of Captain George Julius Dare (1809–1856) and Sarah Shrieve Parke (d. 1879); they had four sons and four daughters. In 1876 the chief executive of the Hongkong Bank, James Greig, was encouraged to resign; Jackson was at first acting manager, and then, at the age of thirty-five, he was confirmed as chief manager in succession to Greig in Hong Kong. He was to serve in this role, with only minor interruptions, until 1902.

With trade in depression and bank-financed projects failing, the Hongkong Bank had decided not to pay shareholders a dividend. All losses had, however, been written off, and the newly appointed Jackson supervised a recovery, while mastering the mounting problems of depreciating silver. He recognized that new capital would be subscribed in large part by those concerned with the bank's sterling performance. His apparently conservative policy, the 'even keel', called for reserves in both silver and sterling appropriate to the bank's liabilities in each, but, anticipating the long-term decline in the value of silver, Jackson managed to preserve his bank's capital, as rival institutions—most notoriously the Oriental Bank Corporation—failed.

Within the bank Jackson fostered a loyal executive staff, which obviated the problem of control in an institution operating twenty-two offices in twelve countries. Well known for his outbreaks of temper, Jackson was equally noted for his personal charitable munificence; he was compassionate, and acknowledged the service role of the bank in carrying deserving customers, both commercial and individual, in difficult times.

Although Jackson served briefly as the first nominee of the general chamber of commerce for a seat in the colony's newly expanded legislative council, on relevant public committees, and finally as the general chamber's chairman, his lasting influence was through the bank. He insisted that the bank serve all nationalities, but as the leading British banker in China he was supportive of British policy. Along with David McLean in London, Ewen Cameron in Shanghai, and E. Guy Hillier in Peking (Beijing), he was able to dominate the China loan market and thus provide a financial dimension to British China policy, while the bank remained a purely commercial enterprise. His bank and board of directors were multinational, his staff and policy British.

On several occasions Jackson attempted to follow China-coast tradition and retire from the East to the London office, but crisis or questionable management forced his recall, and in 1893 he accepted that he would remain as chief executive. During this last period his policies were particularly successful; his retirement in 1902 came at a time when the bank was thriving. The Hongkong Bank's assets had risen during his stewardship from HK$39.1 million to HK$248.8 million; in sterling the increase was not so dramatic, but exchange had fallen by approximately 55 per cent. Published shareholders' funds had reached HK$26 million, more than double the bank's paid-up capital; in addition there were inner reserves of an equivalent amount. Already recognized for his services to China by an 1886 imperial decree, Jackson was created KCMG in 1899 for his contribution to international commerce. He was created a baronet for services to his bank and to Hong Kong in 1902.

Since the Hongkong Bank's head office was in the colony, the London office lacked the contacts normally provided by a City-based board of directors. Instead, a 'consultative committee' had been established; on Jackson's retirement from the East he was appointed to the specially created salaried position of permanent chairman. He was in demand in the City and became, *inter alia*, chairman of the Imperial Bank of Persia (later known as the British Bank of the Middle East) and a director of the London and County (later Westminster) Bank, which acted as the Hongkong Bank's clearing bank. He was also on the board of the Union Discount Company of London, the Royal Exchange Assurance Corporation, the North China Assurance Company, and the Yorkshire Penny Bank. For all his many City positions, however, he kept his office in the Hongkong Bank, where he was regarded with respect and awe, but was frustrated perhaps that neither he nor his committee had in fact any executive role to play.

Although Jackson's most visible achievement was his management of the Hongkong and Shanghai Banking Corporation, which became the symbol of British economic supremacy in the East, he was, as chief executive, also banker to the colonial government and the treasury chest, acting as a key adviser during the turbulent years of mercantile crisis and silver depreciation. He served Hong Kong in a variety of honorary positions including justice of the peace (1876), but his most enduring monument was, in the words of his protégé Sir Charles Addis, 'the standard of commercial morality which he set throughout the Far East' (Addis Papers, PP. MS 14/377, SOAS).

Jackson died of heart failure at his office, 9 Gracechurch Street, in the City of London, on 21 December 1915. He was buried near his country home, Stansted House, at St Mary's parish church, Stansted, Essex, on 24 December.

FRANK H. H. KING

Sources F. H. H. King and others, *The history of the Hongkong and Shanghai Banking Corporation*, 4 vols. (1987–91) • F. H. H. King, ed., *Eastern banking: essays in the history of the Hongkong and Shanghai Banking Corporation* (1983) • G. Jones, *The history of the British Bank of the Middle East*, 1: *Banking and empire in Iran* (1986) • *The Times* (22 Dec 1915), 14f • *The Times* (23 Dec 1915), 11b • *The Times* (27 Dec 1915), 11a • *The Times* (8 March 1916), 11c • *The Times* (24 March 1916), 14e • SOAS, Addis MSS • HSBC Group Archives, London • m. cert. • d. cert.

Archives priv. coll. | HSBC Group Archives, London [especially 'personalities' file] • HSBC Group Archives, London, C. E. King, 'Sir Thomas Jackson, chief manager, Hongkong and Shanghai Banking Corporation, 1876–1902' [script for Radio Hong Kong series 'Hong Kong people', 1984] • SOAS, David McLean MSS • SOAS, Charles S. Addis MSS

Likenesses photograph, 1876–1879?, HSBC Group Archives, London, Midland Bank archives, PHST 29.5 • group portrait, 1886, repro. in King and others, *History of the Hongkong and Shanghai Banking Corporation*, vol. 1 • photographs, 1899, HSBC Group Archives, London, Midland Bank archives, PHST 29.4 and 191.12 • portrait, 1902, repro. in King and others, *History of the Hongkong and Shanghai Banking Corporation*, vol. 1 • London Stereoscopic Co., photograph, pubd 1907–9, NPG [*see illus.*] • H. Barron, portrait, Hong Kong, Hongkong Bank collection; repro. in King and others, *History of the Honkong and Shanghai Banking Corporation*, vol. 1 • Raggi, bronze statue, Statue Square, Hong Kong • photograph (after watercolour miniature), HSBC Group Archives, London, PHST 29.7 • photographs (in later years; after portrait), HSBC Group Archives, London, PHST 29.3

Wealth at death £128,717 8s. 5d.: resworn probate, 3 March 1916, *CGPLA Eng. & Wales*

Jackson, Thomas Alfred (1879–1955), author and communist, was born at 3 Tysoe Street, Clerkenwell, London, on 21 August 1879, the only son among the four children of Thomas Blackwell Jackson, a compositor, and his wife, Alice Nina Baddeley, formerly a domestic servant. His father, a long-standing member of the Compositors' Society, was a stalwart Liberal; his mother, 'deliberately and wilfully anti-progressive'. When Jackson in his teens converted 'in a night' to socialism and atheism, he was 'literally ill for days afterwards', and it was another two years before he felt able to reveal his new beliefs to his parents (memoirs, People's History Museum, Manchester).

To an unusual extent, even for this movement of the printed word, Jackson's socialism was identified with the love of books. Short-sighted from infancy and bookish by inclination, he was one of the last great autodidacts of the British labour movement, his curiosity aroused by G. H. Lewes's *Biographical History of Philosophy*, his scepticism by Victorian agnostics like Thomas Huxley, and his imagination by the classics of English literature and by a love of history. From 1893 to 1899, after an education at Duncombe Road board school, Upper Holloway, he followed his father in serving his apprenticeship as a compositor, but he was not, as was customary, taken on by the firm as a journeyman. There followed a period of uncertain employment, which Jackson attributed to his growing identification with radical causes. It is nevertheless difficult to believe that his escape from a conventional career was entirely contrary to his own wishes.

From about 1909, in any event, Jackson's only employment was of a political character. First making his mark as one of the socialist lecturers so characteristic of the period, he was remembered even by Harry Pollitt, himself no mean orator, as an attraction with whom it was impossible to compete (*Labour Monthly*, January 1951, 43). Around the same time Jackson left the 'impossibilist' Marxist sect, the Socialist Party of Great Britain, to join the Independent Labour Party, and for a short period was employed as an ILP lecturer and organizer in south Wales. Possibly the exigencies of earning a living played a part in this switch of allegiance, but it no more curbed his native irreverence than did his subsequent adhesion to the Communist Party on its formation in 1920.

This was to prove an irrevocable commitment. For eight years (1921–9) Jackson served as a full-time party worker and sometime editor of the *Communist* and the *Workers' Weekly*. Already in 1924 an outspoken critic of the constricted political outlook of party 'Bolshevisers', it was perhaps inevitable that he should then fall victim to the clear-out of the communist old guard which occurred in 1929. Nor did he exactly guard himself against this eventuality when he used the pages of the *Communist Review* (February 1929) to ridicule the 'perspiring concern' of party zealots to brand all 'deviations' with the latest jargon of the Comintern. Formerly a member of its central committee, Jackson never again held a leading position in the Communist Party.

Apart from a spell as a Communist Party propagandist in the 1940s, Jackson now returned to earning a sporadic living as a journalist and lecturer. If communist institutions like the *Daily Worker* and Marx House provided one source of employment, he also retained close links with the world of independent working-class education. A full-time tutor at the North-East Labour College just after the First World War, he remained a regular contributor to the monthly *Plebs*, by this time a relatively unusual form of association for communists. This may explain Jackson's frequent use of a *nom de plume*, but it was only in June 1941 that he finally abandoned the journal because of its toleration of anti-communist, and more especially anti-Soviet, views (*Plebs*, June 1941, 117).

In the same period Jackson had the time to give to longer writings, beginning with his first book, *Dialectics*, published in 1936. In many ways an anachronism, as communism now attracted a swarm of intellectual converts from the universities, this is one of the last great testimonies to British secularist autodidactism. Confident, dogmatic, intellectually curious, and based on a great breadth of reading, its 648 pages, liberally scattered with italics and derisive triple exclamation marks, advanced the scientific and philosophical aspects of Marxism with unselfconscious vigour and exuberance. They also gave voice to the anti-religious views which Jackson had many years earlier propounded through the National Secular Society and more recently, as a communist, through the

party 'front', the League of Militant Atheists. Jackson's other books covered subjects as wide-ranging as Dickens and the Irish independence struggle, and included a work of radical history, *Trials of British Freedom*. Endearingly suggesting his unconventionality, at least for a communist, was the special enthusiasm expressed in his literary journalism for the incongruously mannered world of Jane Austen.

Jackson was notorious for his down-at-heel appearance and inattention to personal hygiene. Perhaps it speaks of his finer qualities that this was not, as in certain similar instances, resented as an affectation. He was married twice: to Katharine Sarah Hawkins, a schoolteacher, who died in January 1927; then, on 15 February 1927, to Lydia Packman, a secretary, the daughter of James Packman, a pianoforte manufacturer. Lydia was an active communist, who died in 1943, leaving the house in which they lived to her sister and thus making Jackson homeless. The elder of his two daughters by his first marriage, Vivien, inherited Jackson's communist beliefs and married the Marxist historian A. L. Morton. It was with them, at the Old Chapel, Clare, Suffolk, that Jackson died on 18 August 1955, leaving behind him a splendid volume of early memoirs, *Solo Trumpet*, and drafts of a successor which could never have passed his party's censorship. He was buried at Clare.

KEVIN MORGAN

Sources T. A. Jackson, *Solo trumpet: some memories of socialist agitation and propaganda* (1953) · T. A. Jackson, memoirs, People's History Museum, Manchester · V. Morton and S. Macintyre, *T. A. Jackson: a centenary appreciation* (1979) · J. Saville and V. Morton, 'Jackson, Thomas Alfred', *DLB*, vol. 4 · S. Macintyre, *A proletarian science: Marxism in Britain, 1917–1933* (1980) · L. J. Macfarlane, *The British communist party: its origin and development until 1929* (1966) · N. Branson, *A history of the communist party of Great Britain, 1927–1941* (1985) · b. cert. · m. cert. [Lydia Packman] · d. cert.
Archives JRL, Labour History Archive and Study Centre, typescript memoirs interim report · People's History Museum, Manchester, Communist Party archives, typescript memoirs | Russian State Archives of Socio-Political History (RGASPI), Moscow, Comintern archives | FILM BFI NFTVA, documentary footage · BFI NFTVA, party political footage
Likenesses photographs, People's History Museum, Manchester

Jackson, Sir Thomas Graham, first baronet (1835–1924), architect, was born on 21 December 1835 in Heath Street, Hampstead, the only son of Hugh Jackson (1799–1881), solicitor, and his wife, Elizabeth (1799–1880), daughter of Thomas Graham Arnold MD of Stamford; he had two sisters. He was educated at Brighton College and he matriculated at Corpus Christi College, Oxford, in 1854, but in the same year was awarded a scholarship at Wadham College. He graduated in 1858 with a third class in *literae humaniores*. He took his MA in 1863 and was elected fellow of Wadham in the following year.

Jackson entered the office of George Gilbert Scott in 1858, and, having served his articles, set up as an architect in London in 1862. Among his earlier designs is the Ellesmere memorial, Walkden, Lancashire, the commission for which he won in competition in 1868. His first major success, however, came in 1876, when he won the competition, limited to five architects, for the new examination schools at Oxford. His career established, he was able to

Sir Thomas Graham Jackson, first baronet (1835–1924), by Hugh Goldwin Riviere, 1900

marry, in 1880, Alice Mary (1846–1900), daughter of William Lambarde DL of Sevenoaks. This meant that he had to resign from his fellowship, but he was made an honorary fellow in 1882. They had two children, Hugh Nicholas (1881–1979) and Basil Hippisley (1887–1976). They lived at first at 11 Nottingham Place, Marylebone, then moved in 1887 to Eagle House, Wimbledon, where Jackson remained until shortly before his death.

No other architect has altered the appearance of Oxford so greatly as Jackson. He went on to design the boys' and girls' high schools, and buildings for Oriel, Hertford (virtual rebuilding, following its refoundation in 1874), Brasenose, Corpus Christi, Trinity, Balliol, Somerville, and Lincoln. He also designed the Radcliffe Science Library, the electrical laboratory, the university cricket pavilion, and a barge for Oriel College, and carried out restoration on the Bodleian Library, St Mary's Church, and Wadham College. Of these buildings the Examinations Schools is the largest, the chapel of Hertford College that which he is said himself to have preferred, and the front of Brasenose College that which met with most general approval at the time. He built about a dozen churches in various parts of the country, notably at Northington, Hampshire, and added to or restored many more. He designed the campanile of the cathedral at Zara in Dalmatia, and his numerous sensitive restorations of old buildings included the underpinning and stabilizing of Winchester Cathedral, in collaboration with the engineer Sir Francis Fox. It was for this work that in 1913 he received the honour, unprecedented for an architect, of being created a baronet.

Like others of Scott's pupils, Jackson adopted an approach to the Gothic style that was more flexible and eclectic than his master's, and he gave particular attention to the reuse of English Renaissance detail, first used for the Examination Schools, and for which the term 'Anglo-Jackson' was coined. Whether he was working in this style, or the Gothic of his training and first practice, he liked to employ unusual processes and materials: Hornblotton church, Somerset, is decorated internally with sgraffito plaster work, the town hall at Tipperary has some coloured decoration externally, and the new buildings at Brighton College have flint walling mingled with terracotta dressings which are derived from Sutton Place. In the domed chapel of Giggleswick School, Yorkshire—his outstanding achievement in buildings connected with schools, of which he designed many—a number of different processes and materials are characteristically combined. Much of his early work was in the arts and crafts tradition, and his other designs included table glass for James Powell & Sons.

Planning was Jackson's weak point, and for this reason he was unsuccessful in the major public competitions which he entered. However, he was an excellent draughtsman, and in an age when architecture was commonly regarded as an art of stylistic decoration, he deserved and won many distinctions. He was elected RA in 1896 (ARA, 1892; treasurer, 1901–12), and was awarded the royal gold medal for architecture in 1910. The universities of Cambridge and Oxford conferred honorary degrees upon him in 1910 and 1911 respectively, the citation from Oxford describing him, to his delight, as 'Artifex Oxoniensissime' (*Recollections*, 272).

The award of the royal gold medal was the sign of a reconciliation between Jackson and the Royal Institute of British Architects, upon whose recommendation the medal is given. Distrusting professionalism in architecture, he had taken a prominent part in the secession from the institute in 1891 of those who opposed the policy of official registration for which the RIBA was then pressing. In his first attacks upon the policy of the institute he was associated with many of his most distinguished confrères, and was joint editor with Richard Norman Shaw of a volume of protesting essays entitled *Architecture: a Profession or an Art* (1892).

Jackson was a scholarly man, and was the author of a number of books, starting with *Modern Gothic Architecture*, published in 1873, and culminating in a series of architectural histories upon which he embarked at the age of seventy-seven: *Byzantine and Romanesque Architecture* (2 vols., 1913), *Gothic Architecture in France, England, and Italy* (2 vols., 1915), and *The Renaissance of Roman Architecture* (3 vols., 1921–3). He retired from practice in 1922 and died at home at 49 Evelyn Gardens, Kensington, on 7 November 1924. He was buried at St Nicholas's Church, Sevenoaks, two days later. He was succeeded as second baronet by his elder son, Hugh Nicholas, and his younger son, Basil Hippisley, who had entered his father's office in 1910, completed his outstanding commissions, and later edited a volume of his father's memoirs.   JAMES BETTLEY

Sources DNB · *Recollections of Thomas Graham Jackson*, ed. B. H. Jackson (1950) · *The Architect*, 112 (1924), 301 · *Architects' Journal* (19 Nov 1924), 758–63 · B. Pite, *The Builder*, 127 (1924), 753 · R. Blomfield, 'The late Sir Thomas G. Jackson', *RIBA Journal*, 32 (1924–5), 49–50 · H. S. Goodhart-Rendel, 'The works of Sir Thomas Graham Jackson', *RIBA Journal*, 33 (1925–6), 466–78 · J. Bettley, *Sir Thomas Graham Jackson, bart., RA, 1835–1924: an exhibition of his Oxford buildings* (1983) · J. Mordaunt Crook, 'T. G. Jackson and the cult of eclecticism', *In search of modern architecture: a tribute to Henry Russell Hitchcock*, ed. H. Searing (1982), 102–20 · J. Bettley, 'T. G. Jackson and the Examination Schools', *Oxford Art Journal*, 6/1 (1983), 57–66 · private information (2004)
Archives Bodl. Oxf., Radcliffe Science Library, corresp. relating to Radcliffe Science Library · Bodl. Oxf., travel journal · Brasenose College, Oxford, drawings of Brasenose College and Frewen Hall · CUL, drawings and plans for Sedgwick Museum · RIBA, drawings · V&A, diary of a journey to Dalmatia, Bosnia, and Herzegovina · Wadham College, Oxford, papers relating to history of Wadham College | Bodl. Oxf., letters to H. W. Acland
Likenesses photograph, c.1897, repro. in ArchR, 1 (1897), 137 · H. G. Riviere, oils, 1900, Wadham College, Oxford [*see illus.*] · S. J. Solomon, oils, 1900, Art Workers' Guild, London · H. Herkomer, group portrait, oils, 1908 (*The council of the Royal Academy*), Tate collection · Elliott & Fry, photograph, 1909, NPG; repro. in *RIBA Journal*, 17 (1910), facing p. 621 · J. Russell & Sons, photograph, NPG
Wealth at death £37,174 15s. 5d.: probate, 3 Jan 1925, CGPLA Eng. & Wales

Jackson, William (1730–1803), musician, painter, and author, was born in Exeter, Devon, on 28 May 1730, the son of an Exeter grocer, also named William Jackson, who squandered his 'little Fortune' (W. Jackson, *Short Sketch*, 58), became a clerk in the counting-house of Thomas Heath, and was later master of the city workhouse. Though he had nothing to bequeath his son, Jackson's father took care with his education. Jackson studied classics from the age of seven and in the following year took up drawing, copying illustrations from George Bickham's *Musical Entertainer* (1737–8) and topographical etchings by Wenceslaus Hollar. His musical studies began about 1742 in the choir at Exeter Cathedral, where the organist (from 1741 to 1753) was John Silvester. After three years he was sent to London to study with John Travers (1703?–1758), organist at the Chapel Royal and himself a pupil of John Christopher Pepusch. During this period Jackson made his first attempts at composition and came into contact with the Academy of Ancient Music (founded by Pepusch and others about 1726). Jackson remembered how he 'squeezed in' (ibid., 60) among the choir for rehearsals of *Judas Maccabaeus* (first performed at Covent Garden on 1 April 1747) and so became acquainted with Handel.

Lack of funds forced Jackson to return to Exeter about 1748. There, while pursuing his studies in a variety of subjects, he began to earn his living as a musician. A year later he found himself a few pounds in debt, but thereafter 'never wanted money in his life' (Rogers, 125). In 1753 he married Mary Bartlett, a milliner, 'a sober, virtuous, good Woman, but as totally unfit for her Husband as he was for Her' (W. Jackson, *Short Sketch*, 62).

1755 saw the publication of Jackson's *Twelve Songs* op. 1; this was followed about 1757 by the first of only two published instrumental works, *Six Sonatas* op. 2. Jackson was passionately committed to national traditions of melody and to vocal settings that eschewed 'descriptive word-painting' in favour of an emphasis on the 'inherent sentiment' of a text (McGrady, 725). Accordingly, secular and sacred vocal works comprise the largest part of his output. His *Elegies* op. 3 of 1760, which were widely appreciated and brought some financial success, were probably written for the series of Bath concerts promoted by Thomas Linley the elder; his subsequent collections of songs include many pieces first heard in Bath. Jackson later recalled that his *Ode to Fancy* op. 8 (c.1770), an oratorio setting of Joseph Warton's poem, had its only satisfactory performance in the city with Elizabeth Linley as solo soprano. His first dramatic work, a setting of John Milton's 'Lycidas' composed to commemorate the death of Edward, duke of York, George III's brother, was performed at Covent Garden and Bath in November 1767. A very successful comic opera, *The Lord of the Manor* op. 12, with a libretto by General John Burgoyne (1722–1792), was produced by Richard Brinsley Sheridan at Drury Lane in December 1780.

Jackson's first attempts at painting landscapes in oil were made about 1757. Though these were later taken for works of Richard Wilson, Jackson lamented a deficiency in the techniques of painting which he said he did not correct until he had reached the advanced age of seventy. His earliest instruction came from Samuel Collins (d. 1768), the Bath miniaturist, through whom he was introduced to Thomas Gainsborough, probably in 1763. Gainsborough exhibited Jackson's portrait at the Royal Academy in 1770. The intimacy between the two men, nourished by Gainsborough's obsessive love of music, is revealed in the surviving letters to Jackson. This animated and uninhibited correspondence shows Gainsborough receiving help with musical problems and giving Jackson lessons in drawing. About 1770 Jackson's interest developed to the point where he considered taking up painting professionally, and in 1771 he exhibited two paintings at the Royal Academy.

The exchanges about art with Gainsborough doubtless provided an important stimulus for Jackson's projected treatise on landscape painting, one of his many 'fine Designs *to be* executed' but 'left undone' (W. Jackson, *Short Sketch*, 101). Other literary projects were, however, brought to fruition. The first of his published writings was the preface to his *Elegies* (1760), and it was succeeded by several other prefaces to his musical works, two collections of miscellaneous essays (*Thirty Letters*, which reached its third edition in 1795; *The Four Ages*, 1798), and *Observations on the Present State of Music in London* (1791). *The Royalist*, a historical novel inspired by Defoe that was much admired by Samuel Rogers, remains undiscovered. Jackson had a number of collaborators, among them Oliver Goldsmith, with whom he planned a periodical modelled on *The Spectator*; John Wolcot (Peter Pindar), who began to supply Jackson with lyrics in the late 1760s; and William Kendall, who provided the text for Jackson's *Fairy Fantasies* op. 16 (c.1790). In 1792 Jackson was instrumental in establishing the Society of Gentlemen at Exeter, a forum for literary and philosophical discussion.

Despite Gainsborough's attempts to persuade him to leave his native city in the late 1760s, Jackson continued to live and work in Exeter. His financial situation was greatly eased in October 1777 when he obtained the post of organist at Exeter Cathedral, which he held until his death and which led him to compose a number of sacred vocal works, notably his service in F. In the summer of that year he took a sketching tour through Devon with his son Thomas (1759–1828), a highly accomplished amateur artist and later a diplomat, and the poet John Bampfylde, whose extraordinary musical abilities Jackson described in a preface prepared for a projected edition of Bampfylde's verse. Jackson's only trip outside England was undertaken in the summer of 1785 when he travelled with his lifelong friend James White (whose nephew John White Abbott was himself a gifted amateur painter) through France to Turin, where Thomas Jackson was then chargé d'affaires. The narrative of the trip, accompanied by an interesting set of sketches, forms a substantial part of Jackson's *A Short Sketch of my Own Life*.

Jackson's marriage to Mary Bartlett produced at least eight children, three of whom survived their father: William (1754–1842), who made his fortune as an employee of the United East India Company; Thomas, the diplomat, who died in Vienna; and Mary (c.1760–1808), who married the painter John *Downman (1750–1824) little more than a year before her death. Late in life, Jackson's liaison with Jane Bradford, the daughter of an Exeter clergyman, produced an illegitimate son, later known as William Elmsley QC (1797–1866), who was born in Bristol. Jane Bradford died in childbirth. Elmsley remained in Bristol until, after his father's death, he was taken to Exeter, where he became the adopted son of his half-brother William Jackson and William's wife, Frances, née Baring. Jackson died of dropsy on 12 July 1803, in Exeter, and was buried in St Stephen's Church, Exeter. A monument there was commissioned by his daughter Mary and designed by John White Abbott. His wife survived him.

Jackson's posthumous reputation was adversely affected as the result of a quarrel with Charles Burney. The two were apparently on reasonably good terms until 1789–90, when Jackson published a two-part review of Burney's *General History of Music* (*Critical Review*, 68.94–103; 70.618–32). Burney, unused to criticism even of the mildest sort, responded with a vehement attack on Jackson's *Observations on the Present State of Music* (*Monthly Review*, October 1791, 196–202) and was evidently still smarting almost thirty years later when he asserted in his article on Jackson in Abraham Rees's *Cyclopaedia* (1819–20) that any good qualities Jackson might have had were 'strongly alloyed by a mixture of selfishness, arrogance, and an insatiable rage for superiority'. Late twentieth-century scholarship has provided a more balanced assessment of Jackson's character and attested to the unusual range of his interests and achievements. PAUL WILLIAMSON

Sources W. Jackson, *A short sketch of my own life* and *Twenty letters*, ed. A. Asfour and P. Williamson, *Gainsborough's House Review* (1996–7), 39–151 • G. Jackson, 'Studien zur Biographie und zum literarischen Nachlass des William Jackson of Exeter, 1730–1803', *English Miscellany*, 22 (1971), 269–332 • R. McGrady, 'Jackson, William', *New Grove*, 2nd edn • *The letters of Thomas Gainsborough*, ed. J. Hayes (2001) • A. Asfour and P. Williamson, '*Ut pictura poesis*: William Jackson and John Bampfylde on the Teign', *Apollo*, 146 (Aug 1997), 37–41 • S. Rogers, commonplace book, UCL, Sharpe MSS 34, 125–7 • R. Lonsdale, *Dr Charles Burney: a literary biography* (1965) • J. Hayes, 'William Jackson of Exeter', *The Connoisseur*, 173 (1970), 17–24 • *DNB* • *IGI* • private information (2004) [David Johnson]
Archives RA, letters and papers
Likenesses T. Gainsborough, oils, 1770, repro. in Jackson, *Short sketch of my own life* • J. Downman, watercolour, 1779, repro. in Jackson, 'Studien zur Biographie' • mezzotint, pubd 1785 (after J. Downman), BM • J. Keenan, oils, 1800, Devon and Exeter Institution, Exeter • mezzotint, pubd 1818 (after Walker), BM, NPG • J. Walker, aquatint, pubd 1819 (after unknown artist), NPG • T. Gainsborough, oils, Exeter City Museum and Art Gallery
Wealth at death £10,000: will, PRO, PROB 10/3637

Jackson, William [pseud. Scrutineer] (1737?–1795), journalist and spy, was born in Dublin, the son of an officer in the prerogative court. After studying at Oxford he was ordained and he moved to London, where he acted as a curate at St Mary-le-Strand and preached at the Tavistock Chapel. However, he never obtained a benefice, and it has been suggested that his failure to succeed as a clergyman led him to abandon an ecclesiastical career in favour of journalism. By the mid-1770s he was editor of the *Public Ledger*. According to one of his obituarists, 'no man, perhaps ever went farther in the boldness of his attacks … The acrimony of his pen soon rendered him conspicuous to the Public' (*The Oracle*, 6 May 1795).

One victim of Jackson's vitriol was the actor Samuel Foote. The memorialist John Taylor suggested that Jackson acted at the instigation of Elizabeth Chudleigh, duchess of Kingston, whom he had served as secretary, but this interpretation has been questioned. What is certain is that Foote satirized Jackson in his comedy *A Trip to Calais* as Dr Viper, and that Jackson responded by accusing Foote of making homosexual advances towards one of his servants. Foote replied by bringing a libel action against Jackson, but he died in 1776 before it could be completed. At about the same time Jackson's wife also died, of breast cancer. Jackson probably went to France at this point with the duchess of Kingston, following her trial for bigamy.

Jackson re-emerged on the London scene in the 1780s. Having previously appeared conservative and hostile to Wilkes, he now emerged as a champion of the American revolutionaries, publishing a reply to Samuel Johnson's *Taxation No Tyranny*, and *The Constitutions of the Several Independent States of America* in 1783. The latter was dedicated to the duke of Portland and should perhaps be seen as a failed attempt at securing political patronage rather than the literary outpourings of a republican convert, although Taylor claimed that Jackson had 'caught the flame of freedom' (Taylor, 2.326). In March 1784 Jackson was installed as editor of the *Morning Post* by John Benjafield, acting on behalf of Pitt's government. Although the paper announced to its readers its intention 'henceforward to be conducted on the most liberal principles' (22 March 1784) its claim to a new impartiality was a hollow one. Under Jackson the *Post* became firmly Pittite and particularly eager to attack Charles James Fox. Jackson wrote a series of letters in the paper, under the pseudonym Scrutineer, which questioned Fox's behaviour in the Westminster election, and he also published a pamphlet entitled *Thoughts on the Causes for the Delay in the Westminster Scrutiny*.

Jackson remained at the *Morning Post* until early 1786, when he was dismissed by one of the proprietors, Richard Tattersall. By 1787 he had involved himself in a new venture as joint partner with John Palmer in the Royalty Theatre. The project was not a success and by 1788 its affairs appear to have been in such a critical state that Jackson was forced to leave the country. Other explanations have also been given of his flight to France. The death of the duchess of Kingston in Paris in August 1788 might have necessitated his assistance in sorting out her property affairs, and it has also been suggested that he went to France on a secret mission to the French government for Pitt. Whatever the reason for his leaving England, it is clear that he stayed in France for several years, and reports of his death were widely circulated in London until his reappearance there in early 1794.

By this time Jackson was acting on behalf of the French government and had been sent to assess the potential for a successful French invasion of England and Ireland. In London he conferred with the leaders of several reform societies, including Horne Tooke, all of whom dismissed his hopes of a revolutionary temperament in Britain. On 3 April 1794 he arrived in Dublin, where he met with more apparent success upon contacting leaders of the United Irishmen, including Archibald Hamilton Rowan and Wolfe Tone. However, he was betrayed to the government by his travelling companion, a lawyer and former employee of the duchess of Kingston named Cockayne. Jackson was arrested on 24 April 1794 and charged with high treason. The discovery of his mission gave the government the pretext it needed to suppress the Dublin Society of United Irishmen, but it also served to publicize the favourable disposition of the French to a possible Irish rising and incited Wolfe Tone, in voluntary exile due to his involvement in the Jackson affair, to travel to France in order to represent the United Irishmen to the French government. In between his arrest and his trial the following year Jackson wrote and published a pamphlet entitled *Observations in Answer to Thomas Paine's 'Age of Reason'* (1795).

Jackson was convicted on Cockayne's evidence in April 1795, despite a spirited defence by United Irishmen lawyers. It has been claimed that Jackson passed up a chance to escape from prison when his cell door was left unlocked and refused to name his co-conspirators, which would also have ensured his freedom. One sympathetic historian attributed this to a 'high sense of honour' (MacNeven, 98). Due to his age the jury recommended mercy but Jackson committed suicide before his sentence was passed, dramatically collapsing in the dock of the court of king's bench from arsenic poisoning as his counsel addressed the court on 30 April 1795. He is supposed to have taken his own life in order to protect a small pension for his second wife, with whom he had had two daughters. Taylor

called him 'a very gallent man, and much favoured by the ladies' (Taylor, 2.325). His obituarist in *The Oracle* was less charitable, and described him as

> above middling stature, of an athletic turn, and manly appearance. With respect to his abilities, they were certainly of a very superior kind ... he was always accounted a good scholar, and an able writer; and ... no one could be more the gentleman ... Yet ... his friendship was always used as a cover for the most sinister views ... no one, perhaps, ever had a smile more at his command, which he admirably suited to the men he had to deal with; always with the most astonishing art and judgment, and frequently with the greatest success.

He was buried on 3 May 1795 in St Michan's cemetery in Dublin.   HANNAH BARKER

Sources L. Werkmeister, 'Notes for a revised life of William Jackson', *N&Q*, 206 (1961), 43–7 [see also pp. 266–7 for postscript] · L. Werkmeister, *The London daily press, 1772–1792* (1963) · N. J. Curtin, *The United Irishmen: popular politics in Ulster and Dublin, 1791–1798* (1994) · W. J. MacNeven, *Pieces of Irish history* (1807) · W. Hindle, *The Morning Post, 1772–1937: portrait of a newspaper* (1937) · J. Taylor, *Records of my life*, 2 vols. (1832) · W. E. H. Lecky, *A history of England in the eighteenth century*, 8 vols. (1879–90) · J. Benjafield, *Statement of facts* (1813) · *DNB*
Likenesses group portrait, coloured lithograph (*The United Irish patriots of 1798*), NPG

Jackson, William (1751–1815), bishop of Oxford, was the younger son of Cyrill (or Cyril) Jackson, physician, and Judith Prescot, his wife, of Stamford, Lincolnshire, and later of York. He was educated at Manchester grammar school from 12 January 1762, and at Westminster School from 1764 to 1768, where he was elected a king's scholar. On 1 June 1768 he matriculated at Oxford as a student of Christ Church, where his tutors included Francis Atterbury, later bishop of Rochester. In 1770 he gained the chancellor's prize for Latin verse, the subject being 'Ars medendi'. He graduated BA in 1772, proceeded MA in 1775, BD in 1783, and DD in 1799. At Christ Church he was for many years actively engaged as tutor, rhetoric reader, and censor. He also became chaplain to William Markham, archbishop of York, whose patronage led him to be appointed prebendary of Southwell on 23 September 1780, prebendary of York on 26 March 1783, and rector of Beeford in the East Riding of Yorkshire. On 19 December 1783 he was elected regius professor of Greek at Oxford, a post he held until 1811, and shortly afterwards one of the curators of the Clarendon Press. From 1783 to 1811 he was preacher to Lincoln's Inn and he published sermons preached before the society on fast and thanksgiving days in 1795 and 1798. He was appointed to a prebend at Bath and Wells on 4 January 1792 and a canonry at Christ Church, Oxford, on 2 August 1799.

Jackson's published sermons numbered half a dozen and are unremarkable in either content or style. Noted for his self-indulgence and port drinking, he lived somewhat in the shadow of his most able older brother Cyril *Jackson (1746–1819), dean of Christ Church 1783–1809. It was only after Cyril refused the offer of the bishopric of Oxford, from his pupil and patron the prince regent, that it was offered to William. Jackson was accordingly consecrated bishop of Oxford on 23 February 1812 and was subsequently appointed clerk of the closet to the king. He died, unmarried, at Cuddesdon, Oxford, on 2 December 1815 and was buried there.

GORDON GOODWIN, rev. ROBERT HOLE

Sources *GM*, 1st ser., 85/2 (1815) · Foster, *Alum. Oxon.* · *Old Westminsters*, vols. 1–2 · *Fasti Angl.* (Hardy) · *Parriana, or, Notices of the Rev. Samuel Parr*, ed. E. H. Barker, 2 vols. (1828–9), vol. 1 · J. F. Smith, ed., *The admission register of the Manchester School, with some notices of the more distinguished scholars*, 1, Chetham Society, 69 (1866)
Archives Christ Church Oxf., Carmen quadragesimalium, MS 421a
Likenesses S. Reynolds, mezzotint, pubd 1818 (after W. Owen), BM, NPG · W. Owen, portrait, Christ Church Oxf.

Jackson, William (1815–1866), composer and choral conductor, born at Masham, Yorkshire, on 9 January 1815, was the son of John Jackson, a miller, of Tanfield. As a child, encouraged by his parents, he taught himself to play the fife and the flute. Having been sent to boarding-school in Pateley Bridge about 1825, he learned the piano and sight-singing. When he was about thirteen he returned home to work at his father's mill. After mending several barrel organs he constructed one himself, with his father's assistance, and then made a five-stop manual organ. He soon taught himself to play fifteen instruments, and studied composition with theory books and scores borrowed from Leeds circulating library. Early compositions included a dozen short anthems that elicited encouragement from Matthew Camidge, the organist of York Minster, and some wind music written for Masham military band, which Jackson began directing about 1829.

Jackson's weekly wage of 3s. 6d. as a journeyman miller was augmented in 1832 by his appointment as organist at Masham church, at £30 per annum. In 1835 he failed to gain the post of organist at Doncaster. He entered into a thirteen-year partnership with Ascough, a tallow chandler of Masham in 1839, the year in which his first publication, the anthem 'For joy let fertile valleys ring', was issued by Novello. The following year the Huddersfield Glee Club awarded him first prize for 'The Sisters of the Sea', which Novello also published, and in 1841 he dedicated a setting of Psalm 103 to the Huddersfield Choral Society. He married Mary Coultman of Leyburn on 27 July 1842. Two years later Novello published his oratorio *The Deliverance of Israel from Babylon*, which was favourably received at performances in Leeds and Bradford in 1847. Other published compositions from this period include a mass in E, songs, glees, psalm tunes, hymns, and anthems, and a slow movement and rondo for piano. Novello issued his second oratorio, *Isaiah*, in 1851. Jackson's *A Singing Class Manual* (1849), the only publication from which he claimed to have derived any profit, shows his interest in John Curwen's tonic sol-fa methods of choral training.

In 1852, in partnership with the singer William Winn, Jackson took over a music business in Cheapside, Bradford, and became organist at St John's Church, from which, in 1856, he transferred to Horton Lane Independent Chapel (Bradford's 'Congregational cathedral'). He was soon invited to direct the Bradford Old Choral Society, and later succeeded Winn as director of the Bradford Choral Union (male voices). At the Bradford festivals of 1853 and 1856 Jackson was chorus master; from 1856 he was conductor of the Festival Choral Society, which, having gained acclaim in Yorkshire and Lancashire, he was invited in 1858 to conduct before the queen at Buckingham Palace. He composed a second setting of Psalm 103 for the 1856 Bradford festival and a cantata, *The Year*, for the 1859 festival. A full service in G was published in 1864. Jackson died at his home, Masham House, Horton Lane, Bradford, on 15 April 1866, without hearing his latest work, *Praise of Music*, a 'symphony' for chorus and orchestra, written for the 1866 festival. He left a widow and nine children, the youngest just five days old. His funeral at Horton Lane Chapel was organized by the Festival Choral Society, and he was interred on 20 April at Undercliffe cemetery. A testimonial fund quickly raised £2000 to support his family, while memorial concerts financed monuments at Undercliffe and Masham. Jackson's second son, William (b. 1853), who composed a few songs and part-songs, died at Ripon on 10 September 1877.

Many of Jackson's works betray his lack of thorough technical training and the limitations of his musical experience. His style is fundamentally indebted to Handel, and, less strongly, to Haydn and Mozart. Traces of later influences are sporadic. His music has, nevertheless, a character and directness that impressed his immediate contemporaries. As a choirmaster he played a leading role in fostering the great Yorkshire choral tradition.

CLIVE BROWN

Sources J. Sutcliffe Smith, *The life of William Jackson (of Masham), the miller musician* (1926) · 'William Jackson, the musical composer', *Eliza Cook's Journal* (23 March 1850), 324–6 · [W. Cudworth], *Musical reminiscences of Bradford* (1885) [repr. from the *Bradford Observer*] · R. V. Taylor, 'Yorkshire musicians', *Yorkshire Weekly Post* (29 Sept 1888) · m. cert. · d. cert. · *CGPLA Eng. & Wales* (1866)
Archives W. Yorks. AS, Bradford, vocal and full scores of music, portrait, and conducting baton, DB 70 C.8
Likenesses photograph, repro. in Sutcliffe Smith, *Life of William Jackson*, frontispiece · portrait, W. Yorks. AS, Bradford, DB 70 C.8
Wealth at death under £2000: administration, 15 June 1866, *CGPLA Eng. & Wales*

Jackson, Sir William Godfrey Fothergill [Bill] (1917–1999), army officer and military historian, was born on 28 August 1917 at Blackpool, the only son and elder of the two children of Colonel Albert Jackson (1887–1956), an officer in the Royal Army Medical Corps, and his wife, Eleanor Mary, née Fothergill (1885–1978). His parents' families originated in Westmorland. His paternal grandfather had been a director of the White Star Line, whose fortunes originated with troop shipping to the Crimean War. His mother's family could be traced back to the Conquest: Sir George de Fothergill was one of William's commanders at the battle of Hastings.

Jackson was educated at Shrewsbury School, the Royal Military Academy, Woolwich (where he was a king's medallist), and King's College, Cambridge, where he obtained an MA in mechanical sciences. He was commissioned into the Royal Engineers in August 1937. In 1940 he was one of the first British soldiers to come under enemy fire, in Norway during the withdrawal to Andalsnes, his gallant handling of the situation earning him a Military Cross. In 1942 in north Africa with 6th armoured division he was badly wounded in the explosion of a truckload of mines. Later he joined General Eisenhower's staff (allied force headquarters) for the invasions of Sicily and Italy. When fully fit he returned to 6th armoured division to lead 8th field squadron through the battles of the Garigliano and Cassino, and the advance past Rome to the Gothic line, winning a bar to his Military Cross and being again wounded.

After a short spell on General Alexander's staff (Fifteenth Army group) Jackson returned to England in early 1945 to attend the Staff College at Camberley. He then went to the Far East, joining Fourteenth Army headquarters planning the reconquest of Malaya. On promotion to lieutenant-colonel he moved to headquarters allied land forces in Singapore to grapple with the multitude of problems in the aftermath of the Japanese surrender, including those of the then Dutch East Indies. He also met his future wife, Joan Mary Buesden (b. 1920), a junior commander in the Auxiliary Territorial Service and a member of his staff. They married on 7 September 1946, and had a son, William Nigel Buesden (b. 1947), and a daughter, Rosemary Joan Fothergill (b. 1950).

Jackson's gift for communication, backed by sharp powers of reasoning and manifest battle experience, made him a natural choice as an instructor. He returned to Camberley in 1948 for two years on the Staff College directing staff and a further two as a company commander at the Royal Military Academy, Sandhurst. He had already started his first book *Attack in the West* (1953), an analysis of Napoleon's first Italian campaign. Two tours at regimental duty were then crowned by his selection as a brevet lieutenant-colonel in 1955. This took him to his first War Office appointment, as assistant adjutant and quartermaster-general war plans. For his work there in the preparations for the Suez expedition of 1956 he was made OBE in 1958. *Seven Roads to Moscow* (1957), a comparative account of the main invasions of Russia, was published at the end of this tour. Command of the recently formed Gurkha engineers in the midst of the Malayan emergency followed.

In 1960 Jackson returned to the Staff College as a colonel heading one of the three divisions. It was then that, among his many gifts, his far-sightedness began to yield dividends for the army in a series of high-pressure and influential jobs: deputy director of army staff duties (1962–4), followed by a brief interlude at the Imperial Defence College; director of the chief of defence staff's Unison exercise (1966–7); and assistant chief of the general staff (operational requirements) (1967–9). Three of his books were published in this period, all harking back to his time in Italy: *The Battle for Italy* (1967), *The Battle for Rome* (1969), and *Alexander of Tunis as a Military Commander* (1971).

Jackson's tour as commander-in-chief, northern command (1970–2), was a breathing space before his final appointment as quartermaster-general and member of the army board (1972–6). Foreseeing the need for economy, he set a trend by moving his own staff and supporting organizations out of London, and setting up the logistic executive at Andover. 'Always ahead of the game (and often ahead of his time)', said Lord Bramall, 'he got quickly to the heart of a problem and was then, with his own clear agenda behind him, able to articulate with the utmost clarity and irrefutable logic, what he felt needed to be done' (Bramall, memorial address). Honours came naturally to such a dedicated professional favoured with an exceptional mind: he was knighted KCB in 1971, and GCB in 1975, and was aide-de-camp (general) to the queen (1974–6), and colonel commandant of the Royal Engineers (1971–6), the Gurkha engineers (1971–6), and the Royal Army Ordnance Corps (1973–8).

In 1978 Jackson was appointed governor and commander-in-chief of Gibraltar. His three-year appointment was extended by one year. In Gibraltar he delighted in his responsibilities, ranging from the detailed administration of the Rock to advocacy of the interests of the Gibraltarians. He became convinced that integration with Spain was neither just nor practicable. During the Falklands War he 'had the delicate task of misleading the Spanish authorities about British strength and intentions, knowing that the Spaniards were in contact with the Argentine government' (*Daily Telegraph*, 16 March 1999). He was later chairman of the Friends of Gibraltar's Heritage (1990–4).

In retirement writing continued to be Jackson's main enthusiasm: more books, letters to the press, military obituaries for *The Times*, and book reviews and articles for service journals. In his lifetime he published, or collaborated in the publication of, some sixteen books including *The Rock of the Gibraltarians* (1988), a history of Gibraltar. In 1977–8 and 1982–7 he was an official military historian at the Cabinet Office, and he co-edited volume 6 of *The Mediterranean and Middle East*, issued in three parts in 1984, 1987, and 1988 as part of the official *History of the Second World War* series. He was twice awarded the Royal United Service Institution's Trench Gascoigne gold medal, for essays published in the institution's *Journal*.

Jackson drove himself hard and was sparing with sleep. To his subordinates he:

> was a man who 'needed to be stood up to' but he always listened to the advice of those who had won his confidence. In spite of his formidable intellect he was a man of great compassion and warmth. His sense of humour was never far below the surface and his audible chuckle often helped ease solutions to problems. (*Royal Engineers Journal*, 128)

He died on 12 March 1999 at the Princess Margaret Hospital, Swindon, Wiltshire, and was buried on 19 March at Huish parish church, Huish, near Oare, Pewsey, Wiltshire. He was survived by his wife of fifty-two years, Joan, and their two children.

GERALD NAPIER

Sources *Royal Engineers Journal*, new ser., 113 (1999), 128–30 · personal record compiled by WGFJ (c.1985), memorial address by FM Lord Bramall, Royal Engineers Library, Jackson papers · unpublished autobiography, priv. coll. [in family possession] · *The Times*

(15 March 1999) • *Daily Telegraph* (16 March 1999) • *The Guardian* (16 March 1999) • *The Independent* (15 March 1999) • *WWW*, 1991–5 • personal knowledge (2004) • private information (2004)

Archives priv. coll., incl. MS autobiography • Royal Engineers, Brompton barracks, Chatham, Kent

Likenesses photograph, *c.*1937, Royal Engineers Library, Chatham • photograph, 1970–79, repro. in *The Times* • photograph, *c.*1972, Royal Engineers Library, Chatham • J. Courtney, oils, 1981, Royal Engineers Headquarters Mess, Chatham • photograph, 1981, repro. in *Daily Telegraph* • oils, priv. coll. • photograph, repro. in *The Guardian* • photograph, repro. in *The Independent*

Wealth at death £1,182,987: probate, 1999, *CGPLA Eng. & Wales*

Jackson, William Lawies, first Baron Allerton (1840–1917), politician, was born at Otley in the West Riding of Yorkshire on 16 February 1840, the eldest son of William Jackson (*d.* 1858), a leather merchant and tanner of Leeds, and his wife, Mary Loise (or Lawies). His education at a private school at Adel and later at the Moravian school at Fulneck was cut short at an early age by his father's financial difficulties. William Jackson had already been obliged to compound with his creditors, and his business was again almost bankrupt when, on his death, Jackson succeeded to it at the age of eighteen. Thanks to a combination of strong will, good health, and unremitting hard work he was soon able to pay off all his father's creditors, and found himself at the head of an unencumbered and very valuable business which, under his continued care, grew to be one of the largest tanning and leather currying concerns in the kingdom. On 10 October 1860 he married Grace (1845–1901), the only daughter of George Tempest of Otley. He was an originator of the Leeds leather fair, and one of the earliest tanners to grapple seriously, and at great cost, with the problem of river pollution. But the momentum of the early years was not sustained: Jackson's sons did not enter the business, and it was closed on his retirement in May 1912.

Jackson became the outstanding figure in Leeds Conservatism, approaching in stature the leading Liberal of the day, James Kitson. He was, in the words of Lord Randolph Churchill, 'the tanner who won Leeds as a Tory' (*Yorkshire Weekly Post*, 7 April 1917). From 1869 to 1881 he represented the Headingley ward on the city council, and at a time of weak leadership by the controlling Liberals instituted successful financial reforms in the running of local utilities through his chairmanship of the finance committee. His nomination as lord mayor in 1895 was a reflection both of that earlier achievement and of a desire to bring back a business élite to local politics after the uninspiring leadership of previous decades. He was awarded the freedom of the city in 1908.

Jackson was Conservative MP for Leeds from 1880 until the redistribution of seats in 1885 after which he represented the north division until 1902, when he was elevated to the peerage as Baron Allerton of Chapel Allerton in Leeds. The historian of Leeds politics has noted that he 'exemplified the combination of religious faith, patriotism and the economic virtues characteristic of someone who built up in Leeds the largest British firm of tanners' (Steele, 335). A firm believer in the economic benefits of empire he was

for most of his career a free-trader, but reluctantly conceded the necessity for tariff reform at the general election of January 1910. His own company had suffered from French tariffs and he had seen German firms which operated in a protected market able to pay the high prices for Indian hides which he could not afford. Arthur Balfour recognized that Jackson might be more than just a provincial success story and he was appointed financial secretary to the Treasury in 1885 in which capacity he served during both Goschen's conversion of the national debt and the Baring crisis of November 1890. His chief secretaryship of Ireland (1891–2) lasted only a few months and was uneventful. He was sworn of the privy council in 1890 and elected FRS the following year.

Jackson was a more than ordinarily silent member of the House of Commons; but he sat on important committees dealing with Indian railways, financial relations between the Indian and home governments, trade, bankruptcy law, and War Office contracts. On all these he did valuable work, and he was also chairman of the royal commission on the coal resources of the United Kingdom (1901–5).

Jackson's most distinctive and unusual contribution to his party was as chairman of the inquiry into the Jameson raid of 1896–7, which examined among other questions whether or not the colonial secretary Joseph Chamberlain had colluded with Rhodes over the disastrous expedition. This called for rather different skills from the solid abilities evident elsewhere in Jackson's career. Chamberlain was helped both by Jackson's apparently ineffective direction of the committee which prevented sustained questioning of witnesses and by his severe editing of some crucial telegrams sent to Rhodes by Flora Shaw, the South African correspondent of *The Times*, which might have implicated Chamberlain. His last important office was that of chairman (1895–1908) of the Great Northern Railway Company, which he successfully defended against the threatened competition of the Great Central Railway, at that time first extended to London; he eventually became chairman of a common purposes committee of the two companies.

After the disastrous failure of the Liberator building society in 1892, Jackson's influence in the city of Leeds enabled him to make a thorough personal investigation into the affairs of building societies, and his proposals for more effective audit and financial control were embodied in the Building Societies Act of 1894. His contribution to Leeds affairs outside the formally political was substantial, especially in matters of education and religion. In the 1880s he served on the council of the newly formed Yorkshire College and played a significant part in its transformation into the University of Leeds, receiving a doctorate of law in 1904 in the first honorary degrees awarded by the university, which he served as treasurer from 1912 to 1917. He had been a mason since 1865 and became provincial grand master of the West Riding masonic order in September 1893. He sat on the board of management of the Leeds Church Extension Society and his memorial service in April 1917 was held in St Matthew's Church, Chapel Allerton, for which he had served as chairman of the building committee. Although he purchased an estate near Doncaster he lived at Allerton Hall in Leeds.

Jackson died after heart illness at his London residence, 41 Cadogan Square, on 4 April 1917 and was buried on 7 April alongside his wife, Grace, who had died on 27 March 1901, in St Matthew's Church, Chapel Allerton. Allerton's title was inherited by his elder son, George Herbert (*b.* 1867); his younger son, Francis Stanley *Jackson (*b.* 1870), was an international cricketer who also had a successful military and political career.   R. C. WHITING

Sources DNB · *Yorkshire Evening News* (4 April 1917) · *Leeds Mercury* (5 April 1917) · *Yorkshire Post* (5 April 1917) · *Yorkshire Weekly Post* (7 April 1917) · *The Times* (5 April 1917) · E. D. Steele, 'Imperialism and Leeds politics, c.1850–1914', *A history of modern Leeds*, ed. D. Fraser (1980), 327–52 · W. G. Rimmer, 'Jackson, William Lawies', *DBB* · J. Butler, *The liberal party and the Jameson raid* (1968) · R. R. James, *Rosebery: a biography of Archibald Philip, fifth earl of Rosebery* (1963) · E. P. Hennock, *Fit and proper persons: ideal and reality in nineteenth-century urban government* (1973) · Burke, *Peerage* · b. cert.
Archives BL, corresp. with A. J. Balfour, Add. MS 49771, *passim* · CKS, letters to Aretas Akers-Douglas · NA Scot., corresp. with A. J. Balfour
Likenesses H. Adlard, stipple, BM · London Stereoscopic Co., photograph, NPG; repro. in R. J. Albery, *Our conservative and unionist statesmen*, 1 (1893) · H. A. Olivier, oils, Museum of British Transport, York · Spy [L. Ward], caricature, chromolithograph, NPG; repro. in *VF* (31 Aug 1899) · photograph (after engraving by Swain), Leeds City Library; repro. in Rimmer, 'Jackson, William Lawies'
Wealth at death under £250,000: probate, 20 April 1917, CGPLA Eng. & Wales

Jackson, Willis, **Baron Jackson of Burnley** (1904–1970), electrical engineer and educationist, was born in Burnley, Lancashire, on 29 October 1904, the only son of Herbert Jackson, parks superintendent, and his wife, Annie Hiley. He was educated at Burnley grammar school. His association with electrical engineering began as an undergraduate at the University of Manchester where he held the Burnley educational committee scholarship (1922–5). The award in 1925 of a BSc with first-class honours and a graduate research scholarship led to research and an MSc in 1926. From 1926 to 1929 he was lecturer in electrical engineering at Bradford Technical College, Yorkshire. A straightforward academic career lay ahead but in 1929 the award of an industrial bursary by the 1851 Exhibition committee enabled Jackson to join the Metropolitan-Vickers Electrical Company and to come under the influence of A. P. M. Fleming. This set Jackson on a life's work embracing both industry and education and inspired him with the wish to bring the two more closely together.

Jackson's first contact with Metropolitan-Vickers was brief and was followed by further academic experience—at Manchester College of Technology (1930–33), and research at Oxford (1933–6) under E. B. Moullin. The Oxford period defined his main technical interest—the behaviour of electrical insulating materials—and provided a major research contribution, the demonstration of dipole rotation in solids and its influence on dielectric

Willis Jackson, Baron Jackson of Burnley (1904–1970), by Walter Bird, 1966

loss, for which he was awarded the DPhil of Oxford and the DSc of Manchester in 1936. In 1938 Jackson married Mary Elizabeth, daughter of Robert Oliphant Boswall DSc, senior lecturer in mechanical engineering at Manchester University; there were two daughters.

Jackson's return to Metropolitan-Vickers as Fleming's personal assistant brought him directly into contact with policy on industrial research and on the training of graduates for industrial careers. This rounded off his extended apprenticeship in industry and academic life. Thirteen years after graduating from the electrotechnics department of Manchester University he returned as its professor. He rapidly established a reputation by the enthusiasm he communicated to students, both in lectures and in tackling projects of an advanced kind. His research group on dielectrics was sufficiently developed by the outbreak of war to be charged, in collaboration with the Signals Research and Development Establishment, with the study of dielectrics needed for radar. Such a study required the development of precise measurements of dielectric properties at centimetre wavelengths and Jackson's group pioneered the use of resonator techniques for this purpose. Theoretical work on the behaviour of waveguide junctions laid the foundations for others to develop. Jackson's wartime group gained an international reputation, largely as a consequence of his shrewd selection of the problems to be tackled, and his drive which infected all his team.

Unwilling to allow the demands of wartime research to diminish his interest in education, Jackson was a major contributor to a remarkably far-sighted document, published in 1942 by the Institution of Electrical Engineers' education and training committee. His anticipation of many of the post-war educational developments was converted to reality during the period 1946–53 when he filled the chair of electrical engineering at the Imperial College of Science and Technology, London. This period, possibly the most fruitful of his career, effected a transformation in all aspects of his department—undergraduate courses, postgraduate courses, and research—creating the most forward-looking electrical engineering university department in the country. His philosophy was essentially simple and is summarized in the quotation from his presidential address to the British Association for the Advancement of Science at Leeds (1967): 'the ultimate purpose of technology and engineering is to apply established scientific principles and other relevant knowledge to productive ends'. All the changes he initiated were directed towards ensuring that his students appreciated this. The majority of the innovations he made—final-year student projects, student colloquia, emphasis on the properties of materials as a major factor in engineering, courses in economics, industrial sociology, and other relevant subjects—became standard but at the time were regarded as revolutionary. His success lay in the skilful selection of staff sympathetic with his views and in giving them his complete support. Research was revitalized and he created lively groups in the fields of control, solid-state electronics, information theory, microwaves, and ultrasonics—subjects all novel at that time.

Election as a fellow of the Royal Society in 1953 in recognition of his research in insulating materials and microwaves completed this phase of Jackson's career. A new challenge was offered by his appointment in 1954 as director of research and education at Metropolitan-Vickers in succession to Fleming. This was a key post, carrying as it did responsibility for the apprentice school—recognized universally as the best of its kind in Britain and the nursery for several generations of distinguished British electrical engineers—and for the research department. Jackson's reorganization of the research department into groups, each directly linked to a product division of the company, bore fruit in the form of designs for advanced products such as mass spectrometers and linear accelerators. Despite such forward-looking innovations, Metropolitan-Vickers could not survive as an independent unit and the formation of a partnership with the British Thompson-Houston Company (BTH) as Associated Electrical Industries was the first of a series of changes leading to the eventual emergence of General Electric as the major British electrical company. By 1961 such changes led to a merger of Metropolitan-Vickers and BTH laboratories. Jackson left industry to return as head of the electrical engineering department at Imperial College, and was pro-rector from 1967.

In 1953 Jackson was appointed as a member of the royal commission on the civil service and thereafter he was continually in demand for public services, especially in the fields of technical education and relations between university and industry. Among many such duties were membership of the University Grants Committee (1955–65), presidency of the British Association for Commercial and Industrial Education (1961–70), and the chairmanship of the industrial research committee of the Federation of British Industry (1958–60). His experience of industry led him to stress repeatedly the need for a comprehensive pattern of technical education, which would supply not only graduate engineers but also craftsmen and technicians to provide essential support. He was therefore opposed to the recommendations of the committee on higher education (chaired by Lord Robbins, 1961–3) for expansion of the universities, fearing that employment opportunities would not increase sufficiently rapidly to meet the aspirations of a greater number of graduates and that concentration on the university sector would lead to a shortage of properly trained technical support staff. The change from colleges of advanced technology to technological universities was one which he especially regretted. Despite his failure to prevent these decisions, he did succeed, by his chairmanship (1956–7), of a special committee of the Ministry of Education on the supply and training of teachers for technical colleges in re-emphasizing the important role of the technical colleges. The recommendations in his report, published in 1957, led, through a new technical teacher training college in Wolverhampton and a residential further education staff college in Blagdon, to a marked improvement in the morale of technical college staff.

Jackson's technical and committee abilities came together through his involvement with the engineering advisory committee of the BBC (1948–53) and as chairman of the postmaster-general's television advisory committee at the period when colour television was being introduced. The technical choice lay between the American NTSC system, the French SECAM, and the German PAL but was complicated by the desire to reach a common European standard. Jackson guided difficult discussion and gained Britain's complete support for PAL at the 1967 meeting of the international radio consultative committee. The rapid introduction of colour television in Britain followed. Despite these exacting tasks, Jackson published many books, articles, and reports.

During the 1960s, technical education was of major concern to the developing countries and Jackson was involved in several new ventures in Africa and India. He played a major part in a collaborative operation, funded in large part by the Commonwealth Office and the Federation of British Industry, which resulted in the creation of a new high-level technological institute in India: the Indian Institute of Technology, Delhi.

As chairman of the scientific manpower committee (1963–4) and of the committee on manpower resources for science and technology, Jackson initiated a series of studies on the factors influencing the supply of trained personnel for industry. He had no illusions regarding the uncertainties inherent in predicting future requirements but succeeded in impressing upon his educational colleagues the importance of meeting such requirements with the resulting creation of several new types of course, particularly at postgraduate level, aimed at bridging the gap between universities and industry.

Jackson deservedly received many recognitions for his work—a knighthood in 1958, a life peerage in 1967, and honorary degrees and fellowships from many British and overseas universities. He was president of the Institution of Electrical Engineers in 1959–60 and of the British Association for the Advancement of Science in 1967.

Jackson brought a vitality and freshness of approach

which was readily communicated to the very wide range of people in industry and education with whom he worked. An unfailing good humour, often extending to a schoolboy-like sense of fun, ensured harmonious personal relations but did not deflect him from pursuing his chosen aims with determination. His load was always a heavy one and although an indication in 1966 that his life would not be long led to some reduction in his commitments, he continued to discharge his duties with his customary high sense of responsibility. On 16 February 1970 he collapsed at his desk in Imperial College; he died the following day.   JOHN BROWN, rev.

Sources D. Gabor and J. Brown, *Memoirs FRS*, 17 (1971), 379–98 · *The Times* (18 Feb 1970) · *The Times* (20 Feb 1970) · *The Times* (23 Feb 1970) · *New Scientist* (26 Feb 1970) · *Institution of Electrical Engineers News* (April 1970), 379–98 · personal knowledge (1981) · private information (1981) · CGPLA Eng. & Wales (1970)
Archives ICL, corresp., papers; autobiographical scrapbook | Sci. Mus., corresp. with Stanley Gill
Likenesses W. Bird, photograph, 1966, NPG [*see illus.*]
Wealth at death £30,339: probate, 26 May 1970, CGPLA Eng. & Wales

Jacob, Arthur (1790–1874), oculist, was born at Knockfin, Maryborough, Queen's county, Ireland, on 13 or 30 June 1790, the second son of John Jacob (1754–1827), surgeon to the Queen's County Infirmary, and his wife, Grace (1765–1835), daughter of Jerome Alley of Donoughmore. He studied medicine with his father, and at Dr Steevens' Hospital, Dublin, under Abraham Colles. Having graduated MD at the University of Edinburgh, he studied at Paris, and then in London under Sir Benjamin Brodie, Sir Astley Cooper, and Sir William Lawrence. In 1819 he returned to Dublin and became demonstrator of anatomy under James Macartney at Trinity College, where his anatomical research gained him a high reputation, and he assembled a valuable collection of specimens which Macartney afterwards sold to the University of Cambridge.

Jacob's name is linked to his discovery in 1816 of the 'Jacob membrane', alleged to be in the layer of rods in the retina, though from the poorly prepared specimens of those days the nature of his discovery is unclear. He published his findings as 'An account of a membrane in the eye, now first described' in *Philosophical Transactions of the Royal Society* (109, 1819, pp. 30–37).

After leaving Macartney, Jacob became one of the founders of the Park Street school of medicine. He married in 1824 Sarah (*d*. 1869), daughter of Coote Carroll of Ballynote, co. Sligo, and with her raised five sons. In 1826 he was elected professor of anatomy in the Royal College of Surgeons in Ireland, and he held the chair until 1869. He was three times chosen president of the college. In 1832, in conjunction with Charles Benson and others, he established the City of Dublin Hospital. With Dr Henry Maunsell in 1839 he started the *Dublin Medical Press*, a weekly journal of medical science, and he edited forty-two volumes between 1839 and 1859. He also took an active part in founding the Royal Medical Benevolent Fund Society of Ireland and the Irish Medical Association.

At the age of seventy-five Jacob retired from the active pursuit of his profession. His fame rests on his anatomical and ophthalmological discoveries. Apart from his discovery of Jacob's membrane, he described 'Jacob's ulcer', and also revived the operation for cataract through the cornea with the curved needle. His publications fall into four groups, of which those dealing with the eye are the most important. Jacob also wrote on anatomy and zoology, and on the therapy of ocular diseases, in which last he held stubbornly to outmoded opinions. In 1869, on the death of his wife, he retired from his professorship and went to live with one of his sons at Newbarnes, Barrow in Furness, Lancashire, where he died on 21 September 1874.

G. C. BOASE, rev. ANITA MCCONNELL

Sources G. Gorin, *History of ophthalmology* (1982), 80 · J. Hirschberg, *The history of ophthalmology*, trans. F. C. Blodi, 8b (1988) · *BMJ* (17 Oct 1874), 511–12 · *Medical Press and Circular*, 69 (1874), 278, 285 · *Medical Times and Gazette* (3 Oct 1874), 405–6 · *The Graphic* (17 Oct 1874), 367, 372 · A. H. Jacob and J. H. Glascott, *An historical and genealogical narrative of the families of Jacob* (1875)
Likenesses S. C. Smith, oils, exh. 1867, Royal College of Surgeons in Ireland, Dublin · portrait, repro. in *The Graphic*
Wealth at death under £450: probate, 27 June 1877, CGPLA Eng. & Wales

Jacob, Benjamin (1778–1829), organist, son of Benjamin Jacob, an amateur violinist, was born in London on 15 May 1778, and was employed as a chorister at Portland Chapel, London, in 1786. He learned the rudiments of music from his father, singing from Robert Willoughby, the harpsichord and organ from William Shrubsole and Matthew Cooke, and at a later date harmony from Samuel Arnold. At the age of ten Jacob became organist of Salem Chapel, Soho; in 1789 organist of Carlisle Chapel, Kennington Lane; and in 1790 organist of Bentinck Chapel, Lisson Grove. In 1791 he was a chorister at the Handel commemoration, and in 1794 he was appointed organist of Surrey Chapel, in succession to John Immyns, the first organist there. An organ (built by Thomas Elliot) had been introduced into Surrey Chapel the previous year, ten years after the opening of the chapel by Rowland Hill (1744–1833). Jacob held the post until 1825, and not only proved himself a very fine performer but also established a series of organ recitals. In 1809 the elder Wesley played alternately with him, and in 1811 William Crotch became his partner for a few years.

Jacob also gave annual public concerts in aid of the Rowland Hill Almshouses, and inaugurated the organs of St Swithin's, London, and Camden Chapel, Camberwell. His connection with Hill ceased, however, after May 1825, when he accepted the post of organist to St John's Church, Waterloo Road, which led to a dispute between the two men, resulting in the publication in 1825 of *A Statement of Facts Relating to the Expulsion of Mr. Jacob from the Organ of Surrey Chapel*. Meanwhile, Jacob had become a member of the Royal Society of Musicians in 1799 and an associate of the Philharmonic Society in 1818. Also in 1818 he had conducted, from the organ and the piano, the Lent oratorios at Covent Garden. The honour of helping to elect an organist for St Paul's, Deptford, was conferred upon him in 1814, leading to his performing similar tasks elsewhere many times thereafter. Also in 1814, he published his one major collection of hymn tunes, entitled *National Psalmody*; this contained twelve original pieces by him as well as a large collection of old church melodies. Jacob remained at St John's Church until his death from consumption on 24 August 1829. He was buried at Bunhill Fields nonconformist burial-ground, London. He left a widow and three daughters: his only son died young.

Jacob's compositions were few and unimportant. Apart from those included in the *National Psalmody*, the best-known were those contained in *Dr. Watts's Divine and Moral Songs, Solos, Duets, and Trios* (1800). Jacob was also represented in *Surrey Chapel Music* (1800? and 1815?). A series of letters addressed to Jacob by Samuel Wesley on the subject of Bach were edited and published by Eliza Wesley in 1875.

L. M. MIDDLETON, *rev.* NILANJANA BANERJI

Sources *New Grove* · Grove, *Dict. mus.* · [Clarke], *The Georgian era: memoirs of the most eminent persons*, 4 (1834), 324 · Brown & Stratton, *Brit. mus.* · D. Baptie, *A handbook of musical biography* (1883) · *Nonconformist Musical Journal* (April–May 1890)

Archives BL, music collections, letters to Samuel Wesley relating to J. S. Bach

Jacob, Sir Claud William (1863–1948), army officer, was born at Mehidpore, Bombay, on 21 November 1863, the son of Lieutenant (later Major-General) William Jacob of the Indian army and his wife, Eliza, daughter of the Revd George Andrew Jacob, headmaster of Christ's Hospital, London. His uncle was Sir George Le Grand Jacob.

Jacob was educated at Sherborne School and the Royal Military College, Sandhurst. He was commissioned second lieutenant in the Worcestershire regiment on 9 September 1882. His regiment arrived in India on 10 January 1883 and when it was stationed at Quetta a year later Jacob transferred to the Indian army. He first saw active service in the 1890 Zhob Valley expedition on the north-west frontier; later he was selected to command the Zhob levy corps, and was responsible for maintaining law and order along the Waziristan and southern Afghan borders and facilitating the collection of revenue in outlying areas where officials needed an escort. At the end of 1901 Jacob participated in the blockade of the Mahsud Waziri tribe, which had committed a series of offences in the settled areas of British India. On 27 August 1894 at Kodaikanal, Madras, Jacob married Clara Pauline (1872–1959), daughter of Joseph Light Wyatt, a missionary in Trichinopoly; she survived him. They had one son, Lieutenant-General Sir (Edward) Ian *Jacob (1899–1993), assistant military secretary to the war cabinet (1939–46) and director-general of the British Broadcasting Corporation. In 1904 Jacob was selected to raise the 106th Hazara pioneers, formed to help improve railway communications along the frontier, which he commanded for the next seven years. Jacob was appointed general staff officer, grade 1 (GSO1) of the Meerut division in 1912, ending a period of thirty years' near continuous service almost entirely on the north-west frontier.

Jacob accompanied the Meerut division when it sailed to France and Flanders, following the outbreak of the First World War, arriving in the autumn of 1914 in time to witness the last stages of the battle of La Bassée. His bravery

Sir Claud William Jacob (1863–1948), by Lafayette, 1926

and insouciance under fire in a critical situation on the Indian corps front just before Christmas 1914 marked him out for promotion. Jacob was appointed to command the Dehra Dun brigade at the beginning of 1915 which he led at Neuve Chapelle in March and at the Aubers Ridge in May. He assumed command of the Meerut division on 6 September 1915 and led it in the costly engagement at Pietre during the battle of Loos. When the Indian corps left for Mesopotamia Jacob remained in France, the only senior Indian army officer of the corps to do so following the personal intervention of Sir Douglas Haig. He took over command of the 21st New Army division on 18 November 1915, was promoted, and later that year was made a CB.

Jacob's efficiency and thoroughness quickly brought his new command to an efficient fighting pitch. Early in 1916 he was wounded, however, by a shell which landed on his headquarters and killed his chief of staff. After a quick recovery he returned to his division in May 1916, but he did not lead it during the opening stages of the battle of the Somme. Instead he commanded a reserve corps, held at the disposal of the commander-in-chief, and was directed to familiarize himself with the dispositions and course of the battle along the whole Somme front.

Jacob was appointed in September 1916 to command the 2nd corps in Fifth Army. On 26 September his troops captured the village of Thiepval which the Germans had declared was impregnable. In the subsequent fighting the 2nd corps secured the Zollern, Stuff, and Schwaben redoubts. At 5.45 a.m. on 13 November, attacking in a thick fog, his command captured St Pierre Divion at comparatively light cost, greatly facilitating the operations of the 5th corps north of the River Ancre. When the Germans conducted a bitterly fought fighting retreat towards the Hindenburg line, his corps advanced past Achiet-le-Grand and beyond St Leger which he reached on 19 March 1917. By these actions Jacob established himself as one of the leading tacticians of Fifth Army. For his services on the Ancre he was promoted KCB in 1917 and made lieutenant-general on 3 June 1917. Jacob's corps, now part of Sir Herbert Plumer's Second Army, took a prominent part in the Passchendaele offensive, and carried out a particularly difficult engagement on the Gheluvelt plateau. During the German spring offensive in 1918 Jacob fought in Flanders and led his corps during the final allied advance which broke German opposition and brought hostilities to an end in November 1918. Jacob was briefly considered as a replacement for Sir Douglas Haig as commander-in-chief during the spring when Lloyd George grew increasingly critical of the latter's leadership. Jacob's corps later formed part of the Army of the Rhine, stationed at Cologne, and he was appointed KCMG in 1919.

In January 1920 Jacob returned to India as chief of the general staff, and on 31 May he was promoted general. He held this important post during the difficult sweeping post-war reorganization of the Indian army. Between 1920 and 1924 Jacob was aide-de-camp to the king and in 1924 he was made a KCSI. In 1924–5 he held the northern command, India, and after the death of Lord Rawlinson in 1925 he served temporarily as commander-in-chief in India. Despite his impeccable credentials for the job this appointment was not confirmed and Jacob returned to England. Between April 1926 and May 1930 he served as secretary of the military department at the India Office. He was appointed GCB in 1926, was promoted field marshal in 1926, and was made GCSI in 1930. Jacob was constable of the Tower of London between 1938 and 1943 and was commandant of the Church Lads' Brigade, in which he was keenly interested, for several years before his death. He was colonel of the 106th Hazara pioneers (1916–33), the Worcestershire regiment (between 1927 and 1938), and, from 1928, the 2nd / 10th Baluch regiment. Jacob died on 2 June 1948, at the age of eighty-four, following an operation in King's College Hospital, Denmark Hill, Camberwell, London.

Jacob was a practical soldier with a high degree of common sense, great thoroughness in method, and the ability to learn from experience. He had a straightforward character, never sought publicity, and his modesty may have kept him from even higher positions. He had an unrivalled knowledge of regimental soldiering, and when in high command possessed the continuous and undiminished confidence of all ranks.　　　　　　T. R. MOREMAN

Sources *The Times* (3 June 1948) · *DNB* · J. E. Edmonds, ed., *Military operations, France and Belgium*, 14 vols., History of the Great War (1922–48) · G. B. Unwin, *History of the blockade of the Mahsud Waziris in 1900–1901* (1904) · J. W. Merewether and F. Smith, *The Indian corps in France* (1917) · J. Willcocks, *With the Indians in France* (1920) · T. Travers, *The killing ground* (1987) · *Army List* · BL OIOC, N/2/80, fol. 44 · *CGPLA Eng. & Wales* (1948)

Archives Bodl. RH, corresp. with C. Walker | FILM IWM FVA, documentary footage · IWM FVA, news footage
Likenesses F. Dodd, charcoal and watercolour drawing, 1917, IWM · W. Stoneman, photograph, 1917, NPG · Lafayette, photograph, 1926, NPG [*see illus.*] · W. Stoneman, photograph, 1938, NPG
Wealth at death £3510 0s. 5d.: probate, 29 July 1948, *CGPLA Eng. & Wales*

Jacob, Edgar (1844–1920), bishop of St Albans, was born at the rectory at Crawley, Hampshire, on 16 November 1844, the fourth son of the evangelical Philip Jacob (*d.* 1884), rector of Crawley and canon (later archdeacon) of Winchester, and his wife, Anna Sophia (*fl.* 1815–1875), eldest daughter of the Hon. Gerard Thomas Noel, canon of Winchester. He was educated at Winchester College and at New College, Oxford, where he matriculated on 16 October 1863 and of which he was a scholar. He obtained a first class in classical moderations (1865) and a third class in *literae humaniores* (1867), proceeding BA (1868) and MA (1870).

Ordained in 1868, Jacob held curacies at Taynton (1868–9) and Witney (1869–71) in Oxfordshire, and then moved to London to be curate in the large parish of St James, Bermondsey (1871–2). There he started to develop his ideas on how to administer such a parish. In 1872 he somewhat reluctantly went to India as domestic chaplain to Robert Milman, bishop of Calcutta and metropolitan of India. However, during the next four years he gained invaluable experience. Much of the work of administering the immense diocese of Calcutta (in those days about two-thirds of India) was gradually handed over to Jacob by the bishop. Milman, although a high-churchman, cultivated good relations with the Church Missionary Society as well as with the Society for the Propagation of the Gospel. Jacob, too, came to appreciate the harmonious way in which these societies and the Bible Society worked together in India. Thus were laid the foundations of his deep interest in missionary work overseas and of his wide sympathy for all Christian agencies engaged in this task.

Following the death of Milman in 1876, Jacob returned to England and was appointed examining chaplain to E. H. Browne, bishop of Winchester, a post he retained under successive bishops until 1896. In 1877 he became the first warden of the Wilberforce Memorial Mission in south London, but the following year the warden and fellows of Winchester College selected him to be vicar of Portsea. There he found a population of over 20,000, a dilapidated and half-empty church, and one curate. On his departure eighteen years later (by which time the population had nearly doubled), there were a magnificent and well-filled parish church, numerous parochial organizations, several mission churches, and twelve curates living in the old vicarage enlarged into a clergy house. The new parish church of St Mary, designed by Sir Arthur Blomfield and consecrated in 1889, was erected at a cost of nearly £50,000, more than half of which was contributed anonymously by Jacob's great friend William Henry Smith, the statesman, bookseller, and philanthropist. It is not too much to say that Jacob's energy and enthusiasm created in Portsea a parochial organization which was widely regarded as a model for the whole Church of England. Indeed eloquent testimony to the value of his work was subsequently given by two of his successors at Portsea, the future archbishops Cosmo Gordon Lang and Cyril Foster Garbett. His views on the pastoral ministry of the church found expression in *The Divine Society* (1890), his Cambridge lectures on pastoral theology.

Jacob was made an honorary canon of Winchester in 1884, an honorary chaplain to Queen Victoria in 1887, a chaplain-in-ordinary in 1890, rural dean of Landport, Hampshire, in 1892, and three years later a proctor in convocation and select preacher at Oxford University. On 25 January 1896 he was consecrated bishop of Newcastle. Although he held the see for only seven years, his organizing and administrative ability soon enlisted the practical support of the leaders of commerce and industry in the north-east in raising large sums of money for diocesan projects. On a wider front he was influential in the passing of the Burial Act of 1901, which he believed allayed the grievances of both Anglicans and nonconformists.

In 1903 Jacob was translated to St Albans, exchanging a compact diocese for one containing the two large counties of Hertfordshire and Essex and 630 benefices. His presence not far from London was greatly desired by the archbishop of Canterbury so that his practical ability could be utilized on such bodies as the ecclesiastical commission and Queen Anne's Bounty. Furthermore the problem of the spiritual care of the rapidly increasing urban population within the diocese consequent on London's expansion elicited his close attention and vigorous response. However, the incessant strain of administering an unwieldy diocese and of raising money for its prospective division impaired his health, and in 1911 he fell seriously ill. After his recovery he saw his efforts crowned in the division of the see in 1914 into the new units of Chelmsford (Essex with London-over-the-border) and St Albans (now comprising Hertfordshire and Bedfordshire). He had desired to be the first bishop of Chelmsford, but continuing poor health necessitated his remaining at St Albans, from which he resigned in December 1919 and retired to Winchester.

Despite carrying for many years a heavy load of parochial and diocesan work at home, Jacob maintained his interest in and advocacy of missionary activity abroad. To a great extent he instigated the board of missions of the province of Canterbury in 1887, of which he became the first secretary. He largely organized the Anglican missionary conference of 1894 and chaired both the foreign missions committee at the 1898 Lambeth conference and the pan-Anglican congress of 1908. When in the upper house of the convocation of Canterbury he moved a resolution in support of the Edinburgh missionary conference of 1910, the bishops gave their unanimous support to his persuasive advocacy.

Bishop Jacob was a great administrator with a well-earned reputation for business capacity and legal acumen, and he employed these gifts for the good of the church at both local and national level. He was of a simple and unpretentious nature, kindly and sympathetic, and his service abroad led him to rise above ecclesiastical partisanship and to strive for co-operation among church people of different persuasions. He never married but relied heavily on the companionship and support of his sister Edith. Shortly after he retired he died at St Cross, Winchester, on 25 March 1920, and was buried in the churchyard of St Albans Cathedral four days later.

K. F. GIBBS, *rev.* STEPHEN GREGORY

Sources J. B. Wainewright, ed., *Winchester College, 1836–1906: a register* (1907) • E. Jacob, *Farewell charge to the clergy and laity of the diocese of St. Albans* (1919) • Crockford (1918–19) • *The Wykehamist* (21 May 1920) • C. F. Garbett, ed., *The work of a great parish* (1915) • *The Guardian* (1 April 1920) • *The Times* (26 March 1920) • *Men and women of the time* (1899) • E. Stock, *The history of the Church Missionary Society: its environment, its men and its work*, 4 vols. (1899–1916) • A. H. Jacob and J. H. Glascott, *An historical and genealogical narrative of the families of Jacob* (1875) • H. Maxwell, *Life and times of the Right Honourable William Henry Smith*, 2 vols. (1893) • Foster, *Alum. Oxon.* • *CGPLA Eng. & Wales* (1920)

Archives LPL, corresp. with Archbishop Benson • W. H. Smith & Son Ltd, Abingdon, Oxfordshire, corresp. with W. H. Smith and others

Likenesses S. P. Hall, group portrait, watercolour (*The bench of bishops, 1902*), NPG • Spy [L. Ward], mechanically reproduced caricature, repro. in *VF* (26 Sept 1906) • Whitlock, postcard, NPG • two photographs, NPG • wood-engraving (after photograph by Whitlock), NPG; repro. in *ILN* (30 Nov 1895)

Wealth at death £24,946 13s. 5d.: probate, 14 July 1920, *CGPLA Eng. & Wales*

Jacob, Edward (1710?–1788), antiquary and naturalist, was born in Canterbury, the eldest son of Edward Jacob (*d.* 1756), surgeon and alderman, who served as mayor of Canterbury in 1727–8, and Jane, daughter of Strangford Violl, vicar of Upminster. About 1735 he moved to Faversham where he lived at 78 Preston Street and practised as a surgeon, following in his father's and grandfather's footsteps. Among his patients was Lord Sondes of Lees Court, Sheldwich. The Jacobs were a long-established east Kent family and several members had served as mayors and magistrates in Sandwich and Dover. Actively interested in local affairs, Jacob was four times mayor of Faversham—in 1749, 1754, 1765, and 1775. On 4 September 1739 he married by licence at the church of All Saints, Eastchurch, Sheppey, Margaret (*bap.* 1709, *d.* 1749), daughter of John and Margaret Rigden of Canterbury, with whom he had no children. Second, he married Mary (1722/3–1803), only daughter of Stephen Long of Sandwich, Kent; they had eleven children, six of whom died in infancy.

Jacob interested himself in the history of Faversham soon after he had moved there, 'having an early propensity to the study of antiquities'. He was elected a fellow of the Society of Antiquaries on 5 June 1755, and in 1774 published *The History of the Town and Port of Faversham*, dedicated to Lord Sondes. He was also one of the first to recognize the significance of rich fossil remains in the clay cliffs of northern Sheppey, where he began collecting examples during the 1740s. This interest led directly to his buying the manor of Nutts in Leysdown on the island. In

1754 he submitted to the Royal Society's *Philosophical Transactions* 'An account of several bones of an elephant found at Leysdown, in the Island of Sheppey'. His *Plantae Favershamienses: a catalogue of … plants growing … about Faversham … with an appendix, exhibiting a short view of the fossil bodies of the adjacect Island of Shepey* appeared in 1777. He also assisted William Boys in *Testacea minuta rariora, or, A collection of the minute … shells … discovered near Sandwich* (1784), lent manuscripts to the Kentish historian Edward Hasted, and commented upon the proofs of Hasted's account of Sheppey. In 1780 he contributed to *Archaeologia* 'Observations on the Roman earthen ware taken from the Pan-Pudding Rock' at Whitstable, Kent, which refuted the views of Thomas Pownall. In 1770 he wrote the preface to a reprint of the first edition of the anonymous domestic tragedy, *Arden of Faversham* (1592).

Jacob died at Faversham on 26 November 1788 and was buried in the parish church, where a mural monument was erected to his memory. He bequeathed the manor of Nutts to his wife, Mary. His third son, **John Jacob** (1765–1840), topographer, was born on 27 December 1765. In 1803 he was living at Roath Court, Glamorgan. In 1815 he moved to Guernsey, where he collected materials for *Annals of some of the British Norman Isles Constituting the Bailiwick of Guernsey*. Part one comprised the Casket lighthouses, Alderney, Sark, Herm, and Jethou, with part of Guernsey, and was printed in a large octavo volume in Paris in 1830. Part two, announced for December 1831, never appeared. He married Anna Maria, daughter of George le Grand, surgeon of Canterbury; they had four daughters and five sons, the youngest of whom was Major-General Sir George le Grand *Jacob (1805–1881). John Jacob died in Guernsey on 21 February 1840.

GORDON GOODWIN, rev. JOHN WHYMAN

Sources A. Winnifrith, *Men of Kent and Kentish Men: biographical notices of 680 worthies of Kent* (1913), 288–9 · J. Whyman, introduction, in E. Jacob, *The history of the town and port of Faversham* (1774); repr. in *History of Faversham* (1974), 7, 8, 13–14, 16–18, 30 · A. Percival, biographical note, in E. Jacob, *The history of the town and port of Faversham* (1774); repr. as *History of Faversham* (1974), 55–61 · P. Hyde, *Thomas Arden in Faversham: the man behind the myth* (1996), 5 · J. Hutchinson, *Men of Kent and Kentish men: a manual of Kentish biography* (1892), 78–9 · J. Simson, *Eminent men of Kent* (1893), 136–7 · E. Hasted, *The history and topographical survey of the county of Kent*, 2nd edn, 6 (1798), 213, 264, 268, 357, 517 · E. Hasted, *The history and topographical survey of the county of Kent*, 2nd edn, 12 (1801), 605, 609 · W. A. Scott Robertson, 'The Church of All Saints, Eastchurch in Sheppey', *Archaeologia Cantiana*, 14 (1882), 374–88, esp. 384 · C. V. Collier, 'Coats of arms in Kent churches: St Mary of Charity, Faversham', *Archaeologia Cantiana*, 22 (1897), 197–208, esp. 205 · G. Culmer, 'Queen Elizabeth's Grammar School, Faversham', *Archaeologia Cantiana*, 47 (1935), 189–97, esp. 196 · F. W. Cook, 'Additional notes on the Horne and Chute families of Appledore', *Archaeologia Cantiana*, 49 (1937), 157–66 · R. Gunnis, 'Signed monuments in Kentish churches', *Archaeologia Cantiana*, 62 (1949), 57–86, esp. 73 · J. Boyle, 'Hasted in perspective', *Archaeologia Cantiana*, 100 (1984), 295–304, esp. 297 · F. H. Panton, 'The finances and government of the city and county of Canterbury in the eighteenth and early nineteenth centuries', *Archaeologia Cantiana*, 109 (1991), 191–246, esp. 196–7, 206n., 219, 221, 237 · J. Boyle, *In quest of Hasted* (1984), 72, 112, 133

Archives Bodl. Oxf., extracts from his MSS

Likenesses C. Hall, line engraving, BM; repro. in E. Jacob, *Plantae Favershamienses* (1777) · portrait, repro. in E. Jacob, *History of Faversham* (1974), facing title-page

Jacob, Edward (1795/6–1841). *See under* Jacob, William (1761/2–1851).

Jacob, Sir George Le Grand (1805–1881), army officer in the East India Company, the fifth son and youngest child of John *Jacob (1765–1840) [*see under* Jacob, Edward (1710?–1788)], and his wife, Anna Maria Le Grand, was born at his father's residence, Roath Court, near Cardiff, on 24 April 1805. His family in 1815 moved to Guernsey. Jacob was educated at Elizabeth College, Guernsey, and by private tutors in France and England, and when about fifteen was sent to London to learn oriental languages under Dr John Borthwick Gilchrist. He obtained an Indian infantry cadetship in 1820, and on the voyage out to Bombay made a close friendship with the political officer and traveller Alexander Burnes. He was posted to the 2nd or grenadier regiment Bombay native infantry (later Prince of Wales's Own) as ensign on 9 June 1821, in which unit he obtained all his regimental steps except the last. He was promoted lieutenant on 10 December 1823, captain on 6 June 1836, major on 1 May 1848, lieutenant-colonel in the 31st Bombay native infantry on 15 November 1853, brevet colonel on 6 December 1856, brigadier-general on 21 July 1858, and major-general on retirement on 31 December 1861.

Jacob passed for interpreter in Hindustani so quickly after arrival in India, that he was complimented in presidency general orders. He afterwards passed in Persian and Marathi. He saw some harassing service with his regiment against the Bhils in the pestiferous Nerbudda jungles, and was subsequently with it in Cutch and at Ukulkote. He took his furlough home in 1831, and in January 1833 was appointed orderly officer at Addiscombe College. While there, at the request of the Oriental Translation Fund, he undertook the translation of the *Ajaib-al-tabakat* ('Wonder of the universe'), a manuscript purchased by Alexander Burnes in the bazaar at Bukhara. Jacob considered the work not worth printing, and his manuscript translation is now in the library of the Asiatic Society, London.

On 18 June 1835 Jacob married Emily, daughter of Colonel Utterton of Heath Lodge, Croydon, and soon afterwards sailed for India. His wife died at sea, and Jacob landed at Bombay in very broken health. He recovered under the care of a brother, William Jacob, then an officer in the Bombay artillery, and in 1836 was appointed second political assistant in Kathiawar, where he was in political charge from 1839 to 1843. His ability in dealing with the disputed Limri succession was noticed by the government; he later described the curious details in his book *Western India*. He was also thanked for his report on the Babriawar people (1843) and for other reports on Kathiawar. Early in 1845 he served as extra aide-de-camp to Major-General Delamotte during the disturbances in the southern Maratha country, and was wounded in the head and arm by a falling rock when in command of the storming party in the assault on the hill fort of Munsuntosh.

In April 1845 Jacob was appointed political agent in Savantvadi. The little state was bankrupt, with its gaols overflowing; but Jacob's judicious measures during a period of six years restored order, retrieved the finances, and reformed abuses. On 8 January 1851 he was made political agent in Cutch, and was sent into Sind as a special commissioner to investigate the case of the unfortunate Mir Ali Murad, khan of Khairpur. He also sat on an inquiry into departmental abuses at Bombay. An account of his travels in Cutch appeared in the 1862 *Proceedings* of the Bombay Geographical Society, later merged in the Asiatic Society of Bombay. His health needing change, Jacob obtained leave, and visited China, Java, Sarawak, and Australia, 'keeping his eyes and ears ever on the alert, always reading, writing, or inquiring—mostly smoking—winning men by his geniality and women by his courteous bearing' (*Overland Mail*, 6 May 1881). On his return he was shipwrecked on a coral reef in Torres Strait, and saved from cannibals by a Dutch vessel. He quitted Cutch for Bombay in December 1856, at first intending to retire; but he served under Outram in the Persian expedition. In Persia he was in command of the native light battalion in the division under Henry Havelock, whom Jacob appears to have regarded as too much of a martinet. He returned with the expeditionary force to Bombay in May 1857.

Acting under the orders of Lord Elphinstone, the governor of Bombay, Jacob arrived at Kolhapur on 14 August, a fortnight after the 27th Bombay native infantry had mutinied there. Four days later he, with a mere handful of troops, quietly disarmed the regiment, and punished the ringleaders. On 4 December following, when the city closed its gates against Jacob's small force which was camped in its lines outside, Jacob promptly blew open one of the gates, put the rebels to flight, tried by drumhead court martial and executed on the spot twenty-one who were convicted of mutiny—eight were blown from the guns, two were hung, and eleven were shot—and held the city until the danger was past. His vigour presumably prevented the uprising from spreading over the whole southern Maratha country and into the nizam's dominions. Jacob was specially thanked in presidency general orders on 8 January 1858. His powers, at first limited to Kolhapur, Savantvadi, and Ratnagiri, were in May 1858 extended to the whole of the southern Maratha country, of which he was appointed special commissioner, the command of the troops with the rank of brigadier-general being subsequently added. After dealing successfully with various local outbreaks, Jacob was sent to Goa to confer with the Portuguese authorities respecting the Savant rebels on the frontier. This service successfully accomplished, he resigned his command. He remained nominally political agent in Cutch up to the date of his leaving India in 1859. James Outram appears to have desired that Jacob should succeed him as member of the council at Calcutta, but he retired with the rank of major-general from 31 December 1861. He was made CB in March 1859, and KCSI in June 1869.

Jacob has been likened in character to his cousin General John Jacob. He had the same fearlessness, the same hatred of red tape and jobbery, and the same genius for understanding and conciliating Asians. His outspoken advocacy of indigenous rights not infrequently offended officials. Throughout his life he was a keen student of the literature of India, and whenever opportunity offered did his best to promote research in Indian history and antiquities. He was one of the earliest copiers of the Asoka inscriptions (250 BC) at Girnar, Kathiawar; and in Cunningham's *Corpus inscriptionum* (1877) are many inscriptions transcribed by Jacob in western India. A list of papers on the history, archaeology, topography, geology, and metallurgy of western India, contributed by Jacob at different times to various publications, is given in the *Journal of the Asiatic Society*, London (new ser., 13, 1881, vii–viii). Some are included in the Royal Society's *Catalogue of Scientific Papers*; but neither list appears complete. In his prime Jacob was a keen sportsman. He shot seven lions in one day in Kathiawar, and his prowess as a shikari was perpetuated in Indian verse. His last twenty years were spent at home under much suffering—a constant struggle with asthma, bronchitis, and growing blindness. His mental vigour remained unimpaired. Helped by his niece and adopted daughter Gertrude Louisa Le Grand Jacob, he wrote his *Western India before and during the Mutinies*, which was published in 1871, and was highly commended by Sir John Kaye. Jacob died at his home, 12 Queensborough Terrace, Bayswater, London, on 27 January 1881, and was buried in Brookwood cemetery, near Woking, Surrey.

H. M. CHICHESTER, rev. JAMES LUNT

Sources East-India Register · Hart's Army List · G. le G. Jacob, *Western India before and during the mutinies* (1871) · *Journal of the Asiatic Society* [London], new ser., 13 (May 1881) · J. W. Kaye and G. B. Malleson, *Kaye's and Malleson's History of the Indian mutiny of 1857–8*, new edn, 6 vols. (1897–8) · T. R. E. Holmes, *A history of the Indian mutiny* (1883) · P. Cadell, *History of the Bombay army* (1938) · F. J. Goldsmid, *James Outram: a biography*, 2 vols. (1880) · *Report on Administration of Public Affairs in Bombay* (1857–8) · Burke, *Peerage* · C. Hibbert, *The great mutiny, India, 1857* (1978) · Boase, *Mod. Eng. biog.*
Archives BL OIOC, papers, MSS Eur F 75
Wealth at death under £9000: probate, 26 Feb 1881, CGPLA Eng. & Wales

Jacob, Giles (*bap.* 1686, *d.* 1744), legal and literary author, was baptized on 22 November 1686 in Romsey, Hampshire, the only son among eight children of Henry Jacob (*d.* 1735), maltster, and his wife, Susanna Thornbery. It is unknown where he received his education, but he later wrote that he received legal training under a 'very eminent attorney' (G. Jacob, *Poetical Register*, 1719, 1.318) and subsequently became steward and secretary to the politician William Blathwayt. This may have been where he gained the experience administering manorial courts that he mentioned in his first guide to legal practice, *The Compleat Court-Keeper*, published in 1713. Jacob was also the compiler at this time of a short chronological guide to statute law, at first published anonymously but later revised and reissued several times under his own name. The success of this table and *The Compleat Court-Keeper* encouraged Jacob to further endeavours, among which the most important was *Lex constitutionis*, published in 1719. It attempted to outline the common and criminal law against the background of the branches of the executive, from the crown to the customs officers. The work was thoroughly researched but has been viewed as less successful as an overview of the constitution than Roger Acherley's *Britannic Constitution* of 1727, its deficiencies attributed by Holdsworth to the speed with which Jacob produced his works.

Although Jacob's lasting reputation was based on his legal writings, his output was far more diverse than this might suggest. In 1714 he published a farce, *Love in a Wood, or, The Country Squire*, admittedly with a legal theme; it was never performed. He experimented with satire in *The Rape of the Smock*, published in 1717, a scatological parody of Alexander Pope's *The Rape of the Lock*. A pornographic work, *Tractatus de hermaphroditis* (1718) followed. In 1719 appeared the first volume of the *Poetical Register*, followed by a second in 1720; the volumes were reissued in 1723. This guide to the lives of contemporary and historical poets involved Jacob in controversy when he criticized John Gay for introducing 'some extraordinary Scenes … which seem'd to trespass on Female Modesty' (Guerinot, 74) in *Three Hours after Marriage*, and then, when attributing the farce *The Confederates* to Joseph Gay, claimed it was written 'to expose the Obscenity and false Pretence to Wit' (ibid.) in the earlier play. *Three Hours after Marriage* had been written by John Gay in collaboration with John Arbuthnot and Pope. Jacob's criticisms of the play were enough to ensure his inclusion in the 1728 edition of *The Dunciad*, book three,

> Jacob, the Scourge of Grammar, mark with awe,
> Nor less revere him, Blunderbuss of Law.

Jacob was probably seen by Pope as a dunce because of his devotion to a culture of litigation that Pope deplored as uncivilized and unnecessary for the truly virtuous. Pope probably regarded Jacob as a minor target but Jacob was understandably aggrieved. On the basis that Pope had read and approved the passages referring to him in the second volume of the *Poetical Register* before publication, Edmund Curll in *The Popiad* accused Pope of writing his own praise, a charge repeated in later years by both Curll and Jacob.

In the meantime Jacob continued to research and write legal books, including *The Student's Companion*, which appeared in 1725. Jacob wrote that this was his favourite book as 'it hath cost me unusual labour' (Holdsworth, *Eng. law*, 12.425). It included study advice and an alphabetical summary of important legal topics. It prepared the way for Jacob's most enduring and successful work, *A New Law Dictionary*, first published in 1729. The dictionary had taken nine years to research and write, and set a new precedent by being the first published guide to English law that combined an abridgement of statute law with a dictionary of legal practice and terminology. *A New Law Dictionary* reached its fifth edition in 1744, the year of Jacob's death; competition from a rival law dictionary by Timothy Cunningham perhaps led to the ninth edition being thoroughly revised by Owen Ruffhead and J. Morgan in 1772. The dictionary was revised again for its eleventh edition in 1797 by Thomas Edlyne Tomlins, whose name supplanted

Jacob's as the author from the twelfth (or second) edition in 1809. However, it was still 'Jacob's Law Dictionary' in which the publisher John Murray acquired a 160th share on 24 June 1807 at a cost of £13, suggesting a total value of £2080. It was the smallest fraction of a copyright which Murray bought that day, but the most expensive, showing how valuable Jacob's work remained over sixty years after his death. Another very successful book was *Every Man his Own Lawyer* (1736), which reached a tenth edition in 1788.

On 2 October 1733 Jacob married Jane Dexter at St Mary Magdalen, Old Fish Street, London; they had at least one child, Jane, born in 1735. By January 1736 Jacob and his family were living in Staines, Middlesex, from where he argued with his brother-in-law Richard Pearce over his father's property in Romsey. He died on 8 May 1744.

MATTHEW KILBURN

Sources Holdsworth, *Eng. law*, vols. 7, 12 · J. D. Cowley, *A bibliography of abridgments, digests, dictionaries and indexes of English law to the year 1800* (1932) · J. Guerinot, *Pamphlet attacks on Alexander Pope, 1711–1744* (1969) · W. Prest, 'Lay legal knowledge in early modern England', *Learning the law: teaching and the transmission of law in England, 1150–1900*, ed. J. A. Bush and A. Wijffels (1999), 303–13 · P. Rogers, *Grub Street: studies in a subculture* (1972) · A. Pope, *The Dunciad*, ed. J. Sutherland (1943), vol. 5 of *The Twickenham edition of the poems of Alexander Pope*, ed. J. Butt (1939–69); 3rd edn [in 1 vol.] (1963); repr. (1965) · Giles Jacob to Richard Pearce, 3 Jan 1736, BL, Add. MS 26775, fol. 97 · J. Latham, notes on ancestry of Giles Jacob, BL, Add. MS 26775, fol. 94–5, 98 · 'Original assignments of copyrights', BL, Add. MS 38730, vol. 3, fols. 98, 127 · *GM*, 1st ser., 14 (1744), 281 · *IGI*

Archives BL, letter to Richard Pearce, Add. MS 26775, fol. 97

Jacob, Gordon Percival Septimus (1895–1984), composer, was born on 5 July 1895 at 44 Victoria Road, Gipsy Hill, Upper Norwood, London, the seventh son and youngest of ten children of Stephen Jacob, an official of the Indian Civil Service stationed in Calcutta, and his wife, Clara Laura Forlong. He was educated at Dulwich College, where his musical gifts were encouraged by performances of early pieces for orchestra and for organ. He joined the army at the outbreak of the First World War and was taken prisoner in 1917. With characteristic resourcefulness he worked his way through a harmony textbook in the camp library and began composing for a camp orchestra of assorted instruments. After demobilization in 1919 and a false start as a student journalist he took a correspondence course which resulted in an ARCM diploma and acceptance as a student at the Royal College of Music in 1920. Here he was a pupil of Charles Villiers Stanford and Ralph Vaughan Williams in composition, of Herbert Howells in theory, and of Adrian Boult in conducting.

Both during and following the war German music was frowned upon, the new French and Russian music (Debussy, Mussorgsky, and early Stravinsky) being favoured in concert programmes. These influences, together with Parry and Elgar, are at the root of Jacob's musical language. It is more difficult to account for Jacob's early skill as an orchestrator. He had a natural curiosity concerning instrumental timbre together with a capacity to analyse, auralize, and organize. At the end of his student course in 1924 he was taken immediately onto the teaching staff of the Royal College of Music, where he remained until his retirement in 1966. In addition to his teaching commitments and examining for the Associated Board of the Royal Schools of Music, he found the time from these earliest years to pour out a ceaseless stream of compositions in every conceivable genre.

At that time choral societies and school choirs could still provide, through the sale of sheet music, a steady income and, while Jacob took advantage of this market, he also had ambitions at a more prestigious level. A viola concerto was first performed at a Prom in 1926, and a piano concerto followed in 1927. The death of a favourite brother in the First World War was the mainspring of the symphony no. 1 of 1928–9. Commissions from festivals and from the many seasonal orchestras then still prevalent in seaside towns provided further opportunities. Leon Goossens gave the first performance of his oboe concerto at a Royal Philharmonic Society concert in 1935, and the *Variations on an Original Theme* was first performed by the Hastings Festival Orchestra in 1937.

During the Second World War Jacob became known to a wider public through his witty arrangements of popular tunes for Tommy Handley's weekly radio comedy show *ITMA*. The epic symphony no. 2 of 1944–5 was described by the composer as 'a meditation on war, suffering and victory'. Four new works appeared in 1951, the year of the Festival of Britain: *Music for a Festival* (for brass and military bands), the horn concerto, the cantata *A Goodly Heritage*, and the flute concerto.

Composers now relied increasingly on fees paid by the Performing Right Society for broadcasts, and in this respect Jacob's place in Britain's musical world seemed assured. However, from 1959, as the BBC began its championship of the avant-garde, an entire generation of composers of Jacob's age and background found itself superseded. As commissions and performances dwindled at home Jacob found his music increasingly popular in Europe and especially in the USA, where his wind-band music had always found favour. He now had a stream of commissions from American universities, and continued into his final years to produce works for the many excellent school orchestras and wind bands in Great Britain that were the product of the new emphasis on instrumental music in education.

Jacob suffered from a cleft palate, a handicap which often coloured his speech with a dry irony that was a delight to his pupils and friends. In 1949 he was awarded the Cobbett medal for chamber music composition. He was a DMus of London University and was appointed CBE in 1968. On 18 December 1924 he married Sidney Wilmot (*b.* 1888/9), daughter of the Revd Arthur Wollaston Gray, of Ipswich. She died in 1958 and on 8 August 1959 he married her niece, Margaret Sidney Hannah, daughter of Cuthbert Arthur Gray, insurance agent of Helions Bumpstead. They had a daughter and a son.

Jacob's place in musical history is as an eclectic, versatile member of the school of Vaughan Williams and Gustav Holst, rather than of the more cosmopolitan group which includes Sir William Walton and Constant Lambert. Pungent and closely argued though much of his music is, its diatonic and often modal lyricism sets it strongly apart from the prevalent style of the succeeding generation of composers, some of whom had been his pupils. He died on 8 June 1984 at his home, 1 Audley Road, Saffron Walden, and was cremated at Cambridge on 14 June. He was survived by his second wife.

ERIC WETHERELL

Sources personal knowledge (2004) · private information (2004) [M. S. H. Jacob] · *CGPLA Eng. & Wales* (1984) · *DNB* · *The Times* (11 June 1984) · *New Grove* · R. S. Pusey, 'Gordon Jacob: a study of the solo works for oboe and English horn and their ensemble literature', diss., Peabody Conservatoire of Music, Johns Hopkins University, Baltimore, 1979 · E. Wetherell, *Gordon Jacob: a centenary biography* (1995) · E. Wetherell, 'Gordon Jacob', *British Music*, 17 (1995), 1–5 · E. Wetherell, 'Gordon Jacob: the windband works', *Winds*, 10/1 (1995), 10–13 · b. cert. · m. certs. · d. cert.
Archives SOUND BL NSA, *Composer's portrait*, 11 Aug 1967, M898W C1 · BL NSA, performance recording
Likenesses J. Pannett, chalk drawing, NPG · photographs, priv. coll.
Wealth at death £73,584: administration with will, 21 Aug 1984, *CGPLA Eng. & Wales*

Jacob, Henry (1562/3–1624), semi-separatist minister, was the son of John Jacob, yeoman, of Cheriton, Kent. According to Anthony Wood he entered St Mary Hall, Oxford, as a commoner or butteler in 1579. He matriculated from that hall on 27 November 1581, aged eighteen, before graduating BA on 16 December 1583, and proceeding MA on 8 July 1586. Later that year he was made precentor of the choir at Corpus Christi College, Oxford.

The next years of his life are obscure, but Jacob did not take up a benefice at Cheriton, as it was once thought, and it is highly unlikely that he became a separatist in the remnant of Robert Browne's congregation at Middleburg, since such a phase is not mentioned by contemporaries, whether friendly or hostile. From *A Defence of the Churches and Ministery of Englande* (1599), a work directed against the separatist Francis Johnson, it appears that Jacob may have been in London in 1596, when Johnson was in the Clink prison. In 1597 a man named Jacob was lecturer in the city parish of St Augustine. Jacob was certainly in London in that year for he attended a sermon given at St Paul's Cross, probably during Lent, by Thomas Bilson, bishop of Winchester, on the subject of Christ's descent into hell. Jacob criticized this in *A Treatise of the Sufferings and Victory of Christ* (1598), and to Bilson's reply he made in 1600 a further riposte, *A Defence of a Treatise*. Both the two pamphlets against Bilson and his critique of Johnson were issued in Middleburg, Zeeland. This is not decisive evidence that Jacob himself had withdrawn there, though if, as has often been suggested, Jacob ministered to the Merchant Adventurers in the town, it was probably in this period. In August 1599 it was reported that a W. Cholmley had been appointed to a post in the Tower of London 'which Henry Jacob lately held' (Burrage, 1.283).

By June 1603 Jacob was living at Wood Street, London, from where he led the puritan campaign to influence the new King James in the direction of a fundamental reform of religion by such means as the famous millenary petition which he helped to draw up, and which concentrated on abuses in the church such as pluralism and non-residence. Jacob hoped to influence Oxford through such figures as Christopher Dale of Merton, a proctor, and Henry Airay, provost of Queen's, but Dale revealed the correspondence to the university authorities, who were able to frustrate his efforts. Condemning Jacob as a schismatic, without consulting convocation they issued on behalf of the university a rebuttal of the proposals for reformation. Later that summer Jacob travelled to Sussex, where he was active in one of the most impressive campaigns of the period. Large numbers were involved, both of clergymen and the laity, among whom were to be found several prominent local gentlemen. The campaign aroused the indignation of Lord Buckhurst, who complained to the king. On 24 September 1603 Archbishop John Whitgift and Bishop Richard Bancroft wrote to Robert Cecil about 'One Jacob, a very insolent person, of much more boldness than either learning or judgement; a man that hath been imprisoned by us for his disobedience … an especial leader in the first petition' in Sussex (Dale, 215–6). It seems that unease over its vigour was a factor in the postponement of the historic Hampton Court conference to January 1604. At that time a gathering appears to have been convened of twenty-seven delegates from various English counties to advise the puritan negotiators. Jacob is listed as one of three who represented London, and it must follow that he had been released from gaol, at least for a time.

The trigger for Jacob's rearrest and imprisonment in the Clink, by Bishop Richard Vaughan of London, was the publication in July or August 1604 in Middleburg of *Reasons Taken out of God's Word*. His response was not the rigid obduracy often adopted by thoroughgoing separatists, but a willingness to appear reasonable in the eyes of the authorities. He had by this time a wife, Sarah, and four young children. Earlier than 4 April 1605, and in order to secure his freedom, he signed a statement prepared by the bishop of London, and promised also not to speak publicly against the government of the church for six months. On his own copy of the subscription, however, Jacob added reservations which make clear that since they had been obtained from him under duress, he was determined to interpret his own words in his own way. There is no conclusive evidence of his whereabouts for the next five years. It cannot be excluded that he was somewhere in the Netherlands at this time, and it is also possible that he was involved in some way in publishing the series of pamphlets by William Bradshaw and others, published secretly by the puritan printer William Jones; his own book *A Christian and Modest Offer of a … Conference* (1606), is certainly part of that series, though most of his works were published by Richard Schilders of Middleburg. On the other hand in February 1605 and again in March 1608 a Mr Jacob is mentioned as tenant of a house in Wood Street, St Alban parish, where Henry Jacob had resided in 1603.

Jacob was certainly in the Netherlands before the end of 1610. His *The Divine Beginning and Institution of Christes True Visible Church* was signed from Leiden on 20 December. It was probably about this time that Jacob had discussions with John Robinson, who was then at Leiden, and with William Ames and Robert Parker. Jacob probably influenced Robinson towards a less exclusive form of separatism than he had hitherto embraced. Jacob signed *A Declaration and Plainer Opening* from Middleburg on 4 September 1611. It is clear that he was still in the Netherlands in mid-1612, for the preface to *An Attestation of Many Learned … Divines* was directed on 18 July to 'my Christian and beloved friends in London and elsewhere in England'. By 1616 Jacob had returned to London, where he and several others covenanted to form the Southwark church of which he became pastor.

Jacob's ideas have given rise to an inordinate amount of controversy, partly because his early views were set out in opposition to the separatists, whereas his later work concentrates fire on the established church. There are continuities, but also a pattern of evolution in his thinking. In 1599, in his work against Johnson, Jacob stressed that though the Church of England was in error in matters such as government and ordination, and ought to reform itself, it was not to be judged as a false church. He continued to accept this throughout his life. However, from 1604, Jacob became increasingly critical of official structures and practices, and in that year, he argued for the first time that salvation would ordinarily be confined to members of visible churches more in keeping with God's law. English martyrs such as Nicholas Ridley and Hugh Latimer had been saved on the basis of their ignorance as to the continuing shortcomings of official protestantism. *Reasons Taken out of Gods Word* was framed as a set of proposals for reform of the individual parishes of the established church, rather than a plea for toleration of voluntary congregations within it; but it opposed authoritarian diocesan and provincial church government irrespective of the forms or mechanisms used in them. There is little sense in the work that (here or earlier) Jacob stood for a presbyterian discipline even of a localized nature, though he conceded the minister's right to restrict the sacraments and did not openly advocate the exclusion of ignorant and scandalous persons from the church altogether. By 1609 all hope of reform was dead, and in *To the Right High and Mightie Prince … an Humble Supplication*, Jacob petitioned the king again in the name of silenced puritan clergymen, for the toleration of 'some churches to be gathered by your majesty's special grace'; he asked that these be granted exemption from the bishops' supervision and placed under 'your subordinate civil magistrates, and so to be for our actions and carriage in the ministry accountable to them' (p. 8).

It has been argued convincingly that Jacob's later views, and the voluntaristic outlook which suffused them, had their roots in late Elizabethan puritanism, a movement too often regarded as synonymous with presbyterianism. The desire for local autonomy expressed in that movement also informs Jacob's writings, notably his view that while synods might play an advisory role, they should never be granted compulsive powers. It is expressed also in the Erastian arguments, notably in *An Humble Supplication*, with which he sought to persuade James I that prelatical privileges were necessarily demeaning to the authority of the state. By this, however, Jacob did not mean to undermine clerical authority in general, but only the authority of clergy, and especially 'lordly prelacy', over other clergy. The preface to *A Christian and Modest Offer* complained that the godly ministers had been silenced by bishops who 'for the maintaining of their own pomp, and for the feeding of their idle bellies, stick not to wrest the sceptre out of the hands of Christ'. Within the sphere of the individual church Jacob strongly defended the powers and authority of the clerical officers, and was unwilling to allow these to be much restrained by the congregation as a whole. The individual congregation, however, joined together on a voluntary basis, was increasingly the basis for his ecclesiological outlook. Thus

> The true visible and ministerial church of Christ is a number of faithful people joined by their willing consent in a spiritual outward society or body politic, ordinarily coming together into one place, instituted by Christ in his New Testament, and having the power to exercise ecclesiastical government and all God's other spiritual ordinances (the means of salvation) in and for itself immediately from Christ. (Jacob, *The Divine Beginning and Institution*, sig. A1)

By 1605 Jacob had come to the view that Christians should join together in a covenant. He never made this a firm imperative, probably because of unwillingness to make a decisive break with the Church of England, but the Southwark church was certainly gathered on the basis of a church covenant. The members

> joined both hands each with other Brother and stood in a ringwise: their intent being declared, H. Jacob and each of the rest made some confession or profession of their faith and repentance … Then they covenanted together to walk in all Gods ways as he had revealed or should make known to them. (Burrage, 2.294)

Jacob had developed a stronger sense of the dangers of the mixing within a single congregation of the godly and the profane, expressed most notably in *A Confession and Protestation of Faith* (1616). But the importance of Jacob's continuing refusal to embrace full separation is attested by the controversies it generated. A former member of Jacob's congregation, Sabine Staresmore, found his application for membership rejected by the separatists on the grounds of the lack of rigour of his former brethren.

Jacob remained pastor of the congregation into the 1620s. His will, signed on 5 October 1622, reveals his intention to leave for Virginia before 31 May the following year. It is believed that he died in the colony about April 1624, though there is no trace of him there. On 5 May 1624 probate was granted to Sarah Jacob, who seems not to have left England. Jacob left his property to his widow and his three children, and an adopted son, whom he seems to have expected to join him later in Virginia. Sarah was in trouble with the authorities as a member of a semi-separatist congregation in 1632 and 1637, but their son Henry *Jacob (*c.*1608–1652) took a different path.

STEPHEN WRIGHT

Sources C. Burrage, *The early English dissenters in the light of modern research, 1550–1641*, 2 vols. (1912) · S. Brachlow, 'The Elizabethan roots of Henry Jacob's churchmanship', *Journal of Ecclesiastical History*, 36 (1985), 228–54 · S. Brachlow, *The communion of saints: radical puritan and separatist ecclesiology, 1570–1625* (1988) · J. von Rohr, 'The congregationalism of Henry Jacob', *Transactions of the Congregational Historical Society*, 19 (1960–64), 107–17 · *Calendar of the manuscripts of the most hon. the marquis of Salisbury*, 24 vols., HMC, 9 (1883–1976), vols. 16–17 · R. W. Dale, *History of English congregationalism*, ed. A. W. W. Dale (1907) · PRO, PROB 11/143, sig. 38, fol. 312v · *Calendar of the manuscripts of Major-General Lord Sackville*, 2 vols., HMC, 80 (1940–66), vol. 1, pp. 102, 154 · M. Tolmie, *The triumph of the saints: the separate churches of London, 1616–1649* (1977) · K. Sprunger, *Dutch puritanism: a history of English and Scottish churches of the Netherlands in the sixteenth and seventeenth centuries* (1982) · B. R. White, *The English separatist tradition* (1971) · *Report on the manuscripts of Lord Montagu of Beaulieu*, HMC, 53 (1900) · Foster, *Alum. Oxon.*

Wealth at death see will, PRO, PROB 11/143, sig. 38

Jacob, Henry (*c.*1608–1652), philologist, was the son of the radical puritan Henry *Jacob (1562/3–1624), and his wife, Sarah, sister of John Dumaresq of Jersey. From 1610 (and perhaps before) the family was at Leiden in Holland. Here the young Henry studied under the Arabist Thomas Erpenius, and 'did in a short time by the help of a natural geny, become the prodigy of his age for philological and oriental learning'. It seems that he remained in Holland even after his father's return, by 1616, to England, and when Henry senior left for Virginia in 1622, the boy did not go with him.

Having arrived in England at an unknown date, Jacob was taken by the vicar of Tottenham, William Bedwell, and 'presented as a great rarity' to William Herbert, earl of Pembroke, chancellor of Oxford University. On 24 November 1628 Pembroke wrote urging that Jacob be created bachelor of arts on the basis of his extensive studies in the Netherlands and his exceptional grasp of oriental languages. The degree was awarded in January 1629. Jacob was admitted to Merton College as a probationary fellow and introduced to scholars such as John Selden, Henry Briggs, and Peter Turner. He helped several Oxford scholars, including Thomas Crosfield, with advice and instruction in Greek and oriental languages, and Samuel Hartlib paid tribute to his teaching in these fields. He is likely also to have contributed to Selden's understanding of Hebrew.

Jacob's progress towards the degree of MA during his year's probation was hindered by his own lack of training in logic and philosophy. The death in 1630 of his patron Pembroke, and his own serious illness, also threatened his future at Oxford. But Archbishop William Laud was persuaded of his 'eminent abilities in the way of philology', and on 20 May 1636 he wrote to the warden and fellows of Merton proposing Jacob for a fellowship. Laud pointed to a clause in the college statutes which enabled his appointment as a lecturer in philology to the junior fellows, a position long unfilled. As a recompense, he proposed that the new fellow would deliver a weekly lecture open to all members of the university, 'upon some title of antiquity, in which he shall compare the Roman, Greek and oriental antiquities one with another' (*Works*, 6.461). Jacob was admitted MA on 31 August, and was employed along the lines suggested. At this time, as John Selden later acknowledged, Jacob acted as his amanuensis. In 1638, though allowed to choose his subject for the weekly lecture, he was asked to give public notice of his choice. Jacob also compiled a catalogue of the increasingly impressive body of Hebrew books and manuscripts at the Bodleian Library.

In June 1641 Jacob was elected superior beadle of divinity and on 1 November 1642 he was created bachelor of physic.

> But his head being always over busy about critical notions (which made him sometimes a little better than crazed) he neglected his duty so much, that he was suspended once if not twice, from his place, and had his beadle's staff taken from him. (Wood, *Ath. Oxon.*, 330)

Permanent deprivation, and expulsion from the college, were imposed by the parliamentary visitors in 1648. Jacob moved to London, where John Selden 'gave him his clothes, and an old scarlet cloak, of which last his friends would mock him, and call him young Selden when they saw it on his back' (ibid.). Wood also says that Jacob irresponsibly left unsecured in Oxford a trunk containing his books and manuscripts, but it is now thought that this was confiscated. At any rate, all Jacob's main works vanished, except *Delphi Phoenicizantes* (1655) and *Philologiae anakalupterion* (1652), published shortly after his death by Jacob's friend Henry Birkhead, whose introduction tells us much of what we know of Jacob's life.

In September 1652 Jacob, '(a harmless, innocent, careless and shiftless person) who by his studies, had brought his body into great indisposition, did some weeks before his end retire, with the advice of friends, to the city of Canterbury'. Here he was looked after by a cousin, William Jacob, a physician, who was able to treat a 'gangrene in his foot' caused by 'going on foot in boots, according to the then mode', but found no means of curing a new infection which quickly followed: 'a tumour breaking out from one of his legs, his radical moisture did, as from a flood gate, violently run forth, and so ended his life, on 5 Nov following about the year of his age 44' (Wood, *Ath. Oxon.*, 1.332). Jacob was buried the next day at All Saints, Canterbury. The doctor related the later appearance in his bedroom of a ghost, which 'laid a cold hand on his face'; awakening, he beheld Henry Jacob, 'with his beard turned up as he used to wear it living' (ibid., 332–3).

STEPHEN WRIGHT

Sources Wood, *Ath. Oxon.*, new edn, 1.328–31 · M. Feingold, 'Oriental studies', *Hist. U. Oxf.* 4: *17th-cent. Oxf.*, 449–503 · G. Martin and J. Highfield, *A history of Merton College, Oxford* (1997) · *The works of the most reverend father in God, William Laud*, 6, ed. J. Bliss (1857) · J. Selden, *Vindiciae … Maris Clausi* (1653), 53 · B. R. White, *The English separatist tradition* (1971)

Jacob, Hildebrand (1692/3–1739), poet, was the only surviving son of Sir John Jacob, third baronet (c.1665–1740), of Bromley, Kent, and Dorothy (c.1662–1749), daughter of Richard Barry, third earl of Barrymore. Sir John was an army officer from 1685 to 1702; he was severely wounded at Killiecrankie and saw active service in Ireland. His infant son Hildebrand received an ensign's commission, dated 1 October 1694, in the 13th regiment of foot, of which his father was colonel. He was promoted lieutenant on 27 January 1706 and was still in the 13th foot in 1715, but it is not known whether he ever saw active service. In 1717 he married Meriel (*bap.* 1690, *d.* 1744), daughter of Sir John Bland, fourth baronet, of Kippax Park, Yorkshire. Their children were Hildebrand [*see below*] and Anne; they lived chiefly at West Wratting, Cambridgeshire.

In 1720 Jacob published anonymously a clever but indelicate poem, *The Curious Maid*, which was sometimes attributed to Prior and was frequently imitated. In the following years he produced a stream of anonymous ribald poems, not all of which he acknowledged in his collected *Works* (1735) (see Foxon). The *Works* were dedicated to James, first Earl Waldegrave, who, as ambassador in Vienna and Paris, had been of service to Jacob during a continental tour, 1728–9, described in 'A Letter from Paris to R. B****, Esq.', published in that collection. Jacob's most substantial work in verse is the forgettable *Brutus the Trojan … an Epic Poem* (1735).

For the stage Jacob wrote *The Fatal Constancy* (1723), a blank-verse tragedy acted six times at Drury Lane, twice by command of the princess of Wales, and *The Nest of Plays* (1738), consisting of three one-act prose comedies, *The Prodigal Reform'd*, *The Happy Constancy*, and *The Trial of Conjugal Love*, whose single performance at Covent Garden on 25 January 1738 was disrupted by protesters against the recent Stage Licensing Act. He also wrote two prose essays on aesthetics: *Of the Sister Arts: an Essay* (1734) and *How the Mind is Rais'd to the Sublime* (1735). He died on 25 May 1739 at Clarges Street, Mayfair, and was buried on 5 June at St Anne's, Soho. His *Chiron to Achilles* (1732) was reprinted in Dodsley's *Collection of Poems*, volume 1 (1748).

Sir Hildebrand Jacob, fourth baronet (1717/18–1790), son of the poet and his wife, Meriel, was baptized on 13 February 1718 at St James, Didsbury, Lancashire, his mother's former home. He matriculated at Oxford (University College) on 25 May 1736, aged eighteen. It was said that he was excelled by few as a general scholar, and 'in knowledge of Hebrew scarcely equalled' (*GM*, 60), but his only recorded academic honour was an Oxford DCL conferred on 8 July 1756. He succeeded to the baronetcy on the death of his grandfather, on 31 March 1740, and made his seat at Overswell, Gloucestershire; he also owned houses in London and Ewelme, Oxfordshire.

It is said that in early life, as soon as the weather was fine and the roads good, Jacob set off with his manservant and very little luggage, 'without knowing whither they were going' (*GM*). When it drew towards evening they enquired at the nearest village

> whether the great man in it was a lover of books, and had a fine library. If the answer was in the negative, they went on farther; if in the affirmative, Sir Hildebrand sent his compliments, that he was come to see him; and there he used to stay till time or curiosity induced him to move elsewhere. (ibid.)

Thus he travelled widely and was rarely obliged to stay at an inn. Though bookish, he seems to have published nothing. 'Thoughts on various subjects', attributed to him in the *Annual Register*, 4 (1761), 195–6, was in fact by his father. He died, unmarried, on 4 November 1790 at Malvern Wells, Worcestershire, and was buried on 22 November at St Anne's, Soho. He left a fortune of well over £45,000.

A. H. BULLEN, *rev.* BRIDGET HILL

Sources GM, 1st ser., 9 (1739), 327 · GM, 1st ser., 60 (1790), 1055 · GEC, *Baronetage*, 4.3–4 · C. Dalton, ed., *English army lists and commission registers, 1661–1714*, 6 vols. (1892–1904), vol. 2, pp. 34, 76, 143; vol. 3, p. 253; vol. 4, pp. 6, 27, 79 · Foster, *Alum. Oxon.*, 1500–1714 · C. Dalton, ed., *George the First's army, 1714–1727*, 1 (1910), 152 · D. Foxon, *English poetry, 1701–1750: a catalogue*, 2 vols. (1975) · W. Van Lennep and others, eds., *The London stage, 1660–1800*, 5 pts in 11 vols. (1960–68), pt 2, 2.7210–21, 760; part 3, 2.698–9 · A. H. Jacob and J. H. Glascott, *An historical and genealogical narrative of the families of Jacob* (1875) · *Pasquin* (8 Feb 1724) · N&Q, 2nd ser., 3 (1857), 76 · N. R. Schweizer, 'Introduction', in J. Hildebrand, *Of the sister arts: an essay* (1734), ed. N. R. Schweizer, Augustan Reprint Society, number 165 (1974), i–x · IGI

Likenesses J. Houbraken, line engraving (after G. Knapton), NPG

Wealth at death over £45,000—Sir Hildebrand Jacob; houses plus contents in London and Ewelme, Oxfordshire: 4 Dec 1790, will, PROB 11/1199, fols. 59v–62v

Jacob, Sir Hildebrand, fourth baronet (1717/18–1790). *See under* Jacob, Hildebrand (1692/3–1739).

Jacob, Sir (Edward) Ian Claud (1899–1993), army officer and broadcasting executive, was born in Quetta, Baluchistan, India, on 27 September 1899, the second of two children of Field Marshal Sir Claud William *Jacob (1863–1948), and his wife, Clara Pauline Wyatt (1872–1959), daughter of the Revd Joseph Light Wyatt, a missionary in Trichinopoly. His elder sister, Aileen, died when she was eight. He was educated at Wellington College and the Royal Military Academy, Woolwich, before joining the Royal Engineers as a second lieutenant in 1918. He subsequently read mechanical sciences at King's College, Cambridge, graduating with a second class degree in 1925. Meanwhile, on 27 August 1924, he married Cecil Bisset Treherne (1902–1991), daughter of Major-General Sir Francis Harper Treherne (1858–1955), of the Red House, Woodbridge, Suffolk. Treherne had been the senior medical officer in Jacob's father's division in France in the First World War, and Jacob had corresponded with Cecil since they were teenagers. He stayed with her family when he returned to Britain from India on his way to Cambridge, and they were married at the end of his first year. They were happily married for sixty-six years, and had two sons, John Claud and William Le Grand.

Jacob was promoted captain in 1929, and in 1931 returned to England to attend the staff college, in an outstanding year which was to produce fifteen generals. From 1934 to 1936 he was a staff officer in the War Office (promoted brevet major in 1935), and from 1936 to 1938 was brigade major in the canal brigade in Egypt. In 1938 he was promoted full major, and appointed military assistant secretary to the committee of imperial defence. The following year he was promoted brevet lieutenant-colonel and appointed assistant military secretary to the war cabinet. From May 1940 he worked closely with the minister of defence (and prime minister), Winston Churchill.

Sir (Edward) Ian Claud Jacob (1899–1993), by Howard Coster, *c.*1953

Churchill liked and respected Jacob, who wrote the official record of all ten of his summit visits to Roosevelt, Chiang Kai-shek, and Stalin. He remained in this post until 1946; he was promoted colonel in 1943, and appointed CBE in 1942, CB in 1944, and KBE in 1946. His experience at the nerve-centre of the war gave him an invaluable insight into world affairs. At the same time it put an end to his professional career as a soldier. 'I knew I could look for no promotion', he said, 'because I had not commanded troops in the field in wartime' (*The Independent*, 26 April 1993). Jacob had to find a civilian job. He retired from the army in 1946, with the rank of acting major-general (later honorary lieutenant-general).

By VE-day the BBC's European service had reached the zenith of its reputation. It had grown into the largest and most trusted foreign-language radio operation in the world. Yet by 1946 it was disintegrating. European statesmen and broadcasters returned to their liberated homelands. Newspapers reclaimed their journalists and universities their dons. Some staff were sent abroad as the vanguard of the BBC's own corps of foreign correspondents. Others joined the United Nations radio department. Moreover, the European service needed a new controller to replace Ivone Kirkpatrick, who had been transferred to the Allied Control Commission for Germany. Kirkpatrick suggested Jacob as his successor. It proved to be an ideal choice. The BBC's director-general, Sir William Haley, needed to arrest the seepage from Bush House, and to restore its morale. He also wanted someone with sufficient authority in Whitehall to stave off further cuts in the grant-in-aid which funded foreign broadcasting. As the new controller of European services Jacob made himself visible and approachable, regularly going to newsrooms and studios to watch the polyglot operation in action.

In 1947 Jacob was put in charge of all overseas broadcasting, with a seat on the newly established board of management, and a strong voice in the overall direction of the BBC. However, his civilian career was interrupted by Churchill's return to Downing Street in October 1951. The prime minister again claimed the defence portfolio for himself and persuaded the BBC to give Jacob leave of absence to become his chief staff officer and deputy military secretary to the cabinet, before setting off for a visit to Washington and Ottawa. On his return Churchill announced that Earl Alexander of Tunis, the retiring governor-general of Canada, would take over the Ministry of Defence. Jacob's enthusiasm was muted. 'Soldiers, however eminent, make bad ministers', he said (*The Independent*, 26 April 1993).

In June 1952 Haley announced that he was leaving the BBC to become editor of *The Times*, following the government's decision to introduce commercial television. Although he had been concerned solely with external broadcasting, Jacob was widely admired and, unlike some of the other contenders for Haley's succession, he had no enemies within the BBC. The governors appointed him director-general in October 1952. Jacob's regime at Broadcasting House (which lasted until 1960) covered a period in which television licences quadrupled, and radio ceased to be the dominant medium. He enlisted the support of the Independent Television Authority in a battle to remove the iniquitous fourteen-day rule. This prevented programmes from discussing any issue due to be debated in parliament during the coming fortnight. As director-general, Jacob cogently presented the case for the rule's abolition. Simultaneously he made sure that audiences were alerted each time the onerous rule had prevented a broadcast. By July 1957 reason, combined with ridicule, had won the battle.

Jacob rejected the notion that items of news should be suppressed because they were 'inconvenient from a short-term political standpoint'. Nor, despite his Whitehall background, did he expect his senior staff meekly to accept governmental direction. When they visited the Foreign Office, he declared, 'They should seek to learn all they can, they should listen to the views expressed, but they should not act on guidance directly from Foreign Office officials without testing it by our long-term standards' (*The Independent*, 26 April 1993). It was under Jacob's direction that the BBC survived the worst threat to its independence. During the Suez crisis of 1956 the prime minister, Sir Anthony Eden, tried to prevent the overseas service from reporting newspaper editorials critical of the bombardment of Egypt. Those who expected Jacob automatically to toe the government line were surprised by his forthright reaction. 'If the BBC is found for the first time to be suppressing significant items of news, its reputation would rapidly vanish', he declared (ibid.). He was summoned to the Foreign Office and told that as a punitive gesture the Bush House grant-in-aid would be cut by £1 million. Jacob and his chairman, Sir Alexander Cadogan, called on R. A. Butler, the lord privy seal, the next day, and managed to get the threatened cut reduced by half. At the time Eden was considering other ways of bringing the BBC to heel. However, during Jacob's absence abroad his stance was stoutly maintained by his deputies. After Eden's resignation that particular threat to BBC editorial independence was lifted.

Jacob played a leading role in the founding of the British Commonwealth International Film Agency, and of the European Broadcasting Union, and was first president of the latter. He retired from the BBC at the end of 1960, having groomed Hugh Carleton Greene to be his successor. He had promoted Greene to the board of management as director of news and current affairs in preference to Tahu Hole, the New Zealander whose malign administration of the BBC news division was widely held to be one of the reasons for the early lead of Independent Television News.

In 1963 Jacob was the principal author of the seminal Ismay–Jacob report on the central organization of defence. The report, commissioned by Harold Macmillan and Peter Thorneycroft and implemented by Earl Mountbatten, led to major changes in the defence establishment. Jacob regarded the production of this report as the most important single act of his career. He held many offices after leaving the BBC. He rescued the Army and Navy Club from oblivion, and subsequently was its chairman for seven years. He became chairman of the Suffolk Police Authority, county councillor for Woodbridge, Suffolk, and deputy lieutenant. He was also chairman of the Covent Garden Authority, a trustee of the Imperial War Museum, a director of Fisons and EMI, chairman of Matthews Holdings, regional director for inner London of Lloyds Bank, and chairman of Sherborne School. He was advanced to GBE in 1960.

As director-general of the BBC, Jacob was overshadowed, metaphorically as well as physically, by those two titans Sir John Reith and Sir Hugh Greene. Yet he successfully piloted the BBC through stormier waters than Reith or Greene ever encountered. He was, in addition, the director-general who brought the BBC into the television age. His friend Sir Charles Richardson published a biography, *From Churchill's Secret Circle to the BBC* (1991), which made substantial use of Jacob's fascinating private diaries. Jacob died of heart failure at his home, the Red House, Cumberland Street, Woodbridge, Suffolk, on 24 April 1993, and was cremated in Woodbridge the next day. A memorial service was held in St Margaret's Church, Westminster Abbey, on 13 October 1993. He was survived by his two sons, his wife, Cecil, having died on 1 January 1991.   LEONARD MIALL

Sources C. Richardson, *From Churchill's secret circle to the BBC* (1991) · *The Independent* (26 April 1993) · *The Times* (26 April 1993) · *Daily Telegraph* (27 April 1993) · personal knowledge (2004) · private information (2004) [W. Le G. Jacob] · A. Briggs, *The history of broadcasting in the United Kingdom*, 4 (1979) · *Ariel* (Dec 1959) [BBC staff magazine] · WWW · Burke, *Peerage* · CGPLA Eng. & Wales (1993)
Archives BBC WAC · CAC Cam., papers · NRA, priv. coll., papers | CAC Cam., letters to Sir W.J. Haley · King's Lond., Liddell Hart C., corresp. with Sir B. H. Liddell Hart · Nuffield Oxf., corresp. with Lord Cherwell | FILM BFI NFTVA, news footage
Likenesses W. Stoneman, photograph, 1947, NPG · H. Coster, photographs, c.1953, NPG [*see illus.*] · W. Stoneman, photograph, 1958, NPG · N. Hepple, oils, c.1965, Army and Navy Club, London · oils, Broadcasting House, London, Council Chamber · photograph, repro. in *The Times* · photograph, repro. in *The Independent*
Wealth at death £272,030: probate, 27 July 1993, CGPLA Eng. & Wales

Jacob, Sir Isaac Hai [Jack] (1908–2000), barrister and jurist, was born on 5 June 1908 in Timtang Road, Shanghai, the third of ten children of Jacob Isaiah Jacob (1863–1935) and his wife, Aziza, *née* Abraham (1887–1976). His father, a Sephardic Jew, had moved from Baghdad to Shanghai to work as an accountant for the wealthy merchant family the Sassoons. He was educated at Shanghai Public School for Boys (1920–25) and emigrated to England at eighteen. From 1927 to 1930 he read for a law degree at London University—initially at the London School of Economics (LSE) and then, on getting a scholarship, at University College (UCL). He obtained first-class honours, and in 1930 was called to the bar at Gray's Inn, which awarded him the Cecil peace prize and an Arden scholarship. Jacob married Rose Mary Jenkins, *née* Samwell (1904–1995), a secretary, in the summer of 1940; they had two sons, both of whom had legal careers. His legal practice at the bar was interrupted for five years by the war. He served in the ranks from 1940, then was commissioned in the Royal Army Ordnance Corps (1942); in the following year he was moved to the War Office, as a staff captain, and there was involved in planning for D-day.

After the war Jacob returned to the bar, where he built up a successful commercial practice specializing in fields such as hire purchase. But in 1957, a depressed time for the bar, he applied for and obtained the position of High Court Queen's Bench master, a minor judicial office dealing with pre-trial litigation. Generally regarded as something of a backwater, for Jacob it became the base from which he established a reputation as the country's leading expert on civil procedure. For some thirty years he worked tirelessly as master, writer, editor, teacher, and reformer. He quickly became involved in preparing the practitioner's bible, the *Annual Practice* (the 'white book', later renamed the *Supreme Court Practice*), of which he was general editor from 1966 to 1990. He also produced new editions of other classic practitioners' texts: the second edition of *Atkin's Encyclopaedia of Court Forms in Civil Proceedings* (1999); the eleventh, twelfth, thirteenth, and fourteenth editions of *Bullen and Leake's Precedents of Pleadings in the Queen's Bench Division of the High Court of Justice* (1959, 1975, 1990, 2001), which became *Bullen, Leake and Jacob's Precedents*; and the nineteenth, twentieth, and twenty-first editions of *Chitty's Queen's Bench Forms* (1965, 1969, 1986), which became *Chitty and Jacob's Queen's Bench Forms*.

In 1975 Jacob became senior master, which by tradition is combined with the role of queen's remembrancer, responsible for testing coins in the Royal Mint and for accepting rent for the City of London in the form of horseshoes and nails. He was appointed queen's counsel in 1976 and knighted in 1979. The best of his essays and conference papers were gathered in *The Reform of Civil Procedural Law and other Essays in Civil Procedure* (1982). In 1986 he gave the annual Hamlyn lectures, the published version of which was his most important publication, with the appropriately sweeping title *The Fabric of English Civil Justice* (1987). Jacob served on, and played a major role as a member of, various official law reform committees, including the Winn committee on personal injuries litigation

(1968), the Payne committee on enforcement of judgment debts (1969), and the working party on the revision of the rules of the Supreme Court (1960–65).

Civil procedure was unknown as a subject for university study in England until the early 1960s, when Jacob co-founded a course in the subject for the LLM programme at London University. He gave the lectures on Monday evenings at UCL for nearly thirty years. His seminars at LSE, accompanying the lectures, were famous for the leading judges, practitioners, and civil servants who participated. From the 1960s he also taught civil procedure at Birmingham University and was actively involved in the foundation and administration of the university's Institute of Judicial Administration. In 1978 he became the first general editor of the *Civil Justice Quarterly*, published by Sweet and Maxwell from the institute at Birmingham, and he served on the institute's committee of management.

After he had retired as queen's bench master, in 1980, Jacob was appointed director of the Institute of Advanced Legal Studies at London University (1986–8). His involvement with legal education extended to law teaching at the former polytechnics and in schools. He was involved in the 1960s in founding the Association of Law Teachers, for non-university teachers, and served both as honorary vice-president and, from 1978, as honorary president of the association.

Sir Jack Jacob died on 26 December 2000 at Bushey House, a retirement home in Bushey, Hertfordshire, where he had moved after the death of his wife in 1995. He was cremated at Golders Green on 10 January 2001. Jacob was a much-loved figure in the law, with an enormous range of friends from many countries. He was appreciated for his engaging personality, for the vast scope of his knowledge of his subject, for his amazing industry, and for his passion for justice. Introducing his Hamlyn lectures he said that for most people English civil justice was a remote, incomprehensible, mystifying, and in some ways terrifying area of the law. What was needed was:

> a breath of fresh air to blow through the corridors of civil justice, to demystify the process, to render it plain and intelligible, to enable not only the experts in other disciplines but also the man in the High Street to understand and appreciate its operation and in this way to bring justice closer to the common people. (Jacob, *The Fabric of English Civil Justice*, 1987, 3–4)

Jack Jacob was that breath of fresh air.

MICHAEL ZANDER

Sources *The Times* (2 Jan 2001) · *The Guardian* (1 Jan 2001) · *The Independent* (12 Jan 2001) · *Civil Justice Quarterly*, 20 (2001), 79–83 · personal knowledge (2004) · private information (2004) [Sir Robin Jacob, son]
Archives London School of Economics
Likenesses C. Cheek, portrait, 1989, U. Lond., Institute of Advanced Legal Studies · photograph, repro. in *The Times* · photograph, repro. in *The Independent*

Jacob, Sir John, first baronet (*bap.* 1597, *d.* 1666), financier, was baptized at Gamlingay, Cambridgeshire, on 12 December 1597, the eldest son of Abraham Jacob (*d.* 1629), a merchant and customs farmer, and his wife, Mary, daughter of Francis Rogers of Dartford in Kent. He was educated at Merton College, Oxford, and on the continent, and in 1620 became secretary to Isaac Wake, the English ambassador at Turin. In 1621 Wake assisted Jacob to secure the post of secretary to the lord treasurer, Lionel Cranfield, earl of Middlesex. Middlesex may have been attracted to Jacob because of his expertise concerning customs, resulting from his work as farmer of the customs on tobacco. Subsequently Jacob became one of the most important customs farmers in the country. The influence of Middlesex probably ensured that he was returned to parliament in 1624 as member for Plympton Erle in Devon, and his presence in the Commons may have been valuable during Middlesex's impeachment. Jacob was unable to prevent his employer's removal from office, but was not adversely affected himself and was confirmed as collector of the pretermitted customs later in the year. By 1627 he had been appointed clerk of the privy council extraordinary, and after his father's death in 1629 joined the farmers of the great customs. He had married, on 2 May 1625, Elizabeth (d. 1632), daughter of John Holliday; they had two sons and a daughter. Subsequently, Jacob was married twice more, in 1632 to Alice, née Clowes (d. 1646), widow of John Eaglesfield, with whom he had two sons and a daughter, and, on 17 April 1651, to Elizabeth (d. 1697), daughter of Sir John Ashburnham of Kent, with whom he had one daughter.

Jacob's willingness to make sizeable loans to the crown, which resulted in his knighthood in 1633, continued during the bishops' wars. He was a successful court candidate at Harwich in elections to the Short Parliament, but the elections for the Long Parliament later in the year revealed the extent to which he had become a controversial figure. Returned at Rye with the assistance of the lord warden of the Cinque Ports, his narrow defeat of two local puritans resulted in a challenge based on allegations of electoral malpractice. His removal from parliament, however, was the result of his role as a monopolist (21 January 1641). During subsequent investigations Jacob and the other customs farmers agreed to compound at £150,000 for loans made to the king in anticipation of customs revenue. This debt was to stay with Jacob for much of his life.

Unlike other monopolists Jacob did not join the king at Oxford during the civil war, although he was widely regarded as a royalist sympathizer. He was briefly imprisoned in 1642 for refusing to contribute to parliament, and was later accused of having sent money to the king. During the 1640s he faced constant pressure for money from both creditors and parliament, by whom he was assessed at £2000, but the financial demands made upon him were hard to meet. Money owed to him by the king was ordered to be paid but never delivered. In January 1648 he was imprisoned again, with debts of nearly £100,000. During the Commonwealth a deal was struck whereby Jacob and the other customs farmers would repay their debt out of an allowance from the proceeds of the act for the sale of crown forests. Although Jacob was released from prison, little money was paid to the government, who eventually decided that he and the others had forfeited the benefit of the act.

After the restoration of Charles II Jacob secured reappointment as a customs farmer but an attempt to return to parliament in 1661 foundered in the absence of a powerful patron. A number of royal grants offered financial relief, however, and he was also rewarded with the appointment as gentleman of the privy chamber in 1664, and with a baronetcy in the following year. By the time of his death, probably at Bromley, Middlesex, in March 1666, Jacob had re-established the family fortunes, and had cleared all but £3000 of his debts. He was buried at Bromley.   J. T. PEACEY

Sources HoP, *Commons, 1690–1715* [draft] · *CSP dom., 1619–60* · *CSP Venice, 1619–23* · GEC, *Baronetage* · W. A. Shaw, ed., *Calendar of treasury books*, [33 vols. in 64], PRO (1904–69) · R. Ashton, *The crown and the money market, 1603–1640* (1960) · CKS, Cranfield papers, U269 · JHC, 2–7 (1640–59) · M. A. E. Green, ed., *Calendar of the proceedings of the committee for advance of money, 1642–1656*, 3 vols., PRO (1888) · E. Sussex RO, Rye corporation records, 47/133, 164 · PRO, PROB 11/320, fol. 105v · M. Prestwich, *Cranfield: politics and profits under the early Stuarts* (1966) · PRO, C/33 234, fol. 765
Archives BL, corresp. with Sir John Harrison, MS Stowe 185 · CKS, Cranfield MSS, U269
Wealth at death £3000 p.a.: PRO, C/33 234, fol. 765

Jacob, John (1765–1840). *See under* Jacob, Edward (1710?–1788).

Jacob, John (1812–1858), army officer in the East India Company, was born on 11 January 1812 at Woolavington-cum-Puriton, Somerset, the seventh child and fifth son of Stephen Long Jacob (1764/5–1851), vicar of Woolavington-cum-Puriton (1806–51) and his wife, Eliza Susanna (d. 1851), eldest daughter of James Bond, vicar of Ashford, Kent. William Stephen *Jacob (1813–1862) was his brother, and Sir George le Grand Jacob (1805–1881) his cousin. Jacob was educated at a dame-school at Milverton, Somerset, at home by his father until 1826, and then was sent to Addiscombe College (1826–8). Jacob was gazetted on 11 January 1828 a second lieutenant in the Bombay artillery. On 26 January 1828 he left England for India, and landed in Bombay six months later. For the next seven years Jacob served with his regiment in the Bombay presidency and was then trusted with a small detached command leading a detachment of Golandaz to Gujarat for training. Jacob spent a short time in civil employ with the provincial administration of Gujarat, boring for water, and on 14 May 1836 was gazetted lieutenant.

Following the outbreak of the First Anglo-Afghan War in 1838 Jacob served with the Bombay column of the army of the Indus under the command of Sir John Keane. He remained with a subsidiary British force posted on the line of communication through Sind for the duration of the war, and was placed in command of a depot for ordnance stores at Fort Bukkur at Sukkur. He briefly led an improvised artillery company during an abortive expedition against the local Baluch hill peoples, who had raided British convoys. In November 1839 he commanded the artillery during a successful expedition under Major

Billamore's command mounted to punish the local people in the hill country to the north of Kachhi. Following this expedition Jacob went to Hyderabad where he met and established a close friendship with Sir James Outram, the political agent for Lower Sind, who selected him for survey work in the Thar Desert. While returning to take up his post with the survey department of Gujarat he successfully reconnoitred the route from Hyderabad to Nuggar Parkur during the hot season at considerable risk to himself. For this service he received the official commendation of the Bombay government. Following an attack on British troops by Marris warriors in October 1840 Jacob left civil employment and returned to Sind, leading a column of reinforcements across the desert to Sukkur. These troops arrived too late to take part in the Brahui campaign and Jacob then briefly served with the 4th troop horse artillery which arrived at the foot of the Bolan Pass in February 1841 *en route* for Quetta. Sir James Outram obtained Jacob's services later that year for survey duty in Kachhi, along the road between Shikarpur to Dadhar. Following this mission in November 1841 Outram selected him to command the Sind irregular horse and as an assistant political agent he was also given as part of his duties political responsibility for Eastern Kachhi. This cavalry regiment had originally been raised in 1839 for service on the 120-mile-long frontier between Sibi and Shikarpur and by 1841 had a strength of 475 men. Jacob was formally gazetted as commandant of the Sind irregular horse on 2 December 1841, and an assistant in the Sind and Baluchistan political agency in charge of the Kachhi frontier early in January 1842. Jacob reorganized his new command, enforced a system of iron discipline, and developed a highly effective system of outposts backed by incessant patrolling by small widely deployed cavalry detachments to counter raids by hostile Baluch warriors that plagued Kachhi and Upper Sind. He proved a brilliant cavalry leader and swordsman on numerous occasions when his men successfully intercepted marauding bands of warriors and restored order in the area. Following the disastrous First Anglo-Afghan War the Sind and Baluchistan political agency was abolished and the Sind irregular horse was withdrawn to Hyderabad. In an official letter to Jacob dated 9 November 1842, written shortly before he left Sind, Outram stated that for the first time Cutchee and Upper Sind had been for a whole year entirely free from the irruptions of the hill peoples which were solely counteracted by the indomitable zeal of Jacob and his officers and men.

The Sind irregular horse returned to Hyderabad in April 1843 and from this base carried out similar duties preventing raiding by fighters from the hills. However, Jacob's hitherto good relationship with Sir Charles Napier, appointed governor following the annexation of Sind, deteriorated when he became embroiled in the bitter acrimony which broke out between Outram and Napier over the origins of the war following the publication of Sir William Napier's *The History of the Conquest of Sind*. Jacob was drawn into the controversy when he openly sided with his old friend and ally Sir James Outram and later published a

rejoinder. When the First Anglo-Sikh War broke out in 1845 Jacob led 'Jacob's horse' as the advance guard of the army of Sind to Bahawalpur, but it arrived too late to see any active service. Despite his now acrimonious relationship with Napier his skill as a military commander of the highly efficient Sind irregular horse meant that in 1846 he was authorized to raise, and was placed in overall command of, an additional Silladar cavalry regiment deployed permanently in Upper Sind. The two combined regiments, comprising 1600 horsemen, were henceforth collectively known as Jacob's horse. Following a raid in force by Bugtis fighters in Upper Sind in December 1846, during which 10,000 cattle were stolen, Napier sent Jacob to Khangarh, where he established his new headquarters, from where operations were mounted to punish the people. He achieved notable success against this people, who were roundly defeated in October 1847 at Zamani, near Shahpur, restoring order to Upper Sind.

Jacob was appointed political superintendent and commandant of the frontier of Upper Sind, as well as retaining overall command of the Sind horse, when Sir Charles Napier finally departed in October 1847. Jacob was faced by a formidable task along an inhospitable desert frontier which stretched from the Punjab as far south as Shahpur in Kachhi. Jacob created a new system of frontier defence, with Jacob's horse holding the entire line of outposts, supported by Baluch scouts, while he was given full magisterial powers and political authority so he could deal directly with the independent peoples and the governments of Khairpur and Kalat. The system of aggressive patrolling, carried out by small detachments of cavalry operating in the belt of desert between the hills and the areas under British administration, once again proved highly successful in preventing raids and helped restore order along the border. A series of reforms were also implemented in Upper Sind by Jacob to bring stability to the area and establish British authority. He oversaw the repair of existing disused irrigation channels and the construction of a network of roads and canals, which were instrumental in enlarging the area under cultivation in the deserts of Upper Sind, whose population steadily increased as a result. Jacob also successfully disarmed every man in the country not in government service, established schemes of revenue collection and magistracy, and began the construction of various public works. He also studied the internal politics of various countries beyond the northwest frontier. In January 1848 he was promoted regimental captain and five months later brevet major. The village of Khangarh became a flourishing town of 12,000 inhabitants and in 1851, in recognition of Jacob's services, by order of Lord Dalhousie, the governor-general, its name was changed to Jacobabad. From 1847 Jacob wrote a series of controversial books and pamphlets on military organization, equipment, and training in India, as well as developing a new pattern of rifle and explosive bullet of his own design. In particular, his criticisms of the lax discipline of the Bengal army caused indignation and resentment.

Jacob worked in close co-operation with Sir Bartle Frere

after the latter was appointed commissioner in Sind in 1851; Frere supported the policy being implemented along the Upper Sind frontier. In 1853–4 Jacob demarcated the Kalat frontier from the western hills to Kashmor. Jacob successfully negotiated a treaty with the khan of Kalat in 1854, to the satisfaction of the government of India. On 13 April 1855 he was promoted lieutenant-colonel, and following the departure of Bartle Frere on furlough to Europe in January 1856 he was appointed acting commissioner in Sind. In recognition of his services in Sind, Jacob was appointed aide-de-camp to Queen Victoria, with the rank of colonel in the army, on 20 March 1856. Jacob, granted the rank of brigadier-general, was given the command of the cavalry division by Sir James Outram when war was declared with Persia. On 13 March 1857 he landed at Bushehr and was given command of the town. When peace was declared following the fall of Muhammarah, Jacob was left in charge of the entire force in Persia until the full terms of the treaty were complied with, after which Bushehr was completely evacuated. For his services in Persia Jacob was mentioned in dispatches and in the *Indian Government Gazette* (7 Nov 1857). Jacob returned to India and landed on 15 October 1857 at Bombay, which was in ferment following the outbreak of the Indian mutiny earlier that year. On 4 November 1857 he set off for Jacobabad to resume his political and military duties on the north-west frontier, where his presence was deemed vital to preserve order. In 1858 Jacob was authorized to raise two infantry regiments, known as Jacob's Rifles, which were armed with a pattern of rifle that he had invented. While on a tour of inspection he was taken ill on 24 November 1857, however, and rode 50 miles to Jacobabad where he refused medical attention and retired to bed.

Jacob died of 'brain fever' at midnight on 5–6 December 1858 at Jacobabad at the age of forty-six, surrounded by his staff and officers of the Sind irregular horse. He was buried the following day without military ceremony in Jacobabad, where his death was mourned by an estimated 10,000 of the city's inhabitants. T. R. MOREMAN

Sources E. T. Lambrick, *John Jacob of Jacobabad* (1960) · A. I. Shand, *General John Jacob* (1900) · L. Pelly, ed., *The views and opinions of General John Jacob* (1858) · E. T. Lambrick, *Sir Charles Napier and Sind* (1952) · P. Napier, *Charles Napier in India* (1991) · *Record book of the Scinde irregular horse* (1853) · [J. Jacob], *Memoir of the first campaign in the hills north of Cutchee, under Major Billamore in 1839–40, by one of his subalterns* (1852) · P. Cadell, *History of the Bombay army* (1938) · H. M. Vibart, *Addiscombe: its heroes and men of note* (1894) · Venn, *Alum. Cant.* · Boase, *Mod. Eng. biog.* · Foster, *Alum. Oxon.*
Archives BL OIOC, papers, MSS Eur. B 114, E 208 · BL OIOC, corresp. and papers, Home misc. series, MS Eur. F 75; MS Eur. F 288 | BL OIOC, letters to Lord Elphinstone, MSS Eur. F 87–89 · SOAS, corresp. with Sir H. Bartle Frere, MS 138373 · W. Yorks. AS, Leeds, letters to Lord Canning
Likenesses T. L. Atkinson, mezzotint, 1859 (after unknown artist), BL OIOC, NPG · M. Thomas, bust, 1884, Shire Hall, Taunton · Atkinson and W. L. Collis, photogravure, repro. in Shand, *General John Jacob* · J. B. Bellasis, watercolour, BL OIOC

Jacob, Joseph (*c*.1667–1722), Independent minister, was born to Quaker parents but early in life he seems to have renounced their beliefs. He was apprenticed to a linen draper in London, where he developed a keen interest in politics, becoming a supporter of civil and religious liberty and championing the cause of William of Orange during the revolution of 1688. After the passing of the Toleration Act in 1689 he proclaimed himself 'a Protestant dissenter of the Congregational persuasion' (Wilson, 1.139) and studied for the ministry under Robert Trail, a learned Presbyterian minister in London. Upon becoming a minister he soon gathered a numerous following and in 1697 he began to give weekly lectures at the meetinghouse of Thomas Gouge in Thames Street. His sermons, however, contained a strong political flavour, which brought censure on him and led to his dismissal.

Jacob's friends opened for him in 1698 a new chapel in Parish Street, Southwark, where he proceeded to establish a 'church more pure than any had been before him' (Jones, 108). It was distinguished by a strict code of conduct and some exclusive rites and characteristics, which included the compulsory growing of moustaches for men and the banning of wigs. Members of his congregation were forbidden to attend worship at another church and forbidden to marry outside the congregation; those not conforming to the new rules were excommunicated, but this harsh treatment offended others too, who withdrew in consequence. By 1702 Jacob's congregation had dwindled away and he was obliged to quit his meeting-house; as an alternative he hired Turners' Hall in Philpot Lane but there he was again castigated for preaching political sermons, pouring scorn on public characters, and ridiculing many worthy ministers. From Turners' Hall he moved to Curriers' Hall, Cripplegate (*c*.1710–1712), where he continued in much the same vein until his congregation once again deserted him.

Jacob died on 26 June 1722 and 'with him died the "reformed" Church of which he was pastor' (Jones, 108). He was buried in Bunhill Fields; his wife, Sarah, and two of his daughters were buried in the same plot. Although a man of some learning he published little: a *Catechism* (1702), *The Covenant to be the Lord's People under Joseph Jacob's Pastoral Charge* (1702), and two or three single sermons from his time at Turners' Hall. He might have made a more lasting impression had he not 'antagonised [so] many people by public outbursts and insistence on eccentric practices' (Wilson, 1.141).

ALEXANDER GORDON, *rev.* M. J. MERCER

Sources J. A. Jones, ed., *Bunhill memorials* (1849) · W. Wilson, *The history and antiquities of the dissenting churches and meeting houses in London, Westminster and Southwark*, 4 vols. (1808–14), vol. 1 · C. Surman, index, DWL · W. Beckett, *A universal biography*, 3 vols. (1835–6) · J. Gorton, *A general biographical dictionary*, new edn, 4 vols. (1851)

Jacob, Joshua (*c*.1802–1877), founder of the White Quakers, was born at Clonmel, co. Tipperary, and was educated at Joseph Tatham's school in Leeds and later in Ballitore, co. Kildare. Having been apprenticed to Adam Calvert, Jacob established himself in 1830 as a grocer in Dublin, and his shop, the Golden Teapot, became famous for its fine tea. In 1829 he married Sarah Fayle and they had three sons. Jacob furnished his home simply, and he demonstrated his own asceticism by smashing in the open street all his mirrors, and protesting against the use of bells, clocks, watches, and newspapers. A birthright member of the Society of Friends, he criticized the comforts of Quaker life, and in 1838 he was disowned by that body. Assisted by Abigail Beale of Irishtown, near Mountmellick, Queen's county, he formed a society of his own, which gained adherents in Dublin, Clonmel, Waterford, and Mountmellick. In 1842 he and his followers began to practise a communal holding of goods. They also appeared in loose, unbleached woollen garments, a costume previously adopted, in 1762, by John Woolman. The new society, commonly called 'White Quakers', held the first of what became yearly meetings in Dublin on 1 May 1843. During these years Jacob issued many (undated) pamphlets and *Some Account of the Progress of the Truth as it is in Jesus*, a publication which appeared at intervals in 1843.

When a bequest of £9000 was used by Jacob for the benefit of his community, he was taken to court and it was held in 1844 that he had misappropriated money to which others were entitled. On his rejection of the judgment he was imprisoned for two years, and the community's property was seized and put up for auction. From prison he issued anathemas against the Irish lord chancellor E. B. Sugden and Edward Litton, master of the Irish court of chancery. After Jacob's release on grounds of ill health in 1846, the White Quakers were active in food distribution during the great famine, but in 1848 the movement disintegrated. The next year Jacob established a community at Newlands, Clondalkin, co. Dublin, formerly the residence of Arthur Wolfe, Viscount Kilwarden. Its members lived in common, abstaining from meat, and using bruised corn instead of flour. On this community's dissolution, Jacob went into business again at Celbridge, co. Kildare. Since 1842 he had lived apart from his wife, who could no longer share his religious views. On her death he married and adopted the religion of a poor Roman Catholic, Catherine Devine, raising six children in that faith. He died in Wales on 15 February 1877, and was buried at Glasnevin cemetery, Dublin, in a plot purchased many years previously for the White Quakers.

ALEXANDER GORDON, rev. TIMOTHY C. F. STUNT

Sources 'Dictionary of Quaker biography', RS Friends, Lond. [card index] · I. Grubb, *Quakers in Ireland, 1654–1900* (1927), 126–9 · J. Smith, ed., *A descriptive catalogue of Friends' books*, 2 (1867), 4 · A. J. Webb, *A compendium of Irish biography* (1878), 260 · private information (1891) · 'Quaker anecdotes', *Journal of the Friends' Historical Society*, 11 (1914), 140

Jacob, Naomi Eleanor Clare [*pseud.* Ellington Gray; *known as* Naomi Ellington Jacob] **(1884–1964)**, writer and actress, was born on 1 July 1884 at 20 High Street, Agnes Gate, Ripon, Yorkshire, the daughter of Samuel Jacob, a German Jew and schoolmaster, and Selina Sara (Nina) Ellington, *née* Collinson (*b.* 1863), a writer who published under the pseudonym Nina Abbott. She had a younger sister. Naomi Jacob's father's ancestors had migrated from Spain to Holland and then Poland, where his grandparents had been killed in the pogroms; Samuel Jacob's father had escaped from Poland to Germany as a boy. The Collinsons, in contrast, were yeomen who had been firmly rooted on the

Naomi Eleanor Clare Jacob (1884–1964), by Bassano, 1939

same plot of land in Yorkshire for over three hundred years. Naomi saw her lively mother as the greatest influence on her, claiming in *Me: Yesterday and To-Day* that she inherited her literary skills from her. Her mother 'had the gift of making whatever she talked of—live' and was also a rebel, a trait she passed on to Naomi (*Yesterday and To-Day*, 143), while she recollected that her father was 'always stern and Teutonic about things that didn't really matter' (ibid., 208). It is thought that he may have been a model for the brutish Yorkshire husbands she repeatedly portrayed in her novels (Jasper, 208). However, she was proud of his Jewish heritage, reacted strongly against antisemitism throughout her life, and warmly portrayed Jewish life in her Gollantz novels.

While Jacob remained very attached to Yorkshire, using the setting and its people as subject matter in her fiction, she hated her schooling in and around Yorkshire. She attended a number of private schools, including Skelfield and Sharow, before moving on to Leeds higher grade school. Her gawky boyish appearance and acerbic manner did not endear her to her teachers, who accused her of 'showing off' (*Yesterday and To-Day*, 33). Ironically, at the age of fifteen, Jacob was forced to take up teaching at a school in Middlesbrough owing to 'family reverses', which may have included her father's death (Jasper, 209). Although she loved children, she 'hated the petty restrictions' of the profession and left it at the age of eighteen to become the secretary of variety performer Marguerite

Broadfoote (*Yesterday and To-Day*, 35). Broadfoote was possibly Jacob's first female lover. It has been suggested that as a young woman Jacob was married for a fortnight, but this was never mentioned in her memoirs (Baker, 302). Thus began her long association with the stage, including performing in vaudeville before the First World War.

Jacob converted to Roman Catholicism when she was about eighteen, having been brought up in the Church of England. She also plunged into socialism (she was a Labour Party campaigner) and the suffrage movement (she joined the Women's Social and Political Union in 1912). At the outbreak of war several of her passions found a focus in the Actresses' Franchise League, a branch of which assigned volunteer tasks to women. Jacob acted as secretary for a toy factory before founding the Three Arts Employment Fund with the purpose of directing actors into war work. During the last two years of the war she served as a captain in the Women's Legion and ran a munitions factory in Willesden, before tuberculosis forced her to enter a sanatorium.

By 1920 Jacob had recovered, returned to the stage, and begun acting in films. (Most notably she appeared with John Gielgud in *The Ringer* in 1936.) She published her first novel, *Jacob Ussher*, a best-seller, in 1925. After rapidly writing several more, Naomi had health troubles again, and in 1930 she was ordered to leave England for a warmer clime. She chose Sirmione on Lake Garda, Italy, where she lived for most of the rest of her life. In 1928 Jacob appeared for the defence of lesbian novelist Radclyffe Hall's *The Well of Loneliness*, and she developed a friendship with Hall and her companion Una Troubridge. They frequently visited Jacob's 'Casa Mickie', (named after the nickname Naomi adopted when she began to express her masculine identity more openly), which she shared intermittently with her lovers Sadie Robinson and later Marjorie Zamble, a married woman with two children.

During the 1930s Jacob embarked on the Gollantz series of novels and achieved widespread recognition with the third volume, *Four Generations* (1934). It chronicles the tribulations of Emmanuel Gollantz, the eldest son of a Jewish antique dealer. Though married for only two years, Emmanuel and his smart wife, Viva, willingly agree to separate and later divorce: she pursues livelier men and he returns to Italy and the great love of his life, Juliet, an opera singer ten years his senior. He experiences a year of bliss with Juliet, before she dies and leaves him with their infant to raise. The novel is essentially a late version of the Edwardian marriage-problem novel, with a modern glaze of frankness and a taste of bitterness. The series as a whole, however, is Edwardian in its assumption of the importance of inherited family traits, with the Gollantz family described as tribal and quixotic.

In 1940, after Italy had entered the Second World War, Jacob was evacuated to England via France and Gibraltar with nothing much except the clothes on her back. She joined the Entertainments National Service Association, and became famous for her flamboyant appearance—signature monocle, crew-cut hair, and First World War

Women's Legion uniform—and humorous performances throughout the Mediterranean and Africa.

On returning to Sirmione following the war, Jacob continued to produce two books per year. Increasingly she nostalgically focused on Yorkshire settings and romantic plots. Typically her alienated heroines make sacrifices, perhaps in loveless, even abusive marriages before their brutish first husbands die and they discover their soulmates, as in *Late Lark Singing* (1957). The best of these novels are well crafted, and contain vividly realized settings and some fine psychological analysis. From the 1930s Jacob also wrote a series of 'Me' memoirs, beginning with *Me: a Chronicle about other People* (1933) and ending with *Me and the Stage* (1964). *Me and the Swans* (1963) recounts her friendship with Hall and Troubridge. In these quirky hybrids of reminiscence, advice, and essays Jacob leaps from interest to interest 'like an elderly gazelle', as she admits: topics include flowers, her beloved cats, travel recommendations, music-hall memories, Italian art, and nuggets of wisdom (*Yesterday and To-Day*, 252). One topic she never broaches in her books (she wrote over seventy) is lesbianism, a sensitive exploration of which might have given her conventional stories greater staying power.

Although Jacob described herself as 'inordinately shy', she loved the limelight and, according to her friend Bransby Williams, was 'a jolly, boisterous laughing companion' (*Yesterday and To-Day* 112, 211). She was short and stocky, a physique she called 'foursquare', and this in combination with her short, brushed-back wavy hair, heavy horn-rimmed glasses, and traditional male attire left an impression not easily forgotten (ibid., 113). Jacob died in Sirmione on 27 August 1964 of a heart attack. Her books still claim a wide readership.

GEORGE MALCOLM JOHNSON

Sources S. J. Kunitz and H. Haycraft, eds., *Twentieth century authors: a biographical dictionary of modern literature* (1942) • M. Jasper, 'Naomi Jacob', *British novelists between the wars*, ed. G. M. Johnson, DLitB, 191 (1998) • N. Jacob, *Me: yesterday and to-day* (1957) • N. Jacob, *Me and the swans* (1963) • S. Cline, *Radclyffe Hall: a woman called John* (1997) • M. Baker, *Our three selves: the life of Radclyffe Hall* (1985) • E. Hamer, *Britannia's glory: a history of twentieth-century lesbians* (1996)
Likenesses Bassano, photograph, 1939, NPG [*see illus.*] • photograph, repro. in Jasper, 'Naomi Jacob', 206 • photograph, repro. in Cline, *Radclyffe Hall*, 210–11 • photographs, repro. in Jacob, *Me*, 128–9
Wealth at death £5000—in England: probate, 19 Nov 1964, CGPLA Eng. & Wales

Jacob, Robert (*d.* 1588), physician, eldest son of Giles Jacob, of London, was entered at Merchant Taylors' School, London, on 21 January 1564. He matriculated as a sizar of Trinity College, Cambridge, on 12 November 1565, proceeded BA in 1569–70, was elected a fellow, and in 1573 commenced MA. He graduated MD at Basel, and was incorporated at Cambridge on 15 May 1579. He became physician to Queen Elizabeth, who in 1581 sent him on a diplomatic mission to the Russian court. Jacob travelled to Russia with Jerome Horsey and became involved in negotiations for Lady Mary Hastings, daughter of the earl of Huntingdon, to become the wife of Tsar Ivan IV. The death of the tsar brought negotiations to an end. Jacob returned to England with Sir Jerome Bowes, the English envoy in Russia, about March 1584. The Russian company, which had initially financed Jacob, charged him with trading on his own account, after he had arranged for a large amount of wax to be sent to England. On 21 May 1583 he was admitted a licentiate of the College of Physicians in London, becoming a candidate on 12 November 1585, and a fellow on 15 March 1586. In the latter year Elizabeth requested that Jacob should return to Russia. Once again he travelled with Horsey. They were accompanied by a midwife, Anna, who had been requested by Boris Godunov to attend the tsarina. Jacob had obviously been forgiven for his transgressions during his first visit, as Godunov claimed that he had 'shewed mercy upon Robarte, pardoned his offences; proclaimed his gracious goodness in all places' (Bond, 293). Jacob died abroad, unmarried, in 1588.

GORDON GOODWIN, rev. MICHAEL BEVAN

Sources J. von Hamel, *England and Russia: comprising the voyages of John Tradescant the Elder, Sir Hugh Willoughby, Richard Chancellor, Nelson, and others to the White Sea*, trans. J. S. Leigh (1854) · E. A. Bond, ed., *Russia at the close of the sixteenth century*, Hakluyt Society, 20 (1856) · Cooper, *Ath. Cantab.*, vol. 2 · Venn, *Alum. Cant.* · Munk, *Roll* · W. M. Richter, 'Analytical and critical reviews: Review I, *History of medicine in Europe*', *British and Foreign Medico-Chirurgical Review*, 30 (Oct 1862), 291 · will, PRO, PROB 11/72, sig. 42 · private information (2004) · M. V. Unkovskaya, 'Anglo-Russian diplomatic relations, 1580–1696', DPhil diss., U. Oxf., 1992

Jacob [*née* Kennedy-Erskine], **Violet Augusta Mary Frederica** (1863–1946), writer, was born on 1 September 1863 at the House of Dun, near Montrose in Angus (Forfarshire), on the east coast of Scotland. She was the eldest of the three surviving children of William Henry Kennedy-Erskine (1828–1870), laird of Dun, and Catherine (1839–1914), daughter of William Jones, landowner, of Henllys, Carmarthenshire, Wales. A brother, John (*b.* 1864), died in infancy, and her younger sister, Millicent Augusta Lilian, born in 1867, died in 1883 at the age of sixteen. Her brother, Augustus John William Henry Kennedy-Erskine (1866–1908), who had succeeded as laird, died and was buried at sea, aged forty-two.

Violet Kennedy-Erskine grew up at Dun, and was educated at home, showing early literary and artistic interests. Her first book, which she also illustrated, was published by Blackwood in 1888, and was a comic narrative poem in Scots, written collaboratively with William Douglas Campbell. This minor work is of much less interest than her later poetry, also mainly in Scots, although it is perhaps her fiction which most strongly justifies Jacob's place in the canon of Scottish literature. Much of her writing draws imaginatively on her early experience of life in Angus, and on knowledge of her family's past. The Erskines of Dun were an ancient family, whose history she later recorded in *The Lairds of Dun* (1931). Lands at Dun purchased by Sir Robert Erskine of that ilk in 1375 belonged to the family until the twentieth century. Several of Jacob's ancestors were notable figures. John Erskine, fifth laird of Dun, a moderator of the general assembly of the Church of Scotland, was active in the emergence of the reformed church in Scotland and friendly with John Knox, although

Violet Augusta Mary Frederica Jacob (1863–1946), by unknown artist

considered moderate by Mary, queen of Scots. The House of Dun, designed by William Adam, was built for David Erskine (*bap.* 1673, *d.* 1758), the thirteenth laird, an eminent Scottish judge who, as a covert Jacobite, espoused different religious and political affiliations from his predecessors. He is the likely model for the character David Logie in what is probably Violet's most significant achievement, her novel *Flemington* (1911); the house, which also appears fictionalized as Balnillo, was acquired by the National Trust for Scotland. Violet's grandmother Augusta was a daughter of the actress Dorothy Jordan and the duke of Clarence (later William IV). These and other aspects of her family history may partly account for her sympathy for the unconventional throughout her work.

On 27 October 1894, at St John's Episcopal Church, Princes Street, Edinburgh, Violet married Arthur Otway Jacob (1867–1936), an Irishman born in Maryborough (now Portlaoise), educated in Dublin, and serving as a lieutenant with the 20th Royal Hussars, a cavalry regiment of the British army. It is not known how the couple met. Arthur Jacob rose to the rank of major, refusing further promotion because he suffered badly from asthma. Their son, Arthur Henry Jacob, known as Harry, was born on 25 August 1895 in Colchester, the site of the regimental barracks.

Arthur Jacob departed with his regiment in 1895 for India, to be stationed at Mhow, an army cantonment town on the plains of Indore state, Central India Agency. Violet and Harry followed soon after. Their years in India were happy ones, recorded by the writer in diaries and letters she sent to her mother, and *Diaries and Letters from India, 1895–1900* was published posthumously in 1990. Violet Jacob responded warmly to local life, learning to speak some Hindustani, and taking a strong interest in Hindu culture. She met various rulers of the Central Indian States, including the maharajas Holkar of Indore and Sindhia of Gwalior. She also had friends and acquaintances among expatriates; one, Adela Nicolson (1865–1904), went on later to publish poetry under the name Laurence Hope. Although Violet Jacob worked as a nurse in the local military hospital at Mhow (and nursed again during wartime), she enjoyed considerable freedom in India, riding on the plains, and collecting and painting plants. Shortly before her death she offered her five volumes of Indian flower paintings to the University of Edinburgh; these were later moved to the Royal Botanical Gardens in Edinburgh.

Arthur Jacob's regiment was posted to South Africa from 1901 to 1902, participating in the last few months of the Second South African War. The Jacobs also went with the hussars to Egypt (1903–4). Susan Tweedsmuir, later married to the writer John Buchan, accompanied her mother to Cairo as a girl, and met Violet Jacob, writing in her autobiography: 'Violet had published a small book of poetry, which made her a little suspect to the military society of Cairo. But her charm and beauty and aptitude for getting on with people helped her to live down even poetry' (Tweedsmuir, 54–5). A painting of Violet Jacob as a young woman shows a large-eyed, pale-skinned beauty, and the poet Hugh MacDiarmid, too, was later to remember her as a charming and handsome woman looking younger than her years (Garden, 10).

Violet Jacob published a volume of poetry in English, *Verses*, in 1905, but while in India had already embarked on her first novel, *The Sheepstealers* (1902). Set in the Welsh borderlands, and based around the Rebecca riots of the 1840s, this was well received on publication, and was compared with the work of Thomas Hardy (in, for instance, *The Spectator*, 13 September 1902). Although the Jacobs lived in various English garrison towns they stayed at Llantomas, near Hay-on-Wye, Herefordshire, around 1908, and seem to have kept rooms there for many years, as Violet had relatives who probably offered the Llantomas house as a base, which the Jacobs used when they were on leave, and after Arthur Jacob's retirement. In 1908 Violet Jacob published two fictional works rooted in the Anglo-Welsh borderlands, a historical novel, *The History of Aythan Waring*, and a slight novella, *Irresolute Catherine*.

Violet Jacob also wrote fiction and poetry for children; an early volume was *The Golden Heart and other Fairy Stories* (1904), while *Tales Told by the Miller* (1909) are for older children. Her writing enabled her to augment the family income, and the quality of her work varies, but her adult Scottish fiction is very fine. *The Interloper* (1904) takes her beloved Angus as its location. Set in the early nineteenth century, the tale of young Gilbert Speid who returns from Spain to his inherited estate near Montrose echoes the work of Scott and Stevenson, and contains some excellent Scots dialogue, while Violet Jacob's style remains distinctively economical and ironic. This historical romance with tragicomic qualities was reprinted in 1912 and again in 1926. *Flemington* (1911) is an even more powerful novel, set mainly in Scotland after the Jacobite defeat at Culloden in 1746, exploring themes of loyalty and betrayal, and the nature of justice. It was described by John Buchan in a letter of 31 December 1911 as 'the best Scots romance since *The Master of Ballantrae*' (National Library of Scotland, MS 27416), and was well received by critics when it first appeared, and again when republished in 1994. The Angus locations are vividly evoked, and the many memorable characters include a sensitive young artist-protagonist, Archie Flemington, his strong and ambitious grandmother Christian, and Skirling Wattie, the legless beggar, whose singing voice suggests the lyrical qualities of Scottish folk culture. Although the narrative is gripping, and lightened by Jacob's wit, it is a sombre work.

Violet Jacob lost her mother in 1914, and the First World War brought further grief. Her son, Harry, died aged twenty, fighting with the Royal Fusiliers at the battle of the Somme in 1916. Around this time she moved around a good deal, writing letters from both Preston and Colchester during the war years. Although drawing strength from her Christian faith, according to Susan Tweedsmuir she never recovered entirely from her son's death. After this she wrote no more novels, but mainly produced poetry and shorter prose.

Many of Violet Jacob's poems were initially published in *Country Life*. Her first collection was *Songs of Angus* (1915), and this was very successful, appealing to exiled Scots, including soldiers, during wartime. The Aberdeenshire vernacular poet Charles Murray, who had emigrated to South Africa, wrote to Violet Jacob admiringly from there. The opening poem of this volume, 'Tam i'the Kirk' has been much anthologized. *More Songs of Angus and Others* (1918) was followed by several more volumes, mainly in Scots. Her poetry was also published in *Northern Numbers* (1920–22) by the young C. M. Grieve (Hugh MacDiarmid), then working as a reporter in Montrose, who called her in the *Scottish Educational Journal* (17 July 1925) 'by far the most considerable of contemporary vernacular poets'. John Buchan included her in his anthology, *The Northern Muse* (1924). Violet Jacob's Scots poetry, which influenced among others Helen Cruickshank, draws on the ballad tradition and folk song; it is skilfully crafted, notable for its handling of structure and metre. *The Scottish Poems of Violet Jacob* (1944) contains some of her best work, and was reprinted several times. Some of her poetry was set to music in the late twentieth century.

In 1920 the Jacobs moved for a time to Ludlow in Shropshire, but still grieving for her son, Violet Jacob found it difficult to settle. Nevertheless, she published a volume of tautly written short stories in 1922, *Tales of my Own Country*, set in Angus, which the Jacobs still visited regularly. In 1977 some further previously uncollected, and mainly unpublished, short stories from the 1920s and 1930s were discovered; the Second World War and paper shortages had blocked their publication. These appeared as *The Lum Hat and other Stories* in 1982, edited by Ronald Garden.

The Jacobs visited India for a second time in 1922–3, accompanying Violet's relation Eilean Sandys-Thomas to her wedding in Bombay. They visited old haunts and explored new ones. Violet Jacob met the begum of Bhopal, then the only woman ruler of an Indian state, and a figure of some consequence, but Violet's diary of this visit remained unpublished at the end of the twentieth century. A young relative considered Violet Jacob herself 'quite a formidable, grand lady' (private information) when he met her in the early 1930s. The Jacobs were now spending their summers at Llantomas and winters abroad, because of Arthur's health. They appear to have spent several months in Liguria, Italy, in 1930, and in 1936 were in the south of France; some watercolours, sketches, and short essays reflect these travels.

Although Violet Jacob received an honorary degree (LLD) from Edinburgh University in 1936, she did not court fame. Only rare photographs of her remain, and she refused the use of her likeness in publicity for her work. She was a very private person, whose published letters and diaries suggest a spirited personality, yet are not very 'personal'. The few extant unpublished letters to friends and acquaintances reveal intermittent glimpses of her inner life. Arthur Jacob's death late in 1936 was a terrible blow; although the couple had enjoyed independent interests it had been a long and happy marriage, and Violet wrote to a friend: 'I hardly know how to stand up to life now, but will try. I have lost what was more than life to me' (Montrose Library, correspondence of David Waterson, MS X/510/8). She moved back to Scotland, living at Marywell House near Kirriemuir in Angus until the end of her life. In these later years she apparently met the poet Marion Angus, but the meeting was not a success.

Violet Jacob died at Marywell House, near Kirriemuir, of heart disease on 9 September 1946 and was buried three days later. *The Scotsman* obituary (11 September 1946) acknowledges her achievements, remarking that she 'was a woman of very strong character, with a delightful sense of humour'. She was not buried in the Erskine burial-ground at the House of Dun, but shared her husband's grave under a modest headstone in the public graveyard at Dun kirk.

CAROL ANDERSON

Sources manuscripts and letters, NL Scot., 'The Lum Hat', MS 27411; typescripts of short stories in the *Lum Hat* collection MS 27412; typescripts or copies of articles and poems; letters from publisher MS 27413; typewritten MSS 'Four Good Years', Indian diaries and letters, 1895–1900 MS 27414; typescript of diaries from India, 1922–3 MS 27415; assorted letters, incl. ones from C. Murray and J. Buchan, and a poem by H. Cruickshank, 'To Violet Jacob…', 1915 MS 27416 · V. Jacob, correspondence of David Waterson, artist in Brechin, Montrose Public Library, MS X/510/8 [13 letters to Mr and Mrs Waterson] · letters to James Christison, librarian at Montrose Public Library, Montrose Public Library · private information (2004) · Erskine of Dun muniments, NA Scot., Accession GD123/230, GD123/232, GD123/237 · R. Garden, 'The Scottish poetry of Violet Jacob', MLitt. diss., U. Aberdeen, 1976 [held in Montrose public library] · V. Jacob, *The lairds of Dun* (1931) · S. Tweedsmuir, *The lilac and the rose* (1952) · *Scots peerage*, vol. 2 · *Scots peerage*, vol. 5 · *The lum hat and other stories: last tales of Violet Jacob*, ed. R. Garden (1982) [introductory biographical material] · *The Scotsman* (11 Sept 1946) · V. Jacob, *Diaries and letters from India, 1895–1900*, ed. C. Anderson [introductory biographical material, incl. much orig. research] · H. MacDiarmid [C. M. Grieve], 'Violet Jacob', *Scottish Educational Journal* (17 July 1925) [repr. in *Contemporary Scottish Studies* (1976) 8–10]

Archives NL Scot., corresp., diaries, and literary MSS · U. Edin., corresp., GEN. 1731/1–3 | Montrose Public Library, letters to James Christison, librarian at Montrose Public Library · Montrose Public Library, letters to Mr and Mrs Waterson, MS X/510/8 · NA Scot., Erskine of Dun muniments, GD 123 · NL Scot., MSS 27411–27416, 26190, 26706

Likenesses photograph, 1922–3, NL Scot., MS. 27415 · W. Lamb, bronze bust, 1925, William Lamb Memorial Studio, Montrose · D. Young, photograph, 1933, House of Dun, Angus · Harris-Brown, oils, Montrose Museum · chalk drawing, Scot. NPG [*see illus.*] · photographs, Montrose Public Library, Montrose Album, vol. 4, LF 1250, LF 1251

Wealth at death £42,296 0s. 7d.: confirmation, 7 March 1947, *CCI*

Jacob, William (1761/2–1851), merchant and writer on the corn trade, was by the early 1790s well established in business as a merchant, in partnership with John Jacob, in premises in Newgate Street, London. According to Joshua Wilson he had become a 'commercial man of considerable credit' and was 'one of the few Englishmen who, in the present day, has carried on a direct trade with South America' (Wilson, 672). Jacob demonstrated his expert knowledge of British trading interests in the Americas during his time in parliament, as member first for Westbury (1806–7) and then for Rye (1808–12), a Treasury seat. While in parliament he also supported the campaign for the abolition of the slave trade, but, it would seem, in the belief that its continuation would lead to overproduction in the colonies rather than on humanitarian grounds.

In 1809 and 1810 Jacob spent six months in Spain, and the letters he wrote from that country were afterwards published as *Travels in the South of Spain* (1811), which was favourably reviewed in the *Edinburgh Review*. Shortly after his return to England he was, in 1810, elected alderman for the ward of Lime Street in the City of London, but the bankruptcy of his business in 1811 caused him to resign this office. He decided not to seek re-election to parliament in the forthcoming general election and instead he settled on his estate at Chesham Lodge, Surrey, where he farmed several hundred acres.

Jacob now became an expert on the European corn trade and British agricultural protection, and between 1814 and 1820 he published several treatises on these subjects. On the death of Arthur Young in 1820 he unsuccessfully applied for the vacant post of secretary to the board of agriculture, but he was appropriately compensated in 1822 by appointment to the office of comptroller of corn returns to the Board of Trade. In this capacity he was sent twice by the British government—in 1825–6 and in 1827—to study agricultural conditions in Germany, Poland, and parts of Russia. The visits were followed by two 'uniquely important' reports (Fairlie, 564) published by the House of

Commons. These were *Report on the Trade in Corn and the Agriculture of Northern Europe* (1826) and *Report on Agriculture and Trade in Corn in some of the Continental States of Northern Europe* (1828). The purpose of these reports was to convince British farmers that there would not be a glut of foreign corn into Britain if the corn laws were relaxed. By achieving this objective, Jacob's reports, and his earlier evidence to the agricultural committee of 1821, helped facilitate the introduction of the sliding scale of corn duties in 1828 and ultimately the repeal of the corn laws in 1846. According to one authority on the corn laws, 'virtually all subsequent observers of agriculture … drew heavily on his reports and were influenced by his conclusions' (ibid., 564 n.).

On the suggestion of William Huskisson, president of the Board of Trade, Jacob undertook an inquiry into the production and trade in precious metals. His findings were published in *An Historical Inquiry into the Production and Consumption of the Precious Metals* (2 vols., 1831). In addition Jacob published several books and pamphlets on economic subjects, contributed to the *Quarterly Review* and *Encyclopaedia Britannica*, and from 1832 to 1838 served as treasurer for the Royal Society of Literature.

Jacob was married, and he and his wife, who died on 18 March 1814, had at least one son, **Edward Jacob** (1795/6–1841), barrister and legal writer. He was educated at Westminster School (1808–11) and Gonville and Caius College, Cambridge, whence he graduated BA (1816) as senior wrangler and first Smith's prizeman. He was elected a fellow of his college and admitted to Lincoln's Inn in 1816; he was called to the bar in 1819 and practised with great success in the chancery court. Appointed a king's counsel on 27 December 1834, he edited several volumes of law reports from the chancery court and published a valuable second edition of R. S. D. Roper's *Treatise on the Law of Property Arising from the Relation between Husband and Wife* in 1826. However, his health suffered from overwork, and he died on 15 December 1841 in Malta, where he had gone to recuperate.

William Jacob retired on a pension from the Board of Trade in 1841, the same year as his son's death. He died at his home at 31 Cadogan Place, Sloane Street, London, on 17 December 1851, aged eighty-nine.

GORDON GOODWIN, rev. M. J. MERCER

Sources J. M. Collinge, 'Jacob, William', HoP, *Commons, 1790–1820* · GM, 1st ser., 84/1 (1814), 416 · GM, 2nd ser., 37 (1852), 523 · Boase, *Mod. Eng. biog.* · S. Fairlie, 'The 19th century corn laws reconsidered', *Economic History Review*, 2nd ser., 18 (1965), 562–75 · EdinR, 55 (1832), 43–61 · EdinR, 18 (1811), 123–52 · J. Wilson, ed., *A biographical index to the present House of Commons* (1808) · Venn, *Alum. Cant.*

Archives BL, Add. MS 38749 · BL, letters to third Lord Hardwicke · BL, letters to Huskisson, Add. MS 38742 · BL, letters to Macvey Napier, Add. MSS 36612–36614

Likenesses M. Gauci, lithograph, 1848 (aged eighty-six; after E. U. Eddis), BM

Jacob, William Stephen (1813–1862), astronomer, the sixth son of Stephen Long Jacob (1764/5–1851), vicar of Woolavington, Somerset, and his wife, Eliza Susannah (d. 1851), the daughter of James Bond, vicar of Ashford in Kent, was born in his father's vicarage on 19 November 1813. His younger brother John *Jacob (1812–1858), his cousin Sir George le Grand Jacob, and several others of his family served in India. William entered Addiscombe College as a cadet in 1828, passed for the engineers, and completed his military education at the Royal Engineer Establishment, Chatham.

On arrival at Bombay in 1831 Jacob was assigned to the trigonometrical survey of the North-Western Provinces. He was promoted lieutenant in 1833 and took charge of the operations in 1836, when he came favourably to the notice of George Everest. He fell ill, and from October 1838 to May 1840 he was on sick leave at the Cape of Good Hope. In 1841 he left Poona to assist Waugh on base-line measurements, but was again taken ill. He went to England in 1843 on a medical certificate, and the following year married Elizabeth (d. 1898), the fourth daughter of Matthew Coates of Gainsborough, with whom he had six sons and two daughters. Jacob and his wife arrived in India in 1845 and settled in Poona, where in 1842 he had built a small brick observatory, with a 5 foot equatorial telescope by Dollond, and had begun compiling a catalogue of double stars. Jacob was employed as assistant superintendent of roads and tanks for Poona, and, unwilling to be transferred to surveys in the Himalaya region, he resigned from the East India Company's service with the rank of captain in January 1848.

Jacob then devoted himself to astronomy. His catalogue of 244 double stars was sent to the Royal Astronomical Society, which elected him a fellow the following year; in the course of this work he computed orbits of several binaries, and in 1847 identified ν Scorpii as a triple star. In March 1849 he was appointed to succeed Thomas Glanville Taylor as astronomer in charge of the East India Company's Madras observatory. Continuing Taylor's programme with his 5 foot transit and 4 foot mural circle, Jacob published his 'Subsidiary catalogue of 1440 stars selected from the British Association catalogue' in the *Madras Observations for 1848–52*. His reobservation of 317 stars from the same collection in 1853–7 showed that large proper motions had erroneously been attributed to them. The same volume contained observations of 250 double stars made with Jacob's own equatorial with a 15 centimetre lens by Lerebours and Secretan of Paris. The Indian government published his work on the mass of Jupiter and Saturn, derived from motions of their satellites, and he noticed in 1852, about the same time as William Lassell, the transparency of Saturn's dusky ring. During the 1850s Jacob also published various sets of magnetical measurements made at Madras, and meteorological observations made at Singapore in 1841–5 and at Dodabetta in 1851–5.

Still troubled by illness, Jacob was in England on sick leave in 1854–5 and again in 1858–9. During these absences Major W. K. Worster of the Madras artillery deputized for him. Worster had requested a transit circle for Madras, similar to that supplied to the Cape observatory, since the existing one had been long in use and damaged by storm, and a clock to go with it. The transit arrived in Madras in March 1859 and it was planned to employ it on observations of planetoids and the faint equatorial stars, for which its construction and geographical location suited it. The following month, however, Jacob left the observatory, and in October 1859 resigned his charge.

Jacob then joined the official expedition to Spain to observe the total solar eclipse of 18 July 1860. His project to erect a mountain observatory at Poona, 5000 feet above sea level, met with the approval of parliament, which voted, in 1862, £1000 towards its equipment. Jacob engaged to work there for three years, with a 9 inch equatorial which he had purchased from Cooke of York. He landed at Bombay on 8 August 1862, but died from a violent liver attack on reaching Poona on 16 August. His death was much regretted for he had been universally admired, both for his considerable mathematical attainments and for his moral qualities as a devoted Christian.

A. M. CLERKE, *rev.* ANITA McCONNELL

Sources *Monthly Notices of the Royal Astronomical Society*, 23 (1862–3), 128–9 · A. H. Jacob and J. H. Glascott, *Historical and genealogical narrative of the families of Jacob* (1875), 22–3 · C. E. Buckland, *Dictionary of Indian biography* (1906), 219 · R. H. Phillimore, ed., *Historical records of the survey of India*, 4 (1958), 448 · *Journal for the History of Astronomy*, 17/4 (1986) [*The Greenwich list of observatories*, ed. D. Howse], esp. 34 · BL OIOC, P/249/43, no. 6 (1855) · Madras public, 1857, BL OIOC, E/4/987 [coll. 15], fols. 766, 963 · W. S. Jacob, 'Micrometrical measure of 120 double or multiple stars, taken at the Honourable East India Company's observatory at Madras, in the years 1856–58', *Memoirs of the Royal Astronomical Society*, 28 (1858–9), 13 · W. S. Jacob, 'Description of a small observatory constructed at Poona in the year 1842', *Monthly Notices of the Astronomical Society of London*, 6 (1843–5), 1 · *CGPLA Eng. & Wales* (1862)

Wealth at death under £12,000 in England: probate, 9 Oct 1862, *CGPLA Eng. & Wales*

Jacobs, George (*d.* 1692). *See under* Salem witches and their accusers (*act.* 1692).

Jacobs, Isaac (1757/8–1835), glass manufacturer, was born in Bristol, probably in Temple parish, one of three children of **Lazarus Jacobs** [Eliezer ben Jacob] (1709?–1796), a Jewish glass cutter born in Frankfurt am Main, Germany, and Mary Hiscocks, of Templecombe, Somerset. In 1774, at the age of sixteen, Isaac became partner in his father's glass-engraving business at 108 Temple Street, Bristol, and at some time thereafter he joined other firms in producing the highly regarded coloured glassware known as Bristol blue glass. A number of Isaac's signed and gilded bowls, decanters, and wineglasses survive today in a variety of public and private collections, including the Victoria and Albert Museum, London, the Ashmolean Museum, Oxford, and the Bristol City Museum.

Bristol's eighteenth-century glass industry was run mainly by manufacturers of west country origin, and the first large consignment of the pigment needed for making Bristol blue glass was imported into Bristol from Saxony by the porcelain manufacturer and chemist William Cookworthy in 1763. Yet Lazarus Jacobs and his son seemed well placed to make their mark on the industry; German engraving techniques were highly sought after, and continental Jews had long been associated with the production of coloured glass.

In 1787 the Jacobs family moved to Avon Street in Temple parish, and then to nearby Great Gardens, in Redcliffe,

a glass-making district and the locus for Bristol's small Jewish community. Isaac and his sisters seem to have been raised as Jews, although a half-sister (the disputed illegitimate child of Lazarus Jacobs by Mary Jones) was baptized into the Church of England about 1767. Lazarus himself was honoured as the Jewish community's most prominent member at the opening of a new synagogue in 1786. Though Isaac married a Christian, Mary MacCreath of Shrewsbury, he retained his Jewish affiliation, and his sisters Hannah and Suky married well-established Jewish merchants.

Following Lazarus Jacobs's death in 1796 Isaac became sole owner of the Temple Street glass manufactory. Lazarus's will does not suggest that the family was wealthy. However, Isaac's good business practices may account for his being able, in 1799, to move his wife and six children to 16 Somerset Square, Redcliffe, a short distance from their glass house. His eldest son, Joseph, was apprenticed to him in 1804, and by the following year Isaac had founded the Non-Such Glass Manufactory; he described himself in 1806 as 'Glass Manufacturer to his Majesty'. Isaac was clearly adept at promoting his business to an increasingly genteel market: 'Specimens', ran one advertisement, 'of the Dessert set which Isaac Jacob had the honour of sending to their Majesties in burnished gold upon royal purple coloured glass may be seen at his manufactory' (Josephs, 111).

In 1809 Jacobs became a freeman of the city of Bristol and moved to Belvedere, a large house that he had commissioned in Weston-super-Mare. In 1812 he was granted a coat of arms, and by 1814 he was a member of the Bristol Commercial Rooms. At the height of his success he was estimated to have been making a gross income of between £15,000 and £20,000 a year. His wares are known to have sold in the United States, and the death of his son Lionel in 1812, in Kingston, Jamaica, suggests that the family business also had West Indian outlets. In 1817 his daughter Matilda married Abraham Alexander, who later became Bristol's first Jewish town councillor. By then, however, Bristol's glass business was in decline and Isaac borrowed heavily to shore up his foundering firm. When in 1820 a loan that he had made to a friend for £2000 was not repaid he was briefly gaoled for debt. In May of the following year he was declared bankrupt amid allegations of fraudulent behaviour (he had named his son and business partner, Joseph Jacobs, as one of his main creditors). Though these charges were eventually dismissed his business was ruined and he sank into ignominious obscurity as a dealer and chapman. He died in 1835 and was buried in the Hebrew burial-ground at St Phillip's, Bristol, which he had purchased for the Jewish community twenty years earlier.

MADGE DRESSER

Sources Z. Josephs, 'Jewish glass-makers', *Transactions of the Jewish Historical Society of England*, 25 (1977) · C. Witt, C. Weeden, and A. Palmer Schwind, *Bristol glass* (1984) · F. Buckley, 'The early glasshouses of Bristol', *Journal of the Society of Glass Technology*, 9 (1925), 36–61 · A. C. Powell, 'Glass-making in Bristol', *Transactions of the Bristol and Gloucestershire Archaeological Society*, 47 (1925), 211–57 · C. H. W. [C. H. Walker], *In the matter of Jacobs, a bankrupt: report of the decision of his honour the lord chancellor upon the petition of John Naylor to* supersede this commission of bankruptcy (1821) · will, 13 April 1796, PRO, PROB 11/1144 [will of Lazarus Jacobs] · Bristol Commercial Rooms, copy of share certificate, Bristol RO, Joseph Bryant Ltd papers, 33302 (107) [copy] · list of contents for town clerk's correspondence, 1768, Bristol RO, bundle 17b · J. Samuel, *Jews in Bristol: the history of the Jewish community in Bristol from the middle ages to the present day* (1997) · counterpart settlement on the marriage of Abraham Alexander with Matilda Jacobs, 25 July 1817, Bristol RO, J. Stewart Esq. papers, 31142 · *The Times* (28 May 1821) · *Felix Farley's Bristol Journal* (26 May 1821); (2 June 1821) · kennedy.soc.surrey.ac. uk/~scs1sp/HWM/bottles/cookwort.htm

Archives Bristol RO, papers
Wealth at death declared bankrupt, 1821: *The Times*

Jacobs, Joseph (1854–1916), historian and folklorist, was born on 29 August 1854 in Sydney, New South Wales, the son of John Jacobs and his wife, Sarah. After attending Sydney grammar school and the University of Sydney, he journeyed to Britain and, in 1873, after a short spell at London University, entered St John's College, Cambridge. While at Cambridge, Jacobs stayed with the family of future Anglo-Jewish historian and foreign affairs activist Lucien Wolf. It was an association that was to prove fruitful. In the early 1880s the two joined the group of northwest London Jewish intellectuals known as the Wanderers—which in 1891 became the Maccabeans—and in 1887 collaborated on the Anglo-Jewish Historical Exhibition and its accompanying catalogue; the following year they jointly produced the *Bibliotheca Anglo-Judaica*.

After graduating from Cambridge as a senior moralist, Jacobs, 'the prince of goodfellows', as Israel Zangwill later described him (*Transactions of the Jewish Historical Society of England*, 131), spent a year in Berlin studying under the renowned Jewish scholars Moritz Lazarus and Moritz Steinschneider. On returning to Britain he furthered his interests in human development as a student of the eugenist Sir Francis Galton. Jacobs then proceeded to carry out a phenological and demographic study of English Jews as a means of confirming his theory that environment rather than biology was the determining factor in the development of racial characteristics. During the 1880s Jacobs published his findings in a series of articles in the *Jewish Chronicle* which he later compiled into two volumes: *Studies in Jewish Statistics* (1891) and *Statistics of the Jewish Population in London* (1894).

Parallel with his scientific studies, the polymath Jacobs was developing his literary talents. He served as secretary of the Society of Hebrew Literature between 1878 and 1884, having in June 1877 published his first literary essay, a study of George Eliot's *Daniel Deronda*, in *Macmillan's Magazine*. Subsequently he published in *The Athenaeum* several articles and obituaries—on Matthew Arnold, Robert Browning, and John Henry Newman—and 'with efficient editorship and masterpieces of introduction' (*Transactions of the Jewish Historical Society of England*, 132) edited several classics, including Jane Austen's *Emma* and the *Arabian Nights*.

However, Jacobs never lost sight of the Jewish past and present. In 1888 he visited Spain—one of the first Jews to do so since the expulsion—and returned with over 1700 documents, which he published as *An Inquiry into the Sources of Spanish-Jewish History* (1893). That he won the approval of the élite in Spain is confirmed by his appointment as a corresponding member of the Royal Spanish Academy. Jacobs was also an ardent student of English Jewish history, and was a founder member and one-time president of the Jewish Historical Society of England. He believed that the Jewish experience, particularly in the historical context, was only one part of a much wider picture and should always be viewed as such. To this end he published a number of articles on the Jews of medieval England in the *Jewish Quarterly Review* and the *Jewish Chronicle*, together with a book on *The Jews of Angevin England* (1893).

The plight of Jewish people in the modern world was not neglected. In January 1882 Jacobs published articles in *The Times* appealing for an end to the persecution of the Jews and the pogroms which had followed the assassination of Tsar Alexander II in 1881; the attention these pieces attracted resulted in the setting up of the Mansion House Committee and Fund to help the Jews of Russia. During the 1880s Jacobs became increasingly aware of the rising tide of 'anti-alien' feeling in England, which coincided with the influx of immigrants from eastern Europe. He sought to dispel some of the myths and stereotyping that were part of the diasporic baggage by producing a volume which would demonstrate that once assimilated Jews made a valuable contribution at all levels of society. The first *Jewish Year Book* appeared in 1896. It was a celebratory and didactic volume in which successful Jews—by birth and/or association—were listed in a style reminiscent of *Burke's Peerage*. Jacobs's apprehensions about antisemitism continued and in 1914 he requested a meeting with G. K. Chesterton to discuss the latter's antisemitic publications and statements.

Joseph Jacobs was a westernized citizen of the Mosaic persuasion who saw no conflict between nationality and religion. Pursuing this belief, and as a way of 'ironing out the ghetto bends', in 1897, together with Leopold Greenberg (editor of the *Jewish Chronicle*, 1907–31), he launched *Young Israel*, a monthly journal for Jewish youth which combined 'the ideals of Englishmen with Jewish values' (Cesarani, 107). Jacobs's separation of the temporal and the spiritual is evident in his attitude to political Zionism and its advocate Theodore Herzl. Jacobs considered that Herzl 'was out of touch with the soul and faith of the Jewish people', and that on a personal level he was 'paltry and materialistic' (*Transactions of the Jewish Historical Society of England*, 142).

In spite of his prolific output, Jacobs still found time to marry Georgina Horne, and they had three children. Perhaps it was the presence of young children around him that encouraged the scholarly Jacobs to turn his attention to the world of folklore and fairy tales. In 1888 he published *The Earliest English Version of the Fables of Bedpai* and one year later an edition of Caxton's *Fables of Aesop*. In 1890, with *English Fairy Tales*, he began a series which was to include *Celtic Fairy Tales* (1892), *Indian Fairy Tales* (1892), *More English Fairy Tales* (1893), and *More Celtic Fairy Tales* (1894). Jacobs was honorary secretary of the International

Folklore Council and editor of *Folklore Magazine*. His work appealed to all ages; as Zangwill said of this side of his talent, his 'books delighted equally the nursery and the drawing room' (*Transactions of the Jewish Historical Society of England*, 138). His final folklore work, *Europa's Fairy Book*, appeared in 1916.

In 1896 Jacobs published a collection of his essays on Jewish history and philosophy under the title *Jewish Ideals*. In that same year he went on a lecture tour of America, where he visited Philadelphia, New York, and Chicago. Four years later that 'laughing joking man always with new projects and theories to pursue' (*Transactions of the Jewish Historical Society of England*, 148) emigrated with his family to New York to take up the position of reviewing editor of the *Jewish Encyclopaedia*, a post he held until 1905. He contributed 400 articles to the work and, in 1906, published a companion under the title *The Jewish Encyclopaedia: a Guide to its Contents, an Aid to its Use*. This was followed by a six-year professorial appointment as English and rhetoric professor at the Jewish Theological Seminary of America in New York. In 1908 Jacobs became a member of the board of editors of the Jewish Publication Society and, in 1913, took on a full-time appointment as editor of the *American Hebrew*, a position he held until his death. In 1915 Jacobs edited the *American Jewish Year Book*. His final literary work, *Jewish Contribution to Civilisation*, was published posthumously in 1919.

Joseph Jacobs was a man of intellect and humour, of insight and scholarliness. A humanist who was always 'bubbling over with fun' (*Transactions of the Jewish Historical Society of England*, 131), he could be scientific 'yet as simple and fresh as a child' (ibid., 140). He had perhaps too many interests; and concentration on one theme, one topic or one discipline, might have produced a weightier, more intellectually reputed and acknowledged scholar and elicited greater respect for his *Wissenschaft des Judentums*. But it would have denied many the joy of his folklore, the benefit of his historical and scientific research and analysis, the urgency of his concerns, and the enthusiasm which he gave to every project.

On 30 January 1916, following a bout of pneumonia, Joseph Jacobs died of heart failure at his home in New Rochelle, New York. He was buried in Mount Hope cemetery, New York.   ANNE J. KERSHEN

Sources R. E. Fierstien, 'Jacobs, Joseph', *ANB* · *Jewish encyclopaedia*, 7 (1912), vol. 7, p. 45 · *Transactions of the Jewish Historical Society of England*, 8 (1915–17), 129–52 [memorial meeting] · *Jewish Year Book* (1896); centenary facs. edn (1996), xv–xxxviii · J. Efron, *Defenders of race* (1994), chap. 4 · *Jewish Chronicle* (11 Feb 1916) · D. Cesarani, *The Jewish Chronicle and Anglo-Jewry, 1841–1991* (1994), 90, 91, 107 · A. Marx, *Essays in Jewish biography* (1947), 251–4 · N. Bentwich, *Solomon Schechter: a biography* (1948), 61–3

Jacobs, Lazarus (1709?–1796). *See under* Jacobs, Isaac (1757/8–1835).

Jacobs, William Wymark (1863–1943), writer, was born in Wapping, London, on 8 September 1863. He was the eldest child of William Gage Jacobs, and his first wife, Sophia Wymark. His father was manager of the South Devon wharf, and the young Jacobs spent much time on Thames-side, growing familiar with the life of the neighbourhood, the *habitués* resident and transient, and the comings and goings of ships. The family was a large one, living on narrow and precarious means, so that W. W. (as he came to be known to his friends) regarded the times when he ran wild in Wapping with his brothers and sisters as happy interludes in a life of nagging discomfort. Almost the only other alleviations of a dreary and restricted childhood were sojourns at a cottage near Sevenoaks, and visits to relatives in rural East Anglia, which permanently endeared country-village life to him, as can be seen in the Claybury stories. Jacobs's mother died when he was very young; he disliked the woman his father later married.

Jacobs was educated at a private school in the City, and later at Birkbeck College, where he made friends with the novelist Pett Ridge. In 1879, at the age of sixteen, he became a boy clerk in the civil service, later becoming a second-division clerk in the savings bank department, where he worked from 1883 until 1899. His work became increasingly a drudgery; but memories of a boyhood of poverty caused him to cling to the safety of a dull and subordinate job until he could feel reasonably sure of earning a living by his pen.

From 1885 Jacobs contributed anonymous and tentative sketches to *Blackfriars*. In the early nineties Jerome K. Jerome accepted a number of his stories for *The Idler* and for *To-Day*, and in 1895 his work was published in the prestigious *Strand Magazine*. These tales—artless, almost naïve—had individuality and gave promise, although as yet tentative, of the humour and mastery of his medium which, in its matured form, ensured Jacobs both livelihood and international repute. In 1896 appeared his first collection of stories, *Many Cargoes*, followed in 1897 by a novelette, *The Skipper's Wooing*, with a moderately successful horror story appended to it, and in 1898 by *Sea Urchins*. The next year he resigned from the civil service and became an author by profession. In 1900 he married Agnes Eleanor, daughter of Richard Owen Williams, bank accountant, of Leystone, Essex: she was a suffragette. They had two sons and three daughters.

On account of his shy, low-voiced address and his gentle melancholy of manner, Jacobs—slight, pale-complexioned, and of almost albino fairness—seemed a smaller man than he really was. In a crowded room he withdrew into self-effacement; but enjoying casual conversation with one or two of his own kind, he talked (as he looked) with a twinkle, and gained stature in proportion as his diffidence fell away.

Jacobs wrote short stories of three kinds: tales about the misadventures of sailors ashore; stories celebrating the unscrupulous ingenuities of the artful dodger of a slow-witted country village; and tales of the macabre. He also wrote seven novels and novelettes, the two best of which, *At Sunwich Port* (1902), and *Dialstone Lane* (1904), display his genius for rendering personalities, comic episodes, and characteristic talk without repeating himself. Popularity as a humorist obscured, even in his heyday, Jacobs's superb technique as a writer of stories. His economy of language, his perpetual understatement, his deadpan manner, together with the suggestion in rapid conversations between his characters of the ludicrous catastrophes which have overtaken or are about to overtake them—these are qualities found only in a master of the writer's craft. In his early stories the characters are impeccably presented, but the tales are mere anecdotes; whereas in *Light Freights* (1901) every moment, from the nonchalant opening to the gentle click of the closing door, is deliberately planned and faultlessly controlled.

In *Light Freights* not only Ginger Dick, Peter Russet, and old Sam Small, but also Bob Pretty, Henery Walker, the bibulous ancient on the bench outside The Cauliflower, and other notabilities of Claybury made their bow. In 1902 came *The Lady of the Barge*, which contained the author's master-tales of horror—'The Monkey's Paw', 'The Well', and 'In the Library'—deftly mixed with seafaring and bucolic absurdities. 'The Monkey's Paw', his most enduring piece of writing, has been frequently anthologized, and was dramatized by L. N. Parker, with whom Jacobs collaborated in writing *Beauty and the Barge* (1904). He wrote a total of eighteen plays, some written in collaboration, and several being dramatizations of his short stories; and published twelve collections of stories, all on the highest level, ending with *Night Watches* (1914).

Jacobs's work after 1914 shows a certain decline. He never published slipshod work, and devised new variations on old themes: it is perhaps indicative that he allowed nothing to be issued in volume form in the seventeen years before he died at Hornsey Lane, Islington, London, on 1 September 1943.

MICHAEL SADLEIR, *rev.* SAYONI BASU

Sources C. Lamerton, *WWJ: a bibliography* (1988) · *The Times* (2 Sept 1943) · G. K. Chesterton, *A handful of authors: essays on books and writers*, ed. D. C. Collins (1953) · M. Drabble, ed., *The Oxford companion to English literature*, 5th edn (1985) · *CGPLA Eng. & Wales* (1943)
Archives BL, corresp. with Society of Authors, Add. MSS 56730, 63276–63277 · Ransom HRC, MSS and letters · University of Bristol Library, literary corresp. | U. Leeds, Brotherton L., letters to Edward Clodd | FILM BFI NFTVA, propaganda footage (Hepworth Manufacturing Company) | SOUND BL NSA, performance recording
Likenesses C. Moore-Park, portrait, 1910, NPG · J. Russell & Sons, photograph, *c.*1915, NPG · W. Tittle, lithograph, 1922, NPG · H. Furniss, pen-and-ink drawing, NPG · D. Low, pencil cartoon, NPG
Wealth at death £24,090 12*s.* 3*d.*: probate, 22 Dec 1943, *CGPLA Eng. & Wales*

Jacobsen, Theodore (*d.* 1772), architect and merchant, the son of the merchant Sir Jacob Jacobsen (*fl. c.*1660–*c.*1700), of north German origin, was born in London. Here his family had been closely involved since at least the 1660s with the running of the Steelyard, the trading centre on Thames Street for the merchants of the Hanseatic League. His uncle, also called Theodore, was the league's agent and housemaster of the Steelyard from 1681 until his death on 17 July 1706. After the death of his brother Jacob in 1735, Theodore Jacobsen ran the family business at the Steelyard. He also began to dabble in architectural design: in 1726 he designed the new headquarters of the East India Company in Leadenhall Street (rebuilt 1799–1800; dem. 1861–2), the building of which was supervised by the experienced architect John James.

For the next forty years Jacobsen balanced his amateur interest in architecture, designing dour, formulaic buildings in an austere Palladian style, with his mercantile career. A design of 1731 for a new building in Threadneedle Street for the Bank of England was rejected in favour of one by George Sampson. In 1740, however, he built himself a house—known as Lonesome Lodge or, later, Tillingbourne—near Abinger in Surrey, where he lived during the summer months until 1763. Although the house was demolished early in the nineteenth century, an engraving survives in the Bodleian Library, Oxford, as does an attribution of the design to Jacobsen by George Vertue in his *Note Books*.

Jacobsen's most famous architectural achievement was the design of the Foundling Hospital in London. Having founded the hospital in 1739, the governors employed the architect John Sanderson to examine possible sites and prepare estimates. However, the task of designing the new building was given to Jacobsen, who joined the governors' ranks. Site management was again entrusted to an expert, in this case the surveyor James Horne (who, like Jacobsen, gave his services free). The hospital's foundation-stone was laid on 16 September 1742, and the new building opened on 1 October 1745—without its projected central chapel, which was begun in May 1747 and not fully completed until 1754. The elevations and interiors of Jacobsen and Horne's two wings were deliberately austere: only in those areas forbidden to the children— the Picture Gallery, Committee Room, and Court Room (provided with an astonishing rococo plaster ceiling by William Wilton)—was elaborate decoration allowed to intrude. Following the needless demolition of the Foundling Hospital in 1926–7, only the southern colonnades and boundary range survive *in situ*. Jacobsen's staircase, together with the major fittings and furnishings of the three principal rooms, was incorporated into John Sheppard's bland Coram Foundation headquarters of 1933–5.

In 1745 Jacobsen was asked to design the Royal Naval Hospital for Sick Sailors at Haslar, near Gosport in Hampshire, which was completed in 1761; it is now demolished, but an engraving of its façade features in the *Gentleman's Magazine* of 1751. Jacobsen's last firmly attributed design was for the main quadrangle of Trinity College, Dublin, built in 1752–9. Once again he relied heavily on the advice and expertise of building professionals, this time Hugh Darley and the architects Henry Keene and John Sanderson. As at the Foundling and Haslar hospitals, the design for Trinity was based on a simple quadrangle with corner pavilions.

Jacobsen died, apparently unmarried, on 25 May 1772 in London, and was buried close to the Steelyard in the family vault of the church of All Hallows-the-Great. His will refers to a portfolio of his own architectural drawings, since lost. The 1742 half-length portrait by William Hogarth, now at the Oberlin Museum in Ohio, USA, shows Jacobsen holding a plan of an unidentified triangular house, for which there is also an elevation in the Victoria and Albert Museum. The full-length portrait by Thomas Hudson of 1746 at the Coram Foundation in London clearly shows him holding a plan and elevation for the Foundling Hospital. S. P. PARISSIEN

Sources Colvin, *Archs.* · R. H. Nichols and F. A. Wray, *The history of the Foundling Hospital* (1935) · S. Parissien, 'The architecture of the Foundling Hospital', *Enlightened self-interest*, ed. S. Harris (1995), 26–31 · B. Nicolson, *The treasures of the Foundling Hospital* (1972) · Vertue, *Note books*, 5.155 · W. Foster, *The East India House* (1924) · Redgrave, *Artists* · P. Norman, 'Notes on the later history of the Steelyard in London', *Archaeologia*, 61 (1908–9), 389–426 · LMA
Archives Coram Foundation Archive, London | Bodl. Oxf., Gough maps, 30, fols. 75–6
Likenesses W. Hogarth, oils, 1742, Oberlin Museum, Ohio · T. Hudson, oils, 1746, Coram Foundation, London

Jacobson, Sydney, Baron Jacobson (1908–1988), newspaper editor and political commentator, was born on 26 October 1908 in Zeerost, Transvaal, the only son and elder child of Samuel and Anna Jacobson, a Jewish couple who had emigrated from Germany and were running an unsuccessful ostrich farm. In the summer of 1914 the family returned to Frankfurt am Main to visit friends and were unfortunate enough to stay on until August, when they were all interned. Jacobson thus obtained his primary education in a German camp, a more humane version of the camps which were to fire his hatred of Germans in the 1930s and 1940s. His father was drowned when the ship in which he was attempting to return to South Africa sank off the south-west coast of England. His mother then took her children to live in Britain with relatives, the family of Lewis Silkin, later a government minister.

Jacobson attended Strand School and then King's College, London, where he obtained a diploma in journalism. He began his journalistic career on weekly papers in Sussex. He soon left for India, however, where he became assistant editor of *The Statesman* (1934–6), a reservist with the Delhi light horse, and a daring steeplechase jockey. On his return to England he worked for the pocket-sized magazine *Lilliput* (1936–9). In 1938 he married Phyllis June (d. 1988), daughter of Frank Steele Buck, stockbroker; they had two sons and one daughter. He enlisted as a private immediately war was declared, was commissioned in the Middlesex regiment, was awarded the MC in 1944 for his resolute defence of a bridge during the 1944 fighting in the Low Countries, and was promoted lieutenant-colonel and given command of his battalion. On demobilization he wrote for *Picture Post* (1945–8) and obtained his first editorship at the *Leader Magazine* (1948–50), a paper which was a journalistic success but a financial failure. Soon after it ceased publication he began his association with the Mirror group, writing first for the *Sunday Pictorial* (1951) under Hugh Cudlipp and then for the *Daily Mirror* as its political editor (1952–62).

The *Daily Mirror* was a noisy, disputatious paper but Jacobson, a quiet man who was erudite, sceptical, and mordant, nevertheless fitted in perfectly. With Cudlipp he produced coruscating attacks on the governments of Churchill, Eden, and Macmillan. Although he was on the far left when young he moved sufficiently to give notable support to Hugh Gaitskell, whose speeches he occasionally helped to write. During the Suez crisis of 1956 Jacobson was instrumental in shifting the *Mirror* from early acquiescence to outright opposition, a policy which reduced its circulation by 70,000. In fact it was prepared to lose many more readers.

When the Mirror group bought Odhams Press in 1961 Jacobson was made editor of the loss-making *Daily Herald* (1962–4), the organ of the Trades Union Congress and the Labour Party. He remained editor (1964–5) after it was transmuted into *The Sun*, a middlebrow paper created to fill what was thought to be a gap in the market but which was proved not to exist. As its losses mounted the paper was sold (almost given away) to Rupert Murdoch in 1969 and Jacobson returned to the *Mirror*, where he became editorial director (1968–74) and later deputy chairman (1973–4) of the group.

In the two general elections of 1974, in February and October, Jacobson was at his peak. Determined that the Labour Party should win, he produced a series of famous poster-type front pages, inspired every leading article, and oversaw all the political stories. With election results as close as they were in both elections, his contributions must have been significant. He had refused a knighthood when he was editing the *Daily Herald*, but after his retirement he accepted the offer of a life peerage in 1975.

Jacobson had hoped to play an active part in the House of Lords, but his later years were affected by ill health. They were also marred by the misfortunes of the Labour Party and by what was happening at the *Daily Mirror*. After Robert Maxwell became its publisher in 1983 Jacobson stopped buying the paper he had served for so long.

Jacobson was a tall, distinguished-looking man with a large nose and sardonic smile. He died on 13 August 1988 in St Albans, Hertfordshire, where his home was at 6 Avenue Road. TERENCE LANCASTER, *rev.*

Sources M. Edelman, *The Mirror: a political history* (1966) · H. Cudlipp, *Walking on the water* (1976) · *The Independent* (16 Aug 1988) · *The Independent* (1 Nov 1988) · *The Times* (15 Aug 1988) · personal knowledge (1996) · private information (1996) · CGPLA Eng. & Wales (1988)
Wealth at death under £70,000: probate, 14 Nov 1988, CGPLA Eng. & Wales

Jacobson, William (1803–1884), bishop of Chester and theologian, son of William Jacobson, a merchant's clerk, and his wife, Judith, née Clarke, was born in Great Yarmouth, Norfolk, on 18 July 1803. His father died shortly after his birth, and as his mother's second husband was a nonconformist, he was sent when about nine to a school at Norwich kept by J. S. Brewer, a baptist, father of John Sherren Brewer. About 1819 he went to Homerton (nonconformist) College, London, where he was taught by Revd William Walford, and in 1822–3 was a student at Glasgow University. In 1823 he was admitted commoner of St Edmund Hall, Oxford. In May 1825 he was elected scholar of Lincoln College (BA in 1827), taking a second class in *literae humaniores*, having received private tuition from C. T. Longley, who became a lifelong friend. Failing to win a fellowship at Exeter College, he was a private tutor

William Jacobson (1803–1884), by Lewis Carroll (Charles Lutwidge Dodgson), 1857

in Ireland until 1829. He then returned to Oxford, obtained the Ellerton theological prize, was elected fellow at Exeter College on 30 June, and proceeded MA. On 6 June 1830 he was ordained deacon, was appointed to the curacy of St Mary Magdalen, Oxford, and was ordained priest the following year. In 1832 he was appointed vice-principal of Magdalen Hall, where he did much to encourage industry and enforce discipline. With a view to preparing an edition of the *Patres apostolici*, which he undertook at the suggestion of Edward Burton, professor of divinity, he travelled to Florence, Rome, and elsewhere to consult manuscripts.

Jacobson vacated his fellowship at Exeter College after his marriage on 23 June 1836 to Eleanor Jane, youngest daughter of Dawson Turner, a banker of Yarmouth, and was an unsuccessful candidate for the headmastership of Harrow in succession to Longley. He remained at Magdalen Hall, and became in 1839 perpetual curate of Iffley. He was made public orator of the university in 1842. Publication of his *Patres apostolici* in 1838 (4th edn, 1863), which was especially important for its treatment of the epistles of St Ignatius, established his reputation for theological learning. This work led to his appointment as regius professor of divinity at Oxford in April 1848, on the recommendation of Lord John Russell, the prime minister, who was further impressed that Jacobson's opinions were 'moderately liberal, and not tory' (Ward, 145). The chair carried with it a canonry of Christ Church, and at that time also the rectory of Ewelme, Oxfordshire. During his tenure he produced a six-volume edition of the works of Robert Sanderson, bishop of Lincoln (1854).

Jacobson was a man of universally acknowledged piety and of simple habits. Although extremely reserved and cautious, he never hesitated to act in accordance with his sense of right, and was a kind and considerate friend. He was a high-churchman of the old scholarly sort; the Oxford Movement exercised no influence on him, and he took no part in it. While his theological lectures, given when he was divinity professor at Oxford, were replete with erudition, they were reckoned unsuited to those attending as a condition of ordination, who comprised the larger part at least of his audience.

In 1865 Jacobson was chairman of Gladstone's election committee at Oxford, and Palmerston, wishing to gain favour with moderate high-churchmen after a series of evangelical appointments, promoted him to the see of Chester on 23 June 1865. He was consecrated on 8 July. He diligently performed his episcopal duties, and in the general administration of his diocese he showed tact and judgement; he continued to live simply, and gave away his money liberally. In his charge at his primary visitation in October 1868 (published) he spoke without reserve on the duty of rubrical conformity. Although personally he had no liking for new or extreme ritual, he made it clearly understood that he would discountenance prosecutions, and that he viewed with displeasure laxity and defect in order. His call to conformity gave offence to the more violent low-churchmen, and in the earlier years of his episcopate he was twice mobbed by Orangemen in Liverpool when on his way to consecrate churches intended for the performance of an ornate service. He established a diocesan conference at Chester (1870), took action to augment benefices, supported the establishment of a house of mercy for prostitutes, and promoted the division of his diocese made by the foundation of the bishopric of Liverpool in 1880. In that year his 'Annotations on the Acts of the Apostles' was published in the Speaker's Commentary. Failure of health caused him to resign his bishopric in February 1884; he was then in his eighty-first year. He died at the episcopal residence, Deeside, on 13 July 1884 and was buried at Chester cemetery. He was survived by his wife and, of their ten children, by three sons and two daughters.   WILLIAM HUNT, *rev.* M. C. CURTHOYS

Sources J. W. Burgon, *Lives of twelve good men*, [new edn], 2 (1889), 238–304 · *Guardian* (13 Aug 1884) · *Saturday Review*, 58 (1884), 83–4 · *The Times* (14 July 1884) · C. W. Boase, ed., *Registrum Collegii Exoniensis*, new edn, OHS, 27 (1894) · W. R. Ward, *Victorian Oxford* (1965) · Gladstone, *Diaries*

Archives BL, corresp. with W. E. Gladstone, Add. MS 44218 · Trinity Cam., letters to Dawson Turner

Likenesses F. Holl, engraving, *c.*1850 (after G. Richmond); copy, priv. coll. · G. Richmond, chalk drawing, 1853, Christ Church Oxf. · L. Carroll [C. L. Dodgson], photograph, 1857, NPG [*see illus.*] · G. Richmond, oils, Hertford College, Oxford · Turner, lithograph (after E. U. Eddis), BM · print (after photograph by J. & C. Watkins), NPG; repro. in *ILN* (2 Sept 1865), 217

Wealth at death £65,280 15s. 4d.: probate, 2 Dec 1884, *CGPLA Eng. & Wales*

Jacombe, Samuel (*bap.* 1628, *d.* 1659). *See under* Jacombe, Thomas (1623/4–1687).

Jacombe, Thomas (1623/4–1687), clergyman and ejected minister, the son of John Jacombe of Burton Lazars, Leicestershire, attended the free school at Melton Mowbray and Newark grammar school. In 1640 he matriculated at Magdalen Hall, Oxford, aged sixteen. Two years later, perhaps as a consequence of the outbreak of civil war, he moved to St John's College, Cambridge. After graduating BA in 1644, he was elected to a fellowship at Trinity College, proceeding MA in 1647. He received presbyterian ordination that year and went to London as the chaplain of Elizabeth Cecil, dowager countess of Exeter (*d.* 1688), third daughter of John Egerton, first earl of Bridgewater, and widow of David Cecil, third earl of Exeter (*d.* 1643). On 10 February 1650 Jacombe was unanimously elected by the vestry to succeed (after an intermission) the sequestrated Michael Jermyn (or Jermin) as rector of St Martin Ludgate, London. On 2 October 1654 Jacombe married Phebe Mellar (*d.* 1674) at St Bride's, London.

Jacombe subsequently became a figure of some standing among London ministers. When Cromwell's ordinance of 22 August 1654 established the commission for the ejection of scandalous ministers Jacombe was appointed one of the ministers to assist the London commissioners. In November of that year he was nominated one of the divines charged to draw up a statement of religious fundamentals which the subcommittee set up to advise Cromwell and the grand committee on religion could put forward as a definition of tolerable religious orthodoxy under the 'Instrument of government', the protectorate's constitution. In March 1660 he became one of the presbyterian commissioners for approbation of ministers (or 'triers'). He was one of the London ministers who, in late 1659 and early 1660, fostered support for the return of the king. Immediately following the Restoration, his churchwarden secured his presentation to the cure of St Martin's under the great seal. During the next eighteen months he was involved in the negotiations surrounding the Restoration ecclesiastical settlement. He was one of the signatories to the address of thanks for the conciliatory Worcester House declaration concerning ecclesiastical affairs presented to the king on 16 November 1660. In 1661 he was created a Cambridge DD by royal mandate. In March that year his disinclination to use the Book of Common Prayer led to a petition from his parishioners to the bishop of London, Gilbert Sheldon, to whom Jacombe pleaded the liberty to tender consciences granted on the eve of the Restoration by the king's declaration of Breda. He was nominated a presbyterian commissioner at the Savoy conference, convened in April in accordance with the Worcester House declaration to discuss revision of the Book of Common Prayer. On 14 April 1661 Pepys heard him preach at St Martin's what he described as 'a lazy sermon, like a presbyterian', and, in conversation after a 'pretty good sermon, though not extraordinary' at St Bride's, Fleet Street, on 16 February 1662, Pepys heard him comment, it

Thomas Jacombe (1623/4–1687), attrib. John Riley

would seem with regret, on the increasing use of the Book of Common Prayer (Pepys, 2.74–5; 3.30). With his presbyterian convictions Jacombe was compelled to withdraw from the established church by the Act of Uniformity, which required of all ministers in the Church of England both episcopal ordination and unfeigned assent and consent to all in the Book of Common Prayer. His morning and afternoon farewell sermons, preached on 17 August, were included in the several collections of farewell sermons published in 1662 and 1663.

Jacombe, who had been a friend of Richard Baxter since at least the mid-1650s and was to accompany him at his trial before Judge George Jeffreys in 1685, was a man of 'sober and moderate Principles' (*Reliquiae Baxterianae*, 3.95) who followed the Baxterian line as a 'Reconciler' in the ecclesiastical politics of the Restoration period. On the understanding that it prohibited only unlawful endeavours to change the government of church or state, Jacombe was one of the few nonconformist ministers who took the Oxford oath imposed by the Five Mile Act of 1665. In 1667 he was, with Baxter and others, one of the addressees of a letter from Dublin nonconformists seeking guidance on terms of communion and in 1671, again with Baxter, he attempted to resolve a dispute within the nonconformist congregation at Hitchin, Hertfordshire. In 1668 and 1675 he was involved, with Thomas Manton, William Bates, and others, in negotiations over comprehension within the established church.

After his ejection Jacombe again acted as chaplain to the dowager countess of Exeter, in whose house in Little Britain, generally every Thursday, he held meetings 'very openly', especially after the fire of London (*Reliquiae*

Baxterianae, 3.19). In the early 1670s Baxter wrote that Jacombe was one that:

> hath still held on Preaching, in the House, and under the Protection of the excellent, sincere, humble, godly, faithful Lady, the Countess Dowager of *Exeter* ... to the utmost of her Power a comfort to all suffering, faithful Ministers and People, and in all this excelling those of her Rank and Generation. (ibid., 3.95)

Jacombe was a member of the London presbyterian delegation which on 28 March 1672 thanked the king for his declaration of indulgence, and he himself applied for a licence to preach at the dowager countess's house and at Haberdashers' Hall, Staining Lane, Cheapside. The licence was issued on 22 April 1672 only for the house in Little Britain. Nevertheless, he preached to the presbyterian congregation meeting at Haberdashers' Hall, in association with its pastor, Lazarus Seaman, and, after Seaman's death in 1675, with his successor, John Howe. For this he was prosecuted in November 1681 and again in April 1683. Under persecution he continued to enjoy the patronage of the dowager countess, living in her house until, having 'for Forty Years faithfully served' her 'in the Affairs of her Soul' (Bates, sig. A2v), he died there of cancer on Easter Sunday, 27 March 1687. He was buried at St Anne, Aldersgate, on 3 April. Bates preached his funeral sermon, publishing it, with a dedication to the dowager countess, as *The Way to the Highest Honour* (1687).

Jacombe was renowned for this 'constant and indefatigable preaching' in London (*Bibliotheca Jacombiana*, preface), becoming 'so universally known, esteem'd and beloved' in the city, claimed Bates in his funeral sermon, 'that his Name is a noble and lasting Elogy' (Bates, 117–18). Defending Jacombe against some slighting remarks in William Sherlock's *Discourse of the Knowledge of Jesus Christ* (1674), his friend Samuel Rolle (or Rolls) asserted that at Trinity twenty-five years before he had been 'in high Repute for his good Life, good Learning, and excellent Gravity', and that as a London minister he had always been 'in very great esteem for his Piety, Parts, Prudence, Sound, Judicious, Practical, Spiritual, Substantial Preaching' (Rolle, 15). His publications derived from this ministry and were of a homiletic nature. They included funeral sermons for Richard Vines (1656) and Thomas Case (1682); *Hosios Enkainismos, or, A Treatise of Holy Dedication* (1668), following the fire of London; *Several Sermons* on Romans 8 (1672), dedicated to the dowager countess, who had requested their publication; and a sermon in each of the morning exercise collections edited by Thomas Case (1660) and Samuel Annesley (1674). These publications are, in the words of Bates, later echoed by Calamy, 'clear, and solid, and affectionate' (Bates, 120; Calamy, *Abridgement*, 2.46), but not distinguished by individuality or literary skill.

Jacombe's first wife died in 1674. On 8 May 1677 he had married at Assington, Suffolk, Amy Forth of Aldermanbury, a widow aged thirty years, the daughter of John Gurdon of Assington. His will of 28 January 1687 mentions a son, William, from his first marriage, and daughters (unnamed). He had been granted a coat of arms on 20 April 1672 and was a person of some substance, leaving property at Brentingby, Leicestershire, and a personal estate of over £2000. His exceptional collection of over 5000 books (catalogued in *Bibliotheca Jacombiana*, 1687), which in his will he said cost him 'neare' £2000, was sold for £1300 by the auctioneer Edward Millington in a sale beginning on 31 October 1687 at the Black Swan, St Paul's Churchyard.

Thomas Jacombe's younger brother, **Samuel Jacombe** (*bap.* 1628, *d.* 1659), clergyman, was baptized at Melton Mowbray on 21 December 1628. He matriculated at Queens' College, Cambridge, in 1644, where he was taught by William Whitaker. He graduated BA in 1648 and MA in 1651, and was created BD in 1658; he was elected to a fellowship at Queens' on 1 March 1648. He was appointed a university preacher. In 1655 he became vicar of St Mary Woolnoth, London. He died, unmarried, on 12 June 1659. His funeral sermon, preached at St Mary Woolnoth on 17 June by his friend Simon Patrick, who had known him since they were both students at Queens', was published as *Divine Arithmetick* (1659) with a dedication to Thomas Jacombe. Although in both Cambridge and London Samuel Jacombe was 'famed for an excellent Preacher' with his 'sweet vein of Eloquence' (Patrick, 64, 67), he published only one sermon, *Moses his Death* (1657), a funeral sermon with some elegies; another sermon was published in the 1660 morning exercise collection edited by Thomas Case. His *Short and Plain Catechism* (1657), however, went through at least seven editions by 1694.

N. H. KEEBLE

Sources W. Bates, *The way to the highest honour: a funeral sermon ... Tho. Jacomb* (1687) · *Bibliotheca Jacombiana* (1687) · S. Patrick, *Divine arithmetick, or, The right art of numbring our dayes* (1659) · *Reliquiae Baxterianae, or, Mr Richard Baxter's narrative of the most memorable passages of his life and times*, ed. M. Sylvester, 1 vol. in 3 pts (1696) · E. Calamy, ed., *An abridgement of Mr. Baxter's history of his life and times, with an account of the ministers, &c., who were ejected after the Restauration of King Charles II*, 2nd edn, 2 vols. (1713), vol. 2, pp. 45–7 · *Calamy rev.* · *Calendar of the correspondence of Richard Baxter*, ed. N. H. Keeble and G. F. Nuttall, 2 (1991), 54, 111–12, 328–31 · Venn, *Alum. Cant.* · W. Kennett, *A register and chronicle ecclesiastical and civil* (1728), 308, 311–12, 398, 403, 407, 502, 505, 546, 852 · G. L. Turner, ed., *Original records of early nonconformity under persecution and indulgence*, 3 vols. (1911–14) · *CSP dom.*, 1660–61, pp. 537, 539; 1680–81, pp. 561, 592, 613; 1682, pp. 609–10 · 'London conventicles in 1683', *Transactions of the Congregational Historical Society*, 3 (1907–8), 364–6 · E. Calamy, *A continuation of the account of the ministers ... who were ejected and silenced after the Restoration in 1660*, 2 vols. (1727), vol. 1, p. 65 · W. Sherlock, *A discourse of the knowledge of Jesus Christ* (1674) · S. Rolle [Rolls], *Prodromus, or, The character of Mr. Sherlock's book* (1674) · Pepys, *Diary* · Foster, *Alum. Oxon.*, 1500–1714 [Thomas Jacome] · J. Nichols, *The history and antiquities of the county of Leicester*, 2/1 (1795), 270–71 · W. Wilson, *The history and antiquities of the dissenting churches and meeting houses in London, Westminster and Southwark*, 4 vols. (1808–14), vol. 3, pp. 13–19 · W. A. Shaw, *A history of the English church during the civil wars and under the Commonwealth, 1640–1660*, 2 vols. (1900) · will of Thomas Jacombe, PRO, PROB 11/387/50 · will of Samuel Jacombe, PRO, PROB 11/294/438 · IGI [St Bride's, Fleet Street, registers, 1653–1714] · BL, Harleian MS 1144, fol. 66 [coat of arms] · DWL, Baxter letters

Likenesses J. Caldwell, line engraving (after J. Riley), NPG · attrib. J. Riley, oils, DWL [*see illus.*]

Wealth at death £2000; plus property; also books sold for £1300 Oct–Nov 1687: will, 1687, PRO, PROB 11/387/50

Jacqueline [Jacqueline of Bavaria], *suo jure* **countess of Hainault**, *suo jure* **countess of Holland, and** *suo jure* **countess of Zeeland** (1401–1436), princess, was born at The Hague, on or shortly before 16 July 1401, the only daughter of Guillaume (VI), count of Hainault, of Holland, and of Zeeland (1365–1417), and of Marguerite (1374–1441), eldest daughter of Philip the Bold, duke of Burgundy. She thus embodied a Burgundian dynastic coup: the double union between the houses of Valois–Burgundy and Wittelsbach–Holland, made in April 1385. Her Wittelsbach ancestry explains frequent references to her as Jacqueline of Bavaria. In June 1406 Jacqueline was betrothed, and on 6 August 1415 married, to Jean, duke of Touraine (b. 1398). Jean succeeded his elder brother Louis as dauphin that December, only to die in April 1417.

The following August, three months after the death of her father, Jacqueline was betrothed to her first cousin John (IV), duke of Brabant (1403–1427). The marriage required a papal dispensation, which was vigorously opposed by Sigismund, king of the Romans, and only confirmed by Martin V in January 1418: the ceremony took place on 8 March. John, however, proved powerless to prevent Jacqueline's uncle, Johann of Bavaria, bishop-elect of Liège, from the forcible pursuit of his claim to Holland and Zeeland, territories long divided by factional politics. By November 1417 the bishop had resigned his see and set himself up as count in Dordrecht, precipitating civil war. John (IV) was unwilling to intervene, agreeing instead to a humiliating truce at Woudrichem in February 1419, the terms of which Jacqueline refused to accept.

When, in April 1420, her husband mortgaged Holland and Zeeland and began to interfere with the management of her household, Jacqueline fled from Brussels to her mother's court in Hainault and began to seek outside assistance. In February 1421 she formally repudiated John (IV) and travelled to Westminster under a safe conduct granted by Henry V who had previously sent envoys to Le Quesnoy to gain her trust, and evidently saw her as a thoroughly useful ally. Jacqueline was provided with a monthly income of £100 on the dower estates of Henry's stepmother, Joan, and was invited to be godmother to the infant Prince Henry. Lured by the prospect of a European adventure, *Humphrey, duke of Gloucester (1390–1447), temporarily abandoned his political ambitions in England in support of Jacqueline's cause. The couple may have married in 1422, but the event was clandestine, and although rumour attributed it to either 13 August or 25 October, after a dispensation had been obtained from the antipope Benedict XIII, neither date can be confirmed. All that can be said with confidence is that the marriage had taken place by the end of January 1423. In October 1424 they landed an army at Calais and swiftly moved to take possession of Hainault: however, they met opposition from Philip the Good, duke of Burgundy, who was now allied to John (IV) and determined to capture the Wittelsbach inheritance for himself. Johann of Bavaria's death in January 1425 gave Philip a freer hand to act against Jacqueline. He launched a counter-invasion of Hainault in April, as a result of which Humphrey abandoned his wife to

Burgundian custody. Jacqueline was taken to Ghent to await a papal pronouncement on the validity of her marriages, but in September escaped to Gouda, where she rallied a faction against the Burgundians and renewed the Dutch civil war in alliance with the bishop of Utrecht.

Jacqueline's entreaties for English aid went largely unanswered, however. Unwilling to offend Philip, the regency council preferred to negotiate a settlement rather than engage Burgundian forces. She was thus left powerless to prevent Philip's assumption of control in Hainault after the death of John (IV) in April 1427. She still maintained a strong position in north Holland, but this was irrevocably weakened in January 1428, when Martin V ruled that her marriage to John (IV) had alone been valid. Humphrey took this opportunity to abandon his costly adventure and to marry his mistress, Eleanor Cobham, in May: now deprived of the English bluff she had been playing, Jacqueline was forced to sue for peace. By the treaty of Delft in July she agreed to recognize Philip as guardian of and heir to all her territories, which were to be administered by a jointly appointed regency council.

Jacqueline, however, refused to accept a quiet life: in the summer of 1432 she contracted a secret marriage with Frank van Borselen (d. 1470), governor of Holland and Zeeland since 1430. This contravened the terms of the treaty, and Borselen was swiftly imprisoned: the situation was resolved only in April 1433, when Jacqueline agreed to an immediate abdication of all her territorial rights and had her marriage confirmed. Thereafter she retreated to her well-appointed castle of Teijlingen, where she was free to indulge a passion for hunting. According to Dutch tradition, she also took up pottery, fashioning a distinctive style of long-necked jar.

Jacqueline died childless on 8 October 1436, after a long illness, presumed consumptive. She had requested burial in her lordship of Sint-Maartensdijk in Zeeland, but her mother insisted on a funeral held later the same month in the court chapel in The Hague, an arrangement which, for once, Jacqueline was unable to defy. Though biographers were later to romanticize her career, few have yet addressed her remarkable strength of character, or her utter refusal to act as a dynastic pawn.

MARTYN ATKINS

Sources F. de Potter, *Geschiedenis van Jacoba van Beieren, 1401–36* (1881) · T. van Riemsdijk, *Het opdracht van het ruwaardschap van Holland en Zeeland aan Philips van Bourgondië* (Amsterdam, 1906) · G. Gysels, 'Le départ de Jacqueline de Bavière de la cour de Brabant, 11 avril 1420', *Miscellanea historica in honorem Leonis van der Essen*, 1 (Brussels, 1947), 413–27 · F. von Löher, *Jakobäa von Baiern und ihre Zeit* (1869) · R. Vaughan, *Philip the Good: the apogee of Burgundy* (1970) · A. G. Jongkees, 'Strijd om de erfenis van Wittelsbach, 1417–33', *Algemene geschiedenis de Nederlanden*, ed. J. A. van Houtte, 3 (1951), 226–52 · G. L. Harriss, *Cardinal Beaufort: a study of Lancastrian ascendancy and decline* (1988) · E. de Dynter, *Chroniques des ducs de Brabant*, ed. P. F. X. de Ram, 3 vols. (1857), 3.342–487 · K. H. Vickers, *Humphrey duke of Gloucester: a biography* (1907) · C. Aurelius, *Die Cronycke van Hollandt, Zeelandt ende Vrieslandt* (1517), fols. 256–276v · *La chronique d'Enguerran de Monstrelet*, ed. L. Douët-d'Arcq, 6 vols. (Paris, 1857–62), vols. 3–5 · 'Rekeninge der testamentoren van wijlen der edelre vorstinnen, vrouwe Jacobs van Beyeren, van Hollant, grauynne van Oistreuant, zaliger gedenckenisse', *Codex*

Diplomaticus Neerlandicae, 2nd ser., 1 (1859), 166–264 · H. P. H. Jansen, *Hoekse en Kabeljauwse twisten* (1966) · E. I. Strubbe and L. Voet, *De chronologie van de middeleeuwen en de moderne tijden in de Nederlanden* (1960)

Likenesses portrait, *c.*1500, Statens Museum for Kunst, Copenhagen, Denmark · portrait, 16th cent., Stadhuis, Sint-Maartensdijk, Zeeland, Denmark · J. C. van Oostzanen, woodcut, before 1519 · J. S. van Leiden, woodcut, repro. in Aurelius, *Chronycke*, fol. 256

Wealth at death approx. £4600: 'Rekeninge der testamentoren van wijlen der edelre vorstinnen', 166–264; Potter, *Geschiedenis*; Löher, *Jakobäa*

Jacques, Josephine Edwina [Hattie] (1922–1980), actress, was born on 7 February 1922 at 125 High Street, Sandgate, Kent, the daughter of Robin Jacques (*d.* 1922), a lieutenant in the army education corps and a former test pilot in the Royal Flying Corps, and his wife, Mary Adelaide Thorn. Her father was killed in a flying accident the year she was born and Jacques and her brother, the book illustrator Robin Jacques (1920–1995), were largely brought up by their grandparents. She attended Godolphin and Latymer Upper School in London, and trained briefly as a hairdresser. She spent two years during the Second World War as a Red Cross nurse, and then as a welder, before making her stage début in 1944 at the Players Theatre in London, singing Victorian songs. The Players was to be her drama school: she acted in plays and revues there, she directed, wrote song lyrics, and developed the persona she was to use in pantomime for years, the large, bossy, but vulnerable fairy queen, which she later said was her favourite part. She toured with the Young Vic company in *The King Stag* as Smeraldina (1947–8), and by 1947 was working regularly in radio. She gained a national audience as the greedy child Sophie Tuckshop, who would regale listeners with terrifying accounts of epic binges, in Tommy Handly's popular series *ITMA* (1948–9). From 1950 to 1954 she appeared with Tony Hancock in Eric Sykes's *Educating Archie*, and subsequently worked on the innovative *Hancock's Half Hour*. Her film career was launched with a series of minor roles in Dickens adaptations—*Nicholas Nickleby* (1948), *Oliver Twist* (1949), *Scrooge* (1951), and *Pickwick Papers* (1953). They reflected her talent for larger-than-life comedy which never lost its grip on humanity, while *Old Mother Riley Meets the Vampire* (1952) showed her in a broader comic mode. On 10 November 1949 she married the actor John *Le Mesurier (1912–1983); they had two children, and were divorced in 1965.

Jacques excelled as a member of a comic team, generous in giving opportunities to fellow actors. Her skills were most evident in two areas. First, there was the BBC television series *Sykes*, which began in 1960 and has a claim to be the first native British sitcom. It starred Eric Sykes as a suburban shopowner living with his sister Hattie, and featured Richard Wattis as their superior neighbour and Deryck Guyler as Corky, the local policeman. Jacques provided a counterpoint to the childlike anarchy of Sykes with her study of a middle-class, slightly pretentious lady struggling to keep her dignity as the men made fools of themselves. Although the plots were undistinguished the

Josephine Edwina [Hattie] **Jacques** (1922–1980), by unknown photographer, 1963

visible teamwork within the quartet ensured a long life for the series, which ended with Jacques's death.

Then there were the *Carry on* films. Made by Peter Rogers and Gerald Thomas between 1958 and 1979, they never pretended to be more than low-budget family entertainment with an edge of vulgarity; they had little plot, relying on slapstick parodies of British institutions such as the National Health Service and the army. Yet they attracted some of the best comic actors of their generation, drawn by the prospect of regular pay for a limited commitment (typically, they were made in about six weeks). Jacques appeared in fourteen of the twenty-eight, and they show a comic talent of extraordinary versatility. In *Sykes* her performance had to be a foil for the main character; in the *Carry Ons* she blossomed. The comedy was superficially grounded in physical types like those on the seaside postcards they sought to emulate—skinny henpecked men, busty blondes, enormous mothers-in-law. Jacques, a large woman, might have found her range limited, but discovered so many variations and shades in her roles that one is hardly aware of a typology at work. In *Sergeant* (1958) she was a no-nonsense army doctor. In *Cabby* (1963) she was the neglected wife of a taxi driver who sets up her own all-woman firm—a truly original piece of comedy exploiting several facets of her comic style. There is her highly individual sexual attractiveness, in a bubblebath sequence where she preens before the mirror in a parody of the cheesecake shots of the day: the humour lies in her highly recognizable awareness of the gap between magazine glamour and reality; however hard she works to become a sensual beauty, her workaholic husband (Sid

James) will never notice. There is a comedy of transformation as Jacques masterminds a battle of wits between
rival cab firms, sending men off on false errands in a series
of assumed voices.

Jacques is enduringly associated with the role of hospital matron, which she played in five *Carry Ons*, often
with Kenneth Williams as chief consultant. The comic
duel between them was for many the high spot of these
films. Both were well aware that they had been cast for
seaside-postcard contrast: both ignored this and stressed
what they shared—authority, embodied in Jacques's size
and bell-like voice and Williams's aristocratic face—an
authority always undercut by the indignity of bodily
desire. In *Carry on Matron* (1972) Williams pursued Jacques,
to be brushed aside like a mosquito. In *Carry on Doctor*
(1968) Jacques was the pursuer, vamping a helpless Williams in a black negligée and a voice which purred like
Eartha Kitt but, at a hint of resistance, took on the steeli-
ness of Margaret Thatcher. The role embodied her particular talent: although often cast in broad comedy, she never
played it broadly, but with an elegance of voice and body
that belied all the clichés about women and weight.

Jacques died suddenly from heart failure on 6 October
1980 at home at 67 Eardley Crescent, Kensington, aged
fifty-eight. At her memorial service at St Paul's, Covent
Garden, Kenneth Williams quoted the Victorian novelist
Mrs Craik on 'the comfort of feeling safe with a person'
(*Kenneth Williams Diaries*, 621) which for him and many
others summed up her qualities as both friend and ensemble actress.   FRANCES GRAY

Sources P. Cornell, M. Day, and K. Topping, *The Guinness book of
classic British TV* (1993) · M. Banks and A. Swift, *The joke's on us: women
in comedy from music hall to the present day* (1987) · S. Wagg, *Because I
tell a joke or two: comedy, politics and social difference* (1998) · *The Kenneth
Williams diaries*, ed. R. Davies (1993) · *The Guardian* (7 Oct 1980) · A. G.
Seaton, 'Hattie Jacques, comedienne', *Annual Obituary* (1980), 594–
6 · b. cert. · m. cert. · d. cert.
Archives FILM BFI NFTVA, 'The unforgettable Hattie Jacques',
ITV, 21 Jan 2000 · BFI NFTVA, performance footage |SOUND BL
NSA, documentary recordings · BL NSA, oral history interview · BL
NSA, performance recordings
Likenesses photograph, 1963, BFI [*see illus.*]
Wealth at death £151,503: probate, 4 March 1981, *CGPLA Eng. &
Wales*

Jacson, Frances Margaretta (1754–1842), novelist, was
born on 13 October 1754 at Bebington rectory, Cheshire,
one of the five surviving children of the Revd Simon
Jacson (1728–1808) and his wife, Anne Fitzherbert (*c.*1729–
1795), elder daughter of Richard Fitzherbert of Somersal
Herbert, Derbyshire. Her elder brothers, Roger and Shallcross, both took holy orders, and in 1771 her father relinquished his living in favour of Roger, the heir, who quickly
became a much respected incumbent. Of the three daughters, Anne (*d.* 1805) married into the Atherton family in
Lancashire, but Frances and her younger sister Maria
Elizabetha *Jacson (1755–1829) remained single, moving
from Bebington with their parents to Stockport and then
to Tarporley, where Simon Jacson took up the rectorship.
There the sisters cared for their father, particularly after

their mother's death in 1795. He became increasingly
infirm, and died in 1808.

It was during their time at Tarporley that the Jacsons
became increasingly concerned about Shallcross, who,
over-fond of drink and horse-racing, had run into debt and
was hardly an ornament to the church or to a respected
clerical family. To help him out of his difficulties the sisters turned to writing, Maria to manuals on botany and
gardening, and Frances to fiction. Her popular first novel,
Plain Sense (1795), was followed in 1797 by *Disobedience*. In
1808 the sisters had to find a new home and after much
uncertainty they gratefully accepted the offer of Somersal
Hall, the beautiful old partly Tudor house lent them for
life by Lord St Helens, a Fitzherbert relation. Shallcross's
troubles soon resurfaced, and at Somersal Frances wrote,
in the same vein as her first two books, *Things by their Right
Names* (1812) and the more accomplished *Rhoda* (1816).
Appalled by her brother's physical and mental state, and
with the help of Roger and Maria Jacson, Frances again
arranged to clear his debts, now amounting to £1760. His
unlooked for death in 1821 was a melancholy release.

A period of calm followed with *Isabella*, Frances's last
book, published in 1823, but then in 1829 Maria fell
gravely ill, and died while the sisters were staying with
friends at Chelford. Returning desolate to Somersal, the
unhappy Frances eventually settled, resuming her social
life among the local gentry and family connections: the
Vernons at Sudbury, the Fitzherberts at Tissington, and
her friends at Ashbourne. Among her many nieces and
nephews, Henry Gally Knight was a special favourite and
kept her in touch with the politics of the time. A firm
whig, she had scant sympathy for the waverings of William IV over the 1832 Reform Bill, recording that 'the
poltroony of the King' and the duplicity of the tories
'shocked every moral feeling' (diary, 18 May 1832).

However immediate a financial purpose her novels
served, Frances Jacson never abandoned her moral feeling. She was a devout Christian and all her novels have a
strong didactic element, as is suggested by the titles of the
first three. All are set in high circles of society, moving
between London (the site of temptation, libertinism, and
schemers) and country estates and parsonages (havens
largely though not entirely beneficial). All feature a heroine, tracing her history through varying circumstances,
some of doubtful probability, but not more so than others
in the genre. Plotting was not Frances Jacson's strength
but what becomes increasingly evident is the author's creative insight into character and motive, exposed through
her accounts of developing relationships, particularly of
courtship and marriage. The rather flat Ellen in *Plain Sense*
excepted, Jacson's lively heroines are convincingly shown
evaluating their surroundings and coming to see the flaws
in their perceptions, or those of others. Moreover, her
minor characters are often presented with highly effective irony, and many of the situations depicted with considerable humour. In *Rhoda*, for example, Jacson outlines
the heroine's growing worldliness, and sympathetically
depicts the workings of her mind as she struggles with
dilemmas; the incompatibilities in Rhoda's marriage with

Sir James Osbourne are both insurmountable and sad. Offset is the clever contrast of the sourness of the marriage of Mr and Mrs Strickland, the latter who 'always admitted truth in the abstract and never practised it in detail' (*Rhoda*, bk 2, 160). Equally skilfully drawn is Mrs Nesbit in *Isabella*, whose self-righteous loquacity makes her a worthy sister to Jane Austen's Mrs Norris.

Frances Jacson died on 17 June 1842 at her home in Somersal and was buried in the Fitzherbert vault there on 24 June. Her only other known writing is a religious pamphlet, *Every Day Christianity* (1816).

Frances Jacson's novels enjoyed considerable contemporary popularity; *Rhoda* was singled out by Maria Edgeworth as superior to Jane Austen's *Emma*, and it was also admired by Sydney Smith, who recommended it to Lady Holland. Although her works have obvious limitations, Jacson's gifts are well worth recognition in any history of the eighteenth- and nineteenth-century English novel. The novels' anonymity was guarded, and her authorship faded into obscurity, so that secure assignment of the novels to her took place only in the late 1990s. Despite the twentieth-century interest in women writers of the past, Jacson has been neglected, probably in part because of an earlier confusion of her works with those of Alethea Lewis (pseudonym Eugenia de Acton). Her eclipse may also be due to the fact that her diaries, written from 1829 until her death, were originally thought to have been written by her brother.   JOAN PERCY

Sources F. Jacson, diaries, 1829–37, Lancs. RO, DX 267–278 · 'Family memorials', MS notebooks · private information (2004) · J. Percy, 'An unrecognised novelist: Frances Jacson (1754–1842)', *British Library Journal*, 23 (1997), 81–97 · Burke, *Gen. GB* (1894) · baptism records, Bebington, Ches. & Chester ALSS · records, Somersal Herbert, Derbys. RO [burial]
Archives Lancs. RO, diaries, DX 267–278
Likenesses H. Edridge, drawing, 1814, priv. coll.; repro. in Percy, 'An unrecognised novelist'

Jacson, Maria Elizabetha (1755–1829), writer on botany, was born at Bebington, Cheshire, the daughter of the Revd Simon Jacson and Anne Fitzherbert. Her family had held land and clerical livings in Cheshire and Derbyshire since the early seventeenth century; Maria grew up in the rectory at Bebington, then lived with her widowed father, privately in Stockport in 1777–87, and later in the rectory at Tarporley, Cheshire. Neither Maria nor her sister Frances *Jacson, a novelist, married. After the death of their father in 1808 the sisters lived in Somersal Hall, an Elizabethan manor house, in Somersal Herbert, Derbyshire, which belonged to a maternal relative.

Maria Jacson had family connections to Enlightenment science culture in the midlands through Erasmus Darwin and her cousin Sir Brooke Boothby of Ashbourne, Derbyshire. Her interest in plants showed itself early in botanical drawing, gardening, and experiments in plant physiology. In 1788 she gave a drawing of a Venus's fly-trap to Darwin, who described her as 'a lady who adds much botanical knowledge to many other elegant acquirements' (Shteir, 114–15). When she was forty-two, induced by family financial circumstances, Maria Jacson began writing for money, and published her first book, *Botanical*

Dialogues, between Hortensia and her Four Children (1797). An introduction to Linnaean botany 'for the use of schools', it takes the form of conversations within a family. The book features a mother who believes in the mental and moral utility of botanical knowledge. Hortensia teaches her children about the Linnaean system of classifying and naming plants, and instructs them about dissecting flowers and examining them under the microscope. In a commendatory note included in the book, Darwin and Boothby praised the author for 'so accurately explaining a difficult science in an easy and familiar manner'. While reviews of the book noted the clarity and elegance of Jacson's exposition, *Botanical Dialogues* was too learned for the juvenile market, and did not go past the first edition.

Probably more a botanist than an educator, Jacson recast her material into a book for general adult readers, under the title *Botanical Lectures* (1804). Shorn of the conversational form and family setting of the earlier title, this book promoted the importance of learning botany from the proper sources and using Latin botanical nomenclature. In the 'Advertisement' Jacson styled her book 'a complete elementary system, which may enable the student of whatever age to surmount those difficulties, which hitherto have too frequently impeded the perfect acquirement of this interesting science'. She situated her own work as introductory to the translation of Linnaeus's *System of Vegetables* (1783) by Erasmus Darwin and the Botanical Society of Lichfield. Jacson's third book, *Sketches of the Physiology of Vegetable Life* (1811), mirrored a shift in focus within early nineteenth-century botany from classification and nomenclature to plant structure and function, and was intended for younger students of physiology. The book reflects wide reading in contemporary botanical literature, as Jacson explores topics such as plant motion, propagation, and analogies between plant and animal functions. She exhorts readers to see for themselves, and describes experiments she conducted on crocus bulbs; her own drawings illustrate the development of bulbs and seeds.

Jacson's books clearly sought to enlarge female education. Nevertheless, the maternal teacher in *Botanical Dialogues* declares that women should:

> avoid obtruding their knowledge upon the public. The world have agreed to condemn women to the exercise of their fingers, in preference to that of their heads; and a woman rarely does herself credit by coming forward as a literary character. (238)

Science books by women were an emergent feature of publishing at the turn of the nineteenth century, and reviewers commented favourably on female author–educators. At the same time, learned women were suspect, and social conventions about female modesty often led women to publish anonymously and to make careful, strategic claims about their expertise. Jacson's books are identified only as 'by a Lady' or 'by the Authoress', or with the initials M. E. J.

In addition to her popular botanical writing, Jacson was an early female horticultural writer, preceding the better-known Jane Loudon by several decades. Her *Florist's manual: hints for the construction of a gay flower-garden with observations on the best method of preventing the depredations of insects* (1816) was directed to women flower growers. Jacson seeks to 'render my sister Florists partakers of my pleasures' to 'enable them more methodically to arrange their flowers, and so to blend their colours, that through most part of the spring and summer months they may procure a succession of enamelled borders' (*Florist's Manual*, 1816, 3–4). The book discusses garden design, including the shape of flowerbeds and placement of a rockery, recommends 'mingled' or mixed beds, and gives a catalogue of suitable herbaceous flowers, bulbs, and grasses. She encourages readers to have a conservatory for spring bulbs. Jacson suggests in her concluding remarks that women can find both horticultural and personal benefit in botany, and hopes to 'induce even a few of my sister Florists to exercise their intellect, or relieve their ennui' through 'the study of vegetable existence'. *Florist's Manual* was Jacson's most successful work; a second, enlarged edition was published with coloured plates in 1822, and a subsequent edition in 1827. John Claudius Loudon cited from it at several points in his *Encyclopedia of Gardening*.

Little is known about Maria Jacson's social circle in later years. Maria Edgeworth recalls meeting the 'gay garden lady' in Lichfield in 1818 (Colvin, 141). Jacson died of a fever at Astle Hall, near Chelford, Cheshire, on 10 October 1829, and was buried at Chelford. ANN B. SHTEIR

Sources A. B. Shteir, *Cultivating women, cultivating science: Flora's daughters and botany in England, 1760–1860* (1996), 108–20 · J. Percy, 'Maria Elizabetha Jacson and her *Florist's manual*', *Garden History*, 20/1 (1992), 45–56 · M. Jacson, *Botanical dialogues* (1797) · *Maria Edgeworth: letters from England, 1813–1844*, ed. C. Colvin (1971), 141

Jaeger, August Johannes (1860–1909), music critic, was born on 18 March 1860 in Düsseldorf, Germany, the second son and the third of the six surviving children of Gottfried Jaeger (1822–1880), a cattle dealer, and his wife, Caroline Obenstintenberg (1826–1910). He was educated at the Düsseldorf Gymnasium and also received tuition in violin and piano, in which instruments he became proficient, although he was forbidden by his father from pursuing a professional musical career. Despite Düsseldorf's longstanding musical traditions, Jaeger left the city in 1878 at the age of eighteen, turning his back, like many others, on Bismarckian authoritarianism in favour of the liberalism of the 'land without music' (Northrop Moore, 48). He settled with his family in London, working as a clerk while continuing to pursue music through choral singing and frequent concertgoing. In particular he followed the Richter concerts, with their revelatory programmes of the most modern orchestral music of the day—particularly Wagner, to whom the young enthusiast became devoted. His first opportunities to experience the music dramas themselves came in 1882, when three complete cycles of *The Ring* were given in London, together with the English premières of *The Mastersingers* and *Tristan*.

In 1890 Jaeger was appointed publishing office manager of Novellos, the leading English music publisher of the time. He gradually became an unofficial musical adviser with a highly individual position, enabling him to pursue a personal mission to discover and encourage new English composers. Ideally placed in a position of some power, he built up a wide network of contacts in support of his efforts, joining the ranks of the critics when he became a staff writer for the *Musical Times*. This enabled him to add campaigning journalism to his direct lobbying of conductors, the Novello's directors, and others, in a determined search for performance and publication opportunities for new composers. Most importantly, he offered direct encouragement and technical advice through detailed and sometimes extended correspondence, where a rigorous critical judgement was fully and frankly exercised, albeit in a warm and personal way; several of his protégés became family friends. But the response from Novellos could be negative and frustrating, as Jaeger tended to be seen as something of an advanced left-winger in an essentially conservative musical establishment slow to embrace the new.

During the 1890s Jaeger did much to establish the reputation of the American Horatio Parker, but his most important efforts during this period were on behalf of Edward Elgar, Walford Davies, and Samuel Coleridge-Taylor, in support of whose highly successful *Hiawatha's Wedding Feast* he gave much specific criticism and advice. Shortly after its first performance, on 22 December 1898 Jaeger married Isabella Donkersley (1864–1938), a former violin student at the Royal College of Music. She combined occasional work as a soloist with teaching, providing extra income to support their two children when Jaeger had to retire early through ill health.

During his career Jaeger actively helped a variety of other young composers, including Cyril Scott, Havergal Brian, Josef Holbrooke, John McEwen, John Foulds, and William Henry Bell; and even such a senior figure as Hubert Parry benefited from his advice. But it is for his work for Elgar, with whom he first made contact in 1897 and with whom he enjoyed an instant rapport, that he is best known. He worked tirelessly to encourage the frequently moody composer, to smooth his path at Novellos, to ensure the accurate production of his scores—often against tight deadlines—and to engineer performances of his works at home and abroad, particularly in Germany. He directly exercised critical judgement over the *Enigma Variations* and *The Dream of Gerontius*, insisting on important changes, and he largely suggested the form and instrumentation of the *Introduction and Allegro for Strings*. In order, too, to prepare the public for the new complexities of Elgar's oratorios, Jaeger wrote lengthy analyses of these works at great labour, although he failed to please the composer by an oversimplistic labelling of leitmotifs. Such efforts further weakened a constitution already at risk from chronic overwork, and lowered resistances exacerbated a family tendency to tuberculosis. Despite treatments at Swiss sanatoria, partly financed by Parry, Jaeger died at his home, 37 Curzon Road, Muswell Hill, on 18 May 1909, aged forty-nine. He was cremated at Golders Green on 22 May.

By temperament Jaeger was essentially an artist, ill-adjusted to the drudgery of office routine, but the exigencies of life put him in a position where his own practical musicianship became subsumed into wider fields; one of the obituaries wrote of 'his genius for discovering genius' (Allen, 283), and Jaeger may be said to have done as much if not more than anyone not a composer or conductor to contribute to the dynamic of the English musical renaissance, albeit from a strongly German perspective. His superbly well-judged suggestions for improvement in Elgar's music remain without parallel in relations between composer and publisher, and his Düsseldorf contacts paved the way for performances of Elgar's music in Germany which established the composer's reputation in his own country as well as in Europe. Elgar recorded deep gratitude for his friend's intimate understanding and encouragement in the celebrated 'Nimrod' movement of the *Enigma Variations*, music which has become a familiar part of English national life and cultural heritage, even if the unmistakably German name of its modest, frail, but determined subject has remained known to comparatively few. And Elgar knew that the movement does not portray the whole man, for he wrote that, in order fully to portray Jaeger's character and temperament, something 'ardent and mercurial' would have been needed.

KEVIN ALLEN

Sources K. Allen, *August Jaeger: portrait of Nimrod* (2000) • J. Northrop Moore, *Elgar and his publishers: letters of a creative life* (1987) • C. Grogan, '"My dear analyst": some observations on Elgar's correspondence with A. J. Jaeger regarding the "Apostles" project', *Music and Letters*, 72 (1991), 48–60 • C. Kent, 'Jaeger, August Johannes', *New Grove*, 2nd edn • E. Elgar, *My friends pictured within* (1949) • m. cert. • d. cert. • *CGPLA Eng. & Wales* (1909) • b. cert. [Isabella Hunter, *née* Donkersley] • d. cert. [Isabella Hunter, wife]
Archives Elgar Birthplace Museum, Broadheath, near Worcester, corresp. • Parry Archive, Shulbrede Priory, Lynchmere, Haslemere, Surrey, corresp. • Worcs. RO, Elgar MSS, corresp. | Royal College of Music, London, Walford Davies papers, corresp. • Yale U., Sanford papers
Likenesses photographs, c.1890–c.1905, repro. in Allen, *August Jaeger* • group portrait, photograph, 1901, repro. in C. Powell, *Edward Elgar: memories of a variation* (1937) • E. T. Holding, photograph, c.1902, repro. in Moore, *Elgar and his publishers* • E. T. Holding, photograph, c.1902, repro. in Elgar, *My friends pictured within*
Wealth at death £242 7s. 2d.: probate, 5 June 1909, *CGPLA Eng. & Wales*

Jaeger, Gustav (1832–1917), physician, zoologist, and dress reformer, was born on 23 June 1832 at Bürg am Kocher, now part of the town of Neuenstadt, Germany, the younger son of Karl Friedrich Jaeger (1794–1842), priest and historian of Schwabia, and his wife, Ulrike (1795–1881), daughter of Pastor Gottlob Friedrich Stang of Kornwestheim. The son and grandson of protestant ministers, Jaeger originally intended to enter the church, but abandoned his studies at the theological seminary in Urach to study medicine and natural sciences at Tübingen. He gained his medical degree in 1856, and in 1858 decided to further his studies in zoology and comparative anatomy at the University of Vienna. Jaeger was much impressed by Darwin's theories of evolution, and he promoted Darwinian ideas in Germany through various influential articles

Gustav Jaeger (1832–1917), by Hermann Brandseph

and scientific papers. His successful work *Deutschlands Tierwelt nach ihren Standorten eingeteilt* (1874) incorporated much of Darwin's thinking on the relevance of ecological factors. While in Vienna he co-founded a zoo, which he directed until 1866. In 1867 he was appointed professor of zoology and anthropology at the Hohenheim Academy, and from 1870 lectured in these subjects at the Royal Polytechnic School, Stuttgart. His first marriage, in 1860, was to Selma Krais (1839–1907), daughter of Pastor Julius Krais of Oferdingen; they had three sons and three daughters. Selma died in 1907, and in the same year Jaeger married Helene Müller.

His anthropological lectures at Stuttgart led Jaeger towards a new field of study. He chose the subject health culture, and as his health was currently poor owing to a sedentary lifestyle following a leg injury, he investigated ways to heal himself. The result of his experiments was his sanitary woollen system, promoted in his book *Die Normalkleidung als Gesundheitsschutz (Mein System)*, published in 1880. Through his zoological studies Jaeger noted that animals were generally healthier than human beings, in spite of permanent exposure to wet and cold, and he concluded that animal wool or hair was the best material for human clothing. His 'system' promoted all-wool clothing, outerwear as well as underwear, which offered three benefits: wool allowed the skin's exhalations to freely pass through, it was a good insulator so the body maintained an even temperature, and, especially when knitted, it fitted the body closely and prevented harmful draughts. The concept of all-wool clothing even extended to the use of woollen bedding. In Jaeger's view, dead vegetable fibres (cotton and linen, and to a lesser degree silk) were unnatural clothing material, unhealthy and unhygienic. Following his system, Jaeger claimed to have restored his own health.

The publication of *Mein System* in 1880, and lectures given in the later 1870s, gained Jaeger many disciples in Germany, Russia, and Britain, where hygienic dress, and dress reform, were already topics of interest and discussion. In 1883 Jaeger licensed Lewis Tomalin, one of his leading supporters in Britain, to open a clothing business in Moor Lane, London, under the name Dr Jaeger's Sanitary Woollen System Co. Ltd, selling pure woollen clothing of all kinds, including garments designed by Jaeger in his specially developed undyed wool stockinet, bearing his trademark. The new company exhibited at the International Health Exhibition held in London in the summer of 1884, gaining much useful publicity. Jaeger published an enlarged *Mein System* in 1885, which was translated into English by Tomalin and published in London in 1887.

Jaeger's theories especially appealed to London's progressive intellectuals, among them Oscar Wilde. William Morris wrote in 1884 to Andreas Scheu, an Austrian political refugee, one of Jaeger's British agents, 'I don't know whether you will be pleased, shocked or amused to hear that Oscar Wilde has gone in for Jägar with enthusiasm' (F. MacCarthy, *William Morris*, 1994, 498). Jaeger's most ardent convert was however George Bernard Shaw, author and playwright, who was making his name in the mid-1880s as a journalist and lecturer on socialist issues, and was a prominent member of the Fabian Society alongside William Morris and Sidney and Beatrice Webb. Shaw's diary for 1885 notes '10 August: Off to dinner at 16, then to J's where I ordered a knitted woollen suit' (*Bernard Shaw: the Diaries*, 1.103). This suit was Jaeger's most eccentric creation, a one-piece combination tunic and trousers, which buttoned up to the neck and on one shoulder, rejecting collar and tie. Shaw achieved a satisfactory notoriety lecturing in this suit; he was likened variously to 'a brown gnome' (ibid., 1.103) and a 'Jaeger Christ' (Holroyd, 1.151). Seen walking down Regent Street in this suit his tall leggy figure and red hair suggested to one observer that he looked 'exactly like a forked radish' (Adburgham, 185).

Although Shaw's enthusiasm as a 'woollener' was exceptional, the business prospered, a second shop opened in Regent Street in the 1890s, and by 1914 branches had opened in Canada, Australia, and New Zealand. During the First World War the company advertised as 'A British company under British control' and in 1920 Dr Jaeger's Sanitary Woollen System Co. Ltd became the Jaeger Co. Ltd. By the late 1920s new management felt that a broader range of merchandise was needed, and a fashion range was introduced alongside the traditional knitted garments. The new Jaeger business, with branches worldwide and which celebrated its centenary in 1983, continues to specialize in elegant, understated classic clothes using mainly woollen fabrics.

Apart from licensing Tomalin to use his name and system, and presumably sharing in its profits, Jaeger probably played little part in the London business and its offshoots. In 1884 he resigned his university posts in Stuttgart and took up practice there as a physician. He revised and republished some of his earlier natural history publications, and a selection from these writings was published in Britain in 1897, translated by H. G. Schlichter, entitled *Problems of Nature: Researches and Discoveries*. Jaeger's death in Stuttgart on 13 May 1917 at the age of eighty-five went unrecognized in the British press, but his name remained synonymous with woollen underwear in Britain for at least half a century, and it continues to identify a chain of fashion shops whose clothes are considered the epitome of restrained 'English' good taste.　　ANTHEA JARVIS

Sources *Neue deutsche Biographie* (1953–) · G. Jaeger, *Dr Jaeger's essays on health-culture*, ed. and trans. L. R. S. Tomalin (1887) · S. M. Newton, *Health, art and reason* (1974) · *Bernard Shaw: the diaries, 1885–1897*, ed. S. Weintraub, 2 vols. (1986), vol. 1 · M. Holroyd, *Bernard Shaw: the search for love*, vol. 1 (1988) · 'Sanitary clothing', *The Times* (4 Oct 1884) · L. Goldsmith, 'Woollen strategies: hygiene, reform and the clothed body—some themes relating to a short history of Jaeger, 1880–1914', MA diss., Royal College of Art, 1997 · P. Johns, 'Gesund, praktisch, schön: dress reform and the reform context in Wilhelmine Germany, 1890–1919', MA diss., Winchester School of Art, U. Southampton, 1997 · A. Adburgham, 'The woollen movement', *Shops and shopping, 1800–1914: where, and in what manner the well-dressed Englishwoman bought her clothes* (1964), 184–7 · P. Symms, 'George Bernard Shaw's underwear', *Costume*, 24 (1990), 94–6
Archives Jaeger & Co., London, company records, trade catalogues, etc. | Gallery of Costume, Manchester, trade catalogues
Likenesses H. Brandseph, photograph, NPG [*see illus.*] · lithograph (after photograph), repro. in *Health Culture* (1902), frontispiece · photograph, Jaeger & Co., archive; repro. in Newton, *Health, art and reason*

Jaeger, Muriel (1892–1969), novelist, was born at 14 Victoria Street, Barnsley, Yorkshire, on 23 May 1892, the daughter of John Edward Jagger (the family appear subsequently to have altered the spelling of their name), an auctioneer and accountant, and his wife, Frances Emma, *née* Hollingsworth. She was educated at Sheffield high school and won a clothworkers' scholarship to Somerville College, Oxford, in 1912 where, following a fashion of the time, she was known as Jim. At Somerville she read English, wrote occasionally for student literary magazines, and became a member of a small Somerville literary circle that called itself, with ironic intent, the Mutual Admiration Society. Her closest friend was her Somerville contemporary Dorothy L. Sayers, an overwhelming personality for whom Jaeger was a match. When they were apart, Sayers wrote affectionately to her friend that she missed 'our loud-voiced arguments' (Coomes, 49). They shared an interest in religion, and Sayers trusted her literary judgement, often trying out ideas on her. Jaeger took an extra year at Oxford, graduating with second-class honours in 1916. She moved to London and in 1917 was working for the Ministry of Food where, as Sayers reported, she developed an expert knowledge of starvation conditions in Germany.

In 1920 Jaeger was hired as a sub-editor of the new feminist journal *Time and Tide*, a good chance for a young woman with her literary ambitions, socialist leanings, and interest in women's education, but the spiky, difficult personality and outspoken views that Sayers so valued proved a liability in a job. Although Jaeger liked the work, she quarrelled with her employers, harsh words were exchanged, and she was discharged. She then went to work for *Vogue*, quickly losing that job under similar circumstances. Sayers remarked that Jaeger had no ability to make herself comfortable, and at least in her early years in London she appears to have been intermittently unhappy and ill. Her difficult personality seems to have been at the root of her troubles; even the loyal Sayers became exasperated, writing that Jaeger made herself unhappy, 'never liking what she's doing at the moment because she thinks she ought to be doing something grander' (*Letters*, 175). By the summer of 1921 she was working hard, writing something which she kept secret, earning no money, and puzzling her friends. Sayers thought she must be receiving a subsidy from her parents and observed: 'I suspect her of a novel' (ibid., 178). Jaeger had time to encourage her friend to write a novel of her own, earning herself the dedication to Sayers's first Lord Peter Wimsey novel, *Whose Body?*: 'To Jim: This book is your fault. If it had not been for your brutal insistence, Lord Peter would never have staggered through to the end of this enquiry' (quoted in Leonardi, 54).

Jaeger's own novel, *The Question Mark*, was published in 1926 by the Hogarth Press. This utopian novel subverted the utopias of William Morris, H. G. Wells, and the American novelist Edward Bellamy by populating them with real people, selfish, idle, and shallow. Although it received good reviews, *The Question Mark* does not have appeared to have sold well, and a second novel published by the Woolfs did no better. In 1929 Jaeger contributed a study of psychology, *Sisyphus*, to the successful Today and Tomorrow series. As her career as a novelist seemed unpromising, she turned to writing non-fiction. In old age she observed that it was a great deal easier for her than fiction, requiring less development of one's 'mental muscles' (Jaeger, 44).

Although Jaeger wrote several plays, two discouraging experiences led her to give that up as well. She chronicles the circumstances which led to her disenchantment with the theatre, whereas the causes of her abandonment of the novel must be inferred. She had what she called 'a curious and painful experience' working with a cast that fought her play, torturing it into something it was not, or so its creator believed (Jaeger, 78). Her second experience was with a play called *Sweet Liberty* (1944) that she co-wrote with her brother. He was killed flying with the RAF shortly after the play was completed, which explains her enormous emotional investment in the project. A satire on the peace negotiations, based on what the Jaegers could

remember about 1918, the play was accepted by a theatre and promptly banned by the lord chamberlain. Fuelled by grief at her brother's death, Jaeger's rage was still burning brightly twenty years later (Jaeger, 87).

It seems probable that Jaeger turned to non-fiction because she tired of the strain her intensely personal reaction to criticism caused her, although economic motives were probably present too. By the time she wrote her last book, *Shepherd's Trade*, in 1965, she had written works of popular history, philosophy, and biography as well as fiction and drama. She had also worked as a publisher's reader and a reviewer, and several chapters in her last book offer advice to aspiring writers. She was feeling her age by then, lamenting the loss of a common frame of literary reference and agreed standards of social conduct, yet her late style was mellower—still sharp, but kindly towards the young writer just starting out. She died, unmarried, at her home, 4 Nevill Park, Tunbridge Wells, Kent, on 21 November 1969.

One of Dorothy L. Sayers's biographers noted the irony 'that it should be Muriel Jaeger, whose own books the world has forgotten, that we have to thank for the reluctant birth of one of the world's most popular detectives' (Brabazon, 2). By the end of the twentieth century this had ceased to be entirely true. Scholars of science fiction on the one hand and feminist scholars on the other, especially those interested in the group known collectively as the Somerville novelists, have all taken an interest in Jaeger: she has been credited with starting a line of thought on utopias that led to Huxley's *Brave New World* (Stableford) and has been included in a group of novelists whose fiction attempts to replace the romantic narrative with one more favourable to women (Leonardi). One scholar has attributed her 'disappearance' to critics' inability to categorize her (Stratton, 68).

A photograph of Jaeger on holiday with Sayers shows a thin woman with untidy hair. She appears to be a person who would be pleasant when relaxed but who perhaps did not relax often. Her friendship with Sayers indicates her ability to form strong friendships and to give support unselfishly when her emotions were engaged. At the same time, it seems likely that she was a difficult individual in many ways; in her writing she often expresses an appreciation of a sense of humour, but her life suggests that she found it impossible to practise. In her book *Experimental Lives, from Cato to George Sand* (1932) Jaeger wrote about a handful of extraordinary people who lived according to principle, rather than expediency. She was also fond of the designation 'opportunist'—most memorably, for Shakespeare. In the absence of much information about her life, it may be permissible to infer that compromise of rigid principles, control of the unruly self, and an opportunism about which she was highly ambivalent but which provided her living were the themes of the life of Muriel Jaeger.   ELIZABETH J. MORSE

Sources M. Jaeger, *Shepherd's trade* (1965) · S. J. Leonardi, *Dangerous by degrees: women at Oxford and the Somerville College novelists*

(1989) · *Somerville College register, 1879–1971* [1972] · *The letters of Dorothy L. Sayers*, ed. B. Reynolds, 1 (1995) · S. Stratton, 'Muriel Jaeger's *The question mark*, a response to Bellamy and Wells', *Foundation: the International Review of Science Fiction*, 29/80 (autumn 2000), 62–9 · B. Stableford, *Scientific romance in Britain, 1890–1950* (1985) · D. Coomes, *Dorothy L. Sayers: a careless rage for life* (1992) · B. Reynolds, *Dorothy L. Sayers: her life and soul* (1993) · J. Brabazon, *Dorothy L. Sayers: the life of a courageous woman* (1981) · J. Clute and P. Nicholls, eds., *The encyclopedia of science fiction* (1993) · Blain, Clements & Grundy, *Feminist comp.* · b. cert. · d. cert. · *CGPLA Eng. & Wales* (1969)

Likenesses photograph, 1920–29 (with D. Sayers), repro. in *Letters*, ed. Reynolds

Wealth at death £15,309: probate, 15 April 1970, *CGPLA Eng. & Wales*

Jænberht (*d.* 792), archbishop of Canterbury, was of Kentish origin. He was abbot of St Peter's and St Paul's (later St Augustine's), Canterbury, from 762. Following the death of Archbishop Bregowine in August 764, Jænberht was consecrated archbishop of Canterbury on 2 February 765, at a church council attended by Offa, king of the Mercians. He received his pallium in 766. The surviving evidence for his career as archbishop arises almost entirely from his relations with Offa, who had already established his influence over the Kentish hierarchy by the time of Jænberht's consecration: there survives a grant by Offa of land in west Kent, made with the consent of Archbishop Bregowine. His control of the kingdom seems to have been checked after the men of Kent fought against him at Otford in 776, and power was exercised there in the following few years by the Kentish king Ecgberht II. However, Offa had recovered his position in Kent by 785.

An explicit indication of Jænberht's poor relationship with Offa comes in a letter that King Cenwulf of the Mercians (*r.* 796–821) sent to Pope Leo III (*r.* 795–816) in 798 seeking the recreation of a single Southumbrian ecclesiastical province after Offa had separated off an archbishopric of Lichfield from that of Canterbury. His predecessor had brought this about, Cenwulf said, 'on account of the enmity he had formed against the venerable Jænberht and the people of Kent' (*English Historical Documents*, 1, no. 204). It has sometimes been suggested that Jænberht supported the Kentishmen against Offa in 776 and was a partisan of Ecgberht II, but there is no certain proof of this. It may have been in the years following Otford, however, that Jænberht issued coins in his own name (bearing the legend 'Ienberht pontifex'). Moreover, at an unknown date Offa confiscated land from Jænberht's kinsman, the Kentish thegn Aldhun.

Differences between Jænberht and Offa may be reflected in the record of the events of 786. In that year there arrived in England two legates sent by Pope Hadrian I (*r.* 772–95), George, bishop of Ostia, and Theophylact, bishop of Todi. In his report to the pope, George of Ostia stated that their purpose had been 'to uproot completely anything harmful and to secure most wholesome fruit'. George's brusque and oblique description of the legates' first meeting with Jænberht, when they 'advised him of those things which were necessary' (*English Historical Documents*, 1, no. 191), contrasts with that of Offa's effusive welcome. It is often thought that the legates' visit was connected in some way with the 'contentious synod' (*ASC*, s.a. 785, *recte* 787) held at Chelsea in the following year, when Hygeberht, bishop of Lichfield, was elevated to archiepiscopal status, his province presumably including the Mercian sees of Lichfield, Leicester, Lindsey, Worcester, and Hereford, and possibly also Dunwich and Elmham in East Anglia. Certainly, Leo III's reply to Cenwulf in 798 shows that Offa had sought Hadrian I's approval of the change, misinforming the pope that it was 'the united wish and unanimous petition' of all the English (*English Historical Documents*, 1, no. 205). However, the date of Offa's appeal is unknown, and it is not clear that the legates' mission was a response to it. They were as much concerned with Northumbria as with the kingdoms of the south, and there are indications that at least some of their canons were drawn up by the Northumbrian cleric Alcuin, who began a glittering career at the court of Charlemagne shortly afterwards. The canons were presented at separate synods in Northumbria and in the south, the latter attended by Jænberht and all the southern bishops, and by Offa.

The year of the creation of the archbishopric of Lichfield also saw the consecration of Offa's son Ecgfrith. It is tempting to think that it was Jænberht's refusal to co-operate in this novel ritual, with its ideological elevation of Offa's dynasty, that prompted the Mercian king to divide the Canterbury province, although it is not known if the cleric who performed the ceremony was the newly created archbishop of Lichfield. But that Jænberht was eventually accommodated into Offa's power structure, however reluctantly, is suggested by coins struck in the late 780s, with the name and title of Jænberht on one side, and those of Offa on the other. In the same period, Offa and Jænberht regularly attended councils together, at Brentford in 781 and annually at Chelsea from 785 to 789. It is striking, however, that Jænberht convened no councils at the regular, but unidentified, synodal meeting place of 'Clofesho', which may indicate that it lay in Mercian territory and that he preferred to keep away from Offa's power base. Jænberht died on 12 August 792. He chose to be buried in the abbey of St Peter and St Paul, bucking the trend for archiepiscopal burial in the Christ Church baptistery established by Archbishop Cuthbert. His successor Æthelheard, a Mercian, was immediately able to secure from Offa a confirmation of the privileges of all the Kentish churches, issued at a council held at 'Clofesho'.

MARIOS COSTAMBEYS

Sources *ASC*, s.a. 763–4 (i.e. 765–6), 773 (i.e. 776), 785 (i.e. 787), 790 (i.e. 792) [text A]; 785 (i.e. 786) [texts D, E] · *AS chart.*, S 105, 1259, 1264 · *English historical documents*, 1, ed. D. Whitelock (1955), nos. 191, 204, 205 · C. Cubitt, *Anglo-Saxon church councils, c.650–c.850* (1995) · S. E. Kelly, ed., *Charters of St Augustine's Abbey, Canterbury, and Minster-in-Thanet*, Anglo-Saxon Charters, 4 (1995) · N. Brooks, *The early history of the church of Canterbury: Christ Church from 597 to 1066* (1984) · P. Wormald, *Legislation and its limits* (1999), vol. 1 of *The making of English law: King Alfred to the twelfth century* (1999–) · P. Grierson and M. Blackburn, *Medieval European coinage: with a catalogue of the* *coins in the Fitzwilliam Museum, Cambridge*, 1: *The early middle ages (5th–10th centuries)* (1986)

Jaffa [*formerly* Jaffe], **Max** (1911–1991), violinist, was born on 28 December 1911 at 25 Goodge Street, London, the son of Israel Jaffe, an immigrant Russian–Jewish tailor then working as a butcher, and his London-born Russian wife, Millie Makoff (d. 1932). On his sixth birthday his father gave him a half-size violin, hoping the boy would later make money from the instrument. He studied for two years under a second-rate teacher, and was about to give up when he was taken to hear Jascha Heifetz's début, and changed his mind. He then took lessons from Wilhelm Sachse, and at the age of thirteen auditioned for the Guildhall School of Music, where his main teacher was Max Mossel. To supplement his scholarship he played in orchestras at Lyons tea houses and as an accompanist to silent films in cinemas, and formed a trio which played in hotels; later he led the orchestras at the Trocadero and Piccadilly hotels, playing the light classics which were to become his stock-in-trade. He won several college prizes, and in October 1931 he graduated from the Guildhall with the gold medal and principal's prize.

Still only nineteen, Jaffa was appointed leader of the Scottish Orchestra (later the Scottish Symphony Orchestra) in November 1931, taking leave from the Piccadilly Hotel, but he did not enjoy the experience, and he returned to London in February 1932 to resume his career with the Piccadilly Salon Orchestra, before going freelance and playing at venues including the Café de Paris and Ciro's, and for film soundtracks. On 7 October 1934 he married Bessie Joseph (b. 1911/12); their daughter, Elizabeth, was born in January 1936, but the couple lived almost separate lives.

During the Second World War, Jaffa served in the Royal Artillery, then as a pilot in the RAF, and later in the Air Transport Auxiliary. He hardly touched the violin during the war, and after demobilization in November 1945 had practically to relearn it with the help of his last teacher, Sasha Lasserson. He joined the Mantovani Orchestra, at the back desk (though he eventually became its leader), was the violin soloist on its bestseller *Charmaine* (1951), and made regular broadcasts with the orchestra for the BBC. In 1948 he bought a Pietro Guarnerius violin of 1704, which became his favourite instrument. He also played with the BBC London Studio Players and occasionally stepped in to the Albert Sandler Trio when Sandler was ill. After Sandler's death in 1948, Jaffa took his place (with the cellist Reginald Kilbey and the pianist Jack Byfield), and the Max Jaffa Trio toured the country, making their first television appearance in 1954. From May 1956 they were regulars on *Music at Ten*, where their lack of scores and scripts lent an air of easy informality to the show. They toured widely and played together until Jack Byfield's death in 1976. Also in 1956, Jaffa became soloist and leader of the BBC Palm Court Orchestra for the popular and long-running radio programme *Grand Hotel*. Jaffa was divorced from his first wife, and on 24 June 1959 he married the singer Jean Grayston (real name Jean Sylvia Gluckstein, b.

1925/6), whom he had met in 1956. They had three daughters.

In 1960 Jaffa began his long association with Scarborough: for twenty-seven years he entertained holidaymakers there during a seventeen-week summer season of concerts given by his fifteen-piece Spa Orchestra. Consisting of light classical pieces, often including more substantial works, these concerts were given in the Grand Hall and broadcast by the BBC. Jaffa had a different programme each night for three weeks, and then repeated the concerts. He received the freedom of the borough of Scarborough in 1986, when, after a mix-up, he gave up the summer seasons. But he did not retire, making broadcasts on BBC Radio 2 while leading the Palm Court Orchestra at the Grand Hotel in Brighton, and toured Britain with a programme entitled 'Max Jaffa—sixty years of music'. During his last performing years he suffered from tinnitus, and he finally retired in 1990. He was appointed OBE in 1982 and was an honorary fellow of the Guildhall School of Music. He published *How to Play the Violin* (1986) and his autobiography, *A Life on the Fiddle* (1991), and made several recordings. Of short stature, always immaculately dressed, Jaffa was a friendly man much loved by his public, his colleagues, and his family. He died peacefully at his home, 31 Elm Tree Road, St John's Wood, London, on 30 July 1991; his second wife, Jean, survived him.

JEAN M. HAIG-WHITELEY

Sources M. Jaffa, *A life on the fiddle* (1991) · *Daily Telegraph* (31 July 1991) · *The Times* (31 July 1991); (1 Aug 1991) · b. cert. · m. certs. · d. cert.
Likenesses BBC photograph, repro. in *The Independent* (1 Aug 1991) · photograph, repro. in *The Times* · photograph, repro. in *Daily Telegraph*
Wealth at death £188,258: probate, 20 March 1992, *CGPLA Eng. & Wales*

Jaffray, Alexander (1614–1673), politician and Quaker leader, was born in Aberdeen in July 1614, a son of Alexander Jaffray (d. 1645), provost of the city, and Magdalen Erskine of Pittodrie (d. 1640). He was educated at Aberdeen grammar school and at schools in Pittodrie and Banchory, and then spent a year at Marischal College, Aberdeen, in 1631–2. On 30 April 1632, while still not eighteen, he married Jean Downe (d. 1644). After his marriage, his father sent him to study law at Edinburgh, where he stayed with his relative Robert Burnet, father of Gilbert Burnet. Jaffray attended the coronation of Charles I in the city in June 1633. He was also sent to England, where he visited London, Cambridge, and Yorkshire. In 1634–5 he spent a number of months in France, staying in Caen and Neufchatel-en-Braye in Normandy. He 'learned so much of the French language, that [he] was able to travel without a guide', and was preserved from the temptations of popery, and 'from the sins of drunkenness and licentiousness, whereunto there was great provocation' (*Diary of … Jaffray*, 44–5).

In 1636 Jaffray finally established his own home with his wife, who had hitherto been living with his parents. At this stage of his life, he later concluded, he was 'very ignorant' of both religious and civil matters. In July 1638, however, when the covenanters visited Edinburgh, the

Jaffrays subscribed the national covenant; they were described as 'great Covenanters' (Spalding, 1.148). Jaffray was made a bailie in Aberdeen in September 1642. After arresting a servant of Sir George Gordon of Haddo for riot, Jaffray was assaulted by Gordon on 1 July 1643 and wounded in the head. Gordon was fined 20,000 merks, and Jaffray received 5000 merks in damages. On 19 March 1644 Gordon, who had joined the royalist rising led by the marquess of Huntly, marched into Aberdeen with sixty horse, captured the Jaffray brothers, and imprisoned them in Strathbogie, Aberdeenshire, and then in Auchendoun Castle, Banffshire; Jaffray's wife died the same month. The brothers were eventually released in early May, and in July Gordon was executed for rebellion against the state. Because of their role in his downfall, the Jaffrays 'leivit under continuall feir of his freindis' (Spalding, 2.251).

Jaffray represented Aberdeen in parliament between 1644 and 1650 and was an active member of several parliamentary committees. In 1644 he took part in fighting with the Irish confederates around Aberdeen. Owing to the city's vulnerability he was given refuge by the Earl Marischal in Dunnottar Castle, Kincardineshire. On leaving the castle one day, he was captured along with the minister, Andrew Cant, and imprisoned for several weeks in Pitcaple, Aberdeenshire. In September 1645 Jaffray and his fellow prisoners managed to overpower their guards and hold the stronghold until they were relieved by friendly forces.

After attending the 1645 parliament at St Andrews, Jaffray sat for three months in Dundee on the parliamentary committee for censuring delinquents. He later regretted that the committee had 'proceeded too rigorously in these things committed to us' (Diary of … Jaffray, 53). On 4 May 1647 he married Sarah Cant (d. 1673), daughter of the covenanter preacher Andrew *Cant (1584/1590–1663). During that year the plague raged in Aberdeen for five or six months, and the family was forced to move for a time to nearby Kingswells. In 1649 Jaffray was one of the covenanter commissioners sent to the Netherlands to negotiate with Charles II. The commissioners returned to the Netherlands in 1650 and succeeded in persuading the young king to take the covenant, so preparing the way for his coronation in Scotland. Jaffray later chided himself for negotiating this deal:

> [I] had so clear convictions of this to be wrong, that I spoke of it to the King himself, desiring him not to subscribe the Covenant, if in his conscience he was not satisfied—and yet went on to close the treaty with him, who, I knew so well, had for his own ends done it against his heart. (Diary of … Jaffray, 55)

The king did not take kindly to this advice, and later used 'sharpe expressions' against Jaffray and his fellow commissioner Alexander Brodie (Diary of Sir Archibald Johnston, ed. Fleming, 42).

On 3 September 1650 Jaffray fought in the battle of Dunbar. He was severely wounded, but after being captured was 'very kindly refreshed' by the English. He remained a prisoner for five or six months, during which time he 'had

good opportunity of frequent conference' with Oliver Cromwell, John Fleetwood, and the independent theologian John Owen. It was at this point that he became convinced that God had judged the covenanters for their alliance with an ungodly king and for their opposition to liberty of conscience. After his release in February 1651 Jaffray returned to Aberdeen, where he was once again elected provost. He also negotiated a surrender of the city to Monck, which allowed it to escape a heavy fine. At a meeting of the protesters in Edinburgh in December 1651 Jaffray bravely submitted a paper containing his analysis of why the covenanter cause was collapsing. John Livingstone and James Guthrie organized a conference with him in an effort to change his mind, but to no avail.

Jaffray now came to believe that he must move beyond presbyterianism. Scotland's godly men had congratulated themselves on being 'as far on as Geneva—yea, in some things beyond her', and mistakenly concluded that the Reformation was complete. In reality, however, it still had some way to go, and Jaffray now believed that the church must be reorganized along independent lines, as his friend John Owen had argued (Diary of … Jaffray, 61). On 24 May 1652 Jaffray and several other independents in Aberdeen wrote to leading presbyterian clergy to explain their new position. A few months later Samuel Rutherford and other presbyterians travelled to Aberdeen for a week-long conference with the Independents, but failed to prevent them from organizing their own congregation in November.

In March 1652 Jaffray had been called by the court of session in Edinburgh to be director of the chancellery, and he took up his new post in June. In July 1653 he was one of five Scots to sit in the short-lived Barebones Parliament. When the parliament was dissolved in December, Jaffray and thirty other MPs remained seated in the house to protest at the dissolution. After returning to Scotland, Jaffray divided his time between Aberdeen and Edinburgh, where he spent six months of the year in his work as director of the chancellery. In 1654 Cromwell and his council awarded Jaffray £1500 sterling to cover the expenses he had incurred in the Netherlands in the negotiations with Charles II—an unusual award which reflected the favour in which Jaffray was held by the regime. In November 1656 he moved his home from Aberdeen to Newbattle, outside Edinburgh, and a year later to Abbey Hill, Edinburgh.

At the Restoration, Jaffray was imprisoned in the Edinburgh Tolbooth, from 20 September 1660 to 17 January 1661. Only when John Middleton, earl of Middleton, moved in parliament that Jaffray be released from imprisonment because of his ill health was he set free on subscribing a bond. He was confined to the city, and threatened with a penalty of £20,000 if he moved beyond the city limits.

Jaffray now found himself increasingly drawn to the Quakers, whose emphasis on Christ within rather than on 'external, outward conformity' seemed to offer a solution to 'my deadness and dullness of heart' (Diary of … Jaffray,

134, 149). In 1662, as a result of the visit of the Quaker William Dewsbury to Scotland, Jaffray converted to Quakerism, and after moving to Inverurie early in 1663 he established a meeting there. The Quakers faced significant persecution, and after a conference with Archbishop James Sharp in 1664 Jaffray was ordered by the high commission to remain 'confined to his own dwelling-house, and keep no meetings therein, nor go any where without the Bishop's license, under the penalty of a fine of 600 merks, Scots money' (*Diary of … Jaffray*, 203). In the mid-1660s his health deteriorated to the extent that death seemed imminent. In September 1668 the bishop of Aberdeen ordered that Jaffray be taken from his house at Kingswells to Banff prison for holding illegal conventicles in his home. Despite being in very poor health Jaffray was imprisoned for more than nine months. In November he wrote to the bishop, warning him to beware of the sin of oppression and persecution, and he was eventually released by order of the privy council. Jaffray died at Kingswells on 7 May 1673 at the age of fifty-nine, having delivered an eloquent Quaker testimony on his deathbed. The next day he was laid to rest in his own burial-ground at Kingswells; his wife survived him only briefly, and died on 24 July that year.

Their son **Andrew Jaffray** (1650–1726), Quaker minister, was born in Kingswells. He married Christian, daughter of Alexander *Skene, with whom he had ten children. He converted to Quakerism in 1673 and became a leading light in the Scottish movement. In the late 1670s he was fined and imprisoned on a number of occasions for keeping conventicles, illegal preaching, and eye-catching prophetic protests against persecution. He accompanied the Quaker apologist Robert Barclay to London in the spring of 1683, and in the 1690s he participated in Quaker missions in Scotland. In 1698 he accompanied his daughter Margaret on a preaching mission in England, and in 1700 Margaret herself toured England and Ireland. After fifty years of Quaker ministry Andrew Jaffray died on 1 February 1726. He was buried in the family burial-ground at Kingswells. JOHN COFFEY

Sources *Diary of Alexander Jaffray*, ed. J. Barclay, 3rd edn (1856) · J. Spalding, *The history of the troubles and memorable transactions in Scotland and England, from 1624 to 1645*, ed. J. Skene, 2 vols., Bannatyne Club, 25 (1828–9) · *The letters and journals of Robert Baillie*, ed. D. Laing, 3 vols. (1841–2) · *Diary of Sir Archibald Johnston of Wariston*, 2, ed. D. H. Fleming, Scottish History Society, 2nd ser., 18 (1919) · *Diary of Sir Archibald Johnston of Wariston*, 3, ed. J. D. Ogilvie, Scottish History Society, 3rd ser., 34 (1940) · *The diary of Alexander Brodie of Brodie*, ed. D. Laing (1863) · F. D. Dow, *Cromwellian Scotland, 1651–1660* (1979) · J. R. Young, *The Scottish parliament, 1639–1661: a political and constitutional analysis* (1996) · J. Nicoll, *A diary of public transactions and other occurrences, chiefly in Scotland, from January 1650 to June 1667*, ed. D. Laing, Bannatyne Club, 52 (1836) · C. H. Firth, ed., *Scotland and the Commonwealth: letters and papers relating to the military government of Scotland, from August 1651 to December 1653*, Scottish History Society, 18 (1895) · J. Besse, *Collections of the sufferings of the people called Quakers* (1753)
Archives Aberdeen City Archives, diary, partly relating to religious experiences · BL, account, 691, fol. 80v · NL Scot., letters, Adv. MSS 35.5.11, fol. 73; 80.1.1, fol. 193 | BL, letters to Charles II, Add. MSS 40132, fol. 1v, 37047, fol. 142

Jaffray, Andrew (1650–1726). *See under* Jaffray, Alexander (1614–1673).

Jagan, Cheddi Berret (1918–1997), president of Guyana, was born on 22 March 1918, the second of eleven children of Indian sugar workers, at Port Mourant plantation in Berbice, British Guiana. His father, a cane cutter at the time of his birth, eventually became the foreman of a gang. His mother worked as a field labourer until he was about nine years old. Jagan's firsthand experience of plantation life gave him a lifelong interest in ameliorating the workers' condition. He received the final years of his secondary education at Queen's College, in the capital, Georgetown, which he entered in 1933 and left in 1935, having obtained a school certificate. Unable to find a suitable job, he went to the United States in 1936, where he took a two year pre-dental course at Howard University, Washington, DC. In 1938 he transferred to Northwestern University's dental school in Chicago and enrolled concurrently at the YMCA College, where he studied social sciences. In 1943 he qualified as a dentist and also graduated with a BSc degree. In August 1943 he married Janet Rosenberg, a student nurse, and returned home later that year to establish a dental practice.

Jagan quickly became involved in the colony's political life. His American education aroused his interest in political matters and his exposure to socialist literature, critical of capitalism, gave him insight into British Guiana's political economy. Jawaharlal Nehru's autobiography, moreover, strengthened his anti-colonial sentiments. In 1945 he became treasurer of the Man-Power Citizens' Association, the first trade union to represent sugar workers, for one year. In 1946 he founded the Political Affairs Committee (PAC) with his wife, Jocelyn Hubbard, a white Marxist, and Ashton Chase, a black trade unionist. Although this organization was Marxist in orientation, it welcomed all shades of political opinion and people committed to self-government. In the following year Jagan was elected to the legislative council, where he directed attention to the social costs of the plantation system to the colony's working classes. His demands, which included adequate taxation of the bauxite and sugar industries, improved housing and health services, and land reform, earned him a working-class following and the hostility of the business community.

By 1950 the leadership of the PAC, which was primarily a forum for discussion, decided to organize a mass-based political party, anticipating the grant of both adult suffrage and internal self-government. It was recognized that such a party would have to extend its appeal beyond the Indian working class. In an attempt to make the new party broadly multiracial Forbes Burnham, a black lawyer, was invited to join the People's Progressive Party (PPP) established in January of that year, as chairman, with Jagan as leader. The party's objectives included political independence and the establishment of a socialist state. In 1953 the PPP won decisively the first elections under adult suffrage, and Jagan took office as minister of agriculture, land, and

Cheddi Berret Jagan (1918–1997), by Maurice Ambler, 1953

mines. On 9 October, 133 days after the PPP's victory, the British governor, Sir Alfred Savage, suspended the constitution after the British had landed troops in Georgetown, claiming that this action averted the establishment of a communist state—a recurring fear during the cold war years. Most important was the economic threat from a government, with significant support across ethnic lines, determined to introduce radical economic reforms which would adversely affect foreign-owned corporations. The British intended to destroy the PPP as a broadly based national movement by isolating the radicals and dividing the anti-colonial forces along ethnic lines. The key to this strategy was Burnham, with support mainly from urban black people, who had challenged Jagan's leadership and was regarded by the colonial administration as a viable socialist alternative to the Marxist Jagan. In 1955 Burnham split the PPP into two factions and in 1957 formed the People's National Congress (PNC). By 1957 a pattern of racial polarization was discernible in Guyanese politics as the African and Indian leadership of separate parties increasingly appealed to ethnic fears to obtain votes.

Following the restoration of responsible government, Jagan's PPP was returned to power in both the 1957 and 1961 elections. Jagan himself served as minister of trade and industry from 1957 to 1961, and as first prime minister of British Guiana, and minister of development and planning from 1961 to 1964. The PPP's third consecutive victory convinced the opposition parties, the PNC and the pro-business United Force (UF), that Jagan's party would dominate electoral politics as long as ethnic loyalty determined voting behaviour. In order to reduce Jagan's support they advocated the introduction of proportional representation. Both parties were opposed to Jagan leading Guyana into independence: the PNC feared ethnic domination, and the UF feared communism. At the height of the cold war the United States also anticipated that an independent Guyana might follow Cuba's example and establish a communist state. President Kennedy concluded, after a 1961 meeting with Jagan, that he would eventually suspend the constitution and muzzle the opposition, and came to see Burnham as the moderate option. Kennedy ordered the Central Intelligence Agency (CIA) to depose Jagan. From early 1962 to mid-1964 the CIA financed the subversion of Jagan's government, by infiltrating the labour unions and fomenting strikes, riots, and interracial violence. At the insistence of Kennedy's administration, the British government delayed Guyana's independence and introduced proportional representation. In the first elections under the new system in 1964 Jagan was replaced by a coalition government of the PNC and the UF which led Guyana to independence in 1966. The PNC won the 1968 elections but only after rigging the vote. This technique, employed in the elections of 1973, 1980, and 1985, perpetuated PNC rule, and made the Indian majority a political minority in Guyana.

Although Jagan had consistently declared his adherence to Marxism, it was never clear whether this involved a Moscow affiliation. However, he declared at a Moscow conference in 1969: 'Not only theory, but practice also, has taught us that this is where we belong' (Manley, 24). His position recognized the efforts of the Western nations to frustrate his radical reforms—a subject treated in his books *Forbidden Freedom* (1954) and *The West on Trial* (1966). Ironically, however, it was Burnham who eventually adopted socialism. Between 1971 and 1976 he nationalized most foreign enterprises, bringing 80 per cent of the economy under state control. Jagan responded to these developments by announcing, in 1975, the PPP's 'critical support' of the PNC regime in a show of leftist solidarity. However, this support overlooked the increasingly repressive nature of the Burnham regime, the concentration of power in the hands of the president after 1980, and the downward spiral of the Guyanese economy.

In October 1992 Jagan returned to power, as president of Guyana—an electoral victory made possible by former president Jimmy Carter's role in ensuring fair elections. With the collapse of the Eastern bloc he was no longer seen as a security threat. He was faced with the task of rebuilding a shattered economy, with a huge international debt, and with boosting morale in a country where massive migration reflected a despair that things would ever improve. In opposition Jagan had modified his earlier positions to include support for a mixed economy. As president he directed his attention to repaying the country's foreign debt. At his death at the Walter Reed Army Medical Center in Washington on 6 March 1997, after he had suffered a heart attack nearly three weeks previously, progress had been made towards that end. He was survived by his wife, one son, and a daughter. He was cremated at Port Mourant, in a ceremony attended by tens of thousands of mourners. Jagan was the first leader in a decolonizing Caribbean to attempt a socialist transformation of plantation society within a parliamentary democracy. That he failed was a reflection of cold war geopolitics and Guyanese ethnic politics.   HOWARD JOHNSON

Sources C. Jagan, *The West on trial: my fight for Guyana's freedom* (1966) • T. J. Spinner, *A political and social history of Guyana, 1945–1983* (1984) • C. Singh, *Guyana: politics in a plantation society* (1988) • Latin America Bureau, *Guyana: fraudulent revolution* (1984) • R. H. Manley, *Guyana emergent: the post-independence struggle for nondependent development* (1979) • F. Furedi, 'Britain's colonial wars: playing the ethnic card', *Journal of Commonwealth and Comparative Politics*, 28 (1990), 70–89 • R. R. Premdas, 'Race, politics, and succession in Trinidad and Guyana', *Modern Caribbean Politics*, ed. A. Payne and P. Sutton (1993), 98–124 • T. Weiner, 'A Kennedy–CIA plot returns to haunt Clinton', *New York Times* (30 Oct 1994) • P. Mars, *Ideology and change: the transformation of the Caribbean left* (1998) • *The Guardian* (7 March 1997) • *The Independent* (7 March 1997) • *Daily Telegraph* (7 March 1997) • C. Jagan, *Forbidden freedom: the story of British Guiana* (1954) • WWW • 'Guyanese President Cheddi Jagan cremated', www.rediff.com/news/mar/13jag.htm, 22 Feb 2000

Archives SOUND BL NSA, *Frankly speaking*, NP446R BDI

Likenesses M. Ambler, photograph, 1953, Hult. Arch. [*see illus.*] • photographs, 1953–63, Hult. Arch. • photograph, repro. in *The Guardian* • photograph, repro. in *Daily Telegraph* • photograph, repro. in *The Independent*

Jaggard, William (*c.*1568–1623), printer and bookseller, was the son of John Jaggard, a London barber–surgeon, and his wife, Bridget. On 20 August 1584 he was apprenticed for eight years from 29 September to the distinguished printer Henry Denham; his brother John was apprenticed to another printer, Richard Tottel, on 29 October. William became a freeman of the Stationers' Company on 6 December 1591. He set up shop as a publisher and on 26 August 1594 married Jayne (or Jane) Uriane (or Vriane; *d.* 1625); a son, Isaac, was baptized on 19 April 1595; three other children, Thomas, Joan, and Alice, figure in his will.

Jaggard's first book was registered with the Stationers' Company on 4 March 1595; he rapidly became a successful businessman. Ill feeling followed his publication in 1599 of *The Passionate Pilgrim*. Ascribed to Shakespeare, this poetical anthology includes versions of sonnets 138 and 144, three extracts from *Love's Labour's Lost*, and other short poems, some by writers other than Shakespeare, others of unknown authorship. In a third edition of 1612 Jaggard added without authority nine poems from *Troia Britannica* (1609) by Thomas Heywood. Heywood, in his *Apology for Actors* (1612), protested and declared Shakespeare 'much offended with M. *Iaggard* (that altogether unknowne to him) presumed to make so bold with his name' (sig. G4r–v). The original title-page was replaced with one that did not mention Shakespeare's name.

Jaggard's career prospered. He seems to have taken at least nine apprentices, the last in November 1622; one, bound in 1610, was John Shakespeare, son of a Warwick butcher. In 1601 Jaggard collaborated with Thomas Pavier

to publish the only book of his own composition, a summary history of the lord mayors of London from Elizabeth's accession until 1601. In the following year he received permission to print playbills (none survive) for Worcester's Men, paying a royalty of 4s. a month to James Roberts, who held the monopoly. In 1604 Jaggard received a lucrative royal commission to print the ten commandments for use in churches throughout the country. In the same year he set up a small printing house of his own in the Barbican. About this time he entered into partnership with Roberts, and two years later he bought and moved into Roberts's larger establishment when Roberts retired from active trade. On 17 December 1610 Jaggard became official printer to the City of London. About 1612 he became blind as a result of syphilis; an account of his treatment is preserved in the British Library (BL, Sloane MS 640). On 23 June 1613 Isaac Jaggard was admitted freeman of the company by patrimony, doubtless to help his father.

In 1619 Jaggard was hired by Pavier (probably in association with Nathaniel Butter and Arthur Johnson) to print a quarto collection of ten plays by and attributed to Shakespeare. He had printed four volumes before the lord chamberlain attempted to stop the venture by ordering the Stationers' Company that no plays belonging to the King's Men were to be printed or reprinted without permission. Pavier and his associates, however, persuaded Jaggard to print the remaining plays with false dates so that they could be passed off as remainders of earlier editions. This fraud caused much editorial confusion until it was exposed as the result of bibliographical detective work by A. W. Pollard, Sir W. W. Greg, and others.

Jaggard is best remembered as printer of the first folio of Shakespeare; printing was completed in late October or early November of 1623, about the time of his death. The colophon names him among those at whose charges the volume was printed, but the title-page (probably printed last) names Isaac, who on 4 November became printer to the City of London 'in the place of William Jaggard his late Father deceased' (CLRO, letter book JJ, fol. 51). Jaggard's will, made on 28 March 1623, appointed his wife, Jane, as executor and Thomas Pavier as one of the overseers of his substantial estate. It was proved on 17 November.

STANLEY WELLS

Sources E. E. Willoughby, *A printer of Shakespeare: the books and times of William Jaggard* (1934) • F. P. Wilson, 'The Jaggards and the first folio of Shakespeare', *TLS* (5 Nov 1925) • F. P. Wilson, 'The first folio of Shakespeare', *TLS* (12 Nov 1925) [letter to the editor] • BL, Sloane MS 640 • letter-books, CLRO, DD; JJ • will, GL, MS 9051/6, fols. 114r–114v • will, GL, MS 9051/6 [Jane Jaggard], fols. 217r–218v

Wealth at death substantial estate: will, GL, MS 9051/6, fols. 114r–114v

Jagger, Charles Sargeant (1885–1934), sculptor, was born at Kilnhurst, Yorkshire, on 17 December 1885, the elder son of Enoch Jagger, colliery manager, and his wife, Mary Elizabeth Sargeant. Educated at Kilnhurst national school and the middle class school, Sheffield, he left aged fourteen to learn the craft of engraving on silver with the Sheffield firm of Messrs Mappin and Webb. Jagger began

Charles Sargeant Jagger (1885–1934), by David Jagger, 1920s?

studying at the Sheffield School of Art in the evenings, eventually becoming a teacher of metal-engraving; this enabled him to give up work at the factory and devote himself to sculpture. In 1907 he won a scholarship to the Royal College of Art, South Kensington. After four years there as student and assistant to Professor Edward Lantéri, a travelling bursary enabled him to study for some months in Rome and Venice. In 1914 he won the Rome scholarship in sculpture, but instead chose to enlist in the Artists' Rifles.

Early in 1915 Jagger passed out with a commission in the 4th battalion of the Worcestershire regiment and was sent to Gallipoli. After recovering from injuries he was transferred to the 2nd battalion, and served in France and Belgium. He was gassed and wounded several times, and won the MC. While convalescing Jagger obtained a commission from the British war memorials committee for a large relief, the *First Battle of Ypres, 1914* (IWM). This was intended for a Hall of Memory which was never completed. Jagger married in 1916 Violet Constance, daughter of Thomas Charles Smith, solicitor's manager, with whom he had one son. They were divorced in 1924. In 1919 the British School at Rome offered Jagger a studio in South Kensington and funding for a year in place of his Rome scholarship. He drew on his experiences at the front to create the bleak and powerful relief *No Man's Land*. The British School paid for this work to be cast in bronze and presented it to the Tate Gallery, London, in 1923.

In 1919 Sir George Frampton, a member of the British School at Rome and national adviser on war memorials, recommended Jagger to the Hoylake and West Kirby war memorial committee. The completed memorial comprised a massive granite base and obelisk flanked by a bronze *Tommy* and *Humanity*. The symbolic qualities of *Humanity* looked back to the work of Sir Alfred Gilbert whom Jagger considered the greatest English sculptor of his day, while the *Tommy* had a realism and vibrance which owed much to Jagger's admiration for Auguste Rodin. The bold modelling of the *Tommy*, combined with the energy and strength the figure conveyed, was an outstanding achievement. The expressiveness of this work was an instant success at the Royal Academy, where it was exhibited in 1921, and resulted in many more commissions. Between 1921 and 1928 Jagger completed war memorials for: S. & J. Watts warehouse (now the Britannia Hotel), Manchester (1921); Southsea, Portsmouth (1921); Bedford (1921); Great Western Railway, Paddington (1922); Brimington (1922); Royal Artillery memorial, Hyde Park corner (1921–5); Anglo-Belgian war memorial, Brussels (1922–3); Nieuwpoort memorial to the missing (1926–8); Tank memorial, Louverval, Cambrai, France (1927–8); and Port Tawfiq, Suez (1927–8). In 1925 Jagger had married, secondly, Evelyn Isabel Wade, with whom he had two daughters.

In the same period Jagger received many other prestigious commissions: a portrait statuette of the prince of Wales (later duke of Windsor) (1922; priv. coll.); a rood for Kelham Chapel, Newark (1927–9; Willen Chapel, Milton Keynes); busts and life-size stone statues of the marquess of Reading and Lord Hardinge of Penshurst for New Delhi (1927–8); and a bronze statue of Sir Ernest Shackleton (1931–2) for the Royal Geographical Society.

Jagger had several private patrons—Sir Alfred Mond, founder of ICI, being the most important. Mond commissioned four massive stone figures symbolic of industries for the company headquarters in Millbank (1928–9) and a decorative low relief, *Scandal*, for the drawing room of Mulberry House, Smith Square (walls decorated by Glyn Philpot). At the height of his career Jagger suddenly died at his home, 67 Albert Bridge Road, Battersea, London, on 16 November 1934. He was survived by his second wife. He left one major work incomplete: a figure, *Christ the King*, for Sir Edwin Lutyens's Metropolitan Cathedral in Liverpool (model, National Museums and Galleries on Merseyside). He had recently completed *Modelling and Sculpture in the Making* for the How To Do It series published by *The Studio* (1933).

The Royal Artillery memorial at Hyde Park corner (with the architect Lionel Pearson) was severely criticized after its unveiling but is now recognized as the outstanding achievement of Jagger's career. It is a highly original conception, with a stone howitzer (known to the troops as Mother) placed on top of a massive sandstone cruciform base. The sides are carved with stone reliefs depicting the artillery in action which are contrasted with four monumental bronze figures. In a daring move, Jagger made one of these a dead soldier. This and other works received awards from the Royal Society of British Sculptors which made him a fellow in 1921. He was elected an associate of the Royal Academy in 1926 and joined the Royal Mint advisory committee on coins, medals, seals, and decorations in 1932.

ANN COMPTON

Sources G. McAllister, 'A rising British sculptor: Charles Sargeant Jagger', *The Studio*, 63 (1914–15), 84–99 · D. S. MacColl, 'Two of the young', *Burlington Magazine*, 40 (1922), 84–90 · C. S. Jagger, 'The sculptor's point of view', *The Studio*, 106 (1933), 251–4 · *Charles Sargeant Jagger memorial exhibition* (1935) [exhibition catalogue, Royal Society of Painters in Water Colours, London, 21 May – 20 June 1935] · archival material, IWM · private information (2004) · *CGPLA Eng. & Wales* (1934) · A. Compton, ed., *Charles Sargeant Jagger: war and peace sculpture* (1985) [exhibition catalogue, IWM, 1 May – 29 Sept 1985, and Mappin Art Gallery, Sheffield, 19 Oct 1985 – 3 Jan 1986] · *DNB*

Archives British School at Rome, MSS · IWM, war artists' archive, MSS, file 240–6

Likenesses D. Jagger, oils, 1917, Graves Art Gallery, Sheffield · D. Jagger, oils, 1920–1929?, NPG [*see illus.*]

Wealth at death £1587 16s. 10d.: probate, 17 Dec 1934, *CGPLA Eng. & Wales*

Jago, James (1815–1893), physician, second son of John Jago, was born on 18 December 1815 at Kigilliack, Budock, near Falmouth, Cornwall. He was educated at the Falmouth classical and mathematical school until about 1833. After a short period of private tuition he entered St John's College, Cambridge, in the Easter term of 1835, and he graduated BA in the mathematical tripos of 1839 as thirty-second wrangler. He then decided on a career in medicine and studied at hospitals in London, Paris, and Dublin. On 16 February 1843 he was incorporated at the University of Oxford from Wadham College, where he graduated BA and BM on 22 June 1843, and DM in 1859.

Jago then began to practise in Truro, and in 1856 he was appointed physician to the Royal Cornwall Infirmary, and he was also connected professionally with the Truro Dispensary. He married, on 24 November 1864, Maria Jones, daughter of Richard Pearce of Penzance; she and their two daughters survived him.

In his early years at Truro, Jago wrote on a range of medical subjects, the most important of which was eye disease, which his mathematical and medical knowledge especially fitted him to discuss. He was also interested in the history and progress of Cornish science and antiquities. Jago was elected a fellow of the Royal Society on 2 June 1870, and in Truro he served from 1873 to 1875 as president of the Royal Institution of Cornwall, a society of which he had been the honorary secretary for many years. He continued to hold the office of vice-president until his death, though he suffered an attack of paralysis about 1885 which left him enfeebled and unable to attend meetings.

Jago died at his home, 1 Robartes Terrace, Truro, on 18 January 1893. D'A. POWER, *rev.* ANITA McCONNELL

Sources E. D., *PRS*, 54 (1893), i–iii · Foster, *Alum. Oxon.* · d. cert. · m. cert.

Wealth at death £11,816 17s. 5d.: probate, 24 Feb 1893, *CGPLA Eng. & Wales*

Jago, Richard (1715–1781), Church of England clergyman and poet, was born on 1 October 1715 in the rectory at Beaudesert, adjoining Henley in Arden, Warwickshire, the third son of the Revd Richard Jago (1679–1741) and Margaret (d. 1745), daughter of William Parker of Henley. The elder Richard Jago came originally from St Mawes, Cornwall, and was rector of Beaudesert from 1709 until his death.

Jago was first taught by his father and learned the rudiments of English verse from William Somervile, the Edston poet, but his formal education was at Solihull School where the headmaster was the Revd Mr Crumpton and where he began a lifelong friendship with his contemporary William Shenstone. On 30 October 1732 he matriculated as a servitor at University College, Oxford, graduating BA in June 1736 and gaining his MA in 1739. He took holy orders and, on leaving Oxford, was appointed curate at Snitterfield, Warwickshire, in 1737. Two years later he became curate of Lapworth. At this period of his life he developed his friendship with Lady Luxborough of The Barrels, Ullenhall, Warwickshire, and introduced her to Shenstone.

On 17 August 1743 Jago married Dorothea Susannah Fancourt (d. 1752), daughter of the Revd Fancourt of Kimcote, Leicestershire, who had been a friend of his father. Their first child, Richard Fancourt, was born in July 1744, and they had two more sons and four daughters. In 1746 Jago was given the livings of Harbury and Chesterton, Warwickshire, and his income was boosted in 1754 when he was given the living of Snitterfield, worth £140 a year, through the influence of Earl Nugent with Dr Madox, bishop of Worcester. He gave up the first two livings in 1771 when he was given the living of the more valuable rectory of Kimcote, worth £300 a year, by Lord Willoughby de Broke. But he retained Snitterfield and remained there for the rest of his life, passing much of his time improving the house and grounds.

From 1747 onwards, as well as bringing up a young family, Jago was active in writing. He wrote an essay on electricity, which was mislaid by Robert Dodsley, and published *A sermon on occasion of a conversation said to have pass'd between one of the inhabitants and an apparition in the churchyard of Harbury* (1755). His second published sermon, *A Christian's Happiness in Death* (1763), marked the death of his patroness, the countess of Coventry. His main interest, however, was in writing poetry. He was something of a perfectionist, insisting on having the final say on any of his published texts. When Shenstone had Dodsley include poems in his *Collection*, volumes 4 (1755) and 5 (1758), without giving Jago the opportunity to check the text, Jago expressed his annoyance. Three poems, 'The Blackbirds', 'The Goldfinches', and 'The Swallows' (1747), display a sentimental attitude to natural life. 'The Blackbirds' was set to music by Mr Isaacs, organist of Worcester Cathedral, and sung by the Revd John Pixell at a Birmingham concert in 1754.

Jago's major work, *Edge Hill, or, The Rural Prospect Delineated and Moralized*, in four books, was first drafted by 1762 and published by James Dodsley in 1767. In this topographical poem he considered not only the local landscape that he loved but also theories about how mountains came into being, his reminiscences of Somervile and Shenstone, and reflections on the earl of Leicester's entertainment of Queen Elizabeth at Kenilworth Castle, ending with an account of the civil war battle of Edgehill in

1642. In 1767 he collaborated with Richard Graves on the preparation of Shenstone's letters for publication, and in 1768 *Labour and Genius, or, The Mill-Stream and the Cascade*, his poem about Shenstone and the Leasowes, was published.

Jago's first wife died in 1752 and in 1759 he married Margaret, daughter of James Underwood of Rugeley, Staffordshire. In 1769 he contributed a roundelay, set to music by Dibdin, to the Shakespeare celebrations organized by Garrick at Stratford upon Avon. At that time he also composed *Adam*, an oratorio compiled from *Paradise Lost*.

Jago died at the vicarage at Snitterfield on 8 May 1781 and was buried in a family vault which he had constructed in the church under the middle aisle. His second wife survived him. In 1784 *Poems Moral and Descriptive*, a collected edition of his poetry edited by John Scott Hylton, was published. The texts included revisions made by Jago towards the end of his life, and the introduction by Hylton portrayed him as a shy, reserved man of middle stature, who was much more relaxed with friends, when his conversation would be sprightly, entertaining, and warm.

F. D. A. BURNS

Sources I. D. Lind, *Richard Jago: a study in eighteenth century localism* (1945) · parish register, Beaudesert, 1715, Warks. CRO [baptism] · parish register, Snitterfield, Warks. CRO · Foster, *Alum. Oxon.* · *DNB* · W. Cooper, *The records of Beaudesert* (1931) · R. M. Ingersley, 'Richard Jago', *Warwickshire poets*, ed. C. H. Poole (1914), 137–46 · *The correspondence of Robert Dodsley, 1733–1764*, ed. J. E. Tierney (1988) · *The letters of William Shenstone*, ed. M. Williams (1939) · R. Jago, *Poems moral and descriptive*, ed. J. S. Hylton (1784) · C. Dibdin, *The overture, songs, airs, and choruses in the jubilee, or, Shakespeare's garland* (1769) · IGI

Archives BL, essays, letters, and other papers, RP 305 [copies] · Bodl. Oxf., sermons and catechetical lectures · Shakespeare Birthplace Trust RO, Stratford upon Avon, letters · U. Birm. L., notebooks and accounts · Yale U., Beinecke L., essays, letters, and other papers | Bodl. Oxf., letters to James Dodsley · Ransom HRC, letters to Robert Dodsley

Wealth at death living of Snitterfield £140 p.a.; living of Kimcote, Leicestershire (1771 onwards) £300 p.a.

Jaillard, Pierre. *See* Bressan, Peter (1663–1731).

Ja Ja of Opobo [*formerly* Jubo Jubagha] (*c*.1821–1891), merchant and king of Opobo, was born in Amaigbo, a village in what became the Orlu division of Nigeria. Cast out from his family (apparently because of an ill-omened physical defect) he was sold as a slave to the coastal state of Bonny and paddled the canoes of the Anna Pepple house, which was engaged in the growing export trade in palm oil. He proved himself an adept, honest, and far-sighted businessman, and progressed through the Bonny trading hierarchy. In 1863, after the head of his house died leaving heavy debts to his British suppliers, Ja Ja accepted the challenge of succeeding him.

Bonny, however, was divided by fierce commercial and political rivalries between its constituent houses, and by 1869 was in a state of civil war, fuelled by European firearms. Defeated in battle, Ja Ja and his associates withdrew and established a strategically sited base in nearby Andoni. Having maintained good relationships with former customers in the palm-growing areas, he enticed

many merchants away from Bonny, led by the Liverpool supercargo C. N. de Cardi, and in 1870 proclaimed the independence of a new state of Opobo. Within three years he had captured the greater part of the Bonny export trade, and secured recognition as king of Opobo by the British consulate.

Enterprising, efficient, handsome, fluent in English, and with a taste for good dry champagne, Ja Ja based his decisions on a hard-headed economic realism. As an entrepreneur he responded to the opportunities on this wild frontier of merchant capitalism with a panache comparable to that of his younger contemporaries Andrew Carnegie and J. D. Rockefeller. By honest and skilful dealings he won the trust of the Igbo and Ibibio communities who controlled the production and marketing of the palm oil that Ja Ja sold in bulk to Liverpool and Glasgow supercargoes at the coast. From this trade his new state derived revenue rising to an estimated £30,000 annually.

Ja Ja was content to operate under the informal structures of British regional authority, represented in the 1870s by an itinerant consul and occasional naval visits, but on his own terms. When in 1884 Consul Edward H. ('Too-Late') Hewett began to collect signatures to printed treaties of protectorate, Ja Ja insisted on amending the text by deleting its reference to freedom of trade. Selective modernization was his aim; though anxious to encourage the benefits of western civilization, including English-language education, he resisted the admission of missionaries, who might undermine traditional religious sanctions which helped to fortify his own authority. Ja Ja began to ship oil directly for sale in Liverpool, but when he judged that this tied up too much working capital he continued to bargain directly with the British merchants.

In 1884 world prices for palm oil fell, and the bargaining became tougher. Five Liverpool firms of the African Association tried to force down the prices which his monopoly enabled him to charge; Ja Ja responded by concentrating his business on the Glasgow house of Miller Brothers. The Liverpool merchants complained to the consul that he was obstructing free trade with the interior—though they knew that none of them had the resources or the skills to go and bargain directly with producers themselves. They persuaded Hewett and others that Ja Ja was making unjustified fiscal and territorial claims. But Lord Salisbury, more judiciously, hesitated to challenge the basis of the *de facto* dominion which Ja Ja had so clearly established.

However, a newly appointed vice-consul, the 27-year-old Harry Johnston (1858–1927), was determined to open the resources of the Nigerian interior to British penetration, without too much respect for Salisbury's scruples. He quickly assembled a dossier of charges against Ja Ja: besides opposing British interpretations of free trade, he was said to be planning to disturb the peace by renewed hostilities against Bonny, and he remained reluctant to accept missionaries. On 5 August 1887 Johnston ordered Ja Ja to raise his restrictions on foreign traders. On 19 September he summoned Ja Ja and gave him an ultimatum: trial at Accra or war and bombardment of Opobo. Realistic and knowing British power, Ja Ja agreed to the trial, went quietly aboard the gunboat *Goshawk*, and was taken to the Gold Coast. Johnston saw the dispute as a simple trial of imperial strength: 'all the native chiefs are watching with interest the long struggle … as either side is victorious they will rule their conduct accordingly' (Hargreaves, 119). Salisbury subsequently described Johnston as 'a resolute but singularly lawless personage' (Oliver, 118); but he backed him nevertheless.

After a manifestly irregular trial in Accra Ja Ja was deported to the West Indies, to St Vincent and later Barbados. A sick man, he received permission to return home in 1891. He died, during his return journey, on 7 July 1891 at Tenerife, Canary Islands. He was buried at Opobo and commemorated by a statue. His vigorous and skilful assertion of independence, though abortive, earned the admiration of African historians of the later twentieth century, as well as of his countrymen in Opobo. He has been portrayed, alternatively, as a hero of Nigerian and of Igbo nationalism.   JOHN D. HARGREAVES

Sources K. Onwuka Dike, *Trade and politics in the Niger delta, 1830–1885* (1956) · C. N. de Cardi, 'A short description of the natives of the Niger Coast protectorate', in M. H. Kingsley, *West African studies* (1899), appx 1 · J. C. Anene, *Southern Nigeria in transition, 1885–1906* (1966) · E. A. Ayandele, *The missionary impact on modern Nigeria, 1842–1914* (1966) · J. D. Hargreaves, *The loaded pause, 1885–1889* (1974), vol. 1 of *West Africa partitioned* · R. Oliver, *Sir Harry Johnston and the scramble for Africa* (1957)
Archives PRO, FO 84 series · PRO, confidential print 5871, FO 403/86
Likenesses photograph, repro. in Kingsley, *West African studies*, 540 · photograph, repro. in M. Crowder, *The story of Nigeria* (1962), 177

Jak. *See* Jackson, Raymond Allen (1927–1997).

Jakobovits, Immanuel, Baron Jakobovits (1921–1999), chief rabbi, was born in Königsberg, East Prussia, on 8 February 1921, the son of Rabbi Julius Jakobovits and his wife, Paula Wreschner. Named after the great Königsberg philosopher Immanuel Kant, he was the scion of a distinguished line of rabbis. Growing up in Berlin, where his father was a *dayan* (judge) in the main rabbinical court, he experienced life under the Nazis and was sent to London in 1936 when aged fifteen. In 1938 his father too fled to Great Britain to become a member of the rabbinical court in London. There Immanuel adjusted to the new language and different Jewish lifestyle within the secure tradition established by Jews in Great Britain. In London he attended the Jewish secondary school, the Yeshiva Etz Chaim, and the more open-minded Jews' College, which prepared its students for the Orthodox ministry. There he obtained his rabbinical diploma in 1944. He received his BA degree from London University and in 1955 his PhD. Earlier, in 1941, aged twenty, he had begun serving as the temporary minister of the Brondesbury Synagogue in north-west London. From 1944 to 1947 he served the South East London Synagogue. He then served the London Great Synagogue from 1947 to 1949. In 1949 he married Amélie Munk, daughter of Rabbi Elie Munk of Paris and member of a distinguished rabbinical family. They had two sons, Julian (*b.* 1950) and Samuel (*b.* 1951), and four daughters,

Immanuel Jakobovits, Baron Jakobovits (1921–1999), by Nick Sinclair, 1992

Esther (*b.* 1953), Jeanette (*b.* 1956), Aviva (*b.* 1958), and Elisheva (*b.* 1966).

Ireland and America In 1949 Jakobovits became the chief rabbi of the Jewish Communities in Ireland, succeeding Rabbi Isaac Herzog, who had accepted a call to Israel. He remained in Ireland, living at 33 Bloomfield Avenue, Dublin, until 1958. In the latter year he accepted the prestigious pulpit of the Fifth Avenue Synagogue in New York city; he was active in all aspects of American Jewish life, giving frequent lectures at Columbia University, Yeshiva College, 92nd Street Young Men's Hebrew Association, and elsewhere. During this period he published *Jewish Medical Ethics* (1966), the standard work in that area, *Jewish Law Faces Modern Problems* (1966), and *Journal of a Rabbi* (1966), which helped establish him as a voice in contemporary Orthodoxy.

When Jakobovits was offered the post of chief rabbi of the United Hebrew Congregations of the British Commonwealth in 1966, he considered the matter carefully. In that year he had advised a younger colleague not to leave the United States for Great Britain: 'The American Jewish community here is the "First Division" of Jewish life', he had told him (personal knowledge). He saw the vitality and the vast resources of American Jewry, in a pattern of polarity with Israel, as a key to survival for world Jewry. At the same time, a return to Great Britain was enticing. He knew that others had been approached before him. Rav Joseph Soloveitchik, the great Boston scholar, a world leader of Jewish thought with no desire for public office, had rejected an approach. The post was then offered to Rabbi Jacob Herzog of Israel, the son of the chief rabbi of Israel and brother of Chaim Herzog, later president of Israel. Herzog accepted the call to Great Britain, but almost immediately withdrew because of ill health. Now the call had come to Jakobovits; and he knew instinctively that it was the right choice for him and for Anglo-Jewry. He loved Great Britain, which he called 'a kingdom of righteousness' (*The Scotsman*); and he respected Anglo-Jewry with all its faults and inner conflicts.

Chief rabbi Almost immediately after his arrival, Jakobovits prevented a split within the United Synagogue from becoming a schism. This was the 'Jacobs affair', when the 'old guard' of traditionalists hounded Rabbi Louis Jacobs, arguably the greatest and most scholarly modern Orthodox rabbi, out of office. The episode caused irreparable harm, and helped create the Masorti movement, equivalent to 'Conservative Judaism' in the United States. Nevertheless Jakobovits re-established personal contacts with Rabbi Jacobs, a more dignified separation took place, and the chief rabbinate as the guiding authority of British Orthodoxy endured and grew under Jakobovits.

In the nineteenth century, the chief rabbis of Great Britain had often come from Germany, and some feared that their tradition of autocratic leadership would be resumed under Jakobovits, but his gentle diplomacy and clear pastoral concerns dispelled such thoughts. His first pastoral tour to almost every Jewish community in the country and their various institutions dispelled all thoughts of remoteness within the chief rabbinate, not least because of the outstanding assistance given Jakobovits by Amélie, his wife. Jakobovits was most concerned with the parlous condition of Jewish education, and set up the Jewish Educational Development Trust (1971) and a network of Jewish schools. A semi-public school, named Immanuel College after him, was the flagship of a group of primary and secondary schools supported by public funds which created a proper system of education, serving more than twice the number of students than had been possible before his arrival. His Orthodox lifestyle gave an additional strength to his family life. On most holidays, the Jakobovits family travelled in a caravan in order to maintain their rigid food laws; and he became president of a caravanning club. Lady Jakobovits was always at his side. Once she asked him whether her father-in-law would have approved of this young French girl whom Immanuel had married. He replied: 'He would have loved you. You have never walked in front of me, or behind me, but always at my side' (private information).

Jakobovits's profound anguish engendered by the Holocaust showed itself in many areas. He refused to visit Germany; although he did accept an invitation from a Catholic conference centre in Aachen to lecture, he gave the lectures in Maastricht, a few miles away in the Netherlands. When the Czech memorial scrolls were moved to Westminster Synagogue, his letter to the centre (10 June 1988) referred to the scrolls as a most precious testimony of Jewish survival. In his poignant note, he added that 'they were organized and catalogued under the instruction of the Nazis by my late uncle, Dr. Tobias Jakobovits … who, after completing this work in 1944, was, together with his wife, deported to Auschwitz where they perished'. Other members of his family too died in the Holocaust. Jakobovits wrote an introduction to a new liturgy for Yom Ha-Shoah, the Holocaust memorial day, *The Six Days of Destruction: Meditations towards Hope*, by Elie Wiesel and Albert Friedlander (1988). He praised it, but expressed his doubts 'about the sanctification of the Holocaust as a cardinal doctrine in contemporary Jewish thought and teaching' (p. xi). He felt that Tisha b'Av, the day of Lamentation for the destructions visited upon the Jews in the past, could encompass the tragedy of the Holocaust.

During the later period of his term of office, the boundary between the traditional community Jakobovits served and the progressive community within Anglo-Jewry became increasingly rigid. In 1973 the chief rabbi could still allow himself to lecture at the Westminster (Reform) Synagogue—though in its social hall, not in its sanctuary. By contrast, his successor, Chief Rabbi Dr Jonathan Sacks, was not permitted by his rabbinic courts and his lay leaders to attend the funeral of his friend, the (Reform) Rabbi Hugo Gryn, which was held in the West London Reform Synagogue. Chief Rabbi Jakobovits was able to maintain friendly links with the leaders of Progressive Judaism, although the informal meetings he held with them and with Christian leaders in his home on Hamilton Terrace were strictly private, and no official notes were taken. The Progressive Jewish communities insisted that the chief rabbi spoke only for the United Synagogue, but recognized and honoured him as a great Jewish leader who did, in fact, serve as a spokesperson for Anglo-Jewry.

Jakobovits's profound devotion and deep ethical concerns represented Judaism at its best, and one newspaper described him as 'the one prelate whose preaching did not, in the views of Mrs. Thatcher, give God a bad name' (*Daily Telegraph*). The fact that his was a Conservative voice in political matters could only underscore the traditional values of Jewish life and the firm structure of Jewish law, which allowed little compromise with the new developments within contemporary legal thinking. His views on family life and fidelity, and his deep understanding of the plight of refugees, which in some ways ran counter to a society built upon a Victorian rejection of outsiders, could be appreciated by all Jews living after the Holocaust. Some had less understanding for his rejection of homosexuality, his strict views on birth control, and his stress on self-help as against receiving help from the state. He disapproved of the 1985 Church of England report *Faith in the City*, which tended to blame the government for the grinding poverty within the inner cities. His own pamphlet *From Doom to Hope* (1986) urged new immigrants to follow the pattern of Jewish immigrants, who had achieved success without government aid. At the same time, his concern for the disadvantaged and weak members of society was in the highest traditions of Judaism and represented all members of the Jewish community. The fact that Margaret Thatcher viewed him as a close friend, relying upon him and bestowing the greatest honours of the land upon him, has to be related to the great service he rendered his country and community. Jakobovits was the first chief rabbi in office to be knighted (in 1981), and the first ever rabbi to enter the House of Lords (with a life peerage, as Baron Jakobovits, in 1988).

Jakobovits's greatness as a moral leader was most evident in his concern for the Palestinian refugees, and in his courageous criticism of the government of Israel throughout his tenure of office. Jakobovits himself was a true lover of Israel, a confirmed Zionist who rejoiced that so many members of his family had settled there. He was also a strong supporter of educational and charitable institutions in that land. Had he not been a discerning critic of some of Israel's policies, he would have been a logical choice to serve as a chief (Ashkenazi) rabbi there; but his prophetic denunciations brought him much abuse, particularly when he declared his opposition to the occupation of the West Bank by the Israelis. Rabbi Shlomo Goren of Israel wanted him 'excommunicated' (*The Guardian*), and called upon Anglo-Jewry 'to spew this dangerous man from our midst' (*Daily Telegraph*). Jakobovits's earlier support of Israel in 1957, at the time of the Six-Day War, was forgotten.

Jakobovits showed his deep concern for Jewish education by founding the Jewish Educational Development Trust. He was president of Jews' College in London, and was involved with most major Jewish organizations in Great Britain and Israel, notably as trustee and governor of the Hebrew University in Jerusalem, the Bar Ilan University in Israel, the Shaare Zedek Hospital in Jerusalem, the Institute of Medicine and Judaism in Jerusalem, and similar organizations. He served as president of the Conference of European Rabbis and president of the Memorial Foundation for Jewish Culture. In recognition of his work in Israel and in the world Jewish community, he received many awards, including the Jerusalem prize (1989); the Katz prize of Israel (1990); and the Templeton prize for progress in religion (1991), often termed the Nobel prize in religion.

Assessment Jakobovits remained true to the Orthodoxy of the nineteenth-century German rabbi Samson Raphael Hirsch. Towards the end of his life he was no longer in tune with the new ultra-fundamentalist thinking that had emerged within Orthodox Jewish life, and could not reach out to those who struggled against secularism and a more vocal progressive section of Anglo-Jewry. In his youth he yearned to be a scientist; and it was he who first coined the term 'Jewish medical ethics'. His wife believed that much of his book on the subject was influenced by his stay in Ireland, where he encountered the Catholic structure of faith and its relationship to science.

As chief rabbi Jakobovits played a special role in Great Britain. The respect given to him rose out of the recognition that he was a man of faith who cared deeply for humanity and stood before all as a witness of God. Tall, impressive, eloquent, he appeared to some as a prophet. On the international scene, he was one of the voices challenging the international arms trade after the Balkan war in 1992. He favoured the acknowledgement of the Palestinian presence in Jerusalem, and suggested that Palestinians be permitted to fly their own flags and assert their identity within the city. He also supported Israeli withdrawal from the occupied areas. At home he was conservative, and his optimistic visions for the future belonged to the world of prayer more than to the world of politics.

Jakobovits died of a brain haemorrhage at 27 Circus Road, Westminster, London, on 31 October 1999, and was survived by his wife, their six children, and thirty-eight grandchildren. A memorial service was held at St John's Wood Synagogue on 16 December 1999. In a world without prophets, this *homo religiosum*, this man of religious faith, was remembered as a presence whose departure left a void in a world where the 'sea of faith' had withdrawn to its outer edges.   ALBERT FRIEDLANDER

Sources I. Jakobovits, *Journal of a rabbi* (1966) • I. Jakobovits, *If only my people … Zionism in my life* (1984) • *The Times* (1 Nov 1999) • *Daily Telegraph* (1 Nov 1999) • *The Guardian* (1 Nov 1999) • *The Independent* (1 Nov 1999) • *The Scotsman* (1 Nov 1999) • *Jewish Chronicle* • *Jewish Yearbook* • archives of the chief rabbi's office, London • RO of the Beth Din (rabbinic court) of the United Synagogue, London • *WWW* • Burke, *Peerage* • private information (2004) [Lady Jakobovits, widow] • personal knowledge (2004) • *CGPLA Eng. & Wales* (2000) • d. cert.

Archives archives of the chief rabbi's office, London • LMA, corresp. and papers • NRA, priv. coll. • RO of the Beth Din (rabbinic court) of the United Synagogue, London

Likenesses N. Sinclair, bromide print, 1992, NPG [*see illus.*] • photograph, repro. in *The Times* • photograph, repro. in *Daily Telegraph* • photograph, repro. in *The Guardian* • photograph, repro. in *The Independent* • photograph, repro. in *The Scotsman* • photographs, Hult. Arch.

Wealth at death £37,661—net: probate, 6 Sept 2000, *CGPLA Eng. & Wales*

Jallow, Momadou Ebrima (1928–1987), trade unionist and Gambian nationalist, was born on 15 June 1928 to parents of mixed Fula, Serahuli, and Wolof stock in Georgetown, McCarthy Island division, in the British protectorate of the Gambia. He later moved to the capital, Bathurst (Banjul), where he married, had several children, and spent most of his life. Following secondary education at St Augustine's School, Bathurst, Jallow joined the civil service as a clerk, first in the education department and then in the income tax division. He also worked in the mid-1950s as a secretary-accountant for private firms in Bathurst. At the urging of friends he formed the Gambia Construction Employees' Society, which led to the creation late in 1956 of the Gambia Workers' Union (GWU), with Jallow as its secretary-general. Although possessing little experience of unionism, Jallow was able in 1958 to negotiate a number of favourable contracts with employers. Late in 1958 he attended a four-month course in trade unionism at Kampala, Uganda, and began to make contacts outside the Gambia. Throughout 1959 he concentrated on building union strength among unskilled labourers—dock workers and daily paid employees. Encouraged by a successful one-day strike for higher wages for its members in February 1960, Jallow and the GWU, in the following January, at the height of the peanut season, conducted the first successful large-scale strike in the Gambia. This strike gained a substantial increase in the wages of daily workers and eventually led to the formation of joint industrial councils for the arbitration of labour disputes. The British government's decision to indict him for taking part in a riot merely increased his popularity among Gambians.

Jallow's decision not to enter politics at this period in Gambian history was crucial, since his popularity might have created a political vehicle that could have challenged the older parties. Partly to retain the support of his union followers, Jallow was critical of all political parties at this point in his career, but at the same time he pressed for rapid constitutional advancement and was considered important enough to attend, as a non-party representative, the constitutional discussions in Bathurst and London in 1961, which preceded the transfer of power. In 1963 Jallow affiliated the GWU with the International Confederation of Free Trade Unions (then in global competition with the communist-sponsored World Federation of Trade Unions for Third World labour support), and in 1964–5 he served as the full-time secretary-general of the African regional office of the International Confederation, with headquarters at Lagos, Nigeria. Dismissed in April 1965, Jallow returned home; there, motivated by a need to re-establish his public prominence, as well as by opposition to presidential rule, he supported the attack of the opposition United Party (UP) on the attempt by the government People's Progressive Party to introduce a republican constitution by means of a referendum in November. Though successful, Jallow's venture into politics lost him support among pro-government workers as well as provoking the hostility of the People's Progressive Party. His relations with the UP soon deteriorated as well, following his decision to stand against the party's leader, P. S. N'Jie, in Bathurst North in 1966, when he was turned down for a safe seat.

Attempts to rebuild Jallow's union reputation after independence through renewed union militancy proved unsuccessful. The general strikes of February 1967 and January 1970 received little support, while those of 1975–6 convinced government that Jallow and the GWU were using industrial action for political ends. Jallow's repeated failure to submit annual accounts of GWU finances, in breach of labour legislation, provided the government with a reason to deregister the union in January 1977. Jallow's professional problems were compounded by personal problems, and he largely retreated from trade union and public life until the time of the failed *coup d'état* of July 1981. His support for the government during the insurrection led to a partial lift in 1983 of the ban on the GWU, but attempts by younger, more militant union leaders to re-engage in industrial action led to the rebanning of the union. Jallow himself, though, enjoyed the support of government, and in 1985 he formed a new trade union, the Gambia Workers' Confederation, which developed ties with a Senegalese trade union confederation, in the spirit of Senegambian co-operation promoted in 1982 by the two governments in the treaty establishing the Senegambia Confederation. Government confidence in Jallow's moderate and supportive public role led it to appoint him a nominated MP two weeks before his death. He died on 23 May 1987 in Banjul, and was buried in the Muslim cemetery, Kanifing, Banjul. Despite his chequered career, Jallow is still regarded as the ablest trade union leader of his time in the Gambia.   ARNOLD HUGHES

Sources A. Hughes and H. Gailey, *Historical dictionary of the Gambia* (1999), 94–5 · A. Hughes and D. Perfect, 'Trade unionism in the Gambia', *African Affairs*, 84/349 (Dec 1989), 559–72 · D. Perfect, 'Organized labour and politics in the Gambia: 1960–85', *LABOUR, Capital and Society*, 19/2 (Nov 1986), 168–99 · 'Gambia's labour leader', *West Africa* [London] (27 May 1961), 569 · 'Jallow's progress', *West Africa* [London] (2 May 1964), 481
Likenesses photographs, repro. in 'Gambia's labour leader'

James I (1394–1437), king of Scots, was the third son of *Robert III (d. 1406), son of *Robert II (1316–1390) and *Annabella, *née* Drummond (d. 1401). He was born at Dunfermline in 1394, probably in late July. His parents were both in middle age, and he had three married sisters and a brother, David *Stewart, then earl of Carrick, who was sixteen. The birth of a new prince would have provided a welcome access of strength for the vulnerable royal dynasty. In early 1394 only the infirm Robert III and his sole surviving son stood between the throne and Robert *Stewart, earl of Fife (later duke of Albany). Ambitious, able, and backed by an extensive family of sons and grandsons, Robert of Fife had recently been lieutenant of the kingdom and still had designs on political power. The rivalry between the two principal branches of the Stewart family would dominate James I's political life and he would never escape its consequences.

Inheritance and influences James's early years were probably spent in the household of his mother in Dunfermline and Scone. Annabella's political interests may well have been perpetuated by the continued links between James and a number of her servants. The queen's death in 1401 seriously weakened the royal dynasty. She had backed the appointment of her eldest son, David, now duke of Rothesay, as lieutenant in 1399 and her absence fatally diminished his position. David's death in custody in early 1402, for which Albany was chiefly responsible, had a massive effect on the young James. When he obtained power in the kingdom in 1424, he brought those responsible for his brother's 'martyrdom' to book and destroyed the Albany Stewarts. David's removal made James heir to the throne, and as such the only alternative to an Albany Stewart succession. Robert III's chief councillors, David Fleming and Henry Sinclair, second earl of Orkney, obtained custody of James and sought to create a following around the prince's person. In 1404 James became twelfth earl of Carrick and was granted the hereditary Stewart lands in Ayrshire and the Clyde as a regality, outside the reach of Albany's lieutenancy; as Robert III's health deteriorated, plans were laid to send James to France, again beyond Albany's control. It was, though, in conflict with the main Douglas kindreds in the south, both the Black and Red branches, that James's custodians came to grief. In early 1406, seeking to extend their influence in Lothian, Fleming and Orkney were trapped by a larger force led by James Douglas of Balvenie (the future seventh earl of Douglas). Fleming was caught and killed, while Orkney took Prince James to the Bass Rock in the Forth. This was no planned departure, and it was only after waiting for over a month that the prince's household finally found a ship going to France. *En route* in late March 1406, the vessel was captured by English pirates off Flamborough Head and James entered captivity. On 4 April Robert III died. Within a fortnight James had become both king of Scots and an English prisoner.

James was absent from Scotland from the age of twelve

James I (1394–1437), coin

until he was thirty. His experience of kingship and politics was largely acquired from England. Although initially kept in custody in the Tower of London and Nottingham Castle and later, after a second period in the Tower, at Pevensey, Kenilworth, and Windsor castles, he was not excluded from court life in England. Henry IV allowed James entry into his household, and from 1419 James had an increased political value for Henry V in France. Between 1420 and Henry's death in 1422 James's activities centred on France, where his presence with English armies was used to justify accusations of treason against the large Scottish forces in French service. He received status and funds in this role and there is no indication of reluctance to back the ambitions of Henry, whom he clearly admired, for the French crown. After residing for a time in Rouen, he returned to England with Henry's funeral cortège in September 1422.

James's relations with his Scottish subjects went beyond serving as justification for their execution by the English king. Throughout his captivity he maintained a small household and was visited by Scots, many of whom established political and personal ties to him which influenced royal policies after 1424. His closest contacts with a Scottish magnate before 1424 were with his fellow captive Murdoch Stewart, son and heir of Robert, duke of Albany, the governor of Scotland in James's absence. While he made token efforts to secure James's release, Albany's dealings with England focused on obtaining the freedom of his son. He had no wish to end his own governorship by engineering the return of the king, and until 1411 styled James only as 'the son of the late king'. When Murdoch was released in 1415, negotiations ended—Henry V's demands had been such as to make a successful outcome very unlikely anyway—and James was left in prison.

James's release came as a result of English action. His connections with Henry V, who knighted him on St George's day 1421, created the impression of sympathy for England. This was further encouraged by his marriage to a member of the Lancastrian dynasty between 10 and 13 February 1424. His bride was *Joan, née Beaufort (d. 1445), niece of Cardinal Henry Beaufort and second cousin of Henry VI. The Scottish king had certainly been influenced by English politics and society. In particular he had seen Henry V's exercise of royal power and the elevation of English prestige in European politics. James would follow the same objectives in his government of Scotland after 1424. He was also affected by English court culture, and his poem The Kingis Quair illustrates both his accomplishment and his English models. The Beauforts hoped that James would continue to act as an ally after his release and their willingness to negotiate forced Murdoch, now duke of Albany, to accept the end of his governorship. Agreements in 1423 at York and London, and in March 1424 at Durham, confirmed James's freedom in return for a ransom of £40,000 (reduced by 10,000 marks, the amount of Queen Joan's dower).

Royal authority and regional lordship In April 1424 James returned to a kingdom which had functioned without assertive kingship for half a century. His own inclinations and experience directed him to exactly this aggressive approach. He also had personal grudges to satisfy. These elements created the grounds for conflict. His early acts as king, including his coronation and first parliament at Scone in May 1424, were designed to emphasize the restoration of royal authority. There was no immediate attempt to challenge existing aristocratic power structures. Instead, recognizing his limited resources, the king sought allies among the Scottish nobility, in particular relying on the powerful Black Douglas earls for support. He made no open move against Albany. The arrest in May of Albany's son Walter was backed by the duke to secure his authority within his family, and the king showed favour to Albany and his third son, Alexander, at his coronation.

The change from this moderate stance was prompted by events in France. The crushing defeat of the Scots army by the English at Verneuil-en-Perche in August 1424 removed a check on James. The deaths of the Scottish leaders, Archibald, fourth earl of Douglas, and John Stewart, earl of Buchan, and many of their adherents weakened the collective resources of the Scottish nobility and created a range of situations for James to exploit. He was quick to react. In early October he met Archibald, fifth earl of Douglas, at Melrose and renewed his alliance with the Black Douglases. From this point James's relationship with the Black Douglases increasingly favoured the crown. Buchan's family, the Albany Stewarts, did not escape so lightly. James began to exert pressure on the late earl's brother, Albany. He wrested Buchan's estates in the north from the family's grasp and arrested Albany's father-in-law, Duncan, earl of Lennox. Lennox's imprisonment may have caused unrest in his earldom, but the king continued to isolate Albany. At Christmas the duke's principal ally, Alexander Stewart, earl of Mar, came to terms with James, encouraged by fear of an alliance between the king and Mar's chief northern rival, Alexander MacDonald, lord of the Isles.

The final clash came at the king's second parliament held at Perth in March 1425. Following an acrimonious debate, which may have dealt with the fate of Albany's son Walter, and in which criticism may also have been voiced of James's dealings with the lord of the Isles, Albany was arrested and his castles were seized. The escape of the duke's youngest son, James, led to open revolt in the Lennox and Argyll, which culminated in the destruction of Dumbarton, but the king remained firm. Gathering his allies at Stirling, he reconvened parliament and presided over an assize of the greatest magnates of the kingdom which sentenced Albany and two of his sons to death. Following their executions James I easily crushed remaining opposition. The execution of Albany was the decisive event of the reign and perhaps the whole of fifteenth-century Scottish politics. The most dramatic assertion of royal power since 1371—the last executions of political opponents took place in 1320—it eliminated the family which had dominated central government since the 1380s. James played on the rights of his office, but the key to the removal of the Albany Stewarts was his handling of the other great magnates. Threats and promises isolated Albany from his peers, who condemned him in parliament.

These magnates had now to face a triumphant king resolved to alter the balance of Scottish political society in his favour. Many found this an uncomfortable experience. The earl of Douglas endured repeated royal interference in his lands in southern Scotland, and his neighbour, George Dunbar, earl of March, was first sidelined and then finally dispossessed by the king. Both these men had backed James in 1424–5, but found he could be an ungrateful master. He was not opposed to the exercise of regional lordship in principal. In the 1420s he allowed the earl of Mar to retain his dominance of northern Scotland, and his own uncle Walter Stewart, earl of Atholl, to extend his influence in Perthshire. Royal pressure on March and on Malise Graham, earl of Strathearn, who was also disinherited by James, was exerted mainly to benefit the king's allies, Atholl and William Douglas, earl of Angus. Yet even such allies felt insecure as the reign went on. James was determined to enforce his control over his kingdom and to establish the royal court as the focus of politics. His tolerance of opposition to royal demands was extremely limited and past service was no guarantee of continued favour to a suspicious and ambitious king.

The king and Gaelic Scotland Nowhere was the conflict between James's view of the kingdom and the reality clearer than in the highlands and islands. In a situation of economic and social crisis and in the absence of effective kingship, power over the Hebrides and the highlands west of Badenoch passed to the semi-independent lordship of the Isles. The relations between these MacDonald lords of the Isles and the early Stewart kings were generally good, and the hostility of clan Donald to the Albany Stewarts made them natural allies of the king. They were rewarded for this by confirmation of their rights in Ross. However,

as lord of the Isles Alexander MacDonald was head of a network of Gaelic kindreds whose activities were associated by lowland commentators with disorder. If James expected Alexander to operate like other magnates in controlling Gaelic military society, he was quickly disappointed. Alexander failed to contain unrest in the far north and west, and may even have fostered it as he sought to extend his own authority. The king's disappointment was encouraged by the earl of Mar, whose career had been built on opposition to the lordship of the Isles. From 1426, following a visit to Mar's estates in Aberdeenshire, James became increasingly hostile towards the lord of the Isles.

James's attitude was characteristically forceful. In a repeat of his treatment of Albany he arrested Alexander of the Isles and fifty of his associates in a council at Inverness in August 1428. Royal aims were flexible. At first he hoped to foment dissension within clan Donald. When that failed he sought to 'educate' the lord of the Isles in his household before freeing him. This policy was disastrous. On his release Alexander rebelled and burnt Inverness. The king replied by leading a huge royal army through Badenoch and Lochaber which defeated the Islesmen and forced Alexander to submit at Holyrood Abbey in August 1429. The campaign and submission marked the high point of James's reign. He had led an army drawn from across the kingdom and humiliated and imprisoned the only remaining rival to his authority. After 1429 he left control of the north in the hands of his lieutenant, Mar. The latter's defeat by the lordship's forces at Inverlochy in 1431 caused an end to any royal attempt to dismantle the lordship of the Isles and forced James to release Alexander, but, with Mar as lieutenant, the king could be sure that royal rights would be recognized in both the lowlands and highlands of northern Scotland. The limits on his resources prevented him from going further and, in the manner of his predecessors, he settled for the exercise of power in the north through a strong deputy.

Royal image and royal resources According to the chronicler Walter Bower (d. 1449), when James returned to his kingdom 'little remained for him to support his state out of the royal rents, lands and possessions' (Bower, 8.241). The situation was exacerbated by a sharp fall in wool exports, and so in customs revenues, after 1400. James's ambitions to increase his power and prestige depended on his ability to increase his resources. Throughout the reign he sought to maximize his income from the customs and crown lands, and contemporaries suspected that his attack on the Albany Stewarts was partly motivated by greed. Certainly the takeover of the family's earldoms and lordships doubled the landed resources of the crown. In the 1420s an even more lucrative means of raising money became available to James. In 1424 parliament agreed to grant him taxation towards payment of the ransom owed to England for his release. The tax seems to have raised almost all of the sum requested (about a quarter of the ransom), but subsequent attempts by the king to obtain taxation met with opposition in parliament and the kingdom. In 1425 and 1427 the estates apparently blocked requests for money and in 1426 only a fraction of the sum agreed in parliament could be gathered. The frequency of James's parliaments in the 1420s and much of the legislation they produced, which led to his reputation as a great lawgiver, stemmed from his efforts to win support for royal taxation.

By 1427 James was aware of the difficulties involved in raising the full ransom. He retained approximately £8000 Scots in his hands and decided to appropriate the money to his own ends. What resulted was a massive increase in royal spending power. He used the funds to purchase the trappings of a Renaissance monarchy. In particular he spent heavily on royal buildings. The castles of Edinburgh and Stirling, only recovered for the crown from powerful magnate keepers in 1424–5, had extensive royal lodgings constructed within their walls, while James's foundation of a charterhouse at Perth may have been partly intended to provide accommodation for the royal court in the burgh, in place of the Blackfriars. However, over £5000 Scots of royal funds was spent on the construction of a new palace at Linlithgow. Rather than a fortress, Linlithgow was a residence designed to display royal status, and by the mid-1430s the palace was a major royal centre. James also lavished money on the furnishings of these residences and on the accoutrements of his household. The other main area of expenditure was military. He bought numerous pieces of artillery from Flanders, including a great cannon named Lion, which were instruments of politics as much as warfare. With such weapons he could pose as a powerful, well-equipped monarch. Similarly, his construction of a Carthusian priory at Perth was intended to raise the prestige of Scottish kingship by imitating European practice, and particularly Henry V's. The Carthusians were introduced to provide a model of monastic behaviour for the Scottish church. Copying Henry V, James attempted to identify renewal of monarchy with the restoration of spiritual standards in the kingdom.

While the Scots were impressed with James's kingship, they clearly thought the price charged was high. His appropriation of the ransom did not end his financial demands. When, in 1431, he was faced with the defeat of his forces in the north at Inverlochy, his appeal for a financial contribution from the estates was met with hostility. Parliament granted the king funds only with safeguards which implied mistrust of his financial probity. The level of resistance forced him to abandon his highland ambitions and resolve his conflicts with the earl of Douglas, the first real setback of the reign. From 1431 James altered his financial methods. Instead of making demands on parliament, he sought to extract contributions from individuals, and especially merchants, who were persuaded to make loans. More significantly, he tried to generate more funds from royal rights and lands. Sheriffs were ordered to increase the profits of justice and the role of royal household officials in raising and administering rents and customs revenue grew. James's attempts to extend the crown's estates were to prove far more serious for him.

Stewart kingship and European monarchy James I began his active reign as a protégé of England. With his Lancastrian connections and wife, he was expected to end Scottish support for the French. But he had no intention of being an English puppet. As with his general approach to kingship, his foreign policy was designed to establish his status and independence as a prince. The elimination of the Scots army at Verneuil freed him from the danger of either French intervention or English interference. Although Scots continued to serve Charles VII of France in small numbers, they acted as useful contacts rather than as an embarrassment to James. As Anglo-French conflict remained finely balanced in the 1420s, his support was sought by both sides. Initially the French made the better offer. In July 1428 a treaty was agreed between James and Charles VII which confirmed earlier Franco-Scottish alliances and betrothed *Margaret of Scotland, James's eldest daughter, to the dauphin Louis. James was to provide a new army for France and would receive estates, including the countship of Saintonge, on fulfilment of the terms.

The French agreement offered James lands and prestige. It also allowed him to halt the ransom payments to England and keep the money raised. The treaty prompted English counter-offers. A marriage between one of James's daughters and Henry VI was proposed in return for a final peace between England and Scotland. The English attempted to play on James's family connections. In early 1429 Queen Joan's uncle Cardinal Henry Beaufort met James at Coldingham in Berwickshire, but James refused to respond to anything other than a direct offer and by the end of the year both sides were making preparations for war. Through early 1430 James skilfully kept his options open, in spite of the opposition of the greatest Scottish marcher magnate, the earl of Douglas. This approach yielded results. James eventually forced the English to accept only a five-year truce from 1431, which did not interfere with the French alliance.

The English were impressed. In July 1433 James's brother-in-law Edmund Beaufort, future duke of Somerset, came to Scotland with a firm offer. In return for peace and the cancellation of the French alliance the English would relinquish their last Scottish strongholds, Roxburgh and Berwick. James summoned a general council with the aim of securing support for this offer, but found himself faced with opposition from his subjects, reluctant to risk breaking their obligation to France. His failure to override his subjects, who may have been suspicious of their king's English connections, led him to seek the conclusion of his agreement with France. As the end of the English truce approached in spring 1436, James sent his daughter Margaret to France with a grand escort. In August he himself prepared to take the field. English military and diplomatic reverses encouraged a plan to take back Roxburgh by force with his imposing artillery train. The campaign was built up as a triumph of royal leadership and power. Its failure due to military incompetence and discord in the Scottish camp dealt a major blow to the standing of the king.

Up to Roxburgh, James's handling of his kingdom's

place in Europe was impressive. He achieved significant gains in prestige and resources without involving himself in Anglo-French conflict. The marriage of Margaret of Scotland to Louis of France hugely boosted the status of the Stewarts. It opened the way for the marriages of the king's younger daughters, Isabella, Eleanor, and Mary, and planned matches for Joanna and Annabella, into European princely families in the 1440s. James also showed an ability to protect his kingdom's interests, beyond relations with England and France. In dealing with the growing crisis in the church caused by the Council of Basel, he maintained a similar balancing act. His aim was to secure and, if possible, extend royal control over the Scottish church and he employed his principal minister, John Cameron, bishop of Glasgow, both as his agent at the council and papal curia and as a buffer between himself and the pope's hostility. When James died in 1437, Scottish churchmen were influential on the council, but he had escaped any serious criticism from the papacy.

The end of the reign The successes won by James in raising the status and power of Stewart monarchy obscured the fragility of his regime. There remained fundamental differences between the king and his greatest subjects on his practice of government. On questions of finance, for example, his attitudes were closer to those of English monarchs, used to annual grants of taxation, than those of his own kingdom, where financial grants to the king were rarely given. Contemporary criticism of his cupidity reflects this difference in experience and it was in attempts to extract funds from parliament that he met most regular opposition. James also wished to introduce something of the power of English royal government into Scotland. This meant a reduction in the authority of the great magnates, who saw the exercise of regional power as intrinsic to their established rights and duties. James's destruction of the Albany Stewarts did not fully secure his position. The survival in exile of James Stewart, Albany's youngest son, was a source of anxiety for a king without a son of his own. The birth of twin sons, Alexander and James, in 1430 was, as a result, the subject of great celebration. James took the opportunity to knight the heirs of many of his household adherents alongside the two babies. These adherents, such as William Crichton and James Douglas of Balvenie, were vital to his government. However, that many retained former bonds with important magnates was a source of weakness. James was served by followers of the earls of Douglas and Atholl, who still sympathized with their old lords.

Despite royal successes, James remained dependent on the backing of the great men of the kingdom. After 1431 his search for funds and attempts to maintain his political predominance put increasing strains on his relationship with many of his most powerful subjects. Between 1432 and 1435 his support for his nephew William, earl of Angus, in the marches led to the escalation of local conflict. In 1434 Angus's rival, the earl of March, was arrested and deprived of his earldom, which James annexed. March and his son attempted to recover their lands with English aid. Although Angus defeated this effort, there

was considerable resentment of royal interference in the marches, which James's failure at Roxburgh exacerbated. The king faced similar problems in the north. The death of Mar without a successor in 1435 threatened to destabilize the whole region from Lochaber to Aberdeen. Instead of seeking to replace Mar's influence, James devoted himself to making financial gains. By the end of 1436 the highland policy which he had followed since 1428 was in tatters. The lord of the Isles had replaced Mar as the dominant magnate in Inverness and Moray, and local landowners in Aberdeenshire were contemplating defiance of the king in the search for effective leadership.

By late 1436 James's approach to kingship had seriously disrupted the internal stability of Scotland. Those magnates who remained were suspicious of royal intentions. The king's frequent arrests of potential enemies without warning must have bred wider anxiety. Even his closest ally among the earls, his uncle Walter Stewart, earl of Atholl, felt insecure. In the 1430s there were indications that James had designs on Atholl's estates in Perthshire, many of which were held only in life-grant. Atholl was in his seventies. His son had died in England as one of the hostages for the payment of James's ransom, a fate far from unique among this group, which may have helped to arouse in many a sense of disenchantment. Atholl's heir was his grandson Robert Stewart, a favourite of the king, but neither was certain of James's continued goodwill and neither was prepared to accept the dismantling of the family's influence and status. Their opportunity came with the general crisis of late 1436.

James I's response to failure at Roxburgh was to override opposition. He was determined to continue with the war and, despite his setback in similar circumstances in 1431, sought taxation to finance it. At the general council which met in late October he encountered concerted dissent, led by Sir Robert Graham, the spokesman for the estates. Graham was a former Albany adherent, a current servant of Atholl, and an articulate critic of James's kingship. Graham attempted to have James removed from active power and, although unsuccessful, his action represented a physical challenge to the king. James had experienced hostility from the estates before. When the council dispersed, he clearly felt the threat was over, and did not identify Graham with any wider faction. When he was in Perth the following February, James took no special precautions. He stayed in the unfortified Blackfriars outside the town walls, where he was removed from much of his household. On the night of 20–21 February 1437 his lodgings were attacked by a group of armed men, led by Robert Graham. The men were former servants of the Albany Stewarts. Their entry into the king's lodging was aided by Robert Stewart, Atholl's grandson, and was only one element of an attempt at a coup. Though James I initially eluded his attackers and put up a desperate fight when cornered, he was overpowered and killed before help could be summoned. He was buried in the Carthusian priory at Perth on 21 February. The assassination was the first part of a determined bid for power by Atholl, which also aimed at securing custody of the new king, the six-year-old *James II. However, the failure to achieve this, and the escape of Queen Joan from Perth to Edinburgh, allowed Atholl's opponents to organize around the person of the young king. After a month-long political crisis Atholl and his principal adherents were rounded up and executed by a regency government led, initially, by the queen.

James I was more than an aggressive politician. He received contemporary praise as a talented musician, an expert in the scriptures, and as a writer, but it was for his ability as a poet that he attracted most attention from later writers. By the early sixteenth century he was known as the author of *The Kingis Quair*, a poem of 197 seven-line verses, dealing principally with the theme of philosophy and fortune after the manner of Boethius. The work, dedicated to Geoffrey Chaucer and John Gower, is an apparently autobiographical account of the king's period of captivity and meeting with his future queen, Joan Beaufort. If James is the author, the poem must date from the period of his personal rule in Scotland. Other verses by the king, mentioned in the early sixteenth century, cannot be identified with anything like the same certainty. Apart from having these intellectual gifts, James was described as a keen archer and jouster, and, while physically short, he was a strong and active wrestler when he returned to Scotland. However, by 1435, when seen by Aeneas Sylvius Piccolomini (the future Pius II), he had become weighed down with fat, though his eyes retained an impression of his energy.

Historiography James I's reign divided contemporaries. The fullest contemporary account of the king came in the last book of Walter Bower's *Scotichronicon*, written in the 1440s. Bower's picture of him as a short but 'incredibly active' and talented man, who readily challenged his magnates to wrestle with him, matches the firsthand description given by Piccolomini of an overweight yet forceful king. Bower's analysis of James's achievements was more complex, but equally influential. From the political turmoil of the 1440s Bower looked back to James as the guardian of peace in Scotland, whose 'energetic justice' inspired fear in all wrongdoers and whose death was a tragedy for the kingdom. However, Bower was aware of the extent of this fear and of the king's ambition. Bower revealed his own and others' sympathy for the fallen house of Albany and his dismay at the greed of James for money and lands. After the general tone of the *Scotichronicon*, such doubts were given only limited space, but Bower hinted at the discomfort among even the king's supporters at the extremism of his policies.

These doubts were given full rein in the so-called *Dethe of the Kynge of Scotis*, a work which although produced in England was contemporary and also drew on reliable Scottish sources. This account of James's death includes criticism of royal taxation and the treatment of Albany. Unlike Bower's work, it makes the suggestion that James's rule amounted to tyranny and that his death could be justified in these terms. The two views of the king, either as a tyrant or as a ruler cut down for his enforcement of law and peace, influenced historians in the subsequent century and a half. While royalist sentiments became increasingly strong in the sixteenth-century histories of John Mair, Hector Boece, John Lesley, and even the usually more critical George Buchanan, the hostile tradition also continued in isolated elements in their accounts, which showed James as arbitrary, vindictive, and greedy. Modern views of his reign have reflected the general alterations in perceptions of late medieval Scotland. Up to the 1960s these took a strongly centralist perspective. E. W. M. Balfour-Melville's biography, written in 1936, focused on the king's legislation as evidence of royal reform of government. The magnates were obstructive and backward-looking, first checking and then destroying the king's attempt to modernize Scotland along the lines of English government. However, more recent studies, notably those of A. A. M. Duncan (1984) and Michael Brown (1994), have produced different conclusions, laying emphasis on James's concern with short-term ends, the violent and despotic way in which these were all too often pursued, and the opposition they provoked.

James I was an able, aggressive, and opportunistic politician. His clear goal was the establishment of a prestigious monarchy, secure from the kinds of challenges which had dogged his father's reign. His means to this end were flexible and unscrupulous. Both means and end aroused hostility as well as support from Scots, unused to such kingship and not sure if the price was worth paying. James's murder was no aberration in Scottish politics; it was a product of the tensions which his rule had created in a kingdom long accustomed to challenging its rulers. His pursuit of royal rights and powers altered the internal structures of the kingdom and created an image of kingship which his successors would follow. That they did not face such entrenched resistance to their authority was James's success. That he was killed and his regime collapsed with him was his failure.   M. H. BROWN

Sources E. W. M. Balfour-Melville, *James I king of Scots* (1936) · M. Brown, *James I* (1994) · A. A. M. Duncan, *James I king of Scots, 1424–1437* (1984) · S. I. Boardman, *The early Stewart kings: Robert II and Robert III, 1371–1406* (1996) · W. Bower, *Scotichronicon*, ed. D. E. R. Watt and others, new edn, 9 vols. (1987–98), vol. 8 · C. A. Barbé, *Margaret of Scotland and the dauphin Louis* (1917) · *A history of greater Britain … by John Major*, ed. and trans. A. Constable, Scottish History Society, 10 (1892) · *The chronicles of Scotland compiled by Hector Boece*, ed. R. W. Chambers, E. C. Batho, and H. W. Husbands, 2 vols., STS, 3rd ser., 10, 15 (1938–41) · M. Connolly, 'The dethe of the kynge of Scotis: a new edition', *SHR*, 71 (1992), 46–69 · J. Wormald, 'Taming the magnates?', *Essays on the nobility of medieval Scotland*, ed. K. Stringer (1985), 270–80 · A. Grant, *Independence and nationhood* (1984) · A. Grant, 'The development of the Scottish peerage', *SHR*, 57 (1978), 1–27 · M. H. Brown, '"That old serpent and ancient of evil days", Walter earl of Atholl and the death of James I', *SHR*, 71 (1992), 23–45 · J. H. Burns, 'Scottish churchmen and the Council of Basle, pt 1', *Innes Review*, 13 (1962), 3–53 · *Recueil des croniques … par Jehan de Waurin*, ed. W. Hardy and E. L. C. P. Hardy, 5 vols., Rolls Series, 39 (1864–91) · Rymer, *Foedera*, 1st edn, 10.322–33 · *The diplomatic correspondence of Richard II*, ed. E. Perroy, CS, 3rd ser., 48 (1933)

Likenesses portrait, 15th/16th cent., NG Scot. · Pinturicchio, wall painting, 1430–70, cathedral library, Siena, Italy · coin, National Museums of Scotland [*see illus.*] · line engraving, BM; repro. in J. Jonston, *Inscriptiones* (1602) · two oil paintings, Scot. NPG · two watercolours, Scot. NPG

James II (1430–1460), king of Scots, was born at Holyrood Abbey, Edinburgh, on 16 October 1430, the younger twin son of *James I (1394–1437) and his spouse, *Joan Beaufort (d. 1445). His elder twin brother, Alexander, died in infancy, and by 22 April 1431 Prince James had been given the courtesy title of duke of Rothesay. There is occasional record of the supply to him of food, drink, and clothes, but little else is known of his early childhood, which seems to have been spent in Edinburgh Castle.

Troubled accession, 1437–1439 James may not have been in Perth at the time of his father's murder there on 21 February 1437, although his mother was certainly present. The murder, occasioned by a plot instigated by Walter Stewart, earl of Atholl, struck fear at the heart of the king's court. There was concern that the conspirators meant to seize the throne, and in the aftermath of the event the queen mother was very anxious about the possible threat to her son. But the conspirators were swiftly pursued and brought to justice, making it easier to effect the coronation of James II at Holyrood Abbey on 25 March 1437, during a parliament held at Edinburgh. It has been noted that James II's steward in his childhood, John Spens of Glendouglas, can no longer be traced after the young king's accession. Spens was a known associate of Atholl, and it is suspected that his disappearance from record is linked to the latter's fate.

The sudden death of James I seems to have thrown the central administration into confusion, a development reflected in the often scanty records of its activities. Government was also affected by the deaths of many of its leading agents, both lay and secular, in the late 1430s, weakening the political leadership of the country. These deaths exacerbated the effects of the executions and forfeitures of the reign of James I, as did the deaths in France of many Scottish barons while fighting against the English. Although there are gaps in the evidence, both chronicles and supplications to the pope for indulgences suggest that there was widespread disorder after the death of James I. Some barons seized the chance to revive dormant claims for lands and titles, presumably in the hope (not always fulfilled) that allies among the minority administration would be complaisant.

Since the king was so young at his accession, it was determined (probably at the May 1437 general council at the latest) that the administrative authority in the realm would be wielded principally by Archibald, fifth earl of Douglas (d. 1439), as regent or lieutenant, with the king's council as the general advisory body. Douglas was a grandson of King Robert III (c.1337–1406); indeed, he was James II's nearest adult male kinsman, and was also the possessor of a huge landed estate. The lieutenancy's exact authority is uncertain, but it was an office of personal prestige. It is doubtful that the king himself had any control of affairs until well into the 1440s: only when negotiations were under way for his own marriage does he appear to have become personally involved. Meanwhile Queen Joan had custody of her son and his sisters, with funds for their maintenance, and may have resided at Edinburgh Castle. The castle's keeper was Sir William

James II (1430–1460), manuscript painting, c.1455 [from the diary of Jörg von Ehingen]

Crichton of that ilk, who was one of the most powerful barons in the kingdom in the late 1430s. His personal authority (confirmed when he became chancellor of the realm in May 1439) was likely to grow while the king was effectively under his control.

Struggles for power, 1439–1445 The death in June 1439 of the earl of Douglas, leaving a teenage heir, seems to have been the trigger for two actions which immediately concerned the king. The first was his mother's marriage to Sir James Stewart, the 'black knight of Lorne'. The second, the direct consequence of the first, was the seizure of Queen Joan and her new spouse on 3 August by Sir Alexander Livingston of Callendar and his associates, and their strict imprisonment in Stirling Castle. They were apparently released only under an agreement sealed during a general council on 4 September 1439, whereby the king was surrendered to the custody of the Livingstons during his minority; James was to remain in Stirling Castle, and the money granted by parliament for his maintenance was handed over to them. To allay suspicions the agreement declared that the Livingstons' actions had been prompted by zeal for the security of the king and his mother, and not by malice. For Crichton this was insupportable, and according to later sources he himself then kidnapped the king and took him to Edinburgh Castle. There on 24 November 1440, probably in association with Livingston, he enticed the young William, sixth earl of

Douglas, to dinner and presided over his execution. The direct male line of the Douglases having died out, the comital title fell to James Douglas, earl of Avondale, an experienced courtier who probably did little to prevent the death of his cousin, knowing the rewards it would bring to his own family.

Avondale was a peripheral figure at court. His own death in 1443 had little effect on the conduct of government, which continued to be dominated by the Crichtons and Livingstons from their bases at Edinburgh and Stirling. The king and court remained mostly at Edinburgh until mid-1442, whereafter Stirling became their chief residence. Administrative continuity was also assured by the emergence of a new generation of principal officials. The course of events after 1443 is often obscure, but William Douglas, who had succeeded as eighth earl of Douglas, far from challenging the government, managed to secure for himself a place within it and may (albeit briefly) have been lieutenant of the realm soon after his succession as earl. Until at least 1450 he was the dominant figure in Scotland, though he depended heavily on the Livingstons for the influence he was able to exert within the institutions of government. In 1444 he co-operated with Alexander Livingston in causing the king to declare a general revocation of all grants of land up to his legitimate age. While it has been argued that the fourteen-year-old king was thereby declaring his majority and thus his freedom from his mother's tutelage, the evidence is open to a different interpretation: it may point to the desire of the three estates to ensure that the royal seals were not being misused to alienate crown possessions to those who temporarily enjoyed the king's favour. The king was still too young to exercise any personal control and he was still in the custody of the Livingstons. But they did not control the great seal, kept by Chancellor Crichton.

Crichton's position was steadily undermined, however, and by 7 September 1444 James Bruce, bishop of Dunkeld, had succeeded him as chancellor. In the following summer Crichton and his associates showed their resentment by occupying Edinburgh Castle and defying forces raised in the king's name, even though parliament was sitting in Edinburgh at the time. The siege was ended by negotiation, and the Crichtons suffered no long-term consequences, but Sir William certainly lost influence as well as high office. Douglas and the Livingstons then capitalized on their success in sidelining Crichton by outmanoeuvring Queen Joan and her allies. Joan's final months are shrouded in obscurity, but on 15 July 1445 she died at Dunbar, where it seems that she and her followers had confined themselves in hope of building support. Her death brought that to an end. The king's feelings about his mother's death are unknown: she had probably been a remote figure to him for several years. In 1450, however, he rewarded a man who had attempted to assist her when she was incarcerated in 1439, suggesting that he recalled that event only too well.

The king's marriage and the fall of the Livingstons, 1445–1450
Principally thanks to the protection and support they received from the earl of Douglas, the Livingstons were approaching the zenith of their power, and it was largely their kin and associates who obtained significant posts in central and local administration. Probably the most important as far as the king is concerned was the creation of that of keeper of the king's person for James Livingston, son and heir of Sir Alexander, an office he held from no later than March 1445 to at least May 1448. The duties of the position are never specified, but the title is probably self-explanatory. It was characteristic of the Livingstons, typical representatives of the new families now establishing themselves at court, that they should have exercised authority by the manipulation, or as in this case the creation, of crown office, in contrast to the long-established magnate families, whose power depended primarily on their landed possessions. Masters of bureaucratic arts, by the late 1440s the Livingstons apparently had a stranglehold on the crown's finances and were firmly in control of day-to-day administration.

Although he had been dismissed in 1444, Sir William (now Lord) Crichton was reinstated as chancellor late in 1447, perhaps in order to forward negotiations for the king's marriage, which had begun in July 1447 with the visit of a Burgundian envoy to Scotland. A foreign spouse was not at all a remarkable prospect—by then all six of James's sisters had been sent abroad for expected marriages—and in April 1448 Crichton was dispatched with two other ambassadors to obtain a suitable bride. The choice fell on *Mary of Gueldres (d. 1463), the niece of Philip the Good, duke of Burgundy. The marriage took place at Holyrood amid great ceremony on 3 July 1449. A Burgundian chronicler remarked upon the dress-style (particularly the unusual headdresses) of the most important Scottish ladies at court, perhaps because it seemed so old-fashioned. The union did much to cement good relations between Scotland and Flanders, countries which already had significant trading links.

It is difficult to avoid the impression that it was the king's marriage which gave him the self-confidence to govern in person. The experienced Crichton was fully restored as chancellor after his return from his embassy and may have capitalized on the king's favour. On 23 September 1449 James Livingston and three others were arrested, followed soon after by Sir Alexander himself and Robert Livingston, the king's comptroller. Deserted by the earl of Douglas, who probably recognized that the young king was becoming a force to be reckoned with, the Livingstons and others whom they had advanced lost their offices. They were tried in parliament in January 1450, and the comptroller and Sir Alexander's son Alexander were executed. The terms of a remission in 1452 suggest that there had been a plot against the king or queen, although there has also been speculation that the Livingstons abused their power for their financial gain. Loyal supporters of the king were prominent among those who received grants of land of those forfeited.

The destruction of the Douglases, 1450–1455 James was now taking an active interest in affairs of government, attested by his signature on documents passing the great or privy seal. The earliest certain example now extant is dated 22

August 1449, and the practice continued intermittently for the rest of the reign. The fall of the Livingstons necessitated some shuffling of offices, and the Crichtons and their associates generally profited from the changes, although the earl of Douglas began to be frequently present at court as well. Since Douglas tenants and clerics closely associated with the family held a number of offices at court, the eighth earl's influence was strong. However, he chose to journey to Rome for the 1450 papal jubilee, and was consequently away from Scotland for six months. In his absence those who had the king's ear began to spread stories about his conduct, to such an extent that the king led an attack on his castles in the south and west of Scotland. But if James hoped to forfeit the earl he was unable to do so. Douglas made a very formal submission to the king at parliament in June 1451, and received back most of his estates, with the remainder following in October 1451.

Peace had been made but tensions persisted. Although this wholehearted gesture by both parties was well received in the kingdom, some remained suspicious. One of the issues was a bond which Douglas had made with the earl of Crawford and Alexander Macdonald, earl of Ross and lord of the Isles. The king was disturbed by it because its terms seem to have implied that the earls were bound to each other's protection and because it lacked any clause excepting the king's actions from this mutual support. Given the troubled course of James's short life to date, it may be argued that he had every justification for fearing the unknown and for forcing Douglas to break his bond.

There is nothing to suggest that the king considered moving first against either of the other sigillants of the bond, despite the seizure by Ross of three crown castles in Inverness-shire in March 1451, apparently encouraged by his father-in-law, James Livingston, who had joined him after escaping from custody in Holyrood Abbey. Action against Ross at that time would have distracted the king from his intended target of Douglas lands; but although Crawford's territory was certainly accessible to attack, James chose to strike at Douglas first. He was more commonly present at court than Crawford, at least up to late 1450, so the king may have had a better understanding of his character and felt that he was more liable to persuasion, especially after the June 1451 submission. Douglas was therefore already indebted to the king to some extent, and the king now sought to press home his advantage.

In spite of the dramatic outcome of Douglas's visit to Stirling in February 1452, there is no evidence that James premeditated an attack on the earl. Nevertheless the power that Douglas and his family enjoyed in the early 1450s was arguably such as to jeopardize the authority of the crown, as James must have appreciated. For his part Douglas knew that something was afoot, and before accepting an invitation to join the king insisted on receiving a safe conduct for himself and his entourage. Only when that was granted did he make his way to Stirling Castle. Against this background of mutual suspicion Douglas found James still in an excitable mood. Their discussions culminated in an after-dinner conversation on the evening of 22 February. The king pressed the earl to break his bond with Crawford and Ross. Douglas refused, whereupon James exclaimed, 'false tratour sen yow will nocht I sall', and stabbed him with a knife; a number of courtiers rushed in to finish the deed, leaving Douglas's body pierced by twenty-six wounds (Craigie, 1.240).

The act was an astonishing one for any monarch. The impulse of fury provoked by Douglas's intransigence had certainly rid James of a thorn in his flesh, but raised the certain prospect of repercussions once the news had broken throughout the land. This was not a time to sit back and await action by others, and James immediately went south to the borders, partly, it seems, to conduct a justice ayre, but also to meet potential Douglas allies who had been cowed into submission.

Meanwhile Earl William's brother James, who became ninth earl of Douglas, made no known response to the killing of the eighth earl until a month had passed; but when he did it was destructive. On 27 March he and his closest associates travelled to Stirling, where they blew out horns against the king and all the lords who were with him at the time of the murder, and they dragged a letter (presumably the dead earl's safe conduct) attached to a board on a horse's tail through the town, which they proceeded to despoil. The king was not present, however; he had set off northwards to confront the earl of Crawford, another sigillant of the contentious bond. The upshot of their meeting was not to Crawford's advantage. His forces clashed with those of the first earl of Huntly at Brechin on 18 May 1452, and Huntly was victorious, having displayed the king's banner and proclaimed that as he was the king's lieutenant the action was in effect the king's own. Crawford and his men yielded, and at parliament at Edinburgh in June 1452 the earl suffered a temporary forfeiture.

This parliament was one of the most important of the reign, in the eyes of contemporaries as well as modern historians. It was here that James would be surrounded for the first time since the Douglas killing by many of his three estates; and that deed could not fail to be discussed. As if to ensure that it would be, under silence of night Douglas attached a letter bearing his own seal and the seals of his brother Hugh, earl of Ormond, and James, Lord Hamilton, to the parliament house door; in it they renounced their allegiance to the king and stated that they would hold their land of him no longer. Although such an act of *diffidatio* broke the fealty owed by a vassal to his lord, Douglas certainly did not look to replace James as king: his protest was directed against the king *as* his lord.

The parliament acquitted the king of evil intent towards the dead earl, but this did not satisfy James, who commanded that under pain of death and loss of lands all capable men should gather south of Edinburgh. In an expedition whose importance is underlined by the postponement of the exchequer audit, normally held about late June or July, James himself led the army so gathered on a raid into the lands where the earls of Douglas traditionally commanded support, according to the contemporary Auchinleck chronicler inflicting destruction on friend as well as foe. However, from the king's point of view the ravages of his host were counter-productive, in that they alienated Douglas tenants whose support he needed to win, and so help to explain why he was unable to ruin the ninth earl. Instead the two men made an agreement. On 28 August 1452 Douglas drew up a bond in which he forgave those who had taken part in the slaying of his brother and agreed to make no bonds which threatened the king. His submission implies that Douglas had decided that in the long run an accommodation with the king would serve him better than confrontation. If not the overwhelming victory he had probably hoped for, it was still a useful boost for James, who in a conciliatory mood sealed a pardon in parliament at this time for the surviving members of the Livingston family, forfeited in 1450.

Perhaps to underline his concern to settle matters with Douglas, the king made a further accord with him in January 1453, under which the earl promised to give manrent and service to the king in return for restoration of certain lands. About the same time the king granted the earl permission to marry his brother's widow, Margaret, the Fair Maid of Galloway, the daughter of the fifth earl of Douglas, if the necessary dispensation was obtained from the pope. Douglas was then accepted back at court, although he seldom attended it. There is little doubt that after the January 1453 accord with the Douglases the kingdom drew a sharp breath of relief, at the end of a remarkable period in the reign.

Despite all this, it became evident that James was still unsettled by thoughts of what Douglas and his followers might do. Douglas too was not inclined to let sleeping dogs lie. He seems to have continued to intrigue with potential supporters; Douglas castles in Morayshire, Kirkcudbrightshire, Lanarkshire, and Linlithgowshire were fortified; and in a wide-ranging series of attacks some of the queen's dower lands and a grange belonging to the king's justiciar, Lord Abernethy, were burnt. The king probably had wind of what was afoot and in March 1455 he responded by besieging and throwing down Douglas's castle of Inveravon, near Linlithgow; then, moving west and south, he began to ravage Douglas and Hamilton lands. By April he had forced Douglas into a desperate and unavailing defence of Abercorn, Linlithgowshire. When Lord Hamilton switched sides because he realized that the king's victory was only a matter of time, Douglas fled to England, paving the way for the final victory for the king's forces over the remnants of Douglas's in a battle at Arkinholm, near Langholm, Dumfriesshire, on 1 May. Douglas's stronghold of Threave Castle, Kirkcudbrightshire, surrendered after a few weeks of siege. Meanwhile the parliament which convened in June had forfeited the refugee earl and his mother and brothers on a charge of treason, and his brother the earl of Ormond was executed. The king's final victory provides a striking demonstration of the effectiveness of royal authority in mobilizing political support against even the greatest magnates.

The conduct of government In the 1450s the king increasingly surrounded himself with men he felt he could trust, and they in turn depended on him for their positions. In the early years of the reign, by contrast, the courtiers had been former adherents of James I and his spouse, or of the earls of Douglas. The king had begun his manoeuvres in the June 1452 parliament, where three men were created earls and seven were created lords of parliament (a title first granted in Scotland in 1445), and the king's council ensured that rewards for service were given to a number of others. Not all of these new lords can thereafter be found frequently at court, but this mass creation clearly showed what was on offer for those prepared to rally to the king. Replenishing his support was crucial to James after he was bereft of long-standing adherents by the death of his chancellor, Lord Crichton, about September 1453 and of two other loyal members of the Crichton family within the following year.

About fifteen leading royal councillors can be identified in the period from 1452 onwards, mostly from the witness-lists to crown charters. They were a mix of clerics and nobles. It is noticeable that the clerics were office-holders and so personally dependent on the king for their authority and prestige, whereas most of the nobles among the regular councillors at this time were not office-holders. This group is certainly much wider than that apparent towards the end of the reign of James I. The king's new noble councillors included Patrick, Lord Glamis, Patrick, Lord Graham, and James Livingston, who became Lord Livingston in 1458: men active in political life before 1450, but whose standing advanced in the 1450s. Livingston's second career certainly has the air of the return of the prodigal son. Despite his disgrace in 1450 and later involvement with his son-in-law the lord of the Isles in attacking royal castles, he was reinstated as chamberlain by May 1454 and by October 1455 was also master of the king's household. William Sinclair, fourth earl of Orkney, at best a fringe figure at court beforehand, became chancellor in 1454. Like Livingston, Orkney was unusual in the late 1450s for being a noble who was also an office-holder.

The presence of senior clerics on the king's regular council attests James's generally cordial relations with the papacy. At the start of the reign the position was complicated by the existence (since 1431) of the Council of Basel, at which there was a lasting official Scottish presence. Into the 1440s ecclesiastical policy was disrupted by a Douglas- and Livingston-led adherence to the anti-pope, Felix V, while most of the clerical leaders were stalwart in their adherence to Eugenius IV, whose cause eventually prevailed. James promoted the candidacies for bishoprics of loyalists such as Ninian Spot, who in 1459 became bishop of Galloway, and Thomas Spens, who preceded Spot in Galloway and was translated to Aberdeen in 1458. Most prominent on the council was George Schoriswood, made bishop of Brechin in 1454, who during the reign advanced from being a minor chancery clerk to chancellor of the realm. Their constant attendance to official duties allowed these men little time for their ecclesiastical duties.

The king also promoted his immediate family. His half-brother John *Stewart (d. 1512) was created earl of Atholl by March 1453, when he can have been barely thirteen years old, and in the late 1450s he was allowed to marry Margaret, successively the widow of the eighth earl of Douglas and divorced from the ninth. Another half-brother, James *Stewart (d. 1499/1500), obtained a favourable marriage into an important Angus family, the Ogilvys, although he did not receive a peerage title until 1470, when he was made earl of Buchan. The king's own sons were also honoured, notwithstanding their extreme youth: David (1455/6–1457) became earl of Moray; John *Stewart (1457?–1479/80) became earl of Mar; and Alexander *Stewart (1454?–1485) became duke of Albany and earl of March.

Justice and parliament James was a monarch keen to be seen as active by his subjects. In the 1450s, especially after the killing of the eighth earl of Douglas in 1452, he made regular perambulations of the realm. Some journeys fitted in with the schedule of justice ayres, at which the king would be present if he could to oversee in person the provision of justice to his subjects. Crown vassals used these appearances by their king to obtain confirmations of their tenure—particularly important for those who had formerly been tenants of the now forfeited Douglases. Other expeditions were clearly made to allow the king to go hunting, a sport he enjoyed greatly. In the 1450s, in particular, there are many references to his preparation for and participation in hunts, for example at Loch Freuchie and Glen Finglas in Perthshire. These perambulations meant that although Edinburgh was certainly the principal centre for the court, it was present there only for a short time each year.

Parliament (encompassing the general council) was important in the reign of James II, and it is evident that the king did not expect to bypass it. Formal legislation does not survive for all the assemblies of the three estates during the reign, but it is known that on average there was at least one meeting of the estates every year (except between mid-1446 and April 1449, when the Livingstons' control of the machinery of government seems to have made parliamentary grants of taxation unnecessary). Equally, only two assemblies between the time of the king's accession and January 1450 were styled parliaments: one in March 1437 when the king was crowned and the other in June–July 1445 when the business included the siege of Edinburgh Castle and the swearing of an oath of loyalty to the king by his subjects.

Although it is hard to assess the effectiveness of legislation passed during the reign, significant matters such as the defence of the borders against England and monetary affairs were often considered. In part furthered by the three estates, an effort was made to lessen the pressure from litigants on the king's council to hear general judicial business. Provision of justice before the king and council was an important responsibility of the monarch, since if the judges-in-ordinary were deficient then people had no other recourse except to the king. Having no salaried judiciary, the king required a co-operative lay baronage and ecclesiastical dignitaries to form his council when legal business occurred, and there was no shortage of difficult cases to confront them. There was pressure on the king and his council to provide justice in a settled place on a regular basis; but this was perhaps not what the king wanted to have his council do. Instead irregular sessions were devised, when a body with equal representation from the three estates sat for about a month in one place before moving to another with a different sederunt. This reactive policy worked, but it was a short-term measure.

James's respect for constitutional forms, even when he exploited them to his own advantage, is shown by the act of annexation passed in the parliament of August 1455. It declared certain lordships and castles to be annexed inalienably to the crown, and enacted that if any of the lands were alienated in future they could be resumed by the crown at any time without compensation. The whole of the customs as they had been in the hands of James I on the day of his death were similarly annexed, and it was provided that future kings were to swear at their coronations to uphold the endowment thus created. No alienations were to be made from it without the consent of parliament. The crown's landed patrimony as covered by this statute extended from the Black Isle in Ross to the kingdom's southern border with England, and had an estimated yearly value of £6500 Scots.

Although it has been argued that the act of annexation was intended to restrict the king's ability to increase the wealth of magnate families while reducing his own, it seems likelier that its purpose was to give statutory form to the crown's landed endowment and, by giving it parliamentary protection, to discourage powerful magnates from attempting to reduce it. It did not, however, stop either James himself or his successors making grants contrary to the terms of the act. The act of annexation was supplemented two months later by a wide-reaching revocation of grants of crown lands which had been made, perhaps by false counsel, during the king's minority. James II was the first Scottish king to use this power of revocation, permitted to a ruler who had reached his 'perfect majority' at the age of twenty-five.

War, diplomacy, and the death of the king, 1455–1460 King James had been knighted at his baptism, and as a determined leader of his armed forces (thereby multiplying his absences from Edinburgh) proved to be the son of his father. He does not seem to have taken part in the set battles which occurred in Scotland during the reign, but his presence at a number of sieges and destructive raids when opposition was encountered can be readily demonstrated. His campaigns outside Scotland included a brief attack on Berwick in June 1455, a very significant raid on Northumberland in July–August 1456, and a further assault on Berwick in February 1457. All these were part of his efforts to encourage the French, in particular, to join a united attack on England. James's position in Scotland may have been stronger by June 1455 and England increasingly in turmoil, but Charles VII was evidently reluctant to commit himself to further warfare with England. In this respect James's foreign diplomacy can scarcely be counted a success. His many sisters had given him a foothold in the European marriage market, but one which he did not handle well: while three of the marriages planned during his reign took place, two of his sisters had to be recalled to have spouses found at home. Yet despite these setbacks, at the end of the 1450s James proposed a marriage alliance with the king of Denmark whose terms included the cession by Denmark to Scotland of her right to Orkney and Shetland. Although this ambitious proposal was then stalled, it was concluded in 1468–9. The general mood prevailing in Scotland at this time is suggested by the parliament of March 1458, which praised the king for causing there to be 'na maisterfull party remanende that may cause ony brekinge in his Realme', but went on to demand that the laws should be upheld (*APS*, 1424–1513, 52)—evidence for satisfaction, but also a warning to James not to take the goodwill of his subjects for granted.

The campaign of 1460 which came to an end shortly after the king's death was set in train by developments in England's civil war. James had intended holding a parliament in Aberdeen in June, an unusual step given that there had been no other meeting of the estates north of Scone for nearly 100 years. But there was a late change of plan, and the parliament was switched to Edinburgh, as the fragility of Henry VI's government became increasingly apparent. Associated with the move, and with James's evident determination to exploit the opportunities presented by English weakness, was the summoning of a general levy to meet shortly after parliament had risen in early July, clearly to enable the army to move south before autumn. In July 1460 there was talk in Bruges of plans for a concerted attack on England by the Yorkist lords from their base at Calais and also James II. Since he had been negotiating with both Lancaster and York, the Scottish king was not likely to be deterred from further action by the capture of Henry VI at Northampton on 10 July and the subsequent establishment of a Yorkist regime, if indeed he knew of it.

The death of the king, in common with those of many of his fellow Stewart kings, was violent and unexpected; but not at the hand of enemies or assassins. On 3 August James was in the middle of the siege of Roxburgh Castle, which had been in English hands since 1346, when a gun that he may have ordered to be fired to celebrate the queen's imminent arrival exploded while he was standing close at hand, inflicting a mortal wound. He is said to have died in Roxburgh's Franciscan friary, before being swiftly buried at Holyrood amid great dolour, but only after his forces had successfully completed the siege. James was just twenty-nine years old. He and his wife, Mary of Gueldres, had four sons and two daughters; the eldest boy, *James III (1452–1488), succeeded him. He also had one illegitimate son. In 1462 Queen Mary, who was closely involved in the government of the realm until her death on 1 December 1463, endowed Trinity College Church, Edinburgh, as a memorial to her husband, probably the instigator of its establishment.

Significance and reputation The unevenness of the surviving documentation hinders the task of the biographer of James II. The crown's own records, partly legal and partly financial, leave important questions unanswered. The sole significant contemporary chronicle, that of Auchinleck, is scrappy and disconnected, and offers few clear opinions about the king or anyone else. Only with the writers of the early sixteenth century and later do distinct impressions of James begin to emerge. They are strikingly and consistently favourable. Thus John Mair presents him as an energetic ruler who overthrew the Douglases as overmighty subjects, waged vigorous war on England, and was mourned like a father at his death. To Robert Lindsay of Pitscottie, James was 'that potent prince' whose killing of Douglas 'brocht his realme to gret tranquillitie' (*Historie and Cronicles*, 1.7–8). The same image was maintained into the nineteenth century and beyond, in accordance with the prevailing view of medieval Scotland as a realm in which strong kingship was needed to subdue feudal anarchy.

Recent historians of later medieval Scotland, however, have suggested that a partnership of crown and nobility formed the normal basis of government, with each side having much to gain from the other in maintaining political stability, rather than relations being characterized by the crown's recurrent efforts to claw back by all available means the acquisitions made by greedy barons during frequent periods of minority rule. The reign of James II, which saw a number of violent deaths among the nobility, headed by that of the eighth earl of Douglas, might appear to contradict the revisionist model. But although it can be argued that the Douglases were more imposed upon than imposing, particularly in the death of the eighth earl, it is probably more realistic to accept that the sheer extent of their power had created an abnormal situation. The background to the conflicts between the Douglas earls and the king was one of considerable mutual suspicion. There were many who wished to maintain good relations; it may be going too far to contend that the Douglases were overmighty subjects whose fall was inevitable, but it is significant that the underlying tension was removed only by their ruin. That James became single-minded in his pursuit of the Douglases, even though he was not bound to succeed and indeed it entailed risks to his life every time he took the field against them, is a further pointer to the threat they posed, or could have posed, to royal power. In other respects the king clearly appreciated the importance of making concessions, not only to court favourites, but also to those who had been disgraced once they showed themselves penitent. The rehabilitations of James Livingston and Lord Hamilton in the 1450s are especially noteworthy.

His bouts of aggression have caused some twentieth-century historians to criticize James II, with references to his 'unprincipled opportunism' and the 'capricious traits of his behaviour' (Dunlop, 209), and to his 'arrogance' and 'wilfulness' towards some of his loyal officers and advisers (Macdougall, 37). It has even been claimed that militarily James was a failure since he was unable to capture either Berwick or Roxburgh, and certainly his life was unfulfilled in that respect. Inevitably his personality remains elusive. But though he is recorded as owning a guitar and playing at cards, while in 1451 men who brought him a camel were paid 52s., it seems clear that he was above all a man of action. His favourite sport was hunting and he was an energetic soldier, as such more interested in improving his fortresses than his palaces. This was in keeping with his view of kingship, which meant to lead, and to be seen to lead, from the front. His unexpected death may have been typical of the man. Perhaps his impulsive qualities should also be seen in the context of his youth, for he was not yet thirty when he died, but historians have often commented that his facial disfigurement, a large fire-red birthmark, seems in keeping with his character. Personality reinforced policy in his style of government. James considered that the most effective way to rule was to be seen by his subjects as often as possible, and he toured his realm ceaselessly. These public displays served him well, and his self-confidence was certainly furthered by his queen's bearing four sons, ensuring the continuation of his dynasty. ALAN R. BORTHWICK

Sources J. M. Thomson and others, eds., *Registrum magni sigilli regum Scotorum / The register of the great seal of Scotland*, 11 vols. (1882–1914) · *APS*, 1424–1567 · *The Asloan manuscript*, ed. W. A. Craigie, 2 vols., STS, new ser., 14, 16 (1923–5) · G. Burnett and others, eds., *The exchequer rolls of Scotland*, 23 vols. (1878–1908), vols. 4–6 · W. Bower, *Scotichronicon*, ed. D. E. R. Watt and others, new edn, 9 vols. (1987–98), vol. 8 · F. J. H. Skene, *Liber pluscardensis*, 2 vols. (1877–80) · A. I. Dunlop, *The life and times of James Kennedy bishop of St Andrews* (1950) · N. Macdougall, *James III: a political study* (1982) · C. McGladdery, *James II* (1990) · M. Brown, *The Black Douglases: war and lordship in late medieval Scotland, 1300–1455* (1998) · E. W. M. Balfour-Melville, *James I king of Scots* (1936) · A. R. Borthwick, 'The king, council and councillors in Scotland, c.1430–1460', PhD diss., U. Edin., 1989 · J. Stevenson, ed., *Letters and papers illustrative of the wars of the English in France during the reign of Henry the Sixth, king of England*, 2 vols., Rolls Series, 22 (1861) · A. I. Dunlop and others, eds., *Calendar of Scottish supplications to Rome, 1418–47*, 5 vols. (1934–83) · F. Downie, 'La voie quelle menace tenir': Annabella Stewart, Scotland, and the European marriage market, 1444–1456', *SHR*, 78 (1999), 170–91 · M. Scott, 'A Burgundian visit to Scotland in 1449', *Costume*, 21 (1987), 16–25 · A. Grant, *Independence and nationhood: Scotland, 1306–1469* (1984) · W. B. D. D. Turnbull, ed., *Extracta e variis cronicis Scocie*, Abbotsford Club, 23 (1842) · R. Nicholson, *Scotland: the later middle ages* (1974), vol. 2 of *The Edinburgh history of Scotland*, ed. G. Donaldson (1965–75) · *A history of greater Britain … by John Major*, ed. and trans. A. Constable, Scottish History Society, 10 (1892) · *The historie and cronicles of Scotland … by Robert Lindesay of Pitscottie*, ed. A. J. G. Mackay, 1, STS, 42 (1899) · *Scots peerage*, vol. 1

Likenesses manuscript painting, c.1455, Württembergische Landesbibliothek, Stuttgart, diary of Jörg von Ehingen, Cod. hist. 4141, s. 97 [*see illus.*] · line engraving, BM; repro. in J. Jonston, *Inscriptiones* (1602) · miniature, V&A · oils, Scot. NPG

James III (1452–1488), king of Scots, was the son of *James II (1430–1460) and *Mary of Gueldres (d. 1463); he was born at St Andrews Castle towards the end of May 1452.

Early years, 1452–1466 The future James III was born into the greatest crisis of his father's reign, the struggle between the crown and the Black Douglases following the killing of William, eighth earl of Douglas, by James II at Stirling on 22 February 1452. The choice of the relative safety of St Andrews Castle for the royal birth is understandable. The Stewart succession and the Douglas threat alike required the birth of a healthy male child, and James II's Golden Charter of June 1452 to Bishop James Kennedy, in whose episcopal castle the royal son and heir was born,

James III (1452–1488), by Hugo van der Goes, c.1480 [kneeling right, with St Andrew (standing) and Prince James (later James IV)]

is perhaps an expression of relief as well as gratitude. The queen continued loyally to consolidate the future of the dynasty by providing her husband with three further sons and a daughter: Alexander *Stewart, duke of Albany and earl of March (1454?–1485), David, earl of Moray (1455/6–1457), John *Stewart, earl of Mar (1457?–1479/80), and Margaret (b. 1459/60). Thus James III was the first Scottish king since the fourteenth century to grow up with brothers close to him in age, a fact which had a significant—possibly crucial—effect on the events of his adult rule.

James was only eight when his father's death at the siege of Roxburgh (3 August 1460) precipitated him into the kingship, and into what would obviously be a lengthy minority. Before his accession we catch only occasional glimpses of James as prince, being toured from one royal palace to another and being considered as a potential bridegroom for the daughter of the Danish king Christian I, in the course of James II's audacious Scoto-Danish foreign negotiations, conducted at Bourges in the summer of 1460. The sudden demise of James II, mortally wounded by the bursting of one of his own cannon at Roxburgh, created a new diplomatic situation; but King James had set the agenda in foreign policy which his son and his ministers were to pursue within the decade, and with considerable success.

A near-contemporary report records a tumult in Edinburgh following James II's death; in fact, however, the new reign got off to a promising start. James III was swiftly crowned at Kelso on 10 August, two days after Roxburgh fell to the Scots. In domestic government there was no real break with the past; most of James II's officers of state remained in post, above all Andrew Stewart, Lord Avondale, who was to serve as chancellor until 1482. The queen mother, Mary of Gueldres, showed a remarkable aptitude for foreign affairs, pursuing her late husband's policy of playing off Lancaster against York in England to secure border gains for Scotland. Thus she gave a temporary refuge to the fugitive Lancastrian rulers, Henry VI and Margaret of Anjou, and thereby acquired Berwick by negotiation in March 1461; then, when it was apparent that the Lancastrian cause in England was lost, Mary of Gueldres astutely changed sides to throw Scottish support behind the victorious Yorkist, Edward IV.

The queen mother's principal rival for control of government, Bishop James Kennedy of St Andrews, disapproved of Mary's pragmatism. Pro-French and Lancastrian by conviction, he was probably the instigator of the abortive Scottish raid on Norham Castle in the summer of 1463, an event attended by the queen mother, Kennedy, and the eleven-year-old James III. Kennedy acquired total control of the king's person when Mary of Gueldres died (1 December 1463), and showed wisdom in domestic policy, taking the king on a northern progress as far as Inverness in 1464; in 1464–5 he reluctantly accepted the need to make a long truce with Yorkist England; and on his death at St Andrews (24 May 1465) he left the adolescent James III in the care of his brother Gilbert, Lord Kennedy.

The Boyd ascendancy, 1466–1469 Kennedy control of royal government was shattered on 9 July 1466, when James III, hunting near Linlithgow after the annual exchequer audit, was seized by a group of magnates headed by Sir Alexander Boyd of Drumcoll, keeper of Edinburgh Castle and the king's household chamberlain, and taken to Edinburgh. The architect of this bloodless coup was Sir Alexander's brother Robert *Boyd, Lord Boyd [see under Boyd family], who used his control of the king to obtain a parliamentary ratification of his family's actions and, more pertinently, his new-found power to obtain promotions for himself and his kin. Boyd became chamberlain, governor of the person of the king and his brothers until James III should reach the age of twenty-one, and keeper of the principal royal castles. Boyd's eldest son, Thomas, was created earl of Arran early in 1467 and, most offensive

of all, was married to the king's elder sister, Mary (b. 1451), in spite of the tears of the adolescent King James [see under Boyd family].

The Boyds' greed proved their undoing. Their one substantial achievement was the treaty of Copenhagen (1468), by which King James was to marry Margaret, daughter of Christian I of Denmark–Norway. King Christian's financial problems meant that he could not afford to pay his daughter's dowry (60,000 Rhenish florins), and protracted negotiations eventually ended in his pawning of the earldom of Orkney and lordship of Shetland to make up the required sum. The marriage of James III and *Margaret of Denmark (1456/7?–1486) took place at Holyrood on 13 July 1469, and coincided with the flight of the Boyds—Thomas, earl of Arran, and his wife, Mary Stewart, and later Robert, Lord Boyd—to Bruges. In a very full assembly of parliament in November 1469 the Boyds were forfeited, and Sir Alexander Boyd of Drumcoll, who had imprudently remained in Scotland, was beheaded. At the age of seventeen James III took control of his government.

Foreign policy James III's adult rule lasted for little short of nineteen years. In certain respects he continued the aggressive policies of his father with some success. Thus he actively sought the aggrandizement of the dynasty at home and abroad. He was concerned from the outset to emphasize the unfettered nature of his power in Scotland: the parliament of November 1469 claimed that the king of Scots had 'ful jurisdictione and fre impire within his realme' (APS, 2.95). With the acquisition of Orkney and Shetland, rapidly annexed by the crown in 1472, and Berwick (since 1461), Scotland had achieved its full territorial extent and James III had a larger stage on which to seek to realize his imperial ambitions. These were not confined to matters of internal jurisdiction, such as the appointment of notaries, but extended to the systematic placement of royal familiars in remote areas of Scotland—for example, Andrew Painter, bishop of Orkney, and Thomas Cochrane, keeper of Kildrummy in Mar—and an obsessive pride in the acquisition of Berwick, where King James for a time installed the royal mint. Above all, in his early years of adult rule, he seems also to have understood the concept of empire in the geographical sense of seeking foreign territories to rule. Between 1471 and 1473 he considered the invasion of Brittany and the acquisition of the duchy of Gueldres through negotiation (as heir to his mother, Mary of Gueldres); and he resurrected a claim, which had its origins in 1428, to the French duchy of Saintonge.

All these foreign schemes proved abortive, and in 1474 the king performed a diplomatic volte-face; abandoning the long-standing Franco-Scottish alliance, he opted instead for a full-scale treaty and marriage alliance with Edward IV of England. Ratified by the Scots on 3 November 1474, this provided for a marriage between James's son and heir, James (b. 17 March 1473), and Cecilia, a daughter of Edward IV (aged five), when both should reach marriageable age; in the meantime the treaty brought James

III immediate financial gain in the shape of annual instalments of the prospective bride's dowry, beginning at the rate of 2000 marks per annum.

With one disastrous exception, the Anglo-Scottish war of 1480–82, James was to pursue a policy of peace and alliance with England for the rest of his life. Further marriage treaties involving the heir to the throne followed, with Anne de la Pole, niece of Richard III, in 1484 (part of a truce agreed at Nottingham in September to conclude the hostilities which had continued intermittently even after the end of open war between England and Scotland in 1482) and with an unspecified daughter of Edward IV in 1486 and 1487; and in 1487 James III himself, now a widower, contemplated marriage with Elizabeth Woodville, Edward IV's widow—a strange proposal, and one hardly calculated to win any kudos for the Scottish king in Tudor England. In March 1484 he had the good sense to renew the discarded French alliance; but in the later seventies his obsequious pursuit of ever stronger links with England, at a time when Edward IV had lost interest in Scotland as an ally—he had made his own highly lucrative deal with Louis XI of France in 1475—left Scotland without friends in Europe, and James himself highly vulnerable to attack not only from England, but from his own subjects.

Patronage and domestic government   For a king with a dynamic and initially volatile foreign policy, James III seems remarkably lacking in energy in the government of his own kingdom. Broadly, though not exclusively, he relied on the support of the great magnates north of Forth—the earls of Argyll, Huntly, and Crawford in particular—yet he was extremely ungenerous in his distribution of rewards for services performed. At the very end of the reign (May 1488) he conferred the dukedom of Montrose, the first non-royal dukedom, on David Lindsay, fifth earl of Crawford, but only to make sure of his continuing loyalty during the rebellion of that year. Significantly, Crawford's son and heir was one of the rebel leaders, that is, on the winning side. As for George Gordon, second earl of Huntly, his service as royal lieutenant in the north, attacking the lands of the forfeited MacDonald earl of Ross in 1476 and taking Dingwall Castle for the crown, was rewarded with a grant of a mere 100 merks' worth of land. This royal parsimony—largely James III's failure to play the patronage game with any success—resulted in Huntly's remaining a committed neutral in the north in 1488 while his king was killed by the rebels in the south.

Magnate apathy, or active hostility, towards James III was clearly a response not only to some of his policies, but also to his style of government. Uniquely among late medieval Scottish kings, he conducted virtually all royal business during his adult rule in Edinburgh, a burgh from which he seems rarely to have moved beyond brief visits to Fife and parts of Lothian. This must have been a conscious decision by King James, possibly connected with his desire, expressed in parliamentary statutes of 1469 and 1471, to encourage appeals from local jurisdictions to sessions of the council held in Edinburgh. The records of the lords of council, many of whom doubled as royal councillors, begin in 1478; and James III reaffirmed the subject's right of direct appeal to the council in January 1488. It must, however, be doubted whether this style of government could possibly work in late medieval Scotland. To most of his subjects James III remained a remote and aloof figure in Edinburgh; although royal justice ayres were held, for example, at Ayr, Cupar, Edinburgh, Haddington, Peebles, Perth, Selkirk, and Stirling, the king was not personally present. Thus local feuds, which could often be settled before or in the wake of a justice ayre headed by the king, continued largely unchecked throughout this reign. Royal slackness in the case of two long-running struggles, the Cunningham–Montgomery feud in northern Ayrshire and the Drummond–Murray contest in Strathearn, produced a polarized society; the rivals raised their local disputes to the level of national politics in 1488, with fatal consequences for the king.

Taxation and finance   Royal slackness in the administration of justice and distribution of patronage was compounded by the king's unpopular methods of raising money. The financial position of the crown during this reign, in spite of falling rents on royal estates, was better than at the time of his two predecessors, largely because of the vast increase in the territorial wealth of the crown—much of it through forfeitures—since 1424. Yet he indulged extensively in one of the most disliked devices to bring in ready cash, the levying of extraordinary taxation in parliament. This he attempted in 1472, 1473, 1479, 1482, 1485, and 1487, amid constant protests and with limited success. Almost equally offensive was another form of casualty, revenue accruing to the crown through the profits of justice. In this case the complaint was that James III was granting remissions, at a price, for serious crimes and so undermining the effectiveness of criminal justice.

James appears to have had little wealth—certainly no annual surplus—in 1479; but in the first audit of treasury revenue after his death (held in February 1492) there was discovered the enormous sum of £24,517 10s. Scots, the equivalent of two years' crown income from normal sources; and it was claimed at the time that this was only a small proportion of the royal treasure. The king seems to have amassed this wealth largely through the introduction of the notorious 'black money' (1480–82, though some of it was still in circulation as late as 1487). This currency, a combination of very base billon and copper, possibly in part a response to a shortage of coin, was probably introduced by James III mainly as a means of clearing debts, while he himself hoarded silver from about 1480 onwards. This was no solution to the long-term financial needs of the crown, but he may have received about £29,000 Scots as profit from a single issue of 'black money'.

The royal Stewart family and the Lauder Bridge crisis   James III was perhaps unfortunate to have brothers close to him in age, something which had not troubled the Stewarts since the late fourteenth century; yet it must be said that his relations with his family were appalling. His elder sister, Mary, widow of the forfeited Thomas Boyd, earl of Arran, was lured back to Scotland, and married to James, first Lord Hamilton. The king's younger sister, Margaret, whom James planned to marry to Anthony Woodville, Lord Rivers, as part of his Anglophile policy, opted to defy her brother and become pregnant by William, third Lord Crichton. The king's three half-uncles, born to James I's widow, Joan Beaufort, following her marriage to Sir James Stewart of Lorne—John, earl of Atholl, James, earl of Buchan, and Andrew, in 1482 bishop-elect of Moray—had varying ambitions, but all three, mistrusting the king, would look to further advancement by opposing him in 1482.

Above all, it was James III's attacks on his brothers Albany and Mar which provoked opposition to his kingship. The much later and much quoted view of the two brothers as men who 'lovit … abill men and goode horse' (*Historie and Cronicles*, 1.162–3), men who were respected by the Scottish nobility in contrast to King James, who is portrayed to his disadvantage as an artistic recluse with no interest in war, probably draws much of its relevance from the king's Anglophile policy of the late 1470s, and Albany's resistance to it. Albany may indeed have served as the natural focus for opposition to the Anglo-Scottish treaty of 1474. In April 1479 his castle of Dunbar was suddenly attacked by the king. Albany fled to France, and in October James III's attempt to have his brother forfeited for treason failed; perhaps significantly, the indictment accused him of abusing his office of march warden by violating the truce with England.

James's younger brother John, earl of Mar, died within a year of Albany's flight, and in mysterious circumstances. At liberty in October 1479, he had certainly been arrested by the following January, and was described as dead and forfeited by July 1480. This was the one crime which later chroniclers all attributed to James; and even the poet Sir David Lindsay of the Mount, who as a young man was employed in the household of James IV, believed that James III was responsible for Mar's death. Thus in the spring of 1480, when King James's Anglophile policy collapsed and war with England broke out, he was plunged into a very dangerous situation: one royal earl dead, a royal duke, whom the Scottish estates refused to forfeit, in exile, royal foreign policy discredited, and a widespread fear, especially in the south, of James's pre-emptive strikes. All these factors combined to create the Lauder crisis of 1482. We cannot be certain how far the large numbers of disaffected Scottish magnates were prepared to support the return of Alexander, duke of Albany, to head the government; probably at least James Livingston, bishop of Dunkeld, Archibald Douglas, earl of Angus, and the shifty James Stewart, earl of Buchan, were in contact with the duke before Lauder, and many others may have given written assurances to Edward IV—Albany's benefactor from early May 1482—that they would support Albany rather than James III.

In the summer of 1482 King James mustered the Scottish host at Lauder to resist the invasion of Albany (styling himself Alexander R.), Richard, duke of Gloucester, and a huge English army. The consequences of a battle would probably have been disastrous for the Scottish king; but before it could happen he was seized at Lauder (22 July) by a group of magnates headed by Buchan and Angus, some of his familiars were hanged over Lauder Bridge (they included Thomas Preston, probably responsible for Mar's imprisonment at Craigmillar in 1479, and Preston's son-in-law Thomas Cochrane, who had been granted the keepership of Kildrummy Castle), and James III was incarcerated in Edinburgh Castle until 29 September. Gloucester negotiated with the king's displaced councillors on his arrival in Edinburgh, but had no access to James himself; eventually the English army withdrew, receiving the surrender of Berwick (August 1482) for what proved to be the last time, and Albany was left to resolve the crisis as best he could.

A complex power struggle ensued. Albany, unacceptable to a majority as king, sought the support of Margaret of Denmark (at Stirling with her sons) as lieutenant-general, returned to Edinburgh, made a show of besieging the castle (29 September), and released James. Attempts to find a settlement followed, with the Stewart half-uncles feathering their own nests—especially Andrew Stewart, who wanted nothing less than the archbishopric of St Andrews and the privy seal—and Albany styling himself lieutenant-general and earl of Mar (October 1482). This last award alienated the earl of Huntly, who reverted to his traditional allegiance and, after an abortive parliament (2–11 December 1482), swung his support behind the king. In the spring of 1483 James III recovered much of his power, Albany's English treasons told against him, and, most important of all, the duke's patron Edward IV died (9 April 1483). Albany's flight was followed by his forfeiture for real rather than imagined treasons (July 1483). Two later efforts at a comeback ended in defeat at Lochmaben (22 July 1484), imprisonment in Edinburgh Castle (summer 1485), a final escape, and Albany's death at a tournament in Paris (late 1485).

The crisis of 1488 and death of the king James III survived 1482–3 partly owing to the timely intervention of loyal northern magnates, but perhaps mainly because there was at the time no credible alternative as king; his eldest son, James, was only nine. By the early months of 1488 much had changed. Queen Margaret of Denmark had died at Stirling (July 1486), and the king's subsequent efforts to have her canonized cannot disguise the fact that he had resented her role in 1482; indeed, rebel propaganda in 1488 claimed that the queen had been poisoned by the royal familiar John Ramsay, a survivor of Lauder. In any event, her death left the thirteen-year-old heir to the throne—fifteen by March 1488—without an influential mentor, and estranged, as his mother had been, from his father.

James III proved the architect of his own downfall. In April 1487 he had obtained from Pope Innocent VIII an indult allowing him eight months' grace, in the case of vacancies in important benefices, to nominate candidates for papal approval; and in 1486 he had received from the same pope the golden rose, a signal mark of papal favour. Armed with these concessions, the king sought to bring the long-running dispute with the Humes over Coldingham Priory (1472–87) to an end by insisting on the suppression of the priory and making resistance to his wishes an act of treason. This demand was the occasion, if not the only cause, of the 1488 rebellion. The Humes, aided by their kin and allies the Hepburns, resisted, and Prince James slipped out of Stirling Castle (2 February 1488) to join them. James III compounded his difficulties by sacking his chancellor, Colin Campbell, first earl of Argyll, and by turning for assistance to his unpopular half-uncles, the men who had imprisoned him in 1482. Pursued from Edinburgh by rebel forces, the king gathered support in Aberdeen, but the northern magnates—Huntly, Erroll, Marischal, and Glamis—were looking for a negotiated settlement with Prince James and the rebels rather than further confrontation. James III did the worst thing possible: he signed an agreement to negotiate (the Aberdeen articles, April 1488), then reneged on his promise and sought to end the rebellion by force. An abortive struggle with the rebels at Blackness (May 1488) ended with James having to give hostages and subsequently escape to Edinburgh. Early in June he advanced to Stirling, having distributed some of his wealth among various supporters to ensure their loyalty; but he died at 'the field of Stirling', later called Sauchieburn, on 11 June 1488, seeking—inappropriately—to emulate Robert I, whose sword he brought to the field. It is uncertain whether he was killed in the battle or afterwards while in flight. Between 25 and 28 June, just after his victorious son's coronation at Scone as James IV, James III was buried at Cambuskenneth Abbey beside his wife, Margaret of Denmark. He left three sons: *James IV (1473–1513), who succeeded him, James *Stewart, duke of Ross (d. 1504), and John, earl of Mar (d. 1503).

The character of the king and reign Defects in James III's governmental style are obvious. Though he had begun his personal rule with advantages denied to his predecessors, he had failed to work at the business of government and to reward his long-suffering supporters. In domestic politics the overall result of this lack of energy or interest was unresolved feuds and a nobility increasingly at odds with, or apathetic towards, the king. Internal dissensions were exacerbated by power struggles among the royal Stewart kin; James III removed his brothers, coerced his sisters, was opposed by his half-uncles and his queen, and ultimately drove his eldest son into the fatal rebellion of 1488. Yet in some ways he set the agenda for his two much more successful successors. The indult from Pope Innocent VIII, confirming the crown's right to nominate to important ecclesiastical benefices, would prove a lucrative source of wealth to James IV and James V; and the Anglo-Scottish alliance of 1474, however flawed in its execution, was the obvious forerunner of the more celebrated treaty of perpetual peace of January 1502.

Near-contemporary and later writers would praise James for his piety and condemn him for his lechery, the latter a remarkably elusive vice in the case of this king, who had no known illegitimate offspring and only one (possible) mistress, a whore called Daisy. Chronicle and record sources alike are in agreement on his continual

acceptance of bad counsel, on his probable role in the removal of his brother Mar, and on his amassing of incalculable wealth. However, George Buchanan is alone among sixteenth-century chroniclers in going so far as to describe the king as a tyrant (as he does in the second volume of his *History*), a claim which probably tells us more about Buchanan's theory of popular sovereignty than it does about James III.

Still more enigmatic is King James's reputation as a major patron of the arts. Such a role would of course fit his concept of himself as a European ruler of significance, a concept reflected in his striking of a medallion at Berwick in 1478 in anticipation of a pilgrimage to Amiens, or his silver coinage of c.1485, on which he is portrayed wearing an imperial crown. However, evidence for royal patronage is scanty, and much of it derives from asides by later chroniclers: Giovanni Ferrerio claimed that William Roger, a royal musician apparently hanged at Lauder in 1482, founded a school of musicians who remembered him as late as 1529; and more famously Robert Lindsay of Pitscottie remarked that James was a recluse who 'delyttit mair in singing and in playing upon instrumentis nor he did in defence of the bordouris or in the ministratioun of justice' (*History and Cronicles*, 1.163). James the recluse is easier to identify than James the musician, though it must be admitted that the treasurer's accounts, the crucial source for casual royal expenditure, are lacking for all but sixteen months of the reign; and the crown undoubtedly employed the services of scholars such as Archibald Whitelaw, John Ireland, and John Reid of Stobo.

Against this it should be said that the king's building programme, a feature of his patronage stressed by later chroniclers, was hardly lavish. There were some additions to Stirling Castle and Linlithgow Palace; and in and around James's favourite burgh, Edinburgh, a royal chapel at Restalrig (1487), some building work at Holyrood, but little else. He does not appear to have made any significant additions to his mother's uncompleted foundation, the collegiate church of the Holy Trinity (1460); and while both James III and Margaret of Denmark are portrayed on separate panels of the great altarpiece, the work of the Flemish artist Hugo van der Goes, which originally stood in that church, recent research would suggest that the altarpiece was commissioned, paid for, and brought to Scotland by Sir Edward Bonkil, provost of Trinity, and not by the king. On balance, then, contemporary evidence, scanty though it is, does not support the image of James III as an important patron of the arts and architecture; certainly his imperial view of Stewart kingship did not find expression in the creation of a glittering Renaissance court. NORMAN MACDOUGALL

Sources J. M. Thomson and others, eds., *Registrum magni sigilli regum Scotorum / The register of the great seal of Scotland*, 11 vols. (1882–1914), vol. 2 · *APS*, 1424–1567 · G. Burnett and others, eds., *The exchequer rolls of Scotland*, 6–9 (1883–6) · *CDS*, vol. 4 · [T. Thomson], ed., *The acts of the lords of council in civil causes, 1478–1495*, 1, RC, 41 (1839) · [T. Thomson], ed., *The acts of the lords auditors of causes and complaints, AD 1466–AD 1494*, RC, 40 (1839) · T. Dickson, ed., *Compota thesaurariorum regum Scotorum / Accounts of the lord high treasurer of*

Scotland, 1 (1877) • *The historie and cronicles of Scotland … by Robert Lindesay of Pitscottie*, ed. A. J. G. Mackay, 1, STS, 42 (1899), 152–212 • J. Lesley, *The history of Scotland*, ed. T. Thomson, Bannatyne Club, 38 (1830) • BL, Royal MS 17 D.xx, fols. 307–308 [pt of a short anonymous chronicle appended to Royal MS of Andrew Wyntoun] • [G. Buchanan], *The history of Scotland translated from the Latin of George Buchanan*, ed. and trans. J. Aikman, 6 vols. (1827–9), vol. 2 • H. Boece, *Scotorum historiae a prima gentis origine*, ed. G. Ferrerio, 2nd edn (Paris, 1574), appx • J. Moir, ed., *Hectoris Boetii Murthlacensium et Aberdonensium episcoporum vitae* (1894) • N. Macdougall, *James III: a political study* (1982) • N. Macdougall, *James IV* (1989) • R. Nicholson, *Scotland: the later middle ages* (1974), vol. 2 of *The Edinburgh history of Scotland*, ed. G. Donaldson (1965–75) • C. McGladdery, *James II* (1990) • N. Macdougall, '"It is I, the earl of Mar": in search of Thomas Cochrane', *People and power in Scotland: essays in honour of T. C. Smout*, ed. R. Mason and N. Macdougall (1992), 28–49 • I. H. Stewart, *The Scottish coinage* (1966) • J. Murray, 'The black money of James III', *Coinage in medieval Scotland, 1100–1600: Second Symposium on Coinage and Monetary History* [Oxford 1977], ed. D. M. Metcalf (1977), 115–30 • L. Campbell, 'Edward Bonkil: a Scottish patron of Hugo van der Goes', *Burlington Magazine*, 126 (1984), 265–74 • W. Angus and A. I. Dunlop, 'The date of the birth of James III', *SHR*, 30 (1951), 199–204

Archives NRA Scotland, accounts of the lord high treasurer • NRA Scotland, A. D. C. • NRA Scotland, family archives on G. D. • NRA Scotland, MS treaties with France • NRA Scotland, records of parliament • NRA Scotland, R. M. S. • NRA Scotland, state papers no. 19 • priv. coll., family archives • PRO, Scots. docs., E 39; E 404 | BL, Add. charters, Add. MSS

Likenesses portrait, *c.*1474, Holyroodhouse, Edinburgh • H. van der Goes, altarpiece, oils on panel, *c.*1480, NG Scot. [*see illus.*] • coin, *c.*1485, NG Scot. • portrait, 1560–99, Scot. NPG • G. Jameson, portrait, 1633 • panel, Scot. NPG • two watercolours (after H. van der Goes), Scot. NPG • watercolour, Scot. NPG

Wealth at death audit of royal treasure in February 1492 produced total of £24,517 10s. 0d. Scots

James IV (1473–1513), king of Scots, was born at Stirling on 17 March 1473, the eldest son of *James III (1452–1488) and his wife, *Margaret of Denmark (1456/7?–1486).

Heir to the throne, 1473–1488 James was at once given the title duke of Rothesay, traditionally borne by the heir to the Scottish throne. He spent his youth at Stirling in the charge of his mother and of his governor, James Shaw of Sauchy.

In October 1474 James was betrothed to Cecilia, youngest daughter of Edward IV, as part of an Anglo-Scottish treaty which represented a major departure from the traditional policy of alliance with France. The dowry of 20,000 marks sterling was paid in advance, by instalments, until 1479, by which date relations between the two countries had deteriorated; Edward IV, after 1475 at peace with France, then raised the stakes by demanding the dispatch of the prince to England, and the cession of Berwick to the English crown. In April 1480 renewal of outright Anglo-Scottish hostilities put an end to the 1474 treaty and its provision for the prince's marriage.

In the aftermath of the Lauder coup of summer 1482, while James III was held captive in Edinburgh Castle, the young prince came into contact with his uncle, the exiled Alexander *Stewart, duke of Albany, who had come to Stirling to obtain the queen's assistance in restoring his position in Scotland. Many participants in the complex negotiations which took place during the king's captivity subsequently fell under royal disfavour and it is possible

James IV (1473–1513), by unknown artist

that James viewed even his eldest son with suspicion thereafter.

In September 1484, as part of James III's renewed attempts to secure a long-term alliance with England, Rothesay was contracted to marry Richard III's niece, Anne de la Pole. That arrangement lapsed with the accession of Henry VII; subsequent marriage proposals centred on the prince's younger brother, James *Stewart, marquess of Ormond: in July 1486 there was no provision for Rothesay, while in November 1487 the provision was at best sketchy, linking the Scottish heir with an unspecified daughter of Edward IV. As the security of Henry VII's throne was not self-evident, and as the prospective brides pertained to the previous dynasty, this omission may have been strategic and sensible: the critical marriage of the heir to the Scottish throne was worth deferring until Henry had a daughter of his own. However, Rothesay may have felt himself sidelined—especially after Ormond, the better to fit him for marriage to an English princess, was in January 1488 raised to the dukedom of Ross.

After the death of the queen in 1486 Rothesay remained with his brothers at Stirling, in what to the fourteen-year-old heir was probably an irksome isolation from the court, and under the continuing guardianship of James Shaw. Shaw was a kinsman of the Humes, influential among a group of nobles hostile to the king. Disaffection turned into outright rebellion when, on 2 February 1488, Shaw delivered the heir to the throne to the king's opponents, not as a helpless victim of events but as a willing participant.

The reasons for the rebellion were mixed and personal: James III had antagonized many influential men, partly by excluding them from his inner council, but in many cases also by individual slights; the prince's motivation fits this general pattern. It is unlikely that the king's enemies were at first united in planning to depose him; certainly Rothesay's declared desire, at least until the later stages, was to have his circumstances raised to befit his rank as heir to the throne. But attitudes hardened during the ensuing military and diplomatic manoeuvres, and when the opportunity arose to make his peace with his father the prince elected to stay with the rebels. James III's death, in or after a minor engagement at Sauchieburn on 11 June 1488, may have been accidental, and was in any case in direct contravention of his son's explicit instructions; but the new king subsequently accepted moral responsibility for the deed by wearing an iron belt, an act of penance which lasted for the rest of his life.

Domestic politics, 1488–1494 James was crowned at Scone on 24 June 1488, and a few days afterwards attended his father's burial at Cambuskenneth, then returned to Stirling, where he attended a mass for his mother. At Stirling, according to Robert Lindsay of Pitscottie, James professed remorse for his part in his father's death to the dean of the Chapel Royal, George Vaus, and imposed on himself the penance of the iron belt; however, it was not until 1496 that he endowed masses for his father's soul.

The king's fellow rebels—especially Patrick Hepburn, second Lord Hailes (shortly afterwards created earl of Bothwell and admiral of Scotland), his kin, and adherents—had assumed immediate control of the offices of state, and proceeded to consolidate their grip on the machinery of government and the administration of patronage. Colin Campbell, earl of Argyll, resumed the chancellorship from which he had been dismissed the previous February. Hailes's uncle, John Hepburn, prior of St Andrews, became keeper of the privy seal, Alexander, master of Hume, became chamberlain, and William Knollis, preceptor of Torphichen, was appointed treasurer. Robert Blackadder, bishop of Glasgow, although not rewarded with office, assumed a prominent role in the council which lasted until his death in 1508. Archibald Douglas, fifth earl of Angus, was named as James's governor, although his place in the government was short-lived, and custody of the king and his brother soon passed to Hailes.

On 21 August 1488 James joined his new councillors at Lanark on justice ayres, which were substantially intended as a show of royal authority and a means of publicly associating that authority with the Hepburns and their allies. James would again attend the ayres early in 1489, and on many occasions subsequently.

The first parliament of the reign convened on 6 October 1488. The parliamentary register provides a unique glimpse of the assembly at work, in its record of a set-piece debate on the causes of Sauchieburn which assigned full responsibility to James III and his 'perverse' councillors. The estates, dominated by the Hepburns and their allies, largely confirmed the new dispositions of power, and conferred legitimacy on the regime, which tightened its hold on government and stepped up the prosecution of the late king's supporters, a process which continued for some months, and especially in the subsequent parliament, held in June 1489. The result was to provoke to rebellion not only a substantial body of James III's former adherents, based in the north and centred around Alexander Gordon, master of Huntly, and Alexander, fourth Lord Forbes, who raised as his standard the late king's bloodstained shirt, but also a powerful group of western magnates, notably Matthew Stewart, master of Lennox, and Robert, second Lord Lyle, who had initially been loyal to the new regime but had become disaffected by the concentration of power in the hands of a small, narrowly based clique. In addition other influential figures such as the earls of Angus and Argyll were either being frozen out by the regime or were wavering in their support for it.

The western lords moved first: in mid-April 1489. Government forces dispatched against them enjoyed initial successes, then settled down to an intermittent two-month siege of Dumbarton Castle, which failed to prevent the northern forces joining the defenders in mid-September and ended only when the rebels emerged and attempted to advance on Stirling, where James was in residence, in an attempt to seize the king's person. This advance was checked by the royal forces at Gartloaning on 11–12 October, with James himself present in the field. However, the effect of this victory was limited and local, and the principal rebels were free to continue their opposition. The siege of Dumbarton rumbled on until December without the castle actually falling; the government was compelled to seek a reconciliation, and, in the parliament which met on 3 February 1490, forfeitures on the principal rebels were reversed and legislation—drafted by a large and representative committee of the estates—included the nomination of a similarly representative minority council.

However, the influence of Bothwell and his associates still predominated, and dissatisfaction persisted, as did the suspicion that James III's treasure had been looted by members of the new government. The mutterings took formal shape in the parliament held on 6 February 1492, where an act all but accused the 1488 government of embezzling the late king's hoard, and charged sheriffs to conduct local investigations as to the fate of the money. Another act resurrected the issue of responsibility for James III's death, and offered rewards for information concerning his killers.

Neither of those acts appears to have had any significant effect, and were probably more the outcome of ill-tempered debates than practical measures. But six months later there began a gradual but far-reaching reshuffle of the minority council, with a weakening of the Hepburn ranks far more drastic than in 1490. Out went Knollis, made a scapegoat for the peculation of the 1488 government, real or imagined; his successor as treasurer was Henry Arnot, abbot of Cambuskenneth—a former supporter of James III. John Hepburn resigned the privy seal to William Elphinstone, another James III man; and on the death of Argyll at the end of 1492 the chancellorship was filled by the earl of Angus. Angus's return from the political wilderness coincided with, and may have been assisted by, James's liaison with the earl's niece, Marion Boyd, daughter of Archibald Boyd of Naristoun, which began about August 1492. Marion Boyd would bear James two children, Alexander *Stewart (b. c.1493; created archbishop of St Andrews in 1504) and Katherine (b. 1494). The affair had ended by late 1495, when the king married Marion off to John Muir of Rowallan.

A priority for the new administration was the imposition of royal authority in the north and west of Scotland. The ineffectiveness of John MacDonald, lord of the Isles, and the disorder caused by power struggles among his kin had culminated in a destructive raid on Inverness in 1491, and drastic retaliation by the Mackenzies, ostensibly in the name of the king. As a first step, in the parliament held in May 1493 the lordship of the Isles was forfeited and its estates annexed to the crown; John MacDonald remained at James's court as a royal pensioner. However, for the crown to establish order—and be able to enjoy the estates of the lordship—it needed to impose effective control over the chieftains. Shortly thereafter James and his council made a brief expedition north to receive oaths of loyalty from the north-western chiefs (probably at Dunstaffnage, on or about 18 August), in some measure to reassure them, and generally to show the young king to his subjects in the west and—after a brief break—in and around Inverness in October and November. For his part James was exposed at first hand to highland culture and the Gaelic tongue, in which he developed an enduring interest.

The government subsequently attempted to maintain a grip on the area by backing first Alexander Macdonald of Islay, then John MacIan of Ardnamurchan, both contenders in the continuing power vacuum. Aware that such loose cannons were uncertain allies without a royal presence in the area James and his council returned to the Isles briefly in May 1494, and in the following July a substantial royal force sailed from Dumbarton to repair, victual, and garrison the castles at Tarbert and Dunaverty.

The daunting of the Isles Even though in March 1494 James had attained the age of twenty-one he appears thus far to have left policy largely to his council: he was present as required, and was no doubt well tutored in the essentials by his advisers, but he did not try to set his own stamp upon it. The government thus remained essentially unchanged, and its policies to a large extent coincided with the interests of its leading members, notably Bothwell until 1492, Angus thereafter. In 1495, however, James himself assumed control of its direction, and the emphasis of policy switched smartly away from domestic concerns towards the international arena. James now returned to the problem of the north and the Isles with impatience, and a more radical response.

Of James's councillors the earl of Argyll was the pre-eminent lord in the north and west, and as such was in theory the crown's natural right-hand man in the area. Earl Archibald, who had succeeded his father in late 1492,

had been excluded from the government largely as a result of Angus's territorial ambitions in the west; now, however, Angus's influence was on the wane, and Argyll, created master of the household in March 1495, came to prominence on the council. At the same time John, Lord Drummond, who had been one of the 1488 rebels but who had also been sidelined under the Angus administration, was restored to favour, being appointed justiciar in or before February of that year. Drummond may have been helped into royal favour by his links, through marriage, to Argyll. But he was probably also assisted by the fact that, at about this time, his daughter, Margaret *Drummond, became the mistress of the king, who publicly maintained her at Stirling from June 1496, and with whom he had a daughter, Margaret. James ended the affair in the following March. Angus remained chancellor until late 1497, when he was succeeded by the second earl of Huntly.

The next expedition to the west followed the pattern of the previous one. In late 1494 James initiated extensive naval and military preparations, and summoned a force which met at Glasgow and, on 5 May 1495, embarked at Dumbarton and sailed via Bute and Kintyre to Mingary Castle, the stronghold of John MacIan of Ardnamurchan. There the chieftains rendered allegiance to the king, who confirmed some of them in their tenure of crown lands following the (routine) general revocation of 26 June 1493.

James returned from the Isles in early June 1495, and his attention then turned to international diplomacy and a military expedition into England. In the meantime, faced with the difficulty of extending royal justice to the former lordship, the council—probably on Argyll's initiative—from October 1496 adopted a new, aggressive policy, one of making chieftains responsible for the execution of summonses on their clan members on pain of themselves being personally summoned as defendants.

In March 1498 James visited the castle he had caused to be built at Kilkerran since his last expedition; then, on 20 March, at Duchal, he issued another general revocation, consequent on his having attained the age of twenty-five. James intended to use this opportunity to draw the highland chieftains systematically into the scheme of royal patronage; accordingly, in May and again in late June, he returned to Kilkerran, on the latter occasion for a six-week stay, along with the council, waiting for the chiefs to render homage and receive confirmation of their lands and titles. But whereas the rhythm of revocation and confirmation was familiar to lowland landholders it was a concept alien to the highland chiefs, some of whom had in any case only recently received—and paid for—such confirmation, and were alarmed by the apparently casual repetition of the process; consequently, few turned up. Underwhelmed and no doubt angry James left Kilkerran in early August, never to return; thereafter he left the settlement of the Isles to others, now with a remit to take more ruthless measures.

The first of those crown agents was MacIan of Ardnamurchan, who in July 1499 sacked the Macdonald stronghold of Finlaggan and captured John Macdonald of Islay and his three sons. In 1494 John of Islay—one of the heirs to the independent lordship—had rebelled against the extension of royal influence in the Isles, and especially in the government's backing of his rivals. He had been summoned for treason, but not taken; now he and his sons were dispatched to Edinburgh, where they were executed.

In April 1500 Argyll was created royal lieutenant within the lordship for three years, and in August 1501 a rather vaguer—and open-ended—lieutenancy was given to Alexander Gordon, newly succeeded to the earldom of Huntly, a highly ambitious magnate who, unburdened by the complex ties of kinship which were already hampering Argyll's effectiveness in the lordship, was able and eager vigorously to extend the crown's authority—and his own advantage—in the region. However the force with which he exercised his commission—including the forcible imposition of new, biddable, crown tenants—exacerbated the unrest fomented by Argyll's brother-in-law Torquil MacLeod of Lewis, and focused on the restoration of the independent lordship in the person of Donald Dubh MacDonald, the young illegitimate grandson of John of the Isles. The death of the latter in January 1503 strengthened the cause of his grandson—then aged about twelve—and by the end of the year the extent of the insurrection, and the lieutenant's evident failure to end it, forced James to summon a parliament, which convened on 15 March 1504. In it James issued another revocation, which this time included not only royal grants, but also statutes thus far promulgated by him or in his name. The estates then approved war plans, the proscription of traitors, and an attempt to make certain chiefs of uncertain loyalty demonstrate their allegiance to the crown.

A fleet was then made ready at Dumbarton, under James's personal supervision; on about 20 April it sailed, under the command of Andrew Wood, to besiege Cairnna-Burgh Castle, beyond Mull, where Donald Dubh was believed to be held. James did not accompany the expedition but kept abreast of developments, initially at Stirling, from where, on 11 May, he dispatched James Hamilton, earl of Arran, to the siege in command of an additional vessel. By late June the castle had been taken—no mean feat—and Argyll placed in charge of it; however Donald Dubh, the object of the exercise, was not there, but was in fact being held by Torquil MacLeod in his stronghold of Stornoway Castle.

The demonstration of James's artillery and naval power, and the threats of forfeiture, gradually brought about the submission of most of the highland chiefs. Torquil MacLeod remained in rebellion: in a parliament convened in February 1506 he was tried and sentenced for treason in his absence; in the following June a force commanded by Huntly sailed to Lewis and by early September Stornoway had fallen, its owner had fled, and Donald Dubh was safely warded in royal custody. Thereafter James was content to delegate royal authority in the highlands to Argyll—after a shaky start—and, above all, to Huntly whose role in pacifying the north had made him vastly and uniquely wealthy and powerful.

Treaty negotiations, 1488–1493 The dominant influence among James's minority government was that of border lords whose regional autonomy benefited enormously from continuing hostility between the English and Scottish kings, and who had thus been opposed to the attempts by James III and his advisers to make a lasting peace with England. Consequently the government which took power in 1488 negotiated with Henry VII only a three-year truce in the interests of immediate security. Meanwhile it succoured Yorkist rebels and sought a renewal of alliance with France, and also a continental bride for James; the October 1488 parliament sanctioned the raising of tax to fund embassies to France, Spain, Denmark, and other countries.

The tax proved hard to collect, and the embassies to Denmark and France were in consequence delayed until early 1492. The Spanish ambassadors, however, came to Scotland in 1489: they initially offered James the hand of the infanta, Katherine, but in this they exceeded their mandate, which was in respect only of an illegitimate daughter of Ferdinand of Aragon, so their embassy was fruitless. The embassy to Denmark renewed what was essentially a trading alliance against Sweden and its ally, Lübeck. The renewal of the Franco-Scottish treaty—which did not provide for a royal marriage—was ratified on 4 March 1492, but effectively became obsolete after 3 November of the same year when, by the treaty of Étaples, England was at peace with France, and Scotland had once again become irrelevant to French foreign policy. By the end of 1492 the pro-French policy of the Bothwell government had lost its appeal, its protagonists had lost their ascendancy in government, and Elphinstone was able to resume his attempts to secure lasting peace with England where he had left off in 1487.

For his part Henry VII was anxious to prevent Scottish support for Yorkist rebels and, after 1491, for the pretender Perkin Warbeck. In the early years of the reign Henry worked covertly with certain Scots—notably the rebels of 1489, the earl of Buchan, John Ramsay (who had been a favourite and trusted agent of James III), and even Angus—who either favoured an alliance with England or who sought outside assistance to recover lost influence in Scotland. But after 1492 it had become clear that the Scottish government was too securely in power to be overturned or destabilized in this manner; consequently in May 1493 Henry VII sought a marriage treaty. The proposed bride was Katherine, a granddaughter of Edmund Tudor, earl of Richmond. Although a kinswoman of the king she was not a princess, and thus was unacceptable to James, who turned elsewhere in the search for a marriage alliance. Nevertheless James's government managed to conclude a series of truces with England which, despite local outbreaks of hostility and one armed incursion, maintained stability between the two kingdoms until 1502.

Armed adventure, 1495–1497 In 1495 James assumed personal rule. Throughout his minority he had interspersed his participation in the business of government with aristocratic outdoor pursuits, notably hawking and the chase; on several occasions he had taken the field against his countrymen in engagements which, however undistinguished, had nevertheless been successful, and had recently mounted an impressive demonstration of military and naval might in the Isles. Now aged twenty-two he was keen to make a vigorous mark both in diplomacy and as a military leader. Henry VII read the signs and ordered strengthening of border defences against a possible (although in this case chimerical) Scottish attack.

Thus, even while many of his closest advisers were working towards long-term peace with England, James was considering giving support to Perkin Warbeck. The threat of such assistance was a bargaining counter in attempts to negotiate a continental marriage treaty, first, in June 1495, with Warbeck's then supporter, the emperor-elect, Maximilian, the intended bride being Maximilian's daughter, Margaret. The mission was unproductive, and in the following month James reopened marriage negotiations with Spain, whose rulers, Ferdinand and Isabella, were seeking an alliance with England against France, had no intention of making a dynastic treaty with Scotland, but hoped by prevarication to keep Scotland from invading England, freeing Henry VII to attack France. By mid-October James had learned this humiliating fact by intercepting the diplomatic bag, and was so piqued that he immediately upped the stakes, receiving Warbeck at court on 20 November as Richard, duke of York, and humiliating the Spanish ambassadors in his presence. In January 1496 Warbeck was married to Katherine Gordon, a daughter of the earl of Huntly; James participated in the jousting which accompanied the wedding, and was lightly but honourably injured in the hand.

While thus dramatically—and expensively—demonstrating his support for the pretender James renewed his efforts to secure a marriage alliance with Ferdinand and Isabella, but without success. At the same time Henry VII, eager to put an end to the threat, renewed his attempts to subvert the impending invasion using the services of his collaborators Buchan, Ramsay, and others, and also to make a lasting peace with Scotland, this time offering a daughter of his own. By this time James had determined on a show of force to demonstrate that he meant business; accordingly, on 20 September 1496, with the king in command and Warbeck in tow, the Scots host crossed into Northumberland. The invasion did nothing for the pretender's cause, and only five days later it was quickly cut short on the approach of the first substantial English force. However, considered as a large-scale border raid it worked rather well, reducing several castles and providing the expected opportunities for plunder; it also allowed James to show himself to foreign rulers and his subjects as a military leader, a role which he played with some bravery and deeply enjoyed.

On 5 November James received word that Henry VII had declared war on him, and he duly prepared to defend the borders. In the event, however, it was not until the following July that Henry, delayed by domestic crisis, was ready to act, by which date James had made extensive preparations, strengthening border strongholds, massing the heavy artillery in which he took such a close interest, and mounting—and personally leading—raids across the border.

In the interim peace negotiations had been conducted, but James wanted a further show of military strength: in July 1497 he sent Warbeck back to Ireland, thus disposing of the major point of contention and simplifying the nature of the contest to one of defending the realm. There ensued a series of sporadic and inconclusive manoeuvres which lasted from 20 July for about a month, enlivened by James IV's challenge to the English commander, Thomas Howard, earl of Surrey, to decide by single combat the fate of Berwick (which was not otherwise relevant to the conflict but had been a sore point with Scottish kings since its capture by the English in 1482), a challenge which was not taken up.

The whole exercise had been immensely costly to both kings. James had been fully stretched both financially and in terms of manpower, and even if it had not ended in military disaster the episode could easily have undone twenty years' painstaking work towards a lasting Anglo-Scottish peace. Yet he had managed to mount a series of audacious raids, and to elude retribution, enhancing his prestige at home and—he hoped—abroad. Henry VII immediately reopened peace negotiations, which resulted in a seven years' truce, concluded on 30 September 1497 and subsequently extended to expire a year after the death of whichever of the two kings outlived the other, and fortified by the nomination of Ferdinand and Isabella as arbitrators.

The Anglo-Scottish treaty and its consequences, 1498–1507 By 1498 the two kings were in broad agreement about a peace treaty cemented by marriage between James and Henry's daughter; the negotiations nevertheless took a further four years to complete. Meanwhile James had other consolations as, in 1498 or 1499, he began a long-lasting liaison with Janet Kennedy, the daughter of John, second Lord Kennedy, and at that time mistress of the earl of Angus. James installed her at Darnaway Castle, and, in or around 1500, she bore him a son, James *Stewart, created earl of Moray in the following year. This relationship continued after James's marriage. Thereafter James had other mistresses of whom one is identifiable: Isabel Stewart, daughter of the earl of Buchan, with whom he had a daughter, Janet.

In 1502 James received a call for military assistance from his uncle King Hans of Denmark, who was faced with revolt in Sweden and Norway; a force of 200 men was duly raised and sent to Denmark, under the command of Alexander, Lord Hume; although, through difficulty in raising the necessary taxation, and in gathering ships and men, the force was smaller than James originally intended; in the event the force did not acquit itself well, and the mission was unsuccessful.

The Anglo-Scottish treaty, which Henry ratified on 24

January 1502 and James on 22 February following, provided for the marriage of James to Henry's eldest daughter, *Margaret (1489–1541); it also specified detailed procedures for dealing with breaches of the peace; significantly, it also bore the intention to seek papal confirmation—granted by Alexander VI on 28 May 1503—and a declaration that whichever king broke the treaty would be excommunicated.

The marriage of James IV and Margaret Tudor was duly celebrated at Holyrood on 8 August 1503, with much pomp and festivity which left the English guests studiedly unimpressed—according to Edward Hall they 'returned into their countrey, gevynge more prayse to the manhoode, than to the good maner and nurture of Scotlande' (Mackie, 112). James, who marked the occasion with gifts to his bride which included a magnificent illuminated book of hours specially made in Flanders (it is now in the Österreichische Nationalbibliothek, Vienna), did not abandon his affairs with other women, and was on one occasion rebuked by the poet William Dunbar for his neglect of 'that sweit meik Rois' (Mackie, 176), but he also gave signs of affection and trust towards his queen. He probably named a ship after her, and on new year's day 1507 gave her a jewelled 'serpent's tongue' as a safeguard against poisoning, and when she was seriously ill shortly afterwards following the birth of their first child he went on pilgrimage to Whithorn to pray for her recovery, and in his will named her regent of the kingdom as long as she remained unmarried. James and Margaret had five children, of whom the first three did not survive infancy: James (b. 21 February 1507, d. 27 February 1508); a girl (b. July 1508, d. the same month); and Arthur (b. October 1509, d. June 1510). The fourth child, *James (later James V) was born on 10 April 1512, and a further son, Alexander, duke of Ross, was born on 30 April 1514, after his father's death.

Before 1504 James's naval building and maintenance centred on Dumbarton, for operations in the Isles. The defences of the eastern seaboard, and other navigation from eastern Scottish ports, were left to private vessels under the capable and largely autonomous direction of the Barton brothers, Andrew, Robert, and John. However, the difficulties of raising sufficient ships for the Danish expedition of 1502 led James to supplement this arrangement by constructing some large ships of his own, using imported French expertise, beginning with the *Margaret*, built at Leith in 1504–5. In May 1504 James was rowed out in a boat to look for the site of what would become the royal dockyard at New Haven of Leith; a further dockyard was constructed at Pool of Airth by 1506. James's great flagship, the *Michael*, was built in 1506–11, and was launched in 1512. The big ships were prestige items on a colossal scale, statements of James's power and confidence. Their construction was a demonstration of continuing amity with France, and in so far as they were intended for national defence, the likely enemy—despite the 1502 treaty—remained England.

For James the year 1507 was a high point in international affairs. The peace with England appeared to be holding, and in February the queen had given birth to a son. On 4 April James received from Pope Julius II the symbolic gifts of a sword and a hat as a mark of papal favour. In that year also James helped to broker a truce between Denmark and Lübeck, and adroitly sidestepped an attempt by Louis XII to secure Scottish armed assistance against the papacy in his Italian wars.

Government and law One of the major achievements of James's reign was the rapid development of the central civil courts. To meet an increasing demand for royal justice the existing parliamentary committee of lords auditors was inadequate; James III's council tried to supplement the auditors' sittings, but by 1487 found themselves swamped by the volume of business. After 1488 the roles were reversed, the council becoming the principal tribunal for which the auditors acted as a clearing-house, and by 1496 the parliamentary committee had fallen into disuse. Between 1497 and 1504 the council reorganized itself in order to hold longer diets or sessions, mostly but not exclusively in Edinburgh, as well as interim sittings wherever the court happened to be. More lords were drafted in and a rota organized; an attempt was also made to schedule hearings in a coherent manner. The place of the session thus reorganized was ratified by an act of the March 1504 parliament.

The lords themselves received a share of fines—a token amount—but were otherwise unpaid. They included a few with legal training, mostly clerics, but mostly and increasingly they were laymen whose practical experience gained in the baronial courts was consolidated and augmented in the course of their work on the council. In 1495 James had sponsored Bishop Elphinstone's foundation of Aberdeen University, which its founder hoped would develop a strong school of law. This did not happen, and it was to Padua and elsewhere on the continent that James's son Alexander, the archbishop-elect, was in 1507 dispatched to further his education. In an attempt to improve the quality of justice in the local courts an act of 1496 required substantial landowners to send their eldest sons to grammar schools and thereafter to university. Although of no immediate systematic effect it sought to encourage an existing and continuing trend among the baronage.

In the early years of his reign James himself attended council sittings when important causes were being heard; this was probably at the behest of his advisers, for the practice ceased after June 1494, at about the time that James started to assert his personal rule, and was not resumed while he was preoccupied with foreign and military affairs. Between January 1503 and April 1505, however, James again attended the lords' meetings, this time sitting in on primarily routine business, and on a day-to-day basis, watching and taking note.

Throughout James's reign, in marked contrast to his father's, the ayres were regularly dispatched around the country dispensing royal justice, sometimes with James himself in attendance. He might intervene decisively in local feuds—notably in the long-running Cunningham–Montgomery conflict in Ayrshire, which was defused, though not ended, by a 1499 judgment in justice ayre—or dispense summary justice to criminals, as at Jedburgh in 1510. Sometimes James's personal touch in administering royal justice assumed more dramatic form, as when, in August 1504, he joined forces with the English warden of the west march, Thomas, second Baron Dacre, for an expedition into Eskdale which interspersed hanging of wrongdoers with falconry and gambling.

In the early years of the reign nine parliaments were held, more than one a year; however, during the eighteen years of his adult rule James summoned only four parliaments. After the parliament of June 1496 there was a gap of nearly eight years until the next, held in March 1504, which was summoned in consequence of the insurrection in the north and west, to provide support for the king in an emergency, one which would probably involve treason proceedings. Thereafter until the end of the reign there were only two more: one held in February 1506, largely to deal with the trial and forfeiture of Torquil MacLeod, the other in May 1509 to acknowledge the viceregal position of the earl of Huntly in the north. When formal business had to be transacted James preferred the more flexible, more quickly convened, and often single issue general councils, or even casually afforced sittings of the daily council, to the wider ranging, cumbersome talking shops which parliaments could so easily become.

There is little evidence that the political nation felt deprived by this state of affairs: James's privy council was broad enough in its composition to accommodate a wide range of interests across estates, regions, and affinities. In the earliest years of the reign it was narrowly based and dominated by the leading political factions, but after 1490 the membership expanded until by 1497 it included representatives of the main regions and political alignments almost as a matter of course. At its core throughout the reign was a small group of the royal officers, notably the keeper of the privy seal, the clerk register, and the director of chancery, officials vital to the smooth administration of patronage.

Beyond the council itself was the wider group of royal familiars from the great magnates to minor servants. James enjoyed informal contact, and a great deal of business would have been transacted, or at least broached, in casual meetings, above all, perhaps, during the games of cards and dice at which James constantly played his courtiers, whether they were in political favour or not. A style of government more different from his father's is hard to imagine.

Crown finances James's reign began with the windfall of James III's massive treasure hoard, which had been secreted in assorted safe places with various custodians; but by 1492 that was all gone, eroded perhaps by embezzlement, but mostly spent on the legitimate expenses of government. The military activities in the early years of the reign, and especially expenditure on ships, ordnance, and fortification, required ready cash; by the mid-1490s James was reduced to pawning valuables

and, in order to defend the borders against English retaliation in 1497, he not only had to invite voluntary donations but also to melt down some personal jewellery.

Traditional means of raising revenue were of little help. Taxation was regularly granted—usually by the estates in parliament—but only for specific purposes like an embassy or military preparations, and sometimes with reluctance, while its collection was often slow and uncertain, especially in the case of ambassadorial levies, where by the turn of the century a succession of fruitless marriage treaty negotiations had engendered what can only be called embassy fatigue among the taxpaying classes. The customs and rents levied in the royal burghs were static, and in any case mostly assigned at source as annuities and other payments to individuals, so very little disposable cash actually reached the crown from that source.

Yet during his reign James, ably served by an increasingly professional team of financial specialists, was able to extract a remarkable amount of additional revenue. Several techniques were used, none of them new, but under James IV applied more extensively and systematically. The crown was able to extract much additional revenue from feudal casualties, specifically from a number of legal niceties which worked in its favour. Notable among those, and most widely detested, was 'recognition', the rule whereby if a tenant alienated without licence more than half the lands he held in feudal tenure the lands so alienated could be resumed by the crown. The crown also extracted considerable sums by way of remissions for crimes, in some instances pursuing individuals for offences committed in the otherwise forgotten past.

Careful resetting of crown leases provided additional revenue, but more substantial increases resulted from the replacement of leases with feu charters, which, in return for a composition and an annual feu duty, gave the feuar a greater measure of tenurial security. The practice was in use even before James III's reign, albeit fairly infrequently, but became common after explicit sanction was given by an act of the March 1504 parliament. Its extensive application in the last decade of the reign gave the crown an immediate increase in revenues, albeit one which declined in real terms as the feu duties remained static. Successive revocations of grants of lands and offices made in the king's name—notably that of March 1498, when James attained the age of twenty-five—also offered prospects of a substantial increase in revenues through the compositions routinely paid for confirmations.

Under James IV increase in royal revenue was matched by a measure of institutional refinement as the Scottish exchequer took significant steps in its development from an event into an institution. James III's exchequer had no regular staff, and its auditors lacked the autonomy, or at least the effective liaison with the king's inner council, necessary to conduct their business with efficiency. However, between July 1488 and 1490 James IV's councillors—determined not only to exercise a tight grip on royal patronage but also, almost obsessively, to track down the late king's treasure and to scrutinize the grants made in the last months of his reign—ran the exchequer effectively as a function of the king's council. By 1492 this hands-on control had ceased, and the composition of the audits once again assumed a less exalted character; but the lasting legacy was that the auditors continued to exercise a greater degree of autonomy than they had done before 1488. It still lacked either a fixed venue or an establishment, but in the course of the reign it acquired a small core of regular staff seconded for the purpose.

The exactions were understandably disliked—the exploitation of feudal casualties especially; but James was sufficiently popular to evade personal blame. Unlike his reclusive father with his secret hoards, moreover, James IV spent visibly, in ways to which his subjects could relate: lavish display at court, notably his wedding in 1503; on ordnance; and, above all, the navy. It is estimated that James's annual disposable revenue increased from about £4500 Scots in 1497 to about £44,500 in 1513; over the same period the annual spending on naval building and maintenance rose from about £140 to over £8700. It is estimated also that in 1513 his annual overspend was around £7000.

Church and state A man of conventionally pious sensibilities, James was reported by John Knox to have presided in person in 1494 at the trial of a number of suspected Lollards from Kyle. By then he was already going on regular pilgrimages, at least once a year to the shrine of St Ninian at Whithorn from 1491, while from October 1493 he also went to that of St Duthac at Tain. The pilgrimages themselves, far from being austerities, were social affairs, attended by friends, courtiers, and musicians; but in this James was not unusual among his contemporaries, and the religious element in these devotions was doubtless sincere.

In 1507 James declared his intention of going on a pilgrimage to the Holy Land, and made some preparations accordingly, but he appears to have dropped the idea after 1508. In and after 1509 James repeatedly expressed a desire to participate in a Europe-wide crusade against the Turks; the idea may have held considerable appeal for him, but the evidence that he actually took practical steps to achieve this is suspect.

James supported the Observantine Friars, founding a house at Stirling in 1495 and probably others elsewhere. Their strict regime impressed him, and he frequently used their Stirling house as a place of retreat. He founded the church of Ladykirk, in Upsettlington, Berwickshire, in thanksgiving for a narrow escape from drowning in the Tweed in 1496 or 1497. In 1501 James erected the Chapel Royal at Stirling as a collegiate church, organized as a cathedral in miniature, and presided over by George Vaus, subsequently styled bishop of Galloway and the Chapel Royal. Its establishment was large enough to give unprecedented scope for the development of polyphonic liturgical music, and it is likely that the earliest works of Robert Carver, who seems to have joined the chapel about 1508, were written for performance there.

Although in James IV's reign laymen were increasingly involved in the royal administration James, like his predecessors, and like other contemporary European monarchs, relied predominantly on clerics as administrators, and consequently was dependent upon the church's career structure to support his civil service. It was therefore of paramount importance to James to have his nominees appointed. By custom, following on from an indult granted by Innocent VIII in 1487 the procedure had developed whereby the king could in normal circumstances nominate his candidate for a cathedral benefice or headship of a major monastery, and the papacy would then provide the nominee to the post. This custom was jealously protected by the crown, and was formally promulgated in a statute of 1493; similarly laws against unauthorized petitions for benefices at Rome and other independent recourse to the papal curia were reiterated in acts of 1488, 1493, and 1496. Throughout the reign, although there were a few contests by individuals well connected at Rome, James had effectively free rein to exploit the church in this way, and unblushingly rewarded his servants with bishoprics, abbacies, and lucrative benefices. Inevitably the church itself suffered, as its resources were diverted from pastoral care, and the charge of religious houses increasingly given to absent commendators.

On 9 January 1492 parliament resolved that the see of Glasgow be elevated to an archbishopric with status equivalent to the diocese of York. There was no sound spiritual or administrative reason for this divisive elevation, which was the result of Bishop Blackadder's personal ascendancy after 1488, and of the simultaneous fall from favour of Archbishop William Scheves of St Andrews. The resulting litigation at Rome mounted by both archbishops was expensive, public, and embarrassing. On Scheves's death in 1497 James took the radical step of appointing to the see of St Andrews his twenty-year-old brother, James, duke of Ross, who even after taking holy orders could not be consecrated until 1507 at the earliest. When Ross died suddenly in January 1504 James appointed his eleven-year-old son Alexander Stewart to the see; Alexander was already destined for the church, and, had he lived, might have turned out to be an admirable archbishop. In any case, between 1497 and 1504 the temporalities of St Andrews were at James's disposal, as was the income from the assorted benefices which the under-age archbishops held as commendators; moreover the likelihood of archiepiscopal intervention in appointments to vacancies was greatly reduced.

Culture and patronage The late fifteenth and early sixteenth centuries in Scotland witnessed a flowering of literary culture, both Latin and vernacular. In James IV's reign this culture became associated with the court, partly as a result of James's own patronage, and partly because his court was frequented by other patrons. This court culture encompassed an eclectic mix reflecting James's own wide-ranging tastes, from clowns and dancers through musicians to poets like Gavin Douglas and William Dunbar and theologians such as John Ireland. Many of the literati were in one capacity or another active in the king's service: James's own secretaries, Archibald Whitelaw and

Patrick Panter, were Latin stylists of international standing.

James was a considerable patron of architecture, for both military and domestic purposes. Thus to strengthen his authority in the west he built a castle at Kilkerran in Kintyre, and he also financed important programmes of works on some of his palaces. Thus at Linlithgow both the public and private apartments were substantially reshaped, and a splendid entrance constructed. A new great hall was built at Edinburgh Castle, with a hammer-beam roof probably derived from English models, though other details show French influence. James had a tower built at Holyrood, while at Stirling he commissioned a towered forework protecting the approaches to the castle, and a new hall within, again with a hammerbeam roof.

Pedro de Ayala, the Spanish ambassador, wrote that James was able to speak Latin very well, French, German, Flemish, Italian, Spanish, and Gaelic. James's hunting and touring brought him into contact with his highland subjects, in whose Gaelic tongue and culture he had an abiding interest: he employed highland musicians and bards to entertain him.

James was fascinated by technological innovation. In 1507 he licensed Walter Chepman and Andrew Millar to set up a printing press in Edinburgh for the publication of laws, statutes, and chronicles, and particularly Scottish liturgical works: he supported Bishop Elphinstone's efforts to develop a Scottish 'use' independent of that of Sarum. Elphinstone's own *Aberdeen breviary* was published in 1509 and 1510. James also devoted much time and money to developing effective artillery, while his intellectual curiosity extended to medicine and to surgery—this included dentistry, James at least once drew a courtier's tooth. More exotically he sponsored the French alchemist John Damian in his whisky-fuelled search for the elixir of life and a famously unsuccessful attempt to fly, and made him abbot of Tongland. But not all his tastes were avant-garde. He shared with most other rulers of his time an enthusiasm for tournaments and other trappings of chivalric culture, both, it would seem, for their own sake and as a means of uniting his court and nobility around himself. Hence the 'counterfutting of the round tabill of King Arthour of Ingland' staged at Edinburgh in early summer 1508 (Macdougall, *James IV*, 295). James jousted enthusiastically, winning a European reputation for himself and his court.

Diplomacy and war, 1507–1513 For much of his reign James made a good showing in international politics; however, from 1507 events began to conspire against him. First, from that year Anglo-Scottish accord, already fairly superficial, began to be challenged by a series of incidents, including the capture and detention of Arran, James's returning ambassador to France, by the English, suspicious of the purpose of that embassy. James treated the English ambassador (the young Thomas Wolsey) in an offhand manner, but managed to persuade him that Scotland would not break its treaty with England; however, the continuing warmth in the diplomatic dealings between James and Louis XII so alarmed Henry VII that he interrogated James's ambassador to France, Gavin Dunbar, when the latter was shipwrecked on his homeward voyage, and also made preparations for the defence of Berwick.

In 1509, on the accession of Henry VIII, the treaty of 1502 was renewed, but the young king's character brought a newly abrasive element into Anglo-Scottish relations, while in the following year Pope Julius II converted the League of Cambrai, founded against Venice, into an anti-French alliance. The amity between Scotland and France continued despite the 1502 treaty, to which James, and many other Scots with him, had no deep attachment. The persisting enmity between France and the papacy, with both of whom Scotland wished to stay friends, was potentially dangerous, and James attempted without success to mediate between the two. There was a steady deterioration in relations between James and Henry, exacerbated by the tone of their correspondence: James's often peevish and intemperate, Henry's contemptuous and arrogant. When in autumn 1511 Henry VIII joined the new Holy League against France, the lethal combination was nearly complete. In an attempt to discourage Henry from attacking his country Louis sought with lavish promises to persuade James to make a new treaty with France which, unlike the 1492 alliance, contained a provision that if England made war on either country the other would make war on England. In July 1512, after much deliberation, and no doubt enraged by the English parliament's reassertion of overlordship in the previous January, James agreed.

One must suppose that James hoped that the mere fact of concluding the treaty would cause Henry VIII to take him more seriously, and that Louis might not require assistance. He almost certainly assumed that even if he acted on the new treaty Julius II would not excommunicate his favoured son. If so he mistook all three men and the complex relationship between them. In February 1513, shortly before he died, Julius issued letters, as he was bound to do by the 1502 treaty, ordering James's excommunication should he attack England. Despite James's strenuous efforts to have it revoked the new pope, Leo X, confirmed this suspended sentence.

Perhaps assuming that James would thus be restrained from attacking England, Henry sailed to France on 30 June 1513. Now honour bound to act on the 1512 treaty James stepped up war preparations, which had been steadily increasing since 1507. Regardless of the sentence of excommunication the war was popular: of the council only Elphinstone and Angus spoke out against it.

On 25 July the Scots fleet, under Arran's command, set sail for France via the Pentland Firth and the west coast. James then dispatched an ultimatum to Henry VIII, who was then engaged in the siege of Thérouanne, and summoned the host. Shortly before 24 August the Scots crossed into Northumberland and within a week had captured Norham Castle, followed by the lesser fortresses of Etal and Ford. They then took up a strong position on Flodden Hill to await the arrival of the English force, one apparently of comparable size (the exact numbers are unrecorded) commanded by the earl of Surrey. On 9 September, after an exchange of challenges, Surrey outmanoeuvred James by threatening to cut off his retreat, so forcing him to abandon his advantageous position and bring his men hastily downhill. James himself insisted on leading the attack, despite the counsel of his nobles that he stay back and direct operations; Ayala had commented that 'he is not a good captain, because he begins to fight before he has given his orders' (Macdougall, *James IV*, 286). The fine and largely new Scottish guns were swiftly overwhelmed by their more skilfully handled English counterparts, while the five massive concentrations of Scottish infantry, equipped with pikes up to 22 feet long, could not keep formation on rough and boggy ground and were broken up by the English foot soldiers, who wielded 8 foot halberds, or brown bills, to deadly effect. After a promising start, when Surrey's brother was nearly killed at the head of his men, a grimly fought battle ended in a shattering defeat for the Scots, who suffered thousands of casualties. Among them were the archbishop of St Andrews, the bishop of the Isles, nine earls, and fourteen lords, and above all King James himself, who is said to have fallen when only a spear's length from Surrey's position at the English rear. His body was sent first to Berwick and later to Richmond, but because he died excommunicate his remains were never accorded a state funeral, and were probably interred in St Paul's Cathedral, London, at an unrecorded date.

Assessment An archetypal lost leader James IV was quickly seen by posterity as a national hero, Sir David Lindsay's 'glore of princelie governyng' (Macdougall, *James IV*, 292), and his reign as a golden age tragically cut short. A considerable corpus of tales grew up around the late king, mostly presenting him as a wise, able, and much loved ruler brought to grief by evil counsel. By the 1950s he had come to be viewed as a renaissance prince, a clever but impractical dilettante whose attitudes, especially towards European politics, were those of a 'moonstruck romantic' (Mackie, 201); but writers at the end of the twentieth century emphasized the traditionally medieval and Scottish aspects of his kingship, gave him more credit for his statecraft, and even attributed the calamity of Flodden to bad luck at the last moment rather than to any deeper defects of judgement. At the beginning of the twenty-first century James IV is usually, almost automatically, cited as Scotland's most successful ruler.

The most familiar image of James—a late sixteenth-century copy by Daniel Mytens of a contemporary original—shows a lean face with retrusive chin, distinctive rather than handsome, but with memorably alert and intelligent eyes. A contemporary portrait, from the book of hours of James and his queen, shows a somewhat fuller face. Ayala described him as of average stature, 'handsome in complexion and shape' (Macdougall, *James IV*, 283), and wrote that he never trimmed his hair or beard, although the beard was shaved off on the day after his marriage.

Ayala, who was in Scotland for little more than a year

during the turbulent, eccentric episode of Perkin Warbeck and its aftermath, expressed several mostly approving opinions on James's character: on his love of war and personal bravery and recklessness, his boundless self-esteem. John Ramsay was more critical, referring to James's wilfulness—a view not inconsistent with Ayala's.

Glimpses of James through the understandably jaundiced eyes of out-of-favour foreign ambassadors reveal the king taking a malicious delight in humiliating them, or otherwise discomfiting them by eccentric, capricious, and even childish behaviour. Such treatment may have been designed to cultivate popularity among rival foreign representatives, and among his own subjects. James's accustomed amusements were probably those recorded in the treasurer's accounts, which show him at play, enjoying the traditional aristocratic sports of hunting and hawking, jousting, gambling at cards and dice, boating, playing golf, watching plays, listening to musicians.

By 1513 James IV was master within his own domains to an extent unmatched by any of his immediate predecessors. He had built up, by Scottish standards, formidable naval and artillery power, which on occasion he used against his subjects; on occasion he also dispensed justice with exemplary violence. But his mastery was based not only or even primarily on the direct exercise of royal power but also on shrewdness in his appraisal of and dealings with his magnates; pragmatic trade-offs with local and personal interests; a significant increase in institutional sophistication; and a considerable degree of personal charm. The charm was exercised not only on courtiers and diplomats, but on the ordinary folk he encountered on his extensive travels on business, pleasure, and pilgrimage. At least among his lowland subjects he was widely popular.

On the whole James showed considerable shrewdness in his dealings with his subjects and other rulers; but this was often limited, and occasionally overruled, by his impetuousness. It is perhaps instructive to compare Henry VII's forbearance in his dealings with the often rash younger king and the ease with which the middle-aged James was provoked by the taunts of Henry's arrogant teenage successor. James's performance in the international arena until 1507 was mercurial rather than assured, but none the less successful, and hardly fits the image of an innocent abroad. However, in the last few years of the reign the ground had shifted: in Louis XII and Julius II James was up against consummate masters of duplicitous statecraft, and consequently he—and Scotland—were in diplomatic terms punching far above their weight.

James would not have allowed himself to be saddled with two incompatible foreign alliances if he had not believed he could get away with it, as he had done when taking similar risks earlier; and even then it was not inevitable that the campaign of 1513 would end in disaster, still less in a disaster on the scale of Flodden. But even if James and his forces had survived the encounter it is likely that troubles of other sorts lay in the immediate future. In particular, the ominous royal overspend, combined with a likely falling off of revenues, might well have produced a rather different sort of calamity; in that case the legend of James IV would have been very different.

T. G. Chalmers

Sources APS, 1424–1567 · T. Dickson and J. B. Paul, eds., *Compota thesaurariorum regum Scotorum / Accounts of the lord high treasurer of Scotland*, 1–4 (1877–1902) · G. Burnett and others, eds., *The exchequer rolls of Scotland*, 23 vols. (1878–1908), vols. 8–13 · J. M. Thomson and others, eds., *Registrum magni sigilli regum Scotorum / The register of the great seal of Scotland*, 11 vols. (1882–1914), vol. 2 · M. Livingstone, D. Hay Fleming, and others, eds., *Registrum secreti sigilli regum Scotorum / The register of the privy seal of Scotland*, 1 (1908), 1488–1529 · [T. Thomson], ed., *The acts of the lords of council in civil causes, 1478–1495*, 1, RC, 41 (1839) · G. Neilson and H. Paton, eds., *Acts of the lords of council in civil causes, 1496–1501*, 2 (1918) · R. K. Hannay, ed., *Acts of the lords of council in public affairs, 1501–1554* (1932) · CDS, vol. 4 · LP Henry VIII, vol. 1, 2nd edn · *The letters of James IV*, ed. R. K. Hannay and R. L. Mackie, Scottish History Society, 3rd ser., 45 (1953) · *The historie and cronicles of Scotland ... by Robert Lindesay of Pitscottie*, ed. A. J. G. Mackay, 3 vols., STS, 42–3, 60 (1899–1911) · P. Hume Brown, *Early travellers in Scotland* (1891) · N. Macdougall, *James III: a political study* (1982) · N. Macdougall, *James IV* (1989) · R. L. Mackie, *King James IV of Scotland* (1958) · R. Nicholson, *Scotland: the later middle ages* (1974), vol. 2 of *The Edinburgh history of Scotland*, ed. G. Donaldson (1965–75) · T. M. Chalmers, 'The king's council, patronage, and governance of Scotland, 1460–1513', PhD diss., U. Aberdeen, 1982 · L. J. Macfarlane, *William Elphinstone and the kingdom of Scotland, 1431–1514: the struggle for order* (1985) · A. Conway, *Henry VII's relations with Scotland and Ireland, 1485–1498* (1932) · J. Wormald, *Court, kirk and community: Scotland, 1470–1625* (1981) · R. Fawcett, *The architectural history of Scotland: Scottish architecture from the accession of the Stewarts to the reformation, 1371–1560* (1994)

Likenesses H. van der Goes, altarpiece, oils on panel, *c.*1480, NG Scot.; *see illus. in* James III (1452–1488) · manuscript illustration, *c.*1503, Österreichische Nationalbibliothek, Vienna · double portrait, 1591 (Seton armorial; with Margaret), NL Scot. · attrib. J. Le Boucq, drawing, Bibliothèque Municipale, Arras · D. Mytens, oils (after earlier work, in or before 1513), priv. coll. · line engraving, BM; repro. in J. Johnston, *Inscriptiones historicae regum Scotorum* (1602) · oils on panel, Scot. NPG [*see illus.*]

James V (1512–1542), by unknown artist, *c.*1540

James V (1512–1542),

king of Scots, was born on 10 April 1512 at Linlithgow Palace, the fourth of the six children of *James IV (1473–1513) and *Margaret (1489–1541), eldest daughter of Henry VII of England and Elizabeth of York. James was the only one of their offspring to survive infancy: two sons and a daughter had already died before he was born, a younger sister died probably in early 1513, and a younger brother, Alexander, duke of Ross (1514–1515), was born after James IV's death and lived for only twenty months.

Flodden and its aftermath, 1512–1515 The marriage of James IV and Margaret Tudor in August 1503 had been intended to cement a treaty of perpetual peace between England and Scotland. However, Scotland also had an 'auld alliance' with France. Following the accession of Henry VIII in 1509 and his subsequent resurrection of English claims to the French crown, Anglo-Scottish relations worsened. The birth of the future James V may have contributed to the tensions because at that time Henry VIII had no children, which made Margaret Tudor and her infant son the nearest heirs to the English throne. Furthermore, by 1513 James IV was pressing Louis XII to acknowledge officially the Scottish place in the English succession, whereas

Henry VIII had committed himself to an anti-French continental alliance. Forced to choose between his two allies, James IV decided to support France against England and in August and September 1513, while Henry VIII was busy invading France, the Scottish host raided Northumberland. On 9 September James IV and many of his magnates were killed in battle at Flodden. Thus James V became king at the tender age of seventeen months and a long minority loomed.

In the aftermath of Flodden the Scots were afraid that the English might invade, and the coronation of the new king at Stirling on 21 September 1513 was therefore hurried and muted. Under the terms of James IV's will Queen Margaret was to be tutrix to her son during her widowhood, and this may have helped to lessen the English threat, since Henry VIII seems to have expected confidently to rule Scotland through his sister. A council of lords was appointed to advise her and in November a general council at Perth requested that John Stewart, fourth duke of Albany, should be sent to Scotland from France by Louis XII. Albany was the son of James III's exiled brother Alexander and his French wife, and was thus the heir presumptive to the Scottish throne after James V's unborn brother. The intention was that Albany would assist the Scots in the next phase of the war but by the spring of 1514, as Queen Margaret retired from public life for the birth of the duke of Ross, France and England were negotiating for peace. The treaty was finalized in August 1514, Scotland was comprehended in the terms without consultation, and Albany remained in France.

During the summer of 1514 factions emerged within the Scottish nobility and Queen Margaret provoked a sharp reaction when she allied herself with the Douglas kindred by her marriage to Archibald Douglas, sixth earl of Angus, in August. She was deprived of her regency powers and retreated to Stirling Castle with her sons while the council renewed requests for Albany to be sent from France. Even Henry VIII was outraged that his sister should contract a second marriage without consulting him, but he soon came to view Angus as a valuable ally against French influence in Scotland. The accession of François I in January 1515 produced a change in French policy. While officially maintaining his predecessor's peace with England, François permitted Albany to go to Scotland in the hope that some advantage might be gained thereby. The duke landed at Dumbarton in May 1515 and was acknowledged as lord governor for the young king in parliament in July. He then gave a powerful demonstration of the widespread support he commanded by leading an army to Stirling and forcing the queen mother to relinquish her custody of the king and his brother.

The minority regimes, 1515–1525 Until 1515 Lord Governor Albany had neither set foot in Scotland nor spoken a word of Scots. He was a peer of the French realm and a valuable agent of French policy. He exercised his governorship in person for only brief periods from May 1515 to June 1517, from November 1521 to October 1522, and from September 1523 to May 1524, and this timetable was dictated largely by French interests, particularly relations with England, rather than Scottish needs. François expected his Scottish allies to threaten the English borders when Henry VIII was planning campaigns in northern France (as he was in 1522–3) and to participate meekly as junior partners in peace treaties when this suited French diplomacy: such deals were forced upon the Scots in 1514–15 and 1525. When Albany was in Scotland he enjoyed considerable support from the magnates and prelates, was able to administer justice equitably, and had sufficient authority to deal with opponents: Lord Hume, an incorrigible rebel, was executed in October 1516, and the troublesome earl of Angus was exiled in France in 1522–4. Albany also obtained the treaty of Rouen from François in 1517 (ratified in 1522). This was an agreement for mutual assistance in the event of English aggression and promised James V one of the French king's daughters as a bride. The duke seems to have taken very seriously his responsibility for the care and education of the young king of Scots, who as an adult would show considerable respect for Albany's views.

When Albany left Scotland in 1517, 1522, and 1524, he tried to leave a balanced council of regency to exercise authority until his return, but invariably the arrangements broke down in his absence. In September 1517 Albany's agent, De la Bastie, was murdered by the Humes in revenge for the execution of 1516, and there followed a period of unrest in which the Hamilton faction of the earl of Arran struggled for supremacy with the Douglas supporters of the earl of Angus. The chaos was epitomized by the Edinburgh brawl of 1520 known as Cleanse the Causeway. During Albany's absence in 1522–3 the Scottish lords found it very difficult to maintain domestic order or to mount an effective defence against English raids. When Albany left again in May 1524 he promised to return before 1 September or forfeit his governorship, but François I was entering a period of uncharacteristically warm relations with Henry VIII and refused to release Albany for service in Scotland. Even before the duke's deadline expired Queen Margaret seized the chance to assert her authority once more. In July she brought James V from Stirling to Edinburgh and 'erected' him as king in his own right (with herself as the power behind the throne), revoked Albany's authority, and redistributed crown appointments; the arrangements were confirmed in parliament on 20 August.

For the time being Margaret commanded considerable magnate support and was also backed by her brother, who paid pensions to her followers, financed the king's royal guard, and started to discuss a possible peace treaty and marriage between James V and Mary Tudor. Yet Henry VIII considered Margaret to be on probation as an English agent in Scotland. He thought her unreliable and was harbouring her estranged husband, the earl of Angus, at the English court, whence the latter had escaped from France in June 1524. As regent, Margaret managed to alienate many lords by relying too heavily on a small group of favourites and by late 1524 she was largely discredited. Henry therefore sent Angus home as his preferred agent in Scotland and from then on channelled English pensions and influence through the Douglases. In February 1525 Angus was readmitted to the Scottish council against Margaret's wishes and in July 1525 a new rota of magnates to keep the king was established. Angus was given custody of James for the three months ending 1 November, when the earl of Arran would replace him, but at the appointed time Angus simply refused to hand over the king. His coup was simple and effective; by maintaining possession of the king, the Douglases were to rule Scotland for nearly three years.

The Scottish records of the period afford only glimpses of the arrangements made for the care and education of the young James V. Albany appointed a rota of trustworthy nobles such as lords Borthwick, Fleming, and Erskine to act as guardians or 'keepers' of the king. They were primarily responsible for security arrangements at the royal lodgings in the castles of Edinburgh, Stirling, and Craigmillar. A team of domestic servants supervised by the king's master usher, Sir David Lindsay of the Mount, catered for his material needs; several chaplains under the master almoner, Sir James Haswell, looked after his spiritual welfare; and grooms and musicians provided training and entertainment. Periodically James received treats and presents such as clothing and miniature weapons from his uncle Henry VIII, the duke of Albany, and other foreign princes, as tokens of their interest in him. In February 1517 Gavin Dunbar, the future archbishop of Glasgow and chancellor, was appointed tutor or 'preceptor' to the young king and he retained this post until he was dismissed by Angus in 1525. In later years the deficiencies of James's education were remarked upon (he struggled with Latin and French) but if, as seems to have been the case, the king had no formal tuition beyond the age of thirteen for political reasons, it may not be fair to blame Dunbar for the problem. James was certainly able to express himself effectively in the Scots language, and is known to have written poetry and to have been a practising musician.

The young king seems to have been a much more able pupil in the field of courtesy and chivalry, however, than in the schoolroom. Sir David Lindsay later claimed some credit for teaching James music, dancing, games, and tales, in his own words:

> Quhen thow wes young, I bure the in myne arme
> Full tenderlie, tyll thow begouth to gang,
> And in thy bed oft happit the full warme,
> With lute in hand, syne sweitlie to the sang:
> Sumtyme, in dansyng, feiralie I flang;
> And, sumtyme, playand fairsis on the flure;
> And, sumtyme on myne office takkand cure;
>
> And, sumtyme, lyke ane feind transfegurate;
> And, sumtyme, like the greislie gaist of gye;
> In divers formis, oft tymes, disfigurate;
> And, sumtyme, disagysit full plesandlye.
> So, sen thy birth, I have continewalye
> Bene ocupyit, and aye to thy plesoure.
> (Works of Sir David Lindsay, 1, 4–5)

The officers of his guard probably would have contributed to James's love of riding, shooting, tennis, archery, sword-play, and other chivalric pursuits. Prominent among these men were Alan Stewart, Andrew Towers, and Robert Borthwick during Albany's regime, Lord Avondale and his brother Henry Stewart (later Lord Methven) during Queen Margaret's ascendancy, and Archibald Douglas of Kilspindie under the earl of Angus. As he grew up it is unlikely that James would have been isolated from other children but it is impossible to say who might have been his classmates and sparring partners. His half-sister, Lady Margaret Douglas (1515–1578), was probably at court between 1525 and 1528 and he seems to have been close to the fourth earl of Huntly, who for a while also had the earl of Angus as his guardian; otherwise his youthful companions are unknown. Although James seems to have derived little benefit from his academic studies, he learned some sharp lessons in practical politics from the upheavals of his minority, which he would put to good use as an adult king.

The Angus hegemony and the coup of 1528 Initially the regime of the earl of Angus had only narrow support within the Scottish realm, but he presented himself as the one man who could bring stability to the borders and lasting peace with England, and this had some appeal to lords who knew that no further help would come from France. His custody of the king was also crucial. An armed rebellion involving Margaret, Arran, and Moray simply dissolved when James was brought to the field of battle near Linlithgow in January 1526, and both Arran and Moray subsequently made an uneasy peace with the Douglases.

However, Margaret would never be reconciled with the man whom she was now determined to divorce, and Archbishop Beaton of St Andrews, who had originally been supportive, quickly became disillusioned with Angus and stepped down as chancellor in June 1526. Even so, a parliament of the same month made Angus's rule legitimate, 'erected' James V as king for a second time, and revoked all grants made under Margaret's regency, thus allowing Angus to control royal patronage. The key offices of state and of the king's household were packed with Douglas supporters and James was isolated; indeed he was effectively a prisoner.

Shortly afterwards Angus took James on a justice ayre to the borders and on 20 July at Darnick, near Melrose, an armed force led by Walter Scott of Buccleuch unsuccessfully attempted to liberate the king from his custodians. James apparently then tried to slip away from Holyrood Palace with the earl of Lennox, to whom he had given a bond promising pre-eminence in a post-Angus government, but this plan was foiled too. Finally, on 4 September Lennox was defeated and killed in battle near Linlithgow in another futile attempt to challenge Douglas power. Thereafter Angus's opponents took no further action, but absented themselves from court and bided their time. Meanwhile, Angus's government became more narrow, partial, and heavy-handed. In August 1527 the earl appointed himself chancellor of the realm, but he was gradually losing control of the royal finances and was finding it difficult to keep order in the borders. Angus presumably imagined that he was indispensable to Henry VIII and therefore secure in his position but he seems to have underestimated the mettle of James V. Throughout 1527 the young king's resentment of his stepfather festered, and by 1528 he was ready to forge an anti-Douglas coalition of his own.

April 1528 was a crucial month. James celebrated his sixteenth birthday on the 10th and clearly began to desire to rule as an adult king. He may also have had a major disagreement with Angus at an Easter session of the council. Furthermore, his mother made public her new marital status. Her divorce from Angus had been pronounced in Rome in March 1527 but the decree did not reach Scotland until April 1528, when she announced that she had taken as her third husband Henry Stewart (c.1495–1553/4), younger brother of Lord Avondale and her favourite of some years. As a magnate of the realm in her own right she needed the king's consent for such a match to be politically acceptable. Angus's reaction was to place Stewart in ward. In the following weeks James clearly struck a deal with his mother independently of Angus. He would accept her remarriage if she would make over to him Stirling Castle, which was part of her jointure as consort of James IV. He planned to use the lofty fortress as a base from which to challenge the rule of Angus.

On 20 May James was in Edinburgh attending a session of the council with Angus. Somehow he managed to escape from the Douglases and by 30 May he was probably in Stirling with Queen Margaret. Between 19 June and 6 July James V established himself at the head of the

Scottish government. Many Douglases were dismissed from office and replaced by men loyal to the king, such as Gavin Dunbar, archbishop of Glasgow and former royal tutor, who became chancellor. Other lords who rallied to the newly assertive monarch included the earls of Arran, Argyll, Eglinton, and Moray, and the abbots of Scone and Cambuskenneth. The new council ordered Angus into ward north of the River Spey and his brother and uncle into ward at Edinburgh Castle; when the Douglases refused to comply they were summonsed for treason and forfeited in their absence in parliament at Edinburgh on 5 September. The king then began a series of largely futile campaigns against key strongholds held by the Douglases such as the castles of Douglas, Newark, and Kilmarnock, the tower of Cockburnspath, and the priory of Coldingham. These actions culminated in the (unsuccessful) siege of Tantallon Castle between 25 October and 5 November. The following day the lords of the council swore a solemn oath to pursue the Douglases to their 'utter destruction' (Hannay, 290). Nevertheless, it was clear that James's attempt to use force against Angus had failed. Instead he made a deal with Henry VIII in December 1528 (ratified in March 1529) allowing the Douglases refuge in England, giving him possession of their Scottish properties, and agreeing a five-year truce between the two realms. Angus finally crossed the border into exile in May 1529. It had taken the king a full year to be rid of his erstwhile guardian.

The assertion of royal authority, 1529–1534 Having demonstrated his determination to be an active adult monarch, James's next priority seems to have been to enforce royal authority and justice throughout the realm. In June 1529 he presided at justice ayres in the borders, where he received bonds and 'pledges' (hostages) for good rule from his lieges. In September he went hunting in the same area and in November he held justice ayres in Dumfries, Galloway, and Ayrshire. Yet lawlessness continued, and in 1530 the king became more energetic. In May two border reivers, William Cockburn of Henderland and Adam Scott of Tushielaw, were executed in Edinburgh, sixteen border magnates were placed in temporary ward, and fifty lairds gave pledges to underlie the law. In July, James led an army on a border raid; he took some prisoners and executed other outlaws, among them the notorious Johnnie Armstrong of Staplegordon. Meanwhile the earl of Moray, as lieutenant of the north, was bringing order to Caithness and Sutherland, and the fourth earl of Argyll, as lieutenant of the west, was failing to control Maclean of Duart and Macdonald of Islay. In 1531 the king planned a show of strength in the west and arranged for an army to gather under his command at Ayr to meet with a force under Moray at Kintail for a joint campaign. The raid seems to have been cancelled when Macdonald and Maclean submitted to the king. James accepted offers of good service from these highland chiefs and dismissed Argyll from his office as chamberlain of Kintyre.

The king's concern that justice should be administered effectively was clearly evident in 1531-2. With Henry VIII pursuing his divorce case and François I maintaining the Anglo-French accord, there was an opportunity for closer ties between the king of Scots and both pope and emperor. At this time Chancellor Dunbar and the royal secretary, Sir Thomas Erskine, seem to have developed a scheme to establish a college of justice as a permanent court of professional judges to hear civil cases, and both Clement VII and Charles V gave their approval. A papal bull of September 1531 authorized taxation of the Scottish clergy to pay for the new institution, on 26 April 1532 James V was admitted to the order of the Golden Fleece, and on 27 May the king presided at the inauguration of the college of justice in Edinburgh. It is possible that the imperial party was still in Edinburgh and witnessed the ceremony, and it is likely that the papal nuncio, Sylvester Darius, was also there. James V was making his mark not only within Scotland but also further afield.

Henry VIII seems to have been alarmed by this evidence of warmth between his nephew, the pope, and the emperor, and decided to test the resolve of the young king. In the summer and autumn of 1532 he urged the earl of Northumberland to goad the Scots: a series of raids provoked reprisals and a border war ensued. James and his council reacted with determination. In October 1532 the earl of Moray was appointed lieutenant-general of the kingdom to command the Scottish host, which was called up in turn from four 'quarters' of the kingdom in the winter and spring of 1532-3. The earl of Bothwell was warded for manifestly treasonable dealings with the earl of Northumberland, and the archbishop of St Andrews was placed under temporary house-arrest on suspicion of communicating with Henry VIII. Furthermore, Hector Maclean of Duart and Alexander Macdonald of Islay were authorized to harry the English by making trouble in Ireland, raiding the Isle of Man, and preying on English ships, two of which were captured and presented to James V. François I was saddened by the hostilities between his two allies and sent an envoy, De Beauvais, to engage in shuttle diplomacy and bring Henry and James to terms. As a result a ceasefire was effected by May 1533, a formal truce agreed in September 1533, and a peace treaty concluded in May 1534.

The French marriages, 1536–1538 James V had been promised a daughter of François I in the treaty of Rouen of 1517, and in the mid-1520s the prospect of marriage with his cousin Mary Tudor had been raised but nothing had been settled. After 1528 James began to pursue actively a marriage that would bring him personal prestige and political advantage and he naturally turned first to France. Yet François was reluctant to jeopardize his delicate relationship with Henry VIII and prevaricated. Mindful of the overtures from emperor and pope, James started to consider alternative candidates from the houses of Habsburg and Medici. Between 1529 and 1535 fifteen ladies from six countries were discussed as potential consorts. Yet as the years passed and no conclusion was reached it became clear that princes were offering prospective brides not out of enthusiasm for a Scottish match but from a desire to disrupt James's negotiations with rival powers if they looked too promising. Therefore in March 1536 James found himself engaged not to one of François's own daughters but to a less prestigious and diplomatically more acceptable alternative, Marie de Bourbon, daughter of the duc de Vendôme. In September James sailed to France to secure his bride, but having inspected her he rejected the match and persuaded François to honour the treaty of Rouen. The French king hesitated until he had gauged the likely English reaction and discovered that Henry was too preoccupied with domestic problems to do more than write a few letters of complaint; the pope was also consulted. The contract of marriage between James V and *Madeleine de Valois (1520–1537) was signed at Blois on 26 November 1536 and the couple were married in Paris on 1 January 1537. The day before the wedding James was given a Parisian royal entry as if he had been the dauphin. This marriage was a triumph not only for the Scottish king but also for the international standing of his realm.

The young couple returned to Scotland in May 1537 but the rigours of the journey and the Scottish climate proved too much for Madeleine's delicate health and she died at Holyrood Palace on 7 July. James immediately requested a replacement from François. Having now obtained the prestige attached to marrying the eldest daughter of a king, James was quite willing to accept a lady of lesser rank as his second wife. Furthermore, François's relationship with Henry VIII was beginning to cool while an imperial friendship was emerging and so the new Scottish match was arranged swiftly. Marie de Lorraine, usually known as *Mary of Guise (1515–1560), daughter of Claude, duc de Guise, and widow of Louis, duc de Longueville, married James V at St Andrews on 17 June 1538. The wedding was intended to symbolize Scottish commitment to the new Catholic alliance which was developing in Europe and threatening to launch a crusade against the 'heretic' king of England. Queen Mary was crowned at Holyrood on 22 February 1540 and gave birth to James, duke of Rothesay, on 22 May at St Andrews. A second son, probably called Robert, duke of Albany, was born at Stirling in April 1541. Both boys died soon afterwards and were buried at Holyrood. A third child was born at Linlithgow Palace on 8 December 1542 and within a few days had ascended the throne as *Mary, queen of Scots (1542–1587). James V also had a considerable illegitimate progeny—including James *Stewart, later first earl of Moray (1531/2–1570), and Robert *Stewart—born of liaisons with at least seven, and perhaps nine, identified mistresses [see James V, mistresses and children of].

James V's court Even before his trip to France, James V had already indicated a desire to emulate the most fashionable developments at the Renaissance courts of Europe, and the time he spent with François I inspired him to even greater efforts. He used the limited resources at his disposal effectively and his cultural patronage propagated multi-layered images of royal power. Continuity with the traditions of his forebears was stressed, but the chivalric, imperial, and humanist themes popular at foreign courts were also adopted enthusiastically.

The architectural patronage of the court was particularly rich and encompassed buildings in the ornate high-Gothic style pioneered in the Burgundian Netherlands, and in a more restrained Italianate classicism borrowed from France. James V's earliest building, a new tower at Holyrood constructed between 1528 and 1532, and a new west range of 1535–6, fell into the former category, as did a new gateway for Linlithgow Palace of 1534 and an entrance tower and south front for Falkland Palace built from 1537. All of these works incorporated crenellations, gun-loops, armorial bearings, gilded weather-vanes, and gargoyles. However, the courtyard façades at Falkland were reconstructed between 1537 and 1541 by French masons in the *François premier* style, while the new palace block at Stirling Castle of about 1540 owes more to the architecture of Louis XII's reign. The 'Stirling heads', a series of carved Renaissance roundels from the ceiling of the king's presence chamber, are of the same period. There is very little portraiture surviving from the court but queens Madeleine and Mary sat for Corneille de Lyon, and a companion piece from the same *atelier* is probably the best contemporary likeness of the king; it suggests an impressive physical presence.

James V was a keen musician. He played the lute, could sight-read vocal scores, and employed a large staff of musicians and minstrels. The consort of viols was first introduced to Scotland under his patronage, as was the French *chanson* style. Composers associated with his court included Robert Carver, John Fethy, and Robert Johnson, but the only surviving piece specifically dedicated to the king is the motet *Si quis diligit me* (c.1530) by David Peebles. The influence of the English and Flemish schools as well as the music of France and Italy can be detected in Scottish compositions of the period and the king employed musicians from all of these countries.

The literary patronage of the court was of a remarkably high quality. During the minority both John Mair and Hector Boece dedicated their histories of Scotland (1521 and 1527 respectively) to the king. Both works were scholarly neo-Latin tomes with humanist influences, but Mair's work, which advocated a union of the realms of England and Scotland, did not find favour with the adult king, who preferred the forthright nationalism of Boece. James commissioned John Bellenden to translate Boece's history and Livy's *History of Rome* into Scots. Many poets were patronized by the king, the most distinguished of them being Sir David Lindsay of the Mount. Eight of Lindsay's earliest surviving poems were written for James and are set at his court. They cast some light on the character of the king, revealing his boisterous nature and his sexual promiscuity; mention is also made of chivalric tournaments, the wedding and funeral of 1537, and even the royal pets. At Epiphany 1540 an interlude written by Lindsay was performed for the king at Linlithgow. It has not survived but seems to have had a heavily anti-clerical tone and to have been a prototype for his play, *Ane Satyre of the Thrie Estaitis* (1552). Anti-clerical poetry was also written at the king's behest by George Buchanan when he was tutor to the eldest Lord James Stewart between 1536 and 1539. The young

Pierre Ronsard visited the Scottish court briefly as a page to Queen Madeleine, and when James was in France Clement Marot and others made poetical offerings.

James V was a dedicated exponent of the cult of chivalry. Jousts and tournaments were staged to mark all the major feasts and celebrations of the reign, and while in Paris James spent much time jousting with the dauphin. He was particularly proud of his membership of the most prestigious European orders of chivalry: the Golden Fleece (1532), the Garter (1535), and St Michael (1536). The insignia of these orders were carved above his new gateway at Linlithgow alongside the emblems of the Scottish Order of the Thistle. James was careful to keep up to date in other aspects of royal symbolism and ceremonial. Scottish kings had depicted themselves on coins, seals, and documents, wearing an arched 'imperial' crown since the reign of James III, but James V was probably the first actually to wear such regalia. The closed crown which is today on display in Edinburgh Castle was remodelled for James V in 1540 and his diadem may have had arches attached to it as early as 1532, to signify that he acknowledged no superior authority in his realm before God.

James V and the church James V's piety was of the conventional rather than convictional kind and his policy towards the church was highly pragmatic. His assumption of royal powers coincided with Henry VIII's divorce case, which led to the English schism and dissolution of the monasteries. With his uncle of England ever eager to coax him into similar policies, James V was able to portray himself as a loyal but embattled son of the church, while exploiting the wealth and power of the Scottish clergy for his own ends. To encourage him to keep faith, the papacy made significant concessions. Much of the clerical taxation granted for the establishment of the college of justice was diverted into the royal palace-building programme without comment, and in 1540 the clergy agreed to contribute £10,000 a year towards the royal household. In 1532 it was recognized that no Scottish case under ecclesiastical jurisdiction could be called to Rome in the first instance, but was to be heard before the king's appointed clerical judges. In 1535 the pope confirmed the crown's right to nominate to vacant benefices and extended the period of nomination (during which the revenues belonged to the king) from eight months to a year. Dispensations were also issued permitting the king's under-age and illegitimate sons to hold five of the most lucrative benefices: the abbeys of Holyrood, Melrose, and Kelso, and the priories of St Andrews and Coldingham. Until the boys reached maturity the king would possess their temporalities. In February 1537, while he was still in France, James received the papal gift of a blessed cap and sword as a mark of particular regard, and there was even a suggestion that the pope was considering reassigning Henry's title of *Fidei defensor* to James, though the latter seems never to have adopted this style officially.

Like many monarchs of the age, James employed large numbers of clerics in his court and government so that ecclesiastical energies were often focused on the king's service rather than on God's. Such prelates as Archbishop Dunbar of Glasgow (chancellor), Abbot Alexander Mylne of Cambuskenneth (president of the college of justice), and Cardinal David Beaton (keeper of the privy seal) had decidedly worldly careers, but James was nevertheless capable of offering patronage to the church as well as exploiting it. He made regular visits and gave gifts to pilgrimage centres including the shrines of St Ninian at Whithorn, St Duthac at Tain, St Adrian on the Isle of May, and the Virgin of Loretto near Musselburgh. He was also an active patron of the Observant Franciscans, the Dominican convent of Sciennes, the abbey of Cambuskenneth, the collegiate church of Restalrig, and Trinity College, Edinburgh. James endowed the Chapel Royal at Stirling with splendid new vestments and ornaments and was on good terms with its staff. The ritual year of the Catholic church largely shaped the itinerary and customs of the Scottish court, and the cycle of feasts and fasts, including the meat-free season of Lent, was rigorously observed.

In spite of this James's personal response to the spread of Lutheranism was rather ambiguous. He seems to have favoured a group of men within his household who would later become known as reformers and to have encouraged some criticism of ecclesiastical corruption by such commentators as Sir David Lindsay and George Buchanan. At the same time he also patronized those of the opposite persuasion and allowed heresy prosecutions to go ahead, sometimes attending in person. The king was present at Holyrood in 1534 when two heretics were executed and one of his kinsmen, Sir James Hamilton of Kincavil, was exiled; and again in 1539 when six men were burned on Castle Hill, a chorister of the Chapel Royal recanted, and Buchanan fled. James's flirtation with reform was probably designed to maintain the simultaneous solicitude of both the pope and Henry VIII, and while he seems to have been willing to enjoy some ribald anti-clerical humour in court entertainments his international profile was consistently Catholic.

James V's government James seems to have regarded it as his primary duty to ensure that Scotland was well governed. His early determination to bring order to the borders and the western and northern isles, to defend his realm from English attacks, and to establish the college of justice has already been noted, and this approach did not waver in subsequent years. Legal reforms continued into the 1530s with acts improving the operation of sheriffs' courts and regulating notaries, and the office of advocate for the poor was revived. James was a restlessly peripatetic monarch, often supervising justice ayres in person and making his presence felt in even the most far-flung corners of the land. In June and July of 1540 he sailed around the entire Scottish coastline from the Firth of Forth to the Firth of Clyde, taking in the Orkneys and the Hebrides. Pledges for good rule were taken from highland chieftains along the way and the first known coastal chart ('rutter') of the Scottish seas was produced. James also encouraged nobles and lairds to fortify the castles and tower houses of the coasts and borders, while spending heavily on new royal fortifications in strategic sites such as Rothesay, Burntisland, Blackness, Tantallon, Crawfordjohn, and

Hermitage Castle in Liddesdale. A new royal arsenal was established in Edinburgh Castle and well stocked with artillery pieces and munitions, while a fleet of warships was constructed virtually from scratch. James was also concerned to stabilize crown finances, which had been 'superexpended' during the minority. Through enforcing his property rights and judicial authority the revenues of the treasury and exchequer were steadily increased throughout the 1530s; to this James added the income obtained from the church, the dowries of his two queens, revenues from the lands of forfeited lords, the profits of crown mining and sheep-farming operations, and taxes levied to support royal embassies and military campaigns. Expenditure on the royal household, pageantry, diplomacy, and defence also increased over time, but James seems to have managed his finances effectively and to have largely lived within his means. This was a remarkable achievement in an age when other monarchs routinely amassed heavy debts.

Although a study of English diplomatic papers and post-Reformation Scottish narratives gives the strong impression that James was unpopular with his nobles, who feared and mistrusted him as a covetous and predatory overlord, a different impression emerges from the surviving records of James V's own government. There, magnates who included the earls of Moray, Huntly, Arran, Argyll, and Eglinton, as well as Lord Maxwell, appear regularly serving on diplomatic, military, administrative, and judicial missions. Four of them (Montrose, Huntly, Eglinton, and Maxwell) along with the two archbishops, were entrusted with regency powers in the absence of the king in France in 1536–7. James was also served well by prelates such as Cardinal Beaton, lawyers such as Sir Thomas Erskine of Brechin, and lairds such as Sir James Kirkcaldy of Grange, all of whom were capable and experienced officers of state. Furthermore, James's reputation for gratuitously prosecuting key magnates in order to benefit from their forfeited estates does not tell the whole story. Cameron has shown that there were sound political reasons for the charges of treason brought against the Douglases in 1528, the earl of Bothwell in 1531, Lady Glamis and the master of Forbes in 1537, Sir James Colville in 1538, and Sir James Hamilton of Finnart in 1540. James might have been prepared to wait for a propitious moment to act, but he would not allow disloyalty to go unpunished. In this he generally had the support of his nobility. Nevertheless, James did benefit personally from these forfeitures, as did such magnates as Huntly and Arran, and the prospect of such gains would not have been unwelcome to any of them.

In foreign affairs James maintained his alliance with France and a cordial relationship with the pope and emperor alongside the peace with England which had been settled in 1534. As the Anglo-French accord broke down in 1537 and François I and Charles V started to consider launching a 'crusade' against the schismatic English realm in 1538–40, relations with Scotland became vital to English diplomacy. Henry sent Sir Ralph Sadler to try to detach James from France, advising that he could profit from a dissolution of the Scottish monasteries and a royal supremacy over the Scottish church. There was also a suggestion that a change of heart by the Scottish king might lead to the recognition of his place in the English succession. Henry hoped that he could meet James in person to resolve their differences, but he was proposing an English venue and the Scottish council feared a kidnap attempt and advised James to decline the invitation. By 1541 Franco-imperial amity had evaporated and Henry, no longer isolated, was negotiating a continental alliance with either François or Charles. He wanted to gauge the Scottish attitude to European developments and had high hopes that James would meet him at York in September. However, James had never formally agreed to attend and when the king of Scots failed to appear Henry, who had travelled to York specifically for the meeting, was exasperated.

The crisis of 1542 In summer 1542 Henry VIII and Charles V agreed to launch a joint attack on France in the following year. Since the king of Scots persisted in his 'auld alliance', Henry needed to secure his northern border before departing for continental adventures. He calculated that a pre-emptive strike would inflict sufficient damage on the Scots to prevent them invading England in support of France, as had happened in 1513. In August 1542 Henry sent Sir Robert Bowes and the earls of Rutland and Angus to Northumberland to prepare for war, with the excuse that the Scottish king was harbouring English rebels and refusing to give redress. James responded by appointing the earl of Huntly as his lieutenant and the Scottish host was put on alert. By the middle of the month a series of border raids was under way and on 24 August an English force was scattered and Bowes captured in a skirmish with Huntly's men at Hadden Rig near Kelso. Henry then appointed the duke of Norfolk, the old victor of Flodden, to be his lieutenant for an invasion of Scotland, as acrimonious peace talks were foundering. The English army was desperately short of supplies and managed to raid only the area around Kelso and Roxburgh between 22 and 28 October before Norfolk returned to Berwick and scaled down his forces. James was determined to repel the English invasion, which he probably thought would head for Edinburgh. Huntly's forces were ordered to gather at Smailholm Tower, while a second army under Moray and the king had reached Lauder by late October. They probably planned to crush Norfolk's force in a pincer movement. Finding that their prey had eluded them and that they in turn were running short of supplies, the Scottish forces were also stood down and James returned to Edinburgh to rethink his strategy.

In November 1542 James decided to take the offensive. Again he divided his forces in two and seems to have disguised his movements to confuse the English. A force under James and Lord Maxwell mustered at Lauder on 20 November, which suggested an attack on the east march, but it then moved swiftly to Langholm in the west while the king based himself at Lochmaben Castle. Meanwhile, the earl of Moray was in charge of another force at Haddington. Cardinal Beaton was also there and the plan seems to have been to await news of successful raids in the west and then to dash across the border at Coldstream and pronounce the papal interdict in an English church. This would have been hugely embarrassing to the English king. However, the plan collapsed on 24 November when a Scottish raiding party in the west was trapped on the edge of a salt marsh by a smaller English force under Sir Thomas Wharton. At the battle of Solway Moss the Scots fought a difficult rearguard action for most of the day, while trying to find a safe crossing of the Esk estuary to take them back home. Eventually they were forced to capitulate, and hundreds of prisoners were taken including the earls of Glencairn and Cassillis, lords Maxwell, Fleming, Gray, Oliphant, and Somerville, and two senior members of the king's own household, Oliver Sinclair of Pitcairn (named in some accounts as the Scottish commander in the battle) and John Ross of Craigie.

Disappointed and humiliated King James returned to Edinburgh to consult his council. He seems to have ordered his lords to prepare for further raids into England while he paid a visit to his pregnant wife at Linlithgow. In the second week of December James fell ill. By 12 December he had retired to Falkland Palace and taken to his bed. At seven o'clock on the morning of 14 December James V appointed Cardinal Beaton, the earls of Moray, Huntly, and Argyll, and Queen Mary to act jointly as tutors and governors to his newly born daughter during her minority in a notarial instrument which was subsequently set aside on a technicality. Later the same day he died. The exact nature of his final illness is unknown. It is often said to have been a nervous collapse, but a virulent disease is more likely and one contemporary account gives a graphic description of deathbed agonies. The body was probably embalmed, and the king's household remained at Falkland during the season of Christmas when solemn mourning was observed. On 7 January the funeral cortège was escorted to Kinghorn by the lieges of Fife and ferried across the Firth of Forth. James V was buried at Holyrood Abbey, Edinburgh, on Monday 8 January 1543 in the presence of the second earl of Arran, lord governor for Mary, queen of Scots.

James V's reputation Many of the official records of the reign of James V are formal, incomplete, and occasionally obscure; some are still unpublished. There are very few contemporary narrative accounts of the reign, and private letters which might illuminate the personality of the king are scarce. Historians have therefore been driven to rely heavily on the English diplomatic record. The accounts of events in Scotland provided for Henry VIII were often produced by envoys who were experienced and knowledgeable eye-witnesses, but rumours of dubious origin were also passed on, and there were undoubtedly moments when they told their master what he wanted to hear. Thus James V's apparent interest in reforming the Scottish church in 1540 was probably exaggerated to please an uncle who hoped to win his co-operation, while stories of the Scottish clergy dominating his council, turning him into a 'priests' king', and sabotaging the proposed summit conference excused the failure of the English policy of persuasion. Similarly, stories of noble disaffection with a greedy and predatory king, James the 'ill-beloved', circulated most energetically during his absence in France in 1536–7 and during the hostilities of 1532–3 and 1542, when Henry was hoping to restore the earl of Angus to power in Scotland. The claim that Cardinal Beaton provided James with a 'black list' of heretical nobles which the king could use to threaten and bully his magnates only surfaced after his death, in March 1543, when the earl of Arran was trying to convince Sir Ralph Sadler that he would rule Scotland in a manner very different from that of his erstwhile monarch.

Some of the most enduring images of James V date from shortly after the Scottish Reformation of 1560. The malice Knox and Buchanan felt for a king who frustrated the advancement of 'true' religion has moulded his reputation. In Knox's *Works* and Buchanan's *History*, James is presented as very much a priests' king, credulous of superstition and idolatry, tolerant of burnings, and susceptible to bribes in the form of cash, lands, and nubile young women. His nobles find him rapacious, suspicious, and intimidating, closeted with bishops and household familiars of low rank; at Lauder in 1542 they steadfastly refuse to invade England in pursuit of the duke of Norfolk, and James angrily accuses them of cowardice; at Solway Moss they mutiny and willingly enter captivity upon hearing that the king's favourite, Oliver Sinclair, has been given military command. The oft-quoted deathbed lament for the loss of Sinclair and the comment that the Stewart crown 'cam wi' a lass and it'l gang wi' a lass' were words placed in James's mouth by Knox (*Works*, 1.90) and also by Pitscottie (*Historie and Cronicles*, 2.406). However, both Knox and Buchanan and the more picturesque accounts of Pitscottie and Leslie acknowledge James's cultural patronage and his interest in law and order. They also recognize his concern for the commons, and suggest that he liked to learn about his subjects by circulating among them incognito. Here is depicted the 'poor man's king', 'the king of the commons', and the origins of the flamboyantly romantic 'gudeman of Ballengeich' presented in Sir Walter Scott's *Tales of a Grandfather*.

James V's reputation has not moved far beyond these late sixteenth-century interpretations. Knox, Leslie, Pitscottie, and Buchanan colour vividly all subsequent accounts by commentators from the seventeenth to the twentieth centuries, including Caroline Bingham's popular biography. However, more recent research has attempted to unravel the history from the mythology by close examination of the surviving record sources, and important studies by W. K. Emond and J. Cameron provide a narrative of the reign which both extends and challenges the analyses of the most successful general histories of the period by Gordon Donaldson and Jenny Wormald. Whereas the latter both judge James very harshly, describing him as rapacious, vindictive, and aggressive, and repeat many of the chroniclers' tales, Cameron presents the adult James as a king who wanted to rule effectively and was determined to enforce his will. The humiliations and frustrations of a long minority were to be set aside and royal authority would be restored. His approach was rational and practical and he borrowed his strategies from earlier Stewart kings, contemporary monarchs, and legal advisers. Had he lived to consolidate and develop the remarkable achievements of the years 1528–42, his historical reputation might have been as glorious as his father's. In the event, his death at the age of thirty cut off in his prime a very promising Renaissance prince.

ANDREA THOMAS

Sources R. K. Hannay, ed., *Acts of the lords of council in public affairs, 1501–1554* (1932) • *APS*, 1424–1567 • J. B. Paul, ed., *Compota thesaurariorum regum Scotorum / Accounts of the lord high treasurer of Scotland*, 4–8 (1902–8) • *LP Henry VIII*, vols. 1–18 • *The letters of James V*, ed. R. K. Hannay and D. Hay (1954) • T. Thomson, ed., *A diurnal of remarkable occurrents that have passed within the country of Scotland*, Bannatyne Club, 43 (1833) • *The works of Sir David Lindsay*, ed. D. Hamer, 4 vols., STS, 3rd ser., 1–2, 6, 8 (1931–6) • J. H. Mackenzie, R. Graham, and J. Mackenzie, eds., *Excerpta e libris domicilii domini Jacobi Quinti Regis Scotorum*, Bannatyne Club, 54 (1836) • *Sixth report*, HMC, 5 (1877–8) • MSS, *libri emptorum* of James V, 1531–43, NA Scot., E 32/2–8 • J. Cameron, *James V: the personal rule, 1528–1542*, ed. N. Macdougall (1998) • W. K. Emond, 'The minority of James V, 1513–1528', PhD diss., U. St Andr., 1988 • A. Thomas, *'Princelie majestie': the court of James V of Scotland, 1528–1542* (2001) • *The works of John Knox*, ed. D. Laing, 6 vols., Wodrow Society, 12 (1846–64) • *The history of Scotland translated from the Latin of George Buchanan*, ed. and trans. J. Aikman, 4 vols. (1827) • J. Lesley, *The history of Scotland*, ed. T. Thomson, Bannatyne Club, 38 (1830) • J. Leslie, *The historie of Scotland*, ed. E. G. Cody and W. Murison, trans. J. Dalrymple, 2 vols. in 4 pts, STS, 5, 14, 19, 34 (1888–95) [1596 trans. of *De origine moribus, et rebus gestis Scotorum libri decem* (Rome, 1578)] • *The chronicles of Scotland*, ed. J. G. Dalyell, 2 vols. (1814) • *The historie and cronicles of Scotland … by Robert Lindesay of Pitscottie*, ed. A. J. G. Mackay, 3 vols., STS, 42–3, 60 (1899–1911) • G. Donaldson, *Scotland: James V to James VII* (1965), vol. 3 of *The Edinburgh history of Scotland* (1965–75) • J. Wormald, *Court, kirk and community: Scotland, 1470–1625* (1992) • E. Bapst, *Les mariages de Jacques V* (Paris, 1889) • *Scots peerage* • C. Bingham, *James V, king of Scots, 1512–1542* (1971) • C. P. Hotle, *Thorns and thistles: diplomacy between Henry VIII and James V, 1528–1542* (1996) • J. Paterson, *James the Fifth or the 'Gudeman of Ballangeich': his poetry and adventures* (1861) • W. Scott, *Tales of a grandfather*, another edn (1872) • S. B. Chrimes, *Henry VII* (1972) • R. J. Knecht, *Renaissance warrior and patron: the reign of Francis I* (1994) • A. L. Murray, ed., 'Accounts of the king's pursemaster, 1539–1540', *Miscellany … X*, Scottish History Society, 4th ser., 2 (1965), 11–51

Archives NA Scot., letter-books • NA Scot., MSS, *libri domicilii* of James V, E 31/1–8 | NA Scot., Tynninghame letter-books

Likenesses attrib. C. de Lyon, oils, *c*.1536 (of James V?), Polesden Lacey, Surrey • attrib. C. de Lyon, oils, *c*.1536–1537 (of James V?), Weiss Gallery, London • double portrait, oils, *c*.1538–1540 (with Mary of Guise), Hardwick Hall, Derbyshire • double portrait, oils, *c*.1538–1540 (with Mary of Guise), Blair Castle, Perthshire • oils, *c*.1538–1540, Royal Collection • oils, *c*.1540, Scot. NPG [*see illus.*] • W. Essex, enamel miniature (after unknown artist), Scot. NPG • oil paintings, Scot. NPG • watercolours, Scot. NPG

Wealth at death left £26,000 Scots contingency fund in treasure chests: Murray, 'Accounts of the king's pursemaster'

James V, mistresses and children of (*act. c.*1529–1592) constitute a notable extension of personality on the part of an early modern British ruler. *James V (1512–1542) had nine known illegitimate children, all born to different mothers. The dates and order of their births are not fully known. Of the two females, **Jean Stewart** (*c*.1530–1588) was the daughter of Elizabeth Beaton, daughter of Sir John Beaton of Creich, and it was probably she—her

maternity given but not her name—who was offered in marriage to Alexander, master of Home, in 1537. In the event she married Archibald Campbell, fifth earl of Argyll (*c*.1532–1573), in 1554; she was divorced from him in June 1573. Her sister Margaret Stewart is obscure, and the name could even be a clerical error for Jean herself, since she was the subject of the same marriage offer to the Homes five years after the first. While there appears to be a preponderance of sons among James's children, unfortunately there is no record of any unacknowledged daughters.

Of the king's sons, **James** [i] **Stewart** (1529–1557) was the son of Elizabeth Shaw, daughter of the laird of Sauchie, and the first beneficiary of the king's policy, inherited from his own father, James IV, of exploiting to his own advantage his control over major church benefices. On the king's appeal to the pope, James [i] became commendator of the abbeys of Kelso and Melrose. James [ii] Stewart [*see* Stewart, James (1531/2–1570)], son of Margaret Erskine [*see below*], wife of Sir Robert Douglas of Lochleven, likewise became commendator of the priory of St Andrews, and later first earl of Moray and regent. John *Stewart (*c*.1531–1563), son of Elizabeth or Katherine Carmichael, daughter of Sir John Carmichael, became commendator of the priory of Coldingham and briefly enjoyed the title Lord Darnley. James [iii] Stewart (*fl*. 1533), son of Christian Barclay, died in infancy. Robert [i] Stewart [*see* Stewart, Robert (1533–1593)] was the son of Euphemia Elphinstone (*b*. 1509, *d*. after 1564), daughter of Alexander, first Lord Elphinstone, who later married John Bruce of Cultmalindie. Robert [i] became commendator of the abbey of Holyrood, and later earl of Orkney. **Robert** [ii] **Stewart** (*d*. 1580) became commendator of the priory of Whithorn; he is said in one near-contemporary source to have been a son of the countess of Sutherland, though no bearer of that title was of an appropriate age. **Adam Stewart** (*d*. 1575), son of Helenor or Elizabeth, daughter of John Stewart, twelfth earl of Lennox, became a monk and pensioner (sometimes erroneously referred to as prior) of the Charterhouse of Perth; his mother subsequently married William Hay, sixth earl of Erroll, and then John Gordon, eleventh earl of Sutherland, and died in 1564.

Whatever the homely reputation of the 'guidman of Ballengeich', James V's known paramours were all drawn from the nobility and lairdly class. Only one, **Margaret Erskine** (*d*. 1572), daughter of John Erskine, fifth Lord Erskine (*d*. 1555), was more than a brief dalliance. She appears in a 'flyting' of Sir David Lindsay, in which the king is castigated for his loose morals, as 'the lady that luffit yow best' (*Works of Sir David Lindsay*, 1.104), and was the model for Dame Sensualitie in Lindsay's *Satyre of the Thrie Estaitis*. In 1536 James appealed to the pope to have her marriage annulled so that he could wed her himself. Had he been successful, then James [ii] could conceivably have been legitimized by the subsequent marriage of his parents and Scottish history would have taken a very different turn. Margaret Erskine was said in later years to have borne ill will against Queen Mary for this reason, though her part in the imprisonment of the queen in her husband's castle of Lochleven in 1567/8 is a matter of dispute. She was a somewhat forbidding companion to the queen during that episode, but is said to have responded to the queen's famous charm.

In their earliest years the children remained at court with their mothers. The four eldest boys—the two surviving Jameses, John, and Robert [i]—then went to school in St Andrews, and James [ii] and John later matriculated at the university. All accompanied the young Queen Mary to France in 1548 and the two university students continued their studies there under the philosopher Pierre Ramus. After returning to Scotland, John, James [ii], and Robert became involved in politics and public affairs and all attended their half-sister during her troubled personal rule. Jean too was a close companion, preferring the court to her husband's domains in the west of Scotland, a fact which put a fatal strain on her marriage. She was present when the queen's secretary David Rizzio was murdered on 9 March 1566.

Neither Jean nor Margaret had children, and all but Robert, earl of Orkney, died comparatively young and produced few descendants. John, Lord Darnley, had one son, Francis *Stewart (1562–1612), who succeeded him as prior of Coldingham and ultimately became the 'madcap' earl of Bothwell. James, earl of Moray, had three daughters, only one of whom had issue, though she was the progenitrix of the continuing Moray line. Adam Stewart died in 1575 in Orkney; his widow is said to have been 'gritlie burdynnit with mony bairnis' (*Registrum secreti sigilli*, 1575–80, no. 1003), though there is knowledge only of Barbara, who married into the Orcadian Halcro family and was responsible for her father's tombstone, carved with the royal arms, which may still be seen in St Magnus Cathedral, Kirkwall.

PETER D. ANDERSON

Sources P. D. Anderson, 'The illegitimate sons of James V', *Robert Stewart, earl of Orkney, lord of Shetland, 1533–93* (1982) · *Scots peerage* · J. Cameron, *James V: the personal rule, 1528–1542*, ed. N. Macdougall (1998) · C. Bingham, *James V, king of Scots* (1971) · A. Fraser, *Mary, queen of Scots* (1969) · R. K. Hannay and D. Hay, eds., *Letters of James V* (1954) · G. Donaldson, 'Stewart builders; the descendants of James V', *The Stewarts*, 16 (1974), 116 · *Twelfth report with an inventory of … Orkney and Shetland*, 1: *Report*, Royal Commission of Ancient and Historical Monuments of Scotland (1946) · M. Livingstone, D. Hay Fleming, and others, eds., *Registrum secreti sigilli regum Scotorum / The register of the privy seal of Scotland*, 8 vols. (1908–82), vols. 3, 7 · *The works of Sir David Lindsay*, ed. D. Hamer, 4 vols., STS, 3rd ser., 1–2, 6, 8 (1931–6)

James VI and I (1566–1625), king of Scotland, England, and Ireland, was born at Edinburgh Castle on 19 June 1566, the only son of *Mary, queen of Scots (1542–1587), and her second husband, Henry *Stewart, Lord Darnley (1545/6–1567).

Baptism and coronation James's birth occurred three months after the conspiracy which led to the savage murder in Mary's presence of her Italian favourite David Riccio, which she chose to believe was aimed at her own life, and that of her unborn son. She was wrong about that; no one was stupid enough to endanger the succession. But it produced the final breakdown of her marriage to the witless drunkard Darnley. Although she was careful

James VI and I (1566–1625), by Daniel Mytens, 1621

to proclaim the child's legitimacy publicly, in the summer and autumn of 1566 she distanced herself further from his father. The last semblance of normality in a deepening political crisis was James's magnificent baptism in the Chapel Royal of Stirling Castle on 17 December, a brilliant court spectacle which showed that in at least one area of monarchy Mary did have considerable skill; but even this was marred by Darnley's highly embarrassing refusal to attend, despite being resident in the castle. Apparently when James was one day old the general assembly of the kirk had sent John Spottiswoode, superintendent of Lothian, to congratulate the queen on the birth and request a protestant baptism for the infant. Given James to hold, Spottiswoode had prayed over him, and asked him to say 'amen'; some kind of gurgling sound from the tactful child seems to have satisfied the godly minister. However, James was baptized a Catholic, with the names Charles James—the first name after his godfather Charles IX, king of France, the second the traditional name of Stewart kings. It showed the greater importance his mother attached to the French than the Scottish monarchy, as did her adoption of the Frenchified version of the family name, Stuart. No one, it appears, agreed with her; it was by the Scottish name James that he was always called.

After the baptism there was no normality. On 14 January 1567 the queen removed herself and her son from Stirling, considered too close to territory dominated by the affinity of James's ambitious grandfather, Matthew *Stewart, thirteenth earl of Lennox, to the relative safety of the palace of Holyrood in Edinburgh. The ailing Darnley, persuaded to leave his father's protection, was also brought to the outskirts of the city, but was murdered at Kirk o'Field on the night of 9–10 February. In March James was taken back to Stirling under the care of his governor, John Erskine, earl of Mar; one last meeting with his mother took place there on 21 April. On 15 May she made her fatal remarriage to the man widely believed to have murdered Darnley, James Hepburn, earl of Bothwell, an act which temporarily united the political nation against her. Having surrendered to confederate lords (including Mar) on 15 June, Mary was incarcerated at Lochleven Castle on the 16th. Under duress and prostrated by a miscarriage, she signed a deed of abdication on 24 July, whereupon James became king. He was crowned as a protestant, still only thirteen months old, on 29 July at Stirling parish church.

The minority, 1567–c.1584 Although the circumstances of James's accession were unusual in Scotland, the youthfulness of the new king was not. Every monarch since 1406 had come to the throne as a minor. James VI was the third successive monarch to have acceded in infancy: his grandfather *James V had been eighteen months old when he became king in 1513; his mother Mary only a week old in 1542. The Stewart kings had a lamentable habit of dying young; the political nation had to cope with the consequences, and cope remarkably well it had done. During minorities the magnates had controlled the affairs of the kingdom. An absence of any aggressive or militant foreign policy meant that war was rare and thus that the Scottish crown did not bear down heavily on its subjects with endless demands for men and money. Hence political tensions were fewer, and at the beginning of James VI's reign the Scottish localities remained autonomous, to what was by then a highly unusual degree. Ties of kinship were still fundamental, written bonds of lordship and allegiance continued to be made, and the blood feud as a force for local stability and the resolution of crime, as well as in its more literally bloody form, was still alive and flourishing.

Previous monarchs had inherited on the death of a king, but Mary remained alive to cause trouble and present a grievous political problem for a further twenty years. This was compounded by the immense problem of religious reformation, new in the minority of Mary but still evolving in that of her son. A nobility, itself divided over religion, had to find a solution to religious crisis, and following the success of the protestant party in 1559–60, increasingly had to do so in the context of a confusion of traditional foreign policy. Many of the Scottish élite became less interested in ties to the 'auld allie', France, as the cornerstone of that policy and began to develop at least a veneer of friendship with the 'auld inemie', England.

In his early years James was very much a background figure, secure in his nursery and schoolroom. The choice of his principal tutor, appointed when he was four, was obvious: George Buchanan, noted European humanist, exponent of resistance theory, and slanderer of his mother, to which attributes could be added a fair degree of sadism; beating 'the Lord's Anointed' was not just a matter of discipline but of satisfaction. At the end of his life the king still had nightmares about Buchanan, although by that time, with Buchanan long dead, he could also express pride in having a tutor of great academic distinction, as he did when complimented by an English courtier on his pronunciation of Latin and Greek. But his tuition was leavened by the presence of his other tutor, the much gentler Peter Young, who later accompanied James to England, and whose son Patrick Young, a leading Greek scholar, became keeper of the king's library. By 1583 James already had a substantial library, based partly on the remnants of Mary's, and partly on the books his tutors bought for him (though Buchanan was apparently too mean to contribute free copies of his own works); it was heavily classical, but also included history, political theory, theology, languages, geography, mathematics—and also, for lighter reading and for sport, romances, bows and arrows, golf clubs, and hunting gloves. Not quite, then, all work and no play, although James's daily educational routine was formidable, producing his famous remark that 'they gar me speik Latin ar I could speik Scotis' (G. F. Warner and J. P. Gilson, *Catalogue of Western Manuscripts in the Old Royal and King's Collections*, 1921, p. xxviii). It was an ordered existence, which despite all its harshness inculcated a love of learning which marked him out in later life as a phenomenon who went well beyond the norm of highly educated early modern kings. His passion for scholarship was utterly natural and deep-rooted.

That ordered existence was in stark contrast to the lack of order in the world outside. The united front against Mary in summer 1567 had dissolved by the end of the year. She escaped from Lochleven in May 1568; but her defeat by her half-brother James Stewart, earl of Moray, at Langside and her lunatic flight to England, which she apparently believed would inspire Elizabeth to restore her to her Scottish throne, left her supporters leaderless. Moray had become regent in 1567; and initially both sides appealed to Elizabeth, in two conferences, at York and Westminster in 1568–9. The astonishing outcome was that although Moray, with great reluctance, produced the casket letters—those letters written, or alleged to have been written, by Mary to Bothwell, making clear her involvement in the Darnley murder—Elizabeth pronounced that nothing had been proved prejudicial to Mary's honour. But it was Moray who went back to Scotland, with £5000 of English money. It was no doubt a realistic assessment of the Scottish political situation, even if it meant Elizabeth paying for her own ambiguity. Moray himself was assassinated in January 1570, and Scotland lurched into a slogging and low-key civil war which dragged on until 1573, when Edinburgh Castle finally fell to the king's party. By then two more of James's regents, his grandfather the earl of Lennox (elected in July 1570) and John Erskine, earl of Mar (elected in September 1571), were dead—Lennox, like Moray, by violence; the fourth regent, James Douglas, fourth earl of Morton, came to office in November 1572.

The 1570s saw rather more political stability, and a switch away from the problem of Mary to the growing division between those who favoured an episcopal reformed church and those who, led by Andrew Melville, utterly rejected any notion of royal supremacy and episcopacy, which was to live on as the major political as well as religious issue of the 1580s and 1590s. Melville himself returned from Geneva in 1574 primarily as an educational reformer, transforming the three universities. But an educational fighter can equally be a religious fighter, and that was what, by 1578, Melville had become, picking up on the strongly anti-Erastian stance of John Knox and his fellow reformers of the 1560s, and going beyond them with his championing of presbyterianism. The struggle was in its infancy under the pro-English Morton, but it was there. Morton himself lost the regency in March 1578, in a messy *coup d'état* led by Colin Campbell, sixth earl of Argyll, and John Stewart, fourth earl of Atholl, with the king as its figurehead, although not in his own estimation; for James, three months short of his twelfth birthday, cheerfully announced his capacity to rule, and followed this up with a spectacular entry into Edinburgh in 1579, in which God and Bacchus both featured prominently, as they would throughout King James's life. It was in September this year that his cousin Esmé Stuart came over from France, to become the king's first 'favourite'. Elevated to the earldom of Lennox (the existing holder of the title, Robert Stewart, bishop of Caithness, having yielded to royal pressure to resign it) in 1580 and then raised to a dukedom in 1581, Lennox was loathed as a pro-French Catholic who enjoyed all too much of the king's favour.

Much has been made of James as the lonely teenager desperate for affection, and no doubt this played a part. But what we are seeing here is the start of a pattern which was repeated in the case of James's other three great favourites: George Gordon, earl of Huntly; and, in England, Robert Carr, earl of Somerset, and George Villiers, duke of Buckingham. James had asserted his kingship, not his loneliness; his authority, not his dependence. Lennox, like his successors, appeared on the scene and demonstrated his usefulness, in this case in the factional struggles surrounding the king, notably in his part in Morton's final downfall. Young though James still was, there were those who were already becoming worryingly aware that the Scottish king might well be an unpredictable force to be reckoned with. In 1578 Elizabeth had had her first unpalatable taste of James's refusal to be browbeaten by the middle-aged and experienced monarch. His response to her furious support of Morton was a letter fulsome in its phraseology, and determined in its refusal to do what she wished. He did promise the queen that the former regent would not be executed, but he did nothing to prevent that eventuality when it occurred in June 1581. It was not Lennox's supposed dominance which provoked Elizabeth's impassioned outburst against 'that false Scots urchin' and his double-dealing (*CSP Spain*, *1580–86*, 207–8),

nor the comments of her ambassadors Henry Carey, Lord Hunsdon, and Thomas Randolph about his perspicacity, fair speeches, and talent for dissimulation, 'wherein he is in his tender years more practised than others forty years older than he' (*CSP Scot.*, *1581–3*, 26). No wonder. Earlier that year that Mary, queen of Scots, had once more made a bid for a return to the political limelight with her proposal for an association where she should rule Scotland as joint monarch with James. Nothing would have suited Elizabeth more than to have the scandalous and discredited queen out of England with the additional advantage of re-creating political instability in Scotland that the proposal for divided sovereignty seemed to promise. James, by contrast, saw no need for guidance from his surrogate mother of England or his real mother of Scotland; he made some personal statements of affection, and stopped decisively there. He interviewed secretly some of the Spanish agents intriguing on Mary's behalf but gave neither help nor encouragement.

There was one final desperate effort to contain James's burgeoning assertion of kingship with the Ruthven raid of 1582. On 28 August a group of hardline presbyterian nobles under William Ruthven, first earl of Gowrie, kidnapped the king and placed him under house arrest in Ruthven Castle. Lennox fled to France, where he died the following May, and for ten months power was exercised by the 'raiders', with the approval of Elizabeth and support from the city of Edinburgh and the general assembly of the kirk. But in June 1583 James escaped and declared his intention to be a 'universal king', above faction (*CSP Scot.*, *1581–3*, 523). With conservatives and moderates at his back and with James Stewart, earl of Arran, emerging as the leader of an administration committed to following an independent middle way, James then showed what that meant by turning savagely on Gowrie, who was executed on 2 May 1584. There was nothing here of his mother's inability to control those who rebelled against her nor the ditherings of Elizabeth over the execution of Thomas Howard, duke of Norfolk, after the rising of the northern earls in 1569 and even the Ridolfi plot of 1571. The circumstances of James's accession, the continuing existence of his mother, the interference by Elizabeth, the religious and political tensions within Scotland: all these had posed serious and novel threats to the prestige and authority of the Scottish crown. None seems seriously to have worried King James. The minority ended on a high note of royal confidence. Arran became chancellor on 15 May and three days later John Maitland of Thirlstane became secretary; important legislation to enhance royal power soon followed. Although Arran fell from office in November 1585 with the return from exile of some of Gowrie's supporters, much of his administration and its outlook survived.

The Scottish personal rule: money and marriage, c.1584–1603

It used to be thought that James's main problem lay in the need to restrain a nobility who for two centuries had enjoyed an unusual level of political control and was far too powerful. But even the peculiarly difficult minority of James VI did not alter the pattern of the minorities. In every case factions such as the Ruthvens grabbed control of the king's person; in every case their efforts were short-lived, and they came to grief. Moreover, the very nature of Scottish society meant that faction-fighting was largely confined to the centre, and did not spill over into the localities. In every reign there were individual aristocratic rogue elephants. James had four: William Ruthven, first earl of Gowrie; his sons John Ruthven, the third earl, and Alexander Ruthven, master of Ruthven, who had the starring parts in the mysterious Gowrie conspiracy of 1600 (see below); and the erratic and unpredictable Francis Stewart, fifth earl of Bothwell, in some ways the equivalent of the second earl of Essex in England, even to the extent of bursting in on his monarch when the latter was still undressed in the bedchamber. But what the history of the Scottish monarchy in the fifteenth and sixteenth centuries shows is that strong nobles wanted strong kings with whom they could link their fortunes and from whom they could receive the rewards obtainable from the greatest patron in the land. This is evocatively manifest in the remarkable custom, which came into existence in the mid-fifteenth century in the second of the minorities, that of James II, whereby kings when they reached majority issued acts of revocation cancelling all minority grants on the ground that they should not be bound by such grants made in their name but over which they had no control. James's own view of the matter is seen in the extent of his appointments of aristocrats to major offices of state, such as John Graham, third earl of Montrose, who became chancellor in 1599, after a period as treasurer beginning in 1584.

The major problems of the reign of James VI were very different. There was a rapid development in Scottish central government. Scotland in 1603 was a very different place from the Scotland of 1580. What is open to debate, though, is how far this was inspired by as well as presided over by the king. It may be that James, with an eye to his English future, wanted a more 'modern', more centralized kingdom from which to launch his English kingship. But that is probably to read back too much from that endlessly misunderstood, decontextualized, and over-quoted phrase plucked from his speech to his English parliament in 1607, 'here I sit and governe it [Scotland] with my Pen, I write and it is done' (James VI and I: Political Writings, 173). This had some truth, in that inevitably absentee government involved government by post, but as a claim to power it would have been nonsense even if made by the most mighty of early modern kings, and it makes no sense at all as a description of how James had ruled his Scottish kingdom before 1603.

There is only one area, indeed, where James's responsibility for the change cannot be doubted: taxation. Scotland suffered as much as England would later do from his hopeless extravagance: any money James had—and it must be admitted that, given the depleted revenues of the Scottish crown, that was not much—he spent. Inevitably there was a sudden increase in expenditure as James emerged from the austere confines of the schoolroom, but the reorganization of the royal household by Lennox

(who like later favourites was generously rewarded by the king) in 1580–81 entailed both a substantial increase in staff (to twenty-four gentlemen of the chamber and a guard of sixty men-at-arms) and a pursuit of recreation and pleasure that scandalized Lennox's enemies in the kirk. In the same period regular taxation was introduced into Scotland for the first time: at a meeting of the convention of estates in February 1581 it was resolved that £40,000 Scots be raised for the country's defence. Years of political stability were in themselves expensive, but also encouraged a hand-to-mouth attitude to running the royal household which was inimical to prudent budgeting. Once stability came the attitude proved difficult to shed and new financial commitments appeared which easily swallowed up the annual pension of £4000 advanced by Elizabeth from 1586. A royal marriage promised a useful dowry but provided the occasion for conspicuous expenditure in the short and longer term.

The idea of a Danish match for James was being discussed from 1581, and a series of negotiations took place between 1585 and 1589. Another possibility, introduced in 1587, was Henri of Navarre's sister Catherine de Bourbon, but the future Henri IV wanted military support in his struggle for the French throne, which James could not or would not give, especially as Henri could not afford a generous dowry. The better choice remained a daughter of the Danish king Frederick II, and James married his younger daughter *Anne (Anna) of Denmark (1574–1619)—with a more acceptable dowry, if one cut down from the outrageous Scottish demand for £1 million Scots to £150,000 Scots. However, this was counterbalanced by the £100,000 Scots levied within Scotland to pay for attendant festivities. With a dash of real romance, James emulated his grandfather James V, who had had a splendid nine-month holiday in France when claiming his bride, François I's daughter Madeleine. When storms prevented Anne coming to Scotland in 1589 following her proxy marriage to him on 20 August, he sailed to Oslo, and had an equally enjoyable if rather shorter holiday, between November 1589 and April 1590, celebrating the marriage ceremony in church on 23 November, travelling about, having intellectual discussions with leading Scandinavian theologians and scientists, and falling in love with his new wife.

Fifteen-year-old Anna, as she was known in Scotland, received a gilded welcome in her new country and a splendid coronation at Holyrood Abbey on 17 May 1590. Subsequently her developed artistic, dramatic, and musical tastes and her dynastic success—five royal children born in Scotland, of whom two sons and a daughter survived to accompany their parents to England—contributed to continuing high expenditure. The baptism of Prince *Henry Frederick (1594–1612) was celebrated with banquets, masques, and tilts and occasioned a levy of £100,000 Scots (an increase of 800 per cent on that levied for James's own baptism). The prince's removal from his mother and placing in the care of the earl of Mar, though well precedented, set a pattern of parallel royal households as well as causing unfortunate friction between Anne and James.

His younger sister *Elizabeth (1596–1662) and younger brother *Charles (1600–1649) were also fostered.

Attempts to increase income met with limited success. Debasement of the coinage between 1583 and 1596 through reduction of its silver content produced a paper profit but exacerbated the inflation which depressed the real income of all European rulers at this period. Improved customs revenues and more efficient collection of fines constituted a drop in the ocean. Various efforts were made by harassed royal officials to control the king and thus address expenditure. Thus in December 1591 the response to his bad-tempered suggestion that his exchequer officials had more care for themselves than for his interests produced by return of post six furious pages in which his shortcomings were clearly laid out. Their fury was entirely understandable: as they complained, for example, the answer to James's naïve question about whether the royal palace of Linlithgow was his wife's or the lord justice clerk's was that thanks to his muddling it was both. A gentler, but equally ineffective, attempt was made in 1596. In a carefully stage-managed piece of play acting his queen (not a lightweight, as traditionally viewed, but a significant player in the factional politics of the decade) presented him with a bag of gold coins at new year. Asked by an astonished king how she had amassed it, she explained that it was a matter of careful household management. James promptly took over her household officials, the eight Octavians. They lasted for less than a year. As the earl of Salisbury and Lionel Cranfield later found, the king had periods of genuine good intentions, but they did not last, caught as he was between the necessity of fiscal control and the demands made on his patronage, for stinginess was a notably unacceptable royal attribute. Hence his request for regular subsidies. The effect was that the government was now pressing on the governed in a new way, and was thus beginning to alter the traditional relationship between centre and locality.

The Scottish personal rule: administration and parliament, c.1584–1603 Beyond this, however, factors other than King James were creating the pressures transforming Scottish central government. One such pressure came from the increasingly literate and ambitious lairds, with their demands for place in court and government, made all the more compelling when the kirk in 1584 pulled its ministers firmly out of state service. The demand was not new. One of James's greatest officials from the lay élite was John Maitland of Thirlestane, secretary and then chancellor, son of Richard Maitland of Lethington, poet and keeper of the privy seal, and brother of Mary's brilliant secretary William Maitland of Lethington. It was a family which can be likened to the Cecils in England, moving in from its local base to make its fortune in crown service, and being rewarded by a peerage and a new level of prestige back in the locality. The Maitlands, Alexander Seton of Fyvie, George Home of Spott, Thomas Hamilton of Binning: these and others like them became prominent in the king's government before 1603, and after 1603 found that James's removal to England meant that an aristocratically minded king now raised them to the peerage, giving them

the dignity and status in the political nation traditionally associated with the landed aristocracy, and in effect creating a *noblesse de robe* which would govern Scotland in his name. Yet the king's attitude to such a change was not entirely clear-cut. Thus after the death of Maitland on 3 October 1595 he removed himself firmly from his capital, going off to Linlithgow to escape the demands of the 'faccaneres' or 'faccioners' at court (*CSP Scot.*, 12.6), with their intriguing and their incessant fascination with the subject of Maitland's successor; and at the same time he was deeply concerned that the death of the earl of Atholl without heirs would leave Perthshire without its natural means of control. This was a highly traditional view of how power in the Scottish state should work. And his solution to the pressure of the factionists, which was to keep the office of chancellor vacant until January 1599, hardly suggests a king primarily interested in the institutional workings of central government. It was, after all, not so much the monarch as his new nobles and the rising breed of professional lawyers whose view of the kingdom of Scotland no longer regarded as acceptable the bonds of lordship and service—maintenance and manrent—and the justice of the feud, in relation either to their Scottish aspirations or, after 1603, to their involvement with James's new kingdom of England which had long rejected both.

Equally the major institutions of government in state and church, parliament and the new and formidable national court of the kirk, the general assembly, forced on the crown a degree of management never before necessary. Scottish parliaments had always been vocal and often highly critical. However, James had to deal with protestants who might be of varying persuasions, but who could all remember the heady days of 1560, when the Reformation Parliament, acting in defiance of the Catholic monarch, brought down the old church. This memory was all the more menacing because of the parliament's astonishing ability to concentrate on the essentials. By contrast with the seven years and numerous acts of Henry VIII's Reformation Parliament, its Scottish equivalent took three weeks and three acts to achieve its aims, leaving the details to be filled in later. As James was later to say, understandably, English parliaments were too long, Scottish parliaments too short. But he undoubtedly understood the significance of the institution. The idea that James I did not know how to manage parliaments makes very little sense when James VI's record is considered. He had one considerable advantage. The Scottish parliament, like European national assemblies, was a joint meeting of the three estates, and the king could be present in person. Moreover, the detailed work on legislation was done by the lords of the articles, an elected committee from the representatives of the three estates. The full parliament assembled and elected the lords of the articles, who settled down to the donkey work; and then the full parliament returned. It used to be thought that this made the Scottish parliament an easy body to manipulate. This is not a mistake which King James ever made; the intrusion of the officers of state as a fourth 'estate', begun in 1567 and increasingly imposed by the king, was a deliberate attempt to impose control, however difficult to sustain in the face of parliamentary criticism and efforts at curtailment. Moreover, the disappearance of the clerical estate, with the *de facto* disappearance of the episcopate between 1592 and 1600, denied the crown much-needed allies in the face of parliamentary support for presbyterian activists within the kirk.

Hence the 1580s and 1590s saw a series of acts which sought to strengthen royal control. The Reformation Parliament of 1560 had seen an unprecedented rush of over 100 lairds to attend, claiming their right under the wholly moribund Shire Election Act of 1428. After 1560 the unchallenged presence of such lairds who chose to turn up, in unpredictable numbers, was an unacceptable headache for the government; and in 1587 the Shire Election Act was duly re-enacted. In 1594 there was a determined onslaught on parliamentary business. Four members of each estate were to meet twenty days before parliament assembled, to receive articles and supplications and sift out frivolous material; only the king was exempt from the twenty-days rule. A long day's work was imposed on them in time of parliament; they were to sit each day from 8 a.m. until 6 p.m. And in the same year, according to the highly critical presbyterian minister David Calderwood, the king asserted his right to vote with the articles. Moreover, while James might casually leave the office of chancellor vacant in the mid-1590s, he had already empowered the chancellor in 1584 to use the sceptre for the ratification of acts, a measure which would have its full relevance after 1603.

Yet this was by no means the whole story. Another indication of James's high sense of his own kingship as early as 1581, when he was fifteen, is that it was in this year that parliament passed his first, admittedly limited, revocations and followed this up with another limited act in 1584; the full general act came in 1587, when he was twenty-one. The 1584 parliament thundered out its endorsement of the king's authority over church and state, and its condemnation of slanderers of the king and—significantly—his parents and progenitors, and specifically attacked the offensive works of Buchanan. At the same time this future divine-right monarch, who was to tantalize and infuriate his English parliament on the subject of king or king-in-parliament as law maker, cheerfully underwrote 'the lawis and actis of parliament (be quhilkis all men ar governit)' (*APS*, 3.293). And in 1587 the king further emphasized the importance and dignity of parliament, in the acts which laid out the rules for the 'riding of parliament' from the palace of Holyroodhouse to the parliament house, and empowered James to design the appropriate robes for each estate. It is not to deny the tensions within the Scottish kingdom to say that, while the records of parliament make them all too clear, they also reflect a certain appealing rumbustiousness with which the king was undoubtedly relaxed, cheerful, and at ease because he was in control without having to assert his royalty too aggressively.

The king and the kirk Rumbustiousness is not, on the other hand, the most notable feature of James's dealings with his kirk, and in particular with its most oppressively godly wing. Yet it is there that his dry, sardonic, and sometimes crude humour is seen to the full, no doubt enhanced by the distinctly humourless approach of his opponents. The extreme presbyterian wing of the kirk was anti-episcopal, hostile, outspoken, and violently critical, using that excellent outlet for media propaganda, the pulpit, to the full; moreover, it denied the king any authority over the kirk, for their king was Christ, and King James 'but a member' (Calderwood, 5.440). Indeed, the struggle with Andrew Melville and his supporters was the major political as well as religious issue of the reign, as well as the main inspiration, even more than the contractual theorizing of Buchanan, for James's own theory about kingship, developed in the late 1590s.

The situation was a good deal less clear-cut, however, than simply King James versus the godly. James charged into lively battle with the extremists, those 'vaine pharasaicall puritanes' (*Basilikon Doron*, 1.39). But there were few who were consistently antagonistic to the king throughout the 1580s and 1590s; there were royal servants, most notably John Maitland of Thirlestane, James's secretary and then chancellor, who could rise to the top in government while being more sympathetic to the presbyterians than was the king himself; there were points on which king and godly, including even Andrew Melville himself, agreed; and above all, while the king might dislike the extremists, it was more because they were extremists—as he said of himself in 1607, he was 'ever for the Medium in every thing' (*James VI and I: Political Writings*, 161)—than because they were to be feared. There was indeed a long-drawn-out struggle for control of the church; and there were times when the king's position looked weak. But these times were few.

As with the state, so with the church. James's emergence from his minority had witnessed a highly confident assertion of royal authority over the kirk. In February 1584 Andrew Melville, summoned before the privy council because of a seditious sermon, denied its competence on the ground that only the general assembly could hear the case; he was ordered into ward, and fled to England, to be followed over the following months by some twenty ministers and academics—along with those nobles who tried unsuccessfully in April to revive the power of the Ruthven faction. This cleared the way for the passing by the parliament which met in May of the Black Acts, which denounced presbyteries; affirmed the authority of bishops, making them in effect answerable to the king rather than the general assembly; asserted the king's supremacy over all matters, secular and ecclesiastical; and—most crucially for the future—insisted on his right to summon general assemblies. These acts have been ascribed to the regime of James Stewart, earl of Arran, who became the leading figure in James's government following the king's escape from the Ruthven raiders in 1583; but there is no reason to question the king's own role in them. They were followed up by the enforcement of subscription to them by generally unwilling ministers. For James Melville, Andrew's nephew, they meant that parliament had created a new pope, and 'sa becum traitors to Chryst' (Melville, 208). And off he went to Newcastle in 1584, to give spiritual succour to the exiled Ruthven faction, invoking Old Testament language in appealing to them as 'valiant warriors and capteanes of the Lords army' (ibid., 178), which no doubt he regarded as sufficient cover for encouragement of armed rebellion.

Yet James's agenda was very far removed from English royal supremacy and from developing ideas of *jure divino* episcopacy. Probably the only person who had any such embryonic ideas was the unfortunate Patrick Adamson, archbishop of St Andrews, whose *Declaration of the Kingis Majesties Intentioun and Meaning toward the Lait Actis of Parliament* (1585) undoubtedly went much further than James's intentions and was, indeed, a considerable embarrassment to the king when the authorship of the tract was ascribed to him; hence the occasion when he toasted his hunting dogs, and especially Tell-true, to whom he would give 'more credence nor either the bishop or Craig' (John Craig, moderate presbyterian and king's minister, but opponent of the Black Acts) (Calderwood, 4.351). The faithful hound was clearly a good deal more acceptable than either excessive supporter or opponent of the acts.

This is hardly surprising. James was undoubtedly threatened as he began his personal rule by the existence of a powerful and vocal party in the kirk, supported by an aristocratic faction sitting just over the border in Newcastle. But the idea of the king and the presbyterians locked throughout his adult rule in perennial and knife-edge combat, which the king only just succeeded in winning, is far too simple. That picture emanates from the bitter and vitriolic invective of three of the extremists: James Melville's autobiography and diary, and the early seventeenth-century histories of David Calderwood (*The True History of the Kirk of Scotland*) and John Row (*The Historie of the Kirk of Scotland*), works all the more bitter and vitriolic because their authors were the losers. Theirs was a highly biased view, which had to depict an extremist king with his acolyte bishops pitted against militant kirkmen fighting for God's true cause, and could therefore give no hint of uncertainties or moderation within the kirk.

What happened, rather, was that James's emergence as an effective adult monarch posed both king and kirk with a problem which had been uniquely absent from the kirk since the success of the reformers in 1560: the role of that king in a kirk hitherto free from effective and consistent royal interference, let alone control. There was indeed a struggle, sometimes tense and sometimes bitter. The language used by the extremists in the kirk was undoubtedly the language of Christian militancy rather than Christian charity, in a particularly graceless form. The king could be equally graceless, but decidedly less humourless; thus 'I will not give a turd for thy preaching' was his response to Robert Gibson, who in a sermon in 1585 likened this persecuting king to Jeroboam, a view no doubt confirmed in Gibson's eyes when he was sent off to ward in Edinburgh

Castle (Calderwood, 4.487). Two years earlier the hectoring lecture by John Davidson about the kirk's concern for his welfare included the dire warning that 'nather ought your Grace to mak light accompt of our threatenings; for there was never one yitt in this realme, in chief authoritie, that ever prospered after the ministers began to threaten him'. The maddening response was that 'the king smiled' (Calderwood, 3.718). Sermons by the godly could certainly be outspoken in the extreme. Gibson, the Melvilles, David Black, and their like were all too willing to attack openly; thus in 1596 Black was brought to trial for announcing from the pulpit that the queen of England was an atheist, and all kings were 'the devils bairns' (Spottiswoode, 3.21). Most famous was the occasion at Falkland in September 1596 when Andrew Melville grabbed the king's sleeve, calling him 'God's sillie [weak] vassal', and telling him that 'thair is twa Kings and twa Kingdomes … Thair is Chryst Jesus the King, and his Kingdome the Kirk, whase subject King James the Saxt is, and of whase kingdome nocht a king nor a lord, nor a heid, bot a member' (Calderwood, 5.440). But while episodes like this would undoubtedly have driven Elizabeth to hysterical fury, the much more pragmatic James could afford to take a cooler line. For they demonstrated that in the struggle for control the king had the upper hand; ministers who acted as spokesmen for the Lord in this way normally found themselves warded or exiled.

James naturally wanted to control the extremists in the kirk; and he had the inestimable advantage that he was the king. Once he was there to challenge the independence which the kirk had enjoyed, it was only the very boldest spirits who would openly defy him; less brave critics muttered and sulked—but ultimately conformed. Yet king and kirkmen had more in common than has been supposed. Indeed, as theologian-king James had a vision of the kirk and a doctrinal belief which in many ways matched that of even the extremists. It has, for example, recently been shown that he was far less enthusiastic about episcopacy than used to be thought; between 1585 and 1600 he did nothing to fill vacant bishoprics. He himself struck a blow at the bishops when, in his act of annexation in 1587, he annexed their temporalities—that 'vile act' as he later, in a different frame of mind, called it (*Basilikon Doron*, 1.79). Moreover, efforts to improve the academic standing of the ministers, their university education reinforced by the dignity of reasonable stipends, stemmed from a shared view, which meant that before 1603 the Scottish ministers were a more respected and better paid breed than their English counterparts, an achievement which continued into the seventeenth century, if the English MP Sir Benjamin Rudyerd's comparison between them in 1628 is to be believed. The origin of the Authorized Version of the Bible lay in his proposal to the general assembly in 1601. It was not followed up; 'yet did not the King let this intention fall to the ground, but after his happy coming to the Crown of England set the most learned Divines of that Church a work for the translation of the Bible' (Spottiswoode, 3.99).

Shared scholarly aspirations are even echoed in the row

between James and Melville in 1596 which, spectacular as it was, does have something of the flavour of impassioned academic debate between two fiery and highly able scholarly opponents. And even Melville himself, in a much less well known role, was prepared to extol Jacobean kingship. He had produced a Latin poem for the coronation of Anne of Denmark in 1590 and again for the baptism of Prince Henry in 1594; the latter specifically looked to James's and Henry's future, addressing James as 'Scoto-Britanno Rege' (Doleman, 61), and anticipating his three poems heralding James's succession to the English throne in 1603. These, along with his highly critical poems about the English church, surely suggest that for Melville, as for David Black, James might not be as godly a prince as they sought, but he and the Scottish kirk were infinitely preferable to the queen of England and her church.

James had his own problems with a monarch violently hostile to presbyterianism among her native subjects yet willing to offer the haven of London, and even its pulpits, to his presbyterian exiles who followed in the footsteps of the continental Reformed congregations of earlier immigrants; Elizabeth's enthusiasm for divinely ordained monarchy and the royal supremacy seems to have been firmly bounded by the English Channel and the Scottish border. But the astonishing rant by Richard Bancroft, chaplain to the lord chancellor and future archbishop of Canterbury, in his Paul's Cross sermon of 1589 against the Scottish presbyterians, and his hysterical outpourings on the same theme in two pamphlets of 1593, *A Survey of the Pretended Holy Discipline* and *Daungerous Positions and Proceedings*, all depicting a king browbeaten by intolerable ministers who appeared to be worse than Catholics, and exaggerating the king's desire for an episcopal church, certainly brought king and kirk together. 'Let not his Majestie nor any prince looke for any better dealing at the handes of any of his [Bancroft's] coat' said John Davidson, trouncing Bancroft for his lack of reverence to King James (D. Laing, ed., *The Miscellany of the Wodrow Society, Volume First*, Wodrow Society, 9, 1844, 508). And in the general assembly of 1590, despite a certain amount of the usual rhetoric in a sermon by James Melville, about 'binding of kings in chains, and the most honourable princes in fetters of yron', the king launched into a speech

> praising God, that he was borne in such a tyme as the tyme of the light of the Gospell, to suche a place as to be king in suche a kirk, the sincerest kirk in the world ... As for our neighbour kirk in England, it is an evill masse in English, wanting nothing but the liftings. I charge you ... to stand to your puritie ... and I, forsuith, as long as I bruike my life and crowne, sall manteane the same.

This brought him the reward that 'the Assemblie so rejoiced, that there was nothing but loud praising of God, and praying for the king for quarter of an houre' (Calderwood, 5.102, 106).

The attack on the English church was not inspired, however, only by Bancroft and the need to please the assembly. Relations between the latter and the king were in any case good owing to a number of factors: James's marriage to the Lutheran princess Anne of Denmark in 1589; his willingness during his absence in Norway and Denmark to claim his bride to allow the godly Robert Bruce, a man whose theological views might have been expected to make him anathema to the king, a place in government; and his choice of him as the minister who crowned and anointed Anne. Moreover, the same hostility towards the English ecclesiastical model surfaced later in the decade. The assembly had by then come to agree with the king about the usefulness of restoring a clerical estate in parliament. Where they disagreed was on who should form that estate. For the assembly it would be ministers elected annually, but the king was moving towards the idea of parliamentary bishops. 'We see him well enough', said Davidson; 'we see the horns of his mitre'. But in 1598 James stated unequivocally to the assembly that 'I minde not ... to bring in Papisticall or Anglican bishopping' (Calderwood, 5.681, 694). This was true enough. The first three parliamentary bishops, appointed in 1600, were nominated by the king and his commissioners and the brethren of the kirk; and even after the restoration of diocesan episcopacy from 1610 the Scottish Jacobean bishop was always a much more low-key figure than his English counterpart.

Crises of the 1590s and the Gowrie conspiracy This, then, is the context in which the two big dramas of 1592 and 1596 must be set. In 1592 parliament passed the Golden Act which gave legal ratification to presbyteries, and annulled several of the Black Acts of 1584. A great triumph for the Melvillians; or was it? It is certainly the case that James was in a comparatively weak position. In February 1592 the Catholic George Gordon, sixth earl (and later first marquess) of Huntly, at feud with the protestant James Stewart, second earl of Moray, in the north-east, caught up with him at Donibristle on the Forth, where he was murdered by Huntly or one of his followers. The kirk now had a lever against a king suspected of complicity, who undoubtedly treated Huntly with an offensive degree of leniency. Moreover, it chose to regard the unreliable Bothwell, who had threatened James in Holyrood in December 1591, as an ally. However, the Golden Act still falls very short of Melvillian victory. The Black Act which had asserted the crown's authority in matters spiritual and temporal was not annulled; and, crucially, the king retained his right to summon and decide on the meeting place of the general assemblies. The state was legislating for the kirk; and the 'concessions' to the crown were very far from minor, as the jubilant presbyterians of 1592 sadly came to realize in the following years when the king took full advantage of his ability to control the meetings of the assembly. The parliament which passed the Golden Act did something else undoubtedly pleasing to James: it forfeited the kirk's great protestant earl, Bothwell.

From the Melvillians' point of view 1596 was even worse; indeed, disastrous. The presbyterian writers, indulging in a good deal of wishful thinking but not much sense of reality, chose to portray 1596 as the year in which God's kirk reached its highest point of perfection, only to be defeated at the end of the year by the violent machinations of King James. But Melville's breathtaking assertions delivered to James in September at Falkland did not deflect the king one whit. Then in November David Black was summoned by the privy council for an undoubtedly seditious sermon preached in October. Like Melville before him, he refused to accept the jurisdiction of the council. Heavy backing from the Melvillians did him no good; he was warded in December. The king then cancelled the assembly due to meet in January 1597, and ordered the commissioners to leave Edinburgh, as they duly did. The Edinburgh ministers carried on the fight, with some lay backing. Rumours of a Catholic rising then produced on 17 December a near riot or, as James preferred, 'the lait tressounable, shamefull and seditious uproare' (*Reg. PCS*, 5.349). That was his excuse for his dramatic departure from Edinburgh with the privy council and the lawcourts. The burgh council of James's capital city promptly saw where its future lay: in a humble apology to the king, and a down payment. The ministers fled, and James returned to Edinburgh. This is supposed to have been the great turning point in James's struggle with the kirk. In fact the events of the year leading up to the spectacular royal gesture do not suggest weakness suddenly giving way to strength; and the gesture itself was the culmination of the policy of dividing the moderates from the extremists, leaving only a small minority—the Edinburgh ministers—to try to orchestrate resistance, with fatal results.

The final crisis of the period, the dark and confusing Gowrie conspiracy of August 1600, apparently had no direct connection with the kirk. The protagonists, John Ruthven, earl of Gowrie, and his brother Alexander were staunch aristocratic supporters of the presbyterians, but their supposed actions had virtually no ministerial backing, before or after the event. It seems likelier than not that their conspiracy was genuine, but because they perished in the course of it the exact truth of the affair is hard to come by and there is much reliance on the account given by James himself, who perceived it as a murder plot. In the early summer of 1600 Gowrie, to whom the king was in debt to the tune of £48,000 Scots, and Alexander, whom gossip had singled out as a favourite of the queen, quitted the court for their country estates. It seems that while there they received correspondence from the king. According to James, early in the morning of 5 August Alexander appeared at Falkland Palace and related to him a story of a treasure trove found by the brothers and now locked up at Gowrie House in Perth. Ultimately persuaded that he must investigate, James left for Perth with what became a large entourage of curious courtiers. On arrival at Gowrie House they found the earl behaving strangely and the household ill-prepared for so large a party. After a delayed and private meal with the brothers, James retired with Alexander Ruthven and Gowrie's chamberlain Andrew Henderson to a small upper room. Both the king and Henderson later testified that Ruthven then locked the door and seized a dagger, threatening James with death in revenge for his part in the execution of William

Ruthven sixteen years earlier. When Alexander left the king in Henderson's keeping and went in search of Gowrie, James thrust his head out of the turret's window, crying treason and murder. Courtiers, who were by this time milling in the garden below in some confusion as to James's whereabouts, rushed up to his aid, and by the time Gowrie, who had gone out into the town, followed them, he found Alexander dead on the stairs. Rampaging into the chamber brandishing two swords, Gowrie stopped short of attacking the king himself and put down his blades. He was then killed instantly, though by whom is unclear.

While it has been argued by some historians that the whole incident stemmed from an intention by James to rid himself of a family with a history of disaffection and treason, there is no evidence to implicate him in any plot. However, he proceeded against the dead brothers with unprecedented ferocity. Following a posthumous trial, they were declared guilty of treason by parliament on 15 November; their property was forfeited to the crown and their descendants disinherited; their bodies were hanged, drawn, quartered, and distributed to strategic locations in Edinburgh and Perth; and the very name of Ruthven was banned. An annual commemoration day on 5 August was also inaugurated, establishing itself sufficiently to be observed later in England too. In the immediate aftermath of the conspiracy only five Edinburgh ministers refused to give thanks to God, as the king commanded, for his safe deliverance; they were duly banished, and four rapidly gave way. This was the final reinforcement of the message delivered to defiant clergy in 1596 that their independent stance would get them nowhere.

Witches and Catholics There were, of course, other problems which rumbled on beneath the dramatic highlights, in an ongoing Greek chorus about witches and Catholics. Witch-hunting did not begin in the 1590s; there had been sporadic outbreaks since the passing of the Witchcraft Act in 1563, and awareness of the demonic pact at least since 1572. James himself had met a notorious witch when he was in Aberdeen in 1589; but neither she nor the witches who were menacing Edinburgh and Haddingtonshire in 1590 seemed to hold much terror or even interest for him. That changed virtually overnight, with the spectacular discovery of a coven at North Berwick [*see* North Berwick witches] which was purportedly in league with the devil to destroy the king, his greatest enemy on earth. This piece of flattery, helpfully relayed by the witches to the king, was not itself the flashpoint; James remained surprisingly sceptical, to the utter indignation of the witches. Their spokeswoman, that stately midwife Agnes Sampson, insisted that they were indeed witches and that she would prove it, which she apparently did by telling James of his conversation with his wife, Anne, on their wedding night in Oslo. Scepticism turned to fear and credulity; and the most famous witch-hunt in Scottish history began.

The Scottish witch was a fearsome and compelling figure, far removed from the stereotypical old and impoverished crone. The North Berwick witches and warlocks ranged in social status from a maidservant and a plough-man to a schoolmaster, to the impressive and dignified Agnes Sampson, to members of the legal and gentry circles of Edinburgh, and even to an earl, Bothwell. James wrote, in his *Daemonologie* of 1597, about the inversion of the coven, the hideous parody by God's Ape of the service prescribed by God; he missed the ironic dimension of that inversion, that tough Scottish witches were no more pre-pared to put up with lengthy sermons from the devil than those who suffered from godly ministers. But it was not just the toughness of the witches that created the fever of persecution, which in 1591–2 and again in 1596–7 spread far beyond the North Berwick case. That was made pos-sible by the creation of legal machinery. Standing commissions of the privy council were set up, the first in 1591 Edinburgh-based, the second in 1592 extended throughout the kingdom, enabling commissioners of the general assembly to choose the nobles, lairds, and bur-gesses who would serve in the localities. This new arrange-ment of 8 June 1592 was established at a time of compara-tive weakness for the crown and temporary ascendancy of the kirk, three days after the passing of the Golden Acts.

The North Berwick witches and his own book on the subject have turned King James into the royal demonolo-gist. It is a much exaggerated reputation. By 1597 the king's scepticism had returned, despite the fact that he was once again plagued by witches, some of whom threat-ened his life. And because the standing commissions meant that 'grite danger may ensew to honnest and fam-ous personis', James revoked them in August 1597 (*Reg. PCS*, 5.409). Thereafter an infuriated kirk, and disap-pointed English subjects who produced witches for his inspection, were faced with lack of belief. When Shake-speare used Macbeth's witches, as recounted by the early sixteenth-century scholar Hector Boece, to flatter the new English king, he wrote a magnificent play; but he mistook his target.

James's record as far as the Catholics were concerned was if anything even worse for many hot protestants; his refusal to persecute Catholics permanently kept up the hackles of the kirk. It also antagonized his sister monarch of England (for reasons of inculcating obedience if not of faith) and her leading ministers, whose persecution of Catholics was intensified in the last twenty years of Eliza-beth's reign, but who would have to deal with a non-persecuting king after 1603. Jesuit missionaries in the north-east faced nothing of the persecution suffered by their counterparts in England. Indeed, towards the end of James's life, when the bishop of the Isles appealed to him to take action against the Jesuits in the western highlands, his sardonic response was that if anyone could civilize the highlanders, even if they were papists, they were wel-come to get on with it. Beginning with Esmé Stuart, duke of Lennox, Catholics had a presence in James's court and government which lasted throughout his life. At least three of the Octavians appointed at the beginning of 1596 to manage the ghastly tangle of his finances had Catholic sympathies. While the king had soon had enough of

household retrenchment and dispensed with their ser-vices, individually they survived in political life. Two of their Catholic or crypto-Catholic members, Alexander Seton of Fyvie and the lord advocate Thomas Hamilton, went on to become earls of Dunfermline and Melrose and, after the earl of Dunbar's death in 1611, the leading poli-ticians in Scotland. Three exiled Catholic bishops were brought into James's favour; one, James Beaton, arch-bishop of Glasgow, he used as his ambassador to France. It was the Catholic poet Alexander Montgomerie who pre-sided over the revival of court culture in the 1580s. Cathol-icism reached the highest circles of court when, some time in 1601–2, the queen herself converted. According to her confessor, when she tremblingly admitted this to the king, the response was not the expected roar of rage, but a plea that she should not allow her new faith to become a political embarrassment. It was James's good fortune that she had the sense not to do so, unlike his son's wife, the overweening and highly embarrassing Henrietta Maria.

Worst of all to the Scottish kirk and the queen of Eng-land were the Scottish Catholic northern earls—Huntly, Francis Hay, ninth earl of Erroll, David Lindsay, eleventh earl of Crawford, and William Douglas, tenth earl of Angus—of whom the greatest, Huntly, was an undoubted favourite of the king; for their activities were on an inter-national scale. In 1589 and again in 1592 they had been in contact with Philip II, offering aid for a renewed Spanish invasion first of England and then of the west coast of Scotland. Their intentions merit serious consideration; they were not just belated examples of the over-mighty aristocracy beloved of older generations of historians, but adherents of the Counter-Reformation seeking support from the mightiest Catholic power, even if with no more success than their counterparts in England, the English northern earls in 1569, or Roberto di Ridolfi. Twice, in 1589 and 1594, the king led his forces against them; on both occasions they refused to fight him. Catholic traitors in Scotland and, for that matter, Scottish witches and two hardline presbyterians, Gowrie and his brother, were, it seems, far less willing to kill their monarch than were Catholic traitors in England.

Under pressure the earls were prepared to trim. Huntly had made a very short-lived conversion to Catholicism in 1588, at the time of his marriage to Henrietta, daughter of Esmé Stuart. Exiled in 1595, Huntly and Erroll came back in 1596 with a promise to make their peace with king and kirk. This was the second of Huntly's four conversions in the course of a very long life; he died a Catholic in 1626. It was also by far the most enjoyable. In June 1597 he and Erroll were solemnly accepted by the kirk in Aberdeen. There then followed a riotous street party, which ended with broken glasses littering the pavements. It is pleasant to record, as an antidote to godly gloom, that some of these glasses had been in the hands of the ministers.

Foreign relations Another Jacobean myth is that James's desperation to succeed Elizabeth meant that he endlessly danced to her tune. It was very much otherwise. Unlike his mother, he was not obsessed by dreams of the English throne, but reverted to the earlier Stewart tradition of an inflated pride in kingship of Scotland, inflated because their kingdom was in fact remote and impoverished, but highly effective in that it encouraged their subjects to think likewise. It was a tradition sustained at the council tables rather than the battlefields of Europe. Given its lack of resources, in men and money, Scotland was fortunate in that none but England had tried to conquer it, and even more fortunate that all would-be conquerors had failed to do so; Scottish pride in successful resistance was reflected time and again in the literature of the period, from the late fourteenth century. That pride also enabled it to become a truly European nation. Its kings made their presence felt on the diplomatic stage; its scholars flocked to European universities; its merchants maintained profitable trade links with mainland Europe and with the Baltic, in which England played a minimal part; its art and culture were heavily influenced by Burgundy, France, and Italy. Jacobean diplomacy therefore involved contact with the Baltic—formalized by James's marriage to Anne of Denmark—the United Provinces, France, Spain, and the papacy; and, despite the howls of the kirk, trade was maintained with France and opened up with Spain. Confessional divisions within Europe now enabled this king, who believed himself to be the leading protestant prince of Europe but was also of a profoundly ecumenical cast of mind, to pursue a very catholic foreign policy, in which he combined friendship with the protestant powers with good relations with the Catholic ones, presenting himself as *rex pacificus*.

James's diplomacy was not always, of course, motivated by lofty ecumenical vision. James was a practising politician. In 1595–6 he engaged in some very shady diplomacy, sending John Ogilvy (Pourie Ogilvy) to Madrid and Rome. There Ogilvy gave out that James had an enthusiasm for the Catholic faith which circumstances made it impossible for him to acknowledge openly. In Rome he overplayed his hand by suggesting that a papal pension might make things easier; understandably the pope was not convinced. But the real intention was to discourage Spain from running a Catholic claimant on Elizabeth's death, and to that extent it succeeded. Rumours that he hoped to convert his Scottish and then his English kingdom lingered on for a decade, and contributed towards dissuading the infanta Isabella from making any move over the English succession.

This is the context into which James's relations with Elizabeth must be set. The child who had roused her rage when in 1578 he sent her a flattering letter which ended with his refusal to take her advice, the 'false Scots urchin' of 1581, did not change; throughout her life her efforts to play a maternal role, advising a young and inexperienced king, were a dismal failure. 'Methink I do but dream', she burst out in fury in 1592 over James's treatment of the northern earls (Calderwood, 5.8). The king did nothing to awaken her; he himself, like his northern earls, was weighing up the advantages of friendship with Spain in that year. Unlike his mother, with her constant nagging about the English succession, James after Mary's death in 1587 knew perfectly well that he was the obvious successor to the childless queen. The propensity of Tudor monarchs for playing around with the succession was the only conceivable threat from Elizabeth. Thus in 1588 James demanded an English dukedom as one of the prices for support against the Armada, in order to remove the taint of being an alien; no dukedom was forthcoming, but neither was the support. But although as late as 1600 Sir Thomas Wilson could record that no one dared mention the Scottish king as a possible successor, and even on her deathbed it is not entirely clear whether Elizabeth did recognize him as her heir, she came very close to admitting reality in 1587, referring to the 'greater prize' which James would get if he did nothing to react to his mother's execution. The king had no pressing need, therefore, to seek her goodwill. Hence in 1584 he could cheerfully turn down the proposed solution to the problem of Mary, that she should be restored to her Scottish throne as joint ruler with James; he enjoyed his kingship, and was far too confident in his own abilities to want to share it with a difficult and damaging woman.

Thus it is not surprising to find that James's interest in the English succession was directed not at Elizabeth but at foreign powers which might intervene, and after the earl of Essex's execution in 1601 at that leading politician Sir Robert Cecil, with whom he kept up a 'secret' correspondence from 1601. He was writing not as a suppliant but as a king, whether in attempting to hoodwink Philip II and the pope or—more worrying to Cecil—making his attitudes all too clear. For he was in contact not only with Cecil but with Henry Percy, ninth earl of Northumberland, and the crypto-Catholic Henry Howard, very much out of favour under Elizabeth. Northumberland's optimistic belief that 'your majestie … will think that your honor in being reputed a king of England will be greater than to be king of scottes' (*Correspondence*, 56), so that James would turn his back on his Scottish subjects, was unfounded, as events of the next few years would show. But Cecilian dominance was also clearly under threat. And not only dominance, for James left him in no doubt about his rejection of Elizabethan and Cecilian policy towards Catholics. Cecil's concern about his reluctance to persecute at least the Jesuits, 'that generation of vipers' (ibid., 33), provoked the response—chilling or magnificent, depending on one's point of view—that:

> I will never allow in my conscience that the blood of any man shall be shed for the diversity of opinion in religion … No! I am so far from any intention of persecution, as I protest to God I reverence their Church as our Mother Church, though clogged with many infirmities and corruptions, besides that I ever did hold persecution as one of the infallible notes of a false church.   (*Letters of James VI and I*, 204–5)

James might be irritated about Elizabeth's relentless longevity, but only because it postponed his English future. His confidence contrasts sharply with the increasing worries of his future English subjects. They, as the grim 1590s wore on, had to live with the knowledge that their ageing monarch might die at any time. At war with Spain and uncertain of what would have been the final irony of the Tudor age, a return to the Wars of the Roses with a dynastic challenge at home—they were far more fearful than King James of what might happen when she did die. The best option was the Scottish king, that king who had already emphatically demonstrated that he was the independent monarch of a separate and independent kingdom, who would be no mere English cipher. An even more striking symbol of his independence was the large and virtually annual pension which that notoriously parsimonious monarch Elizabeth paid to James between May 1586 and December 1602. The 1590s were also a grim decade for the Scots economically, though without the additional burden of war. But in terms of Anglo-Scottish politics all the advantages—and the future—lay with them.

King by the grace of God Throughout his life James was a remarkable phenomenon: a king with an enormous literary output. In this he was unrivalled. Unlike Henry VIII he was his own polemicist; unlike Elizabeth, far more than a translator. His range is astonishing: the poet-king and writer of poetic theory; the new David, with his translation of the Psalms; the theologian; the political theorist as well as practising politician; the speech and letter writer on a huge scale. His harsh education failed to discourage his love of the things of the mind; the king famed to this day for his passion for hunting was, in his own time, equally famed for his passion for retiring into his study for solace and as an escape from relentless and importunate suitors. Several of his holograph manuscripts survive. Perhaps none gives so evocative a picture of the scholar-king as the manuscript of his *Basilikon Doron*. Though it is impressively bound in purple velvet, with the royal initials, the Scottish lion and the thistles stamped on the binding in gold leaf, the inside is a wonderful comedown, a mess such as no teacher or publisher would accept today; the opening of every section reflects graphically the problem of getting started, with the erasures, the inserted scrawls, before the words begin to flow, and all written on sheets which owe nothing to modern standardization of paper size.

Yet for James the disappearance from the bustling world into the study was not a retreat from kingship. Rather, it was an integral part of kingship. Kings impressed their stamp on the culture of their courts. This king made his mark in 1579 with his splendid entry into his capital, for him a symbol of his emergence from regency government. The royal court itself had effectively gone into abeyance during the regency; when he arrived at Holyroodhouse, there was one court poet, Patrick Hume of Polwarth, alone filling the bardic chair in the chimney nuik. That was to change dramatically; the early 1580s witnessed an astonishing flowering of poetry, with a group of poets, Alexander Montgomerie, Hume, William Fowler, John Stewart of Baldynneis, rivalling one another as they vied for the king's favour. But James was not only the royal patron; he was the royal poet—and more than that. In

1584 he produced the *Reulis and Cautelis to be Observit and Eschewit in Scottish Poesie*. This laid down the rules for Scottish poetry—specifically distinguished from English—which would form the basis of the impressive culture of James's court. He was therefore doing far more than patronizing and commissioning those who would produce that culture; he was himself creating it, and legislating for it. The first 'law' this king ever made was his law for Scottish poesie.

It was almost certainly James's most enjoyable piece of legislation. For what he was doing was both kingly and sheer fun. His own poetry showed a light-heartedness which would never really be repeated, teasing Montgomerie—'belovit sandirs maister of oure airt'—for boring everyone by boasting about his horse, which came last in the race; laughing at himself for trying to write when under the influence of Bacchus. More seriously, he and his poets introduced the sonnet, which was much more wide-ranging in its subject matter than the English version; he and they exchanged translations; he wrote a long and moving poem, *The Phoenix*, on the death of Esmé Stuart, and a huge, fast-moving epic on the battle of Lepanto, which this lover of peace clearly greatly enjoyed. Probably in 1589–90, he composed an unfinished poem which beautifully demonstrates his confidence in his kingship:

As I being a King by birth …
& laiking parents, brethren, bairns or any neir of kinn
inkaice of death or absence to suplee my place thairin
& chieflie in so kittill a lande quhaire fue remember can
for to have seine governing thaire a king that vas a man.

Yet these misfortunes, the absence of effective adult rule since the death of his grandfather James V in 1542, were in no way a source of distress. James's belief in God's plan led him to assert that his destiny did not lie in perfidious fortune, and contrast himself with those who 'wandered here and there by gess vith groaping stummelling oft'; 'I may affirme that in my self I proved it to be true' (*Poems*, 2.146–8).

By this time, however, James was writing far less poetry and turning instead to theology. His first biblical commentary, on Revelation, published in 1588, had a preface not by one of his poets, but a minister of the kirk. Its main theme was an attack on Antichrist: the pope, with his minions the Jesuits and his allies the Turks. This shows for the first time an apparent ambivalence in James's approach, which appeared again in his writings after 1603; for his attack hardly squares with his diplomacy and his refusal to persecute Catholics, even after the Gunpowder Plot. In *Lepanto*, published in 1591, he was careful not to award the victory to a Catholic hero over the infidel Turks; God had joined battle with Satan. In his commentary on Revelation he was associating the pope directly with the Turks. Yet this onslaught is perhaps not entirely inconsistent with his more conciliatory approach. He had already carved out his role as poet-king who inspired and presided over a distinguished court. Now he was creating a new image: the theologian-king who would enter directly, as the leading protestant prince of Europe, into the theological debates and divisions of his day. This did not affect his intense dislike of persecution, his growing ecumenism, his awareness of diplomatic considerations. It did enable him to establish the foundations of his approach.

James's next work, the *Meditation on … 1 Chronicles, Ch. 15*, written in 1589, provides a different and more domestic insight, very much reinforcing his practical dealings with the kirk. For when describing the elders, captains, and priests and Levites who accompanied David when he brought the ark of the covenant to Mount Sion, he made a remarkable comment on the second verse of the chapter:

> this is to be marked well of Princes, and of all those of any high calling or degree that hath to do in God's cause. David did nothing in matters appertaining to God without the presence and speciall concurrence of God's ministers, appointed to be spiritual rulers in his Church.   (*Workes*, 84)

This is very far removed from the idea of an endlessly harassed king, prey to the bullying of the Melvillians. He never acknowledged Melvillian claims for the superiority of spiritual rulers. But his vision of the kirk clearly envisaged the king working with the more moderate ministers; and this was producing results already visible in the late 1580s, and very clear in both Scotland and England after 1603.

A postscript to this is James's *Daemonologie* of 1597. Once again he was taking up the great cosmic theme of God's battle with Satan. But it is a curious and flat work, lacking all the verve and style with which this master of prose normally expressed himself; and it gives all the air of having been dashed off in a hurry. It surely reflects his changed attitude to witches. A king involved in one of the great *causes célèbres* of witch-hunting was hardly likely to deny the validity of witchcraft; but he had developed uncertainties, just detectable in his writing, about the validity of individual witches. His work was, he said, designed to resolve doubting hearts. His own heart was surely in doubt; and he signed off on witchcraft.

James's next move took him into the area for which he is best known, the discussion of the nature of kingship itself. In 1598–9 he wrote what are probably his most famous works, and also probably the most misunderstood by later commentators. *Basilikon Doron* and *The Trew Law of Free Monarchies* are, to begin with, not written by James I; those who categorize them in this way make nonsense of them, first because they are the king's mature reflections on his Scottish kingship within a European context—as he himself emphatically stated in the preface to the 1603 edition of *Basilikon Doron*—and second because the author, even when he referred to his tracts after 1603, would never have limited himself or them to the smaller confines of English kingship. Moreover, the distinction between *The Trew Law* and *Basilikon Doron* has been persistently obscured. The first is the theoretic defence of kingship by divine right, with a dash of historical 'fact' to back it up; the second is a practical manual of kingship, written for James's son Henry, and therefore very much in the *speculum principis* genre, with a dash of divine-right theory.

Writing *The Trew Law* brought James straight into the European debate about kingship, a debate begun not by the divine-right theorists but by the Calvinist resistance theorists—the 'monarchomachs'—who argued for contractual kingship and therefore the right of the people, defined either loosely or as the nobility or lesser magistracy, to remove the king if he broke his contract and, if necessary, kill him. The first explosion of this theory had come in the 1550s at the hands of the Marian exiles who included the Scot John Knox. The second, a refined and much more sophisticated version of the first, was produced in the 1570s after the massacre of St Bartholomew, mainly by the Huguenots, but also by Calvin's successor at Geneva, Theodore Beza, and by James's tutor, the Scot George Buchanan. This was answered by Jean Bodin in his *République*. He was followed by a number of writers justifying divine-right theory, including, in 1600, the exiled Catholic Scot William Barclay, who applied it to both king and pope. One of these writers was another Scot, and a king.

Reading the text of *The Trew Law* instantly disposes of the idea espoused by whig historians that James's theory was the product of autocratic, let alone absolutist tendencies. He rejected contractual theory partly on the grounds of history: kings came before parliaments, and therefore were the original law makers; 'and so it follows of necessitie, that the Kinges were the authors & makers of the lawes, and not the laws of Kings' (*Minor Prose Works*, 70). He also picks up on the caution of earlier political theorists, notably Thomas Aquinas, when he argues that even a tyrannical king will not be wholly lustful and lawless, and that removing him may well lead to more disorder as men struggle to find an alternative and set up new laws—an almost prophetic comment on what would happen in 1649—and moreover reiterated the theme that a tyrant is sent by God as punishment for the sins of his people. For that reason the penalty for resistance might be heavy indeed; for it could 'please God to cast such scourges of princes and Instruments of his furie into the fire'. However, he ended his work with an awesome warning, to God-sent tyrants; they would not escape punishment, but

> by the contrary, by remitting them to God (who is their only ordinary judge), I remit them to the sorest and sharpest Scoolemaister that can be devised for them. For the further a king is preferred by God above all other ranks and degrees of men, and the higher that his seate is above theirs: the greater is his obligation to his maker … The highest bench is the sliddriest to sit upon.   (ibid., 81)

There are curious quirks in *The Trew Law*. Arguing against Knox and Melville, as well as Buchanan, meant invoking scripture; James chose to cite Samuel's reminder to the Israelites of the terrible fate that awaited them when God gave them the king they so strenuously desired, a somewhat negative justification of divine-right monarchy. Less grimly, the man waiting for Elizabeth to die could not resist contrasting Scotland favourably with England, one of those societies which had been 'reft by conquest from one to another, as in our neighbour countrie in England (which was never in ours)', so that William the Conqueror 'changed the lawes [and] inverted the order of governement' (*Minor Prose Works*, 71); the concept of the Norman yoke, developed in seventeenth-century England, had an early expression in *The Trew Law*. It was the same need to indulge Scottish humour at the expense of his future kingdom which was to prompt him in 1600 to point out that in changing the beginning of the year to 1 January instead of 25 March he was doing what other civilized countries did; manifestly these did not include England. Once again James's writings are a guide to his political attitudes.

Basilikon Doron is a work of wholly different flavour. It did give a nod to divine-right theory in the first section, in the king's duty to God, when James reminded his son that God 'made you a little God to sitte on his throne, and rule over other men' (*Basilikon Doron*, 1.25). In the second section, however, came the fireworks, with a vitriolic and sardonic attack on the Melvillians, the main target of attack in the book, with their cry for 'paritie' and 'unitie', which meant only division and disruption, and their overweening pride: these puritans, who insisted that 'wee are all but vile worms, & yet wil judge and give law to their king, but will be judged nor controlled by none: surely there is more pride under such a ones black-bonnet nor under great Alexander's Diademe' (ibid., 1.142). Thereafter the book is informed by wit, humour, and sheer common sense. There is very balanced advice on how to treat the nobility, who must not be allowed to become too powerful, but equally must be relied on as 'the armes and executers of your lawes', and as his principal advisers, whose service honours the king (ibid., 1.87). His passage on economic problems shows the layman's lack of understanding, concerning itself too much with high prices and poor quality, and threats of strike action. But he has a well-considered section on the choice of marriage partner, which might fall well short of modern feminist standards, but is remarkably humane. Not surprisingly he advocated peace, but was also prepared to advise on unavoidable war, and the need to be slow in making peace as well as war; but the effect of this is perhaps undermined when his real priority showed up in the amazing recommendation that if the prince had to go to war, he should wear light armour for easier 'away-running', singularly unheroic but also no doubt highly practical (ibid., 1.175). This comes in the third section, 'Indifferent things', whose keynote is archetypal Jacobean moderation, in food, language, and recreation. The prince must eschew pedantry; he must keep himself fit, but not put himself at risk by aspiring to excel at any cost. Hence the advantages of hunting (though hardly a sport without risk).

The first edition of *Basilikon Doron* was extremely private; it ran to seven copies, for specific individuals. But James's enjoyment of and pride in his book are very evident. It was revised in 1601; an English edition flooded the market in spring 1603; and it was a work to which he referred probably more than any of his others. He had every right to enjoy it; the Melvillians were furious. He could take pleasure in writing advice for his son in an affectionate and humorous way, far removed from the hectoring style adopted by Elizabeth when she tried to advise him. It is worth noting, when considering his approach to kingship, that it was the practical manual which he visibly preferred to the theoretic *Trew Law*. It is also worth noting that those modern scholars who have sought to shroud it, along with *The Trew Law*, in the mysteries of state, ignore James's own stated intention. Just as with the *Daemonologie*, so with *Basilikon Doron*; it was, he said, written to explain his kingship of Scotland, the kingdom of which he had experience, and explain it, to great effect, he did.

By the time he was writing these works James had moved beyond the preoccupations with the glories of Scottish poetry which had been so much a feature of the early 1580s. Now the interest had widened. He had inherited an English family of musicians, the Hudsons, from his mother, but they had been absorbed into Scottish court culture. For his marriage celebrations he had asked Elizabeth for six masquers and six torch-bearers, and for English actors, and English actors were invited again in 1594, presumably for the baptism of his son Henry. Then in 1599 Laurence Fletcher and his men arrived in Edinburgh, giving rise to a furious row between a theatre-hating ministry and a theatre-enthusiastic king, which the king won, and, possibly having stayed in Scotland in the interim, they turned up again in 1601, when they went on tour to Dundee and Aberdeen. Fletcher's name headed the list, with Shakespeare's second, in the letters patent to the new King's Men in May 1603; indeed, there is a tantalizing hint that Shakespeare may himself have gone to Scotland with Fletcher. The future king of Britain was already introducing a cross-fertilization of cultures.

The union of the crowns On 24 March 1603 the long-awaited event finally happened: Elizabeth died. The English privy council immediately wrote to James offering him the crown. James's response was to accept it, to thank the English councillors on Elizabeth's behalf for their loyal service, to ask their thanks to God for the blessing about to come among them—a nice example of the mental world of kingship—but to point out that he could not simply rush off from Edinburgh, and therefore would ask them to keep the kingdom ordered and peaceful until his arrival. It was a reasonable enough request. But it produced a frantic response from the English council. For the king's letter had not contained the correct formula authorizing them to act; and so, strictly speaking, at this potentially very tense moment English government went into abeyance until the king wrote two further letters, sending 'out of hand' new commissions as a matter of urgency, and rather tetchily suggesting that they might now do as he had asked (Bodl. Oxf., MS Ashmole 1729, fols. 51, 56). It was an immediate and deeply worrying clash of styles. A Scottish king, unaccustomed to the bureaucratic and civil service mentality and sophistication of England, was being told for the first time that his priority, which was to get things done, came up against an English insistence on getting them done in the right way. It was not a good omen.

Moreover, the abnormal circumstances of James's accession created their own abnormal problems; fixing

JAMES VI AND I

one's interest with the new king was exceptionally difficult when the king was 400 miles away and would take
time to reach his English capital. The unfortunate Robert
Cecil, trapped in London with other privy councillors,
could only watch as others flocked north to greet their
monarch, and do his best to offset their advantage; in particular, strenuous efforts were made to keep Sir Walter
Ralegh away from James. Cecil's quite unrealistic suggestion that James should travel south incognito until he
reached Cecil's brother's seat, Burghley House in Northamptonshire, got the dusty answer that the new king had
no intention of denying York, the second city in the kingdom, a celebration party. He could do nothing to stop
James sending an order for the release of the earl of Southampton, imprisoned in the Tower for his part in the rising
in 1601 of Cecil's major rival Essex. He could only do his
best, pointing out his family's distinguished record of service to the crown, and trying to indicate that by remaining
in London and denying himself the great joy of seeing his
majesty's sweet face he was continuing that service,
unlike those who were rushing out of London in the self-
interested search for patronage. But Cecil's dominance in
Elizabeth's last years had already been threatened by the
warning note that James was no novice in the art of kingship; and it was now further undermined simply by the
political events of spring 1603.

The underlying problem was how the union could be
made to work. There was no shortage of exemplars: the
Spanish *monarchia*, the Scandinavian composite kingdoms, the union of Poland and Lithuania, and the short-
lived unions of Poland and France and Poland and Sweden. All were cited in the flood of tracts on union produced by English and Scots after 1603. It was not
reassuring that the English view was that Scotland should
be incorporated into England, the Scottish that the two
kingdoms should be equal partners. The English approach
had all the extra edge of bitterness that a Scottish king
should do what great English kings had tried and failed to
achieve, unite the kingdoms by annexing Scotland. The
Scots had no intention of allowing their triumph to dissolve into the creation of precisely the situation which the
English had failed to bring about. Moreover, the composite kingdoms of England and Wales and Ireland hardly
provided a model to be followed with any enthusiasm; the
Nine Years' War with Ireland just ended spoke for itself.
All that could be said for 1603, therefore, was that for the
present it averted an English succession crisis. For the
future, fear rather than optimism was the dominant
note.

In the short term, however, the atmosphere was intoxi-
cating. In April and early May 1603 the new king of England travelled south to London, a journey in which, famously, the crowds flocked to meet him; in which, equally
famously, he hanged a thief without due process of law
and doled out knighthoods with a more than lavish hand;
and in which as a prologue to controversies to come, he
was presented with the millenary petition by ministers
hopeful of reform of the church. There was wild enthusiasm for a king, after fifty years of female rule; as the lord

keeper, Thomas Egerton, Lord Ellesmere, wrote in his
notes for his speech at the opening of James's first parliament in 1604, 'In sted of [Elizabeth's] age & orbitye [child-
lessness] … the Kinge of Masture yeres, Experienced in
governments, & behould the Q[ueen]. A ladye … Descended of the moost Royall sept, & progenye etc. ordeyned
to breede & bring fourth kings' (Hunt. L., Bridgewater and
Ellesmere MSS, EL 451, fol. 1). There was huge relief that
the Stuart succession went unchallenged. Even the plague
which hit London in April 1603 apparently failed to undermine the prevailing mood, although it killed nearly a
quarter of the capital's population, halted the frenzied
printing of the new best-seller, *Basilikon Doron*, led to a
postponement of James's state entry into the city, and curtailed attendance at the coronation of the king and queen
at Westminster Abbey on 25 July.

Two days after Elizabeth's death Sir Robert Cotton produced a treatise extolling the name of Britain; as in the
past smaller kingdoms had joined to become the kingdoms of England, France, and Spain, so now the smaller
kingdoms within the British Isles would come together
under the ancient name of Britain; and Cotton rushed to
demonstrate his prestigious Scottish connection with the
house of Bruce, now styling himself Robert Cotton
Bruceus. Poets such as Michael Drayton and Samuel Daniel in England and Alexander Craig and Robert Ayton in
Scotland took up his theme; and the triumphal arches and
pageantry designed by Ben Jonson and Thomas Dekker
reinforced it in James's ceremonial entry into London
when the disappearance of plague allowed the court to
return to the city in March 1604. The costly display funded
by London and its guilds was all very heady, and it both
impressed and alarmed the king.

The veneer of joy and excitement was dangerously thin,
however. 'Never people so happye, yf Wee have grace to
see & feele our owne happiness', said Ellesmere in his
notes for his 1604 speech (Hunt. L., Bridgewater and Ellesmere MSS, EL 151, fol. 1). But public ceremonial of this
order was never to be repeated and the people's grace was
strictly limited. The English might rejoice in a king with
three living children but they had long forgotten the cost
of a royal family; and the purveyance carts which rumbled
along ahead of James's progress through the southern
counties in summer 1603 had their own heightened
unpopularity. There were arguments about whether
Scottish household officials should get the same fees as
English ones. James's attempts on his journey south to
appoint equal numbers of English and Scottish gentlemen of the bedchamber was a failure from the beginning,
provoking the king, as early as May 1603, to create a bedchamber which would remain exclusively Scottish until
1615, to the understandable fury and resentment of his
English subjects. At the same time, the success of Englishmen like Cecil and Henry Howard (created earl of Northampton in 1604) in obtaining formal office in government
to the exclusion of rivals like Sir Walter Ralegh and Sir
John Fortescue exacerbated tensions.

In summer 1603 there were two small and unsuccessful
plots. In late June and early July it emerged that a number

JAMES VI AND I

of Catholics, including William Watson, a mentally unstable priest, and Sir Griffin Markham, a country squire, had conspired to kidnap the king in order to secure concessions for the practice of their religion and the removal of government ministers identified with the persecution of their community during the last years of Elizabeth's reign. This so-called Bye plot failed to attract the high-placed supporters its protagonists had anticipated, and collapsed after internal recriminations and betrayals, but it was soon overshadowed by the Main plot. The latter was first disclosed by George Brooke, who while on trial in July for his involvement in the former, confessed that his elder brother Henry Brooke, eleventh Baron Cobham, had been conspiring with Charles de Ligne, count of Aremberg, to obtain 600,000 crowns from Spain to finance James's overthrow and his replacement with his cousin Lady Arabella Stuart. Cobham in turn implicated Sir Walter Ralegh, who did not subsequently deny he had been attentive to Cobham's schemes: Ralegh's recognition that Cecil was determined to deny him influence with James apparently led him at least to postulate treason. None the less, although found guilty at his trial in November, Ralegh, like Cobham, Markham, and Lord Grey, was ultimately reprieved by the king; lesser men like Watson and Brooke suffered death. More generally a host of small people—saddlers, weavers, and yeomen—were indicted in the southern counties for speaking against the accession of a king whom they regarded as foreign, and therefore no true king of England. In Scotland an already touchy council produced a Scottish translation of the English council's letter to James offering him the throne. And a surly Scotsman, disliking what he regarded as the excessive obsequiousness of the English crowds, muttered sourly that 'this people will spoil a gud king' (A. Wilson, *The History of Great Britain: being the Life and Reign of King James the First*, 1653, 3).

Triple kingship, the union, and the English parliament, 1603–1610 Throughout his reign James brought his Scottish experience to bear on his English rule; his desire for more than the personal union of the crowns dominated English politics for the first five years; and English hatred of the presence of the Scots lasted a good deal longer. In that sense, even when considering the subject from the perspective of London and the English localities, it was a matter of Anglo-Scottish kingship, in a way which it would never be again after 1625, when the dynamics of the 'British problem' changed fundamentally, under rulers who increasingly saw themselves as English. It is therefore impossible to discuss James's kingship of England in isolation; attempts in the past to do so have missed the crucial point about his rule after 1603.

James was a wily and confident king, long experienced in getting what he wanted by a mixture of high demands and negotiation; he did not suddenly lose his touch in 1603. Yet, while he valued the style of Scottish kingship, the English did not; while his political and rhetorical skills are often evident, his aims were too often frustrated. None

the less, those aims might be complex and could be modified. He certainly began by trying to bring the English and the Scots together in court and government, but even his policy here had more than one facet. When he appointed his council in 1603 his main interest lay in expanding the far too narrow, Cecilian-dominated English council of Elizabeth's last years, so that it became more representative; thus he brought on to the council the earls of Cumberland and Northumberland, the former Essex supporter and lord deputy of Ireland Charles Blount, Lord Mountjoy, and the crypto-Catholic Henry Howard, created Lord Howard and then earl of Northampton. In all, his thirteen new councillors more than doubled the Elizabethan council; of these thirteen only five were Scots. And only three Scots held high office. George Home, lord treasurer of Scotland from 1601 and later earl of Dunbar, had a brief spell as chancellor of the exchequer, from 1603 to 1605, before taking up his highly effective and useful position as the politician who was James's link between his two kingdoms, travelling regularly between London and Edinburgh until his death in 1611. Edward Bruce, Lord Kinloss—the man described by Cecil when he arrived in London ahead of the king in 1603 as 'already so good an Englishman'—became master of the rolls (PRO, SP 14/1/18, fol. 38). And Ludovic Stuart, duke of Lennox, son of Esmé Stuart, was steward of the household until his death in 1624.

Moreover, James learned fast. In November 1604 he wrote to Cecil setting out the problem clearly. The English did not welcome the Scots, for they feared loss of office for themselves; but the king could not forget his northern and ancient kingdom. He would no longer, therefore, give Scotsmen place in English government; but he must be allowed to reward them for their service, for he would not—could not—exclude them from his court. Reward meant money and that in itself caused trouble. And there is a vast discrepancy between reality, which was a total of 158 Scotsmen with any sort of position in government and household—indeed, three households, for Queen Anne and Henry, prince of Wales, of course had their separate households—and the despairing English perception of some kind of Scottish takeover, expressed in 1610 by Sir John Holles when he complained about the Scots standing 'like mountains betwixt the beams of his grace and us' (*Portland MSS*, 9.113). Yet the situation created by James was grudgingly accepted.

The four sessions of James's first parliament—March–July 1604, November 1605–May 1606, November 1606–July 1607, February–July/November 1610—were difficult not because of the first Stuart king's failure to control parliament as the last Tudor monarch had done, but because of the new situation created by the union of the crowns, and old problems brought down from Scotland and given a new twist in the English context. Parliament was the major arena in which debates over the nature of the union were fought out, and the issue dominated the sessions of 1604 and 1607. James set out his agenda in his opening speech to the first session. His preferred solution to the problem of multiple kingdoms—or so it appeared—was to unite them, to create, as he said, not just *unus rex*, but also *una lex* and *unus grex*: one king, one law, one people (*James VI and I: Political Writings*, 162). In theory it had the merit of simplicity. In practice it was a hopeless vision. The initial government request for a commission to investigate the union was accepted by MPs in June, but much less palatable was a proposal that James adopt the title of king of Great Britain, the term intended to distinguish Greater from Lesser Britain—Brittany. Despite all the British imagery of the early years of the reign, there was much mere lip-service paid to the idea by leading councillors like Cecil and the lord chancellor, Sir Thomas Egerton. The latter's thoughts were given away in his endorsement to a letter replying to Bacon's which suggested the need for a history of Britain which read 'Sir Francis Bacon touching the story of England' (Hunt. L., Bridgewater and Ellesmere MSS, EL MS 128). Papers arguing against the change were the stuff of parliamentary business, enlarging on the theme that to give up the ancient and glorious name of England would mean that England would lose its identity, at home and abroad. In the meantime, the Commons had their own preoccupations, and the manner in which these were handled did not induce in them an appreciation of Scottish ways of doing things. Time-consuming debate early in the session over the disputed Buckinghamshire election between Sir Francis Goodwin and Sir John Fortescue produced only stalemate. Having witnessed this, James stepped in, quashed the election, and ordered a new one; the Commons publicly praised his wisdom, but behind closed doors complained about his indifference to English conventions. Like a leading privy councillor, the earl of Northumberland, before them, they naïvely saw the solution in telling the new king what English kingship was about. In the context also of disappointed hopes over redress of grievances arising from the unpopular royal rights of wardship and purveyance, the Commons settled down to draft 'The form of apology and satisfaction', a document which detailed relations between them and the crown, and pointed to what had gone wrong. With an attempt at tact, they said that they had not produced such a document before, out of respect for the old queen's age and sex. It purported to be a conservative statement, seeking maintenance of the perceived *status quo*, but still their nerve failed. The apology was never approved by the whole house, and was never presented to the king. This damp squib was not a constitutional milestone on the road to civil war; it was an immediate response to rule by a Scot. But that Scot was not amenable to being told how to be an English king, for he was not an English king. His problem was trying to shift his English subjects into a new perception of themselves. Hence his fury when he heard about the apology. On 7 July he prorogued a parliament which had engendered much hot air but no money for the government of the realm; his closing speech castigated the fools who could not make wise use of their privileges. He showed, too, his frustration at being cut off from the centres of political debate, parliament and council, as he

had not been in Scotland, where he had attended regularly. Admittedly the bicameral English parliament made Scottish practice impossible, for even James could not claim the gift of being in two places at once; but the set speeches to parliament or to deputations of Lords and Commons were no exchange for embroiling himself directly in debate and discussion. His wisdom was endlessly extolled; but to what purpose? As he said to the Commons:

> in my government bypast in Scotland (where I ruled upon men not of the best temper) I was heard not only as a king but as a counsellor. Contrary here nothing but curiosity from morn to night to find fault with my propositions. (PRO, SP 14/8/93)

On 20 October 1604 the king took a step which made him look much more autocratic than he actually was; he assumed the title of king of Great Britain by proclamation. The text was a plea for recognition of the reality of Britain. Shakespeare's 'sceptred isle' of England was now invoked in much more geographically acceptable terms, but not, inevitably, in English ones; nor was the claim that two mighty nations, formerly at war but now at peace, with their shared coastline, language, and religion, had clearly been intended by God to come together in unity. What counted was the side-stepping of parliament. Worse was to come, moreover. On 16 November the king announced that a union currency was to be issued: the first coin would be a twenty-shilling piece called the 'unite'.

When parliament reconvened in late 1605, it was in the wake of events the fall-out from which eclipsed Anglo-Scottish tension but also produced a session dominated by issues other than the union. In the years immediately before Elizabeth's death there had been Catholic Englishmen in Spain desperately trying to persuade the Spanish government to run a Spanish candidate for the English throne, if necessary with military backing. These men included Guy Fawkes and Thomas Winter, two of the thirteen fanatics who were utterly opposed to a protestant succession, no matter whether the future King James would ease the burden of his Catholic subjects. When Spain failed to oblige, they turned to self-help. The plot was being planned in 1604; by the early summer of 1605 the preparations were complete, and the gunpowder stored and ready in the 'cellar' of the House of Lords. It was officially discovered not when William Parker, Lord Monteagle, showed Francis Tresham's anonymous warning letter to Cecil and others on 26 October—but on the night of 4–5 November, on the eve of parliament's reassembling when the lord chamberlain, Thomas Howard, earl of Suffolk, was instructed by the king to have a second look in the Lords, having reported nothing suspicious after the first search. This time he searched properly; the man he had previously met in the cellar—Guy Fawkes—turned out to have a 9 inch match in his pocket; under a pile of coal were the thirty-six barrels of gunpowder. It could hardly have been a more close-run thing. When interrogated, in a pathetic and ineffectual attempt to touch the English xenophobic nerve, Fawkes claimed that they intended to get rid of not only a protestant king but his hated Scots.

The English were, on the whole, relieved that the conspirators had failed. The anniversary of 5 November became an annual holiday, to be celebrated by jollification or sermons, depending on how puritanical was the area. Cecil, who had been created earl of Salisbury that May, harnessed the euphoria among MPs and obtained a vote of subsidies and other levies amounting to about £450,000. Parliamentarians eagerly followed the conspirators' trial on 27 January 1606 and their execution on 30 January, and their relations with the crown seemed set fair. However, in April harmony was threatened when James insisted on a British flag, again by proclamation. His 'Union Jack (Jacobus)' would be flown on British shipping, although English ships would continue to fly the St George's cross, Scottish ones that of St Andrew. The sop to national susceptibilities was not enough. He got his flag, but only after huge rows between the Scottish and English heralds, each trying to outdo the other in making their cross prominent.

By the time the third session of parliament opened in November 1606, the union commissioners had completed their report. The issue again dominated debates. James made a long and very moving speech, appealing to the English to recognize that Scotland was a civilized and governable nation, overplaying his hand in suggesting that it was actually more governable than England, although there was a certain truth in this from his point of view, but also carefully giving recognition to England's predominant place within the British Isles, unlike Scotland which would become as the northern shires, 'seldome seene and saluted by their King' (*James VI and I: Political Writings*, 164). It was a fine piece of rhetoric, careful to combine British kingship with English susceptibilities. But it was directed at the wrong audience. James's union was killed by this parliament. Sir Edwin Sandys damaged it beyond repair by taking up the king's idea of perfect union, and then declaring it impossible to achieve; others were more blunt in delivering the death blow.

Yet despite disquiet about the king's perceived squandering of taxation voted in the previous session, and even about his commitment to the English parliamentary system itself, MPs did make some concessions, accepting the naturalization of the king's Scottish subjects, which was reinforced by the judges' ruling in the carefully fixed Calvin's case of 1608, and accepting free trade between the two kingdoms. The latter was a major concession, achieved in the face of strenuous opposition from the English merchants. It was a messy outcome; it was ramshackle and confused—although that no doubt hardly worried James, a king with little interest in constitutional clarity. It was the best on offer, however, and as only James was really concerned to combine his roles as king of Scotland and king of England, it can hardly be argued that he failed. By pitching his initial demands far too high he was able to scale them down in order to ensure that in practice his Scottish subjects did reasonably well out of the union and his English ones were less unreasonably treated than

they had feared. This did not stop Anglo-Scottish hostility.

Parliament, money, and ministers, 1610–1620 By the time the final session of James's first parliament began in February 1610, mounting royal debts had become the main issue. The problems were deep rooted. Much has been made of the fact that Elizabeth died only £300,000 in debt; the royal debt then steadily escalated under James. The other way of looking at it is to question why the Virgin Queen, with far lighter expenditure than the married king, left so much debt; even though she was at war in the 1590s, it was hardly a ruinously expensive one. Elizabeth had in fact allowed royal revenue to decrease steadily in the course of her reign. Increase in customs revenue had been achieved in the last months of Mary's reign by the upward revision of the book of rates. Elizabeth got the immediate benefit, but did nothing to improve the situation in a period of inflation; customs income stagnated and fell. The same was true of income from land. Crown rents were grievously and sometimes ludicrously undervalued; the beneficiaries included no less a person than William Cecil, Lord Burghley. Moreover, during the war years of the 1590s the queen disposed of capital which was not hers to use in this way, being held in trust for the crown; rather than face up to the demand that parliament should be realistic in financing the war, she sold lands, plate, and jewellery. Cecil was already visibly frantic about the state of royal finance in the 1590s; by 1608, when as earl of Salisbury he succeeded Thomas Sackville, earl of Dorset, as lord treasurer, debt stood at over £1 million. Dorset had made a move towards uprating customs valuations in 1604; now Salisbury revised the book of rates, fifty years after it had last been done. It significantly improved crown revenue from commerce, but drew unpopularity.

Fall in revenue from customs and land had been matched by the falling value of parliamentary subsidy, which made the Commons' generosity of 1605–6 rather less than it seemed. The king therefore turned to ways of raising extra-parliamentary revenue, notably in his impositions on currants from the Levant brought in by the merchant John Bate in 1606, which he claimed to have the right to do on the grounds that trade was a matter of foreign policy, and therefore part of his prerogative. Testing this assertion in the courts with Bate's case brought victory for the king. But it was a very high-risk policy. It raised the spectre, in the worried minds of English MPs, of a king who might free himself of the fiscal restraints imposed by parliament, and follow the lead of contemporary European rulers, whose representative assemblies did not have the power to impose such restraints, and were therefore being the more easily dispensed with. It also brought the prerogative, and especially the extraordinary prerogative, into the open arena of political debate for the first time. Again the nightmare vision of an autocratic king appeared to have some reality. In 1610 it did not help when James ordered all his proclamations to be published in book form, thus appearing to give them more substantive authority than the law allowed.

When parliament assembled that February, Salisbury presented an utterly radical scheme, the great contract, by which the king's debts would be paid off and a regular income guaranteed (a lump sum of £600,000 together with an annual grant of £200,000 was initially suggested). Although the king offered in exchange to sacrifice some of his prerogative sources of income, including the deeply unpopular purveyance, the proposal fell ultimately before the same conservatism. Beneath the inevitable debate over how much money was involved, and the justified fear that whatever James was given would never be enough, lay the profound attachment to the old idea that the king was financed by a willing and loving people, and that he was not a salaried official of the state. The fact that the people were neither willing nor loving enough to meet the financial needs of an early seventeenth-century monarch passed them by. The conservative and conventional minds of English MPs, many of them lawyers, could only see as far as making the existing system work better, and telling the king not to spend so much. Thus in 1604 John Hare's bill on purveyances had done nothing to reform that tired, creaking, inadequate, and thoroughly unpopular way of providing for the royal households, but unrealistically relied on the belief that with the purge of abuses—which did not happen anyway—improvement would automatically follow.

In debates MPs harped on the king's extravagance and his generous grants of crown lands and money, especially to the Scots who had accompanied him south. John Haskyns made an inflammatory if inelegant speech in which he asserted that 'the royal cistern had a leak which till it were stopped, all our consultation to bring money into it was Scots' (Foster, 2.344). James, who by this time had indeed handed out about £90,000 in gifts and over £10,000 a year in pensions to his fellow countrymen, assured MPs that this degree of prodigality would cease, but he suggested that, since Englishmen had already benefited twice as much as Scots from his largesse, they should appreciate a grateful and generous king. Instead parliament turned to attacking impositions and to demanding the abolition, rather than simply the reform, of the court of wards. In the process it raised major legal and constitutional issues over freedom of speech and the extent of MPs' right to question the royal prerogative. Conflicting attitudes were revealed. When James made a speech on the running sore of monopolies which was informed not by English custom but by European examples, the common lawyer and MP Sir Nicholas Fuller came out with an astonishing definition of the role of the Commons: that 'they must tell the king of England what by the laws of England he may do' (Foster, 2.109). The fierily irascible lawyer Sir Edward Coke could not contain himself when James argued that the law was a matter of reason and common sense; no matter his majesty's reason and wisdom, no one could interpret English law without twenty years' training. There was another outburst of royal rage, and Coke apparently sank to his knees, grovelling; but it did not change his attitude.

With the contract now in jeopardy, a frustrated James was impelled to concede discussion of grievances and to promise an act against impositions. Ironically, a reaction to the appalling news of the assassination in May of Henri IV of France also helped belatedly to gain James the appreciation he had sought, and by the time parliament was prorogued in July, he was a fair way towards obtaining a substantial subsidy and £200,000 a year. However, during the recess MPs' enthusiasm waned and they returned in November to unproductive debate. Negotiations on the contract collapsed, and James first prorogued and then dissolved parliament, having gained a mere £100,000 advance and endured much humiliation.

For a time James tried to do without parliament. He survived with the assistance of a £100,000 loan from the city of London and resort to well-worn royal expedients such as the sale of crown lands and monopolies, a rise in the price of wardships, and (in 1611) the levy of a forced loan. A new, and equally unpopular, scheme introduced that year was the sale of baronetcies. But with the death of Salisbury in 1612 the king lost his greatest administrator, and his debts continued to rise. When in 1614 plans for a French marriage for Prince Charles fell through, taking with them the prospect of acquiring a welcome dowry, James was persuaded to call another parliament. In its two-month session, from 5 April to 7 June, the lamentable Addled Parliament passed no bills, but engendered much acrimony. Another attack on Scots in the privy chamber proved the final straw, and James, realizing no money would be forthcoming unless at the price of unacceptable concessions, dissolved a parliament which had achieved nothing. In its aftermath the privy council, as usual deeply worried about the king's finances, debated whether to suggest another. The problem was how to ensure that it would not be a rerun of its predecessor; and Lennox was asked to request that the king should summon parliament in Scotland, for Scotland had never had an Addled Parliament, and might therefore provide a role model. Lennox refused; there was about to be enough trouble in Scotland over the king's new religious policy and he had no desire to allow tensions to be heightened by providing a forum for opposition. Nevertheless, the unthinkable idea that a Scottish parliament might have something to offer an English one had now been expressed; it had much to commend it. The English parliament, by James's reign, was indeed less effective than its Scottish counterpart. Scottish parliaments still got things done. English parliaments increasingly failed to do so, overburdened and overstretched as they were by ever growing pressure of business and compounding the difficulties by their insistence on spending time on talking about custom, precedent, and privilege, issues which hardly ever bothered the Scots except when the lords in parliament squabbled about precedence in order of voting.

In the meantime the king had to live, and thus he had to pursue alternative sources for income. The experiment, launched in December 1614, of allowing Sir William Cockayne to set up an English dyeing industry was supposed to provide the government with an extra £40,000 a year in customs revenues, but it collapsed in 1617 with little to show for it except stagnation in the cloth industry and resentment among its workers. More conventional money-raising expedients were tried, including from 1615 the sale of peerages, but in the end there was nothing for it but to concentrate instead on reducing expenditure. Late in 1617 Lionel Cranfield, a London merchant and surveyor-general of customs, was commissioned to supervise retrenchment. Initially his programme enjoyed some success: the outgoings of the royal household and several government departments were pruned, saving tens of thousands of pounds, and higher returns were realized through more 'efficient' exploitation of customs and of the court of wards. Ultimately, however, James's interest waned, and the plan failed to arrest his rising debts, which by 1620 amounted to nearly £900,000.

Corruption and the court: public and private morality Like parliament, English government was now clearly overstretched, mainly because of the obsessive competition for place in the charmed world of court and government. Whatever the justification for English fears about James's extravagance, he was equally justified in attacking those who criticized that extravagance while demanding largesse for themselves. The attractions of retreat to the study were now enhanced by the welcome opportunity to close the door on importunate suitors; and Salisbury and Cranfield were as much the victims of their rapacity as of James's extravagance. Demand far outstripped supply; and as morally minded Englishmen refused to have any truck with the corrupt venality of the French crown, which staved off the problem with the sale of offices, the situation in England could only become increasingly chaotic. The pernicious practice of reversionary grants was already being adopted in the last years of Elizabeth; by the last years of James, grants were being given of reversions to reversions. Thus the English court presented the unedifying spectacle of containing, in effect, three groups: the fortunate, who held office; the circle of vultures round them waiting for them to resign or die; and a second circle of even more frustrated vultures, waiting for two lives to go. What made it all the worse was that offices were increasingly held for life. Moreover, there was something of an embryonic career structure coming into existence for a few, as able men served first in an office such as clerk of the council, went on to spend time in a foreign embassy, and came back to the pinnacle of success in a major office such as secretary of state. But the passion to gain entrance to Whitehall was not just a matter of major office. Anglo-Scottish tensions reared their head once again when the king preferred a Scotsman who had worked in his Scottish slaughterhouse to the position of keeper of the English slaughterhouse, ousting the English candidate, who was fobbed off with a reversion.

It is in this scrambling, hothouse environment that the notorious royal favourites must be set. Sir Walter Scott introduced the note of immorality; and some modern scholars—notably literary critics—still find the question of James's homosexuality a source of great fascination. There is almost the danger of forgetting that, even if homosexual activity as opposed to homoerotic feeling is ascribed to the king, at the very least, James was bisexual, and succeeded, where his three predecessors had failed, in providing heirs to the throne, which after the previous half-century came as a welcome relief. Moreover, even if seen under the guise of courtly love, the male favourite had had as much of a political role in Elizabeth's court as James's. Whatever the sexual attractions, the main point is that James never allowed his personal feelings to dictate his political ones.

It has already been suggested that Esmé Stuart has loomed too large in the early 1580s, being allowed to crowd out the other things—his poets, the beginnings of his political role—which brought the king out of his harsh childhood. In the late 1580s and 1590s Huntly was favoured when useful, attacked and (in 1596) exiled when not; equally, he had ignored factional pressure after the death of Lord Chancellor Maitland in 1595 and determined to fulfil the role himself. No amount of blandishments from the first great favourite of the English reign, the Scot Robert Carr, who rose to prominence in 1607, persuaded James to appoint one of his clients as secretary in succession to Salisbury in 1612. Carr did accumulate honours and acquire office: he was created Viscount Rochester in 1611 and earl of Somerset in 1613, and between 1612 and 1614 he exercised the functions of secretary of state. In 1613 he and his chosen bride, Lady Frances Howard, also had the all-important backing of the king in Lady Frances's efforts to get her first marriage to the earl of Essex annulled; having successfully forwarded the necessary legal proceedings and squashed the reservations of a discomforted archbishop of Canterbury, James even paid for their wedding that December. However, when in 1615 Somerset reacted to the arrival on the scene of George Villiers by behaving insolently, James put him firmly in his place. Later that year when the king heard rumours of the involvement of the earl and countess in the murder of Somerset's erstwhile adviser Sir Thomas Overbury, favour did not save them from investigation by a royal commission or from subsequent prosecution, conviction, and imprisonment in 1616, although it did save them from death.

Villiers, James's greatest favourite, was appointed cupbearer to the king in 1614 and gentleman of the bedchamber in the following year; thereafter, following the downfall of Somerset, his rise was rapid: knighted and created Viscount Villiers (1616) and successively earl (1617), marquess (1618), and duke (1623) of Buckingham. Perhaps more attention should be paid to the fact that Villiers was brought to James's attention by his wife and by George Abbot, archbishop of Canterbury. Why? No doubt to undermine Somerset and his Howard allies, but this only addresses their objections to a particular favourite. What were the positive advantages they saw to providing the king with a new favourite? To amuse the king? To provide him with someone who, if necessary, would take the rap for unpopular actions or simply take some of the pressure of endless demands for patronage from his shoulders? James might give his favour initially to men of little prominence, but not to political nonentities: to retain favour they had to demonstrate that they were politically useful. Buckingham undoubtedly did, as the patronage networks became increasingly focused on him. That did not mean that the king gave up overall control. The royal chaplain and religious controversialist George Carleton at last stopped being fobbed off with minor bishoprics and got a plum, Chichester, not because his name was on Buckingham's lips, but because James had been impressed with his performance as a delegate at the Synod of Dort. Buckingham's strength was that he knew how to please his royal master. He was, of course, hated by those who failed to benefit from his patronage. There was a good deal less complaining from those who benefited from it. But under the flexible James the patronage networks remained ideologically open. No Jacobean parliament wanted to impeach Buckingham, as Charles I's first two did. It was after 1625, when Buckingham adapted to the new king, Charles I, who had nothing of the flexibility of his father, and when, to compound his increased unpopularity, disastrously went to war with both France and Spain in the same year—1627—that he was seen as a real political menace. Having survived the threat of parliamentary attacks thanks to Charles's protection, Buckingham finally died by the assassin's knife in 1628. James would never have allowed Buckingham the level of power and influence which brought him down.

But the homosexual issue means that Buckingham has remained associated with James; and homosexuality has been a major factor in creating the idea of James's court as sleazy and corrupt. So it must be emphasized that neither in Scotland nor in England were the king's sexual proclivities of as much interest in his day as they later became. And the 'corruption' turns mainly on three episodes: the Overbury murder, which was not a homosexual scandal, and the accounts of two occasions when court entertainment went badly wrong, being swamped by drink; the first was in 1606, when James's brother-in-law Christian IV, king of Denmark—a notorious soak—came to visit, the second in 1618, when the king, grumpy and unwell, spoiled the performance of that year's court masque, and stumped off to bed, whereupon his courtiers, no doubt heartily glad to see the back of him, turned overenthusiastically to the feasting and the drinking. It hardly amounts to 'the' corrupt court. There was, of course, corruption; how could there not have been? The councillors in prison in 1618–19 for financial corruption, chief among them the countess of Somerset's father, the disgraced lord treasurer Thomas Howard, earl of Suffolk, the downfall of the monopolists and no less a person than Sir Francis Bacon in 1621, and even Lionel Cranfield in 1624, all testify to the problems inherent in the factional politics and the intense rivalry for advancement and advantage in the early modern court. But the very fact that men did come to grief in that court indicates that it was not wholly out of control. Nor was it a problem confined only to the English court. It was the additional dimension of the king's favourites, in England far more than in Scotland, which skewed the picture of that court, to a quite unwarranted extent.

Like James himself, all his favourites were married; all had children. The king showed a lot of affection for the wives and children, as he did for his own wife and children. Even if the love between James and Anne had worn thin, by the standards of early modern arranged royal marriages, relations between them remained remarkably good, at least well into the first decade of the seventeenth century and even to some extent in the years before her death in 1619. As for his 'sweet boys', Steenie and Baby Charles, at the end of his life James's letters to them took on a sugary sentimentality which reads unpleasantly by modern standards and, much more to the point, reads very differently from his earlier correspondence (*Letters of James VI and I*, 388–422). This did not mean that he had lost his political grip. But it does suggest, as do his late literary works, an ageing king becoming over-emotional as the confidence with which he had ruled his kingdoms began to fail him.

Triple monarchy: Scotland and Ireland It is all too well known that, despite his promise in 1603 to return to Scotland every three years, James did so only once, in 1617; this has given rise to the idea that after 1603 he turned his back on Scotland, something which his English subjects hoped that he would do but were all too well aware that he did not. He had been, and remained, intensely interested in his Scottish kingdom, in manifest contrast to his mother, for whom Scotland came third on the list of priorities after England and France. In 1605 after the Gunpowder Plot James suggested sending Prince Henry back to Scotland for his safety; in 1607 he was toying with the idea of moving his capital to York. Neither idea found favour in England. Nor did his eventual visit in 1617, which raised considerable opposition; the king had to fight off Buckingham and other courtiers kneeling in his bedchamber and begging him not to go; one of those who accompanied him to Scotland, Sir Anthony Weldon, official of the board of the green cloth and master of the pun, loathed the experience and was probably the author of that vitriolic and witty attack on the northern kingdom, *A Perfect Description of the People and Countrey of Scotland*, finally published in 1659.

But there were compensations for James's personal absence, which eased the path of absentee kingship. The tradition of local autonomy, the repeated experience of minorities, had not entirely disappeared beneath the rapid developments in central government in the 1580s and 1590s. After 1603 James combined the old and the new. To the landed aristocracy who continued to exercise control he promoted a new group: the lairds and lawyers who had risen to prominence at the centre were now given earldoms to enhance their authority as those who would, in effect, govern Scotland—men like Sir George Home of Spott, who became earl of Dunbar, and Alexander Seton of Fyvie, created earl of Dunfermline. Personal contact was maintained for the first eight years after 1603 by Dunbar's regular journeys between Edinburgh and London. Particularly virulent anti-Scottish feeling in 1612 meant that there was no second Dunbar. But James and his Scottish politicians had one great piece of luck; apart from Dunbar, those with whom he had worked in the 1590s lived on until the 1620s, so that personal knowledge and shared political experience were maintained in a way in which they would never be again after 1625. They were reinforced by the new and effective postal system which the king set up when he went to England, cutting the round trip from London to Edinburgh and back to two weeks in winter, ten days in summer; and James's letters, in sharp contrast to Charles's peremptory commands, gave careful thought to the implementation of policy.

Nevertheless, there were evident strains. The Scottish reception of the English council's letter of invitation of 1603 showed an early awareness of the need to protect Scottish interests; but the union appeared to offer more advantage to them than to the English, and if the bandwagon was there, they were delighted to jump on. The visible hostility which greeted their arrival in London naturally soured the Scots; and matters became worse as hostility to James's union policy, even in its scaled-down form, became equally visible. A letter appended to one of the Scottish union tracts, 'Ane wther treatise', adjured James 'to be nevir unmyndfyll of this your first and auldest impyir of Scotland and of your gude subjectis heir' (NL Scot., Advocates MS 31.4.7, fol. 27). The 1604 parliament, discussing the appointment of Scottish commissioners to treat of union, was careful to insist that nothing should be done to prejudice the laws, privileges, offices, and liberties of Scotland and the property rights of the Scots; as the English were hardly likely to rush to acquire Scottish offices and lands, in the way they saw the Scots doing to theirs, this suggests an unnecessary level of paranoia, but the underlying fear of losing out was real enough. By 1607 parliament was writing to the king stating bluntly that James's 'antient and native kingdome' should not be turned into a province, to be governed by a deputy or viceroy as happened in the Spanish *monarchia*; Spain was the explicit example, but the Irish situation can scarcely have passed the Scots by. It was also demanding James's presence; this 'sould alswele as your hairt be equalie divydit betuix us' (*Reg. PCS*, 7.536). They then demanded, in 1610, that copies of foreign treaties should be made available in Edinburgh. They may well have had the king's sympathy over this potential source of neglect; certainly in 1614 Archbishop Abbot was concerned that the idea of a French match had been raised by the Scots, and in the same year Sir Charles Cornwallis, English ambassador to Spain, sought to please James by assuring him that he cared for the Scots 'as he did those of his owne countrey' (PRO, PRO 31/3/47, fols. 245–6). The Scots could still take comfort from the fact that the king of England was their king, be reassured by such things as the Scottish bedchamber that he retained his affection for them and had no wish to lose their presence at his court; but there was no long-term guarantee that this would continue after his death, and all they could do was to assert their position of equality with England as best they could.

On James's side concern about retaining control of his northern kingdom began to topple over into heavy-handedness, certainly in his dealings with parliament and even with his council. In 1608 he demanded to see the voting lists of the council; this, for a king who before 1603 had witnessed the votes for himself, was not as autocratic as it looked, and indeed arguably made it more difficult for James to deal with dissenters than when he had been there in person, but it was a reminder of the greater formality imposed by absentee kingship. Efforts to control parliament, strenuous enough in the 1590s, were also increased. In 1609 he attempted to nominate the lords of the articles himself, but this was politely refused. In 1612, however, he did have some success in nominating the lords to be chosen by the bishops. The 1617 parliament at which he was present saw renewed resistance to nomination by the king, and an effort to control the number of the officers of state who sat on the committee of the articles. Then in 1621 came the high point of royal control. This is a parliament for which the sources are relatively full, and it is quite clear that Thomas Hamilton, at this date earl of Melrose and both secretary of state and president of the court of session, was working at full stretch, lobbying from six in the morning before the lords of the articles met to deliberate at eight. Election to the articles was achieved by the bishops choosing eight nobles, who then chose eight bishops, and together they selected the barons and burgesses. In addition two Englishmen were given Scottish titles so that they could attend and vote; and proxy voting was allowed. The reason for this strenuous management was that the king's religious policy, the five articles of Perth, and a new form of taxation, on annual rents, were coming before parliament. Both were passed, but only just; the combined total of opponents and abstainers outweighed the number who voted for them. James was well aware of just what a close-run matter it had been, turning furiously, and utterly unfairly, on the bishops, the one group who had given him unanimous support. Royal confidence in governing Scotland was not what it had been.

The five articles and the new taxation were not the only contentious issues. As far back as 1581 there had been the idea of introducing commissioners of the peace, in a highly limited form, and this was extended in 1587; but neither found favour among the lairds. After 1603 James tried again. The idea was revived in 1609, and lists of local commissioners were drawn up in 1610, reinforced by officers of state, councillors and senators of the college of justice, some of the great magnates, and the archbishops of St Andrews and Glasgow; clearly the intention was to keep close ties between centre and localities. An even more comprehensive act followed in 1617, extending the powers of the commissioners and bringing them into line with English JPs. 'Anglicization' was neither tactful nor acceptable. In 1611 George Gledstanes, archbishop of St Andrews, himself rejected the scheme, bursting out in fury at a meeting of the council, in a flaming row with Thomas Hamilton, at this date merely a lord of session and king's advocate, 'that the realme had had many hundredth yeires bene weill governed withowt Justices of the Peace' (*Reg. PCS*, 14.621–2). The new JPs tended to use their offices to settle old scores. And by 1625 less than a quarter of the shires had JPs. James was not only losing his confidence; there was an extent to which he was losing his touch. However much he might maintain his interest in his native kingdom, those who had served him before 1603 were now being pushed along new paths.

Paradoxically James had arguably an easier time in Ireland. The lamentable Nine Years' War came to an end in 1603; and royal policy towards Ireland took a very different direction from the experiments and attempts at control of the Tudor monarchs. James approached the problem as a king experienced in ruling a Gaelic area of Scotland and applying rather different methods from those of the lowlands. In 1587 he had relied on a very traditional style of lordship when he introduced the general band, whereby highland and border lords and chiefs of clans would be made responsible, under financial penalty, for the peaceful behaviour of their followers. In 1602 and again in 1605 he had sent Fife gentry west to the Isle of Lewis, to civilize the islesmen; it had been a bloody failure, but it was the beginnings of the policy which later led to the much more wide-ranging plantation of Ulster.

James never subscribed to the harsh and savage view propounded by the poet and administrator in Ireland Edmund Spenser and by the attorney-general of Ireland, Sir John Davies, that the only way to deal with the Irish was by the forcible imposition of English civility. There was no reason why he should do so. Scottish Gaeldom had worried him as king of Scots a great deal less than Gaelic Ireland had worried the Tudors. An English deputy of Ireland was an established official, unparalleled in Scotland, and there to stay. But kings of Scots habitually worked with the earls of Argyll to control the Scottish highlands; and there are some signs that James wanted a similar relationship with that former rebel Hugh O'Neill, earl of Tyrone. The potential for such a working partnership was shattered in 1607 by the dramatic flight of Tyrone and Rury O'Donnell, earl of Tyrconnell. The success in Scotland of the efforts of Argyll and of Colin Mackenzie of Kintail, who became earl of Seaforth for his pains, may well have made the idea of plantation there less urgent than it would be in Ireland, where after 1607 there was no one to fulfil an equivalent role. But in essence the idea was the same, if on a far greater scale. The intention in Lewis had been the mix of lowland and highland Scots, whereas the plantation of Ulster, extensively implemented after 1610, and extended to Wicklow, Wexford, and Carlow in 1611, was a 'British' mix, of Irish, Scots, and English. It was by no means just a protestant mix imposed on Irish Catholics. Border and south-west Catholic Scottish undertakers from a still partially Gaelic area were very successful planters; the protestant Scots Sir George Hamilton of Greenlaw and the earl of Abercorn were very willing to plant Catholics in Strabane.

Another policy shared between the Irish and the Scottish highlanders was the attempt to integrate them more fully into 'British' society through the medium of language. Scottish Gaeldom became something of an embarrassment to King James after 1603; his Gaelic speakers hardly fitted the vision which he was trying to sell to the English of two equal kingdoms with a shared language and culture. In 1609, therefore, he and Andrew Knox, bishop of the Isles, produced the Statutes of Iona, which insisted that the heirs of the chiefs must be educated in the lowlands, and that the chiefs themselves must periodically attend the council; and in 1616 speaking, reading, and writing English became the prerequisite for inheriting land. Gaelic Ireland did not create the same embarrassment. But James had a tendency to reuse his good ideas; and so the eldest sons of the Old English peers were to go to England for their education.

James's one Irish parliament began in 1613 with roaring farce, with a disputed speakership; the Catholic John Everard sat tight in the chair, whereupon his rival Sir John Davies sat on top of him until Everard was removed. Also removed—by the king—was the contentious issue of religion, and as a result this was the easiest parliament which James ever held in any of his three kingdoms, even a subsidy being passed without much difficulty. It would be too much to say, more generally, that his rule of Ireland was either straightforward or wholly successful. But his obvious interest in his Irish kingdom, of which his close attention to the plantation project was a good example, and his refusal to treat it as a colony, as well as his greater understanding of Ireland than his English predecessors had had, combined with lack of fear of it, stood him in very good stead.

Religious matters Unlike modern British monarchs, who in effect show a split personality over religion, belonging to one church in England and another in Scotland, early modern monarchs were expected to preside over religious conformity. This was difficult enough in one kingdom, especially when that kingdom was England, still bound by the ill-defined Elizabethan settlement of 1559; how much more so when there were three kingdoms involved.

James himself was seen in somewhat contradictory terms when he succeeded in 1603; he received both the millenary petition from the puritans, obviously hoping for better things from a more clearly Calvinist monarch than his predecessor and urging moderate reform, and letters from Catholics, looking to him as the son of the 'sainted' Mary, queen of Scots, for relief from their harsh treatment in the last two decades of Elizabeth's reign. Neither was wholly misguided. James had reason to be wary of the leading Elizabethan churchmen, especially Richard Bancroft, by this time bishop of London, whose paranoia about puritans matched that of his queen, and with whom James had crossed swords a decade and more before 1603. What neither John Whitgift, archbishop of Canterbury, nor Bancroft, who succeeded him in 1604, understood was that, despite his battles with the Melvillians, James shared two of the aspirations of his Scottish puritans, decent stipends and a high level of education; by the time he went to England Scottish ministers were pouring out of the Scottish universities. Whitgift and the universities of Oxford and Cambridge were therefore wholly taken aback by his attempt to extend Scottish practice to England, when in 1604 he proposed that the impropriated tithes of the universities should be ploughed back into the church and devoted to clerical education. Challenging three powerful vested interests head on was clearly too much; dons at Oxford and Cambridge were no doubt entirely unwilling to reduce their intake of claret at dinner; and nothing was done.

But there was another Scottish practice which could be introduced into England on a much grander scale than the occasional small debates of Elizabeth's reign: for now it was debate between king and churchmen, as a way forward in trying to resolve religious tensions. Hence in 1604 James summoned the Hampton Court conference. The old idea that this was a line-up by king and bishops against the puritans is not tenable. The reasons why the puritans got less than they had hoped from the conference lay elsewhere. It was held too early in the reign: James was challenging hardline Elizabethan attitudes too soon for success; and he had not yet fully realized how different from his Scottish presbyterians were the English puritans he met at Hampton Court. Hence his furious and famous outburst, 'no bishop, no king'; in the heat of debate, he was surely seeing not John Rainolds and his associates, moderate men all, but in response to Rainolds's unlucky use of the word 'presbytery', seeing Andrew Melville and his extremist supporters. Hence his lack of opposition to Bancroft's extensive deprivations of puritan clerics in 1605–6; deprivation was a weapon he had used in Scotland himself. Nevertheless, Hampton Court was a landmark of importance, in the longer if not the immediate term. For James did come to accept that English puritans were not a continuation of the Scottish threat, not least because his enthusiasm for hunting took him regularly off to Royston in Cambridgeshire, where he met more puritans, and revised his view. Indeed, perhaps too much has been made of that famous outburst. James was a skilled debater, and proud of his skill. Debate, for him, was a matter of impassioned involvement; when he summoned the conference, he was not proposing to preside over a vicarage tea party. Moreover, out of the conference came one outstanding achievement which was undoubtedly of great moment for him. In 1601 he had proposed to the general assembly a new translation of the Bible. He began the process by personally translating the Psalms, but nothing else was done. Now, at Hampton Court, the dream of the new translation of the Bible became reality. The Authorized Version, published in 1611, stands as a lasting monument to Hampton Court, as a masterpiece of English prose which modern versions of the Bible do nothing to rival, and as a shared interest between the aspirations of the puritans and the aspirations of a 'puritanical' king.

The first years of the reign saw not just the theatre of Hampton Court; they also saw the drama of the Gunpowder Plot. James gave out conflicting signals in these years. Scottish Catholics had never troubled him as Scottish puritans had done; and he felt a distaste for persecution. Thus English Catholics did find relief under a king who drastically reduced the recusancy fines, to the deep concern of Cecil (which would give rise to the nonsensical belief that Cecil staged the plot in order to turn James into a persecuting king), the leading churchmen, and his exchequer officials. It was this last group who stopped the rot, when James failed in his attempt, as part of peace negotiations with Spain in 1604, to persuade Spain to pay the recusancy fines; the Spanish preferred to use their money for sweeteners for English protestants. The recusancy fines therefore began to creep up again, but not until after the plot was in being. For the Gunpowder Plot had nothing to do with Catholic hopes being frustrated by King James. Recognizing its real origins, James kept his head and refused to hold English Catholics in general responsible; as the contemporary Jesuit priest John Gerard acknowledged, it was the king who protected them from widespread reprisals. In the twenty-two years of James's English rule only twenty-five Catholics were executed, compared to 189 between 1570 and 1603.

These two events, Hampton Court and the Gunpowder Plot, were the big dramas in the English Jacobean church. James continued to give out what appeared to be conflicting signals: 'puritans' largely ceased to be an issue; Catholics who kept their heads down were left alone. Moreover, despite the king's own Calvinist belief, and the fact that his church was Calvinist in doctrine, his bench of bishops increasingly included Arminians, notably the impressive Lancelot Andrewes, successively bishop of Chichester, Ely, and Winchester. Small wonder that there were concerns about the king, who was seen to prefer theological debate to the imposition of theological conformity; hence the story that Richard Neile (who under James held four bishoprics in succession, culminating in Durham in 1617) orchestrated interruptions to sermons by new preachers, for if the king liked the preacher he would ask him to dinner, debate with him, and give him preferment in the church. But there was a consistency in James: his ecumenical approach, which had led him to propose an ecumenical council in May 1603, and which enabled him to recognize differing religious opinions with interest rather than fear. His court—that supposedly corrupt court—became home to distinguished foreign scholars and churchmen of like mind, most notably Isaac Casaubon. James was a genuinely international Calvinist, strenuously and successfully opposing the appointment of the Dutch Arminian theologian Conradus Vorstius as professor of theology at Leiden in 1612, and in 1618 strongly backing the Synod of Dort, which met in an attempt to resolve the Calvinist–Arminian battle in the Netherlands. However, he never insisted that only Calvinism was acceptable in his church. In the last year of his life he refused to suppress Richard Mountague's contentious anti-Calvinist *A New Gagg for an Old Goose*, instead inviting him to clarify his position, which Mountague did in his *Appello Caesarem*, and this has prompted the suggestion that by then James was departing from his Calvinist faith. It seems more likely that this man of flexible mind, never a hardline and exclusive Calvinist, was adapting to the new problems created by the international crisis of 1618. Thus in the tense world of foreign relations of 1624 the king was not opposed to a cleric who refused to label Catholics as the servants of Antichrist.

Being a member of King James's English church was therefore a great deal more relaxed than being a member of the church of Elizabeth or Charles I. The same was true in his Irish church. James never agreed with that peculiarly unpleasant strand of Calvinist logic which regarded Irish Catholicism as clear evidence of reprobation. The row in 1613 over the speakership came at a tense moment for Irish Catholics, then fearful of losing their place in parliament; they walked out and appealed to the king. James's initial reaction was less than favourable; in July he issued a proclamation stating that he would hear both sides of the argument, but would expect his arbitration, as a prerogative matter, to be final; and this was followed up in May 1614 with a proclamation against popery, which ordered all priests to leave Ireland. He did not pursue it. There was no religious legislation in parliament; the Catholic members returned in a wholly co-operative mood; and once again tension was entirely diffused.

It was a different matter in Scotland. For it was a Calvinist country, like James's English kingdom, but with a much tougher variety of Calvinism. In polity it was a hybrid, containing both bishops and the Calvinist courts, a compromise which existed reasonably successfully under James, for an able bench of bishops dressed like ordinary ministers and worked closely with the church courts. The Jacobean experience shows that the idea that the kirk hated bishops from the beginning is not true. What it hated was the powerful English model later encouraged by Charles I and imposed by him on Scotland; James himself had already spoken against that model. However, while shared Calvinist doctrine accommodated flexibility in polity, it encouraged a drive for greater conformity in worship. The king therefore embarked on the disastrous course of liturgical reform. After the general assembly of August 1616 had agreed to a basket of royal requests and dispersed, James dispatched five articles to be incorporated in the embryonic new canons and liturgy. The five articles of Perth restored, most offensively, the observation of the greater festivals of the Christian year and kneeling at communion. Even Calvin had proposed the abolition of the Christian festivals only until they were no longer associated with popery; yet how the kirk viewed the matter is seen in the fact that only in the mid-twentieth century did Christmas cease to be associated with popery and was adjudged rightly to be celebrated. And kneeling at communion was, of course, idolatry. It almost certainly did not help that James's one visit to Scotland, in 1617, could undoubtedly be seen as an effort to put his personal authority behind the articles, which were not formally presented to the synods until that July. His one concession, the withdrawing of his order to put statues of the apostles in his chapel in Holyroodhouse, did no good. The general assembly which met in November turned down the articles. Early in 1618 the privy council, acting on orders from a furious king, reinforced the article on the religious festivals; and in August a much more carefully managed assembly accepted them all, although with sizeable opposition. In October the privy council ratified the five articles and had them proclaimed publicly. Then came the hard-fought and narrow victory which saw the articles become law in the parliament of 1621, accompanied by James's promise—which he kept—to make no more innovations. He was no longer fighting the Melvillians; their leaders had been summoned to a 'second' Hampton Court conference, in 1606, and exiled. Perhaps he underestimated, therefore, the strength of feeling that Scottish Calvinist practice, unlike what they regarded as watered-down English, made the Scottish church 'one of the most pure kirks under heaven this day', as was claimed in the 1616 confession of faith (*Assemblies of the Kirk of Scotland*, 3.1139). The king threatened that purity. As in some of his secular policies, he appeared to be losing interest in the needs and aspirations of his Scottish kingdom. The man who had so successfully shaped the church that he wanted before 1603 was now losing his grip. Compared to his dealings with the churches of England and Ireland, this was a sad story.

Foreign relations, war in Europe, and the parliaments of the early 1620s As in so much else, James brought to his 'British' kingship his Scottish belief in the importance of Scottish kingship, now enhanced by his new status. Moreover the Stuart dynasty now acquired an importance in European affairs which could not have been attained by the Virgin Queen, simply because the king, having children, could play an important role in dynastic politics. It was the role which entirely suited *rex pacificus*. His first decisive action, in 1604, very much in agreement with Cecil, was to end the Anglo-Spanish war; diplomacy, not war, was to be the keynote of his foreign policy, and a diplomacy which was even-handed, reducing rather than hardening the religious divisions of Europe. His elder son, Henry, a much more militant protestant prince than his father, would have no truck with anything other than a protestant marriage alliance. In fact that suited James very well, and it was indeed realized by the marriage of his daughter Elizabeth to Frederick V, elector palatine; for it could be balanced by an alliance with Catholic Spain, ultimately sealed by the marriage of Prince Charles, heir to the throne since the death of Henry in 1612.

Inevitably, in a kingdom which had been carefully building up for itself a much needed sense of identity based on the ideology of England as God's elect protestant nation, this pacific and balanced policy was hardly popular. Peace with Spain was itself deeply unpopular. Elizabeth, who could be seen as a dismal failure as a militant protestant princess, now became, in the hands of William Camden and that friend and admirer of Philip Sidney, Fulke Greville, who should certainly have known better, the defender of embattled European protestants, compared to her spineless and dangerously pro-Catholic successor. The inglorious and half-hearted intervention in the Netherlands in the 1580s was forgotten; the queen making her nationalist speech in the face of the Armada, at Tilbury in Essex, was remembered. James, on the other hand, refused to act that imagined part of the English king as the military protector of the protestant faith. There was one exception in 1612, when he reluctantly joined the Evangelical Union of the German and Dutch in that brief era when the Catholic League of 1609, the assassination of Henri IV of France in 1610, and the Franco-Spanish alliance of 1611 raised protestant fears. His involvement with the Evangelical Union was short-lived, however: he was distinctly sceptical about the danger posed by the league, formed in reaction to the union's military intervention in Cleves-Jülich to enforce the claims of Lutheran princes to succeed to the duchy whose previous ruler had been a Catholic. What happened in 1613 was much more important than the involvement of 1612. For in that year sure instinct prompted Philip III to send as Spanish ambassador to England that noted bibliophile and scholar Diego Sarmiento de Acuña, count of Gondomar. He began a diplomatic and personal relationship with James which, until its tragic collapse in 1623–4, opened up far more avenues of policy than the king's identification solely with the protestants could ever have done. Spain might have been England's great enemy under Elizabeth, but it had not been Scotland's great enemy under James, who was, symbolically, the sixth of his line to bear the name of the saint associated with the great pilgrimage centre of Compostela. He had taken the novel line, from at least the early 1590s, of preferring Spain to the 'auld ally', France; and after 1603 English susceptibilities were not going to push him into undermining the opportunity of keeping a reasonable level of peace in Europe, which could be achieved by maintaining friendship with the greatest European power. That reasonable level was indeed maintained; only the assassination of Henri IV and the Cleves-Jülich dispute temporarily disturbed it before 1618.

It almost worked. But in 1618 came the Bohemian revolt, and in 1619 James's son-in-law committed the appalling folly of accepting the Bohemian crown, joining the Bohemians in mounting a direct challenge to the emperor Ferdinand II, only to be expelled by the latter's armies a year later. Europe was spiralling down into war; and James, on the grounds of both religion and kinship, was expected by European protestants and a faction of hardline English protestants to take up arms on behalf of the elector. More realistically than either, James regarded Frederick as a dangerous lunatic, writing to him in 1621 to tell him bluntly that if he threatened the stability of Europe and refused to co-operate in seeking a peaceful solution, then the king would disown him. Philip III had already offered a much more acceptable alternative, when he expressed himself willing in 1618 to allow James to arbitrate in the Bohemian problem. Co-operation with the Spanish Habsburgs, who could put pressure on the imperial Habsburgs to restore Frederick to his ancestral Rhineland territories of the Upper Palatinate, was the way forward.

By the end of 1621 there was indeed little alternative. The parliament which opened on 3 January in the context of popular fear of Catholicism whipped up by the crisis in Europe and of an ever-worsening trade depression had at first gone well. In a carefully balanced speech at its opening James had requested the wherewithal to help Frederick, declaring his preference for spending it in peaceful diplomacy, but his readiness to deploy it militarily if absolutely unavoidable. In a rush of enthusiasm the Commons voted two subsidies amounting to about £150,000, but then turned to contentious debate, attacking the privileges of the Merchant Adventurers and notorious monopolists like Sir Giles Mompesson and Sir Francis Mitchel. Next, with the connivance of Cranfield, among others, and the acquiescence of the king, MPs revived the device of impeachment and deployed it against the lord chancellor, Francis Bacon, Viscount St Alban. None the less, the session ended on a note of optimism and during the recess James showed his goodwill, and his own inclinations, by issuing a proclamation cancelling a score of monopolies. He also showed a commitment to economy by promoting Cranfield, ennobled as earl of Middlesex, to the lord treasurership. But when parliament reassembled in November the mood had changed. Harvest failure, floods, and the depth of the trade slump had made MPs wary of voting more money. With the king absent at Newmarket his managers, unsure of their master's precise attitude to war, failed to steer debate in profitable channels. In appending to George Goring's war proposal a petition that Prince Charles marry a protestant the Commons trod on two areas of the king's prorogative. This was an inappropriate meddling in affairs of state, James told them in a letter that December. When on 18 December MPs retaliated by entering a protestation about their privileges in the Commons journal, the king adjourned and then dissolved parliament. In the process he lost a third subsidy, voted but not yet enacted.

Peacemaking now became a necessity, and a Spanish match for Charles the more desirable. In 1622 co-operation with the Habsburgs still looked possible as a conference proposed by James met in Brussels between May and September.

But in 1623 it collapsed. Gondomar now had a powerful rival, the Spanish chief minister Olivares, who was far less favourable to the Spanish match. His views were shared by the prospective bride, the infanta, who objected strongly to being married to a heretic, declaring her preference for a nunnery. Even Philip III, who in 1622 had agreed that Anglo-Spanish forces should fight the emperor if he refused to restore Frederick, lacked the enthusiasm of James and Gondomar for the marriage. In these circumstances Prince Charles made his pre-emptive strike: having left England in February as 'Thomas and John Smith', in March he and Buckingham turned up in Spain. This was a very different matter from the journeys which James V and James VI had made to claim their brides. It was silly and undignified for the prince of Wales and the duke of Buckingham to sneak into Madrid in disguise. It was also very awkward for the Spanish court when their presence became known; for it had just embarked on a period of retrenchment, which had hastily to be forgotten, as the court plunged into an extremely expensive six-month party in their efforts to entertain their English visitors, a party which makes James's own notorious extravagance look positively restrained.

Charles fell in love—and lost (this time at least metaphorically) his political head. In 1622 he had resisted the papal demand for legal toleration of English Catholics as the price for his agreement to issue a dispensation. Once in Spain, he appears to have indicated that James would be prepared to acknowledge the spiritual supremacy of the pope. The sentimentality of James's letters immediately stopped; he utterly repudiated the suggestion. The situation worsened when Gregory XV's dispensation arrived, making demands which were more extreme than those of the Spaniards themselves. The infanta was to have not just her priests but a bishop; and she should not go to England until toleration for English Catholics had been in place for a year. There was no loophole.

Diplomatic politeness was preserved, apart from the quarrels between Olivares and Buckingham. But James recognized defeat. In July 1623 he wrote to Charles, telling him to come home, and hope that the infanta would follow. By then he may well have feared that the Spaniards would keep Charles in Madrid, as a diplomatic weapon. With typical Jacobean hard-headedness, he also told Charles to bring the dowry with him; cash would make up for the lack of the bride. In October a humiliated Charles and Buckingham came back to England, to a rapturous welcome from all those loyal upholders of the protestant cause who could not see—as their feeble king and his devious Spanish ambassador could so clearly see—that upholding the protestant cause in their way would plunge Europe into full-scale and ruinous war. France was now to be the ally, and Charles and Buckingham, enjoying their one brief moment of popularity, cheerfully ignored James's prophetic warning that a parliament might howl for war, but would not be prepared to pay for it. It was they who urged the calling of the parliament which opened in February 1624, and they who led the war party in the Lords. With the council divided between hawks and doves, both played out their rivalries in parliament. James gave an apparently conciliatory inaugural speech soliciting advice on areas of policy he had hitherto guarded to himself—the continuation of negotiations with Spain and the fight against popery—but he later spelled out clearly that war would be possible only if substantial supply were voted. Ironically the session was relatively productive of legislation, although its outcome was inconclusive. Buckingham engineered the impeachment for corruption of Middlesex, now his rival and the leading advocate of peace, but James prorogued parliament on 29 May without the requisite money for a war as yet undeclared. Contrary to his probable intention at the time, it was not recalled.

Leaving aside the question of Spain, in June James made a defensive alliance with the United Provinces, while pursuing the possibility of an anti-Habsburg coalition and a French marriage for Charles. From 1625 fighting in Europe escalated into the major and bloody war which dragged on until 1648. With the departure that January of a mercenary force under Count Mansfeld, destined for the Palatinate, England now made its dismal and short-lived entry into it; as James had foreseen, his southern kingdom had neither the will nor the ability to meet the demands of early seventeenth-century warfare. Possibly James and Gondomar had aimed too high in making the Spanish marriage an essential part of the peaceful solution; it was not, strictly speaking, necessary, for it was the Anglo-Spanish alliance which was essential. But by insisting on the marriage they could be seen to be cutting through the diplomatic manoeuvrings and clarifying the issue. In any case, James and Gondomar had surely been right to resist the calls for war, to seek a diplomatic solution; it is a tribute to the bond between them that they came as close as they did to success. The fact that in the end they failed was a fatally missed opportunity. Many Europeans died because of that failure. And a king of European vision was to die politically bankrupt.

'Tis true I am a cradle king' In the first years of his English rule James's Scottish analysis of divine-right kingship was expanded into direct confrontation with the papacy and its claims of the deposing power over secular rulers. He was now defending European kingship. He began in 1608 with *Triplici nodo, triplex cuneus, or, An Apologie for the Oath of Allegiance*, directed against Pope Paul V and Cardinal Bellarmine. 'Now let us heare the words of his [the pope's] thunder', he wrote, and rushed to demolish them (*James VI and I: Political Writings*, 88). Attacked by Bellarmine for this work, he then raised the stakes and in 1609 addressed the monarchs of Europe in *A Premonition to All Most Mightie Monarches, Kings, Free Princes and States in Christendom*, arguing passionately against papal pretensions to superiority over kings. Finally in 1615 he produced his *Remonstrance for the Right of Kings and the Independence of their Crownes*, which was a broadside against Cardinal Perron and the French clergy for rejecting the oath proposed by the third estate in the uncertain period after Henri IV's assassination on similar lines to the English oath of allegiance introduced after the Gunpowder Plot; thanks to their clergy, the French remained bewitched 'of this pernicious opinion; that Popes may tosse the French King his Throne like a tennis ball, and that killing of Kinges is an acte meritorious to the purchase of the crowne of Martyrdome' (*Political Works of James I*, 170). The lively and effective political polemicist was still there in full measure.

So was the scholar-king, imposing his intellectual tastes on the English court. Pride of place in recognizing the genius of Ben Jonson goes to Anne of Denmark, who first gave him patronage. But James took over, and developed a relationship with the scholar-poet which underpinned the glories of the Jonsonian masque. In 1616, the year in which James's collected works were published, Jonson followed suit with his. James's enthusiasm for Oxford, first displayed in 1604 when he went to the Bodleian Library and declared that if he were not a king, there would be no greater pleasure than in being chained to the library, was now reinforced. When presented with the *Workes*, Oxford bore them in procession to the Bodleian; Cambridge simply accepted a gift to the library, and did not bother. Jonson, Horace and Virgil to James's Augustus, was rewarded in that year with an annual pension, and became poet laureate. But however personally satisfying, James's relationship with Jonson remained just that; there was no English re-creation of the circle of Scottish poets in whom James had taken so much pleasure in his earlier years. And while he had some success in expressing his theological interests with the foundation of a college of divinity in Chelsea, the Oxford and Cambridge monopoly was not broken; the college lasted only until the middle of the seventeenth century.

James never lost his ability to produce the effective phrase. Yet just as the writings before 1603 had reflected his confidence in his Scottish rule, so after 1603, and especially in the later years, they gave expression to something very different: increasing tiredness and disillusion. He wrote less in England, for recreation and enjoyment, and his works came to lack the force and certainty of touch which had characterized his Scottish writing. His 'Epistle dedicatorie' to his 1620 *Meditation upon the 27, 28, 20 Verses of the xxvii Chapter of St Matthew* quite explicitly paints the picture of a king 'being growen in yeares … weary of controversies', and tells us that 'the croun of thornes went never out of my mind, remembring the thorny cares, which a King … must be subject unto'. In this work Buckingham appears in an unfamiliar light. For he offered to be the king's amanuensis, and James's acceptance 'much eased my labour, considering the slownesse, ilnesse and uncorrectnes of my hand' (*James VI and I: Political Writings*, 231–2). That sad self-portrait is very far removed from the active hand which wrote *Basilikon Doron* twenty years earlier, the hand of an author furiously impatient with the difficulty of finding the right words to express the ideas swarming in his brain. The insistent linking of Christ's suffering to the suffering of kings, brought together by the symbol of the crown of thorns, is not only tedious but on occasions comes close to toppling over into a kind of blasphemy. Moreover, James is frankly boring on the difficulty of plaiting a crown of thorns, the etymology of the Greek word *diadema*, the lost recipe for the purple dye of the ancients, and much else besides; and it comes as a shock to find King James a bore.

The slowness of the prose marks it out even from the previous year's *Meditation on the Lords Prayer*, published in 1619. Buckingham appears again, this time as dedicatee. For 'it is a very short and plaine Prayer, and therefore the fitter for a Courtier'; short, because courtiers have little leisure, and especially Buckingham, making himself useful by serving his king, and dealing with 'the uncessant swarme of suitors importunately hanging upon you'; plain, 'since you were not bred a scholler' (*Meditation*, A4). It is very different from the earlier master of taut, pithy prose. Now he rambled, shoving great and small matters together in an increasingly ill-judged mishmash. Even in 1604 his preface to the *Counterblaste to Tobacco* had been far too grand for a treatise on what he himself called mere smoke; he was perhaps beginning to take himself too seriously, to strive too much for effect. The *Meditation on the Lords Prayer* wanders all over the place. Occasionally the old bite flashed out; thus 'And lead us not into temptation' produced:

> the Arminians cannot but dislike the frame of this Petition; for I am sure they would have it, *And suffer us not to be ledde into temptation*, and Vorstius would adde, *as farre, Lord, as is in thy power, for thy power is not infinite*. (ibid., 116)

But the work begins with a vitriolic digression on puritans and Brownists, sectaries; and it includes a couple of hunting stories, a pious reference to his father-in-law, and an attack on 'Tobacco-drunkardes' (ibid., 76) as the epitome of sinners. There is a palpable loss of judgement in these works.

James's last three poems were written in 1622–3. The first, echoing two proclamations in 1615 and 1622, and part of his speech of 1616 to the Star Chamber, adjured the gentry to make themselves deaf to the siren song of London and return to the country. It is therefore an addition to the small group of country house poems, whose status was enhanced when they were declared to be a genre in 1957. Its real target, however, is 'You women that doe London love so well', but whose

> husbands will as kindly you embrace
> without your jewels or your painted face.
> (*Poems*, 2.178, 180)

This poem does retain some of the old vigour. The final one, appealing for the safe return of Jack and Tom (Charles and Buckingham) from Madrid in 1623 has a certain grace and pathos. But his lengthy 'Answere to the Libell called the Comons teares', written between late 1622 and early 1623 is tragic.

> 'Tis true I am a cradle king
> yet doe remember every thinge
> That I have heretofore put out
> and yet begin not for to doubt.
> (ibid., 189)

None the less, begin to doubt James did. The 'Libell' has not survived, but its content is made clear enough in the king's poem. The unpopularity of his Spanish friendship comes out strongly:

> yet you that knowe me all soe well
> why do you push me down to hell
> by making me an Infidell.
> (ibid.)

Control was slipping away:

> And to no use were Councell Tables
> if State affaires were publique bables.
> (ibid., 187)

Where now was the serenity of his poem of 1589–90, his certain dependence on God's plan? The later poem contained perhaps one of the most effective lines he ever wrote: 'God and Kings doe pace together' (ibid., 183). He had little else to pace with. His foreign policy was falling apart, he was faced with increasingly insistent demands that he adopt the role of the protestant prince defending the protestants of Europe, and *rex pacificus* had nothing to offer. So he resorted to threat, to a very untypical appeal to royal rage: 'If once I bend my angry brow … wonder at kings and them obey' (ibid., 191, 183). It was hardly effective; it was, indeed, a despairing cry.

For some time James had suffered from kidney problems and arthritis, and in September 1624 the latter worsened. By March 1625 this had been compounded by a fever, to be followed by a stroke and severe dysentery. James died on 27 March 1625 at Theobalds, Hertfordshire, and was buried in the Henry VII chapel in Westminster Abbey on 5 May. It was a loss keenly felt by his circle of Scottish friends and politicians, who could remember the days of his kingship in Scotland, and now had to face for the first time the heightened chill of absentee monarchy under a king with whom there was no such personal relationship. In England—as the earl of Mar and Kellie, who had grown up beside the king, sadly recorded—the world belonged to Charles and Buckingham. But the sombre magnificence of John Donne's funeral sermon was not just rhetoric; it conjures up the vibrant personality who had gone, and is a reminder that for his English subjects also there was a sense of loss. After his death men looked back on James as the king of scholarship and wit. Even the hostile Weldon described him as very witty; and his table talk was recorded and published, under the variant titles of the sixty *Wittie Observations Gathered from our Late Soveraign King James* (1643) and the 200 *Flores regii, or, Proverbs and aphorisms, divine and morall … spoken by his most excellent majestie James of famous memory* (1627).

But thereafter James's reputation declined. It was the railings of his presbyterian opponents, not the support of his archbishop of St Andrews, John Spottiswoode, in his more anodyne *History of the Church of Scotland* (published posthumously in 1655), which gained ground after 1690, when it began to chime with the inaccurate belief that the kirk had always set its face against bishops. His homosexuality became a moral issue. His writings were regarded as of little value, of note only because they were written by a king. He was divided sharply into James VI and James I, which meant that Scottish historians concentrated on his problems with his over-mighty aristocracy, and English historians with his failure to get on with his English parliaments and to understand the English constitution. Indeed his most extreme critics, the whig historians, detected in him an instinct for absolutism, even tyranny; and in their hands, paradoxically, James I, now separated from James VI, became indissolubly linked to the very different Charles I. In 1956 the critical view reached its final heights in the utterly hostile biography *King James VI and I* by D. H. Willson, that astonishing spectacle of a work whose every page proclaimed its author's increasing hatred for his subject. The Weldon portrait of the disgusting, cowardly pedant, with a conceit which far outweighed his real ability, underpinned it all. It was in fact Weldon who coined the famous phrase 'the wisest fool' in Christendom (wrongly attributed to Henri IV, who never said it), that phrase which has lingered on in popular memory and sadly may continue to do so, even if, as any serious study makes clear, it bears no relation to the reality that was King James.

Recent scholarship has done much to overturn these views; even literary critics have become less hostile, and modern historians see far greater ability in James. He was not a success in every area. He was a financial disaster. His dreams of closer union were not realized, and his efforts to keep his kingdoms out of war in Europe failed. But he was a remarkable man, with a high theoretic sense of his kingship, yet also an adept practical politician, casual, friendly, intellectual, and scholarly. Unlike many of the other multiple kingdoms of early modern Europe, Britain survived, cracks only beginning to show at the end of the twentieth century. That is not, of course, purely because of the particular and in some ways curious skills of the first king of Britain. Its establishment as a viable political entity, which paved the way for its future survival, undoubtedly is. JENNY WORMALD

Sources *Basilicon doron of King James VI*, ed. J. Craigie, 2 vols., STS, 3rd ser., 16, 18 (1944–50) · *Minor prose works of King James VI*, ed. J. Craigie and A. Law, STS, 4th ser., 14 (1982) [includes *The trew law of free monarchies*] · *The poems of James VI of Scotland*, ed. J. Craigie, 2 vols., STS, 3rd ser., 22, 26 (1955–8) · James I, *The workes of the most high and mighty prince, James, by the grace of God kinge of Great Brittaine, France and Ireland* (1616) · James VI and I, *A meditation upon the Lord's prayer* (1619) · *Flores regii, or, Proverbs and aphorisms, divine and morall, as … spoken by his most excellent majesty, James of famous memory king of Great Brittaine* (1627) · *Wittie Observations gathered from our late soveraign king James in his ordinarie discourse* (1643) · *The political works of James I*, ed. C. H. McIlwain (New York, 1918) · *King James VI and I: political writings*, ed. J. P. Sommerville (1994) · [T. Thomson], ed., *The historie and life of King James the Sext*, Bannatyne Club, 13 (1825) · *Correspondence of King James VI of Scotland with Sir Robert Cecil and others in England during the reign of Elizabeth*, ed. J. Bruce, CS, old ser., 78 (1861) · *Letters of King James VI and I*, ed. G. V. P. Akrigg (Berkeley, CA, 1984) · J. Nichols, *The progresses, processions, and magnificent festivities of King James I, his royal consort, family and court*, 4 vols. (1828) · B. Galloway and B. P. Levack, eds., *The Jacobean union: six tracts of 1604*, Scottish History Society, 4th ser., 21 (1985) · *Memoirs of his own life by Sir James Melville of Halhill*, ed. T. Thomson, Bannatyne Club, 18 (1827) · *The autobiography and diary of Mr James Melvill*, ed. R. Pitcairn, Wodrow Society (1842) · *Original letters relating to the ecclesiastical affairs of Scotland*, 2 vols., Bannatyne Club, 92 (1851) · state papers of James I, PRO, SP 14 · E. R. Foster, ed., *Proceedings in parliament, 1610*, 2 vols. (1966) · *Reg. PCS*, 1st ser. · J. Row, *The historie of the Kirk of Scotland*, ed. B. Botfield, 2 pts in 1 vol., Maitland Club (1842) · J. Spottiswoode, *History of the Church of Scotland*, ed. M. Napier and M. Russell, 3 vols., Spottiswoode Society, 6 (1847–51) · J. F. Larkin and P. L. Hughes, eds., *Stuart royal proclamations*, 1 (1973) · B. Bradshaw and J. Morrill, eds., *The British Problem, c.1534–1707: state formation in the Atlantic archipelago* (1996) · L. Barroll, *Anna of Denmark, queen of England* (Philadelphia, 2001) · K. M. Brown, *Bloodfeud in Scotland, 1573–1625: violence, justice and politics in an early modern society* (1986) · K. M. Brown, *Kingdom or province? Scotland and the regal union, 1603–1715* (1992) · *APS* · T. Thomson, ed., *Acts and proceedings of the general assemblies of the Kirk of Scotland*, 3 pts, Bannatyne Club, 81 (1839–45) · D. Calderwood, *The history of the Kirk of Scotland*, ed. T. Thomson and D. Laing, 8 vols., Wodrow Society, 7 (1842–9) · *CSP Scot., 1563–1603* · *CSP Spain, 1580–86* · *The letters of John Chamberlain*, ed. N. E. McClure, 2 vols. (1939) · W. Notestein, F. H. Relf, and H. Simpson, eds., *Commons debates, 1621*, 7 vols. (1935) · *JHC*, 1 (1547–1628) · T. Craig, *De unione regnorum Britanniae tractatus*, Scottish History Society, Edinburgh (1909) · *Calendar of the manuscripts of the most hon. the marquis of Salisbury*, 24 vols., HMC, 9 (1883–1976) · *Report on the manuscripts of the marquis of Downshire*, 6 vols. in 7, HMC, 75 (1924–95), vols. 2–6 · *The manuscripts of his grace the duke of Portland*, 10 vols., HMC, 29 (1891–1931) · J. Wormald, 'James VI and I: two kings or one?', *History*, 68 (1983), 187–209 · J. Wormald, 'The creation of Britain: multiple kingdoms or core colonies', *TRHS*, 6th ser., 2 (1992), 175–94 · P. Croft, *King James* (2003) · G. Burgess, *The politics of the ancient constitution: an introduction to English political thought* (1992) · G. Burgess, *Absolute monarchy and the Stuart constitution* (1996) · T. Cogswell, *The blessed revolution: English politics and the coming of war, 1621–24* (1989) ·

N. Cuddy, 'The revival of the entourage: the bedchamber of James I, 1603–1625', *The English court: from the Wars of the Roses to the civil war*, ed. D. R. Starkey and others (1987), 173–225 · J. Doleman, *King James I and the religious culture of England* (2000) · B. Galloway, *The Union of England and Scotland, 1603–1608* (1986) · K. Fincham, *Prelate as pastor: the episcopate of James I* (1990) · K. Fincham, ed., *The early Stuart church, 1603–1642* (1993) · M. Lee, *John Maitland of Thirlestane* (Princeton, 1959) · M. Lee, *Government by pen: Scotland under James VI and I* (Urbana, IL, 1980) · M. Lee, *Great Britain's Solomon: James VI and I in his three kingdoms* (Urbana, IL, 1990) · P. Lake, *Anglicans and puritans? Presbyterianism and English conformist thought from Whitgift to Hooker* (1988) · B. P. Levack, *The formation of the British state: England, Scotland and the union, 1603–1707* (1987) · R. Lockyer, *Buckingham: the life and political career of George Villiers, first duke of Buckingham, 1592–1628* (1981) · J. Goodare and M. Lynch, eds., *The reign of James VI* (Phantassie, 2000) · R. A. Mason, ed., *Scottish political thought and the Union of 1603* (1994) · D. G. Mullan, *Episcopacy in Scotland: the history of an idea* (1986) · D. G. Mullan, *Scottish puritanism, 1590–1638* (2000) · T. W. Moody and others, eds., *A new history of Ireland, 3: Early modern Ireland, 1534–1691* (1976) · W. B. Patterson, *King James VI and I and the reunion of Christendom* (2000) · L. L. Peck, *Northampton: patronage and politics at the court of James I* (1982) · L. L. Peck, *Court patronage and corruption in early Stuart England* (1990) · L. L. Peck, ed., *The mental world of the Jacobean court* (1991) · C. Russell, *Parliaments and English politics, 1621–1629* (1979) · C. Russell, *The causes of the English civil war* (1990) · K. Sharpe, ed., *Faction and parliament: essays on early Stuart history* (1978) · A. G. R. Smith, ed., *The reign of James VI and I* (1973) · J. P. Sommerville, *Politics and ideology in England, 1603–1640* (1986) · H. Tomlinson, ed., *Before the English civil war: essays on early Stuart politics and government* (1983) · N. Tyacke, *Anti-Calvinists: the rise of English Arminianism, c.1590–1640* (1987)

Archives BL, corresp., Add. MSS 23240–23241 · CUL, corresp. and papers · Dick Institute, Kilmarnock, letters to the Boyd family · Duchy of Cornwall office, London, household accounts · LPL, corresp. and papers · NA Scot., letters · NA Scot., royal letter-book · S. Antiquaries, Lond., papers, incl. establishment lists | BL, Sloane MSS, letters and papers · Hunt. L., letters to the earl of Huntingdon · NA Scot., letters to the dukes of Hamilton · NA Scot., corresp. with the earl of Mar · NA Scot., letters to Sir John Ogilvy · U. Edin. L., corresp. with Queen Elizabeth · W. Sussex RO, letters to the earl of Huntly · Warks. CRO, letters to the wardens of New College, Oxford, and Winchester College

Likenesses L. de Vogelaare, group portrait, oils, c.1567–1568 (*The memorial of Lord Darnley*), Royal Collection, Holyroodhouse, Edinburgh · attrib. A. van Bronckhorst, 1574, Scot. NPG · oils, c.1587, Royal Collection · attrib. A. Vanson, two portraits, oils, 1595, Scot. NPG · W. J. Edwards, engraving, c.1603 (after P. van Somer), Hult. Arch. · silver medal, 1603, Scot. NPG · N. Hilliard, oils, c.1603–1608, Royal Collection; version, V&A · oils, 1604, Scot. NPG · attrib. J. de Critz senior, oils, c.1604–1607, Loseley House, Surrey; versions, Dulwich Picture Gallery, London, NPG, Scot. NPG · N. Hilliard, oils, c.1609–1614, BM · engraving, c.1615, Hult. Arch. · engraving, c.1615 (after Van Dyck), Hult. Arch. · group portrait, engraving, c.1615 (with his family; after engraving by C. de Passe), Hult. Arch. · P. van Somer, oils, 1618, Royal Collection · P. van Somer, oils, c.1620, Royal Collection · D. Mytens, oils, 1621, NPG [*see illus.*] · J. Bushnell, statue, Temple Bar (Theobald's Park), London · A. de Colone, oils, Scot. NPG · M. Colte, statue, Hatfield, Hertfordshire · attrib. R. Lockey, oils (after A. Van Bronckhorst), Scot. NPG, version, Hardwick Hall, Derbyshire · I. Oliver, watercolour on vellum, Scot. NPG; on loan from the Buchanan Society · bronze bust, Whitehall Banqueting House, London · coins, BM · engravings, BM · engravings, Hult. Arch. · line engraving (after A. Vanson), BM; repro. in J. Johnston, *Inscriptiones historicae regum Scotorum* (1602) · medals, BM · oils, Scot. NPG · oils, Scot. NPG; on loan from National Galleries of Scotland · oils, Audley End House and Garden [English Heritage], Essex · pewter badge, Scot. NPG · watercolour, Scot. NPG

James II and VII (1633–1701), king of England, Scotland, and Ireland, was born in St James's Palace, London, on 14

James II and VII (1633–1701), by Sir Godfrey Kneller, 1684

October 1633, the third surviving child and third (but second surviving) son of *Charles I (1600–1649) and his French queen, *Henrietta Maria (1609–1669). At James's baptism, held in St James's on 24 November, one of his sponsors was Frederick Henry, prince of Orange, whose son William, *Mary (1631–1660), James's elder sister, was to marry. Their son, William [*see* William III and II], was destined to be James's nemesis. The other two sponsors were his aunt, *Elizabeth, the queen of Bohemia, and her son *Charles Lewis, the elector palatine, both of whom lived in exile as refugees in the Dutch republic. The European connections of the Stuart dynasty were thus well represented, albeit by proxy, at this ceremony. They were to influence his destiny more than any other contemporaries. James spent nearly a third of his life in two continental exiles. On the second occasion he was driven out of England by his nephew and son-in-law, William of Orange, the husband of his daughter Mary [*see* Mary II].

Childhood At the time, such troubles seemed very remote. James's father was enjoying a relatively stable period between the turbulent encounters with parliament in the 1620s and the civil wars of the 1640s. Some of the assurance of stability can be detected in his making his young son duke of York and Albany shortly after his baptism, and appointing him lord high admiral in 1638. In that year, however, the first rebellion against Charles's rule broke out in Scotland, which brought the period of personal rule to an end. James's childhood was spent mostly in Richmond Palace, where his governor was William Seymour, marquess of Hertford. When in 1642 his father felt unable to remain in London and went to York he summoned Hertford to bring his younger son to join him, despite parliament's having prohibited it. James was subsequently sent to Hull to inform the governor, Sir John Hotham, that the king intended to dine with him the following day. Hotham decided to prevent Charles from entering Hull—a decisive step towards civil war. The king had no alternative but to ask the governor to allow his son to join him, which, in view of parliament's injunction on James's movements, he reluctantly conceded. Father and son then retreated to Beverley.

James was present when his father raised the royal standard at Nottingham, and also at the battle of Edgehill, where he and his brother Charles [see Charles II] came close to being captured by parliamentarian forces. After the battle James accompanied his father to Oxford, where he attended the House of Lords in 1644 at the age of eleven. His two years in the university city were valuable for his education, for he was taught by several fellows of colleges, including Brian Duppa, the deprived bishop of Salisbury, who did more than most Anglican clergymen to keep the ideals of the church alive during the interregnum. How far James progressed in his education after its previous neglect is hard to assess. He seems to have been a reluctant scholar, preferring outdoor pursuits to studying. He did acquire fluent French and some proficiency in music. James does not, however, appear to have made much progress in acquiring knowledge of Anglican doctrine, judging by the basic reading he undertook later to understand it, when assailed by doubts raised by Catholics. After Oxford surrendered to the parliamentarians in 1646 James was taken to London, where his own servants were dismissed from service by his captors, 'not so much as excepting a dwarf whom his Royal Highness was desirous to have retain'd with him' (Life, 1.30). Along with his sister Mary and his younger brother, *Henry, duke of Gloucester, he was placed under the guardianship of the earl of Northumberland at St James's Palace. On hearing that Charles I had been taken prisoner he protested 'how durst any rogues to use his father after that manner', and when his informant threatened to tell Northumberland of his outburst James had to be restrained from firing an arrow at him from a longbow (Turner, 15). He was allowed to visit the captured king, who urged him to be loyal to his elder brother, Charles, and to contrive to join him in France, where he had fled to be with their mother. After two abortive attempts the duke managed to escape in April 1648, despite having promised parliament not to endeavour it again. The undertaking was well planned by Colonel Joseph Bampfield, who advised James to pretend to be playing hide-and-seek with his siblings so that when seeking a hiding place he could slip out of the palace into St James's Park, where the colonel was waiting to escort him to a house near London Bridge. There Bampfield's fiancée, Anne Murray, was ready with girls' clothes specially made for the duke to wear, before boarding a boat to sail down the river to Tilbury. They then transferred to a Dutch ship which conveyed them to Middelburg. On 30 April James arrived at The Hague, to be greeted by his sister Mary and her husband, the prince of Orange.

First exile James spent the rest of 1648 at The Hague. In June he was presented with an opportunity to be his father's lord high admiral in fact as well as in theory, when some parliamentarian seamen mutinied against their officers and put their ships under his command. He sent a message to his brother in Paris requesting his presence. To James's disappointment, after his arrival at The Hague Charles placed the small fleet under Prince Rupert. It was a wise decision, as the fifteen-year-old duke of York had proved unable to exercise authority over it.

At the beginning of 1649 James went to Paris, summoned there by his mother. *En route* he spent nearly a month at the Benedictine monastery at St Armand, his first experience of a Roman Catholic community, which he clearly enjoyed. When he arrived at St Germain-en-Laye in mid-February he learned that his father had been executed. Although his reaction is unknown, the news must have concentrated his mind wonderfully.

James's brother, now that he was Charles II, seems to have decided to assert his independence of their mother, for he moved from St Germain to the Channel Island of Jersey, one of the few possessions of the crown which remained nominally loyal. Charles took James with him, and when he himself went to the Netherlands early in 1650, *en route* for Scotland, he appointed his brother as governor of Jersey. This was the duke's first real experience of command, though he seems to have left its responsibilities to the deputy governor, Sir George Carteret. James's own government of the island ended in September when he returned via the Netherlands to Paris and his mother's court. There was considerable tension between Henrietta Maria and her son on his return. Whether she tried to convert him to Catholicism at this time is not clear. She did, though, try to persuade his younger brother, Henry, duke of Gloucester, to become a Catholic, despite James's protests. There was friction with his mother over his plans to marry the daughter of the duke of Lorraine, an enemy to her country. James ignored her command to stay in Paris and went to see the duke, but the negotiations failed. He then moved from Brussels to The Hague. However, he was refused hospitality from his sister Mary at their mother's instigation. Instead of returning to Paris as Henrietta demanded, he accepted the hospitality of his aunt Elizabeth of Bohemia, who lived at Rhenen in Gelderland. His mother then relented, perhaps because Mary had recently suffered the loss of her husband to smallpox and shortly after his death had given birth to a son, the future William of Orange. At all events James returned to The Hague in January 1651, but moved to Breda when he learned that agents from the English Commonwealth had arrived to negotiate an alliance with the Dutch republic. When he received an order from

Charles to return to Paris and to obey their mother in all matters, except those involving religion, he had no option but to go back to St Germain in June. That September he learned that his brother had been defeated at the battle of Worcester and his fate was unknown. It must have seemed that James might have succeeded him as king already, when to the great relief of the exiled court Charles managed to make his way there from England.

The final collapse of the royal cause at home left the exiles despondent. James was desperately short of money. An attempt to improve his finances by marrying a French heiress failed. By 1652 he had decided that he had no alternative to enlisting in the French army, 'being very desirous of making himself fit one day to serve the King his brother in a useful capacity' (*Memoirs of James II*, 57). Even so, he had to borrow money to equip himself for his new career. The French army was commanded by the vicomte de Turenne, the great Huguenot general, whom James idolized, writing his military *Memoirs* to sing his praises. As a result his own role in the royal army is scarcely mentioned, and there are only occasional glimpses of him in these crucial years. Although they deal with campaigns in the Fronde and in the last stages of the Franco-Spanish war, the *Memoirs* make tedious reading. This is partly because they rarely rise above a detailed narrative of obscure manoeuvres. James delighted in such detail: his account of the revolution of 1688 has significantly more on its military than on its political aspects. He was more a soldier than a politician. Indeed, the question of his grip on politics is raised by the attention to military minutiae which his *Memoirs* and his autobiography document. They record a man who could not discern the wood for the trees.

When James joined the French army his first engagement was in an attack on Etampes, where the Frondeurs were entrenched. He 'was present at this hot attack' and according to Edward Hyde 'behaved himself with extraordinary courage and gallantry' (*Memoirs of James II*, 68; Ashley, 35). The enemy was forced to abandon Etampes and retreat towards Paris. Turenne contrived to outflank them and to install Louis XIII's court in Paris by the end of 1652. During this campaign James became closely attached to the vicomte, acting as lookout for him since Turenne's eyesight was poor.

In the following year James took part in the siege of Mouzon, where he was so conspicuous that he exposed himself to danger. He claimed to have escaped being shot from the walls only because the governor, 'knowing me by my Starr, had forbid his men to fire upon the Company' (*Memoirs of James II*, 48). The fall of Mouzon ended the campaign for that year, and James went back to Paris, again, in Edward Hyde's words, 'full of reputation and honour' (*DNB*). Turenne presumably shared this view, for before the next campaign James was promoted to the rank of lieutenant-general.

During the lull between campaigns James was at the exiled Stuart court, which was riven with intrigue, with Henrietta Maria at loggerheads with Charles. James

inclined to take his brother's side in the dispute, influenced by Sir John Berkeley, whose influence over him his mother disliked. She apparently persuaded Charles that Berkeley was untrustworthy, for he urged James to accept Henry Bennet, whom he felt was more reliable, as his secretary. In spring 1654 the French began to negotiate an alliance with the protectorate of Oliver Cromwell, which led to Charles's leaving France in July. Before going he drew up a list of instructions for James, which indicate the tensions in the royal family. One commanded the duke to 'let nobody persuade you to engage your own person in any attempt or enterprise without first imparting the whole design to me'. Another informed him that their mother had promised Charles not to try to convert their brother Henry to Catholicism. He clearly did not trust her, for he charged Henry to inform James 'if any attempt shall be made upon him to the contrary; in which case you will take the best care you can to prevent his being wrought upon since you cannot but know how much you and I are concerned in it' (Turner, 44). When Henry was sent to a Jesuit college he wrote to his older brothers asking for their help. By then Charles was in Cologne and James at the front. When he eventually returned to the court Henrietta Maria tried to prevent him from seeing Henry unless he promised not to discuss religion when she was not present. James was apparently more sympathetic to his mother's wishes in this regard than was Charles, who had Henry spirited out of her clutches to join him in Germany.

James was in the front line in 1654 at the siege of Arras, where he found himself amid the fighting, some men being killed close by him. He took part in the final assault on the town, which fell to Turenne's troops. At the end of the year James returned to Paris. In May 1655 he wrote to his brother Charles about a Catholic plot to assassinate Oliver Cromwell. Although Charles could not condone assassination James was apparently prepared to consider it, as he did again in the 1690s in the case of William III. So far from endeavouring to topple the English republic the French government concluded a treaty with it in 1655 'by virtue of which', James wrote, 'I was presently to leave the Country' (*Memoirs of James II*, 217).

Yet although there was a clause to that effect, neither Cromwell nor Mazarin insisted on it. The protector would have allowed James to remain in France, and even to serve in the French army provided the service was not in Flanders. Cromwell calculated that such an arrangement would alienate Charles from his brother, which served his foreign policy of hindering a Stuart restoration with foreign arms. The cardinal for his part was anxious to retain the Irish forces under York's command, and sought to employ him in Italy as commander of the army of the duke of Modena. In the event it was at the insistence of Charles, who got Spain to agree to help restore him to the English throne, that James left France to join him in Bruges. James, acting on Turenne's advice, even wrote to Charles to suggest that he would be of more service to the Stuart cause staying in France than joining him in the

Spanish Netherlands. Charles, however, 'far from consenting to the Duke's request, immediately sent him an absolute order to come and join him in Flanders with all possible diligence. He at once obeyed, and the French Court consented' (*Memoirs of James II*, 223). There was clearly disagreement between the two brothers over this and other issues at this time. One was the king's demand that the duke dismiss his secretary, Sir John Berkeley, whom Charles held responsible for James's reluctance to leave the French army. James refused, and though he obeyed Charles's summons to Bruges in September 1656 he insisted that Berkeley accompany him. After his arrival in Bruges he found that Sir Henry Bennet and other courtiers sided with the king in the quarrel, urging him to part with Berkeley. When his sister Princess Mary of Orange visited Bruges in December she took James's side. On this visit Mary was accompanied by her maid of honour Anne Hyde [*see* Anne (1637–1671)], whom he was to marry. With Mary as his ally James determined to keep Berkeley, and left the court with him to return to France. However, when they found that it was not possible to traverse Flanders without being detected, they decided to go to The Hague. This was to be the only occasion when James defied Charles. He sent a letter to his brother apologizing for his defiance, for which he blamed 'violent persons' at court. It was ironic that he should blame evil counsellors for the breach between them, when in the case of their father's opponents he dismissed such arguments as hypocritical. Thus of Sir John Hotham's refusal to admit Charles I into Hull, James observed that he 'fell upon the old common place of declaring against evil counsellors with such canting expressions as were generally in use amongst that party' (*Life*, 1.3). Charles graciously accepted his brother's explanation, permitting him to keep Berkeley as his secretary and sending his rival Bennet to Spain as his envoy. But the gesture of reconciliation was calculated, for Charles made it conditional on James entering the service of Spain. Where previously he had been reluctant to do so and thereby to fight his former comrades in arms, following his return to Bruges early in 1657 he enlisted in the Spanish army.

When James became acquainted with Spanish officers he considered them to be excessively formal and, unlike their French counterparts, incapable of swift reactions to an attack. His preference for his former colleagues became apparent that summer when Turenne laid siege to Mardyck. James took some Horse Guards back to reconnoitre Mardyck, where he engaged in conversation for about an hour with some French officers, who realized who he was when they saw a big greyhound he had previously had with him in France. The duke claimed that this incident showed the civilities which were used between hostile forces on the continent. But it also illustrates his divided loyalties, and his regret that he was no longer serving under Turenne but was actually opposing him. After Mardyck was placed in the hands of an English garrison, under the terms of the Anglo-French treaty, James even contrived to have a conversation with its governor, who to his obvious delight addressed him as 'Your Highness'.

The duke spent the winter of 1657–8 in the Spanish Netherlands. He found himself embarrassed by a proposition put to him by the earl of Bristol, who wished to ingratiate himself with the prince of Condé, that he should place himself under the Frenchman's command. Having commanded the English forces in the service of Spain he was reluctant to be Condé's subordinate, and also to antagonize the Spanish authorities. At the same time he had no wish to alienate Condé. He therefore stalled, even when put under some pressure by Charles. Fortunately Condé himself rejected the scheme.

The campaign of 1658 began with the French investing Dunkirk. The Spanish authorities in Brussels determined to raise the siege, though as James noted they were unable to do so by sea since the English navy controlled the approaches. They therefore resolved to advance towards the town and to camp on the sand dunes east of it. This decision really made them sitting ducks to Turenne's forces. James, who was not present when it was taken, was the first to realize that the Anglo-French army was advancing towards them in battle formation, which he recognized from having fought alongside Turenne. When he informed his Spanish superiors they did not believe him at first, but after Condé supported his opinion they hastily drew up their own forces to resist the attack. The subsequent battle of the Dunes was fought on 14 June. The duke took up a position on the right wing of the Spanish army, facing an onslaught of English troops, who, as he patriotically acknowledged, 'came on with great eagerness and courage' (*Memoirs of James II*, 263). James's cavalry counter-attacked but were beaten back. He rallied them for a second charge but again had to retreat. A similar fate visited the whole front line of the Spanish army, which fled, leaving the field to the French. Turenne went on to take Dunkirk ten days after the battle of the Dunes.

James spent the rest of the summer with the Spaniards putting in order the defences of Nieuport and other towns against a fresh attack from the enemy. He was at Nieuport when he learned that Cromwell had died on 3 September. This news transformed the morale of the Stuart court, which James joined in Brussels. Their hopes of restoration were roused, especially when in 1659 preparations were made for a concerted uprising in several parts of England. Charles and James were waiting to go back home when news came that the general insurrection had been postponed, while only one rising did take place—Sir George Booth's in Cheshire. On hearing of this Charles went to Calais while his brother went to Boulogne, hoping to learn that Booth had been successful, and that this had encouraged others to rebel after all. James was so sanguine that he procured a boat from the lieutenant-governor of Boulogne to convey him across the channel. But Charles brought him news that Booth's rising had not been accompanied by any other. Despairing of sufficient support at home, Charles went to Spain, hoping to get it from the king now that the Franco-Spanish war was coming to an end. Meanwhile James stayed in Boulogne, where Turenne approached him with an offer of French troops for the same purpose. James was delighted by this overture, and was even planning how to use this task force to make a beachhead in Rye when he learned that Booth's rising had been crushed. He therefore withdrew to Brussels in despond. In November he promised to marry Anne Hyde when he discovered that she was pregnant. Charles joined his brother for what must have been a most unmerry Christmas.

Early in 1660 their prospects looked so gloomy that James accepted from the king of Spain the post of high admiral. He was actually preparing to go to take it up 'when that Voyage was happily prevented by the wonderfull changes which were almost daily produced in England' (Memoirs of James II, 291). He was in fact destined to become lord high admiral not of Spain but of his native land. Along with his brother he sailed to England in May to a rapturous welcome. His first exile was over.

Lord high admiral, 1660–1673 The reputation of the restored court as a hotbed of intrigue and immorality was nourished by the scurrilous Memoirs of Count Grammont, in which the duke of York featured as a leading libertine. Despite his marriage to Anne Hyde he was no more faithful to her than Charles II was to his queen. On the contrary, he had a number of mistresses, among them Anne Carnegie, countess of Southesk; Arabella *Churchill (1649–1730), the sister of John Churchill, duke of Marlborough; Frances Jennings, sister of Marlborough's duchess, Sarah; while his longest-lasting liaison was with Catherine *Sedley (1657–1717). 'I do not believe there are two men who love women more than you and I do', Charles II confided to the French ambassador in 1677, 'but my brother, devout as he is, loves them still more' (Turner, 61). Apart from chasing women, hunting foxes appears to have been James's only regular pastime. He hunted at least twice a week, and kept up extensive stables for his hunting horses and kennels for his hounds. He accompanied Charles to Newmarket and other horse races, but apparently did not gamble, and was noted for rarely deviating from strict sobriety.

Nevertheless James's extravagant lifestyle strained the resources of his household to breaking point. At the Restoration he was set up in his own court by his brother. This was a microcosm of the royal court. James had his own treasurer, secretary, and even attorney- and solicitor-general. Below these was the usual retinue of servants associated with the departments of the household such as the bedchamber and the wardrobe. Despite his income from lands in England and Ireland, his investments in commercial enterprises, and his revenues from the Post Office granted by parliament in 1663 and other parliamentary sources and direct subsidies, the duke was chronically in debt. Sir Allen Apsley and Sir Thomas Povey, the household officials in charge of managing his finances, struggled in vain to bring them under control. The root cause was the extravagance of the duke and particularly of his first duchess, Anne. Both had experienced penury in their youth and seemed determined to live high off the hog when they got the chance.

Grammont was not the only observer to portray James as a pleasure-seeker. 'The prince applies himself but little to the affairs of the country and attends to nothing but his pleasures', observed a Venetian in 1661, 'but he is a young man of good spirit, loving and beloved by the King, his brother, and he discharges the office of lord High Admiral' (Turner, 60). Despite his easygoing image, James was no mere figurehead as lord high admiral, but took an active interest in naval affairs. He was assisted in this task by a small navy board of seven men: three commissioners, a treasurer, a surveyor, a comptroller, and a clerk of the acts. The first board included John, Lord Berkeley, Sir William Penn, and Sir Peter Pett as commissioners, Sir George Carteret as treasurer, and Samuel Pepys as clerk of the acts. Pepys indeed is the main source for the workings of this board and James's relations with it, and needs to be read with awareness that the author was by no means impartial. Such entries in his diary as that James was 'concerned to mend things in the navy himself and not leave things to other people' need to be treated with caution (8 July 1668, Pepys, Diary, 9.258). It is in fact virtually impossible to establish what initiatives, if any, the duke took in the activities of those responsible for naval affairs in these years, beyond the fact that he presided over them. Thus there are many letters signed by him in his own Memoirs of the English Affairs Chiefly Naval from the Year 1660 to 1673 (1729) which relate to the most minute details of administration. How far he did anything other than add his signature to these documents cannot be determined. James inherited from the republican regime a navy of over 130 ships, and his main concern was to ensure that it was properly equipped and manned. In selecting officers he preferred to appoint courtiers and gentlemen rather than to promote ordinary seamen or 'tarpaulins', whose loyalty to the restored monarchy was suspect. Their efficiency was to be tested in the second and third Anglo-Dutch wars.

James championed the navy's role in the second Dutch war, which broke out in 1664. While his antagonism towards the Calvinist Dutch republic stemmed perhaps mainly from his religious convictions, he was also convinced that it threatened England's trade. His concern for English commercial interests led him in 1664 to become governor of the Royal Fisheries Company and of the Company of Royal Adventurers trading into Africa. The latter company, having failed to exploit trade with the continent itself, was transformed in 1672 into the Royal African Company, whose principal concern was the slave trade. James became governor of the newly launched company. While these companies challenged the Dutch only indirectly, James fought them head on in 1664 when Charles II granted him colonial rights in America from New England to the Delaware River which encompassed New Netherland. A fleet under Captain Robert Nicholls captured New Amsterdam and renamed it New York in honour of the duke. James became first proprietor of the colony, and allocated the land between the Hudson and Delaware rivers to his former colleagues in the Channel Island of Jersey, Lord Berkeley and Sir Edward Carteret, which they named East and West Jersey. Although the Dutch ceded these colonies to the English at the peace treaty in 1667 they retook them in the third and final war of 1672–4, but then they agreed to recognize the sovereignty of the king of England over them in the treaty of Westminster in 1674.

James was personally involved in the second Dutch war, being on board the *Royal Charles* at the battle of Lowestoft in June 1665. Although he was the nominal admiral of the English fleet, the real commander was Sir William Penn, who was also on board the duke's ship. During a close engagement with the ship of the Dutch admiral Obdam, James's old acquaintance Charles Berkeley, now earl of Falmouth, was killed so near to him that he was spattered with blood. The engagement lasted four hours, ending when Obdam's ship blew up. This brought the battle to an end, the Dutch deciding to retreat to a safe harbour in the Netherlands. The *Royal Charles* pursued them closely until, during the night, Henry Brouckner, a member of James's household staff, took it upon himself to order the crew to wait until the rest of the fleet caught up with them. As a result the Dutch fleet got safely to the Texel. James was so incensed with Brouckner for this that he dismissed him.

James took no further part in the hostilities, being forbidden by his brother Charles from taking such a risk. He did, however, remain as lord high admiral, and was therefore technically responsible for one of the biggest setbacks in English naval history, the burning of the fleet moored at Chatham by the Dutch in 1667. He was not singled out for blame, however, for the lord chancellor, Edward *Hyde, earl of Clarendon, was held responsible. James was not on good terms with Clarendon, who was his father-in-law. Nevertheless he undertook his defence in the House of Lords, even though other peers attached to the court opposed him. James warned the king that their opposition to his chief minister was a dangerous game which could rebound against himself. Charles disregarded his brother's advice, and even sent him to tell Clarendon that he was dismissed. Relations between the two brothers were strained at this time. James disapproved of the secret treaty of Dover which Charles negotiated with Louis XIV in 1670. He was also chagrined by not being consulted when Charles nominated men to the Navy Board. And when England went to war with the Dutch for the third time in 1672 he was concerned that the cost would make the king too dependent upon parliamentary supplies.

James nevertheless took part in the war, being present at the battle of Southwold Bay in May 1672. The Dutch fleet attacked his own ship so fiercely that it was crippled. He transferred to another ship which also became so badly damaged that he had to transfer to a third. The battle ended in stalemate, and the two fleets disengaged. James never took part in a sea battle again. Charles was concerned that in doing so he endangered his life, and put Prince Rupert in charge of the fleet instead. He would have had to lay down his command in 1673 anyway, for James was obliged to resign as lord high admiral then after the passing of the first Test Act, which disqualified Catholics from holding office under the crown.

Catholic claimant The date of James's conversion to Catholicism cannot be pinpointed. During his exile in France he had resisted his mother's attempts to convert him, and protested when she had made similar attempts on his younger brother. At the same time he was impressed by the exemplary lives of many Catholics he met on the continent, and was sympathetic to those in England after the Restoration. During the 1660s he at least outwardly conformed to the Church of England. By 1669, however, he was convinced that only the Roman Catholic faith could procure salvation. In the following summer he was seriously ill, which might have speeded up his conversion, while in August his wife disclosed to him her own. On her death in 1671 James protected her from attempts by Anglicans to declare herself one of them, and he helped to preserve her commitment to the Catholic church. Even then he was not completely committed to it himself, for he kept her conversion a secret, not publishing her reasons for it until 1686. During 1672 he stopped taking communion in the Church of England, even refusing to communicate at Christmas when his brother requested that he join him at an Anglican service. Yet though he resigned as lord high admiral in 1673 when the Test Act made him as a Catholic ineligible to hold the office, he still attended services in the established church until 1676. In that year the pope acknowledged his conversion, and waived his objections to James's second marriage, to *Mary of Modena (1658–1718), which had taken place on 30 September 1673. After 1676 James was completely committed to the Catholic faith. According to his own testimony, what had converted him had been:

> the divisions among Protestants and the necessity of an infallible judge to decide controversies, together with some promises which Christ made to his church in general that the gates of hell should not prevail against it and some others made to St Peter, and there being no person that pretends to infallibility but the Bishop of Rome.   (Bodl. Oxf., Tanner MS 29, fol. 130)

'He concluded the Catholic church to be the sole authoritative voice on earth', observed his Catholic biographer Hilaire Belloc, 'and thenceforward … he not only stood firm against surrender but on no single occasion contemplated the least compromise or by a word would modify the impression made. It is like a rod of steel running through thirty years' (Belloc, 27–8).

Such rigidity alarmed protestants, especially when the hysteria over the so-called Popish Plot, allegedly to assassinate Charles II in order to have James succeed him, erupted in 1678. James was not directly implicated in the plot by Titus Oates, though some of his accomplices were prepared to accuse the duke of plotting the assassination of his own brother. Prospects of the apparent imminent accession of a Catholic to the throne led members of both houses of parliament to try to prevent his succession to the crown. Abortive attempts to pass a bill to that effect were made in three successive parliaments between 1679 and 1681, giving rise to the exclusion crisis. This forced his supporters onto the defensive. Some urged him to renounce Catholicism. On 21 February 1679 the archbishop of Canterbury, William Sancroft, and the bishop of Winchester, George Morley, had a private meeting with him at St James's Palace and begged him to 'quit the communion and guidance of your stepdame the Church of Rome and then return into the bosom of your true, dear and holy mother, the Church of England' (*State Letters of … Clarendon*, 2.268–76). James declined to renounce his religion. Charles II then insisted that he should leave England in order to ease the political tension. In March James went to Brussels, his faith reinforced by this second exile. 'If occasion were', he wrote to a friend, 'I hope God would give me his grace to suffer death for the true Catholic religion as well as banishment' (*Dartmouth MSS*, 1.36).

James was exiled in Brussels until September, when a rumour that his brother was seriously ill had him rushing back to England. There he found that Charles had in fact recovered, and was so opposed to his return that he banished him again, not to the continent but to Edinburgh. The duke went to Scotland as the king's high commissioner from October 1679 to March 1682, spending the period in Edinburgh, apart from a brief return to England in 1680.

James's activities in Scotland, where he was virtual viceroy, earned him the criticism of whig historians who accused him of petty tyranny. Macaulay even depicted him as a brutal sadist who delighted in viewing the sufferings of prisoners undergoing the excruciating torture of the boot. Yet contemporary accounts painted a different picture of the duke acting humanely. Even Bishop Burnet, no admirer of James, observed that 'he advised the bishops to proceed moderately, and to take no notice of conventicles in houses; and that would put an end to those in the fields' (*Bishop Burnet's History*, 2.300). His consulting with the bishops was a continuation of the policy of his predecessor, John Maitland, duke of Lauderdale, who had upheld the episcopalians in Scotland. However, he broke with previous measures of repression against presbyterians, even with regard to the Cameronians, who had fought the king's forces at the battle of Bothwell Bridge shortly before James arrived in the northern kingdom. He even offered to pardon six condemned to death if they would only say the words 'God bless the king', but all but one declined.

'We all remember with joy how well he left us', observed the lord chancellor of Scotland in 1685 looking back on James's sojourn there, 'and by what easie and gentle wayes he brought about the establishment of that unitie' (*Buccleuch MSS*, 146). James in fact built up a considerable body of Scottish support. He employed the patronage at his disposal to foster the growth of the Royal College of Physicians, the Advocates' Library, and the Order of the Thistle. His efforts to encourage supporters of the Stuart monarchy yielded results when he presided over a session of the Scottish parliament in the summer of 1681. 'The duke, finding that he was master of a clear majority', observed Burnet, 'drove on everything fast, and put bills on a very short debate to the vote, which went always as he had a mind to it' (*Bishop Burnet's History*, 2.306). An act was passed making it high treason to attempt to alter the succession to the crown. Another obliged office-holders, members of parliament, and even electors to swear to

uphold the protestant religion. James demanded that the oath should contain a commitment to renounce resistance, to defend all the king's prerogatives, and to repudiate attempts to alter the government in church or state. The ensuing form of words was very complicated, and according to some inconsistent. When the oath was taken it uncovered divisions which James had been anxious to conceal.

By the time he returned to England in March 1682 James felt that he had made a success of ruling Scotland. By contrast Charles had run into great difficulties in England from the exclusionists, which had obliged him to dissolve the third exclusion parliament after a brief session in 1681. James was convinced that the issue was not just about his own succession as a Catholic, but was a scarcely veiled attack on monarchy itself by those who preferred a republic. As he put it to Charles, 'matters were come to such a head that the monarchie must be either more absolute or quite abolished' (*Life*, 1.659–60). He determined to stiffen the king's resolve to get a firmer grip on the political situation following the dissolution of parliament. During the 'tory reaction' of the last four years of Charles's reign James played a major role. 'He directed all our counsels with so absolute an authority', claimed Burnet, 'that the King seemed to have left the government wholly in his hands' (*Bishop Burnet's History*, 3.5). Sir John Reresby agreed that the duke 'did now chiefly manage affairs' (*Memoirs of Sir John Reresby*, 329). James became lord high admiral again in all but name, thereby evading the Test Act. He was also appointed by Charles to a newly formed commission for ecclesiastical appointments, which supervised the promotion of clergymen to bishoprics. As a Catholic, James was not particularly interested in the well-being of the Church of England, but as a Stuart he was concerned to maintain the alliance between church and state which had stood his brother in good stead ever since his restoration. He worked closely with Laurence *Hyde, earl of Rochester, the brother of his first wife, on the commission to elevate high-church clergymen to the episcopacy to ensure a loyal bench of bishops when he became king. The one aspect of the tory reaction which he did not endorse was the enforcement of the laws against Catholics and dissenters. While Charles gave his approval to their strict application James did not share his zeal. When he succeeded to the throne he released many Quakers from gaol, where they had been imprisoned under Charles, and later appointed commissioners to investigate the activities of those who had prosecuted dissenters in the years 1681 to 1685. Those who had acted as informers in order to profit from the fines imposed on nonconformists were obliged to reimburse their victims.

King James II and VII James came to the throne following the death of Charles II on 6 February 1685. After the grim apprehensions of the exclusion crisis his accession came as something of an anticlimax. 'Every thing is very happy here', the earl of Peterborough reported to Sir Justinian Isham:

> Never king was proclaimed with more applause … He has made a speech to the Councell that did charm everybody

concerning his intentions of maintaining the Government as it was established in Church and State. I doubt not but to see a happy reign.   (Northants. RO, Isham correspondence, 1379)

James's first speech to the privy council was extempore. A version of it was recorded by the earl of Nottingham and published with James's approval. He later wished that he had not approved the words 'I shall make it my endeavour to preserve the government in Church and State as it is by law established'. He also regretted not amending the commitment to preserve the Church of England to an undertaking that he would not try to change it (*Life*, 2.4).

James's misgivings arose from the fact that he was intent on changing the status of the Anglican church. It was no longer to be the only established church since, as he told the French ambassador, he also wished to establish Catholicism in England. This went beyond mere toleration to putting it on the same footing as Anglicanism. Thus Catholics were not to enjoy just liberty of conscience and freedom of worship; they were also to be given positions of authority and even power in national and local government. Their proscription, which went back to the reign of Elizabeth I, and had been intensified as recently as that of Charles II, was to be completely lifted. At the outset of his reign, however, James was wary about how to achieve this goal. He hoped he could do so with the co-operation of Anglicans such as the earl of Rochester, whom he made lord treasurer and his chief minister. How difficult it was to be to achieve their acceptance of his schemes, however, was indicated when Rochester refused to accompany the king to the Chapel Royal when he went to mass there.

It was for only a brief honeymoon period, therefore, that James received 'the universal applause and submission of his subjects, every one striving to be as forward as he can to shew his zeal' (*CSP dom.*, *1685*, 8). The king cashed in on his unexpected popularity by calling elections to parliament both in Scotland and in England. Both resulted in handsome majorities for his ministers. James made sure that his coronation took place before the English parliament met, being apparently under the impression that until he was crowned he was only king *de jure* and not *de facto*. The ceremony in Westminster Abbey on 23 April 1685 was presided over by William Sancroft, the archbishop of Canterbury. It followed the liturgy used at Charles II's coronation, though it omitted communion since James as a Catholic could not communicate with the Church of England. Indeed he had openly attended a Catholic service two days after succeeding to the throne, and he avoided processing from the Tower to the abbey as usual probably because he was anxious how his subjects would react to that. Although the ceremony went off peacefully some regarded it as ominous when the crown slipped on the new king's head.

James claimed that he had the parliament of Scotland convene before the English 'to distinguish the confidence he had in the Scotch Nobility and Gentry who had stuck so close to him in his adversitie' (*Life*, 2.10). That it met on 23 April, St George's day and the occasion of his coronation

in Westminster Abbey, might have made this gesture to Scottish public opinion less effective than he intended it to be. Nevertheless his high commissioner in Scotland, the duke of Queensberry, urged the Edinburgh parliament to set an example. It obliged by passing all the acts which James had listed for the lords of the articles. Attendance at field conventicles, or harbouring those who attended them, was made a capital offence. The parliament also voted James generous supplies, granting the excise to him for life which together with other taxes was calculated to raise £60,000 a year.

By contrast there was a rumour that the English parliament, when it met, would not grant the king's supplies for life but only for a limited time, thereby keeping him dependent upon it. This riled James, and in his speech at the opening of parliament on 22 May he expressed his displeasure with any such intention. 'This would be a very improper method to take with me', he warned them; 'the best way to engage me to meet you often is to use me well' (*Life*, 2.14). In the event the Commons voted him the same revenue for life as his predecessor had enjoyed, £1,200,000 a year. There had been complaints that he had continued to collect the customs duties granted to Charles II, but the Commons dutifully gave this a retrospective sanction, although this did not prevent the practice becoming an issue later in the revolution of 1688. When news reached them of the landing in Scotland of Archibald Campbell, earl of Argyll, to raise a rebellion there, and then of the arrival of James Scott, duke of Monmouth, in the west country of England for the same purpose, they granted more money to suppress these uprisings. This increased the total revenue voted in the first session of this parliament to about £2 million a year. Although the emergency supplies would eventually expire, for the immediate future James would not be financially dependent upon parliament after all.

The earl of Argyll landed in Scotland in May and raised his standard in Campbeltown. He published a declaration declaring that James was not the lawful sovereign, and undertook to maintain protestantism, to suppress popery and prelacy, and to form a new government. A second declaration attacked James for

having taken off his mask, and having abandoned and invaded our Religion and Liberties, resolving to enter into the Government and exercise it contrary to law, I think it not only just but my duty to God and my country to use my outmost endeavours to oppose and repress his usurpations and tyranny.   (Greaves, 279)

James's success at building up a body of support in Scotland now paid dividends, for Argyll raised only 2500 men. These were easily suppressed by royal troops. Argyll was captured and taken to Edinburgh, where he was executed without trial, previously having been attainted for refusing to take the oaths passed by the Scottish parliament in 1681.

Monmouth meanwhile had raised his standard at Lyme Regis and declared James a usurper and himself the rightful king. Parliament responded by passing an act of attainder against him, and by voting extra supplies enabling

James to increase his armed forces to 20,000 to deal with the rebellion. The successful crushing of Monmouth's rebellion at Sedgemoor on 5 July left James in a much stronger position than that which he had enjoyed at his accession. Monmouth himself fell into his hands, and was executed on 15 July. James then dispatched Judge George Jeffreys to the west country to try the rebels. Ever since the revolution of 1688 these have been known as the 'bloody assizes'. At the time, however, they seem to have caused little comment, though later the king and the judge tried to put the blame on the other for the bad publicity. Thus James accused Jeffreys of bringing 'great obloquy upon the king's clemency, not only in the number but in the manner too of several executions, and shewing mercy to so few' (*Life*, 2.43). Immediately after his return from the west country, however, Jeffreys was appointed lord chancellor. It seemed as though James's enemies had been routed and he could be king indeed.

James was confident that this was providential. He strongly believed that he had been singled out by providence to be the means of bringing his protestant subjects back to the true faith. 'T'was the devine Providence that drove me early out of my native country', he observed in his private meditations, 'and t'was the same providence ordered it so that I past most of the twelve years I was abroad in Catholike kingdomes, by wch means I came to know what their religion was' (*Papers of Devotion*, 1). When the bid to exclude him from the throne failed James saw in it 'the hand of God' (*Dartmouth MSS*, 1.57). He now saw the crushing of the rebellions of Argyll and Monmouth as providential. In his speech at the opening of the second session of parliament in November he jubilantly exclaimed 'God Almighty be praised by whose blessing that rebellion was suppressed'. James's confidence that providence had blessed his cause led him to employ even more haughty language than that which he had used at the opening of the first session. Wishing to retain the services of Catholics to whom he had granted officers' commissions, he hectored the houses on this score. 'Let no man take exception that there are some officers in the Army not qualified according to the Tests for their employments', he warned:

> I think them now fit to be imployed under me, and will deal plainely with you, that after haveing had the benefit of their services in such a time of need and danger, I will neither expose them to disgrace, nor myself to the want of them, if there should be another rebellion to make them necessary to me. (*Life*, 2.49)

But both Lords and Commons did take exception. They were concerned that the king had put the forces in Scotland under the command of Catholics, and now wished to maintain a standing army in England with popish officers in defiance of the Test Act. They objected to his use of the dispensing power to give them immunity from prosecution, claiming that it was illegal. Their objections led James to prorogue parliament on 20 November until February. In fact the houses were never to meet again in his reign.

The struggles for power in the three kingdoms The suppression of the Argyll and Monmouth rebellions was followed by struggles for power in all James's kingdoms. Ministers committed to the preservation of the status quo in Scotland, England, and Ireland found themselves challenged by rivals who supported the king's Catholic measures.

In Scotland the lord treasurer, William Douglas, duke of Queensberry, was opposed by the chancellor, James Drummond, earl of Perth, and the secretary, John Drummond, earl of Melfort, who was Perth's brother. Perth declared to the king his conversion to Catholicism on a visit to London in 1685, though he kept it secret until early in 1686 when his brother also declared his conversion. When their Catholicism became public knowledge it provoked riots in Edinburgh in January 1686. After two weeks of sporadic violence against Catholics there were rumours of a plot to 'destroy all papists' on 7 February (*Reg. PCS*, 12.92–7; 'A true account concerning the late tumult in Edinburgh'). James took it upon himself to write in Perth's defence and to insist that anybody implicated in the violence should be tortured into confession.

Since Queensberry appeared to have lost control of the capital Perth and Melfort were able to persuade James to dismiss him from his posts of treasurer, governor of Edinburgh Castle, and high commissioner. James appointed commissioners for the Treasury and George Gordon, duke of Gordon, a Catholic, to the governorship. Another Catholic convert, Alexander Stewart, earl of Moray, was made high commissioner. The Drummond brothers now became the king's most trusted Scottish advisers. When a new session of the Scottish parliament opened in April James asked it to pass an act tolerating Catholics. His new advisers, however, failed to procure this. Although a committee was appointed to draw up an act it did not approve of giving Catholics the right to worship, except in private houses, and agreed only to give them liberty of conscience. Even this limited concession to the king's demand met with considerable objections when presented to the full parliament. James consequently prorogued the session. His Catholic advisers had failed to persuade the Scottish parliament to pass an act tolerating their co-religionists. He therefore fell back on his prerogative. Thus he suspended elections in town councils and nominated men to run them.

In England there was a parallel contest between the lord treasurer, Laurence Hyde, earl of Rochester, and the principal secretary of state, Robert Spencer, earl of Sunderland, though it was drawn out longer. Sunderland encouraged a Catholic cabal at court led by Father Edward Petre and the queen. Rochester's influence over James remained formidable, for the king was reluctant to part with the brother of his first wife, not least because the earl had stood firmly by him during the exclusion crisis. In September 1685 the treasurer contrived to get his elder brother, Henry Hyde, earl of Clarendon, appointed as lord lieutenant of Ireland. This was the high water mark of Rochester's ascendancy. He and his rival divided the spoils when George Savile, marquess of Halifax, was dismissed from his posts of lord privy seal and president of the council, Clarendon adding the former to the lord lieutenancy and Sunderland the latter to his secretaryship. But in the year following the prorogation of parliament Sunderland gradually achieved supremacy over the lord treasurer. Early in 1686 he sided with the queen against the king's mistress, Catherine Sedley. Sedley had been made countess of Dorchester, an ennoblement Sunderland attributed to Rochester's influence. When James was challenged about it he backed down and insisted that Sedley should absent herself from court. Rochester also made the error of openly sympathizing with the Huguenots who fled to England from France after the revocation of the edict of Nantes. James himself admired Louis XIV's zeal for the Catholic faith and forbade English ships from bringing Huguenot refugees into England.

The outcome of the case of *Godden* v. *Hales* in 1686 also assisted Sunderland's rise at Rochester's expense. Sir Edward Hales was a Catholic who held a commission in the army in defiance of the Test Act, claiming that he held letters under the great seal dispensing with the statute's obligation to take communion in the Church of England. Hales's own coachman, Godden, brought a collusive action against him to test the validity of this dispensation. It was heard on appeal by the twelve judges of the common-law courts, all but one of whom found in favour of the king's dispensing power. On the authority of this decision James issued dispensations appointing more and more Catholics to places under the crown. In July 1686 four Catholic lords, Arundell, Belasyse, Dover, and Powis, were admitted to the privy council, boosting Sunderland's influence and diminishing Rochester's.

Rochester suffered another blow with the appointment of a commission for ecclesiastical causes, initially introduced to discipline the bishop of London, Henry Compton, for refusing to silence John Sharp, a clergyman in his diocese who had preached an anti-Catholic sermon. The bishop was deprived of all his spiritual functions, which were taken over by the commission. Although Rochester sat on it, along with Sunderland, he had held out for a lesser punishment for the bishop than complete deprivation. Sunderland favoured the harsher treatment which had James's support.

Another sign of Rochester's declining influence was seen in the summer of 1686 when Richard Talbot, whom the king had ennobled as earl of Tyrconnell, returned to Ireland from a visit to England with a commission giving him charge of military matters in Ireland. Tyrconnell proceeded to replace 'English' soldiers with 'Irish natives', many of whom spoke only Gaelic, while Clarendon was instructed to alter the judiciary in favour of Catholics 'of old Irish race'. By September 40 per cent of the officers and 67 per cent of the rank-and-file were Catholics. Clarendon was convinced that Tyrconnell, in collusion with the earl of Sunderland, was undermining his position in England, with the queen as well as with the king, and that his tenure of the lord lieutenancy would soon be terminated.

The final cause of the treasurer's downfall was an abortive attempt by the king to convert him to Catholicism.

Rochester agreed to hear a disputation between Anglican and Catholic divines, but then maintained that the Church of England clergymen had more than held their ground in the exchange. In January 1687 James dismissed him from the Treasury and replaced him with a commission made up of two Catholics and three Anglicans, one of them, Sidney, Lord Godolphin, being the effective head. At the same time Rochester's brother Clarendon was deprived of the lord lieutenancy of Ireland and the privy seal. Two Catholics replaced him, Tyrconnell as virtual lord lieutenant, though he was given the post of lord deputy, and Lord Arundell as lord privy seal. Given complete control on becoming lord deputy, Tyrconnell pursued in earnest the task of turning Ireland into a Catholic stronghold which could assert its independence against a protestant England. He recalled borough charters and issued new ones appointing Catholics as councillors.

North America James's rule over the American colonies as well as in Ireland seemed to portend his plans for England. Following the grant of New Netherland by Charles II to his brother in March 1664 Richard Nicholls was dispatched from England with a fleet to capture it for him. On his arrival off New Amsterdam, Nicholls demanded that Peter Stuyvesant surrender the colony to him. Although the governor was ready to resist the English, the Dutch colonists persuaded him to yield to them. Nicholls then named New Netherland New York in honour of the duke. New Amsterdam was similarly renamed New York city while Orange, a Dutch fort up the Hudson River, became Albany. The duke's claim was not confirmed, however, until after the third and final Anglo-Dutch war (1672–4). The treaty of Westminster concluded the peace with the handing over of the colony.

New York was a proprietary colony under the duke. James ruled his proprietorship as an absolute monarch. William Penn thought his government of New York was a model of what he planned for England 'if the Crown should ever devolve upon his head' (Geiter, 311). Richard Nicholls, who acted as James's deputy governor following the conquest of the colony, introduced into it the so-called 'duke's laws'. These made no mention of elections to an assembly or even to town meetings. Nicholls himself admitted that 'our new laws are not contrived so democratically as the rest'. There was a strong military presence in the colony. New York city became the base for the first regular garrison of soldiers in British America. Following the final surrender of New York to the English in 1674 James appointed an army officer, Sir Edmund Andros, as his deputy. Andros re-established the duke's proprietorship and reinstated the duke's laws. His arbitrary government provoked complaints about military rule and demands in some quarters for a representative assembly. On being informed of these James refused to give in to them, being convinced that to do so would be 'of dangerous consequence, nothing being more known than the aptness of such bodies to assume to themselves many privileges which prove destructive to, or very oft disturb, the peace of the government wherein they are allowed' (R. Ritchie, *The Duke's Province*, 1977, 34, 101–2). Andros, however, found it increasingly difficult to raise taxes without an assembly to consent to them. Since James had invested his own money in the acquisition of New York, spending as much as £2000 to regain it from the Dutch in 1674, he wished not only to recoup his outlay but to make a profit from the colony. The reluctance of the colonists to pay taxes to which they had not consented meant that he was losing rather than making money from his proprietorship of New York. Consequently when Andros went to England in 1681 he was able to persuade the duke that the only way to turn his financial situation round from loss to gain was to summon an assembly. When Colonel Thomas Dongan replaced Andros as governor of New York he was instructed by the duke to convene an assembly there. The first was elected in October 1683 and sat for three weeks. The short session resulted in some important laws for the rights of the colonists. The right to trial by jury and punishments to fit the crime were instituted at this meeting of the assembly. Taxes could be imposed only through the consent of the governor and council. Lands were protected from arbitrary seizure. This bill of rights also included the right of religious freedom so long as those who practised divergent faiths did not disturb the peace of the government. The assembly met again in 1684. In the following year James became king, upon which New York was transformed from a proprietary into a crown colony. Following James II's accession his deputy governor there, Thomas Dongan, dissolved the assembly and called fresh elections for another, which met in October 1685. After a brief session, however, further meetings were called only to be cancelled, until in January 1687 the assembly was dissolved. It never met again under James.

In 1686 James incorporated the colonies of Massachusetts, Connecticut, New Hampshire, and Rhode Island into one jurisdiction, the dominion of New England. Two years later he extended it to New York and New Jersey. In effect it brought into being one vast crown colony extending over the whole area from Maine to the Delaware River. There are signs that it was intended to cover an even greater region. Writs of *quo warranto* demanding justifications of their jurisdictions were issued against the colonies of Maryland and Pennsylvania, including the three lower counties on the Delaware, during the reign of James II. It seemed as though the king wanted to make most of the mainland settlements directly subject to the crown.

In December 1686 Sir Edmund Andros became the governor of the dominion. Andros ruled by decree. Thus he raised taxes without any semblance of representation, provoking resistance from some colonists who, claiming the liberties of Englishmen, protested that taxation could be raised legitimately only with the approval of the suppressed assemblies. Their ringleaders were arrested and thrown into gaol. Andros rigorously enforced the navigation laws, which had been so blatantly disregarded in New England, by allowing only five ports where customs could be cleared. All breaches of the laws were to be tried in Admiralty courts without juries. The selectmen, who were elected to represent the New England towns, were allowed to meet only once a year. For practical purposes

they were superseded by men nominated by Andros himself. Since many were his cronies who did not even reside in New England it was depicted as being 'squeezed by a crew of abject persons fetched from New York' (M. G. Hall, *Edward Randolph and the American Colonies, 1676–1703*, 1960, 108). The entire governing body was replaced subsequent to the revocation of the colony's charter. Edward Randolph, who was appointed as secretary to the dominion, used his position to create a host of new officials, many of them Anglicans who succeeded to the functions formerly carried out by puritans.

James genuinely believed in religious toleration. He had introduced freedom of worship into New York when he became its proprietor. He was determined that those colonists who were members of the Dutch Reformed church should live peaceably with his English subjects. The puritans of Massachusetts were notorious religious bigots, completely intolerant of all sects other than their own. They were particularly severe in their treatment of Quakers. The Massachusetts general court passed laws banning them from proselytizing. Any Friend found trying to convert a puritan was subject to harsh penalties, that for a third offence being death. James insisted upon complete toleration in New England. Although Connecticut had been more tolerant than Massachusetts, the Congregationalists there also resented this policy which effectively disestablished their church. The only New England colony which greeted it with enthusiasm was Rhode Island, where religious toleration was practised. The king was determined to replace the rule of the saints with religious toleration, and instructed Andros to introduce it into the dominion. Andros did so with great zeal. The Congregational church, which was virtually the established church in Massachusetts as it was in Connecticut, was in effect disestablished there too. Its ministers were no longer maintained by local rates. Anglican services were permitted in its churches. On one occasion the Congregationalists who frequented Boston south church had to wait outside while a service was held according to the rites of the Church of England.

Although this experiment in colonial government was undertaken for a variety of reasons, the most pressing motive was undoubtedly defence. Despite the fact that England and France enjoyed peaceful relations in Europe there was friction between them in North America, especially on the frontier between New France and New York. James had been governor of the Hudson's Bay Company from 1683 until he became king, and was aware of conflicting claims between the company and the French in Canada. Indeed the adversary stance adopted by New France to English interests in North America led him to adopt a defensive posture there against the French, notwithstanding the cordial relationship he enjoyed with Louis XIV in European concerns. It is an error to assume that friendly relations implied an alliance. When French and English interests clashed James vigorously defended those of his own country. In 1686 the Compagnie du Nord launched an attack on the Hudson's Bay Company's forts around James Bay. The disputes between the two companies were so serious that Louis XIV sent a special envoy, Bonrepos, to England to resolve them. A draft treaty was drawn up, but it was not until 1687 that a definitive document could be signed by the two sides. Friction continued in North America despite this treaty. Thus in 1687 the French attacked some Indians in the Mohawk River valley allied to the English. It was owing to this attack that James decided to incorporate New York and New Jersey into the dominion of New England. Andros presided over the whole, but his deputy, Dongan, was replaced in New York by Francis Nicholson. Nicholson resumed the crown's rights of government over New Jersey, which the proprietors had exercised since 1680, albeit on dubious authority. As elsewhere in the dominion the assemblies were suspended. The dominion of New England thus acquired many of the characteristics of absolutism which Charles II and James II had established in old England. There was a standing army, censorship of the press, and arbitrary imprisonment.

Toleration The removal of the Hyde brothers, Clarendon and Rochester, and the triumph of Sunderland early in 1687 are usually seen as a major turning-point in James's reign, when he turned from Anglican advisers to rely on Catholics and dissenters. Yet observers had seen Rochester's power slipping to Sunderland over many months. Rochester himself dated his decline from the crushing of Monmouth's rebellion, upon which James had felt able to move more swiftly and boldly to his goal. The king then found the Anglicans reluctant to go along with him, as they were to show in the second session of the parliament. He accused them of being 'like Micannicks in a trade, who are afraid of nothing so much as Interlopers' (*Life*, 2.114). By contrast he found the dissenters more inclined to respond to his overtures. One of the alleged signs of a shift in policy early in 1687 was the king's willingness to work with dissenters when previously he had regarded them as his enemies. However, James had always been ambivalent towards dissent. During the exclusion crisis he regarded them as aligned with those who not only sought to bar him from the succession but to replace the monarchy with a republic. He shared Charles II's view that dissenters who disturbed the peace of the kingdom and took up the 'good old cause' should not be tolerated. Yet also like his brother he could distinguish between disruptive dissenters and those who wished to live peaceably. The former in his view made religion 'only the pretence, and that the real contest was about power and dominion', whereas the latter he regarded as suffering the same unjust persecution as Catholics (ibid., 1.594). When he was attempting to convert his daughter Mary to Catholicism he was 'very severe against the Church of England for its cruelty towards dissenters, saying the dissenters can give as good reason for their separating from [it] as [it] can for [its] departure from Rome' (Bodl. Oxf., Tanner MS 29, fol. 130). He supported Charles II's declarations of indulgence, a policy of religious toleration he himself pursued when he became

king. In February 1686 he issued a proclamation in Scotland allowing Quakers as well as Catholics to worship in their own homes. That spring he pardoned 1200 English Quakers and released them from prison. In May he sent William Penn to The Hague to try to persuade the prince and princess of Orange to support the repeal of the Test Act. Despite the failure of Penn's mission James retained his services, relying on his connections with dissenters to gain their support. Penn seems to have persuaded him that other dissenters as well as the pacifist Quakers would not disturb the peace of the kingdom if granted toleration. It was probably Penn who encouraged the king to get round the failure of both the Scottish and English parliaments to grant relief to Catholics and dissenters by issuing edicts of toleration to them.

The first declaration of indulgence was made in Scotland on 12 February 1687, since Scots had recognized the king's 'sacred, supreme, sovereign and *absolute power* and authority' (*Life*, 2.107). James stressed that the proclamation was based on 'our sovereign authority, prerogative royal and absolute power, which all our subjects are to obey without reserve'. 'Moderate Presbyterians' were allowed to meet in their private houses, while Quakers could 'meet and exercise in their Form in any place or places appointed for their worship'. At the same time the opportunity was taken to 'suspend, stop and disable all laws, or Acts of Parliament … against any of our Roman Catholick subjects' (*By the King a Proclamation … 12 Feb 1687*). Encouraged by what appeared to be a favourable reception for the Scottish proclamation James issued a declaration of indulgence for England and Wales on 4 April, suspending all penal laws against nonconformists.

On 23 April James prorogued parliament a second time until November. Since the fall of Rochester he had interviewed individual peers and members of parliament to ascertain their attitudes to his aim of repealing the penal laws and the first Test Act. The results had been disappointing for the king. Some who opposed him were dismissed. But accounts of dismissals as a result of this 'closeting', as it was called, tended to be exaggerated. 'We doe hear every post of so many persons being out of their employments', Lord Chesterfield observed in March; 'it seems like the account one has after a battle of those who miscarried in the engagement' (BL, Althorp papers H1, Chesterfield to Halifax, 15 March 1687). In fact only six members of the royal household lost their posts. When it became clear that closeting was not going to persuade a majority to support the repeal of the penal laws and Test Act James decided to prorogue parliament until November. He hoped that in the interval the experience of toleration would allay apprehensions sufficiently to persuade a parliamentary majority to repeal them.

Yet unexpectedly James dissolved parliament in July. The timing of the dissolution was apparently owing to his discovering that William of Orange was lobbying MPs to resist the repeal of the penal laws. A Dutch envoy, Dykvelt, had been sent over to England in February to reassure James's opponents that William was opposed to their repeal. At the end of May Dykvelt had a private audience with the king, who instructed him to ask the prince categorically to support his policy of repealing them. When William answered that he was opposed to the policy James replied that he was sorry to find that the prince:

> cannot be for taking off all those laws, and the Tests which are so very severe and hard upon all Dissenters from the Church of England; and since what Mr Dyckvelt said to you from me could not alter your mind as to that, I cannot expect that a letter should prevail with you; so that I shall say no more on that subject now.   (Dalrymple, 2 appx, pt 1, 185)

Aware of Dykvelt's intrigues with his opponents, James decided to dissolve parliament. That summer he took himself off on a canvassing tour of the west country and midlands, visiting a number of towns in a swathe from Portsmouth, through Bristol, to Shrewsbury and then to Oxford. Everywhere he went the king urged the voters to elect 'such parliament men as would concur with him in settling this liberty as firmly as the Magna Charta had been' (*Bishop Burnet's History*, 4.190). The response persuaded James that the prospects for the polls were favourable. 'In most of those places', he claimed, 'they promised to send such members to the ensuing parliament as would be for taking off the penal laws and Test' (*Life*, 2.140).

Oxford, the seven bishops, and the birth of an heir When he was in Oxford on 4 September James summoned the fellows of Magdalen College to an audience at Christ Church. In April he had instructed them to elect as their president a Catholic, Anthony Farmer, but they had defied him by choosing John Hough instead. When summoned to attend the ecclesiastical commissioners to justify their defiance they pleaded that they objected to Farmer not because he was a Catholic but because he was a debauchee. Nevertheless Hough's election had been declared void, and in July James had forbidden the fellows to make any new election 'till we shall signifie our further pleasure, any statute, custom or constitution to the contrary notwithstanding. And so, expecting obedience, herein, we bid you farewell' (*An Impartial Relation*, 13). Farmer's candidacy for the presidency was quietly dropped in view of the evidence of his unsuitability for it, and in his stead James ordered the fellows to elect Samuel Parker, bishop of Oxford. Once again they defied him. When they were summoned to Christ Church he demanded that they choose Parker, warning 'them that refuse to look to it, they shall feel the weight of their sovereign's displeasure' (ibid., 15). The king's browbeating did not cow them, however, for they still refused to obey his orders. The ecclesiastical commission then visited the college and stripped them of their fellowships.

James's high-handed conduct in his dealings with Magdalen College was indicative of a confidence bordering on recklessness that he was bound to gain his ends. He was convinced that his father and brother had failed to achieve theirs because they had shown weakness and that if he remained resolute opposition would be overcome. He was determined to get a parliamentary majority which would repeal the penal laws, to which end he set out to pack the House of Commons with pliant members. In November 1687 he set up a commission to regulate corporations. Over the ensuing months the commissioners carried out a number of purges of boroughs represented in parliament. Some corporations were regulated several times. In many cases Anglicans were removed to be replaced by Catholics and dissenters. The commissions of the peace in the counties were similarly weeded.

How far the exercise would have resulted in a majority in support of the king's policy is a moot point. Public opinion in these months indicates that most of James's subjects were against him. He himself devised a crude test in the form of three questions which justices of the peace, militia officers, and other men holding positions under the crown were required to answer. Would they, if elected to parliament, vote for the repeal of the penal laws? Would they, if they could vote for candidates at the polls, support those in favour of their repeal? Would they support the toleration by living peaceably with those of different persuasions? These began to be circulated in the localities from October 1687, though months elapsed while answers were returned from all over the country. When they did come in they scarcely indicated widespread support. On the contrary only about a quarter answered 'yes' to the first two questions, rather fewer than replied 'no', while the rest evaded answering directly in ways which implied that they were negative. Only the last question elicited overwhelmingly positive responses, indicating that the respondents approved of toleration for non-Anglicans but not of allowing them access to power.

James, however, was detached from these realities in the last year of his reign. When Mary of Modena became pregnant in October 1687 he took it as another sign of divine providence and was confident that his wife would bear a son. This led him to throw caution to the winds and to hurry on his plans to establish Catholicism in England. He persuaded the pope to appoint four vicars-apostolic as bishops *in partibus infidelium*. When Samuel Parker, the bishop of Oxford whom he had foisted on Magdalen College, died in March 1688 he was replaced as president by one of these bishops. A Catholic master was appointed to Sidney Sussex College, Cambridge. It seemed as though the universities were being converted into seminaries for training Catholic priests. There was even a rumour that the vacant archbishopric of York was to be filled by a Catholic.

The birth of a son, *James Francis Edward, on 10 June 1688 was the final confirmation as far as James was concerned that his cause had the blessing of providence. A royal proclamation issued on the day of the prince's birth called for thanksgiving throughout his kingdoms for God's great mercy to the king and his subjects by blessing him with a son. The birth was to be celebrated in London on 17 June and throughout the realm on 1 July. Between the two thanksgiving days, however, the king's belief in providence must have been severely shaken when on 29 June a jury in the court of king's bench acquitted seven bishops of the charge of seditious libel, to universal rejoicing.

The trial had come about because an order in council had been issued in May 1688 requiring the clergy to read the declaration of indulgence in their churches and the bishops to distribute it throughout their dioceses. The archbishop of Canterbury and six bishops presented a petition to James on 18 May asking him not to insist on the distribution and reading of the proclamation. The king admitted to them that he was taken completely by surprise. He accused them of raising 'a standard of rebellion. I never saw such an address'. When the bishops published their petition, while the order in council was widely disregarded, James decided to prosecute them for seditious libel. Because they refused to give recognizances to appear in court he sent them to the Tower, where they spent a week before being bailed by twenty-one peers. At the trial they denied the king's right to issue the declaration of indulgence. Their subsequent acquittal was a great blow to him.

James nevertheless pressed on with his campaign to pack parliament. By September he was so convinced that the regulation of elections for the House of Commons had gone far enough to secure a majority there that he was prepared to make enough peers to give him a majority in the House of Lords too. On 16 September he announced that a general election was to take place. On 26 September he called it off after accepting that the prince of Orange was preparing to invade England.

Revolution Before then James had refused to believe reports that his son-in-law was bent on invading. As late as 10 September the French ambassador wrote to Louis XIV that the English king was beginning to accept that William was getting together a task force to invade England. But James was not finally convinced that the Dutch really were going to invade until 24 September. He not only called off the general election, but abandoned the campaign to pack parliament. The purges of the county militias and commissions of the peace, along with that of the parliamentary boroughs, were reversed, reinstating Anglicans and removing Catholics and dissenters. He also stopped consulting his Catholic advisers and turned instead to the Church of England. On 24 September nine bishops, including four of the seven he had put on trial, were invited to an audience with the king. They presented him with a list of measures they thought to be necessary to restore the constitution in church and state. These included the dismissal of Catholic officials, the abolition of the commission for ecclesiastical causes, the reinstatement of the fellows of Magdalen College, the restoration of borough charters, and the summoning of a free parliament. James responded positively to these points, suspending the commission for ecclesiastical causes, and reinstating the bishop of London and the fellows of Magdalen. 'Nothing seems wanting but a free parliament', one newsletter observed, 'and then I can't see what the Prince will do' (BL, Add. MS 34487, fol. 30).

This was probably why James made these concessions, to wrongfoot William of Orange. If that was his intention, however, it failed to work. For people mistrusted his motives, and so far from denouncing the Orangist intervention in English affairs looked to it to obtain guarantees for the future conduct of their untrustworthy monarch. All thereby came to turn on the outcome of the Dutch invasion. If James won he would be free to act as he pleased. If he lost then, as he informed the French ambassador, he would go into voluntary exile in France, where he had already arranged to send his wife and infant son. Family concerns were intimately involved in the events of 1688. James was outraged that his own daughter and son-in-law were prepared to attack him. He was particularly mortified by the doubts they raised about the legitimacy of the prince of Wales. To establish that he was indeed his son, and had not been smuggled into the queen's bedchamber in a warming pan, he convened an extraordinary meeting of leading dignitaries on 22 October to hear sworn depositions from witnesses to the birth.

James still trusted in divine providence to protect him, especially when William's fleet was driven back to Dutch harbours by a violent storm in mid-October and was pinned in them by contrary winds. 'I see God Almighty continues his Protection to me', he observed on 20 October, 'by bringing the wind westerly again' (*Dartmouth MSS*, 1.169). Then the 'Protestant wind' began to blow from the east, and William was able to make his way down the English Channel to land in Torbay on 5 November.

James initially determined to stay in London and oblige his son-in-law to advance towards the capital. But William stayed in the west country for several days, so that his forces could recuperate from the voyage, and in expectation that they would be joined by deserters from the king's army. A few, led by Edward Hyde, Lord Cornbury, son of the earl of Clarendon, did go over to him while he was at Exeter. Although the numbers that deserted James were not great, and the news that many men actually returned to their posts cheered him, he was sufficiently concerned by the breakdown of discipline in his army to go down to Salisbury to reassert his authority. James arrived there on 19 November. Unfortunately he succumbed to severe nosebleeds, which incapacitated him from giving a firm lead. Instead of inspiring his army to march west, therefore, he agreed at a council of war on 23 November to retreat to London. After this decision more deserters left his army, including Lord Churchill, who went over to William the following night. The loss of Churchill, the future duke of Marlborough, was perhaps the greatest blow to James's morale in the closing weeks of 1688. The desertion of his daughter Anne, however, who went along with Churchill's wife, Sarah, and the bishop of London to join rebels in Nottingham, also unnerved him.

On his return to London James invited all the peers in town to give him their advice. They urged him to call a parliament. On 28 November, therefore, James issued writs for a general election for a parliament to meet in January. He also sent Godolphin, Halifax, and Nottingham to negotiate with William. But all this was a feint. He had already sent his wife and infant son to France and was determined to join them there. On 11 December he fled from the capital, dropping the great seal in the Thames, which effectively stalled the elections. Unfortunately he got only as far as Faversham, where his boat was intercepted by sailors. The next day they took him to the Queen's Arms, where his identity was revealed. News got back to London that the king had been detained by some of his subjects, and a company of guards was sent to rescue him from them. They reached Faversham on 15 December and accompanied the king back to his capital. He was welcomed there by cheering crowds. He took heart at this, and attempted to resume government, even presiding over a meeting of the privy council. Then he received a request from William to remove himself from London. At first the prince recommended Ham House, up river from the City. James, however, preferred to go downstream to Rochester. William agreed to this, seeing in the king's request a plea to let him leave the country, which would be easier to effect from Kent than from Surrey. As James left the capital on 18 December William entered it. James did not take long to escape his Dutch guards, fleeing to France on 23 December. This time he was successful, setting foot on French soil on Christmas day.

Final exile When James joined his wife and son in France Louis XIV gave him accommodation at the château of St Germain-en-Laye. This suited the exiled monarch and his courtiers perfectly. Louis had handsomely refurbished it for James's court, which, contrary to hostile reports from Williamite observers, was not impoverished but maintained a lavish state, in keeping with James's notions of kingly style. Thus he patronized artists and musicians. He could also hunt and pray to his heart's content. Had he had his own way he would probably never have ventured from St Germain again. But the French king intended to send James to Ireland in order to retrieve his crown. Tyrconnell also urged that course of action. 'I beg of you to consider whether you can with honour continue where you are', he wrote, 'when you possess a kingdom of your own plentiful of all things for human life' (Turner, 463). James gave in to this pressure and went to Ireland, landing in Kinsale on 12 March 1689. Tyrconnell joined him at Cork two days later. It soon became clear that their objectives were different. James wanted to use Ireland as a springboard to regain his kingdoms of England and Scotland. To do so meant not alienating his protestant subjects there by becoming too dependent upon Irish Catholics. Tyrconnell on the other hand wanted him to establish himself in Ireland as a Catholic king. The resulting conflicting aims became evident in the calling of an Irish parliament, which met in Dublin on 7 May. The Catholic majority demonstrated its support for Tyrconnell by repealing the Act of Settlement of 1662. This had confirmed the ownership of land following the upheavals of the interregnum, leaving Catholics with less than a quarter of the land in Ireland. The Dublin parliament sought to reverse this settlement and for good measure passed an Act of Attainder against over 2000 protestants. Such vindictiveness stood in sharp contrast to the Toleration Act passed at the same time, in which the parliament paid lip-service to the king's aims.

By convening the Dublin parliament James forfeited his chances of regaining his other kingdoms. At the same time it ensured that the protestants in Ulster would support William III's efforts to reconquer Ireland. The siege of Londonderry was relieved by a force sent from England in August 1689. Later that month the duke of Schomberg landed in Belfast and advanced to Dundalk, eliminating any chance of James using Ireland as a base from which to invade Scotland. This did not necessarily scupper his prospects in Ireland. Schomberg was an octogenarian who was loath to risk a battle. Although James was only fifty-seven, he was no longer the soldier who had served under Turenne. His judgement was called into question by the experienced French diplomat the comte d'Avaux, whom Louis XIV had sent to accompany his ally. But the French king himself did not despair of James, despite Avaux's caustic dispatches. On the contrary he sent reinforcements to James, which arrived in the spring of 1689. William III himself was aware of this, and replaced the aged Schomberg himself. When William landed in Carrickfergus in mid-June, James advanced to meet him at the River Boyne. The battle of the Boyne was fought on 1 July. William defeated James, who threw in the towel and returned to France.

When he returned to France James became a virtual recluse at St Germain. He seems to have regarded his life there as a penance for his former sins. In 1696 he wrote a devotional paper thanking God 'that thou wert pleased to have taken from me my three kingdoms, by which means thou didst awake me out of the lethargy of sin' (*Papers of Devotion*, 61–2). He was convinced that 'Providence had marked out no other way for his salvation except suffering' (*Life*, 2.528). In his advice to his son he pressed upon him the vital importance of being steadfast in his faith, thereby ensuring that he would never regain their former kingdoms for the Stuarts. Yet Jacobites continued to hold out the hope that they would. They backed James's principal advisers, the earl of Melfort and Charles Middleton, earl of Middleton, in their efforts to persuade him to try yet again to recover his crown. James was led to believe that William's regime was so unpopular that his former subjects would welcome his restoration. Now that William had subdued the Irish and concluded the treaty of Limerick in 1691 James lost interest in a fresh attempt to regain his throne from Ireland, and sought to do so by invading England and repeating his brother's restoration in 1660. He hoped to bring this off in 1692, but was thwarted by the English defeat of the French at the naval battle of La Hogue. His hopes were raised again in 1696 with the assassination plot, only to be dashed when the plotters were apprehended. On that occasion he concluded that 'the good Lord did not wish to restore me' (Miller, 238–9).

Jacobites were divided over the best means to obtain the end of another restoration between the so-called 'compounders' and 'non-compounders'. Melfort led the 'non-compounders', who were not prepared to yield any concessions to protestants. Middleton was the leader of the 'compounders', who were adamant that only by offering assurances to the Church of England could James hope to be restored. Yet that would be to acknowledge that the whole of his short reign had been a mistake. Even if James could have brought himself to admit this, which is extremely doubtful, it is hard to see how Anglicans would have trusted him. He himself oscillated between the two positions, siding with Melfort in 1692 and with Middleton in 1693. This gave an impression of wavering and opportunism. In 1696, however, he threw in his lot with those who were prepared to assassinate William III, provoking a backlash of loyalty to the *de facto* king and greatly harming the Jacobite cause.

After the treaty of Ryswick of 1697, in which Louis XIV recognized William III as king of England, James resigned himself to permanent exile. His resignation took the form of austere acts of piety in which he inflicted such mortifications upon himself that his confessor became alarmed for his health. He had suffered his first serious illness in 1695, and thereafter became frailer and frailer until he could be described by the poet Matthew Prior, who visited him in 1698, as being lean and shrivelled. Throughout 1701 he suffered from fainting fits; the last one, which occurred on 22 August, proved fatal. During the two weeks it took him to die he was visited by Louis XIV, who assured James that he would recognize his son as king of England. James died on 5 September. His body was dissected so that parts could be interred in various churches, his brain in the Scots College in Paris and his heart in the nunnery at Chaillot. His corpse was buried in the English Benedictine church in the Faubourg St Jacques, 'provisionally'—until it could be interred in Westminster Abbey. The burial did indeed turn out to be provisional, but for very different reasons. During the French Revolution his tomb was broken up and his body displayed for some months as a tourist attraction. It was then destroyed, although relics which had been removed at the time of his death—his heart, his entrails, hair cuttings, linen dipped in blood, flesh from his right arm—over time were taken to England.

Epilogue 'A great king with strong armies and mighty fleets, a vast treasure and powerful allies fell all at once', Bishop Burnet observed of James II's sudden fall from power. 'And his whole strength, like a spider's web, was so irrevocably broken with a touch, that he was never able to retrieve what for want of judgement and heart he threw up in a day' (*Bishop Burnet's History*, 3.1). This judgement places the responsibility for his downfall on James's own shoulders, implying that if he had possessed the courage to face up to his opponents he might have stayed on his throne. To blame James for his own destiny invites an examination of how far he was responsible for the revolution of 1688.

Burnet was right to attribute to James the main responsibility for the policies carried out in his name, despite the allegation in the bill of rights that he had endeavoured 'to subvert and extirpate the Protestant religion and the laws and liberties of this kingdom ... by the assistance of divers

evil counsellors, judges and ministers employed by him'. Of course James had advisers such as the earls of Rochester and Sunderland, the Catholic Father Petre, and the Quaker William Penn, all of whom were presumably implicated in the bill's indictment. But they were just advisers, for James was determined to be king indeed and to rule as well as reign. It is a mistake to attribute the king's 'policies', to use an anachronistic term, to anybody else.

What his policies were has provoked much debate. James was accused by contemporary critics and by later whig historians of aiming at 'Popery and absolute power'. 'Popery' meant more than Roman Catholicism, signifying the allegiance of Catholics to the pope in Rome—that is, to a foreign potentate who was bent on restoring England to the true faith. James himself was accused of seeking the same end, even by using the royal prerogative to undermine English liberties. For, like all Catholic kings, he was also accused of endeavouring to make himself absolute. A contrary view of James sees him as an enlightened ruler seeking religious toleration. He was not bent on forcing Catholicism on his subjects, but simply sought to achieve toleration for Catholics and other non-Anglicans. His use of the royal prerogative to achieve this was a means to an end, not an end in itself.

James was genuinely committed to religious toleration, but also sought to increase the power of the crown. He wished that all his subjects could be as convinced as he was that the Catholic church was the one true church. He was also convinced that the established church was maintained artificially by penal laws which proscribed nonconformity. If these were removed, and conversions to Catholicism were encouraged, then many would take place. In the event his optimism was misplaced, for few converted. James underestimated the appeal of protestantism in general and the Church of England in particular. His was the zeal and even bigotry of a narrow-minded convert. But he was aware that not everybody would see the light as he had done. Religious toleration was still desirable because it encouraged commerce and helped a nation to prosper. This view was shared by many of his critics. But where James looked back nostalgically to France before the revocation of the edict of Nantes, when toleration and absolutism had gone hand in hand, they tended to look to the United Provinces, where toleration and republicanism combined to create a powerful mercantile economy. James was too autocratic to combine freedom of conscience with popular government. He resisted any check on the monarch's power. That is why his heart was not in the concessions he had to make in 1688. He would rather live in exile with his principles intact than continue to reign as a limited monarch. The fact that he had to make concessions suggests that the English were not prepared to accept the kind of polity James sought to impose upon them. If that were indeed the case then the king's efforts were doomed from the start. Yet they had not shown much resistance to the moves towards arbitrary power which Charles II had made in the last four years of his reign. On the contrary, fears that the exclusion crisis would end in violence made them welcome. Englishmen were far more afraid of a renewal of civil war than they were of absolutism. Charles II used the strengthened royal powers to back up the religious monopoly of intolerant Anglicans rather than to pursue religious toleration, and most of his subjects upheld the king's efforts. But they also showed that they were not averse to religious toleration in their responses to the three questions James put to them. Their replies to the first two, concerning the repeal of the penal laws and Test Act, showed that most were not prepared to support it. Most accounts concentrate on these answers and conclude that the majority of Englishmen were not in favour of toleration. The responses to the third, however, asking if they would 'support the Declaration of Indulgence by living friendly with those of several persuasions as subjects of the same prince and as good Christians ought to do?', were overwhelmingly positive. This showed that James's subjects were convinced that he was not just aiming at religious toleration but sought to empower non-Anglicans and above all his fellow Catholics. Arbitrary power in support of the established church or religious toleration they could stomach. They were prepared to tolerate Catholics as long as they did not represent a political threat, as they showed in the eighteenth century when they left them alone except during the crises of the 'Fifteen and the 'Forty-Five. It was the combination of popery and arbitrary power which they found repugnant. Even then they were reluctant to resist the king until the birth of a son indicated that his regime would be perpetuated. And in the last analysis it took an invasion to persuade them to become revolutionaries. James's project was bound to alienate the majority of his protestant subjects. But that did not mean that its failure was inevitable.

W. A. SPECK

Sources *The memoirs of James II: his campaigns as duke of York, 1652–1660*, ed. A. Lytton Sells (Bloomington, Indiana, 1962) · *The life of James the Second, king of England*, ed. J. S. Clarke, 2 vols. (1816) · *Papers of devotion of James II*, ed. G. Davies (1925) · J. Dalrymple, *Memoirs of Great Britain and Ireland*, 2 vols. (1771–3) · G. Groen van Prinsterer, ed., *Archives, ou, Correspondence inédite de la maison d'Orange-Nassau*, 2nd ser., 5 vols. (Utrecht, 1857–62) · *Négociations de M. le Comte d'Avaux en Irlande, 1689–90*, ed. J. Hogan, 1, IMC (1934) · Marquise Campana de Cavelli, ed., *Les derniers Stuarts à Saint-Germain en Laye*, 2 vols. (Paris, 1871) · R. Morrice, 'Ent'ring book', DWL [to be pubd in 2004 in four vols., ed. M. Goldie, T. Harris, M. Knights, J. Spurr, and S. Taylor] · *Bishop Burnet's History* · corresp. of Paul Barillon, 1681–8, PRO, PRO 31/3/155–178 · *Memoirs of Sir John Reresby*, ed. A. Browning, 2nd edn, ed. M. K. Geiter and W. A. Speck (1991) · *Historical notices of Scotish affairs, selected from the manuscripts of Sir John Lauder of Fountainhall*, ed. D. Laing, 2 vols., Bannatyne Club, 87 (1848) · [James II], *Memoirs of the English affairs chiefly naval from the year 1660 to 1673* (1729) · *CSP dom., 1685–9* · *An impartial relation of the whole proceedings against St Mary Magdalen College* (1688) · *The state letters of Henry earl of Clarendon*, 2 vols. (1763) · Bodl. Oxf., MSS Tanner · BL, Althorp MSS · Northants. RO, Isham papers · *The manuscripts of the earl of Dartmouth*, 3 vols., HMC, 20 (1887–96) · *Reg. PCS*, 3rd ser., vol. 12 · M. Ashley, *James II* (1977) · H. Belloc, *James the Second* (1928) · M. K. Geiter, 'The Restoration crisis and the launching of Pennsylvania, 1679–81', *EngHR*, 112 (1997), 300–18 · R. L. Greaves, *Secrets of the kingdom:*

British radicals from the Popish Plot to the revolution of 1688–89 (1992) · F. C. Turner, *James II* (1948) · J. Callow, *The making of James II: the formative years of a fallen king* (2000) · E. Corp, 'The last years of James II, 1690–1701', *History Today*, 51 (2001), 19–28 · J. Miller, *James II* (2000) · *Report on the manuscripts of his grace the duke of Buccleuch and Queensberry … preserved at Montagu House*, 3 vols. in 4, HMC, 45 (1899–1926)

Archives BL, letters, Add. MS 46412 · BL, Sloane MSS, letters and papers · Bodl. Oxf., corresp. and MSS · Bodl. Oxf., letters as duke of York · CUL, household book, corresp. · Royal Arch., corresp. · TCD, book of devotions · Warks. CRO, household accounts | BL, letters to the duke of Lauderdale, Add. MS 23243 · Hunt. L., letters to the Hastings family · NRA, priv. coll., letters to the duke of Queensberry · priv. coll., letters to William of Orange · Staffs. RO, letters to Lord Dartmouth · W. Sussex RO, letters to the duke of Gordon · Yale U., Beinecke L., letters to Lord Dartmouth [copies]

Likenesses A. Van Dyck, group portrait, oils, 1634?, Galleria Sabauda, Turin · A. Van Dyck, group portrait, oils, 1635, Royal Collection · P. Lely, group portrait, oils, 1637, Royal Collection · C. Johnson, oils, 1639, NPG · P. Lely, oils, 1643, Syon House, Middlesex · W. Dobson, oils, c.1645–1646, Royal Collection · P. Lely, double portrait, oils, 1647 (with Charles I), Syon House, Middlesex · W. Hollar, etching, 1651 (after D. Teniers), BM · attrib. C. Wautier, oils, c.1656–1660, Royal Collection · S. Cooper, miniature, 1661, V&A; version, Badminton House, Gloucestershire · P. Lely, oils, c.1661–1662, Scot. NPG · P. Lely, double portrait, oils, c.1663 (with Anne Hyde), Petworth House, Sussex; version, NPG · S. Cooper, miniature, c.1665, Royal Collection · studio of P. Lely, oils, c.1665, Royal Collection · P. Lely, oils, c.1665–1670, Royal Collection · H. Gascar, oils, c.1672–1673, NMM · P. Lely and B. Gennari, group portrait, oils, c.1674, Royal Collection · G. Kneller, oils, 1684, NPG [*see illus.*] · miniature on vellum, 1684–5 (after G. Kneller), NPG · A. Killigrew, oils, 1685, Royal Collection · attrib. W. Wissing, oils, c.1685–1686, Royal Hospital, Chelsea, London · N. de Largillière, oils, 1686, NMM · J. Smeltzing, pewter medal, 1688, Scot. NPG · S. Le Clerc, copper medal, 1689, Scot. NPG · oils, c.1690, NPG · N. Roettier, silver gilt medal, 1699, Scot. NPG · R. Arondeaux, silver medal, Scot. NPG · G. Kneller, oils, second version, Royal Collection · P. Schenck, mezzotint (after G. Kneller), BM, NPG · P. Schenck, mezzotint (after unknown artist), BM, NPG · R. Sheppard, line engraving (after G. Kneller), BM, NPG · J. Smith, mezzotint (after N de Largillière), BM, NPG · J. Smith, mezzotint (after G. Kneller), BM, NPG · H. Stone or S. Stone, group portrait, oils (after A. Van Dyck), Scot. NPG · H. Stone?, double portrait, oils (after P. Lely), Scot. NPG · G. Valek, mezzotint (after P. Lely), NPG · medals and coins, BM · mezzotint (after unknown artist), NPG · portrait (in first letter of James's charter to port of Kinsale, 1689), Kinsale Museum · terracotta bust, Scot. NPG

James Francis Edward [James Francis Edward Stuart; *styled* James VIII and III; *known as* Chevalier de St George, the Pretender, the Old Pretender] (**1688–1766**), Jacobite claimant to the thrones of England, Scotland, and Ireland, was born at St James's Palace, Westminster, on 10 June 1688, the only surviving son of *James II and VII (1633–1701) and his second wife, Maria Beatrice d'Este of Modena [*see* Mary (1658–1718)]. His birth was highly controversial; his mother had last given birth in 1683 and none of her five earlier children had survived infancy. By the autumn of 1687, when it was generally assumed that the king and queen could not produce healthy children, it was widely feared that James II's policies were directed towards the formal re-establishment of Roman Catholicism as the state religion; in such circumstances the birth of a male heir, who would supersede his protestant half-sisters,

James Francis Edward (1688–1766), by Louis-Gabriel Blanchet, 1741

Princess Mary of Orange [*see* Mary II (1662–1694)] and Princess Anne of Denmark [*see* Anne (1665–1714)], in the succession, would be highly convenient. From the moment the queen's pregnancy was formally announced in November 1687, protestants started a campaign to question its legitimacy and, where possible, avoided the queen's lying-in. Those who were obligated to be present, by virtue of their offices, took pains to stand with their backs to the queen's bed, so they could not be called upon to provide eye-witness testimony. James II attempted in vain to discredit the 'warming pan' fiction (so called after rumours that the child had been smuggled into the queen's chamber in such a device) by publishing the depositions of over seventy witnesses to the birth (*Depositions made in council on Monday, 22 October 1688, concerning the birth of the prince of Wales*), but the nation was prepared to disbelieve any evidence. When the king left London on 17 November to go to Salisbury to confront Prince William of Orange, James was sent to the fortress at Portsmouth, then under the command of his half-brother, James *Fitzjames, duke of Berwick, but as soon as James II had decided to flee to France the prince was returned to London on 9 December, and that night with his mother was taken to Gravesend to embark for Calais. On their arrival Louis XIV ordered that they be transported to the château of St Germain-en-Laye, which was to be the prince's home for the next twenty-four years.

Exile and succession, 1689–1714 During the ensuing Nine Years' War, William III's Roman Catholic allies suggested a compromise which would allow William to remain king for his lifetime, to be succeeded by the prince of Wales. There is no evidence that William had any intention whatsoever of repealing the Act of Settlement of 1689, which barred all Roman Catholics from succession to the throne; Louis XIV, however, desperate for peace, apparently broached the idea with James II, who flatly refused to allow his son to be bred a protestant. When in July 1696 James II established an independent household for his son, he gave the prince's new governor, James Drummond, fourth earl of Perth, an extremely detailed set of rules, the burden of which was to ensure that the prince would not spend one moment without direct adult supervision (*Stuart Papers*, 1.114–17).

On 2/13 September 1701, three days before James II's death, Louis XIV visited St Germain and publicly announced that on the king's death France would recognize his son as king of England, Scotland, and Ireland. This recognition, in contravention of Louis's promises in the treaty of Ryswick (1697), infuriated the English public. In June 1701 parliament had passed an Act of Settlement which vested the succession in the next protestant heir, the dowager Electress Sophia of Hanover 'and the heirs of her body being protestant'. Only a few hours before his death on 8 March 1702, William III assented to an attainder of 'the pretended James III' as well as an act of abjuration of the young prince. During his minority the regency was vested in the prince's mother, Queen Mary, and Jacobite affairs were directed by her closest adviser, Charles, second earl of Middleton; their influence over James remained paramount even after the formal declaration of his majority in June 1706.

A lifetime of repeated failure should not obscure James Francis Edward Stuart's many assets: tenacity of purpose, considerable physical courage, a quick (but not profound) intelligence, and a quiet personal charm (but not the magnetism of his uncle, *Charles II, or of his eldest son, *Charles Edward). Reared largely by Scottish Catholic exiles, James's education had produced a careful, cautious man, very much at home at his writing desk, from which poured thousands of letters. James was susceptible to the influence of favourites in all but one point: he consistently refused to consider renouncing the religion in which he had been reared, even though he fully realized that it precluded his restoration to the British throne.

During the reign of his immensely popular half-sister Queen Anne (1702–1714), there appeared to be little hope of a successful Jacobite uprising in Great Britain; none the less, the French in 1705 sent Lieutenant Nathaniel Hooke to Scotland to explore possibilities there; on his return to France in May 1706 Hooke reported favourably on the possibilities in the northern kingdom. It was the series of military and financial disasters produced by the War of the Spanish Succession (1701–14), however, which impelled the desperate Louis XIV and his ministers to undertake what they regarded as a last throw of the dice, an invasion of Scotland to exploit nationalist discontent there against the Act of Union (1707). Five men-of-war, two transports, and twenty frigates with approximately 4000

French troops under the command of Admiral Claude Forbin were assembled at Dunkirk at the beginning of 1708; on 21 February/3 March James left St Germain secretly and proceeded to Dunkirk, where he arrived two days later. He promptly came down with measles, however, and on the insistence of his physicians the expedition was delayed for one week, finally sailing on 6/17 March. The delay allowed English and Dutch spies in the French ports to alert London and The Hague, and the French found themselves pursued through the channel into the North Sea by a combined Anglo-Dutch fleet under the command of Sir George Byng. The French fleet reached the mouth of the Firth of Forth, but had not seen the bonfires on the coast promised by Scottish Jacobites (most of whom had been arrested) indicating where they should land. Ignoring James's pleas that he, with only his attendants, be allowed to embark in a small boat to land in Fife, Forbin chose to escape Byng's approaching fleet, which he succeeded in doing, returning to Dunkirk with only one ship captured on 27 March/7 April.

On James's return to France, Louis acquiesced in his long-time plea to be allowed to serve militarily, and accordingly he joined the household troops in the army of Flanders, serving with distinction in the battles of Oudenarde (1708) and Malplaquet (1709). The Hague peace negotiations in the spring of 1709 had made it clear that the French would agree to James's expulsion from France as one of the conditions of peace with Great Britain, but Louis was still determined to extract the last ounce of advantage from his support of the Stuarts. In the summer of 1711, instead of being posted again to the army, James was dispatched on a tour of western France in order to raise British apprehensions of another invasion attempt. The advent in August–September 1710 of a new tory government in London, led by Robert Harley, inspired new Jacobite hopes of a Stuart restoration; indeed Harley, in his secret negotiations with the French secretary of foreign affairs, the marquis de Torcy, suggested that James's restoration was his ultimate goal, 'if he thinks like us' in matters of religion. In September 1711, however, the British made it clear that James's expulsion from France was still a prerequisite of peace, although in collusion with Harley (created lord treasurer and earl of Oxford in May 1711) and his secretary of state, Henry St John, Viscount Bolingbroke, Louis and Torcy were able to arrange for James to take up residence in the neighbouring duchy of Lorraine, which he did in February 1713.

After the conclusion of the treaty of Utrecht (1713), Great Britain's erstwhile allies, the whigs, the Electress Sophia, and her eldest son, George Lewis, elector of Hanover, were all convinced that the tory government intended to repeal the Act of Settlement in favour of the Pretender, as James was known. Oxford maintained close contact with James through Torcy and his London agent, the Abbé François Gaultier. At Christmas 1713 Queen Anne became severely ill and for several days seemed likely to die. Her recovery was incomplete, and by January 1714 it was clear that she could not live much longer. It was then that Oxford and Bolingbroke (who by this time were at

each other's throats) secretly and separately requested James to convert to protestantism in order to make a Stuart restoration feasible. James, whose devotion to Roman Catholicism was unalterable, had no difficulty in reaching his decision, nor did he ever regret it. Displaying his full share of Stuart arrogance and lack of remorse, he later informed Torcy: 'I have chosen my own course, therefore it is for others to change their sentiments' (James to Torcy, 27 July 1714 NS, Archives des Affairs Étrangères, CP Angleterre 262, fols. 325–8). With the arrival on 11 March of news of James's refusal to convert (James to Gaultier, 2/13 March 1714, ibid., fols. 311–12; an English translation is printed in Macpherson, 2.525–6), both Oxford and Bolingbroke saw that a restoration attempt was impossible, although for their own purposes they continued to offer pro forma assurances of their sympathies to James and his supporters. On the death of Queen Anne on 1 August 1714 the Jacobites were unable to do anything to hinder the peaceful accession of George I.

The 'Fifteen The establishment of the Hanoverian dynasty ushered in a new whig administration which seemed to be intent on proscribing their tory enemies from all governmental employments. When the new parliament opened in March 1715, it became clear that the government intended to impeach the former tory ministers for their involvement in the Utrecht negotiations. In April 1715 Oxford was sent to the Tower, but Bolingbroke precipitately fled to France, where he joined James openly three months later, being named Jacobite secretary of state and elevated to an earldom in the Jacobite peerage. In August the tory general James Butler, duke of Ormond, also fled to France to escape impeachment. Bolingbroke and Ormond, both in Paris, joined Torcy and James's half-brother, James Fitzjames, duke of Berwick, in planning military intervention in both England and Scotland. Their plans came to grief, however, with the death of Louis XIV on 21 August/1 September 1715. A regency under Louis's nephew, Philippe, duc d'Orléans, was established in the name of Louis XV, and the regent refused to give any material aid to the Jacobites, promising only to regard their activities with a blind eye.

In Scotland, however, events had taken a different turn. On 26 August 1715 John Erskine, twenty-third or sixth earl of Mar, raised the Jacobite standard at Braemar in the highlands. In England the rebellion was quickly crushed; Ormond's attempt to invade the west country failed, largely because the government had arrested most of the prominent Jacobite tories there. On 13 November the crushing government victory at Preston completely extinguished any immediate hope of a rising in northern England. The battle of Sheriffmuir on the same day proved inconclusive militarily, but government forces prevented Mar's army from entering the lowlands of Scotland and kept it bottled up in Perth; in France, however, Sheriffmuir was represented as a great Jacobite triumph. James III had already arranged to go to Scotland; on 28 October he left Bar-le-Duc and, disguised as a French bishop, crossed France, reaching the coast near St Malo on 8

November. For the next eight weeks he roamed the channel coast, waiting fruitlessly for news of a renewed rebellion in England; finally, on 28 December NS he embarked at Dunkirk aboard a small privateer, accompanied by only a few attendants, and on 22 December OS landed at Peterhead on the north-eastern coast of Scotland. There he passed the night, and the next day went to Newburgh, a seat of the Earl Marischal. Passing through Aberdeen in disguise, he journeyed south to Fetteresso, another seat of Marischal's, where he was joined by Mar and a small group of gentlemen from the army at Perth. On Mar's arrival James laid aside his disguise and his arrival in Scotland was publicly announced. A privy council was formed and proclamations were issued in the name of James VIII of Scotland and III of England, one of which appointed his coronation to take place at Scone (which it never did). The magistrates of Aberdeen—Mar's nominees—went to pay him homage, and the episcopal clergy enthusiastically welcomed him. On 2 January 1716 James began his journey south, via Brechin and Glamis, to Dundee, where he made a state entry, the populace receiving him with enthusiasm and no signs of hostility. He then travelled at a leisurely pace to Scone Palace outside Perth, arriving there on 8 January, where he established his court with the observances and etiquette appropriate to royalty. James was reported to be 'a tall lean blak man, loukes half dead alredy, very thine, long faced, and very ill cullored and melancholy' (countess of Lauderdale to duke of Montrose, 14 Jan 1716, Third Report, HMC, 1872, 378).

From the time of his arrival in Scotland, James realized that the military situation was hopeless; while his supporters were rapidly deserting (only about 4000 remained at Perth), the government was reinforcing its position not only with English regiments but also with 5000 Dutch troops. In addition, James had no talent to inspire men en masse. 'If he found himself disappointed with us,' the master of Sinclair later recalled:

> we were tenfold more so in him. We saw nothing in him that looked like spirit. He never appeared with cheerfulness and vigour to animate us. Our men began to despise him; some asked if he could speak. His countenance looked extremely heavy. He cared not to come abroad among us soldiers or to see us handle our arms or do our exercise. (J. Sinclair, A True Account of the Proceedings at Perth, Written by a Rebel, 1716, 20)

The earl of Mar (who had been created a duke in the Jacobite peerage) had already established a complete ascendancy over the Chevalier, and Mar's chief thought now was how to escape the consequences of his rash undertaking. On 28 January news reached Perth that government forces, under the command of the duke of Argyll, were unexpectedly marching through the winter snow towards the highland capital. On the understanding that the army would retire into the highlands to await a spring campaign, the highland chiefs agreed to retreat to Montrose; unbeknown to them, arrangements had secretly been made there for the Chevalier to leave Scotland and sail to France. On 31 January the Jacobite army crossed the Tay on the ice, and by the time they reached Montrose the government forces were two days' march to their rear. On 3

February James wrote to both the regent and Bolingbroke from Montrose, appealing once again for immediate French help but not suggesting that he was preparing to leave Scotland (James to Orléans, 3 Feb 1716, Stuart Papers, 1.54–5). That night, however, in disguise, James slipped onto a waiting French vessel and left Scotland. In his 'letter of adieu to the Scotch' he attempted to justify his precipitate departure and his decision to 'command' Mar to accompany him, but he gave no explanation for leaving the other rebel leaders in ignorance of his plans (ibid., 1.505–7). James's popularity in Scotland was permanently damaged, and virtually all the Scottish exiles (except for his own relatives and dependants) became virulently opposed to the earl of Mar.

Accompanied by only sixteen people, including lords Mar, Drummond, and Melfort, Lieutenant-General Dominick Sheldon, and Sir John Erskine, James landed at Gravelines on 10/21 February 1716. He arrived at St Germain on 26 February and remained in hiding near Paris until 6 March, during which time he abruptly dismissed Bolingbroke from his service, accusing him of treasonable correspondence with England (James to regent, 6 March 1716, Stuart Papers, 2.5). He hoped to re-establish his residence in Lorraine, but Duke Leopold, under pressure from the regent, refused to receive him and, faute de mieux, James was forced to take up residence in the papal enclave of Avignon, where he arrived on 2 April. It was there in October 1716 that he survived traumatic surgery for an anal fistula.

The signature in January 1717 of the triple alliance between Britain, France, and the Dutch Republic, which reiterated the treaty of Utrecht's guarantees of the Hanoverian succession, meant that James could no longer remain in Avignon; on 6 February he began his journey 'beyond the mountains' to the Papal States where, with two short intervals, he spent the remainder of his life. Clement XI (r. 1700–21) grudgingly granted James the Palazzo Muti in Rome, a country home at Albano, and a papal pension of 12,000 Roman crowns (about £3000) p.a., which remained unchanged for the rest of James's life.

The 'Nineteen and marriage In 1717–18 Jacobite hopes centred mainly on Charles XII of Sweden, who was at war with George I as elector of Hanover; hopes that the protestant hero of Europe might intervene in Britain on James's behalf were shattered when Charles XII was killed on 11 December 1718. Meanwhile, however, Giulio, Cardinal Alberoni, had promised to mount a Spanish invasion of Great Britain. On his invitation James left Rome secretly in February 1719 and, after a dangerous voyage, arrived at Madrid in mid-March. Spanish plans called for a large expedition to the west country of 5000 men, and arms for an additional 15,000 to be commanded by the duke of Ormond, and a smaller expedition to Scotland with only two Spanish frigates and 307 men and officers under the command of the Earl Marischal. The main expedition was battered and driven back into port by storms in the Bay of Biscay, but the smaller expedition managed to reach Stornoway in the Isle of Lewis. By contrast to 1715, when nearly 10,000 men had joined 'the cause', now only 1000

Scots rallied to the Jacobite standard, and the government easily suppressed the revolt at Glenshiels on 10 June 1719. Meanwhile James had remained in Madrid, where he was welcomed with royal honours and was assigned the *palacio* Buen Retiro. By early summer, with a series of Spanish reverses at the hands of the British and French, James's presence in Madrid had become an embarrassment and he was unceremoniously advised to return to Rome, which he did in August.

James's search for a bride had begun after the failure of the 'Fifteen, but despite the pleas of his followers he had no intention of considering protestant princesses. After a series of rebuffs by various German and Italian courts, the Chevalier's choice finally fell on Maria Clementina Sobieska [*see* Clementina (1702–1735)], the youngest daughter of Prince James and Hedwig Elizabeth of Neuberg, and granddaughter of King John Sobieski of Poland. A marriage contract signed in July 1718 eventually resulted in James receiving at least 900,000 French livres (approximately £75,000), the largest amount which the exiled Stuarts ever received at one time from one source. At the behest of George I, the emperor Charles VI arrested Clementina and her mother at Innsbruck in October 1718 on their journey to Italy; she was, however, rescued by the Jacobite agent Charles Wogan in April 1719 and arrived in Rome while her fiancé was still in Spain. Immediately after his return, James and Clementina were married on 2 September 1719. To the marriage were born two sons, Charles Edward in December 1720 and *Henry Benedict in March 1725.

In 1722, thanks to the treachery of Mar who confirmed the British government's suspicions, Francis Atterbury, bishop of Rochester, and most leading Jacobite conspirators in England were arrested; Robert Walpole deliberately manipulated the 'Atterbury plot' both to destroy English Jacobitism and to consolidate his own ascendancy. The hysteria manufactured by the government and Atterbury's subsequent attainder and perpetual banishment in 1723 effectively destroyed Jacobitism as a viable political movement in south, but not in north, Britain.

Mar had long before been superseded by his brother-in-law, John Hay, as the Chevalier's principal adviser and confidant. Hay, his wife, Marjorie, and her brother James Murray—all ostensibly protestant—were unquestionably the most important figures in the Jacobite court in the 1720s, which was a growing grievance to James's 'queen'. The breaking point came in November 1725 when James decided to create a separate household for their elder son, Charles Edward, and make Murray the prince's governor. Clementina promptly fled to a Roman convent and appealed to the pope, Benedict XIII, against the domination of protestants in her husband's court and the prospect that her two sons might be educated by them. Common gossip—which quickly spread throughout Europe—held that Clementina's real objection was that Lady Inverness was her husband's mistress. Their separation, which lasted nearly two years, sharply divided the Jacobite movement into 'king's' and 'queen's' factions. Roman society overwhelmingly favoured Clementina, and in

October 1726, exasperated by the pope's hostility, James removed his court from Rome to Bologna (still within the Papal States). A reconciliation was arranged in June 1727, and Clementina was on her way to Bologna when James received word of the sudden death of George I at Osnabrück on 12/23 June. James, accompanied by Inverness, immediately left Italy for Lorraine, hoping that France would be willing to ignore the triple alliance. Leopold of Lorraine once again denied James asylum (Leopold to James, 8 Aug 1727, Stuart papers, RASP 109/46), the government of Louis XV (led by Cardinal Fleury) proved unsympathetic, and James was finally reduced once again to taking up residence in Avignon, where he arrived on 19 August (ibid., RASP 109/186). French pressure on the papacy forced James to return to Bologna in January 1728, where he found his wife in residence. In February of the following year James and his elder son returned to Rome; Clementina and Prince Henry followed in June (ibid., RASP 129/12), and the family remained united until Clementina's death on 18 January 1735.

Later years and reputation James found the reigns of Clement XII (1730–40) and Benedict XIV (1749–58) much more sympathetic than those of earlier pontiffs. When his eldest son, Charles Edward, left Rome for France in 1744 for an abortive invasion attempt, James did everything in his power to raise money for the cause, but was pessimistic about its prospects for success. Nevertheless, he agreed to send his younger son, Henry Benedict, to France in August 1745 to be the ostensible commander of a Franco-Jacobite invasion of England, which never took place. After the collapse of the rising of 1745 and the return of Charles to France in October 1746, his relations with his father and brother deteriorated rapidly. In April 1747, without consulting Charles, James summoned Henry back to Rome, where in July he was created a cardinal. Charles was furious and never forgave his father for what he considered a stab in the back. James's last years, while he gradually failed both in body and mind, were darkened by this estrangement; after the signature of the treaty of Aix-la-Chapelle resulted in Charles's expulsion from France in October 1748, he went into hiding and only occasionally and vaguely communicated with his father. James spent the last decade of his life largely as a bedridden invalid. He died about 9 p.m. on 1 January 1766 at the Palazzo Muti, Rome, and was buried with royal honours in the basilica of St Peter's. In 1819 Pius VII (r. 1800–23) erected a monument by Canova over his tomb and that of his two sons; the prince regent contributed 50 guineas of the cost.

Contemporary characterizations of James vary according to the author's political prejudices. In 1740 the poet Thomas Gray was scathing:

> He is a thin, ill-made man, extremely tall and awkward, of a most unpromising countenance, a good deal resembling King James the Second, and has extremely the air and look of an idiot, particularly when he laughs or prays. The first he does not often, the latter continually.   (Gray to Philip Gray, [10] July 1740, in *The Correspondence of Thomas Gray*, ed. P. Toynbee, L. Whifley, and H. W. Starr, 3 vols., 1971, 1.166–7)

Gray's travelling companion, Horace Walpole, had a somewhat different impression:

> Enthusiasm and disappointment have stamped a solemnity on his person which rather creates pity than respect ... Without the particular features of any Stuart, the Chevalier has the strong lines and fatality of air peculiar to them all. From the moment I saw him, I never doubted the legitimacy of his birth. (H. Walpole, *Memoirs of King George II*, ed. J. Brooke, 3 vols., 1985, 1.195)

An Irishman, Captain Robert O'Flanagan, who accompanied James in 1715 from his departure from Lorraine in October until his embarkation for Scotland in December, recorded:

> I never knew any have better temper, be more familiar and good, always pleased and in good humour, notwithstanding all the crosses and accidents that happen'd during His journey; never the least disquieted, but with the greatest courage and fermness resolved to goe through what He designed on. ... and enfine posessing eminently all the qualityes of a great prince, with those of a most Honest private Gentelman. (Seton, 266)

It has been fashionable among Jacobite historians—among them his biographers Martin Haile (1907), A. and H. Tayler (1934), and Peggy Miller (1971), who focus exclusively on the period covered by the printed Historical Manuscripts Commission Stuart papers—to regard James Stuart as eminently suited to fill the role of a constitutional monarch, at least as it was evolving in the eighteenth century. Such views, however, are superficial, ignoring both his inheritance and his training. James had his full share of Stuart arrogance, wilfulness, ingratitude for the sacrifices of others, and susceptibility to domination by favourites; through his lifelong residence in France and the Papal States, his devotion to an authoritarian church, and a belief in the divine right of monarchs he had only an acquired rather than an innate appreciation of the unwritten limits to the actions of a British sovereign, and his high-handed use of papal police during the last two decades of his life was reminiscent of James II's approach to constitutional and statute law.

EDWARD GREGG

Sources Royal Arch., Stuart papers · *Calendar of the Stuart papers belonging to his majesty the king, preserved at Windsor Castle*, 7 vols., HMC, 56 (1902–23) · BL, Add. MSS 20241–20686 [Cardinal Filippe Gualterio] · BL, Add. MSS 31244–31267 [Cardinals Gualterio-Caprara] · Archives du Ministère des Affaires Étrangères, Paris, Correspondance politique Angleterre, Rome, Lorraine, mémoirs et documents Angleterre · C. Petrie, *The Jacobite movement*, 2 vols. (1948–50) · G. H. Jones, *The mainstream of Jacobitism* (1954) · C. J. Nordmann, *La crise du nord au début du XVIIIᵉ siècle* (Paris, 1962) · J. Macpherson, *Original papers: containing the secret history of Great Britain, from the Restoration, to the accession of the house of Hannover*, 2 vols. (1775) · *The life of James the Second, king of England*, ed. J. S. Clarke, 2 vols. (1816) · G. H. Jones, *Charles Middleton* (1967) · D. Middleton, *Life of Charles, second earl of Middleton* (1957) · *Correspondence of Colonel N. Hooke*, ed. W. D. Macray, 2 vols., Roxburghe Club, 92, 95 (1870–71) · D. Nairne, journal, NL Scot., MS 14266 · G. M. Trevelyan, 'The "Jersey" period of the negotiations leading to the treaty of Utrecht', *EngHR*, 49 (1934), 100–05 · H. N. Fieldhouse, 'Oxford, Bolingbroke and the Pretender's place of residence', *EngHR*, 52 (1937), 443–59 · W. Seton, 'Itinerary of King James II, October to December 1715', *SHR*, 21 (1923–4), 249–66 · H. Tayler, 'The Jacobite papers at Avignon', *Miscellany ... V*, Scottish History Society, 3rd ser., 21 (1933), 294 · *The Jacobite attempt of 1719: letters of James Butler, second duke of Ormonde, relating to Cardinal Alberoni's project for the invasion of Great Britain on behalf of the Stuarts, and to the landing of a Spanish expedition in Scotland*, ed. W. K. Dickson, Scottish History Society, 19 (1895) · E. Gregg, 'The Jacobite career of John, earl of Mar', *Ideology and conspiracy: aspects of Jacobitism, 1689–1759*, ed. E. Cruickshanks (1982) · E. Gregg, 'Power, friends and alliances: the search for the Pretender's bride', *Studies in History and Politics*, 4, ed. K. W. Schweizer (1985), 35–54 · G. V. Bennett, 'Jacobitism and the rise of Walpole', *Historical persepctives*, ed. N. Mackendrick (1974) · F. McLyan, *Charles Edward Stuart* (1988) · B. Fothergill, *The cardinal king* (1955) · N. Woolf, *Medallic records of the Jacobite movement* (1988) · *Third report*, HMC, 2 (1872)

Archives BL, papers · Bodl. Oxf., corresp. and papers, Carte MSS 180–181, 208–212 · Royal Arch. · West Highland Museum, Fort William, letters | Archives du Ministère des Affaires Étrangères, Paris, Mémoirs et documents Angleterre, correspondance politique Angleterre, Rome, Lorraine · BL, letters to F. A. Gualterio, Add. MS 20241–20583, 31255, *passim* · BL, Gualterio-Caprara papers, Add. MSS 20421–20686, 31244–31267 · NA Scot., letters to Admiral Gordon · NL Ire., papers relating to marriage to Maria Clementina Sobieska

Likenesses attrib. N. de Lagillière, oils, 1691, Scot. NPG · N. de Largillière, double portrait, oils, 1695 (with his sister), NPG · F. De Troy, oils, 1701, Scot. NPG · F. De Troy, oils, 1704, Magd. Cam. · studio of A.-S. Belle, oils, *c*.1712, NPG · attrib. F. Trevisani, oils, *c*.1712, Royal Collection · attrib. F. Trevisani, oils, *c*.1718, Stanford Hall, Leicestershire · oils, *c*.1721, Stanford Hall, Leicestershire · oils, *c*.1723–1730, Scot. NPG · A. Masucci, oils, 1735–6 (*Marriage to Clementina Sobieska*), Scot. NPG · A. Masucci and P. L. Ghezzi, oils, 1738–9 (*Baptism of Prince Charles Edward*), Scot. NPG · L.-G. Blanchet, oils, 1741, NPG [*see illus.*] · F. Ponzone?, pen-and-ink drawing, *c*.1741, NPG · Canova, sculpture, 1819, St Peter's, Rome, monument to Stuarts · F. Chereau, print (after A. S. Belle, *c*.1712), BM · G. Edelinck, line engraving (after N. de Largillière, 1692), BM, Scot. NPG · B. Gennari, oils (as an infant), Stonyhurst College, Lancashire · L. Horthemels, line engraving (after A. S. Belle, *c*.1712), BM, NPG · A. Pozzi, ivory bust, Brodick Castle, Isle of Arran · J. Smith, mezzotint (after G. Kneller), BM, NPG · medals, repro. in Woolf, *Medallic record of the Jacobite movement* · medals, BM, NPG

James the Cistercian

James the Cistercian [James the Englishman] (*fl. c.*1270), Cistercian monk and theologian, is said by Bale, Pits, and their followers to have been a doctor of theology of the University of Paris, and subsequently professor first of philosophy and then of theology at the Cistercian Collège St Bernard in Paris about 1270. The college had been founded in 1245. According to the Dominican Pietro di Vicenza, James is also said to have supported Thomas Aquinas in contesting the doctrine of the immaculate conception. Some modern scholars have suggested that he was the James who compiled the *Omne bonum*, an enormous though incomplete encyclopaedia of universal knowledge preserved in British Library, Royal MS 6 E.vi-vii, but this is incorrect. The compiler of this remarkable work was James Palmer, an exchequer clerk who died in 1375. James the Cistercian is reported to have composed a commentary on the Song of Songs, *Conciones in evangelia*, and *Lecturae scholasticae*, but none of these has survived.

DAVID N. BELL

Sources Bale, *Cat.*, 322–3 (iv.36) · C. H. Talbot, 'The English Cistercians and the universities', *Studia Monastica*, 4 (1962), 207–9 · J. C. Russell, 'Dictionary of writers of thirteenth century England', *BIHR*, special suppl., 3 (1936) [whole issue], esp. 54 · L. F. Sandler, *Omne bonum: a fourteenth-century encyclopaedia of universal knowledge* (1996)

James, Alexander Wilson [Alex] (1901–1953), footballer, was born in Caledonian Buildings, Mossend, Lanarkshire, on 14 September 1901, the youngest of six children (four boys and two girls) born to Charles James (1860–1928), railway yard-master, and his wife, Jane Anne Barrie Wilson (*d.* 1924). Both parents were Scottish, his mother hailing from Dundee. He attended the local Bellshill Academy and in 1916 left to work at the Beardsmore steelworks, then producing munitions for the war effort. He was sacked for playing a dangerous prank involving an incendiary device. With his father's help he then obtained a job as a checker on the railways, but his only ambition was to play football.

Owing to his diminutive size (he would never grow taller than 5 feet 6 inches) James at first struggled to succeed. Following a season with the local village side, he played for Orbiston Celtic—Matt Busby's home village team. Then, in 1921, he was invited to join the Glasgow-based Scottish junior club Ashfield, a move that brought him to the notice of league scouts. Following a trial with Motherwell he was lured to Kirkcaldy in Fife to play for second-division Raith Rovers. At Raith James began to develop a distinctive playing style. Though small, he had a surprisingly powerful shot and scored goals in profusion. He also possessed mesmerizing ball skills, although at this stage in his career he was inclined occasionally to over-indulge and waste possession. While at Raith he met Margaret (Peggy) Willis (1909–1992), daughter of the club trainer Dave Willis. Peggy and Alex married in 1924 in Edinburgh and in July 1925 the first of their three children was born, Alex junior; Patricia, their daughter, was to follow in 1927 and a second son, Andrew, was born in 1940.

James remained at Raith for three seasons, and by late 1925 his goalscoring exploits had attracted the attention of English league clubs. Following various tortuous, clandestine negotiations, he was signed by Preston North End, a club attempting to resurrect its once great reputation by investing heavily in Scottish players. In fact, during the four seasons James was at Preston, the club achieved little, though James's international career blossomed. In 1928 he was a member of the famous 'Wembley wizards' Scotland team that thrashed England at Wembley 5–1. The team entered Scottish football folklore, and James became a much sought-after commodity. He was now anxious to cash in on his fame, and more or less forced the Preston club to sell him by conspicuously underperforming on the field of play. There were at least half a dozen clubs anxious to sign him, but only one with sufficient money to do so: Arsenal.

Arsenal's manager, Herbert Chapman, had already spent considerable sums of money attempting to build a side good enough to complement the magnificent new Arsenal stadium, then being constructed at Highbury, north London. James, bought in 1929 for a fee of £9000, though initially less than successful, proved to be the final piece of the jigsaw. Chapman utilized James's football vision and his almost inch-perfect passing accuracy to create a new football team style. He became a deep-lying inside forward, ready to take possession in Arsenal's own

Alexander Wilson James (1901–1953), by James Jarché, 1934

half, then to release speedy wingers (Hulme and Bastin) who swept down either flank before delivering crosses for raiding forwards such as David Jack or Ted Drake, or scored themselves (Bastin held the Arsenal individual scoring record until 1997). James no longer scored many goals himself, but was the fulcrum of one of the most successful, tactically astute teams of the modern era. During his eight seasons at Highbury, Arsenal won the league title four times and established itself as one of the foremost clubs in the land. James's international career was less prolific. During a period when 'Anglo-Scots' (Scottish players employed by English league clubs) were regularly omitted from the national team, James found Scottish international caps hard to come by. He would earn just eight.

James was a flashy, charismatic figure, easily identifiable on the field of play by his baggy shorts and flapping shirt (and perfectly captured for posterity by the great sporting cartoonist of the inter-war years, Tom Webster). Off the field, he was regularly in the news, usually demanding a higher wage or a transfer. James enjoyed the West End lifestyle available to a London-based player and was a regular *habitué* of fashionable cafés and bars. He was a prolific spender and a snappy dresser but was unfortunate to be a sporting star at a time when footballers, though as well known as film stars, were paid a pittance by comparison. He made strenuous efforts to cash in on his 'image': he was a sports demonstrator at Selfridges, he had regular columns in national newspapers and he appeared in advertisements for cigarettes and sports goods. But when he retired in 1937 he had accumulated little, partly because he had no real business acumen. In 1938 he went to Poland to coach the Polish national side—a position he enjoyed but which came to an abrupt end when Germany invaded Poland in August 1939. During the war James served as a gunner in the Royal Artillery's maritime division stationed on the east coast. In 1947 he rejoined Arsenal as a reserve team coach, but he contracted cancer and, after a short illness, died on 1 June 1953 in the Royal Northern Hospital, Holloway, London. He was cremated at Golders Green crematorium.

JOHN HARDING

Sources J. Harding, *Alex James: life of a football legend* (1988) • personal knowledge (2004) • private information (2004) • *DNB*
Likenesses photographs, 1928–61, Hult. Arch. • J. Jarché, photograph, 1934, NPG [*see illus.*] • T. Webster, cartoon drawings, repro. in Harding, *Alex James*, 141, 156 • photograph, Mossend public library, Strathclyde • photograph, Selfridges Archives • photographs, *ILN* Picture Library • photographs, priv. coll. • photographs, repro. in Harding, *Alex James*, 22, 86–7, 150–1

James, Angharad (1677–1749), Welsh-language poet, was born on 16 July 1677 at Gelli Ffrydiau in the parish of Llandwrog, Caernarvonshire, one of six children of James David (*d.* 1712) of Gelli Ffrydiau and his wife, Angharad Humphrey (*d.* 1727). Her education is undocumented but was unusual for a Welshwoman of her time, for as well as learning to read and write she mastered Latin and owned books in that language which later belonged to her descendants. Her Bible and Book of Common Prayer, with annotations in her hand, are still extant. When she was twenty she married a man forty years her senior, William Prichard, or ap Rhisiart (*bap.* 1638, *d.* 1719), and went to live at his substantial farm in Cwm Penamnen, Dolwyddelan, which he held, with another farm and a waulk-mill, from the Gwydir estate. Between 1702 and 1716 the couple had three daughters, Gwen, Margaret, and Catherine, and a son, Dafydd. Because of her husband's age and poor health, much of the responsibility for farming the land as well as managing the home fell on Angharad James's shoulders, and after his death on 2 March 1719 it was hers alone.

Yet James still found time to develop her poetical and musical skills. According to strong local oral traditions, she played the harp and would play dance music for the serving men and maids, in the house but also out in the fields, so that one particular spot was known as Clwt y Ddawns (the dancing place). The fact that some manuscripts name the popular tune to which particular poems are to be sung suggests that she also sang her poems to her own harp accompaniment. No doubt these poems were patterned on such tunes, which would facilitate oral composition while she was engaged on other tasks about the house and farm. Nine poems by her survive, a high score for a Welshwoman before the nineteenth century. At least two of these poems were included in a manuscript volume, 'Llyfr Coch Angharad James', whose present whereabouts is unknown, but whose list of contents, copied by Griffith Williams (Gutun Peris), in 1804, reveals that she

had had access to exemplars of work from the middle ages onwards, including a *cywydd* by the late medieval woman poet Gwerful Mechain. Angharad James was named by Lewis Morris as one of only two women owners of Welsh manuscripts in a list he compiled around 1740, the other being the poet and scribe Margaret Davies (*c.*1700–1785?), who knew and copied work by her.

James's own poems reflect her life experiences. Those in a light-hearted vein include a lively dialogue with her younger sister Began (Margaret), debating whether a younger or an older man makes the best husband, and an invitation to her friend Alis Wiliam of Dolwyddelan to visit her at Cwm Penamnen. In contrast, she also composed touching elegies for her husband and for their son Dafydd, who died at the age of sixteen in 1729, and a poem sadly contemplating giving up the tenancy of her home as she struggled to make ends meet. Copies of her poems can be found in NL Wales, MS 9B, MS 436B, Tanycastell MS 13, J. Glyn Davies MS 25, and Cwrtmawr MS 463B; and Cardiff Central Library, Cardiff MS 64.

James died at Cwm Penamnen in her seventy-third year and was buried on 25 August 1749 in Dolwyddelan parish church, where her gravestone still survives.

CERIDWEN LLOYD-MORGAN

Sources C. Lloyd-Morgan, 'Oral composition and written transmission: Welsh women's poetry from the middle ages and beyond', *Trivium*, 26 (1991), 89–102 • O. Thomas, *Cofiant John Jones, Talsarn* (1874), 24–6 • E. Thomas, *Hynafiaethau, hynodion a hanes Dolwyddelan* (1861) • E. C. Roberts, *Dolwyddelan a'i chymeriadau hynod* [n.d., 1924?] • N. M. Jenkins, '"A'i gyrfa megis Gwerful": bywyd a gwaith Angharad James', *Llên Cymru*, 24 (2001), 79–112 • NL Wales, Facsimile MS 500 [facsimile of annotated pages from the subject's family Bible] • J. E. Jones, 'Bedd Angharad James o Benamnen, Dolwyddelan', *Trafodion Cymdeithas Hanes Sir Gaernarfon*, 46 (1984), 130–37 • Llyfr Gutun Peris, NL Wales, MS 10257B • parish register, St Gwyddelan, Dolwyddelan, 25 Aug 1749 [burial]

James, Arthur Lloyd (1884–1943), phonetician, was born at Pentre, Glamorgan, on 21 June 1884, the son of William James, mining engineer and colliery manager, and his wife, Rachel, *née* Clark. He was educated at Llanelli, the Pontypridd pupil teachers' centre, and University College, Cardiff, where he graduated with third-class honours in French in 1905. After a year or two of teaching he went as an advanced student to Trinity College, Cambridge, and in 1910 graduated in medieval and modern languages, specializing in Old French and Provençal. He then taught French and phonetics at the Islington Training College until the First World War, during which he served with the Royal Engineers.

In 1920 Lloyd James accepted a lectureship in phonetics at University College, London, and entered upon a career of much distinction. He concentrated at first upon the phonetics of English and French, but soon branched out into such fields as the phonetics of Hausa, Yoruba, and other languages of west Africa that he studied with native speakers who happened to be in London. In 1925 he took a prominent part in work for the proposed International Institute for African Languages and Cultures and he had some share in its decision to work especially upon the unification of the orthographies of African languages on a phonetic basis.

In 1927 Lloyd James became the first head of the department of phonetics set up by the School of Oriental Studies in the University of London. This appointment, which began as a lectureship, was raised to a readership in 1930 and a professorship in 1933. It gave Lloyd James much scope for the exercise of his linguistic talents, and the department, which was greatly strengthened by the addition of Ida Ward in 1932, soon became a large and important adjunct to the language departments. A great many students were given an insight into modern methods of acquiring proficiency in exotic spoken languages, and much valuable research into the phonetics of Asian and African languages was carried out.

Lloyd James published a number of works on phonetics, including a very scholarly *Historical Introduction to French Phonetics* (1929). He contributed the article on pronunciation to the fourteenth edition of the *Encyclopaedia Britannica* and he was a frequent broadcaster on speech and language. He also lectured at the Royal Academy of Dramatic Art (1924–33) and acted as adviser on phonetics to the Linguaphone Institute. His wide interests led him, among other things, to undertake some pioneer investigations into the intelligibility of recorded speech, and to devise some phonetic tests for telephone operators. His main work outside the university, however, was done for the BBC. He was, for the term of its existence (1926–40), honorary secretary of the corporation's advisory committee on spoken English, which considered and reported upon words and proper names of difficult or disputed pronunciation. He assembled the evidence, with the assistance of some of the corporation's regular staff, and edited the committee's findings in a series of remarkable booklets on such topics as words of doubtful pronunciation and the place names of the UK. His success in this task led to his appointment in 1929 to train announcers and to act generally as an adviser to the corporation on points of pronunciation not dealt with by the committee. He showed particular ingenuity in devising suitable Anglicizations for those foreign personal and place names with which announcers are apt to be confronted at short notice. In 1938 his position was accorded the official title of linguistic adviser to the BBC. On the outbreak of war he became adviser on radio-telephonic speech to the Royal Air Force and investigated problems involved in transmitting speech between air and ground. He was a member of the Philological Society, the Modern Languages Association, and the International Phonetics Association.

On 11 August 1914 Lloyd James had married Elsie Winifred (1888/9–1941), daughter of Luther Owen, a professional musician, of Llanelli. She was a fellow of the Royal Academy of Music and well known as a violinist. Their only child, David Owen Lloyd James, joined the staff of the BBC. The marriage was a particularly happy one until during the stress and anxieties of war Lloyd James fell a victim to depressive insanity. Fearing separation from, and hardship to, his wife, he took her life in 1941 and his own, in Broadmoor Criminal Lunatic Asylum, Crawthorne, Berkshire, on 24 March 1943. He had been a man of much sociability and highmindedness, with a passion for punctuality and a scrupulous regard for truth.

DANIEL JONES, *rev.* JOHN D. HAIGH

Sources personal knowledge (1959) · *WWW*, 1941–50 · b. cert. · m. cert. · *CGPLA Eng. & Wales* (1943) · d. cert.
Archives SOUND presumed BBC, 'Talking films on speech: King's English'
Likenesses photograph, UCL, department of phonetics and linguistics
Wealth at death £8117 1s. 4d.: administration, 24 June 1943, *CGPLA Eng. & Wales*

James, Bartholomew (1752–1828), naval officer and writer, was born at Falmouth on 28 December 1752, the son of Richard and Joan James. In 1765 he was entered on the cutter *Folkestone* stationed at Bideford; afterwards he served in the *West Indian* and *Lisbon* before being appointed in May 1771 to the sloop *Falcon*, going to the West Indies. After an active commission he came home in the *Falcon* as acting lieutenant in August 1774; but his promotion not being confirmed he again entered the *Folkestone*, and in the following January he moved to the sloop *Wolf* at Penzance.

In October 1775 Bartholomew joined the frigate *Orpheus* which sailed for North America on 30 October and in which he took part in the reduction of New York. In September 1776 he was taken into the *Chatham* by Sir Peter Parker with whom he sailed for Jamaica in January 1778. On arriving on the station James was made acting lieutenant, and appointed to command the *Dolphin*. On 10 August he fell in with a squadron of French frigates, was captured, and sent into Cape François. After eight months he was exchanged and sent back to Port Royal, where the admiral presented him with a commission as lieutenant of the sloop *Porcupine*, which in October 1779 took part in the reduction of the fort of Omoa in the Gulf of Honduras and captured considerable amounts of treasure. This was lost *en route* to England in February 1780.

Later that year in the *Charon* (Captain Thomas Symonds) James took part in the capture of the *Comte d'Artois* (64 guns) and in the defence of Yorktown (1781) before his ship was destroyed. He was taken prisoner following the surrender of Lord Cornwallis; after being sent to England he was exchanged in March 1782. On 19 March 1783 James married Henrietta Pender of Falmouth; they had two daughters, including Henrietta, who became the wife of the admiral Thomas Bull Sulivan.

After a period ashore, James obtained command of a merchant ship in 1785 in which he served principally in the West Indian trade until March 1793, when, hearing news of the war with France, he fitted out a small tender of 40 tons and went to warn outward bound merchant ships. In the summer of 1793 he returned to England, where his ship was taken up by government as a transport for the expedition to the West Indies, and he himself appointed a transport agent and sent to Martinique, the reduction of which was completed by 25 March 1794. Three days later, James was appointed agent for the sale of the produce of the island, which brought him about £3000 in six weeks.

In September 1795 James formed part of the force under Admiral Sir John Jervis in the Mediterranean. Moved to the *Dromedary* early in 1797, James took Commissioner Isaac Coffin to Lisbon. In February 1797 the *Dromedary* and the frigate *Southampton* were chased by a large Spanish fleet. The *Dromedary* was ordered to proceed at once to the Tagus, where James was moved into the brig *Corso* (24 guns), and on 23 March he sailed from Lisbon, with orders to cruise off Tenerife as long as his water and provisions lasted. After a singularly adventurous cruise in which he narrowly escaped capture by the Spanish, he returned to Gibraltar. In January 1798 he was employed in cruising and the protection of trade on the coasts of Spain and Africa as far as Tunis, and he completed his sea service in the following year. From 1803 James had command for some time of the sea fencibles on the coast of Cornwall; but otherwise lived in retirement near Falmouth where he died on 23 May 1828. In addition to his life at sea, James kept a journal which provides insight into the daily life of the navy and for which he gained a degree of fame. The journal was lent by James's family to the children's writer William Henry Giles Kingston who used it to construct his story *Hurricane Hurry* (1874), and it was subsequently edited and published by the naval historian John Laughton in 1896.   J. K. LAUGHTON, rev. NICHOLAS TRACY

Sources *Journal of Rear-Admiral Bartholomew James, 1752–1828*, ed. J. K. Laughton and J. Y. F. Sullivan, Navy Records Society, 6 (1896) · *IGI*

James, Carwyn Rees (1929–1983), rugby player and coach, was born on 2 November 1929 in Rose Villa, Heol yr Ysgol, Cefneithin, Carmarthenshire, the youngest of the four children of Michael James (1891–1972), coalminer, of Beulah, Cardiganshire, and his wife, Anne, *née* Davies (1903–1974). Between 1941 and 1948 he attended Gwendraeth secondary school, where he achieved notable scholastic and sporting success. Nurtured in the performance culture of chapel and eisteddfod, he acquired an early confidence in public speaking matched by written fluency in Welsh, his first language, and English. He was a stylish cricketer and, out of school, an accomplished snooker player, but it was his exceptional ability at rugby that privileged him in a community where athletic and academic prowess were equally esteemed. The captain of the school fifteen as well as head prefect, he won six schoolboy rugby union caps for Wales in 1947 and 1948, and captained the side in the latter year. Lithe and willowy, he was never a robust defender, but his poise, neat footwork, assured handling of the ball, bewildering sidestep, and aptitude for kicking drop goals marked him out for senior honours.

In 1948 James proceeded to the University College of Wales, Aberystwyth, from where he emerged in 1952 with an honours degree in Welsh, a teaching diploma, and the experience of having played both at college and the more bruising local club level; the students' magazine acclaimed 'a born footballer whom one does not hesitate to put in the line of classic Welsh half-backs … pivot of the

attack and tactician-in-chief' (*Y Ddraig*, 34). The two years of national service that followed enabled him to parade his rugby ability on a wider stage and to learn Russian, an asset used by Swansea rugby club when they invited him to join them as player and linguist on a pioneering visit behind the iron curtain to Romania in August 1954.

After briefly teaching at Queen Elizabeth Grammar School, Carmarthen, in 1957 James moved to Llandovery College, an independent boarding-school, where for the next twelve years he taught Welsh and assisted in the coaching of cricket and, especially, rugby. He instilled in his charges an appreciation of the aesthetic beauty as well as the effectiveness of the handling game, where the ball is received and transferred with speed and accuracy to stretch the defence and generally run the opposition off their feet. He was also now in a position to play for Llanelli Rugby Football Club, where his attacking skills and penchant for dropping goals drew the attention of the national selectors. Had his career not run parallel with that of the more durable Cliff Morgan, James would have earned more than the two full Welsh caps he won in 1958, when he made his début with a smartly taken drop goal in the 9–3 win over Australia in January.

A notable player in his own right, it was as an inspiring coach that Carwyn James became a household name in world rugby. In 1967 he coached a west Wales fifteen to perform creditably against the touring All Blacks; two years later and now a lecturer at Trinity College, Carmarthen, he began coaching the Llanelli club, and thus positioned himself to bid for the post of coach to the 1971 British Lions tour of Australia and New Zealand, which he duly secured. The Lions had never won a tour series in New Zealand, and several factors contributed to the 1971 team's historic achievement of two wins, one defeat, and one draw. These included the cornucopia of talent in the back division, built around the Welsh nucleus of such legendary players as Gareth Edwards, Barry John, Gerald Davies, and J. P. R. Williams, reinforced by the brilliance of David Duckham (England) and Michael Gibson (Ireland); the mild New Zealand winter, which camouflaged the Lions' vulnerability at forward while releasing their outstanding backs; and the astute captaincy of John Dawes, and the canny management of Doug Smith. But unquestionably the architect of victory was Carwyn James, whose imaginative coaching methods, meticulous pre-tour preparation, acute analytical rugby brain, deft player management, and emphasis on fast, skilful, attacking rugby won the admiration of even the crustiest New Zealand critics. The following year British audiences saw James work his magic at first hand when on 31 October 1972 he coached his own club, Llanelli, in their centenary year, to a famous 9–3 victory over the visiting All Blacks at Stradey Park, and then inspired the Barbarians, essentially the Lions side of the previous year, to recapture their scintillating brand of open rugby to beat the New Zealanders 23–11 in the last game of the tour in Cardiff on 27 January 1973.

Under James's enlightened coaching Llanelli won Welsh rugby's challenge cup four times in succession in the mid-1970s, then, during a two-year stint in Italy (1977–9), his unfailing Midas touch turned Rovigo into Italian champions. In 1973 he quit the safe haven of Trinity College for the less predictable open seas of freelance journalism and broadcasting, recognizing full well that not only was a realistic academic career now beyond him, but so were any ambitions he might have harboured of coaching the Welsh national side. Petty jealousies, parochialism, and wariness of his intellect reinforced a suspicion of his political views, which he took no pains to disguise: a passionate lover of the Welsh language and its literature, he stood for Plaid Cymru at the Llanelli constituency in the 1970 general election, where he garnered a respectable 8657 votes (about the size of the average crowd at Stradey Park); he rejected the offer of an OBE, and he refused to watch Llanelli—though he coached them—play the Springboks on their controversial 1969 tour of the UK. These factors militated against his admittance to the higher reaches of the Welsh Rugby Union and his becoming national coach, a post he applied for by characteristically setting out terms he knew to be totally unacceptable to the union, but the only ones on which he would consider it. Ironically, Welsh rugby was rescued from the gloom into which it sank in the 1980s and 1990s by appointing as coach the New Zealander Graham Henry, who was not only granted the free hand in selection that had been refused to James, but who also openly acknowledged the inspiration of James's brilliant coaching of the 1971 Lions as a crucial influence on his own rugby thinking.

Carwyn James, a cultivated, sensitive, and essentially private single man in the public, masculine, and frequently insensitive world of rugby football, lost the struggle to contain his personal torments and the constant irritation of a painful skin disease when he died of a heart attack in the Krasnapolsky Hotel in Amsterdam on 10 January 1983. His funeral took place at Cefneithin on 17 January, followed by cremation at Morriston, near Swansea.   GARETH WILLIAMS

Sources A. Richards, *Carwyn: a personal memoir* (1984) · G. Williams, 'Carwyn James', *Heart and soul: the character of Welsh rugby*, ed. H. Richards, P. Stead, and G. Williams (1998) · J. Jenkins, ed., *Carwyn* (1983) [in Welsh] · J. Reason, ed., *The Lions speak* (1972) · *Y Ddraig, the magazine of the University College of Wales, Aberystwyth*, 72/2 (summer 1950) · *The Times* (11 Jan 1983) · *The Times* (14 Jan 1983) · *The Times* (18 Jan 1983) · private information (2004) [D. James]
Archives FILM Broadcasting House, Cardiff, BBC Library | SOUND Broadcasting House, Cardiff, BBC Library
Likenesses photographs, repro. in J. B. G. Thomas, *The illustrated history of Welsh rugby* (1980)
Wealth at death £72,042: probate, 15 March 1983, *CGPLA Eng. & Wales*

James, Charles (d. 1821), army officer and writer, was present in Lisle during the outbreak of the French Revolution, and travelled through France as it spread. He chronicled these events in his *Audi alteram Partem: an extenuation of the conduct of the French revolutionists from 14 July 1789 to 17 January 1793*. He served as a captain in the western regiment of Middlesex militia (later the 2nd Royal West Middlesex militia) in 1793–4, and as captain in the North York militia from 1795 to 1797. On 1 March 1806 he was appointed a

major of the corps of artillery drivers attached to the Royal Artillery. When that rank was abolished in 1812 he was placed on half pay. James died in London on 14 April 1821.

James was a very productive writer, and his many works covered a wide variety of subjects. His poetry included *Petrarch to Laura: a Poetical Epistle* (1787), and a two-volume collection of poems published in 1789, dedicated to the prince of Wales, including pieces written at school in 1775 and at Liège in 1776. Among his military works were *Hints Founded on Facts, or, A View of our Several Military Establishments* (1791), a *Regimental Companion, Containing a Relation of the Duties of every Officer in the British Army* (1799), and a *New and Enlarged Military Dictionary*, with a glossary of French terms (1802). He also wrote volumes advocating the need to improve the regulation of the militia, and on the army's system of court-martial charges.
    H. M. CHICHESTER, *rev.* S. KINROSS

Sources *Army List* · *BL cat.*
Archives BL, corresp. and papers, Add. MS 64951 · NAM, corresp. and papers
Likenesses J. S. Agar, stipple (aged forty-nine; after J. Russell), NPG · M. Bovi, stipple (after J. Russell), BM, NPG

James, Charles Wilson Brega (1906–1978), fashion designer, was born on 18 July 1906 at Agincourt House, Camberley, Surrey, the son of Ralph Ernest Haweis James and his wife, Louise Enders Brega (b. 1874). His father came from a Cornish landowning family, and was a professional soldier, engineer, and instructor at the Royal Military College, Sandhurst. His mother was descended from one of the wealthy founding families of Chicago. Charles James, as he was later to be known, was to retain his English nationality together with the right to reside permanently in America.

After a childhood spent mainly in London, James attended New Beacon School, Sevenoaks (1914–18), and Hopkins School, Lake Placid, New York, USA (1919), before a brief spell at Harrow School in 1919. Although he achieved a certain artistic success, his career at Harrow was terminated after a year for what his father described as idleness, sloppy friends, and sexual escapades. James then spent a year in the architect's office of Samuel Insull, the utilities magnate of Chicago, for whom his father worked. Despite spending much of his time making batik scarves, he absorbed enough of the principles of technical design to provide a credible basis for his subsequent assumption of the role of architect or engineer of fashion.

James's career in fashion began in 1926. Working with a friend, Mme de Launay, he opened a millinery shop, Boucheron, in Chicago, moving briefly to New York in 1929, *en route* for London. He had expanded his range to include garments, made to order as well as retail. Mary Lewis, the fashion buyer for Best & Co., New York, had become a steady patron and was subsequently guarantor of his US work permit. His first London atelier, at 1 Bruton Street, lasted only a year before liquidation, and in the pre-war years James divided his time between London, Paris, and New York.

James's skill with cutting and draping was well suited to the modes of the time and despite constant financial insecurity, eccentric business methods, and unreliable delivery times, both his retail and his wholesale clientele steadily increased. Two of his creations in particular were noteworthy: the Ribbon cape, created in 1937 at a time of financial crisis, and made from Colcombet of St Étienne; old stock ribbons, and his padded jacket of 1938, referred to by Salvador Dalí as the first soft sculpture. Both items became fashion classics, unquestionably original as well as wearable.

In 1939 James left for New York where his first significant commercial association was with Elizabeth Arden, of the cosmetics and fashion firm. In 1944 the partnership was dissolved amid complaints of design piracy from James and of extravagance from Arden. Subsequent contracts with many of the main American wholesale clothing manufacturers tended to run a similar course, despite the undoubted style and popularity of James's work. A lawsuit with Samuel Winston in 1954, though won by James, proved particularly costly to him. James's range was wide, from couture to supermarket uniforms, children's clothes to jewellery and furniture. His dress forms to a revised module were a cherished project. Original models were sold through quality department stores in the US and UK.

Wealthy, socially notable private clients such as Mrs Millicent Huttleston Rogers and Mrs Randolph William Hearst doubled as patrons, ever willing to pay by retainer, and regarding the clothes as works of art, lending them for exhibition and donating them to museums. They shared Cristobal Balenciaga's opinion that James was 'America's greatest couturier, the world's best and only dressmaker who has raised it from an applied art to a pure art form' (Coleman, 9).

The three-dimensional aspect of clothing, the interactions of body mass, movement, and textile, were salient features of James's designs. A significant innovation was his development of master patterns, used in a number of garment contexts over many years. A perfectionist, he developed this aspect with obsessional consistency, and he later claimed that a sleeve had cost him $20,000 and three years' work. His method involved drawing, flat-patterning, and draping on the model and on occasion on himself. He was tireless in exposition, to students, in films, and in exhibitions; and at his insistence preparatory work was given to museums, together with the clothes to which it relates. The designs were recorded in a series of drawings by Antonio Lopez.

James's prices were high and, despite his own claim to be the most expensive dressmaker in the world (Coleman, 84), James never attained the $500,000 turnover that in 1950 he had estimated as necessary for the maintenance of a design studio. There were injections of family money but even chameleon-like changes of corporate identity proved inadequate to protect him from requests for back-taxes, and by 1964 he had retired from the commercial fashion world.

Nevertheless, the New York years ensured James's recognition as a designer of great originality. In 1950 he received the Coty fashion award for 'Great mastery of colour and artistry in draping'; in 1953 the Niemann Marcus award for 'Distinguished services to the industry'; in 1962 a citation from Woolens and Worsteds of America Inc.; and in 1975 the first Guggenheim fine art fellowship awarded to a fashion designer.

James had various male partners but on 8 July 1954 he married Nancy Leigh Gregory; they had a son and a daughter. In 1961 they parted, the family remaining in Chicago and Charles James returning to New York, where his last years were spent sporadically supported by former clients in an apartment in the atmospheric Chelsea Hotel. Cared for by his friend and associate Homer Layne, James was tirelessly willing to work with students and discuss new projects. Despite long-term ill health, the legacy of drug use, diabetes, and kidney disease, he remained superficially unchanged, small, spare, always dark haired, restlessly energetic, endlessly talkative, unforgetful of slights or triumphs, until his death from pneumonia at the Chelsea Hotel, New York on 23 September 1978.

Although a projected autobiography was not completed, the Brooklyn Museum in 1982 organized a major retrospective of his work, and a pioneering study by E. A. Coleman, *The Genius of Charles James*, appeared in 1988.

M. GINSBURG

Sources E. A. Coleman, *The genius of Charles James* (1988) · M. D. Candee, ed., *Current Biography Yearbook* (1956) · personal information (2004) · *Colliers Magazine* (20 Sept 1947)
Archives Brooklyn Museum, New York · priv. coll. · Smithsonian Institution, Washington, DC, National Museum of American History · V&A, department of textiles and dress
Likenesses C. Beaton, photograph, 1932, Sotheby's Collection, Bond Street, London

James, Clara [Claire] (*d.* in or after **1948**), trade unionist and community activist, was born in obscurity in the 1860s: according to her patron, Lilian Gilchrist Thompson, she was orphaned as a child and brought up by an alcoholic employee of her father's. She first came to notice as an activist in the industrial world in 1889, when she joined the Women's Trade Union Association (WTUA). The WTUA was formed in the East End of London after the success of the Bryant and May match girls' strike of 1888, with the aim of establishing self-managed and self-supported unions for women in trades neglected by the more skills-focused Women's Trade Union League. Following dismissal from her job in the confectionery trade for joining a union, James became assistant secretary of the WTUA and a union organizer. As secretary of the Confectioners' Union, she assisted Clementina Black and John Burns to resolve the chocolate makers' strike in 1890. This union failed in 1892, the WTUA annual report suggesting that its demise was partly due to employers' opposition and partly to the notorious difficulty of organizing young girls: juveniles were increasingly employed in this trade. In 1891 Clara James and her friend Amie Hicks were appointed as delegates to the royal commission on labour. They were the only women to give evidence, and they both spoke in favour of women factory inspectors, stipulating that these inspectors should be working women, not ladies. James was also for some time the only woman delegate on the London Trades Council.

Clara James worked as a typist to earn her living, until in 1892 a personal admirer, Lilian Gilchrist Thompson, promised the WTUA a subscription of £70 a year for two years to employ Clara James as an investigator. By 1894 the WTUA was in difficulties, and its fifth annual report noted that Clara James had been unable to organize the box-makers, adding that 'The collapse of the Union did not conclude Miss James' efforts among the boxmakers. She has been constantly among them … and gathered much information which will … be put into a systematic form'. In November 1894 the WTUA was re-formed as the Women's Industrial Council (WIC); James served on the investigation and organization committees. Thompson, who described James as a lively, persuasive personality, paid for her to train as a gymnastics teacher after the two years' subscriptions had expired. James had set up her first working girls' club under the WTUA, where among other activities she organized extremely successful musical drill classes: according to the WTUA's fifth annual report, these classes were emulated by the People's Palace in London's Mile End Road. Clubs for working girls were to occupy much of the rest of her life.

In 1899 the WIC set up the Clubs Industrial Association, which arranged lectures on industrial subjects (including the Factory Acts), social meetings, and citizenship classes for affiliated working girls' clubs. James used her popular physical drill classes to gain the trust of the working girls, and to persuade them to help the women factory inspectors to convict employers in breach of the Factory Acts. The classes in themselves were beneficial to girls physically constrained by factory life, and offered both fun and better health. Margaret Bondfield, later a Labour cabinet minister, was among her pupils. By 1909 James had her own organization, separate from the Clubs Industrial Association, called Working Girls at Play, based at 21 Rochester Square, London: she was the overall organizer of twenty-two clubs and hundreds of girls all over London. Ill health eventually prevented her from continuing as a teacher, and she established a holiday home on Canvey Island. At first it was little more than a campsite, but it was eventually replaced by a house with a self-supporting market garden. From 1925 James served as a parish councillor, justice of the peace, and school governor. She was still alive and in her eighties in 1948 when her former pupil Margaret Bondfield wrote her autobiography.

GERRY HOLLOWAY

Sources L. G. Thompson, *Sidney Gilchrist Thomas: an invention and its consequences* (1940) · M. G. Bondfield, *A life's work* [1948] · J. Bellamy and J. A. Schmiechen, 'Hicks, Amelia (Amy) Jane', *DLB*, vol. 4 · E. Mappen, *Helping women at work: the Women's Industrial Council, 1889–1914* (1985) · C. Black, 'The chocolatemakers' strike', *Fortnightly Review*, 54 (1890), 305–14 · *Women's Trade Union Association Annual Report* (1889–94) · *Women's Industrial Council Annual Report* (1894–1910) · 'Royal commission on labour: minutes of evidence, group C', *Parl. papers* (1892), 35.1060, C. 6708-VI · C. James, 'Working Girls' Club', *Working Girls At Play Reformers Yearbook* (1909), 202 · BLPES, Women's Industrial Council MSS, WIC Box DD2

James, Cyril Lionel Robert (1901–1989), historian and writer, was born on 4 January 1901 in the village of Caroni, Trinidad, the eldest of three children of Robert Alexander James and his wife, Ida Elizabeth (Bessie) Rudder. His paternal grandfather and both maternal grandparents had been migrants from Barbados. His father was a schoolmaster and later headmaster; his mother's love of English literature was a crucial formative influence on James: Shakespeare, Dickens, and the possibly more surprising figure of Thackeray remained aesthetic touchstones throughout his life. Known to friends as Nello, in print, when not using pseudonyms, he was always C. L. R.

The family moved during James's childhood to the larger settlement of Tunapuna—home also to his friend Malcolm *Nurse (1902–1959), subsequently a noted writer and politician under the name George Padmore—and his early education was in his father's own schoolrooms. His was by local standards a comparatively prosperous—indeed, under the influence of the sternly aspiring Robert James, a rigidly conventional—upbringing. But it was also a childhood in a colonial society where slavery remained a living memory, and where people of the James family's colour could achieve even their modestly middle-class status only by exceptional ability and hard work. James certainly had ability, but his application to schoolwork was more questionable: to his father's distress, he increasingly preferred reading and writing fiction, or watching and playing cricket, to his studies. In 1910 he won a scholarship to Queen's Royal College, the island's most prestigious school; but early top grades were not sustained as the teenage James carved his own idiosyncratic path. He knew he did not want to be a teacher or civil servant, or to apply to Oxford or Cambridge, as his father intended, but to be a writer. On graduating from Queen's Royal College, although he found employment as a schoolmaster and private tutor, this was merely a means of paying the rent while he pursued his real interests.

James entered the literary circles centred on pioneer Trinidadian authors Albert Gomes and Alfred Mendes, and first achieved public notice with a short story, 'La divina pastora', published in 1927. Other short stories, essays, and then a novel, *Minty Alley* (written in the summer of 1928, but not published until 1936) followed. His fiction reflected fascination with the world his family spurned, that of the Trinidadian poor and their 'barrack-yard' homes. This was linked, too, with a slowly awakening political consciousness. James became sympathetic to the Trinidad Workingmen's Association and its charismatic leader, Captain A. A. Cipriani: a biography of Cipriani was to be his first published book (1932). From 1927 he was briefly, and unhappily, married to Juanita Samuel Young.

Despite his modest literary success James found colonial Trinidad an increasingly restricting environment. In 1932 came his chance to break from it. He had become friendly with local cricketing hero Learie Constantine,

Cyril Lionel Robert James (1901–1989), by Snowdon, 1983

who had moved to England to play professionally for Lancashire County Cricket Club. Constantine, needing a collaborator for his autobiography *Cricket and I* (1933), invited James to join him there. The solidly working-class Lancashire mill town of Nelson, where the Constantine family lived, seemed an improbable new location for the aspiring Caribbean intellectual. Yet it prompted the next great turn in James's career. Through Constantine, whose broad interests included left-wing politics, James made the acquaintance of local socialist and trade union activists. And from this there rapidly grew an enthusiasm for Marxist, then specifically for Trotskyist, political theory and activity.

James moved to London at the start of 1934 and, while scraping a living as a cricket correspondent for the *Manchester Guardian* and other papers, plunged into political action. He joined both the Independent Labour Party (and, soon, the Trotskyist faction that operated within it) and the small group of West Indian and African émigrés who were agitating from London for colonial independence. To his surprise he discovered that a key member of the latter circle, the pseudonymous George Padmore, was in fact his cousin Malcolm. James also began research in London and Paris for what was to be his most famous book, *The Black Jacobins*, a study of the Haitian revolution, published in 1938. It was not only a major history of those events, but in effect a political manifesto for forthcoming anti-colonial revolt and for Pan-Africanism. This was only the highest peak in James's substantial range of literary activity during the later 1930s: he also published his novel *Minty Alley* (1936), a polemical history of the Communist International, *World Revolution* (1937), a short but pioneering *History of Negro Revolt* (1938), a translation of Boris Souvarine's *Stalin* (1939), numerous political articles, and

of course cricket journalism, while his Haitian work additionally produced a play, *Toussaint L'Ouverture*, performed at the Westminster Theatre in 1936, with Paul Robeson in the title role.

In 1938 James was a delegate to the founding conference of Trotsky's Fourth International in Paris, and then travelled to the United States: partly, it seems, on Trotsky's urging, partly driven by his own restlessness and curiosity. He intended to return to England in time for the 1939 cricket season; but the outbreak of war in Europe extended an American sojourn that was eventually to last fifteen years. For much of that period, he was a full-time political activist: first, for the main US Trotskyist group, the Socialist Workers' Party; then, after seceding from it, working with an even smaller group of like-minded friends in what was labelled the 'Johnson–Forest tendency', 'Johnson' was James's own 'party name', 'Freddie Forest' that of Russian émigré Raya Dunayevskaya. James wrote a mass of political material during these years, both alone and in collaboration with Dunayevskaya and their colleague Grace Lee. Little of this writing has retained lasting interest except among devotees of the minutiae of ultra-left politics; but it included James's *Notes on Dialectics* (1948), an innovative work of Marxist philosophy. Still, James's capacious interests could not be confined in a single political mould: his American years also produced *Mariners, Renegades and Castaways* (1953), a study of Herman Melville, and the remarkable *American Civilization*. The latter, mainly drafted in 1949–50 but never fully completed and published only posthumously in 1992, was far ahead of its time in many ways; not least in its close analysis of 'popular culture'—cinema, comic-books, radio serials, mass-market fiction—as a key to understanding a society.

These were also crucial but turbulent years in James's personal life. In 1939 in Los Angeles he met and fell in love with the eighteen-year-old Constance Webb. It seemed a hopeless infatuation: not only did Constance initially not return his love, she was twenty years his junior, already married, and (still a significant, even dangerous, fact in the USA of the 1940s) she was white, he black. Gradually his affections came to be reciprocated, and he and Constance were married in May 1946. Their son, also C. L. R. James, known as Nobbie, was born in April 1949. Yet theirs remained a stormy relationship, which finally broke down in 1950–51, to James's lasting regret. Although in later life he was married a third time, to Selma Weinstein, there is no doubt that the relationship with Constance was the most important of his life. His many and long letters to her, posthumously published as *Special Delivery* (1996), are deeply poignant documents, as well as providing the most intimate available insight into the workings of James's mind.

In 1952, at the height of the USA's early cold war 'red scare', James was arrested for supposed passport violations, and interned on Ellis Island. The final draft of *Mariners, Renegades and Castaways* was written there, in prison, and included a desperate plea against the injustice of his position. Feeling squeezed between US authorities who called him a communist and communists who thought him a heretic, finally despairing of being able to regularize his resident status in the United States, he headed back to England in the autumn of 1953.

London was to remain James's usual home for the last thirty years of his life, although until the 1980s he travelled more widely than ever before. He was able to revisit the USA many times, lecturing and holding visiting professorships at various American universities. He was a welcome guest in Ghana, whose first post-independence leader Kwame Nkrumah had been a protégé of his—until he expressed publicly his growing disillusion with Nkrumah's authoritarianism. His *Nkrumah and the Ghana Revolution* (1977) traces the enthusiasm, the doubts, the disenchantment, and eventual denunciation—though even at the last James insisted on the political horizons that Nkrumah's project *could* have opened up. In 1958 he relocated to Trinidad, on the invitation of Prime Minister Eric Williams, who had been James's school pupil thirty years before. Williams made him editor of his party's newspaper, *The Nation*, but strains grew between James's radicalism and Williams's more conservative direction. The crisis came over Williams's decision to allow the US Navy to retain a base at Chaguaramas on the island; something James bitterly opposed. He resigned from *The Nation* in March 1960 and was expelled from the party in October, but remained in Trinidad for some time, writing and lecturing. From this period date his books *Modern Politics* (1960), *Party Politics in the West Indies* (1962), and perhaps the most important of his later works, *Beyond a Boundary* (1963), a meditation on the cultural and social meanings of cricket which also included substantial autobiographical elements.

James returned again to England in 1962 but continued to range widely from there, lecturing in Nigeria, Ghana, Tanzania, Uganda, Cuba, and Canada as well as the USA, covering the 1965 England cricket tour of the West Indies for the London *Observer* and *Times* (arriving in Trinidad to watch the test match there, he was promptly placed under house arrest by Eric Williams), and helping initiate the Sixth Pan-African Congress in 1974. He also continued to write extensively on politics, history, literature, and sport, but no substantial new books appeared after the mid-1960s. The major publications of his last years, notably three volumes of essays, *The Future in the Present* (1977), *Spheres of Existence* (1980), and *At the Rendezvous of Victory* (1984), mostly collected earlier work.

In 1981 James finally settled back in London, living in a tiny book-filled apartment at 165 Railton Road, Brixton, above the offices of the magazine *Race Today*, which was run by friends and admirers of his. They cooked and cared for an increasingly frail but still mentally vigorous man who, unable now to travel, instead received a stream of visitors from throughout the world in his bedroom. He continued to watch that world with a keen eye, welcoming with equal enthusiasm the Polish workers' 1980s uprising against communism, the emergence of a new generation of black women writers, and the West Indies' cricketing successes. He died at home of a chest infection, after a short illness, on 31 May 1989. His remains were returned to Trinidad and buried there, in his childhood hometown of Tunapuna.

Very few figures in twentieth-century Caribbean, or British, life and letters have matched the sheer range of James's interests and activities. Revolutionary and aesthete, novelist, historian, literary critic, philosopher, political analyst, and in many eyes the foremost of all writers on cricket, he seemed somehow to bring a unified, intensely personal sensibility to all these spheres. Even if many of his numerous projects never came to full fruition—the unfinished book *American Civilization*, and the autobiography he long planned but never really began, would surely have been his twin masterpieces—he still left a literary and political legacy of remarkable power and continuing influence. STEPHEN HOWE

Sources P. Buhle, ed., *C. L. R. James: his life and work* (1986) · P. Buhle, *C. L. R. James: the artist as revolutionary* (1988) · S. R. Cudjoe and W. E. Cain, eds., *C. L. R. James: his intellectual legacies* (1995) · G. Farred, ed., *Rethinking C. L. R. James* (1996) · A. Grimshaw, *The C. L. R. James archive: a reader's guide* (1991) · P. Henry and P. Buhle, eds., *C. L. R. James's Caribbean* (1992) · K. Worcester, *C. L. R. James: a political biography* (1996) · d. cert.
Archives U. Lond., corresp. and papers | FILM BFI NFTVA, 'C. L. R. James talks to Stuart Hall', Miras Productions, 30 April 1988 · BFI NFTVA, 'A tribute to C. L. R. James, 1901–89', Banding Productions, 21 June 1989 · BFI NFTVA, current affairs footage · BFI NFTVA, documentary footage | SOUND BL NSA, documentary recording
Likenesses Snowdon, photograph, 1983, priv. coll. [*see illus.*]
Wealth at death £21,245: probate, 20 Aug 1989, CGPLA Eng. & Wales

James, David (1839–1893), actor, was born in the Portuguese Jews' Hospital, Mile End Road, Stepney, London, on 13 July 1839, the son of Moses Belasco, a tailor, and his wife, Sophia, *née* Jacobs. He made his first appearance on the stage in a subordinate part at the Princess's Theatre under Charles Kean, but came to notice at the Royalty on 28 September 1863, as the first Mercury in F. C. Burnand's burlesque *Ixion*. The following year he was at the Strand, where he played in burlesque as King Francis in *The Field of the Cloth of Gold* and was the first Archibald Goode, a young lover in H. T. Craven's *Milky White*. In Burnand's *Windsor Castle* he was Will Somers, the Court Jester. Other parts of little importance succeeded, until his reputation rose with his performance on 5 February 1870 of Zekiel Homespun in a revival of Colman's *The Heir-at-Law*. Two months later, in partnership with Henry James Montague and Thomas Thorne, James undertook the management of the Vaudeville, but was unable to appear in the opening performances. Later at the Vaudeville he played Mr Jenkins in James Albery's *Two Roses*, was the original John Tweedie in *Tweedie's Rights*, and Bob Prout in *Apple Blossoms*. He performed Sir Benjamin Backbite in *The School for Scandal* and Goldfinch in Thomas Holcroft's *The Road to Ruin* with brilliant success, Sheridan's masterpiece being performed more than 400 times. His appearance as Perkyn Middlewick, in H. J. Byron's *Our Boys* on 16 January 1875, was his greatest success, and by 18 April 1879 the piece had been given more than a thousand times.

For the next two years James continued to play successful roles in farces and burlesques, including those of

Charles Wills and E. G. Lankester. After the partnership between James and Thorne had come to an end, James joined the Bancrofts at the Haymarket in 1881, playing Lovibond in Tom Taylor's *The Overland Route* and Eccles in T. W. Robertson's *Caste*. In 1885 he undertook the management of the Opera Comique, where he appeared as Blueskin in *Little Jack Sheppard* and Aristides Cassegrain in *The Excursion Train*. In 1886 he was at the Criterion in one of his most successful parts, John Dory in John O'Keeffe's *Wild Oats*, but gradually he had to reduce his performances as a result of failing eyesight. In 1890 he was the sole representative of the original cast when he reappeared in his old part in *Our Boys* at the Criterion. But he was then struck by a serious illness, which kept him from the stage for a year before he was able to take part, in 1893, in revivals at the Vaudeville of *Our Boys* and Lankester's *The Guv'nor*, in which he played Theodore Macclesfield. He was also seen as Moses in *The School for Scandal* and Samuel Coddle in J. B. Buckstone's *Married Life*. He died at his home, 32 St John's Wood Road, on 2 October 1893, leaving his son David James, junior, to continue on the stage. A Mrs David James, presumably his wife, died, aged thirty-eight, in 1881.

James was an admirable comedian in parts in which ripeness and humour were requisite. In John Dory, Perkyn Middlewick, Macclesfield, and other characters in which cheeriness and unction were requisite he had no equal. In his later years he also excelled in such straight parts as Eccles in *Caste* and Stout in Bulwer-Lytton's *Money*.

JOSEPH KNIGHT, *rev.* NILANJANA BANERJI

Sources E. Reid and H. Compton, eds., *The dramatic peerage* [1891]; rev. edn [1892] · C. E. Pascoe, ed., *The dramatic list* (1879) · C. E. Pascoe, ed., *The dramatic list*, 2nd edn (1880) · *The life and reminiscences of E. L. Blanchard, with notes from the diary of Wm. Blanchard*, ed. C. W. Scott and C. Howard, 2 vols. (1891) · P. Hartnoll, ed., *The Oxford companion to the theatre*, 3rd edn (1967) · P. Hartnoll, ed., *The concise Oxford companion to the theatre* (1972) · Hall, *Dramatic ports.* · *Era Almanack and Annual* (1882) · *The Theatre* [various years] · *Sunday Times* [various years] · personal knowledge (1901) · b. cert. · d. cert.

Likenesses Faustin, caricature, chromolithograph cartoon, 12 Dec 1874, NPG · newscutting, Aug 1880 · Elliott & Fry, carte-de-visite, woodburytype, NPG · S. P. Hall, pencil sketch, NPG · caricature, repro. in *Entr'acte* (21 May 1881) · photographs, NPG · prints and caricatures, Harvard TC

Wealth at death £41,594 12s. 1d.: probate, 11 Jan 1894, *CGPLA Eng. & Wales*

James, Edward (1569–1610?), Church of England clergyman and translator, was born in Glamorgan and proceeded to St Edmund Hall, Oxford, where he matriculated on 11 March 1586, when he was sixteen years old. He graduated bachelor of arts from Jesus College, Oxford, on 16 June 1589 and master of arts on 8 July 1592. He was elected a fellow of Jesus College, c.1589–90, and continued to hold his fellowship until c.1596. He appears to have benefited greatly from the patronage of that distinguished scholar, William Morgan, who arrived as bishop of Llandaff in 1595. During Morgan's episcopate James was quickly advanced to become vicar of Caerleon, Monmouthshire, on 2 February 1596, rector of Shirenewton, Monmouthshire, on 8 August 1597, rector of Llangattock-juxta-Usk, Monmouthshire, on 15 April 1598, and vicar of

Llangattock Feibion Afel, Monmouthshire, on 12 July 1599. Later, after Morgan had been translated from Llandaff to St Asaph in 1601, James became vicar of Llangattock-juxta-Neath, Glamorgan, on 23 July 1603 and chancellor of the diocese of Llandaff in 1606. There is no certainty as to the year of his death. J. C. Morrice gave it as 1610; but D. R. Phillips maintained that no successor was appointed until 1620.

The achievement for which James is best remembered is his translation into Welsh of the Book of Homilies, a sequence of twelve set English sermons intended to explain the basics of the Christian faith to congregations lacking a licensed preacher. James published his translation in 1606 under the title, *Pregethau a osodwyd allan trwy awdurdod i 'w darllein ymhob eglwys blwyf a phob capel er adailadaeth i 'r bobl annyscedig. Gwedi eu troi i 'r iaith Gymraeg trwy waith Edward James* ('Sermons set forth by authority to be read in every parish church and chapel for the edification of the unlearned people. Translated into the Welsh language by the work of Edward James'). He derived the inspiration for undertaking this task from his association with Bishop Morgan. The latter gathered about him at his episcopal palace in Matharn a small but industrious group of Welsh littérateurs, of whom the most prominent were Dr John Davies (later of Mallwyd) and Edward James. Although Morgan had left Llandaff in 1601, and was dead (1604) by the time the Welsh version of the homilies was published in 1606, the example of his classic biblical expression exercised a profound influence on James's own style. The latter seems to have owed nothing to the writings of the prolific school of prose authors of medieval Glamorgan. But his own elegant and idiomatic Welsh created a considerable impact not only on worshippers in Welsh churches but also on contemporary poets like Vicar Rhys Prichard. In spite of this, curiously enough, no new edition of the work appeared before 1817, when John Roberts, vicar of Tremeirchion, Flintshire (1775–1829), published his version. Later, in 1847, Morris Williams (Nicander; 1809–1874) ventured on a further edition.

GLANMOR WILLIAMS

Sources Foster, *Alum. Oxon.* · G. Williams, *Grym tafodau tân* (1984) · *DWB* · 'Clerical institutions Wales', NL Wales, MS 1626 · G. J. Williams, *Traddodiad llenyddol Morgannwg* (1948) · C. W. Lewis, 'The literary history of Glamorgan from 1550 to 1770', *Glamorgan county history*, ed. G. Williams, 4: *Early modern Glamorgan* (1974), 535–639 · J. C. Morrice, *Wales in the seventeenth century* (1918) · D. Rhys Phillips, *The history of the Vale of Neath* (1925)

James, Edward (1807–1867), barrister, was born at Manchester, the second son of Frederick William James, merchant, and his wife, Elizabeth, daughter of William Baldwin. He served in a Manchester warehouse for two years, where he gained knowledge which was later to be useful to him in conducting mercantile cases. He matriculated from Magdalen Hall, Oxford, on 3 November 1827, was a scholar of Brasenose from 1829 to 1832, and graduated BA in 1831, and MA in 1834. In 1835 he married Mary, daughter of Edward Mason Crossfield of Liverpool. He was called to the bar at Lincoln's Inn on 16 June the same year, and went on the northern circuit, of which he became leader in

1860. He settled in practice at Liverpool, and was assessor of the court of passage there from 1852 until his death. In November 1853 he was made queen's counsel. He became a bencher of his inn soon afterwards. In 1863 he was gazetted attorney-general and queen's serjeant of the county palatine of Lancaster. By that date he had moved to London. On 14 July 1865, he was returned for Manchester, as a Liberal, and sat until 1867, speaking occasionally on legal subjects and on the reform of the franchise.

James was a sound practical lawyer, with a considerable knowledge of commercial law, especially in its relation to shipping. Too prone to take offence, he brooked no interference in court, and often had unseemly disputes with the judges. James died of typhoid fever, while returning from a holiday in Switzerland, at the Hôtel du Louvre, Paris, on 3 November 1867, and was buried in Highgate cemetery, Middlesex, on 9 November. He was survived by his wife.   G. C. BOASE, *rev.* ERIC METCALFE

Sources *The Times* (5 Nov 1867), 7 · *The Times* (12 Nov 1867), 9 · Foster, *Alum. Oxon.* · *Law Times* (9 Nov 1867), 28 · *Law Times* (16 Nov 1867), 43–4 · *Law Magazine*, new ser., 24 (1867–8), 293–300 · *CGPLA Eng. & Wales* (1868)
Wealth at death under £16,000: probate, 3 Jan 1868, *CGPLA Eng. & Wales*

James, Edward Frank Willis (1907–1984), art patron, was born on 16 August 1907 at Greywalls, Gullane, East Lothian, the youngest of five children of William James (*d.* 1912), landed gentleman, and Evelyn Elizabeth (1869–1929), eldest daughter of Sir Charles Forbes, fourth baronet, of Castle Newe, Aberdeenshire. His father was of American extraction, his mother Scottish. During his mother's childhood she became friendly with the future king and queen, Edward VII and Alexandra. The king became Edward's godfather, and it was often rumoured that he was the father of the boy. Correspondence between Evelyn James and the royal couple suggests that this was most unlikely. There is, however, considerable evidence that Colonel John (Dosie) Brinton may have been Edward's real father; William James was probably left impotent after a severe attack of mumps about 1889. However, James never mentioned that William might not have been his father.

William James died when Edward was only four, leaving him in the hands of the most demanding and possessive of mothers; his childhood and adolescence were eased only by the kindness of Dosie Brinton. Edward was sent to Le Rosey, a private school in Switzerland, and was brought home to attend crammers to prepare him for the Eton College entrance exam. He was there from 1920 to 1924, and won the Geoffrey Gunther memorial drawing prize, presented to him with a flattering commendation by Roger Fry. James went up to Christ Church, Oxford, from 1926 to 1928. He first read history, but in his second year changed to modern languages, doing little of either and leaving Oxford without a degree. But he made his name by the flamboyant decoration of his rooms and by his lavish entertaining.

James published his first book of poems in 1926, the start of a long line of 'vanity' publications which appeared

Edward Frank Willis James (1907–1984), by Sir Cecil Beaton, 1920s

during the next thirty years. He became friends with John Betjeman, subsidizing the Oxford University student newspaper the *Cherwell*, which Betjeman then edited, and in 1931 publishing Betjeman's first book of poems, *Mount Zion*, under the imprint the James Press. Much of his energy at this time was spent in freeing himself from the interference of his mother. Her death in 1929 solved some of his problems, and shortly afterwards the inheritance of huge fortunes from his father and his late uncle Frank created many others.

In his new-found independence, aided by his great wealth, James's eccentricity began to emerge. During a short honorary posting at the British embassy in Rome he mainly distinguished himself by engineering a personal appointment with Mussolini, but the Duce, seeing his youth through the door, refused to see him. In 1928 he had a more fateful meeting in London with the beautiful dancer Ottilie Ethel (Tilly) Losch (*c.*1904–1975). This led to their disastrous marriage in New York in 1931, which deeply affected his future. It has been suggested that Losch agreed to the marriage for financial security, in the certain belief that Edward was homosexual and that the marriage could be rapidly terminated. Living in New York, Losch was overtly unfaithful to James, who sued for divorce; in 1934 she counter-sued for cruelty and homosexuality. There was not a shred of evidence to support her charges and she lost the case. In theory, society at that time ostracized husbands who divorced their wives. James complained that he was cut by old friends, but in reality he was moving into a more bohemian world of artists and composers, spending much of his time on the continent.

In 1931 James, already sensing a coldness in Losch, determined to win back her affections by creating a ballet in which she would be the prima ballerina. The project was finally realized when James met Georges Balanchine in Paris, struggling to launch his new ballet company. With James's money everyone's dream became a reality, and Les Ballets 1933 put on brief performances in Paris and London, with Losch in two starring roles. But she failed to attend the final party James gave for the company at the Savoy. His generous patronage of Les Ballets failed to win back Losch, but it did launch Balanchine on a meteoric career in America, an achievement James seems never to have noticed. However, the Frenchwomen like Marie-Laure de Noailles who had encouraged his patronage led him on to support several important contemporary French composers.

During the 1930s James spent more and more time travelling throughout Europe and renting the beautiful Villa Cimbrone above Ravello which he regarded as his home. He returned to England from time to time for brief stays at his London house, 35 Wimpole Street, bombed during the Second World War, and at West Dean Park and the smaller Monkton House, which Lutyens had built for William James on the nearby South Downs. This nomadic way of life continued thereafter until James's death: from Europe to America to Mexico, to a last few years in Italy.

In the early 1930s James became attracted by contemporary painting and above all by the surrealists and the work of Salvador Dalí. James said he first became aware of Dalí's painting when in 1932, staying with the Noailles at Hyères, he saw the artist's striking portrait of Marie-Laure. Exactly when he first met Dalí is uncertain but was probably at some time in 1933 at Hyères. James was much attracted by the young Catalan painter, and in December 1936 he signed a contract with Dalí, purchasing all the work he produced between June 1937 and June 1938. Dalí claimed later that Edward had all his best work. Dalí's paintings—others acquired at other times—became the crowning glory of James's collection of paintings; many of the best pictures were bought in the 1930s though he continued to collect until late in his life. He also had a fine collection of works by Magritte, de Chirico, Picasso, Paul Delvaux, Pavel Tchelitchew, and Leonora Carrington. James hated to be thought of as a collector—an academic, uncreative word. He liked to think of himself as a creative patron, to some extent involved in the creative process.

Thus motivated, late in 1935 James decided to refurbish Monkton, the Lutyens house he always thought 'too cottagey'. He took Dalí to the first meeting with the architects, Kit Nicholson and Hugh Casson. Casson had said that Dalí mixed the purple colour for the outside walls but thereafter had nothing to do with the 'surrealization' of the house, whose interior was put into the hands of a decorator, Norris Wakefield.

James continued to publish books of poetry and was deeply hurt by Stephen Spender's cutting review in the *New Statesman* of *The Bones of my Hand* (1938). Occasionally James did write moving poetry, but much of his work was too self-conscious. His inspiration in the late 1930s was the beautiful film star Ruth Ford who—though fond of Edward—like Losch was more interested in his wealth and certainly never intended to marry him. In February 1939 Edward sailed for New York, to help with some of Dalí's projects, and did not return to England until 1947.

In 1940 James decided to settle in California, but in May he visited the artists' colony, Taos, made famous by D. H. Lawrence in the 1920s, and was drawn to Los Angeles by the hope of friendship with Aldous Huxley and Gerald Heard, and, on his own written admission, by homosexuality. He found the latter but failed to make friends with Huxley, Heard, or other famous people in Los Angeles. He lived a desultory life in Los Angeles, moving from house to apartment to hotel. Always impractical, and obsessively clean, he covered every surface with tissues until, forced to dispose of them, he pushed them down the lavatory; when it was totally clogged, he tried to clear it by setting fire to the paper, and often the room.

In 1944, staying with a friend in Cuernavaca, James fell in love with Mexico and, more deeply, with Plutarco Gastelum in the local telegraph office. This passion for Mexico and Gastelum filled most of the last chapter of James's life. In 1945 he discovered Xilitla, and in 1947 they bought the first land there, adding to it later. Gastelum married, had children, and built a large house in the village, where Edward lodged in one wing. The mountains rose steeply on one side of their land, with waterfalls running down the slopes. James was enchanted and started by planting thousands of imported orchids. Next he introduced various species of animals but he soon learned that he could not keep them without cages. This led to the idea of enriching the exotic landscape with highly coloured surrealist architecture. With the help of local labour and the practical talents of Gastelum, the Entrance Tower, the Summer Palace, the Plaza San Eduardo, and several other polychromed concrete buildings began to rise high above the shade of the tropical forest. James's imagination created a place of intriguing beauty.

James had long been a tax exile, and his visits to England were limited. Strangely, while trying to curry favour with Huxley, he had written to ask him to help convert West Dean Park into some kind of artistic community. The house was then offered to several institutions, all of which refused it. In November 1964 James gave the house and much of his land to the Edward James Foundation, including the furnishings in the house and the greater part of his art collection. He kept Monkton with 500 acres. It was a munificent gift, but as yet the trust had no precise purpose. It was not until 1969 that Major-General Cyril Lloyd, formerly director-general of the City and Guilds, suggested to the trustees the foundation of an arts and crafts college, which opened in 1971. Strangely, James never mentioned the similar scheme he had suggested to Huxley.

James, at first enthusiastic, never appreciated that the college could not be launched without considerable capital, which could have been raised by the sale of furniture and pictures. When in England he sniped at the college from Monkton, but retired for most of the time to a friend's house in Perinaldo, near San Remo, until, dissatisfied with that, he moved to a nearby restaurant. In early autumn 1984 he became ill there and the ever-patient owner drove him to Paris, where he collapsed on reaching his hotel. Eventually he returned to a nursing home in San Remo where he died on 2 December 1984. He was buried, at his wish, in the arboretum at West Dean.

JOHN LOWE

Sources J. Lowe, *Edward James: poet, patron, eccentric: a surrealist life* (1991) · *A surreal life: Edward James, 1907–1984* (1998) [exhibition catalogue, Royal Pavilion, Brighton, 1998] · E. James, *Swans reflecting elephants: my early years*, ed. G. Melly (1982) · P. Purser, *Where is he now? The extraordinary worlds of Edward James* (1978)

Archives W. Sussex RO, archives · West Dean College, West Sussex archives

Likenesses C. Beaton, photograph, 1920–29, NPG [*see illus.*] · photographs, West Dean College, West Sussex

James, Edwin John (1812–1882), barrister, was the eldest son of John James, solicitor and secondary of the City of London (*d.* 1852), and his wife, Caroline, eldest daughter of Boyce Combe. He was educated at a private school. In early life he frequently acted at a private theatre in Gough Street, Gray's Inn Road, London, and after taking lessons from John Cooper played at the Theatre Royal, Bath. His appearance was against him. It was said that he looked like a prize-fighter (C. Jay, *The Law*, 1868). At the intercession of his parents he left the stage, and on 30 June 1836 was called to the bar at the Inner Temple, and went on the home circuit. Owing to his father's interest he soon acquired an extensive junior practice both civil and criminal. He was engaged in the trial of William Palmer, the 'Rugeley poisoner' in May 1856 and the trial of Simon Bernard for conspiring with Orsini to kill Napoleon III. His speech in defence of Bernard was published in 1858. In dealing with common juries he freely appealed with conspicuous success to their ignorance and prejudices, but his knowledge of law was very limited. In December 1853 he was gazetted a queen's counsel, but his inn did not elect him a bencher. From 1855 to 1861 he acted as recorder of Brighton, and on 25 February 1859 he was returned for Marylebone as a Liberal. He was a steady supporter of Palmerston's government and was described as a reformer, in favour of the ballot and the abolition of church rates. In the autumn of 1860 he travelled to Italy and visited Garibaldi's camp, and was present at the skirmish before Capua on 19 September. On 9 July 1861 he married Marianne, widow of Captain Edward D. Crosier Hilliard of the 10th hussars.

James was now making £7,000 a year, but was heavily in debt. On 10 April 1861 he announced his retirement from the Commons, and soon afterwards withdrew from Brooks's and the Reform Club, its being determined that he owed £100,000. Charges were meanwhile made against his professional character, and on 7 June 1861 the benchers of the Inner Temple commenced an inquiry into his conduct. Among the charges proved were obtaining money by misrepresentation and an apparent attempt to pervert the course of justice (James had borrowed money from a defendant, while acting for the plaintiff in the

Edwin John James (1812–1882), by unknown engraver, pubd 1859 (after John Watkins)

same case). On 18 June 1861 James offered to resign his membership of the bar, but the offer was refused, and on 18 July 1861 he was disbarred. His name was struck off the books of the inn on 20 November.

In the meantime James went to America. He became an American citizen and on 5 November 1861 was admitted to the bar of New York. A notice in the *London Gazette* of 15 July 1862 cancelled his appointment as queen's counsel. When his conduct in England became known in New York, an attempt was made to cancel his membership, but he denied on oath the truth of the charges, the judges were divided in opinion, and the matter was dropped. None the less his career as a barrister was undermined, and April 1865 found him playing at the Winter Garden Theatre, New York. His wife divorced him in January 1863. After returning to London in 1872, he published *The Political Institutions of America and England* and lectured on America at St George's Hall. In 1873 he unsuccessfully petitioned the common-law judges to reconsider his case. In May 1873 he articled himself to a city solicitor and at about the same time again stood as a candidate for Marylebone. He afterwards practised as a legal adviser, came occasionally before the public as a friend of Garibaldi, and wrote magazine articles. Again, he fell into debt, and a subscription was about to be made for him when he died at his home 11 Bayley Street, Bedford Square, London, on 4 March 1882. He was survived by a second wife, Eliza.

G. C. BOASE, *rev.* ERIC METCALFE

Sources *Dod's Parliamentary Companion* · Boase, *Mod. Eng. biog.* · *Law Magazine*, new ser., 12 (1861–2), 263–86 · *Law Magazine*, new ser., 13 (1862), 335–45 · *The Times* (7 March 1882), 10 · *Daily News* (7 March

1882), 5 · *Solicitors' Journal*, 26 (1881–2), 301 · *Law Times* (18 March 1882), 358 · *ILN* (30 April 1859), 429 · *Annual Register* (1862), 140–43 · d. cert.

Archives Herts. ALS, corresp. with Lord and Lady Lytton
Likenesses engraving (after J. Watkins), NPG; repro. in *ILN* (30 April 1859), 429 [*see illus.*] · portrait, repro. in *ILN* (13 Oct 1860), 330
Wealth at death financial difficulty

James, Edwin Oliver (1888–1972), historian of religions and anthropologist, was born at 53 Kelly Street, Kentish Town, London, on 30 March 1888, the only child of William James, a retired draper, and his wife, Sophia Mary, *née* Bowtell. He was educated at University College School, London, and subsequently enrolled in the college in the faculty of science for medicine. He was there for only one year and had to withdraw from his medical studies through shortage of money. He then taught in various schools and in 1911 was ordained in the Church of England, without attending a theological college. He was made a curate in the parish of Low Moor, near Bradford. In the same year, on 25 July, he married Clarese Augusta Copeland (1884–1973). Their only child was a son, Basil. Clarese was from Burgess Hill, Sussex, the only child of William and Clara Copeland. In later life she always accompanied her Tedwin, as she called him, to the many conferences he attended, and was a continual help to him with her knowledge of Spanish and French. When he died she had all his papers destroyed. She died on 16 October 1973. E. O. J., as his colleagues often called him, worked as curate or vicar in parishes, mostly in London and around Oxford, until 1933.

Early in life James had become interested in anthropology and in 1916 was awarded his first degree, a BLitt, together with a diploma in anthropology, from Exeter College, Oxford, under the direction of R. R. Marett. In 1929 he was awarded a PhD by University College, London, under the supervision of the anthropologist G. Elliott Smith; his topic was the cult of the dead. From 1930 to 1933 he was tutor and lecturer in anthropology at Cambridge University. In 1933 he applied for and became the first holder of a chair in the history and philosophy of religion in the University of Leeds. He was also head of the department. In 1934 he received a DLitt from Oxford. He was appointed in 1945 to the chair of philosophy of religion (later history and philosophy of religion) in London University, held at King's College. He retired in 1955 and five years later became chaplain of All Souls College, Oxford, where he remained until his death. That he did not receive a full-time academic post until he was forty-five reflects the fact that in Britain, by contrast with the continent, there were very few posts available in James's subject. For a long time he held the only chair in the country in the history of religions.

James's early academic interests were in science and he was drawn to examine religious phenomena using the tools of critical history, anthropology, sociology, and psychology—disciplines that emerged in the late nineteenth century. From this position he never wavered. But from an early age he had deep religious convictions, exemplified by his attachment to Anglo-Catholicism. His long-term academic aim, in the company of other liberal-minded Christian scholars, was to relate science to the truths of their faith, through an objective study of religious phenomena. This can be seen not only in some of his books, but particularly in an essay in *Essays Catholic and Critical* (1926).

Throughout his life James was a prolific writer, publishing about thirty academic books. The first major work, *Primitive Ritual and Belief*, appeared in 1917, and two years afterwards came *An Introduction to Anthropology*. His last book was *Creation and Cosmology: a Historical and Comparative Inquiry* (1969). One of his best-known works was *Prehistoric Religion* (1957), which was translated into six European languages. Some of his books were related to specific religious institutions: *The Concept of Deity* (1950), *Marriage and Society* (1952), and *The Nature and Function of Priesthood* (1955). *Myth and Ritual in the Ancient Near East* (1958) was particularly influential among scholars. A year later came *The Cult of the Mother Goddess*. *The Origin of Sacrifice* (1933) is still cited by anthropologists nearly seventy years on.

Among the honours bestowed upon him was an honorary DD of St Andrews. He was made fellow of University College, London (1946), and fellow of King's College, London (1950), as well as emeritus professor. For some time he was president of the Folklore Society (also editor of *Folklore* from 1932 to 1958), president of section H (anthropology) of the British Association for the Advancement of Science, and president of the British Association of the History of Religions. He gave courses of lectures in many universities.

During his career James became generally recognized as the doyen of comparative religion in Britain. He had always stressed the importance of the historical and comparative method in studying religious phenomena, and founded the British section of the International Association for the Study of the History of Religions in 1954. At international conferences he was much revered, and about half of the contributions to his Festschrift (*The Saviour God*, ed. S. G. F. Brandon, 1963) came from outside Britain. His encyclopaedic knowledge extended from the earliest religions to those of the present day. Little wonder that he was made editor of various specialist encyclopaedias. When he began writing, comparative religion was often seen as an obscure and dull subject, but by his clarity of style and scope of learning he made it popular in the best sense of the word. Not surprisingly he had an initial interest in the work of Tylor and Frazer but was critical of both for being rigidly evolutionist and for believing that the origins of religion could be established.

In the matter of fieldwork James was more an archaeologist than an anthropologist. He studied the palaeolithic cave paintings of France and early sites in Britain. Although he had to lecture on philosophy in London, he admitted he was neither philosopher nor theologian. Nor was he interested in grand theories: he was very much his own man in comparing the findings of others. He did not attract disciples who might develop his ideas. None the less, James was much liked: his was a warm-hearted, generous nature, coupled with a dry sense of humour. He was totally dedicated to academic life and had few wider interests, save travelling in Europe and those which concerned his faith. His religious convictions however were never obtrusive. He died on 6 July 1972 as the result of an accident in a car park in Oxford—a city which he loved and in which he lived much of his life. He was buried in the cemetery of St Thomas the Martyr, Oxford, where he had spent ten years as vicar of the parish.

W. S. F. PICKERING

Sources WWW, 1971–80 · S. G. F. Brandon, ed., *The Saviour God* (1963) · personal knowledge (2004) · b. cert. · m. cert.
Archives Exeter College, Oxford · Oxf. UA · UCL
Likenesses photograph, repro. in Brandon, *Saviour God* · photographs, priv. coll.

James [*née* Banckes], **Elinor** [Eleanor] (**1644/5–1719**), printer and polemicist, was the daughter of Mary Banckes; the name of her father is not known. By a marriage licence dated 27 October 1662, at the age of seventeen, she married Thomas James (*c.*1640–1709/10), a journeyman printer, in the parish of St Olave, Silver Street, London. The bookseller John Dunton described Thomas James, who set up as a master about 1675, as competent and well-read, but as 'something the better known for being husband to that She-State Politician Mrs. Elianor James' (*Life and Errors*, 1.252–3). The couple had at least four children, of whom two are known to have lived to adulthood: Jane (1670–1733), who married the printer Thomas Ilive and succeeded him after she was widowed; and Sarah (*b.* 1673), who married Robert Saunders. A son, Thomas, about whom little is known, was born in 1665; John Nichols confuses him with the Thomas James who was a letter-founder in Bartholomew Close and the brother of John James the architect. Nichols also erroneously attributes to Elinor a daughter Elizabeth born in 1689. Elinor James continued printing after she was widowed, declaring about 1715, 'I have been in the element of Printing above forty years' (James, *Mrs James's Advice to All Printers*).

Between 1681 and 1716 Elinor James wrote, printed, and distributed more than ninety broadsides and pamphlets addressing political, religious, and commercial concerns. The fact that she either printed or oversaw the printing of her own works had consequences for their material form; she typically entitled her papers *Mrs. James's Advice*, *Mrs. James's Vindication*, and the like, and printed her name in huge letters at the top of her texts. (In fact James may never have 'written' her broadsides at all, but rather composed them directly at the printing press with type.) The papers are addressed to six monarchs, the houses of Lords and Commons, the lord mayor and aldermen of the City of London, and others, and they comment on national events such as the exclusion crisis, the revolution of 1688, the Act of Union, and the Jacobite risings of 1715. James petitioned Charles II against 'sins of the flesh', James II against promoting Catholicism, and William III against taking James II's crown, and her publications describe her apparent interviews with these kings. She also advised City of London leaders on issues ranging from mayoral elections to the enforcement of City by-laws and commented on trade issues such as the management of the

East India and South Sea companies and the economic disadvantages of a free press. In her own time James was satirized as 'London City Godmother' (see, for instance, *A Catalogue of Books to be Sold by Auction at the City-Godmother's in Mincing-Lane*, n.d. [1702]).

James's best-known work, *Mrs. James's Vindication of the Church of England* (1687), provoked at least two rejoinders: the ironic *An Address of Thanks, on Behalf of the Church of England, to Mrs. James* (1687), by an anonymous dissenter, and a verse broadside entitled *Elizabeth Rone's Short Answer to Ellinor James's Long Preamble* (1687). James responded to her critics in *Mrs. James's Defence of the Church of England, in a Short Answer to the Canting Address* (1687). Earlier that year the poet John Dryden referred to James in his preface to *The Hind and the Panther*. She responded, 'As for Mr. Dryden … I do not know him, nor never read his Book, but am told he doth Abuse the Church of England, for which I blame him: For I count it not Wisdom for a Wit, to reflect on that he so lately own'd' (James, *Mrs James's Vindication*, 2).

As the title of her paper *Mrs. Elianor James's Speech to the Citizens of London at Guild-Hall* (1705) suggests, James combined print petitioning with oral activism. Her papers allude to her public political activities at sites such as Guildhall, Whitehall, and Westminster, and her claims are often supported by external evidence. In November 1687 she disrupted a meeting at Grocers' Hall where a nonconformist minister was preaching before the lord mayor, and caused such a disturbance that Robert Spencer, earl of Sunderland, recorded the incident in a newsletter to a fellow peer. In December 1689 she was arrested, tried, and fined for 'distributing scandalous and reflecting papers' condemning William III (Luttrell, 1.617). James wrote more than a dozen works addressing the revolution of 1688, and any one of these might have alarmed the authorities; in *My Lords, I can Assure your Lordships* (1689?), for instance, she urged the Lords to remain loyal to James II, while in *This being your Majesty's Birth-Day* (1689?) she informed William III, 'Not half the Nation thought You would have accepted of the Crown while the King your Father was alive.'

In 1702 James was physically assaulted by the Popish Plot informer Titus Oates. She had publicly provoked Oates by questioning his right to wear canonical garb, and he had responded by smacking her with his cane. Oates was found guilty of assault at the Westminster sessions and ordered to pay a 'considerable fine' but because he was already deeply in debt this was later reduced to 6 marks (about £4) ('Proceedings Against Oates', repr. in *Scarce and Valuable Tracts … Lord Somers*, 4, 1750, 420–22).

In 1710 James served as the executor of her husband's will (proved on 9 May 1710) and she chose to donate his extraordinary personal library of some 3000 books to Sion College. She also donated portraits of Charles I, Charles II, her husband, and herself. The last, labelled 'Eleonora Conjux Thomae James', shows her displaying her *Vindication*. James died some time before 13 July 1719 and was buried on 19 July, probably in St Dunstan-in-the-East, London.

James was among the most prolific and politically active

women writers of the later Stuart period. A middle-class tradeswoman with a printing press in her own home, her works chronicling the national events of a tumultuous period are a unique resource for the recovery of popular female involvement in early modern political culture.

PAULA MCDOWELL

Sources P. McDowell, *The women of Grub Street: press, politics and gender in the London literary marketplace, 1678–1730* (1998) • P. McDowell, ed., *The early modern Englishwoman, essential works: Elinor James* [forthcoming] • E. James, *Mrs. James's vindication of the Church of England, in an answer to a pamphlet entituled, 'A new test of the Church of England's loyalty'* (1687) • E. James, *Mrs. James's defence of the Church of England, in a short answer to the canting address, &c. with a word or two concerning a Quakers good advice* (1687) • E. James, *Mrs. James's advice to all printers in general* (c.1715); repr. in Nichols, *Lit. anecdotes*, 1.306–7 • *An address of thanks, on behalf of the Church of England, to Mris. James* (1687) • Nichols, *Lit. anecdotes*, 1.305–9 • *The life and errors of John Dunton citizen of London*, 2 vols. (1705); repr. (1969), 1.252–3 • W. Reading, *The history of the ancient and present state of Sion-College near Cripplegate, London; and of the London-clergy's library there* (1724) • N. Luttrell, *A brief historical relation of state affairs from September 1678 to April 1714*, 1 (1857), 617 • 'An account of the proceedings against Dr. Titus Oates … July the 2d, 1702, for scandalizing and assaulting Mrs. Eleanor James', *A collection of scarce and valuable tracts … Lord Somers*, 2nd edn, 4 (1814), 420–22 • *A catalogue of books to be sold by auction at the City-Godmother's in Mincing Lane, on the 29th of May next, being the anniversary of the restoration of blessed memory* [n.d.] • E. James, *My Lords, I can assure your Lordships, that you are infinitely admir'd* (1689?) • E. James, *This being your majesty's birth-day, I thought no time more proper than this, to return you thanks* (1689?) • E. James, *Mrs. Elianor James's speech to the citizens of London, at Guild-Hall, relating to their new choice of parliament men* (1705) • E. Rone, *Elizabeth Rone's short answer to Ellinor James's long preamble, or, 'Vindication of the new test, &c.'* (1687) • *Report on the manuscripts of the marquis of Downshire*, 6 vols. in 7, HMC, 75 (1924–95), vol. 1, pt 1, p. 276 • Newgate sessions book, CLRO, SM60 • indictment no. 30, 8 April 1702, LMA, MJ/SR no. 1987 • PROB 11/515, fols. 148v–149r [will of Thomas James] • J. Dryden, 'The hind and the panther', *The works of John Dryden*, ed. {}, 3: *Poems, 1685–1692*, ed. E. Miner and V. A. Dearing (1969), 122 • administration, PRO, PROB 6/95, fol. 166r [Elinor James] • registry of the bishop of London, GL, MS 10091/26 [marriage licence] • E. James, *June the 21th, 1715. Mrs James's reasons, to the lords spiritual and temporal* (1715) • R. H. D'Elboux and W. Ward, eds., *The registers of St Dunstan in the East, London*, pt 3, Harleian Society registers (1958), 86–7 • caveat books, LPL • *A collection of scarce and valuable tracts … Lord Somers*, 4 (1750)

Likenesses oils, c.1700, NPG

James, Eric John Francis, Baron James of Rusholme (1909–1992), headmaster and university administrator, was born on 13 April 1909 near Derby, the younger son of Francis William (Frank) James (1865–1945), of Parkstone, Dorset, commercial traveller for wholesale chemists, and his wife, Lilian (Lily) Taylor (d. 1961), daughter of Robert Taylor, of Whitehaven, who was a governess before her marriage. He was educated at Varndean School, Brighton, Taunton's School, Southampton, and Queen's College, Oxford, where he was an exhibitioner and honorary scholar (1927) and Goldsmith's exhibitioner (1929), played chess for the university, and graduated with first-class honours in natural sciences (chemistry) in 1931, and a DPhil in 1933. On 11 April 1939 he married Cordelia Mary Wintour (b. 1911), only daughter of Major-General FitzGerald Wintour, of Broadstone, Dorset. She was an active magistrate and a member of the Home Office advisory

Eric John Francis James, Baron James of Rusholme (1909–1992), by Elliott & Fry, 1953

panel on the penal system; they had one son, Oliver Francis Wintour (b. 1943), who became professor and head of the department of medicine at Newcastle University.

Early career in education James had hoped to be a surgeon, but limited means led him instead into teaching; he took a temporary post in 1933 at Winchester College, teaching chemistry, and stayed for twelve years. In 1945 he was appointed high master of Manchester grammar school where he remained until 1962. He could have been headmaster of Winchester, but decided that, as an Anglican foundation, it was not suitable for an agnostic. In 1938 he published, with F. Goddard, *Elements of Physical Chemistry*, which became the standard school textbook for many years. Among his later publications were *Science and Education* (in part) (1942), *An Essay on the Content of Education* (1949), *Education and Leadership* (1951), and *Plato's Ideas on Art and Education* (1974).

At Winchester, James exemplified his own belief that a 'scientist should be a man of wide interests in philosophy, literature and the arts' (personal knowledge) by becoming a 'div don' of high repute, that is, taking English, history and divinity; even though an unconcealed agnostic, he was always sympathetic to believers. 'Not to have experienced James on the minor prophets', one pupil said, 'is definitely to have missed something' (*The Independent*). 'He believed deeply in goodness and the power of reason' (Derbyshire, memorial address). He inspired intense personal admiration in pupils, many of whom later became

Nobel prize-winners, professors, teachers, or captains of industry. Enlightened in his modest home by his father, who was devoted to literature, he believed passionately in the teacher as a cultural force, 'opening doors of fulfilment that otherwise pupils could never have attained' (personal knowledge). One boy spoke of James's 'winged words about Jane Austen' (A. H. Brodhurst, *The Times*, 5 June 1992), and another, caught reading Proust in a chemistry lesson, was commended at least for his taste; the next day, turning back from the blackboard, James found every boy had a volume of the Zodiac Proust in his hands. As a bachelor he lived in the 'rough house' whose brilliant, and often merciless, mimicry of colleagues, led by James's abounding vitality of mind and personality, concealed real affection. In particular he passionately admired Spencer Leeson, the headmaster, and, despite the contrast in their beliefs, based much of his own headmastering on Leeson's example and precepts.

At Manchester grammar school James's influence was much greater, because directed towards staff, parents, and governors as well as pupils. He followed Leeson's advice: providing 'spiritual leadership; intellectual distinction; and administrative ability—very definitely in that order', seeing himself as '*primus inter pares* and doing a substantial amount of teaching' (*Spencer Leeson: a Memoir*, 76). His tremendous drive, his belief in lofty academic standards, his devotion to, and excitement about, a school which made possible the best education in the world for clever boys irrespective of their backgrounds ('I've got every sort of boy from the sons of mill workers to the sons of company directors') (personal knowledge)—all these created a great headmastership, one of the most notable of the twentieth century, comparable to that of Arnold of Rugby in the nineteenth century. He found time for everyone and everything until all the school's activities became imbued with his aspiration for excellence. To many of his staff the Chief 'was almost too good to be true. By merely being about the place he brought a vigour to the school which amounted in the course of time to a kind of revolution' (*Ulula*, 83). Always available for discussion, he never pulled rank; wonderfully easy to get on with, he gave colleagues the impression they were a little bit more than his equal. At the same time he was a natural leader—and an exemplar of his vision of masters' needing not only teaching ability but intellectual distinction. His skilful selection of staff on this assumption was vindicated by seventeen of their number achieving headships—in which he was their most important source of wisdom and guidance as they in turn passed on the invaluable lessons learned under his aegis. For one protégé the simplest and best was, wherever possible, to respond positively: 'Why not?' was a hallmark of his attitude to new ideas.

About parents James was somewhat ambivalent: 'one of the most important things a headmaster has to do is to talk to parents about their children' contrasts bizarrely with 'given the choice I should prefer to have been the Head of an orphans' school' (personal knowledge). He spoke clearly about his aims and their responsibilities, expecting the school to achieve the former and parents to fulfil the latter: Manchester grammar school was a ladder giving their sons, from whatever level of society, access to the highest places in the land; and they must play their part, including 'selling their (diseducative) TV sets and buying Plato instead' (ibid.).

As for pupils, some found James distant, even cold and remote, but on others he left an indelible mark, especially those whom he taught chemistry and, memorably, humanities:

> The supreme reward of being ... at MGS was to be taught by Eric James ... This Fabian agnostic took upon himself the Religious Instruction of the Sixth Form. What we got was an awesome trip through the history of Western Thought, after a thoroughgoing grounding in Platonism, the 'Chief' bemoaning the while his ignorance of Classical Greek.
> (*Ulula*, 83)

One boy, asked by the Chief what he was doing alone near the library, said: 'Thinking, Sir'. The cold voice changed instantly: 'Good. Forgive the intrusion' (ibid.). The same pupil wrote: 'I do not miss him. What he was, in the effect he had on the boys of his High Mastership, and what they have passed on to the world, he still is and will be. He gave us our selves' (ibid.).

James's objectives and achievements were clear and pursued relentlessly: scholarship should be an enduring source of satisfaction; equality of opportunity depends not on the ability to pay but on the ability to learn; since clever boys are not little swots but more, not less, likely to be good at other things, the school must give them every opening, including art, music, drama, games, and 'outward Bound-ery', in which Manchester grammar school excelled, with its treks and camps and outdoor centre at Disley. Where some immovable obstacle prevented swift action, as in the development of music, he had the patience to say: 'Where there's death there's hope' (personal knowledge).

James was a member of the University Grants Committee (1949–59) (a very unusual honour for a headmaster at that time), of the BBC's *The Brains Trust* (in the 1950s), of the Central Advisory Council for Education (1957–61), and of the Standing Commission on Museums and Galleries (1958–61), and was chairman of the Headmasters' Conference from 1953 to 1955. His contribution to education was nationally recognized in 1956 when he was knighted, and again in 1959 when he was created a life peer, as Baron James of Rusholme. In the House of Lords as a crossbencher he amply justified these honours by the vigorous part he played in debates relating to those fields where his knowledge and judgement would have full effect.

Creating the University of York In 1962 James left Manchester grammar school to become vice-chancellor of the newly founded University of York. He remained there until his retirement in 1973. York offered new challenges, and by meeting them James created one of the best postwar institutions of higher learning. While he may have run Manchester grammar school as if it were a university, he confessed he could not run York University as if it were a school. First it had to be built, and James played a major role in the architectural plan. Like J. H. Newman he felt its purpose was to help students to think clearly, to confront the perennial problems of human experience, to discuss and evaluate new and difficult ideas, which could often be better achieved by apparently remote than so-called relevant subjects. The buildings therefore had to express the university's total function as a small collegiate campus with a distinctive character: a community of scholars seeking excellence and maintaining tough academic standards; halls of residence as the centre of social and academic life, with a significant element of tutorial teaching and pastoral care; quality of teaching, rather than research, in a limited range rather than a multiplicity of disciplines. The architects regarded James as the perfect client: with the registrar, John West-Taylor, he and they in a rare creative collaboration hammered out the designs for a community in which the physical, social, and intellectual environments were one. James's particular satisfaction was the introduction of a lake, opening out and holding together the whole campus.

Apart from the buildings, how did this man with a dream turn it into reality? By getting good men on the staff, by creating the kind of place where schools sent their best pupils, and by giving them all leadership and unstinted support—'miles of rope' (*The Times*). 'He worked best with and through others' (Derbyshire, memorial address). James made imaginative appointments such as Harry Rée, Alan Peacock, Patrick Nuttgens, Philip Brockbank, and Wilfred Mellers, for whom the early years at York were the 'best time of our professional lives' (ibid.). He wanted open access for applicants who could benefit from what York offered: 'Jude the Obscure need no longer look despairingly at the spires of an inaccessible university, provided he has three good A Levels … and is prepared, if necessary, to do without spires' (personal knowledge).

Students could never claim he was out of touch; those who rejected his pipe-smoking paternalism, and even the International Socialists in 1968 and after, still admired him as always ready to talk, with glasses of Tio Pepe at the ready. His brilliant talents as a chairman, with relieving gifts of humour, held the university together, reconciling, or at least accommodating, conflicting opinions. Above all (and despite giving the impression that he did not care about ordinary people—'I do, only I can't go round saying "I care"') 'he cared profoundly for us all' (*Ulula*, 83).

Other activities Beyond Manchester grammar school and York, James's influence was no less considerable. In the Headmasters' Conference he carried great weight: as chairman, conducting business with outstanding ability and dispatch; as a member, intervening with balanced judgement and common sense. He once flattened in one sentence those who pleaded for the retention of Latin for Oxbridge entrance: 'I cannot believe the whole future of Western civilisation depends upon O level Latin' (personal knowledge). He was a tireless champion of day and direct grant schools. He was an apostle of excellence and an unashamed élitist in an egalitarian age, and many responded gladly to his defence of Plato's ideal of an aristocracy of talent. He believed that in matters of the intellect and

in judgements of value the idea of equality was irrelevant, and he led his grammar school colleagues in the battle for academic standards and selection against the proponents of comprehensive schooling. As a Fabian socialist he did believe in equality of opportunity, but felt that the Labour Party had betrayed its own ideals and experience by destroying the grammar schools while leaving the private schools untouched; many of its leaders had themselves benefited from the direct grant system, which offered opportunity without reference to financial background. Ultimately his campaign failed, and comprehensive schools mostly won the day; even his hopes of keeping a few highly selective schools open to the exceptionally gifted child regardless of financial circumstances were dashed.

Among his fellow vice-chancellors James also found himself in a minority from time to time: while as a former member of the University Grants Committee he had no fears for university freedom from the government's auditing of university finances, his élitist aim to preserve the universities from narrow vocational studies failed. However his 1971 report *The Education and Training of Teachers*, which resulted from his chairmanship of the committee to inquire into the training of teachers (1970–71), won wide acclaim, introducing academic as well as vocational courses and regular in-service training for life: teaching became an all graduate profession, giving practising teachers more opportunity to take responsibility for young recruits. James served also as a member of the Press Council (1963–7) and of the Social Science Research Council (1965–8), and as chairman of the Personal Social Services Council (1973–6). He was a fellow of Winchester College (1963–9), an honorary fellow of the Royal Institute of British Architects (1979), and was awarded honorary degrees by McGill (1957), York (Toronto) (1970), New Brunswick (1974), and York (1974).

As a scientist and an aesthete James was deeply knowledgeable and passionate about alpine plants, and an enthusiastic patron of musicians and artists: the Jameses' gardens were each a miniature botanics; for many in Manchester, to visit the Jameses' house was to discover modern art for the first time; in York he and Lord Harewood introduced the idea of resident musicians (Rostropovich, Bernstein, the Amadeus Quartet) and he brought Herbert Read and Henry Moore—and some of the latter's works—to the campus; through the Royal Fine Arts Commission (which he described as the most civilized body he had ever sat on) (S. Cantacuzino, *The Times*, 23 May 1992), of which he was a member from 1973 to 1976, and chairman from 1976 to 1979, he had a national influence.

Assessment James was remarkable in combining a wonderfully unstuffy and relaxed style with speed of thought and work, ruthless clarity in decision making with insistence on balanced debate, a generous approachability with intolerance of the pretentious and self-important, a commanding intellect with encouragement and freedom for those who worked with him, unwillingness to suffer fools gladly with patience for the vulnerable, the weak and the sincerely simple, and a dominant personality with charming, self-deprecating humour, as much at ease with women as with men. He believed 'the supreme reward of teaching is to realise one is teaching a boy more intelligent than oneself' (*Ulula*, 83), just as he found great pleasure in being forced, by intellectual ingenuity and persistence, to change his mind. Equally, an idea he did not believe in could be deftly sidestepped, as when a government inspector advised that a master should supervise the playground: 'An excellent idea,' he said. 'I'll pass it on to my successor' (personal knowledge). A swift stalker of corridors, he could still put an extraordinary variety of individuals at ease by giving them the impression of time and availability in the comfort of his study. Beneath words of wit there was a will of iron; and behind strong leadership there was willingness to trust and delegate without stint or caveat, so that failure to reciprocate caused him deep hurt. He was very human—so that he delighted in the company of children, for whom he always had a sweet at the ready in his waistcoat pocket—and working with him was great fun. He and his wife, Cordelia, were incomparable hosts, and the cleverer the visitors, the quicker his repartee, the more sparkling his mimicry, and the apter their quotations.

Of medium height, with a small head (going bald on top), piercing blue eyes, a narrow face, sharp and mobile features, and a pipe usually in his mouth, often upside down and readily taken out to emphasize a point with expressive gestures, James was quick to speak and laugh, positive and enthusiastic in his quicksilver responses to others' talk, yet always with an air of meaning business behind his relaxation and ease. Even a sidelong glance from him carried great weight. His oft-imitated voice imbued everything he said with the sense of a rich, confident, and rounded personality. Latterly, loss of sight and lameness afflicted him. His death followed a head injury incurred after stumbling; despite surgery he died three days after the accident, on 16 May 1992 at his home, Penhill Cottage, West Witton, Leyburn, Yorkshire. He was cremated in Darlington on 23 May and his ashes buried in West Witton. He was survived by his wife and son. A celebration of his life was held at York University on 5 October 1992.   ROGER YOUNG

Sources WWW, 1991–5 · Burke, *Peerage* (1969) · *The Times* (19 May 1992) · *Daily Telegraph* (18 May 1992) · *The Guardian* (19 May 1992) · *The Independent* (22 May 1992) · Lord Harewood, B. Saul, G. Aylmer, A. Derbyshire, A. Riddel, and R. Young, addresses given at the memorial celebration of Lord James's life, 5 Oct 1992 · *Ulula* [Manchester grammar school magazine] (1992) · P. Nuttgens, *York University News Sheet* (June 1992) · *Spencer Leeson: a memoir* (1958) · W. Wyatt, *Distinguished by talent* (1958) · personal knowledge (2004) · private information (2004)
Likenesses Elliott & Fry, photograph, 1953, NPG [see illus.] · W. Dring, portrait, University of York · F. Topolski, pen-and-ink sketch, University of York · photograph, repro. in *The Times* (19 May 1992) · photograph, repro. in *The Times* (23 May 1992) · photograph, repro. in *Daily Telegraph* · photograph, repro. in *The Guardian* · photograph, repro. in *The Independent* · photographs, priv. coll.

James, Francis (bap. **1580**, d. **1621**), Latin poet, was baptized on 21 September 1580, in Newport, Isle of Wight, the son of John *James (c.1550–1601), physician, and Elizabeth, daughter and heir of Stephen Caplin. He was a queen's scholar at Westminster School, and in 1598 was elected to a studentship at Christ Church, Oxford, and graduated BA in 1602, MA 1605, BD 1612, and DD on 16 May 1614. According to Wood, James was held 'in great esteem for several specimens of Latin poetry', especially his *Threnodia* of 1612 (Wood, *Ath. Oxon.*, 1.359). If this was ever published as a separate poem, no trace appears to survive; Wood may possibly have a garbled report of his contribution to a collective volume, or verses circulated in manuscript.

James contributed poems to *Oxoniensis academiae funebre officium in memoriam … Elisabethae* (1603), in which he discusses the difficulties of the commemorative genre, while defending its value: 'Talesne exequiae tibi persolvuntur inanes?'—is all this in vain? No, for 'lingua' makes a better bier (James, *Funebre officium*, 134). In the same year, he wrote nine short poems for *Academiae Oxoniensis pietas*, welcoming James I to the English throne. He appears, as a junior MA, in *Musa hospitalis* (1605, sig. D1r), celebrating the royal visit to Christ Church. In *Justa Oxoniensium* (1612) he joins the lamentations for Prince Henry twice, near the end, with a total of four poems (sig. O3v–4r, P1r), managing to include an attack on the Jesuits for plotting to blow up the whole kingdom, while death sought only half, in Prince Henry. Manuscript verses also survive from his Westminster days, 1597, from the Oxford collection for Christian IV, 1606 (BL, Royal MS 12.A.xli, fol. 9; 12.A.xliv, fol. 23b) and in the Bodleian Library.

In his final poem to the new king, James described how, having lost both his parents, he had benefited from Elizabeth's kindness (*Academiae Oxoniensis pietas*, 1603), and hoped that King James would similarly assist. He was subsequently appointed preacher at the Savoy Chapel, London, and from 11 January 1616 also rector of St Matthew's, Friday Street, London, under the king's patronage. He died at Ewhurst, Surrey in 1621 (his will was proved on 9 August), and was buried there; in his will, he had desired to be 'enterred without noyse or pompe'. He left his father's 'greate seale at armes' to his brother Walter, and left his goods, including some modest sums due to him from his parishioners, and an exchequer annuity, to his maid Martha Holt, who had cared for him in his 'tedious and paynefull' illness.   D. K. MONEY

Sources Wood, *Ath. Oxon.*, new edn · Foster, *Alum. Oxon.* · R. Newcourt, *Repertorium ecclesiasticum parochiale Londinense*, 1 (1708) · parish register, 21 Sept 1580, Newport, Isle of Wight [baptism] · E. Ashmole, *The visitation of Berkshire, 1664–6*, ed. W. C. Metcalfe (1882) · W. H. Rylands, ed., *Pedigrees from the visitation of Hampshire … 1530 … 1575 … 1622 … 1634*, Harleian Society, 64 (1913)
Wealth at death probably modest; small sums due to him: will, 1621, PRO, PROB 11/138

James, Frank Linsly (1851–1890), explorer in Africa, was the eldest of three sons born to Daniel James (1800–1876) and his second wife, Mary, daughter of Thomas Hitchcock of New York. James's father was a wealthy Liverpool metal merchant, who had in 1828 migrated from Albany, USA. James himself was born at Liverpool on 21 April 1851, and in consequence of an accident in his early youth was educated at home, acquiring strong literary and artistic tastes. He entered Caius College, Cambridge, in 1870, and in 1874 went to Downing College where he graduated BA in 1877 and MA in 1881. He was admitted at the Inner Temple in 1872 but seems never to have practised law, preferring to travel instead, having spent winters abroad with his sickly younger brother, William Dodge James.

James made his first extended tour in the winter of 1877–8, travelling into the Sudan as far as Berber, going by the Nile and Korosko Desert, and returning across the desert to Dongola. In the following winter he visited India, and was allowed by Sir Samuel Browne to march with his troops up the Khyber Pass to Jalalabad. The next two winters he explored the Basé country in the Sudan, publishing the results in his *Wild Tribes of the Sudan* (1883). Although largely a chronicle of his killing of animals, the book supplied some new geographical information about the Sudan. In the course of the journey he and his party climbed the Tchad-Amba, a high and precipitous mountain occupied by an Abyssinian monastery, and never previously ascended by Europeans. In the winter of 1882–3 James visited Mexico, and on 8 December 1884, after some months spent in cruising along the Somali coast in an Arab dhow, he embarked at Aden for Berbera. Thence he made his way, with his brothers and four others, south into the interior of the Somali country. In spite of previous attempts by Burton, Speke, Hagganmacher, and others, this region had hitherto been unexplored beyond 60 or 70 miles from the coast. James now succeeded in getting as far south as the Webi Shabeelle River, where he found a wide fertile plain which markedly contrasted with the deserts he had traversed. The remarkable feat of taking a caravan of nearly a hundred people and a hundred camels on a thirteen days' journey across the desert was acclaimed by contemporaries, including the Royal Geographical Society of which he was a fellow. Botanical specimens collected during the expedition were presented to Kew, and a collection of lepidoptera was presented to the natural history branch of the British Museum. James published an account of the undertaking in *The Unknown Horn of Africa* ... (1888). This is a far more serious book than his first and was commended for its fine illustrations.

James spent most of 1886, 1887, and 1888 on his yacht, the *Lancashire Witch*, visiting the Persian Gulf, Svalbard, and Novaya Zemlya. In the spring of 1890 he ascended the Niger, and made a series of inland expeditions on the west African coast. On 21 April, his thirty-ninth birthday, he landed from his anchorage off San Benito, about 100 miles north of the Gabon River, and within a mile of the shore was killed by an elephant which he and his friends had wounded. He was buried in Kensal Green cemetery. A home for yacht sailors was established at East Cowes in his memory by his brothers, John Arthur and William Dodge James, and his friends.

As an explorer James was distinguished by his powers of organization and by his tact. In private life he was noted for his generosity with the considerable wealth he had inherited (he left more than £100,000). His literary and artistic tastes were manifested in the fine library and superb collection of eighteenth-century proof engravings which he formed at the house at 14 Great Stanhope Street, London, where he lived with his two brothers. He was also a discriminating scientific collector and published a work on microscopy (St Louis, Missouri, 1887).

THOMAS SECCOMBE, *rev.* ELIZABETH BAIGENT

Sources J. A. James and W. D. James, 'Obituary', in F. L. James, *The unknown Horn of Africa* (1890) · Allibone, *Dict.* · Venn, *Alum. Cant.* · private information (1891) · *Proceedings* [Royal Geographical Society], 7 (1837), 265 · *Proceedings* [Royal Geographical Society], 12 (1842), 426 · *The Times* (29 Dec 1888) · *Saturday Review*, 66 (1888), 591–2

Likenesses portrait, 1890, repro. in James, *Unknown Horn of Africa*

Wealth at death £100,009 5s. 1d.: probate, 14 June 1890, CGPLA Eng. & Wales

James, George (*d.* 1735). *See under* James, John (*c.*1672–1746).

James, George (*d.* 1795), portrait painter, was born in London, the son of a barrister in the Temple, and was a pupil of Arthur Pond. He studied for some time in Italy, where he was first recorded at Naples in 1755, and was three years later in Rome with the painter Jonathan Skelton. After Skelton's death in 1759, James left Rome in 1760 with the painter Biagio Rebecca with whom he established himself in partnership in Dean Street, Soho, London. He became a member of the Incorporated Society of Artists, and exhibited with them from 1761 to 1768 including four Italian subjects, two of which were by Rebecca but shown by James as his own work. Farington noted how the discovery of this 'brought contempt upon James' (Farington, *Diary*, 9.3230). In 1764 he exhibited a painting called *The Death of Abel*. In the same year he sent a large picture of the three ladies Waldegrave, which met with severe criticism. He also exhibited with the Free Society of Artists in 1762–3. In 1770 James was elected an associate of the Royal Academy, and up to 1779 was a regular contributor of portraits to its exhibitions. In 1780 he moved to Bath, where he married 'Miss Boisseur sister to a Mr. Boisseur, a Swiss merchant. She had £15,000' (Farington, *Diary*, 2.305). He practised portrait painting with some success, and in 1789 and 1790 again appeared at the Royal Academy where his last exhibited work was *A Virgin Carrying Water in a Sieve*. Ingamells noted that 'Mrs Piozzi later wrote that James "loved profligate conversation dearly" and like Horace Mann was a "Finger-Twirler" ("meaning a decent word for Sodomites")' (Ingamells, 550). Having inherited house property in Soho, James retired from his profession. Later he moved with his family to Boulogne, where he died early in 1795, after suffering imprisonment during the reign of terror. Farington noted that 'James was a bad painter, but a good mimic, and very entertaining in society by singing humourous songs &c. He also had a talent for drawing caricatures' (Farington, *Diary*, 2.305). While the original contributor of this article noted that his portraits, though carefully painted, were poorly drawn and without character, more recent opinion has been slightly more generous to James: 'At his best—*The Misses Walpole* (exh. Society of Artists 1768)—he is an attractive painter, but he was not much employed' (Waterhouse, 193).

ANNETTE PEACH

Sources Farington, *Diary*, 1.135; 2.305; 6.2251; 9.3230 · J. Ingamells, ed., *A dictionary of British and Irish travellers in Italy, 1701–1800* (1997) · Waterhouse, *18c painters* · DNB

James, George Payne Rainsford (1801–1860), novelist, was born on 9 August 1801 in George Street, Hanover Square, London, the son of Pinkstan James (1766–1830), a physician, and Jean Churnside. James's grandfather Robert *James (*bap.* 1703, *d.* 1776) was a good friend of Samuel Johnson and grew wealthy from his invention of a medication known as James's Powder for Fevers. This medication was enormously popular, though there was a minor scandal when it was believed to have caused the death of Oliver Goldsmith. James's father was also a successful doctor who served as physician to the prince regent. James was educated at the Revd William Carmalt's school at Putney, where he learned to speak French and Italian fluently and also acquired some knowledge of Persian and Arabic. When he was thirteen he was introduced to Lord Byron, who nicknamed him Little Devil because of his headstrong and adventurous personality. In 1815 James joined the British army and only narrowly missed taking part in the battle of Waterloo. He later wrote about this period of his life in 'Extracts from the portfolio of an adventure seeker' which appeared in the American magazine *Harper's Monthly* between March 1853 and August 1855. After being discharged from the army, he decided to try his hand at writing. His earliest surviving work is a series of six tales in imitation of the *Arabian Nights*, which were completed before he was seventeen; they were published in 1832 as *The String of Pearls*. In 1816 he met Washington Irving, who encouraged him in his literary efforts. James did not, however, begin work on his first novel until 1825. Uncertain of its literary merit, he agonized over the first draft for some time, but finally an aunt who had been a schoolmate of Sir Walter Scott's persuaded James to send the manuscript to him. Scott's reply was favourable, and James sent his novel to Henry Colburn; it appeared in 1829 as *Richelieu: a Tale of France*. It was an immediate success, and he was given an advance of £500 for his next work.

James's second novel, published in 1830, was called *Darnley, or, The Field of the Cloth of Gold*, and it was followed in rapid succession by about one romance every nine months for the next eighteen years. Some of his better known works are *Henry Masterson* (1832), *The Gypsy* (1835), *Attila* (1837), *The Man-at-Arms* (1840), *The King's Highway* (1840), *Agincourt* (1844), *Arabella Stuart* (1844), *The Smuggler* (1845), *Henry Smeaton* (1851), and *Ticonderoga* (1854). James specialized in fast-paced historical romances set in a wide variety of places and periods. He came to be nicknamed the Solitary Horseman because so many of his novels opened with a lone rider dramatically galloping into the

George Payne Rainsford James (1801–1860), by Stephen Pearce, 1846

foreground. (Although he was secretly fond of the nickname, he never began a novel with such a scene again after he learned of it.) He took great pains to convince his readers of the historical accuracy of his texts, often quoting directly from his sources in order to prove a point about the customs of a bygone era. When *The Examiner* accused him of shoddy research for *Gowrie* (1848), he published a lengthy pamphlet to prove his thesis that James VI had ordered the murder of John, earl of Gowrie. By modern standards James may have been lacking as a historian, but he took the historical content of his work very seriously and so did his audience, who received much of their knowledge of the past from historical novelists such as James, Sir Walter Scott, Harrison Ainsworth, and Edward Bulwer-Lytton. James also wrote poetry and drama and was an active author and editor of popular historical works. In 1832 he began a study entitled *France in the Lives of her Great Men*, but only one volume appeared—a life of Charlemagne. His *History of the Life of Edward the Black Prince* (1836) resulted in his appointment as historiographer royal to William IV. He also produced *Memoirs of Great Commanders* (1832), *Memoirs of Celebrated Women* (1837), *The Life and Times of Louis XIV* (1838), *Lives of Eminent Foreign Statesmen* (1838–40), *A History of Chivalry* (1843), *The Life of Richard I* (1842–9), *The Life of Henry IV of France* (1847), and *Dark Scenes of History* (1849).

Throughout his literary career James was noted for his astonishing productivity. To those critics who found him to be a purveyor of hackneyed plot he responded in a letter to a friend:

Why is it that I write too fast for that slow beast the Public? Is it because I rise earlier? or because I do it every day and cannot do without it? There are four and twenty hours in the day are there not? Seven for sleep, four for dressing and feeding, four for reading, five for exercise and pleasure and four for writing. I cannot write less than five pages in an hour, which gives at the above calculation six thousand pages in a year of three hundred days.   (MacKenzie, 166)

Despite his constant literary labours he found time for an active family and social life. He married Frances Thomas (d. 1891) on 3 December 1828; they had four children. By all accounts he was a conscientious husband and father, as well as a convivial man who attracted a great many friends.

The 1840s were an active decade for James, as he stood for parliament and became very involved in organizing reform of the copyright laws. His interest in this issue stemmed from the experience of seeing many of his novels published in cheap, unauthorized editions. During this period he also experienced serious financial difficulties. Despite his popularity as an author he failed to accumulate a large fortune, and his problems were increased when he was sued by the engraver of his *Collected Works*. He was forced to pay a sum of several thousand pounds, which virtually ruined him and forced him to emigrate to the United States. On 4 July 1850 he and his family arrived in New York, where he negotiated an arrangement with the publisher James Harper. He then settled in Stockbridge, Massachusetts, where he began a series of successful lectures and befriended Nathaniel Hawthorne and other American writers. In 1851 he published *The Fate*, one of his most successful novels, which was set in the time of James II. It was so highly regarded in the United States that the entire first chapter was read aloud in the supreme court as an accurate description of England in the late seventeenth century.

James also sought a government post to enhance his income, and in 1852 he became British consul in Norfolk, Virginia. Living in Norfolk forced him to confront the institution of slavery, which he initially felt should be abolished. Soon after his arrival a slave ship landed, carrying some black people who had been kidnapped from the West Indies. The slavers intended to sell them, but James defended them as British subjects and got them freed in court. In consequence he became the target of anonymous threats, and his house was attacked eight times. As time went on, however, he gradually moderated his anti-slavery sentiments. In 1856 he published *The Old Dominion, or, The Southampton Massacre*, which featured as its subject the Nat Turner rebellion and which displayed his new anti-abolitionist sentiments. That same year the consul's office was moved to Richmond, and the James family moved with it.

James's health deteriorated during his years in Virginia, as he suffered from gout, leg pains, heart palpitations, and diphtheria. He also began drinking heavily. In 1858, after numerous entreaties for a change of post, he was made British consul in Venice. The move failed to improve his health, however, and in 1859 he began suffering attacks of paralysis. His mental health also declined, and he experienced fits of rage. He gradually sank into a state of depression and incoherence, and he died in Venice on 9 June 1860 and was buried there in the Lido cemetery. His wife moved back to the United States and settled in Eau Claire, Wisconsin. She died on 9 June 1891.

STEPHANIE L. BARCZEWSKI

Sources S. M. Ellis, *The solitary horseman, or, The life and adventures of G. P. R. James* (1927) • R. N. MacKenzie, 'George P. R. James', *British Romantic novelists, 1789–1832*, ed. B. K. Mudge, DLitB, 116 (1992) • J. Meehan, 'The solitary horseman in Virginia: novelist G. P. R. James as British consul, 1852–1858', *Virginia Cavalcade*, 27 (autumn 1977), 58–67 • M. B. Field, *Memories of many men and of some women* (1874) • *EdinR*, 65 (1837), 180–204 • *The Athenaeum* (23 June 1860), 856 • *The Times* (15 June 1860)
Archives Boston PL, poems and corresp. • Hunt. L., letters • LMA, estate, family, and personal papers • Princeton University Library, New Jersey, corresp. and papers • University of Virginia, Charlottesville, papers • Virginia Historical Society, Richmond | BL, business transactions with Richard Bentley, Add. MSS 46612–46649 • BL, corresp. with W. E. Gladstone, Add. MSS 44360–44527, *passim* • BL, letters to Royal Literary Fund, loan 96 • Bodl. Oxf., letters to Sir John Crampton • CUL, letters to the Royal Society of Literature • NA Scot., letters to Harriet Scott • Royal Society of Literature, London, letters to the Royal Society of Literature
Likenesses stipple, 1839, NPG • F. Cruickshank, portrait, 1844 • S. Pearce, oils, 1846, NPG [*see illus.*] • J. C. Armytage, stipple and line print, 1847 (after Cruickshank), NPG
Wealth at death under £800: administration, 17 April 1861, CGPLA Eng. & Wales

James, Sir Henry (1803–1877), surveyor, was the fifth son of John James of Truro, and Jane, daughter of John Hosken of Carines. He was born at Rose in Vale, near St Agnes, Cornwall, in 1803; was educated at the grammar school in Exeter, and at the Royal Military Academy, Woolwich; and was commissioned second lieutenant in the Royal Engineers on 22 September 1826. The following year he was appointed to the Ordnance Survey, on which he served mainly in Ireland. In 1843 he was, on the recommendation of Colonel Thomas Colby, the head of the survey, appointed local superintendent of the geological survey of Ireland under Sir Henry De la Beche, who was not fully satisfied with his work. While in Ireland he showed his ambition by pressing on Thomas Larcom his claim to succeed him as the effective head of the Irish survey. On 7 July 1846 he was transferred to Admiralty employment, and became chief engineer at Portsmouth with charge of the construction works in the dockyard. On 8 September 1847 he was appointed to the commission investigating the use of iron in railway structures. He was made a fellow of the Royal Society on 30 November 1848, and an associate of the Institution of Civil Engineers on 1 May 1849. He returned to the Ordnance Survey in 1850, and had his divisional headquarters at Edinburgh. During part of this year he, like other surveyors, was employed in the Board of Health inquiry into the sanitary state of towns. By 1854 James had married Anne, daughter of Major-General Edward Matson RE, with whom he had two sons and a daughter, who survived him. On 11 July 1854 he succeeded Colonel Hall as superintendent of the Ordnance Survey—it was a contentious appointment to which he was materially aided by his father-in-law and which was treated as an insult by the two more obvious claimants to the post.

On assuming the command of the survey, James found the 'battle of the scales' at its height. Indecision as to scale had produced serious delay, and hundreds of thousands of acres of ground had been surveyed, but not mapped. By 1854 the whole of Ireland, Yorkshire and Lancashire in England, and a few counties in Scotland had been surveyed at a scale of six inches to the mile, but many authorities argued in favour of the scale of 1:2500 or 25.344 inches to the mile. James argued for large-scale maps since these could always be reduced and would prove more economical in the long term. He was a forceful advocate and in the end both the one-inch and six-inch scales were retained for the whole country, and the 1:2500 scale adopted in addition for populous, cultivated, and mining districts. James did not succeed in realizing plans for a cadastral map combined with registration of legal title to land. His preference for large-scale maps can be seen most clearly in Ireland, but he was unable to carry through his schemes for the largest scale plans in that country. The reduction of the plans from one scale to another was much facilitated by the use of photography. James was convinced that this could be done without sensible error, and added a photographic establishment to the survey office at Southampton in 1855. Here all the plans on the 1:2500 scale were reduced to the six-inch scale, with considerable financial savings.

On 22 August 1857 James was appointed director of the topographical and statistical department of the War Office (followed by promotion to colonel in the army on 16 December); the staff employed in the quartermaster-general's office in London were combined with those of the Ordnance Survey, and placed under James's direction. This continued until the Ordnance Survey was transferred from the war department to the office of works in 1870.

While the survey of the country and the duties of the topographical department were under way, related scientific investigations were undertaken. In 1856 observations were made with Airy's zenith sector on the summit of Arthur's Seat, Edinburgh, and at points north and south of that hill, in order to compare the deflection of the plumb line due to the configurations of the ground with the differences between the observed latitudes, and to determine the mean specific gravity of the earth. In 1860 James was knighted in recognition of his services. In 1861 the English triangulation was extended into France and Belgium, in order to establish the connection between the triangulations of the three countries in the best possible manner, with a view to the calculation of the length of the arc of parallel between Orsk on the River Ural in Kazakhstan and the British astronomical station at Feaghmain on the island of Valentia in south-west Ireland. In 1866 the results of the comparisons of the standards of length of England, India, Australia, France, Russia, Prussia, and Belgium were published, all these countries having, on the invitation of the British government, sent their standards for comparison to the Ordnance Survey office at Southampton, where a building and apparatus had been constructed by James for the purpose. The units of measure used in the triangulation of the various countries, and the lengths of the several arcs which had been measured in different parts of the world, were then expressed in terms of the English standard yard and foot, and the elements of the figure of the earth corrected accordingly. In 1867, under James's superintendence, points at Haverfordwest and on Valentia, which had been selected as stations of the great European arc of longitude, were connected with the principal triangulations; and the direction of the meridian was observed at Valentia and compared with the direction as calculated from Greenwich by means of the triangulation connecting Greenwich with Valentia. The lengths of the arcs of parallel from Greenwich to Mount Kemmel in Belgium, from Greenwich to Haverfordwest, and from Greenwich to Valentia were also calculated.

In 1864–5 James arranged for a survey of Jerusalem, which drew on his experience of British sanitary reforms, since its aim was to make the city's water system less hazardous to pilgrims. The survey was made by a party of Royal Engineers under Captain (later Sir) Charles Wilson, whose report was published in 1865, with descriptive notes and photographs. In 1868–9 James approved a survey of Sinai by Captain Wilson and James's nephew, Captain H. S. Palmer RE.

James advocated a new process of map reproduction for which he coined the name 'photozincography', which he later claimed to have discovered. He had a chromocarbon photographic print of a small drawing prepared and successfully transferred to zinc. The new process proved very valuable and it was introduced at the Ordnance Survey office in 1859, under Captain (later Major-General) A. de C. Scott RE, and Lance-Corporal Rider of the photographic establishment at Southampton. Without photozincography it would have been impossible to keep pace with the demand for maps in a variety of scales, and it also allowed substantial gains in accuracy and economy. Its application to maps attracted much attention in continental Europe, whence delegates were sent to Southampton to study the process. The Spanish government was especially interested, and in 1863 the queen of Spain appointed James a commander and Scott a knight of the royal order of Isabella the Catholic. At James's suggestion the method was adopted in the reproduction of the Domesday Book. However, his enthusiasm for photozincography—only one of several idiosyncratic projects that he pursued—caused a regrettable distraction from the real business of surveying and mapping.

James remained at the head of the Ordnance Survey until August 1875, when failing health compelled him to resign. He died on 14 June 1877 at home at 3 Cumberland Terrace, Southampton. The official silence which greeted his resignation and death suggests that his departure was welcome to colleagues since his rule had become tinged with despotism and eccentricity. James was able, ambitious, and opportunistic, wont to take personal credit for his department's achievements. None the less he was an effective advocate for the survey in which he was an enthusiastic believer, and he got things done. He published many scientific and technical papers, on occasion appropriating to himself the work of others. In 1855–6 he began the practice of an annual *Report on the Progress of the*

Ordnance Survey, which he used to full effect as a vehicle for publicity and which has proved a valuable historical record. R. H. VETCH, *rev.* ELIZABETH BAIGENT

Sources W. A. Seymour, ed., *A history of the Ordnance Survey* (1980) · J. H. Andrews, *A paper landscape: the ordnance survey in nineteenth-century Ireland* (1975) · *The old series ordnance survey maps of England and Wales*, Ordnance Survey, 8 vols. (1975–92) [introductions to each vol. by J. B. Harley and others] · private information (1891) · *CGPLA Eng. & Wales* (1877) · d. cert.

Archives Ordnance Survey, Southampton · RS, corresp. · Sci. Mus., note and sketchbook | CUL, letters to Sir George Stokes · Elgin Museum, letters to George Gordon · U. St Andr. L., corresp. with James David Forbes

Likenesses H. James, self-portrait, medal; formerly at ordnance survey office, Dublin, Ireland

Wealth at death under £800: resworn probate, March 1878, *CGPLA Eng. & Wales*

James, Henry, Baron James of Hereford (1828–1911), politician and lawyer, was born on 30 October 1828 at Hereford, the third and youngest son of Philip Turner James, a surgeon, and his wife, Frances Gertrude, daughter of John Bodenham of Presteigne, Radnorshire. He was the first boy admitted to Cheltenham College when it was founded in 1841. On leaving school at the age of seventeen he was apprenticed to a civil engineer in London, but after three years he persuaded his father to let him join the Middle Temple. He was called to the bar in 1852, on the Oxford circuit. Starting without patronage or inherited wealth James steadily built up a lucrative career by concentrating on unfashionable commercial cases, often in obsolete recesses of the legal system. By 1871, as a QC, he was earning £14,000 a year, with a similar income from investments. As a result James, a lifelong bachelor, was able to develop an extensive social and sporting life among the rich and famous, which gave him great personal satisfaction. A keen sportsman, he was president of the MCC in 1889. Edward VII attended his shooting parties.

James was able to embark on a political career while still practising at the bar. He was narrowly defeated as Liberal candidate for Taunton at the 1868 general election, but successfully sustained a bribery petition against his Conservative opponent. He joined the more ebullient Sir William Harcourt below the ministerial gangway, in an attitude of rather self-conscious independence. He did not speak on major measures like Irish church disestablishment or Forster's Education Act, but supported the government's successive attempts to introduce the secret ballot. James was proud of a speech in May 1871 criticizing Gladstone for an insufficiently comprehensive repudiation of women's suffrage, and in March 1873 he again irritated Gladstone by opposing a Treasury proposal to reduce the travelling allowances of county-court judges. He was therefore pleasantly surprised to be made solicitor-general in September 1873, and attorney-general (with Harcourt as his solicitor-general) two months later. He received the traditional knighthood, but before he could start work Gladstone dissolved parliament in January 1874 and lost the election.

The brief ministerial appointment gave useful status to both James and Harcourt during the next six years in

Henry James, Baron James of Hereford (1828–1911), by Bassano, 1893

opposition. They were keen supporters of Lord Hartington, who became Liberal leader in the House of Commons when Gladstone retired at the beginning of 1875, and this allegiance was to be one of the dominant influences on the rest of James's political career. A natural second fiddle, he was never happier than when devilling loyally and assiduously for Hartington, whose exalted social position and whig principles gratified James's personal and political aspirations. Like other Liberal leaders he incurred the queen's displeasure for his opposition to the Royal Titles Bill in 1876, and he was not invited to Windsor until 1891, but thereafter he became a royal favourite.

After the Liberal victory at the general election of April 1880 James, like Harcourt, had expectations of high office in a Hartington government, but when Gladstone became prime minister James returned to the attorney-generalship and remained there until the fall of the government in 1885, when he was sworn of the privy council. His main preoccupations as attorney-general were the Corrupt Practices Act of 1883 and the drafting of the Reform Act of 1884. As a parliamentary speaker his style was over-elaborate, and marred by an embarrassing taste for snatches of bad poetry. But his legal skills were appreciated by Gladstone and James responded loyally, as he had done to Hartington's leadership in opposition. During this period he rejected several offers from Gladstone of judicial appointments, including the mastership of the rolls.

James's two main political loyalties were brought painfully into conflict in 1886 when Hartington took the lead in opposing Gladstone's Irish home-rule proposals. At the general election in November 1885 James successfully contested Bury, in Lancashire, which included a sizeable number of Irish voters. During the campaign he was criticized for his involvement in the drafting of the 1882 Crimes Act, and in return was provoked into an explicit repudiation of home rule. When Gladstone formed his third government in January 1886 he made an emotional and flattering appeal to James not to desert him, and to accept either the lord chancellorship or the Home Office. Hartington did little to dissuade his supporters from joining the government, and it was only after consulting his constituency chairman, who confirmed that James could not hope to be re-elected if he reneged on his pledges, that the latter declined Gladstone's offers.

After this rather unheroic début as a Liberal Unionist James settled into a steady and loyal support of Hartington which was greatly appreciated. When, in December 1886, James was once again offered a judicial appointment Hartington dissuaded him from leaving him 'absolutely alone on our bench'. Unlike G. J. Goschen, who sought to strengthen Hartington's ties with the Conservatives, James was reluctant to accept the permanence of the split in the Liberal Party, and he strongly advised Hartington against accepting Salisbury's invitations, in July and December 1886, to lead a coalition government. James maintained friendly social contacts on both sides of the home-rule divide, including Randolph Churchill, Chamberlain, John Morley, and Harcourt, and sought to reduce the level of bitter mutual recrimination.

In 1888–9 James appeared for *The Times*, supporting Sir Richard Webster, the Conservative attorney-general, before the special judicial commission set up to inquire into the allegations made against Parnell on the basis of the Pigott letters. James had from the outset suspected their authenticity and had persuaded Hartington to have nothing to do with them. During the hearings Pigott's responsibility for forgery was clearly exposed, but in a twelve-day final speech (31 October to 22 November 1889) James successfully shifted the emphasis onto the broader question of Parnell's responsibility for agrarian disorder.

At the end of 1891, following Hartington's elevation to the House of Lords as duke of Devonshire, Chamberlain, rather than James, succeeded as Liberal Unionist leader in the House of Commons. Early in 1892 James became attorney-general to the duchy of Cornwall, and later in the year he received an honorary doctorate of law at Cambridge. At the 1892 general election James retained his seat at Bury in a bitterly fought contest against a Gladstonian Liberal. The breach between the two sides had widened over the years, and in April 1893 James spoke strongly against Gladstone's second Home Rule Bill. In November 1893 he advised the queen against imposing a dissolution of parliament upon Rosebery.

After a meeting with Hartington early in 1895 Chamberlain expansively promised James 'any office you choose' in a forthcoming coalition government, but when Rosebery resigned in June 1895 Salisbury declined to consider James for the lord chancellorship, and instead offered him a judicial post. It was only when Hartington insisted on James's 'strong personal claim', in terms of past services to the Unionist alliance, that he reached the cabinet for the first time, as chancellor of the duchy of Lancaster, with a seat in the House of Lords as Baron James of Hereford. Behind the scenes James continued to play a useful if minor role, particularly in his periods of attendance on the ageing queen, which he enjoyed. From 1896 he was on the judicial committee of the privy council, and from 1898 to 1909 chaired the coal industry conciliation board. Between 1895 and 1902 he was a member of the committee of the privy council appointed to deal with university education in the north of England.

In 1900 Hartington again had to remind Salisbury of the moral obligations arising from past political services when Balfour pressed for James's retirement in the cabinet reshuffle following the 'khaki' election; but in July 1902, when Balfour became prime minister, James, now nearly seventy-four, accepted the inevitable and resigned. Resentment against Balfour underlay his stance during the tariff reform dispute of 1903, although belief in free trade was a lifelong part of his Liberalism. As in 1886 he saw himself as the guardian of Hartington's Liberal conscience, and he helped to persuade his confused and rather reluctant leader to resign from the cabinet and take part in the free-food campaign. He even entertained unrealistic hopes that, if the Balfour government collapsed, Hartington might at last become prime minister.

In 1908 James was gratified when Asquith, who had devilled for him as a young man, became prime minister, and in 1909 he spoke out in the House of Lords against the rejection of the Lloyd George budget. He died on 18 August 1911 at Kingswood Warren, near Epsom, and was buried at Breamore, near Salisbury, which he had made his country home. The peerage became extinct.

James did not achieve the highest levels of distinction either as a lawyer or as a politician, but he was an effective team player, contributing competently behind the scenes to the drafting of legislation and the formulation of policy. He served his political leaders loyally over the years, and his elegant good looks and social charm enabled him to maintain a wide circle of friends in legal, political, artistic, and sporting circles.

PATRICK JACKSON

Sources Lord Askwith, *Lord James of Hereford* (1930) · P. Jackson, *The last of the whigs: a political biography of Lord Hartington* (1994) · Gladstone, *Diaries* · *The Times* (19 Aug 1911) · *Law Journal* (26 Aug 1911)

Archives Herefs. RO, corresp. and papers | BL, corresp. with Henry Campbell-Bannerman, Add. MSS 41232, 41239 · BL, corresp. with Sir Charles Dilke, Add. MS 43892; Add. MS 49610, *passim* · BL, letters to T. H. S. Escott, Add. MS 58782 · BL, corresp. with W. E. Gladstone, Add. MS 44219 · BL, letters to Lord Halsbury, Add. MS 56372 · Bodl. Oxf., corresp. with Sir William and Lewis Harcourt · Bodl. Oxf., corresp. with Lord Kimberley · CAC Cam., corresp. with Lord Randolph Churchill · Chatsworth House, Derbyshire, letters to duke of Devonshire · CKS, letters to Aretas Akers-Douglas · CKS, corresp. with duke and duchess of Cleveland · CKS, letters to Edward Stanhope · Glos. RO, letters to Sir Michael Hicks Beach · LPL, corresp. with Lord Selborne; letters to Lord Selborne · NA

Scot., letters to G. W. Balfour · NL Scot., corresp. with Lord Rosebery · NRA Scotland, priv. coll., letters to Lord Balfour of Burleigh · U. Birm. L., corresp. with Joseph Chamberlain · University of Sheffield, letters to A. J. Mundella

Likenesses Ape [C. Pellegrini], cartoon, 1874, repro. in *VF* · A. Ossani, pastels, 1875, NPG · S. P. Hall, double portrait, pencil, 1889 (with J. G. Biggar), NG Ire. · S. P. Hall, group portrait, pencil, 1889 (*A speech by Michael Davitt M.P.*), NG Ire. · Bassano, photograph, 1893, NPG [*see illus.*] · S. P. Hall, group portrait, pencil (*Charles Stewart Parnell listening to Sir Richard Webster, attorney general and counsel for the Times*), NG Ire. · S. P. Hall, group portrait, pencil (*Sir Richard Webster cross-examining Patrick Delaney*), NG Ire. · S. P. Hall, pencil, NG Ire. · J. St H. Lander, portrait, Middle Temple, London

Wealth at death £177,001 8s. 5d.: probate, 30 Sept 1911, CGPLA Eng. & Wales

James, Henry (1843–1916), writer, was born on 15 April 1843 at 21 Washington Place in New York City, the second of the five children of Henry James (1811–1882), speculative theologian and social thinker, and his wife, Mary, *née* Walsh (1810–1882), daughter of James Walsh, a New York cotton merchant of Scottish descent, and his wife, Elizabeth Robertson Walsh. James was born into a remarkable family. His father, now usually known as Henry James senior, was fifth of the eleven children of William James (*d.* 1832) of Albany, New York, a strict Presbyterian and immigrant from co. Cavan in Ireland who had accumulated, first in the dry goods trade, then in banking and real estate, a sum reported as $3 million, one of the half-dozen largest American fortunes in his time. Henry James senior, who in the course of a wild and rebellious youth had suffered grave burns in an accident and lost his right leg above the knee, had quarrelled with his unyielding father and in 1833 successfully contested a punitive will in order to obtain a yearly income that has been estimated at between $10,000 and $12,500. He had entered the Princeton Theological School in 1835, but turned from its orthodox Calvinism, married Mary Walsh, the sister of a classmate, in 1840, and in 1844, at Windsor in England, suffered a revelatory breakdown. He later termed it a Swedenborgian 'vastation', a confrontation with 'some damnèd shape squatting invisible to me within the precincts of the room, and raying out from his fetid personality influences fatal to life' (*Society the Redeemed Form of Man*, 1879, 160–61). Henry James senior was thereafter inspired by the writings of Swedenborg, but refused fixed adherence to any particular Christian sect and investigated the thought of the French social utopist Charles Fourier. He returned to New York (spending periods staying with his mother and relatives at Albany) and in 1848 settled at 58 West Fourteenth Street. A friend of Emerson and Carlyle, he consolidated his life of lecturing and often unremunerated, sometimes controversial, writing on social and religious subjects.

Early life, 1843–1863 Henry James junior, as he was known until his father's death, had one elder brother, the remarkable psychologist and philosopher William James (1842–1910); his younger siblings were Garth Wilkinson (Wilky; 1845–1883), Robertson (Bob; 1846–1910), and the brilliant diarist and nearly lifelong invalid Alice (1848–1892). Before their restless father took them to Europe in

Henry James (1843–1916), by John Singer Sargent, 1913

1855 for three years of further, peripatetic educational experiments, William and Henry James had already gone through at least ten schools and a dozen assorted teachers, many of them described in *A Small Boy and Others*, James's vivid memoir of 1913: an unnamed Russian lady, Miss Sedgwick, Mrs Lavinia D. Wright, Mlle Delavigne, M. Maurice Vergnès, Richard Puling Jenks, Mrs Daly, and Miss Rogers. The European quest took James and his siblings to tutors and schools in Geneva, London, Paris, and Boulogne—M. Lerambert, Mlle Augustine Danse, the Institution Fézandie, M. Ansiot, the Collège Impérial. In the course of this exposure James later recalled receiving an initiation into European culture, as in the Galerie d'Apollon of the Louvre, where he found 'a general sense of *glory*. The glory meant ever so many things at once, not only beauty and art and supreme design, but history and fame and power, the world in fine raised to the richest and noblest expression' (*Autobiography*, 361). In Boulogne in September 1857 James suffered a near-fatal bout of typhus fever, from which his convalescence took two months; his father described him at this time as 'a devourer of libraries' (Edel, *Life*, 43).

In summer 1858, after an economic depression in America which severely affected the family's income, Henry James senior brought them back to a new home in the refined artistic colony at Newport, Rhode Island, where they were soon neighbours to his friends Edmund and Mary Tweedy, who had adopted Henry James senior's orphaned Temple nieces. After another year of experimental education, from October 1859 to September 1860, in Geneva (the Institution Rochette) and then Bonn, the family returned to Newport, where they remained, at 13

Kay Street, until 1864. At the Revd W. C. Leverett's school James made friends with the equally bookish Thomas Sergeant Perry, future literary critic and historian, while in the studio of the French-trained William Morris Hunt, where William was studying painting, he made friends with the interesting artist and man of the world John La Farge, a reader of Balzac and Browning. From 1860, Perry recalled, the young James:

> was continually writing stories, mainly of a romantic kind. The heroes were for the most part villains, but they were white lambs by the side of the sophisticated heroines, who seemed to have read all Balzac in the cradle and to be positively dripping with lurid crimes. (*Letters*, ed. Lubbock, 1.8)

Literary apprenticeship, 1864–1875 In the autumn of 1862 James enrolled in the Harvard law school, but did not last a full year. In 1863 he was drafted for army service in the civil war, in which his two younger brothers fought, but then was exempted by reason of physical disability—probably through a back strain incurred when helping to extinguish a fire in Newport in 1861. (In chap. 9 of *Notes of a Son and Brother* (1914) James calls the injury 'a horrid even if an obscure hurt', a phrase whose ambiguity has given rise to much excited speculation.) In May 1864 the whole James family moved to 13 Ashburton Place, Boston. In February 1864 the first of James's 112 short stories, 'A Tragedy of Error', was published anonymously in the short-lived *Continental Monthly*, while the first of his enormous tally of critical publications came out in October 1864 in the *North American Review*, edited by the Ruskinian scholar and art critic Charles Eliot Norton and the poet and critic James Russell Lowell. In March 1865 a second story, 'The Story of a Year', appeared under his name in the *Atlantic Monthly*, then edited by the Boston publisher James T. Fields, a magazine with which James was to have a long and close association. The young author thus knew early on several conveniently powerful literary figures; when Norton founded *The Nation* (New York) in 1865 with Edwin L. Godkin, a piece by James was in the first number.

During this period of extremely productive literary apprenticeship, James figured at first more notably as critic than as practitioner, specializing in contemporary French subjects and current Anglo-American fiction, though in 1868 he published six stories (three times what he had managed in any previous year) as well as fifteen reviews. In summer 1866 James met and became friendly with William Dean Howells, novelist, critic, and (luckily for James's career) influential editor. In November 1866 the James family moved again, to 20 Quincy Street, Cambridge, next to Harvard Yard. Between 1866 and 1868 William James and other friends travelled in Europe, leaving the Europhile James reading and writing in Cambridge.

Finally on 27 February 1869 James landed at Liverpool: his turn had come to be financed by the family, for the sake of his bad back and his troubled digestion as well as of his general culture. The well-connected Norton and the female members of his family, including his sister Grace, James's lifelong friend, were in London, and, lodging in Mayfair at 7 Half-Moon Street, James benefited from introductions to such London intellectuals as John Ruskin, William Morris, Leslie Stephen, Frederic Harrison, and Charles Darwin. He toured England and spent some time at Malvern for his constipation before returning to London, where he was charmed by meeting George Eliot, whose work he greatly admired. He spent the summer in Switzerland and in the autumn entered Italy, a country he rapturously enjoyed and which was to loom large in his work and his thinking about civilization. Poor health drove him back to Malvern, where on 26 March 1870 he received word from America of the sudden death, from consumption, of his much loved cousin Mary (Minny) Temple (1845–1870), on whom he based many of his American heroines. Still unwell, he reluctantly returned to the USA a month later, telling Grace Norton, 'It's a good deal like dying' (*Letters*, ed. Edel, 1.233). Forty-four years later he closed *Notes of a Son and Brother* by recalling Minny Temple's death as 'the end of our youth'.

James continued writing—tales, criticism, and now travel pieces (on American resorts) and art criticism (on Boston exhibitions)—and pining for Europe. In 1871 his first novel—*Watch and Ward*, a strange story in which a young girl's guardian becomes her awkward suitor—was published in the *Atlantic* (it did not appear as a book until 1878, and then in heavily revised form). In May 1872 James sailed to Liverpool, this time as companion to his sister, Alice, who was touring to recover from a nervous collapse in 1868, and their mother's sister Catherine Walsh, 'Aunt Kate'. On this visit James wrote a series of travel pieces; for about the next ten years he produced a good deal of travel writing about Europe. He was also writing much short fiction. After seeing off Alice and Aunt Kate in October he went to Paris, and by the end of the year was in Rome, where he stayed until May. He spent the early summer in Switzerland, then went to Homburg in July and returned in October to Italy, where he was joined by his brother William (until February 1874).

It was in Florence in spring 1874 that James began the first novel he would acknowledge, his conscious début: *Roderick Hudson*, for Howells's *Atlantic*. Its 'international' story of an American sculptor and his sponsor in Rome derived much from preoccupations in Hawthorne's *The Marble Faun* (1860), but James's distinctive irony, elegance, and cosmopolitan ease lighten the serious themes of artistic vocation and emotional ambivalence. James returned to the USA in September 1874, but had still not finished the book when its serialization began in January 1875. He was at 111 East 25th Street, New York, for the winter when his first book, *A Passionate Pilgrim, and other Tales*, came out on 31 January 1875—followed on 29 April by *Transatlantic Sketches*, a collection of his travel writings, and in November by the book form of *Roderick Hudson*. He stayed in New York until July 1875 before returning for three months *en famille* at Quincy Street, writing fifty-eight pieces for the New York *Nation* that year.

The move to Europe and success in England, 1875–1881 James was becoming established as an expert on Europe, and on 11 November 1875 he arrived in the French capital, with an appointment as Paris correspondent for the *New York Tribune*. Settling at 29 rue de Luxembourg in the heart of Paris, he at once got to work on his *Tribune* letters—and also began another novel, *The American*, whose confident American millionaire hero, Christopher Newman, tries to marry into the French aristocracy and comes up against an exclusive old world of intrigues, duels, and unfamiliar social codes. While writing it James regularly attended the French theatres and especially the Comédie Française, and also came to know some of the major Parisian writers: Flaubert, Turgenev (of whom he was very fond), Edmond de Goncourt, Alphonse Daudet, and Émile Zola. Most of these he had been reading for years, with on the whole a mixture of admiration for their artistic intensity and severe scepticism about their morality, especially in sexual matters. In June *The American*, much of which was still unwritten, started its run in the *Atlantic*, while James was short of material for the *Tribune* letters; by late July he was writing to his brother William that 'my last layer of resistance to a long-encroaching weariness and satiety with the French mind and its utterance has fallen from me like a garment' (*Correspondence of William James*, 1.271).

With the last instalment of *The American* completed, James crossed the English Channel on 10 December 1876 and quickly settled at 3 Bolton Street in Mayfair, his main residence until 1886. Five years later James recalled in a notebook entry that 'I took possession of London; I felt it to be the right place' (*Notebooks*, 218). Initiated through introductory letters from Norton, J. R. Lowell, and another American friend, the historian and political writer Henry Adams, James was soon a participant observer in London society, dining out constantly and paying many country visits. He was quickly on good terms with, for instance, T. H. Huxley, Richard Monckton Milnes (Lord Houghton), the anthologist F. T. Palgrave, and the editor F. H. Hill, and met Gladstone, Tennyson, and Browning. Apart from a three-month absence in Paris and Italy in the autumn of 1877, James remained in London, busily writing: travel pieces about England, reviews, essays on French writers, and more fiction.

In February 1878 Macmillans published James's first critical volume, *French Poets and Novelists*, an event which marked the beginning of a long association between James and the English publisher. The middle of the year saw the first appearance of two of his freshest and most popular fictions. *Daisy Miller*, the controversial novella about a Europeanized American's comic, then quasi-tragic, misunderstanding of a defiantly innocent Schenectady girl in Europe, appeared (after rejection by *Lippincott's Magazine* of Philadelphia) in Leslie Stephen's *Cornhill Magazine*, James's first showing in a British periodical. It caused a stir in America, where James—whose earlier fiction, though acclaimed, had been criticized as overanalytic—was taken by some to be snobbishly anti-American in his portrayal of Daisy. At the same time *The Europeans* (1878), a brilliant comic short novel about the social and romantic adventures of a Europeanized brother and sister returning to their relations' somewhat

aridly ascetic milieu in mid-century Boston, began its serial run in the *Atlantic*. In 1879 James published a short book on his predecessor, *Hawthorne*, for whose cosmopolitan tone he was attacked in his homeland, and the ironic story 'An International Episode', only his second piece of fiction to be set at all significantly in England, for some parts of which he was denounced by London critics. In the middle of the same year began the serial run of yet another short novel, *Confidence*, a somewhat schematic experiment about men testing women. By this point James could write humorously, to his brother William, that 'I have certainly become a hopeless, helpless, shameless (and you will add, a *bloated*,) cockney' (*Correspondence of William James*, 1.314–15). He told Howells about the same time, though with some exaggeration, that his fame, 'expanding through two hemispheres, is represented by a pecuniary equivalent almost grotesquely small' (Anesko, 134).

This was why James continued to produce at such a rate: to build up a sum sufficient to sustain him while writing a long and ambitious novel, projected for some years, *The Portrait of a Lady*, which would tell the comic, then darkening story of a generous, impulsive American girl, Isabel Archer, going to Europe, inheriting money, and being lured into marriage with a coolly malevolent fortune-hunter. By February 1880, with the aid of three months in Paris, he had written *Washington Square*, an American variation on Balzac's *Eugénie Grandet*, a painfully ironic domestic tragedy set in New York at about the place and time of James's birth. In mid-March 1880 James set about writing *The Portrait of a Lady*, first in Florence, then back in London—delaying a planned return trip to the USA in order to pursue it. The run, simultaneously in *Macmillan's Magazine* in England and in the *Atlantic*, which finally took fourteen instalments, began in October 1880, and James went to Venice to work on it from February to July 1881, not finishing until the end of August. Only in October 1881, then, could James embark for his postponed visit to America, returning to his homeland with a new celebrity. From the family home in Quincy Street he went down to New York and then to Washington, DC, where he planned to spend two or three months—only to be called back by news of his beloved mother's death on 29 January 1882. He stayed on in Boston, writing a dramatization of *Daisy Miller*—with a happy ending, but never produced—until May when he sailed back to England.

A difficult decade, 1882–1890 The rest of the decade held numerous disappointments for James. In mid-September 1882 he left London again for the six-week excursion through rainy French provinces that became *A Little Tour in France* (1884). Shortly after returning he received news of the last illness of his father, and arrived in the USA shortly before Christmas, just too late for the funeral on 21 December. As his father's executor, he stayed on in the small house on Mount Vernon Street to which his widowed father and sister had moved earlier in the year. Howells's provocative essay of November 1882, 'Henry James, jr.', declaring the 'art of fiction' as exemplified by James 'a finer art in our day than it was with Dickens and Thackeray', raised a stir around James both in America and England; such praise made him an easy target for literary and political proponents of other values (such as Theodore Roosevelt). Back in London at the end of August 1883, James began on *The Bostonians*, his large, 'realist', enduringly controversial American novel about ideological conflict in 1870s America, focused as the fierce struggle for the spirit of a gifted young girl. The antagonists are an ardent young Boston spinster seeking intense female friendship and comradeship in the suffrage cause, and a reactionary male lawyer who fought for the defeated south and who wants the girl to acknowledge the domestic satisfactions of traditional marriage as the highest form of female fulfilment.

In February 1884 James was in Paris, seeing something of Daudet, Goncourt, and Zola, the French 'Realists', and declared, in a letter to Howells, his interest in

> the effort & experiment of this little group, with its truly infernal intelligence of art, form, manner—its intense artistic life. They do the only kind of work, to-day, that I respect; & in spite of their ferocious pessimism & their handling of unclean things, they are at least serious and honest. (Anesko, 243)

About this time James made or developed some of his most important artistic friendships: with Edmund Gosse, for instance, a literary ally with whom he remained in close contact until his death; with John Singer Sargent, whom he met in Paris and whom he took trouble to launch on his London career as a portraitist; with Robert Louis Stevenson, who retorted in print to James's 1884 polemic 'The art of fiction', and became a valued intimate until his premature death in the South Seas; with the French novelist and critic Paul Bourget, against whose increasing right-wing snobbery James finally revolted; with Constance Fenimore Woolson, a somewhat deaf and earnest American novelist in Europe whose admiration for James may have led her to entertain hopes of marriage; and with George Du Maurier, illustrator for *Punch* and novelist, whom James liked to visit in Hampstead.

In the spring of 1884 James wrote 'The author of "Beltraffio"', probably basing it on what he knew about the marital situation of J. A. Symonds. It is unclear whether, when James wrote this, the first of a series of brilliant tales of authors and the literary life, he yet knew of Symonds's tormented homosexuality. Late in 1884 James wrote to his friend Grace Norton that 'I shall never marry … I am both happy enough and miserable enough, as it is, and don't wish to add to either side of the account' (*Letters*, ed. Edel, 3.55). Whatever his sexual preferences—as to which there has been much vexed speculation, though little firm evidence survives—James's decision to live as a solitary bachelor clearly fitted in with his high sense of artistic mission (and consequent commercial risk). From November 1884, also, he had taken on responsibility for his invalid sister, Alice, who came to be near him in England. In 'The Lesson of the Master' (1888), James elaborated on art and marriage: the 'master' of fiction in the tale has compromised his artistic integrity, churning out second-rate novels unworthy of his gifts, in order to sustain the high bourgeois comfort of his demanding wife

and children—and this cautionary figure himself warns the aspiring young writer who is James's hero to avoid the same trap.

Before he finished *The Bostonians*, which came out at twice the length contracted, James was already in December 1884 doing research at Millbank prison on the Thames for another realist novel, set among London anarchists, his first with no major American characters—*The Princess Casamassima*. Its fourteen-month publication in the *Atlantic* began, in September 1885, before the thirteen months of *The Bostonians* in *The Century* had ended. 1885 was a bad and busy year for James: in the spring his American publisher J. R. Osgood & Co. went into receivership. James managed to retain the copyright and *The Bostonians* was published by Macmillans in Britain and America (as was *The Princess Casamassima*), but he lost financially, forfeiting the large serialization fee. In May he had to borrow $1000 from his brother William to cover current expenses. Neither of these grandly conceived, exhaustingly composed novels was a critical or financial success.

In November 1885 James took a fourth-floor residential flat in Kensington on a long lease, at 34 De Vere Gardens; when he moved in on 6 March 1886 he was still working on *The Princess Casamassima*, which expanded so that he had to take an extra (unremunerated) instalment and did not finish until July. In December 1886 he went to Italy, where he stayed until late July 1887—visiting Florence and Venice, where he wrote a good number of short works, including 'The Aspern papers' (1888), his celebrated tale of a comically unscrupulous editor scheming to get his hands on a long dead poet's love letters. But the magazines—as if demand for James had been satiated by the two sprawling novels—delayed to publish them. Only one piece of fiction by James was published in 1887, and in January 1888 he confided to Howells that 'I have entered upon evil days' (Anesko, 266). About this time he entered into an arrangement with the pioneering literary agent Alexander Pollock Watt, who handled the affairs of best-selling authors such as Rider Haggard and Walter Besant.

Once back in London, James had begun another novel, *The Tragic Muse*, serialized from January 1889 until May 1890. Intended initially to be half the length of *The Princess Casamassima*, it was in the end even longer. Having put it aside to write *The Reverberator* (1888), a satire on the new journalistic culture of 'personalities' and the threat to privacy, James reconceived it as intertwining two stories, one about the career of an actress, one about a painter who has to confront the opposition of his whole circle and his own doubts about his talent in order to sacrifice a political career and gamble on his vocation. He went to the continent to write—Switzerland, Italy, Paris—in the autumn of 1888. He confessed at this time to his brother William his fatigue with the territory of 'International' contrasts for which he had become known, declaring:

> I aspire to write in such a way that it wd. be impossible to an outsider to say whether I am, at a given moment, an American writing about England or an Englishman writing about America (dealing as I do with both countries,) & so far from being ashamed of such an ambiguity I should be

exceedingly proud of it, for it would be highly civilized. (*Correspondence of William James*, 2.96)

1890 brought a new crisis—Macmillans, out of pocket by James's two previous novels, offered a considerably less advantageous contract for the book version of *The Tragic Muse*, and only Watt's intervention secured a tolerable compromise.

The theatrical years, 1890–1895 By this time James, because of the difficulties in sustaining his income for fiction, had already turned to the theatre, the field in which for several years he sought success. He had already begun a dramatization of his early novel *The American* for Edward Compton's Compton Comedy Theatre, all four acts of which were written by April 1890. In the summer of 1890 James again travelled in Italy, as he did in 1892, and on his return he threw himself into the theatre, rewriting *The American* to fit Compton's requirements and involving himself closely in the production, which opened fairly successfully at Southport on 3 January 1891, then toured the provinces. It received a London première on 26 September 1891, with the pregnant Mrs Compton replaced as the heroine by the remarkable American actress Elizabeth Robins, later a good friend of James. The London critics were respectful, but the run lasted for only seventy performances. (In 1892 James wrote a new final act with an even happier ending to please the Comptons' usual provincial audiences.) During the period that followed, this solitary novelist tried to immerse himself in the collaborative world of the theatre, and projected many plays for different managements and performers, including the American impresario Augustin Daly, only to suffer repeated frustrations. He wrote several more than were ever produced—simultaneously composing a number of short stories, some for Henry Harland's new magazine the *Yellow Book*, in order to bring in an income.

In Paris from March until May 1893, James began a more serious play for the Comptons, concerned with a Catholic hero who renounces the priesthood to save his aristocratic family, then finds that he can make himself happy only at the expense of others and, sacrificing his own interests, returns to his original vocation. The renunciatory ending of *Guy Domville* put off the Comptons, and the play was taken on by the actor–manager George Alexander, and opened at the St James's Theatre on 5 January 1895 in what was the culmination for James of five years' effort in the theatre. He described to William the events after the curtain fell:

> all the forces of civilization in the house waged a battle of the most gallant, prolonged & sustained applause with the hoots & jeers & catcalls of the roughs, whose *roars* (like those of a cage of beasts at some infernal 'Zoo') were only exacerbated (as it were!) by the conflict. It was a charming scene, as you may imagine, for a nervous, sensitive, exhausted author to face. (*Correspondence of William James*, 2.337)

It was reported that rivals had been targeting Alexander, but James's play was the victim, being replaced after thirty-one performances by Alexander's triumphant opening of Oscar Wilde's *The Importance of being Earnest*. The catastrophic arrest of this rival on 5 April 1895 for 'committing unnatural acts' was probably not a consolation.

The return to fiction, 1895–1899 This set-back was the end of James's real theatrical campaign, though he tried again over a decade later and had some minor successes. He returned to fiction with relief, and with a new formal discipline (about scenic construction and the preparation of effects) that gave an experimental edge to his subsequent work. James's enforced awareness of the possible gulf between aesthetic and commercial success gave his tales of the artistic life a darkly ironic, rueful tone. One story in *Terminations* (1895), 'The Altar of the Dead', the tale of a man obsessed with the commemoration of the dead, who are so quickly forgotten in modern London, suggests the effect on James of a terrible succession of personal losses in the preceding years. In March 1888 his old Bostonian friend the painter Lizzie Boott Duveneck had died of pneumonia in Paris, aged forty-two. The young American author Charles Wolcott Balestier, an agent for James in his theatrical affairs, died at twenty-nine of typhoid in Dresden on 6 December 1891 (James went there for the funeral). J. R. Lowell died on 12 August 1891. Alice James, after a painful decline during which she was comforted by James, died of breast cancer on 6 March 1892. The grand old actress and author Fanny Kemble, a long-standing friend, died in 1893. Constance Fenimore Woolson distressingly fell to her death in Venice on 24 January 1894, an apparent suicide. Stevenson died of his tuberculosis in Samoa on 3 December 1894—a blow deeply felt by James.

James made something of a fresh start in 1895: he took up cycling, and began a new phase of fictional productivity. He faced a changed publishing scene, one where many journals appealed to a new mass readership impatient of Jamesian nuance, but also where a new self-consciously refined minority audience, awakened by Ruskin, Pater, Ibsen, Flaubert, Zola, and Tolstoy, was primed for more 'advanced' or difficult art, such as that appearing in the *Yellow Book* or the *Chap-Book* of Chicago. James re-established contact with his old journal the *Atlantic*, which had woundingly rejected the story 'The Pupil' in 1890, and wrote for it *The Spoils of Poynton* (1897, serialized in 1896). The novel concerns a crisis of cultural inheritance: its heroine is caught in the middle when a passionate appreciator of the accumulated treasures of a country house schemes ruthlessly to save them from falling into the hands of philistines. For the *Illustrated London News*, an unusually popular paper for him, James next turned an unproduced, Ibsen-like play, *The Other House*, into a passably sensational novel (1896). To write it, under a looming deadline, he rented a hilltop bungalow in Sussex—Point Hill, Playden, Rye—from May 1896, and when his three months expired was so enchanted by the area he took the vicarage in Rye for two further months. When he returned to London he had already begun *What Maisie Knew* (1897), an imaginative triumph and a technical *tour de force* which takes a topical subject—the possibly damaging effect of divorce on a young child—and renders it from the girl's own point of view.

Trouble with a rheumatic wrist forced James in February 1897 to engage a shorthand stenographer, William MacAlpine. In September 1897 he found that the lease of Lamb House, Rye, a charming redbrick Georgian house he had already admired, was available for £70 a year, and took it on, moving in late in June 1898. By May 1898 James, still justifiably anxious about marketability, had signed up for aid in placing his latest crop of works with a new literary agent, the discreet and reliable James Brand Pinker, who became agent also for Conrad, Wells, and Ford Madox Hueffer, all James's neighbours in Sussex. In 1898 James published a brilliant novella, *In the Cage*, about a young female telegraphist piecing together the intrigues of her upper-class clients, for whom she barely exists; and also one of his great successes, the terrifying and unsettling 'The Turn of the Screw', about the apparent haunting of a governess's young charges by a pair of ghostly servants who may have contaminated their innocence (he had got the germ of the story from Edward White Benson, the archbishop of Canterbury, father of James's friend A. C. Benson). Innocence compromised also dominates James's next novel, *The Awkward Age* (1899, serialized 1898–9), the study, mainly in dialogue, of double standards, bad faith, and malign manipulation in the social circle of a very 'modern' London family. Like much of his work at the period, it was denounced by critics as unpleasant, morbid, and difficult.

After a trip to Europe in spring 1899, James carried on writing at Rye. In August 1899 the freehold of Lamb House became available for £2000 (in fact, £750 and an undertaking to pay the interest on £1250 in mortgages). James leapt at the chance. He let his London flat for a year (later getting rid of the lease) and in December 1900 obtained a bed-sitting-room attached to the Reform Club at 105 Pall Mall. Financially nervous—he wrote to a friend of an 'economic crisis' (*Letters*, ed. Edel, 4.128)—in the autumn of 1899 James projected several different novels for various publishers and editors, redoubling his creative efforts. When *The Soft Side*, containing twelve stories, appeared in August 1900 James had already written at least four of those that would feature in *The Better Sort* (1903). At the start of 1900 he was unable to complete *The Sense of the Past*, a fantastic and complex short novel whose antiquary American hero finds himself transported back to Regency London, and he seems to have made a start on *The Wings of the Dove*, before a short story about emotional vampirism grew into an elaborately fanciful full-length novel, *The Sacred Fount* (published 1901). In May 1900, to meet the new century, James shaved off the now greying beard he had worn for decades.

The 'major phase', 1900–1904 James was now in what F. O. Matthiessen later called his 'major phase', writing in a high, idiosyncratic style characterized by abstraction, ambiguity, dramatic intensity, and unusual demands on the reader's attention. By October 1900 he was working, for Harper's *North American Review*, on another long-projected novel, *The Ambassadors*, an ironic, melancholy, elegant epic of benign misapprehension centring on the epistemological vicissitudes of a fifty-five-year-old New Englander sent on a questionable mission to Paris. He did not finish until the middle of 1901, leaving him only two months before the deadline for delivery of his next contracted novel, *The Wings of the Dove*, to Constable. He asked for an extension until the end of 1901, but in fact, partly because of illness, took until 21 May 1902 over the tragic story, which looks back to James's long dead cousin Minny Temple in its heroine, a fatally ill American heiress who goes to Europe to 'live' before dying and becomes ensnared in a conspiratorial love triangle. He then wrote several more very long stories for *The Better Sort*, a collection which was already at 60,000 words. After this he took up again, and completed by March 1903, a project contracted for several years earlier, *William Wetmore Story and his Friends*, an evocative memorial volume undertaken at the request of the Story family about the mid-century circle of a well-connected (though in James's view artistically negligible) American sculptor and poet living in Rome.

The last of the three novels of the 'major phase', *The Golden Bowl*, was one of two James contracted in April 1903 to deliver by 1904 (the other, *The Sense of the Past* again, never materialized). He also agreed at this time to write a book for Macmillans, a study to be entitled *London Town*, which despite much research by reading and by walking never got beyond notes. Having begun *The Golden Bowl* in April 1903, he did not finally complete it until mid-July 1904. The novel, a tragi-comic multi-faceted story of fortune hunting and adultery, of emotional and financial pressures in the cosmopolitan world of rich Americans in Europe, is in many ways the poetic culmination of James's development, recapitulating themes from his earlier works and achieving a rare complexity in its intricately symmetrical and ironic plotting. All three of James's last major novels confront readers as well as protagonists with situations of high emotional and intellectual difficulty, where sexual betrayal and deep-laid schemes are 'wonderfully' dissimulated beneath glamorous, seductive surfaces of civilized good feeling. In them James counts the cost, often tragic, of the civilization he so values, facing with analytic passion the new configurations of the modern world.

***The American Scene*, and the New York Edition, 1905–1909** Henceforth James's work took on a more retrospective, elegiac tinge. On 24 August 1904 he sailed for New York, twenty-one years after his previous visit, making a trip to his much-changed homeland that was to be financed by a book of travel impressions and (a fresh departure) lecturing. He spent time with his brother William's family at Chocorua, New Hampshire, and Cambridge, Massachusetts, and with his recent but close friend Edith Wharton at Lenox, Massachusetts, but 'the restless analyst', as he called himself in *The American Scene* (1907), saw also New York, Philadelphia, Washington, the south, St Louis, Chicago, Los Angeles, and San Francisco. He was back in Lamb House in mid-July 1905, simultaneously writing *The American Scene*, a dense, brilliant work meditating on America's cultural future, and beginning what would be several years of labour on the monumental New York Edition of the Novels and Tales of Henry James, for which Pinker had negotiated with Scribner, and which eventually appeared between 1907 and 1909 in twenty-four volumes. He selected the works for inclusion (omitting for instance *The Europeans*, *Washington Square*, and *The Bostonians*), intensively revised the earlier ones in particular, collaborated on illustrations with the young American photographer Alvin Langdon Coburn, and wrote the extraordinary prefaces, now classic reflections on the novelist's craft. In October 1905 appeared the revised collection of travel essays, *English Hours*, a model for *Italian Hours*, published in October 1909.

In April 1901 MacAlpine had moved on and been replaced as James's secretary–typist by Mary Weld, who commented, 'He dictated beautifully … Typewriting for him was exactly like accompanying a singer on the piano' (Montgomery Hyde, 152). She married in 1905 during his absence, and in August 1907 James took on Theodora Bosanquet, who knew and admired his fiction, kept a splendid diary, and later wrote a vivid memoir, *Henry James at Work* (1924). In 1908 a play, *The High Bid*, was produced at Edinburgh by Johnston Forbes-Robertson; James was under constant pressure from Scribner about the edition, and also from Harper, to whom he had promised at least one novel—but was also in need of some less deferred payment. In 1908 his literary income was his lowest for twenty-five years. Unfortunately, as Pinker and Scribner discovered too late, the complicated contractual compromises needed to secure use of James's works for the edition from his many publishers prevented the making of profits at all commensurate to the effort James had put in.

Disappointment, illness, America, 1909–1911 This financial disappointment, following years of fairly unremitting effort and a punitive dietary regime according to the system of Horace Fletcher, precipitated minor heart trouble in January 1909. This prevented James's tackling a full-length novel, though he kept at work on further theatrical projects (which, as before, came to little). Early in 1910, more seriously, James was in a state of nervous collapse with digestive problems, and his brother William came over with his wife Alice, despite William's own long-established, and worsening, heart condition. James suffered a series of relapses, and chronic depression, but William went into a dramatic decline. The two brothers travelled back to New Hampshire together only for the elder to die a week later on 26 August. In October 1910 there appeared a final collection of short stories, *The Finer Grain*. James stayed on in Cambridge, Massachusetts, turning one of his rejected plays into a novel (*The Outcry*, 1911). He sailed back to England only in August 1911.

James set to work in London that autumn (avoiding the lonely Rye winters) on what was initially conceived, following conversations with William's widow, as a single family book dealing mainly with William. The project became first *A Small Boy and Others* (1913), a richly associative and imaginative recreation of the complicated family world in which James and his brother William had their childhood (up to James's twelfth year or so). Then in *Notes of a Son and Brother* (1914), making more use of family letters, James brought the account of his father and William up through adolescence and young adulthood to 1870. The difficult, self-reflexive manner of the books, their poetic interest and pleasure in the working of memory, and their constant reversion to the autobiographical make them unique in their kind. They were accorded a warm critical reception.

On 26 June 1912 James received an honorary doctorate at Oxford. On 2 October, just before coming down with agonizing shingles which lasted into 1913, he took a flat at 21 Carlyle Mansions, Cheyne Walk, Chelsea, moving in at the new year. *A Small Boy and Others* was published just in time for his seventieth birthday on 15 April 1913, marked by his British friends with a subscription for a portrait by Sargent (now in the National Portrait Gallery). He sent the publishers *Notes of a Son and Brother* on 6 November; it came out in March 1914, by which time he was at work on another novel, probably *The Ivory Tower* (posthumously published, 1917), which he never completed. He also began in 1914 a third volume of memoirs, never to be finished, and posthumously published as *The Middle Years* (1917).

When the First World War broke out in August, James became passionately engaged with the British cause; he was involved in charitable work for Belgian refugees, later visiting wounded soldiers in hospital. His last collection of essays, *Notes on Novelists*, came out in October 1914. In November he returned to the abandoned *The Sense of the Past*, feeling the present an impossible subject in the shadow of war. He became honorary president of the American Volunteer Motor-Ambulance Corps, and wrote a number of pieces towards the war effort (collected posthumously in *Within the Rim*, 1919), as well as a long preface to *Letters from America* (1916) by his young friend Rupert Brooke, who had died on 23 April 1915. In July 1915 James, partly in protest at America's refusal to enter the war, applied for naturalization in Britain, sponsored by J. B. Pinker, Edmund Gosse, George Prothero, the editor of the *Quarterly Review*, and H. H. Asquith, the prime minister. He took the oath of allegiance on 26 July, to acclaim in Britain and some hostile reaction in the USA. Earlier in the month his uneasy relations with his younger friend H. G. Wells, following the attack on James in Wells's satire *Boon* (1915), had ended with a significant exchange of letters about the principles of literary art.

On 30 July 1915 James was again taken ill with what he told Edith Wharton was 'an interminable gastric crisis of the most vicious and poisonous order' (*Henry James and Edith Wharton: Letters*, 354). He suffered a stroke on 2 December, and thereafter was confused about his whereabouts, though able to be pleased at being appointed to the Order of Merit in the new year's honours of 1916. He died at home at 21 Carlyle Mansions, Cheyne Walk, on 28 February 1916, and by his own wish was cremated, at Golders Green. The funeral was in Chelsea Old Church; James's sister-in-law smuggled his ashes back to America and buried them in the family plot in Cambridge, Massachusetts.

His estate, valued at less than £9000 (exclusive of his share in the family properties in Syracuse), was left to his sister-in-law and thereafter to her children.

Posthumous reputation In politics James was liberal, in religion, seemingly unaligned, and certainly a follower of his father in strong anti-clerical feeling. He lived an extraordinarily full social life. On the other hand, Desmond MacCarthy, struck by James's human detachment, reported him as saying that writing 'is absolute solitude' (Nowell-Smith, 127). His dual role, as immersed social observer and as eremitic devotee of high art, allowed him during more than five decades to produce a vitally developing *œuvre* extraordinarily varied both in subject and in treatment, straddling Victorian, Edwardian, and modernist literary periods, and American, French, and British literary cultures.

Although James's work never attained the wide appeal achieved by some of his friends like Robert Louis Stevenson, George Du Maurier, Mrs Humphry Ward, Edith Wharton, H. G. Wells, Owen Wister, and Hugh Walpole, it has always had a core of influential admirers. On his death James was admiringly commemorated by T. S. Eliot and Ezra Pound, like him American expatriates who made an enormous mark on British literature and culture. James was indeed a strong influence on Eliot's early poetry. His achievement also affected the writing of his friend Edith Wharton, above all in *The Reef* (1912), as well as that of Ford Madox Ford, especially in *The Good Soldier* (1914). Ford had just written *Henry James: a Critical Study* (1913), which Tony Tanner called 'the first really important book on James' (Tanner, 21). One can trace James's influence too in later writers, among them Graham Greene, W. H. Auden, Marguerite Yourcenar, Philip Roth, Cynthia Ozick, Anita Brookner, Barbara Vine, David Lodge, and Kazuo Ishiguro. James has also been important for writers inhabiting worlds more strikingly different from his own, including William Faulkner, Jorge Luis Borges, and Toni Morrison.

On criticism James has exerted a powerful force, both through the example of his fiction, which was first analysed in detail by Joseph Warren Beach in *The Method of Henry James* (1918), and through his brilliant, theoretically astute critical output. There was an early flowering in a highly Jamesian treatise, *The Craft of Fiction* (1921) by Percy Lubbock, a young friend of James's later years who edited *The Letters of Henry James* in 1920. James's importance was granted even by some of those unsympathetic to his approach, like E. M. Forster in his very successful *Aspects of the Novel* (1927), who claimed James's formal preoccupations led him to sacrifice 'human life'. But attacks on him as a mandarin or élitist writer, or from nationalist American critics like Van Wyck Brooks whose *The Pilgrimage of Henry James* (1925) deplored James's expatriation, kept James's reputation at a low ebb in the 1920s and 1930s.

In 1934 the magazine *Hound and Horn* devoted a special issue to James, with contributors including Newton Arvin, R. P. Blackmur, Marianne Moore, Stephen Spender, and Edmund Wilson. To meet the more political bent of the times, several of the writers stressed James's power as a social critic rather than, as had been the earlier tendency, his aesthetic mastery. In 1936 Graham Greene in an essay called 'The private universe' saw something else in James, 'a sense of evil religious in its intensity', and declared, 'He is as solitary in the history of the novel as Shakespeare in the history of poetry.' With the centenary of James's birth in 1943 the poet, critic, and editor Robert Penn Warren devoted a number of the *Kenyon Review* entirely to James, while an essay in the same year by Philip Rahv in *New Republic* described James as 'at once the most and least appreciated figure in American writing'. From this time on there was an ever-increasing flood of writing about James, and major critics like F. O. Matthiessen in America (in *Henry James: the Major Phase*, 1944) and F. R. Leavis in Britain (in *The Great Tradition*, 1948) took his achievement very seriously indeed. With the appearance of Leon Edel's five-volume biography between 1953 and 1972, and the reprinting of much of James's work (much of it by Edel, who became the leading figure in James studies), the centrality of James in the modern literary canon was established. Further biographies have followed, by Fred Kaplan (*Henry James: the Imagination of Genius: a Biography*, 1992) and Sheldon M. Novick (*Henry James: the Young Master*, 1996), as well as countless biographical studies of aspects of James's life and work. Edel also published many of James's letters (in a selection of 1956, then in four volumes published between 1974 and 1984), though in 2001 it was estimated that two-thirds of the novelist's correspondence remained unpublished. Testimony to James's academic status lies in the existence of a large international Henry James Society (based in the USA), and a thriving journal, the *Henry James Review*, as well as numerous websites.

Adaptations of James's work in various forms have proliferated. Despite the relative failure of James's own plays in the theatre, there have been many adaptations of his fiction, one of the more cogent early instances being John L. Balderston's and J. C. Squire's version of the unfinished *The Sense of the Past* as *Berkeley Square* in 1928, which was filmed twice (as *Berkeley Square* by Frank Lloyd in 1933, and later as *I'll Never Forget You* by Roy Ward Baker in 1951). *The Heiress*, a bold reworking of *Washington Square* by Ruth and Augustus Goetz, was immensely successful both as a play in 1947 and in William Wyler's 1949 film starring Ralph Richardson, who had played Dr Sloper in the play's London run, and Olivia de Havilland. In 1959 Michael Redgrave acted with Flora Robson and Beatrix Lehmann in his own subtle adaptation of *The Aspern Papers*.

Less surprising than it might seem, given the prominence of psychological processes in James's fiction, is the number of operatic versions, the earliest being Benjamin Britten's *The Turn of the Screw* (1954). Britten also adapted the tale 'Owen Wingrave' as an opera for television in 1970. Other notable uses of James have included those of Thea Musgrave in *The Voice of Ariadne* (1974), an adaptation of 'The last of the Valerii', and Dominick Argento in *The Aspern Papers*, which received its première on the same night as Philip Hageman's opera based on the same work, 19 November 1988 (the centenary of the novella's original publication in the *Atlantic Monthly*).

The most influential medium for diffusing James's *œuvre* since 1945, albeit mostly without James's own subtlety, has been the screen, cinematic and televisual. The rise of Freudianism in America after the Second World War found material in James's interest in psychology, as seen in *The Heiress* and Martin Gabel's very free Freudian variation on *The Aspern Papers* in *The Lost Moment* (1947). Jack Clayton's British film *The Innocents* (1961) with Deborah Kerr, a fevered adaptation of 'The Turn of the Screw' by Truman Capote and William Archibald, also played up James's melodramatic side. But it was BBC television, broadcasting in the leisurely evenings of the 1960s and 1970s, that adapted James's full-length fiction with least distortion, the highlights being James Cellan Jones's serializations of *The Portrait of a Lady* (1968) and especially *The Golden Bowl* (1972), both four-and-a-half hours long—though in 1977 he and the writer Denis Costanduros produced *The Ambassadors* as a brilliant ninety-five-minute dramatization in the series Play of the Month, with Paul Scofield, Lee Remick, and Delphine Seyrig.

James returned to the cinema in the 1970s with Peter Bogdanovich's serious and thoughtful *Daisy Miller* (1974), and *The Europeans* (1979) by Ismael Merchant and James Ivory, an early manifestation of the 'heritage' cinema that flourished in the 1980s. They followed it with *The Bostonians* (1984), featuring Christopher Reeve and Vanessa Redgrave, and after a gap renewed their engagement with James in a (more fluent) version of *The Golden Bowl* (2000) with Nick Nolte, Uma Thurman, and Kate Beckinsale. At the end of the twentieth century James succeeded Jane Austen in the fashion for film adaptations of classic authors: hence Jane Campion's controversial *The Portrait of a Lady* (1996) with Nicole Kidman; Iain Softley's equally revisionary *The Wings of the Dove* (1997) with Helena Bonham-Carter; and Agnieszka Holland's *Washington Square* (1997) with Jennifer Jason Leigh. James's fiction has also inspired film adaptations further afield: in Spain, Portugal, and Germany, but above all in France, where, notably, François Truffaut made one of his most deeply felt films, *La chambre verte* ('The green room', 1978), based on two James stories.

Such translations of James into forms where he does not actually have to be read kept his name and image in the early twenty-first-century eye, though his work, with its linguistic and epistemological difficulties, and its ironic attitude to mass culture, seems unlikely ever to attain huge popularity. As long as there are reflective readers James will always have his following, and will find different audiences through the rich diversity of themes and modes in his work: of social observation and irony; of cultural history, tracing the turn from the Victorian to the modern world; but also of the 'deeper psychology', as T. S. Eliot called it in 'The Hawthorne aspect' (1918, in *The Question of Henry James*, ed. F. W. Dupee, New York, 1945, 112–19). Through his dedication to fictional experiment, usually directed to presenting his characters' point of view and making their experience more vivid and intimate for the reader, he is a writers' writer. Different Jamesians prefer the early or the late work, and see him as an apologist for the *status quo* or as a 'hater of tyranny' (in Pound's phrase in 'Henry James', 1918, in *Critics on Henry James*, ed. J. Don Vann, 1974, 38–40). The ambiguity of much of his work—in combination with its narrative power, wit, and stylistic beauty—makes it unlikely that debate between different views will subside during the present century.

PHILIP HORNE

Sources M. Anesko, *Letters, fictions, lives: Henry James and W. D. Howells* (1997) · L. Edel and D. H. Laurence, *A bibliography of Henry James: third edition, revised with the assistance of James Rambeau* (1982) · *The complete notebooks of Henry James: the authoritative and definitive edition*, ed. L. Edel and L. H. Powers (1987) · L. Edel, *Henry James: a life* (1985) · *Henry James: letters*, ed. L. Edel, 4 vols. (1974–84) · A. Habegger, *The father: a life of Henry James, sr.* (1994) · P. Horne, *Henry James: a life in letters* (1999) · H. Montgomery Hyde, *Henry James at home* (1969) · H. James, *Autobiography: a small boy and others, notes of a son and brother, the middle years*, ed. F. W. Dupee (1956) · H. James, *The American scene* (1907) · R. W. B. Lewis, *The Jameses: a family narrative* (1991) · *The letters of Henry James*, ed. P. Lubbock, 2 vols. (1920) · S. Nowell-Smith, ed., *The legend of the master* (1947) · *Henry James and Edith Wharton: letters, 1900–1915*, ed. L. H. Powers (1990) · *The correspondence of William James*, ed. I. K. Scrupskelis and E. M. Berkeley, 3 vols. (1992–4) · T. Tanner, ed., *Henry James: modern judgements* (1968) · F. Kaplan, *Henry James: the imagination of genius: a biography* (1992) · S. M. Novick, *Henry James: the young master* (1996) · J. R. Bradley, ed., *Henry James on stage and screen* (2000) [essays by M. Halliwell, P. Swaab, and N. Berry]

Archives Bibliothèque Nationale, Paris · Boston PL · Brown University, Providence, Rhode Island, John Hay Library · Col. U., Rare Book and Manuscript Library, letters, see, NUC MS 70-124 · Col. U. · Colby College, Waterville, Maine, Miller Library · Cornell University, Ithaca, New York, Olin Library · CUL · Dorset County Museum, Dorchester, Dorset Natural History and Archeological Society · Duke U., Perkins L., letters and papers · Eton · FM Cam. · Folger · Harvard TC · Harvard U., Houghton L., corresp., literary MSS, and papers · Harvard U., Houghton L., family papers · King's Cam. · Mass. Hist. Soc. · Middlebury College, Vermont, Abernethy Library · Morgan L. · Pennsylvania State University, University Park, Pattee Library · Ransom HRC, corresp., literary MSS, and papers · Reform Club, London, papers · Rutherford B. Hayes Library, Fremont, Ohio · Smith College, Northampton, Massachusetts · Tate collection · U. Cal., Berkeley, Bancroft Library · U. Glas., Hillhead Library · U. Reading L. · UCL · University of Chicago, Joseph Regenstein Library · University of Southern California, Los Angeles, Doheny Library | BL, corresp. with Lord Gladstone, Add. MS 46018 · BL, corresp. with the MacMillans, Add. MS 54931 · Bodl. Oxf., letters to Christopher Benson · Bodl. Oxf., letters to H. G. Wells · Ches. & Chester ALSS, letters to Rhoda Broughton · Dartmouth College, Hanover, New Hampshire, Baker/Berry Library, letters to Curtis family · Duke U., Perkins L., letters to Sir Edmund Gosse · Harvard U., Houghton L., letters to Theodora Bosanquet; literary MSS · Harvard U., Houghton L., letters to Frances Hodgson Burnett and Mary Cadwalader Jones · Harvard U., Houghton L., letters to Margaret Porter · Hove Central Library, Sussex, letters to Lord and Lady Wolseley · Hunt. L., letters to Edward Prioleau and Margaret Warren · ICL, letters to Thomas Huxley and to Mrs Huxley · NL Scot., corresp. with Sir Graham Balfour and Lord Rosebery · NYPL, Berg collection · Princeton University Library, New Jersey, Firestone Library, Robert H. Taylor collection · Trinity Cam., letters to Mr and Mrs F. W. H. Myers · U. Leeds, Brotherton L., letters mostly to Sir Edmund Gosse · University of Virginia, Charlottesville, Alderman Library, C. Waller Barrett collection · Warks. CRO, letters to Alice Dugdale

Likenesses Elliott & Fry, photograph, 1890–99, University of Virginia, Charlottesville, Alderman Library · W. Rothenstein, drawing, 1897, repro. in Nowell-Smith, *The legend of the master* · W. Rothenstein, lithograph, 1898, NPG · A. Boughton, photographs, 1905, Harvard U., Houghton L. · K. E. McClellan, photographs, 1905,

Smith College, Northampton, Massachusetts; copies, Harvard U., Houghton L. • A. Boughton, photograph, c.1906, Smithsonian Institution, Washington, DC, National Portrait Gallery • A. L. Coburn, photographs, 1906, Harvard U., Houghton L. • A. L. Coburn, photogravure, 1906, NPG; repro. in T. Cooper, *Men of mark: a gallery of contemporary portraits*, 7 vols. (1876–83) • J-E. Blanche, oils, 1908, Smithsonian Institution, Washington, DC, National Portrait Gallery • W. James II, oils, c.1908, Boston Museum of Fine Arts, Massachusetts • J. S. Sargent, charcoal drawing, 1912, Royal Collection • J. S. Sargent, oils, 1913, NPG [*see illus.*] • F. D. Wood, marble bust, 1913, Tate collection • M. Beerbohm, caricature, drawings, National Gallery of Victoria, Melbourne • M. Beerbohm, caricatures, drawings, AM Oxf. • M. Beerbohm, caricatures, drawings, University of Texas, Austin • F. H. D'Avois, photographs, NPG • J. La Farge, oils, Century Association, New York • R. Lehmann, drawing, BM • double portrait, photograph (with William James), NPG • photographs, Harvard U., Houghton L., James family papers

Wealth at death £8961 5s. 2d.: probate, 9 May 1916, CGPLA Eng. & Wales

James, Hugh (1771–1817). *See under* James, John (1729–1785).

James, James [Iago ap Ieuan] (1832–1902), composer of the melody of 'Hen wlad fy nhadau' ('Land of my fathers'), was born on 4 November 1832 at the Ancient Druid inn, Argoed, Bedwellte, Monmouthshire, the only child of Evan James (Ieuan ap Iago; 1809–1878) and his wife, Elizabeth, *née* Stradling, of Caerphilly. In 1850 he married Cecilia, the daughter of Morgan and Joan Miles of Pontypridd, with whom he had two sons and three daughters.

In 1844 Evan James, a weaver, wool merchant, and poet (some of his poems were printed in *Gardd Aberdar*, 1854), moved his family to Pontypridd. It is with that town that father and son are most closely associated, even though James James also lived at other locations in Glamorgan. James James kept public houses, first The Anchor at Walnut Tree Bridge, near Pontypridd, then the Colliers Arms, Mountain Ash, and finally The Swan, Aberaman. He was a harpist but had no reputation as a player. Indeed, his celebrity rests entirely on his contribution to 'Hen wlad fy nhadau'. He composed other works but none was published, and surviving manuscript writings of his show him to be a musician of no particular talent.

The status of 'Hen wlad fy nhadau' was enhanced by several romanticized accounts of the inspirational process that led to father and son writing it. A letter from James published in the *South Wales Daily News* on 17 March 1884 gives the composer's own account, which is disarmingly straightforward. The tune was written by James in January 1856, to words already composed by his father; it was given the title *Glan Rhondda*. In 1858 the harpist Thomas Llewelyn submitted it, with James's permission, to an eisteddfod competition at Llangollen for the best collection of unpublished Welsh airs. The adjudicator of that competition, John Roberts (Owain Alaw), published it in the influential *Gems of Welsh Melody* in 1860. James had given permission for the publication but did not approve minor changes made by Roberts, who also, it appears, was entirely responsible for the harmonies. Performances of the song at various eisteddfods and by touring Welsh choirs quickly popularized it, and by the 1880s it was being used as a national song.

James James [Iago ap Ieuan] (1832–1902), by unknown engraver, pubd 1893

James's letter to the *South Wales Daily News* was stimulated by an extended correspondence in that paper, and its rival publication the *Western Mail*, concerning charges that the song was plagiarized. The allegation was made in the *South Wales Daily News* on 6 March 1884 by Frederick Atkins, an English-born Oxford graduate working in Cardiff as a schoolteacher, who claimed that it was taken 'note for note' from a song called (with numerous variants) *Tiptin o rosin*. The *Western Mail* immediately launched an attack on its rival's Anglicized, establishment, 'anti-Welsh' attitudes, and for two weeks numerous authorities were asked to pass judgement on the authenticity of James's creation. In fact, the two songs have only a passing similarity over a couple of bars. The issue was absurdly inflated and seems to have been worked up by the *Western Mail* to promote its self-appointed, pro-Welsh posture. It did, however, serve to raise the status of the piece even further.

Engravings of James and his father are reproduced in Percy Scholes's article on the composition of 'Hen wlad fy nhadau' which was published in the *National Library of Wales Journal* in 1943. The article also contains a facsimile of the autograph manuscript of the song. James James died at 6 Hawthorn Terrace, Aberdâr, on 11 January 1902. He was buried at Aberdâr cemetery. His death passed without comment in either of the newspapers that had focused so much attention on him in 1884. A memorial by Sir William Goscombe John, dedicated to the memory of James and his father, was unveiled at Ynysangharad Park, Pontypridd, on 23 July 1930. It was paid for by public subscription.

TREVOR HERBERT

Sources DWB • J. E. Lloyd, R. T. Jenkins, and W. L. Davies, eds., *Y bywgraffiadur Cymreig hyd 1940*, 2nd edn (1954) • P. A. Scholes, 'Hen wlad fy nhadau', *National Library of Wales Journal*, 3 (1943–4), 1–10 • *Western Mail* [Cardiff] (4–5 April 1884) • *Western Mail* [Cardiff] (7–9 April 1884) • *South Wales Daily News* (17 March 1884) • *South Wales Daily News* (13 March 1884) • *South Wales Daily News* (8 March 1884) • NL Wales • memorial inscription, Aberdâr cemetery, grave L25/14

Archives NL Wales • Pontypridd Library

Likenesses engraving, NPG; repro. in *The Graphic* (5 Aug 1893) [*see illus.*]

James, Jimmy [*real name* James Casey] (1892–1965), comedian, was born on 20 May 1892 at Portrack Lane, Stockton-on-Tees, co. Durham, the eldest of the family of four sons of Jeremiah Casey, steelworker and clog dancer, and his wife, Polly Gartland. He attended St Mary's School, Stockton-on-Tees, and made his stage début on Teesside in 1904 as Terry the Blue-eyed Irish Boy. After experience with juvenile troupes (Will Netta's Jockeys, Phil Rees's Stable Lads, and Clara Coverdale's Ten to One On), in 1925 he embarked on his own specialist career as a whimsical character comedian. Spotted in Sunderland variety in 1929, he was taken to London where he enjoyed immediate and lasting success, especially at the London Palladium in 1943, and again in 1948 when he saved the show from near disaster when Mickey Rooney flopped. He was extremely popular on the music-hall circuit and played many Blackpool summer seasons, and, although he did radio work and some television and film, it was as a stage comic that he made his lasting impression. Known as 'the comedian's comedian', a host of comic entertainers, from Tony Hancock to Peter Sellars, regarded James as their mentor.

James's humour lay originally in his doughy, ruminant countenance, his gravelly enquiring tones, and the swooping parabola of his distinctive prop, an inevitable cigarette. He basically rang the changes on three sketches, adjusting constantly and subtly in response to his audience in a remarkably sustained, career-long exercise in perceptive improvisation. He was widely regarded as the finest 'timer' of comic material on the light-entertainment circuit. The first of his three sketches—'The Drunk'—was the study, albeit with a couple of marked variants, of an inebriated bridegroom (heralded by James's signature-tune, 'Three O'Clock in the Morning'), locked out on his wedding night. The consummate stage drunk, James, himself a lifelong abstainer, had realized that, unlike the tipsy—whom most actors imitate—the genuinely intoxicated are oblivious to their condition: this was the key to his mastery. The second sketch was 'The Shoe Box', a priceless exercise in lunatic dialogue about the presence of wild animals in the eponymous shoe box. He was accompanied in this most famous of variety sketches by his stooges, the aggressive Hutton Conyers (named after a Yorkshire village) in a voluminous overcoat, and the passive but equally insane Bretton Woods (after the American site of the post-war fiscal agreement) in a shrunken suit and deerstalker hat. The former—'here, are you putting it around that I'm barmy?'—was variously played by his brother-in-law Jack Darby, by his son, Cass James, and, as token to James's attractions as a tutor, by Roy Castle, who yielded up his own career from 1956 to 1959 for the privilege. Jack 'Eli' Casey, a cousin, played Bretton Woods, while Dick Carlton was another recruit to this manic festival. The third sketch, 'The Chipster', which was performed with enormous panache at the 1953 royal command performance, involved a mock lecture on the occupational hazards—the risk of lost digits, the chipster's elbow, the fish-fryer's wink—of preparing chips.

James was married in Scotland in 1921 to Isabelle Darby, a music-hall dancer and singer, who, with his brother Peter, often accompanied him on his perambulations around the theatres, and indeed the racecourses, of provincial Britain. They had an only child, James Casey (Cass James on stage), born in 1922, who later became a light-entertainment producer at the BBC. Failing health and recurring insolvency, the consequence of heavy gambling, marked James's later years. He was declared bankrupt in 1936, 1955, and 1963, and wondered aloud whether he had 'won the official receiver outright': such was the deadpan whimsy off-stage of a creative mind that was as fertile in inventive and straight-faced mockery in private as in public. He never told a joke, on or off stage, and he was restless with the discipline of a script. Rather, he conveyed, in both his professional and personal life, a somewhat melancholy sense of the surreal. He made his last stage appearance early in 1964 and after suffering a heart attack later that year died in Blackpool on 4 August 1965 of pulmonary congestion with various complications. He was buried in Oxbridge cemetery, Stockton-on-Tees. *The Guardian* quoted Jimmy James's thoughtful definition of a genuine comedian as 'a man who says things funnily, not a man who says funny things' (*The Guardian*, 17 Feb 1975); he himself had a fond admiration for the lugubrious Robb Wilton. Each, in an affectionate exchange of mutual compliments, regarded the other as the supreme 'waiter' (that is, exponent of contemplative repose) in the business.

ERIC MIDWINTER

Sources private information (2004) [J. J. Casey] · E. C. Midwinter, *Make 'em laugh: famous comedians and their worlds* (1979) · J. Fisher, *It's a funny way to be a hero* (1973) · R. Busby, *British music hall: an illustrated who's who from 1850 to the present day* (1976)

Archives FILM BFI NFTVA, performance footage |SOUND BBC WAC

Likenesses photographs, Theatre Museum, London · photographs, Trinity College of Music, London, Jerwood Library, Mander and Mitchenson Theatre Collection

James, John (*c*.1550–1601), record-keeper and physician, was the only known child of Richard James (*c*.1524–1581) and Jane Overnone (*b*. *c*.1524), of Newport, Isle of Wight. James matriculated as sizar from Trinity College, Cambridge in 1564, becoming a scholar in 1565. He proceeded BA in 1568; became a fellow in 1569 and MA in 1571; and was licensed to practise medicine in 1575 before receiving his MD in 1578. Travelling to the Netherlands in September 1578 as England's first student at Leiden University medical school, he entered the 'physic line' and successfully incorporated his Cambridge degree into a second MD. Admitted as a candidate (1582), fellow (1584), and censor (1588, 1591, 1594) of the College of Physicians, he became physician to Queen Elizabeth's household in November 1595 at a fee of £50 per annum. Skilled in Spanish and other modern languages, he also served as the queen's reader, and a prebendary of Salisbury Cathedral (1591). He married in 1570 Elizabeth Caplin, with whom he had at least three sons, including the poet Francis *James.

The patronage of the earl of Leicester and Sir Francis

Walsingham, secretary of state, secured James a mastership of requests (1577), to assist Thomas Wilson, Leiden alumnus and 'clerk of the papers', in recovering government documents from private hands. James succeeded Wilson as custodian of the papers in November 1578 at £40 per annum, and often used his proficiency in languages in translating manuscripts. He found the state papers scattered among the shelves and storage chests of an inadequate Whitehall muniment room, on loan to government departments and antiquaries, and 'in the study' of Walsingham's 'post house' in Seething Lane, London. Consequently, he soon joined the council clerk Robert Beale in requesting that 'publicke' papers no longer remain in government officials' homes; and then set about to make an inventory of all of Secretary Walsingham's manuscripts, and to catalogue them in a volume entitled 'Walsingham's table book'. Next, he began using 'docquets of parcels' to itemize all manuscripts and instruments entrusted to departing diplomats, and occasionally provided them with historical briefs of Anglo-European relations, such as his 'Compendium Ansiaticum', which summarized all Anglo-Hanseatic relations, beginning with Edward VI and continuing into Elizabeth's reign.

Now an experienced archivist, James was assigned to examine and confiscate Walsingham's official papers following his death in 1590, only to discover that manuscript collectors had already pilfered the collection. The privy council ordered James to confiscate these essential documents, many of which he successfully retrieved. Still, he grew frustrated with his inadequate staff and muniment room, as well as the lack of a principal secretary of state between 1590 and 1598. He found many of the largely unbound domestic manuscripts in disarray or missing, due to unregistered loans. He also found it time-consuming and exhausting to sort, pack, and deliver 'diverse bookes, letters and other writings for her Majesty's service' when her court was away from Whitehall. Finally, in October 1597, James created order out of chaos by having three rooms built under the decrepit Banqueting House at Whitehall. There he installed manuscript 'presses', storage shelves, and a fireplace for drying documents, and sorted, indexed, and bundled all available letters and papers 'of lesser use' dating from 1550. Following Lord Burghley's death in 1598, his private secretary, Sir Michael Hicks, and James were ordered by the secretary of state, Robert Cecil, to transfer all books and papers from his lordship's Covent Garden house to Sir Robert's Thames-side house in the Strand; they were not deposited in the Whitehall Paper Office, in order to avoid the antiquarian pilferings of that 'engrosser of antiquities', Robert Cotton. For this and other archival services James was paid the considerable sum of £20. The substantial manuscript collections at Hatfield House, Hertfordshire, confirm Cecil's success in protecting his family's papers. However, what neither he nor James knew was that, between Burghley's death and funeral, Hicks had confiscated an equivalent 115 volumes of the treasurer's papers (now the Lansdowne MSS), and carried them off to his country house at Ruckholt, Essex.

James represented St Ives, Cornwall, in the 1584–5 parliament at the behest of the two lords of the borough, Mountjoy and Winchester. He helped to formulate a bill making it treason knowingly to receive or aid Jesuit priests, only to be stunned by John Parry's vehement speech against the bill, and the subsequent discovery of his intent to assassinate the queen. James also scolded the 'undecent forms of speech' of the corrupt and quarrelsome member for Gloucester, Thomas Atkins, who quickly reinterpreted his speech to the satisfaction of the house. Lord Burghley's submission of a bill to the Commons to end fraudulent conveyances incensed James and his colleagues as a violation of house prerogative and procedure, as it allowed victims of such fraud to seek redress in the Star Chamber, instead of the common law courts. Later, James represented Newcastle under Lyme in the reactionary 1593 parliament, which seemed determined to end puritan political power, recently weakened by the deaths of Leicester, Walter Mildmay, Walsingham, and the earl of Warwick. Sitting at the behest of his patron Robert Devereux, earl of Essex, James protested against Archbishop Whitgift's over-zealous drive for religious conformity. He also baulked at the Lords' unprecedented demand for three subsidies of £140,000, in violation of the ancient tradition that such bills must originate in the Commons, and he served on the committee that negotiated a satisfactory compromise. His parliamentary career ended with membership on committees for 'reducing disloyal subjects to their due obedience' and investigating the activities of Staffordshire brewers. The 'Mr. Doctor James' serving on the privileges and subsidy committees of this parliament was the civilian lawyer Francis James.

In December 1599 Elizabeth sent James to a 'desperately sick' earl of Essex with a message of comfort, the written opinions of eight physicians, and a pot of broth. Following the death at Christmas 1600 of Michael Heneage, James was promised the post of keeper of the Tower records, but took sick and died on about 26 January 1601. Soon afterwards his wife successfully petitioned Elizabeth for 'small' pensions for her sons 'to relieve her family's wants'.   F. JEFFREY PLATT

Sources *Calendar of the manuscripts of the most hon. the marquis of Salisbury*, 24 vols., HMC, 9 (1883–1976), vol. 7, p. 431; vol. 9, p. 117; vol. 11, p. 25; vol. 19, p. 506n · APC, 1590–99 · CSP dom., 1598–1601; 1623–5 · S. D'Ewes, ed., *A compleat journal of the votes, speeches and debates ... throughout the whole reign of Queen Elizabeth*, 2nd edn (1693), 340, 349–50, 365, 514, 517 · *Fourth report*, HMC, 3 (1874), 217, 330 · BL, Stowe MSS, no. 162, fols. 1–111 · *Report of the Deputy Keeper of the Public Records*, 30 (1869), 225, 227 · W. P. W. Phillimore and S. Andrews, eds., *Hampshire parish registers* (1912), 5, 8 · HoP, Commons, 1558–1603, 1.361; 2.373–4 · M. H. Cox and G. T. Forrest, *The parish of St Margaret, Westminster*, 2, Survey of London, 13 (1930), 117 · PRO, SP75/2, fols. 128–133 · *Report on the manuscripts of Lord De L'Isle and Dudley*, 2, HMC, 77 (1933), 423 · Munk, *Roll* · Venn, *Alum. Cant.* · Cooper, *Ath. Cantab.*, 2.178 · R. Beale, *A treatise of the office of a councellor and principall secretarie to her ma[jes]tie* (1592) · C. Read, *Mr Secretary Walsingham and the policy of Queen Elizabeth*, 1 (1925), 431 · R. B. Wernham, ed., *List and analysis of state papers, foreign series, Elizabeth I*, 1 (1964), 410–12, 632–3 · PRO, E351/3239 · 'Nicholas Faunt's

Discourse touching the office of the principal secretary of estate, etc. 1592', ed. C. Hughes, *EngHR*, 20 (1905), 499–508, esp. 505 · *DNB* · K. Sharpe, *Sir Robert Cotton, 1586–1631* (1979), 50 · J. E. Neale, *Elizabeth I and her parliaments*, 2: *1584–1601* (New York, 1958), 39–40, 49, 83–8, 245–323, 407

Wealth at death minimal; wife had to beg consideration and pensions for 'sons' from James I: *Calendar of the manuscripts of … the marquess of Salisbury*, HMC, 506 n.

James, John (*d.* 1661), Fifth Monarchist and Seventh Day Baptist preacher, was a native of England, born of poor parents, but his birthplace is unknown. He had little education, and was a ribbon weaver by trade. For some years he earned a living as a small-coal man, but was not strong enough for the work and returned to weaving. He appears to have been of weak frame and diminutive stature. He became a preacher to a congregation of Seventh Day Baptists, who met in Bulstake Alley, Whitechapel. Here he advocated the doctrine of the approaching millennial reign of Christ, where the laws of God would prevail. He employed the fiery rhetoric used by many of the Fifth Monarchists. He preached that Jesus Christ would 'use his people in his hand as his battle-ax and weapon of war for the bringing in the kingdoms of this world into subjection to Him' (*A Narrative*, 34). James's insistence on the literalness of the coming millennium opposed the Quaker spiritualization of such elements, and brought him into conflict with George Fox, who wrote a tract accusing James of having 'spoken reproachfully and backbited the people of God' (Fox, 1).

The stricter censorship brought about by the Restoration meant that religious meetings outside of the established church were banned. James, however, continued to preach, and on 19 October 1661 James and thirty or forty of his congregation were arrested in their meeting-place. James was committed to Newgate, and brought to trial at the king's bench bar on 14, 19, and 22 November. James's arrest was instigated by John Tipler, a journeyman pipemaker, who had taken offence at James's preaching. The indictment was for high treason, 'for compassing and imagining the death of the King' (*A Narrative*, 12) with three separate counts. Sir Robert Foster, the chief justice, with two other judges tried the case. The attorney-general (Sir Geoffrey Palmer) and solicitor-general (Sir Heneage Finch) prosecuted for the crown. James had no formal defence, although he did call his own witnesses who testified that James had not spoken the treasonable words attributed to him by the prosecution. James also spoke in his own defence, denying all the charges laid against him. The prosecution's evidence of the use of treasonable language was conflicting, and they presented no evidence of treasonable action. However, James's adherence to Fifth Monarchist beliefs, and the suspicion that he was involved in Thomas Venner's rising in January 1661, would certainly have gone against him. Contemporary accounts of the trial also suggest that witnesses were intimidated and that the jury was rigged, 'being all pickt men, and most of them knights and gentlemen' (ibid., 14). James was found guilty, and sentenced to be hanged, disembowelled, and quartered.

In the interval between James's conviction and sentence his wife, Elizabeth, petitioned the king telling him of her husband's innocence, but to no avail. The sentence was carried out at Tyburn on 27 November 1661. His head was set up on a pole in Whitechapel, close to the meeting-place of James's congregation. Some of his addresses and a remarkable prayer are contained in *A narrative of the apprehending, commitment, arraignment, condemnation, and execution of John James* (1662; reprinted, nearly in full, in T. B. Howell and T. J. Howell, *A Complete Collection of State Trials*, 33 vols., 1809–28, 6.67–104).

ALEXANDER GORDON, *rev.* JANE BASTON

Sources *A narrative of the apprehending, commitment, arraignment, condemnation, and execution of John James* (1662) · *The last words and actions of John James* (1661) · *Speech and declaration of John James* (1661) · *State trials*, 6.67–104 · B. S. Capp, *The Fifth Monarchy Men: a study in seventeenth-century English millenarianism* (1972) · G. Fox, *I hearing* (1658) · *The Fifth Monarchy, or, Kingdom of Christ, in opposition to the Beast's, asserted* (1659) · private information (2004) [O. Burdick]

James, John (*c.*1672–1746), architect, surveyor, and carpenter, was the eldest son of the Revd John James (*c.*1645–1733). It is clear from his memorial tablet in St Mary's Church, Eversley, Hampshire, that his parents were not Thomas and Elinor James, as was once thought. James's father was educated at the Merchant Taylors' School, London, and St John's College, Oxford. Ordained in 1673, he was elected master or praeceptor of the Holy Ghost School in Basingstoke in the same year. He became vicar of Basingstoke in 1697 and rector of Stratfield Turgis in 1717, where he remained until his death in 1733.

Although the baptisms of twelve of James's siblings are recorded at Basingstoke from 1675 to 1692, that of James himself is not among them and has not been discovered elsewhere. Elizabeth James—probably his mother—was buried at Basingstoke in 1712; his father subsequently married another Elizabeth in 1715, who died a few months after him. James's brother **George James** (*d.* 1735), baptized at Basingstoke on 24 January 1684, was a common councilman and printer to the City of London and resided in Little Britain for many years; another brother, **Thomas James** (*d.* 1738), was baptized on 18 November 1685 and became a letter founder; he recruited the financial assistance and contacts of his architect brother in an unsuccessful venture into block printing. Thomas was succeeded in his foundry business at St Bartholomew, London, in 1736 by his son **John James** (*d.* 1772), baptized on 3 January 1716 and known as the 'last of old English letter-founders'.

It is likely that James received his early education at his father's school in Basingstoke, but it is also possible that he was the John James who attended the Merchant Taylors' School in 1681–2. He did not follow his father to university, and apparently did not travel abroad: the signature of one John James in the visitors' book at Padua University in 1717 does not appear to be his. In a letter of 20 October 1711 James wrote of himself that

> perhaps no person pretending to Architecture among us, Sr. Chr: Wren excepted, has had the Advantage of a better Education in the Latin Italian and French Tongues, a competent share of Mathematicks and Ten Years Instruction in all the practical parts of Building. (Harley MSS, BM Loan 29/217, fol. 556)

This knowledge of building and architecture were acquired during his apprenticeship (1690–97) to Matthew Banckes, the king's master carpenter, through which he also gained the freedom of the City of London. James married Hannah Banckes (d. 1736), Matthew's niece, on 21 May 1697 at St Mary's Church, Teddington.

With Matthew Banckes, James presumably worked at Hampton Court Palace and Chelsea Hospital, and this association with office of works buildings by Wren laid the foundations of his style and circle of contacts with other architects and craftsmen. His earliest recorded independent employment was at the Royal Hospital for Seamen, Greenwich, in 1699, as assistant to the clerk of works, Nicholas Hawksmoor, who was also an important influence on his early work. James became joint clerk of works in 1718, and clerk from 1735, when Hawksmoor resigned. At St Paul's Cathedral, James was recorded as a carpenter in 1707, earning 2s. 6d. a day. He was later appointed master carpenter (1711), then assistant surveyor (1716), and finally surveyor to the cathedral (1724) after the death of Wren. In 1716 he gained the post of surveyor to the commissioners for the 1711 Act for Building Fifty New Churches in London, and thereby received some of his ecclesiastical commissions. He also worked as surveyor to the dean and chapter of Westminster (from 1725) and surveyor of repairs at Westminster Abbey from 1736, when Hawksmoor died. These posts reflect the growing respect for James as an able and experienced professional.

While establishing his career, James supplemented his seasonal income from building by publishing three translations: *Rules and Examples of Perspective* (1707), from Andrea Pozzo's Italian text published in Rome in 1693; *A Treatise of the Five Orders* (two editions, 1708, 1722), from Claude Perrault's French publication of 1683; and *The Theory and Practice of Gardening* (reputedly in three editions, 1712, 1728, and 1743), from Antoine Joseph Dézallier d'Argenville's anonymous original in French of 1709.

James designed both ecclesiastical and secular buildings, mainly in London and the southern counties, and also had an interest in garden design. Of his churches, the most impressive is St George's, Hanover Square, London (1721–5), with his interpretation of the hexastyle portico. Overall, few examples of his built work survive, but others may be seen in engraved form and some scattered examples of his meticulous and beautifully finished drawings record further designs. James has sometimes been seen as a prophet of Palladianism because of his declared admiration for the work of Inigo Jones. However, the qualities he perceived in Jones were plainness and economy, and the style James developed from about 1700 and continued to use was a plain baroque, with clear lines, simple shapes and plans, and a reserved use of the orders, as seen at Herriard, Hampshire, a country house of 1703–6 (dem. 1965), the house for James Johnston at Twickenham of c.1710 (dem. 1927), and his own country house, called Warbrook, in Eversley, Hampshire, built in 1724. His response to English Palladianism was a more conscious use of proportion in both elevations and plans, demonstrated by his work at Wricklemarsh, Blackheath, Kent (1723–4; dem.

1787), and Standlynch, near Downton, Wiltshire (1731–4), now known as Trafalgar House, and his most important surviving domestic work.

James's only son, also John, was born at Greenwich in 1703. He was educated at Oriel College, Oxford, and was called to the bar in 1729. He died in 1733 and was buried at Eversley, where his mother was also buried in 1736. There are no known representations of John James, although Sir James Thornhill intended to include a portrait of him, personifying 'Arithmetique' on the ceiling of the Painted Hall, Greenwich Hospital. James died at Greenwich on 15 May 1746 after a lingering illness and was buried at St Mary's, Eversley, on 21 May. He was survived by his second wife, Mary, to whom, with his daughter-in-law Frances, he left his substantial estate.   SALLY JEFFERY

Sources S. R. Jeffery, 'English Baroque architecture: the work of John James', PhD diss., U. Lond., 1986 · Colvin, *Archs.* · *DNB* · *Collectanea Topographica et Genealogica*, 8 (1843), 64 [text of memorial tablet in St Mary, Eversley] · parish registers, Basingstoke, Eversley and Stratfield Turgis, Hants. RO · parish records, Greenwich and Teddington, LMA · freedom registers, CLRO · records of the Carpenters' Company, GL · Foster, *Alum. Oxon.* · F. J. Baigent and J. E. Millard, *A history of the ancient town and manor of Basingstoke ...: with a brief account of the siege of Basing house, AD 1643–1645*, 2 vols. (1889) · Mrs E. P. Hart, ed., *Merchant Taylors' School register, 1561–1934*, 2 vols. (1936) · E. R. Mores, *A dissertation upon English typographical founders and foundries* (1778) · inventory of George James, PRO, PROB 31 182/691 · BM, Harley MSS, BM Loan 29/217, fol. 556
Archives LPL, corresp. and papers
Wealth at death property at Eversley and Greenwich: will, 1746

James, John (d. 1772). *See under* James, John (c.1672–1746).

James, John (1729–1785), schoolmaster, was born in Thornbarrow, Cumberland, the son of Thomas James. He matriculated from Queen's College, Oxford, on 4 July 1745, aged sixteen, and proceeded BA in 1751 and MA in 1755. In 1754 he became curate of Stanford Dingley, near Reading, and in the following year he was appointed headmaster of St Bees grammar school, near Whitehaven. For seventeen years he enjoyed great success at St Bees, building a flourishing school with a high record of scholarship. On 1 June 1757 he married Ann (Nan) Grayson (1731–1824) of Lamonby Hall and this happiest of marriages produced four sons and three daughters. A combination of very long hours and anxiety to do the best for every boy in his charge wore down his health and in 1771 he accepted the vicarage of Kirkoswald, near Penrith. In the event he held this living only as an absentee (until 1774) since he found the alternative offer of the curacy at Arthuret, near Carlisle, more attractive. He left St Bees in 1772 and from January 1773 was at Arthuret, where in addition to his clerical duties he ran a small private school. In 1782 he was presented to the rectories of Arthuret and Kirkandrews (which he held until his death), and in the same year he returned to Oxford to take his BD and DD degrees.

James was an effective and successful schoolmaster, but his real distinction lies in the survival of a substantial correspondence between him and his son John, and their friends and associates Richard Radcliffe (1727–1793), fellow of Queen's, and Jonathan Boucher (1738–1804), who tutored James's two eldest sons. This correspondence, a selection of which was published by the Oxford Historical Society in 1888, gives a vivid and detailed impression of life and study at Oxford University in the second half of the eighteenth century. James died at Arthuret on new year's day 1785 and was buried in the chancel of the parish church.

The younger **John James** (1760–1786) was James's second child and was born at St Bees on 21 March 1760. He was educated by his father at his schools at St Bees and Arthuret and matriculated from Queen's College, Oxford, on 10 October 1778; he graduated BA in 1782. His letters from Oxford to his father are the most useful of the collection to historians of education, for they describe in great detail the life of the undergraduate. After leaving Oxford, John assisted his father for a time in the school at Arthuret and early in 1783 joined Boucher as his usher in the latter's school at Paddington in London. In 1783 and 1784 he took holy orders as deacon and priest and on 15 April 1784 married Elizabeth Hodgson (d. 1846); they had one daughter. For a short time in 1784 he held the curacy at Paddington and was Boucher's partner in the school, but on his father's death he succeeded as rector of Arthuret and Kirkandrews owing to the influence of Sir James Graham. In November 1785 this 'young man of an amiable disposition, great learning and exemplary piety and virtue' (Evans, xiv) met with a riding accident while on an errand of mercy. He never recovered his health, despite a determined attempt to do so by inducing seasickness, and died 'of a pulmonary complaint' at Brompton, London, on 23 October 1786. He was interred in the Boucher family vault in Paddington church.

Hugh James (1771–1817), the sixth child of John James senior, was born at St Bees on 4 July 1771. He studied medicine in London and Edinburgh and in 1796 commenced practice as a surgeon in Whitehaven. A severe illness suffered in 1798 was accompanied and followed by progressive loss of sight and he abandoned any idea of a career as a surgeon. In 1803 he graduated MD from Edinburgh and subsequently practised as a physician in Carlisle. By 1806 he was completely blind but none the less built up a large and successful practice and was admired as much for his philanthropy in treating poor patients free of charge as for his acknowledged medical skill. His powerful memory enabled him to retain and recollect whatever was read to him and he thereby kept his medical knowledge up to date. He never married but was a cheerful and sociable man who 'went about doing good' (GM, 87/2.286). He died in Carlisle on 20 September 1817 of typhus fever contracted while attending a patient. He was interred in Arthuret parish church. W. R. MEYER

Sources Letters of Richard Radcliffe and John James of Queen's College, Oxford, 1755–83, ed. M. Evans, OHS (1888) · Foster, Alum. Oxon. · GM, 1st ser., 56 (1786), 911 · GM, 1st ser., 87/2 (1817), 285–6 · The story of St Bees, 1583–1939 (1939), 23, 47 · PRO, PROB 11/1146, fols. 353v–355r [will of John James the younger] · DNB
Likenesses D. Gardner, gouache and pastel drawing, Queen's College, Oxford

James, John (1760–1786). See under James, John (1729–1785).

James, John (1811–1867), antiquary, was born at West Witton, Wensleydale, Yorkshire, on 22 January 1811. After receiving a minimal education and working at a lime-kiln, he became clerk, initially to Ottiwell Tomlin, a solicitor at Richmond, Yorkshire, and afterwards to a Bradford solicitor named Tolson. Tolson encouraged him to compile The History and Topography of Bradford (1841), for which 'a continuation and additions' appeared in 1866. After Tolson's death James turned to journalism and antiquarian research, and became the local correspondent at Bradford of the Leeds Times and York Courant. He edited the poems of John Nicholson (1790–1843), the Airedale poet, published in 1844, and those of his friend Robert Story (1795–1860) in 1861. He was elected FSA in 1856, and in 1857 he published a History of the Worsted Manufacture in England from the Earliest Times, which remained the standard account for a generation. In October 1863 his paper 'On the little British kingdom of Elmet and the region of Loidis' was read to the meeting of the British Archaeological Association held at Leeds, and he wrote the entry on Yorkshire for the eighth edition of the Encyclopaedia Britannica. James died on 4 July 1867 at Nether Edge, near Sheffield, and was buried four days later at West Witton.

GORDON GOODWIN, rev. WILLIAM JOSEPH SHEILS

Sources Bradford Observer (11 July 1867) · Bradford Times (6 July 1867) · Sheffield Daily Telegraph (5 July 1867) · Sheffield and Rotherham Independent (6 July 1867) · CGPLA Eng. & Wales (1868)
Archives W. Yorks. AS, Bradford, notebooks
Wealth at death under £300: probate, 9 July 1868, CGPLA Eng. & Wales

James, John Alexander Barbour- (1867–1954), colonial official and author, was born in the Berbice-Courantyne region of British Guiana on 5 June 1867, a son of Bethune James, farmer, and Elizabeth Dunn, both of African descent. A basic education at the Congregational school in Hope Town, Bath School, and Rodborough House School in Berbice enabled him to teach younger children, and fitted him for employment as a clerk in the colony's postal service from around 1892. He studied telegraphy and started a law course by correspondence. At the age of twenty he was appointed a postmaster in Georgetown. As district postmaster at Belfield he organized self-help projects and was active in the Anglican church. He married Caroline Louisa Ethelena Spooner (c.1873–1917) on 1 August 1894; they had eight children, the third named in honour of Governor Walter Sendall, who encouraged black endeavours. Barbour-James's Victoria-Belfield Agricultural Society involved planters, peasant farmers, officials, and teachers.

Barbour-James's ambition to improve his kinfolk in Africa led him to transfer to the Gold Coast postal service in 1902. His family settled at 19 Birkbeck Grove in Acton, Middlesex, around 1904. Three of the children were born in London. In Africa, Barbour-James encouraged agricultural self-help schemes to expand the peasant economy, forming friendships with Caribbeans and Africans including doctors, lawyers, and businessmen. On leave in England he gave lectures and wrote The Agricultural and other Industrial Possibilities of the Gold Coast, published in 1911.

Two daughters and two sons died in 1915; Barbour-James's wife, Caroline, died on 12 March 1917, and their youngest daughter in June 1919. The family moved to 84 Goldsmith Avenue, Acton, when Barbour-James retired in 1918, and were joined by Barbados-born Gold Coast headteacher Edith Rita, *née* Goring (*c*.1880), who married Barbour-James on 19 October 1920 in a ceremony attended by Africans and Caribbeans.

Barbour-James represented black interests in Britain for twenty years. In 1919 he joined a South African delegation to prime minister Lloyd George; he was an official of the African Progress Union during 1918–27, founder of the Association of Coloured Peoples in 1923, and was involved in the League of Coloured Peoples between 1931 and 1947, which was headed by Jamaica-born London doctor Harold Moody. He assisted overseas students, enabled people of different backgrounds to meet, was a guide at the Gold Coast pavilion of the British Empire Exhibition of 1924, attended royal garden parties, was a freemason and a member of the Royal Empire Society and the Conservative Party, and was linked to African and West Indian protest delegations. He wrote to the press, circulated details of positive black achievements, and stressed 'the various and high achievements in culture and arts by full-blooded Negroes of both sexes' (*United Empire*, 13, 1922, 665).

Edith and John Barbour-James went to the West Indies in 1939, where their daughter Muriel was a social worker in Trinidad. This holiday became an exile due to the war. They settled in Georgetown, British Guiana, where he died in 1954.

West Indian recollections of Barbour-James focused on legal disputes over the inheritance of his London property, and his life and role in presenting positive black achievements on three continents were ignored. A younger generation demolished the empire that had found him to be a loyal and efficient servant. The tall, somewhat pompous Barbour-James wore spats decades after that fashion had ended, and his Victorian manners and imperial employment also seemed irrelevant. He had seen negative and positive sides of British imperialism and was prepared to challenge wrongs and to seek reform. He was unable to be disloyal to the system that had made him. JEFFREY GREEN

Sources C. N. Delph and V. Roth, *Who is who in British Guiana, 1938–40*, 2nd edn (1940), 632–3 · *Colonial Office List* (1920), 666 · *Gold Coast Civil Service List* (1917), 133 · *Acton District Post* (22 Oct 1920) · *Barbados Advocate* (6 Feb 1939) · 'Colour question, 1929–1936', RS Friends, Lond. · J. P. Green, 'John Alexander Barbour-James (1867–1954)', *New Community*, 13/2 (autumn 1986), 250–56 · J. P. Green, *Black Edwardians: black people in Britain, 1901–1914* (1998) · m. cert. [E. R. Goring] · private information (2004)
Likenesses photograph, repro. in Green, *Black Edwardians*

James, John Angell (1785–1859), Congregational minister and author, was born on 6 June 1785 at Salisbury Street, Blandford Forum, Dorset, the fourth child and eldest son of the eight children of Joseph James (1753?–1812), linen draper and button maker, and his wife, Sarah (1748?–1807). Another son of theirs, Thomas (1789–1873), became an influential Congregational minister. Since Joseph

John Angell James (1785–1859), by John Cochran (after Henry Room)

James was not a church member, it fell to the mother to instil habits of devotion into her children. John received his elementary education at Blandford and a school conducted by Robert Kell of Wareham, a presbyterian. He was subsequently apprenticed to Bailey, a draper at Poole. It was here that he experienced religious conviction and was encouraged by James Bennett (1774–1862) to undergo preparation for the ministry. In 1802 he entered the academy conducted by David Bogue (1750–1825) at Gosport, supported by a bursary of £30 from the fund provided by Robert Haldane (1764–1842). Since his mother was a General Baptist he had not been baptized in infancy and submitted to the ordinance while at Gosport. In later life James complained that his education had been insufficient to prepare him for his pastoral work. On 18 July 1803, in accordance with the provisions of the Toleration Act, he received at Winchester his licence to preach. In August 1804 he preached at Carrs Lane Chapel, Birmingham, and after receiving a formal call to become its pastor he was ordained on 8 May 1806. He remained minister there until his death. Because of increasing ill health he secured the assistance of R. W. Dale (1825–1895), who became his co-pastor in August 1854 and his successor. On 7 July 1806 James married Frances Charlotte Smith at Edgbaston parish church. She died on 27 January 1819, having had a son and two daughters. On 19 February 1822 John Angell James married Anna Maria, the widow of Benjamin Neale of St Paul's Churchyard. She died on 3 June 1841. Both his wives were wealthy.

James was a significant figure in nineteenth-century

nonconformity because his ministry exemplifies the developments that made it a power in the land. The first seven years of his ministry were uneventful, but from 1813 his influence increased and the new chapel that was opened in 1820 was designed to accommodate 2000 worshippers. The membership when he was ordained was forty, with a congregation of 200, but by 1850 it numbered over 1000. This was due both to his impressive preaching and the changes which he introduced into the life of the church. In 1805 its only meetings were the Sunday services and a Sunday school. Over the years an astonishing number of activities were initiated devoted to missionary and evangelistic work, the promotion of philanthropy among the poor, and the education of over 2000 children. Women took a prominent part in the life of the church as, for example, in the Maternal Society, the Dorcas Society, and the Female Benevolent Society for visiting the sick. Among the fruits of these activities were the founding of two new churches in Birmingham. It was quite usual for the church to raise £1200 a year for these and other good causes, while £23,000 was spent on the buildings during James's ministry. All this shows how Carrs Lane Chapel sought to meet the social and cultural needs of Birmingham and how it had attracted those who had profited from the wealth that was produced by its industries.

In his book *Christian Fellowship* (1822) James argued for closer co-operation between the Congregational churches, and so became one of the founders of the Congregational Union of England and Wales in 1832, a substantial modification of the strict traditional independency of the Congregational churches. In a meeting of the union in 1842 he advocated the formation of a body that would embrace all those of evangelical convictions. This was realized with the formation of the Evangelical Alliance in 1845, of which body he was the first president. His wish to include evangelical Anglicans in this common front explains his antipathy to the militant nonconformity of Edward Miall (1809–1881) as well as his opposition to the formation by him of the Anti-State Church Association in the 1840s. This did not prevent James from criticizing the ways in which the established church impinged upon the liberties of nonconformists, as in his *Dissent and the Church of England* (1834), but he advocated moderation. James shared the diffidence of the older nonconformity in his distaste for active participation in national politics. But his enthusiasm for the work of the London Missionary Society compelled him to realize that the abolition of slavery could only be achieved by political action. Though he was not an enthusiast, he was an activist with regard to public affairs in Birmingham. He was seriously interested in providing for others the educational advantages that had eluded him. Hence the readiness with which he presided over the council of Spring Hill College from its inception in 1839 until his death.

James was a prolific author, as the seventeen volumes of his collected works (1860–64), edited by his son, demonstrate. His moderate Calvinism found expression not in the systematic exposition of doctrine but in promoting practical spiritual and moral guidance. His best-known book was the *Anxious Enquirer*. It was first published in 1834 and became extraordinarily popular. Fifteen editions were published during his lifetime and half a million copies sold, not to mention the translations of the book into a dozen languages. James died on Saturday, 1 October 1859, at his home in Edgbaston, and was buried six days later in a vault before the pulpit in Carrs Lane Chapel, having secured special permission for this from the Home Office.

His son, **Thomas Smith James** (1809–1874), was a lawyer in Birmingham. In addition to editing his father's works, he published *The history of the litigation and legislation respecting presbyterian chapels and charities in England and Ireland* (1867). He died on 3 February 1874, having been twice married. R. TUDUR JONES

Sources *Life and letters of John Angell James*, ed. R. W. Dale (1861) · J. A. James, 'Autobiography', in *Life and letters of John Angell James*, ed. R. W. Dale (1861) · J. Campbell, *John Angell James* (1860) · C. A. Haig, *John Angell James* (1961) · *Christian Witness*, 16 (1859), 490–95 · CGPLA *Eng. & Wales* (1874) [Thomas Smith James]
Archives Birm. CA, letters and papers; corresp. · DWL, corresp. · U. Birm. L., letters relating to proofs, etc.
Likenesses W. Derby, stipple, pubd *c.*1820 (after R. Cooper), NPG · J. Cocheau, engraving (after painting by H. Room), repro. in Campbell, *John Angell James*, frontispiece · J. Cochran, stipple (after H. Room), NPG [*see illus.*] · Coleman, engraving, repro. in *Congregational Magazine* · B. R. Haydon, group portrait, oils (*The Anti-Slavery Society Convention, 1840*), NPG · D. J. Pound, stipple (after photograph by J. Whitlock), NPG · engraving (after Branwhite), repro. in *Evangelical Magazine* · photograph, repro. in *Illustrated News of the World*
Wealth at death under £12,000: resworn probate, Feb 1862, CGPLA *Eng. & Wales* (1859) · under £35,000—Thomas Smith James: probate, 20 Feb 1874, CGPLA *Eng. & Wales*

James, John Haddy (1788–1869), surgeon, the son of William James, a retired Bristol merchant, and his wife, Hannah, *née* Williams, of Sowden House, Lympstone, was born at Maddox Row, Exeter, on 6 July 1788. He attended Exeter grammar school, and was apprenticed in 1803 to Benjamin Johnson, a surgeon apothecary, and, having left early because of Johnson's 'indiscretions', was then apprenticed from 1806 until 1808 to Mr Patch, surgeon to the Devon and Exeter Hospital (James, 1). From 1808 to 1812 he was a student at St Bartholomew's Hospital, London, where he spent a year living with John Abernethy, and then became a house surgeon. James qualified MRCS in 1811, and became assistant surgeon to the 1st Life Guards. He went with his regiment to Ostend in June 1815 and served through the Waterloo campaign and the Paris occupation. The regimental order book of the Life Guards for the day of Waterloo contains the telling injunction that 'Assistant Surgeon James is not in the future to expose himself under fire' (Plarr, 1.605). James kept a journal of his experiences which has since been published.

After leaving the army in June 1816, following two failed attempts James was elected surgeon to the Devon and Exeter Hospital, and at the same time began a general practice in Exeter, with a house in the cathedral close. At the hospital he established a series of lectures on anatomy and physiology, along with a colleague named Barnes, and set up the pathological museum, the catalogue of which occupied much of his spare time. He was a strong advocate of provincial as against exclusively metropolitan medical education, and became one of the original members of the Provincial Medical and Surgical Association (later the British Medical Association). At its Liverpool meeting in 1839 he was chosen to give the retrospective address in surgery, and he was made president of the Exeter meeting in 1842. He became a town councillor of Exeter in 1820, sheriff in 1826, and mayor in 1828; he retired from municipal business when the old corporation was dissolved in 1835.

James was a man of great mental and physical energy who professed tory and staunch high-church principles. He dressed in an old-fashioned way, and in appearance he was:

> of middle height, and compact frame, and very muscular without being large. His features were handsomely and sharply moulded; the eyes blue and soft in expression. He retained, to the very last, a fresh aspect, and even some traces of youthful appearance. (*BMJ*, 319)

In medical matters he was cautious, opinionated, and conservative, and was known as a careful, though not an artistic, surgeon. An assiduous note-taker (he left eleven manuscript volumes of cases written up by himself), he was gifted with a good memory which made his wide experience available to others. James was twice married, first in 1822 to Elizabeth Withal (*d.* 1839), with whom he had eleven children, and again in 1840 to Harriet Hill of Exmouth, who survived him. Only one of his children, his eldest son, a surgeon, died before him.

In 1843 James was nominated as one of the first honorary fellows of the Royal College of Surgeons under its new charter. In 1858 he resigned the surgeoncy of the Devon and Exeter Hospital (his son succeeding him), but he remained until 1868 in his favourite office of curator of the museum, for which he had a house built in its grounds by private subscription in 1853. 'James of Exeter' was well known in the profession at large, partly by the spread of his local fame, and partly as a writer on inflammation, and as one of the few surgeons who had tied the abdominal aorta for aneurysm of the internal iliac artery, though the patient died in less than three hours (*Medico-Chirurgical Transactions*, vol. 14, 1829). His writings on inflammation began in 1818, when he won the Jacksonian prize for an essay on this subject. James frequently quoted John Hunter and M. F. X. Bichat, distinguished between the reparative and other effects of inflammation, and maintained that the extent of the process was limited by the quantity of plastic lymph effused. He published a number of other papers, a complete list of which was published in the *British Medical Journal* (1869, 1.319). His literary activity revived in his last years (1865–9) when, due to failing sight, he occupied himself with dictating the fruits of his experience to an amanuensis, producing several papers this way.

James died on 17 March 1869 at his house in Chichester Place, East Southernhay, Exeter. He was buried in Lympstone churchyard.

CHARLES CREIGHTON, *rev.* PATRICK WALLIS

Sources *BMJ* (3 April 1869), 318–20 · *The Lancet* (3 April 1869) · J. H. James, *Surgeon James's journal*, ed. J. Vansittart (1964) · V. G. Plarr, *Plarr's Lives of the fellows of the Royal College of Surgeons of England*, rev. D'A. Power, 2 vols. (1930) · V. C. Medvei and J. L. Thornton, eds., *The royal hospital of Saint Bartholomew, 1123–1973* (1974)
Archives Devon RO, journal
Likenesses J. Leakey, portrait, Devon and Exeter Hospital, Exeter · portrait, repro. in James, *Surgeon James's journal*, frontispiece
Wealth at death under £25,000: probate, 6 July 1869, *CGPLA Eng. & Wales*

James, John Thomas (1786–1828), bishop of Calcutta and writer on art, was born on 23 January 1786 at Rugby, Warwickshire, the eldest son of Dr Thomas *James (1748–1804), headmaster of Rugby School, and his second wife, Arabella Caldecott (*d.* 1828). He was educated at Rugby School until he was twelve years old, when, by the interest of the earl of Dartmouth, he was placed on the foundation of the Charterhouse. In 1803 he gained the first prize medal given by the Society for the Encouragement of Arts and Sciences for a drawing of Winchester Cathedral. He left the Charterhouse in May 1804, when he was chosen to deliver the annual oration, and entered Christ Church, Oxford. After the death of his father on 23 September 1804, he was granted the dean's studentship by Dr Cyril Jackson. He graduated BA on 9 March 1808, and MA on 24 October 1810.

James continued to reside at Oxford, first as a private tutor and afterwards as student and tutor of Christ Church, until 1813, when he toured northern Europe with Sir James Riddell. After his return he published, in 1816, a *Journal of a Tour in Germany, Sweden, Russia, and Poland, during 1813 and 1814*. Subsequent editions, in two volumes, appeared in 1817 and 1819.

In 1816 James visited Italy, and studied painting at Rome and Naples. On his return to England he entered the church, and resigned his studentship on obtaining the vicarage of Flitton-cum-Silsoe in Bedfordshire. While there he published two works on art—*The Italian Schools of Painting* (1820), and *The Flemish, Dutch, and German Schools of Painting* (1822)—and a theological work entitled *The Semi-Sceptic, or, The Common Sense of Religion Considered* (1825). In 1823 James married Marianne Jane, fourth daughter of Frederick Reeves, of East Sheen, Surrey, and formerly of Mangalore, in the Bombay presidency. The Revd John Acland James was their son. James intended to complete his writings on art with publications on the English, French, and Spanish schools. In 1826 he began the publication of a series of *Views in Russia, Sweden, Poland, and Germany*. These were engraved on stone by himself, and coloured so as to represent originals. Five numbers of these appeared during 1826 and 1827.

Publication of the series was interrupted by James's appointment to the bishopric of Calcutta, vacant owing to the death of Bishop Heber, at the end of 1826. James resigned his vicarage in April 1827. The University of Oxford gave him the degree of DD by diploma on 10 May, and on Whitsunday, 3 June, he was consecrated at Lambeth. He landed at Calcutta on 18 January 1828, and was installed in the cathedral on the following Sunday, the 20th.

After a reorganization of the parishes, on 20 June James commenced a tour of the western provinces of his diocese. He was taken ill *en route* and on returning to Calcutta was ordered to take a sea voyage. He sailed for China on 9 August, but died during the voyage on 22 August 1828. His *Charge Delivered to the Clergy of the Archdeaconry of Calcutta … at the Primary Visitation of … J. T. James … Bishop of Calcutta* was posthumously published in 1829. *The Brief Memoirs … of John Thomas James*, edited by E. James, was published in 1830.
E. J. RAPSON, *rev.* PAUL A. COX

Sources E. James, *Brief memoirs of J. T. James, bishop of Calcutta: particularly during his residence in India; gathered from his letters and papers* (1830) · J. Gorton, *A general biographical dictionary*, new edn, 4 vols. (1851) · will, PRO, PROB 11/1752, sig. 142 · Foster, *Alum. Oxon.*
Archives BL, corresp. with Sir Robert Peel, Add. MSS 40226–40392, *passim*
Likenesses B. R. Faulkner, oils, exh. RA 1828, Christ Church Oxf. · E. Finden, stipple (after J. Slater), BM, NPG

James [*née* Calkin], **Margaret Bernard** (1895–1985), designer, calligrapher, and painter, was born on 23 February 1895 at 22 Holmdale Road, West Hampstead, London, the third of seven children of Harry Bernard Calkin (1861–1926), who married Margaret Agnes Palfrey (1870–1936) in 1890. He was in insurance and became a Lloyds underwriter *c.*1910. Margaret's maternal grandfather, Powell Penry Palfrey, was a noted painter of horses and a heraldic stained-glass designer; her paternal great-grandfather founded the bookbinding firm Robert Riviere & Sons, which later employed her uncle Arthur.

Margaret Calkin was educated at North London Collegiate School (1909–13) and at the Central School of Arts and Crafts (1913–15). She specialized in calligraphy and gilded illumination under Graily Hewitt, and won a queen's scholarship in 1915. She designed and made her own simple clothes, bobbed her hair, and determined to live according to the arts and crafts principle that beauty is a consequence of purpose perfectly fulfilled. In the 1920s she began a lifelong commitment to the ideals and teachings of Christian Science.

During the First World War, Margaret Calkin supervised the art department of the Central London Young Men's Christian Association (YMCA), supplying thousands of items to Red Triangle huts. When the department closed after the war she established her Rainbow Workshop in the same premises and continued to design and produce pictures, soft furnishings, carved signs, memorials, and calligraphy. Her energetic labours were accompanied by a sense of humour and a talent for theatre design and performance.

On 15 June 1922 Margaret Calkin married the architect Charles Holloway James RA FRIBA (1893–1953). He designed a series of houses in Hampstead to accommodate their growing family, always including a workshop for his wife. Their first home—1 Hampstead Way—was linked to the Rainbow Workshop through a carved and painted front-door lintel depicting the ark and rainbow from Calkin's original signboard. The couple were known as Jane and Jimmy James to a wide circle of architects, publishers, and Royal Academicians, who provided Margaret Calkin James with commissions from the Royal Institute of British Architects, Jonathan Cape, the BBC, and Lloyds of London. Her calligraphy was exhibited at the Royal Academy's arts and crafts exhibition (1916) and her book jackets at the 'British Art in Industry' exhibition (RA, 1935). She designed Curwen Press pattern papers and many typographic book covers. Textile patterns designed and printed in and for her own homes exemplify the revival between the wars of hand-blocked printing. Her curtain designs were used in Norwich City Hall, which was designed by the architects C. H. James and S. R. Pierce in 1938.

Calkin James's order book recorded her design jobs; a gap, in 1921–7, signalled her adjustment to family life. She had three children: Brian (1923–1944), Alison (1925–1987), and Elizabeth (b. 1929). She attended design classes inaugurated at Westminster School of Art by E. McKnight Kauffer and merged the stylized geometry of continental modernism with traditional calligraphic skills, hence her striking posters and promotional material for progressive and prestigious clients like Frank Pick (London Passenger Transport Board), Jack Beddington (Shell), and Stephen Tallents (Empire Marketing Board; General Post Office).

Observational drawing and watercolours underpinned all Calkin James's designs. She had three solo shows in London: at Cooling Galleries, New Bond Street, in 1935; at Kensington Art Gallery in 1948; and at St George's Gallery, Cork Street, in 1957. In Chipping Campden, Gloucestershire, during the Second World War she painted flowers and topographical scenes, translating some into prints. Having returned to Hampstead in 1947 her ongoing calligraphic commissions again included memorials of the war dead. Her lino-prints appeared in the Royal Academy summer exhibitions during the 1960s.

A stroke in 1969 deprived Calkin James of speech and the use of her right hand, but not of her delight in experimenting with colour and pattern, thereafter seen in the lively needlepoint samplers stitched with her left hand and exhibited during the International Year of the Disabled (Welwyn, 1981; Central London YMCA, 1982). She died at her home in Welwyn—18 Briary Wood Lane—on 12 February 1985, and was cremated on 16 February. Subsequently her work was exhibited in 'Women Designing: Redefining Design in Britain Between the Wars' (Brighton University, 1994) and then shown nationally from 1996 in the touring retrospective 'At the Sign of the Rainbow'. This exhibition consolidated her reputation, showing her to be a more considerable and indeed consistent designer than had been apparent during her somewhat fragmented career. Examples of her work are held in the Victoria and Albert Museum and the London Transport Museum; samples of her Curwen Press paper designs are in Cambridge University Library.
BETTY MILES

Sources private information (2004) [family] · B. Miles, 'Tradition and modernity? Margaret Calkin James, 1895–1985, and C. H. James, 1893–1953', *Decorative Arts Society Journal*, 20 (1996), 62–78 · B. Miles, 'Margaret Calkin James: designer, calligrapher and painter', *Women designing: redefining design in Britain between the wars,* ed. J. Seddon and S. Worden (1994), 115–22 [exhibition catalogue, University of Brighton Gallery, 7–31 March 1994] • B. Miles, *At the sign of the rainbow: Margaret Calkin James, 1895–1985* (1996) • D. McKitterick, *A new specimen book of Curwen pattern papers* (1987), 62 • A. Simons, 'Lettering in book production', *Lettering of today*, ed. C. G. Holme (1937) • 'The Arts and Crafts Exhibition: pleasure, profit and patriotism', *Glasgow Herald* (31 Nov 1916) • 'At the Sign of the Rainbow', *Queen* (13 Nov 1920) • 'Colour design on the stage', *Architectural Association Journal*, 35/396 (Feb 1920), 247 • 'New talent: the Westminster School of Art', *Commercial Art*, 5/28 (Oct 1928), 179–81 • 'A new telegram envelope', *The Times* (23 July 1935) • *The Times* (10 Feb 1926) • b. cert. • d. cert.

Likenesses photograph, 1935, repro. in Miles, *At the sign of the Rainbow*, 8; priv. coll.

James, Minnie Stewart Rhodes (1865–1903), librarian and author, was born on 7 July 1865 in Aldeburgh, Suffolk, the daughter of Henry Haughton James, late commander in the Indian navy, and his wife, Sophia Helen Courthope. Minnie James was one of the first women in Great Britain to become head of a major library, and was an outspoken proponent of librarianship as a profession for women and of the training of library assistants.

Little is known of James's education and early life until 1887, when she was appointed assistant librarian at the People's Palace, London. She became head librarian in 1889. The People's Palace, located on the Mile End Road, was founded in 1886 to provide technical training and recreation for the people of the East End of London. As she explained in a paper read at the World's Congress of Librarians in Chicago in July 1893, later published in the *Library Journal* in the October of that year, James played an important role in building the collections of the People's Palace Library. Her writings display respect and sympathy for the library's working-class clientele, whom she tried to accommodate by Sunday opening (between 3 p.m. and 10 p.m.) and by the acquisition of novels and other light reading. James left the library, however, in 1894, discouraged by the under-funding of the recreational side of the People's Palace (of which the library was part) in comparison to its technical instruction side. In fact, the library was closed for some years from 1901, although it eventually became the library of Queen Mary College, University of London.

Minnie James next served for a short time as the curator of the Library Association museum, a permanent exhibit of library equipment kept at the Library Bureau in Bloomsbury. The Library Bureau was a branch of the Library Bureau, Boston, Massachusetts, a manufacturer of library equipment founded in 1876 by Melvil Dewey. Known for developing the vertical file system, two-colour typewriter ribbon, and other products, the Library Bureau eventually became a subdivision of the Rand Kardex Bureau. In 1897 James was appointed librarian of the Library Bureau in Boston, Massachusetts, where she remained until her death.

Throughout her career James was active in the Library Association, which she joined in 1889. She was instrumental in getting the Library Association involved in the training of library assistants: she was a founder of the Library Association summer school in library science, first held in 1893, and an active member of the association's education committee and of the Library Assistants Association. She was also active in the American Library Association and in the Massachusetts Library Club.

Well read, liberal-minded, and articulate, James was the author of over twenty-five articles about her work at the People's Palace Library, the need for training of library assistants, and the employment of women in libraries, among other subjects. Her 'The progress of the modern card catalog principle', in *Public Libraries* of May 1902, was reprinted many times. She was particularly concerned with the reluctance of British libraries to hire women, especially in comparison to the United States, where library education was available and women were employed in libraries in much greater numbers: 'Women are peculiarly fitted for such work' she wrote, 'and it is a source of great wonderment to everyone who has considered the subject that so few such women have been employed in British libraries in really responsible positions' (M. James, 'Women librarians and their future prospects', *Library Association Record*, June 1900, 292–3).

About 1900 Minnie James's health began to fail. She spent the spring of 1901 in the Bahamas, producing a paper on the public library system there (it appeared in the *Library Association Record* in 1901). On 5 June 1903 she died of typhoid fever in St Botolph Hospital in Boston. Minnie James was a valued colleague and friend, as evidenced by the many tributes written after her death. The obituary in *Library Journal* (June 1903) noted that, as a woman 'of a most winning vivacity and charm, all who knew her will remember her with affection and will feel her death as a personal loss'.

FERNANDA HELEN PERRONE

Sources A. Clarke, 'Few and far between: women librarians in the nineteenth century', *One hundred years: a collection to celebrate the Library Association centenary* (1977), 25–40 • J. Minto, *A history of the public library movement in Great Britain and Ireland* (1932) • *Library Association Record*, 5 (1903), 326 • *Library Journal*, 28 (June 1903), 320 • M. S. R. James, 'The People's Palace Library', *The Library*, 2 (1890), 341–51 • D. Garrison, *Apostles of culture: the public librarian and American society* (1979) • 'What they read in the East End: an interview with the lady librarian at the People's Palace', *Young Woman*, 1 (1892–3), 411–14 • b. cert.

Likenesses photograph, *c*.1893, repro. in 'What they read in the East End', 411

James, Montague Rhodes (1862–1936), college head, scholar, and author, was born at Goodnestone in Kent on 1 August 1862, the fourth and youngest child of Herbert James (1822–1909) and his wife of fifteen years, Mary Emily Horton (1818–1899). When Monty (as he was familiarly known) was three years old his father, a high-minded country parson, became rector of Great Livermere in Suffolk, near Bury St Edmunds; the love of East Anglia which figures prominently in James's writings was thus begun early. There was some record of achievement and prominence on both sides of the family: the Rhodes Jameses had held substantial interests in Jamaica until the abolition of slavery there in 1807, and Mary Emily's father, Admiral Joshua Sydney Horton, had been a naval hero during the Napoleonic wars.

Montague Rhodes James (1862–1936), by Sir Gerald Kelly, 1936

Education The young Monty was sent to private school at Temple Grove in Surrey (1873–6), where his father had been a pupil and where the headmaster, O. C. Waterfield, was to be a powerful influence, and followed in his father's footsteps also in being elected a king's scholar at Eton College (1876–82). There he flourished, in a context of sympathetic masters and congenial contemporaries; at least one of the former, his tutor H. E. Luxmoore, and several of the latter, notably A. C. Benson, were to become lifelong friends. Easy mastery of the set academic subjects—with mathematics a conspicuous exception—left the precocious schoolboy time to delve into arcane corners of biblical apocrypha and, more important, to avail himself of the nearly unique opportunity offered him by perspicacious authorities to use the college (as distinct from school) library, with its splendid collection of medieval manuscripts and early printed books. The foundations both of his scholarship and of his assumption that scholarship was inseparable from friendships nurtured in select academic settings can be traced to what seem to have been extraordinarily happy years at Eton—to which, as he was candid about saying, his heart always belonged.

Election to a scholarship at King's College, Cambridge, was almost a foregone conclusion. The Cambridge foundation that James entered in 1882 was still heavily Etonian in make-up and ethos, though this was beginning to change. In the ensuing tensions he came to adopt a mediating position, which stood him in good stead when, a

year after having taken his BA in 1886, he was elected to a fellowship in the college and soon found himself dean. For over two decades, until he became provost (and indeed after that, at the provost's lodge), his rooms at King's were a centre of hospitality for those—by no means all from major public schools—who found his blend of donnish affability with a profound if somewhat light-hearted erudition to their taste.

Scholarly interests and research The erudition was bearing early fruit on all three of the branches of learning in which James was to become distinguished. The subject of research that gained him his fellowship was the Apocalypse of Peter, a second-century apocryphon long known about but not fully available until discoveries in Egypt in 1886–7. James had already constructed from patristic and other allusions an outline of what the document would contain, and his surmises were largely borne out when he was able to edit the work (in a joint publication with J. Armitage Robinson, who presented the gospel of Peter) in 1892. Editions of a number of apocryphal pieces followed, principally in two volumes entitled *Apocrypha anecdota* (1893, 1897). Although James was not to become a biblical scholar (extending that term to include students of pseudepigrapha) of the absolute first rank, his contributions were of great importance not only in editions of texts and in numerous articles in the recently founded *Journal of Theological Studies* but also in presentations of the subject in quasi-popular form, through entries in reference works such as Hastings's *Dictionary of the Bible* and, later in his life, in three volumes of translations. These are *The Biblical Antiquities of Philo* (1917), from the pseudo-Philonic *Liber antiquitatum biblicarum*, possibly of the second century; a summary entitled *The lost apocrypha of the Old Testament: their titles and fragments collected, translated, and discussed* (1920); and one of his best-known works, *The Apocryphal New Testament* (1924), a fat collection of all the (then) known 'apocryphal gospels, acts, epistles, and apocalypses' (as the subtitle read), which was standard until J. K. Elliott's collection of the same name appeared in 1993.

The second main branch of James's scholarly interests, those for which he used the umbrella term 'Christian archaeology', began with schoolboy probings into East Anglian and other English churches, and, as expressed in publications, went hand in hand with the extension of those probings on annual (at least) trips to France and with his work at the Fitzwilliam Museum, as assistant director from 1886 and director from 1889 to 1908. A primary thrust of these investigations was iconographic, as in his solving of the puzzle of the mutilated sculptural programme of the lady chapel at Ely (1892). Wall paintings, windows, sculpture, and brasses were elucidated at such places as Canterbury, Malmesbury, Norwich, Peterborough, Bury St Edmunds, and Worcester, and at his own foundations at Eton and King's. Hagiography was another important aspect, the saints in question ranging from the obscure (Urith of Littlehampton) to the dubious (William of Norwich). This combination of interests is seen to advantage in two highly accessible works of his later years, the Great Western Railway volume *Abbeys* (1925) and, in the same spacious format, an East Anglian 'perambulation' entitled *Suffolk and Norfolk* (1930).

The 'descriptive catalogues' The results of teenage browsing into the manuscripts at Eton were jotted into notebooks, as were those from the leisurely scrutinizing of the Fitzwilliam's manuscripts which his position there made convenient. These laid the foundations for the first of the astonishing series of 'descriptive catalogues' of collections of manuscripts in the Cambridge colleges and in several other notable collections, both public and private. (The specifications in the titles vary, but for the most part medieval, and sometimes only medieval Latin, manuscripts are covered.) In a true *annus mirabilis*, there appeared in 1895, as well as many other works, catalogues of the collections not only at Eton and the Fitzwilliam but also at King's, Jesus, and Sidney Sussex. Naturally, these early efforts lack the mastery of some of the later catalogues, but collectively they represent a staggering achievement for a man not yet thirty-five. As was to be true of all his catalogues, their great strength lies in the thoroughness of description of illustration and the ready application of biblical and hagiographic knowledge; where these capacities do not come into play, and above all in some legal and scientific manuscripts, the descriptions can be markedly inadequate. The speed with which the catalogues appeared was facilitated by the willingness of most Cambridge colleges to send the majority of their manuscripts to James's rooms at King's so that he could work on them at leisure there: a practice followed also by the great collector Henry Yates Thompson, many of whose books were catalogued by James in 1898 and 1902, and later by J. Pierpont Morgan for his library in New York (1907).

The series of manuscript catalogues for the Cambridge colleges continued steadily through to 1914, both with the relatively smaller collections and with the two of disproportionate weight and importance, Trinity and Corpus Christi. The catalogue for the very large—roughly 1500 manuscripts—and highly diverse collection at Trinity appeared in four volumes between 1900 and 1905, and shows James at his most expansive in descriptions of its illuminated books, most obviously the Trinity Apocalypse (although the title specifies 'Western manuscripts', the post-medieval books get short shrift). The manuscripts in the Parker Library at Corpus Christi include one of the most valuable collections of Anglo-Saxon manuscripts extant, as well as books of the importance of the Bury Bible and the two-volume Matthew Paris *Chronica maiora*, but James's efforts were somewhat vitiated by a format that tried to reproduce where possible the descriptions of James Nasmith published in 1777: for some 238 of the 538 manuscripts, Nasmith's work, in Latin, is printed first, with James's comments as a kind of gloss. What should have been among his most splendid achievements (2 vols., 1909–12) is thus made often difficult and confusing to use. Other notable catalogues of Cambridge collections include those for Gonville and Caius (2 vols., 1907–8; with

supplement 1914), the McClean collection at the Fitzwilliam Museum (1912, a collection that James had been instrumental in securing), and St John's, arguably the finest of the catalogues (1913). He also completed, largely by 1914, descriptions for catalogues of manuscripts in two notable British collections outside Cambridge, those (Latin manuscripts) at the new John Rylands Library in Manchester (though not published until 1921) and those at Lambeth Palace, most of the work on which was done during the war years, its publication being held up until 1930–32 by the dilatoriness of a putative collaborator for the modern manuscripts.

Cambridge life and the short stories James's life in Cambridge, as fellow and dean of King's and (from 1893) director of the Fitzwilliam, was full and, it appears, massively enjoyable. A more or less conscious decision not to become ordained (although remaining throughout his life a faithful and publicly practising Christian) and an apparently not quite conscious decision not to marry placed at the centre of his life his scholarly work, his academic positions, his family (his father lived until 1909, and there were two brothers and a sister, to all of whom he was reasonably close), and his steadily growing number of friends.

It seems to have been in the context of joint Christmas entertainments with the latter that the first of his ghost stories were written, although it is widely said that their intended audience was the choristers of King's. In any case, a couple were printed in general magazines in the 1890s, and by 1904 James was prevailed on by the publisher Edward Arnold to bring out a collection of eight tales, entitled *Ghost Stories of an Antiquary*. There is no question of apprenticeship here; the first story, 'Canon Alberic's Scrap Book', contains the donnish tone, the massing of verisimilitudinous detail (often of a tongue-in-cheek scholarly sort), and the using of that detail to intensify the terror when it comes that are his trademarks. The popularity of the first collection led to requests for more—among fans were the prince of Wales and Theodore Roosevelt—and (seven) *More Ghost Stories of an Antiquary* appeared in 1911, *A Thin Ghost and other Stories* (five in all) in 1919, and *A Warning to the Curious* (six stories) in 1925. (An omnibus *Collected Ghost Stories* was published in 1931, including four brief pieces written after the latest collection.) Opinions vary vigorously as to favourites among these thirty or so stories, but '"Oh whistle, and I'll come to you, my lad"', 'Casting the Runes', 'The Tractate Middoth', and 'An Uncommon Prayer Book' must certainly be regarded as among the finest in the authenticity of their settings and in the rather satisfying nature of their ghoulish conclusions. There seems to be no evidence that they also reflect conflicts and ambivalences deep inside their author.

Provost of King's and of Eton His election in 1905 to the provostship of King's, although not uncontested and indeed not sought by James himself, was taken almost in his stride. He remained director of the Fitzwilliam until 1908 and continued his multifarious scholarly activities, but there was a great deal of college business to attend to, not all of it congenial. (A particular thorn in his side was John Maynard Keynes, elected to a fellowship in 1906.) To one of his Cambridge experience the vice-chancellorship of the university might have been expected eventually, but James assumed a two-year term in that office unusually early, in 1913; this gave him a year in the post before the First World War broke out. Responsibility for initial wartime arrangements for the university fell heavily on him, and the loss of many of his young friends added to the burden; nor was he sanguine about some of the directions in which he sensed that Cambridge was moving. So it was not surprising that when, towards the war's end, the crown offered him the provostship of Eton, he accepted that less onerous and ostensibly less visible position.

The provostship of Eton was (minimal constitutional duties as head of its corporation aside) pretty much what the holder wanted it to be. In James's case it seems to have been primarily a replication of the aspects of his Cambridge life that he had enjoyed the most: maintaining old friendships, making new ones (especially with the young), and continuing the sorts of scholarly work that most appealed to him. He managed to be amazingly present in the college without seeming to interfere with the headmaster's running of it, and inspired an enduring (and subsequently often expressed) affection among a number of the boys. Although no great feats of published scholarship are primarily the product of the years back at Eton, he maintained a steady production of useful articles, public lectures (notably the 1927 British Academy Schweich lectures, published four years later as *The Apocalypse in Art*), and, most typically, the 'presentation' of important illuminated manuscripts. A number of the latter works appeared as Roxburghe Club publications or in other equally sumptuous formats. A major unfinished project was the cataloguing of the medieval manuscripts at the university library at Cambridge; some draft descriptions, often fragmentary, are all that was accomplished, and the inadequate mid-nineteenth century catalogue still holds the field. On the other hand, the cumulative effect of James's investigations into medieval library catalogues and booklists and into the whole subject summed up by the title of his cheerful pamphlet *The Wanderings and Homes of Manuscripts* (1919) has flourished mightily under the efforts of such successors as N. R. Ker and R. A. B. Mynors (both Etonians).

Final years and reputation James's last years were crowded with honours, especially the Order of Merit, conferred in 1930, as well as honorary doctorates from Oxford and Cambridge. His extensive circle of friends and the prominence of the positions he held would have made him something of a national figure even without his fame as the author of ghost stories. If it is for the latter that he is now most widely known, his scholarly achievement continues to be fundamental in all of the major areas in which he worked. He stands, among the great figures of the British humanistic tradition, on a high peak in terms

of accomplishment and on the very highest in terms of the congeniality of scholarship at its best.

James died, probably of renal failure, on 12 June 1936, while still provost of Eton, and was buried in the parish churchyard there on 15 June. Ten years earlier he had produced an autobiographically uninformative but often hilarious volume of recollections (in tandem with a similar volume by his brother Sydney) called, not surprisingly, *Eton and King's*. Of various memoirs which appeared after his death, the fullest was by his friend S. G. Lubbock (1939), with a classified list of James's writings compiled earlier by A. F. Scholfield, aided by James himself.

RICHARD W. PFAFF

Sources R. W. Pfaff, *Montague Rhodes James* (1980) • L. Dennison, ed., *The legacy of M. R. James* [Cambridge 1995] (2001) • S. G. Lubbock, *A memoir of Montague Rhodes James, with a list of his writings by A. F. Scholfield* (1939) • M. R. James, *Eton and King's: recollections, mostly trivial, 1875–1925* (1926) • M. Cox, *M. R. James: an informal portrait* (1983) • G. McBryde, ed., *Montague Rhodes James: letters to a friend* (1956) • *Montague Rhodes James: three tributes* (1936) • S. Gaselee, 'Montague Rhodes James, 1862–1936', *PBA*, 22 (1936), 418–33 • N. Barker, 'After M. R. James', *Book Collector*, 19 (1970), 7–20

Archives BL, Egerton MS 3141 • CUL, collection of MSS; corresp., bibliographical and antiquarian memoranda, lectures, sermons, etc.; journal and bibliographic notes; lectures and addresses; lecture on Abbey Church, Bury St Edmunds • Eton • FM Cam., notebooks relating to MSS, biblical studies, architecture, classical art and archaeology, iconography, his travels, etc. • King's AC Cam., corresp. and papers | BL, corresp. with Sir Sydney Cockerell, Add. MS 52728 • BL, letters to J. P. Gilson, Add. MSS 47686–47687 • BL, letters to Eric Millar, Add. MSS 54319–54320 • CUL, letters to H. F. Stewart • FM Cam., letters to T. H. Riches • King's AC Cam., letters to Oscar Browning • King's AC Cam., letters to Gwen McBryde • King's AC Cam., letters to Sir J. T. Sheppard • LPL, corresp. with Claude Jenkins • Norfolk RO, letters to Prince Frederick, Duleep Singh • Trinity Cam., letters to Sir Henry Babington Smith

Likenesses W. Strang, chalk drawing, 1909, FM Cam.; repro. in McBryde, ed., *Montague Rhodes James* • M. Saumarez, oils, c.1910, Eton • photograph, 1910, repro. in Lubbock, *Memoir*, frontispiece • O. Edis, photograph, c.1912, NPG • W. Rothenstein, drawing, 1915, King's Cam. • G. Philpot, oils, 1918, King's Cam. • photograph, c.1925, repro. in James, *Eton and King's*, frontispiece • W. Stoneman, photograph, 1930, NPG • H. Coster, photographs, 1930–39, NPG • photograph, c.1932, repro. in Lubbock, *Memoir*, facing p. 42 • G. Kelly, oils, 1936, Eton College [see illus.] • G. Kelly, oils, c.1936, NPG

Wealth at death £3873 1s. 3d.: probate, 4 Aug 1936, CGPLA Eng. & Wales

James, (John) Morrice Cairns, Baron Saint Brides (1916–1989), diplomatist

James, (John) Morrice Cairns, Baron Saint Brides (1916–1989), diplomatist, was born on 30 April 1916 in Finchley, Middlesex, the only son and younger child of Lewis Cairns James, professor of drama and elocution at the Royal College of Music, and his second wife, Catherine Mary, daughter of John Maitland Marshall, of Dulwich, London. He was educated at Bradfield College, Berkshire, and at Balliol College, Oxford, where he obtained second classes in classical honour moderations (1936) and *literae humaniores* (1938). He entered the Dominions Office as an assistant principal in 1939. After war broke out he joined the Royal Navy as an ordinary seaman in 1940, before being commissioned into the Royal Marines in 1941. He subsequently saw action in the Middle East and Sicily, for which he was appointed MBE (military) in 1944, and he was demobilized in the rank of lieutenant-colonel in the following year to return to the Dominions Office (soon to become the Commonwealth Relations Office).

James was a born diplomatist and an outstanding negotiator, whose qualities were made full use of by ministers of both parties, though his easy manner and ready smile concealed a toughness and ambition which did not always endear him to his subordinates. Entries in successive editions of *Who's Who* after his retirement describe his main recreation first as 'exploring the fallibility of contemporary statesmen' and later as 'meeting new and intelligent people'. He appears to have made few lifelong friends among his immediate colleagues, but his new friends invariably found him congenial and sympathetic.

Having joined the civil service before the war, James's promotion when he rejoined it was rapid. After a brief period as first secretary in the high commission in South Africa (1946–7), he became in quick succession head of the Commonwealth Relations Office defence department (1949–51) and then of the establishment department (1951–2). In 1952 he was posted as deputy high commissioner to Lahore, so beginning a unique series of postings to the Indian subcontinent where, with a few breaks, he served successively as deputy and high commissioner in both Karachi and New Delhi. During one of these breaks he accompanied Harold Macmillan on his tour of Asia and the Far East in 1958, and in another made a series of visits to Rhodesia to set up what proved to be the abortive talks between Harold Wilson and Ian Smith in HMS *Tiger* in 1966 and HMS *Fearless* in 1968. Smith's duplicity (or weakness of character) was underlined by the fact that he assured James before the *Tiger* talks that he had 'full and unequivocal powers to settle', but allowed his agreement to be overruled by his cabinet colleagues on his return to Salisbury.

In the Indian subcontinent James initially tended to be identified with Pakistan, where he served as deputy high commissioner in 1955–6 and high commissioner from 1961 to 1966. With his opposite number in India, John Freeman, he was closely involved in the negotiations to settle the Rann of Cutch affair which preceded the outbreak of war between India and Pakistan in 1965, in which the Wilson government gave some evidence of favouring Pakistan. As a result, when James was posted to Delhi as high commissioner in 1968, he faced some initial hostility, though with characteristic aplomb he quickly gained the confidence of Indian ministers.

James's appointment to Delhi came as the culmination of a curious sequence of events. Having been deputy under-secretary of state for two years, he had been appointed permanent under-secretary of state at the Commonwealth Office (formed two years earlier from the amalgamation of the Colonial Office with the Commonwealth Relations Office) in early 1968, but within ten days of his appointment the cup was dashed from his lips by Harold Wilson's announcement that the Commonwealth Office itself was to be amalgamated with the Foreign Office. He thus served as permanent under-secretary of state for only six months, but in compensation was awarded the rare honour for a civil servant of being sworn of the privy council (1968). He ended his career in the diplomatic service as high commissioner to Australia (1971–6). While in the post he had to deal with Australian apprehension over Britain's entry into the European Common Market and with the affair of John Stonehouse, the runaway MP.

James was appointed CMG (1957), CVO (1961), KCMG (1962), and GCMG (1975). In 1977 he received a life peerage, taking the title of Baron Saint Brides and accepting the ceremonial post of king of arms of the Order of St Michael and St George. After his retirement he took up a succession of academic appointments at American universities, including Harvard, the Foreign Policy Research Institute at Philadelphia, and finally the Center for International Security and Arms Control at Stanford, California, where he was remembered with affection and admiration for his work on the Asian–Pacific region and for his encouragement of the younger students.

James was a big man in every way, who in his earlier years waged a cheerful, but not wholly successful, battle with corpulence by swimming whenever he could during his lunch break. He was married twice. His first marriage in 1948, to Elizabeth Margaret Roper Piesse, daughter of Francis Charles Roper Piesse, solicitor and, later, hotelier, came as something of a surprise, many of his colleagues having been under the impression that he had been courting her mother. Of this marriage two daughters and a son were born. Following Elizabeth's death in 1966, he married in 1968 Geneviève Christiane (Jenny) Sarasin, daughter of Robert Henri Houdin, company director. On their return from Australia he moved with her to live in France at La Plotte, Cap St Pierre, St Tropez; he died at St Tropez on 26 November 1989.   DAVID SCOTT, *rev.*

Sources *The Times* (30 Nov 1989) · *WWW* · personal knowledge (1996) · private information (1996) · *CGPLA Eng. & Wales* (1990)
Wealth at death £12,500: probate, 20 July 1990, *CGPLA Eng. & Wales*

James, Reginald William (1891–1964), physicist, was born on 9 January 1891 in London, the elder son of William George Joseph James and his wife, Isabel Sarah, daughter of George Ward, a commercial clerk. Both his father, an umbrella maker and shopkeeper in Praed Street, Paddington, and his mother were keenly interested in natural history and science; not surprisingly James specialized in science at the Polytechnic Day School, Regent Street, and the City of London School. He was awarded a London county council scholarship, an entrance scholarship for natural sciences at St John's College, Cambridge, and the Beaufoy mathematical scholarship in 1909: he entered St John's College as a foundation scholar in October of that year. First classes in both part one (1911) and part two (physics, 1912) of the natural sciences tripos were followed by two disappointingly unproductive years in the Cavendish Laboratory, which was at that time ill-equipped for research and lacked adequate provision for supervision of the beginner. During this five-year period, however, he formed an enduring friendship with another student,

W. L. Bragg, which strongly influenced his later career as a professional physicist.

In July 1914 James was on the point of departure from Cambridge to take up a junior lectureship in Liverpool when by pure chance, and in the most casual way, he was invited to join Shackleton's Antarctic expedition as physicist. His acceptance, without hesitation, represented a clean break from the anticipated regular academic life in favour of adventure which might well—and in the event did—involve severe hardship and danger. The crushing of *Endurance* in the ice in October 1915, and the grim and hazardous existence on Elephant Island which followed until the rescue ship arrived in August 1916, were a severe test for one not accustomed to such harsh conditions. Nevertheless he emerged with honour, having earned the affectionate respect of his companions.

Two years on the western front in the First World War followed. In January 1917, having been commissioned into the Royal Engineers, James joined the sound-ranging section set up in 1915 by Bragg. He played a large part in developing an efficient technique and towards the end of the war was appointed officer in charge of the sound-ranging school, with the rank of captain.

James's entry on a normal academic career was thus delayed for five strenuous years, but his appointment in 1919 as lecturer in physics in Manchester University, where Bragg was the newly appointed professor, was followed by nearly twenty years of successful original research and brilliant teaching, recognized by promotion to senior lecturer in 1921 and reader in experimental physics in 1934.

It would be difficult to exaggerate the importance for X-ray crystallography of James's beautiful quantitative experimental measurements of X-ray reflection (with Bragg and C. H. Bosanquet). When combined with the theoretical studies of C. G. Darwin, D. R. Hartree, and I. Waller they threw a flood of light on the fundamental physics of the process of reflection. At the same time they furnished much more powerful methods than were previously available for the analysis of complex crystal structures. First applied by James and Wood to barium sulphate, their use finally made possible the successful elucidation of the structure of the silicates, the most important constituents of the Earth's crust.

In December 1936, when nearly forty-six, James, who had been long regarded as a confirmed bachelor, switched his domestic life and professional career as suddenly as he had in July 1914: he married, and accepted the chair of physics at Cape Town. His wife was Annie Watson (generally known as Anne), second mistress and senior classics mistress at the Manchester High School for Girls, the only daughter of John Watson, a commercial traveller, of Rochdale. In 1937 they left Manchester for Cape Town, where their three children were born—John Stephen in 1938, David William in 1940, and Margaret Helen in 1943. The marriage was exceedingly happy; deeply devoted to their young family, they had many other interests in common, including James's strong feeling for the classics, derived from his required reading as a schoolboy.

When James took up his professorship in South Africa, the teaching of physics in the department was very good; his major effort was therefore directed to establishing research in crystallography. The papers which began to appear in the international journals were evidence of his success, and members of his team were welcomed as visiting workers in established laboratories overseas. Later, the demands of the higher administration of the university encroached upon his departmental effort; his period of office as acting principal and vice-chancellor coincided with the South Africa government's attack on academic freedom, and James led the fight in its defence. To the thoroughness and total integrity which characterized all his work he now added a degree of political acumen and a high order of statesmanship in meeting conditions not previously encountered in the universities. His wife's support in these troubled times was invaluable, as it was in 1949 during a period of enforced rest following serious heart trouble.

James's book, *The Optical Principles of the Diffraction of X-Rays*, was first published in 1948 and reprinted several times. Masterly in both content and presentation, essential reading for all serious workers in the field, it is a fitting monument to his profound understanding of the fundamental physics on which X-ray crystallography is based.

James's diverse and distinguished career attracted various honours and awards including the Polar medal in 1918 and a Rockefeller research fellowship in Debye's laboratory at Leipzig (1931–2); fellowship of the Royal Society in 1955 was an honour which brought him and his many friends great satisfaction. He was appointed to fellowship of Cape Town University (1949–56) and served a term as president of the Royal Society of South Africa (1950–53); in 1957 the University of the Witwatersrand conferred on him its honorary degree of DSc.

James retired from the chair of physics in December 1956, and from university office as acting principal and vice-chancellor a year later. He died at his home, Brandreth, Mulvihal Road, Rondebosch, near Cape Town on 7 July 1964. A new physics building was completed shortly afterwards, and was named the R. W. James building.

W. H. TAYLOR, *rev.* ISOBEL FALCONER

Sources W. L. Bragg, *Memoirs FRS*, 11 (1965), 115–25 · personal knowledge (1981) · private information (1981) · *CGPLA Eng. & Wales* (1965)

Archives Scott Polar RI, journals

Likenesses B. Dumbleton, oils, 1964, University of Cape Town, R. W. James building · photograph, RS; repro. in Bragg, *Memoirs FRS*, facing p. 115

Wealth at death £1023 in England: probate, 3 May 1965, *CGPLA Eng. & Wales*

James, Richard (*bap.* 1591, *d.* 1638), antiquary, was born at Newport, Isle of Wight, and baptized there on 21 September 1591, the eldest surviving son of Richard James (*d.* 1613), merchant and shipowner, mayor and MP for Newport, and his wife, Averen (*d.* 1615). He had an elder sister, Averen (*bap.* 1586), and a sister Jane who married William Gardyner of Blandford, Dorset. In his papers in the Bodleian Library there is a verse letter 'Ad fratrem suum

Gullielmum Gardinerum' and subscribed 'Tuus et Janae tuae frater amanitissimus R. James'. He had a younger brother, John, a Southampton merchant. John James (c.1550–1601), Queen Elizabeth's physician and another antiquarian, appointed keeper of the records at the Tower of London; Richard Edes (1555–1604), Queen Elizabeth's chaplain; and Thomas James (1572/3–1629), Bodley's first librarian, were among his uncles. James matriculated as a commoner at Exeter College, Oxford, on 6 May 1608 aged sixteen but took a scholarship at Corpus Christi College on 23 September 1608, was admitted BA on 12 October 1611, and MA on 24 January 1615; he was made probationary fellow of Corpus Christi on 30 September 1615. He took holy orders, and graduated BD on 7 July 1624.

Both his debt-ridden father and his mother were dead when in 1616 James was bequeathed £10 per annum by his uncle Dr Edward James, canon of Christ Church and rector of Freshwater, Isle of Wight. Richard James wrote an epitaph to Edward James, 'In mortem optimi avunculi Doctoris Edoardi James, nepotis carmen funebre'. Richard's antiquarian and linguistic interests led to wide-ranging travel in England, Wales, and Scotland, including Shetland, and to Greenland, the North Cape, and Russia. While James was in Russia his uncle Andrew temporarily evicted his nephew's siblings, including Averen, from their home, claiming it for himself, which resulted in court action for repossession. His wife, Elizabeth, died during his absence and was buried at St Margaret's, Westminster, in July 1618.

James never forgot his Isle of Wight origins and family, and often added 'Vectensis' to his name. In 1618 while in Russia as chaplain to Sir Dudley Digges, he wrote in praise of the dolphin, the arms borne by the James family, 'In delphinum insigne Jamesianorum Vectensium'. James left an uncompleted history of the island in Saxon and Norman times, which included a poem on the island's name and the nature of its inhabitants. He worked closely with his uncle Thomas James and refers in his letters to his cousin Elsing. This cousin-by-marriage Henry Elsing (1598–1654) was clerk to parliaments. His second wife, Jane Hardy (née Edes), was James's first cousin.

James was a notable scholar and, in Anthony Wood's judgement, 'tho' humorous, was of a far better judgement than his uncle Thom. James, and had he lived to his age would have surpassed him in published books' (Wood, *Ath. Oxon.*, 2.629). One basis of his scholarship was his command of languages: Anglo-Saxon (he prepared a dictionary), French, Gothic, Greek, Hebrew, Italian, Latin, Russian (he prepared a dictionary), and Spanish. He combined his facility for languages and criticism with an enthusiasm for travel. While in Russia (1618–19), in which as a Russian speaker he acted as interpreter, James assembled materials for the first Anglo-Russian dictionary.

James was away so long that he was believed dead, as his poem 'On my Supposed Death in Russia' indicates. He returned from his extended sojourn in Russia by or in 1620, the year in which his uncle resigned Bodley's librarianship. Thomas used the Bodleian Library in his war

against papists and his resignation was to give him more time for this campaign. Richard joined him and in 1623 was busily engaged on his 'magnum opus', a study of Becket called the 'Decanonizatio Thomae Cantuariensis et suorum'. Such studies required patrons and Thomas, writing to Bishop Ussher in January 1623, referred to Richard's linguistic skill as 'immense and beyond all other men' and extolled his nephew's palaeographic skills. Richard was described as 'both fatherless and motherless, and almost (but for myself), I may say (the more is the pity) friendless'.

The scholarship of the 'Decanonizatio' is unimpeachable; it is 'massive but buoyant, philosophic yet shrewd, controversial nevertheless judicial' (*Poems*, xxix). For six years nephew and uncle worked tirelessly to secure a commission to be appointed by parliament and convocation 'to collate the MSS. of the Fathers in all the Libraries of England with foreign Popish editions, in order that the forgeries in the latter might be detected, and the views of the Roman Catholics in making interpolations, defeated' (Corser, xxii). However, James I's enthusiasm to make the English church a basis for European religious consensus waned, and his death in 1625 elicited Richard James's 'Muses Dirge, Consecrated to the Remembrance of … James, King of Great Brittaine'. Charles I's religious outlook made the hope of a commission on anti-papist writings less likely and with the death of Thomas James in 1629 the enterprise effectively ended. This bereavement brought Richard a windfall on 22 October 1629 when he was presented to Thomas James's sinecure living of Little Mongeham, Kent, his only church preferment, which he resigned in 1635. The lack of ecclesiastical promotion for Richard James may indicate little enthusiasm among the ecclesiastical hierarchy for his intellectual anti-catholicism.

James's circle was wider than the university men with whom he corresponded. Already in 1624 he was employed with Selden to examine the earl of Arundel's marbles, published in 1628 as 'Marmora Arundeliana'. James is here described as 'multijugae doctrinae studiique indefatigabilis'. He met Sir Robert Cotton probably at the Oxford parliament in 1625: they 'held many attitudes and beliefs in common as well as a love of manuscripts and rarities' (Sharpe, 255). James soon offered to help Cotton by making 'some addition to your excellent serraglio of Antiquitie'. Precisely when James 'entered Arundel's entourage' by becoming Cotton's librarian is not known for certain, but was probably c.1625, for in 1630 in dedicating a sermon to Cotton, James asked his patron to receive it kindly 'as you have done me for the space of more than foure yeares' (*Poems*, l–li; Sharpe, 255 and n.2). In November 1628 James, then described as 'an attender on Sir Robert Cotton, a grate lover of his country and hatter of all suche as he supposed enimies to the same', published praise of Felton, 'that worthy patriot' who murdered Buckingham, Charles's favourite. As Cotton's librarian, James instigated systems of acquisitions, exchanges, and loans from the library—some, said his unreliable detractor Simonds D'Ewes, for money. One loan, if such it was, to Oliver St John, was disastrous. This was a 1612 tract on bridling parliaments, which St John circulated among parliamentary leaders (*CSP dom.*, *1629–31*, 110). An explosive reaction from King Charles and his ministers led to the imprisonment of James, Cotton, and others in the Tower and its gatehouse in the autumn of 1629. The prisoners were released, probably on the birth of the prince of Wales in May 1630. St John may have 'planted' the pamphlet to incriminate James and the others, possibly the reason why Cotton apportioned no blame to James for his imprisonment. After Cotton's death James dedicated his 'Defence of Christian religion' (1636) to Cotton's widow.

James 'seems to have served Cotton well' (Sharpe, 85). If he embezzled records for the Cotton Library he did no more than Cotton himself who shamelessly 'borrowed with no intention of returning' manuscripts, and tore out annals for his own collection before returning a monastic document from Thornley Abbey (Tite, 106–7). James's work in the Cotton Library has been underrated. Certainly Cotton took a personal lead in collecting manuscripts and may have chosen the way in which physical rearrangement of the manuscript books in his library was to be reworked from the late 1620s in cases distinguished largely by busts of Roman emperors (ibid., 35–6). However that work was not complete at Cotton's death in 1631 and James carried the work forward for seven years until he died in 1638, for which scant credit has to date been allowed to him.

However, by 1638 'the work of ordering and cataloguing the manuscript collection was largely complete' and 'after 1638 for half a century no one left a mark on the collection in the way that Cotton and James had done' (Tite, 60, 63). If Cotton the collector of manuscripts was the father of the British Library collection, then James's scholarly and administrative work of collecting and identifying manuscripts and supplying contents' lists, which largely stand today, make him the godfather of that collection, a title which, given his protestant purposes, would have appealed to him.

James's published sermons included those on the eucharist, delivered on Easter day at Oxford; on the Lent fast, also in Oxford; and on the apostles preaching (published London, 1629, 1630, 1630); further sermons were published in Oxford in 1632 and 1633. It is possible that James wrote 'On Worthy Master Shakespeare and his Poems', prefixed to the second folio edition of 1632 with the initials J. M. S. (i.e. JaMeS). Corser argues against (1845); Grosart hotly in favour (1880). James was well acquainted with the leading men of letters, including Sir John Eliot, and playwrights such as Ben Jonson to whom his 1631 poem on his 'Staple of News First Presented' was addressed. In 1636 he travelled to Lancashire and stayed with Robert Heywood. He died of quartan fever (malaria) at Sir Thomas Cotton's house in Westminster, where he had lived from the age of thirty-three, and was buried on 8 December 1638 at St Margaret's, Westminster.

James was undoubtedly a leading protestant puritan scholar. However his anti-popery was thwarted by political and religious change; but like his uncle he found himself with one of the greatest libraries of his day at his service. He was, from the description of his detractor D'Ewes, 'a short, red-bearded, high coloured fellow, a master of arts ... an atheistical, profane scholar, but otherwise witty and moderately learned'. His red-bearded countenance was a shared characteristic with his uncle Thomas, as seen in the Bodleian portrait, and Richard was proud of his red hair, offering a poem, 'A Defence of Red Haire', among his works (*Poems*, 213). His fondness for red-haired people may have been a factor in his enthusiasm for the Picts (Stevenson, 116).

James's interest in antiquities and science is seen in allusions to Roman antiquities observed in Cheshire, in his poem about the flood, inspired by finding fossils on English hilltops, and in his enthusiastic correspondence about, and exchange of, antiquities. In Breslau he saw and noted the 1618 comet in Ursa Major which was visible for some two months; Galileo and Kepler observed the same phenomenon. But Richard James was primarily a protestant scholar with encyclopaedic knowledge of texts in many languages. James's interest in Roman and Anglo-Saxon culture and remains, and his antagonism to Norman rule in England, characterized as an attempt to place the British Isles under French rule through the yoke of religion, places him firmly in the tradition of protestant English antiquarians who sought the origins of their faith in texts of the church fathers later corrupted by popish writers, and who sought a native thread throughout. Thus James defends Wyclif and Sir John Oldcastle, Englishmen who sought church reform, in contrast to his 'decanonization' of Becket, a scholarly and much neglected work of 760 pages. Both Richard and his uncle Thomas James were perhaps inspired by James I's notion of the church in England as a basis for European religious consensus. Under Charles I, Richard preached the fruits of his research from the pulpit in Oxford and London, but increasingly limited his active interest in the past to manuscript and material remains of former inhabitants of Britain, hence the appellation (added to the St Margaret's Westminster register in a later hand) following his death as 'That most famous antiquary'.

TOM BEAUMONT JAMES

Sources R. James, *Iter Lancastrense: a poem, written AD 1636, by the Rev. Richard James*, ed. T. Corser, Chetham Society, 7 (1845) · *The poems, etc, of Richard James, BD* (1592–1638), ed. A. B. Grosart (1880) · parish register, Newport, Isle of Wight, 21 Sept 1591, Newport RO [baptism] · *CSP dom.*, *1629–31* · Bodl. Oxf., MSS James · PRO, lawsuit: Andrew James v. Averen James, c. 22/373/21 · A. M. Burke, ed., *Memorials of St Margaret's Church, Westminster* (1914) · C. G. C. Tite, *The manuscript library of Sir Robert Cotton* (1994) · K. Sharpe, 'The intellectual and political activities of Sir Robert Cotton, c. 1590–1631', DPhil diss., U. Oxf., 1975 · F. Psalmon, 'Un ruissant anglais au 16e–17e siècle: Richard James (1592–1638)', *Bulletin de Géographie Historique et Descriptive*, 26 (1911), 232–6 · E. Macgillivray, ed., 'Richard James, 1592–1638: descriptions of Shetland, Orkney and the highlands of Scotland', *Orkney Miscellany*, 1 (1953), 48–56 · D. Stevenson, 'The travels of Richard James in Scotland, c.1615', *Northern Scotland*, 7 (1986–7), 113–18 · DNB · parish register, Westminster, St Margaret's, 8 Dec 1638 [burial]

James, Richard Leon [Dick; *formerly* Isaac Vapnik] (1920–1986), music publisher, was born on 12 December 1920 at 1 Underwood Street, Mile End New Town, Spitalfields, London, the son of Morris Vapnik, master butcher, and his wife, Annie, *née* Puff. Three years after leaving school at fourteen he became a professional vocalist by joining Al Berlin and his band, resident at the Cricklewood Palais in 1937. He used a variety of professional names during his early performing career, including Lee Sheridan. He joined the Royal Army Medical Corps during the Second World War but continued to sing, actually cutting his first disc with Primo Scala's Accordeon [*sic*] Band in 1942. On 28 February 1943 he married Frances Aarons (*b.* 1921), changed his name to Dick James, and appeared with various bands including those run by Henry Hall, Stanley Black, and Cyril Stapleton.

In the early 1950s James decided to become a song-plugger while retaining a recording contract with Parlophone where his recording manager was George Martin. Between 1955 and 1957 he recorded three hit records, all produced by Martin: 'Robin Hood', 'The Ballad of Davy Crockett', and 'Garden of Eden'. 'Robin Hood' was used as the theme tune for the television series starring Richard Green. James's vocal style was pleasant but unremarkable, and in 1959 he consciously took the decision to quit singing professionally. He then worked as assistant to Sidney Bron, the music publisher, following which he formed his own music publishing company, Dick James Music, in September 1961.

After the success of the Beatles' 'Love Me Do', George Martin recommended Dick James to Brian Epstein as potential publisher for the Beatles. Epstein had placed 'Love Me Do' with EMI's publishing arm, Ardmoore and Beechwood, but had been dissatisfied by their lack of promotion. Martin knew that his former vocalist's publishing house was struggling, but suggested to Epstein that a struggling publisher would be more 'hungry'; he also considered James to be a man of integrity. James was able to strike a deal in January 1963 with Epstein (having asked his sixteen-year-old son Stephen about the group the previous evening). Dick James was the archetype of the avuncular impresario—'the ultimate Tin Pan Allyite' (Norman, 73)—and he suggested to Epstein that a company be formed within Dick James Music to cater for the Beatles' own prolific output of songs. Northern Songs, administered by Dick James Music, was thus conceived in January 1963. James had a 55 per cent stake in the company and Epstein and the Beatles the other 45 per cent, which was, in fact, for its day, a reasonably fair-minded contract in music publishing terms.

Dick James Music published 'Please Please Me', but thereafter left all Beatles publishing to Northern Songs. However James's own organization also began to wax powerful in its own right (it soon moved to new, improved headquarters at 71–5 New Oxford Street), with numerous other significant popular music catalogue acquisitions by the mid-1960s. For example, James owned 50 per cent of the Hollies' Gralto Music, of Gerry Marsden's Pacermusic, and the Spencer Davis Group's Spencer Davis Music. These artists were to write and record some of the most successful and enduring pop hits of the decade. James was also a partner in Cookaway Music, formed by songwriters and performers Roger Cook and Roger Greenaway—who scored innumerable hits in the 1960s and 1970s—and was the publishing side of the impresario Larry Page's Page One organization, thereby enjoying a share in the proceeds from the successes of the Troggs. By this time publishers were enjoying profits not so much out of sheet-music sales *per se* but by owning performing rights.

The Beatles remained James's prime concern, however. During the four years after the James and Epstein deal, Lennon and McCartney added more than 100 songs to the company's original (rather meagre) catalogue of fifty-nine songs, despite the fact that their contract demanded only a minimum of six songs per year. DJM, however (as it became known), continued to function as a family business. The only shareholders were Dick James himself, and his accountant Charles Silver. Stephen James, his only son, also worked in the business and became a successful song-plugger in his own right. As the Beatles and Northern Songs claimed more of Dick's attention, Stephen received increased power and was eventually entrusted with the entire day-to-day running of DJM Publishing. He was further entrusted by his father with nurturing songwriting talent, and installed a Studer four-track recording system at New Oxford Street. This studio was made available to all the songwriters and musicians with whom DJM were involved, including a young pianist by the name of Reggie Dwight (later famous as Elton John).

In 1965 James persuaded Beatles manager Brian Epstein to float Northern Songs on the stock exchange and 5 million shares were issued. Charles Silver, the accountant for Northern Songs, was made chairman and he and James—now Northern Songs' managing director—shared 37 per cent. From this moment on it became clear to the Beatles that they would never gain full control of their own compositions, and relationships between James and the Beatles became somewhat strained.

By 1967 Northern Songs was worth millions, but the death of Brian Epstein that year worried the 3000 shareholders of Northern Songs, to whom Dick James owed as much duty as to his own large residual shareholding. He felt that the constant rumours of the Beatles breaking up would send Northern's share price plummeting. James was approached by Sir Lew Grade, head of Associated Television, in 1968 to sell. By March 1969 he had sold his own 23 per cent shareholding to Grade without informing the Beatles. (James and Grade knew each other from years previously: Grade had been James's agent.) Dick James was heavily criticized for this sale, especially because the Beatles themselves also attempted to purchase his shareholding to gain control of their own material. James sold his shareholding to Grade because he (James) was afraid that the Beatles were heading for financial chaos, and feared that incoming manager Allen Klein would some-how manipulate the situation to gain control of Northern Songs for himself.

By 1969 Dick James had become a multi-millionaire, fabulously rich on the songs penned by many of Britain's best young songwriters. He had lost the Beatles but, by 1967, had signed up Elton John and Bernie Taupin in a deal which made over their copyright to Dick James Music. Dick and Stephen James supported this new songwriting duo to the extent of creating a new record label—DJM—for their productions. The subsequent successes of the John–Taupin songwriting partnership were almost to rival those of the Beatles; by 1972, however, with Elton John and his songwriting partner bringing in millions from their songwriting for Dick James Music, they sought release from their contractual obligations. During November 1974 John and Taupin left DJM.

By this time, Dick James had become one of the most distinguished figures in the British entertainment industry. He had become chairman of the Music Publishers Association, and vice-chairman of the Performing Right Society. His company had three times earned the queen's award for industry for its exports and James had person-ally received an Ivor Novello award for services to enter-tainment. He suffered a mild heart attack in 1973 but con-tinued to run the publishing arm of DJM throughout the 1970s. In 1981 he underwent heart bypass surgery and stepped down as managing director of DJM. In 1982 Elton John's manager issued formal notice of court action, chal-lenging the publishing agreement John and Taupin had signed in 1967, claiming a bigger share of the royalties and the ownership of the copyright of their DJM material. On 29 November 1985 Mr Justice Nichols found against DJM, and awarded John and Taupin an increased royalty share; the copyright of their songs, including 'Rocket Man', 'Daniel', and 'Goodbye Yellow Brick Road', however, remained with DJM. In interviews with the trade paper *Music Week* both sides claimed victory.

Although DJM emerged well enough from the battle, the proceedings had made James very frail. Barely three months later, on 1 February 1986, he suffered a massive heart attack at his home, 12 Imperial Court, Prince Albert Road, London, and died before he could be taken to hos-pital. He was buried in London and was survived by his wife.

Dick James was something of an opportunist, but he used his good fortune judiciously and, in a business known for its darker side, resolutely attempted to deal both honourably and fairly with his clientele. Both the sale of Northern Songs in 1968–9 and the High Court epi-sode which brought DJM into the public limelight during the mid-1980s serve to highlight the precarious nature of music publishing, but not the probity of one of the British music industry's great entrepreneurial characters.

MICHAEL BROCKEN

Sources B. Harry, *The ultimate Beatles encyclopedia* (1992) • P. Nor-man, *Elton John* (1991) • *Guinness British hit singles*, 11th edn (1995) • private information (2004) [J. Flannery and S. James] • R. Coleman, *John Lennon* (1984) • 'Dick James, British music publisher', *Annual Obituary* (1986), 113–14 • b. cert. • d. cert.
Archives U. Lpool, Institute of Popular Music | SOUND BL NSA, 'The Dick James story', HC790/1 • BL NSA, performance record-ings • U. Lpool, Institute of Popular Music, Robert Shelton archive
Wealth at death £6,869,792: probate, 1986, *CGPLA Eng. & Wales*

James, Robert (*bap.* 1703, *d.* 1776), physician and inventor of James's fever powder, was baptized on 23 August 1703 at Shenstone, Staffordshire, the son of Edward James of Kinvaston, a major in the army, and his wife, Frances Clarke of Stafford. He was educated at Lichfield grammar school, a younger fellow pupil being Samuel Johnson, and from 1722 at St John's College, Oxford; he graduated BA in 1726. Having studied medicine he became an extra-licentiate of the College of Physicians in 1728 and MD by royal mandate in the University of Cambridge in the same year. He practised at Sheffield and then at Lichfield before moving to Birmingham; there in 1737 he married Mrs Ann Clare, *née* Stephens. Three sons and two daughters sur-vived him, a son Pinkstan being the father of George Payne Rainsford James.

James then settled in London, where he soon estab-lished a fashionable practice. In 1743 he published *A Medi-cinal Dictionary, with a History of Drugs*, a competently writ-ten but largely derivative work. Its main interest lies in the contributions and proposals written by Dr Johnson, a lifelong friend, who in return was helped by James with some medical definitions for his own dictionary. In 1745 James, who that year published *A Treatise on the Gout and Rheumatism*, was admitted to a full licentiate of the College of Physicians. The rest of his life was devoted to the fever powder he had recently invented.

In February 1746 James appointed the publisher and bookseller John Newbery as sales agent for the powders. Newbery, also a wholesale and retail druggist, pushed the remedy enthusiastically, even working puffs for it into some of his books. In consequence the powders became all the rage among the well-to-do, who alone could afford 2*s.* 6*d.* for a pair of doses. They were taken not only against fevers—containing as they did phosphate of lime and oxide of antimony as sweating agents—but also as general pick-me-ups. A veritable pantheon of authors lauded them and their efficacy, Thomas Gray and William Cow-per demurely, Horace Walpole ecstatically, and Richard Cumberland in many stanzas of inflated verse. At Eton College a widespread distribution of the powders sharply reduced the death-rate from fever there, but an attempt in 1759 by an over-zealous admiral on board HMS *Monarque* similarly to dose his exhausted ship's company back to health only led to plentiful burials at sea.

Having taken out a patent, in 1747 James furnished the court of chancery with a description of the contents and the method of manufacture; yet experts soon found these could not make the kind of powder being sold, and indeed the doses varied in quality over time. In 1748 James pub-lished *A Dissertation on Fevers and Inflammatory Distempers*, to which he added an account of the success of his powders 'in the Small-pox, Yellow Fever, Slow Fever, and Rheumat-ism'. An attempt in 1753 to challenge the patent, on the 'madness' in 1788) and for colds, inflicting them also on his family. As late as the 1860s they were to be found in Queen Victoria's medicine chest.

An impetuous and improvident man, James had attractive social gifts and was always happy to enliven a good dinner. In his working life he was a prolific and laborious author and a dabbler in chemical experiments. According to Dr Johnson, he never drew a sober breath during the final twenty years of his life; this scarcely impaired his medical practice as he was extremely adept at concealing his squiffiness. In his Birmingham days he had also been known as an assiduous womanizer, and he persisted in his lechery to an advanced age. When in his sixties he called with his latest doxy to take Dr Johnson for a ride, the latter angrily protested that at their time of life it was indecent to be driving about the streets with a whore. James replied, 'it is very indecent for both of us. But such is my infirmity, that if I go six weeks without a woman, my ballocks swell so that I cannot keep them in my breeches' (Ryskamp and Pottle, 113–14). James died in London, on 23 March 1776 and was survived by his wife.

T. A. B. CORLEY

Sources Boswell, *Life* · A. L. Reade, *Johnsonian gleanings*, 3 (privately printed, London, 1922), 124; 8 (1937), 19; 9 (1939), 225 · *The correspondence and other papers of James Boswell relating to the making of the Life of Johnson*, ed. M. Waingrow (1969), vol. 2 of *The Yale editions of the private papers of James Boswell*, research edn (1966–), 49, 89–90, 247–8 · *Boswell: the ominous years, 1774–1776*, ed. C. Ryskamp and F. A. Pottle (1963), vol. 8 of *The Yale editions of the private papers of James Boswell*, trade edn (1950–89), 113–14 · *The letters of Samuel Johnson*, ed. B. Redford, 1 (1992), 24–7; 2 (1992), 16–18; 4 (1994), 372–3 · 'The Messrs Newbery', *Chemist and Druggist* (15 April 1874), 112–16 · 'An agreement that established a "dynasty"', *Chemist and Druggist* (8 Sept 1956), 254–5 · B. Dickens, 'Dr James's powder: a footnote to eighteenth-century literature', *Life and Letters*, 2 (1929), 36–47 · J. K. Crellin, 'A note on Dr James's fever powder', *Transactions of the British Society for the History of Pharmacy*, 1 (1970–77), 136–43 · *The later correspondence of George III*, ed. A. Aspinall, 5 vols. (1962–70), vol. 3, p. 502n · IGI

Archives MHS Oxf., papers relating to fever powder · Wellcome L., papers relating to fever powder

Likenesses caricature, 1724, repro. in T. Wright, ed., *Caricature history of the Georges* (1876), 230 · W. Walker, line engraving, pubd 1778 (after drawing by P. Scheemakers), RCP Lond. [see illus.]

Robert James (*bap.* 1703, *d.* 1776), by William Walker, pubd 1778 (after Peter Scheemakers)

grounds that the product was copied from one by William Schwanberg, a German, was thrown out.

James's reputation as a doctor was diminished by his and Newbery's strenuous claims for the powders, which only provoked further attacks: in 1760 and 1774 respectively, the physicians Malcolm Flemyng and John Miller circulated warnings about the dangers of attempting to use them as cure-alls. Also in 1774 the death of Oliver Goldsmith, after using the powders, set off a flurry of hostile publicity from William Hawes, who had attended Goldsmith, and John Newbery's son Francis was forced to issue a strong rebuttal. That year James sold to Newbery the right to market his analeptic or restorative pills.

James was not above disseminating some blatant exaggerations about his nostrum. In 1764 he asserted that 1.6 million doses had been sold since 1746, roughly 50,000 packages a year. Newbery's own accounts show that in 1768/9 sales were just under 20,000 packages (valued wholesale at £822), and in 1775 some 38,000 packages, worth about £1600. George III regularly took the powders, both for fevers (including one bout during his period of

James, Sir Robert Vidal Rhodes (1933–1999), historian and politician, was born in India on 10 April 1933, the youngest of four sons and five children of Lieutenant-Colonel William Rhodes James, army officer, and his wife, Violet, *née* Swinhoe. His uncle was Montague Rhodes James, provost of both Eton and King's College, Cambridge, but remembered more for his famous *Ghost Stories of an Antiquary* (1904). Rhodes James was educated at schools in India, at Sedbergh, and at Worcester College, Oxford, where he read modern history and graduated with a second-class degree in 1955. He entered the clerks' office in the House of Commons in 1955, where he remained for nearly ten years. On 18 August 1956 he married Angela Margaret (*b.* 1933/4), teacher, and elder daughter of Ronal Mackay Robertson. They had four daughters.

Rhodes James was a highly capable clerk, but his real interest was in writing history. He made his début in 1959

Sir Robert Vidal Rhodes James (1933–1999), by Douglas Anderson, 1993

with a much praised life of Lord Randolph Churchill. Although highly readable and scholarly, it was replaced by Roy Foster's even more authoritative biography in 1981. But his second venture, the life of Lord Rosebery (1963), was not superseded in his lifetime. It was a brilliantly perceptive work, perhaps the best of all the twenty or so volumes that he wrote. In so far as anyone could explain the springs of action of that glittering, enigmatic, and slightly repellent figure, Rhodes James was able to do so, helped by the generous co-operation of the sixth earl of Rosebery, who gave him the free run of the copious family papers in Barnbougle Castle. He deservedly received the Royal Society of Literature Award. His next book, *Gallipoli* (1965), was also not superseded in his lifetime. He was the first historian to use the unpublished papers which largely conditioned the report of the Dardanelles inquiry in 1917 and threw a critical light on Winston Churchill's role. This may have prompted his next book, *Churchill: a Study in Failure, 1900–1939* (1970). Churchill was still an icon. The title, despite the qualification of the dates, stirred up angry controversy. Perhaps Rhodes James did slightly overstate his case. But the fact remains that before Churchill became a great war leader he had a highly chequered record, even if people disliked being reminded of it.

In 1965 Rhodes James returned to Oxford as a junior research fellow at All Souls and three years later became, until 1973, director of the Institute for the Study of International Organization at Sussex University. After various United Nations consultancies he became in 1973 principal executive officer to the secretary-general, the Austrian Kurt Waldheim, whom he came to detest as a liar about his past as a Nazi sympathizer. He provided Margaret Thatcher with a formidable dossier of the facts when Waldheim came under suspicion in the 1980s. Meanwhile he had resigned from the United Nations to follow a political career. He was deeply disturbed at the chaos in Britain under the Labour regime led by Harold Wilson and James Callaghan. In 1976 he entered parliament as a Conservative at a by-election in Cambridge, a seat which, though never safe, he retained until he retired in 1992. He was an admirably conscientious and highly popular constituency member. But in parliamentary politics he was less at ease. It was a bad moment for a 'one nation' Conservative to enter parliament, and he never quite hit it off with Thatcher, who, as he saw her, was becoming too stridently right-wing for his more liberal tastes. Although he never concealed his own proclivities, indeed proclaimed them with vigour, she allowed him minor preferment as a parliamentary private secretary at the Foreign and Commonwealth Office from 1979 to 1982. He resigned along with Lord Carrington and the rest of the Foreign Office team over the Falklands crisis, though he had no responsibility for the errors that led to that war. He was not given another chance of promotion, and a period as Conservative Party liaison officer for higher and further education ended when he resigned on the question of student loans.

Described by Andrew Roth as 'dark, tall and thin, alternating a lop-sided grin and a troubled look' (*The Guardian*), Rhodes James had an air of intellectual superiority. He was aloof, though always courteous, and something of a loner. He failed to get elected to the 1922 committee, and alienated the tory establishment by describing a memorandum by Sir Keith Joseph as 'negative and philistine' (*The Independent*), and the whips' use of the guillotine as destroying 'the heart and soul of the House … and with it the heart and soul of British democracy' (*Daily Telegraph*). He expected no favour from Thatcher, and John Major was not prepared to go beyond a knighthood in 1991. After a drink or so in Annie's bar Rhodes James would wryly describe himself by the subtitle of his book on Churchill.

Meanwhile, a compulsive writer, Rhodes James continued to pour out books, although quantity led to some loss of quality. His two-volume *The British Revolution, 1880–1939* (1976–7) added little to a well-worn subject. His life of Anthony Eden (1986), written at the request of Eden's widow, was over-defensive on Suez, and his biographies of Albert, prince consort (1983), and George VI (1998) were rather thin. On the other hand his editing of *The Diaries of Sir Henry Channon* (1967) and *Memoirs of a Conservative: J. C. C. Davidson's Memoirs and Papers* (1969) was exemplary. His life of Bob Boothby (1991), for which he received the Angel literary award, was a successful study of that somewhat caddish adventurer, whose liaison with Lady Dorothy Macmillan was treated with candour and tact. He was disappointed over two projects. He believed that he had the go-ahead for the official life of the third marquess of Salisbury, the Victorian prime minister, and for the official history of the firm of Rothschild, but neither came to fruition.

From 1983 to 1992 Rhodes James was a most able and efficient chairman of the History of Parliament Trust. He kept a detailed diary of Thatcher's deposition, which he described as 'an astonishing story', not to be published in his lifetime, 'perhaps never' (*The Independent*). After his retirement from the Commons he set his heart on becoming a life peer but the honour never came his way. He died of cancer at his home, the Stone House, Great Gransden, Sandy, Bedfordshire, on 20 May 1999. He was survived by his wife and their four daughters. A memorial service was held in the chapel of St Mary Undercroft, Palace of Westminster, on 23 November 1999.   ROBERT BLAKE

Sources *The Times* (22 May 1999) · *The Guardian* (22 May 1999) · *Daily Telegraph* (22 May 1999) · *The Independent* (24 May 1999) · *WWW* · personal knowledge (2004) · private information (2004) · m. cert. · d. cert.
Archives CAC Cam., papers relating to Gallipoli campaign | King's Lond., Liddell Hart C., corresp. with Sir B. H. Liddell Hart
Likenesses photograph, 1976, repro. in *The Independent* · photograph, 1987, repro. in *The Times* · D. Anderson, oils, 1993, priv. coll. [*see illus.*] · photograph, repro. in *The Guardian*
Wealth at death under £200,000: probate, 29 Nov 1999, *CGPLA Eng. & Wales*

James, Rolfe Arnold Scott- (1878–1959), journal editor and literary scholar, was born at Stratford upon Avon, Warwickshire, on 21 December 1878, the youngest but one of the two sons and six daughters of the Revd John Scott James, a Congregational minister, and his wife, Elizabeth Barnard. They were an enterprising family whose active careers took them to many parts of the world. Scott-James was educated at Mill Hill School, London (1893–8), and won a scholarship to Brasenose College, Oxford, where he attended from 1898 to 1901. After obtaining a third class in *literae humaniores* (1901) he worked in London at the Canning Town settlement and at Toynbee Hall, where he was greatly influenced by Canon Bartlett.

In 1902 Scott-James joined the staff of the *Daily News*, and was appointed literary editor at the early age of twenty-seven, a post he occupied with notable success for the next six years. He also became a leader writer for the paper, his assistant editor from 1908 being the essayist Robert Lynd. In 1905 he married Violet Eleanor Brooks (*d.* 1942), daughter of Captain Arthur Brooks. They had a son and two daughters, both of the latter being distinguished authors: Marie (*d.* 1956) was a literary critic and Anne a well-known journalist and broadcaster. While at the *Daily News* Scott-James began to display a talent for literary criticism. In 1908 he published *Modernism and Romance*, a study of the then nascent modernist movement which was acclaimed as 'showing clear evidence of instructed taste and balanced judgement' (*The Times*, 5 Nov 1959) and which brought him to the notice of the avant-garde. A further meditation on modernist aesthetics was published in 1913 as *Personality in Literature*, and during the same year he

wrote *The Influence of the Press*, a study of the role of journalism in shaping public opinion.

The Influence of the Press considered the social and political role of the journalist, and Scott-James possessed a strongly developed social conscience. His political sensibility was in part generated by his work at Toynbee Hall, and further nurtured by his time at the *Daily News*, a journal rooted in the liberal and humanitarian tradition. He was a lifelong supporter of the Liberal Party, both in private and through his journalism, and while at the *Daily News* acted upon his political convictions in various capacities. He travelled in Macedonia shortly before the First Balkan War, and from 1903 until 1914 was a member of the executive of the Balkan Committee. Immediately after the sinking of the *Titanic* in April 1912, he sailed to the United States in her sister ship to investigate the case of 500 firemen who had gone on strike in protest against conditions revealed by the sinking of the liner. He was also one of the earliest advocates of the National Theatre, championed the idea in the *Daily News*, and remained a member of the committee until the end of his life.

In 1913 Scott-James left the *Daily News* in order to devote his energies to the foundation of a new paper, which first appeared in March 1914. The *New Weekly* was one of the most vigorous intellectual journals of a period which abounded in new literary enterprises. During his years at the *Daily News* he became acquainted with many of the principal figures of the emergent avant-garde, and his two published studies of modernism had strengthened these connections. He was a close friend of Wyndham Lewis, and within a few months contributors included G. K. Chesterton, E. M. Forster, Thomas Hardy, Arnold Bennett, Hilaire Belloc, Walter de la Mare, W. B. Yeats, and John Galsworthy, who mingled with then lesser-known writers, such as Lewis, Chekhov (newly translated), and Charlotte Mew. The *New Weekly* ran for five months but lost circulation and advertising revenue at an alarming rate. Part of the reason for its failure was the low price: Scott-James's desire to make high modernism financially accessible to all led him to price issues at 2*d*. rather than the usual price of 6*d*., which inevitably meant a corresponding drop in production quality. The *New Weekly* quickly earned a high prestige, but it could not survive the outbreak of the First World War. Scott-James enlisted at the age of thirty-seven and was commissioned in the Royal Garrison Artillery. He served in France, rose to the rank of captain, and in 1918 was awarded the Military Cross.

In the following year Scott-James returned to journalism, working from 1919 to 1930 as leader writer for the *Daily Chronicle*. In 1924 he contributed a report on 'Housing conditions in mining areas' to Lloyd George's survey *Coal and Power*, and four years later he published *The Making of Literature*, based on twenty lectures given at the University of London. The study surveyed the development of criticism and the literary aesthetic from the Periclean age until the twentieth century, arguing for an underlying unity in the creative processes of literature as Scott-James connected his classical education to his understanding of high modernism. In 1931 he published *Personality in Literature, 1913–1931*, a companion to his respected 1913 critical study.

From 1933 to 1935 Scott-James was the leader writer and assistant editor of *The Spectator*, and in 1934 he succeeded Sir John Squire as editor of the *London Mercury*. In the first editorial, Squire had claimed a wider scope than that of any previous English literary magazine, and the journal published poetry, fiction, and *belles-lettres* and also reviewed literature and the arts. Scott-James proved himself 'both an exacting and a receptive editor: he restored the originally high standard of visual presentation' (*DNB*) and continued to broaden the range of contributors. He endeavoured to turn around a flagging publication as far as possible, and he was credited with making a paper predicted to fold in a few months carry on for five years. The *London Mercury* performed the important function of bringing together new and established writers, and its last issue in April 1939 fittingly contained one of its finest contributions, W. H. Auden's 'In Memory of W. B. Yeats'.

In 1940 Scott-James took on a new challenge in an attempt to rescue another failing paper. His was the last editorship of *Britain Today*, at first a fortnightly, later a monthly journal, designed to present a view of Britain in wartime to allies and neutral countries. The paper had to depict a native culture still flowing serenely on, a sharp departure from Scott-James's more usual interest in progressive politics and avant-garde aesthetics. His success at *Britain Today*—by the time it folded in 1954, it had run for 200 issues—added little to his reputation, as during the last fourteen years it had conspicuously avoided divulging the editor's name.

Scott-James's first wife died in 1942, and in 1947 he married Paule Honorine Jeanne Lagarde, daughter of P. E. Lagarde, head of the department of French at the London School of Economics. His final study of modernism, *Fifty Years of English Literature, 1900–1950*, was published in 1951 and displayed the breadth of his reading and literary taste; he also published two short studies of Thomas Hardy (1951) and Lytton Strachey (1955). He was made an OBE (captain) in 1955. After an operation he died at the Royal Free Hospital annex in London on 3 November 1959.

I. S. SCOTT-KILVERT, rev. KATHERINE MULLIN

Sources DNB · A. Palmer, 'An editor', *Review of English Literature*, 8/1 (1967), 85–94 · *The Times* (5 Nov 1959) · WW · CGPLA Eng. & Wales (1960)

Wealth at death £17,158 13s. 4d.: probate, 18 March 1960, CGPLA Eng. & Wales

James, Sidney [Sid; *real name* Sidney Joel Cohen] (1913–1976), actor, was born on 8 May 1913 in Hancock Street, Johannesburg, South Africa, the second of the two sons of Laurie Cohen (b. 1878) and his wife, Reine Solomon. His parents were both Jewish music-hall entertainers who had moved to South Africa from London some years before. For most of his childhood he was raised by relatives in Newcastle, Natal; first as his parents toured with

Sidney James (1913–1976), by unknown photographer

their act, and then after their separation. He attended Hospital Hill primary school in Newcastle and then trade schools in both Newcastle and Johannesburg. From the age of eight, when he began school, he was known as Sidney James, the surname James having been used by his parents in stage routines in England.

James worked as a diamond sorter for a time after leaving school, then in 1930 began work as a hairdresser in a salon operated by his mother. He became very successful at this trade, working also in a salon in Kroonstad, Orange Free State. He met as one of his customers Berthe Sadie (1912–c.1961), known as Toots, the daughter of Joseph Delmont, a wealthy Johannesburg businessman, and they married on 12 August 1936. They were divorced in 1940 largely as a result of James's numerous relationships with other women, a pattern which continued later in his life. His father-in-law had purchased a hairdressing salon for James, but the latter announced his intention of pursuing an acting career and in 1937 joined the Johannesburg Repertory Players. Through this he obtained professional work with the South African Broadcasting Corporation, first in a series of radio children's programmes and then in dramatic roles. He developed a reputation among fellow performers as 'totally dedicated to acting' (Goodwin, 30); he also was known for his heavy drinking and brawling, which contributed to his later battered appearance.

In the Second World War James served with an entertainment unit, where he was commissioned as a second lieutenant and made a producer. During this time, in 1943, he married a dancer, Meg Sergei, *née* Williams (b. 1913). They divorced on 17 August 1952, and on 21 August that year he married Valerie Elizabeth Patsy Assan (b. 1928), an actress who used Ashton as her stage name.

After the war James quickly gained work with the Gwen Ffrangcon-Davies Company in South Africa as a result of his previous acting reputation. As a former serviceman he then obtained a government grant to travel to London to study acting, and arrived there with his wife on Christmas day 1946 with, he said later, only 'a burning ambition to make money' (Goodwin, 53). He obtained a number of small parts in films almost immediately, beginning with *Black Memory* (1947) and *Night Beat* (1948), both crime dramas, and also found radio work. He also worked on the stage, in *Burlesque* in late 1947, and later in more important roles in Cole Porter's *Kiss me Kate* (1951, as one of a pair of inept gangsters), and in *Guys and Dolls*. However, it was the movie industry that kept him most regularly in work in this period, and by the end of 1954 he had appeared in at least forty-seven films. While he still usually played shady characters, his roles had drifted more towards comedy, particularly with parts in *The Lavender Hill Mob* (1951) and *The Titfield Thunderbolt* (1953) for Ealing Studios. It was exactly his type of down-to-earth character that the writers of *Hancock's Half Hour* were seeking in 1954 as a foil for the optimistic dreamer played by Tony Hancock, and James was offered this role on the strength of his movie performances. The show, first on radio (1954–9) and then on television from 1956, was a great success, and the Hancock and James relationship was enormously popular with audiences. However, the partnership ended bitterly in 1960 when Hancock 'began to worry that the success of the show was due to Sid James rather than himself, so he dropped Sid from the show' (Muir, 267). James had continued to make movies in this period, and in 1960 he appeared in *Carry on Constable*, the fourth in the long series of bawdy Carry On films. According to their producer, James soon became the 'anchor man' of the series (Goodwin, 3), playing outlandish characters such as the Rumpo Kid, Sir Sidney Ruff-Diamond, Bill Boosey, and Gladstone Screwer. He appeared in nineteen Carry On productions, and it is for these roles that he is perhaps best remembered.

James also appeared in a number of other television series, such as *Taxi*; the short-lived *East End, West End*; *George and the Dragon* in 1966; and, most successfully, *Bless this House* from 1971 to 1975. With this series and the Carry On films, James became one of the most recognizable and popular British comedy actors of his time. In 1976 he toured Britain with *The Mating Game*. On the opening night at the Empire Theatre in Sunderland, on 26 April 1976, he collapsed on stage with a heart attack, and was pronounced dead on arrival at the Sunderland Royal Infirmary.   MARC BRODIE

Sources *DNB* · C. Goodwin, *Sid James: a biography* (1995) · *The Times* (28 April 1976) · F. Muir, *A Kentish lad*, 2nd edn (1998) · A. Rigelsford, *Carry on laughing: a celebration* (1996) · S. Hibbin and N. Hibbin, *What a carry on* (1988) · *The Kenneth Williams diaries*, ed. R. Davies (1993) · *CGPLA Eng. & Wales* (1976)
Archives FILM BFI NFTVA, *Without walls*, Channel 4, 1 Jan 1993 · BFI NFTVA, 'Carry on darkly', Channel 4, 31 Aug 1998 · BFI NFTVA, 'The unforgettable Sid James', 4 Dec 2000 · BFI NFTVA, news footage · BFI NFTVA, performance footage |SOUND BL NSA, documentary recording · BL NSA, performance recordings
Likenesses photograph, 1949 (with Sam Wanamaker), Hult. Arch. · group portrait, photograph, *c*.1951, Hult. Arch. · group portrait, photograph, *c*.1952, Hult. Arch. · photograph, 1954 (with Alec Guinness), Hult. Arch. · photograph, 1967 (with Joan Sims), Hult. Arch. · photograph, NPG [*see illus.*] · photographs, repro. in Goodwin, *Sid James* · photographs, repro. in Rigelsford, *Carry on laughing*
Wealth at death £68,012: probate, 2 July 1976, *CGPLA Eng. & Wales*

James, Thomas (1572/3–1629), librarian and religious controversialist, was born at Newport, Isle of Wight, probably the youngest child of Richard James and Jane Overnone (d. 1581), who had been married there on 29 June 1549, but who had, according to their son's account many years later, been forced to live beyond the seas in Queen Mary's time. An elder sister, Mary, married Thomas Fleming (1544–1613), later lord chief justice, and it was Fleming who supported James first at Winchester College which he entered at the age of thirteen in 1586, and then at New College, Oxford, where he was admitted a probationer on 30 June 1591. He matriculated on 28 January 1592, was elected a fellow on 30 June 1593, graduated BA on 3 May 1595, and proceeded MA on 5 February 1599.

By this time the first of James's many publications had already appeared. *A Commentary upon the Canticle of Canticles* (1598), a translation of a work by the Italian reformer Antonio Brucioli, and *The Moral Philosophie of the Stoicks* (1598), a translation of a work by Guillaume Du Vair, manifested his linguistic versatility, although Thomas Bodley was later to find fault with James's Hebrew. An edition of Richard Bury's *Philobiblon* was printed at Oxford, also in 1598, and was reissued in the next year with a crude list of manuscripts and a dedication to Thomas Bodley. In it, James promises another catalogue of manuscripts to be published after a journey to Cambridge. By 1599 Bodley had chosen James as librarian for his refounded library, and Bodley's first extant letter, of 24 December that year, is addressed to him at Cambridge. The promised catalogue, *Ecloga Oxonio-Cantabrigiensis* (1600), is a union catalogue of manuscripts in the Oxford and Cambridge college libraries, and in Cambridge University Library. Meanwhile, James had also been engaged upon rearranging and transcribing Oxford's statutes. He was paid £6 13s. 4d. for this in February 1601.

James's appointment as librarian was confirmed by the university on 13 April 1602, at a salary increased that year from £22 13s. 4d. a year to £26 13s. 4d. and in 1613, the year of Bodley's death, to £33 6s. 8d. Bodley's letters to James now became more frequent, and the instructions to the keeper more detailed: 'I can not choose but impart my fansie unto yow in the smallest maters of the Libr[ary]' (*Letters of Sir Thomas Bodley*, no. 50, 8 Oct 1602). There are frequent references to James's brother Edward. Bodley's draft statutes had directed that the librarian should not be 'encombred with mariage', but by September 1601 James had intimated his intention of marrying. Bodley eventually relented, although the move entailed resignation from the New College fellowship and consequent financial loss. James was appointed rector of St Aldates, Oxford, on 14 September 1602 and on 18 October he married Ann Underhill (*bap.* 1581, *d.* 1655), one of a large and prominent Oxford family, in St Thomas's Church. The library opened on 8 November with a procession, and an address by the librarian, but Bodley himself was not present. Remaining in London he bought books for the library there, had them bound to his order and then sent them to Oxford to be

Thomas James (1572/3–1629), attrib. Gilbert Jackson

cataloged and placed by James, who returned manuscript lists to Bodley. The compilation of a general catalogue, printed by Joseph Barnes at Bodley's expense, between June and October 1604, was James's most onerous duty. Published in mid-1605 as *Catalogus librorum bibliothecæ publicæ quam vir ornatissimus Thomas Bodleius … in academia Oxoniensi nuper instituit*, it was dedicated to Prince Henry, from whom Bodley expected more than from King James.

With this task completed and the appointment of an under-keeper in 1606, James turned hopefully to an old preoccupation, the 'collation', the minute examination of the manuscript and printed texts of the church fathers in the belief that Roman Catholic theologians had deliberately falsified them. This had been the theme of James's *Bellum papale* (1600) and indeed was a motive in his early cataloguing of manuscripts. About 1607 he issued as a single sheet *The humble supplication of Thomas James student in divinitie, and keeper of the publike librarie at Oxford, for reformation of the ancient fathers workes, by papists sundrie wayes depraved*, while in 1608 he made use of manuscripts in the Bodleian Library and in Corpus Christi College, Cambridge, to publish an edition of John Wycliffe's proto-reforming work *Two Short Treatises Against the Orders of Begging Friars*. At first his schemes had Bodley's support, but this weakened when Bodley realized that King James's promise of manuscripts from the royal library would not be fulfilled. Nevertheless, he pressed James's claims for preferment with Archbishop Richard Bancroft and his

successor George Abbot. James was made chaplain to Bancroft and appointed rector of Midley in Kent on 6 November 1609. Two autograph (and identically bound) manuscripts in Lambeth Palace Library (MSS 524 and 525) record his gratitude to Bancroft and his hopes of Abbot. In a third manuscript (MS 526) he wrote 'Whence it is clearly proved in what value in this corrupt age manuscripts should be held'. Although Bodley frustrated his hopes of joining the translators of the Bible, James won widespread support in the church for his study of the fathers. A group of theologians was appointed and began work under his direction on 1 July 1610, but ceased, for want of payment, in October 1612. Despite its short life, the group collated fifty-six manuscripts, about half of which were from outside the Bodleian Library. James published in a pamphlet *Bellum Gregorianum* (1610) what he termed 'gustum non fructum', a foretaste of the work. Bodley, however, was contemptuous of 'this so litle fore-running proofe of your greater worke to come' (*Letters of Sir Thomas Bodley*, no. 193, 30 Oct 1610).

James's family grew in these years. Little is known of his eldest children, Thomas and Ann; Francis (*b. c.*1607) followed his father's course to Winchester and New College; Theodore, (*b.* 1609) was later a fellow of Corpus Christi College, Oxford, and his baptism and that of several daughters, Martha (1615), Alice (1616), and Mary (1619), in St Mary Magdalen Church, suggests that the family was then living in that parish.

As a letter of Bodley dated 26 February 1611 makes clear, the agreement of 12 December 1610, between the Stationers' Company of London and the university, for the deposit in the library of the books the stationers printed had been James's idea. Its effect, though far-reaching, was at first vitiated by Bodley's contempt for 'London books', and particularly for plays, and by the stationers' reluctance to keep to the agreement; its enforcement was one of the duties of James's later years as librarian. With Bodley's death on 28 January 1613, James became answerable both for the administration of the library and for the purchase of books to a body of curators. For acquisitions, the curators relied upon the Frankfurt fair catalogues (for the most part, in the London-printed version) and upon experienced booksellers such as John Bill, and later Henry Featherstone.

Meanwhile James was also continuously engaged upon the cataloguing of the library, both upon subject catalogues and upon a new general catalogue. That published in 1605 had been essentially a shelf-list according to the classification of the library, followed by an alphabetical index. He now produced in 1612–13 a new catalogue, in alphabetical order of author or title. It was intended for printing, but absence of funding ensured that it remained in James's autograph. An alphabetical author catalogue was, however, printed and published as *Catalogus universalis librorum in bibliotheca Bodleiana* (1620). The title-page proclaimed James's authorship, although it appeared during the office of his successor, John Rous. His own correspondence shows that he was also much involved in the everyday work of librarianship, such as requests for information and transcriptions.

As building work on the schools quadrangle of the library progressed between 1613 and 1619, James concerned himself with the fabric too. While the overall design can be attributed to Sir Henry Savile, he was certainly responsible for the choice of authors depicted in the painted frieze in the gallery on the top floor. The frieze reflects the contents and arrangement of the library, and James's own reverence for the authors of Greece and Rome, for the church fathers upon whom he had lavished so much zeal, for foreign reformers, and for English protestant divines of his own century.

Meanwhile, James's almost obsessive anti-Catholicism remained unabated, finding expression in such works as *A Treatise of the Corruption of Scripture* (London, 1611) and *The Jesuits Downefall* (Oxford, 1612) and, more practically, in the detection of Jesuits in Oxfordshire. Ecclesiastical preferment also continued to come his way: on 20 October 1617 he was appointed rector of Little Mongeham, Kent.

In 1620 James resigned as Bodley's librarian, and thereafter dedicated himself, notwithstanding the sicknesses of which he complained, to grand schemes of collation, and to that end, to the study of manuscripts. His income, diminished by his resignation, was augmented again by his installation as subdean of Wells on 16 June 1621, but his correspondence is dominated by requests for assistance in paying 'a dozen able schollers' (T. James, *An Explanation or Enlarging of the Ten Articles*, 1625, 31) to peruse the fathers and other ecclesiastical documents supposedly contaminated by the papists. A scheme in ten articles was proposed to the clergy in late 1624 or early 1625 as *The Humble and Earnest Request of Thomas James to the Church of England* and republished as *An Explanation or Enlarging of the Ten Articles* (1625), although, as James wrote on 28 January 1624 to James Ussher, then bishop of Meath, one of his few sympathetic correspondents, 'I have not Encouragement from our Bishops'. However, one work of collation, the *Vindiciae Gregorianae*, appeared in Geneva in 1625, and the access that James had to Sir Robert Cotton's library in order to pursue his researches was no doubt eased by the appointment of his nephew Richard James as Cotton's librarian about that year. A final bolt fired at the papists, *Index generalis librorum prohibitorum à pontificiis*, appeared in 1627.

Little is known of James's last years. When he wrote to Cotton on 11 August 1628 to thank him for petitioning Archbishop Abbot on behalf of his wife and children, he commented that 'long I cannot have the benefitt of this worlde' (BL, Cotton MS Julius C.III, fol. 221). He died in August 1629, and was buried in New College chapel, but the exact site of his grave is unknown. Administration of his estate was granted to his widow, Ann James, on 14 November 1629 in the chancellor's court of Oxford University. An inventory of the same date gives the value of his goods as £219 1s. 10d. His books—which are not specified—were valued at £40. Ann James was buried on 22 June 1655.

In his own time, James was characterized, memorably, and perhaps accurately, by Wood, as 'the most industrious and indefatigable writer against the Papists, that had been educated in Oxon, since the reformation of religion' (Wood, *Ath. Oxon.*, 2.469). Underlying the obsessive vehemence of his anti-Catholicism, there is the fact that many of the patristic and other editions which he attacked were, perhaps more by carelessness than fraudulence, extremely inaccurate, and that James by his insistence on the use of manuscripts, served scholarship well. This service was the greater by his care for the manuscripts in his own library, and by his recording of them elsewhere. With the not always helpful oversight of Thomas Bodley, James was also the first librarian to attempt the organization of knowledge in books and manuscripts into the printed and published catalogues of a large library; the successive catalogues in which he did this were the work of a bibliographical pioneer.   R. JULIAN ROBERTS

Sources *Letters of Sir Thomas Bodley to Thomas James, first keeper of the Bodleian Library*, ed. G. W. Wheeler (1926) · G. W. Wheeler, ed., *Letters addressed to Thomas James* (1933) · indexes to Oxford parish registers, Centre for Oxfordshire Studies · G. W. Wheeler, *The earliest catalogues of the Bodleian Library, Oxford* (1928) · I. Philip, *The Bodleian Library in the seventeenth and eighteenth centuries* (1983) · G. Hampshire, ed., *The Bodleian Library account book, 1613–1646* (1983) · G. W. Wheeler, 'The Bodleian staff, 1600–1612', *Bodleian Quarterly Record*, 2 (1917–19), 279–85 · G. W. Wheeler, 'Thomas James, theologian and Bodley's librarian', *Bodleian Quarterly Record*, 4 (1923–5), 91–5 · G. W. Wheeler, 'A librarian's correspondence', *Bodleian Quarterly Record*, 6 (1929–31), 11–18 · N. R. Ker, 'Thomas James's collation of Gregory, Cyprian and Ambrose', *Bodleian Library Record*, 4 (1952–3), 16–30 · J. N. L. Myres, 'Thomas James and the painted frieze', *Bodleian Library Record*, 4 (1952–3), 30–51 · New College, Oxford, MS 9750, pp. 465, 155 · LPL, MSS 524–526 · registers of archbishops Bancroft and Abbot, LPL · BL, Cotton MS Julius C III, fols. 220, 221 · private information (2004) [T. B. James]
Archives Bodl. Oxf., corresp. and papers, MSS Arch Selden a 75; Ballard 44; Bodley 276, 510, 699, 763; e Mus 38, 40; Rawl. Q e 31 · LPL, collections relating to ecclesiastical history
Likenesses attrib. G. Jackson, oils, Bodl. Oxf. [*see illus.*]
Wealth at death £219 1s. 10d.: inventory, Chancellor's Court, U. Oxf.

James, Thomas (1592/3–1635), explorer and writer, was born in late 1592 or early 1593, a younger son and one of five children of James ap John ap Richard Herbert of the small Wern-y-cwm Manor in Llanwytherin parish, near Abergavenny, Monmouthshire. Little is known of his early life except that he was admitted to the Inner Temple in 1612. He must have had considerable experience of the sea because he was recorded as captain and co-owner of a Bristol-based privateer, the *Dragon* in 1628, before the powerful local Society of Merchant Venturers entrusted him with searching for the north-west passage to Asia. James's expedition was hastily assembled to rival Luke Foxe's similar venture on behalf of London merchants.

On 3 May 1631 James left Bristol in the *Henrietta Maria*, a leaky 70 ton vessel. James took special care in choosing and calibrating a large range of navigation instruments. He deliberately chose a crew of twenty-two young men without Arctic experience in order to ensure dependence on the captain, thereby reducing the prospect of mutiny. The crew was also large enough to make sure the ship could be manhandled through the ice if necessary. James sailed through Hudson Strait and into Hudson Bay, but pack ice prevented him from reaching further than 62°N so he turned south-west, reaching the west coast near Hubbert's Hope on 11 August. He subsequently explored the whole southern shore of Hudson Bay, naming it New South Wales, he labelled its principal river the Severn and named Cape Henrietta Maria after his ship and the queen; the large southern embayment became 'James, His Bay'. Foxe's rival expedition had also been blocked by ice, although it did penetrate slightly further north, to the fringe of the Arctic circle, before turning south into Hudson Bay. The two expeditions met on the south shore on 29 August 1631, but Foxe sailed home rather than facing a winter in the bay.

Worsening ice conditions and storms forced James to search for a place to winter in early October 1631. He chose Charlton Island at the bottom of James Bay, naming it after the king, but was forced to sink his ship to prevent its being battered by ice. After surviving the unimagined cold of winter, the explorers managed to raise the vessel in the late spring but could not leave anchorage until early July. After one more effort to penetrate to the north-west, James found unbroken ice and abandoned the search on 26 July 1632 at approximately 65°30' N, encountering severe ice conditions and storms before his battered ship reached Bristol on 22 October.

The experiences led James to discount any possibility of a commercial passage to Asia through the area he explored, putting forward six convincing reasons for his opinion. His long voyage effectively ended Bristol's interest in the passage.

James's work has often been downplayed by critics. He did not achieve major discoveries but the popular book of his tribulations, *The Strange and Dangerous Voyage of Captain Thomas James* (1633), turned the abortive quest for the north-west passage into an action-packed ordeal of survival. Given the surveying standards of the time, and the often severe climatic conditions he faced, his book and its appendices show an exceptional attention to locational measurement and considerable accuracy in estimating longitude for Charlton Island. James must have been a skilful mariner and capable leader to have survived his eighteen-month journey, losing only three of his inexperienced crew in accidents. His book was not the typical dispassionate daily log of many exploration narratives. It was constructed to provide fast-paced descriptions of the perils faced during his journey, such as the fear of being crushed by icebergs and later pack ice, in which the din of grinding ice floes provided a never-ending assault on the senses—noises that were probably worse in the dark when nothing could be seen; on some days dripping fog enveloped the crew, marooning them in a grey, invisible world from which there seemed no escape; other hazards were provided by frequent storms, dangerous shores, and bone-chilling temperatures, especially between 7 October and 2 July on Charlton Island—problems compounded by the ravages of scurvy and plagues of flies in the early summer.

The book left vivid impressions of James's experiences, and included two poems that were the first composed in the Canadian north. In 1812 these were praised by the poets Robert Southey and Samuel Taylor Coleridge in their book *Omniana*. Coleridge also adapted and used a great deal of James's imagery in his famous poem 'The Rime of the Ancient Mariner'. James's deliberate attention to the difficulties of the journey led many students of exploration to underestimate his achievements, whether in measurement, exploration, or his informative comments about the environment. Important appendices by Cambridge academics provided proof for longitude calculations and a philosophical justification for the primacy of seamen's observations over the speculations of classical scholars. James's literary contributions as a pioneer of Anglo-Welsh and Canadian literature have also been rarely acknowledged, especially the fact that he provided one of the first thrilling, 'man against nature' accounts written about the Canadian north. However, he attributed his many miraculous survivals to God's guiding hand rather than his own skill. He died in 1635 after spending less than two years in distinguished service as captain of a king's ship in the Irish Sea combating piracy. His grave is unknown.

WAYNE K. D. DAVIES

Sources T. James, *The strange and dangerous voyage of Captain Thomas James*, 2nd edn (1740); [new edn], ed. W. A. Kenyon [1975] [repr. Toronto, 1973] · M. Christy, ed., *The voyages of Captain Luke Fox of Hull, and Captain Thomas James of Bristol, in search of the north-west passage, in 1631–32*, 1, Hakluyt Society, 88 (1894); repr. (1981) [repr. 1981; microform] · I. James, *The source of the 'Ancient mariner'* (1890) · C. M. MacInnes, *Captain Thomas James and the north west passage* (1967) · R. Southey and S. T. Coleridge, *Omniana, or, Horae otiosiores* (1812) [repr. 1969] · H. . Helfrich, *Captain Thomas James: fool or hero?* (1972) · P. G. Adams, *Travel literature and the evolution of the novel* (1983) · J. Barrow, *A chronological history of voyages in Arctic regions* (1818) · W. H. Cooke, ed., *Students admitted to the Inner Temple, 1547–1660* [1878], 197

Likenesses line engraving (after unknown portrait), BM, NPG; repro. in T. James, *The strange and dangerous voyage of Captain Thomas James* (1633)

James, Thomas (d. 1738). *See under* James, John (c.1672–1746).

James, Thomas (1748–1804), headmaster, was born on 19 October 1748 at St Ives, Huntingdonshire, the son of Thomas and Mary James of St Ives. Brought up in a well-to-do family, he began his classical education under the Revd John Wheeldon at his school in St Ives and in May 1761 he entered Eton College, where he was elected a king's scholar. He won a reputation for the elegance of his Latin and Greek verses, some of which were printed in the *Musae Etonenses*. He was presented with a copy of Homer's *Iliad* by Mark Akenside in appreciation of his Greek translation of one of the poet's shorter poems, beginning 'Whoever thou art'. In Michaelmas 1767 he matriculated from King's College, Cambridge, where he was a keen student of mathematics as well as classics. He acted as a private tutor to several aristocratic pupils and, at a young age, was elected fellow (1770) and appointed a tutor of his college. He graduated BA in 1771 and MA in 1774. He won in 1772 the first member's prize for a Latin essay awarded to middle bachelors, and in 1773 that awarded to senior bachelors. While an undergraduate he wrote *An Account of King's College Chapel* for the benefit of the recently impoverished chapel clerk, Henry Malden, under whose name it was published in 1769.

In May 1778 James was elected headmaster of Rugby School in succession to the Revd Stanley Burrough. The following month he was ordained priest at Canterbury. The school's constitution had been reformed by an act of parliament in 1777 to provide for salaries for assistant masters, exhibitions, and a new statement of rules and regulations. James took full advantage of these reforms and, together with the assistant master, a fellow Etonian, James Chartes, began to transform the school. The first of several additional schoolrooms was built in 1779 to accommodate the growing number of boys; from only fifty-two boys in 1778 numbers increased to eighty in 1779, 240 in 1790, and the school under James peaked at 245 pupils. He introduced to Rugby the methods of teaching and discipline at Eton which he had recorded when a pupil in his manuscript 'Account of Eton discipline' of 1766. The principal innovations were the tutorial system, by which boys received private lessons with a tutor to prepare for the classes held in the schoolroom; the regulation of school discipline by senior pupils who acted as praeposters, or monitors; and the establishment of dame houses to house the growing number of boarders. He expanded the classical curriculum of Latin and Greek to include history, geography, and mathematics (which he taught himself on Saturday mornings), and allowed two or three half-holidays each week for private tuition in dancing, drawing, and fencing. He also encouraged school sports, principally cricket, swimming, boxing, and fishing, and even built a moveable bathing hut by the river and appointed swimming attendants to look after the boys. A Sunday service was instituted in the school when the number of pupils outgrew the gallery in the parish church and James ensured that the school library was well stocked by persuading boys to donate a book on leaving the school. As Rugby flourished James was able to attract able teachers to the school; by the time he left there were six assistant masters and several writing and arithmetic tutors. Among his more celebrated pupils were Samuel Butler, headmaster of Shrewsbury School, Edward Legge and Richard Bagot, both bishops of Oxford, Charles James Appleby, Stephen Lushington, and Walter Savage Landor. After several tussles with Landor, who was the best classicist but also one of the most audacious pupils in the school, James quietly sent him home rather than expelling him. This episode was typical of his fairness towards the boys, although he never dispensed with the rod; during his headmastership there were only two serious rebellions in the school.

James married twice. On 21 December 1779 he married Elizabeth (*bap.* 1756, *d.* 1784), daughter of John and Elizabeth Mander of Coventry; they had two children, Thomas and Mary. On 27 March 1785 he married Arabella (*d.* 1828), fourth daughter of William Caldecott of Catthorpe, Leicestershire. They had two daughters and four sons, the eldest of whom was John Thomas *James, later bishop of Calcutta. In 1786 James proceeded DD and founded two prizes for Latin declamations by scholars of King's College. He published two works for use in the school, *Compendium of Geography* and *The Principal Propositions of the Fifth Book of Euclid Demonstrated Algebraically* (1791), and two sermons in 1800.

Ill health prevented James from fulfilling his wish to remain a schoolmaster as long as his favourite author, Quintilian, and he resigned his post in 1794. In gratitude towards a headmaster who had transformed Rugby into a leading public school the trustees awarded him an annuity of £80, presented him with a piece of plate, and petitioned the prime minister for a church preferment for him. James was duly appointed in May 1797 to a prebend in Worcester Cathedral and was instituted to the rectory of Harvington in the same county. After a short illness he died on 23 September 1804 at Harvington, and was buried in Worcester Cathedral, where a monument was erected to his memory. Subscriptions from his pupils funded another monument, by Francis Chantrey, with a Latin inscription by Bishop Samuel Butler, which was erected in the chapel of Rugby School in 1824.

GORDON GOODWIN, *rev.* S. J. SKEDD

Sources W. Birch, *The schoolmaster: a tribute to the memory of Thomas James, D.D., with a short memoir prefixed* (1829) · W. H. D. Rouse, *A history of Rugby School* (1898) · Venn, *Alum. Cant.* · R. A. Austen-Leigh, ed., *The Eton College register, 1753–1790* (1921) · *Public characters of 1805* (1805), 242–8 · M. H. Bloxam, *Rugby: the school and the neighbourhood*, ed. W. H. Payne Smith (1889) · [F. Temple], ed., *Rugby School register from 1675 to 1867 inclusive* (1867) · *GM*, 1st ser., 54 (1784), 316 · *GM*, 1st ser., 74 (1804), 982–3 · *IGI* · J. Forster, *Walter Savage Landor: a biography*, 2 vols. (1869), 1.14, 18, 31–2, 195–7 · will, PRO, PROB 11/1420, sig. 108
Archives BL, letters to Samuel Butler, Add. MS 34583 · Rugby School, Warwickshire, letters to Samuel Butler
Likenesses F. Chantrey, marble statue on monument, 1824, Rugby School chapel · N. Houghton, engraving (after miniature by Engleheart)
Wealth at death bequests of several hundred pounds: will, PRO, PROB 11/1420, sig. 108

James, Thomas Smith (1809–1874). *See under* James, John Angell (1785–1859).

James, Walter Charles, first Baron Northbourne (1816–1893), landowner and politician, was born in London on 3 June 1816, the only son and heir of John James (*d.* 1818), minister-plenipotentiary to the Netherlands, and his wife, Emily Jane, daughter of Robert *Stewart, first marquess of Londonderry. He succeeded his grandfather Sir James James (formerly Head), bt, of Langley Hall, Berkshire, as second baronet in 1829. He was educated at Westminster School (1826–33), and then in 1833 went to Christ Church, Oxford, where he obtained second-class honours in classics in 1836, graduating BA that year and proceeding MA in 1840. He married on 17 April 1841 Sarah Caroline (1812–1890), fifth daughter and coheir of Cuthbert Ellison of Hebburn Hall, co. Durham, and his wife, Grace, daughter and coheir of Henry Ibbetson of St Anthony's, Northumberland. Through his marriage he succeeded to the Ellison properties, totalling approximately 4300 acres. He also owned about 2300 acres at Betteshanger, near Sandwich, in Kent.

In 1837, standing as a Conservative, James was elected one of the two MPs for Hull, a seat which he retained until his retirement in 1847. A lay supporter of the Tractarian movement, he became a close friend of W. E. Gladstone, with whom he undertook charitable work in London. He shared Gladstone's Peelite political sympathies and was in favour of free trade, voting in favour of corn-law repeal in the crucial division on 15 May 1846. He joined other Christ Church men as a member of the Canterbury Association, constituted in 1848 to found a Church of England settlement in New Zealand.

James served as sheriff of Kent in 1855, having purchased his family seat, Betteshanger Park, from F. E. Morrice, who had built the house in 1825. James employed the architect George Devey to remodel Betteshanger in a variety of styles and materials to the make the house appear to have developed over the previous four centuries. It was visited by many leading figures of the day from the worlds of politics and the arts, including Gladstone, a family friend to whom he acted as a close political confidant. Gladstone raised him to the peerage as Baron Northbourne on 5 November 1884. A trustee of the National Gallery, Northbourne served in 1880 as a commissioner on the constitution and working of the ecclesiastical courts. He shared with his wife a deep religious conviction, and rebuilt Betteshanger church, where he carved the pulpit and taught at the Sunday school. He died at Betteshanger on 4 February 1893. His son Walter Henry James (1846–1923), Liberal MP for Gateshead from 1874 to 1893, succeeded to his peerage; his daughter Sarah married J. A. Godley, Gladstone's private secretary, in 1871.

ALISON CRESSWELL

Sources *The Times* (6 Feb 1893) · GEC, *Peerage* · Boase, *Mod. Eng. biog.* · H. C. G. Matthew, *Gladstone*, 2 vols. (1986–95) · M. Girouard, 'George Devey in Kent, I', *Country Life*, 149 (1971), 744–7 · Gladstone, *Diaries*
Archives LPL, diary · NRA, priv. coll., corresp. and papers | BL, corresp. with W. E. Gladstone, Add. MSS 44264–44265 · BL, corresp. with Sir Robert Peel, Add. MSS 40426–40599, *passim*
Likenesses portrait, repro. in *Daily Graphic* (9 Feb 1893)
Wealth at death £37,482 15s. 7d.: resworn probate, May 1893, CGPLA Eng. & Wales

James, Walter Haweis (1847–1927), army officer, politician, and military writer, was born on 9 July 1847, the youngest son of H. C. James and his wife, Elizabeth Jane, *née* Page. The family home was Bushmead Hall, Bedford. Educated privately, James entered the Royal Military Academy, Woolwich, and was commissioned in 1867 into the Royal Engineers. He married in 1871 Fanny Eugenia Mabel Caunter, the only daughter of the Revd G. Akehurst, and they had one daughter and three sons.

In 1877 James passed the Staff College course with honours, going on to serve in the War Office intelligence department. Promoted captain in 1879, he served on campaign as a deputy assistant quartermaster-general in the Anglo-Zulu War, but failed to distinguish himself, and retired from the army in 1880 to go into politics.

A staunch Conservative, James contested the parliamentary seat of West St Pancras unsuccessfully in 1885. Between 1889 and 1892 he was a member of the London county council, becoming a whip of the Moderate Party and chairman of the sanitary committee. In 1899 he was made vice-chairman of the Primrose League, on the grand council of which he served for several years.

Re-employed by the army in 1901 at the height of the Second South African War, James served in the War Office as assistant to the permanent under-secretary, being promoted major in 1901 and lieutenant-colonel in 1903. Leaving the army once again, he played a small but significant part in the army reform movement as the author of numerous newspaper and magazine articles, and as editor of the famous Wolseley Series of military textbooks, and established something of a reputation as a military pundit. He published two military books of his own, *Modern Strategy* (1903), intended as a textbook for army officers, and *The Campaign of 1815* (1908).

Part of the conservative mainstream in military thinking as well as in politics, James's works contain some useful insights into war of the period, and are among many which disprove the myth that the armies of Europe had no conception of what awaited them in the First World War. He identified the impact on war made by improved railway and telegraph communications, and by the vastly increased size of armies. He also realized the strength given to the defensive by increased firepower and the increasing impossibility of successful frontal attacks. However, his solution, like that of most of his contemporaries, was to emphasize manoeuvre in the expectation that battle would become more, rather than less, decisive. His military thought, as expressed in *Modern Strategy*, inclines more towards the ideals of Jomini than of Clausewitz.

On 14 September 1914 James was recalled to active service from the reserve for the last time, fulfilling the role of a typical army 'dug-out' officer by working as a general staff officer 2nd grade in the censor's department of the War Office. He retired on 31 May 1918, having reached the age limit. His main post-war achievement was in providing valuable assistance to *The Times* in preparing its *History of the War*.

The family home in later life was 6 St Mary's Mansions, London W2. A member of the Author's Club, James's other recreations were shooting and tennis. He died peacefully of old age on 13 January 1927 in a nursing home in Ealing and was cremated at Golders Green crematorium on 17 January. One of his sons followed him into the army, becoming Lieutenant-Colonel R. H. James.

STEPHEN BADSEY

Sources WWW · *The Times* (15 Jan 1927) · W. H. James, *Modern strategy* (1903) · W. H. James, *The campaign of 1815* (1908)

James, William (1542–1617), bishop of Durham, was the second son of John James of Little Ore, Staffordshire, and Ellen, daughter of William Bolte of Sandbach, Cheshire, where William was born.

William James (1542–1617), by unknown artist

Early career at Oxford and Durham James entered Christ Church, Oxford, in 1559 or 1560, graduated BA in 1563, and proceeded MA in 1565, BTh in 1571, and DTh in 1574. Under letters patent of 29 June 1575 he was appointed rector of Kingham, Oxfordshire, a living which he continued to hold in plurality until 1601. By this time he was already making progress in his academic career. He was theology reader at Magdalen College in 1571 and in the following year he was elected master of University College. In 1573 the chaplain and fellows of the Savoy sought Lord Burghley's support for James's appointment as master of the Savoy on account of his 'wisdom in restoring and bringing to happy quietness the late, wasted, spoiled and indebted University college' (Strype, 4.581). The brevity of James's tenure as an Oxford head suggests considerable special pleading.

Though he was later to be associated with a conservative style of Calvinist churchmanship, it is possible that at this stage James was somewhat more radical in his approach to issues of church government. In 1575 he was one of the signatories of a letter to the earl of Leicester in which a number of Oxford academics defended three fellows of Magdalen who had been summarily dismissed from their fellowships by Lawrence Humphrey, the president of Magdalen, for refusing to take an oath before the election of a new dean of arts. Archdeacon of Coventry from 1577 to 1584, James served twice as vice-chancellor of Oxford, in 1581 and 1590, but received his most significant promotion up to that point when he was made dean of Christ Church on 2 September 1584. The first of his two published sermons, preached before the queen in February 1578, was a vigorous attack on the 'lothsome puddle of Popishe trumperie' and asserted the protestant characteristics of the Church of England which he felt were in danger of 'false undermining' by the increasing influx of seminary priests into England (James, *Sermon Preached before the Queenes Majestie*).

James's career seemed temporarily to stall after his preferment to Christ Church. By that stage he appears to have identified himself with the more conservative elements within Oxford, who associated themselves with the chancellorship of Sir Christopher Hatton, to whom at this stage James was chaplain. Possibly at the behest of Hatton, who was closely involved in the suppression of the anti-episcopal Marprelate tracts, James preached vigorously in defence of episcopacy at Paul's Cross in 1589, when the Marprelate controversy was at its height, dedicating the published version to Hatton. Unsurprisingly, therefore, James enjoyed the support of Archbishop Whitgift. In 1595 the primate and Lord Buckhurst recommended him unsuccessfully to Sir Robert Cecil for the vacant see of Worcester but successfully for the consolation prize of the deanery of Durham. Whitgift had been 'a long and an earnest suitor' for James, whom he considered 'very worthy' (*Salisbury MSS*, 6.117). As dean, James was less active politically than his predecessor Toby Matthew, though he rapidly became a very informative, albeit prolix, correspondent of Cecil. This correspondence concerned not only the extent of Roman Catholic recusancy that he found in Durham but also the scale of poverty and deprivation that the area was suffering as a result of poor harvests, decay of tillage, and plague. In 1598 he was appointed as a commissioner to investigate a complicated dispute concerning the conduct of the grand lease of the mines of Gateshead and Whickham by the mayor and corporation of Newcastle upon Tyne, a commission that he undertook scrupulously. James appeared at this stage to be both a concerned and a conscientious pastor. Unfortunately for James, this image was not to prevail. His conduct of the dean and chapter's relationships with its tenants was castigated in a letter to Cecil, now earl of Salisbury, by a young and politically ambitious Durham gentleman, Henry Anderson of Haswell Grange, who later became a bitter opponent of James as bishop. Unfortunately for the normally mild-mannered James, Anderson was not to be his only enemy in the running of the diocese.

Bishop of Durham The see of Durham became vacant in April 1606 following the promotion of Toby Matthew to York. The manoeuvrings to replace Matthew began early. On 16 January Sir John Ferne, of the council of the north, had written to Salisbury informing him of the death of Archbishop Hutton and recommending both Hutton's replacement by Matthew and Matthew's replacement by James. According to Ferne, James was 'learned, very grave, wise and of honest conversation unreprovable, a stout oppugner of papists' as well as 'an excellent magistrate … in matters of justice most upright and sincere' (*Salisbury*

MSS, 18.22). A week later Adam Newton was writing to Salisbury pointing out that the king had promised him the deanery of Durham, implying that a decision had already been taken to promote James. Nevertheless, no decision was announced for several months. James himself had quickly begun lobbying for promotion to the bishopric in a letter to Salisbury on 8 February, amid a flurry of anti-recusant activity which was likely to appeal to Salisbury in the aftermath of the Gunpowder Plot. By 30 April James had been 'certified by divers friends' of Salisbury's favour, drawing this to the latter's attention in a letter describing the suicide in prison of an arrested recusant (ibid., 18.125). Three weeks later Anderson reported the accurate rumours concerning the promotion of James, though his promotion was not confirmed until September.

At the time, from the point of view of James I and Salisbury, the promotion of William James might have appeared perfectly reasonable. Apart from Anderson's cavilling, they had no reason to suspect the quality of his performance as dean: he was never less than conscientious in his public and religious duties, his record of opposing Catholic recusancy would have enhanced his reputation in Salisbury's eyes, and by 1606 he had had ten years of valuable experience in the diocese. James was not entirely ineffective as diocesan: he was regular in attending sessions of his diocesan ecclesiastical commission, attempted to deal with dilapidated churches in Northumberland, and was also active as a member of the county bench and (for several years) *de facto* lord lieutenant, while Prebendary Peter Smart, at loggerheads with Bishop Richard Neile, wrote of James's episcopate as 'our lesse ceremonious, and more preaching, bishop's time' (Tyacke, 214). But Smart was hardly an impartial witness, and overall James's performance as bishop was undoubtedly weak. As early as 1608 there was implicit criticism of his inadequacy in a sermon preached by Thomas Oxley at a diocesan synod, and there was widespread relief in the diocese at his death.

There were three interconnected reasons for Bishop James's unpopularity. Though a capable administrator, for example, in his discharge of militia responsibilities, he proved politically incapable of defending Durham interests at court and in Westminster. He picked a quarrel with the corporation of Durham which was to cause ill feeling throughout his episcopate. There was dissatisfaction with the performance of some of his officials and clergy. Moreover, his inability to cope satisfactorily with his admittedly difficult task of supervising Lady Arabella Stuart and the disgrace of his patron at court, Salisbury, followed by the latter's death in 1612, left him vulnerable to the counter-attacks of his enemies.

Local difficulties Except for his effective opposition to the despoliation of royal properties by the crown's agents, James's defence of Durham interests was particularly weak. This was most evident in his failure to defend Durham from the extension of the subsidy from which the four far northern counties, Durham, Northumberland, Cumberland, and Westmorland, had hitherto been exempted. The crown's position on this was logical enough. The counties had been exempted from subsidies in order that they might maintain border service. Now that the border had, in effect, disappeared there were no grounds for the maintenance of the privilege. However, the response of the Durham gentry was to seek parliamentary representation, something previously lacking on account of the county's palatine status. To this Bishop James was implacably opposed. It was, moreover, public knowledge that the bishop was beholden to his patron Salisbury for a deal that had been undertaken to exchange property near Durham House, for which Salisbury had provided new stables. In the eyes of the bishop's local opponents this became linked with the controversy over Salisbury's proposed 'great contract', his attempt in 1610 to put the crown's finances on a sound footing, thereby enhancing suspicions of James's conduct.

James's poor relations with his 'crooked and unkind neighbours' (*Salisbury MSS*, 21.224), the corporation of Durham, dogged the whole of his episcopate. The corporation had benefited from a grant by Bishop Matthew in 1602 which had increased their privileges. James clearly thought that this restricted his ability to exercise what remained of his palatine rights. Moreover, the mayor and burgesses had, in James's view, attempted to extend their privileges 'to usurp things never granted and challenge things not grantable' (PRO, SP 14/50/72). In order to regain what James believed to be his rights, he pursued a bitterly contested case in the court of exchequer. Though he was to emerge legally victorious, it proved a Pyrrhic victory, as relationships between diocese and corporation remained blighted until James died, only to be patched up by James's more emollient successor, Richard Neile.

Troubles in parliament and court: death The attack on James and his officials was led by Anderson, whose resentment of the bishop was fully aired during the parliament of 1614. His complaint about James, whose role he intemperately compared with that of the pope, covered the role of clerical justices of the peace and James's opposition to Durham securing representation in the House of Commons. He was also contemptuous about James's conduct of military service within Durham. Furthermore, Anderson's equally intemperate ally William Morton, archdeacon of Durham, launched an attack on both James and his officials in 1616. Morton rather improbably argued that Bishop James was bound, like all of his predecessors, to be perverted by his exercise of the *jura regalia* of the palatinate of Durham. This problem, he further alleged, was reinforced by James's insatiable covetousness.

James's inability to cope with his task of supervising the king's wayward cousin, Lady Arabella Stuart, further weakened his political position. He had been appointed to this unwelcome task in March 1611, presumably on the grounds that, safely ensconced in Durham, Lady Arabella could do little damage to the crown's stability. However, she got no further north than Barnet, after which she attempted to escape to France and was eventually imprisoned in the Tower of London, where she died in 1615. But for James the task of looking after her even briefly had been both expensive and onerous, to the extent that he was forced in January 1612 to go to Bath to recuperate. James certainly blamed Lady Arabella for bringing about his declining health, and the fact that he made a will in April 1611 suggests that his complaints on this score were not without foundation.

These problems, along with the fall of Salisbury, certainly made the bishop vulnerable to the attempts made by Robert Carr, earl of Somerset, to build up his political position in co. Durham. Somerset was appointed lord lieutenant, a position that James himself had coveted. Moreover, James was also anxious about Somerset's links with known Durham recusants. That he was able to survive this potential undermining of his influence owed nothing to his own political stature but was entirely a consequence of Somerset's fall from power in 1615 in scandalous circumstances.

The elderly Bishop James was not able to enjoy his new security for long. In April 1617 he was obliged to offer hospitality to James I on his way to Scotland. Not only was this expensive, but the visit became the stuff of local legend, for it was alleged that the bishop died within three days of the royal visitation on account of the king's criticism of his attitude towards the citizens of Durham. The chronology of the events does not quite fit this interpretation, the bishop dying nineteen days after the king's departure, and such interpretations of the king's possible comments are merely supposition, even though it is clear that the corporation of Durham used the opportunity of the royal visit to make their grievances against the bishop very clear.

James died at Durham on 12 May 1617, of a 'violent fit of stone and stangury', and was buried in his cathedral, though his grave and memorial have disappeared. He had reaffirmed his Calvinist credentials in the preamble to his will, trusting 'to be receyved into his mercie seat with the rest of his electe and chosen Israell' (PRO, PROB 11/129, fol. 462). He had been thrice married. His first wife was Katherine Risby of Abingdon. The identity of his second is unknown. His third was Isabel Atkinson (née Rilley) of Newcastle upon Tyne, and it was their son Francis James who was the principal beneficiary of the bishop's will. James further advanced the interests of his own family by promoting the clerical careers within the palatinate of his nephew William James, his son-in-law Ferdinand Morecroft, and Morecroft's brother George.

MICHAEL TILLBROOK

Sources Calendar of the manuscripts of the most hon. the marquis of Salisbury, 24 vols., HMC, 9 (1883–1976) · state papers domestic, Elizabeth I; James I, PRO, SP 12; SP 14 · exchequer, king's remembrancer, entry books of decrees, series IV, PRO, E126 · exchequer, king's remembrancer, depositions taken by commission, PRO, E134 · W. James, A sermon preached before the queenes majestie at Hampton Courte, the 19 of February laste paste (1578) · W. James, A sermon preached at Paules Crosse the ix of November 1589 (1590) · will, PRO, PROB 11/129, fols. 462 ff. · R. Surtees, The history and antiquities of the county palatine of Durham, 4 vols. (1816–40) · A. Foster, 'The struggle for parliamentary representation for Durham, 1600–41', The last principality, ed. D. Marcombe (1987) · M. J. Tillbrook, 'Aspects of the government and society of county Durham, 1558–1642', PhD diss.,

U. Lpool, 1981 · N. Tyacke, Anti-Calvinists: the rise of English Arminianism, c.1590–1640 (1987) · M. James, Family, lineage and civil society: a study of society, politics and mentality in the Durham region (1974) · C. M. Dent, Protestant reformers in Elizabethan Oxford (1983) · PRO, E126/1, fols. 218–23; E134/8 James I/East 41 · K. Fincham, Prelate as pastor: the episcopate of James I (1990) · R. Welford, History of Newcastle and Gateshead, 3 vols. (1884–7) · J. Strype, Annals of the Reformation and establishment of religion … during Queen Elizabeth's happy reign, new edn, 4 vols. (1824)
Archives Hatfield House, Hertfordshire, Salisbury MSS · PRO, state papers, SP 12, SP 14
Likenesses oils, Christ Church Oxf. [see illus.]

James, William (c.1634–1663), scholar and schoolmaster, was born at Machen, Monmouthshire, son of Henry James (b. c.1602), rector of Machen, and his wife, Barbara (b. 1604), daughter of William Sutton, rector of Blandford St Mary, Dorset. James attended Blandford School, where his uncle the younger William Sutton was master, 'and being extraordinary rath-ripe, and of a prodigious Memory, was entred into his Accedence at five Years of Age' (Wood, Ath. Oxon., 2.324). He was admitted to Westminster School, and in 1646 was elected king's scholar. After failing to obtain election to Christ Church, Oxford, in 1649, he was successful in May 1650 and matriculated on 27 November. He graduated BA on 2 February 1654 and proceeded MA on 30 June 1656.

As early as 1651, James published Eisagōgē in linguam Chaldaeam, a short grammar 'for use at Westminster School'. He wrote English verses prefaced, along with John Dryden's, to John Hoddesdon's Sion and Parnassus (1650), Greek verses prefaced to Henry Stubbs's Horae subsecivae (1651), and Latin verses for Oxford's collection on Cromwell's peace with Holland (1654). He made a Greek translation in 1652 of Terence's Adelphi (Bodl. Oxf., MS Rawl. D. 284, fols. 75–117) and Latin translations in 1652 of Francis Bacon on Queen Elizabeth and on Essex's rebellion and in 1654 of Baltasar Gracián's Hero from John Skeffington's English version (Busby Library MSS, Westminster). His Hebrew–Latin and Arabic–Latin manuscript vocabularies survive (Busby Library MSS); a Greek–Latin one is lost.

James always dedicated his work to Richard Busby— 'Tutor, Parent, Patron'—whose assistant at Westminster School he became while still an undergraduate. The diary James kept from 1 January to 1 May 1655 shows him working on Busby's edition of Martial and much concerned about his health (Bodl. Oxf., MS Rawl. D. 216). Later James makes a shadowy appearance in the undermaster Edward Bagshaw's narrative of his differences with Busby. After degrading Bagshaw to teach 'the Puny-Boyes in the first, second and third Formes', Busby's 'next Plot was to make his Minion and Usher Mr James step over me' (Bagshaw, 3–6). On 29 October 1657 Busby obtained leave from Westminster's governors to make James his personal assistant, and, after Bagshaw's protest failed on 12 November,

> the very next day he brought Mr James into the School, and there with a great deale of Ceremony he placed him above me, employing him, for the most part to teach the fourth Forme, from which I was so lately removed. (ibid., 11)

James would receive £40 p.a. from Busby's own emoluments, at the cost of standing between two forceful characters—'a Trophee erected to my Dishonour' (ibid., 23). Busby complained of Bagshaw's sending a monitor to bid James 'hold his Peace'; Bagshaw admitted telling his scholars 'not to stand up and bow' to James when he entered or left the school (ibid., 15–18). After Bagshaw resigned in May 1658, the governors ruled James's assistantship unstatutable; however, he succeeded Adam Littleton, Bagshaw's successor, as undermaster in 1661. He died, unmarried, in 1663 'to the great Reluctancy of all that knew his admirable Parts' and was buried on 2 July in the south aisle of Westminster Abbey 'near the lowest Door, going into the Cloister' (Wood, *Ath. Oxon.*, 2.324).

HUGH DE QUEHEN

Sources Wood, *Ath. Oxon.*, 2nd edn, 2.324 • *Old Westminsters*, vol. 1 • G. F. R. Barker, *Memoir of Richard Busby* (1895) • F. Madan, *Oxford literature, 1651–1680* (1931), vol. 3 of *Oxford books: a bibliography of printed works* (1895–1931); repr. (1964) • E. Bagshaw, *A true and perfect narrative of the differences between Mr Busby and Mr Bagshawe* (1659) • Foster, *Alum. Oxon.* • J. L. Chester, ed., *The marriage, baptismal, and burial registers of the collegiate church or abbey of St Peter, Westminster*, Harleian Society, 10 (1876)

Archives Bodl. Oxf., Rawl. MSS D.216, D.284 • Westminster School, London

James, Sir William, first baronet (1722–1783), naval officer and director of the East India Company, was born on 5 September 1722 near Haverfordwest, Pembrokeshire. Sir Nathaniel Wraxall, who knew him well, wrote that 'His origin was so obscure as almost to baffle inquiry' (*Historical and Posthumous Memoirs*, 3.168). Most probably he was the son of the miller at Bolton Hill mill, but it has also been said that he was the son of an agricultural labourer and himself a ploughboy. All sources agree that he went to sea, his second wife said at the age of twelve, but there is no unanimity about the course of his early career as a mariner. He may at first have joined a Bristol coaster, but later he is reported as sailing between ports in the southern American colonies and the Caribbean, where he suffered shipwreck and imprisonment by the Spanish. Certainly, he could not have received much in the way of formal education.

It seems clear that James returned to England in the early 1740s, when he is variously reported to have married either the landlady of the Red Cow at Wapping or the widow of the captain of an East Indiaman. It has proved impossible either to confirm or deny the first supposition, but the second appears to have some credence. According to John Pavin Phillips, James was 'introduced when about twenty years of age to the widow of an East India captain, whom he soon after married' (Phillips, 244). Further investigation shows that of five marriages in London between 1742 and 1744 involving men named William James, a putative link with a captain in the East India Company's service is to be found in only one. A William Birch was listed among the company's captains up to 1736 but not thereafter, and an Elizabeth Birch was married at St Anne's, Soho, in Westminster, on 1 May 1744. This marriage would be consistent with Phillips's story, and the subsequent death and burial of Elizabeth James at St

Anne's on 11 August 1753 would have left the way open for a remarriage (see below). Whether coincidentally or not, in later life James had his London residence in Gerrard Street, Soho, which became a popular social centre among East India Company servants. From about 1767 he and his second wife met, and developed a close, valuable friendship with, the author Laurence Sterne, who lived in the area.

James's maritime career starts to fall into shape in 1747 with his appointment as first mate of the company's ship *Hardwicke*, followed by a similar appointment in the *Suffolk* in 1749. He was next given command of the *Guardian*, an armed vessel serving with the Bombay marine. He was senior officer of a small squadron operating between Bombay and Goa with the task of protecting local shipping from the depredations of pirates under the leadership of the Angria family, who occupied much of the coastline and had harassed trade over many years. His convoys were successful in reducing losses, and in 1751 he was promoted to commodore of the Bombay marine, wearing his broad pennant in the *Protector* (44 guns). After three Dutch ships had been attacked in 1754, an operation was mounted in conjunction with the Marathas in March 1755 against Savanadrug ('Severndroog'), one of Tulaji Angria's strongholds. James took his ships into the harbour and closely engaged the fort, which surrendered on 2 April. In November 1755 a naval force commanded by Rear-Admiral Charles Watson arrived in Bombay, and with Colonel Robert Clive and a body of troops also available, the opportunity was taken to remove once and for all the abiding threat of Angria. An expedition sailed from Bombay in February 1756 and the forts at Gheria were attacked in a combined operation. James handled his small squadron skilfully. The forts surrendered and Angria's power was broken with but small loss. In 1757 James was ordered to take news of the outbreak of war with France to Rear-Admiral Watson, by then in the River Hooghly. At this time of year a passage up the Bay of Bengal against the north-east monsoon was considered impracticable. However, by sailing east across the bay to the north-west point of Sumatra and from there up to the Hooghly he made exceptionally good time.

James returned to England in 1759 a wealthy man, his fortune founded on prize money and private commerce. He acquired Park Farm Place, Eltham, in Kent, and married his second wife, Anne (d. 1798), daughter of Edmond Goddard of Hartham, Wiltshire, at St Marylebone, Middlesex, on 15 June 1765; the couple had a son, Edward William, and a daughter, Elizabeth Anne. There is nothing to support the story that he married in India and that a son, Richard, was the first native Asian to succeed to a British title on his father's death. However, there may well have been a natural son. James was first elected a director of the East India Company in 1768 as a supporter of Laurence Sulivan; later, however, he developed an increasingly close association with the earl of Sandwich, whose influence brought him the honours that he enjoyed. He became an elder brother of Trinity House on 22 July 1769 and deputy master on 15 June 1778. He was also appointed a governor of the Royal Hospital at Greenwich. He supported the government in the general court and was anxious to enter parliament. Defeated in a by-election at New Shoreham in 1770, he angled for the governorship of Bombay, but having made his parliamentary aspirations plain in government circles he withdrew his candidature and was elected for West Looe, Cornwall, in the general election of 1774. Two years on he became the company's deputy chairman, the first of three occasions when he held this office. He continued to support Lord North and to co-operate with Sandwich, but his association with Sulivan came under some strain when, under pressure from the government, he voted for the recall of Warren Hastings. Also in 1776 he managed to secure a government contract to provision troops in Canada. He was created a baronet on 27 August 1778 when he was deputy chairman for the second time. He was chairman in 1779. By 1781 James's relationship with Sulivan had improved and he was again chosen as deputy during Sulivan's chairmanship. A year later, in a report from the parliamentary committee on Bengal affairs, both men were alleged to have deliberately misled the committee by altering the company's records. James opposed a motion to print the report and maintained that the charges were without foundation.

Sir William died of a stroke in his house in Gerrard Street, London, on 16 December 1783, the day that his daughter married Thomas Boothby Parkyns, later first Baron Rancliffe. He was buried at Eltham on 22 December. He was succeeded by his son Edward William, who died unmarried in 1792, when the baronetcy became extinct. In 1784 his widow commissioned a triangular Gothic tower (built by Richard Jupp) as a memorial to her husband at the summit of Shooter's Hill, near Blackheath, Kent; it still stands, and is known as Severndroog Castle. James seems never to have shown any inclination to shed light on the first thirty years of his life; he left no tracks, only conjecture.   T. H. BOWYER

Sources DNB • 'Biographical memoir of the late Commodore Sir William James', *Naval Chronicle*, 13 (1805), 89–112 • C. R. Low, *History of the Indian navy, 1613–1863*, 1 (1877), vol. 1, p. 125–51 • J. G. Parker, 'The directors of the East India Company, 1754–1790', PhD diss., U. Edin., 1977 • M. M. Drummond, 'James, William', HoP, *Commons, 1754–90* • J. P. Phillips, 'Sir William James, baronet', *N&Q*, 2nd ser., 12 (1861), 244–5, 402 • *The historical and the posthumous memoirs of Sir Nathaniel William Wraxall, 1772–1784*, ed. H. B. Wheatley, 5 vols. (1884), vol. 3, pp. 167–9 • A. H. Cash, *Laurence Sterne: the later years* (1986) • *The writings and speeches of Edmund Burke*, ed. P. Langford, 5: *India: Madras and Bengal, 1774–1785* (1981) • J. Burke and J. B. Burke, *A genealogical and heraldic history of the extinct and dormant baronetcies of England, Ireland and Scotland*, 2nd edn (1841); repr. (1844) • GEC, *Baronetage* • parish registers, St Anne, Westminster • A. Farrington, *A biographical index of the East India Company maritime service officers, 1600–1834* (1999) • IGI

Archives BL, Hastings papers, Add. MSS 29132–29144 • BL OIOC, Orme collection • NMM, letters to Lord Sandwich

Likenesses J. Reynolds, oils, 1784 (after his painting, 1780–82), NMM • W. Ridley, engraving (after J. Reynolds, 1784), repro. in *Naval Chronicle*, 89 • J. R. Smith, engraving (after J. Reynolds, 1784)

James, William (*fl.* **1760–1771**), topographical painter and picture dealer, of whose parents nothing is known, practised in London, residing for some years in Maiden Lane,

and later at the Golden Head in May's Buildings, St Martin's Lane. He exhibited with the Incorporated Society of Artists, of which he became a member in 1766, from 1761 to 1768, and at the Royal Academy from 1769 to 1771. He was an imitator of Canaletto, and painted views of London, chiefly on the river and in St James's Park, but his works have chiefly an antiquarian interest. Waterhouse noted that 'he is a rather pedestrian imitator of Samuel Scott' (Waterhouse, *18c painters*, 193). His views are hard and mechanical in execution, the ruler being largely used in the lines of the buildings, and the water conventionally treated. In 1768 James sent to the Society of Artists, and in the two following years to the Royal Academy, some views of Egyptian temples, but as he was never out of England these are presumed to have been copies. Seven of his pictures are at Hampton Court. Of these Redgrave noted, 'they are very literal, and entirely without art' (Redgrave, 237). Examples of his work are in the Victoria and Albert Museum, London.

F. M. O'DONOGHUE, *rev.* ANNETTE PEACH

Sources Waterhouse, *18c painters* • Redgrave, *Artists* • Graves, *RA exhibitors* • Mallalieu, *Watercolour artists*, vol. 1

James, William (*d.* **1827**), naval historian, was from 1801 to 1813 an attorney of the supreme court of Jamaica, and practised as a proctor in the vice-admiralty court. In 1812 he was in the United States, and on the declaration of war with Britain was detained. After several months' captivity he escaped, and reached Halifax, Nova Scotia, towards the end of 1813. His attention was thus turned to the details of the war. He sent several letters on it to the *Naval Chronicle* under the signature Boxer, and in March 1816 he published a pamphlet, *An inquiry into the merits of the principal naval actions between Great Britain and the United States*, showing that the American frigates were larger, more heavily armed, and more strongly manned than the British which they had captured; that official United States statements were grossly inaccurate; and that the American victories were to be attributed to superior numerical force. The pamphlet caused considerable excitement in Nova Scotia and the United States, and angry criticisms were published in the American papers. It was falsely asserted that James was an American by birth, that he had been guilty of felony nineteen years before, had been condemned and reprieved, and was now seeking a base revenge on his injured country.

Meantime James had gone to Britain, and in the summer of 1817 published a second edition of his pamphlet, enlarged to virtually a new work, *A full and correct account of the chief naval occurrences of the late war between Great Britain and the United States of America*. In 1818 he followed this with the two-volume work *A full and correct account of the military occurrences of the late war between Great Britain and the United States of America*, and in 1819 by a pamphlet, *Warden refuted, being a defence of the British navy against the misrepresentations of a work recently published at Edinburgh … by D. B. Warden, late consul for the United States at Paris*. In 1819 he began preparing a naval history of the great war, *The naval history of Great*

Britain, from the declaration of war by France in 1793 to the accession of George IV (5 vols., 1822–4). A second edition, in six volumes, was published in 1826.

This last, remarkable, work, which took as its motto *Vérité sans peur*, aimed at an exact account of every operation of naval war during the period named. James consulted not only published works, especially the official narratives, both British and French, but also the logs of the ships, and, whenever possible, the participants themselves. It is, however, a chronicle rather than a history, and is written from an unremittingly British point of view. James's object was to demonstrate that the minor defeats suffered in 1812 did not indicate any weakening of the skill, power, and prestige of the Royal Navy; in order that it might continue to serve as the basis of British foreign policy, James's history was written from a tory perspective, in contrast to the whig slant adopted by his contemporary Edward Brenton. This resulted in the two men's exchanging insults in successive editions of their works.

Although he sought a post or some other act of political patronage, James received little more than block orders from the Admiralty and public thanks for his considerable efforts. James, who resided for his last few years at 12 Chapel Field, South Lambeth, died there on 28 May 1827. His widow, a West Indian, who was unprovided for, received a pension of £100 on the civil list. She had, too, a share in the profits from the sale of the *Naval History*, but for several years these were very small. It was not until 1837 that a third edition was published with additions, including accounts of the First Anglo-Burmese War and the battle of Navarino, by Captain Frederick *Chamier. A full index was published by the Navy Records Society in 1895. James's history served his country well, both as a record of events, and a means of sustaining the reputation of the Royal Navy between Trafalgar and Jutland.

J. K. LAUGHTON, *rev.* ANDREW LAMBERT

Sources *Some official correspondence of George Canning*, ed. E. J. Stapleton, 2 vols. (1887) · T. Roosevelt, *The naval war of 1812* (1882) · *The Times* (31 May 1827) · H. Powell, 'The American naval war, 1812 [2 pts]', *Colburn's United Service Magazine*, 1 (1885), 365–75, 481–91 · *GM*, 1st ser., 97/2 (1827), 281 · H. Furber, 'How William James came to be a naval historian', *American Historical Review*, 38 (1932–3), 74–85

James, William (1771–1837), land agent and railway developer, was born at Henley in Arden, Warwickshire, on 13 June 1771, the son of William James, a solicitor. He was educated at Warwick, and at a school at Winson Green, near Birmingham. After serving his articles he returned about 1797 to Henley in Arden to practise as a solicitor. The main part of his practice was land-agency, and in 1804 he was appointed agent for the earl of Warwick's property necessitating his move to Warwick. In the same year he carried out a plan for the drainage and levelling of Lambeth Marsh in London. A bridge over the Thames, to be erected near the site of the later Waterloo Bridge, formed part of his ambitious scheme. His land-agency and improvement work made James increasingly prosperous, and in 1812 he became a colliery owner in south Staffordshire, and was the first to open the West Bromwich coalfield. He subsequently became chairman of the West

Bromwich Coalmasters' Association, and he was an active promoter of a bill for making a canal from that district to Birmingham. About 1815 he moved his law offices to New Boswell Court, Lincoln's Inn Fields, London, where he carried on one of the largest land-agency businesses in the kingdom. His work involved him in many surveys for the enclosure of commons, and he was also very interested in canal undertakings.

James's connection with the establishment of railways constitutes his chief claim to remembrance. As early as 1806 his attention had been directed to the subject of the horse-worked railways which were well established in the colliery districts of the north of England by the late eighteenth century. James's idea was to extend this system over the country, though the use of steam power as a means of propulsion did not at first occur to him.

During the first two decades of the nineteenth century James actively pursued his idea of an extensive railway network, constructing several short lines of railway in various parts of the country, and proposing and surveying many more. In 1820 he drew up a 'Plan of the lines of the projected central junction railway or tram road', which outlined what was effectively a national railway system using horse-drawn vehicles; this visionary work was not published until 1861. In the autumn of 1821 James paid a first visit to Killingworth colliery and saw George Stephenson's steam locomotive at work. His active mind at once recognized the potential of the machine, and he came to an agreement with Stephenson whereby he would promote the use of Stephenson's engines on new railway lines south of an imaginary line drawn from Liverpool to Hull, in return for a quarter share in the resulting profits. However, as James's railway interests multiplied, his tendency to overstretch himself by taking on too many projects at once began to undermine both his financial and his bodily health. He proved unable to fulfil the commitments he had made in this agreement, and neither he nor Stephenson derived any benefit from it.

Earlier in 1821 James had become involved in the initial stages of the project for constructing a railway between Manchester and Liverpool. He approached Joseph Sandars, a wealthy Liverpool merchant, who was prominently connected with the scheme, and Sandars agreed that he should begin, partly at his own expense, a survey of a proposed route for the railway. The survey was begun in the summer of 1821 and work continued into the following year. Robert Stephenson assisted James in the work, but James was distracted by other projects and the survey was left incomplete after many delays. The route proposed by James was not that eventually adopted, provoking James into a break with the promoters. In May 1824 Sandars informed him that by his delays and broken promises he had 'forfeited the confidence of the subscribers', and James's involvement with the Liverpool and Manchester ceased. The work was completed by George Stephenson, who had the benefit of James's plans and sections. James's early feelings of deep admiration and firm professional and personal friendship with George Stephenson changed to anger and estrangement over this episode and the events that followed. He spent the rest of his life protesting that Stephenson had usurped his rightful claim to be considered the originator of the Liverpool and Manchester Railway and thus a founding father of the railway age. After James's death, George's son Robert Stephenson was prominent among those who gave some public support to this claim, and there can be little doubt that James has indeed never received the recognition he deserved for his pioneering efforts in proposing and surveying railway routes, and in giving early support to the universal use of steam-locomotive traction on railways.

In 1823 James published a report describing in detail a scheme to link London with the strategically important ports of Kent, Sussex, and Hampshire 'by a Line of Engine Railroad'. The scheme was well thought out and soundly based on James's geographical and technical expertise, and showed that he clearly perceived the capabilities of a railway worked by steam locomotives. This report was intended to be the first of a series of twelve reports upon railway communication in various parts of Britain, but the project was halted by James's financial difficulties, and nothing further appeared.

Although James was at one time reported to be worth £150,000 and to be earning £10,000 a year from his practice, his over-ambitious projects, poor health, and, he claimed, the machinations of his rivals, led to his affairs falling into confusion; in 1823 he was declared bankrupt and imprisoned. Shortly afterwards he retired to Bodmin in Cornwall. In 1824 he obtained a patent for hollow rails for railways, but it was of no practical importance. All his efforts to retrieve his position and rescue his reputation were unsuccessful. He had married in 1796 Dinah, daughter of William Tarlton of Botley, with whom he had two sons. With his death at Bodmin on 10 March 1837 his family was left unprovided for. In 1845 an attempt to raise a fund for the benefit of his sons was made, but although Robert Stephenson, Joseph Locke, I. K. Brunel, George Rennie, and other eminent engineers attested to James's vital role in establishing the railway system the scheme failed. In 1858 Robert Stephenson described James, in a letter to Samuel Smiles, as fluent in conversation and 'a ready, dashing writer', but 'no thinker at all in the practical part of the subject he had taken up'.

James's eldest son, **William Henry James** (1796–1873), born at Henley in Arden in March 1796, assisted his father in his survey of the Liverpool and Manchester Railway. He subsequently set up an independent business as an engineer in Birmingham, where he produced experimental steam-driven road vehicles. He took out patents for, among other things, locomotives, steam engines, boilers, railway carriages, and diving apparatus. He invented a multi-tubular boiler for steam engines, in which the tubes were filled with water. This differed from the later boiler, invented by the Stephensons—the prototype for all subsequent railway locomotive boiler design—in which the tubes conducted the heat of the fire to a surrounding jacket filled with water. He died on 16 December 1873 in the Dulwich College almshouses.

R. B. PROSSER, *rev.* RALPH HARRINGTON

Sources E. M. S. Paine [E. M. S. P.], *The two James's and the two Stephensons* (1861) · H. Booth, *Account of the Liverpool and Manchester railway* (1831) · S. Smiles, *Lives of the engineers*, 3 (1862) · R. E. Carlson, *The Liverpool and Manchester railway project, 1821–1823* (1969) · *Mechanics' Magazine*, 31/842 (28 Sept 1839), 447–48 · *Mechanics' Magazine*, 49/1315 (21 Oct 1848), 401–4 · *Mechanics' Magazine*, 49/1315 (21 Oct 1848), 500
Archives Lpool RO, corresp. and papers
Likenesses W. Rolfe, stipple (after Chalon), BM; repro. in *Mechanics' Magazine*, 31 (1839)

James, William Henry (1796–1873). *See under* James, William (1771–1837).

James, Sir William Milbourne (1807–1881), judge, was born in Merthyr Tudful, Glamorgan, the son of Christopher James of Swansea. He was educated at the University of Glasgow, where he graduated MA and afterwards became an honorary LLD. He was called to the bar at Lincoln's Inn in 1831. He read in Fitzroy Kelly's chambers, and attended the Welsh sessions, but specialized in the court of chancery. Ill health forced him to spend two years in Italy before his call and slowed his career; but in time he acquired a large practice. He also became junior counsel to the Treasury in equity, the Office of Woods and Forests, the Inland Revenue, and the board of works. In 1853 he became queen's counsel and succeeded Bethell as vice-chancellor of the duchy of Lancaster.

In 1846 James married Maria (d. 1891), the daughter of William *Otter of Chichester, bishop; they had a son, William Christopher James, later of the 16th lancers, and a daughter, who married Colonel G. Jalis Schwabe. A Liberal in politics, James stood twice as a member of parliament for Derby (the second time in 1859) but was unsuccessful.

In 1866 James was treasurer of Lincoln's Inn and in January 1869 he became a vice-chancellor of the court of chancery and a knight. In 1870 he was made a lord justice of appeal and a privy councillor. He was thought a good judge by his contemporaries, being educated, shrewd, and firm, and was remembered for his terse and clear enunciation of legal principles. The Court of Appeal under him and Lord Justice Mellish was very efficient, and its decisions on the new questions raised by the Companies Acts and the Bankruptcy Act of 1869 were highly regarded.

James was a member of the various commissions on equity procedure, and of the Indian code commission and the army purchase commission. As a member of the judicature commission he was in favour of reform, and urged the total abolition of pleadings. He was also interested in Indian history, and between 1864 and 1869 wrote *The British in India*, published posthumously by his daughter in 1882. James died at his house, 47 Wimpole Street, London, on 7 June 1881. J. A. HAMILTON, *rev.* HUGH MOONEY

Sources *Solicitors' Journal*, 25 (1880–81), 597, 611 · *The Times* (9 June 1881) · *The Times* (15 June 1881) [eulogy by Lord Bramwell]
Likenesses Lock & Whitfield, woodburytype photograph, NPG; repro. in T. Cooper, *Men of Mark: a gallery of contemporary portraits* (1880) · wood-engraving (after photograph by J. Watkins), NPG; repro. in *ILN* (27 March 1869) · wood-engraving, NPG; repro. in *ILN* (18 June 1881)
Wealth at death £43,389 5s. 9d.: resworn probate, July 1882, CGPLA Eng. & Wales (1881)

James, Sir **William Milbourne** (1881–1973), naval officer and writer, was born on 22 December 1881 near Farnborough, the younger son and second of the four children of Major William Christopher James, Scots Greys, and his wife, Effie, daughter of the painter Sir John Everett *Millais of Kensington. W. C. James was the only son of Lord Justice Sir William Milbourne *James. The most notable portrait of William James was done when he was four, sitting for his maternal grandfather; Millais's painting found its way, via the *Illustrated London News*, to Pears soap, which used it as its famous 'Bubbles' advertisement. This nickname remained with James for life.

After Trinity College, Glenalmond, James entered the Royal Naval College, Dartmouth, in 1895. His progress in the service was smooth and by 1913 he was a commander and the executive officer of the new battle cruiser *Queen Mary*, whose captain was the formidable W. R. (Blinker) Hall. Although best-known for their work at naval intelligence, the years of these two officers aboard the *Queen Mary* were also a most creative period, preparing the crew for war and making the vessel the first in the Royal Navy to possess a chapel, cinematograph, bookstall, and laundry. In 1915 James married Dorothy (Robin; *d.* 1971), the youngest daughter of Admiral Sir Alexander *Duff. They had one son and one daughter, who died when she was nineteen.

In March 1916 James became flag commander to Vice-Admiral F. C. D. Sturdee on the *Benbow*, thereby missing the fate of the *Queen Mary*'s crew at Jutland two months later. By the following year he had been promoted captain and appointed to the naval intelligence division, at the request of Hall, who was by then its director. Despite his preference for a post afloat, James clearly enjoyed his work at naval intelligence, whose vital cryptographic service he later described in his book *The Eyes of the Navy: a Biographical Study of Sir R. Hall* (1955). It was during the war that James began his writings, pseudonymously, as a naval poet.

James's career in the inter-war years confirmed his early potential as a staff officer. After a tour on the China station he was appointed deputy director of the Royal Naval Staff College, Greenwich, in 1923 and its director in 1925. During that period he expanded his staff lectures upon the naval side of the American War of Independence into the book *The British Navy in Adversity* (1926), which was for many years the standard work. Another brief spell abroad in the Mediterranean was followed in 1928 by his appointment as naval assistant to the first sea lord and his promotion to rear-admiral. In late 1928 he was chief of staff to the Atlantic Fleet and, from 1930, to the Mediterranean Fleet, both under A. E. M. Chatfield.

In 1932 the plum job of commander of the battle-cruiser squadron came James's way, and he was promoted vice-admiral in 1933. From 1935 to 1938 he was deputy chief of naval staff and centrally involved in Admiralty policy during the critical 'appeasement' years; he was made a full admiral in 1938. After a brief rest, he occupied the important post of commander-in-chief, Portsmouth, between 1939 and 1942, being made a freeman of that city upon his retirement. Appropriately enough, he succeeded Roger Keyes as MP (Unionist) for Portsmouth North in 1943, which he combined with his new post as chief of naval information.

James was not a natural Commons man, although he showed interest in educational as well as naval issues there, and he willingly retired before the 1945 election. He was now, moreover, devoting much more time to talks and writing. *Blue Water and Green Fields*, pieces on the First World War, was published in 1939, and a biography, *Admiral Sir William Fisher*, in 1943. His job as chief of naval information involved constant writing, part of which formed the basis for *The British Navies in the Second World War*, published in 1946—the same year as *The Portsmouth Letters*. Biographies of Nelson (1948), St Vincent (1950), and Admiral Sir Henry Oliver (1956) were published in later years, as was a study of the unhappy relationship between John Ruskin and James's maternal grandmother, Effie Gray. His two most important books in these years were his autobiography, *The Sky was always Blue* (1951), and his book on Hall (1955). Appointed Lees-Knowles lecturer at Cambridge (1947) and naval editor of *Chambers's Encyclopaedia*, the ever-lively James was a source of much information to younger naval historians, as well as being active in youth education and rural matters.

James was appointed CB (1919), KCB (1936), and GCB (1944). He died on 17 August 1973 at Hindhead, Surrey.

PAUL KENNEDY, *rev.*

Sources *The Times* (20 Aug 1973) • W. M. James, *The sky was always blue* (1951) • private information (1986) • *WWW*
Archives CAC Cam., corresp. | FILM BFI NFTVA, news footage
Likenesses J. E. Millais, portrait, *c.*1885, repro. in *ILN*

James, William Owen (1900–1978), plant physiologist, was born on 21 May 1900 at Tottenham, Middlesex, the elder son (there were no daughters) of William Benjamin James (1866–1939), primary school headmaster, of Tottenham, and his wife, Agnes Ursula Collins (1869–1931). He attended Tottenham grammar school from 1910 until 1916 and then joined the flourishing family firm of accountants in Birmingham. He did not enjoy the work and the first of a series of tubercular attacks forced him to leave in 1918. By 1919 he was sufficiently well to attend courses in botany at University College, Reading, where the lectures of Professor Walter Stiles aroused in him an interest in plant physiology, and where, in 1923, he gained a first-class BSc (London). He then secured a training grant for research at Cambridge under Frederick Blackman, and was awarded his Cambridge PhD in 1927. From Cambridge, James joined the research team of Vernon Blackman at Imperial College, working largely at Rothamsted, where the team had field plots.

In 1927 James joined the staff of Arthur Tansley, professor of botany at Oxford, as a demonstrator. At that time the department's buildings were quite inadequate for experimental botany and funds were scanty. Acting with characteristic resourcefulness James, his technician, and some research students themselves converted an old lecture room into a reasonably spacious and well-equipped research laboratory. From the start his imaginatively prepared lectures and practical classes greatly impressed able students. Many sought to work for a research degree under his supervision, and he was soon also attracting graduates from other universities. In April 1928 James married Gladys Macphail, a fellow botany student at Reading, and daughter of Ernest William Redfern of Leeds and his wife, Charlotte Elizabeth, née Lowe. The couple lived in Islip, near Oxford, and had two daughters (born in 1930 and 1932).

By the mid-1930s plant respiration had become James's major interest, and his high reputation as a research scientist and expositor rests largely on his achievements in this field. His health remained good until the late 1930s when he had a further serious tubercular attack and spent some time in a sanatorium. During the Second World War, with the help of his wife and numbers of undergraduate and research students, James explored the feasibility of the home cultivation of certain medicinal plants and the collection by members of the public of medically useful material of wild plants such as foxglove. The success of his efforts led to national recognition of the Oxford Medicinal Plants Scheme and later to departmental research on the biosynthesis of plant alkaloids. In 1946 he became reader in botany.

In 1959 James became professor of botany at Imperial College, London. In his new post he sought to broaden the scope of the teaching and research by increasing emphasis on intracellular and ultrastructural studies. He retired in 1967 and was made emeritus professor. In 1969 he was elected an honorary fellow of Imperial College. Towards the end of 1977 he and his wife decided, because of his failing health, to join their two daughters in New Zealand. He died peacefully in his sleep, after a stroke, on 15 September 1978, in Wellington. He was survived by his wife.

Over the course of his career James produced a stream of publications, all written in a clear and simple style. He was, for many years, editor of the *New Phytologist*, and was elected FRS in 1952. He was remembered by many for his distinction as a person. Despite his frail physique and the inescapable concern over his health James had always been quite active in his pleasant Islip garden and played his part in village life. He carried himself with almost military erectness, and his sharp features and piercing blue eyes warned that he was not to be trifled with. His pungency of expression suggested a formidable personality. Yet his students and colleagues were well aware of another side to his nature, and to his close friends he revealed a basic warmth and kindliness.

A. R. CLAPHAM, rev. PETER OSBORNE

Sources A. R. Clapham and J. L. Harley, *Memoirs FRS*, 25 (1979), 337–64 · personal knowledge (1986) · *WWW*, 1971–80
Archives University of Sheffield, corresp. with Arthur Roy Clapham

Jameson, Andrew, Lord Ardwall (1845–1911), judge, was born at Ayr on 5 July 1845, the eldest son of Andrew Jameson, barrister and sheriff of Aberdeen and Kincardine (who had earlier revised the Maltese constitution), and his

wife, Alexander, daughter of Alexander Colquhoun Campbell. He was educated at Mr Oliphant's school, Edinburgh, and at Edinburgh Academy, and graduated MA from the University of St Andrews in 1865. He took the law classes at Edinburgh University and, after working for a short time with a firm of solicitors, he was called to the Scottish bar on 19 May 1870. He married, on 29 July 1875, Christian Robison (d. 1940), daughter of John Gordon Brown and niece of Walter McCullough. It was from her uncle that she inherited the Galloway estate of Ardwall, from which Jameson later took his courtesy title. They had three sons and a daughter, to whom Jameson was at all times friend rather than Victorian paterfamilias.

Jameson acquired a considerable practice, usually being briefed for the defence. He had all the attributes of a brilliant barrister—he could transform a mass of complex material into the most straightforward points, he was an assiduous learner, he had a quite remarkable memory, and he was immensely painstaking. He also had a highly successful style of cross-examination, befriending rather than browbeating the witness, while his jury speeches were a model of forensic advocacy. He came to be viewed, with Comrie Thomson, as the best jury counsel in Parliament House, and in 1883 he was appointed junior counsel to the Office of Woods and Forests.

Jameson's first judicial appointment came on 27 April 1886, when he was appointed sheriff of the borders. Four years later he was transferred to the northern counties in place of Alexander Low, who had been raised to the bench of the Court of Session. On 27 October 1891 Jameson was appointed to the premier sheriffdom—Perthshire. He sat at Perth for thirteen years, and his legal abilities, coupled with his practical knowledge of agriculture and business affairs, led to his being judged effective and distinguished in the post. In 1897 Jameson was among the first Scottish barristers in private practice to take silk (until then the honour could be bestowed only upon Scotsmen who were law officers, former law officers, or deans of faculty). During his time as sheriff Jameson conducted a number of important government inquiries and frequently acted as arbiter in industrial disputes. In August 1901 he was appointed, in succession to Lord James of Hereford, chairman of the board of conciliation of the Coalowners' and Scottish Miners' Federation, in which role he enjoyed great success.

Jameson eventually grew impatient to hold high judicial office, but finally, on 31 December 1904, he was raised to the bench of the Court of Session on the resignation of Lord Traynor, taking the courtesy title of Lord Ardwall. Lord Low wrote to him: 'never in my memory has there been such unanimity of opinion that the right man has been put in the right place'. He sat in the outer house for two years. He was apt to be rather impetuous in his early days, but his natural sagacity soon corrected this. He was especially at home in technical and commercial cases, as he had always had a great thirst for knowledge and had acquired, over time, a considerable command of many technical subjects.

In 1905 Lord Ardwall was made an honorary doctor of

laws by St Andrews University, and in January 1907 he succeeded Lord Kyllachy in the inner house, where, it is generally agreed, his best work was done. His strong dissent, later upheld by the House of Lords, in *North British Railway Co. v. Budhill Coal and Sandstone Co.* (1909), had important effects on the prices to be paid to landowners by railway companies in compulsory purchase cases. After an illness of about six months he died, of dropsy, on 21 November 1911 at his city house, 14 Moray Place, Edinburgh. He was buried in Anwoth churchyard, near Gatehouse, Kirkcudbrightshire.

Politically Jameson began as a Gladstonian Liberal, but severed all links with the party in 1885 over Irish home rule, becoming a staunch unionist and chairman of the West Edinburgh Unionist Association. He admired Joseph Chamberlain and his gospel of imperial unity, and advocated a Bismarckian 'blood and iron' approach to foreign affairs. In religion he was a staunch Free Churchman, and served as an elder of St George's, Edinburgh, but he was firmly in favour of establishment and hoped always to see one great national church.

In matters personal Jameson learned much from his father, particularly his religion and his strenuous rectitude. But he was no puritan; according to Buchan, 'he was at all times like a rosy Scots laird than the conventional tight-lipped lawyer'. He was noted too for his kindness to the needy, as when he directed that his fees as arbiter in the coalminers' wage disputes be given to the Royal Infirmary, and he knew nothing of ill will, 'coming down upon the enemy like a mountain … and then inviting him to dinner'. In his free time he lived the life of the tenant farmer, having leased Ardwall from his wife. He enjoyed walking, shooting, and especially fishing, was an expert on claret, and blended his own whisky. He was also the second president of the Edinburgh Sir Walter Scott Association.   NATHAN WELLS

Sources J. Buchan, *Andrew Jameson, Lord Ardwall* (1913) · *Scottish Law Review*, 27 (1911), 264–5 · F. J. Grant, ed., *The Faculty of Advocates in Scotland, 1532–1943*, Scottish RS, 145 (1944)

Likenesses G. Reid, portrait, repro. in Buchan, *Andrew Jameson*, frontispiece · G. Reid, two portraits; formerly at 14 Moray Place, Edinburgh, 1912

Wealth at death £47,704 8s.: confirmation, 27 Jan 1912, *CCI*

Jameson [*née* Murphy], **Anna Brownell** (1794–1860), writer and art historian, was born on 19 May 1794 at Dublin, the first of the five daughters of Denis Brownell *Murphy (d. 1842), Irish miniature artist, and his English wife, Johanna, known as Minnie (d. 1854). In 1798 the Murphy family emigrated to Whitehaven in Cumberland, moving to Newcastle upon Tyne in 1802 where they lived over the shop of Miller the bookseller and publisher. A year later they were in Hanwell and in 1806 settled in London near Pall Mall. In this prosperous period (1802–6) Denis Murphy employed a governess to educate his daughters. Miss Yokeley left the family when Anna was eleven or twelve years old, and Anna took over the education of her sisters from this time. Her formal working life began in 1810 when she was employed as governess to the family of the marquess of Winchester where she remained for four

Anna Brownell Jameson (1794–1860), by David Octavius Hill and Robert Adamson, 1843–8

years. She subsequently worked as a governess, for the Rowles family of Bradbourne Park, Kent, from 1819 to 1821, and from 1821 to 1825 for the Littleton family (later Lord and Lady Hatherton) of Teddesley in Staffordshire.

In 1825 Anna Brownell Murphy married Robert Sympson Jameson (1798–1854), a barrister. The couple had met in the winter of 1820–21. Robert was the boyhood friend of Hartley Coleridge and had excellent literary connections, at one stage acting as legal agent for Charles Lamb. The marriage was probably already foundering when he was appointed puisne judge to Dominica in 1829. They reunited briefly in 1833, when Robert Jameson took up an appointment as attorney-general of Upper Canada in the same year. In 1837 he was appointed vice-chancellor of the court of chancery, retiring with a pension in 1850. They had no children. For whatever reason, Jameson chose not to accompany Robert to either Dominica or Canada. Her subsequent journey to Canada in 1836–7 at his request was probably designed to facilitate his promotion to vice-chancellor, which carried an increased income, rather than a serious attempt at reconciliation. When Jameson returned to England in 1838 Robert had drawn up a formal paper agreeing that they live apart and to pay her £300 annually. The cause of the marriage breakdown, while the subject of some speculation, appears to have been incompatibility of temperament.

In her thirty-year literary career Anna Jameson's major

publications were non-fiction prose, including art criticism, Shakespearian criticism, travel writing, history, and biography. Almost all her work was about women and, she claimed, designed for women readers and although she was never a feminist, her writing nevertheless developed a feminist polemic. She travelled extensively in Germany and Italy and her works are informed by her links with both those countries. Throughout her career her publications received often lengthy, sometimes laudatory reviews by contemporary writers, including Mary Shelley, Charles Kingsley, John Wilson (Christopher North), and Geraldine Jewsbury.

Anna Jameson's first publication, *The Diary of an Ennuyée* (1826), was first issued anonymously as *A Lady's Diary*. The melodramatic plot of a heroine dying for love is completely submerged by the same heroine's vibrant, humorous descriptions of travel and art in Italy. Jameson never attempted fiction again. The book created a minor sensation when it was discovered not to be a true story, as this account by Fanny Kemble in 1828 indicates: 'The *Ennuyée*, one is given to understand, dies, and it was a little vexatious to behold her sitting on a sofa in a very becoming state of blooming *plumptitude*' (Macpherson, 44). Kemble describes Jameson as an 'attractive-looking young woman, with a skin of that dazzling whiteness which generally accompanies reddish hair' and a face 'capable of a marvellous power of concentrated feeling' (ibid., 45). Thomas Carlyle was less impressed, describing her in 1834 as a 'little, hard, proud, redhaired, freckled, fierce-eyed, square-mouthed woman; shrewd, harsh, cockneyish-irrational' (*Collected Letters*, 7.150).

However, Carlyle also calls her the 'celebrated Mrs. Jamieson', an epithet achieved through the success of *Characteristics of Women, Moral, Poetical and Historical* (1832), later more popularly known as *Shakespeare's Heroines*. Of her five major works published to 1834, including *The Loves of the Poets* (1829), *Memoirs of Celebrated Female Sovereigns* (1831), and *Visits and Sketches at Home and Abroad* (1834), *Characteristics* established her reputation. Gerard Manley Hopkins would later rank Jameson equally with Schlegel, Coleridge, and Lamb as a Shakespearian critic of note (Thomas, 72). Her second travel book, *Winter Studies and Summer Rambles in Canada* (1838), confirmed her literary reputation and remained in print at the end of the twentieth century. It was in this work that she first began to write more openly about the condition of women.

The five-volume series *Sacred and Legendary Art*, beginning with the two volumes of that title (1848), followed by *Legends of the Monastic Orders* (1850), *Legends of the Madonna* (1852), and *The History of Our Lord* published posthumously in 1864 (completed by Lady Elizabeth Eastlake), confirmed Jameson as an art critic of note, following her earlier guidebooks to the public and private galleries of London and *Memoirs of the Early Italian Painters* (1845). *Sacred and Legendary Art* remained in print until the 1920s, despite Ruskin's infamous attack in *Praeterita* some twenty-five years after her death claiming she 'was absolutely without knowledge or instinct of painting (and had no sharpness of insight even for anything else)' (*Works*, 35.374). Obituaries in *The Athenaeum*, the *Art-Journal*, and the *Gentleman's Magazine* regarded this series as 'the greatest literary labour of a busy life', 'books which have become standard works in Art-literature', and maintained that as 'an art-critic Mrs. Jameson was almost unrivalled'. She was effectively the first professional female art critic, and throughout her career she also contributed articles and reviews to a variety of respected British journals.

Jameson became a mentor to a younger generation of women writers and artists, in particular the influential feminists Barbara Bodichon and Bessie Rayner Parkes. Jameson's last major publications were two lectures inspired by her association with these women and their feminist activities, *Sisters of Charity, Catholic and Protestant, Abroad and at Home* (1855) and *The Communion of Labour: a Second Lecture on the Social Employments of Women* (1856).

Anna Jameson struggled for money and position all her adult life. Her father seems to have been struggling financially from about 1828, and her two unmarried sisters, Eliza and Charlotte, never earned sufficient money to keep themselves, despite attempting many projects. Jameson remained the family's only substantial breadwinner. When the financial affairs of her sister Louisa's husband collapsed in 1839, Jameson added their eldest daughter, Gerardine, to her dependants. She was occasionally forced to sell her copyrights to raise cash quickly. Early in 1851 Jameson was nominated for a pension of £100 from her majesty's pension list. William Makepeace Thackeray and John Murray III were her trustees. After her husband's death in 1854 and the discovery that she had been written out of his will in favour of a married couple in Toronto who had cared for him, Jameson's friends subscribed to a fund which produced an annuity of £100.

Anna Jameson led a peripatetic life, residing at various addresses with friends and relations in London, most notably at 51 Wimpole Street, where she came to know both Elizabeth Barrett and Robert Browning, and on the continent staying with Ottilie von Goethe, and later with the Brownings in Italy. When the Brownings eloped in 1846 Jameson was working in Paris; Elizabeth's frail strength had failed by the time they reached Paris and Robert called on their mutual friend for assistance. This was so effective they begged her to travel with them to Pisa. Jameson's letters to Lady Byron written on this journey provide an eye-witness account of one of the most famous literary elopements in history. The Brownings remained among Jameson's most devoted friends, addressing her always with affection as Mona Nina or Aunt Nina. The two women in particular thoughtfully critiqued each other's work and celebrated each other's triumphs. From 1842 to 1856 Jameson's most permanent London address was the home of her mother and sisters at Broomfield Place, Ealing. Jameson's mother died in 1854 and the sisters moved to 16 Chatham Place, Brighton, in 1856.

Anna Jameson died on 17 March 1860 at her rooms at 57 Conduit Street, London, having contracted bronchial pneumonia after working long hours in the British Library and walking home in a snowstorm. She was buried with her parents at Kensal Green cemetery, London. In a biographical sketch-cum-obituary Harriet Martineau wrote that a future generation would learn 'that in ours was a restless, expatiating, fervent, unreasoning, generous, accomplished Mrs. Jameson ... a great benefit to her time from her zeal for her sex and for Art' (Martineau, 435). JUDITH JOHNSTON

Sources C. Thomas, *Love and work enough: the life of Anna Jameson* (1967) · G. Macpherson, *Memoirs of the life of Anna Jameson*, ed. M. O. W. Oliphant (1878) · *Letters of Anna Jameson to Ottilie von Goethe*, ed. G. H. Needler (1939) · J. Johnston, *Anna Jameson: Victorian, feminist, woman of letters* (1997) · *Anna Jameson: letters and friendships*, ed. B. S. Erskine (1915) · H. Martineau, *Biographical sketches, 1852–1868*, 2nd edn (1869) · *The collected letters of Thomas and Jane Welsh Carlyle*, ed. C. R. Sanders and K. J. Fielding, 7 (1977) · *The works of John Ruskin*, ed. E. T. Cook and A. Wedderburn, library edn, 39 vols. (1903–12), vol. 35 · d. cert. · A. Jameson, 'Revelation of childhood', *Commonplace book* (1854) · unpublished MS letters to and from Jameson

Archives BL, corresp. with Sir Robert Peel, Add. MSS 40532, 40541, 40601 · Bodl. Oxf., corresp. with Lady Byron and notebook · Girton Cam., letters to Bessie Rayner Parkes · Goethe und Schiller Archiv, Weimar, Germany, Ottilie von Goethe collection · NL Scot., letters to George Combe · Staffs. RO, letters to Lord Hatherton and Lady Hatherton · Wellesley College, Massachusetts, Browning corresp.

Likenesses D. B. Murphy, miniature, 1810, repro. in Erskine, ed., *Anna Jameson* · C. Vogel, drawing, 1839, Staatliche Kunstsammlungen, Dresden, Kupferstichkabinett · D. O. Hill and R. Adamson, photograph, 1843–8, NPG [*see illus.*] · J. Gibson, marble bust, 1862, NPG; repro. in Erskine, ed., *Anna Jameson* · H. Adlard, stipple (after D. B. Murphy), repro. in Macpherson, *Memoirs* · H. P. Briggs, oils, repro. in Thomas, *Love and work enough* · W. Hensel, drawing, National Gallery, Berlin, Hensel album, vol. 13 · W. Hensel, drawing, National Gallery, Berlin · D. O. Hill, photograph, Scot. NPG · R. G. Lane, lithograph (after H. P. Briggs, c.1835), BM, NPG; repro. in Thomas, *Love and work enough*

Wealth at death under £1500: probate, 17 May 1860, CGPLA Eng. & Wales

Jameson, James Sligo (1856–1888), naturalist and traveller in Africa, was born on 17 August 1856 at the Walk House, Alloa, Clackmannanshire, son of Andrew Jameson, a land agent of Irish stock, and his wife, Margaret (d. 1856), daughter of James Cochrane of Glen Lodge, Sligo. After elementary education at Dreghorn boarding-school, near Edinburgh, from 1868 Jameson studied under Dr Leonard Schmitz at the International College, Isleworth, and subsequently read for the army. However, in 1877 he decided to travel and set off for Borneo via Ceylon and Singapore. In Borneo, Jameson was the first to discover the black pern, a kind of honey buzzard, and he returned home with a fine collection of birds, butterflies, and beetles. Towards the end of 1878 he went out to South Africa in search of big game, and hunted on the edges of the Kalahari Desert. In the early part of 1879 he returned to Potchefstroom, from where, despite the disaffection of the Boers, he reached the Zambezi district of the interior, trekking along the Great Marico River and up the Limpopo. Together with H. Collison he next passed through the 'Great Thirst Land' into the country of the Matabele (Ndebele), whose king received them hospitably. They were joined by the African hunter F. C. Selous and pushed on into Mashonaland, hunting lions and rhinoceroses; the party also confirmed the confluence of the Umvuli and

James Sligo Jameson (1856–1888), by unknown engraver, pubd 1890

Umnyati rivers. In 1881 Jameson returned to England with a collection of large hunting trophies as well as ornithological, entomological, and botanical specimens. 'This expedition to Mashona', wrote Bowdler Sharpe, 'added a great deal to our knowledge of the birds of South-East Africa'.

In 1882–3, accompanied by his brother John Andrew, Jameson went on a shooting expedition to the Rocky Mountains. Spain and Algeria were visited in 1884, and on his return home in February 1885 he married Ethel (b. c.1867), daughter of Sir Henry Marion Durand.

Jameson joined the Emin Pasha Relief Expedition under the direction of Henry Morton Stanley in 1887, contributing £1000 to the funds, and serving as naturalist. The expedition reached Banana at the mouth of the Congo on 18 March. In June he was left as second in command of the rear column under Major Walter Barttelot, at Yambuya on the Aruwhimi River, while Stanley's party pushed further into the interior in search of Emin. The chief, Tippu Tip, had promised Stanley to send to Yambuya men and carriers. Thus reinforced Jameson and his companions were to follow Stanley with stores. However, Tippu Tip failed to keep his word, and in August Jameson visited the chief at the Stanley Falls on the upper Congo without result. No news from Stanley reached the camp, and subsequently a third of the rear column died. In the spring of 1888 Jameson revisited Tippu at Kasongo, 300 miles higher up the Congo River than the Stanley Falls.

While returning with Tippu to the falls in May, Jameson witnessed at the house of the chief of the settlement of Riba Riba some native dances. Tippu told him that the festivities usually concluded with a banquet of human flesh. Jameson expressed himself incredulous, but gave the performers six handkerchiefs, which they clearly regarded as a challenge to prove their cannibal habits. A girl of ten years old was promptly killed and dismembered in Jameson's presence. Jameson declares in his diary that 'I could not bring myself to believe that it was anything save a ruse to get money out of me, until the last moment' but he admits that later in the day he tried to 'make some small sketches of the scene' (Jameson, 291). After Jameson's death and the conclusion of the expedition Stanley published the story in *The Times* (8 November 1890), and represented that Jameson almost directly invited the girl's murder, and made sketches on the spot. Stanley obtained his information from William Bonny, one of Jameson's companions at Yambuya, and from Assad Farran, Jameson's Syrian interpreter. Although it seems unlikely that Jameson actually invited the sacrifice it remains unclear whether or not he could have intervened to stop it. At the very least, most of his contemporaries regarded him as being guilty of callousness, especially in sketching the scene.

On arriving at Yambuya on 31 May 1888 Jameson prepared for the evacuation of the camp, which took place on 11 June. Tippu had finally sent 400 Manyema to act as carriers, but they proved insubordinate, and Barttelot, having divided the expedition into two, hastened forward (15 June) and left Jameson to follow with the loads at greater leisure. On 19 July Barttelot was shot dead at Banalia. On receiving this disastrous news Jameson hurried to Unaria, and thence to Stanley Falls, where he arrived on 1 August. Six days later he was present at the trial and execution of Sanga, Barttelot's murderer, and obtained the promise of Tippu Tip, who seemed alone able to control the tribal followers, to accompany the expedition in the search for Stanley, under conditions, which it was necessary to submit to the committee at home. Jameson offered to pay £20,000 out of his own purse rather than allow the expedition to be abandoned. In order to place himself in communication with England, he left Stanley Falls on 8 August to go down the Congo to Bangala, where Herbert Ward, a member of Major Barttelot's party, was known to be awaiting telegrams from the Emin committee. The weather was bad; on 10 August Jameson contracted a chill which developed into haematuric fever, and on 17 August, the day after his arrival at Bangala, he died. On the 18th he was buried on an island in the Congo River opposite the village.

A small but valuable collection of birds and insects which Jameson made at Yambuya was sent to Britain in 1890. The bulk of his collections remained with his widow, but a valuable portion of the ornithological collections was placed by Captain Shelley, to whom Jameson gave it, in the Natural History Museum, London. His diary of the Emin Pasha expedition, edited by his wife, was published in 1891 as *The Story of the Rear Column*. Of slight build, Jameson was to all appearance scarcely strong enough for the rough work of his last expedition. Stanley once regarded him as a 'nice fellow … sociable and good' (Stanley, 1.74). Jameson's wife and two daughters survived him.   M. G. WATKINS, rev. ANDREW GROUT

Sources J. S. Jameson, *The story of the rear column of the Emin Pasha relief expedition*, ed. Mrs J. S. Jameson [1891] · I. R. Smith, *The Emin Pasha relief expedition, 1886–1890* (1972) · F. McLynn, *Stanley: sorcerer's apprentice* (1991) · H. M. Stanley, *In darkest Africa*, 2 vols. (1890) · J. M. Jadot, 'Jameson J. S., 1856–1888', in *Biographie coloniale belge*, Académie Royale des Sciences Coloniales, 4 (1955), 433–7 · private information (1891) · *Journal et correspondance du major Edmund Musgrave Barttelot*, ed. W. G. Barttelot (Paris, 1891) · J. R. Troup, *With Stanley's rear column* (1890) · T. Heazle Parke, *My personal experiences in equatorial Africa* (1891) · Gallery of Natural History, Piccadilly, *Exhibition of the Jameson trophies* (1888) · *The Athenaeum* (6 Oct 1888), 453 · *The Times* (22 Sept 1888) · *The Times* (7 Dec 1890) · *The Times* (24 Dec 1890) · 'Mr H. M. Stanley and his officers', *Times Weekly Edition* (14 Nov 1890), 2–6 · 'Stanley's rear column', *Times Weekly Edition* (14 Nov 1890), 10–11 · 'Stanley's rear column', *Times Weekly Edition* (21 Nov 1890), 2–8, 13 · 'The story of the rear guard', *Times Weekly Edition* (5 Dec 1890), 13 · CGPLA Eng. & Wales (1889)

Archives U. Oxf., Pitt Rivers Museum, corresp., diaries, and papers relating to his involvement with Emin Pasha relief expedition

Likenesses photograph, repro. in Jameson, *Story of the rear column*, frontispiece · wood-engraving, NPG; repro. in *ILN* (22 Nov 1890) [*see illus.*]

Wealth at death £33,053 17s. 6d.: resworn probate, May 1889, CGPLA Eng. & Wales (1887)

Jameson, John (*bap.* 1740, *d.* 1823), Irish whiskey distiller, was baptized on 5 October 1740 in Alloa, Clackmannanshire, one of the children of William Jameson (*b.* 1718) of Alloa, and his wife, Helen Horne, of Thormaneau, Kinross-shire. In 1768 he married Margaret (1753–1815), eldest daughter of John Haig, whisky distiller, of The Gartlands, Alloa, and his wife, Margaret Stein, of Kennetpans, Clackmannanshire, from another important lowland distilling family, the first regular exporters of Scotch whisky to London. They had eight sons and eight daughters. Jameson was sheriff-clerk of Clackmannanshire from about 1770 until his death.

Some time in the late 1770s Jameson visited Dublin, a flourishing centre of production of Irish whiskey despite the heavy excise duties, and about 1780 he bought a share in a small distillery in Bow Street, which according to a tradition repeated by Alfred Barnard, who toured the Irish distilleries in the 1880s, belonged to three wealthy men, a baronet, a general, and an 'honourable'. Jameson later established two of his sons, John and William, in the business. By 1800 the younger John Jameson was running the distillery, and after his marriage in 1802 to Isabella, daughter of John Stein, who also had a distillery in Bow Street, he took this over too. The title John Jameson & Son dates from 1810. By then the firm was operating a 1256 gallon still, and by 1821 it was the second largest distillery in Ireland. William Jameson ran another of John Stein's distilleries, in Marrowbone Lane, which became Jameson and Stein in 1802, with a 1206 gallon still. William died in 1802, and left his distillery to a third and younger brother, James, later a director and deputy governor of the Bank of Ireland, and the firm became James Jameson & Co. A fourth of Jameson's sons, Andrew, who had a small distillery at Enniscorthy, co. Wexford, was the grandfather of Guglielmo Marconi, inventor of wireless telegraphy. The Jamesons continued to marry members of the Haig family: Jameson's grandson John Jameson married Anne Haig, and two of their sons, including the eldest, another John Jameson, went on to marry daughters of John Haig of Fife. James Jameson's grandson also married a Haig.

The Jamesons became the most important distilling family in Ireland, despite rivalry between the Bow Street and Marrowbone Lane distilleries. John Jameson senior died on 3 December 1823.   ANNE PIMLOTT BAKER

John Jameson (*bap.* 1740, *d.* 1823), by Sir Henry Raeburn

Sources A. Barnard, *The whisky distilleries of the United Kingdom* (1887), 353–6 · J. Laver, *The house of Haig* (1958), 13–21 · Burke, *Gen. Ire.* (1976) · E. B. McGuire, *Irish whiskey: a history of distilling, the spirit trade, and excise controls in Ireland* (1973), 340, 372–4 · *The history of a great house: the origin of John Jameson whiskey* (1924) · M. Magee, *1000 years of Irish whiskey* (1980) · D. Thomson, 'Raeburn': the art of Sir Henry Raeburn, 1756–1823 (1997), 180 [exhibition catalogue, Royal Scot. Acad., 1 Aug 1997 – 5 Oct 1997, and NPG, 24 Oct 1997 – 1 Feb 1998] · b. cert.
Likenesses H. Raeburn, oils, NG Ire. [*see illus.*]

Jameson [Jamieson], **John Paul** (1659–1700), Roman Catholic priest and antiquary, was born in Aberdeen, the son of John Jameson, trader, and his wife, Joanna Blackburn (*d.* 1680). The family was of some note, as in 1684 their daughter Jane married the city provost's son. Having been converted to Catholicism, Jameson journeyed to Paris and on to Rome, where he entered the Scots College in late 1677. Despite illness he studied rhetoric for one year and philosophy for three, then after four years of theology defended his theses and graduated doctor in February 1685. In May 1685, having been ordained priest, he went to the seminary in Padua, recommended by the Roman agent of the Scottish clergy, William Leslie, to the cardinal bishop, who appointed him to succeed the professor of theology there, also named William Leslie (later bishop of Laibach). The prefect of studies in the seminary, Thomas Nicolson, planned to send Jameson to Paris to work on Scottish history, as Jameson had shown a bent for this. In October 1685, however, at the request of Cardinal Carlo Barberini, he entered the cardinal's household in Rome. Towards the end of 1687 he arrived in Scotland to work as a priest, first at Huntly, and he continued to minister in Scotland until his death.

Yet it is as a dedicated worker on Scottish history that Jameson is best-known, largely through the laudatory citations in William Nicolson's *Scottish Historical Library* (1702) and from Bishop Robert Keith's commendation, for Jameson's projected history of Scotland was never published. In Rome he unearthed and transcribed materials in Barberini's library and in the Vatican deposits, including letters of Queen Mary Stewart, papal bulls and briefs, extracts from the consistorial records, and a copy of Ferrerius's history of the abbots of Kinloss. At some point, almost certainly during residence at the Scots College in Paris when returning to Scotland, he worked in France, for Nicolson cites a manuscript volume found by him there and Thomas Innes later commented on his zealous searches in Italy and France. Some of his papers were deposited in the Paris college. He later compiled for Innes a cartulary of the church in Aberdeen, no doubt during his years there. Besides using previously unknown sources Jameson made detailed critical notes on printed versions of Bede's *History*, the *Chronicle of Melrose*, the early part of John Spottiswood's *History*, and Sir James Melville's *Memoirs*, as well as on George Martine's unpublished 'Reliquiae Divi Andreae'. One can see in his work the influence of the Parisian Maurist historians. His character and spirituality have also earned high praise.

In August 1688 Jameson was to be found at Elgin, though only fragments of information have survived about his activities in the following years. According to one source in 1690 he had been living with the earl of Dunfermline and at the revolution was imprisoned in the Elgin tolbooth, but was freed by the earl and was apparently with him in his armed resistance to the new regime. Other sources have him in prison in 1689–90, at Elgin first, then Aberdeen. In 1692 he was on parole and confined to the city of Aberdeen, where he ministered to the Catholics. He was still there in 1695 and very ill. In 1697–9 he was in various places in the lowlands and in very poor health; from October 1699 he was in Edinburgh, where he died on 25 March 1700.

THOMPSON COOPER, *rev.* MARK DILWORTH

Sources W. Clapperton, 'Memoirs of Scotch missionary priests', Scottish Catholic Archives, Edinburgh, CC 1/9, no. 35 · J. F. S. Gordon, ed., *The Catholic church in Scotland* (1874), 567–8, 628–9 · W. Nicolson, *The Scottish historical library* (1702), 82, 130, 182, 196, 211, 213–15, 224–5, 347–50 · P. J. Anderson, ed., *Records of the Scots colleges at Douai, Rome, Madrid, Valladolid and Ratisbon*, New Spalding Club, 30 (1906), 119 · M. Dilworth, 'The Scottish mission in 1688–1689', *Innes Review*, 20 (1969), 68–79, esp. 72, 76 · Robert Sibbald compilation, NL Scot., Adv. MS 33.3.25, fols. 25–8 · T. Innes, *A critical essay on the ancient inhabitants of the northern parts of Britain, or Scotland*, 2 (1729), 578–9 · [J. Robertson], ed., *Concilia Scotiae*, 1 (1866), clxvi–clxvii · W. Forbes-Leith, ed., *Memoirs of Scottish Catholics*, 2 vols. (1909), vol. 2, p. 165
Archives NL Scot., transcripts, Adv. MS 33. 3. 25 [fols. 26–8 very possibly in Jameson's hand]

Jameson, Sir Leander Starr, baronet (1853–1917), medical practitioner and colonial administrator, was born on 9 February 1853 at 5 Charlotte Street, Edinburgh, the

Sir Leander Starr Jameson, baronet (1853–1917), by George
Charles Beresford, 1914

youngest of eleven children of Robert William *Jameson
(1805–1868), writer to the signet, poet, playwright, radical
freethinker, supporter of colonial settlement, and campaigner against slavery and the corn laws—and brother of
Robert *Jameson (1774–1854), geologist—and his wife,
Christian, daughter of Major-General John Pringle of
Symington, Midlothian, and his wife, Christian Watson.
Christian Pringle possessed, according to Jameson's official biographer, Ian Colvin, a 'strong sense of duty', which
'corrected, as far as possible, the effects of her husband's
rashness' (Colvin, 1.5). Soon afterwards his father gave up
the practice of law and, under the patronage of the whig
earl of Stair, from 1855 was editor of the *Wigtownshire Free
Press* in Stranraer. In 1860 he used a legacy to acquire two
small provincial newspapers, the *Suffolk and Essex Free Press*
and the *Essex and Suffolk News*, both published at Sudbury,
moving with his family to Suffolk and later London. Soon
after, he sold the papers at a loss. He died in Kensington on
10 December 1868. Jameson grew up one of the 'genteel
poor'.

Early years and medical practice Leander, called Lanner by
his brothers, was a precocious child. After drinking a glass
of sherry at the age of six he is said to have declared, 'Now
I feel as if I could go and do everything' (Colvin, 1.6). He
was educated at Sudbury grammar school in Suffolk, at
the Godolphin School in Hammersmith (opened in 1856,
it closed in 1900 and was replaced by the Godolphin and
Latymer School for Girls), and from 1870 at University College, Gower Street, London. There, with a loan from his

eldest brother, Tom, a naval surgeon, he studied medicine, doing his clinical training at University College Hospital. He graduated BS (1875) and MD (1877), and was
elected MRCS (1875). He won silver medals for anatomy,
medicine, and surgery and the Atkinson Morley surgical
scholarship, though Sir George Buckston Browne, his
medical supervisor, recalled his performance as 'undistinguished'. As resident surgeon of University College Hospital, Jameson seemed destined for a solid career in surgery, but he embarked instead on a life of adventure. He
travelled first to Paris, where he witnessed the commune,
and afterwards to the United States.

In 1878 an elderly American physician, Dr James Perrott
Prince, with a large practice in Kimberley, Cape Colony,
advertised at University College, London, for a partner,
and Jameson was accepted for the post. His health was not
good, and the south African climate was believed beneficial for those with lung complaints. Moreover, three of his
brothers had already settled there; one of them, Julius,
had sent home an uncut diamond. Kimberley was a boom
diamond-mining town where medical practitioners' skills
were in demand, and the partnership was a profitable one.
Jameson reputedly made £5000 from it and £10,000 from
private practice within a few years of his arrival. He drove
'a very smart victoria with two very fast black horses'
(Colvin, 1.27). In 1879 he was appointed one of the first
three consultant medical officers in Kimberley, and two
years later he bought Prince's share of the practice, which
was largely concerned with the care of African minework-
ers. In 1882, however, Jameson and several colleagues
were accused by Dr Hans Sauer, medical officer for Griqua-
land West, of first diagnosing and then concealing an outbreak of smallpox, so that mining operations would not
be hampered by a quarantine programme. Sauer and
Jameson sued each other for libel and both were awarded
identical sums in damages. In spite of this, Jameson continued to enjoy the popular title of the Doctor (British
newspapers later called him Dr Jim). He gambled heavily
at poker and whist. Short, slim, lively, charming, laconic,
and reportedly a 'ladies' man', Jameson nevertheless had
no intention of marrying, 'never', as he put it, 'having felt
in the least inclined that way' (Colvin, 1.38).

Soon after arriving in Kimberley, Jameson became a
friend of Cecil Rhodes and is believed to have encouraged
him to stand for the Cape parliament in 1881. Their friendship became particularly close after 1886 when Jameson
attended Rhodes's injured secretary and dearest friend,
Neville Pickering. After Pickering's death (16 October
1886) Rhodes moved into Jameson's untidy bungalow.
Jameson was Rhodes's closest friend, confidant, and 'alter
ego' (Rotberg, *The Founder*, 126). Ostensibly they had little
in common. Rhodes repeatedly proclaimed his visionary
schemes, while Jameson was reserved, but, according to
the American engineer John Hays Hammond, their ill
health put both of them 'always under the strain against
time' (Rotberg, 'Who was responsible?', 141). Jameson
later recalled that he fell under the power of Rhodes's personality almost immediately on meeting, but his support
for Rhodes's northward expansionist plans took some

persuasion. Once swayed, however, he became the energetic instrument of Rhodes's vision. His interests now became political rather than medical. He shunned involvement in the local branch of the British Medical Association, and although he remained on the medical register of Cape Colony until 1911, he increasingly confined his practice to a few patients in his immediate political circle.

Mashonaland and Matabeleland Jameson's first mission for Rhodes was in April 1889 to Lobengula, king of the Ndebele (Matabele), to persuade him not to cancel his October 1888 mineral concession to Charles Dunell Rudd and his associates—a concession crucial to Rhodes's plans. Jameson was unsuccessful on this occasion and had to make a second journey in October, when he stayed for three months and treated the king's gout with morphia injections, and his sore eyes with ointments. Lobengula began to trust him and made him an *induna* and confirmed the Rudd concession. With the British South Africa Company's incorporation by royal charter, the preparations for the occupation of Mashonaland were now nearing completion, but Lobengula repudiated the agreement. In April 1890 Jameson made a third visit, ensuring that the pioneer column could advance unharmed through Lobengula's domain. Jameson accompanied the column, organized by Frank Johnson and commanded by Lieutenant-Colonel Graham Pennefather, on its occupation of Mashonaland.

In September 1890, while the pioneers established an administrative capital in Mashonaland at Fort Salisbury, Jameson made two expeditions into Mozambique territory claimed by the Portuguese. He tried, unsuccessfully, to gain a coastline on the Indian Ocean through treaties with local chiefs, and he was arrested briefly by the Portuguese authorities. In April 1891 he returned to Mashonaland where, with a strong force of company police with machine-guns, without fighting, he successfully turned back the Adendorff party of trekboers. Jameson became increasingly impatient with the company administrator, Archibald Colquhoun, whom he regarded as a pedantic bureaucrat. Colquhoun believed that the actions of Jameson and Johnson threatened relations with African chiefs and the Portuguese, and once threatened to arrest him, but Jameson's frontier pragmatism had Rhodes's confidence, and he was appointed to succeed Colquhoun, as chief magistrate and administrator, in September 1891.

Jameson's major task was to develop quickly the resources of Mashonaland, but company retrenchment reduced his administrative staff to a mere twenty men in a territory of approximately 110,000 square miles. The rule of law, particularly in relation to African property rights, did not figure highly among Jameson's priorities as it had with Colquhoun. He promulgated regulations without Colonial Office authorization, tolerated settler assaults on Africans, and upheld the allegedly excessive violence against recalcitrant chiefs by his magistrate Captain Charles Frederick Lendy as a necessary assertion of sovereignty against overwhelming numbers of Africans and the overlordship of Lobengula. Arguably, he had little

choice. The boundary between company territory and Lobengula's domains was vague and interpreted differently by both sides. With slender military resources, regular frontier patrols were impossible, and Jameson was forced to rely on unruly settlers for defence in time of emergency. He shared Rhodes's view that a confrontation with Lobengula was inevitable, but, as the reduction of the company's military resources indicated, neither expected such a showdown to be imminent. Jameson had initially tolerated punitive Ndebele raids against Lobengula's disobedient vassals, but later attempted to gain the king's recognition of the company's rights over both black and white inhabitants of Mashonaland. Both sides attempted to exercise restraint, but a mood of suspicion developed. Frequent Ndebele raids began to undermine the company's claim to uphold peace and order in Mashonaland, the very basis of its justification for the imposition of a hut tax on the African population.

By July 1893 hostilities seemed unavoidable; but Jameson, requiring a clear *casus belli*, attempted to censor all news—including telegraphic communications—coming out of Mashonaland, so that the company would be clearly regarded as a victim of Lobengula's tyranny. Sir Henry Loch, the British high commissioner, agreed with Rhodes that force was necessary, partly in an attempt to impose a restraining Colonial Office influence over the company. In the Victoria agreement of 14 August 1893 with the settlers, Jameson promised each volunteer for war against the Ndebele a generous grant of land, 'loot' cattle, and mining claims in Matabeleland. A skirmish between company police and the Ndebele reported on 30 September provided him with the required justification for an invasion (the Matabele (Ndebele) campaign of 1893), and he accompanied the invasion force commanded by Major Patrick William Forbes. Matabeleland was conquered rapidly and added to Jameson's responsibilities. He spent much of the following year establishing townships, schools, roads, magistrates' courts, and a system of native administration. A popular hero in Britain, he was made a CB in 1894. In the same year an order in council reorganized the company's government, vesting all real power in Jameson as administrator.

The Jameson raid and its aftermath As administrator in Southern Rhodesia, Jameson had enormous responsibilities and was in practice allowed almost unlimited initiative. Administration bored him, and his chaotic regime was characterized by ignorance, neglect, irresponsibility, and unscrupulousness. He made regulations, then broke them. Probably most harmful was his land alienation. He irresponsibly and lavishly granted vast areas, notably to Sir John Willoughby, fifth baronet—his military adviser and later commander of the raid—and others of the 'Honourable and military element' (Keppel-Jones, 369), without requiring occupation or farming. Most was acquired by absentee speculators. William Henry (later Sir William) Milton, the civil servant appointed in 1896 after the raid to reorganize the administration, wrote in September 1896:

> Everything official here is in an absolutely rotten condition
> … Jameson has given nearly the whole country away to the

Willoughbys, Whites and others of that class … It is perfectly sickening to see the way in which the country has been run for the sake of hob-nobbing with Lord this and the Honble that. I think Jameson must have been off his head for some time before the raid.   (Ranger, 104)

Milner wrote to Chamberlain in December 1897, 'land was alienated in the most reckless manner' (ibid.). Moreover, Jameson's regime, and especially its seizure of land and cattle, harmed the indigenous people—Milner wrote in November 1897, 'the blacks have been scandalously used' (Headlam, 178)—and largely caused the Matabele and Shona uprisings.

From October 1894 Jameson became drawn into the conspiracy to foment an Uitlander rebellion on the Witwatersrand to overthrow Kruger's government. Sir Henry Loch originally proposed such a rising, but Rhodes and Jameson took it up in earnest, believing that the use of company forces would limit the 'imperial factor' and spare Britain embarrassment. In October 1895 the Colonial Office transferred to the company a strip of territory along the Bechuanaland border over which Jameson was appointed resident commissioner. From here he established contact with the Johannesburg reformers. By 28 December it was clear to Rhodes that the rising would have to be postponed, but Jameson, having cut the telegraph wires, was beyond reach. Believing that firm action would spur the Uitlanders into rebellion, and encouraged by his recent success against the Ndebele, Jameson's gambler's instinct prevailed. On his own initiative he launched his raid from Pitsani into Transvaal on 29 December 1895 with a force of 511 police and volunteers, but, hopelessly outnumbered by Boer forces, he was forced to surrender to General Cronjé on 2 January 1896 at Doornkop, 14 miles from Johannesburg. Rhodes said, 'Old Jameson has upset my apple-cart' (Colvin, 2.125). By agreement between the Transvaal and British governments, Jameson and five of his officers were handed over to the British authorities. In London, at the Old Bailey, he was tried and convicted on a charge of violating the Foreign Enlistment Act of 1870 and sentenced to fifteen months' imprisonment. Incarcerated in Holloway prison, brooding and suffering from gallstones, Jameson was released by the end of the year on the grounds of serious illness, probably malaria. At the British parliamentary select committee of inquiry in 1897 he attempted to carry the entire blame for the raid, and declared: 'I also know that if I had succeeded I should have been forgiven' (Colvin, 2.165). However, a select committee of the Cape parliament had already placed most of the responsibility firmly on Rhodes. Jameson nevertheless earned the admiration of many imperialists, among them the poet laureate, Alfred Austin, whose much criticized ballad 'Jameson's Ride' celebrated the event.

After an extended vacation in Europe, Jameson returned to south Africa in 1899, where he became a strong supporter of Milner's 'forward policy' against Kruger. Soon after the outbreak in October 1899 of the Second South African War he travelled from Rhodesia to Ladysmith where he remained trapped throughout the siege

(November 1899–February 1900). He helped treat the wounded, nursed his servant who had typhoid, and himself became seriously ill with dysentery. By the time of the relief he was apparently near death, and according to Colvin, 'his physique was broken by Ladysmith' (Colvin, 1.192).

In May 1900 Jameson was elected unopposed to replace Rutherfoord Harris as member of the Cape house of assembly for Kimberley. He became a director of De Beers, and of the British South Africa Company in 1902. Initially he was received coldly by his fellow parliamentarians, but he later won over some of them with a maiden speech asking that they forgive the 'blunder' of the raid.

Parliamentary career and south African unification Although Jameson's raid had resulted in the political, but not economic, fall of Rhodes, their friendship remained as strong as ever. In 1901 he toured Europe and Egypt with Rhodes, whom he nursed throughout his final illness until his death on 26 March 1902. Jameson then threw himself more energetically into his parliamentary career, becoming the leader of the Progressive Party in March 1902. Little united the Progressives except the Rhodes legend, of which Jameson was custodian, but in the general election which followed the fall of Sir Gordon Sprigg it gained a narrow majority of five, owing to the disenfranchisement of Cape rebels, and Jameson became prime minister in February 1904. His ministry was wholly English-speaking and strongly supported the promotion of British immigration and the strengthening of imperial ties. He did not, however, oppose the pardoning of Cape rebels in 1904, and he won opposition support for his irrigation law and his encouragement of bilingualism in schools and the civil service, even if Afrikaner language activists remained dissatisfied. Widespread fears about white poverty were assuaged by his School Board Act of 1905, which provided for primary education for white children and restricted coloured children to mission schools, and his Chinese Exclusion Act. His Representation Act of 1905 was, contrary to Afrikaner expectations, generally regarded as equitable. In 1904 Jameson's influence as Rhodes trustee was crucial in gaining financial backing for the establishment of Rhodes University College in Grahamstown.

In 1907 Jameson attended the conference of colonial premiers in London; there, together with Alfred Deakin of Australia and Sir Joseph Ward of New Zealand, he championed closer imperial co-operation against the more cautious Sir Wilfrid Laurier of Canada and General Louis Botha of the Transvaal. Nevertheless, Jameson came to regard Botha as central to south African unification and the two became close friends. While in London he was sworn of the privy council. The Progressive Party was now renamed the Unionist Party, reflecting Jameson's central objective. He increasingly preached a policy of reconciliation with Afrikaners. He encouraged the high commissioner, Lord Selborne, to prepare his 'Memorandum', and he joined F. S. Malan in proposing a motion for federation in the Cape assembly. At the Inter-colonial Conference of 1908 he won further Afrikaner support for his suggestion that the historic name of the Orange Free State be restored.

In spite of these successes, achieved with a waning parliamentary majority, Jameson's ministry was overwhelmed by the severe financial depression in Cape Colony and the need for retrenchment. In 1908 the Unionists were defeated in the legislative council elections, and Jameson was succeeded as prime minister by John X. Merriman. He nevertheless retained great influence in the negotiations leading to union. He abandoned his earlier support for a federal constitution and now sought a complete realignment of politics around Botha, whom he regarded as more likely to promote imperial interests than Merriman. He believed that a 'best-man cabinet' would finally bury Anglo-Afrikaner racialism in a unitary state and, together with Sir Percy Fitzpatrick, he did much to appease British south African anxiety about their political future in the Union. In 1909 his ideas were well received by Botha when he accepted Jameson's invitation to holiday at Nairn in Scotland. Through a further series of meetings with Transvaal and Natal political leaders, Jameson gained the further support of British south Africans for his scheme, but former President Steyn would not be won over by Jameson's charm. At the national convention he became regarded, along with Botha, as a leading opponent of the 'miserable old racial divisions' between Boer and Briton. He opposed discriminatory labour policies and any change in the 'colour blind' Cape franchise under union, although this was probably due more to his need to woo black and coloured voters than to any innate liberalism.

Ireland, final years, and reputation With Botha's political freedom limited by Afrikaner nationalist sensitivities, there was no place for Jameson in the first Union cabinet in 1910, and he became leader of the opposition in the national assembly, having unified progressive elements across the dominion into a single Unionist Party. He remained hopeful of an Anglo-Afrikaner realignment around Botha. He was made a baronet in 1911, and in 1912 he resigned the party leadership, gave up his parliamentary seat on grounds of ill health, and settled in England. In 1913 he succeeded James Hamilton, second duke of Abercorn, as president of the British South Africa Company and became largely concerned with the future of the Rhodesias. In 1913–14 he toured Southern Rhodesia, where, appealing to imperial patriotism, he attempted to persuade the settlers to look to a post-war amalgamation of the Rhodesias rather than, as expected, entry into the Union. By 1916, however, many settlers rejected this as a cost-saving device and began to consider the alternatives of responsible government and membership of the Union.

In spite of declining health, Jameson still retained some of his taste for intrigue. In 1914, in marked contrast to Rhodes's earlier support of Charles Stewart Parnell and Irish home rule, Jameson entered the fringes of the conspiracy to support the Ulster loyalist revolt against home rule orchestrated by Lord Milner and Sir Edward Carson, who had acted as junior counsel in his trial for the raid. To

Milner and Jameson's admirer Kipling the loyalists were, like Uitlanders, another band of beleaguered kinsfolk whose security demanded the same kind of desperate measures which Jameson had personified in the raid. After the outbreak of war Jameson occasionally joined Carson, Milner, and other leading political figures at meetings of the Monday Night Club, and he chaired a War Office committee on British prisoners of war. Following the Easter rising of 1916 he was briefly considered by Walter Long as a suitable chief secretary for Ireland, and as chairman of a committee to consider a federal solution to the Irish problem. In 1917 the British government, drawing on the South African precedent, organized an Irish convention to reconcile loyalists and constitutional nationalists; Jameson visited Dublin to discuss its proceedings with Lord Dunraven, his last political undertaking. In his last years he resided at 2 Great Cumberland Place, Hyde Park, London. He died there on 26 November 1917 after a short but painful illness. On 29 November his remains were interred in a vault at Kensal Green cemetery, London. In 1920 they were taken to Southern Rhodesia, and on 22 May were reburied close to Rhodes's grave in the Matopo Hills near Bulawayo.

Many of Jameson's political dealings were beyond the bounds of conventional morality, but, like his heroes Robert Clive and Rhodes, he believed his approach was justified by the extraordinary demands of life on the imperial frontier. He was impulsive, ambitious, and often shallow, yet he was also capable of profound personal devotion to family and close political associates. Jameson ranks alongside Rhodes and Alfred Beit as a chief architect of Rhodesia, and was a founder of the Union of South Africa, but for all his impulsiveness and lack of self-doubt, he was characteristically a follower of 'men of vision' such as Rhodes and Botha rather than a leader in his own right, even if he inspired loyalty in those under his authority. He provided Kipling with the inspiration for his poem 'If'. Lord Blake has written of Jameson that 'In spite of all that has been written about him, this mercurial, unscrupulous, intrepid, reckless, restless, tireless medical man is one of the great enigmas of his time' (Blake, 56).

DONAL LOWRY

Sources 'Jameson', *West London Observer* (11 Jan 1896) · 'The Rt. Hon. Sir Starr Jameson: death of the chartered company's president', *African World* (Dec 1917) · I. D. Colvin, *The life of Jameson*, 2 vols. (1922) · T. R. H. Davenport, 'Jameson', *DSAB* · E. Dicey, 'The new Cape premier', *Fortnightly Review*, 81 (1904) · G. Seymour Fort, *Dr Jameson* (1908) · Imperialist [J. R. Maguire], *Cecil Rhodes: a biography and appreciation with personal reminiscences by Dr Jameson* (1897) · *DNB* · R. Rotberg, 'Who was responsible? Rhodes, Jameson and the raid', *The Jameson raid*, ed. J. Carruthers (1996) · W. T. Stead, 'Dr Jameson: prime minister of the Cape', *Review of Reviews*, 29 (1904) · E. van Heyningen, 'Leander Starr Jameson', *The Jameson raid*, ed. J. Carruthers (1996) · P. Cuthbert, 'The administration of Dr Jameson as prime minister of the Cape Colony, 1904–1908', MA diss., University of Cape Town, 1950 · M. R. Siepman, 'An analytical survey of the political career of Leander Starr Jameson, 1900–1912', PhD diss., University of Natal, Durban, 1979 · R. Blake, *A history of Rhodesia* (1977) · R. Brown, 'Aspects of the struggle for Mashonaland', *The Zambesian past*, ed. E. Stokes and R. Brown (1966) · W. H. Brown, *On the South African frontier* (1899) · E. H. Burrows, *A history of* *medicine in South Africa* (1958) · J. Butler, *The liberal party and the Jameson raid* (1968) · J. R. D. Cobbing, 'Lobengula, Jameson and the occupation of Mashonaland', *Rhodesian History*, 4 (1973) · A. R. Colquhoun, *From Dan to Beersheba* (1908) · J. Cooper-Chadwick, *Three years with Lobengula* (1894) · A. Digby, '"A medical El Dorado": colonial medical incomes and practice at the Cape', *Social History of Medicine*, 8 (1995) · J. Dobson and C. Wakeley, *Sir George Buckston Browne* (1957) · J. S. Galbraith, *Crown and charter: the early years of the British South Africa Company* (1974) · J. S. Galbraith, 'Engine without a governor: the early years of the British South Africa Company', *Rhodesian History*, 1 (1970) · F. E. Garrett and E. J. Edwards, *The story of an African crisis* (1897) · J. P. Fitzpatrick, *The Transvaal from within* (1899) · S. Glass, *The Matabele War* (1968) · W. K. Hancock, *Smuts*, 1: *The sanguine years, 1870–1919* (1962) · D. O. Helly and H. Callaway, 'Journalism as active politics: Flora Shaw, *The Times* and South Africa', *The South African War reappraised*, ed. D. Lowry (2000) · J. Hofmeyr and J. P. Cope, *South Africa* (1931) · H. M. Hole, *The making of Rhodesia* (1926) · H. M. Hole, *Old Rhodesian days* (1926) · H. M. Hole, *The Jameson raid* (1930) · F. Johnson, *Great days* (1940) · J. Kendle, *Colonial and imperial conferences, 1887–1911* (1967) · J. Kendle, *Walter Long, Ireland and the Union, 1905–1920* (1992) · A. Keppel-Jones, *Rhodes and Rhodesia: the white conquest of Zimbabwe, 1884–1902* (Kingston, ON, 1987) · A. Leonard, *How we made Rhodesia* (1896) · *Selections from the correspondence of J. X. Merriman*, ed. P. Lewsen, 4 vols. (1960–69) · B. K. Long, *Drummond Chaplin: his life and times in Africa* (1941) · A. Lycett, *Rudyard Kipling* (1999) · G. Martin, 'Imperial federation', *Reappraisals in British imperial history*, ed. G. Martin and R. Hyam (1975) · P. Maylam, *Rhodes, the Tswana and the British, 1885–1899* (1980) · J. Meintjes, *General Louis Botha* (1970) · L. Michell, *The life of the Rt. Hon. C. J. Rhodes, 1853–1902* (1910) · J. T. Molteno, *Further South African reminiscences* (1926) · C. Palley, *The constitutional history and law of Southern Rhodesia* (1966) · G. Pyrah, *Imperial policy and South Africa* (1955) · J. Rose Innes, *Autobiography* (1949) · R. Rotberg, *The founder: Cecil Rhodes and the pursuit of power* (1988) · S. Samkange, *The origins of Rhodesia* (1968) · H. Sauer, *Ex Africa* (1937) · K. Sayce, *A town called Victoria* (1978) · A. T. Q. Stewart, *The Ulster crisis* (1968) · L. M. Thompson, *The unification of South Africa, 1902–1910* (1960) · P. Stigger, 'Volunteers and the profit motive in the Anglo-Ndebele war, 1893', *Rhodesian History*, 2 (1971) · M. Tamarkin, *Cecil Rhodes and the Cape Afrikaners* (1996) · S. Taylor, *The mighty Nimrod: a life of Frederick Courtney Selous* (1989) · D. R. Torrance, *The strange death of the liberal empire: Lord Selborne in South Africa* (1996) · J. van der Poel, *The Jameson raid* (1951) · P. Warhurst, *Anglo-Portuguese relations in south-central Africa, 1890–1900* (1962) · W. A. Wills and L. T. Collingbridge, *The downfall of Lobengula* (1894) · T. O. Ranger, *Revolt in Southern Rhodesia, 1896–1897: a study in African resistance* (1967) · Boase, *Mod. Eng. biog.* · E. Walton, *The inner history of the South African Convention* (1912) · E. Longford, *Jameson's raid* (1983) · R. F. Currey, *Rhodes University, 1904–1970: a chronicle* (1977) · *The Milner papers*, ed. C. Headlam, 1: *South Africa, 1897–1899* (1931) · private information (2004) [UCL] · *CGPLA Eng. & Wales* (1918)

Archives National Archives of Zimbabwe, Harare, corresp. and papers, JA 1–2 · National Archives of Zimbabwe, Harare, British South Africa Company, Cape Town (Kimberley) Office, out letters, CT 2/5/1–2 | BL, letters to Lady Milner, Add. MS 63591 · Bodl. RH, Jameson raid, MS Afr. s. 2206 · Bodl. RH, Rhodes (miscellaneous) papers, MSS Afr. s. 8, s. 641; t. 5, t. 6, t. 14 · Bodl. RH, Rhodes papers, MSS Afr. s. 227–228 · Bodl. RH, Rhodes (supplementary) papers, MS Afr. s. 229 · Bodl. RH, South Africa, MSS Afr. s. 13–15 · Bodl. RH, South Africa (Bower), MSS Afr. s. 63, 1279 · Bodl. RH, South Africa (British South Africa Company), MSS Afr. s. 70–84 · Bodl. RH, South Africa (Colvin), MS Afr. s. 229A · Bodl. RH, South Africa (Godman), MS Afr. s. 8, fols. 106–7 · Bodl. RH, South Africa (Grey), MS Afr. s. 424, fols. 479–81 · Bodl. RH, South Africa (Hamilton), MS Afr. s. 19 · Bodl. RH, South Africa (Low), MS Afr. t. 22, fols. 60–77 · Bodl. RH, South Africa (R. White), MSS Afr. s. 220–224 · Bodl. RH, Transvaal, micr. Afr. 156 (4) · Bodl. RH, Transvaal (Bower), micr. Afr. 411 · Bodl. RH, Transvaal (British South Africa Company) (B), MS Dep. Monk Bretton 86 · Bodl. RH, Transvaal (Lloyd), MS Afr. s. 424, fols. 560–

62 · Bodl. RH, Zimbabwe, MS Afr. s. 8 (1–5) · Derbys. RO, corresp. with P. L. Gell · National Archives of Zimbabwe, Harare, Lobengula corresp., LO 1/1/1 · Richmond Local Studies Library, London, letters to D. Sladen, SLA/72

Likenesses H. von Herkomer, oils, 1895 · G. C. Beresford, photograph, 1914, NPG [*see illus.*] · G. C. Beresford, photograph, NPG · D. C. Boonzaaier, caricatures, University of Cape Town · A. S. Boyd, caricatures, University of Cape Town · F. C. Gould, caricatures, University of Cape Town · M. Jameson, oils, NPG · M. Prior, pencil sketch (*After the battle of Doornkop, near Johannesburg. Doctor Jameson and his men being escorted to Pretoria by the Boer army*) · Spy [L. Ward], caricature, repro. in *VF* (9 April 1896) · J. Tweed, death mask · G. Witch, pencil sketch · marble bust, Bodl. RH · photograph, NPG

Wealth at death £45,082 18s. 10d.: administration with will, 16 Jan 1918, *CGPLA Eng. & Wales*

Jameson, Margaret Ethel [Storm] (1891–1986), novelist, was born on 8 January 1891 in Whitby in the North Riding of Yorkshire, the eldest in the family of three daughters and one son of William Storm Jameson, sea captain, and his wife (who was also his stepsister), Hannah Margaret, daughter of George Gallilee, shipbuilder. As a child she accompanied her parents on several voyages, which marked the beginning of a lifelong passion for travel. Yet despite her self-imposed exile from Whitby, the harbour town remained central to her imagination and to many of her novels.

Her parents' marriage was unhappy and Storm Jameson's early life was dominated by her high-tempered, bitter mother whom she both feared and loved, and who encouraged her to receive an academic education. After being taught privately and at Scarborough municipal school for a year, she won one of three county scholarships which enabled her to take a place at Leeds University, where she read English for three years, graduating in 1912 with a first-class degree. A research scholarship allowed her to go to London, first to University College, then to King's College. She was awarded her MA in 1914 for a thesis on modern European drama, which was published in 1920 as *Modern Drama in Europe*.

On 15 January 1913 Jameson married Charles Dougan Clarke, schoolmaster, whom she had met in her second year at Leeds; he was the son of Charles Granville Clarke, doctor of medicine, an American Quaker. Their son, Charles William Storm, was born on 20 June 1915. The pair were temperamentally ill-matched and the marriage soon foundered, though they did not divorce until 1925. Meanwhile Jameson had begun the extraordinarily prolific career of 'une machine à faire des livres', as she once described herself. The author of forty-five novels, numerous pamphlets, essays, and reviews, she freely admitted that she wrote too much, fuelled by her enormous energy and driven by the need to make money. Generous and spendthrift, constantly moving house and travelling in Europe whenever she could afford it, her career was shaped from the outset by her financial circumstances, which remained precarious throughout her life.

After refusing a job on *The Egoist*, which went to Rebecca West, Jameson worked successively for an advertising agency, the *New Commonwealth*, and Alfred Knopf, the American publisher, but after 1928 most of her income

Margaret Ethel [Storm] Jameson (1891–1986), by Howard Coster, 1930s

was derived from writing. Her first novel, *The Pot Boils* (1919), was widely reviewed and her popularity increased with the publication of the Mary Hervey trilogy, *The Triumph of Time* (1927–31), which charted the fortunes of the Whitby shipbuilding community between 1841 and 1923. Jameson was by now happy in her personal life, having in 1926 married the historian and novelist Guy Patterson Chapman (1889–1972), the son of George Walter Chapman, official receiver in bankruptcy. Chapman shared her love of France and tolerated her 'mania against domestic life' to the extent of living with her in a hotel for six years when he became professor of modern history at Leeds in 1945.

In 1930 Jameson began consciously to change her writing style in emulation of Stendhal. The result was three novellas about women, including the remarkably imagined meditations of an elderly prostitute in *A Day Off* (1933). Shortly afterwards she began a Balzacian quintet, *The Mirror in Darkness* (1934), which was based on the autobiographical figure of Mary Hervey Russell. Her own dissatisfaction as well as poor reviews caused her to abandon the series in 1936, though the related *The Journal of Mary Hervey Russell* (1945) and *The Black Laurel* (1947) are among her best novels, together with those inspired by her knowledge of Europe and love of France: *Cousin Honoré* (1940), *Europe to Let* (1940), and *Cloudless May* (1943).

During the 1930s Jameson became passionately involved in issues of social justice and anti-fascism. Between 1938 and 1944 she was president of the English section of PEN, for which she worked tirelessly on behalf of exiled European writers, earning herself a place on the 'Berlin death list'. After the war, though she continued to write indefatigably, her reputation as a novelist declined and the reprinting of some of her books by Virago Press in the 1980s did little to revive interest in her work. She noted her eclipse without resentment in her autobiography, *Journey from the North* (2 vols., 1969–70), which contains a memorably honest self-portrait of the author as well as harrowing accounts of bereavement and war.

Jameson liked to remember that her Nordic ancestors had been peasants of the sea whom she resembled in her restlessness and endurance, as she did in her looks. Her large, long-sighted eyes were grey-blue, set in a round high-cheekboned face. Sensual and physically strong, she experienced a series of romantic and sexual obsessions until the time of her second marriage. She received few public honours, though her honorary DLitt from Leeds University (1943) gave her pleasure, as did her honorary membership of the American Academy and Institute of Arts and Letters. She died on 30 September 1986 in Cambridge.   JUDITH PRIESTMAN, *rev.*

Sources *The Times* (7 Oct 1986) · S. Jameson, *Journey from the north*, 2 vols. (1969–70) · *CGPLA Eng. & Wales* (1987)
Archives CAC Cam., diary of a visit to Poland · King's Cam. | Bodl. Oxf., Thompson MSS · King's Cam., letters to Rosamund Lehmann · King's Lond., Liddell Hart C., corresp. with Sir B. H. Liddell Hart · University of Bristol Library, Lady Chatterley MSS
Likenesses H. Coster, photographs, 1930–39, NPG [*see illus.*] · G. Argent, photograph, 1970, NPG
Wealth at death £161,528: probate, 13 Jan 1987, *CGPLA Eng. & Wales*

Jameson [*formerly* Coster]**, Rex** [*performing name* Mrs Shufflewick] **(1924–1983),** comedian and female impersonator, was born at Southend-on-Sea on 11 June 1924 of unknown parentage. Dumped as a baby on a police station doorstep, he was taken in and fostered by a Mrs Coster whose surname he initially adopted. One of a line of children she brought up, Jameson was not close to her and she took no interest in his career.

During the Second World War Jameson was in the number 4 gang show unit posted to the Middle East in 1946. In Cairo he became—ominously for both—the drinking companion of the comedian Tony Hancock. After demobilization he joined Alfred Denville's theatre company in Harrow but was sacked after one season for falling down drunk on stage. Renamed Rex Jameson—doubtless after the whisky—he became part of the resident revue team at London's Windmill Theatre.

Jameson's principal variety turn was as a *risqué* vicar. When he approached BBC radio in 1949, such an act was clearly unsuitable. He changed the character to a tipsy, shabby-genteel woman but the *Variety Bandbox* producer, Bryan Sears, was still dubious, fearing the act was too visual. However, so obvious was Jameson's talent that he got his first wireless opportunity on 4 May 1950 as Mrs Shufflewick, and Shufflewick he henceforth remained: his agent (Joe Collins) insisted on his being thus billed and publicized without mention of his real name or sex. Soon a household name, Mrs Shufflewick was frequently heard on such shows as *Midday Music Hall* and *Variety Playhouse* throughout the 1950s and early 1960s. He also became a television star in *Evans Above* (1954) with Norman Evans and *It's a Great Life* (1955–6). He was a draw in variety and summer shows and a popular pantomime dame.

After playing at the London pub the Waterman's Arms, Jameson appeared for the same producer, Dan Farson, in what was probably the high spot of his career, *Nights at the Comedy* (1964), co-starring Jimmy James. Harold Hobson, the distinguished *Sunday Times* theatre critic, was wildly enthusiastic about Mrs Shufflewick's act: 'She is overwhelmingly and shatteringly funny. She manifests that heart-warming honest vulgarity we hear so much about … she is also very relevant to the serious theatre' (Farson, 160). With self-destruction setting in, Rex disappeared to Nottingham in the late 1960s. After he returned to London in the 1970s he played only small variety dates and pubs. (He became a gay cult and a somewhat reluctant participant in seedy drag shows.)

His star status gone, Rex was paid appallingly for such engagements—£5 or just a bottle of whisky. Then he met Patrick Newley who became his manager in 1972 and arranged better terms. Sadly, most of this income went on drink, betting, and personal generosity, and his life in north London was almost that of a dosser. However, he became established at the Black Cap, Camden Town (where his improvised duologues with the voluminous, vituperative drag queen Marc Fleming were quite inspired). He appeared at numerous other venues—notably the Nashville, West Kensington—and co-starred with Dorothy Squires at Lewisham and the London Palladium (1976–8), when he invariably stole the show with his masterly audience control. After one appearance in *Looks Familiar* (1971) Rex was barely seen again on television.

In contrast with the sad indiscipline of Rex Jameson's personal life, his Mrs Shufflewick was a joyful, meticulously crafted creation with superb diction—ultra refined cockney marinated in gin—timing her lines (Harold Hobson again) 'more accurately than Mussolini did his trains' (Farson, 160). Who, having seen her, could forget that tiny fragile creature teetering up to the microphone—dress, hat, gloves, and handbag all in clashing shades of pink, with her scrawny fur: 'Untouched pussy, practically unobtainable in the West End of London' (private information)? Her face, with its pop eyes and red-tipped nose, was that of a solemn clown—suddenly and delightfully breaking into a wide, wicked grin.

Demurely, formally, Shufflewick would launch into some long, rambling saga of outrageous behaviour. The most celebrated began with her indulging in a huge, Homeric drinking bout with a sailor in her local and ended with her stark naked on top of a number 29 bus. 'Shuff's' humour was decidedly Rabelaisian but did not offend; this was partly because of her touching bewilderment in the face of life's grotesqueries, partly because of her delicately pedantic speech: 'I am broadminded to the point of obscenity' (private information). Above all it was because one could not but warm to this battered elf, a miniature genius, in the front rank of music-hall character comedians.

The off-stage Rex Jameson was a quiet little loner in a Chairman Mao cap and a zoot suit, carrying Mrs Shufflewick's accoutrements in a brown-paper carrier bag. He was generous and exceedingly humorous, with a devoted circle of friends and no enemies. Occasionally he would succumb to black, alcohol-induced depressions, feeling himself a failure professionally and privately. Bisexual, he was ashamed of his puny physique and baldness and seemed incapable of forming a stable relationship. But on normal days he was, wrote Patrick Newley, 'Happy go lucky—a sort of impish pixie'. Above all he knew he was gifted, and he worked until the end, which came quickly in 1983 when, walking between two 'gigs', he collapsed in a doorway—an eerie echo of his foundling origins. Jameson died in the Royal Free Hospital, Camden, on 5 March 1983. His funeral at Golders Green was attended by over 500 people—including top show-business names.   JONATHAN CECIL

Sources private information (2004) [Patrick Newley and Mrs Jonathan Cecil] · D. Farson, *Marie Lloyd and music hall* (1972) · J. Fisher, *Funny way to be a hero* (1973) · R. Hudd, *Roy Hudd's cavalcade of variety acts* (1997) · *The Times* (11 March 1983) · d. cert.
Archives BBC WAC, interview with Michael Pointon, 39502 | SOUND BBC WAC, interview with Michael Pointon, 39502
Likenesses photograph, repro. in Hudd, *Roy Hudd's cavalcade*

Jameson, Robert (1774–1854), geologist and natural historian, was born on 11 July 1774 in Leith, the third son in the family of twelve of Thomas Jameson (c.1750–1802), a soap maker of Shetland ancestry, and his wife, Catherine Paton (1750–1794) of Leith. The boredom of grammar school led Jameson to an interest in natural history that proved to be lifelong. Dissuaded from going to sea, he instead attended the University of Edinburgh (1789–96), taking classes in medicine among other subjects. John Walker's lectures on natural history in 1792–3 and a London visit to naturalists and institutions there in 1793 led Jameson to give up medicine without graduating.

In 1794 Jameson and his younger brother Andrew (1779–1861) visited their father's homeland of Shetland. Four years later Robert published the results of that journey as *An Outline of the Mineralogy of the Shetland Islands, and of the Island of Arran* (1798). Further journeys led to publication of *Mineralogy of the Scottish Isles* (1800), an augmented revision of the 1798 work, now including studies of the Orkneys. In both books Jameson adopted a Neptunist position, favouring the agency of water in rock formation—in opposition to the Plutonism of James Hutton, whose theory emphasized the internal heat of the earth.

Now fully committed to natural history, in 1800 Jameson travelled to Germany for coursework in mineralogy and geology under the renowned teacher Abraham Gottlob Werner (also a Neptunist) at the Bergakademie, Freiberg, in Saxony. Forced by his father's death to return to Scotland, Jameson assisted Dr Walker (who was by then blind and very ill) with his classes. After visiting his

Robert Jameson (1774–1854), by Frederick Schenck (after W. Stewart)

brother Andrew, a minister in Dumfriesshire, for several months, Jameson published *A Mineralogical Description of Dumfriesshire* (intended as one of a series) in 1805. In it, he attempted to apply Werner's geological theory to the topography of Scotland and was criticized in the *Edinburgh Review* by James Headrick for having done so.

When Walker died, on 31 December 1803, Jameson succeeded to the Edinburgh chair of natural history, a post he held with distinction for the rest of his life. For more than fifty years he lectured regularly on meteorology, hydrology, mineralogy, geology, botany, zoology, and anthropology. Between 1804 and 1808 he published the most important of his books, a three-volume *System of Mineralogy* based on the teachings of Werner. His equally Wernerian *Treatise on the External Character of Minerals* appeared in 1805 (rev. edn, 1816) and a *Manual of Mineralogy* in 1821. In 1808 Jameson founded the Wernerian Natural History Society, of which he remained president for life.

Following its appearance in 1811–12, the geological theory of Georges Cuvier (which derived in part from Werner's) also attracted Jameson, who contributed prefaces and notes to successive editions of its preliminary discourse, as *Essay on the Theory of the Earth*, translated by Robert Kerr (d. 1813). After Kerr's death the translation was entirely in Jameson's hands, and was much augmented by him in the fifth edition of 1827. The edition was Jameson's second most important work as a geologist, though superseded by Lyell's uniformitarianist *Principles of Geology* three years later. However, between 1813 and 1830, Jameson's version of Cuvier was the most influential popular geology in Britain.

Jameson's role as keeper of the natural history museum at Edinburgh University was both productive and controversial. When originally placed under his care in 1804, its collections were in such poor shape that many specimens could only be discarded. Jameson energetically replaced and enlarged the museum's holdings, secured many valuable additions, and successfully obtained new and larger quarters for the museum as a whole. By the time of his death in 1854 it contained 40,000 rocks and minerals, 10,000 fossils, and 8000 birds, together with numerous crania, skeletons, fishes, reptiles, invertebrates, insects, recent shells, casts, drawings, models, maps, and instruments. In 1826, however, a royal commission investigating the university and its museum received numerous complaints (primarily from members of the Royal Society of Edinburgh) that Jameson arbitrarily restricted admission to the museum and limited its geological and mineralogical exhibits to those which reflected his Wernerian bias. These complaints were probably well founded: James Hutton's rock collection, for instance, remained packed in the same boxes in which it had arrived.

Jameson was first editor of the *Memoirs of the Wernerian Society* (from 1811). Between 1819 and 1824 he founded and co-edited the *Edinburgh Philosophical Journal* with David Brewster. After 1824 Jameson alone continued it as the *Edinburgh New Philosophical Journal*, a distinguished publication remarkably open to important new ideas, even when they contradicted Jameson's own positions. He was also associated with *Blackwood's Edinburgh Magazine*.

Despite his editorial openness, Jameson's numerous writings tended strongly to take sides, usually on behalf of Werner and Cuvier. As a medical student he had presented two papers attacking the geological theory of James Hutton. Though John Playfair, in his *Illustrations of the Huttonian Theory* (1802), cited Jameson's *Scottish Isles* three times, Jameson replied the same year with three papers attacking Playfair. When the three volumes of Charles Lyell's *Principles of Geology* (1830–33) appeared, Jameson opposed them in his correspondence. Even so, his forthright changes of mind were exceptional. Jameson accepted the efficacy of some present-day geological causes in 1808, gave up his belief in the deluge before Buckland and Sedgwick did, and presided over the discrediting of Werner by his own students and in his own journal. He accepted extensive glaciation before Agassiz did, and by 1833 had adopted large parts of the Huttonian theory he had once so vehemently opposed.

During a long and productive lifetime Jameson distinguished himself as a keeper of the Edinburgh University museum and its library, greatly expanding each; as a teacher for fifty years, with many distinguished pupils; as an editor of some consequence; and as an author of numerous books and papers. In addition to works on geology, he wrote or edited various works dealing with travel, geography, history, and ornithology.

Recollections of Jameson present a wiry, thin, sometimes unkempt figure of enormous industry, achievement, and influence, though not one of genius. Autocratic yet humble, stubborn yet fair-minded, intimidating yet friendly, familial yet unmarried, he strove throughout his life to resolve the inherent contradictions on which his mind and self were built. Jameson died on 19 April 1854 and was buried at Warriston cemetery in Edinburgh on 28 April. DENNIS R. DEAN

Sources L. Jameson, *Edinburgh New Philosophical Journal*, 57 (1854), 1–49 · *DNB* · D. R. Dean, *James Hutton and the history of geology* (1992) · private information (2004) · *DSB* · A. C. Chitnis, 'The University of Edinburgh's Natural History Museum and the Huttonian–Wernerian debate', *Annals of Science*, 26 (1970), 85–94 · J. M. Sweet and C. D. Waterston, 'Robert Jameson's approach to the Wernerian theory of the earth, 1796', *Annals of Science*, 23 (1967), 81–95 · J. M. Sweet, 'Robert Jameson's Irish journal, 1797', *Annals of Science*, 23 (1967), 97–126 · J. M. Sweet, 'Robert Jameson in London, 1793', *Annals of Science*, 19 (1963), 81–116 · R. Jameson, *System of mineralogy*, 3: *Elements of geognosy* (1808); repr. with introduction by J. M. Sweet as *The Wernerian theory of the Neptunian origin of rocks* (1976) · J. Headrick, review, *EdinR*, 6 (1805), 228–45 · J. Ritchie, 'A double centenary—two notable naturalists, Robert Jameson and Edward Forbes', *Proceedings of the Royal Society of Edinburgh*, 66B (1955–7), 29–58 · J. M. Sweet, *Scottish Genealogist*, 16 (1969), 1–18

Archives JRL, lecture notes · NA Scot., lecture notes · NL Scot., lecture notes · U. Edin. L., corresp. and papers · U. Glas. L., catalogue of minerals · U. St Andr. L., lecture notes · Wellcome L., lecture notes | Glos. RO, letters to Daniel Ellis · NL Scot., corresp. with John Gibson Lockhart · U. St Andr. L., corresp. with James David Forbes · UCL, letters to George Greenough

Likenesses G. Watson, oils, in or after 1800, Scot. NPG · J. Jenkins, stipple, 1832 (after K. Macleary), BM, NPG; repro. in W. Jerdan, *National portrait gallery of illustrations and eminent personages*, 3 (1832) · sketch, 1850, NL Scot. · engraving, 1854 (after G. Watson), repro. in *Edinburgh New Philosophical Journal* · Lizars, etching (after P. M.), BM, NPG; repro. in J. G. Lockhart, *Peter's letters to his kinsfolk* (1819) · F. Schenck, lithograph (after W. Stewart), NPG [*see illus.*] · bust, U. Edin. L. · miniature

Jameson, Robert William (1805–1868), newspaper editor and author, born at Leith, Scotland, was the youngest son of Thomas Jameson, merchant, and nephew of Robert *Jameson, mineralogist. He was educated at the high school and university of Edinburgh, became a writer to the signet, and practised for many years in Edinburgh. In 1835 he married Christina or Christian Pringle, third daughter of Major-General Pringle of Symington, Midlothian, and they had eleven children, the youngest of whom was the medical practitioner and colonial administrator Sir Leander Starr *Jameson.

In his public life Jameson was a strong radical, and prominent in the reform, anti-slavery, and anti-corn law movements. He was one of the first members of the reformed town council of Edinburgh and Sir John Campbell, later lord chancellor, said that Jameson was the best hustings speaker he ever heard. Jameson was also a writer, and published 'Nimrod', a poem in blank verse (1848), *The Curse of Gold*, a novel (1854), and a tragedy, *Timoleon*, which was acted at the Theatre Royal, Edinburgh, in 1852, and published shortly after, reaching a second edition in the same year.

In 1855 Jameson went to live at Stranraer as editor of the *Wigtownshire Free Press*, and remained there until 1861, when he moved to England, residing first at Sudbury and

afterwards in London. He died at his home, 12 Earl's Court Terrace, Kensington, on 10 December 1868, and was survived by eight of his children.

[ANON.], *rev.* NILANJANA BANERJI

Sources *The Times* (12 Dec 1868) · T. Cooper, ed., *The register, and magazine of biography, a record of births, marriages, deaths and other genealogica and personal occurrences*, 1 (1869), 124–5

Wealth at death under £100: resworn probate, April 1869, CGPLA Eng. & Wales

Jameson, William (*fl.* 1689–1720), university teacher and religious controversialist, was born blind; nothing is known of his parents or background. He may have been William Gemisoune, a student at Glasgow University in 1676, and he may also have been a theology bursar there in 1691. Jameson, who was noted for his learning, first appears as an author in 1689. His blindness would not have precluded study at university, where examinations were oral, nor would his religious affiliations, as a Presbyterian, have stood in the way of his studies, for students in the Scottish system did not swear an oath of allegiance. With the removal of James VII and the establishment of a Presbyterian settlement of religious government the universities were purged of Episcopalians not willing to adhere to the new regime. Presbyterian propagandists such as Jameson saw career prospects opened up. When he failed to get a regency post in 1690 the faculty offered him work in giving weekly Latin lectures on civil and ecclesiastical history, for 200 merks per annum. He continued in this post until the 1720s, when the crown provided additional grants to the university to pay him. Though listed as a professor in some documents he never took part in the university administration, and he should properly be seen as an early example of the modern paid lecturer.

Jameson's writings reflect his continued promotion of Presbyterian views based in the initial triumph of the covenanting party. His first work, *Verus patroclus* of 1689, attacked Quakerism. In *Nazianem Quelela et votum justum: the Fundamentals of the Hierarchy Examined and Disproved* (1697) he refuted hierarchy in church government, and he continued his attack on Episcopalianism with *Roma racoviana et racovia Romana* in 1702. In 1705 he entered the controversy over the Cyprianic bishop between the new principal of Edinburgh University, Gilbert Rule, and the nonjuring Bishop John Sage, with his *Cyprianus Isotimus*. In *The Sum of the Episcopal Controversy* (1713) he sourced his covenanting beliefs in God's covenant with Isaiah. His *Spicilegia antiquitatum Ægypti* (1720) was an attempt to coalesce religious and profane history. Since the Toleration Act of 1712 Presbyterian zeal had lessened, and after 1720 Jameson disappears from view. However, his *Fundamentals of the Hierarchy* continued to be widely read, by figures such as the geologist and evangelical Hugh Miller, well into the nineteenth century.

JAMES TAIT, *rev.* CAMPBELL F. LLOYD

Sources C. Innes, ed., *Munimenta alme Universitatis Glasguensis / Records of the University of Glasgow from its foundation till 1727*, 4 vols., Maitland Club, 72 (1854) · J. D. Mackie, *The University of Glasgow, 1451–1951: a short history* (1954) · J. Coutts, *A history of the University of*

Glasgow (1909) • W. P. Dickson, *Address to the classes of the faculty of theology* (1880)

Archives NL Scot., lectures and notes | U. Edin. L., corresp. with Robert Wodrow

Jameson, William (1796–1873), botanist, was born in Edinburgh on 3 October 1796, the son of William Jameson, a writer to the signet, and his wife, the daughter of John Spottiswoode, a merchant of Edinburgh. From 1814 to 1817 Jameson studied medicine at the University of Edinburgh where he attended the classes of Thomas Charles Hope and Robert Jameson in chemistry and natural history respectively. He graduated MD in 1818, receiving his diploma from the Royal College of Surgeons of Edinburgh. In the same year he became surgeon on a whaling vessel and visited Baffin Bay and botanized on Hare (or Waygat) Island. In 1818–19 he again matriculated in medicine at Edinburgh, and attended lectures on mineralogy. In April 1820 he made his second voyage to Baffin Bay, visiting Duck Island (in lat. 74° N); later that year he sailed for South America as a ship's surgeon, reaching Callao, Peru, in June 1821.

Jameson decided to remain in Peru, first in Lima and then from 1822 to 1826 at Guayaquil. Following an attack of yellow fever he moved to the better climate of Quito, Ecuador, where he lived intermittently for much of the rest of his life. During his first year in Quito he practised medicine, then, in late 1827, he was elected professor of chemistry and botany in the Universidad Central. In 1832 he was appointed chief assayer to the Quito mint. As the result of a government commission in 1835 to investigate the mineral resources of the country Jameson opened and managed silver mines in Azogues, where he lived until 1840. He then returned to his posts at Quito, but, finding the remuneration insufficient and complaining of government corruption, the following year he resumed his medical practice in Guayaquil. In June 1846, at the request of the new president, he returned to his posts at Quito; he held the chair of chemistry until 1858 and that of botany until 1860, when he became an agent of the Ecuador Land Company. He was appointed director of the mint in 1861, in addition to his posts as assayer and treasurer, but again complained about the difficulty in obtaining his rightful salaries.

In 1864 the government appointed Jameson to prepare a synopsis of the flora of Ecuador, of which two volumes and part of a third were printed at Quito in 1865 under the title *Synopsis plantarum aequatoriensium*, but the work was never completed. A new edition, including some pages of autobiography, was published at Quito in 1940.

While in Ecuador Jameson married, had three sons and one daughter, and converted to Roman Catholicism. In late 1869 he travelled to Argentina where his sons had settled, and stayed there for two years before making his way to Edinburgh. He returned to Ecuador via Valparaiso in 1873, but was seized with fever shortly after his arrival in Quito, and died there on 22 June 1873. His funeral was attended by the president of Ecuador.

Jameson had long corresponded with British and other botanists, including William and Joseph Hooker, Sir William Jardine, and J. H. Balfour, and he sent to Britain many new species of plants, among which those of anemone, gentian, and the moss *Dicranum* bear his name. A genus of ferns described by Hooker and Greville is also called *Jamesonia*. In recognition of his services to science, in 1866 Jameson was created a *caballero* by Isabella II of Spain. He was the author of nine papers, mainly on botanical subjects, but the *Synopsis* was his only important work.

ANDREW GROUT

Sources M. J. Anderson, 'William Jameson and the Quito mint', *Proceedings of the XIth International Numismatic Congress*, [Brussels 1991], ed. M. Hoc, 4 (1993), 147–50 • *Gardeners' Chronicle* (7 Dec 1872), 1622 • *Transactions of the Botanical Society* [Edinburgh], 12 (1873), 19–28 • F. A. Stafleu and R. S. Cowan, *Taxonomic literature: a selective guide*, 2nd edn, 2, Regnum Vegetabile, 98 (1979), 421 • Desmond, *Botanists*, rev. edn, 379 • *Gardeners' Chronicle* (23 Aug 1873), 1151 • *Journal of Botany, British and Foreign*, 11 (1873), 318–19 • G. Jameson, *Synopsis plantarum aequatoriensium*, new edn (1940), 5–10 • R. K. Greville, 'Description of a new species of Potentilla, from the west coast of Greenland', *Memoirs of the Wernerian Natural History Society*, 3 (1821), 416–36 • *Catalogue of scientific papers*, Royal Society, 19 vols. (1867–1925) • M. Anderson, *A numismatic history of Ecuador* (2001), appx [on William Jameson]

Archives Harvard U., Gray Herbarium, papers • Linn. Soc. • RBG Kew, MSS • Warrington Library

Likenesses R. J. Lane, print, 1841, BM, NPG • A. Salas, oils, 1842, RBG Kew • photograph (in later life), repro. in M. Acosta-Solis, *Naturalistas y viajeros científicos que han contribuido al conocimiento florístico y fito-geográfico del Ecuador* (1968) • portrait, Hunt Institute for Botanical Documentation, Pittsburgh, Pennsylvania

Jameson, William (1815–1882), army surgeon and botanist, was born at Leith, Midlothian, went to the high school at Edinburgh, and then studied medicine at the local university where his uncle, Robert Jameson, was professor of natural history. He qualified as LRCS in 1836 and was appointed assistant surgeon in the Bengal medical service in August 1838. After arrival in Calcutta Jameson was temporarily appointed curator of the museum of the Asiatic Society of Bengal. Before long, however, he was posted to a battery of artillery at Cawnpore. In 1841 he was civil surgeon at Ambala, and in the same year led an expedition to the River Indus to assess the effects of recent severe flooding. Jameson was foiled in his attempt to reach the reputed source of the flooding when he and his Sikh escort were captured in the hills west of Peshawar. Through the intervention of the Sikh government he was freed after four months' imprisonment at Kohat. Despite losing his notebooks and specimens he was able to make a report on the geology and zoology of the Punjab and part of Afghanistan (published in the *Journal of the Asiatic Society of Bengal*, 12, 1843, 183–227).

In 1842 Jameson succeeded Hugh Falconer as superintendent of the garden at Saharanpur, where he concentrated on the propagation of horticultural plants for private gardens, public parks, and military cantonments. He established tea plantations in northern India, and tried to convince villagers that tea could be grown as a hardy crop, not requiring much care. He introduced American maize to Kumaon and Garhwal and experimented with growing flax. He contributed five articles, mainly zoological, to the

Journal of the Asiatic Society of Bengal and nine articles, mostly on economic crops, to the *Journal of the Agri-Horticultural Society of India.*

Jameson was promoted to surgeon in April 1852 and to surgeon-major in February 1859. He retired on 31 December 1875 and started a tea plantation at Dehra Dun in northern India. The viceroy made him a companion of the Indian Empire in January 1878 in recognition of his services. He died at Dehra Dun on 18 March 1882, leaving a widow, and two sons who served in the staff corps of the Indian army.　　　　　　　　　　　　　　RAY DESMOND

Sources H. Cleghorn, *Transactions of the Botanical Society* [Edinburgh], 14 (1883), 288–95 · R. Desmond, *The European discovery of the Indian flora* (1992) · I. H. Buckill, *Chapters on the history of botany in India* (Calcutta, 1965)

Archives RBG Kew, Indian plant specimens · RBG Kew, letters · RBG Kew, map · RBG Kew, specimens · U. Edin. L., family corresp.

Jameson, Sir (William) Wilson (1885–1962), medical officer and medical adviser, was born at Craigie, Perth, on 12 May 1885, the second of the three children and elder son of John Wilson Jameson (1814–1891) and his second wife, Isabella Milne (1852–1947). His father, who was joint manager of a bank in Perth, died when Jameson was six, and his mother, who had been a schoolteacher and came from Aberdeen, returned there for the sake of its educational opportunities. After ten years at the grammar school, in 1902 Jameson entered King's College in Aberdeen University; he graduated in arts in 1905 before transferring to Marischal College to qualify MB, ChB, with distinction, in 1909. He had been a notable athlete at school, but played only golf thereafter. He was president of the students' representative council in 1907, revealing the diplomatic ability which was to characterize his later life.

After qualifying Jameson went to London, where he spent a year in resident posts at the Prince of Wales General Hospital. He then worked for two years on tuberculosis at the City of London Hospital for Diseases of the Chest, at Victoria Park. He obtained the MD from Aberdeen University, with commendation, in 1912, his thesis dealing with the treatment of pulmonary tuberculosis. After a year at Eastbourne in general practice he returned to London, as an assistant medical officer to the Hackney Hospital, in 1913; he also worked at St George's Home in Chelsea in 1914. He became a member of the Royal College of Physicians in 1913 and obtained the DPH in 1914 after attending a part-time course at University College, London. Professor H. R. Kenwood chose Jameson from that course as an assistant lecturer in the department, and Jameson thus entered the first of the three phases of his main medical work.

From 1915 to 1919 Jameson was in the Royal Army Medical Corps, working mainly on hygiene and laboratory services, and serving in France and Italy. After demobilization he returned to the teaching of public health at University College, and in 1920 he became medical officer of health for Finchley and deputy medical officer of health for Marylebone. The first edition of his *Synopsis of Hygiene*, with F. T. Marchant, was published in 1920. In 1922 he was called to the bar by the Middle Temple. In 1925 he became medical officer of health for Hornsey, and in 1926 he was appointed lecturer at Guy's Hospital.

Jameson continued to teach at University College until in 1929 he took up the post of first professor of public health at the London School of Hygiene and Tropical Medicine, the first independent postgraduate school in London University. This institution gave fresh impetus to the teaching of preventive medicine and medical administration throughout the world. Jameson became its dean in 1931 and contributed more than anyone to its success. He travelled widely in North America, Burma, Malaya, west and east Africa, and Europe. The reputation of his brilliant group of colleagues, including W. W. C. Topley, P. A. Buxton, R. T. Leiper, Graham Wilson, Major Greenwood, and A. B. Hill, as well as that of Jameson himself, brought students from all over the world to Jameson's own course for the diploma in public health as well as to other courses. Jameson was a fine teacher and his course was particularly broadly based. In other fields of medicine in London he also became influential in discussions which prepared the way for necessary changes in the organization of British medicine.

The outbreak of war in 1939 temporarily brought the diploma course to an end, and Jameson had to deal with the evacuation of the departments of the school which, among its other activities, was to contribute so much to the Emergency Public Health Laboratory Service. In 1940 Jameson acted as part-time medical adviser to the Colonial Office; this brought him in contact with Malcolm MacDonald, who became minister of health in May 1940, and who in November of that year invited Jameson to become chief medical officer, on the retirement of Sir Arthur MacNalty.

Jameson remained chief medical officer of the Ministry of Health and of the Board of Education until 1950. His responsibilities were concerned with the nation's health, and he helped to develop the emergency services required to deal with casualties and other civilian needs arising from the large movements of people, particularly children, and from wartime conditions. His report on the nation's health during the six years of the war was published in 1946. It was difficult to maintain services in such conditions, but there were two great contributions which were largely inspired by Jameson. One was the special attention given to the nutrition of children and expectant mothers, for which Jameson chaired an advisory committee to the Ministry of Food. The other was the introduction of a nationwide scheme for immunization against diphtheria, which not only prevented the epidemic increase which might have been expected in wartime but actually brought about the near-elimination of the disease.

As a member of the Goodenough committee (1942–4) Jameson made a major contribution to the planned reorganization of medical education which took place after the war. During the war his personal influence was directed towards better public information on health, on such subjects as immunization, tuberculosis, and venereal disease, on which he was one of the first people to broadcast, and on the problem of controlling the prevalence of the head louse and the itch mite.

The Ministry of Health, consequent upon the publication of the Beveridge report in 1942, produced a plan for a national health service, in a white paper in February 1944. From then until the introduction of the National Health Service in 1948 there was constant negotiation and preparation. Jameson's was one of the most important influences in these developments and he remained chief medical officer through the difficult transition period until the service was nearly two years old. At no time was Jameson's capacity for attracting the support of leading figures in the profession and obtaining their confidence more manifest or more important. That the health service was established without a final breach between the government and the medical profession was perhaps as much due to Jameson as to anyone.

After he retired in 1950 Jameson became medical adviser to the King Edward's Hospital Fund for London, and in the next ten years he influenced most of the important educational work of the fund—in hospital administration, nursing administration, and catering—through his direct participation and through teaching. He gained universal esteem in an organization in which the medical influence had previously been almost entirely that of the leading consultants in London teaching hospitals. He did more than anyone to broaden the interests of the fund and to lead it into supporting some of the less glamorous and yet extremely important areas of hospital work. Despite periods of ill health he continued working even after the death of his first wife in 1958; he finally retired in 1960.

Jameson was elected FRCP in 1930, knighted in 1939 while still at the London School of Hygiene and Tropical Medicine, and appointed KCB (1943) and GBE (1949) while at the Ministry of Health. He received a number of honorary degrees, was Harveian orator and Bisset Hawkins medallist of the Royal College of Physicians, and received the Lasker award of the American Public Health Association. He was master of the Society of Apothecaries and he received the United States medal of freedom.

Wilson Jameson was of middle height and modest presence, with a high forehead and an air of unfailing benignity. He was cool, persuasive, and always lucid; his friendly voice never lost its Aberdonian intonation. He made many friends in the medical and other circles in which he moved, but his intimates were few. His students and colleagues held him in admiration and affection, the justification for which he was never able to understand. He did not want the honours that were heaped upon him. His remark that 'It's a terrible thing to have a sense of your own dignity' could never have been made of him, but in his generation no member of his own profession had a greater right to that dignity.

In 1916 Jameson married Pauline Frances (d. 1958), daughter of James Paul Helm, sheep farmer. He had met her while he was still a medical student. They had two daughters. On 6 February 1959 he married Constance Helen Scotland (b. 1906/7), a nurse, daughter of Dr Herbert Dobie. Jameson died in University College Hospital, London, on 18 October 1962. His second wife survived him. A memorial service was held at St James's, Piccadilly, on 31 October. GEORGE E. GODBER

Sources N. Goodman, *Wilson Jameson, architect of national health* (1970) · private information (1981) · personal knowledge (2004) · *CGPLA Eng. & Wales* (1962) · m. cert., 1959
Likenesses W. Stoneman, photograph, 1941, NPG · photograph, repro. in Goodman, *Wilson Jameson*
Wealth at death £17,894 15s. 9d.: probate, 28 Nov 1962, *CGPLA Eng. & Wales*

Jamesone, George (1589/90–1644), portrait painter, was born in Aberdeen between the autumn of 1589 and the summer of 1590, the third son and fourth child of a master mason, Andrew Jamesone, and his wife, Marjory Anderson. Both of these families were prosperous and well established in the city. Jamesone had two brothers, Andrew and David, who died young, David before 1607 and Andrew in 1613. His younger brother William became a lawyer and practised in Edinburgh until his death in 1632.

A great part of Jamesone's significance resides in the fact that he is the earliest British-born painter of whom it is possible to give a completely rounded picture, of both his life and his work. His achievement has to be seen in the context of the dominance of the art of portraiture in Britain by artists from the continent during the sixteenth and seventeenth centuries.

In 1612 Jamesone began an eight-year apprenticeship as a painter in Edinburgh. This rather unusual step, at a relatively late age, may have been made possible because his elder brother Andrew was still alive and the likely successor to his father's business. Jamesone's master, John Anderson, who was probably a relative, was a decorative painter—at a time when painted interiors were common in larger Scottish houses—and it remains unclear by what precise means Jamesone evolved into a portrait painter. Although he is known to have visited London in later life, there is no evidence of travels to the continent.

From 1620, when he painted Sir Paul Menzies, provost of Aberdeen (Marischal College, Aberdeen), he went on to establish a substantial practice as a portrait painter which brought him considerable wealth and contemporary fame. His practice soon extended from the burgess and academic circles of Aberdeen to encompass the northern aristocracy, and eventually that of the entire country. During the 1620s he must have experienced some competition from Adam de Colone, and he may well have been influenced by the more cosmopolitan manner of that Netherlandish-trained artist. By comparison with de Colone, his technical methods were fragile, and the resultant damage to many of his paintings has made his qualities difficult to assess. Two of his finest surviving paintings belong to this decade, the portraits of Mary Erskine, Countess Marischal (1626; National Gallery of Scotland, Edinburgh), and the young James Graham, future marquess of Montrose (1629; priv. coll.). These have a fresh, atmospheric, even 'modern', quality that distinguishes

George Jamesone (1589/90–1644), self-portrait, *c*.1642–3

them from other native British painters of the late Jacobean and Caroline periods.

About 1625 Jamesone married Isobel Tosche (*b*. 1608?), who seems to have brought considerable property to the marriage. By 1630 they had rights to five dwelling houses in Aberdeen, though they presumably lived in the rather grand house (now destroyed) on the north side of Schoolhill which Jamesone had inherited from his father in 1607. The couple are known to have had five sons and four daughters. None of the sons survived for long. Of the two daughters who reached adulthood, Marjory (the firstborn) and Mary, the former married an advocate, John Alexander. Isobel Tosche remarried after Jamesone's death and lived until 1680.

From 1633 until his death Jamesone's working life centred on Edinburgh, where he leased premises on the north side of the High Street, near the Netherbow Gate. In the former year he was commissioned by the council of Edinburgh to provide a variety of work to decorate the city for the triumphal entry of Charles I—an event orchestrated by William Drummond of Hawthornden. Some of the work was decorative history painting, but the main part was a series of 'fancy' portraits of the king's ancestors, of which a number survive.

This work inspired a major patron in the mid-1630s, Sir Colin Campbell of Glenorchy, who commissioned another series of Scottish kings and queens, portraits of his female ancestors, and a number of portraits of eminent contemporaries to whom Campbell was related. In addition, he commissioned the large *Glenorchy Family-Tree* (Scot. NPG), which falls between the decorative and portrait traditions. At the same time, on 6 April 1636, Jamesone took his only recorded apprentice, the nineteen-year-old Londoner John Michael Wright.

Jamesone's consciousness of the status he had attained in the latter part of his life was expressed both by his creation of an ornamental garden in Aberdeen and by a self-portrait in his workroom, in which he is surrounded by his paintings and the accoutrements of success (Scot. NPG). At the same time he acquired two estates outside

Aberdeen—in effect, the result of two large loans to Gilbert Hay, earl of Erroll and lord high constable of Scotland. He also became embroiled in the political troubles of the times, acting as a diplomat for Aberdeen to the forces of the covenant. This led to his imprisonment in Edinburgh as a 'delinquent' for a number of months in 1639.

This turmoil, as well as a lack of rivals, led to a deterioration of Jamesone's work in the final years of his life. His death occurred at some time after September 1644, when Montrose sacked Aberdeen, and before 11 December of the same year, when his surviving daughters were served as his heirs. Not for the first time he was praised in contemporary Latin verse, this time in a lamentation by David Wedderburn, an indication of the near-mythic national status that Jamesone had attained in his own lifetime.

DUNCAN THOMSON

Sources D. Thomson, *The life and art of George Jamesone* (1974) · D. Thomson, *Painting in Scotland, 1570–1650* (1975) [exhibition catalogue, Scot. NPG, 21 Aug – 21 Sept 1975]
Likenesses G. Jamesone, self-portrait, oils, *c*.1637, Aberdeen Art Gallery · G. Jamesone, self-portrait, oils, *c*.1642–1643, Scot. NPG [*see illus.*] · A. Jamesone, etching, 1728 (after G. Jamesone), BM · G. Jamesone, self-portrait, oils, Scot. NPG
Wealth at death owned five properties in Aberdeen, and two estates outside the city: Thomson, *The life and art*

Jamieson, Christina (1864–1942), writer and suffragist, was born on 30 June 1864 at Cruisdale, Sandness, Shetland, the second of the seven children of Robert Jamieson (1827–1899), schoolmaster, and Barbara Laing (1838–1923), daughter of a schoolmaster and land surveyor. Jamieson received her education at the school in Sandness, where her father was headmaster, and she acted for a while as a pupil teacher there. Several of her brothers went on to become eminent academics on the mainland, but she remained in Shetland for most of her life.

Robert Jamieson was a contributor of articles and stories to *The Scotsman*, and his daughter followed suit. In the late 1890s she began to write short stories and factual pieces for weekly and other papers, sometimes under the *nom de plume* John Cranston. These writings were usually about her native islands, and often had a strong antiquarian content. She continued to write throughout her life, often in a robust Shetland dialect.

When Robert Jamieson died in 1899, Jamieson and her mother moved to Lerwick. They eventually lived in Twagios House, a large eighteenth-century building at the south side of the town, and for several years Jamieson used it as a base for her suffragist activities. She helped to found the Shetland Women's Suffrage Society in 1909 and guided its affiliation to the National Union of Women's Suffrage Societies. She designed a local banner, and helped to carry it in processions as far afield as London. Her other main contribution to the movement was literary and oratorical: she wrote numerous pro-suffrage items for the local press, lectured on the movement's history to the Lerwick Literary and Debating Society in March 1909, and published a pamphlet based on the lecture (*Sketch of Votes for Women*, 1909). In 1910 she wrote a moving article on the economic and emotional plight of the women of Shetland (*Shetland Times*, 22 and 29 January 1910).

Jamieson's party political adherence is unknown, but she was often friendly to unpopular causes. About 1900 she wrote an essay with sympathetic remarks about pro-Boers (Shetland Archives, MS D.18/32/23), and she befriended and assisted local socialists in the inter-war period. In the 1920s and 1930s she shared Twagios House with her nephew Bertie Jamieson, an active communist. During the First World War she played an important and, as far as her sex was concerned, unique part in public life in the islands: in 1916 she became a member of Lerwick school board, and in 1918 she became interim chairman of it. She was also a member of the county committee on secondary education, and eventually of the education authority. In all these forums she was a forthright speaker.

In her later years Jamieson devoted her attention to antiquarian and folklore matters. In 1930 she founded the Shetland Folklore Society, which specialized in recreating old Shetland dances for audiences in Lerwick and throughout the islands. Jamieson's kitchen at Twagios was the site of many of these performances. In 1931 she encouraged the education authority to prepare a 'Shetland Book' for local scholars (a project which came to fruition in 1967). With the antiquarian E. S. Reid Tait, and with the assistance of her nephew Bertie Jamieson, she transcribed for publication extracts from the old kirk session minutes of her native parish of Walls and Sandness. These were published as *The Hjaltland Miscellany*, volumes 2 and 3 (1937 and 1939); volume 2 contains superb introductory essays by Jamieson. Jamieson had emigrated to New Zealand in 1935 to live with a brother, in a fruitless search for relief from asthma. She died at Nelson, New Zealand, on 23 March 1942. BRIAN SMITH

Sources *Shetland Times* (4 June 1942) · *Shetland News* (6 June 1942) · misc. MSS, Shetland Archives, D. 18/38 · L. Leneman, *A guid cause: the women's suffrage movement in Scotland* (1995) [rev. 1995]
Archives Shetland Archives, Lerwick, corresp. and papers
Likenesses photograph, repro. in Leneman, *A guid cause*, 85

Jamieson, George Auldjo (1828–1900), accountant, was born at Castle Hill, Aberdeen, on 1 May 1828, the son of James Jamieson MD, a former naval surgeon. He was educated at Aberdeen grammar school and he graduated from Aberdeen University in 1846. After working in an Aberdeen law firm, he moved to Edinburgh, around 1849, to join his uncle, George Auldjo Esson, in the accountancy firm Lindsay and Esson. Jamieson was soon made a partner and his rapid progress was confirmed when, in 1854, he became a founder member of the Society of Accountants in Edinburgh. In 1879 he was appointed judicial factor in the Orr-Ewing case, notable for its resolution of conflicts between Scots and English law. Jamieson's adept handling of the issues, as well as his appointment as one of the liquidators of the City of Glasgow Bank in 1878, enhanced his growing reputation as one of Scotland's leading chartered accountants.

During the 1880s and 1890s, with Edinburgh maturing

George Auldjo Jamieson (1828–1900), by Sir George Reid

as an international financial centre, Jamieson and many of his fellow chartered accountants led the way in directing Scottish capital abroad. Jamieson's personal involvement in foreign investment also grew at this time, and by his death he owned shares in overseas enterprises probated at £51,500.

A significant aspect of Jamieson's business career was his involvement with the Arizona Copper Company, formed in 1882 to purchase mines in a desolate part of the south-western United States. Despite initial optimism, difficulties mounted, and amid rumours of share-rigging by the original board, calls for a man of proven integrity to head the firm led to Jamieson being appointed chairman in November 1883. He guided the firm through a major financial reconstruction and modernization programme, and by 1892, when he toured America, it was firmly set on a course of rising profitability, with accumulated dividends amounting to more than £6 million by 1918.

Jamieson was undoubtedly one of the most successful and influential Scottish chartered accountants in the late nineteenth century. He was a director of numerous companies by the late 1890s, including the Royal Bank of Scotland and the North British and Mercantile Insurance Company, both at the heart of Scotland's close-knit financial community, and was president of the Society of Accountants in Edinburgh, 1882–8. He appears to have been conservative in many respects, and deliberated long over complex issues, but he was also capable of great energy and acumen, as displayed in his overseas investment activities.

A wide knowledge of financial affairs brought him on to a number of royal commissions, including those on mining royalties (1889) and on company law (1895). In 1860 he was elected a fellow of the Royal Society of Edinburgh, and in 1887 he attended the Manchester meeting of the British Association, contributing two papers on finance.

Jamieson was for a long period chairman of Edinburgh West Conservative Association, and in 1885 unsuccessfully stood as parliamentary candidate for Edinburgh West. In 1889 he entered Edinburgh city council as member for St Luke's ward, a seat he held until his death, and at various times was chairman of the council's law committee. He was also a commissioner of supply for the city and county of Edinburgh, in which capacity he was an ardent opponent of the municipal takeover of gas, tramway, and electric lighting operations.

Jamieson was married twice—to Mary Jane Souter Robertson, and afterwards to Susan Helena Oliphant. He had five sons (one of whom died in the Second South African War) and two daughters. Religion played a strong part in his life and he was a member and office bearer of St John's Episcopal Church, Edinburgh, as well as chancellor of the episcopal diocese of Aberdeen. He also supported a number of charitable organizations such as the Edinburgh Association for Incurables.

Jamieson died suddenly at the New Club, Edinburgh, on the evening of 18 July 1900, following an influenza attack. He was buried on 21 July at Dean cemetery, Edinburgh, in a ceremony attended by the earls of Aberdeen and Haddington, and the municipal corporation of Edinburgh. He was survived by his second wife.

CHRISTOPHER J. SCHMITZ

Sources *The Scotsman* (20 July 1900) · R. Brown, *A history of accounting and accountants* (1905) · J. A. Stewart, *Pioneers of a profession: chartered accountants to 1879* (1977) · W. T. Jackson, *The enterprising Scot: investors in the American west after 1873* (1968) · annual returns of capital, shareholders, and directors, Arizona Copper Co. Ltd, 1882–1900, NA Scot., BT2/1144, 1375 · A. R. Davidson, *The history of the Faculty of Actuaries in Scotland, 1856–1956* (1956)

Likenesses G. Reid, oils, Institute of Chartered Accountants, Edinburgh [*see illus.*]

Wealth at death £154,023 3s. 2d.: confirmation, 6 Nov 1900, *CCI* · £1800: additional estate, 10 Dec 1900, *CCI* · £8746 5s.: additional estate, 30 Jan 1901, *CCI* · £3375 7s. 6d.: additional estate, 16 June 1903, *CCI* · £16,373 6s. 6d.: additional estate, 28 Jan 1908, *CCI*

Jamieson, John (1759–1838), antiquary and philologist, was born in Glasgow on 5 March 1759, the son of the Revd John Jamieson, an Anti-Burgher minister, and his wife, *née* Cleland. He was educated at a school kept by his father's precentor (to 1765), at the Latin Grammar School, Glasgow (1765–6), and at home (1766–8). At the age of nine he entered Glasgow University, where his interest in language was furthered by the teaching of the Revd George Muirhead, professor of humanity—'and to it I may most probably ascribe that partiality for philological and etymological research in which I have ever since had so much pleasure' (Johnstone, x). From 1773 he studied the necessary course in theology with the Associate Presbytery of Glasgow, and in 1780 he was licensed to preach; shortly afterwards he was appointed minister to a congregation in Forfar, where he remained for seventeen years. There, on 21 July 1781, he married Charlotte Watson, daughter of Robert Watson of Shielhill, Forfarshire. Their marriage lasted fifty-five years and they had seventeen children.

Jamieson's evangelical and polemical writings attracted attention, and he was called to Edinburgh by the Nicolson Street congregation of Anti-Burghers; he became their minister in 1797. He became widely known and respected for his scholarship and social worth. His deep convictions were balanced by ecumenical sympathies, and he was deeply gratified in 1820 by the union of the closely related Secessionist sects the Burghers and the Anti-Burghers, a reconciliation largely due to his own suggestion and guidance.

In 1788, in recognition of his ability and attainments, after replying to Priestley's *History of Early Opinions* in his own *Vindication of the Doctrine of Scripture* (2 vols., 1795), Jamieson received from the college of New Jersey the degree of DD. His other honours included membership of the Society of Scottish Antiquaries, of the Royal Physical Society of Edinburgh, of the American Antiquarian Society of Boston, United States, and of the Copenhagen Society of Northern Literature. He was also a royal associate of the first class of the Royal Society of Literature instituted by George IV.

Jamieson's chief work, the *Etymological Dictionary of the Scottish Language*, appeared, with an elaborate preliminary dissertation, in two volumes in 1808. While Jamieson was in Forfar an interview with the Danish scholar Grim Thorkelin, professor of antiquities in Copenhagen, had suggested this work. His special knowledge and great industry enabled him to complete it almost single-handedly, with Thomas Ruddiman's glossary to Gavin Douglas's translation of the *Aeneid* as a basis. He prepared a valuable abridgement in 1818 (reissued in 1846 with a prefatory memoir by John Johnstone), and by further industry and perseverance, aided by numerous devoted volunteers, he added two supplementary volumes in 1825. The work was reissued with additions in 1840. It is somewhat weak in philology, but is generally admirable in definition and illustration, and provides 'accurately referenced quotations, usually in chronological order' (McArthur, 902); it exhibits a rare grasp of folklore and important provincialisms. The introductory dissertation, ingeniously supporting an obsolete theory regarding the Gothic influence on the Scottish language, has long had a merely antiquarian interest. The revised edition (1879–87), by John Longmuir and David Donaldson, had a high philological as well as literary value.

Jamieson's other works included *Socinianism Unmasked* (1786); a poem, *The Sorrows of Slavery* (1789); *Sermons on the Heart* (2 vols., 1791); *Congal and Fenella, a Tale* (1791); *Remarks on Rowland Hill's Journal* (1799), which answered his attacks on the Secessionist churches; *Important Trial in the Court of Conscience* (1806); *A Historical Account of the Ancient Culdees of*

Iona (1811), published, through Walter Scott's active generosity, by James Ballantyne (*Letters of Sir Walter Scott*, 3.437; 1.39 n. 1); and *Hermes Scythicus* (1814), which expounded affinities between the Gothic (Germanic) and the classical tongues.

Apart from juvenile efforts Jamieson likewise wrote on such diverse themes as rhetoric, cremation, and the royal palaces of Scotland, besides publishing occasional sermons. In 1820 he issued in two volumes well-edited versions of Barbour's *Bruce* and Blind Harry's *Wallace*, which Scott commended to his friends (*Letters of Sir Walter Scott*, 3.437, 480, 522). He also prepared extensive autobiographical notes, on which others drew. The Revd Andrew Somerville, who knew him well, wrote of 'his extensive learning, his urbane deportment, his entertaining conversation, and his consistency of character' (Somerville, xxv).

Jamieson outlived his wife, who died about 1836, and all but three of his children; his second son, Mr Robert Jamieson, died in 1835 after displaying brilliant promise at the Scottish bar. After a period of bilious and nervous attacks he died on 12 July 1838 at his house in George's Square, Edinburgh, and is thought to have been buried in the city. To Sir Walter Scott, Jamieson was 'an excellent good man and full of auld Scottish cracks' (*Journal*, 176).

T. W. BAYNE, rev. JOHN D. HAIGH

Sources J. Johnstone, 'Preface' and 'Memoir of Dr. Jamieson', in J. Jamieson, *A dictionary of the Scottish language*, ed. J. Johnstone (1846), v–vi, ix–xvi · A. Somerville, 'Preface' and 'Memoir', in J. Jamieson, *Reality of the gracious influence of the Holy Spirit* (1844) · *The journal of Sir Walter Scott*, ed. W. E. K. Anderson (1972), 176–8, 522 · *The letters of Sir Walter Scott*, ed. H. J. C. Grierson and others, centenary edn, 12 vols. (1932–79) · 'Scottish dictionaries', *The Oxford companion to the English language*, ed. T. McArthur (1992), 901–3 · F. J. Hausmann and others, eds., *Wörterbücher: ein internationales Handbuch zur Lexikographie / Dictionaries: an international encyclopedia of lexicography*, 2 (Berlin, 1989), 1984 · W. Anderson, *The Scottish nation*, 2 (1866) · T. Thomson, ed., *A biographical dictionary of eminent Scotsmen*, rev. edn (1868), 2.386–7 · IGI
Archives BL, letters to Lord Spencer · Bodl. Oxf., letters to Richard Heber · NL Scot., corresp. with Sir Robert Liston
Likenesses J. Kay, caricature, etching, 1799, BM · E. Mitchell, line engraving, BM, NPG; repro. in *Theological and Biblical Magazine* (1804) · W. Yellowlees, portrait, Scot. NPG
Wealth at death pension of 100 guineas: Johnstone, 'Memoir'

Jamieson, John Paul. See Jameson, John Paul (1659–1700).

Jamieson, Robert (1772?–1844), antiquary and ballad collector, was a native of Moray, and, after graduating from King's College, Aberdeen, in 1793, was appointed an assistant classical teacher at Macclesfield, Cheshire, in 1796. There he designed a collection of Scottish ballads and was engaged on it for several years after 1800, in England and while working as a tutor in Riga, 1805–9. He announced his work in the *Scots Magazine* in 1803, mentioning at the same time his indebtedness to the friendship of Sir Walter Scott. He published in 1806 two volumes entitled *Popular ballads and songs, from tradition, manuscript, and scarce editions, with translations of similar pieces from the antient Danish language and a few originals by the editor*.

Scott, who held a high opinion of Jamieson, emphasized in his 1830 essay on popular poetry prefaced to later editions of his *Border Minstrelsy* Jamieson's discovery of the undoubted kinship between Scandinavian and Scottish ballads, 'a circumstance which no antiquary had before so much as suspected'. Jamieson owed this discovery to the Icelandic antiquary G. J. Thorkelin's gift to him of *Kaempe viser* (ed. Peder Syv, Copenhagen, 1695), a volume of Danish heroic ballads. His long letter to Scott on the subject, which forms an essay on comparative literature unparalleled at the time in this field, is included in the second volume of his *Popular Ballads and Songs*. Like Scott's *Border Minstrelsy* (1802–3), many of Jamieson's *Ballads* derive from manuscript transcripts made by Mrs Brown, widow of the minister of Falkland, Fife. They are annotated with scholarship and taste; and in the original section Jamieson's own lyrics 'The Quern Lilt' and 'My Wife's a Winsome Wee Thing' secure for him a place among minor Scottish singers. In addition to his *Popular Ballads* Jamieson edited with Henry Weber and Sir Walter Scott *Illustrations of Northern Antiquities* (1814); in 1818 he prepared a new edition of Edward Burt's *Letters from the North* (1818), to which Scott again contributed.

In 1809 Jamieson became, through Scott's influence, assistant to the depute-clerk-register in the General Register House, Edinburgh, and he held the post until about 1843, when he was appointed one of the poor brethren of the Charterhouse in London. He broke with Scott in 1821 over his failure to secure the post of keeper of the Advocates' Library, Edinburgh. Jamieson died in the Charterhouse on 24 September 1844.

T. W. BAYNE, rev. HARRIET HARVEY WOOD

Sources Thorkelin correspondence, U. Edin. L., MS La. III. 379 · NL Scot., Jamieson MSS · T. Constable, *Archibald Constable and his literary correspondents*, 1 (1873) · P. J. Anderson, ed., *Roll of alumni in arts of the University and King's College of Aberdeen, 1596–1860* (1900) · Nichols, *Illustrations*, vols. 7–8 · *The letters of Sir Walter Scott*, ed. H. J. C. Grierson and others, centenary edn, 12 vols. (1932–79) · G. Neilson, 'A bundle of ballads', *Essays and Studies by Members of the English Association*, 7 (1921) · E. H. Harvey Wood, 'Letters to an antiquary: literary correspondence of G. J. Thorkelin (1752–1829)', PhD diss., U. Edin., 1972 · H. Harvey Wood, 'Scott and Jamieson: the relationship between two ballad collectors', *Studies in Scottish Literature*, 9 (1971–2), 2–3, 71–96 · d. cert.
Archives BL, letters to Edward Hawkins · NL Scot., letters to Archibald Constable; corresp. with Sir Walter Scott · U. Edin. L., corresp. with Grimr Thorkelin

Jamieson, Robert (1791/2–1861), merchant, traded to South America, Brazil, India, and China. He is variously described as being of Liverpool, Glasgow, and London, but certainly traded from the City of London between 1836 and 1861. He sought to open up west African rivers to navigation and commerce, particularly in palm oil. His schooner, the *Warree*, went to the Niger in 1838. In 1839 he built and equipped the steamer *Ethiope*, which, under the command of John Beecroft, explored several west African rivers, including the Fermoso and particularly the distributaries of the Niger to higher points, in some instances, than had previously been reached. Narratives of these explorations were communicated by Jamieson to the Royal Geographical Society and afterwards published in its *Journal*. When the Melbourne ministry resolved to send the African Colonization Expedition to the Niger,

Jamieson denounced the scheme in two *Appeals* (1840 and 1841). The expedition broke up, through disease and disaster, in September 1841, and on 25 October most of the surviving colonists and their ship, the *Albert*, were rescued by the *Ethiope*. Jamieson pointed out the fulfilment of his prophecies in a *Sequel to Two Appeals* (1843). In 1859 he published *Commerce with Africa*, emphasizing the inadequacy of treaties for the suppression of the African slave trade, and urging the use of the land route from the Cross River to the Niger, to avoid the swamps of the delta where Europeans so easily succumbed to malaria. In 1840 he was offered, but declined, a vice-presidency of the Institut d'Afrique of France. He died at 18 Gloucester Square, London, on 5 April 1861, leaving a substantial fortune.

Described by contemporaries as a philanthropist, Jamieson was a shrewd businessman who recognized Beecroft as the most likely person to open up the Niger area to trade and who had the means to promote his ideas. He argued for the suppression of the slave trade but none the less his interests remained primarily commercial.

JAMES TAIT, rev. ELIZABETH BAIGENT

Sources J. Beecroft, 'On Benin and the upper course of the River Quorra or Niger', *Journal of the Royal Geographical Society*, 11 (1840), 184–90 · J. Beecroft, 'Account of a visit to the capital of Benin', *Journal of the Royal Geographical Society*, 11 (1840), 190–92 · *GM*, 3rd ser., 10 (1861), 588–9 · R. I. Murchison, *Proceedings* [Royal Geographical Society], 5 (1860–61), 160 · K. O. Dike, *Trade and politics in the Niger delta, 1830–1885* (1956) · Boase, *Mod. Eng. biog.* · *The Times* (8 April 1861) · d. cert. · *CGPLA Eng. & Wales* (1861)
Wealth at death £90,000: probate, 21 June 1861, *CGPLA Eng. & Wales*

Jamieson, Robert (1802–1880), Church of Scotland minister, was born in Edinburgh on 3 January 1802, the son of Robert Jamieson, a baker. He was educated at Edinburgh high school and matriculated at Edinburgh University, intending to study for the medical profession. Before he had completed his course, however, he decided to enter the Church of Scotland ministry; he trained at the Divinity Hall, and was licensed as a preacher by the presbytery of Biggar, Lanarkshire, on 13 February 1827. He was ordained minister of the parish of Weststruther, in the presbytery of Lauder, Berwickshire, on 22 April 1830. On 1 June 1830 he married his cousin Eliza (*d.* 1889), daughter of George Jamieson, a baker; they had six sons and four daughters, several of whom died young.

Jamieson remained at Weststruther until 23 November 1837, when he was translated to Currie, in the presbytery of Edinburgh, to which he was presented by the city magistrates. During the controversies preceding the Disruption of 1843 he was among those attempting to prevent a schism, arguing that the reforms demanded could be implemented without endangering the established church. When John Forbes, minister of St Paul's, Glasgow, resigned his charge to join the Free Church, Jamieson was appointed as his successor by the magistrates of Glasgow, and was admitted as minister on 14 March 1844. The University of Glasgow conferred a DD upon him on 17 April 1848. For many years Jamieson was active in ecclesiastical business, and in 1872 he was unanimously chosen moderator of the general assembly. In appearance, Jamieson was

thin and of medium height; his features were described as 'marked and bold' (Smith, 265). He was a learned and accurate preacher, whose sermons rarely exceeded the forty minutes he allocated to them; a contemporary claimed, however, that his habit of preaching without notes made his meaning obscure, and also condemned the 'loud monotony' of his delivery (ibid., 263–4). Jamieson devoted himself to the guidance of young men studying for the ministry and his students' classes were influential throughout the church. His publications included *Eastern Manners Illustrative of the Old and New Testaments* (3 vols., 1836–8), *Manners and Trials of the Primitive Christians* (1840), and (in conjunction with E. H. Bickersteth) *The Holy Bible* (1861–5). Jamieson died in Glasgow on 26 October 1880; his wife survived him.

A. H. MILLAR, rev. ROSEMARY MITCHELL

Sources *Fasti Scot.* · *Glasgow Herald* (27 Oct 1880) · J. Smith, *Our Scottish clergy*, 1st ser. (1848), 259–65 · private information (1891)
Wealth at death £2336 8s. 8d.: confirmation, 8 Dec 1880, *CCI*

Jamieson, Thomas Hill (1843–1876), librarian, was born on 21 August 1843 at Bonnington, Forfarshire, the son of Peter Jamieson, a shoemaker, and his wife, Janet Hill, and was educated at the burgh and parochial school of Arbroath. He became a pupil teacher at Bonnington. In 1862 he went to Edinburgh, where he attended the high school and subsequently the university. While still at college he acted as a sub-editor of *Chambers's Etymological Dictionary*. In 1867 he was appointed assistant to Samuel Halkett, keeper of the Advocates' Library. During Halkett's illness Jamieson effectively assumed the keepership, and following Halkett's death in April 1871 he was appointed to the post on 3 June 1871, having submitted a remarkable set of testimonials in support of his candidacy. The work of printing the new catalogue, of which the first part had appeared in 1863, passed into his care. In order to hasten completion of this great project, begun in 1853, it was decided that the biographical information relating to each author listed should be omitted. Although good progress was made during Jamieson's time in office, the catalogue was not completed until two years after his death. Jamieson was assisted in this task by Jón A. Hjaltalín. In 1872 he wrote a prefatory notice for an edition of Archie Armstrong's *Banquet of Jests*, and in 1874 he published an edition of Alexander Barclay's translation of Sebastian Brandt's *Ship of Fools*, to which he contributed an introduction discussing Brandt and his writings, as well as a lengthy *Notice of the Life and Writings of Alexander Barclay*, with a bibliography of his work. He married, on 11 June 1872, Jane Alison Kilgour; they had two children. The fire which occurred in the Advocates' Library on 9 March 1875, in which 551 volumes were destroyed and some three thousand others damaged, roused him to exertions apparently beyond his strength, and he died at his home, 7 Gillespie Crescent, Edinburgh, on 9 January 1876, aged only thirty-two. According to his former chief at Chambers, writing in a testimonial, Jamieson was a 'born librarian'. Scholars valued, in particular, his knowledge of the manuscript collection of the Faculty of Advocates, then still much neglected. As George Burnett, lord Lyon king of arms, wrote in his testimonial, Jamieson had interested himself in, and understood, matters connected with manuscripts 'which would be the despair of any ordinary librarian'. G. C. BOASE, *rev.* IAIN GORDON BROWN

Sources *The Scotsman* (10 Jan 1876), 5–6 · *Edinburgh Courant* (10 Jan 1876), 8 · *Testimonials in favour of Thomas Hill Jamieson, candidate for the office of keeper of the Advocates' Library* (privately printed, 1871) · P. Cadell and A. Matheson, eds., *For the encouragement of learning: Scotland's National Library, 1689–1989* (1989), 212, 295 · I. G. Brown, *Building for books: the architectural evolution of the Advocates' Library, 1689–1925* (1989), 168 · *CGPLA Eng. & Wales* (1876)
Wealth at death £790 5s. 8d.: probate, 11 Feb 1876, NA Scot., SC 70/1/176, 966

Jamrach, Charles [Johann Christian Carl] (1815–1891), dealer in wild animals, the son of Johann Gottlieb Jamrach (d. c.1840), a dealer in birds and shells, was born in Hamburg or Memel in March 1815. Having moved to England, Jamrach took over his father's London-based business on the latter's death, and made himself famous among naturalists and entertainers alike as an importer, breeder, and exporter of all kinds of animals. Zoos and circuses relied on him. 'When a few years ago Mr Barnum was burnt out, the void thus made in "the Greatest show on Earth" was to a large extent filled from [Jamrach's] establishment at 180 St George Street East' (*The Era*, 12 Sept 1891, 16). He attracted a good deal of press attention and was admired for his courage when he struggled with a runaway tiger in 1857. Jamrach showed particular interest in breeding long-coated Persian greyhounds, Japanese pigs, and Madagascan cats. In later years his exploitation of animals became less profitable because of competition, and he diversified, importing large quantities of Eastern curiosities.

Jamrach married, first, Mary Athanasio, the daughter of a Neapolitan or French Canadian; second, Ellen Downing; and, last, Clara Salter. There were children by his first two marriages. A son, Albert Edward Jamrach, also became a dealer in wild animals. Jamrach died on 6 September 1891 at his home, Beaufort Cottage, Wellington Road, Bow. BRENDA ASSAEL

Sources *The Era* (12 Sept 1891), 16 · *The Times* (6 Sept 1891) · *The Times* (9 Sept 1891) · *DNB* · d. cert.
Wealth at death £7160 0s. 8d.: probate, 21 Oct 1891, *CGPLA Eng. & Wales*

Jane [*née* Jane Seymour] (1508/9–1537), queen of England, third consort of Henry VIII, was probably born at Wolf Hall, Wiltshire, the eldest daughter of ten children of Sir John Seymour (1476?–1536) of Wolf Hall, soldier and courtier, and Margery Wentworth (d. 1550), eldest daughter of Sir Henry Wentworth of Nettlestead, Suffolk.

Background and appearance at court The Seymours were descended from Guy de St Maur, who is said to have accompanied William the Conqueror to England, although authenticated members of the family date only from the thirteenth century. Through the Wentworths, Jane claimed royal blood through descent from Edward III. She was one of ten children, of whom three sons and a daughter died unmarried. Her surviving siblings included

Jane [Jane Seymour] (1508/9–1537), by Hans Holbein the younger, 1536–7

Edward *Seymour, later duke of Somerset (d. 1552); Henry (d. 1578); Thomas *Seymour, who became Baron Seymour of Sudeley (d. 1549); Elizabeth, who married first Sir Anthony Ughtred, second, Gregory, son of Thomas Cromwell, earl of Essex, and third, William Paulet, first marquess of Winchester; and Dorothy, who married Sir Clement Smith.

Nothing is known of Jane's early life and education, but she was probably taught by her father's chaplain at Wolf Hall. While accounts of her beauty differ with the eye of the beholder, most contemporaries agree that she was above average in intelligence. The imperial ambassador, Eustace Chapuys, described her as 'of middle stature and no great beauty, so fair that one would call her rather pale than otherwise' and added that she was inclined to be proud and haughty (*LP Henry VIII*, 10, no. 901). She first appeared at court about 1529 and served as a lady-in-waiting to both Katherine of Aragon and Anne Boleyn. *Henry VIII (1491–1547) honoured the Seymour family with a visit to Wolf Hall in September 1535. Although it has been suggested that this was the first meeting between the king and Jane, a letter from Chapuys dated 13 October 1534 refers to an unnamed young lady to whom the king was attached and says that her credit was increasing as that of Queen Anne declined. There is very little doubt that this was Jane. Chapuys adds that the lady in question had recently sent a message to Princess Mary telling her to take good heart because her tribulations would end very soon.

Courtship and marriage On 10 February 1536 Chapuys reported that after Queen Anne's miscarriage in January 1536 Henry had sent 'great presents' to Jane, but he later reported that she refused a purse of money and a letter sent by him. On 1 April he recorded that Jane had fallen to her knees, begging a messenger to tell Henry:

> to consider that she was a well-born damsel, the daughter of good and honourable parents, without blame or reproach of any kind; there was no treasure in this world that she valued as much as her honour, and on no account would she lose it, even if she were to die a thousand deaths. That if the king wished to make her a present of money, she requested him to reserve it for such a time as God would be pleased to send her some advantageous marriage. (*CSP Spain, 1536–8*, no. 84)

Jane's response increased the king's affection for her, encouraging him to praise her virtue and promise to speak to her only in the presence of her family. Henry subsequently installed Jane's brother Edward, who was a gentleman of the privy chamber, and his second wife, Anne, in rooms vacated by Thomas Cromwell in Greenwich Palace so that he and Jane could meet more discreetly and conveniently. While Queen Anne was in the Tower awaiting trial, Jane stayed with Sir Nicholas Carew at Beddington, Surrey, and then at Hampton to be nearer the king.

Archbishop Cranmer issued a dispensation from prohibitions of affinity for Jane to marry Henry on 19 May (also the day of Anne's execution), because they were fifth cousins. The couple were betrothed the following day, and a private marriage took place on 30 May 1536 in the queen's closet at Whitehall. Coming as it did after the death of Queen Katherine and the execution of Queen Anne, there could be no doubt of the lawfulness of Henry's marriage to Jane. The new queen was introduced at court during Whitsuntide festivities and appeared before the Londoners in June when she accompanied Henry to the Mercers' Hall to watch the setting of the ceremonial city watch. No coronation followed the wedding, and plans for an autumn coronation were laid aside because of an outbreak of plague at Westminster; Jane's pregnancy undoubtedly eliminated any possibility of a later coronation.

Queenship Henry VIII gave Jane not only jewellery but also a jointure of lands and lordships in several counties, including Suffolk Place, Southwark, as her London residence, in all valued at £938 6s. 3d. In July 1536 parliament inserted Jane's issue into a new Act of Succession (28 Hen. VIII c.7), which also provided for future wives and empowered the king to name his successor by either letters patent or by will.

Although Jane made no attempt to promote a faction, the Seymour family benefited from the marriage. Her brother Edward was created Viscount Beauchamp in 1536, earl of Hertford in 1537, and became a privy councillor on 22 May 1537. After his sister's marriage Thomas was made a gentleman of privy chamber and knighted in 1537. Both brothers received generous grants of land from the king. Jane's sister Elizabeth married Gregory, son and heir of Cromwell, who described the queen as the 'most virtuous and veriest gentlewoman that liveth' (*LP Henry VIII*, 11, no. 29). Jane promoted reconciliation between Henry and Princess Mary, but it was not achieved until after the marriage, when Mary (who was also under pressure from Cromwell, and indeed from Henry himself) made a complete submission to her father and in July 1536 met him for the first time in almost three years. Subsequently Jane befriended Mary as well as Elizabeth.

During the 1530s the Seymours were neither committed anti-papalists nor protestants. No surviving evidence shows that Jane patronized clerics of any persuasion, but Luther was informed that she was an enemy of the gospel, and her sympathy with Mary could suggest that she was conservative in religion. On the other hand, the reformer Miles Coverdale printed her initials at the head of the dedication across the name of Anne Boleyn in an edition of his English Bible. According to hearsay that has been widely quoted, Jane begged the king to save the abbeys during the Pilgrimage of Grace but was warned not to meddle in politics.

During her short reign, Jane enjoyed court life to the full. In July 1536 the royal couple travelled from London to Rochester, Canterbury, and Dover, where they met Arthur Plantagenet, Lord Lisle, and his wife, who had come from Calais. When Henry began the autumn hunting season, Jane joined him. She and the king rode in an elaborate procession through London in December accompanied by the nobility and the imperial ambassador. Streets along the route were colourfully hung with arras and cloth of gold. Jane suffered a great personal loss when her father died on 21 December, but there is no evidence that she went home for his funeral. She kept her only Christmas as queen with Henry at Greenwich with mirth and high celebration. Jane enjoyed a friendly relationship with Lord Lisle and his wife, a couple whose surviving letters illuminate social life of the early Tudor period. Lady Lisle sought preferment for her daughters at court, while her husband obtained plump quail for the queen at Calais, which his agent had roasted for presentation. The duke of Norfolk sought her favour with a generous gift of gold taken from a dissolved monastery. As her pregnancy progressed, Jane developed a craving for cucumbers, which were provided by Princess Mary.

Childbearing and death The queen's pregnancy was made known in February 1537, and news of the quickening of her child was celebrated on Trinity Sunday (27 May). On 16 September Jane officially withdrew from court life to her chamber at Hampton Court to await the birth of the baby. An uneventful pregnancy was followed by a difficult labour that lasted two days and three nights, after which she gave birth to a healthy son at about 2 a.m. on 12 October. The king joined Jane on the evening following the child's birth. The infant's name, Edward, was chosen because of his birth on the eve of the feast of the translation of St Edward the Confessor. During the reign of Elizabeth the Roman Catholic historian Nicholas Sander popularized the story of Edward's caesarean birth, a fabrication that survived into the twentieth century. Sixteenth-century women were unlikely to survive caesarean delivery, whereas Jane not only survived but initially appeared to be making a normal recovery.

Prince Edward was baptized in the royal chapel at Hampton Court on 15 October. Queen Jane received guests seated in the antechamber of the chapel, but according to protocol neither she nor Henry attended the actual ceremony. The godfathers were Archbishop Cranmer and the duke of Norfolk while Princess Mary was godmother. The queen's brother Edward carried the four-year-old Princess Elizabeth, the infant's other half-sister, to the baptism. Although attendance was restricted, 300 guests were present. On 18 October Edward was proclaimed prince of Wales, duke of Cornwall, and earl of Carnarvon.

Queen Jane received the last rites of the church two days after the christening. A rally gave false hope of her recovery, but the king cancelled a hunting trip to Esher. On 24 October the queen's life was in danger and her almoner, Robert Aldrich, bishop of Carlisle, administered extreme unction and notified the king. Most historians have assumed that she developed puerperal fever, something for which there was no effective treatment, though at the time the queen's attendants were blamed for allowing her to eat unsuitable food and to take cold. An alternative medical opinion suggests that Jane died because of retention of parts of the placenta in her uterus. That condition could have led to a catastrophic haemorrhage several days after delivery of the child. What is certain is that septicaemia developed, and she became delirious. After being queen for less than eighteen months Jane died just before midnight on 24 October, aged twenty-eight. It is not known whether Henry was at her side when she died, but he was at Hampton Court. The grief-stricken king writing to the king of France told how 'Divine Providence has mingled my joy with the bitterness of the death of her who brought me this happiness' (*LP Henry VIII*, 12/2, no. 972). As many as 1200 masses were said for Jane in the city of London alone.

Memorials and images Queen Jane was the first English queen to die in 'good estate' since the death of Henry VII's consort Elizabeth of York in 1503. Burial required an elaborate ritual in which the queen's body was purged and then eviscerated and embalmed. Encased in lead and sealed in a wooden coffin, the corpse remained in the presence chamber at Hampton Court until 31 October. Throughout this period a vigil was maintained by ladies and gentlemen of the household. On 1 November, All Saints' day, the bier on which the coffin rested was carried by torchlight to the chapel where a new watch was mounted. The funeral procession set off for burial at Windsor on 12 November. She was interred in St George's Chapel on the following day. Since by tradition the king did not appear, Jane's chief mourner was Princess Mary.

The period of mourning at court extended until Christmas, and Henry did not cease wearing black until 2 February 1538. The king planned a great monument in Jane's memory, but it was never built. Her image is, however, preserved in a number of paintings, including a sketch and a finished portrait by Holbein.

Jane's motto, 'Bound to obey and serve', which in its submissive tone resembled the mottoes of Elizabeth of York and Katherine of Aragon, sheds light on her personality and consequent success as queen. Unlike Anne Boleyn, Jane was docile, represented no ideology, led no court faction, and conspicuously deferred to the king in public, although she was the unchallenged mistress behind the closed door of her household. Jane further separated herself from Anne both in her style of dress, by rejecting the French hood, and in favouring other more traditional English usages. Perhaps Jane's greatest strength lay in what one historian called her 'good-natured imperturbability' (Loades, 95). She left posterity an indelible impression of perfection and was remembered by Henry as the wife with whom he had been uniquely happy. When Henry died in 1547 he was buried with Jane at Windsor.

BARRETT L. BEER

Sources P. M. Gross, *Jane, the quene: third consort of King Henry VIII* (1999) · D. Loades, *Henry VIII and his queens* (1997) · A. Fraser, *The wives of Henry VIII* (1992) · W. Seymour, *Ordeal by ambition: an English family in the shadow of the Tudors* (1972) · *LP Henry VIII*, vols. 7–13 · *CSP Spain, 1534–8* · GEC, *Peerage*, new edn, 12/1.59–65 · E. W. Ives, *Anne Boleyn* (1986) · J. Loach, *Edward VI*, ed. G. Bernard and P. Williams (1999) · J. J. Scarisbrick, *Henry VIII* (1968) · R. Michell, *The Carews of Beddington* (1981) · N. Sander, *The rise and progress of the English Reformation* (1827) · M. St C. Byrne, ed., *The Lisle letters*, 6 vols. (1981) · *DNB*

Likenesses H. Holbein the younger, oils, 1536–7, Kunsthistorisches Museum, Vienna [*see illus.*] · portrait, *c.*1545 (*The family of Henry VIII*), Royal Collection · N. Hilliard, miniature (after H. Holbein the younger), Royal Collection · H. Holbein, chalk sketch, Royal Collection · H. Holbein the younger, oils, Mauritshuis, The Hague; repro. in Scarisbrick, *Henry VIII* · Hornebolte, miniature · Van Leemput, group portrait, Royal Collection; repro. in Gross, *Jane*

Wealth at death £938 6s. 3d.: Gross, *Jane*

Jane, (John) Frederick Thomas (1865–1916), author, journalist, and illustrator, was born in Richmond, Surrey, on 6 August 1865, the eldest of four sons and three daughters of the Revd John Jane, later vicar of Upottery, Devon, and his wife, Caroline, daughter of the Revd James Frederick Todd, vicar of Liskeard. The family had a nautical ancestry: in the sixteenth century the merchant John Jane sailed with the navigator John Davis to the Arctic; Captain Henry Jane commanded HMS *Seahorse* during the war of 1739–48.

At Exeter School, Jane demonstrated a liking for practical jokes that was to endure for his lifetime, and also a socially unpopular talent for manufacturing explosives. His father intended him for an army career, but that and a project for farming in the colonies came to nothing; by 1885 he was living hand to mouth in Holborn as an illustrator and journalist.

In August 1889 Jane was commissioned by *Pictorial World* to cover a month of naval manoeuvres, preceded by an inspection of the combined fleets at Spithead by the German emperor Wilhelm II. Jane was able to sketch nearly one hundred ships, as well as paying off his mess bill by painting decorative panels in his host ship's wardroom. From then onwards, 'Fred. T. Jane' became a recognized signature on bold black and white illustrations in a number of books and magazines; so realistic was the picture in the *Illustrated London News* of the torpedoing of the ironclad *Blanco Encalada* in the Chilean Revolutionary War of 1891 that a legend grew that Jane had been present at the action.

Aircraft, television, and laser holograms were recognizably foreshadowed in a series of Jane's drawings, 'Guesses at Futurity', in the *Pall Mall Magazine*, 1894–5. Jane became a successful novelist with *Blake of the 'Rattlesnake'* (1895), followed by science-fiction titles *The Incubated Girl* (1896), *To Venus in Five Seconds* (1897), and *The Violet Flame* (1899), which featured an armament with the characteristics of a nuclear weapon. Jane was married twice: first, in 1892, to Alice (*c*.1870–1908), daughter of Hamilton Beattie; they had a daughter. In 1909 he married Edith Frances Muriel (*b*. 1882), daughter of Lieutenant Henry Chase Carré RN, and the marriage produced another daughter.

As early as 1882, inspired by the Mediterranean Fleet's bombardment of Alexandria, Jane had conceived the idea of a warship sketchbook, provisionally entitled 'Ironclads of the world'. This bore fruit in 1898 with the publication of *Jane's All the World's Fighting Ships* (shortened to *Jane's Fighting Ships* in 1905), with details of all major surface warships; this was to be used as a ship recognition and intelligence aid by all sides in many future naval conflicts. The edition of 1903 contained an article, '*Invincible*: an ideal warship for the British navy', by Vittorio Cuniberti, which foreshadowed the main features of the dreadnought class of battleships. In 1909 the first edition was published of what became *Jane's All the World's Aircraft*. Jane is credited with inventing the rules of a naval war game complete with scale models of warships.

In 1906 Jane stood unsuccessfully as an independent 'navy before party' parliamentary candidate for Portsmouth. The years 1908–9 were dramatic: on the look-out for spies, Jane abducted a German who seemed to be acting suspiciously in Portsmouth, and deposited him in the duke of Bedford's animal park at Woburn. The publicity generated by this exploit produced letters denouncing other suspected spies which Jane handed to the War Office, thus assisting what was to become MI5. As a practical joke, he kidnapped by car the socialist MP Victor Grayson, who was due to address a Portsmouth meeting; a similar plan to kidnap Winston Churchill failed when travel arrangements were altered.

To his chagrin, Jane was not appointed to any official position during the First World War, and had to be content with privately supporting naval recruiting and propaganda. Fred T. Jane died of a heart attack following severe influenza at 26 Clarence Esplanade, Southsea, on 8 March 1916, and was buried at Highland Road cemetery, Southsea, two days later. Publications carrying his name still provide authoritative data on the production of military equipment throughout the world. The word 'Jane' features in the *Collins English Dictionary* as a noun indicating completeness and reliability.

ROBERT HUTCHINSON, *rev.*

Sources *The Times* (10 March 1916) · C. Andrew, *Secret service: the making of the British intelligence community* (1985) · *WWW* · private information (1993) · *CGPLA Eng. & Wales* (1916) · R. Brooks, *Fred T. Jane: an eccentric visionary* (1997)
Archives Portsmouth Museum and Record Service, letters, PCRO 8 38A
Likenesses portraits, repro. in Brooks, *Fred T. Jane*, frontispiece, 82, 136
Wealth at death £4681 17s. 4d.: probate, 19 June 1916, *CGPLA Eng. & Wales*

Jane, Joseph (*d*. 1658), politician and controversialist, was born in Liskeard, Cornwall, to an influential Cornish family (the family coat of arms was argent, a lion rampant azure between three escallops gules). The identity of his mother is unknown. His father, Thomas Jane, was first a 'Steward' in 1604–5 and then mayor of Liskeard in 1621; and his grandfather may have been the John Jane who died in Liskeard in 1603. There is no evidence that Joseph attended university, though his son William *Jane became canon of Christ Church, Oxford. Joseph Jane was elected MP for the borough for the 1625 parliament and in 1631, and in 1635–6 he was mayor of Liskeard.

In 1640 Jane was elected burgess of Liskeard to serve in the Long Parliament. He was one of several Cornish MPs who voted against the act of attainder against the earl of Strafford on 21 April 1641. His sympathies were unwaveringly royalist: he retired to the king's parliament at Oxford in 1643, and was the same year appointed one of the king's commissioners in Cornwall. There he tried to raise Cornish forces for the king's cause, though he had limited success in persuading them to leave the county in order to defend Devon. On 22 January 1644 he was discharged and disabled from sitting in the house for his desertion of service and adherence to the king (*JHC*, 3.374). Charles I spent six nights at Jane's house in Cornwall in August 1644, and a further night on 4 September. It was probably about this time that Jane composed a 'Relation of the state of the parties in Cornwall in 1642' (Bodl. Oxf., MS Clarendon 2074), a manuscript combining a narrative account with political advice. Edward Hyde had this in his possession while writing the *History*. In 1645 Jane's son William was born; he had at least one other son and a daughter. His wife's identity is unknown.

Jane was one of John Arundell's officers at the siege of Pendennis Castle from April to August 1646, and appears as a signatory to a desperate appeal for help addressed to the prince of Wales. After the surrender of Pendennis Castle on 17 August 1646 Jane went into exile and began to suffer financially. His estate was listed as sequestered on 24 April 1648, though he did not initially offer to compound. In the later 1640s, perhaps as late as 1649, he served under Sir John Grenville at Scilly; by September 1649 he was operating as an intelligencer to Edward Nicholas, secretary to the council of the exiled Charles Stuart. In 1650 he was appointed a clerk to Charles's council, a post he apparently held until his death. His main residence in exile was The Hague, though correspondence also survives from Caen, Dort, and, dated 1658, from Bruges. One letter of August 1650 locates him at Mr Browne's the English bookseller, at The Hague; another in December 1654 at Mr Fargison's, Scotland Arms, Molle Street, The Hague.

Jane maintained a steady and frequent supply of news, some in code, to Nicholas at Paris, Utrecht, and Brussels. He gathered his news from printed newsbooks and pamphlets from Britain, and by word of mouth from travellers and merchants. He would gloss this news with political interpretation and his sense of the weight of public opinion, both in Britain and in Anglophone communities in the Netherlands and elsewhere. Among the opinions he expressed was his disapproval of Charles Stuart taking the covenant in 1649: 'if the repug[n]ancy of their [presbyterian] principles to kingly government were tolerable, yet I think a man may without rashness or bigottery affirme that it's an ill exchange to gayne a kingdome by rooting upp religion and piety' (Warner, 1.137). Throughout his correspondence his contempt for presbyterians—whom he blamed for the downfall of monarchy—almost matched the opprobrium with which he referred to varieties of nonconformist religious faith.

Jane's sole extant polemical contribution to the royalist cause is his response to Milton, the anonymous *Eikon aklastos, the image unbroaken: a perspective of the impudence, falshood, vanitie, and prophannes, published in a libell entitled Eikonoklastes against Eikon basilike* (1651). Written as animadversions on Milton's *Eikonoklastes*, as a work of propaganda it is weak, neither eloquent nor well reasoned nor sharply rebarbative. Its prose is leaden, its syntax clumsy and repetitive; though some of its antipathetic comments on the radicalism of Milton's politics are well judged. Edward Hyde wrote to Nicholas that 'The King has a singular good esteem of Joseph Jane and of his book', and claimed that notice was taken of *Eikon aklastos* in London (*Clarendon State Papers*, 2.136, 170). Jane had earnest ambitions as a polemicist. By January 1653 he was pressing senior figures to endorse a translation of his tract into French; in 1654 he believed that a Jersey man had undertaken to do this. In September 1654 he wrote to Nicholas that 'I was told by Mr Edgman some yeres since, that one had undertaken to translate my booke into French and that was ready for the presse; what the hinderance is I never understood' (Warner, 3.42–3). He had hoped to combat Milton on a Europewide stage, though his friends and associates had their doubts about this. Hyde wrote to Nicholas in January 1653 'Nothing is heard of Milton's book being translated into French; though Jo. Jane be really an able man, are his writings, if translated, weighty enough to gain credit in other languages?' (*Clarendon State Papers*, 2.171). Hyde's doubts carried weight. Nor was the English edition a commercial success. A bookseller reissued unsold sheets in 1660 as *Salmasius his Dissection and Confutation of the Diabolical Rebel Milton*, with a new title-page and an address to the reader, intending to pass it off as the work of Claude de Saumaise.

Jane may have made other polemical contributions. Nicholas sent to Hyde in December 1652 'a print of Mr. Jos. Jane touching the interest of these countries in the restitution of the King' (Warner, 1.321). Jane was also keen in 1654 to write a response to a defence of the protectorate which he had seen, a Latin translation of an English original. He intended to respond to the original and have his response translated into Latin, his philological skills evidently not suiting him to the task of royal apologist (ibid., 2.108–9, 145–6). Nicholas informed him that 'Mr. Cha. will write you what he thinks of an answer to "the reasons of Cromwell's present government", to which I can say nothing, not having seen the book' (*CSP dom.*, 1654, 408). Jane was apparently not encouraged and no subsequent references to the project are extant. In June 1655 he sent to Nicholas a draft of a proposed royal declaration concerning the terms of a Restoration, in which he cautioned against offering to concede too many particulars (Warner, 2.349).

Financial hardship from 1650 onwards led to hints that Jane was culpable of financial misdealings. Nicholas petitioned for the settlement of a bill exchanged by Jane, which Jane denied. Another of Nicholas's correspondents picked up a similar theme in 1657. In 1652 Jane learned that his sequestered Cornish estate was for sale, and on 17 November he petitioned the committee for compounding, claiming with thorough disingenuity that he had submitted to parliamentary ordinances, and begging for relief on terms of the articles of war. On 5 July 1653 his property, sold to John Trethewy, was discharged from sequestration (the phrase is ambiguous, but it suggests that his petition was unsuccessful). Expression of concern over financial hardship crept into his correspondence with Nicholas, which climaxed in April 1658 in wounded declarations when he was not remembered in Charles's lists of moneys for members of his council, though the other two clerks had been rewarded. At this time his daughter was resident with Nicholas at Brussels, owing to difficulties Jane was experiencing in providing for and removing her. He sought and failed to obtain patronage from the princess royal. There is some indication that Nicholas and others thought that Jane took advantage of his position, though he may have been Mr Jane 'the waterman' (*CSP dom.*, 1657–8, 345, 347, 357) to whom Hyde sent modest sums. None the less, over eight years of correspondence a degree of intimacy developed between Jane and Nicholas; their wives exchanged greetings, and sought each other's company, and informal final paragraphs creep into their letters. Nicholas even requested that Jane deliver his will to his wife in the event of his death. And, despite misgivings, the epithet 'honest' was applied to him by several exiled royalists.

On 9 September 1658 Nicholas wrote to Hyde that 'Honest Mr. Jane is dangerously sick at Middleborrow' (*Clarendon State Papers*, 4.77); news was sent to him from Middleburgh on 14 September that 'honest' Jane, presumed to be of a 'great age', was dead (Warner, 4.68).

JOAD RAYMOND

Sources *The Nicholas papers*, ed. G. F. Warner, 4 vols., CS, new ser., 40, 50, 57, 3rd ser., 31 (1886–1920) · *Calendar of the Clarendon state papers preserved in the Bodleian Library*, ed. O. Ogle and others, 5 vols. (1869–1970) · *CSP dom.*, 1650–59 · M. Coate, *Cornwall in the great civil war and interregnum, 1642–1660*, 2nd edn (1963) · M. A. E. Green, ed., *Calendar of the proceedings of the committee for compounding … 1643–1660*, 5 vols., PRO (1889–92) · 'Relation of the state of the parties', Bodl. Oxf., MS Clarendon 2074 · Boase & Courtney, *Bibl. Corn.* · J. Polsue, *A complete parochial history of the county of Cornwall*, 4 vols. (1867–72) · *JHC*, 3 (1642–4) · archdeaconry of Cornwall, wills and administrations, pt 1 (1929)
Archives BL, letters of Sir Edward Nicholas, Egerton MSS 2533–2562

Jane, Thomas (*c*.1438–1500), bishop of Norwich, originated from Milton Abbas, Dorset, entered Winchester College in 1449, and in 1454 proceeded to New College, Oxford, where he was a fellow (1456–72). He was a bachelor in civil and canon law by 1464, and a doctor of canon law by 1469, when he was sub-warden of his college and commissary of the chancellor of the university. About this time he became official of Thomas Kemp, bishop of London, who now became Jane's main patron, giving him much preferment, including, in succession, the prebends of Reculverland, Rugmere, and Brownswood in St Paul's Cathedral, and in 1480 the archdeaconry of Essex. In 1472, on resigning his first benefice, the rectory of Little Burstead, Essex, he was presented by Anne, duchess of Exeter, Edward IV's sister, to the chapelry of Foulness, and by the prior and convent of the Cluniac monastery of that place to the vicarage of Prittlewell (both livings also in Essex). In 1473 Jane resigned the vicarage and, dispensed to hold incompatible benefices, was admitted to the rectories of Winterbourne Strickland, near his Dorset home, and of Hayes, Middlesex, and the vicarage of Ashwell, Hertfordshire, keeping Ashwell and Hayes for more than ten years. Other benefices that he held for short periods in the 1480s included St Bride's in London and the vicarages of St Sepulchre Holborn and Walden, Essex. Jane's standing as a leading canon lawyer does much to explain his advancement, and is simply demonstrated by commissions received from the archbishop of Canterbury, the pope (although Rome also received complaints about his judicial activities), and Oxford University; and, in 1495–6, by his grace to incorporate at Cambridge University, where he was regarded as a *precipium Judicem* ('distinguished judge'; *Grace Book B, 1488–1511*, 119). In 1489 he was Bishop Kemp's executor, and one of those nominated by the chapter of St Paul's to act as the archbishop's official in the London diocese during the vacancy of the see. Although not in fact chosen in 1489, he served as Archbishop John Morton's official during the succeeding vacancy (1496). By 1493 he was a member of the privy council deputed to hear cases in the embryonic court of requests. In 1496 he was appointed canon of Wells Cathedral (with the prebend of Combe Terciadecima) and of St George's Chapel, Windsor, and dean of the Chapel Royal; and he became a canon of Salisbury Cathedral (with the prebend of Fordington and Writhlington) in 1497.

Two years later Jane became bishop of Norwich, being provided on 14 June and consecrated on 20 October 1499.

He had appointed his vicar-general by 4 August, and reached Norwich no later than the spring of 1500. He was travelling round the eastern part of his diocese, perhaps undertaking his primary visitation, when he seems to have succumbed to the pestilence then raging through the country. His hurried will, requesting burial in his cathedral if he should die within 16 miles of Norwich, was made on 20 July; and he was dead by 27 August. Jane was a benefactor to New College and Syon Abbey, a friend to Merton College, and probably contributed to the building of St Mary's Church, Oxford.

EDMUND VENABLES, *rev.* ROSEMARY C. E. HAYES

Sources NCC will registers, 1499–1500, Norfolk RO, Norwich episcopal records, vol. 23 (1499–1500); vol. 24 (1500) [vol. 23 is the only known surviving record of his episcopate] · London episcopal registers, GL, 9531/7–8: 1450–1501 · wills of bishops Kemp and Jane, PRO, PROB 11/8, 12 · Chancery records · *CEPR letters*, vols. 13–17 · *The register of John Morton, archbishop of Canterbury, 1486–1500*, ed. C. Harper-Bill, 1–2, CYS, 75, 78 (1987–91) · H. E. Salter, ed., *Registrum cancellarii Oxoniensis, 1434–1469*, 2, OHS, 94 (1932) · I. S. Leadam, ed., *Select cases in the court of requests, AD 1497–1569*, SeldS, 12 (1898) · M. Bateson, ed., *Grace book B*, 1 (1903) · BL, Cotton MS Cleopatra E.iii · H. E. Salter, ed., *Registrum annalium collegii Mertonensis, 1483–1521*, OHS, 76 (1923) · H. Anstey, ed., *Epistolae academicae Oxon.*, 2, OHS, 36 (1898) · *Registrum Thomae Bourgchier … 1454–1486*, ed. F. R. H. Du Boulay, CYS, 54 (1957) · Emden, *Oxf.*, vol. 2 · *Fasti Angl., 1300–1541* · T. F. Kirby, *Winchester scholars: a list of the wardens, fellows, and scholars of … Winchester College* (1888) · D. Baldwin, *The Chapel Royal: ancient and modern* (1990)
Archives GL, registers, GL 9531/7–8 · Norfolk RO, Norwich episcopal records, NCC will registers, vol 23 (1499–1500); vol. 24 (1500)
Likenesses seal, repro. in 'Descriptive catalogue of the seals of the bishops of Norwich, AD 850 to Reformation', *Norfolk Archaeology*, 1 (1947), 205–23
Wealth at death residue of estate to be spent relieving poverty of household and for good of his soul: will, PRO, PROB 11/12

Jane, William (*bap.* 1645, *d.* 1707), Church of England clergyman, was born at Liskeard, Cornwall, where he was baptized on 22 October 1645. His father, Joseph *Jane (*d.* 1658), a much respected clerk of Charles II's privy council in exile, sent him to Westminster School, an institution that retained its Anglican royalist sympathies. He was admitted commoner of Christ Church, Oxford, by the dean, Dr George Morley, who assigned Henry Bold as his tutor. He matriculated on 5 December 1660, and was Bostock exhibitioner, before being elected student on 29 April 1661. He graduated BA on 16 June 1664, and proceeded MA on 21 May 1667, BD on 11 November 1674, and DD on 4 July 1679. He lived in Oxford for the remainder of his life. After ordination he became lecturer at Carfax church. He held a variety of college offices, including the senior censorship (1672–3), and attracted the patronage of the aristocratic Henry Compton, canon of Christ Church, who, on being promoted bishop of Oxford in 1674, chose him to preach his consecration sermon (6 December) and appointed him his chaplain. Following Compton's translation to London, Jane was made rector of Wennington, Essex (1678), prebendary of Chamberlainswood and canon treasurer of St Paul's Cathedral (1679), and archdeacon of Middlesex (1679, resigned 1686). Even so, his services were considered too valuable to the rulers of the university to let him leave Oxford.

William Jane (*bap.* 1645, *d.* 1707), by William Gandy, 1706

On 5 July 1678 Charles II, acting at the instance of Morley (now bishop of Winchester), Compton, and John Fell, dean of Christ Church, nominated Jane to succeed to Richard Allestree's Christ Church canonry, on the understanding that he would also succeed him as regius professor of divinity, which Jane did in May 1680. The preferment placed him at the head of the university's most influential faculty. Although he enjoyed his predecessor's approbation Jane lacked Allestree's scholarly distinction, yet he could be relied upon to uphold the teaching of the restored Church of England against its Roman Catholic and nonconformist adversaries. Esteemed 'a Calvinist with respect to doctrine' (Calamy, 1.275), he was strongly attached to the rites and ceremonies of the 1662 prayer book, on which the life of Restoration Oxford was centred.

Jane's rapid promotion brought him to the attention of parliament. He was invited to preach before the House of Commons. In his sermon, delivered on 11 April 1679, he warned against the dangers of protestant fanaticism, and censured 'the apostate principles of the Leviathan', which put self-preservation above all other considerations. Though he was thanked by the house and asked to print his sermon, the majority of MPs chose not to heed his warning. With the rest of the university Jane set his face against whig demands to exclude the king's heir, the Catholic James, duke of York, from the throne. He evolved into a thorough-paced tory.

In June 1680 Jane, anxious to preserve Oxford's reputation as a bastion of protestantism, was to the fore in disciplining Francis Nicholson for preaching 'Popish doctrine' in a university sermon. In the same year he became rector of Newland, Oxfordshire. Of greater political

moment, he drew up the Oxford decree of 21 July 1683, in which the university anathematized twenty-seven propositions, judged to contain 'damnable doctrines'. Drawn from the publications of whigs, dissenters, Hobbists, and papists, they were denounced as being 'destructive of the kingly government, the safety of His Majestie's person, the public peace, the laws of nature and bonds of humane society'. Promulgated in the wake of the Rye House plot, the decree was in intention and effect a reassertion of loyalty to the *jure divino* rule of the house of Stuart, and a timely affirmation of James's birthright. Passive obedience was declared an obligation on all subjects, 'absolute and without exception', and the moral right to resist the God-given sovereign categorically denied. The publication of the decree in Latin and in English contributed to the rout of whiggery in the last years of Charles II's reign.

Jane greeted James II's accession enthusiastically, and drafted the university's loyal address on 21 February 1685. On 2 May he received the deanery of Gloucester as his reward. All continued well in Oxford until late 1686. The emergence of the Catholic challenge, headed by the converts Obadiah Walker and John Massey, threw the university into turmoil. The nomination of Massey to the deanery of Christ Church catapulted Jane and his brethren of the chapter into direct opposition to the king's Catholicizing policies. Their attempt to invoke the law against Massey by instigating proceedings in the court of king's bench in January 1687 was halted by James's intervention. Jane formally opposed the royal chaplains' attempt to convert the king's former brother-in-law, Lawrence Hyde, earl of Rochester. When in May the Oxford clergy were faced by a demand from their diocesan, Dr Samuel Parker, to thank James for his edict of toleration, Jane openly and successfully led the opposition. At Gloucester he supported Bishop Robert Frampton in a similar refusal to address. In 1688 he and his Christ Church colleague Henry Aldrich, together with the earls of Clarendon and Rochester, rallied behind the newly elected chancellor of Oxford, James, duke of Ormond, in resisting the king's will.

Like Compton, Jane welcomed William of Orange's invasion in November 1688 as a godsend. He approved Aldrich's offer of the university's plate to the prince at Hungerford in December, and made little mourn at James II's expulsion from Whitehall. In countenancing dynastic revolution, Jane contravened the very principles on which he had framed the decree of 1683, and made himself the butt of learned wits—the Latinized form of his name, Janus, recalling the two-faced, double-dealing deity of classical antiquity. However, he and other high-churchmen soon came to rue the king's dethronement as William, once possessed of James's throne, showed less affection for their church than had his predecessor. The enactment of toleration in 1690 robbed the state church of its legal monopoly and seriously aggravated the legacy of ecclesiastical discontent left over from the previous reign.

Realizing too late that their opposition to James's policies had emancipated their whig and nonconformist enemies, Jane and his allies were driven to fight a rearguard action: first, in the 1689 commission of divines summoned by William to revise the prayer book with a view to satisfying nonconformist objections, and second in convocation. In October Jane opposed the removal of readings from the Apocrypha, supported Bishop Thomas Sprat in questioning the legality of the commission, and finally withdrew. Before the proposals were submitted to convocation Jane conspired with the tory earls of Rochester and Clarendon to draw up a plan of opposition. When convocation met on 21 November, he was elected, by 55 votes to 28, prolocutor of the lower house of clergy, in opposition to the ex-dissenter and whig John Tillotson, the court candidate. He emphasized the meaning of his victory, when presented to Compton, president of the upper house, by pointedly throwing back at him the words which had been emblazoned on the bishop's colours when he rose in support of William of Orange: 'Nolumus leges Angliae mutari' ('we refuse to alter the laws of England'). It was the opening move in a campaign which defeated the government's efforts to force through comprehension at the expense of traditional Anglicanism.

In Oxford Jane continued his defence of established religion, and drew up the university decree of 19 August 1690 condemning Arthur Bury's *Naked Gospel* and its reductionist view of Christianity. He opposed the spread of unorthodoxy, Socinianism, and unitarianism especially, and lent support to tory attempts to restrict the further erosion of the Church of England's ascendancy. Although he had been appointed a royal chaplain following the revolution of 1688, he refused to sign the 1696 association in defence of William's person, so disillusioned had he become with his government.

Queen Anne's accession in 1702 brought a general improvement in Anglican tory fortunes, but still no bishopric for Jane, who soldiered on as regius professor with the aid of his deputy, George Smalridge. He was not liked by Aldrich's successor, the megalomanic Dean Francis Atterbury, who tried without success to get rid of him by preferring him elsewhere. Jonathan Trelawny, the tory bishop of Exeter, collated him to the chancellorship of his cathedral in February 1703, which Jane exchanged for the precentorship in May 1704 (resigned 1706). He died, unmarried, at Christ Church on 23 February 1707, and was buried in Christ Church. His will was proved at Oxford on 10 November. He published only four sermons.

Jane was a conspicuous example of a Restoration cleric whose outlook had been forged against the backdrop of the eclipse of the Church of England in the 1650s. As an Anglican loyalist he strove to answer the needs of the re-established church by defending its doctrinal authority and its privileged position in society, both of which, he believed, would be safe under the protection of the Stuart monarchy. It was his singular misfortune to see the harmony of church and state relations shattered by the ambitions of the Catholic King James and his whig-backed supplanter, William.   R. A. P. J. BEDDARD

Sources Wood, *Ath. Oxon.*, new edn · *The life and times of Anthony Wood*, ed. A. Clark, 5 vols., OHS, 19, 21, 26, 30, 40 (1891–1900) · *Judicium et decretum universitatis Oxonienses, latum in convocatione habita Julii 21 an. 1683, contra quosdam perniciosos libros et propositiones impias* (1683) · R. A. Beddard, 'Tory Oxford', *Hist. U. Oxf.* 4: *17th-cent. Oxf.*, 863–906 · R. A. Beddard, 'James II and the Catholic challenge', *Hist. U. Oxf.* 4: *17th-cent. Oxf.*, 907–54 · E. Calamy, *An historical account of my own life, with some reflections on the times I have lived in, 1671–1731*, ed. J. T. Rutt, 2 vols. (1829) · G. Every, *The high church party, 1688–1718* (1956) · G. V. Bennett, *The tory crisis in church and state* (1975)
Archives Christ Church Oxf. · Gloucester Cathedral · Oxf. UA | Bodl. Oxf., Ballard MSS, Rawl. MSS, Tanner MSS · PRO, state papers, SP 29, SP 31, SP 44
Likenesses W. Gandy, oils, 1706, Bodl. Oxf. [*see illus.*]

Janes, Emily (1846–1928), women's welfare activist, was born on 14 February 1846 at Tring, Hertfordshire, the eldest daughter of George Janes and Martha Stevens, the daughter of William Stevens of Cheddington, Buckinghamshire. She was educated at a private school at Chesham, Buckinghamshire, and began philanthropic work in Apsley, Bedfordshire, by undertaking voluntary parish duties including the management of clubs. From 1877 to 1878 she was diocesan secretary of the St Albans branch of the Girls Friendly Society, and for a year from 1880 she was matron at the Magdalen Hospital in Streatham. Up to this point she worked on a voluntary basis.

In 1882 Emily Janes was introduced by Louisa Hubbard (1836–1906) to (Jane) Ellice Hopkins (1836–1904), and for the next four years she worked as Ellice Hopkins's private secretary, campaigning for the amendment of laws relating to the protection of girls. This work led to the formation of Ladies' Associations for the Care of Friendless Girls: groups of women united by an awareness of a need to help and support young women and girls. From 1886 to 1895 Emily Janes worked as the honorary organizing secretary for the association. She was also a member of the National Vigilance Association, formed in 1885 'to repress criminal vice and public immorality'.

From 1886 onwards Emily Janes was funded by a group of friends who were keen to help her continue what they saw as her valuable and strenuous work. Her workload for 1891 was described in her obituary:

> In a year of 365 days, to speak at 170 meetings at most of which she was forced to undertake the whole burden and responsibility (no other speaker being provided), to attend committees, to spend on an average not less than three hours daily in correspondence, to travel hundreds of miles to and fro over a network of railways and upon every kind of road, in almost every sort of conveyance, and to be constantly called upon for advice in almost every kind of difficulty and distress, means a strain on heart, voice and brain which only exceptional devotion could carry on. (*National Council of Women News*)

Aware that the great deal of philanthropic work being undertaken by women was unco-ordinated, Louisa Hubbard in 1890 wrote and circulated a suggestion for the formation of a Central Conference Council (CCC) to establish co-ordinating conferences of women workers. It was set up in 1891 with Emily Janes as its honorary organizing secretary, lecturer, and editor of its quarterly journal, the *Threefold Chord*. At a conference held in Nottingham in 1895, the CCC reformed as the National Union of Women

Workers (NUWW), again with Emily Janes as its organizing secretary and editor of its journal, initially titled *An Occasional Paper*. From that time until 1917 Emily Janes worked tirelessly for the NUWW.

Emily Janes was clearly effective in her role of organizing secretary: in 1895 there were 10 branches of the NUWW, by 1918 there were 130. Throughout her working life she played a pivotal role in the organization of women undertaking philanthropic work, inspiring those who worked with her by her abilities and energy. Her success was felt to be due 'to her thorough grasp of the social questions of the day, and the practical common sense with which she discussed them'. She had:

> a tact and a quiet force of character that drew people towards her and was to be of the highest value in bringing about the formation of those local associations which were for years the chief object of her travels through the country. (Pratt, 106)

Emily Janes described the world in which she worked in her paper 'On the associated work of women in religion and philanthropy', which appeared in 1893 in Angela Burdett-Coutts's publication *Woman's Mission*. In 1898 she took over from Louisa Hubbard as editor of the *Englishwoman's Yearbook and Directory*.

In 1917 age and ill health compelled Emily Janes to resign as organizing secretary of the NUWW, but she continued to attend meetings and remained on the executive committee as a vice-president. Emily Janes never married. In 1910 she described her interests as reading, music, and conversation. She was living at 31 Tanza Road, Hampstead, London, in 1910, moving later to 90 Hampstead Way, Hendon, Hertfordshire, and then, towards the end of her life, to Hastings in Sussex.

Some time before her death Emily Janes had become completely paralysed. She died on 26 October 1928 at her home, Dunclutha, Hastings; a memorial service was held at Christ Church, Westminster, on 16 November 1928.

SERENA KELLY

Sources *National Council of Women News* (Dec 1928) • E. A. Pratt, *A woman's work for women* (1893) • *WW* • E. Janes, 'On the associated work of women in religion and philanthropy', *Woman's mission: a series of congress papers on the philanthropic work of women*, ed. Baroness Burdett-Coutts [A. G. Burdett-Coutts] (1893), 131–48
Likenesses photograph (in old age), repro. in *National Council of Women News*

Janeway, James (1636–1674), nonconformist minister, fourth of the nine sons of William Janeway (d. 1654), curate of Lilley and later rector of Kelshall (both in Hertfordshire), and younger brother of John *Janeway, was born about the end of 1636 at Lilley. He matriculated at Christ Church, Oxford, on 1 April 1656 and graduated BA on 12 October 1659. Janeway was ordained deacon at Oxford on 1 January 1661. After university, he lived in the house of a Mrs Stringer at Windsor, as tutor to her son George. Edmund Calamy includes him in his list of those ministers 'ejected or silenced' by the Act of Uniformity of 1662, but there is no evidence that he had taken any position in the established church.

Janeway seems to have first acted as a nonconformist preacher in London during the plague year, 1665. Following the issue of Charles II's declaration of indulgence, he was licensed on 11 April 1672 as a presbyterian at his house in Salisbury Street, Bermondsey. A meeting-house was built for him in Jamaica Row, Rotherhithe, Surrey, where he became very popular. Richard Baxter commented on how well known Janeway was in London and characterized him as 'a *humble*, a *serious*, a *peaceable*, and an *industrious* spirit: his heart … set on the work of God, and the winning of Souls' (J. Janeway, *Saints Incouragement to Diligence in Christs Service*, 1674, preface, sigs. a3–a3v). After the withdrawal of the indulgence Janeway's meeting-house was wrecked by a band of troopers, but rebuilt on a larger scale. On two occasions Janeway escaped arrest.

Like others of his family (his brothers Abraham and John both died in their twenties), James Janeway became consumptive. He died on 16 March 1674, 'in the 38 yeare of his age', leaving a widow, Hannah, and was buried on 20 March in the church of St Mary Aldermanbury, near the grave of his brother Abraham. Funeral sermons were preached by Nathaniel Vincent and John Ryther.

In his funeral sermon Vincent remarked that Janeway would commend 'the old Puritan strictness and circumspection, and bewail the excesses and licentiousness of professors!' (Vincent, 33), and Janeway's publications do place him firmly in the tradition of evangelistic and practical puritan divinity:

> Christians, be not in the least disheartened but rather quickned; quit you like men, be strong; behold the cross, win it and wear it; let nothing discourage thee, methinks that far more exceeding and eternal weight of glory should make all hinderances insignificant. (*Saints Incouragement*, 59)

This exhortation is a catena of familiar texts and homiletic commonplaces. The book from which it comes, Janeway's *Saints Incouragement to Diligence in Christs Service* (1674), is an admonition to sinners to reform and an exhortation to zealous conscientiousness in the converted, in their performance of duties, in introspective scrutiny of their spiritual condition, and in meditation upon God's providences. This book was prefaced by Baxter, and Janeway shared with Baxter and with other puritans a fascination with everyday experience and with the course of human lives. His homiletic fervour is consequently combined with an attentiveness to the circumstantial and material. His writings never let go their grasp on fact; they are habitually anecdotal and biographical. His *Token for children: being an exact account of the conversion, holy and exemplary lives, and joyful deaths of several young children* (1672; part II, 1673), intended to rescue children from their 'miserable condition by Nature' and 'from falling into everlasting Fire' (*Token for children*, pref., sigs. A4v, A7v), consists of histories of exceptional piety in the young, their authenticity and reliability confirmed by details of time and place and the identification both of the children and of witnesses and informants. The posthumous *Mr. James Janeway's legacy to his friends containing twenty seven famous instances of Gods providences in and about sea dangers* (1674), prefaced by Ryther, shows a similar concern to set accurately reported experience in a providential context.

These and others of Janeway's works went into several editions. Most popular of all, with seven editions by 1698 and at least another twelve during the next two centuries, was *Invisibles, realities, demonstrated in the holy life and triumphant death of Mr. John Janeway* (1673), again prefaced by Baxter. Prompted by 'some Reverend, Learned and Holy men' (Baxter presumably among them), Janeway wrote this life of his brother as an antidote to atheism, impiety, and the derision of godliness. Focusing upon the frequency and warmth of his brother's private devotions, his meditative introspection, and (though John was never ordained) his pastoral commitment to others, Janeway constructs an exemplary puritan saint whose 'sweetness of temper declares the beauty of Religion' (*Invisibles, Realities*, 23). With its contention that for John Janeway 'Christ was at the end and bottom of every thing' (ibid., 7) attested by the inclusion of many letters and other documents, it was this work which secured the posthumous reputation of one who during his lifetime 'made no great noise in the world' (ibid., 36). Janeway may also have been the author of a life of his brother Abraham, extant in manuscript (Bodl. Oxf., MS Rawl. D.110).

N. H. KEEBLE

Sources E. Calamy, ed., *An abridgement of Mr. Baxter's history of his life and times, with an account of the ministers, &c., who were ejected after the Restauration of King Charles II*, 2nd edn, 2 vols. (1713), vol. 2, p. 838 · E. Calamy, *A continuation of the account of the ministers ... who were ejected and silenced after the Restoration in 1660*, 2 vols. (1727), vol. 1, p. 533, vol. 2, pp. 962–5 · Calamy rev. · *Saints memorials, or, Words fitly spoken ... being a collection of divine sentences ... by Edmund Calamy, Joseph Caryl, Ralph Venning, James Janeway* (1673) · N. Vincent, *The saints triumph over the last enemy* (1674) · W. Urwick, *Nonconformity in Hertfordshire* (1884), 658–9 · Foster, *Alum. Oxon.* · G. L. Turner, ed., *Original records of early nonconformity under persecution and indulgence*, 2 (1912), 979 · W. Wilson, *The history and antiquities of the dissenting churches and meeting houses in London, Westminster and Southwark*, 4 vols. (1808–14), vol. 2, pp. 347–8 · Wood, *Ath. Oxon.*, new edn, 3.1006; 4.218

Archives Bodl. Oxf., MS life of his brother Abraham Janeway, MS Rawlinson D.110

Likenesses line engraving, BM, NPG · portrait, repro. in J. Janeway, *Mr. James Janeway's legacy to his friends* (1674), frontispiece · portrait, repro. in Calamy and others, *Saints memorials*, frontispiece

Janeway, John (1633–1657), scholar and writer on religion, was born at Lilley, Hertfordshire, on 27 October 1633 and was baptized there on 4 December, the second son of William Janeway (d. 1654), curate of the parish. His brother James *Janeway (1636–1674) was after the Restoration pastor of a presbyterian congregation at Rotherhithe, and in 1673 issued a life of John. When John was about eleven the family moved to Aspenden, Hertfordshire, and at about the same time he was admitted to St Paul's School, where he became proficient in Latin and Greek and developed interests in arithmetic and Hebrew. He was elected to a foundation scholarship at Eton College after taking a brilliant oral examination in several subjects; his grasp of 'the Hebrew tongue ... was looked upon as beyond precedent' (Gardiner, 1.43). While still enrolled at Eton, Janeway spent three months at Oxford as a pupil in mathematics of Seth Ward. He was admitted as a scholar to King's College,

Cambridge, where he matriculated in 1651 and graduated BA in 1655. He did not marry, and was a fellow of King's College from 1654 until his death.

At Cambridge Janeway was converted to a demanding puritan outlook, a religion of the head and of the heart. Aged only eighteen or nineteen, he wrote to an elderly minister of the need for 'daily close walking with God'; this was:

> a bitter sweet duty, bitter to corrupt nature, but sweet to the regenerate part if performed ... I charge it upon you with humility and tenderness, that God have a least half an hour allowed him for this exercise: oh, this most precious, soul ravishing, soul perfecting duty! (Janeway, 14)

He was sustained in such feelings by a group in the college which met together for spiritual exercises and discussion. Before graduating, however, Janeway left the college to attend his father, who was terminally ill, at Kelshall, Hertfordshire. After his return to Cambridge the active members of the discussion club left one by one, and the atmosphere became less fervid. Isolated, Janeway seems to have concentrated on his solitary studies and this, if his brother is to be believed, served to 'inflict an unhealable wound to his bodily constitution' (ibid., 38). Briefly he acted as a tutor in the household of Dr Thomas Coxe, but was forced by ill health to abandon the work, retreating into the care of his family at Kelshall.

Here Janeway had a dream in which he witnessed the coming of the day of judgement:

> I heard terrible cracks of thunder, and saw dreadful lightnings; the foundations of the earth did shake, and the heavens were rolled together as a garment; yea all things visible were in a flame; methought I saw the graves opened, and the earth and sea giving up their dead; methought I beheld millions of angels and Christ coming in the clouds.

Then God appeared on his throne:

> his garments were white as snow, and the hair of his head was like pure wool ... and I cried out 'I have waited for thy salvation, O God', and so I mounted into the air, to meet my Lord in the clouds. (Janeway, 96)

Not long after, in June 1657, now almost blind, John Janeway died of tuberculosis in the presence of seven brothers and two sisters. He was buried in the church of Kelshall, where in 1823 a monument was erected to his memory.

STEPHEN WRIGHT

Sources J. Janeway, *Invisibles, realities, demonstrated in the holy life and triumphant death of Mr John Janeway, fellow of King's College* (1673) · Venn, *Alum. Cant.* · W. Sterry, ed., *The Eton College register, 1441–1698* (1943) · M. McDonnell, ed., *The registers of St Paul's School, 1509–1748* (privately printed, London, 1977) · R. B. Gardiner, ed., *The admission registers of St Paul's School, from 1748 to 1876* (1884) · W. Urwick, *Nonconformity in Hertfordshire* (1884) · will, PRO, PROB 11/250 [William Janeway, father], quire 395, fols. 180v–181r

Janiewicz, Feliks. *See* Yaniewicz, Felix (1762–1848).

Janner, Barnett, Baron Janner (1892–1982), politician and lawyer, was born on 20 June 1892 in Lucknick (now Luocke), in the province of Kovno (Kaunas), Lithuania, the first of three surviving children of Joseph Vitum-Janner (d. 1932), a shopkeeper, and his wife, Gertrude (Gittel), *née* Zweck, of Telz (Telsiai), Lithuania. His parents brought him to Britain at the age of nine months and his earliest memories were of childhood in Barry, Glamorgan, where his father opened a furniture shop. His mother died in 1902 while giving birth to twins (who both died shortly after); the loss affected him deeply and marred his later childhood.

Janner was educated at Holton Road School in Barry and, from the age of thirteen, at Barry county school to which he won a scholarship of 6*d.* a week. The headmaster of the school, Major Edgar Evans, was a formative influence. In 1911 he won a scholarship to University College, Cardiff, where he studied English, mathematics, and other subjects, gaining a BA honours degree in 1914. While a student, he eked out his scholarship by teaching at the Cardiff School of Commerce, known as Bloggs School.

Janner's family was Jewish and moderately orthodox. He later wrote, 'Being of an unusual religion the family was known as a kind of mascot'. The family observed the laws of *kashrut* and the sabbath. Some Yiddish was spoken in the home but Janner never learned more than the rudiments of spoken Hebrew. Throughout his life he was intensely loyal to his Jewish origins. He served as treasurer of the Barry Dock Jewish community (of nine families) in 1911 and as a student was active in support of Zionism.

After graduating, Janner continued his studies in law and became articled to the Cardiff firm of solicitors Sidney, Jenkins, and Howell. In March 1916 he enlisted in the Royal Garrison Artillery but was not called up until August 1917. In November he was posted to the western front and served as a gunner near Noordschoote and in the Amiens sector. In August 1918, at Carnoi, his battery was bombarded with mustard-gas shells. Janner was temporarily blinded but his life was saved by a comrade who fixed on his gas mask when he was already unconscious. The gassing left him with a 'chest condition' that troubled him intermittently for the rest of his life. Otherwise, he remained generally healthy although he took little exercise.

Upon demobilization Janner returned to Cardiff and set up as a solicitor. He also entered politics, contesting the municipal election in 1921 as a candidate for the Comrades of the Great War. In 1924 he fought central ward in Cardiff, the first of several unsuccessful attempts as a Liberal. Meanwhile he engaged in Jewish affairs, securing election in 1926 to the Board of Deputies of British Jews, the main representative body of the community. He also began to play a prominent role in the English Zionist Federation and by 1930 was a member of its executive.

In 1927 Janner married Elsie Sybil (1905–1994), daughter of Joseph and Henrietta Cohen, at the Hampstead synagogue. She was born in Newcastle but grew up in London where her father owned a furniture store. The marriage produced two children, Greville Ewan, later Lord Janner of Braunstone (*b.* 1928), and Ruth, later Lady Morris of Kenwood (*b.* 1932).

At the 1929 general election Janner stood unsuccessfully as the Liberal candidate for the parliamentary seat of Cardiff Central. Later that year he moved to London and bought a house in Hendon. He worked as a solicitor and as company secretary to two new companies established by his father-in-law.

In December 1930 Janner contested the Whitechapel and St George's by-election for the Liberals. This was a constituency with a large concentration of Jewish voters and Janner made much of his opposition to the government's recently issued white paper on Palestine. His campaign was partly funded by the Zionist-inspired Palestine Protest Committee. He narrowly lost the by-election but in the general election ten months later he gained the seat, becoming a Liberal MP at thirty-nine. Devoted to Whitechapel, he maintained the practice far into old age of visiting all the synagogues in the district every year on the eve of the day of atonement.

Although a conscientious constituency member, Janner was unable in 1935 to resist the electoral tide that swept away most remaining Liberal MPs. Standing as a Liberal and anti-fascist candidate, he was defeated by his Labour opponent. During the next decade he practised as a solicitor in Holborn and concentrated on Jewish and Zionist affairs. He joined the Labour Party in 1936 and was soon after adopted as prospective candidate for West Leicester.

In the Labour landslide of 1945 he defeated the sitting member, Harold Nicolson. Janner held the constituency (renamed Leicester North West in 1950) until 1970. Throughout his parliamentary career he took a particular interest in safeguarding the rights of tenants. In 1959 he was successful in obtaining passage of a private member's bill for the restriction of offensive weapons—the 'Flick-Knife Bill'. He was the first, in 1949, to raise in the House of Commons the question of British adhesion to the Genocide Convention; he was rebuffed but continued to press the issue until Britain finally ratified the convention in 1970. He never sought—and was never offered—office.

Janner became best-known as a leader of the Jewish community. In 1940 he was elected chairman of the English Zionist Federation and from 1950 to 1970 served as its president. In 1955 he was elected president of the Board of Deputies of British Jews. The Suez crisis the following year brought a severe conflict of loyalties, particularly after his party leader, Hugh Gaitskell, denounced British–Israeli 'collusion'. Janner joined five other Jewish Labour MPs in abstaining in some (not all) key parliamentary votes. He found himself fiercely criticized by fellow Jews but survived a vote of confidence at the board of deputies. In 1964, however, he suffered a humiliating defeat in his attempt to secure election to a fourth term as president. He nevertheless remained very active in Jewish causes. In particular, he helped organize the evacuation to Britain in 1967 of the last remaining Jews in Aden.

In 1961 Janner was knighted 'for services to the Jewish community'—the first to be honoured for this reason. He called it the proudest moment of his life. In 1970 he became a life peer as Baron Janner of the city of Leicester. He was succeeded in his Commons seat by his son, Greville, who, also like him, became president of the Board of Deputies of British Jews.

In physique Janner was imposing, a large, heavy-set man with a head shaped 'rather like an egg' (Janner, 5). He had no joint in the fourth finger of his left hand. He was dog-matic, large-hearted, emotional, financially scrupulous, a champion of the underdog. He was a good dancer. His attitudes and dress were formal and Victorian. An old-fashioned, sonorous, sometimes long-winded but nevertheless effective orator, he continued to speak in the House of Lords and from Jewish platforms until shortly before his death. Janner died on 4 May 1982 at his home, 45 Morpeth Mansions, Morpeth Terrace, London. He was buried two days later in Willesden cemetery. The village of Gan Ner (a play on his name) was founded in his memory in Israel.   BERNARD WASSERSTEIN

Sources E. Janner, *Barnett Janner: a personal portrait* (1984) · C. Bermant, *Troubled Eden: an anatomy of British Jewry* (1969) · private information (2004) [family] · personal knowledge (2004) · *Jewish Chronicle* (23 March 2001)
Archives FILM BFI NFTVA, party political footage
Likenesses J. Epstein, bust, 1965 · R. Sallon, cartoon, priv. coll.
Wealth at death £67,461: probate, 20 Aug 1982, *CGPLA Eng. & Wales*

Janssen, Bernard (*fl.* 1616–1627). *See under* Johnson family (*per. c.*1570–*c.*1630).

Janssen, Sir Theodore, first baronet (*c.*1658–1748), financier, born in Angoulême, France, was the eldest son of Abraham Janssen, a Huguenot of Walloon descent, and a merchant and paper manufacturer of Angoulême, and his wife, Henrietta Manigault. He was probably educated in the Netherlands and, reputed to be worth £20,000, settled in London in 1683. He was naturalized on 26 June 1685 and quickly made his reputation in the City. On 26 January 1698 he married Williamza (Williamson) Henley (*d.* 1731), the daughter of Sir Robert Henley, a wealthy MP. None of their five sons left legitimate sons; two of their daughters were connected through marriage with the lords Baltimore and the earls of Essex. Janssen was knighted on 1 May 1696 and received his baronetcy on 11 March 1715. He sat as a whig MP for Yarmouth, Isle of Wight, from 12 April 1717 until he was expelled on 23 January 1721.

At the height of his prosperity Janssen invested in property in Westminster and Dorset, bought one of the new town houses, number 20, in aristocratic Hanover Square, London, and for his country seat bought the manor of Wimbledon, Surrey, where he already held some property. He built a new house in the Palladian style at Wimbledon and planned a garden ornamented with his beloved trees and classical statues.

Janssen's extensive contacts in France, north Italy, and Amsterdam eased his mercantile and financial activities. The range of his commercial interests cannot be documented but is partly reflected in the books he owned and in particular the tract he wrote in 1713, 'General maxims in trade, particularly applied to the commerce between Great Britain and France'. He was a founder member of the Bank of England in 1694 when he was one of only twelve to invest £10,000, and he was a key director during the first critical years and later. He took an interest in other companies, including the South Sea Company, set up in 1711, organized loans for individuals, and dealt in

securities. But the profits which may most have contributed to the fortune of nearly £300,000 which he had built up by 1720 were probably derived from his services to the government, nearly continuously between 1688 and 1713 involved in wars with France. Either as a member of syndicates or alone he remitted vast sums, sometimes at short notice and reduced commission, for the subsistence of the army in Flanders and the subsidies for continental allies.

Janssen was a cultured and thoughtful man with many interests. He was closely involved in a prestigious though loss-making publication undertaken by the recently established Cambridge University Press: a three-volume edition of Suidas's Greek–Latin lexicon with text, annotated, in parallel columns. He supplied the paper and eventually agreed to cover three-fifths of the cost. His own classical studies were reflected by the many texts and translations in his library. A detailed list of his books (more than 560 volumes) drawn up in 1721 includes many reference works and religious and philosophical studies, as well as literary, historical, and some scientific works. Books on architecture and gardening reflected his current interests.

Janssen was a cautious and highly respected man, proud of his reputation for honesty. Yet like thousands of others he was drawn into the speculation which followed fraudulent dealings in South Sea Company shares. After rising from 128 in January 1720 to 950 by 1 July the value of shares collapsed in the autumn, falling to 155 by 15 December when the House of Commons assembled to investigate and punish those held responsible. Janssen was not one of the committee responsible for mismanagement but he had in February 1719 again accepted nomination as a director. He was then over sixty, possibly reluctant to investigate malpractices he must surely have suspected. He faced in person a hostile House of Commons on 23 January 1721, when he was expelled from the house, and later was disqualified for life from public office. He was released from custody in order to prepare the inventory of all his assets on 1 June 1720 and income and expenditure between then and 20 March 1721. This lengthy and detailed document is the major source for the study of his activities, since he left no personal papers.

Janssen's estate was valued at £243,000, of which the House of Commons agreed on 2 June 1721, by 134 votes to 118, that he should be allowed to keep £50,000, later raised by £9000. His estates were given up on 20 September 1721 and sold for £88,700 between 1723 and 1729. He seems ultimately to have been able to retain over £90,000, which amount allowed him to buy back some of the Dorset estates, the house in Hanover Square, and his new house and garden at Wimbledon. He was to let these two houses, lease a smaller London property, and make his Wimbledon home in the house he had first held there.

Little is known of Janssen's later activities. He was in partnership with Stephen Theodore Janssen (1705–1777), the son who shared his interests. His son, from 1766 the fourth and last baronet, became a member and then master of the Stationers' Company (1749–51), an alderman (1748–65), and lord mayor (1754–5).

Janssen died intestate, aged about ninety, on 22 September 1748 and was buried on 28 September in the churchyard of St Mary, Wimbledon. The originals of a miniature of him and the painting of the house he built, from which slides were made for what is now the Wimbledon Society in the 1920s, have not been traced; the portrait by Sir Godfrey Kneller of Lady Janssen, who died on 2 September 1731, is in private hands. They are all reproduced in the article on Janssen in the *Proceedings of the Huguenot Society* (26, 1994–7, 264–88).   ELSPETH VEALE

Sources *Sir Theodore Janssen, kt., bart., his particular and inventory, containing the particulars of all and singular the lands, tenements and hereditaments, goods, chattels, debts and personal estate … (1721)* · The estates of the South Sea directors as sold, 1722?–1730, Bodl. Oxf., MSS Med. F. 1.5–6 [2 vol. collection of 341 sale catalogues] · 'The case of Sir Theodore Janssen', 1721?, GL [broadsheet] · T. Janssen, 'General maxims in trade, particularly applied to the commerce between Great Britain and France', *A collection of scarce and valuable tracts … Lord Somers*, ed. W. Scott, 2nd edn, 13 (1815), 287–99 · W. A. Shaw, ed., *Calendar of treasury books*, [33 vols. in 64], PRO (1904–69), esp. vols. 8–26 · *JHC*, 19 (1718–21) · E. Veale, 'Sir Theodore Janssen, Huguenot and merchant of London, *c*.1658–1748', *Proceedings of the Huguenot Society*, 26 (1994–7), 264–88 [fully documented] · J. Carswell, *The South Sea Bubble*, rev. edn (1993) · P. G. M. Dickson, *The financial revolution in England: a study in the development of public credit, 1688–1756* (1967); repr. (1993) · private information · *GM*, 1st ser., 18 (1748), 428 · W. Minet and S. Minet, eds., 'Libre des tesmoignages de l'Eglise de Threadneedle Street, 1669–1789', *Publications of the Huguenot Society of London*, 21 (1909) [whole issue], esp. 145 · *Publications of the Huguenot Society of London*, 18 (1911) · W. A. Littedale, ed., *The registers of Christ Church, Newgate, 1538 to 1754*, Harleian Society, register section, 21 (1895), 216 · W. Musgrave, *Obituary prior to 1800*, ed. G. J. Armytage, 3, Harleian Society, 46 (1900) · *London Magazine*, 17 (1748), 429, 476–7 · [A. W. Hughes Clarke], ed., *The parish register of Wimbledon, co. Surrey*, Surrey RS, 8 (1924)
Archives Bank of England Archive, City of London · NRA, priv. coll., papers about South Sea Company | BL, South Sea Company MSS, Add. MSS 25494–25581 · HLRO, South Sea Company MSS, parchment collection, boxes 155, 156, 167
Likenesses miniature, repro. in Veale, 'Sir Theodore Janssen', 272

Janssen Van Ceulen, Cornelius. *See* Johnson, Cornelius (*bap*. 1593, *d*. 1661).

Janyns, Henry (*fl*. 1453–1483), master mason, was probably the son of Robert Janyns senior, master mason of the tower of Merton College chapel, Oxford (begun 1448), and warden of the masons at Eton College from 1449. By 1453/4 John Clerk was the warden at Eton and Henry Janyns was his apprentice. Under Clerk's will of 1459 Henry was left his master's tools and designs, together with 26*s*. 8*d*. in cash. Apart from a possible reference to him in 1463/4 in connection with carvings for the gatehouse at Merton, he is next heard of in 1478, by which time he was master mason of Edward IV's new chapel of St George in Windsor Castle. Probably in charge since 1475, when work began, he is last mentioned in 1483. In 1481 a house of his at Burford was leased for use by the king's masons, who were no doubt occupied in the nearby Taynton quarries which supplied practically all the stone for the chapel.

St George's Chapel was the most ambitious new church begun in late fifteenth-century England. Of cathedral format but restricted scale, its main sources are the two outstanding church buildings of the preceding century, the choir of St Peter's Abbey, Gloucester (now the cathedral), and the nave of Canterbury Cathedral. The exceptionally consistent use of flattened four-centred arches imparts a distinctive rigour and elegance to the elevations, and the fan vaults in the aisles display complete mastery of the problems of designing a vault type which was much used in the Oxford region.

Robert Janyns junior (*d*. 1506), master mason, probably Henry's son, is first recorded in 1499 as master mason of the extension to the king's lodging in Windsor Castle known as Henry VII's Tower. Its outstanding feature is its multi-tier bay windows of complex form, some of which change plan at each level. Robert probably succeeded Henry Janyns as master mason of St George's Chapel, but there is unfortunately no documentary evidence for the identity of the holder of this post during his lifetime. He is also the master mason most likely to have designed Henry VII's most important architectural commission, the lady chapel built at Westminster Abbey from 1503. The main elevations and many other aspects of the design show a thorough understanding both of the originality of St George's and of its indebtedness to earlier designs. The attribution of the Westminster chapel to Robert Vertue, which has sometimes been advanced, founders on the dissimilarity of its vaults to those at Bath Abbey, which are Vertue's only documented and extant work. Robert Janyns's short and simple will, proved on 9 October 1506, shows that Burford was his home town.

CHRISTOPHER WILSON

Sources J. Harvey and A. Oswald, *English mediaeval architects: a biographical dictionary down to 1550*, 2nd edn (1984), 159–60 · H. M. Colvin and others, eds., *The history of the king's works*, 6 vols. (1963–82), vol. 1, pp. 215, 282; vol. 2, pp. 884–5; vol. 3, pp. 26, 214, 304 and n., 307–8, 313–14 · W. H. St J. Hope, *Windsor Castle: an architectural history*, 1 (1913), 237–47; 2 (1913), 375–406, 585–6 · C. Wilson, 'The designer of Henry VII's chapel, Westminster Abbey', *The reign of Henry VII* [Harlaxton 1993], ed. B. Thompson (1995), 133–56

Janyns, Robert, junior (*d*. 1506). *See under* Janyns, Henry (*fl*. 1453–1483).

Japhet, Saemy (1858–1954), merchant banker, was born on 2 May 1858 at Frankfurt am Main, Germany, the son of a teacher of Hebrew. In late 1873, straight from high school in Germany, he joined the small Frankfurt private bank of Emile Schwarzschild as an office junior. After a short stint in the army, he returned to become his firm's stock exchange representative, and in 1880 he established his own stockbroking firm of S. Japhet. Japhet married, and he and his wife, Marie (1862–1932), had at least three daughters.

Japhet operated in a small way, from his home and with no staff until the late 1880s, executing orders in Frankfurt for clients elsewhere. His transactions came to embrace placings of securities with syndicates of clients and friends and the flotation of private businesses. His handling of the sale of a Frankfurt brewery in 1887 apparently met with such success that, according to his own account, 'from now onwards numerous projects were entrusted to me' (Japhet, 44).

In 1886 Japhet first visited London, which 'made an enormous impression upon me and became henceforth the goal towards which I was drawn' (Japhet, 40). Initially his capital was sufficient to finance only a Berlin branch in 1891, and he went to live in that city. Powerful friends were now made, not least staff of the Deutsche Bank, which provided especially favourable settlement arrangements in London; these proved 'an enormous help' (ibid., 61). Notwithstanding an imperfect knowledge of English, Japhet opened a London branch in 1896 with £15,000 capital. He ran it on cautious lines, eschewing 'so-called proper business—ie we should drop commission business and concentrate on stock dealings on our own account and on financial transactions' (ibid., 73). 'Arbitrage' in stocks was central to his London operations, which gradually became much more important and profitable than his continental branches.

In 1900 Japhet moved permanently to London, where his business 'developed splendidly' (Japhet, 76). His willingness to allow outsiders to take large interests in his firm, notably the powerful financiers Sir Basil Zaharoff and Sir Ernest Cassel in 1902 and 1910 respectively, was remarkable. Of the firm's capital of £400,000 in 1910, half had been contributed by Cassel, who was responsible for introducing a number of important clients to the firm.

Japhet's memoirs, published privately in 1931, are largely silent about his First World War experiences, but his continental business was surely gravely damaged and his German origins must have drawn opprobrium. His house's culture was strongly German, his staff being largely German nationals who conducted business in their native language. An ambiguity was underlined in his 1954 *Times* obituary which spoke of unquestioned loyalty to Britain yet affection for Germany during 1914 to 1918.

Japhet recognized in 1918 that much pre-war business had been permanently lost. He then developed Japhets into a leading London merchant bank, S. Japhet & Co. Ltd, specializing in financing German business. His achievement was remarkable. He again showed willingness to introduce resources from outside, through the recruitment of leading German bankers. A securities business continued alongside banking, however; and the firm's significance was underlined in 1919 when, along with two other established London houses, it disposed of securities valued at £10 million received by the British government as reparations.

Like many of his competitors, Japhet failed to anticipate Germany's 1931 economic collapse, which almost overwhelmed his house, cutting its balance sheet in half by 1938. During Japhet's lifetime the business never really recovered; it resigned temporarily from the prestigious Accepting Houses Committee in 1942. His other activities were restricted to support of the Jewish community. He was a long-serving chairman of Jews' College, treasurer of the Home and Hospital for Jewish Incurables, and was a founder of the Jewish communal centre at Woburn House, London, in 1932. He supported fully the establishment of a Jewish state based upon Palestine and was a director of the Palestine Corporation. In 1937 he published the text of a public lecture he had given, *Impressions from Jewish History in Connection with the Mediterranean*.

Japhet remained chairman of S. Japhet & Co. and attended the office at 60 London Wall three times weekly until shortly before his death, aged ninety-five, on 2 February 1954, at his home, 122 North Gate, London. He had stayed for far too long but, in doing so, was typical of his generation. Immediately after his death, his firm was given new impetus in consequence of its sale to the Charterhouse group.

Saemy Japhet was characterized by great charm and humour; Montagu Norman, governor of the Bank of England, told him, apparently, 'you must have many friends … because everyone speaks well of you' (Japhet, 40). However, his remarkably candid memoirs reveal that his charm was allied to keen ambition.   JOHN ORBELL

Sources S. Japhet, *Recollections of my business life* (1931) · L. Dennett, *The Charterhouse Group, 1925–1979: a history* (1979) · *The Times* (3 Feb 1954) · *CGPLA Eng. & Wales* (1954) · d. cert.
Likenesses photograph, repro. in Dennett, *Charterhouse group*, 72
Wealth at death £28,924 10s. 1d.: probate, 20 May 1954, *CGPLA Eng. & Wales*

Japp, Alexander Hay [*pseud.* H. A. Page] (1836–1905), author and publisher, born at Dun, near Montrose, Forfarshire, on 27 December 1836, was the youngest son of Alexander Japp, a carpenter, and his wife, Agnes Hay. After his father's early death, Japp's mother moved the family to Montrose, where Japp attended Milne's school. At eighteen he became a bookkeeper with Messrs Christie & Sons, tailors, at Edinburgh. Three years later he moved to London, and for two years was employed in the East India department of Smith, Elder & Co. Due to illness he returned to Scotland, where he worked for Messrs Grieve and Oliver, Edinburgh hatters, and in his leisure time in 1860–61 attended classes at the university in metaphysics, logic, and moral philosophy. He became a double prizeman in rhetoric and received from Professor W. E. Aytoun a special certificate of distinction, but he did not graduate. At Edinburgh he frequently socialized with young artists, among whom was John Pettie. He began a career in journalism, and edited the *Inverness Courier* and the *Montrose Review*. On 13 March 1863 he married, at Montrose, Elizabeth Paul Falconer (1837/8–1888), a milliner, daughter of John Falconer, a stoneware merchant, of Laurencekirk, Kincardineshire. They had seven children, of whom a son and two daughters survived.

After returning to London to settle in 1864, Japp joined the *Daily Telegraph* for a short time. He also acted as general literary adviser to the publishing firm of Alexander Strahan (afterwards William Isbister & Co.). From 1869 to 1879 he assisted in editing their periodicals *Good Words* and *Sunday Magazine*, and from 1866 to 1872 the *Contemporary Review*, while Dean Alford was editor. He also assisted Robert Carruthers in the third edition of *Chambers's Encyclopaedia*, and his services were acknowledged by his being made LLD at Glasgow in 1879. In 1880 he was elected FRSE.

In October 1880 Japp started his own publishing firm under the name Marshall, Japp & Co., at 17 Holborn Viaduct, where he published his own work. Ill health and insufficient capital led him to turn his venture over to T. Fisher Unwin in 1882. From that year until 1888 he was literary adviser to the firm of Hurst and Blackett. Following the death of his wife from cancer in 1888, he married Eliza Love (d. 1912), who was of Scottish descent.

Japp was a versatile and prolific writer, writing under seven known pseudonyms (some of which appear to be variations on his own name and birthplace) as well as in his own name. As E. Conder Gray, A. N. Mount Rose, and A. F. Scot he published fiction, verse, and other works centring on religious themes, benevolence, and moral instruction. Under a double pseudonym he issued in 1878 a semi-autobiographical fiction, *Lights on the Way: some Tales within a Tale* (by 'the late J. H. Alexander, B.A., with explanatory note by H. A. Page'). He published *Noble Workers: a Book of Examples for Young Men* (1875), also as H. A. Page. As the editor Benjamin Orme he issued *Treasure-Book of Devotional Reading* (1866) and *Treasure-Book of Consolation* (1880). His collection of biographical sketches entitled *German Life and Literature* (1880), published under his own name, indicates that he knew German. Two works also published under his own name reflect an anti-Darwinian position: *Our Common Cuckoo, and other Parasitical Birds, …* (1899), a criticism of the Darwinian view of parasitism; and *Darwin Considered Mainly as Ethical Thinker, Human Reformer and Pessimist* (1901), a criticism of the theory of natural selection. *Three Great Teachers of our own Time: an Attempt to Deduce the Spirit and Purpose animating Carlyle, Tennyson and Ruskin* (1865) was also issued under his own name; of this, Ruskin wrote to Smith Williams: 'It is the only time that any English or Scotch body has really seen what I am driving at—seen clearly and decisively'. As H. A. Page he published *The Memoir of Nathaniel Hawthorne* (1872; with several uncollected contributions to American periodicals) and an analytical study of Henry David Thoreau, *Thoreau: his Life and Aims* (1878). His chief work, however, was on Thomas De Quincey. Through James Hogg, the Edinburgh publisher, he made the acquaintance of De Quincey's daughters, who provided him with the manuscripts from which he published, as H. A. Page, *Thomas De Quincey: his Life and Writings, with Unpublished Correspondence* (2 vols., 1877; 2nd edn, 2 vols., 1879; rev. edn under his own name, 1 vol., 1890), *De Quincey Memorials: being Letters and Other Records here first Published* (2 vols., 1891), and *Posthumous Works of Thomas De Quincey* (vol. 1, 1891; vol. 2, 1893)—the last two publications under his own name. Comparison of these works with manuscripts extant in the National Library of Scotland, the Wordsworth Library at Grasmere, and the Bodleian Library at Oxford reveals a wilful mishandling of material on Japp's part as editor. He cut manuscripts into fragments, altered dates, merged unrelated documents, and added his own text to the manuscript, thereby obscuring De Quincey's work.

Japp made the acquaintance of Robert Louis Stevenson at Braemar in August 1881, his conversation appealing to both Stevenson and his father. Stevenson read the early chapters of *Treasure Island* (at that time called 'The Sea Cook') to Japp, who was given the manuscript and who negotiated its publication in *Young Folks*. Subsequently Stevenson and Japp corresponded on intimate terms; Japp's last work, *Robert Louis Stevenson: a Record, an Estimate, and a Memorial* (1905), in which he draws attention to Stevenson's fascination with psychological complexities and heightened capacity for dreaming, was the result of their friendship. Editors of the collected edition of Stevenson's letters claim that Japp's portrait is highly inaccurate. As with De Quincey, Japp merged unrelated letters and padded out his reminiscences with much irrelevant matter.

From 1884 until 1900 Japp lived at Elmstead, near Colchester, where he cultivated his taste for natural history. From 1884 to 1901 he was also a member of the newly founded National Liberal Club. He moved back to London for three years but finally settled at Coulsdon, Surrey, in September 1903. While there he contributed to the *Weekly Budget* under the pseudonym Rupert II and worked on a study of social life in the middle ages, as well as a study of Hebrew rites and customs, having taught himself Hebrew when he was past fifty. Japp died of heart failure on 29 September 1905 at Dunrose, Coulsdon, and was buried on 4 October in Abney Park cemetery in Coulsdon; he was survived by his second wife. His contemporaries described him as a man of strong will and democratic tendency; they noted his almost morbidly sensitive temperament and sympathy for the suffering and oppressed (*Weekly Budget*, 7 Oct 1905). Japp had originally intended to devote himself to the ministry. His religious faith in the transformation of human suffering carried through to his last words: 'light may unexpectedly arise in the darkness' (ibid.). At his death he left an extensive collection of books and manuscripts, auctioned by Sothebys in 1926.

G. LE G. NORGATE, rev. LAURA E. ROMAN

Sources *Weekly Budget* (7 Oct 1905) · S. Whitman, *Westminster Gazette* (12 Oct 1905) · *The Times* (2 Oct 1905) · *Montrose Review* (6 Oct 1905) · W. I. Addison, ed., *The matriculation albums of the University of Glasgow from 1728 to 1858* (1913) · I. F. Mayo, *Recollections of what I saw, what I lived through, and what I learned, during more than fifty years of social and literary experience* (1910), 117–70 · J. Hogg, ed., *De Quincey and his friends* (1895), 2–70 [also preface] · sale catalogue (1926), 74–7 [Sothebys, London, 15–16 Feb 1926] · *Stevenson's letters*, ed. S. Colvin (1899), 2.45–6, 51–3, 74–5 · *The letters of Robert Louis Stevenson*, ed. B. A. Booth and E. Mehew, 3 (1994), 217, 218n., 223n., 226n., 227–8, 230, 272–4, 305 · De Quincey MSS, Bodl. Oxf., MS Eng. lett. 461, fols. 88–121 · Wordsworth Library, Grasmere, De Quincey MSS, 1989:161.27–83 · NL Scot., De Quincey MS 10998, fols. 142–3 · b. cert. · m. cert. · d. cert. [Elizabeth Falconer Japp] · *CGPLA Eng. & Wales* (1905)

Likenesses W. McTaggart, portrait, 1857, priv. coll.

Wealth at death £7431 0s. 4d.: administration, 29 Nov 1905, *CGPLA Eng. & Wales*

Jaques, John

Jaques, John (1823–1898), sports and games manufacturer, was born in London, the only son of John Jaques (1795–1877), an ivory- and wood-turner of Leather Lane in the City of London, and his wife, Ann. In adolescence he was apprenticed into the family firm of T. and J. Jaques, founded in 1795 by his grandfather, Thomas Jaques (1765–

1844), which moved its headquarters in 1838 from Leather Lane to 102 Hatton Garden, London. Eventually the firm was renamed Jaques & Son.

The firm's fortunes were built on handcrafted bowling woods, false teeth made from hippopotamus ivory, and elegant chess sets of a new standard design, named after a leading Victorian player, Edward Staunton. The younger John Jaques expanded the product range to include a variety of indoor games, demonstrating his ingenuity as an inventor: *Happy Families*, *Tiddly-Winks*, *Ludo*, and *Snakes and Ladders*, staples of domestic entertainment for well over a century.

The most important change came in 1851 when Jaques exhibited a croquet set at the Great Exhibition in London and became the game's most influential popularizer. During the next two decades croquet spread extremely rapidly, not least in British India, proving ideal for a newly affluent upper middle class seeking to play gentle games on private lawns; it also offered a very useful, socially controlled and partly chaperoned addition to the marriage mart. Jaques codified the rules in what long remained the standard work, his *Croquet, the Laws and Regulations of the Game*, first published in 1864. He married Harriet Ingram (1823–1898), the daughter of Nathaniel Cooke, proprietor of the *Illustrated London News*; they had six daughters and two sons, one of whom continued the innovatory traditions of the firm. John Jaques was made a freeman of the City of London in 1869 and played a prominent role in one of the City livery companies, the Turners. John Jaques died on 3 April 1898 at his home, Hillside, Duppas Hill, Croydon, Surrey. He was survived by his wife.

By that time the business had already passed into the control of his second son, also **John Jaques** (1862–1937), sports and games manufacturer, who was born on 3 September 1862 at 4 Caroline Place, St Pancras, London. He joined the firm in 1884 and was a keen sportsman and an all-round athlete. He maintained the firm's base in domestic games but directed output towards other burgeoning middle-class sports after croquet declined in the later 1870s, after the rapid spread of lawn tennis. That sport was catered for by the firm, together with cricket, archery, football, and badminton, which experienced an Edwardian surge in popularity. Croquet also revived in this sporting boom, as did bowls. John Jaques responded to that by introducing mechanized production of bowling woods, and Jaques's bowls became the game's standard for a long time. There were also additions to the range of board games, including a short-lived response to the 1890s bicycling boom, *Wheeling*, which involved moving lead figures of cyclists along a stylized route through the Thames valley.

In the longer term the most significant of Jaques's innovations was *Gossima*, later renamed *Ping-Pong*. It was an indoor game, playable on dinner tables. It boomed in the early 1900s, although Jaques's product soon found a rival in the similar *Table Tennis*, produced by other manufacturers with slightly different rules. It then lost popularity rapidly until it re-emerged after the First World War as a staple of youth club provision.

In 1901 Jaques married Mimie Constable Roberts, who died in the following year giving birth to a son, John Jaques. In 1917 he married Irene Amy Dodgson, the niece of Lewis Carroll; they had nine children, and she survived him. The firm's integrity in a fickle and competitive market was strengthened by incorporation as a private limited liability company in 1899 when John became a salaried managing director at £400 a year; in 1912 outside investors were allowed in but never to such an extent that Jaques family control was threatened. John Jaques died on 14 January 1937 at his home, Croft Cottage, 5 Forest Road, Branksome Park, near Bournemouth. He left his descendants a very well-established firm, combining innovation and a strong product line rooted in the quality of its Victorian staples.

J. R. LOWERSON

Sources Jaques 150th anniversary (typescript), John Jaques & Son Ltd, 361 White Horse Road, Thornton Heath, London · *John Jaques, 1795–1995* (John Jaques & Son Ltd, 1995) · private information (2004) · *Truth* (19 Dec 1901) · *The rules of Ping-Pong* (1901) · PRO, BT 31/31693, co. 61539 · games, Worthing Museum, West Sussex · J. Lowerson, *Sport and the English middle classes, 1870–1914* (1993) · *CGPLA Eng. & Wales* (1898) · *CGPLA Eng. & Wales* (1937) · b. cert. [John Jaques (1862–1937)] · d. cert. [John Jaques (1862–1937)]
Wealth at death £88,382 17s. 9d.: resworn probate, Aug 1898, *CGPLA Eng. & Wales* · £32,599 16s. 10d.—John Jaques (1862–1937): resworn probate, 30 April 1937, *CGPLA Eng. & Wales*

Jaques, John (1862–1937). *See under* Jaques, John (1823–1898).

Jarché, James [Jimmy] (1890–1965), photographer, was born on 8 September 1890 at 131 Commercial Road, Mile End, London, the son of Arnold Jarché (or Jarchy; d. 1901) and his wife, Amelie Solomon. His parents were Jewish, and had been born in France. Jarché himself had his bar mitzvah but became non-observant. His father, Arnold, had a photographic studio in Rotherhithe, trading as Jarchy: the business prospered and additional premises were opened in Tower Bridge Road and in Balham. The young Jarché assisted his father and, as well as taking conventional portraits for cartes-de-visite, worked with the Rotherhithe police, photographing corpses recovered from the Thames.

Jarché was a reluctant schoolboy and was expelled from St Olave's Grammar School. He was sent after his father's early death in 1901 to a boarding-school in Ramsgate, which he left without attaining academic distinction. On his return to Rotherhithe he joined Grange Park wrestling club and in 1909 became a world amateur wrestling middleweight champion. By this time his mother, who had been running the photographic studios since the death of his father, decided it was time for Jarché to take gainful employment.

His first work was for the *Daily Telegraph*, cycling around the London suburbs photographing schools inside and out. After this his mother apprenticed him (for £30) to a Bond Street photographer. This ended abruptly when the chief operator boxed his ears for asking questions. This was unwise because Jarché, a fit wrestling champion, sent him tumbling down the stairs. Jarché left and his mother in a fury recovered the apprenticeship payment. He began his Fleet Street career with a photograph of ragamuffins playing leapfrog in Southwark Park, sold at his mother's suggestion to the *Daily Mirror*, which paid him half a guinea. When he applied for a post at the *Mirror* the legendary Guy Bartholomew sent him on to Mr Warhurst of World's Graphic Press. Jarché wrote of Warhurst: 'I can never be grateful enough to him … I met a man in a million, who played in my life the combined parts of Father Christmas, fairy godmother, guide, critic, and friend' (Jarché, *People*, 21).

During the First World War Jarché served in France, rising to the rank of company sergeant-major of the 1st army corps school for physical training and bayonet training. On leave in 1917, he went to the White Lion, Epping, Essex, where his wife, Elsie Gladys, *née* Jezzard (1893/4–1971), whom he had married on 18 August 1914, was living with her parents, who ran the pub. There he made his first photographic scoop: a Zeppelin illuminated by searchlights bursting into flames. It made the front page of the *Daily Sketch*. Prior to this, the closest he had come to a scoop was a picture of Winston Churchill at the Sydney Street siege in 1911, of which he said: 'an agency man, standing by me, got a better shot' (Jarché, *People*, 70).

In 1912 Jarché joined the *Sketch*, where he remained until 1929. Unfortunately all records and negatives from his time there were destroyed in 1957. Jarché's autobiography, *People I Have Shot* (1934), covers some of his scoops in those years, but was written more to provide entertainment than as a serious history. The book does document the influence on him of probably the greatest Fleet Street art editor, Hannen Swaffer. 'Swaff' had a magical intuition for newspaper photographs and layout that distinguished every paper he worked on, and Jarché was employed with him on the *Sketch*, *The Graphic* and the *Daily Herald*. At the *Herald*, which was taken over by Odhams Press in 1928 as a Labour Party and TUC newspaper, Swaff was art editor and Jarché the leading photographer, heading a talented team that included Edward Malindine. Jarché's Odhams Press years, which were among his most fruitful, are relatively well documented. The *Daily Herald* glass negatives are now held at the National Museum of Photography, Film, and Television at Bradford. The rolls of miniature film, mostly from *Weekly Illustrated*, are now with Popperfoto in Northamptonshire.

Jarché was a one-shot photographer, whether what he was photographing was a visit by the king of Serbia or a cup final. His exposure of twenty-five plates at one TUC meeting was—for him and for the time—exceptional. Frequently he would outsmart his Fleet Street colleagues but when he was in with the pack it was said that he had the sharpest elbows to manoeuvre into the best position. He used a large-plate camera; the advantage in using plates for a scoop-hungry cameraman was that a wet plate straight from the developing tank could be put in a horizontal enlarger and a print speedily made.

Jarché's autobiography became a requiem for one era of Fleet Street. In the year that it was published (1934) the *Weekly Illustrated* first appeared. It was started by Odhams from the ashes of a failed socialist weekly, *The Clarion*, and heralded the death of the scoop and the rise of the picture story.

For Jarché, the transition was uneasy; he became chief photographer at the *Illustrated*, where Tom Hopkinson, a sub-editor who had transferred from *The Clarion*, found his work sometimes uninspired though at other times brilliant and well seen. The output of Jarché and his fellow photographers was huge. In one twelve-month period he produced 190 picture stories, including seven in one week during November 1934. The *Weekly Illustrated* built up a healthy circulation of a quarter of a million.

Jarché spent his wartime years in the Middle East as a British war correspondent, producing some of his best work for the *Herald* and *Weekly Illustrated*, of which the latter received favoured treatment, as it was much less critical of government policy than its rival, *Picture Post*. Before the USA entered the war he was also an official photographer for *Life* magazine. He relished the two uniforms with which he was issued, particularly the American one, as it gave him priority with London taxis. His wartime negatives are kept at the Imperial War Museum in a *Life* magazine file.

After the war Jarché returned to Odhams Press, but the world of Fleet Street was changing. The *Daily Herald* was in decline, despite a Labour government being in power, as were the illustrated weeklies, perhaps because of the spread of television. The last great success for *Weekly Illustrated* and the *Herald* was the coronation of Elizabeth II which, ironically, resulted in the end of Jarché's career on both papers. He was given a privileged place in Westminster Abbey, and the story is that he shot permitted black and white film for Odhams Press as well as a parallel series in colour which he sold as a freelance. As a result, it is said, he was sacked from Odhams, losing his pension six months before his retirement. He then joined the *Daily Mail* for six years before retiring in 1959.

Jarché's final flourish was a triumph. Before the war he had worked for the film manufacturers Ilford Ltd, using their infra-red film. After his retirement Ilford employed him to tour camera clubs with his lecture 'People I have shot'. His talks were a runaway success, thanks to the combination of funny anecdotes and his finest photographs to illustrate them.

Jarché died at his north London home, 20 Rosecroft Avenue, Hampstead, on 6 August 1965 and was cremated at the Golders Green crematorium. He was survived by his wife and their daughter, Joan, who married Jack Suchet, a distinguished Harley Street gynaecologist who had worked with Alexander Fleming on the development of penicillin. COLIN OSMAN

Sources J. Jarché, *People I have shot* (1934) · MSS, unpublished autobiography · D. Smith, *James Jarché, press picture pioneer* (1980) · D. Jeffrey, *Feeling for the past: photojournalism* [exhibition catalogue, Hayward Gallery, London, 1979–81] · *Creative Camera*, 211 (July–Aug 1982) · *Creative Camera*, 247–8 (July–Aug 1985) · private information (2004) [family] · b. cert. · m. cert. · d. cert.
Archives IWM · National Museum of Photography, Film, and Television, Bradford | Popperfoto, Northamptonshire, archive

Likenesses A. Jarché, portrait (as a child), repro. in Jarché, *People I have shot*, facing p. 12 · J. Jarché, self-portraits, repro. in Jarché, *People I have shot*, 124, 140 [examples]

Wealth at death not a large estate: private information (2004) [family]

Jardine, Alexander (*d.* 1799), army officer and author, was the illegitimate son of Sir Alexander Jardine, fourth baronet (1712–1790), army officer, of Applegirth, Dumfries. He entered the Royal Artillery in 1755 and the Royal Military Academy, Woolwich, in 1757, and in 1773 was promoted captain-lieutenant. In 1769 his observations of the sun's eclipse of 3 June at Gibraltar were published in the Royal Society's *Philosophical Transactions*. In 1771, still at Gibraltar, he conceived the idea of a liberal society, founded in 1772 at Woolwich, to advance mathematical and experimental knowledge in artillery, to unify military theory and practice, and to consider reforms of military education and training. Also in 1771 he was sent from Gibraltar on a mission to the emperor of Morocco. His active military career ended in 1776, when he became a British agent in Spain, gathering intelligence for four years in sometimes dangerous conditions. He was transferred to the invalid artillery, where he eventually rose to lieutenant-colonel in 1794.

Jardine published his observations from Morocco, Spain, France, Portugal, and Jersey in *Letters from Barbary, France, Spain, Portugal &c* (2 vols., 1788), although Robert Southey dismissed this work as conveying 'much thought in a most uninteresting manner' (*Letters of Robert Southey*, 8). Its larger theme is government and society, but it is notable for its defence of sexual equality and advocacy of greater similarity in education and dress between the sexes. Its political theme resurfaces in more radical form in *An Essay on Civil Government, or, Society Restored* (1793). The title essay is by Antonio Borghesi, but Jardine contributed the rest, arguing for rational justice's incompatibility with private property and for freethinking and intellectual liberty. This work reflects the influence of his friends, among them William Godwin, David Williams, the American Joel Barlow, and the South American revolutionary Francisco Miranda. In 1791 Jardine was appointed British consul to Galicia. *En route* in 1793 his ship was boarded by a French frigate and a privateer from Jersey, but he eventually arrived in north-western Spain. In 1795 he was host to Southey, who described his impressions in *Letters Written during a Short Residence in Spain and Portugal* (1797).

Jardine was married to a Spaniard, and Southey noted that their marriage accorded with Jardine's quaint whim 'for making cross breeds to improve the human species' (*New Letters of Robert Southey*, 1.218). They had at least five children, of whom three (a son on army service in India and two daughters) died within a short period in 1792. Jardine died in Portugal on 8 April 1799, following a protracted illness and his expulsion from Spain.

H. M. CHICHESTER, *rev.* J. DYBIKOWSKI

Sources Bodl. Oxf., MSS Abinger b.227/2, c.532/4, e.199–201, e.273/2 · *Archivo del General Miranda*, 6 (1930) · petition from Jardine to Pitt, 1784, PRO, MS 30/8/148, fols. 96–101 · *Minutes of the Proceedings of the Royal Artillery Institution*, 1 (1858), xvii–xxxii · R. Southey, *Letters written during a short residence in Spain and Portugal* (1797) · J. Dybikowski, 'Society restored and its authors', *Enlightenment and Dissent*, 11 (1992), 107–14 · *New letters of Robert Southey*, ed. K. Curry, 1 (1965), 218 · *Letters of Robert Southey*, ed. M. Fitzgerald (1912) · J. Kane, *List of officers of the royal regiment of artillery from the year 1716 to the year 1899*, rev. W. H. Askwith, 4th edn (1900), 9, 9A · A. Jardine, letter to Joseph Johnson, 6 June 1792, U. Edin. L., MS La II 432/158 · *Boswell, laird of Auchinleck, 1778–1782*, ed. J. W. Reed and F. A. Pottle (1977), vol. 11 of *The Yale editions of the private papers of James Boswell*, trade edn (1950–89), 352 · Jardine to Joseph Banks, 12 June 1783, RBG Kew, Banks correspondence, I.142 · review of *Letters on political liberty*, *Monthly Review*, 66 (1782), 551–5 · *London Chronicle* (12–14 Nov 1793), 472 · *London Chronicle* (19–21 Nov 1793), 496 · GEC, *Baronetage* · *GM*, 1st ser., 61 (1791), 590 · *Royal Kalendar* (1791) · *Royal Kalendar* (1799) · *Army List* (1792) · A. Jardine, *Cartas de España*, ed. and trans. J. F. Pérez Berenguel (2001)

Archives Bodl. Oxf., Abinger deposit

Jardine, David (1794–1860), magistrate and legal historian, was born at Pickwick, Wiltshire, the eldest of the three children of David Jardine (1766–1797), minister at the Trim Street Unitarian Chapel, Bath, and his wife, the daughter of George Webster of Hampstead. He matriculated at the University of Glasgow in 1810 and graduated MA in 1813. He was admitted to the Middle Temple on 17 April 1817 and called to the bar on 7 February 1823. He joined the western circuit and practised as a special pleader both on circuit and at the Bristol and Somerset sessions. He became recorder of Bath in 1837.

In 1833 Jardine was appointed a member of the royal commission of inquiry into municipal corporations. The commissioners were to consider nine areas (called circuits) and Jardine was assigned to the midland circuit with Peregrine Bingham the younger. The commission sat until 1835 and Jardine signed a supplementary report, which appeared in 1837, on the corporation of London and the City companies. In 1836 he was also appointed one of six law commissioners, filling the vacancy created by the resignation that year of John Austin. Set up in 1833, the commission operated on classical Benthamite principles and was authorized to codify the criminal law, both common and statute law. The last report signed by Jardine was the sixth, for he ceased to take part in the proceedings of the commission after his appointment in 1839 as a Metropolitan Police magistrate at Bow Street.

Jardine's appointment as a police magistrate coincided with the passing of the Metropolitan Police Courts Act (2 & 3 Vict. c. 71). Although section 9 of that act determined the police magistrates' salaries at £1200 per annum, the government fixed them at £1000. Some measure of the high esteem in which Jardine was held by the legal profession is provided by a discussion of police magistrates' stipends in the *Law Magazine, or, Quarterly Review of Jurisprudence*; the writer said: 'The only plausible apology for the reduced salary is, that the government have notwithstanding secured the services of such men as Mr. Long and Mr. Jardine' (*Law Magazine*, 21, 1839, 489). Jardine discharged his duties at Bow Street with distinction until 8 September 1860. He died at his home, at The Heath, Weybridge,

Surrey, on 13 September 1860, from bronchial pneumonia. His wife, Sarah, died on 6 October, also at Weybridge.

Robert James Ball's ridiculing of Jardine's abilities in his satirical poem *Justices' Justice* (1845) must be treated with reserve. Ball had been the complainant in a case of assault where Jardine had fined the defendant 10s., a penalty which he, Ball, regarded as derisory.

Jardine published a number of books, some of which drew on his experience as a magistrate; others reflected his legal-historical interests. Of the former, a good example is his *Remarks on the Expediency of Requiring the Presence of Accused Persons at Coroners' Inquests* (1846). In that study he argues for limiting a coroner's powers to the investigation of the cause of a death rather than widening them to include the functions of a detective. Jardine saw that accused persons could be deprived of a fair trial if at the inquest they were required to put forward their defence against a charge of murder or manslaughter and were subject to cross-examination.

Jardine the popular historian appears in the *Life of Lord Somers* (1833), which Jardine contributed to *Lives of Eminent Persons* in the Library of Useful Knowledge. He was an active member of the Society for the Diffusion of Useful Knowledge between 1828 and 1831. His legal and historical interests were united in his studies of the Gunpowder Plot and also in his edition of *Criminal Trials* (1832–3), published in two volumes in the Library of Entertaining Knowledge. In the *Trials* Jardine improved the text of T. B. Howell's *A Complete Collection of State Trials* (1816–26) by collating it with the original documents. ROGER TURNER

Sources *Annual Register* (1860), 453 · W. I. Addison, ed., *The matriculation albums of the University of Glasgow from 1728 to 1858* (1913), 247 · Prefatory memoir, *Sermons by the late Rev. David Jardine*, ed. J. P. Estlin, 2 vols. (1798) · R. J. Ball, *Justices' justice: a satire* (1845) · *GM*, 3rd ser., 9 (1860), 565 · d. cert.

Archives UCL, letters to Society for the Diffusion of Useful Knowledge

Wealth at death under £14,000: probate, 16 Nov 1860, *CGPLA Eng. & Wales*

Jardine, Douglas Robert (1900–1958), cricketer, was born on 23 October 1900 in Malabar Hill, Bombay, the only son of Malcolm Robert Jardine (1869–1947) and his wife, Alison, daughter of Dr Robert Moir, physician.

Family, Winchester, and Oxford Jardine's parentage was Scottish on both sides and his father, while at Fettes College, Edinburgh, was regarded as one of the best schoolboy cricketers Scotland had produced. Malcolm Jardine captained Oxford University and played briefly for Middlesex before making his career at the Bombay bar and becoming in 1915 advocate-general of Bombay. The son, at the age of nine, was sent home to be brought up in St Andrews by his aunt and was befriended by the scholar and cricket devotee Andrew Lang. He was educated at Norris Hill preparatory school, near Newbury, where he had a thorough grounding in cricket and where he saved up 6d. a week to buy C. B. Fry's book on batsmanship. Winchester College—its austere code heightened by wartime

Douglas Robert Jardine (1900–1958), by Herbert Olivier, 1934

deprivations—taught Jardine the virtue of self-reliance. At both schools he developed his particular qualities as a leader. At Norris Hill not a match was lost in 1914 (and only one drawn) under his captaincy. Five years later, as captain of Winchester, his authoritarian approach was matched by the 997 runs (average 66.46) he made and by his tactical astuteness, especially in the defeat of Eton. He played for the public schools at Lord's and, of all the schoolboys in 1919, he had 'the soundest defence, the greatest patience and the best judgement' (*Wisden*, 1920, 260).

Jardine, by now tall and already patrician in his bearing, went up to New College, Oxford, in 1919 and secured his blue as a freshman. His 96 not out in the closing stages of the match against the 1921 Australian tourists won him praise for his driving. More significantly, the innings created the mythology that he resented the Australians for not playing an extra over to let him get his century. The Christ Church score-board did not, however, record individual scores and it is doubtful whether either he or they knew his exact score. Two years later it was an Australian, R. H. Bettington, who was elected to the university captaincy to which Jardine might have aspired. In neither happening lies his later antipathy towards Australians. He left Oxford in 1923, having scored 1381 runs, won a blue at real tennis, and obtained a fourth class in modern history.

Surrey and England batsman A residential qualification led to Jardine's playing for Surrey. In a powerful batting side he established himself at number 5. He was able to adapt himself to the needs of a situation and the whims of an eccentric captain in P. G. H. Fender. His classic driving was in the tradition of an older generation of amateur bats-men, to which he added strong back-play and exact aware-ness of the position of the stumps. These technical qual-ities were strengthened by powers of concentration and determination. Playing for an England eleven against the Australians in 1926, he saw Harold Larwood take seven for 95 in a devastating spell which was significant in the light of later events. In both 1927 and 1928 Jardine topped the national batting averages, at 91.09 and 87.15 respectively. A century for the gentlemen against the players at Lord's was 'in the manner of the master' (*The Times*, 14 July 1927). A year later he made 193 in the same fixture at the Oval.

Jardine played the first of his twenty-two test matches, against the West Indians, in 1928 and toured Australia in 1928–9. He played a sound part in England's 4–1 victory over Australia and had a tour average of 64.88. At Adelaide he and W. R. Hammond set a record of 262 for an England third-wicket stand against Australia, which remains unbeaten. On personal grounds, however, the tour proved to be the groundstone of his later troubles. His Harlequin cap—symbol of class and imperialism to a sensitive soci-ety—brought a fierce response by what he himself called 'partial and unintelligent barracking' (Chapman and others, 215). *Wisden*'s comment that to Australian crowds barracking 'was part of their day's enjoyment' (*Wisden*, 1930, 659) was a view that Jardine never came to appreci-ate. It had been unfortunate that he had fielded on the boundary and been vulnerable to the crowds.

Captain of England: 'bodyline' Although Jardine had quali-fied as a solicitor in 1926, he had never practised and he had earned his living, rather unenthusiastically, as a bank clerk. He played little between his return from Australia and his appointment as the England captain in 1931 against New Zealand and, a year later, for the inaugural test against India. In the four tests, as captain, he averaged 79.00. On his batting form he was an undoubted candidate to go with the Marylebone Cricket Club (MCC) to Australia in 1932, but his selection as captain received a more mixed reception, although he had captained Surrey that year. *The Times* felt 'his claim had yet to be proved' (*The Times*, 11 June 1932), while his old cricket master at Winchester, E. R. Wil-son (who had himself toured Australia in 1920–21), observed that Jardine might win back the Ashes but could lose a dominion.

In what proved to be the most bitter tour in cricket his-tory Jardine was the architect of victory and the harbinger of controversy. To beat Australia, England had to combat Donald Bradman, who had averaged 139.00 when Austra-lia had regained the Ashes in 1930. Jardine invited the Not-tinghamshire fast bowlers H. Larwood and W. Voce to dine with him in London. There they discussed how leg the-ory—an acceptable bowling tactic—might be employed on the hard Australian wickets and, in particular, against Bradman. Leg theory itself was a form of attack in which a field was set employing several fielders on the leg side, most of whom would be behind the wicket. In defending a ball pitched on or outside the leg stump, a batsman might give a catch. In itself, it has its place in cricket history, but as recently as the summer of 1932 Pelham Warner had

criticized its use in the bowling of W. E. Bowes of York-shire to Surrey's Jack Hobbs: 'These things lead to reprisals, and when they begin goodness knows where they will end' (*Morning Post*, 22 Aug 1932). Accurate, short-pitched bowling, such as Bowes had employed, was a dan-ger to batsmen. Jardine had played in the match and liked what he saw. Warner, in due course, would have his words thrown back at him by the Australian press.

The possibilities of using this form of attack Jardine—with Larwood, Voce, and Bowes all in his party—privately contemplated on the voyage out. As an individual, he remained aloof and remote from the players. Neither Warner—who as chairman of selectors had chosen Jar-dine and who was himself chosen as manager—nor the players were aware of Jardine's thinking. During the first test, at Sydney, the word 'bodyline' was used by the *Mel-bourne Herald* to describe Larwood's bowling because of its speed, its accuracy, and the threat to the body posed by a short-pitched ball. Jardine commented to the press, 'these so-called new tactics are nothing new at all' (Douglas, 126). After a win apiece, matters came to a head in the third test at Adelaide in January 1933. All went well on the first day since England were batting. After their dismissal for 341, the Australians went in to bat at 3 p.m. on the second after-noon. In his second over Larwood hit the Australian cap-tain, W. M. Woodfull, over the heart, though he had not bowled 'leg theory'. In his next over, having set a leg-side field, he knocked Woodfull's bat out of his hand. A crowd of some 50,000 that Saturday, 14 January 1933, was noisily antagonistic as the magisterial Jardine—in the Harlequin cap and scarf which aroused so much enmity—deter-minedly set his leg-side field for his bowlers. The threat of a pitch invasion was very real. Even members in the enclosure 'rose to their feet blood-red in the face' (Mason, 112). At the end of the day Warner visited the Australian dressing-room. In essence Woodfull said to him: 'I don't want to speak to you, Mr Warner. There are two teams out there; one is playing cricket, the other is not. It is too great a game to spoil. The matter is in your hands' (Howat, 117).

When play resumed after the weekend the Australian wicket-keeper, W. A. Oldfield, was also hit. The ball had pitched on the off side (with an off-side field) and he exon-erated Larwood from blame. The match took its course and England won by 338 runs but what happened on the field was less significant than what resulted off it. Before the match was over a cable had gone from the Australian board of control, on 18 January, to MCC. 'Body-line bowl-ing has assumed such proportions as to menace the best interest of the game, making protection of the body by the batsmen the main consideration … In our opinion it is unsportsmanlike' (*Wisden*, 1934, 328). It was the first of an exchange of twelve cables between the two authorities which ended on 14 December 1933.

The press in both countries took up standpoints both for and against Jardine while MCC cabled their congratula-tions to him on winning the third test. The players—though there would be some backsliding in the months and years to come—declared loyalty to their captain. Not until the word 'unsportsmanlike' was withdrawn would

Jardine agree to play the fourth test. England duly won the series 4–1 but their success had put a severe strain on relations between the mother country and its dominion.

With the wider political and economic issues raised by the crisis Jardine was not directly involved. The burden fell on the manager, Warner. Yet for a broad understanding of the events of 1932–3 some comment is called for. While the cricket world was concerned with the allegations of unsportsmanship, the political and economic one—from an Australian angle—feared for the success of government loan conversions. Both at federal and state level (South Australia) coalition governments were vulnerable to the world economic crisis. The Australian federal government, under J. A. Lyons, was seeking a £17 million conversion loan on the London stock exchange. This was at risk since a British public, whose cricketers were being accused of unsportsmanlike play, would hardly be sympathetic. Nor would the Treasury be likely to approve a new overseas issue. To an Australia needing capital investment the consequences were alarming.

The British government—itself a national coalition under Ramsay MacDonald—avoided direct involvement and there is no record in cabinet minutes of the matter being discussed. But J. H. Thomas, the dominions secretary, held a meeting at which MCC, the governor of South Australia, Sir Alexander Hore-Ruthven (later Lord Gowrie)—on leave at the time—and the attorney-general were present. Thomas was later to say that nothing caused him such trouble, during his years in office, as the cricket crisis. Someone who played an important intermediary role—thus avoiding governments in direct confrontation—was E. T. Crutchley, the head of the British mission in Canberra. He and Warner dealt directly with one another. With the withdrawal of the word 'unsportsmanlike' a truce was reached between MCC and the Australian board of control. The long-term implications for Anglo-Australian cricketing relations were resolved later. An interesting comment on South Australian attitudes of the time may be found in the papers of Lord Gowrie (MS 2852, 2nd ser., National Library, Canberra). There is some irony in the fact that Jardine, the bank clerk, had thrown into confusion banking negotiations at international level. The man—cricket apart—was content to live his life at a low-key level.

But Jardine's return to England was anything but low-key. He received a hero's welcome from the public and an invitation from MCC to captain England against the West Indies in 1933. His 127 in the second test at Old Trafford was made against the bowling of Learie Constantine and E. A. Martindale, who employed the same tactics as Larwood had done in Australia. Jardine 'probably played it better than any other man in the world' (*Wisden*, 1934, 31). He had already been appointed the England captain by MCC for the 1933–4 tour of India. At a time of strong anti-British feeling in India it was important to avoid any repetition of the events of the year before. But Jardine's conduct proved the antithesis of that in Australia. In speech after speech he praised players and supporters alike and was proud to be in the land of his birth. As diplomatist,

captain, and player (he averaged 73.66 in the tests) he was an outstanding success. Yet while still in India he cabled to the London *Evening Standard* that he had 'neither the intention nor the desire to play cricket against Australia' (*Evening Standard*, 31 March 1934) in the forthcoming series. He cannot have known that a confidential letter from Hore-Ruthven had urged Pelham Warner to use his influence to prevent 'the selection of a man of Jardine's temperament as captain' (Gowrie MSS, MS 2852, 2nd ser. 5 Feb 1934, National Library of Australia, Canberra).

Retirement and marriage MCC were saved from having to make an embarrassing decision. Jardine had also informed Surrey he would not be available as captain in 1934. At the age of thirty-three his career in first-class cricket was virtually over. He would play only three more matches over the next fourteen years. He had retired at the peak of his ability, having made 14,848 runs (average 46.83), including thirty-five centuries, and averaged 48.00 in test cricket. He remained marginalized from cricket at the highest level and the stigma of his identification with 'bodyline' lingered. Even the possibility of his returning to Australia in 1936 as a journalist reporting the next MCC tour filled Lord Gowrie, now the governor-general, with dismay.

On 14 September 1934 Jardine married Irene Margaret Peat (b. 1908/9) at St George's, Hanover Square, London. The responsibilities he assumed seem the best explanation for his giving up first-class cricket. His father-in-law, Sir William Henry Peat, an eminent accountant, was anxious he should practise his profession as a solicitor but Jardine was content to continue as a bank clerk, augmenting his income by writing and reporting on cricket. His book *In Quest of the Ashes* (1933) was very much a legalistic defence of 'bodyline'; it emphasizes the support his players gave him and makes no reference at all to the difficult relationship he had with Warner, the manager.

There is a sense in which the rest of Jardine's public life remained unfulfilled. After being commissioned in the Royal Berkshire regiment in 1939 and returning from Dunkirk in 1940, his qualities of leadership were not called upon. He spent most of the war years as a provisions officer in India. In the post-war years he was briefly employed as a company secretary before becoming a director of the Scottish Australian Company. After some hesitation he went to Australia in 1953 on the company's business and was well received; he even lunched with the prime minister. He continued, out of financial necessity, to do some cricket reporting and broadcasting. His books included *Cricket: how to Succeed* (1936), written as a textbook for the National Union of Teachers.

Jardine was a devoted family man, and spent much time with his wife and four children. With no cricket mountains to climb and no ambitions beyond financial security, he mellowed. Club cricketers with whom he played saw him as modest and self-effacing. Instances abound of good deeds done secretly to those in need. There was a humanity not apparent in his days of fame. To the qualities of courage and conviction were added charm and warmth.

Douglas Jardine died of cancer on 18 June 1958 in a clinic

at Montreux, Switzerland. His body was cremated and the ashes scattered in the mountains at Cross Craig, Perthshire. There were generous tributes to his memory. Warner, despite the events of 1932–3, wrote that he would have picked Jardine 'as England captain every time' (*Wisden*, 1959, 933). Three weeks after his death D. R. Jardine's eleven played two first-class matches against Oxford and Cambridge. Jardine, president of the Oxford University Cricket Club (1955–7), had raised the sides just before his death. The epilogue was not inappropriate to one who had once declared that cricket, with the classics, were the most important things in life.　　　GERALD M. D. HOWAT

Sources C. Douglas, *Douglas Jardine* (1984) · D. R. Jardine, *In quest of the ashes* (1933) · L. Le Quesne, *The bodyline controversy* (1983) · B. Harris, *Jardine justified* (1933) · R. Sissons and B. Stoddart, *Cricket and empire: the 1932–33 bodyline tour of Australia* (1984) · D. Frith, *Bodyline autopsy: the full story of the most sensational test cricket series, England v Australia 1932–3* (2002) · *The Times* (20 June 1958) · *Wisden* (1928) · *Wisden* (1934) · *Wisden* (1959) · G. Howat, *Plum Warner* (1987) · A. P. F. Chapman and others, *The game of cricket* (1930) · D. R. Jardine, *Ashes and dust* (1934) · D. R. Jardine, *Cricket: how to succeed* (1936) · R. Mason, *Ashes in the mouth* (1982) · m. cert. · *CGPLA Eng. & Wales* (1958) · P. Bailey, P. Thorn, and P. Wynne-Thomas, *Who's who of cricketers*, rev. edn (1993)
Archives NL Aus., Gowrie MSS, MS 2852 ser. 2 | FILM BBC WAC · BFI NFTVA, news footage · BFI NFTVA, sports footage · priv. coll.
Likenesses photographs, 1926–56, Hult. Arch. · cartoon, c.1930, Lord's, London, Marylebone Cricket Club Museum; repro. in Chapman and others, *The game of cricket* · photograph, 1930, repro. in Chapman and others, *The game of cricket* · photograph, c.1930, Marylebone Cricket Club Museum, Lord's, London; repro. in Chapman and others, *The game of cricket* · photograph, c.1930, repro. in Mason, *Ashes in the mouth* · H. Olivier, oils, 1934, Marylebone Cricket Club Museum, Lord's, London [*see illus.*]
Wealth at death £71,274 9s. 8d.: probate, 1 Aug 1958, *CGPLA Eng. & Wales*

Jardine, George (1742–1827), university professor and administrator, was born at Wandal, in Lanarkshire, the son of William Jardine, a landholder in that county, and his wife, the daughter of the landowning Weir of Birkwood. He attended his local parish school at Lamington before entering Glasgow University in 1760; his master of arts degree was awarded in 1765. He attended the divinity course and by 1770 had been licensed to preach in the Church of Scotland's presbytery of Linlithgow. He remained in the Church of Scotland throughout his life and represented the presbytery of Hamilton at the general assembly of the Church of Scotland. In 1770 he left for Paris, as tutor to the sons of Baron Mure of Caldwell. There he met Helvetius and D'Alembert, using introductions gained for him by Baron Mure from David Hume. Having returned to Scotland in 1773 he applied for the chair of humanity at Glasgow University but was not successful. In 1774 he was appointed professor of Greek and assistant professor of logic. On 6 July 1776 he married Janet Lindsay (d. 1815), from Glasgow, with whom he had one son, John Jardine (d. 1850), advocate. In 1787 he finally became sole professor of logic at Glasgow.

Jardine was responsible for a number of changes and reforms in curricular and administrative aspects of the university. His aims were to improve the reputation of the institution well in advance of royal commissions visiting the Scottish universities in the 1820s. This was despite the fact that he enjoyed many privileges: he had a free house, influence over the university administration, and a share in income from student fees. Yet he had been appointed as an assistant to Professor Clow, which exposed him to iniquities of the university sinecure system and meant that Jardine did the work while Clow sat in comfortable retirement. Once Clow had died Jardine assumed full office, but his awareness of this practice led him to promote the standardization of written successions to professorships in the 1790s. He also opposed the practice of professors' holding pluralities where they were also acting as church ministers, and took exception to both Principal Taylor and Principal Macfarlan holding ministries in Glasgow. As clerk to the faculty of the university he was responsible for re-establishing some order in the university finances. He organized the lucrative sale of the university patronage of Govan and encouraged the university to buy the city observatory. In the early 1800s he was involved in regulating and raising student fees at the university. He also promoted the interests of the university in the Glasgow medical school and acted as secretary at the Glasgow Royal Infirmary (of which he was one of the founders) for twenty years, from 1792.

In his own subject Jardine also instituted changes. He lectured in English, and through the introduction of a system of daily examination of students he was able to assist them to progress effectively. The results of these changes were increased class numbers, from an average of 50 to nearly 200, and, while some of his colleagues were disparaging, Jardine maintained the respect of his students. He published his *Outlines of Philosophical Education* (1818; 2nd edn, 1825) towards the end of his life, while his *Lectures on Logic and Belles Lettres* was republished from the 1790s through to the 1820s. Jardine retired in 1824 and lived at his estate of Hallside, near Hamilton. Having been taken ill at the general assembly in Edinburgh in 1826 he died on 28 January the following year. He had been in many respects a quiet reformer and improver who succeeded in increasing the status of the University of Glasgow by persevering at regulating and improving conditions for both students and staff.

JAMES TAIT, rev. CAMPBELL F. LLOYD

Sources Chambers, *Scots.* (1835) · *Blackwood*, 21 (1827) · W. I. Addison, *A roll of graduates of the University of Glasgow from 31st December 1727 to 31st December 1897* (1898) · W. I. Addison, ed., *The matriculation albums of the University of Glasgow from 1728 to 1858* (1913) · J. Coutts, *A history of the University of Glasgow* (1909) · J. D. Mackie, *The University of Glasgow, 1451–1951: a short history* (1954) · Chambers, *Scots.* (1868–70) · J. Geyer-Kordesch and F. Macdonald, *Physicians and surgeons in Glasgow* (1999) · IGI · inventory, PRO, SC 36/48/20/674-5
Archives NL Scot., corresp. with Mure family · U. Glas. L., letters to Robert Hunter
Likenesses J. Graham Gilbert, oils (after Raeburn), Hunterian Art Gallery, Glasgow · T. Hodetts, engraving (after oils by J. Graham Gilbert), U. Glas.

Jardine, James (1776–1858), civil engineer, was born on 13 November 1776 at Applegarth, Dumfriesshire, the third

James Jardine (1776–1858), by unknown artist

child of James Jardine, farmer, and his wife, Elspeth Rodgerson. Having shown great ability in mathematics at Dumfries Academy, he went to Edinburgh with an introduction from his teacher to John Playfair, professor of mathematics at the university, where he attended classes but did not graduate. Playfair warmly befriended Jardine and obtained for him employment as a teacher of mathematics. His many pupils included Professor Dugald Stewart's son Matthew, Henry John Temple (afterwards Lord Palmerston), and Lord John Russell.

Before 1809 Jardine, on Playfair's advice, had begun to practise as a civil engineer and by 1811 had opened an office at 54 Princes Street, Edinburgh. In 1809 he observed levels in the Tay with reference to salmon stake nets. As a consequence of this research Jardine was the first to determine, by observations of the tides over a great extent of coast, the mean level of the sea and to show the symmetry of the undisturbed tidal wave above and below that level and the effect of a river current in disturbing that symmetry. These were deemed to be 'discoveries of high importance, both scientific and practical' (Waller, 12.1042, notice by W. J. M. Rankine). In 1810 on the recommendation of Thomas Telford, with whom he was to become closely associated over three decades, Jardine accurately determined the levels and output of springs in the Pentland hills. This work eventually led, in consultation with Telford, to his greatest and best-known achievement, supplying Edinburgh with a plentiful supply of water from Crawley spring and a newly constructed reservoir at Glencorse, via an iron aqueduct. The Scotsman described these works in 1825 as some of the most extensive, perfect, and complete ever executed at that time. Jardine was engineer

to the water company from 1819 to 1846, his last major improvement being Threipmuir Reservoir, near Balerno. Other water-supply schemes on which he was consulted included Perth, Dumfries, Glasgow, Cobbinshaw Reservoir, and Leslie. He was also employed on several important law cases involving hydraulics. In 1830 he was consulted on the River Leven improvement and safely lowered the level of the loch. From 1831 to 1849 he acted as the project's commissioner.

Jardine's other work in Edinburgh included road layout, retaining walls and foundations, often associated with the architectural projects of William Playfair and others, and major drainage of the remainder of the North Loch and the meadows. Jardine also had a considerable practice in the improvement of communications throughout Scotland, at first on canal work, followed by pre-steam locomotion road and railway projects. In 1813–14 he surveyed and estimated costs for the Annandale Canal and the continuation of John Rennie's high-level Union Canal line via the south and east of Edinburgh to Leith docks. Neither scheme was implemented. In 1818 he advised on a proposed deviation of the Union Canal line through Callendar Park near Falkirk. (He was not responsible for the construction of the Union Canal as suggested in his *Dictionary of National Biography* entry.) From 1825 to 1830 Jardine directed extensive surveys and prepared estimates for a railway between Edinburgh and Glasgow but his proposals, although seriously considered, were not adopted.

In 1826 Jardine was appointed engineer for the Edinburgh and Dalkeith—or Innocent as it was later known—Railway and by 1831 he had designed and supervised the construction of the line. At its Edinburgh end this had an inclined plane operated by steam engine and the first public railway tunnel in Scotland and, near Dalkeith, Glenesk Bridge. The tunnel and bridge, both impressive structures, have survived. Although horse-operated, the line was commercially successful both as a mineral and passenger railway, and for a number of years prior to its adaptation for steam locomotion in the mid-1840s carried more passengers per mile than the Liverpool and Manchester Railway. In 1827 Jardine also became engineer for the Ardrossan and Johnstone Railway which, although underfunded, was opened from Ardrossan to Kilwinning in 1831. In 1835 he surveyed the Nith valley line. In autumn 1830, with the success of steam locomotion on the Liverpool and Manchester Railway, horse traction projects became outdated, which was unfortunate for Jardine, who had two lines nearing completion. He played little part in the subsequent development of railways, but continued to be employed on river navigation and harbour improvement work. This included projects at Saltcoats, the Tay, the Forth ferries, the Earl Grey and King William IV docks at Dundee in consultation with Telford, and with other improvements at Perth, Leith, and Eyemouth. In addition he undertook the evaluation of metal lighthouse proposals for Skerryvore.

At Telford's request Jardine furnished calculations for the pioneering Menai suspension bridge in 1821, and he was a leading bridge engineer in Scotland. In addition to railway structures in iron, timber, and stone, his work included masonry bridges at Threave, Almond (near Perth), at and south of Dalkeith, and over the realigned River Leven. Unexecuted masonry projects included a five-span design for Dean Bridge, Edinburgh and a 160 ft span at Coulternose over the Findhorn. Jardine's scientifically based designs were influenced by Telford's practice but were more refined in some respects. For masonry bridges he adopted exceptionally small arch-ring depths, which combined with the adoption of arch-rings which reduced in depth towards the crown, low rise arches, and longitudinal walls within hollow spandrels, economized on materials and minimized weight on the foundations. Rankine assessed Jardine's work as 'all models of skilful design and solid construction' and his masonry 'worthy of the study of every engineer' (Waller, 12.1042).

Jardine had a national reputation as a scientific engineer. He played an important part in determining the proportions of the old and diverse Scottish weights and measures to the imperial standards. In 1811 he determined the length of the ell as 37.0598 inches at 62 °F. In 1824, after the passing of the act for establishing the imperial standards weights and measures, he became a member of the commission which examined all the old weights and measures in use in Scotland and conducted his enquiries 'with extreme precision'. Jardine was elected to fellowship of the Royal Society of Edinburgh in 1812, the Geological Society in 1816, and to membership of the Institution of Civil Engineers and the Society of Civil Engineers in 1820 and 1827 respectively. He was a director of the Edinburgh Astronomical Institution and its astronomer from 1815 to 1825.

From 1826 Jardine operated his practice from his house at 18 Queen Street, Edinburgh, where he died from senile debility on 20 June 1858 following an attack of bronchitis. He had remained a bachelor, but had a daughter, Ann, from a relationship with Margaret McGee. Ann Jardine (b. 1825) married her cousin Alexander Jardine, who practised as a surveyor and civil engineer at 18 Queen Street from 1844 to 1858. Rankine commented from personal knowledge that although Jardine's manner 'was somewhat eccentric and cynical, he secured the warm regard of his intimate friends amongst whom were many of the highest eminence in science' (Waller, pt 12). Jardine was buried at Warriston cemetery, Edinburgh.

ROLAND PAXTON

Sources J. F. Waller, ed., *The imperial dictionary of universal biography*, 3 vols. in 16 pts (1857–63) · *The Scotsman* (26 June 1858), suppl. 252 · R. W. Jardine, 'James Jardine and the Edinburgh Water Company', *Transactions* [Newcomen Society], 64 (1992–3), 121–30 · J. Colston, *The Edinburgh and District water supply* (1890) · J. Jardine, *Dundee Harbour: report respecting the extension of the docks* (1830) · A. W. Skempton, *British civil engineering, 1640–1840: a bibliography of contemporary printed reports, plans, and books* (1987) · R. A. Paxton, *Three letters from Thomas Telford* (1968) · *The Post Office Edinburgh directory* [annuals] · *Edinburgh almanacks* · private information (2004) · *The Scotsman*, 9 (1825) · d. cert.

Archives NA Scot., register of house plans

Likenesses P. Park, marble bust, 1842, Scot. NPG · etching (after G. Aikman), repro. in Colston, *Edinburgh and District water supply*, facing p. 38 · watercolour drawing, Scot. NPG [*see illus.*]

Wealth at death approx. £400

Jardine, John (1716–1766), Church of Scotland minister, was born on 3 January 1716 at Lochmaben, Dumfriesshire, to Robert Jardine (d. 1749), minister of Lochmaben, and Janet Rannie (d. 1778). He was educated at the University of Edinburgh, where he became intimate with Hugh Blair, William Robertson, and other divinity students who would later be among the leaders of the moderate party in the Church of Scotland. He received his licence to preach from the presbytery of Lochmaben on 7 September 1736, and in 1741 was presented by the crown to the parish of Liberton, near Edinburgh, where he was ordained, on 30 July, assistant and successor to the elderly Samuel Semple, who died the following January. It was apparently during the five years between licensing and ordination that Jardine gained the favour of Charles Erskine of Alva, then lord advocate of Scotland and later, as Lord Tinwald, lord justice clerk. According to Jardine's family friend, Alexander Carlyle, Tinwald gave Jardine the political management of the burgh of Lochmaben when he was just twenty-nine years old, and in that capacity he acquired a 'dexterity in managing men' which he later applied to Edinburgh politics (*Autobiography*, ed. Burton, 491–2).

On 7 February 1744 Jardine married Jean Drummond (d. 1766), the eldest daughter of George *Drummond, who served often as provost of Edinburgh and managed the city for the third duke of Argyll and his Scottish *sous-ministre*, Lord Milton, in the aftermath of the Jacobite uprising of 1745. During that conflict Jardine travelled with the duke of Cumberland's army and reported the latest news directly to Milton. His experiences led to a life-long project to write a history of the 'Forty-Five', which was well under way by 1748; the work was believed by one contemporary to be 'far advanced, if not finished' by the time of Jardine's death, but it never appeared, perhaps because its revelations of the 'wanton cruelties perpetrated by the Duke of Cumberland' would have been deemed 'highly offensive' (Somerville, 92–3). Like Tinwald and Drummond, Jardine had strong anti-Jacobite sentiments, and a review that he published in the *Edinburgh Review* in 1755 insinuating that the *Scots Magazine* had been soft on Jacobitism during the uprising sparked an indignant defence by the editors.

Owing to political management by Drummond and the Argyll interest, Jardine was called to Lady Yester's Church, Edinburgh, on 26 July 1750, even though the Saltoun papers reveal that two other ministers were known to be more popular among the clergy and elders of the town (NL Scot., Saltoun MS 17602, fols. 188–9). He was translated to the Tron Church in 1754. In Edinburgh he initially allied himself with the evangelical minister Alexander Webster but soon switched to the moderate party that was emerging under the leadership of William Robertson. He regularly served the moderates through his influence with Milton and especially Drummond, and in the Drysdale 'Bustle' of 1762–4 he helped to manage, and probably instigated, the moderates' plan to reclaim for the town council the right to present clergymen to vacant Edinburgh churches without the involvement of the town's ministers and elders. He also joined with the Robertson circle to produce the short-lived *Edinburgh Review* of 1755–6, to which he is believed to have contributed eight anonymous reviews. Jardine was a member of numerous Edinburgh clubs during the last decade of his life, including the anti-Jacobite Revolution Club; the Select Society and its offshoot, devoted to promoting the reading and speaking of English in Scotland; the St Giles Society; and the patriotic *Poker Club. He was a particular friend of David Hume, who once wrote from Fontainebleau of his yearning for 'the plain roughness of the *Poker*, and particularly the sharpness of Dr Jardine, to correct and qualify so much lusciousness' (*Letters*, 1.410–11).

At 6 feet 2 inches tall, with a large frame, Jardine could be an imposing figure, but like his father, who was well known for buffoonery, he enjoyed playing the jester among friends. Carlyle said he 'had much drollery and wit, though but little learning' and an artful manner in politics (*Autobiography*, ed. Burton, 289). Thomas Somerville added that he had a 'benevolent heart' and effectively superintended charitable institutions in Edinburgh (Somerville, 91). Jardine excelled at using patronage to obtain sinecures, including appointment as a royal chaplain in ordinary in September 1759, as a dean of the Chapel Royal in August 1761, and as dean of the Order of the Thistle in January 1763—the last giving rise to John Maclaurin's quip about

> The P[rovos]t, who dances, you know, to the whistle
> Of that arch-politician, the D[ea]n of the T[hist]le.
> (Sher, 'Drysdale "Bustle"', 189)

He also received an honorary DD degree from the University of St Andrews on 20 November 1758. In 1753, and again in 1762, Jardine was an unsuccessful candidate for the principalship of Edinburgh University.

Jardine's life ended dramatically on 30 May 1766, when he collapsed in the general assembly just as the moderates were dealing the final blow to their opponents in the schism overture affair. His death was followed just four months later by that of his wife, who had recently given birth to their fifth child, Henry (1766–1851), later a writer to the signet, a baronet, and the king's remembrancer. A daughter, Janet (1762–1840), married in 1782 George Home Drummond of Blair Drummond, the only son and heir of Henry Home, Lord Kames.   RICHARD B. SHER

Sources *The autobiography of Dr Alexander Carlyle of Inveresk, 1722–1805*, ed. J. H. Burton (1910) · J. Mackintosh, ed., *The Edinburgh Review, for the year 1755*, 2nd edn (1818) · *The letters of David Hume*, ed. J. Y. T. Greig, 2 vols. (1932) · W. C. Lehmann, *Henry Home, Lord Kames, and the Scottish Enlightenment* (1971) · E. C. Mossner, *The life of David Hume*, 2nd edn (1980) · F. Douglass and W. Murray, 'Extract of a letter to the author of *The Edinburgh Review*, occaisioned by his remarks on the history of the rebellion', *Scots Magazine*, 17 (1755), 432–3 · 'On the East India company's Mutiny Bill', *Scots Magazine*, 17 (1755), 27–9 · *Fasti Scot.*, new edn, 1.140–41 · R. B. Sher, *Church and university in the Scottish Enlightenment: the moderate literati of Edinburgh* (1985) · R. B. Sher, 'Moderates, managers and popular politics in mid-eighteenth-century Edinburgh: the Drysdale "bustle" of the 1760s', *New perspectives on the politics and culture of early modern Scotland*, ed. J. Dwyer, R. A. Mason, and A. Murdoch (1982), 179–209 ·

T. Somerville, *My own life and times, 1741–1814*, ed. W. Lee (1861) · *DNB*
Archives BL, Newcastle MSS, Add. MS 32895, fols. 134–6 · NL Scot., Minto MSS (Sir Gilbert Elliot) · NL Scot., Saltoun MSS (Lord Milton) · U. Edin. L., sermons and papers

Jardine, Sir Robert, first baronet (1825–1905), East India merchant and politician, was born on 24 May 1825, the fourth and youngest son (of six children) of David Jardine, farmer, of Muirhousehead, Applegarth, Dumfriesshire, and Rachel, daughter of William Johnston, farmer, of Linns, Dumfriesshire. Roby, as he was known, was educated at Merchiston College, Edinburgh, and learned trade and banking at the London firm of Magniac, Smith & Co. By the mid-1840s the firm of Jardine, Matheson & Co., founded a decade earlier by his uncle, Dr William Jardine, and James Matheson, had established its headquarters in the newly acquired colony of Hong Kong, where it was the leading merchant house.

The young Jardine arrived at Hong Kong in 1845, following his brothers, Andrew, Joseph, and David, all of whom had gone out to the Far East. Their uncle's business was an agency house, engaged in buying and selling commodities for clients, as well as dealing in tea and providing shipping and banking services. Opium, which had figured prominently in the rise of the family's fortunes in China, continued to be of major importance in the firm's operations. However, Robert Jardine's primary commercial activity involved Jardines' teas. Against the background of a booming international trade in the new treaty ports of China and the turbulence of the far-reaching Taiping uprising, he spent a portion of each of his years in China purchasing teas at Foochow (Fuzhou). He became a partner in Jardine Matheson in 1852 and later a partner in the separate London house of Matheson & Co. (formerly Magniac, Smith & Co.).

When the boom of the 1850s and early 1860s in China burst in 1865, with many British firms failing, Jardine, Matheson & Co. also found itself in difficulties because of its loans to unstable firms. Although he had retired from the Far East, Robert Jardine had inherited much of the Jardine family's interest in the firm, because his brothers David and Joseph had died childless. In the financial crisis he became in effect a creditor for loan capital to the firm's working partners in the Far East. Consequently his resources were vital to the survival of Jardine, Matheson & Co., and he was reinstated as a governing partner.

Robert Jardine continued as a partner in both the Hong Kong and London firms from the 1860s to the end of his life, but he now concentrated on politics, sports, and farming. His cousin William Keswick (a grandson of Jean Jardine, the founder's sister) became a partner in Jardine Matheson in 1862 and rose to be *taipan* by 1874. They enjoyed a good working relationship, as both had experience in the Far East, and Jardine allowed Keswick to take full charge of the management of the firm.

In 1865 Jardine entered the Commons as the member for Ashburton, in Devon, a seat held earlier by his uncle, William Jardine from 1841 to 1843. However, his parliamentary career was interrupted in 1867 when that seat was absorbed into a larger constituency. Jardine married Margaret Seton Buchanan on 4 April 1867. Twenty-one years his junior, she was the eldest daughter of John Buchanan of Leny, Perthshire. Just eleven months later he was desolated by her death, at the age of twenty-one, on 7 March 1868, not long after the birth of their only child, Robert.

In the following year, while he was in Yorkshire recovering from the shock of his wife's death, Jardine was sought out by prominent Liberals from Dumfries, who persuaded him to be their candidate for the Dumfries burghs, and he won the seat. In 1874 he agreed to stand for the county of Dumfries, but lost by a small margin. Nevertheless, he remained popular among the Liberals of Dumfriesshire, and a close relationship developed between Jardine and the prominent Liberal leader (and future prime minister), Lord Rosebery, with whom he shared interests in the empire and in horse-racing.

Political success returned in 1880, when Jardine was again elected for Dumfriesshire, and that success was repeated in 1885 when he stood for election as Sir Robert Jardine, baronet, having been honoured by the queen in July of that year for his public service. It was to be his last campaign as a Liberal, for he went with the Unionists following the split of the Liberal Party over home rule in 1886. Sir Robert defeated the Liberal candidate for Dumfriesshire in 1886 and remained in the Commons until 1892. In a parliamentary career of twenty-one years, he gave painstaking attention to local matters but seldom spoke in the Commons. *Vanity Fair* described him as 'a Liberal Unionist who sets a good example in an age of talk by not troubling the House with much speaking' (23 Aug 1890).

On the Victorian sporting scene, Jardine was notable for his lively interest in horse-racing and in coursing. His passion for horse-racing was first stirred in China, and once home he allied with his cousin John Johnstone of Halleaths to maintain the Sheffield Lane stud. Bearing their dark blue and silver colours, their racehorse Pretender won the Derby and the Two Thousand Guineas in 1869; their horses also won the Queen's Vase at Ascot on two occasions, and many other major races.

Among Jardine's estates the two greatest properties were Castlemilk, Lockerbie, inherited from his unmarried brother Joseph, and Lanrick Castle, Perthshire, inherited from his unmarried brother Andrew. At Castlemilk he demolished the Georgian house and built a grand Victorian mansion, designed by the Scottish architect David Bryce. On that estate he maintained a farm of 850 acres. Widely recognized as a very successful breeder of prize-winning Galloway cattle, he was also an excellent landlord, kind-hearted, genial, and interested in the welfare of his tenantry.

Jardine died at Castlemilk, in the evening, on 17 February 1905, after several years of declining health. He was buried on 21 February in a quiet spot beneath the ivy-covered ruins of old St Mungo's in Lockerbie, not far from the new church he had built for the parish. His son, Robert William Buchanan Jardine, succeeded to the baronetcy

and inherited the entire Jardine family interest in Jardine, Matheson & Co. But the heir took no active interest in the firm, and William Keswick found it necessary to restructure Jardine, Matheson & Co. as a limited liability company in 1906. Six years later, Jardine, Matheson & Co. purchased the Matheson family's share in the London firm. Thereafter, Jardine successors—most notably the Keswicks—preserved the dynastic management of the two firms.   RICHARD J. GRACE

Sources M. Keswick, ed., *The thistle and the jade: a celebration of 150 years of Jardine, Matheson & Co.* (1982) · *Dumfries and Galloway Standard and Advertiser* (18 Feb 1905) · *Dumfries and Galloway Standard and Advertiser* (22 Feb 1905) · *The Times* (18 Feb 1905) · J. Junior, 'Statesman no. 572, Sir Robert Jardine', *VF* (23 Aug 1890), 163 · *Dumfries and the Highland Show* (1910) · *DNB* · b. cert.

Archives CUL

Likenesses H. T. Wells, portrait, exh. RA 1876 · Spy [L. Ward], cartoon, repro. in *VF* (1890) · photograph, repro. in Keswick, ed., *The thistle and the jade*, 36 · photograph, repro. in *Dumfries and the Highland Show*

Wealth at death £1,114,489 8s.: confirmation, 15 July 1905, *CCI*

Jardine, William (1784–1843), physician and merchant, was born on 24 February 1784 at Broadholm, a farm near Lochmaben, Dumfriesshire, the third son and the sixth of seven children of Andrew Jardine, farmer, and Elizabeth Johnstone. Educated in medicine at the University of Edinburgh, he obtained a diploma from the Royal College of Surgeons, Edinburgh, in March 1802.

In that same month Jardine secured a position with the East India Company as ship's surgeon's mate aboard the *Brunswick*, bound for India. Captured by the French and shipwrecked in 1805, Jardine was repatriated that autumn and returned to the East India Company's service as ship's surgeon. 'Privilege tonnage', a benefit accorded ships' officers, allowed him a measure of cargo space for private trade. When profits from such trade far surpassed his wages as ship's surgeon, his career interests shifted.

Returning from Canton (Guangzhou) in May 1817, Jardine gave up medicine for commerce, which he learned from Thomas Weeding, a London merchant and East India Company agent. He sailed for Bombay in 1818, and in succeeding years travelled between Bombay and Canton, as supercargo on the *Sarah*, of which he was co-owner. At Bombay in 1820, he met a fellow Scot, James Matheson, who was speculating in the opium trade. In time their names would identify the biggest British trading concern in the Far East.

From 1820 until 1839 Jardine was resident in China. At Canton his early success, as commercial agent for opium merchants in India, led to his admission in 1825 as a full partner of Magniac & Co., and by 1826 he was controlling that firm's Canton operations. Shortly thereafter, Matheson joined him, and in 1832 Magniac & Co. was reconstituted as Jardine, Matheson & Co.

At Canton, foreign merchants were required to conduct business only through the small group of commercial intermediaries known as the Hong merchants. However, by 1834 Jardine, Matheson & Co., known as 'the Princely Hong', was regularly operating beyond the traditional

William Jardine (1784–1843), by Thomas Goff Lupton (after George Chinnery)

British trade with the Hong merchants of Canton, speculating in smuggled opium and piece goods. Their own fleet of ships, flying the company flag of a white diagonal cross on a blue field (Scotland's cross of St Andrew with colours reversed), were the fastest ocean-going vessels in the Far East.

By the mid-1830s, William Jardine was the most influential British figure at Canton and was already a celebrated name in the commercial world of London. Yet he was by then past fifty and anxious to retire from China. However, his return to England was delayed for several years because of his worries about the unstable debt situation among the Hong merchants, as he felt obliged to keep close watch on the safety of his firm's assets.

Peking ordered the opium importers to be expelled in 1836, but Jardine refused to leave. The pressure intensified and opium sales were at a standstill by 1838 when Lin Zexu was appointed imperial commissioner in Canton. Shortly before Lin's arrival, Jardine retired from Canton, in January 1839, intending a leisurely trip home via Bombay and Suez. But startling news awaited him at Naples. Lin had confiscated 20,000 cases of British-owned opium, worth £2 million. Jardine hastened to London, arriving early in September, and immediately prepared to press the foreign secretary, Palmerston, for a forceful response to Lin's actions.

Jardine's consultations with Palmerston began late that month and extended into 1840. He advised a military and naval action involving seizure of one or more Chinese islands for British commerce. Then a negotiation could be conducted along the lines 'You take my opium—I take your Islands in return—we are therefore Quits,—& thenceforth if you please let us live in friendly Communion and good fellowship' (Jardine to Palmerston, 5 Dec 1839, Broadlands Papers, MM/CH/5). Palmerston's subsequent policy adhered closely to Jardine's advice. The British expeditionary force seized Hong Kong in 1841, and the Chinese ports opened to British commerce by the treaty of Nanking (Nanjing) (1842) corresponded generally to Jardine's recommendations.

During the period of the First Opium War (1839–42), Jardine joined the London banking firm of Magniac, Smith & Co. (renamed Magniac Jardine in 1841), which handled London affairs for British merchants in Asia; and he successfully stood for election to parliament as the whig candidate for Ashburton, Devon, a town with interests in the woollen export trade to China. In the Commons he seldom spoke, but in 1842, after the treaty of Nanking had secured Hong Kong and opened five new 'treaty ports', Palmerston, acknowledging Jardine's counsel, credited him with a major role in the success of British policy towards China.

Jardine embodied a complex amalgam of shrewd political judgement, raw business 'savvy', and philanthropic inclinations (he contributed to the Morrison Education Society for free education in Chinese and English for Chinese youths, and he provided money for medical treatment for poor Chinese). Among the Chinese he was known as the 'Iron-Headed Rat', referring to an incident at Canton when he was struck on the head by a club and shrugged off the attack. His stern personality and disdain for idleness were reflected in his practice of keeping only one chair in his office, on which he sat while visitors stood.

Jardine was an advocate of free trade, as the East India Company monopoly was expiring; yet he was willing to collaborate with his major rival, Lancelot Dent, to reduce the growing number of vessels competing in the opium trade along the coast. In 1835 he wrote to one of his ship captains, who was selling opium to coastal smugglers: 'If you could manage matters so as to make the Mandarins attack every one but your own party it would have good effect.' (Jardine to Capt. J. Rees, 9 March 1935, private letterbook, C4/4, Jardine Matheson Archive, Cambridge).

Jardine saw opium as the only source of ready Chinese currency, with which to trade in silk, tea, and other items. In 1830 he described the opium trade as 'the safest and most gentlemanlike speculation I am aware of' (Jardine to R. Rolfe, 6 April 1830, private letterbook, C4/1, Jardine Matheson Archive, Cambridge); and he later argued that it was Chinese buyers, rather than British merchants, who were doing the smuggling. He told a parliamentary committee in 1840 that once the money was received and the Chinese buyer got his opium from the ships offshore, then it was the buyer's business what became of the opium.

Jardine never married. However, his private correspondence suggests that he had once had a liaison with a Mrs Ratcliffe, who lived in Kent, and that a young woman named Matilda Jane Ratcliffe, who was provided for in his estate, may have been their daughter. Upon returning to London he joined the Oriental Club and resided at Upper Belgrave Street.

In 1841 he purchased the estate of Lanrick in Perthshire. This property and his shares in the London and Hong Kong firms were bequeathed to his nephews. He died in Upper Belgrave Street, London, on 27 February 1843, following a prolonged, painful illness resulting from a tumour, which necessitated his confinement to a water bed in the final months of his life. He was buried on 14 April 1843 in the churchyard at Lochmaben, where his grave is marked by a tall obelisk, rivalling in size the statue of Robert the Bruce in the town centre, about a hundred yards away.

RICHARD J. GRACE

Sources CUL, Jardine, Matheson & Co. MSS · A. R. Williamson, *Eastern traders* (1975) · 'Select committee on trade with China', *Parl. papers* (1840), vol. 7, no. 359 · Palmerston (Broadlands) MSS, U. Southampton L. · M. Keswick, ed., *The thistle and the jade* (1982) · J. K. Fairbank, *Trade and diplomacy on the China coast, 1842–1854* (1964) · P. W. Fay, *The Opium War* (1975) · M. Greenberg, *British trade and the opening of China, 1800–42* (1951) · 'Biographical particulars', *Jardine, Matheson & Co. afterwards Jardine, Matheson & Co. Limited: an outline of the history of a China house ... 1832–1932*, ed. J. Steuart (privately printed, Hong Kong, 1934) · private information (2004) · *Dumfries and Galloway Standard* (26 April 1843) · W. Johnstone, *The bard and the belted knight* (1867) [incl. obit. from *Dumfries Courier*, 1843]

Archives CUL

Likenesses G. Chinnery, portrait, priv. coll.; repro. in Keswick, ed., *The thistle* · T. G. Lupton, engraving (after G. Chinnery), NPG [*see illus.*] · portrait, Jardine, Matheson & Co. Ltd

Wealth at death interests in Jardine, Matheson, and Magniac Jardine; estate of Lanrick in Perthshire

Jardine, Sir William, of Applegirth, seventh baronet (1800–1874), naturalist, was born on 23 February 1800 in Edinburgh, the eldest son of Sir Alexander Jardine of Applegirth, sixth baronet (1771/2–1821), and Jane Dorcas Maule. He was brought up at Jardine Hall, an estate with 5538 acres in Dumfriesshire. He went to Edinburgh high school, and in 1815 transferred to York before entering Edinburgh University in 1817 to read literature and medicine. On 28 June 1820 Jardine married Jean (known as Jane) Home Lizars, the daughter of Daniel Lizars of Edinburgh and sister of the engraver William Home *Lizars (1788–1859). Soon after their wedding the couple went for about nine months to Paris, where Jardine continued his studies. There were seven children of the marriage.

Jardine's studies included anatomy, geology, ornithology, botany, and ichthyology. He was a keen sportsman, hunting with the Stirling and Linlithgow foxhounds, shooting deer and birds, and fishing the Annan, which flowed through the grounds of Jardine Hall. Between 1832 and 1835 he fished the Tweed, a period during which he leased out Jardine Hall and rented The Holmes at St Boswell's, Roxburghshire, as an economy measure. Jardine's determination to solve the history of the life cycles of trout and salmon led to his collection of specimens from many English lakes and Scottish lochs, especially on a tour of Sutherland made with his brother John, P. J. Selby, James Wilson, and Dr Robert Kaye Greville in 1834. In

1838–41 he issued *British Salmonidae* with his own finely etched plates. His expertise was utilized in 1860 when he was appointed to the royal commission which surveyed the salmon fisheries of England and Wales.

Jardine travelled widely, visiting Paris (where he attended classes in anatomy and natural history) in 1820, the continent (with Selby) in 1825, Ireland in 1845, and Bermuda, Barbados, Trinidad, and Jamaica in 1860–61. His voluminous correspondence with naturalists all over the world was very fruitful in obtaining specimens of birds, many new to science, for description in his several ornithological books, and expanding his museum collection.

The first of Jardine's publications was *Illustrations of Ornithology*, issued jointly with Selby in 1827–35. The two friends, with the physician and naturalist George *Johnston (1797–1855), then edited the *Magazine of Zoology and Botany* from its inception in 1836. Jardine also began to edit the series of forty small volumes in the immensely successful *Naturalist's Library*, designed to be affordable by the general public. Between 1833 and 1845 Jardine wrote fifteen of the texts himself, and several of the biographies of naturalists which preceded each text. He also edited Gilbert White's *Selborne* in 1829 (an edition which brought this text to prominence following a period of obscurity) and Alexander Wilson's *American Ornithology* in 1832, adding a biography of his fellow Scot. Jardine was supported financially in his publishing by William Lizars, who also printed the etchings.

Jardine was a member of several natural history societies in Edinburgh, Berwickshire, Northumberland, and Dumfriesshire, and frequently acted as their president and contributed articles to their journals. Between 1855 and 1864 he was joint editor of the *Edinburgh New Philosophical Journal*. He was a fellow of the Linnean Society and the royal societies of London and Edinburgh, was awarded the degree of LLD by Edinburgh University in 1862, and was elected an honorary member of the Royal Scottish Academy in 1826. He exhibited his oil paintings at the academy and in art shows at Newcastle and Dumfries.

Jardine met the zoologist Hugh Edwin Strickland (1811–1853) at the Glasgow meeting of the British Association for the Advancement of Science in 1840. Strickland was one of the supporters, with Jardine, of the Ray Society instigated by Johnston in 1844. The following year Strickland married Catherine Dorcas Maule (1825–1888), Jardine's second daughter. She assisted both her father and her husband with drawings of birds, some reproduced anastatically in Jardine's *Contributions to Ornithology* (1848–53). Strickland was fatally wounded when struck by a train while geologizing near Clarborough Tunnel in 1853. Jardine wrote a memoir of his life and was deeply affected by the tragedy. He had already suffered by the building of the Caledonian railway line which, despite protracted opposition from Jardine in 1839–45, was ultimately routed through his grounds at Jardine Hall.

Jardine influenced the next generation of naturalists, whom he welcomed to his extensive museum, which contained 6000 species of birds. In Scotland he was also influential in local affairs, being one of the convenors of the

Church of Scotland, justice of the peace, commissioner of supply, and deputy lieutenant for Dumfriesshire in 1841. Jane, Lady Jardine, died in 1871 and shortly after, on 18 November 1871, Jardine married Hyacinthe, daughter of the Revd W. S. Symonds. Jardine died on 21 November 1874 at Sandown on the Isle of Wight. He was buried in the grounds of Applegarth kirk on 27 November.

CHRISTINE E. JACKSON

Sources H. Gladstone, 'Sir William Jardine', Royal Scottish Museum, Edinburgh · W. H. Mullens and H. K. Swann, *A bibliography of British ornithology from the earliest times to the end of 1912* (1917) · J. H., *Berwickshire Naturalists' Club*, 7 (1876), 402–6 · *Proceedings of the Royal Society of Edinburgh*, 9 (1875–8), 20–22 · J. Pitman, *Manuscripts in the Royal Scottish Museum Edinburgh*, 1: *William Jardine papers* (1981) · H. B. McCall, *Some old families: a contribution to the genealogical history of Scotland* (1890) · W. MacDowells, *History of the burgh of Dumfries* (1867) · Jardine graves, Applegarth, Dumfriesshire

Archives Bath Central Library · Linn. Soc. · NA Scot., corresp. and papers · National Museum of Scotland, Edinburgh, corresp. and papers · NHM, letter-book · NL Scot., letters · NRA Scotland, priv. coll. · U. Edin. L., corresp., journals, and papers | American Philosophical Society, Philadelphia, letters to Thomas Eyton · Bath Royal Literary and Scientific Institution, letters to Leonard Blomefield · Linn. Soc., letters to William Swainson · RBG Kew, letters to Sir William Hooker · RBG Kew, letter to Sir William Master · U. Cam., department of zoology, corresp. with Prideaux Selby

Likenesses photographs, *c.*1864–1872, Royal Scottish Museum, Edinburgh · W. H. Lizars, pencil drawing, Scot. NPG · T. H. Maguire, lithograph, BM, NPG; repro. in T. H. Maguire, *Portraits of honorary members of the Ispwich Museum* (1852) · line drawing, repro. in S. Devlin-Thorp, ed., *One hundred medical and scientific fellows of the Royal Society of Edinburgh, selected from 1783 to 1832* (1981) · oils, Scot. NPG · wood-engraving (after photograph by Maull & Co.), NPG; repro. in *ILN* (26 Dec 1876)

Wealth at death £14,256 15s. 1d.: confirmation, 19 Feb 1875, NA Scot., SC 15/41/15, 1153–1160

Jarlath. *See* Iarlaithe (*supp. d.* 481).

Jarman, (Michael) Derek Elworthy (1942–1994), filmmaker, painter, and campaigner for homosexual rights, was born on 31 January 1942 at the Victoria Nursing Home, Pinner Hill, Middlesex, the elder child of Wing Commander Lancelot Elworthy Jarman (1907–1986), RAF officer, and his wife, Elizabeth Evelyn (Betts; 1918–1978), daughter of Harry Litten Puttock, tea merchant, and his wife, Moselle Reuben. His father's RAF postings saw a succession of temporary homes—the Villa Zuassa (Lake Maggiore), RAF Oakington, RAF Abingdon, Curry Mallet Manor, Karachi—until his father left the RAF in July 1958 and built himself a house, Merryfield, at 42 Murray Road, Northwood. Jarman attended Hordle preparatory school from 1950 to 1954 and then Canford Hall until 1960. At Canford he developed a love for the Dorset coast, which featured as settings in future films, and of painting, influenced by the art master, Robin Noscoe. A place at the Slade School of Fine Art was deferred because he had agreed with his father that he would do an 'academic' degree first. He studied English, history, and the history of art at King's College, London, from 1960 to 1963. The influence of Nicholas Pevsner persisted in Jarman's exhaustive and exhausting knowledge of London architecture.

Jarman attended the Slade from 1963 to 1967, where his

(Michael) Derek Elworthy Jarman (1942–1994), by David Thompson, 1992

personal tutor was Maurice Feild. There he preferred the screenings of the film course, started by Sir William Coldstream in 1960, and his specialization in theatre design, run by Peter Snow, to the then prevailing mode of teaching painting. But he was occupied with painting throughout his life. He won the Peter Stuyvesant foundation prize at the Young Contemporaries (1967), showed regularly at the Lisson Gallery and the Edward Totah, the Karsten Schubert, and the Richard Salmon galleries, and had retrospectives at the Institute of Contemporary Arts, London (1984), the Manchester City Art Gallery (1992), and, posthumously, at the Barbican Art Gallery (1996). He was also nominated for the Turner prize in 1986. Even when almost blind, with the assistance of Piers Clemmet and Karl Lydon he still managed to produce paintings in Richard Salmon's studio.

But stage design first beckoned: in 1968 Jarman designed sets for Frederick Ashton's *Jazz Calendar* at the Royal Opera House and John Gielgud's *Don Giovanni* at the London Coliseum. The lack of critical success of the latter, in particular, turned his attention away from ballet. A chance encounter in 1970 led to his involvement in the designs for Ken Russell's film *The Devils* (1971) and *Savage Messiah* (1972). Introduced to Super-8 filming by Marc Balet, an architectural student in Warhol's circle, he made his first film, *Electric Fairy*, in 1970, assisted by Andrew Logan. In 1971 he purchased his own Nizo Super-8 camera: not only was it cheaper than conventional film, but it permitted an escape from the restraints imposed by conventional cinematographic procedures. His subsequent films showed a catholic range of influence—Fleming's *The Wizard of Oz*, Pasolini (P.P.P. was often referred to in Jarman's diaries), Anger, Warhol, Le Grice, and Lopushansky among others. His reading of Jung's *Sermons to the Dead* influenced his integration of past and present, dream and reality. His films also shared other characteristics—a love of tableaux, a static camera, filming through coloured gels, the blowing up of Super-8 to 35 mm gauge, superimposition, retardation, re-incorporation of pre-existing footage, narrative imposed in the editing room, the use of a mixture of amateur and professional actors, and an iconographic repertoire of masks, mirrors, bonfires, and derelict banks of the Thames. Lack of money enforced some of these—many of the films were made on shoe-string budgets, and some as tax dodges.

Sebastiane (1975), the story of the early Christian martyr, co-directed by Paul Humfrees, featured explicit male nudity and homo-eroticism (but in the obscurity of a learned language, Latin): its showing on Channel 4 in 1982 led to a media furore, which thereafter frequently dogged Jarman. *Jubilee* (1977), financed by James Whaley, paralleled the worlds of queens Elizabeth I and II: its home-made qualities suited the 'punk' ethic and its cast included 'Jordan' (Pamela Rooke) and Toyah Wilcox, who also appeared in *The Tempest* (1979). The 1980s saw a seven-year struggle to finance and make *Caravaggio*. Meanwhile Jarman designed a performance in Florence of *The Rake's Progress* (1982), and for the Micha Bergese ballet *Mouth of the Night* (1984), and produced films for Genesis P. Orridge's group, Throbbing Gristle. From 1982 he made a series of pop 'promos' for Marianne Faithfull, Marc Almond, The Smiths, Bryan Ferry, and the Pet Shop Boys. In 1984 he made the 16 mm short, *Imagining October*, inspired by a visit to Russia, and he also published the autobiographical *The Dancing Ledge*. His film *The Angelic Conversation* (1985), again blown up to 35 mm, was based on a gay interpretation of Shakespeare's sonnets, and was financed by Peter Sainsbury's British Film Institute production board. 1986 finally saw the production of *Caravaggio*, his first 35 mm film, and his first casting of the actress Tilda Swinton. *The Last of England* (1987), an eschatological exploration in Super-8 of Thatcher's Britain, *War Requiem* (1989), *Edward II* (1991), and *Wittgenstein* (1993) followed. *Glitterbug*, the last film made from his Super-8 footage from 1971 to 1986, was effectively directed by James McKay.

Jarman was a passionate supporter of gay rights and was closely involved in the campaign to repeal clause 28 of the Local Government Bill (1987) and to lower the age of consent for homosexuals. He took the side of the more militant OutRage rather than of Stonewall: in 1991 he publicly denounced the actor Ian McKellen for accepting a knighthood from what Jarman saw as a repressive, homophobic government. Diagnosed HIV positive on 22 December 1986, he made this public a month later, on radio. His last years were frenetic with activity, recorded in a series of journals: *Modern Nature* (1991), *At your Own Risk* (1992), and the posthumously published *Smiling in Slow Motion* (2000). These journals also recorded the construction of a garden at Prospect Cottage, Dungeness, Kent, bought in 1987 with money left by his father. Together with his partner Keith Collins (the H.B. of Jarman's diaries), Howard Sooley, Peter Fillingham, and Karl Lydon, he developed a unique garden in an extreme and inhospitable environment; it provided the setting of his 1990 film *The Garden*. As the secondary symptoms and opportunistic infections of AIDS—tuberculosis of the liver, cytomegalovirus, and bacillary angiomatosis—began to set in, necessitating long spells in hospital, the tall, strong, saturnine Jarman with characteristic flapping arms, hovering from foot to foot, grew frail, and finally blind. His abstract film, *Blue* (1993), with a blank, Yves-Kleinian blue screen, a soundtrack compiled from diaries and poetry about the struggle with AIDS, and music by Simon Fisher Turner, was a testimony to the stoicism with which he faced this blow and transformed it into art. He died of bronchopneumonia at St Bartholomew's Hospital, London, on 19 February 1994 and was buried in St Clement's churchyard, New Romney, Kent, on 2 March 1994.   STEPHEN BURY

Sources A. Peake, *Derek Jarman* (1999) • J. C. Parkes and others, *Derek Jarman: a portrait*, ed. R. Wollen (1996) • M. O'Pray, *Derek Jarman: dreams of England* (1996) • D. Jarman, *Up in the air: collected film scripts* (1996) • D. Jarman, *Last of England* (1987) • D. Jarman, *The dancing ledge* (1984) • D. Jarman, *Modern nature: the journals of Derek Jarman* (1991) • D. Jarman, *At your own risk: a saint's testament* (1992) • D. Jarman, *Smiling in slow motion* (2000) • *Derek Jarman's garden, with photographs by Howard Sooley* (1995) • *The Guardian* (21 Feb 1994) • *The Independent* (21 Feb 1994) • *The Times* (21 Feb 1994) • b. cert. • d. cert. **Archives** BFI, corresp. and papers • priv. coll., Jarman estate | UCL, Slade School of Art archives | FILM Basilisk Communications, London • BFI NFTVA, 'Clause and Effect', 1988 • BFI NFTVA, 'Books by my bedside', ITV, 4 Jan 1989 • BFI NFTVA, 'Derek Jarman — you know what I mean', Channel 4, 11 May 1989 • BFI NFTVA, 'Derek Jarman — a portrait', BBC 2, 25 Jan 1991 • BFI NFTVA, 'There we are John …', Berlin Film Festival, 1994 • BFI NFTVA, *The late show*, BBC2, 15 March 1993 • BFI NFTVA, 'A night with Derek II', Channel 4, 20 Feb 1995 • BFI NFTVA, documentary footage | SOUND BL NSA, ICA in conversation, 7 Feb 1984, BD1 • BL NSA, 'Calling the shots', B8267/02 • BL NSA, 'Derek Jarman: a portrait', V51601 • BL NSA, documentary recordings • BL NSA, performance recordings **Likenesses** M. Laye, photograph, 1986, repro. in *The Independent* • I. Rank-Broadley, bronze medallion, 1991, NPG • D. Thompson, photograph, 1992, NPG [see illus.] • M. Clark, oil on card, 1993, NPG • H. Sooley, photograph, 1993, repro. in Peake, *Derek Jarman*, facing p. 307 • H. Sooley, photograph, 1993, repro. in *The Independent* • H. Sooley, photograph, repro. in *Derek Jarman's garden*, 78 • H. Sooley, photograph, repro. in Peake, *Derek Jarman*, facing p. 459 • photograph, repro. in *The Times* **Wealth at death** £144,667: probate, 18 Oct 1994, CGPLA Eng. & Wales

Jarman [*married name* Ternan], **Frances Eleanor** [Fanny] (1802–1873), actress, was born in Hull on 8 February 1802, the daughter of John Jarman, a lawyer turned actor who was prompter in the Yorkshire touring company of Tate Wilkinson, and his second wife, Martha Maria Mottershed (d. 1849), who acted under the name of Miss Errington. She was baptized in Doncaster in November 1804, having already made her earliest stage appearances as the baby in *Pizarro* and in 'Monk' Lewis's *The Bleeding Nun*. Once she could walk she began to play roles such as the Duke of York in *Richard III* and Fleance in *Macbeth*, and while still a child performed with both Sarah Siddons and Dorothy Jordan. Wilkinson's company was disbanded in 1813, and nothing more is known of her father after this date. In 1814 her mother joined the Bath theatre company, and here Fanny worked throughout her childhood years, moved on to principal parts, and established herself as a favourite, appearing mainly in Shakespeare—she played Juliet to her mother's Nurse—and adaptations of Scott. She had good features, a graceful and dignified stage manner, and a sweet voice, and she sang well. She made a highly successful appearance at the Crow Street Theatre

Frances Eleanor Jarman (1802–1873), by Maria Ternan (Mrs Rowland Taylor)

Shakespeare and Byron, but his acting was judged 'forcible rather than finished' in his native Dublin, where he played Shylock and Rob Roy in 1833. Macready took a poor view of both his talent and his character, and as a tragedian he was hampered by being short and stout; but after an energetic courtship he and Fanny Jarman were married, on 21 September 1834, and at once sailed for America, where they toured for the next three years, their success being largely attributable to her talent. A daughter, also Fanny [see Trollope, Frances Eleanor, under Ternan, Ellen Lawless] was born in 1835 aboard a paddle steamer; a second, Maria, followed after their return to England in 1837, and a third, Ellen Lawless *Ternan, in 1839. In this year the family moved to Newcastle upon Tyne, where Ternan became manager of the Theatre Royal, his wife was the principal actress—still sometimes billed as 'late Miss Jarman'—and their eldest daughter began her brilliant career as a child performer. In 1842 a son was born who lived only a few months; at the same time Ternan began to show signs of illness. In 1844 he collapsed, and for two years his wife and children worked to support him in the asylum at Bethnal Green, touring wherever they could find work in England and Ireland. His death from 'general paralysis' came in 1846, when his wife was appearing at the Surrey Theatre with Macready, who did what he could to assist the family.

Mother and daughters continued to tour, and appeared with (among others) Fanny Kemble, Madame Vestris, and Charles Mathews. Mrs Ternan played Juliet to the Romeo of Charlotte Cushman, the American actress who made a speciality of male roles. In the early 1850s she worked with Samuel Phelps at Sadler's Wells and in 1853 took part in a royal command performance at Windsor. By 1855 the family was settled at Park Cottage, Northampton Park, in north London, and Mrs Ternan, Fanny, and Maria were all working for Charles Kean at the Princess's Theatre. In 1857 Mrs Ternan was recommended by the manager Alfred Wigan to Charles Dickens, who invited her, together with Maria and Ellen, to join him in his amateur production of Wilkie Collins's melodrama *The Frozen Deep*, to be performed in Manchester.

The friendship with Dickens, who interested himself in the whole family, was responsible for an improvement in their situation. Mrs Ternan was able to give up work and travel to Italy with Fanny, who wished to become an opera singer. A substantial house at 2 Houghton Place, Ampthill Square (near Mornington Crescent), was given—almost certainly by Dickens—to the elder daughters in 1859 and then, a year later, when she reached the age of twenty-one, transferred to Ellen. All were living there in April 1861 when Mrs Ternan described herself as an 'annuitant' in the census. She was not, however, in London for the wedding of Maria in 1863, and in June 1865 she was travelling with Dickens and Ellen on a train returning from France, which crashed at Staplehurst. The following year she returned to the stage, as blind Alice in Fechter's Lyceum production of *The Master of Ravenswood*, and in *The Corsican Brothers*, and in the same year attended the wedding of her daughter Fanny to Thomas Adolphus Trollope

in Dublin in 1822, followed by a tour of Ireland, during which she narrowly escaped abduction and rape. For the next four years she continued to tour in England and Ireland, and in 1824 appeared in Dublin with W. C. Macready, which was the beginning of a long professional collaboration and personal friendship.

In 1827 Fanny Jarman appeared at Covent Garden as Juliet to the Romeo of Charles Kemble and as Ophelia to his Hamlet; she was also seen as Portia to the Shylock of Edmund Kean, with whom she had previously acted in Bath, and Desdemona to his Othello. Her nervousness at facing the London audience made her almost inaudible at first, and, although she played major roles for three seasons and also appeared at the Lyceum, she did not entirely convince the London critics. She was described as picturesque rather than passionate in tragedy, correct and elegant, but with 'something wanting'. When she visited Scotland in the summer, the Edinburgh critics were very much more enthusiastic. Christopher North (John Wilson), one of the most influential, considered her superior to both Fanny Kemble and Fanny Kelly. When she was replaced at Covent Garden by Fanny Kemble in 1829, she moved to Scotland, where, in 1831, she met **Thomas Lawless Ternan** (1790–1846) and performed with him in *Comus*.

Ternan, the son of a Dublin grocer, joined the Kent circuit as an aspiring actor in 1808. He had a passion for in Paris. In the winter of 1867–8 she visited the Trollopes in Florence with Ellen, while Dickens was in America. Her last years were spent in Oxford, at The Lawn, St Giles's Road East, the comfortable home of her daughter Maria; she died of acute bronchitis on 30 October 1873.

CLAIRE TOMALIN

Sources C. Tomalin, *The invisible woman: the story of Nelly Ternan and Charles Dickens* (1990) · d. cert.
Likenesses I. W. Slater, lithograph, pubd 1829, BM, Harvard TC · M. Ternan, drawing, V&A [*see illus.*] · drawing (as a young actress), priv. coll. · group portrait, photograph (with daughters, in old age), priv. coll. · portraits, repro. in Tomalin, *Invisible woman* · prints, Harvard TC

Jarmay, Sir John Gustav (1856–1944), industrial chemist, was born on 31 December 1856, the son of Gustav de Jármay, a pharmacist of Pest, Hungary. He was educated at private schools in Hungary and at the Technische Hochschule in Zürich, where he had the good fortune to be a pupil of Georg Lunge. Although Lunge inspired many chemists who later became distinguished in theoretical fields, he was experienced in the chemical industry as well, having spent a long time in England in work connected with alkali manufacture. Jarmay followed his example and came early to England, to study for a while in Manchester. There he came to the notice of H. E. Roscoe, whom Lunge had known. Like Lunge, Roscoe saw the need to promote scientifically trained men into the chemical industry and he encouraged Jarmay to take the first step on his long industrial career with Greenall, Whitley & Co., brewers of Warrington. Two years later Jarmay began a connection with Brunner, Mond & Co. which was to last the rest of his active life. This leading enterprise had been set up by John Tomlinson Brunner and Ludwig Mond in 1873, becoming a limited company in 1881. Like other British chemical companies it had often to recruit foreign chemists; Brunner admired Roscoe's work, and encouraged his students, so Jarmay had a double virtue in his eyes. He became a manager for the company at Winnington in 1880. On 2 June 1882 Jarmay married Charlotte Elizabeth (d. 1938), daughter of George Wyman, a surgeon. She was very active in the work of the Red Cross in Cheshire during the First World War and was made an OBE in 1919. They had one son, who became a farmer.

The key to Jarmay's success was the ammonia-soda process, which had been developed to a high degree of efficiency by Solvay in Belgium, who then licensed Brunner, Mond to use it. With Brunner providing the financial acumen and Mond the chemical insight, their team was well set to advance. It was just the situation in which Jarmay could exercise his own talents and in 1884 he established himself as a leading figure in the company by patenting, with Mond, a process for purifying crude bicarbonate of soda (a main product of the ammonia-soda process). He made many inventions on his own for which he was granted more than forty patents. He rose rapidly, from a junior managerial position to chief technical manager and to membership, in 1889, of the board of directors.

Jarmay's life revolved around the development of a number of technical processes, the most important being the manufacture of soda (sodium carbonate), a substance central to many manufactures, such as soap and glass, all of which were being made within easy reach of the Brunner, Mond factories. After Mond's death in 1909 Jarmay was largely responsible for the technical progress not only of Brunner, Mond but of other companies with which he was connected. At the outbreak of war in 1914 it became apparent that the country was seriously short of explosives, and a massive industrial effort was made to remedy this. The important Brunner, Mond contribution was led by Jarmay. He served on a government committee dealing with high explosives, to such good effect that in 1918, on the recommendation of Lord Moulton (who had been minister of munitions), he was made KBE.

The British industrial scene changed greatly as a consequence of the war, not only because of events within the United Kingdom but also because of what was happening in Europe and the world at large. New techniques developed abroad had to be studied, and one of these was the fixation of atmospheric nitrogen in which the German chemists, Haber and Bosch, had made a revolution. Jarmay did something towards introducing the process into the UK, but younger men were now ready to lead. When the rationalization of the chemical industry led to the formation in 1926 of Imperial Chemical Industries, into which Brunner, Mond was absorbed, Jarmay might have been expected to be appointed to its board but he was not. He spent the last twenty years of his life in industrial activity but never quite at its centre. He was, however, able to enjoy the recreations which had coloured much of his life, keeping up his mountaineering and his hunting as long as he could. In the company of H. E. Roscoe, Mond, and others he took part in the discussions which led in 1881 to the foundation of the Society of Chemical Industry and maintained his connection with that and with the Institute of Chemistry and the Chemical Society. He enjoyed life and was noted for his hospitality. In group photographs of company staff he appears as an upright figure, bearded and commanding.

Jarmay set up another home in Italy but returned to England on the outbreak of war in 1939. He died at his home, 1 Lothair Villas, Hatfield on 22 August 1944.

FRANK GREENAWAY

Sources *The Times* (24 Aug 1944) · *Journal of the Society of Chemical Industry* (July 1931), 116 [jubilee number] · *Journal of the Institute of Chemistry* (1944), 186 · *Fifty years of progress: the story of the Castner-Kellner Alkali Company*, Castner-Kellner Alkali Co. [1945] · J. I. Walls, *The first fifty years of Brunner Mond, 1873–1923* (1923) · F. D. Miles, *A history of research in the Nobel division of ICI* (1955) · student records, Technische Hochschule, Zürich, Archives · *WW* · m. cert. · d. cert.
Likenesses group portraits, photographs, repro. in Castner-Kellner Alkali Company, *Fifty years of progress*
Wealth at death £21,883 8s. 4d.: probate, 16 Jan 1945, *CGPLA Eng. & Wales*

Jarrett, Sir Clifford George (1909–1995), civil servant, was born in Dover on 10 December 1909, the older child and only son of George Henry Jarrett (1881–1974), a photographer, and his wife, Kate Ellen, *née* Elgar (1883–1963). His childhood was disrupted by the First World War. In

Sir Clifford George Jarrett (1909–1995), by Elliott & Fry

1917, while his father was in the army, a German air raid on Dover made the family home uninhabitable. He moved with his mother and sister to Canterbury, where he entered the Payne Smith elementary school. In 1919, after his father was demobilized, the family returned to Dover. There, he later acknowledged, a superb deputy head and good teaching at St Mary's elementary school helped him to win a scholarship in 1920 to Dover County School for Boys, where he became captain of his house and company quartermaster-sergeant in the cadet corps. In 1927 he won an open scholarship to Sidney Sussex College, Cambridge.

Before starting at Cambridge Jarrett taught himself German; he wished to read modern languages, and the county school had taught only French. He went up to Sidney Sussex College in October 1928, graduating in 1931 with a double first in the modern languages tripos. The college extended his scholarship for another year to enable him to read for the history tripos and prepare for the civil service examination. He came first in the administrative class examination of 1932, and joined the Home Office. He soon found it, in his own words, 'rather stuffy', and in 1934 he successfully responded to an Admiralty appeal for experienced assistant principals. It was the start of a departmental career culminating in his appointment twenty-seven years later as the last secretary of the Admiralty.

Jarrett's ability was quickly recognized. Between 1936 and 1938 he was private secretary to two parliamentary secretaries, followed by two years as head of the political section, in which, as the Second World War began, his main task was to monitor breaches of international law by the Germans. When A. V. Alexander succeeded Churchill as first lord in May 1940 Jarrett was appointed his principal private secretary—the most important post in the department for a junior civil servant. It was a tribute to his intellect, character, and stamina that he held it for four years of war, living in the Admiralty building and frequently working a fifteen-hour day. In May 1944 he was promoted to a less demanding post; but he was shortly moved twice to gain experience in other departmental areas, followed by a brief assignment in Ottawa and Washington. In 1946, at the early age of thirty-seven, he was promoted again, to be the under-secretary in charge of all civilian personnel. Four years later he was promoted once more, becoming the sole deputy secretary under Sir John Lang, the secretary of the Admiralty since 1947. It was not, in Jarrett's view, an entirely satisfactory post since important issues had to be considered by the secretary while lesser matters could usually be handled by the under-secretaries. But special tasks fell to him, notably the negotiation in 1955 of the Simonstown naval agreement; and, in a period marked by constant reorganization and retrenchment, and also by such emergencies as the Korean War and the Suez crisis, Jarrett's acute mind and steady hand were invaluable. After eleven years as heir apparent he succeeded Lang as secretary in 1961. It was not to be for long. In 1964 the prime minister, Harold Macmillan, created the unified Ministry of Defence, abolishing separate service departments and redeploying their permanent secretaries to other departments. It was the end of the Admiralty, and its last secretary became permanent secretary of the Ministry of Pensions and National Insurance.

Jarrett took the transition in his stride. His colleagues were impressed by his friendly approach and by his speed in absorbing the intricacies of a fresh field of administration. The newly elected Labour government introduced a succession of departmental changes which he handled with quiet authority: a merger with the Supplementary Benefits Commission, then in 1968 a further merger with the Ministry of Health, thus establishing the Department of Health and Social Security with Jarrett as its first permanent secretary. His secretary of state, Richard Crossman, described him in his *Diaries* as 'that big, bluff fellow with his blue eyes, his uncomplicated exterior, and his extraordinary competence' (Crossman, 732); but some other references were disparaging. Jarrett was not alone, however, in finding working relations difficult, and official colleagues took the view that his calm and wise leadership carried the department skilfully through difficult years in the National Health Service and a major attempt to reform the pensions system. The end of Jarrett's career was marred by a personal rift with Crossman, when the latter's strong objection led to the refusal of his request to accept, after retirement, a directorship in the pensions industry. Although pressed to stay longer by Sir Keith Joseph, after a government change in May, he retired as planned in July 1970.

Hard-working as ever, Jarrett remained busy in the subsequent decade. A lifelong pipe smoker, he chaired the Tobacco Research Council, and also a review of the medical services of the armed forces; and he served as a trustee of the National Maritime Museum. He particularly valued his chairmanship of the Dover Harbour Board from 1971 to 1980, during which he saw through a £50 million port expansion programme—a satisfying conclusion to a life which began in Dover more than seventy years earlier.

Jarrett was appointed CBE in 1945 and CB in 1949, being advanced to KBE in 1956. He was twice married: in 1933 to Hilda Alice (1909–1975), daughter of Reginald Goodchild, and in 1978 to Mary Evelyn, a medical librarian (b. 1929), daughter of Charles Beacock. There was one son and two daughters of the first marriage. In 1976 he moved from Chislehurst to 1 the Coach House, Derry Hill, Menston, near Ilkley, Yorkshire, where he died on 9 July 1995; he was cremated on 13 July at Rawdon, Leeds, and his ashes were committed to the waters of Dover harbour three days later. His second wife survived him.

PATRICK NAIRNE

Sources *The Times* (19 July 1995) · *Daily Telegraph* (14 July 1995) · Dame Mildred Riddlesdell, memorial service address, 1995 · personal knowledge (2004) · private information (2004) · R. H. S. Crossman, *The diaries of a cabinet minister*, 3 vols. (1975–7) · T. Dalyell, *Dick Crossman—a portrait* (1989) · P. Hennessy, *Whitehall* (1989) · *WWW* · Burke, *Peerage* · b. cert. · d. cert.
Likenesses Elliott & Fry, photograph, NPG [*see illus.*] · photograph, repro. in *The Times* · photograph, repro. in *Daily Telegraph*
Wealth at death £68,235: probate, 16 Oct 1995, *CGPLA Eng. & Wales*

Jarrett, Cyril Beaufort [*name in religion* Bede] (**1881–1934**), Dominican friar, was born at Blackheath, London, on 22 August 1881, the fifth of the six sons of Henry Sullivan Jarrett (1839–1919), an officer in the Indian army, and his wife, Agnes Delacour Beaufort (1850–1930), whose father, Francis, was in the Indian Civil Service and whose grandfather was the hydrographer Sir Francis Beaufort. Cyril Jarrett's parents lived in India and returned to England in retirement in 1896 to settle at East Grinstead in Sussex. Most of Cyril's childhood was spent with his paternal grandmother, Mrs Thomas Jarrett, at Woodchester Park, Gloucestershire. It was here that he first encountered the Dominicans who served the Catholic church at Woodchester and had a community there. His father was a Roman Catholic by birth, his mother a convert, and it was to Stonyhurst, the Jesuit school in Lancashire, that he went in 1891. On leaving Stonyhurst in 1898 he joined the Dominicans. All his brothers followed their father into the army. Clothed in the Dominican habit on 24 September 1898 and taking the name Bede he did his noviciate and philosophy at Woodchester Priory and continued his theological studies at Hawkesyard Priory in Staffordshire. He made his solemn profession there on 20 September 1902 and was ordained priest on 15 December 1904 at Woodchester, having already been resident at the Benedictine Hunter-Blair's Hall at Oxford for a term. The universities had just been opened to Roman Catholics and he was the first Dominican to be sent to Oxford since the Reformation. He graduated, with first-class honours, in the modern history

school in 1907. His studies were completed at Louvain where he successfully completed his lectorate in theology in a year.

The constitutions of the Dominican order, emphasizing fraternity rather than hierarchy, are notably democratic and office depends on election by the brethren at every level. The talented young friar can make his influence felt very quickly. Bede Jarrett, despite his academic prowess, was denied a quiet life of scholarship. In June 1914, after a number of years combining historical and pastoral work in London, he was elected prior of the Dominican London house at Haverstock Hill. He was to spend the rest of his life in one office of responsibility or another. On 5 September 1916 he was elected prior provincial, the regional superior, in the first scrutiny of the election, with twelve votes out of a possible seventeen. He was the youngest provincial in the order. He was re-elected provincial in 1920, 1924, and 1928. In 1932 he was elected prior of the Oxford house, his own foundation.

The administrative tasks of a Dominican provincial include the annual visitation of his province (based at the Dominican priory in London) as well as attending the worldwide general chapters of his order. In 1926 Jarrett received two votes at the general chapter in the election for master-general, the order's head. In 1929, with twenty-four votes in the first scrutiny and thirty-one in the second (the elected Martin Gillet received forty-six), Jarrett was runner-up and failed to become the first English master-general. During his provincialate the province increased in numbers, from 124 in 1916 to 183 in 1932, and in foundations. Jarrett, following St Dominic, his model in so much, believed in dispersing rather than hoarding his manpower. By 1932 the province had acquired a large new mission at Stellenbosch in South Africa (1917) to add to its commitments in Grenada in the West Indies, was on the way to starting a new mission to Persia, and had a new monastery of nuns (at Headington, Oxford), a new school at Laxton in Northamptonshire, and two major new houses of friars at Edinburgh (1931) and Oxford.

Oxford had been the principal academic centre of the Blackfriars, as the Dominicans were popularly called, in the middle ages, and the idea of a renewed Dominican presence at Oxford was not Jarrett's own—as early as 1911 a substantial bequest had been made to make such a house possible—but it was his drive and money-making skills (taking him on preaching tours to the USA in 1923, 1928, and 1933) which made it a reality. Financial management was not his forte, appropriately enough for a mendicant friar vowed to apostolic poverty, and the precarious state of the province's finances was not allowed to get in the way of bringing the Dominicans and their Thomist theology back to the university. The foundation stone of the new Blackfriars was laid by Cardinal Bourne with the other English cardinal, Gasquet, preaching on 15 August 1921, 700 years to the day since the first Dominicans had come to Oxford. The house, in St Giles', and its spacious chapel were opened in 1929 not as a permanent private hall of the university like those of the Benedictines or

Jesuits but as a self-sufficient Dominican *studium* with its own teachers, students, and Dominican personality.

The foundation of Blackfriars and the other initiatives which he made as provincial, which included organizing a continuing series of public lectures in London under the auspices of the University of London (from 1921) and the launching (in 1919) of an English Dominican academic journal, *Blackfriars*, reflected a growing self-confidence and a substantial change of emphasis among the English Dominicans, a rediscovery of the central role of teaching and preaching in the order's charism and a move away from a predominantly parochial ministry. It was a return to origins but motivated as much by evangelical zeal as by romantic nostalgia. Jarrett felt confident that the Dominican way and the theology of St Thomas Aquinas could provide as coherent a system for the modern epoch as they had for the later middle ages. The flowering of the Dominican ideal in the English province in the three decades after Jarrett's death owed much to Jarrett's conviction that the Dominicans could flourish at the heart of English intellectual life.

Jarrett's writings reflected his vision. They were principally historical and devotional but included some volumes of printed sermons and retreat addresses. His historical work concerned itself principally with the middle ages and in its demythologizing of anti-Catholic stereotypes, and in presenting a broad view it had something in common with the writings of Christopher Dawson. His first two important works were *Medieval Socialism* (1913) and *St Antonino and Medieval Economics* (1914) which placed the Dominicans in their wider historical context. His *Social Theories of the Middle Ages* (1926) and *A History of Europe* (1929) attempted a clear synthesis while *The English Dominicans* (1921) and his life of St Dominic (1924) brought his order to a wider English audience. Among his devotional works were *Meditations for Layfolk* (1915), *Living Temples* (1919), *The Space of Life between* (1930), *The House of Gold* (1931) and *No Abiding City* (1934).

Bede Jarrett was about 5 feet 9 or 10 inches. His hair was always kept short, not cropped, and retained its colour, brown, until death, with a little circle of baldness at the crown, a natural tonsure. He was a man of great energy, always brisk in his work, despite the leisurely, carefree image he cultivated, and despite his ecclesiastical work and numerous publications he was readily available to many people both as a preacher and as a friend. He had a quiet demeanour. Jarrett rediscovered the medieval notion of *gratia praedicationis*, that the consequence of grace is to make the word spoken by the preacher a 'graceful', attractive word, which will win favour with those who hear it. His gift for friendship amounted to genius and he remained both loyal and unpossessive in his relationships. In all the friendships of this latter-day Ailred of Rievaulx divine love was at the heart. 'Since he is the object of our creation, though, perhaps we did not realise it, in all our youthful dreamings and hungers it was really for God that we yearned, really God that we desired' (Wykeham-George and Mathew, 160). Jarrett died at the Hospital of St John and St Elizabeth in London on 17 March

1934 following a stroke and a prolonged period of weakness and exhaustion. He was buried on 22 March at Woodchester following requiems at London and Oxford. His grave was marked by a simple stone.

Dominic Aidan Bellenger

Sources B. Bailey, S. Tugwell, and A. Bellenger, eds., *Letters of Bede Jarrett* (1989) · K. Wykeham-George and G. Mathew, *Bede Jarrett of the order of Preachers* (1952) · W. Gumbley, *Obituary notices of the English Dominicans from 1555 to 1952* (1955) · A. White, 'Father Bede Jarrett, OP, and the renewal of the English Dominican province', *Opening the scrolls: essays in Catholic history in honour of Godfrey Anstruther*, ed. D. A. Bellenger (1987), 216–34 · A. Nichols, *Dominican gallery: portrait of a culture* (1997) · private information (2004) [Bede Bailey, OP]
Archives Dominican Priory, Edinburgh, English province of the Order of Preachers archives
Likenesses photograph, repro. in Wykeham-George and Mathew, *Bede Jarrett*

Jarrett, Rebecca (1846–1928), prostitute and social purity activist, was probably born in London on 3 March 1846, the youngest of thirteen children whose father had a ropewalk and shop off the Old Kent Road. Claiming public attention during just one year, when she was co-accused in 1885 with W. T. Stead and Bramwell Booth in the notorious Eliza Armstrong case, Jarrett's true story is lost in mists of deception, melodrama, and Victorian seduction narrative.

Jarrett's father left home when she was young, and the strain of supporting the family caused Mrs Jarrett to turn to drink. By the time Rebecca was twelve years old her mother was taking her to the disreputable Cremorne Gardens in Chelsea and selling her to men. At the trial Jarrett, aged thirty-nine, was described as of unprepossessing appearance, walking with a limp, tall, with a dark, sallow complexion, and almost black hair; but in her memoirs she described her youthful self as 'tall, with very fair hair, blue eyes, a good looker, who rejoiced in a necklace of great blue beads'.

When a brother returned from sea, finding his mother an alcoholic and his sister a prostitute he turned Rebecca out of the house; she lost touch with her family for many years. By sixteen she was managing an accommodation brothel which rented rooms by the hour. For twenty years she moved around the country living off men, drinking heavily, and keeping brothels in Bristol, Manchester, and Marylebone, London; she may also have had several children. These activities were interspersed with laundry work—during which she suffered a hip injury which left her with a limp.

In 1884 Rebecca Jarrett was staying with a man friend in Northampton, dangerously ill from drink. When she fainted outside a Salvation Army meeting, a determined captain 'saved' her. She was sent to London for ten weeks' drying-out in Whitechapel Hospital, where Catherine Booth herself prayed with her. Because she was being hunted by previous colleagues in vice, Jarrett was sent in 1885 to sanctuary with Josephine Butler, whose husband was a canon of Winchester Cathedral. Jarrett proved successful at rescue work among prostitutes in Portsmouth, and the Butlers helped her set up her own rescue home at Hope Cottage, Winchester.

Because of public concern for the morals of young girls, a parliamentary bill to raise the female age of consent above thirteen had been proposed for several years but without success. In 1885 W. T. Stead, editor of the *Pall Mall Gazette*, joined forces with Bramwell Booth of the Salvation Army to force public opinion to alter this stalemate. To further their melodramatic plan, they asked Butler to find a procurer who could provide a virgin of thirteen. She recommended Jarrett, who unwillingly agreed on the understanding that it would 'save the poor little children' in the long run (Jarrett).

In June Jarrett bought Eliza Armstrong from her mother for £5, although in court Mrs Armstrong swore she sent Eliza into domestic service. Certified *virgo intacta*, Eliza stayed overnight with Jarrett in a London brothel; on the following day they crossed the channel to a French brothel. She was not, in fact, interfered with sexually, and was returned unharmed to her family in August.

Stead wrote the story up sensationally in the *Pall Mall Gazette* under the title 'The maiden tribute of modern Babylon', and a scandalized public opinion forced the government to push the Criminal Law Amendment Act through, raising the female age of consent to sixteen years. But to satisfy the prudish, Rebecca Jarrett, Stead, Bramwell Booth, and others were arrested for abduction and assault, appearing at the Old Bailey in November 1885. A farrago of accusations and lies was unravelled, but the judge decided that the case turned on the fact that Eliza had been taken by Jarrett without the consent of her father, which was an illegal act whatever the good intentions of the accused. When Jarrett broke down under cross-examination, telling stories about her past that were proved false, the defence collapsed; Stead served three months in Holloway and Jarrett went to Millbank for six months.

Jarrett's hard times were not over on release from gaol in April 1886. She still had alcoholic relapses, and criminal acquaintances made it impossible for her to continue her rescue work. Briefly in 1886–7 she tried a new start in Canada, but this did not work as she was drinking again. Finally, she settled in 1889 with the Salvation Army in Mare Street, Hackney, where Bramwell Booth considered her subsequent life 'has amply proved the sincerity of her repentance, as she is still with the Army, enjoying a happy old age free from the bondage of the past'. She died on 20 February 1928 at 259 Mare Street, Hackney, and was buried with Salvation Army honours at Abney Park cemetery on 23 February. Ironically, years later it was discovered that Eliza Armstrong's parents had never married, so the father's consent was immaterial and the crown case should have failed.   BEVERLEY GREY

Sources R. Jarrett, 'Short memoirs', *c.*1926, Salvation Army archives · J. E. Butler, *Rebecca Jarrett* (1885–6) · W. T. Stead, 'The Eliza Armstrong case: proceedings at Bow Street', *Pall Mall Gazette* (3 Oct 1885) · *War Cry*, 1885–6, Salvation Army, London, archives [letters and newspaper cuttings] · *War Cry*, 1923, Salvation Army, London, archives [letters and newspaper cuttings] · 'The passing of Rebecca Jarrett', *War Cry* (10 March 1928) · B. Booth, *Echoes and memories*, another edn (1977) · J. R. Walkowitz, *City of dreadful delight: narratives of sexual danger in late-Victorian London* (1992) · F. Whyte, *The life of W. T. Stead*, 2 vols. (1925) · A. Plowden, *The case of Eliza Armstrong* (1974) · A. Stafford, *The age of consent* (1964) · M. Pearson, *The age of consent* (1972) · G. Petrie, *A singular iniquity* (1971) · d. cert.
Archives Salvation Army, London, archives
Likenesses photograph (in old age), repro. in *War Cry* (10 March 1928) · sketch, repro. in *Pall Mall Gazette*, special issues (Nov–Dec 1885)

Jarrett, Thomas (1805–1882), oriental linguist, was educated at St Catharine's College, Cambridge, where he graduated BA in 1827 as thirty-fourth wrangler, and seventh in the first class of the classical tripos. In the following year he was elected a fellow of his college, where he resided as classical and Hebrew lecturer until 1832. He was ordained priest in 1830, and in 1832 he was presented by his college to the rectory of Trunch, North Walsham, Norfolk. In 1831 he was elected to the professorship of Arabic at Cambridge, and held the chair until 1854, when he was appointed regius professor of Hebrew and canon of Ely.

As a linguist Jarrett was chiefly remarkable for the extent and variety of his knowledge. He knew at least twenty languages, and taught Hebrew, Arabic, Sanskrit, Persian, Gothic, and indeed almost any language for which he could find a student. Much of his time was spent in the transliteration of oriental languages into the roman character, according to his own system. In his *A New Way of Marking the Sounds of English without Change of Spelling* (1858) he offered a solution to the problem of spelling and pronunciation by a system of printing English with diacritical marks to show the sound of each vowel. He had illustrated this system already in his *The Holy Gospel and the Acts of the Apostles; so Printed as to Show the Sound of each Word without Change of Spelling* (1857).

Jarrett's other works include *An Essay on Algebraic Development* (1831), intended to illustrate and apply a system of algebraic notation submitted by him to the Cambridge Philosophical Society in 1827, and printed in the third volume of their *Transactions*; *A Grammatical Index to the Hebrew Text of Genesis* (1830); and *A Hebrew–English and English–Hebrew Lexicon* (1848). He also published an edition of Virgil with all the quantities marked (1866); *Nalopākhyānam*, or the Sanskrit text of the story of Nala transliterated into roman characters (1875); and *The Hebrew Text of the Old Covenant Printed in a Modified Roman Alphabet* (1882). He also prepared transliterated editions, which were never published, of the Ramayana, the Shahnamah, and the Koran.

Jarrett died at Trunch rectory on 7 March 1882, and was survived by his wife, Sarah Hume Jarrett. He left his library to St Catharine's.

E. J. RAPSON, *rev.* JOHN D. HAIGH

Sources private information (1891) [Professor Cowell] · *BL cat.* · Crockford (1880) · Venn, *Alum. Cant.*, 2/3 · *CGPLA Eng. & Wales* (1882)
Wealth at death £12,705 1s. 6d.: probate, 9 May 1882, *CGPLA Eng. & Wales*

Jarrold, Thomas (1770–1853), physician, was born in Manningtree, Essex, on 1 December 1770. He was educated at Edinburgh University, where he is said to have taken the degree of MD in 1802, though his name does not appear in the published list of graduates. He was in medical practice at Stockport, Cheshire, in 1806, and soon afterwards moved to Manchester. Jarrold was a member of the city's literary and philosophical society, to which he read a number of papers. He published on medicine, psychology, and anthropology. Among his works were *Dissertations on Man* (1806); a critique of Malthus's *Essay on the Principle of Population*, which drew on his own experience as a doctor in an industrial area; and *A Letter to Samuel Whitbread, M.P. ... on the Poor Laws* (1807). In *Instinct and Reason Philosophically Investigated* (1836), Jarrold claimed to have defined the boundary between the opposing faculties of the work's title, but in the preface to his last work, *Education of the People* (1847), he was obliged to admit that this self-perceived breakthrough had attracted little notice.

Jarrold was twice married, first to Susanna, who died on 12 March 1817, aged fifty-one; his second wife, details of whom are unknown, died in Norwich in 1886, aged ninety-one. His son Edgar T. Jarrold died in New York on 25 February 1890. Jarrold himself died at Greenhill Street, Greenhays, Manchester, on 24 June 1853, and was buried at the Congregational chapel in Grosvenor Street, Manchester.   C. W. SUTTON, *rev.* H. J. SPENCER

Sources *Cheshire Notes and Queries*, 2nd. ser., 3 (1888) · J. P. Earwaker, ed., *Local gleanings relating to Lancashire and Cheshire*, 2 vols. (1875–8) · private information (1891) [T. Jarrold, daughter; W. I. Wild] · Boase, *Mod. Eng. biog.* · Allibone, *Dict.* · R. H. I. Palgrave, ed., *Dictionary of political economy*, 3 vols. (1894–9)

Jarrott, Charles (1877–1944), racing motorist, was born at 25 Hendon Street, Pimlico, London, on 26 March 1877, the son of Robert Jarrott, a blacksmith's labourer, and his wife, Martha Rosser. He had three elder sisters. Said to have been educated at schools in London and Cambridge, he was articled to a firm of solicitors. He began motoring in 1896 and witnessed the London to Brighton run (14 November 1896) to celebrate the emancipation of the motor car following the passage of the Light Locomotives Act. In 1897 he became secretary to the Motor Car Club, the organizers of the run. After giving up the law, he entered the motor trade and formed the English De Dion Bouton Co. in 1899, visiting the USA to report on the machines being manufactured there. In 1900 he went into partnership with Harvey du Cros in the English Panhard Levassor Motor Co., and in 1902 with William Malesbury Letts formed Charles Jarrott and Letts Ltd, sole agents for De Dietrich and Oldsmobile, as well as selling Crossley and Bugatti cars. He retired from the partnership in 1909.

A contemporary of Selwyn Edge, Jarrott was one of the earliest racing drivers in Britain, racing motor tricycles, cycles, and cars. He took part in fifty races in 1899, and won the Motor Car Club's 5 mile championship on a De Dion tricycle in 8 minutes 11 seconds and the 10 mile cycle scratch race in 17 minutes 22 seconds. In a match with a famous trotting horse, Gold Ring, over a mile on a grass track, after giving the horse a 250 yards start he won easily. He gave up motor cycle racing to concentrate on racing in cars, and took part in what were later described as 'Homeric inter-country races' on the continent in the

Charles Jarrott (1877–1944), by unknown photographer [seated on the De Dion Bouton *Spider*]

early twentieth century (*Autocar*, 21). Driving a Panhard, he competed in the Paris–Berlin race of June 1901 and the Paris–Vienna race of June 1902.

Jarrott's greatest feat was on 31 July 1902 when, after starting thirty-fourth, he won the Circuit des Ardennes in Belgium, the first circuit race ever held. Driving a 70 hp Panhard six times round the course of 53.5 miles, he covered 321 miles in 5 hours 53 minutes, an average speed of 54 m.p.h. The secret of his success was obsessional concentration. Also in 1902 he beat the kilometre record on the Welbeck track with a time of 28.5 seconds (78 m.p.h.). In May 1903 he took part in the Paris–Madrid race and, driving a Napier, represented England (along with Edge and J. W. Stocks) in the Gordon Bennett race held in Ireland (2 July 1903) but had to retire owing to an accident in which he broke a collar bone. His last race on the continent was in the Gordon Bennett race in Germany in June 1904, after which he gave up racing to concentrate on his business. He described his racing exploits in a classic book, *Ten Years of Motors and Motor Racing* (1906; later editions 1912, 1928, 1956), in which he celebrated the good fellowship and sporting spirit among the early drivers, and regretted the growing commercialization of motor sport.

Jarrott married on 12 August 1903 Violet Aline (1869/70–1945), the divorced wife of James Francis Harry St Clair-Erskine, fifth earl of Rosslyn; she was the daughter of Robert Charles de Grey Vyner of Gautby Hall, Lincolnshire. She shared her husband's enthusiasm for automobilism, and drove a 16 hp Dietrich at motor gatherings in 1905.

Jarrott was one of the pioneers who developed the motor car for general road use. In the foreword to the 1928 reprint of his book he commented, 'the motor vehicle has dominated the world. It has altered the whole aspect of our lives'. His holy grail was the open road. After being fined £5 by Lincolnshire magistrates in 1898 for driving a motor vehicle in excess of 12 m.p.h., he became one of the leaders of the movement to protect motorists from what he regarded as legal persecution by 'horsey' JPs and police who used 'unEnglish' methods against them. He organized cycle patrols to warn motorists of police speed traps on the London to Brighton road, and was a founder in 1905 of the Automobile Association. In 1922 he succeeded Sir William Joynson-Hicks to become the association's third chairman, but resigned in 1924 over the failure of the planned amalgamation with the Royal Automobile Club, of which he had also been a member since its foundation. He was an officer of several other motoring bodies, and was a founder of the Olympia motor show. A founder member of the Royal Aero Club, he was inspector of transport for the Royal Flying Corps during the First World War, and held the rank of lieutenant-colonel; he was mentioned in dispatches three times and appointed OBE in 1918.

From 1935 until his death Jarrott was general secretary of the Royal Society of St George. He died of bronchopneumonia in St Stephen's Hospital, Chelsea, London, on 4 January 1944, and was cremated at Golders Green.

ELIZABETH ELLEN BENNETT

Sources *Autocar*, 89 (14 Jan 1944), 21, 29 • *The Times* (7 Jan 1944), 6 • C. Jarrott, *Ten years of motors and motor racing, 1896–1906* (1928) • *Motoring Annual and Motorist's Year Book* (1907) • *Who's who in the motor trade* • Kelly, *Handbk* (1942) • H. Barty-King, *The AA: a history of the first 75 years of the Automobile Association, 1905–1980* (1980) • b. cert. • m. cert. • d. cert. • census returns, 1881 • 'Rosslyn', GEC, *Peerage* • 'Letts, Sir William Malesbury', *DBB*
Archives Veteran Car Club of Great Britain Library, Ashwell, Hertfordshire
Likenesses L. Ward, drawing, repro. in Jarrott, *Ten years of motors*, frontispiece • photograph, Veteran Car Club of Great Britain [*see illus.*] • photographs, repro. in C. Jarrott, *Ten years of motors*
Wealth at death £911 11s. 6d.: probate, 9 June 1944, CGPLA Eng. & Wales

Jarry, Francis (1733–1807), army officer and military educationist, was born in France. According to the French war ministry he entered the Prussian army, where he became a captain and engineer; he was promoted major on 28 October 1763, and colonel on 30 March 1790. The German war ministry, however, could find no trace of any officer of that name in the records of the Prussian army. Jarry claimed to have been instructed in the art of war by Frederick the Great of Prussia in person, and after the Seven Years' War, in which he was wounded several times, to have been appointed by the king as commandant of the Prussian École de Guerre, an appointment he held until 1776, when ill health caused him to return to France. He re-entered Prussian service in 1790 but resigned in 1791.

Jarry is said to have entered the service of France at the invitation of General Dumouriez, who described him as 'one of the cleverest officers in any service' (Le Marchant, 117–18). He was created a chevalier of the order of St Louis on 19 June 1791, was admitted colonel and adjutant-general in the French army on 6 July 1791, and became

maréchal de camp on 27 May 1792. He served under Marshal Luckner against the Austrians in 1792, and displeased the national government by burning part of the suburbs of Courtrai on 29 June 1792 because they were sheltering enemy troops. He left the French service on 16 August 1792, following the overthrow of the monarchy.

From 1793 to 1799 Jarry was a prolific writer of often voluminous papers on the military and political situation in Europe which he addressed to imperial and British diplomats and members of the British government. Lord Grenville considered him 'a man of information and talent' (*Fortescue MSS*, 2.409), while Lord St Helens at The Hague thought him 'by far the most judicious, clearheaded and unprejudiced of the emigrants in this part of the world' (ibid., 2.622). The British employed him in 1794 in intelligence gathering and as an adviser to the army in the Low Countries.

Jarry settled in London after the British army returned from the continent in 1795. He became acquainted with the third duke of Portland, and was military tutor to one of the duke's sons, Lord William Henry Cavendish-Bentinck. Jarry's proposals to the duke of York, the commander-in-chief, for a school for training officers became linked with a more ambitious scheme produced by John Gaspard Le Marchant, then lieutenant-colonel in the 7th light dragoons. The duke agreed in 1798 that Jarry should lecture on staff duties to voluntary classes of young officers at a house in High Wycombe, Buckinghamshire, which was rented for the purpose. Jarry's position was formalized on 4 January 1799, when he was appointed commandant of the Royal Military College (he became commandant of its senior department on 1 July 1801, when a junior department was created at Marlow). The college opened at High Wycombe on 4 May 1799, and additional teachers were later appointed; the number of officers attending during Jarry's time there averaged twenty-five. Instruction in staff duties was unprecedented in the British army, although the rudimentary knowledge of military science among British officers (and their limited French, in which Jarry, who spoke little English, lectured) meant that not all his pupils could profit from his instruction. The work included reconnaissance, sketching, and planning marches; officers undertook schemes in the field and had to prepare their proposals in the form of orders. Some of the alumni from High Wycombe served with distinction as staff officers in Egypt and the Peninsula, confirming the value of the college and the principles of Jarry's teaching.

Jarry's most influential published work was *Instruction concernant le service de l'infanterie en campagne* (1801), translated by order of the duke of York in 1803 as *Instruction Concerning the Duties of Light Infantry in the Field*. This contained valuable observations on the tactics of the 'small war', the employment of outposts and skirmishers, the importance of reconnaissance, and the relationship between officers and their men. With Francis de Rottenburg's *Regulations for the Exercise of Riflemen and Light Infantry* (1791) it was 'to form the basis of British light infantry training for the whole of the Napoleonic Wars and many decades beyond'

(Gates, 105). The *Treatise on the Marches and Movements of Armies* (1807), translated from one of Jarry's manuscripts, contained both theory and practical advice.

Jarry was a man of high professional ability, of easy and refined manners, and of the most unassuming disposition, but his lean, bent form and his many eccentricities, including carelessness of dress, exposed him to persecution at the hands of some idlers among his pupils. Among their practical jokes was the destruction of all the models made by him for instruction in field-works. This deeply wounded him. Cookery and gardening were his special hobbies. At the time of the peace of Amiens his position appears to have been so uncomfortable that he asked permission to return to France, where his wife, Anna Zabina Jarry, whom he had not seen since 1789, was ill, but permission was refused. He was appointed inspector-general of instruction on 25 June 1806, but his ill health, which had already restricted his activities in 1804, compelled him to resign in August. He was not allowed to return to France, as he requested, while the war continued. He died at High Wycombe on 15 March 1807, and was buried there. After some delay, pensions of £100 a year were given to his widow and two daughters, who had come to England and were left unprovided for.   J. E. O. SCREEN

Sources A. R. Godwin-Austen, *The staff and the Staff College* (1927) · R. H. Thoumine, *Scientific soldier: a life of General Le Marchant, 1766–1812* (1968) · D. Le Marchant, *Memoirs of the late Major-General Le Marchant* (1841); repr. (1997) · 'Commissioners of military enquiry: tenth report', *Parl. papers* (1810), 9.189, no. 78 [Royal Military College] · 'Select committee on Sandhurst Royal Military College', *Parl. papers* (1854–5), 12.311, no. 317 · D. Gates, *The British light infantry arm, c.1790–1815* (1987) · BL, Pelham MSS, Add. MSS 33101, 33109–33112 · BL, Dropmore MSS, Add. MS 59036 · *The manuscripts of J. B. Fortescue*, 10 vols., HMC, 30 (1892–1927), vol. 2 · R. Glover, *Peninsular preparation: the reform of the British army, 1795–1809* (1963) · Count de Caire, *Observations sur un ouvrage de M. de Jarry, ayant pour titre, 'Projet de formation de l'armée française'* (Paris, 1790) · PRO, WO 1/943 · private information (1891) · PRO, PROB 6/183, fol. 620, administration · *DNB*

Archives BL, letters to Lord Grenville, Add. MS 59036 · BL, Pelham MSS, Add. MSS 33101, 33109–33112 · PRO, Royal Military College, WO 1/943 · Royal Military College, Sandhurst, Le Marchant MSS, memoir in French on military instruction given at Royal Military College, High Wycombe, packet 13.11

Likenesses T. Birch, portrait, *c.*1803 (after pencil sketch), repro. in Godwin-Austen, *The staff and the Staff College*

Wealth at death £300: administration, PRO, PROB 6/183, fol. 620

Jars, Gabriel (1732–1769). *See under* Industrial spies (*act. c.*1700–*c.*1800).

Jarvis, Claude Scudamore (1879–1953), colonial governor and orientalist, born at Forest Gate, London, on 20 July 1879, was the son of John Bradford Jarvis, an insurance clerk, and his wife, Mary Harvey. He does not seem to have been educated with any profession in mind, and at the age of seventeen he joined the merchant navy as an apprentice, sailing from Shadwell to Sydney and back by way of Cape Horn. But on the outbreak of the Second South African War in 1899 he enlisted in the imperial yeomanry as a trooper, and on his return to England in 1902 was gazetted to the 3rd battalion, the Dorsetshire regiment (special

Claude Scudamore Jarvis (1879–1953), by unknown photographer

reserve). He married in 1903 Mabel Jane, daughter of Charles Hodson of the American embassy, London; they had one daughter.

In the First World War Jarvis served in France, Egypt, and Palestine, reached the rank of major, and acquired a good knowledge of Arabic. Egypt was then a British protectorate, and its desert borders had become of considerable military importance, on the east as the main theatre of operations against Turkey, and on the west through Turkish subversion of the Senussi tribesmen. It was against the latter that a disproportionate number of troops were employed against what proved to be a largely mythical enemy. It was to reduce this commitment that the British high commissioner, Sir Reginald Wingate, succeeded in persuading the Egyptian government to establish a frontiers administration, and Jarvis was among the first selected for this service, subsequently to be described by him as brought into the world by British influence and afterwards treated with studied neglect by Egypt.

Nevertheless it was in this unpromising atmosphere that Jarvis achieved remarkable success, gaining not only the confidence of the tribal Arabs whom he governed but that of the Egyptian government who, if they were niggardly in their financial aid, trusted him and gave him support. His first appointment was to the western desert, followed by the governorship of the oases of the Libyan desert, but he was then transferred in 1922 to the eastern desert as governor of Sinai where he remained until he retired voluntarily in 1936, when he was appointed CMG.

Unfettered by bureaucratic control, and with what seemed to be a hopelessly inadequate budget, Jarvis became a legendary figure. His knowledge of Arabic, and of Bedouin customs and law, enabled him to settle tribal feuds, not only among the tribes under his official control, but their feuds with the neighbouring tribes in Transjordan and Saudi Arabia. He virtually obliterated banditry, and contributed effectively to Egypt's efforts to suppress the drug traffic by the desert routes. He made a special study of the wanderings of the Israelites in the Exodus, and traced the remains of what, before the Arab conquest, must have been a flourishing Roman and later Byzantine settlement in the north of Sinai. There, by damming the

Wadi Gedeirat (Kadesh Barnea of the Bible), and restoring the old stone channels, he transformed a small swampy waterhole into several hundred acres of olive and fruit trees.

Jarvis was a botanist and naturalist of considerable skill, in addition to being a practical agriculturist, and a watercolourist of some merit. He was among the last of the Englishmen in the great tradition of the early members of the Indian Civil Service whose usually single-handed contribution to the then isolated areas under their charge will probably not be forgotten.

Jarvis's retirement opened the final phase in his career. He joined the staff of *Country Life*, where his 'A countryman's notes', with their knowledge of agriculture and wildlife and their delightful anecdotes, gained a wide and appreciative readership for fourteen years until his death. He lectured frequently, and the Royal Central Asian Society awarded him the Lawrence memorial medal in 1938. He was a prolific author, writing not only on his experiences in Sinai and its history, but on Arab customs and agriculture, and sometimes in a lighter and satirical vein on the British in the Middle East. His best-known works were *Yesterday and Today in Sinai* (1931), *Three Deserts* (1936), *Deserts and Delta* (1938), *Arab Command* (1942), *Heresies and Humours* (1943), and his autobiography, *Half a Life* (1943). Jarvis was small in stature, with great charm and wit both in speaking and writing which enabled him to invest the animals, birds, and fishes which he knew so well with almost human characteristics. He died at his home, Chele Orchard, Ringwood, Hampshire, on 8 December 1953.   RONALD WINGATE, *rev.*

Sources The Times (10 Dec 1953) · Country Life, 114 (1953), 2026 · personal knowledge (1971) · private information (1971) · *CGPLA Eng. & Wales* (1954)
Likenesses photograph, repro. in *Country Life* [*see illus.*]
Wealth at death £16,009 4s. 1d.: probate, 3 April 1954, *CGPLA Eng. & Wales*

Jarvis, Edward Kem (*bap.* 1805, *d.* 1853), judge and philanthropist, was baptized on 15 March 1805 at Ratcliffe Culey parish church, Hinckley, Leicestershire, the only child of Joseph Jarviss (*fl.* 1785–1830), Atherstone postmaster and innkeeper, and his wife, Mary (*fl.* 1785–1810), daughter of John Sands, publican, of Congerstone, and his wife, Melinda. Jarvis's parents were midlanders. The Jarvis ancestry included the parliamentarian Purefoy (later Jervis) family of Caldecote (Warwickshire) and Fenny Drayton (Leicestershire) and Swynfen Jervis, the ancestor of the earls of St Vincent. His first two names acknowledge the benefaction and bequest left to his father, Joseph, by Edward Kem (*d.* 1800), yeoman of Attleborough and Armitage, who could trace his origins back to the Northumbrian D'Umfrevilles and Talboys as well as Baron De Kyme of Lincolnshire [*see* Kem, Joseph].

Jarvis's early life is unknown: he may have been educated at the locally endowed Queen Elizabeth Grammar School before moving to Hinckley in 1819. In 1826 he joined the legal practice of Charles Jervis (a distant relative whose business was established before 1800). On 16

September 1828 he married Rebecca Brown, *née* Tomlinson (*b.* 1791), a blind widow. From 1829 Jarvis's name appeared annually in the *Law List* as a solicitor. By 1838 he was listed as clerk to the Hinckley magistrates' court and parish auditor. His chief claim to fame derives from his meticulous and thought-provoking evidence to the royal commission into the conditions of the frame-work knitters in 1844. In hosiery's 'golden age' (1781–1811), Hinckley had contributed 2400 pairs of stockings for British troops on the continent in 1793. But the industry was very vulnerable to market changes, and by 1829, 66 per cent of the town's people were on poor relief. By the time the commission's report was published Leicestershire's hosiery goods were uncompetitive in their traditional foreign markets because of the progressive American and German manufacturers.

Jarvis's evidence stated that he had been one of two or three local manufacturers who did not practise the pernicious truck system of payment of workers in kind, often in goods of inferior quality. He had set up his own knitting company where no frame rents or standing charges were levied, and even offered his workers stone breaking in the slack times, but their hands were too soft from the intricate loomwork. The project failed because local framework knitters disliked the regular routine of his factory. Jarvis also told of how he had called various meetings to set up local funds to help suppress the 'truck'. His evidence also provided details of the profiteering devices adopted by other local manufacturers. As a lawyer, Jarvis was litigious and resourceful and by 1846 his outstanding ability saw him promoted to judge of Hinckley and Market Bosworth. As a judge, he disliked imprisoning firsttime offenders, preferring to fine the truck operator £5 for a first offence, and £10 for the second before invoking his powers of incarceration. By 1851 he had been made a perpetual commissioner for the poor.

On 1 January 1853 Jarvis died of a heart attack at his home, 4 The Borough, Hinckley; he was buried in a vault beneath the floor of St Mary's Church, Hinckley, on 7 January. A shield-shaped brass plaque with the initials EKJ was affixed to the wall near the bell-tower entrance. His will records investments, cattle, real estate, and property in Hinckley, Barwell, and Burbage, which he left to his wife.   ALAN F. COOK

Sources will of Edward Kem Jarvis, PRO, PROB 11/2179, fols. 304, 305 · *Report of the commissioner appointed to inquire into the condition of the frame-work knitters* (1845), appx to the report, pt 1, 205–14 · *Clarke's New Law List* (1828–40) · *Law List* (1841–8) · *Law List* (1849–53) · will of Edward Kem, Lichfield Joint RO, PROB 1800 B/C/11 · *Leicester Chronicle* (8 Jan 1853) · *Leicester Chronicle* (15 Jan 1853) · *Leicester Journal* (7 Jan 1853) · *Leicester Advertiser* (8 Jan 1853) · census returns, 1841, PRO, HO 107/602, p. 21; 1851, HO 107/2092, p. 2 · 'John Huskisson serves notice to quit a house in Hinckley to a Miss Ann Davison, niece of Mrs Edward Kem Jarvis. Edward Kem Jarvis and his wife must leave by 5th Mar 1829', Warks. CRO, Cross Collection, nos. 539, 540 · W. White, *History, gazetteer, and directory of Leicestershire, and the small county of Rutland* (1846) · A. J. Pickering, *The cradle and home of the hosiery trade* (1940) · parish registers, Hinckley, Ratcliffe Culey, and Congerstone, Leics. RO · parish registers, Atherstone, Warks. CRO · *VCH Leicestershire*, vol. 3 · B. Burke, *A genealogical history of the dormant, abeyant, forfeited and extinct peerages of* the British empire, new edn (1883) • S. A. Royle, 'The "spiritual destruction is excessive—the poverty overwhelming": Hinckley in the mid-nineteenth century', *Leicestershire Archaeological and Historical Society Transactions*, 54 (1978–9), 51–60 • Pigot, *Trade directory, Warwickshire* (1828–9) • 'Jervis of Staffordshire', Harleian Society, 63 (1912), 140 • A. R. Maddison, ed., *Lincolnshire pedigrees*, 4 vols., Harleian Society, 50–52, 55 (1902–6), vol. 2, pp. 571–2, vol. 4, pp. 1274–6 [De Kyme of Lincolnshire]

Jarvis, John Arthur (1872–1933), swimmer, was born at 6 Crown Street, Leicester, on 24 February 1872, one of the ten children of John Jarvis and his wife, Elizabeth Glover. Like his father he became a painter and decorator, and ran his own business from Morledge Street, Leicester. Jarvis started swimming when he was eleven years old and began racing at sixteen on joining Leicester swimming club. He won his first midland titles in 1893 (440 yards and 880 yards), and successfully defended them annually until 1907. He won his first of twenty-four national titles in 1897, when he beat the holder, J. H. Tyers, by 30 yards over 1 mile. Jarvis spent the winter training in the open at Kibworth alongside his professional rival Joey Nutall. Both used an orthodox right overarm side-stroke but developed a special kick which became known as the Jarvis–Nutall kick. Many regarded Jarvis's 1 mile win as a fluke but in the following year he retained the title and lowered Tyers's record of 26 min. 46.5 sec. set in 1896 by 9.2 sec.

Jarvis went on to dominate world middle- and long-distance swimming between 1898 and 1902. He held all the national middle-distance titles (440 yards, 500 yards, 880 yards, and 1 mile) between 1898 and 1901 and won the long-distance title on seven successive occasions from 1898 to 1904. He made his international reputation during numerous European tours at the turn of the century, and won a plethora of so-called 'world championships' in, among other places, Italy, Germany, Austria, France, and the Netherlands. Moreover, he was in magnificent form at the 1900 Olympiad in Paris. Swimming in the River Seine, he won the 1000 metres by an astonishing 1 min. 13.2 sec. and the 4000 metres by over 10.5 min. He also won the 100 metres (unlisted in the official record). Distance prevented Britain competing in the 1904 Olympiad in St Louis and Jarvis was past his best by the 1906 intercalated Olympic games in Athens, although he won three medals (silver for the mile and bronze for the 400 metres and the 4x250 metres team race). He competed in the 1908 games in London but, aged thirty-six, failed to reach the 1500 metres final. Perhaps his most satisfying and most publicized achievement was winning the inaugural 15 mile 'swim though London' from Richmond to Blackfriars in 1907, which attracted thirty-four of the world's finest long-distance swimmers. He was also a very good water polo player, and although he never represented Great Britain in the Olympic games, he played fourteen times for England between 1894 and 1904.

Jarvis won at least 108 titles between 1897 and 1906 in Britain and Europe against the world's finest swimmers. He set numerous world records, although none was officially recognized by the Fédération Internationale de Natation Amateure. He had a reputation for offering tips

and advice to novices and rivals alike. These were developed and published in *The Art of Swimming with Notes on Water Polo and Aids to Life-Saving* (1902), which he wrote with assistance from W. H. Clarke, a Leicester printer, who described Jarvis as 'a modest and good natured champion' (*The Art of Swimming*, 97).

On his retirement from swimming, Jarvis was respectfully referred to as 'professor' and became involved in swimming administration and officiating, and in life-saving teaching. He served on the midland executive committee and the council of the Amateur Swimming Association. Moreover, his wife (whose name is unknown) was 'one of the most ardent workers for swimming in the Midlands' and the first female midland president in 1927 (*Swimming Times*, 201). All three of his daughters became swimming teachers and one of his sisters, Clara, was a well-known coach at Leicester ladies' swimming club. Moreover, his great-great-niece, the yachtswoman Debbie Jarvis, competed at the Olympic games in 1992. Latterly he moved to London, and lived at 5 Derby Street, St Pancras. Jarvis died at University College Hospital, London, on 9 May 1933.   PETER BILSBOROUGH

Sources I. Buchanan, *British Olympians: a hundred years of gold medallists* (1991) • P. Besford, *Encyclopaedia of swimming* (1971) • R. D. Binfield, *The story of the Olympics* (1948) • *Amateur Swimming Association handbook* (1906) • *Swimming Times* (June 1933) • P. Gilbey, 'Mr Leicester's diary', *Leicester Mercury* (19 Aug 1992) • P. Gilbey, 'Mr Leicester's diary', *Leicester Mercury* (22 July 1992) • b. cert. • d. cert.
Likenesses photograph, repro. in C. M. Daniels, H. Johansson, and A. Sinclair, *How to swim and save life* (1907) • photograph, repro. in *Leicester Mercury* (12 July 1992) • photograph, repro. in Besford, *Encyclopaedia of swimming* • photographs, repro. in J. A. Jarvis, *The art of swimming with notes on water polo and aids to life-saving* (1902)

Jarvis, Sir John Layton [Jack] (1887–1968), racehorse trainer, was born in Newmarket, Suffolk, on 28 December 1887, the third and youngest son of William Arthur Jarvis, racehorse trainer, and his wife, Norah, daughter of James Godding, also a racehorse trainer. Jarvis was educated at Cranleigh School, Surrey. On leaving school he served his apprenticeship as a jockey with his father, and rode the winner of the Cambridgeshire Handicap (Hackler's Pride) at the age of sixteen. His increasing weight put an end to his career as a jockey. He then assisted his father, accompanying the horses to meetings until he set up as a trainer himself in 1914. In that year he married Ethel Edina, daughter of Thomas Leader, a racehorse trainer of Newmarket. They had one daughter.

Within a few years Jack Jarvis, as he was known, provided a steady stream of winners. His first major success was in 1921, with the colt Ellangowan, in the Two Thousand Guineas. Jarvis provided winners for the same race in both 1928 (Flamingo) and 1939 (Blue Peter). The One Thousand Guineas also fell to his horses three times—in 1924 to Plack, in 1934 to Campanula, and in 1953 to Happy Laughter. Jarvis won the St Leger once, in 1931 with Sandwich. His horses also won the Derby twice, in 1939 and 1944 (Blue Peter and Ocean Swell). From 1922 until his death he trained for the fifth earl of Rosebery and his son, the sixth earl.

Jarvis knew best how to train middle-distance horses

and stayers, but he was also a skilled handler of faster horses. He trained to great advantage the outstanding sprinters Honeyway and Royal Charger. Jarvis set himself the highest standards, working his horses as hard as himself. It was often said that his horses consequently looked on the light-framed side, but it was a tribute to his profound equine understanding that they were capable of winning in spring, mid-season, and autumn, thus confounding the paddock critics, who decried them by saying they were 'over the top'.

Jarvis was a forthright person and left no doubt about his views. He was somewhat quick-tempered, but his bark was worse than his bite, and altercations would be over as quickly as they started. He could be kind, and was always keen to help those, especially the young, who wished to make their way. He went annually to South Africa, where he appreciated the warmer climate. There he made many close friends and came to hear of a young jockey, John Gorton, who was employed by Lord Rosebery on Jarvis's suggestion and rode a Rosebery horse, Sleeping Partner, to victory in 1969 in the Epsom Oaks.

Jarvis was always meticulous, in his stables and in his other activities. He served on committees in the town, and, for several years, until advised against it for medical reasons, was on the town council in Newmarket. Among his relaxations were shooting and hare-coursing. He won the Waterloo cup, the most cherished coursing prize, with Jovial Judge, and the Barbican cup with Junior Journalist. Also a pigeon fancier, his bird was winner one year, and runner-up the next, in the Lerwick race. Jarvis regularly attended functions at the Subscription Rooms, Newmarket's racing club. In 1967 he was knighted for his services to racing. He died on 19 December 1968 at his home in Newmarket, on the eve of a visit to South Africa.

K. M. NORMAN, rev.

Sources J. Jarvis, *They're off* (1969) · personal knowledge (1981) · private information (1981) · *The Times* (20 Dec 1968)
Archives FILM BFI NFTVA, documentary footage
Wealth at death £218,021: probate, 7 Jan 1969, *CGPLA Eng. & Wales*

Jarvis, Samuel (*d.* 1784), organist and composer, was blind from birth. He studied the organ with Dr John Worgan, and became organist successively to the Foundling Hospital and to St Sepulchre in the City of London. His compositions included *Six Songs for Harpsichord, Violin and German Flute* (1764), and *Twelve Songs* (*c*.1785), edited after his death in 1784 by one of his pupils, John Groombridge.

L. M. MIDDLETON, rev. K. D. REYNOLDS

Sources E. van der Straeten, 'Jarvis, Samuel', Grove, *Dict. mus.* (1927) · B. Matthews, ed., *The Royal Society of Musicians of Great Britain: list of members, 1738–1984* (1985)

Jasper, Ronald Claud Dudley (1917–1990), liturgical scholar and historian, was born on 17 August 1917 at 4 York Terrace, Ford, Devonport, Devon, the only child of Claud Albert Jasper (1882–1974), a shipwright, and his wife, Florence Lily, *née* Curtis (1885–1957). Educated first at Ford primary school and Plymouth College, he then read history at Leeds University and obtained a second-class degree in 1938. Responding to a call to ordination, he went to the College of the Resurrection at Mirfield, Yorkshire, to prepare for the priesthood, while completing an MA on constitutional history, which he gained with distinction. However, the academic world was not beckoning and on ordination he became curate of Ryhope in the diocese of Durham (1940–42).

From the beginning of Jasper's time there, the bishop, A. T. P. Williams, himself a distinguished historian, kept a benevolent eye on this young man with historical interests. At the first opportunity he sent him to Durham as a curate of St Oswald's (1942–3). On 10 August 1943 he married Ethel (Betty) Wiggins (*b.* 1919), a domestic science teacher, and daughter of David Wiggins, a solicitor's managing clerk; they had a daughter, and a son who became principal of St Chad's College, Durham, and later professor and dean of divinity at the University of Glasgow. After a period as priest in charge of Langley Park and Esh (1943–5) and then curate in charge of St Giles, Durham (1945–6), two years as chaplain of University and Hatfield colleges in Durham (1946–8) gave him the opportunity for further serious study, and the result was a Leeds BD (1950) and *Prayer Book Revision in England, 1800–1900* (1954), the first of his many books. During this time he was also encouraged by Colin Dunlop, bishop of Jarrow, who used him as a lecturer at his clergy schools. In 1954 Bishop Dunlop, who had become dean of Lincoln, was asked by the archbishops of Canterbury and York to chair a commission 'to consider all matters of liturgical concern referred to it by the archbishops', and was given a free hand in choosing his team. Having identified a young priest of talent he included Jasper, who was vicar of Stillington, co. Durham (1948–55), and who became succentor of Exeter Cathedral (1955–60).

The archbishop of York, Donald Coggan, who succeeded Dunlop on the liturgical commission in 1960, decided he must give up its chairmanship and persuaded Jasper to take it on. By this time Jasper had left Exeter, had obtained his DD (1961) from Leeds, and was lecturing in liturgy at King's College, London (lecturer 1960–67, reader 1967–8), and acquiring a reputation as an ecclesiastical biographer, with a life of Arthur Cayley Headlam, bishop of Gloucester (1960), and a biography of George Bell, bishop of Chichester (1967), in progress. 'I was doing the very things in life I had always wanted to do and to take on the Commission would involve a serious disruption', he said at the time. But he realized that his study of the papers of Walter Frere, bishop of Truro (*Walter Howard Frere: his Correspondence on Liturgical Revision and Construction*, 1954), who had been much involved in the abortive 1927–8 prayer book revision, as well as his earlier researches, had given him a unique insight into the pitfalls awaiting those brave enough to attempt this kind of work in the Church of England. He also glimpsed the possibilities of ecumenical liturgical co-operation. He therefore assumed the chairmanship of the commission in 1964, a position he held until 1981.

Jasper was responsible for convincing Archbishop

Michael Ramsey to invite the mainstream British churches to form the joint liturgical group, set up in 1963. Jasper served as its secretary and diligent facilitator until his retirement in 1984. During that time he edited a series of books which greatly influenced the revision of most denominational service books in Britain. His ecumenical vision was further widened when, in 1966, he was appointed an official observer to the Concilium Liturgicum, set up to work out the implications of the Second Vatican Council's *Constitution on the Sacred Liturgy* (1963). From this work emerged the need for a forum at which the dilemmas of those engaged in liturgical revision in English-speaking countries could be shared. Roman Catholics were particularly anxious to be involved, being engaged in the problem of producing liturgical texts in the vernacular. The result was the International Consultation on English Texts (1967–74). In 1969 Jasper was elected president of the Societas Liturgica, the international ecumenical society for liturgical study and research formed in 1967. At the same time he was engaged in all the major works of liturgical revision in the Church of England, of which the *Alternative Service Book* (1980) was to be the fruition. In this work he was much supported by the scholarship of Geoffrey John Cuming (1917–1988) and Edward Charles Whitaker (1916–1988). Whitaker was an example of the now almost extinct breed of parson-scholar, hardly venturing beyond his native Cumbria, yet having an international reputation for his work on Christian initiation. Cuming also spent many years as a parish priest, but succeeded Jasper at King's, London in 1968. At his death Cuming was described as 'standing in the first rank of liturgists worldwide'.

Jasper was a canon of Westminster (1968–75), archdeacon of Westminster (1974–5), and dean of York (1975–84). At York he saw through a liturgical reordering of the nave and significant work in the lady chapel and the Zouche Chapel. He pressed for a traffic-free Deansgate and implemented the rescue, conservation, and restoration of the fifteenth-century St William's College. His time at York came to a dramatic conclusion. A lightning bolt struck the minster and the subsequent fire, which destroyed the roof and vault of the south transept, occurred on 9 July 1984, four days before his retirement.

Under Jasper's leadership major changes in the worship of the Church of England were inaugurated. Not all have been popular, but he courageously orchestrated change from a historian's knowledge of its inevitability and from a liturgist's appreciation of modern scholarship, never forgetting his ministry in the pit villages of co. Durham and never allowing the church's worship to become recherché or arcane. He retired to Ripon in Yorkshire and produced *The Development of the Anglican Liturgy, 1662–1980* (1989), an overview of liturgical development in England. He received the honorary degree of DLitt at Susquehanna University, Pennsylvania, in 1976 and was appointed CBE in 1981.

Jasper was of average height, had a slim build, and was always neatly and smartly dressed. He was one of those rare clergymen who took care in his choice of clothes when not in clerical dress. In his later years he lived at 3 Westmount Close, Ripon. He died on 11 April 1990 in Harrogate District Hospital. His funeral was held in York Minster on 18 April and his ashes laid to rest in the Zouche Chapel on 1 June 1990. DONALD GRAY

Sources D. Gray, *Ronald Jasper: his life, his work and the ASB* (1997) · D. Gray, 'E. C. Whitaker', 'G. J. Cuming', 'R. C. D. Jasper', *They shaped our worship*, ed. C. Irvine (1998), 145–60 · D. Gray, 'Dr Ronald Jasper and the liturgical commission', *Annual Report* [Friends of York Minster], 62 (1991) · *The Times* (12 April 1990) · *The Times* (4 June 1990) · *The Independent* (14 April 1990) · K. Stevenson, 'Geoffrey John Cuming, 1917–1988', *The liturgy of St Mark*, ed. G. J. Cuming (1990) · personal knowledge (2004) · private information (2004) · *WWW*, 1991–5 · *CGPLA Eng. & Wales* (1990) · b. cert. · d. cert.
Archives LPL, liturgical corresp. and papers | Church of England Record Centre, London, Church of England Liturgical Commission MSS
Likenesses photograph, St William's College, York
Wealth at death under £115,000: probate, 23 July 1990, *CGPLA Eng. & Wales*

Jast, Louis Stanley (1868–1944), librarian, was born on 20 August 1868 in George Street, Halifax, Yorkshire, the third son of Stefan Louis de Jastrzebski (*b.* 1823), originally of Zebrzydowice, Poland, and his wife, Elizabeth Morgan, of Franche, Kidderminster. Jastrzebski served in the Polish Legion under Kossuth and fled to England in 1849, eventually becoming a tobacconist in George Street, Halifax. Jast's eldest brother, later known as Bogdan Edwards (1860–1923), became a medical officer of health, and the other brother, Thaddeus de Jastrzebski (1862–1930), was assistant registrar general. Jast shortened his surname in 1895.

Jast acquired a love for literature from his parents' books. He attended Park Chapel and was educated at Field's academy, Halifax. After failing the civil service examination, he became an assistant at Halifax Public Library in April 1887 at 10s. a week, often working ten hours each day. He was soon in charge of a branch library. He became interested in eastern philosophy, often giving talks on the subject to local societies, and was made a fellow of the Theosophical Society in 1889.

In July 1892 Jast was appointed from fifty-five applicants the first librarian of Peterborough Public Library at £100 per annum. As was normal, the library was closed access, but Jast decided to classify the books according to the Dewey classification, a revelation to him that librarianship could be one of the 'fine arts that ... reduce chaos to order' (Fry and Munford, 8). The classification was used in his printed catalogue, only the second such to use Dewey in England. Jast soon became known in the Library Association for his support of classified rather than dictionary catalogues. In 1896 he wrote *The up-to-Date Guide to Peterborough Cathedral, City and Neighbourhood*.

In July 1892 Jast was appointed chief librarian of Croydon Public Library, where the controversial 'open-access' system, as practised at Clerkenwell under James Duff Brown, had already been introduced. Shortly afterwards he addressed the Library Association on his belief in detailed—or 'explanatory'—cataloguing to aid users, and in the need to sweep away illiberal regulations.

Jast revolutionized Croydon Public Library by introducing the telephone (unheard of in most libraries), extending and making publicly accessible the reference library, and initiating a readers' bulletin, lectures, reading circles, and much more. Ernest Savage wrote of him: 'our chief had a single aim—to win the support of the public by improving the libraries until they were among the best in the country. To us he made library work interesting' (Fry and Munford, 21). He was a large man with a broad face, sallow complexion, and a handlebar moustache: 'I knew the meaning of personality in management', wrote Savage, 'of a chief who rose in the morning not to the bureaucratic routine of another day, but eager and fighting fit to drive things along to victory' (ibid.).

Jast became friendly with James Duff Brown and contributed to his journal, *Library World*, particularly on classification matters. Together they founded the Pseudonyms, a librarians' dining club whose proceedings were regularly (if not factually) reported in *Library World* (Jast was Orlando Furioso). Jast also wrote frequently for the *Library Association Record* and the *Library Review*.

As acting (later permanent) honorary secretary of the Library Association from 1904, Jast attended the American Library Association conference of that year in St Louis, where he spoke on extension work, followed by a tour of public libraries; this resulted in a series of appreciative articles. He made a return visit in 1913. He was active in Library Association affairs, particularly supporting a professional register. In 1915 he resigned to become deputy librarian of Manchester Public Library, as from 1 December, assuming the chief librarianship in April 1920. The reference library was contained in huts in Piccadilly outside the old Royal Infirmary, whose out-patients department was used for library administration. In 1919 he opened the commercial library (he had advocated technical libraries in 1903, in the *Library Association Record*).

At Library Association meetings Jast met (Ethel) Winifred *Austin (1873–1918) of the National Library for the Blind. They agreed to marry, but she died in 1918, a tragedy marked by his play, *The Lover and the Dead Woman*, staged in 1918 by the Unnamed Society, a drama club which he had helped to found in 1916, a forerunner of the Manchester Library Theatre. He also wrote poetry. A later successful, mystical play was *Shah Jahan* (published 1934). His theatrical writings were collected in 1923 and published as *The Lover and the Dead Woman, and Five other Plays in Verse*.

In 1920 Jast belonged to a luncheon club where he met his future wife, Millicent Beatrice Murby (1873–1951), a civil servant—at that time a health inspector—who had formerly worked for the Post Office. She had been a member of the executive committee of the Fabian Society, with H. G. Wells and George Bernard Shaw. Millicent was an amateur actress and produced Jast's plays. She wrote a Fabian pamphlet, *The Common Sense of the Woman Question* (1908). They married in 1925.

The various departments of the public library gradually expanded into temporary premises, and land was bought next to the town hall for what was to become the famous circular Central Library, though Jast retired before its completion. His plans, influenced by American models, appeared in *The Planning of a Great Library* (1926). An unusual feature was the four-tier bookstack at the centre of the building. Jast was so wedded to the idea of reference services that a lending department was added only after his retirement in 1931. He created a book exchange service between the branches, developed 'young people's rooms', and provided a mobile library service, among other innovations.

On retirement the Jasts moved to The Cedars, Beckington, near Bath, and in 1939 to Twickenham. His belief in society's vital need for libraries was expressed in his collected papers, published as *Libraries and Living* (1932), and *The Library and the Community* (1939), for general readers. At the outbreak of war the Jasts moved temporarily to Penzance where he wrote *What it all Means* (1941), a popular guide to theosophy. They returned to Twickenham to live at Penrhyn House, 3 Riverdale Road, where Jast died suddenly on Christmas day 1944. His widow died on 14 January 1951; they had no children.   K. A. MANLEY

Sources W. G. Fry and W. A. Munford, *Louis Stanley Jast* (1966) · *Library Association Record*, 47 (1945) · *Collected letters: Bernard Shaw*, ed. D. H. Laurence, 4 vols. (1965–88), vol. 2

Archives Man. CL, Manchester Archives and Local Studies, corresp. and papers · NL Scot., corresp.

Likenesses photograph, c.1930, Man. CL; repro. in Fry and Munford, *Louis Stanley Jast*

Wealth at death £945 7s. 0d.: probate, 10 Feb 1945, CGPLA Eng. & Wales

Jay, Douglas Patrick Thomas, Baron Jay (1907–1996), politician, was born at the Tower House, Plum Lane, Woolwich, London, on 23 March 1907, the son of Edward Aubrey Hastings Jay, barrister, and his wife, Isobel Violet, née Craigie. His father represented Woolwich on the London county council as a Municipal Reformer (conservative), and was chairman of the education committee. He was educated at Winchester College and was a scholar of New College, Oxford, where he obtained first-class honours in *literae humaniores* in 1929. He was a fellow of All Souls College, Oxford, from 1930 to 1937 and from 1968 until his death. In 1933 he married Margaret Christian, eldest daughter of James Clerk Maxwell Garnett, with whom he had two sons and two daughters. The marriage was dissolved in 1972, in which year he married Mary Lavinia, daughter of Hugh Lewis Thomas.

After leaving Oxford Jay worked as a journalist successively on *The Times*, *The Economist*, and the *Daily Herald*, where he was City editor from 1937 to 1940. In the 1930s he was active, together with Hugh Dalton, Hugh Gaitskell, and Evan Durbin, in developing policies for the next Labour government. During the Second World War he was a temporary civil servant at the Ministry of Supply (1940–43) and the Board of Trade (1943–5). On the election of the Labour government in July 1945, he became personal assistant to the prime minister, Clement Attlee. He was elected MP for Battersea North in July 1946 and held the seat until his retirement from the House of Commons at the 1983 general election. He was economic secretary to the Treasury from 1947 to 1950 and financial secretary to

Douglas Patrick Thomas Jay, Baron Jay (1907–1996), by Elliott & Fry, 1949

the Treasury from 1950 to 1951. He was sworn of the privy council in 1951. He entered the cabinet as president of the Board of Trade in 1964, and held the post until 1967. A politician of unquestionable integrity, and of the highest intellectual calibre, though lacking in personal charisma, Jay was significant in the history of the Labour Party for three reasons. The first was his attempt to reconcile socialism with Keynesianism. Second, he exercised considerable influence on his close friend and fellow Wykehamist Hugh Gaitskell, chancellor of the exchequer from 1950 to 1951 and leader of the Labour Party from 1955 to 1963. Third, he was probably the most consistent socialist opponent of British participation in any form of European economic integration involving supranational institutions.

The high unemployment of the 1920s and 1930s was socialism's best recruiting sergeant. Keynes's *General Theory* (1936) was a threat to the Labour Party because it purported to demonstrate that full employment could be realized by managing capitalism, and without recourse to socialism. Some socialists, such as G. D. H. Cole and Aneurin Bevan, doubted that Keynes's demonstration was foolproof. Others, such as Evan Durbin, questioned whether Keynes's ideas could be implemented without serious inflationary side-effects. Jay, in his book *The Socialist Case*, first published in 1937, accepted Keynes's argument that full employment could be achieved by managing 'total effective demand'. He therefore emphasized equality as the principal argument for socialism. 'In most

modern societies one of the chief reasons why the poor are very poor is that the rich are very rich … poverty cannot be removed without some mitigation of inequality' (D. Jay, *The Socialist Case*, 1947, 3). While supporting the need for the nationalization of coal and the major utilities, he thought that socialists were in error in their obsession with nationalization:

> Socialists have been mistaken in making ownership of the means of production instead of ownership of inherited property the test of socialization. … It is not the ownership of the means of production as such, but ownership of large inherited incomes, which ought to be eliminated.
> (ibid., 195)

Unlike most other contemporary socialists, he valued the activity of the individual entrepreneur. 'Great entrepreneurs … are of a value so great that it would be impossible to overpay them' (ibid., 116). Later Jay came to accept that he had underestimated the inflationary consequences of demand management. But in his rejection of nationalization as the core of socialism, he anticipated later socialist revisionists.

There were three young economists in the Attlee government who acquired great influence owing mainly to the declining health of Sir Stafford Cripps, who, in November 1947, had succeeded Dalton as chancellor of the exchequer. The three were Harold Wilson, Hugh Gaitskell, and Douglas Jay. They regarded full employment as the principal achievement of the Labour government but were sensitive to the threat constituted by the dollar shortage, by the liberalization of trade under American pressure, and by the 1948 American recession. Jay, together with Gaitskell, played a leading role in persuading the Attlee government, including a reluctant chancellor, to devalue sterling in September 1949. They had concluded that the UK's lack of competitiveness could prejudice full employment and that economic planning could not operate sufficiently rapidly to prevent it. Wilson, they both thought, played an equivocal role in pressing the case for devaluation, and this was one source of the distrust subsequently manifested towards Wilson by both Jay and Gaitskell. Gaitskell and Jay also attempted to devise a system of international economic relations that would defend full employment in Britain against the impact of external events. There would be two worlds, one based on the sterling area (which could for this purpose include western Europe) and the other based on the dollar area. The use of gold and dollars would be permitted only in relations with the dollar area. Unfortunately for their scheme, western Europe exhibited a higher tolerance of unemployment than was considered politically acceptable in the UK. The deflationary policies pursued by western European countries resulted in surpluses in their trade with the UK, which they wished discharged in gold and dollars, of which Britain was desperately short. This refusal to co-operate with Jay's plan was a source of his deep and lifelong hostility to economic integration with western Europe. Jay believed that, to guarantee full employment, the UK must retain control of its own economic destiny, including the right to limit the import of manufactured goods whenever the balance of payments required it.

On 2 June 1950 Jay represented the chancellor, Stafford Cripps, who was on holiday, at the cabinet meeting that finally decided to reject British participation in the Schuman plan for the creation of a European Coal and Steel Community. The previous day an ultimatum had been received from Paris demanding to know by the evening of 2 June whether or not the British would join the negotiations to establish the community. Jay's resentment at French impertinence emerges in his autobiography, published thirty years later:

> The ultimatum is not explicable except on the assumption that the French were determined to keep future moves for so-called 'European Unity' under French control, and exclude the British at least until such time as the whole arrangement had been so devised as to promote French interests and where possible to damage this country.   (Jay, 200)

The French ultimatum followed two weeks of telegraphic exchanges during which they had attempted to persuade the British to take part and during which no British minister had thought it worthwhile to cross the channel to determine whether British anxieties could be assuaged. But, for Jay, the French objective had been to damage Britain. Jay's antipathy to European economic integration never softened. He was an influence in determining Gaitskell's opposition to Macmillan's 1961 application to join the EEC on the terms that appeared to be emerging. As president of the Board of Trade, he opposed the 1967 decision of the Wilson government to apply for membership. Wilson removed him from office, ostensibly on the grounds of age but probably even more because of his implacable opposition to the British application. Three months later General de Gaulle delivered his second 'Non'. Jay had served three leaders of the Labour Party, Attlee, Gaitskell, and Wilson. For the first two he had nothing but admiration, for the third little but contempt. Thereafter, whether during the governments of Heath or of Wilson, Jay remained adamantly in the forefront of the opponents of British membership of the EEC; he was chairman of the Common Market Safeguards Campaign from 1970 to 1977. In his view the argument against membership had been reinforced by the community's adoption of the common agricultural policy, because it would cut Britain off from cheap sources of food, including from the Commonwealth, and thus make British manufacture less competitive.

Jay was one of the intellectual leaders of Labour's right wing. After Labour's defeat at the 1959 general election, he bravely, or perhaps insensitively, speculated publicly about the desirability of changing the party's name in order to transform its proletarian image. He thereby incurred deep left-wing hostility. It was one idea which did not command Gaitskell's assent, though Gaitskell was suspected of encouraging Jay to fly the kite. One effect of Jay's inflexible rejection of the EEC was to divide, and weaken, the right of the Labour Party. When, in 1981, many 'European' Gaitskellites defected from the Labour Party to form the Social Democratic Party, Jay was not one of them: his own concerns about the direction of Labour Party policy in the early 1980s were submerged by the principal passion of his political life, to keep Britain free of European entanglements.

Jay was created a life peer in 1987. He died in Minster Lovell, Oxfordshire, where he lived, on 6 March 1996 and was buried in the churchyard there. He was survived by both wives and the four children of his first marriage. Peter Jay (b. 1937), the economist, diplomatist, and broadcaster, is his son from his first marriage.

EDMUND DELL

Sources D. Jay, *Change and fortune: a political record* (1980) · P. M. Williams, *Hugh Gaitskell: a political biography* (1979) · B. Brivati, *Hugh Gaitskell* (1996) · H. Wilson, *The labour government, 1964–1970: a personal record* (1971) · K. O. Morgan, *Callaghan: a life* (1997) · E. Dell, *The Schuman plan and the British abdication of leadership in Europe* (1995) · B. Pimlott, *Harold Wilson* (1992); repr. (1993) · P. Ziegler, *Harold Wilson: the authorised life* (1993) · *The Times* (7 March 1996) · *The Independent* (6 March 1996) · *The Guardian* (7 March 1996) · *Daily Telegraph* (7 March 1996) · *WWW* · b. cert.
Archives NRA, priv. coll., papers · NRA, priv. coll., corresp. with his agent and constituency labour party | BLPES, corresp. with J. E. Meade · Bodl. Oxf., corresp. with Lord Attlee · U. Leeds, Brotherton L., corresp. with Henry Drummond-Wolff
Likenesses Elliott & Fry, photograph, 1949, NPG [*see illus.*] · photograph, 1964, Hult. Arch. · photograph, repro. in *The Times* · photograph, repro. in *The Independent* · photograph, repro. in *The Guardian* · photograph, repro. in *Daily Telegraph*
Wealth at death £198,573: probate, 22 May 1996, *CGPLA Eng. & Wales*

Jay, Edith Katherine Spicer [*pseud.* E. Livingston Prescott] (1847–1901), writer and philanthropist, was born on 6 March 1847 at 11 Norfolk Street, Park Lane, London, the daughter of Samuel Jay (1800/1–1881), barrister, and his wife, Elizabeth Maria Jane Spicer. Both sides of Jay's family had army connections. On her father's side she was the great-niece of Major Alexander Livingston of the 12th dragoons, a decorated hero in the Peninsular War; on her mother's side she was the granddaughter of Colonel Spicer of the 2nd Life Guards and lieutenant-colonel in the Queen's Bays. Jay was also related to Lord Farnborough and to Sir George Prescott, bt, of Theobald's Park, Hertfordshire.

When Jay started publishing her books—mostly fiction with military settings—her pen-name, E. Livingston Prescott, paid allegiance to two of her forebears. The name also concealed her sex—she was, after all, entering the indubitably masculine world of Kipling's poetry and fiction—and reviewers tended to assume she was a man. Jay published at least eighteen books, several of them posthumously, between 1896 and 1904. Most were novels or collections of tales. Representative titles suggest some of Jay's fictional interests: *The Rip's Redemption: a Trooper's Story* (1897); *Scarlet and Steel: some Modern Military Episodes* (1897); *Red-Coat Romances* (1898). Her plots often turn on the reformation of characters whose flaws include drunkenness and abuse of authority. She was especially exercised by the practice of flogging military prisoners. Reviewers' assessments of her fiction range from 'very cleverly written' (*New York Times*, 17 May 1896) to 'these books do violence to every principle of good novel-writing' (*The Dial*, 93).

Jay's involvement with the army went beyond her family and her fiction. She served as honourable lady superintendent of the London Soldiers' Home and Guards' Home until her health failed. When in hopes of alleviating her health problems she moved to Sandgate on the Kent coast, Jay made her home available to the troopers stationed at nearby Shorncliffe camp at what she called 'Cavalry Circle'. She also appointed army men as two of the three executors of her will.

Jay's commitment to worthy causes testifies to the generosity of her spirit. In addition to her work for the London Soldiers' Home and Guards' Home, she willed pictures and the royalties from her books after her death to the Home for Incurables, Streatham Common. She left bequests to the Bridge of Hope Mission, London, to the National Society for the Prevention of Cruelty to Children, and to the Royal Society for the Prevention of Cruelty to Animals. Not forgetting her army friends, she willed legacies to the Papillon Soldiers' Institute, Sandgate, and to the Soldiers' Christian Association. She was also associated with the Religious Tract Society, which published two of her books after her death, and with the Willow Dene Mission in Clapham.

For over ten years Jay suffered from rheumatoid arthritis; she finally died from renal and cardiac arrest at her home, Channel Bower, Riviera, Sandgate, on 3 December 1901. So moved by her death were the soldiers of Shorncliffe camp that extraordinary arrangements were made for her to be buried on 9 December in the military cemetery there. Her coffin, draped in the Union Jack, was carried from her home to the burial-grounds accompanied by Sandgate coastguards and soldiers of the 3rd provisional regiment of dragoons. Shopkeepers along the route of the procession drew their blinds. According to her wish, a Bible was placed in her grave.   JOHN H. SCHWARZ

Sources will, proved 14 May 1902, Sandgate, Kent • 'The soldiers' friend', *Folkestone Herald* (7 Dec 1901) • 'Funeral of the authoress of *Scarlet and steel*', *Folkestone Herald* (14 Dec 1901) • b. cert. • d. cert. • *The Times* (9 March 1847) [birth announcement] • *The Times* (6 Dec 1901) • *WWW*, 1961–70 • private information (2004) [Elizabeth Boardman] • *British Museum general catalogue of printed books … to 1955*, BM, 20 (1963) • Blain, Clements & Grundy, *Feminist comp.* • *New York Times* (17 May 1896) [review of *A mask and a martyr*] • W. N. Payne, review of *The apotheosis of Mr Tyrawley* and *A mask and a martyr*, *The Dial*, 21 (1896), 93 • *IGI*

Likenesses photograph, repro. in *The Bookman*, 14 (June 1898)

Wealth at death £12,745 8s. 7d.: probate, 14 May 1902, *CGPLA Eng. & Wales*

Jay, (Jane) Isabella Lee (1842/3–1919). *See under* Women artists in Ruskin's circle (*act.* 1850s–1900s).

Jay, John (1745–1829), revolutionary and politician in the United States of America, was born on 12 December 1745 in New York city, the sixth son of Peter Jay, merchant and gentleman, and Mary van Cortlandt. He was of French Huguenot descent through his father and Dutch through his mother. He was a lifelong Anglican/Episcopalian. After

private tutoring John Jay earned a BA at King's College in 1764 and went on to study law in the office of Benjamin Kissam. He began legal practice in 1768. Never a man for popular politics or street radicalism, he took very little part in the gathering revolutionary movement in his native city. Through his mother he was linked to one of New York's great landlord families. His marriage, on 28 April 1774, to Sarah van Brugh Livingston (d. 1801) connected him to another. It also connected him to the American movement, in which the Livingstons were more involved than any other great New York family. Jay began to take a role that was strong in the political sense of opposing British policies but conservative in the sense of minimizing social change. He was joined in this project by a remarkable group of young fellow New Yorkers, most of them King's College graduates and lawyers, including Robert R. Livingston II, Gouverneur Morris, and Egbert Benson, and by the Albany landlord Philip Schuyler.

Jay emerged into public life in 1774, as Americans from New Hampshire to Georgia responded to the strong punishment visited by Britain upon Boston and Massachusetts for the Boston Tea Party (December 1773). He served on New York city's committee of correspondence, the first continental congress, which worked out a coherent American policy of resistance, and in its successor second continental congress, which took on the attributes of government after the American War of Independence broke out on 19 April 1775. Jay was no firebrand, agreeing with most New York leaders that independence needed to be put off as long as possible. But he never considered loyalism. At independence he returned to New York, joining its revolutionary convention, organizing a political police force, and writing the major part of the constitution that the state adopted in April 1777. The document expressed the views of his sort of men perfectly, providing for an upper legislative house intended to protect property interests and a strong governorship and court system. Jay himself became chief justice of the state, holding the office until 1779. However, his return to congress in December 1778 marked a shift of his interests to the national stage.

Almost immediately upon returning to congress Jay was chosen as its president (10 December 1778), which made him nominally the American head of state. He continued in that post until 27 September 1779, when congress elected him American minister to Madrid. He arrived in Spain on 22 January 1780 and found that his task was exceedingly difficult. Unlike their French cousins, the Spanish Bourbons would not recognize American independence (though they entered the war as French allies). He found his presence barely tolerated by foreign minister Count Floridablanca. Jay did secure a Spanish government loan that allowed him to pay off American debts that had been contracted in expectation of his success at doing so. He also learned the complexities of the diplomatic web in which the Americans were enmeshed, thanks to Spain's treaty claims upon France.

After the American victory at Yorktown, Virginia, reduced Britain's capacity to fight, Benjamin Franklin, the

American minister in Paris, called for Jay's help in negotiating the peace treaty. Jay arrived in the French capital on 23 June 1782, joining Franklin and John Adams on the American team. He may have had a hand there in undermining plans by Franklin to acquire Canada as part of the settlement; he certainly was in contact during the negotiations with Lord Shelburne, the British prime minister. But Jay and Adams together persuaded Franklin not to subordinate the American negotiators to the French foreign minister Vergennes, despite instructions from congress and Vergennes's own expectations. The resulting treaty was very favourable to the Americans, giving them title to the whole territory south of the Great Lakes, the upper St Lawrence, and Quebec, east of the Mississippi, and north of Florida.

Jay returned to New York on 24 July 1784, where he found himself elected by congress as secretary for foreign affairs. He held that post until Thomas Jefferson became secretary of state under President Washington on 22 March 1790. His task was very difficult. The United States owed money to the Dutch and the French and to Europeans who had served in its army. It wanted recognition from the European powers and access to its former markets in the British West Indies. No longer British, its ships had no protection from north African navies. Britain would not withdraw from the posts it held along the Canadian line, though these were on American soil. Spain controlled Florida, whose northern boundary was ill defined, and the mouth of the Mississippi, which meant that it controlled the commerce of the trans-Appalachian American interior.

Jay's achievement in office was primarily that he did not let a bad situation become worse. His extended negotiations with Spanish minister Gardoqui on the Mississippi and southern boundary problems ultimately came to little. Although Jay bore the full responsibilities assigned to a European foreign minister, he had to carry out his duties without a strong government to back him. Even enforcing the terms of the peace treaty with Britain proved difficult, particularly its requirement that the states end their persecution of former loyalists.

Not surprisingly Jay supported the growing movement that sought to weaken the power of the separate states. He was not a member of the federal convention that wrote the United States constitution in 1787 but he joined convention delegates Alexander Hamilton and James Madison in writing *The Federalist*, the series of eighty-five essays signed Publius and addressed to 'the considerate citizens of the State of New York', on the theoretical strengths and the practical advantages of the new constitution. He was the junior member of the team, penning the five essays which dealt with foreign affairs. He also took a strong role in New York state's ratifying convention which met at Poughkeepsie in July 1788. Despite *The Federalist*, the convention had a strong majority against the constitution. Its supporters' task was eased by ratification in New Hampshire and Virginia while the convention was debating, which changed the question from whether the constitution would take effect to whether New York would take

part. Jay gets credit for persuading 'soft' anti-federalists to vote for ratification 'in full confidence' of subsequent amendments rather than conditional upon such amendments.

President Washington named Jay as the first chief justice of the United States supreme court, over which he presided from 1789 until 1794. His major contribution to American constitutional law came in *Chisholm* v. *Georgia* (1793), which upheld the principle that a citizen of one state could sue the government of another state. His ruling was later overturned by the eleventh amendment to the constitution. While chief justice he frequently advised Washington, especially on foreign affairs, and he drafted Washington's proclamation of American neutrality between warring Britain and France in 1793.

The following year Washington sent Jay to London to negotiate a treaty that would remove British troops from forts on American soil along the Canadian boundary, end Royal Navy impressment from American ships, and settle commercial and debt difficulties. Jay's hand was weakened by British knowledge of the minimal American position, and the treaty's main achievement was removal of the troops while violating American obligations under international law to France and offending American supporters of the French Revolution. When its terms became known it proved highly unpopular, but it none the less was ratified and put into effect.

While Jay was in England he won New York's gubernatorial election of 1795. Most historians agree that he actually had won a majority of votes for governor in the previous election three years earlier but that electoral fraud had kept him out of office then. Now, in an ironic reversal of the strong nationalism he had displayed in congress, in foreign service, and on the supreme court, he resigned the chief justiceship to take control of his state. His two terms as governor were uneventful, except at the very end in 1800, when he scornfully dismissed a suggestion by Alexander Hamilton that he make use of legal technicalities in order to keep New York's electoral college votes from going to Thomas Jefferson and thus keep Jefferson out of the presidency. He always was a strong opponent of slavery. He freed the slaves who came to him by inheritance and marriage, and when he was drafting New York's constitution of 1777 he sought unsuccessfully to include a clause providing for gradual emancipation. He was a founding member of the New York Manumission Society in 1784 and as governor he signed into law the bill for gradual emancipation that the state legislature adopted in 1795. After 1800 Jay left public life and lived quietly as a widower at Bedford, Westchester county until his death there of 'palsy' on 17 May 1829.

EDWARD COUNTRYMAN

Sources F. Monaghan, *John Jay* (1935) · R. B. Morris, ed., *John Jay*, 2 vols. (1975) · R. B. Morris, *The peacemakers: the great powers and American independence* (1965) · R. B. Morris, *John Jay, the nation, and the court* (1967) · R. B. Morris, *Witnesses at the creation* (1985) · W. Jay, *The life of John Jay* (1833) · S. F. Bemis, *Jay's treaty*, rev. edn (1962) · J. A. Combs, 'Jay, John', *ANB*
Archives Col. U. | BL, corresp. with Lord Grenville, Add. MS 59049

Likenesses G. Stuart, oils, 1783, Frick Art Reference Library, New York

Jay, John (1805–1872), building and civil engineering contractor, was born on 22 January 1805 at Buckingham (now Buckenham Parva), Norfolk. Nothing is known about his parents, but he had a younger brother, who survived him, and a sister. He married Esther Wilson (1806–1888) on 25 May 1826 at St Matthew's, Bethnal Green, where he was then living; they are known to have had three daughters, two of whom, unmarried, survived Jay, and a son who predeceased them.

Described in earlier London commercial directories as a carpenter, by 1839 Jay was a 'builder' capable of handling a £20,000 railway construction contract (London Viaduct, Eastern Counties Railway), though whence he derived the necessary capital is unknown. As a large-scale general contractor, Jay executed both public buildings and railway works during the 1840s. St Michael's Church, Stockwell (1840–41), was followed by the Infant Orphan Asylum, Wanstead (1841–3). In 1847 he put in tenders (unsuccessfully) totalling £700,000 for building the North Kent Railway, and the Ashford–Hastings line. By 1850 he had acquired wharves and premises (rateable value, £557) at Macclesfield Road North, Finsbury, adjoining the Regent's Canal, and undertook the building of 343 houses on the nearby Packington estate leased from the Clothworkers' Company by James Rhodes, land that included brickfields. In 1854 when Jay petitioned that further leases should be made direct to him, the company's clerk observed that 'he is a man of considerable wealth and responsibility' (Clothworkers' Co. MSS, Packington Estate, bundle J).

In 1849 Jay had secured the contract for building the Great Northern Railway from King's Cross to the southern end of the tunnel under Copenhagen Fields against such experienced railway contractors as Brassey and Peto and Betts, despite the line engineer's warning that it would be 'highly objectionable and hazardous to the completion of the works to accept a tender at the low prices offered by Mr Jay' (PRO, RAIL 236/271, 201–2). His use of steam engines enabled a thousand cubic yards of soil to be removed from the cutting daily. This contract was quickly followed by those for the 45 acre King's Cross goods station, and for the passenger terminus (1851, £123,500), where he had a thousand men working on two immense sheds 800 ft long, 105 ft wide and 71 ft high, the double-span arched roof then the largest of its kind in the world. Paid in a conventional mix of cash and bonds, Jay insisted that he be allowed the contract price for his brickwork even after the brick excise tax was abolished in 1850. Although not in the international league of railway contractors, Jay, working relatively close to his London base, was a powerful competitor. In 1853 he was appointed contractor for the eastern portion of the Metropolitan underground railway (which was not started until 1860 for lack of capital); he took the largest shareholding (£100,000), from which he sought to be relieved in 1858, implying that his resources were then stretched. It was at this time that he sold the unbuilt parts of his Packington estate holdings.

Throughout the 1850s Jay had numerous contracts in hand. The King's Cross works completed, in 1852 he secured that for continuing the new houses of parliament (at £152,333), and was building St Olave's Grammar Schools, Southwark (nearly £24,000). Despite a 44 per cent increase in his prices, the basis of his contract, he won the next stage at Westminster (£94,929), as well as large warehouse contracts in the City (where he also rebuilt Clothworkers' Hall, 1856–8, £33,846), and Colchester Station for the Eastern Counties Railway. At Westminster he refused to exchange his prices contract for the more popular lump sum form; he completed the clock and Victoria towers (where the ironwork of the cresting bears his name)—works involving the most advanced building technology—together with the Old Palace Yard front. The superior quality of his materials and workmen was commented on, and according to his obituary he was 'widely known as a liberal and considerate employer, and a businessman of uprightness and integrity' (Islington Gazette). He won the friendship of the government surveyor, Henry Arthur Hunt, who became one of his executors. About 1860 the Jay family, with four resident servants, moved to Highbury Park House, Islington, standing in its own grounds.

On completing the structure of the palace at Westminster in 1861, Jay sought more lucrative undertakings. With at least one further substantial contract for City warehouses in his pocket, he took up his long-deferred Metropolitan Railway work, completed in 1863, which proved extremely laborious and cost about £250,000 a mile. His last large contracts embraced both work on the Palmerston government's fortifications programme, including casemented barracks at Portland, and the £600,000 Hither Green–Tonbridge section of the South Eastern Railway. He appears to have retired from business about 1870, and died at his residence, Ashford House, Hornsey, London, on 28 December 1872, 'much esteemed for his social qualities and his genial bearing' (Islington Gazette). Jay, his wife, and his son were all buried beneath a richly carved sarcophagus in Abney Park cemetery, Stoke Newington, London; the chapel there, built in 1840, is Jay's first known building. M. H. PORT

Sources census returns, 1841, 1861, 1871 · L. Popplewell, *A gazetteer of the railway contractors and engineers of South East England, 1830–1914* (1983) · parish register (marriages), St Matthew, Bethnal Green, London, 1826 · parish register (baptisms), St Luke's, Old Street, 1828 · parish register (baptisms), All Hallows, London Wall, 1838 · parish register (baptisms), All Hallows, London Wall, 1843 · court minutes and Packington estate papers, Clothworkers' Company · PRO, RAIL 236/70, p. 303; 236/271, pp. 201–2; 231/239, pp. 96, 114 · M. H. Port, ed., *The Houses of Parliament* (1976) · list of tenders, *The Builder*, 13–24 (1855–66) · list of tenders, *The Builder*, 1 (1843), 459 · list of tenders, *The Builder*, 17 (1859), 400 · *Railway Times* (19 April 1856), 494 · *Railway Times* (21 Aug 1858), 1017 · M. H. Port, *Six hundred new churches: a study of the church building commission, 1818–1856, and its church building activities* (1961) · *London Directory* (1836–72) · *Civil Engineer and Architect's Journal* (1861), 28 · *Civil Engineer and Architect's Journal* (1863), 98 · inscriptions on sarcophagus, Abney Park cemetery, Stoke Newington · Finsbury rate books, 1850–59 · *Islington Gazette* (7 Jan 1873) · d. cert.

Wealth at death under £30,000: probate, 5 Feb 1873, CGPLA Eng. & Wales

Jay, John George Henry (1770–1849), violinist, was born on 27 November 1770, the son of Stephen Jay of Leytonstone, Essex, possibly the 'eminent dancing-master' referred to by Hawkins (p. 853 n.). He studied the violin and composition under John Hindmarsh and Francis Phillips and completed his education on the continent. After returning to England in 1800 he established himself as a teacher and became an excellent violinist. He was engaged by a Mrs Cannon, of Little Chelsea in London, as the resident instructor in music of the young ladies at her seminary, where he remained, possibly until his death. Jay was awarded a BMus from Magdalen Hall, Oxford, in 1809, and obtained the degree of DMus from Trinity Hall, Cambridge, in 1811. He was also made an honorary member of the Royal Academy of Music, where his eldest daughter was a student and a fine performer on the harp. His second daughter was a pianist, and his son, John (1812–1889), was a good violinist. Jay's compositions include a *Phantasia and Two Sonatas* for piano (1800), *Six Waltzes for Pianoforte, with Flute Accompaniment* op. 22 (1817), and songs. He died in Chelsea on 29 August 1849. DAVID J. GOLBY

Sources [J. S. Sainsbury], ed., *A dictionary of musicians*, 2 vols. (1824) · J. Hawkins, *A general history of the science and practice of music*, new edn, 2 (1853), 853 n. · *The Times* (31 Aug 1849), 7 · Venn, *Alum. Cant.* · Grove, *Dict. mus.*

Jay, (Arthur) Osborne Montgomery (1858–1945), Church of England clergyman and social commentator, was born on 14 April 1858 at Landour, north India, the second son of the Revd William James Jay and Harriet, daughter of Martin Rawling of St Ives, Huntingdonshire. His parents had married in 1850 just as William was about to take up a position as chaplain to the Bengal establishment, which he held until his return to England in 1860. From 1860 to 1866 William was chaplain of the East India Hospital, Poplar, and Osborne's connections with the East End of London went back to his childhood. In 1865, however, William was presented to the rectory of Elvedon, Suffolk, by the maharaja Duleep Singh, and Osborne was sent to boarding-school in Leamington Spa, where he remained until about 1870. From Leamington Spa he proceeded to Eton College, and in 1876 to St Catharine's, Cambridge, in the footsteps of his brother William (who was a pensioner there from 1874 until 1878). Osborne was also admitted pensioner on 1 September 1876 and took his BA in 1880. In 1881 he was ordained deacon in the diocese of London. Later Osborne remembered that he became curate of 'the mother church of East London, Old Stepney', which was Holy Trinity, Stepney, in that same year. In 1882 he took priest's orders and in 1883 became an MA of the University of Cambridge.

From 1883 until 1886 Jay was in charge of a college mission in Stepney. He described in one of his books (*Life in Darkest London*, 1891, 12) how 'on the closing of this enterprise [he was] living in a dismal street near Ratcliff Highway, close to the famous "Tiger-Bay", drawing a stipend from the Bishop of Bedford's Fund … and looking for fresh opportunities of work'. Then the bishop of London offered him the living of Holy Trinity, Shoreditch, with £200 a year and a deal 'of hard work to be done, and that

for many years to come'. In December 1886 Jay accepted the living, which was on the boundary between Shoreditch and Bethnal Green. Within the parish was the notorious Old Nichol. When Jay entered the parish there was no church building; instead services were held in the loft of a stable. He was supported by a grant from Magdalen College, Oxford. Within ten years he had raised £25,000 to build a church, social club, lodging house, and gymnasium. He campaigned (successfully) for the London county council to demolish the slums of the Old Nichol and replace them with an estate of model dwellings (known as the Boundary Street estate). Jay was much annoyed that the former slum dwellers were not rehoused in this estate but were forced to move themselves and their slums elsewhere. When he read Arthur Morrison's *Tales of Mean Streets* (1894) he promptly wrote and invited the novelist to come and live in the parish and experience at first hand the life of the Old Nichol, which contrasted with the boring respectability of the mean streets. Morrison accepted the invitation, and the Old Nichol became the Jago of his novel *Child of the Jago*; in the novel the character of Father Sturt was modelled closely upon Jay. Jay told his own story in three books, *Life in Darkest London* (1891), *The Social Problem and its Solution* (1893), and *A Story of Shoreditch* (1896). Jay, in other respects a humane man, advised that the criminal elements of society (the population of the Old Nichol) could not be reformed and that, therefore, they should be forcibly removed to penal settlements where they should serve life sentences and be forbidden to procreate. This, he believed, would have the effect of wiping out the strain of criminality from the British population.

In the late 1890s Ernest Aves commented that Jay was, with the exception of the bishop of Stepney, the 'best known man associated with the Church in Bethnal Green'. He went on to describe Jay's ministry, which he reckoned to be successful as measured both by attendance and by the success of his clubs. In contrast to many churches, more than half of the congregation at Holy Trinity consisted of men. Aves contrasted Jay's muscular brand of Christianity and his personal appearance—'he looks like a prize fighter'—with his aestheticism and his high-churchmanship. He had never 'had the gloves on in his life' and 'in his buildings he has attached very great importance, and has secured great richness in design, compactness, and great aesthetic beauty. He is a High churchman, and estimates very highly the parish system of the church of England. He thinks that one "should clean ones' own doorstep" and that useful work has to be concentrated in the way which strict adherence to the parochial system alone makes possible' (Ernest Aves's report on district IX, Booth Collection). In the interview upon which Aves's report was based, George Duckworth described Jay as 'a voluble and discursive talker' and described how he had roused considerable opposition in the neighbouring parishes.

Jay never married and, when interviewed by Duckworth, admitted that he did not get on well with women. He remained at Holy Trinity, Shoreditch, until

1921. In that year he retired to Great Malvern, in Worcestershire, where he died of 'senile cerebral degeneration' at his home, Thornbury, Avenue Road, on 14 January 1945. ROSEMARY O'DAY

Sources Ernest Aves's report on district IX, BLPES, Booth MSS · George Duckworth's interview with Osborne Jay, BLPES, Booth MSS, B228 · Venn, *Alum. Cant.* · O. Jay, *Life in darkest London* (1891) · O. Jay, *The social problem and its solution* (1893) · O. Jay, *A story of Shoreditch* (1896) · A. Morrison, *A child of the Jago* (1896) · d. cert.
Likenesses photograph, BLPES, Booth collection, B228
Wealth at death £33,654 9s. 6d.: probate, 25 April 1945, CGPLA Eng. & Wales

Jay, William (1769–1853), Congregational minister, was born on 6 May 1769 at Tisbury, Wiltshire, the only son in the family of five children of a stonemason. In 1783 he began working for his father on the building of Fonthill Abbey, for William Beckford. After Cornelius Winter had preached at Tisbury he invited Jay to come to his academy in Marlborough to train for the ministry. Winter's theological training concentrated on practical evangelism, and his students were expected to preach in the surrounding villages, which Jay began to do at the age of about sixteen. After leaving Marlborough in 1788 he preached a series of sermons to large crowds at Surrey Chapel, London, for the Revd Rowland Hill. He was minister at Christian Malford, near Chippenham, and then at the Hotwells, Clifton, where he officiated in Hope Chapel, belonging to Lady Maxwell.

On 6 January 1791 Jay married Anne, daughter of the Revd Edward Davies, non-resident rector of Coychurch, Glamorgan, and curate of Batheaston, near Bath. They had three sons and three daughters. She died in 1845, and on 2 September 1846 he married Marianna Jane (d. 1857), daughter of George Head of Bradford; according to his son, Cyrus Jay, she was seventy-two at the time of the marriage.

On 30 January 1791 Jay was ordained pastor of Argyle Chapel at Bath, and remained there for sixty-two years. In Bath he became very popular, one of the most fashionable preachers of his day. His sermons, delivered in a sonorous voice, were noted for their clarity and directness. As well as preaching in Bath, he went to Surrey Chapel, London, for six-week periods, for many years. A teetotaller from 1833, he was a supporter of the temperance movement. Some of his writings had a large circulation, including *The Domestic Minister's Assistant* (1820), a manual of family prayer, *The Mutual Duties of Husbands and Wives* (1801), which ran to six editions, *Morning Exercises in the Closet* (1829), which went to ten editions, and *Evening Exercises* (1831).

Jay resigned on 30 January 1853, and was widely criticized when he tried to interfere in the choice of his successor. He died at 4 Percy Place, Bath, on 27 December 1853, and was buried in Snow Hill cemetery, Bath, on 3 January 1854. A tablet was erected in his memory in Argyle Chapel. G. C. BOASE, *rev.* ANNE PIMLOTT BAKER

Sources *The autobiography and reminiscences of the Revd William Jay*, ed. G. Redford and J. A. James (1854) · R. Tudur Jones, *Congregationalism in England, 1662–1962* (1962) · C. Jay, *Recollections of William Jay* (1859) · *Congregational Year Book* (1855), 219–21 · D. W. Lovegrove,

Established church, sectarian people: itinerancy and the transformation of English dissent, 1780–1830 (1988) · S. Couling, *History of the temperance movement in Great Britain and Ireland* (1862), 314–15
Archives Bath Central Library, letters, mainly to Charles Godwin
Likenesses J. Goldar, print, 1789, repro. in Jay, *Recollections* · R. Hancock, stipple, pubd 1799 (after J. Hutchinson), NPG · S. E. Covell, wax medallion, 1812, NPG · W. Holl, stipple (after R. Evans), BM, NPG; repro. in W. Jerdan, *National portrait gallery of illustrious and eminent personages of the nineteenth century, with memoirs*, 5 vols. (1830–34) · J. Thomson, stipple (after W. Etty), BM, NPG; repro. in *European Magazine* (1819) · engraving (after W. Etty), repro. in Redford and James, eds., *The Autobiography and reminiscences of the Revd William Jay*, frontispiece · oils, NPG · portrait (aged eighty-four), repro. in Jay, *Recollections*, frontispiece · portrait, repro. in *European Magazine* (Jan 1819), 5–8 · portrait, repro. in *The Pulpit*, 1 (1824), 436, 455 · portrait, repro. in W. C. Taylor, *National Portrait Gallery*, 4 (1846), 107–8 · portrait, repro. in Wilson, *Memoir of William Jay* (1854)

Jaye, Henry (b. in or before **1580**, d. in or before **1641**), musical instrument maker, came from an unknown family. He would have had to finish an apprenticeship, begun at the age of about fourteen, in order to advertise his name on an instrument's label. Such labels, which show that Jaye lived and worked in Southwark, London, survive in viols dated between 1611 and 1667; Francis Galpin reported one from 1610. Since few manual workers of this period would still have been active at the age of eighty-seven, since there is a consistency of style between the earliest and the latest instruments, and since the latest work shows no evidence of being the work of an old man, there may have been two Henry Jayes, possibly father and son. This would echo their distinguished predecessors, John Rose, father and son, who worked in nearby Bridewell.

Thomas Mace listed Jaye in 1676 among the five most admired viol makers. More instruments by, or attributed to, Jaye survive than for any other English luthier of his time or earlier. His reputation is currently sustained by both this large quantity and its high quality. A bass viol of 1619 (priv. coll., London) is probably the best-preserved English stringed instrument from before the Restoration. All surviving Jaye instruments are viols but he may also have made violins and, as some authors have claimed, lutes, though none is known. No death date for Henry Jaye has come to light, although he was dead by 1641. MICHAEL FLEMING

Sources M. Fleming, 'Viol-making in England, c.1580–1660', PhD diss., Open University, 2001 · P. Tourin, *Viollist: a comprehensive catalogue of historical viole da gamba in public and private collections* (privately printed, Duxbury, VT, 1979) · T. Mace, *Musick's monument* (1676), 245 · F. W. Galpin, *Old English instruments of music*, 4th edn (1965), 67 · CLRO, REP 27, fol. 310 · W. Henley, *Universal dictionary of violin and bow makers*, 1 vol. edn (1973) · G. Hart, *The violin: its famous makers and their imitators* (1880) · H. Poidras, *Critical & documentary dictionary of violin makers* (1928) · *New Grove* · B. W. Harvey, *The violin family and its makers in the British Isles: an illustrated history and directory* (1995)

Jayne, Francis John (1845–1921), bishop of Chester, was born on 1 January 1845 at Llanelli, Brecknockshire, the eldest son of John Jayne JP (d. 1873), a colliery owner, of Panty-beili House, Llanelli, and his second wife, Elisabeth

Francis John Jayne (1845–1921), by Bassano

Haines. He was educated at Rugby School, where he distinguished himself both in his academic studies and in sport. In 1863 he entered Wadham College, Oxford, and was soon rowing in the college boat. He gained a first class in classical moderations in 1865, a first in *literae humaniores* in the summer of 1867, and at the end of that year a first in jurisprudence and modern history. In 1868 he became a fellow of Jesus College, Oxford, where he also served between 1871 and 1879 as lecturer in modern history.

In 1870 Jayne took holy orders and he ministered, while continuing to reside in Jesus College, as curate of St Clement's Church in Oxford, an evangelical establishment in an area of the city 'dominated by the brewing interest'. He resigned his curacy when he was appointed to a tutorship at the new Keble College in 1871. In the same year he also took up a lectureship at Wadham College. He resigned his fellowship at Jesus College in 1873, following his marriage in 1872 to Emily Sarah, eldest daughter of Watts John Garland and sister of Mary Garland, who in 1886 married A. G. Edwards, later bishop of St Asaph and archbishop of Wales. Frank and Emily Jayne had six sons and three daughters. Those who knew Jayne at Oxford recalled him as a handsome and athletic man, 'with hair falling oddly over his brow'. His shyness, which increased with age, gave him the reputation of being something of an enigma, albeit an enigma 'with decided promise' (*Manchester Guardian*).

With the strong backing of the bishop of Oxford and the

warden of Keble, Jayne secured the post of principal of St David's College, Lampeter, and he was sworn into office on 25 February 1879. At Lampeter Jayne found much to do. His predecessor, Llewelyn Lewellin, had presided with an amiable lethargy over the college since its opening in 1827. During his years at Lampeter Jayne reformed the college in many ways: new statutes were promulgated, the college chapel was rebuilt, affiliation to Oxford and Cambridge was achieved, a new two-year course for the licence in divinity was introduced, a new hall of residence was built for the increasing number of students (60 at his arrival and more than 120 at his departure), sporting facilities were improved, and in 1884 the College School was opened to provide sound education for entrants to the college itself.

Jayne, who was unsuccessful in his candidature for the principalship of King's College, London, in 1883, was criticized by some for his lack of Welsh and for his autocratic control of the staff, to which he appointed such distinguished scholars as E. H. Culley, John Owen, Hastings Rashdall, T. F. Tout, and Hugh Walker, but there is some truth in the observation that his headship of Lampeter was the greatest success of his life. He deserves to be remembered as 'the second founder' of the college. Jayne maintained his links with Lampeter after his return to England, moving a resolution in the House of Lords in 1893 that the charter of the University of Wales should not receive the royal assent until such portions had been omitted which precluded the inclusion of Lampeter as a constituent college of the university. He also played a significant part in the struggle against the disestablishment of the Church of England in Wales.

On 29 September 1886 Jayne resigned the principalship of Lampeter on his appointment to the vicarage of Leeds. During his relatively brief tenure of this influential office he set the parochial finances on a sound footing at a time when many of the wealthier inhabitants were moving out into the suburbs. He achieved notable success in establishing special monthly services for men, he built a club house for the athletes in the Parish Church Recreation Club, and he adapted the ante-chapel of the church for weekday services. He had long since widened his churchmanship from the evangelicalism of St Clement's, Oxford, and the high-church tradition of Leeds appealed greatly to him. However, he never forgot the comment of Cosmo Lang, a curate of Leeds, in *Church and Town for Fifty Years* (1891) that 'even then [Jayne] seemed to have learned Napoleon's art of covering a mistake by a new appearance of success'. In later years, when Lang was archbishop of York, Jayne would never stay at Bishopthorpe, the archbishop's residence, during meetings of the bishops of the northern province.

In September 1888 Lord Salisbury invited Jayne to accept nomination to the see of Chester, and he was consecrated on 24 February 1889, the youngest bishop in the Church of England, embarking on what was to be the longest tenure of the bishopric of Chester in its history. He refused nomination to Durham in 1890 on the grounds that he had not been long enough in his new diocese. Jayne was content to devote his immense energies with total dedication—he scarcely ever took a holiday—to Chester, ultimately at the cost of his health, building on the foundations laid by his episcopal predecessors William Jacobson and William Stubbs, both of whom stood in the same ecclesiastical tradition as Jayne himself now did. The days of building churches were almost at an end by Jayne's episcopate; his main priority was to increase clerical stipends.

Jayne's strength lay in administration; in the pulpit he was 'interesting rather than eloquent' (*Manchester Guardian*). He was relatively unknown in the wider church outside his diocese, and he published very little: an edition of Richard Baxter's *Self Review* (1910) and an edition, with a long introduction, of pronouncements by other church leaders under the title *Anglican pronouncements upon Auricular Confession and Fasting Communion* (1912). Extracts from some of his charges were published as an appendix to *Anglican Essays* by various authors (1923).

The diocese of Chester under Jayne was renowned for being remarkably free from tensions produced by extremes of churchmanship, with some allegations that Jayne took great care to appoint safe and diligent men to important posts, rather than risking visionaries whose zeal might create problems. Jayne approved of those who shared his own devotion to the Book of Common Prayer, but he had little patience with the 'self-authorized eclecticism' and 'ardent congregationalism' of the few definite Anglo-Catholics, and his opposition to them increased as he became older and they became more Romanist. With nonconformists he was on good terms. He favoured some modification of the damnatory clauses of the Athanasian creed, but he was opposed to any revision of the 1662 holy communion service.

Jayne's concern about the misuse of alcohol led him to found the People's Refreshment House Association Limited in an attempt to reform the management of public houses in line with the Göteborg system favoured by Joseph Chamberlain. Ultimately the association owned 130 inns and hotels.

An illness early in 1918 compelled Jayne to consider resigning his see at the end of that year, although in the event he remained bishop of Chester until a breakdown forced him to leave office on 1 May 1919. He never recovered his strength in retirement. He died at his home at The Quarry, Oswestry on 23 August 1921, and was buried at Bowden in Cheshire on 26 August. **D. T. W. PRICE**

Sources B. St G. Drennan, *The Keble College centenary register, 1870–1970* (1970) · D. T. W. Price, *A history of Saint David's University College Lampeter*, 1: *To 1898* (1977) · C. G. Lang, ed., *Church and town for fifty years* (1891) · *VCH Cheshire*, vol. 3 · *The Times* (25 Aug 1921) · *Manchester Guardian* (25 Aug 1921) · *Yorkshire Post* (25 Aug 1921) · *Chester Diocesan Gazette* (May 1919) · *Chester Diocesan Gazette* (Oct 1921)
Archives NRA, priv. coll., letters to first duke of Westminster
Likenesses Bassano, photograph, NPG [*see illus.*] · S. P. Hall, group portrait, watercolour (*The bench of bishops, 1902*), NPG · C. W. Walton, drawing, bishop's palace, Chester · wood-engraving (after photograph by H. Woods of Leeds), NPG; repro. in *ILN* (6 Oct 1888) · oils, St David's University College, Lampeter
Wealth at death £5518 4s. 11d.: probate, 20 Sept 1921, *CGPLA Eng. & Wales*

Jeacocke, Caleb (1705/6–1786), orator, was born in London, where he was apprenticed to a baker and opened his own shop on the High Street in the St Giles-in-the-Fields area of the city. A diligent businessman with a flair for figures, he was elected to the Skinners' Company, became the director of the Hand-in-Hand fire office, and was said to have worked on the accounts of 'some of the greatest Men in the Kingdom' (*History*, 128). Jeacocke also attended the Monday evening meetings of the Robin Hood Society, a London debating club of up to sixty members who engaged in free and often frank discussion on a predetermined subject. Jeacocke's skill as a speaker was such that he is reported to have outwitted Edmund Burke and celebrated MPs on numerous occasions. About 1742 he was appointed the society's president, and charged with regulating and summarizing debates according to club rules. That this responsibility now fell to a baker was the source of some humour in mid-century depictions of the society. Writing in the *Covent Garden Journal*, Henry Fielding claimed to have received his bread rolls wrapped in a copy of the society's agenda, while a 1752 engraving depicts Jeacocke balancing a loaf of bread atop his wig. When Oliver Goldsmith attended a meeting early in the following decade he was impressed by the president's commanding presence and suggested that Jeacocke might be taken for a lord chancellor. 'No, no,' came the reply from Goldsmith's companion Samuel Derrick, 'only for a master of the rolls' (Forster, 1.288). Jeacocke resigned his office after nineteen years to become JP for Middlesex; at the same time he also turned his talents to writing, publishing *A Vindication of the Moral Character of the Apostle Paul* in 1765. Described in the society's history as lacking the 'variegated Hues that make so pleasing an Appearance in the Biographer's Page', Jeacocke none the less received a glowing testimony. A man of great philanthropy and learning who combined austerity without melancholy and cheerfulness without merriment, it was claimed that he 'has been talked of … in every City and Town in England' (*History*, 127). Jeacocke died, aged eighty, on 7 January 1786 at his house on Denmark Street, London.

GORDON GOODWIN, *rev.* PHILIP CARTER

Sources *The history of the Robin Hood Society* (1764) · R. J. Allen, *The clubs of Augustan London* (1933) · J. Forster, *The life and times of Oliver Goldsmith*, [new edn], 2 vols. (1885) · *GM*, 1st ser., 56 (1786), 84, 180
Likenesses group portrait, engraving, 1752 (Robin Hood Society), repro. in Allen, *Clubs* · C. Cotton sen., portrait, St Giles-in-the-Field, London

Jeaffreson, John Cordy (1831–1901), writer and archivist, was born at Framlingham, Suffolk, on 14 January 1831, the second son and ninth child of William Jeaffreson (1790–1865), surgeon, and his wife, Caroline, *née* Edwards (1795–1863). He was named after his mother's uncle, John Cordy (1762–1828) of Woodbridge, a dealer and landowner. Jeaffreson attended successively the grammar schools at Woodbridge and Botesdale between 1840 and 1845, and was then apprenticed to his father as a surgeon. In 1846, however, he renounced surgery and in June 1848, after the crisis of a serious illness, matriculated from Pembroke College, Oxford, with the intention of taking orders. His undergraduate friends included Henry Kingsley and Arthur Locker, and he graduated BA in 1852. Soon after, he moved to London, having decided to write, and to support himself by teaching. In 1856 he entered Lincoln's Inn, and was called to the bar in 1859. He did not practise, but he enlarged his social circle through the life of the inns of court. He also became an assiduous clubman.

In 1854 Jeaffreson published *Crewe Rise*, the first of a near dozen three-volume novels which appeared over the next thirty years. In 1856 he began to write regularly for *The Athenaeum*, and felt able to give up teaching. His novels were adequately successful, but he had turned also to a series of historical and literary studies, the first of which, *Novels and Novelists from Elizabeth to Victoria*, appeared in 1858. It was followed by *A Book about Doctors* (1860), conceived as anecdotal social history. The formula had a wide appeal, and *A Book about Lawyers* (1866), *A Book about the Clergy* (1870), *Brides and Bridals* (1872), and *A Book about the Table* all sold well. A continuing flow of novels and a commissioned life of Robert Stephenson (1864) left him still with much energy for social life and travel. On 2 October 1860, at St Sepulchre's, Newgate Street, Jeaffreson married Arabella Ellen (*b*. 1839), the only surviving daughter of William Eccles FRCS (*d*. 1847) of Old Broad Street; they had one daughter, Caroline (1861–1909).

Jeaffreson's circle included Sir Thomas Duffus Hardy, deputy keeper of the public records since 1861, and the founder of the Royal Commission on Historical Manuscripts, which was established in 1869. In 1871 Hardy surprised Jeaffreson by suggesting that he should become one of the commission's inspectors, and offering to train him in palaeography. Jeaffreson accepted the proposition with some misgivings, and spent two years in the Public Record Office transcribing documents under Hardy's tuition. In 1874 he went to inspect the manuscripts of the Revd Edmund Field, chaplain of Lancing College, and the contents of the parish chest at Mendlesham in Suffolk, to prepare his first reports for the commission, which were published in 1876.

Over the next eleven years Jeaffreson reported on twenty-seven other collections, twelve of them in private hands, four held in counties by clerks of the peace, and the other eleven the records of municipal corporations, including major holdings at Chester (1881), Ipswich (1883), Leicester (1881), King's Lynn (1887), and Great Yarmouth (1883). Beyond his formal reports, which provided inventories of the records with introductory commentaries and extracts, he also published an index to the records at Leicester (1881), and four volumes of calendars and transcripts of Middlesex county records (1886–92). His work on the original letters collected by Alfred Morrison led on to lives of Byron (1883) and Shelley (1888), and to *Lady Hamilton and Lord Nelson* (1888) and *The Queen of Naples and Lord Nelson* (1889), which all attracted scholarly criticism.

Jeaffreson's was a felicitous appointment, and he rendered a real service to historical studies, despite Sir Sidney Lee's observation that his archival work 'exhibited many traces of his lack of historical training' (*DNB*). Jeaffreson necessarily learned his history from his work. There was

at the time no system of historical studies to match the palaeographical and diplomatic advice which Hardy provided, and the physical condition of the archives was also daunting. The older material almost everywhere was ill-housed, disordered, and dirty, and identifying and arranging it was at least as formidable a task as selecting illustrative material and preparing the reports. Despite its flaws, even a century later the work of Jeaffreson and his colleagues has not been entirely superseded.

Jeaffreson published *A Book of Recollections* in 1894, but in his last years he was incapable of literary work. His autobiography is ebullient, like his other writings, and remorseless in anecdote. He accepted and propagated Duffus Hardy's mistaken belief that he had been deprived of the deputy keepership in 1838 by the ill faith of Sir Francis Palgrave, but in general the book is a lively account of literary society in Victorian London. Jeaffreson died at his home at Portsdown Mansions, Portsdown Road, Maida Vale, London, on 2 February 1901, and was buried in Paddington old cemetery, Willesden Lane. He was survived by his wife and their daughter, who died, unmarried, in 1909.

G. H. MARTIN

Sources J. C. Jeaffreson, *A book of recollections*, 2 vols. (1894) · *DNB* · J. D. Cantwell, *The Public Record Office, 1838–1958* (1991) · *Ninth report*, 1, HMC, 8 (1883) · G. H. Martin, 'The borough and the merchant community of Ipswich, 1317–1422', DPhil diss., U. Oxf., 1955 · d. cert.

Archives Bodl. Oxf., corresp. · City Westm. AC, corresp. · PRO, corresp. as an HMC inspector, HMC 1 · Suffolk RO, Ipswich, corresp. | BL, letters to T. J. Wise, As MS A 4144 · U. Edin. L., corresp. with J. O. Halliwell-Phillips

Likenesses M. Hector (Mrs Robb), oils, 1901, Ipswich Museum, Suffolk

Wealth at death £4776 2*s*. 5*d*.: probate, 26 Feb 1901, *CGPLA Eng. & Wales*

Jeake, Samuel (1623–1690), lawyer and nonconformist preacher, was born in Rye on 9 October 1623, son of Henry Jeake (*b*. *c*.1600), a baker in Rye, and his wife, Anne (*d*. 1639), daughter of the Sussex minister John Pierson, and was baptized on 12 October. Jeake's education is obscure, but his godly milieu in his formative years is illustrated by material preserved in his letter-book, including various letters of pious exhortation relating both to his mother's circle and his own.

Jeake himself emerged to prominence in the religious controversies in the town of Rye between 1640 and 1642. His enthusiasm for the parliamentary cause during the civil war is revealed by his letter-book, while in 1647 he orchestrated a joint letter to Lord General Fairfax in which the parliamentary victory in the war was seen as an opportunity for reform. Further letters illustrate the negotiations preceding his marriage to Frances Hartridge (*d*. 1654) in 1651, in which she submitted five 'propositions' to her suitor, including a demand for 'libertie of conscience' once married (Hunter and others, xvii). Only one son, Samuel *Jeake (1652–1699), survived infancy.

Hints survive concerning Jeake's intellectual and professional activities in the years around 1650. It was evidently at this time that he began the book on arithmetic that was to be published posthumously in 1696 by his son as *Logistikēlogia, or, Arithmetick surveighed and reviewed*. His interest in astrology is documented by surviving manuscripts, as is his skill in calligraphy, which he probably deployed professionally. That he had by now begun a legal career is suggested by his commentary on his horoscope in 1648 that 'the use of a pen may be hinted to the native, to Administer publicke affaires, for Ingrossments, Conveyances, Draughts, &c. if not an office of that kind' (Hunter and others, xix).

During the 1650s Jeake moved to a central position in Rye affairs. In 1651 he became town clerk, and his efficient execution of this office throughout the interregnum is witnessed by the official records of Rye corporation; from 1653 to 1656 he also served as registrar for births, deaths, and marriages under the terms of the Cromwellian Marriage Act. In addition, notes survive at Rye Museum of sermons that he preached in Rye in 1655–6.

At the Restoration Jeake lost his job as town clerk, while in 1662 he and other active supporters of the parliamentary regime were deprived of their voting rights. But he continued to play a prominent role in the town's religious affairs, acting as leader of its nonconformist congregation, which in 1669 was said to meet at his house; notes on sermons that he gave survive from the 1660s. In addition, profuse letters of religious controversy that he wrote at this time are preserved in his letter-book, which also contains letters offering spiritual advice to his co-religionists.

For the 1660s and early 1670s Jeake's everyday correspondence survives—as against the spiritually significant letters that he vouchsafed to his letter-book—and this reveals his legal work in and around Rye. Indeed, in 1682 one of his political opponents in the town described him as 'an amphibious creature between an attorney and a scrivener and has for many years been employed in most of the contracts and conveyances of the town and adjacent country' (Hunter and others, xx). His continuing interest in municipal affairs is indicated by his best-known book, *The Charters of the Cinque Ports*, which was said when it was published in 1728 to have been 'wrote in 1678' (ibid.).

In the years following the Restoration Jeake drew up the extant catalogue of his library, an extraordinary assemblage of about 2100 items which combined a remarkable holding of the radical pamphlets of the civil war and interregnum with learned works on a wide range of subjects, including an extensive selection of theological works as well as books on literature, law, mathematics, science, and magic. It is an outstanding example of a library of an unusual type, built up by a provincial, independent-minded book collector remote from the culture of church and university. Though the library itself has long since been dispersed, and only a few dozen items from it are known, the catalogue—to which Jeake and his son continued to add throughout his life—provides a vivid record of its former glories. A context for the library is provided by what we know of the lively intellectual milieu to which Jeake belonged, including John Allin, vicar of Rye from 1653 to 1662, who kept in touch with Jeake and his friends by profuse correspondence after moving to London; Richard Hartshorne (d. 1680), the local schoolmaster, whose daughter was to marry Jeake's son; and Philip Frith, a surgeon-apothecary, himself a book collector, whose holdings were bequeathed to the younger Jeake and added to the library following Frith's death in 1670.

For Jeake, the 1670s and 1680s were dominated by the mounting persecution of the nonconformists in Rye as elsewhere; as leader of the local conventicle, he was an obvious target. Though excommunicated in 1676, he played an active role in Rye politics during the exclusion crisis, reaching a climax with a defiant interview with Charles II on 7 September 1681; in it, Jeake invoked the law, and the king replied that 'if he were so much for Law, he should have it', ordering Jeake to be prosecuted and his meeting suppressed (Hunter and Gregory, 157). In the following year, with the court party on the ascendant in Rye, the threat of persecution was such that Jeake fled to London. His enforced leisure appears to have been devoted largely to the compilation of an elaborate treatise on the chronology of the world from the creation to the flood, which he left unfinished at his death.

Though encouraged by his son to return to Rye in 1686, Jeake did so only in 1687, thereafter reverting for the last three years of his life to his role as leader of the nonconformist congregation in the town. In August 1690 there was even a suggestion that he might once again become town clerk, with the younger Jeake acting as deputy: but earlier that summer Jeake had begun to suffer from a succession of ailments that within a few months were to prove fatal. On 31 August that year he preached his last sermon, and he died on 3 October, bequeathing all his possessions to his son.

MICHAEL HUNTER

Sources T. W. W. Smart, 'A biographical sketch of Samuel Jeake, senr., of Rye', *Sussex Archaeological Collections*, 13 (1861), 57–79 • T. W. W. Smart, 'A notice of the Rev. John Allin, vicar of Rye, AD 1653–1662; an ejected minister', *Sussex Archaeological Collections*, 31 (1881), 123–56 • M. Hunter and others, eds., *A radical's books: the library catalogue of Samuel Jeake of Rye, 1623–90* (1999) • M. Hunter and A. Gregory, eds., *An astrological diary of the 17th century: Samuel Jeake of Rye, 1652–99* (1988) • S. Jeake, *Logistekēlogia, or, Arithmetick surveighed and reviewed* (1696) • S. Jeake, *The charters of the Cinque Ports* (1728) • W. Holloway, *The history and antiquities of the ancient town and port of Rye* (1847), 550 ff. • A. Fletcher, *A county community in peace and war: Sussex, 1600–1660* (1975), chaps. 3, 6 • M. Allison, 'Puritanism in mid 17th-century Sussex: Samuel Jeake of Rye', *Sussex Archaeological Collections*, 125 (1987), 125–38

Archives East Sussex County RO, Lewes, corresp., letter-book, FRE 4223 • Rye Museum, East Sussex, Selmes and Jeake MSS

Wealth at death £540: Hunter and Gregory, eds., *Astrological diary*

Jeake, Samuel (1652–1699), merchant and astrologer, was born on 4 July 1652 at Rye, Sussex, the first son of Samuel *Jeake the elder (1623–1690), lawyer and nonconformist preacher, and his wife, Frances Hartridge (d. 1654), daughter of Thomas and Mary Hartridge. His siblings all died in infancy, and as an only son he lived alone with his father until his marriage in 1680. His father was a major figure in the religious life of Rye and took charge of his son's upbringing and education, instilling strong puritan principles in him. He learned grammar, logic, rhetoric, mathematics, and general knowledge; his schoolbooks, written in a neat script, are extant. His reading on religious and more miscellaneous topics—largely from books in his father's remarkable library—is documented in his diary.

In 1674 Jeake began to pursue a career in trade, encouraged by his father, who put up the capital which supported his initial ventures. By this time he had already begun to earn money by scrivening, an occupation he continued to ply, but during the mid-1670s he became increasingly involved in trade with France, importing cloth, and exporting fish and other local produce. This trade was abruptly halted by the trade embargo imposed by parliament in 1678, which caused severe problems for Jeake and other small businessmen. Instead, he turned to other activities, particularly moneylending, including the loan of money on ships, and negotiating bills of exchange. He also traded in hops from 1678 and wool from 1680 onwards, as well as reverting to trade in French cloth when it was safe to do so. The result of this diversification was to place his financial affairs on a sounder basis. His finances also benefited from his marriage in 1680 to Elizabeth, daughter of Barbara Hartshorne, widow of Richard Hartshorne, former schoolmaster of Rye, who brought with her a dowry of £1000.

Jeake's fortunes remained vulnerable, however. In the 1680s he had to contend with the pressures imposed by the persecution of nonconformists, which resulted in his father being exiled from Rye. In the 1690s there was a fresh outbreak of war with France. As a result, though he continued to trade in hops and other commodities in the Rye area, he increasingly shifted his commercial operations to London, attracted by the financial experimentation that characterized the metropolis in the 1690s. He speculated in stock in the East India Company and other, more novel ventures such as the Lustring Company, which was devoted to the manufacture of glossy black silk. He also invested in the Million Adventure (which guaranteed basic annuities and offered the chance to win supplementary ones); and, from 1694 onwards, he invested substantial sums of money in the Bank of England, in which his holdings reached a peak of £2500 in December 1697.

Jeake's career as a merchant was accompanied by a deep fascination with astrology, an interest he shared with his father, though the younger man pursued it with a single-mindedness not paralleled in the older. Already in 1668 Jeake had sufficient astrological skill to draw up an elaborate analysis of his birth chart, and his astrological activity flowered in the 1670s, when, in addition to further such analyses, he compiled two treatises on the principles of astrology. In 1670 he also prepared a collection juxtaposing biographical data about friends and relatives with their natal charts, evidently in an attempt to generalize about planetary influences, while from 1670 to 1677 he compiled an elaborate weather diary—both of them typical of the activities of astrological reformers of the day.

From the 1680s Jeake embarked on a much more unusual venture, an attempt to test and improve the rules of astrology by close attention to his own life. Between 1687 and 1692 he composed a work entitled 'Astrological experiments exemplified', which correlated data about his affairs during a single year, 1687–8, and their astrological circumstances, attempting to derive 'Theoremes' from this. His *Diary*, which he wrote up in its final form in 1694, on the basis of memoranda that he had begun to keep in 1666, represents a further stage in his astrological studies, intended partly to settle the controversy among astrologers as to what was the best method of calculating the 'measure of time' (by which allowance was made for a person's age in interpreting the directions in their natal chart), and partly to investigate the 'astrall causes' of events in his life. The diary shows a fascination with the astrological circumstances of 'accidents' which befell him, while he also appears to have hoped for an astrological explanation of the incidence of ague and other illnesses that afflicted him and which he recorded in detail. In the last few years of his life, using data collected in the diary, he began work on a surpassingly detailed analysis of his natal chart, which was also intended to elucidate the issue of the measure of time.

With the exception of his diary (published in 1988), Jeake's writings were not published and therefore had no influence. However, they typify the impulse in his period to test and refine astrological principles through careful empirical investigation. They are also revealing of a genuine compatibility between astrology and Jeake's mercantile career, since it is clear that, apart from his disinterested concern with the reliability of astrological principles, he found astrology useful in helping him to make decisions about his commercial affairs. In addition his interest in the system of secondary causation offered by astrology reflected the changing nature of his religiosity, which became noticeably more comfortable and worldly as his life progressed, despite his strong puritan background.

It was, however, unfortunate for Jeake that the tide of educated opinion was turning against astrology, as he must have been brutally reminded by the response of the astronomer royal, John Flamsteed, to a query raised on Jeake's behalf by his neighbour, John Harris FRS, vicar of Winchelsea. Commenting on an error that 'your Ingenious sober and candid freind Mr Jeake' had made in his calculations, Flamsteed went on to 'take Occasion from his Mistake to shew him how he may Imploy his time much better then in the study of Astrology' (*Astrological Diary*, 50). Yet Jeake's astrological concern with his own life has preserved a vivid picture of his lifestyle and preoccupations through the various autobiographical documents he prepared. Though no portrait of him survives, his diary entry for his nineteenth birthday, 4 July 1671, even describes his appearance: 'My Face pale & lean, Forehead high; Eyes grey, Nose large, Teeth bad & distorted' (ibid., 117). In addition, the diary gives a telling and almost endearing picture of a conscientious, methodical, self-preoccupied figure, and of his intellectual style and milieu.

Jeake and his wife, Elizabeth, had six children, of whom four survived infancy. One of these, a third Samuel Jeake, jurat of Rye and projector, devised a system of shorthand published in *Philosophical Transactions* in 1748; of two of the others, Barbara and Francis, portraits survive at Brickwall, Northiam, where there is also a portrait of his wife. Jeake died, apparently of a stroke, at Rye, Sussex, on 22 November 1699 and was buried there the following day. His wife subsequently married Joseph Tucker, a gentleman from Buxted, Sussex, who had settled in Rye.

MICHAEL HUNTER

Sources *An astrological diary of the seventeenth century: Samuel Jeake of Rye, 1652–99*, ed. M. Hunter and A. Gregory (1988) · M. Hunter and others, eds., *A radical's books: the library catalogue of Samuel Jeake of Rye, 1623–90* (1999) · *In obitum vere deploratum Samuelis Jeake, Gent. (qui obiit 22 Novembris, 1699) Carmen Lugubre* (1700) [broadsheet] · Bank of England subscription book, general court minutes, and stock ledger, Bank of England, London, Bank of England archives · W. Holloway, *The history and antiquities of the ancient town and port of Rye* (1847), 550–79 · T. W. W. Smart, 'A biographical sketch of Samuel Jeake, senr., of Rye', *Sussex Archaeological Collections*, 13 (1861), 57–79 · S. Jeake, 'The elements of a *short hand*', *PTRS*, 45 (1748), 345–51 · Nichols, *Lit. anecdotes*, 9.700
Archives Bank of England Archive, London · E. Sussex RO, corresp. and papers · E. Sussex RO, ledger | Rye Museum, Sussex, Selmes MSS
Wealth at death over £2500: Bank of England, London, archives, bank stock ledger, 1, 145; 2, 637

Jean, Philippe (1755–1802), miniature painter, was born at St Ouen, Jersey, on 30 November 1755, the son of Nicolas Jean and his wife, Marie, *née* Grandin. He married, first, Anne Noel (d. 1787), with whom he had a son, the miniature painter Roger Jean, and second, Marie de Ste Croix, with whom he had three daughters. He served in the navy under Admiral Lord Rodney, during the cessation of naval hostilities he practised as a miniature painter, and finally he adopted that profession. He was a frequent exhibitor at the Royal Academy from 1787 to 1803 and was patronized by the duke of Gloucester, whose portrait he painted in miniature as well as those of the duchess and her children. He also painted full-length portraits of George III and of Queen Charlotte. Some of his miniatures were engraved.

Jean's painting style varied considerably as he appears to have emulated other contemporary miniaturists. This inconsistency did not interfere with his success as a miniaturist; one Royal Academy critic described him as an 'ingenious foreigner', dated 1788. Foskett noted that 'one of his finest miniatures' was that of the marine painter, Dominic Serres (NPG; Foskett, *Miniatures: Dictionary and Guide*, 576). Jean also painted a miniature of the landscape painter Paul Sandby (exh. 'British Portrait Miniatures', exhibition cat., Edinburgh International Festival, 1965). Three of his miniatures were exhibited at the Holburne Museum of Art, Bath (1999).

Jean lived for many years in Hanover Street, Hanover Square, London, but died at Hempstead, in Kent, on 12 September 1802.

L. H. CUST, *rev.* EMMA RUTHERFORD

Sources D. Foskett, *A dictionary of British miniature painters*, 2 vols. (1972) · B. S. Long, *British miniaturists* (1929) · C. H. Collins Baker, notes on artists, NPG, archive · Royal Academy catalogues (1787–1803) · T. L. Propert (Burlington Fine Arts Club exh. catalogue, 1889) · R. Bayne-Powell, ed., *Catalogue of portrait miniatures in the Fitzwilliam Museum, Cambridge* (1985) · G. Reynolds, *English portrait miniatures* (1952) · D. Foskett, *Collecting miniatures* (1979) · D. Foskett, *Miniatures: dictionary and guide* (1987) · *IGI* · A. Sumner and R. Walker, *Secret passion to noble fashion: the world of the portrait miniature* (1999) [exhibition catalogue, Holburne Museum of Art, Bath]
Likenesses Hoppner, portrait, 1795, priv. coll. · P. Jean, self-portrait, exh. Burlington Fine Arts Club 1889

Jeanes, Henry (1611–1662), Church of England clergyman, was born at Allansay, Somerset, the son of Christopher Jeanes of Kingston in the same county. He matriculated plebeian from New Inn Hall, Oxford, in 1626, and graduated BA in 1630 (incorporated at Cambridge in 1632). According to Wood he became 'a most noted and ready disputant' during his years as a student, and he proceeded MA from Oxford in 1633 (Wood, *Ath. Oxon.*, 3.590). He subsequently studied at Hart Hall and took holy orders, gaining a reputation as a learned preacher within the university.

On 5 August 1635 Jeanes was presented by Sir John Windham to the rectory of Beer Crocombe and Capland, Somerset. He was ordained priest on 20 September following and was later also appointed vicar of Kingston. According to Calamy, Jeanes underwent a complete retreat from a zealous high-church position, becoming a strenuous defender of presbyterianism, and perhaps this accounts for his flight from Somerset during the early part of the civil war. Taking refuge at Chichester he and his family, of whom no further details are known, were warmly received by the local citizens.

On 13 February 1647 Jeanes replaced the sequestered Walter Raleigh as rector of Chedzoy, Somerset, where he remained for the rest of his life. In the following year he was a signatory to the attestation of the Somerset ministers in support of their presbyterian brethren in the Westminster assembly in London. During the 1650s he is said to have prepared a number of young men for university, tutoring them privately in his home. Wood recounts that Jeanes:

> was a most excellent philosopher, a noted metaphysician, … well grounded in polemical divinity … also a scholastical man, a contemner of the world, generous, free-hearted, jolly, witty, and facetious … All which qualities do very rarely or seldom meet in men of the presbyterian persuasion. (Wood, *Ath. Oxon.*, 3.591)

Jeanes was the author of a number of treatises and was embroiled in a range of theological disputes. His 1653 work, *The Want of Church-Government No Warrant for a Totall Omission of the Lord's Supper*, argued against the practice of foregoing the Lord's supper altogether in the absence of church discipline, opposing what he saw as an alarming drift towards sectarianism. His arguments were disputed by the Independent Francis Fulwood, leading to an exchange of pamphlets between the two men. Jeanes was also involved in pamphlet disputes with the minister Henry Hammond concerning church festivals, signing with the cross, and paedobaptism, and with Jeremy Taylor on the subject of original sin.

In 1662 Jeanes was prosecuted at the assizes, most likely for refusing to read the Book of Common Prayer. However, he was not ejected from Chedzoy as he died at Wells in Somerset in August 1662, the month preceding the mass ejection of the interregnum clergy, and was buried in Wells Cathedral. John Owen reported a rumour that Jeanes conformed to the Restoration church prior to his death and died 'sadly and desperately', but the accuracy of the story is unknown.　　　　　　J. WILLIAM BLACK

Sources *Calamy rev.* · *DNB* · Wood, *Ath. Oxon.*, new edn, 3.590 · H. Jeanes, *A second part of the mixture scholastical divinity* (1656) [dedication] · Foster, *Alum. Oxon.* · Venn, *Alum. Cant.* · W. M. Lamont, *Godly rule: politics and religion, 1603–60* (1969), 147–9

Jeans, Sir James Hopwood (1877–1946), mathematician and astronomer, was born on 11 September 1877 at 29 Kew Road, Birkdale, Lancashire, the only son of William Tulloch Jeans, parliamentary journalist, and his wife, Martha Ann Hopwood. On his father's side there was a strong newspaper tradition: both his grandfather and his great-grandfather had owned newspapers. His mother came from a strongly evangelical family, and this made for a rather strict and unhappy childhood. However, he shared a liking for walking with his father, and the latter, who wrote two popular science books, encouraged his son's intellectual interests.

Jeans was numerate from an early age. He could tell the time at the age of three, and enjoyed memorizing strings of numbers. His greatest enthusiasm was reserved for clocks. From early on he took pleasure in drawing them and in working out how they operated. When he was three years old his family moved to Tulse Hill, London. From 1890 he attended the nearby Merchant Taylors' School. His mathematical abilities rapidly became evident, and he also developed his skill in playing the piano and the organ. In 1896 he went up to Trinity College, Cambridge, as a scholar to read mathematics. He and his fellow undergraduate, G. H. Hardy, were advised to take part one of the tripos in two years rather than the normal three. He thrived on the challenge, and in 1898 was bracketed second wrangler. His work for part two was interrupted by tuberculosis of the knees and wrists, which required him to spend considerable time in two sanatoriums. He was not finally cured until 1903. Despite this he was awarded a first class in part two in 1900, followed by an Isaac Newton studentship and a Smith's prize. In 1901 he was elected a fellow of his college, and in 1904 was appointed a university lecturer in mathematics.

During his stay in the sanatoriums Jeans extended the interest in molecular motions that he had demonstrated in his Smith's prize essay. He published the result in 1904 as the *Dynamical Theory of Gases*. This reigned for many years as a standard textbook on the topic, and was rewritten and republished in 1940 as *An Introduction to the Kinetic Theory of Gases*. Jeans's prime concern in his Smith's prize essay had been the equipartition of energy in a dynamical system of interacting bodies. From an examination of matter alone, he then went on to consider a system containing both matter and radiation. In 1905 he published a correction to a solution given by Lord Rayleigh for the

Sir James Hopwood Jeans (1877–1946), by Philip A. de Laszlo, 1924

wavelength distribution of black body radiation. The resulting Rayleigh–Jeans law indicated that at equilibrium almost all energy would radiate at short wavelengths. This was contradicted by Max Planck's empirically successful model, which posited energy quantization, violating the rules of classical thermodynamics. To save classical principles Jeans argued that the observed Planck distribution might be a steady state which slowly gave way to his predicted short wavelength pattern.

In the autumn of 1904 Jeans applied for the vacant chair of mathematics at the University of Aberdeen. He was not appointed but in the following summer, while attending a meeting of the British Association in Cape Town, he received the offer of a chair in applied mathematics from the president of Princeton University, Woodrow Wilson. He stayed at Princeton for only four years, but it proved to be a busy time of his life. In 1906 he was elected a fellow of the Royal Society at the early age of twenty-eight. In 1907 he married Charlotte Tiffany Mitchell, daughter of Alfred Mitchell, explorer, of New London, Connecticut, and related to the well-known Tiffany family of New York. During his stay in the United States he also published two successful textbooks: *Theoretical Mechanics* (1906) and *Mathematical Theory of Electricity and Magnetism* (1908).

Jeans returned to England in 1909 and in the following year was appointed Stokes lecturer in applied mathematics at Cambridge University. In 1912 he retired from this post in order to devote his entire time to research and writing. His wife was well-to-do (and, in due course, he obtained considerable income from his popular works). In 1914 he produced a *Report on Radiation and the Quantum Theory* for the Physical Society of London, which, unlike his 1905 work, denied that classical principles could even transiently allow the Planck distribution of black body radiation, thus underlining the radical contrast with the new quantum approach. However, astronomy was now becoming the main focus of his interest. In 1917 he gave the Bakerian lecture to the Royal Society on 'The configurations of rotating compressible masses', and in the same year was awarded the Adams prize of the University of Cambridge for an essay on 'Problems of cosmogony and stellar dynamics', published as a book in 1919. Both these texts dealt with the shapes taken up by rotating, gravitating bodies: a problem of fundamental importance that had already been tackled by some of the leading mathematicians, including Jeans's former colleague at Cambridge, Sir George Darwin. As the title of his Adams prize essay indicates, Jeans had long been interested in stellar motions, as well as rotations. Here his concern with the microscopic and macroscopic came together, as the theory developed for molecules in a gas was applied to collections of stars.

In June 1917 Jeans started a long dispute on stellar structure with the professor of astronomy at Cambridge, Arthur Eddington. Jeans attacked Eddington's model of internal radiative equilibrium and, on the basis of the high degree of ionization within stars, queried the link between star mass and luminosity. In early 1918 at the Royal Astronomical Society, the forum for their increasingly tetchy debates, Jeans countered Eddington's pulsation model for cepheid variable stars with a theory of periodic explosions. The arguments between the two on this and other matters went on for some years, and became sufficiently famous that some joined the Royal Astronomical Society primarily in order to listen to their debates. During the early 1920s Jeans judged gravitational condensation the only energy source in stars; then after Eddington's 1924 account of radioactive annihilation, Jeans conceded that this might also be an energy source and applied it to idiosyncratic accounts of liquid stellar cores. He summarized this research in *Astronomy and Cosmogony* (1928), his swansong in original investigations.

In 1919 Jeans was awarded a royal medal of the Royal Society and elected an honorary secretary of the society. His major achievement during his period of office was to enhance the prestige of the *Proceedings of the Royal Society A* (which published research in the physical sciences). Prior to his time most of the important papers in physics had appeared elsewhere: from now on, the *Proceedings* became an important source of new research information. The decade of the 1920s brought him a range of other honours. In 1922 he was awarded the gold medal of the Royal Astronomical Society. He subsequently became president (1925–7), presenting it in 1926 with £1000 for an annual lecture—called the George Darwin lecture—to be given by an overseas scientist. He won the Hopkins prize of the Cambridge Philosophical Society for 1921–4; the citation

mentioned his work on the theory of gases, on radiation, and on the evolution of stellar systems. He gave the Halley lecture at Oxford in 1922, the Guthrie lecture of the Physical Society of London in 1923, and the Rouse Ball lecture at Cambridge in 1925. He was knighted in 1928 for his services to science, including those to the Royal Society (where he ceased to be secretary in the following year).

In 1928 Jeans's *Astronomy and Cosmogony* came to the attention of S. C. Roberts, the secretary of Cambridge University Press, who appreciated the general interest of its subject matter and the attraction of Jeans's writing style. He persuaded Jeans to write a popular account, *The Universe around Us*, which was published by the press in 1929. One stimulus for Jeans had been the success of Eddington's attempt at this kind of writing in the previous year. The success of his own publication led to a series of popular books during the remainder of his life; these took precedence over original research. His popularity as a writer depended partly on his topic—new, thought provoking views of the universe—and partly on his style, which combined an authoritative knowledge of the subject with a vivid turn of phrase. In 1930 he gave the Rede lecture at Cambridge. An expanded version was published simultaneously as *The Mysterious Universe*. His conclusion has often been quoted: 'the Great Architect of the Universe now begins to appear as a pure mathematician'. One result of these books was that he came to be in great demand as a lecturer and broadcaster.

Ever since his days at Princeton Jeans had maintained close contacts with colleagues in the United States, especially with G. E. Hale, the founder of the Mount Wilson observatory in California. In 1923 he was accorded the rare honour of being appointed a research associate of the observatory, which encouraged further visits to the USA. In 1931 he was awarded the Franklin medal of the Franklin Institute in Philadelphia. He also became a foreign member of the National Academy of Sciences in Washington. In the 1930s Jeans also visited India, taking over the presidency of the jubilee meeting of the Indian Science Congress when Lord Rutherford died. He was awarded the Mukerjee medal in 1937 followed by the Calcutta medal in 1938.

At home Jeans received a succession of new honours. In 1934 he became president of the British Association for its meeting in Aberdeen, taking over unexpectedly when the president-elect, Sir William Hardy, died suddenly. In the following year the Royal Institution decided to establish a professorship of astronomy. Jeans, who had given the institution's Christmas lectures in 1933, was invited to fill the post. He held it until shortly before his death. Jeans was vice-president of the Royal Society in 1938–40, and in 1941 was made an honorary fellow of his old college at Cambridge. The Merchant Taylors' Company admitted him to its honorary freedom, and he was the recipient of honorary degrees from many universities: Aberdeen, Benares, Calcutta, Dublin, Johns Hopkins, Manchester, Oxford, and St Andrews. He received the ultimate accolade of the Order of Merit in 1939.

Music remained one of Jeans's great interests throughout his life. When he moved to Cleveland Lodge, Dorking, in 1918, he installed an organ and often played on it for hours at a time. His wife died in 1934 after an extended illness. The following year he met Susanne (Susi) [see Jeans, Susanne (1911–1993)], daughter of Oskar and Jekaterina Hock of Vienna. She was already, at the age of twenty-four, an internationally recognized organist. The two were married in Vienna on 30 September 1935 after a week's engagement. Jeans installed a second organ at Cleveland Lodge for his wife's use. The two separate organ rooms were well insulated for sound, so that Jeans and his wife could practise whenever they wished without disturbing each other. Jeans became a director of the Royal Academy of Music in 1937, and the following year, at his wife's instigation, published a semi-popular book, *Science and Music*.

In terms of personality Jeans tended to hold himself aloof, and could be both supercilious and sarcastic. However, those who knew him best believed a significant factor in this was his innate shyness. This may also have been reflected in his extreme unwillingness to play the organ in front of others. At the same time he was hard-working and businesslike with excellent lecturing abilities. Both during his lifetime and since it has been felt that, though an outstanding mathematician, he sometimes lacked a physical feel for the situations he was trying to describe mathematically. In this respect he has been seen as less successful than his contemporary, Eddington. To some extent, this is unfair: not only has some of Jeans's work had an important impact on astronomy, but, in addition, Eddington—as Jeans thought—was not always right. Nevertheless, more recent re-evaluation of Jeans's contributions has tended still to emphasize the value of the mathematical formulation, rather than the physical insight.

During the First World War Jeans lived at various addresses in Sussex and Surrey. In the Second World War, Cleveland Lodge, his Surrey home, was requisitioned by the military, so the family moved to Somerset. Jeans had a heart problem in 1917, but seemed to have fully recovered in the inter-war years. Illness struck again in Somerset, and early in 1945 he experienced a coronary thrombosis. Again he seemed to make a good recovery, but a second attack followed in the autumn. On 16 September 1946, not long after his post-war return to Cleveland Lodge, Jeans died. He was buried in the churchyard at nearby Mickleham, Surrey. He was survived by his second wife, one daughter from his first marriage, and two sons and one daughter from his second marriage.   A. J. MEADOWS

Sources E. A. Milne, *Sir James Jeans* (1952) · E. A. Milne, *Monthly Notices of the Royal Astronomical Society*, 107 (1947), 46–53 · E. A. Milne, *Obits. FRS*, 5 (1945–8), 573–89 · election certificate, RS · b. cert.
Archives RS, corresp. and papers | BL, corresp. of him and his wife with Marie Stopes, Add. MS 58543 · California Institute of Technology, Pasadena, archives; corresp. with George Hale · Nuffield Oxf., corresp. with Lord Cherwell · Ransom HRC, letters to Sir Owen Richardson
Likenesses W. Stoneman, photograph, 1922, NPG · P. A. de Laszlo, photograph, 1924, RS [see illus.] · H. Coster, photographs, 1930–39, NPG · P. A. de Laszlo, portrait, priv. coll. · photograph, RAS · three photographs, RS
Wealth at death £256,054 9s. 1d.: probate, 11 Dec 1946, *CGPLA Eng. & Wales*

Jeans, Ronald (1887–1973), playwright, was born on 10 May 1887 at 26 Shrewsbury Road, Oxton, Birkenhead, the younger son of Sir Alexander Grigor Jeans (1849–1924), founder and managing editor of the *Liverpool Post and Mercury*, and his wife, Ellen Gallon (d. 1889). Educated at the Loretto School, Jeans for a time studied art at the Slade School of Fine Art before entering a stockbroker's office in Liverpool. During his stockbroking years Jeans, early smitten by the stage, also wrote dramatic criticism for his father's newspaper. He met Alec Rea, another theatrical enthusiast, and the pair began campaigning for an experimental repertory season in Liverpool. Basil Dean, then involved with a similar venture in Manchester, approached them with what Jeans later called 'a cut and dried plan for putting the season into practice' (R. Jeans, undated appreciation of A. Rea, Theatre Museum, London).

Thus was born in 1910 the Liverpool Repertory Theatre (LRT), dedicated to classic and contemporary works unlikely to be on offer in the West End or on tour. Jeans saw to it that his father's newspaper covered the experimental season, and the LRT in Williamson Square was launched in 1911. Threatened with closure in 1914 by the outbreak of war, it survived until 1916 as a 'commonwealth' owned by the company and the staff. It was only the second such venture in Great Britain and far outlasted the first. Rea was its director for six years, Dean its original producer, and Jeans soon its outstanding author.

Jeans's career as playwright lasted almost fifty years. Between the 1930s and 1955 he was one of the West End's most reliable sources of undemanding, expertly crafted social comedy. But aside from his role as innovator in the repertory movement, his greatest significance was as an early master of writing for intimate revue, arguably Britain's major contribution to twentieth-century theatre. He had written several witty romantic comedies for the Liverpool Repertory before his first revue, *Hullo, Repertory!*, during the spring season of 1915. The revue had a short London season and, after several more revues for LRT, Jeans was hired by the West End impresario André Charlot to write the second edition of *Tabs* (1918). By the time Charlot's *Buzz Buzz* opened after the armistice, Jeans had established himself at the head of the second generation of revue sketch-writers. *Buzz Buzz*, with 613 performances, became the longest-running British intimate revue. On 6 June 1917 Jeans married Margaret Evelyn Wise; they had a son and daughter and remained married until Jeans's death.

The qualities that Jeans, as an admirer of literary drama, brought to revue differed markedly from those of the previous master, Harry Grattan. As a performer Grattan was on the bill of the first royal variety performance (1912). His speciality was 'turns' featuring direct and chatty communication with an audience, combined with a keen sense of the absurd. Jeans was a sharp observer of modern manners, an expert chronicler of what he later called 'the state of mind of the public of today … A revue should give the audience at any time during the run the feeling that it was written last night' (Review of *Streamline*, 31 Aug 1934, file of R. Jeans, Theatre Museum). His sketches (at least eight in any production), usually gently ironic, managed the standard elements of plot and characterization, a beginning, middle, end and sometimes a moral—all in five to seven minutes, frequently capped by a startling, appropriate 'twist'. He brought the same qualities to his occasional lyric-writing.

Jeans also adapted two French plays for Charlot. His was the 'safe pair of hands' helping Noël Coward's first revue effort for Charlot (*London Calling*, 1923). Jeans and Dion Titheradge shared credit for *Charlot's London Revue*, the 1924 compilation which overjoyed New York and eventually changed the course of American musical revue. During this period Jeans moved from London to Brighton, his home until his death. From 1926 he was more often employed by Jack Hulbert, a graduate of Charlot revues, and by Charles B. Cochran, Charlot's chief rival. Although he never completely abandoned revue, Jeans had already moved away in 1930 with *Lean Harvest*, a basically serious study of marriage, and *Can the Leopard …?* (1931). The latter, a star vehicle for Gertrude Lawrence, who had performed many Jeans sketches for Charlot, is typical of Jeans's full-length dramatic work. Staged at the Theatre Royal, Haymarket (nearly all Jeans's plays opened at major West End houses), it unfolded in three acts the problems encountered by an orderly husband (Ian Hunter) and his untidy but lovable wife, concluding that the husband was wrong to attempt to change her. One reviewer noted 'Since [Noel Coward's] *Private Lives* [1930] it seems the ambition of every dramatist to show how he can turn out an entertaining play about nothing' (undated review, c.1931, R. Jeans, Theatre Museum). With perhaps unintended irony, considering Jeans's sketch-writing, it was also noted that: 'films now make us expect to have in 5 minutes what the stage takes three-quarters of an hour to show' (ibid.).

In 1938 Jeans, a solid member of London's theatrical establishment, joined Michael Macowan and the playwright J. B. Priestley in converting the Westminster Theatre into the London Mask Company. Its manifesto insisted that:

> there should be in London a permanent theatre with a policy, character and company of its own, where intelligent playgoers can always be sure of finding a first-class play at very much lower prices than is charged by the West End theatre. (Marshall, 211)

Jeans had high hopes for the nurturing of new writing talent, but the Mask was disbanded during the Second World War. Still, its first season included Shakespeare and Eugene O'Neill, while Priestley's *Music at Night* (1939) was the first play produced in London after the outbreak of war. During the war Jeans ran his own cinema for the entertainment of armed forces personnel. Jeans re-formed the Mask Theatre briefly in 1947.

After the war Jeans's career as craftsman of three-act light comedies resumed. *The Young Wives' Tale* at the Savoy Theatre (1949) was another tale of apparent marital incompatibility wrapped in a contemporary 'situation'— the housing shortage. It was created for two major film stars, Naunton Wayne and Joan Greenwood. Within twenty-four hours of its opening the producer reported full booking three months ahead. Jeans was following precepts set forth in his own prescriptive *Writing for the Theatre* (1949). He insisted that it was better to have a trivial subject competently constructed and carried out than to have a genuinely inspired dramatic notion undramatically and crudely realized. In addition to *Writing for the Theatre*, he was responsible for nine booklets of revue sketches and two volumes of chat and reminiscence.

Jeans continued to turn out charming, superficially topical comedies. *Grace and Favour* (1954) was a somewhat fresher examination of a Kensington dowager's insistence upon managing all aspects of the lives of those who depend upon her, finally being outmanoeuvred by two young lovebirds, one a rogue and the other an ingenious ingénue. The arrival of a new generation of writers less interested in well-made plays than in truth-telling (generally assumed to have begun with John Osborne's *Look Back in Anger*, 1956, quickly followed by Harold Pinter and Arnold Wesker) hastened Jeans's oblivion, though his plays remained viable for a certain playgoer and continued to be produced through 1958. Jeans repaired to Brighton and died at 14 Eaton Gardens, Hove, on 16 May 1973.

JAMES ROSS MOORE

Sources H. R. Shaw, unpublished profile, 5 Aug 1959, Liverpool Daily Post and Echo Library · J. R. Moore, 'An intimate understanding: British musical revue, 1890–1920', PhD diss., University of Warwick, 2000 · *Liverpool Daily Post* (17 May 1973) · *The Times* (17 May 1973) · *Daily Telegraph* (17 May 1973) · N. Marshall, *The other theatre* (1947) · G. W. Goldie, *The Liverpool Repertory Theatre, 1914–1934* (1935) · S. Mander and R. Mitchenson, *The theatres of London* (1975) · *CGPLA Eng. & Wales* (1973) · file of R. Jeans, Theatre Museum, London, and V&A NAL · d. cert.

Archives Theatre Museum, London · V&A NAL | BL, lord chamberlain's collection · BL, corresp. with League of Dramatists, Add. MS 63397

Wealth at death £84,131: probate, 27 June 1973, *CGPLA Eng. & Wales*

Jeans [*née* Hock], **Susanne** [Susi], **Lady Jeans** (1911–1993), organist and musicologist, was born on 25 January 1911 in Vienna, the eldest of the four children of Oskar Hock, the director of a paper mill in Bohemia, and his wife, Jekaterina, who came from a military family. She entered the Vienna Music Academy in 1925, studying the piano and theory with the composer Franz Schmidt, and in 1927 began to play the organ, taking lessons with Franz Schütz. Her interest in baroque organs began in 1929, when she heard the 1710 Silbermann organ in Freiburg Cathedral in Saxony, and was overwhelmed by the beauty of the sound and the clarity of the articulation. After gaining her diploma from the academy in 1931, she gave her first important organ recital in the Grosser Musikvereinssaal in Vienna in December 1931, giving the first performance of Franz Schmidt's prelude and fugue in G, before moving to

Leipzig in 1932 to study at the Kirchenmusikalisches Institut with Karl Straube, cantor of the Thomaskirche. In 1933 Charles-Marie Widor, professor of organ at the Paris Conservatoire, invited her to study with him.

Hock made her first recital tour of England in 1934, returning in 1935, when she was a soloist at the Handel festival in Cambridge, playing German baroque music on the organ of St John's College. After an invitation in July 1935 to play at a party at Cleveland Lodge, Westhumble, near Dorking, the home of the mathematician and astronomer Sir James Hopwood *Jeans (1877–1946), whose first wife had died in 1934, she married Jeans on 30 September 1935; they had two sons and one daughter. Sir James Jeans was a very good organist himself, possessing a large three-manual Romantic organ of 1924, and after their marriage he added a new organ room and installed a 1936 Eule organ for Susi, the first neo-baroque organ in England: the two organ rooms were soundproofed so that they could play without disturbing each other. She built up a collection of keyboard instruments, including an English chamber organ of 1796, a two-manual and pedal harpsichord (for a long time the only one in England), and a working model of a seventeenth-century water organ.

During the Second World War Cleveland Lodge was requisitioned and the family moved to Somerset; then in 1946 Susi Jeans's husband died. After this she resumed her solo career. While her authentic performances and broadcasts of English organ music of the seventeenth and eighteenth centuries were an important influence on organ building and playing in England, she did not confine herself to early music, and at the inauguration of the Royal Festival Hall organ in 1954 she played Max Reger's 'Was Gott tut, das ist wohlgetan'. She also introduced English audiences to works by twentieth-century Austrian composers, including Franz Schmidt, Walter Pach, and Augustinus Kropfreiter. She had first performed in the United States in 1937, and she continued to make concert tours of North America, Australia, and Europe, also giving masterclasses and seminars; in 1967 she was organist in residence at the University of Colorado. She was elected an honorary fellow of the Royal College of Organists in 1966.

Jeans's short piece 'In praise of tremulants' (*MT*, 1950) was the first of many articles she contributed to English and German scholarly journals, mainly concerning seventeenth- and eighteenth-century keyboard music and its performance and ornamentation; her topics ranged from the pedal clavichord to seventeenth-century musicians mentioned in the Sackville papers, seventeenth-century water-blown organs, the Easter psalms of Christ's Hospital, and the painted organ case in Gloucester Cathedral. Her editions of keyboard music include the complete keyboard works of the Exeter organist John Lugge (*c*.1587–*c*.1647), on which she collaborated with John Steele, published in 1990; *Voluntary for Organ in C* by Benjamin Rogers (1613/14–1698), published in 1962; and *Four Inventions* by H. N. Gerber (1702–1775), published in 1974. In 1972 she lectured at Cornell University on Sir Isaac Newton's studies in music theory. She became increasingly worried about the state of the few old organs remaining in English churches and historic houses, and in 1969 founded the Organ Preservation Society, which saved many organs which would otherwise have been destroyed or altered; the organs were then repaired without altering the pipework or the action, in order to preserve their tone and voicing.

In 1954 Susi Jeans started the Mickleham and Westhumble festival, renamed the Boxhill festival in 1966: this took place in the music room at Cleveland Lodge every year until 1992, concentrating on works by neglected composers of the Renaissance and baroque periods and on newly discovered pieces by better-known composers. In 1978 she founded the annual Cleveland Lodge summer school for English organ music, which she directed. Before she died, she offered Cleveland Lodge to the Royal School of Church Music, although she had never been a church organist herself, and in 1996 the organization moved there. Her pupils included many who became leading organists, including Peter Hurford, David Lumsden, and George Guest.

Despite living in England for nearly sixty years, Susi Jeans never lost her strong Austrian accent. Tall and elegant (she had trained as a fashion model in Austria), she loved skiing and mountaineering, and climbed the Matterhorn twice. She died at Cleveland Lodge on 7 January 1993. Her funeral service was held at Mickleham parish church on 16 January. In 1993 the Lady Susi Jeans Centre for Organ Historiography was founded at the University of Reading.   ANNE PIMLOTT BAKER

Sources R. Judd, ed., *Aspects of keyboard music: essays in honour of Susi Jeans* (1992) · G. Oldham, 'Susi Jeans: a seventieth birthday tribute', *MT*, 122 (1981), 47–9 · 'Lady Jeans at 70: a conversation with Gillian Weir', *Organists' Review*, 67/2 (1982), 9–14 · E. A. Milne, *Sir James Jeans* (1952) · *The Times* (23 Jan 1993) · *The Organ*, 72 (spring 1993), 54 · *New Grove*, 2nd edn · d. cert. · *WW* · *The Times* (11 Jan 1993)
Archives BL, music manuscripts and papers, MSS Mus. 88–96 · U. Reading, Lady Susi Jeans Centre for Organ Historiography
Likenesses J. D. Sharp, photograph, repro. in *The Times* · portrait, repro. in Judd, ed., *Aspects of keyboard music*, frontispiece

Jearsey, William (*d.* 1690), merchant and East India Company servant, was the younger son of John Jearsey (*d.* 1653), brewer of Cheshunt, Hertfordshire, and his wife, Mary (*d.* 1661).

Little is known about Jearsey's early career. In 1650 he served on board a privately owned ship on a voyage from the Indian port of Masulipatam to Pegu in Burma. That there is no mention of him in the East India Company's records suggests that Jearsey was not a company servant at his departure, but probably worked his way out to Asia. Furthermore he is not mentioned in his father's will (15 October 1652), indicating a possible break between father and son.

Between 1653 and 1655 Jearsey served the East India Company at Siriam in Burma and was probably head of the English factory there. When the directors decided to close the factory and recall its personnel, he refused to leave. He delayed his departure until 1657, apparently using the company's money in his private trading ventures. His conduct led to conflicts with the directors in

London as well as with the council at Fort St George. He was dismissed and lived for some time as a free merchant in Madras. About 1658 Jearsey married Catherine (*d*. 1688), a Dutchwoman about whom further details are unknown aside from her abilities as a merchant in her own right.

In 1662 Jearsey was reconciled with the East India Company and was appointed chief of the factory in Masulipatam, at that time the second most important English settlement on the Coromandel coast after Madras. Devoting himself to his work, Jearsey became a prominent merchant in Masulipatam and a leading figure in the promotion of English private trade in Asia. His mercantile adventures were extensive and directed towards markets in the Bay of Bengal and Persia. Hitherto, historians have claimed that Jearsey obtained his investment capital from embezzling the company's funds, but he had an additional source of income. Between 1662 and 1669 he played an important part in establishing the Anglo-Indian diamond trade. As the leading English commissioner in India, he administered substantial amounts of money and bought diamonds on behalf of merchants in the City of London, charging a 7 per cent commission. In the late 1660s he appears to have run into financial difficulties, prompting him to cheat the London merchants by using their money in his private trade before purchasing diamonds and taking 12 per cent in commission instead of the normal 7 per cent (letter-book of John Chomley, 31 January 1668). Owing to their ensuing mistrust, the diamond merchants stopped using him as commissioner in 1669. The same year he was dismissed from the company's service and charged with embezzlement. Both were fatal blows to his private situation and substantially reduced his private trading activities. On the arrival of his successor Richard Mohun in July 1670, Jearsey refused to hand over the factory's account books. In November, suspecting that Jearsey was attempting to conceal his embezzlement, Mohun warned him to produce the accounts immediately or have his estate seized in order to meet the company's claims. When he did not comply, some of his ships were seized and goods confiscated. In March 1671 he left Masulipatam and began his journey towards Madras, 'with his Colours flying, Drum, Trumpets, Pipes and Horns sounding' as if he still had the esteem of the company. Although he lived in Madras as a free merchant for the following twenty years and was regarded as a man of substance, he never recovered his leading position among the English private merchants. In spite of ongoing requests from London, Jearsey never furnished the accounts from Masulipatam; instead, he sued the company for having illegally seized his property. This case lasted several years and ended in October 1685, when the council at Madras, unable to prove his embezzlement, offered him a compensation of 3000 pagodas.

During his life in India William Jearsey acquired a mixed reputation. He was a skilful merchant, but also insubordinate with a fiery temperament, capable of any action in order to protect his position. Upon his being appointed chief of the factory in Masulipatam in 1662, the directors praised his honesty and abilities, but the diamond merchant John Chomley claimed 'by Mr. Jearsey's own friends' to have learned that 'he will promise you faire but perform little' (letter-book of John Chomley, 27 Dec 1665). During Sir Edward Winter's usurpation of the government in Madras in 1665, Jearsey actively supported the rightfully appointed agent George Foxcroft. His actions impressed the directors and probably contributed to Jearsey's being allowed to remain in India after his dismissal. His wife, Catherine, died in September 1688 and was buried in St Mary's churchyard in Madras. Jearsey died a little over two years later, in December 1690, and was buried beside her. The couple had no children and there is no record of a will. He left no fortune although he lived more than forty years in India.   SØREN MENTZ

Sources L. M. Anstey, 'Some Anglo-Indian worthies of the seventeenth century: William Jearsey', *Indian Antiquary*, 34 (1905), 164–76 · S. Mentz, 'English private trade on the Coromandel coast: diamonds and country trade', *Indian Economic and Social History Review*, 33 (1996), 155–73 · letter-book of John Chomley, N. Yorks. CRO, 2 CG · H. D. Love, *Vestiges of old Madras, 1640–1800*, 4 vols. (1913), vol. 1 · will, proved, Jan 1661 [M. Jearsey] · will, proved, 19 May 1653 [J. Jearsey]

Jeavons, Thomas (*bap.* **1795**, *d.* **1867**), engraver, was baptized on 10 February 1795 at St Martin's, Birmingham, a younger son of Benjamin Jeavons and his wife, Ann. He worked with William Radclyffe and gained experience in landscape engraving, at which he later excelled. His earliest plates of note were the thirteen engraved after J. P. Neale for the first series of his *Views of the Seats of Noblemen* (1818–24). Most if not all of his later work was engraved on steel, and he did six plates for William Brockedon's *Illustrations of the Passes of the Alps* (2 vols., 1827–9) and nine for T. Rose's *Westmorland, Durham and Northumberland* and *Cumberland* (1832). He engraved regularly for T. Roscoe's *Landscape Annual* from 1830 and L. Ritchie's *Heath's Picturesque Annual* from 1832, after W. H. Bartlett, Thomas Allom, and others. He also engraved four plates after J. M. W. Turner for *Friendship's Offering* (1830) and *Turner's Annual Tour* (1833–5). About 1834 he began working for the publishers G. Virtue, with engravings for three of W. Beattie's books, and H. Fisher. His only contribution to the *Art Journal* was *Dutch Boats in a Calm*, after E. W. Cooke (1849), from the Vernon Gallery. From about 1845 onwards he engraved more than forty prints of Brighton for W. Grant, a newsagent, of 5 Castle Square, after local artists. His plates were signed 'T. Jeavons', 'Thos Jeavons', or just 'Jeavons'. During the 1860s he retired to Welshpool, Montgomeryshire, where he died on 26 November 1867 after a short illness. His estate was valued at under £300 when declared by the executor, his widow, Mary.   B. HUNNISETT

Sources *Art Journal*, 27 (1865), 31, 62 · *Art Journal*, 30 (1868), 9 · Redgrave, *Artists* · *Exhibition catalogue*, Royal Birmingham Society of Artists (1877), 7, 28 · IGI · St Catherine's index, 1867 · *CGPLA Eng. & Wales* (1867)
Wealth at death under £300: administration, 11 Dec 1867, *CGPLA Eng. & Wales*

Jebb, Ann (1735–1812). *See under* Jebb, John (1736–1786).

Jebb [*née* Noble], **Cynthia**, Lady Gladwyn (1898–1990), political hostess and diarist, was born on 20 November 1898 at The Grove, Jesmond Dene, Newcastle upon Tyne, the younger daughter and youngest of the four children of Sir Saxton William Armstrong Noble, third baronet (1863–1942) of Ardmore and Ardardan, civil engineer and businessman, and his wife, Celia Brunel, *née* James (1871–1962), daughter of Arthur James, schoolmaster, of Eton College. A weak baby, thought likely to die, she was baptized immediately. Her paternal grandfather was Sir Andrew *Noble, first baronet, chairman of the powerful armament and shipbuilding firm Armstrong Whitworth, based in Newcastle. Her mother's maternal grandfather was Isambard Kingdom *Brunel, the celebrated engineer. An aura of opulence and energy pervaded the houses in which she spent her early youth, fostered by her high-minded mother. Her father (who succeeded to the baronetcy on the death of his elder brother in 1937) represented Armstrongs in London, and the family resided at Kent House, Knightsbridge (decorated with murals by the Spanish artist Sert), and at Wretham Hall, near Thetford (designed for them by Reginald Blomfield). In 1912 she was sent to Northlands, a small girls' school at Englefield Green, Surrey, where she received an informal education based on literature and music; this was supplemented by stimulating conversation at home and fortified by her excellent memory.

Cynthia Noble came out into society in the aftermath of the First World War, in which her brother Marc had been killed. She continued to live with her parents, galvanizing them in keeping up their round of entertainment, but also developed her own circle of friends, including Walter Turner, the Australian musicologist. On 22 January 1929 she married (Hubert Miles) Gladwyn *Jebb (1900–1996), a rising diplomat in the foreign service. They had a son, Miles (*b*. 1930), and two daughters, Vanessa (*b*. 1931) and Stella (*b*. 1933). In 1932 she accompanied her husband to Rome, where he had been posted as a secretary in the British embassy. In 1935 they returned to London, where over the next fifteen years he was appointed to a succession of increasingly important posts in the Foreign Office, being knighted in 1949. Cynthia Jebb had no regrets about not being sent abroad during this difficult period. Together with her husband she coped with the challenges of the Second World War from an attic flat in Mount Street, stimulated by a diversity of interesting and influential people who passed through Mayfair in those years, including many émigrés from occupied Europe. After the war, although most of their friends were upper-class people who deeply resented the penal taxes, the Jebbs traversed the political divide without incongruity through their contact with prominent politicians of the left.

In 1950 Gladwyn Jebb was posted to New York as the British representative on the Security Council of the United Nations, where he achieved popular fame during the Korean crisis, being lionized by New York society. Cynthia Jebb was able to exploit this wave of Anglophilia with her sharp social sense and charm of manner. These talents were perfectly suited for the six years of her husband's

Cynthia Jebb, Lady Gladwyn (1898–1990), by unknown photographer

ambassadorship to France (1954–60). She entered with zest into the Parisian beau monde, and was able to establish herself as one of the leading hostesses. She revelled in the quick and clever conversation of the French, and was herself authoritative on many subjects in French art and history. She ran the ambassadorial residence with a meticulous attention to detail, and closely supervised the arrangements for several royal and prime-ministerial visits at a time when the British embassy was of great political importance in Paris, especially during the Suez crisis and the collapse of the Fourth Republic. On their departure from Paris President de Gaulle gave a magnificent dinner in their honour.

In 1960 Gladwyn Jebb retired from the foreign service and was granted a peerage, as Baron Gladwyn. Cynthia Gladwyn selected a mansion flat in Whitehall Court as their London residence. From there she continued an active social life, supportive of her husband's position on the front bench of the Liberal Party in the House of Lords. At Bramfield Hall, their house in Suffolk, she annually gave a large lunch party during the Aldeburgh festival. In 1976 her book *The Paris Embassy* was published by Collins. Her elegant text and impressive research into the historic mansion and its ambassadorial incumbents received critical acclaim. In 1996, six years after her death, *The Diaries of Cynthia Gladwyn*, edited by her son, was published by Constable. The diaries covered the period 1946–69, and provided a remarkable feminine insight into the social and diplomatic world of the post-war era, displaying a strong visual sense. She was engagingly frank about the people she encountered, with pronounced likes and dislikes, her vignettes of politicians such as Eden, Butler, and Macmillan being particularly acute.

Throughout their long marriage Cynthia Gladwyn greatly helped her husband, and was adept at smoothing feathers ruffled by his brusqueness towards fools and bores. She was a prominent example of those British diplomatic wives who, before the days of female diplomats, provided, albeit in a minor way, a feminine participation in overseas representation. Her approach was entirely personal and intuitive, and part of her skill was to avoid entering into political discussions, but rather to set the scene for discussions by others, and the mood for confidences and revelations. She was remembered for her sparkle and vivacity, and her sense of intimate enjoyment and affectionate friendship. She was neat and petite; her hair turned grey when young, but she wisely never dyed it. Her conversation was composed of a delicate blend of intelligence and mischief, and she exuded charm and gaiety, her laughter enchanting and her speech of bell-like clarity. But her innate shrewdness, as revealed in her diaries, was often masked by a desire to please her interlocutor. She always made the most of things, and the most trivial matters were often transformed into sources of interest and fun. From her youth she always wanted to shine, and this she continued to do until her last years, her skin unwrinkled and looking half her age, a stunning effect achieved by a rigorous maintenance of personal standards. She was highly competitive and supremely self-confident. She died at Bramfield Hall, Halesworth, on 21 September 1990, of stomach cancer, and her ashes were placed in the Brunel tomb in Kensal Green cemetery. She was survived by her husband and their three children. MILES JEBB

Eglantyne Jebb (1876–1928), by unknown photographer

Sources C. Gladwyn, *The Paris embassy* (1976) · *The diaries of Cynthia Gladwyn*, ed. M. Jebb (1996) · *Daily Telegraph* (22 Sept 1990) · Burke, *Peerage* · personal knowledge (2004) · b. cert. · d. cert. · A. Noble, *Noble of Ardmore and Ardkinglas* (1971)

Likenesses photograph, NPG [*see illus.*] · portraits, repro. in *Diaries*, ed. Jebb, jacket and pp. 288–9

Jebb, Dorothy Frances. *See* Buxton, Dorothy Frances (1881–1963).

Jebb, Eglantyne (1876–1928), philanthropist, was born on 25 August 1876 at The Lyth, Ellesmere, Shropshire. She was the third daughter and fourth child in a close-knit family of seven born to Arthur Trevor Jebb (1839–1894), of Ellesmere, a country landowner, and his wife, Eglantyne Louisa Jebb (1845–1925), a distant cousin of her husband and a sister of Sir Richard Claverhouse Jebb. Both parents felt a strong social conscience. Educated at home, Eglantyne enjoyed a happy childhood and her parents were fond. She went up to Lady Margaret Hall, Oxford, in 1895, 'slim and tall, with delicate features, brilliant colouring, copper-red hair' (D. G. and R. M. W., 31). She arrived with (in her own words) a mania for books and little desire for friends or creature comforts, making an impact on contemporaries with her spartan carpetless

room, and left in 1898 after taking second-class honours in modern history. It was probably Charlotte Toynbee's influence which encouraged her to spend a year in London at Stockwell Training College for Elementary Teachers. Then in 1899 she went to St Peter's church school, Marlborough, for more than a year, but poor health forced her to leave. Her repeated illnesses stemmed from thyroid deficiency, but as a young woman she seems also to have seriously lacked self-confidence and any clear sense of direction. She returned to live with her mother, who had settled in Cambridge after her husband's death in 1894.

Eglantyne loved riding or walking alone in the Cambridgeshire countryside, and seized opportunities for staying in remote places to write. 'Personal relations never came to her as a matter of course' (D. G. and R. M. W., 33). After another set-back in 1902, when her affection for a man was not reciprocated, she took lessons in economics from Mary Paley Marshall in 1903 and became active in social work. Serving as honorary secretary of the local branch of the Charity Organization Society (COS) until 1908, she compiled her *Cambridge: a Brief Study in Social Questions* (1906) with help from her many local contacts. It was practical manual and reflective treatise all in one. Continuously analytic, lucid, compassionate, and often self-reproaching, the book includes maps, statistics, and ample information which aimed to find the quickest route to 'the New Cambridge', and it breathes throughout an acute sense of personal responsibility for social problems. Though it propagated the COS programme in seeking cures rather than palliatives, it resembled Florence, Lady Bell's study of Middlesbrough (1907) in making an imaginative effort to situate the alleged defects of the poor within the discouraging context of their lives. Nor did it shrink from criticizing the rich. It reflects the author's anxious belief in a mutual responsibility central to the concept of citizenship, together with her family's Shropshire-based cultivation of close relations between rich and poor.

It is, in short, an impressive book, yet for Eglantyne herself it brought no immediate dividend: until 1914 she busied herself with poetry, wrote a novel (*The Ring Fence*) which remained unpublished because it was too long, accompanied her ailing mother to European health resorts, engaged in personal charity, and, with her sister Lill [see Wilkins, Louisa], worked for the Agricultural Organization Society to encourage smallholdings. Ever conscious of social duty and of the need to bridge the class divide, she was oppressed by a sense of personal failure—a casualty, we would now say, of the meagre career opportunities open to the cultivated Edwardian woman. By this time her brother-in-law Charles Roden Buxton had become a strong influence, supplanting with Liberalism her inherited Conservative allegiance. It was his influence that in 1913 after the Second Balkan War led her to embark on relief work among peasants in Macedonia, and on her return she energetically promoted the Macedonian relief fund. In the First World War she helped her youngest sister, Dorothy *Buxton, to edit weekly 'Notes from the foreign press' in the *Cambridge Magazine*, hoping thereby to moderate the wartime polarization between two 'sides'. The millions of children in Europe who starved at the end of the war were indisputably, in COS terminology, 'deserving cases'; Eglantyne and Dorothy launched the Fight the Famine Council, parent in 1919 of the Save the Children Fund, in an almost apolitical humanitarian impulse which painstakingly transcended national and political loyalties.

Hitherto Eglantyne's career had been moulded by the claims and enthusiasms of friends and relatives: now she had a cause of her own, the fund. It claimed the rest of her life, and she drove it forward from temporary expedient to permanent campaign with her powerful combination of personal energy, flair for publicity, astute political and diplomatic skill, and personal approaches to prominent people. With her, as with others, an early training in the COS tended to inculcate principles which later bore unexpected fruit—in this case drawing together religious inspiration and systematic social science, but for an international rather than a domestic purpose. Seeking as she did to raise charity to a higher power, the word 'supranational' was often on Jebb's lips. It was she who in 1923 worked out the text of the 'Children's charter', with its high social and economic aspirations for child welfare. Successfully resisting statist variants of the charter (she opposed family allowances, for instance), she stressed the overriding need to educate the parent, the volunteer, and

the teacher in humane values. The League of Nations unanimously adopted it on 26 September 1924 as the declaration of Geneva, whence much of her later work was done. A year later she was made an assessor to the league's advisory council for the protection of children. She published a booklet of poems on children's sufferings, *The Real Enemy*, interspersed with explanatory footnotes, in 1928. Yet the children she had remembered when making her last will in the previous year were all Jebbs: her nieces and her god-daughter, together with her sister Louie and her brother Richard. Throughout her life, her family was the formative influence upon her. In 1928 she fell ill and on 17 December she died at 22 chemin des Cottages, Geneva, Switzerland; on 20 December she was buried in St George's cemetery, Geneva.

Eglantyne's sister Dorothy collected her poems into a booklet in 1929: *Post tenebras lux*. Eglantyne's essay *Save the Child!* (1929), written just before her health broke down and never revised by her, was also published posthumously, and testifies to the reflectiveness and intelligence that informed her ideals. Dorothy's long-held intention of writing Eglantyne's biography was never acted upon. Nor is it clear that those who immediately identified Eglantyne as a saint, her health undermined by self-sacrifice, did her subsequent reputation much service. With Eglantyne Jebb, as with Josephine Butler, there was a complex interaction—impossible now precisely to recapture—between fluctuations in personal health, unhappiness in personal life, belief in woman's distinctive moral power, an almost obsessive preoccupation with the need to rectify injustice, and a religious commitment harnessed to what later seemed largely secular causes. To identify both women as saints is to risk sentimentalizing them and to downplay the deep reflectiveness and intelligence inspiring their humanitarian concern and shining out from parts of Jebb's *Save the Child!* 'If we obey self-interest on Monday we shall forget altruism on Tuesday', she declared, deploring 'the fatal duality in our creed' between the principle of service governing private relations and 'the belief that self-interest should govern our public relations'. Her almost Hobsonian argument about the domestic moral and social impact of events overseas deserved fuller scope, but like other humanitarian pioneers she experienced all the tension between three reforming strategies: responding to the urgent claims of suffering, constructively harnessing indignation at injustice, and engaging in the hard thought about means and ends that can alone render indignation effective.

BRIAN HARRISON

Sources R. Symonds, 'Eglantyne Jebb and the world's children (1876–1928)', *Far above rubies: the women uncommemorated by the Church of England* (1993), 69–91 • F. M. Wilson, *Rebel daughter of a country house: the life of Eglantyne Jebb, founder of the Save the Children Fund* (1967) • D. G. and R. M. W., 'Eglantyne Jebb (1876–1928)', *Brown Book* (1929), 31–5 • *DNB* • *CGPLA Eng. & Wales* (1929)
Archives Save the Children, London, corresp. and papers relating to Save the Children Fund
Likenesses photographs, Save the Children Archives, London [see illus.]

Wealth at death £10,323 16s. 2d.: probate, 12 April 1929, *CGPLA Eng. & Wales*

Jebb, (Hubert Miles) Gladwyn, first Baron Gladwyn (1900–1996), diplomatist, was born in Firbeck, near Rotherham, Yorkshire, on 25 April 1900, the only son and the oldest of three children of Sydney Jebb (1871–1950), of Firbeck Hall, and later of the Manor House, Haslemere, Surrey, landowner, and his first wife, Rose Eleanor (c.1879–1962), third daughter of Major-General Hugh Chichester, of the Royal Artillery. His father was an unusual man; Sir Richard Claverhouse Jebb, a cousin from another branch of the family, was a famous Greek scholar, but Sydney had been forced by his father to go into the army. When serving in India he inherited the family's Yorkshire property, and he then resigned his commission, came home, married, and devoted himself to a study of the classics in the intervals of country pursuits. He was a brilliant shot. After settling in Yorkshire he interested himself in politics and stood unsuccessfully as Conservative candidate for the Holmfirth division of the West Riding in 1905. His failure to win the seat was a great blow to his morale and his marriage broke up two years later, though he and his wife were not divorced until 1933. Jebb and his sisters were then brought up by their mother in London, with holidays in Devon.

(Hubert Miles) Gladwyn Jebb, first Baron Gladwyn (1900–1996), by Dorothy Wilding, 1951

Education and early career Jebb was educated at Sandroyd preparatory school, followed by Eton College (1913–18) and Magdalen College, Oxford (1919–22). Evidently he was slow to acquire self-confidence both intellectually and socially, but he much enjoyed his last year at Eton and specially benefited from being tutored by Aldous Huxley, who first opened his eyes to the pleasures of the mind. His short service as a cadet in the army in 1918 with the household brigade officers' battalion also helped him to grow up. He fell on his feet at Magdalen, stimulated by some interesting and agreeable contemporaries as well as by some outstanding tutors, including Francis Fortescue 'Sligger' Urquhart and Lewis Namier. His university career was crowned by the achievement of first-class honours in history in 1922. For a time he was tempted to follow an academic career, but when he tried and failed to win a fellowship of All Souls he decided to take the diplomatic service examination. To his chagrin his French proved not quite good enough and he was ploughed on the first attempt. On the second try a year later he passed in top. Jebb then made what he himself described as a shaky start as a young third secretary in the legation at Tehran from October 1924 under the formidable Sir Percy Loraine, who seems to have taken against him from the outset, regarding Jebb as insufficiently deferential and also unwilling to take trouble over the humdrum tasks that fell to him. His situation was improved by the arrival of a new counsellor (his immediate superior) in the person of Harold Nicolson, and he eventually finished his tour in reasonably good standing, having just managed to avoid getting into some serious scrapes. When he arrived back in London in May 1927 he was, however, still uncertain whether or not to stay on in the service or to try his luck in a different career.

Jebb developed rapidly during his next period of service in the Foreign Office. At first as a bachelor he moved in Bloomsbury circles, partly through his friendship with Harold Nicolson, and he adopted a mildly left-wing political attitude. Then, on 22 January 1929, he married Cynthia Noble [see Jebb, Cynthia (1898–1990)], younger daughter and the youngest of the four children of Sir Saxton William Armstrong Noble, third baronet (1863–1942), of Ardmore and Ardardan Noble, and his wife, Celia Brunel, née James (d. 1962). Cynthia—a great-granddaughter of Isambard Kingdom *Brunel—was known in social circles as a 'pocket Venus', and Jebb began to entertain and to be entertained. He then proved a great success as private secretary to the (Labour) parliamentary under-secretary, Hugh Dalton, who was responsible for the handling of parliamentary business, including the editing of replies to Foreign Office parliamentary questions. It was largely as a result of Jebb's deft management of this tricky assignment that he was rewarded with a posting to Rome in November 1931. There he had his first taste of the potential threat to British interests represented by an Italy where Mussolini was beginning to pursue dangerously irresponsible policies, including a military adventure in Ethiopia. Jebb was disturbed at the apparently undecided drift of British and French policy at a time when Mussolini was moving into even closer relations with Germany.

On Jebb's return to the Foreign Office in November 1935 he was sufficiently well placed to take a vigorous part in the discussion within the department between 1935 and 1939 about the policy which might best defend British interests in the face of the increasingly aggressive moves of Nazi Germany and fascist Italy. His standing in the office, especially when he became private secretary first to Sir Robert Vansittart and then to Sir Alexander Cadogan, from December 1937 to August 1940, was evidently growing fast, and although still only a junior first secretary he was the author of several well-argued papers that contributed to the formulation of policy. His view in 1937 was that Italy should be in effect bought off and thus kept on Britain's side, instead of being allowed to slide into the arms of the Germans, but writing in 1972 he admitted that this proposal—like many other intelligent ideas suggested by anguished Foreign Office officials in those desperate years before the Second World War—was not politically feasible at the time. This was the period when from the best of motives Chamberlain was leading a virtually unarmed Britain to the brink of disaster. Jebb shared with his Foreign Office colleagues the sense of humiliation and frustration that was then suffered by most of those who knew anything about foreign affairs and understood the feeble state of British armed forces.

The Second World War and reconstruction It was as private secretary to Sir Alexander Cadogan (and not, it seems, an adequately self-effacing one) that Jebb witnessed the early days of General de Gaulle's activities in London as leader of the Free French after the fall of France in 1940. Acting as Cadogan's representative he had the exacting task of persuading the general to accept some last-minute amendments to the text of a BBC broadcast to France on 26 June 1940. He subsequently had many other opportunities to meet the general, whom he greatly admired, but he also recognized the damage that de Gaulle did to those who attempted to help him. Shortly after this he was invited by Hugh Dalton, newly appointed minister of economic warfare in Churchill's coalition government, to be the chief executive of the Special Operations Executive (SOE), which was charged with the task of stimulating and supporting the Resistance in occupied territories. In the first two years of SOE's existence Jebb won golden opinions from Dalton and he proved to be a robust and fearless champion of SOE in the murkier corridors of Whitehall, where both the Foreign Office and the Secret Intelligence Service (SIS) were often obstructive to the new organization. After Dalton's transfer to another department, Jebb was superseded, to his annoyance, by Sir Charles Hambro in May 1942, but clearly Jebb would not have been on the same wavelength as Dalton's successor, Lord Selborne, who was generally regarded as somewhat slow witted.

From this dark world of intrigue and subversion Jebb was then translated to an entirely new sphere, and one which he came to regard as being in accordance with his own natural propensity. At first as head of the economic and reconstruction department of the Foreign Office, and later in all the interconnected tasks of preparing for the post-war world, Jebb was one of the most influential of the handful of British ministers and officials who helped to shape the immediate future. His boldness in denouncing the ill-thought-out ramblings of some of his superiors had sometimes to be curbed for the sake of good manners within the Whitehall community; but in general his own fertility of ideas—combined with common sense and by now considerable intellectual self-assurance—enabled him to identify most of the feasible ideas and to throw out the bad ones. As the great power of the United States began to make itself felt, he was increasingly brought into consultation by the leading US politicians and officials, and he was closely involved in the post-war planning that took place in 1944 and 1945. He was present at all the great allied conferences—Tehran, Yalta, Potsdam—and he played a key role in the discussions at Dumbarton Oaks that preceded the approval of the United Nations charter at San Francisco in 1945. He was the natural choice as executive secretary of the preparatory commission of the United Nations, from August 1945, and as acting secretary-general of the United Nations when the first assembly met at Church House in London in February 1946, pending the appointment of the first United Nations secretary-general in the person of the Norwegian foreign minister, Trygve Lie. Jebb was still only a counsellor in his own service, but on resuming duty in the Foreign Office in March 1946 he was very soon promoted to be assistant under-secretary of state (deputy under-secretary from February 1949) and he became one of the most trusted lieutenants of the foreign secretary, Ernest Bevin. For the next four years he was to be at Bevin's elbow, helping him to negotiate the alliance of western Europe and the United States embodied in NATO and buttressed by the Marshall plan. It was this that constituted the alternative settlement of the post-war world following the collapse in 1947 of the attempt to include the Soviet Union in a co-operative world system. It was probably the time when Jebb was able to contribute most to the formulation of British foreign policy. He was made CB in 1947 and KCMG in 1949 (having been appointed CMG in 1942).

The United Nations and the Paris embassy In June 1950 Jebb was appointed to succeed Cadogan as British representative at the United Nations in New York. In some ways he found it hard to abandon a central role in policy making and to accept the otherwise enticing prospect of being promoted to grade one of the service while still barely fifty. At the time of his appointment it was not at all clear how important or prominent a role he would play. As things turned out he had to hasten his departure for New York because of the outbreak of the Korean War. He then, and to his surprise, achieved considerable and even somewhat embarrassing publicity in the United States, where television had just become available on a national scale. The attack of North Korea on South Korea in June 1950 was the first occasion on which the newly established United Nations was confronted by the challenge of an act of aggression. The Security Council then acted as the aegis for the armed resistance led by the United States and supported by what was then called the 'free world'. Fortunately the Soviet Union had absented themselves from the Security Council as a protest against the presence of nationalist China, and could not therefore exercise their veto when the key resolution was passed. Realizing their mistake they instructed their representative, Yakub

Malik, to return to the council and to attempt in every possible way to obstruct UN actions. Jebb thus found himself, as the articulate representative of the United States' main ally, cast in the role of a champion taking up Malik's challenge. His calm demeanour and icy sarcasm when dealing with Malik's interventions were very much to the taste of his American television viewers. Although genuinely surprised at his sudden leap into star status, Jebb admitted in his memoirs that he was gratified by his success and especially pleased by the generous praise then given to him by Bevin and by his senior colleagues in the Foreign Office. Indeed he wrote that 'I have never had a year that I enjoyed more than 1950' (Jebb, 248).

In 1953 the foreign secretary, Anthony Eden, offered Jebb the Paris embassy on the retirement of Sir Oliver Harvey. Jebb would have preferred to be permanent under-secretary, for which he thought he was better suited by talents and inclination, but Eden thought otherwise, and his view was shared by many of Jebb's friends and colleagues who considered him to be far from ideal as permanent under-secretary while admirably suited to the role of British ambassador to France, in which he would be supported by his wife, Cynthia, an exceptionally brilliant hostess. Jebb and his wife arrived in Paris in April 1954 for a tour of duty that was to last over six years. When he arrived the Fourth Republic was wrestling with the problems of Indo-China, Tunisia, and, above all, Algeria. Then there was the French failure to ratify the European Defence Community and Eden's successful initiative in creating the Western European Union; the Suez crisis in 1956; the queen's state visit to Paris in 1957; the near-revolutionary events of 1958 over Algeria that inaugurated the Fifth Republic and de Gaulle's return; the general's brilliant state visit to London in the spring of 1960; and finally the failed U2 summit of that year in Paris. Jebb left France on his retirement in October 1960. While in Paris he had loyally and effectively carried out the government's policies vis-à-vis the French with some success. On Suez he was not consulted, perhaps because he would have advised strongly against the secret collusion with the French and Israelis to attack Egypt. He did his best to support Macmillan's 'summitry', albeit with some misgivings, and he was not too downcast at its failure in 1960. With de Gaulle he succeeded in establishing a singular personal rapport, though as he himself admitted this counted for nothing in influencing the general's policy. He came to believe that in order to affect de Gaulle's actions it was necessary to face him with the firmest opposition. In his view the general was pursuing a European policy that was directly threatening British interests (as became manifest in 1963 after Jebb had left France, when the French government vetoed the first British application to join the EC). Nevertheless the general gave Jebb and his wife a magnificent send-off, which Jebb found very moving. His admiration of de Gaulle as a man and as a statesman seems to have been mutual; on two occasions after Jebb's retirement de Gaulle took the initiative in arranging a talk, although well aware of Jebb's opposition to the policy he was then pursuing.

Personality and final years Jebb was a tall, well-built man of commanding presence, rather redoubtable on first encounter. Many people found his manner somewhat arrogant or even contemptuous. At meetings he sometimes caused unwitting offence by derisively laughing at views which he regarded as foolish. He had little small talk but was a lively and convivial host and guest, especially in small parties among old friends. To his intimates he was known to be a warm friend and a loyal colleague. In later years he became very fond of life in the country at his house in Suffolk, where he much enjoyed gardening and also cooking. Until very late in life he was an outstandingly good shot and an expert angler.

Jebb was made GCMG in 1954 and GCVO in 1957, and, after his retirement from the diplomatic service in 1960, he became a hereditary peer as the first Baron Gladwyn. He became an active participant in public discussion of foreign policy issues in the House of Lords, at Chatham House, and in a number of other forums in Europe, such as the Western European Union assembly in Paris, and also in the United States. He was an early advocate of Britain's joining the EEC and he played a leading part in its affairs. After the British general election and change of government in 1964 he decided to join the Liberal Party. He was for a time deputy leader of the party in the House of Lords, and was Liberal spokesman on foreign affairs in the Lords for over twenty years. He also became closely associated with Roy Jenkins, Lord Jenkins of Hillhead, in the Campaign for Europe. During this first decade of his retirement he was prolific in speeches, articles, letters to the newspapers, and in books on various aspects of European affairs, and he exercised considerable influence on UK foreign policy. He never hesitated to express a view, not only on Europe but, for example, as a fierce opponent of the 'star wars' concept. He was for a time chairman of the Atlantic Treaty Association and a governor of the Atlantic Institute. He was also a nominated member of the European parliament from 1973 to 1975, and he won a considerable reputation in that body. His main publications were: *Is Tension Necessary?* (1959), *Peaceful Coexistence* (1962), *The European Idea* (1966), *Halfway to 1984* (1967), *De Gaulle's Europe* (1969), *Europe after de Gaulle* (1970), and *The Memoirs of Lord Gladwyn* (1972). The last Gladwyn book was his wife's, *The Paris Embassy* (1976), a sparkling account of the famous house in the Faubourg St Honoré and its incumbents. Gladwyn was very pleased with its success.

Gladwyn remained active both physically and mentally until an advanced age, continuing to contribute to foreign affairs debates and writing articles or letters to the newspapers. He mellowed somewhat as time went on and faced the last years of his long life with fortitude; he never became querulous or a burden on others. He and his wife had a son, Miles Alvery Gladwyn (b. 1930), and two daughters, Vanessa Mary (b. 1931) and Stella Candida (b. 1933), who were married respectively to Hugh Thomas (later Lord Thomas of Swynnerton), a historian, and Baron Joël de Rosnay, a scientist. He was proud that both sons-in-law came to achieve intellectual distinction. When his wife died in 1990 he was sad but philosophical; she had been an important support during his life. After his wife's death he was grateful for the kindness and consideration of his son, especially in his last years. He also found great pleasure in the company of his grandchildren and great-grandchildren. Gladwyn regarded himself in his heyday as an ideas man, as indeed he was. Some of his ideas were in advance of their time, but he could take satisfaction from the fact that many of them were to be accepted later in whole or in part as being the best way forward for Britain. Perhaps Bevin's alleged comment on him is still the most appropriate: 'Whatever you may say about Gladwyn, he ain't never dull' (Jebb, 228). He was justly described in *The Times* as 'the outstanding diplomat of his generation' (*The Times*). He died as a result of a stroke at his home, Bramfield House, Halesworth, Suffolk, on 24 October 1996. A memorial service was held at St Margaret's, Westminster, at which the address was given by Lord Jenkins of Hillhead. His banner, as a knight grand cross of the Order of St Michael and St George, hangs in St Andrew's Church at Bramfield, Halesworth, in Suffolk, where he was buried. He was survived by his two daughters and his son, who inherited the peerage.   ALAN CAMPBELL

Sources H. M. G. Jebb [Lord Gladwyn], *The memoirs of Lord Gladwyn* (1972) · *WWW* [forthcoming] · private information (2004) [family] · personal knowledge (2004) · *The diaries of Sir Alexander Cadogan*, ed. D. Dilks (1971) · *The Second World War diary of Hugh Dalton, 1940–1945*, ed. B. Pimlott (1986) · *The Times* (25 Oct 1996) · *The Independent* (26 Oct 1996) · *Daily Telegraph* (25 Oct 1996) · *FO List* · Burke, *Peerage*
Archives Bodl. Oxf., transcript of interview concerning early days of UN · CAC Cam., corresp., diaries, notebooks, and papers | BLPES, corresp. with Hugh Dalton · Nuffield Oxf., corresp. with Lord Cherwell | SOUND Bodl. Oxf., MS Eng c 4647 [transcript of 1983 interview]
Likenesses group portrait, photograph, 1944 (with European Advisory Commission), Hult. Arch. · D. Wilding, photograph, 1951, NPG [see illus.] · V. Thomas, oils (in his eighties), priv. coll. · photograph, repro. in *The Times* · photograph, repro. in *The Independent* · photograph, repro. in *Daily Telegraph*
Wealth at death £656,118: probate, 13 Feb 1997, CGPLA Eng. & Wales

Jebb, John (1736–1786), religious and political reformer, was born on 16 February 1736 at Southampton Street, Covent Garden, London, the eldest son of Dr John Jebb (*d.* 1787), dean of Cashell, Ireland, and Ann, daughter of Daniel Gansel of Donyland Hall, near Colchester in Essex. His father was an intimate friend of David Hartley, for whose work Jebb had a lifelong admiration. He was educated at schools in Drogheda, Carlow, and Dublin in Ireland, and at schools at Shrewsbury, Stand near Manchester, Leicester, and Chesterfield in England.

Education and early career Jebb began his university studies at Trinity College, Dublin, where he was admitted a pensioner on 7 July 1753, but he soon moved to Peterhouse, Cambridge, and was admitted a pensioner there on 9 November 1754. His academic abilities were evident in his being placed as second wrangler when he graduated as a bachelor in January 1757 and, after taking his MA in 1760, he was awarded a fellowship at Peterhouse. Like most fellows he was ordained (deacon 1762, priest 1763) and clerical preferment soon followed with the bestowal of the

John Jebb (1736–1786), by Charles Knight, pubd 1782

vicarage of Gamlingay, Bedfordshire, which he soon resigned, and the rectory of Ovington, Norfolk, in 1764. He later served as curate of St Andrew's Church, Cambridge; vicar of Flixton, Suffolk; rector of the joint parishes of Cross and Homersfield; and chaplain to Robert, earl of Harborough.

The financial independence that such livings brought Jebb probably helps to explain his marriage on 29 December 1764 to Ann Torkington [*see below*], a step which meant the resignation of his fellowship. However, he maintained his connection with the university by acting as a private tutor; his expertise in the mathematical sciences, which dominated the curriculum, is evident in the publication in 1765 of the *Excerpta quaedam e Newtoni principiis philosophiae naturalis, cum notis variorum*. This work, whose co-authors were Jebb, the Revd Robert Thorpe of Peterhouse, and the Revd George Wollaston of Sidney Sussex, provided a lucid exposition of those sections of Newton's *Principia* which dealt with the system of the world, and was popular in late eighteenth-century Cambridge as a textbook.

Questioning the Trinity Together with his work as a tutor in the mathematical sciences Jebb gave lectures on the Greek New Testament from 1768. In doing so he had the support of Edmund Law, master of Jebb's college, Peterhouse, from 1756 to 1768 (the year in which he became bishop of Carlisle) and, like Jebb, a thoroughgoing whig in both his religious and political opinions. Among those who graduated from Peterhouse during Law's mastership were such colleagues of Jebb in the cause of political and religious reform as Henry Cavendish, Sir James Lowther, George Tierney, and Capel Lofft. It was the aim of Edmund Law 'to recover the simplicity of the gospel from beneath that load of unauthorized additions, which … [had been] heaped upon it' (M. L. Clarke, *Paley: Evidences for the Man*, 1974, 14)—a goal shared by Jebb in his lectures and theological writings more generally. Within the university, however, Jebb's lectures were regarded with disfavour as promoting Socinianism and, from 1770, some colleges forbade their undergraduates attending. Indeed, he himself acknowledged that in his lectures he 'maintained steadily the proper unity of God; and that he alone should be the object of religious worship' (*Works*, 1.106). But, as he urged in his pamphlet *A Short Account of Theological Lectures* (1770), such a 'right of private judgment' was his entitlement as one 'born to the enjoyment of civil and religious liberty' (ibid., 1.5). These lectures on the New Testament confirmed a reputation for radicalism which had already been established in 1769 when Jebb had refused to endorse an address from the university supporting the prime-ministership of the duke of Grafton, the chancellor of Cambridge, then under attack from John Wilkes and his fellow political reformers.

Jebb's questioning of the traditional doctrine of the Trinity, which had made his lectures contentious, helps to explain why it was that from 1771 he devoted himself to promoting the abolition of clerical subscription. It was a cause, he maintained in a series of letters to the *Whitehall Evening Post*, that represented the natural extension of the principles of religious liberty embodied in the Reformation. The object of this movement was to abolish the requirement that clergy of the established church should subscribe to the Thirty-Nine Articles, the credal statement of the Church of England; instead it was proposed that they should simply declare a belief in the scriptures. At the initiative of Jebb and two other Cambridge liberal divines, Francis Blackburne and Theophilus Lindsey, a petition was drawn up following a meeting at the Feathers tavern, the Strand, London. The document, with 250 signatures, was presented to parliament, where a motion in its support was defeated on 6 February 1772 by 217 votes to 71. The proposal met with the energetic opposition of Edmund Burke, who argued that the articles should 'remain fixed and permanent like our civil constitution' in order to 'preserve the body ecclesiastical from tyranny and despotism' (W. Cobbett, ed., *The Parliamentary History of England*, 36 vols., 1806–20, 17.255).

Nothing daunted, Jebb continued to maintain publicly that the Thirty-Nine Articles were 'exquisitely nonsensical, and the authority of imposing them … destitute of all rational foundation' (*Works*, 3.72). Such views he advanced in an open letter to Bishop John Green of Lincoln, in which he also vented his anger on Green as one who was 'inflated with pride, and with insolence insupportable' since, in Jebb's view, he had compromised his own beliefs in political and religious liberty in order to retain high ecclesiastical office. The bishops more generally Jebb castigated as being 'the firm and steady supporters of civil and religious despotism' (ibid., 3.75).

Although defeated in his attempt to persuade parliament to abolish subscription, Jebb had some limited success in this same cause within his own university. As part of his anti-subscription drive he published four letters in 1771 urging undergraduates to ponder the implications of the articles before subscribing to them as they were required to do before graduating. Such publications formed part of the background to the successful passage through the university senate on 23 June 1772 of a motion abolishing the requirement that those graduating should subscribe to the articles. Instead a graduate was simply required to declare that he was '*bona fide* a member of the Church of England as by law established' (Winstanley, 313).

University reformer Emboldened by such a success Jebb attempted to institute a reform of the university's curriculum with the establishment of annual examinations. Such was the practice at Trinity College, Dublin (which also dispensed with the subscription requirement), where Jebb had first begun his university studies. Within Cambridge such annual examinations had been established at St John's but by proposing to hand such functions to the university Jebb was seen as challenging the power of the colleges. Although the proposal had sufficient support to establish a syndicate of the senate to examine it, the attempt to institute annual examinations was fairly narrowly defeated by 14 to 9 on 21 October 1773. Never one to accept defeat, Jebb then attempted to propose less sweeping reforms which would ensure that undergraduates drawn from the privileged ranks of the nobility and fellow-commoners were required to undergo examination and that all other students be examined in their second year. But on 19 April 1774 these measures were also defeated, as was an attempt at a further compromise on 28 October 1774. Before leaving the university in September 1776 he made a last attempt in February 1776 to revive his plans for an annual examination but, predictably, the result was another clear defeat. By this time he had so many enemies in Cambridge that his advocacy of a measure was likely to ensure its downfall. As one undergraduate wrote on 25 February 1776:

> Mr Jebb is to propose his graces for the public examination tomorrow for the last time, but I believe without any hope of success, for he is so obnoxious a person himself that every plan or proposal, however good in itself, provided it comes from him, is sure to be rejected. (Winstanley, 329)

Quite apart from the antagonism that Jebb had stirred up in his attempt to reform the deeply conservative university, his standing within Cambridge had been gravely undermined. For in September 1775 he had taken the momentous step of resigning his livings since he could no longer accept the doctrines of the established church. As he made clear in his public letter on the subject, his chief objection was the doctrine of the Trinity which, he wrote, 'is equally contrary to sound reason and the holy scriptures' (*Works*, 2.206). He also regarded the requirement to subscribe to the articles as an unwarranted intrusion on protestant liberty, contending that 'the Bible only, ought to be considered as an all-sufficient directory to the preacher' (ibid., 2.214). Although he was invited by Lindsey to join him in establishing a Unitarian chapel, Jebb turned to the study of medicine. He attended anatomical lectures before he left Cambridge and in March 1777 received a doctorate of physic from St Andrews. After having been admitted as a licentiate of the Royal College of Physicians on 25 June 1777, he built up a successful London practice based at Craven Street, though his radicalism denied him a post at a London hospital. He also contributed to the medical literature with a pamphlet on paralysis of the lower extremities (1782).

Political reformer Residence in the capital brought with it the opportunity to become more closely involved in the cause of political reform, which was stimulated by the American War of Independence. This was a natural progression from Jebb's earlier preoccupation with ecclesiastical reform for it was his belief 'that religious and civil liberty go hand in hand' (Works, 3.158). He sympathized with the cause of the American colonists and, as early as 21 November 1774, wrote to a friend to rejoice 'that the americans continue to proceed with so much bravery and prudence', adding that 'Locke had shewn me who are the real rebels, in a contest of this kind' (ibid., 1.85–6). Such was the depth of his opposition to Britain's prosecution of the war that he was one of the organizers of a meeting of the city of Westminster called to express the need for 'the correction of the gross abuses in the expenditure of public money' (ibid., 1.146). This same meeting, at Jebb's urging, moved that Charles James Fox should act as their MP as one who was 'the steady opponent of an administration aiming at rendering the king despotic' (ibid., 1.154). However, Jebb was later to be disillusioned with Fox when he formed a coalition with Lord North in 1782.

To widen the movement for political reform Jebb actively assisted Major John Cartwright in establishing in 1780 the Society for Promoting Constitutional Information, the aim being, as Jebb put it, 'to diffuse, among the commonalty of this island, the knowledge of those political rights and privileges, which are immediately connected with the enjoyment of civil liberty' (Works, 3.362). As he indicated in a letter to his fellow reformer Christopher Wyvill, these included 'Equal representation, sessional [annual] parliaments, and the universal right of [male] suffrage'. Characteristically he regarded Wyvill's attempts to obtain less sweeping reforms by reducing the number of government posts as much too timid, and admonished him in 1781 that 'the spirit of accommodation will ruin all' (ibid., 1.167). Wyvill and Jebb also differed on the latter's view that extra-parliamentary conventions should have the right to suspend the powers of parliament if it refused to enact the reforms for which the society stood. Invoking this principle, he had advised the freeholders of Middlesex in 1779 that 'if such combined assemblies should in solemn council, declare, that the present House of Commons was dissolved, such declaration would be truly constitutional' (ibid., 2.479).

The extent of Jebb's radicalism was also evident in his support for the volunteer cause in Ireland, where he had family connections. On 19 November 1784 he wrote in defence of the need to organize along military lines since 'Recent events shew the necessity of an exertion of the inquisitorial power of the people' (Works, 1.206). Consistent with his abhorrence of religious tests he also attacked the penal laws against Roman Catholics in Ireland, arguing that 'confining the enjoyment of civil privileges, within the pale of a particular communion, is equally intolerant and unwise' (ibid., 2.543). Along with his attempts to institute constitutional change Jebb was closely involved in moves to overhaul other aspects of the unreformed social order. Thus he took a close interest in the reform of the criminal law and indeed was admitted to Lincoln's Inn on 9 November 1780, though he does not appear to have practised law. Closely connected with this was his publication in 1785 of a pamphlet urging the need for prison reform. In it he advocated such practical reforms as better light and ventilation to prevent disease along with the general principle that 'the restraint of liberty' be kept 'as mild as the circumstances will admit' (ibid., 2.564). In his writings he urged the view that 'Women are not dealt with justly by the laws of the land' (ibid., 2.180) and he was also an opponent of the slave trade.

Although increasingly immersed in the cause of political and social reform, Jebb remained convinced that the most basic need of all was the reform of the religious establishment—the cause which had first set him on the path of radicalism. '[T]he evils of government and the want of felicity in the governed', he wrote, '… arise from the want of a moral and religious principle, which the religion of the gospel, unvailed in its native excellence can alone afford' (Works, 1.189). To achieve such ends Jebb was one of the founders of the Society for Promoting the Knowledge of the Scriptures which was established on 29 September 1783 at Essex Street—the site of a Unitarian chapel founded by Theophilus Lindsey. The liturgy there was based on one that had been drawn up (but never used) by Samuel Clarke early in the eighteenth century, with modifications by Lindsey and 'his friends Dr Jebb, Mr Tyrwhitt, and a few other learned and liberal members of the university of Cambridge' (Belsham, 103). Jebb regularly attended the chapel, along with such other notable political and religious radicals as Benjamin Franklin, Sir George Savile, and Joseph Priestley. Jebb's warm sympathy with Priestley's theological views is evident in the notes he contributed to the latter's Harmony of the Gospels. In turn Priestley dedicated his Doctrine of Philosophical Necessity (1777) to Jebb with an encomium praising him for his 'ardent zeal for the cause of civil and religious liberty in their full extent' (Works, 1.129–30).

Along with such theological interests Jebb continued to take an interest in the promotion of science and was made a fellow of the Royal Society in 1779—science and theology being closely linked in his mind as complementary paths to the mind of the creator. Thus, while at Cambridge, he had urged his students to regard 'the Newtonian system, as the strongest, and, indeed, only rational demonstration of the existence of a deity' (*Works*, 1.15). He died at his house in Parliament Street, London, on 2 March 1786 and was buried on 9 March in unconsecrated ground in Bunhill Fields. There is a portrait of him by Hoppner and an engraving by J. Young which forms the frontispiece of his work on prisons.

Ann Jebb [*née* Torkington] (1735–1812) was born on 9 November 1735 at Ripton-Kings, Hutingdonshire, the eldest daughter of the Revd James Torkington, rector of Little Stukely in Huntingdonshire, and Lady Dorothy Sherard, daughter of Philip, second earl of Harborough. She appears to have been educated at home but achieved a high standard of fluency in both her conversation and her writings. She was in warm sympathy with her husband's views and wrote in their support: during the subscription controversy she addressed a series of letters to the *London Chronicle* from 1772 to 1774 under the *nom de plume* Priscilla, and she also published articles in the *Whitehall Evening Post* urging the need for annual examinations at Cambridge. When Jebb resigned his livings he had, as her biographer Meadley puts it, the 'hearty concurrence of Mrs Jebb, who deemed no duty superior … to preserving the integrity of his own mind' (Meadley, 600). Following their move to London she joined with her husband in the cause of political reform and, like him, was active in such causes as opposition to Britain in the American War of Independence, support for the widening of the franchise, and the removal of discriminatory laws against Roman Catholics. Following Jebb's death in 1786 she remained closely involved with his circle of political and religious radicals, though she came to regret 'the increasing divisions amongst the friends of liberty' (ibid., 666). She and Jebb had no children. Of a delicate constitution, and an invalid for much of her life, Ann Jebb died at her house in Half-Moon Street, London, on 20 January 1812, and was buried alongside her husband in Bunhill Fields.

JOHN GASCOIGNE

Sources *The works, theological, medical, political and miscellaneous of John Jebb*, ed. J. Disney, 3 vols. (1787) · *Life and correspondence of Joseph Priestley*, ed. J. T. Rutt, 2 (1832) · *Anecdotes of the life of Richard Watson*, ed. R. Watson (1817) · G. Dyer, *History of the university and colleges of Cambridge*, 2 vols. (1814) · Nichols, *Lit. anecdotes*, 8.114, 571; 9.659 · T. Belsham, *Memoirs of the late Reverend Theophilus Lindsey* (1812) · W. Turner, *Lives of eminent Unitarians*, 2 vols. (1840–43) · D. A. Winstanley, *Unreformed Cambridge: a study of certain aspects of the university in the eighteenth century* (1935) · G. W. M. [G. W. Meadley], 'Memoirs of Mrs Jebb', *Monthly Repository*, 7 (1812), 597–604, 661–71 · J. Gascoigne, *Cambridge in the age of the Enlightenment* (1989) · *DNB* · *GM*, 1st ser., 56 (1786), 267–8 · *GM*, 1st ser., 82/1 (1812), 94
Archives DWL, notebooks and papers incl. lectures on the Greek New Testament | Mass. Hist. Soc., corresp. with John Adams · N. Yorks. CRO, corresp. with Christopher Wyvill
Likenesses C. Knight, stipple, pubd 1782, BM, NPG [*see illus.*] · J. Young, engraving, pubd 1786 (after J. Hoppner), BM · J. K. Sherwin, line engraving, 1787 (after bust by J. Flaxman), BM, NPG · J. Hoppner, oils

Jebb, John (1775–1833), Church of Ireland bishop of Limerick, Ardfert, and Aghadoe, was the younger son of John Jebb, alderman of Drogheda, co. Louth, and his second wife, Alicia Forster. He was born at Drogheda on 27 September 1775. His grandfather Richard Jebb had come to Ireland from Mansfield, Nottinghamshire, where the family had been settled for several generations. His father experienced financial difficulties and Jebb at two years old was entrusted to his aunt, Mrs M'Cormick. In 1782 he returned to his father at Leixlip, co. Kildare, and went to school in the nearby village of Celbridge. His elder brother, Richard [*see below*], who succeeded in 1788 to the estate of Sir Richard Jebb, undertook the cost of his education. He was sent to the Londonderry grammar school, where he formed a lifelong friendship with the theological writer Alexander Knox. In 1791 he entered Trinity College, Dublin, where he obtained a scholarship in 1794, a BA in 1796, and proceeded MA in 1801. He lived with his brother, who on their father's death in 1796 gave him £2000. He was an active member of the historical society, and the experience he acquired from taking part in its proceedings well equipped him for public debate. In February 1799 he was ordained deacon by Matthew Young, bishop of Clonfert. In July 1799 he obtained through Knox the curacy of Swanlinbar, co. Cavan, and was ordained priest in the following December by Charles Brodrick, bishop of Kilmore. In December 1801 he was instituted by Brodrick, archbishop of Cashel, to the curacy of Mogorban, co. Tipperary. In 1805 he became Brodrick's examining chaplain of candidates for ordination.

Jebb visited England with Knox in 1809, and made the acquaintance of Samuel Wilberforce and Hannah More. In the course of the summer he was appointed to the rectory of Abington, co. Limerick, where Charles Forster, later his biographer, was curate. In 1812 he was thrown from a gig and dislocated his left shoulder, an accident made more serious by the ineptitude of a village bone-setter. He was in London in 1815, and again in 1820, when he published an *Essay on Sacred Literature*, which helped to establish his scholarly reputation. At the end of 1820 he became archdeacon of Emly, and in February 1821 accumulated the degrees of BD and DD. During the riots which followed the agricultural depression of 1822 his was said to have been the only quiet parish in the district; and he was even asked by the local priest to use his influence with local Roman Catholics to keep the peace. He was appointed bishop of Limerick, Ardfert, and Aghadoe in December 1822, succeeding Thomas Elrington in the post.

Jebb attempted to raise the educational standards of his clergy by introducing an examination and study course for candidates for holy orders. On 10 July 1824 he made a speech in the House of Lords on the Tithe Commutation Bill, which Wilberforce described as 'one of the most able ever delivered in parliament' and which was seen as a powerful defence of the position of the Irish establishment. In 1827, while at Limerick, he suffered a stroke and was unable to continue with his duties as bishop. He left Ireland, spending most of his time in Leamington, Warwickshire, with Forster, his chaplain, as his companion and occupied himself with writing. A second stroke in 1829 confined him to his chair, but he was still able to use his pen. In 1830 he moved to East Hill, Wandsworth, London. In 1832 he began to have liver problems. He died unmarried at East Hill on 9 December 1833 and was buried in St Paul's churchyard, Clapham.

Jebb's thought and works were a synthesis of Catholic tradition and evangelical fervour. In conjunction with Knox he anticipated elements of the thought of the Tractarian or Oxford Movement, which began about the date of his death. John Henry Newman, in letters dated between 1833 and 1836, expressed his sympathy with Jebb's views on daily services and frequent communions, but it would be an exaggeration to suggest, as some scholars of the 1880s did, that he was the chief inspiration for the leaders of the Oxford Movement. Jebb's published works were influential and helped him to be elected a fellow of the Royal Society. They include *Sermons on Subjects Chiefly Practical* (1815), *An Essay on Sacred Literature* (1820), and *Practical Theology* (1830). *Thirty Years' Correspondence with Alexander Knox* was published posthumously in 1834. He also edited, among other works, Dr Townson's *Practical Discourses* (1828) and part of Knox's *Literary Remains* (1834–7).

Richard Jebb (1766–1834), judge, was born at Drogheda, the elder brother of John Jebb. While a student at Lincoln's Inn he inherited, in 1787, the property of his cousin, Sir Richard Jebb. He was called to the Irish bar in 1789. He supported the union, and published *A Reply to a Pamphlet Entitled 'Arguments For and Against an Union'* (1799), which attracted attention, and led the English government to offer him a seat in the united parliament, which he declined. He was appointed successively king's counsel, and third and second serjeant, and in December 1818 fourth justice of the Irish court of king's bench. He married Jane Louisa, eldest daughter of John Finlay, MP for Dublin; they had five sons, including John *Jebb (1805–1886), and a daughter. He died suddenly at his house at Rostrevor, co. Down, on 3 September 1834, when a soda water bottle exploded in his mouth.

ALEXANDER GORDON, *rev.* DAVID HUDDLESTON

Sources C. Forster, *The life and letters of John Jebb* (1836) · J. B. Leslie, *Ardfert and Aghadoe clergy and parishes* (1940) · J. Wills, *Lives of illustrious and distinguished Irishmen*, 6 vols. (1839–47) · *GM*, 2nd ser., 1 (1834), 223–5 · *Letters and correspondence of John Henry Newman during his life in the English church*, ed. A. Mozley, 2 vols. (1891), vol. 1, pp. 440, 470 · P. B. Nockles, *The Oxford Movement in context: Anglican high churchmanship, 1760–1857* (1994) · W. A. Phillips, ed., *History of the Church of Ireland*, 3 vols. (1933–4) · D. Bowen, *The protestant crusade in Ireland, 1800–70* (1978) · H. Cotton, *Fasti ecclesiae Hibernicae*, 1 (1845), 333–4 · *GM*, 2nd ser., 2 (1834), 532–3
Archives PRO NIre., Jebb and Heyland MSS, D/4058 · Representative Church Body Library, Dublin, corresp. · TCD, corresp. | BL, corresp. with Alexander Knox, Add. MSS 41163–41166 · Derbys. RO, corresp. with Sir R. J. Wilmot-Horton · N. Yorks. CRO, corresp. with Christopher Wyvill
Likenesses G. Richmond, pencil drawing, 1832, NG Ire. · G. Adcock, stipple, pubd 1834, NPG · E. H. Baily, sculpture, Limerick Cathedral, co. Limerick, Ireland · T. Lupton, mezzotint (aged fifty-one; after T. Lawrence), BM, NPG

Jebb, John (1805–1886), Church of England clergyman and religious writer, was born in Dublin, the eldest son of Richard *Jebb (1766–1834), judge [*see under* Jebb, John (1775–1833)], and his wife, Jane Louisa Finlay. His father

was the elder brother of Dr John Jebb, bishop of Limerick. He was educated at Winchester College and at Trinity College, Dublin, and graduated BA in 1826, MA in 1829, and BD in 1862; he also became DD. Having held for a short time the rectory of Dunerlin in Ireland, he was appointed prebendary of Donoughmore in Limerick Cathedral in 1832, and instituted to the rectory of Peterstow, near Ross, Herefordshire, in 1843. He was appointed prebendary of Preston Wynne in Hereford Cathedral in 1858, and was praelector from 1863 to 1870, when he was appointed canon residentiary. *A Literal Translation of the Book of Psalms*, which he published in two volumes in 1846, gave him some standing as a Hebrew scholar and he was appointed one of the revisers of the Old Testament; however, he soon resigned the post in the belief that the plan proposed by his colleagues involved unnecessary change of the Authorized Version. He died at his home, Peterstow rectory, on 8 January 1886. Richard Claverhouse *Jebb was his nephew and executor.

Jebb published many sermons and pamphlets, especially on cathedrals. His chief works of substance are *The Divine Economy of the Church* (1840), *The Church Service of the United Church of England and Ireland* (1843), and *The rights of the Irish branch of the United Church of England and Ireland considered on fundamental principles, human and divine* (1868).

THOMAS SECCOMBE, *rev.* H. C. G. MATTHEW

Sources *The Times* (13 Jan 1886) · *The Athenaeum* (16 Jan 1886), 104 · *The letters and diaries of John Henry Newman*, ed. C. S. Dessain and others, [31 vols.] (1961–) · H. Cotton, *Fasti ecclesiae Hibernicae*, 1–5 (1845–60)
Archives LPL, corresp. · TCD, corresp.
Wealth at death £8399 7s. 10d.: administration, 23 March 1886, CGPLA Eng. & Wales

Jebb, Sir Joshua (1793–1863), prison administrator, was born in Chesterfield on 8 May 1793, the eldest son of Joshua Jebb (1769–1845) of Walton, Derbyshire, and his wife, Dorothy, the daughter of General Henry Gladwin of Stubbing Court, Derbyshire. Destined for a military career, he attended the Royal Military Academy at Woolwich and was commissioned as a second lieutenant in the Royal Engineers on 1 July 1812. Promoted first lieutenant on 21 July 1813, he embarked for Canada the following October. Here he served first on the frontier of Lower Canada and subsequently in the campaign in the United States during the autumn of 1814. He was present at the battle of Plattsburg and was thanked in general orders. On his return from Canada in 1820 he was stationed at Woolwich and then at Hull. In December 1827 he set sail for the West Indies, where he was promoted second captain on 26 February 1828. Invalided home the following September, he married his first wife, Mary Legh (d. 1850), daughter of William Burtinshaw Thomas of Highfield, Derbyshire, on 14 June 1830. On 11 February 1831 he was appointed adjutant of the Royal Sappers and Miners at Chatham. His promotion to first captain came on 10 January 1837.

Although continuing to carry out military duties, from 1837 Jebb was increasingly involved in civilian tasks. On 10 March 1838 he was appointed by the lord president of the council to conduct inquiries into the grants of charters of incorporation to Bolton and Sheffield. He was made a member of the commission on the Birmingham municipal boundary on 21 May 1838. But the bulk of his civilian work related to his secondment to advise the Home Office on the building of prisons.

Jebb's initial secondment was made towards the end of 1837 for a period of six months. Convinced of the value of the separate system of prison discipline by two of the new inspectors of prisons, William Crawford and Whitworth Russell, the home secretary sought an officer of engineers to advise and guide the conversion of old buildings and the construction of new. One of the first conversions which Jebb supervised was that of Parkhurst, on the Isle of Wight, from a military hospital to a juvenile prison. In May 1839 Jebb was made a visitor at the prison. On 20 September that year his secondment to the Home Office was put on a more permanent footing and he was relieved of his remaining military duties; however, he retained his rank, and was promoted major on 23 November 1841 and lieutenant-colonel on 16 April 1847.

Much of Jebb's early work for the Home Office concerned the construction of the new penitentiary of Pentonville, which opened in 1842 with Jebb as one of its commissioners. Two years later he was appointed to the newly created position of surveyor-general of prisons, and he published *Modern Prisons: their Construction and Ventilation*. In the same year, following evidence to a royal commission that military prisoners were generally disruptive in the civilian prisons where they were held, it was decided to establish prisons exclusively for military offenders. These were to be supervised by a new inspector-general of military prisons, and Jebb was appointed to this post also, on 27 December 1844.

As surveyor-general of prisons Jebb had a wide remit; he was responsible for the conversion and construction of government prisons, and also for some administration. He was consulted by local authorities on prison design and construction, and, given the broad and somewhat nebulous range of his tasks, some local authorities sought his advice on much wider issues of punishment. Jebb was happy to respond to all and any such queries, and this brought him into conflict with the prison inspectorate, particularly Crawford and Russell, with whom he had ideological differences. The two were ideologues for whom the separate system appeared the ultimate reformative for offenders. Jebb took a more utilitarian attitude, and while he acknowledged the value of a limited period of solitary confinement for offenders, he believed also in the idea of punishment as a deterrent. Moreover, he recognized opportunities for profit in convict labour and, as a military officer, he saw the advantage of using such labour to improve Britain's defences. These ideas were developed in a report which he presented in November 1846 in response to the home secretary's request that he work out the practical details of both the end of transportation and the use of the hulks for keeping convicts engaged on public works. The first concrete manifestation of the report was Portland Prison, built between 1847 and 1849, which became the model for public-works prisons; it was followed by a refurbished Dartmoor, and new prisons at Portsmouth and Chatham.

Jebb's principal critics and rivals in the prison inspectorate, Crawford and Russell, both died in 1847. On 1 May 1849 his appointment as commissioner of Pentonville was renewed. At the beginning of 1850 he opted to quit military service on full pay and continue his civilian employment. In August he was appointed as chairman of the directors of convict prisons, a new body designed to supervise the management of these institutions; the directors were responsible to the home secretary and independent of the prison inspectorate. His wife, with whom he had a son and three daughters, died that same year. On 5 September 1854 he married Lady Amelia Rose Pelham (d. 1884), the daughter of Thomas *Pelham, second earl of Chichester, who was himself a significant influence on national penal policy; the marriage and the cordial relations with his father-in-law appear to have strengthened Jebb's professional position.

Recognition of his public service came on 25 March 1859 when he was created KCB. He had been given the honorary rank of colonel on 28 November 1854, and received that of major-general on 6 July 1860. In addition to his prison duties during 1861 and 1862 he served on a series of commissions considering the construction of Thames embankments and communications across the metropolis. He died suddenly, while travelling on an omnibus in the Strand to his offices in Parliament Street, on 26 June 1863.

CLIVE EMSLEY

Sources L. Radzinowicz and R. Hood, *A history of English criminal law and its administration from 1750*, 5: *The emergence of penal policy in Victorian and Edwardian England* (1986) • S. McConville, *A history of English prison administration*, 1: *1750–1877* (1981) • E. Stockdale, 'The rise of Joshua Jebb, 1837–1850', *British Journal of Criminology*, 16 (1976), 164–70 • Burke, *Gen. GB* • *CGPLA Eng. & Wales* (1863) • *The Times* (27 June 1863)
Archives BLPES, personal and family corresp. and papers | W. Sussex RO, letters to duke of Richmond
Likenesses wood-engraving, pubd 1863 (after engraving), NPG; repro. in *ILN* (11 July 1863) • P. Macdowell, bust, 1865, Bethnal Green Museum, London
Wealth at death under £30,000: probate, 18 Aug 1863, *CGPLA Eng. & Wales*

Jebb, Julian Alvery Marius (1934–1984), journalist and television producer, was born on 2 April 1934 at Hawkesyard Priory, Rugeley, Staffordshire, the youngest of the four children of Reginald Douglas (Rex) Jebb (1883–1977) schoolmaster and journalist, and his wife, Eleanor Philippa (1899–1979), daughter of Hilaire *Belloc (1870–1953) and his wife, Elodie. He was brought up in the Belloc family home, Kingsland, near Horsham, Sussex, its rooms lined with some ten thousand books, richly redolent of candle-grease and his grandfather's Catholicism. Jebb was educated at Downside School (1947–52) and King's College, Cambridge (1953–6), where he co-edited the magazine *Granta* with Jonathan Gathorne-Hardy and performed in reviews with the Cambridge Footlights. His childhood and education pointed him towards a career as a novelist, but after spasmodic attempts to write fiction his contribution to English artistic life was channelled into reviews of novels and films, and his own arts documentaries made for BBC television. He was always a devoted enthusiast and promoter of talents.

After leaving Cambridge Jebb worked for the Catholic weekly *The Tablet* and the literary agent Stephen Aske. In Germany he produced and acted in English-language plays for Radio Bremen. In the sixties he taught English in Rome. He travelled in Spain and Greece, leading the expatriate life, the typewriter set up by the open window, the Aegean beyond. Such money as he earned tended to be spent rapidly and generously. He was homosexual, but the claims of close friendship suited him better than the uncertain territory of love affairs.

In 1967 Jebb joined the arts department of BBC television as an assistant producer. He co-produced a series of literary programmes, flourishing in the friendlier climate of those times, with BBC2 only recently started, and a mission to put writers on the screen, spearheaded by the young Melvyn Bragg. By means of a quotation guessing game, called *Take it or Leave it*, which was devised by Brigid Brophy, Jebb, through contacts and friendships, introduced a number of writers to the television studio for the first time. Participants included Anthony Burgess, John Bayley, Iris Murdoch, Cyril Connolly, A. S. Byatt, Philip Toynbee, and Mary McCarthy. He conducted the first studio interview with the painter Francis Bacon and made interview-based documentaries with Christopher Isherwood, John Osborne, Patricia Highsmith, and Anthony Powell. In 1969 he filmed 'Tennyson on the Isle of Wight' with John Betjeman, the best of several collaborations with the poet laureate. His longer documentaries on Virginia Woolf, the Mitford sisters, and Dame Edna Everage (Barry Humphries) drew on a lively affection for his subjects. It was the only way he knew how to work. In those days the BBC was happy to retain on the staff someone who had a wide-ranging knowledge and enjoyment of the arts—literature, opera, ballet, painting, films of all kinds, the pop culture of television (not rock music, however): Jebb cheerfully crossed the boundaries of critical definitions. He was an excellent radio broadcaster and in some respects had more in common with the old-style producers of Radio 4, but he found himself entranced with the new world of television. Unfortunately the medium did not nurture his abilities, even if the excitement of programme making convinced him that he was fully stretched. The weeks before his death were marked by increasing despair at the callous treatment he felt he had received. He was a literary amateur working in a world increasingly dominated by career-driven professionals.

Jebb was a brilliant mimic with a wonderful vein of fantasy, but a haunting sense of failure increasingly plagued him. No one could halt the inroads of alcohol and pills, which undermined his health and work. Finally, on 31 October 1984, he killed himself at his flat, 171 Ladbroke Grove, London, with an overdose of heminevrin. He had, as a pained and angry Germaine Greer wrote, been given so much and thrown it all away. Sadly a rare gift for friendship and promoting the talents of others had undermined the will-power needed for his own survival.

In 1993 a memoir, called *A Dedicated Fan*, was published. It includes interviews with Evelyn Waugh (*Paris Review*, 1962, a sparkling performance) and Elizabeth Bowen, unpublished journals, personal memories from friends, family, and a number of writers including V. S. Naipaul, Alison Lurie, Patricia Highsmith, A. S. Byatt, Caroline Blackwood, Paul Theroux, Frances Partridge, Patrick Leigh Fermor, Antonia Fraser, Barry Humphries, Melvyn Bragg, Jonathan Gathorne-Hardy, and Elaine Dundy.

TRISTRAM POWELL

Sources T. Powell and G. Powell, eds., *A dedicated fan* (1993) · b. cert. · d. cert.
Archives priv. coll., letters, etc. | FILM BBC, television programmes | SOUND BBC Radio
Likenesses D. Hill, painting · photographs, repro. in Powell and Powell, eds., *A dedicated fan*
Wealth at death £53,540: administration, 20 Feb 1986, *CGPLA Eng. & Wales*

Jebb, Sir Richard, first baronet (*bap.* **1729**, *d.* **1787**), physician, son of Samuel *Jebb (1693/4–1772), physician, was born at Stratford, Essex, and baptized there on 30 October 1729. He entered St Mary Hall, Oxford, in 1747; but being a nonjuror he could not graduate in that university, and proceeded to Aberdeen, where he joined Marischal College and graduated MD on 23 September 1751. He took rooms in Parliament Street, London, and slowly built a practice.

> He did a little business; he talked of a little more. But he disdained any of the Common Quackery, and all its shabby expedients. He never went into common tricks of calling for himself: he never frequented public places for the purpose of being fetched out. (*GM*, 642–3)

Jebb could also be less than deferential to patients. He was admitted a licentiate of the Royal College of Physicians on 24 March 1755. He was physician to the Westminster Hospital from 1754 to 1762, when on 7 May he was elected physician to St George's Hospital. He went to Italy to attend the duke of Gloucester, and became a favourite of George III, who granted him a crown lease of 385 acres of Enfield Chase in Middlesex. He built on it a small house named Trent Place, enclosed it with a fence, and kept deer. In 1771 he was elected a fellow, *speciali gratia*, of the Royal College of Physicians; in 1774 he delivered the Harveian oration, and was censor in 1772, 1776, and 1781. He was created a baronet on 4 September 1778, and was FRS (1765) and FSA. In 1768 the growth in his private practice led him to resign his hospital appointment, and in the three years 1779–81 his fees amounted to 20,000 guineas. In 1780 he was appointed physician to the prince of Wales, and in 1786 to the king.

Jebb was tall and thin, and fond of wine and music. John Wilkes and the poet Charles Churchill were his friends, and Jebb paid for the education of Churchill's son. His professional reputation was high, although John Coakley Lettsom, who knew him well, wrote:

> I loved that man with all his eccentricity. He had the bluntness, but not the rudeness, of Radcliffe. He had the medical perception, but not the perseverance and temporizing politeness, of Warren. In every respect, but fortune, superior to Turton; or to Baker, but in classical

learning; and yet he was the unhappy slave of unhappy passions. His own sister is, and has long been, in a madhouse; the same fate attends his cousin, and a little adversity would have placed poor Sir Richard there also. There was an impetuosity in his manner, a wildness in his look, and sometimes a strange confusion in his head, which often made me tremble for his sensorium. He had a noble, generous heart, and a pleasing frankness among his friends; communicative of experience among the faculty, and earnest for the recovery of his patients, which he sometimes manifested by the most impetuous solicitude. Those who did not well know him, he alarmed; those who did, saw the unguarded and rude ebullition of earnestness for success. (Munk, *Roll*)

In June 1787, while attending two of the princesses, Jebb was attacked by fever. He was attended by Richard Warren and Henry Revell Reynolds, but died at 2 a.m. on 4 July 1787 at his house in Great George Street, Westminster, and was buried in the west cloister of Westminster Abbey. He was unmarried. A *Catalogue of the Genuine Library of the Late Sir Richard Jebb* was published in 1788.

NORMAN MOORE, rev. MICHAEL BEVAN

Sources Munk, *Roll* · *GM*, 1st ser., 57 (1787), 642–3, 834 · Foster, *Alum. Oxon.* · *The record of the Royal Society of London*, 4th edn (1940) **Likenesses** attrib. J. Zoffany, oils, RCP Lond. **Wealth at death** over £7200; incl. Enfield Chase estate: *GM*

Jebb, Richard (1766–1834). *See under* Jebb, John (1775–1833).

Jebb, Richard (1874–1953), publicist and theorist on imperial themes, was born at The Lyth, Ellesmere, Shropshire, on 16 October 1874, the second son in the family of two sons and five daughters of Arthur Trevor Jebb (1839–1894), landowner, and his wife, Eglantyne Louisa (a distant cousin), daughter of Robert Jebb of Killiney, Ireland. The philanthropists Eglantyne *Jebb and Dorothy Frances *Buxton, and the agricultural administrator Louisa *Wilkins, were his sisters. His uncle was the classical scholar Sir Richard Jebb. His family had been landowners in Wales and Shropshire. He was educated at Marlborough College and at New College, Oxford, where he obtained second classes in classical honour moderations (1895) and *literae humaniores* (1897). His interest in the British empire was stimulated by a schoolmaster's setting for a Latin essay prize a subject involving imperial federation. He won the prize, and made the empire his principal concern for the rest of his life.

Jebb intended to join the Indian Civil Service, but while he was at Oxford his father and his only brother died, and he inherited the family estate, which provided him with an income for the rest of his life. On 29 September 1900 he married Margaret Ethel (d. 1949), daughter of George Lewthwaite of Littlebank, Settle, with whom he had two sons and one daughter. The years 1898–1901 were spent in travel abroad, mainly in the self-governing colonies. He made many journeys on a bicycle, including a honeymoon trip the length of the north island of New Zealand. The colonial experience gave him material for his propositions about colonial nationalism, the subject which he quickly made his own.

In 1905 Jebb published *Studies in Colonial Nationalism*, the book which brought him into public notice. A fervent follower of the tariff reform movement of Joseph Chamberlain, he began to write leaders and articles for the *Morning Post* under the editorship of his friend Fabian Ware; in 1906 he wrote articles for it during the course of a journey through Canada, Australia, New Zealand, and South Africa.

At the general election of January 1910 Jebb made his only attempt to enter parliament, contesting the seat of East Marylebone as a Unionist with tariff-reform beliefs; the official Unionist candidate won, with a Liberal second and Jebb third. He took no further part in party politics, confining himself to local bodies: he was a magistrate and served on the Shropshire county council from 1923 to 1934. He continued to express firm opinions in letters to newspapers, but seems to have lost faith in parliamentary institutions, even toying with fascism and social credit. In the First World War he served from 1914 to 1919 in the King's Shropshire light infantry, mostly in Britain, and in the Second World War he commanded the Ellesmere company of the Home Guard.

Jebb's books included the two-volume *The Imperial Conference* (1911), *The Britannic Question* (1913), *The Empire in Eclipse* (1926), and *His Britannic Majesty* (1935). In May 1914 he had apparently financed a journal, the *Britannic Review*, but it did not survive the outbreak of war in August. *The Imperial Conference* received much public notice, but the other books did not.

Jebb's ideas were relatively simple. He saw that there was a sentiment which he called colonial nationalism, which was not merely separatism, but a complex of local feeling and attachment to Britain. Imperial federationists and the Round Table group headed by Lionel Curtis did not understand the strength of this sentiment: their proposals, not taking account of it, would therefore fail. Jebb favoured a system of alliance or partnership between Britain and what came to be known as the dominions: he approved of separate dominion navies in co-operation with the Royal Navy; he wanted tariff reform and imperial preference as means of binding the dominions more closely; and he wanted the Imperial Conference turned into a continuous body handling large defence and economic questions. Jebb died peacefully at his home, The Lyth, on 25 June 1953.   J. D. MILLER, rev.

Sources J. D. B. Miller, *Richard Jebb and the problem of empire* (1956) · J. Eddy and D. Schreuder, eds., *The rise of colonial nationalism* (1988) **Archives** NL Aus., corresp. · U. Lond., Institute of Commonwealth Studies, corresp. and papers | BLPES, corresp. with Tariff Commission · NL Aus., corresp. with Alfred Deakin **Wealth at death** £60,274 12s. 3d.: administration with will, 29 Oct 1953, *CGPLA Eng. & Wales*

Jebb, Sir Richard Claverhouse (1841–1905), Greek scholar, was the eldest of the four children of Robert Jebb, an Irish barrister, and his wife, Emily Harriet (d. 1883), third daughter of Heneage Horsley, dean of Brechin; he derived his second name from Claverhouse, near Dundee,

Sir Richard Claverhouse Jebb (1841–1905), by Window & Grove

where he was born on 27 August 1841. His family had been prominent in Nottinghamshire since the reign of Elizabeth I. His great-great-grandmother, whose daughter married Samuel Jebb (b. 1670), was the sister of John De Witt, the grand pensionary of Holland, who was murdered in 1672; her father Jacob had come to England to drain the fens of Lincolnshire. Samuel's son Richard went from Mansfield to Drogheda in Ireland early in the eighteenth century. One of his sons, Richard, was an Irish judge and another, John Jebb, was bishop of Limerick; Richard *Jebb [see under Jebb, John (1775–1833)] was the grandfather of Sir Richard.

Jebb's early life was spent in or near Dublin; but in 1850 the family moved to Killiney, 9 miles off. He was at school at St Columba's College, Rathfarnham, and later at Charterhouse, which had not yet moved to Godalming. In 1858 he matriculated at Trinity College, Cambridge. As an undergraduate he led an active social life, and at first had no wish for an academic career. But he was notably successful in his studies, winning the Porson prize in 1859, the Craven scholarship in 1860, and the first chancellor's medal in 1862, and graduating in 1862 as senior classic. In 1863 he was elected fellow of Trinity College.

During the next few years Jebb continued his social activities; the remark of W. H. Thompson, master of Trinity, that 'what time he can spare from the adornment of his person he devotes to the neglect of his duties' (Read, 104), though not seriously intended, must have had a grain of truth. With his friends he travelled to Egypt and Syria, later visiting France and Germany. But he must have worked hard at this time. In 1869 he became public orator

of the university, and he augmented his income by writing leaders for The Times. He published elementary editions of the Electra (1867) and the Ajax (1868) of Sophocles, and a text, with commentary, of the Characters of Theophrastus (1870). The last work was slight by the standards of contemporary German scholarship, but showed something of the polished style and high intelligence of his later productions; a new edition revised by Sir John Sandys came out in 1909. In 1873 he brought out the first edition of his Translations into Greek and Latin Verse, including a rendering of Browning's Abt Vogler into the metre of Pindar's fourth Pythian ode. Although they show greater smoothness and regularity than most Greek archaic and classical poetry, contrasting in this respect with the translations of H. A. J. Munro, these versions are a remarkable performance.

In 1870 Jebb made the acquaintance of an American lady, Mrs Slemmer (1840–1930), born Caroline Lane Reynolds, daughter of John Reynolds, rector of St James Episcopal Church, Evansburgh, Pennsylvania, and his wife, Eleanor Evans. She was the widow of General Adam Slemmer, who had done distinguished service in the American Civil War. After her husband's early death Mrs Slemmer, armed with a general letter of introduction from General William T. Sherman, came to visit cousins in England, and while staying with one of these in Cambridge enjoyed very great social success. Mrs Slemmer was in the unanimous opinion of all who knew her a great beauty, with auburn hair and a deep rich voice; she was also highly cultivated and exceptionally intelligent. Even people whom all others found difficult surrendered to her. By her own testimony she received during her life thirty-seven proposals of marriage, including one from Commodore Cornelius Vanderbilt; a number of these were made during her first visit to Cambridge in 1870. After her return to America she kept up a correspondence with Jebb, and soon after she had come back to England in 1874 the two were married on 18 August.

There was a striking contrast in character between Jebb and his wife, as can be seen from the two books which are the main sources for their lives. Lady Jebb's life of her husband, published two years after his death, contains some not uninteresting letters written by him to a female cousin early in his career and others written to his future wife after her return to America in 1870. But the tone is one of bland encomium, and the latter part of the book, consisting largely of lists of committees, honours, and public activities, makes dull reading. Not so With Dearest Love to All: the Life and Letters of Lady Jebb, by her niece Mary Bobbitt Read (1960). Lady Jebb's letters from England to her sister Ellen Du Puy in America, and later from America to her niece Lady Darwin in England, are most unlike the Life, being candid, witty, and often extremely entertaining.

Jebb was exceptionally sensitive, not to say nervous; his wife wrote to her sister that he had 'wit without humour'. She, on the other hand, was a dashing talker, completely free from inhibitions, and a fascinating and dominating figure in any group; her grand-niece Gwen Raverat wrote that 'poor Uncle Dick was the least considered in the Jebb household' (Raverat, 91). But with those who knew him well Jebb could be a sympathetic and entertaining companion, and he was devoted to his wife, whose qualities perfectly complemented his own. The couple led an active social life. As a young man Jebb had known Thackeray, and he was great friends with Thackeray's daughter Lady Ritchie, as he was with Sir Leslie Stephen. He knew Browning, had at least one memorable conversation with George Eliot, and was intimate with Tennyson, who dedicated to him his poem *Demeter and Persephone*:

Bear witness you, that yesterday
From out the ghost of Pindar in you
Roll'd an Olympian.

He was on friendly terms with Benjamin Jowett, and sometimes visited him in Oxford.

In 1875 Jebb was elected to the chair of Greek in the University of Glasgow. He had a competitor for the chair, Lewis Campbell, professor of Greek at St Andrews, a fine scholar and a Scot, but the powerful support of Sir William Thomson, later Lord Kelvin, carried the day. Jebb kept a house in Cambridge, and spent about half the year away from Glasgow, and it is possible that Campbell would have been a better choice for this particular post. Though Jebb took great trouble over his lectures, he lacked the gifts of an orator, and he was less suited to dealing with the Glasgow undergraduates than with those at Cambridge. But he discharged his duties with great conscientiousness, and won high regard in Glasgow. He and his wife several times travelled on the continent together. In 1884 he visited America for the first time, and spoke at Harvard; in the different social climate Jebb was able to relax, and the visit was a great success. It was repeated in 1891, when he lectured at Johns Hopkins.

In 1876 Jebb brought out the two volumes of *The Attic Orators from Antiphon to Isaeus*. The book was attacked by J. P. Mahaffy for its excessive dependence on the *Attische Beredsamkeit* of Friedrich Blass. This was not altogether fair, since Jebb would have been wrong not to have made full use of this important book; but it is true that though Jebb's work gave a clear and elegant account of its subject, useful to English readers, it did little to advance knowledge. In 1879 he followed it with a volume of selections called *The Attic Orators*, with a useful commentary. Jebb took a great interest in modern Greece, which he first visited in 1876. He taught the language one day a week in Glasgow, and in 1880 brought out a small book called *Modern Greece*; he received from the king of Greece the order of the Saviour. He was active in planning an 'English' school for classical studies in Athens and on 25 June 1883 organized a large meeting at Marlborough House to raise funds for what became the British School at Athens. He contributed to the series of the English Men of Letters an excellent short book on Richard Bentley; although he had less in common with Bentley than his first biographer, Bishop Monk, he contrived to do him justice. His *Homer: an Introduction to the Iliad and Odyssey* (1887) is a small book that is still worth reading; he rightly warned against

Schliemann's naïve interpretation of his great discoveries. More importantly, in 1880 he began work on his edition of Sophocles, the first three volumes of which (*Oedipus Tyrannus*, 1883; *Oedipus at Colonus*, 1885; *Antigone*, 1888) appeared while he was still at Glasgow. The first two initially appeared with notes in Latin, but Jebb wisely allowed Matthew Arnold to persuade him to use English.

In 1889 the death of B. H. Kennedy at last allowed Jebb to leave Glasgow and occupy the regius chair of Greek at Cambridge, for which he was ideally suited. Here he brought out the last four volumes of his edition of Sophocles (*Philoctetes*, 1890; *Women of Trachis*, 1892; *Electra*, 1894; *Ajax*, 1896). He had intended to produce an eighth volume containing the fragments, but broke off in order to deal with the papyrus of Bacchylides, which reached the British Museum in 1896 and was published in 1897. The Sophoclean fragments were edited (1917) by A. C. Pearson, making use of notes left by Jebb. Two other works that were posthumously published were his *Essays and Addresses* (1907) and his valuable translation of Aristotle's *Rhetoric*, brought out by Sir John Sandys in 1909.

Jebb's famous edition of Sophocles has certain deficiencies: he lacked the comprehensive learning of some of his German contemporaries; he fatally swallowed the misguided metrical theories of J. H. H. Schmidt; and he sometimes glossed over a difficulty that he should have tackled. He cannot be said to have made an important contribution to the constitution of the text, a fact that may account for the low regard for him entertained by Housman, who wrote in a private letter 'Jebb is the Lewis Morris of scholarship', and of Eduard Fraenkel, who preferred to Jebb's Sophocles the edition published earlier by Lewis Campbell. But he had, as J. D. Denniston wrote, 'a very fine feeling for Greek', and his English style, which has reminded some of Addison, enabled him to express the most delicate nuances of the poet's meaning. He wrote at a time when textual emendation had been carried too far, even by distinguished scholars, and again and again he was able to show why the text was sound and why Sophocles had written precisely those words and no others. Wilamowitz wrote in 1924 that Jebb's interpretations of Sophocles would remain alive so long as people continued to make a serious effort to understand the language of that difficult writer, and these words seem as true today as when he wrote them. Jebb's principal aim, as Wilamowitz observed, was to convey to readers the nature of the poet's style.

Another major work is Jebb's edition of Bacchylides, with commentary, which appeared in 1905, the year of his death. In his translation and commentary he did for the lesser poet Bacchylides what he had done for Sophocles. Like the edition of Sophocles, the edition of Bacchylides remains after almost a century necessary reading for any serious student of that author.

No one played a greater part than Jebb in the foundation of the Society for the Promotion of Hellenic Studies and of the British School at Athens, and when the British Academy was established in 1902 he was one of the original fellows. Jebb was an active defender of the humanities, who warned against the tendency, very marked in his time, particularly in Germany, to try too hard to make them scientific. Jebb was a Christian, who followed Arnold in believing that Hellenism provided a necessary counter-weight to Hebraism.

Jebb received honorary degrees from Edinburgh, Cambridge, Dublin, Bologna, and Oxford; he was a fellow of London University and a corresponding member of the German Institute of Archaeology. He succeeded W. E. Gladstone as professor of ancient history to the Royal Academy, and was a trustee of the British Museum. He gave the Rede lecture at Cambridge and the Romanes lecture at Oxford. After declining it in 1897 he accepted the honour of knighthood in 1900, and in 1905 he was appointed to the Order of Merit.

In 1891 Jebb, standing as a Conservative, was elected MP for Cambridge University, and was re-elected in 1892, 1895, and 1900. He spoke fairly often, served on several royal and parliamentary commissions, and was active in the resistance to the proposal to disestablish the Anglican church in Wales. It is possible to regret that he gave so much time to public activities, which must have imposed a severe strain. In 1905 he travelled to South Africa to preside over the educational section of the meeting of the British Association, and soon after his return to England his health, never robust, broke down completely. He died at his home, Springfield, Newnham, Cambridge, on 9 December 1905, and was buried in St Giles's Church. His portrait, painted by Sir George Reid in 1903, is in Trinity College. 'It is a faithful likeness', according to one who knew him, 'but the sitter was suffering from hay fever at the time, and the expression is consequently harassed'.

HUGH LLOYD-JONES

Sources C. Jebb, *Life and letters of Sir Richard Claverhouse Jebb* (1907) · A. W. Verrall, 'The scholar and critic', in C. Jebb, *Life and letters of Sir Richard Claverhouse Jebb* (1907), 427–87 · *The Times* (11 Dec 1905) · *The Athenaeum* (16 Dec 1905), 836 · R. Y. Tyrrell, 'Sir Richard Claverhouse Jebb, 1841–1905', *PBA*, [2] (1905–6), 443–8 · H. Tennyson, *Alfred Lord Tennyson: a memoir by his son*, 2 vols. (1897) · M. E. G. Duff, *Notes from a diary, 1889–1901* (1901–5) · J. E. Sandys, *A history of classical scholarship*, 3 (1908), 413–15 · U. von Wilamowitz-Moellendorff, 'Sophoclis fabulae', *Deutsche Literaturzeitung*, 45 (1924), 2315–18 [repr. in *Kleine Schriften* 1 (2nd edn, 1971)] · G. Raverat, *Period piece* (1952) · M. Bobbitt Read, *With dearest love to all: the life and letters of Lady Jebb* (1960) · H. Waterhouse, *The British School at Athens* (1986)
Archives Amherst College, Massachusetts, corresp., notebooks, and literary MSS · King's Lond., corresp., notebooks, diary and papers relating to Greek history | BL, letters to T. H. S. Escott, Add. MS 58783 · BL, corresp. with Macmillans · U. Leeds, Brotherton L., letters to Sir Edmund Gosse · U. St Andr. L., letters to Wilfrid Ward
Likenesses G. Reid, oils, 1903, Trinity Cam. · C. A. Shaw, photograph, *c*.1905, NPG · Spy [L. Ward], chromolithograph, caricature, NPG; repro. in *VF* (20 Oct 1904) · B. Stone, photograph, NPG · Window & Grove, photograph, NPG [*see illus.*] · oils, British Academy, London · photograph, repro. in Jebb, *Life and letters*
Wealth at death £5703 13s. 6d.: probate, 16 Jan 1906, *CGPLA Eng. & Wales*

Jebb, Samuel (1693/4–1772), physician and scholar, was born probably at Mansfield, Nottinghamshire, the second son of Samuel Jebb, a maltster. He was educated at Mansfield grammar school, and became a sizar at Peterhouse, Cambridge, on 15 June 1709, aged fifteen. He graduated BA in January 1713. He was intended for the church, but being a nonjuror he was unable to take orders. He remained at Cambridge at least until 1718, when he became librarian to Jeremy Collier in London and began to occupy himself with literary work. In 1722 he started a classical periodical, *Bibliotheca Literaria*, which was intended to appear every two months. Ten numbers were issued from 1722 to 1724. Possibly the death of Collier in 1726 had something to do with Jebb's change of profession, for on the advice of Dr Richard Mead he commenced the study of medicine, attending Mead's private practice, and also learning chemistry and pharmacy from Mr Dillingham, an apothecary of Red Lion Square. About 1727 he married a relative of Dillingham's wife; they had several children, one of whom was the physician, Sir Richard *Jebb. Jebb took the degree of MD at Rheims on 12 March 1728 and set up as a physician at Stratford-le-Bow, Middlesex, where he combined medical practice with his literary work. His publications were chiefly editions and translations, in particular editions of Roger Bacon's *Opus maius* (1733) and of the Greek rhetorician Aristides (1722–30), and he published no original work on medicine. He did not become a licentiate of the College of Physicians until 1751. A few years before his death he retired with a moderate fortune to Chesterfield, Derbyshire, where he died on 9 March 1772.

J. F. PAYNE, rev. CLAIRE L. NUTT

Sources Munk, *Roll* · Nichols, *Lit. anecdotes*, 1.160, 436, 480; 8.366 · Nichols, *Illustrations*, 5.398–400 · Venn, *Alum. Cant.*
Archives Bodl. Oxf., letters to Thomas Brett
Wealth at death 'a moderate fortune': Munk, *Roll*

Jeejeebhoy, Sir Jamsetjee, first baronet (1783–1859), businessman and philanthropist, was born at Bombay on 15 July 1783. He was the son of Merwanjee Maneckjee Jeejeebhoy (d. 1799) and Jeeveebai Cowassi (d. 1799), weavers, of Nowsaree, a small town in the princely state of Baroda. In 1799 he was apprenticed to his cousin, Merwanjee Maneckjee, a merchant, and acted as a clerk on a voyage to China. On 1 March 1803 he married Awabaee Framjee (1793–1870), daughter of Framjee Pestonjee, a Bombay merchant, who was also engaged in trade with China. As partner of his father-in-law he made four more voyages to China. On the return voyage from Canton (Guangzhou) in 1804 the ship in which he sailed formed one of the fleet of merchantmen under the command of Sir Nathaniel Dance, which routed a squadron of French warships under Admiral Linois. During a subsequent voyage Jeejeebhoy was captured by the French and taken to the Cape of Good Hope. After losing all his property and suffering many hardships he obtained a passage in a Danish vessel bound for Calcutta, and returned to Bombay in 1807.

From this time, Jeejeebhoy's career as a successful merchant developed rapidly. In 1821–2 Jeejeebhoy's firm was able to establish a dominant position in the China import trade, using the British Far Eastern house of Jardine Matheson as its chief agents, and by 1822 Jeejeebhoy had built

Sir Jamsetjee Jeejeebhoy, first baronet (1783–1859), by unknown artist

up a fortune of Rs20 million. He also enjoyed good relations with the British merchant community of Bombay, and in particular with Charles Forbes (founder of the important British agency house of Forbes Forbes Campbell). Having established himself as a successful and wealthy merchant, Jeejeebhoy became a leading figure in the Bombay Parsi business community, and an important pioneer in the creation of Bombay as a leading modern commercial city: in 1835 he became a founder director of the first savings bank of Bombay, in 1842 he became a member of the European-dominated harbour committee and port trust, and in 1843 he became the only Indian director of the Bombay Bank. Having made a substantial fortune, Jeejeebhoy became, from the early 1820s onwards, a major philanthropist. Over the course of his life he gave over Rs30,000 to a wide variety of public and private causes: he provided famine relief, financed public works, and founded hospitals, schools, and scholarship funds. His best-known foundations were the Jamsetjee Jeejeebhoy Hospital and the Jamsetjee Jeejeebhoy School of Art.

Jeejeebhoy was an important reformer of his own Parsi community. He opposed the domination of the Parsi *panchayat* by priests, and was instrumental in reorganizing it along less hierarchical lines. He was also a supporter of women's education. His interest in education received governmental recognition when, in 1842, he was appointed to the board of education. He was also a member of the senate of Bombay University when it was established in 1857.

Jeejeebhoy also took a strong interest in political life. Though not a nationalist in the modern sense of the term, he was an early advocate of the promotion of Indians into the British-dominated administrative élite. He became the first honorary president of the highly influential Indian political organization the Bombay Association at its foundation in 1852. As the proprietor of the *Bombay Courier* and of the *Bombay Times* (later the *Times of India*), he played a leading role in the political mobilization of the business and intellectual élites of western India. He was, however, a firm supporter of British rule in India. In 1842 he received a knighthood and in 1857 he was created the first Indian baronet. He distinguished himself by his loyalty during the mutiny of 1857, and by the generous contributions which he made afterwards for the relief of its casualties in India. He died on 14 April 1859, and was succeeded in the baronetcy by his eldest son, Cursetjee, who in 1860 assumed the name of his father. The second baronet died on 17 June 1908; his remains were disposed of according to Parsi rites.   E. J. RAPSON, rev. A.-M. MISRA

Sources J. H. Wadia, *The life of Sir Jamsetjee Jeejeebhoy, first baronet* (1950) · J. R. P. Mody, *Jamsetjee Jeejeebhoy: the first Indian knight and baronet, 1783–1859* (1989) · G. A. Natesan, *Famous Parsees: biographical and critical sketches* · *Bombay Gazetteer* (15 April 1959) · C. E. Dobbin, *Urban leadership in western India: politics and communities in Bombay city, 1840–1885* (1972)
Likenesses Baron Marochetti, bronze statue, Kent's Corner, Bombay, India · portrait, Oriental Club, London [*see illus.*]
Wealth at death Rs2,500,000: Mody, *Jamsetjee Jeejeebhoy* (1959), 157

Jeens, Charles Henry (1827–1879), engraver, was born on 19 October 1827, at Uley in Gloucestershire, the son of Henry and Matilda Jeens. On 1 March 1855 he married Harriet Deborah Nesbitt at St Pancras Old Church, London; there is no record of any children. He was taught his trade by John Brain (*fl.* 1836–1879) in the 1840s, and went on to study under William Greatbach (1802–*c*.1885). Most, if not all, of his plates were engraved on steel, many after contemporary artists, and his best work was done as a figure and portrait engraver; at least sixty-seven portraits of British nationals are known by him. His earliest independent plate was probably *Lord William Russell—1683*, after A. Johnston, for the *Art Journal* (1854). Greatbach almost certainly introduced Jeens to the publisher Virtue, who later regarded him as 'among the best and most efficient helps on our staff of figure engravers' (*Art Journal*, 42, 1880, 39). Jeens engraved seventeen plates for the periodical between 1854 and 1879, six of which, issued between 1855 and 1860, were also published in 600 proof impressions to form S. C. Hall's *The Royal Gallery of Art* (1854–60). A proof before letters of an 1876 *Art Journal* plate, *The Parting*, after J. D. Watson, was offered for £40 in 1997; its original purchase price was probably 1 guinea. Also for Virtue, Jeens engraved vignettes of two battles after E. Armitage and M. A. Hayes for E. H. Nolan's *The Illustrated History of the British Empire in India* (1858–60).

About 1860 Jeens became associated with Macmillan &

Co., for whose Golden Treasury series and other publications he produced many vignettes and portraits, among the latter a series of 'scientific worthies', issued in the periodical *Nature*. These earned him notice as one of the miniaturists of engravers, and in some ways a follower of Bartolozzi. In the 1860s he undertook work for the postage stamp engravers and printers Perkins, Bacon & Co., and is credited with engraving the 1*d.* Antigua stamp designed by E. H. Corbould (August 1862). In 1863 Jeens completed for the Art Union of London the plate commenced by H. C. Shenton from F. R. Dicksee's *A Labour of Love*, because of Shenton's failing eyesight. *Joseph and Mary*, after E. Armitage, was published by the same society in 1877; *Stolen by Gipsies—the Rescue*, after J. B. Burgess, was finished after Jeens's death by L. Stocks and issued to subscribers in 1883.

In 1867 Jeens was elected a member of the Graphic Society, and in 1868 he engraved a plate for Queen Victoria's *Leaves from the Journal of our Life in the Highlands from 1848 to 1861*. *Rebekah and Eliezer*, after H. Vernet, appeared in an illustrated edition of the Bible published by J. G. Murdoch, in 1878, the frontispiece to W. H. Pater's *Studies in the History of the Renaissance* in 1873, and a rare landscape vignette as the title-page of George Eliot's *Middlemarch* published by Blackwood in 1875. Representative of his best work is *Armado and Jacquematta*, after J. Holmes, engraved for the first volume of The Royal Shakespeare, published by Cassell in 1883. For the print publisher Colnaghi he engraved *Lady Hamilton with the Spinning-Wheel* after G. Romney. He signed his plates 'C. H. Jeens'. Jeens died at 67 St Paul's Road, Camden Square, London, after a long illness, on 22 October 1879, aged fifty-two, leaving a widow, and less than £3000 in his will.

F. M. O'DONOGHUE, rev. B. HUNNISETT

Sources *Art Journal*, 16 (1854), 152 · *Art Journal*, 23 (1861), 256 · *Art Journal*, 29 (1867), 29 · *Art Journal*, 42 (1880), 39 · *Art Journal*, new ser., 2 (1882), 286 · H. Delaborde, *Engraving: its origin, processes and history* (1886), 314 · *Engraved Brit. ports.*, 6.637 · index of deaths, General Register Office for England · IGI · CGPLA *Eng. & Wales* (1880)
Archives BM, department of prints and drawings, volume of vignette proofs
Wealth at death under £3000: probate, 18 Feb 1880, CGPLA *Eng. & Wales*

Jeeves, Percy (1888–1916), cricketer, was born on 5 March 1888 at Common Side, Soothill Nether, near Dewsbury, Yorkshire, the son of Edwin Jeeves, railway porter, and his wife, Nancy Garforth. The family moved to Goole in 1901 and in the following year Jeeves left Alexander Street School and played in the Goole first eleven. Although he successfully answered an advertisement for a professional at Hawes cricket club, he was unsuccessful in a Yorkshire trial in 1910. R. V. Ryder, Warwickshire's secretary, noted his abilities and he joined the county ground staff in 1911, the year in which Warwickshire won the county championship. While waiting to qualify, Jeeves played for Moseley in the Birmingham league but was permitted to make his county début against the Australians (1912).

Jeeves's first full season for Warwickshire (1913), in which he topped the bowling averages, was 'nothing short of a triumph' (*Wisden*, 1914, 199). Three successive matches in August were especially significant. Against Worcestershire his seven for 34 were the best figures of his career, while his 86 not out against Yorkshire proved to be his highest score. In the third match, against Gloucestershire at Cheltenham, the spectators included P. G. Wodehouse, an enthusiast for the game. The writer had been casting round for a name to give to the fictional 'gentleman's gentleman' whom he was creating in his mind. In settling on Jeeves he identified the cricketer with a figure who, from 1916 onwards, would have literary immortality.

Jeeves did well again in 1914 and *Wisden* was fulsome, seeing him 'as one of the great bowlers of the future' (*Wisden*, 1915, 123). He had been selected for the Players against the Gentlemen and his four wickets for 44 in the second innings had brought his side an unexpected victory. The season ended abruptly shortly after the outbreak of war on 4 August. In Warwickshire's last match, against Surrey, Jeeves clean bowled Tom Hayward twice and Jack Hobbs to help his side in a defeat of the reigning county champions. With his medium-fast away-swingers he took, in his career, 199 wickets (average 20.03) while scoring 1204 runs as a late-order attacking batsman.

Jeeves joined the Royal Warwickshire regiment and was killed in action in France on the Somme at High Wood, Montauban, on 22 July 1916. In the view of P. F. Warner he had been an England bowler of the future.

GERALD M. D. HOWAT

Sources *Wisden* (1913–15) · *Wisden* (1917) · S. Santall, 'A chat with Percy Jeeves', *Cricket* (15 Nov 1913), 59 · L. B. Duckworth, *The story of Warwickshire cricket … 1882–1972* (1974) · R. Brooke, ed., *Warwickshire cricketers, 1843–1973* (1973) · F. Donaldson, *P. G. Wodehouse* (1982) · P. Bailey, P. Thorn, and P. Wynne-Thomas, *Who's who of cricketers*, rev. edn (1993) · C. Martin-Jenkins, *World cricketers: a biographical dictionary* (1996) · b. cert. · d. cert. · CGPLA *Eng. & Wales* (1916)
Likenesses photograph, 1913, repro. in Santall, 'A chat with Percy Jeeves' · two photographs, 1913–14, Ken Kelly Collection
Wealth at death £223 1s. 2d.: administration, 20 Oct 1916, CGPLA *Eng. & Wales*

Jeffcock, Parkin (1829–1866), mining engineer, was born at Cowley Manor on 27 October 1829, the second child and elder son of John Jeffcock of Cowley, Derbyshire, and his wife, Catherine, *née* Parkin. Although at first intended for Oxford and the church, he was articled in 1850, after some training at the College for Civil Engineers, Putney, to George Hunter, a colliery viewer and engineer of Durham. Making rapid progress in his profession, in 1857 he became partner of J. T. Woodhouse, a mining engineer and agent of Derby; in 1860 he took up residence at Duffield, near Derby. He greatly distinguished himself in 1861 by the bravery he displayed in attempting to rescue the men and boys confined in a coal pit at Clay Cross during an inundation. In 1863, and again in 1864, he examined and reported on the Moselle coalfield, near Saarbrücken in Germany. On 12 December 1866 he learned, while at his house at Duffield, that the Oaks pit, near Barnsley, was on fire; Jeffcock went there at once, and with three others descended to make a complete exploration of the mine. One of the party returned to the surface to send down volunteers, but Jeffcock remained below directing such life-saving operations as could be carried on during the night of 12 December. Before further help arrived on the following morning a second explosion had killed Jeffcock and, with a single exception, the whole band of volunteers, thirty in number. The mine was sealed down, and Jeffcock's body was not recovered until 5 October 1867, when it was buried in Ecclesfield churchyard. A church, named St Saviour's, built as a memorial to Jeffcock at Mortomley, near Sheffield, was completed in 1872 at a cost of £3000.

THOMAS SECCOMBE, *rev.* ROBERT BROWN

Sources J. T. Jeffcock, *Parkin Jeffcock, civil and mining engineer* (1867) • *Derby Mercury* (19 Dec 1866) • *Derby Mercury* (26 Dec 1866) • private information (1891) • Boase, *Mod. Eng. biog.*
Likenesses photograph, repro. in Jeffcock, *Parkin Jeffcock*, frontispiece
Wealth at death under £9000: probate, 10 April 1867, *CGPLA Eng. & Wales*

Jefferay, Sir John (*c.*1523–1578), judge, was born at Chiddingly in Sussex, the elder of the two sons of Richard Jefferay (*d.* 1554) and his wife, Elizabeth, daughter of Robert Whitfield of Wadhurst. The family had been landowners and office-holders in the parish from the 1470s; Richard Jefferay's father, John (*d.* 1513), was commemorated by a brass in Chiddingly church. Both brothers entered Gray's Inn; John was admitted in 1544, called to the bar in 1546, and elected an ancient in 1552. In 1553 he married Alice (*d.* 1570), daughter of John Apsley of London. Probably through the influence of Sir Ambrose Cave, chancellor of the duchy of Lancaster, he sat as MP for Clitheroe in 1563, and was described as 'a favourer of religion', that is, a supporter of the Elizabethan religious settlement. He sat for the duchy borough of East Grinstead in 1571 and for the county of Sussex from 1572.

Jefferay became a serjeant-at-law in April 1567 and queen's serjeant on 15 October 1572; in the following year he began to ride the western circuit with Roger Manwood as a justice of assize. He was appointed a justice of the court of queen's bench on 15 May 1576 and the chief baron of the court of exchequer on 12 October 1577, when he was knighted. In Sussex he was a JP by 1564 and chairman of the bench of the eastern division from January 1569. He greatly augmented the family's landholdings in Chiddingly and by the 1570s was lord of several manors, but he nevertheless chose copyhold land on which to build a new mansion between 1573 and 1574; the property already included a pigeon-house, a conduit-house for the supply of water, and a park of 80 acres, to which Thomas Sackville, Lord Buckhurst, had sent six live does in 1570. His punning motto, *Je fray ce que diray* ('I shall do what I say') was in the eighteenth century still to be seen in the glass of the window of the great hall. His relationship with his powerful Pelham neighbours was close, sometimes uncomfortably so. His mansion was held of their manor of Laughton, and he lent his support in their struggle to wrest control of the Dicker Common from the crown. In 1575 the duchy's lessee Anthony Smyth accused Jefferay of confederacy with Sir John Pelham, to whom he gave free

legal advice; Jefferay had been 'very froward and prone … to bolster and cloak with his credit all the riots and routs … both with his counsel and money' (BL, Add. MS 33187, fol. 171). One of his last acts in Sussex was to draft an arbitration award between Pelham and one of his manorial tenants.

Jefferay's will, drawn up in July 1576, has a preamble thanking God for his first wife, 'a good portion and great comfort unto me, doubling my years and filling the same in peace'. Seven of his eight children were dead, and he accepted these losses as 'great callings and warnings … to prepare for death'. His second wife, Mary, was also dead by May 1577 when he contracted to marry another Mary, eldest daughter of George Goring of Ovingdean, within a year. He died in Coleman Street ward, London, on 13 May 1578 and was buried at Chiddingly. His widow, Mary, who later married John Hotham, was granted letters of administration on 29 May 1578. His surviving daughter, Elizabeth, aged fifteen at his death, proved Jefferay's will on achieving her majority in 1584, after the death of her stepmother. In 1585 she married Sir Edward Montagu of Boughton in Northamptonshire, the son of the judge of the same name (*d.* 1557). On his death in 1611 Montagu provided a lavish monument at Chiddingly for her and her parents, in which Sir John is prominently featured. Although the Montagus occasionally lived there, the days of Chiddingly Place as a gentry residence were over almost as soon as they had begun. The mansion ceased to be occupied by its owners and gradually degenerated into a tenanted farm, a long history of neglect punctuated only by episodes of demolition. About 1605 the Montagus' daughter Elizabeth married Robert Bertie, Lord Lindsey; in 1634 they sold the whole Jefferay inheritance in Sussex for £8300 to Sir Thomas Pelham of Laughton.

Jefferay left no reports and was rarely mentioned in those of his colleagues. His short career on the bench left little mark on the law, but he was remembered in anecdote. In 1610 Edward Coke cited Jefferay's inability to prevent a school from operating on the floor beneath his London study, which had been made untenable by the 'gabber de boys'. In a character sketch published in Lloyd's *State Worthies* almost a century after his death Jefferay was described as 'the plodding student', whose qualities were:

> inclination, method, religion with that just and composed mind which attends it, and a great happiness in all four faculties that make a lawyer—sharp invention and clear apprehension, judgement, memory, and a prompt and ready delivery set out with ingenuity and gravity … His gesture and habit was grave but not affected … Modest he was, but not fondly bashful … His humility begat affableness; his affableness, society; that, conference; conference, parts; and they acquaintance; and that, practice; and practice, experience; experience, renown; and that, preferment. (Lloyd, 221–3)

CHRISTOPHER WHITTICK

Sources HoP, *Commons, 1558–1603*, 2.374–5 • Baker, *Serjeants* • M. A. Lower, 'Parochial history of Chiddingly', *Sussex Archaeological Collections*, 14 (1862), 218–28 • BL, Pelham archive, esp. Add. Ch 29640, 29873, 29902, 29921–29923; Add. MS 33186, fols. 4–13, 235, 342–6; 33187, fols. 168–78; 33084, fol. 6 • BL, Add. MS 25209, fol.

211v · inquisition post mortem, PRO, C142/191/77, 106 · PRO, DL 1/100/I and J 4, 104/I and J 6 · will, PRO, PROB 11/67 · J. S. Cockburn, ed., *Calendar of assize records: Sussex indictments, Elizabeth I* (1975) · D. Lloyd, *State worthies* (1670), 221–3 · monument, Chiddingly church, Sussex

Archives BL, Pelham archive, deeds of his estate at Chiddingly in Sussex, Add. Ch 29529–32739

Likenesses portrait, 1571, priv. coll. · effigy on monument, 1612, Chiddingly church, Sussex · portrait (aged forty-eight; after unknown artist, 1571), priv. coll.

Wealth at death land at Chiddingly in Sussex assessed at £30 in 1576 subsidy: typescript at PRO of return in private hands

Jefferies, Joyce (c.1570–1650), moneylender and diarist, was probably born at Ham or Home Castle, Clifton upon Teme, Worcestershire, the only child of Henry Jefferies (d. in or before 1608), gentleman, of that seat and his wife, Anne (d. 1617), daughter of Thomas Barnaby of Bockleton, Worcestershire. Anne was the widow of Johannes Coningsby (d. 1567) of Nene Solars, Shropshire, with whom she had two children, Katherine (d. 1640) and the travel writer Humfrey *Coningsby (1567–1610/11), also of Nene Solars.

Jefferies, who never married, inherited successive legacies from her father, her mother, her half-brother Humfrey Coningsby, and her cousin Thomas Coningsby (d. 1625), to whom (along with the rest of the Coningsby family) she was very close. She employed this wealth principally by lending money as a professional activity. Though she was probably thus engaged well prior to 1638 (earlier documentation having been destroyed in a fire of 1886), she meticulously recorded her transactions thereafter in a financial diary (BL, Egerton MS 3054) which is the chief source for her life and professional activity.

The first twenty-two folios of the account book list moneys received for loans along with the details of the loan agreement. Folios 25–73 record, with revealing annotations, all personal and household expenses. The amount of cash on hand is never indicated, so that Jefferies's precise worth cannot be known. Yet her annual income from loans ranged from a low point of £264 in 1643–4 (when the civil war had interrupted her living arrangements and the lives of many of her clients) and a peak of £658 (on £5890 lent out) in 1638–9. Loans extended as mortgages reached as high as £800, though most conventional loans were for between £10 and £50. Borrowers include friends and relatives on the one hand and perfect strangers, some from as far away as London, on the other. Her lending activity displays elements both of the traditional moral economy—in which people lent to kin and neighbours at low rates and permissive expectation of timely returns—and of the impersonal, rational, and more thoroughly capitalistic outlook.

By 1634, and probably considerably earlier, Jefferies had established her principal residence in Hereford. She lived there first in a rented house; from 1640 in one she bought on Widemarsh Street near the city gate, and finally, when this was torn down in efforts to defend the city during the war, briefly in one she had built for herself in 1643–4. Yet, as Hereford often found itself in the path of rival armies, she spent most of the time between September 1642 and 1648 in self-imposed exile from that city, seeking safety with relatives in surrounding areas of Herefordshire and Worcestershire.

Jefferies by no means allowed spinsterhood to preclude an active engagement in the society of her time and place. Even when living away from her home, she maintained a household and small staff, and frequently visited and was visited by a wide circle of relatives and friends. She tended to keep company and do business especially with other women, and was especially solicitous of and generous to her female relatives and their children. She also maintained close associations with Hereford city and parish officials. Jefferies was also highly literate (keeping the diary herself except when too ill), purchased books and paintings, and followed the news of the day quite closely. Something of the range of her interests and of her political and religious outlook can be inferred from her purchases. She bought two pamphlets on the death of Ben Jonson, whose death she lamented in her diary, a book on the 'untimely death' of Mary, queen of Scots, and two books by Bishop Joseph Hall. She also purchased pictures of the earl of Strafford and Archbishop Laud. Her last recorded expenditure suggests a strongly optimistic outlook: though probably near eighty years of age and in ill health she paid to mend a pair of shoes. She died in 1650, between 3 April, when she made a codicil to her will, and 9 November, when the will was proved. She was buried by her own request in Clifton upon Teme with other members of the Coningsby family. ROBERT TITTLER

Sources R. Tittler, 'Money-lending in the west midlands: the activities of Joyce Jefferies, 1638–1649', *Historical Research*, 67 (1994), 249–63 · R. Tittler, 'Joyce Jefferies and the possibilities of spinsterhood', *Townspeople and nation: English urban experiences, 1540–1640* (2001), chap. 8 · J. Jefferies, account book, BL, Egerton MS 3054 · will, PRO, Family Record Centre, PROB 11/214, fols. 174–5 · F. R. James, 'The diary of Joyce Jefferies, a resident of Hereford during the civil war', *Transactions of the Woolhope Naturalists' Field Club* (1921–3), xlix-lx · J. Webb, 'Some passages in the life and character of a lady resident in Herefordshire and Worcestershire during the civil war', *Archaeologia*, 37 (1857), 189–223 · R. G. Griffiths, 'Joyce Jefferies of Ham Castle', *Transactions of the Worcestershire Archaeological Society*, new ser., 10 (1933), 1–32; new ser., 11 (1933), 1–13 · W. P. W. Phillimore, ed., *The visitation of the county of Worcester made in the year 1569*, Harleian Society, 27 (1888), 58 · A. T. Butler, ed., *The visitation of Worcestershire, 1634*, Harleian Society, 90 (1938)

Archives BL, Egerton MS 3054

Wealth at death est. over £5000; incl. £1408 14s. 8d. owed to her at death: J. Jefferies, account book, BL, Egerton MS 3054

Jefferies, (John) Richard (1848–1887), writer and mystic, was born on 6 November 1848 at the Jefferies Farm at Coate, in the parish of Chiseldon, near Swindon in Wiltshire, the first son and second of five children of James Luckett Jefferies (1816–1896), dairyman, and his wife, Elizabeth (1817–1895), daughter of Charles Gyde, printer, and his wife, Elizabeth, *née* Estcourt.

Ancestry and early life Jefferies was proud of his descent from many generations of Wiltshire and Gloucestershire farmers, but his was country blood with a difference, for the family had strong connections with the London printing trade. In 1816 Richard's grandfather John Jefferies had

(John) **Richard Jefferies** (1848–1887), by London Stereoscopic Co.

reluctantly resigned his position as overseer with the Fleet Street printer Richard Taylor to take over the family mill and bakery in the market town of Swindon. The family also owned a small estate in the nearby hamlet of Coate, consisting of a labourer's cottage (to which John Jefferies added a dwelling house about 1823) and 39 acres of pasture. The farm was managed by Richard's father, James, after his marriage in Islington in 1844 to Elizabeth Gyde, daughter of Taylor's binder and manager Charles Gyde, whose family came from Painswick in Gloucestershire. An original but unbusinesslike man, James spent more time embellishing his garden and orchard than running the farm. Lacking capital, he was further handicapped by a charge placed on his will by his father, who died in 1868. James took out a mortgage of £1500 to pay off legacies to two sisters and began to slide into debt. In 1877 the creditors foreclosed, the farm was sold, and James ended his days as an odd-job gardener in Bath.

James's wife, always known as Betsy, was a kind, nervous, town-bred woman not happy living in the country. Their first-born child, Ellen, was killed by a runaway horse at the age of five. Richard, their second child, was sent to live between the ages of four and nine with an aunt and uncle, the Harrilds, at Sydenham in Kent, where he attended preparatory school. Thomas Harrild was a successful Fleet Street printer. With his aunt Ellen (*née* Gyde) the boy formed a close friendship. On his return home he attended various small private schools in Swindon but showed little promise. After leaving school at fifteen he did no farm work and spent much of his time poking about the hedgerows with a gun, gaining a reputation as an idler. In 1864 he and his cousin James Cox ran away to France, planning to march to Moscow and back. Their French took them no further than Picardy. Instead of returning home they next tried for America, perhaps fired by the tales of Jefferies's father, who had worked his passage to America as a boy of sixteen, but in Liverpool were detained by the police when they tried to pawn their watches and sent back to Swindon in disgrace. Superficially idle, Jefferies was living in a ferment of undefined ideas and aspirations. He was by now a voracious, eclectic reader: J. Fenimore Cooper's 'Leather-Stocking Tales', Longfellow, the *Odyssey*, Goethe's *Faust*, *Don Quixote*, the *Arabian Nights*, Thomas Percy's *Reliques of Ancient English Poetry*, and Shakespeare's poems were among his favourite books. When he was about eighteen he began to read the ancient classics in Bohn's translations.

Years of struggle, 1866–1876 In March 1866 Jefferies joined the *North Wilts Herald*, a Swindon-based tory newspaper, where his first published work appeared in the shape of satirical poems, sensational tales, and laborious local histories. Jefferies became an antiquary interested in the prehistoric relics of his vicinity which he said was 'alive with the dead' (letter to Ellen Harrild, 21 July 1867). He was the first to identify a small stone circle of recumbent sarsens in Day House Lane. 1866 was also the year when he began to resort to the downs near Coate in search of spiritual renewal. Liddington Hill with its 'cassel' or Iron Age hill fort became a favourite haven. Here and elsewhere Jefferies experienced moments of intense communion with sun, sky, earth, and distant sea, when he lost all sense of separate existence and became absorbed into the being of the universe. In September 1867 and July 1868 Jefferies was ill with what are now known to have been the first symptoms of tuberculosis. On 28 August he reported to his aunt that his legs were 'as thin as a grasshopper's'. A holiday in Brussels in September 1870 earned him the nickname of 'the Belgian Lamp-Post'.

On 14 November 1872 Jefferies first came into prominence with a long letter in *The Times* on the Wiltshire labourer. The letter appeared in the wake of the publicity attending the formation of the National Agricultural Labourers' Union under Joseph Arch. Jefferies's letter, which was followed by two others, championed the tenant farmer and adopted a condescending attitude towards the labourer. But though partisan, the letters were models of clear, forceful exposition and attracted notice. Jefferies became regarded as an authority on farming matters, about which he contributed articles to *Fraser's Magazine* and other publications in the mid-1870s. His chief energies, however, were directed to winning fame and fortune as a novelist. *The Scarlet Shawl* (1874), *Restless Human Hearts* (3 vols., 1875), and *World's End* (3 vols., 1877), published by William Tinsley, publisher of Thomas Hardy's early novels, were critical and commercial failures but fortified Jefferies's imagination in a way that the admirably practical farming articles for *Fraser's* could not.

On 8 July 1874 at Holy Cross Church, Chiseldon, Jefferies married Jessie, *née* Baden (1853–1926), daughter of a neighbouring farmer, Andrew Baden, of Day House. In 1875 the couple moved to 22 Victoria Street (now 93 Victoria Road) in Old Swindon, where their first child, Richard Harold, was born on 3 May.

Years of success, 1877–1880 Early in 1877 Jefferies moved to 2 Woodside Terrace, (now 296) Ewell Road, Tolworth, Surrey, to be nearer his London editors. The separation from his native Wiltshire spurred his memory and on 4 January 1878 in the *Pall Mall Gazette* appeared the first of a series of twenty-four anonymous articles entitled 'The gamekeeper at home' which were published in volume form later that year by Smith, Elder, & Co. Subtitled 'Sketches of natural history and rural life' and based on Haylock, keeper on the Burderop estate near Coate, *The Gamekeeper at Home* was an immediate success and quickly ran through several editions. Reviewers hailed the author as the new Gilbert White and praised the charm and exactness of the natural descriptions. Drawing on his Wiltshire memories, Jefferies poured them forth in a series of titles redolent of the countryside—*Wild Life in a Southern County* (1879), *The Amateur Poacher* (1879), *Hodge and his Masters* (2 vols., 1880), and *Round about a Great Estate* (1880), which Q. D. Leavis called 'one of the most delightful books in the English language' (Leavis, 440). These works established Jefferies as the foremost country writer of his day. Edward Thomas wrote:

> No one English writer before had had such a wide knowledge of labourers, farmers, gamekeepers, poachers, of the fields, and woods, and waters, and the sky above them, by day and night … When he wrote these books—*The Amateur Poacher* and its companions—he had no rival, nor have they since been equalled in purity, abundance, and rusticity. (Thomas, 320)

In Tolworth, where a daughter, Jessie Phyllis, was born on 6 December 1880, Jefferies also published *Greene Ferne Farm* (1880), a slight but charming pastoral novel, and two children's stories which have become classics. *Wood Magic* (2 vols., 1881), dedicated to his son Harold, is a satirical fable about a Battle of the Birds which ends on a mystical note with the wind whispering 'There never was a yesterday … and there never will be to-morrow. It is all one long to-day' (chap. 17). *Bevis* (3 vols., 1882), for many the best boys' book ever written, recreates large tracts of Jefferies's childhood at Coate whose reservoir, transformed into a New Sea, is the setting of the adventures of Bevis and his friend Mark. The novel celebrates the unconscious education imbibed in the open air and records Bevis's visionary moments, when he feels out to sun and stars and is lost in 'the larger consciousness of the heavens' (chap. 35). All these works, which represented an astonishing outburst of creativity, a Proustian recapture of *temps perdu*, were based on Wiltshire memories. The first book in which Jefferies explored his immediate surroundings in north Surrey was *Nature Near London* (1883), a collection of articles on the theme of the richness of wild life to be found in the London suburbs. A new strain of observation is apparent in these essays, a more subtle, delicate, tender, and microscopic eye not afraid to linger over fleeting effects of colour, form, and atmosphere.

Illness and final years In December 1881 Jefferies had again been ill, with an anal fistula. In 1882 after four painful operations he moved to West Brighton in Sussex to convalesce, first to 3 Lorna Road, then (between March and April

1883) to Savernake, 8 (now 87) Lorna Road. The recovery of a chalk grassland landscape, the presence of the sea, always a potent force in his imagination, and the shadow cast by his illness combined to inspire Jefferies to write his spiritual autobiography, *The Story of my Heart* (1883). There he recorded the moments of ecstasy, visions of eternity, and dreams of a world freed from want and needless toil that had come to him alone on the Marlborough Downs, by the Sussex sea, and in London. A failure on publication, the book remains the cornerstone of his work, a classic of English mysticism saluted by William James as 'Jefferies's wonderful and splendid mystic rhapsody' (W. James, *The Varieties of Religious Experience*, 1902, 425).

A visit to Somerset in June 1883 inspired *Red Deer* (1884) which Jefferies described as 'a minute account of the natural history of the wild deer of Exmoor and of the mode of hunting them' (letter to C. J. Longman, 22 Aug 1883). In Sussex Jefferies published *The Life of the Fields* (1884) and *The Open Air* (1885), which contain some of his best and most characteristic essays. These include impassioned meditations like 'The pageant of summer', 'Sunlight in a London square', 'The pigeons at the British Museum', and 'Wild flowers'; pieces of close, almost scientific, observation like 'The hovering of the kestrel' and 'Birds climbing the air'; and Zola-esque tales like 'One of the new voters', about a reaper who works fourteen hours a day in the August sun, where Jefferies exposes the degradation and hardship behind the scenes of rural life. Jefferies also published two novels: *The Dewy Morn* (2 vols., 1884) is notable for its chaste but sensuous heroine Felise and its mordant satire of the vacuous squire Cornleigh and his do-gooding wife Letitia. Q. D. Leavis called *The Dewy Morn* 'one of the few real novels between *Wuthering Heights* and *Sons and Lovers*' and said that in it Jefferies 'goes further than any Victorian novelist towards the modern novel' (Leavis, 445). In the futurist *After London* (1885) England has reverted to nature, society relapsed into barbarism, the Thames valley flooded to become an inland sea, and London lies buried beneath a miasmal swamp. The opening section is remarkable for its remorseless Thucydidean power.

In April 1885 Jefferies's health finally broke down. In summer 1886 he vomited blood. His savings went on doctors' fees, and in November he accepted a grant of £100 from the Royal Literary Fund. In March 1887 he had another haemorrhage and could not even dictate. Yet in these years, during which he wrestled manfully with his three great giants of Disease, Despair, and Poverty, Jefferies produced much of his finest work. Essays like 'Hours of spring', 'Nature and books', 'Winds of heaven', 'Walks in the wheat-fields', 'Nature in the Louvre', and the valedictory 'My old village'—collected by his widow and published posthumously in *Field and Hedgerow* (1889)—extend the boundaries of the form as practised by Addison, Hazlitt, and Lamb, and in their emotional vigour anticipate D. H. Lawrence. Fittingly, among the last pieces Jefferies wrote was the preface to a new edition of White's *The Natural History of Selborne* (1887). The final work published in his lifetime was the autobiographical novel *Amaryllis at the Fair* (1887), memorable for its portrait of the farmer Iden, based on Jefferies's father, with his muddling ways and heroic individuality.

After Brighton Jefferies was nowhere long. From 24 June 1884 he lived at 14 Victoria (now 59 Footscray) Road, Eltham, Kent, where his twenty-month-old son, Richard Oliver Launcelot, who had been born in Brighton on 18 July 1883, died suddenly of meningitis. Jefferies was so distressed that he was unable to attend the funeral. Jefferies was then briefly at Rehoboth Villa (now Brook View House), Jarvis Brook, Rotherfield, Sussex, before moving to The Downs, high on Crowborough Hill, and finally to Sea View (now Jefferies House), the Bottom of the Sack (now Jefferies Lane), Goring by Sea, where he died on 14 August 1887, aged thirty-eight, of chronic fibroid phthisis (a form of tuberculosis) and exhaustion. He was buried on 20 August at Broadwater cemetery, Worthing.

Jefferies was a tall, thin, bearded, and slightly stooping figure with brown hair, broad intellectual brow, clear blue eyes, somewhat drooping eyelids, and calm meditative expression. He was a man of simple tastes and regular habits who found his deepest joy in the solitary contemplation of nature. Otherwise he was perfectly content with his family. Proud and reserved, he did not mix in literary society but maintained amicable relations with his editors Frederick Greenwood, C. J. Longman, Oswald Crawford, and C. P. Scott and later in life became friendly with the artist J. W. North.

Posthumous influence　Richard Jefferies is among the purest and most sensitive observers of nature England has produced. Blessed with exquisite senses, he responds to the beauty of the visible world with passion, tenderness, and joy but without sentimentality. He teaches humankind to observe what is about it, to delight in the common sights and sounds of nature. The reader comes to see the world through Jefferies's eyes and his or her life is immeasurably enriched. No writer transports the reader outdoors with such immediacy and Jefferies's work belies his own aphorism: 'The sheaf you may take home with you, but the wind that was among it stays without' ('The July grass', *Field and Hedgerow*). Few writers, at least in prose, have articulated the hidden, spiritual aspect of nature with such haunting power. 'The clearness of the physical is allied to the penetration of the spiritual vision' (Thomas, 49). Jefferies wrote as much about people as about nature and his country books are an indispensable source for the rural history of late nineteenth-century England. *Hodge and his Masters* (1880) in particular presents a magnificent panoramic view of a southern English farming community at the start of what came to be known as the great agricultural depression. A reliable, fair commentator unrivalled for the breadth of his knowledge of the countryside, Jefferies is the central figure in the whole rural tradition, a Janus looking back to the cruder, more spacious world of the early nineteenth century and forward to the troubled introspection of George Sturt (George Bourne), Edward Thomas, and Henry Williamson. Jefferies was also a considerable novelist, an important bridge between Hardy and D. H. Lawrence, and a prose artist of bewitching power, the master of a simple, flowing,

apparently effortless style. 'His writing never reaches after effect and seems unconscious of achieving any; he is therefore the best possible model' (Leavis, 443). Not least, he inspired one of the finest literary biographies in the language, by Edward Thomas. As Jefferies wrote of Iden (*Amaryllis at the Fair*, chap. 26): 'It was his genius to make things grow … [he was] a sort of Pan, a half-god of leaves and boughs, and reeds and streams, a sort of Nature in human shape, moving about and sowing Plenty and Beauty.'

ANDREW ROSSABI

Sources E. Thomas, *Richard Jefferies: his life and work* (1909) · H. R. Matthews and P. Treitel, *The forward life of Richard Jefferies: a chronological study* (1994) · G. Miller and H. R. Matthews, *Richard Jefferies: a bibliographical study* (1993) · Q. D. Leavis, 'Lives and works of Richard Jefferies', *Scrutiny*, 6/4 (March 1938), 435–46 · BL, Richard Jefferies Collection, Add. MS 58822A, B [20A, B correspondence of Jefferies with members of his family and various publishers] · W. J. Keith, *Richard Jefferies: a critical study* (1965) · W. J. Keith, 'Richard Jefferies', *The rural tradition: a study of the non-fiction prose writers of the English countryside* (1974), 127–47 · W. Besant, *The eulogy of Richard Jefferies* (1888) · H. S. Salt, *Richard Jefferies: a study* (1894) · O. Crawfurd, 'Richard Jefferies: field-naturalist and litterateur', *The Idler*, 13 (Oct 1898), 289–301 · J. Luckett [F. C. Hall], 'The forbears of Richard Jefferies', *Country Life*, 23 (14 March 1908), 373–6 · R. H. Jefferies, 'Memories of Richard Jefferies', *Concerning Richard Jefferies, by various writers*, ed. S. J. Looker (1944), 17–27 · R. Ebbatson, 'Richard Jefferies', *Lawrence and the nature tradition: a theme in English fiction 1859–1914* (1980), 127–64 · 'Jefferies at Goring', *Richard Jefferies: a tribute by various writers*, ed. S. J. Looker (1946), 143–56 · [L. M. Phillips], *EdinR*, 210 (1909), 221–43 · L. V. Grinsell, 'The archaeological contribution of Richard Jefferies', *Transactions of the Newbury District Field Club*, 8 (1940), 216–26 · P. K. Robins, 'Richard Jefferies at Tolworth', *Richard Jefferies Society Journal*, 6 (spring 1997), 14–19 · J. Hall, 'A personal reminiscence of Richard Jefferies', *Country Life*, 26 (18 Dec 1909), 870–71 · A. Delattre, 'The Jefferies saga', unpublished typescript, 1992, Archives of the Richard Jefferies Society · A. Smith, 'The Gydes, the Jefferies and the Harrilds', unpublished typescript, 1984, Archives of the Richard Jefferies Society

Archives BL, corresp., literary MSS, and autograph notebooks, Add. MSS 58803–58832 · Devizes Museum, Wiltshire Archaeological and Natural History Society | BL, Archive of the Royal Literary Fund, loan 96 M1077/1–145 · Richard Jefferies Museum, Coate, Wiltshire

Likenesses J. G. Barrable, photograph, 1862, BL · attrib. F. C. Hall, photograph, 1872, repro. in G. Toplis, ed., *The early fiction of Richard Jefferies* (1896) · M. Thomas, plaster, 1890 (after marble bust), NPG · M. Thomas, marble effigy on monument, 1891 (unveiled 1892), Salisbury Cathedral · P. Nutt, acrylic, 1985 (after photograph), Richard Jefferies Museum, Coate, Wiltshire · Elliott & Fry, photograph, priv. coll. · London Stereoscopic Co., photo-mezzotype, BL, NPG [*see illus.*] · W. Strang, etching (after photograph by London Stereoscopic and Photographic Company, 1879), repro. in R. Jefferies, *Field and hedgerow*, large paper edn (1889) · bust, Taunton shire hall

Wealth at death £184 12*s.*: administration, 3 Sept 1887, *CGPLA Eng. & Wales*

Jefferson, Sir Geoffrey (1886–1961), neurosurgeon, was born at 27 Barrett Street, Stockton-on-Tees, co. Durham, on 10 April 1886, the eldest of the six children of Arthur John Jefferson (1857–1915), a general practitioner and surgeon in Rochdale, and his wife, Cecilia, *née* James (d. 1946), of Stockton, who was formerly a nurse. Jefferson attended Rochdale collegiate school from 1895 and Manchester grammar school from 1899, but his performance as a classicist was undistinguished. However, in 1904, on changing to scientific subjects in order to read medicine at Manchester University, he showed his potential and was inspired by the professor of anatomy, Grafton Elliot Smith. Jefferson was awarded scholarships in anatomy and physiology and qualified in 1909, passing the London MB BS with honours and a distinction in surgery. After house appointments at the Manchester Royal Infirmary he worked as a demonstrator in anatomy and began his first studies on the nervous system. He obtained his FRCS in 1911. During further house appointments in London, Jefferson obtained the London MS with the gold medal in 1913.

Gertrude May Flumerfelt (1882–1961), a Canadian medical student to whom he had become engaged, persuaded Jefferson that his future lay in Canada. They were married in Victoria, British Columbia, on 17 January 1914 and set up a joint practice in general surgery and medicine. But wishing to contribute to the war effort they returned to England in February 1916. Jefferson was appointed a surgeon to the Anglo-Russian hospital in St Petersburg, where he arrived in May 1916. In June he was sent to Lutsk on the eastern front; there he commanded a surgical unit and was awarded the medal of the Russian order of St George. He returned to St Petersburg in December, and to England in June 1917. He was then in very poor health, and was posted to a hospital in Manchester until he was fit enough to join the 14th general hospital at Wimereux, near Boulogne, in April 1918. Head and spinal injuries were placed under his care, though no specialized unit was established. The war having ended he returned home in January 1919.

After a short period, during which Jefferson studied the wounds in brain specimens he had sent home from France, he obtained an appointment as a general surgeon to the Salford Royal Hospital. In order to further his neurosurgical experience he visited Harvey Cushing in Boston in 1924. Jefferson, joined later by Hugh Cairns in London and Norman Dott in Edinburgh, then began to establish specialized neurosurgery in Britain. The Society of British Neurological Surgeons was founded in 1926 as a result of his efforts and Jefferson served two terms as its president. Also in 1926 he was appointed to Manchester Royal Infirmary as a surgeon with a special interest in the nervous system. Jefferson's reputation as a teacher and lecturer grew steadily, and papers on head wounds, injuries of the spine, and epilepsy soon established his international reputation. Most important among these were two on fractures of the atlas vertebra, which acquired the eponymous title of Jefferson's fracture. His later work covered a wide field in which his studies on the effects of raised intracranial pressure and the clinical manifestations of aneurysms and tumours in the neighbourhood of the optic chiasm and cavernous sinus were important. Jefferson was particularly interested in the extra-sellar extensions of pituitary tumours, the subject of his Sherrington lecture, which was published as The Invasive Adenomas of the Pituitary (1955).

Jefferson also wrote a number of biographical papers, but is remembered more for the so-called meditations, the range of which can be gleaned from titles such as Meditations on Sources of Knowledge, The Mind of Mechanical Man (his Liston oration), Scepsis scientifica, The Localization of the Soul, On Being Happy and Liking it, or, A Postscript to Aristotle (1949). His Selected Papers was published in 1960.

In 1933 Jefferson became a visiting surgeon to the National Hospital for Nervous Diseases in London, attending just once a fortnight. He was later offered a full consultant appointment there but hesitated to accept. When Manchester University created a chair in neurosurgery for him in 1939, the first of its kind in Britain, he ceased working in London. He had resigned from his Salford appointment in 1935. With the onset of the Second World War, Jefferson, as consultant adviser to the ministries of Health and Pensions, had responsibility for organizing civilian neurosurgical facilities throughout the United Kingdom. For this he was rewarded by a CBE in 1943. In that year he was sent on a mission to the United States. He was a member of the brain injuries committee of the Medical Research Council during the war, and of the council itself from 1948 to 1952, when he became chairman of the clinical research committee. Jefferson was largely responsible for planning the future of neurosurgery in post-war Britain.

Jefferson was honoured with fellowships of the Royal Society and the Royal College of Physicians in 1947, and a knighthood in 1950. He did not stop work on retirement in 1951. Always in demand to speak at congresses abroad and meetings at home, he travelled often, when his health would allow, for he had frequent illnesses. He gave numerous eponymous lectures, some being of a semiphilosophical nature, and received a number of honorary degrees and honorary memberships of societies. Whatever Jefferson said was worth hearing, and was spoken in his own unusual manner. He had a compendious knowledge of neuro-anatomy and neurophysiology which, with his love of literature, was the key to his success as a surgeon and speaker. Tall and slowly spoken, he had a presence, occasional disregard for the feelings of others, and no idea of time. His comments were often very humorous, apt, perspicacious, and sometimes devastating; his aphorisms were legendary and his authority unquestioned.

Jefferson died in Manchester Royal Infirmary on 29 January 1961, shortly after returning to England from the United States, where he had suffered a severe heart attack. He was cremated in Manchester on 3 February. Lady Jefferson, who had been founder and director of the family welfare service in Manchester, died within a fortnight of her husband. They had a daughter and two sons, of whom one became a neurologist and the other a neurosurgeon. The Jefferson Memorial Library was opened at the Manchester Royal Infirmary in 1971.   PETER H. SCHURR

Sources P. H. Schurr, So that was life: a biography of Sir Geoffrey Jefferson (1997) · priv. coll. [family archive] · M. Harmer, The forgotten hospital (1982) · G. Jefferson, Selected papers (1960) · F. M. R. Walshe, Memoirs FRS, 7 (1961), 127–35 · G. F. Rowbotham, British Journal of Surgery, 48 (1961), 586–8 · R. H. O. B. Robinson and W. R. Le Fanu, Lives of the fellows of the Royal College of Surgeons of England, 1952–1964

(1970), 212–13 • W. Brockbank, *The honorary medical staff of the Manchester Royal Infirmary, 1830–1948* (1965) • J. Hardman, 'Professor Jefferson as a teacher', *Manchester University Medical School Gazette*, 25 (1946), 52–5 • R. Platt, *Annual address to the Royal College of Physicians* (1961) • A. Jefferson, 'Sir Geoffrey Jefferson, 1886–1961', *Neurosurgical giants: feet of clay and iron*, ed. P. C. Bucy (1985), 231–8 • personal knowledge (2004) • private information (2004) • b. cert. • *CGPLA Eng. & Wales* (1961)

Archives Manchester Royal Infirmary, Jefferson Memorial Library • priv. coll., family archive • Wellcome L., papers | JRL, letters to the *Manchester Guardian* • U. Edin. L., corresp. with N. M. Dott

Likenesses photograph, 1949, NPG • photograph, 1949, RS • F. Deane, oils, *c.*1950, Manchester Royal Infirmary, Jefferson Memorial Library • G. Kelly, oils, 1955, RCS Eng., London; on loan • photograph (after Kelly), Manchester Royal Infirmary, University Department of Medical Illustration

Wealth at death £17,708 12s. 9d.: probate, 1 March 1961, *CGPLA Eng. & Wales*

Jefferson, Samuel (1808–1846), topographer, was born at Basingstoke, Hampshire, on 28 October 1808, the fourth son of Joseph Jefferson (1766–1824), pastor of the Independent chapel there, and his wife, Jane. His father, who was a native of Wigton, Cumberland, published several antiquarian works. Samuel Jefferson returned to Cumberland and married Mary, daughter of Thomas Porthouse, at Wigton on 17 August 1836.

While living in Carlisle as a bookseller, Jefferson wrote and published topographical guides to Carlisle and the surrounding areas. His major work was an intended multivolume history of Cumberland, of which only the volumes on Leath ward (1840) and Allerdale ward above Derwent (1842) were completed. Previous historians of the county had paid scant attention to church history and architecture, deficiencies that Jefferson remedied, particularly by using hitherto unpublished manuscript sources in the Carlisle Dean and Chapter Library. Jefferson's topographical work made him little money, however, and financial difficulties, compounded by failing health, forced him to seek work in London. He acted for six months as assistant to Mr Bell, a bookseller in Fleet Street, and latterly wrote for Sharpe's *London Magazine* until his health finally failed. He died of pulmonary consumption on 5 February 1846 in the Caledonian Road, Pentonville, and was survived by his wife and five children.

ANGUS J. L. WINCHESTER

Sources *GM*, 2nd ser., 25 (1846), 546–7 • F. J. Baigent and J. E. Millard, *A history of the ancient town and manor of Basingstoke …: with a brief account of the siege of Basing house,* AD *1643–1645*, 2 vols. in 1 (1889), 543–5 • PRO, RG 4/2106, fol. 62*v* • Cumbria AS, PR 36/266, 276

Jefferson, Thomas (1732–1807), actor and theatre manager, was born in a farm near Carthorpe in the North Riding of Yorkshire on 31 January 1732. After his mother's early death, instead of following his father into farming, he was articled to a Yorkshire attorney. Shortly before his fifteenth birthday he moved to London, probably still in the employ of an attorney, but was soon in thrall to the theatre. It is possible that David Garrick, having watched or heard of his amateur début at the Haymarket playhouse, advised him to work in the provincial theatre to prepare him for membership of the Drury Lane company, and it was probably while he was acting on the Kent circuit in 1751 that he met and married Elizabeth May, the daughter of an officer in the merchant navy. The bride's father's attempt to keep his daughter off the stage failed, and it was as a couple that the Jeffersons were engaged at Drury Lane for five seasons from October 1753. Their modest status is represented in his roles as Guildenstern in *Hamlet*, the duke of Burgundy in *King Lear*, and Count Paris in *Romeo and Juliet*, and hers as Lady Macduff in *Macbeth*, but their reliability was appreciated by Garrick and the senior actors. It earned them, in 1758, an invitation to join Spranger Barry and Henry Woodward in a new theatrical enterprise in Dublin. They were lucky to get there. The *Dublin Trader*, in which they embarked on 27 October 1758, struck a sandbar, and the Jeffersons were among the passengers who elected to abandon ship. The few who remained on board included the actor Theophilus Cibber and the equilibrist Anthony Maddox: they were among the drowned when the ill-fated packet sank in a storm.

The Jeffersons acted in Dublin from 1758 until 1763, and may have toured in Ireland for a further year. They are next heard of in Exeter, where Jefferson entered into joint management of the theatre. He remained in management for the rest of his active life, and was particularly associated with the Plymouth circuit from 1765 to 1796, but he had no intention of abandoning acting. Management gave him access to leading roles, feeding an appetite which he was happy to gratify away from home. In 1767, a year after the sudden death of his first wife, he rejoined Garrick at Drury Lane, and remained in the company until Garrick retired in 1776. He had graduated to stronger roles—Claudius in *Hamlet*, Orsino in *Twelfth Night*, Jaques in *As You Like It*—but it was as the foil to Garrick's sprightly heroes in contemporary comedies that he proved most valuable. He was a stalwart member of London's finest theatre. He was also a man of uncommon entrepreneurial energy. While retaining his interest in the Plymouth circuit, he managed, jointly with the dancer Simon Slingsby, the Richmond assembly rooms and theatre in the summers of 1774–7, and from 1778 to 1779 he was one of three lessees of the Bristol Theatre Royal, though this seems to have been a less than glorious bid to raise the status of his Plymouth stock company.

Jefferson was already suffering recurrent attacks of gout, and it may have been for reasons of health that he settled in Plymouth from 1780. He continued to manage theatrical affairs from his house next door to the playhouse in Frankfort Place, acting when health and circumstance allowed (he starred himself as King Lear at Exeter on 17 December 1784). By the time he surrendered his theatrical interests in 1796 there were complaints that he had outstayed his welcome, but Plymouth signalled its respect by awarding him an annual theatrical benefit, which continued until at least 1805. In his last years he was left disabled, and largely confined to his Plymouth home. It was probably there that he died in January 1807, in sufficient poverty to earn for his widow the award of £10 from the Drury Lane Actors' Fund.

Jefferson had married his second wife, Rebecca Bainbridge, in Exeter Cathedral on 27 December 1766, less than six months after the death of his first wife. Of their five children, the three who survived infancy became actors, but it was through Joseph (*c*.1760–1832), the second son of Jefferson's first marriage, that the Jefferson theatrical dynasty was most famously established. Joseph emigrated to America with his Scottish wife, and their seven children all became actors. The third son, also Joseph, married an actress, and their son, Joseph Jefferson III, became an international star through his playing of Rip Van Winkle in Dion Boucicault's dramatization of Washington Irving's story. Through her marriage to B. L. Farjeon, the eldest daughter of this Joseph Jefferson restored the dynasty to England. Three of the Farjeon children, Eleanor (1881–1965), Joseph Jefferson (1883–1955), and Herbert (1887–1945), included plays among their voluminous writings.   PETER THOMSON

Sources Highfill, Burnim & Langhans, *BDA* · J. Bernard, *Retrospections of the stage*, ed. W. B. Bernard, 2 vols. (1830) · T. Wilkinson, *The wandering patentee, or, A history of the Yorkshire theatres from 1770 to the present time*, 4 vols. (1795) · G. W. Stone, ed., *The London stage, 1660–1800*, pt 4: *1747–1776* (1962) · K. Barker, *The Theatre Royal, Bristol, 1766–1966* (1974) · *Monthly Mirror* (July 1804)
Likenesses W. Ridley, engraving (after Vanderburg), repro. in *Monthly Mirror*

Jefferson, Thomas (1743–1826), revolutionary politician and president of the United States of America, was born on 13 April 1743 at Shadwell, Albemarle county, Virginia, the first son and third child of the ten children of Peter Jefferson (1708–1757), planter, surveyor, and office-holder, and Jane, *née* Randolph (1720–1776). In 1745 Jefferson and his family moved to Tuckahoe, on the James River in Goochland county, 60 miles from his birthplace, where Peter Jefferson managed the estate and served as guardian of the children of his friend, and his wife's cousin, Colonel William Randolph. Having returned to Albemarle in 1752, Thomas Jefferson made the county his lifelong home, first at his father's Shadwell plantation and then, beginning at 1770, at his own Monticello, located nearby.

Background and early years Peter Jefferson's large holdings in land and slaves helped make him a prominent figure in Albemarle, marked by his selection as justice of the peace and militia officer, and election to the colony's house of burgesses (1754–5). Peter Jefferson is best remembered for his then definitive map of Virginia, prepared in collaboration with fellow surveyor and mathematics professor Joshua Fry, first published in London in 1751 and reprinted many times, most notably in Thomas Jefferson's *Notes on the State of Virginia* (1787). Although he was not a learned man himself, Peter Jefferson recognized the importance of a good education for his son, and placed Thomas in the home of the Revd William Douglas in St James parish, Northam, where he studied until 1757. After Peter Jefferson's death Thomas continued his studies under the Revd James Maury, a much more accomplished classicist, who lived closer to Shadwell in Albemarle county. Peter Jefferson left his first son more than 5000 acres—including the

Thomas Jefferson (1743–1826), by Rembrandt Peale, 1800

Shadwell estate, which remained under his mother's control until her death—a sizeable number of slaves, a small library of forty volumes, and a leading position in local society. Thomas Jefferson acknowledged his father's important influence on his early development, but said virtually nothing about his mother, through whom he was related to the socially prominent Randolph family.

Young Jefferson proved to be a precocious student. Recognizing the limits to his aspirations in a newly developed backcountry region, he persuaded the executors of his father's will to allow him to continue his studies at the College of William and Mary in Williamsburg, the provincial capital. His years at the college (1760–62) and studying law under George Wythe (1762–5), then emerging as a leading figure at the Virginia bar, were formative ones. Although he found most of his instructors dull, he soon fell under the influence of William Small, a mathematics professor who had recently arrived from Scotland; Small in turn introduced Jefferson to Wythe and Governor Francis Fauquier. Jefferson recalled in his *Autobiography* (1821) that he and these three enlightened men formed 'a partie quarree', and that he had learned much from their 'habitual conversations' at the governor's palace. Wythe was Jefferson's most important mentor, preparing him for a successful career as a lawyer, cut short by the imperial crisis, and as a legislator and legal reformer.

Jefferson was the quintessentially ambitious provincial, irresistibly drawn toward the metropolis. The ease with which he reached the pinnacle of provincial society, in the conviviality of Governor Fauquier's intimate circle, pointed him toward the larger world beyond Virginia which he first glimpsed in the books he eagerly consumed in rural Albemarle. After he completed his studies Jefferson proceeded to consolidate his prominent position in the colony through his extensive legal practice and first forays in politics. But his early dissatisfaction with the mediocrity of William and Mary anticipated the more comprehensive misgivings about the social and cultural state of the province as a whole that later inspired his efforts as a republican reformer. Jefferson's provincial cosmopolitanism also inspired a patriotic, idealized vision of the British empire that would make him into a revolutionary.

Jefferson enhanced his financial prospects through marriage on 1 January 1772 to the young widow Martha Wayles Skelton (1748–1782), daughter of John Wayles, a prosperous slave-trading merchant. When Wayles died in 1773, Jefferson and his fellow heirs decided to divide the estate before liquidating creditors' claims. It would prove to be a fateful decision. Although he gained immediate access to 135 slaves, more than tripling the size of his workforce, the outbreak of the revolution made it impossible to disentangle himself from his father-in-law's indebtedness to British merchants, a burden that afflicted Jefferson for the rest of his life, colouring his thinking about public finance and the continuing threat of British economic power to American independence. He brought his new wife to live at the site of his new home, Monticello, on a hilltop overlooking Shadwell, the family estate on the Rivanna, where his mother continued to live until her death in 1776.

Origins of a revolutionary politician In the next few years Jefferson curtailed his far-flung legal practice, concentrating instead on his career as a prominent planter and politician. His position in the county oligarchy was secured by his appointment to the county court as a justice of the peace and as lieutenant (chief commander) of the county militia; in 1769 Albemarle voters elected him to the Virginia house of burgesses, where he would represent the county for the remainder of the colonial period.

Jefferson's rapid ascent to the top rungs of the provincial ruling class was not unusual for the scion of a successful planter, with connections through his mother to the associated first families of Virginia. Coming from a new county on the province's periphery, where the local oligarchy was still consolidating its position and competition for office was limited, also proved a boon to Jefferson's career prospects. But it was the deepening crisis over the future of British imperial rule in the American provinces that gave him the opportunity to develop and display his talents as a polemicist and statesman. The imperial crisis transformed the county gentleman with a vested interest in the status quo and a characteristic sense of class privilege into a radical revolutionary.

Explanations for Jefferson's radical turn usually emphasize his responsiveness to the various strains of Enlightenment thought that he encountered in his rapidly expanding personal library. He was certainly extraordinarily studious, as his fellow burgesses recognized when naming him to key committees charged with justifying the province's opposition to imperial policy. But the advanced positions Jefferson staked out in the imperial crisis, most notably in his famous pamphlet *The Summary View of the Rights of British America* (1774), did not challenge the provincial social order. His great contribution was instead to translate the corporate claims and class interests of Virginia's ruling élite into the more capacious language of English and universal natural rights. In retrospect his differences with more conservative fellow revolutionaries— for instance, on land policy or on state support for the established Anglican church—loomed ever larger, distinguishing the precocious 'democrat' from his 'aristocratic' foes. Yet his enthusiasm for the revolution was an expression of his provincial patriotism, not of social radicalism. In his subsequent career as a republican reformer Jefferson could envision the transformation of his 'country's' political and constitutional order precisely because of his confidence in the durability of provincial society—and of his own class position.

Jefferson was ambitious in a characteristically provincial way. If few members of the Virginian gentry matched his erudition, they applauded his efforts to secure provincial rights and gain the respect of metropolitan Britons in the great debate over the imperial constitution. The principles Jefferson invoked in this debate were staples of British Enlightenment thought, adapted to the peculiar needs of anxious provincials who feared imminent political degradation and economic exploitation. As a lawyer he was particularly attracted to an idealized conception of the English common-law tradition and 'ancient constitution' that grounded law in the custom and consent of local communities, and imposed constitutional constraints on monarchical authority. Jefferson's historical understanding of the ongoing struggles between king and commons that produced the modern British constitution was widely shared by British whigs. His less conventional celebration of English liberty before the Norman conquest reflected the need to establish a primitive pedigree for American freedom in the right of expatriation exercised by colonial settlers in the New World, and before them by the Anglo-Saxon settlers of ancient Britain. This imaginative rewriting of British and colonial American history authorized challenges to the new ministerial orthodoxy of parliamentary sovereignty, justifying the convergent efforts of British radicals to purge the constitution of its accumulated corruptions, and of provincial patriots to reform the imperial relationship. Jefferson's faith in the possibility of progressive improvement emerged in tandem with deep anxieties about the potential loss of provincial and individual rights, a counterpoint of hope and fear that defined his political thought and career.

Jefferson's *Summary View*, drafted as instructions for Virginia's delegates to the first continental congress in Philadelphia but not officially adopted by the house of burgesses, framed the imperial crisis in terms of the implied contractual obligations of George III to his loyal American subjects. Although this controversial pamphlet was published anonymously, Jefferson's authorship was soon widely known, and led to his selection to the second congress in 1775. A poor public speaker, the Virginian did not play a conspicuous role in congressional deliberations. His writing skills earned him several choice writing assignments, however, including the original draft of the 'Declaration of the causes and necessity of taking up arms' (July 1775) and the American Declaration of Independence (4 July 1776). The principles Jefferson so eloquently invoked in the second paragraph of the Declaration of Independence:

> that all men are created equal; that they are endowed by their creator with inherent and inalienable rights; that among these are life, liberty, and the pursuit of happiness: that to secure these rights, governments are instituted among men, deriving their just powers from the consent of the governed

would later be taken as the authoritative expression of the new nation's republican creed, and therefore as the source of Jefferson's lasting reputation. But contemporaneous responses focused the declaration's justification for rebellion in its exhaustive rehearsal of the British monarch's 'long train of abuses' against his American subjects. In its outraged sense of betrayal Jefferson perfectly articulated the revolutionaries' provincial mentality, identifying them with their 'British brethren' while simultaneously proclaiming that 'the circumstances of our emigration and settlement' made them a separate, effectively independent people, even before George III's efforts to establish 'an absolute Tyranny' over them. The challenge for Jefferson was to conjure into existence an American 'people' who were entitled to resist the king's 'injuries and usurpations' and then to determine their own political destiny according to the familiar axioms of social contract theory (Jefferson, *Papers*, 1.429–33).

Jefferson in Virginia Jefferson's authorship of the declaration was not well known at the time, nor was it yet recognized as 'American scripture' (Maier). Convinced that the establishment of republican governments in the separate states constituted the chief business of the American War of Independence, and that a more perfect union of the states would naturally follow, Jefferson would rather have been in Virginia where he might have exercised more influence over the drafting of the state's revolutionary constitution. When Jefferson finally did arrive in Williamsburg in October to begin his tenure as a member of the new house of delegates (1776–9), he spearheaded the reform and codification of Virginia's laws. The revisal of the laws reveals the full range of Jefferson's concerns as a republican reformer, from provisions for universal education (rejected by the house) and gradual emancipation of Virginia's slaves (never reported) to ultimately successful bills for abolishing primogeniture and entail, and guaranteeing religious freedom. Jefferson later wrote that 'these bills, passed or reported … form[ed] a system by which every fibre would be eradicated of antient or future aristocracy' (Jefferson, *Writings*, ed. Peterson, 44). Only a few of the 126 bills reported by the committee were enacted before Jefferson's fellow legislators elevated him to the governorship (1779–81). Lacking effective constitutional powers, he failed to resist a British expeditionary force led by turncoat Benedict Arnold when it invaded the

state in 1780, driving the state government out of Richmond, and Jefferson from his home in Charlottesville. Although suggestions that he was personally responsible for this débâcle were eventually refuted by the legislature, the embittered Jefferson left office under a cloud.

During the subsequent brief interlude from public life Jefferson devoted his energies to responding to a set of queries circulated by François Marbois, secretary to the French legation at Philadelphia, to leading figures throughout America, seeking comprehensive information on the population, manners, institutions, resources, and history of all the members of the far-flung American union. No one was better equipped to assess Virginia's circumstances and prospects, and none of the recipients of the queries in the other states produced anything comparable. Later published as *Notes on the State of Virginia* (French edition, 1785; English edition, 1787), Jefferson's only published book includes his most comprehensive and illuminating commentaries on various controversial questions, including the institution of slavery. Although it was designed to promote Virginia's future economic development, the *Notes* also reflects the republican reformer's misgivings about the progress of the revolution in Virginia.

Jefferson's extended discussion of the state's constitution underscored some of its 'capital defects', including the disproportionate power of the legislature, legislative malapportionment, and the weakness of the executive; most critically the constitution itself had not been drafted by a proper constitutional convention, nor ratified by a vote of the people (Jefferson, *Notes*, 118). An equally long response to Marbois's query on laws includes some of the most fascinating and controversial material in the entire manuscript, most notably the famous treatment of race and slavery. Jefferson juxtaposed the rule of law for white Virginians to the despotic, lawless enslavement of Afro-Virginians, arguing that the only resolution to this unjust state of affairs was to emancipate and expatriate Virginia's slaves and then 'declare them a free and independant people'. Colonization was necessary because racial co-existence was impossible; emancipation without expatriation would produce 'convulsions which will probably never end but in the extermination of one or the other race'. Differences between the two races were 'fixed in nature'; black people, Jefferson suspected, were 'inferior' in mental capacities (ibid., 138, 143). In his brief account of manners, Jefferson returned to the institution of slavery, this time emphasizing its demoralizing effects on the master class: 'the whole commerce between master and slave is a perpetual exercise of the most boisterous passions' (ibid., 162). Even when Jefferson was not addressing the slavery problem directly, he was obsessed with threats to freedom and equality. In his discussion of manufactures, for instance, he concluded that Virginia should leave its 'work-shops … in Europe', so avoiding the kind of servile dependence that advanced manufactures and a degraded working population entailed (ibid., 165).

Although he was an accomplished writer, Jefferson was always reluctant to publish under his own name. This characteristic reticence was reinforced in the case of the *Notes* by his anxiety that Virginians at home would object to his critical treatment of their constitution and his even more devastating commentary on slavery. His wariness about his countrymen's response (at first he proposed to circulate the *Notes* only among the presumably enlightened students at William and Mary), suggested that the republican millennium he envisioned might be postponed indefinitely.

Coming at a moment when Jefferson's career radically shifted focus, from the republican reform of Virginia's institutions to the promotion of the new nation's interests and image during his years as a diplomat in Paris, the *Notes* illuminates Jefferson's hopes and fears for the ultimate outcome of the American War of Independence. This period also constituted a pivotal moment in Jefferson's personal life. Martha Jefferson never recovered from a difficult sixth pregnancy, and her death in September 1782 left her distraught widower to care for three surviving daughters—Martha (1772–1836), Mary (1778–1804), and Lucy (1782–1784). This traumatic loss prepared Jefferson to leave Monticello and return to public life. He was supposed to join the American delegation at the Paris peace talks in 1782, but his departure was postponed when news arrived that negotiations ending the revolution and recognizing American independence had been successfully concluded. While awaiting his diplomatic assignment, Jefferson represented Virginia in congress for a few eventful months (1783–4).

The major problem before the confederation government was the organization and development of the new national domain in the Northwest Territory that came into existence when Virginia ceded its claims to the region in March 1784. Jefferson had already given much thought to the problem of new state formation, including a provision for the creation of new states in his proposed draft of the Virginia state constitution of 1776. As a leading advocate of the long-delayed Virginia cession, he was well prepared to take the lead in drafting the first congressional ordinances for western government and land sales. Jefferson's brief tenure as a congressman gave him a good sense of the weaknesses of a confederation that had no effective controls over fractious member states. This concern deepened over his years in Paris.

American minister to France Jefferson finally sailed from Boston in July 1784 to take up his new responsibilities as American minister to France, accompanied by daughter Martha (Mary stayed with relatives in Virginia, but joined her father in Paris in 1786). He soon found that America was not in a strong position to negotiate further treaty agreements with France and other European powers that would promote American commercial and political interests. He also found that his predecessor, Benjamin Franklin, who had been lionized by Parisian polite society, would be a very hard act to follow. Jefferson was always somewhat awkward in public settings and, though a master of the written language, he was not a fluent French speaker.

Yet Jefferson's frustrations as a diplomat did not diminish his enjoyment of this period in his life. To the contrary, his official inactivity provided ample scope for the studious Jefferson to pursue his intellectual interests and to cultivate friendships within the great Enlightenment 'republic of letters'. Distance from his native country gave him new perspectives that would have a profound effect on the rest of his career. The opening phases of the French Revolution, from Jefferson's perspective the ultimate tribute to the revolutionary achievement of the Americans, were particularly exhilarating for him, giving rise to some of his most radical political ideas, including the concept of generational sovereignty, 'that the earth belongs in usufruct to the living', developed in his famous letter of 6 September 1789 to James Madison (Jefferson, *Papers*, 15.392–8).

During his years in France (1784–9) Jefferson had the leisure to explore Europe and its institutions, observing the inner workings of the ancient regime and clarifying some of his fundamental principles. He was convinced that a great moral and political division separated the Old World from the New. However seductive its attractions might be to Jefferson, he recognized that European civilization exacted enormous human costs: by abolishing despotic rule and the popular ignorance that sustained it, the American revolution constituted a great leap forward for mankind.

Jefferson found the opportunity to hold forth on the new nation's moral superiority irresistible. But this did not stop him from savouring the delights of refined and civilized life in the great European metropolis. New scenes and sensations enabled the grieving widower to explore dormant aspects of his own emotional life. His passionate, possibly sexual relationship with the artist Maria Cosway was only one of many close, sentimentally satisfying friendships he made with European women and men. At this time Jefferson also probably initiated a long-term sexual relationship with his slave Sally Hemings (1773?–1835?), the half-sister of his deceased wife, Martha.

Jefferson was still in Europe while James Madison and his colleagues were crafting a proposal for a stronger federal government in America. Jefferson's cautious responses to the plan, particularly his concern about the omission of a bill of rights, that 'palladium' of liberty to which 'the people are entitled … against every government on earth', anticipated his subsequent emphasis on strict construction of the constitution as a member of President Washington's cabinet and then as the leader of the anti-administration republican opposition (Jefferson to Madison, 20 Dec 1787, Jefferson, *Papers*, 12.440). If Jefferson recovered his emotional equilibrium during his protracted European interlude, he also prepared himself for a career of intense partisan political activity by reaffirming and strengthening his most fundamental ideological commitments.

National politician When Jefferson sailed from France in October 1789, he hoped to attend to personal business in

Virginia—most urgently, to sort out his tangled financial affairs—before returning to his post in Paris. But an invitation awaited him from George Washington to join the new president's cabinet as secretary of state. Washington finally succeeded in persuading the reluctant Jefferson to accept his offer in February 1790; Jefferson joined the new government in New York in late March. Jefferson had every reason to believe that he would play a decisive role in the first Washington administration. As secretary of state he would play a key role in formulating the new nation's foreign policy. Because the new government presumably would earn more respect from foreign powers than its predecessor, he would be able to follow through on diplomatic initiatives that had been thwarted during his Paris years. But Jefferson's cabinet colleague treasury secretary Alexander Hamilton had already set the tone for the administration well before Jefferson's arrival. Hamilton's 'Report on the public credit' (delivered to congress on 14 January 1790) outlined a bold financial policy for servicing federal and state revolutionary war debts. The need for assuring a steady flow of revenue, primarily through import duties on Anglo-American trade, dictated a conciliatory commercial policy toward Britain, thus severely curtailing the new nation's—and Jefferson's—diplomatic options. Implementation of Hamilton's financial plan, including the establishment of a national bank, depended on an expansive definition of the federal government's powers under the new federal constitution. For the emerging 'republican' opposition the resulting 'consolidation' of authority threatened to obliterate the state governments and to transform the federal government into an American version of the British imperial regime that the revolution had overthrown. The British character of the new regime, the foreign policy tilt toward Britain, and the dominating presence of Hamilton himself made the nonpartisan Jefferson into a party leader in spite of himself.

Jefferson's certainty in the righteousness of his own position was reinforced by contemporary events in Europe, where the expanding conflict between republican France and the counter-revolutionary coalition revealed to Jefferson the identical battle line between progressive and reactionary forces that seemed to be unfolding in America. Jefferson's political principles took on their mature form during the great struggles over foreign policy divisions between Anglophile federalists and Francophile republicans. But Jefferson's affinity for France also led to political embarrassments that tarnished the republican cause, and sustained the federalists in power through the 1790s. The pattern was set when Citizen Edmond Genêt, minister from the French republic, made a sensational tour across the country in 1793, distributing military commissions and rousing popular support for the French cause in defiance of Washington's neutrality proclamation (22 April 1793). Federalists could link republicanism with challenges to legitimate, constituted authority, a charge that would continue to resonate after Jefferson withdrew from the cabinet at the end of 1793, for instance when rebellious western farmers resisted the excise on whisky in 1794 or when the Kentucky and Virginia legislatures challenged the constitutionality of federal laws in 1798.

Jefferson's retirement to Monticello proved to be brief. As the runner-up to John Adams in the 1796 presidential contest, Jefferson became vice-president, finding himself once again in the position of partisan opponent of the administration he ostensibly served. Adams and the federalists prospered as federalist diplomatic successes preempted the threat of war with Britain and opened the Mississippi to American commerce, thus fostering a booming economy. Meanwhile, French anger at John Jay's 'English treaty' led to a rapid deterioration of Franco-American relations and French depredations on American shipping that led to an undeclared war. During this quasi-war (1798–1800) the republicans' traditional tilt toward France proved to be a tremendous liability. The republican challenge was to sever the French connection and adopt a plausibly neutral stance; then, as Jefferson counselled his allies, republicans should bide their time, waiting for the 'reign of witches' to subside as federalist warmongers overplayed their hand (Jefferson to John Taylor of Caroline, 4 June 1798, Jefferson, *Writings*, ed. Lipscomb and Bergh, 10.46). If the quasi-war ever became full blown, then peace-loving, tax-averse Americans would recover their senses; if the administration launched a sustained assault on its domestic enemies, liberty-loving republicans would remember why they had fought the revolution in the first place.

Jefferson's counsels of patience betrayed mounting desperation; for the time being the republicans could do little more than wait. The recourse to the state legislatures was counter-productive: Kentucky and Virginia would find themselves standing alone if they followed through on their disunionist threats. Yet, in the republicans' darkest hour, federalists were divided over appropriate preparations for war and, finally and fatally, over Adams's ultimately successful peace negotiation with France that led to the convention of 1800. As the threat of war diminished, federalists were hard-pressed to justify the 'war' against domestic dissidents that they had launched under the aegis of the Aliens and Sedition Acts of 1798.

President of the United States Jefferson hailed his elevation to the presidency in the election of 1800 as a return to the revolutionary principles of 1776. His experiences as opposition party leader in the dark days of federalist rule had not taught him to accept the legitimacy of party competition: aristocratic high federalists were, in his mind, clearly hostile to republican self-government. Jefferson's understanding of partisan conflict in the 1790s as a clash of fundamentally opposed philosophies and systems was reinforced by the global struggle between revolutionary republicanism and monarchical reaction that had been initiated by the French Revolution. Rumours that embittered federalists meant to steal the election after Jefferson and his running mate, Aaron Burr, received the same number of votes in the electoral college (votes for president and vice-president were not distinguished until ratification of the twelfth amendment in 1804) heightened the sense of crisis in the months before Jefferson's inauguration in March 1801. Because of the deadlock the election was thrown into the old house of representatives, controlled by federalists, that had been elected in 1798. A federalist caucus decided to support the more pliable Burr, but could not muster sufficient state votes to resolve the deadlock. Finally, after thirty-six ballots, a few key federalists relented, perhaps recognizing that their defiance of the popular will (republican voters in 1800 believed they were voting for Jefferson) would precipitate a genuine constitutional crisis and jeopardize the survival of the union. Some federalists, including Jefferson's nemesis Alexander Hamilton, were also persuaded that the Virginian would not tamper with the basic structure of the federal regime and that federalist interests would be best served by graceful acquiescence in his election.

In his inaugural address of 4 March 1801 Jefferson asserted that the republicans' 'federal and republican principles' would henceforth be the standard of patriotic Americanism, inviting his erstwhile opponents to recant their heresies and join the new national consensus (Jefferson, *Writings*, ed. Peterson, 493). Jefferson believed that the tide had turned, irrevocably: the new republican administration would not have to resort to the kind of repressive measures that federalists had so eagerly and foolishly embraced in 1798. Confident that the revolution was now secure, Jefferson projected a moderate and conciliatory posture: under the able administration of treasury secretary Albert Gallatin, Hamilton's financial system remained intact, but would no longer serve as the engine of consolidation; internal taxes were repealed and import revenues were used to reduce the national debt (from $83 million to $57 million by 1809). Nor were federalists driven *en masse* from appointive offices in the federal bureaucracy, though Jefferson was attentive to the needs of republican loyalists in making new appointments. Republican animosity toward the federalist judges led to repeal of the Judiciary Act of 1801, which had expanded the federal court system, and to controversial efforts to impeach particularly obnoxious incumbents such as John Pickering of New Hampshire (convicted and removed in March 1804) and Samuel Chase of Maryland (acquitted in March 1805). Jefferson's revolution did not result in wholesale purges of political enemies. But federalists learned to play by the new rules of the game, and many, finding Jefferson much less dangerous to the established order than their own campaign rhetoric had led them to fear, were drawn into the republican ranks.

The success of the republicans' 'revolution of 1800' was not measured by the violence of its retaliation against the federalists, but by growing majorities in both houses of congress and by Jefferson's landslide re-election in 1804. As the nation grew more republican it expanded in size. The administration's greatest coup, the Louisiana Purchase of 1803, doubled the extent of American territory and removed the danger of a destabilizing French presence in the Mississippi valley. When Jefferson delivered his second inaugural address in March 1805, the new nation's prospects could not have been more favourable.

Yet the vulnerability of Jefferson's achievement would soon become apparent. American peace and prosperity were dependent on maintaining a neutral position in the Napoleonic wars that were engulfing the Atlantic world. The European war opened up extraordinary new opportunities to American producers and shippers, but it also put them at grave risk: the belligerent powers showed little respect for 'neutral rights' when their own vital interests were at stake. Jefferson found that threats of commercial sanctions against the belligerents, culminating in the ill-fated embargo of 1807–9, were ineffective, even counter-productive. By the end of his presidency the possibility of war seemed increasingly strong—with either Britain or France, or both.

Jefferson's problems in his second term were not confined to foreign affairs. American foreign policy had always been inextricably linked to sectional tensions and centrifugal tendencies in the American federal union. Aaron Burr's western 'conspiracy' of 1806 illuminates these connections. Jefferson was convinced that his former vice-president was guilty of treason against the United States, but it was by no means clear that Burr contemplated disunion, filibustering into Spanish territory, or a combination of the two, or neither. Jefferson's relentless pursuit of Burr, culminating in the adventurer's trial for treason (he was acquitted), revealed how anxious the president was about the very survival of the union.

Jefferson's old enemies gained a new lease of life as opposition to his foreign and domestic policies grew. Meanwhile republicans were divided, with 'old republican' purists aligning themselves against moderates who tilted too much toward federalist heresies. These divisions, which originated late in Jefferson's first term, became more pronounced as republicans looked toward the presidential succession. Insurgent old republicans rallied around James Monroe; moderates around James Madison, Jefferson's secretary of state and heir apparent. Some republicans thought that the only hope for the survival of the party and the union was that Jefferson agree to serve a third term. By 1809, however, the 65-year-old Jefferson, enduring one of the worst phases of his political career, longed to return to private life.

Retirement Jefferson never left Virginia after retiring to Monticello, his mountain top home, in March 1809. Although he kept up a far-flung correspondence and took a keen interest in national politics under the administrations of his Virginian allies James Monroe and James Madison (1809–25), Jefferson focused his energies on his home, his ever-expanding family, and his agricultural enterprises. With the vindication of American independence in the Anglo-American War of 1812–14, Jefferson's reputation quickly rebounded from the political and diplomatic set-backs of his second term. Swarms of admiring visitors came to pay homage, driving the Sage of Monticello into periodic exile at his Poplar Forest plantation in Bedford county, 70 miles away.

Popular adulation was undoubtedly gratifying to Jefferson: ambitious young public men sought his counsel, aspiring authors sent their books for his endorsement, and an adoring white family basked in his genial presence. Daughter Martha and her husband, Thomas Mann Randolph, provided Jefferson with twelve grandchildren, eleven still living at his death. Meanwhile, Jefferson's liaison with Sally Hemings produced four unrecognized children who lived to maturity: Beverley (b. 1798, d. after 1822), Harriet (b. 1801, d. after 1822), Madison (1805–1877), and Eston (1808–1856). Notwithstanding recurrent physical complaints, these were among Jefferson's happiest years. For the first time since his tenure as American minister in Paris, Jefferson could indulge his many intellectual interests. Rising above partisan conflict, he could take a more dispassionate, philosophical view of the controversial questions that had led to his estrangement from fellow revolutionaries such as John Adams who had betrayed 'aristocratic' tendencies. But Jefferson did not lose his intellectual edge in retirement. To the contrary, his reflections on political and constitutional theory offered him the opportunity to reaffirm and deepen his commitment to the fundamental principles that had guided him throughout his career. Jefferson's retrospective view was often distorted and self-serving, but the story he told about the new nation's history and about his own history as a nation-maker was inspiring and influential. Jefferson's prophetic vision, seemingly confirmed by his country's glorious ascent, transformed him into an American icon in his own lifetime.

Yet all was not well in Jefferson's world. Sectional divisions over the spread of slavery in the Missouri controversy (1819–21) presented the most obvious danger, but Jefferson was equally troubled by supreme court decisions such as *McCulloch v. Maryland* (1819) that pointed toward the consolidation of power in the federal government. Jefferson's dire financial situation, exacerbated by a depression in 1819 that was particularly devastating to overextended staple producers, made him acutely sensitive to threats to the economic interests and political power of his class and region. Jefferson's solicitude for his fellow slave-holders made him increasingly suspicious of the motives of anti-slavery activists whose humanitarian professions masked a great danger, that Virginia and the other slave states would themselves be enslaved by an all-powerful central government. Although he continued to advocate the compensated emancipation and colonization of slaves, Jefferson's hopes for this great panacea were undercut by doubts about the good faith of his fellow Americans. With no prospect for an effective solution to the slavery problem Jefferson did nothing to disentangle himself from the peculiar institution—beyond providing for the freedom of his mixed-race children.

When Jefferson confronted fundamental challenges to the republican legacy of the American revolution, he was forced to question the value and purpose of his whole public life. The oscillation between vaulting hopes and bleak moments of despair that characterized his political life thus echoed through his retirement. Yet there was always consolation in the long historical perspective: the sons of the commonwealth educated at Jefferson's new University of Virginia (established in Charlottesville in 1817) would redeem the revolutionary legacy; the rising generation would, somehow, deal with the problem of slavery; and American independence would be an inspiration to oppressed peoples everywhere, 'arousing men to burst the chains under which monkish ignorance and superstition had persuaded them to bind themselves' (Jefferson to Roger Weightman, 24 June 1826, Jefferson, *Writings*, ed. Lipscomb and Bergh, 16.182).

Jefferson was eighty-three years old when he died at Monticello on 4 July 1826, the fiftieth anniversary of American independence. He was buried at Monticello on the following day. At his direction the following epitaph was inscribed on his tombstone: 'Here was buried Thomas Jefferson, Author of the Declaration of American Independence, of the Statute of Virginia for religious freedom & Father of the University of Virginia' (Jefferson, *Writings*, ed. Peterson, 706).

Reputation Jefferson was always concerned with his place in history, and his tombstone inscription correctly identified the sources of his future fame. During the deepening sectional crisis that was prefigured in the Missouri controversy, some northern abolitionists celebrated Jefferson as an early leader in the struggle against slavery, underscoring the progressive implications of his famous statement in the Declaration of Independence that 'all men are created equal'. As Jefferson's stock rose to the north, southern defenders of slavery tended to dismiss him as a radical egalitarian, echoing charges made by federalist critics in his lifetime. This pattern of celebration and condemnation, driven by contemporaneous political divisions, continued to define Jefferson's reputation throughout American history.

The American Civil War brought the Jefferson image into sharp focus. President Abraham Lincoln invoked Jefferson's moral authority in justifying the federal government's great moral crusade to save the union and ultimately to abolish slavery. At the same time, however, more critical commentators argued that Jefferson's ideas about states' rights, most famously set forth in his Kentucky resolutions (1798), justified the secession of the southern states and were ultimately responsible for the carnage of the war. When the war's wounds finally began to heal in the late nineteenth century (and the nation's commitment to securing the civil rights of former slaves diminished), Jefferson's reputation revived. His hostility to political centralization and his patriotic commitment to his 'country', Virginia, made him an increasingly popular figure among libertarian and agrarian conservatives. The 'liberal' Jefferson only returned to the fore as twentieth-century reformers made him the patron saint of their struggles for democracy, culminating in Franklin D. Roosevelt's campaign to give big government a Jeffersonian gloss in the New Deal.

Jefferson's worldwide reputation reflects his perceived role as a prophet of democracy, but his reputation in the United States has been complicated by the politics of race. In their efforts to rekindle the egalitarian creed of Lincoln and the abolitionists, leaders of the civil rights movement invoked Jefferson and his Declaration of Independence.

Opponents of integration responded by emphasizing Jefferson's commitments to slavery and local self-government, mirroring criticism from radicals who stressed the discrepancy between his anti-slavery sentiments and his failure to take significant steps against the institution—or to free more than a handful of his own slaves. In recent years, however, the debate over Jefferson's anti-slavery credentials has lost some of its urgency: with the consolidation of the civil rights revolution, Jefferson has become a less controversial figure.

Responses to the revelations in 1997 of Jefferson's liaison with Sally Hemings suggest that in this case the discrepancy between profession—Jefferson always strongly opposed race-mixing—and practice worked to the advantage of his reputation. For Americans who continue to revere Jefferson as a democratic icon the Hemings relationship neutralized the virulent racism of his *Notes on … Virginia*, revealing a fundamental accord between sexual impulses and natural rights principles.   P. S. ONUF

Sources *The papers of Thomas Jefferson*, ed. J. P. Boyd and others, 27 vols. (1950–) · *The writings of Thomas Jefferson*, ed. A. A. Lipscomb and A. E. Bergh, 20 vols. (1903–4) · *The writings of Thomas Jefferson*, ed. P. L. Ford, 10 vols. (1892–9) · *Writings / Thomas Jefferson*, ed. M. D. Peterson (1984) · T. Jefferson, *Notes on the state of Virginia*, ed. W. Peden (1954) · D. Malone, *Jefferson and his time*, 6 vols. (1948–81) · M. D. Peterson, *Thomas Jefferson and the new nation: a biography* (1970) · A. Burstein, *The inner Jefferson: portrait of a grieving optimist* (1995) · J. J. Ellis, *American sphinx: the character of Thomas Jefferson* (1997) · P. S. Onuf, ed., *Jeffersonian legacies* (1993) · P. S. Onuf, *Jefferson's empire: the language of American nationhood* (2000) · J. Fliegelman, *Declaring independence: Jefferson, natural language, and the culture of performance* (1993) · P. Maier, *American scripture: making the Declaration of Independence* (1997) · F. McDonald, *The presidency of Thomas Jefferson* (1976) · A. Gordon-Reed, *Thomas Jefferson and Sally Hemings: an American controversy* (1997) · A. Helo, 'Thomas Jefferson's republicanism and the problem of slavery', PhD diss., Tampere University, 1999 · R. M. S. McDonald, 'Jefferson and America: episodes in image formation', PhD diss., University of North Carolina, 1998
Archives BL, letter-book · L. Cong., papers · Mass. Hist. Soc., papers · Missouri Historical Society, St Louis, papers · University of Virginia, Charlottesville, papers | L. Cong., James Madison papers · L. Cong., James Monroe papers
Likenesses R. Peale, portrait, 1800, White House, Washington, DC [*see illus.*] · portraits, Charlottesville, Virginia; repro. in A. L. Bush, *The life portraits of Thomas Jefferson*, new edn (1987)
Wealth at death $112,500 assets; $107,273.63 in debts (not finally settled until 1878): will, *Writings*, ed. Ford, vol. 10, pp. 392–6; Malone, *Jefferson*, vol. 6, pp. 511–12

Jeffery, Dorothy. *See* Pentreath, Dorothy (*bap.* 1692, *d.* 1777).

Jeffery, George Barker (1891–1957), mathematician and educationist, was born in Lambeth, London on 9 May 1891, the son of George Jeffery, corresponding clerk, and his wife, Elizabeth McDonald McKenzie. He was educated at Strand School, King's College, London, and Wilson's Grammar School, Camberwell. In 1909 he entered University College, London, for a two-year course, followed by a year at the London Day Training College. He then returned to University College as a research student and assistant to L. N. G. Filon and obtained his BSc in 1912. In the same year his first research paper was communicated to the Royal Society. In 1914 Filon went away on war service and Jeffery,

aged twenty-three, was left in charge of the department. In 1915 he married Elizabeth Schofield; they had one son and two daughters. Jeffery was a Quaker and in 1916 spent a short time in prison as a conscientious objector but was later allowed to do work of national importance. In 1919 he returned to the college, again as an assistant to Filon.

During this time Jeffery published a series of papers on the mathematical functions which occur in the solution of Laplace's equation and on the theory of viscous flow. He was particularly interested in the general solution of Laplace's equation given by E. T. Whittaker in 1902. He used this formula as a means of obtaining relations between spherical harmonics, cylindrical harmonics, and other such functions which occur in the solution of Laplace's equation. In fluid motion his object was to obtain exact solutions of the Navier–Stokes equation, and he discovered a number of new and interesting types of flow. His point of view was very practical: he was looking for exact solutions of definite physical problems.

In 1921 Jeffery became university reader in mathematics and in 1922 professor of mathematics at King's College, London, but in 1924 he returned to University College as Astor professor of pure mathematics. His researches at this time were mainly inspired by Einstein's theory of relativity, and he published a small book, *Relativity for Physics Students* (1924). He was elected FRS in 1926. In the years following the war he published a series of original papers in rapid succession. They were entirely in the field of applied mathematics in which his real scientific interest lay. (He made no further original contribution to pure mathematics.) He was becoming increasingly absorbed in the problems of college and university administration, and even in applied mathematics his original work came to an early end. In all he published twenty-one original papers, the last in 1929.

Jeffery had many activities outside the work of his own department. He was Swarthmore lecturer to the Society of Friends (1934); president of the London Mathematical Society (1935–7), of the London Society for the Study of Religion (1937–8), and of the Mathematical Association (1947); and a vice-president of the Royal Society (1938–40). He became a member of the senate of London University in 1935 and in 1939 chairman of the matriculation and school examination council of the university. In 1948 he became chairman of the South-West Middlesex Hospital management committee.

In 1939 a section of University College, London, moved to Bangor where Jeffery acted as pro-provost. When the war was over the college returned to London. Soon afterwards he resigned his chair to become director of the Institute of Education and entered upon what was in some ways the most successful period of his life. In 1945 London University accepted responsibility for the training of teachers in more than thirty colleges, many in the London area, but others scattered over the south-east of England. The shaping of the scheme for the whole area was almost entirely due to Jeffery who produced a comprehensive plan in two days of concentrated work.

Through its colonial department the Institute of Education had strong overseas interests, especially among west African students, and Jeffery became interested in the problems of west African education. In December 1949 he visited west Africa to report upon a proposal for an examination council, spending eight weeks in Nigeria, the Gold Coast, Sierra Leone, and the Gambia. In his report (March 1950) he recommended the foundation of a west African examination council to control all the examinations in the area. In the next year Jeffery led a study group which visited west Africa for six months at the same time as another group was visiting east and central Africa. Presumably the west African section of the report *African Education: a Study of Educational Policy and Practice in British Tropical Africa* (1953) was largely Jeffery's work. Subsequently he paid an annual visit to west Africa to keep in touch with the work of the Examinations Council of which he was the founder. He also visited Russia with a study group and contributed to a report on the country's schools and training of teachers.

Jeffery was also much interested in craftsmanship. He was descended from a family of wheelwrights and was himself an expert cabinet-maker: several tables in the staff common room at University College were made by him. Late in life he took up silversmithing and registered his own hallmark with the Goldsmiths' Company. From 1952 he was dean of the College of Handicraft. It was while driving home from the annual conference of this college, on 27 April 1957, that he died from a sudden seizure on the Great North Road near Woolmer Green, Hertfordshire. He was survived by his wife.   E. C. TITCHMARSH, rev.

Sources CGPLA Eng. & Wales (1957) · WWW · E. C. Titchmarsh, *Memoirs FRS*, 4 (1958), 129–37 · private information (1971) · personal knowledge (1971)
Likenesses W. Stoneman, photograph, 1944, NPG · W. Stoneman, black and white photograph, RS · W. Stoneman, black and white photograph, repro. in Titchmarsh, *Memoirs FRS*
Wealth at death £5416 4s. 11d.: probate, 3 July 1957, CGPLA Eng. & Wales

Jeffery, John (1647–1720), Church of England clergyman, was born on 20 December 1647 of poor parents in the parish of St Laurence, Ipswich. He showed such an early disposition for learning and piety that his father had him educated at Ipswich grammar school, and in 1664, with the support of family friends, he entered St Catharine's College, Cambridge, as a sizar. He studied under John Echard, graduating BA in 1669 and proceeding MA in 1672; he was created DD in 1696. He was ordained deacon on 19 March 1671, becoming curate of Dennington, Suffolk, where he gained a reputation for scholarship and preaching. In 1678 a visitor from Norwich was so impressed with his sermon that he persuaded the curate to take part in an open contest before the parishioners of St Peter Mancroft (the most important parish in that city) to elect a new rector. He was unanimously elected by them. Having acquired sufficient income he married Sarah (d. 1705), sister of John Ireland, apothecary and alderman, of Great Yarmouth, about 1679. They had a son who died in infancy

and four daughters. Sarah, the eldest, married William Blomefield of Martlesham, Suffolk, and Anna-Penelope married Samuel *Salter, vicar of St Stephen's, Norwich (later archdeacon of Norfolk), in 1708. Elizabeth married the Revd John Wrench in 1710, and Mary never married. In 1710 Jeffery married Susan Ganning (d. 1748), but there were no further children.

Jeffery won the friendship and regard of many influential persons in Norwich, including the physician and author Sir Thomas Browne, who was his parishioner; John Sharp, dean of Norwich (afterwards archbishop of York); and Sir Edward Atkyns, lord chief baron of the exchequer. Atkyns spent his vacations in Norwich and offered Jeffery an apartment in his house. He also took him to London and introduced him to John Tillotson, preacher of Lincoln's Inn (who frequently engaged Jeffery to preach for him), and the Cambridge Platonist Benjamin Whichcote. Although Jeffery never sought preferment he also became rector of Kirton and vicar of Falkenham, Suffolk, on the recommendation of Sharp in 1687. On 13 April 1694 Tillotson, by then archbishop of Canterbury, appointed Jeffery archdeacon of Norwich, and would have promoted him further, but died in the same year. Jeffery later claimed to have been 'as much mortified at receiving preferment, as some have been at missing it' (Salter, li).

Jeffery published many sermons and tracts after 1689, and supported Francis Burges's fledgeling local press in Norwich after 1701, sending at least nine of his works to be printed there rather than in London. These included commemoration and funeral sermons, an exposition on the catechism, proposals to the clergy concerning the reformation of manners, and *Forms of Prayer … [and] Exercises of Devotion* (1706). Although he wrote *The Dangerous Imposture of Quakerism* (1699, answered by Richard Ashby in the same year), Jeffery was usually an enemy of religious controversy, as it was apt 'to produce more heat than light' (Salter, xxvi). He disliked, and took no great part in, the acrimonious political and ecclesiastical disputes between the upper and lower houses of the Canterbury convocation (1700–17). After marrying his second wife he ceased to attend, arguing (from Deuteronomy 24: 5) 'that when a man has taken a new wife, he shall not be obliged to go out to war' (Salter, xxvii–xxviii). Jeffery was also the editor of other men's works, having been chosen by the executors of Benjamin Whichcote to publish his works. Likewise he was selected by the daughter of Sir Thomas Browne to edit a manuscript omitted from the collection of her father's posthumous writings in 1712. This was published under the title *Christian Morals* in 1716.

John Jeffery died quietly on 1 April 1720 and was buried four days later in the chancel of St Peter Mancroft. His grandson Samuel *Salter [see under Salter, Samuel] published a collected edition of his published and unpublished works with a memoir in 1751. Jeffery was a hardworking, mild-mannered man who spent his life 'framing and perfecting a scheme of religion, for his own and his hearers' use, agreeable to the holy scriptures; without respect to what any sect or church had done before'

(Salter, xvi). He was an early riser: and 'for thirty years together never studied fewer hours, than the common labourer works in a day' (Salter, xv).   DAVID STOKER

Sources S. Salter, 'A memoir', *A complete collection of the sermons and tracts written by John Jeffery, D. D.*, ed. S. Salter (1751), 2v · *GM*, 1st ser., 21 (1751), 266–8 · [J. Chambers], *A general history of the county of Norfolk*, 2 vols. (1829), 1142–3 · T. Birch, *The life of the Most Reverend Dr John Tillotson, lord archbishop of Canterbury*, 2nd edn (1753), 299–300 · F. Blomefield and C. Parkin, *An essay towards a topographical history of the county of Norfolk*, 5 vols. (1739–75), vol. 2, pp. 462–621 · A. Chalmers, ed., *The general biographical dictionary*, new edn, 32 vols. (1812–17) · D. Stoker, 'Printing at the Red Well: an early Norwich press through the eyes of contemporaries', *The mighty engine: the printing press at work*, ed. P. Isaac and B. McKay (2000), 29–38, 97–106 · F. L. Huntley, *Sir Thomas Browne* (1962), 225–6 · Nichols, *Lit. anecdotes*, 3.221–3
Archives Norfolk RO, MS notes on Epistles to the Galations and Romans
Likenesses L. Seeman, oils · A. Walker, line engraving (after L. Seeman), BM, NPG; repro. in Salter, ed., *Complete collection*

Jeffery, Thomas (1698–1729), Presbyterian minister and religious writer, was born in Trinity parish, Exeter, on 26 July 1698 and baptized at the Exeter Bow Presbyterian Meeting by George Trosse on 14 August, the first of nine children of Thomas Jeffery (*b.* 1667) and his second wife, Susanna. The Jefferys were prominent Exeter merchants and dissenters. His grandfather Andrew Jeffery, fuller, of St Mary Major was fined £20 in November 1670 for an illegal assembly at his house and, following James II's declaration of indulgence in 1685, he was one of three principal undertakers of the building of James's Meeting in James Street, Exeter. Jeffery's father became a leading member of the James's Meeting and was on the Committee of Thirteen that raised money to pay the ministers of the three meetings in Exeter: St James's, Little, and Bow. He was also treasurer and one of four trustees of James's Meeting from 1705. His substantial property holdings and investments in the city enabled him to take up £1199 of South Sea stock in 1720.

Given his family background, it was natural that the young Thomas Jeffery train for the ministry at the nonconformist Exeter academy conducted by Joseph Hallett II (1656–1722). Jeffery may have subsequently assisted Hallett in his Exeter ministry. At the outbreak of controversy over the orthodoxy of the Exeter ministers and the principle of subscription, the trustees of James's Meeting, who feared that both their authority and the credit of nonconformity were at stake, locked the doors against the non-subscribers James Peirce and Joseph Hallett II. However, approximately 300 worshippers continued to support the barred ministers and in 1720 followed them to a new, specially constructed meeting-house at the Mint. Despite his father's position on the orthodox side of the controversy, Jeffery, who sided with the non-subscribers, in 1726 succeeded Peirce as one of the two ministers of the Mint Meeting. Shortly afterwards he was called to Little Baddow, Essex, but remained there only until 1728 before returning shortly before his death to his native city.

During these later years Jeffery was an active writer. In 1725 he gave learned support to Samuel Chandler, William Whiston, Thomas Sherlock, and other opponents of

Anthony Collins, the deist, in two works, a *Review of the Controversy* and *True Grounds and Reasons of the Christian Religion*. The latter was described by the nonconformist author John Leland as an 'ingenious treatise' and by Collins himself as the work of an 'ingenious author' (J. Leland, *A View of the Principal Deistical Writers*, 2 vols., 1754–6, 1.119). Jeffery also wrote *Christianity Proved from Holy Scripture* and in 1728 *Christianity the Perfection of All Religion, Natural and Revealed*. Benjamin Kennicott praised his works, and Jeffery is described in Philip Doddridge's *Family Expositor* as having 'handled the subject of prophecy and the application of it in the New Testament more studiously perhaps than anyone since the time Eusebius wrote his *Demonstratio evangelica*' (DNB).

Jeffery died, unmarried, in Exeter on 29 July 1729, aged thirty-one.   PATRICK WOODLAND

Sources ledger, Devon RO, Jeffery family papers, MS 61/6/1 · PRO, MS and Exeter Bow Meeting Presbyterian register, RG4/965 · J. Watkins, *The universal biographical dictionary*, new edn (1821) · J. Youings, *Tuckers Hall, Exeter: the history of a provincial city company through five centuries* (1968) · A. Brockett, *Nonconformity in Exeter, 1650–1875* (1962) · A. Warne, *Church and society in eighteenth century Devon* (1969) · R. Newton, *Eighteenth-century Exeter* (1984) · IGI · J. Murch, *A history of the Presbyterian and General Baptist churches in the west of England* (1835) · W. Musgrave, *Obituary prior to 1800*, ed. G. J. Armytage, 3, Harleian Society, 46 (1900) · DNB
Archives Devon RO, family ledger

Jefferys, James (1751–1784), historical draughtsman, was born in Maidstone, Kent, on 19 May 1751 and was baptized at All Saints', Maidstone, on 28 May 1751, the son of William Jefferys (1723?–1805), painter, and his wife, Parnell. He attended the free school in Maidstone, and was given basic artistic training by his father, who was a coach-painter and artist based in the area. Jefferys moved to London about 1771 where he was apprenticed to the leading engraver William Woollett (1735–1785). On 14 November 1772 he entered the Royal Academy Schools, and may have worked with John Hamilton Mortimer, whose drawing style he imitated. During the early 1770s he exhibited a number of subject pictures, mainly drawings, at the Society of Artists of Great Britain. In 1774 he won the Royal Academy's top prize for a historical painting with his *Seleus and Stratonice* and a gold palette from the Society of Arts for a drawing, *The Deluge* (a version is in the Royal Academy). In 1774 Jefferys and the sculptor Charles Banks (brother of Thomas Banks) were put forward by Sir Joshua Reynolds for the travel scholarships offered to two students of the Royal Academy by the Society of Dilettanti. In the event the society sent only Jefferys, together with an artist of their own choice, William Pars. Jefferys left England in July 1775, and arrived in Rome on 7 October. The scholarship was for a period of three years, but Edward Edwards noted that he was in Italy for four, and nothing definite is known of him until 1781, when he is recorded in England. He is not known to have produced finished paintings during his time abroad, but his drawings of often violent classical scenes were seen and admired by fellow artists. Their emphatically linear style and heroic conception show a continuing debt to the example of Mortimer and the draughtsmanship of James Barry (1741–

1806). Nancy Pressly has identified Jefferys as the 'Master of the Giants' (Pressly, 'James Jefferys'), the artist responsible for a group of claustrophobic and grotesquely distorted figure studies (examples are in the V&A and the British Museum, London), some dated 1779. The attribution is not universally accepted.

Little is known of Jefferys's work following his return to London. A group of drawings illustrating the Revd Charles Davy's annotated edition of Chaucer's *Canterbury Tales* (Houghton Library, Harvard) is dated September 1781. Davy was rector of Onehouse, Suffolk, and the drawings were probably executed during a stay there. His only other known work from this later period was a painting, the *Siege of Gibraltar*, exhibited at the Royal Academy in 1783. The original painting is in Maidstone Museum and an engraving of it was made by Woollett and completed by his pupil John Emes and published in 1789. Jefferys died prematurely from a fever at his lodgings at Meard's Court, Soho, London, on 31 January 1784. He was apparently unmarried. Until his work was rediscovered in the 1970s, many of his drawings circulated as works by James Barry or John Hamilton Mortimer, which they resemble closely. Important examples are at Maidstone Museum and Art Gallery, the Victoria and Albert Museum, and the Royal Academy, London. Although highly derivative in style, these are now recognized as exemplary of the violently imaginative mannerism typical of British neo-classicism.

Martin Myrone

Sources E. Edwards, *Anecdotes of painters* (1808); facs. edn (1970) · T. Clifford and S. Legouix, *Burlington Magazine*, 118 (1976), 148–57 · T. Clifford and S. Legouix, *The rediscovery of an artist: the drawings of James Jefferys, 1751–1784* (1976) [exhibition catalogue, V&A, Feb–May 1976] · J. Sunderland, 'Two self-portraits by James Jefferys?', *Burlington Magazine*, 119 (1977), 274–80 · N. Pressly, 'James Jefferys and the Master of the Giants', *Burlington Magazine*, 119 (1977), 280–84 · M. Butlin, 'The rediscovery of an artist', *Blake Newsletter* (spring 1977), 123–4 · N. L. Pressly, *The Fuseli circle in Rome: early Romantic art of the 1770s* (New Haven, CT, 1979) [exhibition catalogue, Yale U. CBA, 12 Sept – 11 Nov 1979] · J. Ingamells, ed., *A dictionary of British and Irish travellers in Italy, 1701–1800* (1997) · minutes of the council and of the general assembly, RA

Likenesses J. Jefferys, self-portrait, pen-and-ink drawing, 1773–5, NPG · J. Jefferys, self-portrait, pen-and-ink drawing, c.1774–1775, Yale U. CBA · W. Jefferys, porte crayon painting, National Book League; watercolour copy, Maidstone Museum, Kent [crayon portrait on loan to Maidstone Museum]

Jefferys [*née* Davies], **Margaret** [Margot] (1916–1999), medical sociologist, was born on 1 November 1916 in Madras, India, the second of three daughters and third among the four children of (James) Arthur Davies, barrister and principal of the Law College in Madras, and his wife, Margaret Dorothea, *née* Mayhew. Although registered Margaret after her mother she was always known as Margot both in her family and publicly. When she was five the family returned to England, settling in Berkhamsted where she later went to Berkhamsted High School for Girls. Bright, good at sports, and rebellious, she intended to be a physical education teacher. However, during a year with a family in Switzerland her political awareness increased and in 1935 she went to the London School of Economics, where she specialized in modern economic history and was

taught by H. I. Beales, Eileen Power, and R. H. Tawney; she graduated with a first-class degree in 1938. Imbued by her parents with a strong sense of social justice she joined the Communist Party.

At the London School of Economics Davies met and from her second year lived with James Bavington Jefferys (b. 1913/14); they married on 31 May 1941. He was the son of John Herbert Jefferys. After graduating he had been briefly employed as a research economist in the civil service, but from 1940 they both worked in Coventry, he in a tank factory and she in an aircraft factory. From 1944 they were back in London, Margot Jefferys teaching part time for the Workers Educational Association. She gave birth to twins Peter and Steve in 1944 (Steve died when two days old) and a second son, also Steve, in 1945. She and her husband were divorced in 1959. She retained her married name after her divorce.

From 1947 to 1950 Jefferys was a researcher at the Ministry of Works for Jacob Bronowski, chief scientific adviser, who highly commended her field, statistical, and analytic work when she applied to Bedford College for a post as a research assistant. Her research at Bedford led to her first book, *Mobility and the Labour Market* (1954). In 1953 John Brotherston, then reader in public health, recruited her to the London School of Hygiene and Tropical Medicine to teach public health students. Fred Martin and Ann Cartwright were recruited in the same week. She quickly developed a close personal and professional friendship with Cartwright that lasted throughout her life. *An Anatomy of Social Welfare* (1965), written at that time, arose from her survey of social welfare staff and clients, including health services, in Buckinghamshire.

Observing the constraints upon social scientists working in medical schools Jefferys moved back to Bedford College in 1965 as director of the social research unit (funded by the Department of Health). The University of London gave her a readership, followed in 1968 by a personal chair in medical sociology—the first time a professorship of medical sociology had been created in the UK. Following the recommendations of the royal commission on medical education in 1968, she was invited to develop sociology as applied to medicine for London medical students. She founded an intercalated degree in medical sociology so that medical students could take an honours degree alongside their medical education. In 1969, with George Brown, she established an MSc in medical sociology, which became internationally renowned. Gradually medical sociology teaching became established in medical schools throughout the UK.

In 1970 the Department of Health and Social Security funded a ground-breaking study of general practice, with Jefferys as project director. This twelve-year study involved several medical practices and many researchers; she wrote up the findings with Hessie Sachs as *Rethinking General Practice: Dilemmas in Primary Medical Care* (1983). The project concluded in 1982, the year Jefferys retired.

Characteristically Jefferys not only remained active in retirement but also continued to do innovative work. She headed a new research initiative on ageing for the Social

Science Research Council; she interviewed old people, which she greatly enjoyed, and edited *Growing Old in the Twentieth Century* (1989); and from 1992 to 1997 she was visiting professor at the centre of medical law and ethics at King's College, London, working on ethics in health and social care, especially in relation to the elderly.

Held in high esteem by both sociologists and medical professionals, Jefferys received many honours, including fellowship of the Faculty of Public Health Medicine (1984) and honorary fellowship of the Royal College of General Practitioners (1988). She considered her career and the developments she was involved in 'serendipitous'. To whatever serendipity there may have been she added dedication to her subject, rigorous scholarship, and an ability to 'seize the moment' to overcome setbacks. A founder of the discipline of medical sociology she also contributed to important professional and public reforms in health care. She was held in high affection by many— doctors, nurses, and sociologists alike—to whom she was a guide, mentor, and friend. She was particularly helpful to women, conscious of the disadvantages and difficulties they faced. A woman of great strength with a large capacity for friendship, she was full of fun, loving, and generous with her time, money, house, skill, and knowledge; and her careful critiques—sometimes sharp—were always to the point. She was also a family woman, a devoted mother and grandmother who delighted in watching her children and grandchildren grow and develop. She died of cancer of the pancreas in the company of her family at her home, 32 Bisham Gardens, Highgate, London, on 3 March 1999.　　　　MEG STACEY

Sources M. Jefferys, 'Serendipity: an autobiographical account of the career of a medical sociologist in Britain', *Medical sociologists at work*, ed. R. Elling and M. Sokolowska (1978) · *The Independent* (12 March 1999) · *The Guardian* (17 March 1999) · *The Times* (13 April 1999) · *Medical Sociology News*, 25/2 (1999), 45–60 · personal knowledge (2004) · private information (2004) · parish register, Madras, India, St George's, 29 Nov 1916 [baptism] · m. cert. · d. cert.
Likenesses photograph, repro. in *The Independent* · photograph, repro. in *The Guardian*

Jefferys, Thomas (*c*.1719–1771), engraver, cartographer, and publisher, was the son of Henry Jefferys, a cutler. At the time of his apprenticeship to Emanuel Bowen in 1735 his family was living in Clerkenwell, London. No further detail of the family has been traced, although his contemporaries, the brass-founder Josiah Jefferys and the goldsmith Nathaniel Jefferys, are thought to have been his brothers. Despite the existence of two maps of London bearing Jefferys's name and dated 1732 and 1735 respectively, his independent career did not begin until about 1744, at which date he became a freeman of the Merchant Taylors' Company. His earliest atlas was *The Small English Atlas*, produced with Thomas Kitchin in 1748–9, and his earliest distinctive work was the engraving of several plans of the manufacturing towns of the midlands, including Samuel Bradford's Coventry (1750) and Birmingham (1751) and the plan of Wolverhampton (1751) by Isaac Taylor. His family may perhaps have been connected with this area.

Thomas Jefferys (*c*.1719–1771), by Paul Sandby, *c*.1765

Originally from Red Lion Street, Clerkenwell, but by 1750 settled at well-known premises at the corner of St Martin's Lane, London, Jefferys is remembered in particular for some of the most important eighteenth-century maps of the Americas, a series given cohesion and impetus by the preliminary hostilities and eventual outbreak of the Seven Years' War. Among many individual works of note were Joshua Fry's and Peter Jefferson's 1751 survey of Virginia, engraved and published by Jefferys in 1753, and Joseph Blanchard's and Samuel Langdon's New Hampshire (1761), the first published map of the state. The culmination of this concentration of work was the atlas published in association with Robert Sayer as *A General Topography of North America* in 1768. Posthumous collections were published by Sayer in 1775 as *The American Atlas*, *The North-American Pilot*, including important charts by James Cook, and *The West-India Atlas*, for which a collection of working drafts survives in the British Library (BL Maps 188.o.2).

Jefferys's status was underlined by his publication of many of the key geographical texts of the period. His *The Conduct of the French, with Regard to Nova Scotia* of 1754 lays the ground for British claims, evincing detailed knowledge of the 'geographical slight of hand' of recent French maps (p. 52). Jefferys also published the London edition of *The Journal of Major George Washington* (1755) and, among many substantial works, *A Description of the Spanish Islands … of the West Indies* (1762), with charts based on captured Spanish originals. The end of hostilities saw a shift of emphasis to more domestic mapping and Jefferys was the engraver of the map of Devon (1765) by Benjamin Donn that gained the first award made by the Society of Arts in its effort to improve technical standards of large-scale county mapping. Jefferys's contribution in this area was considerable, with his own large-scale surveys of six counties.

Jefferys was appointed geographer to George III in December 1760. His apprentices and assistants included Isaac Taylor, John Ainslie, John Spilsbury, Thomas Donald, and John Lodge. Aside from his own publications he produced many maps for the books and magazines of the period, as well as a wide range of other engraved material, including some early geographical board games. He stocked a large selection of prints and was also a major importer of the best and most recent maps from overseas. As the leading map supplier of his day he was a principal figure in the emergence of London as an international centre of cartographic enterprise.

Notwithstanding his achievement, Jefferys was declared bankrupt in November 1766. He spoke only of 'a train of unforseen accidents' (Harley, 28), but the root cause of this set-back was almost certainly an investment beyond his resources in undertaking the large-scale county surveys. Much of his stock was sold by auction and his business was saved only by the help of friends. Principal among these must have been Sayer, with whom Jefferys visited Paris in 1768, perhaps intent on restoring his fortunes: the two men were charged by the French police with the possession of a quantity of indecent prints.

Little is known of Jefferys's private life. He is probably the 'Thomas Jefferey' received into the Baptist communion of the Barbican Chapel in 1742, a place of worship associated with both Bowen and Kitchin. If so, it is recorded that he later belonged to the Pinners' Hall congregation, conducted by James Foster. Details of his marriage remain untraced, but he and his wife, Elizabeth, baptized four sons and three daughters at St Martin-in-the-Fields between 1753 and 1766. Jefferys died on 20 November 1771 and was buried at St Martin-in-the-Fields on 23 November. His will leaves only the sum of £20, his debts, and his remaining effects to his widow and four surviving children. His eldest son, also Thomas (b. 1755), apprenticed to Jefferys in 1769, continued the business in a partnership with William Faden that endured until the younger Jefferys reached his majority in 1776. Two sketches of Jefferys by Paul Sandby are preserved, in the Royal Collection and at the British Museum. Both show him asleep on a chair, the former with a convivial bottle placed nearby, but the humour of these amiable likenesses probably derives from their showing the energetic Jefferys in far from typical pose.   LAURENCE WORMS

Sources J. B. Harley, 'The bankruptcy of Thomas Jeffreys: an episode in the economic history of eighteenth-century map-making', *Imago Mundi*, 20 (1966), 27–48 • M. S. Pedley, 'Maps, war and commerce: business correspondence with the London map firm of Thomas Jefferys and William Faden', *Imago Mundi*, 48 (1996), 161–73 • R. A. Skelton and R. V. Tooley, 'The marine surveys of James Cook in North America, 1758–1768', *Map Collectors' Circle*, 37 (1967) • *BL cat.* • *British Library map library catalogue* (1998) [CD-ROM] • parish registers, St Martin-in-the-Fields, London • records of the Merchant Taylors' Company, GL • M. Pedley, 'Gentlemen abroad: Jefferys and Sayer in Paris', *Map Collector*, 37 (1986), 20–23 • D. Hodson, *County atlases of the British Isles published after 1703: a bibliography*, 3 (1997) • IGI • PRO, PROB 11/972, sig. 444
Archives BL
Likenesses P. Sandby, drawing, c.1765, Royal Collection [see illus.] • P. Sandby, sketch, c.1765, BM
Wealth at death £20; debts; remaining effects: will, PRO, PROB 11/972, sig. 444

Jeffes, Simon Harry Piers (1949–1997), musician and composer, was born at the Montalan Nursing Home, Crawley, Sussex, on 19 February 1949, the son of James Henry Elliston Jeffes, a research chemist, and his wife, Anne Hope Madeline, *née* Clutterbuck. Jeffes spent part of his childhood in Canada before returning with his family to Britain, where he attended school in Devon. He started to play the guitar at the age of thirteen and then studied classical guitar, piano, and music theory. He took classes at the music department of Chiswick Polytechnic and planned to go on to music college, but found academic study not to his liking. Although he played in avant-garde ensembles such as the Omega Players, he soon rejected the notions of experimental composition then current in the British classical music establishment. Inspiration came to him instead from the minimalist styles of what later became known as 'world music', most notably from Japan and Zimbabwe.

In 1972 Jeffes went on holiday in the south of France and suffered a bout of food poisoning. The story goes that as he lay in bed he had a strange recurring vision of a concrete hotel-like building. In each room people were engaged in various activities—making love and listening to music for example—that were being performed joylessly in a place 'which had no heart'. The following day he felt better and went to the beach. A poem came to him. It began 'I am the proprietor of the Penguin Cafe. I will tell you things at random'. The poem went on to stress the value of chance in human life and in composing music. Thus the idea of the Penguin Café Orchestra (PCO) began to germinate. Jeffes envisaged it as a house band for an imaginary café, which, instead of playing soulless avant-garde music, would play the sort of music played by 'imagined wild, free, mountain people creating sounds of a subtle dreamlike quality' (Penguin Café Orchestra website).

In 1973 Jeffes collected some friends to form the first PCO, mixing together sounds from a novel selection of instruments—including guitar, quatro, violin, rubber band, ring modulator, and bongos. This eclectic instrumentation was balanced by strong melodies and hooklines, a characteristic of the PCO sound that gave the music an appeal far beyond the egg-headed *cognoscenti* of modern classical music. The ensemble's first album (simply entitled *Music from the Penguin Café Orchestra*) emerged in 1976 on the Obscure label curated by Brian Eno, the doyen of the late twentieth-century popular music leftfield in Britain.

In a bid to boost his income Jeffes oversaw early recordings by The 101ers, Joe Strummer's pub-rock band, before the advent of the punk rock standard-bearers The Clash. He thereby came to the attention of the Sex Pistols' manager Malcolm McLaren, who asked him to create the string arrangement for Sid Vicious's comic version of 'My Way'. He also taught African drumming techniques to McLaren's then protégés Adam and the Ants; thus infused with a powerful rhythmic backbone, they, and their offshoot Bow Wow Wow, went on to enjoy enormous success in the pop market.

By the mid-1980s the Penguin Café Orchestra had released two more albums: *Penguin Café Orchestra* (1981) and *Broadcasting from Home* (1984). At that time the PCO featured musicians such as the violinist Geoffrey Richardson, formerly of the progressive rock group Caravan. A fourth album, *Signs of Life*, was released in 1987, by which time Jeffes's music had begun to ooze into the mainstream through an unexpected route. The track 'Music for a Found Harmonium'—composed by Jeffes on a semi-functioning instrument discovered on a street in Tokyo—was used in a television campaign which followed the launch of *The Independent* newspaper. Jeffes's compositions were also used in the advertisements for Hobnobs biscuits, the Eurostar rail service ('Perpetuum mobile'), and IBM computers. Perhaps his best-known composition was 'Telephone and Rubber Band', in which a telephone ring tone forms an insistent riff, which soundtracked the Mercury One-2-One mobile phone company television advertisements.

In 1988 Jeffes arranged some of the PCO's music for full-scale orchestra for the Royal Ballet's *Still Life at the Penguin Café*, which was choreographed by David Bintley. A live album, recorded at the Royal Festival Hall in London and entitled *When in Rome*, was released in the same year. Jeffes thrived in the live arena: he introduced his compositions with an unforced informality, and made light work of the occasional drunken heckler with pithy put-downs. The playful titles of many of his pieces—'Salty bean Fumble', for example—betokened a refreshing reluctance to take himself or his work too seriously.

Jeffes also worked with the Japanese composer Ryuichi Sakamoto, who like himself had successfully vaulted the divide between pop and classical music, and the Senegalese musician Baaba Maal. The 1993 PCO album *Union Call* featured such novelties as dripping taps as well as the violinist Nigel Kennedy. After re-recording some of his favourite tracks on a live studio album, *Concert Program* (1995), Jeffes moved with his partner (and PCO cellist) Helen Jane Liebmann to Wadeford, Somerset, where they built a new studio. Sadly, work on new material was cut short by his untimely death, at St Margaret's Somerset Hospice, Heron Drive, Bishops Hull, Taunton, of a brain tumour on 11 December 1997. He was survived by Helen and by a son, Arthur.

A posthumous solo album, the self-descriptive *Piano Music*, appeared in 2000, and in the following year came a four-CD PCO retrospective. Two PCO compilation albums, entitled *Preludes, Airs and Yodels—a Penguin Café Primer* (1996) and *A Short History* (2001), provide an invaluable introduction to the work of a genre-defying musical talent.   DOMINIC MACLAINE

Sources *The Independent* (18 Dec 1997) · *The Times* (13 Dec 1997) · *The Guardian* (15 Dec 1997) · b. cert. · d. cert. · *CGPLA Eng. & Wales* (1998) · www.penguincafe.com [Penguin Café Orchestra official website], Jan 2002
Likenesses photograph, repro. in *The Independent* · photograph, repro. in *The Times* · photograph, repro. in *The Guardian* · photographs, www.penguincafe.com
Wealth at death £1,130,324: probate, 1998, *CGPLA Eng. & Wales*

Jeffrey. *See also* Geoffrey, Jefferay, Jeffery, Jeffray.

Jeffrey, Alexander (1806–1874), antiquary, was born near Lilliesleaf, Roxburghshire, the fourth son of a farm steward or bailiff, who belonged to the Anti-Burgher branch of the secession church. He was a studious youth, but left school at an early age, became a solicitor's clerk at first in Melrose and afterwards in Edinburgh, and was later an assistant in the town clerk's office at Jedburgh. In 1838 he obtained admission as a practitioner in the sheriff court of Roxburghshire, and subsequently became the most popular and successful agent, especially in criminal cases, in the sheriff courts of Roxburgh and Selkirk. He lived at Jedburgh, and died there on 29 November 1874. His wife had died in 1872.

Despite his professional industry Jeffrey was well read in general literature, and as an enthusiastic archaeologist was elected a member of the Scottish Society of Antiquaries. His chief work, *The History and Antiquities of Roxburghshire* (4 vols., 1857–64), was an expanded version of an earlier (1836) account. To the *Transactions* of the Berwickshire Naturalists' Club, of which he was a member, he contributed two topographical papers on Jedburgh and Ancrum respectively. He also published a small guide to the scenery and antiquities of Jedburgh (n.d.).

[ANON.], *rev.* H. C. G. MATTHEW

Sources *The Scotsman* (30 Nov 1874) · private information (1891)
Wealth at death £186 5s. 6d.: confirmation, 31 March 1876

Jeffrey, Francis, Lord Jeffrey (1773–1850), writer and judge, was born on 23 October 1773 at 7 Charles Street, off George Square, Edinburgh, the elder son and third of five children of George Jeffrey (1742–1812), depute clerk in the Court of Session, and Henrietta, daughter of John Louden, a farmer near Lanark. His father was a respectable, conservative, and gloomy man; his mother, of a cheerful temperament and greatly loved by her family, died in 1786.

Early years and education Jeffrey was, according to his friend Henry Cockburn, 'the tiniest possible child, but dark and vigorous' (Cockburn, *Life*, 1.3). He grew into a bookish boy, with no interest in physical exercise. He entered Edinburgh high school in 1781, a year after Walter Scott and a year before Henry Brougham. At the age of thirteen he caught a glimpse of Robert Burns, and some time later helped to carry a drunken James Boswell to bed. In 1787 he went to the University of Glasgow to study law. However, his father forbade him to hear the lectures of its most eminent professor, John Millar, the liberal legal theorist, and so from 1789 he continued his education under the more orthodox David Hume and Robert Dick at the University of Edinburgh. In 1791 he proceeded to Queen's College, Oxford. Like many Scottish students, he found life there uncongenial. He left after a year. The one legacy from his stay was his accent. He cast off his Scots, at least

Francis Jeffrey, Lord Jeffrey (1773–1850), by Sir Henry Raeburn, in or before 1812

for public purposes, and acquired a high-pitched pronunciation which grated on most contemporaries. 'The laddie has clean tint his Scotch, and found nae English', said Lord Braxfield (Omond, 2.301).

Jeffrey returned to Edinburgh to finish reading for the bar, to which he was admitted on 16 December 1794. He began to practise, with little success. But he continued, as he had all through his student days, to devote much energy to literary composition, of essays, verse, and attempts at drama. He would 'never be a great man, unless it be as a poet' (Cockburn, *Life*, 1.69), he had written to a sister while at Oxford. In particular, he began to put together his thoughts on politics, in a spirit of philosophical whiggery bound to meet disapproval from his colleagues, as from his father, at a time of growing conservatism among the Scottish elites. It appeared nowhere more strongly than in the faculty of advocates, which during these years deposed a whig, Henry Erskine, from its deanship and saw one of its members, Thomas Muir, transported for sedition, after a trial which the horrified Jeffrey watched from the public gallery. He could thus expect no preferment, nor even many briefs, and only earned about £100 a year. In 1795 he tried his luck in London, but introductions to various editors got him nowhere. Back in Edinburgh, where he had a flat at 18 Buccleuch Place, he continued to improve himself by attending lectures at the university nearby, especially on political economy. Many more of his idle hours he passed away in entertainment: in the Friday Club, which he frequented for forty years, or in the Speculative Society,

which attracted all the city's bright young men and where, to his ultimate advantage, he fell in with others of like mind.

On 1 November 1801 Jeffrey married a second cousin, Catherine Wilson, daughter of the professor of ecclesiastical history in the University of St Andrews. They set themselves up at 62 Queen Street. They had a son in September 1802, who survived only a month. Catherine Jeffrey herself died on 8 August 1805. Jeffrey's second wife was Charlotte Wilkes of New York, great-niece of John Wilkes, the radical agitator. She was another relative of Jeffrey's, his paternal uncle having married John Wilkes's sister. Their family had emigrated to America whence, with her banker father, Charlotte Wilkes toured Europe in 1810. She met Jeffrey then, and he followed her after she went back to the United States in 1813, despite the war going on with Great Britain at the time. They married on 1 October 1813, almost as soon as he landed in her native city. 'Almost the whole happiness of his life flowed from this union' (Cockburn, *Life*, 2.306). He took the opportunity of travelling to Washington to have interviews with president James Madison and the secretary of state, James Monroe, before returning to Edinburgh. There the Jeffreys lived at 92 George Street, and rented a country house, Craigcrook, at the back of Corstorphine Hill just outside the city. They had one child, Charlotte, who married William Empson in 1838.

Jeffrey could keep such exalted American company because he had meanwhile won fame. By the time of his first marriage it was obvious to him that he could scarcely live off the law. He had that year done credit to himself as a legal assessor at the general assembly of the Church of Scotland, where he regularly continued to appear afterwards, usually pleading on the side of the evangelical party. But more lucrative briefs were still some way off and would only come with his growing renown outside his profession. He never gave up hope of success in it, and always turned down offers of employment which would have taken him away for good from the courts of Edinburgh. But for the time being even the political changes of 1801—when Henry Dundas retired from the management of Scotland and the country's patronage was opened up somewhat—did not benefit Jeffrey. After failing to win the very minor office of reporter in the Court of Session, Jeffrey decided in some desperation that he must try to earn his bread from writing. But he now happened to have a number of friends—the Revd Sydney Smith, Henry Brougham, and Francis Horner—with similar concerns. Smith was apparently the one who, during a meeting in Jeffrey's flat, proposed that they should found the *Edinburgh Review*.

The *Edinburgh Review* If Smith took the lead, this was at the outset a co-operative venture in which they all dealt with both copy and proofs. They would meet at the printer's, just off the High Street, Smith apparently insisting that they went singly and by back approaches to the office. But the original arrangements turned out to be too awkward and, well before Smith left Scotland early in 1803,

Jeffrey became the editor responsible. Archibald Constable, the imperious publisher of Scott and other literary lions, bore the cost of starting up the publication on condition that the young men should produce the four initial monthly numbers for nothing. The first issue, of 750 copies, appeared on 2 October 1802 and sold out almost at once. Of the third issue, 2500 copies were printed. Constable then agreed to pay 10 guineas a sheet, a fee already handsome by the standards of the day, but this was raised afterwards to a minimum of 16 guineas. Jeffrey reckoned that the average income during the quarter-century of his editorship lay between 20 and 25 guineas per issue, and he himself received £50. This innovative generosity kept the *Edinburgh Review* going and maintained its quality long after the circle of founders had dispersed. Cockburn remarked that it 'drew authors from dens where they would otherwise have starved, and made Edinburgh a literary mart, famous with strangers, and the pride of its own citizens'. Sales rose steadily, to 7000 within five years, and more than 14,000 by the mid-1820s (Cockburn, *Life*, 2.70–6).

The *Edinburgh Review* had an influence on opinion and taste far beyond its circulation. It popularized, though it also vulgarized, the teachings of the Scottish Enlightenment, and it helped to transform them into Victorian orthodoxies. Under Jeffrey's editorship, it also marked an epoch in the history of the periodical. Though not the first to bear the title of review, it was the direct parent of the genre as the vehicle of bourgeois culture that it became in the course of the nineteenth century, in Britain and other countries. If the genre afterwards declined, it left to the higher journalism of the modern age much of the same ethos: clever, probing, irreverent. Cockburn said that the venture burst upon a public that seemed to be waiting for something of the kind. News of public events, even of the excitements of war, had until then been conveyed through boring reprints of official documents and dispatches in a press often subsidized by the government. Jeffrey gave more graphic and objective accounts, on which he editorialized judiciously. Again, almost the only way for the reading public to find out about the latest books had been through publishers' puffs, which were no more reliable then than later. The *Edinburgh Review*, by contrast, offered independent criticism, even if in Jeffrey's case it has not stood the test of time. Altogether, this new type of periodical marked the emergence of a middle-class public opinion, culturally and politically aware, which was now served by an organ that could articulate and promote its interests.

The *Edinburgh Review* first came out in wartime, and while the wars went on Jeffrey expressed his political views cautiously. He showed no such restraint in his literary judgements, which were savage to the point of being sensational, and made his reputation. On one occasion they were even the cause of a threat to his life. In 1806 Thomas Moore, after Jeffrey had criticized a supposedly immoral tendency in his *Epistles, Odes and other Poems*, heard that he was on a visit to London and challenged him to a duel. They met at Chalk Farm. Neither had the faintest idea how to go about fighting. The Bow Street runners had anyway been informed. They arrived in the nick of time and, after arresting the pair, found that Jeffrey's pistol contained no bullet. Both were bound over to keep the peace, and they later became friends, with Moore even contributing to the *Edinburgh Review*.

Influential though he became, Jeffrey failed to appreciate some of the best and most enduring literature of his time. He could see no virtue, for example, in the English lake poets; he dismissed William Wordsworth's 'The Excursion' with the terse comment that it 'would never do' (*Edinburgh Review*, xxiii, 1814, 3); his attack on Lord Byron's first collection provoked the latter's satire, 'English bards and Scotch reviewers'; and he overstated the case for Scott's 'Marmion':

> To write a modern romance of chivalry seems to be such a phantasy as to build a modern abbey or an English pagoda. For once, however, it may be excused as a pretty caprice of genius, but a second production of the same sort is entitled to less indulgence, and imposes a sort of duty to drive the author from so idle a task, by a fair exposition of the faults which are, in a manner, inseparable from its expression. (*Edinburgh Review*, xii, 1808, 278)

His choice of the word 'faults' shows Jeffrey's lack of sympathy with, indeed incomprehension of, romantic sensibility. He remained in aesthetic matters a man of the eighteenth century, holding to standards of correctness in literature which he identified with artificial diction and deliberate design.

According to Thomas Carlyle, this influence was baleful, though there can have been nothing personal in the stricture: Jeffrey lent him money and made a special friend of his wife. In his *Reminiscences* Carlyle warmly characterized this 'delicate, attractive, dainty little figure … uncommonly bright black eyes, instinct with honesty, intelligence, and kindly fire, rounded brow, delicate oval face full of rapid expression, figure light, nimble, pretty though small, perhaps hardly five feet in height'. But Carlyle added that he found Jeffrey's conversation better than his writing, especially if, as was evidently still the case sometimes, he spoke Scots:

> Here is a man whom they have kneaded into the shape of an Edinburgh Reviewer, and clothed the soul of in whig formulas … but he might have been a beautiful Goldoni, too, or something better in that kind, and given us beautiful comedies, and aerial pictures, true and poetic, of Human Life, in a far other way.

Carlyle then went so far as to call Jeffrey 'a potential Voltaire', yet he had turned out 'not deep enough, pious or reverent enough to have been great in Literature'. In the end, Carlyle felt forced to condemn his benefactor as a man who had reduced criticism to banality:

> Democracy, the gradual uprise and rule in all things of roaring, million-headed, unreflecting, darkly suffering, darkly sinning Demos come to call old superiors to account, at its maddest of tribunals: nothing in my time has so forwarded this as Jeffrey and his once-famous *Edinburgh Review*. (Carlyle, 2.14ff.)

Even with allowance for Carlyle's habitual exaggeration, it may be conceded that Jeffrey's blend of artistic timidity and liberal politics fostered a conventional bourgeois respectability. He himself confirmed it in urging his readers 'to adopt a style of literary and political principles, which was rooted, not in eternal principles, but in the ordinary experience of ordinary literate and responsible men living in the modern age' (*Edinburgh Review*, xxxiii, 1823, 237).

As for the political principles, the *Edinburgh Review* would come to identify them with the whig party. At first it did not do so explicitly, though Jeffrey never made any secret of his commitment to such liberal causes as Roman Catholic emancipation, or of his scepticism about the war with France. Equally, he was strong on political economy, and made the *Edinburgh Review* a channel for diffusing its doctrines. Two of his most frequent contributors, Brougham and Horner, had sat with him at the feet of Dugald Stewart in the lecture halls of Edinburgh, and Stewart was himself a pupil of Adam Smith. But they did not regard *The Wealth of Nations* as a tablet of stone. They noted how Britain had now acquired an industrial economy and a global empire, in a commercial system where commodities from the periphery fed manufactures at the centre. The account of free trade which they then developed was fairly modest in scope compared to the conceptions prevailing later in the century. But here Jeffrey consciously maintained the broad-minded outlook of the Scottish Enlightenment, baulking at the logical rigour and crude accountancy of the emerging utilitarian school in England.

As a political position, there was nothing too suspect in any of this, and a high tory like Scott happily wrote for the early numbers of the *Edinburgh Review*, while Henry Dundas read them with attention and commended the editor's reasoning. Only in 1808, when Jeffrey printed, and according to Cockburn wrote, a notorious article, 'Don Pedro Cevallos on the French usurpation in Spain', did he really begin to flaunt whig colours. Scott was so angry with this attack on British strategy in the Peninsula that he cancelled his subscription and launched the *Quarterly Review* as a patriotic rival. Jeffrey now set out to elaborate his politics in print, if still guardedly enough to avert any threats of censorship. But he was ready to tackle even such a sensitive subject as the French Revolution. It seemed to him that it had been an expression of genuine grievance which had no other outlet, and that savage repression of similar unhappiness in Britain would be the worst response imaginable. Thus, when disruption of trade during the war caused unemployment and unrest at home, he was the only leading whig to posit a link between economic distress and the need for reform.

Legal and political career Peace in 1815 failed of itself to relieve the country's economic problems, but on the contrary plunged it into a terrible depression, marked by workers' protests which the government vigorously suppressed. Jeffrey, now at last sought after for some of the biggest legal cases, specialized for the defence at the state trials by which the Scottish authorities played their part in executing policy. They took a hard line in prosecutions of radicals, and a none too scrupulous one, with ample use

of informers and agents provocateurs. In a series of dramatic scenes in the courtrooms during 1817, Jeffrey exposed this sharp practice with such skill that juries became reluctant to convict and the whole official campaign against radicalism backfired. He was less successful in defending rebels involved in the 'radical war' of 1820, a small-scale proletarian uprising in the west of Scotland; three men were found guilty and hanged.

Jeffrey's professional activity was a natural extension of what he had been preaching in the *Edinburgh Review*. There he argued that there was a danger of the people losing their allegiance to British constitutionalism, and that it fell to the whigs to save the situation. They had a duty not only to oppose executive abuse, as they had ever done, but to curb the radical forces which prompted it as well. In a straight contest with the ruling class, Jeffrey reckoned, the people were bound to win. So he urged the whigs to ally themselves with radical leaders, restrain their demands, guide them through orderly channels, and halt any slide towards revolution. This meant a departure from the aristocratic whiggery of old, though not a break. Jeffrey saw aristocracy as a mark of all civilized society, and was himself if anything anti-democratic. He still drew a distinction between the right to vote, which was not for everybody, and civil liberty, which was. Parliamentary reform would be preferable, but even an unreformed parliament might guarantee civil liberty so long as it met frequently and criticized without restraint.

Jeffrey had inherited from David Hume and Adam Smith a science of politics. What is striking about his development of it is his stress on the practice and style of discourse necessary to make enlightened ideas work in an era of confused and often violent conflicts. It was something of a retreat from the creative audacity of the Scottish Enlightenment proper, and altogether different from the portentous political philosophy current in Europe. Yet, while highly pragmatic, it was intellectual enough not to fall into mere expediency.

Jeffrey himself became a politician. He won his first office with election to the rectorship of the University of Glasgow in 1820. He began to appear regularly on public platforms calling for various reforming measures. Rising whigs agreed with him on the need to bridge the gap between their staid leadership at Westminster and their potential support in the country. The *Edinburgh Review* was the mouthpiece for this programme, and it acquired a remarkable authority in the prelude to its triumph in 1832. Nowhere was that truer than on Jeffrey's native heath, where to wide applause he mounted a systematic and telling critique of the Scottish system of political management. The managers sought to appease the reviewers with patronage, but these were not disarmed. While other whigs accepted appointments to the Scottish bench, Jeffrey declined. In July 1829, however, he was elected without official opposition as dean of the faculty of advocates. He moved to his last and grandest house in Edinburgh, at 24 Moray Place, and took the opportunity to retire as editor of the *Edinburgh Review*, handing over to Macvey Napier.

When the general election of 1830 brought the whigs to power, Jeffrey was appointed lord advocate. With Cockburn as solicitor-general, and Thomas Kennedy, MP for the Ayr burghs, he constituted a reform committee for Scotland and within days sent proposals to the cabinet. It was necessary for Jeffrey to be in the House of Commons, but his efforts to get elected cost him £10,000. He was first chosen for the Perth burghs, was unseated on a technicality, and was then returned for Malton, Yorkshire. Between coming in and going out, he had been able to introduce the first Scottish Reform Bill in March 1831. It lapsed, however, when the English bill was defeated and the ministry had once more to go to the country. Jeffrey seized the chance to challenge the tories in their stronghold of Edinburgh, standing against a cadet of the Dundas family. More than 17,000 citizens petitioned the town council in his favour, but it rejected him by 17 votes to 14. He was returned again for the Perth burghs. He introduced his second Reform Bill in July. It was only to receive the royal assent, after many further vicissitudes, more than a year later. Though it increased the Scottish electorate from 4000 to 65,000, it was in some respects a cautious measure and in others a sloppy one. Now that Jeffrey could actually do something about reform, he was mainly concerned with not going too far towards democracy. He and especially his draftsman, Cockburn, showed besides a rather silly contempt for the Scots feudal law which made a minefield of the suffrage but which had to be mastered if a moderate measure was to work. Instead, hasty and ill-considered compromises allowed abuses to persist, while deliberately conservative elements in the package meant that aristocratic control of the counties continued. Numerous blemishes in the working of Jeffrey's reformed system were to appear, for which he has to be held largely to account.

However, Jeffrey enjoyed a personal triumph when he went back to Edinburgh and was comfortably elected one of its MPs, along with his fellow whig, James Abercromby. Reappointed lord advocate as well, he proceeded straight to reform of the notoriously corrupt Scottish burgh councils. Although eventually successful, he was shocked at the difficulty of the task. Cockburn had already observed: 'I fear for him in Parliament—nearly sixty years of age, a bad trachea, inexperience and a great reputation are bad foundations for success in the House of Commons' (*Journal*, 16). Now Jeffrey saw at first hand some of the deficiencies of his reformed system. It did not, for example, suppress the importunity of Scots for official patronage. The only difference was that liberals now demanded all the jobs previously reserved for tories. Raised expectations similarly increased the demand for legislation. Jeffrey, who unlike the former managers was not a member of the cabinet, could never persuade it to give him enough time. He had to work there either through the capricious Brougham, who vaunted himself on familiarity with Scottish affairs but did nothing about them, or through the home secretary, Lord Melbourne, who viewed them with languid indifference and was ready only with excuses for inaction. Most of Jeffrey's business was

referred to committees of Scots MPs, whose bickering constantly thwarted him. Cockburn wrote: 'He was left to the mercies of every county, city, parish, public body or person, who had an interest or a fancy to urge' (Cockburn, *Life*, 2.355). Since no degree of industry or complaisance seemed to satisfy his countrymen, Jeffrey found his position impossibly burdensome. Frustrated and disillusioned, he got out of parliament by appointing himself to the Scottish bench. He took his seat on the bench as Lord Jeffrey on 7 June 1834.

According to Cockburn, Jeffrey was a popular judge—patient, painstaking, and candid, but too voluble and unpredictable, keeping up a 'running margin of questions, suppositions and comments' (Cockburn, *Life*, 2.422). The most notable verdict he had to deliver came in the Auchterarder case of 1838, in the long dispute over lay patronage in the Church of Scotland which was to lead to the Disruption in 1843. On the appeal to the Court of Session he found, in the minority, for the evangelical defendants. At the Disruption, when one-third of the ministers seceded from the kirk, he famously declared: 'I am proud of my country. In not another land in the world would such a thing have been done' (2.431).

After an illness, Jeffrey's workload was reduced by transfer to a lower division of the court in 1842. He continued to preside over a sociable table, improved his country house and garden, and kept in touch with literary trends. He gave advice to young authors, made a friend of Charles Dickens, whose novels brought tears to his eyes, and revised the proofs of the first two volumes of Thomas Macaulay's *History of England*. He remained lively enough, though steadily weakening. He died on 26 January 1850 and was buried quietly four days later in the Dean cemetery, Edinburgh, at a spot chosen by himself. His wife survived him only briefly, and died on 18 May, to be interred beside him.

MICHAEL FRY

Sources H. Cockburn, *Life of Lord Jeffrey, with a selection from his correspondence*, 2 vols. (1852) · *Journal of Henry Cockburn: being a continuation of the 'Memorials of his time', 1831–1854*, 2 vols. (1874) · F. Jeffrey, *Contributions to the Edinburgh Review*, 4 vols. (1844) · G. W. T. Omond, *The lord advocates of Scotland from the close of the fifteenth century to the passing of the Reform Bill*, 2 vols. (1883) · J. Clive, *Scotch reviewers: the Edinburgh Review, 1802–1815* (1957) · J. A. Greig, *Francis Jeffrey of the Edinburgh Review* (1948) · T. Carlyle, *Reminiscences*, ed. J. A. Froude, 2 vols. (1881) · NA Scot., SC 70/1/72, p. 48

Archives Hunt. L., letters · Mitchell L., Glas., corresp. · NL Scot., corresp; diaries of journies; journals, etc.; legal notes; letter-books; letter-books as lord advocate; letters; answers to memorials and queries relating to encroachments on works of Sir Walter Scott; journal of his visit to the United States | Birm. CA, corresp. with Gregory Watt · BL, corresp. with John Allen, Add. MS 52181 · BL, corresp. with Lord Holland, Add. MS 51644 · BL, letters to Macrey Napier, Add. MSS 34611–34626 *passim* · BL OIOC, corresp. with Mountstuart Elphinstone, Eur. MS F 88, boxes 3C, D, G-H · BLPES, letters to Francis Horner · Glos. RO, letters to Daniel Ellis · Heriot-Watt University archives, letters to Sir James Gibson-Craig · NA Scot., letters to Sir John Dalrymple · NL Scot., corresp. with Thomas Carlyle and Jane Carlyle · NL Scot., corresp. with Henry Cockburn; letters to Henry Cockburn; corresp, with Archibald Constable; corresp. with Lord Dunfermline; letters to James Reddie; corresp. with Thomas Spring Rice; letters to Andrew Rutherfurd; letters to Sir Walter Scott · NRA, priv. coll., corresp. with William Creech · NRA, priv. coll., letters to Lord Moncreiff ·

NRA, priv. coll., letters to Sir John Sinclair · U. Durham L., letters to Earl Grey · U. Edin. L., letters to George Wilson · U. Edin., New Coll. L., letters to Thomas Chalmers · U. Glas. L., letters to J. P. Muirhead · U. Reading L., letters to Thomas Moore · UCL, letters to Lord Brougham and Henry Brougham · W. Sussex RO, letters to duke of Richmond · William Patrick Library, Glasgow, letters to Peter Mackenzie

Likenesses J. Henning, wax medallion, 1801, Scot. NPG · J. Henning, chalk drawing, 1806, Scot. NPG · W. Evans, stipple, pubd c.1812 (after H. Raeburn), NPG · H. Raeburn, portrait, in or before 1812; Sothebys, New York, 4 June 1980, lot 159 [*see illus.*] · W. Nicholson, watercolour, 1816, Abbotsford House, Selkirkshire · S. Joseph, plaster bust, 1822, Scot. NPG · J. Pairman, oils, 1823, Scot. NPG · A. Geddes, oils, 1826, NPG · S. Cousins, mezzotint, 1830 (after C. Smith), NG Ire. · J. Steell, marble statue, 1855, Parliament House, Edinburgh · W. Bewick, chalk drawing, Scot. NPG · B. W. Crombie, pencil and watercolour study, Scot. NPG; repro. in W. S. Douglas, *Modern Athenians* (1882) · G. Hayter, mezzotint (after J. E. Coombs), NPG · G. Hayter, mezzotint (after J. Sartain), NPG · J. Linnell, pencil drawing, NPG · P. Park, marble bust, NPG · C. Smith, oils, Scot. NPG

Wealth at death £11,613 0s. 5d.: inventory, 11 Jan 1851, NA Scot., SC 70/1/72, p. 48

Jeffrey, John. *See* Jefferay, Sir John (c.1523–1578).

Jeffreys. *See also* Jefferies, Jefferys, Jeffreys, Jeffries, Jeffryes.

Jeffreys, Bertha, Lady Jeffreys (1903–1999). *See under* Jeffreys, Sir Harold (1891–1989).

Jeffreys, Christopher (c.1642–1693). *See under* Jeffreys, George (c.1610–1685).

Jeffreys, George (c.1610–1685), composer and organist, was possibly born in or near Weldon, Northamptonshire, and descended, according to Anthony Wood, from the family of Matthew Jeffries (*fl. c.*1590), a vicar-choral at Wells Cathedral. Nothing is known of his parents or early life, but he appears to have had connections with the Hatton family of Kirby Hall, Northamptonshire, from at least 1631. That year he set verses by Richard Hatton, and by 1633 he was working as a secretary and steward for Richard Hatton's cousin Sir Christopher Hatton (created Baron Hatton in 1643). Both Richard and Christopher Hatton were students at Cambridge, but there is no record that Jeffreys attended the university himself; he did however compose some of the music for Peter Hausted's comedy *The Rival Friends* that was performed at Cambridge in March 1632 in the presence of the king and queen. In 1637 Jeffreys married Mary Peirs, the widowed daughter of Thomas Mainwaring, rector of Weldon and Dene, and his wife, Elizabeth Salwey. They had two children: Christopher [*see below*] and Mary.

During the civil war, owing to the patronage of Hatton, Jeffreys went to Oxford and there gained his only professional musical appointment as organist to Charles I. After the capitulation of Oxford and Baron Hatton's move to France in November 1646, Jeffreys returned to his family in the village of Weldon, near Kirby Hall, and continued to serve Lady Hatton, who had remained in England.

For someone employed only briefly as a fully fledged musician, Jeffreys's output, spread over fifty years, is impressive. His surviving compositions consist of 7 instrumental fantasias, 13 Italian madrigals, 16 English songs, 63 Latin motets, 6 Latin canticles, 2 Latin mass movements, 28 English anthems or devotional pieces, and 4 settings of texts from the English communion service. Forty-eight of his small-scale Italianate *concertato* pieces date from before 1648, and some could have been composed as early as 1638. It was undoubtedly Jeffreys's exposure to the Italian music in the Hatton music collection—particularly the small-scale *concertato* motets written by contemporaries of Monteverdi—which led to his most successful compositions; his anthems, devotional songs, and motets show a complete assimilation of the Italian *seconda prattica* style, especially with regard to melodic shape and the expressive use of dissonance. No other pre-Commonwealth composer showed such a wholehearted commitment to the *stile nuovo* and, as such, George Jeffreys must be recognized as the main pioneer of Italianate sacred music in England.

By the time of the Restoration, Jeffreys had acquired some land of his own in Weldon, and, no longer dependent solely on the employment and patronage of the Hatton family, continued to compose. Although his name appears twice in James Clifford's text anthology *The divine services and anthems usually sung in the cathedrals and collegiate choires in the Church of England* (1663), only one of his works was published during his lifetime, the two-voice motet *Erit gloria domini*, which appeared in John Playford's *Cantica sacra … the Second Sett* (1674). His latest surviving manuscript is a copy of three of Purcell's *Sonnata's of III Parts* published in 1683; Jeffreys must therefore have copied the sonatas during the last two years of his life.

Jeffreys died at Weldon on 1 July 1685, having possibly outlived his wife, and was buried at St Mary's Church, Weldon. His manuscripts were dispersed and his pioneering achievements of the 1640s were soon forgotten. Only at the close of the twentieth century was Jeffreys's remarkable contribution to English seventeenth-century music acknowledged.

Jeffreys's son, **Christopher Jeffreys** (c.1642–1693), was educated at Westminster School and Christ Church, Oxford, graduating BA in 1663 and proceeding MA in 1666. His friend Anthony Wood described him as being skilled at the organ and the virginals or harpsichord. He travelled to Spain, but his father's attempts to gain for him a position in the ambassador's suite on the strength of his musical abilities were unsuccessful. Later he married Anna Brydges, sister of James, eighth Baron Chandos, and lived with his father at Weldon; one of their four children was the poet George *Jeffreys (1678–1755). Jeffreys himself died in 1693.   JONATHAN P. WAINWRIGHT

Sources P. Aston, 'George Jeffreys and the English Baroque', DPhil diss., University of York, 1970 · R. Thompson, 'George Jeffreys and the *stile nuovo* in English sacred music: a new date for his autograph score, British Library Add. MS 10338', *Music and Letters*, 70 (1989), 317–41 · J. P. Wainwright, *Musical patronage in seventeenth-century England: Christopher, first Baron Hatton (1605–70)* (1997) · letter of Jeffreys to Lady Hatton, 1665, BL, Add. MS 29550, fols. 232–3, 236v · P. Aston, 'George Jeffreys', *MT*, 110 (1969), 772–6 · P. Aston, 'Tradition and experiment in the devotional music of George Jeffreys', *Proceedings of the Royal Musical Association*, 99 (1972–3), 105–15 ·

K. Bergdolt, 'The sacred music of George Jeffreys', PhD diss., University of Cincinnati, 1976 · H. W. Shaw, 'Extracts from Anthony à Wood's *Notes on the lives of musicians* hitherto unpublished', *Music and Letters*, 15 (1934), 157–62 · *The life and times of Anthony Wood*, ed. A. Clark, 5 vols., OHS, 19, 21, 26, 30, 40 (1891–1900) · Wood, *Ath. Oxon.*, new edn · J. Hawkins, *A general history of the science and practice of music*, new edn, 3 vols. (1875) · *DNB* · will, Northants. RO
Wealth at death see will, proved 31 July 1685, Northants. RO

Jeffreys, George, first Baron Jeffreys (1645–1689), judge, was born on 15 May 1645, son of John Jeffreys (1608–1691) and Margaret, *née* Ireland, at his family's home of Acton Park near Wrexham in Denbighshire and just a few miles from Chester. He was one of at least nine children born into a family notable for its royalism; his grandfather had been one of the justices for north Wales, but his father pursued no professional calling.

Education and early career, 1645–1678 Jeffreys began his formal schooling with Thomas Chaloner, who had been expelled from the headship of Shrewsbury School by parliamentary forces in 1645. In November 1652 he enrolled with his brothers at Shrewsbury, where he remained until 1659. He then moved to London, studying first at St Paul's School and, from 1661 to 1662, at Westminster School. He entered Trinity College, Cambridge, in March 1662, but left without a degree for the Inner Temple in May 1663.

Late in his student years at the Temple, Jeffreys began his search for a wife from a family of means. Believing he had found such a woman, he courted her with the help of her companion, Sarah Neesham (*bap.* 1644, *d.* 1678). But once his letters to the young woman were discovered her father ended their amours and dismissed Neesham. Jeffreys, now appreciating qualities that he had overlooked, proposed to Neesham instead. Though she brought a dowry of only £300—modest for one of his pretensions—they were married at All Hallows Barking on 23 May 1667. They established themselves in a house on Coleman Street, near the Guildhall. Theirs was reportedly a happy union, from which came seven children before it was ended by Sarah's death on 14 February 1678. Jeffreys referred to this marriage as the happiest phase of his life.

Jeffreys was called to the bar on 22 November 1668. Operating from expensive chambers in King's Bench Walk, he staked his future on opportunities provided by the courts of London. Appearing regularly before Middlesex sessions both in Hicks Hall and at the Old Bailey, he quickly became known as a master of cross-examination. He took care to ingratiate himself with less prominent Londoners, especially with the attorneys who were so important in feeding business to barristers. He also cultivated friendships with prominent merchants and leaders in City politics such as Sir Robert Clayton, later lord mayor, and Alderman John Jeffreys, and received favourable attention from Sir Matthew Hale, soon to become the chief justice of king's bench. When he was only twenty-five he obtained his first public legal office upon his election as common serjeant of London on 17 March 1671. With office came an impressive house in Aldermanbury, near St Mary's Church. Holding a prominent legal office also gave a boost to business, and he now began to argue

George Jeffreys, first Baron Jeffreys (1645–1689), by John Michael Wright, 1675

cases in royal courts as well as City ones. In the early 1670s his appearances in the reports and records of the courts of Westminster Hall were surprisingly rare compared with those of barristers like William Williams or Francis Winnington, who, like Jeffreys, later became prominent in politics as well as law. But in the mid-1670s Jeffreys's pleadings in the kingdom's leading courts increased. By 1680 his reputation for powerful courtroom advocacy had made him one of the most active barristers in king's bench.

As early as 1672 Jeffreys began to wheedle his way into the good graces of prominent courtiers. He did this initially by using his office as a way of providing information about City politics. He may well have been the author of a report for the king in 1672 concerning the political leanings of City leaders. Later in the 1670s he cultivated the support of the earl of Danby and of the Catholic royal mistress, the duchess of Portsmouth, by offering intelligence about possible parliamentary actions that might affect the crown. On 14 September 1677 the king knighted Jeffreys and made him a king's counsel; in the following January he became a bencher of his inn.

Jeffrey's wealth grew with his prominence. By the end of the 1660s he had been able to invest in at least one shipping venture and in a farm in his native Denbighshire. But his first major purchase of property came in 1676 when he bought Temple Bulstrode and 800 acres surrounding it in Buckinghamshire; he continued to buy land in the neighbourhood in subsequent years. Bulstrode provided the setting for the 33-year-old barrister to receive the ultimate honour when the king and the duchess of Portsmouth dined with him in August 1678. Charles reportedly drank his host's health no less than seven times. Keen observers knew that this indicated further advancement. When the recordership of London became vacant, the king made clear to London his preference for Jeffreys, whom the City obediently elected on 22 October 1678.

Recorder of London, 1678–1680 Jeffreys first appeared in a judicial capacity on 11 December 1678 when he sat as recorder in the Old Bailey. An unusually full account of the session was printed, perhaps with Jeffreys's encouragement. Though sitting on the bench, he could not resist continuing to play the advocate, a tendency that, for good and ill, was apparent throughout his years as a judge. Thus when the jury failed to return a guilty verdict against a prisoner accused of child rape—the jurors complaining that the evidence was largely hearsay—Jeffreys 'labour'd to satisfy them of the manifestness of the proof', ultimately changing their minds (*Exact Account*, 15). He also relished the recorder's responsibility to pronounce sentence as he lectured those convicted for their wickedness.

Jeffreys's elevation to London's highest legal office had come just as Titus Oates unleashed the storm of bigotry called the Popish Plot. Jeffreys thus opened the treason case in king's bench against Edward Coleman, though the main work of prosecution fell to others. In the following month, Jeffreys sat with those presiding in the Old Bailey trial of William Ireland. Again he played a less prominent role than other actors until time came for him, as recorder, to pronounce sentence. Jeffreys unleashed his fury on Catholicism, recommending that the condemned rely 'upon the merits of a crucified saviour, and not upon your masses, tricks or trumperies'. But Jeffreys also noted that he did not mean 'to inveigh against all persons that profess the Romish religion; for there are many that are of that persuasion, that do abhor those base principles of murdering kings and subverting governments' (*State trials*, 7.138). Thus from the outset of the Popish Plot hysteria Jeffreys took care to distinguish between Catholics generally and traitors specifically. Perhaps owing to this care, the duke of York asked Jeffreys in January 1679 to serve as his solicitor-general, which gave him 'a very uneasy time in the City' (Knights, 277n.). That month a fire swept through the Temple. Jeffreys ordered gunpowder and directed the destruction of a group of buildings, thereby stopping the flames before they engulfed the Temple Church and moved into Fleet Street.

His first wife having died early in 1678, Jeffreys married again at St Mary Aldermanbury—where his first wife lay buried—on 10 June 1679. His new wife was Anne (1657–1703), the widow of Sir John Jones of Glamorgan and daughter of Sir Thomas Bludworth, a wealthy merchant, former lord mayor, and Jeffreys's long-time London ally. This was a less happy match for both of them, and one mocked in the press, which attacked Jeffreys's new wife for her alleged dalliances with others. Three days after the ceremony Jeffreys resumed his seat in the Old Bailey to try a group of Jesuits for treason. On the following day he presided in the trial of Richard Langhorn, a barrister with chambers near his own, on the same charge. Jeffreys

expressed his particular regret for Langhorn as he pronounced sentence.

Throughout the trials of 1679 Jeffrey's part remained the same: when presiding in the Old Bailey, doing little more than pronounce sentence, and when pleading in king's bench, leaving the lion's share of the prosecution to others such as Sir John Maynard, Sir Francis Winnington, and Sir William Jones, ardent whigs eager to pursue the plot. As judge or as prosecutor Jeffreys was a moderate in a year of immoderation. He certainly doubted sooner than others the tales of Titus Oates. This became most apparent when Jeffreys sat in the Old Bailey in July 1679 during the trial of the queen's physician, Sir George Wakeman, a Catholic accused of plotting to poison the king. He rebuked Oates for the lies he had told and Wakeman walked free.

The atmosphere in parliament was changing rapidly. Many of the lawyers with whom Jeffreys had teamed in these early prosecutions, especially Winnington and Jones, as well as other prominent barristers—George Pollexfen, George Treby, and William Williams—now led those in the Commons who attacked the duke of York while Jeffreys's support of him increased. In October 1679, when Jones's opposition to the crown made it impossible for him to continue as attorney-general, rumours arose that Jeffreys would receive the office, though this did not happen. Late in the year, with parliament in abeyance, many in London planned to petition the king to summon parliament so that pursuit of the plot, and of York, might continue. Jeffreys reportedly told the City's aldermen that petitioning 'was bordering upon treason, and the beginning of rebellion' (Knights, 277n.). Though their advice varied slightly, he and Sir Francis North both recommended that the king issue a proclamation condemning petitioning, which he did. The struggle between petitioners for parliament—increasingly called whigs—and those who 'abhorred' such petitions—tories—was now engaged. In April 1680 Jeffreys, joined by Westminster MP Sir Francis Wythens, presented the king with an abhorrence of petitions signed by citizens of London and Westminster.

Part of the battle between petitioners and addressers, in which Jeffreys played such a public part, was fought in court. He thus prosecuted Benjamin Harris in February 1680 for his pamphlet *An Appeal from the Country to the City*, which criticized the ongoing prorogation of parliament. Jeffreys complained that it was 'as base a piece as ever was contrived in hell, either by papists, or the blackest rebel that ever was' (*State trials*, 7.927). There was little Harris's counsel could do. The jury's initial verdict, that Harris was guilty only of selling the book, was ultimately changed to guilt for seditious libel after some chastisement from Jeffreys. Days later Jeffreys, with the help of John Holt, prosecuted the dissenting bookseller Francis Smith, likewise charged with seditious libel for his pamphlet condemning Wakeman's acquittal. Smith had pleaded not guilty but, complaining of sickness, he did not attend his trial. Just as witnesses were about to be sworn, his wife, accepting advice of counsel, confessed his fault and Smith was fined.

In July Jeffreys prosecuted Henry Care, also for seditious libel, contending that much had been done of late to criticize the government in the name of protecting the nation from 'popery'. Jeffreys made the usual attacks on Catholicism, but added that 'in case any man will be transported with zeal because he is of a party, and under pretence of endeavoring to suppress popery, should support a party, that man ought to be detected' (ibid., 7.1115). This was not only a denunciation of whiggery, but of party division itself. Yet these were nothing if not partisan proceedings, as amply testified by the fact that William Williams, now Jeffreys's most important foe, served as defence counsel in all three cases. The courtroom crowd's noisy negative reaction to Jeffreys in all these trials was another sign of the increasingly poisoned atmosphere he confronted.

Though his actions alienated Jeffreys from the City's whig-leaning leadership, he remained their recorder and presided at Guildhall sessions in the summer of 1680. But all his efforts at elections in July could not prevent the victory of Sir Patience Ward as lord mayor and Henry Cornish and Slingsby Bethel as sheriffs. Jeffreys now fought with these whig sheriffs over the power to name jurors. The struggle became acute in September when Francis Smith was again charged with seditious libel for another pamphlet. The grand jury—carefully selected by the sheriffs—returned the indictment 'ignoramous'. But Jeffreys insisted on presenting the same indictment to the Old Bailey sessions; again, it was dismissed. Jeffreys could do little but scold them for finding against the evidence. He then remanded Smith to the next sessions, doing all he could to obstruct Smith's efforts to get a copy of the indictment against him.

With parliament finally about to reconvene late in 1680, Jeffreys's days in London were clearly numbered. None other than William Williams presided now as speaker of the House of Commons, where articles of impeachment were prepared against a number of judges. A petition had circulated in the City in September calling for Jeffreys's dismissal as recorder. The Commons too, on 13 November, accused Jeffreys of 'murdering petitions' and thereby betraying the rights of subjects, and thus joined calls for his removal as recorder. Jeffreys seemed destined to join the list of others now under impeachment. Adding a populist punch to the attack, on Queen Elizabeth's accession day, 17 November, London crowds burnt pictures of Jeffreys and other abhorrers along with pictures of the pope. On 2 December 1680 Jeffreys tendered his resignation as recorder. On the following day George Treby, another whig leader in the Commons, was elected in his place.

Chief justice of Chester, 1680–1683 London's aldermen voted to pay Jeffreys £200 for his services and appointed a committee to tabulate how much he was owed for his expenses in improving his house, a City property. More astonishing, he was not evicted; he remained there several years more. But losing the recordership indicated that Jeffreys's most important ties to the City, where he had built his career, were now cut. Compensation for the loss of City office could come only through further royal preferment. Owing largely to the intervention of the duchess of Portsmouth, preferment had already come. On 30 April 1680 the king had named Jeffreys chief justice of the palatine courts at Chester. On 12 May 1680 he also took the oaths of a king's serjeant.

At Chester, Jeffreys combined ever more boldly his unique brand of judicial advocacy with political advocacy in the interest of the king and his embattled heir. He was also a commendable judge when matters without a political cast came before him. Henry Booth, later Lord Delamere, complained in parliament of Jeffreys's comportment in Chester, condemning his tendency to treat those before him with too much levity or scorn and alleging that he did not work hard enough to go through the long dockets of cases before him. Such charges had more partisan bias than justification behind them. Surviving plea rolls show that Jeffreys was assiduous in performing his duties at Chester. They also show him gaining extensive experience in civil litigation to add to his command of criminal process. But his work in the city included much more than able handling of the usual run of court business. His deep involvement in local politics resulted from his familial connection to the area and from the fact that two of his most important enemies in parliament—both of whom had helped to drive him from his recorder's place—were Henry Booth, a leading figure in Cheshire politics and heir to the barony of Delamere, and Williams, Chester's recorder and the speaker of the House of Commons.

Like Jeffreys, Williams was one of the great courtroom advocates of the age. These two Welsh lawyers clashed often. In June 1681 Jeffreys prosecuted Edward Fitzharris for treason; Williams worked with Treby, Winnington, and Pollexfen to provide an ultimately unsuccessful defence. Williams joined the same trio in 1683 to defend Sir Patience Ward from charges of perjury. Jeffreys again conducted the prosecution. They represented opposing sides in lesser-known actions too. In 1681 Williams represented John Sherwin, an alleged frequenter of conventicles, when he sought a writ of mandamus from king's bench to order his admission to an alderman's place in Nottingham. Jeffreys advised Sherwin's corporate foes.

For Jeffreys 1681 was a year of increased responsibilities in the royal interest. That spring the king appointed him to the City militia and lieutenancy. In August Jeffreys conducted the prosecution for treason of Stephen College at Oxford. Jeffreys summarized by playing on one of his favourite themes: 'God forbid any person, Protestant or other, should attempt the life of the king, and the subversion of our religion, and by styling themselves by the name of Protestants, should excuse themselves from any such crimes' (State trials, 8.703–4). Jeffreys was chosen by the county's other magistrates to chair Middlesex sessions. He used this post to harass dissenters, whom he increasingly reviled for their whig sympathies. At quarter sessions in October his charge inveighed 'against the papists and dissenters, equally ranking them as mischievous to church and state' (Luttrell, 1.132). At the same sessions he tussled again with the sheriffs over the appointment of jurors, a battle he fought—and won—with the king's clear blessing. For all his vigorous service Charles II on 17 November 1681 made Jeffreys a baronet.

Jeffreys remained just as busy in the politically charged courtroom proceedings of 1682 and 1683. He prosecuted the whig leader Lord Grey of Warke for his liaison with his young sister-in-law, Lady Henrietta Berkeley; Williams provided Grey's unsuccessful defence. Jeffreys represented the king's perfumer in his *scandalum magnatum* action against London's whiggish sheriff, Thomas Pilkington, winning an £800 judgment. More important, he appeared for the duke of York in a similar suit against Pilkington, for saying that the duke 'had burnt the city, and was now come to cut the citizens' throats' (Luttrell, 1.240). Damages in this instance came to £100,000: Pilkington had been destroyed. In May 1683 Pilkington was sued along with other former whig sheriffs Samuel Shute, Slingsby Bethel, and Henry Cornish, Lord Grey, and others, for a riot at the previous sheriffs' election. All were heavily fined. Days later Jeffreys won a judgment against former lord mayor Sir Patience Ward for his alleged perjury in Pilkington's earlier trial for *scandalum magnatum*. In both cases Williams led a vigorous but ultimately unsuccessful defence against Jeffreys's prosecution. In the following month Jeffreys gained the first conviction for the Rye House plot when he helped to prosecute Lord Russell for treason.

1682 and 1683 were also marked by conflicts with Williams at Chester. In September 1682 the duke of Monmouth received a clamorous welcome there from Williams's friends and much of Chester's populace. But Jeffreys arrived soon thereafter to preside at assizes. Many were charged with riot for the display during Monmouth's visit, but a Chester grand jury returned 'ignoramous'. Jeffreys quickly wrote to London, suggesting that a commission of oyer and terminer be sent by which he could try the rioters. When it was opened in court Williams denied the legality of Jeffreys's special commission, and in a stirring speech referring to Chester's ancient chartered privileges, condemned the proceedings, to no avail; Jeffreys's new jurors found the riot. His work done, Jeffreys rode to Macclesfield where he received the freedom. Williams's mention of the charter was perhaps a tactical blunder. By this time, London's charter was under legal assault by *quo warranto*. Judgment was given against London in June 1683. The stage was now set for similar legal action against England's other incorporated towns. Williams's power base in Chester was one of the first targets.

In July 1683 an information in the nature of *quo warranto* was filed against Chester's corporation. In the following month, when 'loyal' Cestrians and area gentry subscribed an address to the king submitting to the *quo warranto*, Williams convinced the corporation to reject the address. But by the time that Jeffreys went to Chester for the assizes in September, the Rye House plot had been revealed. Chester's grand jury duly condemned the plotters and then presented more than two dozen local leaders, including Booth, for having presented an address concerning the succession and the Popish Plot. Jeffreys bound them all to keep the peace, thus leaving a legal sword of Damocles hanging over them to compel political obedience. But at the setting of Chester's Christmas watch in 1683, Williams gave another powerful speech opposing surrender of their charter, which his foes thought was their only hope of political safety.

Some in the corporation seemed ready to join Williams in the fight, but a majority voted in the following month not to appear in court to the *quo warranto*: in effect, a surrender of their charter. Undaunted, Williams and his allies still planned to make a courtroom appearance against the *quo warranto*. The remainder of the corporation, afraid of the consequences of further opposition to the king, petitioned the chief justice of king's bench not to accept their appearance. The chief justice, now Jeffreys himself, agreed to refuse Williams's effort to plead. Chester's charter was thus forfeit in February 1684. Williams and his friends were removed from the corporation by the new charter granted in the following year. Given that Williams had played such an important part in Jeffreys's loss of London's recordership in 1680, Jeffreys perhaps took some pleasure in returning the favour.

Chief justice of king's bench, 1683–1685 Charles II reportedly had his doubts but, with strong encouragement from the earl of Sunderland, appointed Jeffreys chief justice of king's bench on 28 September 1683. Days later Jeffreys was sworn of the privy council as well. Many felt misgivings, including leading tories like Sir Francis North, now lord keeper, and Baron Guilford. John Evelyn said Jeffreys was 'reputed the most ignorant, though the most daring' (Evelyn, *Diary*, 4.342). Jeffreys's worsening health, the result of the stone in his bladder, did little to diminish his daring as he became master in that court, where he cared little what his lesser colleagues on the bench thought. For good and ill, Jeffreys never failed to impress. Even Roger North, rarely kind to Jeffreys in his biography of his brother Lord Guilford, had to confess that 'When he was in temper and matters indifferent came before him he became the seat of justice better than any other I saw in his place' (North, 1.288). Thus many naysayers would be silenced, though others would only be enraged when Jeffreys presided in matters more than indifferent.

The treason trial of Algernon Sidney, held just days after Jeffreys took his place on the bench, was hardly a matter indifferent. None other than William Williams counselled Sidney, the most celebrated of the Rye House plotters. Sidney engaged Jeffreys in a dispute over the indictment during his arraignment. During trial Sidney continued to press on legal more than factual arguments in a way that clearly challenged Jeffreys's command of the situation. Their greatest struggle came over the rule requiring two witnesses to treason. This resulted in Jeffreys's famed pronouncement '*scribere est agere*' (*State trials*, 9.889). Sidney's unpublished 'Discourses' thus served as a second witness to Lord Howard's testimony against Sidney. The jury took less than half an hour to find his guilt. Before delivering sentence Jeffreys delivered his own verdict on Sidney's book, 'in which there is scarce a line, but what contains the rankest treason' (ibid., 9.902).

John Hampden's trial for his part in the Rye House plot followed early in 1684. Charged with a misdemeanour—sedition—rather than with a felony, since only one witness could be found, Hampden was permitted counsel. He chose Williams. From the start, when Williams began challenging proposed jurors, Jeffreys hounded him from the bench. Like Jeffreys, Williams could strain the law in hopes of winning a point; unlike Jeffreys, he could not control the proceedings. His efforts to disparage the witness—again, Lord Howard—or to introduce questionable evidence were for naught. Hampden was convicted and fined £40,000.

Perhaps the most notorious of the Rye House proceedings over which Jeffreys presided was that of Sir Thomas Armstrong. Armstrong, a friend of Monmouth, had fled to the Netherlands after the plot was uncovered but was captured and returned. While abroad he had been outlawed and thus the court was now entitled to proceed immediately to pronounce judgment against him. But Armstrong argued that he was due a trial since he had been out of the country when outlawed. Jeffreys, unconvinced, was ready to proceed to sentence when Armstrong's daughter shouted out that she had a statute supporting her father's contention. Jeffreys said 'We do not use to have women plead in the Court of King's Bench. Pray be at quiet' (*State trials*, 10.110). Armstrong picked up the argument, but Jeffreys would hear nothing of it. Armstrong died six days later, one of his quarters being sent for display in Stafford, which he had represented in parliament.

Throughout his time in king's bench Jeffreys handled a long string of prosecutions for *scandalum magnatum* and seditious libel. Many of these were brought at the suit of the duke of York, and the most spectacular culminated in a £100,000 fine on Titus Oates in June 1684. About the same time the publisher Francis Smith was fined £500 and sentenced to the pillory for his pamphlet *The Raree Show*. Numerous others in the book trade suffered a similar fate.

Contrary to common suggestions Jeffreys presided often and ably in civil cases. Lady Ivy's case—a complex property dispute—heard in June 1684, was reportedly one of the longest trials in memory. Jeffreys's long summary was widely admired, even by his detractors. A more important matter occupied Jeffreys off and on for nearly his entire two years as chief justice. This was the *East India Company* v. *Thomas Sandys* for the latter's violation of the company's exclusive trading privileges. The leading lawyers of the day were briefed—Holt, Sawyer, Finch, Pollexfen, Treby, and Williams—the last three arguing against the company's claims. Williams's arguments were the most important. He had contended that the company's charter, by granting exclusive powers to the company, diminished the king's own authority: 'as this great and mighty charter is penned, it doth not only invest the Company, but divest the king of his prerogative' (*State trials*, 10.496). Jeffreys observed drily:

> Mr. Williams (always a friend to the king's prerogative), in tenderness and care thereof, seemed to be surprised by the inconsiderate extravagancy of the grant; and would have us believe, that he was afflicted with the dismal consequences that must necessarily ensue by the king's parting with so great a prerogative. (ibid., 10.520)

Williams also argued that the king should consult parliament in a matter of such importance. This cut too close to the political bone. Jeffreys, reminded of the struggles of 1679 to 1681, replied:

> God be praised, it is in the king's power to call and dissolve parliaments, when and how he pleases … Mr. Williams would do well to save himself the trouble of advising the king of what things are fit for him to consult with his parliament about. (ibid., 10.534)

Jeffreys repeatedly singled out Williams's arguments, sniping at him as he made his legal points in summation, but also showing his respect by according Williams's ideas so much care in rebuttal. Like Williams, Jeffreys relied not only on a full command of English precedents, but also on extensive reading in the works of Grotius and in civil law, with a touch of Cicero added for good measure. Concluding that the company's charter was indeed good as derived from the king's prerogative, Jeffrey had delivered a judgment displaying impressive erudition.

As a royal justice Jeffreys presided at assizes too. For his first assize in February 1684 he chose the western circuit, where he carried instructions from the privy council to take the region's political temperature. The London *quo warranto* decision now long past, this was also the period when towns by the score were surrendering their charters in return for new ones that typically left those of whiggish sympathies out of the corporations. Thus another of Jeffreys's tasks was to encourage further surrenders. He did this ever more effectively when he rode the northern circuit in July. Jeffreys found an enthusiastic if fawning reception everywhere he went as drums played, guns boomed in salute, and town leaders bowed to him across the north. Pontefract, Carlisle, York, Berwick, and Durham were just some of the towns that offered up their charters in hopes that by doing so they would receive new ones with favourable terms owing to Jeffreys's influence. Townsmen underscored their hopes of his patronage by making him a freeman or choosing him as their high steward or recorder. Colonial and company charters were forfeit as well, and in these too Jeffreys played the crucial role.

Some were clearly concerned by Jeffreys's growing power, and none more than Lord Keeper Guilford. Guilford had been the early architect of the crown's chartering policy, but Jeffreys was clearly driving it to the point where even good tories like Guilford worried that Jeffreys would alienate many who would otherwise be strong friends of the crown. But Jeffreys pressed on. When he returned from the north in autumn 1684 he brought with him a list he had collected of Catholics gaoled there and suggested to the king in the privy council that he grant a general pardon to them. Guilford, alone of the councillors present, opposed him, and the matter was allowed to drop. But the rivalry between Jeffreys and Guilford only sharpened, all the more so since Jeffreys now lobbied to have the great seal for himself.

1685 and the western assizes Charles II had died and had been replaced by his brother by the time Jeffreys rode his next circuit. Jeffreys, long the duke of York's most vigorous supporter, stood to gain by his ascent to the throne as James II. His role at court immediately grew. In one of James's first privy council meetings, Jeffreys advised that James continue collecting revenues that parliament had granted only for the lifetime of Charles II, advice James readily accepted despite questions about its legality raised by Guilford. As Jeffreys left for the eastern circuit early in March 1685 he knew a new parliament was in the offing and that political business on the circuit would be far more important than the usual business of hearing cases at *nisi prius*. Upon concluding his circuit, Jeffreys went to Bulstrode. There he undertook intensive efforts to shape the outcome of elections across Buckinghamshire, though he achieved little, as whigs won the county seats and those for most of the boroughs.

Early in May Titus Oates, in prison for his inability to pay the huge fine levied on him in the previous year, returned to Westminster Hall to stand trial before Jeffreys on two counts of perjury for his testimony in the Popish Plot trials. Oates made the intriguing argument that his evidence had been countenanced then by the bench and so must be now. Jeffreys replied thoughtfully, explaining that judges rule only in matters of law, not of fact:

> A judge's opinion is of value in points of law that arise upon facts found by juries, but are [*sic*] no evidence of the fact: for judges only do presume the fact to be true as it is found by the jury.

In turn, juries only found fact based on sworn evidence. Thus, Jeffreys explained, 'I must tell you, there is no doubt, but that those juries did every one of them believe the evidence you gave, or they would not have convicted the prisoners' (*State trials*, 10.1144). If there had been a wrongful verdict, it could have happened only as a result of Oates's testimony. Oates was readily convicted on both counts and fined and sentenced to severe whippings, perpetual imprisonment, and appearances in the pillory on dates marking the anniversaries of the occasions that he lied in court. Though Jeffreys condemned anyone 'that should take away the lives of their fellow-creatures by perjury', he had handled these trials with care (ibid., 10.1212). It is a testament to the integrity of his conduct that Oates failed in 1689 to have this judgment reversed by parliament.

James raised Jeffreys to the peerage as first Baron Jeffreys of Wem on 16 May 1685, Jeffreys taking his title from a Shropshire manor he had acquired the year before. Three days later he took his seat in the House of Lords when the new parliament opened. Jeffreys made arrangements to ride the home circuit for the next assizes; he then left for Tunbridge Wells in hopes that the waters would alleviate the increasing pain he suffered from the stone. While there in early July he learned of Monmouth's rebellion and that the king had decided that Jeffreys and four other judges would be sent on assizes to the west instead, carrying with them two special commissions by which they would try the rebels captured after the battle of Sedgemoor.

Jeffreys remained in Tunbridge until late August. He then returned to London to meet the other judges and to begin their circuit. Throughout September—beginning at Winchester and proceeding through Salisbury, Dorchester, Exeter, Taunton, Bristol, and Wells—Jeffreys and his four brethren justices held regular assizes and conducted trials under their special commissions. The first case heard was among those that raised the greatest odium in later years, the trial of Lady Alice Lisle, accused of treason for accepting a few of the rebels into her house after their defeat. The elderly widow was a clear object for pity. Jeffreys, always one to examine witnesses aggressively, was reportedly especially vicious on this occasion, though the only surviving account of the trial is of questionable reliability. Lisle was convicted and sentenced to die though Jeffreys delayed execution to give her time to appeal to the king for mercy. One of the central points to remember concerning the western assizes of 1685 is that it was James who pointedly denied mercy in this and scores of other instances that September.

In the weeks following, Jeffreys and his colleagues conducted routine assize business and ploughed through astonishingly long dockets of accused traitors. Process, in keeping with contemporary norms, was hasty. Enormous pressure was exerted, not only by the judges, but by Henry Pollexfen, the whiggish lawyer who served as lead counsel throughout, for rebels to confess in hopes they would be spared. Many did confess; their sentences were usually commuted to transportation to the West Indies, the increasingly common practice by the 1680s for convicted felons of all kinds. Of course Jeffreys had always been rigorous in sedition and treason trials, and he was at least as zealous as ever in his work in the west. But throughout the proceedings he remained in constant contact with James and Lord Treasurer Sunderland, informing them of the verdicts and supplying names of convicts for possible pardons. That so few pardons were forthcoming, and that so much vigour was used in trying them in the first place, resulted principally from the energy with which James wanted the rebels pursued. Though a final reckoning may not be computed precisely, the evidence suggests that about 2600 prisoners were detained on charges connected to the rebellion, nearly half of whom confessed. 1381 were tried; most were convicted and sentenced to die. Of these approximately 200 were executed; most of the remainder, plus most that had confessed, were transported to the West Indies. These had been vicious judicial proceedings in an age that replied viciously to rebellion. In the context of other risings—for instance, those of 1536, 1569, 1715, and 1745—it is difficult to see these results as anything but ones reached according to ideas of justice prevailing throughout the period.

On 8 September Jeffreys received news at Dorchester that Lord Keeper Guilford had died. An important political foe and the last obstacle to his elevation had been removed. Jeffreys immediately wrote to Sunderland underscoring his long-standing hopes that his master would give him the great seals, not by the lesser title of lord keeper, but as lord chancellor.

Lord chancellor On 28 September 1685, the day when Jeffreys returned to London, James made him lord chancellor. Jeffreys moved to the chancellor's grand house in Great Queen Street by Lincoln's Inn Fields and named his close friend and cousin, Sir John Trevor, master of the rolls, second only to the chancellor in that court. Jeffreys first presided in his new court on 23 October. He normally sat in chancery three days each week during term. He was not one of that court's great jurists, but he managed its business competently. Perhaps more remarkable, none of his decrees was later reversed. He undertook a programme of minor reforms, cracking down on corrupt court clerks and insisting that successful defendants receive full costs as a way of discouraging vexatious actions.

As chancellor, and as one of the king's most important advisers, Jeffreys found that demands on him sharpened. So did the pain in his bladder. The heavy drinking that many contemporaries noted seems to have increased throughout 1686 and 1687 in response to his discomfort. But Jeffreys remained active on all fronts. Bulstrode, having burnt down a few years earlier, had been rebuilt by early 1686, and there Jeffreys went in February to convalesce after a serious vomiting fit. In April 1687, his illness worsening again, he moved from the chancellor's residence to a house in Duke Street, by St James's Park, in order to be closer to Whitehall. There he added an extra room in which he could hear chancery matters without leaving home.

But presiding as a judge was the least of Jeffreys's concerns. Rather, his part in politics consumed most of his energy. On 9 November 1685 he first sat on the woolsack in the House of Lords, which he had entered as a member only six months earlier, and where he now helped to guide the king's parliamentary agenda. James also made Jeffreys president of the ecclesiastical commission when he revived that defunct court in July 1686. In his work on the commission, one can see Jeffreys's unease grow as he was compelled to discipline the clergy of the Church of England in pursuit of a royal policy that increasingly favoured Catholics. This was evident in the first case heard by the commission, that of Henry Compton, bishop of London, who had refused a royal command to dismiss a clergyman who had preached against Catholicism. Compton was suspended. Jeffreys also presided when various fellows of Magdalen College, Oxford, and other colleges were punished for refusing to accept James's appointment of Catholics to their ranks.

Jeffreys's discomfort only grew as James sought toleration for his co-religionists by remodelling county benches, the lieutenancy, and urban corporations in 1687 and 1688. The new commissions and charters by which these changes were made had to pass the great seal held by Jeffreys as chancellor. He thus oversaw a process by which his tory allies lost local office, only to be replaced by dissenters and Catholics. None the less, Jeffreys performed his master's wishes. In doing so, and in particular, in remodelling the borough corporations, Jeffreys was assisted by his nemesis, Sir William Williams, recently made a baronet and brought into government as solicitor-general in one of the more remarkable political turnabouts of the late seventeenth century.

For all his compliance with the king's methods, Jeffreys's influence waned as the influence of Catholic advisers rose at court. In April 1687 Jeffreys refused to sign James's first declaration of indulgence. By August, rumours were about that he might be relieved of office, but shortly thereafter he accompanied the king and queen on a tour of the west, and his position appeared secure.

1688 began with Jeffreys again sinking into illness, this time prompted by a cold acquired when he went in state to his parish church in Aldermanbury at Christmas to receive the Anglican eucharist. He was unable to take his place in court as Hilary term opened, though he soon recovered and resumed his heavy schedule. In June, Jeffreys examined the seven bishops before the privy council, where they were accused of seditious libel for presenting a petition by which they questioned the legality of the dispensing power James employed when issuing his declaration of indulgence. Jeffreys advised that the bishops not be prosecuted, but other counsel prevailed. Jeffreys blamed Catholic members of the council and foretold the trouble that would ensue.

Still, Jeffreys remained in the king's good graces. The chancellor was present when the prince of Wales was born, and in July 1688, when Jeffreys's fifteen-year-old son John married Lady Charlotte, the thirteen-year-old daughter and heir of Philip Herbert, seventh earl of Pembroke, the king attended the celebrations at Bulstrode. Late in August the king returned to Bulstrode for dinner. But it took another month for Jeffreys to convince James to reverse his policies in order to counter the threat posed by the prince of Orange's looming invasion. James did issue a proclamation that he intended no harm to the established church and expressed his intention to meet leading Anglicans who had been out of influence for the last few years. But even now, James proved halting, pulled as he was in the other direction by his Catholic advisers. None the less, Jeffreys convinced James to restore the charter of London in early October; Jeffreys himself carried it back to the City through cheering crowds. He also prevailed with the king to restore the charters of other towns rechartered in the 1680s and to reverse the changes he had made to the personnel of county government. But these actions, announced on 14 October—the king's birthday—during a dinner for leading lawyers at Jeffreys's home, had come too late to save either king or chancellor.

The Tower, 1688–1689 Jeffreys sensed trouble. At the end of October he made a settlement of most of his property on his wife and son, asking that his whiggish friends Sir Robert Clayton and Henry Pollexfen serve as trustees. Days later Sunderland was dismissed from office, leaving Jeffreys ever more isolated as William of Orange landed in England. On 17 November Jeffreys joined a small group that witnessed the king's will. James then left for Salisbury, hoping to stop William's advance on London. Before leaving he put the government in the hands of five councillors, headed by Jeffreys. Meanwhile, Jeffreys sent his wife and children to Leatherhead in Surrey. Throughout these early days of crisis, he still managed to preside in chancery.

When James returned to London at the end of the month he summoned his remaining councillors and asked their advice about whether to convene a parliament. Jeffreys and others advised him to do so. On the following day James ordered Jeffreys to issue the necessary writs, and then asked him to move into apartments in Whitehall so that the king could have the great seal nearby; before leaving his house in Duke Street, Jeffreys made a point of settling all his outstanding debts. In the midst of this chaos, he also received news that his two year-old daughter Anne was dying. He went to her immediately and was there when she died, after which he quickly returned to the capital.

Jeffreys sat briefly in chancery on 8 December. Later that day James summoned him, asking that he bring the great seal and the parliamentary writs with him. These Jeffreys turned over to the king. In the early hours of the 11th, before James slipped out of London he burnt the writs; as he fled, he threw into the Thames the great seal Jeffreys had worked so hard to gain. When Jeffreys learned later that morning that the king had gone, he decided immediately to leave as well. Avoiding his house, he made his way to the docks at Wapping and boarded a collier bound for Hamburg, shaved his eyebrows, and put on the clothes of a sailor. Hearing that the ship might be searched, he went ashore on the following day. By that afternoon constables knew he was at the sign of the Red Cow. Only the arrival of the militia ensured Jeffreys's protection from the mob's anger once his identity had been confirmed. He was taken first to the lord mayor at the Grocers' Hall and finally to the Tower. On the following day the lords of the new council signed a warrant committing him for treason. Jeffreys was interrogated in the days ahead about the whereabouts of the parliamentary writs and the great seal, though he could honestly answer that he had no idea where they might be.

Jeffreys's health declined steadily throughout his winter in the Tower. He lingered until mid-April, when he sent for his wife and son and received the sacrament and spiritual counsel from the bishop of Gloucester. On 15 April he made his will. Much of the work of settling his property having been done in October, his will is more memorable for the penitence and pleas for forgiveness it contains, all of which he sought through the rites of the Church of England, 'the best Church in the world'. He died on 18 or 19 April 1689, surviving sources providing conflicting dates of his death in the Tower; he was a month short of his forty-fourth birthday. Though a warrant was issued for the release of his body to his family, it was instead laid in the Tower chapel of St Peter, reportedly next to the duke of Monmouth. Not until 2 November 1693 were his remains removed to St Mary Aldermanbury, London, and placed by those of his first wife, as he had requested. Of the eight children Jeffreys had with his second wife, only

three girls survived. Two girls and a boy, John, survived from his first marriage, four other boys having predeceased Jeffreys. Jeffreys's titles and properties descended to **John Jeffreys**, second Baron Jeffreys (*bap.* 1673, *d.* 1702). He was baptized at St Mary Aldermanbury on 16 July 1673, educated at Westminster School, 'and is said to have exceeded even his father in his powers of drinking' (*DNB*). John took his seat in the House of Lords on 12 November 1694 and was reportedly one of those responsible for ensuring that John Dryden received a public rather than a private funeral. John Jeffreys died on 9 May 1702, when the barony became extinct. From his marriage in 1688 to Lady Charlotte Herbert (*d.* 1733), his only surviving child was Henrietta Louisa, who married Thomas Fermor, first earl of Pomfret [*see* Fermor, Henrietta Louisa (1698–1761)].

Reputation The fury unleashed on the first Baron Jeffreys after his death was even worse than any he felt during his life. His effigy was gibbeted and burnt by a London mob later in 1689. Though dead, he was excepted from a general act of pardon the following year. Some in parliament tried as well to pass a bill of attainder by which his titles and estates would be lost, though this failed. Most important, pamphlets of all kinds poured scorn upon him. In particular John Tutchin's mythologizing account, *The Western Martyrology, or, The Bloody Assizes* (1689), permanently attached 'bloody' to the western assizes of 1685 and thus to Jeffreys's own name. This all but obliterated the memory of any finer qualities the judge may actually have possessed.

Such qualities did exist. If sometimes given to spectacular bouts of drink and gluttony, Jeffreys was little different from many of his detractors. He was a witty and convivial companion and a loyal friend. Though he held intense ideological and partisan attachments, men like Sir Robert Clayton and Henry Pollexfen remained his friends to the last; contemporary diaries show him interacting regularly, even casually, in London, Chester, and elsewhere with those of decidedly different views. Surviving financial records suggest that he collected a handsome library; his opinions show that he read what was on the shelves. While rightly famous for badgering witnesses, especially in the more spectacular political crimes that came before him, Jeffreys simply performed with greater zeal than others the judicial function as it was understood in his age, that of judge as chief examiner as well as arbiter of the law.

But Jeffreys is better known for his caricature than for his character. Tutchin's sensational pamphlet formed the foundation of other writings that rushed from the press in the years following; these in turn coloured most portraits of Jeffreys through the eighteenth and nineteenth centuries. For all Macaulay's rhetorical power, the flawed human being that was Jeffreys is nowhere recognizable in his *History*. Not until the late nineteenth century, with the publication of H. B. Irving's *Judge Jeffreys* (1898), was it possible to take Jeffreys seriously again as a person or as a lawyer. More careful accounts followed in the twentieth century, namely those of G. W. Keeton, *Lord Chancellor Jeffreys and the Stuart Cause* (1965), and Montgomery Hyde, *Judge Jeffreys*

(2nd edn, 1948). But no amount of thoughtful revision can change the fact that Jeffreys could be a nightmare to behold when moved by ideological passion and righteous anger during political trials.

Two qualities in Jeffreys stood out: his professional ability and his loyalty and strength of conviction. This was a volatile mix at a time when political survival required the kind of pliability that made it possible for Jeffreys's rival, William Williams, to move from whig leadership to the inner circle of James II's government and back again. None the less, Jeffreys possessed a wealth of those things all litigants want in an advocate: enormous erudition and verbal ability joined to tenacity. F. E. Smith, Lord Birkenhead, writing in the 1920s, noted 'There must, on the whole, have been something quite exceptional about his ability or he would neither have risen so fast nor have been hated so heartily' (Smith, 70). Admirers and detractors agreed that Jeffreys was one of the forensic masters in an age filled with brilliant courtroom performers. But the same qualities that made him magnificent at the bar were problematic on the bench. He allowed his tongue free rein in a way which, even by prevailing standards, was excessive, especially against defendants before him on allegations of sedition and treason. Never a profound jurist, Jeffreys was none the less a learned justice who managed his court effectively. Virtually no complaints survive of his conduct as a judge in civil proceedings.

It was loyalty that destroyed Jeffreys. His commitment to serve his king kept him at his post even longer than the king stayed at his. Like all tories, Jeffreys was loyal to the Church of England too and believed in its social and political primacy: a fact poignantly acknowledged by his will. Unlike most tories, Jeffreys placed his loyalty to the crown above his loyalty to the church when James II's policies forced him to choose. Reviled by whigs, and by 1688 rejected by tories, Jeffreys could only hope to die peacefully once he was deserted by his king. This he managed to do; his reputation fared less well.   PAUL D. HALLIDAY

Sources M. H. Hyde, *Judge Jeffreys*, 2nd edn (1948) · G. W. Keeton, *Lord Chancellor Jeffreys and the Stuart cause* (1965) · Foss, *Judges* · F. E. Smith, earl of Birkenhead, *Fourteen English judges* (1926), 70–98 · J. B. Williamson, *The history of the Temple, London* (1924), 589–601 · *CSP dom., 1683–91* · *Third report*, HMC, 2 (1872) · *Fourth report*, HMC, 3 (1874) · *Fifth report*, HMC, 4 (1876) · *Seventh report*, HMC, 6 (1879) · *Ninth report*, 3 vols., HMC, 8 (1883–4), vols. 1–2 · *Calendar of the manuscripts of the marquess of Ormonde*, new ser., 8 vols., HMC, 36 (1902–20), vols. 5–6 · *The manuscripts of S. H. Le Fleming*, HMC, 25 (1890) · N. Luttrell, *A brief historical relation of state affairs from September 1678 to April 1714*, 6 vols. (1857) · *Burnet's History of my own time*, ed. O. Airy, new edn, 2 vols. (1897–1900) · J. Scott, *Algernon Sidney and the Restoration crisis, 1677–1683* (1991) · M. Knights, *Politics and opinion in crisis, 1678–81* (1994) · D. Lemmings, *Gentlemen and barristers: the inns of court and the English bar, 1680–1730* (1990) · *The life and times of Anthony Wood*, ed. A. Clark, 2, OHS, 21 (1892); 3, OHS, 26 (1894) · J. G. Muddiman, ed., *The bloody assizes* (1929) · E. M. Thompson, ed., *Correspondence of the family of Hatton*, 2 vols., CS, new ser., 22–3 (1878) · Evelyn, *Diary* · *An exact account of the trials … Old Bailey … Decemb. 11. 1678* (1678) · Sainty, *Judges* · R. North, *The lives of … Francis North … Dudley North … and … John North*, ed. A. Jessopp, 3 vols. (1890) · Sainty, *King's counsel* · will, PRO, PROB 11/400, fols. 309–11 · *State trials* · *DNB*

Archives Bucks. RLSS, papers · GL, corresp. and papers · NL Wales, letters and papers | BL, letters to Lord Hatton, Add. MSS 29551–29559

Likenesses J. M. Wright, oils, 1675, NPG [*see illus.*] · attrib. W. W. Claret, oils, *c.*1678–1680, NPG · G. Kneller, oils, *c.*1685, Harvard U., law school · G. Kneller, oils, 1686, Erddig, Wrexham · A. Wivell, mezzotint, pubd 1819 (after G. Kneller), BM, NPG · R. White, two line engravings (after G. Kneller), BM · portrait, Durham Castle

Wealth at death see will, PRO, PROB 11/400, fols. 309–11

Jeffreys, George (1678–1755), poet and translator, was born probably at Little Weldon, Northamptonshire, the son of Christopher *Jeffreys (*c.*1642–1693) [*see under* Jeffreys, George] and Anna Brydges, sister of James Brydges, eighth Baron Chandos. He was thus the grandson of his namesake George *Jeffreys (*c.*1610–1685), organist and composer. Jeffreys was educated at Westminster School and at Trinity College, Cambridge, where he was admitted as a pensioner on 12 November 1694. On 23 April 1697 he became a scholar there, and became first a minor then a major fellow of the college. During his time there he also served as *lector linguae Latinae* (1704), as sub-orator, and as senior taxor of the university (1707). In 1709 he vacated his fellowship, declining to take orders in the English church. He came to London and was called to the bar, although he seems never to have practised. He was secretary to Dr Hartstonge, bishop of Derry, between 1714 and 1717, and held a post in the custom house at London.

Jeffreys' earliest known works are orations delivered at Cambridge in 1702 and 1704, but he also wrote two tragedies for the professional stage. *Edwin*, a tragedy acted at Lincoln's Inn Fields, was published in 1724, having allegedly earned its author over £1000. *Merope*, another tragedy by Jeffreys, was not such a success on the stage, where the audience were dismissed on the second night without a performance: however, it too was printed, in 1731, the year it was performed. There is a strong resemblance between Jeffreys' play and Voltaire's tragedy *Merope*, written in December 1737, although the situation is complicated since both are in turn adaptations of Scipione Maffei's verse drama *La Merope* (1713). Voltaire certainly knew Jeffreys' adaptation, since he criticizes it in his preface. For his part Jeffreys saw these criticisms as Voltaire's attempt to disguise his reliance on his version, adding that Voltaire 'dignifies his own whims by the name of *French delicacy*' (G. Jeffreys, *Miscellanies*, 1754, ix).

In 1736 Jeffreys published two poems, *Father Francis and Sister Constance*, a versified version of a story printed in *The Spectator*, and *Chess*, a translation from Vida which had benefited from the comments of Alexander Pope. Both of these reappeared, along with the plays, and an oratorio entitled *The Triumph of Truth*, in *Miscellanies in Verse and Prose* (1754), which represents in effect his collected works. The collection also includes poems that he had published in the *Gentleman's Magazine* for 1752 and 1753, as well as others which indicate the breadth of his literary activities: extempore epigrams, translations from Latin and French, and an epilogue to Thomas Southerne's *Money the Mistress*. The collection also includes verses 'To Mr Addison, on his Tragedy of Cato', which had appeared anonymously before the play when it was printed. The oratorio, and indeed the collection as a whole, is dedicated to the marquess of Carnarvon. The collection includes lavish commendatory verses by John Duncombe (1729–1786), who seems to have been a close friend: Jeffreys contributed versions of several of Horace's odes to Duncombe's translation of Horace, and was the dedicatee of at least one of Duncombe's translated versions. In addition, letters to and from Jeffreys, and an essay by him on the use of monosyllables in versification, appear in Duncombe's *Collection of Letters* (1773).

According to his obituarist, Jeffreys passed most of his life at leisure in the houses of his relations, the dukes of Chandos. He died on 17 August 1755.

MATTHEW STEGGLE

Sources *GM*, 1st ser., 25 (1755), 381 · *DNB* · *The complete works of Voltaire*, ed. W. H. Barber and U. Kölving, 17 (1991)

Jeffreys, Sir Harold (1891–1989), geophysicist, was born on 22 April 1891 in Fatfield, co. Durham, the only child of Robert Hall Jeffreys, headmaster of the village school at Fatfield, and his wife, Elizabeth Mary, schoolteacher, daughter of William Sharpe. His parents both came from families living near Morpeth, Northumberland. Jeffreys was educated at Rutherford College and Armstrong College (both in Newcastle upon Tyne) and at St John's College, Cambridge, of which he was a scholar. He obtained a first class in part one (1911) and was a wrangler in part two (1913) of the mathematical tripos. He was awarded the Smith's prize in 1915. Inspired by the work of Sir George Darwin on tides he began research in celestial mechanics. He was elected a fellow of St John's in 1914, retaining his fellowship until his death. He obtained a Durham DSc in 1917.

During the First World War Jeffreys worked in the Cavendish Laboratory, Cambridge, on wartime problems, from 1915 to 1917. He then went to the Meteorological Office from 1917 to 1922, returning to Cambridge as lecturer in mathematics in 1922. He won the Adams prize in 1927. He became reader in geophysics in 1931 and was elected Plumian professor of astronomy and experimental philosophy in 1946, retiring in 1958. On 6 September 1940 he married Bertha Swirles, mathematician. There were no children of the marriage.

Jeffreys worked in five branches of mathematics: hydrodynamics, celestial mechanics, seismology and the physics of the interior of the earth, probability, and pure mathematics. His wartime work led him to study fluid dynamics. He demonstrated the importance of eddy viscosity, identified by G. I. Taylor, in geophysical fluid motions, classified winds by their dynamical origins, and established the essential role of cyclones in the general circulation of the atmosphere. He was the first to identify the importance of viscosity in boundary conditions. He studied the mechanism for the generation of surface waves on water and developed the work of J. W. Strutt (third Baron Rayleigh) on the initiation of convection.

Jeffreys had early realized the importance of seismology, which occupied him from 1921 to the end of his life, for investigating the interior of the earth, for which he established three major structural features. In 1921, with Dorothy Wrinch, he showed from records of an explosion in the Rhineland that the crust of the earth had at least two layers above the mantle; the study also demonstrated the value of explosions as seismic sources. In 1927 Jeffreys showed that the earth must have a dense core which must be effectively liquid, and this was amply confirmed subsequently. His third major discovery was the division between the upper and lower mantle of the earth, which he attributed to a change of crystal structure of olivine to a denser form at high pressure. He spent many years on calculations of travel times of seismic waves over the earth, and produced the Jeffreys-Bullen tables, first published in 1940, and still used in routine identification of earthquake epicentres and as reference times for both comparison with observations and calculations of models of the interior of the earth. Jeffreys also made many contributions to the theory of elastic waves.

Working mostly by himself and with few research students, Jeffreys wrote extensively on the dynamics of the earth and the solar system. In the years before artificial satellites were launched he analysed observations of gravity on the surface of the earth, another very laborious numerical project, and derived a consistent set of dynamical parameters of the earth and the moon. He studied the variations in the rotation of the earth and showed that the slowing down of the earth's rotation, found astronomically, was probably due to eddy viscosity in shallow seas, another result that later seemed fully confirmed. Those studies, and his theoretical work on the effect of the liquid core on the earth's rotation, dominated the subject.

Jeffreys's book *The Earth* (1924) was the first systematic account of the physical state of the earth as a whole and had a profound influence on generations of geophysicists through its many successive editions. Jeffreys was not uncontroversial, and indeed he was involved in a number of major debates which seem to have called forth his tersest writing. In particular he always opposed the ideas of continental drift and plate tectonics, although it was he who first pointed out that the earth's crust was just the upper layer of a rigid lithosphere about 100 km thick, and he was a keen advocate (1936) of systematic studies of the floor of the oceans. Although his most significant work in geophysics was completed before the technical revolutions of artificial satellites, marine geophysics, and new methods of seismology changed the face of geophysics in the middle of the twentieth century, his major results were the foundation of subsequent developments. He showed, above all, how rigorous methods of classical mechanics should be applied to the study of the structure of the earth and the planets.

He had an early interest in scientific inference and, later, prompted by statistical problems arising from his work on seismic travel times, he constructed a comprehensive corpus of methods for estimation and tests of significance according to Bayesian principles. His *Theory of Probability* (1939), which presented a formal algebra of probability on an axiomatic basis, with many applications in various branches of physics, became very influential.

Much of his original work in pure mathematics was incorporated in *Methods of Mathematical Physics* (1946, with his wife). His most important contributions were to the study of operational methods for the solution of differential equations and to asymptotic methods.

Jeffreys was elected a fellow of the Royal Society in 1925 and was president of the Royal Astronomical Society in 1955–7. He was a foreign member of a number of academies, among them the US Academy of Science, the Accademia Nazionale dei Lincei (Rome), and the royal academies of Sweden and Belgium. He was awarded, besides other prizes, the gold medal of the Royal Astronomical Society (1937), a royal medal (1948) and the Copley medal (1960) of the Royal Society, the Vetlesen prize of Columbia University (1962), the Guy medal of the Royal Statistical Society (1963), and the Wollaston medal of the Geological Society (1964). He received five honorary degrees and was knighted in 1953.

Jeffreys had wide interests within and beyond science. Besides some prophetic papers on physics and stellar structure, he wrote on the ecology of co. Durham and the Breckland and on psychology. He was a skilled photographer; a large collection of his negatives was given to St John's College. He was for many years active in national and international astronomical and geophysical societies. Undoubtedly one of the distinctive personalities of Cambridge in his time, he was difficult to talk to and was known for his intensive smoking and for his bicycling everywhere. Yet he was very sociable, dined regularly in his college, sang tenor for many years in the Cambridge Philharmonic choir, and greatly enjoyed the dinners of the Royal Astronomical Society Club. He was somewhat over medium height and spare of frame. He wore glasses, had a small moustache, and was usually dressed informally, often wearing shorts in hot weather. Jeffreys died in Cambridge on 18 March 1989.

Jeffreys's wife, **Bertha Jeffreys**, Lady Jeffreys (1903–1999), mathematician, was born on 22 May 1903 at 22 St Michael's Mount, Northampton, the daughter of William Alexander Swirles, a commercial traveller in leather, and his wife, Harriet, *née* Blaxley, later a primary school teacher. She was a cousin of Michael Stewart, Baron Stewart of Fulham. She was educated at Northampton School for Girls and, from 1921, read mathematics at Girton College, Cambridge, where she graduated with first-class honours. Her postgraduate research on quantum theory, partly under R. H. Fowler, and partly at Göttingen under Max Born and Werner Heisenberg, gained her a PhD in 1929. A series of teaching posts at Manchester, Bristol, London, and again Manchester preceded her return in 1938 to Girton, where she was fellow and lecturer in mathematics, and from 1949 director of studies in mathematics. After her marriage to Jeffreys in 1940 she continued to publish on quantum theory, but expanded her interests to include seismology. She took an active role in the life of Girton, where she was vice-mistress from 1966 to 1969, and, although never one to suffer fools gladly, always offered a warm welcome at her house to her and her husband's pupils and former students—friendships repaid

when about 140 people attended her ninetieth birthday party. Music was an important element in her life (she was a talented pianist and cellist), as was women's education generally. She died at 160 Huntingdon Road, Cambridge, on 18 December 1999, following a stroke.

ALAN COOK, *rev.*

Sources A. Cook, *Memoirs FRS*, 36 (1990), 303–33 · H. Jeffreys and B. Swirles, eds., *Collected papers of Sir Harold Jeffreys on geophysics and other sciences*, 6 vols. (1973–7) · M. A. K. and D. H. G., 'Sir Harold Jeffreys', *Annual Report* [Geological Society of London] (1989), 34–5 · J. A. Hudson, *Astronomy and Geophysics*, 41 (2000), 3.36–3.37 · *The Independent* (22 Dec 1999) · m. cert. · b. cert. [Bertha Swirles] · d. cert. [Bertha Jeffreys]
Archives St John Cam., papers | CAC Cam., corresp. with Sir Edward Bullard
Likenesses photograph, repro. in *Memoirs FRS* · portrait, St John Cam.
Wealth at death £635,235: probate, 2 Aug 1989, *CGPLA Eng. & Wales*

Jeffreys, Sir Jeffrey (*c*.1652–1709), politician and merchant, was the third son of Walter (or Watkin) Jeffreys of Llywel, Brecknockshire. He is reported to have been 'educated and adopted' by his rich bachelor uncle, Alderman John *Jeffreys of London. When, in the late 1670s, Jeffrey married Sarah (*d.* 1725), daughter of Nicholas Dawes, goldsmith and citizen of London, his alderman uncle provided a significant share of the property or commitments covered by the marriage contract. Jeffreys studied law at the Inner Temple and was called to the bar in 1676. However, upon the death in 1680 of his uncle's partner, Thomas Colclough, he left the law and became a half-share partner in his uncle's merchant house, the largest importer of tobacco and the most important North American merchant company in the kingdom.

When John Jeffreys died in 1688, he left his remaining half of the business to Jeffrey's younger brother John, later an MP, but much of his metropolitan real estate to Jeffrey. With the start of the War of the League of Augsburg in 1689, the two partner brothers decided that in such hazardous times the likely rewards of the Chesapeake trade were not sufficiently attractive, and fairly rapidly withdrew their name from that commerce. Jeffrey Jeffreys, however, retained correspondents in the Chesapeake and was for a number of years in the early 1690s the London agent for Virginia; it is therefore possible that his firm retained some interest in the Chesapeake trade carried on by other firms. He was admitted to the Eastland Company in 1690 and thus was able in the 1690s to export tobacco to Riga and elsewhere in the Baltic, as well as to Spain. He tentatively returned to the tobacco-import trade with the peace of 1697, but detailed import data after that date have not survived. Although they withdrew from the Chesapeake, the brothers continued and expanded their late uncle's trade in the West Indies, including Barbados, Jamaica, and the Leeward Islands (for which Jeffrey Jeffreys was London agent, 1690–97). Their firm also had contracts for victualling the navy in Jamaica and remitting funds to the garrison in New York. The brothers further supported their Caribbean trade by continuing their uncle's active interest in the slave-trading Royal African

Company, and both served as 'assistants' (directors) in the company—Jeffrey in 1684–6 and 1692–8, John in 1690–91 and 1693. During the war, letters of marque were issued for ten vessels in which Jeffreys was interested, the largest being the *Hannibal*, 450 tons, 100 men, 36 guns, which was leased to the Royal African Company in 1693. The other nine had crews too small for privateers and were probably also used in the slave trade or in Jeffreys's West Indian contract work. During the period 1702–9 Jeffreys, as a licensed 'separate trader', sent three private ventures to the west African coast. He was also a shareholder in the East India Company (c.1690–91) but was not conspicuously involved in the struggle between the old and new companies in the ensuing decade.

Unlike his uncle, Jeffreys was interested in a more prominent public activity than the merely philanthropic service he gave as a commissioner for the Greenwich Hospital in 1695 or even the lieutenancy commission to which he and his brother John were named in 1689. From the heiress of the (unrelated) Colonel John Jeffreys of Brecon, he purchased The Priory there. This significant acquisition facilitated his return to parliament as a tory for the borough of Brecon in every parliament between 1690 and his death in 1709, except for that of 1698–1701, when his petition against a hostile return was rejected by the House of Commons. In parliament Jeffreys was particularly active on colonial and commercial questions. He continued his family's tory loyalties, an affiliation consistent with his association with the Royal African Company and the old East India Company. Nevertheless, as a merchant he found it prudent to mute his partisanship. After his death, both his son Nicholas and his daughter Sarah married into the whig Eyles family.

Jeffreys's political activity did not at first extend to the City of London, but in 1699, by which time he was thought to be worth £300,000, he was elected sheriff. He surprised the City then by agreeing to serve, instead of fining to be excused as his uncle had done when elected alderman in 1660. In 1699 he was also knighted as sheriff and elected master of the Grocers' Company (1699–1701). This sudden spurt of activity was followed by his election as a common councillor for Aldgate ward (1700–01) and alderman for Portsoken ward in 1701. The lieutenancy commissioners named him colonel of the Yellow regiment of the trained bands in 1707, but forced him out the next year when they refused to accept the lesser officers he had nominated. He stood unsuccessfully for the mayoralty in 1703 but, it was thought at the time, would have been elected in 1709 had he not then been on his deathbed.

Jeffreys inherited from his uncle a large town house on unusually extensive grounds in St Mary Axe. (After his death, his heirs cleared the property for the construction of Jeffreys Square.) For his greater comfort, he purchased Roehampton House, Surrey, from the estate of the countess of Devonshire. Here he resided until his death, which occurred at Marlborough on 25 October 1709, while he was returning home from a visit to Bath. He left extensive real estate, including several thousand acres acquired in Brecknockshire and the inherited prebendary lease (from

St Paul's Cathedral) of the manor of Kentish Town outside London, including a demesne of 210 acres. Sir Jeffrey and his wife, who died in 1725, raised two sons and six daughters. On the death without male issue of both sons, Edward (1680–1740) and Nicholas (1683–1747), Jeffreys's real estate passed to Nicholas's daughter and heir, Elizabeth, who in 1749 was to marry the rising lawyer, Charles Pratt, later lord chancellor and first Earl Camden. On the Kentish Town demesne lands their son, the first Marquess Camden, developed the neighbourhood known as Camden Town, where Jeffreys Street and Brecknock Road recall the former owner. JACOB M. PRICE

Sources *Le Neve's Pedigrees of the knights*, ed. G. W. Marshall, Harleian Society, 8 (1873) • T. Jones, *A history of the county of Brecknock*, rev. edn, rev. J. R. Bailey, first Baron Glanusk, 4 vols. (1909–30) • J. M. Price, *Perry of London: a family and a firm on the seaborne frontier, 1615–1753* (1992) • K. G. Davies, *The Royal African Company* (1957) • letters of marque declarations, PRO, HCA/26/1–3 • N. Luttrell, *A brief historical relation of state affairs from September 1678 to April 1714*, 6 vols. (1857) • J. R. Woodhead, *The rulers of London, 1660–1689* (1965) • L. M. Penson, *The colonial agents of the British West Indies* (1924) • R. W. K. Hinton, *The Eastland trade and the common weal in the seventeenth century* (1959) • D. Lysons, *The environs of London*, 4 vols. (1792–6) • F. A. Inderwick and R. A. Roberts, eds., *A calendar of the Inner Temple records*, 5 vols. (1896–1936) • *The names of the Lords and other commissioners for Greenwich Hospital* (1695) • *CSP dom.*, 1689–90; 1700–02 • Jeffreys v. Vassall, PRO, C.7/191/80 • will, PRO, PROB 11/511, sig. 247
Wealth at death wealthy; reportedly £300,00 in 1699

Jeffreys, John (c.1614–1688), merchant, was the third of six sons of Edward Jeffreys (d. 1642) of Llywel, Brecknockshire, a minor country gentleman of an ancient if decayed family. (The merchant is often confused with the unrelated Colonel John Jeffreys (1623–1689), of The Priory, Brecon, MP, brother of Herbert Jeffreys, lieutenant-governor of Virginia.) As a younger son in a family of limited resources, he was in 1632 placed apprentice with a merchant member of the London Grocers' Company. From the beginning of his independent activity, he devoted his attention primarily to the Virginia tobacco trade, then just beginning to be of commercial importance. In the 1630s and 1640s the London customs records show him importing modest amounts of tobacco from Virginia. His emergence as a leader in the trade came in the dynamic 1650s following the adoption of the Navigation Act and the reconquest of royalist Virginia by a parliamentary fleet. (Though a royalist by sentiment, he was not above contracting to carry Cromwell's Irish prisoners to Virginia.) From at least the 1650s, he conducted his business in partnership with Thomas Colclough (1619–1680) from a Staffordshire gentry family. By 1660–61 Jeffreys was sufficiently prominent to be named (as a representative of the Chesapeake trade) a member of a panel of merchants advising the lords of a committee of council on foreign trade. His tobacco-import business was great enough for him to lose a reported £20,000 in leaf in the great fire of 1666. Thereafter, until his death in 1688, his firm was indisputably the leading importer of tobacco in London and in the country. As tobacco was the major commodity returned from North America, this made it the leading English merchant house trading to the continental colonies.

Jeffreys also developed other trades of significant volume, if less important to him than tobacco. The London port book for 1686 shows him importing wine and raisins from Spain and Madeira, as well as iron and hemp from the Baltic (probably in return for tobacco) and linen from Hamburg. The last was probably intended for re-export to North America or the West Indies, whence he had also developed a significant import trade in sugar and logwood.

As early as the 1650s, Jeffreys and Colclough maintained a 'principal factor' in Virginia, who supervised the selling and buying of lesser factors acting on commission. This basic trade was supplemented by a commission (or consignment) trade with local merchants, merchant planters, and a few greater planters in the tobacco colonies. The company was the London correspondent of governor Lord Howard of Effingham and of leading planter or merchant planter families such as the Chicheleys, Lees, Ludwells, and Wormeleys. Jeffreys was also active in the tobacco re-export trades. In the 1670s and 1680s, he and Alderman Jacob Lucie of London, an Eastland merchant, had contracts to supply tobacco to the monopolist Royal Tobacco Company of Sweden. These contracts involved them in frequent recourse to English ministers for help in obtaining payment from the monopoly company and from Andre Onkell, their factor in Stockholm. They were helped in getting such assistance not only by the fact that both were good tories, but also in part because Jeffreys was very close to his fellow Welshman, the secretary of state, Sir Leoline Jenkins, who admitted, 'I have subsisted 4 or 5 years in my Employment abroad by the Credit he [Jeffreys] gave me.' (CSP dom., 1680–81, 52). Also relevant for Jeffreys's American trades was his election in the 1670s as 'assistant' (director) of the slave-trading Royal African Company. In the 1680s his collaborator Lucie was both an assistant and deputy governor of this company, while Jeffreys's nephews were to continue this participation in the 1690s. Since the Royal African Company was reluctant to ship slaves to Virginia on its own account, the Jeffreys and their associates contracted in the 1670s and 1680s to buy from the company whole shiploads of slaves delivered by it in Virginia.

Jeffreys's status in the London trading world was acknowledged by his election as master of the Grocers' Company in 1661. The year before, he had been elected alderman for Bread Street ward but paid £820 to be permitted to resign immediately. His family associations were all ultra-royalist and later tory but he may have judged a non-political stance commercially necessary. Tobacco was a highly taxed commodity and all who dealt in it had to be on civil terms with those in authority. Jeffreys on occasion spoke for the whole trade as well as for his private concerns. In 1685, for example, he led a delegation of the London Chesapeake trade testifying before the House of Commons (in committee of the whole) against the proposed new tobacco impost. Even so, in his old age Jeffreys accepted inclusion in the London lieutenancy commission of 1685. His closest competitor in his last

years, Micaiah Perry, also avoided public office except for the lieutenancy.

When Thomas Colclough died in 1680, Jeffreys replaced him as partner with his own nephew Jeffrey *Jeffreys, son of his brother Walter (or Watkin) of Llywel. Like most successful merchants of his day, Alderman John Jeffreys accumulated considerable real estate both in his native county and in England, particularly in Gloucestershire and in and around London—including the manor of Kentish Town. He was unmarried and following his death at Llywel on 5 November 1688 (the day William III landed in England), his will transferred most of his real estate in Brecknockshire to Lewis, son of his brother Thomas, and to Edward and Evan, the elder two sons of his brother Walter. The other half of his London firm was left to John, Walter's youngest son. His real estate in England went to his nephews Jeffrey and John, who were continuing his London business. A sister and other relatives were also remembered but the most interesting bequests were £2000 to Lord Chancellor Jeffreys (who was no relation), and another £2000 to his lordship's eldest son, John, the alderman's godson. Thus John Jeffreys's will suggests much about both his wealth and his adherence to his family's tory loyalties.

JACOB M. PRICE

Sources T. Jones, A history of the county of Brecknock, rev. edn, rev. J. R. Bailey, first Baron Glanusk, 4 vols. (1909–30) · J. M. Price, The tobacco adventure to Russia: enterprise, politics, and diplomacy in the quest for a northern market for English colonial tobacco, 1676–1722 (1961) · J. M. Price, Perry of London: a family and a firm on the seaborne frontier, 1615–1753 (1992) · Le Neve's Pedigrees of the knights, ed. G. W. Marshall, Harleian Society, 8 (1873) · B. Fleet and L. O. Duvall, eds., Virginia colonial abstracts, 34 vols. (1937–49); repr. in 3 vols. (1988) · L. O. Duvall, ed., Virginia colonial abstracts, 2nd ser. (1951) · CSP dom., 1680–81, 52; 1685 · will, PRO, PROB 11/393; sentence, PROB 11/401, sig. 168 · K. G. Davies, The Royal African Company (1957) · CSP col., –1689 · G. J. Armytage and W. H. Rylands, eds., Staffordshire pedigrees, Harleian Society, 63 (1912) · J. R. Woodhead, The rulers of London, 1660–1689 (1965) [satisfactory for Thomas Colclough, inaccurate on John Jeffries] · London port book, PRO, E.190/78/1 · London port book, PRO, E.190/143/1 [see also E.190/38/5, 43/5, 50/1–2, 56/1, 68/1]

Jeffreys, John, second Baron Jeffreys (bap. 1673, d. 1702). See under Jeffreys, George, first Baron Jeffreys (1645–1689).

Jeffreys, John Gwyn (1809–1885), lawyer and conchologist, was born at Swansea on 18 January 1809, the eldest of four children of John Jeffreys (d. 1815), solicitor, and Martha Tringham. He was educated at Swansea grammar school, from whose master, Evan Griffiths, he received his first lessons in shell collecting. At seventeen he was articled to a local solicitor. After many successful years in his profession at Swansea, he was called to the bar of Lincoln's Inn in 1856, when he moved to London to practise in the court of chancery and before parliamentary committees. On 21 April 1840 he married Ann Nevill (d. 1881) of Llangennech Park, Carmarthenshire; they had six children.

Jeffreys retired from practice in 1866, and purchased Ware Priory in Hertfordshire, a fine old house, which became a meeting-place for many British and foreign naturalists. He was JP for the counties of Glamorgan, Brecon, and Hertfordshire, deputy lieutenant for Hertfordshire and high sheriff of the same county in 1877. He was elected a fellow of the Linnean Society in 1829, and a fellow of the Royal Society in 1840. The University of St Andrews awarded him the honorary degree of LLD in 1840. He did much work in the British Association, of which he was local treasurer at the Swansea meeting of 1848, vice-president in 1880, and president of the biological section in 1877. For many years he acted as treasurer of the Linnean and Geological societies, and of the Royal Society Club. After the death of his wife in 1881 he moved to Kensington, where he remained until his death.

Jeffreys is best known for his work on British and Mediterranean Mollusca, on which he wrote more than one hundred papers; the first, 'A synopsis of the pneumonobranchous Mollusca of Great Britain', appeared in the *Transactions of the Linnean Society of London* for 1828. Of his many publications, his chief work was *British Conchology* (5 vols., 1862–9).

Jeffreys was led to undertake deep-sea dredging by his belief, fostered by the work of Edward Forbes, that the molluscs of the present day were the direct descendants of those which lived in British seas during the late Tertiary and early Pleistocene periods, and that relics of those times would be found in deep, cold water. While engaged in his profession his time for collecting specimens was very limited; but he paid a visit to Shetland for this purpose in 1841 and again in 1848. At first he joined George Barlee, one of the old school of conchologists, sharing the expenses and the specimens obtained, while Barlee did the collecting. He made a lengthy collecting trip to the Mediterranean coast between Nice and Genoa in 1855, finding species that apparently linked the British and Mediterranean faunas. Near and after retirement he devoted himself more fully to scientific work, and, in company with Edward Waller, the Revd A. M. Norman, and other naturalists, spent six summers between 1861 and 1868 dredging in deep water around and north of Shetland, mainly using the yacht *Osprey*. The results showed that Scandinavian relics of the glaciations mixed with a few species of the warmer Tertiary at Shetland, indicating the climatic changes that had occurred, and that the British fauna had a long and continuous history that could be elucidated by dredging.

In 1869 Jeffreys joined the Royal Navy surveying ship *Porcupine*, assigned to deep-sea explorations organized by W. B. Carpenter and Charles Wyville Thomson. With Jeffreys in charge of the first cruise, she dredged to 1476 fathoms off the west coast of Ireland, the deepest dredging to that date. Always in search of rare or new species of Mollusca that would throw light on the history of the European fauna, in 1870 Jeffreys went in *Porcupine* to dredge the deep sea in the Bay of Biscay and off the Portuguese coast. In 1871 he visited the United States, and in 1875 did more dredging on board the Royal Navy ship *Valorous* in Baffin Bay during the British Arctic expedition under G. S. Nares. In 1878 and 1879, with the invertebrate zoologist A. M. Norman, he dredged off the Norwegian coast, and in 1880 the two naturalists, on the invitation of the French government, took part in an expedition on board *Le Travailleur* for deep-sea dredging in the Bay of Biscay.

Jeffreys' magnificent collection of European Mollusca, which abounded in type specimens, was purchased two years before his death for the Smithsonian Institution, rather than the British Museum, and taken to the United States. His work as a highly talented amateur zoologist and collector bridged the eras of Edward Forbes and of HMS *Challenger* in the 1870s, when British marine science expanded and began to professionalize. Jeffreys had the talents of a field naturalist and the organizing ability of a man of affairs. Although, even as an anti-Darwinian, Jeffreys contributed to the solution of biogeographic problems, his main interests were narrower, in the collection and description of rare molluscs. At this he was an acknowledged master. He died of apoplexy at his home at 1 The Terrace, Kensington, London, on 24 January 1885.

W. J. HARRISON, rev. ERIC L. MILLS

Sources letters, priv. coll. [Prof. David Gwyn Jeffreys, Bexhill-on-Sea, Sussex] · scientific correspondence of Joshua Alder and Alfred Merle Norman, 1826–1911, NHM, general and zoology library, 7 vols. · 'J. Gwyn Jeffreys, LLD', *Biography and Review* (Oct 1881), 373–8 · W. B. Carpenter, *PRS*, 38 (1884–5), xiv–xvii · E. L. Mills, 'Edward Forbes, John Gwyn Jeffreys, and British dredging before the *Challenger* expedition', *Journal of the Society of the Bibliography of Natural History*, 8 (1976–8), 507–36 · 'John Gwyn Jeffreys', *Nature*, 31 (1884–5), 317–18 · Boase, *Mod. Eng. biog.*, 2.72 · C. Matheson, 'John Gwyn Jeffreys: a famous Glamorgan naturalist', *Stewart Williams's Glamorgan historian*, ed. S. Williams, 8 [1972], 29–35 · A. Waren, *Marine Mollusca described by John Gwyn Jeffreys: with the location of the type material* (1980) · D. Heppell, 'Jeffreys, John Gwyn', *DSB*, 7.91–2

Archives priv. coll. · Smithsonian Institution, Washington, DC, corresp. and papers | Bath Royal Literary and Scientific Institution, letters to Leonard Blomefield · Bodl. Oxf., Radcliffe Science Library, annotated copy of *British conchology* · Elgin Museum, Elgin, letters to Gordon · NHM, letters to Joshua Alder and/or Alfred Merle Norman; letters to Otto Morch · U. Edin. L., letters to Sir Charles Lyell

Likenesses Maull & Fox, photograph, RS · photograph, priv. coll. · wood-engraving, NPG; repro. in *ILN* (7 Feb 1885), 147

Wealth at death £51,308: probate, 2 March 1885, *CGPLA Eng. & Wales*

Jeffreys, Julius (1800–1877), surgeon and inventor of the respirator, was born on 14 September 1800 at Hall Place, Bexley, Kent, the fourth son and tenth child of the sixteen born to Richard Jeffreys (1762–1830), rector of Throcking, Hertfordshire, from 1786 to 1830, and of Parndon, Essex, and his wife, Sarah, daughter of the Revd Jonathan Gilder and his wife, Elizabeth Sanders. Revd Jeffreys rented Hall Place from Sir Francis Dashwood in 1795 and ran a school there until 1802. From 1802 to 1810 Julius Jeffreys lived in India, where his father, a fine example of clerical pluralism and absenteeism, had taken the post of chaplain to the East India Company. He was educated mainly by his father, who was described by his eldest son as a profound mathematician and classicist. After studying medicine at Edinburgh and London, Jeffreys became a member of the Royal College of Surgeons, London, on 1 March 1822. He immediately applied to the East India Company for the post of assistant surgeon to the Bengal presidency. After landing in Calcutta he was first attached to the general hospital; a cholera epidemic was raging in the region and he was thrown in head first, with 200 in his care.

Jeffreys had already published two papers which revealed his interest in the application of physics to medicine (published in 1822 as *An Inquiry into the Comparative Forces of the Extensor and Flexor Muscles Connected with the Joints of the Human Body*); these were well received and Jeffreys now set himself to study the effects of the Indian climate on health. The British made no concessions to climatic differences. Regiments drilled during the hottest time of the day; anything less was considered effeminate, with the result that between a third and a half of the troops were in hospital with heatstroke at any one time, and there were many deaths. Jeffreys designed installations for the cooling of dwellings, using the evaporation of water and a quadratic pump of his own design, which he called 'the refrigerator', an early use of the word. He studied airflow through the solar topee and insisted that it should not be hermetically sealed to the head. He showed also, contrary to the current belief that rarefaction of the atmosphere made it dangerous to live at an altitude above 4000 feet, that the climate of the hill country was superior even to that of England. His report advocating convalescent centres at places such as Simla, where at that time there was only one house, was widely distributed; it was the first step towards the establishment of hill stations, and the annual move from the plains to the hills and back again.

Jeffreys served most of his time in Uttar Pradesh. On 1 July 1826 he married Ellen Penelope Dougan (1803–1835?), daughter of John Dougan and his wife, Clarissa, *née* Squire, and during the next six years they had three sons and twin daughters. Jeffreys transferred to the civil establishment in 1827, and interested himself in the development of local resources; he set up factories for the manufacture of pottery, brickware, and saltpetre, and used kilns of his own design. For these endeavours he was commended by the governor-general, Lord Bentinck. Jeffreys published a long article advocating that much of the wealth that was being drained from India should instead be reinvested for the development of agriculture and industry; entitled 'On the natural resources of India', it was published in *The Asiatic Journal and Monthly Register* in 1835 (vol. 17, 137–49 and 229–43; and vol. 18, 65–77). Jeffreys refused the superintendentship of the East India Company's main opium factory on moral and religious grounds, and, his health failing, he returned to England with his family in late 1835. There is a family tradition, but no documentary evidence, that his wife died in childbirth during the voyage.

After returning home Jeffreys found his eldest sister with advanced pulmonary disease, and he was struck as he went about by the prevalence of cough and the irritating effect of cold air. This led first to the design of the volute humidifier, subsequently used by John Snow as the basis for his ether and chloroform inhalers, and then to the invention of the device which he called 'the respirator'. This was a mask consisting of layers of fine wire lattices insulated from one another, which enabled the collection of warmth and moisture during exhalation, and

the transfer of both to the incoming breath; it was described by Jeffreys in *Observations upon the Construction and Design of the Respirator* (1836). The mask was so effective that Jane Carlyle, who suffered from a weak chest, described it as a most wonderful acquisition, which 'has the property of making all the air which goes down one's throat as warm as summer air' (Carlyle, 71–2). It was mentioned also by Ruskin, and, towards the end of the century, by George Gissing, in his novel *New Grub Street*.

To safeguard his design from inferior imitations, and to secure some return in order to support his family, Jeffreys patented his invention (no. 6988, 1836), and advertised it in *The Times* and the *Morning Post*. This brought him into conflict with the medical profession, ostensibly for ethical but also for financial reasons. Medical practitioners were losing income, because patients could buy a respirator over the counter and save the cost of regular visits to the surgery for a bottle of linctus. Jeffreys defended himself vigorously against these attacks, stating that he would rather live on the returns from intellectual property which was bringing great benefit to the public than on income gained from prescribing ineffective rubbish; and, he pointed out, even peers of the realm held patents.

In 1841 Jeffreys was elected a fellow of the Royal Society. During the early 1840s he campaigned against the increasing importation and use of opium, and against atmospheric pollution. For some months he filtered all the air entering his home in Bayswater, and showed that it was heavily contaminated with horse droppings. He advocated that houses, including the new House of Commons, should be ventilated from above downwards, bringing fresh air straight to the lungs rather than contaminating it first with dirt and dust from the floor. His views on a healthy environment were conveyed in a series of eleven papers, in which he conceptualized, apparently for the first time, the idea that the breathing passages are actually outside the body, and so can be subjected to a different atmosphere from that to which the skin is exposed; 'On artificial climates for the restoration and preservation of health' was published in the *London Medical Gazette* in 1841–2 (vol. 29, 814–22ff.). Jeffreys stressed the importance of heat lost by radiation, and he designed an economical stove which would both improve ventilation and replace this loss. He researched and published on the physiology of lung volumes, making at least two major contributions, and proposed a nomenclature which remained in use for a century, but for which John Hutchinson, inventor of the spirometer, who speedily adopted it, received all the credit (J. Jeffreys, *Views upon the Statics of the Human Chest*, 1843). This book also contains an early and very perceptive critique of Liebig's recently published metabolic theories.

Towards the end of the decade he became involved, through the Valpy family, in-laws of his sister Caroline, with the early settlers in New Zealand, and encouraged his son, John Julius Jeffrys, to emigrate. On 8 April 1851 Jeffreys married Jane Mary Graham (1819/20–1902), daughter of James Graham, a merchant of Glasgow, with whom he had five children. In the early 1850s he patented a much improved system for launching ships' lifeboats, which it is claimed saved a number of lives. During the Crimean War he failed to interest the War Office in his invention of an armour-piercing shell. With much prescience, he strongly advocated the fire-proofing of battleships. In 1858 he published *The British Army in India*, in which he distilled all his experience and thoughts on the preservation of health in a hot climate. At about this time he was also working on the design of a refrigerator for the transport of meat from the Antipodes.

Jeffreys died at his home, 9 Park Villas West, Queen's Road, Richmond, Surrey, on 13 May 1877. He was buried in Richmond cemetery four days later. Jeffreys embodied all the qualities which we associate with the Victorians. He was inventive, enterprising, entrepreneurial, and philanthropic. There is no doubt that the respirator was very effective in the palliation of bronchitis and lung disease. It was exhibited at the London International Exhibition of 1862 and was widely advertised in the pharmaceutical press until the end of the nineteenth century; many tens of thousands of the devices were sold, so it is surprising that it is no longer remembered. However, the idea was rediscovered in 1956, and the heat-and-moisture exchanger (HME), which works on the identical principle, is now in everyday use in the intensive care units of hospitals all over the world.

DAVID ZUCK

Sources Jeffreys file, BL OIOC, L/MIL/9/374/f106–10 · E. Jeffreys, *A confutative biographical notice of Julius Jeffreys, FRS, FGS* (1855) · *East-India Register and Directory* (1823–35) · 'New instrument for preventing and relieving pulmonary affections', *The Lancet* (14 Jan 1837), 567–9 · A. Carlyle, ed., *New letters and memorials of Jane Welsh Carlyle*, 1 (1903), 71–2 · G. L. Cumming, 'Rev. Charles Jeffreys', *The advance guard*, ed. G. T. Griffiths (1973), 12–32 · *The illustrated catalogue of the industrial department: British division*, 2 (1862), class 13, pp. 133–4 [exhibition catalogue, International Exhibition, London, 1862] · D. Zuck, 'Julius Jeffreys, pioneer of humidification', *Proceedings of the History of Anaesthesia Society*, 8b (1990), 70–80 · D. Zuck, 'Julius Jeffreys and the physiology of lung volumes', *Proceedings of the History of Anaesthesia Society*, 10 (1991), 55–61 · D. G. Crawford, *A history of the Indian medical service, 1600–1913*, 2 vols. (1914) · D. McDonald, *Surgeons twoe and a barber* (1950) · private information (2004) · parish register (birth), Bexley, Kent · parish register (marriage), Barony, Glasgow, 1851 · d. cert. · burial register, Richmond cemetery
Archives BL OIOC · Hall Place, Bexley, Kent · RS · University of Otago, Dunedin, New Zealand, Hocken Library
Likenesses oils, priv. coll.
Wealth at death under £2000: resworn probate, June 1878, CGPLA Eng. & Wales (1877)

Jeffries, Sir Charles Joseph (1896–1972), civil servant, was born on 7 May 1896 at 112 Stondon Park, Lewisham, the eldest son of Charles David Jeffries, a company secretary, and his wife, Margaret Sarah Baird. He was educated at Malvern College, and won a classical demyship (scholarship) to Magdalen College, Oxford, in 1913, but never took it up. In 1915 he was commissioned as second lieutenant in the Wiltshire regiment, and was invalided out of the army in 1917, his voice permanently damaged by the effects of gas, and joined the Colonial Office. In 1921 he married Myrtle, daughter of Dr J. H. Bennett; they had three daughters.

At the Colonial Office, Jeffries worked with Ralph Furse, who in 1929 encouraged Leo Amery, secretary of state for the colonies, to set up the colonial services committee, chaired by Warren Fisher, permanent secretary of the Treasury and head of the civil service, to consider the structure of the colonial services, with particular attention to recruitment. Before 1930 there was no such thing as a colonial service, though the term was used to refer to British officers in the public services of the colonies, appointed and employed by the individual colonial governments. It was felt that in order to attract good recruits there was a need for a more attractive career structure, with appointments made by the secretary of state, who would control promotion, with opportunities extending over the whole of the colonial empire, and no longer limited to the colony to which an officer was first posted. In 1930 the Warren Fisher report, called 'the Magna Carta of the modern Colonial Service' by Jeffries (*The Colonial Empire and its Civil Service*, 55), recommended unification into a single colonial service, and a new colonial service personnel division was set up, responsible for the selection and training of recruits into the upper grades of the colonial service. Jeffries, as an assistant secretary and establishment officer, was in charge of one of the two departments, and he was given the job of putting the principle of unification into practice, while Furse, as director of recruitment, was in charge of the other department. He began by setting up the colonial administrative service in 1932, and by the outbreak of war unification was largely completed, with the creation of a chain of unified services, including the colonial medical service (1934), the colonial forest service (1935), the colonial veterinary service (1935), the colonial police service (1937), and the colonial mines service (1938). The remaining services were set up after the war, the last being the colonial research service in 1949. For each of these, a list of 'scheduled' posts was drawn up, with standard salaries and conditions of employment, designed for expatriate officers. These were senior grade posts, requiring a university degree or a professional qualification; junior grade posts were mainly filled by local people in the colonies, and were not scheduled. The idea was to establish a pool of officers, selected by the secretary of state, available for posting where required, though they continued to be paid by the colonial governments, and not by the British government. Jeffries became an assistant under-secretary of state in 1939, and was created KCMG in 1943.

Jeffries was a member of the Devonshire committee, which sat from 1944 to 1945, set up to consider training for all branches of the post-war colonial service. The committee included representatives from the universities of Oxford, Cambridge, and London, including Douglas Veale, registrar of Oxford University, with whom Jeffries was to work closely in the foundation of Queen Elizabeth House, Oxford, in 1954, as a Commonwealth centre. He was involved in setting up the 'Devonshire courses', introduced in 1946. In 1947 Jeffries became joint deputy under-secretary of state, and head of the personnel division. Despite the success of the recruitment campaign immediately after the war, with 3000 new appointments by mid-1947, by the early 1950s recruitment was falling and there was a large number of resignations, as local politicians in the colonies began to display their hostility to expatriate officers. Ceylon had gained her independence in 1947, and leaders in the Gold Coast and Nigeria, where there were many expatriate officers, were pressing to follow suit, and many lost confidence in the will or power of the secretary of state to interfere. They were concerned about their salaries and pensions as local power shifted from the governors to local leaders, while a career in the colonial service seemed less attractive to potential new recruits: in 1953, only half of the vacant administrative posts were filled. As early as 1941 Jeffries had chaired a committee which recommended the recognition of the principle that the British government should be responsible for securing suitable terms for British officers employed by the colonial territories, but this was turned down in 1944, to Jeffries's great disappointment: he came to believe that this decision was a turning point in the history of the colonial service. Although few in the early 1950s could predict that progress to political independence would be so rapid—and the colonial service continued to recruit in the expectation that the colonies would need expatriate staff for many years to come—it was clear that change was needed, and in 1954 the colonial service became Her Majesty's overseas civil service (HMOCS). It was hoped that under this new structure existing staff would be content to remain, and new staff would continue to be recruited, but after 1956 the transfer of power in one colony after another removed the responsibility for staffing the public services from the British government.

Jeffries retired in 1956. He published several books about the colonial service, including *The Colonial Empire and its Civil Service* (1938), *Partners for Progress: the Men and Women of the Colonial Service* (1949), *The Colonial Police* (1952), and *Whitehall and the Colonial Service: an Administrative Memoir, 1939–1956* (1972). A member of the Church of England, he was concerned with the question of Christian unity, and his religious publications included *Nebuchadnezzar's Image: a Layman's Thoughts on Christian Disunion* (1947), and *Christian Unity: a Layman's Challenge* (1967), the latter an article he wrote for *The Times*, reprinted with a selection of readers' letters. He was a member of the house of laity of the church assembly from 1950 to 1955, and also vice-president of the United Society for the Propagation of the Gospel, a member of the governing body of the Society for Promoting Christian Knowledge, and a member of the general committee of the British and Foreign Bible Society. He served as honorary secretary of the Corona Club (founded in 1900 by Joseph Chamberlain for past and present colonial officers) from 1921 to 1949.

Jeffries died on 11 December 1972 in Beckenham Hospital, Beckenham, Kent.   ANNE PIMLOTT BAKER

Sources C. Jeffries, *Whitehall and the colonial service: an administrative memoir, 1939–1956* (1972) · C. Jeffries, *Partners for progress: the men and women of the colonial service* (1949) · C. Jeffries, *The colonial empire and its civil service* (1938) · R. D. Furse, *Aucuparius: recollections of a recruiting officer* (1962) · R. Heussler, *Yesterday's rulers: the making of the British colonial service* (1963) · *The Times* (13 Dec 1972) · *WW* · b. cert. · d. cert. · A. Kirk-Greene, *On crown service* (1999)
Archives Bodl. Oxf., memoir of visit to West Africa
Likenesses photograph, repro. in *The Times*

Jeffryes, Elizabeth (1727–1752), murderer, was born in July 1727 in Bridgnorth, Shropshire, one of three children and the only daughter of Francis Jeffryes, a boat builder 'in a reputable Way of Life' (*Authentick Memoirs*, 2). When she was five years old, Elizabeth was sent to live with her uncle Joseph Jeffryes in Walthamstow, Essex. The latter, who was childless and had 'acquired a considerable Fortune' as a butcher, raised her as his own daughter, making her heir to the bulk of his estate (*Authentick Trylas*, 2). When, at about the age of twenty-two, Elizabeth began a 'criminal Commerce' (*Authentick Memoirs*, 5) with one of her uncle's servants, a young man by the name of John Swan (c.1725–1752), the elder Jeffryes 'threatened to alter his will, and cut her off, if she did not alter her Conduct' (*Authentick Trylas*, 8). Elizabeth, fearing she would 'be ruined and beggared' (it was rumoured that she believed she was pregnant with Swan's child), began to conspire with her lover to murder her uncle (*Authentick Memoirs*, 3).

The couple approached one Thomas Mathews, a rather disreputable character who had worked briefly as a servant on the Jeffryes estate, offering him £700 to 'knock that old miser his master on the head'. But, as Mathews later claimed, he baulked at committing murder; and, on 3 July 1751, upon his telling Swan and Miss Jeffryes that he 'could not find it in his heart to do it', he witnessed Swan go upstairs with a loaded pistol, and shortly afterwards heard gunfire (*GM*, 121–2). Some forty minutes later, Elizabeth, dressed only in her shift, and seeming 'very much affrighted', jumped from her bedroom window, rousing the neighbourhood with an 'outcry' of 'Murder! Fire! Thieves' Jeffryes was found in bed, mortally wounded, apparently the victim of 'rogues' who had broken into the house (ibid., 123).

While suspicion initially fell upon Mathews, the latter was no sooner apprehended then he implicated Swan and Jeffryes, who were arrested and tried at the Chelmsford assizes on 11 March 1752: Swan for the murder of his master; Jeffryes as an accessory to the crime. After deliberating for over an hour, the jury brought them both in guilty, a verdict which was received with 'great Satisfaction' by the 'amazing Concourse of People in the Court' (*Daily Advertiser*, 13 March 1752).

After her condemnation Jeffryes confessed to the crime, admitting that she had been plotting her uncle's 'Destruction' ever since she had, two years previously, begun to suspect he would 'alter [his will] in favour' of a maid with whom she had 'catch'd … [him] in Bed' (*Authentick Memoirs*, 7). More shocking still was Jeffryes's claim to have been, at the age of fifteen, 'debauched' by her uncle, by whom she had twice become pregnant—miscarrying once, and the second time losing the baby after he 'gave her Things to cause an Abortion' (ibid., 5–6).

Elizabeth Jeffryes's claim that she had been 'induced to

do what she did' by 'all the ill-usage she had met with' seems to have been little credited by contemporaries. We are told that 'Miss was of a very vicious and wicked Inclination naturally', and had moreover on at least one occasion proven 'very willing to prostitute herself' (*Authentick Memoirs*, 6–7, 13). In the various accounts of her life, Elizabeth was cast not as a victim of incest, but as a grasping and treacherous woman who had 'enticed and persuaded' Swan to commit a murder for which he had very little stomach (*Whole Tryal*, 18). And, while it was conceded that Jeffryes's 'Person' was 'tolerable'—her figure shapely and her complexion 'fresh'—contemporaries could not refrain from adding that there was 'something indelicate in her Mein and Countenance' (*Read's Weekly Journal*; *London Evening-Post*, 12–14 March 1752).

But while Jeffryes was reported to have sworn, gambled, and drunk 'very excessively' in prison, in public she played the part of the frail female to perfection (*Authentick Memoirs*, 8), fainting and falling into 'fits' at both her arraignment and trial. On 28 March 1752, when she and Swan were executed near Epping Forest before 'an innumerable Multitude of Spectators', Jeffryes's 'Distress' was such that the more 'polished' of the onlookers 'were melted into Tears', and even the 'low People … seemed much afflicted' (*Read's Weekly Journal*). Jeffryes not only 'swooned away' while being drawn to the gallows, but was 'so insensible' that she had to be supported while the noose was fastened about her neck (*Authentick Memoirs*, 12; *General Advertiser*). The two lovers, whose affections had cooled since their arrest and who scarcely spoke at the place of execution (where Jeffryes had denied Swan the 'Favour' of a farewell kiss), were united in death: they were hanged on either end of the same rope, causing 'them both to twist round' so that Jeffryes 'expired' with her 'Head in Swan's Bosom' (*Daily Advertiser*, 30 March 1752). After her execution, Jeffryes's body was 'put into her coffin, and delivered to her friends' (*London Evening-Post*, 28–31 March 1752); she was presumably buried in her family plot in Bridgnorth, where her parents were still living at the time of her death.   ANDREA MCKENZIE

Sources Authentick memoirs of the wicked life and transactions of Elizabeth Jeffryes, Spinster (1752) · The authentick tryals of John Swan, and Elizabeth Jeffryes, for the murder of Mr. Joseph Jeffryes of Walthamstow in Essex (1752) · The authentick trylas at large of John Swan and Elizabeth Jeffryes (1752) · The tryal of Thomas Colley at the assizes at Hertford … likewise a narrative of the cruel murder of Mr. Joseph Jeffryes (1751) · The whole tryal of John Swann, and Elizabeth Jeffries, 2nd edn (1752) · Genuine letters that pass'd between Miss Blandy and Miss Jeffries (1752) · London Evening-Post (12 March 1752) · London Evening-Post (13 March 1752) · London Evening-Post (14 March 1752) · London Evening-Post (24 March 1752) · London Evening-Post (25 March 1752) · London Evening-Post (26 March 1752) · London Evening-Post (28 March 1752) · London Evening-Post (29 March 1752) · London Evening-Post (30 March 1752) · London Evening-Post (31 March 1752) · Daily Advertiser [London] (13 March 1752) · Daily Advertiser [London] (30 March 1752) · General Advertiser (30 March 1752) · GM, 1st ser., 22 (1752), 121–4 · Read's Weekly Journal, or, British Gazetteer (4 April 1752)
Likenesses portrait, repro. in Authentick memoirs of … Elizabeth Jeffryes
Wealth at death signed over most of estate from uncle to Mr McCoon: Authentick memoirs, 10

Jegon, John (1550–1618), bishop of Norwich, was born at Coggeshall, Essex on 6 December 1550, the elder son of Robert Jegon (d. in or before 1558) and his wife, Joan, née Whyte (d. 1607). Joan's father, John, was a weaver and clothmaker of the town. From the local grammar school Jegon matriculated at Queens' College, Cambridge, on 25 October 1567. On graduating BA in 1572 he was elected a fellow, and became successively tutor and vice-president of the college and a proctor in the university. In 1590 he was nominated by the crown to the mastership of Corpus Christi College. The fellows there had other plans but reluctantly complied, telling the university's chancellor, Lord Burghley, that they only did so 'for that our statute so in part requireth, and your last letters seem to command' (*CSP dom.*, 1581–90, 682). By bringing with him several of his pupils from Queens', Jegon soon justified the royal choice, freeing the college from financial difficulties and raising academic standards. In 1593 he showed his colours by signing the formal protest against William Barret's sermon attacking Calvinistic doctrine. As vice-chancellor on four occasions between 1596 and 1601 he vigorously maintained the rights and privileges of the university. In doing so he earned the dislike of the townsmen, of whose treatment of him he complained in letters to Burghley.

Jegon's last preferments came swiftly to him as one of the queen's chaplains-in-ordinary. On 22 July 1601 he was installed dean of Norwich, and on 20 February 1603 was consecrated bishop there in succession to William Redman. Archbishop Whitgift was anxious that his chaplain Benjamin Carrier, a senior fellow of Corpus Christi, should succeed to the vacant mastership, but although Jegon appeared to favour the plan, he contrived the election of his own younger brother, Thomas, a fellow there since 1587, much to Whitgift's indignation.

Jegon came in as a new broom. He claimed £194 from Redman's executors to put the Norwich palace in good repair. The chaotic records of the see were soon put in good order by Anthony Harison, a lawyer from Cambridge who served the bishop as an excellent secretary throughout his tenure. Harison's *Registrum vagum* records much of the business of the whole diocese, save that the record for the archdeaconry of Sudbury is lost. Jegon was quick to interrogate his officials from the chancellor down to the commissaries with their registrars, and by August 1602 had signed orders for the 'present suppressing of the multitude and iniquity of apparitors in my several jurisdictions, against whom I have received many foul complaints' (Collinson, *Elizabethan Puritan Movement*, 451). Suspending the offenders summarily, he only reinstated those prepared to forswear bribery and extortion. In this heyday of Jacobean Calvinism he addressed his clergy in a notably courteous and tactful manner, supporting them in their preaching ministry. He co-operated with 'knights and worthy gentlemen' and townspeople to establish market-day lectures in such places as Swaffham, where he was told that the inhabitants were 'more rude than easily will bee believed' being 'utterlie destitute of preaching ministers' (Collinson, *Religion of Protestants*, 78). Nicholas

John Jegon (1550–1618), by unknown artist, 1601

Bownde, one of the staunchest puritan ministers in his diocese, expressed general approbation for Jegon when he wrote 'how readie we are, and shall be, to yeild obedience to all your lordship's godly proceedings', blessing God, 'not only for your comming among us, but much more for your continuance with, and over us' (Bownde, sig. ¶5–6).

Probably in 1606 Jegon married Dorothy, daughter of Richard *Vaughan, bishop of London. Between 1607 and 1617 they had two sons, Robert and John (both educated at Corpus Christi), and two daughters, Dorothy and Joan. In 1614 fire caused by the negligence of the brewhouse servants destroyed the thatched parts of Ludham House, Jegon's country seat. Instead of rebuilding Ludham, Jegon built himself a house at Aylsham, which his critics regarded as too remote from Norwich. Unflattering contemporary verses, collected by Harison, were later printed by Francis Blomefield. Too much credence has been given to these doggerel caricatures. They describe Jegon as a small corpulent man; he was considered a harsh disciplinarian, and by some people illiberal for one of such ample wealth. The historian of Corpus Christi states that he was 'so noted for a monied man, that the king sent to borrow £100 of him by way of loan' (Masters' History, 146). There was probably at least some truth in these charges. Jegon's portrait, dated 1601, shows that he was not handsome; he enforced conformity among the clergy of his diocese; and

there is evidence that not all the complaints of covetousness and parsimony were wide of the mark. He maintained a modest-sized household of about twenty-five servants, not one of whom was remembered in his will, and charged what were regarded as high fees for ordinations and institutions to benefices. None the less, Thomas Fuller may have been nearer the truth than Jegon's adversaries when he described the bishop as 'A most serious man and grave governour; yet withall of a most facetious disposition; so that it was hard to say whether his counsel was more grateful for the soundness, or his company more acceptable for the pleasantness thereof' (Fuller, *Worthies*, 1.346).

Failing in health in his latter years, Jegon was granted leave of absence from parliament. He died at Aylsham on 13 March 1618, and was buried in the chancel of that church. His monument has no effigy. On 29 April 1620 his widow married Sir Charles Cornwallis, of Beeston, Norfolk, formerly ambassador to Spain, as his third wife. The bishop's son and heir, Robert, built a house on the large estate he was bequeathed at Buxton, Norfolk. His father also left him all his books in Hebrew, Greek, Latin, and English. In the civil war Robert Jegon was in trouble as a royalist. His brother, John, had he lived to be twenty-one, would have had his estate at Thorndon in Suffolk, but he died in 1631 and was buried with his father. In 1632 Jegon's elder daughter, Dorothy, married Robert Gosnold, gentleman, of Otley, Suffolk.   J. M. BLATCHLY

Sources Venn, *Alum. Cant.*, 1/2.466 · P. Collinson, *The religion of protestants* (1982), 78–9, 92 · P. Collinson, *The Elizabethan puritan movement* (1967); repr. (1982), 210, 450–51 · *The Registrum vagum of Anthony Harison*, ed. T. F. Barton, 2 vols., Norfolk RS, 32–3 (1963–4) · F. Blomefield and C. Parkin, *An essay towards a topographical history of the county of Norfolk*, [2nd edn], 11 vols. (1805–10), 3.562–3 · *Masters' History of the college of Corpus Christi and the Blessed Virgin Mary in the University of Cambridge*, ed. J. Lamb (1831) · A. Campling, ed., *East Anglian pedigrees*, 1; Harleian Society, 91 (1939), 120–21 · K. Fincham, *Prelate as pastor: the episcopate of James I* (1990) · N. Bownde, *The holy exercise of fasting* (1604) · *CSP dom.*, 1581–90 · PRO, PROB 11/131, fols. 228v–229v · F. G. Emmison, ed., *Essex wills*, 8 (1993) · J. Bevlatsky, 'The Elizabethan episcopate: patterns of life and expenditure', *Princes and paupers in the English church, 1500–1800*, ed. R. O'Day and F. Heal (1981), 111–27 · Fuller, *Worthies* (1811)

Archives CUL, corresp. and papers

Likenesses oils, 1601, CCC Cam. [*see illus.*] · oils, Norwich Cathedral · two line engravings, BM, NPG

Wealth at death estates at Aylsham and Buxton, Norfolk, and Thorndon, Suffolk: will, proved 17 Nov 1618, PRO, PROB 11/131, fols. 228v–229v

Jehner [*later* Jenner], **Isaac** (1750–1818), portrait painter and engraver, was born on 2 December 1750 in Queen's Head Court, Great Windmill Street, Westminster, London, the last of eighteen children (nine with each of two wives) of Johan Jehner (1700–1752). Born in Hesse-Cassel and apprenticed as a gunsmith, Johan Jehner's journeyman years led him to Paris and then London, where he arrived in 1722. With the considerable profit from that trade he turned to silver planishing, in which he excelled. He delighted in making statuary and, being a sociable man, he was a founder member of a club of artists. Jehner's mother died, also in 1752, leaving the seven surviving children orphaned. Jehner was well cared for, but in the course of a lively childhood suffered two fractured thighs; incorrectly treated, he was left with such deformed legs that he was dwarfed and disabled for life.

Aged twenty, Jehner replied to an advertisement for an apprentice to learn to draw, and was accepted and articled, although his master was about to retire. Jehner, however, stayed with him until 1775, when the master gave him furniture and money to start up in business. Jehner's diminutive size made it hard to find work, but he was soon employed by William Pether. He married on 2 June 1777 Elizabeth, daughter of William Payne, staymaker, of Plymouth.

At this time the print trade was extremely competitive. Jehner decided to improve his skills in portraiture, which hitherto he had practised only in crayon and watercolour. He resolved to learn the use of oils and, hearing that the Flemish schools were the best, he and his wife travelled to Lille soon after their marriage. There Jehner became acquainted with Marmaduke Gwynn of Garth, Brecknockshire, who, besides immediately buying prints from Jehner, recommended him to the Royal Academy of the city, to save him needing to buy his freedom. He set out to return to Britain with Gwynn, but was delayed at Calais over a matter of his passport. A brief commission to draw a map for Colonel Pearson further detained him; in November 1779 he arrived in London, where his son Isaac was born on 1 January 1780.

In May Jehner went to Exeter, hoping for another map commission but, when this failed to materialize, he opened a drawing school there. Soon he moved to Plymouth, establishing a drawing school at Plymouth Dock. In 1781 he was made a freemason in Fortitude lodge, where he painted a canopy for the master, and engraved a number of mezzotints of fellow masons. Another son was born in February 1781. Invited to Saltash, he painted an altarpiece of Moses and Aaron. A third son, John William Jehner, born in November 1784, was sent to sea and died of yellow fever at Martinique, aged thirteen.

Jehner spent five years, from 1785 to 1790, at Bristol, where he produced two mezzotints of Hogarth altarpieces at St Mary Redcliffe; in 1787 he opened a shop at Bath. Needing a steadier income, he returned to the metropolis and took employment in the Polygraphic Society, which manufactured partly printed copies of oil paintings at Woolwich Common. While there he developed a method of painting on silk in emulation of stained glass. The Polygraphic was destroyed by fire in January 1793, at which time Jehner returned to central London, and had his two elder boys working with him. In 1806 he published a short autobiography entitled *Fortune's Football*. He died in 1818.

TIMOTHY CLAYTON and ANITA MCCONNELL

Sources Dodd's history of English engravers, BL, Add. MS 33402, fols. 148–9, 'Isaac Jehner' · I. Jehner, *Fortune's football* (1806) · Thieme & Becker, *Allgemeines Lexikon* · parish register, St James, Piccadilly, City Westm. AC · parish register, Rame-by-Plymouth, Plymouth and West Devon Record Office, Plymouth · parish register, Brighton, St Nicolas, E. Sussex RO
Likenesses I. Jehner, self-portrait, mezzotint, pubd 1818, BM

Jekyll [*née* Graham**], Dame Agnes** (1861–1937), philanthropist and political hostess, was born on 12 October 1861 in Largs, Ayrshire, the sixth daughter of William *Graham (1817–1885), Liberal MP and art collector, and his wife, Jane Catherine (1819/20–1899), daughter of John Loundes of Arthurlie, Renfrewshire. From her parents she acquired many of the attributes she was to perfect later in life, notably the gift of hospitality. Her father was a patron of the Pre-Raphaelite painters and this led to her interest in the arts. She inherited his deep political convictions and Christian faith. From her mother, an accomplished pianist, she inherited a great appreciation of music. She was educated at home by governesses, and stated that she had attended classes at King's College, London; these were probably the early lectures for ladies organized by King's College in Kensington from 1878 onwards.

On 29 December 1881 Agnes married Sir Herbert Jekyll (1846–1932), a captain (later colonel) in the Royal Engineers; he was a brother of the artist Gertrude Jekyll. Marriage brought her new spheres in which to practise her hostessing skills. She always travelled with her husband on his postings, including to Dublin, where he was private secretary to two lords lieutenant (the earl of Carnarvon, 1885–6, and Lord Houghton, 1892–5), Paris, where he was commissioner for the British section of the Paris Exhibition in 1900, and Gibraltar for the War Office. Such was her devotion to her husband that she left her one-year-old first-born with her parents while she accompanied him during his inspections of fortifications in Ceylon and Singapore. Their daughters, Barbara and Pamela, married Bernard Cyril Freyberg, first Baron Freyberg, and Reginald McKenna respectively.

Agnes Jekyll's husband was assistant secretary at the Board of Trade from 1901 to 1911, and they entertained at their home, Munstead House, Busbridge, Godalming, Surrey. The Asquiths (who knew her as Aggie) were among their guests. During the First World War, as chairman of St John of Jerusalem's warehouse for hospital supplies, Clerkenwell, she worked unstintingly in organizing and maintaining supplies to numerous hospitals and convalescent homes. She prided herself on answering every demand for supplies promptly. She was also one of the first to volunteer to provide an ambulance service when London was subject to air raids. In recognition of her war work she was created DBE on 1 January 1918.

Agnes Jekyll also brought her considerable organizational skills to the public sphere particularly for the benefit of those of her own sex who were in some sort of trouble. For ten years she was chair of the visiting committee of the Borstal Institution for Girls at Aylesbury and would often serve on juries in order to do her best for girls and women who stood in the dock. In 1925 she was made a magistrate on the Guildford bench and sat regularly on the panel of the children's court. She also served from 1884 to the time of her death as a member of the East End maternity hospital committee. A 'mistress of all domestic lore' (*The Times*, 29 Jan 1937, 16), she promoted housekeeping skills. Her *Kitchen Essays* (1922) brought together a series of articles she had written for *The Times* through which she initiated many into the secrets of successful domestic management.

Agnes Jekyll's life of public service was typical of many of the women of her class and generation. While not professionally trained to run public institutions she was able to apply many of the skills and values commonly associated with the private domestic sphere to the problems of society. While she was hailed as an exceptionally able amateur, it was remarked that had she been a man she would have been 'a great public servant' (*The Times*, 3 Feb 1937, 16). She outlived her husband by five years, dying in her sleep at Munstead House on 28 January 1937. Her funeral took place at Busbridge church on 1 February 1937. CORDELIA MOYSE

Sources *The Times* (29 Jan 1937), 16 · *The Times* (2 Feb 1937), 15 · *The Times* (3 Feb 1937), 16 · B. Freyberg and P. McKenna, eds., *Ne oublie* (1937) · *WWW* · m. cert. · d. cert. · F. Jekyll, *Gertrude Jekyll: a memoir* (1934) · Burke, *Gen. GB* (1914) [Graham of Hilston Park] · *H. H. Asquith: letters to Venetia Stanley*, ed. M. Brock and E. Brock (1982)
Likenesses photograph, repro. in Freyberg and McKenna, eds., *Ne oublie*, frontispiece
Wealth at death £72,564 11s. 2d.: probate, 30 April 1937, *CGPLA Eng. & Wales*

Jekyll, Elizabeth (*bap.* 1624, *d.* 1653). *See under* Jekyll, John (1611–1690).

Jekyll, Gertrude (1843–1932), artist and garden designer, was born at 2 Grafton Street, London, on 29 November 1843, and baptized at St George's, Hanover Square, the fifth of seven children and the second daughter of Edward Joseph Hill Jekyll (1804–1876), a retired captain in the Grenadier Guards, and his wife, Julia (1813–1895), the daughter of the banker Charles Hammersley. Her forebears included Joseph Jekyll (1753–1837), master in chancery and solicitor-general to the prince of Wales (later George IV); John Jekyll (1674–1732), collector of customs for the port of Boston, with an estate in Stow, Massachusetts, USA; Sir Joseph Jekyll (1662–1738), master of the rolls; Thomas Jekyll (1570–1652), secretary of the King's Bench and licensed to bear arms; and William Jekyll (1470–1539), purveyor of forage for the king's horse. This notable lineage enabled Gertrude Jekyll, in a philological duel with Logan Pearsall Smith, to revive the old word 'armigerous' and he to refer to her as an armigerous 'old Amazon' (Smith, 63–4).

Early life and training Jekyll was educated by her parents and by German and French governesses at home at Bramley House in Surrey, where the family lived from 1848 until 1868. Here she met scientists, engineers, musicians, artists, members of parliament, and archaeologists, including Michael Faraday, Felix Mendelssohn, Sir Charles Newton, Sir Henry Layard, and Sir Gilbert Lewis, many of whom she sketched. Here, too, she had her first garden, with her sister Caroline Jekyll (1837–1928), and learned practical skills in her father's workshop. In 1861 she enrolled with her friend and fellow student Susan Muir-Mackenzie at the National School of Art in South Kensington. She was taught anatomy by John Marshall, botanical drawing and ornament by Christopher Dresser, and colour harmony by Richard Redgrave. From 1865 her

Gertrude Jekyll (1843–1932), by Sir William Nicholson, 1920

paintings, upon which John Ruskin commented favourably, were exhibited at the Royal Academy and the Society of Female Artists.

In 1868 the family moved to Wargrave Hill, overlooking the River Thames in Berkshire. Although the landscape was not to her liking because it was based on chalk and not the sand of the Surrey Weald, with its woods and heathlands, Gertrude Jekyll's painting, craft, interior decoration, and gardening activities, begun at Bramley House, increased and their quality was instantly recognized. George Leslie RA, remarked on both the range and quality of her accomplishments:

> Clever and witty in conversation, active and energetic in mind and body, and possessed of artistic talents of no common order … there is hardly any useful handicraft the mysteries of which she has not mastered—carving, modelling, house painting, carpentry, smith's works, *repoussé* work. Gilding, wood inlaying, embroidery, gardening, and all manner of herb and flower knowledge and culture, everything being carried on with perfect method and completeness. (Leslie, 35)

Artist, craftwork, and interior decoration In 1869 Jekyll visited William Morris and, although not part of the arts and crafts movement, was imbued by its spirit of the unity of the arts. For her this unity was not just an artistic concept but was fundamental to her special skills in homemaking, which she applied throughout her life. In his memoir Sir Herbert Baker wrote:

> her outstanding possession was the power to see, as a poet, the art and creation of home-making as a whole in relation to Life; the best simple English country life of her day, frugal, yet rich in beauty and comfort; in the building and furnishing and their homely craftsmanship, in the garden uniting the house with surrounding nature; all in harmony and breathing the spirit of its creator. (Baker, 15–16)

Between 1867 and 1893 she visited the artist G. F. Watts, sat to him 'for arms' (F. Jekyll, 87), and asserted after one visit that she felt she had been 'in paradise' (Blunt, 207).

Miss Jekyll's craft and garden work was sought by a

growing band of clients, whether it was a window box for a mechanic in Rochdale in 1870, or in the same year the architectural drawings, details, and plantings for Phillimore's Spring at Crazies Hill, north of Wargrave in Berkshire, a tablecloth, designed and embroidered for Lord Leighton, or quilts for him and for Edward Burne-Jones. In 1871 she painted the fish casts for Frank Buckland's Economic Fish Museum. She received commissions for interior design work and execution from the duke of Westminster in 1875 and also from Lord Ducie. At Eaton Hall, newly enlarged and modernized by Alfred Waterhouse, not only did she design and partly work with members of the Royal School of Embroidery the panels for the turret doors and the tapestry in the drawing-room, but she also advised on the furnishing. In addition she designed and made the gates for the entrance to Eaton Hall and earned a reputation as an art blacksmith. Her most comprehensive interior design work was for Jacques Blumenthal, a composer of popular songs and pianist to Queen Victoria, and his wife, Leonie, at 43 Hyde Park Gate, London. Here from 1871 she designed and executed the wall decorations of orange trees and peacocks and the ceilings of orange leaves. She also designed and made the quilted curtains and carried out the inlay work and the arrangement of the furnishings. At Le Chalet, the Blumenthals' home in Switzerland, an inner circle of friends spent evenings singing some of Gertrude Jekyll's translations of songs in German to the accompaniment of the pianist Lionel Benson, whose caricatures of her as a ballerina and singer of French *chansons* convey an unexpected aspect of her character. Through the Blumenthals, Jekyll met Barbara Bodichon, *née* Leigh-Smith, the artist and co-founder of Girton College, Cambridge and Bedford College, London, and the impressionist Hercules Brabazon, about whom she averred in 1906 that 'nobody has helped me more than Mr. Brabazon to understand and enjoy the beauty of colour and of many aspects concerning the fine arts' (Massingham, 107). During the winter of 1873–4, Miss Jekyll, Brabazon, and Frederic Walker stayed with Barbara Bodichon and her husband in Algiers. Watercolours of the landscapes, plants, buildings, and people in and around Algiers fill the pages of Gertrude Jekyll's albums at the Surrey History Centre in Woking, Surrey.

Plant collecting and breeding Gertrude Jekyll was profoundly affected by the plants, vegetation, landscapes, and architecture of the Mediterranean, which she had first seen in 1863 and 1864 when she accompanied Charles and Mary Newton to Turkey, Rhodes, and Greece. She collected plants from countries around the Mediterranean—Greece and Turkey in 1863–4, Italy in 1872 and 1876, and Capri in 1883—using a specially designed pick, and sent them back to England, where she tested them for their hardiness and utility as garden plants. From Capri she collected *Lithospermum rosmarinifolium*, *Crocus imperati*, *Smilax aspera*, a procumbent form of *Rosmarinus officinalis*, *Rosa sempervirens*, and *Campanula fragilis*; from Switzerland, *Primula villosa*, and from the Pyrenees, *Fritillaria pyrenaica*. Plants of Mediterranean origin became a characteristic feature of her garden designs and were grown close to the

house and against garden walls that afforded some protection during the English winter. She grew many irids from the Mediterranean, including the blue and white *Iris unguicularis* (*I. stylosa*) (collected and introduced by Edwyn Arkwright), as well as aromatic shrubs such as rosemary and lavender, and, if the English climate had permitted, would have grown out of doors agaves, aloes, opuntias, and bougainvilleas, which she had seen and painted in Algeria, for their bold and striking foliage and distinctive flowers. Her sister Caroline gardened on the Mediterranean coast and created a famous garden on the Guidecca in Venice from 1884 using a rich palette of Mediterranean plants. Two of her brothers were also able gardeners: Walter (1849–1929) showed what could be done following his sister's principles of garden design using tropical and subtropical plants in his garden in the Blue Mountains in Jamaica, and Herbert (1846–1932) maintained and enriched the garden she had laid out and planted at Munstead House, Surrey, after their mother's death in 1895.

Since 1863 Gertrude Jekyll had been collecting plants from the wild in Britain and throughout Europe, and from cottage gardens, and improving them. Many of the forms she bred were given to friends, some of whom, such as George Paul of Messrs Paul & Son, the Old Nurseries, Cheshunt, introduced them commercially and exhibited them in the Royal Horticultural Society's rooms. Miss Jekyll selected and bred more than thirty herbaceous annuals, biennials, and perennials and dwarf shrubs. Six were highly commended or received the award of merit from 1896 and continued to receive awards well after her death. For example, *Primula* 'Munstead bunch' received a bronze Banksian medal from the Royal Horticultural Society in 1900, and *Lavandula angustifolia* 'Munstead' in 1963. Although she took care to guard against loss by sending plants to botanic gardens, such as Kew, most have not survived. Only eight of the plants she bred are still available: *Aquilegia vulgaris* 'Munstead white', *Lavandula angustifolia* 'Munstead', *Nigella damascena* 'Miss Jekyll', *Primula* 'Munstead bunch', *Pulmonaria angustifolia* 'Munstead blue', *Sedum telephium* 'Munstead red', *Vinca minor* 'Gertrude Jekyll', and *Viola hispida* 'Jackanapes'. (The origins of the cultivar names are given in Tooley and Arnander, 130ff.) More than ten years before receiving her first awards for plant breeding Gertrude Jekyll was arranging displays of spring flowers at the Royal Horticultural Society and entering them successfully in the floral committee section to be judged; in 1885 she received a bronze medal for her display of daffodils and primroses. It came as no surprise therefore that she was one of only two women (the other was Ellen Willmott) to be awarded in 1897 the Victoria medal of honour of the Royal Horticultural Society by the president, Sir Trevor Lawrence. It was perhaps an even greater honour and pleasure for her to be referred to as the Queen of Spades by Dean Reynolds Hole, who responded on her behalf at the ceremony.

Garden designer In 1875 Miss Jekyll met William Robinson at the offices of *The Garden* and from 1881 began contributing articles to his journal. Her obituarist attributed to Miss

Jekyll and William Robinson 'not only the complete transformation of English horticultural method and design, but also that wide diffusion of knowledge and taste which has made us almost a nation of gardeners' (*The Times*, 10 Dec 1932, 12). In 1876 Miss Jekyll's father died, and her mother commissioned John James Stevenson, one of the leading architects of the Queen Anne style and an adherent of the Society for the Protection of Ancient Buildings founded by William Morris, Philip Webb, and others, to design a home for herself and her daughter on Munstead Heath, Surrey. Gertrude Jekyll laid out the garden. It was made up from many elements, including a parterre, a pergola, a bank of Scotch briars, an alpine garden, a grove of azaleas, an auricula garden, an orchard, a hardy flower border, a reserve garden, and a kitchen garden. There were lawns running into the heath, grass walks, and rhododendron plantings. It was the precursor of the garden of her own home, Munstead Wood, built in 1895 across the lane from Munstead House. This garden broke the mould of the Victorian flower garden, and a contemporary visitor noted that it was laid out in 'quite an unconventional way' (Goldring, 191). The garden designer, author, and student of Kew, William Goldring, visited Munstead House in 1882 and described the hardy flower border:

> the brilliancy of the border … was beyond anything we had hitherto seen in the way of hardy flowers—as different from the ordinary mixed border as night from day … The great point in this border is the grouping of the colours in broad masses, all being blended as to produce one harmonious whole. (ibid.)

Distinguished gardeners and botanists, including Dean Reynolds Hole, William Robinson, G. F. Wilson, Sir Michael Foster, F. W. Burbidge, Sir Joseph Hooker, James and Harry Mangles, Theresa Earle, Ellen Willmott, Sir Frederick Moore, the Revd C. Wolley Dod, Peter Barr, Max Leichtlin, Sir Thomas Hanbury, Dr Alexander Wallace, Mrs E. V. Boyle, Beatrix Farrand, and Edith Wharton, repaired to both Munstead House and Munstead Wood to see the gardens. Henri Correvon, the director of Le Jardin Alpin d'Acclimatation in Geneva, visited Munstead in 1894 and noted that the garden had 'deservedly attained a universal reputation for excellence' (Correvon, 167).

Drawing on close observation of nature, plants and gardens, hard labour, and much practice, Miss Jekyll applied to the designs and plantings of gardens 'the sensitive artistry and skill of hand hitherto devoted to her painting and handcrafts' (Hussey, 23). For Gertrude Jekyll, 'the first purpose of a garden is to be a place of quiet beauty such as will give delight to the eye and repose and refreshment to the mind' (Jekyll, 'Garden design on old-fashioned lines', 383–4). Much of her inspiration for laying out ground came from nature. However, in her first book, *Wood and Garden: Notes and Thoughts, Practical and Critical, of a Working Amateur*, published in 1899, she wrote that:

> no artificial planting can equal that of Nature, but one may learn from it the great lesson of the importance of moderation and reserve, of simplicity of intention, of directness of purpose, and the inestimable value of the quality called 'breadth' in painting. For planting ground is

painting a landscape with living things, and as I hold that good gardening ranks within the bounds of the fine arts, so I hold that to plant well needs an artist of no mean capacity. And his difficulties are not slight ones, for his living pictures must be right from all points, and in all lights. (Jekyll, *Wood and Garden*, 156–7)

Gertrude Jekyll's principles of gardening were enunciated earlier in 1896 in the *Edinburgh Review*, and to these she kept faith for the next thirty-five years, both in her garden at Munstead Wood and in more than 400 commissions in Great Britain (166 in Surrey alone) and in Ireland, France, Germany, Yugoslavia, and the United States of America. She subscribed neither to the formal school of landscape gardening, as exemplified in the work of Sir Reginald Blomfield and William Andrews Nesfield, nor to the free school of her friend William Robinson. She selected the best from both schools, extolling their most worthy properties. The principles of garden design that she followed comprised six articles: by forming and respecting quiet spaces of lawn, unbroken by flower beds or any encumbrance; by the simple grouping of noble types of hardy vegetation, whether their beauty be that of flower, foliage, or general aspect; by putting the right thing in the right place—a matter which involves both technical knowledge and artistic ability; by employing restraint and proportion in the manner of numbers and/ or quantity—to use enough and not too much of any one thing at a time; by grouping plants in sequences of good colouring and with due regard to their form and stature and season of blooming, or of autumnal beauty of foliage; and by seeing how to join house to garden and garden to woodland. The book that she wrote in 1908, *Colour in the Flower Garden*, exemplifies and is the practical outcome of these principles.

At about the same time Jekyll established, with the help of her Swiss gardener Albert Zumbach, a plant nursery at Munstead Wood. This was not only for economic reasons, to supply both plants and planting plans to her clients, but also to ensure their availability so that the right pictorial effect was realized and plant substitution, sometimes practised by her clients' gardeners, avoided. As late as 1932 she was promoting her nursery to the actress Amy Barnes-Brand in the following terms: 'I have a splendid list of good hardy plants, and bigger plants and at lower prices than the nurseries' (Tooley and Arnander, 120). The plant nursery was run by her for thirty-five years, until 1932. Each year thousands of plants were dispatched: for Sir George Sitwell's garden at Renishaw 1250 plants were sent in February and March 1910; for Roger Fry's garden at Durbins in Guildford a single consignment of plants dispatched in May 1911 numbered 600; and at the end of the year more than 3000 plants were sent to a client in Berkhamsted. After her death the nursery was run by her nephew Francis Jekyll (1882–1965) for a further nine years.

Gertrude Jekyll's clients included friends and relatives, government departments (including the War Graves Commission), publishers (Edward Hudson), newspaper owners (Lord Northcliffe), mill owners (Sir Amos Nelson and J. T. Hemingway), bankers (Otto Falk), local authorities (for example, the borough of Godalming), university colleges (including Newnham College and Girton College, Cambridge), churches (such as St Edmund's and the Wesleyan church, Godalming), schools (Charterhouse), hospitals (King Edward VII Sanatorium, Midhurst, Sussex), and charities (the National Trust), as well as some of the most distinguished public servants in the country such as Lord Curzon, Lord Lytton, Lord Revelstoke, and Reginald McKenna. She designed flower borders in suburban gardens and reached a large popular audience through her articles in *The Garden*, *Gardening Illustrated*, the *Daily Mail*, and the *Daily Express*.

Most (247) of Miss Jekyll's garden designs and planting plans were commissions received directly from clients, but others (153) came from collaborations with distinguished architects, such as her friend Sir Edwin Lutyens, Sir Robert Lorimer, Oliver Hill, Sidney Barnsley, Sir Herbert Baker, Morley Horder, L. Rome Guthrie, and M. H. Baillie Scott, and provincial architects such as Walter Brierley. While most of the architects with whom she collaborated provided her with outline plans of the garden ground, with Lutyens the plans were dynamic and interactive. Lutyens regularly visited her at Munstead Wood, for which he was the architect, referring to it as 'Plazzoh' or 'Bumpstead' and to her as 'Bumps'. He provided the detailed drawings for the garden and Jekyll the planting plans that softened, enriched, and emphasized his hard ground effects. Hestercombe, Somerset (1904), is the best example of this brilliant partnership, with Jekyll's planting enhancing and complementing the lines of perspective, the changes of level, the water features, the surprise views, and the sequestered bowers of the new garden that wraps around the house, all created with the craftsmanship and natural materials that both had seen together in the vernacular architecture of Surrey. The Jekyll–Lutyens garden at Hestercombe exploits the site with glimpses of the eighteenth-century designed landscape, further enhanced by plantings of the now-drained serpentine lake margins by Miss Jekyll and long views of the Blackdown Hills to the south. The working relationship between Jekyll and Lutyens was summed up by Miss Jekyll herself in a comment to Betty Balfour: 'Bumps told Betty that the difference between working with Nedi and Lorimer was as between quicksilver and suet' (RIBA, Lutyens Papers, LuE/4/10/7 (i–) Ap 12, 1901).

The gardens Miss Jekyll designed have to a great extent been lost, although some—such as her own garden at Munstead (1882); Hestercombe (1904); Lindisfarne Castle, Holy Island, Northumberland (1911); the Old Manor House, Upton Grey, near Winchfield in Hampshire (1908); and the Old Glebe House, Woodbury, Connecticut, USA (1926)—have been restored. The rich record she kept in plans, letters, writings, and photographs she took to illustrate articles and books (and six volumes of annotated photographs in the College of Environmental Design, University of California) permit, however, a glimpse of her genius as 'the greatest *artist* in horticulture and garden planting' (Hussey, 23).

Author Gertrude Jekyll wrote fourteen books, three of which were published by Longmans and the rest by Country Life, but her prodigious output of articles (more than 1138) in the gardening journals from 1881 to 1932, on a wide range of topics and illustrated with her photographs from Munstead House and Munstead Wood, bears witness to her desire to communicate ideas and information based on observation and practice to a large and interested public. A series of articles on flowers and plants in the house formed the basis of *Flower Decoration in the House* (1907), and the series on garden and woodland in the *Guardian Newspaper* served as the basis for the first book she wrote, *Wood and Garden* (1899).

These articles and books contain apposite and economical notes on the cultural requirements and pictorial effects of individual plants or plant associations. Plants tested successfully for their hardiness, such as *Romneya coulteri* and *Carpenteria california*, are often described. Gertrude Jekyll was probably the first to flower successfully out of doors the giant lily, *Cardiocrinum giganteum* (*Lilium giganteum*). She was responsible for introducing the giant hogweed, *Heracleum mantegazzianum*, in woodland plantings around Britain, and between 1911 and 1932 she wrote several articles about this proscribed plant, which she described thus: 'this grand plant has an appearance of greater refinement and beauty … and the mien of a specially proud and sumptuous plant' (Jekyll, 'Bog gardens', 670), as well as including it in planting plans such as those for Blagdon in Northumberland. There were articles on gardens that she and others had designed, such as Millmead, Surrey; Sandbourne, Worcestershire; Frant Court, Kent; and Warley, Essex, and articles on women as gardeners. Descriptions of tools she had designed included picks, trowels, labels, and the rolling steps. There were unexpected articles on railway gardening, gardening on corrugated iron, the rot pit, and the topiary cat cut in yew at Munstead Wood. She collected tools and old articles of cottage furniture and equipment throughout west Surrey, which were subsequently donated to Guildford Museum, and she wrote about them and the life and ways of country folk in *Old West Surrey* (1904). During her lifetime, the books she wrote were often reprinted and continued to be sought. In the 1970s and 1980s they were reissued, and they continue to be a source of inspiration.

In 1920 Sir Edwin Lutyens persuaded Gertrude Jekyll to sit for her portrait to William Nicholson. She agreed provided it was not during the hours of daylight. So she was painted by lamplight while she rested, and during the daylight hours William Nicholson painted her Balmoral boots. Of her portrait, now in the National Portrait Gallery, she referred to herself as a 'passive auxiliary' and wished 'it could have represented a more beautiful object' (F. Jekyll, 188).

The painting of her (men's) Balmoral boots is in the Tate collection; the boots had been bought by Gertrude Jekyll in Paris in 1883, at the time she had acquired a pair for William Robinson, and remained in continual use for almost fifty years, repaired and patched. In 1900 she wrote:

> no carpenter likes a new plane; no house painter likes a new brush. It is the same with clothes; the familiar ease can only come of use and better acquaintance. I suppose no horse likes a new collar; I am quite sure I do not like new boots. (Jekyll, *Home and Garden*, 119)

Gertrude Jekyll's ideas on gardening and planting have been remarkably persistent, spanning many years in three centuries. Her ideas do not rely on fashion, but are based on practice and experience communicated in English that was 'direct, simple and discriminating' (Hussey, 23). In July 1904 she admitted to Edwin Lutyens that 'she gloried at the idea of the children being in the studio and would give up all her garden for paddling!!' (RIBA, LuE, 28 July 1904). Fortunately she did not, and the fruits of a long, talented, creative, and industrious life as an artist, gardener, and craftsman are manifest in her paintings, garden designs, photographs, books, and journal articles.

Gertrude Jekyll received few awards. Following the Victoria medal of honour in 1897, the Royal Horticultural Society awarded her the Veitch gold medal in 1929, and in the same year she received from the Massachusetts Horticultural Society the George Robert White medal of honor. She died at Munstead Wood on 8 December 1932 and was buried in the churchyard of St John the Baptist, Busbridge, Surrey, on 12 December. She was unmarried. As she stood at the open door of Munstead Wood in 1932 Logan Pearsall Smith recalled her as 'some ancient, incredibly aristocratic rhinoceros gazing gravely out from amid a tangle of river reeds' (Smith, 64). In his life of Lutyens, Christopher Hussey described her as 'earthy and practical and determined … short, stout, myopic, downright … a frightening, but kind, wise old lady' (p. 23).　　MICHAEL TOOLEY

Sources [G. Jekyll], 'Gardens and garden craft', *EdinR*, 184 (1896), 161–84; repr. as G. Jekyll, 'The idea of a garden', *A gardener's testament: a selection of articles and notes by Gertrude Jekyll*, ed. F. Jekyll and G. C. Taylor (1982), 18–56 · G. Jekyll, *Wood and garden* (1899) · G. Jekyll, *Colour schemes in the flower garden* (1914) · F. Jekyll, *Gertrude Jekyll: a memoir* (1934) · F. Jekyll and C. G. Taylor, eds., *A gardener's testament: a selection of articles and notes by Gertrude Jekyll* (1937) · G. Jekyll, 'Garden design on old-fashioned lines', *Black's gardening dictionary* (1921), 383–4 · *The Times* (10 Dec 1932) · M. J. Tooley and P. Arnander, eds., *Gertrude Jekyll: essays on the life of a working amateur* (1995) · M. J. Tooley, ed., *Gertrude Jekyll: artist, gardener, craftswoman* (1984) · J. B. Tankard and M. A. Wood, *Gertrude Jekyll at Munstead Wood: writing, horticulture, photography, homebuilding* (1996) · B. Massingham, *Miss Jekyll: portrait of a great gardener* (1966) · S. Festing, *Gertrude Jekyll* (1991) · F. Gunn, *Lost gardens of Gertrude Jekyll* (1991) · R. Bisgrove, *The gardens of Gertrude Jekyll* (1992) · J. Brown, *Gardens of a golden afternoon: the story of a partnership, Edwin Lutyens and Gertrude Jekyll* (1982) · H. Baker, *Architecture and personalities* (1944) · W. Blunt, *England's Michelangelo: a biography of George Frederic Watts O.M. R.A.* (1975) · H. Correvon, 'The alpine gardens at Warley, Essex', *The Garden*, 45 (1894), 167–8 · J. Edwards, 'Gertrude Jekyll: prelude and fugue', *Gertrude Jekyll: artist, gardener, craftswoman*, ed. M. J. Tooley (1984), 25–40 · W. Goldring, 'Munstead, Godalming', *The Garden*, 22 (1882), 191–3 · C. Hussey, *The life of Sir Edwin Lutyens* (1950) · G. Jekyll, *Home and garden* (1900); repr. (1982), 167 · G. Jekyll, 'Bog gardens', *Country Life*, 29 (1911), 670–71 · G. D. Leslie, *Our river: personal reminiscences of an artist's life on the River Thames* (1881) · L. P. Smith, *Reperusals and re-collections* (1936)

Archives Godalming Museum, Godalming, Surrey, account books, notebooks, artefacts, watercolours [copy of item 3] · U. Cal., Berkeley, College of Environmental Design, Reef Point Gardens collection of designs, plans, corresp., photographs | BL, letters to A. W. Rowe, Add. MS 45926 · Canadian Centre for Architecture, Montreal, letters to Edwin Landseer Lutyens · English Heritage, Swindon, National Monuments Record, drawings, planting designs, and other papers [microfilm, copies] · Hove Central Library, Sussex, letters to Lady Wolseley · RBG Kew, letters to Royal Botanical Society · Royal Horticultural Society, London, Lindley Library, letters to Mrs Brand · Royal Horticultural Society, London, corresp. with William Robinson · Surrey HC, corresp. and plans mostly of gardens in Surrey · Surrey HC, presentation copy of *Gertrude Jekyll: a memoir*, and letters to F. W. Cobb · Surrey HC, sketchbooks, MS of *Old west Surrey* and related papers · University of Illinois, corresp. with Helen Allingham

Likenesses three photographs, 1862–1923, repro. in Tooley and Arnander, eds., 1 · attrib. W. Nicholson, cartoon, pencil and charcoal, 1920, repro. in Tooley and Arnander, eds., *Gertrude Jekyll*, 5 · W. Nicholson, oils, 1920, NPG [*see illus.*]

Wealth at death £20,091 8s. 8d.: 11 Feb 1933, *CGPLA Eng. & Wales*

Jekyll, John (1611–1690), local politician and religious radical, was born on 21 September 1611 at Bocking, Essex, the fourth son of the eight children of Thomas *Jekyll (1570–1652), lawyer and antiquary, and Elizabeth Leake (1575–1658). John was apprenticed as a fishmonger in 1629: he became a freeman in 1637, but seems to have set up business as a haberdasher. In the 1640s he was using business trips to the north-east and south-west to help provision the parliamentary army. He happened to be in Bristol in July 1643 when it fell to the royalists; he was recognized as 'the greatest Roundhead in all the parish' (Osborn MS b.221, p. 3), arrested, and released on the personal intervention of Sir Lewis Dyve. The parish in question must be that of St Stephen Walbrook, in the City of London, where Jekyll was resident from 1643 with other radical merchants such as the Huguenot Peter Houblon, and where in 1650 he became churchwarden. With the minister, Thomas Watson, who was to become a lifelong friend, he took an active part in Christopher Love's presbyterian plot. He was subjected to fines and threats, and reluctantly testified against Love, who was executed as the leader. A penitent letter from Jekyll to Love was printed in *Loves Name Lives* (1651). His first wife, Elizabeth Ward [*see below*], died in March 1653, leaving him with five young children. He remarried on 20 December that year, his second wife being Tryphena Hill (*d.* in or before 1692), widow of Richard Hill. Five more children were baptized between 1654 and 1662.

When Thomas Watson was ejected in 1662 Jekyll stayed on as a member of the vestry-meeting at St Stephen Walbrook. He was a member of common council for London for the years 1661–2, 1668–70, and 1681, serving on important committees and becoming extremely influential in the City: he was also active in the Fishmongers' Company from 1668 to 1688. With James Hayes he was arrested for riot during the protests against the second Conventicle Act in 1670, although the lord mayor admitted that Jekyll was merely trying to protect Thomas Watson from arrest for preaching. Hayes and Jekyll, in turn, had the lord mayor, Samuel Starling, arrested, and they took their case, which became a *cause célèbre*, to the Commons, where, despite Andrew Marvell's speech in their favour, they lost. Jekyll's essentially nonconformist allegiance, despite his occasional conformity, is indicated by the fact that he sent at least two of his sons to nonconformist academies.

Jekyll's allegiance appears to have been consistently presbyterian. He was a friend of the presbyterian poet Robert Wild; he sent a copy of the declaration of indulgence to Wild in March 1672 and in return Wild published *A letter from Dr Robert Wild to his friend Mr J. J. upon occasion of his majesty's declaration for liberty of conscience*. It is to be assumed that Jekyll shared Wild's cynicism about the declaration. During the 1670s he acted as a 'vicar-general' or 'solicitor-general' (the terms are those of his enemies) to the four nonconformist churches in Bristol. The Baptist congregation at Broadmead wrote to him during a particularly heavy persecution in 1675, and his friends in the House of Lords wrote a threatening letter to the tory mayor of Bristol in response. The following year a dissenting mayor was elected, and Jekyll invited him to London to meet the duke of York: 'No man has more influence and favour here then Mr. Jekell', rejoiced the new mayor. Bishop Guy Carleton of Bristol, however, had a rather different opinion: 'The ch: hath not a more malicious adversarie, nor the king a worse subject', he wrote to Gilbert Sheldon (Tanner MS 40, fol. 37).

Jekyll's substantial haberdasher's shop in Walbrook had been destroyed in the great fire, but although he staked out new foundations he does not seem to have reopened his business there. He moved to St Lawrence Lane, near the Guildhall, where he is recorded as having ten hearths in the hearth tax assessment of 1672. He became an active member of the vestry-meeting at St Lawrence Jewry. Jekyll lost his seat on common council in December 1681, when tory George Evans wrote to secretary of state Leoline Jenkins 'The loyal party in Cheap Ward have totally routed the ill-principled Common Councilmen, Mr. Jekill being the rankest' (*CSP dom.*, 1681, 637). He signed the monster petition for the recall of parliament in 1680 and served on a whig grand jury in 1681.

With Henry Cornish, Algernon Sidney, and other influential whigs, Jekyll was arrested for rioting at the controversial election of sheriffs in midsummer 1682, which was the climax of the exclusion crisis for the City. Information given to the government indicates that he was considered to be a conspirator in the Rye House plot. Jekyll visited Algernon Sidney just before his execution and reported that Sidney had locked the sheriffs into his cell and harangued them (*House of Lords MSS*, 3.51). During the 'Battle for the City', when Charles demanded the surrender of the city charter in 1683, a satirical pamphlet, *News from the Guild-Hall*, represents Jekyll as bankrolling the campaign for its defence, along with the radical Francis Jenks and one of the Houblon brothers. Although he was arrested during the Monmouth rebellion, he was immediately released on petition to James II. Jekyll testified for Henry Cornish at his trial later in 1685 for involvement in the Rye House plot, but did not impress the judge, who considered Jekyll implicated in the conspiracy.

Soon after the accession of James II, a royal proclamation ordered those who had been involved in printing and who were not members of the Stationers' Company to switch liveries forthwith and become subject to Stationers' Company regulation or cease printing. The names of Jekyll and his son John were top of the list. They did not join the Stationers' Company, and presumably their printing presses fell silent. Jekyll was subsequently removed from the court of the Fishmongers' Company in the years of James II's crackdown on dissenters, 1685–6. No more is known of Jekyll until the revolution, when in 1689 at the age of seventy-seven, he again stood as lord chamberlain of the City, seventeen years after his first attempt. He was again unsuccessful. William III, the same year, overturned his conviction with those of the other 'rioters' at the Guildhall shrieval elections.

Jekyll died in 1690 and was buried in St Stephen Walbrook on 23 September with his first wife. He left most of his substantial estate to his second wife, who survived him by two years, and his favourite son, Thomas *Jekyll, his eldest surviving son with Elizabeth. Thomas and Sir Joseph *Jekyll, his youngest son from his marriage to Tryphena and future master of the rolls, were his executors.

Jekyll's first wife, **Elizabeth Jekyll** [*née* Ward] (*bap.* 1624, *d.* 1653), was baptized on 18 July 1624 at St Christopher's in the parish of St Mary Woolchurch, London, the daughter of George Ward (1587–1646) and Elizabeth Ward (*d.* 1652), who had powerful family connections in the City. She married John Jekyll some time before 1643, when her diary begins. Cast in puritan providential style, the diary, now in the Beinecke Library at Yale University (Osborn MS b.221), charts her husband's involvement in the parliamentary cause, the births of seven children, deliverances of her family from accident, and parliamentary victories in the course of the first civil war. It also includes family records, religious meditations, and some poetry. The most sustained meditation, composed in 1652, lists the afflictions of her life, ending with her husband's imprisonment for involvement in the presbyterian plot, and accounts for them in terms of punishment for her own sin. The diary (which is clearly a copy as it adds, in the same hand, Alicia Lisle's 'dying speech' from the aftermath of the Monmouth rebellion) breaks off with a short entry on 13 January 1653. On 26 March 1653 Elizabeth was buried in the south aisle of St Stephen Walbrook, a week after the infant to whom she had given birth.

ELIZABETH R. CLARKE

Sources E. Jekyll, diary, Yale U., Beinecke L., Osborn MS b.221 · J. R. Woodhead, *The rulers of London, 1660–1689* (1965), 98 · W. B. Bannerman and W. B. Bannerman, jun., eds., *The registers of St Stephen's, Walbrook, and of St Benet Sherehog, London*, 1, Harleian Society, register section, 49 (1919) · W. C. Metcalfe, ed., *The visitation of Essex* (1878) · G. S. De Krey, 'The first Restoration crisis: conscience and coercion in London, 1667–73', *Albion*, 25 (1993), 567 · *State trials*, 5.111–23; 9.187–267; 11.433 · *CSP dom.*, 1670–77; 1681; 1683 · *The visitation of London, anno Domini 1633, 1634, and 1635, made by Sir Henry St George*, 1, ed. J. J. Howard and J. L. Chester, Harleian Society, 15 (1880), vol. 1, p. 176 · Fishmongers' Company great minute book, 1666–99, GL, MS 5570/5 · vestrybook St Stephen Walbrook, St Lawrence Jewry, GL · Bodl. Oxf., MS Tanner 40, fol. 37 · A. Grey, ed., *Debates of the House of Commons, from the year 1667 to the year 1694*, new edn, 10 vols. (1769), vol. 1, pp. 295–307 · R. Hayden, ed., *The records of a church in Christ in Bristol, 1640–1687*, Bristol RS, 27 (1974), 177 · will, PRO, PROB 11/401/155 · 'A posting book for receipts of money for staking out of foundations in the ruins of the City of London', P. Mills and J. Oliver, *The survey of building sites in the City of London after the great fire of 1666* (1967), vol. 1, p. 78 · *The manuscripts of the House of Lords*, 4 vols., HMC, 17 (1887–94), vol. 3 · CLRO, MS Rep 90, fols. 81v–82r · R. Morrice, 'Ent'ring book', DWL, vol. 1, pp. 315, 476 · information from Dr Mark Knights's database of Monster Petition signatories · private information (2004) [G. S. De Krey] · private information (2004) [J. Reynolds]

Wealth at death £9000?: will, proved 7 Oct 1690, PRO, PROB 11/401, sig. 155

Jekyll, Sir Joseph (*bap.* 1662, *d.* 1738), lawyer and politician, was baptized on 3 October 1662 at St Stephen Walbrook, London. Little is known of his early upbringing, but his social origins were within the middling sort. He was the fourth son of John *Jekyll (1611–1690), a radical dissenting politician and haberdasher, and his second wife, Tryphena or Tryfenia (*d.* in or before 1692), the widow of Richard Hill. Thomas *Jekyll (1646–1698) was his half-brother. Joseph Jekyll attended Islington nonconformist seminary before entering the Middle Temple in 1680. He was called to the bar in 1687. Through his association with the Middle Temple and work as a lawyer he cultivated the important patronage of Lord Chancellor Somers. By 1697 Jekyll had married Somers's second sister, Elizabeth (*d.* 1745); they had no children.

With the active support of Somers, Jekyll was appointed to the bench as chief justice of Chester in June 1697; he was knighted on 12 December the same year. His legal career was distinguished as he ascended the ranks of the crown's legal and judicial administration. In 1700 he was created serjeant-at-law, was a queen's serjeant from 1702 to 1714, and was made prime serjeant by George I in 1714. In 1725 he briefly served as first commissioner of the great seal. Jekyll was an active counsel in appellate proceedings before the House of Lords. In the 1706/7 session of parliament alone he presented fourteen civil cases before the Lords. In 1717, the same year he was appointed to the privy council, Jekyll resigned his position of chief justice to become master of the rolls, a position he held until his death. As master of the rolls Jekyll defended chancery from charges of arbitrariness. His decisions and decrees provided a more careful and systematic formulation of chancery's status as a court of conscience, ensuring that discretionary authority under conscience was limited. As Jekyll determined in the case of *Cowper* v. *Cowper* in 1734: 'discretion is a science, not to act arbitrarily according to men's wills and private affections, so the discretion which is exercised here is to be governed by the rules of law and equity' (D. Lieberman, *The Province of Legislation Determined*, 1989, 80).

Jekyll's parliamentary career was also initiated with the assistance of his brother-in-law. As a nominee of Somers in 1697 he was elected for Eye and held the seat until 1713. From 1713 to 1722 Jekyll represented Lymington. In 1722 he was returned for Reigate and would represent this constituency without contest until death. In the House of Commons, Jekyll was a hardworking and conscientious legislator. The *Journals of the House of Commons* reveal that his attendance was frequent and that he regularly served on committees. He drafted numerous bills and statutes both privately and for the government as master of the rolls. Much of his parliamentary work related to his legal expertise and he played a significant role in Commons proceedings that pertained to issues of jurisprudence, common law, or impeachment. Jekyll played a prominent role in many of the highly charged partisan parliamentary inquiries and trials of the period. In 1701 he defended Somers in the impeachment proceedings revolving around the partition treaties and 'penned all messages and answers' (D. Hayton, ed., *The Parliamentary Diary of Sir Richard Cocks*, 1996, 162) brought to the Commons for his brother-in-law. In 1710 Jekyll drafted the articles and managed the impeachment of Dr Sacheverell, delivering the opening and closing statements in the proceedings. In 1715 Jekyll served on a secret parliamentary committee to prepare impeachment proceedings against the leaders of the fallen tory government, but refused to support impeaching Robert Harley, earl of Oxford, and James Butler, duke of Ormond, because the proceedings 'were so slightly founded and straining the law' (*Portland MSS*, 5.512). With the collapse of the South Sea Bubble in 1720 he successfully pressured the government to instigate another secret committee of the Commons to investigate corrupt practices of ministers and company directors. Jekyll was learned in parliamentary procedure and studied closely the rules, orders, and precedents in the Commons. In debate he was often quick to flaunt his legal pedigree, behaviour that was often perceived as arrogant. In the debate surrounding the disputed Marlborough election in 1735 Jekyll, well in his seventies and speaking after midnight, 'threw out a defiance to any man who understood the law to contradict him' causing Lord Hervey to recollect that his 'desire of appearing in the right, more than the desire of being so, forced him often in parliament to balance in points where vanity wore the appearance of integrity' (R. Sedgwick, ed., *Lord Hervey's Memoirs*, 1931, 418–19).

As a member of Somers's stable of six to seven MPs Jekyll was considered one of the junto whig leaders and star debaters in the Commons prior to 1715. But Jekyll was also sympathetic to country issues, supporting bills against bribery and corruption in elections, anticipating his independence from the court whigs after the Hanoverian succession. Under Walpole he generally voted against the government and has been regarded by authorities as an independent or patriot whig and 'somewhat quixotic opposition leader' (P. Langford, *The Excise Crisis*, 1975, 72), who refused to ally with the tories and in fact voted with the government during the excise crisis. Indeed, his last recorded speech in parliament in 1738 was a country inspired plea for reducing the standing army because 'a mutiny of the army is more dangerous than a mob of the people' (Cobbett, *Parl. hist.*, 10.447).

In the Hanoverian period Jekyll's legislative activity was chiefly informed by his desire for moral reform and his anticlerical sentiments. He served as a parliamentary leader for the moralist lobby of members of the Society for Promoting Christian Knowledge, the Society for the Propagation of the Gospel, and the Georgia Society, and was an advocate for the Georgia settlement, where Jekyll Island bears his name. He supported or drafted legislation to ban duelling and lotteries, to censor the stage, to reform the poor law, and to build hospitals, workhouses, and houses of correction. He was most famous for his drafting and sponsorship of the Gin Act in 1736, which sought to regulate retailers of spirits in order to limit drunkenness, and was the occasion for much public disorder. Also in 1736 Jekyll authored the Quaker Tithe Bill and the Mortmain Act to limit the alienation of land to religious institutions. In 1719 he defended the repeal of the Occasional Conformity Act and in 1736 called the Test Act 'a prostitution of the Sacrament … that deprives [his majesty] of the service of some of his faithfullest subjects' (Taylor and Jones, 133). Jekyll took Anglican communion to maintain his government positions under the Test Acts but his legislative activities and his friendships with freethinkers such as William Whiston and Alured Clarke, reveal his dissenting sympathies and perhaps faith. At his death he left money to the widows and orphans of dissenting ministers and also to his chaplain.

Jekyll amassed a considerable fortune in land and investments. In Surrey he purchased estates in Bletchingley and Oxted and inherited from Somers the manors of Reigate and Howleigh in addition to the estate of Brookmans in Hertfordshire. He also owned property in Lincoln's Inn Fields. He owned extensive shares in the Bank of England and in the South Sea and East India companies; his will bequeathed £20,000 of these stocks to the sinking fund after his wife's death. Jekyll was charitable in nature and built a new market hall in Reigate, and served as governor of a number of London hospitals and president of the Westminster Infirmary. On his death from 'mortification of the bowels' (*DNB*) at Brookmans on 19 August 1738 it was noted that he had a 'hatchet face and surly look, always looking grave and speaking sententiously … [but] … was reckoned a great patron of the freethinkers … and a generous man' (*Egmont Diary*, 2.507). He was buried on 1 September 1738 in the Rolls Chapel, London.

TIM KEIRN

Sources W. Sachse, *Lord Somers: a political portrait* (1975) • R. R. Sedgwick, 'Jekyll, Sir Joseph', HoP, *Commons, 1715–54* • L. Davison, 'Experiments in the social regulation of industry: the Gin Act', *Stilling the grumbling hive: the response to social and economic problems in England, 1689–1750*, ed. L. Davison and others (1992), 25–48 • W. Hooper, *Reigate: its story through the ages* (1945) • P. Clark, 'The "Mother Gin" controversy in early eighteenth century England', *TRHS*, 5th ser., 38 (1988), 63–84 • *Tory and whig: the parliamentary papers of Edward Harley, third earl of Oxford, and William Hay, MP for Seaford, 1716–1753*, ed. S. Taylor and C. Jones (1998) • I. R. Christie, *British 'non-elite' MPs, 1715–1820* (1995) • G. S. Holmes, *British politics in the age of Anne*, rev. edn (1987) • C. Gerrard, *The patriot opposition to Walpole: politics, poetry, and national myth, 1725–1742* (1994) • J. Hoppitt and J. Innes, eds., *Failed legislation: 1660–1800* (1997) • Baker, *Serjeants*, 60, 116, 451, 520 • C. Robbins, *The eighteenth-century commonwealthman* (1959), 280 • will, PRO, PROB 11/691 • N. Luttrell, *A brief historical relation of state affairs from September 1678 to April 1714*, 6 vols. (1857) • *DNB* • *The manuscripts of his grace the duke of Portland*, 10

vols., HMC, 29 (1891–1931), vol. 5 • *Manuscripts of the earl of Egmont: diary of Viscount Percival, afterwards first earl of Egmont*, 3 vols., HMC, 63 (1920–23), vol. 2 • P. Watson and S. M. Wynne, 'Jekyll, Sir Joseph', HoP, *Commons, 1690–1715*
Archives BL, letters to the earl of Hardwicke, Add. MSS 35359, 35586, 35909 • Surrey HC, Somers MSS
Likenesses G. Vertue, line engraving, 1731 (after M. Dahl), BM, NPG • M. Dahl, oils, Middle Temple, London; version, Royal Courts of Justice, London
Wealth at death £20,000 of stock; £32,000 to a variety of friends, associates, and distant relatives; estates in Surrey and Hertfordshire; house and property in Lincoln's Inn Fields: will, PRO, PROB 11/691

Jekyll, Joseph (1754–1837), lawyer and politician, was born on 1 January 1754, the only son of Captain Edward Jekyll RN (*d.* 1776) of Haverfordwest, Pembrokeshire, and his wife, Elizabeth, the daughter of Thomas Walter of Killiver, Carmarthenshire, and the widow of John Williams of Pont-hywel, Carmarthenshire. Little is known of Jekyll's childhood, but he attended Westminster School from 1766 to 1770 and matriculated at Christ Church, Oxford, on 1 February 1771, whence he graduated BA in 1774 (MA, 1777). After graduation he spent a year in France, mostly at Blois, with the object of acquiring the French language. While in France he got to know several significant figures in French society, including the duchesse du Barry and the duc and duchesse de Choiseul. He returned to England in February 1776 and was called to the bar at Lincoln's Inn in May 1778.

Jekyll went on to practise on the western circuit and supplemented his legal earnings by writing pieces for newspapers such as the *Morning Chronicle* and the *Evening Statesman*. Commenting on his ability as a barrister, John Scott, first earl of Eldon, later wrote that Jekyll:

> in his practice as a common lawyer, was very successful, as many others have been, in diverting the attention of jurymen at county assizes, from thinking seriously in serious proceedings, by introducing observations and jokes, tending to turn all that was passing into the ridiculous. (Twiss, 1.351)

In 1782 there appeared in two volumes the *Letters of the Late Ignatius Sancho*, a former slave, to which was appended an anonymous 'Memoir' by Jekyll, which was not acknowledged overtly until the one-volume fifth edition of 1803. According to Jekyll, 'previous to the publication in 1782 Dr Johnson had promised to write the Life of Ignatius Sancho, which afterwords he neglected to do', whereupon Jekyll provided one 'in imitation of Dr Johnson's style' (*Letters of the late Ignatius Sancho*, introduction, vi).

On 20 August 1787 Jekyll was returned to the House of Commons for the borough of Calne, Wiltshire, upon the interest of William Petty, first marquess of Lansdowne. According to one of Lansdowne's biographers, 'the choice of Jekyll seems to have been largely influenced by an attack made in the House of Commons by [Richard Brinsley] Sheridan', which prompted Lansdowne to comment: 'if I go on in any political line, I foresee I must consider of some connection in a law line, who may be ready to answer such *bavardage*' (Fitzmaurice, 2.288). Whether

Joseph Jekyll (1754–1837), by George Dance, 1796

or not this was Lansdowne's motivation for returning Jekyll, his decision to do so was partly responsible for stimulating one of Lansdowne's circle, the philosopher Jeremy Bentham, to heights of indignation. In an extraordinary and lengthy letter of August 1787, Bentham chastised Lansdowne for his choice of men to represent his interest in parliament when better men such as himself were neglected. Bentham reserved particular ire for the return of Jekyll. He was prepared to agree that Jekyll was 'a very pretty poet, a man without his equal, perhaps for small talk and ready wit and repartee and powers of entertainment adapted to the taste of fashionable circles', but nevertheless he was a man wholly unfit for the role he had been handed in parliament or indeed any role 'in which there may occasionally be a demand for serious knowledge'. Despite this vitriolic outburst, Jekyll and Bentham appear to have been on relatively good terms subsequently, with Bentham sending Jekyll copies of his publications on occasion.

In parliament Jekyll followed the inclinations of his patron Lord Lansdowne and in his early years there voted in support of the ministry of William Pitt the younger, an old acquaintance from the bar. In 1790 he made another visit to Paris, where he moved in the circles of the leading figures of the early phase of the revolution, notably the comte de Mirabeau. While there Jekyll was responsible, if an anecdote that John Wilkes told to Lord Eldon is to be believed, for encouraging the revolutionaries to believe that they were enforcing the English constitution in France. In the same year Jekyll was elected a fellow of the

Royal Society (3 June) and a fellow of the Society of Antiquaries (16 December). By 1792, following his patron's move into opposition to the Pitt ministry, he had become a regular speaker in parliament on the opposition side of the Commons, and the latter part of the 1790 parliament saw him opposing the war with France, voting in favour of parliamentary reform, and criticizing measures such as the suspension of habeas corpus (1794) and the acts against treason and seditious meetings (1795) which the Pitt ministry introduced to control domestic radicalism. At the end of the parliamentary session of 1795 Jekyll was listed in the diary of Charles Abbot, the future speaker, as one of the most active members of the house. Abbot found him:

> first rate for convivial wit and pleasantry, and admired by all … but positively without weight even in his own party; rancorous in language, feeble in argument, and empty of ideas; few people applaud his rising, and everybody is glad when he sits down. (*Diary and Correspondence*, 1.24)

The parliament of 1790–96 was to be Jekyll's most active period as an MP, and his contributions to debate became less frequent particularly after 1801 and the fall of Pitt's first ministry.

On 20 August 1801 Jekyll married Maria, the daughter of Hans Sloane of South Stoneham, Hampshire, with whom he had two sons and a daughter. By the time of Pitt's return to power in 1804 he had been drawn into the circle of the prince of Wales (later George IV), and in February 1805 he became the prince's solicitor-general and took silk as a king's counsel. In the same year he became a bencher of the Inner Temple, to which he had transferred in 1795; he went on to be reader (1814) and treasurer (1816). During his tenure of the latter office he was responsible for restoring the Temple church, a building about which he had published a volume in 1811.

In the later years of his public life Jekyll devoted himself more to the law than to politics. In June 1815, through the intervention of the prince regent, he achieved a position that he had long desired, that of master in chancery. The lord chancellor at the time, Lord Eldon, had been extremely reluctant to appoint Jekyll (who since 1812 had been the prince's attorney-general) to a mastership in chancery on the grounds that his lack of previous experience in chancery work meant that he was 'totally unfit to discharge the duties of that office' (Twiss, 2.268)—an opinion with which Sir Samuel Romilly concurred. None the less, the prince regent called at Eldon's home, where the chancellor was bedridden with gout, and refused to leave until Eldon acquiesced in Jekyll's appointment, an appointment which caused 'great offence … to the gentlemen at the Chancery Bar' (ibid., 2.266). Nevertheless, as Lord Eldon later conceded, 'Jekyll got on capitally' as master in chancery, as a 'consciousness of his own want of ability led him in all difficult cases to consult two or three other Masters in Chancery; and, being guided by two or three experienced heads, he never got wrong' (ibid., 2.269). This appointment brought to a close Jekyll's parliamentary career, and he vacated his seat in February 1816. He retired from his mastership in March 1823 and spent his retirement entertaining the dinner tables of London. He died at his home in New Street, Spring Gardens, on 8 March 1837. If he is remembered by later generations, it is chiefly as a wit. It has to be said, however, that his wit, which consisted in large measure of excruciating puns, has not lasted well.   STEPHEN M. LEE

Sources R. G. Thorne, 'Jekyll, Joseph', HoP, *Commons, 1790–1820* · *The public and private life of Lord Chancellor Eldon, with selections from his correspondence*, ed. H. Twiss, 3 vols. (1844) · *Letters of the late Ignatius Sancho, an African*, 5th edn (1803); facs. repr. with introduction by P. Edwards (1968) · J. Jekyll, *Correspondence of Mr. Joseph Jekyll with his sister-in-law, Lady Gertrude Sloane Stanley, 1818–1838*, ed. A. Bourke (1894) · *The correspondence of Jeremy Bentham*, 4, ed. A. T. Milne (1981) · *GM*, 2nd ser., 8 (1837), 208 · *Life of William, earl of Shelburne … with extracts from his papers and correspondence*, ed. E. G. P. Fitzmaurice, 2nd edn, 2 vols. (1912) · *The diary and correspondence of Charles Abbot, Lord Colchester*, ed. Charles, Lord Colchester, 3 vols. (1861) · S. Romilly, *Memoirs of the life of Sir Samuel Romilly*, 3 vols. (1840) · *The correspondence of George, prince of Wales, 1770–1812*, ed. A. Aspinall, 8 vols. (1963–71) · *The Farington diary*, ed. J. Greig, 8 vols. (1922–8) · *The journal of Elizabeth, Lady Holland, 1791–1811*, ed. earl of Ilchester [G. S. Holland Fox-Strangways], 2 vols. (1908) · L. B. Namier, 'Jekyll, Joseph', HoP, *Commons, 1754–90*
Archives BL, letters to Lord Holland and Lady Holland, Add. MS 51594 · BL, letters to Sir James Scarlett and others, index of MSS, V, 1985 · Dorset RO, letters to Nathaniel Bond, D367
Likenesses G. Dance, pencil drawing, 1796, NPG [*see illus.*] · J. Sayers, double portrait, caricature, etching, 1798 (with Lord Lansdowne), NPG · T. Lawrence, portrait, *c.*1816–1817, repro. in Jekyll, *Correspondence* · W. Say, mezzotint, pubd 1818 (after T. Lawrence), BM, NPG

Jekyll, Thomas (1570–1652), antiquary, was born on 12 January 1570 in the parish of St Helen, Bishopsgate, London, the third of five sons of John Stocker Jekyll (*d.* 1598), attorney, of Clement's Inn, London, latterly of Bocking, Essex, and Mary (*d.* 1617), daughter of Nicholas Barnehouse, burgess and white tanner of Bristol. He became an attorney of Clifford's Inn, London, and subsequently a secondary of the king's bench. Before 1603 he married Elizabeth (1575–1658), daughter of Richard Leake, of a legal family, of Norton Twycross, Leicestershire, and his wife, Elizabeth Hyll, and had five sons and three daughters, of whom the second child was baptized at Bocking in 1604; one of his sons was John *Jekyll (1611–1690).

It is likely that Jekyll consorted with members of the Society of Antiquaries which flourished between about 1588 and about 1608. Although his name does not appear in surviving lists, it was apparently believed by his grandson Nicholas Jekyll of Castle Hedingham, Essex, as quoted by Arthur Collins in 1735, that Thomas Jekyll 'was of the Club of Antiquaries with Camden, Selden, Sir Robert Cotton, and others' (*Dartmouth MSS*). Certainly from 1611 to 1642 he 'liv'd in great familiarite with Dr. John Barkham, Dean of Bocking, who was very well verst in the knowledge of antiquity' (Essex RO, T/P195/14, Holman's Bocking notes, 88). In 1627, the year he became chief clerk of the paper office of king's bench, the preamble to a confirmation of armorials describes Jekyll as a 'Lover of Antiquities … and the Mathematical Sciences … acquainted with Camden and other famous Antiquaries of that time' (BL, Add. MSS 12225, fol. 121). At the heralds' visitation of Essex in 1632, Jekyll was allowed to simplify a

coat of arms granted to his great-grandfather, William Jekyll. At the same time his claim to quarter Barnehouse, Stocker, and Britrixton was recognized. His memory was still recalled in Bocking early in the next century:

> Though he was no Lord of any Manor in this Towne, nor in his life time made any great figure in the world, as loving a recluse and studious way of Life, yet deserves a Remembrance … he settled here, and lived at the corner House of Church Lane. (Essex RO, T/P195/14, 86)

Jekyll assembled—and in some cases compiled—much manuscript material relating to the history of East Anglia, especially Essex. Whether he intended to publish a county history seems uncertain.

Jekyll died in Bocking on 17 August 1652. His widow, who was granted administration of his estate on 13 May 1653, survived until 6 March 1657. Both were buried in the chancel of Bocking church, where their youngest son, Nicholas Jekyll (*d.* 1683), also of Clifford's Inn, and of Castle Hedingham, Essex, erected an informative memorial tablet.

Jekyll had apparently made no provision for the future of his large collection of manuscripts. In the event, by circuitous routes, they passed into various collections at the Bodleian Library and the British Library, some of them at the latter's foundation in 1753. Meanwhile several local historians made significant use of them. William Holman (*d.* 1730), nonconformist minister and researcher, listed some of them in 1715, while Nicholas Tindal used them for the two small parts of his intended history of Essex which appeared in 1732. Nathaniel Salmon (*d.* 1742), who bought a substantial number of them in the 1730s, brought out from 1738 to 1742 sections of a *History of Essex from the Collections of Thomas Jekyll and Others*, amounting to 460 pages but still appreciably incomplete. Philip Morant of Colchester was heavily dependent on Jekyll's work for his *History of Essex* (1768), acknowledging in the preface his own and others' debt in the remark that Jekyll was 'the person who laid the first foundation' of all their work.

                                                      J. S. REYNOLDS

Sources C. F. D. Sperling, *Essex Review*, 3 (1894), 245–61 · Holman's Bocking notes, Essex RO, T/P195/14, 86–8, 106–7 · Bocking burial register, 1655–70, Essex RO, D/P268/1/2 · BL, Add MSS 12225, B.2 (Aspidora Segariana), fol. 121 · J. H. Baker, *The legal profession and the common law: historical essays* (1986), 81–5 · Bodl. Oxf., MS Rawl. Essex 1, vol. 1, fols. 77, 82, 83; Essex 22 (Jekyll family) · *First register of St Mary's Church, Bocking*, ed. J. J. Goodwin (1903) · J. Guillim, *A display of heraldry*, 6th edn (1724), 158–9 · *An inventory of the historical monuments in Essex*, Royal Commission on Historical Monuments (England), 1 (1916), 32 · W. C. Metcalfe, ed., *The visitations of Essex*, 1, Harleian Society, 13 (1878), 427 · P. Morant, *The history and antiquities of the county of Essex*, 2 vols. (1768) · PRO, PROB 6/30, fol. 40 [administration to Jekyll's widow] · PRO, PROB 11/36 [N. Barnehouse, will] · A. R. Wagner, *English genealogy* (1960), 319, 330 · A. P. Burke, *Family records* (1897), 347–50 · *The manuscripts of the earl of Dartmouth*, 3 vols., HMC, 20 (1887–96), vol. 1, p. 328
Archives BL, collections for a history of Essex, Add. MSS 19985–19989 | All Souls Oxf., Holman's list of some of Jekyll's MSS, 1715, no. 297 · BL, Egerton MSS · BL, Harley MSS · BL, Stowe MSS · Bodl. Oxf., Holman collection · Bodl. Oxf., Rawl. MSS · Essex RO, Chelmsford, Holman MSS

Jekyll, Thomas (1646–1698), Church of England clergyman, was born on 16 July 1646 and baptized on 3 August

1646 in the parish of St Stephen Walbrook, London, the eldest son of John *Jekyll (1611–1690), a freeman of the Fishmongers' Company but by trade a wealthy haberdasher, and his first wife, Elizabeth *Jekyll, *née* Ward (*bap.* 1624, *d.* 1653) [*see under* Jekyll, John]. The lawyer and politician Sir Joseph *Jekyll was his stepbrother. He entered Merchant Taylors' School, London, in 1652 and was admitted commoner of Trinity College, Oxford, on 4 September 1663. Jekyll graduated BA on 4 July 1667 and proceeded MA on 11 May 1670. He was ordained deacon by the bishop of Lincoln on 18 December 1670. In 1671 he became vicar of Rowde in Wiltshire. The London Haberdashers' Company had presented him to its lectureship at Newland, Gloucestershire, by February 1678 when the parish register recorded the baptism of Triphena, the first of his three children baptized there; two sons, Thomas and Richard, followed in March 1679 and June 1680. These were probably not the first children born to Thomas and his wife Elizabeth: his son and heir John evidently had already been baptized elsewhere. By 1682 he had returned to London as minister of the New Church in the parish of St Margaret, Westminster. Jekyll remained close to his nonconformist father, who in his will, made in 1683, acknowledged that his 'dutifulnesse and obedience hath been a renewed and continued comfort to mee' (will, PRO, PROB 11/401, sig. 155, fol. 170v).

Jekyll's published sermons present a clergyman who viewed his vocation as a moral crusade against the impiety and the cultured apostasy which in his opinion had generated the beast of party politics. But his career may not have been as politically quiescent as his sermons protest. Given his father's presbyterianism and close connections with the whig political machine in London, it was not surprising that Thomas took a solidly whig line. Despite attacking party politics as the product of impiety he seems to have entered partisan debate, albeit repeatedly stressing his moderation to defend himself from its heats. While at Rowde, Jekyll preached in Bristol twice a year, 'In obedience to the Commands of a Person, to whom I am beholden for a very Liberal Education, and a great deal more too' (Jekyll, *Peace and Love*, 'To the reader', sig. A2r), this being possibly a reference to an unknown Bristol patron, but more probably to his father; the latter had longstanding links with the city, having been captured there when it fell to the royalists in 1643, and in the 1670s acting as a London agent for its nonconformist congregations. These sermons routinely offended some of his auditors. Before preaching there on 31 January 1675 he was mobbed, sent to the mayor, and accused of serious, even capital, crimes. To vindicate himself Jekyll published the sermons which he claimed he was to deliver there, *Peace and Love, Recommended and Perswaded* (1675). These denied God's intent to fulfil his prophecies of conflict, denied man's role in effecting them, and recommended the 'golden rule'. Such antimillennialism and his apparently nonpartisan moral criticisms made Jekyll useful to his whig patrons between 1678 and 1682, but even in print he could not always resist criticizing the government.

A sermon he delivered at Newland privately on the fast day of 22 December 1680 safely affirmed the reality of the Popish Plot, but it also insinuated that Catholics about Newland were being tolerated and indulged far beyond the limits retained for protestant nonconformists, and charged that local authorities were not even searching Catholics' houses for arms. Upon hearing of the sermon the local JP sent the vicar of Newland to Jekyll in order to explain himself, and Jekyll again resorted to print to distance himself from the 'faction' sympathetic to whigs, republicans, and protestant nonconformists (Jekyll, *Popery*, preface, sig. A4v). Preaching before the exclusionist and dissenter lord mayor of London Sir Patience Ward on 25 September 1681, Jekyll only lamented the controversies surrounding toleration, comprehension, and further reformation of the church, and vowed to 'leave all things of this nature to my superiors' (Jekyll, *Righteousness and Peace*, 28). But less than a year later, Jekyll found himself even more clearly at the centre of whig activity. He was scheduled to preach at St Michael Cornhill on 21 April 1682, before a feast that would be attended by the whig leaders the earl of Shaftesbury, the duke of Monmouth, and the earl of Essex at Haberdashers' Hall, the home of Jekyll's patrons. On 19 April the privy council at Whitehall banned the feast as a seditious assembly, and on 21 April it placed four companies of trained bands, constables, and watchmen throughout the City. No trouble ensued, but Jekyll took no chances. Having been publicly identified with the whigs he delivered what he claimed was the intended April sermon at the New Church on 29 May, the king's birthday, the anniversary of the Restoration and a tory holiday which in 1682 was 'kept more strict then formerly' (Luttrell, 1.190). Jekyll protested that he was not a man of 'those dangerous Anti-monarchical Principles as some men would endeavour to make the World believe', but it is impossible to know how far the sermon Jekyll had originally planned was indeed the sermon that he delivered in May and published as *True Religion Makes the Best Loyalty* (Jekyll, *True religion*, 40). It identified rebellion, faction, and regicide as popish inventions, and declared protestantism and English government to be inseparable; Jekyll urged his audience to venerate the king as sacred and submit to him in the spirit of the primitive Christians.

Jekyll's defensiveness in print reveals the success of the tory smear campaign against the whigs; he published his sermons in the 1670s and 1680s to distance himself from his patrons, and in each case their settings were far more controversial than the printed sermons themselves. If Jekyll had something to hide, print helped him do so. Concerned with the rise of Catholic schools following the accession of James II, and mindful to imitate his influential neighbour, Thomas Tenison, rector of St Martin-in-the-Fields, Jekyll founded an Anglican school for fifty poor children, which was financed by the parishioners of the New Church. In 1694 he proceeded DD from Sidney Sussex College, Cambridge. He was a supporter of the philanthropic and moral reform movements of the 1690s. In 1697 he delivered a sermon, *Publick Charity*, before the lord mayor and governors of the City hospitals, and in the following year he preached to the societies for the reformation of manners.

Jekyll died in London in the first week of October 1698. He was able to die spiritually prepared, calling his friends, wife, and children to him one by one, 'and giving each of them such advice as a dying Friend, Husband and father, and a dying Christian, would give to those whom he affectionately loved' (Williams, 22). By his deathbed will, made on 2 October, he made careful provision for his family. By then he had three sons and five daughters (two of the latter had been baptized at St Margaret's, Westminster, in June 1683 and July 1684) and, concerned that 'my estate is but small and my Children many', he directed that no mourning gifts be distributed to his kin. To his 'most dear and beloved wife (one of the best of women)' he left his whole estate (will, PRO, PROB 11/447, fol. 292r). After her death all his children (apart from one daughter who had already received her marriage portion) were to receive £500 apiece, with the proviso that any who proved undutiful to their mother would receive only 5 s. He was buried in the New Church on 7 October. The conflict over his successor at the New Church began the next day, the impropriation being worth £300 per annum.

Jekyll's funeral sermon was delivered by his friend John Williams, bishop of Chichester. Williams and another bishop, White Kennett, remembered Jekyll not for his earlier sermons and the political climate which compelled him to publish them, but for his service to the school which he founded and with which he remained involved for the rest of his life. The catechism he produced for the school's use, *A Brief and Plain Exposition of the Church-Catechism*, first published in 1690, had gone through four editions by 1700.   BURKE GRIGGS

Sources Foster, *Alum. Oxon.* · Wood, *Ath. Oxon.*, new edn, 4.681–3 · will, PRO, PROB 11/447, sig. 216 [Thomas Jekyll] · will, PRO, PROB 11/401, sig. 155 [John Jekyll, father] · IGI · N. Luttrell, *A brief historical relation of state affairs from September 1678 to April 1714*, 6 vols. (1857), vols. 1, 4 · *DNB* · T. Jekyll, *Peace and love, recommended and perswaded* (1675) · J. Williams, *A sermon preach'd at the funeral of … Thomas Jekyll* (1698) · T. Jekyll, *Popery a great mystery of iniquity* (1681) · T. Jekyll, *Righteousness and peace the best means to prevent ruin* (1681) · T. Jekyll, *True religion makes the best loyalty* (1682) · T. Jekyll, *Publick charity* (1697) · T. Jekyll, *A sermon preach'd at St Mary-le-Bow, June 27, 1698, before the societies, for reformation of manners in the city of London and Westminster* (1698) · J. Spurr, *The Restoration Church of England* (1992) · T. Harris, *London crowds in the reign of Charles II* (1987) · D. Cressy, *Bonfires and bells: national memory and the protestant calendar in Elizabethan and Stuart England* (1989)

Wealth at death see will, PRO, PROB 11/447, sig. 216

Jelf, George Edward (1834–1908), Church of England clergyman and author, was born on 29 January 1834 in Berlin, the eldest son of the seven children of Richard William *Jelf (1798–1871) and Emmy, Countess Schlippenbach (1802–1878), lady-in-waiting to Frederica, duchess of Cumberland. His father was tutor to Prince George of Cumberland and subsequently principal of King's College, London. His uncle was the scholar William Edward Jelf; his younger brothers were the Hon. Sir Arthur Richard Jelf, judge of the High Court, and Colonel Richard Henry Jelf,

governor of the Royal Military Academy, Woolwich. Educated at preparatory schools at Hammersmith and Brighton, Jelf was admitted to Charterhouse in 1847, and matriculated at Christ Church, Oxford, on 2 June 1852. He held a studentship at Christ Church from 1852 to 1861, and won a first class in classical moderations in 1854. He graduated BA with a third class in *literae humaniores* in 1856 (MA 1859, DD 1907). In 1857 he entered Wells Theological College, and was ordained deacon in 1858 and priest in 1859. He held curacies at St Michael's, Highgate (1858–60) and St James's, Clapton (1860–66), and a senior curacy at Aylesbury (1866–8). On the presentation of Roundell Palmer, first earl of Selborne, he became vicar of the newly constituted parish of Blackmoor, Hampshire, in 1868, and in 1874 he accepted from Lord Braybrooke the living of Saffron Walden. In 1878 he was made an honorary canon of St Albans.

Jelf's long connection with Rochester began with his appointment in 1880 to a residentiary canonry, a position he held for twenty-seven years. He continued his parish work at Saffron Walden until 1882, and from 1883 to 1889 he had charge of St Mary's, Chatham; subsequently he devoted himself to mission work in the diocese, although he was forced to take on extra duties to supplement his income. Following a brief tenure of the rectory of Wiggonholt, near Pulborough (1896–7), Jelf accepted the incumbency of the proprietary chapel of St German's, Blackheath, where he enjoyed comparative freedom from parochial responsibilities. In 1904 he resigned this benefice and retired to Rochester. But in 1907 he was appointed master of Charterhouse. His health, however, failed soon after moving to London.

Jelf married in 1861 Fanny (d. 1865), daughter of G. A. Crawley of Highgate. They had one son, who survived him, and three daughters, who all died of scarlet fever in 1871. He remarried in 1876; his new wife was Katherine Frances, younger daughter of prebendary C. B. Dalton, vicar of St Michael's, Highgate, who survived him. They had three sons and four daughters.

A moderate high-churchman, Jelf was a trusted friend and godson of Edward Bouverie Pusey, whose *Christus consolator* (1883) he edited. From 1895 he acted as proctor in convocation for the dean and chapter of Rochester, where he was active in promoting missions, religious education, and clergy training. His concerns were pastoral and devotional rather than academic, and he exercised considerable influence as a popular preacher and missioner, and through his numerous popular homiletic publications, of which the most important are *The Secret Trials of the Christian Life* (1873), *The Rule of God's Commandments* (1878), *The Consolations of the Christian Seasons* (1880), *Work and Worship* (1888), *Mother, Home and Heaven* (1891), and *Sound Words, their Form and Spirit* (1907).

Jelf died on 19 November 1908 at the master's lodge, Charterhouse. The funeral service was held at Charterhouse on 23 November, and he was buried in Highgate cemetery. On the same day a memorial service was held in Rochester Cathedral.   G. S. WOODS, *rev.* PETER DAVIE

Sources K. F. Jelf, *George Edward Jelf: a memoir* (1909) · *The Times* (20 Nov 1908) · *The Guardian* (25 Nov 1908) · *Chatham and Rochester News* (21 Nov 1908) · R. Palmer, first earl of Selborne, *Memorials. Part II: personal and political, 1865–1895*, ed. S. M. Palmer, 2 vols. (1898)
Archives Bodl. Oxf., letters to Kitty Bickersteth, poem · LPL, corresp. with Lord Selborne
Likenesses photograph, repro. in Jelf, *George Edward Jelf*, frontispiece
Wealth at death £6458 10s. 10d.: probate, 12 Dec 1908, CGPLA Eng. & Wales

Jelf, Richard William (1798–1871), college head, born on 25 January 1798, at Gloucester, was the second son of Sir James Jelf (1763–1842), and his wife, Mary (d. 1850), daughter of George Kidman. He was brother of William Edward *Jelf. His father was a partner in the Gloucester Old Bank, and mayor of Gloucester in 1814, the year of his knighthood. Jelf was educated at Eton College, where he began a lifelong friendship with E. B. Pusey. In December 1816 he matriculated from Christ Church, Oxford, where he graduated BA (with a second class in classics) in 1820, MA in 1823, BD in 1831, and DD in 1839. In 1820 he was elected fellow of Oriel, he took holy orders in 1821, and in 1823 he became one of the tutors. He was master of the schools in 1824 and classical examiner in 1825. After being for a short time private tutor to Sir George Nugent, Jelf was in 1826 appointed, on the recommendation of Charles Lloyd, bishop of Oxford, to the position of preceptor to Prince George, duke of Cumberland, afterwards king of Hanover (1851–66). He held this office for thirteen years, residing much at Berlin before his pupil's father became king of Hanover (February 1837). In 1830 he was appointed canon of Christ Church, Oxford. He married on 17 July 1830 Emmy, Countess Schlippenbach (1802–1878), tenth child of Carl, Count Schlippenbach. They had seven children, the eldest of whom was the clergyman and author George Edward *Jelf. His wife was lady-in-waiting to Frederica, duchess of Cumberland.

Jelf never took a prominent part in the Oxford Movement, but was so much respected for his impartiality that both his friend Pusey and Newman addressed to him their respective letters on the interpretation of the Thirty-Nine Articles, advocated in Tract 90 (1841), and he attempted to act as a mediator in some of the disputes connected with the movement. In 1842 he preached a sermon before the university, which was published with the title *Via media, or, The Church of England our Providential Path between Romanism and Dissent*, a reassertion of the traditional Anglican position in the face of Tractarian innovations. The following year he was appointed one of the six doctors to examine and report on Pusey's sermon, with the result that Pusey was suspended from preaching for two years. Jelf gave the Bampton lectures at Oxford in 1844, his subject being 'An inquiry into the means of grace, their mutual connection and combined use, with especial reference to the Church of England'. He became a frequent contributor to the *English Review*, a high-church periodical, edited by William Palmer (1803–1885).

In 1844 Jelf succeeded John Lonsdale as principal of King's College, London. The first decade of his administration was one of prosperity for the college. His principal achievement was the founding of a theological department in 1846. In 1848 he published an edition of Bishop Jewel's works in eight volumes. He became involved in a serious controversy when F. D. Maurice, the professor of theology, published his *Theological Essays* in 1853. Jelf, who was determined to maintain the high-church character of the college, condemned Maurice's views, and the council deprived Maurice of his professorship. Though much criticized, Jelf handled Maurice with more patience than was often acknowledged. In 1861 he took a leading part in the proceedings in convocation against the authors of *Essays and Reviews*.

During Jelf's last years as principal, King's College was in decline and facing mounting debt. His resignation in 1868 followed a report by the college council which implied criticism of his administration. He was for many years proctor in convocation for the chapter of Christ Church, and also sub-almoner to the queen. After his resignation from King's College, he lived in the house attached to his canonry at Oxford, where he died on 19 September 1871. He left behind him a series of *Lectures on the Thirty-Nine Articles*, which were edited after his death, in 1873, by his son-in-law, the Revd J. R. King.

W. A. GREENHILL, *rev.* M. C. CURTHOYS

Sources *The Guardian* (20 Sept 1871) · Boase, *Mod. Eng. biog.* · G. C. Richards and C. L. Shadwell, *The provosts and fellows of Oriel College, Oxford* (1922) · I. Ellis, *Seven against Christ: a study of 'Essays and reviews'* (1980) · F. J. C. Hearnshaw, *The centenary history of King's College, London, 1828–1928* (1929) · P. B. Nockles, *The Oxford Movement in context: Anglican high churchmanship, 1760–1857* (1994) · *GM*, 1st ser., 100/2 (1830), 175
Archives BL, corresp. with W. E. Gladstone, Add. MSS 44362–44413, *passim* · LPL, corresp. with A. C. Tait · Pusey Oxf., letters to T. Henderson · Pusey Oxf., letters to E. B. Pusey
Likenesses T. H. Maguire, lithograph, pubd 1850, BM
Wealth at death under £25,000: probate, 13 Oct 1871, CGPLA Eng. & Wales

Jelf, William Edward (1811–1875), Church of England clergyman and classical scholar, born in the city of Gloucester on 3 April 1811, was fifth son of Sir James Jelf (1763–1842), and his wife, Mary (d. 1850), daughter of George Kidman; he was brother of Richard William *Jelf. He was educated at Eton College, then matriculated from Christ Church, Oxford, in July 1829, and was elected a student on the nomination of E. B. Pusey in the same year. He gained a first class in classics at the Easter examination, 1833, graduated BA in 1833, MA in 1836, and BD in 1844, and was ordained in 1834. From 1836 to 1849 he was tutor of Christ Church, and for a time was senior censor. He was master of the schools, 1839; classical examiner, 1840, 1841, 1855, and 1856; proctor of the university, 1843; select preacher, 1855; and classical moderator, 1862, 1863. Although he discharged his duties conscientiously, faults of temper and manner rendered him as proctor and senior censor (university and college disciplinary offices respectively) unpopular with undergraduates. Their noisy protest against his regime as proctor, at the Oxford encaenia ceremony in 1843, was unusually vehement.

Jelf had a higher reputation as a classical tutor, Algernon Freeman-Mitford (first Baron Redesdale) being among his grateful pupils. His most important literary work was his Greek grammar, first published in two volumes, in 1842–5, with the title, *A Grammar of the Greek Language, Chiefly from the German of Raphael Kühner*. It was at once recognized as a substantial improvement on existing Greek grammars in the English language, and passed through at least five editions. In the later editions Jelf's own part of the work became so extensive that he thought himself justified in omitting Kühner's name from the title-page. His *Notes to Aristotle's Ethics* (1856) was less well received, hostile reviewers (who included Mark Pattison in the *Saturday Review*, 8 March 1856) pointing out its origin in the routine teaching in Oxford lectures and its preoccupation with 'petty construings and bald technicalities'.

Jelf left Oxford in 1849, relinquishing his studentship at Christ Church, to become vicar of Carleton, near Skipton, in Yorkshire (a college living). He married, on 5 July 1849, Maria Katherine, daughter of John Hayes Petit (1771–1822), of Coton Hall, Alveley, Shropshire. They had six children. He remained at Carleton until 1854, when he moved to Cae'rdeon, near Barmouth, in north Wales. He held no church preferment there, but officiated in a church built on his own property, which was eventually consecrated and endowed as a district church in 1875.

Jelf was, like his brother, an orthodox high-churchman of the pre-Tractarian sort. In 1857 he delivered the Bampton lectures at Oxford on 'The Christian faith comprehensive and definite', and he contributed to *Faith and Peace* (1862) the orthodox retort to the liberal *Essays and Reviews*. He attacked Frederick Temple's contribution to the latter collection for attempting to assert the supremacy of reason over scripture. Latterly, in a number of publications, he fiercely attacked ritualism (1873)—describing himself as 'a high churchman of the old school'—secession to Rome (1873), confession (1875), and the practices of the Roman Catholic church (posthumously in 1876). He left the materials for a commentary on the first epistle of John, which was published with the Greek text in 1877, under the editorship of W. Webster.

The last few months of Jelf's life were passed at Hastings Lodge, Hastings, where he died on 18 October 1875. His wife survived him.

W. A. GREENHILL, rev. M. C. CURTHOYS

Sources *The Guardian* (27 Oct 1875) · *The Guardian* (3 Nov 1875) · Foster, *Alum. Oxon.* · W. E. Jelf, *Remarks on some criticisms in the Guardian* (1856) · Lord Redesdale [A. B. Freeman-Mitford], *Memories*, 2 vols. (1915) · W. Tuckwell, *Reminiscences of Oxford*, 2nd edn (1907) · *CGPLA Eng. & Wales* (1875) · m. cert. · M. G. Brock and M. C. Curthoys, eds., *Nineteenth-century Oxford*, pt 1 (1997)
Archives BL, corresp. with W. E. Gladstone, Add. MSS 44366–44390
Wealth at death under £18,000: probate, 2 Dec 1875, *CGPLA Eng. & Wales*

Jelfe, Andrews (*c*.1690–1759), masonry contractor and architect, was one of at least two sons of William Jelfe (*c*.1660–1721), a carpenter, of South Weald, Essex, and his wife, Mary, *née* Andrews (*c*.1668–1748). On 2 August 1704 he was apprenticed to Edward Strong junior, one of a family of Burford-based masons who had profited greatly from the rebuilding of London after the great fire. In 1705 the

Strongs took the chief masonry contract for the construction of Blenheim Palace, where their foreman was Christopher Cass. Cass later joined with Joshua Fletcher (*d*. 1725), foreman to Henry Banks, who had taken another masonry contract at Blenheim, but after Fletcher's death he formed another partnership with Strong and Jelfe. Strong withdrew in 1728, but Cass and Jelfe continued in partnership until the former's death, whereupon Jelfe inherited a well-established business with a considerable workforce. He married and had at least two sons and a daughter.

The partners' business was founded less upon the increasing number of brick and timber houses in the West End of London (which enriched many contemporary bricklayers and carpenters), than upon the concurrent increase in public buildings, for which stone, usually Portland, was invariably regarded as more appropriate than brick. The largest proportion of these were churches, built under the Fifty New Churches Act of 1711 and still being constructed as late as 1730, when Cass and Jelfe sought payment for their work at St Alfege, Greenwich, and St George, Hanover Square. Cass gained the contracts for a number of buildings designed by James Gibbs (one of the surveyors to the Fifty New Churches commission), notably St Martin-in-the-Fields Church, the Senate House of Cambridge University, and the Fellows' Building of King's College, Cambridge. They set up a yard in Cambridge whence they rebuilt Waresley church, Huntingdon, refronted Trinity Hall, and refloored the chapel of Magdalene College.

The Cambridge yard also ran a quarry at Burwell and dispatched clunch from it, with other (finished) work, by river. In 1734–5 it employed a total of twenty-eight men, although never more than twelve at any time, and an average of about six. After Cass died it only undertook small jobs, including gravestones, marble tables, and chimneypieces. When John Ogle, the foreman, died in 1735, Jelfe closed it altogether, although he had undertaken masonry work at a few private houses in the area, including Gogmagog Hall, Exning Park, Hinchingbrooke Hall, and Abington Lodge. Private commissions thereafter were presumably executed from the yard which he obtained from the Westminster Bridge commissioners, approximately on the site of Big Ben. They included an ionic temple at Shirburn Castle, Oxfordshire, in 1741, carved ornament at Holkham Hall, Norfolk, in 1742, and masonry at Woodcote Park, Surrey, in 1753. They also included work on four houses belonging to the architect Nicholas Hawksmoor, and his gravestone in Shenley churchyard, Hertfordshire. However, these contracts were small by comparison to those he had undertaken with Cass; on Sir Robert Walpole's new stables at Houghton Hall, Norfolk, for instance, they had employed sixty-nine men in 1733–5, while simultaneously running another contract at Wolterton Hall in the same county, for Sir Robert's brother, Lord Walpole.

Jelfe had, however, developed contacts with central government, initially the armed forces. Five years after obtaining his freedom of the City as a mason he began to be employed as a surveyor or architect for the Board of Ordnance, whose services, in the aftermath of the rebellion of 1715, were much in demand. From 1716 to 1719 he provided the board's drawing office in the Tower of London with 'draughts of buildings and fortifications'. From 1719 to 1727 he held the post of architect to the board. In this capacity he was posted first to the north of the country, completing the barracks designed by Hawksmoor at Berwick and by James Smith at Kilwhimen and Inversnaid. He designed further fortifications at Edinburgh Castle and built barracks at Bernera, Blackness, Dumbarton, Stirling, Ruthven, Inverness, and Fort William. In 1720 he was transferred to the western division, where he supervised the construction of the gun wharf and its officers' houses at Morice Yard, Devonport, possibly to his own design, but considerably influenced by Hawksmoor. At Pendennis Castle, Falmouth, he measured and made up accounts in 1722. In 1727 he was replaced by James Gibbs as architect to the board, but it continued to employ him as a masonry contractor. In 1734 he repaired the fortifications of Portsmouth Town, the governor's house, powder magazine, the storehouse and storekeeper's house in the gun wharf there, and the breakwater at Calshot Castle. In 1735 he undertook the masonry work in converting St Thomas's Tower at the Tower of London into an infirmary.

By that date Jelfe had largely replaced his income from the Board of Ordnance with earnings from the Board of Works. He had held a post in the office of works even before he began to provide designs for the Ordnance; from 1715 to 1718 he had been clerk of works at Newmarket Palace and from 1715 to 1728 he had been clerk itinerant, but the works did not offer him any masonry contracts during the 1720s. His first contract from that source was for the Hermitage in Richmond Park, built for Queen Caroline in 1730 to the design of William Kent. Kent was the architect of nearly all the Board of Works' buildings of which Jelfe was the masonry contractor—the Cumberland apartment at Hampton Court Palace (1732), the stable in the Royal Mews (1732-3), the Treasury building (1733-7), Queen Caroline's Library at St James's Palace (1736-7), Queen Caroline's sarcophagus beneath Henry VII's chapel (1737), and the Horse Guards' Building (1750-59). Only the additional knights' stalls in Henry VII's Chapel, Westminster Abbey, formed in 1733, and the keeper's house in the Royal Mews, built in 1750, were designed by other architects, probably Henry Flitcroft in the first case, and certainly James Paine in the second.

Jelfe's third source of income from public works was provided by the construction of Westminster Bridge, in which he had earlier displayed considerable commercial interest. In 1726 he obtained the masonry contract for the proposal designed by Thomas Ripley. When that proposal was revived in 1736, Jelfe petitioned to be allowed to build a trial pier. In 1737 he was among those who provided the technical evidence on Ripley's design. He was prepared to work to it, but equally prepared to work to the design put forward in 1738 by Charles Labelye, and eventually executed. For this purpose he went into partnership with Samuel Tufnell, master mason of Westminster Abbey, and between June 1738 and February 1750 they took out ten different contracts to build the bridge, stage by stage, including parapets, semi-octagonal domed recesses on the footway, paving, the paving of the newly laid-out Parliament Street (which approached it from the north-west), and the repair of the pier, which had sunk in the course of construction, to the delight of the press. Jelfe encountered still greater difficulties in procuring a constant supply of Portland stone, increased by the freezing of the Thames in 1741, impressment of seamen for the war with Spain, and the deviousness of the quarry owners at Weymouth. As the masonry contractor at Houghton he was known to Sir Robert Walpole, and a peremptory letter from the Treasury to the quarry owners (who were crown tenants) ameliorated that problem.

Jelfe was not a significant building speculator. He may have been part of the 'Christopher Cass & Co.' who worked on Lord Bristol's house in St James's Square in 1732, and he executed masonry for Sir John Evelyn at his house in St James's Place in 1740. Otherwise his only known London houses were for the commissioners of Westminster Bridge. In 1740 he leased land surplus to that needed for the construction of the western approach, between Bridge Street and New Palace Yard. On this he built thirteen houses (including an inn), his only known speculation, undertaken together with the architect Roger Morris. In 1748 Jelfe acquired the freehold, eventually bequeathing it to his elder son, Captain Andrews Jelfe RN. In 1750 he built a house in Abingdon Buildings (later Abingdon Street) as an office for the commissioners, and it is possible that he built other houses in this street and Parliament Street.

Jelfe took five apprentices, Peter Phillips (1728), Thomas Gaffer or Gayfere (1734), Thomas Waterfall (1739), George Banks (1739), and William Jelfe (1739). He had an evidently trusted foreman at Houghton, Henry Bowman, whom he may have inherited from Cass. Thomas Roper, one of his Cambridge masons, was sent to Portland to be Jelfe's agent at the quarries during the construction of Westminster Bridge. Gayfere (c.1721–1812), son of a Westminster mason (and later the father of an antiquarian-minded architect), was immediately employed to audit the accounts of the Cambridge yard; later he was Jelfe's foreman on Westminster Bridge, and in 1766 he became master mason to Westminster Abbey in succession to Tufnell. William Jelfe (c.1725–71) was the orphaned son of Jelfe's younger brother William (c.1694–1726), a goldsmith and clockmaker in the City. At Andrews Jelfe's death he was in partnership with his nephew William, and he left him his stock-in-trade, all his tools, and a 21-year lease of the Westminster yard. William Jelfe continued his business, working for both the Board of Works and the Board of Ordnance, and executed masonry at Stourhead, Wiltshire, to Flitcroft's design.

Jelfe, who died in 1759, was lucky to have a poor dependant to continue his business. For his children he had higher ambitions. In 1747 he had bought Pendell or Pondhill House at Bletchingley, Surrey, a decent gentry house dating from about 1650. He left this to his eldest son, together with the thirteen houses between Bridge Street and Old Palace Yard, Westminster. In 1738 he had lived in the parish of St Martin-in-the-Fields, but in 1756 he occupied a house on the east side of Old Palace Yard adjacent to his yard; he left this to his daughter Elizabeth, who was married to the timber merchant Griffin Ransom, plus the freehold of his yard and its buildings, and £10,000 above the £5000 he was bound to pay her by her marriage articles. To his younger son, William, 'who has proved very idle & extravagant' (Colvin, *Archs.*, 543), he left £10,000 and £5000 in trust. Captain Andrews Jelfe and Francis Tregagle were the trustees and the former was the residuary legatee.

Jelfe is of interest for more than his evidently successful business career. He designed some of the buildings whose masonry he executed, particularly those for the Board of Ordnance, for which he employed the simplified Roman style developed by Hawksmoor and Sir John Vanbrugh; he is alleged also to have designed the court house at Rye, Sussex (1743), built largely at the expense of the borough's MPs, Phillips Gybbon and Admiral of the Fleet Sir John Norris. He was a friend of the antiquary William Stukeley (who drew a portrait of him), and he provided Stukeley, who was vicar of All Saints', Stamford, with designs for at least one of his friends there. While working in Scotland in 1719 he supplied Stukeley with measured drawings of the Roman monument known as Arthur's O'on, and while at Plymouth in 1722 he promised Stukeley measured drawings of the Roman amphitheatre at Dorchester. He may have designed the granite monument to Christopher Cass in the burial-ground of St John's Westminster, which resembles a Roman tomb. He almost certainly designed the sarcophagus, also of granite, which he erected to the memory of his family in South Weald churchyard and which also has an antique appearance. His will directed that he was to be buried under or near it.

RICHARD HEWLINGS

Sources Colvin, *Archs.* • R. Gunnis, *Dictionary of British sculptors, 1660–1851* (1953), 88–9, 218, 401 • H. M. Colvin and others, eds., *The history of the king's works*, 3 (1975) • R. J. B. Walker, *Old Westminster Bridge: the bridge of fools* (c.1979) • HoP, *Commons, 1715–54*, 2.93, 298, 418 • U. Lambert, *Blechingley: a parish history*, 1 (1921), 316–17 • A. G. Grimwade, *London goldsmiths, 1697–1837: their marks and lives, from the original registers at Goldsmiths' Hall* (1976) • S. Piggott, *William Stukeley: an eighteenth-century antiquary* (1950), 59–60, 164 • R. Hastings, *Antiques* (Jan 1934), 15–16 • *The parish of St James, Westminster*, 1/2, Survey of London, 30 (1960), 516 • S. H. A. H., ed., *The diary of John Hervey, first earl of Bristol* (1894), 132ff • will of Andrews Jelfe
Archives BL, letter-book, Add. MS 27587
Likenesses portrait, Bodl. Oxf., MS. Eng. Misc. e.136 (fol.30)
Wealth at death over £30,000: will

Jellett, John Hewitt (1817–1888), college head, the son of Morgan Jellett, a clergyman, was born at Cashel in co. Tipperary on 25 December 1817, and educated at Trinity College, Dublin, of which he became a fellow in 1840. He graduated BA in 1838, MA in 1843, BD in 1866, and DD on 1 March 1881. He was admitted into priest's orders in 1846. He married Dora, daughter of James Morgan of Tivoli, co. Cork.

In 1848 Jellett was elected to the chair of natural philosophy at Trinity College, Dublin, and in 1868 he was appointed a commissioner of Irish national education. A year later the Royal Irish Academy elected him president. In 1870, on the death of Dr Thomas Luby, he was co-opted by the senior fellows of Trinity College as a member of their board. Gladstone's government appointed Jellett provost of Trinity in February 1881; in the same year he was awarded one of the royal medals of the Royal Society. After the disestablishment of the Church of Ireland he was active in the general synod. He was an able mathematician, and wrote *A Treatise of the Calculus of Variations* in 1850, *A Treatise on the Theory of Friction* in 1872 (the latter being regarded as a classic work), and several papers on pure and applied mathematics, as well as articles in the *Transactions* of the Royal Irish Academy. His theological essays, sermons, and religious treatises included *An Examination of some of the Moral Difficulties of the Old Testament* (1867), and *The Efficacy of Prayer* (1878).

As provost Jellett was remembered for his fine presence and keen glance, though also perhaps for a want of humility. He died at the provost's house, Trinity College, Dublin, on 19 February 1888, and was buried in Mount Jerome cemetery on the 23rd. His son, William Morgan Jellett (1857–1936), a barrister, was Unionist MP for Dublin University in 1919–22; his youngest daughter, Eva Jellett, was in 1904 among the first women to be admitted as graduates of Trinity College, Dublin.

G. C. BOASE, rev. M. C. CURTHOYS

Sources *The Times* (21 Feb 1888), 10 • *The Times* (24 Feb 1888), 5 • *Freeman's Journal* [Dublin] (20 Feb 1888), 3 • *Freeman's Journal* [Dublin] (24 Feb 1888), 3 • *ILN* (7 May 1881), 453–4 • *The Graphic* (10 March 1888), 234, 240 • Boase, *Mod. Eng. biog.* • Burtchaell & Sadleir, *Alum. Dubl.* • WWBMP • R. B. McDowell and D. A. Webb, *Trinity College, Dublin, 1592–1952: an academic history* (1982) • CGPLA Eng. & Wales (1888)
Likenesses portrait, 1888, repro. in *The Graphic*, 240 • S. Purser, oils, 1889, TCD • oils (after photograph by Chancellor of Dublin), TCD • portrait, repro. in *ILN*, 453 • wood-engraving (after photograph by Chancellor of Dublin), NPG; repro. in *ILN*
Wealth at death £5873 10s.: probate, 5 April 1888, CGPLA Eng. & Wales

Jellett, Mary Harriett [Mainie] (1897–1944), painter and writer on art, was born on 20 April 1897 at 36 Fitzwilliam Square, Dublin, and baptized at St Anne's Church, Dawson Street, the eldest of the four daughters of William Morgan Jellett (1857–1936) and Janet McKensie Stokes (*b.* 1874). Her father was a successful barrister from a Huguenot family that had settled in Ireland in the seventeenth century. Her paternal grandfather, John Hewitt *Jellett (1817–1888), was provost of Trinity College, Dublin. Her mother's family migrated from Wiltshire in the seventeenth century and had made a distinguished contribution to public life in Ireland in engineering and medicine; her maternal grandfather, William *Stokes (1804–1878), was a renowned chest physician. Mainie Jellett (as she was known) was educated, as were all the daughters, at home by tutors or governesses, and it was not until she entered art school that she experienced outside education. Musically gifted, she played the piano well from an early age, performing with her mother and other members of the

Mary Harriett Jellett (1897–1944), by unknown photographer

family at musical soirées. She studied at the Leinster School of Music under Mabel Länder, and regularly won prizes at *feis ceoil* competitions. She also studied painting as a child. Though this eclectic system of education inspired her, and provided a secure and comfortable childhood, she was surrounded by the tensions of Ireland's political circumstances as well as the cultural ferment occasioned by a literary and artistic revival led by William Butler Yeats and Lady Augusta Gregory. This political activity was represented in practical ways in the family by Mainie's father. He was energetically active in the southern unionist tradition and was directly involved in the party's organization and affairs; he served as an MP at Westminster, holding the Dublin University seat.

At the age of twelve Mainie began to study art under May Manning, a serious project which lasted five years and led directly to her enrolment in the Metropolitan School of Art, where briefly she was a pupil of Sir William Orpen. A career in music was considered, but preferring a creative rather than an interpretative involvement in art, she chose to go on with artistic studies. In 1917 she moved to the Westminster School of Art in London, where she studied under Walter Sickert and Walter Bayes. Under Sickert's direction, she later wrote, 'drawing and composition came alive to me and I began to understand the work of the Old Masters' (MacCarvill, 47).

Mainie Jellett produced an outstanding body of student drawings, watercolours, and paintings. In 1919 she won the Taylor prize in the annual Royal Dublin Society competition with a painting entitled *Peace* (priv. coll.), celebrating the end of the First World War. She held an exhibition in company with Lillian Davidson in Dublin in 1920 that was favourably noticed in the *Irish Times*: 'There is a

joyful note in Miss Jellett's pictures that appeal to the eye. The artist revels in the seashore and conveys her impression in lucid style' (Arnold, 43). There is some evidence that both artists came increasingly under the influence of Jack Yeats.

Although she felt drawn to a professional career as an artist, which inevitably would have meant teaching as well as painting and exhibiting work, Jellett was not entirely satisfied with what she had achieved. She decided to study with the cubist painter André Lhote in Paris, and spent part of 1920 and 1921 in his atelier. From there, in December 1921, she moved to study with Albert Gleizes and spent a fruitful year embracing the principles of abstract cubism, which the French cubist painter was then working out. She was accompanied by her friend Evie *Hone (1894–1955) during these studies. Hone was a lifelong companion of Jellett's; a sufferer from infantile paralysis, and permanently disabled, she became both friend and working companion in the spread of Irish modernism.

In 1923 Jellett, having completed almost ten years studying art, returned to a very changed Dublin, capital of an independent Ireland. She was full of the intellectual and creative turmoil of new ideas and new directions. Together with Hone, she made an immediate and profound impact on the city (likened to the Athens of Pericles) and its cultural life by exhibiting a joint show entirely of abstract works. With Jellett's *Decoration* (NG Ire.)—the crucial work of the exhibition—modernism in Ireland began. Ten years before the arrival of abstraction in England, Dublin saw the full-blooded fruits of French studies in the works of these two young painters. The city took it badly. A serious controversy developed, splitting critics and collectors into two opposed groups.

Through the 1920s and into the 1930s Mainie Jellett, working a good deal in the company of Evie Hone, continued painting works of abstraction in a city unreconciled to this kind of art. Jellett in particular applied her fine analytical mind to the philosophy behind abstraction, and her abilities reflected and shaped the serious and often confrontational situations which her work invoked. She was a powerful campaigner for the art in which she believed, while at the same time respecting all painters and supporting their right to public interest and support. The pattern of work and study pursued during these years by Jellett and Hone, who usually travelled together, was to return to France and spend time each summer with Albert Gleizes. They were consciously part of a small international movement with concerns embracing philosophical and religious beliefs and ideas as well as the principles of abstraction, then very new. As Jellett explained, in a lecture on 3 February 1926, they endeavoured:

to penetrate beneath the exterior forms of nature, and to discover her natural laws and to construct accordingly. A picture should be a miniature universe, with all its forms interdependent, as the organization of the universe itself … A picture should be as complete as the human body so that the removal of any of its members would upset the equilibrium of the whole … You will not find blue sea and white clouds and waves, which make you feel you want to bathe and remind you of hot summer days; but instead, if you can look at these pictures with an open mind and without prejudice, they will give you a sensation of their own, resulting from the abstract qualities of the good or bad harmony of form and colour, balance and movement. They will affect you through your eyes and thence to your brain, the same way music affects you through your ear and thence to your brain. (Arnold, 94)

The possibility of a career as a painter in Paris was always there, but Mainie Jellett felt a moral obligation to her own country, newly forging ideas and artistic activity under the governments of first W. T. Cosgrave and then Eamon de Valera. The family had at first felt isolated. Southern unionists were deserted by the unionists of the separated six counties in the north-east of Ireland and rapidly became a political anachronism. This affected Mainie's father most of all; the rest of the family soon acclimatized to the predominantly Roman Catholic state. Mainie Jellett took on adult pupils, taught children, lectured widely, and contributed to broadcast debates on the subject of modern art. She led a movement of Irish modernism that was vigorous and combative. Her art, which had gone through markedly varied stages of development—from the fluid representational work of the Sickert period, through the angular representational cubism of Lhote, to abstraction—now developed further. The strict rules of the 1920s gave way to flowing and brilliant colours, and to a combination of softness and strength which characterized her mature output—as in, for example, *Abstract Composition* (c.1931; Crawford Municipal Gallery of Modern Art, Cork) and *Abstract Composition* (c.1931; priv. coll. reproduced in Arnold, 127, pl. 187). In 1931 she was a founder figure of the international movement Abstraction-Création, an exhibiting society based in Paris, and she became the associate of other friends of Albert Gleizes, including Robert and Sonia Delaunay. By the early 1930s two of her sisters had married and moved away from home, where family ties were exceptionally close and supportive. Then in 1936 her father died. The two had enjoyed a close and loving relationship: at Christmas 1932 he had written to her in Paris, 'No present that I could give you would convey what I feel. The unspoken word is sometimes more elegant than volumes of talk. You are the very best' (Arnold, 77). Throughout this period she exhibited regularly every two years.

Jellett believed in 'the necessity of a highly developed sense of craftsmanship; every artist should be capable of executing adequately whatever job he is entrusted with' (MacCarvill, 98). She designed cubist rugs which were woven by family members and also by the Dun Emer Guild, established by the Yeats sisters, Elizabeth (Lollie) and Susan (Lily). As the arts and crafts movement in Ireland took inspiration from Celtic art, Jellett responded to the similar capacity of Chinese art to transcend various media. She wrote to Gleizes in 1936:

I was staying with a friend on the rocks [of Achill Island in the west of Ireland] near the sea, the peace and aloofness from the confusion and scrambling of the world of the moment was wonderful—one had the same feeling in the Chinese exhibition [at the Royal Academy, London, 1935] … there was a natural rhythm running through the works as a whole, which caught you up and led you quickly on. (Arnold, 152)

This invigorating experience led Jellett to reintroduce into her work landscape and figure studies that derive much of their economy and fluidity from the Chinese tradition in painting. Gratified that the Second World War, far from exercising a dispiriting effect on art, led to a burgeoning round of artistic events and exhibitions, Jellett supported a new venture, the White Stag Group of modernist painters and sculptors, who had a great impact in the city. She also worked towards the setting up of an alternative annual show of paintings in rivalry with the rather staid classicism of the Royal Hibernian Academy. Known as the Irish Exhibition of Living Art, the first exhibition was held in 1943 and was a huge success. Unfortunately, Mainie became ill at the end of that year, and was misdiagnosed as suffering from tuberculosis, then widespread. Though it would not have made a great deal of difference, treatment being so difficult, she was, in fact, suffering from cancer. She died at 96 Lower Lesson Street, Dublin, on 16 February 1944 at the age of forty-six, and was buried at St Fintan's, Howth, co. Dublin. Apart from the short periods when she studied art in London and Paris, she spent the whole of her life living in the same house. The writer Elizabeth Bowen recalled that Jellett's

dynamicism [*sic*] … was at first found unfriendly, destructive, even repellent. She had gone so far as to go, it seemed, out of view. A mystique without the familiar softness, expressing itself in the ice of abstract terms, and the apparent subjugation of the soul to the intellect, took some accepting. (Arnold, 203)

Her painting *I have Trodden the Wine Press Alone* (1943; NG Ire.), whose title is a quotation from Isaiah, is a fitting emblem of Jellett's life.   BRUCE ARNOLD

Sources B. Arnold, *Mainie Jellett and the modern movement in Ireland* (1991) • E. MacCarvill, *Mainie Jellett, the artist's vision: lectures and essays on her art* (1958) • d. cert. • *Mainie Jellett, 1897–1944* (1991) [exhibition catalogue, Irish Museum of Modern Art, Dublin, 7 Dec 1991 – 22 March 1992]
Archives priv. coll.
Likenesses photograph, priv. coll. [*see illus.*]
Wealth at death £1384 14*s*. 8*d*.: administration, 1944, *CGPLA Éire*

Jellicoe [*née* Mullin], **Anne William** (1823–1880), educationist, born in Mountmellick, Queen's county, was the daughter of William Mullin (1796–1826), a Quaker schoolmaster, and his wife, Margaret Thompson (1801–1840). Little is known about her early life. Orphaned by the time she was seventeen years of age, she married John Jellicoe (d. 1862), a flour miller, in 1846 and they moved to Clara, King's county, in 1848. It was here, in the aftermath of the famine, that she began her first attempt to provide some kind of paid work for women. She set up an embroidery school for sewed muslin in 1850 and for lace crochet work in 1853, arranging for the export of the work to Glasgow. Both were gone by 1856, but the experience convinced her that women's work would remain limited and poorly paid until women were better educated. This conviction was reinforced when she moved to Dublin with her husband in 1858. Once again she came up against great poverty, this time in the Liberties area of the city. She helped revive Cole Alley infant school, run by the Quakers for poor children of all creeds, by going into homes and persuading mothers to send their children to this school.

When the Social Science Association met in Dublin for the first time in 1861, Anne Jellicoe was asked to prepare a paper on the working conditions of women factory workers in Dublin. Out of this came the first society in Ireland for the employment of women, which she founded with the help of Ada Barbara Corlett. Called the Irish Society for Promoting the Employment of Educated Women, after the London society of the same name, it soon became known as the Queen's Institute. Its committee of twenty-eight men from the professional and business life of the city and thirty-eight women, mostly titled ladies of the highest social standing, restricted the institute to working only with middle-class women. The assumption that these 'distressed gentlewomen' were educated and therefore easily trained proved to be a major stumbling-block to the institute's progress. Its first phase, 1861–6, was one of only limited success in the employment of women—the most successful classes being those directly linked to jobs, such as the sewing-machine class, law writing, and the work of telegraph clerks. It was only during the institute's second stage, 1866–80, when it became involved in girls' secondary and higher education, that it became much more successful. Ironically this occurred only after Anne Jellicoe had left the Queen's Institute in 1864 because of its refusal to start a training course for governesses.

Widowed in 1862, Anne Jellicoe continued her educational work. She decided to set up a training college for teachers, but was persuaded by Archbishop Chenevix Trench, the newly appointed archbishop of Dublin, to base her new college on the model of Queen's College, London. Alexandra College, Dublin, founded in 1866, became the first institution in Ireland to aspire to a university-type education for women over fifteen years of age. It had close links with the University of Dublin from the beginning, as the fellows and professors of Trinity College both taught and set the written examinations in Alexandra College. The range of subjects covered (theology, history, English language and literature, French, German, Italian, Latin, geography, arithmetic, algebra, geometry, natural science, mental and moral philosophy, music, and drawing) also raised it above the ordinary level of girls' second level schools in Ireland. In the period 1880–1904 it prepared girls for the degrees of the Royal University of Ireland, and was also in the vanguard of the movement to persuade Trinity College, Dublin, to open its degrees to women, which finally occurred in 1904. Anne Jellicoe was lady superintendent of the college, remaining at its head until her death, judiciously guiding it through the early years, when acceptance of the need for women's higher education was by no means universal.

In April 1869 Anne Jellicoe founded the Governess Association of Ireland, to help 'promote the higher education of ladies as teachers' by founding studentships and exhibitions in schools and colleges. While the association never reached its full potential due to lack of funds, it did further the higher education of women by persuading Trinity College, Dublin, to establish examinations for women, first held in 1870. It also brought Anne Jellicoe into contact with Maria Grey, who came to both Belfast and Dublin in January 1872 to spread her ideas about the high school movement for girls. Both women shared a passionate conviction in the right of women to higher education, but feared that their efforts to gain public sympathy and funds for this cause might be endangered by the emerging women's suffrage movement. As a result Anne Jellicoe remained outside any of the political delegations of the 1870s which lobbied for reform of girls' secondary and higher education, and did not take any active part in the campaign to win the suffrage for women.

The founding of Alexandra School in 1873 to act as a feeder to the college was another testimony to Anne Jellicoe's vision. She believed that the college could not survive financially without a school, and this was proved true in the 1880s, during a general depression, when the school's profits allowed the college to continue despite heavy losses. Although the Queen's Institute had both a school and college it did not survive beyond 1880, and this seems to have been due to its attempts to cater for every conceivable examination, while striving to retain its technical origins.

A very shy woman with a keen sense of humour, Anne Jellicoe once remarked that 'action is more my forte than speech-making' (A. Jellicoe, *A Few Words Addressed to the Students Representative Body, Alexandra College, 5 March 1878*, 1878). She ceased to be a member of the Society of Friends at about the time of her husband's death, becoming a member of the Church of Ireland. She loved music and art and was wont, as a friend remarked, on gala days, 'to go about, not in garb of drabs or greys, but with a brilliant red shawl which mostly trailed on the ground after her' (*Alexandra College Jubilee Record, 1866–1916*, 1916, 11–12). Anne Jellicoe died at her brother's house, 13 South Road, Birmingham, on 18 October 1880, and was buried on 21 October at the Friends' burial-ground, Rosenallis, Mountmellick.

A. V. O'CONNOR

Sources Alexandra College Archives, Dublin · *Englishwoman's Review*, 11 (15 Nov 1880), 517–19 · *Alexandra College Magazine*, 28 (June 1906), 5–7 · letters from Mrs Grey to Mrs Jellicoe, 21 Jan 1872–25 June 1874, Alexandra College, Dublin · minute book of Governess Association of Ireland, April 1869–Nov 1884, Alexandra College, Dublin · A. B. Corbett, 'Twenty years history of the Queen's Institute and College, Dublin', *Journal of the Women's Education Union*, 9/107 (15 Nov 1881), 170–72 · *Alexandra College Jubilee Record, 1866–1916* (1916) · d. cert. · *Irish Times* (22 Oct 1880) · *Freeman's Journal* [Dublin] (22 Oct 1880)

Archives Alexandra College, Milltown, Dublin, papers

Likenesses painting, c.1839–1840 (aged sixteen/seventeen years), Alexandra College, Milltown, Dublin · painting, c.1870–1880, Alexandra College, Milltown, Dublin

Jellicoe, (John) Basil Lee (1899–1935), housing reformer and Church of England clergyman, was born on 5 February 1899 at Chailey, Sussex, the elder son of Thomas Harry Lee Jellicoe, rector of Chailey, and his wife, Bethia Theodora, youngest daughter of Sir John Boyd, of Maxpoffle,

Roxburgh, lord provost of Edinburgh from 1888 to 1891. His father was a cousin of J. R. Jellicoe, first Earl Jellicoe.

From an early age Jellicoe's heart was set upon the vocation of the priesthood. Through the generosity of his godmother, Mrs Hepburn, he was educated at Haileybury and at Magdalen College, Oxford. A few months before the end of the First World War he left Oxford to join the Royal Naval Volunteer Reserve and served for a short time in the Mediterranean. In 1920 he resumed his studies at Oxford and was ordained deacon in 1922 and priest in 1923.

Brought up in the Tractarian tradition, it was the social implications of sacramental Christianity which determined Jellicoe's outlook; as a schoolboy he had made a speech on Christian socialism to the Oddfellows at a village inn. For politics or social reform as such he had but little interest; it was the theological aspect of these matters in their direct relation to human beings which aroused in him an urgent desire to demonstrate the efficacy of the Christian gospel. This he achieved, not only by means of the great enterprises which he inspired, but also through the influence of his character and convictions on all types of people, especially the young. 'No man', wrote William Temple, 'ever so luminously exemplified the sacramental quality of the Christian religion as did Basil Jellicoe.' His opportunity came at an early age when in 1921, while still a layman, he was given charge of the Magdalen College mission in the Somers Town district of St Pancras, London. In that overcrowded area, where more than 22,000 people were living at an average of two to three persons per room, Jellicoe realized that the value of clubs and camps was merely palliative; the fundamental need was better housing. The evils resulting from slum conditions were to him 'the devil's work' and he described Somers Town as 'a gigantic theft'. So, towards the end of 1924, largely as a result of his initiative, the St Pancras House Improvement Society was formed to rehouse existing tenants. Beginning with a share capital of £250 it became the vanguard of a widespread campaign of voluntary housing. By 1930 the society's capital had reached £160,000, and some hundreds of the poorest families in London had been rehoused in blocks of flats at low but economic rents.

Jellicoe found the Magdalen College mission disorganized and heavily in debt. When in 1927 he resigned the headship owing to ill health he left it not only free of debt but in a flourishing condition. Indeed, the *New Survey of London Life and Labour* published by the London School of Economics in the early 1930s referred to the splendid work of the Magdalen College mission in St Pancras. After his resignation he continued his work for housing in Somers Town and elsewhere, notably in the Isle of Dogs, London.

Jellicoe's ambition was not limited to the rehousing of the poor; it was to demonstrate the possibility of a Christian motive and environment for all human activities through the consecration of life to the service of God. A public house under Christian management was among the projects which he initiated.

In 1931 Jellicoe visited Canada, where his sermons and speeches made a profound impression. Illness frequently intervened during the last ten years of his short life, and he died, unmarried, in a nursing home at Uxbridge, on 24 August 1935.   PERCY MARYON-WILSON, *rev.*

Sources *The Times* (26 Aug 1935) · K. Ingram, *Basil Jellicoe* (1936) · personal knowledge (1949) · *New survey of London life and labour*, 9 vols. (1930–35) · private information (1949)
Likenesses H. Carr, oils (after photographs), St Pancras Housing Association, London · photographs, St Pancras Housing Association, London

Jellicoe, Sir Geoffrey Alan (1900–1996), landscape architect, was born on 8 October 1900 at 70 Wynnstay Gardens, Chelsea, London, the younger son of George Edward Jellicoe, publisher's manager, and later publisher, and his wife, Florence Waterson, *née* Waylett. His parents separated when he was about fourteen and he lived alone with his mother, his teenage older brother having been swept into fighting in the First World War. He attended Cheltenham College as an exhibitioner, seeing as little of his father as possible, and money was scarce. His mother was an artist who had been trained at the Slade School; later in life she went on to create a series of free style embroidery pictures.

From January 1919 until 1923 Jellicoe attended the Architectural Association School of Architecture in Bloomsbury, London. He then travelled with Jock Shepherd, a fellow student, in Italy, where they collected material for their classic book, *Italian Gardens of the Renaissance* (1925). The book was illustrated by Shepherd's exquisite plans and cross-sections, based on Jellicoe's survey drawings: 'We suddenly realised we were into an extraordinary field of discovery, because as the drawing began to appear on paper, one realised the beauty of the actual plan and how it related to the site' (Harvey, *Reflections*, 4). So started Jellicoe's lifelong and stimulating journey of discovery of landscape design, a field in which he was pre-eminent throughout his long and active life. In 1930 he was a Bernard Webb scholar at the British School in Rome.

Soon after their return from Italy Jellicoe and Shepherd set up in practice together, but in 1931 Jellicoe started his own practice at 40 Bloomsbury Square, London, feeling the need to break free from Shepherd's dominance as a designer. He continued to write: he had published *Gardens and Design* (1927) with Shepherd, and (as sole author) he published *Baroque Gardens of Austria* in 1932. He also taught at the Architectural Association (1929–34). He soon had interesting design opportunities. He built the international style Cheddar Gorge Caveman Restaurant (1934), the roof of which was a glass floored pool. He created several landscapes for private clients, often co-operating with Russell Page as planting designer; one of these was the Royal Lodge, Windsor, for the duke and duchess of York. An important work was extensive new formal gardens at Ditchley Park (1935–9) for Ronald and Nancy Tree, clients who, followed by their son Michael, remained patrons for fifty years. As well as several faithful clients there were other strands of continuity in Jellicoe's richly varied career. He always lived by Highgate Hill in London, and his office was always in Bloomsbury.

Sir Geoffrey Alan Jellicoe (1900–1996), by Anne-Katrin Purkiss, 1990

On 11 July 1936 Jellicoe married Ursula Pares [**Ursula** [Susan] **Jellicoe** (1907–1986)], who had joined the office as secretary, drawn by her interest in the arts. They enjoyed a happy and fruitful fifty-year marriage and professional co-operation, in which Susan gradually built up a distinct oeuvre of her own. She had secretarial qualifications, was fluent in French, German, and Italian, and had been working as personal secretary to the managing director of the Anglo-Continental Bank. She must have seemed surprisingly high-powered to have wanted to become secretary to so small a practice, even one run by someone so lively. Susan was born on 30 June 1907 at 18 Gambier Terrace, Liverpool, one of the six children of Professor Sir Bernard *Pares (1867–1949), historian and co-founder of the School of Slavonic and East European Studies at London University, and his wife, Margaret Ellis (Daisy), née Dixon (1879–1964). Her early childhood was in Liverpool, then on the Wirral. From 1920 to 1925 she attended St Paul's Girls' School while living with her mother and grandparents in Belsize Park (her parents having separated in 1919). She was a graceful, artistic child, a beautiful classical dancer, and loved singing and music throughout her life. During the Second World War she worked in the Ministry of Information and distinguished herself by revealing analysis of aerial photography. From their marriage until 1984 the Jellicoes lived in a narrow Georgian house with a long garden at 19 Grove Terrace, Parliament Hill Fields. There were no children of the marriage.

Jellicoe did much to promote the profession of landscape architecture. In 1929 he was a founder member of the Institute of Landscape Architects (later, to his delight, broadened into the Landscape Institute). From 1939 to 1949 he was the institute's president, keeping it alive through the arduous years of war. He edited the institute's *Journal* from 1941 to 1945. He was busy during the war on emergency housing and other mainly architectural work, including immediate restoration of areas wrecked by bombs. He recorded 'That whenever a bomb fell ... I thought this means another thousand or two in one's pocket! This was so horrible that ... that was why one financed landscape during the war' by passing on all money from this source to the Institute of Landscape Architects (Harvey, *Reflections*, 10). This was typical of his strong sense of honour, integrity, and generosity, which left him at the end of his long and successful life with few accumulated resources other than a collection of pictures and numerous admiring friends and colleagues. During the same period he was also principal of the Architectural Association School (1939–42), a task he found exhausting and unrewarding. In 1948 he chaired an international conference for landscape architects in London and Cambridge, at the conclusion of which representatives from sixteen countries founded the International Federation of Landscape Architects, later a worldwide organization. Jellicoe was elected first president (1948–54) and was thereafter honorary president for life.

Jellicoe continued to run a practice until 1973, from about 1954 in partnership with the architect Francis Coleridge. Much of the work of the practice was architectural, and the design of buildings was certainly the primary source of income. For the period 1943–73 Michael Spens ascribed eighty-three works to Jellicoe, of which eighteen were abortive designs and five were in Northern Rhodesia (1947–52). Several of his landscape works during this period were seminal in character, expressive of ideas which only later became widely accepted. Hope cement works in the Peak District (1943) was a fifty-year plan for the development and restoration of an industrial site and quarry. A rooftop café and water garden were created at Harvey's department store in Guildford (1956–7). At Hemel Hempstead linear water gardens gave delight to those moving into the shopping centre from town car parks (1959). Waste spoil was shaped into curvaceous hills at Park Royal (1959) and Harwell (1960). A plan for the centre of Gloucester included building height restrictions to safeguard views of the cathedral tower (1961).

During the same period Jellicoe started to collect contemporary pictures, first influenced by Frederick Gibberd, with whom he travelled each year to study important landscapes. He served on the Royal Fine Arts Commission (1954–68) and greatly enjoyed his period as a trustee of the Tate Gallery (1967–74). This led to warm friendships with Henry Moore and Ben Nicholson, whose work he greatly admired.

For many years Jellicoe was interested in the subconscious in landscape design, an idea he explored more deeply in creating the Kennedy Memorial at Runnymede (1964). 'It gave me my first serious opportunity to put a subconscious idea into a work, so that it is more important and more lasting than the purely visual impression the eye receives' (Harvey, *Reflections*, 17). Everything seen is underlain by an allegorical unseen meaning; the granite setts represent the multitude of pilgrims on their way upwards, the woodlands the cycle of life, the slightly curved memorial stone appears to float above the ground. The place is indeed peaceful and inspiring. Jellicoe's three volumes of *Studies in Landscape Design* (1960, 1966, and 1970) explored connections between artworks, landscapes, and hidden ideas, connections later summarized in his Guelph lectures (1983). His designs too developed in controlled and sophisticated use of more abstract forms combined with traditional, exemplified by the central pool at Wisley (1971–2), and the exquisite Shute gardens for Michael and Lady Anne Tree (1970–80).

In 1973 'the partnership ceased, I closed the office and one retired to one's home where one thought one would probably lead a quiet old age. *The Landscape of Man* was the last major work one ever hoped to do and that was published in 1975', Jellicoe later recalled (Harvey, *Reflections*, 23–4). *The Landscape of Man* proved a seminal work. Geoffrey and Susan Jellicoe wrote this great book together, starting in 1957, Susan taking many of its photographs. It was an exploration of examples of man's shaping of the environment worldwide throughout time, opening with the words: 'The world is moving into a phase when landscape design may well be recognised as the most comprehensive of the arts'.

Susan Jellicoe had by this time established herself as an important figure in the world of landscape architecture. She was elected honorary associate of the Landscape Institute in 1968. She possessed a remarkable aptitude in quickly mastering and then excelling in any subject of interest to her. She had become a fine plantsman, and prepared planting schemes for many of her husband's landscapes. She was also an excellent black and white landscape photographer, her photographs appearing in several books in which she collaborated. These included *Modern Private Gardens* (1968) and *The Use of Water in Landscape Architecture* (1971), both with her husband; three books with Lady Marjory Allen, including *Town Gardens to Live in* (1977); and *The Gardens of Mughal India* (1972), with text by Sylvia Crowe and Sheila Haywood. She was an active member of the Garden History Society. She was editor of the magazine *Landscape Design* for twenty years, and also chairman of the Landscape Institute's journal committee, which was responsible for this magazine. She edited the *Observer*'s gardening panel from 1961 to 1965. In 1985 she was awarded an honorary doctorate by the University of Sheffield and was invested at home a few days before her death. She was a gifted cook and the Jellicoes frequently entertained visitors of all ages at 19 Grove Terrace. She died at the Arkley Nursing Home, Wood Street, Barnet, Hertfordshire, on 1 August 1986, of Parkinson's disease, and was cremated on 10 August at Golders Green, London.

From the age of eighty Jellicoe's creativity enjoyed a final passionate flowering, continuing even during Susan's last years, when he nursed her devotedly. They had moved in 1984 to a small modern flat with a wonderful view over Hampstead Heath, at 14 High Point, Highgate, designed in 1936 by Lubetkin and Tecton. He seemed to be happier working on his own without the pressures involved in managing an office. With an ever-smiling round face and bouncy demeanour he would brief younger colleagues on how to carry out his designs on site. Previously an uninspiring draughtsman, he started to produce large exquisite drawings in stipple and irregular ink line, enlivened with patches of colour; he would spend his morning over a drawing board in a tiny room in the flat. He was elected a Royal Academician in 1991 and held an exhibition there in 1994. 'I have a perfectly clear philosophy now in one's old age, that one can do good through one's work, which means that through this I should like everybody to experience life at a much deeper level than that of the visible world' (Harvey, *Reflections*, 29). He read widely and was greatly interested in Jung's theories about the subconscious. 'Like the portrait painter, the landscape designer needs to be a psychologist first and a technician afterwards. He needs to dig into the subconscious' (Parkin and Fieldhouse, 7–11).

Jellicoe's gardens at Sutton Place, Guildford (1980–86), for Stanley Seeger included a romantic lake, walled gardens on both sides of the house, a characteristic long walk leading to a 'Magritte Walk', with strange optical scale effects, and a beautifully placed sculpted wall by Ben Nicholson. The whole was an inspiration. He designed landscape town plans for Modena and Brescia in Italy, the botanical and historical Moody Gardens for Galveston, Texas, and the Atlanta Historical Gardens in Georgia. Irrepressibly he produced numerous large detailed drawings in his own hand for these projects. Though in his last few years he became unable to leave home, he entertained visitors with a flood of ideas. At his well-attended ninetieth birthday party he delivered an inspiring and forward-looking speech in response to citations by others about the past. He subsequently set about founding the Landscape Foundation to promote new ideas in landscape design.

Jellicoe was honoured by Landscape Architects' gold medals worldwide, American (1981), British (1985), and Australian (1990). He received the Royal Horticultural Society's Victoria medal of honour in 1995. In 1961 he was appointed CBE and in 1979 knighted. He worked on cheerfully until a year before his death, on 17 July 1996, at the Check House Nursing Home, Beer Street, Seaton, Devon, of heart failure. He was cremated on 25 July at Golders Green, London. In Kathryn Moore's words, he left 'a distinctive body of work, showing the development of his ideas across a turbulent century. He also leaves us with an enduring impression of energy, passion and enthusiasm' (Harvey, *LDT Monograph*, 151).   HAL MOGGRIDGE

Sources S. Harvey, ed., *Reflections on landscape* (1987), 1–29 [from interviews by I. C. Laurie and M. Lancaster] · M. Spens, *The complete landscape designs and gardens of Geoffrey Jellicoe* (1994) · G. Collens, S. Crowe, and H. Moggridge, 'A tribute to Susan Jellicoe', *Landscape Design* (Oct 1986), 12–13 · S. Harvey, ed., *LDT monograph no. 1: Geoffrey*

Jellicoe (1998) • S. Parkin and K. Fieldhouse, 'Geoffrey Jellicoe', *Landscape Design* (Sept 1996), 7–11 • K. Wells and N. Edwards, *Sir Geoffrey Alan Jellicoe* (University of Guelph, 1983) • *The Guardian* (19 July 1996) • *The Times* (20 July 1996) • *The Independent* (19 July 1996) • *Daily Telegraph* (19 July 1996) • *WWW* • b. cert. [Geoffrey Ann Jellicoe] • m. cert. • d. cert. [Geoffrey Alan Jellicoe] • private information (2004) • personal knowledge (2004) [Ann Jellicoe Mayne, Andrew Pares]
Archives Library of the Landscape Institute, London, drawings and photographs • RIBA BAL, original drawings for *Italian gardens of the Renaissance* | Tate collection, corresp. with Ben Nicholson
Likenesses H. Palmer, photograph with drawing, 1989, repro. in Spens, *Complete landscape designs*, frontispiece • A. K. Purkiss, photograph, 1990, NPG [*see illus.*] • double portrait, photograph (with Ursula (Susan) Jellicoe), repro. in Harvey, ed., *LDT monograph no. 1* • photograph, repro. in *The Times* • photograph, repro. in *Daily Telegraph* • photograph, repro. in Wells and Edwards, *Sir Geoffrey Alan Jellicoe* • photograph, repro. in G. Jellicoe, *The Guelph lectures on landscape design* (1983) • photograph, repro. in Harvey, ed., *Reflections on landscape* • photographs, repro. in Harvey, ed., *LDT monograph no. 1*
Wealth at death £155,166: probate, 1997, *CGPLA Eng. & Wales* • £169,461—Ursula (Susan) Jellicoe: probate, 1986, *CGPLA Eng. & Wales*

Jellicoe, John Rushworth, first Earl Jellicoe (1859–1935), naval officer, was born at Southampton on 5 December 1859, the second of four sons of John Henry Jellicoe (1825–1914), a captain in the Royal Mail Steam Packet Company, and his wife, Lucy Henrietta (*d.* 17 Oct 1916), daughter of Dr John Rushworth Keele, also of Southampton. The powerful combination of his father's career and the location of the family ensured that Jellicoe became familiar with ships and the sea at an early age. His family tree included seven naval officers, notably his maternal great-grandfather, Admiral Sir Philip *Patton, a contemporary of Nelson, and he had several relatives in the service throughout his career. However, his father's occupation was of only moderate social status, at a time when the officer corps of the Royal Navy was increasingly aristocratic. In consequence Jellicoe's career was reflected merit; he exploited a promotion system based on examinations in which mathematical expertise was vital, to propel him into positions where attention to detail, hard work, and an equable temperament would ensure success. After preparatory school in Southampton, he spent a year at Field House School, Rottingdean, where he mastered the foundations of mathematics that both built his career, and provided a key insight into the man.

Early career, 1872–1897 In 1872 Jellicoe was nominated for the Royal Navy by Captain Robert Hall, a friend of his father, who was then naval secretary to the Admiralty. He joined the cadet training ship HMS *Britannia*, moored in the River Dart, in the summer of that year, coming second out of thirty-nine cadets. He was then only 4 feet 6 inches tall, and would remain of slight stature throughout his life. Aboard *Britannia* his mathematical skill and small-boat experience gave him an advantage over his contemporaries, and he passed out at the top of his term in the summer of 1874. This early success explains why he spent so much of his seagoing career aboard flagships. With first-class certificates in all subjects he was immediately

John Rushworth Jellicoe, first Earl Jellicoe (1859–1935), by James Russell & Sons, *c.*1910

promoted midshipman. In September he joined the wooden steam frigate *Newcastle*, one of six fully rigged frigates in the flying squadron which roamed the globe for the next two and a half years. By the time the *Newcastle* returned to Plymouth in early 1877 he had learnt the art of square-rigged ship handling, seen the seaports of several continents, and grown 5 inches. In July he joined the ironclad *Agincourt*, flagship of the channel squadron, which was shortly afterwards sent out to reinforce the Mediterranean Fleet, under Admiral Sir Geoffrey Hornby. Soon after arriving the fleet passed up the Dardanelles into the Sea of Marmora, and Jellicoe was given numerous responsible tasks, commanding boats, carrying messages, and finally commanding the sailing sloop *Cruiser* with the admiral aboard. Despite these activities he passed third out of the 103 candidates for the rank of sub-lieutenant, gained a first-class certificate in seamanship at Malta, and first-class certificates at the Royal Naval College, Greenwich, and at the gunnery and torpedo schools at Portsmouth. This success entitled him to immediate promotion, but the reward was delayed for six months, during which time he served as signal sub-lieutenant of the Mediterranean flagship *Alexandra*. In September 1880 he was promoted, returning home to devote himself to gunnery, then the dominant specialization of the navy. He rejoined the *Agincourt* in February 1881, to complete his time as a watch-keeping officer. In May 1882 his ship returned to the

Mediterranean, following the Egyptian nationalist revolt. After active service ashore Jellicoe returned to the Royal Naval College, Greenwich, in mid-1882, winning first prize for theoretical work, and continuing his unbroken run of examination success at the gunnery and torpedo schools. In May 1884 he qualified as a gunnery lieutenant, and was immediately appointed to the staff of the gunnery school *Excellent* by her captain, John Arbuthnot Fisher. From this point Jellicoe's career was dominated by this dynamic, ambitious, and ruthless man. Clearly Fisher saw something of himself in Jellicoe: hard work, commitment, and technical excellence. In 1885 Fisher was appointed flag captain to Admiral Hornby, who commanded a Baltic fleet assembled to deter Russian aggression against Afghanistan. Jellicoe, the junior lieutenant of the *Excellent*, was his personal staff officer. After Hornby's fleet was dispersed Jellicoe joined the old turret ship *Monarch* in September 1885 as gunnery lieutenant, moving to the new battleship *Colossus* in April 1886. Here he invented the competitive naval field-gun exercise, later carried out at the Royal Tournament every year, to stimulate interest in gunnery. In December he returned to the *Excellent* as an experimental officer, being involved in the adoption of quick-firing medium-calibre guns, which radically altered the nature of war at sea. The Naval Defence Act of 1889 provided a major sustained increase in the level of naval spending, notably the construction of ten battleships and forty-two cruisers. This placed an enormous burden on Fisher, as director of naval ordnance, and he had Jellicoe transferred to Whitehall as his assistant. Here Jellicoe encountered administrative paper work that often kept him at the office until midnight. Promoted commander in June 1891 he left the Admiralty to become executive officer of the new battleship *Sans Pareil* (Captain Arthur *Wilson), joining the Mediterranean Fleet. The following year Jellicoe was moved to the flagship *Victoria*, at the request of the commander-in-chief, Admiral Sir George *Tryon. On 22 June 1893 the *Victoria* sank off Tripoli after being rammed by *Camperdown*, an accident caused by the failure of any subordinate officer to query an order given by Tryon which was impossible to execute. At the time Jellicoe, suffering from Malta fever, was confined to bed. Going on deck after the collision he was fortunate not to share the fate of 358 of his shipmates. Such was Jellicoe's standing in the service that he was appointed to *Ramillies* (Captain Francis Bridgeman), the flagship of the new commander-in-chief, Admiral Sir Michael Culme-Seymour, along with Lieutenant Hugh Evan-Thomas, and many other officers who would hold key appointments in the First World War. Flagships have always produced a disproportionate percentage of the senior officers of the next generation, but the *Ramillies* was unusual, even by the standards of the day. Selected to lay the ghost of Sir George Tryon, and in particular of his controversial command style that emphasized initiative and simple permissive instructions, Culme-Seymour and his staff elevated the science of precision fleet handling to new levels, suppressing the individuality of the captains and junior

admirals with a plethora of flag signals. The ship was also a centre for all manner of sporting prowess, from rowing and sailing to coaling ship, field-gun drill, and polo. In later life Jellicoe would recall this period of his life with particular pleasure. When he wanted examples of command style Jellicoe looked to Culme-Seymour, and later Wilson, rather than the more flexible Fisher, or the brilliant Tryon, with whom he served but briefly. As Andrew Gordon (in *The Rules of the Game*) has demonstrated, this commission was the foundation of command attitudes that bedevilled the Royal Navy in the First World War. In 1896 Jellicoe missed an opportunity for early promotion when Culme-Seymour refused a request that he command gunboats on the Nile during Kitchener's advance into Sudan. Culme-Seymour feared that Jellicoe's predisposition to Malta fever would lead to a more serious illness. Instead the promotions went to Commander Stanley Colville and Lieutenant David Beatty. In December 1896 Jellicoe returned to England, and was promoted captain on 1 January 1897, serving for a year on the ordnance committee. This involved several visits to Scotland where he stayed with Sir Charles Cayzer.

China and Admiralty, 1897–1910 Jellicoe returned to sea in late 1897 as flag captain to Admiral Sir Edward *Seymour, commander-in-chief on the China station, in *Centurion*. The defeat of China by Japan in 1894 had exposed the weakness of the Celestial empire, and encouraged the predatory instincts of the major powers. The activity of the great powers led to a violent reaction among the Chinese, largely encouraged by the dowager empress. The anti-Western movement, commonly referred to as the 'Boxers', began systematic attacks on Europeans, their embassies, and Christian converts in May 1900, leading the British ambassador at Peking (Beijing) to telegraph for assistance on the 28th. Although Seymour had no troops, he assembled a force from the various national squadrons then lying off the mouth of the Peiho (Beihe) River. On 5 June Jellicoe went ahead to assess the most effective method of advance. With the river choked by sandbanks, and the road little more than a track, the railway was the only option, though a vulnerable one. On 10 June, 2129 seamen and marines were landed, 915 of whom were British. So small a force would be effective only if the Chinese army did not join the Boxers, and the railway remained open. After passing Tientsin (Tianjin) the expedition was unable to advance or retreat; the Chinese army, now openly hostile, had destroyed the railway. On 19 June Seymour abandoned the railway, loaded the wounded onto sampans and retreated. The allies had to clear every village on their route, and on 21 June Jellicoe was hit in the chest while leading such an attack. Although the wound was initially considered fatal, and Jellicoe characteristically took the trouble to write his will, he was evacuated with the rest of the force and made a full recovery. He would carry the rifle bullet in his left lung for the rest of his life. Returning to his post afloat Jellicoe accumulated considerable experience of foreign armed forces, and was particularly impressed by the professionalism of the German navy. Created CB in 1900, he had demonstrated leadership, courage, and administrative talent. There could be no doubt that he would reach the top of his profession. The *Centurion* paid off in August 1901.

Returning to the Admiralty in March 1902 as assistant to the third sea lord and controller, Admiral Sir William May, Jellicoe spent much of his time visiting shipyards, often in Glasgow, where he renewed his friendship with the Cayzer family. In July 1902 he married Sir Charles Cayzer's second daughter, Florence Gwendoline. Despite his late start Jellicoe found married life very much to his taste. The future Lady Jellicoe provided an outgoing and often outspoken personality and uncommon energy that complemented his altogether different character.

After a year commanding the cruiser *Drake*, where he adopted the gunnery reforms developed by Captain Percy Scott, Jellicoe was recalled to the Admiralty in November 1904 as director of naval ordnance, by Fisher, newly installed as first sea lord. He was now part of the technical brains trust that developed the epochal all-big-gun battleship *Dreadnought*. For this work he was made a CVO. At this time he corresponded frequently with his friend from the China station and fellow gunnery enthusiast, Captain William Sowden Sims USN, the American inspector of target practice. This period marked the pinnacle of Jellicoe's technical career. In February 1907 he was promoted rear-admiral, and in August he was appointed second in command of the Atlantic Fleet with his flag in the pre-dreadnought battleship *Albermarle*. In October he was knighted and invested as KCVO. His year afloat included an early experience of long-range battle practice. His return to the Admiralty as controller, after only one year afloat, reflected the reality of the naval situation. Faced by the challenge of the imperial German navy Fisher wanted to deter war by a combination of numerical superiority and aggressive posturing. However, the Liberal government elected in 1906 was anxious to reduce defence spending, and cut back the naval programmes that would have maintained the advantage secured by the sudden appearance of the *Dreadnought*. Consequently Fisher needed his best brains at the Admiralty to win the naval race, not at sea preparing to fight a war he was anxious to avoid. As a result Jellicoe spent relatively little time at sea between 1900 and 1914, and even less in positions of ultimate authority. If Fisher really saw him as a second Nelson—he declared, 'Sir John Jellicoe is the future Nelson—he is incomparably the ablest sea Admiral we have' in October 1911 (Marder, *Fear God*, 2.397)—then he made a serious error in keeping him at Whitehall for so much of his career. Jellicoe helped to secure the naval programme of 1908–9, when eight battleships were ordered. These ships made a vital difference, winning the naval race and providing a numerical edge at Jutland. By contrast his efforts to improve the effectiveness of armour-piercing shells for long-range fire were incomplete when he left office, and remained so until after Jutland. Jellicoe knew that Fisher's much vaunted ships were actually inferior to their German opposite numbers on a ship-for-

ship basis, notably with less armour and internal subdivision. The British ships were far cheaper than their German equivalents. This was the real cost of winning the naval race on constrained budgets.

Fleet command and Admiralty, 1910–1914 In December 1910 Jellicoe, as acting vice-admiral, took command of the Atlantic Fleet, aboard the pre-dreadnought *Prince of Wales*. The following year he became second in command of the Home Fleet, under Sir George *Callaghan, with his flag in the dreadnought *Hercules* to gain some experience of dreadnought fleets. His old captain from *Ramillies*, Francis Bridgeman, warned Fisher that Jellicoe was too anxious, and undertook too much himself.

> At present he puts himself in the position of a glorified gunnery lieutenant. This will not do when he gets a big fleet. He must trust his staff and captains and if they don't fit he must kick them out. (Marder, *Fear God*, 2.418–19)

This failing reflected both the nature of the man, and the cultural conditioning of the past two decades. Although he could see flaws in everything and everyone, Jellicoe lacked the ruthlessness to sack the incompetents, made too many allowances for old friends, and did too much of everyone else's work. Even the hard lessons of war would not change him.

In December 1912 he returned to the Admiralty as second sea lord, with responsibility for manning and discipline. Even out of office Fisher continued to pull the strings of Jellicoe's career: in 1912 he persuaded the new first lord, Winston Churchill, to make a wholesale clearance of the navy list, to place Jellicoe in the supreme command afloat in 1914, the year he had long anticipated war would break out. In the interval Fisher tried, with limited success, to coach him in the virtues of independent squadron tactics. He used them as a subordinate in the 1912 manoeuvres, but never as a commander-in-chief. Jellicoe also supervised the trials of Percy Scott's director firing system, and played a (historically) controversial part in approving the adoption of Captain Frederick Dreyer's fire-control system. In 1913 he took temporary command of the 'hostile' fleet in the annual manoeuvres, exploiting favourable rules to get the better of Sir George Callaghan's 'British' fleet. However, this success afloat was a temporary distraction; Jellicoe was increasingly occupied by the threat of German mines, U-boats, mass torpedo attacks, and Zeppelin scouting. He shared Fisher's opinion that the North Sea was no place for a battlefleet, and yet objected to his mentor's schemes which were intended to draw the German fleet into battle by threatening to occupy the Baltic, or stage large-scale amphibious operations.

Crisis and war, 1914–1916 After a period of sick leave on the continent Jellicoe returned to London in July 1914 to find himself appointed second in command of the Grand Fleet, which contained all the modern battleships. It had been intended that he would succeed Callaghan in October, but the July crisis hastened the process. After arriving at Scapa Flow Jellicoe was ordered to relieve Callaghan, a step against which he protested vehemently, not once but four times. Finally on 4 August he went aboard the *Iron*

Duke, and took command. Churchill and Prince Louis of Battenberg had completed Fisher's plan. The step was more bold than brilliant, for Callaghan had the confidence of the entire service, the worship of his fleet, and a wealth of experience. Furthermore, despite Churchill's claims, he was in fine health, unlike Jellicoe. Had the fleet been forced into battle at any time before the end of the year Callaghan's abrupt dismissal would have seemed, in retrospect, to have been among Churchill's worst decisions of the year. Had Jellicoe been left in place as second in command he could have developed his grasp of the fleet under less trying circumstances, profited from the wisdom of the older man, and arrived at the supreme command in better health. This he recognized, and far from grasping at the high command went far beyond mere common decency in his attempts to stave off his fate.

Jellicoe took command aged fifty-five, a small (5 feet 6 inches), wiry man of quick and precise movements.

> His mind was a well-ordered filing system of detail, reflected by his small, neat person, the tight mouth, and the watchful brown eyes that looked out steadily past the prominent nose. His manner was cool, controlled, and always polite.
> (Barnett, 109)

He would need all of his qualities for the campaign that would follow. In the strategy designed by Fisher, and developed by the secretary of the committee of imperial defence, Maurice Hankey, the Grand Fleet would control the war, denying Germany contact with the outside world, cutting her trade, and crippling her economy by blockade. There was no need to seek out the enemy battlefleet, because the Grand Fleet already held all the strategic advantages; it was up to the Germans to seek battle at a time and place of Jellicoe's choosing if they wanted to change matters. This they would be reluctant to do, for the inner logic of the Tirpitz plan, and the end of the naval race in 1912, a crushing British victory, had left their fleet inferior to the British. The whole structure reflected the genius of one man, Fisher, and he had selected the calm, controlled Jellicoe for the most tedious task. One has to conclude that he knew his man, and did not mean the Nelson comparison to be taken too literally.

In the first months of the war Jellicoe's prime concern was to preserve his occasionally slender margin of superiority, at a time when his main base at Scapa Flow lacked any security against submarines. Elements of the fleet were detached, his ships suffered from a rash of technical problems, and their vulnerability was emphasized by the loss of the modern dreadnought *Audacious* to a single mine on 27 October. Well aware of German technical prowess Jellicoe kept his fleet at sea for long periods, learning how to handle the largest fleet yet assembled. His natural caution, allied to years of conditioning, made him an arch centralizer. This tendency was reinforced by the low opinion he held of many of his key subordinates, and resulted in the production of the stifling 'Grand Fleet battle orders', a massive compendium intended to allow the fleet to be controlled by flag signals. They 'verged upon an attempt to foresee and provide for all contingencies' (Patterson, *Jellicoe*, 67). He was reducing the possibilities of a fleet battle to a single scenario.

Lacking the hard test of battle, and the ruthlessness that characterized Fisher's career, Jellicoe patiently built up his fleet, his base, and his methods, settling into a routine. In essence he developed a system to work with limitations that he either could not, or in the case of junior commanders, would not, deal with. By reducing his squadron commanders to signal-driven automata he reduced the chances both of defeat, and of victory. In October 1914 he secured Admiralty acquiescence for his reluctance to go too far south, or chase a fleeing enemy too closely for fear of mines. Although the whole world expected a big battle, replaying Trafalgar, Jellicoe knew that the high seas fleet was far better than Villeneuve's scratch force, while his own fleet lacked the battle experience, initiative, and drive that had enabled Nelson to overwhelm his enemy. In falling back on rigid control systems Jellicoe was, unknowingly, replaying an earlier period of British naval activity, when similar rules had been introduced to avoid costly errors by inexperienced officers.

By mid-1915 Jellicoe's margin of superiority over the German fleet was large enough to cover refits and still leave him with a markedly larger battlefleet. German battle cruiser raids on such important military targets as the seaside resorts of Scarborough and Great Yarmouth had failed to bring on the detached squadron action they sought. Despite the boredom and bleak surroundings of Scapa the morale of the Grand Fleet held up well, a major effort being put into sports, entertainment, and other activities. Once again Jellicoe earned the lifelong devotion of his officers and men by his thoughtful and humane leadership. What little glory fell to the Royal Navy in the North Sea in the first two years of war went to the Battle-Cruiser Fleet under Vice-Admiral Sir David Beatty, leaving the Grand Fleet to practise ship handling, squadron manoeuvres, and gunnery, waiting for *Der Tag*.

The battle of Jutland, 1916 Their chance came at the end of May 1916, when the new German commander-in-chief, Admiral Reinhard Scheer, adopted a more aggressive policy. He planned to sortie into the North Sea, setting a submarine ambush, and seeking an engagement with a portion of Jellicoe's fleet. However, Scheer did not realize that British naval intelligence was reading his wireless signals, and was able to forewarn Jellicoe that something was happening, if not the exact details. Consequently Jellicoe put to sea late on 30 May, long before Scheer, and arranged to rendezvous with Beatty off the Jutland peninsula at 2 p.m. the following afternoon. Yet the Admiralty mishandled critical intelligence on the composition and location of the German fleet, giving him no reason to suspect that the whole German fleet had left harbour. Consequently Jellicoe did not hurry to the rendezvous. The Admiralty would be equally negligent on the following day, failing to send the powerful Harwich flotilla to join him. His subordinates compounded his problems by failing to relay tactical information on a day when no one could hope to obtain a full picture of events.

At 2.20 p.m. one of Beatty's light cruisers reported contact with the enemy, and Jellicoe then increased to full speed. At 2.35 p.m., long before the two main fleets came into contact, their advanced forces, Beatty's Battle-Cruiser Fleet and Vice-Admiral Franz Hipper's first scouting group, were in action. In his anxiety to engage the retreating enemy Beatty lost touch with his supporting force, the four very powerful fast battleships of Vice-Admiral Hugh Evan-Thomas's 5th battle squadron, and compromised the fire-control analysis of his ships. When the battle cruisers opened fire at 3.48 p.m. Hipper's five ships, with the advantage of better light conditions, outshot Beatty's six, one of which exploded. Although Evan-Thomas managed to regain contact by 4.06 p.m., another of Beatty's ships exploded twenty minutes later. Both ships were destroyed after shells penetrated their turrets, the flash of exploding ammunition passing down into the magazine, igniting hundreds of tons of volatile high explosive. The flash travelled down the magazine hoists because the battle cruisers had removed the safety interlocks to increase their rate of fire, to compensate for poor gunnery. Jellicoe did not know of these losses until after the battle.

When the leading ships of Scheer's main fleet were sighted at 4.33 p.m. Beatty turned north, leading Hipper and Scheer towards Jellicoe, who was coming south at 20 knots. Aboard the *Iron Duke* he was largely blind; only the reports from Commodore William *Goodenough's 2nd cruiser squadron, which was with Beatty's force, were particularly accurate. Consequently he did not know the exact bearing on which the enemy was steering, or when he could expect to encounter them. In addition he was uncertain as to the exact number of ships the Germans had brought out, and their order of sailing. However, there had never been any doubt in his mind that he would deploy his six columns of sailing into a single line ahead on the port column, a manoeuvre he ordered at 6.14 p.m. This would secure the best light conditions for gunnery, place his most powerful ships in the van, with his flagship one-third distance from the head of the line, and position his fleet between Scheer and the German bases. Just before the two fleets came into contact, the 3rd battle-cruiser squadron (Rear-Admiral Sir Horace Hood) drove Hipper's battle cruisers off course, denying Scheer his only chance to obtain any tactical information, before Hood's flagship blew up. The sudden appearance of Scheer's leading units to the south-west, not the south as expected, was a shock, but Jellicoe already had the Grand Fleet into line with the visibility in their favour in time for a classic crossing the T manoeuvre, enabling his leading ships to open fire at 6.23 p.m. and inflict serious damage on the three leading German battleships. In the poor visibility Scheer could not see his enemy, but realized that he had no option but to retreat, and he ordered a complex and risky manoeuvre, the 'battle-turn-away', which required all his ships to reverse course together. In poor and inconsistent visibility Jellicoe was not aware of the manoeuvre, and was never able to form a comprehensive impression of the battle.

At 7.10 p.m. Scheer, having inexplicably reversed course, was once again hammered by the Grand Fleet. The gunnery of *Iron Duke* (Captain Frederick Dreyer) was particularly good. Once again Scheer turned away and fled into the combination of haze, coal smoke, and cordite fumes that shrouded the battlefield. This time Scheer covered his retreat with a massed torpedo attack, something Jellicoe had long feared. He responded, as he had always intended, by turning his fleet away, to outrun the torpedoes and present the minimum target. There were no hits, but Scheer escaped.

Twice Jellicoe had briefly been able to fight the battle he wanted, a medium-range gunnery duel with his fleet in line ahead engaging the enemy who had very few guns bearing. This maximized his strength in heavy guns, exploited his simple fire-control calculators, and avoided the need for lower level initiative. However, poor visibility, lack of time, and defective armour-piercing shells denied him victory that day. He made no effort to regain contact with Scheer. Believing night actions were a lottery he would wait until the morning. Confident that he had outfought Scheer and outmanoeuvred him, to secure the critical advantage of laying between Scheer and his bases he only had to hold his position to produce a 'glorious first of June' to eclipse Lord Howe's victory. He did not attempt to keep contact with the German fleet, or divide his fleet to cover the two routes by which Scheer could return to Germany through the minefields. Placing his destroyer flotillas astern of the battle fleet to avoid friendly fire incidents Jellicoe continued towards the southern route. By 10 p.m. the Admiralty knew that Scheer had ordered a Zeppelin reconnaissance over the northern route, the Horn's Reef, for the following dawn, but failed to pass on the information. As if that were not enough Scheer was then able to push through the rear of the British fleet, often in clear sight of battleship captains, junior admirals, and other commanders, who failed to engage, and assumed that Jellicoe could also see what was happening. Despite heavy firing and some serious losses among light craft, Jellicoe was never made aware of the situation. The following morning he was left to cruise around a battlefield strewn with wreckage and corpses. Scheer had escaped. Jellicoe had lost a unique opportunity to have a positive impact on the course of the war. Churchill famously said that he was the only man who could have lost the war in an afternoon. He could also have helped to shorten it by destroying the high seas fleet, and Scheer gave him three chances to do just that. While the advance to Jutland was strategically aggressive, the battle being fought far closer to the German ports than it was to Scapa, Jellicoe lacked the remorseless urge to victory, and linked hatred of the enemy, that dominated Nelson's career. He was the safe choice to command the Grand Fleet, a task for which Nelson was never considered suitable.

The aftermath of Jutland After the battle the German government claimed a momentous victory, on the spurious grounds that they had sunk more British ships than they had lost. This led to some public criticism of the admiral and his fleet. In fact the Grand Fleet had a greater margin of superiority over the high seas fleet after the battle than it had possessed before, as many of the German ships would be in dockyard hands for months. More significantly Jellicoe realized that there would be no more major fleet actions, the Germans having been too roughly handled to risk another Jutland. Henceforth the naval challenge would come from the U-boats. Once the reality of what had occurred at Jutland had been accepted, namely that the British had won a significant strategic victory, confirming their dominance of the world's oceans, the ignorant attacks subsided. The initial success of German propaganda ultimately rebounded on them. However, even before his dispatch had been completed, Jellicoe had further cause for self-doubt: on 5 June the cruiser *Hampshire* sank after striking a mine shortly after leaving Scapa on a route he had advised; among those lost was the secretary of state for war, Lord Kitchener.

The lessons of the battle were studied in detail by Grand Fleet committees, notably the adequacy of protection against long-range fire, and the performance of armour-piercing shells. Grand Fleet battle orders were modified, introducing a few new alternatives, but in essence they remained centralized. Jellicoe was anxious to reduce the chance that the battle cruisers could become engaged with the enemy too far ahead of the battle fleet. At the Admiralty the handling of signals intelligence was improved and integrated into the naval staff. The package of reforms, improvements, and modifications that were put in place greatly enhanced the combat effectiveness of the Grand Fleet. As Arthur Marder argued, 'His true greatness as a fleet commander lay in his capitalisation on the lessons of Jutland' (Marder, *From the Dreadnought*, 3.285).

There was even another chance of battle. On 19 August Scheer sortied in an attempt to draw Jellicoe into another submarine ambush. This time the nervous German admiral was misled by his Zeppelins, and there was no contact, although Jellicoe lost two cruisers to submarines. Thereafter both he and Beatty agreed that the fleet should not go further south than the site of the Jutland battle, relying on the blockade to bring the Germans to give battle under circumstances favourable to the British. The Admiralty concurred in this sound policy. Having failed to alter the balance of heavy surface forces the Germans switched their submarines back to attacking merchant shipping on 6 October, although still under restrictions agreed with the United States. This deprived Scheer of the only 'leveller' that would warrant another sortie, and condemned the Grand Fleet to two more years of waiting. However, the problem would from now on be only a part of Jellicoe's remit. If he had been stretched to the limit of his capacity, and rather beyond his education and experience, as commander-in-chief of the Grand Fleet, Jellicoe was about to face an altogether more imposing set of demands.

Admiralty and U-boat threat, 1916–1918 Jellicoe left the Grand Fleet with a heavy heart on 28 November, and arrived at the Admiralty on 4 December 1916 to relieve the uninspiring technocrat Admiral Sir Henry *Jackson as first sea lord. He had accepted the call to the highest office,

like so much else, from a sense of duty, but without enthusiasm. In his new post Jellicoe was responsible for advising the cabinet on the overall direction of the war at sea; his primary task was to combat the submarine threat to merchant shipping. Although Jellicoe was widely regarded as the one man capable of meeting the challenge, Fisher did not think he would be able to deal with politicians. In addition Jellicoe was exhausted and in poor health, problems which stemmed from his style of leadership and approach to command, and only exacerbated his natural caution. The impact of the renewed German campaign was immediate, and it was only a question of time before the Germans adopted unrestricted attacks. Having failed to secure victory on land, and suffering heavy attrition at Verdun and in the Somme, the German high command decided to shift its main effort to the sea. The commanders were convinced they could defeat Britain by unrestricted U-boat warfare in six month, sinking enough tons of shipping to starve Britain out of the war and bring down the entire alliance. If they were correct, the intervention of the United States would be too late. Unrestricted U-boat warfare began on 1 February 1917. Within two months shipping losses had reached the staggering level of 800,000 tons per month, while the U-boats seemed to be immune.

Jellicoe had no simple answer to the U-boats. He argued that the problem had to be considered as a whole and a range of measures taken to deal with it. He installed a new set of sea lords, added a fifth, and created an anti-submarine division of the naval staff with a mandate to co-ordinate all relevant activity. In addition he added a trade division to the naval intelligence department, opening the prospect of integrating shipping, ports, inland transport, and import priorities into an overall policy. This new division was headed by Rear-Admiral Alexander Duff, a trusted Grand Fleet officer. Unfortunately for Jellicoe the new naval staff proved far from harmonious—junior officers critical of Duff and Jellicoe passed information and opinions to the secretary of the committee of imperial defence, Maurice Hankey, as a conduit to the prime minister, Lloyd George. Lloyd George was also receiving criticism of Jellicoe and the Admiralty from the Grand Fleet. Ultimately the system of convoying merchant ships with warship escorts would prove decisive—denying the U-boats the chance to attack without risking their own destruction. Jellicoe has been widely criticized for not adopting this measure more quickly, a charge that presupposes the concept was generally accepted, easy to introduce, and risk free. In fact Jellicoe, as might be expected, moved cautiously, introducing convoy on the Scandinavian and French coal trade routes in January and February 1917. When these experiments proved successful he regularized the routes in mid-April, and added a new convoy route between Gibraltar and Britain. In his *War Memoirs* Lloyd George claimed that his visit to the Admiralty on 30 April 1917 forced the Admiralty to adopt the convoy; but this, like much else in the book, was spurious. In fact he spent most of the time playing with Jellicoe's young daughters. His well-known anxiety for action may have provided a stimulus, but this had been effective long before the end of April. Duff's report in favour of the convoy had already been issued on the 26th.

Shortly afterwards Lloyd George sent Sir Eric Geddes to the Admiralty as a civilian controller of shipbuilding and procurement, and a harbinger of his efforts to gain control of naval policy. Throughout 1917 there was a widespread, if unfocused feeling that the Admiralty and the navy were lacking initiative and drive. This reflected a complete ignorance of the effectiveness of the blockade in strangling the German economy, confining the conflict to Europe, and securing access to the resources of manpower, finished goods, and raw materials of the rest of the world. As in the major wars of the past the long-drawn-out struggle of attrition provided few moments of glory to punctuate the tedium. Jellicoe, a convinced 'Westerner' in grand strategy, believed that victory could only be achieved by defeating the Germans in home waters, and in France. He prepared a major amphibious operation for the Belgian coast, to be carried out if Field Marshal Haig's Paschendaele offensive reached key targets. The offensive, aimed at German U-boat bases in Belgium, had been largely developed in response to the submarine threat. When it failed the amphibious operations were cancelled.

As Fisher had anticipated Jellicoe proved to be less effective at Whitehall and in cabinet meetings than he had been aboard the *Iron Duke*. He was undemonstrative, lacked oratorical gifts, and was characteristically cautious, tending towards outright pessimism, an approach that was diametrically opposed to that of Lloyd George. The continuing high level of merchant-ship losses did nothing to improve his standing. He had already put in place the convoy system as the critical element in an all-round approach to meeting the threat, but the ultimate success of his measures would only become clear with the benefit of post-war analysis. He lacked the high-level social contacts, outgoing personality, and political sense to be a great first sea lord. Lloyd George disliked both his gloomy perspective and his refusal to join attacks on Haig. Haig repaid his professional loyalty by intriguing against him with everyone who would listen, from the king and Sir Max Aitken to Asquith. However, Lloyd George lacked the political strength to sack Jellicoe in July 1917, restricting himself to replacing his strongest supporter, the first lord, Sir Edward *Carson, with Geddes, who was very much the prime minister's man. In September Geddes brought Admiral Sir Rosslyn *Wemyss to the Admiralty as deputy first sea lord. Then at 6 p.m. on Christmas eve 1917 Geddes sacked Jellicoe, choosing his moment to reduce the amount of adverse publicity. The other sea lords threatened to resign as a body, but were dissuaded by Jellicoe and the civilian members of the Admiralty. Whether Jellicoe should have been replaced, and his weariness, ill health, and gloom suggest he was due for a well-earned rest, the manner of his dismissal was deeply offensive both to the man and to the service. That he never complained of his treatment reflected his immense personal dignity.

Assessment of Jellicoe as first sea lord Jellicoe's legacy as first sea lord was the system that defeated the U-boats in 1918. He also remedied the defects shown up at Jutland, improving magazine safety and armour-piercing shells; maintained the successful naval strategy against pressure from ill-advised politicians, at the time when American entry into the war allowed the blockade to be made more rigorous; and established excellent relations with the new belligerent, through his long-standing friendship with their senior officer in Europe, Admiral William Sims USN. There had been no glory and little reward in his year at Whitehall, but he had done his duty to the best of his ability. He was still an arch centralizer, reluctant to delegate, and unable to avoid immersion in trivia that should have been handled at a far lower level. In attending to these comforting reminders of happier days he neglected the higher direction of the war and the vital business of cabinet level co-operation. His successor immediately divested himself of all such routine tasks, without adversely affecting the conduct of the war.

On 15 January 1918 he was ennobled as Viscount Jellicoe of Scapa. He had already received the GCVO and the Order of Merit in 1916, to which he would add a variety of foreign orders and decorations, the freedom of several cities, and honorary degrees. He devoted his new found freedom to writing a narrative of his war. The first volume, *The Grand Fleet, 1914–1916*, was published in 1919; *The Crisis of the Naval War* appeared in 1920. Although useful sources they were limited by the need for secrecy, and the lack of any sense of deep personal involvement. In May 1918 it was proposed that he should become allied commander-in-chief in the Mediterranean, but the Italian government refused to entrust their battle fleet to a foreign officer. Through an oversight neither he nor Fisher were invited to witness the surrender of the high seas fleet on 20 November 1918. In 1918 his only son, George Patrick John Rushworth, later second Earl Jellicoe, was born. He was the last of his six children, one of his daughters dying in infancy. In January 1919 Jellicoe received the thanks of both houses of parliament, a grant of £50,000, and promotion to admiral of the fleet.

Post-war, 1918–1935 In August 1918 the dominion prime ministers had urged the Admiralty to send a senior officer to advise them on the creation of dominion navies. These were to be independent, but linked to the Royal Navy. They favoured Jellicoe for the mission. Both the Admiralty and the admiral would have preferred a single imperial navy, but this was not an option. Jellicoe received little guidance from an Admiralty board which was probably only too pleased to send him round the world at that time. He left England on 21 February 1919, aboard the battle cruiser *New Zealand*. He viewed Japan as the likely future enemy, and advised that a 100 per cent superiority would be required on account of the vast distances involved. He called for a powerful fleet to be based in the Far East; Australia and New Zealand would contribute ships, while India paid for cruisers and smaller vessels and the Royal Navy provided the battle fleet. He recognized that a lack of dock and base facilities was the major weakness of the imperial position. He stressed the need for the officer corps of all the navies to be integrated, using the Royal Navy as the common standard. While he was warmly received everywhere, and worked hard on his reports, Jellicoe's mission was eccentric to the post-war planning of the Admiralty and was overtaken by the Washington treaty of 1922, which crippled British and dominion seapower. The Singapore naval base, the Royal Indian Navy and the New Zealand division were the enduring legacies of the tour. After a visit to the United States he hauled down his flag for the last time at Spithead on 4 February 1920.

On his return to Britain Jellicoe was drawn into the growing controversy over the conduct and consequences of Jutland. Wemyss had ordered a purely narrative account to be prepared, but when Beatty replaced him as first sea lord on 1 November 1919, he objected to certain passages that he felt did not do full justice to the Battle-Cruiser Fleet. When Jellicoe was shown Beatty's amendments he refused to take up his appointment as governor-general of New Zealand until he was satisfied that they would not be published. Unable to resolve the clash between Beatty's perceptions and Jellicoe's evidence the Admiralty postponed publication. Beatty then commissioned a naval staff appreciation, which turned out to be strongly pro-Beatty, and not particularly accurate. Even when toned down for publication in 1924 as the *Admiralty Narrative* this document remained divisive. Jellicoe considered it grossly inaccurate. He particularly resented the treatment of his lifelong friend Hugh Evan-Thomas, who had been blamed for allowing the distance between his squadron and the battle cruisers to become too great on two vital occasions. Evan-Thomas, distressed by the document, had a stroke. Jellicoe believed the fault, on both occasions, was due to Beatty's incompetent signal staff. When the *Official History of Naval Operations* reached Jutland (in 1922 with volume 3), Sir Julian Corbett's careful account was criticized for being written from Jellicoe's perspective, and minimizing the importance of forcing the battle to a decisive conclusion. In truth Corbett understood the strategy of the North Sea, and the role of the battle, far better than his critics. Jellicoe kept out of the public controversy, and although he did prepare a revised edition of *The Grand Fleet*, which contained more criticism of Beatty, refuting the major points raised by the *Admiralty Narrative*, the market for such books was exhausted.

Between 1920 and 1924 Jellicoe was governor-general of New Zealand, where he built on the popularity evident in 1919, and modernized the way in which the office was exercised, making himself accessible to all. Typically he was always busy either travelling, speaking, working, sailing, or playing golf. Much as he enjoyed the post he declined a further term in order to take his children back to Britain for their education. He left New Zealand in November 1924, being elevated to earl in the following June in recognition of his services.

Unfortunately the Jutland controversy flared up again with Admiral Bacon's *The Jutland Scandal*, a violently pro-Jellicoe account, the translation of the German official account, which also favoured Jellicoe, and Churchill's version, which leant heavily on the *Admiralty Narrative* and was highly critical of his caution. Only in 1927 did something like a consensus begin to emerge, to be revisited from time to time from that day to this. Jutland retains an enduring fascination, both as the only full-scale naval battle of the dreadnought era, and as one of history's great talking points.

The next battle for Jellicoe was with Lloyd George's version of the decision to adopt the convoy, which Sir Henry Newbolt was about to repeat in volume five of the *Official History*. When the relevant volume of Lloyd George's *War Memoirs* appeared in 1934 Jellicoe responded with a new account of 1917, *The Submarine Peril*, which came out in the same year.

When he returned to Britain Jellicoe remained devoted to public service, dividing his time between London county council, the Empire Service League, the Boy Scouts, the National Rifle Association, and four years as president of the British Legion. These were all active roles, and it was typical that he should have caught a chill while planting poppies on 9 November 1935, and then attended an Armistice day service in defiance of medical advice. The chill developed into pneumonia and he died at his home, 39 Egerton Gardens, Chelsea, on 19 November. He was buried at St Paul's Cathedral on 25 November, alongside Nelson and Collingwood.

Assessment From relatively humble origins Jellicoe rose to the top of a profession dominated by birth, wealth, and privilege. He did so on ability and determination. His precise, mathematical intellect emphasized control, the reduction of risk, and the management of what could not be controlled. As a commander he was self-reliant, but lacked the ability to delegate, or to sack. He shunned publicity, and took more satisfaction from the devotion of the lower deck than the acclaim of the press. His loyalty to his subordinates was legendary, although not always merited. He ignored public attacks on his own conduct, but responded firmly to criticism of those under his command. He had a quiet, reserved manner, immense reserves of dignity (seen to the greatest advantage in the Jutland debate of the 1920s), and a very personal style of command which secured the lifelong love of all those who served him. The same character traits meant that he lacked the hard-edged, ruthless careerist ambition that so marked his mentor, Fisher, and the overt charisma of his successor Beatty. Fisher had predicted that Jellicoe would be a second Nelson. But he was wrong. Jellicoe was not touched by the genius or the passion that made Nelson unique. He was a very fine officer of outstanding ability who had the singular misfortune to meet his defining moment without the benefit of an intelligent education in the higher direction of war, or any worthwhile prior experience. Even then he did not lose his battle: he only failed to make it decisive, a failure that has given rise to more controversy than any naval battle in history. Under the direction of a strategist of genius, Fisher, he would have been provided with a better understanding of his role, but the Admiralty regime of Sir Arthur Balfour and Admiral Jackson lacked energy and vision, and the navy was assigned a largely passive role in the British war effort by a cabinet ignorant of its real strength.

For all his essential humanity and dignity Jellicoe remains a controversial figure. His public actions between 1914 and 1917 are at the core of debates on the pre-1914 Royal Navy, Jutland, and the introduction of the convoy. These are major issues and will be discussed for as long as naval history is written. Those who wish to criticize him have to address the structural failings of the pre-1914 Royal Navy, which emphasized a very limited range of skills as the key to success, and failed to educate the men who would have to lead the service in wartime. Jellicoe was not a genius. He was asked to do the impossible in two posts, and he did his best. It is unlikely that any of his contemporaries would have done better; most, when tested, proved far less capable. In summary it was not just the one afternoon when he could have lost the war; the critical period stretched from 4 August 1914 to 24 December 1917. For three and a half years he bore a crushing burden of responsibility, well aware of the many disadvantages under which the Royal Navy laboured. Twice he defeated the naval challenge of imperial Germany. He deserves his place alongside the heroes of another age.

ANDREW LAMBERT

Sources A. T. Patterson, *Jellicoe* (1969) · R. Bacon, *The life of Earl Jellicoe* (1936) · *The Jellicoe papers*, ed. A. T. Patterson, 2 vols., Navy RS, 108, 111 (1966–8) · A. J. Marder, *From the Dreadnought to Scapa Flow: the Royal Navy in the Fisher era, 1904–1919*, 5 vols. (1961–70) · *Fear God and dread nought: the correspondence of Admiral of the Fleet Lord Fisher of Kilverstone*, ed. A. J. Marder, 3 vols. (1952–9) · A. Gordon, *The rules of the game: Jutland and British naval command* (1996) · C. Barnett, *The swordbearers* (1963) · J. Goldrick, *The king's ships were at sea* (1984) · F. C. Dreyer, *The sea heritage: a study in maritime warfare* (1955) · S. W. Roskill, *Admiral of the fleet Earl Beatty: the last naval hero, an intimate biography* (1980) · J. T. Sumida, *In defence of naval supremacy: finance, technology and British naval policy, 1889–1914* (1989) · S. W. Roskill, *Hankey, man of secrets*, 1 (1970) · Burke, *Peerage* · GEC, *Peerage* · *CGPLA Eng. & Wales* (1936)
Archives BL, corresp. and papers, Add. MSS 48989–49052 | BL, corresp. with Arthur James Balfour, Add. MSS 49714, *passim* · BL, corresp. with Lord Keyes · Bodl. Oxf., letters to Herbert Asquith · CAC Cam., letters to A. Hurd; corresp. with Lord Fisher · HLRO, letters to Herbert Samuel · IWM, letters to Admiral de Chavis · LPL, letters to H. R. L. Sheppard · NL Aus., corresp. with Lord Novar · NMM, letters to David Beatty; corresp. with Sir Julian Corbett, Sir Alexander Duff, R. H. Gibson · PRO, admiralty archives · PRO NIre., corresp. with Edward Carson, D1507 | FILM BFI NFTVA, actuality footage; documentary footage
Likenesses J. Russell & Sons, photograph, *c.*1910, Hult. Arch. [*see illus.*] · F. Dodd, charcoal and watercolour drawing, 1917, IWM · G. Philpot, oils, 1918, IWM · W. Stoneman, photograph, 1925, NPG · E. Kapp, drawing, 1928, Barber Institute of Fine Arts, Birmingham · H. A. Pigram, plaster bust, 1928, IWM · W. T. Monnington, oils, 1932–4, NMM · R. G. Eves, oils, 1935, NPG · Mrs A. Broom, photograph, NPG · A. S. Cope, group portrait, oils (*Naval officers of World War I, 1914–18*), NPG · R. G. Eves, oils, HMS *Excellent*, Portsmouth · D. Low, pencil sketches, NPG · W. Macmillan, bronze bust, Trafalgar Square, London · Spy [L. Ward], caricature, NPG; repro. in *VF* (26 Dec 1906)
Wealth at death £13,370 18*s.* 0*d.*: probate, 7 Feb 1936, *CGPLA Eng. & Wales*

Jellicoe, Ursula, Lady Jellicoe (1907–1986). *See under* Jellicoe, Sir Geoffrey Alan (1900–1996).

Jemmat [*née* Yeo], **Catherine** (*bap.* 1714, *d.* 1766?), memoirist, was baptized on 12 November 1714 at St Thomas the Apostle, Exeter, the eldest of three children of John Yeo (*d.* 1756), a half-pay admiral, and his first wife. The family moved to Plymouth shortly after her birth. She is known for her *Memoirs* (2 vols., 1762; 2nd edn, 1765), the chief source of information about her life. There, she describes her father as an indifferent sailor and, at home, 'a bashaw, whose single nod of disapprobation struck terror into the whole family' (Jemmat, *Memoirs*, 1.5). Her mother died when she was five or six years old and, within months, her father had married 'a giggling girl of nineteen' (ibid., 1.10); they had five children, four of whom died. Catherine Yeo was sent to a boarding-school for a time; she describes herself as 'endow'd with a quick genius, and a propensity to learn whatever was in the reach of my capacity' (ibid., 1.16). She left the boarding-school 'to learn plain work, under the care of three gentlewomen' (ibid., 1.17), and eventually returned to her father's house.

Much of Catherine's *Memoirs* describes the tensions between her own 'giddy and romantic' nature (Jemmat, *Memoirs*, 1.118–19) and her father's desire to arrange a financially advantageous marriage for her. She characterizes herself as being 'used to the gaiety of public places; to a perpetual round of company' (ibid., 2.4), and the first volume of her *Memoirs* is largely devoted to accounts of her numerous suitors. But Catherine also implies that her father resorted to domestic violence in his efforts to control her choice of husband, for she characterizes his behaviour as 'insupportable, and such as I had much rather the reader would guess at … than I should attempt further to illustrate' (ibid., 1.96). She does describe being 'lock'd … up for two months' in order to be kept apart from one of her suitors, 'during which space, I never saw a creature but the person who brought me victuals; I was neither suffered to have pen, ink, or paper' (ibid., 1.52). Finally, she 'resolved to marry the first person who should propose himself to me' (ibid., 1.166).

Catherine's resolution resulted in marriage to a Mr Jemmat, a Plymouth silk mercer. He claimed to have 'a pretty fortune of about three thousand pounds, well laid out in business' (Jemmat, *Memoirs*, 2.1), and offered his 'affection and fortune' as a means of escape 'from the tyranny of a relentless father' (ibid., 2.7–8). After their marriage they returned to Jemmat's home and business in Plymouth: the house was 'an hog-sty' (ibid., 2.33), and Jemmat himself alcoholic and physically abusive, with 'no intentions to settle in the world, or to obtain the reputation of an upright man' (ibid., 2.33). She described their marriage:

> night after night, like a poor submissive slave, have I laid my lordly master in his bed, intoxicated and insensible: day after day have I received blows and bruises for my reward: in short, I thought I had married a man, I found I had married a monster. (ibid., 2.57)

She also soon learned that Jemmat married her in order 'to extort money from my father to pay his creditors, who were very numerous and pressing' (ibid., 2.34); when her father refused to comply, Jemmat finally went bankrupt within three years of their marriage. By this time, Catherine Jemmat had given birth to a daughter. Despite the intervention of her friends, Admiral Yeo refused to help his daughter, with the result that she was 'thrown upon the wide world for support' (ibid., 2.58).

Catherine Jemmat employs many of the stock defences of the eighteenth-century woman writer to justify her entrance into print. At one point she laments her own romantic streak which led her to reject a marriage proposal from an

> eminent tradesman … had I been but worldly enough to have suppressed my want of regard, and to have acted like the modern young ladies, I might now have been driven in a coach and six, instead of driving myself a quill. (Jemmat, *Memoirs*, 1.119–20)

But elsewhere she suggests something more than financial motives for her *Memoirs*. She is 'induc[ed] to … resigning the needle for the pen' in order '[t]o arraign my words, thoughts, and actions, with the minutest truth, at the tribunal of publick justice' (ibid., 1.3). Jemmat confesses that her reputation has been irretrievably damaged, but at the end of her *Memoirs* she is at pains to demonstrate that she has not 'act[ed] beneath the dignity of my sex', and provides evidence from her acquaintances in order to 'shew the opinion that every one that knew me had of my father and husband's behaviour' (ibid., 2.59).

Almost nothing is known of Catherine Jemmat's life beyond the events described in her *Memoirs*. In 1762 the first edition of her *Memoirs* was published by subscription, with an extensive list of subscribers. A second edition appeared in 1765. Her *Miscellanies, in Prose and Verse* was published in 1766, again by subscription. She explains in her introduction that the collection 'does not consist wholly of originals', and includes pieces by friends as well as some previously published material. Modern scholars have been reluctant to ascribe any sections of the *Miscellanies* to Jemmat herself. Her death was reported in the *London Magazine* in November 1766. Two further editions of both her *Memoirs* and *Miscellanies* appeared in 1771.

JEANNE WOOD

Sources C. Jemmat, *The memoirs of Mrs. Catherine Jemmat, daughter of the late Admiral Yeo of Plymouth, written by herself*, 2nd edn, 2 vols. (1765) · C. Jemmat, *Miscellanies, in prose and verse* (1766) · parish register, Exeter, St Thomas the Apostle, 1714 [baptism] · *London Magazine*, 35 (1766), 599 · R. Lonsdale, 'Catherine Jemmat (née Yeo)', *Eighteenth-century women poets: an Oxford anthology*, ed. R. Lonsdale (1989), 234–5; pbk edn (1990) · Blain, Clements & Grundy, *Feminist comp.* · J. Todd, ed., *A dictionary of British and American women writers, 1660–1800* (1984)

Jemmat, William (d. 1678), Church of England clergyman and author, was born in Reading, Berkshire, one of at least two sons of William Jemmat (d. 1609), brewer, of St Giles's parish, and his wife, Elizabeth (1568/9–1650). His father, who died intestate in August 1609, had probably served as warden of the High ward of Reading borough in 1597–8; Elizabeth Jemmat married John Grove on 17 April 1615. William was educated at Reading Free Grammar School before entering Magdalen College, Oxford, in 1610. He

graduated BA in 1614 and proceeded MA from Magdalen Hall three years later.

Jemmat's career over the next thirty years can be reconstructed only partially. After being ordained he spent some time in Reading, where he married a local woman, Anne Pocock, on 11 October 1619 at St Giles's Church. That year he published *A Mappe of Rome*, an edition of five sermons preached by Thomas Taylor, a celebrated preacher who had often visited the town in Jemmat's younger days. However, it seems likely Jemmat did not stay in Reading long; no baptisms of his children in St Giles's parish are recorded. He was described as 'preacher at Lechlade' (Gloucestershire) in his own *A Spirituall Trumpet: Exciting and Preparing to the Christian Warfare* (1624), and Anthony Wood records another sermon preached there in December 1625 at the funeral of Mistress Bathurst and published as *Corona pietatis: the Memorial of the Just* (1627), although no known copy survives. About 1626 Jemmat became a licensed lecturer at Isleworth, Middlesex; Bishop William Laud of London in January 1632 permitted him 'to lecture … every afternoon' (Davies, 137). He continued to edit Taylor's works, publishing his *Christs Victorie* (1633), *Christ Revealed* (1635), and *The Principles of Christian Practice* (1635). Isleworth probably remained his home for fourteen years until, as was alleged in a petition presented by some parishioners to parliament in 1641, he was ejected by the vicar, William Grant.

By the time he published *A Watch-Word for Kent* (1643) Jemmat had been 'ordered by parliament to be preacher' at Faversham, while in *The Rock* (1644) he is described as 'pastor of Nettlestead' in the same county. In 1647 he was back at Isleworth, acting as interim vicar, and it was as preacher there and 'a cordial friend' of the late John Preston that he published *An Abridgement of Dr Preston's Works* (1648). On 20 December that year he was appointed under the great seal to succeed his brother John, who had been buried ten days earlier, as vicar of St Giles, Reading; he was instituted there in June 1649. The last of his editions of Taylor's work, *Moses and Aaron*, was published in 1653. He is also said to have translated part of Thomas Goodwin's works into Latin; the resulting publication appeared at Heidelberg in 1658.

At the Restoration Jemmat remained in post, 'much followed and admired by those of his persuasion' (Wood, *Ath. Oxon.*, 3.1147), taking the oath of allegiance and supremacy on 23 January 1661. His final work, *A Practical Exposition of the Historical Prophesie of Jonah*, was issued in 1666. At some point he leased a plot of land in the parish, which he bequeathed to his wife in his will, dated 6 September 1677. By this date he had four surviving sons, Samuel, John, Laurence, and Gideon, and two daughters, Margaret Stedman and Sarah Chandler. In the event that his wife survived him, he named Margaret as executor in order to 'provide for and cherish her mother' (PRO, PROB 11/256, fol. 24). Wood claims that he gave a legacy of books to the parish, but Jemmat divided these equally between Samuel and John; it was probably his father who gave the books recorded in a churchwardens' inventory of 1637. Jemmat died on 28 January 1678 and was buried in the chancel of his parish church three days later. Margaret Stedman proved the will on 11 March. JOAN A. DILS

Sources Wood, *Ath. Oxon.*, new edn, 3.1147 · Foster, *Alum. Oxon.*, *1500–1714* [William Jemmet] · will, PRO, PROB 11/256, fol. 24 · parish register, Reading, St Giles, 1564–99, 1599–1636, 1636–1730, Berks. RO, D/P96/1/1, 2, 3 · parish register, Reading, St Giles, 17 Aug 1609, Berks. RO, D/P96/1/2 [burial, William Jemmat, father] · parish register, Reading, St Giles, 22 March 1650, Berks. RO, D/P96/1/3 [burial, Elizabeth Jemmat, mother] · parish register, Reading, St Giles, 31 Jan 1678, Berks. RO, D/P96/13 [burial] · bond of administration and probate inventory of William Jemmat, father, 27 Feb 1610, Berks. RO, D/A1/198/63 · L. Harman, *The parish of St Giles-in-Reading* (1946), 57–8 · *ESTC* · J. M. Guilding, ed., *Reading records: diary of the corporation*, 1 (1892), 444 · *JHL*, 10 (1647–8), 635 · C. Coates, *The history and antiquities of Reading* (1802), 352–4 · *Reg. Oxf.*, 2/3.327 · *Walker rev.*, 260 · J. Davies, *The Caroline captivity of the church: Charles I and the remoulding of Anglicanism, 1625–1641* (1992), 137
Wealth at death books, lease of a barn and 'some ground' in Reading: will, PRO, PROB 11/256, fol. 24

Jemmy Button (*b.* **1815/16**, *d.* in or after **1855**). *See under* Exotic visitors (*act. c.*1500–c.1855).

Jempson, (Arthur) John (1904–1981), road haulier, was born at Strand Quay, Rye, Sussex, on 14 September 1904, the eldest son in a family of two sons and four daughters of Arthur Jempson (1877–1955) and his wife, Ruth Palmer (1876–1956), daughter of a seed merchant. The parents were Strict Baptists. Arthur Jempson had acquired a small haulage business from an uncle in the late nineteenth century, and the family home was next to rented stables where the firm's few horses and vehicles were kept. John Jempson went to local schools but left aged thirteen to join his father at a time of acute wartime labour shortage. As a schoolboy he was accustomed to delivering and collecting goods in his spare time, so he soon mastered the details of what was essentially a local business.

Young Jempson's interests were in motors, however, and he soon owned his own motor cycle, which he used for both work and pleasure. In 1924, aged twenty, he persuaded his reluctant father to lend him £145 to buy a Ford Model T, which he ran himself as part of the business, sharing the proceeds with his father. Capable of carrying 30 cwt, though supposed to carry no more than 20, and faster than horse-drawn vehicles, this small motor lorry had greater earning capacity, but involved much more work for its owner–driver, as he shovelled stone, or loaded sacks, which then weighed up to 2.25 cwt each. Living simply with his parents, he soon built up a business, and was able to repay his father's loan within six months. In March 1926 he paid £800 for a 6 ton Thornycroft; other motor lorries soon followed. John Jempson made the transition to employer, though he continued to drive one of the larger lorries (with a mate) until 1934, with one of his sisters taking orders, and holding the office together, which she continued to do until her death. By 1934 seasonal traffic in fruit and hops, and all-year traffic in building materials, had been developed over the longer distance to London, providing door-to-door service at railway rates. Return freight, if available, was brought back the same day from the London docks. By 1937 turnover neared £14,000, and

father and son could pay themselves not only their £6 per week wages but also £608 each out of the year's profit of £2776. John Jempson had become a man of substance in control of a flourishing business. On 9 June 1938, aged thirty-three, he married Adah Ruth Ashby, the daughter of a prosperous Romney Marsh farmer. They had a son and a daughter and lived at Romney Marsh until 1943, when they moved to Rye.

Nationalization of road haulage proved advantageous for John Jempson. He agreed to manage the Rye depot of British Road Services, of which his former business was the nucleus, and was later promoted traffic superintendent at Tenterden, where he got to know new customers. On denationalization he put in a successful bid for the Rye depot, buying back a much larger business for considerably less than he had extracted in compensation earlier. This must have given him much satisfaction as a lifelong Conservative. Rapid economic—and therefore traffic—growth followed during the 1950s. The firm's profits allowed vehicles to be replaced by larger, faster, and more efficient models. By 1960, with this transformed fleet of only twenty-five lorries, revenue had grown by nearly 50 per cent, and costs by only 20 per cent. The firm was turned into a limited company, but was still wholly owned by Jempson and his wife. Economic conditions in the following years were less propitious, but by 1965 Jempson, then sixty-one, felt able to hand over day-to-day running to his 22-year-old son.

Like his father, Jonathan Jempson had driven lorries in his holidays, but his father's success had bestowed benefits John himself had never had; Tonbridge School, followed by a degree in commerce at Edinburgh. Jonathan's outlook was rather different from that of his cautious father. He also believed in borrowing money to make more of opportunities and accelerate growth, and this new policy was very successful. By the early 1980s the company was running sixty up-to-date vehicles.

John Jempson died at St Helen's Hospital, Ore, Hastings, Sussex, on 21 October 1981, survived by his wife. He was buried in Rye cemetery on 26 October. He had built up a business by careful and unceasing effort from small beginnings over forty long years; he handed it on to a son who was prepared to build on his success. THEO BARKER

Sources T. Barker, *The transport contractors of Rye* (1982) · private information (2004) · T. C. Barker and C. I. Savage, *An economic history of transport in Britain* (1974)
Archives John Jempson & Sons Ltd, Rye
Wealth at death £292,298: probate, 31 March 1982, *CGPLA Eng. & Wales*

Jenison, Francis [*known as* Count Jenison Walworth] (**1764–1824**), diplomatist, the son of Francis Jenison of Walworth, Heighington parish, co. Durham, was born at Walworth, where his ancestors had long resided, on 8 February 1764. The family withdrew to the continent in 1776, and settled at Heidelberg. The younger Francis became a page of honour and an officer of the guards of the elector palatine of Bavaria, and was afterwards a colonel in the service of Hesse-Darmstadt. At the beginning of the war in

1793 he was sent to the court of St James as envoy from Hesse-Darmstadt, and arranged for the employment of Hessian troops in British pay. After the marriage of the princess royal of England, Charlotte Augusta (1766–1828) with Prince Frederick, afterwards king of Württemberg, in 1797, Jenison was made high chamberlain of the household at Stuttgart, a post he held until the death of the king in 1816. He was at one time Bavarian minister at Naples. Jenison had a son from his first marriage, who was Bavarian envoy at Naples. His second wife was Mary, eldest daughter of Topham *Beauclerk, the friend of Dr Johnson, with whom he had a family of six, who survived him. He died at Heidelberg in 1824.

H. M. CHICHESTER, rev.

Sources GM, 1st ser., 94/1 (1824), 637

Jenison, Robert (bap. **1583**, d. **1652**), clergyman, was baptized at St Nicholas's, Newcastle, on 6 January 1583, the son of Ralph Jenison, a member of the governing élite who died in 1597 during his mayoral year, and his wife, Margaret, widow of Andrew Bewick, another member of the élite. Having attended the town's grammar school, Robert was admitted to Emmanuel College, Cambridge, where his tutor was the puritan Samuel Ward, with whom Jenison was to correspond until Ward's death. Jenison graduated BA in 1605 and proceeded MA from St John's in 1608, where he was a fellow and took his BD in 1616. He was briefly chaplain to the earl of Kent, but at the latter's death in 1614 returned to his fellowship.

Jenison returned to Newcastle in 1619 as master of St Mary Magdalene's Hospital, and on 22 June married at St Nicholas's, Newcastle, Anne, daughter of William Bonner. By 1622 he had been appointed lecturer at All Saints, when the corporation granted him an annual salary of £100, raised to £140 in 1625. The diocese was firmly in the hands of the Arminians at this time and supporters were placed in the vicarage. Although the parish was divided Jenison was not troubled by the courts despite his strong Calvinist leanings, which he had revealed in The Christian's Apparelling by Christ (1625, with an epistle to the reader by the eminent preacher Richard Sibbes), and his doubts over ceremonial, which he conveyed privately to Ward. Jenison saw himself as a conformist and took his DD in 1628, but he became increasingly uncomfortable with authority. Taking up a common theme in puritan writing, he saw England as undergoing divine chastisement for its sins, publishing his views in The Citie's Safety (1630). In 1631 local disagreements became public and on Good Friday he preached a sermon challenging Arminian practices which attracted the attention of the high commission, though no action was taken. Religion divided the community and in 1635 the future regicide John Blakiston, among others, was prosecuted for attending Jenison's sermons rather than services at his parish church. A severe outbreak of plague decimated the town in 1636–7, and Jenison wrote a vivid account, characteristically entitled Newcastle's call to her neighbours … to take warning by her sins and sorrows lest this overflowing scourge of pestilence reach even unto them, to which

he appended statistical details of the epidemic. The outbreak of the bishops' war heightened tensions in the town, and some puritans were suspected of treating with the Scottish covenanters. The high commission moved against Jenison in March 1639 and, though no evidence of disloyalty was found against him, he was finally deprived in September of that year for nonconformity.

In 1640 Jenison withdrew to Danzig, from where in a letter to Ward he described Newcastle as 'that wretched and unthankful town'. While there he published a collection of sermons, including the Good Friday one of 1631, but, following the sequestration of the Arminian vicar Yeldred (or Yeldard) Alvey, was invited back to his home town on 2 April 1645 as preacher. From that time he was the senior minister in the town, secured the appointment of most of the other clergy, administered the solemn league and covenant to the town, and was frequently consulted by the corporation. By this date his position had moved to a determined presbyterian one, declared in his The Return of the Sword (1648), and he set about establishing a classis system in the town. His health began to fail from 1647 and the town secured assistants to cover his preaching duties, but he remained active and was among those clergy who protested against the preaching of Socinian doctrines by Robert Everard in 1651. He died in Newcastle on 6 November 1652 and was buried there in St Nicholas's Church on 8 November, being survived by his second wife, Barbara (d. 1673), daughter of Samuel Sanderson of Hedleythorpe. He was succeeded as preacher by an Independent, Samuel Hammond, but his overall impact on the community was best expressed by an opponent who, complaining to Laud about a puritan preacher at Sunderland, wrote that there would soon be a proverb 'that Sunderland is Husbandied as Newcastle is Jenisonied' (Howell, Puritans and Radicals, 112).

WILLIAM JOSEPH SHEILS

Sources R. Howell, Puritans and radicals in north England: essays on the English revolution (1984) · R. Howell, Newcastle upon Tyne and the puritan revolution: a study of the civil war in north England (1967) · R. Welford, ed., History of Newcastle and Gateshead, 3: Sixteenth and seventeenth centuries (1887) · J. Brand, The history and antiquities of the town and county of the town of Newcastle upon Tyne, 2 vols. (1789) · [W. Greenwell], ed., Wills and inventories from the registry at Durham, 2, SurtS, 38 (1860) · Memoirs of the life of Mr Ambrose Barnes, ed. [W. H. D. Longstaffe], SurtS, 50 (1867)

Jenison [alias Freville, Beaumont], **Robert** (**1590–1656**), Jesuit, was born at Walworth, co. Durham, the eldest son of William Jenison esquire of Walworth Castle, and Jane Scurlock, daughter of Barnabas Scurlock esquire of Ireland, and grandson to Thomas Jenison, auditor-general of Ireland. He was admitted a student of Gray's Inn on 9 March 1615, was subsequently educated in the English College at St Omer, and joined the Society of Jesus in 1617 or 1619. He continued his studies at the Liège seminary and was ordained priest in 1622 and sent to England. His name appears in Gee's list of priests and Jesuits in and about London in 1623. His ordinary alias was Freville but he is also mentioned under the assumed name of Beaumont among the Jesuits seized by Humphrey Cross and other pursuivants at Clerkenwell in March 1628. In 1645 he became rector of the house of probation at Ghent, and in 1649 returned as missioner to the Hampshire district, where he probably died on 10 (or 13) October 1656.

THOMPSON COOPER, *rev.* G. BRADLEY

Sources T. M. McCoog, *English and Welsh Jesuits, 1555–1650*, 2 vols., Catholic RS, 74–5 (1994–5), 178 · Gillow, *Lit. biog. hist.*, 3.610 · A. M. C. Forster, 'A Durham family: Jenisons of Walworth', *Biographical Studies*, 3 (1955–6), 2–15 · H. Foley, ed., *Records of the English province of the Society of Jesus*, 5 (1879), 632–3; 7 (1882–3), 400–01 · P. Caraman, ed., *The years of siege: Catholic life from James I to Cromwell* (1966), 35–7

Jenison, Robert (*b.* 1648/9), informer, was the second of four sons of John Jenison (1622/3–1680), of High Walworth, Durham, and his first wife, Catherine Ironmonger (*bap.* 1615, *d.* in or before 1666). He is said to have been aged seventeen in 1666. Like his brothers he was educated at Douai, but was then admitted to Gray's Inn on 17 June 1676, as his father's heir. His elder brother, Thomas, was a Jesuit and thus precluded from inheriting the family estate. In September 1678 Thomas Jenison was among the first wave of suspects arrested when the Popish Plot broke.

Robert Jenison seems to have been involved in the investigations surrounding the Popish Plot following a letter to his friend Robert Bowes written from Reading in December 1678. According to his own account Jenison was persuaded to convert to protestantism in 1679 and reveal what he knew of the plot after reading the defence of William Ireland, in which Ireland denied being in London during August 1678, a denial which was backed up by many Catholic witnesses from Staffordshire. Jenison was able to contradict this story, claiming to have seen Ireland in London on 19 August. He made several depositions before Edmund Warcup, a Middlesex JP, in June and July 1679, which were duly published by order of the privy council. He was thus on hand on 18 July to appear at the trial of Sir George Wakeham, as a witness to prove the veracity of the plot. Jenison made a credible witness, owing to his background as 'a gentleman of family and estate' (*Bishop Burnet's History*, 2.191), and Lord Chief Justice Scroggs was evidently delighted to find another witness to disprove Ireland's alibi, which he had maintained to the scaffold. Jenison made two further depositions before Warcup in early August and appeared before the privy council at Hampton Court on 7 August. He now proceeded to divulge more of the plot to kill Charles II, actually naming the 'four ruffians' deputed to do the deed. Furthermore, he revealed that his family's priest, John Smith, could corroborate certain details. Warrants were duly issued for arrest of the four men. Jenison quickly authorized the printing of *The narrative of Robert Jenison* (1679), penning a dedication to the earl of Shaftesbury.

Meanwhile, in late September 1679 Jenison's elder brother died in Newgate. Following the death of his father in 1680, the family estates were divided according to a chancery decree, Jenison succeeding to the estate at High Walworth, which he sold to a distant relative, Ralph Jenison of Elswick, Northumberland. Other estates went to John Jenison's son by his second marriage.

Jenison was now fully committed to the whigs. He appeared for Sir William Waller at the Westminster election of September 1679, and when parliament finally met in October 1680, he was called upon to give evidence on the plot to the Commons on 9 November, just prior to the second reading debate on the Exclusion Bill. He was again called upon to prove the existence of the plot at the trial of Lord Stafford on 30 November. In April 1682 it was reported that Jenison 'spoke of his royal highness [York] things unbecoming any man but a hellish Whig' (*CSP dom.*, 1682, 169). With the tory reaction in full cry in June 1682, neither Jenison nor Titus Oates felt it prudent to attend the trial in king's bench of Dennis Kearney, one of the four 'ruffians', who had surrendered himself in November 1681, and the case was dismissed.

Jenison fled abroad on James II's accession and was not to be found when Oates wished to use him as a defence witness at his trial for perjury in May 1685. In 1686 he approached the English envoy in Amsterdam, Bevil Skelton, in an attempt to obtain a pardon because of his need 'to put in order my entangled affairs' (BL, Add. MS 41818, fol. 237), and in return he even offered to raise a hundred men in England or the Netherlands for the king.

In the early 1690s Jenison sent a begging letter to Lady Clinton bemoaning his ill luck in being persecuted for giving evidence in the Popish Plot. According to his version of events, having taken refuge in the Netherlands 'for my support I sold the greater part of my estate and the remainder being £230 per annum was illegally given away by Judge Allibone' (BL, Add. MS 70500, fol. 336). He had an application pending for support at the Treasury, but was now destitute and dependent on the charity of people like the countess of Shaftesbury and Lady Russell. Nothing further is heard of him and his date of death is unknown.

STUART HANDLEY

Sources R. Surtees, *The history and antiquities of the county palatine of Durham*, 4 vols. (1816–40), vol. 3 · J. Foster, ed., *Pedigrees recorded at the visitations of the county palatine of Durham* (1887), 189 · *The narrative of Robert Jenison of Gray's Inn* (1679) · *Bishop Burnet's History*, vol. 2 · N. Luttrell, *A brief historical relation of state affairs from September 1678 to April 1714*, 6 vols. (1857), vol. 1 · *CSP dom.*, 1679–82 · J. Kenyon, *The Popish Plot* (1972) · BL, Add. MS 70500, fol. 336 · BL, Add. MS 41818, fol. 237 · K. H. D. Haley, *The first earl of Shaftesbury* (1968) · J. Foster, *The register of admissions to Gray's Inn, 1521–1889, together with the register of marriages in Gray's Inn chapel, 1695–1754* (privately printed, London, 1889), 323 · IGI · DNB

Jenison, Thomas (*c.*1525–1587), administrator, was the eldest son of Robert Jenison of Yokeflete, Yorkshire, a minor country gentleman, and Agnes, daughter of William Wren of the Isle of Ely. Probably during the late 1540s or early 1550s he married Elizabeth, daughter of Edward Birch of Sandon in Bedfordshire, groom-porter to Henry VIII; they had five sons and a daughter. Skilful in money matters, he received his first important government posting early in 1550 when he was sent with Sir Richard Cotton to take accounts in the north of England. In order to further his career he moved to London, leasing property in the parish of St Giles Cripplegate, and he was subsequently made auditor of the court of admiralty. Despite his youth, on 10 February 1551 he was named auditor-general of Ireland for life—possibly, it has been suggested, at the behest of the lord deputy, Sir Anthony St Leger—and he removed himself to Dublin. Shortly afterwards the Irish financial administration fell into disrepute, and in 1553 he was suspended from office during a major investigation, charged with various misdemeanours, including misappropriation of crown funds and failure to make account of the revenues of the realm. Although he procured a royal pardon in October 1553, by 24 February 1555 he had been dismissed, described in a document of that date as the 'late auditor of Ireland' (*CPR, 1554–5*, 104). He reacted badly to this set-back, in April 1556 being required to enter a recognizance of £100,000 in which he undertook not to pester or intimidate his replacement.

In 1560, his indiscretions apparently forgotten, Jenison became comptroller of the works, keeper of the stores, and clerk of the check at Berwick, a position he retained for many years. Eventually in 1566, on the recommendation of the new lord deputy, Sir Henry Sidney, he returned to Ireland to resume the auditor-generalship. He was thereafter commissioned to audit the accounts of successive vice-treasurers of Ireland and other officials, to recover the queen's Irish debts, and to make inquisitions of forfeited lands. Old habits, however, died hard. Repeatedly the London government requested Jenison to produce regular accounts, only for him to procrastinate and delay. In March 1574 the privy council wrote to express its frustration that, far from advertising them of Irish finance on a monthly basis, as he had agreed, Jenison had yet to complete the audit of accounts that had been due three years previously. Again in 1578 letters were dispatched demanding that he complete the audit of 1574. Such censure went unheeded and he continued to work at a snail's pace. It is a curious fact that he excited little criticism from Dublin Castle while Sir Henry Sidney retained an influence over the Irish administration; indeed Sidney actively protected him, granting him three general pardons between 1575 and 1578.

It was only with Sidney's final recall in 1578 that derogatory comments were made about Jenison, by the likes of the lord chancellor of Ireland William Gerard, Edward Fitton, and Edward Waterhouse, who suspected him of exaggerating the scale of the queen's debts in Ireland—presumably, they hinted, for the benefit of Sidney and himself. Having followed Sidney home to England in 1578 he delayed his return to Dublin for two years, until August 1580, by which time Sidney's friend Lord Grey of Wilton had been appointed to the Irish lord deputyship. Growing ill health, however, characterized by repeated attacks of gout, severely limited Jenison's activities following his return, so that another important audit was delayed. Accusations of recusancy directed against his eldest son, combined with ongoing suspicions of his own financial impropriety, added to his difficulties, but even so it was not until the spring of 1587 that the privy council finally agreed upon his replacement as auditor. He died a few months afterwards, on 17 November 1587, still in office, his passing regretted by few; in the words of the then lord deputy, Sir John Perrot, he had 'lived like a hog and died like a dog' (*CSP Ire., 1586–8*, 475).

Immediately upon his decease trunkloads of account rolls, mainly concerning army captains, were removed from his rooms—allegedly on his authorization—in order to prevent their falling into the hands of his successor; the practice of presenting regular audits of the Irish accounts only commenced after his demise. Like many officials in Ireland he often pleaded penury yet profited from his career in the country; he was able to purchase the Walworth estate in Durham and rebuild the castle there as a new family seat. There is little doubt that he died a rich man. According to his will, at the time of his death he held both freehold and leasehold property in Yorkshire, Gloucestershire, Northamptonshire, Somerset, and Caernarvonshire, as well as houses in Dublin, Berwick, and London. At his death his chief concern was the obstinate religious stance of his eldest son, William, whom he had disinherited for defying his command not to marry the daughter of a prominent Irish recusant spokesman. Accordingly his second son, John Jenison, inherited the bulk of his English and Welsh lands after 1587, leaving William to found a Catholic branch of the family in co. Kildare.

DAVID EDWARDS

Sources *CSP Ire., 1586–8* · PRO, state papers, Ireland, SP 63 · will, PRO, PROB 11/72, fols. 65r–66r · *The Irish fiants of the Tudor sovereigns*, 4 vols. (1994) · *APC, 1550–52, 1554–5, 1574–5* · *CPR, 1553–5; 1566–78* · J. Hogan and N. McNeill O'Farrell, eds., *The Walsingham letter-book, or, Register of Ireland, May 1578 to December 1579*, IMC (1959) · B. Dietz, 'Jenison, William I', HoP, *Commons, 1558–1603*, 2.375–6 · S. G. Ellis, *Tudor Ireland: crown, community, and the conflict of cultures, 1470–1603* (1985) · C. Brady, *The chief governors: the rise and fall of reform government in Tudor Ireland, 1536–1588* (1994) · T. Ó Laidhin, ed., *Sidney state papers, 1565–70*, IMC (1962) · A. J. Sheehan, 'Irish revenues and English subventions, 1559–1622', *Proceedings of the Royal Irish Academy*, 90C (1990), 35–65 · *CSP for., 1560–61*

Jenkes, Henry (*d.* 1697), Church of England clergyman and author, was admitted in 1642 to King's College, Aberdeen, where, described as *Anglo-Borussus*, he was a pupil of Alexander Middleton. He graduated MA in 1646 and was admitted, apparently by incorporation, to Emmanuel College, Cambridge, in the same year. He was a senior fellow of Gonville and Caius College from 25 March 1653 until his death and was one of the fellows who obtained letters from Charles II confirming him in his place at the Restoration, when presumably he received episcopal ordination. Jenkes acted as Greek lecturer (1674–8), Hebrew lecturer (1678–90), catechist (1691–7), and, for several years, dean and chaplain. In 1687 he served as a university proctor. He was incorporated at Oxford on 13 July 1669. Jenkes was elected FRS in 1674 but was inactive and was among those expelled in 1682. He succeeded William Croone as Gresham professor of rhetoric on 21 October 1670, resigning on 2 October 1676.

Jenkes was a friend of Ralph Cudworth, with whom he wrote a commendation for Pannoni's edition of *Isocratis Orationes duae* (1676), and of Henry More, with whom he appears to have discussed the manuscript of *Enchiridion ethicum* (More to Worthington, 10 May 1665; Worthington,

36.172–3). He corresponded with Philip van Limborch in the Netherlands and Jean le Clerc travelled to Cambridge to meet him and Cudworth and More. Jenkes died in his college in August 1697 and was buried at St Michael's, Cambridge, on 1 September. In his will his books were left to James Halman (d. 1702), fellow and later master of Gonville and Caius. Among these was the manuscript of his 'Rationale biblicum', for which there was an agreement with Richard Chiswell the publisher, though there is no evidence that it actually appeared. Jenkes's *The Christian Tutor* (1683), addressed to James King in the East Indies, is a conventional guide to Christian morality, including a reading list citing contemporary theologians such as Cudworth and More, and works of geography. He also contributed a brief preface to the 1684 edition of Étienne de Courcelles *Synopsis ethuces*. Jenkes is credited (by Ward) with a work called 'The Christian dial' of which there appears to be no trace.   JOHN STEPHENS

Sources J. Venn and others, eds., *Biographical history of Gonville and Caius College*, 1: *1349–1713* (1897) · J. Venn, *Caius College* (1901) · L. Simonutti, 'Reason and toleration: Henry More and Philip van Limborch', *Henry More (1614–1687): tercentenary studies*, ed. S. Hutton (1990), 201–18 · L. Simonutti, *Arminianesimo e Tolleranza nel Seicento Olandese: il carteggio Ph van Limborch, J. le Clerc* (Florence, 1980) · R. L. Colie, *Light and enlightenment: a study of the Cambridge Platonists and the Dutch Arminians* (1957) · *The diary and correspondence of Dr John Worthington*, ed. J. Crossley and R. C. Christie, 2 vols. in 3, Chetham Society, 13, 36, 114 (1847–86) · *DNB*
Archives University of Amsterdam, Limborch's letter-book 'Epistolae ad Anglos'
Wealth at death very little; mainly books and chattels: Venn, *Caius College*, vol. 1, p. 387

Jenkin, Charles Frewen (1865–1940), civil engineer and university teacher, was born at Claygate, Surrey, on 24 September 1865, the second son of Henry Charles Fleeming *Jenkin (1833–1885), electrical engineer, and his wife, Anne (d. 1921), only child of Alfred Austin, permanent secretary to the office of works. Jenkin was educated at Edinburgh Academy and at Edinburgh University, where he assisted his father, then professor of engineering, before entering Trinity College, Cambridge, to read mathematics—there being no engineering courses. On graduating in 1886 he entered the engineering workshops of Mather and Platt in Manchester, from where he moved to the London and North Western Railway works at Crewe, supported by a Miller scholarship from the Institution of Civil Engineers.

In 1889 Jenkin married Mary Oswald, youngest daughter of Donald Mackenzie, Lord Mackenzie, a Scottish judge. Their sons Charles (1890–1939) and Conrad (1894–1916) predeceased him; a daughter, May (b. 1892), and his wife survived him. Jenkin took up the post of mechanical assistant superintendent to the Royal Gunpowder Factory at Waltham Abbey in 1891, where he designed machinery for a new cordite factory. He later worked for Nettlefolds at their Newport steelworks (1893–8), then spent ten years with Siemens Brothers, first at Charlton, then as works manager and head of Siemens's railway department at Stafford. While enthusiastic about the technical side of engineering, he found its commercial side less appealing than research.

Jenkin had spent his early family holidays among the islands off the west coast of Scotland and he was a lover of the sea and ships. He combined this with an interest in botany and zoology, becoming an authority on sponges. He took over from Professor A. E. Minchin the task of classifying the calcareous sponges brought back from the National Antarctic Expedition of 1901–4; his first publications were on this subject and his name was given to a genus—Jenkina—of these creatures. Among his other leisure pursuits he taught himself medieval French and Spanish, as well as Italian, Portuguese, and Catalan.

In 1907 a new chair of engineering science was founded at Oxford University, to which Jenkin was elected. He was initially associated with New College but his salary was paid by Brasenose, to which he migrated with a fellowship in 1912. Teaching commenced in 1908 in the face of considerable opposition from senior staff at the university. For some years Jenkin was handicapped by insufficient staff, space, and equipment: not until 1914 was his department collected into one building. With the outbreak of the First World War Jenkin became a lieutenant in the Royal Naval Volunteer Reserve and worked in the Admiralty air department. When the Royal Flying Corps and the Royal Naval Air Service amalgamated early in 1918 as the Royal Air Force, he joined the aircraft production department of the Ministry of Munitions, and with the rank of lieutenant-colonel directed a group responsible for the preparation of specifications for every kind of aircraft material. At the time many fundamental questions of the strength and properties of materials used in aircraft construction remained unanswered; Jenkin's work led to their quantification, whereby the previous generous safety factors could be considerably reduced, with consequent savings of weight and materials. The results were published in 1918 as *Report on Materials of Construction used in Aircraft and Aircraft Engines*.

On his return to Oxford after the war Jenkin continued the research begun during hostilities. His main concern was with fatigue and on the effects of cracks and notches on the strength of machine parts. In particular with several co-workers he advanced the understanding of corrosion fatigue. Introducing a novel method of testing in which the specimen itself was made the reed of an acoustic resonator, he was able to subject metals to stress reversals at frequencies up to 20,000 Hz—a rate far higher than had been usual. Many of Jenkin's research projects were allied to consultancies, and were thus external in nature. He was chairman of the materials subcommittee of the Aeronautical Research Committee, and from 1924 he chaired the structures investigation committee of the Building Research Board at Watford. The engineering department at Oxford never attracted many students, and funding for apparatus remained meagre. Jenkin retired from Oxford in 1929, moved to St Albans, and transferred his work to the Building Research Station at Watford, where he took a modest position until a heart condition forced his retirement in 1933.

Jenkin's achievements were recognized by his appointment as CBE in 1919 and an honorary LLD in the University of Edinburgh in 1927. The Institution of Civil Engineers, which he joined as an associate in 1891, elected him to full membership in 1912 and awarded him a Telford medal and premium, and a Watt medal. He was elected an associate of the Institution of Electrical Engineers in 1899, transferring to membership in 1901. He became FRS in 1931. Jenkin suffered a series of heart attacks in 1933, but lived until increasing pain culminated in his death at his home, 25 Battlefield Road, St Albans, on 23 August 1940. His funeral and burial took place at St Albans Abbey on 27 August.   R. V. SOUTHWELL, *rev.* ANITA McCONNELL

Sources R. V. Southwell, *Obits. FRS*, 3 (1939–41), 575–85 · J. Morrell, *Science at Oxford, 1914–1939: transforming an arts university* (1997), 94–8 · *Journal of the Institution of Civil Engineers*, 15 (1940–41), 72 · *The Engineer* (30 Aug 1940), 140 · *Engineering* (30 Aug 1940), 174 · *The Times* (26 Aug 1940), 7d · *The Times* (28 Aug 1940), 7b · M. Bunton, *A revision of the classification of the calcareous sponges* (1963) · C. F. Jenkin, 'Presidential address', section G, *Report of the British Association for the Advancement of Science* (1920), 124–34 · b. cert. · d. cert.
Likenesses photograph, repro. in Southwell, *Obits. FRS*
Wealth at death £8587 10s. 4d.: probate, 23 Dec 1940, *CGPLA Eng. & Wales*

Jenkin, (Henry Charles) Fleeming (1833–1885), electrical engineer and university teacher, was born on 25 March 1833 near Dungeness, Kent, the only child of Captain Charles Jenkin RN (1801–1885), a coastguard, and his wife, Henrietta Camilla *Jenkin (c.1807–1885), a novelist. A vagrant childhood saw Fleeming (pronounced 'Fleming'), as he was generally known, commence school in 1841 in Jedburgh prior to attending Edinburgh Academy (from 1843) where J. C. Maxwell was his senior and P. G. Tait his classmate. Forced by poverty into leaving for continental Europe in 1846, the Jenkin family headed first to Frankfurt, and then, in 1847, to Paris, where Fleeming acquired French and became attuned to mathematics. In 1848, while sympathizing with Parisian revolutionaries, the liberal minded family left for Genoa, again to witness social disturbances. Enrolling as the first protestant student of the university, Fleeming studied natural philosophy. 'Signor Flaminio', having mastered Italian, graduated as master of arts with first-class honours in 1850 and began employment in Philip Taylor's Genoese locomotive workshop.

After returning to Britain in 1851 Jenkin began a three-year apprenticeship at Fairbairn's works in Manchester, after which he undertook six months' railway surveying in Switzerland. In 1855, foreseeing emigration to Canada or Australia, he became draughtsman at Penn's steam engine works in Greenwich. Joining Liddell and Gordon a year later, however, Jenkin became deeply involved in marine telegraph engineering through Lewis Gordon's association with the cable manufacturer R. S. Newall of Birkenhead. Thanks to Gordon, who found him to be 'a young man of remarkable ability' (*Papers, Literary, Scientific*, 1.C/V), Jenkin transferred to Newall's in 1857 as philosophical assistant, and gained an introduction to William Thomson (they first met in Glasgow early in 1859) who

(Henry Charles) Fleeming Jenkin (1833–1885), by unknown photographer

became a lifelong friend. On 26 February 1859 Jenkin married Anne (d. 1921), only child of Alfred Austin (1805–1884) and his wife, Eliza *née* Barron (d. 1885), into whose Westminster circle he had entered (bearing an introductory letter from Mrs Elizabeth Gaskell of Manchester) in 1855. Together they had three sons, Austin Fleeming (1861–1910), Charles Frewen *Jenkin (1865–1940), and Bernard Maxwell (1867–1951). In 1860 Jenkin left Newall's, filed his first joint patent with Thomson, and (a year later) formed a partnership with H. C. Forde (1827–1897) that laid a Lowestoft–Norderney cable for Reuters in 1865.

At Newall's Jenkin had tested the first Atlantic and Red Sea telegraph cables, whose subsequent failures led to a parliamentary enquiry into construction procedures. Furnishing evidence in December 1859 Jenkin urged an alliance of standardized practice with theory, a conclusion the joint committee strongly endorsed. In December 1866 he assured readers of the *North British Review* that 'deep-sea cables are no longer gambling ventures, but legitimate speculations' (*Papers, Literary, Scientific*, 2.231). Jenkin experienced seasickness from his first telegraph cruise in 1858 to his last in 1873, during which time he advised British governments on telegraph nationalization, and served Reuters, the French Atlantic, and the German Union telegraph companies. In 1861 the *Encyclopaedia Britannica* (8th edition) published Jenkin's Birkenhead investigations, the first measurements in absolute units of the specific resistance of the insulator gutta-percha.

Representing Thomson at the 1861 British Association (BA) meeting in Manchester, Jenkin was instrumental in forming a committee (of which he was appointed secretary) to determine a convenient unit and standard of electrical resistance. Apart from editing the committee's *Reports* (1862–9), from 1865 Jenkin distributed the approved standards. As Thomson's lieutenant he undertook, with Maxwell, the classic experiments that led Thomson to ascribe the BA ohm largely 'to Jenkin's zeal' (*Papers, Literary, Scientific*, 1.clviii). Following Jenkin's presidency of the mechanical section at Edinburgh's meeting in 1871, he published *Magnetism and Electricity* in 1873. Thomson hailed this textbook (soon translated into Italian and German) as the first to contain British Association quantitative methods.

In 1865 Jenkin signed a patent pooling agreement with Thomson and C. F. Varley, to which he primarily contributed business acumen, securing the patents 'a freedom from litigation remarkable in so valuable a property' (*PICE*, 367). Jenkin was elected FRS aged thirty-two, and in 1866 he accepted the chair of civil engineering at University College, London. Coincident with his patents suddenly paying well, Jenkin was appointed professor of engineering at the University of Edinburgh in 1868. Securing the new chair, despite competition from Macquorn Rankine, further relieved Jenkin of financial worries. He dissolved his partnership with Forde in favour of one with Thomson. Jenkin took his teaching very seriously, and among his students were three future professors, J. A. Ewing, C. Michie Smith, and his middle son, Charles Frewen Jenkin. Another pupil, Robert Louis Stevenson, regarded 'any professor as a joke, and Fleeming as a particularly good joke'. A short man, 'markedly plain' and 'boyishly young in manner', the disputatious Jenkin was unprepossessing, but none the less a strict disciplinarian (*Papers, Literary, Scientific*, 1.cxxxii).

Jenkin's long vacations were not periods of undisturbed contemplation, nor was his work as an educator bound by classroom walls. Besides professional business he appeared before the Samuelson select committee on scientific instruction (1868) and the Devonshire commission on scientific instruction (1870), and was on the directorate of the Watt Institution of Edinburgh. At the Royal Scottish Society of Arts (January 1869) he advocated science schools, emphasized the value (within a curriculum modelled on German practice) of mechanical drawing for skilled workmen, and urged all universities professing to prepare engineers to institute engineering degrees.

In all, Jenkin filed thirty-five British patents and put his name to some forty published papers, mainly discussing telegraphic matters, although his critical faculty ranged across literature and the arts. His home theatricals, indeed, became a social event of the Edinburgh spring. A sceptic turned undogmatic churchman, within his article on 'Lucretius and the atomic theory' (*North British Review*, 1868) Jenkin cited physical laws as evidence of a divine lawgiver.

In 1867 the *North British Review* published Jenkin's critique on 'Darwin and the *Origin of Species*'. Darwin himself, confessing to J. D. Hooker in January 1869, found it 'of

more real use … than any other essay or review' (*More Letters*, 2.379). Jenkin offered his lay audience an eloquent exposition of Thomson's abstruse cosmical thermodynamics. This countered Darwin's acceptance of an 'indefinite, if not infinite' (*Papers, Literary, Scientific*, 1.235) age of the earth, a belief founded upon the uniformitarian geology of Lyell. With Jenkin's entertainingly clear views on variability and the efficiency of natural selection, Darwin declared himself convinced (in correspondence with A. R. Wallace in January 1869) of the need for clarifications he had already drafted for his *Origin of Species* (*Life and Letters*, 2.288). Darwin's fifth (August 1869) and sixth (February 1872) editions cite Jenkin's anonymously published article.

Jenkin's paper, 'Trade unions: how far legitimate?' (*North British Review*, 1868), began his distinguished five-paper contribution to political economy. He advanced modern wage theory and introduced the graphical method into British economic literature. Observing that contemporary economists failed to acknowledge Jenkin's priority, J. A. Schumpeter (in 1954) summarized Jenkin as 'an economist of major importance, whose main papers … form an obvious stepping stone between J. S. Mill and [Alfred] Marshall' (Schumpeter, 837).

Moved, in autumn 1877, to campaign for healthy houses, Jenkin's public lectures during early 1878 inspired Edinburgh's Sanitary Protection Association, modelled on Fairbairn's Steam Boiler Users' Association. Jenkin was consultant engineer, and many cities, including London and Glasgow, followed suit within five years.

In 1882 Jenkin filed the first of some dozen patents for telpherage, a system for the economical overhead electrical conveyance of bulky materials. With professors Ayrton and Perry the Telpherage Company was formed in 1883, and Jenkin outlined his intentions in a demonstrative lecture before the Society of Arts in May 1884. A telpher line was opened at Glynde, Sussex, in October 1885, and Jenkin received a posthumous gold medal at the International Inventions Exhibition (1885).

A member of the Institution of Civil Engineers (from 1868) and the Institution of Mechanical Engineers (from 1875), Jenkin served as juror at exhibitions in London (1862) and Paris (1878), and represented Britain at the Paris International Congress on Electrical Standards (1883). In 1879 he was elected vice-president of the Royal Society of Edinburgh, whose highest distinction—the Keith gold medal—he had earned for his paper 'On the application of graphic methods to the determination of the efficiency of machinery' (published in their *Transactions*, 28, 1877). He received the degree of LLD from the University of Glasgow in 1883. Jenkin's father and mother both died in February 1885. After a trifling, and apparently successful, operation upon his foot, Fleeming Jenkin fell unconscious and died, at his home, 3 Great Stuart Street, Edinburgh, of blood poisoning on 12 June 1885. He was buried at Stowting, Kent.   GARETH E. BARKLEY

Sources *Papers, literary, scientific, &., by the late Fleeming Jenkin, F.R.S., LL.D., professor of engineering at the University of Edinburgh*, ed.

S. Colvin and J. A. Ewing, 2 vols. (1887) • G. Cookson and C. A. Hempstead, *A Victorian scientist and engineer: Fleeming Jenkin and the birth of electrical engineering* (2000) • C. Smith and M. N. Wise, *Energy and empire: a biographical study of Lord Kelvin* (1989) • *PICE*, 82 (1884–5), 365–77 • C. A. Hempstead, 'An appraisal of Fleeming Jenkin, 1833–1885, electrical engineer', *History of Technology*, 13 (1991), 119–44 • S. W. Morris, 'Fleeming Jenkin and *The origin of species*: a reassessment', *British Journal for the History of Science*, 27 (1994), 313–43 • *The life and letters of Charles Darwin, including an autobiographical chapter*, ed. F. Darwin, rev. edn, 3 vols. (1888) • *More letters of Charles Darwin*, ed. F. Darwin and A. C. Seward, 2 vols. (1903) • J. A. Schumpeter, *History of economic analysis* (1954) • A. D. Browlie and M. F. L. Prichard, 'Professor Fleeming Jenkin, 1833–1885: pioneer in engineering and political economy', *Oxford Economic Papers*, 15 (1963), 204–16 • A. W. Ewing, *The man of room 40: the life of Sir Alfred Ewing* (1939) • B. Lightman, ed., *Victorian science in context* (1997) • D. L. Hull, *Darwin and his critics: the reception of Darwin's theory of evolution by the scientific community* (1973) • D. R. Oldroyd, *Darwinian impacts, an introduction to the Darwinian revolution* (1980) • P. Vorzimmer, 'Charles Darwin and blending inheritance', *Isis*, 54 (1963), 371–90 • d. cert. • *CCI* (1885) • election certificate, RS
Archives NRA, priv. coll., corresp. and papers • RS, letters and papers | CUL, department of manuscripts and university archives, corresp. with Lord Kelvin • U. Glas. L., letters mainly to Lord Kelvin
Likenesses portraits, *c*.1860–1880, repro. in Cookson and Hempstead, *Victorian scientist and engineer*; priv. coll. • portrait, *c*.1870, repro. in Cookson and Hempstead, *Victorian scientist and engineer*, 96; priv. coll. • J. Moffat, photograph, repro. in Colvin and Ewing, eds., *Papers, literary, scientific*, vol. 1, inside front cover • photogravure, NPG [*see illus.*]
Wealth at death £18,116 17*s*. 5*d*.: confirmation, 29 Oct 1885, *CCI* • £3034 10*s*. 7*d*.: additional estate, 9 Feb 1886, *CCI*

Jenkin [*née* Jackson], **Henrietta Camilla** (*c*.1807–1885), novelist, was born in Jamaica, the only daughter of Robert Jackson, a colonial administrator of Kingston, Jamaica, and his wife, Susan Campbell, a Scottish woman. Little is known of her early life, but in 1832 she married Charles Jenkin (1801–1885), midshipman (afterwards captain) in the Royal Navy, and they had a son, Henry Charles Fleeming *Jenkin (1833–1885), who was born near Dungeness, Kent. She began to write under pressure of poverty; Robert Louis Stevenson later noted in a memoir of her son that she had written for no motive other than money. Her first novels were published in the 1840s and included *Wedlock* (1841), *The Smiths* (1843), and *Lost and Won, or, The Love Test* (1846). The Jenkins were forced by their financial circumstances to live in Europe from 1847 to 1851, living in Paris from 1847 to 1848, and then moving to Genoa, where she associated with Ruffini and other liberals.

In 1858 Jenkin published *Violet Bank and its Inmates*, which met with little success, but her next novel, *Cousin Stella, or, Conflict* (1859) generated both sales and controversy, and made Jenkin's reputation. A love story set in the Jamaica of her childhood, it has slavery as a key issue, and has graphic depictions of white brutality. Her next novel, *Who Breaks, Pays* (1861), was lighter in tone, and set in 1840s Italy. It was followed by several other novels, including *Skirmishing* (1862), and *Once and Again* (1865), a novel set in Paris.

In 1868 Jenkin's son was appointed to a professorship in engineering at Edinburgh University, and she lived with him after this, becoming a favourite in the city's society.

Her health began to fail in 1875, and she died of paralysis and bronchitis at 1 Manchester Park, Edinburgh, on 8 February 1885, three days after her husband.

M. CLARE LOUGHLIN-CHOW

Sources R. L. Stevenson, *Memoir of Fleeming Jenkin* (1912) • J. Sutherland, *The Longman companion to Victorian fiction* (1988) • Blain, Clements & Grundy, *Feminist comp.* • *DNB* • d. cert.
Archives NRA, priv. coll., corresp.
Likenesses H. C. F. Jenkin, portrait, repro. in Stevenson, *Memoir*

Jenkin, (Alfred) Kenneth Hamilton (1900–1980), social historian and industrial archaeologist, was born at Green Lane, Redruth, Cornwall, on 29 October 1900, the only child of Alfred Hamilton Jenkin, solicitor (*d*. 1919), and his wife, Amy Louisa, *née* Keep. Born into a family connected with mining since the mid-eighteenth century, he took a special interest in the mines and mining people of his native county from an early age. He was educated privately, then at school in Stoke Bishop, at Sherborne School (one term), Clifton College, and University College, Oxford, graduating BA with second class honours in English in 1922 and BLitt in 1924 for a thesis on Richard Carew, the Cornish antiquary.

Settling in St Ives, Jenkin began freelance writing, lecturing, and broadcasting. His first book, *The Cornish Miner* (1927), established him as a historian and writer, and became a standard work. Numerous books and articles followed on various aspects of Cornish life and also on copper smelting and slate quarrying in Wales, salt production in Cheshire, bell founding in Loughborough, steel smelting in Sheffield, and coalmining from the Forest of Dean to Scotland. The result of many years of research and mine-walking led to his monumental *Mines and Miners of Cornwall* in 16 parts (1961–70), *Wendron Tin* (1978), and two books on Devon mines.

On 15 July 1926 Jenkin married Luned Marion Jacobs (*b*. 1904), the second daughter of William Wymark *Jacobs, the humorous writer. They had two daughters. The marriage was dissolved in 1939. On 22 January 1948 he married Elizabeth Elsie Lenton (*d*. 1977), formerly the wife of Stanley Lenton, and daughter of Clement Philip Le Sueur, shipping agent. Apart from absences while studying and a few months in London he lived all his life in Cornwall, in Redruth, St Ives, and Mullion, returning to Redruth in 1954. He died at Treliske Hospital, Truro, on 20 August 1980, and was buried beside his second wife in St Euny's parish churchyard, Redruth.

During a busy and active life Jenkin was a founder member of the Cornish gorsedd in 1928, and was given the bardic name of Lef Stenoryon, Voice of the Tinners. He helped to found the St Ives and Mullion Old Cornwall societies, as well as the Federation of Old Cornwall Societies, of which he was secretary and later president and life vice-president. He served on the council of the Royal Institution of Cornwall for half a century, during which time he became its president and life vice-president. In recognition of his devotion to historical research the council twice granted him the institution's Jenner medal. In 1935 he was a founder member of the Cornish Engines Preservation Society, now the Trevithick Society, and on his retirement in 1974 after long service on its committee he was awarded the Trevithick gold medal. In the 1950s, with others, he persuaded the Cornwall county council to set up a county record office, now one of the country's finest, serving on its committee until his death. In 1974 he became a fellow of the Society of Antiquaries. Finally, in 1978, as a recognition of his contribution to the literature and social and economic history of Cornwall and to Cornish scholarship, Exeter University conferred on him the honorary degree of DLitt.

A tall, spare figure, Jenkin was an accomplished and witty speaker, and a friendly and very likeable person. He was happy at any time to discuss matters Cornish, and to share his findings with others. He divided his great collection of books, manuscripts, and maps between the local studies library in Redruth, the Royal Institution of Cornwall Library, and the county record office, both in Truro, each of which has a collection bearing his name.

JUSTIN BROOKE

Sources *Oration delivered by the public orator of Exeter University, Professor C. F. Parker, on the conferment of the degree of honorary doctor of letters, 7th July 1978* (1978) · private information (2004) [J. H. Heseltine; B. Sinclair; R. Phillips] · *The Cornishman* (26 May 1966) · *Kelly's directory for Cornwall* (1923), 395; (1935), 156 · *West Briton* (7 Nov 1974) · Cornwall RO, A. K. H. Jenkin MSS · Redruth Local Studies Library, A. K. H. Jenkin MSS · *The Times* (27 Oct 1980) · *Mining World* (12 March 1932) · b. cert. · m. certs. · d. cert. · personal knowledge (2004)
Archives Cornwall RO · Redruth Local Studies Library | Royal Institution of Cornwall, MSS
Likenesses L. Fuller, oils, *c.*1970, Redruth Local Studies Library
Wealth at death £210,056: probate, 13 Oct 1980, *CGPLA Eng. & Wales*

Jenkin, Robert (*bap.* 1656, *d.* 1727), college head and religious controversialist, was born on the Isle of Thanet, Kent, and was baptized at Minster on the Isle of Thanet on 31 January 1656, the son of Thomas Jenkin, a yeoman of Thanet with a good estate, and his wife, Mary. Of his brothers, Henry became rector of South Runcton, Norfolk, and John served as a judge in Ireland until the revolution of 1688. Robert was educated at the King's School, Canterbury, and then at St John's College, Cambridge, where he matriculated in 1674. There his tutor was Francis Roper, who would refuse the oaths to William and Mary in 1690. After graduating BA in 1678 Jenkin was admitted to a fellowship on the foundress's foundation in March 1680, proceeding MA in the following year.

Retaining his fellowship, Jenkin entered holy orders and was presented by Francis Turner, bishop of Ely, to the vicarage of Waterbeach, Cambridgeshire. Soon afterwards he became chaplain to Bishop John Lake who in 1688 collated him to the precentorship of Chichester Cathedral. Lake's exertions in publishing his opposition to the king's ecclesiastical policy later led to his incarceration in the Tower as one of the seven bishops; his chaplain proved no less assiduous in publishing his opposition to popery. His *An Historical Examination of the Authority of General Councils* (1688), licensed by Archbishop Sancroft, assailed the fashionable Gallicanism which had become a hallmark of King James's Roman Catholic apologists. In its preface Jenkin ridiculed a convoluted fable by the poet laureate, John Dryden, *The Hind and the Panther*. Jenkin's book was a formidable work, the scholarship of which transcended its immediate polemical context, as its inclusion in Bishop Edmund Gibson's compendious *Preservative Against Popery* (1738) suggests.

Following the flight of James II, events in the autumn of 1688 led high-churchmen to favour a regency, and, like his brother John, whose career came to an end with the collapse of Tyrconnell's regime in Ireland, Robert was unable to take the oaths of allegiance to the new monarchs. During this period he remained Lake's chaplain, serving as amanuensis and signatory to the bishop's deathbed profession of his continued adherence to the doctrines of passive obedience, now caricatured by its opponents as a Jacobite shibboleth rather than a defining characteristic of the established church. The immediate flurry of hostile commentaries the declaration provoked prompted Jenkin's anonymously published *A Defence of the Profession* (1690), in which he championed Lake as having 'done his glorious part to save the Church twice in the space of one year' (p. 59). Jenkin was careful to distinguish the nonjuring and actively Jacobite positions, explaining the former as a case of conscience compelled by an oath to a monarch who continued to demand his subjects' allegiance. This important emphasis helps to explain Jenkin's reconciliation with the establishment following King James's death, which may thus be fairly ascribed to a consistent application of principle rather than opportunistic apostasy.

In 1691 Jenkin relinquished his preferments but, like many other St John's men, was able to retain his college fellowship since the necessary mechanism for expulsion, a visitation, could be initiated only through the vote of a majority of the fellowship. The previous year the earl of Exeter, a leading nonjuring layman, had made him his chaplain, and he was still living at the earl's seat at Burghley, Lincolnshire, as late as 1698.

Jenkin spent his retirement engaged in writings on topics of allegiance and faith. He was one of a series of nonjurors who exposed the unseemly implications of William Sherlock's hapless intervention to end the schism in *The Title of a Thorough Settlement Examined* (1691), the remorseless and austere argumentative style of which is well characterized by its introduction's enquiry 'Whether the thorough Settlement of an Usurper doth entitle him to the Allegiance of the Subjects; over whom his Usurpation is thoroughly settled, though the rightful King … demand their Allegiance', a question which the tract went on to resolve in the negative. This was to prove Jenkin's last contribution to the nonjuring cause. Following the treaty of Ryswick in 1697 he strongly implied, to the evident perturbation of another St John's fellow, that he would consider his duty of allegiance extinguished in the event of King James's relinquishing his title.

1696 saw the publication of what was to prove Jenkin's most successful work, *The Reasonableness and Certainty of the Christian Religion*. Dedicated to his patron the earl of Exeter, three separate editions appeared by 1708, with a

French translation appearing in Amsterdam. Among its *bêtes noires* were the Socinian John Locke and the deist Charles Blount, but its polite style and lucid simplicity rather than any polemical animus account for its popularity. As late as 1795 John Plumptre thought it sufficiently serviceable against the assaults of republican atheism to form the substance of his own treatise on the same topic. Jenkin's *A Brief Confutation of the Pretences Against Natural and Revealed Religion* followed in 1702, a dialogue between atheist and believer which attacked the shallowness of the fashionable will-o'-the-wisp deism. In the preface Jenkin contended that the 'Atheistical and Prophane' had generally 'been treated as Men of Parts and Learning', whereas his satirical exposé sought to demonstrate 'the Contradictions and Absurdities of Atheism' (sig. A2r). In both form and treatment Jenkin thus modestly anticipated George Berkley's *Alciphron*. Writings in a similar vein, exposing Locke and William Whiston, Pierre Bayle and Jacques Basnage, followed.

The death of King James in 1701 inaugurated an extensive correspondence with George Hickes, the leading proponent of perpetuating the nonjuring separation through the consecration of priests, whose exhaustive attempts to allay Jenkin's formidable doubts as to the legitimacy of the prince of Wales, James Francis Edward, are collected in Richard Rawlinson's manuscripts in the Bodleian Library. Jenkin's formal deed of renunciation came with his admission to the degree of DD in 1709, a requirement of which was subscription to the oaths. Nevertheless, he retained his nonjuring links, living about this time with the family of Thomas Thynne, Lord Weymouth, at Longleat, Wiltshire. On the death of Humphrey Gower, whom he also succeeded as the Lady Margaret professor of divinity, Jenkin became master of St John's College in 1711. Reckoned at this time 'the Modestest man in the World' by the nonjuror Hilkiah Bedford, he was suddenly wealthy, with an aggregate from both offices estimated to be £400 per annum (*Remarks*, 3.141). Most of Jenkin's difficult tenure would be spent alone: his wife, Susannah (1666/7–1713), daughter of William Hatfield, an alderman and merchant of Lynn, Norfolk, died prematurely in 1713 aged forty-six.

The appointment of Jenkin had augured well: his experience and affinity seemed likely to secure the future of the discreet handful of nonjurors which the college fellowship retained. The Hanoverian succession, however, witnessed a new clamour for tighter regulation of the universities. Legislation of 1715 compelled colleges to register evidence of their fellows' subscription to the state oaths; the penalty for noncompliance was ejection of the nonjurors and the filling of any ensuing vacancies with government nominees. Thus, the colleges' policy of 'judicious inactivity' could no longer be maintained (Findon, 120). A beneficiary of the previous indulgence of St John's now found himself in the invidious position of having to decide the future of the short file of his nonjuring peers. On 27 January 1717 'an election was held, and the veteran Nonjuring fellows were replaced, together with four others who had entered the college since 1689' (ibid., 121).

The nonjuring antiquary Thomas Hearne, hitherto on amicable terms, was characteristically severe in his report, claiming Jenkin was 'much blamed for doing it, he being afraid of the Governm[en]t' (*Remarks*, 6.55). Thomas Baker was the most celebrated casualty, and in his private writings registered his surprise and disappointment at Jenkin's compliance. Both critics overestimated the master's room for manoeuvre. The episode thus cast a shadow over Jenkin's administration and unfairly left him open to charges of political apostasy and personal betrayal.

Some years before his death Jenkin's mind failed, and he went to live with his brother at the rectory in South Runcton, Norfolk, where he died on 7 April 1727. Jenkin's demise initiated a singularly bitter contest for the mastership of his college. He was buried in Holme Chapel in South Runcton, where a mural monument with a Latin inscription was erected to his memory. Two of his children, Henry and Sarah, died prematurely in the same year. Jenkin was survived by a daughter, also called Sarah.

D. A. BRUNTON

Sources T. Baker, *History of the college of St John the Evangelist, Cambridge*, ed. J. E. B. Mayor, 2 vols. (1869), vol. 1, pp. 300, 323; vol. 2, p. 305 · *GM*, 1st ser., 49 (1779), 287, 350 · *Remarks and collections of Thomas Hearne*, ed. C. E. Doble and others, 11 vols., OHS, 2, 7, 13, 34, 42–3, 48, 50, 65, 67, 72 (1885–1921) · Nichols, *Lit. anecdotes*, 1.76; 4.240–52; 5.109; 7.197 · J. C. Findon, 'The nonjurors and the Church of England, 1689–1716', DPhil diss., U. Oxf., 1978 · BL, Add. MSS 5831, fols. 119–21; 5873, fol. 5; 5850, fols. 215–19; 5852, fol. 13; 32096, fols. 25–38 · Bodl. Oxf., MS Rawl. D. 836, fol. 251 · Bodl. Oxf., MS Eng. hist. b. 2, fols. 29–37 · W. K. Clay, *History of Waterbeach* (1861), 66 · J. S. Sidebotham, *Memorials of the King's School, Canterbury* (1865), 17, 46–7 · DNB · Venn, *Alum. Cant.* · *Fasti Angl.* (Hardy), vol. 1

Archives Bodl. Oxf., corresp. with Hickes

Jenkins, Albert Edward (1895–1953), rugby player, was born at 39 Mount Pleasant, Llanelli, Carmarthenshire, on 11 March 1895, the son of William James Jenkins, a gas works labourer, and his wife, Margaret Hughes. Nothing is known of his early years beyond the fact that he played local rugby with a team called the Seaside Stars. During the First World War he served in France with the 38th (Welsh) infantry division, for whom he also played rugby at full-back. On his return to Llanelli in 1919 he moved to centre three-quarter to become one of the outstanding players of his era and a rugby legend who never attained the proper international recognition to which many, far beyond his home town, believed he was entitled.

A series of impressive club performances soon brought Jenkins to the attention of the Welsh selectors and he won his first cap on 17 January 1920 against England at Swansea. On that occasion he played a subordinate role to his co-centre, Jerry Shea of Newport, who scored a remarkable sixteen points in Wales's 19–5 victory. Having retained his place for the away game against Scotland in February, Jenkins converted his own try to supply Wales's only points in a 9–5 defeat. Five weeks later, on 13 March 1920, Jenkins produced a sensational performance in his country's 28–4 victory over Ireland on a waterlogged Cardiff Arms Park, scoring a try, two conversions, and a dropped goal in a personal tally of eleven points, as well as carving innumerable openings for his wing and club-mate

Bryn Williams, who scored three tries. The following year, against Scotland at Swansea on 5 February 1921, Jenkins, frustrated by his team's inability to make any impression on the Scots' eleven-point lead, took the game into his own hands by subjecting the Scottish posts to a ferocious barrage of drop kicks and pot-shots. After he had narrowed the Scottish lead to three points with two colossal drop goals (at that time worth four points each) the crowd, already surging along the touchline, invaded the field, bringing play to a halt. For ten minutes the Scots were able to regain their breath as officials, helped by the Welsh players, cleared the pitch. Once play was eventually resumed, Scotland regained the initiative and when soon afterwards Jenkins was carried off with a leg injury, Welsh hopes of victory evaporated.

Despite frequent attempts to lure him north by rugby league scouts, Batley's being particularly persistent, Jenkins remained loyal to Llanelli, whom he captained in 1921–2 and for three seasons in 1923–6. The 1920s, in many respects a grim decade for Welsh club and international rugby, saw Llanelli, a west Wales tinplate town less severely affected by the prolonged coal strike and subsequent depression in the valleys of Glamorgan and Monmouthshire, enjoy considerable success. They lost only narrowly (8–3) to the invincible 1924 All Blacks, who had already defeated Wales 19–0, and they beat the New Zealand Maoris of 1926 by three points to nil. In 1927–8 the 'Scarlets' became Welsh club champions, and that season supplied seven players to the Welsh team. Albert Jenkins was central to their achievements: he was among the six Llanelli players who secured Wales's first post-war victory over Scotland by thirteen points to nil at Murrayfield in February 1928, and was one of the seven 'Scarlets' selected to face Ireland at Cardiff the following month. Jenkins was appointed captain (he had captained Wales once before, against Ireland in 1923) and scored a try, but Wales lost 13–10 and he was never selected again. He rarely played well away from Llanelli's Stradey Park, but the fourteen international caps he won between 1920 and 1928 were scant recognition of his gifts, which were acknowledged as much outside Wales as within it, and his country's poor international record in this period testifies to the national selectors' perversity in overlooking his erratic but match-winning ability.

As a player, Jenkins had all the attributes except perhaps that of fine judgement. He was a prodigious kicker who could punt, drop- and place-kick enormous distances with accuracy. His squat, sturdy frame made him look shorter than his 5 feet 8 inches, while his meaty shoulders, barrel chest, and powerful thighs tapered down to a sprinter's calves, narrow ankles, and small, balletic feet. But no ballet dancer was as strong on the burst as Albert Jenkins: 'when a special effort was called for his head would go back with a characteristic mannerism—a danger signal— and he would go full tilt for the line with the acceleration, skill and power of a stampeding rhino' (*Llanelly Mercury*, 8 Oct 1953). At 12½ stone, his speed off the mark and determination as a runner who swerved rather than side-stepped, made him very difficult to stop. He was also a devastating tackler who could force an entire back division across field until the hapless winger received both the ball and Jenkins at the same time and was hurled into touch. His passing too was noted for its timing and accuracy, but his judgement as to whether to pass was not always reliable.

In a ten-year club career that ended against Swansea on 26 January 1929 Jenkins scored a total of 966 points for Llanelli, including 121 tries. Idolized by his community, where he was corporate property and known to all and sundry by his first name (and as 'Jinks' to his team-mates), Albert Jenkins was essentially a modest man who shunned the limelight. He was an authentic working-class hero who was able to walk from his home to the Stradey Park ground, the one sphere where he cast off his habitual taciturnity to become truly articulate and where he found stability and reassurance as he shifted uneasily from one occupation to another as docker, coal-trimmer, and tinplater. Always immaculate in appearance, on retiring from the game his involvement with it ceased and he rarely returned to the scene of so many of his triumphs. After a long illness he died at Llanelli and District General Hospital on 7 October 1953 and was buried in the town's Box cemetery on 12 October. He was survived by two sons and a daughter.   GARETH WILLIAMS

Sources G. Hughes, *One hundred years of scarlet* (1983) · G. Hughes, *The Scarlets: a history of Llanelli rugby football club* (1986?) · D. Smith and G. Williams, *Fields of praise: the official history of the Welsh Rugby Union, 1881–1981* · J. B. G. Thomas, *Great rugger players* (1955) · *Llanelly Mercury* (8 Oct 1953) · *Llanelly Mercury* (15 Oct 1953) · R. Harding, *Rugby reminiscences and opinions* (1929) · CGPLA Eng. & Wales (1953) · b. cert.

Likenesses drawing, repro. in Hughes, *The Scarlets*, facing p. 104 · photograph, repro. in Hughes, *One hundred years*, 154

Wealth at death £1691 17s. 4d.: probate, 28 Oct 1953, CGPLA Eng. & Wales

Jenkins, Arthur (1882–1946), politician, was born on 3 February 1882 at Varteg, Abersychan, Monmouthshire, the son of Thomas Jenkins (1855/6–1929), a coalminer, and his wife, Eliza Perry. He was educated at Varteg board school before leaving, aged twelve, to work in Viponds colliery, Varteg. He involved himself in the South Wales Miners' Federation (SWMF) and in the Pontypool and district trades and labour council, becoming its secretary. He continued with his education through evening classes and discussion groups, and in 1908 won the Eastern Valley Miners' scholarship to Ruskin College, Oxford. In 1909 Jenkins was one of the Ruskin 'strikers' who supported the radical principal, Dennis Hird, in a dispute over the teaching of Marxism, and left the college for the Central Labour College (initially in Oxford, later in London).

In 1910 Jenkins spent ten months studying in company with his friend Frank Hodges, the future miners' leader, at the Foyer de l'Ouvrier, Paris, before returning to Monmouthshire to work underground (at the Tirpentwys and Blaensychan collieries) and conduct evening classes at Garndiffaith. On 2 October 1911 he married Harriet (Hattie) Harris (1885/6–1953), the orphaned daughter of the manager of the Bessemer plant at Blaenafon, who was then working in a Pontypool music shop, and they had two sons, one stillborn (1915) and Roy, later Lord Jenkins (1920–2003). A keen sportsman, Arthur Jenkins played cricket, rugby, and soccer into his late twenties.

In 1918 Jenkins became deputy miners' agent for the Eastern Valley district of the SWMF, and in 1921 agent. He subsequently served on the executive council of the SWMF and, between 1934 and 1936, as the union's vice-president, playing an important part (alongside James Griffiths) in the struggle against company and non-unionism. In 1918 he was elected councillor for the Abersychan urban district council, and in 1919 he was elected to the Monmouthshire county council, of which he later became an alderman and chairman (1932–3). He also served on the national executive committee of the Labour Party (1925–9, 1931–3, 1935–7), and was a magistrate, a member of the County Councils Association, and a member of the royal commission on licensing appointed in 1929. In November 1926 he was sentenced to nine months' imprisonment for riotous assault and incitement to riot, following a violent clash between striking miners and police at the Quarry level, near Crumlin. There was little doubt at the time, and even less afterwards, that the police fabricated evidence against him and that the sentence was disproportionate. The conviction was seen as unjust and vindictive even by political opponents and coal owners.

In 1935 Jenkins was elected Labour MP for Pontypool against Conservative opposition, winning two-thirds of the votes cast, a share that rose to 77 per cent in 1945. In parliament he spoke regularly, authoritatively, and sometimes movingly on questions concerning the coal industry, unemployment, and poverty, and had extensive interests in education and foreign affairs (in which, as a strong believer in collective security, he opposed the rearmament programme in the late 1930s). During the Second World War he was chairman of the local appeal board at the Royal Ordnance Factory, Glascoed; in consequence of the fact that he was an MP, this appointment required the passage of a special indemnity act.

Being a man of considerable personal charm and 'great intellectual power' and a 'very accomplished platform speaker' (Francis, Howells, and Tucker), Jenkins could communicate beyond the Labour Party's natural constituency to middle-class audiences. In 1937 he was made parliamentary private secretary to Clement Attlee (member of the war cabinet and lord privy seal from 1940), who became a close friend, and in March 1945, during the wartime coalition, Jenkins was appointed parliamentary secretary to the Ministry of Town and Country Planning (under William Shepherd Morrison); then, in the Attlee government, he was parliamentary secretary to the Ministry of Education (under Ellen Wilkinson). Had his health not been poor a cabinet post might have been his reward in 1945, but he was forced to retire from the government that October. He died on 25 April 1946 at St Thomas's Hospital, Lambeth, London, from uraemia and an enlarged prostate. Although 'quietly agnostic' (Jenkins, 66), he was buried in Trevethin churchyard, Pontypool, following an Anglican service, on 29 April 1946. A clock in his memory

was subsequently erected by public subscription in Pontypool park.

Arthur Jenkins was a humane and sincere politician and a dedicated constituency MP and family man, who inspired respect and affection from members of all mainstream political parties. That he was 'moderate and sensible' (Jones, 95), 'eminently respectable' (Coldrick, Egan, and Lewis), and 'mild-mannered' (Francis and Smith, 64) was not always to his advantage in the often vigorously contested atmosphere of the south Wales coalfield, and explains why commentators and historians have underestimated his contribution. CHRIS WILLIAMS

Sources R. Jenkins, *A life at the centre* (1991) · H. Francis, K. Howells, and C. Tucker, interview, U. Wales, South Wales Miners' Library, South Wales Coalfield collection, AUD/16 [date of interview probably late 1970s or early 1980s] · W. Coldrick, D. Egan, and R. Lewis, interview, 24 Sept 1973, U. Wales, South Wales Miners' Library, South Wales Coalfield collection, AUD/339 · *The Times* (27 April 1946) · *South Wales Argus* (26 April 1946) · *Free Press of Monmouthshire* (3 May 1946) · *The Labour who's who* (1927) · H. Francis and D. Smith, *The fed: the south Wales miners in the twentieth century* (1980), (1998) · G. H. Armbruster, 'The social determination of ideologies: being a study of a Welsh mining community', PhD diss., U. Lond., 1940 · F. Hodges, *My adventures as a labour leader* (1925) · *Western Mail* (1926) · *Western Mail* (1935) · *Western Mail* (1945) · *South Wales Argus* (1926) · *South Wales Argus* (1935) · *South Wales Argus* (1945) · *Free Press of Monmouthshire* (1926) · *Free Press of Monmouthshire* (1935) · *Free Press of Monmouthshire* (1945) · *Hansard 5C* (1935–46), vol. 751, col. 1361 · A. Crane, B. Derrick, and E. Donovan, *Pontypool's heritage in pictures and postcards* (1989) · T. Jones, *Whitehall diary*, vol 2: *1926–1930* (1969) · b. cert. · m. cert. · d. cert.

Archives priv. coll., diaries | Bodl. Oxf., corresp. with Clement Attlee · JRL, Labour History Archive and Study Centre, corresp., LP/MIN/19/30–43 | SOUND U. Wales, Swansea, South Wales Miners' Library, South Wales Coalfield collection, interviews

Likenesses photograph, Hult. Arch. · photograph, repro. in Francis and Smith, *Fed*, following p. 108 · photograph, repro. in Crane, Derrick, and Donovan, *Pontypool's heritage*, following p. 111 · photograph, repro. in *Free Press of Monmouthshire* (22 Nov 1935), 5 · photograph, repro. in *South Wales Argus* (3 July 1945), 3 · photograph, repro. in *South Wales Argus* (26 July 1945), 4 · photograph, repro. in *South Wales Argus* (26 April 1946), 3 · photographs, repro. in Jenkins, *Life at the centre*, following p. 130

Wealth at death £1631 16s. 1d.: administration, 1947, CGPLA Eng. & Wales

Jenkins, Claude (1877–1959), historian and Church of England clergyman, claimed to have been born on 26 May 1877 (his birth certificate counter-claimed 24 May) in Handsworth, Staffordshire, the eldest son of Oswald Jenkins, cashier and later land agent, and his wife, Sarah, daughter of William Palmer. He was a foundation scholar at King Edward's School, Birmingham, and was elected to a classical exhibition at New College, Oxford, in 1896. He obtained second classes in classical honour moderations (1898), *literae humaniores* (1900), and theology (1901), and was awarded a Liddon exhibition in 1900 and a Denyer and Johnson scholarship in 1902. After studying palaeography with Robinson Ellis, he assisted C. H. Turner with a projected edition of Eusebius; his research in France and Italy yielded his edition of catena fragments of Origen (*Journal of Theological Studies*, 9/34, January 1908, 231–47; 9/35, April 1908, 353–72; 9/36, July 1908, 500–14). For a year he taught at Magdalen College School, and after ordination in 1903 became curate of St Martin-in-the-Fields and assistant chaplain at Charing Cross Hospital. His abilities impressed A. C. Headlam, principal of King's College, London, who secured lectureships in ecclesiastical history (1905–11) and patristics (1911–18) for him and made him sub-editor (1903–18) and later joint editor (1921–7) of the *Church Quarterly Review*.

In 1910, with Headlam's support, Jenkins became librarian of Lambeth Palace Library, where he extended the foundations of his immense erudition. Constitutionally disinclined to surrender preferment, being, as he once observed, 'of a modest if not of a retiring disposition' (private information), he remained librarian until 1952. He was chaplain to Archbishop Randall Davidson from 1911 and helped to revise the coronation service, but was not closely involved in church affairs. In 1918 he became professor of ecclesiastical history at King's, where he wished to integrate historical studies with the collections at Lambeth, and in 1931 professor of ecclesiastical history at London University. He was canon of Canterbury from 1929 to 1934, when he was appointed regius professor of ecclesiastical history and canon of Christ Church, Oxford. He published little except a few articles and reviews, notably his devastating critique of A. S. Barnes's *Bishop Barlow and Anglican Orders* (1922) (*Journal of Theological Studies*, 24/93, 1922, 1–32). His learning, which was perhaps too diffuse, was that of the antiquarian rather than the historian.

At Christ Church Jenkins's eccentricities, which became celebrated, recalled an earlier generation. With his low-crowned hat and antiquated clerical costume, his broad scholarship and unenthusiastic divinity, his uncompromising insistence on ancient rights (especially in chapter), his belief that land and 'the funds' were the only proper investment for the college and industrial shares a new form of the South Sea Bubble, he seemed to have stepped out of the eighteenth century. In term he usually lectured continuously three mornings a week, often to an audience of one, an ancient alarm clock reminding him to change the subject, perhaps from the Paston letters to the puritans or from Greek epigraphy to the Oxford Movement. He was very discursive: his lectures on Augustine, the date of whose birth he was still discussing at the end of term, contrived to include a list of books on the law of tort. Similarly his sermons were memorable less for their theology than for digressions ranging from the price of second-hand books to a dramatic reading from *Macbeth*. In the late 1950s the congregation was startled to be apostrophized with the words, 'Those of you who remember the siege of Mafeking' (private information). His only luxury was the purchase of books, which filled his canonical lodgings almost to the point of impenetrability—even the bath contained the files of the *Church Quarterly Review*—but his library was unsystematic and lacked bibliographical distinction.

Often exasperating to colleagues, he was always courteous and never bore personal rancour. He delighted in the young and was assiduous in attendance at the Oxford Union, where he was senior librarian. In private life he was very generous, and gave a large sum anonymously to St Edmund Hall, the first £10,000 characteristically arriving in a dirty used envelope. He led a remarkably frugal existence but his idiosyncrasies, which embraced the recycling of cigar butts, were from preference rather than parsimony. Said to have an equal aversion to women and cats, he left most of his library to a women's college, St Anne's. To Christ Church senior common room he bequeathed a fund for the purchase of snuff, of which he was inordinately fond. He died at 1 Clarence Road, Tunbridge Wells, on 17 January 1959 while on holiday.

E. G. W. BILL, rev.

Sources *The Times* (19 Jan 1959) · *WWW* · private information (1993) · personal knowledge (1993) · *CGPLA Eng. & Wales* (1959) · b. cert.
Archives Bodl. Oxf., Faculty Office register [transcripts] · Christ Church Oxf., corresp. and papers · LPL, corresp. and papers | LPL, corresp. with Lord Gladstone · LPL, corresp. with Montagu Rhodes James
Likenesses H. Roland White, photograph, *c*.1957, Christ Church Oxf. · photograph, 1957, Christ Church Oxf. · photograph, Christ Church Oxf.
Wealth at death £29,250 5*s.* 11*d.*: probate, 4 June 1959, *CGPLA Eng. & Wales*

Jenkins, (David) Clive (1926–1999), trade unionist, was born on 2 May 1926 at 4 Maesycwrt Terrace, Port Talbot, Glamorgan, the youngest son of David Samuel Jenkins (*d.* *c*.1940), a railway clerk, and his wife, Miriam Hughes, *née* Harris. His brother Thomas Harris (Tom) Jenkins (*b.* 1920) was also a trade unionist, and served as general secretary of the Transport Salaried Staffs' Association from 1977 to 1982. He was educated at Port Talbot Central Boys' School and Port Talbot county school, leaving at the age of fourteen on the death of his father to work in a local metal laboratory, where he was trained to be a metallurgist. Despite his comparative lack of formal education, he enjoyed rapid promotion; within three years he was put in charge of the laboratory, becoming a tin-plate nightshift foreman in 1945. He also took a precocious interest in trade unionism and was branch secretary for the small Association of Scientific Workers by the age of eighteen. Two years later his career as a full-time union official began when he was appointed an assistant divisional secretary in the midlands of the Association of Supervisory Staffs, Executives, and Technicians (ASSET), based in Birmingham. His rise to prominence within the small union was meteoric. By the time he was twenty-eight he was one of the union's national officers and he cut his teeth recruiting white-collar staff at London's Heathrow airport. In 1957 he was appointed deputy general secretary, and in 1961 he succeeded Harry Knight as the union's general secretary.

During the next twenty years, through the 1960s and 1970s, Jenkins was one of the most colourful trade union leaders of his generation. He became the often shameless and ebullient beneficiary of a social revolution in what had been a rather staid trade union world dominated by male manual workers. More than anybody else he made trade unionism respectable among the often stuffy, conservative, but aspiring ranks of Britain's white-collar salariat. In his *Who's Who* entry he included 'organising the

(David) Clive Jenkins (1926–1999), by Liam Woon, 1985

middle classes' among his few hobbies. With his entrepreneurial energies, he articulated and sought to practise, with a shrewd use of marketing techniques, an almost American style of business unionism.

The union's growth was phenomenal. In 1960 it could claim only 20,000 members. Eight years later, as a result of a merger with another union, it was reborn as the Association of Scientific, Technical, and Managerial Staffs (ASTMS) and by 1980 could claim to represent 500,000 white-collar staff, in manufacturing and the services sector. Jenkins's personality was crucial in the union's extraordinary expansion. A lover of the good life—with two homes and a taste for fine food, claret, hand-made suits, and foreign travel—he was the first trade union leader to become a millionaire, largely through shrewd property investments. Inevitably he grew into an object of envy and distaste for many in the labour movement. For much of his time as a trade union leader he was treated as something of an irritant. His irrepressible sense of fun and fertile mind hardened over the years as he tried to grow more serious, but he also became more self-important and pompous.

Jenkins was married twice. On 1 March 1955, in Lyngby-Taarback, Denmark, he married Jean Lynn, an American communist, to enable her to achieve UK residential status. The marriage was dissolved in January 1963, and on 12 February the same year he married Moira McGregor Jenkins (b. 1931/2), formerly Hilley, the daughter of James McGregor Maguire, a bank official. She was a divorcee five years younger than Jenkins who had adopted his surname by deed poll before their marriage. They had one son and one daughter.

For years the trade union establishment kept Jenkins off the ruling general council of the Trades Union Congress (TUC). Not until September 1974 did he secure a place on that body when a special section was created to accommodate him. He was chairman of the TUC general council in 1987–8 and served on most of its leading committees. He also served on a number of public bodies during the 1970s, including the board of the National Research Development Corporation (1974–80) and the British National Oil Corporation (1979–82), and was a member of the Bullock committee on industrial democracy (1975) and the Wilson committee to review the functioning of financial institutions (1977–80).

Jenkins could be a serious thinker. On the left wing of the Labour Party for most of his life after a brief flirtation with communism, he gave up prospects of a career as a politician after failing to secure the party's parliamentary nomination for Shoreditch and Finsbury in 1963. He turned into a persistent critic of successive Labour governments in their efforts to restrain wage inflation in the national economic interest. His efforts reflected the demands of his acquisitive members for higher pay and benefits, most of whom had no political sympathies for Labour. Jenkins believed in import controls, state ownership of industry, and the need for more training and education. He wrote a number of books about trade unionism, the future of work, and the impact of technology on employment, and he was an admirer of Swedish manpower planning. For a long time he opposed British membership of the European Common Market.

Nevertheless his strongly held left-wing opinions never prevented Jenkins from seizing any opportunities available to him to advance his union's ambitions. He was quite prepared initially to use the Industrial Relations Act of 1971 during its short life, despite official TUC policy to boycott its operations. Although his union was never able to establish a strong position in the Labour Party, with most of its members refusing to pay the political levy, Jenkins also played an increasingly important role in its affairs, especially after its defeat in the general election of May 1979. His efforts perhaps did more harm than good. It was under his influence that Labour decided to abandon its method for the election of party leader by its members of parliament alone and to include the trade unions and constituency associations in the process through the creation of an electoral college. In 1980 he helped to persuade Michael Foot to stand successfully for the party leadership, and was his stalwart defender until Labour's disastrous defeat at the polls three years later. He was also able to make sure Neil Kinnock secured the succession as party leader by getting his union's executive to nominate him within hours of Foot's resignation on election night. His critics believed he was too much of a manipulator, who was able with wit and intelligence to over-influence fellow union leaders. He even attempted unsuccessfully to have Len Murray removed as TUC general secretary in 1983. His reputation for behind-the-scenes intrigue was exaggerated, but it did him a great deal of harm at a time when the labour movement was engulfed in self-destructive conflicts.

During the early 1980s Jenkins's union lost members heavily in the economic recession and its influence declined. In 1987 ASTMS was merged with TASS (the Technical, Administrative, and Supervisory Section of the

Amalgamated Union of Engineering Workers) to form the Manufacturing, Science, and Finance Union (MSF), with Jenkins as its joint general secretary. But two years later he retired and (his second marriage having ended in divorce) went off to Tasmania with a girlfriend, Sherie Nadoo, to open a restaurant and campaign for the preservation of miniature fairy penguins. He returned to England in 1990 (the year in which he published his autobiography, *All Against the Collar*), but he was never able to re-establish himself as a public figure and became a rather isolated and embittered man. He died at Kingston Hospital, Kingston upon Thames, on 22 September 1999, of chronic liver disease and multi-organ failure, survived by the son and daughter of his second marriage. ROBERT TAYLOR

Sources C. Jenkins, *All against the collar* (1990) · *The Times* (23 Sept 1999) · *Daily Telegraph* (23 Sept 1999) · *The Independent* (23 Sept 1999) · *The Guardian* (23 Sept 1999) · *The Scotsman* (23 Sept 1999) · *WWW* · personal knowledge (2004) · private information (2004) · b. cert. · decree nisi (1963) · m. cert. (1963) · d. cert.

Archives U. Warwick Mod. RC, diaries, corresp., and papers | SOUND BL NSA, current affairs recordings · BL NSA, documentary recordings

Likenesses photograph, 1967, repro. in *The Times* · photograph, 1974, repro. in *The Independent* · L. Woon, photograph, 1985, NPG [*see illus.*] · photograph, 1988, repro. in *Daily Telegraph* · photograph, repro. in *The Guardian*

Jenkins, David (1582–1663), royalist judge, was the son of Jenkin Richard of Hensol, in the parish of Pendeulwyn, Glamorgan, where he was born. He became a commoner of St Edmund Hall, Oxford, in 1597 and took a BA degree on 4 July 1600.

Early legal career Admitted to Gray's Inn on 5 November 1602 Jenkins was called to the bar in 1609. Although mentioned in law reports of London cases at about the same time, Jenkins on 15 May 1615 obtained a patent for the office of king's attorney for the counties of Carmarthen, Cardigan, Pembroke, Brecknock, and Radnor, which he held jointly with Walter Rumsey until 1631, and alone thereafter until May 1636. Having been selected reader at Barnard's Inn in 1620 he became an antient of Gray's Inn in May 1622, but he was fined £20 for refusing to read in 1625, and 'because he sent the Readers of the House a peremtory answere in prescribinge rules and orders to them' (Fletcher, 1.270) was barred from reading or being called to the bench in the future. A descendant of well-established gentry stock Jenkins had no doubt already established the lucrative practice in south Wales that subsequently made him one of the wealthiest landowners in Glamorgan.

The royalist judge According to biographical details that he published himself in 1647, Jenkins opposed royal financial exactions of the 1630s such as ship money and grants of patents of monopoly; in addition in 1640 he was heavily involved in proceedings with the ecclesiastical court of high commission for opposing the excesses of one of the bishops. Nevertheless he also mentioned that two of the principal enforcers of Caroline policy, William Noy and Sir John Bankes, were 'pleased to make often use of me' (*Works*, 3), apparently by asking him to vet proposals made to the king by various projectors, although these activities

Here JENKINS stands, who thundring from the TOWER
Shook the bold Senats Legiflative Power,
Six of whose words twelve Reames of votes exceed
As mountaines mov'd by graines of muftard-feed;
Thus gasping Lawes were rescu'd from the Snare.
He that will saue a Crowne must Know and dare
J. Berkenhead.

David Jenkins (1582–1663), by William Marshall, pubd 1648

have left little trace in contemporary documents. Claiming that the position cost him much more than it was worth, Jenkins was appointed against his will as puisne justice on the Carmarthen circuit of the court of great sessions in March 1643, but by then his adherence to the royalist cause, which soon became his trademark, must already have been evident. In the late summer of 1643 he was involved in raising money to support the siege of Gloucester, and he indicted several parliamentarians, including Sir Richard and Erasmus Phillips and Major-General Langhorne, for high treason while presiding at the great sessions. *The Kingdom's Weekly Intelligencer* accused him of encouraging atrocities alleged to have been committed in Pembrokeshire in September 1644 by Irish troops led by the royalist commander in south Wales, Colonel Charles Gerrard, and Aubrey famously described Jenkins riding into battle himself in 'forlorne-hope, with his long rapier drawn' (*Brief Lives*, 2.5). Apparently present at Swansea at the time of its capitulation to parliament he fled towards the end of 1645 to Hereford, where he was taken prisoner along with a large number of other prominent royalists, and was eventually placed in the Tower of London. An unsubstantiated newspaper report claimed that one of his captors found that he had £6000 in gold with him, which he had carried from one garrison to the next, but refused to use to further the king's cause.

The House of Commons ordered that a charge be drawn up against Jenkins in January 1646, but there was little progress with his case until April 1647. By then he had firmly established the positions on which he would take his stand. Brought before a Commons committee chaired by Miles Corbet on the 10th, he refused to answer any question put to him, handing over instead a written statement which argued that without the presence of the king, parliament had no power to try him. Jenkins denied that it was treason not to obey the two houses of parliament, because 'the supreame and onely power by the Lawes of this Land is in the King' (*Works*, 62). According to the laws of the land, he could be examined only by the king's writ, patent, or commission, not by a mere ordinance of parliament: 'I cannot be examined by you, without a power derived by his Majesty' (ibid., 66). Discovering that his statement had been misrepresented and published 'to the good people' of London as his recantation, by the end of April Jenkins printed it as his own *Vindication*. This was the first among a barrage of cheaply printed tracts that appeared during spring and summer 1647 and then continued at a slower pace over the course of the next eighteen months. Frequently describing their author as 'a prisoner in the Tower', the works in part sustained Jenkins's claim that, since the two houses without the king had no powers to administer justice, he could be tried only by a jury at common law.

But Jenkins also aimed more broadly. Several works addressed to the parliamentary army attempted to create divisions among the soldiers about whether to seek an accommodation with the king. Claiming to have considered the problems raised by the army's desire for an indemnity for crimes committed during the course of the war, Jenkins pointed out that soldiers were unlikely to get much sympathy if they were brought before local juries, and that an indemnity passed as an ordinance of the two houses would have much less authority than a proper one that was based on the consent of the king in parliament. In addition, his *A Discourse Touching the Inconveniencies of a Long Continued Parliament* (17 June 1647) argued that, among other things, a 'perpetual parliament' was contrary to the Triennial Act, and *A Scourge for the Directorie and the Revolting Synod* (October 1647) expressed his anxiety about proposals to discard the Book of Common Prayer, a development he feared would leave ignorant rural parishioners without any spiritual sustenance other than that provided by the rantings of mechanic preachers.

Lex terrae A recurrent theme in Jenkins's work was his view that before 1640 both the civil and ecclesiastical government of the country had worked well. The address to the members of Gray's Inn and other 'professors of the law' (*Works*, 1), with which he prefaced his most comprehensive work, *Lex terrae* (April 1647), stressed his longstanding study of the common law, and explained that since the 'commonwealth hath flourished for some ages past in great splendour and happiness' (ibid.) thanks to the existence of the laws of the land, he was quite happy to make himself a sacrifice to their defence. *Lex terrae* displays considerable legal learning, and Jenkins took special delight in pointing out discrepancies between parliament's actions and the writings of their 'oracle' (ibid., 40), Sir Edward Coke. Nevertheless his effectiveness as a polemicist lay in the way he set out his position as a series of logical propositions that were supported, but not overwhelmed, by the citation of authorities. His principal point was that 'The king of England hath his title to the crown and to his kingly office and power, not by way of trust, from the two Houses of Parliament, or from the People, but by inherent Birth-right, from God, Nature and the Law' (ibid., A3v). Hence any legal act from the appointment of justices of the peace to the making of legislation could be done only with the explicit authority of the king. Jenkins's most penetrating point was that parliament's repeated claims to be acting in the name of the king, or that the king's power was 'virtually' (ibid., 24) present in the proceedings of the two houses was false. The common law and parliament were corporate bodies that were incomplete without the king; the Lords and Commons in fact acknowledged the absence of the king every time they sent propositions for a settlement to him. The attempt to solve this problem by arguing that the king was virtually present in parliament involved making an unwarranted distinction between the person of the king and his crown or authority, a false 'damned opinion' (ibid., A3v) that Jenkins traced to the treasons of the Despensers in the reign of Edward II.

The impact of Jenkins's arguments can be measured by the fact that his 'odious charges upon parliament and those that supported it in the war' (Parker, preface) brought forth a very quick reply from Henry Parker, who attempted to address the problem of the 'virtual' presence of royal power in parliament by claiming that parliament's position was that it acknowledged the king as 'our Supreme Governor over all Persons and in all causes' (ibid., 5), but that he had been declared in no condition to govern because he had taken up arms against parliament. Nor in any case was the king above the safety of the people, which was the end of the law, and, indeed, paramount to law itself. In conclusion Parker expressed a wish that Jenkins would 'lick up againe his black infamous execrable reproaches so filthily vomited out' (ibid., 6), but the judge was undaunted. According to a letter of 19 June 1647 addressed to the House of Commons by the parliamentary committee at Usk, a recently suppressed royalist uprising in Glamorgan had been 'contrived by Jenkins and other delinquents in the Tower' (*DNB*). On 22nd June an order was passed in the House of Commons that Jenkins and his publishers should be prosecuted in the king's bench for his scandalous books and pamphlets; a powerful legal team including Corbet, William Prynne, and John Bradshaw were appointed to assist in the process. Described as a prisoner for high treason, Jenkins was moved by order of the house from the Tower to Newgate prison in September 1647, but his case progressed so slowly that the solicitor-general had to be reminded the following January to proceed against him with 'effect and speed' (*JHC*, 5.437).

Tried for sedition At this point Jenkins himself caused further outrage by refusing to give an answer at the chancery bar in connection with a private suit that had been brought against him, exclaiming that it was not a proper court of justice since the seal it used was not the great seal of England, but a counterfeit one. On 22 February 1648 he was once again brought to the bar of the house facing charges of levying war against parliament, writing treasonous pamphlets, and other seditious practices. Though he removed his hat, Jenkins refused to kneel at the bar according to the custom of the house, and he is reported to have used 'very contemptuous words and reproaches against the houses, and the power of parliament' (*The Trial of Judge Jengins*, A3). According to a hostile published account, when he came out of the chamber he took off his hat and addressed the soldiers and others at the door, giving them his blessing, and reminding them to 'Protect the Laws of the Kingdom' (ibid.). The house fined him £1000 for his contempt. After hearing several witnesses as to the matter of fact an ordinance of attaint was passed against him and Serjeant John Wilde was charged with sending it up to the House of Lords. Another, uncorroborated, account alleged that Jenkins indignantly refused an offer of a free pardon and a pension of £1000 p.a. if he submitted to parliamentary authority. In any event he continued to publish pamphlets concerning his case as well as a collection of his principal controversial *Works*, which was adorned with an engraved portrait of the author. In April 1648 a 'loyal subject' published three poems in his honour, one of which included the lines:

A British Lawyer (in the Lawes well grounded)
By lawlesse madmen in a Jayle impounded;
Belov'd, not having any good mans hate,
A well known Champion gainst th'usurping State.
(*Verses*, 6)

Early in October 1648 Jenkins was removed from Newgate to Wallingford Castle, where he appears to have written a letter on the 12th to King Charles, which urged him to sign the treaty of Newport. Though the letter is said to have been intercepted its substance was published in *The declaration of David Jenkins … concerning the parliament's army, with a copy of his letter to his dread soveraign the king*. In March 1649 the House of Commons voted that he should be tried, this time ordering that an indictment be drawn up against him that could be put before Welsh judges in the country. Once again, however, the case stalled, and in April Jenkins published his last important polemical work, *God and the king, or, The divine constitution of the supreme magistrate; especially in the kingdom of England*. Still maintaining that the critical question was whether supreme authority was vested in the houses of parliament or in the king, Jenkins drew more heavily on the scriptures than in his previous works to provide the answer. Since magistracy involved power over life and death, it was evident that such authority could come only from God. The houses of parliament

represented the people, but the king was the only representative of God, and therefore the king must have the greater power. He finished by referring to the works of Coke to illustrate the point that parliamentary depositions of kings were treasonous.

Jenkins was yet again threatened with the scaffold when he was named in the spring of 1650 on a list of several prisoners that the Rump Parliament considered executing in retaliation for the assassination of Anthony Ascham in Spain, but in the end no action was taken. Though resolved to be 'hanged with the Bible under one arme and Magna Charta under the other' (*Brief Lives*, 2.6), Jenkins was reprieved when Henry Martin reminded the house that it would do more harm than good to their cause to make a martyr of him. Moved from Wallingford to Windsor Castle in 1652 he was finally discharged and allowed to go to Gray's Inn on 12 January 1657, and afterwards, though still under surveillance, lived for a while at Oxford. 'Amidst the Sound of Drums and Trumpets, surrounded with an odious Multitude of Barbarians, broken with old Age and Confinement in Prisons, where my Fellow Subjects grown wild with Rage detained me for fifteen Years', Jenkins used the period of his confinement to write *Rerum judicatarum centurix octo*, a compilation of judicial decisions made in exchequer chamber between 1275 and 1613. Jenkins said that he intended the work to be useful to all who studied the laws of England by rendering more certain the scattered decisions of former ages. His method was to give a short statement of each case and the decision, along with a marginal reference to the authority from which it was taken, only occasionally offering a commentary of his own. First published in French and Latin in 1661 the text was translated as *Eight Centuries of Reports* and was twice reprinted in the eighteenth century. Three other works (*Pacis consultum …; an Exact Method for Keeping a Court of Survey*; and *Some Difficult Questions in Law*) published under his name in 1657 were disclaimed by Jenkins and are very unlikely to be authentic.

In 1660 Jenkins was made a bencher at Gray's Inn and, according to Anthony Wood and John Aubrey, himself claimed that he would have been rewarded for his sufferings by being made a judge of Westminster Hall if he had given Lord Chancellor Clarendon money for the position. Since Wood was expelled from Oxford University because of the allegation, and Clarendon's works are curiously silent about Jenkins and his exploits, it is unclear what truth there is in it. Having recovered his estate (worth some £1500 p.a.), which had been sequestrated in 1652, Jenkins was evidently content to return to Hensol, where he became a patron of bards. He and his wife, Cecil, daughter of Sir Thomas Aubrey, had four sons and six daughters, and Jenkins is also said to have encouraged the early studies of Sir Leoline Jenkins, a relation by marriage. He died on 6 December 1663, probably at Hensol, and was buried at Cowbridge. Though Jenkins had no monument Wood eulogized him as 'a vigorous maintainer of the rights of the crown, a heart of oak, and a pillar of the law' (Wood, *Ath. Oxon.*, 3.644).   CHRISTOPHER W. BROOKS

Sources R. J. Fletcher, ed., *The pension book of Gray's Inn*, 2 vols. (1901–10) · *The works of that grave and learned lawyer Judge Jenkins, prisoner in Newgate upon divers statuttes, concerning the liberty, and freedome of the subject* (1648) · *The trial of Judge Jengins at the House of Commons barre upon an impeachement of high-treason, on Munday last, February 21, 1647. With heads of the charge read against him and his Anslwer. Also the votes of the House of Commons thereupon* (1648) · *State trials*, vol. 4 · D. Jenkins, *God and king, or, The divine constitution of the supreme magistrate; especially in the kingdom of England* (1649) · *Brief lives, chiefly of contemporaries, set down by John Aubrey, between the years 1669 and 1696*, ed. A. Clark, 2 vols. (1898) · G. Williams, ed., *Glamorgan county history*, 4: *Early modern Glamorgan* (1974) · H. P. [H. Parker], 'An answer to the poysonus sedicious paper of Mr David Jenkins' (1647) [E 386(14)] · *JHC*, 5 (1646–8) · *Verses in honour of the revernd and learned judge of the law, Judge Jenkin: the sole author of his sovereign's rights, England laws and the people's liberty* (1648) · W. R. Williams, *The history of the great sessions in Wales, 1542–1830* (privately printed, Brecon, 1899) · Wood, *Ath. Oxon.*, new edn, 3.643–8

Likenesses W. Marshall, line engraving, BM, NPG; repro. in *Works* (1648) [*see illus.*] · line engraving (after W. Marshall), BM, NPG; repro. in *The works of the eminent … Judge Jenkins* (1681)

Wealth at death very wealthy; est. to be £1500 p.a.

Jenkins, David Llewelyn, Baron Jenkins (1899–1969), judge, was born at Exmouth, Devon, on 8 April 1899, the third son and fifth of the seven children of Sir John Lewis Jenkins KCSI (1857–1912), a civil servant in India, and his wife, Florence Mildred (*d.* 1956), daughter of Sir Arthur Trevor KCSI, and niece of W. S. Trevor. His father's father was a farmer in Carmarthenshire. His mother was a granddaughter of Captain R. S. Trevor of the 3rd Bengal cavalry who was murdered with Sir William Macnaghten in Kabul in 1841 and whose widow was eventually able to return by way of India to England with her seven surviving children, an eighth, born in captivity, having died in India shortly after release.

Although his ancestry on both sides was Welsh and his family was predominantly associated with the Indian service, Jenkins never had a home in either Wales or India. His father had bought a house in Exmouth as a home for his family; there the children seem to have spent an exceedingly happy childhood in the care of their mother, when she was not in India, and at other times of an aunt. Their father joined them during his periods of home leave once in every three years. In 1912, following Sir John's death, the family moved to Kew.

In the same year Jenkins won a scholarship at Charterhouse School, where he became a fine schoolboy classical scholar, won all the prizes open to him, and became head of the school. He gained a domus exhibition in classics at Balliol College, Oxford, but was shortly afterwards called up for military service. Commissioned in July 1918, he was in France with the 12th (service) battalion of the rifle brigade for a few weeks before the armistice was signed. Demobilized early in 1919 he went up to Balliol, where he obtained a first class in classical honour moderations (1920) and a second in *literae humaniores* (1922). He was a Craven scholar and *proxime accessit* for the Ireland in 1919 and *proxime accessit* for the Hertford in 1920.

In spite of the long family connections with India, it did not attract Jenkins, although his brothers Sir Evan and Sir Owain Jenkins both had distinguished careers there. While still at Charterhouse Jenkins had decided that he wished to go to the bar. He became a student member of Lincoln's Inn while an undergraduate and secured a Tancred studentship. He was called to the bar in 1923 and became a pupil of J. E. Harman (father of the future Lord Justice Harman), thus gaining the advantage of seeing one of the largest and most varied junior Chancery practices of the day. Harman died suddenly near the end of the pupillage and Charles Harman and Jenkins together dealt with winding up his practice. After a period in the chambers of Edward Beaumont, Jenkins was invited to move to J. H. Stamp's chambers at 11 New Court, of which Raymond Evershed, a Balliol friend and later master of the rolls, was already a member. Jenkins devilled extensively for Stamp, who was standing junior counsel to the Inland Revenue, built up a sound junior practice of his own at the Chancery bar, and took silk in 1938.

Jenkins's career as a leader was soon interrupted by the Second World War in which he held a temporary commission in the Royal Army Service Corps, serving for a time as adjutant of a training unit with the temporary rank of major. In 1943 he transferred to the political warfare executive branch of the Foreign Office under Sir Robert Bruce Lockhart who, when Jenkins returned to the bar in 1945, wrote that in the 'mercurial atmosphere' of the branch Jenkins's 'even temperament and dispassionate judgement' had been of great value.

Jenkins returned to the bar rather apprehensively, but his experience of revenue work with Stamp led to his being frequently selected to lead for the Inland Revenue and this was a type of work in which he excelled. In 1946 he was appointed attorney-general of the duchy of Lancaster. In 1947 he was promoted to the Chancery bench and two years later to the Court of Appeal. During his ten years there his judicial excellence was demonstrated by the remarkable regularity with which any dissenting judgment of his was upheld in the House of Lords. In 1959 he was appointed a lord of appeal in ordinary.

Jenkins was a shy man, his manner somewhat withdrawn, but among friends he was the best of company. His figure was slight and he retained the spareness of his youth, conjuring up the image of some slim and cautiously intent bespectacled bird. Behind his glasses were a pair of markedly humorous and observant eyes. His wit was incisive, good humoured, and irreverent towards conventional judgments. On becoming a judge he applied for a grant of arms, and is reported to have proposed as his motto the injunction 'Up Jenkins'. At the Foreign Office, when his colleagues were seeking to encapsulate in a single sentence the cause for which the allies were fighting, after a moment's reflection Jenkins exclaimed: 'I have it: To make the world SHAEF for democracy.'

Jenkins's quality as a judge, like his wit, closely resembled that of Lord Bowen, his Victorian predecessor. Among his contemporaries he excelled in penetrating analysis and lucid exposition. He had probably the best judicial brain of his day.

Jenkins served for some time as chairman of the lord chancellor's Law Reform Committee and presided over a number of other important committees concerned with law reform. These included the leasehold committee which reported in 1950, and notably the company law committee, whose report in 1962 was Jenkins's last and probably his most notable contribution to law reform. In the following year ill health compelled him to retire. He died after a long sad illness in London on 21 July 1969.

Jenkins never married. He was a bencher of Lincoln's Inn (1945), an honorary fellow of Balliol (1950), a governor (1953–65) of Sutton's Hospital in Charterhouse, and chairman for some years of the Tancred studentship trustees. He was knighted in 1947, sworn of the privy council in 1949, and made a life peer in 1959.

DENYS B. BUCKLEY, *rev.*

Sources personal knowledge (1981) · private information (1981) · *The Times* (23 July 1969) · Burke, *Peerage* (1967)
Likenesses N. Hepple, group portrait, oils (*Court of appeal in 1958*), Lincoln's Inn, London · N. Hepple, group portrait, oils (*The short adjournment*), Lincoln's Inn, London
Wealth at death £79,439: probate, 2 Sept 1969, *CGPLA Eng. & Wales*

Jenkins, Ebenezer Evans (1820–1905), Wesleyan Methodist minister and missionary, born at Exeter on 10 May 1820, was the second son of John Jenkins, cabinet maker, and his wife, Mary Evans, a Welshwoman. His parents were Methodists. Educated at Exeter grammar school, he showed literary leanings and soon became assistant master in William Pengelly's school. He resolved on the Methodist ministry, and was ordained in 1845 and sent out to Madras. Stationed at first at Mannargudi, he was able by September 1846 to prepare a Tamil sermon. After a move to Negapatam, he settled, about 1848, at Black Town Chapel, Madras, and soon started the Royapettah School (later College) there, the oldest Wesleyan educational institution in India. He married Eliza Drewett in Madras in 1850; she died in 1869, and on 19 October 1871 he married Margaret Heald, daughter of Dr Peter Wood of Southport. She died in childbirth in 1875. Jenkins was absent (1855–7) from India on account of his health during the mutiny, but in 1857 he returned as chairman of the Madras district, continuing to minister in his old chapel, which he enlarged. He persuaded the missionary committee to start the Hyderabad mission in 1862, and a volume of his sermons was published at Madras in 1863. But Jenkins's health again failed, and after returning home by way of Australia, where he gave many lectures, he was appointed superintendent of the Hackney circuit in 1865. He at once gained a high reputation as a preacher and speaker through the country, and made several foreign tours in an official capacity, speaking at the Evangelical Alliance convention at New York in 1873, and in 1875–6 and again in 1884–5 visiting missions in China, Japan, and India. From 1877 to 1888 he was a general secretary of the Wesleyan Methodist Missionary Society, remaining an honorary secretary until his death. At the conferences of 1889 and 1890 he indignantly defended the Wesleyan missionaries in India against the charges of luxury and aloofness brought against them by Hugh Price Hughes and others. In 1880 he was president of the Wesleyan conference. Jenkins's last years were spent in Southport, where he died at 14 Scarisbrick Street on 19 July 1905. He was buried at Norwood cemetery in Southport.

CHARLOTTE FELL-SMITH, *rev.* TIM MACQUIBAN

Sources J. H. Jenkins, *Ebenezer E. Jenkins* (1906) · *The Times* (20 July 1905) · W. Hill, *An alphabetical arrangement of all the Wesleyan-Methodist ministers, missionaries, and preachers*, rev. J. P. Haswell, 9th edn (1862) · *Minutes of the Methodist conference* · G. G. Findlay and W. W. Holdsworth, *The history of the Wesleyan Methodist Missionary Society*, 5 vols. (1921–4) · N. B. Harmon, ed., *The encyclopedia of world Methodism*, 2 vols. (1974) · m. cert. · d. cert.
Likenesses wood-engraving (after photograph by Done & Co. of Baker Street), NPG; repro. in *ILN* (31 July 1880)
Wealth at death £1515 19s. 4d.: probate, 21 Sept 1905, *CGPLA Eng. & Wales*

Jenkins, Sir (Thomas) Gilmour (1894–1981), civil servant, was born at 25 Llantwit Road, Neath, Glamorgan, on 18 July 1894, the son of Thomas Jenkins, a civil servant in the Inland Revenue, and his wife, Letitia Annie Parker, *née* Keane. He was educated at Rutlish School, South Wimbledon. In 1913 he joined the civil service in the Exchequer and Audit Department as an examiner, and took an external BSc degree at London University in 1916. On 1 November 1916 he married Evelyne Mary (1891/2–1976), the daughter of Charles Henry Nash, provision merchant. They had two children: a son, Alexander James Keane (b. 1923), and a daughter, Patricia Mary Keane (b. 1928).

In the First World War Jenkins was commissioned in the Royal Garrison Artillery in 1917; he was awarded the Military Cross and bar, both in 1918. On demobilization he joined the Board of Trade. There he served mainly on the marine side of the department, concerned with regulating the safety of British merchant shipping and seamen's conditions. He became an assistant secretary in 1934 and principal assistant secretary in 1937, and was UK government delegate to the marine sessions of the international labour conferences at Geneva in 1935 and 1936. On the outbreak of war in 1939 a separate Ministry of Shipping took over the shipping divisions of the Board of Trade, and he became second secretary there. The almost immediate reorganization of the ministry under a director-general (Sir Cyril Hurcomb) somewhat reduced the status of the secretary and second secretary; but in 1941 Jenkins became deputy director-general, in charge of the shipping side of what was now the Ministry of War Transport. Thus he was involved in the main issues of shipping policy in the war—making sure that shipping was provided for essential imports, and that conflicting demands were scaled down to meet the shipping resources available— though these were largely handled by the director-general himself. Jenkins was made a CB in 1941, and KBE in 1944, taking the style Sir Gilmour Jenkins.

In 1946 Jenkins was promoted to permanent secretary, taking charge of the work of the Allied Control Commission for Germany, and when that became part of the Foreign Office in 1947 he was briefly joint permanent under-secretary of state there. In the same year he returned to the Ministry of Transport as permanent secretary. In 1948 he was made a KCB. When the work of the Ministry of

Civil Aviation was transferred to the transport department in 1953, he remained as permanent secretary of the restyled Ministry of Transport and Civil Aviation; he retired in 1959.

As permanent secretary Jenkins was able to oversee the broad lines of the transport department's policies without detailed intervention. But his long shipping background disposed him to regard the shipping side as the department's most important charge, at a time when increasingly this was ceasing to be true, as British shipping was no longer as dominant in world shipping or in the country's economic life as it had been before 1939. His knowledge and experience of shipping matters, however, paid off when in 1956 he took direct charge of the department's work in the Suez crisis, arranging to provide merchant shipping which could transport troops and equipment for the campaign itself. But he was not eager to grapple with the increasing problems of the country's inland transport, including the need for a major programme of new road improvements, and for measures to meet the decline of the railways. Nor did he involve himself to any great extent in civil aviation matters when these were transferred to the department. A lack of dynamism from the top in dealing with these increasingly important fields of government activity left his successor with much to do in redirecting the department. Jenkins had perhaps lost some of his earlier drive, and may have stayed on too long.

A book, *The Ministry of Transport and Civil Aviation*, was published under Jenkins's name in 1959. Outside official work his main interest was in music. From conducting civil service choirs, he established a place in the musical world, becoming a close friend of the composer Ralph Vaughan Williams and his second wife, Ursula (with whom he lived during the week, returning to his home at Goldhanger, near Maldon in Essex, at the weekends), as well as of Gerald Finzi. He was vice-president and an honorary fellow of the Royal Academy of Music and a member of the London Philharmonic Orchestra council.

White-haired and white-moustached, Jenkins's appearance and manner was distinguished, and very much that of the high official; but with it he was approachable and friendly. His wife died in 1976. He himself died in a residential home, Weald Hall, Mayfield Lane, Wadhurst, Sussex, on 9 September 1981.   GEOFFREY WARDALE

Sources personal knowledge (2004) · b. cert. · m. cert. · d. cert. · Burke, *Peerage* (1967) · C. Brock, *Rutlish School: the first hundred years* (1995) · records, U. Lond. · NAM · exchequer and audit records, London · C. B. A. Behrens, *Merchant shipping and the demands of war* (1955) · U. Vaughan Williams, *RWV: a biography of Ralph Vaughan Williams* (1964)
Archives SOUND BL NSA, oral history interview
Wealth at death £47,826: probate, 3 March 1982, *CGPLA Eng. & Wales*

Jenkins, Harold (1909–2000), literary scholar and university teacher, was born on 19 July 1909 at Shenley Church End, Shenley, Buckinghamshire, the eldest son of Henry Jenkins (1878–1932), a dairyman, and his wife, Mildred, *née* Carter, who were cousins. Harold had an elder and a

younger sister, and two younger brothers. Educated at a local school from the age of three, he won a free place in 1920 at what became Wolverton grammar school. Scholarships enabled him to proceed in 1927 to University College, London, where he read English language and literature. He graduated in 1930 with first-class honours, winning both the George Morley medal in English literature and the prestigious George Smith studentship (1930–31). The subsequent award of the Quain studentship enabled him to continue his studies for another five years, during which he also taught. His MA thesis (1933) on the Elizabethan dramatist Henry Chettle, supervised by W. W. Greg, was published in revised form as *The Life and Work of Henry Chettle* in the following year. After a year as William Noble fellow in the University of Liverpool he took up a lecturership in English in 1936 at the University of the Witwatersrand, South Africa, where he stayed until 1945. His Witwatersrand DLitt thesis (1945) appeared in revised form as *Edward Benlowes (1602–76): Biography of a Minor Poet* (1952). In 1939 he married Gladys Puddifoot (1908–1984), whom he had met as a student. She became a respected historian and was an ideal partner, sharing his scholarly interests and bringing him much happiness until her death in a road accident in 1984. There were no children.

Returning to London as lecturer at University College in 1945, Jenkins was promoted reader in the following year, and in 1954 took up the chair of English at Westfield College. During the 1950s he wrote brilliant essays on *Twelfth Night* and *As You Like It*, and a classic study, *The Structural Problem in Henry IV* (1956), delivered as his inaugural lecture at Westfield College. In 1958 he became joint general editor with Dr Harold Brooks of the Arden Shakespeare, for which he undertook to edit *Hamlet*. From 1955 onwards he published a series of authoritative bibliographical and critical studies on the play, including his British Academy lecture *Hamlet and Ophelia* (1963).

In 1967 Jenkins was appointed regius professor of rhetoric and English literature in the University of Edinburgh. It was not a happy move; he retired early and returned to London in 1971 to work on his still uncompleted edition of *Hamlet*. It did not see the light until 1982. It is a monument to the tenets of the 'new bibliography' established in the early years of the century by Greg and others: comprehensive in scope, minute in its exploration of detail, scrupulous in acknowledging disagreement, judicious in its editorial decisions, and written with the fastidious elegance—and occasional acerbity—of which Jenkins was a master. But by the time it appeared, the scholarly climate was changing; editors were paying more attention to the theatre—Jenkins's edition boasts neither stage history nor illustrations—and the foundations of the new bibliography were wobbling. The edition has been greatly admired, but it would have been even more enthusiastically acclaimed had it appeared ten years earlier.

In later life Jenkins received several prizes and honours including the fellowship of the British Academy in 1989. A volume in his honour, *Fanned and Winnowed Opinions*, including essays by friends along with a memoir and a list of publications, appeared in 1987. For over forty years Jenkins served on the council of the Malone Society, of which he was elected president in 1989, and for which he edited Chettle's *Tragedy of Hoffman* (1951).

Jenkins was a marvellous teacher, erudite, lucid in exposition, with a remarkable capacity to carry his hearers along on the tide of his own enthusiasm. Students remember with admiration and affection the sprightly vivacity of his tutorials and the exuberance of his lecturing style, whether on Restoration comedy, eighteenth-century poetry, or Shakespeare. His intercollegiate lectures on Shakespeare's tragedies in the early 1960s were greeted, to his evident surprise and gratification, with a standing ovation. Dapper in appearance, usually sporting a bow-tie, he was the most courteous of men, crisply and wittily articulate in conversation, fastidiously discriminating in his choice of words, positive in his opinions, but sensitive to disagreement in others.

Jenkins's sharpness of mind stayed with him to the end, but failing eyesight and hearing along with the after-effects of a stroke ultimately quenched his appetite for life. He died at home, at Red House, Skinners Lane, Ashtead, Surrey, on 4 January 2000, bequeathing his books to Queen Mary and Westfield College, which also houses his literary papers. STANLEY WELLS

Sources WW · E. A. J. Honigmann, 'Harold Jenkins, 1909–2000', *PBA*, 111 (2001), 548–68 · personal knowledge (2004) · J. W. Mahon and T. A. Pendleton, eds., *Fanned and winnowed opinions: Shakspearean essays presented to Harold Jenkins* (1987)
Archives Queen Mary College, London, books and literary papers
Likenesses photograph, repro. in Honigmann, 'Harold Jenkins'
Wealth at death £822,880: probate, 2 May 2000, *CGPLA Eng. & Wales*

Jenkins, Henry [*called* the Modern Methuselah] (*d.* 1670), claimant to extreme old age, was a native of Ellerton upon Swale, Yorkshire. He subsisted as a labourer and fisherman. Latterly he gained a livelihood by begging, and to attract attention regaled his patrons with anecdotes of his younger days. He claimed to have been born about 1501 and to have been sent at the time of the battle of Flodden (1513) to North Allerton with a horse-load of arrows for the army. He also claimed to have been employed in his younger days as butler to Lord Conyers, whose carouses with Marmaduke, abbot of Fountains Abbey, he recollected. He had sworn, he said, as a witness in a cause at York assizes to 120 years. In April 1667 he appeared in a tithe cause between Charles Anthony, vicar of Catterick, and Calvert Smithson, a parishioner, and then claimed to be 157 years old. His notoriety is due to a letter published in *Philosophical Transactions* (1696) by Miss Ann Savile of Bolton-on-Swale, who interviewed him in 1662 or 1663, when he claimed to be 162 or 163. Charles Anthony, who conducted Jenkins's funeral at Bolton, where he was buried on 9 December 1670, merely described him in the register as 'a very aged and poore man'. Jenkins's wife had predeceased him by only a very few years, having been buried at Bolton on 27 January 1668.

In 1743 an obelisk to Jenkins's memory was erected in Bolton churchyard. In the church a black marble tablet was placed, recording that he lived to the 'amazing age of 169'. The debate regarding Jenkins, who was known as the Modern Methuselah, was energetically conducted in *Notes and Queries* throughout the nineteenth century and up to 1945. His fame in Yorkshire persisted thereafter and he is mentioned in numerous guidebooks to the region.

GORDON GOODWIN, *rev.* ELEANOR O'KEEFFE

Sources A. Savile, letter, *PTRS*, 19 (1695–7), 266–8 · C. Clarkson, *The history of Richmond in the county of York* (1821) · W. Grainge, *Three wonderful Yorkshire characters* (1864) · W. J. Thoms, *The longevity of man* (1879) · G. B. Wood, *Yorkshire villages* (1971) · 'Longevity', *N&Q*, 3rd ser., 8 (1865), 64, 157, 327 · W. J. Thoms, 'Henry Jenkins's alleged longevity', *N&Q*, 4th ser., 5 (1870), 487 · 'Henry Jenkins', *N&Q*, 7th ser., 11 (1891), 484 · 'Henry Jenkins: super-centenarian', *N&Q*, 176 (1939), 383–5; 177 (1939), 12–13 · B. l'Anson, 'Henry Jenkins', *N&Q*, 189 (1945), 18–19
Likenesses R. Page, engraving, repro. in H. Wilson, ed., *Wonderful characters: memoirs and anecdotes of remarkable persons*, 1 (1826) · T. Worlidge, etching (after Walker), BM, NPG
Wealth at death very poor: Clarkson, *History of Richmond*

Jenkins, John (1591×6?–1678), composer, was born at Maidstone, Kent. He was possibly born either in late 1591 or 1592 as the eldest son of Henry Jenkins (*d.* 1617), carpenter and freeman of Maidstone, and his wife, Anne Jordaine (*d.* 1623)—a date indicated by a monumental inscription which records him as aged eighty-six in October 1678 and implied by his proficiency in playing the bass viol in 1603. Otherwise, he may have been born—probably in 1596—as the couple's second son, and younger brother of Henry Jenkins, who was baptized in May 1595 (an alternative deduced from the order in which the brothers were mentioned in their parents' wills and Anne Jenkins's specific reference to Henry junior as 'my eldest son'). A gap in the Maidstone baptism register from March 1588 to November 1593 makes verification impossible, but it may be that the former is correct: when the wills were made John Jenkins had probably long left Maidstone, and an error may have been made in the nuncupative transmission of his mother's last wishes. It is clear, however, that the household was involved in music-making, and perhaps instrument making too: the inventory of Henry Jenkins senior's goods included seven viols and violins, a bandora, and, cytherne, and he bequeathed an instrument to each of his sons, including a bandora to John.

Jenkins probably became apprenticed to a professional musician in the household of a gentleman, and from Lady Anne Clifford's note in her diary that she 'learned to sing and play on the bass viol of Jack Jenkins, my aunt's boy' (Sackville-West, 16), it seems that in 1603 he was resident with Lady Anne Dudley, widow of Ambrose Dudley, earl of Warwick, at Northall, Hertfordshire, or at her town house 'in or neere Broadstreet', London. By the countess's will, dated 11 October 1603, Jenkins received a £10 annuity, administered by her brother William Russell. This annuity was renewed in Russell's own will of 1612.

By this time Jenkins is likely to have completed his apprenticeship, and the death of Lord William may have provided an opportune moment for him to break with the Russell family. He found a new patron in Thomas Derham, who had recently acquired substantial estates at West Dereham, Norfolk. While Derham, a lawyer, had witnessed Russell's will, it is equally plausible that Jenkins's contact with the family came rather through Thomas's father, Baldwin Derham (d. 1610), a former master of the Mercers' Company with links to Maidstone's flourishing textile manufacture.

No more is known of Jenkins until early 1634, when he took a prominent part among the instrumentalists performing the extravagant inns of court masque *The Triumph of Peace*. This was given before the king and queen at Whitehall on 3 February 1634 and again on 13 February at Merchant Taylors' Hall. On 4 March Jenkins signed a receipt for £10 for his services. His presence at the event alongside the cream of the king's musicians indicates that he was known to them and already highly esteemed. 'He was once', wrote his pupil Roger North, 'carryed to play on the viol afore King Charles I, which he did in his voluntary way, with wonderful agility, and odd humours … And when he had done the King sayd he did wonders upon an inconsiderable instrument' (Wilson, 295).

It seems likely that Jenkins was based in London during the 1630s, but North recorded that, with the disbanding of the court in 1642, he left the city, 'and past his time at gentlemen's houses in the country where musick was of the family … I never heard that he articled with any gentleman where he resided, but accepted what they gave him' (Wilson, 344).

During the 1640s Jenkins was patronized by the Derhams and by the L'Estrange family of Hunstanton. Several of Jenkins's holograph music manuscripts from the library of Sir Nicholas L'Estrange (1604–1655) are extant; annotations in them show that many of the pieces were written at West Dereham and Hunstanton between about 1640 and 1645. Both families were royalist and jointly active in support of Charles I at the siege of King's Lynn. Jenkins himself wrote a pictorial instrumental piece, 'Newark Seidge', commemorating a more successful royalist venture, while his song 'When fair Aurora' looked for 'tidings of peace and Blessings in a King'. When his friend William Lawes was killed fighting for the king at Chester, Jenkins contributed an elegy to the memorial volume *Choice Psalmes* (1648).

The title-page of Edward Benlowes's *Theophila* (1652) states that several parts were set by Jenkins. The composer may also have had contact with Sir Robert Bolles at Scampton, where Christopher Simpson resided: Jenkins wrote commendations for Simpson's *The Division-Violist* (1659) and later for his *Compendium of Practical Musick* (1667). By 1654 he was staying intermittently with the North family at Kirtling, Cambridgeshire. A large collection of music by Jenkins (Bodl. Oxf., MSS Mus. Sch.) was made for the family. Roger North considered that 'besides his musicall excellences, he was an accomplisht, ingenious person, and so well behaved, as never to give offence, and wherever he went was allwais welcome and courted to stay' (Wilson, 344).

On 19 June 1660 Jenkins was sworn as a theorbo player among the royal musicians. Although he retained the place until March 1678, he seems to have retired from court about 1663, at which point the fees paid to him at Kirtling doubled. A letter dated 25 May 1668 (PRO, E406/50, fol. 92) shows him still there, and although, according to North, he was not musically productive and was 'withall, obnoxious to great infirmitys, he was taken care of as a friend' (Wilson, 344). His last years were spent at Kimberley, Norfolk, with Sir Philip Wodehouse, where he died on 27 October 1678. He was buried in the chancel of the church there two days later. No will seems to be extant, although a letter from his executors is preserved (PRO, E406/50, fol. 158), showing that arrears due from his court fees were to be shared between his colleague and friend John Lilly and 'Johanna Wheeler' of Stepney, perhaps his landlady. He died, as North put it, 'not poor but capable to leav, as he did, hansome remembrances to some of his freinds' (Wilson, 344).

Jenkins was a prolific composer of instrumental music, where his supreme achievement lies in more than 100 fantasias for viol consorts, and in the rather later series of fantasia-suites for strings and organ. Although content to retain the forms evolved by previous generations, his gifts of lyrical invention were unsurpassed and were allied to distinctive imaginative exploration of key and instrumental colour. Many works from the 1630s and 1640s incorporate virtuoso passages ('divisions') for all the string players. Throughout his life Jenkins also wrote great quantities of simple but attractive dance pieces, ideal for amateurs; many of these were published in the collections by John Playford and others. His vocal music is relatively insignificant. As a performer he was famed as a lutenist (although no lute music by him is known) and violist, especially on the bass and lyra viols. Many of his pieces for lyra viol solo or in consort are extant. North wrote that Jenkins 'had a vivacious spirit and often proffered at poetry' (Wilson). A few poems by him survive, including one in memory of Dudley North, who died in December 1666.

ANDREW ASHBEE

Sources A. Ashbee, *The harmonious music of John Jenkins*, vol. 1 (1992) · J. Wilson, *Roger North on music* (1959) · A. Ashbee, ed., *Records of English court music*, 1 (1986) · A. Ashbee, ed., *Records of English court music*, 5 (1991) · A. Ashbee, ed., *Records of English court music*, 8 (1995) · *The life and times of Anthony Wood*, ed. A. Clark, 1, OHS, 19 (1891) · *The diary of Lady Anne Clifford* (1923) [with introductory note by V. Sackville-West] · M. Lefkowitz, 'The Longleat papers of Bulstrode Whitelocke: new light on Shirley's *Triumph of peace*', *Journal of the American Musicological Society*, 18 (1965), 42–60 · A. Sabol, 'New documents on Shirley's masque *The triumph of peace*', *Music and Letters*, 47 (1966), 10–26 · A. Ashbee and P. Holman, eds., *John Jenkins and his time: studies in English consort music* (1996) · A. Ashbee, 'Jenkins, John', *New Grove* · CKS, PRC 28/9, fol. 294; PRC 44, fol. 260; PRC 45, fol. 329 · PRO, PROB 11/103, fol. 13 (will of Anne, countess of Warwick); PROB 11/122, fol. 86 (will of William Russell); E406/50 · Longleat House, Wiltshire, Whitelocke MSS, parcel II

Archives BL, holograph MSS, Add. MSS 23779, 29290, 31428 · Bodl. Oxf., MS Mus. Sch. C. 88, 184.c.8; MS North e.37 · Christ Church Oxf., Mus 1005 · Newberry Library, Chicago, Case MS VM.1.A.18.j.52c · PRO, signature, LC9/195, fol. 21r · Royal College of Music, London, MS 921 | Longleat House, Wiltshire, Whitelocke papers, parcel II, no. 6, signature

Wealth at death died 'not poor but capable to leav, as he did, hansome remembrances to some of his freinds'; presumably only that part of Jenkins's estate relating to court and notice of other bequests was omitted because irrelevant to court officials: Wilson, *Roger North*, 344; Ashbee, *The harmonious music*, 320–21; PRO, E406/50, fol. 158

Jenkins, John Edward (1838–1910), politician and satirist, born at Bangalore, Mysore, India, on 28 July 1838, was the eldest son of Dr John Jenkins (1813–1898), a Wesleyan missionary, and his wife, Harriette (d. 1875), the daughter of James Shepstone of Clifton. After some years first in Malta and then in Cornwall, in 1847 his father moved to Canada, where he eventually became minister of St Paul's Presbyterian Church, Montreal, and moderator of the general assembly. After having been educated at the High School, Montreal, at McGill College, and later at the University of Pennsylvania, Jenkins went to London, and was called to the bar at Lincoln's Inn on 17 November 1864. In 1867 he married Hannah Matilda, the daughter of Philip Johnstone of Belfast; they had five sons and two daughters. In 1870 Jenkins was retained by the Aborigines Protection and Anti-Slavery Society to observe the proceedings of the royal commission of inquiry into indentured labour in British Guiana. He visited the colony and became the champion of the Indian indentured labourers there; in 1871 he published *The Coolie: his Rights and Wrongs*. His zeal for social reform led him away from his profession, and in 1870 he suddenly became famous as the anonymous author of *Ginx's Baby, his Birth and other Misfortunes*, a satire on the struggles of rival sectarians for the religious education of an abandoned child, which attracted much attention and influenced the religious compromise in the Education Act of 1870.

Jenkins was a strong imperialist, and in 1871 he organized a conference on colonial questions which met at Westminster under his chairmanship. His inaugural address was entitled 'The colonies and imperial unity, or, The barrel without the hoops'. The conference prompted the Imperial Federation movement, and led in 1874 to Jenkins's appointment as first agent-general in London for the dominion of Canada, an office which he held for only two years. His imperialism did not, however, hinder him from protesting against the act by which Queen Victoria became empress of India in 1876, when he published anonymously *The Blot on the Queen's Head*. Jenkins was an ardent radical with political ambitions. After unsuccessfully contesting Stafford and Truro as an advanced Liberal, he was during his absence in Canada returned at the general election of 1874 as member of parliament for Dundee, a seat he retained until the dissolution of 1880. At a by-election in January 1881 he unsuccessfully contested Edinburgh as an independent Liberal. His dislike for Gladstone's imperial policies later overcame his radicalism in home politics, and in 1885 he attempted to win back his seat for Dundee as a Conservative, but he failed both then and in 1896.

Jenkins made some largely unsuccessful attempts to repeat the popular success of *Ginx's Baby*, and his novels included *Lord Bantam*, a satire on a young aristocrat in democratic politics (2 vols., 1871); *Little Hodge*, supporting

the agitation led by Joseph Arch on behalf of the agricultural labourer (1872); *Lutchmee and Dilloo*, a tale of West Indian life (3 vols., 1877); and *Pantalas and what they did with him*, the original story of the 'Elephant Man' (Joseph Carey Merrick) (1897). *The Devil's Chain* (1876), a polemic against alcohol, was the most successful of these later works, and was very widely read. Jenkins was from 1886 editor of the *Overland Mail* and the *Homeward Mail*, newspapers of which his brother-in-law, Sir Henry Seymour King, was the proprietor. From the beginning of King's political career Jenkins acted as his parliamentary secretary.

Jenkins died in London on 4 June 1910, after some years' suffering from paralysis.

R. E. Graves, *rev.* Lynn Milne

Sources *Morning Post* (6 June 1910) · *The Times* (6 June 1910) · *Overland Mail* (10 June 1910) · *WWW* · J. S. Moir, 'Jenkins, John', *DCB*, vol. 12 · J. Sutherland, *The Longman companion to Victorian fiction* (1988)

Jenkins, John Gwili (1872–1936), poet and theologian, was born on 8 October 1872 at Hendy, Llanedi, Carmarthenshire, the fifth of nine children of John Jenkins (1829–1899), a tin-plate worker, and his wife, Elizabeth, née Davies (1842–1926). He attended the village school at Hendy, being engaged as a pupil teacher from 1887 to 1890, and then entered the Gwynfryn School, Ammanford, a preparatory school that catered mainly for nonconformist ministerial candidates. He was a student at the Baptist College and the University College, Bangor, in 1892–5, but his preoccupation with eisteddfod competition in poetry led to a serious neglect of his studies. He spent a year as a student at University College, Cardiff, in 1895–6, before returning to the Gwynfryn as an assistant to the master, Watcyn Wyn.

Jenkins wrote under the bardic name Gwili, a name which, as Edward Thomas remarked in a pen portrait of his friend, he took from the stream flowing beside his boyhood home, 'whose sound was ever in his ears' (Thomas). The bardic name was later incorporated into the name under which his published work appeared. He won early renown as a poet in the free metres, notably in winning the crown at the national eisteddfod of Wales at Merthyr Tudful in 1901. But apart from eisteddfod compositions he wrote other verse at this time, and indeed all the work included in his collected poems, *Caniadau* (1934), had been completed by 1906. It includes lyric poems and, notably, a poem to the Virgin Mary, a sensitive composition on a subject that might not have been expected to commend itself to a poet of a distinctly protestant adherence in that period. Several of his hymns have been received into the canon of Welsh hymnology. His English verse was collected in his volume *Poems* (1920). In his literary criticism, while acknowledging the requirements of form and refinement in expression, he laid emphasis on the virtue of subject matter that respected the realities of human experience in its entirety, thereby striking a chord with poets of a younger generation who later found his critical judgement a source of encouragement as they made their breach with older conventions.

Jenkins was never ordained as the pastor of a church,

but he earned respect as a preacher, though his advanced views and the rigour of his argument, no less than the rapidity of his delivery, earned him greater favour among his more percipient hearers. In his published work in scriptural criticism he conveyed his disquiet at the widening gulf between modern biblical scholarship and the outmoded teaching to which the congregations were largely confined. Increasingly concerned, however, at his lack of formal teaching in Christian doctrine he entered Jesus College, Oxford, in 1905 and graduated with a second-class degree in theology in 1908. No new vocational opportunity presented itself and he returned to the Gwynfryn as the school's master for seven years but, fortified by his academic experience, he resumed his scriptural studies with new vigour. In the preface to a volume on the prophets of the Old Testament examined in the setting of the history of Israel, *Llin ar lin* (1909), he expressed his regret at the churches' continued adherence to 'the doctrine of reserve' under which the benefits of recent scriptural scholarship were deliberately withheld so as to maintain orthodox belief. Commentaries on Isaiah and the epistles to the Thessalonians, written in collaboration, were among the studies which gradually brought contemporary exegesis within the reach of Welsh-language readers.

Jenkins's liberal theology was matched by a concern that the nonconformist churches' lack of sympathy with those in Welsh society who nurtured socialist aspirations would lead to a damaging alienation. In lectures to branches of the Independent Labour Party in 1909–10, though not formally associated with the movement, he urged the acceptance of an essential consonance of the search for social justice with the teaching of the New Testament. The First World War created new tensions and, as editor of the Welsh Baptist weekly *Seren Cymru*, he maintained a consistent critical commentary throughout its duration while still respecting the need to represent the varied viewpoints appropriate to a denominational journal. The issue of recruitment to the forces, exacerbated by the active participation of some ministers of religion in furthering the government's call to arms, and then the issue of conscription, both matters of deep concern, brought forth a sequence of cogently argued editorials. Problems of labour and capitalism in turn drew comments that signalled Jenkins's repudiation of the Welsh denominations' accord with the Liberal Party. In his immediate response to the Easter rising, virtually alone among Welsh commentators, he viewed the events in Dublin not as a regrettable reverse for the war effort but as a tragedy that underlined the government's failure in its responsibility to allow the Irish nation to order its own affairs. His writings on war, labour, and nationality marked a singular contribution to serious discussion during an acute crisis of conscience in Welsh nonconformity.

With the school at Gwynfryn unable to withstand the coming of war, Jenkins was relieved to be able to accept an invitation to join Professor Thomas Powel as an assistant in the department of Welsh language and literature at University College, Cardiff. By then he was married (the marriage having taken place on 22 August 1910) to Mary Elizabeth (*b.* 1877/8), daughter of Thomas Lewis, an ironfounder; they had two daughters. At Oxford he had availed himself of the classes of Professor John Rhys in Celtic philology and literature and he took with enthusiasm to his new task of teaching complemented by research in medieval Welsh religious prose, a field in which he was awarded the degree of BLitt in 1918. Powel's retirement and the end of the war brought changes in the department, however, and in 1919 Jenkins accepted a position as librarian of the Salesbury Library, the Welsh collection at the college. Frustrated, but resolved to turn his appointment to good advantage, he applied himself to studies in the field in which he would find fulfilment thereafter. In 1923, now over fifty years of age, he was appointed professor of New Testament Greek at the Baptist College, Bangor, a position that brought him membership of the faculty of theology at the University College. His dedicated application is reflected in two very substantial scholarly works. *Arweiniad i'r Testament Newydd* (1928), an introduction to the New Testament, provided a comprehensive and enduring work of theological scholarship conceived on a vastly greater scale than anything hitherto attempted in the Welsh language. *Hanfod duw a pherson Crist* (1931) provided a detailed exposition of doctrine in the protestant tradition as it was revealed in the adherence of the Welsh congregations and the academies from the teaching of the early eighteenth century to contemporary liberal theology. He was awarded the degree of DLitt by the University of Oxford the next year.

In 1931 Jenkins's immense contribution to the literary activity of the national eisteddfod was recognized by his election as archdruid of Wales. Assiduous discharge of numerous obligations continued unabated, but the strain took its toll. He died at his home, 38 College Road, Bangor, on 16 May 1936 and was buried on 20 May in the graveyard of the Congregational church, Capel Tŷ Newydd, Llanedi, Carmarthenshire, on the hillside above the village where he had spent his boyhood and the river that had given him the name by which he was affectionately known. He was survived by his wife.   J. B. Smith

Sources NL Wales, J. Gwili Jenkins papers · E. C. Jones, *Cofiant a phregethwr* (1937) · J. B. Smith, 'J. Gwili Jenkins, 1872–1936', *Transactions of the Honourable Society of Cymmrodorion* (1973), 191, 214 · *Seren Cymru* (29 May 1936) [commemorative edition at time of death] · *Seren Cymru* (3 Nov 1972) [commemorative edition at time of centenary of birth] · *The Times* (18 May 1936) · *DWB*, 434–5 · E. Thomas, *Horae solitariae* (1902), 153–4 · m. cert. · *CGPLA Eng. & Wales* (1936)
Archives NL Wales, corresp. and papers | NL Wales, letters to Wil Ifan
Likenesses photograph, *c.*1931, priv. coll.
Wealth at death £2147 1s. 5d.: resworn probate, 11 Aug 1936, *CGPLA Eng. & Wales*

Jenkins, Joseph (*fl.* 1702–1736). *See under* Jenkins, Joseph (1743–1819).

Jenkins, Joseph (1743–1819), Particular Baptist minister, was born at Wrexham, Denbighshire, the son of Evan Jenkins (1712–1752), former pastor of the Old Meeting at

Wrexham. Benefiting from the charity of Thomas Llewellyn, he was sent to London when sixteen to learn Greek and Hebrew under Mr Walker. In 1761 he was awarded one of Dr John Ward's exhibitions to King's College, Aberdeen, where he graduated in 1765. His theological views were not yet settled, and it was only after serving as tutor in the household of the Revd Samuel Stennett's sister that he became associated with the church in Little Wild Street, Lincoln's Inn Fields. There he was baptized on 6 April 1766 by Stennett, whose funeral sermon he later preached. Jenkins joined Stennett's church and served for a short while as afternoon lecturer of the Seventh Day Baptist church meeting at Currier's Hall. It was the Little Wild Street Church that set him apart for the ministry.

Three years later Jenkins returned to Wrexham, and he exercised for a time some pastoral authority over an Independent church in Common Hall Lane, Chester. In 1773 he was ordained to the pastorate of the Old Meeting, the Baptist–Independent church formerly under his father's guidance, and published his confession of faith at Shrewsbury. Many curious notices of his pastorate at Wrexham are recorded in the church book he kept during most of his stay there. For example, they clearly indicate his early adoption of the practice of infant dedication, and that the church had a number of country members with special needs, some of whom were subsequently dismissed and formed the Baptist church in Chester, using the premises of the former Independent church, where Jenkins had once been pastor. A declaration of faith in 1773 refers to the Baptist–Independent church in Wrexham. By 1778 it was stipulated that the minister was to be of 'the Antipaedobaptist persuasion', and emphasized that the church should be trinitarian and Calvinist in doctrine. While it was recognized that historically the church had been one of 'open or mixt-communion', two Independents admitted in 1776 were required to indicate that they would not prevent the appointment of an Antipaedobaptist minister. Attempts to prevent Presbyterians from using the Old Meeting graveyard were unsuccessful and their rights of access had to be conceded after litigation in 1788.

During his Wrexham ministry Jenkins was an important member of the Midland Association of Particular Baptist Churches, being appointed in 1792 to write the circular letter to the member-churches. In 1790 he received the degree of DD from the University of Edinburgh. The suggestion that in 1791 he served as interim president of the Bristol Academy following Caleb Evans's death is erroneous, for this position was filled by Joseph Hughes, though Jenkins was considered as a candidate for Evans's Broadmead pastorate, the congregation failing to agree on him. In 1795 he became minister of the new Baptist church in Blandford Street, London, but he only stayed two years because of the insufficient income.

Jenkins married Mary Fossey (1755/6–1791), with whom he had five children, only two of whom—Mary (1781–1845) and William, a draper, wool merchant, and trustee of the Old Meeting-House in Wrexham—survived into adulthood. He remarried shortly after his first wife's death on 6 July 1791, and had a further daughter, Sarah Load, who was born on 15 June 1793. In 1798 he succeeded Joseph Swain in the Wednesday evening lectureship at Devonshire Square, and in the pastorate of the Particular Baptist church in East Street, Walworth, where he exercised the ministry until he retired in December 1818. He then planted a new church in Alfred Place, Old Kent Road, with a number of former East Street members. Jenkins published many separate sermons and devotional works as well as tracts in defence of believers' baptism and against anti-trinitarianism. A. N. Palmer, though reckoning him 'honest, good and pious', labels him an inflexible disciplinarian and 'a rigid doctrinarian clad in impenetrable mail from head to foot' (Palmer, 105). He died of apoplexy in Walworth on 21 February 1819 and was buried in Bunhill Fields.

Jenkins is not to be confused with another **Joseph Jenkins** (*fl.* 1702–1736), General Baptist minister. His first ministry was as assistant at White's Alley, Moorfields, which had been abruptly left pastorless in 1699. He served at Hart Street, Covent Garden (1702–9), and at High Hall, West Smithfield (1709–16). The High Hall congregation dissolved in 1716 and many of his congregation followed him to his new charge at Duke Street, Southwark, which he served until 1731. He also acted as secretary to the short-lived Hanover Coffee House group that in 1714 sought to bring Particular and General Baptists closer together, and thereafter became a prominent signatory of petitions from the London dissenting clergy to the crown. He also signed the petition from an equal number of London Baptists and Quakers to their opposite numbers in Northamptonshire, pleading with them not to engage in 'verbal gladitorial conflict' (Ivimey, 3.141). He is recorded as living in poverty in 1736.   J. H. Y. BRIGGS

Sources J. Ivimey, *A history of the English Baptists*, 4 vols. (1811–30), vol. 3 · A. N. Palmer, *A history of the town and parish of Wrexham*, 3: *A history of the older nonconformity of Wrexham* [1888] · G. V. Price, *The old meeting* (1932) · *Baptist Quarterly*, 21 (1965–6), 234 · *DNB*

Archives NL Wales, commonplace book | BL, corresp. with John Rippen, Add. MS 25387, fol. 322

Likenesses J. Fittler, line engraving, pubd 1805 (after J. F. Burrell), BM · portrait, repro. in *Baptist Annual Register* (1801), 26 · portrait, repro. in *Sermons*, 2 vols. (1779)

Jenkins, Joseph John (*bap.* 1812, *d.* 1885), engraver and watercolour painter, was baptized John Joseph Jenkins on 1 March 1812 at St Pancras Old Church, London, the son of Joseph and Sarah Jenkins, *née* Pledger. He had one brother. His early life was spent at Manor Court, Walworth, Surrey, where his father was an engraver. At the age of fourteen he started engraving plates for books and journals. He also studied at the artists' school in Clipstone Street, London. From 1825 he exhibited prints, engraved after old masters and from his own work, at the Royal Academy, Suffolk Street, and at the British Institution. Eventually a chest complaint forced him to abandon engraving, and he turned instead to watercolour painting.

Jenkins was elected in 1842 a member of the New Water-colour Society, where he exhibited fifty-seven drawings before he resigned in 1847; he was elected two years later to the more prestigious Old Watercolour Society. From 1854 to 1864 he served—with considerable success—as the secretary to the society, years in which it was at the height of its reputation. It was Jenkins who instigated the first ever special private views for the press. He himself exhibited 271 pictures with the society, a relatively modest number. His usual signature was 'Jos. J. Jenkins'. In his early years Jenkins tended to produce sentimental genre and figure work, particularly with a French theme, and his pictures had titles such as *Chit-Chat* and *Evangeline at Prayer*. Later in his career he exhibited English landscapes, which are superior. These were frequently subtitled *Study from Nature*, and examples include *A Yorkshire Beck* (1865, Victoria and Albert Museum) and *Larpool Beck, Near Whitby* (1867, Yale U. CBA). His pictures sold for up to £100.

Joe Jenkins was an immensely sociable man who in his spare time enjoyed gossip, cards, and tobacco. He spent many years collecting materials for a history of the art of watercolour painting in Britain and of the Old Watercolour Society. In 1852 he advertised for information in *The Times*, and also had questionnaires printed. Eventually ill health prevented him from carrying out the work; instead he handed over his papers to John Lewis Roget, who used them for his *History of the 'Old Water-Colour' Society*, which was published in 1891. A passport issued in France in 1846 describes Jenkins as 175 centimetres in height, with chestnut-coloured hair, grey eyes, a medium nose and mouth, no beard, a round chin, and an oval face. A photograph dating from around 1865 shows a careworn face with a drooping moustache and deep-set eyes.

Jenkins remained unmarried but lived with his brother, Henry, a lawyer, until the latter's death in 1871. Most of his life was spent in a small area: he moved from 56 Red Lion Street to 8 Caroline Street, and then in 1859 from 5 Newman Street to 35 Upper Charlotte Street. Finally in 1874 he settled at 67 Hamilton Terrace, St John's Wood, where he died on 9 March 1885, 'having long been afflicted by bodily suffering', as *The Times* obituary of 13 March stated. He was buried in London. He left an estate valued at £15,386. His will is evidence of his wide circle of friends, for in it he names thirty-five beneficiaries, twenty-four of them women. He also left £1000 and a number of watercolours and etchings to the Royal Watercolour Society. A studio sale of Jenkins's work was held at Christies on 1 March 1886.　　　　　　　　　　　　　　SIMON FENWICK

Sources J. L. Roget, *A history of the 'Old Water-Colour' Society*, 2 vols. (1891) · Royal Watercolour Society, Jenkins MSS · S. Fenwick and G. Smith, eds., *The business of watercolour: a guide to the archives of the Royal Watercolour Society* (1997) · *The Athenaeum* (21 March 1885), 217 · *CGPLA Eng. & Wales* (1885) · IGI · *The Times* (13 March 1885)
Archives BM, Royal Watercolour Society
Likenesses J. Watkins, photograph, c.1865, Royal Watercolour Society, London · Cundall & Fleming, carte-de-visite, NPG · wood-engraving (after photograph by H. S. Melville), NPG; repro. in *ILN* (28 March 1885)
Wealth at death £15,386 13s. 0d.: probate, 1 April 1885, *CGPLA Eng. & Wales*

Jenkins, Sir Lawrence Hugh (1857–1928), judge in India, was born at The Priory, Cardigan, on 22 December 1857, the younger son of Richard David Jenkins, solicitor, of Cilbronnau, Cardiganshire, and the only child of his second marriage with Elizabeth, daughter of Thomas Lewis, of Machynlleth, surgeon in the Royal Navy. He was educated at Cheltenham College (February 1869 to July 1877)—where he rowed and played football for the college—and University College, Oxford, where he matriculated in October 1877, and gained first class in jurisprudence (BA 1881). He was admitted at Lincoln's Inn on 11 November 1879 and called to the bar on 17 November 1883. He practised on the Chancery side until 1896, when he became a puisne judge of the high court at Calcutta.

On 19 April 1892 Jenkins married Catherine Minna, second daughter of Andrew Brown Kennedy, sugar planter, of Sea Cow Lake, Natal. She survived him with one son who died unmarried in 1930; a daughter died in infancy. In 1899 Jenkins was promoted chief justice of the high court of judicature, Bombay, and knighted. During his tenure he was an active member of the committee which, under Sir Henry Erle Richards, revised the code of civil procedure, the new draft receiving legislative approval in 1908. In 1903 he was made KCIE.

In 1908, invited by John Morley (Liberal secretary of state for India, 1905–10), Jenkins returned to England to join the Council of India. There his strong Liberal sympathies contributed to his exceptional position in Morley's confidence, and he had a large part in drafting the 1909 Morley–Minto reforms. Morley valued Jenkins's 'highly competent legal guidance' (Morley, 260) and wrote that he was:

> one of the two or three most valuable men of my Council. He is a remarkably clear-headed man, with a copious supply of knowledge in law, as well as of political imagination … a fine fellow … of immense value to me about Reforms.
> (ibid., 270–71, 286, 303)

Although Morley was reluctant to lose his services, in 1909 Jenkins was appointed chief justice of Bengal at the request of the viceroy, Lord Minto.

Shortly after Jenkins's appointment, there was a revival of revolutionary terrorism in Bengal. Difficult and complicated conspiracy cases came before him, and in view of his well-known sympathy with constitutional reform, his judicial conduct received both ignorant criticism and undiscerning praise. He tried to temper justice with mercy, particularly to young offenders, whom he felt were often the tools of older men. A conspicuous example was the Khulna conspiracy case (1911), when he released on probation some schoolboys and university students who had been convicted of an offence more serious than those for which such a course was provided in the criminal procedure code. Allegedly the initiative came from Jenkins, though it did not appear in the report. When government, alarmed at the impossibility of getting convictions in face of the terrorization of witnesses, took powers under the Defence of India Act to intern suspects without trial, it applied to Jenkins for a high court judge to advise on the evidence in confidential reports; but this Jenkins refused

Sir Lawrence Hugh Jenkins (1857–1928), by Sir William Quiller Orchardson, 1909

to permit, holding that it would compromise the judicial office. He realized judicial criticism of the executive might be unjust to officials who from the circumstances could not be heard in their own defence. A notable example may be seen on comparing Jenkins's judgment with those of his two fellow judges in the Musalmanpara bomb case (1915), when the police evidence, which all three judges suspected, but the other two condemned, was subsequently shown to be substantially true. Jenkins enjoyed in this period the confidence of men of varied opinions and positions from the governor downwards. A keen freemason, he was district grandmaster for Bombay and Bengal.

In 1915 Jenkins retired, and in 1916 was appointed, though without allowances, to the judicial committee of the privy council. He took little part in its work, and the judgments of the board delivered by him were few. He usually attended the committee's autumn session and his judicial eminence received public recognition in 1924 when he was appointed to the board, under Lord Dunedin, to delimit the Northern Ireland boundary. Failing health and London fogs made him increasingly prefer the occupations of a country gentleman at his home, Cilbronnau, near Cardigan, Cardiganshire, where he was chairman of quarter sessions.

Jenkins's legal equipment when he first went to India was a keen dialectical mind, a thorough grasp of English equity principles, and a power of expressing himself in clear and forcible English. He soon added a mastery of Indian law and custom astonishing in one who did not visit India until his thirty-ninth year and then served only in Presidency towns; many of his finest judgments enlightened dark questions of Hindu law. The same ability rapidly to acquire a grasp of unfamiliar legal principles was exemplified when the outbreak of war in 1914 brought him cases in prize. His unpublished official opinions as chief justice on proposals for improvement of the law and similar topics are also noteworthy. He was business-like in administration, and men he chose for high responsibility justified his choice. A sociable man, Jenkins successfully devoted himself to breaking down the barriers then separating British and Indians, especially in the Presidency towns. He came to know the leading Indian moderate politicians, and sympathized with their aims. It was his advice which led the National Congress to elect (Lord) Sinha to its presidency in 1915.

Jenkins died at Ealing, London, on 21 October 1928.

S. V. FitzGerald, *rev.* Roger T. Stearn

Sources *The Times* (3 Oct 1928) · *Calcutta Weekly Notes* (April 1911) [notes portion] · *Calcutta Weekly Notes*, 19 (1915), 923 [reports] · *Calcutta Weekly Notes* (Nov 1928) [notes portion] · private information (1937) · E. S. Skirving, ed., *Cheltenham College register, 1841–1927* (1928), 220 · Foster, *Alum. Oxon., 1715–1886* · Burke, *Peerage* (1904) · *WWW, 1916–28* · W. P. Baildon, ed., *The records of the Honorable Society of Lincoln's Inn: admissions*, 1 (1896) · J. Foster, *Men-at-the-bar: a biographical hand-list of the members of the various inns of court*, 2nd edn (1885) · J. Morley, *Recollections*, 2 vols. (1917) · D. A. Hamer, *John Morley: liberal intellectual in politics* (1968) · S. E. Koss, *John Morley at the India Office, 1905–1910* (1969) · B. R. Nanda, *Gokhale: the Indian moderates and the British raj* (1977) · P. Hees, *The bomb in Bengal: the rise of revolutionary terrorism in India, 1900–1910* (1993) · J. M. Brown, *Modern India: the origins of an Asian democracy*, 2nd edn (1994)

Archives NL Wales, corresp. and personal papers, MSS 1464–1471, 1546, 1551–1556, 1567–1569 | BL OIOC, letters to Lord Morley, Eur. MS D 573 · CUL, corresp. with Lord Hardinge

Likenesses W. Q. Orchardson, oils, 1909, NMG Wales [*see illus.*] · W. Stoneman, photograph, 1918, NPG

Jenkins, Sir Leoline (1625–1685), lawyer and diplomat, was born in Llantrithyd, Glamorgan, the son of Leoline or Lewellyn Jenkins, a yeoman of modest estate from Llanblethian in Glamorgan, who was recognized as being 'honest, prudent and industrious' (Wynne, 1.1). John Aubrey noted Jenkins's father as a 'good plaine Countrey-man, a copy holder of sir John Aubrey' (*Brief Lives*, 174). Wood claimed that he was a 'poore taylor' (*Life and Times of Anthony Wood*, 3.162). His son remained unmarried and seems to have had no known relationships with women.

Early life Jenkins, assisted by the patronage of Sir John Aubrey, was educated locally at Cowbridge grammar school, a foundation that he would later acquire, financially endow, and bequeath to Jesus College, Oxford. Jenkins went up to Jesus, a college which had a great influence on his life, in June 1641, where an academic or clerical career seemed to beckon. His tutor was Henry Vaughan. His biographer and friend, William Wynne, noted that during his years as a student Jenkins was of 'settled Gravity and serious deportment' with a 'passion for reading', traits that he retained throughout his life (Wynne, 1.2). Jenkins was religiously inclined and continued throughout his life to be a staunch believer in the

Sir Leoline Jenkins (1625–1685), by Herbert Tuer, 1679

doctrines of the Church of England. The church was central to his life and, he believed, 'established by God's providence and lawes [as a] true ... member of Christ's Catholique Church, which hee hath purchased with his blood' (PRO, PROB 11/381, fol. 217).

Jenkins's studies at Oxford were interrupted by the civil war and he briefly took up arms for the royalists. He was forced to leave Oxford by 1648–9 and soon returned to Glamorgan, from where he continued his association with Aubrey, as well as Francis Mansell, principal of Jesus College. Additionally Jenkins was introduced to Gilbert Sheldon, whom he afterwards described as his 'incomparable patron' (PRO, PROB 11/381, fol. 224). Jenkins took up the post as tutor to Aubrey's eldest son, as well as other young men at Llantrithyd, but soon afterwards he was indicted for allegedly keeping a seditious seminary and he was constrained to leave the area after Aubrey's house was sequestrated.

By May 1651 Jenkins had returned to Oxford with his pupils and settled in a house owned by Sampson White in the High Street, commonly known as Welsh Hall. Jenkins later recalled that the 'Church itself might be said to have retir'd to that upper chamber' (Jenkins, 20–22, 25). He was also a member of John Fell's congregation in Oxford and in 1654 was involved in a collection of money for exiled bishops of the Church of England. Unsympathetic to republican and Cromwellian Oxford and facing the hostility of the new Oxford authorities Jenkins retired abroad. He subsequently spent three years in France, the Netherlands, and Germany as a tutor to various pupils. It was noted that he used the 'old Roman system of education',

seeking his pupils' goodwill and friendship as well as their education (Wynne, 1.vi). In 1658 he was invited by Sir William Whitmore to live at Appleby in Shropshire, where he retired to study civil law until the Restoration.

Work at Oxford and in the law With the Restoration Jenkins returned to Oxford and was elected a fellow of his college. Jenkins took the degree of DCL in 1661 and on Mansell's retirement in that same year he was elected principal of Jesus, holding the office until 1673. He was responsible for much of the college's reorganization and was regarded by many as a second founder. He made generous donations to it, paying for, among other matters, a new library and the completion of the building of the quadrangle at the cost of £1440. He attended to college discipline and was a staunch defender of its rights and privileges. Jenkins continued as a vigorous supporter of the church; indeed some claimed he was so high church that he was even disposed to popery, but in reality this seems to have been merely malicious gossip. He was certainly doctrinaire in his devotions, being thought of 'excellent Piety and unaffected Devotion' (Wynne, 1.lix).

In 1662 Jenkins was appointed deputy professor of civil law, but with the help of Sheldon he moved to London to practise. In 1668 he was admitted to Doctors' Commons and was appointed assistant to the dean of the court of arches. In March 1665, with the beginning of the Second Anglo-Dutch War, Jenkins was appointed judge-assistant to the judge of the Admiralty John Exton. He took on the bulk of the work and the office itself after the death of Exton, and he remained judge of the Admiralty throughout the reign. He was noted for his success there, with even foreign governments calling upon him for rulings on points of maritime law. Jenkins proved to be independent and quite often refused to follow the government line. Pepys thought him a 'very excellent man both for judgement, temper (yet majesty enough) and by all men's reports not to be corrupted' (Pepys, 8.133). Jenkins's views were often sought on laws of neutrality and prize law and he had a hand in making the set of rules for prizes. In 1668 he drafted the proclamation of neutrality. His work as a judge of the Admiralty was significant for the history of prize law and it was claimed by later generations that he was one of the principal architects of this branch of international law. He was also made a judge of the prerogative court of Canterbury in January 1669.

Diplomacy With suitable patronage and his legal background Jenkins became more prominent in the late 1660s and the early 1670s and found himself chosen for a number of diplomatic missions. In 1669 he was knighted for his negotiations with the French over the estate of the queen mother. The king of France had caused her jewels and other goods to be sealed when she died in Paris. Jenkins was sent for and was able to deal successfully with the administration of the will and points of law. During his travels in the depth of winter 1669 he 'was frozen almost to death and had they not rub'd or anointed him with brandy he might have lost his life' (*Life and Times of Anthony Wood*, 3.163). Jenkins acted as a commissioner for the rather desultory negotiations for a possible union with Scotland in the autumn of 1670, although he was plainly antipathetic to the actual project itself. In 1671 he entered parliament as member for Hythe. His career in the House of Commons was never influential, but he was a reliable court supporter, albeit noted for his lacklustre speeches. He subsequently sat as a member for Oxford University in 1679–85, where he had also acted as a justice of the peace. In 1672 he became one of the managers of the university press.

In 1673 Jenkins was made a plenipotentiary, alongside Sir Joseph Williamson, to the congress meeting at Cologne. The congress, arranged by the Swedish government, was intended to bring peace to Europe by arranging for the great powers involved in the Third Anglo-Dutch War of 1672 to meet, but it is unlikely that it ever had any chance of success. Louis XIV used it as a delaying tactic in a war that had gone seriously wrong in 1673 when the French army became bogged down in the flooded fields of the Netherlands. Robert Spencer, earl of Sunderland, who was to have been the third plenipotentiary for the English side, never thought it worthwhile actually to arrive in Cologne, and after a series of sterile negotiations the congress broke up in February 1674. Both Williamson and Jenkins were relatively inexperienced in the power politics of the day. Some thought that they had been sent on a fools' errand and a sarcastic 'report went that a schoolmaster and the chief gazeteir were sent by the king of England on an embassie' (*Life and Times of Anthony Wood*, 3.163). Williamson seems to have used the congress as much for its social ambience as for learning diplomacy, while Jenkins at least gained the diplomatic experience that was of use to him in later years. In their personal relations the two men were not visibly close: Williamson was very much Arlington's man, and Jenkins reported critically on his fellow plenipotentiary to Danby. It was also claimed that Williamson frequently slighted or ignored Jenkins in the negotiations. Nevertheless, with Williamson on shore while at Brill on the journey north after the congress, Jenkins managed to force a Dutch man-of-war to strike the flag to his ambassadorial yacht, much to Williamson's 'great mortification when he heard of it' (Wynne, 1.xxiii).

As Jenkins had proved dependable in his dealings he was again sought as a plenipotentiary and mediator to the Congress of Nijmegen from 1675 to 1679. Here he worked closely with Sir William Temple. Even before the negotiations began he had again made his mark, forcing some Dutch men-of-war to lower their flag to his yacht. He reached Nijmegen in January 1676. While the bulk of the negotiations fell on him when Temple was recalled in June 1677 little else took place at the congress until the marriage of William of Orange and Princess Mary. Temple claimed that as a diplomatic negotiator Jenkins was timid, indecisive, and lacked resource, but his knowledge of international and civil law proved useful in negotiations there. However, with Louis XIV once more manipulating the congress much of Jenkins's good work proved futile. A separate peace between the French and the Dutch was concluded in August 1678, with the Spanish in September,

and in February 1679 with the empire. With no recognition of Jenkins and Temple by the imperial ambassadors the pair withdrew.

Jenkins was appointed resident ambassador to the Netherlands on 14 February 1679 and then sole representative to the congress on 20 February. He was finally recalled on 11 July 1679 and had reached London by August that year, being graciously received by Charles II for all his services. Jenkins had even been independent minded enough in the course of his sojourn in Nijmegen to refuse a gift of a miniature set in diamonds from Louis XIV. Though he was urged to accept by Colbert, he believed the French king had acted in bad faith throughout.

Secretary of state Jenkins had been briefly discussed as a possible secretary of state on Williamson's resignation from the office in 1679, but Temple was preferred over him, though he refused the position. In 1680 Jenkins came into the privy council. With difficulty he was then persuaded by Sunderland to accept the office of a secretary of state. Sunderland thought him 'a very good man … useful and firm' and was keen to see Jenkins in the government (BL, Add. MS 32680, fol. 264). Jenkins accordingly became secretary of state in the place of Sir William Coventry on 26 April 1680. According to one source he was only 'in the last resort most absolutely resigned to his Majesty's will and disposition' (*Ormonde MSS*, 4.578). Jenkins proved a staunch tory in all his dealings, as well as a strong defender of the Church of England and his university. Labelled 'thrice vile' by Shaftesbury, the place of church and king in his politics was not in doubt in this era of political conflict (Jones, 236). 'It is from the church I have learnt my duty to the king', he noted, and ''tis to her I shall always endeavour to approve myself' (PRO, SP 63/341, 10).

As a secretary of state Jenkins was neither an innovator nor a real policy maker, but his workman-like attitude to his heavy workload as secretary and in his dealings with the secretariat in all quarters, as well as his faithfulness on questions of the royal prerogative, meant that his industry was well used. North noted him as 'the most faithful drudge of a secretary that ever the Court had' (*Lives*, 1.301). In the Commons Jenkins remained an ungainly speaker, being thought heavy in his discourse and laboured in points of debate. Solidly tory in outlook he had neither Sunderland's quickness of mind nor Arlington's personal connections with his monarch. As a result while Jenkins remained a capable administrative secretary of state he was not a politician of the first rank. He was, however, a principled and natural anti-exclusionist, disliking the idea of exclusion in terms of his own high-church standpoint, his previous service to the crown, and the needs of the nation, as well as seeing it as contrary to natural justice. Government, he thought, had its 'original, not from the people, but from God' and Jenkins believed that such a means of settling the problem of James by exclusion would reduce the crown to an elective monarchy for 'When God gives us a king in His wrath, it is not in our power to change him' (Grey, 7.419, 446). He also claimed that the bill was against religion, government, and the wisdom of the nation. Despite this Jenkins made some attempts to resolve the crisis by trying to persuade James to return to the Church of England.

In his relations with the House of Commons Jenkins clumsily came into conflict with it on two major occasions in December 1680 and March 1681. In the first instance the arrest and imprisonment of Peter Norris, a self-important Scot keen to uncover more of the Popish Plot, led to complaints against Jenkins of illegal and arbitrary actions; these were later dropped. In the second instance Jenkins was ordered by the Commons to carry up the impeachment of Fitzharris to the Lords in the third Exclusion Parliament. He responded by saying:

> This had not been put upon me but for the character I bear. I look upon it as a reflection on the king my master, and though I know how to value my life and liberty, do what you will I will not go. (*Ormonde MSS*, 7.22)

The resulting calls for his withdrawal and a great deal of noise in the Commons eventually forced Jenkins to submit to the will of the Commons and to express regret for his unparliamentary language.

Following the collapse of the whigs at the Oxford parliament Jenkins was involved in the uncovering of whig plots, especially that of Rye House in 1683. In the Rye House conspiracy Jenkins marshalled the evidence given to him by Keeling and others. His investigations of the plot were sober and largely judicious, if slightly more legally minded than many in the government wished to see. He testified (although largely unsuccessfully) against Shaftesbury in his trial of November 1681 and also played a part in the election of the tory sheriffs in 1682. He had been uncertain about intervening when the whigs seized the positions in 1680, but by 1682 his position was less ambiguous. Although he took little pleasure in the affair Jenkins was also involved in the *quo warranto* proceedings against the City of London. He expressed his dislike of these events in a letter to the duke of York, fearing that agitation and discontent would result. However Jenkins also acted as a conduit for the court's links with City tories. After four years as a secretary of state, 'wasted by his zeal and application', Jenkins resigned on 4 April 1684 (Wynne, 1.xlix). In the main his resignation was due to ill health, but there is little doubt that Jenkins was relieved to be out of the political fray. He retired to his home in Hammersmith. In March 1685 he was made a privy councillor once more and a member of parliament for Oxford, but seems not to have attended either body owing to his continued illness. Jenkins died at 3 o'clock on the morning of 1 September 1685 at his home in Hammersmith. His body was transported to Oxford in great solemnity and lay in state at the divinity school. The funeral was attended by most of the Oxford élite and the coffin, carried by six doctors of civil law, was taken to Jesus College chapel for burial, as he had requested. After a funeral service and a 'very solemn … dolefull anthem' (*Life and Times of Anthony Wood*, 3.162) he was buried in the chapel on 17 September near the grave of Dr Mansell with much pomp. Jenkins left the majority of his estate to the college.

Conclusion In his life Jenkins proved worthy, economical, and temperate. He never married and seems to have been a serious minded man who was as devoted to the monarchy as to his church and his college. His conscientious and morally upright nature was well known. He even refused his own brother a post well within his gift, noting that 'Providence had sufficiently enabled him to provide for himself, without burthening the Publick with his relations' (Wynne, 1.lxxi). Jenkins had little by way of leisure pursuits and was somewhat conservative and rigid in his outlook. His religion was, as with his politics, high church; he was one who urged the early promotion of the future nonjurors Francis Turner and Thomas Ken. Noted for being early to his bed and early to rise, Jenkins's attitude led to many in the court of Charles II to view him as both uninteresting and lacking any of the usual court affectations. If he was proud of anything then it was his Welsh background and one curious French courtier who asked for a specimen of his native language received the reply: 'Nid wrth ei big y mae adnabod cyffylog' ('You can't tell a woodcock by its beak'). While in office he tended to shun the king's more salacious relationships and, unlike others at court, he specifically avoided the duchess of Portsmouth's lodgings. Continually dressed in black, Jenkins's own 'nature turn[ed] away from all the noise and glittering of a court' (*Ormonde MSS*, 4.578). Charles II, however, did discover that his abstemious secretary was immoderately amused by bawdy stories and thus he frequently told him coarse jests in the hopes of making the sober Jenkins laugh.

ALAN MARSHALL

Sources *The life and times of Anthony Wood*, ed. A. Clark, 5 vols., OHS, 19, 21, 26, 30, 40 (1891–1900) · W. Wynne, *The life of Sir Leoline Jenkins*, 2 vols. (1724) · will, PRO, PROB 11/381, fols. 217–226v · L. Jenkins, *The life of Francis Mansell DD, principal of Jesus College in Oxford* (1854) · Pepys, *Diary* · BL, Add. MS 32680, fol. 264 · J. R. Jones, 'Shaftesbury's "worthy men": a whig view of the parliament of 1679', *BIHR*, 30 (1957), 232–41 · PRO, SP 63/341 · R. North, *The lives of … Francis North … Dudley North … and … John North*, new edn, 3 vols. (1826) · A. Grey, ed., *Debates of the House of Commons, from the year 1667 to the year 1694*, new edn, 10 vols. (1769) · *Calendar of the manuscripts of the marquess of Ormonde*, new ser., 8 vols., HMC, 36 (1902–20), vols. 4, 7 · E. G. Hardy, *Jesus College* (1899) · F. M. G. Evans, *The principal secretary of state: a survey of the office from 1558 to 1680* (1923) · D. J. Llewelyn Davies, 'The development of prize law under Sir Leoline Jenkins', *Transactions of the Grotius Society*, 21 (1935) · D. J. Llewelyn Davies, 'Enemy property and ultimate destination during the Anglo-Dutch Wars 1664–7 and 1672–4', *The British Year Book of International Law*, 15 (1934) · *Aubrey's Brief lives*, ed. O. L. Dick (1949)

Archives All Souls Oxf., papers · BL, corresp., Add. MSS 9801–9802 · Bodl. Oxf., devotional papers · Bodl. Oxf., MSS Rawl. A–C · Jesus College, Oxford, papers relating to him, CXLVIII · Yale U., anecdotes of persons and places in France | BL, corresp. with Henry Coventry, Add. MSS 25119–25123 · BL, letters to John Ellis, Add. MS 28896 · BL, letters to Laurence Hyde, Add. MSS 15901–15902 · BL, letters to Robert Southwell, Add. MS 34346 · BL, corresp. with William Trumbull · BL, Harley MSS, corresp. with Joseph Williamson · Bodl. Oxf., corresp. with Joseph Williamson · NL Wales, letters to Richard Bulstrode · PRO, state papers Charles II, SP 29 · PRO, Sir Joseph Williamson's Collection, SP 9 State Papers Misc. · Yale U., letters to Edmund Poley

Likenesses H. Tuer, oils, 1679, NPG [*see illus.*] · H. Tuer, oils, second version, Jesus College, Oxford · E. Vandergucht, line engraving (after H. Tuer), BM, NPG; repro. in Wynne, *Life*

Wealth at death land, tenements, and estates across southern England and Wales; majority of estate left to Jesus College, Oxford, increasing their annual revenue by £700; additional sums given to raise allowances for a number of the fellows and master of the college; also bequests to brother as well as servants: will, PRO, PROB 11/381, fols. 217–226*v*

Jenkins, Peter George James (1934–1992), journalist and author, was born on 11 May 1934 at 5 Penn Road, Beaconsfield, Buckinghamshire, the elder child and only son of Kenneth Edmund Jenkins (1906–1993), a pharmaceutical chemist, and his wife, Joan Evelyn Croger (1907–1981), a teacher. From 1938 he grew up at Bury St Edmunds, where his father kept a leading chemist's shop, and from 1945 was a boarder at the nearby Methodist school, Culford. Though his parents were outsiders (Welsh and Londoner) and he was to develop Labour sympathies, his upbringing—he later wrote—was so like Margaret Thatcher's that 'I know [her]': he knew at first hand the shopkeeper's sense that the 1945 Labour victory was the triumph of Antichrist. He too had longed to flee 'the excruciating tedium of petty bourgeois life in a small provincial town' (Jenkins, *Mrs Thatcher's Revolution*, 82–4).

His early years were marked by estrangement from his alcoholic father—part of a family conflict that was to end in his parents' separation. After two years' national service in the Royal Navy (1952–4), which briefly commissioned him sub-lieutenant, he read history at Trinity Hall, Cambridge, taking a first in part one and in part two a second (division one). Because his father (who wanted him to settle in Bury as a solicitor) would not help to maintain him at Cambridge, he launched as an undergraduate into freelance journalism. He had long wanted to write; after a year in the United States on a Harkness fellowship, in 1958 he joined the *Financial Times*, where gifted young reporters were set to producing quick, well-researched background articles.

Jenkins made his mark and, in 1960, became deputy to the labour correspondent of *The Guardian*, John Cole, whose job he took over in 1963. Also in 1960, he married the first of his two wives, each descended from the 'intellectual aristocracy' but distinguished in her own right. With Charlotte Strachey (1935–1970), a woman of fine-drawn beauty but frail health, he lived to begin with in a milieu part intellectual, part raffish. Through both family background and closeness to Newmarket, he had a lifelong passion for horse racing and, at first, a marked gambling streak; he fancied at one time becoming a gentleman jockey, often dressed like a bookmaker, and enjoyed the cockles-and-champagne aspect of the sport. The purchase of a house in then barely gentrifying Crescent Grove, Clapham, and the birth of a daughter, marked a settling down, but Charlotte developed Hodgkin's disease and, after thirty months' distressing illness, died on 2 April 1970. He then married on 28 December 1970 Mary Louisa (Polly) Toynbee (*b*. 1946), altogether a stronger person, who herself became a leading journalist and author;

Peter George James Jenkins (1934–1992), by Herbie Knott, 1987 [telephoning his election copy from Neil Kinnock's Islwyn constituency, south Wales]

they had two daughters and a son, and combined busy careers with many friendships and a warm, hospitable family life.

Writing on labour affairs while trade unions were still an estate of the realm lay at the heart of serious political journalism. Jenkins did far more than report industrial disputes. He won a series of resounding scoops on matters then important: the draft report (1963) of the National Economic Development Council on incomes policy, another—damning—draft report on the newspaper industry, George Brown's preference for devaluation over deflation (1966), Harold Wilson's attempt to create a legal framework for industrial relations. The last was the subject of a vigorous, revealing instant history, *The Battle of Downing Street* (1970); Jenkins's witty handling was typified by his dubbing James Callaghan, instrumental in preserving the unions' hold over the Labour Party, 'the keeper of the cloth cap'. He got these stories from ministers and senior officials who liked and respected him as an equal; few—Richard Crossman was one—tried to manipulate him. Scoops apart, he learned the art of piecing together bits of information to understand what was going on in Whitehall.

To keep him, *The Guardian* in 1967 matched the *Sunday Times*'s offer to make him political columnist; he became policy editor from 1974. His interests were in the world at large; he modelled himself, as far as British conditions allowed, on Walter Lippmann's famous column, writing two, three, or four times a week. His main themes were the relative decline of Britain, which he felt keenly, and the need, throughout Europe but especially in the Labour Party, to replace the socialist ideal with social democracy, combining liberal economics with the pursuit of collective social goals. His close friend Anthony Crosland inspired this consistent belief, as did the example of West Germany; Jenkins was a fixture at the annual Anglo-German Königswinter conference and strongly supported British commitment to the European Community. In the 1980s he both influenced and was influenced by the 'gang of four' who founded the Social Democratic Party. Though he became an outstanding analyst of British politics, he could drop everything to report vividly what the people in the street (or the picket line) had to say.

A stint as Washington correspondent (1972–4) brought out his courage: before the Watergate scandal broke, he wrote that Richard Nixon's re-election 'should be viewed with repugnance and deep foreboding'; it would confirm American society in its 'deform[ation] by callousness, brutality and greed' and obscure 'the simple moral fact that killing people—even Asians—is wrong' (Jenkins, *Anatomy of Decline*, 49–51). He showed similar courage in opposing the Falklands War: 'by what gigantic lack of proportion' was the loss of the islands 'to be seen as a major national humiliation?' (Taylor, 232).

By the 1980s Jenkins's writing had shed some of its irreverent wit and acquired gravitas. Restless at *The Guardian*, he found little satisfaction at the *Sunday Times* (1985–7) but bloomed again as associate editor of the new *Independent*. He started reviewing plays (for *The Spectator*, 1979–81) and writing them. *Illuminations* (1980), about a Crosland-like politician, had a short run; though often effective, it was old-fashioned in construction. A television comedy series, *Struggle* (1983), made fun of the 'loony left'—observable in his home borough of Lambeth in London. With a long-standing interest in visual art and in Italy, he wrote for the revisionist journal *Modern Painters* and bought a house in Umbria. He became a prison visitor. His chief interest remained writing about politics. In a penetrating book, *Mrs Thatcher's Revolution* (1987), he argued that although Thatcherism was more style than ideology, and the changes wrought were part of a European trend, the prime minister had significantly changed British society by curbing the unions and dispelling the sense of decline. What was now needed was to enlarge the rights of the citizen as consumer, parent, tenant, and patient. With this in Jenkins's mind went continuing scepticism about the Labour Party; in 1992 he considered voting Conservative. If he had lived he would doubtless have rallied to Labour under Tony Blair, but while he was at the height of his powers a lung disease, fibrosing alveolitis, failed to respond to treatment; he died in University College Hospital, London, on 27 May 1992, and was buried at Putney Vale on 1 June.

Jenkins was of striking appearance, short, top-heavy (soon tubby), with a large head and expressive features, dark eyes, and thick eyebrows often puckered in amusement. He was unusually spontaneous: his moods showed. His sense of fun and enjoyment communicated itself—summed up by the motto on his gravestone, 'seize the day'; so at times did his impatience or his justified sense of his own worth. By some he was disliked, by others loved; few were indifferent to a personality with a strong tang.

JOHN ROSSELLI

Sources personal knowledge (2004) · personal information (2004) · *Anatomy of decline: the political journalism of Peter Jenkins*, ed. B. Brivati and R. Cockett (1995) · G. Taylor, *Changing faces: a history of The Guardian, 1956–1988* (1993) · *The Times* (28 May 1992) · *The Guardian* (28 May 1992) · *The Guardian* (29 May 1992) · *The Guardian* (3 April 1970) · A. Hetherington, *Guardian years* (1981) · *WWW* · P. Jenkins, *Mrs Thatcher's revolution* (1987) · A. Neil, *Full disclosure* (1996) · G. Cleverley, *The Fleet Street disaster* (1976) · M. Cockerell, P. Hennessy, and D. Walker, *Sources close to the prime minister* (1984) · S. Raven, *'Is there anybody there?' said the traveller: memories of a private nuisance* (1990) · b. cert. · d. cert. · Burke, *Peerage*

Archives priv. coll., notebooks | *The Independent* offices, Canary Wharf, London, archives · JRL, *Manchester Guardian* archives | SOUND BL NSA, current affairs recordings · BL NSA, performance recordings

Likenesses J. Bratby, oils, 1980–84, priv. coll. · H. Knott, photograph, 1987, priv. coll. [*see illus.*] · photographs, priv. coll. · portrait, repro. in *The Guardian* (28 May 1992)

Wealth at death £75,123: probate, 5 Feb 1993, CGPLA Eng. & Wales

Jenkins, Rhys (1859–1953), engineer and historian of engineering, was born on 29 September 1859 at Mountain Ash, Glamorgan, the son of Thomas Jenkins, an engineer. He was educated at the Alderman Davies School, Neath, and in 1874 commenced a four-year apprenticeship with Richard Nevil, engineer and ironfounder, at the Empire ironworks, Llanelli. He remained with the firm for another two years as a draughtsman. In 1880 he obtained a post in the drawing office of John Fowler & Co. at Leeds and then a similar position with Greenwood and Batley Ltd in the same city. At this time he attended evening classes at the Yorkshire College, which later became the University of Leeds. In December 1881 he moved to Richard Hornsby & Sons of Grantham and in June 1883 to Marshall, Sons & Co. of Gainsborough.

The 1883 Patents Act introduced the requirement that every patent application be referred to an examiner. The Patent Office thus found it necessary to recruit a staff of examiners and Rhys Jenkins was one of the first batch of entrants. Having passed the qualifying examination in scientific subjects he was appointed assistant examiner on 1 July 1884. Shortly after securing this position, on 28 August 1884, he married Charlotte Ann Morgan (d. 1936). They had two sons, both of whom became civil engineers.

Jenkins joined the Institution of Mechanical Engineers as a graduate in 1880 when he was still with his first employer and was transferred to full membership in 1886. As his career in the Patent Office progressed he was promoted to deputy examiner from 1 April 1903, examiner from 1 October 1904, and senior examiner from 1 July 1914. He retired on 31 December 1919 having reached a senior position in the Patent Office as one of sixteen senior examiners in the total examining staff of nearly three hundred. However, his major contribution to scholarship was made in his spare-time studies of the history of engineering and industry.

From the time of his first appointment in the Patent Office Jenkins began the systematic collection of notes, transcripts, and extracts from printed and manuscript sources relating to engineering history. The classification and arrangement of this material occupied his leisure hours over the next sixty years and it is now in the Science Museum Library. He was the author of two books on road transport and he contributed many articles to various journals, notably a series in *The Engineer* between 1917 and 1920 under the title 'Links in the history of engineering'.

In September 1919 a conference was held in Birmingham to commemorate the centenary of the death of James Watt and it was at this meeting that the idea of forming a society devoted to the study of the history of engineering was suggested. Jenkins was involved from the outset as a member of the committee which planned the inaugural meeting in London on 4 June 1920, at which was founded the society which became the Newcomen Society for the study of the History of Engineering and Technology. The society was launched at a general meeting on 5 November 1920 and Jenkins read a paper at its second meeting on 27 January 1921, the first of his thirty-one major contributions to the society's *Transactions*. At the first annual general meeting on 15 December 1921 he was elected a vice-president and he served as president for the sessions of 1924–5 and 1925–6. One of the aims of the committee organizing the 1919 James Watt centenary commemoration was to produce a memorial book and this was achieved in *James Watt and the Steam Engine*, by Jenkins and H. W. Dickinson (1927). After the founding of the Newcomen Society almost all Jenkins's researches were published in that society's *Transactions*. In 1936, as a tribute to him, the Newcomen Society published a volume of his collected papers entitled *Links in the History of Engineering and Technology from Tudor Times*, comprising twenty-six of his pre-1920 articles which had appeared in various technical and antiquarian journals.

Shortly after his retirement from the Patent Office Rhys Jenkins moved to Hermitage, near Newbury, Berkshire, and in 1936, after the death of his wife, to Hastings, Sussex, to live with his younger son. Although he rarely attended meetings of the Newcomen Society in his later years he continued to contribute papers and his wide knowledge was available to help others. He was very quiet and unassuming but was always listened to with the greatest respect. In appearance he was described as small, very neat, and bearded, with very blue twinkling eyes. He died at 53 West Hill, Hastings, on 27 January 1953.

R. T. SMITH

Sources *Transactions* [Newcomen Society], 28 (1951–3), 285–6 · *The Engineer* (6 Feb 1953), 213 · *Engineering* (6 Feb 1953), 181–2 · *The Times* (28 Jan 1953) · Newcomen Society minute books and records · Institution of Mechanical Engineers membership records · m. cert. · d. cert.

Archives Sci. Mus.
Likenesses photograph, repro. in *Transactions* [Newcomen Society], pl. 1 · photograph, repro. in *Engineering*, 181
Wealth at death £4340 2s. 11d.: probate, 4 March 1953, *CGPLA Eng. & Wales*

Jenkins, Sir Richard (1785–1853), East India Company servant, was born at Cruckton, Shropshire, on 18 February 1785, the eldest son of Richard Jenkins (1760–1797) of Bicton, Shropshire, and Harriet Constantina (d. 1832), daughter of George Ravenscroft of Wrexham. In 1798 Jenkins was nominated as a writer on the East India Company's Bombay establishment, and he went to India in 1800. He distinguished himself at the company's college at Fort William, Calcutta; his abilities in mastering Arabic and Persian were soon noted. Jenkins's career began as an assistant in the office of the governor-general, Lord Wellesley, which became the nursery for a new generation of particularly able administrators such as Charles Metcalfe and Jenkins himself. At about this time Jenkins established his acquaintance with Mountstuart Elphinstone. The two men shared a love of literature and sport; Elphinstone noted Jenkins's zeal for learning, and once recorded that 'I find Jenkins being here a great defence against dejection and utter indolence. Besides the pleasure of his company, I am prevented by shame from giving up any study I have begun with him' (Colebrooke, 1.166).

Jenkins was very rare among members of the company's political service in seeking to educate himself in international law and diplomacy as a practical background to the conduct of his duties. He once noted:

> It has long been my wish to form a collection for a Diplomatic Library … I am aware that the most useful kind of work for a diplomatic character are the memoirs and correspondence of public ministers, [which are] almost the only fund of practical knowledge on the subject … mere etiquettes and formalities may undoubtedly be reduced to rules in Europe but books which treat of them can be of little use in India. (Fisher, 92)

That these remarks were made in 1810, well into Jenkins's Indian career, underlines that he never lost his interest in the value of constant self-instruction. Jenkins once identified the qualities required by a successful political officer as:

> a knowledge of the languages, and an acquaintance with the manners and habits of the Natives, highly necessary for a diplomatic man, he unites with these qualifications a degree of mildness and temper, particularly calculated to succeed in business with natives and to ensure their confidence and good opinion. (Fisher, 98)

In 1804 Jenkins began his field career as first assistant to resident Josiah Webbe at the court of Daulat Rao Sindhia, the maharaja of Gwalior, at a critical time when Sindhia was intriguing with the other Maratha chiefs against the company. Webbe died in November 1804 and Jenkins acted as resident pending the arrival of Sir Barry Close as Webbe's successor. Jenkins's diplomatic position steadily worsened as Sindhia's hostility to the company increased. By the end of January 1805 the acting resident had become a virtual prisoner and by May seemed to be under threat of imminent death, though Elphinstone noted that 'Nothing can be more admirable than the unsubdued spirit which Jenkins shows in his despatches' (Colebrooke, 1.131). Fortunately for Jenkins he was released before negotiations with Sindhia, which produced a treaty in November 1805.

In 1807 Jenkins became resident at Nagpur (formally appointed from 1810), where he came to spend the bulk of his Indian career. Wellesley's campaigns had curtailed but not eliminated Maratha power. Jenkins closely followed events in central India, was suspicious of Maratha intentions, and advocated a more interventionist policy to Wellesley's successors as governor-general. He told a fellow resident that 'I would even destroy [Maratha] power altogether … [We] have the experience of the past to guide us', and was convinced of the superiority of British rule (Fisher, 215–16).

The remaining Maratha chiefs soon determined on a further struggle for independence from the company. Hostilities broke out again at Nagpur in 1817. Jenkins had already anticipated trouble, and had concentrated about 1400 British troops on the Sitabaldi hills. On 26 November this force was attacked by a much larger contingent of the Nagpur army: the battle spanned two days, and Jenkins was in the thick of the action. The result was a company victory, and Jenkins's conduct was mentioned in despatches and praised in parliament by Canning, then president of the Board of Control. Although the raja of Nagpur, Appa Sahib, was restored to his throne he soon renewed intrigues with the peshwa, and Jenkins, acting at the very limits of official policy, was instrumental in his further deposition in 1818 in favour of a royal grandson. The new raja came under the close tutelage of the resident, so Jenkins established what was almost direct British rule until he devised a treaty (1826–7) to govern Nagpur's future relations with the company. It was also at this time that he gathered material for his *Report on the Territories of the Rajah of Nagpore* (1827), an important analytical document of the period.

In 1828 Jenkins retired from company service and returned to England. On 31 March 1824 he had married Elizabeth Helen Spottiswoode, whose father was also in the company service. The couple had at least three sons and two daughters; some sources suggest that their family numbered nine. Jenkins and his family took up residence at Abbeyforegate in Shrewsbury, and renewed his interest in his home area. In the 1830 general election he successfully stood as a tory candidate for the city. He was returned again the following year, but thereafter stood down until 1837, when he was again returned after a spirited campaign. After the dissolution of 1841 Jenkins retired from parliamentary life. He was also a magistrate and deputy lieutenant for Shropshire, and a magistrate for Middlesex. In 1838 he was appointed a knight grand cross in the Order of the Bath, an honour never before granted to an Indian administrator below the rank of governor.

Shortly after his return from India, Jenkins was elected a director of the East India Company, and subsequently served as deputy chairman (1838) and chairman (1839). He maintained a close interest in Indian affairs, and many in Shropshire came to benefit from his company patronage.

He brought to the court of directors a sympathetic view of Wellesley's tenure as governor-general.

Sir Richard died on 30 December 1853 at his house, Gothic Cottage, at Blackheath, Kent. His remains were returned to Shrewsbury and were buried on 6 January 1854 in the family vault at Bicton.   DAVID J. HOWLETT

Sources GM, 2nd ser., 41 (1854), 197–9 · T. E. Colebrooke, *Life of the Honourable Mountstuart Elphinstone*, 2 vols. (1884) · M. H. Fisher, *Indirect rule in India: residents and the residency system, 1764–1858* (1991) · C. A. Bayly, *Indian society and the making of the British empire* (1988), vol. 2/1 of *The new Cambridge history of India*, ed. G. Johnson · Burke, *Gen. GB* (1914)

Archives BL OIOC, letter-books and papers, Eur. MSS E 111–112, F 34 · BL OIOC, Home misc. series, corresp. relating to India · Cleveland Public Library, Cleveland, Ohio | BL OIOC, letters to Lord Amherst, Eur. MS F 140

Jenkins, Robert (*d.* 1743), merchant naval officer, was in 1731 master of the brig *Rebecca* bound for Jamaica which was boarded on 9 April by a Spanish coastguard off Havana. Jenkins was half-strangled and beaten by the Spanish, who wished to get him to reveal suspected hidden contraband. After failing to discover anything, the Spanish commander cut off part of Jenkins's ear, 'bidding him to carry it to his Master King George' (*Political State of Great Britain*, 11). The *Rebecca* was plundered and, as Rear-Admiral Stewart informed the Spanish governor of Havana on 12 September 1731, left 'with the intent that she should perish in her passage' (PRO, Adm 1/231). Despite its poor condition the ship arrived in the Thames on 11 June and Jenkins's case was reported in the press along with other allegations of Spanish intimidation at a time of worsening relations between Britain and Spain over navigation rights and suspected smuggling. Rear-Admiral Stewart specifically mentioned the case to the Spanish governor as part of a series of complaints for which he demanded satisfaction. However, it was not until 1738 that the impact of the Jenkins episode was fully felt in the wake of new criticisms of Spain. On 17 March the House of Commons resolved to examine a petition of several merchants trading to America complaining of Spanish depredations. Jenkins was ordered to attend the committee on 22 March. In the event he did not attend, but his plight was a powerful motif for the pro-war opposition to Robert Walpole's ministry. Cultural events relating to the Jenkins incident included a masquerade performed in February 1739 which featured a

> Spaniard, very richly dressed, who called himself knight of the Ear; as a Badge of which order he wore on his Breast the form of a Star, whose Points seem'd ting'd with Blood, on which was painted an Ear, and round it, written in Capital letters the word Jenkins. (GM, 9.103)

The Anglo-Spanish war which finally broke out in 1739 owed very little to the *Rebecca* incident though Jenkins's ear continued to serve as a potent symbol of political rights and Spanish cruelty. The identity of the Spanish commander who had perpetrated the crime was eagerly sought in order that his capture would prove an equally symbolic revenge. At least two Spanish captains were suspected of being Jenkins's tormentor, and their capture in 1740 and 1742 was heralded as fitting justice. Little more is known of Jenkins's professional or private life except that he became the captain of an East-Indiaman and died in Bombay in 1743 while commanding the *Harrington*.

J. K. LAUGHTON, *rev.* RICHARD HARDING

Sources A. Boyer, *The political state of Great Britain*, 42 (1731), 9–11 · *GM*, 1st ser., 1 (1731), 265 · *GM*, 1st ser., 9 (1739), 103 · *JHC*, 22 (1737–41), 94, 102 [16–17 March 1737] · L. Cong., manuscript division, Vernon-Wager MSS, microfilm 92, frames 456–65 · BL OIOC, L/MAR/B 654 D · PRO, Adm 1/231

Jenkins, Robert Thomas [*pseud.* Idris Thomas] (1881–1969), historian and writer, was born on 31 August 1881 at 13 Tennyson Street, Liverpool, the only child of Robert Jenkins (*d.* 1888) and Margaret, *née* Thomas (*d.* 1887). His father, a bookkeeper, and mother were natives of north Wales. In 1884 the family moved to Bangor, the father being appointed clerk to Cadwaladr Davies, registrar of the newly established University College. Jenkins, whose first language was English, attended a dame-school at Castle Bank, Bangor, until 1888. His mother died in 1887, his father in 1888, and he was brought up by his maternal grandmother and her husband in Bala, Merioneth, his education continuing at the Bala board school up to 1893, and thereafter at Bala grammar school, where he was well grounded in Latin, Greek, and Welsh. In 1898 he gained a scholarship to the University College of Wales at Aberystwyth, where he read English under Charles Harold Herford, who sparked his interest in the eighteenth century, and in 1901 gained first-class honours. With a sizarship at Trinity College, Cambridge, he spent three years studying history as well as English.

Straitened circumstances dictated that Jenkins became a history teacher, briefly at Llandysul, then at the county school at Brecon, from 1904 to 1917, and then at Cardiff High School for Boys until 1930. While in Brecon, on 31 December 1907 he married his first wife, Mary Davies (1877/8–1946), daughter of Evan Davies, a builder. On moving to Cardiff they lived at Lôn-y-dail in Rhiwbeina Garden Village, next door to W. J. Gruffydd, who in 1922 established *Y Llenor*, the leading Welsh literary periodical, which offered Jenkins an outlet up to the 1950s for his essays. It was in Rhiwbeina that he did his most original scholarly work, his *Hanes Cymru yn y ddeunawfed ganrif* ('History of Wales in the eighteenth century') in 1928. Its nineteenth-century sequel, his *Hanes Cymru yn y bedwaredd ganrif ar bymtheg, 1789–1843*, was published in 1933. He also became known to a wider public with two collections of essays, published in 1930, *Yr apêl at hanes* ('The appeal to history') and *Ffrainc a'i phobl* ('France and her people'), and as an immensely popular public lecturer, having conquered a serious speech impediment.

In 1930 Jenkins was appointed independent lecturer in Welsh history at the University College of North Wales, Bangor; he was appointed professor in 1945 and retired in 1948. In 1931 he edited (with his former pupil from Brecon Professor William Rees) *The Bibliography of Welsh History*, editing also the history and law section of the journal the *Bulletin of the Board of Celtic Studies* from 1937 onwards. In 1937 he published a scholarly study of the Independent cause at Llanuwchllyn near Bala, and in 1938 *The Moravian Brethren in North Wales*. In 1938 he became assistant editor of the projected *Dictionary of Welsh Biography*, being co-editor of the Welsh version, *Y bywgraffiadur Cymreig* (1953), and sole editor of the English version (1959). He gained the degree of DLitt in 1939. During the Second World War, using the pen-name Idris Thomas, he was co-editor of *Cofion Cymru*, the journal for Welsh-speakers in the forces overseas, and using this pen-name published a short novel, *Ffynhonnau Elim*, in 1945. He had already in 1943 published an excellent historical novel, *Orinda* (about the poet Katherine Philips), under his own name. He co-operated with Helen Ramage in 1951 to write *The History of the Honourable Society of Cymmrodorion, 1751–1951*. He was awarded the honorary degree of LLD by the University of Wales in 1956, and made a CBE in the same year.

After Jenkins's retirement further essays were published as the collections *Casglu ffyrdd* (1956) and *Ymyl y ddalen* (1957), and essays on Methodist history were collected in *Yng nghysgod Trefeca* (1968), in which year was published his autobiography covering the years from 1881 to 1930, *Edrych yn ôl*. His first wife died in 1946, and on 16 December 1947 he married Myfanwy Wyn Williams (*b.* 1904), daughter of Richard Williams. In retirement he continued to live at Rhuddallt, Sili-wen, in Upper Bangor, and it was there he died on 11 November 1969; he was buried in the Bangor cemetery. Some collections of his essays appeared after his death, *Cyfoedion* in 1974 and *Cwpanaid o dê a diferion eraill* in 1997.

Jenkins is however essentially a writer of the period of *Y Llenor* from the 1920s to the 1950s. His style is deliberately un-Victorian, humorous, discursive, parenthetic, and conversational. He wrote much on religious history, especially Methodism—he was a lifelong Calvinistic Methodist—but he did so in a jaunty, secular, and often debunking way. He had a great range of styles, at times academic, at others turning to the novel, and yet again to the light essay, and even writing brilliantly for children, as he did in 1933 with his *Y ffordd yng Nghymru* ('The way in Wales'), where roadways are used to illustrate Welsh history. Wearing his learning lightly, he often used his essays as a vehicle for discussing ideas. He was above all an entertaining master of Welsh prose, at a time of rapid maturing and modernization of Welsh-language culture in the 1920s and 1930s, making historical criticism and debate of central importance to that culture. PRYS MORGAN

Sources A. Llywelyn-Williams, 'Llyfryddiaeth R. T. Jenkins', *Journal of the Welsh Bibliographical Society*, 10 (1966–71), 107–15 · G. F. Nuttall, 'Dr R. T. Jenkins's articles in the *Dictionary of Welsh biography*', *Journal of the Welsh Bibliographical Society*, 10 (1966–71), 178–93 · R. T. Jenkins, *Edrych yn ôl* (1968) [memoirs 1881–1930] · A. Llywelyn-Williams, *R. T. Jenkins* (1977) · J. G. Williams, 'Jenkins, Robert Thomas', *Y bywgraffiadur Cymreig, 1951–1970*, ed. E. D. Jones and B. F. Roberts (1997) · M. Stephens, ed., *The new companion to the literature of Wales*, rev. edn (1998) · *Y Traethodydd*, 125 (1970), 63–109 · G. F. Nuttall, 'The genius of R. T. Jenkins', *Transactions of the Honourable Society of Cymmrodorion* (1977), 181–94 · E. D. Jones, *Transactions of the Honourable Society of Cymmrodorion* (1969), 346–9 · G. Williams, *Taliesin*, 21 (1970), 13–25 · d. cert.

Archives U. Wales, Bangor, papers | NL Wales, letters, incl. some to Thomas Iorwerth Ellis · NL Wales, letters to W. J. Gruffydd [in Welsh]

Likenesses photograph, repro. in Jenkins, *Edrych yn ôl*, frontispiece

Jenkins, Thomas (1722–1798), art dealer, painter, and banker, was probably born in December 1722 in Sidbury, Devon, one of the two sons of William Jenkins. His brother, William, later became vicar of Sidbury and rector of Upottery. Possibly they were the William and Thomas Jenkins who were baptized the sons of William Jenkins and Sarah at Honiton-on-Otter on 20 February 1717 and 10 December 1722 respectively. Ashby states that 'Thomas Jenkins was actually born in Rome', adding that 'various entries in the parish registers of S. Maria del Popolo at Rome (in which his name appears, curiously misspelt) point to the date of his birth being in reality 1722' (Ashby, 488). No more precise record appears to have come to light, however, and it remains possible that Ashby based this statement on the source to which Brinsley Ford referred when he later noted that 'In the Archivo del Vicariato, Stato del Anime S. Maria del Popolo Jenkins's age in 1758 is given as 36 and it says he is son of William J.' (Brinsley Ford archive). Joseph Farington stated that 'Mr. Jenkins, of Rome, was born at Sidbury near Sidmouth in Devonshire … [He] was apprentice[d] to a Mr. Hake, a clothier, at Honiton, and absconded from his apprenticeship from dislike to the business' (Farington, *Diary*, 2.391).

Painter Jenkins is believed to have studied in London under the portrait painter Thomas Hudson, who was a native of Devon. In 1750 or 1751 he left to study history painting in Italy, travelling from Venice to Rome with his friend Richard Wilson, the landscape painter, and the art collector William Lock of Norbury. In 1752 and 1753 Wilson and Jenkins lodged in piazza di Spagna, and it is during this period that Wilson made the portrait drawing of Jenkins now in the Pierpont Morgan Library, New York. Jenkins's early work in Rome includes portraits of Francesco Geminiani (priv. coll.) engraved by Valentine Green (1777), and Thomas Brand (1753; ex Christies, 18 June 1976), who introduced Wilson and Jenkins to William Legge, second earl of Dartmouth, and Frederick North, later second earl of Guilford, known as Lord North. Jenkins painted their portraits and Dartmouth also commissioned from him a *Nymph* and some drawings. Of Jenkins's history paintings little is known. He received 40 sequins for a picture commissioned by Stephen Beckingham entitled *Time Discovering Truth: an Allegorical Subject*; a copy drawn by Nikolaus Mosman (BM) records his *Hagar and Ishmael*. When he dispatched two of his landscapes to England in March 1754 they formed part of a shipment including marbles, columns, and classical antiquities, as well as old master paintings, prints, and drawings Jenkins had acquired for Lord Dartmouth. The varied contents of this consignment reveal that Jenkins was exploring alternative means to secure an income and indicate where his future prosperity lay. He continued, however, to be described as a painter in parish registers of Rome until 1773, having been elected to the Accademia Clementina in Bologna in 1760, and to the Florentine academy and the Accademia di San Luca, Rome, in 1761.

Art dealer In 1758 Jenkins had moved to a Rome address on the Corso in the parish of San Lorenzo in Lucina which he shared with Wilson's pupil John Plimer or Plimmer (*d.* 1760). By this time he was more active as a dealer in art and antiquities than as a painter. Through the offices of his friend Thomas Hollis he had been elected a fellow of the Society of Antiquaries in London in 1757, and his letters and drawings held by the society, later described by S. R. Pierce in an article in the society's journal, provide an important account of contemporary excavations in Italy. Accused by 'a Scottish faction' of accruing an unreasonable profit on a bust he had sold, he was threatened with banishment by the government of Rome (Ingamells, 554). With the support of Cardinal Alessandro Albani, Lord Dartmouth, and Lord North, he survived this attack on his reputation, though he continued to be subjected to imputations of damaging the prospects of fellow artists and even of spying: 'take care how you keep company with one Jenkins … he is a Spy in Rome for our Government' (ibid., 554).

While some of these disputes arose from tensions between the Catholic Jacobite and protestant British communities in Rome, less easily explained away are the accounts, of which many survive, of the doubtful honesty of Jenkins's dealing in both painting and antiquities. In 1761, by which time he had been admitted to Albani's powerful circle which included the philosopher and art theorist Johann Joachim Winckelmann and the painter Anton Raphael Mengs, James Adam observed that Jenkins '"plays his cards to admiration" having sold last winter "no less than £5000 worth of pictures &ca. to the English of which every person of any knowledge is convinced he put £4000 in his pocket"' (ibid., 554). In 1765 he sold to the collector William Weddell a large quantity of paintings and sculpture, including the Barberini Venus. The torso of this antique figure had been found by Gavin Hamilton in the Barberini Palace. He sold it 'at a moderate price' (Ford, 416) to Jenkins, who added to it another antique head he had acquired from Joseph Nollekens before letting it go to Weddell for about 1000 guineas. Farington's comment, thirty years later, that 'Jenkins … obtained from the late Mr. Weddell of Yorkshire, £2000, and an annuity of £100 for his life, for a statue of Venus' perhaps indicates that the story became embellished in the re-telling (Farington, *Diary*, 2.439, 12 Dec 1795).

Nollekens recalled that in the 1760s Jenkins was:

> supplying foreign visitors with Intaglios and Cameos made by his own people, that he kept in a part of the Coliseum, fitted up for 'em to work in slyly by themselves … he sold 'em as fast as they made 'em. (Ingamells, 555)

His clients found his sales technique convincing, however, and it was noted that he parted with some objects in tears. Notwithstanding his sharp dealing, Jenkins's clients included Charles Townley, James Hugh Smith Barry, and Henry Blundell. After about 1780, when war with France closed sea routes to England, he sold paintings and antiquities to Empress Catherine II of Russia (who later refused to deal with him), Prince Stanislaus Poniatowski, and others of the Russian, Polish, German, and Austrian nobility.

Agent and banker Jenkins moved again in 1765 to a larger house on the opposite side of the Corso, later extending it. It was from here that, as Jenkins's guest, the duke of Gloucester watched the start of the Corso dei Cavalli, a lively horse race, in 1772. With his increasing wealth, Jenkins's power and influence at the papal court became more potent. In 1772 he escorted Sir William Hamilton to an informal audience with Pope Clement XIV, with whom he was on good terms. In the absence of an official British presence in Rome, Jenkins fulfilled the role of unofficial representative to the Holy See. He also acted as cicerone to British and European royal and aristocratic families on the grand tour. The duke of Cumberland dined with him in 1774. In the following year he took luxurious apartments in a villa at Castel Gandolfo outside Rome, described by Father John Thorpe (also a dealer) as 'a sort of trap' for wealthy young Englishmen who wished to buy antiquities (Ingamells, 555).

According to the artist Thomas Jones, by Christmas 1776 Jenkins had almost superseded Barazzi as principal banker to the English in Rome. For almost ten years he was Angelica Kauffman's banker and during that time she painted a double portrait of Jenkins and his niece, Anna Maria (1790; NPG). In addition to being his client, Charles Townley also engaged in business with Jenkins and acted as his agent in London for many English collectors. Their correspondence from 1768 to 1798, over 1000 sheets, is in the Townley manuscripts collection in the British Museum. Jenkins was involved in several excavation projects, and also received a share of findings from those undertaken by Gavin Hamilton. In 1785 he purchased the entire collection of antiquities of the Villa Negroni, and sold the principal pieces, including a *Caryatid* (BM), to Townley. Bernini's *Neptune and Triton* (V&A), also part of the collection, he sold to Sir Joshua Reynolds, president of the Royal Academy. The 'Jenkins vase' (NMG Wales) he acquired as an antique well-head from the Caraffa collection in Naples about 1769. It was converted into a vase by his restorers and sold in the 1770s to Smith Barry.

Later years In 1793 Sir William Forbes wrote that 'Jenkins had long been a sort of Introductor to British travellers residing in Rome, where there being no British ambassador, Mr Jenkins may be said to have done the honours of the nation' (Ingamells, 556). From the 1770s onwards he also received royal visitors from Russia and Sweden to see his collections. His personal fortune was said to be £100,000. In 1788 Jenkins had returned to England, where he purchased an estate in the parish of Sidbury and further land in the parish of Axmouth. To his family he was generous and supportive: his nephew John, a painter, had come to live with him in Rome in 1778, and another, James, arrived in 1781 and entered his uncle's banking business. His niece Anna Maria returned with him to Rome in 1788 and married his neighbour Giovanni Martinez in 1794. Jenkins left Italy in 1798 as a result of the French invasion. He took with him his collection of gems

and cameos but the rest of his collection was left behind. In his extensive will he left most of his property to his brother's children, two other nephews, William and Thomas, being the principal heirs. At Florence on 16 March 1798 he made a codicil annulling his nomination of Nicolas Castelli (of the banking firm Castelli & Co. to whom he transferred his banking business) as executor of his will 'as all my effects in Rome have been confiscated by the ffrench' (will). Though he reduced the legacies he left to the sculptors Christopher Hewetson and Carlo Albacini in amount, his reference to them in the codicil reveals a concern to memorialize their close friendship, despite the loss of his property in Rome. Jenkins died, according to Redgrave, shortly after landing at Yarmouth after a storm at sea. His will was proved in London on 6 November 1798. Having apportioned his property Jenkins was moved to comment:

> what I feel most particularly sensible of is that the property I have has been by the Blessing of God fairly & justly acquired which gives me reason to hope it will prosper with my heirs—to whom I most seriously recommend to do all the Good in their power to act not only with Justice but with humanity to all—it being impossible for any person to be content who does not do his duty *An honest Mind is a Perpetual Feast.* (will)

'Through his energy and urbanity, and regrettably through his duplicity, Thomas Jenkins became the richest and most influential figure of the English colony in Rome during the second half of the eighteenth century' (Ford, 416).

ANNETTE PEACH

Sources B. Ford, 'Thomas Jenkins: banker, dealer and unofficial agent', *Apollo*, 99 (1974), 416–25 · J. Ingamells, ed., *A dictionary of British and Irish travellers in Italy, 1701–1800* (1997) · G. Vaughan, 'Jenkins, Thomas', *The dictionary of art*, ed. J. Turner (1996) · will, PRO, PROB, 11/1315, fols. 60v–67r · Farington, *Diary* · Brinsley Ford archive, Paul Mellon Centre for Studies in British Art, London · T. Ashby, 'Thomas Jenkins in Rome', *Papers of the British School at Rome*, 6/8 (1913), 487–511 · S. R. Pierce, 'Thomas Jenkins in Rome: in the light of letters, records and drawings at the Society of Antiquaries in London', *Antiquaries Journal*, 45 (1965), 200–29 · Redgrave, *Artists* · IGI · Waterhouse, *18c painters* · A. Wilton and I. Bignamini, eds., *Grand tour* (1996) [exhibition catalogue, Tate Gallery, London]

Archives RA, letters and papers | BL, letters to second Earl Spencer

Likenesses R. Wilson, chalk drawing, *c.*1753, Morgan L. · A. Kauffman, double portrait, oils, 1790 (with his niece, Anna Maria Jenkins), NPG · A. Maron, oils, 1791, Accademia di San Luca, Rome

Wealth at death lost most property and fortune after the French invaded Italy, 1797–8

Jenkins, Sir William (1871–1944), politician, was born at Afon Vale, Glyncorrwg, near Cymmer, Glamorgan, on 8 January 1871, the son of Miles Jenkins (1842–1909), a miner, and his wife, Anne Davies (*d.* 1913). He was educated at Glyncorrwg national school before leaving, aged eleven, to work on the Rhondda and Swansea Bay Railway. A year later he entered the mines, working as a collier boy at the Avon Hill colliery, Abergwynfi. He became an active trade unionist and was appointed lodge secretary in 1890 before becoming a check-weigher in 1898 at Cymmer drift mine. Notwithstanding the demands of underground labour, he continued to study at evening classes and to lead boys' classes at a Sunday school. A Welsh-speaking nonconformist, he became precentor and deacon of Hebron Congregational Chapel, Cymmer, and, as a talented tenor singer, won prizes at eisteddfods and later became an eisteddfod conductor (he was also chairman of the Port Talbot national eisteddfod in 1932, and vice-chairman of the Neath national eisteddfod in 1934). On 2 November 1895 he married Mary Hannah Evans (1872–1952) of Cwmafon, Glamorgan, the daughter of William Evans, a coalminer. They had five children.

In 1900 Jenkins was elected to the Glyncorrwg school board. Following its supersession, he won in 1904 a place on the Glyncorrwg urban district council, which he retained until his death, chairing the council on three occasions (in 1908, 1927, and 1944). In 1906 he was appointed secretary for the Western Miners' Association; from 1907 to 1922 he was a member of the south Wales coal conciliation board, and he also served (from 1910 to 1924) as an executive council member of the South Wales Miners' Federation. In 1922, following his election to parliament, he was appointed chief agent for the Afan Valley Miners' Association, and he continued to be involved with the coal industry, attending international miners' conferences across Europe. Jenkins was also a pioneer of the co-operative movement in the locality and was managing secretary of the first federal co-operative society in south Wales. In 1914 he was made a magistrate, later chairing the Port Talbot petty sessions.

Jenkins's greatest contribution was made on the Glamorgan county council, to which he was elected in 1906. He was made chairman of the education committee in 1918, served as council chairman from 1919 to 1921 (as the Labour Party took control of the county council for the first time), and was elected to the aldermanic benches in 1920. He was devoted to widening access to education, and has been credited with increasing secondary school provision, as well as with multiplying the number of scholarships, grants, and loans allowing working-class children to extend their education. A member of the council of the University of Wales and of the Central Welsh Board, he was also chairman of the Glamorgan School for the Blind. In 1934 he became chairman of the Federation of Education Authorities of Wales, and in 1938 chairman of the County Council Association of England and Wales. A highly knowledgeable administrator, he dominated the Glamorgan county council (one of never more than three contemporary Labour-controlled county councils in England and Wales) from the end of the First World War to his death.

Jenkins was selected as the Labour Party candidate to fight the Neath constituency at the general election of 1922; he unseated the National Liberal MP J. Hugh Edwards, amassing a majority of 6235. At five subsequent general elections Jenkins was unopposed twice and polled over 60 per cent of the vote on all other occasions. During the Labour government of 1924 he served as parliamentary private secretary to the postmaster-general, Vernon Hartshorn, but otherwise enjoyed an unremarkable parliamentary career, serving as chairman of the ways and means committee and presiding over the House of Commons on an occasional basis. As a conscientious backbench MP he was popular across all parties, speaking rarely but enjoying the 'companionship and social life' of parliament as well as being active in the London Welsh Dining Club (*Western Mail*, 9 Dec 1944). His knighthood (1931) was awarded largely for his service to local government.

Jenkins died at his home, 3 Mount Pleasant in Cymmer, in the Afan valley, on 8 December 1944 and was buried at Cymmer cemetery three days later. A clubbable figure with an interest in bowls and golf, he was a humorous raconteur. Left-wing critics saw him as personifying the rise of the Labour Party to the status of the Welsh political establishment. In the minds of those who voted for him, however, and of Jenkins himself, this was the point of his contribution. For a child born into the manual working class, the achievement of becoming an MP and a prominent county councillor could be seen as representing a democratic and popular triumph, whereby the voice of the people (and particularly of the coalminers) might be heard on the national stage. Their ambition was limited and simple, but also attainable: to inherit the existing political system and to turn it (gradually, imperfectly, but still significantly) to their own ends.   CHRIS WILLIAMS

Sources *The Times* (9 Dec 1944) · *Daily Herald* (9 Dec 1944) · *Western Mail* (9 Dec 1944) · *Neath Guardian* (15 Dec 1944) · G. Elwyn Jones, 'Education in Glamorgan since 1700', *Glamorgan County history*, vol. 6: *Glamorgan society, 1780–1980*, ed. P. Morgan (1988), 326–7 · *Western Mail* (1 Jan 1931) · *Neath Guardian* · South Wales Miners' Federation minute books, 1910–24, U. Wales, South Wales Miners' Library [printed] · private information (2004) [Emlyn Davies, son-in-law] · b. cert. · m. cert. · d. cert. · *Western Mail* (Oct 1922) · *Western Mail* (Nov 1922) · *Western Mail* (Nov 1923) · *Western Mail* (Dec 1923) · *Western Mail* (May 1929) · *Western Mail* (Oct 1931)

Likenesses group portrait, photograph (as MP), South Wales Coalfield collection, PHO/ED/1/9 · photograph, repro. in *Afar Uchaf: the Journal of the Cymer Afar and District Historical Society*, 8 (1985), 45 · photograph, repro. in *Western Mail* (1 Jan 1931) · photograph, repro. in *Western Mail* (17 Nov 1922)

Wealth at death £7,358 2s. 9d.: probate, 1945, *CGPLA Eng. & Wales*

Jenkinson, Anthony (1529–1610/11), traveller and writer, was born at Market Harborough, Leicestershire, on 8 October 1529, the second son of William Jenkinson (d. 1565/6), the owner of several inns and considerable property, and his wife, Elizabeth (d. after 1572). Trained for a mercantile career, he travelled extensively from 1546 through Europe and most of the Mediterranean basin countries and the main islands. In 1553 he received special licence from Suleiman the Magnificent at Aleppo in Syria to trade with the Turks. Appointed in 1557 captain-general of a convoy of four ships by the Muscovy Company as successor to Willoughby and Chancellor, Jenkinson sailed to Russia with the returning ambassador Osip Nepea in order to explore eastern trade routes. He spent four months at the company's north Russian factories before proceeding to Moscow where he received much hospitality from tsar Ivan IV, the 'Terrible', at banquets held on Christmas day and on 4 January 1558.

In April 1558 Jenkinson left Moscow with letters of safe conduct, travelling south by waterways, down the Volga and through Russia's newly conquered territories to the port of Astrakhan. A month's perilous navigation of the Caspian Sea brought him to Mangyshlak on the north-east coast. From here his group travelled south-east overland for four months, crossing Tartar lands and enduring great hardship and danger, graphically described by Jenkinson, before wintering at Bukhara. Convinced by enquiries made of caravan merchants that this central Asian crossroads offered no prospect for the Muscovy Company's eastern trade, and forced by the political situation to renounce his intention of travelling on to Persia, Jenkinson, accompanied by six Tartar ambassadors and twenty-five Russian slaves he freed, retraced his steps, returning to Moscow at length in September 1559. He was fêted by the tsar and sailed back to England when the navigation route reopened in 1560.

On 21 November 1560 Anthony Jenkinson, who 'hath ben as furre … in all ptes as ever anye e[n]gelisheman hathe ben … to the comforte of our engellishe merchants', was made a freeman of the Mercers' Company by redemption gratis ('Repertorys or acts of court'). Two years later his map of Russia was published with a dedication to his patron Sir Henry Sidney, most of which was incorporated by Ortelius in his famous atlas, *Theatrum orbis terrarum* (1570). The prototype map, engraved by Nicholas Reynolds, edited by Clement Adams, printed possibly at Antwerp, and acquired in 1988 by Wrocław University Library in Poland, is the earliest known surviving map (1562) engraved by an Englishman.

After reporting back to the Muscovy Company, Jenkinson immediately prepared for a follow-up expedition through Russia to Persia. Carrying the new Queen Elizabeth's letters of recommendation to Ivan and the sophy of Persia, he reached Moscow in August 1561, but the tsar's remarriage and an obstructive court secretary delayed his audience with Ivan until March 1562. Entrusted with a secret commission by him, he pursued his journey through Russia in the Persian ambassador's company, giving a vivid account of his reception at Shemakha by the Shirvan ruler Abdul-khan who supplied him with safe-conduct letters to the Persian court at Quazvin. A recent treaty between Persia and Turkey compelled him to change his trade plans, and he spent the winter months a virtual prisoner before he was allowed to return to Shirvan where he obtained favourable terms for English merchants. He reached Moscow on 20 August 1563 and soon afterwards delivered special messages from Abdul-khan and the Georgian king to the tsar who, delighted by the way in which Jenkinson had discharged his commissions, readily granted a significant extension of trade privileges to the Muscovy Company. He set sail for London in July 1564, having established an excellent rapport with Ivan and paved the way for trade to Persia.

In May 1565 Jenkinson petitioned to explore a north-east passage to the Far East, debating the issue with Humphrey Gilbert before the queen and the privy council that winter without result. He was awarded a life annuity of £40 in July 1566 for services to the crown, but a royal assignment in September to clear the North Sea of pirates and prevent the earl of Bothwell from landing in Scotland to support Mary Stuart ended on an ambiguous note. Shortly afterwards the Muscovy Company was authorized to dispatch Jenkinson on a third mission to Russia. His main task as special envoy was to remove an obstacle that had arisen to the trade privileges granted in 1564. On arrival in northern Russia in June 1566 he sent an elk and wrote a letter to William Cecil about the country's wars with Poland and Sweden, mentioning Ivan's great cruelty towards the noblemen and gentry he suspected of plotting against him. When Jenkinson presented Ivan with Elizabeth's letter on 1 September 1566, the tsar, instead of responding directly to her request to reaffirm the trade privileges, wrote her a letter on 6 September asking for technical experts to strengthen his war campaigns.

Although Jenkinson's very brief travel notes fail to indicate when he left Russia, it is clear that he sailed back early in October 1566, regaining London by mid-December. Reconstructed documentation also shows that Ivan's conditional response led to Jenkinson's return in the summer of 1567, conveying Elizabeth's letter of 18 May in which she confirmed that she was sending him back with the requisite technicians. With consummate skill, Jenkinson managed to negotiate a considerable extension of the trade privileges and to consolidate the Muscovy Company's absolute monopoly in the White Sea area. Having taken leave of Ivan on 22 September 1567, Jenkinson returned to England by sea with the tsar's letter dated 11 September and a separate secret message which he delivered to Elizabeth in November. In them Ivan stressed his desire for a political alliance, mediated by Jenkinson at ambassadorial level, and a mutual refuge pact for both monarchs in each other's countries. The inference is that Jenkinson, a highly accurate reporter, deliberately omitted mention of the two separate but linked missions in his travel memorandum for reasons of state security, concealing the fact that English specialists had been sent to place Russia on a stronger war footing.

On 26 January 1568 Anthony Jenkinson married Judith Marshe at St Michael, Wood Street, London. She was the daughter of John *Marshe (c.1516–1579) and his wife, Alice, whose father, William Gresham, was a cousin of Sir Thomas Gresham. Marshe, an original member of the Muscovy Company in 1555, governor of the Merchant Adventurers, an MP for London, and warden of the Mercers' Company, shared many trade associations with his son-in-law. Jenkinson was granted a coat of arms with a crest featuring a heraldic sea horse on 14 February 1569. His travels and voyages are comprehensively summarized in the preamble which refers, for instance, to the Caspian Sea and 'dyvers contreys there abowt, to the old cosmographers utterly unknowne' (Morgan and Coote, 1.c–ciii). He and his wife were living in a house in Aldersgate Street,

St John Zachary parish, London, by 1570; four of their six daughters and one of five sons survived.

As a result of a breakdown in the reciprocal defence treaty, caused by Thomas Randolph's mission to Russia in 1568, Ivan revoked the Muscovy Company's trading privileges. Jenkinson was appointed ambassador in May 1571 with the remit to recoup them. He reached north Russia by ship late that July, but was confined by plague quarantines for six and a half months at Kholmogory, an English factory centre south-east of Archangel. From here he penned another letter to William Cecil, now Lord Burghley, describing the plague and the Crimean Tartars' devastation of Moscow and other parts of Russia in May 1571, giving yet more instances of atrocities perpetrated on Ivan's orders. Received by Ivan on 23 March 1572, Jenkinson transmitted three of Elizabeth's letters to him, both sides raising matters for discussion at a second meeting held on 13 May. Jenkinson's instructions were to reinstate the trade privileges by hinting verbally at a political alliance without committing anything concrete to writing. In the event he succeeded admirably, all privileges were restored, and the tsar gave 'Anthony' full credit for the results. In September Jenkinson returned to England, having sailed from Russia on 23 July—a brilliant culmination to a career which won him a permanent place in the history of Anglo-Russian relations.

Over the next decade Jenkinson was much preoccupied with business and property matters. In February 1573 he and John Marshe were appointed to a feodaries' commission of the court of wards and liveries, responsible for the city of London circuit, and in 1574 he acted as a key deponent in a dispute about some inherited property in Warwickshire. When Martin Frobisher returned in 1577 from his first voyage to discover a north-west trade passage, Jenkinson, who subscribed to the Cathay Company, was commissioned to help equip his second expedition, also participating in the work of a commission which reported on the ore brought back from Frobisher's third voyage in 1578 and assayed at Muscovy House. Humphrey Gilbert, knighted in 1570, who had proposed Frobisher for his voyages, paid tribute to Jenkinson in his *Discourse of a Discovery for a New Passage to Cataia* (1576) as 'a man of rare vertue, great travaile, and experience' (Hakluyt, 606–7). Jenkinson was a member, and Marshe the president, of the Spanish Company incorporated in June 1577. In July Jenkinson and his colleague Daniel Rogers were sent on a special assignment to the north-west German port of Emden in an attempt to resolve with Danish commissioners the vexed question of tolls for navigating the northern sea route to the White Sea. At the end of 1577 he acquired Sywell Manor near Northampton from John Marshe, purchasing additional surrounding property and estate during 1579. In 1583 the queen granted him 200 acres of arable land and 300 acres of pastureland at Sywell, with licence to build.

Jenkinson's precise and vivid travel accounts, reproduced in Hakluyt's *Principal Navigations* (1589 and 1598–1600), have been widely circulated by English and foreign anthologies. But claims originating with William Ross in 1939, and repeated by W. J. F. Hutcheson in 1950 and Margaret Morton in 1960, that on his return from Russia Jenkinson had an illegitimate daughter, Anne Beck or Whateley, who was a gifted writer and who in 1582 was thwarted in her hopes of marriage to William Shakespeare, have found no favour with scholars.

In 1606 Jenkinson decided to sell Sywell Manor and moved 11 miles north to Ashton, occupying the manor house, probably as a crown lessee. His wife had predeceased him when, badly afflicted with palsy, he drew up his will on 13 November 1610. He was buried on 16 February 1611 at Holy Trinity Church in Teigh, on Rutland's border with Leicestershire, by its rector Zachary Jenkinson, his nephew and executor.   JOHN H. APPLEBY

Sources E. Delmar Morgan and C. H. Coote, eds., *Early voyages and travels to Russia and Persia by Anthony Jenkinson and other Englishmen* (1886) · M. B. G. Morton, *The Jenkinson story* (1962) · H. R. Huttenbach, 'Anthony Jenkinson's 1566 and 1567 missions to Muscovy', *Canadian-American Slavic Studies*, 9/2 (1975), 179–203 · H. R. Huttenbach, 'The search for new archival material for ambassador Jenkinson's mission to Muscovy in 1571–72', *Canadian-American Slavic Studies*, 6/3 (1972), 416–36 · *Map Collector*, 48 (1989), 38–9 · PRO, C24/113 · parish register, St Michael, Wood Street, GL, MS 6530 · *CPR*, 1575–8 · *CPR*, 1572–5 · H. Miller, 'Marshe, John', HoP, *Commons, 1509–58*, 2.576–7 · A. N. Panin-Pavlov, 'Anthony Jenkinson's travels in Russia (Cheboksary)', *From Harborough to Tartary* (2000) [exhibition catalogue, Harborough Museum, 2000] · J. Foster and W. H. Rylands, eds., *Grantees of arms named in docquets and patents to the end of the seventeenth century*, Harleian Society, 66 (1915) · E. G. R. Taylor, *Tudor geography, 1485–1583* (1930) · 'Repertorys or acts of court, 1560–1595', *Mercers' Company* · R. Hakluyt, *The principal navigations, voyages, traffiques and discoveries of the English nation*, 2nd edn, 3 vols. (1598–1600) · parish register, Teigh, Holy Trinity, 16 Feb 1611, Leics. RO, DE 3855/1 [burial] · W. J. Fraser Hutcheson, 'letter to editor', *Evesham Journal and Four Shires Advertiser* (31 Dec 1949)

Likenesses N. Hilliard, miniature, 1588, V&A; close variant sold at Christie's, 3 March 1993, as Shakespeare's portrait

Wealth at death great personal estate; also lands, houses, and property: Morton, *Jenkinson story*, 299–300

Jenkinson, Charles, first earl of Liverpool (1729–1808),

politician, was born at Winchester on 26 April 1729, the eldest son of Charles Jenkinson (1693–1750), an army officer, and his wife, Amarantha Cornwall (d. 1785), the daughter of Captain Wolfran Cornwall RN. Despite being born into a well-connected Oxfordshire gentry family, Jenkinson, as the son of a younger son, had his own way to make in the world. His cousin Sir Robert Jenkinson held the baronetcy, first granted in 1661; four of his immediate ancestors had represented the county as tories. On his mother's side, he was related to the Cornwalls of Herefordshire: his cousin (and brother-in-law) Charles Wolfran Cornwall was speaker of the House of Commons from 1780 to 1789. His father, a colonel, died when Jenkinson was twenty-one, leaving an estate at Burford. After attending Charterhouse School and University College, Oxford, Jenkinson decided to enter the church, and in 1753 was offered the living of Hanwell, near Banbury, by Sir Jonathan Cope, another relative; however, at a very late stage in the negotiation he withdrew and abandoned that career. He took a prominent part in the hotly contested Oxfordshire election of 1754, writing squibs and lampoons for the whigs. This may have whetted his appetite

Charles Jenkinson, first earl of Liverpool (1729–1808), by George Romney, 1786–8

for politics. It certainly brought him into close contact with the Oxfordshire whig grandees Marlborough, Macclesfield, and, especially, Harcourt. They arranged for him to be employed as unpaid secretary to Lord Holdernesse, secretary of state for the north, to introduce him to the business of foreign affairs. In November 1756 he asked George Grenville to intercede for him with Pitt for a post as under-secretary, enclosing the draft of a pamphlet on the militia, later published as *A Discourse on the Establishment of a National and Constitutional Force in England*. Although the application failed, the contacts remained valuable. Jenkinson stayed in post, wrote copiously to Grenville, published in 1758 a *Discourse on the Conduct of Great Britain with Respect to Neutral Nations* (which was an important issue during the Seven Years' War), and in 1760 was given a pension of £250 per annum until he could be better provided for.

The follower of Bute When Lord Bute took office as secretary of state in 1761, Jenkinson became an under-secretary. On 24 March he wrote to Grenville: 'I am absolutely in love with Lord Bute: his goodness shows itself to me more and more every day' (*Grenville Papers*, 1.359). A fortnight later he was brought into parliament for Cockermouth, a borough under the control of Sir James Lowther, one of Bute's followers and his future son-in-law. When Bute became first lord of the Treasury in 1762, Jenkinson stayed with him as private secretary, with a sinecure at the Ordnance in lieu of salary and the reversion of the

collectorship of the customs inwards for the port of London. Lowther turned out to be a demanding patron: 'he seems to rely very much on me in all his public concerns', remarked Jenkinson innocently as early as June 1761. But through Lowther he made the acquaintance of John Robinson, the Lowthers' man of business in the north-west, and the two, with much in common, became life-long friends. Since Jenkinson was hard-working and assiduous, his career was now launched, though he was less successful in the House of Commons, where his manner was uneasy. James Harris, commenting on an important speech in February 1766 against repealing the Stamp Act, praised its content and argument, but added that, 'from defect of voice, it was ill-heard' (HoP, *Commons*). In 1770 the excitable Tommy Townshend deplored Jenkinson's 'pompous manner', but when he declared that it was unbecoming in a gentleman 'risen from the situation he had done', he met with a smart riposte: 'my rise is from as old a family as his own', replied Jenkinson, 'I have risen by industry, by attention to duty, and by every honourable means I could devise' (Namier, 1.15). Wraxall, who sat in the house with Jenkinson later, wrote that 'no ray of wit, humour or levity pervaded his speeches. All was fact and business' (*Memoirs of … Wraxall*, 1.419).

Political difficulties When Grenville replaced Bute in 1763, Jenkinson was appointed one of the secretaries to the Treasury, with responsibility for patronage, elections, and parliamentary management. But Grenville's growing suspicion of Bute's continuing influence made his relations with Jenkinson awkward, and by the end of the ministry they were on cool terms. He left office with Grenville in 1765 but was given the auditorship to the princess of Wales to tide him over—presumably through Bute's intervention. He was in opposition to the Rockingham ministry and did not at first hold office in the Pitt–Grafton ministry, but in December 1766 was made a lord of the Admiralty. Grenville regarded this as a betrayal and gave orders to his porter not to admit Jenkinson in future. A year later Jenkinson transferred to the Treasury board, which was more suited to his interests. In one of Lowther's many reshuffles of his members, he was moved in January 1767 to Appleby, which strengthened his links with Robinson, a native of the borough, who owned a fine house there. But the lack of a secure parliamentary seat made life difficult, especially after Lowther moved into opposition. This may have prompted Jenkinson to one of the few injudicious moves of his life. On a parliamentary vacancy in February 1768 he put himself forward for the University of Oxford, where the franchise was in the doctors and masters of arts. He was forced to withdraw but came forward again the following month at the general election. Since the university had a fondness for Oxfordshire gentlemen, his candidature was not implausible, but his zeal on behalf of the whigs in 1754 had not been forgotten by the university tories. They raised the cry of government interference and Jenkinson was well beaten by Francis Page, a stolid and unremarkable tory gentleman: 'the cry of independence was so general', reported Jenkinson's chief supporter, 'that all were to be proscribed that did not vote for

Page' (HoP, *Commons*). Some compensation for the failure of 'a scheme which I own I have very much to heart' (*Hist. U. Oxf.* 5: *18th-cent. Oxf.*, 155) came in 1773 when, at North's installation as chancellor, Jenkinson received an honorary DCL. In 1769 he was dismayed to discover that Lowther, who had lost his own seat for Cumberland, might expect him to retire to make room. Although that crisis was averted, he took the first opportunity to find a safer seat, and in August 1772 transferred to the Treasury borough of Harwich: 'I have for some time had a squabble with Sir James', he explained to a friend (HoP, *Commons*).

Jenkinson married on 9 February 1769 Amelia Watts (1750/51–1770), the daughter of William Watts, formerly governor of Fort William in Bengal, and his wife, Frances Crook. They had one child, Robert Banks *Jenkinson, the future prime minister, who was born on 7 June 1770. Amelia Jenkinson died a month later, on 7 July, aged nineteen. On 22 June 1782 Jenkinson married Catherine Cope (1744–1827), the widow of Sir Charles Cope and the youngest daughter of Sir Cecil Bisshopp, sixth baronet, and his wife, Anne Boscawen. Their son, Charles Cecil Cope *Jenkinson, succeeded his half-brother as third earl of Liverpool, and their daughter, Charlotte, married James Walter, first earl of Verulam.

In the early 1770s Jenkinson's upwards progress slowed. The new prime minister, Lord North, was a good man of business, a much better debater than Jenkinson, and younger. Princess Augusta's death in 1772 robbed Jenkinson of his position at her court, and in January 1773 he left the Treasury board to make room for Charles James Fox, taking the joint vice-treasurership of Ireland, where his patron Lord Harcourt was serving as lord lieutenant. He was appointed to the privy council in February 1773, and in 1775, in exchange for the Irish vice-treasurership, he gained the clerkship of the Pells, an Irish sinecure worth more than £2000 per annum. It looked as if he had settled for comfortable obscurity, and he took time off to travel on the continent and in Ireland. But in December 1778 North made him secretary at war, an important post during the American conflict and one which brought close contact with the king. He was now at the very centre of North's group of intimates and, together with Robinson, took on responsibility for sustaining the prime minister's morale and reporting to the king. His closeness to George III, his Bute antecedents, and his self-effacing manner fuelled the opposition's suspicion that he was an *éminence grise*: 'Jenkinson governs every thing', Burke assured Rockingham in 1775 (*Correspondence*, 3.89), and two years later Jenkinson himself wrote deprecatingly to Harcourt that 'the world are so obliging as to give me credit of much more influence than I really have' (*Jenkinson Papers*, xxiv–xxv). His next career move should have been the chancellorship of the exchequer, but the king was reluctant to see North hand over those duties in case it encouraged him to abandon all the others, despite North's assurance that Jenkinson was 'the fittest person to have the direction of the finances of this country' (*Correspondence*, ed. Fortescue, 4.264, letter no. 2512). His duties ran much wider than those strictly of his office: in August 1779 he was employed

in proposals for Ireland and in November the king asked his advice on the prospects for a coalition. In October 1779 North pressed strongly for his inclusion in the cabinet, but this did not take place, possibly because Jenkinson himself was not willing. In 1781 there was a sharp disagreement over raising six regiments in Ireland, to which Jenkinson objected strongly: his resignation was talked of, but the cabinet gave way. In December 1781 he was considered as a possible successor to Lord George Germain as American secretary but refused it, perhaps because his post at the war office brought in £5000 per annum, but possibly because there was not much left of America to be secretary of. He was still in office when North's ministry collapsed.

Supporter of Pitt In the confused months that followed, Jenkinson lay low, deliberately absenting himself from the House of Commons. When Shelburne formed his ministry in July 1782 Jenkinson was not given any post, but the king wrote urgently that he should offer 'every degree of assistance' (HoP, *Commons*). This helped to persuade Robinson to assist Shelburne with his parliamentary expertise. Jenkinson voted for Shelburne's peace preliminaries in February 1783 and was consulted by the king in March in a desperate attempt to avoid a coalition ministry. With Shelburne gone, Jenkinson transferred his hopes to William Pitt. He spoke and voted against the India Bill in November 1783, was sharply attacked by Fox for supporting an 'infernal spirit of intrigue' (Cobbett, *Parl. hist.*, 24, 1783, 219), and on 5 December wrote to Robinson that the king 'sees the bill in all the horrors that you and I do' (*Abergavenny MSS*, 61). But although Pitt's fledgeling ministry in December 1783 was desperately short of administrative talent, Jenkinson received no offer. 'I am ready to accept office', he wrote to Robinson on 24 December, and a week later that 'I have not heard a word from Mr. Pitt ... he has not even paid me this small mark of attention' (ibid., 64). 'Fears and doubts', replied Robinson gnomically, 'makes difficulties to your having office at this moment' (HoP, *Commons*). Jenkinson was pilloried in the opposition's satire *The Rolliad* as 'the Reverend Jenky', arch-conspirator. Once again his progress seemed to have stalled. In December 1784, after Pitt's great election victory in the spring, he told Robinson: 'I do not choose to give up the game as yet entirely' (*Abergavenny MSS*, 69). Meanwhile he worked on his *Collection of Treaties between Great Britain and the Powers from 1648 to 1783*, which came out in 1785.

But a spectacular recovery was at hand. Jenkinson had continued to speak occasionally on Pitt's side in the Commons and he was too useful to be abandoned. First, in March 1784, he was made an honorary member of the Board of Trade. Next he was consulted by Pitt about the Irish commercial propositions brought forward in the summer of 1785. On 8 January 1786 the king agreed to creating him a peer in due course. Fox, in a debate on India in June 1786, made a severe and sustained attack on Jenkinson's secret power, insisting that 'it continues to spread its baleful influence on the measures of government of this nation' (Cobbett, *Parl. hist.*, 26, 1786, 81), but few seriously believed that Jenkinson manipulated Pitt. On 21 August

1786 he was made Baron Hawkesbury—the name of one of his Gloucestershire estates: two days later he became the first president of the new Board of Trade and the following month he was appointed chancellor of the duchy of Lancaster. He held the posts for seventeen and eighteen years respectively. In 1789 he inherited the Jenkinson baronetcy from his cousin and in 1791 was brought into the cabinet.

Baron Hawkesbury and the earl of Liverpool Until Hawkesbury's later years, when he was sorely crippled by rheumatoid arthritis, he was one of the workhorses of the administration. He defended Eden's commercial treaty with France in 1787, though, having begun his career before Smith's *The Wealth of Nations* appeared in 1776, his approach to trade remained mercantilist and he was less taken with free-trade notions than Pitt. He was particularly concerned with the negotiation of Jay's treaty with the USA in 1794. In 1795 he was promised an earldom and in May 1796 became earl of Liverpool. He declined the lord privy seal in 1798. The following year when his son Lord Hawkesbury was appointed master of the Royal Mint, he wrote that 'many reforms are to be made there, in which I have been and shall be principally employed' (*Later Correspondence of George III*, 3.192, n. 3). By this time he was 'old Liverpool', and in 1800 he wrote that 'I am so very ill with the rheumatism ... that I cannot walk at all except on plain ground and have had no rest for some nights' (ibid., 3.450, n. 3). His last reported intervention in debate was in May 1800 in support of the union with Ireland. In 1801 his son, the future prime minister, joined him in the cabinet as foreign secretary, though Liverpool's attendance was by now spasmodic. In April 1801 the king wrote charmingly to his new foreign secretary: 'I wish to know how *my friend* the Earl of Liverpool continues, and wish he may be acquainted how perfectly I am satisfied with his eldest son's tallents, assiduity and good temper' (ibid., 3.519). Liverpool gave up the chancellorship in November 1803 and the Board of Trade in May 1804. His *Treatise on the Coins of the Realm* was published in 1805. In an offer to resign the chancellorship in 1803 he had written of 'this last act of my political life' that he had been 'solely and separately attached to his Majesty not only from duty but from affectionate inclination (if I may venture to use such an expression), during a period of almost fifty years' (ibid., 125, n. 3). Although he was often caricatured and satirized as leader of the 'King's friends', few historians now believe that any organized group existed or that their behaviour was unconstitutional. He has been described as foreshadowing a modern civil servant, unattached to party, but there was much in Liverpool of his tory ancestry, a sense of personal loyalty to the monarch, and he was a man of the past as well as of the future.

Liverpool's appearance encouraged many of the prejudices against him. Lank and lean, blinking nervously with eyes cast down, wringing his hands, he was the very image of a plotter. But Mrs Piozzi, though admitting that he was 'eminently ugly', found him 'a very particularly agreeable man, unaffectedly good-humoured, and pleasant in his voice and manner' (*Memoirs of ... Wraxall*, 1.418). Liverpool

died at his London home, 26 Hertford Street, Mayfair, on 17 December 1808 and was buried at Hawkesbury, Gloucestershire, on 30 December. JOHN CANNON

Sources *The Jenkinson papers, 1760–1766*, ed. N. S. Jucker (1949) · *The correspondence of King George the Third from 1760 to December 1783*, ed. J. Fortescue, 6 vols. (1927–8) · *The manuscripts of the marquess of Abergavenny*, Lord Braye, G. F. Luttrell, HMC, 15 (1887) · J. Brooke, 'Jenkinson, Charles', HoP, *Commons* · *The Grenville papers: being the correspondence of Richard Grenville ... and ... George Grenville*, ed. W. J. Smith, 4 vols. (1852–3) · Cobbett, *Parl. hist.*, 24.219; 26.81 · *Parliamentary papers of John Robinson, 1774–1784*, ed. W. T. Laprade, CS, 3rd ser., 33 (1922) · *Additional Grenville papers, 1763–1765*, ed. J. R. G. Tomlinson (1962) · *The Croker papers: the correspondence and diaries of ... John Wilson Croker*, ed. L. J. Jennings, 3 vols. (1884) · *The historical and the posthumous memoirs of Sir Nathaniel William Wraxall, 1772–1784*, ed. H. B. Wheatley, 5 vols. (1884) · B. Bonsall, *Sir James Lowther and Cumberland and Westmorland elections, 1754–75* (1960) · E. W. Harcourt, ed., *The Harcourt papers*, 14 vols. (privately printed, London, [1880–1905]) · L. B. Namier, *The structure of politics at the accession of George III*, 2 vols. (1929) · R. G. Robson, *The Oxfordshire election of 1754* (1949) · *The later correspondence of George III*, ed. A. Aspinall, 5 vols. (1962–70) · W. R. Ward, *Georgian Oxford: university politics in the eighteenth century* (1958) · *Hist. U. Oxf. 5: 18th-cent. Oxf.* · *The correspondence of Edmund Burke*, ed. T. W. Copeland and others, 10 vols. (1958–78) · parish register, Winchester, St Thomas's, 16 May 1729 [baptism]
Archives BL, corresp. and papers, Add. MSS 38190–38475, 38489, 38564–38578, 38580, 59772, 61818; loan 72 · Duke U., Perkins L., corresp. and papers | Birm. CA, letters to the Boulton family · BL, corresp. with Lord Auckland, Add. MSS 34412–34457 · BL, corresp. with Sir Joseph Banks · BL, letters to Lord Grenville, Add. MS 58935 · BL, corresp. with George Grenville, Add. MS 57809 · BL, letters to duke of Leeds, Add. MSS 28061–28067 · CKS, corresp. with duke of Dorset · CKS, letters to William Pitt · Hunt. L., letters to Lord Percy · N. Yorks. CRO, letters to Lord Bolton · NA Scot., corresp. with Charles Erskine · PRO, corresp. with Sir Henry Clinton, PRO30/55 · PRO, letters to William Pitt, PRO30/8 · Rothamsted Experimental Station Library, corresp. with Sir Joseph Banks · Sheff. Arch., corresp. with Edmund Burke · Yale U., Farmington, Lewis Walpole Library, letters to Edward Weston
Likenesses G. Romney, oils, 1786–8, NPG [*see illus.*] · J. Murphy, mezzotint, 1788 (after G. Romney), BM, NPG · H. Edridge, drawing, 1802; formerly in the possession of S. Foljambe, 1891 · J. Flaxman, Wedgwood medallion, Wedgwood museum, Barlaston, Staffordshire · line engraving, BM, NPG; repro. in *European Magazine* (1785) · oils (after G. Romney, *c.*1786–1788), University College, Oxford

Jenkinson, Charles (1887–1949), housing reformer and Church of England clergyman, was born on 25 June 1887 at 93 Sussex Street, Poplar, London, one of the eight children of Charles Jenkinson, a stonemason, and his wife, Mary Ann Elizabeth, *née* Evans. Of west country stock, he spent his childhood and youth in the East End of London, where his father, working spasmodically as a docker, struggled to support his large family. Indeed because of domestic overcrowding, Charles was brought up by a grandmother and bachelor uncle at 78 Sussex Street, Poplar. He received an elementary education at Tarrance Street council school, where he gained a reputation as a studious boy with an amazing memory for facts. He left at fourteen to begin a career in bookkeeping to help with the family budget.

As a chorister and later music librarian Jenkinson regularly attended St Stephen's Church, Poplar, and later went to help as a Sunday school teacher at a mission hall in a depressed neighbourhood in the parish of St James-the-

Less, Bethnal Green. There he led a successful agitation for the suppression of pew rents, and championed the cause of the Church Socialist League, helping to organize a week's mission to promote its aims at which Ramsay Mac-Donald and Conrad Noel were guest speakers; he joined the Independent Labour Party in 1908. He became increasingly disillusioned by contemporary business ethics and the prospect of a career in commerce, and when Noel became vicar of Thaxted in 1909 Jenkinson joined him as his lay secretary. He also championed farm workers in their campaign to improve their living conditions, becoming secretary of the North-West Essex Federation of the National Agricultural Labourers' and Rural Workers' Union, and served as an election agent supporting the Revd Edward George Maxted's candidature for the Essex county council.

On the eve of the First World War, 28 July 1914, Jenkinson married Emily Cecilia Caton (b. 1882/3?) of Thaxted, the daughter of Waller Caton, a labourer. Their son was born in 1915. During the war Jenkinson, a pacifist, joined the Royal Army Medical Corps, gaining a reputation as a first-class medical orderly and winning the respect of all ranks, to whom he was affectionately known as Jenks. However, he suffered arrest with other conscientious objectors for resisting peremptory transfer to the infantry by over-zealous army officials, but was later released and his reputation restored after a public campaign had highlighted the injustice of their treatment.

During his war service Jenkinson gained a working knowledge of Latin and Greek through private study, and immediately after his demobilization from the army in April 1919 he began studying for a law degree at Fitzwilliam Hall, Cambridge, 'in order that his wits might be sharpened', he wryly observed to a friend, 'to help him to wage a more successful battle against the devil in man' (Hammerton, 31) and as preparation for subsequent ministerial training; he graduated in 1921. His eclectic religious views derived from an early acquaintance with an earnest evangelicalism, which emphasized the importance of religious experience, and an attraction to Christian socialism and Catholic modernism, which recognized the primacy of social justice and the richness and beauty of the Catholic heritage of worship. His opinions defied ecclesiastical labelling and were already well developed when in 1921 he entered Ripon Hall, Oxford, a theological college, where he defended the modernist principal, Henry Dewsbury Alves Major, against allegations of heresy relating to the doctrine of the resurrection. Jenkinson had been strongly influenced by the Christian socialist ideas of F. D. Maurice and the ecclesiological views of Percy Dearmer, and subsequently also developed a passionate support for the ordination of women and Anglican and Free Church reunion. He also sought to minimize distinctions between the clergy and the laity, even shunning the use of the clerical collar, but he was fond of wearing cassock and gown with Canterbury cap and later would occasionally rush away from Sunday evening worship without removing his cassock to address political meetings.

After ordination and a curacy at Barking, Jenkinson requested appointment to 'the hardest parish in the country' (Hammerton, 61) and was appointed vicar of St John and St Barnabas, Holbeck, in 1927, the oldest suburb in Leeds and at the time one of its worst slums. In many ways Leeds had been dilatory in its housing reform: the council had been reluctant to take advantage of the subsidies available for council house building in the 1920s and slow to react to the Greenwood Housing Act of 1930, even failing to produce the requisite housing survey and five-year plan for slum clearance and rehousing within the specified period. Jenkinson, encouraged by a growing concern within the Church of England about the plight of slum-dwellers, gained election from the North Holbeck ward to Leeds city council in November 1930 and campaigned vigorously for housing reform in his pamphlet *Sentimentality or Common Sense?*, which received the support of local clergy of the Leeds ruri-decanal chapter in June 1931. A special resolution tabled by Jenkinson to appoint a subcommittee to enquire into housing policy was adopted by the Conservative-controlled Leeds city council. Jenkinson and two other Labour councillors, however, considered the resulting report inadequate and issued in 1933 their minority report, *Housing Policy in the City of Leeds*, a closely argued, ninety-page printed document with an impressive array of statistics, which proposed that slum dwellings be cleared at an annual rate of 3000 until 1948, that a housing committee be established, and that a housing director be appointed. Its proposals gained wide circulation as a Labour Party twopenny booklet *Decent Houses for All*, and provided the blueprint for the brilliant housing programme of the Labour-controlled council from 1933 to 1936. Under the energetic leadership of Jenkinson, as first chairman of the new housing committee, the council succeeded in meeting its ambitious target of rehousing some 6000 slum dwellers in two years.

The most contentious and innovative aspect of the programme was a differential rent scheme which proved enormously beneficial to poorer tenants and helped to ensure that ultimately 85 per cent of slum-dwelling families were rehoused on new green-field estates or in the new Quarry Hill flats, the most renowned city-owned working-class housing development in the country, comprising 938 flats of varying sizes, occupying a 26 acre site close to the city centre. Jenkinson was hailed by his supporters as 'Good old Jenky, t' best booger i' Leeds' (*Leeds Weekly Citizen*, 26 July 1935) and Leeds soon became 'the Mecca of all housing reformers' (Hammerton, 84). However, he encountered bitter opposition from some quarters, and the Conservatives accused Labour of 'the Red Ruin of the City' and regained control of the council in November 1935, Jenkinson himself losing his seat in 1936.

Jenkinson welcomed the respite from politics to supervise the historic move of his own congregation from Holbeck to a new estate at Belle Isle. An essentially practical man, he was eager to don a boiler suit to help to decorate his new church and equip its congregation for mission. A tall, bespectacled figure with a ruddy complexion and a steadfast and composed look in his penetrating eyes, he exhibited a Spartan lifestyle, wearing for many years an old overcoat purchased for a shilling in a church jumble sale. His most cherished possessions were his books and his bicycle, and he was most characteristically remembered, soft-collared and flannel-trousered, hurtling through the streets of Leeds, with his coat-tails flapping in the wind. Neither Cambridge nor Oxford, nor indeed Yorkshire, made the slightest impression on his native Cockney accent and his speech was characterized by its high-pitched rapid delivery. A doughty debater, he displayed immense physical and mental energy, his natural modesty giving way in later years to a greater assertiveness, an intolerance of opposition, and an occasional brusqueness. His wife had already undergone the hardship of supporting him through university, theological college, and an East End curacy, and her devoted companionship was crucial in sustaining Jenkinson in his remarkable ministry.

During his seven years' absence from Leeds city council, Jenkinson served from 1941 on a Labour Party subcommittee set up to consider post-war housing and town planning. In 1943 he returned to the council and in 1947 became leader of the Labour group, chairman of the finance and parliamentary committee, and an alderman, assuming responsibility for implementing the city's post-war housing policy. He received national recognition for his outstanding contribution to housing development in his appointment by the president of the Board of Trade as a member of an advisory committee to produce specifications for utility furniture in 1942, as a member of the Central Housing Advisory Committee in 1947, and as chairman of the Stevenage New Town Development Corporation in September 1948. Exploratory surgery in May 1949 revealed inoperable cancer, and he died in Leeds General Infirmary on 3 August 1949, survived by his wife and son. He was cremated at Lawnswood crematorium, Leeds, on 6 August.

Effusive tributes appeared in the *Manchester Guardian* and *The Times*, which acknowledged him as 'one of the most forceful advocates of slum clearance' of his day (*The Times*, 4 August, 1949). At a memorial service at Leeds parish church the vicar of Leeds recognized the ideal of compassionate Christian service which lay at the heart of Jenkinson's achievement. His slum clearance and rehousing initiatives which transformed Leeds between 1933 and 1939 from a notorious centre of inferior back-to-back housing into a city with an internationally acclaimed, innovative housing authority constituted a remarkable achievement for an Anglican priest who continued to engage in his parish ministry, demonstrating the public role a strong clergyman could still play within the local community in Britain in the 1930s.

JOHN A. HARGREAVES

Sources H. J. Hammerton, *This turbulent priest: the story of Charles Jenkinson, parish priest and housing reformer* (1952) · A. Ravetz, *Model estate: planned housing at Quarry Hill, Leeds* (1974) · R. Lloyd, *The Church of England, 1900–65* (1966) · *The Times* (4 Aug 1949) · *Manchester Guardian* (4 Aug 1949) · *Yorkshire Evening News* (3 Aug 1949) · *Yorkshire Post* (4 Aug 1949) · A. Hastings, *A history of English Christianity, 1920–1985* (1987) · D. Fraser, ed., *A history of modern Leeds* (1980) · J. Reynolds and K. Laybourn, *Labour heartland: a history of the labour party in West Yorkshire during the inter-war years, 1918–39* (1987) · b. cert. · m. cert. · d. cert.
Archives Local History Library, Leeds, press cuttings file · W. Yorks. AS, Leeds, city of Leeds labour party minutes
Likenesses T. Johnston, cartoon, repro. in Hammerton, *This turbulent priest*, facing p. 80 · photographs, repro. in Hammerton, *This turbulent priest*
Wealth at death £957 8s. 3d.: administration, 6 Jan 1950, *CGPLA Eng. & Wales*

Jenkinson, Charles Cecil Cope, third earl of Liverpool (1784–1851), politician, born on 29 May 1784, was the second son of Charles *Jenkinson, first earl of Liverpool (1729–1808), and his second wife, Catherine Cope, *née* Bisshopp (1744–1827), the widow of Sir Charles Cope. He went to sea before he was ten years old, and served in the navy in 1794–7 and again in 1801, but having left the service matriculated at Christ Church, Oxford, on 23 April 1801. He did not take a degree, but became a précis writer at the Foreign Office. In 1804 he was briefly secretary to his half-brother Robert Banks *Jenkinson (when home secretary) and was then, in 1804–7, attaché at Vienna; he served as a volunteer in the Austrian army at Austerlitz. On inheriting the Pitchford estate of his cousin Adam Ottley in Shropshire, he decided to enter parliament. The influence of his half-brother—then warden of the Cinque Ports—secured his election in 1807 for Sandwich. In 1812 he was elected for Bridgnorth, and he sat for East Grinstead from 1818 to December 1828, a seat where his half-sister, the duchess of Dorset, was influential (HoP, *Commons*). On 10 October 1807 he was appointed parliamentary under-secretary for the Home department, and in 1809–10 he was under-secretary of state for war and the colonies. He was a strong opponent of Catholic emancipation (though he voted for it in 1829). He supported his half-brother's administration but was not a prominent or important politician.

Jenkinson married, on 19 July 1810, Julia Evelyn Medley, only child and heir of Sir George Shuckburgh Evelyn and his second wife, Julia Annabella. She died, aged twenty-three, in 1814 having borne Jenkinson three daughters. One of these, Catherine, was a lady-in-waiting to the duchess of Kent, mother of Princess (later Queen) Victoria, who used to stay quite frequently at Buxted Park, Sussex, and at Pitchford.

On 4 December 1828, on the death of his half-brother, Jenkinson succeeded as third earl of Liverpool. He was nominated lord steward of the household in Sir Robert Peel's administration on 3 September 1841, and sworn of the privy council. The same year (on 15 June) he was created DCL by the University of Oxford. He voted for corn-law repeal in 1846 just before he resigned his office owing to ill health. He died suddenly of heart disease on 3 October 1851 at Buxted Park and was buried there on the 10th. His baronetcy passed on his death to a cousin, Sir Charles Jenkinson. The earldom, which became extinct, was revived in 1905.

W. A. J. ARCHBOLD, rev. H. C. G. MATTHEW

Sources *The Times* (6 Oct 1851) · *The Times* (7 Oct 1851) · *GM*, 2nd ser., 2 (1852), 538 · GEC, *Peerage* · HoP, *Commons*
Archives BL, corresp. and papers; corresp., logbook, and papers, Add. MSS 38190, 38195–38196, 38303, 38372, 38381, 38475, 38477, 38479, 38576 · NL Wales, diary, letter-books, corresp., and papers | BL, corresp. with Sir Robert Peel, Add. MSS 40227–40582 · NA Scot., letters to Sir Charles Augustus Murray · NL Wales, letters to Louisa Lloyd
Likenesses Ross, miniature, priv. coll. · portrait, priv. coll.; formerly at Buxted Park in nineteenth century

Jenkinson, Francis John Henry (1853–1923), librarian and bibliographer, born at Forres, Morayshire, on 20 August 1853, was the elder son of John Henry Jenkinson (1823–1914), younger brother of Sir George Samuel Jenkinson, eleventh baronet, of Hawkesbury, Gloucestershire, and of his wife, Alice Henrietta (*d.* 1859), daughter of Sir William Gordon Gordon-Cumming, second baronet, of Altyre and Gordonstoun, Morayshire, and sister of Roualeyn George Gordon-Cumming.

Jenkinson grew up in Reading, and after elementary education at Woodcote, near Henley-on-Thames, entered Marlborough College under G. G. Bradley in 1865. In 1872 he went up to Trinity College, Cambridge, was elected a scholar, and in 1876 graduated in the first class of the classical tripos. In 1878 he was elected a fellow, and from 1881 to 1889 he was a college lecturer in classics. Never robust, as an undergraduate he developed his interests in archaeology and natural history, especially entomology. He was also introduced to Henry Bradshaw, who encouraged him to study early printing and whose papers he edited (1889). Jenkinson became Bradshaw's most apt and faithful pupil, basing both his bibliographical work and his eventual career on his master's example. When Bradshaw died suddenly in 1886, many assumed that Jenkinson would succeed him as university librarian; instead he gave his support to William Robertson Smith, whose subsequent election to the chair of Arabic again left the librarianship vacant.

Jenkinson was elected university librarian in 1889. Although in retrospect many considered his term of office as one of consolidation, in fact he oversaw much change. In this he was ably helped by H. G. Aldis, bibliographer of Scottish books and (in 1899) the first to be appointed to a new post of secretary. A proposal that the library should join with the British Museum and the Bodleian Library to buy the manuscripts of Sir Thomas *Phillipps proved abortive. But the gift by Lord Morley in 1902 of most of Lord Acton's library brought the largest single collection ever received in Cambridge; Jenkinson took a personal interest in sorting the books and trying to make good imperfect sets, and, as part of the extra staff engaged to catalogue so large a collection, appointed the first woman to the library. In 1898, the gift of most of the contents of the Cairo genizah brought over 140,000 fragments dating mainly from the tenth to the thirteenth centuries: special provision had to be made for their investigation, principally by Solomon Schechter. In efforts to find new space the Woodwardian museum of geology was converted into bookstacks; and the university embroiled itself in two separate campaigns to build in the library's eastern court.

Francis John Henry Jenkinson (1853–1923), by John Singer Sargent, 1915

To have done so would have brought only very temporary relief, and though Jenkinson was despondent at losing opportunities for space he took little public part in the debates. Some relief was obtained by the reallocation of adjacent offices, and by the decision (unwelcome to Jenkinson) in 1905 to remove most of the law books to the new specialist library established under the will of Rebecca Flower Squire (*d.* 1898). By 1921 he recognized that the university library would have to move to an entirely new location, and by his death the university was looking towards the site on which Scott's new building was opened in 1934.

Jenkinson's contemporaries spoke of him as a saint. None questioned his benevolent temper, and scholars throughout Europe repeatedly acknowledged his generosity and skills. Doubts of his energies were dispelled by his determined and successful orchestration of the defence of the right of Cambridge and Oxford to copies of new publications, when proposed legislation in 1910–11 threatened their interests. From 1915 Jenkinson threw his energy into collecting the literature, and particularly the ephemera, of the war, on a worldwide basis; he thereby established an archive which began to be properly appreciated only many years after his death.

Jenkinson's edition (1908) of the seventh-century Hiberno-Latin poem *Hisperica famina* was based on work begun by Bradshaw. As a bibliographer, Jenkinson concentrated on fifteenth-century printing and on early printing in Cambridge, developing many of his ideas in correspondence and conversation with Edward Gordon Duff and Robert Proctor. His single Sandars lecture (1908, published in *The Library* in 1926) consisted of a meticulous examination of the early printing of Ulrich Zell, in Cologne. Under his aegis, a catalogue of the library's early English printed books was compiled by Charles Sayle and published in 1900–07; but Jenkinson himself made little progress with cataloguing the library's incunabula.

Jenkinson was a passionate listener to music. Tall, delicately featured, and with a sweep of hair that he hated to get wet, he made a striking subject for J. S. Sargent's portrait of 1915. In 1902 he received the honorary degree of DLitt from Oxford. He was married twice: first, on 6 July 1887, to Marian Wetton (d. 1888), fifth daughter of Champion Wetton of Joldwynds, near Gomshall, Surrey, and sister-in-law of C. V. Stanford; and second, on 2 April 1902, at Crowborough to Margaret Stewart (1859–1933), daughter of Ludovick Charles Stewart. He had no children. He died on 21 September 1923 at a nursing home, The Nook, Hampstead, following an operation, and was buried at Trumpington.   DAVID MCKITTERICK

Sources H. F. Stewart, *Francis Jenkinson: a memoir* (1926) · 'A list of the incunabula collected by George Dunn', *Transactions of the Bibliographical Society: Supplement*, 3 (1923) · H. Scott, 'Francis Jenkinson', *Nature*, 112 (1923), 516 · J. C. T. Oates, *A catalogue of the fifteenth-century printed books in the University Library, Cambridge* (1954) · S. C. Reif, 'Jenkinson and Schechter at Cambridge: an expanded and updated assessment', *Jewish Historical Studies*, 32 (1990–92), 279–316 · Venn, *Alum. Cant.* · private information (1995) · *CGPLA Eng. & Wales* (1923)
Archives CUL, corresp., diaries, travel journals and papers · U. Cam., Museum of Zoology, corresp. and notebooks | CUL, corresp., incl. letters to H. F. Stewart; letters to E. G. Duff · NRA, priv. coll., letters to Sir Norman Moore · Royal Entomological Society of London, letters to C. J. Wainwright
Likenesses J. S. Sargent, oils, 1915, CUL [*see illus.*]
Wealth at death £16,593 18s. 11d.: probate, 30 Nov 1923, *CGPLA Eng. & Wales*

Jenkinson, Sir (Charles) Hilary (1882–1961), archivist, was born at Streatham, London, on 1 November 1882, the youngest of the six children of William Wilberforce Jenkinson, land agent, and his wife, Alice Leigh Bedale. He was a nephew of the librarian F. J. H. Jenkinson. He was educated at Dulwich College (1895–1901) and at Pembroke College, Cambridge, where he was a scholar and graduated with first-class honours in classics (1904). He entered the Public Record Office at the beginning of 1906, and after a formative period of training under C. G. Crump he worked chiefly on the arrangement and classification of records of the medieval exchequer. In 1912 he was put in charge of the literary search room with a general instruction to reorganize its services in the light of the criticisms made in the first report of the royal commission on public records (1910–19). His work there and in the reorganization after 1922 of the repairing department and of the repository to which he moved from the search room in 1929 probably constitutes his most valuable contribution to the office and its users. He was appointed secretary and principal assistant keeper in 1938, and was deputy keeper from 1947 until his retirement in 1954. During these years plans were made for the wartime dispersal of a great part of the records to temporary accommodation in the country and for their safe return afterwards, for the acquisition of buildings at Ashridge in Hertfordshire to supplement the storage at headquarters, and for the establishment of the intermediate repository at Hayes in Middlesex to meet the needs of departments in housing non-current records and preparing them for transfer to the Public Record Office. A photographic service was brought into being and new forms of publication were planned with the co-operation of a consultative committee of historians, but Jenkinson was unable to play the part he would have chosen in the reorganization of the office which followed the publication, shortly after his retirement, of the report of the Grigg committee on departmental records (1954).

On 11 August 1910 Jenkinson married Alice Violet (d. 1960), daughter of Andrew Knox Rickards. There were no children. His wife made many contributions to the Victoria county history of Bedfordshire, her own county. In 1915 Jenkinson was commissioned in the Royal Garrison Artillery, and he served in France and Belgium from 1916 to 1918. He was then employed as GSO3 at the War Office until he was demobilized in 1920. During part of the Second World War he was lent to the War Office to advise on the protection of archives in occupied enemy territory, and served in Italy and Germany.

Jenkinson's extra-official interests were directly related to his work. Within a few years of the start of his official career he had become honorary secretary of the Surrey Archaeological Society and had taken a leading part in founding the Surrey Record Society, whose volumes, edited on principles laid down by him as general editor and designed to provide reliable texts of documents of local history, with introductions setting out their administrative context, have earned a high place among record publications. He also became associated with his colleague Charles Johnson in the work on medieval handwritings which was published in 1915 under the title *English Court Hand*. This was followed by various papers on post-medieval scripts culminating in his *Later Court Hands in England from the Fifteenth to the Seventeenth Century* (1927). From 1911 to 1935 he was the Maitland memorial lecturer at Cambridge, his subject being English palaeography and diplomatic from the Norman conquest to 1485, and from 1920 he was lecturer and from 1925 until 1947 reader in diplomatic and archives at King's College, London. Between 1920 and 1925 he also lectured on palaeography and archives for the new school of librarianship at University College, London. His *Manual of Archive Administration*, undertaken for the Carnegie Foundation, was published in 1922 and reissued with some revision in 1937. This pioneer work had a unique influence on the development and practice of record keeping in England, and through it and his many lectures and other writings on the topic he merited the description 'doyen of archivists' given him by a French colleague.

For some years before 1932 the need for an influential national organization committed to promoting the preservation and accessibility to students of documents in local or private custody and at risk of dispersal or destruction had exercised the minds of many interested people. After prolonged negotiations and discussions, in which Jenkinson took a prominent part, the British Records Association was formed. As joint secretary until 1947 and afterwards vice-president he directed its policy and was its chief propagandist. Among the achievements for which he and the association could fairly claim a share of the credit were the establishment of local record offices throughout the country and the inauguration of university diploma courses in archives for the training of staff. Jenkinson was himself instrumental in persuading the University of London to enlarge the school of librarianship at University College into a school of librarianship and archives, with separate diploma courses for each branch. He himself gave the inaugural lecture of the archives course with the title 'The English archivist: a new profession'. In 1943 he formulated through the British Records Association proposals for legislation to control local and private archives. For the most part they proved to be too controversial and had to be abandoned, but out of them came the establishment of the National Register of Archives which later took permanent form as a branch of the Historical Manuscripts Commission. On being appointed deputy keeper of the public records he became executive historical manuscripts commissioner and chairman of the directorate of the national register, and after his retirement as deputy keeper, the commission, register, and association retained his active interest.

Over the years Jenkinson formed friendships with archivists in many countries and had a high reputation among them. He was the British representative on the committee set up in 1948 under the auspices of UNESCO to draft proposals for an International Council on Archives, and when the new council was formed he was elected one of its vice-presidents.

In the course of his lifetime Jenkinson played a leading part in establishing in England principles which should govern the care of records, in rousing public interest in their preservation, and in providing for the professional training of their custodians, who should be, as he preferred to call them, archivists rather than amateurs with antiquarian tastes. His gift for personal relationships undoubtedly went far to promote the cause he had at heart, although his pursuit of perfection betrayed him into a doctrinaire advocacy of ideas and practices which created difficulties and brought frustration. He was generous in the help he gave to students and old pupils, and his official contacts often developed into personal friendships. He was a delightful host, a connoisseur of good food and wine, an ardent gardener, and an amateur of eighteenth-century domestic architecture and furnishing, cultivating at home the feeling for good craftsmanship and interest in its methods which displayed itself in his official publications on seals and the binding of Domesday Book.

Jenkinson was for many years a prominent fellow of the Society of Antiquaries, and he was also a fellow of the Royal Historical Society, and president of the Jewish Historical Society and the Society of Archivists. He was appointed CBE in 1943 and was knighted in 1949, and was an honorary fellow of University College, London, and an honorary LLD of Aberdeen (1949). He died on 5 March 1961 at St Thomas Home, St Thomas's Hospital, London, and was buried at Horsham, Sussex, on 10 March.

H. C. JOHNSON, rev.

Sources H. C. Johnson, biographical memoir, *Studies presented to Sir Hilary Jenkinson*, ed. J. C. Davies (1957) · R. Somerville, *Archives*, 5 (1961–2), 49–51 · *The Times* (7 March 1961) · *The Times* (11 March 1961) · T. L. Ormiston, ed., *Dulwich College register, 1619 to 1926* (1926) · R. Ellis, 'Recollections of Sir Hilary Jenkinson', *Journal of the Society of Archivists*, 4 (1970–73), 261–75 · A. E. J. Hollaender, ed., *Essays in memory of Sir Hilary Jenkinson* (1962) · J. D. Cantwell, *The Public Record Office, 1838–1958* (1991) · R. Ellis, 'Jenkinson, Sir Hilary', *ALA world encyclopedia of library and information services*, ed. R. Wedgeworth (1980) · *CGPLA Eng. & Wales* (1961)
Archives PRO, corresp., papers and MS collection, 30/75 · UCL, corresp. and notes
Likenesses W. Stoneman, photograph, 1944, NPG · sketch, repro. in *The Times* (7 March 1961)
Wealth at death £12,886 3s. 6d.: probate, 19 April 1961, *CGPLA Eng. & Wales*

Jenkinson, John Banks (1781–1840), bishop of St David's, was born at Winchester on 2 September 1781, the second son of John Jenkinson (c.1734–1805) and his wife, Frances (d. 1811), daughter of Rear-Admiral John Barker of Guildford. John Jenkinson, the father, a brother of Charles *Jenkinson, first earl of Liverpool, was a colonel in the army, joint secretary for Ireland, and gentleman usher to Queen Charlotte. John Banks Jenkinson was educated at Winchester College, where he was elected scholar in 1793. On 22 December 1800 he matriculated from Christ Church, Oxford, graduated BA in 1804, and proceeded MA in 1807 and DD in 1817. His advancement in the church was assisted by his cousin, the second earl of Liverpool, the prime minister. He became prebendary of Worcester on 30 August 1808, rector of Leverington, Cambridgeshire, on 8 July 1812, dean of Worcester on 28 November 1817, and master of St Oswalds, Worcester, on 8 January 1818. He married, on 8 April 1813, Frances Augusta, daughter of Augustus Pechell of Berkhamsted, Hertfordshire.

On 23 July 1825 Jenkinson was elected bishop of St David's, and on 4 August 1825 was appointed canon of Durham. On 13 June 1827 he became dean of Durham, and held the deanery, then worth the huge sum of £9000 a year, with his bishopric for the remainder of his life, dividing his time between Durham and Abergwili. In the House of Lords he voted for Catholic emancipation in 1829 and for the Reform Bill in 1832, having abstained in the previous year. He was closely involved in the foundation of Durham University (1832) by the Durham chapter, who were anxious to forestall radical attacks on their great wealth, though his enthusiasm for the project waned as the costs grew. He was also visitor of St David's College, Lampeter, which opened in 1827. He died at Great Malvern on 7 July 1840, and was buried on 13 July in Worcester Cathedral. Jenkinson was a man of amiable disposition, and possessed a fine library; he maintained a school for the children of the poor at Carmarthen, which usually contained

150 scholars, and spent lavishly on improvements to his palace at Abergwili to create employment for the poor. He published a few separate sermons. He was survived by his wife, two sons, and two daughters. The eldest son, George Samuel Jenkinson, succeeded his uncle, Sir Charles, as eleventh baronet in 1855.

W. A. J. ARCHBOLD, *rev.* M. C. CURTHOYS

Sources *GM*, 2nd ser., 14 (1840), 321–2 • O. Chadwick, *The Victorian church*, 1 (1966) • E. A. Varley, *The last of the prince bishops: William Van Mildert and the high church movement of the early nineteenth century* (1992)
Archives U. Durham L., corresp. with Charles Thorp relating to University of Durham

Jenkinson, Sir Mark Webster (1880–1935), accountant, was born on 31 July 1880, at 263 Pearl Street, Ecclesall Bierlow, Yorkshire, one of seven sons of Mark Jenkinson (1856–1942), rent collector and later estate agent, and his wife, Hannah Elizabeth Mansell. Educated at Wesley College, Sheffield, he was first prizeman in the finals of the Institute of Chartered Accountants (1901) and afterwards became a fellow (1908). His early accountancy career was promoted by the Sheffield dignitary George Franklin. During this period he compiled *Book-Keeping for Retail Grocers* (1905), *Cost Accounts for Small Manufacturers* (1907), and textbooks on factory costing, auditing, and commercial organization.

The convulsion of war pitched Webster Jenkinson from prosperous provincial obscurity. In September 1915 he was recruited to the Ministry of Munitions as director of factory accounting. Later he received the status of deputy director-general and was appointed controller of the department of factory audits and costs (1917). Following the armistice he was chief liquidator of contracts at the ministry, until March 1920. Each of these posts involved high responsibilities and a heavy burden of work; he saved his country hundreds of millions of pounds. In peace time he served on departmental committees on night work in the bread baking trade (1919), on the high cost of building working-class dwellings (1921), and on army administration (1923–4). In acknowledgement of his work in reforming military accountancy, and of his assistance to the private armaments sector, he was created KBE (5 June 1926).

Jenkinson's route to eminence among European private armaments manufacturers was circuitous. In 1921 he was recruited by the industrialist Dudley Docker to become secretary of a private investment bank, the Electric and Railway Finance Corporation (Elrafin). Docker had an important interest in Vickers, the armaments combine, which had embarked on rash post-war diversifications. In June 1925 the Vickers board, confronted with financial crisis, accepted an advisory committee on reconstruction comprising Docker, his friend Reginald MacKenna, and Sir William Plender. Their report (published in December 1925 and almost wholly Jenkinson's work) recommended that Vickers's assets be written down by over £12 million, and that it dispose of many peripheral subsidiaries.

Jenkinson left Elrafin to join the Vickers board in 1926, and with the help of Sir Basil Zaharoff he succeeded Sir Vincent Caillard as financial controller in 1927. He thus became a leading proponent of the industrial rationalization movement and a new player in the great game of international armaments. The arrangement reached in 1928 between Vickers and Cammell Laird whereby their rolling-stock interests were combined in the Metropolitan-Cammell Company and their steelworks united in the English Steel Corporation was the most crucial part of Jenkinson's strategy of recovery. The sale of Metropolitan-Vickers Electrical in 1928 was also important. The merger of Vickers's shipyards and engineering factories with those of Armstrong Whitworth, to form Vickers Armstrong, in 1927, mattered less to Jenkinson. The Cammell Laird arrangement marked a high point of the industrial rationalization movement. In 1929 Jenkinson published *Some Aspects of Rationalisation*.

Both Vickers's board and its management were reformed at Jenkinson's instigation. He believed that rationalized companies should have two directorates: the 'control' board, chiefly comprising non-executive outsiders; and 'executive' boards, for the operating managers of the different divisions. Vickers became a holding company with directors in overall control; executive responsibility was devolved to three management boards (armaments and shipbuilding; finance management; and industrial management). The purity and accuracy of accounts was a passion with Jenkinson, who introduced a masterful new system of accountancy controls throughout Vickers and urged that every public company should be obliged to employ an official to explain its accounts intelligibly to shareholders.

Vickers's interwar contracts for foreign armaments were with minor powers for whom financial facilities such as payment by instalments were often more important than the technical performance of the weaponry. Jenkinson played an indispensable part in preparing and superintending the financial provisions of such sales. He also expedited the liquidation or reduction of Vickers's investments in overseas arsenals and shipyards. An optimist about the possibilities of civil aviation, particularly for goods transportation, he supported the development of Vickers Aviation after 1928. He had non-executive responsibilities in the midlands colliery and metallurgical interests of the earl of Dudley, and advised the board of Birmingham Small Arms during its crisis of 1932.

On 27 March 1930 Jenkinson testified to the committee on finance and industry chaired by Lord Macmillan. Basing his recommendations on Vickers's misfortunes since 1918, he advocated the formation of a financial trust with capital invested in gilt-edged securities to provide capital for industry and to involve financiers in industrial management; industrial banks to promote the rationalization of different industrial sectors; and a contracts' guarantee scheme to enable British manufacturers to take overseas contracts on deferred terms. In 1931 he was a member of the committee on national economy chaired by Sir George May; its exaggerated prediction of budget deficits and recommendations of cuts in social service spending precipitated the fall of the Labour government and the formation of a peace-time coalition.

Webster Jenkinson was a clear-headed, methodical man who knew what he wanted. His appearance was ordinary, except for intelligent eyes and a moustache of a type later made notorious by Hitler. He was a devout admirer of Victorian values and comforts, including Victorian cooking. Some of his more Belgravian colleagues at Vickers found his accent and attitudes rather too redolent of Sheffield; this was ungrateful, for Jenkinson gave his life for the company. After warnings that he was overworking, he died of heart disease, on 4 November 1935, at his home, Woodside, Smallfield, Surrey; he was buried on 7 November at Ecclesall church, Sheffield. Apparently unmarried, he was for many years the companion of Mrs Nina Stokes, who was his co-executor and chief beneficiary under his will dated 1924. RICHARD DAVENPORT-HINES

Sources *Financial Times* (5 Nov 1935) · *The Times* (5 Nov 1935) · CUL, Vickers MSS · R. P. T. Davenport-Hines, *Dudley Docker: the life and times of a trade warrior* (1984) · R. P. T. Davenport-Hines, 'Vickers as a multinational before 1945', *British multinationals: origins, management and performance*, ed. G. Jones (1986), 43–67 · R. P. T. Davenport-Hines, ed., *Markets and bagmen: studies in the history of marketing and British industrial performance, 1830–1939* (1986) · J. D. Scott, *Vickers: a history* (1962) · *CGPLA Eng. & Wales* (1936) · b. cert. · Burke, *Peerage* · *The Times* (6 Nov 1935)
Archives CUL, Vickers archives · PRO, Board of Trade MSS, Jenkinson memorandum on steel industry, July 1929, BT 56/2 · PRO, Ministry of Munitions MSS, Jenkinson's evidence, 20 Jan 1919, to McKinnon Wood committee on royal ordnance factories, Mun 4/6375
Likenesses photograph, *c.*1928, repro. in *DBB*
Wealth at death £10,905 15s. 10d.: probate, 22 Jan 1936, *CGPLA Eng. & Wales*

Jenkinson, Robert Banks, second earl of Liverpool (**1770–1828**), prime minister, was born on 7 June 1770, the eldest son of Charles *Jenkinson, first earl of Liverpool (1729–1808), MP, and his first wife, Amelia (1750/51–1770), daughter of William Watts, governor of Fort William and president of the council in Bengal. Jenkinson's mother died on 7 July 1770, shortly after his birth, and in 1782 his father married again. Charles Jenkinson's second wife was Catherine (1744–1827), widow of Sir Charles Cope, bt; they had two children, Charles Cecil Cope *Jenkinson, later third earl of Liverpool, and Charlotte.

Upbringing and education Jenkinson was baptized on 29 June 1770 at St Margaret's Church, Westminster. As a small motherless child he spent much time with his grandmother Amarantha Cornwall at Winchester and for a time attended a school there. His regular education began at a private school at Parson's Green, Fulham. In September 1783 he was sent to board at Charterhouse School, where his father had been a foundation scholar forty years earlier. He remained there nearly four years, his educational progress being carefully monitored by his father, who ensured that in addition to the classics and mathematics he studied the more unconventional subjects of French, history, European politics, and political economy. It is obvious that Charles Jenkinson was ambitious for his first-born son and impressed on him from an early age the expectations of his family that he would

Robert Banks Jenkinson, second earl of Liverpool (1770–1828), by Sir Thomas Lawrence, *c.*1820

have an eminent career in public life. From Charterhouse he proceeded without a break to Christ Church, Oxford, where he matriculated on 27 April 1787. Though not yet seventeen, he struck observers as having an unusually wide knowledge, particularly of European history and politics, with a touch of intellectual conceit and considerable powers of self-expression. He was also, perhaps because of his father's constant supervision and the absence of a mother's affection, emotionally immature and lacking in natural self-confidence, though conciliatory and good-natured. At Christ Church, where he was an industrious and sober student, he took part for a time in a small debating society which included George Canning and Lord Henry Spencer. Canning, of whose talents he was a warm admirer, became one of his closest companions. It was the start of a lifelong friendship. It was, however, an uneven relationship. Canning was jealous of Jenkinson's more fortunate background and found in the latter's moral seriousness and emotional sensitivity easy targets for ridicule.

In the summer of 1789 Jenkinson spent four months in Paris to perfect his French and enlarge his social experience. His French tutor described him as well informed, well behaved, and amiable, though deficient in social poise and self-confidence. Another critic, the Abbé Barthelemy, discerned beneath his simplicity and kindness a reassuring firmness of character. In July Jenkinson was an eyewitness of the storming of the Bastille; it was his first, and disagreeable, taste of revolution. He returned to

Oxford for three months to complete his terms of residence and in May 1790 was created master of arts, the usual procedure for peers' sons. In the general election the following month his father's influence secured his return in two boroughs, Appleby (a constituency under the influence of the Lowther family) and Rye (a pocket borough). The independence of the latter was preferred; but being still under age, he refrained from taking his seat and spent the following winter and early spring in an extended tour of the continent which took in the Netherlands and Italy. It is not clear exactly when he entered the Commons but as his twenty-first birthday was not reached until almost the end of the 1791 session, it is possible that he waited until the following year.

Early parliamentary career In February 1792 Jenkinson was entrusted by the prime minister with the reply to Whitbread's critical motion on the government's Russian policy and made a successful début as a Commons debater. He delivered several other speeches during the session, including one against the abolition of the slave trade, which reflected his father's strong opposition to Wilberforce's campaign. In July he went abroad again (according to French newspapers as an agent of the ministry) and sent back to his father useful reports on the state of the Austrian and Prussian armies on the French frontier. Returning home for the early meeting of parliament necessitated by the government's defence precautions, he spoke strongly against Fox's motion in December 1792 calling for peaceful negotiations with France. After war broke out he became one of the staunchest supporters of the government's military policy despite the ridicule heaped on his suggestion in a debate of April 1794 that the soundest strategy might be to strike at the heart of the enemy and march on Paris. His services were recognized by his appointment in April 1793 to the Board of Control set up by Pitt's India Act of 1784.

In the patriotic defence movement which followed the outbreak of hostilities Jenkinson was one of the first of the junior ministers to enlist in the militia. In 1794 he became a colonel in the Cinque Ports fencibles and his assiduity in his military duties led to frequent absences from the Commons. In 1796 his regiment was sent to Scotland and he was quartered for a time in Dumfries. His parliamentary attendance also suffered from his mutinous reaction when his father angrily opposed his projected marriage with Lady (Theodosia) Louisa Hervey, daughter of the earl of Bristol. After Pitt and the king had intervened on his behalf, the wedding finally took place at Wimbledon on 25 March 1795. In June 1796, when his father was created earl of Liverpool, he took the courtesy title of Lord Hawkesbury, by which he was known until his father's death in 1808. Three years later he was promoted to the mastership of the Royal Mint and membership of the Board of Trade.

Foreign secretary, 1801–1804 When Pitt unexpectedly resigned in February 1801, Hawkesbury's first instinct was to go out with him. He had supported Irish union, had apparently no strong views on Catholic emancipation,

and favoured carrying on the war, though privately critical of its conduct. Nevertheless, he was persuaded by Pitt not to retire and instead took the daunting post of foreign secretary in the depleted administration led by Addington. His three years in that office did little to enhance his reputation. The peace with France, to which the ministers were committed, was reached with the treaty of Amiens (March 1802) after long, difficult negotiations; but mutual distrust delayed its full implementation. When the government abruptly renewed hostilities in May 1803, it was without a single ally on the continent. The hard line taken with France probably owed more to the older members of the cabinet than to the foreign secretary. Nevertheless, the impression was created that Hawkesbury's conduct of diplomacy had not been a success, even though his parliamentary speeches vindicating the government's policy earned much praise. The main charges against him were slowness in transacting business and awkwardness in dealing with people, especially foreign representatives. There were many interested parties ready to exploit the criticisms. His predecessor at the Foreign Office, Lord Grenville, despite Hawkesbury's initially conciliatory overtures, had become increasingly hostile. Another enemy was Count Vorontsov, Russian ambassador and Grenville's personal friend, with whom Hawkesbury's relations seem to have been particularly difficult. Senior British diplomats disliked his youth and inexperience; and Canning's resentment at Pitt's supersession embraced Hawkesbury as well as Addington.

In the Lords, and home secretary With his parliamentary support crumbling, the prime minister asked Hawkesbury at the end of 1803 to move to the Lords to counter Grenville's bitter attacks. It was with great reluctance that Hawkesbury left the Commons, where he was generally regarded as the most effective speaker on the front bench. He was created Baron Hawkesbury. When Pitt replaced Addington he offered Hawkesbury the Home department with the leadership of the Lords, which, with some hesitation, he accepted in May 1804. Although it was politically inexpedient for Pitt to retain him at the Foreign Office, he clearly regarded Hawkesbury as an indispensable member of his new administration, not only because of his influence in the Lords but also because he had come to have a high opinion of his knowledge and judgement. In June, however, following a wounding reference by Canning in the House of Commons to his removal from the Foreign Office, Hawkesbury tendered his resignation, feeling that he had been left unsupported by the prime minister. Pitt subsequently made amends for this in parliament and privately made it clear to both men that, if forced, he would prefer to part with Canning rather than lose Hawkesbury.

Although his tenure of the Home department was clouded by the fact that it was widely regarded as a demotion, its routine business at least enabled Hawkesbury to strengthen his already good relations with the king; and he declined a proposal by Pitt to transfer to the Admiralty in 1805 after Melville's resignation. Outside his department he found a congenial role as mediator between past and present colleagues. It was he who on behalf of the cabinet started the negotiations with Addington that led to the latter's return to office early in 1805. The ministry, however, lacked a firm political basis and on Pitt's death in January 1806 the cabinet decided to resign. The king offered the premiership to Hawkesbury and, when he wisely refused, pressed on him the wardenship of the Cinque Ports previously held by Pitt. Acceptance of this lucrative sinecure exposed Hawkesbury to much public criticism.

In opposition for the first time, Hawkesbury acted with Castlereagh and others in keeping together a nucleus of Pittite politicians as a possible alternative set of ministers for the king rather than as a direct opposition to the new Grenville administration. When it abruptly resigned in 1807, Hawkesbury and the former lord chancellor, Eldon, were called in for consultation by the king. Hawkesbury's advice, as agreed among the Pittites, was for the appointment of the elderly Lord Portland as a compromise prime minister, with Perceval as leader in the Commons. In the ministry thus formed he returned to his former post as home secretary and once again acted as the chief conciliatory influence within the government. It was a function made increasingly necessary by the passivity and ill health of Lord Portland and the deepening rivalry among Canning, Castlereagh, and Perceval. When in the summer of 1809 cabinet disunity could no longer be contained, Hawkesbury ranged himself firmly with Castlereagh and Perceval against Canning. He did more perhaps than any member of the cabinet to ensure the continuation in office under Perceval of the rump of the old Portland ministry.

Lord Liverpool, and secretary for war Perceval's immediate task was to fill the two secretaryships of state left vacant by the resignations of Canning and Castlereagh. Lord Liverpool (as Hawkesbury had now become by the death of his father in December 1808) was unwilling to go back to the Foreign Office where he felt that there had been an unfair campaign against him; but Perceval insisted on his acceptance of the almost equally unattractive secretaryship for war, which had an alarming record of failure and mismanagement throughout the war, culminating in the disaster at Corunna in January 1809. Liverpool's first step on taking up his new post was to elicit from Wellington a strong enough statement of his ability to resist a French attack to persuade the cabinet to commit themselves to the maintenance of his small force in Portugal. Only the determination of the government in fact upheld the Peninsular strategy in the face of their pessimistic parliamentary supporters and a defeatist whig opposition.

With limited reserves of men and money, and a clumsy apparatus of army administration, Liverpool needed time to build up Wellington's army. But he assured its commander that he had the full confidence of the cabinet and that they would not dissipate their resources on any subsidiary strategy. Despite Wellington's initial distrust and frequent grumbling, Liverpool remained calm and conciliatory, though he had to emphasize to his impatient general the importance of not risking the actual existence of the only army in the field the country possessed. By hard departmental work the force in the peninsula was raised by January 1811 to 48,000, substantially more than the 33,000 the cabinet had agreed to in 1809. By the time Liverpool left the War Office he had dispatched some 25,000 additional troops to Portugal and annual expenditure on the Peninsular campaign had risen from a planned £3 million to £6 million in 1810 and £9 million in 1811. Liverpool felt he had made a success of his post and had no wish to leave it while the war lasted. When, during the negotiations with Castlereagh early in 1812, it transpired that the latter wanted to go back to his old office, there was no desire in the cabinet to make a change. Lord Mulgrave told Plumer Ward that 'Lord Liverpool was too good a War Secretary to be spared there' (R. Plumer Ward, *Memoirs*, 1850, 1.428).

Prime minister After the prolonged regency crisis had been overcome by the recruitment of Castlereagh and Sidmouth early in 1812, the ministry was again thrown into disarray by Perceval's assassination the following May. The cabinet proposed Liverpool as his successor with Castlereagh as leader in the Commons. But after an adverse vote in the Lower House they subsequently tendered their resignations. The prince regent, however, found it impossible to construct an alternative coalition and in the end confirmed Liverpool as prime minister on 8 June. The reasons for the cabinet's choice of Liverpool are not difficult to guess. During the previous decade he had shown himself a good colleague, an efficient administrator, and an outstanding debater. In difficult times he had remained cheerful and courageous. He had stayed in the mainstream of the Pittite party and within it had been an unselfish and unifying figure. On more than one occasion he had been ready to sacrifice personal advantage in order to keep the government going. He had been liked and trusted by George III; and by the time the prince regent assumed full powers in February 1812 he had come to regard Liverpool as more congenial than Perceval or Addington, and more trustworthy than Canning.

Many of the government's troubles in parliament had been caused by the rigid line taken by Perceval on Catholic claims and the unpopular orders in council. Liverpool's first actions as prime minister were to announce the neutrality of the ministry over the Catholic issue and to revoke the orders in council, a pacific gesture which came just too late to prevent an American declaration of war. In the cabinet he cemented the alliance with the Addington party by appointing Sidmouth to the Home Office and Vansittart as chancellor of the exchequer. In July he made a prolonged but unsuccessful attempt to bring back Canning, which broke down on the latter's insistence on having the leadership of the Commons as well as the Foreign Office. Confident it would be recognized that he had made fair offers to Canning, Liverpool then took the unusual step of calling an early general election in the hope of gaining a more favourable House of Commons. He also perhaps wished to weaken what he called the 'third party' of Canning and Wellesley which in his mind constituted a greater danger to the government than the whig opposition. His appreciation of Canning's value remained unaltered. Two years later, when the ministry's position had become unassailable, Liverpool gave him a special mission to Lisbon with a private assurance of the first cabinet vacancy, and meanwhile appointed to minor offices several of his followers, including Huskisson.

In the summer of 1814 the prominent part played by Britain in the overthrow of Napoleon was marked by the presence of the allied monarchs in London and the award of the Garter to the prime minister. At the peace negotiations which followed, Liverpool's main concern was to obtain a European settlement that would ensure the independence of the Netherlands, Spain, and Portugal and confine France inside her pre-war frontiers without damaging her national integrity. For that he was ready to return all British colonial conquests except a few of special strategic importance. Within this broad framework he gave Castlereagh a wide discretion at the Congress of Vienna. He was realistically aware, however, of the limitations of British influence on the settlement in eastern Europe and made it his task to emphasize to the foreign secretary the restrictions on British policy created by parliament, public opinion, and lack of financial resources. Nevertheless, he gave prompt approval for Castlereagh's bold initiative in making the defensive alliance with Austria and France in January 1815, partly out of loyalty to his distant colleague, partly because he did not think it would actually lead to war.

Post-war policies The coming of peace ended the patriotic enthusiasm which had simplified the task of parliamentary management. When the powerful agricultural lobby in parliament demanded protection, Liverpool yielded to political necessity. Under governmental supervision the notorious corn law of 1815 was passed prohibiting the import of foreign wheat until the domestic price reached 80s. a quarter. Liverpool, in principle a free-trader, would have preferred a sliding scale but he accepted the bill as a temporary measure to ease the transition to peacetime conditions. His chief economic problem was finance. Interest on the national debt, grossly swollen by the enormous expenditure of the final war years, together with continuing liabilities such as war pensions, absorbed the greater part of normal revenue. The refusal of the Commons in 1816 to continue the wartime income tax left ministers with no immediate alternative but to go on with the ruinous system of borrowing to meet necessary annual expenditure.

The social and political disturbances in the country in 1816 and 1817 led the home secretary to press for instant legislation. Liverpool preferred to collect evidence and obtain the backing of the country gentry. The reports of the secret committees he obtained in 1817 pointed to the existence of an organized network of disaffected political societies, especially in the manufacturing areas. Though in retrospect the evidence before the committees can be seen to have been biased and exaggerated, it convinced both the cabinet and parliament. Liverpool told Peel that the disaffection in the country seemed even worse than in

1794. The resulting legislation included a temporary suspension of habeas corpus in cases of alleged treason; but this summary power of arrest and detention (which Liverpool agreed in the Lords was 'a most odious one') was sparingly used. Other legislation that session showed that the government was not indifferent to the social distress which made the political agitation appear so dangerous.

In August 1819 the handling by local magistrates of the Peterloo meeting at Manchester was privately admitted by the prime minister to have been imprudent; but he thought they had acted in good faith and had to be supported. He was opposed, however, to any further action until in the autumn the whig leaders tried to make political capital out of the incident in a series of county protest meetings. It was this which persuaded him to dismiss Earl Fitzwilliam, lord lieutenant of Yorkshire, who had helped to organize the protest in his county, and to call an early meeting of parliament. Legislation was now unavoidable but Liverpool was less concerned with Hunt and the other radical agitators, who were left to the ordinary processes of the law, than with the growth of seditious journals, the dilatoriness of legal machinery, and the frightening novelty of huge open-air political meetings. The legislation laid before parliament, notorious to posterity as the Six Acts, was designed to deal with these problems. But it was kept studiously moderate and both the home secretary and many government supporters were critical of its leniency. Liverpool, however, was anxious not to encroach more than was necessary on the traditional liberty of the subject. Apart from the temporary powers (which were not renewed when they expired) to search for arms and prohibit mass meetings, he could claim with some justice that there was nothing in the Six Acts that violated the fundamental principles of the constitution.

The reputation of the government sank even lower with the queen's affair in 1820. The initial refusal of the cabinet to accede to George IV's wish, on becoming king, for a divorce, nearly led to the dismissal of the prime minister. Only when compromise negotiations with Caroline failed, and she made a public arrival in London, did Liverpool reluctantly introduce a bill to deprive her of her titles and annul the marriage. The sensational hearing in the Lords in the autumn was conducted by him with dignity and restraint; but weakening parliamentary support forced him to drop first the divorce clause and finally the whole bill. It was the worst point in his long premiership. The king took soundings with prominent whigs and the end of the ministry was confidently expected. Even so, though emotionally harassed, Liverpool stood firm on his refusal to provide Caroline with a royal palace or reinsert her name in the liturgy. He let it be known that this was a moral issue on which he was prepared to leave office and the following session the House of Commons rallied to his support.

Though it was delayed by the events of 1820 Liverpool had already started his government on the road to recovery. He had long felt that their concessions to the endless demands for retrenchment and lower taxation were harming the machinery of the state and that the only remedy for their financial straits lay in ending inflation and returning to balanced budgeting. By 1818 he had probably decided in favour of restoring the gold standard, though his colleagues were divided and the timing was difficult. An unexpected change of mind by the Bank of England in favour of an inquiry accelerated the decision. The currency committees he secured in 1819 recommended a return to cash payments by 1823—a target actually reached in 1821. His other policy objective proved more difficult. The cabinet, stiffened by Liverpool's insistence that they must at last stand and fight, agreed in 1819 to use the sinking fund, and raise an additional £3 million in new taxes, to create a budget surplus which they hoped would continue for the next three years. Fortified by the recommendation of the ministerial-dominated committee of finance that, in principle, government revenue should exceed expenditure by a clear annual surplus of £5 million, the cabinet in the end saw its innovatory budget of 1819 accepted by the Commons. It was the turning point in the post-war history of the ministry and Liverpool had been ready to stake its existence on the issue. 'If we cannot carry what has been proposed,' he told the apprehensive lord chancellor, 'it is far, far better for the country that we should cease to be the Government' (H. Twiss, *Life of Lord Chancellor Eldon*, 1844, 2.39).

Ministerial changes, 1822 The steady recovery of authority by the ministry after 1821 enabled Liverpool to make a number of ministerial changes that he had long been contemplating. His primary object was to strengthen the front bench in the Commons and conciliate the Grenville faction, the only remaining element of the old Pittite following which still remained aloof. Peel replaced the ageing Lord Sidmouth at the Home Office and Grenville, though himself too old for office, was gratified by a dukedom for Lord Buckingham, the Irish lord lieutenancy for Lord Wellesley, a cabinet seat for Wynn, and minor appointments for other members of the group. The future of Canning, who had earned royal displeasure by resigning in protest over the queen's divorce bill, was settled by his appointment as governor-general of India. Castlereagh's suicide in August 1822, however, reopened the issue in circumstances of even greater acrimony. Only after a severe battle of wills with the king was Liverpool able to secure Canning's succession to Castlereagh's 'whole inheritance'—the Foreign Office and the leadership of the Commons. Later in the year the altered balance of power in the administration was reflected in the promotion of two junior Canningite ministers, Robinson to the chancellorship of the exchequer and Huskisson to the presidency of the Board of Trade. Although these piecemeal and partly fortuitous changes enhanced the public standing of the government, they materially weakened the unity of the cabinet which had been its principal source of strength.

Catholic emancipation and cabinet conflict One source of disunion was Catholic emancipation. In 1805, in his first important statement of his views on the subject, Liverpool had argued that the special relationship of the monarch with the Church of England, and the refusal of Roman Catholics to take the oath of supremacy, justified their exclusion from political power. The decision of 1812 to remove the issue from collective cabinet policy, followed in 1813 by the defeat of Grattan's Roman Catholic Relief Bill, brought a period of relative calm. As an individual member of the House of Lords Liverpool supported marginal concessions such as the admittance of English Roman Catholics to the higher ranks of the armed forces, the magistracy, and the parliamentary franchise; but he remained opposed to their participation in parliament itself. In the 1820s pressure from the liberal wing of the Commons and the rise of the Catholic Association in Ireland revived the controversy. By the date of Sir Francis Burdett's Catholic Relief Bill in 1825 Liverpool was probably already anticipating the ultimate victory of the emancipation party, though he was determined to take no responsibility for the measure. The success of the bill in the Commons in April, followed by Peel's tender of resignation, finally persuaded Liverpool that it was time to retire. The speech he made against the bill in the Lords in May, though couched in unusually strong terms, he regarded as a dying effort. When Canning made a formal proposal that the cabinet should take up the issue, Liverpool was convinced that his administration had come to its end. It was in fact that fearful prospect which induced the cabinet to continue with the old principle of neutrality. This in turn deprived both Liverpool and Peel of any ground for resignation.

Agriculture and the corn laws This conflict within the cabinet, largely hidden from the public, was in ironic contrast to the support the ministry now enjoyed in the country and the continued success of its economic policies. The government-inspired committee on foreign trade in 1820 and 1821 reaffirmed the principles of free trade which Liverpool had outlined to the Lords in a wide-ranging speech of May 1820. The budgets of 1824 and 1825 constituted the first free-trade budgets of the century, encouraging home consumption and lowering the cost of raw materials. Liverpool himself was in favour of an even more drastic reduction in indirect taxation and an actual increase in direct taxation; but although it was politically inexpedient to put forward such revolutionary ideas, the government pursued a policy of using its budget surpluses to finance a programme of simplifying and lowering tariffs rather than of cutting direct taxes still further, as Canning and some government supporters would have liked.

Agriculture remained a problem because good harvests between 1819 and 1822 had brought down prices and evoked a cry for greater protection. Though politically significant, because of the powerful landed interest in parliament, the issue remained for Liverpool one of economic principle. In an important speech of February 1822 he denied that agricultural distress was caused by high taxation, emphasized the interdependence of agriculture, commerce, and manufacture, and argued that the remedy for agricultural depression lay in expanding the market and promoting greater consumption of its products in the population at large. The sudden rise in wheat prices in 1825, which made the cabinet authorize an emergency release of bonded grain, hardened his determination to revise the unsatisfactory corn law of 1815. Liverpool's plan, accepted by the cabinet at the end of 1826, provided for a sliding scale of duties, pivoting round a 'remunerative price' for wheat of 60s. a quarter, with duties on foreign imports ending entirely when the domestic price reached 70s. Though he was denied the opportunity to put this through parliament in the 1827 session as planned, it was the substance of the act passed by Wellington's ministry in 1828.

Liverpool's economic and political outlook That the Liverpool administration was the first to pursue a coherent economic programme was largely due to the fact that Liverpool was the first prime minister to have a coherent economic philosophy. It owed much to the early tutelage of his father and his youthful study of Adam Smith. In principle he deprecated the intervention of the legislature in the economy of the country. 'Government or Parliament never meddle with these matters at all,' he wrote in 1819, 'but they do harm more or less' (Yonge, 2.416). Britain had become great, he told the Lords in 1820, not because of but despite its protectionist system. Free trade was therefore the right direction for policy even if in the absolute sense it was not immediately or perhaps ever attainable. Financially he was a monetarist. In the crisis of 1825 he refused to meet the Bank of England's wish to suspend cash payments. In his view the only sound remedy for overborrowing was a rise in interest rates. He was not, however, a doctrinaire exponent of *laissez-faire*. He supported the elder Peel's act to protect children in cotton mills and in 1818 assisted the movement for church building in manufacturing towns with a government grant of £1 million.

In his general political outlook Liverpool was guided by the traditional aristocratic concept of duty to the state. The task of government, he held, was to keep the balance between the great interests and to consider the needs of all classes of the community. While he knew that government could not in the long run maintain itself without the support of public opinion, he thought it had a duty to disregard popular clamour when pursuing the long-term interests of the nation. He distrusted calls for parliamentary reform since he believed that this would strengthen the influence of the volatile urban electorate. The country gentry, though not always amenable to government control, represented to him a more stable element in the constitution.

As prime minister Liverpool upheld the authority of his office and the integrity of the cabinet against the capricious interference of the crown. Within the cabinet he led through persuasion, tact, and moderation. He never allowed his administration to degenerate into a collection of departments and exercised a close supervision of all its main branches. There can be little doubt that he, not Huskisson, was the dominant influence in economic policy;

and though he was accused of being led by Canning in foreign policy, the record of his career supports his contention that on its basic principles—distrust of the congress system, avoidance of permanent alliances and commitments in mainland Europe, and encouragement of national independence and liberal regimes among the smaller continental states—he and Canning thought alike.

As a parliamentarian Liverpool was among the best debaters in either house. His speeches were characterized by clarity, command of detail, and objectivity; and he had the rare quality of always doing justice to the arguments of his opponents. His more elevated sphere in the House of Lords and his unostentatious style of leadership concealed from the public the crucial importance of his position in the administration, even though his honesty and blameless private life earned their respect. Among his colleagues, however, there was general recognition that his unrivalled experience in high office, his administrative skills, his prudence and common sense, and his ability to get the best out of ministers of diverse views and temperaments, made him indispensable to the existence of the government. His long period at the head of affairs, surpassed only by Walpole and the younger Pitt, was proof of his qualities as prime minister, as was, in a different way, the immediate breakup of the cabinet after his retirement.

Appearance, health, and second marriage A lanky, awkward figure when young, Liverpool in later life was a serious-looking man, fairly tall, with strong chin and long nose, and what Mrs Arbuthnot described as an '*untidy* look and slouching way of standing'. His health had never been robust and for many years he had suffered from a painful form of thrombophlebitis in his left leg. It is evident that there was a general vascular weakness affecting his heart and pulse-rate which was only temporarily relieved by his regular visits to Bath. After the death of his wife in June 1821, which affected him profoundly, there was an observable deterioration in his physical condition. In coming to difficult decisions, and in time of personal crisis, he displayed increasing irritability and nervous agitation. Beneath his phlegmatic appearance he had an anxious temperament and had always been easily moved to tears. In private life he preferred the company of women to that of men. On 24 September 1822 he married Mary Chester, a friend and long-standing companion of his first wife; his early remarriage was an indication of his need for a peaceful domestic refuge. He entertained little, and among politicians Coombe House (near Kingston upon Thames) was rated as one of the duller houses to visit. Despite the soberness of his own household, however, he was by no means an unsociable guest elsewhere.

Illness, retirement, death, and estate On 17 February 1827 at Fife House (his riverside residence in Whitehall since 1810) Liverpool suffered a severe cerebral haemorrhage and in March the king was obliged to seek a successor. There was another minor stroke in July after which he lingered on at Coombe until a third and fatal attack on 4 December 1828.

He was buried in Hawkesbury parish church, Gloucestershire, beside his father and his first wife. He had no children and his main landed estate with his titles passed to his stepbrother Cecil Jenkinson. His personal estate was registered at under £120,000. Liverpool was not, by contemporary standards, a rich man; and he had been a generous supporter of public charities and impoverished relatives. There is no reason to disbelieve the statement of his official biographer, C. D. Yonge, that he left office poorer than he entered it. He had a well-stocked library, was knowledgeable on the history and literature of the previous century, took considerable interest in the arts, and was a patron both of contemporary British painters and of the two great sculptors Chantrey and Canova. But neither these aesthetic tastes nor the improvements he made to his modest country house at Coombe Wood, which he had purchased in 1801, led him into any great extravagance. His major contribution to the arts was the part he played in the foundation of the National Gallery and the provision of a government grant to acquire for it J. J. Angerstein's great collection of paintings and his house in Pall Mall in 1824.

Subsequent reputation In the nineteenth century Liverpool's reputation suffered partly because of his modest personality, partly because Victorian opinion tended to date the period of liberalism and enlightened government from the Reform Act of 1832. Though the *Dictionary of National Biography* observed that 'history has hardly done justice to Liverpool's solid though not shining talents', another half-century passed before a start was made in reassessing his historical importance. It was a slow process. Sir Charles Petrie's popular account *Lord Liverpool and his Times* appeared in 1954 but until 1984 there was no specific modern biography to place beside Yonge's dull but indispensable three-volume study. It was through more general historical writing that a gradual shift of opinion first became discernible. Disraeli's flippant label of the 'Arch-Mediocrity' was discarded and even the later concept of a deliberate reconstruction of the ministry in 1821 to allow a new 'liberal toryism' to emerge was increasingly regarded as an artificial imposition on the underlying continuity of policy and personnel present in the administration.

The security measures taken between 1817 and 1820 were recognized as a relatively moderate response—by contemporary standards—to a difficult situation, and Liverpool's desire to encroach as little as possible on constitutional liberties received belated acknowledgement. Attention has also been given to the sincere and tolerant Christianity which underlay his genuine concern for the poor and enabled him to deal sympathetically with religious parties as diverse as the high-church Hackney phalanx, the evangelical British and Foreign Bible Society, and the Wesleyan Methodists. His academic free-trade principles are seen to have been tempered by humanitarian considerations, a realistic view of the actual state of the economy, a shrewd diagnosis of political possibilities, and a regard for national strength. Even with these limitations, the work of the 1819–27 years is accepted as comparable with that of any other administration of the century.

Liverpool failed to find a solution for the disruptive issue of Catholic emancipation. That apart, he showed great and continuing ability in dealing with a succession of problems which in intensity and variety have rarely fallen to the lot of a single prime minister. His success was the more striking since he never possessed effective control of the House of Commons nor enjoyed the steady support of a constitutionally still influential monarch. Indeed, the royal family added substantially to his difficulties. Although his administration belonged, in structure and membership, to what might be called the *ancien régime* in British politics, he was paradoxically the first in a line of creative prime ministers who helped to shape the Victorian state. For his financial and commercial policies alone he deserves to rank with Peel and Gladstone.

NORMAN GASH

Sources C. D. Yonge, *The life and administration of Robert Banks, second earl of Liverpool*, 3 vols. (1868) · N. Gash, *Lord Liverpool* (1984) · N. Gash, 'Lord Liverpool: a private view', *History Today*, 30/5 (1980), 35–40 · N. Gash, 'The tortoise and the hare: Liverpool and Canning', *History Today*, 32/3 (1982), 12–19 · J. E. Cookson, *Lord Liverpool's administration: the crucial years, 1815–1822* (1975) · 'Jenkinson, Robert Banks, second earl of Liverpool', HoP, *Commons* · GEC, *Peerage* · W. R. Brook, *Lord Liverpool and liberal toryism* (1941) · B. Hilton, *Corn, cash, commerce: the economic policies of the tory governments, 1815–1830* (1977) · B. Hilton, 'The political arts of Lord Liverpool', *TRHS*, 5th ser., 38 (1988), 147–70 · Burke, *Peerage*

Archives BL, corresp., Add. MS 74091 · BL, corresp. and papers, loan 72 · BL, corresp. and papers, Add. MSS 38190–38475, 38489, 38564–38578, 38580, 59772, 61818 · Harrowby Manuscript Trust, Sandon Hall, Staffordshire, letters to Lord Harrowby · PRO, letters and papers, PRO 30/29 | BL, corresp. with Sir Joseph Banks · BL, corresp. with Lord Bathurst, MS loan 57 · BL, letters to Lord Bexley, Add. MSS 31231–31232 · BL, corresp. with Lord Grenville, Add. MS 58936 · BL, corresp. with third earl of Hardwicke, Add. MSS 35395–35765, *passim* · BL, corresp. with John Charles Herries, Add. MS 57367 · BL, corresp. with William Huskisson, Add. MSS 38737–38748 · BL, corresp. with Prince Lieven, Add. MSS 47287–47293 · BL, corresp. with Moore family, Add. MS 57545 · BL, corresp. with Sir A. Paget, Add. MS 48389 · BL, letters to Sir Robert Peel, Add. MSS 40181, 40304–40305 · BL, corresp. with Comte de Puisaye, etc., Add. MS 7981 · BL, corresp. with Lord Wellesley, Add. MSS 37295–37310, *passim* · BL, letters to Sir James Willoughby Gordon, Add. MS 49476 · BL, corresp. with C. P. Yorke, Add. MS 45036 · Cambs. AS, Huntingdon, letters to duke of Manchester · CKS, corresp. with Lord Camden; corresp. with Lord Cornwallis etc., letters to William Pitt etc. · Cumbria AS, Carlisle, letters to first earl of Lonsdale · Devon RO, corresp. with Lord Sidmouth · Duke U., corresp. and papers · Durham RO, corresp. with Lord Londonderry · Hunt. L., letters to Lord Beresford · Kent Archives Office, Camden MSS · Kent Archives Office, Pitt MSS · Lambton Park, Chester-le-Street, co. Durham, corresp. with first earl of Durham · LPL, letters to Archbishop Manners-Sutton · NA Scot., corresp. with Lord Melville · NL Scot., corresp. with Sir Alexander Cochrane; corresp. with Sir Thomas Graham; corresp. with Robert Liston; corresp. with Lord Melville · Northumbd RO, Newcastle upon Tyne, letters to Lord Wallace · NRA, priv. coll., letters to William Adams · NRA, priv. coll., letters to Lord Eldon · NRA, priv. coll., corresp. with Spencer Perceval · NRA, priv. coll., letters to second earl Spencer · PRO, letters to William Pitt, PRO 30/8 · PRO NIre., corresp. with second earl of Caledon, D2431–2433 · PRO NIre., corresp. with Lord Castlereagh, D3030 · Royal Arch., letters to George III · Sheff. Arch., letters to Lady Erne; letters to Lord Fitzwilliam · Suffolk RO, Bury St Edmunds, letters to first marquis of

Bristol · SUL, Wellington MSS · Surrey HC, corresp. with Henry Goulburn · TCD, corresp. with Lord Donoughmore · U. Hull, Brynmor Jones L., corresp. with T. Perronet Thompson · U. Nott. L., corresp. with duke of Newcastle; letters to duke of Portland · U. Southampton L., corresp. with Lord Palmerston · UCL, letters to Lord Brougham · W. Yorks. AS, Leeds, corresp. with George Canning

Likenesses T. Lawrence, portrait, c.1796, priv. coll. · J. Hoppner, portrait, c.1807, priv. coll. · H. H. Meyer, mezzotint, pubd 1815 (after J. Hoppner), NPG · J. Nollekens, marble bust, 1816, Royal Collection · T. Lawrence, oils, c.1820, Royal Collection [see illus.] · C. Turner, mezzotint, pubd 1826, BM, NPG · T. Lawrence, oils, exh. RA 1827, NPG · T. Lawrence, portrait, pubd 1845 (after J. R. Jackson), NPG · B. F. Hardenberg, bust, Ickworth House, Park and Garden, Suffolk · G. Hayter, group portrait, oils (The trial of Queen Caroline, 1820), NPG · G. Hayter, oils, Weston Park, Shropshire · K. A. Hickel, group portrait, oils (The House of Commons, 1793), NPG

Wealth at death under £120,000 personal estate

Jenks, Benjamin (bap. 1648, d. 1724), Church of England clergyman, was baptized in Eaton under Heywood, Shropshire, on 23 May 1648, the son of its vicar, John Jenks or Jenkes (1604/5–1695), and his wife, Joyce (d. 1680). Jenks matriculated from Queen's College, Oxford, on 1 July 1664 and graduated BA in 1668. In that same year he became curate of Harley in Shropshire. The patron of the living, Francis, Lord Newport (later first earl of Bradford), made Jenks rector of Harley and also of the nearby parish of Kenley as well as his personal chaplain. Jenks remained minister at Harley until his death.

The maiden name of Jenks's first wife was Baugh; they had a son (who died in infancy) and a daughter. After his first wife's death Jenks married Mary Andrews, née Hunt, the widow of a minister, in June 1705. The couple had no children. Jenks died on 10 May 1724 and was buried four days later in the chancel of the church at Harley. A monument there, inscribed with his coat of arms, marked his good and faithful service to the parish for fifty-six years.

Jenks's publications began with A Thanksgiving Sermon Preach'd upon the Fifth of November, 1689 (1689), celebrating both the anniversary of the foiling of the Gunpowder Plot and James II's downfall, and his later Sermon Preach'd at Harley marked William III's safe return to England in 1697. Jenks developed moralizing messages in several of his writings, lecturing against swearing, lewdness, and lust, and people trusting in their own opinions rather than in God (A Letter to a Gentleman of Note, Guilty of Common Swearing, 1690; The Glorious Victory of Chastity, 1707; Submission to the Righteousness of God, 1700). In 1710 he published a translation of the Roman Catholic Bellarmine's writings on the eternal satisfaction of the saints (Ouranography, or, Heaven Opened).

Jenks's most popular works were his books of prayer. The preliminary work in this series was a manual on the proper form and method of prayer, entitled The Liberty of Prayer Asserted (1695), from which followed Prayers and Offices of Devotion (1697), The Bell Rung to Prayers (1699), and The Poor Man's Ready Companion (1713), the latter being a smaller and less expensive form of his family prayer book. Jenks also published several volumes of meditations, in 1701 and 1704, dealing with a wide variety of Christian topics and themes. In the 1704 edition he expressed his

desire 'that even after my Decease, I may still be Preaching by these Papers' (A Second Century of Meditations, 1703, 1), a hope which was achieved in the reprinting of several of his works in the later eighteenth century, and especially in more than thirty-five editions and reprints of his Prayers and Offices, published into the late nineteenth century.

WARREN JOHNSTON

Sources Letters from the Rev. Mr. Job Orton; and the Rev. Sir James Stonhouse, bart. M.D. to the Rev. Thomas Stedman, M.A. vicar of St Chad's Shrewsbury (1800), 16–19 · Foster, Alum. Oxon., 1500–1714 [Benjamin Jenks] · DNB · Eaton-under-Heywood register, Shropshire Parish Register Society, diocese of Hereford, 19, pt 3 (1940) · 'The register of Harley', Shropshire Parish Register Society: diocese of Hereford, 2 (1901), 1–26 · 'The register of Kenley', Shropshire Parish Register Society: diocese of Hereford, 2 (1901), 81–146 · T. R. Horton, ed., The registers of Harley, Shropshire (privately printed, London, 1899), 3 · G. E. Cokayne and E. A. Fry, eds., Calendar of marriage licences issued by the faculty office, 1632–1714, British RS, 33 (1905), 214

Jenks, Clarence Wilfred (1909–1973), international lawyer and director-general of the International Labour Organization, was born on 7 March 1909 in Bootle, Lancashire, the son of Richard Jenks, an officer in the merchant navy, and his wife, Alice Sophia Craig. Jenks's father was lost at sea when Jenks was eleven and he effectively became head of the family. This early assumption of responsibility could explain his positive, energetic, and constructive outlook as well as the close relationship he maintained with his mother for the rest of her life.

Jenks's early education was in state schools in Liverpool. In 1926 he won an open scholarship to Gonville and Caius College, Cambridge, where, from the outset, he showed that strong interest in history, politics, international relations, and law which was to characterize his whole career. He became treasurer of the British Universities League of Nations Society as well as chairman of the Cambridge University League of Nations Union. He was twice awarded a scholarship at the Institute of International Studies at Geneva, a city in which he was to spend much of his life. In 1930 he was elected president of the Cambridge Union. He was called to the bar by Gray's Inn in 1936.

In 1949 Jenks married Jane Louise Broverman, a daughter of Frederick S. Broverman of New York, who provided him with a tranquil home and unfailing social support. They had two sons, Craig and Bruce, both of whom inherited their father's international interests and outlook.

Jenks combined what amounted to virtually two separate, albeit closely linked, careers. In formal terms he spent the whole of his working life as an official of the International Labour Office—the secretariat of the International Labour Organization (ILO)—which he entered immediately on obtaining his law degree at Cambridge. He was soon made a permanent member of the legal staff and gradually advanced until he reached the position of principal legal adviser.

The work of the ILO, perhaps more than that of any other international organization, is reflected in legal texts: conventions regulating a wide range of matters affecting conditions of labour; reports of committees, including those scrutinizing, and even adjudicating on, the performance by members of their convention obligations; and resolutions of the general conference. In the preparation of these documents Jenks's skills were much in demand. His contribution went beyond mere technical drafting. It embraced the imaginative formulation and active negotiation of policy solutions to the many new problems confronting the organization. His knowledge of the constitutional aspects of international institutions was unrivalled. At the end of the Second World War he was the principal architect of the revision of the ILO constitution and his help was widely sought in structuring the family of United Nations specialized agencies that emerged at that time.

Eventually Jenks's special standing, going beyond that accorded to a distinguished and experienced lawyer, was recognized by his appointment first as assistant director-general, then as deputy director-general. In 1970 he became director-general, a post he held until his death in 1973.

Jenks's creative work in the ILO was illuminated by an almost passionate devotion to his vision of the objectives and higher good of the organization. He saw in the protection of the interests of all workers (a category he interpreted very broadly) a major component of the rapidly developing field of the international protection of human rights. His insistence on the independence of the international public service and his firm adherence to principle brought him early in his period as director-general into such direct conflict with the United States that for a while that country withdrew its support from the organization. In 1973 he vigorously, and successfully, opposed an initiative in the general conference which would have had Israel condemned for alleged breaches of its obligations of membership without the protection of prior judicial process.

Despite the intensity and demands of his official commitments, but without detracting from his performance of them, Jenks also established himself as one of the most prominent and prolific writers on international law of his time. He sought to give permanent academic expression not only to points of international law arising in the course of his official work, but also to many other matters of major importance in the international legal field. His book-length article in 1945 entitled 'Some constitutional problems of international organization' (*British Yearbook of International Law*, 22) was for long the unrivalled source of instruction on that subject for professionals and academics alike. He also wrote on legal subjects related to the ILO, such as the international protection of trade union rights and law, freedom, and welfare. He demonstrated his foresight and speculative ability by producing in 1965 a volume on space law so early in the development of space activities that some thought him almost unduly imaginative. Although he did not have much direct involvement in international adjudication, he published in 1964 a major study on that subject, *The Prospects of International Adjudication*.

Jenks was greatly sought after as a lecturer, but the rapid and intense manner of his delivery made little allowance for the frailty of his audiences who could not always fully grasp the significance of what they were hearing. During the period when he was assistant director-general of the ILO he declined to allow himself to be considered for almost certain election to one of the world's most prestigious chairs of international law. By reason, as he put it, 'of public duty and international public spirit by which I have felt bound', he could not, 'consistently with the proper discharge of duties arising from past years, leave [his] present post on [his] own initiative at a time as difficult, but as potentially fruitful, as that through which we are now passing' (private letter, Jenks archive).

Jenks was a member of the Institut de Droit International, during the 1973 session of which in Rome he died of a heart attack on 9 October. He was buried in Geneva on 15 October.   ELIHU LAUTERPACHT

Sources DNB · personal knowledge (2004) · private information (2004) · International Labour Office, Geneva, Switzerland, Jenks archive · *CGPLA Eng. & Wales* (1974) · *WWW* · *The Times* (11 Oct 1973) · *British Yearbook of International Law*, 46 (1972–3), xi–xxx
Archives International Labour Office, Geneva, Switzerland, MSS
Likenesses B. Rubbra, portrait · photograph, repro. in *British Yearbook of International Law*
Wealth at death £8849 in England and Wales: administration with will, 26 April 1974, *CGPLA Eng. & Wales*

Jenks, Edward (1861–1939), jurist and writer, was born in Stockwell, London, on 20 February 1861, the eldest of the four sons of Robert Jenks, a furniture dealer in the City of London, and his second wife, Isobel Frances, daughter of Edward Jones of Nottingham, furniture manufacturer. He was educated at Dulwich College from 1874 to 1877 but left at sixteen to be articled to a solicitor. In 1883, the year after he qualified, the death of his mother put money at his disposal, and so made it possible for him to enter King's College, Cambridge. A brilliant law student and the recipient of several prizes, he was placed first in the law tripos of 1886, and the next year was bracketed second in the history tripos. Concurrently he read for the bar, to which he was called by the Middle Temple in 1887, having won the Barstow scholarship of the inns of court that year. He became director of studies in law and history at Jesus College, Cambridge, in 1888–9, when he was elected a fellow of King's College, Cambridge.

Later the same year Jenks left England to become dean of the faculty of law in the University of Melbourne. In 1890, soon after his arrival, he married Annie Ingham, of Leeds, who had followed him from England. She died the next year after giving birth to a son. By nature pugnacious, Jenks was soon engaged in public controversy with John Madden, the vice-chancellor, over university administration. This did not distract him from collecting material for *The Government of Victoria* (*Australia*), published in 1891, a pioneer work of merit, nor prevent his winning the Yorke prize at Cambridge in 1891 for an essay *The History of the Doctrine of Consideration in English Law* published in 1892.

In November 1891 Jenks resigned his post in Melbourne to return to England where in 1892 he was elected to a chair in the recently instituted faculty of law at University College, Liverpool. In 1895 this became the Queen Victoria chair of law in the University of Manchester, of which University College, Liverpool, was part. He was an efficient but rather schoolmasterly teacher. During his four years at Liverpool (1892–6) Jenks championed the cause of humanism in legal education against the view, which then prevailed among the leaders of the profession, that a solicitor was perfectly equipped if he had learned the technique of his trade. Jenks entered the fray with zest and, despite, as he put it, 'years of much trial and occasional despondency' (Lee, 405) succeeded in attracting at least some students to subjects of intellectual interest but little immediate practical value, such as international and constitutional law and jurisprudence.

In 1896 Jenks left Liverpool to become reader in English law in the University of Oxford and a tutor of Balliol College. In these capacities he made his mark as a sound and stimulating teacher but he and A. V. Dicey shared responsibility for Oxford's rejection of the Squire endowment for a law library, against which they campaigned vigorously, and which went instead to Cambridge. His *Law and Politics in the Middle Ages* was published in 1898 (2nd edn, 1913) and in 1900 there appeared a manual entitled *A History of Politics* which had a large sale and was translated into Japanese. An original enterprise begun during this period was *A Digest of English Civil Law*, arranged at the suggestion of Dr Felix Meyer of Berlin in a form similar to the German civil code which had come into force in 1900. It was produced by Jenks as editor with the assistance of four other Oxford lawyers. Appearing in parts between 1905 and 1917 and in a consolidated edition in 1921, the 'Jenkische Kodifikation', as it was called in Germany, embodied his talent for classification and pithy phrasing. It made the impenetrable forest of English private law, as the dean of the Paris faculty put it, accessible for the first time to foreign lawyers. Translated into both French and German, it led to his being given an honorary doctorate in Paris. In Britain, however, though it ran to a third edition in 1937, the work fell flat.

In 1903 Jenks left Oxford for London on his appointment as director of legal studies to the Law Society, a position which he held for twenty-one years. Here the challenge was similar to that in Liverpool, but on a nationwide scale. Jenks fought with indomitable courage and played a large part in inducing provincial universities in England to collaborate with their local law societies to provide law schools for articled clerks. In his article 'The myth of Magna Carta' (*Independent Review*, November 1904), he caused a stir by attacking the view that the charter was the foundation of English liberties. His *Short History of English Law*, which resembled W. S. Holdsworth's history on a small scale, came out in 1912 and ran to six editions. Then in 1924 he transferred his activities to the new chair of English law in the University of London, attached to the London School of Economics, where, encouraged by Lord Atkin, he compiled *The Book of English Law*. This introductory work was seen by both as a step towards securing the recognition of the teaching of law as a feature in a general liberal education—an aim that has not been fulfilled.

Jenks quirkishly took the London degree of LLB in 1909 and in his forty-ninth year obtained a first class.

When his five-year tenure as professor expired in 1929 Jenks made his home at Bishop's Tawton, near Barnstaple, where he continued to take a keen interest in public affairs and, in particular, in the Workers' Educational Association and the League of Nations Union, visiting Geneva annually when the assembly of the league was in session. Boating and tramping were among the hobbies he listed in *Who's Who*.

An activity in which Jenks took a prominent part was the foundation in 1909 of the Society of Public Teachers of Law, of which he was secretary from 1909 to 1919. Though known at the time as 'Jenks's trade union', its main aim, in which it had some modest success, was less to bargain for better conditions for law teachers than to uphold academic values in legal education.

Apart from Paris in 1929 Jenks received honorary degrees from the universities of Wales in 1928 and Bristol in 1933 and was elected FBA in 1930. In 1898 he married as his second wife Dorothy Mary, fourth daughter of Sir William Bower Forwood, of Liverpool, who with their son and daughter survived him. The son of his first marriage won the Military Cross and was killed in action in 1917. He himself died at his home, Tawton House, Bishop's Tawton, on 10 November 1939.

Indefatigable in both mind and body, and obstinate to a fault in maintaining a view once formed, Jenks's varied writings in law and history were less the product of original research than sustained attempts to spread a knowledge of English law and its history. Unsurprisingly, they have not stood the test of time; but their author was the person most responsible for raising the professional and academic standing of teachers of law in the early part of the twentieth century, for making English private law accessible to continental lawyers of that period, and for ensuring that the education of solicitors was less narrowly technical than, left to itself, the profession would have chosen.   TONY HONORÉ

Sources DNB · preface, *A digest of English civil law*, ed. E. Jenks and others, 2nd edn, 2 vols. (1921) · R. W. Lee, 'Edward Jenks, 1861–1939', *PBA*, 26 (1940), 399–423 [incl. bibliography] · *WWW, 1929–40* · *The Times* (13 Nov 1939) · CGPLA Eng. & Wales (1940)
Archives BL, corresp. with Society of Authors, Add. MS 56732 · King's AC Cam., letters to Oscar Browning
Likenesses F. Bennett, oils, 1925, College of Law, London · photograph, repro. in *PBA*, facing p. 399
Wealth at death £21,856 0s. 7d.: resworn probate, 9 Feb 1940, CGPLA Eng. & Wales

Jenks, Francis (*bap.* 1640, *d.* 1686), linen draper and whig activist, was the son of Herbert Jencks, esquire, of New Hall, Shropshire, and his wife, Elizabeth. He was baptized at Eaton under Heywood, Shropshire, on 5 November 1640. Apprenticed in 1658 to a member of the London Fishmongers' Guild, Jenks married Sarah Walwyn, daughter of the famous Leveller William Walwyn, then a physician in Sutton, Surrey, in 1666. In March 1674 the couple baptized a child named Walwyn for his maternal grandfather, an indication, perhaps, of Jenks's respect for his father-in-law. Jenks was by then established in the London parish of St Michael, Cornhill, for which he served on the common council in 1676.

Jenks first gained notoriety on 24 June 1676 as a speaker in common hall, the annual assembly of liverymen who elected the sheriffs of London and Middlesex. He was already associated with the civic opposition that had emerged in 1675, and his speech rehearsed several country themes. He moved that the lord mayor be directed to call a common council so that the corporation could petition Charles II for a new parliament. Indeed, he suggested that the recent lengthy prorogation of the Cavalier Parliament constituted a technical dissolution. He also voiced widespread fears about Louis XIV and popery, playing upon the anxieties of many citizens about mounting commercial competition from France.

Jenks was actually acting as a mouthpiece for the duke of Buckingham, to whom he had been introduced by his friend John Wildman, another one-time Leveller. Jenks's speech, Buckingham hoped, would stimulate further demands for a new parliament from the counties. Instead, it brought Jenks a summons to appear before the king in council, where he informed Charles that every London citizen 'had liberty to debate whatever he thinks for the service of the King and the good of the City' (*CSP dom.*, 1676–7, 194). Jenks's refusal to answer questions about his relationship to Buckingham earned him three months in the Gatehouse, but his imprisonment raised further contentious issues. The incarceration of a citizen for making a motion in common hall was condemned by some as a dangerous challenge to the 'common liberty of Englishmen' (ibid., 256). Jenks's civic friends also asserted the authority of the common hall electorate and of their representatives in common council over the lord mayor and aldermen, a position which Jenks himself advocated.

Denied bail, Jenks 'molest [ed] all judicatures' from the Gatehouse (*Poems and Letters of Andrew Marvell*, 2.348). He demanded his freedom by means of habeas corpus or a writ of mainprize, thereby generating arguments that would contribute to the Habeas Corpus Amendment Act of 1679. A contemporary satirist characterized him as the 'Rational Attorney General' of the civic opposition, one who 'speaks all oracle' in his lofty visions of 'an Utopian State' (BL, Add. MS 34362, fol. 13). Jenks had secured his freedom by the time Buckingham made the same arguments about the dissolution of parliament to the House of Lords at the beginning of the February 1677 session. Jenks then rushed his patron into hiding as the Lords condemned him; and he was also with Buckingham when the duke appeared at the Tower to surrender.

Jenks's association with Buckingham, his passionate rhetoric, and his membership in the Green Ribbon Club kept him at the centre of opposition in the capital throughout the crisis of 1678–83. He was a promoter of a city petition for a new parliament in January 1679, and he signed a petition in support of a protestant succession in May 1679. He was discussed as a possible MP for the corporation prior to both parliamentary elections of that year, but he lacked the wealth and stature of the successful anti-court candidates. His advancement for sheriff of London and Middlesex in 1679 was more realistic. Although the expenses of the shrievalty were beyond his means, his supporters intended to raise a public subscription to sustain him in office. They hoped thereby to make the shrievalty more accessible to ordinary men of ability. The scheme may have had the backing of the duke of Monmouth, whose city agent, Sir Thomas Armstrong, was observed in conference with Jenks about this time. However, the prospect of a popular tribune as sheriff—indeed, of a 'Puppet Sheriff', who might become 'Pensioner to the meanest Trades-man of his Party'—so horrified city loyalists that they carried a poll against Jenks for an Anglican alderman (*Venn and his Mermydons*, 3). Yet the spirit of 'Jenkism', or the political assertiveness of ordinary citizens, which was 'reckoned up as one of the Cities new Heresies', had not been defeated (*Vindicator Vindicated*, 2). When the whig Slingsby Bethel served as London sheriff for 1680–81, his much ridiculed frugality in office was, like Jenks's 1679 candidacy, intended to open the shrievalty to citizens of middling rank.

In January 1680 Jenks assisted the rabidly anti-Catholic Middlesex justice Sir William Waller in the public disgrace of Colonel Thomas Blood, notorious as the one-time stealer of the crown jewels. Acting on behalf of the imprisoned earl of Danby, Blood had encouraged a pair of Irish adventurers to destroy Buckingham with an accusation of sodomy. However, Jenks and Buckingham's attorney turned the accusers against Blood, who was convicted of suborning witnesses. When Waller's somewhat irregular proceedings against Blood led to his replacement as a JP, Jenks found himself prosecuted for seditious words in claiming that the king's discharge of Waller was an affront to justice.

Jenks was highly visible as a whig organizer and agitator in the 1682–3 contest for political control of the corporation. He encouraged sheriffs Thomas Pilkington and Samuel Shute to proceed with a poll, against mayoral command, on behalf of whig shrieval candidates at the 24 June 1682 common hall. For this action he was, with other civic whig leaders, indicted for a riot, eventually found guilty, and fined 300 marks. When the king in council suppressed the election of the whig candidates and ordered a new choice, Jenks attempted to read the 1642 parliamentary regulation of the privy council to the common hall. In October 1682 he served as scrutineer for the whigs in the disputed mayoral election for 1682–3. When the loyalist-dominated aldermanic bench sought to adjust the poll results in favour of the tory candidate, Jenks denied that the aldermen 'had anything to do' with polls in common hall (*Exact Account of the Proceedings at Guild-Hall*). And when the loyalist lord mayor declared the election of a tory successor, Jenks 'stepped upon the hustings and told the lord mayor that he made a false report' (Newdigate newsletters, Folger, L.c.1292, 26 Oct 1682).

One informer reported in July 1682 that he had 'often' heard Jenks encourage the London whigs to 'take [up] immediate arms against the Government' (*CSP dom.*, 1682, 237). The linen draper's name appears in other early accounts of illicit whig designs as well: four years earlier a search of his house had turned up a pamphlet advocating resistance under some circumstances. The extent to which Jenks became involved in the whig conspiracies of 1682–3 is unclear, however. Three different informants implicated Jenks during the government's investigation of these conspiracies in the summer of 1683. Conspirator Colonel John Rumsey declared that he had heard that Jenks favoured the 'lopping point' or assassination of Charles II (*CSP dom.*, *July–Sept 1683*, 237). But another suspected conspirator reported that Jenks had turned 'politician' of late, appearing 'more calm' and not appearing 'so much in company as formerly' (*CSP dom.*, *Jan–June 1683*, 185). Examined before the privy council, Jenks seemingly acknowledged awareness of the conspiracies while distancing himself from them. Confirming his long-term association with leading plotter Richard Goodenough, he nevertheless claimed that 'what he has done was concerning the rights of the City and that he shunned everything else' (*CSP dom.*, *July–Sept 1683*, 79).

Given his political record, Jenks was not surprisingly confined at the time of Monmouth's rebellion in 1685; and he was one of the last of several hundred detained Londoners to be freed. In that year he also acquired part of the grounds of Buckingham's Wallingford House, in the West End, in payment for a debt. He began to build upon this property before his death the following year; he was buried on 9 December 1686. Legal objections to the construction work had not been resolved. Sarah Jenks soon remarried: the Leveller's daughter and the agitator's widow became the spouse of Anglican divine Dr John Williams, who was subsequently bishop of Chichester.

GARY S. DE KREY

Sources CSP dom., 1676–7, 180, 184–5, 193–4, 253–6, 388–9, 454, 564; 1677–8, 22; 1678, 313; 1679–80, 63, 240, 584–5; 1680–81, 462–4, 585, 666; 1682, 237, 295, 462, 573; Jan–June 1683, 66, 105, 185, 301, 356; July–Sept 1683, 5, 11–12, 71, 79, 237, 329 • State trials, 6.1189–1208; 9.252, 261–2, 388–9 • An account of the proceedings at Guild-Hall, London, at the Tolke-Moot [1676] • Mr Francis Jenk's speech: spoken in a common hall [n.d., 1679?] • BL, Add. MS 34362, fol. 13 • The poems and letters of Andrew Marvell, ed. H. Margoliouth, rev. P. Legouis, 3rd edn, 2 (1971), 345, 348 • GL, MSS 1993, 1998, 3589 • J. R. Woodhead, The rulers of London, 1660–1689 (1965), 98 • Venn and his mermydons, or, The linen-draper capotted (1679) • The vindicator vindicated, or, A surrejoynder on behalf of Sir Thomas Player (1679) • An exact account of the proceedings at Guild-hall (1682) • Newdigate newsletter, 15 Sept 1679, Folger, L.c.836; 4 Oct 1679, Folger, L.c.844; 26 Oct 1682, Folger, L.c.1292 • PRO, Prerogative court of Canterbury wills, PROB 11/365, qu. 13 [will of William Walwyn, repr. in The writings of William Walwyn, ed. J. R. McMichael and B. Taft (1989), 537–8] • A. Marshall, Intelligence and espionage in the reign of Charles II, 1660–1685 (1994), 216–23 • K. H. D. Haley, The first earl of Shaftesbury (1968), 409–10, 412, 416–17, 425–6, 440, 499 • M. Knights, Politics and opinion in crisis, 1678–1681 (1994), 187–8, 205, 221–2, 223, 266 • CLRO, Alchin B/33/15 • CLRO, Assessment Box 25 • court of lieutenancy minute book, 1684–7, CLRO, fol. 24 • R. Morrice, 'Ent'ring book', DWL, Morrice MS P, 500 • Magd. Cam., Pepys Library, Pepys MS 2895 (miscellaneous, vii), fols. 489–91 • L. Cong., manuscript division, London newsletters collection, 6.274 (23 Sept 1679); 8.211 (15 July 1682) • A letter from J. B. alias Oldcutt, to his friend Mr. Jenks (1679) • An account of the proceedings at the Guild-Hall of the city of London [1679] • London's choice of citizens to represent them in the ensuing parliament (1679) • R. H., Remarks on some eminent passages in the life of the famed Mr. Blood (1680), 12–14 • A paper delivered to the lord mayor and court of aldermen (1682) • G. Villiers, A speech made by the duke of Buckingham, the first day of the session of the parliament, State tracts: being a collection of several treatises relating to the government (privately printed, London, 1689) [1677] • W. A. Shaw, ed., Calendar of treasury books, 8, PRO (1923), 951, 1000, 1055, 1378, 1398 • Seventh report, HMC, 6 (1879), 475–6, 478 [Verney] • The manuscripts of S. H. Le Fleming, HMC, 25 (1890), 128 • J. L. Chester, ed., The parish registers of St Michael, Cornhill, London, Harleian Society, register section, 7 (1882), 147 • C. E. Pike, ed., Selections from the correspondence of Arthur Capel, earl of Essex, 1675–1677, CS, 3rd ser., 24 (1913), 61, 63, 64, 69–70 • E. M. Thompson, ed., Correspondence of the family of Hatton, 1, CS, new ser., 22 (1878), 133 • N. Luttrell, A brief historical relation of state affairs from September 1678 to April 1714, 1 (1857), 227, 263 • HoP, Commons, 1660–90 • M. Knights, 'London petitions and parliamentary politics in 1679', Parliamentary History, 12 (1993), 41

Jenks [alias Metcalfe], **Silvester** (1656–1714), Roman Catholic priest, was born on 1 January 1656, the only son of Benjamin Jenks (d. c.1665) and Elizabeth Jenks (d. 1683) of Worcester. He was educated at the English College in Douai where he took the missionary oath on 15 August 1675 in the assumed name of Metcalfe, and gained his doctorate of divinity in 1680 while he was teaching philosophy in the college and four years before his ordination to the priesthood (on 23 September 1684). He returned to England on 23 September 1686. For a short time he lived with Lady Mary Yate at Harvington Hall, Worcestershire, who had contributed to the cost of his education at Douai. On his progress from Bath to Chester James II assisted at mass in the new chapel at Worcester on 24 August 1687, in the course of which Jenks happened to preach the third of a series of sermons on transubstantiation. Impressed, the king appointed him a preacher royal and Jenks moved to London, where he received £60 p.a. from the exchequer for his services to the court. Three other royal sermons survive, all from 1688: two delivered at Whitehall (on St George's day and Corpus Christi), the other at Windsor on 26 August.

At the revolution a warrant for his arrest forced Jenks to live abroad, but he returned to England some time before 1698 to act as chaplain to the Ireland family of Albrighton, Shropshire, then living in London. Later, after a brief visit to Louvain, he moved, with the recently widowed Mrs Ireland, back to Albrighton. In 1699 Jenks was pleased to be elected to the chapter and named titular archdeacon of Surrey and Kent. Following the death of the chapter secretary, John Rogers (alias Ward), strenuous efforts were made to persuade Jenks to accept the vacancy, but he steadfastly refused, preferring to stand by the now distressed Ireland family.

> The death of her husband, the solitude of the country, the perplexities of a widow's administration, the threats of a protestant heir and the difficulties of a son's defence and education make her now much more inclined to melancholy and to scruples than before. In a word, I have been so kindly used by my friends in their prosperity that (though they would give me leave) I cannot upon any terms be so ill-natured, so ungrateful, so uncharitable as to leave them in their adversity. (S. Jenks, letter, 28 March 1703, in Anstruther, 3.116)

As early as 1703 Jenks was being mentioned as a future bishop, but it was not until the death of Bishop James

Smith of the northern district in 1711 that his name was put forward. After a considerable delay, explained partly by the current bad feeling between secular and regular clergy, Rome decided in favour of Jenks in a congregation held on 13 August 1713, which Pope Clement XI approved eleven days later. His brief of appointment was drawn up on 20 September, but its delivery was delayed and Jenks, who had already suffered a stroke, died at Holborn, London, on 15 December 1714, apparently unaware of his elevation to the episcopate. He was buried at St Pancras two days later.

Dodd says that 'he was a person of singular qualifications' (Dodd, 3.487) and especially remarkable for his clearness of thought and style and his agreeable conversation. In addition to his published sermons Jenks wrote several books on spirituality and some unpublished treatises, and despite his reticence occasionally ventured into polemics, instanced by his outburst in 1707 against John Sargeant, whom he accused of slandering himself and the chapter, and an attack on Jansenism in 1710. However, he had little appetite for public life.

> I keep my name to myself, and my reason is, because I love a quiet life. I ever looked upon it as the greatest blessing a bad world can afford, and am persuaded that being private is the easiest and securest way of being quiet. Besides, I see no good there is in being talked of, either well or ill. The one is good for nothing, but to make a man vain; the other is apt to make him vexed.   (S. Jenks, *Blind Obedience*, 1699, preface)

THOMPSON COOPER, rev. D. MILBURN

Sources G. Anstruther, *The seminary priests*, 4 vols. (1969–77), vol. 2, pp. 288–9; vol. 3, pp. 114–17 · Gillow, *Lit. biog. hist.*, 3.616–21 · B. Hemphill, *The early vicars apostolic of England, 1685–1750* (1954), 40–43 · C. Dodd [H. Tootell], *The church history of England, from the year 1500, to the year 1688*, 3 (1742), 486

Archives BL, letter-book, Add. MS 29612 · St Edmund's College, Ware, papers, MS 131 | Ushaw College, Durham, Ushaw collection of MSS, corresp., I f. 353

Likenesses J. le Pouter, engraving, repro. in S. Jenks, *The blind obedience of an humble penitent*

Wealth at death a man of few means; some small bequests: Anstruther, *Seminary priests*, vol. 3, p. 117

Jenkyn, William (*bap.* 1613, *d.* 1685), nonconformist minister, was baptized on 3 December 1613 at All Saints', Sudbury, Suffolk, where his father, William Jenkyn (*d.* 1618), was vicar.

A puritan upbringing Jenkyn's family was a model of puritanism. His father, the son of the landed Robert Jenkyn of Folkestone in Kent, was disinherited for his puritan beliefs. His mother was the daughter of Richard Rogers, the godly preacher of Wethersfield in Essex, and the granddaughter of John Rogers, one of the protestants martyred in the reign of Mary Tudor. After his father's death in 1618 he lived with his grandfather. However, in 1623 his mother, now remarried, fearing for William's soul, took him back to provide a godly education. Jenkyn was trained for the ministry and matriculated as a pensioner from St John's College, Cambridge, at Easter 1628, putting himself under the supervision of Anthony Burgess. He graduated BA in 1632 and migrated with Burgess

in April 1634 to Emmanuel College, where he proceeded MA in 1635.

In 1639 Jenkyn was chosen as the lecturer to the London parish of St Nicholas Acons, and he stayed in that post until 27 January 1641, when he was elected rector of St Leonard's, Colchester. However, he returned to London in 1642 and on 1 February 1643 replaced Edward Finch at the vicarage of Christchurch, Newgate Street. He was also elected as the lecturer at Dr William Gouge's parish of St Anne Blackfriars.

An impassioned presbyterian Jenkyn was one of the most impassioned presbyterians in London, and from 1645 Christchurch was a centre of presbyterian zeal. He instituted the presbyterian system, and the parish elected five ruling elders including the godly publisher William Greenhill and the puritan activist John Vicars. The London presbyterian ministers also chose Christchurch as the site for Thomas Edwards's weekly lecture against heresy; these lectures later became the basis of his infamous heresiography *Gangraena*. Jenkyn was a key member of the presbyterian London provincial assembly, sitting on its grand committee. With such fiery company it is unsurprising that he emerged as one of London presbyterianism's principal controversialists. In particular he engaged in a long and bitter printed dispute with John Goodwin, the sectarian vicar of St Stephen, Coleman Street. Jenkyn accused Goodwin of encouraging the expansion of heresy and social disorder; in return Goodwin charged Jenkyn with spreading intolerant bigotry. Jenkyn also signed the London ministers' *Testimony* (1648) against the toleration of heterodox belief.

The rise of the New Model Army in the late 1640s, and of its supporters in parliament, caused Jenkyn and his fellow presbyterians to believe that heretics were perverting the cause of the solemn league and covenant. His zealous stance against the army and for the covenant led him to be summoned by the House of Commons on 2 October 1647 to explain why he had preached in support of the City's stance against the army and parliament. When Colonel Pride ejected the presbyterian members of parliament in December 1648, and the army put the king on trial and considered instituting the Leveller *Agreement of the People* as the constitution of the new republic, Jenkyn was appalled. He was one of the signatories to the London ministers' *Serious and Faithful Representation* calling on Lord General Fairfax to reverse the revolution. He also signed the *Vindication* defending the ministers' intervention in the politics of the revolution.

Resistance to the Commonwealth After the execution of Charles I Jenkyn became a vocal opponent of the republic. He refused to take the oath of engagement and preached against the new regime, calling it a work of sin. Jenkyn refused to observe days of national fasting ordered by the republican parliament, and was consequently summoned by the committee for plundered ministers on 27 June 1650. He appeared with his fellow presbyterian James Cranford; they defended themselves by arguing that they had prayed 'for the privileges of Parliament … according to the Covenant' (*Mercurius Politicus*, 4, 27 June – 4 July 1650, 50–52). Jenkyn left unrepentant, but was ordered to appear before the committee again a few days later for further refusing to preach at a state fast. Unsurprisingly, the committee ordered his sequestration and, as an extra insult, imposed the heretical Fifth Monarchist firebrand Christopher Feake on the parish of Christchurch.

In spring 1651 Jenkyn was arrested with many of his presbyterian compatriots for his complicity in the City presbyterian plot to restore the exiled Charles II to the throne. This plot envisaged restoring Charles through the might of the Scots army, thus ensuring the presbyterian settlement in England. Parliament used the failure of the plot to silence the London presbyterian ministry. In August 1651 Jenkyn's friend Christopher Love was executed, his brother-in-law Thomas Cawton was forced to flee to exile in the Netherlands, and Jenkyn escaped with his life only because he agreed to sign a submissive recantation drawn up by Dr John Arthur of Clapham. The petition was presented to parliament on 15 October. Jenkyn and his fellow presbyterians were discharged by order of the speaker on 16 October and released two days later. Despite his recantation Jenkyn took the opportunity to preach a pro-covenant sermon on 5 November at Edmund Calamy's church of St Mary Aldermanbury on 'the danger thou runnest into by apostatising from God' (Jenkyn, *Sermon*, 19). Love's execution forced Jenkyn to shy away from contention for the rest of the Commonwealth period. Although his sequestration was removed with his release, he did not eject Feake and instead preached at Christchurch on Sunday mornings.

Protectorate preacher With the dissolution of the republic and the creation of the Cromwellian protectorate Jenkyn appears to have been publicly rehabilitated. In 1654 he was elected to replace William Gouge as minister at St Anne Blackfriars; he commenced this employment by preaching Gouge's funeral sermon. He probably returned to Christchurch at some time in the mid-1650s when Feake was ejected, but he was not officially reinstituted until 18 June 1658. The younger Edmund Calamy noted that Jenkyn 'was very cautious of touching upon anything that might give umbrage to the government, when he knew so many eyes were upon' and preached a series of expository sermons on the epistle of Jude. Perhaps in recognition of his compliance he was awarded the honour of preaching before the protectorate parliament on 24 September 1656.

Despite his public rehabilitation Jenkyn remained committed to the presbyterian cause. He wrote against the Quakers and was a signatory to the *Serious Exhortation of the Ministers of London* of 1660 warning the City's congregations of the twin dangers of heresy and popery. In the same year he was made a commissioner for the approbation of ministers by the restored Long Parliament.

Restoration nonconformist Jenkyn probably welcomed the restoration of Charles II but soon fell out with the new monarchical regime. He was summoned before the council for not praying for the king in January 1662 and refused

to conform to the Act of Uniformity in the following August. Joining the London ministers in preaching farewell sermons to the parishes of London, he offered his parishioners two sermons. The topic of each reveals his attitude to the policy of the new bishops. The morning sermon was on Hebrews 11: 38 and observed that 'A godly man sees a very great worth and excellence in the people of God in the midst of all the trouble and persecution that can befall them'. The afternoon sermon, on Exodus 3: 2–5, took as its symbol the ever-burning bush to show that the true church would continue despite its tribulations.

Jenkyn refused to settle into nonconformist retirement and joined many of his former London presbyterian brethren in preaching at conventicles. In 1663 he preached at the house of Mr Clayton in Wood Street, at Mr Angell's house in Newgate Market, and at the Rose and Crown in Blowe Bladder Street. He was also involved in the organization of nonconformity, being the treasurer of the public stock taken to support City ministers, and was friendly with the nonconformist patron Lord Wharton. With the passing of the first Conventicle Act in 1664 he retired to his house at Kings Langley in Hertfordshire, preaching every Sunday. Such was Jenkyn's notoriety among the cavalier-Anglican élite that Lord Fanshawe, the lord lieutenant of Hertfordshire, required a bond of £2000 from him in 1666 to keep the peace. This did not stop his ministry, however, and he is recorded as having preached in St Albans and Watford in 1669.

The late 1660s saw disagreements among the presbyterians over whether to negotiate reconciliation with the Anglican Church of England or to concentrate on building a strong nonconformist alternative. Jenkyn was one of the most vociferous opponents of reconciliation. In September 1668 Dr Thomas Manton, the leader of the pro-reconciliation presbyterians, informed the Worcestershire preacher Richard Baxter that Jenkyn had been excluded from comprehension talks with the Anglicans, 'he having spoken … against all endeavours of Comprehension' (Keeble and Nuttall, 2.66). Despite this division the presbyterians remained friendly with one another, Baxter admiringly describing Jenkyn as a 'sententious, elegant preacher', and in 1675 the two men provided a joint epistle to a work by Richard Garbut (*Reliquiae Baxterianae*, pt 3, 94).

The king's indulgence of 1672 allowed Jenkyn to return to London, and he was the first nonconformist licensed, registering as a presbyterian preacher at Horne Alley in Aldersgate Street. He was chosen as one of the joint presbyterian and Independent Pinner's Hall lecturers, and his congregation built a meeting-house in Jewin Street. He was also a preacher at the nonconformist morning exercises. Resisting the occasional disturbance of soldiers, Jenkyn stayed with his congregation after the revocation of the indulgence in 1673. He also remained a sharp critic of the Church of England. In 1675 he used the funeral of his old friend Dr Lazarus Seaman to preach a sermon against Anglican hypocrisy. This incited argument and in particular a Latin controversy with Robert Grove, later bishop of Chichester. Jenkyn's wife, Elizabeth Lovekin, died in 1675, the couple having had ten children.

Last years In 1682, after the exclusion crisis, the government once again attacked nonconformist gatherings. Jenkyn refused to stop preaching and was arrested, appearing before the Guildhall sessions on 16 November to receive a fine of £40. On 2 September 1684 he was present at a prayer meeting where he gathered with the ministers John Flavel, John Reynolds, and Francis Keeling and a small congregation. This meeting was disturbed by soldiers, who arrested Jenkyn when he paused to allow a lady to escape on the stairs of the meeting-house. He was taken before Sir James Edwards and Sir James Smith, two of the City's aldermen, who administered the Oxford oath in support of the Anglican Church of England. Naturally Jenkyn refused the oath, and the aldermen, refusing the option of a fine, committed Jenkyn to Newgate gaol. Although attempts were made to secure his release on medical grounds, the Anglican establishment was committed to keeping him imprisoned, even denying him the chance to take the comfort of prayer with visitors or his family. As he lamented of his plight, 'A man might be as effectively murder'd in Newgate as at Tyburn'.

Jenkyn died in Newgate gaol on 19 January 1685 after four months of imprisonment and was buried in the nonconformist cemetery at Bunhill Fields. His daughter Elizabeth, who married Thomas Juyce, vicar of Kings Langley, and was described by the younger Calamy as 'a high spirited, tho' a very worthy and pious woman', gave out mourning rings bearing the inscription 'William Jenkyn, Murdered in Newgate' (*Nonconformist's Memorial*, 1.112). In 1715 she erected a monument to him, describing him as a prisoner and martyr. Jenkyn was also survived by his second wife, the widowed Frances Hollyburton (*née* Lucas). His son William was executed at Taunton on 30 September 1685 as a supporter of Monmouth's rebellion; a second daughter, Anne Gurdon, also survived him.

E. C. VERNON

Sources The nonconformist's memorial ... originally written by ... Edmund Calamy, ed. S. Palmer, 2 vols. (1775) • Calamy rev. • J. Quick, 'Icones sacrae Anglicae', DWL, RNC 38.34 • minutes of the London provincial assembly, DWL, MS 201: 12–13 • W. Jenkyn, The busie bishop (1647) • W. Jenkyn, Celeusma, seu, Clamor ad theologos hierarche Anglicanae (1679) • W. Jenkyn, A sermon preached ... Nov 5, 1651 (1651) • JHC, 5 (1646–8) • E. C. Vernon, 'The Sion College conclave and London presbyterianism during the English revolution', PhD diss., U. Cam., 1999 • Venn, Alum. Cant. • D. Neal, History of the puritans (1822) • [E. Calamy], A compleat collection of farewell sermons (1663) • IGI • Calendar of the correspondence of Richard Baxter, ed. N. H. Keeble and G. F. Nuttall, 2 vols. (1991) • Reliquiae Baxterianae, or, Mr Richard Baxter's narrative of the most memorable passages of his life and times, ed. M. Sylvester, 1 vol. in 3 pts (1696) • will, PRO, PROB 11/383, fols. 108v–109v

Likenesses G. Burder, line engraving (after Gibson), NPG

Wealth at death over £300 in chattels and personalty: will, PRO, PROB 11/383, fols. 108v–109v

Jenkyns, Henry (1795–1878), Church of England clergyman and classical scholar, was born on 22 June 1795, eighth of the nine children of John Jenkyns (1753–1824),

vicar of Evercreech, Somerset, and Jane (*d.* 1825), daughter of James Banister, a Bristol merchant. The eldest child was Richard *Jenkyns, master of Balliol College. Henry Jenkyns was educated at Eton College and at Corpus Christi College, Oxford, where he was a scholar (1813–18). He took a double first in 1816, and graduated BA in 1817 (MA 1819, BD and DD 1841).

Oriel College, at that time academically dominant in Oxford, elected Jenkyns to a fellowship in 1818, which he held until 1835. He played his part in college affairs (he was treasurer in 1831) and politics—leading a faction which opposed the appointment of John Henry Newman as dean in 1833—but he was never a college tutor. Throughout the twenties he was private tutor to two sons of Charles Manners Sutton, speaker of the House of Commons, and he was frequently absent from Oxford with them at Eton or Westminster. His only substantial publication, an edition of the *Remains* of Thomas Cranmer, appeared in 1833. At that time Oxford's conservative churchmen were bent on inflating the reputations of the protestant martyr-bishops, and Cranmer's *Remains* was scholarly propaganda in that campaign. The four volumes are meticulously edited, but Jenkyns's no-popery sentiments are apparent in his long preface and footnotes.

In 1833 Jenkyns became the first professor of Greek and classical literature at the University of Durham. His brother-in-law Thomas Gaisford, dean of Christ Church and a former canon of Durham, was instrumental in his appointment. On 31 March 1834 Jenkyns married his second cousin Harriet (1807–1876), daughter of Henry *Hobhouse. They had four daughters and four sons. He was a leading member of the tiny senate which guided the University of Durham through its formative years, and was sub-warden for eight periods between 1840 and 1860. He was acting professor of divinity from 1835, but did not resign as professor of Greek and classical literature until 1840. The inaugural lecture he gave in 1834, published as *A Lecture on the Advantages of Classical Studies*, is remarkable for its prolixity and lack of substance. But his divinity teaching lectures, a systematic two-year course on church history, dogmatic theology, and forms of worship, were models of clarity, organization, and orthodoxy which attracted migrants from Oxford and Cambridge. According to Fowler, Jenkyns commanded the admiration and respect of his students. Although somewhat cold and aloof, he had a caustic sense of humour which occasionally enlivened the otherwise rigid decorum of his lecture room. The lectures were not published, but several sets of notes taken from them survive at Durham in the university library.

Jenkyns was collated to the third stall in Durham Cathedral in 1839, the last canon of Durham to be installed before the Ecclesiastical Commissioners Act of 1840 reduced the value of such dignities, and he was formally appointed professor of divinity in 1840. It was intended that the canonry should eventually be annexed to and support the professorship, but the two were not formally linked until later. In 1864 he resigned his professorship and retired to Botley Hill, Bishop's Waltham, near Southampton. He was nevertheless able to enjoy the unreformed emoluments of his golden stall (nearly £4000 per annum) until his death. He voluntarily surrendered £1000 per annum to cover the cost of his replacement as professor but, controversially, he continued to enjoy in retirement a net income which was three times as much as his successor would ever earn. He died at Botley Hill on 2 April 1878, and was buried next to his wife in the graveyard of Curdridge church.   JOHN JONES

Sources Balliol Oxf., Jenkyns MSS · additional Jenkyns material, incl. correspondence on family and collections, Balliol Oxf. · J. T. Fowler, *Durham University: earlier foundations and present colleges* (1904) · *The letters and diaries of John Henry Newman*, ed. C. S. Dessain and others, [31 vols.] (1961–), vol. 3, pp. 58–64 · *Evidence taken by the Durham University commissioners under the Durham University Act, 1861* (1863), 27 Feb 1862 · *The Times* (20 Oct 1864) · *The Times* (22 Oct 1864) · *The Times* (27 Oct 1864) · A. S. Havens, 'Henry Jenkyns on the Thirty-nine Articles: a study in nineteenth-century Anglican confessionalism', MA diss., U. Durham, 1982 · C. E. Whiting, *The University of Durham, 1832–1932* (1932), 91–2
Archives Balliol Oxf., corresp. and papers | U. Durham, sets of notes taken from Jenkyns's lectures
Likenesses group portrait, silhouette, *c.*1800 (as a small boy with family), priv. coll.; copy, Jenkyns MSS · H. Robinson, engraving (after drawing by G. Newton), Durham Cath. CL; copy at Oriel College, Oxford · oils, U. Durham, Castle Hall · photograph, Durham Cath. CL
Wealth at death £40,410 18s. 6d.: probate, 4 July 1878, *CGPLA Eng. & Wales*

Jenkyns, Richard (1782–1854), college head, born at Evercreech, Somerset, and baptized there on 21 December 1782, was the eldest son of John Jenkyns (1753–1824), prebendary of Wells, and his wife, Jane Banister (d. 1825). He was admitted as a commoner to Balliol College, Oxford, in 1800, and was soon afterwards elected scholar. John Randolph, bishop of Oxford, took a close interest in his career. In 1803, soon after he reached the statutable age of twenty, he was elected fellow against a strong field of competitors. He graduated BA in 1804, MA in 1806, and BD and DD in 1819, and acted as public examiner in 1811–12. He was appointed tutor of his college in 1813, bursar in 1814, and on 23 April 1819 was elected master. Jenkyns held his father's living at Evercreech from 1821 to 1825, succeeding also to his rectory of Pinder and prebend at Wells, both of which he retained from 1824 to 1845. He married on 25 April 1835 Troth, the only child of Grey Germyn Grove, of Pool Hall, Shropshire.

Jenkyns's ability and learning were moderate, but his devotion to the college and his zeal for its interests made his mastership remarkably successful. At his death Balliol could claim to rank as the first college in Oxford. The change was chiefly due to the substitution of open competition for the old system under which scholars were elected on the simple nomination of each fellow in his turn. The first election to open scholarships took place in 1828, and the new practice was confirmed by a visitatorial decree in 1834. The credit of this reform has been generally ascribed to Jenkyns, but he himself afterwards said that he had done no more than acquiesce in it with the

gravest doubts as to the probability of its success. The college, however, undoubtedly greatly benefited by his exertions in obtaining fellows and scholars of ability and in raising the standard required from commoners on admission. His appointments to tutorships were also testimony to his astute judgement of individuals. The assumption of severity with which he covered a kind and indulgent disposition, the pompous appearance of his short figure, his strange accent and the eccentricity of his sayings, gave him an important place in the memories of members of his college, and led to many comic anecdotes of which he was the hero. His strictness during his tenure as university vice-chancellor between 1824 and 1828, however, brought him temporary unpopularity.

A staunch protestant and conservative, Jenkyns belonged to the 'high and dry' school of churchmanship. His antipathy to the Tractarian movement was legendary. He was one of the six doctors who condemned Pusey's sermon in 1843. In the same year he successfully vetoed Pugin's plans for rebuilding Balliol College in the Gothic style. He greatly feared the influence on undergraduates of the Tractarian fellow, W. G. Ward, and forced his resignation from his mathematical lectureship in 1844; he was, as a member of the hebdomadal board, a party to the proceedings against Ward in 1845. Peel appointed Jenkyns to the deanery of Wells on 4 June 1845, having established that this preferment could be held in conjunction with the mastership of Balliol so as not to precipitate the election of a new head of the college. Until his death Jenkyns divided his time between the two offices. Known to be one of the wealthiest men in the university, he died, childless, on 6 March 1854 at the master's lodgings, Balliol College, Oxford.   EDWIN CANNAN, *rev.* M. C. CURTHOYS

Sources J. Jones, *Balliol College: a history, 1263–1939* (1988) · J. Jones, 'Sound religion and useful learning', *Balliol studies*, ed. J. Prest (1982) · Boase, *Mod. Eng. biog.* · *GM*, 2nd ser., 3 (1835), 654 · *GM*, 2nd ser., 41 (1854), 425 · W. R. Ward, *Victorian Oxford* (1965) · W. Ward, *W. G. Ward and the Oxford Movement* (1890)
Archives Balliol Oxf., corresp. and papers | BL, letters to Philip Bliss, Add. MSS 34572–34581 · BL, corresp. with Lord Grenville, Add. MS 59415 · BL, corresp. with Sir Robert Peel, Add. MSS 40373–40568 · LPL, corresp. with A. C. Tait · Wells Cathedral, corresp. with Henry Hobhouse and papers
Likenesses F. Cruickshank, watercolour drawing, exh. RA 1839, Balliol Oxf. · H. P. Briggs, oils, exh. RA 1841, Balliol Oxf. · T. Lupton, engraving, 1842 (after H. P. Briggs)

Jennens, Charles (1700/01–1773), patron of the arts and librettist, was born probably at Gopsall Hall, Leicestershire, the son of Charles Jennens (*bap.* 1662, *d.* 1747), gentleman and JP, son of the Birmingham ironmaster Humphrey Jennens, and his second wife, Elizabeth Burdett (1667–1707/8), daughter of Sir Robert Burdett, bt, of Bramcote, Warwickshire, and his wife, Mary, born Pigot, of Thrumpton, Nottinghamshire. With his first wife Charles Jennens sen. had another son, who died in infancy in 1705; with his second he had two more sons and three daughters. Jennens was educated at Balliol College, Oxford; he matriculated on 16 February 1716, aged fifteen.

Charles Jennens (1700/01–1773), by Thomas Hudson, 1747

Subsequently he divided his time between the Leicester-shire estate of Gopsall (736 acres), which his grandfather had purchased in 1685, and London, initially his brother-in-law's house in Queen Square and later his own house in Ormond Street.

The guiding principles of Jennens's life were protestant Christianity and the Stuart cause. Unlike his father but like some other members of his family he was a nonjuror, and became one of the major patrons of nonjurors and Jacobites of his generation. Excluding himself from public office, he devoted much of his time, taste, and wealth to vigorous engagement in, and patronage of, arts and letters. A member of the circle of Handel's admirers which included the fourth earl of Shaftesbury and James Harris, he had catholic but decisive musical tastes. He was one of the first owners of a pianoforte in England, and he had an organ made to Handel's specification (now at Great Packington church, Warwickshire). A constant and generous subscriber to Handel's published works, he amassed the largest contemporary collection of the composer's works, in print and manuscript. He also acquired part of Cardinal Ottoboni's music library and other Italian music manuscripts (lending them to Handel, who used them), and he encouraged contemporary English composers by subscribing to and collecting their works. He left his unparalleled music library to his second cousin, the third earl of Aylesford, also a collector. Sold off from 1873, the Aylesford collection is preserved mainly in Manchester Public Library.

Jennens's modern fame rests chiefly on his collaboration with Handel. He first offered Handel a libretto in 1735; he wrote for no other composer (all his librettos were published anonymously). He was Handel's best English librettist. *Messiah* (1741–2) was not only his libretto but his brainchild (conceived in 1739). His librettos of *Saul* (1738–9) and *Belshazzar* (1744–5) show an impressive gift for dramatic structure and characterization and the ability to wield political analogies adroitly. He prompted James Harris to draft the libretto of *L'allegro ed il penseroso* (1740–41, selections from Milton's poems), which he and Handel completed, Jennens supplying the words for the concluding *Il moderato* at Handel's request. He also possibly compiled or advised on the text of *Israel in Egypt* (1738–9). During the composition of *Saul* Handel incorporated some crucial alterations which Jennens suggested. Though the relationship of librettist and composer, both strongly opinionated and touchy men, could be tempestuous, they remained good friends, Jennens commissioning Thomas Hudson's 'Gopsall' portrait of Handel (1756) and Handel bequeathing Jennens two paintings.

During his lifetime Jennens was better known for his picture and sculpture collection, one of only four commoners' collections listed in Thomas Martyn's survey of the twenty best English art collections, *The English Connoisseur* (1766). It comprised over 500 items and manifested his religious commitment, his loyalty to the deposed Stuart royal family, his enthusiasm for Italian art, and his patronage, in later life, of English artists. At Gopsall, which he inherited in 1747 (with thirty-four other properties in six counties), he apparently employed William and David Hiorn and James Paine, and transformed the Jacobean house into a magnificent, richly decorated, late-Palladian mansion (dem. 1951). He lavished equal attention on the garden layout and buildings, reputedly at a cost of over £80,000. The chief feature of the grounds was the monument (1764) to the classical scholar Edward Holdsworth (1684–1746), a close friend and fellow nonjuror whose work on Virgil he had assisted and published; an Ionic rotunda by Paine and the Hiorn brothers (rediscovered in 1992) over a cenotaph by Richard Hayward was surmounted by Roubiliac's *Religion* or *Fides Christiana* (cenotaph and statue, Belgrave Hall Museum, Leicester). The composition is iconographically subtle and complex, the inscription eloquent of Jennens's abiding nonjuring principles, and the statue not only unique in Roubiliac's output but 'unlike anything else in England' (Bindman and Baker, 122).

Jennens was sensitive and depressive, possibly manic-depressive. (His younger brother Robert, a promising Middle Templar, dramatically committed suicide when Jennens was twenty-eight, the victim, it was thought, of despair arising from religious doubts.) He never married. His shyness and irascibility, coupled with his great wealth, earned him resentment. Posthumous derogation of his abilities derives mainly from abusive allegations by George Steevens, who justifiably envied Jennens's final engagement with dramatic literature, his scrupulous and forward-looking editions of *King Lear*, *Hamlet*, *Othello*, *Macbeth*, and *Julius Caesar* (1770–74): the first appearance of each play in a single volume and with textual variants in footnotes. His superb library, particularly rich in classical and theological publications and Shakespeare incunabula, was dispersed in an abysmally catalogued sale in 1918.

Jennens died at Gopsall Hall on 20 November 1773 and was interred in the family vault at Nether Whitacre church, Warwickshire, where his monument records his generous bequests to religious charities. His chief beneficiary was his niece Esther Hanmer's son Penn Assheton Curzon (1757–1797), who married Lady Sophia Charlotte Howe, eldest daughter of Richard, Earl Howe, and on her father's death Baroness Howe in her own right. Jennens's portraits preserve the privacy which he seems to have preferred to the ostentation which his detractors attributed to him; they barely suggest his strong character and abilities.   RUTH SMITH

Sources R. Smith, 'The achievements of Charles Jennens', *Music and Letters*, 70 (1989), 161–90 · D. Bindman and M. Baker, *Roubiliac and the eighteenth-century monument: sculpture as theatre* (1995) · R. Smith and R. Williams, 'Jennens, Charles', *The dictionary of art* (1996) · *Music and theatre in Handel's world: the family papers of James Harris, 1732–1780*, ed. D. Burrows and R. Dunhill (2002) · R. Smith, 'Handel's English librettists', *The Cambridge companion to Handel*, ed. D. Burrows (1997), 92–108 · J. Nichols, *The history and antiquities of the county of Leicester*, 4/2 (1811), 856–9 · Foster, *Alum. Oxon.* · will, Leics. RO, DG/22/5/8 [transcript]

Archives Hants. RO, corresp. with Edward Holdsworth · Hants. RO, corresp. with James Harris · RIBA, drawings collection, drawings for Gopsall, Gopsall Box, folders K10/1–15 · Warks. CRO, Aylesford and Newdigate Papers, material relating to subject and subject's family

Likenesses W. Hoare?, oils, *c.*1738, priv. coll. · T. Hudson, oils, *c.*1745, FM Cam. · T. Hudson, oils, 1747, priv. coll. [*see illus.*] · M. Chamberlain, oils, *c.*1770, Hants. RO · N. Dance, oils, 1770, priv. coll.

Wealth at death Gopsall Hall, Leicestershire, its contents and park (736 acres); thirty-four other properties in Derbyshire, Leicestershire, Nottinghamshire, Staffordshire, Warwickshire, and Worcestershire; Aylesford collection of eighteenth-century music MSS; £28,350: total bequests; £36 p.a.: annuities: will

Jennens, Sir William (*bap.* 1634, *d.* 1704?), naval officer, was baptized on 27 June 1634, the ninth and youngest son of Sir John Jennens or Jennyns (1596–1642), MP for St Albans in 1628 and 1640–42, and his wife, Alice Spencer. He was an uncle of Sarah Churchill, future duchess of Marlborough. He married Diana Steward of Hampshire, who was a shadowy government informer in the 'Hampton Court plot', apparently a scheme to assassinate Oliver Cromwell discussed by exiled royalists, with whom she had briefly associated, in the Low Countries in 1655. They had at least three children, William and Ambrose, who served at sea with their father in the 1670s and 1680s (William subsequently commanded a French privateer in 1693), and a daughter, Agnetta. Little is known of Jennens's career before the Restoration but he was nominated lieutenant of the *Newcastle* on 22 February 1660 and served in the summer guard that year. He served as lieutenant of the *Adventure* in 1661–2, and of the *Gloucester* and *Portland* in 1664. The Second Anglo-Dutch War brought him his first command, the fourth-rate *Ruby*, in which he served at the battle of Lowestoft (3 June 1665) and the Four Days' Fight (1–4 June 1666), in which he was wounded. It

was his bravery in the latter engagement, along with the patronage of Prince Rupert, which brought him a knighthood and the command of the third-rate *Lion*, in which he served at the St James's day fight on 25 July 1666. He was second in command under Sir Robert Holmes of the raid on Dutch shipping at Terschelling in August.

From this point on, Jennens's promising naval career began to lurch from one crisis to another, the consequences of an abrasive personality which made Pepys describe him as 'a proud, idle fellow' (Pepys, 9.430). His command of the *Sapphire* in 1667–8 brought accusations of cowardice during the Dutch raid on the Medway and of administrative irregularities during a subsequent Mediterranean cruise. His command of the *Princess* in the Mediterranean in 1670–71 led to his dismissal from the service for keeping his wife aboard during the voyage, contrary to order, and he was also sentenced to a year and a day in the Marshalsea prison. The Third Anglo-Dutch War brought him back into the service, first as a captain in the admiral's regiment in 1672, then as captain of the second-rate *Victory* in 1673, in which he fought and was wounded at the battle of the Texel on 11 August, and briefly as captain of the *Gloucester*. He subsequently commanded the *French Ruby* in the mobilization of 1678 and the guardship *Royal James* at Portsmouth in 1678–9. The guardship command again led him into a series of clashes with Pepys: Jennens was reprimanded for keeping women aboard and for plundering wine from Dutch vessels wrecked on the Isle of Wight. During this period his attempts to gain alternative employment also brought mixed results. He was abroad between 1676 and 1678 and offered his services (unsuccessfully) to the French navy. From 1678 onwards he was involved in developing the patent for the first Turkish baths or 'bagnios' in London, although this only led him into a series of protracted lawsuits with his erstwhile partners. It also led him into financial difficulties, or so he alleged in a letter of 1684 to the Navy Board which typifies his erratic and self-centred character:

> gentlemen, the state of my affairs is in truth thus, the bagnio in Long Acre is engaged for £1400; money is called for … [unless] I have my bills to get the money, I shall be turned out of doors before ten days. My bills are my blood … pray be not sorry for me when it is too late to help me.   (PRO, ADM 106/371, no. 481)

Jennens diversified his commercial activities in 1685 by taking out a patent for 'preserving by liquors all sorts of flesh, foul and fish' (*CSP dom.*, 1685, 114). In 1686 he took command of the guardship *Jersey* at Portsmouth, but was severely reprimanded and fined by a court martial in 1688 for a drunken brawl at a dinner with a fellow captain. During the crisis later that year, he commanded the *Rupert* and (briefly) the *Warspite*, and was the leading critic of the fleet's strategy of not actively seeking out the invasion force of William of Orange.

A further series of clashes with authority led to Jennens giving up his command and early in 1689 he followed James II into exile, despite the fact that he always continued to adhere to protestantism. During the 1690 and 1691 campaigns he served aboard the French flagship, interrogating British prisoners and sending Jacobite propaganda ashore, and took part in the planning of the projected Franco-Jacobite invasion of 1692. Jennens made a surprise visit to England in 1698 in an unsuccessful attempt to obtain a pardon; the government quickly deported him, perhaps fortunately for Jennens as his creditors had been alerted to his return, and this attempt to betray the Jacobites as well ruled out any return to France. He turned up at Lisbon in 1699 and offered his services to the Portuguese crown. Although the French ambassador was if anything even more hostile to Jennens than his pro-Portuguese English counterpart, describing him as 'a very pernicious man, and capable of any ill design' (PRO, SP Portugal, 89/17, fol. 347), the old captain seems to have been successful: one eighteenth-century list notes that Sir William Jennens died at Lisbon in 1704, 'chief engineer' to the king of Portugal (Hardy, 14).   J. D. DAVIES

Sources Pepys, *Diary* · J. R. Powell and E. K. Timings, eds., *The Rupert and Monck letter book, 1666*, Navy RS, 112 (1969) · PRO, ADM MSS · *CSP dom., 1664–91* · BL, Add. MS 42586, fols. 93–4 · 'Jennyns, Sir John', HoP, *Commons* [draft] · J. Hardy, *A chronological list of the captains of his majesty's Royal Navy* (1779), 14 · Bodl. Oxf., MSS Rawl. A34, A178, A181 · PRO, SP Portugal, 89/17 · *The manuscripts of the House of Lords*, new ser., 12 vols. (1900–77) · *The manuscripts of the earl of Dartmouth*, 3 vols., HMC, 20 (1887–96) · *Report on the manuscripts of Allan George Finch*, 5 vols., HMC, 71 (1913–2003), vols. 1–2 · J. D. Davies, *Gentlemen and tarpaulins: the officers and men of the Restoration navy* (1991) · parish register, Hertfordshire, St Albans Abbey, 1634, Herts. ALS [baptism] · PRO, C 8/281, no. 47
Archives PRO, Admiralty MSS

PICTURE CREDITS